# Collins
# French
# Dictionary

William Collins' dream of knowledge for all began with the publication of his first book in 1819. A self-educated mill worker, he not only enriched millions of lives, but also founded a flourishing publishing house. Today, staying true to this spirit, Collins books are packed with inspiration, innovation, and practical expertise. They place you at the centre of a world of possibility and give you exactly what you need to explore it.

Language is the key to this exploration, and at the heart of Collins Dictionaries is language as it is really used. New words, phrases, and meanings spring up every day, and all of them are captured and analysed by the Collins Word Web. Constantly updated, and with over 2.5 billion entries, this living language resource is unique to our dictionaries.

Words are tools for life. And a Collins Dictionary makes them work for you.

**Collins. Do more.**

# Collins
# French
# Dictionary

**HarperCollins Publishers**
Westerhill Road
Bishopbriggs
Glasgow
G64 2QT
Great Britain

Sixth Edition 2010

Reprint 10 9 8 7 6 5 4

© HarperCollins Publishers 1997, 2000, 2004, 2006, 2007, 2010

ISBN 978-0-00-732315-9

Collins® is a registered trademark of HarperCollins Publishers Limited

www.collinslanguage.com

A catalogue record for this book is available from the British Library

HarperCollins Publishers, 10 East 53rd Street, New York, NY 10022

COLLINS FRENCH CONCISE DICTIONARY.
Fifth US Edition 2010

ISBN 978-0-06-199863-8

www.harpercollins.com

HarperCollins books may be purchased for educational, business, or sales promotional use. For information, please write to: Special Markets Department, HarperCollins Publishers, 10 East 53rd Street, New York, NY 10022

Dictionary and grammar text typeset by Thomas Callan

Printed in Italy by LEGO Spa, Lavis (Trento)

This book is set in Collins Fedra, a typeface specially created for Collins dictionaries by Peter Bil'ak

**Acknowledgements**
We would like to thank those authors and publishers who kindly gave permission for copyright material to be used in the Collins Word Web. We would also like to thank Times Newspapers Ltd for providing valuable data.

Pierre-Henri Cousin
Lorna Sinclair Knight
Jean-François Allain
Catherine E. Love

OTHER CONTRIBUTORS/
AUTRES COLLABORATEURS
Megan Thomson
Cécile Aubinière-Robb
Harry Campbell
Keith Foley
Janet Gough
Jean-Benoît Ormal-Grenon
Laurent Jouet

EDITORIAL STAFF/
SECRÉTARIAT DE RÉDACTION
Genevieve Gerrard

SERIES EDITOR/
COLLECTION DIRIGÉE PAR
Rob Scriven

EDITORIAL MANAGEMENT/
CHEF DE PROJET
Gaëlle Amiot-Cadey

# Table des matières

# Contents

**LES MARQUES DEPOSÉES**
Les termes qui constituent à notre connaissance une marque déposée ont été désignés comme tels.
La présence ou l'absence de cette désignation ne peut toutefois être considérée comme ayant valeur juridique.

**NOTE ON TRADEMARKS**
Words which we have reason to believe constitute trademarks have been designated as such. However, neither the presence nor the absence of such designation should be regarded as affecting the legal status of any trademark.

# Introduction

You may be starting French for the first time, or you may wish to extend your knowledge of the language. Perhaps you want to read and study French books, newspapers and magazines, or perhaps simply have a conversation with French speakers. Whatever the reason, whether you're a student, a tourist or want to use French for business, this is the ideal book to help you understand and communicate. This modern, user-friendly dictionary gives priority to everyday vocabulary and the language of current affairs, business, computing and tourism, and, as in all Collins dictionaries, the emphasis is firmly placed on contemporary language and expressions.

## How to use the dictionary

Below you will find an outline of how information is presented in your dictionary. Our aim is to give you the maximum amount of detail in the clearest and most helpful way.

## Entries

A typical entry in your dictionary will be made up of the following elements:

## Phonetic transcription

Phonetics appear in square brackets immediately after the headword. They are shown using the International Phonetic Alphabet (IPA), and a complete list of the symbols used in this system can be found on pages xii and xiii.

## Grammatical information

All words belong to one of the following parts of speech: noun, verb, adjective, adverb, pronoun, article, conjunction, preposition.

Nouns can be singular or plural and, in French, masculine or feminine. Verbs can be transitive, intransitive, reflexive or impersonal. Parts of speech appear in *italics* immediately after the phonetic spelling of the headword. The gender of the translation appears in *italics* immediately following the key element of the translation.

Often a word can have more than one part of speech. Just as the English word **chemical** can be an adjective or a noun, the French word **rose** can be an adjective ("pink") or a feminine noun ("rose"). In the same way the verb **to walk** is sometimes transitive, ie it takes an object ("to walk the dog") and sometimes intransitive, ie it doesn't take an object ("to walk to school"). To help you find the meaning you are looking for quickly and for clarity of presentation, the different part of speech categories are separated by a right facing triangle ▷.

## Meaning divisions

Most words have more than one meaning. Take, for example, **punch** which can be, amongst other things, a blow with the fist or an object used for making holes. Other words are translated differently depending on the context in which they are used. The transitive verb **to roll up**, for example, can be translated by "rouler" or "retrousser" depending on what it is you are rolling up. To help you select the most appropriate translation in every context, entries are divided according to meaning. Different meanings are introduced by an "indicator" in *italics* and in brackets. Thus, the examples given above will be shown as follows:

> **punch** n (*blow*) coup m de poing; (*tool*) poinçon m
> **roll up** vt (*carpet, cloth, map*) rouler; (*sleeves*) retrousser

Likewise, some words can have a different meaning when used to talk about a specific subject area or field. For example, **bishop**, which we generally use to mean a high-ranking clergyman, is also the name of a chess piece. To show English speakers which translation to use, we have added "subject field labels" in *italics*, starting with a capital letter, and in brackets, in this case (*Chess*):

> **bishop** n évêque m; (*Chess*) fou m

Field labels are often shortened to save space. You will find a complete list of abbreviations used in the dictionary on pages x and xi.

## Translations

Most English words have a direct translation in French and vice versa, as shown in the examples given above. Sometimes, however, no exact equivalent exists in the target language. In such cases we have given an approximate equivalent, indicated by the sign ≈. An example is **National Insurance**, the French equivalent of which is "Sécurité Sociale". There is no exact equivalent since the systems of the two countries are quite different:

> **National Insurance** n (*Brit*) ≈ Sécurité Sociale

On occasion it is impossible to find even an approximate equivalent. This may be the case, for example, with the names of types of food:

> **mince pie** n *sorte de tarte aux fruits secs*

Here the translation (which doesn't exist) is replaced by an explanation. For increased clarity the explanation, or "gloss", is shown in *italics*.

It is often the case that a word, or a particular meaning of a word, cannot be translated in isolation. The translation of **Dutch**, for example, is "hollandais(e), neérlandais(e)". However, the phrase **to go Dutch** is rendered by "partager les frais".

Even an expression as simple as **washing powder** needs a separate translation since it translates as "lessive (en poudre)", not "poudre à laver". This is where your dictionary will prove to be particularly informative and useful since it contains an abundance of compounds, phrases and idiomatic expressions.

## Levels of formality and familiarity

In English you instinctively know when to say "I don't have any money" and when to say "I'm broke" or "I'm a bit short of cash". When you are trying to understand someone who is speaking French, however, or when you yourself try to speak French, it is important to know what is polite and what is less so, and what you can say in a relaxed situation but not in a formal context. To help you with this, on the French–English side we have added the label (*inf*) to show that a French meaning or expression is colloquial, while those meanings or expressions which are vulgar are given an exclamation mark (*inf!*), warning you they can cause serious offence. Note also that on the English–French side, translations which are vulgar are followed by an exclamation mark in brackets.

## Keywords

Words labelled in the text as KEYWORDS, such as **be** and **do** or their French equivalents **être** and **faire**, have been given special treatment because they form the basic elements of the language. This extra help will ensure that you know how to use these complex words with confidence.

## Cultural information

Entries which appear distinguished in the text by a column of dots explain aspects of culture in French and English-speaking countries. Subject areas covered include politics, education, media and national festivals, for example **Assemblée nationale**, **baccalauréat**, **BBC** and **Hallowe'en**.

# Abréviations

# Abbreviations

| | | |
|---|---|---|
| abréviation | *ab(b)r* | abbreviation |
| adjectif, locution adjectivale | *adj* | adjective, adjectival phrase |
| administration | *Admin* | administration |
| adverbe, locution adverbiale | *adv* | adverb, adverbial phrase |
| agriculture | *Agr* | agriculture |
| anatomie | *Anat* | anatomy |
| architecture | *Archit* | architecture |
| article défini | *art déf* | definite article |
| article indéfini | *art indéf* | indefinite article |
| automobile | *Aut(o)* | the motor car and motoring |
| aviation, voyages aériens | *Aviat* | flying, air travel |
| biologie | *Bio(l)* | biology |
| botanique | *Bot* | botany |
| anglais britannique | *Brit* | British English |
| chimie | *Chem* | chemistry |
| cinéma | *Ciné, Cine* | cinema |
| commerce, finance, banque | *Comm* | commerce, finance, banking |
| informatique | *Comput* | computing |
| conjonction | *conj* | conjunction |
| construction | *Constr* | building |
| nom utilisé comme adjectif | *cpd* | compound element |
| cuisine | *Culin* | cookery |
| article défini | *def art* | definite article |
| déterminant: article; adjectif démonstratif *ou* indéfini etc | *dét* | determiner: article, demonstrative etc |
| économie | *Écon, Econ* | economics |
| électricité, électronique | *Élec, Elec* | electricity, electronics |
| en particulier | *esp* | especially |
| exclamation, interjection | *excl* | exclamation, interjection |
| féminin | *f* | feminine |
| langue familière (! emploi vulgaire) | *fam(!)* | colloquial usage (! particularly offensive) |
| emploi figuré | *fig* | figurative use |
| (verbe anglais) dont la particule est inséparable | *fus* | (phrasal verb) where the particle is inseparable |
| généralement | *gén, gen* | generally |
| géographie, géologie | *Géo, Geo* | geography, geology |
| géométrie | *Géom, Geom* | geometry |
| langue familière (! emploi vulgaire) | *inf(!)* | colloquial usage (! particularly offensive) |
| infinitif | *infin* | infinitive |
| informatique | *Inform* | computing |
| invariable | *inv* | invariable |
| irrégulier | *irrég, irreg* | irregular |
| domaine juridique | *Jur* | law |

# Abréviations     Abbreviations

| | | |
|---|---|---|
| grammaire, linguistique | *Ling* | grammar, linguistics |
| masculin | *m* | masculine |
| mathématiques, algèbre | *Math* | mathematics, calculus |
| médecine | *Méd, Med* | medical term, medicine |
| masculin *ou* féminin | *m/f* | masculine *or* feminine |
| domaine militaire, armée | *Mil* | military matters |
| musique | *Mus* | music |
| nom | *n* | noun |
| navigation, nautisme | *Navig, Naut* | sailing, navigation |
| nom *ou* adjectif numéral | *num* | numeral noun *or* adjective |
| | *o.s.* | oneself |
| péjoratif | *péj, pej* | derogatory, pejorative |
| photographie | *Phot(o)* | photography |
| physiologie | *Physiol* | physiology |
| pluriel | *pl* | plural |
| politique | *Pol* | politics |
| participe passé | *pp* | past participle |
| préposition | *prép, prep* | preposition |
| pronom | *pron* | pronoun |
| psychologie, psychiatrie | *Psych* | psychology, psychiatry |
| temps du passé | *pt* | past tense |
| quelque chose | *qch* | |
| quelqu'un | *qn* | |
| religion, domaine ecclésiastique | *Rel* | religion |
| | *sb* | somebody |
| enseignement, système scolaire et universitaire | *Scol* | schooling, schools and universities |
| singulier | *sg* | singular |
| | *sth* | something |
| subjonctif | *sub* | subjunctive |
| sujet (grammatical) | *su(b)j* | (grammatical) subject |
| superlatif | *superl* | superlative |
| techniques, technologie | *Tech* | technical term, technology |
| télécommunications | *Tél, Tel* | telecommunications |
| télévision | *TV* | television |
| typographie | *Typ(o)* | typography, printing |
| anglais des USA | *US* | American English |
| verbe (auxiliare) | *vb (aux)* | (auxiliary) verb |
| verbe intransitif | *vi* | intransitive verb |
| verbe transitif | *vt* | transitive verb |
| zoologie | *Zool* | zoology |
| marque déposée | ® | registered trademark |
| indique une équivalence culturelle | ≈ | introduces a cultural equivalent |

# Transcription phonétique

| Consonnes | | Consonants |
|---:|:---:|:---|
| *poupée* | p | *puppy* |
| *bombe* | b | *baby* |
| *tente thermal* | t | *tent* |
| *dinde* | d | *daddy* |
| *coq qui képi* | k | *cork kiss chord* |
| *gag bague* | g | *gag guess* |
| *sale ce nation* | s | *so rice kiss* |
| *zéro rose* | z | *cousin buzz* |
| *tache chat* | ʃ | *sheep sugar* |
| *gilet juge* | ʒ | *pleasure beige* |
| | tʃ | *church* |
| | dʒ | *judge general* |
| *fer phare* | f | *farm raffle* |
| *valve* | v | *very rev* |
| | θ | *thin maths* |
| | ð | *that other* |
| *lent salle* | l | *little ball* |
| *rare rentrer* | ʀ | |
| | r | *rat rare* |
| *maman femme* | m | *mummy comb* |
| *non nonne* | n | *no ran* |
| *agneau vigne* | ɲ | |
| | ŋ | *singing bank* |
| *hop!* | h | *hat reheat* |
| *yeux paille pied* | j | *yet* |
| *nouer oui* | w | *wall bewail* |
| *huile lui* | ɥ | |
| | x | *loch* |

| Divers | | Miscellaneous |
|---:|:---:|:---|
| pour l'anglais: le "r" final se prononce en liaison devant une voyelle | ʳ | in English transcription: final "r" can be pronounced before a vowel |
| pour l'anglais: précède la syllabe accentuée | ' | in French wordlist: no liaison before aspirate "h" |

**NB:** p, b, t, d, k, g sont suivis d'une aspiration en anglais.
p, b, t, d, k, g are not aspirated in French.

En règle générale, la prononciation est donnée entre crochets après chaque entrée. Toutefois, du côté anglais-français et dans le cas des expressions composées de deux ou plusieurs mots non réunis par un trait d'union et faisant l'objet d'une entrée séparée, la prononciation doit être cherchée sous chacun des mots constitutifs de l'expression en question.

# Phonetic transcription

| Voyelles | | Vowels |
|---|---|---|
| ici vie lyrique | i i: | heel bead |
| | ɪ | hit pity |
| jouer été | e | |
| lait jouet merci | ɛ | set tent |
| plat amour | a æ | bat apple |
| bas pâte | ɑ ɑː | after car calm |
| | ʌ | fun cousin |
| le premier | ə | over above |
| beurre peur | œ | |
| peu deux | ø əː | urgent fern work |
| or homme | ɔ | wash pot |
| mot eau gauche | o ɔː | born cork |
| genou roue | u | full hook |
| | uː | boom shoe |
| rue urne | y | |

| Diphtongues | | Diphthongs |
|---|---|---|
| | ɪə | beer tier |
| | ɛə | tear fair there |
| | eɪ | date plaice day |
| | aɪ | life buy cry |
| | au | owl foul now |
| | əu | low no |
| | ɔɪ | boil boy oily |
| | uə | poor tour |

| Nasales | | Nasal vowels |
|---|---|---|
| matin plein | ɛ̃ | |
| brun | œ̃ | |
| sang an dans | ɑ̃ | |
| non pont | ɔ̃ | |

**NB:** La mise en équivalence de certains sons n'indique qu'une ressemblance approximative.

The pairing of some vowel sounds only indicates approximate equivalence.

In general, we give the pronunciation of each entry in square brackets after the word in question. However, on the English-French side, where the entry is composed of two or more unhyphenated words, each of which is given elsewhere in this dictionary, you will find the pronunciation of each word in its alphabetical position.

# French verb forms

1 Present participle 2 Past participle 3 Present 4 Imperfect 5 Future 6 Conditional
7 Present subjunctive 8 Impératif

**acquérir** 1 acquérant 2 acquis 3 acquiers,
acquérons, acquièrent 4 acquérais
5 acquerrai 7 acquière
**ALLER** 1 allant 2 allé 3 vais, vas, va, allons,
allez, vont 4 allais 5 irai 6 irais 7 aille
**asseoir** 1 asseyant 2 assis 3 assieds,
asseyons, asseyez, asseyent 4 asseyais
5 assiérai 7 asseye
**atteindre** 1 atteignant 2 atteint 3 atteins,
atteignons 4 atteignais 7 atteigne
**AVOIR** 1 ayant 2 eu 3 ai, as, a, avons, avez,
ont 4 avais 5 aurai 6 aurais 7 aie, aies, ait,
ayons, ayez, aient
**battre** 1 battant 2 battu 3 bats, bat, battons
4 battais 7 batte
**boire** 1 buvant 2 bu 3 bois, buvons, boivent
4 buvais 7 boive
**bouillir** 1 bouillant 2 bouilli 3 bous,
bouillons 4 bouillais 7 bouille
**conclure** 1 concluant 2 conclu 3 conclus,
concluons 4 concluais 7 conclue
**conduire** 1 conduisant 2 conduit 3 conduis,
conduisons 4 conduisais 7 conduise
**connaître** 1 connaissant 2 connu 3 connais,
connaît, connaissons 4 connaissais
7 connaisse
**coudre** 1 cousant 2 cousu 3 couds, cousons,
cousez, cousent 4 cousais 7 couse
**courir** 1 courant 2 couru 3 cours, courons
4 courais 5 courrai 7 coure
**couvrir** 1 couvrant 2 couvert 3 couvre,
couvrons 4 couvrais 7 couvre
**craindre** 1 craignant 2 craint 3 crains,
craignons 4 craignais 7 craigne
**croire** 1 croyant 2 cru 3 crois, croyons,
croient 4 croyais 7 croie
**croître** 1 croissant 2 crû, crue, crus, crues
3 croîs, croissons 4 croissais 7 croisse
**cueillir** 1 cueillant 2 cueilli 3 cueille,
cueillons 4 cueillais 5 cueillerai 7 cueille
**devoir** 1 devant 2 dû, due, dus, dues 3 dois,
devons, doivent 4 devais 5 devrai 7 doive

**dire** 1 disant 2 dit 3 dis, disons, dites,
disent 4 disais 7 dise
**dormir** 1 dormant 2 dormi 3 dors, dormons
4 dormais 7 dorme
**écrire** 1 écrivant 2 écrit 3 écris, écrivons
4 écrivais 7 écrive
**ÊTRE** 1 étant 2 été 3 suis, es, est, sommes,
êtes, sont 4 étais 5 serai 6 serais 7 sois,
sois, soit, soyons, soyez, soient
**FAIRE** 1 faisant 2 fait 3 fais, fais, fait,
faisons, faites, font 4 faisais 5 ferai
6 ferais 7 fasse
**falloir** 2 fallu 3 faut 4 fallait 5 faudra
7 faille
**FINIR** 1 finissant 2 fini 3 finis, finis, finit,
finissons, finissez, finissent 4 finissais
5 finirai 6 finirais 7 finisse
**fuir** 1 fuyant 2 fui 3 fuis, fuyons, fuient
4 fuyais 7 fuie
**joindre** 1 joignant 2 joint 3 joins, joignons
4 joignais 7 joigne
**lire** 1 lisant 2 lu 3 lis, lisons 4 lisais 7 lise
**luire** 1 luisant 2 lui 3 luis, luisons 4 luisais
7 luise
**maudire** 1 maudissant 2 maudit
3 maudis, maudissons 4 maudissait
7 maudisse
**mentir** 1 mentant 2 menti 3 mens,
mentons 4 mentais 7 mente
**mettre** 1 mettant 2 mis 3 mets, mettons
4 mettais 7 mette
**mourir** 1 mourant 2 mort 3 meurs,
mourons, meurent 4 mourais 5 mourrai
7 meure
**naître** 1 naissant 2 né 3 nais, naît,
naissons 4 naissais 7 naisse
**offrir** 1 offrant 2 offert 3 offre, offrons
4 offrais 7 offre
**PARLER** 1 parlant 2 parlé 3 parle, parles,
parle, parlons, parlez, parlent 4 parlais,
parlais, parlait, parlions, parliez, parlaient
5 parlerai, parleras, parlera, parlerons,

parlerez, parleront **6** parlerais, parlerais, parlerait, parlerions, parleriez, parleraient **7** parle, parles, parle, parlions, parliez, parlent **8** parle! parlons! parlez!

**partir** **1** partant **2** parti **3** pars, partons **4** partais **7** parte

**plaire** **1** plaisant **2** plu **3** plais, plaît, plaisons **4** plaisais **7** plaise

**pleuvoir** **1** pleuvant **2** plu **3** pleut, pleuvent **4** pleuvait **5** pleuvra **7** pleuve

**pourvoir** **1** pourvoyant **2** pourvu **3** pourvois, pourvoyons, pourvoient **4** pourvoyais **7** pourvoie

**pouvoir** **1** pouvant **2** pu **3** peux, peut, pouvons, peuvent **4** pouvais **5** pourrai **7** puisse

**prendre** **1** prenant **2** pris **3** prends, prenons, prennent **4** prenais **7** prenne

**prévoir** *like* **voir** **5** prévoirai

**RECEVOIR** **1** recevant **2** reçu **3** reçois, reçois, reçoit, recevons, recevez, rerçoivent **4** recevais **5** recevrai **6** recevrais **7** reçoive

**RENDRE** **1** rendant **2** rendu **3** rends, rends, rend, rendons, rendez, rendent **4** rendais **5** rendrai **6** rendrais **7** rende

**résoudre** **1** résolvant **2** résolu **3** résous, résout, résolvons **4** résolvais **7** résolve

**rire** **1** riant **2** ri **3** ris, rions **4** riais **7** rie

**savoir** **1** sachant **2** su **3** sais, savons, savent

**4** savais **5** saurai **7** sache **8** sache! sachons! sachez!

**servir** **1** servant **2** servi **3** sers, servons **4** servais **7** serve

**sortir** **1** sortant **2** sorti **3** sors, sortons **4** sortais **7** sorte

**souffrir** **1** souffrant **2** souffert **3** souffre, souffrons **4** souffrais **7** souffre

**suffire** **1** suffisant **2** suffi **3** suffis, suffisons **4** suffisais **7** suffise

**suivre** **1** suivant **2** suivi **3** suis, suivons **4** suivais **7** suive

**taire** **1** taisant **2** tu **3** tais, taisons **4** taisais **7** taise

**tenir** **1** tenant **2** tenu **3** tiens, tenons, tiennent **4** tenais **5** tiendrai **7** tienne

**vaincre** **1** vainquant **2** vaincu **3** vaincs, vainc, vainquons **4** vainquais **7** vainque

**valoir** **1** valant **2** valu **3** vaux, vaut, valons **4** valais **5** vaudrai **7** vaille

**venir** **1** venant **2** venu **3** viens, venons, viennent **4** venais **5** viendrai **7** vienne

**vivre** **1** vivant **2** vécu **3** vis, vivons **4** vivais **7** vive

**voir** **1** voyant **2** vu **3** vois, voyons, voient **4** voyais **5** verrai **7** voie

**vouloir** **1** voulant **2** voulu **3** veux, veut, voulons, veulent **4** voulais **5** voudrai **7** veuille **8** veuillez!

For additional information on French verb formation see pages 6-131 of Grammar section.

# Les nombres

# Numbers

| | | |
|---|---|---|
| un (une) | 1 | one |
| deux | 2 | two |
| trois | 3 | three |
| quatre | 4 | four |
| cinq | 5 | five |
| six | 6 | six |
| sept | 7 | seven |
| huit | 8 | eight |
| neuf | 9 | nine |
| dix | 10 | ten |
| onze | 11 | eleven |
| douze | 12 | twelve |
| treize | 13 | thirteen |
| quatorze | 14 | fourteen |
| quinze | 15 | fifteen |
| seize | 16 | sixteen |
| dix-sept | 17 | seventeen |
| dix-huit | 18 | eighteen |
| dix-neuf | 19 | nineteen |
| vingt | 20 | twenty |
| vingt et un (une) | 21 | twenty-one |
| vingt-deux | 22 | twenty-two |
| trente | 30 | thirty |
| quarante | 40 | forty |
| cinquante | 50 | fifty |
| soixante | 60 | sixty |
| soixante-dix | 70 | seventy |
| soixante-et-onze | 71 | seventy-one |
| soixante-douze | 72 | seventy-two |
| quatre-vingts | 80 | eighty |
| quatre-vingt-un (-une) | 81 | eighty-one |
| quatre-vingt-dix | 90 | ninety |
| cent | 100 | a hundred, one hundred |
| cent un (une) | 101 | a hundred and one |
| deux cents | 200 | two hundred |
| deux cent un (une) | 201 | two hundred and one |
| quatre cents | 400 | four hundred |
| mille | 1000 | a thousand |
| cinq mille | 5000 | five thousand |
| un million | 1000000 | a million |

# Les nombres

premier (première), 1<sup>er</sup> (1<sup>ère</sup>)
deuxième, 2<sup>e</sup> *or* 2<sup>ème</sup>
troisième, 3<sup>e</sup> *or* 3<sup>ème</sup>
quatrième, 4<sup>e</sup> *or* 4<sup>ème</sup>
cinquième, 5<sup>e</sup> *or* 5<sup>ème</sup>
sixième, 6<sup>e</sup> *or* 6<sup>ème</sup>
septième
huitième
neuvième
dixième
onzième
douzième
treizième
quartorzième
quinzième
seizième
dix-septième
dix-huitième
dix-neuvième
vingtième
vingt-et-unième
vingt-deuxième
trentième
centième
cent-unième
millième

# Numbers

first, 1st
second, 2nd
third, 3rd
fourth, 4th
fifth, 5th
sixth, 6th
seventh
eighth
ninth
tenth
eleventh
twelfth
thirteenth
fourteenth
fifteenth
sixteenth
seventeenth
eighteenth
nineteenth
twentieth
twenty-first
twenty-second
thirtieth
hundredth
hundred-and-first
thousandth

## L'heure

*quelle heure est-il?*
  *il est ...*

minuit
une heure (du matin)
une heure cinq
une heure dix
une heure et quart
une heure vingt-cinq
une heure et demie,
  une heure trente
deux heures moins vingt-cinq,
  une heure trente-cinq
deux heures moins vingt,
  une heure quarante
deux heures moins le quart,
  une heure quarante-cinq
deux heures moins dix,
  une heure cinquante
midi
deux heures (de l'après-midi),
  quatorze heures
sept heures (du soir),
  dix-sept heures

*à quelle heure?*
à minuit
à sept heures

dans vingt minutes
il y a un quart d'heure

## The time

*what time is it?*
  *it's ...*

midnight, twelve p.m.
one o'clock (in the morning), one (a.m.)
five past one
ten past one
a quarter past one, one fifteen
twenty-five past one, one twenty-five
half-past one,
  one thirty
twenty-five to two,
  one thirty-five
twenty to two,
  one forty
a quarter to two,
  one forty-five
ten to two,
  one fifty
twelve o'clock, midday, noon
two o'clock (in the afternoon),
  two (p.m.)
seven o'clock (in the evening),
  seven (p.m.)

*(at) what time?*
at midnight
at seven o'clock

in twenty minutes
fifteen minutes ago

# La date

aujourd'hui
demain
après-demain
hier
avant-hier
la veille
le lendemain

le matin
le soir
ce matin
ce soir
cet après-midi
hier matin
hier soir
demain matin
demain soir
dans la nuit du samedi au
    dimanche
il viendra samedi
le samedi
tous les samedis
samedi passé *ou* dernier
samedi prochain
samedi en huit
samedi en quinze
du lundi au samedi
tous les jours
une fois par semaine
une fois par mois
deux fois par semaine
il y a une semaine *ou* huit jours
il y a quinze jours
l'année passée *ou* dernière
dans deux jours
dans huit jours *ou* une semaine
dans quinze jours
le mois prochain
l'année prochaine

*quel jour sommes-nous?*
le 1er/24 octobre 2007


en 2007
mille neuf cent quatre-vingt seize
44 av. J.-C.
14 apr. J.-C.
au XIXe (siècle)
dans les années trente
il était une fois ...

# The date

today
tomorrow
the day after tomorrow
yesterday
the day before yesterday
the day before, the previous day
the next *or* following day

morning
evening
this morning
this evening
this afternoon
yesterday morning
yesterday evening
tomorrow morning
tomorrow evening
during Saturday night, during the
    night of Saturday to Sunday
he's coming on Saturday
on Saturdays
every Saturday
last Saturday
next Saturday
a week on Saturday
a fortnight *or* two weeks on Saturday
from Monday to Saturday
every day
once a week
once a month
twice a week
a week ago
a fortnight *or* two weeks ago
last year
in two days
in a week
in a fortnight *or* two weeks
next month
next year

*what day is it?*
the 1st/24th of October 2007,
    October 1st/24th 2007

in 2007
nineteen ninety-six
44 BC
14 AD
in the nineteenth century
in the thirties
once upon a time ...

# Aa

**A, a** [ɑ] *nm inv* A, a ▷ *abr* = **anticyclone; are;**
(*ampère*) amp; (*autoroute*) ≈ M (Brit); **A comme
Anatole** A for Andrew (Brit) *ou* Able (US); **de a à
z** from a to z; **prouver qch par a + b** to prove
sth conclusively
**a** [a] *vb voir* **avoir**

 MOT-CLÉ

**à** [a] (*à* + *le* = **au**, *à* + *les* = **aux**) *prép* **1** (*endroit,
situation*) at, in; **être à Paris/au Portugal** to be
in Paris/Portugal; **être à la maison/à l'école** to
be at home/at school; **à la campagne** in the
country; **c'est à 10 m/km/à 20 minutes (d'ici)**
it's 10 m/km/20 minutes away
**2** (*direction*) to; **aller à Paris/au Portugal** to go
to Paris/Portugal; **aller à la maison/à l'école**
to go home/to school; **à la campagne** to the
country
**3** (*temps*): **à 3 heures/minuit** at 3 o'clock/
midnight; **au printemps** in the spring; **au
mois de juin** in June; **au départ** at the start, at
the outset; **à demain/la semaine prochaine!**
see you tomorrow/next week!; **visites de 5
heures à 6 heures** visiting from 5 to *ou* till 6
o'clock
**4** (*attribution, appartenance*) to; **le livre est à
Paul/à lui/à nous** this book is Paul's/his/ours;
**donner qch à qn** to give sth to sb; **un ami à
moi** a friend of mine; **c'est à moi de le faire**
it's up to me to do it
**5** (*moyen*) with; **se chauffer au gaz** to have gas
heating; **à bicyclette** on a *ou* by bicycle; **à la
main/machine** by hand/machine; **à la
télévision/la radio** on television/the radio
**6** (*provenance*) from; **boire à la bouteille** to
drink from the bottle
**7** (*caractérisation, manière*): **l'homme aux yeux
bleus** the man with the blue eyes; **à la russe**
the Russian way; **glace à la framboise**
raspberry ice cream
**8** (*but, destination*): **tasse à café** coffee cup;
**maison à vendre** house for sale; **problème à
régler** problem to sort out
**9** (*rapport, évaluation, distribution*): **100 km/unités
à l'heure** 100 km/units per *ou* an hour; **payé à**
l'heure paid by the hour; **cinq à six** five to six
**10** (*conséquence, résultat*): **à ce qu'il prétend**
according to him; **à leur grande surprise**
much to their surprise; **à nous trois nous
n'avons pas su le faire** we couldn't do it even
between the three of us; **ils sont arrivés à
quatre** four of them arrived (together)

**Å** *abr* (= *Ångstrom*) Å *ou* A
**AB** *abr* = **assez bien**
**abaissement** [abɛsmɑ̃] *nm* lowering; pulling
down
**abaisser** [abese] *vt* to lower, bring down;
(*manette*) to pull down; (*fig*) to debase; to
humiliate; **s'abaisser** *vi* to go down; (*fig*) to
demean o.s.; **s'~ à faire/à qch** to stoop *ou*
descend to doing/to sth
**abandon** [abɑ̃dɔ̃] *nm* abandoning; deserting;
giving up; withdrawal; surrender,
relinquishing; (*fig*) lack of constraint; relaxed
pose *ou* mood; **être à l'~** to be in a state of
neglect; **laisser à l'~** to abandon
**abandonné, e** [abɑ̃dɔne] *adj* (*solitaire*) deserted;
(*route, usine*) disused; (*jardin*) abandoned
**abandonner** [abɑ̃dɔne] *vt* to leave, abandon,
desert; (*projet, activité*) to abandon, give up;
(*Sport*) to retire *ou* withdraw from; (*Inform*) to
abort; (*céder*) to surrender, relinquish;
**s'abandonner** *vi* to let o.s. go; **s'~ à** (*paresse,
plaisirs*) to give o.s. up to; **~ qch à qn** to give sth
up to sb
**abasourdir** [abazurdiʀ] *vt* to stun, stagger
**abat** *etc* [aba] *vb voir* **abattre**
**abat-jour** [abaʒuʀ] *nm inv* lampshade
**abats** [aba] *vb voir* **abattre** ▷ *nmpl* (*de bœuf, porc*)
offal *sg* (Brit), entrails (US); (*de volaille*) giblets
**abattage** [abataʒ] *nm* cutting down, felling
**abattant** [abatɑ̃] *vb voir* **abattre** ▷ *nm* leaf, flap
**abattement** [abatmɑ̃] *nm* (*physique*)
enfeeblement; (*moral*) dejection, despondency;
(*déduction*) reduction; **~ fiscal** ≈ tax allowance
**abattis** [abati] *vb voir* **abattre** ▷ *nmpl* giblets
**abattoir** [abatwaʀ] *nm* abattoir (Brit),
slaughterhouse
**abattre** [abatʀ(ə)] *vt* (*arbre*) to cut down, fell;
(*mur, maison*) to pull down; (*avion, personne*) to

shoot down; (*animal*) to shoot, kill; (*fig: physiquement*) to wear out, tire out; (: *moralement*) to demoralize; **s'abattre** *vi* to crash down; **s'~ sur** (*pluie*) to beat down on; (: *coups, injures*) to rain down on; **~ ses cartes** (*aussi fig*) to lay one's cards on the table; **~ du travail** *ou* **de la besogne** to get through a lot of work

**abattu, e** [abaty] *pp de* **abattre** ▷ *adj* (*déprimé*) downcast

**abbatiale** [abasjal] *nf* abbey (*church*)

**abbaye** [abei] *nf* abbey

**abbé** [abe] *nm* priest; (*d'une abbaye*) abbot; **M l'~** Father

**abbesse** [abɛs] *nf* abbess

**abc, ABC** [abese] *nm* alphabet primer; (*fig*) rudiments *pl*

**abcès** [apsɛ] *nm* abscess

**abdication** [abdikasjɔ̃] *nf* abdication

**abdiquer** [abdike] *vi* to abdicate ▷ *vt* to renounce, give up

**abdomen** [abdɔmɛn] *nm* abdomen

**abdominal, e, -aux** [abdɔminal, -o] *adj* abdominal ▷ *nmpl*: **faire des abdominaux** to do exercises for the stomach muscles

**abécédaire** [abesedɛR] *nm* alphabet primer

**abeille** [abɛj] *nf* bee

**aberrant, e** [abɛRɑ̃, -ɑ̃t] *adj* absurd

**aberration** [abɛRasjɔ̃] *nf* aberration

**abêtir** [abetiR] *vt* to make morons (*ou* a moron) of

**abêtissant, e** [abetisɑ̃, -ɑ̃t] *adj* stultifying

**abhorrer** [abɔRe] *vt* to abhor, loathe

**abîme** [abim] *nm* abyss, gulf

**abîmer** [abime] *vt* to spoil, damage; **s'abîmer** *vi* to get spoilt *ou* damaged; (*fruits*) to spoil; (*tomber*) to sink, founder; **s'~ les yeux** to ruin one's eyes *ou* eyesight

**abject, e** [abʒɛkt] *adj* abject, despicable

**abjurer** [abʒyRe] *vt* to abjure, renounce

**ablatif** [ablatif] *nm* ablative

**ablation** [ablasjɔ̃] *nf* removal

**ablutions** [ablysjɔ̃] *nfpl*: **faire ses ~** to perform one's ablutions

**abnégation** [abnegasjɔ̃] *nf* (self-)abnegation

**aboie** *etc* [abwa] *vb voir* **aboyer**

**aboiement** [abwamɑ̃] *nm* bark, barking *no pl*

**aboierai** *etc* [abwajəRe] *vb voir* **aboyer**

**abois** [abwa] *nmpl*: **aux ~** at bay

**abolir** [abɔliR] *vt* to abolish

**abolition** [abɔlisjɔ̃] *nf* abolition

**abolitionniste** [abɔlisjɔnist(ə)] *adj, nm/f* abolitionist

**abominable** [abɔminabl(ə)] *adj* abominable

**abomination** [abɔminasjɔ̃] *nf* abomination

**abondamment** [abɔ̃damɑ̃] *adv* abundantly

**abondance** [abɔ̃dɑ̃s] *nf* abundance; (*richesse*) affluence; **en ~** in abundance

**abondant, e** [abɔ̃dɑ̃, -ɑ̃t] *adj* plentiful, abundant, copious

**abonder** [abɔ̃de] *vi* to abound, be plentiful; **~ en** to be full of, abound in; **~ dans le sens de qn** to concur with sb

**abonné, e** [abɔne] *nm/f* subscriber; season ticket holder ▷ *adj*: **être ~ à un journal** to subscribe to *ou* have a subscription to a periodical; **être ~ au téléphone** to be on the (tele)phone

**abonnement** [abɔnmɑ̃] *nm* subscription; (*pour transports en commun, concerts*) season ticket

**abonner** [abɔne] *vt*: **s'abonner à** to subscribe to, take out a subscription to

**abord** [abɔR] *nm*: **être d'un ~ facile** to be approachable; **être d'un ~ difficile** (*personne*) to be unapproachable; (*lieu*) to be hard to reach *ou* difficult to get to; **de prime ~, au premier ~** at first sight; **d'~** *adv* first; **tout d'~** first of all

**abordable** [abɔRdabl(ə)] *adj* (*personne*) approachable; (*marchandise*) reasonably priced; (*prix*) affordable, reasonable

**abordage** [abɔRdaʒ] *nm* boarding

**aborder** [abɔRde] *vi* to land ▷ *vt* (*sujet, difficulté*) to tackle; (*personne*) to approach; (*rivage etc*) to reach; (*Navig: attaquer*) to board; (: *heurter*) to collide with

**abords** [abɔR] *nmpl* surroundings

**aborigène** [abɔRiʒɛn] *nm* aborigine, native

**Abou Dhabî, Abu Dhabî** [abudabi] *nm* Abu Dhabi

**aboulique** [abulik] *adj* totally lacking in willpower

**aboutir** [abutiR] *vi* (*négociations etc*) to succeed; (*abcès*) to come to a head; **~ à/dans/sur** to end up at/in/on

**aboutissants** [abutisɑ̃] *nmpl voir* **tenants**

**aboutissement** [abutismɑ̃] *nm* success; (*de concept, projet*) successful realization; (*d'années de travail*) successful conclusion

**aboyer** [abwaje] *vi* to bark

**abracadabrant, e** [abRakadabRɑ̃, -ɑ̃t] *adj* incredible, preposterous

**abrasif, -ive** [abRazif, -iv] *adj, nm* abrasive

**abrégé** [abReʒe] *nm* summary; **en ~** in a shortened *ou* abbreviated form

**abréger** [abReʒe] *vt* (*texte*) to shorten, abridge; (*mot*) to shorten, abbreviate; (*réunion, voyage*) to cut short, shorten

**abreuver** [abRœve] *vt* to water; (*fig*): **~ qn de** to shower *ou* swamp sb with; (*injures etc*) to shower sb with; **s'abreuver** *vi* to drink

**abreuvoir** [abRœvwaR] *nm* watering place

**abréviation** [abRevjasjɔ̃] *nf* abbreviation

**abri** [abRi] *nm* shelter; **à l'~** under cover; **être/se mettre à l'~** to be/get under cover *ou* shelter; **à l'~ de** sheltered from; (*fig*) safe from

**Abribus®** [abRibys] *nm* bus shelter

**abricot** [abRiko] *nm* apricot

**abricotier** [abRikɔtje] *nm* apricot tree

**abrité, e** [abRite] *adj* sheltered

**abriter** [abRite] *vt* to shelter; (*loger*) to accommodate; **s'abriter** *vi* to shelter, take cover

**abrogation** [abRɔgasjɔ̃] *nf* (*Jur*) repeal, abrogation

**abroger** [abRɔʒe] *vt* to repeal, abrogate

**abrupt, e** [abʀypt] *adj* sheer, steep; *(ton)* abrupt

**abruti, e** [abʀyti] *nm/f (fam)* idiot, moron

**abrutir** [abʀytiʀ] *vt* to daze; *(fatiguer)* to exhaust; *(abêtir)* to stupefy

**abrutissant, e** [abʀytisã, -ãt] *adj (bruit, travail)* stupefying

**abscisse** [apsis] *nf* X axis, abscissa

**absence** [apsãs] *nf* absence; *(Méd)* blackout; *(distraction)* mental blank; **en l'~ de** in the absence of

**absent, e** [apsã, -ãt] *adj* absent; *(chose)* missing, lacking; *(distrait: air)* vacant, faraway ▷ *nm/f* absentee

**absentéisme** [apsãteism(ə)] *nm* absenteeism

**absenter** [apsãte]: **s'absenter** *vi* to take time off work; *(sortir)* to leave, go out

**abside** [apsid] *nf (Archit)* apse

**absinthe** [apsɛ̃t] *nf (boisson)* absinth(e); *(Bot)* wormwood, absinth(e)

**absolu, e** [apsɔly] *adj* absolute; *(caractère)* rigid, uncompromising ▷ *nm (Philosophie)*: **l'~** the Absolute; **dans l'~** in the absolute, in a vacuum

**absolument** [apsɔlymã] *adv* absolutely

**absolution** [apsɔlysjɔ̃] *nf* absolution; *(Jur)* dismissal *(of case)*

**absolutisme** [apsɔlytism(ə)] *nm* absolutism

**absolvais** *etc* [apsɔlvɛ] *vb voir* **absoudre**

**absorbant, e** [apsɔʀbã, -ãt] *adj* absorbent; *(tâche)* absorbing, engrossing

**absorbé, e** [apsɔʀbe] *adj* absorbed, engrossed

**absorber** [apsɔʀbe] *vt* to absorb; *(gén Méd: manger, boire)* to take; *(Écon: firme)* to take over, absorb

**absorption** [apsɔʀpsjɔ̃] *nf* absorption

**absoudre** [apsudʀ(ə)] *vt* to absolve; *(Jur)* to dismiss

**absous, -oute** [apsu, -ut] *pp de* **absoudre**

**abstenir** [apstəniʀ]: **s'abstenir** *vi (Pol)* to abstain; **s'~ de qch/de faire** to refrain from sth/from doing

**abstention** [apstãsjɔ̃] *nf* abstention

**abstentionnisme** [apstãsjɔnism(ə)] *nm* abstaining

**abstentionniste** [apstãsjɔnist(ə)] *nm* abstentionist

**abstenu, e** [apstəny] *pp de* **abstenir**

**abstiendrai** [apstjɛ̃dʀe], **abstiens** *etc* [apstjɛ̃] *vb voir* **abstenir**

**abstinence** [apstinãs] *nf* abstinence; **faire ~** to abstain *(from meat on Fridays)*

**abstint** *etc* [apstɛ̃] *vb voir* **abstenir**

**abstraction** [apstʀaksjɔ̃] *nf* abstraction; **faire ~ de** to set *ou* leave aside; **~ faite de ...** leaving aside ...

**abstraire** [apstʀɛʀ] *vt* to abstract; **s'abstraire** *vi*: **s'~ (de)** *(s'isoler)* to cut o.s. off (from)

**abstrait, e** [apstʀɛ, -ɛt] *pp de* **abstraire** ▷ *adj* abstract ▷ *nm*: **dans l'~** in the abstract

**abstraitement** [apstʀɛtmã] *adv* abstractly

**abstrayais** *etc* [apstʀɛjɛ] *vb voir* **abstraire**

**absurde** [apsyʀd(ə)] *adj* absurd ▷ *nm* absurdity; *(Philosophie)*: **l'~** absurd; **par l'~** ad absurdio

**absurdité** [apsyʀdite] *nf* absurdity

**abus** [aby] *nm (excès)* abuse, misuse; *(injustice)* abuse; **~ de confiance** breach of trust; *(détournement de fonds)* embezzlement

**abuser** [abyze] *vi* to go too far, overstep the mark ▷ *vt* to deceive, mislead; **s'abuser** *vi (se méprendre)* to be mistaken; **~ de** *vt (force, droit)* to misuse; *(alcool)* to take to excess; *(violer, duper)* to take advantage of

**abusif, -ive** [abyzif, -iv] *adj* exorbitant; *(punition)* excessive; *(pratique)* improper

**abusivement** [abyzivmã] *adv* exorbitantly; excessively; improperly

**AC** *sigle f* = **appellation contrôlée**

**acabit** [akabi] *nm*: **du même ~** of the same type

**acacia** [akasja] *nm (Bot)* acacia

**académicien, ne** [akademisjɛ̃, -ɛn] *nm/f* academician

**académie** [akademi] *nf (société)* learned society; *(école: d'art, de danse)* academy; *(Art: nu)* nude; *(Scol: circonscription)* ≈ regional education authority; **l'A~ (française)** the French Academy; *see note*

**ACADÉMIE FRANÇAISE**

The *Académie française* was founded by Cardinal Richelieu in 1635, during the reign of Louis XIII. It is made up of forty elected scholars and writers who are known as "les Quarante" or "les Immortels". One of the *Académie's* functions is to keep an eye on the development of the French language, and its recommendations are frequently the subject of lively public debate. It has produced several editions of its famous dictionary and also awards various literary prizes.

**académique** [akademik] *adj* academic

**Acadie** [akadi] *nf*: **l'~** the Maritime Provinces

**acadien, ne** [akadjɛ̃, -ɛn] *adj* Acadian, of *ou* from the Maritime Provinces

**acajou** [akaʒu] *nm* mahogany

**acariâtre** [akaʀjɑtʀ(ə)] *adj* sour(-tempered) *(Brit)*, cantankerous

**accablant, e** [akablã, -ãt] *adj (témoignage, preuve)* overwhelming

**accablement** [akabləmã] *nm* deep despondency

**accabler** [akable] *vt* to overwhelm, overcome; *(témoignage)* to condemn, damn; **~ qn d'injures** to heap *ou* shower abuse on sb; **~ qn de travail** to overburden sb with work; **accablé de dettes/soucis** weighed down with debts/cares

**accalmie** [akalmi] *nf* lull

**accaparant, e** [akapaʀã, -ãt] *adj* that takes up all one's time *ou* attention

**accaparer** [akapaʀe] *vt* to monopolize; *(travail etc)* to take up (all) the time *ou* attention of

**accéder** [aksede]: **~ à** *vt (lieu)* to reach; *(fig: pouvoir)* to accede to; *(: poste)* to attain; *(accorder:*

*requête*) to grant, accede to

**accélérateur** [akseleʀatɶʀ] *nm* accelerator

**accélération** [akseleʀasjɔ̃] *nf* speeding up; acceleration

**accéléré** [akseleʀe] *nm*: **en** ~ (*Ciné*) speeded up

**accélérer** [akseleʀe] *vt* (*mouvement, travaux*) to speed up ▷ *vi* (*Auto*) to accelerate

**accent** [aksɑ̃] *nm* accent; (*inflexions expressives*) tone (of voice); (*Phonétique, fig*) stress; **aux ~s de** (*musique*) to the strains of; **mettre l'~ sur** (*fig*) to stress; ~ **aigu/grave/circonflexe** acute/grave/ circumflex accent

**accentuation** [aksɑ̃tɥasjɔ̃] *nf* accenting; stressing

**accentué, e** [aksɑ̃tɥe] *adj* marked, pronounced

**accentuer** [aksɑ̃tɥe] *vt* (*Ling: orthographe*) to accent; (: *phonétique*) to stress, accent; (*fig*) to accentuate, emphasize; (: *effort, pression*) to increase; **s'accentuer** *vi* to become more marked *ou* pronounced

**acceptable** [akseptabl(ə)] *adj* satisfactory, acceptable

**acceptation** [akseptasjɔ̃] *nf* acceptance

**accepter** [aksepte] *vt* to accept; (*tolérer*): ~ **que qn fasse** to agree to sb doing; ~ **de faire** to agree to do

**acception** [aksepsjɔ̃] *nf* meaning, sense; **dans toute l'~ du terme** in the full sense *ou* meaning of the word

**accès** [akse] *nm* (*à un lieu, Inform*) access; (*Méd*) attack; (: *de toux*) fit, bout ▷ *nmpl* (*routes etc*) means of access, approaches; **d'~ facile/ malaisé** easily/not easily accessible; **donner ~ à** (*lieu*) to give access to; (*carrière*) to open the door to; **avoir ~ auprès de qn** to have access to sb; **l'~ aux quais est interdit aux personnes non munies d'un billet** ticket-holders only on platforms, no access to platforms without a ticket; ~ **de colère** fit of anger; ~ **de joie** burst of joy

**accessible** [aksesibl(ə)] *adj* accessible; (*personne*) approachable; (*livre, sujet*): ~ **à qn** within the reach of sb; (*sensible*): ~ **à la pitié/l'amour** open to pity/love

**accession** [aksesjɔ̃] *nf*: ~ **à** accession to; (*à un poste*) attainment of; ~ **à la propriété** home-ownership

**accessit** [aksesit] *nm* (*Scol*) ≈ certificate of merit

**accessoire** [akseswaʀ] *adj* secondary, of secondary importance; (*frais*) incidental ▷ *nm* accessory; (*Théât*) prop

**accessoirement** [akseswaʀmɑ̃] *adv* secondarily; incidentally

**accessoiriste** [akseswaʀist(ə)] *nm/f* (*TV, Ciné*) property man/woman

**accident** [aksidɑ̃] *nm* accident; **par** ~ by chance; ~ **de parcours** mishap; ~ **de la route** road accident; ~ **du travail** accident at work; industrial injury *ou* accident; ~**s de terrain** unevenness of the ground

**accidenté, e** [aksidɑ̃te] *adj* damaged *ou* injured (in an accident); (*relief, terrain*) uneven; hilly

**accidentel, le** [aksidɑ̃tɛl] *adj* accidental

**accidentellement** [aksidɑ̃tɛlmɑ̃] *adv* (*par hasard*) accidentally; (*mourir*) in an accident

**accise** [aksiz] *nf*: **droit d'~(s)** excise duty

**acclamation** [aklamasjɔ̃] *nf*: **par** ~ (*vote*) by acclamation; **acclamations** *nfpl* cheers, cheering *sg*

**acclamer** [aklame] *vt* to cheer, acclaim

**acclimatation** [aklimatasjɔ̃] *nf* acclimatization

**acclimater** [aklimate] *vt* to acclimatize; **s'acclimater** *vi* to become acclimatized

**accointances** [akwɛ̃tɑ̃s] *nfpl*: **avoir des** ~ **avec** to have contacts with

**accolade** [akɔlad] *nf* (*amicale*) embrace; (*signe*) brace; **donner l'~ à qn** to embrace sb

**accoler** [akɔle] *vt* to place side by side

**accommodant, e** [akɔmɔdɑ̃, -ɑ̃t] *adj* accommodating, easy-going

**accommodement** [akɔmɔdmɑ̃] *nm* compromise

**accommoder** [akɔmɔde] *vt* (*Culin*) to prepare; (*points de vue*) to reconcile; ~ **qch à** (*adapter*) to adapt sth to; **s'accommoder de** to put up with; (*se contenter de*) to make do with; **s'~ à** (*s'adapter*) to adapt to

**accompagnateur, -trice** [akɔ̃paɲatɶʀ, -tʀis] *nm/f* (*Mus*) accompanist; (*de voyage*) guide; (*de voyage organisé*) courier; (*d'enfants*) accompanying adult

**accompagnement** [akɔ̃paɲmɑ̃] *nm* (*Mus*) accompaniment; (*Mil*) support

**accompagner** [akɔ̃paɲe] *vt* to accompany, be *ou* go *ou* come with; (*Mus*) to accompany; **s'accompagner de** to bring, be accompanied by

**accompli, e** [akɔ̃pli] *adj* accomplished

**accomplir** [akɔ̃pliʀ] *vt* (*tâche, projet*) to carry out; (*souhait*) to fulfil; **s'accomplir** *vi* to be fulfilled

**accomplissement** [akɔ̃plismɑ̃] *nm* carrying out; fulfilment (*Brit*), fulfillment (*US*)

**accord** [akɔʀ] *nm* (*entente, convention, Ling*) agreement; (*entre des styles, tons etc*) harmony; (*consentement*) agreement, consent; (*Mus*) chord; **donner son** ~ to give one's agreement; **mettre deux personnes d'~** to make two people come to an agreement, reconcile two people; **se mettre d'~** to come to an agreement (with each other); **être d'~** to agree; **être d'~ avec qn** to agree with sb; **d'~!** OK!, right!; **d'un commun** ~ of one accord; ~ **parfait** (*Mus*) tonic chord

**accord-cadre** [akɔʀkadʀ(ə)] (*pl* **accords-cadres**) *nm* framework *ou* outline agreement

**accordéon** [akɔʀdeɔ̃] *nm* (*Mus*) accordion

**accordéoniste** [akɔʀdeɔnist(ə)] *nm/f* accordionist

**accorder** [akɔʀde] *vt* (*faveur, délai*) to grant; (*attribuer*): ~ **de l'importance/de la valeur à qch** to attach importance/value to sth; (*harmoniser*) to match; (*Mus*) to tune; **s'accorder** *vi* to get on together; (*être d'accord*) to agree; (*couleurs, caractères*) to go together, match; (*Ling*) to agree; **je vous accorde que ...** I grant you that ...

**accordeur** [akɔRdœR] *nm* (*Mus*) tuner
**accoster** [akɔste] *vt* (*Navig*) to draw alongside; (*personne*) to accost ▷ *vi* (*Navig*) to berth
**accotement** [akɔtmɑ̃] *nm* (*de route*) verge (*Brit*), shoulder; ~ **stabilisé/non stabilisé** hard shoulder/soft verge *ou* shoulder
**accoter** [akɔte] *vt*: ~ **qch contre/à** to lean *ou* rest sth against/on; **s'~ contre/à** to lean against/on
**accouchement** [akuʃmɑ̃] *nm* delivery, (child)birth; (*travail*) labour (*Brit*), labor (*US*); ~ **à terme** delivery at (full) term; ~ **sans douleur** natural childbirth
**accoucher** [akuʃe] *vi* to give birth, have a baby; (*être en travail*) to be in labour (*Brit*) *ou* labor (*US*) ▷ *vt* to deliver; ~ **d'un garçon** to give birth to a boy
**accoucheur** [akuʃœR] *nm*: (**médecin**) ~ obstetrician
**accoucheuse** [akuʃøz] *nf* midwife
**accouder** [akude]: **s'accouder** *vi*: **s'~ à/contre/sur** to rest one's elbows on/against/on; **accoudé à la fenêtre** leaning on the windowsill
**accoudoir** [akudwaR] *nm* armrest
**accouplement** [akupləmɑ̃] *nm* coupling; mating
**accoupler** [akuple] *vt* to couple; (*pour la reproduction*) to mate; **s'accoupler** *vi* to mate
**accourir** [akuRiR] *vi* to rush *ou* run up
**accoutrement** [akutRəmɑ̃] *nm* (*péj*) getup (*Brit*), outfit
**accoutrer** [akutRe] (*péj*) *vt* to do *ou* get up; **s'accoutrer** to do *ou* get o.s. up
**accoutumance** [akutymɑ̃s] *nf* (*gén*) adaptation; (*Méd*) addiction
**accoutumé, e** [akutyme] *adj* (*habituel*) customary, usual; **comme à l'~e** as is customary *ou* usual
**accoutumer** [akutyme] *vt*: ~ **qn à qch/faire** to accustom sb to sth/to doing; **s'accoutumer à** to get accustomed *ou* used to
**accréditer** [akRedite] *vt* (*nouvelle*) to substantiate; ~ **qn (auprès de)** to accredit sb (to)
**accro** [akRo] *nm/f* (*fam*: = *accroché(e)*) addict
**accroc** [akRo] *nm* (*déchirure*) tear; (*fig*) hitch, snag; **sans** ~ without a hitch; **faire un** ~ **à** (*vêtement*) to make a tear in, tear; (*fig*: *règle etc*) to infringe
**accrochage** [akRɔʃaʒ] *nm* hanging (up); hitching (up); (*Auto*) (minor) collision; (*Mil*) encounter, engagement; (*dispute*) clash, brush
**accroche-cœur** [akRɔʃkœR] *nm* kiss-curl
**accrocher** [akRɔʃe] *vt* (*suspendre*): ~ **qch à** to hang sth (up) on; (*attacher*: *remorque*) to hitch sth (up) to; (*heurter*) to catch; to hit; (*déchirer*): ~ **qch (à)** to catch sth (on); (*Mil*) to engage; (*fig*) to catch, attract ▷ *vi* to stick, get stuck; (*fig*: *pourparlers etc*) to hit a snag; (*plaire*: *disque etc*) to catch on; **s'accrocher** *vi* (*se disputer*) to have a clash *ou* brush; (*ne pas céder*) to hold one's own, hang in in (*fam*); **s'~ à** (*rester pris à*) to catch on;

(*agripper*, *fig*) to hang on *ou* cling to
**accrocheur, -euse** [akRɔʃœR, -øz] *adj* (*vendeur*, *concurrent*) tenacious; (*publicité*) eye-catching; (*titre*) catchy, eye-catching
**accroire** [akRwaR] *vt*: **faire** *ou* **laisser** ~ **à qn qch/que** to give sb to believe sth/that
**accroîs** [akRwa], **accroissais** *etc* [akRwasɛ] *vb* *voir* **accroître**
**accroissement** [akRwasmɑ̃] *nm* increase
**accroître** [akRwatR(ə)] *vt*, **s'accroître** *vi* to increase
**accroupi, e** [akRupi] *adj* squatting, crouching (down)
**accroupir** [akRupiR]: **s'accroupir** *vi* to squat, crouch (down)
**accru, e** [akRy] *pp de* **accroître**
**accu** [aky] *nm* (*fam*: = *accumulateur*) accumulator, battery
**accueil** [akœj] *nm* welcome; (*endroit*) reception (desk); (: *dans une gare*) information kiosk; **comité/centre d'~** reception committee/centre
**accueillant, e** [akœjɑ̃, -ɑ̃t] *adj* welcoming, friendly
**accueillir** [akœjiR] *vt* to welcome; (*loger*) to accommodate
**acculer** [akyle] *vt*: ~ **qn à** *ou* **contre** to drive sb back against; ~ **qn dans** to corner sb in; ~ **qn à** (*faillite*) to drive sb to the brink of
**accumulateur** [akymylatœR] *nm* accumulator, battery
**accumulation** [akymylasjɔ̃] *nf* accumulation; **chauffage/radiateur à** ~ (night-)storage heating/heater
**accumuler** [akymyle] *vt* to accumulate, amass; **s'accumuler** *vi* to accumulate; to pile up
**accusateur, -trice** [akyzatœR, -tRis] *nm/f* accuser ▷ *adj* accusing; (*document*, *preuve*) incriminating
**accusatif** [akyzatif] *nm* (*Ling*) accusative
**accusation** [akyzasjɔ̃] *nf* (*gén*) accusation; (*Jur*) charge; (*partie*): **l'~** the prosecution; **mettre en** ~ to indict; **acte d'~** bill of indictment
**accusé, e** [akyze] *nm/f* accused; (*prévenu(e)*) defendant ▷ *nm*: ~ **de réception** acknowledgement of receipt
**accuser** [akyze] *vt* to accuse; (*fig*) to emphasize, bring out; (: *montrer*) to show; **s'accuser** *vi* (*s'accentuer*) to become more marked; ~ **qn de** to accuse sb of; (*Jur*) to charge sb with; ~ **qn/qch de qch** (*rendre responsable*) to blame sb/sth for sth; **s'~ de qch/d'avoir fait qch** to admit sth/having done sth; to blame o.s. for sth/for having done sth; ~ **réception de** to acknowledge receipt of; ~ **le coup** (*aussi fig*) to be visibly affected
**acerbe** [asɛRb(ə)] *adj* caustic, acid
**acéré, e** [aseRe] *adj* sharp
**acétate** [asetat] *nm* acetate
**acétique** [asetik] *adj*: **acide** ~ acetic acid
**acétone** [asetɔn] *nf* acetone
**acétylène** [asetilɛn] *nm* acetylene

**ach.** *abr* = **achète**

**acharné, e** [aʃaʀne] *adj* (*lutte, adversaire*) fierce, bitter; (*travail*) relentless, unremitting

**acharnement** [aʃaʀnəmɑ̃] *nm* fierceness; relentlessness

**acharner** [aʃaʀne]: **s'acharner** *vi*: **s'~ sur** to go at fiercely, hound; **s'~ contre** to set o.s. against; to dog, pursue; (*malchance*) to hound; **s'~ à faire** to try doggedly to do; to persist in doing

**achat** [aʃa] *nm* buying *no pl*; (*article acheté*) purchase; **faire l'~** to buy, purchase; **faire des ~s** to do some shopping, buy a few things

**acheminement** [aʃminmɑ̃] *nm* conveyance

**acheminer** [aʃmine] *vt* (*courrier*) to forward, dispatch; (*troupes*) to convey, transport; (*train*) to route; **s'acheminer vers** to head for

**acheter** [aʃte] *vt* to buy, purchase; (*soudoyer*) to buy, bribe; **~ qch à** (*marchand*) to buy *ou* purchase sth from; (*ami etc: offrir*) to buy sth for; **~ à crédit** to buy on credit

**acheteur, -euse** [aʃtœʀ, -øz] *nm/f* buyer; shopper; (*Comm*) buyer; (*Jur*) vendee, purchaser

**achevé, e** [aʃve] *adj*: **d'un ridicule ~** thoroughly *ou* absolutely ridiculous; **d'un comique ~** absolutely hilarious

**achèvement** [aʃevmɑ̃] *nm* completion, finishing

**achever** [aʃve] *vt* to complete, finish; (*blessé*) to finish off; **s'achever** *vi* to end

**achoppement** [aʃɔpmɑ̃] *nm*: **pierre d'~** stumbling block

**acide** [asid] *adj* sour, sharp; (*ton*) acid, biting; (*Chimie*) acid(ic) ▷ *nm* acid

**acidifier** [asidifje] *vt* to acidify

**acidité** [asidite] *nf* sharpness; acidity

**acidulé, e** [asidyle] *adj* slightly acid; **bonbons ~s** acid drops (*Brit*), ≈ lemon drops (*US*)

**acier** [asje] *nm* steel; **~ inoxydable** stainless steel

**aciérie** [asjeʀi] *nf* steelworks *sg*

**acné** [akne] *nf* acne

**acolyte** [akɔlit] *nm* (*péj*) associate

**acompte** [akɔ̃t] *nm* deposit; (*versement régulier*) instalment; (*sur somme due*) payment on account; (*sur salaire*) advance; **un ~ de 10 euros** 10 euros on account

**acoquiner** [akɔkine]: **s'acoquiner avec** *vt* (*péj*) to team up with

**Açores** [asɔʀ] *nfpl*: **les ~** the Azores

**à-côté** [akote] *nm* side-issue; (*argent*) extra

**à-coup** [aku] *nm* (*du moteur*) (hic)cough; (*fig*) jolt; **sans ~s** smoothly; **par ~s** by fits and starts

**acoustique** [akustik] *nf* (*d'une salle*) acoustics *pl*; (*science*) acoustics *sg* ▷ *adj* acoustic

**acquéreur** [akeʀœʀ] *nm* buyer, purchaser; **se porter/se rendre ~ de qch** to announce one's intention to purchase/to purchase sth

**acquérir** [akeʀiʀ] *vt* to acquire; (*par achat*) to purchase, acquire; (*valeur*) to gain; (*résultats*) to achieve; **ce que ses efforts lui ont acquis** what his efforts have won *ou* gained (for) him

**acquiers** *etc* [akjɛʀ] *vb voir* **acquérir**

**acquiescement** [akjɛsmɑ̃] *nm* acquiescence, agreement

**acquiescer** [akjese] *vi* (*opiner*) to agree; (*consentir*): **~ (à qch)** to acquiesce *ou* assent (to sth)

**acquis, e** [aki, -iz] *pp de* **acquérir** ▷ *nm* (accumulated) experience; (*avantage*) gain ▷ *adj* (*voir acquérir*) acquired; gained; achieved; **être ~ à** (*plan, idée*) to be in full agreement with; **son aide nous est ~e** we can count on *ou* be sure of his help; **tenir qch pour ~** to take sth for granted

**acquisition** [akizisjɔ̃] *nf* acquisition; (*achat*) purchase; **faire l'~ de** to acquire; to purchase

**acquit** [aki] *vb voir* **acquérir** ▷ *nm* (*quittance*) receipt; **pour ~** received; **par ~ de conscience** to set one's mind at rest

**acquittement** [akitmɑ̃] *nm* acquittal; payment, settlement

**acquitter** [akite] *vt* (*Jur*) to acquit; (*facture*) to pay, settle; **s'acquitter de** to discharge; (*promesse, tâche*) to fulfil (*Brit*), fulfill (*US*), carry out

**âcre** [akʀ(ə)] *adj* acrid, pungent

**âcreté** [akʀəte] *nf* acridness, pungency

**acrimonie** [akʀimɔni] *nf* acrimony

**acrobate** [akʀɔbat] *nm/f* acrobat

**acrobatie** [akʀɔbasi] *nf* (*art*) acrobatics *sg*; (*exercice*) acrobatic feat; **~ aérienne** aerobatics *sg*

**acrobatique** [akʀɔbatik] *adj* acrobatic

**acronyme** [akʀɔnim] *nm* acronym

**Acropole** [akʀɔpɔl] *nf*: **l'~** the Acropolis

**acrylique** [akʀilik] *adj, nm* acrylic

**acte** [akt(ə)] *nm* act, action; (*Théât*) act; **actes** *nmpl* (*compte-rendu*) proceedings; **prendre ~ de** to note, take note of; **faire ~ de présence** to put in an appearance; **faire ~ de candidature** to submit an application; **~ d'accusation** charge (*Brit*), bill of indictment; **~ de baptême** baptismal certificate; **~ de mariage/naissance** marriage/birth certificate; **~ de vente** bill of sale

**acteur** [aktœʀ] *nm* actor

**actif, -ive** [aktif, -iv] *adj* active ▷ *nm* (*Comm*) assets *pl*; (*Ling*) active (voice); (*fig*): **avoir à son ~** to have to one's credit; **actifs** *nmpl* people in employment; **mettre à son ~** to add to one's list of achievements; **~ toxique** toxic asset; **l'~ et le passif** assets and liabilities; **prendre une part active à qch** to take an active part in sth; **population active** working population

**action** [aksjɔ̃] *nf* (*gén*) action; (*Comm*) share; **une bonne/mauvaise ~** a good/an unkind deed; **mettre en ~** to put into action; **passer à l'~** to take action; **sous l'~ de** under the effect of; **l'~ syndicale** (the) union action; **un film d'~** an action film *ou* movie; **~ en diffamation** libel action; **~ de grâce(s)** (*Rel*) thanksgiving

**actionnaire** [aksjɔnɛʀ] *nm/f* shareholder

**actionner** [aksjɔne] *vt* to work; to activate; to operate

**active** [aktiv] *adj f voir* **actif**

**activement** [aktivmɑ̃] *adv* actively

**activer** [aktive] *vt* to speed up; (*Chimie*) to activate; **s'activer** *vi* (*s'affairer*) to bustle about; (*se hâter*) to hurry up

**activisme** [aktivism(ə)] *nm* activism

**activiste** [aktivist(ə)] *nm/f* activist

**activité** [aktivite] *nf* activity; **en** ~ (*volcan*) active; (*fonctionnaire*) in active life; (*militaire*) on active service

**actrice** [aktʀis] *nf* actress

**actualiser** [aktɥalize] *vt* to actualize; (*mettre à jour*) to bring up to date

**actualité** [aktɥalite] *nf* (*d'un problème*) topicality; (*événements*): **l'**~ current events; **les** ~**s** (*Ciné, TV*) the news; **l'**~ **politique/sportive** the political/ sports *ou* sporting news; **les** ~**s télévisées** the television news; **d'**~ topical

**actuel, le** [aktɥɛl] *adj* (*présent*) present; (*d'actualité*) topical; (*non virtuel*) actual; **à l'heure** ~**le** at this moment in time, at the moment

**actuellement** [aktɥɛlmɑ̃] *adv* at present, at the present time

**acuité** [akɥite] *nf* acuteness

**acuponcteur, acupuncteur** [akypɔ̃ktœʀ] *nm* acupuncturist

**acuponcture, acupuncture** [akypɔ̃ktyʀ] *nf* acupuncture

**adage** [adaʒ] *nm* adage

**adagio** [ada(d)ʒjo] *adv, nm* adagio

**adaptable** [adaptabl(ə)] *adj* adaptable

**adaptateur, -trice** [adaptatœʀ, -tʀis] *nm/f* adapter

**adaptation** [adaptɑsjɔ̃] *nf* adaptation

**adapter** [adapte] *vt* to adapt; **s'adapter (à)** (*personne*) to adapt (to); (: *objet, prise etc*) to apply (to); ~ **qch à** (*approprier*) to adapt sth to (fit); ~ **qch sur/dans/à** (*fixer*) to fit sth on/into/to

**addenda** [adɛ̃da] *nm inv* addenda

**Addis-Ababa** [adisababa], **Addis-Abeba** [adisabəba] *n* Addis Ababa

**additif** [aditif] *nm* additional clause; (*substance*) additive; ~ **alimentaire** food additive

**addition** [adisjɔ̃] *nf* addition; (*au café*) bill

**additionnel, le** [adisjɔnɛl] *adj* additional

**additionner** [adisjɔne] *vt* to add (up); **s'additionner** *vi* to add up; ~ **un produit d'eau** to add water to a product

**adduction** [adyksjɔ̃] *nf* (*de gaz, d'eau*) conveyance

**adepte** [adɛpt(ə)] *nm/f* follower

**adéquat, e** [adekwa, -at] *adj* appropriate, suitable

**adéquation** [adekwɑsjɔ̃] *nf* appropriateness; (*Ling*) adequacy

**adhérence** [adeʀɑ̃s] *nf* adhesion

**adhérent, e** [adeʀɑ̃, -ɑ̃t] *nm/f* (*de club*) member

**adhérer** [adeʀe] *vi* (*coller*) to adhere, stick; ~ **à** (*coller*) to adhere *ou* stick to; (*se rallier à: parti, club*) to join; to be a member of; (: *opinion, mouvement*) to support

**adhésif, -ive** [adezif, -iv] *adj* adhesive, sticky ▷ *nm* adhesive

**adhésion** [adezjɔ̃] *nf* (*à un club*) joining; membership; (*à une opinion*) support

**ad hoc** [adɔk] *adj* ad hoc

**adieu, x** [adjø] *excl* goodbye ▷ *nm* farewell; **dire** ~ **à qn** to say goodbye to sb; **dire** ~ **à qch** (*renoncer*) to say *ou* wave goodbye to sth

**adipeux, -euse** [adipø, -øz] *adj* bloated, fat; (*Anat*) adipose

**adjacent, e** [adʒasɑ̃, -ɑ̃t] *adj*: ~ (**à**) adjacent (to)

**adjectif** [adʒɛktif] *nm* adjective; ~ **attribut** adjectival complement; ~ **épithète** attributive adjective

**adjectival, e, -aux** [adʒɛktival, -o] *adj* adjectival

**adjoignais** *etc* [adʒwaɲɛ] *vb voir* **adjoindre**

**adjoindre** [adʒwɛ̃dʀ(ə)] *vt*: ~ **qch à** to attach sth to; (*ajouter*) to add sth to; ~ **qn à** (*personne*) to appoint sb as an assistant to; (*comité*) to appoint sb to, attach sb to; **s'adjoindre** *vt* (*collaborateur etc*) to take on, appoint

**adjoint, e** [adʒwɛ̃, -wɛ̃t] *pp de* **adjoindre** ▷ *nm/f* assistant; **directeur** ~ assistant manager

**adjonction** [adʒɔ̃ksjɔ̃] *nf* (*voir adjoindre*) attaching; addition; appointment

**adjudant** [adʒydɑ̃] *nm* (*Mil*) warrant officer; ~- **chef** ≈ warrant officer 1st class (*Brit*), ≈ chief warrant officer (*US*)

**adjudicataire** [adʒydikatɛʀ] *nm/f* successful bidder, purchaser; (*pour travaux*) successful tenderer (*Brit*) *ou* bidder (*US*)

**adjudicateur, -trice** [adʒydikatœʀ, -tʀis] *nm/f* (*aux enchères*) seller

**adjudication** [adʒydikɑsjɔ̃] *nf* sale by auction; (*pour travaux*) invitation to tender (*Brit*) *ou* bid (*US*)

**adjuger** [adʒyʒe] *vt* (*prix, récompense*) to award; (*lors d'une vente*) to auction (off); **s'adjuger** *vt* to take for o.s.; **adjugé!** (*vendu*) gone!, sold!

**adjurer** [adʒyʀe] *vt*: ~ **qn de faire** to implore *ou* beg sb to do

**adjuvant** [adʒyvɑ̃] *nm* (*médicament*) adjuvant; (*additif*) additive; (*stimulant*) stimulant

**admettre** [admɛtʀ(ə)] *vt* (*visiteur, nouveau-venu*) to admit, let in; (*candidat: Scol*) to pass; (*Tech: gaz, eau, air*) to admit; (*tolérer*) to allow, accept; (*reconnaître*) to admit, acknowledge; (*supposer*) to suppose; **j'admets que** ... I admit that ...; **je n'admets pas que tu fasses cela** I won't allow you to do that; **admettons que** ... let's suppose that ...; **admettons** let's suppose so

**administrateur, -trice** [administratœʀ, -tʀis] *nm/f* (*Comm*) director; (*Admin*) administrator; ~ **délégué** managing director; ~ **judiciaire** receiver

**administratif, -ive** [administʀatif, -iv] *adj* administrative ▷ *nm* person in administration

**administration** [administʀɑsjɔ̃] *nf* administration; **l'A**~ ≈ the Civil Service

**administré, e** [administʀe] *nm/f* ≈ citizen

**administrer** [administʀe] *vt* (*firme*) to manage, run; (*biens, remède, sacrement etc*) to administer

**admirable** [admiʀabl(ə)] *adj* admirable, wonderful

**admirablement** [admiʀabləmɑ̃] *adv* admirably
**admirateur, -trice** [admiʀatœʀ, -tʀis] *nm/f* admirer
**admiratif, -ive** [admiʀatif, -iv] *adj* admiring
**admiration** [admiʀasjɔ̃] *nf* admiration; **être en ~ devant** to be lost in admiration before
**admirativement** [admiʀativmɑ̃] *adv* admiringly
**admirer** [admiʀe] *vt* to admire
**admis, e** [admi, -iz] *pp de* **admettre**
**admissibilité** [admisibilite] *nf* eligibility; admissibility, acceptability
**admissible** [admisibl(ə)] *adj* (*candidat*) eligible; (*comportement*) admissible, acceptable; (*Jur*) receivable
**admission** [admisjɔ̃] *nf* admission; **tuyau d'~** intake pipe; **demande d'~** application for membership; **service des ~s** admissions
**admonester** [admɔnɛste] *vt* to admonish
**ADN** *sigle m* (= *acide désoxyribonucléique*) DNA
**ado** [ado] *nm/f* (*fam*: = *adolescent(e)*) adolescent, teenager
**adolescence** [adɔlesɑ̃s] *nf* adolescence
**adolescent, e** [adɔlesɑ̃, -ɑ̃t] *nm/f* adolescent, teenager
**adonner** [adɔne]: **s'adonner à** *vt* (*sport*) to devote o.s. to; (*boisson*) to give o.s. over to
**adopter** [adɔpte] *vt* to adopt; (*projet de loi etc*) to pass
**adoptif, -ive** [adɔptif, -iv] *adj* (*parents*) adoptive; (*fils, patrie*) adopted
**adoption** [adɔpsjɔ̃] *nf* adoption; **son pays/sa ville d'~** his adopted country/town
**adorable** [adɔʀabl(ə)] *adj* adorable
**adoration** [adɔʀasjɔ̃] *nf* adoration; (*Rel*) worship; **être en ~ devant** to be lost in adoration before
**adorer** [adɔʀe] *vt* to adore; (*Rel*) to worship
**adosser** [adose] *vt*: **~ qch à** *ou* **contre** to stand sth against; **s'~ à** *ou* **contre** to lean with one's back against; **être adossé à** *ou* **contre** to be leaning with one's back against
**adoucir** [adusiʀ] *vt* (*goût, température*) to make milder; (*avec du sucre*) to sweeten; (*peau, voix, eau*) to soften; (*caractère, personne*) to mellow; (*peine*) to soothe, allay; **s'adoucir** *vi* to become milder; to soften; to mellow
**adoucissement** [adusismɑ̃] *nm* becoming milder; sweetening; softening; mellowing; soothing
**adoucisseur** [adusisœʀ] *nm*: **~ (d'eau)** water softener
**adr.** *abr* = **adresse**; **adresser**
**adrénaline** [adʀenalin] *nf* adrenaline
**adresse** [adʀɛs] *nf* (*voir adroit*) skill, dexterity; (*domicile, Inform*) address; **à l'~ de** (*pour*) for the benefit of
**adresser** [adʀese] *vt* (*lettre: expédier*) to send; (: *écrire l'adresse sur*) to address; (*injure, compliments*) to address; **~ qn à un docteur/bureau** to refer *ou* send sb to a doctor/an office; **~ la parole à qn** to speak to *ou* address sb; **s'adresser à** (*parler à*)

to speak to, address; (*s'informer auprès de*) to go and see, go and speak to; (: *bureau*) to enquire at; (*livre, conseil*) to be aimed at
**Adriatique** [adʀijatik] *nf*: **l'~** the Adriatic
**adroit, e** [adʀwa, -wat] *adj* (*joueur, mécanicien*) skilful (*Brit*), skillful (*US*), dext(e)rous; (*politicien etc*) shrewd, skilled
**adroitement** [adʀwatmɑ̃] *adv* skilfully (*Brit*), skillfully (*US*), dext(e)rously; shrewdly
**AdS** *sigle f* = **Académie des Sciences**
**ADSL** *sigle m* (= *asymmetrical digital subscriber line*) ADSL; **avoir l'~** to have broadband
**aduler** [adyle] *vt* to adulate
**adulte** [adylt(ə)] *nm/f* adult, grown-up ▷ *adj* (*personne, attitude*) adult, grown-up; (*chien, arbre*) fully-grown, mature; **l'âge ~** adulthood; **formation/film pour ~s** adult training/film
**adultère** [adyltɛʀ] *adj* adulterous ▷ *nm/f* adulterer/adulteress ▷ *nm* (*acte*) adultery
**adultérin, e** [adylteʀɛ̃, -in] *adj* born of adultery
**advenir** [advəniʀ] *vi* to happen; **qu'est-il advenu de ...?** what has become of ...?; **quoi qu'il advienne** whatever befalls *ou* happens
**adventiste** [advɑ̃tist(ə)] *nm/f* (*Rel*) Adventist
**adverbe** [advɛʀb(ə)] *nm* adverb; **~ de manière** adverb of manner
**adverbial, e, -aux** [advɛʀbjal, -o] *adj* adverbial
**adversaire** [advɛʀsɛʀ] *nm/f* (*Sport, gén*) opponent, adversary; (*Mil*) adversary, enemy
**adverse** [advɛʀs(ə)] *adj* opposing
**adversité** [advɛʀsite] *nf* adversity
**AELE** *sigle f* (= *Association européenne de libre-échange*) EFTA (= *European Free Trade Association*)
**AEN** *sigle f* (= *Agence pour l'énergie nucléaire*) ≈ AEA = **Atomic Energy Authority**
**aérateur** [aeʀatœʀ] *nm* ventilator
**aération** [aeʀasjɔ̃] *nf* airing; (*circulation de l'air*) ventilation; **conduit d'~** ventilation shaft; **bouche d'~** air vent
**aéré, e** [aeʀe] *adj* (*pièce, local*) airy, well-ventilated; (*tissu*) loose-woven; **centre ~** outdoor centre
**aérer** [aeʀe] *vt* to air; (*fig*) to lighten; **s'aérer** *vi* to get some (fresh) air
**aérien, ne** [aeʀjɛ̃, -ɛn] *adj* (*Aviat*) air *cpd*, aerial; (*câble, métro*) overhead; (*fig*) light; **compagnie ~ne** airline (company); **ligne ~ne** airline
**aérobic** [aeʀɔbik] *nf* aerobics *sg*
**aérobie** [aeʀɔbi] *adj* aerobic
**aéro-club** [aeʀɔklœb] *nm* flying club
**aérodrome** [aeʀɔdʀɔm] *nm* airfield, aerodrome
**aérodynamique** [aeʀɔdinamik] *adj* aerodynamic, streamlined ▷ *nf* aerodynamics *sg*
**aérofrein** [aeʀɔfʀɛ̃] *nm* air brake
**aérogare** [aeʀɔgaʀ] *nf* airport (buildings); (*en ville*) air terminal
**aéroglisseur** [aeʀɔglisœʀ] *nm* hovercraft
**aérogramme** [aeʀɔgʀam] *nm* air letter, aerogram(me)
**aéromodélisme** [aeʀɔmɔdelism(ə)] *nm* model aircraft making

**aéronaute** [aeʀɔnot] *nm/f* aeronaut

**aéronautique** [aeʀɔnotik] *adj* aeronautical ▷ *nf* aeronautics *sg*

**aéronaval, e** [aeʀɔnaval] *adj* air and sea *cpd*

**Aéronavale** [aeʀɔnaval] *nf* ≈ Fleet Air Arm (*Brit*), ≈ Naval Air Force (*US*)

**aéronef** [aeʀɔnɛf] *nm* aircraft

**aérophagie** [aeʀɔfaʒi] *nf*: **il fait de l'~** he suffers from abdominal wind

**aéroport** [aeʀɔpɔʀ] *nm* airport; **~ d'embarquement** departure airport

**aéroporté, e** [aeʀɔpɔʀte] *adj* airborne, airlifted

**aéroportuaire** [aeʀɔpɔʀtɥeʀ] *adj* of an *ou* the airport, airport *cpd*

**aéropostal, e, -aux** [aeʀɔpɔstal, -o] *adj* airmail *cpd*

**aérosol** [aeʀɔsɔl] *nm* aerosol

**aérospatial, e, -aux** [aeʀɔspasjal, -o] *adj* aerospace ▷ *nf* the aerospace industry

**aérostat** [aeʀɔsta] *nm* aerostat

**aérotrain** [aeʀɔtʀɛ̃] *nm* hovertrain

**AF** *sigle fpl* = **allocations familiales** ▷ *sigle f* (*Suisse*) = **Assemblée fédérale**

**AFAT** [afat] *sigle m* (= *Auxiliaire féminin de l'armée de terre*) *member of the women's army*

**affabilité** [afabilite] *nf* affability

**affable** [afabl(ə)] *adj* affable

**affabulateur, -trice** [afabylatœʀ, -tʀis] *nm/f* storyteller

**affabulation** [afabylɑsjɔ̃] *nf* invention, fantasy

**affabuler** [afabyle] *vi* to make up stories

**affacturage** [afaktyʀaʒ] *nm* factoring

**affadir** [afadiʀ] *vt* to make insipid *ou* tasteless

**affaiblir** [afebliʀ] *vt* to weaken; **s'affaiblir** *vi* to weaken, grow weaker; (*vue*) to grow dim

**affaiblissement** [afeblismɑ̃] *nm* weakening

**affaire** [afeʀ] *nf* (*problème, question*) matter; (*criminelle, judiciaire*) case; (*scandaleuse etc*) affair; (*entreprise*) business; (*marché, transaction*) (business) deal, (piece of) business *no pl*; (*occasion intéressante*) good deal; **affaires** *nfpl* affairs; (*activité commerciale*) business *sg*; (*effets personnels*) things, belongings; **~s de sport** sports gear; **tirer qn/se tirer d'~** to get sb/o.s. out of trouble; **ceci fera l'~** this will do (nicely); **avoir ~ à** (*comme adversaire*) to be faced with; (*en contact*) to be dealing with; **tu auras ~ à moi!** (*menace*) you'll have me to contend with!; **c'est une ~ de goût/d'argent** it's a question *ou* matter of taste/money; **c'est l'~ d'une minute/heure** it'll only take a minute/an hour; **ce sont mes ~s** (*cela me concerne*) that's my business; **toutes ~s cessantes** forthwith; **les ~s étrangères** (*Pol*) foreign affairs

**affairé, e** [afeʀe] *adj* busy

**affairer** [afeʀe]: **s'affairer** *vi* to busy o.s., bustle about

**affairisme** [afeʀism(ə)] *nm* (political) racketeering

**affaissement** [afɛsmɑ̃] *nm* subsidence; collapse

**affaisser** [afese]: **s'affaisser** *vi* (*terrain, immeuble*) to subside, sink; (*personne*) to collapse

**affaler** [afale]: **s'affaler** *vi*: **s'~ dans/sur** to collapse *ou* slump into/onto

**affamé, e** [afame] *adj* starving, famished

**affamer** [afame] *vt* to starve

**affectation** [afɛktɑsjɔ̃] *nf* (*voir affecter*) allotment; appointment; posting; (*voir affecté*) affectedness

**affecté, e** [afɛkte] *adj* affected

**affecter** [afɛkte] *vt* (*émouvoir*) to affect, move; (*feindre*) to affect, feign; (*telle ou telle forme etc*) to take on, assume; **~ qch à** to allocate *ou* allot sth to; **~ qn à** to appoint sb to; (*diplomate*) to post sb to; **~ qch de** (*de coefficient*) to modify sth by

**affectif, -ive** [afɛktif, -iv] *adj* emotional, affective

**affection** [afɛksjɔ̃] *nf* affection; (*mal*) ailment; **avoir de l'~ pour** to feel affection for; **prendre en ~** to become fond of

**affectionner** [afɛksjɔne] *vt* to be fond of

**affectueusement** [afɛktɥøzmɑ̃] *adv* affectionately

**affectueux, -euse** [afɛktɥø, -øz] *adj* affectionate

**afférent, e** [afeʀɑ̃, -ɑ̃t] *adj*: **~ à** pertaining *ou* relating to

**affermir** [afɛʀmiʀ] *vt* to consolidate, strengthen

**affichage** [afiʃaʒ] *nm* billposting, billsticking; (*électronique*) display; **"~ interdit"** "stick no bills", "billsticking prohibited"; **~ à cristaux liquides** liquid crystal display, LCD; **~ numérique** *ou* **digital** digital display

**affiche** [afiʃ] *nf* poster; (*officielle*) (public) notice; (*Théât*) bill; **être à l'~** (*Théât*) to be on; **tenir l'~** to run

**afficher** [afiʃe] *vt* (*affiche*) to put up, post up; (*réunion*) to put up a notice about; (*électroniquement*) to display; (*fig*) to exhibit, display; **s'afficher** *vi* (*péj*) to flaunt o.s.; **"défense d'~"** "stick no bills"

**affichette** [afiʃɛt] *nf* small poster *ou* notice

**affilé, e** [afile] *adj* sharp

**affilée** [afile]: **d'~** *adv* at a stretch

**affiler** [afile] *vt* to sharpen

**affiliation** [afiljɑsjɔ̃] *nf* affiliation

**affilié, e** [afilje] *adj*: **être ~ à** to be affiliated to ▷ *nm/f* affiliated party *ou* member

**affilier** [afilje] *vt*: **s'affilier à** to become affiliated to

**affiner** [afine] *vt* to refine; **s'affiner** *vi* to become (more) refined

**affinité** [afinite] *nf* affinity

**affirmatif, -ive** [afiʀmatif, -iv] *adj* affirmative ▷ *nf*: **répondre par l'affirmative** to reply in the affirmative; **dans l'affirmative** (*si oui*) if (the answer is) yes ..., if he does (*ou* you do *etc*) ...

**affirmation** [afiʀmɑsjɔ̃] *nf* assertion

**affirmativement** [afiʀmativmɑ̃] *adv* affirmatively, in the affirmative

**affirmer** [afiʀme] *vt* (*prétendre*) to maintain, assert; (*autorité etc*) to assert; **s'affirmer** *vi* to assert o.s.; to assert itself

9

**affleurer** [aflœʀe] *vi* to show on the surface
**affliction** [afliksjɔ̃] *nf* affliction
**affligé, e** [afliʒe] *adj* distressed, grieved; **~ de** (*maladie, tare*) afflicted with
**affligeant, e** [afliʒɑ̃, -ɑ̃t] *adj* distressing
**affliger** [afliʒe] *vt* (*peiner*) to distress, grieve
**affluence** [aflyɑ̃s] *nf* crowds *pl*; **heures d'~** rush hour *sg*; **jours d'~** busiest days
**affluent** [aflyɑ̃] *nm* tributary
**affluer** [aflye] *vi* (*secours, biens*) to flood in, pour in; (*sang*) to rush, flow
**afflux** [afly] *nm* flood, influx; rush
**affolant, e** [afɔlɑ̃, -ɑ̃t] *adj* terrifying
**affolé, e** [afɔle] *adj* panic-stricken, panicky
**affolement** [afɔlmɑ̃] *nm* panic
**affoler** [afɔle] *vt* to throw into a panic; **s'affoler** *vi* to panic
**affranchir** [afʀɑ̃ʃiʀ] *vt* to put a stamp *ou* stamps on; (*à la machine*) to frank (*Brit*), meter (*US*); (*esclave*) to enfranchise, emancipate; (*fig*) to free, liberate; **s'affranchir de** to free o.s. from; **machine à ~** franking machine, postage meter
**affranchissement** [afʀɑ̃ʃismɑ̃] *nm* franking (*Brit*), metering (*US*); freeing; (*Postes: prix payé*) postage; **tarifs d'~** postage rates
**affres** [afʀ(ə)] *nfpl*: **dans les ~ de** in the throes of
**affréter** [afʀete] *vt* to charter
**affreusement** [afʀøzmɑ̃] *adv* dreadfully, awfully
**affreux, -euse** [afʀø, -øz] *adj* dreadful, awful
**affriolant, e** [afʀijɔlɑ̃, -ɑ̃t] *adj* tempting, enticing
**affront** [afʀɔ̃] *nm* affront
**affrontement** [afʀɔ̃tmɑ̃] *nm* (*Mil, Pol*) clash, confrontation
**affronter** [afʀɔ̃te] *vt* to confront, face; **s'affronter** to confront each other
**affubler** [afyble] *vt* (*péj*): **~ qn de** to rig *ou* deck sb out in; (*surnom*) to attach to sb
**affût** [afy] *nm* (*de canon*) gun carriage; **à l'~ (de)** (*gibier*) lying in wait (for); (*fig*) on the look-out (for)
**affûter** [afyte] *vt* to sharpen, grind
**afghan, e** [afgɑ̃, -an] *adj* Afghan
**Afghanistan** [afganistɑ̃] *nm*: **l'~** Afghanistan
**afin** [afɛ̃]: **~ que** *conj* so that, in order that; **~ de faire** in order to do, so as to do
**AFNOR** [afnɔʀ] *sigle f* (= *Association française de normalisation*) *industrial standards authority*
**a fortiori** [afɔʀsjɔʀi] *adv* all the more, a fortiori
**AFP** *sigle f* = **Agence France-Presse**
**AFPA** *sigle f* = **Association pour la formation professionnelle des adultes**
**africain, e** [afʀikɛ̃, -ɛn] *adj* African ▷ *nm/f*: **Africain, e** African
**afrikaans** [afʀikɑ̃] *nm, adj inv* Afrikaans
**Afrique** [afʀik] *nf*: **l'~** Africa; **l'~ australe/du Nord/du Sud** southern/North/South Africa
**afro** [afʀo] *adj inv*: **coupe ~** afro hairstyle ▷ *nm/f*: **Afro** Afro
**afro-américain, e** [afʀoameʀikɛ̃, -ɛn] *adj* Afro-American

**AG** *sigle f* = **assemblée générale**
**ag.** *abr* = **agence**
**agaçant, e** [agasɑ̃, -ɑ̃t] *adj* irritating, aggravating
**agacement** [agasmɑ̃] *nm* irritation, aggravation
**agacer** [agase] *vt* to pester, tease; (*involontairement*) to irritate, aggravate; (*aguicher*) to excite, lead on
**agapes** [agap] *nfpl* (*humoristique: festin*) feast
**agate** [agat] *nf* agate
**AGE** *sigle f* = **assemblée générale extraordinaire**
**âge** [ɑʒ] *nm* age; **quel ~ as-tu?** how old are you?; **une femme d'un certain ~** a middle-aged woman, a woman who is getting on (in years); **bien porter son ~** to wear well; **prendre de l'~** to be getting on (in years), grow older; **limite d'~** age limit; **dispense d'~** special exemption from age limit; **troisième ~** (*période*) retirement; (*personnes âgées*) senior citizens; **l'~ ingrat** the awkward *ou* difficult age; **~ légal** legal age; **~ mental** mental age; **l'~ mûr** maturity, middle age; **~ de raison** age of reason
**âgé, e** [ɑʒe] *adj* old, elderly; **~ de 10 ans** 10 years old
**agence** [aʒɑ̃s] *nf* agency, office; (*succursale*) branch; **~ immobilière** estate agent's (office) (*Brit*), real estate office (*US*); **~ matrimoniale** marriage bureau; **~ de placement** employment agency; **~ de publicité** advertising agency; **~ de voyages** travel agency
**agencé, e** [aʒɑ̃se] *adj*: **bien/mal ~** well/badly put together; well/badly laid out *ou* arranged
**agencement** [aʒɑ̃smɑ̃] *nm* putting together; arrangement, laying out
**agencer** [aʒɑ̃se] *vt* to put together; (*local*) to arrange, lay out
**agenda** [aʒɛ̃da] *nm* diary
**agenouiller** [aʒnuje]: **s'agenouiller** *vi* to kneel (down)
**agent** [aʒɑ̃] *nm* (*aussi*: **agent de police**) policeman; (*Admin*) official, officer; (*fig: élément, facteur*) agent; **~ d'assurances** insurance broker; **~ de change** stockbroker; **~ commercial** sales representative; **~ immobilier** estate agent (*Brit*), realtor (*US*); **~ (secret)** (secret) agent
**agglo** [aglo] *nm* (*fam*) = **aggloméré**
**agglomérat** [aglɔmeʀa] *nm* (*Géo*) agglomerate
**agglomération** [aglɔmeʀasjɔ̃] *nf* town; (*Auto*) built-up area; **l'~ parisienne** the urban area of Paris
**aggloméré** [aglɔmeʀe] *nm* (*bois*) chipboard; (*pierre*) conglomerate
**agglomérer** [aglɔmeʀe] *vt* to pile up; (*Tech: bois, pierre*) to compress; **s'agglomérer** *vi* to pile up
**agglutiner** [aglytine] *vt* to stick together; **s'agglutiner** *vi* to congregate
**aggravant, e** [agʀavɑ̃, -ɑ̃t] *adj*: **circonstances ~es** aggravating circumstances

**aggravation** [agʀavɑsjɔ̃] nf worsening, aggravation; increase

**aggraver** [agʀave] vt to worsen, aggravate; (Jur: peine) to increase; **s'aggraver** vi to worsen; ~ **son cas** to make one's case worse

**agile** [aʒil] adj agile, nimble

**agilement** [aʒilmɑ̃] adv nimbly

**agilité** [aʒilite] nf agility, nimbleness

**agio** [aʒjo] nm (bank) charges pl

**agir** [aʒiʀ] vi (se comporter) to behave, act; (faire quelque chose) to act, take action; (avoir de l'effet) to act; **il s'agit de** it's a matter ou question of; it is about; (il importe que): **il s'agit de faire** we (ou you etc) must do; **de quoi s'agit-il?** what is it about?

**agissements** [aʒismɑ̃] nmpl (gén péj) schemes, intrigues

**agitateur, -trice** [aʒitatœʀ, -tʀis] nm/f agitator

**agitation** [aʒitɑsjɔ̃] nf (hustle and) bustle; (trouble) agitation, excitement; (politique) unrest, agitation

**agité, e** [aʒite] adj (remuant) fidgety, restless; (troublé) agitated, perturbed; (journée) hectic; (mer) rough; (sommeil) disturbed, broken

**agiter** [aʒite] vt (bouteille, chiffon) to shake; (bras, mains) to wave; (préoccuper, exciter) to trouble, perturb; **s'agiter** vi to bustle about; (dormeur) to toss and turn; (enfant) to fidget; (Pol) to grow restless; **"~ avant l'emploi"** "shake before use"

**agneau, x** [aɲo] nm lamb; (toison) lambswool

**agnelet** [aɲlɛ] nm little lamb

**agnostique** [agnɔstik] adj, nm/f agnostic

**agonie** [agɔni] nf mortal agony, death pangs pl; (fig) death throes pl

**agonir** [agɔniʀ] vt: ~ **qn d'injures** to hurl abuse at sb

**agoniser** [agɔnize] vi to be dying; (fig) to be in its death throes

**agrafe** [agʀaf] nf (de vêtement) hook, fastener; (de bureau) staple; (Méd) clip

**agrafer** [agʀafe] vt to fasten; to staple

**agrafeuse** [agʀaføz] nf stapler

**agraire** [agʀɛʀ] adj agrarian; (mesure, surface) land cpd

**agrandir** [agʀɑ̃diʀ] vt (magasin, domaine) to extend, enlarge; (trou) to enlarge, make bigger; (Photo) to enlarge, blow up; **s'agrandir** vi to be extended; to be enlarged

**agrandissement** [agʀɑ̃dismɑ̃] nm extension; enlargement; (photographie) enlargement

**agrandisseur** [agʀɑ̃disœʀ] nm (Photo) enlarger

**agréable** [agʀeabl(ə)] adj pleasant, nice

**agréablement** [agʀeabləmɑ̃] adv pleasantly

**agréé, e** [agʀee] adj: **concessionnaire ~** registered dealer; **magasin ~** registered dealer('s)

**agréer** [agʀee] vt (requête) to accept; ~ **à** vt to please, suit; **veuillez ~ ...** (formule épistolaire) yours faithfully

**agrég** [agʀeg] nf (fam) = **agrégation**

**agrégat** [agʀega] nm aggregate

**agrégation** [agʀegɑsjɔ̃] nf highest teaching diploma in France; see note

● **AGRÉGATION**
●
● The *agrégation*, informally known as the
● "*agrég*", is a prestigious competitive
● examination for the recruitment of
● secondary school teachers in France. The
● number of candidates always far exceeds
● the number of vacant posts. Most teachers
● of 'classes préparatoires' and most
● university lecturers have passed the
● *agrégation*.

**agrégé, e** [agʀeʒe] nm/f holder of the *agrégation*

**agréger** [agʀeʒe] : **s'agréger** vi to aggregate

**agrément** [agʀemɑ̃] nm (accord) consent, approval; (attraits) charm, attractiveness; (plaisir) pleasure; **voyage d'~** pleasure trip

**agrémenter** [agʀemɑ̃te] vt: ~ **(de)** to embellish (with), adorn (with)

**agrès** [agʀɛ] nmpl (gymnastics) apparatus sg

**agresser** [agʀese] vt to attack

**agresseur** [agʀesœʀ] nm aggressor

**agressif, -ive** [agʀesif, -iv] adj aggressive

**agression** [agʀesjɔ̃] nf attack; (Pol, Mil, Psych) aggression

**agressivement** [agʀesivmɑ̃] adv aggressively

**agressivité** [agʀesivite] nf aggressiveness

**agreste** [agʀɛst(ə)] adj rustic

**agricole** [agʀikɔl] adj agricultural, farm cpd

**agriculteur, -trice** [agʀikyltœʀ, -tʀis] nm/f farmer

**agriculture** [agʀikyltyʀ] nf agriculture; farming

**agripper** [agʀipe] vt to grab, clutch; (pour arracher) to snatch, grab; **s'agripper à** to cling (on) to, clutch, grip

**agroalimentaire** [agʀɔalimɑ̃tɛʀ] adj farming cpd ▷ nm: **l'~** agribusiness

**agronome** [agʀɔnɔm] nm/f agronomist

**agronomie** [agʀɔnɔmi] nf agronomy

**agronomique** [agʀɔnɔmik] adj agronomic(al)

**agrumes** [agʀym] nmpl citrus fruit(s)

**aguerrir** [ageʀiʀ] vt to harden; **s'aguerrir (contre)** to become hardened (to)

**aguets** [agɛ] : **aux ~** adv: **être aux ~** to be on the look-out

**aguichant, e** [agiʃɑ̃, -ɑ̃t] adj enticing

**aguicher** [agiʃe] vt to entice

**aguicheur, -euse** [agiʃœʀ, -øz] adj enticing

**ah** [ɑ] excl ah!; **ah bon?** really?, is that so?; **ah mais ...** yes, but ...; **ah non!** oh no!

**ahuri, e** [ayʀi] adj (stupéfait) flabbergasted; (idiot) dim-witted

**ahurir** [ayʀiʀ] vt to stupefy, stagger

**ahurissant, e** [ayʀisɑ̃, -ɑ̃t] adj stupefying, staggering, mind-boggling

**ai** [e] vb voir **avoir**

**aide** [ɛd] nm/f assistant ▷ nf assistance, help; (secours financier) aid; **à l'~ de** with the help ou aid of; **aller à l'~ de qn** to go to sb's aid, go to help sb; **venir en ~ à qn** to help sb, come to sb's assistance; **appeler (qn) à l'~** to call for help (from sb); **à l'~!** help!; **~ de camp** *nm* aide-de-camp; **~ comptable** *nm* accountant's assistant; **~ électricien** *nm* electrician's mate; **~ familiale** *nf* mother's help, ≈ home help; **~ judiciaire** *nf* legal aid; **~ de laboratoire** *nm/f* laboratory assistant; **~ ménagère** *nf* ≈ home help; **~ sociale** *nf* (*assistance*) state aid; **~ soignant, e** *nm/f* auxiliary nurse; **~ technique** *nf* ≈ VSO (*Brit*), ≈ Peace Corps (*US*)

**aide-éducateur, -trice** [ɛdmedykatœʀ, tʀis] *nm/f* classroom assistant

**aide-mémoire** [ɛdmemwaʀ] *nm inv* (key facts) handbook

**aider** [ede] *vt* to help; **~ à qch** to help (towards) sth; **~ qn à faire qch** to help sb to do sth; **s'aider de** (*se servir de*) to use, make use of

**aide-soignant, e** [ɛdswajɑ̃, ɑ̃t] *nm/f* auxiliary nurse

**aie** *etc* [ɛ] *vb voir* **avoir**

**aïe** [aj] *excl* ouch!

**AIEA** *sigle f* (= *Agence internationale de l'énergie atomique*) IAEA (= *International Atomic Energy Agency*)

**aïeul, e** [ajœl] *nm/f* grandparent, grandfather/grandmother; (*ancêtre*) forebear

**aïeux** [ajø] *nmpl* grandparents; forebears, forefathers

**aigle** [ɛgl(ə)] *nm* eagle

**aiglefin** [ɛgləfɛ̃] *nm* = **églefin**

**aigre** [ɛgʀ(ə)] *adj* sour, sharp; (*fig*) sharp, cutting; **tourner à l'~** to turn sour

**aigre-doux, -douce** [ɛgʀədu, -dus] *adj* (*fruit*) bitter-sweet; (*sauce*) sweet and sour

**aigrefin** [ɛgʀəfɛ̃] *nm* swindler

**aigrelet, te** [ɛgʀəlɛ, -ɛt] *adj* (*goût*) sourish; (*voix, son*) sharpish

**aigrette** [ɛgʀɛt] *nf* (*plume*) feather

**aigreur** [ɛgʀœʀ] *nf* sourness; sharpness; **~s d'estomac** heartburn *sg*

**aigri, e** [ɛgʀi] *adj* embittered

**aigrir** [egʀiʀ] *vt* (*personne*) to embitter; (*caractère*) to sour; **s'aigrir** *vi* to become embittered; to sour; (*lait etc*) to turn sour

**aigu, ë** [egy] *adj* (*objet, arête*) sharp, pointed; (*son, voix*) high-pitched, shrill; (*note*) high(-pitched); (*douleur, intelligence*) acute, sharp

**aigue-marine** [ɛgmaʀin] (*pl* **aigues-marines**) *nf* aquamarine

**aiguillage** [egɥijaʒ] *nm* (*Rail*) points *pl*

**aiguille** [egɥij] *nf* needle; (*de montre*) hand; **~ à tricoter** knitting needle

**aiguiller** [egɥije] *vt* (*orienter*) to direct; (*Rail*) to shunt

**aiguillette** [egɥijɛt] *nf* (*Culin*) aiguillette

**aiguilleur** [egɥijœʀ] *nm*: **~ du ciel** air traffic controller

**aiguillon** [egɥijɔ̃] *nm* (*d'abeille*) sting; (*fig*) spur, stimulus

**aiguillonner** [egɥijɔne] *vt* to spur *ou* goad on

**aiguiser** [egize] *vt* to sharpen, grind; (*fig*) to stimulate; (: *esprit*) to sharpen; (: *sens*) to excite

**aiguisoir** [egizwaʀ] *nm* sharpener

**aïkido** [ajkido] *nm* aikido

**ail** [aj] *nm* garlic

**aile** [ɛl] *nf* wing; (*de voiture*) wing (*Brit*), fender (*US*); **battre de l'~** (*fig*) to be in a sorry state; **voler de ses propres ~s** to stand on one's own two feet; **~ libre** hang-glider

**ailé, e** [ele] *adj* winged

**aileron** [ɛlʀɔ̃] *nm* (*de requin*) fin; (*d'avion*) aileron

**ailette** [ɛlɛt] *nf* (*Tech*) fin; (: *de turbine*) blade

**ailier** [elje] *nm* (*Sport*) winger

**aille** *etc* [aj] *vb voir* **aller**

**ailleurs** [ajœʀ] *adv* elsewhere, somewhere else; **partout/nulle part ~** everywhere/nowhere else; **d'~** *adv* (*du reste*) moreover, besides; **par ~** *adv* (*d'autre part*) moreover, furthermore

**ailloli** [ajɔli] *nm* garlic mayonnaise

**aimable** [ɛmabl(ə)] *adj* kind, nice; **vous êtes bien ~** that's very nice *ou* kind of you, how kind (of you)!

**aimablement** [ɛmabləmɑ̃] *adv* kindly

**aimant¹** [ɛmɑ̃] *nm* magnet

**aimant², e** [ɛmɑ̃, -ɑ̃t] *adj* loving, affectionate

**aimanté, e** [ɛmɑ̃te] *adj* magnetic

**aimanter** [ɛmɑ̃te] *vt* to magnetize

**aimer** [eme] *vt* to love; (*d'amitié, affection, par goût*) to like; (*souhait*): **j'aimerais ...** I would like ...; **s'aimer** to love each other; to like each other; **je n'aime pas beaucoup Paul** I don't like Paul much, I don't care much for Paul; **~ faire qch** to like doing sth, to like to do sth; **aimeriez-vous que je vous accompagne?** would you like me to come with you?; **j'aimerais (bien) m'en aller** I should (really) like to go; **bien ~ qn/qch** to like sb/sth; **j'aime mieux Paul (que Pierre)** I prefer Paul (to Pierre); **j'aime mieux** *ou* **autant vous dire que** I may as well tell you that; **j'aimerais autant** *ou* **mieux y aller maintenant** I'd sooner *ou* rather go now; **j'aime assez aller au cinéma** I quite like going to the cinema

**aine** [ɛn] *nf* groin

**aîné, e** [ene] *adj* elder, older; (*le plus âgé*) eldest, oldest ▷ *nm/f* oldest child *ou* one, oldest boy *ou* son/girl *ou* daughter; **aînés** *nmpl* (*fig: anciens*) elders; **il est mon ~ (de 2 ans)** he's (2 years) older than me, he's (2 years) my senior

**aînesse** [ɛnɛs] *nf*: **droit d'~** birthright

**ainsi** [ɛ̃si] *adv* (*de cette façon*) like this, in this way, thus; (*ce faisant*) thus ▷ *conj* thus, so; **~ que** (*comme*) (just) as; (*et aussi*) as well as; **pour ~ dire** so to speak, as it were; **~ donc** and so; **~ soit-il** (*Rel*) so be it; **et ~ de suite** and so on (and so forth)

**aïoli** [ajɔli] *nm* = **ailloli**

**air** [ɛʀ] *nm* air; (*mélodie*) tune; (*expression*) look, air; (*atmosphère, ambiance*): **dans l'~** in the air (*fig*); **prendre de grands ~s (avec qn)** to give o.s. airs (with sb); **en l'~** (up) into the air; **tirer en l'~** to fire shots in the air; **paroles/menaces**

en l'~ idle words/threats; **prendre l'~** to get some (fresh) air; *(avion)* to take off; **avoir l'~ triste** to look *ou* seem sad; **avoir l'~ de qch** to look like sth; **avoir l'~ de faire** to look as though one is doing, appear to be doing; **courant d'~** draught *(Brit)*, draft *(US)*; **le grand ~** the open air; **mal de l'~** air-sickness; **tête en l'~** scatterbrain; **~ comprimé** compressed air; **~ conditionné** air-conditioning

**airbag** [ɛʀbag] *nm* airbag

**aire** [ɛʀ] *nf (zone, fig, Math)* area; *(nid)* eyrie *(Brit)*, aerie *(US)*; **~ d'atterrissage** landing strip; landing patch; **~ de jeu** play area; **~ de lancement** launching site; **~ de stationnement** parking area

**airelle** [ɛʀɛl] *nf* bilberry

**aisance** [ɛzɑ̃s] *nf* ease; *(Couture)* easing, freedom of movement; *(richesse)* affluence; **être dans l'~** to be well-off *ou* affluent

**aise** [ɛz] *nf* comfort ▷ *adj*: **être bien ~ de/que** to be delighted to/that; **aises** *nfpl*: **aimer ses ~s** to like one's *(creature)* comforts; **prendre ses ~s** to make o.s. comfortable; **frémir d'~** to shudder with pleasure; **être à l'~** *ou* **à son ~** to be comfortable; *(pas embarrassé)* to be at ease; *(financièrement)* to be comfortably off; **se mettre à l'~** to make o.s. comfortable; **être mal à l'~** *ou* **à son ~** to be uncomfortable; *(gêné)* to be ill at ease; **mettre qn à l'~** to put sb at his *(ou* her) ease; **mettre qn mal à l'~** to make sb feel ill at ease; **à votre ~** please yourself, just as you like; **en faire à son ~** to do as one likes; **en prendre à son ~ avec qch** to be free and easy with sth, do as one likes with sth

**aisé, e** [eze] *adj* easy; *(assez riche)* well-to-do, well-off

**aisément** [ezemɑ̃] *adv* easily

**aisselle** [ɛsɛl] *nf* armpit

**ait** [ɛ] *vb voir* **avoir**

**ajonc** [aʒɔ̃] *nm* gorse *no pl*

**ajouré, e** [aʒuʀe] *adj* openwork *cpd*

**ajournement** [aʒuʀnəmɑ̃] *nm* adjournment; deferment, postponement

**ajourner** [aʒuʀne] *vt (réunion)* to adjourn; *(décision)* to defer, postpone; *(candidat)* to refer; *(conscrit)* to defer

**ajout** [aʒu] *nm* addition; **merci pour l'~** thanks for the add

**ajouter** [aʒute] *vt* to add; **~ à** *(accroître)* to add to; **s'ajouter à** to add to; **~ que** to add that; **~ foi à** to lend *ou* give credence to

**ajustage** [aʒystaʒ] *nm* fitting

**ajusté, e** [aʒyste] *adj*: **bien ~** *(robe etc)* close-fitting

**ajustement** [aʒystəmɑ̃] *nm* adjustment

**ajuster** [aʒyste] *vt (régler)* to adjust; *(vêtement)* to alter; *(arranger)*: **~ sa cravate** to adjust one's tie; *(coup de fusil)* to aim; *(cible)* to aim at; *(adapter)*: **~ qch à** to fit sth to

**ajusteur** [aʒystœʀ] *nm* metal worker

**alaise** [alɛz] *nf* = **alèse**

**alambic** [alɑ̃bik] *nm* still

**alambiqué, e** [alɑ̃bike] *adj* convoluted, overcomplicated

**alangui, e** [alɑ̃gi] *adj* languid

**alanguir** [alɑ̃giʀ]: **s'alanguir** *vi* to grow languid

**alarmant, e** [alaʀmɑ̃, -ɑ̃t] *adj* alarming

**alarme** [alaʀm(ə)] *nf* alarm; **donner l'~** to give *ou* raise the alarm; **jeter l'~** to cause alarm

**alarmer** [alaʀme] *vt* to alarm; **s'alarmer** *vi* to become alarmed

**alarmiste** [alaʀmist(ə)] *adj* alarmist

**Alaska** [alaska] *nm*: **l'~** Alaska

**albanais, e** [albanɛ, -ɛz] *adj* Albanian ▷ *nm (Ling)* Albanian ▷ *nm/f*: **Albanais, e** Albanian

**Albanie** [albani] *nf*: **l'~** Albania

**albâtre** [albɑtʀ(ə)] *nm* alabaster

**albatros** [albatʀos] *nm* albatross

**albigeois, e** [albiʒwa, -waz] *adj* of *ou* from Albi

**albinos** [albinos] *nm/f* albino

**album** [albɔm] *nm* album; **~ à colorier** colouring book; **~ de timbres** stamp album

**albumen** [albymɛn] *nm* albumen

**albumine** [albymin] *nf* albumin; **avoir** *ou* **faire de l'~** to suffer from albuminuria

**alcalin, e** [alkalɛ̃, -in] *adj* alkaline

**alchimie** [alʃimi] *nf* alchemy

**alchimiste** [alʃimist(ə)] *nm* alchemist

**alcool** [alkɔl] *nm*: **l'~** alcohol; **un ~** a spirit, a brandy; **~ à brûler** methylated spirits *(Brit)*, wood alcohol *(US)*; **~ à 90°** surgical spirit; **~ de prune** *etc* plum *etc* brandy

**alcoolémie** [alkɔlemi] *nf* blood alcohol level

**alcoolique** [alkɔlik] *adj, nm/f* alcoholic

**alcoolisé, e** [alkɔlize] *adj* alcoholic

**alcoolisme** [alkɔlism(ə)] *nm* alcoholism

**alcootest®, alcotest®** [alkɔtɛst] *nm (objet)* Breathalyser®; *(test)* breath-test; **faire subir l'alco(o)test à qn** to Breathalyse® sb

**alcôve** [alkov] *nf* alcove, recess

**aléas** [alea] *nmpl* hazards

**aléatoire** [aleatwaʀ] *adj* uncertain; *(Inform, Statistique)* random

**alémanique** [alemanik] *adj*: **la Suisse ~** German-speaking Switzerland

**ALENA** [alena] *sigle m (= Accord de libre-échange nord-américain)* NAFTA (= *North American Free Trade Agreement)*

**alentour** [alɑ̃tuʀ] *adv* around (about); **alentours** *nmpl* surroundings; **aux ~s de** in the vicinity *ou* neighbourhood of, around about; *(temps)* around about

**alerte** [alɛʀt(ə)] *adj* agile, nimble; *(style)* brisk, lively ▷ *nf* alert; warning; **donner l'~** to give the alert; **à la première ~** at the first sign of trouble *ou* danger; **~ à la bombe** bomb scare

**alerter** [alɛʀte] *vt* to alert

**alèse** [alɛz] *nf (drap)* undersheet, drawsheet

**aléser** [aleze] *vt* to ream

**alevin** [alvɛ̃] *nm* alevin, young fish

**alevinage** [alvinaʒ] *nm* fish farming

**Alexandrie** [alɛksɑ̃dʀi] *n* Alexandria

**alexandrin** [alɛksɑ̃dʀɛ̃] *nm* alexandrine

**alezan, e** [alzɑ̃, -an] *adj* chestnut

a

**algarade** [algaʀad] *nf* row, dispute
**algèbre** [alʒɛbʀ(ə)] *nf* algebra
**algébrique** [alʒebʀik] *adj* algebraic
**Alger** [alʒe] *n* Algiers
**Algérie** [alʒeʀi] *nf*: **l'~** Algeria
**algérien, ne** [alʒeʀjɛ̃, -ɛn] *adj* Algerian ▷ *nm/f*: **Algérien, ne** Algerian
**algérois, e** [alʒeʀwa, -waz] *adj* of *ou* from Algiers ▷ *nm*: **l'A~** (*région*) the Algiers region
**algorithme** [algɔʀitm(ə)] *nm* algorithm
**algue** [alg(ə)] *nf* seaweed *no pl*
**alias** [aljas] *adv* alias
**alibi** [alibi] *nm* alibi
**aliénation** [aljenasjɔ̃] *nf* alienation
**aliéné, e** [aljene] *nm/f* insane person, lunatic (*péj*)
**aliéner** [aljene] *vt* to alienate; (*bien, liberté*) to give up; **s'aliéner** *vt* to alienate
**alignement** [aliɲmɑ̃] *nm* alignment, lining up; **à l'~** in line
**aligner** [aliɲe] *vt* to align, line up; (*idées, chiffres*) to string together; (*adapter*): **~ qch sur** to bring sth into alignment with; **s'aligner** *vi* (*soldats etc*) to line up; **s'~ sur** (*Pol*) to align o.s. with
**aliment** [alimɑ̃] *nm* food; **~ complet** whole food
**alimentaire** [alimɑ̃tɛʀ] *adj* food *cpd*; (*péj: besogne*) done merely to earn a living; **produits ~s** foodstuffs, foods
**alimentation** [alimɑ̃tasjɔ̃] *nf* feeding; supplying, supply; (*commerce*) food trade; (*produits*) groceries *pl*; (*régime*) diet; (*Inform*) feed; **~ (générale)** (general) grocer's; **~ de base** staple diet; **~ en feuilles/en continu/en papier** form/stream/sheet feed
**alimenter** [alimɑ̃te] *vt* to feed; (*Tech*): **~ (en)** to supply (with), feed (with); (*fig*) to sustain, keep going
**alinéa** [alinea] *nm* paragraph; **"nouvel ~"** "new line"
**aliter** [alite]: **s'aliter** *vi* to take to one's bed; **infirme alité** bedridden person *ou* invalid
**alizé** [alize] *adj, nm*: **(vent) ~** trade wind
**allaitement** [alɛtmɑ̃] *nm* feeding; **~ maternel/au biberon** breast-/bottle-feeding; **~ mixte** mixed feeding
**allaiter** [alɛte] *vt* (*femme*) to (breast-)feed, nurse; (*animal*) to suckle; **~ au biberon** to bottle-feed
**allant** [alɑ̃] *nm* drive, go
**alléchant, e** [aleʃɑ̃, -ɑ̃t] *adj* tempting, enticing
**allécher** [aleʃe] *vt*: **~ qn** to make sb's mouth water; to tempt sb, entice sb
**allée** [ale] *nf* (*de jardin*) path; (*en ville*) avenue, drive; **~s et venues** comings and goings
**allégation** [alegasjɔ̃] *nf* allegation
**allégé, e** [aleʒe] *adj* (*yaourt etc*) low-fat
**alléger** [aleʒe] *vt* (*voiture*) to make lighter; (*chargement*) to lighten; (*souffrance*) to alleviate, soothe
**allégorie** [alegɔʀi] *nf* allegory
**allégorique** [alegɔʀik] *adj* allegorical
**allègre** [alɛgʀ(ə)] *adj* lively, jaunty (*Brit*); (*personne*) gay, cheerful

**allégresse** [alegʀɛs] *nf* elation, gaiety
**allegretto** [al(l)egʀɛt(t)o] *adv, nm* allegretto
**allegro** [al(l)egʀo] *adv, nm* allegro
**alléguer** [alege] *vt* to put forward (as proof *ou* an excuse)
**Allemagne** [aləmaɲ] *nf*: **l'~** Germany; **l'~ de l'Est/Ouest** East/West Germany; **l'~ fédérale (RFA)** the Federal Republic of Germany (FRG)
**allemand, e** [almɑ̃, -ɑ̃d] *adj* German ▷ *nm* (*Ling*) German ▷ *nm/f*: **Allemand, e** German; **A~ de l'Est/l'Ouest** East/West German
**aller** [ale] *nm* (*trajet*) outward journey; (*billet*): **~ (simple)** single (*Brit*) *ou* one-way ticket; **~ (et) retour (AR)** (*trajet*) return trip *ou* journey (*Brit*), round trip (*US*); (*billet*) return (*Brit*) *ou* round-trip (*US*) ticket ▷ *vi* (*gén*) to go; **~ à** (*convenir*) to suit; (*forme, pointure etc*) to fit; **cela me va** (*couleur*) that suits me; (*vêtement*) that suits me; that fits me; (*projet, disposition*) that suits me, that's fine *ou* OK by me; **~ à la chasse/pêche** to go hunting/fishing; **~ avec** (*couleurs, style etc*) to go (well) with; **je vais le faire/me fâcher** I'm going to do it/to get angry; **~ voir/chercher qn** to go and see/look for sb; **comment allez-vous?** how are you?; **comment ça va?** how are you?; (*affaires etc*) how are things?; **ça va? — oui (ça va)!** how are things? — fine!; **pour ~ à** how do I get to; **ça va (comme ça)** that's fine (as it is); **il va bien/mal** he's well/not well, he's fine/ill; **ça va bien/mal** (*affaires etc*) it's going well/not going well; **tout va bien** everything's fine; **ça ne va pas!** (*mauvaise humeur etc*) that's not on!, hey, come on!; **ça ne va pas sans difficultés** it's not without difficulties; **~ mieux** to be better; **il y va de leur vie** their lives are at stake; **se laisser ~** to let o.s. go; **s'en aller** *vi* (*partir*) to be off, go, leave; (*disparaître*) to go away; **~ jusqu'à** to go as far as; **ça va de soi, ça va sans dire** that goes without saying; **tu y vas un peu fort** you're going a bit (too) far; **allez!** go on!; come on!; **allons-y!** let's go!; **allez, au revoir!** right *ou* OK then, bye-bye!
**allergène** [alɛʀʒɛn] *nm* allergen
**allergie** [alɛʀʒi] *nf* allergy
**allergique** [alɛʀʒik] *adj* allergic; **~ à** allergic to
**allez** [ale] *vb voir* **aller**
**alliage** [aljaʒ] *nm* alloy
**alliance** [aljɑ̃s] *nf* (*Mil, Pol*) alliance; (*mariage*) marriage; (*bague*) wedding ring; **neveu par ~** nephew by marriage
**allié, e** [alje] *nm/f* ally; **parents et ~s** relatives and relatives by marriage
**allier** [alje] *vt* (*métaux*) to alloy; (*Pol, gén*) to ally; (*fig*) to combine; **s'allier** *vi* to become allies; (*éléments, caractéristiques*) to combine; **s'~ à** to become allied to *ou* with
**alligator** [aligatɔʀ] *nm* alligator
**allitération** [aliteʀasjɔ̃] *nf* alliteration
**allô** [alo] *excl* hullo, hallo
**allocataire** [alɔkatɛʀ] *nm/f* beneficiary
**allocation** [alɔkasjɔ̃] *nf* allowance; **~ (de) chômage** unemployment benefit; **~ (de)**

**logement** rent allowance; **~s familiales** ≈ child benefit *no pl*; **~s de maternité** maternity allowance

**allocution** [alɔkysjɔ̃] *nf* short speech

**allongé, e** [alɔ̃ʒe] *adj* (*étendu*): **être ~** to be stretched out *ou* lying down; (*long*) long; (*étiré*) elongated; (*oblong*) oblong; **rester ~** to be lying down; **mine ~e** long face

**allonger** [alɔ̃ʒe] *vt* to lengthen, make longer; (*étendre: bras, jambe*) to stretch (out); (*sauce*) to spin out, make go further; **s'allonger** *vi* to get longer; (*se coucher*) to lie down, stretch out; **~ le pas** to hasten one's step(s)

**allouer** [alwe] *vt*: **~ qch à** to allocate sth to, allot sth to

**allumage** [alymaʒ] *nm* (*Auto*) ignition

**allume-cigare** [alymsigaʀ] *nm inv* cigar lighter

**allume-gaz** [alymgɑz] *nm inv* gas lighter

**allumer** [alyme] *vt* (*lampe, phare, radio*) to put *ou* switch on; (*pièce*) to put *ou* switch the light(s) on in; (*feu, bougie, cigare, pipe, gaz*) to light; (*chauffage*) to put on; **s'allumer** *vi* (*lumière, lampe*) to come *ou* go on; **~ (la lumière** *ou* **l'électricité)** to put on the light

**allumette** [alymɛt] *nf* match; (*morceau de bois*) matchstick; (*Culin*): **~ au fromage** cheese straw; **~ de sûreté** safety match

**allumeuse** [alymøz] *nf* (*péj*) tease (*woman*)

**allure** [alyʀ] *nf* (*vitesse*) speed; (: *à pied*) pace; (*démarche*) walk; (*maintien*) bearing; (*aspect, air*) look; **avoir de l'~** to have style *ou* a certain elegance; **à toute ~** at top *ou* full speed

**allusion** [alyzjɔ̃] *nf* allusion; (*sous-entendu*) hint; **faire ~ à** to allude *ou* refer to; to hint at

**alluvions** [alyvjɔ̃] *nfpl* alluvial deposits, alluvium *sg*

**almanach** [almana] *nm* almanac

**aloès** [alɔɛs] *nm* (*Bot*) aloe

**aloi** [alwa] *nm*: **de bon/mauvais ~** of genuine/ doubtful worth *ou* quality

⬤ MOT-CLÉ

**alors** [alɔʀ] *adv* **1** (*à ce moment-là*) then, at that time; **il habitait alors à Paris** he lived in Paris at that time; **jusqu'alors** up till *ou* until then
**2** (*par conséquent*) then; **tu as fini? alors je m'en vais** have you finished? I'm going then
**3** (*expressions*): **alors? quoi de neuf?** well *ou* so? what's new?; **et alors?** so (what)?; **ça alors!** (well) really!
▷ *conj*: **alors que 1** (*au moment où*) when, as; **il est arrivé alors que je partais** he arrived as I was leaving
**2** (*pendant que*) while, when; **alors qu'il était à Paris, il a visité ...** while *ou* when he was in Paris, he visited ...
**3** (*tandis que*) whereas, while; **alors que son frère travaillait dur, lui se reposait** while his brother was working hard, HE would rest

**alouette** [alwɛt] *nf* (sky)lark

**alourdir** [aluʀdiʀ] *vt* to weigh down, make heavy; **s'alourdir** *vi* to grow heavy *ou* heavier

**aloyau** [alwajo] *nm* sirloin

**alpaga** [alpaga] *nm* (*tissu*) alpaca

**alpage** [alpaʒ] *nm* high mountain pasture

**Alpes** [alp(ə)] *nfpl*: **les ~** the Alps

**alpestre** [alpɛstʀ(ə)] *adj* alpine

**alphabet** [alfabɛ] *nm* alphabet; (*livre*) ABC (book), primer

**alphabétique** [alfabetik] *adj* alphabetic(al); **par ordre ~** in alphabetical order

**alphabétisation** [alfabetizɑsjɔ̃] *nf* literacy teaching

**alphabétiser** [alfabetize] *vt* to teach to read and write; (*pays*) to eliminate illiteracy in

**alphanumérique** [alfanymeʀik] *adj* alphanumeric

**alpin, e** [alpɛ̃, -in] *adj* (*plante etc*) alpine; (*club*) climbing

**alpinisme** [alpinism(ə)] *nm* mountaineering, climbing

**alpiniste** [alpinist(ə)] *nm/f* mountaineer, climber

**Alsace** [alzas] *nf*: **l'~** Alsace

**alsacien, ne** [alzasjɛ̃, -ɛn] *adj* Alsatian

**altercation** [altɛʀkɑsjɔ̃] *nf* altercation

**alter ego** [altɛʀego] *nm* alter ego

**altérer** [alteʀe] *vt* (*faits, vérité*) to falsify, distort; (*qualité*) to debase, impair; (*données*) to corrupt; (*donner soif à*) to make thirsty; **s'altérer** *vi* to deteriorate; to spoil

**altermondialisme** [altɛʀmɔ̃djalism] *nm* anti-globalism

**altermondialiste** [altɛʀmɔ̃djalist] *adj, nm/f* anti-globalist

**alternance** [altɛʀnɑ̃s] *nf* alternation; **en ~** alternately; **formation en ~** sandwich course

**alternateur** [altɛʀnatœʀ] *nm* alternator

**alternatif, -ive** [altɛʀnatif, -iv] *adj* alternating ▷ *nf* alternative

**alternativement** [altɛʀnativmɑ̃] *adv* alternately

**alterner** [altɛʀne] *vt* to alternate ▷ *vi*: **~ (avec)** to alternate (with); **(faire) ~ qch avec qch** to alternate sth with sth

**Altesse** [altɛs] *nf* Highness

**altier, -ière** [altje, -jɛʀ] *adj* haughty

**altimètre** [altimɛtʀ(ə)] *nm* altimeter

**altiport** [altipɔʀ] *nm* mountain airfield

**altiste** [altist(ə)] *nm/f* viola player, violist

**altitude** [altityd] *nf* altitude, height; **à 1000 m d'~** at a height *ou* an altitude of 1000 m; **en ~** at high altitudes; **perdre/prendre de l'~** to lose/ gain height; **voler à haute/basse ~** to fly at a high/low altitude

**alto** [alto] *nm* (*instrument*) viola ▷ *nf* (*contr*)alto

**altruisme** [altʀɥism(ə)] *nm* altruism

**altruiste** [altʀɥist(ə)] *adj* altruistic

**aluminium** [alyminjɔm] *nm* aluminium (*Brit*), aluminum (*US*)

**alun** [alœ̃] *nm* alum

**alunir** [alyniʀ] *vi* to land on the moon

a

15

**alunissage** [alynisaʒ] nm (moon) landing
**alvéole** [alveɔl] nm ou f (de ruche) alveolus
**alvéolé, e** [alveɔle] adj honeycombed
**AM** sigle f = **assurance maladie**
**amabilité** [amabilite] nf kindness; **il a eu l'~ de**
he was kind ou good enough to
**amadou** [amadu] nm touchwood, amadou
**amadouer** [amadwe] vt to coax, cajole; (adoucir)
to mollify, soothe
**amaigrir** [amegʀiʀ] vt to make thin ou thinner
**amaigrissant, e** [amegʀisɑ̃, -ɑ̃t] adj: **régime ~**
slimming (Brit) ou weight-reduction (US) diet
**amalgame** [amalgam] nm amalgam; (fig: de
gens, d'idées) hotch-potch, mixture
**amalgamer** [amalgame] vt to amalgamate
**amande** [amɑ̃d] nf (de l'amandier) almond; (de
noyau de fruit) kernel; **en ~** (yeux) almond cpd,
almond-shaped
**amandier** [amɑ̃dje] nm almond (tree)
**amanite** [amanit] nf (Bot) mushroom of the genus
Amanita; **~ tue-mouches** fly agaric
**amant** [amɑ̃] nm lover
**amarre** [amaʀ] nf (Navig) (mooring) rope ou line;
**amarres** nfpl moorings
**amarrer** [amaʀe] vt (Navig) to moor; (gén) to
make fast
**amaryllis** [amaʀilis] nf amaryllis
**amas** [amɑ] nm heap, pile
**amasser** [amɑse] vt to amass; **s'amasser** vi to
pile up, accumulate; (foule) to gather
**amateur** [amatœʀ] nm amateur; **en ~** (péj)
amateurishly; **musicien/sportif ~** amateur
musician/sportsman; **~ de musique/sport** etc
music/sport etc lover
**amateurisme** [amatœʀism(ə)] nm
amateurism; (péj) amateurishness
**Amazone** [amazɔn] nf: **l'~** the Amazon
**amazone** [amazɔn] nf horsewoman; **en ~** sidesaddle
**Amazonie** [amazɔni] nf: **l'~** Amazonia
**ambages** [ɑ̃baʒ]: **sans ~** adv without beating
about the bush, plainly
**ambassade** [ɑ̃basad] nf embassy; (mission): **en ~**
on a mission
**ambassadeur, -drice** [ɑ̃basadœʀ, -dʀis] nm/f
ambassador/ambassadress
**ambiance** [ɑ̃bjɑ̃s] nf atmosphere; **il y a de l'~**
everyone's having a good time
**ambiant, e** [ɑ̃bjɑ̃, -ɑ̃t] adj (air, milieu)
surrounding; (température) ambient
**ambidextre** [ɑ̃bidɛkstʀ(ə)] adj ambidextrous
**ambigu, ë** [ɑ̃bigy] adj ambiguous
**ambiguïté** [ɑ̃biguite] nf ambiguousness no pl,
ambiguity
**ambitieux, -euse** [ɑ̃bisjø, -øz] adj ambitious
**ambition** [ɑ̃bisjɔ̃] nf ambition
**ambitionner** [ɑ̃bisjɔne] vt to have as one's aim
ou ambition
**ambivalent, e** [ɑ̃bivalɑ̃, -ɑ̃t] adj ambivalent
**amble** [ɑ̃bl(ə)] nm: **aller l'~** to amble
**ambre** [ɑ̃bʀ(ə)] nm: **~ (jaune)** amber; **~ gris**
ambergris

**ambré, e** [ɑ̃bʀe] adj (couleur) amber; (parfum)
ambergris-scented
**ambulance** [ɑ̃bylɑ̃s] nf ambulance
**ambulancier, -ière** [ɑ̃bylɑ̃sje, -jɛʀ] nm/f
ambulanceman/woman (Brit), paramedic (US)
**ambulant, e** [ɑ̃bylɑ̃, -ɑ̃t] adj travelling,
itinerant
**âme** [ɑm] nf soul; **rendre l'~** to give up the
ghost; **bonne ~** (aussi ironique) kind soul; **un
joueur/tricheur dans l'~** a gambler/cheat
through and through; **~ sœur** kindred spirit
**amélioration** [ameljɔʀasjɔ̃] nf improvement
**améliorer** [ameljɔʀe] vt to improve;
**s'améliorer** vi to improve, get better
**aménagement** [amenaʒmɑ̃] nm fitting out;
laying out; development; **aménagements** nmpl
developments; **l'~ du territoire** = town and
country planning; **~s fiscaux** tax adjustments
**aménager** [amenaʒe] vt (agencer: espace, local) to
fit out; (: terrain) to lay out; (: quartier, territoire) to
develop; (installer) to fix up, put in; **ferme
aménagée** converted farmhouse
**amende** [amɑ̃d] nf fine; **mettre à l'~** to
penalize; **faire ~ honorable** to make amends
**amendement** [amɑ̃dmɑ̃] nm (Jur) amendment
**amender** [amɑ̃de] vt (loi) to amend; (terre) to
enrich; **s'amender** vi to mend one's ways
**amène** [amɛn] adj affable; **peu ~** unkind
**amener** [amne] vt to bring; (causer) to bring
about; (baisser: drapeau, voiles) to strike; **s'amener**
vi (fam) to show up, turn up; **~ qn à qch/à faire**
to lead sb to sth/to do
**amenuiser** [amənɥize]: **s'amenuiser** vi to
dwindle; (chances) to grow slimmer, lessen
**amer, amère** [amɛʀ] adj bitter
**amèrement** [amɛʀmɑ̃] adv bitterly
**américain, e** [ameʀikɛ̃, -ɛn] adj American ▷ nm
(Ling) American (English) ▷ nm/f: **Américain, e**
American; **en vedette ~e** as a special guest
(star)
**américaniser** [ameʀikanize] vt to Americanize
**américanisme** [ameʀikanism(ə)] nm
Americanism
**amérindien, ne** [ameʀɛ̃djɛ̃, -ɛn] adj
Amerindian, American Indian
**Amérique** [ameʀik] nf America; **l'~ centrale**
Central America; **l'~ latine** Latin America; **l'~
du Nord** North America; **l'~ du Sud** South
America
**Amerloque** [amɛʀlɔk] nm/f (fam) Yank, Yankee
**amerrir** [ameʀiʀ] vi to land (on the sea); (capsule
spatiale) to splash down
**amerrissage** [ameʀisaʒ] nm landing (on the
sea); splash-down
**amertume** [amɛʀtym] nf bitterness
**améthyste** [ametist(ə)] nf amethyst
**ameublement** [amœbləmɑ̃] nm furnishing;
(meubles) furniture; **articles d'~** furnishings;
**tissus d'~** soft furnishings, furnishing fabrics
**ameuter** [amøte] vt (badauds) to draw a crowd
of; (peuple) to rouse, stir up
**ami, e** [ami] nm/f friend; (amant/maîtresse)

boyfriend/girlfriend ▷ adj: **pays/groupe ~** friendly country/group; **être (très) ~ avec qn** to be (very) friendly with sb; **être ~ de l'ordre** to be a lover of order; **un ~ des arts** a patron of the arts; **un ~ des chiens** a dog lover; **petit ~/ petite ~e** (fam) boyfriend/girlfriend

**amiable** [amjabl(ə)]: **à l'~** adv (Jur) out of court; (gén) amicably

**amiante** [amjɑ̃t] nm asbestos

**amibe** [amib] nf amoeba

**amical, e, -aux** [amikal, -o] adj friendly ▷ nf (club) association

**amicalement** [amikalmɑ̃] adv in a friendly way; (formule épistolaire) regards

**amidon** [amidɔ̃] nm starch

**amidonner** [amidɔne] vt to starch

**amincir** [amɛ̃siʀ] vt (objet) to thin (down); **s'amincir** vi to get thinner ou slimmer; **~ qn** to make sb thinner ou slimmer

**amincissant, e** [amɛ̃sisɑ̃, -ɑ̃t] adj slimming

**aminé, e** [amine] adj: **acide ~** amino acid

**amiral, -aux** [amiʀal, -o] nm admiral

**amirauté** [amiʀote] nf admiralty

**amitié** [amitje] nf friendship; **prendre en ~ to** take a liking to; **faire** ou **présenter ses ~s à qn** to send sb one's best wishes; **~s** (formule épistolaire) (with) best wishes

**ammoniac** [amɔnjak] nm: **(gaz) ~** ammonia

**ammoniaque** [amɔnjak] nf ammonia (water)

**amnésie** [amnezi] nf amnesia

**amnésique** [amnezik] adj amnesic

**Amnesty International** [amnɛsti-] n Amnesty International

**amniocentèse** [amnjosɛ̃tɛz] nf amniocentesis

**amnistie** [amnisti] nf amnesty

**amnistier** [amnistje] vt to amnesty

**amocher** [amɔʃe] vt (fam) to mess up

**amoindrir** [amwɛ̃dʀiʀ] vt to reduce

**amollir** [amɔliʀ] vt to soften

**amonceler** [amɔ̃sle] vt: **s'amonceler** to pile ou heap up; (fig) to accumulate

**amoncellement** [amɔ̃sɛlmɑ̃] nm piling ou heaping up; accumulation; (tas) pile, heap, accumulation

**amont** [amɔ̃]: **en ~** adv upstream; (sur une pente) uphill; **en ~ de** prép upstream from; uphill from, above

**amoral, e, -aux** [amɔʀal, -o] adj amoral

**amorce** [amɔʀs(ə)] nf (sur un hameçon) bait; (explosif) cap; (tube) primer; (: contenu) priming; (fig: début) beginning(s), start

**amorcer** [amɔʀse] vt to bait; to prime; (commencer) to begin, start

**amorphe** [amɔʀf(ə)] adj passive, lifeless

**amortir** [amɔʀtiʀ] vt (atténuer: choc) to absorb, cushion; (bruit, douleur) to deaden; (Comm: dette) to pay off, amortize; (: mise de fonds, matériel) to write off; **~ un abonnement** to make a season ticket pay (for itself)

**amortissable** [amɔʀtisabl(ə)] adj (Comm) that can be paid off

**amortissement** [amɔʀtismɑ̃] nm (de matériel)

writing off; (d'une dette) paying off

**amortisseur** [amɔʀtisœʀ] nm shock absorber

**amour** [amuʀ] nm love; (liaison) love affair, love; (statuette etc) cupid; **un ~ de** a lovely little; **faire l'~** to make love

**amouracher** [amuʀaʃe]: **s'amouracher de** vt (péj) to become infatuated with

**amourette** [amuʀɛt] nf passing fancy

**amoureusement** [amuʀøzmɑ̃] adv lovingly

**amoureux, -euse** [amuʀø, -øz] adj (regard, tempérament) amorous; (vie, problèmes) love cpd; (personne): **~ (de qn)** in love (with sb) ▷ nm/f lover ▷ nmpl courting couple(s); **tomber ~ de qn** to fall in love with sb; **être ~ de qch** to be passionately fond of sth; **un ~ de la nature** a nature lover

**amour-propre** [amuʀpʀɔpʀ(ə)] (pl **amours-propres**) nm self-esteem

**amovible** [amɔvibl(ə)] adj removable, detachable

**ampère** [ɑ̃pɛʀ] nm amp(ere)

**ampèremètre** [ɑ̃pɛʀmɛtʀ(ə)] nm ammeter

**amphétamine** [ɑ̃fetamin] nf amphetamine

**amphi** [ɑ̃fi] nm (Scol fam: = amphithéâtre) lecture hall ou theatre

**amphibie** [ɑ̃fibi] adj amphibious

**amphibien** [ɑ̃fibjɛ̃] nm (Zool) amphibian

**amphithéâtre** [ɑ̃fiteatʀ(ə)] nm amphitheatre; (d'université) lecture hall ou theatre

**amphore** [ɑ̃fɔʀ] nf amphora

**ample** [ɑ̃pl(ə)] adj (vêtement) roomy, ample; (gestes, mouvement) broad; (ressources) ample; **jusqu'à plus ~ informé** (Admin) until further details are available

**amplement** [ɑ̃pləmɑ̃] adv amply; **~ suffisant** ample, more than enough

**ampleur** [ɑ̃plœʀ] nf scale, size; extent, magnitude

**ampli** [ɑ̃pli] nm (fam: = amplificateur) amplifier, amp

**amplificateur** [ɑ̃plifikatœʀ] nm amplifier

**amplification** [ɑ̃plifikasjɔ̃] nf amplification; expansion, increase

**amplifier** [ɑ̃plifje] vt (son, oscillation) to amplify; (fig) to expand, increase

**amplitude** [ɑ̃plityd] nf amplitude; (des températures) range

**ampoule** [ɑ̃pul] nf (électrique) bulb; (de médicament) phial; (aux mains, pieds) blister

**ampoulé, e** [ɑ̃pule] adj (péj) pompous, bombastic

**amputation** [ɑ̃pytasjɔ̃] nf amputation

**amputer** [ɑ̃pyte] vt (Méd) to amputate; (fig) to cut ou reduce drastically; **~ qn d'un bras/pied** to amputate sb's arm/foot

**Amsterdam** [amstɛʀdam] n Amsterdam

**amulette** [amylɛt] nf amulet

**amusant, e** [amyzɑ̃, -ɑ̃t] adj (divertissant, spirituel) entertaining, amusing; (comique) funny, amusing

**amusé, e** [amyze] adj amused

**amuse-gueule** [amyzgœl] nm inv appetizer,

**a**

17

snack

**amusement** [amyzmɑ̃] nm (voir amusé) amusement; (voir amuser) entertaining, amusing; (jeu etc) pastime, diversion

**amuser** [amyze] vt (divertir) to entertain, amuse; (égayer, faire rire) to amuse; (détourner l'attention de) to distract; **s'amuser** vi (jouer) to amuse o.s., play; (se divertir) to enjoy o.s., have fun; (fig) to mess around; **s'~ de qch** (trouver comique) to find sth amusing; **s'~ avec** ou **de qn** (duper) to make a fool of sb

**amusette** [amyzɛt] nf idle pleasure, trivial pastime

**amuseur** [amyzœʀ] nm entertainer; (péj) clown

**amygdale** [amidal] nf tonsil; **opérer qn des ~s** to take sb's tonsils out

**amygdalite** [amidalit] nf tonsillitis

**AN** sigle f = **Assemblée nationale**

**an** [ɑ̃] nm year; **être âgé de** ou **avoir 3 ans** to be 3 (years old); **en l'an 1980** in the year 1980; **le jour de l'an, le premier de l'an, le nouvel an** New Year's Day

**anabolisant** [anabɔlizɑ̃] nm anabolic steroid

**anachronique** [anakʀɔnik] adj anachronistic

**anachronisme** [anakʀɔnism(ə)] nm anachronism

**anaconda** [anakɔ̃da] nm (Zool) anaconda

**anaérobie** [anaeʀɔbi] adj anaerobic

**anagramme** [anagʀam] nf anagram

**ANAH** sigle f = **Agence nationale pour l'amélioration de l'habitat**

**anal, e, -aux** [anal, -o] adj anal

**analgésique** [analʒezik] nm analgesic

**anallergique** [analɛʀʒik] adj hypoallergenic

**analogie** [analɔʒi] nf analogy

**analogique** [analɔʒik] adj (Logique: raisonnement) analogical; (calculateur, montre etc) analogue; (Inform) analog

**analogue** [analɔg] adj: **~ (à)** analogous (to), similar (to)

**analphabète** [analfabɛt] nm/f illiterate

**analphabétisme** [analfabetism(ə)] nm illiteracy

**analyse** [analiz] nf analysis; (Méd) test; **faire l'~ de** to analyse; **une ~ approfondie** an indepth analysis; **en dernière ~** in the last analysis; **avoir l'esprit d'~** to have an analytical turn of mind; **~ grammaticale** grammatical analysis, parsing (Scol)

**analyser** [analize] vt to analyse; (Méd) to test

**analyste** [analist(ə)] nm/f analyst; (psychanalyste) (psycho)analyst

**analyste-programmeur, -euse** [analist-] (pl **analystes-programmeurs, -euses**) nm/f systems analyst

**analytique** [analitik] adj analytical

**analytiquement** [analitikmɑ̃] adv analytically

**ananas** [anana] nm pineapple

**anarchie** [anaʀʃi] nf anarchy

**anarchique** [anaʀʃik] adj anarchic

**anarchisme** [anaʀʃism(ə)] nm anarchism

**anarchiste** [anaʀʃist(ə)] adj anarchistic ▷ nm/f anarchist

**anathème** [anatɛm] nm: **jeter l'~ sur, lancer l'~ contre** to anathematize, curse

**anatomie** [anatɔmi] nf anatomy

**anatomique** [anatɔmik] adj anatomical

**ancestral, e, -aux** [ɑ̃sɛstʀal, -o] adj ancestral

**ancêtre** [ɑ̃sɛtʀ(ə)] nm/f ancestor; (fig): **l'~ de** the forerunner of

**anche** [ɑ̃ʃ] nf reed

**anchois** [ɑ̃ʃwa] nm anchovy

**ancien, ne** [ɑ̃sjɛ̃, -ɛn] adj old; (de jadis, de l'antiquité) ancient; (précédent, ex-) former, old ▷ nm (mobilier ancien): **l'~** antiques pl ▷ nm/f (dans une tribu etc) elder; **un ~ ministre** a former minister; **mon ~ne voiture** my previous car; **être plus ~ que qn dans une maison** to have been in a firm longer than sb; (dans la hiérarchie) to be senior to sb in a firm; **~ combattant** exserviceman; **~ (élève)** (Scol) ex-pupil (Brit), alumnus (US)

**anciennement** [ɑ̃sjɛnmɑ̃] adv formerly

**ancienneté** [ɑ̃sjɛnte] nf oldness; antiquity; (Admin) (length of) service; seniority

**ancrage** [ɑ̃kʀaʒ] nm anchoring; (Navig) anchorage; (Constr) anchor

**ancre** [ɑ̃kʀ(ə)] nf anchor; **jeter/lever l'~** to cast/weigh anchor; **à l'~** at anchor

**ancrer** [ɑ̃kʀe] vt (Constr) to anchor; (fig) to fix firmly; **s'ancrer** vi (Navig) to (cast) anchor

**andalou, -ouse** [ɑ̃dalu, -uz] adj Andalusian

**Andalousie** [ɑ̃daluzi] nf: **l'~** Andalusia

**andante** [ɑ̃dɑ̃t] adv, nm andante

**Andes** [ɑ̃d] nfpl: **les ~** the Andes

**Andorre** [ɑ̃dɔʀ] nf Andorra

**andouille** [ɑ̃duj] nf (Culin) sausage made of chitterlings; (fam) clot, nit

**andouillette** [ɑ̃dujɛt] nf small andouille

**âne** [ɑn] nm donkey, ass; (péj) dunce, fool

**anéantir** [aneɑ̃tiʀ] vt to annihilate, wipe out; (fig) to obliterate, destroy; (déprimer) to overwhelm

**anecdote** [anɛkdɔt] nf anecdote

**anecdotique** [anɛkdɔtik] adj anecdotal

**anémie** [anemi] nf anaemia

**anémié, e** [anemje] adj anaemic; (fig) enfeebled

**anémique** [anemik] adj anaemic

**anémone** [anemɔn] nf anemone; **~ de mer** sea anemone

**ânerie** [ɑnʀi] nf stupidity; (parole etc) stupid ou idiotic comment etc

**anéroïde** [aneʀɔid] adj voir **baromètre**

**ânesse** [ɑnɛs] nf she-ass

**anesthésie** [anɛstezi] nf anaesthesia; **sous ~** under anaesthetic; **~ générale/locale** general/local anaesthetic; **faire une ~ locale à qn** to give sb a local anaesthetic

**anesthésier** [anɛstezje] vt to anaesthetize

**anesthésique** [anɛstezik] adj anaesthetic

**anesthésiste** [anɛstezist(ə)] nm/f anaesthetist

**anfractuosité** [ɑ̃fʀaktɥozite] nf crevice

**ange** [ɑ̃ʒ] nm angel; **être aux ~s** to be over the moon; **~ gardien** guardian angel

**angélique** [ãʒelik] *adj* angelic(al) ▷ *nf* angelica
**angelot** [ãʒlo] *nm* cherub
**angélus** [ãʒelys] *nm* angelus; *(cloches)* evening bells *pl*
**angevin, e** [ãʒvɛ̃, -in] *adj* of *ou* from Anjou; of *ou* from Angers
**angine** [ãʒin] *nf* sore throat, throat infection; **~ de poitrine** angina (pectoris)
**angiome** [ãʒjom] *nm* angioma
**anglais, e** [ãglɛ, -ɛz] *adj* English ▷ *nm* (*Ling*) English ▷ *nm/f*: **Anglais, e** Englishman/woman; **les A~** the English; **filer à l'~e** to take French leave; **à l'~e** (*Culin*) boiled
**anglaises** [ãglɛz] *nfpl* (*cheveux*) ringlets
**angle** [ãgl(ə)] *nm* angle; (*coin*) corner; **~ droit/obtus/aigu/mort** right/obtuse/acute/dead angle
**Angleterre** [ãglətɛʀ] *nf*: **l'~** England
**anglican, e** [ãglikã, -an] *adj, nm/f* Anglican
**anglicanisme** [ãglikanism(ə)] *nm* Anglicanism
**anglicisme** [ãglisism(ə)] *nm* anglicism
**angliciste** [ãglisist(ə)] *nm/f* English scholar; (*étudiant*) student of English
**anglo...** [ãglɔ] *préfixe* Anglo-, anglo(-)
**anglo-américain, e** [ãglɔamerikɛ̃, -ɛn] *adj* Anglo-American ▷ *nm* (*Ling*) American English
**anglo-arabe** [ãglɔaʀab] *adj* Anglo-Arab
**anglo-canadien, ne** [ãglɔkanadjɛ̃, -ɛn] *adj* Anglo-Canadian ▷ *nm* (*Ling*) Canadian English
**anglo-normand, e** [ãglɔnɔʀmã, -ãd] *adj* Anglo-Norman; **les îles ~es** the Channel Islands
**anglophile** [ãglɔfil] *adj* anglophilic
**anglophobe** [ãglɔfɔb] *adj* anglophobic
**anglophone** [ãglɔfɔn] *adj* English-speaking
**anglo-saxon, ne** [ãglɔsaksɔ̃, -ɔn] *adj* Anglo-Saxon
**angoissant, e** [ãgwasã, -ãt] *adj* harrowing
**angoisse** [ãgwas] *nf*: **l'~** anguish *no pl*
**angoissé, e** [ãgwase] *adj* anguished; (*personne*) full of anxieties *ou* hang-ups (*fam*)
**angoisser** [ãgwase] *vt* to harrow, cause anguish to ▷ *vi* to worry, fret
**Angola** [ãgɔla] *nm*: **l'~** Angola
**angolais, e** [ãgɔlɛ, -ɛz] *adj* Angolan
**angora** [ãgɔʀa] *adj, nm* angora
**anguille** [ãgij] *nf* eel; **~ de mer** conger (eel); **il y a ~ sous roche** (*fig*) there's something going on, there's something beneath all this
**angulaire** [ãgylɛʀ] *adj* angular
**anguleux, -euse** [ãgylø, -øz] *adj* angular
**anhydride** [anidʀid] *nm* anhydride
**anicroche** [anikʀɔʃ] *nf* hitch, snag
**animal, e, -aux** [animal, -o] *adj, nm* animal; **~ domestique/sauvage** domestic/wild animal
**animalier** [animalje] *adj*: **peintre ~** animal painter
**animateur, -trice** [animatœʀ, -tʀis] *nm/f* (*de télévision*) host; (*de music-hall*) compère; (*de groupe*) leader, organizer; (*Ciné: technicien*) animator
**animation** [animasjɔ̃] *nf* (*voir animé*) busyness; liveliness; (*Ciné: technique*) animation; **animations** *nfpl* (*activité*) activities; **centre d'~**

≈ community centre
**animé, e** [anime] *adj* (*rue, lieu*) busy, lively; (*conversation, réunion*) lively, animated; (*opposé à inanimé, aussi Ling*) animate
**animer** [anime] *vt* (*ville, soirée*) to liven up, enliven; (*mettre en mouvement*) to drive; (*stimuler*) to drive, impel; **s'animer** *vi* to liven up, come to life
**animosité** [animozite] *nf* animosity
**anis** [ani] *nm* (*Culin*) aniseed; (*Bot*) anise
**anisette** [anizɛt] *nf* anisette
**Ankara** [ãkaʀa] *n* Ankara
**ankyloser** [ãkiloze]: **s'ankyloser** *vi* to get stiff
**annales** [anal] *nfpl* annals
**anneau, x** [ano] *nm* ring; (*de chaîne*) link; (*Sport*): **exercices aux ~x** ring exercises
**année** [ane] *nf* year; **souhaiter la bonne ~ à qn** to wish sb a Happy New Year; **tout au long de l'~** all year long; **d'une ~ à l'autre** from one year to the next; **d'~ en ~** from year to year; **l'~ scolaire/fiscale** the school/tax year
**année-lumière** [anelymjɛʀ] (*pl* **années-lumières**) *nf* light year
**annexe** [anɛks(ə)] *adj* (*problème*) related; (*document*) appended; (*salle*) adjoining ▷ *nf* (*bâtiment*) annex(e); (*de document, ouvrage*) annex, appendix; (*jointe à une lettre, un dossier*) enclosure
**annexer** [anɛkse] *vt* to annex; **s'annexer** (*pays*) to annex; **~ qch à** (*joindre*) to append sth to
**annexion** [anɛksjɔ̃] *nf* annexation
**annihiler** [aniile] *vt* to annihilate
**anniversaire** [anivɛʀsɛʀ] *nm* birthday; (*d'un événement, bâtiment*) anniversary ▷ *adj*: **jour ~** anniversary
**annonce** [anɔ̃s] *nf* announcement; (*signe, indice*) sign; (*aussi*: **annonce publicitaire**) advertisement; (*Cartes*) declaration; **~ personnelle** personal message; **les petites ~s** the small *ou* classified ads
**annoncer** [anɔ̃se] *vt* to announce; (*être le signe de*) to herald; (*Cartes*) to declare; **je vous annonce que ...** I wish to tell you that ...; **s'annoncer bien/difficile** *vi* to look promising/difficult; **~ la couleur** (*fig*) to lay one's cards on the table
**annonceur, -euse** [anɔ̃sœʀ, -øz] *nm/f* (*TV, Radio: speaker*) announcer; (*publicitaire*) advertiser
**annonciateur, -trice** [anɔ̃sjatœʀ, -tʀis] *adj*: **~ d'un événement** presaging an event
**Annonciation** [anɔ̃sjasjɔ̃] *nf*: **l'~** (*Rel*) the Annunciation; (*jour*) Annunciation Day
**annotation** [anɔtasjɔ̃] *nf* annotation
**annoter** [anɔte] *vt* to annotate
**annuaire** [anɥɛʀ] *nm* yearbook, annual; **~ téléphonique** (telephone) directory, phone book
**annuel, le** [anɥɛl] *adj* annual, yearly
**annuellement** [anɥɛlmã] *adv* annually, yearly
**annuité** [anɥite] *nf* annual instalment
**annulaire** [anɥlɛʀ] *nm* ring *ou* third finger
**annulation** [anylasjɔ̃] *nf* cancellation; annulment; quashing, repeal

19

**annuler** [anyle] vt (rendez-vous, voyage) to cancel, call off; (mariage) to annul; (jugement) to quash (Brit), repeal (US); (résultats) to declare void; (Math, Physique) to cancel out; **s'annuler** to cancel each other out

**anoblir** [anɔbliʀ] vt to ennoble

**anode** [anɔd] nf anode

**anodin, e** [anɔdɛ̃, -in] adj harmless; (sans importance) insignificant, trivial

**anomalie** [anɔmali] nf anomaly

**ânon** [anɔ̃] nm baby donkey; (petit âne) little donkey

**ânonner** [anɔne] vi, vt to read in a drone; (hésiter) to read in a fumbling manner

**anonymat** [anɔnima] nm anonymity; **garder l'~** to remain anonymous

**anonyme** [anɔnim] adj anonymous; (fig) impersonal

**anonymement** [anɔnimmɑ̃] adv anonymously

**anorak** [anɔʀak] nm anorak

**anorexie** [anɔʀɛksi] nf anorexia

**anorexique** [anɔʀɛksi] adj, nm/f anorexic

**anormal, e, -aux** [anɔʀmal, -o] adj abnormal; (insolite) unusual, abnormal

**anormalement** [anɔʀmalmɑ̃] adv abnormally; unusually

**ANPE** sigle f (= Agence nationale pour l'emploi) national employment agency (functions include job creation)

**anse** [ɑ̃s] nf handle; (Géo) cove

**antagonisme** [ɑ̃tagɔnism(ə)] nm antagonism

**antagoniste** [ɑ̃tagɔnist(ə)] adj antagonistic ▷ nm antagonist

**antan** [ɑ̃tɑ̃]: **d'~** adj of yesteryear, of long ago

**antarctique** [ɑ̃taʀktik] adj Antarctic ▷ nm: **l'A~** the Antarctic; **le cercle A~** the Antarctic Circle; **l'océan A~** the Antarctic Ocean

**antécédent** [ɑ̃tesedɑ̃] nm (Ling) antecedent; **antécédents** nmpl (Méd etc) past history sg; **~s professionnels** record, career to date

**antédiluvien, ne** [ɑ̃tedilyvjɛ̃, -ɛn] adj (fig) ancient, antediluvian

**antenne** [ɑ̃tɛn] nf (de radio, télévision) aerial; (d'insecte) antenna (pl -ae), feeler; (poste avancé) outpost; (petite succursale) sub-branch; **sur l'~** on the air; **passer à/avoir l'~** to go/be on the air; **deux heures d'~** two hours' broadcasting time; **hors ~** off the air; **~ chirurgicale** (Mil) advance surgical unit

**antépénultième** [ɑ̃tepenyltjɛm] adj antepenultimate

**antérieur, e** [ɑ̃teʀjœʀ] adj (d'avant) previous, earlier; (de devant) front; **~ à** prior ou previous to; **passé/futur ~** (Ling) past/future anterior

**antérieurement** [ɑ̃teʀjœʀmɑ̃] adv earlier; (précédemment) previously; **~ à** prior ou previous to

**antériorité** [ɑ̃teʀjɔʀite] nf precedence (in time)

**anthologie** [ɑ̃tɔlɔʒi] nf anthology

**anthracite** [ɑ̃tʀasit] nm anthracite ▷ adj: **(gris) ~ charcoal (grey)**

**anthropologie** [ɑ̃tʀɔpɔlɔʒi] nf anthropology

**anthropologue** [ɑ̃tʀɔpɔlɔg] nm/f

anthropologist

**anthropomorphisme** [ɑ̃tʀɔpɔmɔʀfism(ə)] nm anthropomorphism

**anthropophage** [ɑ̃tʀɔpɔfaʒ] adj cannibalistic

**anthropophagie** [ɑ̃tʀɔpɔfaʒi] nf cannibalism, anthropophagy

**anti...** [ɑ̃ti] préfixe anti...

**antiaérien, ne** [ɑ̃tiaeʀjɛ̃, -ɛn] adj anti-aircraft; **abri ~** air-raid shelter

**antialcoolique** [ɑ̃tialkɔlik] adj anti-alcohol; **ligue ~** temperance league

**antiatomique** [ɑ̃tiatɔmik] adj: **abri ~** fallout shelter

**antibiotique** [ɑ̃tibjɔtik] nm antibiotic

**antibrouillard** [ɑ̃tibʀujaʀ] adj: **phare ~** fog lamp

**antibruit** [ɑ̃tibʀɥi] adj inv: **mur ~** (sur autoroute) sound-muffling wall

**antibuée** [ɑ̃tibɥe] adj inv: **dispositif ~** demister; **bombe ~** demister spray

**anticancéreux, -euse** [ɑ̃tikɑ̃seʀø, -øz] adj cancer cpd

**anticasseur, anticasseurs** [ɑ̃tikɑsœʀ] adj: **loi/ mesure ~(s)** law/measure against damage done by demonstrators

**antichambre** [ɑ̃tiʃɑ̃bʀ(ə)] nf antechamber, anteroom; **faire ~** to wait (for an audience)

**antichar** [ɑ̃tiʃaʀ] adj antitank

**antichoc** [ɑ̃tiʃɔk] adj shockproof

**anticipation** [ɑ̃tisipasjɔ̃] nf anticipation; (Comm) payment in advance; **par ~** in anticipation, in advance; **livre/film d'~** science fiction book/film

**anticipé, e** [ɑ̃tisipe] adj (règlement, paiement) early, in advance; (joie etc) anticipated, early; **avec mes remerciements ~s** thanking you in advance ou anticipation

**anticiper** [ɑ̃tisipe] vt to anticipate, foresee; (paiement) to pay ou make in advance ▷ vi to look ou think ahead; (en racontant) to jump ahead; (prévoir) to anticipate; **~ sur** to anticipate

**anticlérical, e, -aux** [ɑ̃tikleʀikal, -o] adj anticlerical

**anticoagulant, e** [ɑ̃tikɔagylɑ̃, -ɑ̃t] adj, nm anticoagulant

**anticolonialisme** [ɑ̃tikɔlɔnjalism(ə)] nm anticolonialism

**anticonceptionnel, le** [ɑ̃tikɔ̃sɛpsjɔnɛl] adj contraceptive

**anticonformisme** [ɑ̃tikɔ̃fɔrmism(ə)] nm nonconformism

**anticonstitutionnel, le** [ɑ̃tikɔ̃stitysjɔnɛl] adj unconstitutional

**anticorps** [ɑ̃tikɔʀ] nm antibody

**anticyclone** [ɑ̃tisiklɔn] nm anticyclone

**antidater** [ɑ̃tidate] vt to backdate, predate

**antidémocratique** [ɑ̃tidemɔkʀatik] adj antidemocratic; (peu démocratique) undemocratic

**antidépresseur** [ɑ̃tidepʀɛsœʀ] nm antidepressant

**antidérapant, e** [ɑ̃tideʀapɑ̃, -ɑ̃t] adj nonskid

**antidopage** [ātidɔpaʒ], **antidoping** [ātidɔpiŋ] adj (lutte) antidoping; (contrôle) dope cpd

**antidote** [ātidɔt] nm antidote

**antienne** [ātjɛn] nf (fig) chant, refrain

**antigang** [ātigāg] adj inv: **brigade ~** commando unit

**antigel** [ātiʒɛl] nm antifreeze

**antigène** [ātiʒɛn] nm antigen

**antigouvernemental, e, -aux** [ātiguvɛʀnəmātal, -o] adj antigovernment

**Antigua et Barbude** [ātigaebaʀbyd] nf Antigua and Barbuda

**antihistaminique** [ātiistaminik] nm antihistamine

**anti-inflammatoire** [ātiɛ̃flamatwaʀ] adj anti-inflammatory

**anti-inflationniste** [ātiɛ̃flɑsjɔnist(ə)] adj anti-inflationary

**antillais, e** [ātijɛ, -ɛz] adj West Indian

**Antilles** [ātij] nfpl: **les ~** the West Indies; **les Grandes/Petites ~** the Greater/Lesser Antilles

**antilope** [ātilɔp] nf antelope

**antimilitarisme** [ātimilitaʀism(ə)] nm antimilitarism

**antimilitariste** [ātimilitaʀist(ə)] adj antimilitarist

**antimissile** [ātimisil] adj antimissile

**antimite, antimites** [ātimit] adj, nm: **(produit) ~(s)** mothproofer, moth repellent

**antimondialisation** [ātimɔ̃djalizasjɔ̃] nf antiglobalization

**antinucléaire** [ātinykleɛʀ] adj antinuclear

**antioxydant** [ātiɔksidā] nm antioxidant

**antiparasite** [ātipaʀazit] adj (Radio, TV) antiinterference; **dispositif ~** suppressor

**antipathie** [ātipati] nf antipathy

**antipathique** [ātipatik] adj unpleasant, disagreeable

**antipelliculaire** [ātipelikylɛʀ] adj anti-dandruff

**antiphrase** [ātifʀaz] nf: **par ~** ironically

**antipodes** [ātipɔd] nmpl (Géo): **les ~** the antipodes; (fig): **être aux ~ de** to be the opposite extreme of

**antipoison** [ātipwazɔ̃] adj inv: **centre ~** poison centre

**antipoliomyélitique** [ātipɔljɔmjelitik] adj polio cpd

**antiquaire** [ātikɛʀ] nm/f antique dealer

**antique** [ātik] adj antique; (très vieux) ancient, antiquated

**antiquité** [ātikite] nf (objet) antique; **l'A~** Antiquity; **magasin/marchand d'~s** antique shop/dealer

**antirabique** [ātiʀabik] adj rabies cpd

**antiraciste** [ātiʀasist(ə)] adj antiracist, antiracialist

**antireflet** [ātiʀəflɛ] adj inv (verres) antireflective

**antirépublicain, e** [ātiʀepyblikɛ̃, -ɛn] adj antirepublican

**antirides** [ātiʀid] adj (crème) antiwrinkle

**antirouille** [ātiʀuj] adj inv: **peinture ~** antirust paint; **traitement ~** rustproofing

**antisémite** [ātisemit] adj anti-Semitic

**antisémitisme** [ātisemitism(ə)] nm antiSemitism

**antiseptique** [ātisɛptik] adj, nm antiseptic

**antisocial, e, -aux** [ātisɔsjal, -o] adj antisocial

**antispasmodique** [ātispasmɔdik] adj, nm antispasmodic

**antisportif, -ive** [ātispɔʀtif, -iv] adj unsporting; (hostile au sport) antisport

**antitétanique** [ātitetanik] adj tetanus cpd

**antithèse** [ātitɛz] nf antithesis

**antitrust** [ātitʀœst] adj inv (loi, mesures) antimonopoly

**antituberculeux, -euse** [ātitybɛʀkylø, -øz] adj tuberculosis cpd

**antitussif, -ive** [ātitysif, -iv] adj antitussive, cough cpd

**antivariolique** [ātivaʀjɔlik] adj smallpox cpd

**antiviral, e, -aux** [ātiviʀal, o] adj (Méd) antiviral

**antivirus** [ātiviʀys] nm (Inform) antivirus (program)

**antivol** [ātivɔl] adj, nm: **(dispositif) ~** antitheft device; (pour vélo) padlock

**antonyme** [ātɔnim] nm antonym

**antre** [ātʀ(ə)] nm den, lair

**anus** [anys] nm anus

**Anvers** [āvɛʀ] n Antwerp

**anxiété** [āksjete] nf anxiety

**anxieusement** [āksjøzmā] adv anxiously

**anxieux, -euse** [āksjø, -øz] adj anxious, worried; **être ~ de faire** to be anxious to do

**AOC** sigle f (= Appellation d'origine contrôlée) guarantee of quality of wine; see note

> ● **AOC**
> ●
> ● AOC ("appellation d'origine contrôlée") is
> ● the highest French wine classification. It
> ● indicates that the wine meets strict
> ● requirements concerning vineyard of
> ● origin, type of grape, method of production
> ● and alcoholic strength.

**aorte** [aɔʀt(ə)] nf aorta

**août** [u] nm August; voir aussi **juillet; Assomption**

**aoûtien, ne** [ausjɛ̃, -ɛn] nm/f August holidaymaker

**AP** sigle f = **Assistance publique**

**apaisant, e** [apɛzā, -āt] adj soothing

**apaisement** [apɛzmā] nm calming; soothing; (aussi Pol) appeasement; **apaisements** nmpl soothing reassurances; (pour calmer) pacifying words

**apaiser** [apeze] vt (colère) to calm, quell, soothe; (faim) to appease, assuage; (douleur) to soothe; (personne) to calm (down), pacify; **s'apaiser** vi (tempête, bruit) to die down, subside

**apanage** [apanaʒ] nm: **être l'~ de** to be the privilege ou prerogative of

**aparté** [apaʀte] nm (Théât) aside; (entretien) private conversation; **en ~** adv in an aside (Brit);

(*entretien*) in private

**apartheid** [apaʀtɛd] *nm* apartheid

**apathie** [apati] *nf* apathy

**apathique** [apatik] *adj* apathetic

**apatride** [apatʀid] *nm/f* stateless person

**APCE** *sigle f* (= *Agence pour la création d'entreprises*) business start-up agency

**apercevoir** [apɛʀsəvwaʀ] *vt* to see; **s'apercevoir de** *vt* to notice; **s'~ que** to notice that; **sans s'en ~** without realizing *ou* noticing

**aperçu, e** [apɛʀsy] *pp de* **apercevoir** ▷ *nm* (*vue d'ensemble*) general survey; (*intuition*) insight

**apéritif, -ive** [apeʀitif, -iv] *adj* which stimulates the appetite ▷ *nm* (*boisson*) aperitif; (*réunion*) (pre-lunch *ou* -dinner) drinks *pl*; **prendre l'~** to have drinks (before lunch *ou* dinner) *ou* an aperitif

**apesanteur** [apəzɑ̃tœʀ] *nf* weightlessness

**à-peu-près** [apøpʀɛ] *nm inv* (*péj*) vague approximation

**apeuré, e** [apœʀe] *adj* frightened, scared

**aphasie** [afazi] *nm* aphasia

**aphone** [afɔn] *adj* voiceless

**aphorisme** [afɔʀism(ə)] *nm* aphorism

**aphrodisiaque** [afʀɔdizjak] *adj, nm* aphrodisiac

**aphte** [aft(ə)] *nm* mouth ulcer

**aphteuse** [aftøz] *adj f:* **fièvre ~** foot-and-mouth disease

**à-pic** [apik] *nm* cliff, drop

**apicole** [apikɔl] *adj* beekeeping *cpd*

**apiculteur, -trice** [apikyltœʀ, -tʀis] *nm/f* beekeeper

**apiculture** [apikyltyʀ] *nf* beekeeping, apiculture

**apitoiement** [apitwamɑ̃] *nm* pity, compassion

**apitoyer** [apitwaje] *vt* to move to pity; **~ qn sur qn/qch** to move sb to pity for sb/over sth; **s'~ (sur qn/qch)** to feel pity *ou* compassion (for sb/ over sth)

**ap.J.-C.** *abr* (= *après Jésus-Christ*) AD

**APL** *sigle f* (= *aide personnalisée au logement*) housing benefit

**aplanir** [aplaniʀ] *vt* to level; (*fig*) to smooth away, iron out

**aplati, e** [aplati] *adj* flat, flattened

**aplatir** [aplatiʀ] *vt* to flatten; **s'aplatir** *vi* to become flatter; (*écrasé*) to be flattened; (*fig*) to lie flat on the ground; (: *fam*) to fall flat on one's face; (: *péj*) to grovel

**aplomb** [aplɔ̃] *nm* (*équilibre*) balance, equilibrium; (*fig*) self-assurance; (: *péj*) nerve; **d'~** *adv* steady; (*Constr*) plumb

**APN** *sigle m* (*appareil photo(graphique) numérique*) digital camera

**apocalypse** [apɔkalips(ə)] *nf* apocalypse

**apocalyptique** [apɔkaliptik] *adj* (*fig*) apocalyptic

**apocryphe** [apɔkʀif] *adj* apocryphal

**apogée** [apɔʒe] *nm* (*fig*) peak, apogee

**apolitique** [apɔlitik] *adj* (*indifférent*) apolitical; (*indépendant*) unpolitical, non-political

**apologie** [apɔlɔʒi] *nf* praise; (*Jur*) vindication

**apoplexie** [apɔplɛksi] *nf* apoplexy

**a posteriori** [apɔsteʀjɔʀi] *adv* after the event, with hindsight, a posteriori

**apostolat** [apɔstɔla] *nm* (*Rel*) apostolate, discipleship; (*gén*) evangelism

**apostolique** [apɔstɔlik] *adj* apostolic

**apostrophe** [apɔstʀɔf] *nf* (*signe*) apostrophe; (*appel*) interpellation

**apostropher** [apɔstʀɔfe] *vt* (*interpeller*) to shout at, address sharply

**apothéose** [apoteoz] *nf* pinnacle (of achievement); (*Mus etc*) grand finale

**apothicaire** [apotikɛʀ] *nm* apothecary

**apôtre** [apotʀ(ə)] *nm* apostle, disciple

**apparaître** [apaʀɛtʀ(ə)] *vi* to appear ▷ *vb copule* to appear, seem

**apparat** [apaʀa] *nm:* **tenue/dîner d'~** ceremonial dress/dinner

**appareil** [apaʀɛj] *nm* (*outil, machine*) piece of apparatus, device; (*électrique etc*) appliance; (*politique, syndical*) machinery; (*avion*) (aero)plane (*Brit*), (air)plane (*US*), aircraft *inv*; (*téléphonique*) telephone; (*dentier*) brace (*Brit*), braces (*US*); **~ digestif/reproducteur** digestive/reproductive system *ou* apparatus; **l'~ productif** the means of production; **qui est à l'~?** who's speaking?; **dans le plus simple ~** in one's birthday suit; **~ (photographique)** camera; **~ numérique** digital camera

**appareillage** [apaʀɛjaʒ] *nm* (*appareils*) equipment; (*Navig*) casting off, getting under way

**appareiller** [apaʀeje] *vi* (*Navig*) to cast off, get under way ▷ *vt* (*assortir*) to match up

**appareil photo** [apaʀɛjfɔtɔ] (*pl* **appareils photos**) *nm* camera

**apparemment** [apaʀamɑ̃] *adv* apparently

**apparence** [apaʀɑ̃s] *nf* appearance; **malgré les ~s** despite appearances; **en ~** apparently, seemingly

**apparent, e** [apaʀɑ̃, -ɑ̃t] *adj* visible; (*évident*) obvious; (*superficiel*) apparent; **poutres ~es** exposed beams

**apparenté, e** [apaʀɑ̃te] *adj:* **~ à** related to; (*fig*) similar to

**apparenter** [apaʀɑ̃te]: **s'apparenter à** *vt* to be similar to

**apparier** [apaʀje] *vt* (*gants*) to pair, match

**appariteur** [apaʀitœʀ] *nm* attendant, porter (*in French universities*)

**apparition** [apaʀisjɔ̃] *nf* appearance; (*surnaturelle*) apparition; **faire son ~** to appear

**appartement** [apaʀtəmɑ̃] *nm* flat (*Brit*), apartment (*US*)

**appartenance** [apaʀtənɑ̃s] *nf:* **~ à** belonging to, membership of

**appartenir** [apaʀtəniʀ]: **~ à** *vt* to belong to; (*faire partie de*) to belong to, be a member of; **il lui appartient de** it is up to him to

**appartiendrai** [apaʀtjɛ̃dʀe], **appartiens** *etc* [apaʀtjɛ̃] *vb voir* **appartenir**

**apparu, e** [apaʀy] *pp de* **apparaître**

**appas** [apɑ] *nmpl* (*d'une femme*) charms

**appât** [apɑ] *nm* (*Pêche*) bait; (*fig*) lure, bait
**appâter** [apɑte] *vt* (*hameçon*) to bait; (*poisson, fig*) to lure, entice
**appauvrir** [apovʀiʀ] *vt* to impoverish; **s'appauvrir** *vi* to grow poorer, become impoverished
**appauvrissement** [apovʀismɑ̃] *nm* impoverishment
**appel** [apɛl] *nm* call; (*nominal*) roll call; (: *Scol*) register; (*Mil: recrutement*) call-up; (*Jur*) appeal; **faire ~ à** (*invoquer*) to appeal to; (*avoir recours à*) to call on; (*nécessiter*) to call for, require; **faire** *ou* **interjeter ~** (*Jur*) to appeal, lodge an appeal; **faire l'~** to call the roll; to call the register; **indicatif d'~** call sign; **numéro d'~** (*Tél*) number; **produit d'~** (*Comm*) loss leader; **sans ~** (*fig*) final, irrevocable; **~ d'air** in-draught; **~ d'offres** (*Comm*) invitation to tender; **faire un ~ de phares** to flash one's headlights; **~ (téléphonique)** (tele)phone call
**appelé** [aple] *nm* (*Mil*) conscript
**appeler** [aple] *vt* to call; (*Tél*) to call, ring; (*faire venir: médecin etc*) to call, send for; (*fig: nécessiter*) to call for, demand; **~ au secours** to call for help; **~ qn à l'aide** *ou* **au secours** to call to sb for help; **~ qn à un poste/des fonctions** to appoint sb to a post/assign duties to sb; **être appelé à** (*fig*) to be destined to; **~ qn à comparaître** (*Jur*) to summon sb to appear; **en ~ à** to appeal to; **s'appeler: elle s'appelle Gabrielle** her name is Gabrielle, she's called Gabrielle; **comment ça s'appelle?** what is it *ou* that called?
**appellation** [apelasjɔ̃] *nf* designation, appellation; **vin d'~ contrôlée** "appellation contrôlée" wine, *wine guaranteed of a certain quality*
**appelle** *etc* [apɛl] *vb voir* **appeler**
**appendice** [apɛ̃dis] *nm* appendix
**appendicite** [apɑ̃disit] *nf* appendicitis
**appentis** [apɑ̃ti] *nm* lean-to
**appert** [apɛʀ] *vb*: **il ~ que** it appears that, it is evident that
**appesantir** [apzɑ̃tiʀ]: **s'appesantir** *vi* to grow heavier; **s'~ sur** (*fig*) to dwell at length on
**appétissant, e** [apetisɑ̃, -ɑ̃t] *adj* appetizing, mouth-watering
**appétit** [apeti] *nm* appetite; **couper l'~ à qn** to take away sb's appetite; **bon ~!** enjoy your meal!
**applaudimètre** [aplodimɛtʀ(ə)] *nm* applause meter
**applaudir** [aplodiʀ] *vt* to applaud ▷ *vi* to applaud, clap; **~ à** *vt* (*décision*) to applaud, commend
**applaudissements** [aplodismɑ̃] *nmpl* applause *sg*, clapping *sg*
**applicable** [aplikabl(ə)] *adj* applicable
**applicateur** [aplikatœʀ] *nm* applicator
**application** [aplikasjɔ̃] *nf* application; (*d'une loi*) enforcement; **mettre en ~** to implement
**applique** [aplik] *nf* wall lamp
**appliqué, e** [aplike] *adj* (*élève etc*) industrious, assiduous; (*science*) applied
**appliquer** [aplike] *vt* to apply; (*loi*) to enforce; (*donner: gifle, châtiment*) to give; **s'appliquer** *vi* (*élève etc*) to apply o.s.; **s'~ à** (*loi, remarque*) to apply to; **s'~ à faire qch** to apply o.s. to doing sth, take pains to do sth; **s'~ sur** (*coïncider avec*) to fit over
**appoint** [apwɛ̃] *nm* (extra) contribution *ou* help; **avoir/faire l'~** (*en payant*) to have/give the right change *ou* money; **chauffage d'~** extra heating
**appointements** [apwɛ̃tmɑ̃] *nmpl* salary *sg*, stipend
**appointer** [apwɛ̃te] *vt*: **être appointé à l'année/au mois** to be paid yearly/monthly
**appontage** [apɔ̃taʒ] *nm* landing (*on an aircraft carrier*)
**appontement** [apɔ̃tmɑ̃] *nm* landing stage, wharf
**apponter** [apɔ̃te] *vi* (*avion, hélicoptère*) to land
**apport** [apɔʀ] *nm* supply; (*argent, biens etc*) contribution
**apporter** [apɔʀte] *vt* to bring; (*preuve*) to give, provide; (*modification*) to make; (*remarque*) to contribute, add
**apposer** [apoze] *vt* to append; (*sceau etc*) to affix
**apposition** [apozisjɔ̃] *nf* appending; affixing; (*Ling*) **en ~** in apposition
**appréciable** [apʀesjabl(ə)] *adj* (*important*) appreciable, significant
**appréciation** [apʀesjɑsjɔ̃] *nf* appreciation; estimation, assessment; **appréciations** *nfpl* (*avis*) assessment *sg*, appraisal *sg*
**apprécier** [apʀesje] *vt* to appreciate; (*évaluer*) to estimate, assess; **j'~ais que tu ...** I should appreciate (it) if you ...
**appréhender** [apʀeɑ̃de] *vt* (*craindre*) to dread; (*arrêter*) to apprehend; **~ que** to fear that; **~ de faire** to dread doing
**appréhensif, -ive** [apʀeɑ̃sif, -iv] *adj* apprehensive
**appréhension** [apʀeɑ̃sjɔ̃] *nf* apprehension
**apprendre** [apʀɑ̃dʀ(ə)] *vt* to learn; (*événement, résultats*) to learn of, hear of; **~ qch à qn** (*informer*) to tell sb (of) sth; (*enseigner*) to teach sb sth; **tu me l'apprends!** that's news to me!; **~ à faire qch** to learn to do sth; **~ à qn à faire qch** to teach sb to do sth
**apprenti, e** [apʀɑ̃ti] *nm/f* apprentice; (*fig*) novice, beginner
**apprentissage** [apʀɑ̃tisaʒ] *nm* learning; (*Comm, Scol: période*) apprenticeship; **école** *ou* **centre d'~** training school *ou* centre; **faire l'~ de qch** (*fig*) to be initiated into sth
**apprêt** [apʀɛ] *nm* (*sur un cuir, une étoffe*) dressing; (*sur un mur*) size; (*sur un papier*) finish; **sans ~** (*fig*) without artifice, unaffectedly
**apprêté, e** [apʀete] *adj* (*fig*) affected
**apprêter** [apʀete] *vt* to dress, finish; **s'apprêter** *vi*: **s'~ à qch/à faire qch** to prepare for sth/for doing sth
**appris, e** [apʀi, -iz] *pp de* **apprendre**
**apprivoisé, e** [apʀivwaze] *adj* tame, tamed

**apprivoiser** [apʀivwaze] *vt* to tame
**approbateur, -trice** [apʀɔbatœʀ, -tʀis] *adj*
approving
**approbatif, -ive** [apʀɔbatif, -iv] *adj* approving
**approbation** [apʀɔbasjɔ̃] *nf* approval; **digne**
**d'~** (*conduite, travail*) praiseworthy,
commendable
**approchant, e** [apʀɔʃɑ̃, -ɑ̃t] *adj* similar, close;
**quelque chose d'~** something similar
**approche** [apʀɔʃ] *nf* approaching; (*arrivée,*
*attitude*) approach; **approches** *nfpl* (*abords*)
surroundings; **à l'~ du bateau/de l'ennemi** as
the ship/enemy approached *ou* drew near; **l'~**
**d'un problème** the approach to a problem;
**travaux d'~** (*fig*) manoeuvrings
**approché, e** [apʀɔʃe] *adj* approximate
**approcher** [apʀɔʃe] *vi* to approach, come near
▷ *vt* (*vedette, artiste*) to come close to, approach;
(*rapprocher*): **~ qch (de qch)** to bring *ou* put *ou*
move sth near (to sth); **~ de** *vt* to draw near to;
(*quantité, moment*) to approach; **s'approcher de**
*vt* to approach, go *ou* come *ou* move near to;
**approchez-vous** come *ou* go nearer
**approfondi, e** [apʀɔfɔ̃di] *adj* thorough, detailed
**approfondir** [apʀɔfɔ̃diʀ] *vt* to deepen; (*question*)
to go further into; **sans ~** without going too
deeply into it
**appropriation** [apʀɔpʀijɑsjɔ̃] *nf* appropriation
**approprié, e** [apʀɔpʀije] *adj*: **~ (à)** appropriate
(to), suited (to)
**approprier** [apʀɔpʀije] *vt* (*adapter*) adapt;
**s'approprier** *vt* to appropriate, take over
**approuver** [apʀuve] *vt* to agree with; (*autoriser:*
*loi, projet*) to approve, pass; (*trouver louable*) to
approve of; **je vous approuve entièrement/ne**
**vous approuve pas** I agree with you entirely/
don't agree with you; **lu et approuvé** (read
and) approved
**approvisionnement** [apʀɔvizjɔnmɑ̃] *nm*
supplying; (*provisions*) supply, stock
**approvisionner** [apʀɔvizjɔne] *vt* to supply;
(*compte bancaire*) to pay funds into; **~ qn en** to
supply sb with; **s'approvisionner** *vi*: **s'~ dans**
**un certain magasin/au marché** to shop in a
certain shop/at the market; **s'~ en** to stock up
with
**approximatif, -ive** [apʀɔksimatif, -iv] *adj*
approximate, rough; (*imprécis*) vague
**approximation** [apʀɔksimasjɔ̃] *nf*
approximation
**approximativement** [apʀɔksimativmɑ̃] *adv*
approximately, roughly; vaguely
**appt** *abr* = **appartement**
**appui** [apɥi] *nm* support; **prendre ~ sur** to lean
on; (*objet*) to rest on; **point d'~** fulcrum; (*fig*)
something to lean on; **à l'~ de** (*pour prouver*) in
support of; **à l'~** *adv* to support one's
argument; **l'~ de la fenêtre** the windowsill,
the window ledge
**appuie** *etc* [apɥi] *vb voir* **appuyer**
**appui-tête, appuie-tête** [apɥitɛt] *nm inv*
headrest

**appuyé, e** [apɥije] *adj* (*regard*) meaningful;
(*: insistant*) intent, insistent; (*excessif: politesse,*
*compliment*) exaggerated, overdone
**appuyer** [apɥije] *vt* (*poser*): **~ qch sur/contre/à**
to lean *ou* rest sth on/against/on; (*soutenir:*
*personne, demande*) to support, back (up) ▷ *vi*: **~**
**sur** (*bouton, frein*) to press, push; (*mot, détail*) to
stress, emphasize; (*chose: peser sur*) to rest
(heavily) on, press against; **s'appuyer sur** *vt* to
lean on; (*compter sur*) to rely on; **s'~ sur qn** to
lean on sb; **~ contre** (*toucher: mur, porte*) to lean *ou*
rest against; **~ à droite** *ou* **sur sa droite** to bear
(to the) right; **~ sur le champignon** to put
one's foot down
**apr.** *abr* = **après**
**âpre** [ɑpʀ(ə)] *adj* acrid, pungent; (*fig*) harsh;
(*lutte*) bitter; **~ au gain** grasping, greedy
**après** [apʀɛ] *prép* after ▷ *adv* afterwards; **deux**
**heures ~** two hours later; **~ qu'il est parti/**
**avoir fait** after he left/having done; **courir ~**
**qn** to run after sb; **crier ~ qn** to shout at sb;
**être toujours ~ qn** (*critiquer etc*) to be always on
at sb; **~ quoi** after which; **d'~** *prép* (*selon*)
according to; **d'~ lui** according to him; **d'~ moi**
in my opinion; **~ coup** *adv* after the event,
afterwards; **~ tout** *adv* (*au fond*) after all; **et**
**(puis) ~?** so what?
**après-demain** [apʀɛdmɛ̃] *adv* the day after
tomorrow
**après-guerre** [apʀɛgɛʀ] *nm* post-war years *pl*;
**d'~** *adj* post-war
**après-midi** [apʀɛmidi] *nm ou f inv* afternoon
**après-rasage** [apʀɛʀazaʒ] *nm inv*: (**lotion**) **~**
after-shave (lotion)
**après-shampooing** [apʀɛʃɑ̃pwɛ̃] *nm inv*
conditioner
**après-ski** [apʀɛski] *nm inv* (*chaussure*) snow boot;
(*moment*) après-ski
**après-soleil** [apʀɛsɔlej] *adj inv* after-sun *cpd*
▷ *nm* after-sun cream *ou* lotion
**après-vente** [apʀɛvɑ̃t] *adj inv* after-sales *cpd*
**âpreté** [ɑpʀəte] *nf* (*voir âpre*) pungency;
harshness; bitterness
**à-propos** [apʀopo] *nm* (*d'une remarque*) aptness;
**faire preuve d'~** to show presence of mind, do
the right thing; **avec ~** suitably, aptly
**apte** [apt(ə)] *adj*: **~ à qch/faire qch** capable of
sth/doing sth; **~ (au service)** (*Mil*) fit (for
service)
**aptitude** [aptityd] *nf* ability, aptitude
**apurer** [apyʀe] *vt* (*Comm*) to clear
**aquaculture** [akwakyltyʀ] *nf* fish farming
**aquaplanage** [akwaplanaʒ] *nm* (*Auto*)
aquaplaning
**aquaplane** [akwaplan] *nm* (*planche*) aquaplane;
(*sport*) aquaplaning
**aquaplaning** [akwaplaniŋ] *nm* aquaplaning
**aquarelle** [akwaʀɛl] *nf* (*tableau*) watercolour
(*Brit*), watercolor (*US*); (*genre*) watercolo(u)rs *pl*,
aquarelle
**aquarelliste** [akwaʀelist(ə)] *nm/f* painter in
watercolo(u)rs

**aquarium** [akwaʀjɔm] *nm* aquarium
**aquatique** [akwatik] *adj* aquatic, water *cpd*
**aqueduc** [akdyk] *nm* aqueduct
**aqueux, -euse** [akø, -øz] *adj* aqueous
**aquilin** [akilɛ̃] *adj m*: **nez ~** aquiline nose
**AR** *sigle m* = **accusé de réception**; **lettre/paquet**
**avec AR** = recorded delivery letter/parcel; *(Aviat,*
*Rail etc)* = **aller (et) retour** ▷ *abr (Auto)* = **arrière**
**arabe** [aʀab] *adj* Arabic; *(désert, cheval)* Arabian;
*(nation, peuple)* Arab ▷ *nm (Ling)* Arabic ▷ *nm/f*:
**Arabe** Arab
**arabesque** [aʀabɛsk(ə)] *nf* arabesque
**Arabie** [aʀabi] *nf*: **l'~** Arabia; **l'~ Saoudite** *ou*
**Séoudite** Saudi Arabia
**arable** [aʀabl(ə)] *adj* arable
**arachide** [aʀaʃid] *nf* groundnut (plant); *(graine)*
peanut, groundnut
**araignée** [aʀeɲe] *nf* spider; **~ de mer** spider
crab
**araser** [aʀɑze] *vt* to level; *(en rabotant)* to plane
(down)
**aratoire** [aʀatwaʀ] *adj*: **instrument ~**
ploughing implement
**arbalète** [aʀbalɛt] *nf* crossbow
**arbitrage** [aʀbitʀaʒ] *nm* refereeing; umpiring;
arbitration
**arbitraire** [aʀbitʀɛʀ] *adj* arbitrary
**arbitre** [aʀbitʀ(ə)] *nm (Sport)* referee; *(: Tennis,*
*Cricket)* umpire; *(fig)* arbiter, judge; *(Jur)*
arbitrator
**arbitrer** [aʀbitʀe] *vt* to referee; to umpire; to
arbitrate
**arborer** [aʀbɔʀe] *vt* to bear, display; *(avec*
*ostentation)* to sport
**arborescence** [aʀbɔʀesɑ̃s] *nf* tree structure
**arboricole** [aʀbɔʀikɔl] *adj (animal)* arboreal;
*(technique)* arboricultural
**arboriculture** [aʀbɔʀikyltyʀ] *nf* arboriculture;
**~ fruitière** fruit (tree) growing
**arbre** [aʀbʀ(ə)] *nm* tree; *(Tech)* shaft; **~ à cames**
*(Auto)* camshaft; **~ fruitier** fruit tree; **~**
**généalogique** family tree; **~ de Noël**
Christmas tree; **~ de transmission** *(Auto)*
driveshaft
**arbrisseau, x** [aʀbʀiso] *nm* shrub
**arbuste** [aʀbyst(ə)] *nm* small shrub, bush
**arc** [aʀk] *nm (arme)* bow; *(Géom)* arc; *(Archit)* arch;
**~ de cercle** arc of a circle; **en ~ de cercle** *adj*
semi-circular
**arcade** [aʀkad] *nf* arch(way); **~s** arcade *sg*,
arches; **~ sourcilière** arch of the eyebrows
**arcanes** [aʀkan] *nmpl* mysteries
**arc-boutant** [aʀkbutɑ̃] *(pl* **arcs-boutants**) *nm*
flying buttress
**arc-bouter** [aʀkbute]: **s'arc-bouter** *vi*: **s'~**
**contre** to lean *ou* press against
**arceau, x** [aʀso] *nm (métallique etc)* hoop
**arc-en-ciel** [aʀkɑ̃sjɛl] *(pl* **arcs-en-ciel**) *nm*
rainbow
**archaïque** [aʀkaik] *adj* archaic
**archaïsme** [aʀkaism(ə)] *nm* archaism
**archange** [aʀkɑ̃ʒ] *nm* archangel

**arche** [aʀʃ(ə)] *nf* arch; **~ de Noé** Noah's Ark
**archéologie** [aʀkeɔlɔʒi] *nf* arch(a)eology
**archéologique** [aʀkeɔlɔʒik] *adj*
arch(a)eological
**archéologue** [aʀkeɔlɔg] *nm/f* arch(a)eologist
**archer** [aʀʃe] *nm* archer
**archet** [aʀʃɛ] *nm* bow
**archevêché** [aʀʃəveʃe] *nm* archbishopric;
*(palais)* archbishop's palace
**archevêque** [aʀʃəvɛk] *nm* archbishop
**archi...** [aʀʃi] *préfixe (très)* dead, extra
**archibondé, e** [aʀʃibɔ̃de] *adj* chock-a-block
(Brit), packed solid
**archiduc** [aʀʃidyk] *nm* archduke
**archiduchesse** [aʀʃidyʃɛs] *nf* archduchess
**archipel** [aʀʃipɛl] *nm* archipelago
**archisimple** [aʀʃisɛ̃pl(ə)] *adj* dead easy *ou*
simple
**architecte** [aʀʃitɛkt(ə)] *nm* architect
**architectural, e, -aux** [aʀʃitɛktyʀal, -o] *adj*
architectural
**architecture** [aʀʃitɛktyʀ] *nf* architecture
**archive** [aʀʃiv] *nf* file; **archives** *nfpl* archives
**archiver** [aʀʃive] *vt* to file
**archiviste** [aʀʃivist(ə)] *nm/f* archivist
**arçon** [aʀsɔ̃] *nm voir* **cheval**
**arctique** [aʀktik] *adj* Arctic ▷ *nm*: **l'A~** the
Arctic; **le cercle A~** the Arctic Circle; **l'océan**
**A~** the Arctic Ocean
**ardemment** [aʀdamɑ̃] *adv* ardently, fervently
**ardent, e** [aʀdɑ̃, -ɑ̃t] *adj (soleil)* blazing; *(fièvre)*
raging; *(amour)* ardent, passionate; *(prière)*
fervent
**ardeur** [aʀdœʀ] *nf* blazing heat; *(fig)* fervour,
ardour
**ardoise** [aʀdwaz] *nf* slate
**ardu, e** [aʀdy] *adj* arduous, difficult; *(pente)*
steep, abrupt
**are** [aʀ] *nm* are, 100 square metres
**arène** [aʀɛn] *nf* arena; *(fig)*: **l'~ politique** the
political arena; **arènes** *nfpl* bull-ring *sg*
**arête** [aʀɛt] *nf (de poisson)* bone; *(d'une montagne)*
ridge; *(Géom etc)* edge *(where two faces meet)*
**arg.** *abr* = **argus**
**argent** [aʀʒɑ̃] *nm (métal)* silver; *(monnaie)*
money; *(couleur)* silver; **en avoir pour son ~** to
get value for money; **gagner beaucoup d'~** to
earn a lot of money; **~ comptant** (hard) cash; **~**
**liquide** ready money, (ready) cash; **~ de poche**
pocket money
**argenté, e** [aʀʒɑ̃te] *adj* silver(y); *(métal)* silver-
plated
**argenter** [aʀʒɑ̃te] *vt* to silver(-plate)
**argenterie** [aʀʒɑ̃tʀi] *nf* silverware; *(en métal*
*argenté)* silver plate
**argentin, e** [aʀʒɑ̃tɛ̃, -in] *adj* Argentinian,
Argentine ▷ *nm/f*: **Argentin, e** Argentinian,
Argentine
**Argentine** [aʀʒɑ̃tin] *nf*: **l'~** Argentina, the
Argentine
**argentique** [aʀʒɑ̃tik] *adj (appareil-photo)* film *cpd*
**argile** [aʀʒil] *nf* clay

**argileux, -euse** [aʀʒilø, -øz] *adj* clayey
**argot** [aʀgo] *nm* slang; *see note*

● **ARGOT**
●
● *Argot* was the term originally used to
● describe the jargon of the criminal
● underworld, characterized by colourful
● images and distinctive intonation and
● designed to confuse the outsider. Some
● French authors write in *argot* and so have
● helped it spread and grow. More generally,
● the special vocabulary used by any social or
● professional group is also known as *argot*.

**argotique** [aʀgɔtik] *adj* slang *cpd*; *(très familier)*
slangy
**arguer** [aʀgɥe]: ~ **de** *vt* to put forward as a
pretext *ou* reason; ~ **que** to argue that
**argument** [aʀgymã] *nm* argument
**argumentaire** [aʀgymãtɛʀ] *nm* list of sales
points; *(brochure)* sales leaflet
**argumentation** [aʀgymãtasjɔ̃] *nf (fait
d'argumenter)* arguing; *(ensemble des arguments)*
argument
**argumenter** [aʀgymãte] *vi* to argue
**argus** [aʀgys] *nm guide to second-hand car etc prices*
**arguties** [aʀgysi] *nfpl* pettifoggery *sg* (Brit),
quibbles
**aride** [aʀid] *adj* arid
**aridité** [aʀidite] *nf* aridity
**arien, ne** [aʀjɛ̃, -ɛn] *adj* Arian
**aristocrate** [aʀistɔkʀat] *nm/f* aristocrat
**aristocratie** [aʀistɔkʀasi] *nf* aristocracy
**aristocratique** [aʀistɔkʀatik] *adj* aristocratic
**arithmétique** [aʀitmetik] *adj* arithmetic(al)
▷ *nf* arithmetic
**armada** [aʀmada] *nf (fig)* army
**armagnac** [aʀmaɲak] *nm* armagnac
**armateur** [aʀmatœʀ] *nm* shipowner
**armature** [aʀmatyʀ] *nf* framework; *(de tente etc)*
frame; *(de corset)* bone; *(de soutien-gorge)* wiring
**arme** [aʀm(ə)] *nf* weapon; *(section de l'armée)*
arm; **armes** *nfpl* weapons, arms; *(blason)* (coat
of) arms; **les ~s** *(profession)* soldiering *sg*; **à ~s
égales** on equal terms; **en ~s** up in arms;
**passer par les ~s** to execute (by firing squad);
**prendre/présenter les ~s** to take up/present
arms; **se battre à l'~ blanche** to fight with
blades; ~ **à feu** firearm; ~**s de destruction
massive** weapons of mass destruction
**armé, e** [aʀme] *adj* armed; ~ **de** armed with
**armée** [aʀme] *nf* army; ~ **de l'air** Air Force; **l'~
du Salut** the Salvation Army; ~ **de terre** Army
**armement** [aʀməmã] *nm (matériel)* arms *pl*,
weapons *pl*; *(: d'un pays)* arms *pl*, armament;
*(action d'équiper: d'un navire)* fitting out; ~**s
nucléaires** nuclear armaments; **course aux ~s**
arms race
**Arménie** [aʀmeni] *nf*: **l'~** Armenia
**arménien, ne** [aʀmenjɛ̃, -ɛn] *adj* Armenian
▷ *nm (Ling)* Armenian ▷ *nm/f*: **Arménien, ne**
Armenian

**armer** [aʀme] *vt* to arm; *(arme à feu)* to cock;
*(appareil-photo)* to wind on; ~ **qch de** to fit sth
with; *(renforcer)* to reinforce sth with; ~ **qn de** to
arm *ou* equip sb with; **s'armer de** to arm o.s.
with
**armistice** [aʀmistis] *nm* armistice; **l'A~**
≈ Remembrance (Brit) *ou* Veterans (US) Day
**armoire** [aʀmwaʀ] *nf* (tall) cupboard; *(penderie)*
wardrobe (Brit), closet (US); ~ **à pharmacie**
medicine chest
**armoiries** [aʀmwaʀi] *nfpl* coat of arms *sg*
**armure** [aʀmyʀ] *nf* armour *no pl*, suit of armour
**armurerie** [aʀmyʀʀi] *nf* arms factory; *(magasin)*
gunsmith's (shop)
**armurier** [aʀmyʀje] *nm* gunsmith; *(Mil, d'armes
blanches)* armourer
**ARN** *sigle m* (= *acide ribonucléique*) RNA
**arnaque** [aʀnak] *nf*: **de l'~** daylight robbery
**arnaquer** [aʀnake] *vt* to do *(fam)*, swindle; **se
faire ~** to be had *(fam)* ou done
**arnaqueur** [aʀnakœʀ] *nm* swindler
**arnica** [aʀnika] *nm*: **(teinture d')~** arnica
**arobase** [aʀobaz] *nf (Inform)* "at" symbol, @;
**"paul ~ société point fr"** "paul at société dot fr"
**aromates** [aʀɔmat] *nmpl* seasoning *sg*, herbs
(and spices)
**aromathérapie** [aʀɔmateʀapi] *nf* aromatherapy
**aromatique** [aʀɔmatik] *adj* aromatic
**aromatisé, e** [aʀɔmatize] *adj* flavoured
**arôme** [aʀom] *nm* aroma; *(d'une fleur etc)*
fragrance
**arpège** [aʀpɛʒ] *nm* arpeggio
**arpentage** [aʀpãtaʒ] *nm* (land) surveying
**arpenter** [aʀpãte] *vt* to pace up and down
**arpenteur** [aʀpãtœʀ] *nm* land surveyor
**arqué, e** [aʀke] *adj* arched; *(jambes)* bow *cpd*,
bandy
**arr.** *abr* = **arrondissement**
**arrachage** [aʀaʃaʒ] *nm*: ~ **des mauvaises
herbes** weeding
**arraché** [aʀaʃe] *nm (Sport)* snatch; **obtenir à l'~**
*(fig)* to snatch
**arrache-pied** [aʀaʃpje]: **d'~** *adv* relentlessly
**arracher** [aʀaʃe] *vt* to pull out; *(page etc)* to tear
off, tear out; *(déplanter: légume)* to lift; *(: herbe,
souche)* to pull up; *(bras etc: par explosion)* to blow
off; *(: par accident)* to tear off; **s'arracher** *vt*
*(article très recherché)* to fight over; ~ **qch à qn** to
snatch sth from sb; *(fig)* to wring sth out of sb,
wrest sth from sb; ~ **qn à** *(solitude, rêverie)* to drag
sb out of; *(famille etc)* to tear *ou* wrench sb away
from; **se faire ~ une dent** to have a tooth out *ou*
pulled (US); **s'~ de** *(lieu)* to tear o.s. away from;
*(habitude)* to force o.s. out of
**arraisonner** [aʀɛzɔne] *vt* to board and search
**arrangeant, e** [aʀãʒã, -ãt] *adj* accommodating,
obliging
**arrangement** [aʀãʒmã] *nm* arrangement
**arranger** [aʀãʒe] *vt* to arrange; *(réparer)* to fix,
put right; *(régler)* to settle, sort out; *(convenir à)* to
suit, be convenient for; **s'arranger** *vi* *(se mettre*

d'accord) to come to an agreement *ou*
arrangement; (*s'améliorer: querelle, situation*) to be
sorted out; (*se débrouiller*): **s'~ pour que ...** to
arrange things so that ...; **je vais m'~** I'll
manage; **ça va s'~** it'll sort itself out; **s'~ pour
faire** to make sure that *ou* see to it that one can
do

**arrangeur** [aʀɑ̃ʒœʀ] *nm* (*Mus*) arranger
**arrestation** [aʀɛstɑsjɔ̃] *nf* arrest
**arrêt** [aʀɛ] *nm* stopping; (*de bus etc*) stop; (*Jur*)
judgment, decision; (*Football*) save; **arrêts** *nmpl*
(*Mil*) arrest *sg*; **être à l'~** to be stopped, have
come to a halt; **rester** *ou* **tomber en ~ devant**
to stop short in front of; **sans ~** without
stopping, non-stop; (*fréquemment*) continually;
**~ d'autobus** bus stop; **~ facultatif** request
stop; **~ de mort** capital sentence; **~ de travail**
stoppage (of work)

**arrêté, e** [aʀete] *adj* (*idées*) firm, fixed ▷ *nm*
order, decree; **~ municipal** ≈ bylaw, byelaw
**arrêter** [aʀete] *vt* to stop; (*chauffage etc*) to turn
off, switch off; (*Comm: compte*) to settle; (*Couture:
point*) to fasten off; (*fixer: date etc*) to appoint,
decide on; (*criminel, suspect*) to arrest; **s'arrêter** *vi*
to stop; (*s'interrompre*) to stop o.s.; **~ de faire**
to stop doing; **arrête de te plaindre** stop
complaining; **ne pas ~ de faire** to keep on
doing; **s'~ de faire** to stop doing; **s'~ sur** (*choix,
regard*) to fall on

**arrhes** [aʀ] *nfpl* deposit *sg*
**arrière** [aʀjɛʀ] *nm* back; (*Sport*) fullback ▷ *adj inv*:
**siège/roue ~** back *ou* rear seat/wheel; **arrières**
*nmpl* (*fig*): **protéger ses ~s** to protect the rear; **à
l'~** *adv* behind, at the back; **en ~** *adv* behind;
(*regarder*) back, behind; (*tomber, aller*) backwards;
**en ~ de** *prép* behind

**arriéré, e** [aʀjeʀe] *adj* (*péj*) backward ▷ *nm*
(*d'argent*) arrears *pl*
**arrière-boutique** [aʀjɛʀbutik] *nf* back shop
**arrière-cour** [aʀjɛʀkuʀ] *nf* backyard
**arrière-cuisine** [aʀjɛʀkɥizin] *nf* scullery
**arrière-garde** [aʀjɛʀgaʀd(ə)] *nf* rearguard
**arrière-goût** [aʀjɛʀgu] *nm* aftertaste
**arrière-grand-mère** [aʀjɛʀgʀɑ̃mɛʀ] (*pl* **-s**) *nf*
great-grandmother
**arrière-grand-père** [aʀjɛʀgʀɑ̃pɛʀ] (*pl* **arrière-
grands-pères**) *nm* great-grandfather
**arrière-grands-parents** [aʀjɛʀgʀɑ̃paʀɑ̃] *nmpl*
great-grandparents
**arrière-pays** [aʀjɛʀpei] *nm inv* hinterland
**arrière-pensée** [aʀjɛʀpɑ̃se] *nf* ulterior motive;
(*doute*) mental reservation
**arrière-petite-fille** [aʀjɛʀpətitfij] (*pl* **arrière-
petites-filles**) *nf* great-granddaughter
**arrière-petit-fils** [aʀjɛʀpətifis] (*pl* **arrière-
petits-fils**) *nm* great-grandson
**arrière-petits-enfants** [aʀjɛʀpətizɑ̃fɑ̃] *nmpl*
great-grandchildren
**arrière-plan** [aʀjɛʀplɑ̃] *nm* background; **d'~** *adj*
(*Inform*) background *cpd*
**arriérer** [aʀjeʀe]: **s'arriérer** *vi* (*Comm*) to fall into
arrears

**arrière-saison** [aʀjɛʀsezɔ̃] *nf* late autumn
**arrière-salle** [aʀjɛʀsal] *nf* back room
**arrière-train** [aʀjɛʀtʀɛ̃] *nm* hindquarters *pl*
**arrimer** [aʀime] *vt* to stow; (*fixer*) to secure,
fasten securely
**arrivage** [aʀivaʒ] *nm* arrival
**arrivant, e** [aʀivɑ̃, -ɑ̃t] *nm/f* newcomer
**arrivée** [aʀive] *nf* arrival; (*ligne d'arrivée*) finish; **~
d'air/de gaz** air/gas inlet; **courrier à l'~**
incoming mail; **à mon ~** when I arrived
**arriver** [aʀive] *vi* to arrive; (*survenir*) to happen,
occur; **j'arrive!** (I'm) just coming!; **il arrive à
Paris à 8 h** he gets to *ou* arrives in Paris at 8; **~ à
destination** to arrive at one's destination; **~ à**
(*atteindre*) to reach; **~ à (faire) qch** (*réussir*) to
manage (to do) sth; **~ à échéance** to fall due;
**en ~ à faire ...** to end up doing ..., get to the
point of doing ...; **il arrive que ...** it happens
that ...; **il lui arrive de faire ...** he sometimes
does ...

**arrivisme** [aʀivism(ə)] *nm* ambition,
ambitiousness
**arriviste** [aʀivist(ə)] *nm/f* go-getter
**arrogance** [aʀɔgɑ̃s] *nf* arrogance
**arrogant, e** [aʀɔgɑ̃, -ɑ̃t] *adj* arrogant
**arroger** [aʀɔʒe]: **s'arroger** *vt* to assume
(without right); **s'~ le droit de ...** to assume
the right to ...
**arrondi, e** [aʀɔ̃di] *adj* round ▷ *nm* roundness
**arrondir** [aʀɔ̃diʀ] *vt* (*forme, objet*) to round;
(*somme*) to round off; **s'arrondir** *vi* to become
round(ed); **~ ses fins de mois** to supplement
one's pay
**arrondissement** [aʀɔ̃dismɑ̃] *nm* (*Admin*)
≈ district
**arrosage** [aʀozaʒ] *nm* watering; **tuyau d'~**
hose(pipe)
**arroser** [aʀoze] *vt* to water; (*victoire etc*) to
celebrate (over a drink); (*Culin*) to baste
**arroseur** [aʀozœʀ] *nm* (*tourniquet*) sprinkler
**arroseuse** [aʀozøz] *nf* water cart
**arrosoir** [aʀozwaʀ] *nm* watering can
**arrt** *abr* = **arrondissement**
**arsenal, -aux** [aʀsənal, -o] *nm* (*Navig*) naval
dockyard; (*Mil*) arsenal; (*fig*) gear,
paraphernalia
**art** [aʀ] *nm* art; **avoir l'~ de faire** (*fig: personne*) to
have a talent for doing; **les ~s** the arts; **livre/
critique d'~** art book/ critic; **objet d'~** objet
d'art; **~ dramatique** dramatic art; **~s
martiaux** martial arts; **~s et métiers** applied
arts and crafts; **~s ménagers** home economics
*sg*; **~s plastiques** plastic arts
**art.** *abr* = **article**
**artère** [aʀtɛʀ] *nf* (*Anat*) artery; (*rue*) main road
**artériel, le** [aʀteʀjɛl] *adj* arterial
**artériosclérose** [aʀteʀjɔskleʀoz] *nf*
arteriosclerosis
**arthrite** [aʀtʀit] *nf* arthritis
**arthrose** [aʀtʀoz] *nf* (*degenerative*)
osteoarthritis
**artichaut** [aʀtiʃo] *nm* artichoke

**article** [aʀtikl(ə)] nm article; (Comm) item, article; **faire l'~** (Comm) to do one's sales spiel; **faire l'~ de** (fig) to sing the praises of; **à l'~ de la mort** at the point of death; **~ défini/indéfini** definite/indefinite article; **~ de fond** (Presse) feature article; **~s de bureau** office equipment; **~s de voyage** travel goods ou items

**articulaire** [aʀtikylɛʀ] adj of the joints, articular

**articulation** [aʀtikylɑsjɔ̃] nf articulation; (Anat) joint

**articulé, e** [aʀtikyle] adj (membre) jointed; (poupée) with moving joints

**articuler** [aʀtikyle] vt to articulate; **s'articuler (sur)** vi (Anat, Tech) to articulate (with); **s'~ autour de** (fig) to centre around ou on, turn on

**artifice** [aʀtifis] nm device, trick

**artificiel, le** [aʀtifisjɛl] adj artificial

**artificiellement** [aʀtifisjɛlmɑ̃] adv artificially

**artificier** [aʀtifisje] nm pyrotechnist

**artificieux, -euse** [aʀtifisjø, -øz] adj guileful, deceitful

**artillerie** [aʀtijʀi] nf artillery, ordnance

**artilleur** [aʀtijœʀ] nm artilleryman, gunner

**artisan** [aʀtizɑ̃] nm artisan, (self-employed) craftsman; **l'~ de la victoire/du malheur** the architect of victory/of the disaster

**artisanal, e, -aux** [aʀtizanal, -o] adj of ou made by craftsmen; (péj) cottage industry cpd, unsophisticated

**artisanalement** [aʀtizanalmɑ̃] adv by craftsmen

**artisanat** [aʀtizana] nm arts and crafts pl

**artiste** [aʀtist(ə)] nm/f artist; (Théât, Mus) artist, performer; (: de variétés) entertainer

**artistique** [aʀtistik] adj artistic

**artistiquement** [aʀtistikmɑ̃] adv artistically

**aryen, ne** [aʀjɛ̃, -ɛn] adj Aryan

**AS** sigle fpl (Admin) = **assurances sociales** ▷ sigle f (Sport: = Association sportive) ≈ FC (= Football Club)

**as** vb [a] voir **avoir** ▷ nm [ɑs] ace

**a/s** abr (= aux soins de) c/o

**ASBL** sigle f (= association sans but lucratif) non-profit-making organization

**asc.** abr = **ascenseur**

**ascendance** [asɑ̃dɑ̃s] nf (origine) ancestry; (Astrologie) ascendant

**ascendant, e** [asɑ̃dɑ̃, -ɑ̃t] adj upward ▷ nm influence; **ascendants** nmpl ascendants

**ascenseur** [asɑ̃sœʀ] nm lift (Brit), elevator (US)

**ascension** [asɑ̃sjɔ̃] nf ascent; climb; **l'A~** (Rel) the Ascension; (: jour férié) Ascension (Day); see note; **(île de) l'A~** Ascension Island

● **L'ASCENSION**
●
● The fête de l'Ascension is a public holiday in
● France. It always falls on a Thursday, usually
● in May. Many French people take the
● following Friday off work too and enjoy a
● long weekend.

**ascète** [asɛt] nm/f ascetic

**ascétique** [asetik] adj ascetic

**ascétisme** [asetism(ə)] nm asceticism

**ascorbique** [askɔʀbik] adj: **acide ~** ascorbic acid

**ASE** sigle f (= Agence spatiale européenne) ESA (= European Space Agency)

**asepsie** [asɛpsi] nf asepsis

**aseptique** [asɛptik] adj aseptic

**aseptisé, e** [asɛptize] (péj) adj sanitized

**asexué, e** [asɛksɥe] adj asexual

**asiatique** [azjatik] adj Asian, Asiatic ▷ nm/f: **Asiatique** Asian

**Asie** [azi] nf: **l'~** Asia

**asile** [azil] nm (refuge) refuge, sanctuary; (Pol): **droit d'~** (political) asylum; (pour malades, vieillards etc) home; **accorder l'~ politique à qn** to grant ou give sb political asylum; **chercher/trouver ~ quelque part** to seek/find refuge somewhere

**asocial, e, -aux** [asɔsjal, -o] adj antisocial

**aspect** [aspɛ] nm appearance, look; (fig) aspect, side; (Ling) aspect; **à l'~ de** at the sight of

**asperge** [aspɛʀʒ(ə)] nf asparagus no pl

**asperger** [aspɛʀʒe] vt to spray, sprinkle

**aspérité** [aspeʀite] nf excrescence, protruding bit (of rock etc)

**aspersion** [aspɛʀsjɔ̃] nf spraying, sprinkling

**asphalte** [asfalt(ə)] nm asphalt

**asphyxiant, e** [asfiksjɑ̃, -ɑ̃t] adj suffocating; **gaz ~** poison gas

**asphyxie** [asfiksi] nf suffocation, asphyxia, asphyxiation

**asphyxier** [asfiksje] vt to suffocate, asphyxiate; (fig) to stifle; **mourir asphyxié** to die of suffocation ou asphyxiation

**aspic** [aspik] nm (Zool) asp; (Culin) aspic

**aspirant, e** [aspiʀɑ̃, -ɑ̃t] adj: **pompe ~e** suction pump ▷ nm (Navig) midshipman

**aspirateur** [aspiʀatœʀ] nm vacuum cleaner, hoover®

**aspiration** [aspiʀasjɔ̃] nf inhalation, sucking (up); drawing up; **aspirations** nfpl (ambitions) aspirations

**aspirer** [aspiʀe] vt (air) to inhale; (liquide) to suck (up); (appareil) to suck ou draw up; **~ à** vt to aspire to

**aspirine** [aspiʀin] nf aspirin

**assagir** [asaʒiʀ] vt, **s'assagir** vi to quieten down, sober down

**assaillant, e** [asajɑ̃, -ɑ̃t] nm/f assailant, attacker

**assaillir** [asajiʀ] vt to assail, attack; **~ qn de** (questions) to assail ou bombard sb with

**assainir** [aseniʀ] vt to clean up; (eau, air) to purify

**assainissement** [asenismɑ̃] nm cleaning up; purifying

**assaisonnement** [asɛzɔnmɑ̃] nm seasoning

**assaisonner** [asɛzɔne] vt to season; **bien assaisonné** highly seasoned

**assassin** [asasɛ̃] nm murderer; assassin

**assassinat** [asasina] nm murder; assassination

**assassiner** [asasine] vt to murder; (surtout Pol) to assassinate

**assaut** [aso] *nm* assault, attack; **prendre d'~** to (take by) storm, assault; **donner l'~ (à)** to attack; **faire ~ de** (*rivaliser*) to vie with *ou* rival each other in

**assèchement** [asɛʃmɑ̃] *nm* draining, drainage

**assécher** [aseʃe] *vt* to drain

**ASSEDIC** [asedik] *sigle f* (= *Association pour l'emploi dans l'industrie et le commerce*) unemployment insurance scheme

**assemblage** [asɑ̃blaʒ] *nm* assembling; (*Menuiserie*) joint; **un ~ de** (*fig*) a collection of; **langage d'~** (*Inform*) assembly language

**assemblée** [asɑ̃ble] *nf* (*réunion*) meeting; (*public, assistance*) gathering; assembled people; (*Pol*) assembly; (*Rel*): **l'~ des fidèles** the congregation; **l'A~ nationale (AN)** the (French) National Assembly; *see note*

● **ASSEMBLÉE NATIONALE**
●
● The *Assemblée nationale* is the lower house of
● the French Parliament, the upper house
● being the "Sénat". It is housed in the Palais
● Bourbon in Paris. Its members, or "députés"
● are elected every five years.

**assembler** [asɑ̃ble] *vt* (*joindre, monter*) to assemble, put together; (*amasser*) to gather (together), collect (together); **s'assembler** *vi* to gather, collect

**assembleur** [asɑ̃blœʀ] *nm* assembler, fitter; (*Inform*) assembler

**assener, asséner** [asene] *vt*: **~ un coup à qn** to deal sb a blow

**assentiment** [asɑ̃timɑ̃] *nm* assent, consent; (*approbation*) approval

**asseoir** [aswaʀ] *vt* (*malade, bébé*) to sit up; (*personne debout*) to sit down; (*autorité, réputation*) to establish; **s'asseoir** *vi* to sit (o.s.) up; to sit (o.s.) down; **faire ~ qn** to ask sb to sit down; **asseyez-vous!, assieds-toi!** sit down!; **~ qch sur** to build sth on; (*appuyer*) to base sth on

**assermenté, e** [asɛʀmɑ̃te] *adj* sworn, on oath

**assertion** [asɛʀsjɔ̃] *nf* assertion

**asservir** [asɛʀviʀ] *vt* to subjugate, enslave

**asservissement** [asɛʀvismɑ̃] *nm* (*action*) enslavement; (*état*) slavery

**assesseur** [asesœʀ] *nm* (*Jur*) assessor

**asseyais** *etc* [aseje] *vb voir* **asseoir**

**assez** [ase] *adv* (*suffisamment*) enough, sufficiently; (*passablement*) rather, quite, fairly; **~!** enough!, that'll do!; **~/pas ~ cuit** well enough done/underdone; **est-il ~ fort/rapide?** is he strong/fast enough?; **il est passé ~ vite** he went past rather *ou* quite *ou* fairly fast; **~ de pain/livres** enough *ou* sufficient bread/books; **vous en avez ~?** have you got enough?; **en avoir ~ de qch** (*en être fatigué*) to have had enough of sth; **travailler ~** to work (hard) enough

**assidu, e** [asidy] *adj* assiduous, painstaking; (*régulier*) regular; **~ auprès de qn** attentive towards sb

**assiduité** [asidɥite] *nf* assiduousness, painstaking regularity; attentiveness; **assiduités** *nfpl* assiduous attentions

**assidûment** [asidymɑ̃] *adv* assiduously, painstakingly; attentively

**assied** *etc* [asje] *vb voir* **asseoir**

**assiégé, e** [asjeʒe] *adj* under siege, besieged

**assiéger** [asjeʒe] *vt* to besiege, lay siege to; (*foule, touristes*) to mob, besiege

**assiérai** *etc* [asjeʀe] *vb voir* **asseoir**

**assiette** [asjɛt] *nf* plate; (*contenu*) plate(ful); (*équilibre*) seat; (*de colonne*) seating; (*de navire*) trim; **~ anglaise** assorted cold meats; **~ creuse** (soup) dish, soup plate; **~ à dessert** dessert *ou* side plate; **~ de l'impôt** basis of (tax) assessment; **~ plate** (dinner) plate

**assiettée** [asjete] *nf* plateful

**assignation** [asiɲasjɔ̃] *nf* assignation; (*Jur*) summons; (: *de témoin*) subpoena; **~ à résidence** compulsory order of residence

**assigner** [asiɲe] *vt*: **~ qch à** to assign *ou* allot sth to; (*valeur, importance*) to attach sth to; (*somme*) to allocate sth to; (*limites*) to set *ou* fix sth to; (*cause, effet*) to ascribe *ou* attribute sth to; **~ qn à** (*affecter*) to assign sb to; **~ qn à résidence** (*Jur*) to give sb a compulsory order of residence

**assimilable** [asimilabl(ə)] *adj* easily assimilated *ou* absorbed

**assimilation** [asimilasjɔ̃] *nf* assimilation, absorption

**assimiler** [asimile] *vt* to assimilate, absorb; (*comparer*): **~ qch/qn à** to liken *ou* compare sth/sb to; **s'assimiler** *vi* (*s'intégrer*) to be assimilated *ou* absorbed; **ils sont assimilés aux infirmières** (*Admin*) they are classed as nurses

**assis, e** [asi, -iz] *pp de* **asseoir** ▷ *adj* sitting (down), seated ▷ *nf* (*Constr*) course; (*Géo*) stratum (*pl* -a); (*fig*) basis (*pl* bases), foundation; **~ en tailleur** sitting cross-legged

**assises** [asiz] *nfpl* (*Jur*) assizes; (*congrès*) (annual) conference

**assistanat** [asistana] *nm* assistantship; (*à l'université*) probationary lectureship

**assistance** [asistɑ̃s] *nf* (*public*) audience; (*aide*) assistance; **porter** *ou* **prêter ~ à qn** to give sb assistance; **A~ publique (AP)** *public health service*; **enfant de l'A~ (publique)** child in care; **~ technique** technical aid

**assistant, e** [asistɑ̃, -ɑ̃t] *nm/f* assistant; (*d'université*) probationary lecturer; **les assistants** *nmpl* (*auditeurs etc*) those present; **~e sociale** social worker

**assisté, e** [asiste] *adj* (*Auto*) power assisted ▷ *nm/f* person receiving aid from the State

**assister** [asiste] *vt* to assist; **~ à** *vt* (*scène, événement*) to witness; (*conférence*) to attend, be (present) at; (*spectacle, match*) to be at, see

**association** [asɔsjasjɔ̃] *nf* association; (*Comm*) partnership; **~ d'idées/images** association of ideas/images

**associé, e** [asɔsje] *nm/f* associate; (*Comm*)

partner
**associer** [asɔsje] *vt* to associate; ~ **qn à** *(profits)*
to give sb a share of; *(affaire)* to make sb a
partner in; *(joie, triomphe)* to include sb in; ~ **qch**
**à** *(joindre, allier)* to combine sth with; **s'associer**
*vi* to join together; *(Comm)* to form a
partnership ▷ *vt (collaborateur)* to take on (as a
partner); **s'~ à** to be combined with; *(opinions,
joie de qn)* to share in; **s'~ à** *ou* **avec qn pour faire**
to join (forces) *ou* join together with sb to do
**assoie** *etc* [aswa] *vb voir* **asseoir**
**assoiffé, e** [aswafe] *adj* thirsty; *(fig)*: ~ **de** *(sang)*
thirsting for; *(gloire)* thirsting after
**assoirai** [aswaʀe], **assois** *etc* [aswa] *vb voir*
**asseoir**
**assolement** [asɔlmɑ̃] *nm* (systematic) rotation
of crops
**assombrir** [asɔ̃bʀiʀ] *vt* to darken; *(fig)* to fill
with gloom; **s'assombrir** *vi* to darken; *(devenir
nuageux, fig: visage)* to cloud over; *(fig)* to become
gloomy
**assommer** [asɔme] *vt* *(étourdir, abrutir)* to knock
out, stun; *(fam: ennuyer)* to bore stiff
**Assomption** [asɔ̃psjɔ̃] *nf*: **l'~** the Assumption;
*see note*

⦿ **L'ASSOMPTION**
⦿
⦿ The *fête de l'Assomption*, more commonly
⦿ known as "le 15 août" is a national holiday
⦿ in France. Traditionally, large numbers of
⦿ holidaymakers leave home on 15 August,
⦿ frequently causing chaos on the roads.

**assorti, e** [asɔʀti] *adj* matched, matching;
**fromages/légumes ~s** assorted cheeses/
vegetables; ~ **à** matching; ~ **de** accompanied
with; *(conditions, conseils)* coupled with; **bien/
mal ~** well/ill-matched
**assortiment** [asɔʀtimɑ̃] *nm (choix)* assortment,
selection; *(harmonie de couleurs, formes)*
arrangement; *(Comm: lot, stock)* selection
**assortir** [asɔʀtiʀ] *vt* to match; **s'assortir** *vi* to
go well together, match; ~ **qch à** to match sth
with; ~ **qch de** to accompany sth with; **s'~ de**
to be accompanied by
**assoupi, e** [asupi] *adj* dozing, sleeping; *(fig)*
(be)numbed; *(sens)* dulled
**assoupir** [asupiʀ]: **s'assoupir** *vi* *(personne)* to
doze off; *(sens)* to go numb
**assoupissement** [asupismɑ̃] *nm (sommeil)*
dozing; *(fig: somnolence)* drowsiness
**assouplir** [asupliʀ] *vt* to make supple, soften;
*(membres, corps)* to limber up, make supple; *(fig)*
to relax; *(: caractère)* to soften, make more
flexible; **s'assouplir** *vi* to soften; to limber up;
to relax; to become more flexible
**assouplissant** [asuplisɑ̃] *nm* (fabric) softener
**assouplissement** [asuplismɑ̃] *nm* softening;
limbering up; relaxation; **exercices d'~**
limbering up exercises
**assourdir** [asuʀdiʀ] *vt (bruit)* to deaden, muffle;

*(bruit)* to deafen
**assourdissant, e** [asuʀdisɑ̃, -ɑ̃t] *adj (bruit)*
deafening
**assouvir** [asuviʀ] *vt* to satisfy, appease
**assoyais** *etc* [aswajɛ] *vb voir* **asseoir**
**assujetti, e** [asyʒeti] *adj*: ~ **(à)** subject (to);
*(Admin)*: ~ **à l'impôt** subject to tax(ation)
**assujettir** [asyʒetiʀ] *vt* to subject, subjugate;
*(fixer: planches, tableau)* to fix securely; ~ **qn à**
*(règle, impôt)* to subject sb to
**assujettissement** [asyʒetismɑ̃] *nm* subjection,
subjugation
**assumer** [asyme] *vt (fonction, emploi)* to assume,
take on; *(accepter: conséquence, situation)* to accept
**assurance** [asyʀɑ̃s] *nf (certitude)* assurance;
*(confiance en soi)* (self-)confidence; *(contrat)*
insurance (policy); *(secteur commercial)*
insurance; **prendre une ~ contre** to take out
insurance *ou* an insurance policy against; ~
**contre l'incendie** fire insurance; ~ **contre le
vol** insurance against theft; **société d'~**,
**compagnie d'~s** insurance company; ~
**maladie (AM)** health insurance; ~ **au tiers**
third party insurance; ~ **tous risques** *(Auto)*
comprehensive insurance; **~s sociales (AS)**
≈ National Insurance *(Brit)*, ≈ Social Security
*(US)*
**assurance-vie** [asyʀɑ̃svi] *(pl* **assurances-vie***)* *nf*
life assurance *ou* insurance
**assurance-vol** [asyʀɑ̃svɔl] *(pl* **assurances-vol***)*
*nf* insurance against theft
**assuré, e** [asyʀe] *adj (victoire etc)* certain, sure;
*(démarche, voix)* assured, (self-)confident;
*(certain)*: ~ **de** confident of; *(Assurances)* insured
▷ *nm/f* insured (person); ~ **social** ≈ member of
the National Insurance *(Brit)* *ou* Social Security
*(US)* scheme
**assurément** [asyʀemɑ̃] *adv* assuredly, most
certainly
**assurer** [asyʀe] *vt (Comm)* to insure; *(stabiliser)* to
steady, stabilize; *(victoire etc)* to ensure, make
certain; *(frontières, pouvoir)* to make secure;
*(service, garde)* to provide, operate; ~ **qch à qn**
*(garantir)* to secure *ou* guarantee sth for sb;
*(certifier)* to assure sb of sth; ~ **à qn que** to assure
sb that; **je vous assure que non/si** I assure you
that that is not the case/is the case; ~ **qn de** to
assure sb of; ~ **ses arrières** *(fig)* to be sure one
has something to fall back on; **s'assurer**
**(contre)** *vi (Comm)* to insure o.s. (against); **s'~
de/que** *(vérifier)* to make sure of/that; **s'~ (de)**
*(aide de qn)* to secure; **s'~ sur la vie** to take out
life insurance; **s'~ le concours/la
collaboration de qn** to secure sb's aid/
collaboration
**assureur** [asyʀœʀ] *nm* insurance agent; *(société)*
insurers *pl*
**Assyrie** [asiʀi] *nf*: **l'~** Assyria
**astérisque** [asteʀisk(ə)] *nm* asterisk
**astéroïde** [asteʀɔid] *nm* asteroid
**asthmatique** [asmatik] *adj* asthmatic
**asthme** [asm(ə)] *nm* asthma

**asticot** [astiko] *nm* maggot

**asticoter** [astikɔte] *vt (fam)* to needle, get at

**astigmate** [astigmat] *adj (Méd: personne)* astigmatic, having an astigmatism

**astiquer** [astike] *vt* to polish, shine

**astrakan** [astʀakɑ̃] *nm* astrakhan

**astral, e, -aux** [astʀal, -o] *adj* astral

**astre** [astʀ(ə)] *nm* star

**astreignant, e** [astʀɛɲɑ̃, -ɑ̃t] *adj* demanding

**astreindre** [astʀɛ̃dʀ(ə)] *vt*: ~ **qn à qch** to force sth upon sb; ~ **qn à faire** to compel *ou* force sb to do; **s'astreindre à** to compel *ou* force o.s. to

**astringent, e** [astʀɛ̃ʒɑ̃, -ɑ̃t] *adj* astringent

**astrologie** [astʀɔlɔʒi] *nf* astrology

**astrologique** [astʀɔlɔʒik] *adj* astrological

**astrologue** [astʀɔlɔg] *nm/f* astrologer

**astronaute** [astʀɔnot] *nm/f* astronaut

**astronautique** [astʀɔnotik] *nf* astronautics *sg*

**astronome** [astʀɔnɔm] *nm/f* astronomer

**astronomie** [astʀɔnɔmi] *nf* astronomy

**astronomique** [astʀɔnɔmik] *adj* astronomic(al)

**astrophysicien, ne** [astʀɔfizisjɛ̃, -ɛn] *nm/f* astrophysicist

**astrophysique** [astʀɔfizik] *nf* astrophysics *sg*

**astuce** [astys] *nf* shrewdness, astuteness; *(truc)* trick, clever way; *(plaisanterie)* wisecrack

**astucieusement** [astysjøzmɑ̃] *adv* shrewdly, cleverly, astutely

**astucieux, -euse** [astysjø, -øz] *adj* shrewd, clever, astute

**asymétrique** [asimetʀik] *adj* asymmetric(al)

**AT** *sigle m* (= *Ancien Testament*) OT

**atavisme** [atavism(ə)] *nm* atavism, heredity

**atelier** [atəlje] *nm* workshop; *(de peintre)* studio

**atermoiements** [atɛʀmwamɑ̃] *nmpl* procrastination *sg*

**atermoyer** [atɛʀmwaje] *vi* to temporize, procrastinate

**athée** [ate] *adj* atheistic ▷ *nm/f* atheist

**athéisme** [ateism(ə)] *nm* atheism

**Athènes** [atɛn] *n* Athens

**athénien, ne** [atenjɛ̃, -ɛn] *adj* Athenian

**athlète** [atlɛt] *nm/f (Sport)* athlete; *(costaud)* muscleman

**athlétique** [atletik] *adj* athletic

**athlétisme** [atletism(ə)] *nm* athletics *sg*; **faire de l'~** to do athletics; **tournoi d'~** athletics meeting

**Atlantide** [atlɑ̃tid] *nf*: **l'~** Atlantis

**atlantique** [atlɑ̃tik] *adj* Atlantic ▷ *nm*: **l'(océan) A~** the Atlantic (Ocean)

**atlantiste** [atlɑ̃tist(ə)] *adj, nm/f* Atlanticist

**Atlas** [atlɑs] *nm*: **l'~** the Atlas Mountains

**atlas** [atlɑs] *nm* atlas

**atmosphère** [atmɔsfɛʀ] *nf* atmosphere

**atmosphérique** [atmɔsfeʀik] *adj* atmospheric

**atoll** [atɔl] *nm* atoll

**atome** [atom] *nm* atom

**atomique** [atɔmik] *adj* atomic, nuclear; *(usine)* nuclear; *(nombre, masse)* atomic

**atomiseur** [atɔmizœʀ] *nm* atomizer

**atomiste** [atɔmist(ə)] *nm/f (aussi:* **savant,**

**ingénieur** *etc* **atomiste)** atomic scientist

**atone** [atɔn] *adj* lifeless; *(Ling)* unstressed, unaccented

**atours** [atuʀ] *nmpl* attire *sg*, finery *sg*

**atout** [atu] *nm* trump; *(fig)* asset; *(: plus fort)* trump card; **"~ pique/trèfle"** "spades/clubs are trumps"

**ATP** *sigle f* (= *Association des tennismen professionnels*) ATP (= *Association of Tennis Professionals*) ▷ *sigle mpl* = **arts et traditions populaires**; **musée des ~** ≈ folk museum

**âtre** [ɑtʀ(ə)] *nm* hearth

**atroce** [atʀɔs] *adj* atrocious, horrible

**atrocement** [atʀɔsmɑ̃] *adv* atrociously, horribly

**atrocité** [atʀɔsite] *nf* atrocity

**atrophie** [atʀɔfi] *nf* atrophy

**atrophier** [atʀɔfje]: **s'atrophier** *vi* to atrophy

**attabler** [atable]: **s'attabler** *vi* to sit down at (the) table; **s'~ à la terrasse** to sit down (at a table) on the terrace

**ATTAC** *sigle f* (= *Association pour la Taxation des Transactions pour l'Aide aux Citoyens*) ATTAC, organization critical of globalization originally set up to demand a tax on foreign currency speculation

**attachant, e** [ataʃɑ̃, -ɑ̃t] *adj* engaging, likeable

**attache** [ataʃ] *nf* clip, fastener; *(fig)* tie; **attaches** *nfpl (relations)* connections; **à l'~** *(chien)* tied up

**attaché, e** [ataʃe] *adj*: **être ~ à** *(aimer)* to be attached to ▷ *nm (Admin)* attaché; **~ de presse/ d'ambassade** press/embassy attaché; **~ commercial** commercial attaché

**attaché-case** [ataʃekɛz] *nm inv* attaché case (Brit), briefcase

**attachement** [ataʃmɑ̃] *nm* attachment

**attacher** [ataʃe] *vt* to tie up; *(étiquette)* to attach, tie on; *(souliers)* to do up ▷ *vi (poêle, riz)* to stick; **s'attacher** *vi (robe etc)* to do up; **s'~ à** *(par affection)* to become attached to; **s'~ à faire qch** to endeavour ou try to do sth; **~ qch à** to tie ou fasten ou attach sth to; **~ qn à** *(fig: lier)* to attach sb to; **~ du prix/de l'importance à** to attach great value/attach importance to

**attaquant** [atakɑ̃] *nm (Mil)* attacker; *(Sport)* striker, forward

**attaque** [atak] *nf* attack; *(cérébrale)* stroke; *(d'épilepsie)* fit; **être/se sentir d'~** to be/feel on form; **~ à main armée** armed attack

**attaquer** [atake] *vt* to attack; *(en justice)* to bring an action against, sue; *(travail)* to tackle, set about ▷ *vi* to attack; **s'attaquer à** *vt* to attack; *(épidémie, misère)* to tackle, attack

**attardé, e** [ataʀde] *adj (passants)* late; *(enfant)* backward; *(conceptions)* old-fashioned

**attarder** [ataʀde]: **s'attarder** *vi (sur qch, en chemin)* to linger; *(chez qn)* to stay on

**atteignais** *etc* [atɛɲɛ] *vb voir* **atteindre**

**atteindre** [atɛ̃dʀ(ə)] *vt* to reach; *(blesser)* to hit; *(contacter)* to reach, contact, get in touch with; *(émouvoir)* to affect

**atteint, e** [atɛ̃, -ɛ̃t] *pp de* **atteindre** ▷ *adj (Méd)*: **être ~ de** to be suffering from ▷ *nf* attack; **hors**

**d'~e** out of reach; **porter ~e à** to strike a blow at, undermine

**attelage** [atlaʒ] *nm* (*de remorque etc*) coupling (*Brit*), (trailer) hitch (*US*); (*animaux*) team; (*harnachement*) harness; (: *de bœufs*) yoke

**atteler** [atle] *vt* (*cheval, bœufs*) to hitch up; (*wagons*) to couple; **s'atteler à** (*travail*) to buckle down to

**attelle** [atɛl] *nf* splint

**attenant, e** [atnã, -ãt] *adj*: **~ (à)** adjoining

**attendant** [atãdã]: **en ~** *adv* (*dans l'intervalle*) meanwhile, in the meantime

**attendre** [atãdʀ(ə)] *vt* to wait for; (*être destiné ou réservé à*) to await, be in store for ▷ *vi* to wait; **je n'attends plus rien (de la vie)** I expect nothing more (from life); **attendez que je réfléchisse** wait while I think; **s'~ à (ce que)** (*escompter*) to expect (that); **je ne m'y attendais pas** I didn't expect that; **ce n'est pas ce à quoi je m'attendais** that's not what I expected; **~ un enfant** to be expecting a baby; **~ de pied ferme** to wait determinedly; **~ de faire/d'être** to wait until one does/is; **~ que** to wait until; **~ qch de** to expect sth of; **faire ~ qn** to keep sb waiting; **se faire ~** to keep people (*ou us etc*) waiting; **en attendant** *adv voir* **attendant**

**attendri, e** [atãdʀi] *adj* tender

**attendrir** [atãdʀiʀ] *vt* to move (to pity); (*viande*) to tenderize; **s'attendrir (sur)** to be moved *ou* touched (by)

**attendrissant, e** [atãdʀisã, -ãt] *adj* moving, touching

**attendrissement** [atãdʀismã] *nm* (*tendre*) emotion; (*apitoyé*) pity

**attendrisseur** [atãdʀisœʀ] *nm* tenderizer

**attendu, e** [atãdy] *pp de* **attendre** ▷ *adj* long-awaited; (*prévu*) expected ▷ *nm*: **~s reasons adduced for a judgment**; **~ que** *conj* considering that, since

**attentat** [atãta] *nm* (*contre une personne*) assassination attempt; (*contre un bâtiment*) attack; **~ à la bombe** bomb attack; **~ à la pudeur** (*exhibitionnisme*) indecent exposure *no pl*; (*agression*) indecent assault *no pl*; **~ suicide** suicide bombing

**attente** [atãt] *nf* wait; (*espérance*) expectation; **contre toute ~** contrary to (all) expectations

**attenter** [atãte]: **~ à** *vt* (*liberté*) to violate; **~ à la vie de qn** to make an attempt on sb's life; **~ à ses jours** to make an attempt on one's life

**attentif, -ive** [atãtif, -iv] *adj* (*auditeur*) attentive; (*soin*) scrupulous; (*travail*) careful; **~ à** paying attention to; (*devoir*) mindful of; **~ à faire** careful to do

**attention** [atãsjõ] *nf* attention; (*prévenance*) attention, thoughtfulness *no pl*; **mériter ~** to be worthy of attention; **à l'~ de** for the attention of; **porter qch à l'~ de qn** to bring sth to sb's attention; **attirer l'~ de qn sur qch** to draw sb's attention to sth; **faire ~ (à)** to be careful (of); **faire ~ (à ce) que** to be ou make sure that; **~!** careful!, watch!, watch *ou* mind (*Brit*) out!; **~,**

**si vous ouvrez cette lettre** (*sanction*) just watch out, if you open that letter; **~, respectez les consignes de sécurité** be sure to observe the safety instructions

**attentionné, e** [atãsjone] *adj* thoughtful, considerate

**attentisme** [atãtism(ə)] *nm* wait-and-see policy

**attentiste** [atãtist(ə)] *adj* (*politique*) wait-and-see ▷ *nm/f* believer in a wait-and-see policy

**attentivement** [atãtivmã] *adv* attentively

**atténuant, e** [atenɥã, -ãt] *adj*: **circonstances ~es** extenuating circumstances

**atténuer** [atenɥe] *vt* to alleviate, ease; (*diminuer*) to lessen; (*amoindrir*) to mitigate the effects of; **s'atténuer** *vi* to ease; (*violence etc*) to abate

**atterrer** [ateʀe] *vt* to dismay, appal

**atterrir** [ateʀiʀ] *vi* to land

**atterrissage** [ateʀisaʒ] *nm* landing; **~ sur le ventre/sans visibilité/forcé** belly/blind/forced landing

**attestation** [atestasjõ] *nf* certificate, testimonial; **~ médicale** doctor's certificate

**attester** [ateste] *vt* to testify to, vouch for; (*démontrer*) to attest, testify to; **~ que** to testify that

**attiédir** [atjediʀ]: **s'attiédir** *vi* to become lukewarm; (*fig*) to cool down

**attifé, e** [atife] *adj* (*fam*) got up (*Brit*), decked out

**attifer** [atife] *vt* to get (*Brit*) *ou* do up, deck out

**attique** [atik] *nm*: **appartement en ~** penthouse (flat (*Brit*) *ou* apartment (*US*))

**attirail** [atiʀaj] *nm* gear; (*péj*) paraphernalia

**attirance** [atiʀãs] *nf* attraction; (*séduction*) lure

**attirant, e** [atiʀã, -ãt] *adj* attractive, appealing

**attirer** [atiʀe] *vt* to attract; (*appâter*) to lure, entice; **~ qn dans un coin/vers soi** to draw sb into a corner/towards one; **~ l'attention de qn** to attract sb's attention; **~ l'attention de qn sur qch** to draw sb's attention to sth; **~ des ennuis à qn** to make trouble for sb; **s'~ des ennuis** to bring trouble upon o.s., get into trouble

**attiser** [atize] *vt* (*feu*) to poke (up), stir up; (*fig*) to fan the flame of, stir up

**attitré, e** [atitʀe] *adj* qualified; (*agréé*) accredited, appointed

**attitude** [atityd] *nf* attitude; (*position du corps*) bearing

**attouchements** [atuʃmã] *nmpl* touching *sg*; (*sexuels*) fondling *sg*, stroking *sg*

**attractif, -ive** [atʀaktif, -iv] *adj* attractive

**attraction** [atʀaksjõ] *nf* attraction; (*de cabaret, cirque*) number

**attrait** [atʀɛ] *nm* appeal, attraction; (*plus fort*) lure; **attraits** *nmpl* attractions; **éprouver de l'~ pour** to be attracted to

**attrape** [atʀap] *nf voir* **farce**

**attrape-nigaud** [atʀapnigo] *nm* con

**attraper** [atʀape] *vt* to catch; (*habitude, amende*) to get, pick up; (*fam: duper*) to take in (*Brit*), con

**attrayant, e** [atʀɛjɑ̃, -ɑ̃t] *adj* attractive
**attribuer** [atʀibɥe] *vt* (*prix*) to award; (*rôle, tâche*) to allocate, assign; (*imputer*) ~ **qch à** to attribute sth to, ascribe sth to, put sth down to; **s'attribuer** *vt* (*s'approprier*) to claim for o.s.
**attribut** [atʀiby] *nm* attribute; (*Ling*) complement
**attribution** [atʀibysjɔ̃] *nf* (*voir attribuer*) awarding; allocation, assignment; attribution; **attributions** *nfpl* (*compétence*) attributions; **complément d'~** (*Ling*) indirect object
**attristant, e** [atʀistɑ̃, -ɑ̃t] *adj* saddening
**attrister** [atʀiste] *vt* to sadden; **s'~ de qch** to be saddened by sth
**attroupement** [atʀupmɑ̃] *nm* crowd, mob
**attrouper** [atʀupe]: **s'attrouper** *vi* to gather
**au** [o] *prép voir* **à**
**aubade** [obad] *nf* dawn serenade
**aubaine** [obɛn] *nf* godsend; (*financière*) windfall; (*Comm*) bonanza
**aube** [ob] *nf* dawn, daybreak; (*Rel*) alb; **à l'~** at dawn *ou* daybreak; **à l'~ de** (*fig*) at the dawn of
**aubépine** [obepin] *nf* hawthorn
**auberge** [obɛʀʒ(ə)] *nf* inn; ~ **de jeunesse** youth hostel
**aubergine** [obɛʀʒin] *nf* aubergine (*Brit*), eggplant (*US*)
**aubergiste** [obɛʀʒist(ə)] *nm/f* inn-keeper, hotel-keeper
**auburn** [obœʀn] *adj inv* auburn
**aucun, e** [okœ̃, -yn] *adj, pron* no; (*positif*) any ▷ *pron* none; (*positif*) any(one); **il n'y a ~ livre** there isn't any book, there is no book; **je n'en vois ~ qui ...** I can't see any which ..., I (can) see none which ...; ~ **homme** no man; **sans ~ doute** without any doubt; **sans ~e hésitation** without hesitation; **plus qu'~ autre** more than any other; **plus qu'~ de ceux qui ...** more than any of those who ...; **en ~e façon** in no way at all; ~ **des deux** neither of the two; ~ **d'entre eux** none of them; **d'~s** (*certains*) some
**aucunement** [okynmɑ̃] *adv* in no way, not in the least
**audace** [odas] *nf* daring, boldness; (*péj*) audacity; **il a eu l'~ de ...** he had the audacity to ...; **vous ne manquez pas d'~!** you're not lacking in nerve *ou* cheek!
**audacieux, -euse** [odasjø, -øz] *adj* daring, bold
**au-dedans** [odədɑ̃] *adv, prép* inside
**au-dehors** [odəɔʀ] *adv, prép* outside
**au-delà** [odla] *adv* beyond ▷ *nm*: **l'~** the hereafter; ~ **de** *prép* beyond
**au-dessous** [odsu] *adv* underneath; below; ~ **de** *prép* under(neath), below; (*limite, somme etc*) below, under; (*dignité, condition*) below
**au-dessus** [odsy] *adv* above; ~ **de** *prép* above
**au-devant** [odvɑ̃]: ~ **de** *prép*: **aller ~ de** to go (out) and meet; (*souhaits de qn*) to anticipate
**audible** [odibl(ə)] *adj* audible
**audience** [odjɑ̃s] *nf* audience; (*Jur: séance*) hearing; **trouver ~ auprès de** to arouse much interest among, get the (interested)

attention of
**audimat®** [odimat] *nm* (*taux d'écoute*) ratings *pl*
**audio-visuel, le** [odjovizɥɛl] *adj* audio-visual ▷ *nm* (*équipement*) audio-visual aids *pl*; (*méthodes*) audio-visual methods *pl*; **l'~** radio and television
**auditeur, -trice** [oditœʀ, -tʀis] *nm/f* (*à la radio*) listener; (*à une conférence*) member of the audience, listener; ~ **libre** unregistered student (*attending lectures*), auditor (*US*)
**auditif, -ive** [oditif, -iv] *adj* (*mémoire*) auditory; **appareil ~** hearing aid
**audition** [odisjɔ̃] *nf* (*ouïe, écoute*) hearing; (*Jur: de témoins*) examination; (*Mus, Théât: épreuve*) audition
**auditionner** [odisjɔne] *vt, vi* to audition
**auditoire** [oditwaʀ] *nm* audience
**auditorium** [oditɔʀjɔm] *nm* (*public*) studio
**auge** [oʒ] *nf* trough
**augmentation** [ɔgmɑ̃tasjɔ̃] *nf* (*action*) increasing; raising; (*résultat*) increase; ~ **(de salaire)** rise (in salary) (*Brit*), (pay) raise (*US*)
**augmenter** [ɔgmɑ̃te] *vt* to increase; (*salaire, prix*) to increase, raise, put up; (*employé*) to increase the salary of, give a (salary) rise (*Brit*) *ou* (pay) raise (*US*) to ▷ *vi* to increase; ~ **de poids/volume** to gain (in) weight/volume
**augure** [ɔgyʀ] *nm* soothsayer, oracle; **de bon/mauvais ~** of good/ill omen
**augurer** [ɔgyʀe] *vt*: ~ **qch de** to foresee sth (coming) from *ou* out of; ~ **bien de** to augur well for
**auguste** [ɔgyst(ə)] *adj* august, noble, majestic
**aujourd'hui** [oʒuʀdɥi] *adv* today; **aujourd'hui en huit/quinze** a week/two weeks today, a week/two weeks from now; **à dater** *ou* **partir d'aujourd'hui** from today('s date)
**aumône** [omon] *nf* alms *sg* (*pl inv*); **faire l'~ (à qn)** to give alms (to sb); **faire l'~ de qch à qn** (*fig*) to favour sb with sth
**aumônerie** [omonʀi] *nf* chaplaincy
**aumônier** [omonje] *nm* chaplain
**auparavant** [oparavɑ̃] *adv* before(hand)
**auprès** [opʀɛ]: ~ **de** *prép* next to, close to; (*recourir, s'adresser*) to; (*en comparaison de*) compared with, next to; (*dans l'opinion de*) in the opinion of
**auquel** [okɛl] *pron voir* **lequel**
**aura** *etc* [ɔʀa] *vb voir* **avoir**
**aurai** *etc* [ɔʀe] *vb voir* **avoir**
**auréole** [ɔʀeɔl] *nf* halo; (*tache*) ring
**auréolé, e** [ɔʀeɔle] *adj* (*fig*): ~ **de gloire** crowned with *ou* in glory
**auriculaire** [ɔʀikylɛʀ] *nm* little finger
**aurons** *etc* [ɔʀɔ̃] *vb voir* **avoir**
**aurore** [ɔʀɔʀ] *nf* dawn, daybreak; ~ **boréale** northern lights *pl*
**ausculter** [ɔskylte] *vt* to sound
**auspices** [ɔspis] *nmpl*: **sous les ~ de** under the patronage *ou* auspices of; **sous de bons/mauvais ~** under favourable/unfavourable auspices
**aussi** [osi] *adv* (*également*) also, too; (*de*

33

*comparaison*) as ▷ *conj* therefore, consequently; ~
**fort que** as strong as; **lui** ~ (*sujet*) he too; (*objet*)
him too; ~ **bien que** (*de même que*) as well as
**aussitôt** [osito] *adv* straight away,
immediately; ~ **que** as soon as; ~ **envoyé** as
soon as it is (*ou* was) sent; ~ **fait** no sooner done
**austère** [ɔstɛʀ] *adj* austere; (*sévère*) stern
**austérité** [ɔsteʀite] *nf* austerity; **plan/budget**
**d'**~ austerity plan/budget
**austral, e** [ɔstʀal] *adj* southern; **l'océan A**~ the
Antarctic Ocean; **les Terres A~es** Antarctica
**Australie** [ɔstʀali] *nf*: **l'**~ Australia
**australien, ne** [ɔstʀaljɛ̃, -ɛn] *adj* Australian
▷ *nm/f*: **Australien, ne** Australian
**autant** [otɑ̃] *adv* so much; (*comparatif*): ~ **(que)**
as much (as); (*nombre*) as many (as); ~ **(de)** so
much (*ou* many); as much (*ou* many);
**n'importe qui aurait pu en faire** ~ anyone
could have done the same *ou* as much; ~ **partir**
we (*you etc*) may as well leave; ~ **ne rien dire**
best not say anything; ~ **dire que** ... one might
as well say that ...; **fort** ~ **que courageux** as
strong as he is brave; **il n'est pas découragé**
**pour** ~ he isn't discouraged for all that; **pour** ~
**que** *conj* assuming, as long as; **d'**~ *adv*
accordingly, in proportion; **d'**~ **plus/mieux**
**(que)** all the more/the better (since)
**autarcie** [otaʀsi] *nf* autarky, self-sufficiency
**autel** [ɔtɛl] *nm* altar
**auteur** [otœʀ] *nm* author; **l'**~ **de cette**
**remarque** the person who said that; **droit d'**~
copyright
**auteur-compositeur** [otœʀkɔ̃pozitœʀ] *nm/f*
composer-songwriter
**authenticité** [ɔtɑ̃tisite] *nf* authenticity
**authentifier** [ɔtɑ̃tifje] *vt* to authenticate
**authentique** [ɔtɑ̃tik] *adj* authentic, genuine
**autiste** [otist] *adj* autistic
**auto** [oto] *nf* car; **~s tamponneuses** bumper
cars, dodgems
**auto...** [oto] *préfixe* auto..., self-
**autobiographie** [otɔbjɔgʀafi] *nf* autobiography
**autobiographique** [otɔbjɔgʀafik] *adj*
autobiographical
**autobronzant** [otɔbʀɔ̃zɑ̃] *nm* self-tanning
cream (*or* lotion *etc*)
**autobus** [otɔbys] *nm* bus
**autocar** [otɔkaʀ] *nm* coach
**autochtone** [otɔktɔn] *nm/f* native
**autocollant, e** [otɔkɔlɑ̃, -ɑ̃t] *adj* self-adhesive;
(*enveloppe*) self-seal ▷ *nm* sticker
**auto-couchettes** [otɔkuʃɛt] *adj inv*: **train** ~ car
sleeper train, motorail® train (*Brit*)
**autocratique** [otɔkʀatik] *adj* autocratic
**autocritique** [otɔkʀitik] *nf* self-criticism
**autocuiseur** [otɔkwizœʀ] *nm* (*Culin*) pressure
cooker
**autodéfense** [otɔdefɑ̃s] *nf* self-defence;
**groupe d'**~ vigilante committee
**autodétermination** [otɔdetɛʀminasjɔ̃] *nf* self-
determination
**autodidacte** [otɔdidakt(ə)] *nm/f* self-taught

person
**autodiscipline** [otɔdisiplin] *nf* self-discipline
**autodrome** [otɔdʀom] *nm* motor-racing
stadium
**auto-école** [otɔekɔl] *nf* driving school
**autofinancement** [otɔfinɑ̃smɑ̃] *nm* self-
financing
**autogéré, e** [otɔʒeʀe] *adj* self-managed,
managed internally
**autogestion** [otɔʒɛstjɔ̃] *nf* joint worker-
management control
**autographe** [otɔgʀaf] *nm* autograph
**autoguidé, e** [otɔgide] *adj* self-guided
**automate** [otɔmat] *nm* (*robot*) automaton;
(*machine*) (automatic) machine
**automatique** [otɔmatik] *adj, nm* automatic; **l'**~
(*Tél*) ≈ direct dialling
**automatiquement** [otɔmatikmɑ̃] *adv*
automatically
**automatisation** [otɔmatizasjɔ̃] *nf* automation
**automatiser** [otɔmatize] *vt* to automate
**automédication** [otɔmedikasjɔ̃] *nf* self-
medication
**automitrailleuse** [otɔmitʀajøz] *nf* armoured
car
**automnal, e, -aux** [otɔnal, -o] *adj* autumnal
**automne** [otɔn] *nm* autumn (*Brit*), fall (*US*)
**automobile** [otɔmɔbil] *adj* motor *cpd* ▷ *nf*
(motor) car; **l'**~ motoring; (*industrie*) the car *ou*
automobile (*US*) industry
**automobiliste** [otɔmɔbilist(ə)] *nm/f* motorist
**autonettoyant, e** [otɔnɛtwajɑ̃, -ɑ̃t] *adj*: **four** ~
self-cleaning oven
**autonome** [otɔnɔm] *adj* autonomous
**autonomie** [otɔnɔmi] *nf* autonomy; (*Pol*) self-
government, autonomy; ~ **de vol** range
**autonomiste** [otɔnɔmist(ə)] *nm/f* separatist
**autoportrait** [otɔpɔʀtʀɛ] *nm* self-portrait
**autopsie** [otɔpsi] *nf* post-mortem
(examination), autopsy
**autopsier** [otɔpsje] *vt* to carry out a post-
mortem *ou* an autopsy on
**autoradio** [otɔʀadjo] *nf* car radio
**autorail** [otɔʀaj] *nm* railcar
**autorisation** [otɔʀizasjɔ̃] *nf* permission,
authorization; (*papiers*) permit; **donner à qn l'**~
**de** to give permission to, authorize sb to;
**avoir l'**~ **de faire** to be allowed *ou* have
permission to do, be authorized to do
**autorisé, e** [otɔʀize] *adj* (*opinion, sources*)
authoritative; (*permis*): ~ **à faire** authorized *ou*
permitted to do; **dans les milieux ~s** in official
circles
**autoriser** [otɔʀize] *vt* to give permission for,
authorize; (*fig*) to allow (of), sanction; ~ **qn à**
**faire** to give permission to sb to do, authorize
sb to do
**autoritaire** [otɔʀitɛʀ] *adj* authoritarian
**autoritarisme** [otɔʀitaʀism(ə)] *nm*
authoritarianism
**autorité** [otɔʀite] *nf* authority; **faire** ~ to be
authoritative; **~s constituées** constitutional

authorities

**autoroute** [ɔtɔʀut] nf motorway (Brit), expressway (US); ~ **de l'information** (Tél) information highway

**autoroutier, -ière** [ɔtɔʀutje, -jɛʀ] adj motorway cpd (Brit), expressway cpd (US)

**autosatisfaction** [ɔtɔsatisfaksjɔ̃] nf self-satisfaction

**auto-stop** [ɔtɔstɔp] nm: **l'~** hitch-hiking; **faire de l'~** to hitch-hike; **prendre qn en ~** to give sb a lift

**auto-stoppeur, -euse** [ɔtɔstɔpœʀ, -øz] nm/f hitch-hiker, hitcher (Brit)

**autosuffisant, e** [ɔtɔsyfizɑ̃, -ɑ̃t] adj self-sufficient

**autosuggestion** [ɔtɔsygʒɛstjɔ̃] nf autosuggestion

**autour** [otuʀ] adv around; **~ de** prép around; (environ) around, about; **tout ~** adv all around

🔵 MOT-CLÉ

**autre** [otʀ(ə)] adj **1** (différent) other, different; **je préférerais un autre verre** I'd prefer another ou a different glass; **d'autres verres** different glasses; **se sentir autre** to feel different; **la difficulté est autre** the difficulty is ou lies elsewhere

**2** (supplémentaire) other; **je voudrais un autre verre d'eau** I'd like another glass of water

**3**: **autre chose** something else; **autre part** somewhere else; **d'autre part** on the other hand

▷ pron **1**: **un autre** another (one); **nous/vous autres** us/you; **d'autres** others; **l'autre** the other (one); **les autres** the others; (autrui) others; **l'un et l'autre** both of them; **ni l'un ni l'autre** neither of them; **se détester l'un l'autre/les uns les autres** to hate each other ou one another; **d'une semaine/minute à l'autre** from one week/minute ou moment to the next; (incessamment) any week/minute ou moment now; **de temps à autre** from time to time; **entre autres** among other things

**2** (expressions): **j'en ai vu d'autres** I've seen worse; **à d'autres!** pull the other one!

**autrefois** [otʀəfwa] adv in the past

**autrement** [otʀəmɑ̃] adv differently; (d'une manière différente) in another way; (sinon) otherwise; **je n'ai pas pu faire ~** I couldn't do anything else, I couldn't do otherwise; **~ dit** in other words; (c'est-à-dire) that is to say

**Autriche** [otʀiʃ] nf: **l'~** Austria

**autrichien, ne** [otʀiʃjɛ̃, -ɛn] adj Austrian ▷ nm/f: **Autrichien, ne** Austrian

**autruche** [otʀyʃ] nf ostrich; **faire l'~** (fig) to bury one's head in the sand

**autrui** [otʀɥi] pron others

**auvent** [ovɑ̃] nm canopy

**auvergnat, e** [ɔvɛʀɲa, -at] adj of ou from the Auvergne

**Auvergne** [ɔvɛʀɲ(ə)] nf: **l'~** the Auvergne

**aux** [o] prép voir **à**

**auxiliaire** [ɔksiljɛʀ] adj, nm/f auxiliary

**auxquels, auxquelles** [okɛl] pron voir **lequel**

**AV** sigle m (Banque: = avis de virement) advice of bank transfer ▷ abr (Auto) = **avant**

**av.** abr (= avenue) Av(e)

**avachi, e** [avaʃi] adj limp, flabby; (chaussure, vêtement) out-of-shape; (personne): **~ sur qch** slumped on ou across sth

**avais** etc [avɛ] vb voir **avoir**

**aval** [aval] nm (accord) endorsement, backing; (Géo): **en ~** downstream, downriver; (sur une pente) downhill; **en ~ de** downstream ou downriver from; downhill from

**avalanche** [avalɑ̃ʃ] nf avalanche; **~ poudreuse** powder snow avalanche

**avaler** [avale] vt to swallow

**avaliser** [avalize] vt (plan, entreprise) to back, support; (Comm, Jur) to guarantee

**avance** [avɑ̃s] nf (de troupes etc) advance; (progrès) progress; (d'argent) advance; (opposé à retard) lead; being ahead of schedule; **avances** nfpl overtures; (amoureuses) advances; **une ~ de 300 m/4 h** (Sport) a 300 m/4 hour lead; **(être) en ~** (to be) early; (sur un programme) (to be) ahead of schedule; **on n'est pas en ~!** we're kind of late!; **être en ~ sur qn** to be ahead of sb; **d'~, à l'~, par ~** in advance; **~ (du) papier** (Inform) paper advance

**avancé, e** [avɑ̃se] adj advanced; (travail etc) well on, well under way; (fruit, fromage) overripe ▷ nf projection; overhang; **il est ~ pour son âge** he is advanced for his age

**avancement** [avɑ̃smɑ̃] nm (professionnel) promotion; (de travaux) progress

**avancer** [avɑ̃se] vi to move forward, advance; (projet, travail) to make progress; (être en saillie) to overhang; to project; (montre, réveil) to be fast; (: d'habitude) to gain ▷ vt to move forward, advance; (argent) to advance; (montre, pendule) to put forward; (faire progresser: travail etc) to advance, move on; **s'avancer** vi to move forward, advance; (fig) to commit o.s.; (faire saillie) to overhang; to project; **j'avance (d'une heure)** I'm (an hour) fast

**avanies** [avani] nfpl snubs (Brit), insults

**avant** [avɑ̃] prép before ▷ adv: **trop/plus ~** too far/further forward ▷ adj inv: **siège/roue ~** front seat/wheel ▷ nm front; (Sport: joueur) forward; **~ qu'il parte/de partir** before he leaves/leaving; **~ qu'il (ne) pleuve** before it rains (ou rained); **~ tout** (surtout) above all; **à l'~** (dans un véhicule) in (the) front; **en ~** adv forward(s); **en ~ de** prép in front of; **aller de l'~** to steam ahead (fig), make good progress

**avantage** [avɑ̃taʒ] nm advantage; (Tennis): **~ service/dehors** advantage ou van (Brit) ou ad (US) in/out; **tirer ~ de** to take advantage of; **vous auriez ~ à faire** you would be well-advised to do, it would be to your advantage to do; **à l'~ de qn** to sb's advantage; **être à son ~**

to be at one's best; **~s en nature** benefits in kind; **~s sociaux** fringe benefits

**avantager** [avɑ̃taʒe] vt (*favoriser*) to favour; (*embellir*) to flatter

**avantageux, -euse** [avɑ̃taʒø, -øz] adj attractive; (*intéressant*) attractively priced; (*portrait, coiffure*) flattering; **conditions avantageuses** favourable terms

**avant-bras** [avɑ̃bʀɑ] nm inv forearm

**avant-centre** [avɑ̃sɑ̃tʀ(ə)] nm centre-forward

**avant-coureur** [avɑ̃kuʀœʀ] adj inv (*bruit etc*) precursory; **signe ~** advance indication ou sign

**avant-dernier, -ière** [avɑ̃dɛʀnje, -jɛʀ] adj, nm/f next to last, last but one

**avant-garde** [avɑ̃gaʀd(ə)] nf (*Mil*) vanguard; (*fig*) avant-garde; **d'~** avant-garde

**avant-goût** [avɑ̃gu] nm foretaste

**avant-hier** [avɑ̃tjɛʀ] adv the day before yesterday

**avant-poste** [avɑ̃pɔst(ə)] nm outpost

**avant-première** [avɑ̃pʀəmjɛʀ] nf (*de film*) preview; **en ~** as a preview, in a preview showing

**avant-projet** [avɑ̃pʀɔʒe] nm preliminary draft

**avant-propos** [avɑ̃pʀɔpo] nm foreword

**avant-veille** [avɑ̃vɛj] nf: **l'~** two days before

**avare** [avaʀ] adj miserly, avaricious ▷ nm/f miser; **~ de compliments** stingy ou sparing with one's compliments

**avarice** [avaʀis] nf avarice, miserliness

**avarié, e** [avaʀje] adj (*viande, fruits*) rotting, going off (*Brit*); (*Navig: navire*) damaged

**avaries** [avaʀi] nfpl (*Navig*) damage sg

**avatar** [avataʀ] nm misadventure; (*transformation*) metamorphosis

**avec** [avɛk] prép with; (*à l'égard de*) to(wards), with ▷ adv (*fam*) with it (*ou* him *etc*); **~ habileté/ lenteur** skilfully/slowly; **~ eux/ces maladies** with them/these diseases; **~ ça** (*malgré ça*) for all that; **et ~ ça?** (*dans un magasin*) anything ou something else?

**avenant, e** [avnɑ̃, -ɑ̃t] adj pleasant ▷ nm (*Assurances*) additional clause; **à l'~** adv in keeping

**avènement** [avɛnmɑ̃] nm (*d'un roi*) accession, succession; (*d'un changement*) advent; (*d'une politique, idée*) coming

**avenir** [avniʀ] nm: **l'~** the future; **à l'~** in future; **sans ~** with no future, without a future; **carrière/politicien d'~** career/politician with prospects ou a future

**Avent** [avɑ̃] nm: **l'~** Advent

**aventure** [avɑ̃tyʀ] nf: **l'~** adventure; **une ~** an adventure; (*amoureuse*) an affair; **partir à l'~** to go off in search of adventure; (*au hasard*) to go where one's fancy takes one; **roman/film d'~** adventure story/film

**aventurer** [avɑ̃tyʀe] vt (*somme, réputation, vie*) to stake; (*remarque, opinion*) to venture; **s'aventurer** vi to venture; **s'~ à faire qch** to venture into sth

**aventureux, -euse** [avɑ̃tyʀø, -øz] adj adventurous, venturesome; (*projet*) risky,

chancy

**aventurier, -ière** [avɑ̃tyʀje, -jɛʀ] nm/f adventurer ▷ nf (*péj*) adventuress

**avenu, e** [avny] adj: **nul et non ~** null and void

**avenue** [avny] nf avenue

**avéré, e** [aveʀe] adj recognized, acknowledged

**avérer** [aveʀe]: **s'avérer** vr: **s'~ faux/coûteux** to prove (to be) wrong/expensive

**averse** [avɛʀs(ə)] nf shower

**aversion** [avɛʀsjɔ̃] nf aversion, loathing

**averti, e** [avɛʀti] adj (well-)informed

**avertir** [avɛʀtiʀ] vt: **~ qn (de qch/que)** to warn sb (of sth/that); (*renseigner*) to inform sb (of sth/ that); **~ qn de ne pas faire qch** to warn sb not to do sth

**avertissement** [avɛʀtismɑ̃] nm warning

**avertisseur** [avɛʀtisœʀ] nm horn, siren; **~ (d'incendie)** (fire) alarm

**aveu, x** [avø] nm confession; **passer aux ~x** to make a confession; **de l'~ de** according to

**aveuglant, e** [avœglɑ̃, -ɑ̃t] adj blinding

**aveugle** [avœgl(ə)] adj blind ▷ nm/f blind person; **les ~s** the blind; **test en (double) ~** (double) blind test

**aveuglement** [avœgləmɑ̃] nm blindness

**aveuglément** [avœglemɑ̃] adv blindly

**aveugler** [avœgle] vt to blind

**aveuglette** [avœglɛt]: **à l'~** adv groping one's way along; (*fig*) in the dark, blindly

**avez** [ave] vb voir **avoir**

**aviateur, -trice** [avjatœʀ, -tʀis] nm/f aviator, pilot

**aviation** [avjasjɔ̃] nf (*secteur commercial*) aviation; (*sport, métier de pilote*) flying; (*Mil*) air force; **terrain d'~** airfield; **~ de chasse** fighter force

**aviculteur, -trice** [avikyltœʀ, -tʀis] nm/f poultry farmer; bird breeder

**aviculture** [avikyltyʀ] nf (*de volailles*) poultry farming

**avide** [avid] adj eager; (*péj*) greedy, grasping; **~ de** (*sang etc*) thirsting for; **~ d'honneurs/ d'argent** greedy for honours/money; **~ de connaître/d'apprendre** eager to know/learn

**avidité** [avidite] nf eagerness; greed

**avilir** [aviliʀ] vt to debase

**avilissant, e** [avilisɑ̃, -ɑ̃t] adj degrading

**aviné, e** [avine] adj drunken

**avion** [avjɔ̃] nm (*aero*)plane (*Brit*), (air)plane (*US*); **aller (quelque part) en ~** to go (somewhere) by plane, fly (somewhere); **par ~** by airmail; **~ de chasse** fighter; **~ de ligne** airliner; **~ à réaction** jet (plane)

**avion-cargo** [avjɔ̃kaʀgo] nm air freighter

**avion-citerne** [avjɔ̃sitɛʀn(ə)] nm air tanker

**aviron** [aviʀɔ̃] nm oar; (*sport*): **l'~** rowing

**avis** [avi] nm opinion; (*notification*) notice; (*Comm*): **~ de crédit/débit** credit/debit advice; **à mon ~** in my opinion; **je suis de votre ~** I share your opinion, I am of your opinion; **être d'~ que** to be of the opinion that; **changer d'~** to change one's mind; **sauf ~ contraire** unless you hear to the contrary; **sans ~ préalable**

without notice; **jusqu'à nouvel ~** until further notice; **~ de décès** death announcement

**avisé, e** [avize] *adj* sensible, wise; **être bien/mal ~ de faire** to be well-/ill-advised to do

**aviser** [avize] *vt* (*voir*) to notice, catch sight of; (*informer*): **~ qn de/que** to advise *ou* inform *ou* notify sb of/that ▷ *vi* to think about things, assess the situation; **s'~ de qch/que** to become suddenly aware of sth/that; **s'~ de faire** to take it into one's head to do

**aviver** [avive] *vt* (*douleur, chagrin*) to intensify; (*intérêt, désir*) to sharpen; (*colère, querelle*) to stir up; (*couleur*) to brighten up

**av. J.-C.** *abr* (= *avant Jésus-Christ*) BC

**avocat, e** [avɔka, -at] *nm/f* (*Jur*) ≈ barrister (*Brit*), lawyer; (*fig*) advocate, champion ▷ *nm* (*Culin*) avocado (pear); **se faire l'~ du diable** to be the devil's advocate; **l'~ de la défense/partie civile** the counsel for the defence/plaintiff; **~ d'affaires** business lawyer; **~ général** assistant public prosecutor

**avocat-conseil** [avɔkakɔ̃sɛj] (*pl* **avocats-conseils**) *nm* ≈ barrister (*Brit*)

**avocat-stagiaire** [avɔkastaʒjɛʀ] (*pl* **avocats-stagiaires**) *nm* ≈ barrister doing his articles (*Brit*)

**avoine** [avwan] *nf* oats *pl*

◯ MOT-CLÉ

**avoir** [avwaʀ] *nm* assets *pl*, resources *pl*; (*Comm*) credit; **avoir fiscal** tax credit
▷ *vt* **1** (*posséder*) to have; **elle a deux enfants/une belle maison** she has (got) two children/a lovely house; **il a les yeux bleus** he has (got) blue eyes
**2** (*éprouver*): **qu'est-ce que tu as?, qu'as-tu?** what's wrong?, what's the matter?; *voir aussi* **faim, peur** *etc*
**3** (*âge, dimensions*) to be; **il a 3 ans** he is 3 (years old); **le mur a 3 mètres de haut** the wall is 3 metres high
**4** (*fam: duper*) to do, have; **on vous a eu!** you've been done *ou* had!
**5**: **en avoir contre qn** to have a grudge against sb; **en avoir assez** to be fed up; **j'en ai pour une demi-heure** it'll take me half an hour; **n'avoir que faire de qch** to have no use for sth
▷ *vb aux* **1** to have; **avoir mangé/dormi** to have eaten/slept; **hier je n'ai pas mangé** I didn't eat yesterday
**2** (*avoir+à +infinitif*): **avoir à faire qch** to have to do sth; **vous n'avez qu'à lui demander** you only have to ask him; **tu n'as pas à me poser des questions** it's not for you to ask me questions
▷ *vb impers* **1**: **il y a** (+*singulier*) there is; (+*pluriel*) there are; **qu'y-a-t-il?, qu'est-ce qu'il y a?** what's the matter?, what is it?; **il doit y avoir une explication** there must be an explanation; **il n'y a qu'à ...** we (*ou* you *etc*) will just have to ...; **il ne peut y en avoir qu'un** there can only be one
**2** (*temporel*): **il y a 10 ans** 10 years ago; **il y a 10 ans/longtemps que je le connais** I've known him for 10 years/a long time; **il y a 10 ans qu'il est arrivé** it's 10 years since he arrived

**avoisinant, e** [avwazinɑ̃, -ɑ̃t] *adj* neighbouring

**avoisiner** [avwazine] *vt* to be near *ou* close to; (*fig*) to border *ou* verge on

**avons** [avɔ̃] *vb voir* **avoir**

**avortement** [avɔʀtəmɑ̃] *nm* abortion

**avorter** [avɔʀte] *vi* (*Méd*) to have an abortion; (*fig*) to fail; **faire ~** to abort; **se faire ~** to have an abortion

**avouable** [avwabl(ə)] *adj* respectable; **des pensées non ~s** unrepeatable thoughts

**avoué, e** [avwe] *adj* avowed ▷ *nm* (*Jur*) ≈ solicitor (*Brit*), lawyer

**avouer** [avwe] *vt* (*crime, défaut*) to confess (to)
▷ *vi* (*se confesser*) to confess; (*admettre*) to admit; **~ avoir fait/que** to admit *ou* confess to having done/that; **~ que oui/non** to admit that that is so/not so

**avril** [avʀil] *nm* April; *voir aussi* **juillet**

**axe** [aks(ə)] *nm* axis (*pl* axes); (*de roue etc*) axle; **dans l'~ de** directly in line with; (*fig*) main line; **~ routier** trunk road, main road

**axer** [akse] *vt*: **~ qch sur** to centre sth on

**axial, e, -aux** [aksjal, -o] *adj* axial

**axiome** [aksjom] *nm* axiom

**ayant** [ɛjɑ̃] *vb voir* **avoir** ▷ *nm*: **~ droit** assignee; **~ droit à** (*pension etc*) person eligible for *ou* entitled to

**ayons** *etc* [ɛjɔ̃] *vb voir* **avoir**

**azalée** [azale] *nf* azalea

**Azerbaïdjan** [azɛʀbaidʒɑ̃] *nm* Azerbaijan

**azimut** [azimyt] *nm* azimuth; **tous ~s** *adj* (*fig*) omnidirectional

**azote** [azɔt] *nm* nitrogen

**azoté, e** [azɔte] *adj* nitrogenous

**AZT** *sigle m* (= *azidothymidine*) AZT

**aztèque** [aztɛk] *adj* Aztec

**azur** [azyʀ] *nm* (*couleur*) azure, sky blue; (*ciel*) sky, skies *pl*

**azyme** [azim] *adj*: **pain ~** unleavened bread

# Bb

**B, b** [be] *nm inv* B, b ▷ *abr* = **bien**; **B comme Bertha** B for Benjamin (*Brit*) *ou* Baker (*US*)
**BA** *sigle f* (= *bonne action*) good deed
**baba** [baba] *adj inv*: **en être ~** (*fam*) to be flabbergasted ▷ *nm*: **~ au rhum** rum baba
**babil** [babi] *nm* prattle
**babillage** [babija3] *nm* chatter
**babiller** [babije] *vi* to prattle, chatter; (*bébé*) to babble
**babines** [babin] *nfpl* chops
**babiole** [babjɔl] *nf* (*bibelot*) trinket; (*vétille*) trifle
**bâbord** [babɔʀ] *nm*: **à** *ou* **par ~** to port, on the port side
**babouin** [babwɛ̃] *nm* baboon
**baby-foot** [babifut] *nm inv* table football
**Babylone** [babilɔn] *n* Babylon
**babylonien, ne** [babilɔnjɛ̃, -ɛn] *adj* Babylonian
**baby-sitter** [babisitœʀ] *nm/f* baby-sitter
**baby-sitting** [babisitiŋ] *nm* baby-sitting; **faire du ~** to baby-sit
**bac** [bak] *nm* (*Scol*) = **baccalauréat**; (*bateau*) ferry; (*récipient*) tub; (: *Photo etc*) tray; (: *Industrie*) tank; **~ à glace** ice-tray; **~ à légumes** vegetable compartment *ou* rack
**baccalauréat** [bakalɔʀea] *nm* ≈ A-levels *pl* (*Brit*), ≈ high school diploma (*US*); *see note*

**bâche** [baʃ] *nf* tarpaulin, canvas sheet
**bachelier, -ière** [baʃəlje, -jɛʀ] *nm/f* holder of the *baccalauréat*
**bâcher** [baʃe] *vt* to cover (with a canvas sheet *ou* a tarpaulin)
**bachot** [baʃo] *nm* = **baccalauréat**
**bachotage** [baʃɔta3] *nm* (*Scol*) cramming
**bachoter** [baʃɔte] *vi* (*Scol*) to cram (for an exam)

**bacille** [basil] *nm* bacillus
**bâcler** [bakle] *vt* to botch (up)
**bacon** [bekɔn] *nm* bacon
**bactéricide** [bakteʀisid] *nm* (*Méd*) bactericide
**bactérie** [bakteʀi] *nf* bacterium
**bactérien, ne** [bakteʀjɛ̃, -ɛn] *adj* bacterial
**bactériologie** [bakteʀjɔlɔ3i] *nf* bacteriology
**bactériologique** [bakteʀjɔlɔ3ik] *adj* bacteriological
**bactériologiste** [bakteʀjɔlɔ3ist(ə)] *nm/f* bacteriologist
**badaud, e** [bado, -od] *nm/f* idle onlooker
**baderne** [badɛʀn(ə)] *nf* (*péj*): **(vieille) ~** old fossil
**badge** [bad3(ə)] *nm* badge
**badigeon** [badi3ɔ̃] *nm* distemper; colourwash
**badigeonner** [badi3ɔne] *vt* to distemper; to colourwash; (*péj*: *barbouiller*) to daub; (*Méd*) to paint
**badin, e** [badɛ̃, -in] *adj* light-hearted, playful
**badinage** [badina3] *nm* banter
**badine** [badin] *nf* switch (*stick*)
**badiner** [badine] *vi*: **~ avec qch** to treat sth lightly; **ne pas ~ avec qch** not to trifle with sth
**badminton** [badmintɔn] *nm* badminton
**BAFA** [bafa] *sigle m* (= *Brevet d'aptitude aux fonctions d'animation*) *diploma for youth leaders and workers*
**baffe** [baf] *nf* (*fam*) slap, clout
**Baffin** [bafin] *nf*: **terre de ~** Baffin Island
**baffle** [bafl(ə)] *nm* baffle (board)
**bafouer** [bafwe] *vt* to deride, ridicule
**bafouillage** [bafuja3] *nm* (*fam*: *propos incohérents*) jumble of words
**bafouiller** [bafuje] *vi, vt* to stammer
**bâfrer** [bafʀe] *vi, vt* (*fam*) to guzzle, gobble
**bagage** [baga3] *nm*: **~s** luggage *sg*, baggage *sg*; **faire ses ~s** to pack (one's bags); **~ littéraire** (stock of) literary knowledge; **~s à main** hand-luggage
**bagarre** [bagaʀ] *nf* fight, brawl; **il aime la ~** he loves a fight, he likes fighting
**bagarrer** [bagaʀe]: **se bagarrer** *vi* to (have a) fight
**bagarreur, -euse** [bagaʀœʀ, -øz] *adj* pugnacious ▷ *nm/f*: **il est ~** he loves a fight
**bagatelle** [bagatɛl] *nf* trifle, trifling sum (*ou* matter)

**Bagdad, Baghdâd** [bagdad] n Baghdad
**bagnard** [baɲaʀ] nm convict
**bagne** [baɲ] nm penal colony; **c'est le ~** (fig) it's forced labour
**bagnole** [baɲɔl] nf (fam) car, wheels pl (Brit)
**bagout** [bagu] nm glibness; **avoir du ~** to have the gift of the gab
**bague** [bag] nf ring; **~ de fiançailles** engagement ring; **~ de serrage** clip
**baguenauder** [bagnode]: **se baguenauder** vi to trail around, loaf around
**baguer** [bage] vt to ring
**baguette** [bagɛt] nf stick; (cuisine chinoise) chopstick; (de chef d'orchestre) baton; (pain) stick of (French) bread; (Constr: moulure) beading; **mener qn à la ~** to rule sb with a rod of iron; **~ magique** magic wand; **~ de sourcier** divining rod; **~ de tambour** drumstick
**Bahamas** [baamas] nfpl: **les (îles) ~** the Bahamas
**Bahreïn** [baʀɛn] nm Bahrain ou Bahrein
**bahut** [bay] nm chest
**bai, e** [bɛ] adj (cheval) bay
**baie** [bɛ] nf (Géo) bay; (fruit) berry; **~ (vitrée)** picture window
**baignade** [bɛɲad] nf (action) bathing; (bain) bathe; (endroit) bathing place
**baigné, e** [beɲe] adj: **~ de** bathed in; (trempé) soaked with; (inondé) flooded with
**baigner** [beɲe] vt (bébé) to bath ▷ vi: **~ dans son sang** to lie in a pool of blood; **~ dans la brume** to be shrouded in mist; **se baigner** vi to go swimming ou bathing; (dans une baignoire) to have a bath; **ça baigne!** (fam) everything's great!
**baigneur, -euse** [beɲœʀ, -øz] nm/f bather ▷ nm (poupée) baby doll
**baignoire** [beɲwaʀ] nf bath(tub); (Théât) ground-floor box
**bail, baux** [baj, bo] nm lease; **donner** ou **prendre qch à ~** to lease sth
**bâillement** [bɑjmɑ̃] nm yawn
**bâiller** [bɑje] vi to yawn; (être ouvert) to gape
**bailleur** [bajœʀ] nm: **~ de fonds** sponsor, backer; (Comm) sleeping ou silent partner
**bâillon** [bɑjɔ̃] nm gag
**bâillonner** [bɑjɔne] vt to gag
**bain** [bɛ̃] nm (dans une baignoire, Photo, Tech) bath; (dans la mer, une piscine) swim; **costume de ~** bathing costume (Brit), swimsuit; **prendre un ~** to have a bath; **se mettre dans le ~** (fig) to get into (the way of) it ou things; **~ de bouche** mouthwash; **~ de foule** walkabout; **~ de pieds** footbath; (au bord de la mer) paddle; **~ de siège** hip bath; **~ de soleil** sunbathing no pl; **prendre un ~ de soleil** to sunbathe; **~s de mer** sea bathing sg; **~s(-douches) municipaux** public baths
**bain-marie** [bɛ̃maʀi] (pl **bains-marie**) nm double boiler; **faire chauffer au ~** (boîte etc) to immerse in boiling water
**baïonnette** [bajɔnɛt] nf bayonet; (Élec): **douille à ~** bayonet socket; **ampoule à ~** bulb with a bayonet fitting
**baisemain** [bɛzmɛ̃] nm kissing a lady's hand
**baiser** [beze] nm kiss ▷ vt (main, front) to kiss; (fam!) to screw (!)
**baisse** [bɛs] nf fall, drop; (Comm): **"~ sur la viande"** "meat prices down"; **en ~** (cours, action) falling; **à la ~** downwards
**baisser** [bese] vt to lower; (radio, chauffage) to turn down; (Auto: phares) to dip (Brit), lower (US) ▷ vi to fall, drop, go down; **se baisser** vi to bend down
**bajoues** [baʒu] nfpl chaps, chops
**bal** [bal] nm dance; (grande soirée) ball; **~ costumé/masqué** fancy-dress/masked ball; **~ musette** dance (with accordion accompaniment)
**balade** [balad] nf walk, stroll; (en voiture) drive; **faire une ~** to go for a walk ou stroll; to go for a drive
**balader** [balade] vt (traîner) to trail around; **se balader** vi to go for a walk ou stroll; to go for a drive
**baladeur** [baladœʀ] nm personal stereo; **~ numérique** MP3 player
**baladeuse** [baladøz] nf inspection lamp
**baladin** [baladɛ̃] nm wandering entertainer
**balafre** [balafʀ(ə)] nf gash, slash; (cicatrice) scar
**balafrer** [balafʀe] vt to gash, slash
**balai** [balɛ] nm broom, brush; (Auto: d'essuie-glace) blade; (Mus: de batterie etc) brush; **donner un coup de ~** to give the floor a sweep; **~ mécanique** carpet sweeper
**balai-brosse** [balebʀɔs] (pl **balais-brosses**) nm (long-handled) scrubbing brush
**balance** [balɑ̃s] nf (à plateaux) scales pl; (de précision) balance; (Comm, Pol): **~ des comptes** ou **paiements** balance of payments; (signe): **la B~** Libra, the Scales; **être de la B~** to be Libra; **~ commerciale** balance of trade; **~ des forces** balance of power; **~ romaine** steelyard
**balancelle** [balɑ̃sɛl] nf garden hammock-seat
**balancer** [balɑ̃se] vt to swing; (lancer) to fling, chuck; (renvoyer, jeter) to chuck out ▷ vi to swing; **se balancer** vi to swing; (bateau) to rock; (branche) to sway; **se ~ de qch** (fam) not to give a toss about sth
**balancier** [balɑ̃sje] nm (de pendule) pendulum; (de montre) balance wheel; (perche) (balancing) pole
**balançoire** [balɑ̃swaʀ] nf swing; (sur pivot) seesaw
**balayage** [balɛjaʒ] nm sweeping; scanning
**balayer** [baleje] vt (feuilles etc) to sweep up, brush up; (pièce, cour) to sweep; (chasser) to sweep away ou aside; (radar) to scan; (: phares) to sweep across
**balayette** [balɛjɛt] nf small brush
**balayeur, -euse** [balɛjœʀ, -øz] nm/f road sweeper ▷ nf (engin) road sweeper
**balayures** [balɛjyʀ] nfpl sweepings
**balbutiement** [balbysimɑ̃] nm (paroles) stammering no pl; **balbutiements** nmpl (fig:

b

*débuts*) first faltering steps

**balbutier** [balbysje] *vi*, *vt* to stammer

**balcon** [balkɔ̃] *nm* balcony; (*Théât*) dress circle

**baldaquin** [baldakɛ̃] *nm* canopy

**Bâle** [bɑl] *n* Basle *ou* Basel

**Baléares** [baleaʀ] *nfpl*: **les** ~ the Balearic Islands

**baleine** [balɛn] *nf* whale; (*de parapluie*) rib; (*de corset*) bone

**baleinier** [balenje] *nm* (*Navig*) whaler

**baleinière** [balenjɛʀ] *nf* whaleboat

**balisage** [balizaʒ] *nm* (*signaux*) beacons *pl*; buoys *pl*; runway lights *pl*; signs *pl*, markers *pl*

**balise** [baliz] *nf* (*Navig*) beacon, (marker) buoy; (*Aviat*) runway light, beacon; (*Auto, Ski*) sign

**baliser** [balize] *vt* to mark out (with beacons *ou* lights *etc*)

**balistique** [balistik] *adj* (*engin*) ballistic ▷ *nf* ballistics

**balivernes** [balivɛʀn(ə)] *nfpl* twaddle *sg* (*Brit*), nonsense *sg*

**balkanique** [balkanik] *adj* Balkan

**Balkans** [balkɑ̃] *nmpl*: **les** ~ the Balkans

**ballade** [balad] *nf* ballad

**ballant, e** [balɑ̃, -ɑ̃t] *adj* dangling

**ballast** [balast] *nm* ballast

**balle** [bal] *nf* (*de fusil*) bullet; (*de sport*) ball; (*du blé*) chaff; (*paquet*) bale; (*fam: franc*) franc; ~ **perdue** stray bullet

**ballerine** [balʀin] *nf* ballet dancer; (*chaussure*) pump, ballerina

**ballet** [balɛ] *nm* ballet; (*fig*): ~ **diplomatique** diplomatic to-ings and fro-ings

**ballon** [balɔ̃] *nm* (*de sport*) ball; (*jouet, Aviat, de bande dessinée*) balloon; (*de vin*) glass; ~ **d'essai** (*météorologique*) pilot balloon; (*fig*) feeler(s); ~ **de football** football; ~ **d'oxygène** oxygen bottle

**ballonner** [balɔne] *vt*: **j'ai le ventre ballonné** I feel bloated

**ballon-sonde** [balɔ̃sɔ̃d] (*pl* **ballons-sondes**) *nm* sounding balloon

**ballot** [balo] *nm* bundle; (*péj*) nitwit

**ballottage** [balɔtaʒ] *nm* (*Pol*) second ballot

**ballotter** [balɔte] *vi* to roll around; (*bateau etc*) to toss ▷ *vt* to shake *ou* throw about; to toss; **être ballotté entre** (*fig*) to be shunted between; (: *indécis*) to be torn between

**ballottine** [balɔtin] *nf* (*Culin*): ~ **de volaille** meat loaf made with poultry

**ball-trap** [baltʀap] *nm* (*appareil*) trap; (*tir*) clay pigeon shooting

**balluchon** [balyʃɔ̃] *nm* bundle (of clothes)

**balnéaire** [balneɛʀ] *adj* seaside *cpd*

**balnéothérapie** [balneoteʀapi] *nf* spa bath therapy

**BALO** *sigle m* (= *Bulletin des annonces légales obligatoires*) ≈ Public Notices (*in newspapers etc*)

**balourd, e** [baluʀ, -uʀd(ə)] *adj* clumsy ▷ *nm/f* clodhopper

**balourdise** [baluʀdiz] *nf* clumsiness; (*gaffe*) blunder

**balte** [balt] *adj* Baltic ▷ *nm/f*: **Balte** native of the Baltic States

**baltique** [baltik] *adj* Baltic ▷ *nf*: **la (mer) B~** the Baltic (Sea)

**baluchon** [balyʃɔ̃] *nm* = **balluchon**

**balustrade** [balystʀad] *nf* railings *pl*, handrail

**bambin** [bɑ̃bɛ̃] *nm* little child

**bambou** [bɑ̃bu] *nm* bamboo

**ban** [bɑ̃] *nm* round of applause, cheer; **être/ mettre au ~ de** to be outlawed/to outlaw from; **le ~ et l'arrière-~ de sa famille** every last one of his relatives; ~**s (de mariage)** banns, bans

**banal, e** [banal] *adj* banal, commonplace; (*péj*) trite; **four/moulin** ~ village oven/mill

**banalisé, e** [banalize] *adj* (*voiture de police*) unmarked

**banalité** [banalite] *nf* banality; (*remarque*) truism, trite remark

**banane** [banan] *nf* banana

**bananeraie** [banaŋʀe] *nf* banana plantation

**bananier** [banaŋje] *nm* banana tree; (*bateau*) banana boat

**banc** [bɑ̃] *nm* seat, bench; (*de poissons*) shoal; ~ **des accusés** dock; ~ **d'essai** (*fig*) testing ground; ~ **de sable** sandbank; ~ **des témoins** witness box; ~ **de touche** dugout

**bancaire** [bɑ̃kɛʀ] *adj* banking, bank *cpd*

**bancal, e** [bɑ̃kal] *adj* wobbly; (*personne*) bow-legged; (*fig: projet*) shaky

**bandage** [bɑ̃daʒ] *nm* bandaging; (*pansement*) bandage; ~ **herniaire** truss

**bande** [bɑ̃d] *nf* (*de tissu etc*) strip; (*Méd*) bandage; (*motif, dessin*) stripe; (*Ciné*) film; (*Radio, groupe*) band; (*péj*): **une** ~ a bunch *ou* crowd of; **par la** ~ in a roundabout way; **donner de la** ~ to list; **faire** ~ **à part** to keep to o.s.; ~ **dessinée (BD)** strip cartoon (*Brit*), comic strip; ~ **magnétique** magnetic tape; ~ **passante** (*Inform*) bandwidth; ~ **perforée** punched tape; ~ **de roulement** (*de pneu*) tread; ~ **sonore** sound track; ~ **de terre** strip of land; ~ **Velpeau**® (*Méd*) crêpe bandage

**bandé, e** [bɑ̃de] *adj* bandaged; **les yeux ~s** blindfold

**bande-annonce** [bɑ̃danɔ̃s] (*pl* **bandes-annonces**) *nf* (*Ciné*) trailer

**bandeau, x** [bɑ̃do] *nm* headband; (*sur les yeux*) blindfold; (*Méd*) head bandage

**bandelette** [bɑ̃dlɛt] *nf* strip of cloth, bandage

**bander** [bɑ̃de] *vt* to bandage; (*muscle*) to tense; (*arc*) to bend ▷ *vi* (*fam!*) to have a hard on (!); ~ **les yeux à qn** to blindfold sb

**banderole** [bɑ̃dʀɔl] *nf* banderole; (*dans un défilé etc*) streamer

**bande-son** [bɑ̃dsɔ̃] (*pl* **bandes-son**) *nf* (*Ciné*) soundtrack

**bandit** [bɑ̃di] *nm* bandit

**banditisme** [bɑ̃ditism(ə)] *nm* violent crime, armed robberies *pl*

**bandoulière** [bɑ̃duljɛʀ] *nf*: **en** ~ (slung *ou* worn) across the shoulder

**Bangkok** [bɑ̃ŋkɔk] *n* Bangkok

**Bangladesh** [bɑ̃gladɛʃ] *nm*: **le** ~ Bangladesh

**banjo** [bɑ̃(d)ʒo] *nm* banjo

**banlieue** [bɑ̃ljø] nf suburbs pl; **quartiers de ~** suburban areas; **trains de ~** commuter trains

**banlieusard, e** [bɑ̃ljøzaʀ, -aʀd(ə)] nm/f suburbanite

**bannière** [banjɛʀ] nf banner

**bannir** [baniʀ] vt to banish

**banque** [bɑ̃k] nf bank; (activités) banking; **~ des yeux/du sang** eye/blood bank; **~ d'affaires** merchant bank; **~ de dépôt** deposit bank; **~ de données** (Inform) data bank; **~ d'émission** bank of issue

**banqueroute** [bɑ̃kʀut] nf bankruptcy

**banquet** [bɑ̃kɛ] nm (de club) dinner; (de noces) reception; (d'apparat) banquet

**banquette** [bɑ̃kɛt] nf seat

**banquier** [bɑ̃kje] nm banker

**banquise** [bɑ̃kiz] nf ice field

**bantou, e** [bɑ̃tu] adj Bantu

**baptême** [batɛm] nm (sacrement) baptism; (cérémonie) christening, baptism; (d'un navire) launching; (d'une cloche) consecration, dedication; **~ de l'air** first flight

**baptiser** [batize] vt to christen; to baptize; to launch; to consecrate, dedicate

**baptiste** [batist(ə)] adj, nm/f Baptist

**baquet** [bakɛ] nm tub, bucket

**bar** [baʀ] nm bar; (poisson) bass

**baragouin** [baʀagwɛ̃] nm gibberish

**baragouiner** [baʀagwine] vi to gibber, jabber

**baraque** [baʀak] nf shed; (fam) house; **~ foraine** fairground stand

**baraqué, e** [baʀake] adj well-built, hefty

**baraquements** [baʀakmɑ̃] nmpl huts (for refugees, workers etc)

**baratin** [baʀatɛ̃] nm (fam) smooth talk, patter

**baratiner** [baʀatine] vt to chat up

**baratte** [baʀat] nf churn

**Barbade** [baʀbad] nf: **la ~** Barbados

**barbant, e** [baʀbɑ̃, -ɑ̃t] adj (fam) deadly (boring)

**barbare** [baʀbaʀ] adj barbaric ▷ nm/f barbarian

**Barbarie** [baʀbaʀi] nf: **la ~** the Barbary Coast

**barbarie** [baʀbaʀi] nf barbarism; (cruauté) barbarity

**barbarisme** [baʀbaʀism(ə)] nm (Ling) barbarism

**barbe** [baʀb(ə)] nf beard; **(au nez et) à la ~ de qn** (fig) under sb's very nose; **quelle ~!** (fam) what a drag ou bore!; **~ à papa** candy-floss (Brit), cotton candy (US)

**barbecue** [baʀbəkju] nm barbecue

**barbelé** [baʀbəle] nm barbed wire no pl

**barber** [baʀbe] vt (fam) to bore stiff

**barbiche** [baʀbiʃ] nf goatee

**barbichette** [baʀbiʃɛt] nf small goatee

**barbiturique** [baʀbityʀik] nm barbiturate

**barboter** [baʀbɔte] vi to paddle, dabble ▷ vt (fam) to filch

**barboteuse** [baʀbɔtøz] nf rompers pl

**barbouiller** [baʀbuje] vt to daub; (péj: écrire, dessiner) to scribble; **avoir l'estomac barbouillé** to feel queasy ou sick

**barbu, e** [baʀby] adj bearded

**barbue** [baʀby] nf (poisson) brill

**Barcelone** [baʀsəlɔn] n Barcelona

**barda** [baʀda] nm (fam) kit, gear

**barde** [baʀd(ə)] nf (Culin) piece of fat bacon ▷ nm (poète) bard

**bardé, e** [baʀde] adj: **~ de médailles etc** bedecked with medals etc

**bardeaux** [baʀdo] nmpl shingle no pl

**barder** [baʀde] vt (Culin: rôti, volaille) to bard ▷ vi (fam): **ça va ~** sparks will fly

**barème** [baʀɛm] nm scale; (liste) table; **~ des salaires** salary scale

**barge** [baʀʒ] nf barge

**baril** [baʀil] nm (tonneau) barrel; (de poudre) keg

**barillet** [baʀijɛ] nm (de revolver) cylinder

**bariolé, e** [baʀjɔle] adj many-coloured, rainbow-coloured

**barman** [baʀman] nm barman

**baromètre** [baʀɔmɛtʀ(ə)] nm barometer; **~ anéroïde** aneroid barometer

**baron** [baʀɔ̃] nm baron

**baronne** [baʀɔn] nf baroness

**baroque** [baʀɔk] adj (Art) baroque; (fig) weird

**baroud** [baʀud] nm: **~ d'honneur** gallant last stand

**baroudeur** [baʀudœʀ] nm (fam) fighter

**barque** [baʀk(ə)] nf small boat

**barquette** [baʀkɛt] nf small boat-shaped tart; (récipient: en aluminium) tub; (: en bois) basket

**barracuda** [baʀakyda] nm barracuda

**barrage** [baʀaʒ] nm dam; (sur route) roadblock, barricade; **~ de police** police roadblock

**barre** [baʀ] nf (de fer etc) rod; (Navig) helm; (écrite) line, stroke; (Danse) barre; (niveau): **la livre a franchi la ~ des 1,70 euros** the pound has broken the 1.70 euros barrier; (Jur): **comparaître à la ~** to appear as a witness; **être à ou tenir la ~** (Navig) to be at the helm; **coup de ~** (fig): **c'est le coup de ~!** it's daylight robbery!; **j'ai le coup de ~!** I'm all in!; **~ fixe** (Gym) horizontal bar; **~ de mesure** (Mus) bar line; **~ à mine** crowbar; **~s parallèles/asymétriques** (Gym) parallel/asymmetric bars

**barreau, x** [baʀo] nm bar; (Jur): **le ~** the Bar

**barrer** [baʀe] vt (route etc) to block; (mot) to cross out; (chèque) to cross (Brit); (Navig) to steer; **se barrer** vi (fam) to clear off

**barrette** [baʀɛt] nf (pour cheveux) (hair) slide (Brit) ou clip (US); (broche) brooch

**barreur** [baʀœʀ] nm helmsman; (aviron) coxswain

**barricade** [baʀikad] nf barricade

**barricader** [baʀikade] vt to barricade; **se ~ chez soi** (fig) to lock o.s. in

**barrière** [baʀjɛʀ] nf fence; (obstacle) barrier; (porte) gate; **la Grande B~** the Great Barrier Reef; **~ de dégel** (Admin: on roadsigns) no heavy vehicles -- road liable to subsidence due to thaw; **~s douanières** trade barriers

**barrique** [baʀik] nf barrel, cask

**barrir** [baʀiʀ] vi to trumpet

**bar-tabac** [baʀtaba] nm bar (which sells tobacco and stamps)

**baryton** [baʀitɔ̃] *nm* baritone
**bas, basse** [bɑ, bɑs] *adj* low; (*action*) low, ignoble
▷ *nm* (*vêtement*) stocking; (*partie inférieure*): **le ~
de** the lower part *ou* foot *ou* bottom of ▷ *nf* (*Mus*)
bass ▷ *adv* low; (*parler*) softly; **plus ~** lower
down; more softly; (*dans un texte*) further on,
below; **la tête ~se** with lowered head; (*fig*)
with head hung low; **avoir la vue ~se** to be
short-sighted; **au ~ mot** at the lowest estimate;
**enfant en ~ âge** infant, young child; **en ~**
down below; at (*ou* to) the bottom; (*dans une
maison*) downstairs; **en ~ de** at the bottom of;
**de ~ en haut** upwards; from the bottom to the
top; **des hauts et des ~** ups and downs; **un ~
de laine** (*fam: économies*) money under the
mattress (*fig*); **mettre ~** *vi* (*animal*) to give birth;
**à ~ la dictature!** down with dictatorship!; **~
morceaux** (*viande*) cheap cuts
**basalte** [bazalt(ə)] *nm* basalt
**basané, e** [bazane] *adj* (*teint*) tanned, bronzed;
(*foncé; péj*) swarthy
**bas-côté** [bakote] *nm* (*de route*) verge (*Brit*),
shoulder (*US*); (*d'église*) (side) aisle
**bascule** [baskyl] *nf*: (**jeu de**) **~** seesaw; (**balance
à**) **~** scales *pl*; **fauteuil à ~** rocking chair;
**système à ~** tip-over device; rocker device
**basculer** [baskyle] *vi* to fall over, topple (over);
(*benne*) to tip up ▷ *vt* (*aussi*: **faire basculer**) to
topple over; to tip out, tip up
**base** [bɑz] *nf* base; (*Pol*): **la ~** the rank and file,
the grass roots; (*fondement, principe*) basis (*pl
bases*); **jeter les ~s de** to lay the foundations of;
**à la ~ de** (*fig*) at the root of; **sur la ~ de** (*fig*) on
the basis of; **de ~** basic; **à ~ de café** *etc* coffee *etc*
-based; **~ de données** (*Inform*) database; **~ de
lancement** launching site
**base-ball** [bɛzbol] *nm* baseball
**baser** [bɑze] *vt*: **~ qch sur** to base sth on; **se ~
sur** (*données, preuves*) to base one's argument on;
**être basé à/dans** (*Mil*) to be based at/in
**bas-fond** [bafɔ̃] *nm* (*Navig*) shallow; **bas-fonds**
*nmpl* (*fig*) dregs
**basilic** [bazilik] *nm* (*Culin*) basil
**basilique** [bazilik] *nf* basilica
**basket** [baskɛt] *nm*, **basket-ball** [baskɛtbol] *nm*
basketball
**baskets** [baskɛt] *nfpl* (*chaussures*) trainers (*Brit*),
sneakers (*US*)
**basketteur, -euse** [baskɛtœʀ, -øz] *nm/f*
basketball player
**basquaise** [baskɛz] *adj f* Basque ▷ *nf*: **B~** Basque
**basque** [bask(ə)] *adj*, *nm* (*Ling*) Basque ▷ *nm/f*:
**Basque** Basque; **le Pays ~** the Basque country
**basques** [bask(ə)] *nfpl* skirts; **pendu aux ~ de
qn** constantly pestering sb; (*mère etc*) hanging
on sb's apron strings
**bas-relief** [baʀəljɛf] *nm* bas-relief
**basse** [bɑs] *adj f*, *nf* *voir* **bas**
**basse-cour** [baskuʀ] (*pl* **basses-cours**) *nf*
farmyard; (*animaux*) farmyard animals
**bassement** [basmɑ̃] *adv* basely
**bassesse** [basɛs] *nf* baseness; (*acte*) base act

**basset** [basɛ] *nm* (*Zool*) basset (hound)
**bassin** [basɛ̃] *nm* (*cuvette*) bowl; (*pièce d'eau*) pond,
pool; (*de fontaine, Géo*) basin; (*Anat*) pelvis;
(*portuaire*) dock; **~ houiller** coalfield
**bassine** [basin] *nf* basin; (*contenu*) bowl, bowlful
**bassiner** [basine] *vt* (*plaie*) to bathe; (*lit*) to
warm with a warming pan; (*fam: ennuyer*) to
bore; (: *importuner*) to bug, pester
**bassiste** [basist(ə)] *nm/f* (*double*) bass player
**basson** [basɔ̃] *nm* bassoon
**bastide** [bastid] *nf* (*maison*) country house (*in
Provence*); (*ville*) walled town (*in SW France*)
**bastion** [bastjɔ̃] *nm* (*aussi fig, Pol*) bastion
**bas-ventre** [bavɑ̃tʀ(ə)] *nm* (lower part of the)
stomach
**bât** [bɑ] *nm* packsaddle
**bataille** [bataj] *nf* battle; **en ~** (*en travers*) at an
angle; (*en désordre*) awry; **~ rangée** pitched
battle
**bataillon** [batajɔ̃] *nm* battalion
**bâtard, e** [bɑtaʀ, -aʀd(ə)] *adj* (*enfant*)
illegitimate; (*fig*) hybrid ▷ *nm/f* illegitimate
child, bastard (*péj*) ▷ *nm* (*Boulangerie*) ≈ Vienna
loaf; **chien ~** mongrel
**batavia** [batavja] *nf* ≈ Webb lettuce
**bateau, x** [bato] *nm* boat; (*grand*) ship ▷ *adj inv*
(*banal, rebattu*) hackneyed; **~ de pêche/à
moteur/à voiles** fishing/motor/sailing boat
**bateau-citerne** [batositɛʀn(ə)] *nm* tanker
**bateau-mouche** [batomuʃ] *nm* (passenger)
pleasure boat (*on the Seine*)
**bateau-pilote** [batopilɔt] *nm* pilot ship
**bateleur, -euse** [batlœʀ, -øz] *nm/f* street
performer
**batelier, -ière** [batəlje, -jɛʀ] *nm/f* ferryman/-
woman
**bâti, e** [bɑti] *adj* (*terrain*) developed ▷ *nm*
(*armature*) frame; (*Couture*) tacking; **bien ~**
(*personne*) well-built
**batifoler** [batifɔle] *vi* to frolic *ou* lark about
**batik** [batik] *nm* batik
**bâtiment** [bɑtimɑ̃] *nm* building; (*Navig*) ship,
vessel; (*industrie*): **le ~** the building trade
**bâtir** [bɑtiʀ] *vt* to build; (*Couture: jupe, ourlet*) to
tack; **fil à ~** (*Couture*) tacking thread
**bâtisse** [bɑtis] *nf* building
**bâtisseur, -euse** [bɑtisœʀ, -øz] *nm/f* builder
**batiste** [batist(ə)] *nf* (*Couture*) batiste, cambric
**bâton** [bɑtɔ̃] *nm* stick; **mettre des ~s dans les
roues à qn** to put a spoke in sb's wheel; **à ~s
rompus** informally; **~ de rouge (à lèvres)**
lipstick; **~ de ski** ski stick
**bâtonnet** [bɑtɔnɛ] *nm* short stick *ou* rod
**bâtonnier** [bɑtɔnje] *nm* (*Jur*) ≈ President of the
Bar
**batraciens** [batʀasjɛ̃] *nmpl* amphibians
**bats** [ba] *vb* *voir* **battre**
**battage** [bataʒ] *nm* (*publicité*) (hard) plugging
**battant, e** [batɑ̃, -ɑ̃t] *vb* *voir* **battre** ▷ *adj*: **pluie
~e** lashing rain ▷ *nm* (*de cloche*) clapper; (*de
volets*) shutter, flap; (*de porte*) side; (*fig: personne*)
fighter; **porte à double ~** double door;

**tambour** ~ briskly

**batte** [bat] *nf* (*Sport*) bat

**battement** [batmã] *nm* (*de cœur*) beat; (*intervalle*) interval (*between classes, trains etc*); ~ **de paupières** blinking *no pl* (of eyelids); **un ~ de 10 minutes, 10 minutes de** ~ 10 minutes to spare

**batterie** [batʀi] *nf* (*Mil, Élec*) battery; (*Mus*) drums *pl*, drum kit; ~ **de cuisine** kitchen utensils *pl*; (*casseroles etc*) pots and pans *pl*; **une ~ de tests** a string of tests

**batteur** [batœʀ] *nm* (*Mus*) drummer; (*appareil*) whisk

**batteuse** [batøz] *nf* (*Agr*) threshing machine

**battoir** [batwaʀ] *nm* (*à linge*) beetle (*for laundry*); (*à tapis*) (carpet) beater

**battre** [batʀ(ə)] *vt* to beat; (*pluie, vagues*) to beat *ou* lash against; (*œufs etc*) to beat up, whisk; (*blé*) to thresh; (*cartes*) to shuffle; (*passer au peigne fin*) to scour ▷ *vi* (*cœur*) to beat; (*volets etc*) to bang, rattle; **se battre** *vi* to fight; ~ **la mesure** to beat time; ~ **en brèche** (*Mil: mur*) to batter; (*fig: théorie*) to demolish; (: *institution etc*) to attack; ~ **son plein** to be at its height, be going full swing; ~ **pavillon britannique** to fly the British flag; ~ **des mains** to clap one's hands; ~ **des ailes** to flap its wings; ~ **de l'aile** (*fig*) to be in a bad way *ou* in bad shape; ~ **la semelle** to stamp one's feet; ~ **en retraite** to beat a retreat

**battu, e** [baty] *pp de* **battre** ▷ *nf* (*chasse*) beat; (*policière etc*) search, hunt

**baud** [bo(d)] *nm* baud

**baudruche** [bodʀyʃ] *nf*: **ballon en** ~ (toy) balloon; (*fig*) windbag

**baume** [bom] *nm* balm

**bauxite** [boksit] *nf* bauxite

**bavard, e** [bavaʀ, -aʀd(ə)] *adj* (very) talkative; gossipy

**bavardage** [bavaʀdaʒ] *nm* chatter *no pl*; gossip *no pl*

**bavarder** [bavaʀde] *vi* to chatter; (*indiscrètement*) to gossip; (: *révéler un secret*) to blab

**bavarois, e** [bavaʀwa, -waz] *adj* Bavarian ▷ *nm ou f* (*Culin*) bavarois

**bave** [bav] *nf* dribble; (*de chien etc*) slobber, slaver (*Brit*), drool (*US*); (*d'escargot*) slime

**baver** [bave] *vi* to dribble; to slobber, slaver (*Brit*), drool (*US*); (*encre, couleur*) to run; **en** ~ (*fam*) to have a hard time (of it)

**bavette** [bavɛt] *nf* bib

**baveux, -euse** [bavø, -øz] *adj* dribbling; (*omelette*) runny

**Bavière** [bavjɛʀ] *nf*: **la** ~ Bavaria

**bavoir** [bavwaʀ] *nm* (*de bébé*) bib

**bavure** [bavyʀ] *nf* smudge; (*fig*) hitch; blunder

**bayer** [baje] *vi*: ~ **aux corneilles** to stand gaping

**bazar** [bazaʀ] *nm* general store; (*fam*) jumble

**bazarder** [bazaʀde] *vt* (*fam*) to chuck out

**BCBG** *sigle adj* (= *bon chic bon genre*) ≈ preppy

**BCG** *sigle m* (= *bacille Calmette-Guérin*) BCG

**bcp** *abr* = **beaucoup**

**BD** *sigle f* = **bande dessinée**; (= *base de données*) DB

**bd** *abr* = **boulevard**

**b.d.c.** *abr* (*Typo*: = *bas de casse*) l.c.

**béant, e** [beã, -ãt] *adj* gaping

**béarnais, e** [beaʀnɛ, -ɛz] *adj* of *ou* from the Béarn

**béat, e** [bea, -at] *adj* showing open-eyed wonder; (*sourire etc*) blissful

**béatitude** [beatityd] *nf* bliss

**beau, bel, belle, beaux** [bo, bɛl] *adj* beautiful, lovely; (*homme*) handsome ▷ *nf* (*Sport*) decider ▷ *adv*: **il fait** ~ the weather's fine ▷ *nm*: **avoir le sens du** ~ to have an aesthetic sense; **le temps est au** ~ the weather is set fair; **un** ~ **geste** (*fig*) a fine gesture; **un** ~ **salaire** a good salary; **un** ~ **gâchis/rhume** a fine mess/nasty cold; **en faire/dire de belles** to do/say (some) stupid things; **le** ~ **monde** high society; ~ **parleur** smooth talker; **un** ~ **jour** one (fine) day; **de plus belle** more than ever, even more; **bel et bien** well and truly; (*vraiment*) really (and truly); **le plus** ~ **c'est que** ... the best of it is that ...; **c'est du** ~! that's great, that is!; **on a** ~ **essayer** however hard *ou* no matter how hard we try; **il a** ~ **jeu de protester** *etc* it's easy for him to protest *etc*; **faire le** ~ (*chien*) to sit up and beg

MOT-CLÉ

**beaucoup** [boku] *adv* **1** a lot; **il boit beaucoup** he drinks a lot; **il ne boit pas beaucoup** he doesn't drink much *ou* a lot

**2** (*suivi de plus, trop etc*) much, a lot, far; **il est beaucoup plus grand** he is much *ou* a lot *ou* far taller

**3**: **beaucoup de** (*nombre*) many, a lot of; (*quantité*) a lot of; **pas beaucoup de** (*nombre*) not many, not a lot of; (*quantité*) not much, not a lot of; **beaucoup d'étudiants/de touristes** a lot of *ou* many students/tourists; **beaucoup de courage** a lot of courage; **il n'a pas beaucoup d'argent** he hasn't got much *ou* a lot of money; **il n'y a pas beaucoup de touristes** there aren't many *ou* a lot of tourists

**4**: **de beaucoup** by far

▷ *pron*: **beaucoup le savent** lots of people know that

**beau-fils** [bofis] (*pl* **beaux-fils**) *nm* son-in-law; (*remariage*) stepson

**beau-frère** [bofʀɛʀ] (*pl* **beaux-frères**) *nm* brother-in-law

**beau-père** [bopɛʀ] (*pl* **beaux-pères**) *nm* father-in-law; (*remariage*) stepfather

**beauté** [bote] *nf* beauty; **de toute** ~ beautiful; **en** ~ *adv* with a flourish, brilliantly

**beaux-arts** [bozaʀ] *nmpl* fine arts

**beaux-parents** [bopaʀã] *nmpl* wife's/husband's family, in-laws

**bébé** [bebe] *nm* baby

**bébé-éprouvette** [bebeepʀuvɛt] (*pl* **bébés-éprouvette**) *nm* test-tube baby

**bec** [bɛk] *nm* beak, bill; (*de plume*) nib; (*de cafetière etc*) spout; (*de casserole etc*) lip; (*d'une clarinette etc*)

**b**

mouthpiece; (fam) mouth; **clouer le ~ à qn**
(fam) to shut sb up; **ouvrir le ~** (fam) to open
one's mouth; **~ de gaz** (street) gaslamp; **~
verseur** pouring lip
**bécane** [bekan] nf (fam) bike
**bécarre** [bekaʀ] nm (Mus) natural
**bécasse** [bekas] nf (Zool) woodcock; (fam) silly
goose
**bec-de-cane** [bɛkdəkan] (pl **becs-de-cane**) nm
(poignée) door handle
**bec-de-lièvre** [bɛkdəljɛvʀ(ə)] (pl **becs-de-lièvre**)
nm harelip
**béchamel** [beʃamɛl] nf: **(sauce) ~** white sauce,
bechamel sauce
**bêche** [bɛʃ] nf spade
**bêcher** [beʃe] vt (terre) to dig; (personne: critiquer)
to slate; (: snober) to look down on
**bêcheur, -euse** [beʃœʀ, -øz] adj (fam) stuck-up
▷ nm/f fault-finder; (snob) stuck-up person
**bécoter** [bekɔte]: **se bécoter** vi to smooch
**becquée** [beke] nf: **donner la ~ à** to feed
**becqueter** [bɛkte] vt (fam) to eat
**bedaine** [bədɛn] nf paunch
**bédé** [bede] nf (fam) = **bande dessinée**
**bedeau, x** [bədo] nm beadle
**bedonnant, e** [bədɔnɑ̃, -ɑ̃t] adj paunchy,
potbellied
**bée** [be] adj: **bouche ~** gaping
**beffroi** [befʀwa] nm belfry
**bégaiement** [begɛmɑ̃] nm stammering,
stuttering
**bégayer** [begeje] vt, vi to stammer
**bégonia** [begɔnja] nm (Bot) begonia
**bègue** [bɛg] nm/f: **être ~** to have a stammer
**bégueule** [begœl] adj prudish
**beige** [bɛʒ] adj beige
**beignet** [bɛɲɛ] nm fritter
**bel** [bɛl] adj m voir **beau**
**bêler** [bele] vi to bleat
**belette** [bəlɛt] nf weasel
**belge** [bɛlʒ(ə)] adj Belgian ▷ nm/f: **Belge**
Belgian; see note

**Belgique** [bɛlʒik] nf: **la ~** Belgium
**Belgrade** [bɛlgʀad] n Belgrade
**bélier** [belje] nm ram; (engin) (battering) ram;
(signe): **le B~** Aries, the Ram; **être du B~** to be
Aries
**Bélize** [beliz] nm: **le ~** Belize
**bellâtre** [belɑtʀ(ə)] nm dandy
**belle** [bɛl] adj f, nf voir **beau**
**belle-famille** [bɛlfamij] (pl **belles-familles**) nf
(fam) in-laws pl
**belle-fille** [bɛlfij] (pl **belles-filles**) nf daughter-
in-law; (remariage) stepdaughter
**belle-mère** [bɛlmɛʀ] (pl **belles-mères**) nf

mother-in-law; (remariage) stepmother
**belle-sœur** [bɛlsœʀ] (pl **belles-sœurs**) nf sister-
in-law
**belliciste** [belisist(ə)] adj warmongering
**belligérance** [beliʒeʀɑ̃s] nf belligerence
**belligérant, e** [beliʒeʀɑ̃, -ɑ̃t] adj belligerent
**belliqueux, -euse** [belikø, -øz] adj aggressive,
warlike
**belote** [bəlɔt] nf belote (card game)
**belvédère** [bɛlvedeʀ] nm panoramic viewpoint
(or small building there)
**bémol** [bemɔl] nm (Mus) flat
**ben** [bɛ̃] excl (fam) well
**bénédiction** [benediksjɔ̃] nf blessing
**bénéfice** [benefis] nm (Comm) profit; (avantage)
benefit; **au ~ de** in aid of
**bénéficiaire** [benefisjɛʀ] nm/f beneficiary
**bénéficier** [benefisje] vi: **~ de** to enjoy; (profiter)
to benefit by ou from; (obtenir) to get, be given
**bénéfique** [benefik] adj beneficial
**Bénélux** [benelyks] nm: **le ~** Benelux, the
Benelux countries
**benêt** [bənɛ] nm simpleton
**bénévolat** [benevɔla] nm voluntary service ou
work
**bénévole** [benevɔl] adj voluntary, unpaid
**bénévolement** [benevɔlmɑ̃] adv voluntarily
**Bengale** [bɛ̃gal] nm: **le ~** Bengal; **le golfe du ~**
the Bay of Bengal
**bengali** [bɛ̃gali] adj Bengali, Bengalese ▷ nm
(Ling) Bengali
**Bénin** [benɛ̃] nm: **le ~** Benin
**bénin, -igne** [benɛ̃, -iɲ] adj minor, mild;
(tumeur) benign
**bénir** [beniʀ] vt to bless
**bénit, e** [beni, -it] adj consecrated; **eau ~e** holy
water
**bénitier** [benitje] nm stoup, font (for holy water)
**benjamin, e** [bɛ̃ʒamɛ̃, -in] nm/f youngest child;
(Sport) under-13
**benne** [bɛn] nf skip; (de téléphérique) (cable) car; **~
basculante** tipper (Brit), dump ou dumper truck
**benzine** [bɛ̃zin] nf benzine
**béotien, ne** [beɔsjɛ̃, -ɛn] nm/f philistine
**BEP** sigle m (= Brevet d'études professionnelles) school-
leaving diploma, taken at approx. 18 years
**BEPC** sigle m (= Brevet du premier cycle) former
school certificate (taken at approx. 16 years)
**béquille** [bekij] nf crutch; (de bicyclette) stand
**berbère** [bɛʀbeʀ] adj Berber ▷ nm (Ling) Berber
▷ nm/f: **Berbère** Berber
**bercail** [bɛʀkaj] nm fold
**berceau, x** [bɛʀso] nm cradle, crib
**bercer** [bɛʀse] vt to rock, cradle; (musique etc) to
lull; **~ qn de** (promesses etc) to delude sb with
**berceur, -euse** [bɛʀsœʀ, -øz] adj soothing ▷ nf
(chanson) lullaby
**BERD** [bɛʀd] sigle f (= Banque européenne pour la
reconstruction et le développement) EBRD
**béret** [beʀɛ], **béret basque** [beʀɛbask(ə)] nm
beret
**bergamote** [bɛʀgamɔt] nf (Bot) bergamot

**b**

**berge** [bɛʀʒ(ə)] nf bank
**berger, -ère** [bɛʀʒe, -ɛʀ] nm/f shepherd/
shepherdess; ~ **allemand** (chien) alsatian (dog)
(Brit), German shepherd (dog) (US)
**bergerie** [bɛʀʒəʀi] nf sheep pen
**bergeronnette** [bɛʀʒəʀɔnɛt] nf wagtail
**béribéri** [beʀibeʀi] nm beriberi
**Berlin** [bɛʀlɛ̃] n Berlin; ~-**Est/-Ouest** East/West
Berlin
**berline** [bɛʀlin] nf (Auto) saloon (car) (Brit),
sedan (US)
**berlingot** [bɛʀlɛ̃go] nm (emballage) carton
(pyramid shaped); (bonbon) lozenge
**berlinois, e** [bɛʀlinwa, -waz] adj of ou from
Berlin ▷ nm/f: **Berlinois, e** Berliner
**berlue** [bɛʀly] nf: **j'ai la** ~ I must be seeing
things
**bermuda** [bɛʀmyda] nm (short) Bermuda shorts
**Bermudes** [bɛʀmyd] nfpl: **les (îles)** ~ Bermuda
**Berne** [bɛʀn(ə)] n Bern
**berne** [bɛʀn(ə)] nf: **en** ~ at half-mast; **mettre
en** ~ to fly at half-mast
**berner** [bɛʀne] vt to fool
**bernois, e** [bɛʀnwa, -waz] adj Bernese
**berrichon, ne** [beʀiʃɔ̃, -ɔn] adj of ou from the
Berry
**besace** [bəzas] nf beggar's bag
**besogne** [bəzɔɲ] nf work no pl, job
**besogneux, -euse** [bəzɔɲø, -øz] adj hard-
working
**besoin** [bəzwɛ̃] nm need; (pauvreté): **le** ~ need,
want; **le** ~ **d'argent/de gloire** the need for
money/glory; ~**s (naturels)** nature's needs;
**faire ses** ~**s** to relieve o.s.; **avoir** ~ **de qch/faire
qch** to need sth/to do sth; **il n'y a pas** ~ **de
(faire)** there is no need to (do); **au** ~, **si** ~ **est** if
need be; **pour les** ~**s de la cause** for the
purpose in hand
**bestial, e, -aux** [bɛstjal, -o] adj bestial, brutish
▷ nmpl cattle
**bestiole** [bɛstjɔl] nf (tiny) creature
**bétail** [betaj] nm livestock, cattle pl
**bétaillère** [betajɛʀ] nf livestock truck
**bête** [bɛt] nf animal; (bestiole) insect, creature
▷ adj stupid, silly; **les** ~**s** (the) animals;
**chercher la petite** ~ to nit-pick; ~ **noire** pet
hate, bugbear (Brit); ~ **sauvage** wild beast; ~ **de
somme** beast of burden
**bêtement** [bɛtmɑ̃] adv stupidly; **tout** ~ quite
simply
**Bethléem** [bɛtleɛm] n Bethlehem
**bêtifier** [betifje] vi to talk nonsense
**bêtise** [betiz] nf stupidity; (action, remarque)
stupid thing (to say ou do); (bonbon) type of mint
sweet (Brit) ou candy (US); **faire/dire une** ~ to
do/say something stupid
**béton** [betɔ̃] nm concrete; **(en)** ~ (fig: alibi,
argument) cast iron; ~ **armé** reinforced concrete;
~ **précontraint** prestressed concrete
**bétonner** [betɔne] vt to concrete (over)
**bétonnière** [betɔnjɛʀ] nf cement mixer
**bette** [bɛt] nf (Bot) (Swiss) chard

**betterave** [bɛtʀav] nf (rouge) beetroot (Brit), beet
(US); ~ **fourragère** mangel-wurzel; ~ **sucrière**
sugar beet
**beugler** [bøgle] vi to low; (péj: radio etc) to blare
▷ vt (péj: chanson etc) to bawl out
**Beur** [bœʀ] adj, nm/f see note

○ ● **BEUR**
○
○ ● Beur is a term used to refer to a person born
● ● in France of North African immigrant
● ● parents. It is not racist and is often used by
● ● the media, anti-racist groups and second-
● ● generation North Africans themselves. The
● ● word itself comes from back slang or
● ● "verlan".

**beurre** [bœʀ] nm butter; **mettre du** ~ **dans les
épinards** (fig) to add a little to the kitty; ~ **de
cacao** cocoa butter; ~ **noir** brown butter (sauce)
**beurrer** [bœʀe] vt to butter
**beurrier** [bœʀje] nm butter dish
**beuverie** [bœvʀi] nf drinking session
**bévue** [bevy] nf blunder
**Beyrouth** [beʀut] n Beirut
**Bhoutan** [butɑ̃] nm: **le** ~ Bhutan
**bi...** [bi] préfixe bi..., two-
**Biafra** [bjafʀa] nm: **le** ~ Biafra
**biafrais, e** [bjafʀɛ, -ɛz] adj Biafran
**biais** [bjɛ] nm (moyen) device, expedient; (aspect)
angle; (bande de tissu) piece of cloth cut on the
bias; **en** ~, **de** ~ (obliquement) at an angle; (fig)
indirectly
**biaiser** [bjeze] vi (fig) to sidestep the issue
**biathlon** [bjatlɔ̃] nm biathlon
**bibelot** [biblo] nm trinket, curio
**biberon** [bibʀɔ̃] nm (feeding) bottle; **nourrir au**
~ to bottle-feed
**bible** [bibl(ə)] nf bible
**bibliobus** [biblijɔbys] nm mobile library van
**bibliographie** [biblijɔgʀafi] nf bibliography
**bibliophile** [biblijɔfil] nm/f book-lover
**bibliothécaire** [biblijɔtekɛʀ] nm/f librarian
**bibliothèque** [biblijɔtɛk] nf library; (meuble)
bookcase; ~ **municipale** public library
**biblique** [biblik] adj biblical
**bic®** [bik] nm Biro®
**bicarbonate** [bikaʀbɔnat] nm: ~ **(de soude)**
bicarbonate of soda
**bicentenaire** [bisɑ̃tnɛʀ] nm bicentenary
**biceps** [bisɛps] nm biceps
**biche** [biʃ] nf doe
**bichonner** [biʃɔne] vt to groom
**bicolore** [bikɔlɔʀ] adj two-coloured (Brit), two-
colored (US)
**bicoque** [bikɔk] nf (péj) shack, dump
**bicorne** [bikɔʀn(ə)] nm cocked hat
**bicyclette** [bisiklɛt] nf bicycle
**bidasse** [bidas] nm (fam) squaddie (Brit)
**bide** [bid] nm (fam: ventre) belly; (Théât) flop
**bidet** [bidɛ] nm bidet
**bidoche** [bidɔʃ] nf (fam) meat

**bidon** [bidɔ̃] *nm* can ▷ *adj inv* (*fam*) phoney
**bidonnant, e** [bidɔnɑ̃, -ɑ̃t] *adj* (*fam*) hilarious
**bidonville** [bidɔ̃vil] *nm* shanty town
**bidule** [bidyl] *nm* (*fam*) thingamajig
**bielle** [bjɛl] *nf* connecting rod; (*Auto*) track rod
**biélorusse** [bjelɔʀys] *adj* Belarussian ▷ *nm/f*:
  **Biélorusse** Belarussian
**Biélorussie** [bjelɔʀysi] *nf* Belorussia

🔘 MOT-CLÉ

**bien** [bjɛ̃] *nm* **1** (*avantage, profit*): **faire le bien** to
do good; **faire du bien à qn** to do sb good; **ça
fait du bien de faire** it does you good to do;
**dire du bien de** to speak well of; **c'est pour
son bien** it's for his own good; **changer en
bien** to change for the better; **le bien public**
the public good; **vouloir du bien à qn** (*vouloir
aider*) to have sb's (best) interests at heart; **je te
veux du bien** (*pour mettre en confiance*) I don't
wish you any harm
  **2** (*possession, patrimoine*) possession, property;
**son bien le plus précieux** his most treasured
possession; **avoir du bien** to have property;
**biens (de consommation** *etc*) (consumer *etc*)
goods; **biens durables** (consumer) durables
  **3** (*moral*): **le bien** good; **distinguer le bien du
mal** to tell good from evil
  ▷ *adv* **1** (*de façon satisfaisante*) well; **elle travaille/
mange bien** she works/eats well; **aller** *or* **se
porter bien** to be well; **croyant bien faire, je/
il …** thinking I/he was doing the right thing, I/
he …
  **2** (*valeur intensive*) quite; **bien jeune** quite
young; **bien assez** quite enough; **bien mieux**
(very) much better; **bien du temps/des gens**
quite a time/a number of people; **j'espère bien
y aller** I do hope to go; **je veux bien le faire**
(*concession*) I'm quite willing to do it; **il faut
bien le faire** it has to be done; **il y a bien deux
ans** at least two years ago; **il semble bien que**
it really seems that; **peut-être bien** it could
well be; **aimer bien** to like; **Paul est bien
venu, n'est-ce pas?** Paul HAS come, hasn't
he?; **où peut-il bien être passé?** where on
earth can he have got to?
  **3** (*conséquence, résultat*): **si bien que** with the
result that; **on verra bien** we'll see; **faire bien
de …** to be right to …
  ▷ *excl* right!, OK!, fine!; **eh bien!** well!; (*c'est*)
**bien fait!** it serves you (*ou* him *etc*) right!; **bien
sûr!, bien entendu!** certainly!, of course!
  ▷ *adj inv* **1** (*en bonne forme, à l'aise*): **je me sens
bien, je suis bien** I feel fine; **je ne me sens pas
bien, je ne suis pas bien** I don't feel well; **on
est bien dans ce fauteuil** this chair is very
comfortable
  **2** (*joli, beau*) good-looking; **tu es bien dans
cette robe** you look good in that dress
  **3** (*satisfaisant*) good; **elle est bien, cette
maison/secrétaire** it's a good house/she's a
good secretary; **c'est très bien (comme ça)** it's

fine (like that); **ce n'est pas si bien que ça** it's
not as good *ou* great as all that; **c'est bien?** is
that all right?
  **4** (*moralement*) right; (*: personne*) good, nice;
(*respectable*) respectable; **ce n'est pas bien de …**
it's not right to …; **elle est bien, cette femme**
she's a nice woman, she's a good sort; **des gens
bien** respectable people
  **5** (*en bons termes*): **être bien avec qn** to be on
good terms with sb

**bien-aimé, e** [bjɛ̃neme] *adj, nm/f* beloved
**bien-être** [bjɛ̃nɛtʀ(ə)] *nm* well-being
**bienfaisance** [bjɛ̃fəzɑ̃s] *nf* charity
**bienfaisant, e** [bjɛ̃fəzɑ̃, -ɑ̃t] *adj* (*chose*) beneficial
**bienfait** [bjɛ̃fɛ] *nm* act of generosity,
  benefaction; (*de la science etc*) benefit
**bienfaiteur, -trice** [bjɛ̃fɛtœʀ, -tʀis] *nm/f*
  benefactor/benefactress
**bien-fondé** [bjɛ̃fɔ̃de] *nm* soundness
**bien-fonds** [bjɛ̃fɔ̃] *nm* property
**bienheureux, -euse** [bjɛ̃nœʀø, -øz] *adj* happy;
  (*Rel*) blessed, blest
**biennal, e, -aux** [bjenal, -o] *adj* biennial
**bien-pensant, e** [bjɛ̃pɑ̃sɑ̃, -ɑ̃t] *adj* right-
  thinking ▷ *nm/f*: **les ~s** right-minded people
**bien que** [bjɛ̃k(ə)] *conj* although
**bienséance** [bjɛ̃seɑ̃s] *nf* propriety, decorum *no
  pl*; **les ~s** (*convenances*) the proprieties
**bienséant, e** [bjɛ̃seɑ̃, -ɑ̃t] *adj* proper, seemly
**bientôt** [bjɛ̃to] *adv* soon; **à ~** see you soon
**bienveillance** [bjɛ̃vɛjɑ̃s] *nf* kindness
**bienveillant, e** [bjɛ̃vɛjɑ̃, -ɑ̃t] *adj* kindly
**bienvenu, e** [bjɛ̃vny] *adj* welcome ▷ *nm/f*: **être
le ~/la ~e** to be welcome ▷ *nf*: **souhaiter la ~e à**
to welcome; **~e à** welcome to
**bière** [bjɛʀ] *nf* (*boisson*) beer; (*cercueil*) bier; **~
blonde** lager; **~ brune** brown ale; **~ (à la)
pression** draught beer
**biffer** [bife] *vt* to cross out
**bifteck** [biftɛk] *nm* steak
**bifurcation** [bifyʀkasjɔ̃] *nf* fork (*in road*); (*fig*)
  new direction
**bifurquer** [bifyʀke] *vi* (*route*) to fork; (*véhicule*) to
  turn off
**bigame** [bigam] *adj* bigamous
**bigamie** [bigami] *nf* bigamy
**bigarré, e** [bigaʀe] *adj* multicoloured (*Brit*),
  multicolored (*US*); (*disparate*) motley
**bigarreau, x** [bigaʀo] *nm* *type of cherry*
**bigleux, -euse** [biglø, -øz] *adj* (*fam: qui louche*)
  cross-eyed; (*: qui voit mal*) short-sighted; **il est
  complètement ~** he's as blind as a bat
**bigorneau, x** [bigɔʀno] *nm* winkle
**bigot, e** [bigo, -ɔt] (*péj*) *adj* bigoted ▷ *nm/f* bigot
**bigoterie** [bigɔtʀi] *nf* bigotry
**bigoudi** [bigudi] *nm* curler
**bigrement** [bigʀəmɑ̃] *adv* (*fam*) fantastically
**bijou, x** [biʒu] *nm* jewel
**bijouterie** [biʒutʀi] *nf* (*magasin*) jeweller's
  (shop) (*Brit*), jewelry store (*US*); (*bijoux*)
  jewellery, jewelry

**bijoutier, -ière** [biʒutje, -jɛʀ] *nm/f* jeweller (*Brit*), jeweler (*US*)

**bikini** [bikini] *nm* bikini

**bilan** [bilɑ̃] *nm* (*Comm*) balance sheet(s); (*annuel*) end of year statement; (*fig*) (net) outcome; (: *de victimes*) toll; **faire le ~ de** to assess; to review; **déposer son ~** to file a bankruptcy statement; **~ de santé** (*Méd*) check-up; **~ social** *statement of a firm's policies towards its employees*

**bilatéral, e, -aux** [bilateʀal, -o] *adj* bilateral

**bilboquet** [bilbɔkɛ] *nm* (*jouet*) cup-and-ball game

**bile** [bil] *nf* bile; **se faire de la ~** (*fam*) to worry o.s. sick

**biliaire** [biljɛʀ] *adj* biliary

**bilieux, -euse** [biljø, -øz] *adj* bilious; (*fig: colérique*) testy

**bilingue** [bilɛ̃g] *adj* bilingual

**bilinguisme** [bilɛ̃gɥism(ə)] *nm* bilingualism

**billard** [bijaʀ] *nm* billiards *sg*; (*table*) billiard table; **c'est du ~** (*fam*) it's a cinch; **passer sur le ~** (*fam*) to have an (*ou* one's) operation; **~ électrique** pinball

**bille** [bij] *nf* ball; (*du jeu de billes*) marble; (*de bois*) log; **jouer aux ~s** to play marbles

**billet** [bijɛ] *nm* (*aussi:* **billet de banque**) (bank)note; (*de cinéma, de bus etc*) ticket; (*courte lettre*) note; **~ à ordre** *ou* **de commerce** (*Comm*) promissory note, IOU; **~ d'avion/de train** plane/train ticket; **~ circulaire** round-trip ticket; **~ doux** love letter; **~ de faveur** complimentary ticket; **~ de loterie** lottery ticket; **~ de quai** platform ticket; **~ électronique** e-ticket

**billetterie** [bijɛtʀi] *nf* ticket office; (*distributeur*) ticket dispenser; (*Banque*) cash dispenser

**billion** [biljɔ̃] *nm* billion (*Brit*), trillion (*US*)

**billot** [bijo] *nm* block

**bimbeloterie** [bɛ̃blɔtʀi] *nf* (*objets*) fancy goods

**bimensuel, le** [bimɑ̃sɥɛl] *adj* bimonthly, twice-monthly

**bimestriel, le** [bimɛstʀijɛl] *adj* bimonthly, two-monthly

**bimoteur** [bimɔtœʀ] *adj* twin-engined

**binaire** [binɛʀ] *adj* binary

**biner** [bine] *vt* to hoe

**binette** [binɛt] *nf* (*outil*) hoe

**binoclard, e** [binɔklaʀ, -aʀd(ə)] (*fam*) *adj* specky ▷ *nm/f* four-eyes

**binocle** [binɔkl(ə)] *nm* pince-nez

**binoculaire** [binɔkylɛʀ] *adj* binocular

**binôme** [binom] *nm* binomial

**bio** [bjo] *adj* (*fam*) = **biologique**; (*produits, aliments*) organic

**bio...** [bjɔ] *préfixe* bio...

**biocarburant** [bjokaʀbyʀɑ̃] *nm* biofuel

**biochimie** [bjoʃimi] *nf* biochemistry

**biochimique** [bjoʃimik] *adj* biochemical

**biochimiste** [bjoʃimist(ə)] *nm/f* biochemist

**biodégradable** [bjodegʀadabl(ə)] *adj* biodegradable

**biodiversité** [bjodivɛʀsite] *nf* biodiversity

**bioéthique** [bjoetik] *nf* bioethics *sg*

**biographe** [bjɔgʀaf] *nm/f* biographer

**biographie** [bjɔgʀafi] *nf* biography

**biographique** [bjɔgʀafik] *adj* biographical

**biologie** [bjɔlɔʒi] *nf* biology

**biologique** [bjɔlɔʒik] *adj* biological

**biologiste** [bjɔlɔʒist(ə)] *nm/f* biologist

**biomasse** [bjomas] *nf* biomass

**biopsie** [bjɔpsi] *nf* (*Méd*) biopsy

**biosphère** [bjɔsfɛʀ] *nf* biosphere

**biotechnologie** [bjotɛknɔlɔʒi] *nf* biotechnology

**bioterrorisme** [bjotɛʀɔʀism] *nm* bioterrorism

**bioterroriste** [bjotɛʀɔʀist] *nm/f* bioterrorist

**biotope** [bjɔtɔp] *nm* biotope

**bipartisme** [bipaʀtism(ə)] *nm* two-party system

**bipartite** [bipaʀtit] *adj* (*Pol*) two-party, bipartisan

**bipède** [bipɛd] *nm* biped, two-footed creature

**biphasé, e** [bifaze] *adj* (*Élec*) two-phase

**biplace** [biplas] *adj, nm* (*avion*) two-seater

**biplan** [biplɑ̃] *nm* biplane

**bique** [bik] *nf* nanny goat; (*péj*) old hag

**biquet, te** [bikɛ, -ɛt] *nm/f*: **mon ~** (*fam*) my lamb

**BIRD** [biʀd] *sigle f* (= *Banque internationale pour la reconstruction et le développement*) IBRD

**biréacteur** [biʀeaktœʀ] *nm* twin-engined jet

**birman, e** [biʀmɑ̃, -an] *adj* Burmese

**Birmanie** [biʀmani] *nf*: **la ~** Burma

**bis, e** [bi, biz] *adj* (*couleur*) greyish brown ▷ *adv* [bis]: **12 ~ 12a** *ou* A ▷ *excl, nm* [bis] encore ▷ *nf* (*baiser*) kiss; (*vent*) North wind; **faire une** *ou* **la ~e à qn** to kiss sb

**bisaïeul, e** [bizajœl] *nm/f* great-grandfather/great-grandmother

**bisannuel, le** [bizanɥɛl] *adj* biennial

**bisbille** [bisbij] *nf*: **être en ~ avec qn** to be at loggerheads with sb

**Biscaye** [biske] *nf*: **le golfe de ~** the Bay of Biscay

**biscornu, e** [biskɔʀny] *adj* crooked; (*bizarre*) weird(-looking)

**biscotte** [biskɔt] *nf* (breakfast) rusk

**biscuit** [biskɥi] *nm* biscuit (*Brit*), cookie (*US*); (*gateau*) sponge cake; **~ à la cuiller** sponge finger

**biscuiterie** [biskɥitʀi] *nf* biscuit manufacturing

**bise** [biz] *adj f, nf voir* **bis**

**biseau, x** [bizo] *nm* bevelled edge; **en ~** bevelled

**biseauter** [bizote] *vt* to bevel

**bisexué, e** [bisɛksɥe] *adj* bisexual

**bisexuel, le** [bisɛksɥɛl] *adj, nm/f* bisexual

**bismuth** [bismyt] *nm* bismuth

**bison** [bizɔ̃] *nm* bison

**bisou** [bizu] *nm* (*fam*) kiss

**bisque** [bisk(ə)] *nf*: **~ d'écrevisses** shrimp bisque

**bissectrice** [bisɛktʀis] *nf* bisector

**bisser** [bise] *vt* (*faire rejouer: artiste, chanson*) to encore; (*rejouer: morceau*) to give an encore of

**bissextile** [bisɛkstil] *adj*: **année ~** leap year

47

**bistouri** [bisturi] *nm* lancet
**bistre** [bistr(ə)] *adj* (*couleur*) bistre; (*peau, teint*) tanned
**bistro, bistrot** [bistro] *nm* bistro, café
**BIT** *sigle m* (= *Bureau international du travail*) ILO
**bit** [bit] *nm* (*Inform*) bit
**biterrois, e** [biterwa, -waz] *adj* of *ou* from Béziers
**bitte** [bit] *nf*: ~ **d'amarrage** bollard (*Naut*)
**bitume** [bitym] *nm* asphalt
**bitumer** [bityme] *vt* to asphalt
**bivalent, e** [bivalɑ̃, -ɑ̃t] *adj* bivalent
**bivouac** [bivwak] *nm* bivouac
**bizarre** [bizar] *adj* strange, odd
**bizarrement** [bizarmɑ̃] *adv* strangely, oddly
**bizarrerie** [bizarri] *nf* strangeness, oddness
**blackbouler** [blakbule] *vt* (*à une élection*) to blackball
**blafard, e** [blafar, -ard(ə)] *adj* wan
**blague** [blag] *nf* (*propos*) joke; (*farce*) trick; **sans ~!** no kidding!; ~ **à tabac** tobacco pouch
**blaguer** [blage] *vi* to joke ▷ *vt* to tease
**blagueur, -euse** [blagœr, -øz] *adj* teasing ▷ *nm/f* joker
**blair** [bler] *nm* (*fam*) conk
**blaireau, x** [blero] *nm* (*Zool*) badger; (*brosse*) shaving brush
**blairer** [blere] *vt*: **je ne peux pas le ~** I can't bear *ou* stand him
**blâmable** [blɑmabl(ə)] *adj* blameworthy
**blâme** [blɑm] *nm* blame; (*sanction*) reprimand
**blâmer** [blɑme] *vt* (*réprouver*) to blame; (*réprimander*) to reprimand
**blanc, blanche** [blɑ̃, blɑ̃ʃ] *adj* white; (*non imprimé*) blank; (*innocent*) pure ▷ *nm/f* white, white man/woman ▷ *nm* (*couleur*) white; (*linge*): **le ~** whites *pl*; (*espace non écrit*) blank; (*aussi:* **blanc d'œuf**) (egg-)white; (*aussi:* **blanc de poulet**) breast, white meat; (*aussi:* **vin blanc**) white wine ▷ *nf* (*Mus*) minim (*Brit*), half-note (*US*); (*fam: drogue*) smack; **d'une voix blanche** in a toneless voice; **aux cheveux ~s** white-haired; **le ~ de l'œil** the white of the eye; **laisser en ~** to leave blank; **chèque en ~** blank cheque; **à ~** *adv* (*chauffer*) white-hot; (*tirer, charger*) with blanks; **saigner à ~** to bleed white; **~ cassé** off-white
**blanc-bec** [blɑ̃bɛk] (*pl* **blancs-becs**) *nm* greenhorn
**blanchâtre** [blɑ̃ʃɑtr(ə)] *adj* (*teint, lumière*) whitish
**blancheur** [blɑ̃ʃœr] *nf* whiteness
**blanchir** [blɑ̃ʃir] *vt* (*gén*) to whiten; (*linge, fig: argent*) to launder; (*Culin*) to blanch; (*fig: disculper*) to clear ▷ *vi* to grow white; (*cheveux*) to go white; **blanchi à la chaux** whitewashed
**blanchissage** [blɑ̃ʃisaʒ] *nm* (*du linge*) laundering
**blanchisserie** [blɑ̃ʃisri] *nf* laundry
**blanchisseur, -euse** [blɑ̃ʃisœr, -øz] *nm/f* launderer
**blanc-seing** [blɑ̃sɛ̃] (*pl* **blancs-seings**) *nm* signed blank paper

**blanquette** [blɑ̃kɛt] *nf* (*Culin*): ~ **de veau** veal in a white sauce, blanquette de veau
**blasé, e** [blaze] *adj* blasé
**blaser** [blaze] *vt* to make blasé
**blason** [blazɔ̃] *nm* coat of arms
**blasphémateur, -trice** [blasfematœr, -tris] *nm/f* blasphemer
**blasphématoire** [blasfematwar] *adj* blasphemous
**blasphème** [blasfɛm] *nm* blasphemy
**blasphémer** [blasfeme] *vi* to blaspheme ▷ *vt* to blaspheme against
**blatte** [blat] *nf* cockroach
**blazer** [blazɛr] *nm* blazer
**blé** [ble] *nm* wheat; ~ **en herbe** wheat on the ear; ~ **noir** buckwheat
**bled** [blɛd] *nm* (*péj*) hole; (*en Afrique du Nord*): **le ~** the interior
**blême** [blɛm] *adj* pale
**blêmir** [blemir] *vi* (*personne*) to (turn) pale; (*lueur*) to grow pale
**blennorragie** [blenɔraʒi] *nf* blennorrhoea
**blessant, e** [blɛsɑ̃, -ɑ̃t] *adj* hurtful
**blessé, e** [blese] *adj* injured ▷ *nm/f* injured person, casualty; **un ~ grave, un grand ~** a seriously injured *ou* wounded person
**blesser** [blese] *vt* to injure; (*délibérément: Mil etc*) to wound; (*souliers etc, offenser*) to hurt; **se blesser** to injure o.s.; **se ~ au pied** *etc* to injure one's foot *etc*
**blessure** [blesyr] *nf* injury; wound
**blet, te** [blɛ, blɛt] *adj* overripe
**blette** [blɛt] *nf* = **bette**
**bleu, e** [blø] *adj* blue; (*bifteck*) very rare ▷ *nm* (*couleur*) blue; (*novice*) greenhorn; (*contusion*) bruise; (*vêtement: aussi:* **bleus**) overalls *pl* (*Brit*), coveralls *pl* (*US*); **avoir une peur ~e** to be scared stiff; **zone ~e** ≈ restricted parking area; **fromage ~** blue cheese; **au ~** (*Culin*) au bleu; ~ (**de lessive**) ≈ blue bag; ~ **de méthylène** (*Méd*) methylene blue; ~ **marine/nuit/roi** navy/midnight/royal blue
**bleuâtre** [bløɑtr(ə)] *adj* (*fumée etc*) bluish, blueish
**bleuet** [bløɛ] *nm* cornflower
**bleuir** [bløir] *vt, vi* to turn blue
**bleuté, e** [bløte] *adj* blue-shaded
**blindage** [blɛ̃daʒ] *nm* armo(u)r-plating
**blindé, e** [blɛ̃de] *adj* armoured (*Brit*), armored (*US*); (*fig*) hardened ▷ *nm* armoured *ou* armored car; (*char*) tank
**blinder** [blɛ̃de] *vt* to armour (*Brit*), armor (*US*); (*fig*) to harden
**blizzard** [blizar] *nm* blizzard
**bloc** [blɔk] *nm* (*de pierre etc, Inform*) block; (*de papier à lettres*) pad; (*ensemble*) group, block; **serré à ~** tightened right down; **en ~** as a whole; wholesale; **faire ~** to unite; ~ **opératoire** operating *ou* theatre block; ~ **sanitaire** toilet block; ~ **sténo** shorthand notebook
**blocage** [blɔkaʒ] *nm* (*voir bloquer*) blocking; jamming; freezing; (*Psych*) hang-up

**bloc-cuisine** [blɔkkɥizin] (*pl* **blocs-cuisines**) *nm* kitchen unit

**bloc-cylindres** [blɔksilɛ̃dʀ(ə)] (*pl* **blocs-cylindres**) *nm* cylinder block

**bloc-évier** [blɔkevje] (*pl* **blocs-éviers**) *nm* sink unit

**bloc-moteur** [blɔkmɔtœʀ] (*pl* **blocs-moteurs**) *nm* engine block

**bloc-notes** [blɔknɔt] (*pl* **blocs-notes**) *nm* note pad

**blocus** [blɔkys] *nm* blockade

**blog, blogue** [blɔg] *nm* blog

**blogging** [blɔgiŋ] *nm* blogging

**bloguer** [blɔge] *vi* to blog

**blond, e** [blɔ̃, -ɔ̃d] *adj* fair; (*plus clair*) blond; (*sable, blés*) golden ▷ *nm/f* fair-haired *ou* blond man/woman; **~ cendré** ash blond

**blondeur** [blɔ̃dœʀ] *nf* fairness; blondness

**blondin, e** [blɔ̃dɛ̃, -in] *nm/f* fair-haired *ou* blond child *ou* young person

**blondinet, te** [blɔ̃dinɛ, -ɛt] *nm/f* blondy

**blondir** [blɔ̃diʀ] *vi* (*personne, cheveux*) to go fair *ou* blond

**bloquer** [blɔke] *vt* (*passage*) to block; (*pièce mobile*) to jam; (*crédits, compte*) to freeze; (*personne, négociations etc*) to hold up; (*regrouper*) to group; **~ les freins** to jam on the brakes

**blottir** [blɔtiʀ]: **se blottir** *vi* to huddle up

**blousant, e** [bluzɑ̃, ɑ̃t] *adj* blousing out

**blouse** [bluz] *nf* overall

**blouser** [bluze] *vi* to blouse out

**blouson** [bluzɔ̃] *nm* blouson (jacket); **~ noir** (*fig*) = rocker

**blue-jean** [bludʒin], **blue-jeans** [bludʒins] *nm* jeans

**blues** [bluz] *nm* blues *pl*

**bluet** [blyɛ] *nm* = **bleuet**

**bluff** [blœf] *nm* bluff

**bluffer** [blœfe] *vi, vt* to bluff

**BNF** *sigle f* = **Bibliothèque nationale de France**

**boa** [bɔa] *nm* (*Zool*): **~ (constricteur)** boa (constrictor); (*tour de cou*) (feather *ou* fur) boa

**bobard** [bɔbaʀ] *nm* (*fam*) tall story

**bobèche** [bɔbɛʃ] *nf* candle-ring

**bobine** [bɔbin] *nf* (*de fil*) reel; (*de machine à coudre*) spool; (*de machine à écrire*) ribbon; (*Élec*) coil; **~ (d'allumage)** (*Auto*) coil; **~ de pellicule** (*Photo*) roll of film

**bobo** [bobo] *nm* sore spot

**bobsleigh** [bɔbslɛg] *nm* bob(sleigh)

**bocage** [bɔkaʒ] *nm* (*Géo*) bocage, farmland criss-crossed by hedges and trees; (*bois*) grove, copse (*Brit*)

**bocal, -aux** [bɔkal, -o] *nm* jar

**bock** [bɔk] *nm* (*beer*) glass; (*contenu*) glass of beer

**body** [bɔdi] *nm* body(suit); (*Sport*) leotard

**bœuf** [bœf, *pl* bø] *nm* ox, steer; (*Culin*) beef; (*Mus: fam*) jam session

**bof** [bɔf] *excl* (*fam: indifférence*) don't care!, meh; (: *pas terrible*) nothing special

**Bogota** [bɔgɔta] *n* Bogotá

**bogue** [bɔg] *nf* (*Bot*) husk ▷ *nm* (*Inform*) bug

**Bohème** [bɔɛm] *nf*: **la ~** Bohemia

**bohème** [bɔɛm] *adj* happy-go-lucky, unconventional

**bohémien, ne** [bɔemjɛ̃, -ɛn] *adj* Bohemian ▷ *nm/f* gipsy

**boire** [bwaʀ] *vt* to drink; (*s'imprégner de*) to soak up; **~ un coup** to have a drink

**bois** [bwa] *vb voir* **boire** ▷ *nm* wood; (*Zool*) antler; (*Mus*): **les ~** the woodwind; **de ~, en ~** wooden; **~ vert** green wood; **~ mort** deadwood; **~ de lit** bedstead

**boisé, e** [bwaze] *adj* woody, wooded

**boiser** [bwaze] *vt* (*galerie de mine*) to timber; (*chambre*) to panel; (*terrain*) to plant with trees

**boiseries** [bwazʀi] *nfpl* panelling *sg*

**boisson** [bwasɔ̃] *nf* drink; **pris de ~** drunk, intoxicated; **~s alcoolisées** alcoholic beverages *ou* drinks; **~s non alcoolisées** soft drinks

**boit** [bwa] *vb voir* **boire**

**boîte** [bwat] *nf* box; (*fam: entreprise*) firm, company; **aliments en ~** canned *ou* tinned (*Brit*) foods; **~ de sardines/petits pois** can *ou* tin (*Brit*) of sardines/peas; **mettre qn en ~** (*fam*) to have a laugh at sb's expense; **~ d'allumettes** box of matches; (*vide*) matchbox; **~ de conserves** can *ou* tin (*Brit*) (of food); **~ crânienne** cranium; **~ à gants** glove compartment; **~ aux lettres** letter box, mailbox (*US*); (*Inform*) mailbox; **~ à musique** musical box; **~ noire** (*Aviat*) black box; **~ de nuit** night club; **~ à ordures** dustbin (*Brit*), trash can (*US*); **~ postale (BP)** PO box; **~ de vitesses** gear box; **~ vocale** voice mail

**boiter** [bwate] *vi* to limp; (*fig*) to wobble; (*raisonnement*) to be shaky

**boiteux, -euse** [bwatø, -øz] *adj* lame; wobbly; shaky

**boîtier** [bwatje] *nm* case; (*d'appareil photo*) body; **~ de montre** watch case

**boitiller** [bwatije] *vi* to limp slightly, have a slight limp

**boive** *etc* [bwav] *vb voir* **boire**

**bol** [bɔl] *nm* bowl; (*contenu*): **un ~ de café** *etc* a bowl of coffee *etc*; **un ~ d'air** a breath of fresh air; **en avoir ras le ~** (*fam*) to have had a bellyful

**bolée** [bɔle] *nf* bowlful

**boléro** [bɔleʀo] *nm* bolero

**bolet** [bɔlɛ] *nm* boletus (mushroom)

**bolide** [bɔlid] *nm* racing car; **comme un ~** like a rocket

**Bolivie** [bɔlivi] *nf*: **la ~** Bolivia

**bolivien, ne** [bɔlivjɛ̃, -ɛn] *adj* Bolivian ▷ *nm/f*: **Bolivien, ne** Bolivian

**bolognais, e** [bɔlɔɲɛ, -ez] *adj* Bolognese

**Bologne** [bɔlɔɲ] *n* Bologna

**bombance** [bɔ̃bɑ̃s] *nf*: **faire ~** to have a feast, revel

**bombardement** [bɔ̃baʀdəmɑ̃] *nm* bombing

**bombarder** [bɔ̃baʀde] *vt* to bomb; **~ qn de** (*cailloux, lettres*) to bombard sb with; **~ qn directeur** to thrust sb into the director's seat

**bombardier** [bɔ̃baʀdje] *nm* (*avion*) bomber; (*aviateur*) bombardier

**b**

**bombe** [bɔ̃b] *nf* bomb; (*atomiseur*) (aerosol) spray; (*Équitation*) riding cap; **faire la ~** (*fam*) to go on a binge; **~ atomique** atomic bomb; **~ à retardement** time bomb

**bombé, e** [bɔ̃be] *adj* rounded; (*mur*) bulging; (*front*) domed; (*route*) steeply cambered

**bomber** [bɔ̃be] *vi* to bulge; (*route*) to camber ▷ *vt*: **~ le torse** to swell out one's chest

○ MOT-CLÉ

**bon, bonne** [bɔ̃, bɔn] *adj* **1** (*agréable, satisfaisant*) good; **un bon repas/restaurant** a good meal/restaurant; **être bon en maths** to be good at maths

**2** (*charitable*): **être bon (envers)** to be good (to), to be kind (to); **vous êtes trop bon** you're too kind

**3** (*correct*) right; **le bon numéro/moment** the right number/moment

**4** (*souhaits*): **bon anniversaire** happy birthday; **bon courage** good luck; **bon séjour** enjoy your stay; **bon voyage** have a good trip; **bon week-end** have a good weekend; **bonne année** happy New Year; **bonne chance** good luck; **bonne fête** happy holiday; **bonne nuit** good night

**5** (*approprié*): **bon à/pour** fit to/for; **bon à jeter** fit for the bin; **c'est bon à savoir** that's useful to know; **à quoi bon (...)?** what's the point *ou* use (of ...)?

**6** (*intensif*): **ça m'a pris deux bonnes heures** it took me a good two hours; **un bon nombre de** a good number of

**7**: **bon enfant** *adj inv* accommodating, easy-going; **bonne femme** (*péj*) woman; **de bonne heure** early; **bon marché** cheap; **bon mot** witticism; **pour faire bon poids ...** to make up for it ...; **bon sens** common sense; **bon vivant** jovial chap; **bonnes œuvres** charitable works, charities; **bonne sœur** nun

▷ *nm* **1** (*billet*) voucher; (*aussi*: **bon cadeau**) gift voucher; **bon de caisse** cash voucher; **bon d'essence** petrol coupon; **bon à tirer** pass for press; **bon du Trésor** Treasury bond

**2**: **avoir du bon** to have its good points; **il y a du bon dans ce qu'il dit** there's some sense in what he says; **pour de bon** for good

▷ *nm/f*: **un bon à rien** a good-for-nothing

▷ *adv*: **il fait bon** it's *ou* the weather is fine; **sentir bon** to smell good; **tenir bon** to stand firm; **juger bon de faire ...** to think fit to do ...

▷ *excl* right!, good!; **ah bon?** really?; **bon, je reste** right, I'll stay; *voir aussi* **bonne**

**bonasse** [bɔnas] *adj* soft, meek

**bonbon** [bɔ̃bɔ̃] *nm* (boiled) sweet

**bonbonne** [bɔ̃bɔn] *nf* demijohn; carboy

**bonbonnière** [bɔ̃bɔnjɛR] *nf* sweet (*Brit*) *ou* candy (*US*) box

**bond** [bɔ̃] *nm* leap; (*d'une balle*) rebound, ricochet; **faire un ~** to leap in the air; **d'un seul ~** in one bound, with one leap; **~ en avant**

(*fig: progrès*) leap forward

**bonde** [bɔ̃d] *nf* (*d'évier etc*) plug; (: *trou*) plughole; (*de tonneau*) bung; bunghole

**bondé, e** [bɔ̃de] *adj* packed (full)

**bondieuserie** [bɔ̃djøzRi] *nf* (*péj: objet*) religious knick-knack

**bondir** [bɔ̃diR] *vi* to leap; **~ de joie** (*fig*) to jump for joy; **~ de colère** (*fig*) to be hopping mad

**bonheur** [bɔnœR] *nm* happiness; **avoir le ~ de** to have the good fortune to; **porter ~ (à qn)** to bring (sb) luck; **au petit ~** haphazardly; **par ~** fortunately

**bonhomie** [bɔnɔmi] *nf* good-naturedness

**bonhomme** [bɔnɔm] (*pl* **bonshommes** [bɔ̃zɔm]) *nm* fellow ▷ *adj* good-natured; **un vieux ~** an old chap; **aller son ~ de chemin** to carry on in one's own sweet way; **~ de neige** snowman

**boni** [bɔni] *nm* profit

**bonification** [bɔnifikasjɔ̃] *nf* bonus

**bonifier** [bɔnifje]: **se bonifier** *vi* to improve

**boniment** [bɔnimɑ̃] *nm* patter *no pl*

**bonjour** [bɔ̃ʒuR] *excl, nm* hello; (*selon l'heure*) good morning (*ou* afternoon); **donner** *ou* **souhaiter le ~ à qn** to bid sb good morning *ou* afternoon

**Bonn** [bɔn] *n* Bonn

**bonne** [bɔn] *adj f voir* **bon** ▷ *nf* (*domestique*) maid; **~ à toute faire** general help; **~ d'enfant** nanny

**bonne-maman** [bɔnmamɑ̃] (*pl* **bonnes-mamans**) *nf* granny, grandma, gran

**bonnement** [bɔnmɑ̃] *adv*: **tout ~** quite simply

**bonnet** [bɔnɛ] *nm* bonnet, hat; (*de soutien-gorge*) cup; **~ d'âne** dunce's cap; **~ de bain** bathing cap; **~ de nuit** nightcap

**bonneterie** [bɔnɛtRi] *nf* hosiery

**bon-papa** [bɔ̃papa] (*pl* **bons-papas**) *nm* grandpa, grandad

**bonsoir** [bɔ̃swaR] *excl* good evening

**bonté** [bɔ̃te] *nf* kindness *no pl*; **avoir la ~ de** to be kind *ou* good enough to

**bonus** [bɔnys] *nm* (*Assurances*) no-claims bonus

**bonze** [bɔ̃z] *nm* (*Rel*) bonze

**boomerang** [bumRɑ̃g] *nm* boomerang

**boots** [buts] *nfpl* boots

**borborygme** [bɔRbɔRigm(ə)] *nm* rumbling noise

**bord** [bɔR] *nm* (*de table, verre, falaise*) edge; (*de rivière, lac*) bank; (*de route*) side; (*de vêtement*) edge, border; (*de chapeau*) brim; **(monter) à ~** (to go) on board; **jeter par-dessus ~** to throw overboard; **le commandant de ~/les hommes du ~** the ship's master/crew; **du même ~** (*fig*) of the same opinion; **au ~ de la mer/route** at the seaside/roadside; **être au ~ des larmes** to be on the verge of tears; **virer de ~** (*Navig*) to tack; **sur les ~s** (*fig*) slightly; **de tous ~s** on all sides; **~ du trottoir** kerb (*Brit*), curb (*US*)

**bordeaux** [bɔRdo] *nm* Bordeaux ▷ *adj inv* maroon

**bordée** [bɔRde] *nf* broadside; **une ~ d'injures** a volley of abuse; **tirer une ~** to go on the town

**bordel** [bɔRdɛl] *nm* brothel; (*fam!*) bloody (*Brit*)

ou goddamn (US) mess (!) ▷ *excl* hell!

**bordelais, e** [bɔʀdəlɛ, -ɛz] *adj* of *ou* from Bordeaux

**border** [bɔʀde] *vt* (*être le long de*) to border, line; (*garnir*): **~ qch de** to line sth with; to trim sth with; (*qn dans son lit*) to tuck up

**bordereau, x** [bɔʀdəʀo] *nm* docket, slip

**bordure** [bɔʀdyʀ] *nf* border; (*sur un vêtement*) trim(ming), border; **en ~ de** on the edge of

**boréal, e, aux** [bɔʀeal, -o] *adj* boreal, northern

**borgne** [bɔʀɲ(ə)] *adj* one-eyed; **hôtel ~** shady hotel; **fenêtre ~** obstructed window

**bornage** [bɔʀnaʒ] *nm* (*d'un terrain*) demarcation

**borne** [bɔʀn(ə)] *nf* boundary stone; (*aussi*: **borne kilométrique**) kilometre-marker, ≈ milestone; **bornes** *nfpl* (*fig*) limits; **dépasser les ~s** to go too far; **sans ~(s)** boundless

**borné, e** [bɔʀne] *adj* narrow; (*obtus*) narrow-minded

**Bornéo** [bɔʀneo] *nm*: **le ~** Borneo

**borner** [bɔʀne] *vt* (*délimiter*) to limit; (*limiter*) to confine; **se ~ à faire** to content o.s. with doing; to limit o.s. to doing

**bosniaque** [bɔznjak] *adj* Bosnian ▷ *nm/f*: **Bosniaque** Bosnian

**Bosnie** [bɔsni] *nf* Bosnia

**Bosnie-Herzégovine** [bɔsniɛʀzegɔvin] *nf* Bosnia-Herzegovina

**bosnien, ne** [bɔznjɛ̃, -ɛn] *adj* Bosnian ▷ *nm/f*: **Bosnien, ne** Bosnian

**Bosphore** [bɔsfɔʀ] *nm*: **le ~** the Bosphorus

**bosquet** [bɔskɛ] *nm* copse (*Brit*), grove

**bosse** [bɔs] *nf* (*de terrain etc*) bump; (*enflure*) lump; (*du bossu, du chameau*) hump; **avoir la ~ des maths** *etc* to have a gift for maths *etc*; **il a roulé sa ~** he's been around

**bosseler** [bɔsle] *vt* (*ouvrer*) to emboss; (*abîmer*) to dent

**bosser** [bɔse] *vi* (*fam*) to work; (: *dur*) to slog (hard) (*Brit*), slave (away)

**bosseur, -euse** [bɔsœʀ, -øz] *nm/f* (hard) worker, slogger (*Brit*)

**bossu, e** [bɔsy] *nm/f* hunchback

**bot** [bo] *adj m*: **pied ~** club foot

**botanique** [bɔtanik] *nf* botany ▷ *adj* botanic(al)

**botaniste** [bɔtanist(ə)] *nm/f* botanist

**Botswana** [bɔtswana] *nm*: **le ~** Botswana

**botte** [bɔt] *nf* (*soulier*) (high) boot; (*Escrime*) thrust; (*gerbe*): **~ de paille** bundle of straw; **~ de radis/d'asperges** bunch of radishes/asparagus; **~s de caoutchouc** wellington boots

**botter** [bɔte] *vt* to put boots on; (*donner un coup de pied à*) to kick; (*fam*): **ça me botte** I fancy that

**bottier** [bɔtje] *nm* bootmaker

**bottillon** [bɔtijɔ̃] *nm* bootee

**bottin** ® [bɔtɛ̃] *nm* directory

**bottine** [bɔtin] *nf* ankle boot

**botulisme** [bɔtylism(ə)] *nm* botulism

**bouc** [buk] *nm* goat; (*barbe*) goatee; **~ émissaire** scapegoat

**boucan** [bukɑ̃] *nm* din, racket

**bouche** [buʃ] *nf* mouth; **une ~ à nourrir** a

mouth to feed; **les ~s inutiles** the non-productive members of the population; **faire du ~ à ~ à qn** to give sb the kiss of life (*Brit*), give sb mouth-to-mouth resuscitation; **de ~ à oreille** confidentially; **pour la bonne ~** (*pour la fin*) till last; **faire venir l'eau à la ~ to** make one's mouth water; **~ cousue!** mum's the word!; **~ d'aération** air vent; **~ de chaleur** hot air vent; **~ d'égout** manhole; **~ d'incendie** fire hydrant; **~ de métro** métro entrance

**bouché, e** [buʃe] *adj* (*flacon etc*) stoppered; (*temps, ciel*) overcast; (*carrière*) blocked; (*péj: personne*) thick; (*trompette*) muted; **avoir le nez ~** to have a blocked(-up) nose

**bouchée** [buʃe] *nf* mouthful; **ne faire qu'une ~ de** (*fig*) to make short work of; **pour une ~ de pain** (*fig*) for next to nothing; **~s à la reine** chicken vol-au-vents

**boucher** [buʃe] *nm* butcher ▷ *vt* (*pour colmater*) to stop up; to fill up; (*obstruer*) to block (up); **se boucher** (*tuyau etc*) to block up, get blocked up; **se ~ le nez** to hold one's nose

**bouchère** [buʃɛʀ] *nf* butcher; (*femme du boucher*) butcher's wife

**boucherie** [buʃʀi] *nf* butcher's (shop); (*métier*) butchery; (*fig*) slaughter, butchery

**bouche-trou** [buʃtʀu] *nm* (*fig*) stop-gap

**bouchon** [buʃɔ̃] *nm* (*en liège*) cork; (*autre matière*) stopper; (*fig: embouteillage*) holdup; (*Pêche*) float; **~ doseur** measuring cap

**bouchonner** [buʃɔne] *vt* to rub down ▷ *vi* to form a traffic jam

**bouchot** [buʃo] *nm* mussel bed

**bouclage** [buklaʒ] *nm* sealing off

**boucle** [bukl(ə)] *nf* (*forme, figure, aussi Inform*) loop; (*objet*) buckle; **~ (de cheveux)** curl; **~ d'oreilles** earring

**bouclé, e** [bukle] *adj* curly; (*tapis*) uncut

**boucler** [bukle] *vt* (*fermer: ceinture etc*) to fasten; (: *magasin*) to shut; (*terminer*) to finish off; (: *circuit*) to complete; (*budget*) to balance; (*enfermer*) to shut away; (: *condamné*) to lock up; (: *quartier*) to seal off ▷ *vi* to curl; **faire ~** (*cheveux*) to curl; **la boucle** (*Aviat*) to loop the loop

**bouclette** [buklɛt] *nf* small curl

**bouclier** [buklije] *nm* shield

**bouddha** [buda] *nm* Buddha

**bouddhisme** [budism(ə)] *nm* Buddhism

**bouddhiste** [budist(ə)] *nm/f* Buddhist

**bouder** [bude] *vi* to sulk ▷ *vt* (*chose*) to turn one's nose up at; (*personne*) to refuse to have anything to do with

**bouderie** [budʀi] *nf* sulking *no pl*

**boudeur, -euse** [budœʀ, -øz] *adj* sullen, sulky

**boudin** [budɛ̃] *nm* (*Culin*) black pudding; (*Tech*) roll; **~ blanc** white pudding

**boudiné, e** [budine] *adj* (*doigt*) podgy; (*serré*): **~ dans** (*vêtement*) bulging out of

**boudoir** [budwaʀ] *nm* boudoir; (*biscuit*) sponge finger

**boue** [bu] *nf* mud

**bouée** [bwe] *nf* buoy; (*de baigneur*) rubber ring; **~**

**(de sauvetage)** lifebuoy; (*fig*) lifeline

**boueux, -euse** [bwø, -øz] *adj* muddy ▷ *nm* (*fam*) refuse (*Brit*) *ou* garbage (*US*) collector

**bouffant, e** [bufã, -ãt] *adj* puffed out

**bouffe** [buf] *nf* (*fam*) grub, food

**bouffée** [bufe] *nf* puff; ~ **de chaleur** (*gén*) blast of hot air; (*Méd*) hot flush (*Brit*) *ou* flash (*US*); ~ **de fièvre/de honte** flush of fever/shame; ~ **d'orgueil** fit of pride

**bouffer** [bufe] *vi* (*fam*) to eat; (*Couture*) to puff out ▷ *vt* (*fam*) to eat

**bouffi, e** [bufi] *adj* swollen

**bouffon, ne** [bufõ, -ɔn] *adj* farcical, comical ▷ *nm* jester

**bouge** [buʒ] *nm* (*bar louche*) (low) dive; (*taudis*) hovel

**bougeoir** [buʒwaʀ] *nm* candlestick

**bougeotte** [buʒɔt] *nf*: **avoir la** ~ to have the fidgets

**bouger** [buʒe] *vi* to move; (*dent etc*) to be loose; (*changer*) to alter; (*agir*) to stir ▷ *vt* to move; **se bouger** (*fam*) to move (oneself)

**bougie** [buʒi] *nf* candle; (*Auto*) spark(ing) plug

**bougon, ne** [bugõ, -ɔn] *adj* grumpy

**bougonner** [bugɔne] *vi, vt* to grumble

**bougre** [bugʀ(ə)] *nm* chap; (*fam*): **ce** ~ **de** ... that confounded ...

**boui-boui** [bwibwi] *nm* (*fam*) greasy spoon

**bouillabaisse** [bujabɛs] *nf* type of fish soup

**bouillant, e** [bujã, -ãt] *adj* (*qui bout*) boiling; (*très chaud*) boiling (hot); (*fig: ardent*) hot-headed; ~ **de colère** *etc* seething with anger *etc*

**bouille** [buj] *nf* (*fam*) mug

**bouilleur** [bujœʀ] *nm*: ~ **de cru** (home) distiller

**bouillie** [buji] *nf* gruel; (*de bébé*) cereal; **en** ~ (*fig*) crushed

**bouillir** [bujiʀ] *vi* to boil ▷ *vt* (*aussi*: **faire bouillir**: *Culin*) to boil; ~ **de colère** *etc* to seethe with anger *etc*

**bouilloire** [bujwaʀ] *nf* kettle

**bouillon** [bujõ] *nm* (*Culin*) stock *no pl*; (*bulles, écume*) bubble; ~ **de culture** culture medium

**bouillonnement** [bujɔnmã] *nm* (*d'un liquide*) bubbling; (*des idées*) ferment

**bouillonner** [bujɔne] *vi* to bubble; (*fig*) to bubble up; (*torrent*) to foam

**bouillotte** [bujɔt] *nf* hot-water bottle

**boulanger, -ère** [bulãʒe, -ɛʀ] *nm/f* baker ▷ *nf* (*femme du boulanger*) baker's wife

**boulangerie** [bulãʒʀi] *nf* bakery, baker's (shop); (*commerce*) bakery; ~ **industrielle** bakery

**boulangerie-pâtisserie** [bulãʒʀipɑtisʀi] (*pl* **boulangeries-pâtisseries**) *nf* baker's and confectioner's (shop)

**boule** [bul] *nf* (*gén*) ball; (*pour jouer*) bowl; (*de machine à écrire*) golf ball; **roulé en** ~ curled up in a ball; **se mettre en** ~ (*fig*) to fly off the handle, blow one's top; **perdre la** ~ (*fig: fam*) to go off one's rocker; ~ **de gomme** (*bonbon*) gum(drop), pastille; ~ **de neige** snowball; **faire** ~ **de neige** (*fig*) to snowball

**bouleau, x** [bulo] *nm* (silver) birch

**bouledogue** [buldɔg] *nm* bulldog

**bouler** [bule] *vi* (*fam*): **envoyer** ~ **qn** to send sb packing; **je me suis fait** ~ (*à un examen*) they flunked me

**boulet** [bulɛ] *nm* (*aussi*: **boulet de canon**) cannonball; (*de bagnard*) ball and chain; (*charbon*) (coal) nut

**boulette** [bulɛt] *nf* ball

**boulevard** [bulvaʀ] *nm* boulevard

**bouleversant, e** [bulvɛʀsã, -ãt] *adj* (*récit*) deeply distressing; (*nouvelle*) shattering

**bouleversé, e** [bulvɛʀse] *adj* (*ému*) deeply distressed; shattered

**bouleversement** [bulvɛʀsəmã] *nm* (*politique, social*) upheaval

**bouleverser** [bulvɛʀse] *vt* (*émouvoir*) to overwhelm; (*causer du chagrin à*) to distress; (*pays, vie*) to disrupt; (*papiers, objets*) to turn upside down, upset

**boulier** [bulje] *nm* abacus; (*de jeu*) scoring board

**boulimie** [bulimi] *nf* bulimia; compulsive eating

**boulimique** [bulimik] *adj* bulimic

**boulingrin** [bulɛ̃gʀɛ̃] *nm* lawn

**bouliste** [bulist(ə)] *nm/f* bowler

**boulocher** [bulɔʃe] *vi* (*laine etc*) to develop little snarls

**boulodrome** [bulɔdʀɔm] *nm* bowling pitch

**boulon** [bulõ] *nm* bolt

**boulonner** [bulɔne] *vt* to bolt

**boulot** [bulo] *nm* (*fam: travail*) work

**boulot, te** [bulo, -ɔt] *adj* plump, tubby

**boum** [bum] *nm* bang ▷ *nf* party

**bouquet** [bukɛ] *nm* (*de fleurs*) bunch (of flowers), bouquet; (*de persil etc*) bunch; (*parfum*) bouquet; (*fig*) crowning piece; **c'est le** ~! that's the last straw!; ~ **garni** (*Culin*) bouquet garni

**bouquetin** [buktɛ̃] *nm* ibex

**bouquin** [bukɛ̃] *nm* (*fam*) book

**bouquiner** [bukine] *vi* (*fam*) to read

**bouquiniste** [bukinist(ə)] *nm/f* bookseller

**bourbeux, -euse** [buʀbø, -øz] *adj* muddy

**bourbier** [buʀbje] *nm* (*quag*)mire

**bourde** [buʀd(ə)] *nf* (*erreur*) howler; (*gaffe*) blunder

**bourdon** [buʀdõ] *nm* bumblebee

**bourdonnement** [buʀdɔnmã] *nm* buzzing *no pl*, buzz; **avoir des** ~**s d'oreilles** to have a buzzing (noise) in one's ears

**bourdonner** [buʀdɔne] *vi* to buzz; (*moteur*) to hum

**bourg** [buʀ] *nm* small market town (*ou* village)

**bourgade** [buʀgad] *nf* township

**bourgeois, e** [buʀʒwa, -waz] *adj* (*péj*) ≈ (upper) middle class; bourgeois; (*maison etc*) very comfortable ▷ *nm/f* (*autrefois*) burgher

**bourgeoisie** [buʀʒwazi] *nf* ≈ upper middle classes *pl*; bourgeoisie; **petite** ~ middle classes

**bourgeon** [buʀʒõ] *nm* bud

**bourgeonner** [buʀʒɔne] *vi* to bud

**Bourgogne** [buʀgɔɲ] *nf*: **la** ~ Burgundy ▷ *nm*: **bourgogne** Burgundy (wine)

**bourguignon, ne** [buʀɡiɲɔ̃, -ɔn] *adj* of *ou* from Burgundy, Burgundian; **bœuf ~** bœuf bourguignon

**bourlinguer** [buʀlɛ̃ɡe] *vi* to knock about a lot, get around a lot

**bourrade** [buʀad] *nf* shove, thump

**bourrage** [buʀaʒ] *nm* (*papier*) jamming; **~ de crâne** brainwashing; (*Scol*) cramming

**bourrasque** [buʀask(ə)] *nf* squall

**bourratif, -ive** [buʀatif, -iv] *adj* filling, stodgy

**bourre** [buʀ] *nf* (*de coussin, matelas etc*) stuffing

**bourré, e** [buʀe] *adj* (*rempli*): **~ de** crammed full of; (*fam: ivre*) pickled, plastered

**bourreau, x** [buʀo] *nm* executioner; (*fig*) torturer; **~ de travail** workaholic, glutton for work

**bourrelé, e** [buʀle] *adj*: **être ~ de remords** to be racked by remorse

**bourrelet** [buʀlɛ] *nm* draught (*Brit*) *ou* draft (*US*) excluder; (*de peau*) fold *ou* roll (of flesh)

**bourrer** [buʀe] *vt* (*pipe*) to fill; (*poêle*) to pack; (*valise*) to cram (full); **~ de** to cram (full) with, stuff with; **~ de coups** to hammer blows on, pummel; **~ le crâne à qn** to pull the wool over sb's eyes; (*endoctriner*) to brainwash sb

**bourricot** [buʀiko] *nm* small donkey

**bourrique** [buʀik] *nf* (*âne*) ass

**bourru, e** [buʀy] *adj* surly, gruff

**bourse** [buʀs(ə)] *nf* (*subvention*) grant; (*porte-monnaie*) purse; **sans ~ délier** without spending a penny; **la B~** the Stock Exchange; **~ du travail** ≈ trades union council (regional headquarters)

**boursicoter** [buʀsikɔte] *vi* (*Comm*) to dabble on the Stock Market

**boursier, -ière** [buʀsje, -jɛʀ] *adj* (*Comm*) Stock Market *cpd* ▷ *nm/f* (*Scol*) grant-holder

**boursouflé, e** [buʀsufle] *adj* swollen, puffy; (*fig*) bombastic, turgid

**boursoufler** [buʀsufle] *vt* to puff up, bloat; **se boursoufler** *vi* (*visage*) to swell *ou* puff up; (*peinture*) to blister

**boursouflure** [buʀsuflyʀ] *nf* (*du visage*) swelling, puffiness; (*de la peinture*) blister; (*fig: du style*) pomposity

**bous** [bu] *vb voir* **bouillir**

**bousculade** [buskylad] *nf* (*hâte*) rush; (*poussée*) crush

**bousculer** [buskyle] *vt* to knock over; to knock into; (*fig*) to push, rush

**bouse** [buz] *nf*: **~ (de vache)** (cow) dung *no pl* (*Brit*), manure *no pl*

**bousiller** [buzije] *vt* (*fam*) to wreck

**boussole** [busɔl] *nf* compass

**bout** [bu] *vb voir* **bouillir** ▷ *nm* bit; (*extrémité: d'un bâton etc*) tip; (: *d'une ficelle, table, rue, période*) end; **au ~ de** at the end of, after; **au ~ du compte** at the end of the day; **pousser qn à ~** to push sb to the limit (of his patience); **venir à ~ de** to manage to finish (off) *ou* overcome; **~ à ~** end to end; **à tout ~ de champ** at every turn; **d'un ~ à l'autre, de ~ en ~** from one end to the other; **à ~**

**portant** at point-blank range; **un ~ de chou** (*enfant*) a little tot; **~ d'essai** (*Ciné etc*) screen test; **~ filtre** filter tip

**boutade** [butad] *nf* quip, sally

**boute-en-train** [butɑ̃tʀɛ̃] *nm inv* live wire (*fig*)

**bouteille** [butɛj] *nf* bottle; (*de gaz butane*) cylinder

**boutiquaire** [butikɛʀ] *adj*: **niveau ~** shopping level

**boutique** [butik] *nf* shop (*Brit*), store (*US*); (*de grand couturier, de mode*) boutique

**boutiquier, -ière** [butikje, -jɛʀ] *nm/f* shopkeeper (*Brit*), storekeeper (*US*)

**boutoir** [butwaʀ] *nm*: **coup de ~** (*choc*) thrust; (*fig: propos*) barb

**bouton** [butɔ̃] *nm* (*de vêtement, électrique etc*) button; (*Bot*) bud; (*sur la peau*) spot; (*de porte*) knob; **~ de manchette** cuff-link; **~ d'or** buttercup

**boutonnage** [butɔnaʒ] *nm* (*action*) buttoning(-up); **un manteau à double ~** a coat with two rows of buttons

**boutonner** [butɔne] *vt* to button up, do up; **se boutonner** to button one's clothes up

**boutonneux, -euse** [butɔnø, -øz] *adj* spotty

**boutonnière** [butɔnjɛʀ] *nf* buttonhole

**bouton-poussoir** [butɔ̃puswaʀ] (*pl* **boutons-poussoirs**) *nm* pushbutton

**bouton-pression** [butɔ̃pʀesjɔ̃] (*pl* **boutons-pression**) *nm* press stud, snap fastener

**bouture** [butyʀ] *nf* cutting; **faire des ~s** to take cuttings

**bouvreuil** [buvʀœj] *nm* bullfinch

**bovidé** [bɔvide] *nm* bovine

**bovin, e** [bɔvɛ̃, -in] *adj* bovine ▷ *nm*: **~s** cattle

**bowling** [boliŋ] *nm* (tenpin) bowling; (*salle*) bowling alley

**box** [bɔks] *nm* lock-up (garage); (*de salle, dortoir*) cubicle; (*d'écurie*) loose-box; (*aussi*: **box-calf**) box calf; **le ~ des accusés** the dock

**boxe** [bɔks(ə)] *nf* boxing

**boxer** [bɔkse] *vi* to box ▷ *nm* [bɔksɛʀ] (*chien*) boxer

**boxeur** [bɔksœʀ] *nm* boxer

**boyau, x** [bwajo] *nm* (*corde de raquette etc*) (cat) gut; (*galerie*) passage(way); (narrow) gallery; (*pneu de bicyclette*) tubeless tyre ▷ *nmpl* (*viscères*) entrails, guts

**boyaux** [bwajo] *nmpl* (*viscères*) entrails, guts

**boycottage** [bɔjkɔtaʒ] *nm* (*d'un produit*) boycotting

**boycotter** [bɔjkɔte] *vt* to boycott

**BP** *sigle f* = **boîte postale**

**brabançon, ne** [bʀabɑ̃sɔ̃, -ɔn] *adj* of *ou* from Brabant

**Brabant** [bʀabɑ̃] *nm*: **le ~** Brabant

**bracelet** [bʀaslɛ] *nm* bracelet

**bracelet-montre** [bʀaslɛmɔ̃tʀ(ə)] *nm* wristwatch

**braconnage** [bʀakɔnaʒ] *nm* poaching

**braconner** [bʀakɔne] *vi* to poach

**braconnier** [bʀakɔnje] *nm* poacher

**brader** [bʀade] vt to sell off, sell cheaply
**braderie** [bʀadʀi] nf clearance sale; (par des particuliers) ≈ car boot sale (Brit), ≈ garage sale (US); (magasin) discount store; (sur marché) cutprice (Brit) ou cut-rate (US) stall
**braguette** [bʀagɛt] nf fly, flies pl (Brit), zipper (US)
**braillard, e** [bʀɑjaʀ, -aʀd] adj (fam) bawling, yelling
**braille** [bʀɑj] nm Braille
**braillement** [bʀɑjmɑ̃] nm (cri) bawling no pl, yelling no pl
**brailler** [bʀɑje] vi to bawl, yell ▷ vt to bawl out, yell out
**braire** [bʀɛʀ] vi to bray
**braise** [bʀɛz] nf embers pl
**braiser** [bʀeze] vt to braise; **bœuf braisé** braised steak
**bramer** [bʀame] vi to bell; (fig) to wail
**brancard** [bʀɑ̃kaʀ] nm (civière) stretcher; (bras, perche) shaft
**brancardier** [bʀɑ̃kaʀdje] nm stretcher-bearer
**branchages** [bʀɑ̃ʃaʒ] nmpl branches, boughs
**branche** [bʀɑ̃ʃ] nf branch; (de lunettes) side(-piece)
**branché, e** [bʀɑ̃ʃe] adj (fam) switched-on, trendy ▷ nm/f (fam) trendy
**branchement** [bʀɑ̃ʃmɑ̃] nm connection
**brancher** [bʀɑ̃ʃe] vt to connect (up); (en mettant la prise) to plug in; ~ **qn/qch sur** (fig) to get sb/sth launched onto
**branchies** [bʀɑ̃ʃi] nfpl gills
**brandade** [bʀɑ̃dad] nf brandade (cod dish)
**brandebourgeois, e** [bʀɑ̃dəbuʀʒwa, -waz] adj of ou from Brandenburg
**brandir** [bʀɑ̃diʀ] vt (arme) to brandish, wield; (document) to flourish, wave
**brandon** [bʀɑ̃dɔ̃] nm firebrand
**branlant, e** [bʀɑ̃lɑ̃, -ɑ̃t] adj (mur, meuble) shaky
**branle** [bʀɑ̃l] nm: **mettre en ~** to set swinging; **donner le ~ à** to set in motion
**branle-bas** [bʀɑ̃lba] nm inv commotion
**branler** [bʀɑ̃le] vi to be shaky, be loose ▷ vt: ~ **la tête** to shake one's head
**braquage** [bʀakaʒ] nm (fam) stick-up, hold-up; (Auto): **rayon de ~** turning circle
**braque** [bʀak] nm (Zool) pointer
**braquer** [bʀake] vi (Auto) to turn (the wheel) ▷ vt (revolver etc): ~ **qch sur** to aim sth at, point sth at; (mettre en colère): ~ **qn** to antagonize sb, put sb's back up; ~ **son regard sur** to fix one's gaze on; **se braquer** vi: **se ~ (contre)** to take a stand (against)
**bras** [bʀa] nm arm; (de fleuve) branch ▷ nmpl (fig: travailleurs) labour sg (Brit), labor sg (US), hands; ~ **dessus ~ dessous** arm in arm; **à ~ raccourcis** with fists flying; **à tour de ~** with all one's might; **baisser les ~** to give up; ~ **droit** (fig) right hand man; ~ **de fer** arm-wrestling; **une partie de ~ de fer** (fig) a trial of strength; ~ **de levier** lever arm; ~ **de mer** arm of the sea, sound
**brasero** [bʀazeʀo] nm brazier

**brasier** [bʀazje] nm blaze, (blazing) inferno; (fig) inferno
**Brasilia** [bʀazilja] n Brasilia
**bras-le-corps** [bʀalkɔʀ]: **à ~** adv (a)round the waist
**brassage** [bʀasaʒ] nm (de la bière) brewing; (fig) mixing
**brassard** [bʀasaʀ] nm armband
**brasse** [bʀas] nf (nage) breast-stroke; (mesure) fathom; ~ **papillon** butterfly(-stroke)
**brassée** [bʀase] nf armful; **une ~ de** (fig) a number of
**brasser** [bʀase] vt (bière) to brew; (remuer: salade) to toss; (: cartes) to shuffle; (fig) to mix; ~ **l'argent/les affaires** to handle a lot of money/business
**brasserie** [bʀasʀi] nf (restaurant) bar (selling food), brasserie; (usine) brewery
**brasseur** [bʀasœʀ] nm (de bière) brewer; ~ **d'affaires** big businessman
**brassière** [bʀasjɛʀ] nf (baby's) vest (Brit) ou undershirt (US); (de sauvetage) life jacket
**bravache** [bʀavaʃ] nm blusterer, braggart
**bravade** [bʀavad] nf: **par ~** out of bravado
**brave** [bʀav] adj (courageux) brave; (bon, gentil) good, kind
**bravement** [bʀavmɑ̃] adv bravely; (résolument) boldly
**braver** [bʀave] vt to defy
**bravo** [bʀavo] excl bravo! ▷ nm cheer
**bravoure** [bʀavuʀ] nf bravery
**BRB** sigle f (Police: = Brigade de répression du banditisme) ≈ serious crime squad
**break** [bʀɛk] nm (Auto) estate car (Brit), station wagon (US)
**brebis** [bʀəbi] nf ewe; ~ **galeuse** black sheep
**brèche** [bʀɛʃ] nf breach, gap; **être sur la ~** (fig) to be on the go
**bredouille** [bʀəduj] adj empty-handed
**bredouiller** [bʀəduje] vi, vt to mumble, stammer
**bref, brève** [bʀɛf, bʀɛv] adj short, brief ▷ adv in short ▷ nf (voyelle) short vowel; (information) brief news item; **d'un ton ~** sharply, curtly; **en ~** in short, in brief; **à ~ délai** shortly
**brelan** [bʀəlɑ̃] nm: **un ~** three of a kind; **un ~ d'as** three aces
**breloque** [bʀəlɔk] nf charm
**brème** [bʀɛm] nf bream
**Brésil** [bʀezil] nm: **le ~** Brazil
**brésilien, ne** [bʀeziljɛ̃, -ɛn] adj Brazilian ▷ nm/f: **Brésilien, ne** Brazilian
**bressan, e** [bʀesɑ̃, -an] adj of ou from Bresse
**Bretagne** [bʀətaɲ] nf: **la ~** Brittany
**bretelle** [bʀətɛl] nf (de fusil etc) sling; (de vêtement) strap; (d'autoroute) slip road (Brit), entrance ou exit ramp (US); **bretelles** nfpl (pour pantalon) braces (Brit), suspenders (US); ~ **de contournement** (Auto) bypass; ~ **de raccordement** (Auto) access road
**breton, ne** [bʀətɔ̃, -ɔn] adj Breton ▷ nm (Ling) Breton ▷ nm/f: **Breton, ne** Breton

**breuvage** [bʀœvaʒ] nm beverage, drink

**brève** [bʀɛv] adj f, nf voir **bref**

**brevet** [bʀəvɛ] nm diploma, certificate; ~ **(d'invention)** patent; ~ **d'apprentissage** certificate of apprenticeship; ~ **(des collèges)** school certificate, taken at approx. 16 years

**breveté, e** [bʀəvte] adj patented; (diplômé) qualified

**breveter** [bʀəvte] vt to patent

**bréviaire** [bʀevjɛʀ] nm breviary

**BRGM** sigle m = **Bureau de recherches géologiques et minières**

**briard, e** [bʀijaʀ, -aʀd(ə)] adj of ou from Brie ▷ nm (chien) briard

**bribes** [bʀib] nfpl bits, scraps; (d'une conversation) snatches; **par** ~ piecemeal

**bric** [bʀik]: **de** ~ **et de broc** adv with any old thing

**bric-à-brac** [bʀikabʀak] nm inv bric-a-brac, jumble

**bricolage** [bʀikɔlaʒ] nm: **le** ~ do-it-yourself (jobs); (péj) patched-up job

**bricole** [bʀikɔl] nf (babiole, chose insignifiante) trifle; (petit travail) small job

**bricoler** [bʀikɔle] vi to do odd jobs; (en amateur) to do DIY jobs; (passe-temps) to potter about ▷ vt (réparer) to fix up; (mal réparer) to tinker with; (trafiquer: voiture etc) to doctor, fix

**bricoleur, -euse** [bʀikɔlœʀ, -øz] nm/f handyman/woman, DIY enthusiast

**bride** [bʀid] nf bridle; (d'un bonnet) string, tie; **à** ~ **abattue** flat out, hell for leather; **tenir en** ~ to keep in check; **lâcher la** ~ **à, laisser la** ~ **sur le cou à** to give free rein to

**bridé, e** [bʀide] adj: **yeux** ~**s** slit eyes

**brider** [bʀide] vt (réprimer) to keep in check; (cheval) to bridle; (Culin: volaille) to truss

**bridge** [bʀidʒ(ə)] nm bridge

**brie** [bʀi] nm Brie (cheese)

**brièvement** [bʀijɛvmɑ̃] adv briefly

**brièveté** [bʀijɛvte] nf brevity

**brigade** [bʀigad] nf squad; (Mil) brigade

**brigadier** [bʀigadje] nm (Police) ≈ sergeant; (Mil) bombardier; corporal

**brigadier-chef** [bʀigadjeʃɛf] (pl **brigadiers-chefs**) nm ≈ lance-sergeant

**brigand** [bʀigɑ̃] nm brigand

**brigandage** [bʀigɑ̃daʒ] nm robbery

**briguer** [bʀige] vt to aspire to; (suffrages) to canvass

**brillamment** [bʀijamɑ̃] adv brilliantly

**brillant, e** [bʀijɑ̃, -ɑ̃t] adj brilliant; bright; (luisant) shiny, shining ▷ nm (diamant) brilliant

**briller** [bʀije] vi to shine

**brimade** [bʀimad] nf vexation, harassment no pl; bullying no pl

**brimbaler** [bʀɛ̃bale] vb = **bringuebaler**

**brimer** [bʀime] vt to harass; to bully

**brin** [bʀɛ̃] nm (de laine, ficelle etc) strand; (fig): **un** ~ **de** a bit of; **un** ~ **mystérieux** etc (fam) a weeny bit mysterious etc; ~ **d'herbe** blade of grass; ~ **de muguet** sprig of lily of the valley; ~ **de paille** wisp of straw

**brindille** [bʀɛ̃dij] nf twig

**bringue** [bʀɛ̃g] nf (fam): **faire la** ~ to go on a binge

**bringuebaler** [bʀɛ̃gbale] vi to shake (about) ▷ vt to cart about

**brio** [bʀijo] nm brilliance; (Mus) brio; **avec** ~ brilliantly, with panache

**brioche** [bʀijɔʃ] nf brioche (bun); (fam: ventre) paunch

**brioché, e** [bʀijɔʃe] adj brioche-style

**brique** [bʀik] nf brick; (fam) 10 000 francs ▷ adj inv brick red

**briquer** [bʀike] vt (fam) to polish up

**briquet** [bʀikɛ] nm (cigarette) lighter

**briqueterie** [bʀiktʀi] nf brickyard

**bris** [bʀi] nm: ~ **de clôture** (Jur) breaking in; ~ **de glaces** (Auto) breaking of windows

**brisant** [bʀizɑ̃] nm reef; (vague) breaker

**brise** [bʀiz] nf breeze

**brisé, e** [bʀize] adj broken; ~ **(de fatigue)** exhausted; **d'une voix** ~**e** in a voice broken with emotion; **pâte** ~**e** shortcrust pastry

**brisées** [bʀize] nfpl: **aller ou marcher sur les** ~ **de qn** to compete with sb in his own province

**brise-glace, brise-glaces** [bʀizglas] nm inv (navire) icebreaker

**brise-jet** [bʀizʒɛ] nm inv tap swirl

**brise-lames** [bʀizlam] nm inv breakwater

**briser** [bʀize] vt to break; **se briser** vi to break

**brise-tout** [bʀiztu] nm inv wrecker

**briseur, -euse** [bʀizœʀ, -øz] nm/f: ~ **de grève** strike-breaker

**brise-vent** [bʀizvɑ̃] nm inv windbreak

**bristol** [bʀistɔl] nm (carte de visite) visiting card

**britannique** [bʀitanik] adj British ▷ nm/f: **Britannique** Briton, British person; **les B~s** the British

**broc** [bʀo] nm pitcher

**brocante** [bʀɔkɑ̃t] nf (objets) secondhand goods pl, junk; (commerce) secondhand trade; junk dealing

**brocanteur, -euse** [bʀɔkɑ̃tœʀ, -øz] nm/f junk shop owner; junk dealer

**brocart** [bʀokaʀ] nm brocade

**broche** [bʀɔʃ] nf brooch; (Culin) spit; (fiche) spike, peg; (Méd) pin; **à la** ~ spit-roasted, roasted on a spit

**broché, e** [bʀɔʃe] adj (livre) paper-backed; (tissu) brocaded

**brochet** [bʀɔʃɛ] nm pike inv

**brochette** [bʀɔʃɛt] nf skewer; ~ **de décorations** row of medals

**brochure** [bʀɔʃyʀ] nf pamphlet, brochure, booklet

**brocoli** [bʀɔkɔli] nm broccoli

**brodequins** [bʀɔdkɛ̃] nmpl (de marche) (lace-up) boots

**broder** [bʀɔde] vt to embroider ▷ vi: ~ **(sur des faits ou une histoire)** to embroider the facts

**broderie** [bʀɔdʀi] nf embroidery

**bromure** [bʀɔmyʀ] nm bromide

**broncher** [bʀɔʃe] vi: **sans ~** without flinching, without turning a hair

**bronches** [bʀɔʃ] nfpl bronchial tubes

**bronchite** [bʀɔʃit] nf bronchitis

**broncho-pneumonie** [bʀɔ̃kɔpnømɔni] nf broncho-pneumonia no pl

**bronzage** [bʀɔ̃zaʒ] nm (hâle) (sun)tan

**bronze** [bʀɔ̃z] nm bronze

**bronzé, e** [bʀɔ̃ze] adj tanned

**bronzer** [bʀɔ̃ze] vt to tan ▷ vi to get a tan; **se bronzer** to sunbathe

**brosse** [bʀɔs] nf brush; **donner un coup de ~ à qch** to give sth a brush; **coiffé en ~** with a crewcut; **~ à cheveux** hairbrush; **~ à dents** toothbrush; **~ à habits** clothesbrush

**brosser** [bʀɔse] vt (nettoyer) to brush; (fig: tableau etc) to paint; to draw; **se brosser** vt, vi to brush one's clothes; **se ~ les dents** to brush one's teeth; **tu peux te ~!** (fam) you can sing for it!

**brou** [bʀu] nm: **~ de noix** (pour bois) walnut stain; (liqueur) walnut liqueur

**brouette** [bʀuɛt] nf wheelbarrow

**brouhaha** [bʀuaa] nm hubbub

**brouillage** [bʀujaʒ] nm (d'une émission) jamming

**brouillard** [bʀujaʀ] nm fog; **être dans le ~** (fig) to be all at sea

**brouille** [bʀuj] nf quarrel

**brouillé, e** [bʀuje] adj (fâché): **il est ~ avec ses parents** he has fallen out with his parents; (teint) muddy

**brouiller** [bʀuje] vt to mix up; to confuse; (Radio) to cause interference to; (: délibérément) to jam; (rendre trouble) to cloud; (désunir: amis) to set at odds; **se brouiller** vi (ciel, vue) to cloud over; (détails) to become confused; **se ~ (avec)** to fall out (with); **~ les pistes** to cover one's tracks; (fig) to confuse the issue

**brouillon, ne** [bʀujɔ̃, -ɔn] adj disorganized, unmethodical ▷ nm (first) draft; **cahier de ~** rough (work) book

**broussailles** [bʀusaj] nfpl undergrowth sg

**broussailleux, -euse** [bʀusajø, -øz] adj bushy

**brousse** [bʀus] nf: **la ~** the bush

**brouter** [bʀute] vt to graze on ▷ vi to graze; (Auto) to judder

**broutille** [bʀutij] nf trifle

**broyer** [bʀwaje] vt to crush; **~ du noir** to be down in the dumps

**bru** [bʀy] nf daughter-in-law

**brucelles** [bʀysɛl] nfpl: **(pinces) ~** tweezers

**brugnon** [bʀynɔ̃] nm nectarine

**bruine** [bʀɥin] nf drizzle

**bruiner** [bʀɥine] vb impers: **il bruine** it's drizzling, there's a drizzle

**bruire** [bʀɥiʀ] vi (eau) to murmur; (feuilles, étoffe) to rustle

**bruissement** [bʀɥismɑ̃] nm murmuring; rustling

**bruit** [bʀɥi] nm: **un ~** a noise, a sound; (fig: rumeur) a rumour (Brit), a rumor (US); **le ~** noise; **pas/trop de ~** no/too much noise; **sans ~** without a sound, noiselessly; **faire du ~** to make a noise; **~ de fond** background noise

**bruitage** [bʀɥitaʒ] nm sound effects pl

**bruiteur, -euse** [bʀɥitœʀ, -øz] nm/f sound-effects engineer

**brûlant, e** [bʀylɑ̃, -ɑ̃t] adj burning (hot); (liquide) boiling (hot); (regard) fiery; (sujet) red-hot

**brûlé, e** [bʀyle] adj (fig: démasqué) blown; (: homme politique etc) discredited ▷ nm: **odeur de ~** smell of burning

**brûle-pourpoint** [bʀylpuʀpwɛ̃]: **à ~** adv point-blank

**brûler** [bʀyle] vt to burn; (eau bouillante) to scald; (consommer: électricité, essence) to use; (feu rouge, signal) to go through (without stopping) ▷ vi to burn; (jeu): **tu brûles** you're getting warm ou hot; **se brûler** to burn o.s.; to scald o.s.; **se ~ la cervelle** to blow one's brains out; **~ les étapes** to make rapid progress; (aller trop vite) to cut corners; **~ (d'impatience) de faire qch** to burn with impatience to do sth, be dying to do sth

**brûleur** [bʀylœʀ] nm burner

**brûlot** [bʀylo] nm (Culin) flaming brandy; **un ~ de contestation** (fig) a hotbed of dissent

**brûlure** [bʀylyʀ] nf (lésion) burn; (sensation) burning no pl, burning sensation; **~s d'estomac** heartburn sg

**brume** [bʀym] nf mist

**brumeux, -euse** [bʀymø, -øz] adj misty; (fig) hazy

**brumisateur** [bʀymizatœʀ] nm atomizer

**brun, e** [bʀœ̃, -yn] adj brown; (cheveux, personne) dark ▷ nf (cigarette) cigarette made of dark tobacco; (bière) ≈ brown ale, ≈ stout

**brunâtre** [bʀynɑtʀ(ə)] adj brownish

**brunch** [bʀœntʃ] nm brunch

**Brunei** [bʀynei] nm: **le ~** Brunei

**brunir** [bʀyniʀ] vi: **se brunir** to get a tan ▷ vt to tan

**brushing** [bʀœʃiŋ] nm blow-dry

**brusque** [bʀysk(ə)] adj (soudain) abrupt, sudden; (rude) abrupt, brusque

**brusquement** [bʀyskəmɑ̃] adv (soudainement) abruptly, suddenly

**brusquer** [bʀyske] vt to rush

**brusquerie** [bʀyskəʀi] nf abruptness, brusqueness

**brut, e** [bʀyt] adj raw, crude, rough; (diamant) uncut; (soie, minéral, Inform: données) raw; (Comm) gross ▷ nf brute; **(champagne) ~** brut champagne; **(pétrole) ~** crude (oil)

**brutal, e, -aux** [bʀytal, -o] adj brutal

**brutalement** [bʀytalmɑ̃] adv brutally

**brutaliser** [bʀytalize] vt to handle roughly, manhandle

**brutalité** [bʀytalite] nf brutality no pl

**brute** [bʀyt] adj f, nf voir **brut**

**Bruxelles** [bʀysɛl] n Brussels

**bruxellois, e** [bʀysɛlwa, -waz] adj of ou from Brussels ▷ nm/f: **Bruxellois, e** inhabitant ou native of Brussels

**bruyamment** [bʀɥijamɑ̃] adv noisily

**bruyant, e** [bʀɥijɑ̃, -ɑ̃t] adj noisy

**bruyère** [bʀyjɛʀ] *nf* heather

**BT** *sigle m* (= *Brevet de technicien*) *vocational training certificate, taken at approx. 18 years*

**BTA** *sigle m* (= *Brevet de technicien agricole*) *agricultural training certificate, taken at approx. 18 years*

**BTP** *sigle mpl* (= *Bâtiments et travaux publics*) *public buildings and works sector*

**BTS** *sigle m* (= *Brevet de technicien supérieur*) *vocational training certificate taken at end of two-year higher education course*

**BU** *sigle f* = **Bibliothèque universitaire**

**bu, e** [by] *pp de* **boire**

**buanderie** [bɥɑ̃dʀi] *nf* laundry

**Bucarest** [bykaʀɛst] *n* Bucharest

**buccal, e, -aux** [bykal, -o] *adj*: **par voie ~e** orally

**bûche** [byʃ] *nf* log; **prendre une ~** (*fig*) to come a cropper (*Brit*), fall flat on one's face; **~ de Noël** Yule log

**bûcher** [byʃe] *nm* pyre; bonfire ▷ *vi* (*fam: étudier*) to swot (*Brit*), grind (*US*) ▷ *vt* to swot up (*Brit*), cram

**bûcheron** [byʃʀɔ̃] *nm* woodcutter

**bûchette** [byʃɛt] *nf* (*de bois*) stick, twig; (*pour compter*) rod

**bûcheur, -euse** [byʃœʀ, -øz] *nm/f* (*fam: étudiant*) swot (*Brit*), grind (*US*)

**bucolique** [bykɔlik] *adj* bucolic, pastoral

**Budapest** [bydapɛst] *n* Budapest

**budget** [bydʒɛ] *nm* budget

**budgétaire** [bydʒetɛʀ] *adj* budgetary, budget *cpd*

**budgétiser** [bydʒetize] *vt* to budget (for)

**buée** [bɥe] *nf* (*sur une vitre*) mist; (*de l'haleine*) steam

**Buenos Aires** [bwenɔzɛʀ] *n* Buenos Aires

**buffet** [byfɛ] *nm* (*meuble*) sideboard; (*de réception*) buffet; **~ (de gare)** (*station*) buffet, snack bar

**buffle** [byfl(ə)] *nm* buffalo

**buis** [bɥi] *nm* box tree; (*bois*) box(wood)

**buisson** [bɥisɔ̃] *nm* bush

**buissonnière** [bɥisɔnjɛʀ] *adj f*: **faire l'école ~** to play truant (*Brit*), skip school

**bulbe** [bylb(ə)] *nm* (*Bot, Anat*) bulb; (*coupole*) onion-shaped dome

**bulgare** [bylgaʀ] *adj* Bulgarian ▷ *nm* (*Ling*) Bulgarian ▷ *nm/f*: **Bulgare** Bulgarian, Bulgar

**Bulgarie** [bylgaʀi] *nf*: **la ~** Bulgaria

**bulldozer** [buldozœʀ] *nm* bulldozer

**bulle** [byl] *adj, nm*: **(papier) ~** manil(l)a paper ▷ *nf* bubble; (*de bande dessinée*) balloon; (*papale*) bull; **~ de savon** soap bubble

**bulletin** [byltɛ̃] *nm* (*communiqué, journal*) bulletin; (*papier*) form; (*: de bagages*) ticket; (*Scol*) report; **~ d'informations** news bulletin; **~ météorologique** weather report; **~ de naissance** birth certificate; **~ de salaire** pay slip; **~ de santé** medical bulletin; **~ (de vote)** ballot paper

**buraliste** [byʀalist(ə)] *nm/f* (*de bureau de tabac*) tobacconist; (*de poste*) clerk

**bure** [byʀ] *nf* homespun; (*de moine*) frock

**bureau, x** [byʀo] *nm* (*meuble*) desk; (*pièce, service*) office; **~ de change** (foreign) exchange office *ou* bureau; **~ d'embauche** ≈ job centre; **~ d'études** design office; **~ de location** box office; **~ des objets trouvés** lost property office (*Brit*), lost and found (*US*); **~ de placement** employment agency; **~ de poste** post office; **~ de tabac** tobacconist's (shop), smoke shop (*US*); **~ de vote** polling station

**bureaucrate** [byʀokʀat] *nm* bureaucrat

**bureaucratie** [byʀokʀasi] *nf* bureaucracy

**bureaucratique** [byʀokʀatik] *adj* bureaucratic

**bureautique** [byʀotik] *nf* office automation

**burette** [byʀɛt] *nf* (*de mécanicien*) oilcan; (*de chimiste*) burette

**burin** [byʀɛ̃] *nm* cold chisel; (*Art*) burin

**buriné, e** [byʀine] *adj* (*fig: visage*) craggy, seamed

**Burkina-Faso** [byʀkinafaso] *nm*: **le ~(-Faso)** Burkina Faso

**burlesque** [byʀlɛsk(ə)] *adj* ridiculous; (*Littérature*) burlesque

**burnous** [byʀnu(s)] *nm* burnous

**Burundi** [buʀundi] *nm*: **le ~** Burundi

**bus** *vb* [by] *voir* **boire** ▷ *nm* [bys] (*véhicule, aussi Inform*) bus

**busard** [byzaʀ] *nm* harrier

**buse** [byz] *nf* buzzard

**busqué, e** [byske] *adj*: **nez ~** hook(ed) nose

**buste** [byst(ə)] *nm* (*Anat*) chest; (*: de femme*) bust; (*sculpture*) bust

**bustier** [bystje] *nm* (*soutien-gorge*) long-line bra

**but** [by] *vb voir* **boire** ▷ *nm* (*cible*) target; (*fig*) goal, aim; (*Football etc*) goal; **de ~ en blanc** point-blank; **avoir pour ~ de faire** to aim to do; **dans le ~ de** with the intention of

**butane** [bytan] *nm* butane; (*domestique*) calor gas® (*Brit*), butane

**buté, e** [byte] *adj* stubborn, obstinate ▷ *nf* (*Archit*) abutment; (*Tech*) stop

**buter** [byte] *vi*: **~ contre** *ou* **sur** to bump into; (*trébucher*) to stumble against ▷ *vt* to antagonize; **se buter** *vi* to get obstinate, dig in one's heels

**buteur** [bytœʀ] *nm* striker

**butin** [bytɛ̃] *nm* booty, spoils *pl*; (*d'un vol*) loot

**butiner** [bytine] *vi* to gather nectar

**butor** [bytɔʀ] *nm* (*fig*) lout

**butte** [byt] *nf* mound, hillock; **être en ~ à** to be exposed to

**buvable** [byvabl(ə)] *adj* (*eau, vin*) drinkable; (*Méd: ampoule etc*) to be taken orally; (*fig: roman etc*) reasonable

**buvais** *etc* [byvɛ] *vb voir* **boire**

**buvard** [byvaʀ] *nm* blotter

**buvette** [byvɛt] *nf* refreshment room *ou* stall; (*comptoir*) bar

**buveur, -euse** [byvœʀ, -øz] *nm/f* drinker

**buvons** *etc* [byvɔ̃] *vb voir* **boire**

**BVP** *sigle m* (= *Bureau de vérification de la publicité*) *advertising standards authority*

**Byzance** [bizɑ̃s] *n* Byzantium

**byzantin, e** [bizɑ̃tɛ̃, -in] *adj* Byzantine

**BZH** *abr* (= *Breizh*) Brittany

# Cc

**C, c** [se] *nm inv* C, c ▷ *abr* (= *centime*) c; (= *Celsius*) C;
**C comme Célestin** C for Charlie

**c'** [s] *pron voir* **ce**

**CA** *sigle m* = **chiffre d'affaires**; **conseil
d'administration**; **corps d'armée** ▷ *sigle f* =
**chambre d'agriculture**

**ça** [sa] *pron* (*pour désigner*) this; (: *plus loin*) that;
(*comme sujet indéfini*) it; **ça m'étonne que** it
surprises me that; **ça va?** how are you?; how
are things?; (*d'accord?*) OK?, all right?; **ça alors!**
(*désapprobation*) well!, really!; (*étonnement*)
heavens!; **c'est ça** that's right

**çà** [sa] *adv*: **çà et là** here and there

**cabale** [kabal] *nf* (*Théât, Pol*) cabal, clique

**caban** [kabɑ̃] *nm* reefer jacket, donkey jacket

**cabane** [kaban] *nf* hut, cabin

**cabanon** [kabanɔ̃] *nm* chalet, (country) cottage

**cabaret** [kabaʀɛ] *nm* night club

**cabas** [kabɑ] *nm* shopping bag

**cabestan** [kabɛstɑ̃] *nm* capstan

**cabillaud** [kabijo] *nm* cod *inv*

**cabine** [kabin] *nf* (*de bateau*) cabin; (*de plage*)
(beach) hut; (*de piscine etc*) cubicle; (*de camion,
train*) cab; (*d'avion*) cockpit; ~ **(d'ascenseur)** lift
cage; ~ **d'essayage** fitting room; ~ **de
projection** projection room; ~ **spatiale** space
capsule; ~ **(téléphonique)** call *ou* (tele)phone
box, (tele)phone booth

**cabinet** [kabinɛ] *nm* (*petite pièce*) closet; (*de
médecin*) surgery (*Brit*), office (*US*); (*de notaire etc*)
office; (: *clientèle*) practice; (*Pol*) cabinet; (*d'un
ministre*) advisers *pl*; **cabinets** *nmpl* (*w.-c.*) toilet
*sg*; ~ **d'affaires** business consultants' (bureau),
business partnership; ~ **de toilette** toilet; ~ **de
travail** study

**câble** [kɑbl(ə)] *nm* cable; **le** ~ (*TV*) cable
television, cablevision (*US*)

**câblé, e** [kɑble] *adj* (*fam*) switched on; (*Tech*)
linked to cable television

**câbler** [kɑble] *vt* to cable; ~ **un quartier** (*TV*) to
put cable television into an area

**cabosser** [kabɔse] *vt* to dent

**cabot** [kabo] *nm* (*péj: chien*) mutt

**cabotage** [kabɔtaʒ] *nm* coastal navigation

**caboteur** [kabɔtœʀ] *nm* coaster

**cabotin, e** [kabɔtɛ̃, -in] *nm/f* (*péj: personne*

*maniérée*) poseur; (: *acteur*) ham ▷ *adj* dramatic,
theatrical

**cabotinage** [kabɔtinaʒ] *nm* playacting; third-
rate acting, ham acting

**cabrer** [kabʀe]: **se cabrer** *vi* (*cheval*) to rear up;
(*avion*) to nose up; (*fig*) to revolt, rebel; to jib

**cabri** [kabʀi] *nm* kid

**cabriole** [kabʀijɔl] *nf* caper; (*gymnastique etc*)
somersault

**cabriolet** [kabʀijɔlɛ] *nm* convertible

**CAC** [kak] *sigle f* = **Compagnie des agents de
change**; **indice** ~ ≈ FT index (*Brit*), ≈ Dow Jones
average (*US*)

**caca** [kaka] *nm* (*langage enfantin*) pooh; (*couleur*):
~ **d'oie** greeny-yellow; **faire** ~ (*fam*) to do a pooh

**cacahuète** [kakaɥɛt] *nf* peanut

**cacao** [kakao] *nm* cocoa (powder); (*boisson*) cocoa

**cachalot** [kaʃalo] *nm* sperm whale

**cache** [kaʃ] *nm* mask, card (*for masking*) ▷ *nf*
hiding place

**cache-cache** [kaʃkaʃ] *nm*: **jouer à** ~ to play
hide-and-seek

**cache-col** [kaʃkɔl] *nm* scarf

**cachemire** [kaʃmiʀ] *nm* cashmere ▷ *adj*: **dessin**
~ paisley pattern; **le C-** Kashmir

**cache-nez** [kaʃne] *nm inv* scarf, muffler

**cache-pot** [kaʃpo] *nm inv* flower-pot holder

**cache-prise** [kaʃpʀiz] *nm inv* socket cover

**cacher** [kaʃe] *vt* to hide, conceal; ~ **qch à qn** to
hide *ou* conceal sth from sb; **se cacher** to hide;
to be hidden *ou* concealed; **il ne s'en cache pas**
he makes no secret of it

**cache-sexe** [kaʃsɛks] *nm inv* G-string

**cachet** [kaʃɛ] *nm* (*comprimé*) tablet; (*sceau: du roi*)
seal; (: *de la poste*) postmark; (*rétribution*) fee; (*fig*)
style, character

**cacheter** [kaʃte] *vt* to seal; **vin cacheté** vintage
wine

**cachette** [kaʃɛt] *nf* hiding place; **en** ~ on the sly,
secretly

**cachot** [kaʃo] *nm* dungeon

**cachotterie** [kaʃɔtʀi] *nf* mystery; **faire des ~s**
to be secretive

**cachottier, -ière** [kaʃɔtje, -jɛʀ] *adj* secretive

**cachou** [kaʃu] *nm*: **pastille de** ~ cachou (*sweet*)

**cacophonie** [kakɔfɔni] *nf* cacophony, din

**cacophonique** [kakɔfɔnik] *adj* cacophonous
**cactus** [kaktys] *nm* cactus
**c.-à-d.** *abr* (= *c'est-à-dire*) i.e.
**cadastre** [kadastʀ(ə)] *nm* land register
**cadavéreux, -euse** [kadaveʀø, -øz] *adj* (*teint, visage*) deathly pale
**cadavérique** [kadaveʀik] *adj* deathly (pale), deadly pale
**cadavre** [kadavʀ(ə)] *nm* corpse, (dead) body
**Caddie®** [kadi] *nm* (supermarket) trolley
**cadeau, x** [kado] *nm* present, gift; **faire un ~ à qn** to give sb a present *ou* gift; **faire ~ de qch à qn** to make a present of sth to sb, give sb sth as a present
**cadenas** [kadnɑ] *nm* padlock
**cadenasser** [kadnase] *vt* to padlock
**cadence** [kadɑ̃s] *nf* (*Mus*) cadence; (: *rythme*) rhythm; (*de travail etc*) rate; **cadences** *nfpl* (*en usine*) production rate *sg*; **en ~** rhythmically; in time
**cadencé, e** [kadɑ̃se] *adj* rhythmic(al); **au pas ~** (*Mil*) in quick time
**cadet, te** [kadɛ, -ɛt] *adj* younger; (*le plus jeune*) youngest ▷ *nm/f* youngest child *ou* one, youngest boy *ou* son/girl *ou* daughter; **il est mon ~ de deux ans** he's two years younger than me, he's two years my junior; **les ~s** (*Sport*) the minors (15–17 years); **le ~ de mes soucis** the least of my worries
**cadrage** [kadʀaʒ] *nm* framing (*of shot*)
**cadran** [kadʀɑ̃] *nm* dial; **~ solaire** sundial
**cadre** [kadʀ(ə)] *nm* frame; (*environnement*) surroundings *pl*; (*limites*) scope ▷ *nm/f* (*Admin*) managerial employee, executive ▷ *adj*: **loi ~** outline *ou* blueprint law; **~ moyen/supérieur** (*Admin*) middle/senior management employee, junior/senior executive; **rayer qn des ~s** to discharge sb; to dismiss sb; **dans le ~ de** (*fig*) within the framework *ou* context of
**cadrer** [kadʀe] *vi*: **~ avec** to tally *ou* correspond with ▷ *vt* (*Ciné, Photo*) to frame
**cadreur, -euse** [kadʀœʀ, -øz] *nm/f* (*Ciné*) cameraman/woman
**caduc, -uque** [kadyk] *adj* obsolete; (*Bot*) deciduous
**CAF** *sigle f* (= *Caisse d'allocations familiales*) family allowance office
**caf** *abr* (*coût, assurance, fret*) cif
**cafard** [kafaʀ] *nm* cockroach; **avoir le ~** to be down in the dumps, be feeling low
**cafardeux, -euse** [kafaʀdø, -øz] *adj* (*personne, ambiance*) depressing, melancholy
**café** [kafe] *nm* coffee; (*bistro*) café ▷ *adj inv* coffee *cpd*; **~ crème** coffee with cream; **~ au lait** white coffee; **~ noir** black coffee; **~ en grains** coffee beans; **~ en poudre** instant coffee; **~ tabac** *tobacconist's or newsagent's also serving coffee and spirits*; **~ liégeois** *coffee ice cream with whipped cream*
**café-concert** [kafekɔ̃sɛʀ] (*pl* **cafés-concerts**) *nm* (*aussi:* **caf'conc'**) *café with a cabaret*
**caféine** [kafein] *nf* caffeine
**cafétéria** [kafeteʀja] *nf* cafeteria

**café-théâtre** [kafeteatʀ(ə)] (*pl* **cafés-théâtres**) *nm* *café used as a venue by (experimental) theatre groups*
**cafetière** [kaftjɛʀ] *nf* (*pot*) coffee-pot
**cafouillage** [kafujaʒ] *nm* shambles *sg*
**cafouiller** [kafuje] *vi* to get in a shambles; (*machine etc*) to work in fits and starts
**cage** [kaʒ] *nf* cage; **~ (des buts)** goal; **en ~** in a cage, caged up *ou* in; **~ d'ascenseur** lift shaft; **~ d'escalier** (stair)well; **~ thoracique** rib cage
**cageot** [kaʒo] *nm* crate
**cagibi** [kaʒibi] *nm* shed
**cagneux, -euse** [kaɲø, -øz] *adj* knock-kneed
**cagnotte** [kaɲɔt] *nf* kitty
**cagoule** [kagul] *nf* cowl; hood; (*Ski etc*) cagoule
**cahier** [kaje] *nm* notebook; (*Typo*) signature; (*revue*): **~s** journal; **~ de revendications/doléances** list of claims/grievances; **~ de brouillons** rough book, jotter; **~ des charges** specification; **~ d'exercices** exercise book
**cahin-caha** [kaɛ̃kaa] *adv*: **aller ~** to jog along; (*fig*) to be so-so
**cahot** [kao] *nm* jolt, bump
**cahoter** [kaɔte] *vi* to bump along, jog along
**cahoteux, -euse** [kaɔtø, -øz] *adj* bumpy
**cahute** [kayt] *nf* shack, hut
**caïd** [kaid] *nm* big chief, boss
**caillasse** [kajas] *nf* (*pierraille*) loose stones *pl*
**caille** [kaj] *nf* quail
**caillé, e** [kaje] *adj*: **lait ~** curdled milk, curds *pl*
**caillebotis** [kajbɔti] *nm* duckboard
**cailler** [kaje] *vi* (*lait*) to curdle; (*sang*) to clot; (*fam*) to be cold
**caillot** [kajo] *nm* (blood) clot
**caillou, x** [kaju] *nm* (little) stone
**caillouter** [kajute] *vt* (*chemin*) to metal
**caillouteux, -euse** [kajutø, -øz] *adj* stony; pebbly
**cailloutis** [kajuti] *nm* (*petits graviers*) gravel
**caïman** [kaimɑ̃] *nm* cayman
**Caïmans** [kaimɑ̃] *nfpl*: **les ~** the Cayman Islands
**Caire** [kɛʀ] *nm*: **le ~** Cairo
**caisse** [kɛs] *nf* box; (*où l'on met la recette*) cashbox; (: *machine*) till; (*où l'on paye*) cash desk (*Brit*), checkout counter; (: *au supermarché*) checkout; (*de banque*) cashier's desk; (*Tech*) case, casing; **faire sa ~** (*Comm*) to count the takings; **~ claire** (*Mus*) side *ou* snare drum; **~ éclair** express checkout; **~ enregistreuse** cash register; **~ d'épargne (CE)** savings bank; **~ noire** slush fund; **~ de retraite** pension fund; **~ de sortie** checkout; *voir* **grosse**
**caissier, -ière** [kesje, -jɛʀ] *nm/f* cashier
**caisson** [kesɔ̃] *nm* box, case
**cajoler** [kaʒɔle] *vt* to wheedle, coax; to surround with love and care, make a fuss of
**cajoleries** [kaʒɔlʀi] *nfpl* coaxing *sg*, flattery *sg*
**cajou** [kaʒu] *nm* cashew nut
**cake** [kɛk] *nm* fruit cake
**CAL** *sigle m* (= *Comité d'action lycéen*) pupils' action group seeking to reform school system
**cal** [kal] *nm* callus
**cal.** *abr* = **calorie**

**C**

**calamar** [kalamaʀ] *nm* = **calmar**
**calaminé, e** [kalamine] *adj (Auto)* coked up
**calamité** [kalamite] *nf* calamity, disaster
**calandre** [kalɑ̃dʀ(ə)] *nf* radiator grill; *(machine)* calender, mangle
**calanque** [kalɑ̃k] *nf* rocky inlet
**calcaire** [kalkɛʀ] *nm* limestone ▷ *adj (eau)* hard; *(Géo)* limestone *cpd*
**calciné, e** [kalsine] *adj* burnt to ashes
**calcium** [kalsjɔm] *nm* calcium
**calcul** [kalkyl] *nm* calculation; **le ~** *(Scol)* arithmetic; **~ différentiel/intégral** differential/integral calculus; **~ mental** mental arithmetic; **~ (biliaire)** (gall)stone; **~ (rénal)** (kidney) stone; **d'après mes ~s** by my reckoning
**calculateur** [kalkylatœʀ] *nm*, **calculatrice** [kalkylatʀis] *nf* calculator
**calculé, e** [kalkyle] *adj*: **risque ~** calculated risk
**calculer** [kalkyle] *vt* to calculate, work out, reckon; *(combiner)* to calculate; **~ qch de tête** to work sth out in one's head
**calculette** [kalkylɛt] *nf* (pocket) calculator
**cale** [kal] *nf (de bateau)* hold; *(en bois)* wedge, chock; **~ sèche** *ou* **de radoub** dry dock
**calé, e** [kale] *adj (fam)* clever, bright
**calebasse** [kalbas] *nf* calabash, gourd
**calèche** [kalɛʃ] *nf* horse-drawn carriage
**caleçon** [kalsɔ̃] *nm* pair of underpants, trunks *pl*; **~ de bain** bathing trunks *pl*
**calembour** [kalɑ̃buʀ] *nm* pun
**calendes** [kalɑ̃d] *nfpl*: **renvoyer aux ~ grecques** to postpone indefinitely
**calendrier** [kalɑ̃dʀije] *nm* calendar; *(fig)* timetable
**cale-pied** [kalpje] *nm inv* toe clip
**calepin** [kalpɛ̃] *nm* notebook
**caler** [kale] *vt* to wedge, chock up; **~ (son moteur/véhicule)** to stall (one's engine/vehicle); **se ~ dans un fauteuil** to make o.s. comfortable in an armchair
**calfater** [kalfate] *vt* to caulk
**calfeutrage** [kalføtʀaʒ] *nm* draughtproofing (Brit), draftproofing (US)
**calfeutrer** [kalføtʀe] *vt* to (make) draughtproof (Brit) *ou* draftproof (US); **se calfeutrer** *vi* to make o.s. snug and comfortable
**calibre** [kalibʀ] *nm (d'un fruit)* grade; *(d'une arme)* bore, calibre (Brit), caliber (US); *(fig)* calibre, caliber
**calibrer** [kalibʀe] *vt* to grade
**calice** [kalis] *nm (Rel)* chalice; *(Bot)* calyx
**calicot** [kaliko] *nm (tissu)* calico
**calife** [kalif] *nm* caliph
**Californie** [kalifɔʀni] *nf*: **la ~** California
**californien, ne** [kalifɔʀnjɛ̃, -ɛn] *adj* Californian
**califourchon** [kalifuʀʃɔ̃]: **à ~** *adv* astride; **à ~ sur** astride, straddling
**câlin, e** [kɑlɛ̃, -in] *adj* cuddly, cuddlesome; tender
**câliner** [kɑline] *vt* to fondle, cuddle
**câlineries** [kɑlinʀi] *nfpl* cuddles

**calisson** [kalisɔ̃] *nm* diamond-shaped sweet or candy made with ground almonds
**calleux, -euse** [kalø, -øz] *adj* horny, callous
**calligraphie** [kaligʀafi] *nf* calligraphy
**callosité** [kalozite] *nf* callus
**calmant** [kalmɑ̃] *nm* tranquillizer, sedative; *(contre la douleur)* painkiller
**calmar** [kalmaʀ] *nm* squid
**calme** [kalm(ə)] *adj* calm, quiet ▷ *nm* calm(ness), quietness; **sans perdre son ~** without losing one's cool *ou* calmness; **~ plat** *(Navig)* dead calm
**calmement** [kalməmɑ̃] *adv* calmly, quietly
**calmer** [kalme] *vt* to calm (down); *(douleur, inquiétude)* to ease, soothe; **se calmer** *vi* to calm down
**calomniateur, -trice** [kalɔmnjatœʀ, -tʀis] *nm/f* slanderer; libeller
**calomnie** [kalɔmni] *nf* slander; *(écrite)* libel
**calomnier** [kalɔmnje] *vt* to slander; to libel
**calomnieux, -euse** [kalɔmnjø, -øz] *adj* slanderous; libellous
**calorie** [kalɔʀi] *nf* calorie
**calorifère** [kalɔʀifɛʀ] *nm* stove
**calorifique** [kalɔʀifik] *adj* calorific
**calorifuge** [kalɔʀifyʒ] *adj* (heat-)insulating, heat-retaining
**calot** [kalo] *nm* forage cap
**calotte** [kalɔt] *nf (coiffure)* skullcap; *(gifle)* slap; **la ~** *(péj: clergé)* the cloth, the clergy; **~ glaciaire** icecap
**calque** [kalk(ə)] *nm (aussi*: **papier calque**) tracing paper; *(dessin)* tracing; *(fig)* carbon copy
**calquer** [kalke] *vt* to trace; *(fig)* to copy exactly
**calvados** [kalvados] *nm* Calvados *(apple brandy)*
**calvaire** [kalvɛʀ] *nm (croix)* wayside cross, calvary; *(souffrances)* suffering, martyrdom
**calvitie** [kalvisi] *nf* baldness
**camaïeu** [kamajø] *nm*: **(motif en) ~** monochrome motif
**camarade** [kamaʀad] *nm/f* friend, pal; *(Pol)* comrade
**camaraderie** [kamaʀadʀi] *nf* friendship
**camarguais, e** [kamaʀgɛ, -ɛz] *adj* of *ou* from the Camargue
**Camargue** [kamaʀg] *nf*: **la ~** the Camargue
**cambiste** [kɑ̃bist(ə)] *nm (Comm)* foreign exchange dealer, exchange agent
**Cambodge** [kɑ̃bodʒ] *nm*: **le ~** Cambodia
**cambodgien, ne** [kɑ̃bodʒjɛ̃, -ɛn] *adj* Cambodian ▷ *nm/f*: **Cambodgien, ne** Cambodian
**cambouis** [kɑ̃bwi] *nm* dirty oil *ou* grease
**cambré, e** [kɑ̃bʀe] *adj*: **avoir les reins ~s** to have an arched back; **avoir le pied très ~** to have very high arches *ou* insteps
**cambrer** [kɑ̃bʀe] *vt* to arch; **se cambrer** *vi* to arch one's back; **~ la taille** *ou* **les reins** to arch one's back
**cambriolage** [kɑ̃bʀijɔlaʒ] *nm* burglary
**cambrioler** [kɑ̃bʀijɔle] *vt* to burgle (Brit), burglarize (US)
**cambrioleur, -euse** [kɑ̃bʀijɔlœʀ, -øz] *nm/f*

burglar

**cambrure** [kɑ̃bʀyʀ] nf (du pied) arch; (de la route) camber; ~ **des reins** small of the back

**cambuse** [kɑ̃byz] nf storeroom

**came** [kam] nf: **arbre à ~s** camshaft; **arbre à ~s en tête** overhead camshaft

**camée** [kame] nm cameo

**caméléon** [kameleɔ̃] nm chameleon

**camélia** [kamelja] nm camellia

**camelot** [kamlo] nm street pedlar

**camelote** [kamlɔt] nf rubbish, trash, junk

**camembert** [kamɑ̃bɛʀ] nm Camembert (cheese)

**caméra** [kameʀa] nf (Ciné, TV) camera; (d'amateur) cine-camera

**caméraman** [kameʀaman] nm cameraman/-woman

**Cameroun** [kamʀun] nm: **le ~** Cameroon

**camerounais, e** [kamʀunɛ, -ɛz] adj Cameroonian

**caméscope®** [kameskɔp] nm camcorder

**camion** [kamjɔ̃] nm lorry (Brit), truck; (plus petit, fermé) van; (charge): ~ **de sable/cailloux** lorry-load (Brit) ou truck-load of sand/stones; ~ **de dépannage** breakdown (Brit) ou tow (US) truck

**camion-citerne** [kamjɔ̃sitɛʀn(ə)] (pl **camions-citernes**) nm tanker

**camionnage** [kamjɔnaʒ] nm haulage (Brit), trucking (US); **frais/entreprise de ~** haulage costs/business

**camionnette** [kamjɔnɛt] nf (small) van

**camionneur** [kamjɔnœʀ] nm (entrepreneur) haulage contractor (Brit), trucker (US); (chauffeur) lorry (Brit) ou truck driver; van driver

**camisole** [kamizɔl] nf: ~ **(de force)** straitjacket

**camomille** [kamɔmij] nf camomile; (boisson) camomile tea

**camouflage** [kamuflaʒ] nm camouflage

**camoufler** [kamufle] vt to camouflage; (fig) to conceal, cover up

**camouflet** [kamuflɛ] nm (fam) snub

**camp** [kɑ̃] nm camp; (fig) side; ~ **de nudistes/ vacances** nudist/holiday camp; ~ **de concentration** concentration camp

**campagnard, e** [kɑ̃paɲaʀ, -aʀd(ə)] adj country cpd ▷ nm/f countryman/woman

**campagne** [kɑ̃paɲ] nf country, countryside; (Mil, Pol, Comm) campaign; **en ~** (Mil) in the field; **à la ~** in/to the country; **faire ~ pour** to campaign for; ~ **électorale** election campaign; ~ **de publicité** advertising campaign

**campanile** [kɑ̃panil] nm (tour) bell tower

**campé, e** [kɑ̃pe] adj: **bien ~** (personnage, tableau) well-drawn

**campement** [kɑ̃pmɑ̃] nm camp, encampment

**camper** [kɑ̃pe] vi to camp ▷ vt (chapeau etc) to pull ou put on firmly; (dessin) to sketch; **se ~ devant** to plant o.s. in front of

**campeur, -euse** [kɑ̃pœʀ, -øz] nm/f camper

**camphre** [kɑ̃fʀ(ə)] nm camphor

**camphré, e** [kɑ̃fʀe] adj camphorated

**camping** [kɑ̃piŋ] nm camping; **(terrain de) ~** campsite, camping site; **faire du ~** to go

camping; **faire du ~ sauvage** to camp rough

**camping-car** [kɑ̃piŋkaʀ] nm caravanette, camper (US)

**camping-gaz®** [kɑ̃piŋgaz] nm inv camp(ing) stove

**campus** [kɑ̃pys] nm campus

**camus, e** [kamy, -yz] adj: **nez ~** pug nose

**Canada** [kanada] nm: **le ~** Canada

**canadair®** [kanadɛʀ] nm fire-fighting plane

**canadien, ne** [kanadjɛ̃, -ɛn] adj Canadian ▷ nm/f: **Canadien, ne** Canadian ▷ nf (veste) fur-lined jacket

**canaille** [kanɑj] nf (péj) scoundrel; (populace) riff-raff ▷ adj raffish, rakish

**canal, -aux** [kanal, -o] nm canal; (naturel) channel; (Admin): **par le ~ de** through (the medium of), via; ~ **de distribution/télévision** distribution/television channel; ~ **de Panama/ Suez** Panama/Suez Canal

**canalisation** [kanalizasjɔ̃] nf (tuyau) pipe

**canaliser** [kanalize] vt to canalize; (fig) to channel

**canapé** [kanape] nm settee, sofa; (Culin) canapé, open sandwich

**canapé-lit** [kanapeli] (pl **canapés-lits**) nm sofa bed

**canaque** [kanak] adj of ou from New Caledonia ▷ nm/f: **Canaque** native of New Caledonia

**canard** [kanaʀ] nm duck

**canari** [kanaʀi] nm canary

**Canaries** [kanaʀi] nfpl: **les (îles) ~** the Canary Islands, the Canaries

**cancaner** [kɑ̃kane] vi to gossip (maliciously); (canard) to quack

**cancanier, -ière** [kɑ̃kanje, -jɛʀ] adj gossiping

**cancans** [kɑ̃kɑ̃] nmpl (malicious) gossip sg

**cancer** [kɑ̃sɛʀ] nm cancer; (signe): **le C~** Cancer, the Crab; **être du C~** to be Cancer; **il a un ~** he has cancer

**cancéreux, -euse** [kɑ̃seʀø, -øz] adj cancerous; (personne) suffering from cancer

**cancérigène** [kɑ̃seʀiʒɛn] adj carcinogenic

**cancérologue** [kɑ̃seʀɔlɔg] nm/f cancer specialist

**cancre** [kɑ̃kʀ(ə)] nm dunce

**cancrelat** [kɑ̃kʀəla] nm cockroach

**candélabre** [kɑ̃delɑbʀ(ə)] nm candelabrum; (lampadaire) street lamp, lamppost

**candeur** [kɑ̃dœʀ] nf ingenuousness

**candi** [kɑ̃di] adj inv: **sucre ~** (sugar-)candy

**candidat, e** [kɑ̃dida, -at] nm/f candidate; (à un poste) applicant, candidate

**candidature** [kɑ̃didatyʀ] nf candidacy; application; **poser sa ~** to submit an application, apply; ~ **spontanée** unsolicited job application

**candide** [kɑ̃did] adj ingenuous, guileless, naïve

**cane** [kan] nf (female) duck

**caneton** [kantɔ̃] nm duckling

**canette** [kanɛt] nf (de bière) (flip-top) bottle; (de machine à coudre) spool

**canevas** [kanva] nm (Couture) canvas (for tapestry work); (fig) framework, structure

**caniche** [kaniʃ] nm poodle
**caniculaire** [kanikylɛʀ] adj (chaleur,jour) scorching
**canicule** [kanikyl] nf scorching heat; midsummer heat, dog days pl
**canif** [kanif] nm penknife, pocket knife
**canin, e** [kanɛ̃, -in] adj canine ▷ nf canine (tooth), eye tooth; **exposition ~e** dog show
**caniveau, x** [kanivo] nm gutter
**cannabis** [kanabis] nm cannabis
**canne** [kan] nf (walking) stick; **~ à pêche** fishing rod; **~ à sucre** sugar cane; **les ~s blanches** (les aveugles) the blind
**canné, e** [kane] adj (chaise) cane cpd
**cannelé, e** [kanle] adj fluted
**cannelle** [kanɛl] nf cinnamon
**cannelure** [kanlyʀ] nf fluting no pl
**canner** [kane] vt (chaise) to make ou repair with cane
**cannibale** [kanibal] nm/f cannibal
**cannibalisme** [kanibalism(ə)] nm cannibalism
**canoë** [kanɔe] nm canoe; (sport) canoeing; **~ (kayak)** kayak
**canon** [kanɔ̃] nm (arme) gun; (Hist) cannon; (d'une arme: tube) barrel; (fig) model; (Mus) canon ▷ adj: **droit ~** canon law; **~ rayé** rifled barrel
**cañon** [kaɲɔ̃] nm canyon
**canonique** [kanɔnik] adj: **âge ~** respectable age
**canoniser** [kanɔnize] vt to canonize
**canonnade** [kanɔnad] nf cannonade
**canonnier** [kanɔnje] nm gunner
**canonnière** [kanɔnjɛʀ] nf gunboat
**canot** [kano] nm boat, ding(h)y; **~ pneumatique** rubber ou inflatable ding(h)y; **~ de sauvetage** lifeboat
**canotage** [kanɔtaʒ] nm rowing
**canoter** [kanɔte] vi to go rowing
**canoteur, -euse** [kanɔtœʀ, -øz] nm/f rower
**canotier** [kanɔtje] nm boater
**Cantal** [kɑ̃tal] nm: **le ~** Cantal
**cantate** [kɑ̃tat] nf cantata
**cantatrice** [kɑ̃tatʀis] nf (opera) singer
**cantilène** [kɑ̃tilɛn] nf (Mus) cantilena
**cantine** [kɑ̃tin] nf canteen; (réfectoire d'école) dining hall
**cantique** [kɑ̃tik] nm hymn
**canton** [kɑ̃tɔ̃] nm district (consisting of several communes); see note; (en Suisse) canton

● **CANTON**
●
● A French canton is the administrative
● division represented by a councillor in the
● "Conseil général". It comprises a number of
● "communes" and is, in turn, a subdivision
● of an "arrondissement". In Switzerland the
● cantons are the 23 autonomous political
● divisions which make up the Swiss
● confederation.

**cantonade** [kɑ̃tɔnad]: **à la ~** adv to everyone in general; (crier) from the rooftops

**cantonais, e** [kɑ̃tɔnɛ, -ɛz] adj Cantonese ▷ nm (Ling) Cantonese
**cantonal, e, -aux** [kɑ̃tɔnal, -o] adj cantonal, = district
**cantonnement** [kɑ̃tɔnmɑ̃] nm (lieu) billet; (action) billeting
**cantonner** [kɑ̃tɔne] vt (Mil) to billet (Brit), quarter; to station; **se ~ dans** to confine o.s. to
**cantonnier** [kɑ̃tɔnje] nm roadmender
**canular** [kanylaʀ] nm hoax
**CAO** sigle f (= conception assistée par ordinateur) CAD
**caoutchouc** [kautʃu] nm rubber; **~ mousse** foam rubber; **en ~** rubber cpd
**caoutchouté, e** [kautʃute] adj rubberized
**caoutchouteux, -euse** [kautʃutø, -øz] adj rubbery
**CAP** sigle m (= Certificat d'aptitude professionnelle) vocational training certificate taken at secondary school
**cap** [kap] nm (Géo) cape; headland; (fig) hurdle; watershed; (Navig): **changer de ~** to change course; **mettre le ~ sur** to head ou steer for; **doubler** ou **passer le ~** (fig) to get over the worst; **Le C~** Cape Town; **le ~ de Bonne Espérance** the Cape of Good Hope; **le ~ Horn** Cape Horn; **les îles du C~ Vert** (aussi: **le Cap-Vert**) the Cape Verde Islands
**capable** [kapabl(ə)] adj able, capable; **~ de qch/ faire** capable of sth/doing; **il est ~ d'oublier** he could easily forget; **spectacle ~ d'intéresser** show likely to be of interest
**capacité** [kapasite] nf (compétence) ability; (Jur, Inform, d'un récipient) capacity; **~ (en droit)** basic legal qualification
**caparaçonner** [kapaʀasɔne] vt (fig) to clad
**cape** [kap] nf cape, cloak; **rire sous ~** to laugh up one's sleeve
**capeline** [kaplin] nf wide-brimmed hat
**CAPES** [kapɛs] sigle m (= Certificat d'aptitude au professorat de l'enseignement du second degré) secondary teaching diploma; see note

● **CAPES**
●
● The French CAPES ("certificat d'aptitude au
● professorat de l'enseignement du second
● degré") is a competitive examination sat by
● prospective secondary school teachers after
● the 'licence'. Successful candidates become
● fully qualified teachers ("professeurs
● certifiés").

**capésien, ne** [kapesjɛ̃, -ɛn] nm/f person who holds the CAPES
**CAPET** [kapɛt] sigle m (= Certificat d'aptitude au professorat de l'enseignement technique) technical teaching diploma
**capharnaüm** [kafaʀnaɔm] nm shambles sg
**capillaire** [kapilɛʀ] adj (soins, lotion) hair cpd; (vaisseau etc) capillary; **artiste ~** hair artist ou designer
**capillarité** [kapilaʀite] nf capillary action
**capilotade** [kapilɔtad]: **en ~** adv crushed to a

pulp; smashed to pieces

**capitaine** [kapitɛn] *nm* captain; ~ **des pompiers** fire chief (*Brit*), fire marshal (*US*); ~ **au long cours** master mariner

**capitainerie** [kapitɛnʀi] *nf* (*du port*) harbour (*Brit*) *ou* harbor (*US*) master's (office)

**capital, e, -aux** [kapital, -o] *adj* major; fundamental; (*Jur*) capital ▷ *nm* capital; (*fig*) stock; asset ▷ *nf* (*ville*) capital; (*lettre*) capital (letter) ▷ *nmpl* (*fonds*) capital *sg*, money *sg*; **les sept péchés capitaux** the seven deadly sins; **peine ~e** capital punishment; ~ **(social)** authorized capital; ~ **d'exploitation** working capital

**capitaliser** [kapitalize] *vt* to amass, build up; (*Comm*) to capitalize ▷ *vi* to save

**capitalisme** [kapitalism(ə)] *nm* capitalism

**capitaliste** [kapitalist(ə)] *adj*, *nm/f* capitalist

**capiteux, -euse** [kapitø, -øz] *adj* (*vin, parfum*) heady; (*sensuel*) sensuous, alluring

**capitonnage** [kapitɔnaʒ] *nm* padding

**capitonné, e** [kapitɔne] *adj* padded

**capitonner** [kapitɔne] *vt* to pad

**capitulation** [kapitylasjɔ̃] *nf* capitulation

**capituler** [kapityle] *vi* to capitulate

**caporal, -aux** [kapɔʀal, -o] *nm* lance corporal

**caporal-chef** [kapɔʀalʃɛf, kapɔʀo-] (*pl* **caporaux-chefs**) *nm* corporal

**capot** [kapo] *nm* (*Auto*) bonnet (*Brit*), hood (*US*)

**capote** [kapɔt] *nf* (*de voiture*) hood (*Brit*), top (*US*); (*de soldat*) greatcoat; ~ **(anglaise)** (*fam*) rubber, condom

**capoter** [kapɔte] *vi* to overturn; (*négociations*) to founder

**câpre** [kɑpʀ(ə)] *nf* caper

**caprice** [kapʀis] *nm* whim, caprice; passing fancy; **caprices** *nmpl* (*de la mode etc*) vagaries; **faire un ~** to throw a tantrum; **faire des ~s** to be temperamental

**capricieux, -euse** [kapʀisjø, -øz] *adj* capricious; whimsical; temperamental

**Capricorne** [kapʀikɔʀn] *nm*: **le ~** Capricorn, the Goat; **être du ~** to be Capricorn

**capsule** [kapsyl] *nf* (*de bouteille*) cap; (*amorce*) primer; cap; (*Bot etc, spatiale*) capsule

**captage** [kaptaʒ] *nm* (*d'une émission de radio*) picking-up; (*d'énergie, d'eau*) harnessing

**capter** [kapte] *vt* (*ondes radio*) to pick up; (*eau*) to harness; (*fig*) to win, capture

**capteur** [kaptœʀ] *nm*: ~ **solaire** solar collector

**captieux, -euse** [kapsjø, -øz] *adj* specious

**captif, -ive** [kaptif, -iv] *adj*, *nm/f* captive

**captivant, e** [kaptivɑ̃, -ɑ̃t] *adj* captivating

**captiver** [kaptive] *vt* to captivate

**captivité** [kaptivite] *nf* captivity; **en ~** in captivity

**capture** [kaptyʀ] *nf* capture, catching *no pl*; catch

**capturer** [kaptyʀe] *vt* to capture, catch

**capuche** [kapyʃ] *nf* hood

**capuchon** [kapyʃɔ̃] *nm* hood; (*de stylo*) cap, top

**capucin** [kapysɛ̃] *nm* Capuchin monk

**capucine** [kapysin] *nf* (*Bot*) nasturtium

**Cap-Vert** [kabvɛʀ] *nm*: **le ~** Cape Verde

**caquelon** [kaklɔ̃] *nm* (*ustensile de cuisson*) fondue pot

**caquet** [kakɛ] *nm*: **rabattre le ~ à qn** to bring sb down a peg or two

**caqueter** [kakte] *vi* (*poule*) to cackle; (*fig*) to prattle

**car** [kaʀ] *nm* coach (*Brit*), bus ▷ *conj* because, for; ~ **de police** police van; ~ **de reportage** broadcasting *ou* radio van

**carabine** [kaʀabin] *nf* carbine, rifle; ~ **à air comprimé** airgun

**carabiné, e** [kaʀabine] *adj* violent; (*cocktail, amende*) stiff

**Caracas** [kaʀakas] *n* Caracas

**caracoler** [kaʀakɔle] *vi* to caracole, prance

**caractère** [kaʀaktɛʀ] *nm* (*gén*) character; **en ~s gras** in bold type; **en petits ~s** in small print; **en ~s d'imprimerie** in block capitals; **avoir du ~** to have character; **avoir bon/mauvais ~** to be good-/ill-natured *ou* tempered; ~ **de remplacement** wild card (*Inform*); ~**s/seconde (cps)** characters per second (cps)

**caractériel, le** [kaʀakteʀjɛl] *adj* (*enfant*) (emotionally) disturbed ▷ *nm/f* problem child; **troubles ~s** emotional problems

**caractérisé, e** [kaʀakteʀize] *adj*: **c'est une grippe/de l'insubordination ~e** it is a clear(-cut) case of flu/insubordination

**caractériser** [kaʀakteʀize] *vt* to characterize; **se ~ par** to be characterized *ou* distinguished by

**caractéristique** [kaʀakteʀistik] *adj*, *nf* characteristic

**carafe** [kaʀaf] *nf* decanter; carafe

**carafon** [kaʀafɔ̃] *nm* small carafe

**caraïbe** [kaʀaib] *adj* Caribbean; **les Caraïbes** *nfpl* the Caribbean (Islands); **la mer des C~s** the Caribbean Sea

**carambolage** [kaʀɑ̃bɔlaʒ] *nm* multiple crash, pileup

**caramel** [kaʀamɛl] *nm* (*bonbon*) caramel, toffee; (*substance*) caramel

**caraméliser** [kaʀamelize] *vt* to caramelize

**carapace** [kaʀapas] *nf* shell

**carapater** [kaʀapate]: **se carapater** *vi* to take to one's heels, scram

**carat** [kaʀa] *nm* carat; **or à 18 ~s** 18-carat gold

**caravane** [kaʀavan] *nf* caravan

**caravanier** [kaʀavanje] *nm* caravanner

**caravaning** [kaʀavaniŋ] *nm* caravanning; (*emplacement*) caravan site

**caravelle** [kaʀavɛl] *nf* caravel

**carbonate** [kaʀbɔnat] *nm* (*Chimie*): ~ **de soude** sodium carbonate

**carbone** [kaʀbɔn] *nm* carbon; (*feuille*) carbon, sheet of carbon paper; (*double*) carbon (copy)

**carbonique** [kaʀbɔnik] *adj*: **gaz ~** carbon dioxide; **neige ~** dry ice

**carbonisé, e** [kaʀbɔnize] *adj* charred; **mourir ~** to be burned to death

**carboniser** [kaʀbɔnize] *vt* to carbonize; (*brûler*

63

*complètement*) to burn down, reduce to ashes
**carburant** [kaʀbyʀɑ̃] *nm* (motor) fuel
**carburateur** [kaʀbyʀatœʀ] *nm* carburettor
**carburation** [kaʀbyʀasjɔ̃] *nf* carburation
**carburer** [kaʀbyʀe] *vi* (*moteur*): **bien/mal ~** to be
    well/badly tuned
**carcan** [kaʀkɑ̃] *nm* (*fig*) yoke, shackles *pl*
**carcasse** [kaʀkas] *nf* carcass; (*de véhicule etc*)
    shell
**carcéral, e, -aux** [kaʀseʀal, -o] *adj* prison *cpd*
**carcinogène** [kaʀsinɔʒɛn] *adj* carcinogenic
**cardan** [kaʀdɑ̃] *nm* universal joint
**carder** [kaʀde] *vt* to card
**cardiaque** [kaʀdjak] *adj* cardiac, heart *cpd* ▷ *nm/f*
    heart patient; **être ~** to have a heart condition
**cardigan** [kaʀdigɑ̃] *nm* cardigan
**cardinal, e, -aux** [kaʀdinal, -o] *adj* cardinal
    ▷ *nm* (*Rel*) cardinal
**cardiologie** [kaʀdjɔlɔʒi] *nf* cardiology
**cardiologue** [kaʀdjɔlɔg] *nm/f* cardiologist,
    heart specialist
**cardio-vasculaire** [kaʀdjɔvaskylɛʀ] *adj*
    cardiovascular
**cardon** [kaʀdɔ̃] *nm* cardoon
**carême** [kaʀɛm] *nm*: **le C~** Lent
**carence** [kaʀɑ̃s] *nf* incompetence, inadequacy;
    (*manque*) deficiency; **~ vitaminique** vitamin
    deficiency
**carène** [kaʀɛn] *nf* hull
**caréner** [kaʀene] *vt* (*Navig*) to careen; (*carrosserie*)
    to streamline
**caressant, e** [kaʀɛsɑ̃, -ɑ̃t] *adj* affectionate;
    caressing, tender
**caresse** [kaʀɛs] *nf* caress
**caresser** [kaʀese] *vt* to caress, stroke, fondle;
    (*fig: projet, espoir*) to toy with
**cargaison** [kaʀgɛzɔ̃] *nf* cargo, freight
**cargo** [kaʀgo] *nm* cargo boat, freighter; **~ mixte**
    cargo and passenger ship
**cari** [kaʀi] *nm* = **curry**
**caricatural, e, -aux** [kaʀikatyʀal, -o] *adj*
    caricatural, caricature-like
**caricature** [kaʀikatyʀ] *nf* caricature; (*politique
    etc*) (satirical) cartoon
**caricaturer** [kaʀikatyʀe] *vt* (*personne*) to
    caricature; (*politique etc*) to satirize
**caricaturiste** [kaʀikatyʀist(ə)] *nm/f*
    caricaturist, (satirical) cartoonist
**carie** [kaʀi] *nf*: **la ~** (**dentaire**) tooth decay; **une
    ~** a bad tooth
**carié, e** [kaʀje] *adj*: **dent ~e** bad *ou* decayed
    tooth
**carillon** [kaʀijɔ̃] *nm* (*d'église*) bells *pl*; (*de pendule*)
    chimes *pl*; (*de porte*): **~ (électrique)** (electric)
    door chime *ou* bell
**carillonner** [kaʀijɔne] *vi* to ring, chime, peal
**caritatif, -ive** [kaʀitatif, -iv] *adj* charitable
**carlingue** [kaʀlɛ̃g] *nf* cabin
**carmélite** [kaʀmelit] *nf* Carmelite nun
**carmin** [kaʀmɛ̃] *adj inv* crimson
**carnage** [kaʀnaʒ] *nm* carnage, slaughter
**carnassier, -ière** [kaʀnasje, -jɛʀ] *adj*

carnivorous ▷ *nm* carnivore
**carnation** [kaʀnasjɔ̃] *nf* complexion;
    **carnations** *nfpl* (*Peinture*) flesh tones
**carnaval** [kaʀnaval] *nm* carnival
**carné, e** [kaʀne] *adj* meat *cpd*, meat-based
**carnet** [kaʀnɛ] *nm* (*calepin*) notebook; (*de tickets,
    timbres etc*) book; (*d'école*) school report; (*journal
    intime*) diary; **~ d'adresses** address book; **~ de
    chèques** cheque book (*Brit*), checkbook (*US*); **~
    de commandes** order book; **~ de notes** (*Scol*)
    (school) report; **~ à souches** counterfoil book
**carnier** [kaʀnje] *nm* gamebag
**carnivore** [kaʀnivɔʀ] *adj* carnivorous ▷ *nm*
    carnivore
**Carolines** [kaʀɔlin] *nfpl*: **les ~** the Caroline
    Islands
**carotide** [kaʀɔtid] *nf* carotid (artery)
**carotte** [kaʀɔt] *nf* (*aussi fig*) carrot
**Carpates** [kaʀpat] *nfpl*: **les ~** the Carpathians,
    the Carpathian Mountains
**carpe** [kaʀp(ə)] *nf* carp
**carpette** [kaʀpɛt] *nf* rug
**carquois** [kaʀkwa] *nm* quiver
**carre** [kaʀ] *nf* (*de ski*) edge
**carré, e** [kaʀe] *adj* square; (*fig: franc*)
    straightforward ▷ *nm* (*de terrain, jardin*) patch,
    plot; (*Navig: salle*) wardroom; (*Math*) square; **~
    blanc** (*TV*) "adults only" symbol; (*Cartes*): **~
    d'as/de rois** four aces/kings; **élever un
    nombre au ~** to square a number; **mètre/
    kilomètre ~** square metre/kilometre; **~ de soie**
    silk headsquare *ou* headscarf; **~ d'agneau** loin
    of lamb
**carreau, x** [kaʀo] *nm* (*en faïence etc*) (floor) tile,
    (wall) tile; (*window*) pane; (*motif*) check,
    square; (*Cartes: couleur*) diamonds *pl*; (: *carte*)
    diamond; **tissu à ~x** checked fabric; **papier à
    ~x** squared paper
**carrefour** [kaʀfuʀ] *nm* crossroads *sg*
**carrelage** [kaʀlaʒ] *nm* tiling; (tiled) floor
**carreler** [kaʀle] *vt* to tile
**carrelet** [kaʀlɛ] *nm* (*poisson*) plaice
**carreleur** [kaʀlœʀ] *nm* (floor) tiler
**carrément** [kaʀemɑ̃] *adv* (*franchement*) straight
    out, bluntly; (*sans détours, sans hésiter*) straight;
    (*nettement*) definitely; **il l'a ~ mis à la porte** he
    threw him straight out
**carrer** [kaʀe]: **se carrer** *vi*: **se ~ dans un
    fauteuil** to settle o.s. comfortably *ou* ensconce
    o.s. in an armchair
**carrier** [kaʀje] *nm*: (**ouvrier**) **~** quarryman,
    quarrier
**carrière** [kaʀjɛʀ] *nf* (*de roches*) quarry; (*métier*)
    career; **militaire de ~** professional soldier;
    **faire ~ dans** to make one's career in
**carriériste** [kaʀjeʀist(ə)] *nm/f* careerist
**carriole** [kaʀjɔl] *nf* (*péj*) old cart
**carrossable** [kaʀɔsabl(ə)] *adj* suitable for
    (motor) vehicles
**carrosse** [kaʀɔs] *nm* (horse-drawn) coach
**carrosserie** [kaʀɔsʀi] *nf* body, bodywork *no pl*
    (*Brit*); (*activité, commerce*) coachwork (*Brit*), (car)

body manufacturing; **atelier de ~** (*pour réparations*) body shop, panel beaters' (yard) (*Brit*)
**carrossier** [kaʀɔsje] *nm* coachbuilder (*Brit*), (car) body repairer; (*dessinateur*) car designer
**carrousel** [kaʀuzɛl] *nm* (*Équitation*) carousel; (*fig*) merry-go-round
**carrure** [kaʀyʀ] *nf* build; (*fig*) stature
**cartable** [kaʀtabl(ə)] *nm* (*d'écolier*) satchel, (school)bag
**carte** [kaʀt(ə)] *nf* (*de géographie*) map; (*marine, du ciel*) chart; (*de fichier, d'abonnement etc, à jouer*) card; (*au restaurant*) menu; (*aussi:* **carte postale**) (post)card; (*aussi:* **carte de visite**) (visiting) card; **avoir/donner ~ blanche** to have/give carte blanche *ou* a free hand; **tirer les ~s à qn** to read sb's cards; **jouer aux ~s** to play cards; **jouer ~s sur table** (*fig*) to put one's cards on the table; **à la ~** (*au restaurant*) à la carte; **~ à circuit imprimé** printed circuit; **~ à puce** smartcard, chip and PIN card; **~ bancaire** cash card; **C~ Bleue®** debit card; **~ de crédit** credit card; **~ d'état-major** ≈ Ordnance (*Brit*) *ou* Geological (*US*) Survey map; **la ~ grise** (*Auto*) ≈ the (car) registration document; **~ d'identité** identity card; **~ jeune** young person's railcard; **~ mémoire** (*d'appareil photo numérique*) memory card; **~ perforée** punch(ed) card; **~ routière** road map; **~ de séjour** residence permit; **~ SIM** SIM card; **~ téléphonique** phonecard; **la ~ verte** (*Auto*) the green card; **la ~ des vins** the wine list
**cartel** [kaʀtɛl] *nm* cartel
**carte-lettre** [kaʀtəlɛtʀ(ə)] (*pl* **cartes-lettres**) *nf* letter-card
**carte-mère** [kaʀtəmɛʀ] (*pl* **cartes-mères**) *nf* (*Inform*) mother board
**carter** [kaʀtɛʀ] *nm* (*Auto: d'huile*) sump (*Brit*), oil pan (*US*); (*: de la boîte de vitesses*) casing; (*de bicyclette*) chain guard
**carte-réponse** [kaʀt(ə)ʀepɔ̃s] (*pl* **cartes-réponses**) *nf* reply card
**cartésien, ne** [kaʀtezjɛ̃, -ɛn] *adj* Cartesian
**Carthage** [kaʀtaʒ] *n* Carthage
**cartilage** [kaʀtilaʒ] *nm* (*Anat*) cartilage
**cartilagineux, -euse** [kaʀtilaʒinø, -øz] *adj* (*viande*) gristly
**cartographe** [kaʀtɔgʀaf] *nm/f* cartographer
**cartographie** [kaʀtɔgʀafi] *nf* cartography, map-making
**cartomancie** [kaʀtɔmɑ̃si] *nf* fortune-telling, card-reading
**cartomancien, ne** [kaʀtɔmɑ̃sjɛ̃, -ɛn] *nm/f* fortune-teller (*with cards*)
**carton** [kaʀtɔ̃] *nm* (*matériau*) cardboard; (*boîte*) (cardboard) box; (*d'invitation*) invitation card; (*Art*) sketch; cartoon; **en ~** cardboard *cpd*; **faire un ~** (*au tir*) to have a go at the rifle range; to score a hit; **~ (à dessin)** portfolio
**cartonnage** [kaʀtɔnaʒ] *nm* cardboard (packing)
**cartonné, e** [kaʀtɔne] *adj* (*livre*) hardback, cased
**carton-pâte** [kaʀtɔ̃pat] *nm* pasteboard; **de ~** (*fig*) cardboard *cpd*

**cartouche** [kaʀtuʃ] *nf* cartridge; (*de cigarettes*) carton
**cartouchière** [kaʀtuʃjɛʀ] *nf* cartridge belt
**cas** [kɑ] *nm* case; **faire peu de ~/grand ~ de** to attach little/great importance to; **le ~ échéant** if need be; **en aucun ~** on no account, under no circumstances (whatsoever); **au ~ où** in case; **dans ce ~** in that case; **en ~ de** in case of, in the event of; **en ~ de besoin** if need be; **en ~ d'urgence** in an emergency; **en ce ~** in that case; **en tout ~** in any case, at any rate; **~ de conscience** matter of conscience; **~ de force majeure** case of absolute necessity; (*Assurances*) act of God; **~ limite** borderline case; **~ social** social problem
**Casablanca** [kazablɑ̃ka] *n* Casablanca
**casanier, -ière** [kazanje, -jɛʀ] *adj* stay-at-home
**casaque** [kazak] *nf* (*de jockey*) blouse
**cascade** [kaskad] *nf* waterfall, cascade; (*fig*) stream, torrent
**cascadeur, -euse** [kaskadœʀ, -øz] *nm/f* stuntman/girl
**case** [kɑz] *nf* (*hutte*) hut; (*compartiment*) compartment; (*pour le courrier*) pigeonhole; (*de mots croisés, d'échiquier*) square; (*sur un formulaire*) box
**casemate** [kazmat] *nf* blockhouse
**caser** [kɑze] *vt* (*mettre*) to put; (*loger*) to put up; (*péj*) to find a job for; to marry off; **se caser** *vi* (*personne*) to settle down
**caserne** [kazɛʀn(ə)] *nf* barracks
**casernement** [kazɛʀnəmɑ̃] *nm* barrack buildings *pl*
**cash** [kaʃ] *adv*: **payer ~** to pay cash down
**casier** [kɑzje] *nm* (*à journaux etc*) rack; (*de bureau*) filing cabinet; (*: à cases*) set of pigeonholes; (*case*) compartment; pigeonhole; (*: à clef*) locker; (*Pêche*) lobster pot; **~ à bouteilles** bottle rack; **~ judiciaire** police record
**casino** [kazino] *nm* casino
**casque** [kask(ə)] *nm* helmet; (*chez le coiffeur*) (hair-)dryer; (*pour audition*) (head-)phones *pl*, headset; **les C~s bleus** the UN peacekeeping force
**casquer** [kaske] *vi* (*fam*) to cough up, stump up (*Brit*)
**casquette** [kaskɛt] *nf* cap
**cassable** [kɑsabl(ə)] *adj* (*fragile*) breakable
**cassant, e** [kɑsɑ̃, -ɑ̃t] *adj* brittle; (*fig*) brusque, abrupt
**cassate** [kasat] *nf*: **(glace) ~** cassata
**cassation** [kasasjɔ̃] *nf*: **se pourvoir en ~** to lodge an appeal; **recours en ~** appeal to the Supreme Court
**casse** [kas] *nf* (*pour voitures*): **mettre à la ~** to scrap, send to the breakers (*Brit*); (*dégâts*): **il y a eu de la ~** there were a lot of breakages; (*Typo*): **haut/bas de ~** upper/lower case
**cassé, e** [kɑse] *adj* (*voix*) cracked; (*vieillard*) bent
**casse-cou** [kɑsku] *adj inv* daredevil, reckless; **crier ~ à qn** to warn sb (*against a risky undertaking*)
**casse-croûte** [kɑskʀut] *nm inv* snack

65

**casse-noisettes** [kɑsnwazɛt], **casse-noix**
[kɑsnwa] *nm inv* nutcrackers *pl*
**casse-pieds** [kɑspje] *adj, nm/f inv* (*fam*): **il est ~,
c'est un ~** he's a pain (in the neck)
**casser** [kɑse] *vt* to break; (*Admin*: *gradé*) to
demote; (*Jur*) to quash; (*Comm*): **~ les prix** to
slash prices; **se casser** *vi* to break; (*fam*) to go,
leave ▷ *vt*: **se ~ la jambe/une jambe** to break
one's leg/a leg; **à tout ~** fantastic, brilliant; **se
~ net** to break clean off
**casserole** [kɑsʁɔl] *nf* saucepan; **à la ~** (*Culin*)
braised
**casse-tête** [kɑstɛt] *nm inv* (*fig*) brain teaser;
(*difficultés*) headache (*fig*)
**cassette** [kɑsɛt] *nf* (*bande magnétique*) cassette;
(*coffret*) casket; **~ numérique** digital compact
cassette; **~ vidéo** video
**casseur** [kɑsœʁ] *nm* hooligan; rioter
**cassis** [kasis] *nm* blackcurrant; (*de la route*) dip,
bump
**cassonade** [kasɔnad] *nf* brown sugar
**cassoulet** [kasulɛ] *nm* *sausage and bean hotpot*
**cassure** [kɑsyʁ] *nf* break, crack
**castagnettes** [kastaɲɛt] *nfpl* castanets
**caste** [kast(ə)] *nf* caste
**castillan, e** [kastijã, -an] *adj* Castilian ▷ *nm*
(*Ling*) Castilian
**Castille** [kastij] *nf*: **la ~** Castile
**castor** [kastɔʁ] *nm* beaver
**castrer** [kastʁe] *vt* (*mâle*) to castrate; (*femelle*) to
spay; (*cheval*) to geld; (*chat, chien*) to doctor (*Brit*),
fix (*US*)
**cataclysme** [kataklism(ə)] *nm* cataclysm
**catacombes** [katakɔ̃b] *nfpl* catacombs
**catadioptre** [katadjɔptʁ(ə)] *nm* = **cataphote**
**catafalque** [katafalk(ə)] *nm* catafalque
**catalan, e** [katalã, -an] *adj* Catalan, Catalonian
▷ *nm* (*Ling*) Catalan
**Catalogne** [katalɔɲ] *nf*: **la ~** Catalonia
**catalogue** [katalɔg] *nm* catalogue
**cataloguer** [katalɔge] *vt* to catalogue, list; (*péj*)
to put a label on
**catalyse** [kataliz] *nf* catalysis
**catalyser** [katalize] *vt* to catalyze
**catalyseur** [katalizœʁ] *nm* catalyst
**catalytique** [katalitik] *adj* catalytic
**catamaran** [katamaʁã] *nm* (*voilier*) catamaran
**cataphote** [katafɔt] *nm* reflector
**cataplasme** [kataplasm(ə)] *nm* poultice
**catapulte** [katapylt(ə)] *nf* catapult
**catapulter** [katapylte] *vt* to catapult
**cataracte** [kataʁakt(ə)] *nf* cataract; **opérer qn
de la ~** to operate on sb for a cataract
**catarrhe** [kataʁ] *nm* catarrh
**catarrheux, -euse** [kataʁø, -øz] *adj* catarrhal
**catastrophe** [katastʁɔf] *nf* catastrophe,
disaster; **atterrir en ~** to make an emergency
landing; **partir en ~** to rush away
**catastropher** [katastʁɔfe] *vt* (*personne*) to
shatter
**catastrophique** [katastʁɔfik] *adj* catastrophic,
disastrous

**catch** [katʃ] *nm* (all-in) wrestling
**catcheur, -euse** [katʃœʁ, -øz] *nm/f* (all-in)
wrestler
**catéchiser** [kateʃize] *vt* to indoctrinate; to
lecture
**catéchisme** [kateʃism(ə)] *nm* catechism
**catéchumène** [katekymɛn] *nm/f* catechumen,
*person attending religious instruction prior to baptism*
**catégorie** [kategɔʁi] *nf* category; (*Boucherie*):
**morceaux de première/deuxième ~** prime/
second cuts
**catégorique** [kategɔʁik] *adj* categorical
**catégoriquement** [kategɔʁikmã] *adv*
categorically
**catégoriser** [kategɔʁize] *vt* to categorize
**caténaire** [katenɛʁ] *nf* (*Rail*) catenary
**cathédrale** [katedʁal] *nf* cathedral
**cathéter** [katetɛʁ] *nm* (*Méd*) catheter
**cathode** [katɔd] *nf* cathode
**cathodique** [katɔdik] *adj*: **rayons ~s** cathode
rays; **tube/écran ~** cathode-ray tube/screen
**catholicisme** [katɔlisism(ə)] *nm* (Roman)
Catholicism
**catholique** [katɔlik] *adj, nm/f* (Roman) Catholic;
**pas très ~** a bit shady *ou* fishy
**catimini** [katimini]: **en ~** *adv* on the sly, on the
quiet
**catogan** [katɔgã] *nm* bow (*tying hair on neck*)
**Caucase** [kokaz] *nm*: **le ~** the Caucasus
(Mountains)
**caucasien, ne** [kokazjɛ̃, -ɛn] *adj* Caucasian
**cauchemar** [koʃmaʁ] *nm* nightmare
**cauchemardesque** [koʃmaʁdɛsk(ə)] *adj*
nightmarish
**causal, e** [kozal] *adj* causal
**causalité** [kozalite] *nf* causality
**causant, e** [kozã, -ãt] *adj* chatty, talkative
**cause** [koz] *nf* cause; (*Jur*) lawsuit, case; brief;
**faire ~ commune avec qn** to take sides with
sb; **être ~ de** to be the cause of; **à ~ de** because
of, owing to; **pour ~ de** on account of; owing to;
**(et) pour ~** and for (a very) good reason; **être
en ~** (*intérêts*) to be at stake; (*personne*) to be
involved; (*qualité*) to be in question; **mettre en
~** to implicate; to call into question; **remettre
en ~** to challenge, call into question; **c'est hors
de ~** it's out of the question; **en tout état de ~**
in any case
**causer** [koze] *vt* to cause ▷ *vi* to chat, talk
**causerie** [kozʁi] *nf* talk
**causette** [kozɛt] *nf*: **faire la** *ou* **un brin de ~** to
have a chat
**caustique** [kostik] *adj* caustic
**cauteleux, -euse** [kotlø, -øz] *adj* wily
**cautériser** [koteʁize] *vt* to cauterize
**caution** [kosjɔ̃] *nf* guarantee, security; deposit;
(*Jur*) bail (bond); (*fig*) backing, support; **payer la
~ de qn** to stand bail for sb; **se porter ~ pour
qn** to stand security for sb; **libéré sous ~**
released on bail; **sujet à ~** unconfirmed
**cautionnement** [kosjɔnmã] *nm* (*somme*)
guarantee, security

**cautionner** [kosjɔne] *vt* to guarantee; (*soutenir*) to support
**cavalcade** [kavalkad] *nf* (*fig*) stampede
**cavale** [kaval] *nf*: **en ~** on the run
**cavalerie** [kavalʀi] *nf* cavalry
**cavalier, -ière** [kavalje, -jɛʀ] *adj* (*désinvolte*) offhand ▷ *nm/f* rider; (*au bal*) partner ▷ *nm* (*Échecs*) knight; **faire ~ seul** to go it alone; **allée** *ou* **piste cavalière** riding path
**cavalièrement** [kavaljɛʀmɑ̃] *adv* offhandedly
**cave** [kav] *nf* cellar; (*cabaret*) (cellar) nightclub ▷ *adj*: **yeux ~s** sunken eyes; **joues ~s** hollow cheeks
**caveau, x** [kavo] *nm* vault
**caverne** [kavɛʀn(ə)] *nf* cave
**caverneux, -euse** [kavɛʀnø, -øz] *adj* cavernous
**caviar** [kavjaʀ] *nm* caviar(e)
**cavité** [kavite] *nf* cavity
**Cayenne** [kajɛn] *n* Cayenne
**CB** [sibi] *sigle f* (= *citizens' band, canaux banalisés*) CB = **carte bancaire**
**CC** *sigle m* = **corps consulaire; compte courant**
**CCI** *sigle f* = **Chambre de commerce et d'industrie**
**CCP** *sigle m* = **compte chèque postal**
**CD** *sigle m* (= *chemin départemental*) secondary road, ≈ B road (Brit); (= *compact disc*) CD; (= *comité directeur*) steering committee; (*Pol*) = **corps diplomatique**
**CDD** *sigle m* (= *contrat à durée déterminée*) fixed-term contract
**CDI** *sigle m* (= *Centre de documentation et d'information*) school library; (= *contrat à durée indéterminée*) permanent *ou* open-ended contract
**CD-ROM** [sederɔm] *nm inv* (= *Compact Disc Read Only Memory*) CD-Rom
**CDS** *sigle m* (= *Centre des démocrates sociaux*) political party
**CE** *sigle f* (= *Communauté européenne*) EC; (*Comm*) = **caisse d'épargne** ▷ *sigle m* (*Industrie*) = **comité d'entreprise**; (*Scol*) = **cours élémentaire**

🔵 MOT-CLÉ

**ce, cette** [sə, sɛt] (*devant nm* **cet** + *voyelle ou h aspiré*; *pl* **ces**) *adj dém* (*proximité*) this; these *pl*; (*non-proximité*) that; those *pl*; **cette maison(-ci/là)** this/that house; **cette nuit** (*qui vient*) tonight; (*passée*) last night
▷ *pron* **1**: **c'est** it's, it is; **c'est petit/grand/un livre** it's *ou* it is small/big/a book; **c'est un peintre** he's *ou* he is a painter; **ce sont des peintres** they're *ou* they are painters; **c'est le facteur** *etc* (*à la porte*) it's the postman *etc*; **qui est-ce?** who is it?; (*en désignant*) who is he/she?; **qu'est-ce?** what is it?; **c'est toi qui lui as parlé** it was you who spoke to him
**2**: **c'est que**: **c'est qu'il est lent/qu'il n'a pas faim** the fact is, he's slow/he's not hungry
**3** (*expressions*): **c'est ça** (*correct*) that's it, that's right; **c'est toi qui le dis!** that's what YOU say!; *voir aussi* **c'est-à-dire**; *voir* **-ci**; **est-ce que**;

**n'est-ce pas**
**4**: **ce qui, ce que** what; (*chose qui*): **il est bête, ce qui me chagrine** he's stupid, which saddens me; **tout ce qui bouge** everything that *ou* which moves; **tout ce que je sais** all I know; **ce dont j'ai parlé** what I talked about; **ce que c'est grand!** it's so big!

**CEA** *sigle m* (= *Commissariat à l'énergie atomique*) ≈ AEA (= *Atomic Energy Authority*) (Brit) ≈ AEC = **Atomic Energy Commission** (US)
**CECA** [seka] *sigle f* (= *Communauté européenne du charbon et de l'acier*) ECSC (= European Coal and Steel Community)
**ceci** [səsi] *pron* this
**cécité** [sesite] *nf* blindness
**céder** [sede] *vt* to give up ▷ *vi* (*pont, barrage*) to give way; (*personne*) to give in; **~ à** to yield to, give in to
**cédérom** [sederɔm] *nm* CD-ROM
**CEDEX** [sedɛks] *sigle m* (= *courrier d'entreprise à distribution exceptionnelle*) accelerated postal service for bulk users
**cédille** [sedij] *nf* cedilla
**cèdre** [sɛdʀ(ə)] *nm* cedar
**CEE** *sigle f* (= *Communauté économique européenne*) EEC
**CEI** *sigle f* (= *Communauté des États indépendants*) CIS
**ceindre** [sɛ̃dʀ(ə)] *vt* (*mettre*) to put on; (*entourer*): **~ qch de qch** to put sth round sth
**ceinture** [sɛ̃tyʀ] *nf* belt; (*taille*) waist; (*fig*) ring; belt; circle; **~ de sauvetage** lifebelt (Brit), life preserver (US); **~ de sécurité** safety *ou* seat belt; **~ (de sécurité) à enrouleur** inertia reel seat belt; **~ verte** green belt
**ceinturer** [sɛ̃tyʀe] *vt* (*saisir*) to grasp (round the waist); (*entourer*) to surround
**ceinturon** [sɛ̃tyʀɔ̃] *nm* belt
**cela** [səla] *pron* that; (*comme sujet indéfini*) it; **~ m'étonne que** it surprises me that; **quand/où ~?** when/where (was that)?
**célébrant** [selebʀɑ̃] *nm* (*Rel*) celebrant
**célébration** [selebʀɑsjɔ̃] *nf* celebration
**célèbre** [selebʀ(ə)] *adj* famous
**célébrer** [selebʀe] *vt* to celebrate; (*louer*) to extol
**célébrité** [selebʀite] *nf* fame; (*star*) celebrity
**céleri** [sɛlʀi] *nm*: **~(-rave)** celeriac; **~ (en branche)** celery
**célérité** [seleʀite] *nf* speed, swiftness
**céleste** [selɛst(ə)] *adj* celestial; heavenly
**célibat** [seliba] *nm* celibacy, bachelor/ spinsterhood
**célibataire** [selibatɛʀ] *adj* single, unmarried ▷ *nm/f* bachelor/unmarried *ou* single woman; **mère ~** single *ou* unmarried mother
**celle, celles** [sɛl] *pron voir* **celui**
**cellier** [selje] *nm* storeroom
**cellophane®** [selɔfan] *nf* cellophane
**cellulaire** [selylɛʀ] *adj* (*Bio*) cell *cpd*, cellular; **voiture** *ou* **fourgon ~** prison *ou* police van; **régime ~** confinement
**cellule** [selyl] *nf* (*gén*) cell; **~ (photo-électrique)**

electronic eye
**cellulite** [selylit] *nf* cellulite
**celluloïd®** [selylɔid] *nm* Celluloid
**cellulose** [selyloz] *nf* cellulose
**celte** [sɛlt(ə)], **celtique** [sɛltik] *adj* Celt, Celtic

⭕ MOT-CLÉ

**celui, celle** [səlɥi, sɛl] (*mpl* **ceux,** *fpl* **celles**) *pron*
**1: celui-ci/là, celle-ci/là** this one/that one;
**ceux-ci, celles-ci** these (ones); **ceux-là, celles-là** those (ones); **celui de mon frère** my
brother's; **celui du salon/du dessous** the one
in (*ou* from) the lounge/below
**2: celui qui bouge** the one which *ou* that
moves; (*personne*) the one who moves; **celui
que je vois** the one (which *ou* that) I see;
(*personne*) the one (whom) I see; **celui dont je
parle** the one I'm talking about
**3** (*valeur indéfinie*): **celui qui veut** whoever
wants

**cénacle** [senakl(ə)] *nm* (literary) coterie *ou* set
**cendre** [sɑ̃dʀ(ə)] *nf* ash; **~s** (*d'un foyer*) ash(es),
cinders; (*volcaniques*) ash *sg*; (*d'un défunt*) ashes;
**sous la ~** (*Culin*) in (the) embers
**cendré, e** [sɑ̃dʀe] *adj* (*couleur*) ashen; (**piste**) **~e**
cinder track
**cendreux, -euse** [sɑ̃dʀø, -øz] *adj* (*terrain,
substance*) cindery; (*teint*) ashen
**cendrier** [sɑ̃dʀije] *nm* ashtray
**cène** [sɛn] *nf*: **la ~** (Holy) Communion; (*Art*) the
Last Supper
**censé, e** [sɑ̃se] *adj*: **être ~ faire** to be supposed
to do
**censément** [sɑ̃semɑ̃] *adv* supposedly
**censeur** [sɑ̃sœʀ] *nm* (*Scol*) deputy head (*Brit*),
vice-principal (*US*); (*Ciné, Pol*) censor
**censure** [sɑ̃syʀ] *nf* censorship
**censurer** [sɑ̃syʀe] *vt* (*Ciné, Presse*) to censor; (*Pol*)
to censure
**cent** [sɑ̃] *num* a hundred, one hundred; **pour ~**
(%) per cent (%); **faire les ~ pas** to pace up and
down ▷ *nm* (*US, Canada, partie de l'euro etc*) cent
**centaine** [sɑ̃tɛn] *nf*: **une ~ (de)** about a
hundred, a hundred or so; (*Comm*) a hundred;
**plusieurs ~s (de)** several hundred; **des ~s (de)**
hundreds (of)
**centenaire** [sɑ̃tnɛʀ] *adj* hundred-year-old
▷ *nm/f* centenarian ▷ *nm* (*anniversaire*) centenary
**centième** [sɑ̃tjɛm] *num* hundredth
**centigrade** [sɑ̃tigʀad] *nm* centigrade
**centigramme** [sɑ̃tigʀam] *nm* centigramme
**centilitre** [sɑ̃tilitʀ(ə)] *nm* centilitre (*Brit*),
centiliter (*US*)
**centime** [sɑ̃tim] *nm* centime; **~ d'euro** euro
cent
**centimètre** [sɑ̃timɛtʀ(ə)] *nm* centimetre (*Brit*),
centimeter (*US*); (*ruban*) tape measure,
measuring tape
**centrafricain, e** [sɑ̃tʀafʀikɛ̃, -ɛn] *adj* of *ou* from
the Central African Republic

**central, e, -aux** [sɑ̃tʀal, -o] *adj* central ▷ *nm*: **~
(téléphonique)** (telephone) exchange ▷ *nf*: **~e
d'achat** (*Comm*) central buying service; **~e
électrique/nucléaire** electric/nuclear power
station; **~e syndicale** group of affiliated trade
unions
**centralisation** [sɑ̃tʀalizasjɔ̃] *nf* centralization
**centraliser** [sɑ̃tʀalize] *vt* to centralize
**centralisme** [sɑ̃tʀalism(ə)] *nm* centralism
**centraméricain, e** [sɑ̃tʀameʀikɛ̃, -ɛn] *adj*
Central American
**centre** [sɑ̃tʀ(ə)] *nm* centre (*Brit*), center (*US*); **~
commercial/sportif/culturel** shopping/
sports/arts centre; **~ aéré** outdoor centre; **~
d'appels** call centre; **~ d'apprentissage**
training college; **~ d'attraction** centre of
attraction; **~ de gravité** centre of gravity; **~ de
loisirs** leisure centre; **~ d'enfouissement des
déchets** landfill site; **~ hospitalier** hospital
complex; **~ de tri** (*Postes*) sorting office; **~s
nerveux** (*Anat*) nerve centres
**centrer** [sɑ̃tʀe] *vt* to centre (*Brit*), center (*US*) ▷ *vi*
(*Football*) to centre the ball
**centre-ville** [sɑ̃tʀəvil] (*pl* **centres-villes**) *nm*
town centre (*Brit*) *ou* center (*US*), downtown
(area) (*US*)
**centrifuge** [sɑ̃tʀify3] *adj*: **force ~** centrifugal
force
**centrifuger** [sɑ̃tʀify3e] *vt* to centrifuge
**centrifugeuse** [sɑ̃tʀify3øz] *nf* (*pour fruits*) juice
extractor
**centripète** [sɑ̃tʀipɛt] *adj*: **force ~** centripetal
force
**centrisme** [sɑ̃tʀism(ə)] *nm* centrism
**centriste** [sɑ̃tʀist(ə)] *adj, nm/f* centrist
**centuple** [sɑ̃typl(ə)] *nm*: **le ~ de qch** a hundred
times sth; **au ~** a hundredfold
**centupler** [sɑ̃typle] *vi, vt* to increase a
hundredfold
**CEP** *sigle m* = **Certificat d'études (primaires)**
**cep** [sɛp] *nm* (vine) stock
**cépage** [sepa3] *nm* (type of) vine
**cèpe** [sɛp] *nm* (edible) boletus
**cependant** [səpɑ̃dɑ̃] *adv* however, nevertheless
**céramique** [seʀamik] *adj* ceramic ▷ *nf* ceramic;
(*art*) ceramics *sg*
**céramiste** [seʀamist(ə)] *nm/f* ceramist
**cerbère** [sɛʀbɛʀ] *nm* (*fig: péj*) bad-tempered
doorkeeper
**cerceau, x** [sɛʀso] *nm* (*d'enfant, de tonnelle*) hoop
**cercle** [sɛʀkl(ə)] *nm* circle; (*objet*) band, hoop;
**décrire un ~** (*avion*) to circle; (*projectile*) to
describe a circle; **~ d'amis** circle of friends; **~ de
famille** family circle; **~ vicieux** vicious circle
**cercler** [sɛʀkle] *vt*: **lunettes cerclées d'or** gold-
rimmed glasses
**cercueil** [sɛʀkœj] *nm* coffin
**céréale** [seʀeal] *nf* cereal
**céréalier, -ière** [seʀealje, -jɛʀ] *adj* (*production,
cultures*) cereal *cpd*
**cérébral, e, -aux** [seʀebʀal, -o] *adj* (*Anat*)
cerebral, brain *cpd*; (*fig*) mental, cerebral

**cérémonial** [seʀemɔnjal] *nm* ceremonial
**cérémonie** [seʀemɔni] *nf* ceremony;
 **cérémonies** *nfpl* (*péj*) fuss *sg*, to-do *sg*
**cérémonieux, -euse** [seʀemɔnjø, -øz] *adj*
 ceremonious, formal
**cerf** [seʀ] *nm* stag
**cerfeuil** [seʀfœj] *nm* chervil
**cerf-volant** [seʀvɔlɑ̃] *nm* kite; **jouer au ~** to fly
 a kite
**cerisaie** [səʀizɛ] *nf* cherry orchard
**cerise** [səʀiz] *nf* cherry
**cerisier** [səʀizje] *nm* cherry (tree)
**CERN** [seʀn] *sigle m* (= *Centre européen de recherche
 nucléaire*) CERN
**cerné, e** [seʀne] *adj*: **les yeux ~s** with dark rings
 *ou* shadows under the eyes
**cerner** [seʀne] *vt* (*Mil etc*) to surround; (*fig*:
 *problème*) to delimit, define
**cernes** [seʀn(ə)] *nfpl* (dark) rings, shadows
 (under the eyes)
**certain, e** [seʀtɛ̃, -ɛn] *adj* certain; (*sûr*): **~ (de/
 que)** certain *ou* sure (of/ that); **d'un ~ âge** past
 one's prime, not so young; **un ~ temps** (quite)
 some time; **sûr et ~** absolutely certain; **~s** *pron*
 some
**certainement** [seʀtɛnmɑ̃] *adv* (*probablement*)
 most probably *ou* likely; (*bien sûr*) certainly, of
 course
**certes** [seʀt(ə)] *adv* admittedly; of course;
 indeed (yes)
**certificat** [seʀtifika] *nm* certificate; **C~
 d'études (primaires)** *former school leaving
 certificate* (*taken at the end of primary education*); **C~
 de fin d'études secondaires** school leaving
 certificate
**certifié, e** [seʀtifje] *adj*: **professeur ~** qualified
 teacher; (*Admin*): **copie ~e conforme (à
 l'original)** certified copy (of the original)
**certifier** [seʀtifje] *vt* to certify, guarantee; **~ à
 qn que** to assure sb that, guarantee to sb that; **~
 qch à qn** to guarantee sth to sb
**certitude** [seʀtityd] *nf* certainty
**cérumen** [seʀymɛn] *nm* (ear)wax
**cerveau, x** [seʀvo] *nm* brain; **~ électronique**
 electronic brain
**cervelas** [seʀvəla] *nm* saveloy
**cervelle** [seʀvɛl] *nf* (*Anat*) brain; (*Culin*) brain(s);
 **se creuser la ~** to rack one's brains
**cervical, e, -aux** [seʀvikal, -o] *adj* cervical
**cervidés** [seʀvide] *nmpl* cervidae
**CES** *sigle m* (= *Collège d'enseignement secondaire*)
 ≈ (junior) secondary school (*Brit*), ≈ junior high
 school (*US*)
**ces** [se] *adj dém voir* **ce**
**césarienne** [sezaʀjɛn] *nf* caesarean (*Brit*) *ou*
 cesarean (*US*) (section)
**cessantes** [sesɑ̃t] *adj fpl*: **toutes affaires ~**
 forthwith
**cessation** [sesasjɔ̃] *nf*: **~ des hostilités**
 cessation of hostilities; **~ de paiements/
 commerce** suspension of payments/trading
**cesse** [ses]: **sans ~** *adv* continually, constantly;

continuously; **il n'avait de ~ que** he would not
 rest until
**cesser** [sese] *vt* to stop ▷ *vi* to stop, cease; **~ de
 faire** to stop doing; **faire ~** (*bruit, scandale*) to put
 a stop to
**cessez-le-feu** [seselfø] *nm inv* ceasefire
**cession** [sesjɔ̃] *nf* transfer
**c'est** [sɛ] *voir* **ce**
**c'est-à-dire** [setadiʀ] *adv* that is (to say);
 (*demander de préciser*): **c'est-à-dire?** what does
 that mean?; **c'est-à-dire que ...** (*en conséquence*)
 which means that ...; (*manière d'excuse*) well, in
 fact ...
**CET** *sigle m* (= *Collège d'enseignement technique*)
 (*formerly*) technical school
**cet** [sɛt] *adj dém voir* **ce**
**cétacé** [setase] *nm* cetacean
**cette** [sɛt] *adj dém voir* **ce**
**ceux** [sø] *pron voir* **celui**
**cévenol, e** [sevnɔl] *adj* of *ou* from the Cévennes
 region
**cf.** *abr* (= *confer*) cf, cp
**CFAO** *sigle f* (= *conception de fabrication assistée par
 ordinateur*) CAM
**CFC** *sigle mpl* (= *chlorofluorocarbures*) CFC
**CFDT** *sigle f* (= *Confédération française démocratique du
 travail*) trade union
**CFF** *sigle m* (= *Chemins de fer fédéraux*) Swiss railways
**CFL** *sigle m* (= *Chemins de fer luxembourgeois*)
 Luxembourg railways
**CFP** *sigle m* = **Centre de formation
 professionnelle** ▷ *sigle f* = **Compagnie française
 des pétroles**
**CFTC** *sigle f* (= *Confédération française des travailleurs
 chrétiens*) trade union
**CGC** *sigle f* (= *Confédération générale des cadres*)
 management union
**CGPME** *sigle f* = **Confédération générale des
 petites et moyennes entreprises**
**CGT** *sigle f* (= *Confédération générale du travail*) trade
 union
**CH** *abr* (= *Confédération helvétique*) CH
**ch.** *abr* = **charges; chauffage; cherche**
**chacal** [ʃakal] *nm* jackal
**chacun, e** [ʃakœ̃, -yn] *pron* each; (*indéfini*)
 everyone, everybody
**chagrin, e** [ʃagʀɛ̃, -in] *adj* morose ▷ *nm* grief,
 sorrow; **avoir du ~** to be grieved *ou* sorrowful
**chagriner** [ʃagʀine] *vt* to grieve, distress;
 (*contrarier*) to bother, worry
**chahut** [ʃay] *nm* uproar
**chahuter** [ʃayte] *vt* to rag, bait ▷ *vi* to make an
 uproar
**chahuteur, -euse** [ʃaytœʀ, -øz] *nm/f* rowdy
**chai** [ʃɛ] *nm* wine and spirit store(house)
**chaîne** [ʃɛn] *nf* chain; (*Radio, TV*) channel;
 (*Inform*) string; **chaînes** *nfpl* (*liens, asservissement*)
 fetters, bonds; **travail à la ~** production line
 work; **réactions en ~** chain reactions; **faire la
 ~** to form a (human) chain; **~ alimentaire** food
 chain; **~ compacte** music centre; **~ d'entraide**
 mutual aid association; **~ (haute-fidélité** *ou*

69

**hi-fi**) hi-fi system; ~ **(de montage** *ou* **de fabrication)** production *ou* assembly line; ~ **(de montagnes)** (mountain) range; ~ **de solidarité** solidarity network; ~ **(stéréo** *ou* **audio)** stereo (system)

**chaînette** [ʃɛnɛt] *nf* (small) chain

**chaînon** [ʃɛnɔ̃] *nm* link

**chair** [ʃɛR] *nf* flesh ▷ *adj*: **(couleur)** ~ flesh-coloured; **avoir la ~ de poule** to have goose pimples *ou* goose flesh; **bien en ~** plump, well-padded; **en ~ et en os** in the flesh; ~ **à saucisses** sausage meat

**chaire** [ʃɛR] *nf* (*d'église*) pulpit; (*d'université*) chair

**chaise** [ʃɛz] *nf* chair; ~ **de bébé** high chair; ~ **électrique** electric chair; ~ **longue** deckchair

**chaland** [ʃalɑ̃] *nm* (*bateau*) barge

**châle** [ʃɑl] *nm* shawl

**chalet** [ʃalɛ] *nm* chalet

**chaleur** [ʃalœR] *nf* heat; (*fig*) warmth; fire, fervour (*Brit*), fervor (*US*); heat; **en ~** (*Zool*) on heat

**chaleureusement** [ʃalœRøzmɑ̃] *adv* warmly

**chaleureux, -euse** [ʃalœRø, -øz] *adj* warm

**challenge** [ʃalɑ̃ʒ] *nm* contest, tournament

**challenger** [ʃalɑ̃ʒɛR] *nm* (*Sport*) challenger

**chaloupe** [ʃalup] *nf* launch; (*de sauvetage*) lifeboat

**chalumeau, x** [ʃalymo] *nm* blowlamp (*Brit*), blowtorch

**chalut** [ʃaly] *nm* trawl (net); **pêcher au ~** to trawl

**chalutier** [ʃalytje] *nm* trawler; (*pêcheur*) trawlerman

**chamade** [ʃamad] *nf*: **battre la ~** to beat wildly

**chamailler** [ʃamaje]: **se chamailler** *vi* to squabble, bicker

**chamarré, e** [ʃamaRe] *adj* richly brocaded

**chambard** [ʃɑ̃baR] *nm* rumpus

**chambardement** [ʃɑ̃baRdəmɑ̃] *nm*: **c'est le grand ~** everything has been (*ou* is being) turned upside down

**chambarder** [ʃɑ̃baRde] *vt* to turn upside down

**chamboulement** [ʃɑ̃bulmɑ̃] *nm* disruption

**chambouler** [ʃɑ̃bule] *vt* to disrupt, turn upside down

**chambranle** [ʃɑ̃bRɑ̃l] *nm* (door) frame

**chambre** [ʃɑ̃bR(ə)] *nf* bedroom; (*Tech*) chamber; (*Pol*) chamber, house; (*Jur*) court; (*Comm*) chamber; federation; **faire ~ à part** to sleep in separate rooms; **stratège/alpiniste en ~** armchair strategist/mountaineer; ~ **à un lit/ deux lits** single/twin-bedded room; ~ **pour une/deux personne(s)** single/double room; ~ **d'accusation** court of criminal appeal; ~ **d'agriculture (CA)** *body responsible for the agricultural interests of a département*; ~ **à air** (*de pneu*) (inner) tube; ~ **d'amis** spare *ou* guest room; ~ **de combustion** combustion chamber; ~ **de commerce et d'industrie (CCI)** chamber of commerce and industry; ~ **à coucher** bedroom; **la C~ des députés** the Chamber of Deputies, ≈ the House (of Commons) (*Brit*), ≈ the

House of Representatives (*US*); ~ **forte** strongroom; ~ **froide** *ou* **frigorifique** cold room; ~ **à gaz** gas chamber; ~ **d'hôte** ≈ bed and breakfast (*in private home*); ~ **des machines** engine-room; ~ **des métiers (CM)** *chamber of commerce for trades*; ~ **meublée** bedsit(ter) (*Brit*), furnished room; ~ **noire** (*Photo*) dark room

**chambrée** [ʃɑ̃bRe] *nf* room

**chambrer** [ʃɑ̃bRe] *vt* (*vin*) to bring to room temperature

**chameau, x** [ʃamo] *nm* camel

**chamois** [ʃamwa] *nm* chamois ▷ *adj*: **(couleur)** ~ fawn, buff

**champ** [ʃɑ̃] *nm* (*aussi Inform*) field; (*Photo: aussi:* **dans le champ**) in the picture; **prendre du ~** to draw back; **laisser le ~ libre à qn** to leave sb a clear field; ~ **d'action** sphere of operation(s); ~ **de bataille** battlefield; ~ **de courses** racecourse; ~ **d'honneur** field of honour; ~ **de manœuvre** (*Mil*) parade ground; ~ **de mines** minefield; ~ **de tir** shooting *ou* rifle range; ~ **visuel** field of vision

**Champagne** [ʃɑ̃paɲ] *nf*: **la ~** Champagne, the Champagne region

**champagne** [ʃɑ̃paɲ] *nm* champagne

**champenois, e** [ʃɑ̃pənwa, -waz] *adj* of *ou* from Champagne; (*vin*): **méthode ~e** champagne-type

**champêtre** [ʃɑ̃pɛtR(ə)] *adj* country *cpd*, rural

**champignon** [ʃɑ̃piɲɔ̃] *nm* mushroom; (*terme générique*) fungus; (*fam: accélérateur*) accelerator, gas pedal (*US*); ~ **de couche** *ou* **de Paris** button mushroom; ~ **vénéneux** toadstool, poisonous mushroom

**champion, ne** [ʃɑ̃pjɔ̃, -ɔn] *adj, nm/f* champion

**championnat** [ʃɑ̃pjɔna] *nm* championship

**chance** [ʃɑ̃s] *nf*: **la ~** luck; **une ~** a stroke *ou* piece of luck *ou* good fortune; (*occasion*) a lucky break; **chances** *nfpl* (*probabilités*) chances; **avoir de la ~** to be lucky; **il a des ~s de gagner** he has a chance of winning; **il y a de fortes ~s pour que Paul soit malade** it's highly probable that Paul is ill; **bonne ~!** good luck!; **encore une ~ que tu viennes!** it's lucky you're coming!; **je n'ai pas de ~** I'm out of luck; (*toujours*) I never have any luck; **donner sa ~ à qn** to give sb a chance

**chancelant, e** [ʃɑ̃slɑ̃, -ɑ̃t] *adj* (*personne*) tottering; (*santé*) failing

**chanceler** [ʃɑ̃sle] *vi* to totter

**chancelier** [ʃɑ̃səlje] *nm* (*allemand*) chancellor; (*d'ambassade*) secretary

**chancellerie** [ʃɑ̃sɛlRi] *nf* (*en France*) ministry of justice; (*en Allemagne*) chancellery; (*d'ambassade*) chancery

**chanceux, -euse** [ʃɑ̃sø, -øz] *adj* lucky, fortunate

**chancre** [ʃɑ̃kR(ə)] *nm* canker

**chandail** [ʃɑ̃daj] *nm* (thick) jumper *ou* sweater

**Chandeleur** [ʃɑ̃dlœR] *nf*: **la ~** Candlemas

**chandelier** [ʃɑ̃dəlje] *nm* candlestick; (*à plusieurs branches*) candelabra

**chandelle** [ʃɑ̃dɛl] *nf* (tallow) candle; (*Tennis*):

faire une ~ to lob; (*Aviat*): **monter en** ~ to climb vertically; **tenir la** ~ to play gooseberry; **dîner aux** ~**s** candlelight dinner

**change** [ʃɑ̃ʒ] *nm* (*Comm*) exchange; **opérations de** ~ (foreign) exchange transactions; **contrôle des** ~**s** exchange control; **gagner/perdre au** ~ to be better/worse off (for it); **donner le** ~ **à qn** (*fig*) to lead sb up the garden path

**changeant, e** [ʃɑ̃ʒɑ̃, -ɑ̃t] *adj* changeable, fickle

**changement** [ʃɑ̃ʒmɑ̃] *nm* change; ~ **de vitesse** (*dispositif*) gears *pl*; (*action*) gear change

**changer** [ʃɑ̃ʒe] *vt* (*modifier*) to change, alter; (*remplacer, Comm, rhabiller*) to change ▷ *vi* to change, alter; **se changer** *vi* to change (o.s.); ~ **de** (*remplacer: adresse, nom, voiture etc*) to change one's; ~ **de train** to change trains; ~ **d'air** to get a change of air; ~ **de couleur/direction** to change colour/direction; ~ **d'idée** to change one's mind; ~ **de place avec qn** to change places with sb; ~ **de vitesse** (*Auto*) to change gear; ~ **qn/qch de place** to move sb/sth to another place; ~ (**de bus** *etc*) to change (buses *etc*); ~ **qch en** to change sth into

**changeur** [ʃɑ̃ʒœR] *nm* (*personne*) moneychanger; ~ **automatique** change machine; ~ **de disques** record changer, autochange

**chanoine** [ʃanwan] *nm* canon

**chanson** [ʃɑ̃sɔ̃] *nf* song

**chansonnette** [ʃɑ̃sɔnɛt] *nf* ditty

**chansonnier** [ʃɑ̃sɔnje] *nm* cabaret artist (*specializing in political satire*); (*recueil*) song book

**chant** [ʃɑ̃] *nm* song; (*art vocal*) singing; (*d'église*) hymn; (*de poème*) canto; (*Tech*): **posé de** *ou* **sur** ~ placed edgeways; ~ **de Noël** Christmas carol

**chantage** [ʃɑ̃taʒ] *nm* blackmail; **faire du** ~ to use blackmail; **soumettre qn à un** ~ to blackmail sb

**chantant, e** [ʃɑ̃tɑ̃, -ɑ̃t] *adj* (*accent, voix*) sing-song

**chanter** [ʃɑ̃te] *vt, vi* to sing; ~ **juste/faux** to sing in tune/out of tune; **si cela lui chante** (*fam*) if he feels like it *ou* fancies it

**chanterelle** [ʃɑ̃tRɛl] *nf* chanterelle (*edible mushroom*)

**chanteur, -euse** [ʃɑ̃tœR, -øz] *nm/f* singer; ~ **de charme** crooner

**chantier** [ʃɑ̃tje] *nm* (building) site; (*sur une route*) roadworks *pl*; **mettre en** ~ to start work on; ~ **naval** shipyard

**chantilly** [ʃɑ̃tiji] *nf voir* **crème**

**chantonner** [ʃɑ̃tɔne] *vi, vt* to sing to oneself, hum

**chantre** [ʃɑ̃tR(ə)] *nm* (*fig*) eulogist

**chanvre** [ʃɑ̃vR(ə)] *nm* hemp

**chaos** [kao] *nm* chaos

**chaotique** [kaɔtik] *adj* chaotic

**chap.** *abr* (= *chapitre*) ch

**chapardage** [ʃapaRdaʒ] *nm* pilfering

**chaparder** [ʃapaRde] *vt* to pinch

**chapeau, x** [ʃapo] *nm* hat; (*Presse*) introductory paragraph; ~! well done!; ~ **melon** bowler hat; ~ **mou** trilby; ~**x de roues** hub caps

**chapeauter** [ʃapote] *vt* (*Admin*) to head, oversee

**chapelain** [ʃaplɛ̃] *nm* (*Rel*) chaplain

**chapelet** [ʃaplɛ] *nm* (*Rel*) rosary; (*fig*): **un** ~ **de** a string of; **dire son** ~ to tell one's beads

**chapelier, -ière** [ʃapəlje, -jɛR] *nm/f* hatter; milliner

**chapelle** [ʃapɛl] *nf* chapel; ~ **ardente** chapel of rest

**chapellerie** [ʃapɛlRi] *nf* (*magasin*) hat shop; (*commerce*) hat trade

**chapelure** [ʃaplyR] *nf* (dried) breadcrumbs *pl*

**chaperon** [ʃapRɔ̃] *nm* chaperon

**chaperonner** [ʃapRɔne] *vt* to chaperon

**chapiteau, x** [ʃapito] *nm* (*Archit*) capital; (*de cirque*) marquee, big top

**chapitre** [ʃapitR(ə)] *nm* chapter; (*fig*) subject, matter; **avoir voix au** ~ to have a say in the matter

**chapitrer** [ʃapitRe] *vt* to lecture, reprimand

**chapon** [ʃapɔ̃] *nm* capon

**chaque** [ʃak] *adj* each, every; (*indéfini*) every

**char** [ʃaR] *nm* (*à foin etc*) cart, waggon; (*de carnaval*) float; ~ (**d'assaut**) tank

**charabia** [ʃaRabja] *nm* (*péj*) gibberish, gobbledygook (*Brit*)

**charade** [ʃaRad] *nf* riddle; (*mimée*) charade

**charbon** [ʃaRbɔ̃] *nm* coal; ~ **de bois** charcoal

**charbonnage** [ʃaRbɔnaʒ] *nm*: **les** ~**s de France** the (French) Coal Board *sg*

**charbonnier** [ʃaRbɔnje] *nm* coalman

**charcuterie** [ʃaRkytRi] *nf* (*magasin*) pork butcher's shop and delicatessen; (*produits*) cooked pork meats *pl*

**charcutier, -ière** [ʃaRkytje, -jɛR] *nm/f* pork butcher

**chardon** [ʃaRdɔ̃] *nm* thistle

**chardonneret** [ʃaRdɔnRɛ] *nm* goldfinch

**charentais, e** [ʃaRɑ̃tɛ, -ɛz] *adj ou* from Charente ▷ *nf* (*pantoufle*) slipper

**charge** [ʃaRʒ(ə)] *nf* (*fardeau*) load; (*explosif, Élec, Mil, Jur*) charge; (*rôle, mission*) responsibility; **charges** *nfpl* (*du loyer*) service charges; **à la** ~ **de** (*dépendant de*) dependent upon, supported by; (*aux frais de*) chargeable to, payable by; **j'accepte, à** ~ **de revanche** I accept, provided I can do the same for you (in return) one day; **prendre en** ~ to take charge of; (*véhicule*) to take on; (*dépenses*) to take care of; ~ **utile** (*Auto*) live load; (*Comm*) payload; ~**s sociales** social security contributions

**chargé** [ʃaRʒe] *adj* (*voiture, animal, personne*) laden; (*fusil, batterie, caméra*) loaded; (*occupé: emploi du temps, journée*) busy, full; (*estomac*) heavy, full; (*langue*) furred; (*décoration, style*) heavy, ornate ▷ *nm*: ~ **d'affaires** chargé d'affaires; ~ **de cours** ≈ lecturer; ~ **de** (*responsable de*) responsible for

**chargement** [ʃaRʒəmɑ̃] *nm* (*action*) loading; charging; (*objets*) load

**charger** [ʃaRʒe] *vt* (*voiture, fusil, caméra*) to load; (*batterie*) to charge ▷ *vi* (*Mil etc*) to charge; **se** ~ **de** *vt* to see to, take care of; ~ **qn de qch/faire qch** to give sb the responsibility for sth/of doing sth; to put sb in charge of sth/doing sth;

se ~ **de faire qch** to take it upon o.s. to do sth

**chargeur** [ʃaʁʒœʁ] nm (dispositif: d'arme à feu) magazine; (: Photo) cartridge; ~ **de batterie** (Élec) battery charger

**chariot** [ʃaʁjo] nm trolley; (charrette) waggon; ~ **élévateur** fork-lift truck

**charisme** [kaʁism(ə)] nm charisma

**charitable** [ʃaʁitabl(ə)] adj charitable; kind

**charité** [ʃaʁite] nf charity; **faire la** ~ to give to charity; to do charitable works; **faire la** ~ **à** to give (something) to; **fête/vente de** ~ fête/sale in aid of charity

**charivari** [ʃaʁivaʁi] nm hullabaloo

**charlatan** [ʃaʁlatɑ̃] nm charlatan

**charlotte** [ʃaʁlɔt] nf (Culin) charlotte

**charmant, e** [ʃaʁmɑ̃, -ɑ̃t] adj charming

**charme** [ʃaʁm(ə)] nm charm; **charmes** nmpl (appas) charms; **c'est ce qui en fait le** ~ that is its attraction; **faire du** ~ to be charming, turn on the charm; **aller** ou **se porter comme un** ~ to be in the pink

**charmer** [ʃaʁme] vt to charm; **je suis charmé de …** I'm delighted to …

**charmeur, -euse** [ʃaʁmœʁ, -øz] nm/f charmer; ~ **de serpents** snake charmer

**charnel, le** [ʃaʁnɛl] adj carnal

**charnier** [ʃaʁnje] nm mass grave

**charnière** [ʃaʁnjɛʁ] nf hinge; (fig) turning-point

**charnu, e** [ʃaʁny] adj fleshy

**charogne** [ʃaʁɔɲ] nf carrion no pl; (fam!) bastard (!)

**charolais, e** [ʃaʁɔlɛ, -ɛz] adj of ou from the Charolais

**charpente** [ʃaʁpɑ̃t] nf frame(work); (fig) structure, framework; (carrure) build, frame

**charpenté, e** [ʃaʁpɑ̃te] adj: **bien** ou **solidement** ~ (personne) well-built; (texte) well-constructed

**charpenterie** [ʃaʁpɑ̃tʁi] nf carpentry

**charpentier** [ʃaʁpɑ̃tje] nm carpenter

**charpie** [ʃaʁpi] nf: **en** ~ (fig) in shreds ou ribbons

**charretier** [ʃaʁtje] nm carter; **de** ~ (péj: langage, manières) uncouth

**charrette** [ʃaʁɛt] nf cart

**charrier** [ʃaʁje] vt to carry (along); to cart, carry ▷ vi (fam) to exaggerate

**charrue** [ʃaʁy] nf plough (Brit), plow (US)

**charte** [ʃaʁt(ə)] nf charter

**charter** [tʃaʁtœʁ] nm (vol) charter flight; (avion) charter plane

**chasse** [ʃas] nf hunting; (au fusil) shooting; (poursuite) chase; (aussi: **chasse d'eau**) flush; **la** ~ **est ouverte** the hunting season is open; **la** ~ **est fermée** it is the close (Brit) ou closed (US) season; **aller à la** ~ to go hunting; **prendre en** ~, **donner la** ~ **à** to give chase to; **tirer la** ~ (**d'eau**) to flush the toilet, pull the chain; ~ **aérienne** aerial pursuit; ~ **à courre** hunting; ~ **à l'homme** manhunt; ~ **gardée** private hunting grounds pl; ~ **sous-marine** underwater fishing

**châsse** [ʃas] nf reliquary, shrine

**chassé-croisé** [ʃasekʁwaze] (pl **chassés-croisés**) nm (Danse) chassé-croisé; (fig) mix-up (where people miss each other in turn)

**chasse-neige** [ʃasnɛʒ] nm inv snowplough (Brit), snowplow (US)

**chasser** [ʃase] vt to hunt; (expulser) to chase away ou out, drive away ou out; (dissiper) to chase ou sweep away; to dispel, drive away

**chasseur, -euse** [ʃasœʁ, -øz] nm/f hunter ▷ nm (avion) fighter; (domestique) page (boy), messenger (boy); ~ **d'images** roving photographer; ~ **de têtes** (fig) headhunter; ~**s alpins** mountain infantry

**chassieux, -euse** [ʃasjø, -øz] adj sticky, gummy

**châssis** [ʃasi] nm (Auto) chassis; (cadre) frame; (de jardin) cold frame

**chaste** [ʃast(ə)] adj chaste

**chasteté** [ʃastəte] nf chastity

**chasuble** [ʃazybl(ə)] nf chasuble; **robe** ~ pinafore dress (Brit), jumper (US)

**chat¹** [ʃa] nm cat; ~ **sauvage** wildcat

**chat²** [tʃat] nm (Internet: salon) chat room (: conversation) chat

**châtaigne** [ʃatɛɲ] nf chestnut

**châtaignier** [ʃatɛɲe] nm chestnut (tree)

**châtain** [ʃatɛ̃] adj inv chestnut (brown); (personne) chestnut-haired

**château, x** [ʃato] nm castle; ~ **d'eau** water tower; ~ **fort** stronghold, fortified castle; ~ **de sable** sand castle

**châtelain, e** [ʃatlɛ̃, -ɛn] nm/f lord/lady of the manor ▷ nf (ceinture) chatelaine

**châtier** [ʃatje] vt to punish, castigate; (fig: style) to polish, refine

**chatière** [ʃatjɛʁ] nf (porte) cat flap

**châtiment** [ʃatimɑ̃] nm punishment, castigation; ~ **corporel** corporal punishment

**chatoiement** [ʃatwamɑ̃] nm shimmer(ing)

**chaton** [ʃatɔ̃] nm (Zool) kitten; (Bot) catkin; (de bague) bezel; stone

**chatouillement** [ʃatujmɑ̃] nm (gén) tickling; (dans le nez, la gorge) tickle

**chatouiller** [ʃatuje] vt to tickle; (l'odorat, le palais) to titillate

**chatouilleux, -euse** [ʃatujø, -øz] adj ticklish; (fig) touchy, over-sensitive

**chatoyant, e** [ʃatwajɑ̃, -ɑ̃t] adj (reflet, étoffe) shimmering; (couleurs) sparkling

**chatoyer** [ʃatwaje] vi to shimmer

**châtrer** [ʃatʁe] vt (mâle) to castrate; (femelle) to spay; (cheval) to geld; (chat, chien) to doctor (Brit), fix (US); (fig) to mutilate

**chatte** [ʃat] nf (she-)cat

**chatter** [tʃate] vi (Internet) to chat

**chatterton** [ʃatɛʁtɔn] nm (ruban isolant: Élec) (adhesive) insulating tape

**chaud, e** [ʃo, -od] adj (gén) warm; (très chaud) hot; (fig: félicitations) hearty; (discussion) heated; **il fait** ~ it's warm; it's hot; **manger** ~ to have something hot to eat; **avoir** ~ to be warm; to be hot; **tenir** ~ to keep hot; **ça me tient** ~ it keeps me warm; **tenir au** ~ to keep in a warm place;

**rester au ~** to stay in the warm
**chaudement** [ʃodmɑ̃] *adv* warmly; *(fig)* hotly
**chaudière** [ʃodjɛʀ] *nf* boiler
**chaudron** [ʃodʀɔ̃] *nm* cauldron
**chaudronnerie** [ʃodʀɔnʀi] *nf (usine)*
  boilerworks; *(activité)* boilermaking; *(boutique)*
  coppersmith's workshop
**chauffage** [ʃofaʒ] *nm* heating; **~ au gaz/à
  l'électricité/au charbon** gas/electric/solid
  fuel heating; **~ central** central heating; **~ par
  le sol** underfloor heating
**chauffagiste** [ʃofaʒist(ə)] *nm (installateur)*
  heating engineer
**chauffant, e** [ʃofɑ̃, -ɑ̃t] *adj*: **couverture ~e**
  electric blanket; **plaque ~e** hotplate
**chauffard** [ʃofaʀ] *nm (péj)* reckless driver; road
  hog; *(après un accident)* hit-and-run driver
**chauffe-bain** [ʃofbɛ̃] *nm* = **chauffe-eau**
**chauffe-biberon** [ʃofbibʀɔ̃] *nm* (baby's) bottle
  warmer
**chauffe-eau** [ʃofo] *nm inv* water heater
**chauffe-plats** [ʃofpla] *nm inv* dish warmer
**chauffer** [ʃofe] *vt* to heat ▷ *vi* to heat up, warm
  up; *(trop chauffer: moteur)* to overheat; **se
  chauffer** *vi (se mettre en train)* to warm up; *(au
  soleil)* to warm o.s.
**chaufferie** [ʃofʀi] *nf* boiler room
**chauffeur** [ʃofœʀ] *nm* driver; *(privé)* chauffeur;
  **voiture avec/sans ~** chauffeur-driven/self-
  drive car; **~ de taxi** taxi driver
**chauffeuse** [ʃoføz] *nf* fireside chair
**chauler** [ʃole] *vt (mur)* to whitewash
**chaume** [ʃom] *nm (du toit)* thatch; *(tiges)* stubble
**chaumière** [ʃomjɛʀ] *nf* (thatched) cottage
**chaussée** [ʃose] *nf* road(way); *(digue)* causeway
**chausse-pied** [ʃospje] *nm* shoe-horn
**chausser** [ʃose] *vt (bottes, skis)* to put on; *(enfant)*
  to put shoes on; *(soulier)* to fit; **~ du 38/42** to take
  size 38/42; **~ grand/bien** to be big-/well-fitting;
  **se chausser** to put one's shoes on
**chausse-trappe** [ʃostʀap] *nf* trap
**chaussette** [ʃosɛt] *nf* sock
**chausseur** [ʃosœʀ] *nm (marchand)* footwear
  specialist, shoemaker
**chausson** [ʃosɔ̃] *nm* slipper; *(de bébé)* bootee; **~
  (aux pommes)** (apple) turnover
**chaussure** [ʃosyʀ] *nf* shoe; *(commerce)*: **la ~** the
  shoe industry *ou* trade; **~s basses** flat shoes; **~s
  montantes** ankle boots; **~s de ski** ski boots
**chaut** [ʃo] *vb*: **peu me ~** it matters little to me
**chauve** [ʃov] *adj* bald
**chauve-souris** [ʃovsuʀi] *(pl* **chauves-souris**) *nf*
  bat
**chauvin, e** [ʃovɛ̃, -in] *adj* chauvinistic; jingoistic
**chauvinisme** [ʃovinism(ə)] *nm* chauvinism;
  jingoism
**chaux** [ʃo] *nf* lime; **blanchi à la ~** whitewashed
**chavirer** [ʃaviʀe] *vi* to capsize, overturn
**chef** [ʃɛf] *nm* head, leader; *(patron)* boss; *(de
  cuisine)* chef; **au premier ~** extremely, to the
  nth degree; **de son propre ~** on his *ou* her own
  initiative; **général/commandant en ~**

general-/commander-in-chief; **~ d'accusation**
  *(Jur)* charge, count (of indictment); **~ d'atelier**
  (shop) foreman; **~ de bureau** head clerk; **~ de
  clinique** senior hospital lecturer; **~
  d'entreprise** company head; **~ d'équipe** team
  leader; **~ d'état** head of state; **~ de famille**
  head of the family; **~ de file** *(de parti etc)* leader;
  **~ de gare** station master; **~ d'orchestre**
  conductor (Brit), leader (US); **~ de rayon**
  department(al) supervisor; **~ de service**
  departmental head
**chef-d'œuvre** [ʃɛdœvʀ(ə)] *(pl* **chefs-d'œuvre**)
  *nm* masterpiece
**chef-lieu** [ʃɛfljø] *(pl* **chefs-lieux**) *nm* county
  town
**cheftaine** [ʃɛftɛn] *nf* (guide) captain
**cheik, cheikh** [ʃɛk] *nm* sheik
**chemin** [ʃəmɛ̃] *nm* path; *(itinéraire, direction, trajet)*
  way; **en ~, ~ faisant** on the way; **~ de fer**
  railway (Brit), railroad (US); **~ de fer** by rail;
  **les ~s de fer** the railways (Brit), the railroad
  (US); **~ de terre** dirt track
**cheminée** [ʃəmine] *nf* chimney; *(à l'intérieur)*
  chimney piece, fireplace; *(de bateau)* funnel
**cheminement** [ʃəminmɑ̃] *nm* progress; course
**cheminer** [ʃəmine] *vi* to walk (along)
**cheminot** [ʃəmino] *nm* railwayman (Brit),
  railroad worker (US)
**chemise** [ʃəmiz] *nf* shirt; *(dossier)* folder; **~ de
  nuit** nightdress
**chemiserie** [ʃəmizʀi] *nf* (gentlemen's)
  outfitters'
**chemisette** [ʃəmizɛt] *nf* short-sleeved shirt
**chemisier** [ʃəmizje] *nm* blouse
**chenal, -aux** [ʃənal, -o] *nm* channel
**chenapan** [ʃənapɑ̃] *nm (garnement)* rascal; *(péj:
  vaurien)* rogue
**chêne** [ʃɛn] *nm* oak (tree); *(bois)* oak
**chenet** [ʃənɛ] *nm* fire-dog, andiron
**chenil** [ʃənil] *nm* kennels *pl*
**chenille** [ʃənij] *nf (Zool)* caterpillar; *(Auto)*
  caterpillar track; **véhicule à ~s** tracked vehicle,
  caterpillar
**chenillette** [ʃənijɛt] *nf* tracked vehicle
**cheptel** [ʃɛptɛl] *nm* livestock
**chèque** [ʃɛk] *nm* cheque (Brit), check (US); **faire/
  toucher un ~** to write/cash a cheque; **par ~** by
  cheque; **~ barré/sans provision** crossed (Brit) /
  bad cheque; **~ en blanc** blank cheque; **~ au
  porteur** cheque to bearer; **~ postal** post office
  cheque, ≈ giro cheque (Brit); **~ de voyage**
  traveller's cheque
**chèque-cadeau** [ʃɛkkado] *(pl* **chèques-
  cadeaux**) *nm* gift token
**chèque-repas** *(pl* **chèques-repas**) [ʃɛkʀəpa],
  **chèque-restaurant** *(pl* **chèques-restaurant**)
  [ʃɛkʀɛstɔʀɑ̃] *nm* ≈ luncheon voucher
**chéquier** [ʃekje] *nm* cheque book (Brit),
  checkbook (US)
**cher, -ère** [ʃɛʀ] *adj (aimé)* dear; *(coûteux)*
  expensive, dear ▷ *adv*: **coûter/payer ~** to cost/
  pay a lot ▷ *nf*: **la bonne chère** good food; **cela**

**coûte ~** it's expensive, it costs a lot of money; **mon ~, ma chère** my dear

**chercher** [ʃɛRʃe] vt to look for; (gloire etc) to seek; **~ des ennuis/la bagarre** to be looking for trouble/a fight; **aller ~** to go for, go and fetch; **~ à faire** to try to do

**chercheur, -euse** [ʃɛRʃœR, -øz] nm/f researcher, research worker; **~ de** seeker of; hunter of; **~ d'or** gold digger

**chère** [ʃɛR] adj f, nf voir **cher**

**chèrement** [ʃɛRmɑ̃] adv dearly

**chéri, e** [ʃeRi] adj beloved, dear; **(mon) ~** darling

**chérir** [ʃeRiR] vt to cherish

**cherté** [ʃɛRte] nf: **la ~ de la vie** the high cost of living

**chérubin** [ʃeRybɛ̃] nm cherub

**chétif, -ive** [ʃetif, -iv] adj puny, stunted

**cheval, -aux** [ʃəval, -o] nm horse; (Auto): **~ (vapeur) (CV)** horsepower no pl; **50 chevaux (au frein)** 50 brake horsepower, 50 b.h.p.; **10 chevaux (fiscaux)** 10 horsepower (for tax purposes); **faire du ~** to ride; **à ~ on** horseback; **à ~ sur** astride, straddling; (fig) overlapping; **~ d'arçons** vaulting horse; **~ à bascule** rocking horse; **~ de bataille** charger; (fig) hobby-horse; **~ de course** race horse; **chevaux de bois** (des manèges) wooden (fairground) horses; (manège) merry-go-round

**chevaleresque** [ʃəvalRɛsk(ə)] adj chivalrous

**chevalerie** [ʃəvalRi] nf chivalry; knighthood

**chevalet** [ʃəvalɛ] nm easel

**chevalier** [ʃəvalje] nm knight; **~ servant** escort

**chevalière** [ʃəvaljɛR] nf signet ring

**chevalin, e** [ʃəvalɛ̃, -in] adj of horses, equine; (péj) horsy; **boucherie ~e** horse-meat butcher's

**cheval-vapeur** [ʃəvalvapœR, ʃəvo-] (pl **chevaux-vapeur**) nm voir **cheval**

**chevauchée** [ʃəvoʃe] nf ride; cavalcade

**chevauchement** [ʃəvoʃmɑ̃] nm overlap

**chevaucher** [ʃəvoʃe] vi (aussi: **se chevaucher**) to overlap (each other) ▷ vt to be astride, straddle

**chevaux** [ʃəvo] nmpl voir **cheval**

**chevelu, e** [ʃəvly] adj with a good head of hair, hairy (péj)

**chevelure** [ʃəvlyR] nf hair no pl

**chevet** [ʃəvɛ] nm: **au ~ de qn** at sb's bedside; **lampe de ~** bedside lamp

**cheveu, x** [ʃəvø] nm hair ▷ nmpl (chevelure) hair sg; **avoir les ~x courts/en brosse** to have short hair/a crew cut; **se faire couper les ~x** to get ou have one's hair cut; **tiré par les ~x** (histoire) far-fetched

**cheville** [ʃəvij] nf (Anat) ankle; (de bois) peg; (pour enfoncer une vis) plug; **être en ~ avec qn** to be in cahoots with sb; **~ ouvrière** (fig) kingpin

**chèvre** [ʃɛvR(ə)] nf (she-)goat; **ménager la ~ et le chou** to try to please everyone

**chevreau, x** [ʃəvRo] nm kid

**chèvrefeuille** [ʃɛvRəfœj] nm honeysuckle

**chevreuil** [ʃəvRœj] nm roe deer inv; (Culin) venison

**chevron** [ʃəvRɔ̃] nm (poutre) rafter; (motif) chevron, v(-shape); **à ~s** chevron-patterned; (petits) herringbone

**chevronné, e** [ʃəvRɔne] adj seasoned, experienced

**chevrotant, e** [ʃəvRɔtɑ̃, -ɑ̃t] adj quavering

**chevroter** [ʃəvRɔte] vi (personne, voix) to quaver

**chevrotine** [ʃəvRɔtin] nf buckshot no pl

**chewing-gum** [ʃwiŋɡɔm] nm chewing gum

Ⓞ MOT-CLÉ

**chez** [ʃe] prép **1** (à la demeure de) at; (: direction) to; **chez qn** at/to sb's house ou place; **chez moi** at home; (direction) home
**2** (à l'entreprise de): **il travaille chez Renault** he works for Renault, he works at Renault('s)
**3** (+profession) at; (: direction) to; **chez le boulanger/dentiste** at ou to the baker's/dentist's
**4** (dans le caractère, l'œuvre de) in; **chez les renards/Racine** in foxes/Racine; **chez les Français** among the French; **chez lui, c'est un devoir** for him, it's a duty
▷ nm inv: **mon chez moi/ton chez toi** etc my/your etc home ou place

**chez-soi** [ʃeswa] nm inv home

**Chf. cent.** abr (= chauffage central) c.h

**chiadé, e** [ʃjade] adj (fam: fignolé, soigné) wicked

**chialer** [ʃjale] vi (fam) to blubber; **arrête de ~!** stop blubbering!

**chiant, e** [ʃjɑ̃, -ɑ̃t] adj (fam!) bloody annoying (vulgar: Brit) damn annoying; **qu'est-ce qu'il est ~!** he's such a bloody pain! (!)

**chic** [ʃik] adj inv chic, smart; (généreux) nice, decent ▷ nm stylishness; **avoir le ~ de ou pour** to have the knack of ou for; **de ~** adv off the cuff; **~!** great!, terrific!

**chicane** [ʃikan] nf (obstacle) zigzag; (querelle) squabble

**chicaner** [ʃikane] vi (ergoter): **~ sur** to quibble about

**chiche** [ʃiʃ] adj (mesquin) niggardly, mean; (pauvre) meagre (Brit), meager (US) ▷ excl (en réponse à un défi) you're on!; **tu n'es pas ~ de lui parler!** you wouldn't (dare) speak to her!

**chichement** [ʃiʃmɑ̃] adv (pauvrement) meagrely (Brit), meagerly (US); (mesquinement) meanly

**chichi** [ʃiʃi] nm (fam) fuss; **faire des ~s** to make a fuss

**chichis** [ʃiʃi] (fam) nmpl fuss sg

**chicorée** [ʃikɔRe] nf (café) chicory; (salade) endive; **~ frisée** curly endive

**chicot** [ʃiko] nm stump

**chien** [ʃjɛ̃] nm dog; (de pistolet) hammer; **temps de ~** rotten weather; **vie de ~** dog's life; **couché en ~ de fusil** curled up; **~ d'aveugle** guide dog; **~ de chasse** gun dog; **~ de garde** guard dog; **~ policier** police dog; **~ de race** pedigree dog; **~ de traîneau** husky

**chiendent** [ʃjɛ̃dɑ̃] nm couch grass

**chien-loup** [ʃjɛ̃lu] (pl **chiens-loups**) nm

wolfhound

**chienne** [ʃjɛn] *nf* (she-)dog, bitch

**chier** [ʃje] *vi* (*fam!*) to crap (!), shit (!); **faire ~ qn** (*importuner*) to bug sb; (*causer des ennuis à*) to piss sb around (!); **se faire ~** (*s'ennuyer*) to be bored rigid

**chiffe** [ʃif] *nf*: **il est mou comme une ~, c'est une ~ molle** he's spineless *ou* wet

**chiffon** [ʃifɔ̃] *nm* (piece of) rag

**chiffonné, e** [ʃifɔne] *adj* (*fatigué: visage*) worn-looking

**chiffonner** [ʃifɔne] *vt* to crumple, crease; (*tracasser*) to concern

**chiffonnier** [ʃifɔnje] *nm* ragman, rag-and-bone man; (*meuble*) chiffonier

**chiffrable** [ʃifRabl(ə)] *adj* numerable

**chiffre** [ʃifR(ə)] *nm* (*représentant un nombre*) figure; numeral; (*montant, total*) total, sum; (*d'un code*) code, cipher; **~s romains/arabes** roman/arabic figures *ou* numerals; **en ~s ronds** in round figures; **écrire un nombre en ~s** to write a number in figures; **~ d'affaires (CA)** turnover; **~ de ventes** sales figures

**chiffrer** [ʃifRe] *vt* (*dépense*) to put a figure to, assess; (*message*) to (en)code, cipher ▷ *vi*: **~ à, se ~ à** to add up to

**chignole** [ʃiɲɔl] *nf* drill

**chignon** [ʃiɲɔ̃] *nm* chignon, bun

**chiite** [ʃiit] *adj* Shiite ▷ *nm/f*: **Chiite** Shiite

**Chili** [ʃili] *nm*: **le ~** Chile

**chilien, ne** [ʃiljɛ̃, -ɛn] *adj* Chilean ▷ *nm/f*: **Chilien, ne** Chilean

**chimère** [ʃimɛR] *nf* (wild) dream, pipe dream, idle fancy

**chimérique** [ʃimeRik] *adj* (*utopique*) fanciful

**chimie** [ʃimi] *nf* chemistry

**chimio** [ʃimjɔ], **chimiothérapie** [ʃimjɔteRapi] *nf* chemotherapy

**chimique** [ʃimik] *adj* chemical; **produits ~s** chemicals

**chimiste** [ʃimist(ə)] *nm/f* chemist

**chimpanzé** [ʃɛ̃pɑ̃ze] *nm* chimpanzee

**chinchilla** [ʃɛ̃ʃila] *nm* chinchilla

**Chine** [ʃin] *nf*: **la ~** China; **la ~ libre, la république de ~** the Republic of China, Nationalist China (*Taiwan*)

**chine** [ʃin] *nm* rice paper; (*porcelaine*) china (vase)

**chiné, e** [ʃine] *adj* flecked

**chinois, e** [ʃinwa, -waz] *adj* Chinese; (*fig: péj*) pernickety, fussy ▷ *nm* (*Ling*) Chinese ▷ *nm/f*: **Chinois, e** Chinese

**chinoiserie** [ʃinwazRi], **chinoiseries** *nf(pl)* (*péj*) red tape, fuss

**chiot** [ʃjo] *nm* pup(py)

**chiper** [ʃipe] *vt* (*fam*) to pinch

**chipie** [ʃipi] *nf* shrew

**chipolata** [ʃipɔlata] *nf* chipolata

**chipoter** [ʃipɔte] *vi* (*manger*) to nibble; (*ergoter*) to quibble, haggle

**chips** [ʃips] *nfpl* (*aussi*: **pommes chips**) crisps (Brit), (potato) chips (US)

**chique** [ʃik] *nf* quid, chew

**chiquenaude** [ʃiknod] *nf* flick, flip

**chiquer** [ʃike] *vi* to chew tobacco

**chiromancie** [kiRɔmɑ̃si] *nf* palmistry

**chiromancien, ne** [kiRɔmɑ̃sjɛ̃, -ɛn] *nm/f* palmist

**chiropracteur** [kiRɔpRaktœR] *nm*, **chiropraticien, ne** [kiRɔpratisjɛ̃, -ɛn] *nm/f* chiropractor

**chirurgical, e, -aux** [ʃiRyRʒikal, -o] *adj* surgical

**chirurgie** [ʃiRyRʒi] *nf* surgery; **~ esthétique** cosmetic *ou* plastic surgery

**chirurgien** [ʃiRyRʒjɛ̃] *nm* surgeon; **~ dentiste** dental surgeon

**chiure** [ʃjyR] *nf*: **~s de mouche** fly specks

**ch.-l.** *abr* = **chef-lieu**

**chlore** [klɔR] *nm* chlorine

**chloroforme** [klɔRɔfɔRm(ə)] *nm* chloroform

**chlorophylle** [klɔRɔfil] *nf* chlorophyll

**chlorure** [klɔRyR] *nm* chloride

**choc** [ʃɔk] *nm* impact; shock; crash; (*moral*) shock; (*affrontement*) clash ▷ *adj*: **prix ~** amazing *ou* incredible price/prices; **de ~** (*troupe, traitement*) shock *cpd*; (*patron etc*) high-powered; **~ opératoire/nerveux** post-operative/nervous shock; **~ en retour** return shock; (*fig*) backlash

**chocolat** [ʃɔkɔla] *nm* chocolate; (*boisson*) (hot) chocolate; **~ chaud** hot chocolate; **~ à cuire** cooking chocolate; **~ au lait** milk chocolate; **~ en poudre** drinking chocolate

**chocolaté, e** [ʃɔkɔlate] *adj* chocolate *cpd*, chocolate-flavoured

**chocolaterie** [ʃɔkɔlatRi] *nf* (*fabrique*) chocolate factory

**chocolatier, -ière** [ʃɔkɔlatje, -jɛR] *nm/f* chocolate maker

**chœur** [kœR] *nm* (*chorale*) choir; (*Opéra, Théât*) chorus; (*Archit*) choir, chancel; **en ~** in chorus

**choir** [ʃwaR] *vi* to fall

**choisi, e** [ʃwazi] *adj* (*de premier choix*) carefully chosen; select; **textes ~s** selected writings

**choisir** [ʃwaziR] *vt* to choose; (*entre plusieurs*) to choose, select; **~ de faire qch** to choose *ou* opt to do sth

**choix** [ʃwa] *nm* choice; selection; **avoir le ~** to have the choice; **je n'avais pas le ~** I had no choice; **de premier ~** (*Comm*) class *ou* grade one; **de ~** choice *cpd*, selected; **au ~** as you wish *ou* prefer; **de mon/son ~** of my/his *ou* her choosing

**choléra** [kɔleRa] *nm* cholera

**cholestérol** [kɔlesteRɔl] *nm* cholesterol

**chômage** [ʃomaʒ] *nm* unemployment; **mettre au ~** to make redundant, put out of work; **être au ~** to be unemployed *ou* out of work; **~ partiel** short-time working; **~ structurel** structural unemployment; **~ technique** lay-offs *pl*

**chômer** [ʃome] *vi* to be unemployed, be idle; **jour chômé** public holiday

**chômeur, -euse** [ʃomœR, -øz] *nm/f* unemployed person, person out of work

**chope** [ʃɔp] *nf* tankard

**choper** [ʃope] (*fam*) *vt* (*objet, maladie*) to catch

**choquant, e** [ʃɔkɑ̃, -ɑ̃t] *adj* shocking

**choquer** [ʃɔke] vt (offenser) to shock; (commotionner) to shake (up)

**choral, e** [kɔRal] adj choral ▷ nf choral society, choir

**chorégraphe** [kɔRegRaf] nm/f choreographer

**chorégraphie** [kɔRegRafi] nf choreography

**choriste** [kɔRist(ə)] nm/f choir member; (Opéra) chorus member

**chorus** [kɔRys] nm: **faire ~ (avec)** to voice one's agreement (with)

**chose** [ʃoz] nf thing ▷ nm (fam: machin) thingamajig ▷ adj inv: **être/se sentir tout ~** (bizarre) to be/feel a bit odd; (malade) to be/feel out of sorts; **dire bien des ~s à qn** to give sb's regards to sb; **parler de ~(s) et d'autre(s)** to talk about one thing and another; **c'est peu de ~** it's nothing much

**chou, x** [ʃu] nm cabbage ▷ adj inv cute; **mon petit ~** (my) sweetheart; **faire ~ blanc** to draw a blank; **feuille de ~** (fig: journal) rag; **~ à la crème** cream bun (made of choux pastry); **~ de Bruxelles** Brussels sprout

**choucas** [ʃuka] nm jackdaw

**chouchou, te** [ʃuʃu, -ut] nm/f (Scol) teacher's pet

**chouchouter** [ʃuʃute] vt to pet

**choucroute** [ʃukRut] nf sauerkraut; **~ garnie** sauerkraut with cooked meats and potatoes

**chouette** [ʃwɛt] nf owl ▷ adj (fam) great, smashing

**chou-fleur** [ʃuflœR] (pl **choux-fleurs**) nm cauliflower

**chou-rave** [ʃuRav] (pl **choux-raves**) nm kohlrabi

**choyer** [ʃwaje] vt to cherish; to pamper

**CHR** sigle m = **Centre hospitalier régional**

**chrétien, ne** [kRetjɛ̃, -ɛn] adj, nm/f Christian

**chrétiennement** [kRetjɛnmɑ̃] adv in a Christian way ou spirit

**chrétienté** [kRetjɛ̃te] nf Christendom

**Christ** [kRist] nm: **le ~** Christ; **christ** (crucifix etc) figure of Christ; **Jésus ~** Jesus Christ

**christianiser** [kRistjanize] vt to convert to Christianity

**christianisme** [kRistjanism(ə)] nm Christianity

**chromatique** [kRɔmatik] adj chromatic

**chrome** [kRom] nm chromium; (revêtement) chrome, chromium

**chromé, e** [kRome] adj chrome-plated, chromium-plated

**chromosome** [kRɔmozom] nm chromosome

**chronique** [kRɔnik] adj chronic ▷ nf (de journal) column, page; (historique) chronicle; (Radio, TV): **la ~ sportive/théâtrale** the sports/theatre review; **la ~ locale** local news and gossip

**chroniqueur** [kRɔnikœR] nm columnist; chronicler

**chrono** [kRɔnɔ] nm (fam) = **chronomètre**

**chronologie** [kRɔnɔlɔʒi] nf chronology

**chronologique** [kRɔnɔlɔʒik] adj chronological

**chronologiquement** [kRɔnɔlɔʒikmɑ̃] adv chronologically

**chronomètre** [kRɔnɔmetR(ə)] nm stopwatch

**chronométrer** [kRɔnɔmetRe] vt to time

**chronométreur** [kRɔnɔmetRœR] nm timekeeper

**chrysalide** [kRizalid] nf chrysalis

**chrysanthème** [kRizɑ̃tɛm] nm chrysanthemum

**CHU** sigle m (= Centre hospitalo-universitaire) ≈ (teaching) hospital

**chu, e** [ʃy] pp de **choir**

**chuchotement** [ʃyʃɔtmɑ̃] nm whisper

**chuchoter** [ʃyʃɔte] vt, vi to whisper

**chuintement** [ʃɥɛ̃tmɑ̃] nm hiss

**chuinter** [ʃɥɛ̃te] vi to hiss

**chut** excl [ʃyt] sh! ▷ vb [ʃy] voir **choir**

**chute** [ʃyt] nf fall; (de bois, papier: déchet) scrap; **la ~ des cheveux** hair loss; **faire une ~ (de 10 m)** to fall (10 m); **~s de pluie/neige** rain/snowfalls; **~ (d'eau)** waterfall; **~ du jour** nightfall; **~ libre** free fall; **~ des reins** small of the back

**Chypre** [ʃipR] nm Cyprus

**chypriote** [ʃipRiɔt] adj, nm/f = **cypriote**

**-ci, ci-** [si] adv voir **par**; **ci-contre**; **ci-joint** etc ▷ adj dém: **ce garçon~/-là** this/that boy; **ces femmes~/-là** these/those women

**CIA** sigle f CIA

**cial** abr = **commercial**

**ciao** [tʃao] excl (fam) (bye-)bye

**ci-après** [siapRɛ] adv hereafter

**cibiste** [sibist(ə)] nm CB enthusiast

**cible** [sibl(ə)] nf target

**cibler** [sible] vt to target

**ciboire** [sibwaR] nm ciborium (vessel)

**ciboule** [sibul] nf (large) chive

**ciboulette** [sibulɛt] nf (small) chive

**ciboulot** [sibulo] nm (fam) head, nut; **il n'a rien dans le ~** he's got nothing between his ears

**cicatrice** [sikatRis] nf scar

**cicatriser** [sikatRize] vt to heal; **se cicatriser** to heal (up), form a scar

**ci-contre** [sikɔ̃tR(ə)] adv opposite

**CICR** sigle m (= Comité international de la Croix-Rouge) ICRC

**ci-dessous** [sidəsu] adv below

**ci-dessus** [sidəsy] adv above

**ci-devant** [sidəvɑ̃] nm/f inv aristocrat who lost his/her title in the French Revolution

**CIDJ** sigle m (= Centre d'information et de documentation de la jeunesse) careers advisory service

**cidre** [sidR(ə)] nm cider

**cidrerie** [sidRəRi] nf cider factory

**Cie** abr (= compagnie) Co

**ciel** [sjɛl] nm sky; (Rel) heaven; **ciels** nmpl (Peinture etc) skies; **cieux** nmpl sky sg, skies; (Rel) heaven sg; **à ~ ouvert** open-air; (mine) opencast; **tomber du ~** (arriver à l'improviste) to appear out of the blue; (être stupéfait) to be unable to believe one's eyes; **C~!** good heavens!; **~ de lit** canopy

**cierge** [sjɛRʒ(ə)] nm candle; **~ pascal** Easter candle

**cieux** [sjø] nmpl voir **ciel**

**cigale** [sigal] nf cicada

**cigare** [sigaR] nm cigar

**cigarette** [sigaRɛt] nf cigarette; **~ (à) bout**

**filtre** filter cigarette
**ci-gît** [siʒi] adv here lies
**cigogne** [sigɔɲ] nf stork
**ciguë** [sigy] nf hemlock
**ci-inclus, e** [siɛ̃kly, -yz] adj, adv enclosed
**ci-joint, e** [siʒwɛ̃, -ɛ̃t] adj, adv enclosed; **veuillez trouver ~** please find enclosed
**cil** [sil] nm (eye)lash
**ciller** [sije] vi to blink
**cimaise** [simɛz] nf picture rail
**cime** [sim] nf top; (montagne) peak
**ciment** [simɑ̃] nm cement; **~ armé** reinforced concrete
**cimenter** [simɑ̃te] vt to cement
**cimenterie** [simɑ̃tʀi] nf cement works sg
**cimetière** [simtjɛʀ] nm cemetery; (d'église) churchyard; **~ de voitures** scrapyard
**cinéaste** [sineast(ə)] nm/f film-maker
**ciné-club** [sineklœb] nm film club; film society
**cinéma** [sinema] nm cinema; **aller au ~** to go to the cinema ou pictures ou movies; **~ d'animation** cartoon (film)
**cinémascope**® [sinemaskɔp] nm Cinemascope®
**cinémathèque** [sinematɛk] nf film archives pl ou library
**cinématographie** [sinematɔgʀafi] nf cinematography
**cinématographique** [sinematɔgʀafik] adj film cpd, cinema cpd
**cinéphile** [sinefil] nm/f film buff
**cinérama**® [sineʀama] nm: **en ~** in Cinerama®
**cinétique** [sinetik] adj kinetic
**cingalais, cinghalais, e** [sɛ̃galɛ, -ɛz] adj Sin(g)halese
**cinglant, e** [sɛ̃glɑ̃, -ɑ̃t] adj (propos, ironie) scathing, biting; (échec) crushing
**cinglé, e** [sɛ̃gle] adj (fam) crazy
**cingler** [sɛ̃gle] vt to lash; (fig) to sting ▷ vi (Navig): **~ vers** to make ou head for
**cinq** [sɛ̃k] num five
**cinquantaine** [sɛ̃kɑ̃tɛn] nf: **une ~ (de)** about fifty; **avoir la ~** (âge) to be around fifty
**cinquante** [sɛ̃kɑ̃t] num fifty
**cinquantenaire** [sɛ̃kɑ̃tnɛʀ] adj, nm/f fifty-year-old
**cinquantième** [sɛ̃kɑ̃tjɛm] num fiftieth
**cinquième** [sɛ̃kjɛm] num fifth
**cinquièmement** [sɛ̃kjɛmmɑ̃] adv fifthly
**cintre** [sɛ̃tʀ(ə)] nm coat-hanger; (Archit) arch; **plein ~** semicircular arch
**cintré, e** [sɛ̃tʀe] adj curved; (chemise) fitted, slim-fitting
**CIO** sigle m (= Comité international olympique) IOC (= International Olympic Committee); (= centre d'information et d'orientation) careers advisory centre
**cirage** [siʀaʒ] nm (shoe) polish
**circoncis, e** [siʀkɔ̃si, -iz] adj circumcized
**circoncision** [siʀkɔ̃sizjɔ̃] nf circumcision
**circonférence** [siʀkɔ̃feʀɑ̃s] nf circumference

**circonflexe** [siʀkɔ̃flɛks(ə)] adj: **accent ~** circumflex accent
**circonlocution** [siʀkɔ̃lɔkysjɔ̃] nf circumlocution
**circonscription** [siʀkɔ̃skʀipsjɔ̃] nf district; **~ électorale** (d'un député) constituency; **~ militaire** military area
**circonscrire** [siʀkɔ̃skʀiʀ] vt to define, delimit; (incendie) to contain; (propriété) to mark out; (sujet) to define
**circonspect, e** [siʀkɔ̃spɛkt] adj circumspect, cautious
**circonspection** [siʀkɔ̃spɛksjɔ̃] nf circumspection, caution
**circonstance** [siʀkɔ̃stɑ̃s] nf circumstance; (occasion) occasion; **œuvre de ~** occasional work; **air de ~** fitting air; **tête de ~** appropriate demeanour (Brit) ou demeanor (US); **~s atténuantes** mitigating circumstances
**circonstancié, e** [siʀkɔ̃stɑ̃sje] adj detailed
**circonstanciel, le** [siʀkɔ̃stɑ̃sjɛl] adj: **complément/proposition ~(le)** adverbial phrase/clause
**circonvenir** [siʀkɔ̃vniʀ] vt to circumvent
**circonvolutions** [siʀkɔ̃vɔlysjɔ̃] nfpl twists, convolutions
**circuit** [siʀkɥi] nm (trajet) tour, (round) trip; (Élec, Tech) circuit; **~ automobile** motor circuit; **~ de distribution** distribution network; **~ fermé** closed circuit; **~ intégré** integrated circuit
**circulaire** [siʀkylɛʀ] adj, nf circular
**circulation** [siʀkylasjɔ̃] nf circulation; (Auto): **la ~** (the) traffic; **bonne/mauvaise ~** good/bad circulation; **mettre en ~** to put into circulation
**circulatoire** [siʀkylatwaʀ] adj: **avoir des troubles ~s** to have problems with one's circulation
**circuler** [siʀkyle] vi to drive (along); to walk along; (train etc) to run; (sang, devises) to circulate; **faire ~** (nouvelle) to spread (about), circulate; (badauds) to move on
**cire** [siʀ] nf wax; **~ à cacheter** sealing wax
**ciré** [siʀe] nm oilskin
**cirer** [siʀe] vt to wax, polish
**cireur** [siʀœʀ] nm shoeshine boy
**cireuse** [siʀøz] nf floor polisher
**cireux, -euse** [siʀø, -øz] adj (fig: teint) sallow, waxen
**cirque** [siʀk(ə)] nm circus; (arène) amphitheatre (Brit), amphitheater (US); (Géo) cirque; (fig: désordre) chaos, bedlam; (: chichis) carry-on
**cirrhose** [siʀoz] nf: **~ du foie** cirrhosis of the liver
**cisaille** [sizaj], **cisailles** nf(pl) (gardening) shears pl
**cisailler** [sizaje] vt to clip
**ciseau, x** [sizo] nm: **~ (à bois)** chisel ▷ nmpl (pair of) scissors; **sauter en ~x** to do a scissors jump; **~ à froid** cold chisel
**ciseler** [sizle] vt to chisel, carve
**ciselure** [sizlyʀ] nf engraving; (bois) carving

**Cisjordanie** [sisʒɔʀdani] *nf:* **la** ~ the West Bank (of Jordan)
**citadelle** [sitadɛl] *nf* citadel
**citadin, e** [sitadɛ̃, -in] *nm/f* city dweller ▷ *adj* town *cpd*, city *cpd*, urban
**citation** [sitasjɔ̃] *nf* (*d'auteur*) quotation; (*Jur*) summons *sg*; (*Mil: récompense*) mention
**cité** [site] *nf* town; (*plus grande*) city; ~ **ouvrière** (workers') housing estate; ~ **universitaire** students' residences *pl*
**cité-dortoir** [sitedɔʀtwaʀ] (*pl* **cités-dortoirs**) *nf* dormitory town
**cité-jardin** [siteʒaʀdɛ̃] (*pl* **cités-jardins**) *nf* garden city
**citer** [site] *vt* (*un auteur*) to quote (from); (*nommer*) to name; (*Jur*) to summon; ~ **(en exemple)** (*personne*) to hold up (as an example); **je ne veux** ~ **personne** I don't want to name names
**citerne** [sitɛʀn(ə)] *nf* tank
**cithare** [sitaʀ] *nf* zither
**citoyen, ne** [sitwajɛ̃, -ɛn] *nm/f* citizen
**citoyenneté** [sitwajɛnte] *nf* citizenship
**citrique** [sitʀik] *adj:* **acide** ~ citric acid
**citron** [sitʀɔ̃] *nm* lemon; ~ **pressé** (fresh) lemon juice; ~ **vert** lime
**citronnade** [sitʀɔnad] *nf* lemonade
**citronné, e** [sitʀɔne] *adj* (*boisson*) lemon-flavoured (*Brit*) *ou* -flavored (*US*); (*eau de toilette*) lemon-scented
**citronnelle** [sitʀɔnɛl] *nf* citronella
**citronnier** [sitʀɔnje] *nm* lemon tree
**citrouille** [sitʀuj] *nf* pumpkin
**cive** [siv] *nf* chive
**civet** [sivɛ] *nm* stew; ~ **de lièvre** jugged hare
**civette** [sivɛt] *nf* (*Bot*) chives *pl*; (*Zool*) civet (cat)
**civière** [sivjɛʀ] *nf* stretcher
**civil, e** [sivil] *adj* (*Jur, Admin, poli*) civil; (*non militaire*) civilian ▷ *nm* civilian; **en** ~ in civilian clothes; **dans la** ~ in civilian life
**civilement** [sivilmɑ̃] *adv* (*poliment*) civilly; **se marier** ~ to have a civil wedding
**civilisation** [sivilizasjɔ̃] *nf* civilization
**civilisé, e** [sivilize] *adj* civilized
**civiliser** [sivilize] *vt* to civilize
**civilité** [sivilite] *nf* civility; **présenter ses ~s** to present one's compliments
**civique** [sivik] *adj* civic; **instruction** ~ (*Scol*) civics *sg*
**civisme** [sivism(ə)] *nm* public-spiritedness
**cl.** *abr* (= *centilitre*) cl
**clafoutis** [klafuti] *nm* batter pudding (*containing fruit*)
**claie** [klɛ] *nf* grid, riddle
**clair, e** [klɛʀ] *adj* light; (*chambre*) light, bright; (*eau, son, fig*) clear ▷ *adv:* **voir** ~ to see clearly ▷ *nm:* **mettre au** ~ (*notes etc*) to tidy up; **tirer qch au** ~ to clear sth up, clarify sth; **bleu** ~ light blue; **pour être** ~ so as to make it plain; **y voir** ~ (*comprendre*) to understand, see; **le plus** ~ **de son temps/argent** the better part of his time/money; **en** ~ (*non codé*) in clear; ~ **de lune** moonlight

**claire** [klɛʀ] *nf:* (**huître de**) ~ fattened oyster
**clairement** [klɛʀmɑ̃] *adv* clearly
**claire-voie** [klɛʀvwa]: **à** ~ *adj* letting the light through; openwork *cpd*
**clairière** [klɛʀjɛʀ] *nf* clearing
**clair-obscur** [klɛʀɔpskyʀ] (*pl* **clairs-obscurs**) *nm* half-light; (*fig*) uncertainty
**clairon** [klɛʀɔ̃] *nm* bugle
**claironner** [klɛʀɔne] *vt* (*fig*) to trumpet, shout from the rooftops
**clairsemé, e** [klɛʀsəme] *adj* sparse
**clairvoyance** [klɛʀvwajɑ̃s] *nf* clear-sightedness
**clairvoyant, e** [klɛʀvwajɑ̃, -ɑ̃t] *adj* perceptive, clear-sighted
**clam** [klam] *nm* (*Zool*) clam
**clamer** [klame] *vt* to proclaim
**clameur** [klamœʀ] *nf* clamour (*Brit*), clamor (*US*)
**clan** [klɑ̃] *nm* clan
**clandestin, e** [klɑ̃dɛstɛ̃, -in] *adj* clandestine, covert; (*Pol*) underground, clandestine; **passager** ~ stowaway
**clandestinement** [klɑ̃dɛstinmɑ̃] *adv* secretly; **s'embarquer** ~ to stow away
**clandestinité** [klɑ̃dɛstinite] *nf:* **dans la** ~ (*en secret*) under cover; (*en se cachant: vivre*) underground; **entrer dans la** ~ to go underground
**clapet** [klapɛ] *nm* (*Tech*) valve
**clapier** [klapje] *nm* (*rabbit*) hutch
**clapotement** [klapɔtmɑ̃] *nm* lap(ping)
**clapoter** [klapɔte] *vi* to lap
**clapotis** [klapɔti] *nm* lap(ping)
**claquage** [klakaʒ] *nm* pulled *ou* strained muscle
**claque** [klak] *nf* (*gifle*) slap; (*Théât*) claque ▷ *nm* (*chapeau*) opera hat
**claquement** [klakmɑ̃] *nm* (*de porte: bruit répété*) banging; (: *bruit isolé*) slam
**claquemurer** [klakmyʀe]: **se claquemurer** *vi* to shut o.s. away, closet o.s
**claquer** [klake] *vi* (*drapeau*) to flap; (*porte*) to bang, slam; (*coup de feu*) to ring out ▷ *vt* (*porte*) to slam, bang; (*doigts*) to snap; **elle claquait des dents** her teeth were chattering; **se** ~ **un muscle** to pull *ou* strain a muscle
**claquettes** [klakɛt] *nfpl* tap-dancing *sg*
**clarification** [klaʀifikasjɔ̃] *nf* (*fig*) clarification
**clarifier** [klaʀifje] *vt* (*fig*) to clarify
**clarinette** [klaʀinɛt] *nf* clarinet
**clarinettiste** [klaʀinetist(ə)] *nm/f* clarinettist
**clarté** [klaʀte] *nf* lightness; brightness; (*d'un son, de l'eau*) clearness; (*d'une explication*) clarity
**classe** [klɑs] *nf* class; (*Scol: local*) class(room); (: *leçon*) class; (: *élèves*) class, form; **1ère/2ème** ~ 1st/2nd class; **un (soldat de) deuxième** ~ (*Mil: armée de terre*) private (soldier); (: *armée de l'air*) ≈ aircraftman (*Brit*), ≈ airman basic (*US*); **de** ~ luxury *cpd*; **faire ses ~s** (*Mil*) to do one's (recruit's) training; **faire la** ~ (*Scol*) to be a *ou* the teacher; to teach; **aller en** ~ to go to school; **aller en** ~ **verte/de neige/de mer** to go to the countryside/skiing/to the seaside with the

school; ~ **préparatoire** *class which prepares students for the Grandes Écoles entry exams; see note;* ~ **sociale** social class; ~ **touriste** economy class

⊚ **CLASSES PRÉPARATOIRES**
⊚
⊚ *Classes préparatoires* are the two years of
⊚ intensive study which coach students for
⊚ the competitive entry examinations to the
⊚ "grandes écoles". These extremely
⊚ demanding courses follow the
⊚ "baccalauréat" and are usually done at a
⊚ "lycée". Schools which provide such classes
⊚ are more highly regarded than those which
⊚ do not.

**classement** [klɑsmɑ̃] *nm* classifying; filing; grading; closing; *(rang: Scol)* place; *(: Sport)* placing; *(liste: Scol)* class list (in order of merit); *(: Sport)* placings *pl*; **premier au ~ général** *(Sport)* first overall

**classer** [klɑse] *vt (idées, livres)* to classify; *(papiers)* to file; *(candidat, concurrent)* to grade; *(personne: juger: péj)* to rate; *(Jur: affaire)* to close; **se ~ premier/dernier** to come first/last; *(Sport)* to finish first/last

**classeur** [klɑsœʀ] *nm* file; *(meuble)* filing cabinet; ~ **à feuillets mobiles** ring binder

**classification** [klasifikasjɔ̃] *nf* classification

**classifier** [klasifje] *vt* to classify

**classique** [klasik] *adj* classical; *(habituel)* standard, classic ▷ *nm* classic; classical author; **études ~s** classical studies, classics

**claudication** [klodikasjɔ̃] *nf* limp

**clause** [kloz] *nf* clause

**claustrer** [klostʀe] *vt* to confine

**claustrophobie** [klostʀɔfɔbi] *nf* claustrophobia

**clavecin** [klavsɛ̃] *nm* harpsichord

**claveciniste** [klavsinist(ə)] *nm/f* harpsichordist

**clavicule** [klavikyl] *nf* clavicle, collarbone

**clavier** [klavje] *nm* keyboard

**clé, clef** [kle] *nf* key; *(Mus)* clef; *(de mécanicien)* spanner *(Brit)*, wrench *(US)* ▷ *adj*: **problème/position** ~ key problem/position; **mettre sous ~** to place under lock and key; **prendre la ~ des champs** to run away, make off; **prix ~s en main** *(d'une voiture)* on-the-road price; *(d'un appartement)* price with immediate entry; ~ **de sol/de fa/d'ut** treble/bass/alto clef; **livre/film** *etc* **à ~** *book/film etc in which real people are depicted under fictitious names;* **à la ~** *(à la fin)* at the end of it all; ~ **anglaise** = **clé à molette**; ~ **de contact** ignition key; ~ **à molette** adjustable spanner *(Brit)* ou wrench, monkey wrench; ~ **USB** USB key; ~ **de voûte** keystone

**clématite** [klematit] *nf* clematis

**clémence** [klemɑ̃s] *nf* mildness; leniency

**clément, e** [klemɑ̃, -ɑ̃t] *adj (temps)* mild; *(indulgent)* lenient

**clémentine** [klemɑ̃tin] *nf (Bot)* clementine

**clenche** [klɑ̃ʃ] *nf* latch

**cleptomane** [klɛptɔman] *nm/f* = **kleptomane**

**clerc** [klɛʀ] *nm*: ~ **de notaire** *ou* **d'avoué** lawyer's clerk

**clergé** [klɛʀʒe] *nm* clergy

**clérical, e, -aux** [kleʀikal, -o] *adj* clerical

**cliché** [kliʃe] *nm (Photo)* negative; print; *(Typo)* (printing) plate; *(Ling)* cliché

**client, e** [klijɑ̃, -ɑ̃t] *nm/f (acheteur)* customer, client; *(d'hôtel)* guest, patron; *(du docteur)* patient; *(de l'avocat)* client

**clientèle** [klijɑ̃tɛl] *nf (du magasin)* customers *pl*, clientèle; *(du docteur, de l'avocat)* practice; **accorder sa ~ à** to give one's custom to; **retirer sa ~ à** to take one's business away from

**cligner** [kliɲe] *vi*: ~ **des yeux** to blink (one's eyes); ~ **de l'œil** to wink

**clignotant** [kliɲɔtɑ̃] *nm (Auto)* indicator

**clignoter** [kliɲɔte] *vi (étoiles etc)* to twinkle; *(lumière: à intervalles réguliers)* to flash; *(: vaciller)* to flicker; *(yeux)* to blink

**climat** [klima] *nm* climate

**climatique** [klimatik] *adj* climatic

**climatisation** [klimatizasjɔ̃] *nf* air conditioning

**climatisé, e** [klimatize] *adj* air-conditioned

**climatiseur** [klimatizœʀ] *nm* air conditioner

**clin d'œil** [klɛ̃dœj] *nm* wink; **en un clin d'œil** in a flash

**clinique** [klinik] *adj* clinical ▷ *nf* nursing home, (private) clinic

**clinquant, e** [klɛ̃kɑ̃, -ɑ̃t] *adj* flashy

**clip** [klip] *nm (pince)* clip; *(vidéo)* pop *(ou promotional)* video

**clique** [klik] *nf (péj: bande)* clique, set; **prendre ses ~s et ses claques** to pack one's bags

**cliquer** [klike] *vi (Inform)* to click; ~ **deux fois** to double-click

**cliqueter** [klikte] *vi* to clash; *(ferraille, clefs, monnaie)* to jangle, jingle; *(verres)* to chink

**cliquetis** [klikti] *nm* jangle; jingle; chink

**clitoris** [klitɔʀis] *nm* clitoris

**clivage** [klivaʒ] *nm* cleavage; *(fig)* rift, split

**cloaque** [klɔak] *nm (fig)* cesspit

**clochard, e** [klɔʃaʀ, -aʀd(ə)] *nm/f* tramp

**cloche** [klɔʃ] *nf (d'église)* bell; *(fam)* clot; *(chapeau)* cloche (hat); ~ **à fromage** cheese-cover

**cloche-pied** [klɔʃpje]: **à ~** *adv* on one leg, hopping (along)

**clocher** [klɔʃe] *nm* church tower; *(en pointe)* steeple ▷ *vi (fam)* to be *ou* go wrong; **de ~** *(péj)* parochial

**clocheton** [klɔʃtɔ̃] *nm* pinnacle

**clochette** [klɔʃɛt] *nf* bell

**clodo** [klɔdo] *nm (fam:* = *clochard)* tramp

**cloison** [klwazɔ̃] *nf* partition (wall); ~ **étanche** *(fig)* impenetrable barrier, brick wall *(fig)*

**cloisonner** [klwazɔne] *vt* to partition (off), to divide up; *(fig)* to compartmentalize

**cloître** [klwatʀ(ə)] *nm* cloister

**cloîtrer** [klwatʀe] *vt*: **se cloîtrer** to shut o.s. away; *(Rel)* to enter a convent *ou* monastery

**clonage** [klonaʒ] *nm* cloning

**clone** [klon] *nm* clone

**cloner** [klone] vt to clone
**clope** [klɔp] (fam) nm ou f fag (Brit), cigarette
**clopin-clopant** [klɔpɛ̃klɔpɑ̃] adv hobbling along; (fig) so-so
**clopiner** [klɔpine] vi to hobble along
**cloporte** [klɔpɔʀt(ə)] nm woodlouse
**cloque** [klɔk] nf blister
**cloqué, e** [klɔke] adj: **étoffe ~e** seersucker
**cloquer** [klɔke] vi (peau, peinture) to blister
**clore** [klɔʀ] vt to close; **~ une session** (Inform) to log out
**clos, e** [klo, -oz] pp de **clore** ▷ adj voir **maison; huis; vase** ▷ nm (enclosed) field
**clôt** [klo] vb voir **clore**
**clôture** [klotyʀ] nf closure, closing; (barrière) enclosure, fence
**clôturer** [klotyʀe] vt (terrain) to enclose, close off; (festival, débats) to close
**clou** [klu] nm nail; (Méd) boil; **clous** nmpl = **passage clouté; pneus à ~s** studded tyres; **le ~ du spectacle** the highlight of the show; **~ de girofle** clove
**clouer** [klue] vt to nail down (ou up); (fig): **~ sur/ contre** to pin to/against
**clouté, e** [klute] adj studded
**clown** [klun] nm clown; **faire le ~** (fig) to clown (about), play the fool
**clownerie** [klunʀi] nf clowning no pl; **faire des ~s** to clown around
**club** [klœb] nm club
**CM** sigle f = **chambre des métiers** ▷ sigle m = **conseil municipal**; (Scol) = **cours moyen**
**cm.** abr (= centimètre) cm
**CMU** sigle f (= couverture maladie universelle) system of free health care for those on low incomes
**CNAT** sigle f (= Commission nationale d'aménagement du territoire) national development agency
**CNC** sigle m (= Conseil national de la consommation) national consumers' council
**CNDP** sigle m = **Centre national de documentation pédagogique**
**CNE** sigle m (= Contrat nouvelles embauches) less stringent type of employment contract for use by small companies
**CNED** sigle m (= Centre national d'enseignement à distance) ≈ Open University
**CNIL** sigle f (= Commission nationale de l'informatique et des libertés) board which enforces law on data protection
**CNIT** sigle m (= Centre national des industries et des techniques) exhibition centre in Paris
**CNJA** sigle m (= Centre national des jeunes agriculteurs) farmers' union
**CNL** sigle f (= Confédération nationale du logement) consumer group for housing
**CNRS** sigle m = **Centre national de la recherche scientifique**
**c/o** abr (= care of) c/o
**coagulant** [kɔagylɑ̃] nm (Méd) coagulant
**coaguler** [kɔagyle]: **se coaguler** vi to coagulate
**coaliser** [kɔalize]: **se coaliser** vi to unite, join forces

**coalition** [kɔalisjɔ̃] nf coalition
**coasser** [kɔase] vi to croak
**coauteur** [kɔotœʀ] nm co-author
**coaxial, e, -aux** [kɔaksjal, -o] adj coaxial
**cobaye** [kɔbaj] nm guinea-pig
**cobra** [kɔbʀa] nm cobra
**coca®** [kɔka] nm Coke®
**cocagne** [kɔkaɲ] nf: **pays de ~** land of plenty; **mât de ~** greasy pole (fig)
**cocaïne** [kɔkain] nf cocaine
**cocarde** [kɔkaʀd(ə)] nf rosette
**cocardier, -ière** [kɔkaʀdje, -jɛʀ] adj jingoistic, chauvinistic; militaristic
**cocasse** [kɔkas] adj comical, funny
**coccinelle** [kɔksinɛl] nf ladybird (Brit), ladybug (US)
**coccyx** [kɔksis] nm coccyx
**cocher** [kɔʃe] nm coachman ▷ vt to tick off; (entailler) to notch
**cochère** [kɔʃɛʀ] adj f voir **porte**
**cochon, ne** [kɔʃɔ̃, -ɔn] nm pig ▷ nm/f (péj: sale) (filthy) pig; (: méchant) swine ▷ adj (fam) dirty, smutty; **~ d'Inde** guinea-pig; **~ de lait** (Culin) sucking pig
**cochonnaille** [kɔʃɔnaj] nf (péj: charcuterie) (cold) pork
**cochonnerie** [kɔʃɔnʀi] nf (fam: saleté) filth; (: marchandises) rubbish, trash
**cochonnet** [kɔʃɔnɛ] nm (Boules) jack
**cocker** [kɔkɛʀ] nm cocker spaniel
**cocktail** [kɔktɛl] nm cocktail; (réception) cocktail party
**coco** [kɔko] nm voir **noix**; (fam) bloke (Brit), dude (US)
**cocon** [kɔkɔ̃] nm cocoon
**cocorico** [kɔkɔʀiko] excl, nm cock-a-doodle-do
**cocotier** [kɔkɔtje] nm coconut palm
**cocotte** [kɔkɔt] nf (en fonte) casserole; **ma ~** (fam) sweetie (pie); **~ (minute)®** pressure cooker; **~ en papier** paper shape
**cocu** [kɔky] nm cuckold
**code** [kɔd] nm code; **se mettre en ~(s)** to dip (Brit) ou dim (US) one's (head)lights; **~ à barres** bar code; **~ de caractère** (Inform) character code; **~ civil** Common Law; **~ machine** machine code; **~ pénal** penal code; **~ postal** (numéro) postcode (Brit), zip code (US); **~ de la route** highway code; **~ secret** cipher
**codéine** [kɔdein] nf codeine
**coder** [kɔde] vt to (en)code
**codétenu, e** [kɔdetny] nm/f fellow prisoner ou inmate
**codicille** [kɔdisil] nm codicil
**codifier** [kɔdifje] vt to codify
**codirecteur, -trice** [kɔdiʀɛktœʀ, -tʀis] nm/f co-director
**coéditeur, -trice** [kɔeditœʀ, -tʀis] nm/f co-publisher; (rédacteur) co-editor
**coefficient** [kɔefisjɑ̃] nm coefficient; **~ d'erreur** margin of error
**coéquipier, -ière** [kɔekipje, -jɛʀ] nm/f team-mate, partner

**coercition** [kɔɛRsisjɔ̃] nf coercion
**cœur** [kœR] nm heart; (Cartes: couleur) hearts pl; (: carte) heart; (Culin:) ~ **de laitue/d'artichaut** lettuce/artichoke heart; (fig:) ~ **du débat** heart of the debate; ~ **de l'été** height of summer; ~ **de la forêt** depths pl of the forest; **affaire de** ~ love affair; **avoir bon** ~ to be kind-hearted; **avoir mal au** ~ to feel sick; **contre** ou **sur son** ~ to one's breast; **opérer qn à** ~ **ouvert** to perform open-heart surgery on sb; **recevoir qn à** ~ **ouvert** to welcome sb with open arms; **parler à** ~ **ouvert** to open one's heart; **de tout son** ~ with all one's heart; **avoir le** ~ **gros** ou **serré** to have a heavy heart; **en avoir le** ~ **net** to be clear in one's own mind (about it); **par** ~ by heart; **de bon** ~ willingly; **avoir à** ~ **de faire** to be very keen to do; **cela lui tient à** ~ that's (very) close to his heart; **prendre les choses à** ~ to take things to heart; **à** ~ **joie** to one's heart's content; **être de tout** ~ **avec qn** to be (completely) in accord with sb
**coexistence** [kɔɛgzistɑ̃s] nf coexistence
**coexister** [kɔɛgziste] vi to coexist
**coffrage** [kɔfRaʒ] nm (Constr: dispositif) form(work)
**coffre** [kɔfR(ə)] nm (meuble) chest; (coffre-fort) safe; (d'auto) boot (Brit), trunk (US); **avoir du** ~ (fam) to have a lot of puff
**coffre-fort** [kɔfRəfɔR] (pl **coffres-forts**) nm safe
**coffrer** [kɔfRe] vt (fam) to put inside, lock up
**coffret** [kɔfRɛ] nm casket; ~ **à bijoux** jewel box
**cogérant, e** [kɔʒeRɑ̃, -ɑ̃t] nm/f joint manager/manageress
**cogestion** [kɔʒestjɔ̃] nf joint management
**cogiter** [kɔʒite] vi to cogitate
**cognac** [kɔɲak] nm brandy, cognac
**cognement** [kɔɲmɑ̃] nm knocking
**cogner** [kɔɲe] vi to knock, bang; **se cogner** vi to bump o.s.
**cohabitation** [kɔabitasjɔ̃] nf living together; (Pol, Jur) cohabitation
**cohabiter** [kɔabite] vi to live together
**cohérence** [kɔeRɑ̃s] nf coherence
**cohérent, e** [kɔeRɑ̃, -ɑ̃t] adj coherent
**cohésion** [kɔezjɔ̃] nf cohesion
**cohorte** [kɔɔRt(ə)] nf troop
**cohue** [kɔy] nf crowd
**coi, coite** [kwa, kwat] adj: **rester** ~ to remain silent
**coiffe** [kwaf] nf headdress
**coiffé, e** [kwafe] adj: **bien/mal** ~ with tidy/untidy hair; ~ **d'un béret** wearing a beret; ~ **en arrière** with one's hair brushed ou combed back; ~ **en brosse** with a crew cut
**coiffer** [kwafe] vt (fig) to cover, top; ~ **qn** to do sb's hair; ~ **qn d'un béret** to put a beret on sb; **se coiffer** vi to do one's hair; to put on a ou one's hat
**coiffeur, -euse** [kwafœR, -øz] nm/f hairdresser ▷ nf (table) dressing table
**coiffure** [kwafyR] nf (cheveux) hairstyle, hairdo; (chapeau) hat, headgear no pl; (art): **la** ~ hairdressing

**coin** [kwɛ̃] nm corner; (pour graver) die; (pour coincer) wedge; (poinçon) hallmark; **l'épicerie du** ~ the local grocer; **dans le** ~ (aux alentours) in the area, around about; locally; **au** ~ **du feu** by the fireside; **du** ~ **de l'œil** out of the corner of one's eye; **regard en** ~ side(ways) glance; **sourire en** ~ half-smile
**coincé, e** [kwɛ̃se] adj stuck, jammed; (fig: inhibé) inhibited, with hang-ups
**coincer** [kwɛ̃se] vt to jam; (fam) to catch (out); to nab; **se coincer** vi to get stuck ou jammed
**coïncidence** [kɔɛ̃sidɑ̃s] nf coincidence
**coïncider** [kɔɛ̃side] vi: ~ **(avec)** to coincide (with); (correspondre: témoignage etc) to correspond ou tally (with)
**coin-coin** [kwɛ̃kwɛ̃] nm inv quack
**coing** [kwɛ̃] nm quince
**coït** [kɔit] nm coitus
**coite** [kwat] adj f voir **coi**
**coke** [kɔk] nm coke
**col** [kɔl] nm (de chemise) collar; (encolure, cou) neck; (de montagne) pass; ~ **roulé** polo-neck; ~ **de l'utérus** cervix
**coléoptère** [kɔleɔptɛR] nm beetle
**colère** [kɔlɛR] nf anger; **une** ~ a fit of anger; **être en** ~ **(contre qn)** to be angry (with sb); **mettre qn en** ~ to make sb angry; **se mettre en** ~ to get angry
**coléreux, -euse** [kɔleRø, -øz] adj, **colérique** [kɔleRik] ▷ adj quick-tempered, irascible
**colibacille** [kɔlibasil] nm colon bacillus
**colibacillose** [kɔlibasiloz] nf colibacillosis
**colifichet** [kɔlifiʃɛ] nm trinket
**colimaçon** [kɔlimasɔ̃] nm: **escalier en** ~ spiral staircase
**colin** [kɔlɛ̃] nm hake
**colin-maillard** [kɔlɛ̃majaR] nm (jeu) blind man's buff
**colique** [kɔlik] nf diarrhoea (Brit), diarrhea (US); (douleurs) colic (pains pl); (fam: personne ou chose ennuyeuse) pain
**colis** [kɔli] nm parcel; **par** ~ **postal** by parcel post
**colistier, -ière** [kɔlistje, -jɛR] nm/f fellow candidate
**colite** [kɔlit] nf colitis
**coll.** abr = **collection**; (= collaborateurs): **et** ~ et al
**collaborateur, -trice** [kɔlabɔRatœR, -tris] nm/f (aussi Pol) collaborator; (d'une revue) contributor
**collaboration** [kɔlabɔRasjɔ̃] nf collaboration
**collaborer** [kɔlabɔRe] vi to collaborate; (aussi: **collaborer à**) to collaborate on; (revue) to contribute to
**collage** [kɔlaʒ] nm (Art) collage
**collagène** [kɔlaʒɛn] nm collagen
**collant, e** [kɔlɑ̃, -ɑ̃t] adj sticky; (robe etc) clinging, skintight; (péj) clinging ▷ nm (bas) tights pl
**collatéral, e, -aux** [kɔlateRal, -o] nm/f collateral
**collation** [kɔlasjɔ̃] nf light meal
**colle** [kɔl] nf glue; (à papiers peints) (wallpaper)

paste; (*devinette*) teaser, riddle; (*Scol fam*) detention; **~ forte** superglue®
**collecte** [kɔlɛkt(ə)] *nf* collection; **faire une ~** to take up a collection
**collecter** [kɔlɛkte] *vt* to collect
**collecteur** [kɔlɛktœʀ] *nm* (*égout*) main sewer
**collectif, -ive** [kɔlɛktif, -iv] *adj* collective; (*visite, billet etc*) group *cpd* ▷ *nm*: **~ budgétaire** mini-budget (*Brit*), mid-term budget; **immeuble ~** block of flats
**collection** [kɔlɛksjɔ̃] *nf* collection; (*Édition*) series; **pièce de ~** collector's item; **faire (la) ~ de** to collect; **(toute) une ~ de ...** (*fig*) a (complete) set of ...
**collectionner** [kɔlɛksjɔne] *vt* (*tableaux, timbres*) to collect
**collectionneur, -euse** [kɔlɛksjɔnœʀ, -øz] *nm/f* collector
**collectivement** [kɔlɛktivmɑ̃] *adv* collectively
**collectiviser** [kɔlɛktivize] *vt* to collectivize
**collectivisme** [kɔlɛktivism(ə)] *nm* collectivism
**collectiviste** [kɔlɛktivist(ə)] *adj* collectivist
**collectivité** [kɔlɛktivite] *nf* group; **la ~** the community, the collectivity; **les ~s locales** local authorities
**collège** [kɔlɛʒ] *nm* (*école*) (secondary) school; *see note*; (*assemblée*) body; **~ électoral** electoral college

**collégial, e, -aux** [kɔleʒjal, -o] *adj* collegiate
**collégien, ne** [kɔleʒjɛ̃, -ɛn] *nm/f* secondary school pupil (*Brit*), high school student (*US*)
**collègue** [kɔlɛg] *nm/f* colleague
**coller** [kɔle] *vt* (*papier, timbre*) to stick (on); (*affiche*) to stick up; (*appuyer, placer contre*): **~ son front à la vitre** to press one's face to the window; (*enveloppe*) to stick down; (*morceaux*) to stick ou glue together; (*fam: mettre, fourrer*) to stick, shove; (*Scol fam*) to keep in, give detention to ▷ *vi* (*être collant*) to be sticky; (*adhérer*) to stick; **~ qch sur** (ou paste ou glue) sth on(to); **~ à** to stick to; (*fig*) to cling to
**collerette** [kɔlʀɛt] *nf* ruff; (*Tech*) flange
**collet** [kɔlɛ] *nm* (*piège*) snare, noose; (*cou*): **prendre qn au ~** to grab sb by the throat; **~ monté** *adj inv* straight-laced
**colleter** [kɔlte] *vt* (*adversaire*) to collar, grab by the throat; **se ~ avec** to wrestle with

**colleur** [kɔlœʀ] *nm*: **~ d'affiches** bill-poster
**collier** [kɔlje] *nm* (*bijou*) necklace; (*de chien, Tech*) collar; **~ (de barbe), barbe en ~** narrow beard along the line of the jaw; **~ de serrage** choke collar
**collimateur** [kɔlimatœʀ] *nm*: **être dans le ~** (*fig*) to be in the firing line; **avoir qn/qch dans le ~** (*fig*) to have sb/sth in one's sights
**colline** [kɔlin] *nf* hill
**collision** [kɔlizjɔ̃] *nf* collision, crash; **entrer en ~ (avec)** to collide (with)
**colloque** [kɔlɔk] *nm* colloquium, symposium
**collusion** [kɔlyzjɔ̃] *nf* collusion
**collutoire** [kɔlytwaʀ] *nm* (*Méd*) oral medication; (*en bombe*) throat spray
**collyre** [kɔliʀ] *nm* (*Méd*) eye lotion
**colmater** [kɔlmate] *vt* (*fuite*) to seal off; (*brèche*) to plug, fill in
**Cologne** [kɔlɔɲ] *n* Cologne
**colombage** [kɔlɔ̃baʒ] *nm* half-timbering; **une maison à ~s** a half-timbered house
**colombe** [kɔlɔ̃b] *nf* dove
**Colombie** [kɔlɔ̃bi] *nf*: **la ~** Colombia
**colombien, ne** [kɔlɔ̃bjɛ̃, -ɛn] *adj* Colombian ▷ *nm/f*: **Colombien, ne** Colombian
**colon** [kɔlɔ̃] *nm* settler; (*enfant*) boarder (*in children's holiday camp*)
**côlon** [kɔlɔ̃] *nm* colon (*Méd*)
**colonel** [kɔlɔnɛl] *nm* colonel; (*de l'armée de l'air*) group captain
**colonial, e, -aux** [kɔlɔnjal, -o] *adj* colonial
**colonialisme** [kɔlɔnjalism(ə)] *nm* colonialism
**colonialiste** [kɔlɔnjalist(ə)] *adj, nm/f* colonialist
**colonie** [kɔlɔni] *nf* colony; **~ (de vacances)** holiday camp (*for children*)
**colonisation** [kɔlɔnizasjɔ̃] *nf* colonization
**coloniser** [kɔlɔnize] *vt* to colonize
**colonnade** [kɔlɔnad] *nf* colonnade
**colonne** [kɔlɔn] *nf* column; **se mettre en ~ par deux/quatre** to get into twos/fours; **en ~ par deux** in double file; **~ de secours** rescue party; **~ (vertébrale)** spine, spinal column
**colonnette** [kɔlɔnɛt] *nf* small column
**colophane** [kɔlɔfan] *nf* rosin
**colorant** [kɔlɔʀɑ̃] *nm* colo(u)ring
**coloration** [kɔlɔʀasjɔ̃] *nf* colour(ing) (*Brit*), color(ing) (*US*); **se faire faire une ~** (*chez le coiffeur*) to have one's hair dyed
**coloré, e** [kɔlɔʀe] *adj* (*fig*) colo(u)rful
**colorer** [kɔlɔʀe] *vt* to colour (*Brit*), color (*US*); **se colorer** *vi* to turn red; to blush
**coloriage** [kɔlɔʀjaʒ] *nm* colo(u)ring
**colorier** [kɔlɔʀje] *vt* to colo(u)r (in); **album à ~** colouring book
**coloris** [kɔlɔʀi] *nm* colo(u)r, shade
**coloriste** [kɔlɔʀist(ə)] *nm/f* colo(u)rist
**colossal, e, -aux** [kɔlɔsal, -o] *adj* colossal, huge
**colosse** [kɔlɔs] *nm* giant
**colostrum** [kɔlɔstʀɔm] *nm* colostrum
**colporter** [kɔlpɔʀte] *vt* to peddle
**colporteur, -euse** [kɔlpɔʀtœʀ, -øz] *nm/f*

hawker, pedlar

**colt** [kɔlt] *nm* revolver, Colt®

**coltiner** [kɔltine] *vt* to lug about

**colza** [kɔlza] *nm* rape(seed)

**coma** [kɔma] *nm* coma; **être dans le ~** to be in a coma

**comateux, -euse** [kɔmatø, -øz] *adj* comatose

**combat** [kɔ̃ba] *vb voir* **combattre** ▷ *nm* fight; fighting *no pl*; **~ de boxe** boxing match; **~ de rues** street fighting *no pl*; **~ singulier** single combat

**combatif, -ive** [kɔ̃batif, -iv] *adj* with a lot of fight

**combativité** [kɔ̃bativite] *nf* fighting spirit

**combattant** [kɔ̃batɑ̃] *vb voir* **combattre** ▷ *nm* combatant; *(d'une rixe)* brawler; **ancien ~** war veteran

**combattre** [kɔ̃batʀ(ə)] *vi* to fight ▷ *vt* to fight; *(épidémie, ignorance)* to combat

**combien** [kɔ̃bjɛ̃] *adv (quantité)* how much; *(nombre)* how many; *(exclamatif)* how; **~ de** how much; how many; **~ de temps** how long, how much time; **c'est ~?, ça fait ~?** how much is it?; **~ coûte/pèse ceci?** how much does this cost/weigh?; **vous mesurez ~?** what size are you?; **ça fait ~ en largeur?** how wide is that?

**combinaison** [kɔ̃binɛzɔ̃] *nf* combination; *(astuce)* device, scheme; *(de femme)* slip; *(d'aviateur)* flying suit; *(d'homme-grenouille)* wetsuit; *(bleu de travail)* boilersuit (Brit), coveralls *pl* (US)

**combine** [kɔ̃bin] *nf* trick; *(péj)* scheme, fiddle (Brit)

**combiné** [kɔ̃bine] *nm (aussi:* **combiné téléphonique**) receiver; *(Ski)* combination (event); *(vêtement de femme)* corselet

**combiner** [kɔ̃bine] *vt* to combine; *(plan, horaire)* to work out, devise

**comble** [kɔ̃bl(ə)] *adj (salle)* packed (full) ▷ *nm (du bonheur, plaisir)* height; **combles** *nmpl (Constr)* attic *sg*, loft *sg*; **de fond en ~** from top to bottom; **pour ~ de malchance** to cap it all; **c'est le ~!** that beats everything!, that takes the biscuit! (Brit); **sous les ~s** in the attic

**combler** [kɔ̃ble] *vt (trou)* to fill in; *(besoin, lacune)* to fill; *(déficit)* to make good; *(satisfaire)* to gratify, fulfil (Brit), fulfill (US); **~ qn de joie** to fill sb with joy; **~ qn d'honneurs** to shower sb with honours

**combustible** [kɔ̃bystibl(ə)] *adj* combustible ▷ *nm* fuel

**combustion** [kɔ̃bystjɔ̃] *nf* combustion

**COMECON** [kɔmekɔn] *sigle m* Comecon

**comédie** [kɔmedi] *nf* comedy; *(fig)* playacting *no pl*; **jouer la ~** *(fig)* to put on an act; **la C~ française**; *see note*; **~ musicale** musical

**comédien, ne** [kɔmedjɛ̃, -ɛn] *nm/f* actor/actress; *(comique)* comedy actor/actress, comedian/comedienne; *(fig)* sham

**comestible** [kɔmɛstibl(ə)] *adj* edible; **comestibles** *nmpl* foods

**comète** [kɔmɛt] *nf* comet

**comice** [kɔmis] *nm*: **~ agricole** agricultural show

**comique** [kɔmik] *adj (drôle)* comical; *(Théât)* comic ▷ *nm (artiste)* comic, comedian; **le ~ de qch** the funny *ou* comical side of sth

**comité** [kɔmite] *nm* committee; **petit ~** select group; **~ directeur** management committee; **~ d'entreprise (CE)** works council; **~ des fêtes** festival committee

**commandant** [kɔmɑ̃dɑ̃] *nm (gén)* commander, commandant; *(Mil: grade)* major; *(: armée de l'air)* squadron leader; *(Navig)* captain; **~ (de bord)** *(Aviat)* captain

**commande** [kɔmɑ̃d] *nf (Comm)* order; *(Inform)* command; **commandes** *nfpl (Aviat etc)* controls; **passer une ~ (de)** to put in an order (for); **sur ~** to order; **~ à distance** remote control; **véhicule à double ~** vehicle with dual controls

**commandement** [kɔmɑ̃dmɑ̃] *nm* command; *(ordre)* command, order; *(Rel)* commandment

**commander** [kɔmɑ̃de] *vt (Comm)* to order; *(diriger, ordonner)* to command; **~ à** *(Mil)* to command; *(contrôler, maîtriser)* to have control over; **~ à qn de faire** to command *ou* order sb to do

**commanditaire** [kɔmɑ̃ditɛʀ] *nm* sleeping (Brit) *ou* silent (US) partner

**commandite** [kɔmɑ̃dit] *nf*: **(société en) ~** limited partnership

**commandite**r [kɔmɑ̃dite] *vt (Comm)* to finance, back; to commission

**commando** [kɔmɑ̃do] *nm* commando (squad)

 MOT-CLÉ

**comme** [kɔm] *prép* **1** *(comparaison)* like; **tout comme son père** just like his father; **fort comme un bœuf** as strong as an ox; **joli comme tout** ever so pretty

**2** *(manière)* like; **faites-le comme ça** do it like this, do it this way; **comme ça on n'aura pas d'ennuis** that way we won't have any problems; **comme ci, comme ça** so-so, middling; **comment ça va? — comme ça** how are things? — OK; **comme on dit** as they say

**3** *(en tant que)* as a; **donner comme prix** to give as a prize; **travailler comme secrétaire** to work as a secretary

**4**: **comme quoi** *(d'où il s'ensuit que)* which shows that; **il a écrit une lettre comme quoi il ...** he's written a letter saying that ...

**5**: **comme il faut** *adv* properly

C

▷ *adj* (*correct*) proper, correct
▷ *conj* **1** (*ainsi que*) as; **elle écrit comme elle parle** she writes as she talks; **comme si** as if **2** (*au moment où, alors que*) as; **il est parti comme j'arrivais** he left as I arrived **3** (*parce que, puisque*) as, since; **comme il était en retard, il ...** as he was late, he ...
▷ *adv*: **comme il est fort/c'est bon!** he's so strong/it's so good!; **il est malin comme c'est pas permis** he's as smart as anything

**commémoratif, -ive** [kɔmemɔʀatif, -iv] *adj* commemorative; **un monument ~** a memorial
**commémoration** [kɔmemɔʀɑsjɔ̃] *nf* commemoration
**commémorer** [kɔmemɔʀe] *vt* to commemorate
**commencement** [kɔmɑ̃smɑ̃] *nm* beginning, start, commencement; **commencements** *nmpl* (*débuts*) beginnings
**commencer** [kɔmɑ̃se] *vt* to begin, start, commence ▷ *vi* to begin, start, commence; **~ à** *ou* **de faire** to begin *ou* start doing; **~ par qch** to begin with sth; **~ par faire qch** to begin by doing sth
**commensal, e, -aux** [kɔmɑ̃sal, -o] *nm/f* companion at table
**comment** [kɔmɑ̃] *adv* how; **~?** (*que dites-vous*) (I beg your) pardon?; **~!** what! ▷ *nm*: **le ~ et le pourquoi** the whys and wherefores; **et ~!** and how!; **~ donc!** of course!; **~ faire?** how will we do it?; **~ se fait-il que ...?** how is it that ...?
**commentaire** [kɔmɑ̃tɛʀ] *nm* comment; remark; **~ (de texte)** (*Scol*) commentary; **~ sur image** voice-over
**commentateur, -trice** [kɔmɑ̃tatœʀ, -tʀis] *nm/f* commentator
**commenter** [kɔmɑ̃te] *vt* (*jugement, événement*) to comment (up)on; (*Radio, TV*: *match, manifestation*) to cover, give a commentary on
**commérages** [kɔmeʀaʒ] *nmpl* gossip *sg*
**commerçant, e** [kɔmɛʀsɑ̃, -ɑ̃t] *adj* commercial; trading; (*rue*) shopping *cpd*; (*personne*) commercially shrewd ▷ *nm/f* shopkeeper, trader
**commerce** [kɔmɛʀs(ə)] *nm* (*activité*) trade, commerce; (*boutique*) business; **le petit ~** small shop owners *pl*, small traders *pl*; **faire ~ de** to trade in; (*fig: péj*) to trade on; **chambre de ~** Chamber of Commerce; **livres de ~** (account) books; **vendu dans le ~** sold in the shops; **vendu hors-~** sold directly to the public; **~ en** *ou* **de gros/détail** wholesale/retail trade; **~ électronique** e-commerce; **~ équitable** fair trade; **~ intérieur/extérieur** home/foreign trade
**commercer** [kɔmɛʀse] *vi*: **~ avec** to trade with
**commercial, e, -aux** [kɔmɛʀsjal, -o] *adj* commercial, trading; (*péj*) commercial ▷ *nm*: **les commerciaux** the commercial people
**commercialisable** [kɔmɛʀsjalizabl(ə)] *adj* marketable
**commercialisation** [kɔmɛʀsjalizɑsjɔ̃] *nf* marketing
**commercialiser** [kɔmɛʀsjalize] *vt* to market
**commère** [kɔmɛʀ] *nf* gossip
**commettant** [kɔmetɑ̃] *vb voir* **commettre** ▷ *nm* (*Jur*) principal
**commettre** [kɔmetʀ(ə)] *vt* to commit; **se commettre** *vi* to compromise one's good name
**commis¹** [kɔmi] *nm* (*de magasin*) (shop) assistant (*Brit*), sales clerk (*US*); (*de banque*) clerk; **~ voyageur** commercial traveller (*Brit*) *ou* traveler (*US*)
**commis², e** [kɔmi, -iz] *pp de* **commettre**
**commisération** [kɔmizeʀɑsjɔ̃] *nf* commiseration
**commissaire** [kɔmisɛʀ] *nm* (*de police*) ≈ (police) superintendent (*Brit*), ≈ (police) captain (*US*); (*de rencontre sportive etc*) steward; **~ du bord** (*Navig*) purser; **~ aux comptes** (*Admin*) auditor
**commissaire-priseur** [kɔmisɛʀpʀizœʀ] (*pl* **commissaires-priseurs**) *nm* (official) auctioneer
**commissariat** [kɔmisaʀja] *nm*: **~ (de police)** police station; (*Admin*) commissionership
**commission** [kɔmisjɔ̃] *nf* (*comité, pourcentage*) commission; (*message*) message; (*course*) errand; **commissions** *nfpl* (*achats*) shopping *sg*; **~ d'examen** examining board
**commissionnaire** [kɔmisjɔnɛʀ] *nm* delivery boy (*ou* man); messenger; (*Transports*) (forwarding) agent
**commissure** [kɔmisyʀ] *nf*: **les ~s des lèvres** the corners of the mouth
**commode** [kɔmɔd] *adj* (*pratique*) convenient, handy; (*facile*) easy; (*air, personne*) easy-going; (*personne*): **pas ~** awkward (to deal with) ▷ *nf* chest of drawers
**commodité** [kɔmɔdite] *nf* convenience
**commotion** [kɔmosjɔ̃] *nf*: **~ (cérébrale)** concussion
**commotionné, e** [kɔmosjɔne] *adj* shocked, shaken
**commuer** [kɔmɥe] *vt* to commute
**commun, e** [kɔmœ̃, -yn] *adj* common; (*pièce*) communal, shared; (*réunion, effort*) joint ▷ *nf* (*Admin*) commune, ≈ district; (: *urbaine*) ≈ borough; **communs** *nmpl* (*bâtiments*) outbuildings; **cela sort du ~** it's out of the ordinary; **le ~ des mortels** the common run of people; **sans ~e mesure** incomparable; **être ~ à** (*chose*) to be shared by; **en ~** (*faire*) jointly; **mettre en ~** to pool, share; **peu ~** unusual; **d'un ~ accord** of one accord; with one accord
**communal, e, -aux** [kɔmynal, -o] *adj* (*Admin*) of the commune, ≈ (district *ou* borough) council *cpd*
**communard, e** [kɔmynaʀ, -aʀd(ə)] *nm/f* (*Hist*) Communard; (*péj*: *communiste*) commie
**communautaire** [kɔmynotɛʀ] *adj* community *cpd*
**communauté** [kɔmynote] *nf* community; (*Jur*): **régime de la ~** communal estate settlement
**commune** [kɔmyn] *adj f, nf voir* **commun**

**communément** [kɔmynemã] *adv* commonly
**Communes** [kɔmyn] *nfpl* (*en Grande-Bretagne*: *parlement*) Commons
**communiant, e** [kɔmynjã, -ãt] *nm/f* communicant; **premier ~** child taking his first communion
**communicant, e** [kɔmynikã, -ãt] *adj* communicating
**communicatif, -ive** [kɔmynikatif, -iv] *adj* (*personne*) communicative; (*rire*) infectious
**communication** [kɔmynikasjɔ̃] *nf* communication; **~ (téléphonique)** (telephone) call; **avoir la ~ (avec)** to get *ou* be through (to); **vous avez la ~** you're through; **donnez-moi la ~ avec** put me through to; **mettre qn en ~ avec qn** (*en contact*) to put sb in touch with sb; (*au téléphone*) to connect sb with sb; **~ interurbaine** long-distance call; **~ en PCV** reverse charge (*Brit*) *ou* collect (*US*) call; **~ avec préavis** personal call
**communier** [kɔmynje] *vi* (*Rel*) to receive communion; (*fig*) to be united
**communion** [kɔmynjɔ̃] *nf* communion
**communiqué** [kɔmynike] *nm* communiqué; **~ de presse** press release
**communiquer** [kɔmynike] *vt* (*nouvelle, dossier*) to pass on, convey; (*maladie*) to pass on; (*peur etc*) to communicate; (*chaleur, mouvement*) to transmit ▷ *vi* to communicate; **~ avec** (*salle*) to communicate with; **se ~ à** (*se propager*) to spread to
**communisme** [kɔmynism(ə)] *nm* communism
**communiste** [kɔmynist(ə)] *adj, nm/f* communist
**commutateur** [kɔmytatœʀ] *nm* (*Élec*) (change-over) switch, commutator
**commutation** [kɔmytasjɔ̃] *nf* (*Inform*): **~ de messages** message switching; **~ de paquets** packet switching
**Comores** [kɔmɔʀ] *nfpl*: **les (îles) ~** the Comoros (Islands)
**comorien, ne** [kɔmɔʀjɛ̃, -ɛn] *adj ou* from the Comoros
**compact, e** [kɔ̃pakt] *adj* dense; compact
**compagne** [kɔ̃paɲ] *nf* companion
**compagnie** [kɔ̃paɲi] *nf* (*firme, Mil*) company; (*groupe*) gathering; (*présence*): **la ~ de qn** sb's company; **homme/femme de ~** escort; **tenir ~ à qn** to keep sb company; **fausser ~ à qn** to give sb the slip, slip *ou* sneak away from sb; **en ~ de** in the company of; **Dupont et ~, Dupont et Cie** Dupont and Company, Dupont and Co; **~ aérienne** airline (company)
**compagnon** [kɔ̃paɲɔ̃] *nm* companion; (*autrefois*: *ouvrier*) craftsman; journeyman
**comparable** [kɔ̃paʀabl(ə)] *adj*: **~ (à)** comparable (to)
**comparaison** [kɔ̃paʀɛzɔ̃] *nf* comparison; (*métaphore*) simile; **~ (de)** in comparison (with); **par ~ (à)** by comparison (with)
**comparaître** [kɔ̃paʀɛtʀ(ə)] *vi*: **~ (devant)** to appear (before)

**comparatif, -ive** [kɔ̃paʀatif, -iv] *adj, nm* comparative
**comparativement** [kɔ̃paʀativmã] *adv* comparatively; **~ à** by comparison with
**comparé, e** [kɔ̃paʀe] *adj*: **littérature** *etc* **~e** comparative literature *etc*
**comparer** [kɔ̃paʀe] *vt* to compare; **~ qch/qn à** *ou* **et** (*pour choisir*) to compare sth/sb with *ou* and; (*pour établir une similitude*) to compare sth/sb to *ou* and
**comparse** [kɔ̃paʀs(ə)] *nm/f* (*péj*) associate, stooge
**compartiment** [kɔ̃paʀtimã] *nm* compartment
**compartimenté, e** [kɔ̃paʀtimãte] *adj* partitioned; (*fig*) compartmentalized
**comparu, e** [kɔ̃paʀy] *pp de* **comparaître**
**comparution** [kɔ̃paʀysjɔ̃] *nf* appearance
**compas** [kɔ̃pa] *nm* (*Géom*) (pair of) compasses *pl*; (*Navig*) compass
**compassé, e** [kɔ̃pase] *adj* starchy, formal
**compassion** [kɔ̃pasjɔ̃] *nf* compassion
**compatibilité** [kɔ̃patibilite] *nf* compatibility
**compatible** [kɔ̃patibl(ə)] *adj*: **~ (avec)** compatible (with)
**compatir** [kɔ̃patiʀ] *vi*: **~ (à)** to sympathize (with)
**compatissant, e** [kɔ̃patisã, -ãt] *adj* sympathetic
**compatriote** [kɔ̃patʀijɔt] *nm/f* compatriot, fellow countryman/woman
**compensateur, -trice** [kɔ̃pãsatœʀ, -tʀis] *adj* compensatory
**compensation** [kɔ̃pãsasjɔ̃] *nf* compensation; (*Banque*) clearing; **en ~** in *ou* as compensation
**compensé, e** [kɔ̃pãse] *adj*: **semelle ~e** platform sole
**compenser** [kɔ̃pãse] *vt* to compensate for, make up for
**compère** [kɔ̃pɛʀ] *nm* accomplice; fellow musician *ou* comedian *etc*
**compétence** [kɔ̃petãs] *nf* competence
**compétent, e** [kɔ̃petã, -ãt] *adj* (*apte*) competent, capable; (*Jur*) competent
**compétitif, -ive** [kɔ̃petitif, -iv] *adj* competitive
**compétition** [kɔ̃petisjɔ̃] *nf* (*gén*) competition; (*Sport*: *épreuve*) event; **la ~** competitive sport; **être en ~ avec** to be competing with; **la ~ automobile** motor racing
**compétitivité** [kɔ̃petitivite] *nf* competitiveness
**compilateur** [kɔ̃pilatœʀ] *nm* (*Inform*) compiler
**compiler** [kɔ̃pile] *vt* to compile
**complainte** [kɔ̃plɛ̃t] *nf* lament
**complaire** [kɔ̃plɛʀ]: **se complaire** *vi*: **se ~ dans/parmi** to take pleasure in/in being among
**complaisais** *etc* [kɔ̃plɛzɛ] *vb voir* **complaire**
**complaisamment** [kɔ̃plɛzamã] *adv* kindly; complacently
**complaisance** [kɔ̃plɛzãs] *nf* kindness; (*péj*) indulgence; (: *fatuité*) complacency; **attestation de ~** *certificate produced to oblige a patient etc*; **pavillon de ~** flag of convenience
**complaisant, e** [kɔ̃plɛzã, -ãt] *vb voir* **complaire**

85

▷ *adj* (*aimable*) kind; obliging; (*péj*) accommodating; (: *fat*) complacent

**complaît** [kɔ̃plɛ] *vb voir* **complaire**

**complément** [kɔ̃plemɑ̃] *nm* complement; (*reste*) remainder; (*Ling*) complement; ~ **d'information** (*Admin*) supplementary *ou* further information; ~ **d'agent** agent; ~ (**d'objet**) **direct/indirect** direct/indirect object; ~ (**circonstanciel**) **de lieu/temps** adverbial phrase of place/time; ~ **de nom** possessive phrase

**complémentaire** [kɔ̃plemɑ̃tɛʀ] *adj* complementary; (*additionnel*) supplementary

**complet, -ète** [kɔ̃plɛ, -ɛt] *adj* complete; (*plein: hôtel etc*) full ▷ *nm* (*aussi:* **complet-veston**) suit; **au** (**grand**) ~ all together

**complètement** [kɔ̃plɛtmɑ̃] *adv* (*en entier*) completely; (*absolument: fou, faux etc*) absolutely; (*à fond: étudier etc*) fully, in depth

**compléter** [kɔ̃plete] *vt* (*porter à la quantité voulue*) to complete; (*augmenter*) to complement, supplement; to add to; **se compléter** *vi* (*personnes*) to complement one another; (*collection etc*) to become complete

**complexe** [kɔ̃plɛks(ə)] *adj* complex ▷ *nm* (*Psych*) complex, hang-up; (*bâtiments*): ~ **hospitalier/industriel** hospital/industrial complex

**complexé, e** [kɔ̃plɛkse] *adj* mixed-up, hung-up

**complexité** [kɔ̃plɛksite] *nf* complexity

**complication** [kɔ̃plikasjɔ̃] *nf* complexity, intricacy; (*difficulté, ennui*) complication; **complications** *nfpl* (*Méd*) complications

**complice** [kɔ̃plis] *nm* accomplice

**complicité** [kɔ̃plisite] *nf* complicity

**compliment** [kɔ̃plimɑ̃] *nm* (*louange*) compliment; **compliments** *nmpl* (*félicitations*) congratulations

**complimenter** [kɔ̃plimɑ̃te] *vt*: ~ **qn** (**sur** *ou* **de**) to congratulate *ou* compliment sb (on)

**compliqué, e** [kɔ̃plike] *adj* complicated, complex, intricate; (*personne*) complicated

**compliquer** [kɔ̃plike] *vt* to complicate; **se compliquer** *vi* (*situation*) to become complicated; **se ~ la vie** to make life difficult *ou* complicated for o.s

**complot** [kɔ̃plo] *nm* plot

**comploter** [kɔ̃plɔte] *vi, vt* to plot

**complu, e** [kɔ̃ply] *pp de* **complaire**

**comportement** [kɔ̃pɔʀtəmɑ̃] *nm* behaviour (*Brit*), behavior (*US*); (*Tech: d'une pièce, d'un véhicule*) behavio(u)r, performance

**comporter** [kɔ̃pɔʀte] *vt* to be composed of, consist of, comprise; (*être équipé de*) to have; (*impliquer*) to entail, involve; **se comporter** *vi* to behave; (*Tech*) to behave, perform

**composant** [kɔ̃pozɑ̃] *nm* component, constituent

**composante** [kɔ̃pozɑ̃t] *nf* component

**composé, e** [kɔ̃poze] *adj* (*visage, air*) studied; (*Bio, Chimie, Ling*) compound ▷ *nm* (*Chimie, Ling*) compound; ~ **de** made up of

**composer** [kɔ̃poze] *vt* (*musique, texte*) to compose; (*mélange, équipe*) to make up; (*faire partie de*) to make up, form; (*Typo*) to (type)set ▷ *vi* (*Scol*) to sit *ou* do a test; (*transiger*) to come to terms; **se ~ de** to be composed of, be made up of; ~ **un numéro** (*au téléphone*) to dial a number

**composite** [kɔ̃pozit] *adj* heterogeneous

**compositeur, -trice** [kɔ̃pozitœʀ, -tʀis] *nm/f* (*Mus*) composer; (*Typo*) compositor, typesetter

**composition** [kɔ̃pozisjɔ̃] *nf* composition; (*Scol*) test; (*Typo*) (type)setting, composition; **de bonne ~** (*accommodant*) easy to deal with; **amener qn à ~** to get sb to come to terms; ~ **française** (*Scol*) French essay

**compost** [kɔ̃pɔst] *nm* compost

**composter** [kɔ̃pɔste] *vt* to date-stamp; to punch

**composteur** [kɔ̃pɔstœʀ] *nm* date stamp; punch; (*Typo*) composing stick

**compote** [kɔ̃pɔt] *nf* stewed fruit *no pl*; ~ **de pommes** stewed apples

**compotier** [kɔ̃pɔtje] *nm* fruit dish *ou* bowl

**compréhensible** [kɔ̃pʀeɑ̃sibl(ə)] *adj* comprehensible; (*attitude*) understandable

**compréhensif, -ive** [kɔ̃pʀeɑ̃sif, -iv] *adj* understanding

**compréhension** [kɔ̃pʀeɑ̃sjɔ̃] *nf* understanding; comprehension

**comprendre** [kɔ̃pʀɑ̃dʀ(ə)] *vt* to understand; (*se composer de*) to comprise, consist of; (*inclure*) to include; **se faire ~** to make o.s. understood; to get one's ideas across; **mal ~** to misunderstand

**compresse** [kɔ̃pʀɛs] *nf* compress

**compresser** [kɔ̃pʀese] *vt* to squash in, crush together; (*Inform*) to zip

**compresseur** [kɔ̃pʀesœʀ] *adj m voir* **rouleau**

**compressible** [kɔ̃pʀesibl(ə)] *adj* (*Physique*) compressible; (*dépenses*) reducible

**compression** [kɔ̃pʀesjɔ̃] *nf* compression; (*d'un crédit etc*) reduction

**comprimé, e** [kɔ̃pʀime] *adj*: **air ~** compressed air ▷ *nm* tablet

**comprimer** [kɔ̃pʀime] *vt* to compress; (*fig: crédit etc*) to reduce, cut down

**compris, e** [kɔ̃pʀi, -iz] *pp de* **comprendre** ▷ *adj* (*inclus*) included; ~**?** understood?, is that clear?; ~ **entre** (*situé*) contained between; **la maison ~e/non ~e, y/non ~ la maison** including/excluding the house; **service ~** service (charge) included; **100 euros tout ~** 100 euros all inclusive *ou* all-in

**compromettant, e** [kɔ̃pʀɔmetɑ̃, -ɑ̃t] *adj* compromising

**compromettre** [kɔ̃pʀɔmetʀ(ə)] *vt* to compromise

**compromis** [kɔ̃pʀɔmi] *vb voir* **compromettre** ▷ *nm* compromise

**compromission** [kɔ̃pʀɔmisjɔ̃] *nf* compromise, deal

**comptabiliser** [kɔ̃tabilize] *vt* (*valeur*) to post; (*fig*) to evaluate

**comptabilité** [kɔ̃tabilite] *nf* (*activité, technique*) accounting, accountancy; (*d'une société: comptes*) accounts *pl*, books *pl*; (: *service*) accounts office *ou* department; ~ **à partie double** double-entry book-keeping

**comptable** [kɔ̃tabl(ə)] *nm/f* accountant ▷ *adj* accounts *cpd*, accounting

**comptant** [kɔ̃tɑ̃] *adv*: **payer** ~ to pay cash; **acheter** ~ to buy for cash

**compte** [kɔ̃t] *nm* count, counting; (*total, montant*) count, (right) number; (*bancaire, facture*) account; **comptes** *nmpl* accounts, books; (*fig*) explanation *sg*; **ouvrir un** ~ to open an account; **rendre des ~s à qn** (*fig*) to be answerable to sb; **faire le** ~ **de** to count up, make a count of; **tout** ~ **fait** on the whole; **à ce ~-là** (*dans ce cas*) in that case; (*à ce train-là*) at that rate; **en fin de** ~ (*fig*) all things considered, weighing it all up; **au bout du** ~ in the final analysis; **à bon** ~ at a favourable price; (*fig*) lightly; **avoir son** ~ (*fig: fam*) to have had it; **pour le** ~ **de** on behalf of; **pour son propre** ~ for one's own benefit; **sur le** ~ **de qn** (*à son sujet*) about sb; **travailler à son** ~ to work for oneself; **mettre qch sur le** ~ **de qn** (*le rendre responsable*) to attribute sth to sb; **prendre qch à son** ~ to take responsibility for sth; **trouver son** ~ **à qch** to do well out of sth; **régler un** ~ (*s'acquitter de qch*) to settle an account; (*se venger*) to get one's own back; **rendre** ~ (**à qn**) **de qch** to give (sb) an account of sth; **tenir** ~ **de qch** to take sth into account; ~ **tenu de** taking into account; ~ **en banque** bank account; ~ **chèque(s)** current account; ~ **chèque postal (CCP)** Post Office account; ~ **client** (*sur bilan*) accounts receivable; ~ **courant (CC)** current account; ~ **de dépôt** deposit account; ~ **d'exploitation** operating account; ~ **fournisseur** (*sur bilan*) accounts payable; ~ **à rebours** countdown; ~ **rendu** account, report; (*de film, livre*) review; *voir aussi* **rendre**

**compte-gouttes** [kɔ̃tgut] *nm inv* dropper

**compter** [kɔ̃te] *vt* to count; (*facturer*) to charge for; (*avoir à son actif, comporter*) to have; (*prévoir*) to allow, reckon; (*tenir compte de, inclure*) to include; (*penser, espérer*): ~ **réussir/revenir** to expect to succeed/return ▷ *vi* to count; (*être économe*) to economize; (*être non négligeable*) to count, matter; (*valoir*): ~ **pour** to count for; (*figurer*): ~ **parmi** to be *ou* rank among; ~ **sur** to count (up)on; ~ **avec qch/qn** to reckon with *ou* take account of sth/sb; ~ **sans qch/qn** to reckon without sth/sb; **sans** ~ **que** besides which; **à** ~ **du 10 janvier** (*Comm*) (as) from 10th January

**compte-tours** [kɔ̃ttuʀ] *nm inv* rev(olution) counter

**compteur** [kɔ̃tœʀ] *nm* meter; ~ **de vitesse** speedometer

**comptine** [kɔ̃tin] *nf* nursery rhyme

**comptoir** [kɔ̃twaʀ] *nm* (*de magasin*) counter; (*de café*) counter, bar; (*colonial*) trading post

**compulser** [kɔ̃pylse] *vt* to consult

**comte, comtesse** [kɔ̃t, kɔ̃tɛs] *nm/f* count/ countess

**con, ne** [kɔ̃, kɔn] *adj* (*fam!*) bloody (*Brit*) *ou* damned stupid (!)

**concasser** [kɔ̃kase] *vt* (*pierre, sucre*) to crush; (*poivre*) to grind

**concave** [kɔ̃kav] *adj* concave

**concéder** [kɔ̃sede] *vt* to grant; (*défaite, point*) to concede; ~ **que** to concede that

**concentration** [kɔ̃sɑ̃tʀasjɔ̃] *nf* concentration

**concentrationnaire** [kɔ̃sɑ̃tʀasjɔnɛʀ] *adj* of *ou* in concentration camps

**concentré** [kɔ̃sɑ̃tʀe] *nm* concentrate; ~ **de tomates** tomato purée

**concentrer** [kɔ̃sɑ̃tʀe] *vt* to concentrate; **se concentrer** to concentrate

**concentrique** [kɔ̃sɑ̃tʀik] *adj* concentric

**concept** [kɔ̃sɛpt] *nm* concept

**concepteur, -trice** [kɔ̃sɛptœʀ, -tʀis] *nm/f* designer

**conception** [kɔ̃sɛpsjɔ̃] *nf* conception; (*d'une machine etc*) design

**concernant** [kɔ̃sɛʀnɑ̃] *prép* (*se rapportant à*) concerning; (*en ce qui concerne*) as regards

**concerner** [kɔ̃sɛʀne] *vt* to concern; **en ce qui me concerne** as far as I am concerned; **en ce qui concerne ceci** as far as this is concerned, with regard to this

**concert** [kɔ̃sɛʀ] *nm* concert; **de** ~ *adv* in unison; together

**concertation** [kɔ̃sɛʀtasjɔ̃] *nf* (*échange de vues*) dialogue; (*rencontre*) meeting

**concerter** [kɔ̃sɛʀte] *vt* to devise; **se concerter** *vi* (*collaborateurs etc*) to put our (*ou* their *etc*) heads together, consult (each other)

**concertiste** [kɔ̃sɛʀtist(ə)] *nm/f* concert artist

**concerto** [kɔ̃sɛʀto] *nm* concerto

**concession** [kɔ̃sesjɔ̃] *nf* concession

**concessionnaire** [kɔ̃sesjɔnɛʀ] *nm/f* agent, dealer

**concevable** [kɔ̃svabl(ə)] *adj* conceivable

**concevoir** [kɔ̃svwaʀ] *vt* (*idée, projet*) to conceive (of); (*méthode, plan d'appartement, décoration etc*) to plan, design; (*enfant*) to conceive; **maison bien/mal conçue** well-/badly-designed *ou* -planned house

**concierge** [kɔ̃sjɛʀʒ(ə)] *nm/f* caretaker; (*d'hôtel*) head porter

**conciergerie** [kɔ̃sjɛʀʒəʀi] *nf* caretaker's lodge

**concile** [kɔ̃sil] *nm* council, synod

**conciliable** [kɔ̃siljabl(ə)] *adj* (*opinions etc*) reconcilable

**conciliabules** [kɔ̃siljabyl] *nmpl* (*private*) discussions, confabulations (*Brit*)

**conciliant, e** [kɔ̃siljɑ̃, -ɑ̃t] *adj* conciliatory

**conciliateur, -trice** [kɔ̃siljatœʀ, -tʀis] *nm/f* mediator, go-between

**conciliation** [kɔ̃siljasjɔ̃] *nf* conciliation

**concilier** [kɔ̃silje] *vt* to reconcile; **se concilier qn/l'appui de qn** to win sb over/sb's support

**concis, e** [kɔ̃si, -iz] *adj* concise

**concision** [kɔ̃sizjɔ̃] *nf* concision, conciseness

**concitoyen, ne** [kɔ̃sitwajɛ̃, -ɛn] *nm/f* fellow citizen

C

**conclave** [kɔ̃klav] *nm* conclave
**concluant, e** [kɔ̃klyɑ̃, -ɑ̃t] *vb voir* **conclure** ▷ *adj* conclusive
**conclure** [kɔ̃klyʀ] *vt* to conclude; *(signer: accord, pacte)* to enter into; *(déduire)*: ~ **qch de qch** to deduce sth from sth; ~ **à l'acquittement** to decide in favour of an acquittal; ~ **au suicide** to come to the conclusion *(ou (Jur)* to pronounce) that it is a case of suicide; ~ **un marché** to clinch a deal; **j'en conclus que** from that I conclude that
**conclusion** [kɔ̃klyzjɔ̃] *nf* conclusion; **conclusions** *nfpl (Jur)* submissions; findings; **en** ~ in conclusion
**concocter** [kɔ̃kɔkte] *vt* to concoct
**conçois** [kɔ̃swa], **conçoive** *etc* [kɔ̃swav] *vb voir* **concevoir**
**concombre** [kɔ̃kɔ̃bʀ(ə)] *nm* cucumber
**concomitant, e** [kɔ̃kɔmitɑ̃, -ɑ̃t] *adj* concomitant
**concordance** [kɔ̃kɔʀdɑ̃s] *nf* concordance; **la** ~ **des temps** *(Ling)* the sequence of tenses
**concordant, e** [kɔ̃kɔʀdɑ̃, -ɑ̃t] *adj (témoignages, versions)* corroborating
**concorde** [kɔ̃kɔʀd(ə)] *nf* concord
**concorder** [kɔ̃kɔʀde] *vi* to tally, agree
**concourir** [kɔ̃kuʀiʀ] *vi (Sport)* to compete; ~ **à** *vt (effet etc)* to work towards
**concours** [kɔ̃kuʀ] *vb voir* **concourir** ▷ *nm* competition; *(Scol)* competitive examination; *(assistance)* aid, help; **recrutement par voie de** ~ recruitment by (competitive) examination; **apporter son** ~ **à** to give one's support to; ~ **de circonstances** combination of circumstances; ~ **hippique** horse show; *voir* **hors-concours**
**concret, -ète** [kɔ̃kʀɛ, -ɛt] *adj* concrete
**concrètement** [kɔ̃kʀɛtmɑ̃] *adv* in concrete terms
**concrétisation** [kɔ̃kʀetizasjɔ̃] *nf* realization
**concrétiser** [kɔ̃kʀetize] *vt* to realize; **se concrétiser** *vi* to materialize
**conçu, e** [kɔ̃sy] *pp de* **concevoir**
**concubin, e** [kɔ̃kybɛ̃, -in] *nm/f (Jur)* cohabitant
**concubinage** [kɔ̃kybinaʒ] *nm (Jur)* cohabitation
**concupiscence** [kɔ̃kypisɑ̃s] *nf* concupiscence
**concurremment** [kɔ̃kyʀamɑ̃] *adv* concurrently; jointly
**concurrence** [kɔ̃kyʀɑ̃s] *nf* competition; **jusqu'à** ~ **de** up to; ~ **déloyale** unfair competition
**concurrencer** [kɔ̃kyʀɑ̃se] *vt* to compete with; **ils nous concurrencent dangereusement** they are a serious threat to us
**concurrent, e** [kɔ̃kyʀɑ̃, -ɑ̃t] *adj* competing ▷ *nm/f (Sport, Écon etc)* competitor; *(Scol)* candidate
**concurrentiel, le** [kɔ̃kyʀɑ̃sjɛl] *adj* competitive
**conçus** [kɔ̃sy] *vb voir* **concevoir**
**condamnable** [kɔ̃danabl(ə)] *adj (action, opinion)* reprehensible
**condamnation** [kɔ̃danasjɔ̃] *nf (action)* condemnation; sentencing; *(peine)* sentence;

conviction; ~ **à mort** death sentence
**condamné, e** [kɔ̃dane] *nm/f (Jur)* convict
**condamner** [kɔ̃dane] *vt (blâmer)* to condemn; *(Jur)* to sentence; *(porte, ouverture)* to fill in, block up; *(malade)* to give up (hope for); *(obliger)*: ~ **qn à qch/à faire** to condemn sb to sth/to do; ~ **qn à deux ans de prison** to sentence sb to two years' imprisonment; ~ **qn à une amende** to impose a fine on sb
**condensateur** [kɔ̃dɑ̃satœʀ] *nm* condenser
**condensation** [kɔ̃dɑ̃sasjɔ̃] *nf* condensation
**condensé** [kɔ̃dɑ̃se] *nm* digest
**condenser** [kɔ̃dɑ̃se]: **se condenser** *vi* to condense
**condescendance** [kɔ̃desɑ̃dɑ̃s] *nf* condescension
**condescendant, e** [kɔ̃desɑ̃dɑ̃, -ɑ̃t] *adj (personne, attitude)* condescending
**condescendre** [kɔ̃desɑ̃dʀ(ə)] *vi*: ~ **à** to condescend to
**condiment** [kɔ̃dimɑ̃] *nm* condiment
**condisciple** [kɔ̃disipl(ə)] *nm/f* school fellow, fellow student
**condition** [kɔ̃disjɔ̃] *nf* condition; **conditions** *nfpl (tarif, prix)* terms; *(circonstances)* conditions; **sans** ~ *adj* unconditional ▷ *adv* unconditionally; **sous** ~ **que** on condition that; **à** ~ **de** *ou* **que** provided that; **en bonne** ~ in good condition; **mettre en** ~ *(Sport etc)* to get fit; *(Psych)* to condition (mentally); **~s de vie** living conditions
**conditionnel, le** [kɔ̃disjɔnɛl] *adj* conditional ▷ *nm* conditional (tense)
**conditionnement** [kɔ̃disjɔnmɑ̃] *nm (emballage)* packaging; *(fig)* conditioning
**conditionner** [kɔ̃disjɔne] *vt (déterminer)* to determine; *(Comm: produit)* to package; *(fig: personne)* to condition; **air conditionné** air conditioning; **réflexe conditionné** conditioned reflex
**condoléances** [kɔ̃dɔleɑ̃s] *nfpl* condolences
**conducteur, -trice** [kɔ̃dyktœʀ, -tʀis] *adj (Élec)* conducting ▷ *nm/f (Auto etc)* driver; *(d'une machine)* operator ▷ *nm (Élec etc)* conductor
**conduire** [kɔ̃dɥiʀ] *vt (véhicule, passager)* to drive; *(délégation, troupeau)* to lead; **se conduire** *vi* to behave; ~ **vers/à** to lead towards/to; ~ **qn quelque part** to take sb somewhere; to drive sb somewhere
**conduit, e** [kɔ̃dɥi, -it] *pp de* **conduire** ▷ *nm (Tech)* conduit, pipe; *(Anat)* duct, canal
**conduite** [kɔ̃dɥit] *nf (en auto)* driving; *(comportement)* behaviour (Brit), behavior (US); *(d'eau, de gaz)* pipe; **sous la** ~ **de** led by; ~ **forcée** pressure pipe; ~ **à gauche** left-hand drive; ~ **intérieure** saloon (car)
**cône** [kon] *nm* cone; **en forme de** ~ cone-shaped
**conf.** *abr* = **confort**; **tt** ~ all mod cons (Brit)
**confection** [kɔ̃fɛksjɔ̃] *nf (fabrication)* making; *(Couture)*: **la** ~ the clothing industry, the rag trade *(fam)*; **vêtement de** ~ ready-to-wear *ou*

off-the-peg garment
**confectionner** [kɔ̃fɛksjɔne] *vt* to make
**confédération** [kɔ̃federɑsjɔ̃] *nf* confederation
**conférence** [kɔ̃ferɑ̃s] *nf* (*exposé*) lecture;
(*pourparlers*) conference; ~ **de presse** press
conference; ~ **au sommet** summit
(conference)
**conférencier, -ière** [kɔ̃ferɑ̃sje, -jɛʀ] *nm/f*
lecturer
**conférer** [kɔ̃fere] *vt*: ~ **à qn** (*titre, grade*) to confer
on sb; ~ **à qch/qn** (*aspect etc*) to endow sth/sb
with, give (to) sth/sb
**confesser** [kɔ̃fese] *vt* to confess; **se confesser** *vi*
(*Rel*) to go to confession
**confesseur** [kɔ̃fesœʀ] *nm* confessor
**confession** [kɔ̃fesjɔ̃] *nf* confession; (*culte:*
*catholique etc*) denomination
**confessionnal, -aux** [kɔ̃fesjɔnal, -o] *nm*
confessional
**confessionnel, le** [kɔ̃fesjɔnɛl] *adj*
denominational
**confetti** [kɔ̃feti] *nm* confetti *no pl*
**confiance** [kɔ̃fjɑ̃s] *nf* confidence, trust; faith;
**avoir ~ en** to have confidence ou faith in, trust;
**faire ~ à** to trust; **en toute ~** with complete
confidence; **de ~** trustworthy, reliable; **mettre**
**qn en ~** to win sb's trust; **vote de ~** (*Pol*) vote of
confidence; **inspirer ~ à** to inspire confidence
in; ~ **en soi** self-confidence; *voir* **question**
**confiant, e** [kɔ̃fjɑ̃, -ɑ̃t] *adj* confident; trusting
**confidence** [kɔ̃fidɑ̃s] *nf* confidence
**confident, e** [kɔ̃fidɑ̃, -ɑ̃t] *nm/f* confidant/
confidante
**confidentiel, le** [kɔ̃fidɑ̃sjɛl] *adj* confidential
**confidentiellement** [kɔ̃fidɑ̃sjɛlmɑ̃] *adv* in
confidence, confidentially
**confier** [kɔ̃fje] *vt*: ~ **à qn** (*objet en dépôt, travail etc*)
to entrust to sb; (*secret, pensée*) to confide to sb;
**se confier à qn** to confide in sb
**configuration** [kɔ̃figyʀɑsjɔ̃] *nf* configuration,
layout; (*Inform*) configuration
**configurer** [kɔ̃figyʀe] *vt* to configure
**confiné, e** [kɔ̃fine] *adj* enclosed; (*air*) stale
**confiner** [kɔ̃fine] *vt*: ~ **à** to confine to; (*toucher*)
to border on; **se ~ dans** ou **à** to confine o.s. to
**confins** [kɔ̃fɛ̃] *nmpl*: **aux ~ de** on the borders of
**confirmation** [kɔ̃fiʀmɑsjɔ̃] *nf* confirmation
**confirmer** [kɔ̃fiʀme] *vt* to confirm; ~ **qn dans**
**une croyance/ses fonctions** to strengthen sb
in a belief/his duties
**confiscation** [kɔ̃fiskɑsjɔ̃] *nf* confiscation
**confiserie** [kɔ̃fizʀi] *nf* (*magasin*) confectioner's
ou sweet shop (*Brit*), candy store (*US*);
**confiseries** *nfpl* (*bonbons*) confectionery *sg*,
sweets, candy *no pl*
**confiseur, -euse** [kɔ̃fizœʀ, -øz] *nm/f*
confectioner
**confisquer** [kɔ̃fiske] *vt* to confiscate
**confit, e** [kɔ̃fi, -it] *adj*: **fruits ~s** crystallized
fruits ▷ *nm*: ~ **d'oie** potted goose
**confiture** [kɔ̃fityʀ] *nf* jam; ~ **d'oranges**
(orange) marmalade

**conflagration** [kɔ̃flagʀɑsjɔ̃] *nf* cataclysm
**conflictuel, le** [kɔ̃fliktɥɛl] *adj* full of clashes ou
conflicts
**conflit** [kɔ̃fli] *nm* conflict
**confluent** [kɔ̃flyɑ̃] *nm* confluence
**confondre** [kɔ̃fɔ̃dʀ(ə)] *vt* (*jumeaux, faits*) to
confuse, mix up; (*témoin, menteur*) to confound;
**se confondre** *vi* to merge; **se ~ en excuses** to
offer profuse apologies, apologize profusely; ~
**qch/qn avec qch/qn d'autre** to mistake sth/sb
for sth/sb else
**confondu, e** [kɔ̃fɔ̃dy] *pp de* **confondre** ▷ *adj*
(*stupéfait*) speechless, overcome; **toutes**
**catégories ~es** taking all categories together
**conformation** [kɔ̃fɔʀmɑsjɔ̃] *nf* conformation
**conforme** [kɔ̃fɔʀm(ə)] *adj*: ~ **à** (*en accord avec*) in
accordance with, in keeping with; (*identique à*)
true to; **copie certifiée ~** (*Admin*) certified copy;
~ **à la commande** as per order
**conformé, e** [kɔ̃fɔʀme] *adj*: **bien ~** well-formed
**conformément** [kɔ̃fɔʀmemɑ̃] *adv*: ~ **à** in
accordance with
**conformer** [kɔ̃fɔʀme] *vt*: ~ **qch à** to model sth
on; **se ~ à** to conform to
**conformisme** [kɔ̃fɔʀmism(ə)] *nm* conformity
**conformiste** [kɔ̃fɔʀmist(ə)] *adj, nm/f*
conformist
**conformité** [kɔ̃fɔʀmite] *nf* conformity;
agreement; **en ~ avec** in accordance with
**confort** [kɔ̃fɔʀ] *nm* comfort; **tout ~** (*Comm*) with
all mod cons (*Brit*) ou modern conveniences
**confortable** [kɔ̃fɔʀtabl(ə)] *adj* comfortable
**confortablement** [kɔ̃fɔʀtabləmɑ̃] *adv*
comfortably
**conforter** [kɔ̃fɔʀte] *vt* to reinforce, strengthen
**confrère** [kɔ̃fʀɛʀ] *nm* colleague; fellow member
**confrérie** [kɔ̃fʀeʀi] *nf* brotherhood
**confrontation** [kɔ̃fʀɔ̃tɑsjɔ̃] *nf* confrontation
**confronté, e** [kɔ̃fʀɔ̃te] *adj*: ~ **à** confronted by,
facing
**confronter** [kɔ̃fʀɔ̃te] *vt* to confront; (*textes*) to
compare, collate
**confus, e** [kɔ̃fy, -yz] *adj* (*vague*) confused;
(*embarrassé*) embarrassed
**confusément** [kɔ̃fyzemɑ̃] *adv* (*distinguer, ressentir*)
vaguely; (*parler*) confusedly
**confusion** [kɔ̃fyzjɔ̃] *nf* (*voir confus*) confusion;
embarrassment; (*voir confondre*) confusion;
mixing up; (*erreur*) confusion; ~ **des peines** (*Jur*)
concurrency of sentences
**congé** [kɔ̃ʒe] *nm* (*vacances*) holiday; (*arrêt de*
*travail*) time off *no pl*, leave *no pl*; (*Mil*) leave *no pl*;
(*avis de départ*) notice; **en ~** on holiday; off
(work); on leave; **semaine/jour de ~** week/day
off; **prendre ~ de qn** to take one's leave of sb;
**donner son ~ à** to hand ou give in one's notice
to; ~ **de maladie** sick leave; ~ **de maternité**
maternity leave; ~ **payés** paid holiday ou leave
**congédier** [kɔ̃ʒedje] *vt* to dismiss
**congélateur** [kɔ̃ʒelatœʀ] *nm* freezer, deep
freeze
**congélation** [kɔ̃ʒelɑsjɔ̃] *nf* freezing; (*de l'huile*)

congealing
**congeler** [kɔ̃ʒle]: **se congeler** vi to freeze
**congénère** [kɔ̃ʒenɛʀ] nm/f fellow (bear ou lion
etc), fellow creature
**congénital, e, -aux** [kɔ̃ʒenital, -o] adj
congenital
**congère** [kɔ̃ʒɛʀ] nf snowdrift
**congestion** [kɔ̃ʒɛstjɔ̃] nf congestion; ~
**cérébrale** stroke; ~ **pulmonaire** congestion of
the lungs
**congestionner** [kɔ̃ʒɛstjɔne] vt to congest;
(Méd) to flush
**conglomérat** [kɔ̃glɔmeʀa] nm conglomerate
**Congo** [kɔ̃go] nm: **le** ~ (pays, fleuve) the Congo
**congolais, e** [kɔ̃gɔlɛ, -ɛz] adj Congolese ▷ nm/f:
**Congolais, e** Congolese
**congratuler** [kɔ̃gʀatyle] vt to congratulate
**congre** [kɔ̃gʀ(ə)] nm conger (eel)
**congrégation** [kɔ̃gʀegasjɔ̃] nf (Rel)
congregation; (gén) assembly; gathering
**congrès** [kɔ̃gʀɛ] nm congress
**congressiste** [kɔ̃gʀesist(ə)] nm/f delegate,
participant (at a congress)
**congru, e** [kɔ̃gʀy] adj: **la portion ~e** the
smallest ou meanest share
**conifère** [kɔnifɛʀ] nm conifer
**conique** [kɔnik] adj conical
**conjecture** [kɔ̃ʒɛktyʀ] nf conjecture,
speculation no pl
**conjecturer** [kɔ̃ʒɛktyʀe] vt, vi to conjecture
**conjoint, e** [kɔ̃ʒwɛ̃, -wɛ̃t] adj joint ▷ nm/f
spouse
**conjointement** [kɔ̃ʒwɛ̃tmɑ̃] adv jointly
**conjonctif, -ive** [kɔ̃ʒɔ̃ktif, -iv] adj: **tissu** ~
connective tissue
**conjonction** [kɔ̃ʒɔ̃ksjɔ̃] nf (Ling) conjunction
**conjonctivite** [kɔ̃ʒɔ̃ktivit] nf conjunctivitis
**conjoncture** [kɔ̃ʒɔ̃ktyʀ] nf circumstances pl; **la**
~ (**économique**) the economic climate ou
situation
**conjoncturel, le** [kɔ̃ʒɔ̃ktyʀɛl] adj: **variations/
tendances ~les** economic fluctuations/trends
**conjugaison** [kɔ̃ʒygɛzɔ̃] nf (Ling) conjugation
**conjugal, e, -aux** [kɔ̃ʒygal, -o] adj conjugal;
married
**conjugué, e** [kɔ̃ʒyge] adj combined
**conjuguer** [kɔ̃ʒyge] vt (Ling) to conjugate; (efforts
etc) to combine
**conjuration** [kɔ̃ʒyʀasjɔ̃] nf conspiracy
**conjuré, e** [kɔ̃ʒyʀe] nm/f conspirator
**conjurer** [kɔ̃ʒyʀe] vt (sort, maladie) to avert;
(implorer): ~ **qn de faire qch** to beseech ou
entreat sb to do sth
**connais** [kɔnɛ], **connaissais** etc [kɔnɛsɛ] vb voir
**connaître**
**connaissance** [kɔnɛsɑ̃s] nf (savoir) knowledge no
pl; (personne connue) acquaintance; (conscience)
consciousness; **connaissances** nfpl knowledge
no pl; **être sans** ~ to be unconscious; **perdre/
reprendre** ~ to lose/regain consciousness; **à
ma/sa** ~ to (the best of) my/his knowledge;
**faire** ~ **avec qn** ou **la** ~ **de qn** (rencontrer) to meet

sb; (apprendre à connaître) to get to know sb; **avoir
~ de** to be aware of; **prendre ~ de** (document etc)
to peruse; **en ~ de cause** with full knowledge
of the facts; **de** ~ (personne, visage) familiar
**connaissant** etc [kɔnɛsɑ̃] vb voir **connaître**
**connaissement** [kɔnɛsmɑ̃] nm bill of lading
**connaisseur, -euse** [kɔnɛsœʀ, -øz] nm/f
connoisseur ▷ adj expert
**connaître** [kɔnɛtʀ(ə)] vt to know; (éprouver) to
experience; (avoir) to have; to enjoy; ~ **de nom/
vue** to know by name/sight; **se connaître** vi to
know each other; (soi-même) to know o.s.; **ils se
sont connus à Genève** they (first) met in
Geneva; **s'y ~ en qch** to know about sth
**connasse** [kɔnas] nf (fam!) stupid bitch (!) ou
cow (!)
**connecté, e** [kɔnɛkte] adj (Inform) on line
**connecter** [kɔnɛkte] vt to connect; **se
connecter à Internet** to log onto the internet
**connerie** [kɔnʀi] nf (fam!) stupid (Brit) ou
damn-fool (US) thing to do ou say
**connexe** [kɔnɛks(ə)] adj closely related
**connexion** [kɔnɛksjɔ̃] nf connection
**connivence** [kɔnivɑ̃s] nf connivance
**connotation** [kɔnɔtasjɔ̃] nf connotation
**connu, e** [kɔny] pp de **connaître** ▷ adj (célèbre)
well-known
**conque** [kɔ̃k] nf (coquille) conch (shell)
**conquérant, e** [kɔ̃keʀɑ̃, -ɑ̃t] nm/f conqueror
**conquérir** [kɔ̃keʀiʀ] vt to conquer, win
**conquerrai** etc [kɔ̃kɛʀʀe] vb voir **conquérir**
**conquête** [kɔ̃kɛt] nf conquest
**conquière, conquiers** etc [kɔ̃kjɛʀ] vb voir
**conquérir**
**conquis, e** [kɔ̃ki, -iz] pp de **conquérir**
**consacrer** [kɔ̃sakʀe] vt (Rel): ~ **qch (à)** to
consecrate sth (to); (fig: usage etc) to sanction,
establish; (employer): ~ **qch à** to devote ou
dedicate sth to; **se consacrer à qch/faire** to
dedicate ou devote o.s. to sth/to doing
**consanguin, e** [kɔ̃sɑ̃gɛ̃, -in] adj between blood
relations; **frère** ~ half-brother (on father's side);
**mariage** ~ intermarriage
**consciemment** [kɔ̃sjamɑ̃] adv consciously
**conscience** [kɔ̃sjɑ̃s] nf conscience; (perception)
consciousness; **avoir/prendre ~ de** to be/
become aware of; **perdre/reprendre** ~ to lose/
regain consciousness; **avoir bonne/mauvaise
~** to have a clear/guilty conscience; **en (toute)** ~
in all conscience
**consciencieux, -euse** [kɔ̃sjɑ̃sjø, -øz] adj
conscientious
**conscient, e** [kɔ̃sjɑ̃, -ɑ̃t] adj conscious; ~ **de**
aware ou conscious of
**conscription** [kɔ̃skʀipsjɔ̃] nf conscription
**conscrit** [kɔ̃skʀi] nm conscript
**consécration** [kɔ̃sekʀasjɔ̃] nf consecration
**consécutif, -ive** [kɔ̃sekytif, -iv] adj consecutive;
~ **à** following upon
**consécutivement** [kɔ̃sekytivmɑ̃] adv
consecutively; ~ **à** following on
**conseil** [kɔ̃sɛj] nm (avis) piece of advice, advice no

pl; (assemblée) council; (expert): ~ **en
recrutement** recruitment consultant ▷ adj:
**ingénieur-~** engineering consultant; **tenir ~**
to hold a meeting; to deliberate; **donner un ~**
ou **des ~s à qn** to give sb (a piece of) advice;
**demander ~ à qn** to ask sb's advice; **prendre ~
(auprès de qn)** to take advice (from sb); ~
**d'administration (CA)** board (of directors); ~
**de classe** (Scol) meeting of teachers, parents and class
representatives to discuss pupils' progress; ~ **de
discipline** disciplinary committee; ~ **général**
regional council; see note; ~ **de guerre** court-
martial; **le ~ des ministres** ≈ the Cabinet; ~
**municipal (CM)** town council; ~ **régional**
regional board of elected representatives; ~ **de
révision** recruitment ou draft (US) board

⊛ **CONSEIL GÉNÉRAL**
⊛
⊛ Each "département" of France is run by a
⊛ Conseil général, whose remit covers personnel,
⊛ transport infrastructure, housing, school
⊛ grants and economic development. The
⊛ council is made up of "conseillers
⊛ généraux", each of whom represents a
⊛ "canton" and is elected for a six-year term.
⊛ Half of the council's membership are
⊛ elected every three years.

**conseiller¹** [kɔ̃seje] vt (personne) to advise;
(méthode, action) to recommend, advise; ~ **qch à
qn** to recommend sth to sb; ~ **à qn de faire qch**
to advise sb to do sth
**conseiller², -ière** [kɔ̃seje, -ɛʀ] nm/f adviser; ~
**général** regional councillor; ~ **matrimonial**
marriage guidance counsellor; ~ **municipal**
town councillor; ~ **d'orientation** (Scol) careers
adviser (Brit), (school) counselor (US)
**consensuel, le** [kɔ̃sɑ̃sɥɛl] adj consensual
**consensus** [kɔ̃sɛ̃sys] nm consensus
**consentement** [kɔ̃sɑ̃tmɑ̃] nm consent
**consentir** [kɔ̃sɑ̃tiʀ] vt: ~ **(à qch/faire)** to agree
ou consent (to sth/to doing); ~ **qch à qn** to grant
sb sth
**conséquence** [kɔ̃sekɑ̃s] nf consequence,
outcome; **conséquences** nfpl consequences,
repercussions; **en ~** (donc) consequently; (de
façon appropriée) accordingly); **ne pas tirer à ~** to
be unlikely to have any repercussions; **sans ~**
unimportant; **de ~** important
**conséquent, e** [kɔ̃sekɑ̃, -ɑ̃t] adj logical,
rational; (fam: important) substantial; **par ~**
consequently
**conservateur, -trice** [kɔ̃sɛʀvatœʀ, -tʀis] adj
conservative ▷ nm/f (Pol) conservative; (de
musée) curator
**conservation** [kɔ̃sɛʀvasjɔ̃] nf retention;
keeping; preservation
**conservatisme** [kɔ̃sɛʀvatism(ə)] nm
conservatism
**conservatoire** [kɔ̃sɛʀvatwaʀ] nm academy;
(Écologie) conservation area

**conserve** [kɔ̃sɛʀv(ə)] nf (gén pl) canned ou tinned
(Brit) food; **~s de poisson** canned ou tinned (Brit)
fish; **en ~** canned, tinned (Brit); **de ~** (ensemble)
in concert; (naviguer) in convoy
**conservé, e** [kɔ̃sɛʀve] adj: **bien ~** (personne) well-
preserved
**conserver** [kɔ̃sɛʀve] vt (faculté) to retain, keep;
(habitude) to keep up; (amis, livres) to keep;
(préserver, Culin) to preserve; **se conserver** vi
(aliments) to keep; (aussi: **"conserver au frais"**)
"store in a cool place"
**conserverie** [kɔ̃sɛʀvəʀi] nf canning factory
**considérable** [kɔ̃sideʀabl(ə)] adj considerable,
significant, extensive
**considération** [kɔ̃sideʀasjɔ̃] nf consideration;
(estime) esteem, respect; **considérations** nfpl
(remarques) reflections; **prendre en ~** to take
into consideration ou account; **ceci mérite ~**
this is worth considering; **en ~ de** given,
because of
**considéré, e** [kɔ̃sideʀe] adj respected; **tout
bien ~** all things considered
**considérer** [kɔ̃sideʀe] vt to consider; (regarder)
to consider, study; ~ **qch comme** to regard sth
as
**consigne** [kɔ̃siɲ] nf (Comm) deposit; (de gare) left
luggage (office) (Brit), checkroom (US); (punition:
Scol) detention; (: Mil) confinement to barracks;
(ordre, instruction) instructions pl; ~
**automatique** left-luggage locker; **~s de
sécurité** safety instructions
**consigné, e** [kɔ̃siɲe] adj (Comm: bouteille,
emballage) returnable; **non ~** non-returnable
**consigner** [kɔ̃siɲe] vt (note, pensée) to record;
(marchandises) to deposit; (punir: Mil) to confine
to barracks; (: élève) to put in detention; (Comm)
to put a deposit on
**consistance** [kɔ̃sistɑ̃s] nf consistency
**consistant, e** [kɔ̃sistɑ̃, -ɑ̃t] adj thick; solid
**consister** [kɔ̃siste] vi: ~ **en/dans/à faire** to
consist of/in/in doing
**consœur** [kɔ̃sœʀ] nf (lady) colleague; fellow
member
**consolation** [kɔ̃sɔlasjɔ̃] nf consolation no pl,
comfort no pl
**console** [kɔ̃sɔl] nf console; ~ **graphique** ou **de
visualisation** (Inform) visual display unit, VDU;
~ **de jeux** games console
**consoler** [kɔ̃sɔle] vt to console; **se ~ (de qch)** to
console o.s. (for sth)
**consolider** [kɔ̃sɔlide] vt to strengthen,
reinforce; (fig) to consolidate; **bilan consolidé**
consolidated balance sheet
**consommateur, -trice** [kɔ̃sɔmatœʀ, -tʀis] nm/f
(Écon) consumer; (dans un café) customer
**consommation** [kɔ̃sɔmasjɔ̃] nf consumption;
(Jur) consummation; (boisson) drink; ~ **aux 100
km** (Auto) (fuel) consumption per 100 km,
≈ miles per gallon (mpg), ≈ gas mileage (US); **de
~** (biens, société) consumer cpd
**consommé, e** [kɔ̃sɔme] adj consummate ▷ nm
consommé

91

**consommer** [kɔ̃sɔme] vt (personne) to eat ou drink, consume; (voiture, usine, poêle) to use, consume; (Jur) to consummate ▷ vi (dans un café) to (have a) drink
**consonance** [kɔ̃sɔnɑ̃s] nf consonance; **nom à ~ étrangère** foreign-sounding name
**consonne** [kɔ̃sɔn] nf consonant
**consortium** [kɔ̃sɔRsjɔm] nm consortium
**consorts** [kɔ̃sɔR] nmpl: **et ~** (péj) and company, and his bunch ou like
**conspirateur, -trice** [kɔ̃spiRatœR, -tRis] nm/f conspirator, plotter
**conspiration** [kɔ̃spiRasjɔ̃] nf conspiracy
**conspirer** [kɔ̃spiRe] vi to conspire, plot; **~ à** (tendre à) to conspire to
**conspuer** [kɔ̃spɥe] vt to boo, shout down
**constamment** [kɔ̃stamɑ̃] adv constantly
**constance** [kɔ̃stɑ̃s] nf permanence, constancy; (d'une amitié) steadfastness; **travailler avec ~** to work steadily; **il faut de la ~ pour la supporter** (fam) you need a lot of patience to put up with her
**constant, e** [kɔ̃stɑ̃, -ɑ̃t] adj constant; (personne) steadfast ▷ nf constant
**Constantinople** [kɔ̃stɑ̃tinɔpl(ə)] n Constantinople
**constat** [kɔ̃sta] nm (d'huissier) certified report (by bailiff); (de police) report; (observation) (observed) fact, observation; (affirmation) statement; **~ (à l'amiable)** (jointly agreed) statement for insurance purposes
**constatation** [kɔ̃statasjɔ̃] nf noticing; certifying; (remarque) observation
**constater** [kɔ̃state] vt (remarquer) to note, notice; (Admin, Jur: attester) to certify; (dégâts) to note; **~ que** (dire) to state that
**constellation** [kɔ̃stelasjɔ̃] nf constellation
**constellé, e** [kɔ̃stele] adj: **~ de** (étoiles) studded ou spangled with; (taches) spotted with
**consternant, e** [kɔ̃stɛRnɑ̃ -ɑ̃t] adj (nouvelle) dismaying; (attristant, étonnant: bêtise) appalling
**consternation** [kɔ̃stɛRnasjɔ̃] nf consternation, dismay
**consterner** [kɔ̃stɛRne] vt to dismay
**constipation** [kɔ̃stipasjɔ̃] nf constipation
**constipé, e** [kɔ̃stipe] adj constipated; (fig) stiff
**constituant, e** [kɔ̃stitɥɑ̃, -ɑ̃t] adj (élément) constituent; **assemblée ~e** (Pol) constituent assembly
**constitué, e** [kɔ̃stitɥe] adj: **~ de** made up ou composed of; **bien ~** of sound constitution; well-formed
**constituer** [kɔ̃stitɥe] vt (comité, équipe) to set up, form; (dossier, collection) to put together, build up; (éléments, parties: composer) to make up, constitute; (représenter, être) to constitute; **se ~ prisonnier** to give o.s. up; **se ~ partie civile** to bring an independent action for damages
**constitution** [kɔ̃stitysjɔ̃] nf setting up; building up; (composition) composition, make-up; (santé, Pol) constitution
**constitutionnel, le** [kɔ̃stitysjɔnɛl] adj constitutional

**constructeur** [kɔ̃stRyktœR] nm manufacturer, builder
**constructif, -ive** [kɔ̃stRyktif, -iv] adj (positif) constructive
**construction** [kɔ̃stRyksjɔ̃] nf construction, building
**construire** [kɔ̃stRɥiR] vt to build, construct; **se construire** vi: **l'immeuble s'est construit très vite** the building went up ou was built very quickly
**consul** [kɔ̃syl] nm consul
**consulaire** [kɔ̃sylɛR] adj consular
**consulat** [kɔ̃syla] nm consulate
**consultant, e** [kɔ̃syltɑ̃, -ɑ̃t] adj consultant
**consultatif, -ive** [kɔ̃syltatif, -iv] adj advisory
**consultation** [kɔ̃syltasjɔ̃] nf consultation; **consultations** nfpl (Pol) talks; **être en ~** (délibération) to be in consultation; (médecin) to be consulting; **aller à la ~** (Méd) to go to the surgery (Brit) ou doctor's office (US); **heures de ~** (Méd) surgery (Brit) ou office (US) hours
**consulter** [kɔ̃sylte] vt to consult ▷ vi (médecin) to hold surgery (Brit), be in (the office) (US); **se consulter** vi to confer
**consumer** [kɔ̃syme] vt to consume; **se consumer** vi to burn; **se ~ de chagrin/douleur** to be consumed with sorrow/grief
**consumérisme** [kɔ̃symeRism(ə)] nm consumerism
**contact** [kɔ̃takt] nm contact; **au ~ de** (air, peau) on contact with; (gens) through contact with; **mettre/couper le ~** (Auto) to switch on/off the ignition; **entrer en ~** (fils, objets) to come into contact, make contact; **se mettre en ~ avec** (Radio) to make contact with; **prendre ~ avec** (relation d'affaires, connaissance) to get in touch ou contact with
**contacter** [kɔ̃takte] vt to contact, get in touch with
**contagieux, -euse** [kɔ̃taʒjø, -øz] adj contagious; infectious
**contagion** [kɔ̃taʒjɔ̃] nf contagion
**container** [kɔ̃tenɛR] nm container
**contamination** [kɔ̃taminasjɔ̃] nf infection; contamination
**contaminer** [kɔ̃tamine] vt (par un virus) to infect; (par des radiations) to contaminate
**conte** [kɔ̃t] nm tale; **~ de fées** fairy tale
**contemplatif, -ive** [kɔ̃tɑ̃platif, -iv] adj contemplative
**contemplation** [kɔ̃tɑ̃plasjɔ̃] nf contemplation; (Rel, Philosophie) meditation
**contempler** [kɔ̃tɑ̃ple] vt to contemplate, gaze at
**contemporain, e** [kɔ̃tɑ̃pɔRɛ̃, -ɛn] adj, nm/f contemporary
**contenance** [kɔ̃tnɑ̃s] nf (d'un récipient) capacity; (attitude) bearing, attitude; **perdre ~** to lose one's composure; **se donner une ~** to give the impression of composure; **faire bonne ~ (devant)** to put on a bold front (in the face of)
**conteneur** [kɔ̃tnœR] nm container; **~ (de**

**bouteilles)** bottle bank
**conteneurisation** [kɔ̃tnœʀizasjɔ̃] *nf*
containerization
**contenir** [kɔ̃tniʀ] *vt* to contain; *(avoir une capacité de)* to hold; **se contenir** *vi (se retenir)* to control o.s. *ou* one's emotions, contain o.s.
**content, e** [kɔ̃tɑ̃, -ɑ̃t] *adj* pleased, glad; ~ **de** pleased with; **je serais ~ que tu ...** I would be pleased if you ...
**contentement** [kɔ̃tɑ̃tmɑ̃] *nm* contentment, satisfaction
**contenter** [kɔ̃tɑ̃te] *vt* to satisfy, please; *(envie)* to satisfy; **se ~ de** to content o.s. with
**contentieux** [kɔ̃tɑ̃sjø] *nm (Comm)* litigation; *(: service)* litigation department; *(Pol etc)* contentious issues *pl*
**contenu, e** [kɔ̃tny] *pp de* **contenir** ▷ *nm (d'un bol)* contents *pl*; *(d'un texte)* content
**conter** [kɔ̃te] *vt* to recount, relate; **en ~ de belles à qn** to tell tall stories to sb
**contestable** [kɔ̃tɛstabl(ə)] *adj* questionable
**contestataire** [kɔ̃tɛstatɛʀ] *adj (journal, étudiant)* anti-establishment ▷ *nm/f* (anti-establishment) protester
**contestation** [kɔ̃tɛstasjɔ̃] *nf* questioning, contesting; *(Pol)*: **la ~** anti-establishment activity, protest
**conteste** [kɔ̃tɛst(ə)]: **sans ~** *adv* unquestionably, indisputably
**contesté, e** [kɔ̃tɛste] *adj (roman, écrivain)* controversial
**contester** [kɔ̃tɛste] *vt* to question, contest ▷ *vi (Pol: gén)* to protest, rebel (against established authority)
**conteur, -euse** [kɔ̃tœʀ, -øz] *nm/f* story-teller
**contexte** [kɔ̃tɛkst(ə)] *nm* context
**contiendrai** [kɔ̃tjɛ̃dʀe], **contiens** etc [kɔ̃tjɛ̃] *vb voir* **contenir**
**contigu, ë** [kɔ̃tigy] *adj*: ~ **(à)** adjacent (to)
**continent** [kɔ̃tinɑ̃] *nm* continent
**continental, e, -aux** [kɔ̃tinɑ̃tal, -o] *adj* continental
**contingences** [kɔ̃tɛ̃ʒɑ̃s] *nfpl* contingencies
**contingent** [kɔ̃tɛ̃ʒɑ̃] *nm (Mil)* contingent; *(Comm)* quota
**contingenter** [kɔ̃tɛ̃ʒɑ̃te] *vt (Comm)* to fix a quota on
**contins** etc [kɔ̃tɛ̃] *vb voir* **contenir**
**continu, e** [kɔ̃tiny] *adj* continuous; **(courant) ~** direct current, DC
**continuation** [kɔ̃tinɥasjɔ̃] *nf* continuation
**continuel, le** [kɔ̃tinɥɛl] *adj (qui se répète)* constant, continual; *(continu)* continuous
**continuellement** [kɔ̃tinɥɛlmɑ̃] *adv* continually; continuously
**continuer** [kɔ̃tinɥe] *vt (travail, voyage etc)* to continue (with), carry on (with), go on with; *(prolonger: alignement, rue)* to continue ▷ *vi (pluie, vie, bruit)* to continue, go on; *(voyageur)* to go on; **se continuer** *vi* to carry on; ~ **à** *ou* **de faire** to go on *ou* continue doing
**continuité** [kɔ̃tinɥite] *nf* continuity;

continuation
**contondant, e** [kɔ̃tɔ̃dɑ̃, -ɑ̃t] *adj*: **arme ~e** blunt instrument
**contorsion** [kɔ̃tɔʀsjɔ̃] *nf* contortion
**contorsionner** [kɔ̃tɔʀsjɔne]: **se contorsionner** *vi* to contort o.s., writhe about
**contorsionniste** [kɔ̃tɔʀsjɔnist(ə)] *nm/f* contortionist
**contour** [kɔ̃tuʀ] *nm* outline, contour; **contours** *nmpl (d'une rivière etc)* windings
**contourner** [kɔ̃tuʀne] *vt* to bypass, walk *ou* drive) round
**contraceptif, -ive** [kɔ̃tʀasɛptif, -iv] *adj, nm* contraceptive
**contraception** [kɔ̃tʀasɛpsjɔ̃] *nf* contraception
**contracté, e** [kɔ̃tʀakte] *adj (muscle)* tense, contracted; *(personne: tendu)* tense, tensed up; **article ~** *(Ling)* contracted article
**contracter** [kɔ̃tʀakte] *vt (muscle etc)* to tense, contract; *(maladie, dette, obligation)* to contract; *(assurance)* to take out; **se contracter** *vi (métal, muscles)* to contract
**contraction** [kɔ̃tʀaksjɔ̃] *nf* contraction
**contractuel, le** [kɔ̃tʀaktɥɛl] *adj* contractual ▷ *nm/f (agent)* traffic warden; *(employé)* contract employee
**contradiction** [kɔ̃tʀadiksjɔ̃] *nf* contradiction
**contradictoire** [kɔ̃tʀadiktwaʀ] *adj* contradictory, conflicting; **débat ~** (open) debate
**contraignant, e** [kɔ̃tʀɛɲɑ̃, -ɑ̃t] *vb voir* **contraindre** ▷ *adj* restricting
**contraindre** [kɔ̃tʀɛ̃dʀ(ə)] *vt*: ~ **qn à faire** to force *ou* compel sb to do
**contraint, e** [kɔ̃tʀɛ̃, -ɛ̃t] *pp de* **contraindre** ▷ *adj (mine, air)* constrained, forced ▷ *nf* constraint; **sans ~e** unrestrainedly, unconstrainedly
**contraire** [kɔ̃tʀɛʀ] *adj, nm* opposite; ~ **à** contrary to; **au ~** *adv* on the contrary
**contrairement** [kɔ̃tʀɛʀmɑ̃] *adv*: ~ **à** contrary to, unlike
**contralto** [kɔ̃tʀalto] *nm* contralto
**contrariant, e** [kɔ̃tʀaʀjɑ̃, -ɑ̃t] *adj (personne)* contrary, perverse; *(incident)* annoying
**contrarier** [kɔ̃tʀaʀje] *vt (personne)* to annoy, bother; *(fig)* to impede; to thwart, frustrate
**contrariété** [kɔ̃tʀaʀjete] *nf* annoyance
**contraste** [kɔ̃tʀast(ə)] *nm* contrast
**contraster** [kɔ̃tʀaste] *vt, vi* to contrast
**contrat** [kɔ̃tʀa] *nm* contract; *(fig: accord, pacte)* agreement; ~ **de travail** employment contract
**contravention** [kɔ̃tʀavɑ̃sjɔ̃] *nf (infraction)*: ~ **à** contravention of; *(amende)* fine; *(PV pour stationnement interdit)* parking ticket; **dresser ~ à** *(automobiliste)* to book; to write out a parking ticket for
**contre** [kɔ̃tʀ(ə)] *prép* against; *(en échange)* (in exchange) for; **par ~** on the other hand
**contre-amiral, -aux** [kɔ̃tʀamiʀal, -o] *nm* rear admiral
**contre-attaque** [kɔ̃tʀatak] *nf* counterattack
**contre-attaquer** [kɔ̃tʀatake] *vi* to

counterattack

**contre-balancer** [kɔ̃tʀəbalãse] *vt* to counterbalance; *(fig)* to offset

**contrebande** [kɔ̃tʀəbãd] *nf (trafic)* contraband, smuggling; *(marchandise)* contraband, smuggled goods *pl*; **faire la ~ de** to smuggle

**contrebandier, -ière** [kɔ̃tʀəbãdje, -jɛʀ] *nm/f* smuggler

**contrebas** [kɔ̃tʀəba]: **en ~** *adv* (down) below

**contrebasse** [kɔ̃tʀəbas] *nf* (double) bass

**contrebassiste** [kɔ̃tʀəbasist(ə)] *nm/f* (double) bass player

**contre-braquer** [kɔ̃tʀəbʀake] *vi* to steer into a skid

**contrecarrer** [kɔ̃tʀəkaʀe] *vt* to thwart

**contrechamp** [kɔ̃tʀəʃã] *nm (Ciné)* reverse shot

**contrecœur** [kɔ̃tʀəkœʀ]: **à ~** *adv* (be)grudgingly, reluctantly

**contrecoup** [kɔ̃tʀəku] *nm* repercussions *pl*; **par ~** as an indirect consequence

**contre-courant** [kɔ̃tʀəkuʀã]: **à ~** *adv* against the current

**contredire** [kɔ̃tʀədiʀ] *vt (personne)* to contradict; *(témoignage, assertion, faits)* to refute; **se contredire** *vi* to contradict o.s.

**contredit, e** [kɔ̃tʀədi, -it] *pp de* **contredire** ▷ *nm*: **sans ~** without question

**contrée** [kɔ̃tʀe] *nf* region; land

**contre-écrou** [kɔ̃tʀekʀu] *nm* lock nut

**contre-enquête** [kɔ̃tʀãkɛt] *nf* counter-inquiry

**contre-espionnage** [kɔ̃tʀɛspjɔnaʒ] *nm* counter-espionage

**contre-exemple** [kɔ̃tʀɛgzãpl(ə)] *nf* counter-example

**contre-expertise** [kɔ̃tʀɛkspɛʀtiz] *nf* second (expert) assessment

**contrefaçon** [kɔ̃tʀəfasɔ̃] *nf* forgery; **~ de brevet** patent infringement

**contrefaire** [kɔ̃tʀəfɛʀ] *vt (document, signature)* to forge, counterfeit; *(personne, démarche)* to mimic; *(dénaturer: sa voix etc)* to disguise

**contrefait, e** [kɔ̃tʀəfɛ, -ɛt] *pp de* **contrefaire** ▷ *adj* misshapen, deformed

**contrefasse** [kɔ̃tʀəfas], **contreferai** *etc* [kɔ̃tʀəfʀe] *vb voir* **contrefaire**

**contre-filet** [kɔ̃tʀəfilɛ] *nm (Culin)* sirloin

**contreforts** [kɔ̃tʀəfɔʀ] *nmpl* foothills

**contre-haut** [kɔ̃tʀəo]: **en ~** *adv* (up) above

**contre-indication** [kɔ̃tʀɛ̃dikasjɔ̃] *nf* contraindication

**contre-indiqué, e** [kɔ̃tʀɛ̃dike] *adj (Méd)* contraindicated

**contre-interrogatoire** [kɔ̃tʀɛ̃teʀɔgatwaʀ] *nm*: **faire subir un ~ à qn** to cross-examine sb

**contre-jour** [kɔ̃tʀəʒuʀ]: **à ~** *adv* against the light

**contremaître** [kɔ̃tʀəmɛtʀ(ə)] *nm* foreman

**contre-manifestant, e** [kɔ̃tʀəmanifɛstã, -ãt] *nm/f* counter-demonstrator

**contre-manifestation** [kɔ̃tʀəmanifɛstasjɔ̃] *nf* counter-demonstration

**contremarque** [kɔ̃tʀəmaʀk(ə)] *nf (ticket)* pass-out ticket

**contre-offensive** [kɔ̃tʀɔfãsiv] *nf* counteroffensive

**contre-ordre** [kɔ̃tʀɔʀdʀ(ə)] *nm* = **contrordre**

**contrepartie** [kɔ̃tʀəpaʀti] *nf* compensation; **en ~** in compensation; in return

**contre-performance** [kɔ̃tʀəpɛʀfɔʀmãs] *nf* below-average performance

**contrepèterie** [kɔ̃tʀəpɛtʀi] *nf* spoonerism

**contre-pied** [kɔ̃tʀəpje] *nm (inverse, opposé):* **le ~ de ...** the exact opposite of ...; **prendre le ~ de** to take the opposing view of; to take the opposite course to; **prendre qn à ~** *(Sport)* to wrong-foot sb

**contre-plaqué** [kɔ̃tʀəplake] *nm* plywood

**contre-plongée** [kɔ̃tʀəplɔ̃ʒe] *nf* low-angle shot

**contrepoids** [kɔ̃tʀəpwa] *nm* counterweight, counterbalance; **faire ~** to act as a counterbalance

**contrepoil** [kɔ̃tʀəpwal]: **à ~** *adv* the wrong way

**contrepoint** [kɔ̃tʀəpwɛ̃] *nm* counterpoint

**contrepoison** [kɔ̃tʀəpwazɔ̃] *nm* antidote

**contrer** [kɔ̃tʀe] *vt* to counter

**contre-révolution** [kɔ̃tʀəʀevɔlysjɔ̃] *nf* counter-revolution

**contre-révolutionnaire** [kɔ̃tʀəʀevɔlysjɔnɛʀ] *nm/f* counter-revolutionary

**contresens** [kɔ̃tʀəsãs] *nm* misinterpretation; *(mauvaise traduction)* mistranslation; *(absurdité)* nonsense *no pl*; **à ~** *adv* the wrong way

**contresigner** [kɔ̃tʀəsiɲe] *vt* to countersign

**contretemps** [kɔ̃tʀətã] *nm* hitch, contretemps; **à ~** *adv (Mus)* out of time; *(fig)* at an inopportune moment

**contre-terrorisme** [kɔ̃tʀəteʀɔʀism(ə)] *nm* counter-terrorism

**contre-terroriste** [kɔ̃tʀəteʀɔʀist(ə)] *nm/f* counter-terrorist

**contre-torpilleur** [kɔ̃tʀətɔʀpijœʀ] *nm* destroyer

**contrevenant, e** [kɔ̃tʀəvnã, -ãt] *vb voir* **contrevenir** ▷ *nm/f* offender

**contrevenir** [kɔ̃tʀəvniʀ]: **~ à** *vt* to contravene

**contre-voie** [kɔ̃tʀəvwa]: **à ~** *adv (en sens inverse)* on the wrong track; *(du mauvais côté)* on the wrong side

**contribuable** [kɔ̃tʀibɥabl(ə)] *nm/f* taxpayer

**contribuer** [kɔ̃tʀibɥe]: **~ à** *vt* to contribute towards

**contribution** [kɔ̃tʀibysjɔ̃] *nf* contribution; **les ~s** *(bureaux)* the tax office; **mettre à ~** to call upon; **~s directes/indirectes** direct/indirect taxation

**contrit, e** [kɔ̃tʀi, -it] *adj* contrite

**contrôlable** [kɔ̃tʀolabl(ə)] *adj (maîtrisable: situation, débit)* controllable; *(alibi, déclarations)* verifiable

**contrôle** [kɔ̃tʀol] *nm* checking *no pl*, check; supervision; monitoring; *(test)* test, examination; **perdre le ~ de son véhicule** to lose control of one's vehicle; **~ des changes** *(Comm)* exchange controls; **~ continu** *(Scol)* continuous assessment; ~ **d'identité** identity check; ~ **des naissances** birth control; ~ **des prix** price control

**contrôler** [kɔ̃tʀole] vt (vérifier) to check; (surveiller) to supervise; to monitor, control; (maîtriser, Comm: firme) to control; **se contrôler** vi to control o.s.

**contrôleur, -euse** [kɔ̃tʀolœʀ, -øz] nm/f (de train) (ticket) inspector; (de bus) (bus) conductor/tress; ~ **de la navigation aérienne**, ~ **aérien** air traffic controller; ~ **financier** financial controller

**contrordre** [kɔ̃tʀɔʀdʀ(ə)] nm counter-order, countermand; **sauf** ~ unless otherwise directed

**controverse** [kɔ̃tʀɔvɛʀs(ə)] nf controversy

**controversé, e** [kɔ̃tʀɔvɛʀse] adj (personnage, question) controversial

**contumace** [kɔ̃tymas]: **par** ~ adv in absentia

**contusion** [kɔ̃tyzjɔ̃] nf bruise, contusion

**contusionné, e** [kɔ̃tyzjɔne] adj bruised

**conurbation** [kɔnyʀbasjɔ̃] nf conurbation

**convaincant, e** [kɔ̃vɛ̃kɑ̃, -ɑ̃t] vb voir **convaincre** ▷ adj convincing

**convaincre** [kɔ̃vɛ̃kʀ(ə)] vt: ~ **qn (de qch)** to convince sb (of sth); ~ **qn (de faire)** to persuade sb (to do); ~ **qn de** (Jur: délit) to convict sb of

**convaincu, e** [kɔ̃vɛ̃ky] pp de **convaincre** ▷ adj: **d'un ton** ~ with conviction

**convainquais** etc [kɔ̃vɛ̃kɛ] vb voir **convaincre**

**convalescence** [kɔ̃valesɑ̃s] nf convalescence; **maison de** ~ convalescent home

**convalescent, e** [kɔ̃valesɑ̃, -ɑ̃t] adj, nm/f convalescent

**convenable** [kɔ̃vnabl(ə)] adj suitable; (décent) acceptable, proper; (assez bon) decent, acceptable; adequate, passable

**convenablement** [kɔ̃vnabləmɑ̃] adv (placé, choisi) suitably; (s'habiller, s'exprimer) properly; (payé, logé) decently

**convenance** [kɔ̃vnɑ̃s] nf: **à ma/votre** ~ to my/your liking; **convenances** nfpl proprieties

**convenir** [kɔ̃vniʀ] vt to be suitable; ~ **à** to suit; **il convient de** it is advisable to; (bienséant) it is right ou proper to; ~ **de** (bien-fondé de qch) to admit (to), acknowledge; (date, somme etc) to agree upon; ~ **que** (admettre) to admit that, acknowledge the fact that; ~ **de faire qch** to agree to do sth; **il a été convenu que** it has been agreed that; **comme convenu** as agreed

**convention** [kɔ̃vɑ̃sjɔ̃] nf convention; **conventions** nfpl (convenances) convention sg, social conventions; **de** ~ conventional; ~ **collective** (Écon) collective agreement

**conventionnalisme** [kɔ̃vɑ̃sjɔnalism(ə)] nm (des idées) conventionality

**conventionné, e** [kɔ̃vɑ̃sjɔne] adj (Admin) applying charges laid down by the state

**conventionnel, le** [kɔ̃vɑ̃sjɔnɛl] adj conventional

**conventionnellement** [kɔ̃vɑ̃sjɔnɛlmɑ̃] adv conventionally

**conventuel, le** [kɔ̃vɑ̃tɥɛl] adj monastic; monastery cpd, conventual, convent cpd

**convenu, e** [kɔ̃vny] pp de **convenir** ▷ adj agreed

**convergent, e** [kɔ̃vɛʀʒɑ̃, -ɑ̃t] adj convergent

**converger** [kɔ̃vɛʀʒe] vi to converge; ~ **vers** ou **sur** to converge on

**conversation** [kɔ̃vɛʀsasjɔ̃] nf conversation; **avoir de la** ~ to be a good conversationalist

**converser** [kɔ̃vɛʀse] vi to converse

**conversion** [kɔ̃vɛʀsjɔ̃] nf conversion; (Ski) kick turn

**convertible** [kɔ̃vɛʀtibl(ə)] adj (Écon) convertible; **(canapé)** ~ sofa bed

**convertir** [kɔ̃vɛʀtiʀ] vt: ~ **qn (à)** to convert sb (to); ~ **qch en** to convert sth into; **se** ~ **(à)** to be converted (to)

**convertisseur** [kɔ̃vɛʀtisœʀ] nm (Élec) converter

**convexe** [kɔ̃vɛks(ə)] adj convex

**conviction** [kɔ̃viksjɔ̃] nf conviction

**conviendrai** [kɔ̃vjɛ̃dʀe], **conviens** etc [kɔ̃vjɛ̃] vb voir **convenir**

**convier** [kɔ̃vje] vt: ~ **qn à** (dîner etc) to (cordially) invite sb to; ~ **qn à faire** to urge sb to do

**convint** etc [kɔ̃vɛ̃] vb voir **convenir**

**convive** [kɔ̃viv] nm/f guest (at table)

**convivial, e** [kɔ̃vivjal] adj (Inform) user-friendly

**convocation** [kɔ̃vɔkasjɔ̃] nf (voir convoquer) convening, convoking; summoning; invitation; (document) notification to attend; summons sg

**convoi** [kɔ̃vwa] nm (de voitures, prisonniers) convoy; (train) train; ~ **(funèbre)** funeral procession

**convoiter** [kɔ̃vwate] vt to covet

**convoitise** [kɔ̃vwatiz] nf covetousness; (sexuelle) lust, desire

**convoler** [kɔ̃vɔle] vi: ~ **(en justes noces)** to be wed

**convoquer** [kɔ̃vɔke] vt (assemblée) to convene, convoke; (subordonné, témoin) to summon; (candidat) to ask to attend; ~ **qn (à)** (réunion) to invite sb (to attend)

**convoyer** [kɔ̃vwaje] vt to escort

**convoyeur** [kɔ̃vwajœʀ] nm (Navig) escort ship; ~ **de fonds** security guard

**convulsé, e** [kɔ̃vylse] adj (visage) distorted

**convulsif, -ive** [kɔ̃vylsif, -iv] adj convulsive

**convulsions** [kɔ̃vylsjɔ̃] nfpl convulsions

**cookie** [kuki] nm (Inform) cookie

**coopérant** [kɔɔpeʀɑ̃] nm ≈ person doing Voluntary Service Overseas (Brit), ≈ member of the Peace Corps (US)

**coopératif, -ive** [kɔɔpeʀatif, -iv] adj, nf co-operative

**coopération** [kɔɔpeʀasjɔ̃] nf co-operation; (Admin): **la C-** ≈ Voluntary Service Overseas (Brit) ou the Peace Corps (US) (done as alternative to military service)

**coopérer** [kɔɔpeʀe] vi: ~ **(à)** to co-operate (in)

**coordination** [kɔɔʀdinasjɔ̃] nf coordination

**coordonnateur, -trice** [kɔɔʀdɔnatœʀ, -tʀis] adj coordinating ▷ nm/f coordinator

**coordonné, e** [kɔɔʀdɔne] adj coordinated ▷ nf (Ling) coordinate clause; **coordonnés** nmpl

(*vêtements*) coordinates; **coordonnées** *nfpl*
(*Math*) coordinates; (*détails personnels*) address,
phone number, schedule *etc*; whereabouts;
**donnez-moi vos ~** (*fam*) can I have your details
please?
**coordonner** [kɔɔʀdɔne] *vt* to coordinate
**copain, copine** [kɔpɛ̃, kɔpin] *nm/f* mate (*Brit*),
pal ▷ *adj*: **être ~ avec** to be pally with
**copeau, x** [kɔpo] *nm* shaving; (*de métal*) turning
**Copenhague** [kɔpənag] *n* Copenhagen
**copie** [kɔpi] *nf* copy; (*Scol*) script, paper;
exercise; **~ certifiée conforme** certified copy;
**~ papier** (*Inform*) hard copy
**copier** [kɔpje] *vt, vi* to copy; **~ sur** to copy from
**copieur** [kɔpjœʀ] *nm* (photo)copier
**copieusement** [kɔpjøzmã] *adv* copiously
**copieux, -euse** [kɔpjø, -øz] *adj* copious, hearty
**copilote** [kɔpilɔt] *nm* (*Aviat*) co-pilot; (*Auto*) co-
driver, navigator
**copinage** [kɔpinaʒ] *nm*: **obtenir qch par ~** to
get sth through contacts
**copine** [kɔpin] *nf voir* **copain**
**copiste** [kɔpist(ə)] *nm/f* copyist, transcriber
**coproduction** [kɔpʀɔdyksjɔ̃] *nf* coproduction,
joint production
**copropriétaire** [kɔpʀɔpʀijetɛʀ] *nm/f* co-owner
**copropriété** [kɔpʀɔpʀijete] *nf* co-ownership,
joint ownership; **acheter en ~** to buy on a co-
ownership basis
**copulation** [kɔpylasjɔ̃] *nf* copulation
**copyright** [kɔpiʀajt] *nm* copyright
**coq** [kɔk] *nm* cockerel, rooster ▷ *adj inv* (*Boxe*):
**poids ~** bantamweight; **~ de bruyère** grouse; **~
du village** (*fig*: *péj*) ladykiller; **~ au vin** coq au
vin
**coq-à-l'âne** [kɔkalan] *nm inv* abrupt change of
subject
**coque** [kɔk] *nf* (*de noix, mollusque*) shell; (*de bateau*)
hull; **à la ~** (*Culin*) (soft-)boiled
**coquelet** [kɔklɛ] *nm* (*Culin*) cockerel
**coquelicot** [kɔkliko] *nm* poppy
**coqueluche** [kɔklyʃ] *nf* whooping-cough; (*fig*):
**être la ~ de qn** to be sb's flavour of the month
**coquet, te** [kɔkɛ, -ɛt] *adj* appearance-conscious;
(*joli*) pretty
**coquetier** [kɔktje] *nm* egg-cup
**coquettement** [kɔkɛtmã] *adv* (*s'habiller*)
attractively; (*meubler*) prettily
**coquetterie** [kɔkɛtʀi] *nf* appearance-
consciousness
**coquillage** [kɔkijaʒ] *nm* (*mollusque*) shellfish *inv*;
(*coquille*) shell
**coquille** [kɔkij] *nf* shell; (*Typo*) misprint; **~ de
beurre** shell of butter; **~ d'œuf** *adj* (*couleur*)
eggshell; **~ de noix** nutshell; **~ St Jacques**
scallop
**coquillettes** [kɔkijɛt] *nfpl* pasta shells
**coquin, e** [kɔkɛ̃, -in] *adj* mischievous, roguish;
(*polisson*) naughty ▷ *nm/f* (*péj*) rascal
**cor** [kɔʀ] *nm* (*Mus*) horn; (*Méd*): **~ (au pied)** corn;
**réclamer à ~ et à cri** to clamour for; **~ anglais**
cor anglais; **~ de chasse** hunting horn

**corail, -aux** [kɔʀaj, -o] *nm* coral *no pl*
**Coran** [kɔʀã] *nm*: **le ~** the Koran
**coraux** [kɔʀo] *nmpl de* **corail**
**corbeau, x** [kɔʀbo] *nm* crow
**corbeille** [kɔʀbɛj] *nf* basket; (*Inform*) recycle bin;
(*Bourse*): **la ~ =** the floor (of the Stock Exchange);
**~ de mariage** (*fig*) wedding presents *pl*; **~ à
ouvrage** work-basket; **~ à pain** breadbasket; **~
à papier** waste paper basket *ou* bin
**corbillard** [kɔʀbijaʀ] *nm* hearse
**cordage** [kɔʀdaʒ] *nm* rope; **cordages** *nmpl* (*de
voilure*) rigging *sg*
**corde** [kɔʀd(ə)] *nf* rope; (*de violon, raquette, d'arc*)
string; (*trame*): **la ~** the thread; (*Athlétisme,
Auto*): **la ~** the rails *pl*; **les ~s** (*Boxe*) the ropes; **les
(instruments à) ~s** (*Mus*) the strings, the
stringed instruments; **semelles de ~** rope
soles; **tenir la ~** (*Athlétisme, Auto*) to be in the
inside lane; **tomber des ~s** to rain cats and
dogs; **tirer sur la ~** to go too far; **la ~ sensible**
the right chord; **usé jusqu'à la ~** threadbare; **~
à linge** washing *ou* clothes line; **~ lisse**
(climbing) rope; **~ à nœuds** knotted climbing
rope; **~ raide** tightrope; **~ à sauter** skipping
rope; **~s vocales** vocal cords
**cordeau, x** [kɔʀdo] *nm* string, line; **tracé au ~**
as straight as a die
**cordée** [kɔʀde] *nf* (*d'alpinistes*) rope, roped party
**cordelière** [kɔʀdəljɛʀ] *nf* cord (belt)
**cordial, e, aux** [kɔʀdjal, -o] *adj* warm, cordial
▷ *nm* cordial, pick-me-up
**cordialement** [kɔʀdjalmã] *adv* cordially,
heartily; (*formule épistolaire*) (kind) regards
**cordialité** [kɔʀdjalite] *nf* warmth, cordiality
**cordillère** [kɔʀdijɛʀ] *nf*: **la ~ des Andes** the
Andes cordillera *ou* range
**cordon** [kɔʀdɔ̃] *nm* cord, string; **~ sanitaire/de
police** sanitary/police cordon; **~ littoral**
sandbank, sandbar; **~ ombilical** umbilical cord
**cordon-bleu** [kɔʀdɔ̃blø] *adj, nm/f* cordon bleu
**cordonnerie** [kɔʀdɔnʀi] *nf* shoe repairer's *ou*
mender's (shop)
**cordonnier** [kɔʀdɔnje] *nm* shoe repairer *ou*
mender, cobbler
**cordouan, e** [kɔʀduã, -an] *adj* Cordovan
**Cordoue** [kɔʀdu] *n* Cordoba
**Corée** [kɔʀe] *nf*: **la ~** Korea; **la ~ du Sud/du
Nord** South/North Korea; **la République
(démocratique populaire) de ~** the
(Democratic People's) Republic of Korea
**coréen, ne** [kɔʀeɛ̃, -ɛn] *adj* Korean ▷ *nm* (*Ling*)
Korean ▷ *nm/f*: **Coréen, ne** Korean
**coreligionnaire** [kɔʀəliʒjɔnɛʀ] *nm/f* fellow
Christian/Muslim/Jew *etc*
**Corfou** [kɔʀfu] *n* Corfu
**coriace** [kɔʀjas] *adj* tough
**coriandre** [kɔʀjãdʀ(ə)] *nf* coriander
**Corinthe** [kɔʀɛ̃t] *n* Corinth
**cormoran** [kɔʀmɔʀã] *nm* cormorant
**cornac** [kɔʀnak] *nm* elephant driver
**corne** [kɔʀn(ə)] *nf* horn; (*de cerf*) antler; (*de la
peau*) callus; **~ d'abondance** horn of plenty; **~**

**de brume** (*Navig*) foghorn
**cornée** [kɔʀne] *nf* cornea
**corneille** [kɔʀnɛj] *nf* crow
**cornélien, ne** [kɔʀneljɛ̃, -ɛn] *adj* (*débat etc*) where love and duty conflict
**cornemuse** [kɔʀnəmyz] *nf* bagpipes *pl*; **joueur de ~** piper
**corner**[1] [kɔʀnɛʀ] *nm* (*Football*) corner (kick)
**corner**[2] [kɔʀne] *vt* (*pages*) to make dog-eared ▷ *vi* (*klaxonner*) to blare out
**cornet** [kɔʀnɛ] *nm* (*paper*) cone; (*de glace*) cornet, cone; **~ à pistons** cornet
**cornette** [kɔʀnɛt] *nf* cornet (*headgear*)
**corniaud** [kɔʀnjo] *nm* (*chien*) mongrel; (*péj*) twit, clot
**corniche** [kɔʀniʃ] *nf* (*de meuble, neigeuse*) cornice; (*route*) coast road
**cornichon** [kɔʀniʃɔ̃] *nm* gherkin
**Cornouailles** [kɔʀnwaj] *nf(pl)* Cornwall
**cornue** [kɔʀny] *nf* retort
**corollaire** [kɔʀɔlɛʀ] *nm* corollary
**corolle** [kɔʀɔl] *nf* corolla
**coron** [kɔʀɔ̃] *nm* mining cottage; mining village
**coronaire** [kɔʀɔnɛʀ] *adj* coronary
**corporation** [kɔʀpɔʀasjɔ̃] *nf* corporate body; (*au Moyen-Âge*) guild
**corporel, le** [kɔʀpɔʀɛl] *adj* bodily; (*punition*) corporal; **soins ~s** care *sg* of the body
**corps** [kɔʀ] *nm* (*gén*) body; (*cadavre*) (dead) body; **à son ~ défendant** against one's will; **à ~ perdu** headlong; **perdu ~ et biens** lost with all hands; **prendre ~** to take shape; **faire ~ avec** to be joined to; to form one body with; **~ d'armée (CA)** army corps; **~ de ballet** corps de ballet; **~ constitués** (*Pol*) constitutional bodies; **le ~ consulaire (CC)** the consular corps; **~ à ~** *adv* hand-to-hand ▷ *nm* clinch; **le ~ du délit** (*Jur*) corpus delicti; **le ~ diplomatique (CD)** the diplomatic corps; **le ~ électoral** the electorate; **le ~ enseignant** the teaching profession; **~ étranger** (*Méd*) foreign body; **~ expéditionnaire** task force; **~ de garde** guardroom; **~ législatif** legislative body; **le ~ médical** the medical profession
**corpulence** [kɔʀpylɑ̃s] *nf* build; (*embonpoint*) stoutness (*Brit*), corpulence; **de forte ~** of large build
**corpulent, e** [kɔʀpylɑ̃, -ɑ̃t] *adj* stout (*Brit*), corpulent
**corpus** [kɔʀpys] *nm* (*Ling*) corpus
**correct, e** [kɔʀɛkt] *adj* (*exact*) accurate, correct; (*bienséant, honnête*) correct; (*passable*) adequate
**correctement** [kɔʀɛktəmɑ̃] *adv* accurately; correctly; adequately
**correcteur, -trice** [kɔʀɛktœʀ, -tʀis] *nm/f* (*Scol*) examiner, marker; (*Typo*) proofreader
**correctif, -ive** [kɔʀɛktif, -iv] *adj* corrective ▷ *nm* (*mise au point*) rider, qualification
**correction** [kɔʀɛksjɔ̃] *nf* (*voir corriger*) correction; marking; (*voir correct*) correctness; (*rature, surcharge*) correction, emendation; (*coups*) thrashing; **~ sur écran** (*Inform*) screen editing;

**~ (des épreuves)** proofreading
**correctionnel, le** [kɔʀɛksjɔnɛl] *adj* (*Jur*): **tribunal ~** ≈ criminal court
**corrélation** [kɔʀelasjɔ̃] *nf* correlation
**correspondance** [kɔʀɛspɔ̃dɑ̃s] *nf* correspondence; (*de train, d'avion*) connection; **ce train assure la ~ avec l'avion de 10 heures** this train connects with the 10 o'clock plane; **cours par ~** correspondence course; **vente par ~** mail-order business
**correspondancier, -ière** [kɔʀɛspɔ̃dɑ̃sje, -jɛʀ] *nm/f* correspondence clerk
**correspondant, e** [kɔʀɛspɔ̃dɑ̃, -ɑ̃t] *nm/f* correspondent; (*Tél*) person phoning (*ou* being phoned)
**correspondre** [kɔʀɛspɔ̃dʀ(ə)] *vi* (*données, témoignages*) to correspond, tally; (*chambres*) to communicate; **~ à** to correspond to; **~ avec qn** to correspond with sb
**Corrèze** [kɔʀɛz] *nf*: **la ~** the Corrèze
**corrézien, ne** [kɔʀezjɛ̃, -ɛn] *adj* of *ou* from the Corrèze
**corrida** [kɔʀida] *nf* bullfight
**corridor** [kɔʀidɔʀ] *nm* corridor, passage
**corrigé** [kɔʀiʒe] *nm* (*Scol*) correct version; fair copy
**corriger** [kɔʀiʒe] *vt* (*devoir*) to correct, mark; (*texte*) to correct, emend; (*erreur, défaut*) to correct, put right; (*punir*) to thrash; **~ qn de** (*défaut*) to cure sb of; **se ~ de** to cure o.s. of
**corroborer** [kɔʀɔbɔʀe] *vt* to corroborate
**corroder** [kɔʀɔde] *vt* to corrode
**corrompre** [kɔʀɔ̃pʀ(ə)] *vt* (*dépraver*) to corrupt; (*acheter: témoin etc*) to bribe
**corrompu, e** [kɔʀɔ̃py] *adj* corrupt
**corrosif, -ive** [kɔʀɔzif, -iv] *adj* corrosive
**corrosion** [kɔʀɔzjɔ̃] *nf* corrosion
**corruption** [kɔʀypsjɔ̃] *nf* corruption; bribery
**corsage** [kɔʀsaʒ] *nm* (*d'une robe*) bodice; (*chemisier*) blouse
**corsaire** [kɔʀsɛʀ] *nm* pirate, corsair; privateer
**corse** [kɔʀs(ə)] *adj* Corsican ▷ *nm/f*: **Corse** Corsican ▷ *nf*: **la C~** Corsica
**corsé, e** [kɔʀse] *adj* vigorous; (*café etc*) full-flavoured (*Brit*) *ou* -flavored (*US*); (*goût*) full; (*fig*) spicy; tricky
**corselet** [kɔʀsəlɛ] *nm* corselet
**corser** [kɔʀse] *vt* (*difficulté*) to aggravate; (*intrigue*) to liven up; (*sauce*) to add spice to
**corset** [kɔʀsɛ] *nm* corset; (*d'une robe*) bodice; **~ orthopédique** surgical corset
**corso** [kɔʀso] *nm*: **~ fleuri** procession of floral floats
**cortège** [kɔʀtɛʒ] *nm* procession
**cortisone** [kɔʀtizɔn] *nf* (*Méd*) cortisone
**corvée** [kɔʀve] *nf* chore, drudgery *no pl*; (*Mil*) fatigue (duty)
**cosaque** [kɔzak] *nm* cossack
**cosignataire** [kɔsiɲatɛʀ] *adj, nm/f* co-signatory
**cosinus** [kɔsinys] *nm* (*Math*) cosine
**cosmétique** [kɔsmetik] *nm* (*pour les cheveux*) hair-oil; (*produit de beauté*) beauty care product

C

**cosmétologie** [kɔsmetɔlɔʒi] *nf* beauty care
**cosmique** [kɔsmik] *adj* cosmic
**cosmonaute** [kɔsmɔnot] *nm/f* cosmonaut, astronaut
**cosmopolite** [kɔsmɔpɔlit] *adj* cosmopolitan
**cosmos** [kɔsmɔs] *nm* outer space; cosmos
**cosse** [kɔs] *nf* (*Bot*) pod, hull
**cossu, e** [kɔsy] *adj* opulent-looking, well-to-do
**Costa Rica** [kɔstaʀika] *nm*: **le ~** Costa Rica
**costaricien, ne** [kɔstaʀisjɛ̃, -ɛn] *adj* Costa Rican ▷ *nm/f*: **Costaricien, ne** Costa Rican
**costaud, e** [kɔsto, -od] *adj* strong, sturdy
**costume** [kɔstym] *nm* (*d'homme*) suit; (*de théâtre*) costume
**costumé, e** [kɔstyme] *adj* dressed up
**costumier, -ière** [kɔstymje, -jɛʀ] *nm/f* (*fabricant, loueur*) costumier; (*Théât*) wardrobe master/mistress
**cotangente** [kɔtɑ̃ʒɑ̃t] *nf* (*Math*) cotangent
**cotation** [kɔtasjɔ̃] *nf* quoted value
**cote** [kɔt] *nf* (*en Bourse etc*) quotation; quoted value; (*d'un cheval*): **la ~ de** the odds *pl* on; (*d'un candidat etc*) rating; (*mesure: sur une carte*) spot height; (: *sur un croquis*) dimension; (*de classement*) (classification) mark; reference number; **avoir la ~ to** be very popular; **inscrit à la ~** quoted on the Stock Exchange; **~ d'alerte** danger *ou* flood level; **~ mal taillée** (*fig*) compromise; **~ de popularité** popularity rating
**coté, e** [kɔte] *adj*: **être ~** to be listed *ou* quoted; **être ~ en Bourse** to be quoted on the Stock Exchange; **être bien/mal ~** to be highly/poorly rated
**côte** [kot] *nf* (*rivage*) coast(line); (*pente*) slope; (: *sur une route*) hill; (*Anat*) rib; (*d'un tricot, tissu*) rib, ribbing *no pl*; **~ à ~** *adv* side by side; **la C~ (d'Azur)** the (French) Riviera; **la C~ d'Ivoire** the Ivory Coast; **~ de porc** pork chop
**côté** [kote] *nm* (*gén*) side; (*direction*) way, direction; **de chaque ~ (de)** on each side of; **de tous les ~s** from all directions; **de quel ~ est-il parti?** which way *ou* in which direction did he go?; **de ce/de l'autre ~** this/the other way; **d'un ~ ... de l'autre ~ ...** (*alternative*) on (the) one hand ... on the other (hand) ...; **du ~ de** (*provenance*) from; (*direction*) towards; **du ~ de Lyon** (*proximité*) near Lyons; **du ~ gauche** on the left-hand side; **de ~** *adv* sideways; on one side; to one side; aside; **laisser de ~** to leave on one side; **mettre de ~** to put on one side, put aside; **de mon ~** (*quant à moi*) for my part; **à ~** *adv* (right) nearby; beside next door; (*d'autre part*) besides; **à ~ de** beside; next to; (*fig*) in comparison to; **à ~ (de la cible)** off target, wide (of the mark); **être aux ~s de** to be by the side of
**coteau, x** [kɔto] *nm* hill
**côtelé, e** [kotle] *adj* ribbed; **pantalon en velours ~** corduroy trousers *pl*
**côtelette** [kotlɛt] *nf* chop
**coter** [kɔte] *vt* (*Bourse*) to quote

**coterie** [kɔtʀi] *nf* set
**côtier, -ière** [kotje, -jɛʀ] *adj* coastal
**cotisation** [kɔtizasjɔ̃] *nf* subscription, dues *pl*; (*pour une pension*) contributions *pl*
**cotiser** [kɔtize] *vi*: **~ (à)** to pay contributions (to); (*à une association*) to subscribe (to); **se cotiser** to club together
**coton** [kɔtɔ̃] *nm* cotton; **~ hydrophile** cotton wool (*Brit*), absorbent cotton (*US*)
**cotonnade** [kɔtɔnad] *nf* cotton (fabric)
**Coton-Tige**® [kɔtɔ̃tiʒ] *nm* cotton bud®
**côtoyer** [kotwaje] *vt* to be close to; (*rencontrer*) to rub shoulders with; (*longer*) to run alongside; (*fig: friser*) to be bordering *ou* verging on
**cotte** [kɔt] *nf*: **~ de mailles** coat of mail
**cou** [ku] *nm* neck
**couac** [kwak] *nm* (*fam*) bum note
**couard, e** [kwaʀ, -aʀd(ə)] *adj* cowardly
**couchage** [kuʃaʒ] *nm voir* **sac**
**couchant** [kuʃɑ̃] *adj*: **soleil ~** setting sun
**couche** [kuʃ] *nf* (*strate: gén, Géo*) layer, stratum (*pl* -a); (*de peinture, vernis*) coat; (*de poussière, crème*) layer; (*de bébé*) nappy (*Brit*), diaper (*US*); **~ d'ozone** ozone layer; **couches** *nfpl* (*Méd*) confinement *sg*; **~s sociales** social levels *ou* strata
**couché, e** [kuʃe] *adj* (*étendu*) lying down; (*au lit*) in bed
**couche-culotte** [kuʃkylɔt] (*pl* **couches-culottes**) *nf* (plastic-coated) disposable nappy (*Brit*) *ou* diaper (*US*)
**coucher** [kuʃe] *nm* (*du soleil*) setting ▷ *vt* (*personne*) to put to bed; (: *loger*) to put up; (*objet*) to lay on its side; (*écrire*) to inscribe, couch ▷ *vi* (*dormir*) to sleep, spend the night; **~ avec qn** to sleep with sb, go to bed with sb; **se coucher** *vi* (*pour dormir*) to go to bed; (*pour se reposer*) to lie down; (*soleil*) to set, go down; **à prendre avant le ~** (*Méd*) take at night *ou* before going to bed; **~ de soleil** sunset
**couchette** [kuʃɛt] *nf* couchette; (*de marin*) bunk
**coucheur** [kuʃœʀ] *nm*: **mauvais ~** awkward customer
**couci-couça** [kusikusa] *adv* (*fam*) so-so
**coucou** [kuku] *nm* cuckoo ▷ *excl* peek-a-boo
**coude** [kud] *nm* (*Anat*) elbow; (*de tuyau, de la route*) bend; **~ à ~** *adv* shoulder to shoulder, side by side
**coudée** [kude] *nf*: **avoir ses ~s franches** (*fig*) to have a free rein
**cou-de-pied** [kudpje] (*pl* **cous-de-pied**) *nm* instep
**coudoyer** [kudwaje] *vt* to brush past *ou* against; (*fig*) to rub shoulders with
**coudre** [kudʀ(ə)] *vt* (*bouton*) to sew on; (*robe*) to sew (up) ▷ *vi* to sew
**couenne** [kwan] *nf* (*de lard*) rind
**couette** [kwɛt] *nf* duvet, (continental) quilt; **couettes** *nfpl* (*cheveux*) bunches
**couffin** [kufɛ̃] *nm* Moses basket; (straw) basket
**couilles** [kuj] *nfpl* (*fam!*) balls (!)
**couiner** [kwine] *vi* to squeal

**coulage** [kulaʒ] *nm* (*Comm*) loss of stock (*due to theft or negligence*)

**coulant, e** [kulā, -āt] *adj* (*indulgent*) easy-going; (*fromage etc*) runny

**coulée** [kule] *nf* (*de lave, métal en fusion*) flow; **~ de neige** snowslide

**couler** [kule] *vi* to flow, run; (*fuir: stylo, récipient*) to leak; (*sombrer: bateau*) to sink ▷ *vt* (*cloche, sculpture*) to cast; (*bateau*) to sink; (*fig*) to ruin, bring down; (: *passer*): **~ une vie heureuse** to enjoy a happy life; **se ~ dans** (*interstice etc*) to slip into; **faire ~** (*eau*) to run; **faire ~ un bain** to run a bath; **il a coulé une bielle** (*Auto*) his big end went; **~ de source** to follow on naturally; **~ à pic** to sink *ou* go straight to the bottom

**couleur** [kulœʀ] *nf* colour (*Brit*), color (*US*); (*Cartes*) suit; **couleurs** *nfpl* (*du teint*) colo(u)r *sg*; **les ~s** (*Mil*) the colo(u)rs; **en ~s** (*film*) in colo(u)r; **télévision en ~s** colo(u)r television; **de ~** (*homme, femme*) colo(u)red; **sous ~ de** on the pretext of; **de quelle ~** of what colo(u)r

**couleuvre** [kulœvʀ(ə)] *nf* grass snake

**coulisse** [kulis] *nf* (*Tech*) runner; **coulisses** *nfpl* (*Théât*) wings; (*fig*): **dans les ~s** behind the scenes; **porte à ~** sliding door

**coulisser** [kulise] *vi* to slide, run

**couloir** [kulwaʀ] *nm* corridor, passage; (*d'avion*) aisle; (*de bus*) gangway; (: *sur la route*) bus lane; (*Sport: de piste*) lane; (*Géo*) gully; **~ aérien** air corridor *ou* lane; **~ de navigation** shipping lane

**coulpe** [kulp(ə)] *nf*: **battre sa ~** to repent openly

**coup** [ku] *nm* (*heurt, choc*) knock; (*affectif*) blow, shock; (*agressif*) blow; (*avec arme à feu*) shot; (*de l'horloge*) chime; stroke; (*Sport*) stroke; shot; blow; (*fam: fois*) time; (*Échecs*) move; **~ de coude/genou** nudge (with the elbow)/ with the knee; **à ~s de hache/marteau** (hitting) with an axe/a hammer; **~ de tonnerre** clap of thunder; **~ de sonnette** ring of the bell; **~ de crayon/pinceau** stroke of the pencil/brush; **donner un ~ de balai** to sweep up, give the floor a sweep; **donner un ~ de chiffon** to go round with the duster; **avoir le ~** (*fig*) to have the knack; **être dans le/hors du ~** to be/not to be in on it; **boire un ~** to have a drink; **d'un seul ~** (*subitement*) suddenly; (*à la fois*) at one go; in one blow; (: *tu vois*) you see); **du ~** so (you see); **du premier ~** first time *ou* go, at the first attempt; **du même ~** at the same time; **à ~ sûr** definitely, without fail; **après ~** afterwards; **~ sur ~** in quick succession; **être sur un ~** to be on to something; **sur le ~** outright; **sous le ~ de** (*surprise etc*) under the influence of; **tomber sous le ~ de la loi** to constitute a statutory offence; **à tous les ~s** every time; **il a raté son ~** he missed his turn; **pour le ~** for once; **~ bas** (*fig*): **donner un ~ bas à qn** to hit sb below the belt; **~ de chance** stroke of luck; **~ de chapeau** (*fig*) pat on the back; **~ de couteau** stab (of a knife); **~ dur** hard blow; **~ d'éclat** (great) feat; **~ d'envoi** kick-off; **~ d'essai** first attempt; **~ d'état** coup d'état; **~ de feu** shot; **~ de filet**

(*Police*) haul; **~ de foudre** (*fig*) love at first sight; **~ fourré** stab in the back; **~ franc** free kick; **~ de frein** (sharp) braking *no pl*; **~ de fusil** rifle shot; **~ de grâce** coup de grâce; **~ du lapin** (*Auto*) whiplash; **~ de main: donner un ~ de main à qn** to give sb a (helping) hand; **~ de maître** master stroke; **~ d'œil** glance; **~ de pied** kick; **~ de poing** punch; **~ de soleil** sunburn *no pl*; **~ de téléphone** phone call; **~ de tête** (*fig*) (sudden) impulse; **~ de théâtre** (*fig*) dramatic turn of events; **~ de vent** gust of wind; **en ~ de vent** (*rapidement*) in a tearing hurry

**coupable** [kupabl(ə)] *adj* guilty; (*pensée*) guilty, culpable ▷ *nm/f* (*gén*) culprit; (*Jur*) guilty party; **~ de** guilty of

**coupant, e** [kupā, -āt] *adj* (*lame*) sharp; (*fig: voix, ton*) cutting

**coupe** [kup] *nf* (*verre*) goblet; (*à fruits*) dish; (*Sport*) cup; (*de cheveux, de vêtement*) cut; (*graphique, plan*) (cross) section; **être sous la ~ de** to be under the control of; **faire des ~s sombres dans** to make drastic cuts in

**coupé, e** [kupe] *adj* (*communications, route*) cut, blocked; (*vêtement*): **bien/mal ~** well/badly cut ▷ *nm* (*Auto*) coupé ▷ *nf* (*Navig*) gangway

**coupe-circuit** [kupsiʀkɥi] *nm inv* cutout, circuit breaker

**coupe-feu** [kupfø] *nm inv* firebreak

**coupe-gorge** [kupgɔʀʒ(ə)] *nm inv* cut-throats' den

**coupe-ongles** [kupɔ̃gl(ə)] *nm inv* (*pince*) nail clippers; (*ciseaux*) nail scissors

**coupe-papier** [kuppapje] *nm inv* paper knife

**couper** [kupe] *vt* to cut; (*retrancher*) to cut (out), take out; (*route, courant*) to cut off; (*appétit*) to take away; (*fièvre*) to take down, reduce; (*vin, cidre*) to blend; (: *à table*) to dilute (with water) ▷ *vi* to cut; (*prendre un raccourci*) to take a short-cut; (*Cartes: diviser le paquet*) to cut; (: *avec l'atout*) to trump; **se couper** *vi* (*se blesser*) to cut o.s.; (*en témoignant etc*) to give o.s. away; **~ l'appétit à qn** to spoil sb's appetite; **~ la parole à qn** to cut sb short; **~ les vivres à qn** to cut off sb's vital supplies; **~ le contact** *ou* **l'allumage** (*Auto*) to turn off the ignition; **~ les ponts avec qn** to break with sb; **se faire ~ les cheveux** to have *ou* get one's hair cut

**couperet** [kupʀɛ] *nm* cleaver, chopper

**couperosé, e** [kupʀoze] *adj* blotchy

**couple** [kupl(ə)] *nm* couple; **~ de torsion** torque

**coupler** [kuple] *vt* to couple (together)

**couplet** [kuplɛ] *nm* verse

**coupleur** [kuplœʀ] *nm*: **~ acoustique** acoustic coupler

**coupole** [kupɔl] *nf* dome, cupola

**coupon** [kupɔ̃] *nm* (*ticket*) coupon; (*de tissu*) remnant; roll

**coupon-réponse** [kupɔ̃ʀepɔ̃s] (*pl* **coupons-réponses**) *nm* reply coupon

**coupure** [kupyʀ] *nf* cut; (*billet de banque*) note; (*de journal*) cutting; **~ de courant** power cut

**cour** [kuʀ] *nf* (*de ferme, jardin*) (court)yard; (*d'immeuble*) back yard; (*Jur, royale*) court; **faire la ~ à qn** to court sb; **~ d'appel** appeal court (*Brit*), appellate court (*US*); **~ d'assises** court of assizes, ≈ Crown Court (*Brit*); **~ de cassation** final court of appeal; **~ des comptes** (*Admin*) revenue court; **~ martiale** court-martial; **~ de récréation** (*Scol*) schoolyard, playground

**courage** [kuʀaʒ] *nm* courage, bravery

**courageusement** [kuʀaʒøzmɑ̃] *adv* bravely, courageously

**courageux, -euse** [kuʀaʒø, -øz] *adj* brave, courageous

**couramment** [kuʀamɑ̃] *adv* commonly; (*parler*) fluently

**courant, e** [kuʀɑ̃, -ɑ̃t] *adj* (*fréquent*) common; (*Comm, gén: normal*) standard; (*en cours*) current ▷ *nm* current; (*fig*) movement; trend; **être au ~ (de)** (*fait, nouvelle*) to know (about); **mettre qn au ~ (de)** (*fait, nouvelle*) to tell sb (about); (*nouveau travail etc*) to teach sb the basics (of), brief sb (about); **se tenir au ~ (de)** (*techniques etc*) to keep o.s. up-to-date (on); **dans le ~ de** (*pendant*) in the course of; **~ octobre** *etc* in the course of October *etc*; **le 10 ~** (*Comm*) the 10th inst.; **~ d'air** draught (*Brit*), draft (*US*); **~ électrique** (electric) current, power

**courbature** [kuʀbatyʀ] *nf* ache

**courbaturé, e** [kuʀbatyʀe] *adj* aching

**courbe** [kuʀb(ə)] *adj* curved ▷ *nf* curve; **~ de niveau** contour line

**courber** [kuʀbe] *vt* to bend; **~ la tête** to bow one's head; **se courber** *vi* (*branche etc*) to bend, curve; (*personne*) to bend (down)

**courbette** [kuʀbɛt] *nf* low bow

**coure** *etc* [kuʀ] *vb voir* **courir**

**coureur, -euse** [kuʀœʀ, -øz] *nm/f* (*Sport*) runner (*ou* driver); (*péj*) womanizer/manhunter; **~ cycliste/automobile** racing cyclist/driver

**courge** [kuʀʒ(ə)] *nf* (*Bot*) gourd; (*Culin*) marrow

**courgette** [kuʀʒɛt] *nf* courgette (*Brit*), zucchini (*US*)

**courir** [kuʀiʀ] *vi* (*gén*) to run; (*se dépêcher*) to rush; (*fig: rumeurs*) to go round; (*Comm: intérêt*) to accrue ▷ *vt* (*Sport: épreuve*) to compete in; (*risque*) to run; (*danger*) to face; **~ les cafés/bals** to do the rounds of the cafés/dances; **le bruit court que** the rumour is going round that; **par les temps qui courent** at the present time; **~ après qn** to run after sb, chase (after) sb; **laisser ~ qn** to let things alone; **faire ~ qn** to make sb run around (all over the place); **tu peux (toujours) ~!** you've got a hope!

**couronne** [kuʀɔn] *nf* crown; (*de fleurs*) wreath, circlet; **~ funéraire** *ou* **mortuaire** (funeral) wreath

**couronnement** [kuʀɔnmɑ̃] *nm* coronation, crowning; (*fig*) crowning achievement

**couronner** [kuʀɔne] *vt* to crown

**courons** [kuʀɔ̃], **courrai** *etc* [kuʀe] *vb voir* **courir**

**courre** [kuʀ] *vb voir* **chasse**

**courriel** [kuʀjɛl] *nm* email; **envoyer qch par ~** to email sth

**courrier** [kuʀje] *nm* mail, post; (*lettres à écrire*) letters *pl*; (*rubrique*) column; **qualité ~** letter quality; **long/moyen ~** *adj* (*Aviat*) long-/medium-haul; **~ du cœur** problem page; **~ électronique** electronic mail, E-mail

**courroie** [kuʀwa] *nf* strap; (*Tech*) belt; **~ de transmission/de ventilateur** driving/fan belt

**courrons** *etc* [kuʀɔ̃] *vb voir* **courir**

**courroucé, e** [kuʀuse] *adj* wrathful

**cours** [kuʀ] *vb voir* **courir** ▷ *nm* (*leçon*) lesson; class; (*série de leçons*) course; (*cheminement*) course; (*écoulement*) flow; (*avenue*) walk; (*Comm*) rate; price; (*Bourse*) quotation; **donner libre ~ à** to give free expression to; **avoir ~** (*monnaie*) to be legal tender; (*fig*) to be current; (*Scol*) to have a class *ou* lecture; **en ~** (*année*) current; (*travaux*) in progress; **en ~ de route** on the way; **au ~ de** in the course of, during; **le ~ du change** the exchange rate; **~ d'eau** waterway; **~ élémentaire (CE)** 2nd and 3rd years of primary school; **~ moyen (CM)** 4th and 5th years of primary school; **~ préparatoire** ≈ infants' class (*Brit*), ≈ 1st grade (*US*); **~ du soir** night school

**course** [kuʀs(ə)] *nf* running; (*Sport: épreuve*) race; (*trajet: du soleil*) course; (: *d'un projectile*) flight; (: *d'une pièce mécanique*) travel; (*excursion*) outing; climb; (*d'un taxi, autocar*) journey, trip; (*petite mission*) errand; **courses** *nfpl* (*achats*) shopping *sg*; (*Hippisme*) races; **faire les** *ou* **ses ~s** to go shopping; **jouer aux ~s** to bet on the races; **à bout de ~** (*épuisé*) exhausted; **~ automobile** car race; **~ de côte** (*Auto*) hill climb; **~ par étapes** *ou* **d'étapes** race in stages; **~ d'obstacles** obstacle race; **~ à pied** walking race; **~ de vitesse** sprint; **~s de chevaux** horse racing

**coursier, -ière** [kuʀsje, -jɛʀ] *nm/f* courier

**court, e** [kuʀ, kuʀt(ə)] *adj* short ▷ *adv* short ▷ *nm*: **~ (de tennis)** (tennis) court; **tourner ~** to come to a sudden end; **couper ~ à** to cut short; **à ~ de** short of; **prendre qn de ~** to catch sb unawares; **pour faire ~** briefly, to cut a long story short; **ça fait ~** that's not very long; **tirer à la ~e paille** to draw lots; **faire la ~e échelle à qn** to give sb a leg up; **~ métrage** (*Ciné*) short (film)

**court-bouillon** [kuʀbujɔ̃] (*pl* **courts-bouillons**) *nm* court-bouillon

**court-circuit** [kuʀsiʀkɥi] (*pl* **courts-circuits**) *nm* short-circuit

**court-circuiter** [kuʀsiʀkɥite] *vt* (*fig*) to bypass

**courtier, -ière** [kuʀtje, -jɛʀ] *nm/f* broker

**courtisan** [kuʀtizɑ̃] *nm* courtier

**courtisane** [kuʀtizan] *nf* courtesan

**courtiser** [kuʀtize] *vt* to court, woo

**courtois, e** [kuʀtwa, -waz] *adj* courteous

**courtoisement** [kuʀtwazmɑ̃] *adv* courteously

**courtoisie** [kuʀtwazi] *nf* courtesy

**couru, e** [kuʀy] *pp de* **courir** ▷ *adj* (*spectacle etc*) popular; **c'est ~ (d'avance)!** (*fam*) it's a safe bet!

**cousais** *etc* [kuzɛ] *vb voir* **coudre**

**couscous** [kuskus] *nm* couscous

**cousin, e** [kuzɛ̃, -in] *nm/f* cousin ▷ *nm* (*Zool*) mosquito; **~ germain** first cousin
**cousons** *etc* [kuzɔ̃] *vb voir* **coudre**
**coussin** [kusɛ̃] *nm* cushion; **~ d'air** (*Tech*) air cushion
**cousu, e** [kuzy] *pp de* **coudre** ▷ *adj*: **~ d'or** rolling in riches
**coût** [ku] *nm* cost; **le ~ de la vie** the cost of living
**coûtant** [kutɑ̃] *adj m*: **au prix ~** at cost price
**couteau, x** [kuto] *nm* knife; **~ à cran d'arrêt** flick-knife; **~ de cuisine** kitchen knife; **~ à pain** bread knife; **~ de poche** pocket knife
**couteau-scie** [kutosi] (*pl* **couteaux-scies**) *nm* serrated(-edged) knife
**coutelier, -ière** [kutəlje, -jɛʀ] *adj*: **l'industrie coutelière** the cutlery industry ▷ *nm/f* cutler
**coutellerie** [kutɛlʀi] *nf* cutlery shop; cutlery
**coûter** [kute] *vt* to cost ▷ *vi*: **~ à qn** to cost sb a lot; **~ cher** to be expensive; **~ cher à qn** (*fig*) to cost sb dear *ou* dearly; **combien ça coûte?** how much is it?, what does it cost?; **coûte que coûte** at all costs
**coûteux, -euse** [kutø, -øz] *adj* costly, expensive
**coutume** [kutym] *nf* custom; **de ~** usual, customary
**coutumier, -ière** [kutymje, -jɛʀ] *adj* customary; **elle est coutumière du fait** that's her usual trick
**couture** [kutyʀ] *nf* sewing; dress-making; (*points*) seam
**couturier** [kutyʀje] *nm* fashion designer, couturier
**couturière** [kutyʀjɛʀ] *nf* dressmaker
**couvée** [kuve] *nf* brood, clutch
**couvent** [kuvɑ̃] *nm* (*de sœurs*) convent; (*de frères*) monastery; (*établissement scolaire*) convent (school)
**couver** [kuve] *vt* to hatch; (*maladie*) to be sickening for ▷ *vi* (*feu*) to smoulder (*Brit*), smolder (*US*); (*révolte*) to be brewing; **~ qn/qch des yeux** to look lovingly at sb/sth; (*convoiter*) to look longingly at sb/sth
**couvercle** [kuvɛʀkl(ə)] *nm* lid; (*de bombe aérosol etc, qui se visse*) cap, top
**couvert, e** [kuvɛʀ, -ɛʀt(ə)] *pp de* **couvrir** ▷ *adj* (*ciel*) overcast; (*coiffé d'un chapeau*) wearing a hat ▷ *nm* place setting; (*place à table*) place; (*au restaurant*) cover charge; **couverts** *nmpl* place settings; cutlery *sg*; **~ de** covered with *ou* in; **bien ~** (*habillé*) well wrapped up; **mettre le ~** to lay the table; **à ~** under cover; **sous le ~ de** under the shelter of; (*fig*) under cover of
**couverture** [kuvɛʀtyʀ] *nf* (*de lit*) blanket; (*de bâtiment*) roofing; (*de livre, fig: d'un espion etc, Assurances*) cover; (*Presse*) coverage; **de ~** (*lettre etc*) covering; **~ chauffante** electric blanket
**couveuse** [kuvøz] *nf* (*à poules*) sitter, brooder; (*de maternité*) incubator
**couvre** *etc* [kuvʀ(ə)] *vb voir* **couvrir**
**couvre-chef** [kuvʀəʃef] *nm* hat
**couvre-feu, x** [kuvʀəfø] *nm* curfew

**couvre-lit** [kuvʀəli] *nm* bedspread
**couvre-pieds** [kuvʀəpje] *nm inv* quilt
**couvreur** [kuvʀœʀ] *nm* roofer
**couvrir** [kuvʀiʀ] *vt* to cover; (*dominer, étouffer: voix, pas*) to drown out; (*erreur*) to cover up; (*Zool: s'accoupler à*) to cover; **se couvrir** *vi* (*ciel*) to cloud over; (*s'habiller*) to cover up, wrap up; (*se coiffer*) to put on one's hat; (*par une assurance*) to cover o.s.; **se ~ de** (*fleurs, boutons*) to become covered in
**cover-girl** [kɔvœʀg[ʷɔeʀl] *nf* model
**cow-boy** [kobɔj] *nm* cowboy
**coyote** [kɔjɔt] *nm* coyote
**CP** *sigle m* = **cours préparatoire**
**CPAM** *sigle f* (= *Caisse primaire d'assurances maladie*) health insurance office
**cps** *abr* (= *caractères par seconde*) cps
**cpt** *abr* = **comptant**
**CQFD** *abr* (= *ce qu'il fallait démontrer*) QED = **quod erat demonstrandum**
**CR** *sigle m* = **compte rendu**
**crabe** [kʀab] *nm* crab
**crachat** [kʀaʃa] *nm* spittle *no pl*, spit *no pl*
**craché, e** [kʀaʃe] *adj*: **son père tout ~** the spitting image of his (*ou* her) father
**cracher** [kʀaʃe] *vi* to spit ▷ *vt* to spit out; (*fig: lave etc*) to belch (out); **~ du sang** to spit blood
**crachin** [kʀaʃɛ̃] *nm* drizzle
**crachiner** [kʀaʃine] *vi* to drizzle
**crachoir** [kʀaʃwaʀ] *nm* spittoon; (*de dentiste*) bowl
**crachotement** [kʀaʃɔtmɑ̃] *nm* crackling *no pl*
**crachoter** [kʀaʃɔte] *vi* (*haut-parleur, radio*) to crackle
**crack** [kʀak] *nm* (*intellectuel*) whiz kid; (*sportif*) ace; (*poulain*) hot favourite (*Brit*) *ou* favorite (*US*)
**Cracovie** [kʀakɔvi] *n* Cracow
**cradingue** [kʀadɛ̃g] *adj* (*fam*) disgustingly dirty, filthy-dirty
**craie** [kʀɛ] *nf* chalk
**craignais** *etc* [kʀɛɲɛ] *vb voir* **craindre**
**craindre** [kʀɛ̃dʀ(ə)] *vt* to fear, be afraid of; (*être sensible à: chaleur, froid*) to be easily damaged by; **~ de/que** to be afraid of/that; **je crains qu'il (ne) vienne** I am afraid he may come
**crainte** [kʀɛ̃t] *nf* fear; **de ~ de/que** for fear of/ that
**craintif, -ive** [kʀɛ̃tif, -iv] *adj* timid
**craintivement** [kʀɛ̃tivmɑ̃] *adv* timidly
**cramer** [kʀame] *vi* (*fam*) to burn
**cramoisi, e** [kʀamwazi] *adj* crimson
**crampe** [kʀɑ̃p] *nf* cramp; **~ d'estomac** stomach cramp
**crampon** [kʀɑ̃pɔ̃] *nm* (*de semelle*) stud; (*Alpinisme*) crampon
**cramponner** [kʀɑ̃pɔne]: **se cramponner** *vi*: **se ~ (à)** to hang *ou* cling on (to)
**cran** [kʀɑ̃] *nm* (*entaille*) notch; (*de courroie*) hole; (*courage*) guts *pl*; **~ d'arrêt/de sûreté** safety catch; **~ de mire** bead
**crâne** [kʀɑn] *nm* skull
**crâner** [kʀɑne] *vi* (*fam*) to swank, show off
**crânien, ne** [kʀɑnjɛ̃, -ɛn] *adj* cranial, skull *cpd*,

101

**brain** cpd
**crapaud** [kʀapo] nm toad
**crapule** [kʀapyl] nf villain
**crapuleux, -euse** [kʀapylø, -øz] adj: **crime ~** villainous crime
**craquelure** [kʀaklyʀ] nf crack; crackle no pl
**craquement** [kʀakmɑ̃] nm crack, snap; (du plancher) creak, creaking no pl
**craquer** [kʀake] vi (bois, plancher) to creak; (fil, branche) to snap; (couture) to come apart, burst; (fig) to break down, fall apart; (: être enthousiasmé) to go wild ▷ vt: **~ une allumette** to strike a match
**crasse** [kʀas] nf grime, filth ▷ adj (fig: ignorance) crass
**crasseux, -euse** [kʀasø, øz] adj filthy
**crassier** [kʀasje] nm slag heap
**cratère** [kʀatɛʀ] nm crater
**cravache** [kʀavaʃ] nf (riding) crop
**cravacher** [kʀavaʃe] vt to use the crop on
**cravate** [kʀavat] nf tie
**cravater** [kʀavate] vt to put a tie on; (fig) to grab round the neck
**crawl** [kʀol] nm crawl
**crawlé, e** [kʀole] adj: **dos ~** backstroke
**crayeux, -euse** [kʀɛjø, -øz] adj chalky
**crayon** [kʀɛjɔ̃] nm pencil; (de rouge à lèvres etc) stick, pencil; **écrire au ~** to write in pencil; **~ à bille** ball-point pen; **~ de couleur** crayon; **~ optique** light pen
**crayon-feutre** [kʀɛjɔ̃føtʀ(ə)] (pl **crayons-feutres**) nm felt(-tip) pen
**crayonner** [kʀɛjɔne] vt to scribble, sketch
**CRDP** sigle m (= Centre régional de documentation pédagogique) teachers' resource centre
**créance** [kʀeɑ̃s] nf (Comm) (financial) claim, (recoverable) debt; **donner ~ à qch** to lend credence to sth
**créancier, -ière** [kʀeɑ̃sje, -jɛʀ] nm/f creditor
**créateur, -trice** [kʀeatœʀ, -tʀis] adj creative ▷ nm/f creator; **le C~** (Rel) the Creator
**créatif, -ive** [kʀeatif, -iv] adj creative
**création** [kʀeasjɔ̃] nf creation
**créativité** [kʀeativite] nf creativity
**créature** [kʀeatyʀ] nf creature
**crécelle** [kʀesɛl] nf rattle
**crèche** [kʀɛʃ] nf (de Noël) crib; see note; (garderie) crèche, day nursery

○ **CRÈCHE**
○
○ In France the Christmas crib (crèche) usually
○ contains figurines representing a miller, a
○ wood-cutter and other villagers as well as
○ the Holy Family and the traditional cow,
○ donkey and shepherds. The Three Wise Men
○ are added to the nativity scene at Epiphany
○ (6 January, Twelfth Night).

**crédence** [kʀedɑ̃s] nf (small) sideboard
**crédibilité** [kʀedibilite] nf credibility
**crédible** [kʀedibl(ə)] adj credible

**crédit** [kʀedi] nm (gén) credit; **crédits** nmpl funds; **acheter à ~** to buy on credit ou on easy terms; **faire ~ à qn** to give sb credit; **~ municipal** pawnshop; **~ relais** bridging loan
**crédit-bail** [kʀedibaj] (pl **crédits-bails**) nm (Écon) leasing
**créditer** [kʀedite] vt: **~ un compte (de)** to credit an account (with)
**créditeur, -trice** [kʀeditœʀ, -tʀis] adj in credit, credit cpd ▷ nm/f customer in credit
**credo** [kʀedo] nm credo, creed
**crédule** [kʀedyl] adj credulous, gullible
**crédulité** [kʀedylite] nf credulity, gullibility
**créer** [kʀee] vt to create; (Théât: pièce) to produce (for the first time); (: rôle) to create
**crémaillère** [kʀemajɛʀ] nf (Rail) rack; (tige crantée) trammel; **direction à ~** (Auto) rack and pinion steering; **pendre la ~** to have a house-warming party
**crémation** [kʀemasjɔ̃] nf cremation
**crématoire** [kʀematwaʀ] adj: **four ~** crematorium
**crématorium** [kʀematɔʀjɔm] nm crematorium
**crème** [kʀɛm] nf cream; (entremets) cream dessert ▷ adj inv cream; **un (café) ~** ≈ a white coffee; **~ chantilly** whipped cream, crème Chantilly; **~ fouettée** whipped cream; **~ glacée** ice cream; **~ à raser** shaving cream; **~ solaire** sun cream
**crémerie** [kʀemʀi] nf dairy; (tearoom) teashop
**crémeux, -euse** [kʀemø, -øz] adj creamy
**crémier, -ière** [kʀemje, -jɛʀ] nm/f dairyman/-woman
**créneau, x** [kʀeno] nm (de fortification) crenel(le); (fig, aussi Comm) gap, slot; (Auto): **faire un ~** to reverse into a parking space (between cars alongside the kerb)
**créole** [kʀeɔl] adj, nm/f Creole
**crêpe** [kʀɛp] nf (galette) pancake ▷ nm (tissu) crêpe; (de deuil) black mourning crêpe; (ruban) black armband (ou hatband ou ribbon); **semelle (de) ~** crêpe sole; **~ de Chine** crêpe de Chine
**crêpé, e** [kʀepe] adj (cheveux) backcombed
**crêperie** [kʀepʀi] nf pancake shop ou restaurant
**crépi** [kʀepi] nm roughcast
**crépir** [kʀepiʀ] vt to roughcast
**crépitement** [kʀepitmɑ̃] nm (du feu) crackling no pl; (d'une arme automatique) rattle no pl
**crépiter** [kʀepite] vi to sputter, splutter, crackle
**crépon** [kʀepɔ̃] nm seersucker
**CREPS** [kʀɛps] sigle m (= Centre régional d'éducation physique et sportive) ≈ sports ou leisure centre
**crépu, e** [kʀepy] adj frizzy, fuzzy
**crépuscule** [kʀepyskyl] nm twilight, dusk
**crescendo** [kʀeʃɛndo] nm, adv (Mus) crescendo; **aller ~** (fig) to rise higher and higher, grow ever greater
**cresson** [kʀesɔ̃] nm watercress
**Crète** [kʀɛt] nf: **la ~** Crete
**crête** [kʀɛt] nf (de coq) comb; (de vague, montagne) crest
**crétin, e** [kʀetɛ̃, -in] nm/f cretin

**crétois, e** [kʀetwa, -waz] *adj* Cretan
**cretonne** [kʀətɔn] *nf* cretonne
**creuser** [kʀøze] *vt* (*trou, tunnel*) to dig; (*sol*) to dig a hole in; (*bois*) to hollow out; (*fig*) to go (deeply) into; **ça creuse** that gives you a real appetite; **se ~ (la cervelle)** to rack one's brains
**creuset** [kʀøzɛ] *nm* crucible; (*fig*) melting pot, (severe) test
**creux, -euse** [kʀø, -øz] *adj* hollow ▷ *nm* hollow; (*fig: sur graphique etc*) trough; **heures creuses** slack periods; off-peak periods; **le ~ de l'estomac** the pit of the stomach
**crevaison** [kʀəvɛzɔ̃] *nf* puncture, flat
**crevant, e** [kʀəvɑ̃, -ɑ̃t] *adj* (*fam: fatigant*) knackering; (: *très drôle*) priceless
**crevasse** [kʀəvas] *nf* (*dans le sol*) crack, fissure; (*de glacier*) crevasse; (*de la peau*) crack
**crevé, e** [kʀəve] *adj* (*fam: fatigué*) worn out, dead beat
**crève-cœur** [kʀɛvkœʀ] *nm inv* heartbreak
**crever** [kʀəve] *vt* (*papier*) to tear, break; (*tambour, ballon*) to burst ▷ *vi* (*pneu*) to burst; (*automobiliste*) to have a puncture (*Brit*) *ou* a flat (tire) (*US*); (*abcès, outre, nuage*) to burst (open); (*fam*) to die; **cela lui a crevé un œil** it blinded him in one eye; **~ l'écran** to have real screen presence
**crevette** [kʀəvɛt] *nf*: **~ (rose)** prawn; **~ grise** shrimp
**CRF** *sigle f* (= *Croix-Rouge française*) French Red Cross
**cri** [kʀi] *nm* cry, shout; (*d'animal: spécifique*) cry, call; **à grands ~s** at the top of one's voice; **c'est le dernier ~** (*fig*) it's the latest fashion
**criant, e** [kʀijɑ̃, -ɑ̃t] *adj* (*injustice*) glaring
**criard, e** [kʀijaʀ, -aʀd(ə)] *adj* (*couleur*) garish, loud; (*voix*) yelling
**crible** [kʀibl(ə)] *nm* riddle; (*mécanique*) screen, jig; **passer qch au ~** to put sth through a riddle; (*fig*) to go over sth with a fine-tooth comb
**criblé, e** [kʀible] *adj*: **~ de** riddled with
**cric** [kʀik] *nm* (*Auto*) jack
**cricket** [kʀikɛt] *nm* cricket
**criée** [kʀije] *nf*: **(vente à la) ~** (sale by) auction
**crier** [kʀije] *vi* (*pour appeler*) to shout, cry (out); (*de peur, de douleur etc*) to scream, yell; (*fig: grincer*) to squeal, screech ▷ *vt* (*ordre, injure*) to shout (out), yell (out); **sans ~ gare** without warning; **~ grâce** to cry for mercy; **~ au secours** to shout for help
**crieur, -euse** [kʀijœʀ, -øz] *nm/f*: **~ de journaux** newspaper seller
**crime** [kʀim] *nm* crime; (*meurtre*) murder
**Crimée** [kʀime] *nf*: **la ~** the Crimea
**criminalité** [kʀiminalite] *nf* criminality, crime
**criminel, le** [kʀiminɛl] *adj* criminal ▷ *nm/f* criminal; murderer; **~ de guerre** war criminal
**criminologie** [kʀiminɔlɔʒi] *nf* criminology
**criminologiste** [kʀiminɔlɔʒist(ə)] *nm/f* criminologist
**criminologue** [kʀiminɔlɔg] *nm/f* criminologist
**crin** [kʀɛ̃] *nm* hair *no pl*; (*fibre*) horsehair; **à tous**

**~s, à tout ~** diehard, out-and-out
**crinière** [kʀinjɛʀ] *nf* mane
**crique** [kʀik] *nf* creek, inlet
**criquet** [kʀikɛ] *nm* grasshopper
**crise** [kʀiz] *nf* crisis (*pl* crises); (*Méd*) attack; fit; **~ cardiaque** heart attack; **~ de foi** crisis of belief; **~ de foie** bilious attack; **~ de nerfs** attack of nerves
**crispant, e** [kʀispɑ̃, -ɑ̃t] *adj* annoying, irritating
**crispation** [kʀispasjɔ̃] *nf* (*spasme*) twitch; (*contraction*) contraction; tenseness
**crispé, e** [kʀispe] *adj* tense, nervous
**crisper** [kʀispe] *vt* to tense; (*poings*) to clench; **se crisper** to tense; to clench; (*personne*) to get tense
**crissement** [kʀismɑ̃] *nm* crunch; rustle; screech
**crisser** [kʀise] *vi* (*neige*) to crunch; (*tissu*) to rustle; (*pneu*) to screech
**cristal, -aux** [kʀistal, -o] *nm* crystal; **cristaux** *nmpl* (*objets*) crystal(ware) *sg*; **~ de plomb** (lead) crystal; **~ de roche** rock-crystal; **cristaux de soude** washing soda *sg*
**cristallin, e** [kʀistalɛ̃, -in] *adj* crystal-clear ▷ *nm* (*Anat*) crystalline lens
**cristalliser** [kʀistalize] *vi, vt,* **se cristalliser** *vi* to crystallize
**critère** [kʀitɛʀ] *nm* criterion (*pl* -ia)
**critiquable** [kʀitikabl(ə)] *adj* open to criticism
**critique** [kʀitik] *adj* critical ▷ *nm/f* (*de théâtre, musique*) critic ▷ *nf* criticism; (*Théât etc: article*) review; **la ~** (*activité*) criticism; (*personnes*) the critics *pl*
**critiquer** [kʀitike] *vt* (*dénigrer*) to criticize; (*évaluer, juger*) to assess, examine (critically)
**croasser** [kʀɔase] *vi* to caw
**croate** [kʀɔat] *adj* Croatian ▷ *nm* (*Ling*) Croat, Croatian
**Croatie** [kʀɔasi] *nf*: **la ~** Croatia
**croc** [kʀo] *nm* (*dent*) fang; (*de boucher*) hook
**croc-en-jambe** [kʀɔkɑ̃ʒɑ̃b] (*pl* crocs-en-jambe) *nm*: **faire un ~ à qn** to trip sb up
**croche** [kʀɔʃ] *nf* (*Mus*) quaver (*Brit*), eighth note (*US*); **double ~** semiquaver (*Brit*), sixteenth note (*US*)
**croche-pied** [kʀɔʃpje] *nm* = **croc-en-jambe**
**crochet** [kʀɔʃɛ] *nm* hook; (*clef*) picklock; (*détour*) detour; (*Boxe*): **~ du gauche** left hook; (*Tricot: aiguille*) crochet hook; (: *technique*) crochet; **crochets** *nmpl* (*Typo*) square brackets; **vivre aux ~s de qn** to live *ou* sponge off sb
**crocheter** [kʀɔʃte] *vt* (*serrure*) to pick
**crochu, e** [kʀɔʃy] *adj* hooked; claw-like
**crocodile** [kʀɔkɔdil] *nm* crocodile
**crocus** [kʀɔkys] *nm* crocus
**croire** [kʀwaʀ] *vt* to believe; **~ qn honnête** to believe sb (to be) honest; **se ~ fort** to think one is strong; **~ que** to believe *ou* think that; **vous croyez?** do you think so?; **~ être/faire** to think one is/does; **~ à, ~ en** to believe in
**croîs** *etc* [kʀwa] *vb voir* **croître**
**croisade** [kʀwazad] *nf* crusade

**croisé, e** [kʀwaze] *adj* (*veston*) double-breasted ▷ *nm* (*guerrier*) crusader ▷ *nf* (*fenêtre*) window, casement; **~e d'ogives** intersecting ribs; **à la ~e des chemins** at the crossroads

**croisement** [kʀwazmã] *nm* (*carrefour*) crossroads *sg*; (*Bio*) crossing; crossbreed

**croiser** [kʀwaze] *vt* (*personne, voiture*) to pass; (*route*) to cross, cut across; (*Bio*) to cross ▷ *vi* (*Navig*) to cruise; **~ les jambes/bras** to cross one's legs/fold one's arms; **se croiser** *vi* (*personnes, véhicules*) to pass each other; (*routes*) to cross, intersect; (*lettres*) to cross (in the post); (*regards*) to meet; **se ~ les bras** (*fig*) to twiddle one's thumbs

**croiseur** [kʀwazœʀ] *nm* cruiser (*warship*)

**croisière** [kʀwazjɛʀ] *nf* cruise; **vitesse de ~** (*Auto etc*) cruising speed

**croisillon** [kʀwazijɔ̃] *nm*: **motif/fenêtre à ~s** lattice pattern/window

**croissais** *etc* [kʀwasɛ] *vb voir* **croître**

**croissance** [kʀwasãs] *nf* growing, growth; **troubles de la ~** growing pains; **maladie de ~** growth disease; **~ économique** economic growth

**croissant, e** [kʀwasã, -ãt] *vb voir* **croître** ▷ *adj* growing; rising ▷ *nm* (*à manger*) croissant; (*motif*) crescent; **~ de lune** crescent moon

**croître** [kʀwatʀ(ə)] *vi* to grow; (*lune*) to wax

**croix** [kʀwa] *nf* cross; **en ~** *adj, adv* in the form of a cross; **la C~ Rouge** the Red Cross

**croquant, e** [kʀɔkã, -ãt] *adj* crisp, crunchy ▷ *nm/f* (*péj*) yokel, (country) bumpkin

**croque-madame** [kʀɔkmadam] *nm inv* toasted cheese sandwich with a fried egg on top

**croque-mitaine** [kʀɔkmitɛn] *nm* bog(e)y-man (*pl* -men)

**croque-monsieur** [kʀɔkməsjø] *nm inv* toasted ham and cheese sandwich

**croque-mort** [kʀɔkmɔʀ] *nm* (*péj*) pallbearer

**croquer** [kʀɔke] *vt* (*manger*) to crunch; to munch; (*dessiner*) to sketch ▷ *vi* to be crisp *ou* crunchy; **chocolat à ~** plain dessert chocolate

**croquet** [kʀɔkɛ] *nm* croquet

**croquette** [kʀɔkɛt] *nf* croquette

**croquis** [kʀɔki] *nm* sketch

**cross** [kʀɔs], **cross-country** [kʀɔskuntʀi] (*pl* **-(-countries)**) *nm* cross-country race *ou* run; cross-country racing *ou* running

**crosse** [kʀɔs] *nf* (*de fusil*) butt; (*de revolver*) grip; (*d'évêque*) crook, crosier; (*de hockey*) hockey stick

**crotale** [kʀɔtal] *nm* rattlesnake

**crotte** [kʀɔt] *nf* droppings *pl*; **~!** (*fam*) damn!

**crotté, e** [kʀɔte] *adj* muddy, mucky

**crottin** [kʀɔtɛ̃] *nm*: **~ (de cheval)** (horse) dung *ou* manure

**croulant, e** [kʀulã, -ãt] *nm/f* (*fam*) old fogey

**crouler** [kʀule] *vi* (*s'effondrer*) to collapse; (*être délabré*) to be crumbling

**croupe** [kʀup] *nf* croup, rump; **en ~** pillion

**croupier** [kʀupje] *nm* croupier

**croupion** [kʀupjɔ̃] *nm* (*d'un oiseau*) rump; (*Culin*) parson's nose

**croupir** [kʀupiʀ] *vi* to stagnate

**CROUS** [kʀus] *sigle m* (= *Centre régional des œuvres universitaires et scolaires*) students' representative body

**croustade** [kʀustad] *nf* (*Culin*) croustade

**croustillant, e** [kʀustijã, -ãt] *adj* crisp; (*fig*) spicy

**croustiller** [kʀustije] *vi* to be crisp *ou* crusty

**croûte** [kʀut] *nf* crust; (*du fromage*) rind; (*de vol-au-vent*) case; (*Méd*) scab; **en ~** (*Culin*) in pastry, in a pie; **~ aux champignons** mushrooms on toast; **~ au fromage** cheese on toast *no pl*; **~ de pain** (*morceau*) crust (of bread); **~ terrestre** earth's crust

**croûton** [kʀutɔ̃] *nm* (*Culin*) crouton; (*bout du pain*) crust, heel

**croyable** [kʀwajabl(ə)] *adj* believable, credible

**croyais** *etc* [kʀwajɛ] *vb voir* **croire**

**croyance** [kʀwajãs] *nf* belief

**croyant, e** [kʀwajã, -ãt] *vb voir* **croire** ▷ *adj*: **être/ne pas être ~** to be/not to be a believer ▷ *nm/f* believer

**Crozet** [kʀɔze] *n*: **les îles ~** the Crozet Islands

**CRS** *sigle fpl* (= *Compagnies républicaines de sécurité*) state security police force ▷ *sigle m* member of the CRS

**cru, e** [kʀy] *pp de* **croire** ▷ *adj* (*non cuit*) raw; (*lumière, couleur*) harsh; (*description*) crude; (*paroles, langage: franc*) blunt; (: *grossier*) crude ▷ *nm* (*vignoble*) vineyard; (*vin*) wine ▷ *nf* (*d'un cours d'eau*) swelling, rising; **de son (propre) ~** (*fig*) of his own devising; **monter à ~** to ride bareback; **du ~** local; **en ~e** in spate

**crû** [kʀy] *pp de* **croître**

**cruauté** [kʀyote] *nf* cruelty

**cruche** [kʀyʃ] *nf* pitcher, (earthenware) jug

**crucial, e, -aux** [kʀysjal, -o] *adj* crucial

**crucifier** [kʀysifje] *vt* to crucify

**crucifix** [kʀysifi] *nm* crucifix

**crucifixion** [kʀysifiksjɔ̃] *nf* crucifixion

**cruciforme** [kʀysifɔʀm(ə)] *adj* cruciform, cross-shaped

**cruciverbiste** [kʀysivɛʀbist(ə)] *nm/f* crossword puzzle enthusiast

**crudité** [kʀydite] *nf* crudeness *no pl*; harshness *no pl*; **crudités** *nfpl* (*Culin*) mixed salads (*as hors-d'œuvre*)

**crue** [kʀy] *nf voir* **cru**

**cruel, le** [kʀyɛl] *adj* cruel

**cruellement** [kʀyɛlmã] *adv* cruelly

**crûment** [kʀymã] *adv* (*voir cru*) harshly; bluntly; crudely

**crus, crûs** *etc* [kʀy] *vb voir* **croire**; **croître**

**crustacés** [kʀystase] *nmpl* shellfish

**crypte** [kʀipt(ə)] *nf* crypt

**CSA** *sigle f* (= *Conseil supérieur de l'audiovisuel*) French broadcasting regulatory body, ≈ IBA (Brit), ≈ FCC (US)

**cse** *abr* = **cause**

**CSEN** *sigle f* (= *Confédération syndicale de l'éducation nationale*) group of teachers' unions

**CSG** *sigle f* (= *contribution sociale généralisée*) supplementary social security contribution in aid of the underprivileged

**CSM** *sigle m* (= *Conseil supérieur de la magistrature*)

French magistrates' council

**Cte** *abr* = **Comtesse**

**CU** *sigle f* = **communauté urbaine**

**Cuba** [kyba] *nm*: **le ~** Cuba

**cubage** [kybaʒ] *nm* cubage, cubic content

**cubain, e** [kybɛ̃, -ɛn] *adj* Cuban ▷ *nm/f*: **Cubain, e** Cuban

**cube** [kyb] *nm* cube; (*jouet*) brick, building block; **gros ~** powerful motorbike; **mètre ~** cubic metre; **2 au ~ = 8** 2 cubed is 8; **élever au ~** to cube

**cubique** [kybik] *adj* cubic

**cubisme** [kybism(ə)] *nm* cubism

**cubiste** [kybist(ə)] *adj, nm/f* cubist

**cubitus** [kybitys] *nm* ulna

**cueillette** [kœjɛt] *nf* picking, gathering; harvest *ou* crop (of fruit)

**cueillir** [kœjiʀ] *vt* (*fruits, fleurs*) to pick, gather; (*fig*) to catch

**cuiller, cuillère** [kɥijɛʀ] *nf* spoon; **~ à café** coffee spoon; (*Culin*) ≈ teaspoonful; **~ à soupe** soup spoon; (*Culin*) ≈ tablespoonful

**cuillerée** [kɥijʀe] *nf* spoonful; (*Culin*): **~ à soupe/café** tablespoonful/teaspoonful

**cuir** [kɥiʀ] *nm* leather; (*avant tannage*) hide; **~ chevelu** scalp

**cuirasse** [kɥiʀas] *nf* breastplate

**cuirassé** [kɥiʀase] *nm* (*Navig*) battleship

**cuire** [kɥiʀ] *vt*: **(faire) ~** (*aliments*) to cook; (*au four*) to bake; (*poterie*) to fire ▷ *vi* to cook; (*picoter*) to smart, sting, burn; **bien cuit** (*viande*) well done; **trop cuit** overdone; **pas assez cuit** underdone; **cuit à point** medium done; done to a turn

**cuisant, e** [kɥizɑ̃, -ɑ̃t] *vb voir* **cuire** ▷ *adj* (*douleur*) smarting, burning; (*fig: souvenir, échec*) bitter

**cuisine** [kɥizin] *nf* (*pièce*) kitchen; (*art culinaire*) cookery, cooking; (*nourriture*) cooking, food; **faire la ~** to cook

**cuisiné, e** [kɥizine] *adj*: **plat ~** ready-made meal *ou* dish

**cuisiner** [kɥizine] *vt* to cook; (*fam*) to grill ▷ *vi* to cook

**cuisinette** [kɥizinɛt] *nf* kitchenette

**cuisinier, -ière** [kɥizinje, -jɛʀ] *nm/f* cook ▷ *nf* (*poêle*) cooker; **cuisinière électrique/à gaz** electric/gas cooker

**cuisis** *etc* [kɥizi] *vb voir* **cuire**

**cuissardes** [kɥisaʀd] *nfpl* (*de pêcheur*) waders; (*de femme*) thigh boots

**cuisse** [kɥis] *nf* (*Anat*) thigh; (*Culin*) leg

**cuisson** [kɥisɔ̃] *nf* cooking; (*de poterie*) firing

**cuissot** [kɥiso] *nm* haunch

**cuistre** [kɥistʀ(ə)] *nm* prig

**cuit, e** [kɥi, -it] *pp de* **cuire** ▷ *nf* (*fam*): **prendre une ~** to get plastered *ou* smashed

**cuivre** [kɥivʀ(ə)] *nm* copper; **les ~s** (*Mus*) the brass; **~ rouge** copper; **~ jaune** brass

**cuivré, e** [kɥivʀe] *adj* coppery; (*peau*) bronzed

**cul** [ky] *nm* (*fam!*) arse (*Brit !*), ass (*US !*), bum (*Brit*); **~ de bouteille** bottom of a bottle

**culasse** [kylas] *nf* (*Auto*) cylinder-head; (*de fusil*) breech

**culbute** [kylbyt] *nf* somersault; (*accidentelle*) tumble, fall

**culbuter** [kylbyte] *vi* to (take a) tumble, fall (head over heels)

**culbuteur** [kylbytœʀ] *nm* (*Auto*) rocker arm

**cul-de-jatte** [kydʒat] (*pl* **culs-de-jatte**) *nm/f* legless cripple

**cul-de-sac** [kydsak] (*pl* **culs-de-sac**) *nm* cul-de-sac

**culinaire** [kylinɛʀ] *adj* culinary

**culminant, e** [kylminɑ̃, -ɑ̃t] *adj*: **point ~** highest point; (*fig*) height, climax

**culminer** [kylmine] *vi* to reach its highest point; to tower

**culot** [kylo] *nm* (*d'ampoule*) cap; (*effronterie*) cheek, nerve

**culotte** [kylɔt] *nf* (*de femme*) panties *pl*, knickers *pl* (*Brit*); (*d'homme*) underpants *pl*; (*pantalon*) trousers *pl* (*Brit*), pants *pl* (*US*); **~ de cheval** riding breeches *pl*

**culotté, e** [kylɔte] *adj* (*pipe*) seasoned; (*cuir*) mellowed; (*effronté*) cheeky

**culpabiliser** [kylpabilize] *vt*: **~ qn** to make sb feel guilty

**culpabilité** [kylpabilite] *nf* guilt

**culte** [kylt(ə)] *adj*: **livre/film ~** cult film/book ▷ *nm* (*religion*) religion; (*hommage, vénération*) worship; (*protestant*) service

**cultivable** [kyltivabl(ə)] *adj* cultivable

**cultivateur, -trice** [kyltivatœʀ, -tʀis] *nm/f* farmer

**cultivé, e** [kyltive] *adj* (*personne*) cultured, cultivated

**cultiver** [kyltive] *vt* to cultivate; (*légumes*) to grow, cultivate

**culture** [kyltyʀ] *nf* cultivation; growing; (*connaissances etc*) culture; **(champs de) ~s** land(s) under cultivation; **~ physique** physical training

**culturel, le** [kyltyʀɛl] *adj* cultural

**culturisme** [kyltyʀism(ə)] *nm* body-building

**culturiste** [kyltyʀist(ə)] *nm/f* body-builder

**cumin** [kymɛ̃] *nm* (*Culin*) cumin

**cumul** [kymyl] *nm* (*voir cumuler*) holding (*ou* drawing) concurrently; **~ de peines** sentences to run consecutively

**cumulable** [kymylabl(ə)] *adj* (*fonctions*) which may be held concurrently

**cumuler** [kymyle] *vt* (*emplois, honneurs*) to hold concurrently; (*salaires*) to draw concurrently; (*Jur: droits*) to accumulate

**cupide** [kypid] *adj* greedy, grasping

**cupidité** [kypidite] *nf* greed

**curable** [kyʀabl(ə)] *adj* curable

**Curaçao** [kyʀaso] *n* Curaçao ▷ *nm*: **curaçao** curaçao

**curare** [kyʀaʀ] *nm* curare

**curatif, -ive** [kyʀatif, -iv] *adj* curative

**cure** [kyʀ] *nf* (*Méd*) course of treatment; (*Rel*) cure, ≈ living; presbytery, ≈ vicarage; **faire une ~ de fruits** to go on a fruit cure *ou* diet; **faire**

une ~ **thermale** to take the waters; **n'avoir ~ de** to pay no attention to; ~ **d'amaigrissement** slimming course; ~ **de repos** rest cure; ~ **de sommeil** sleep therapy *no pl*

**curé** [kyʀe] *nm* parish priest; **M le ~ ≈** Vicar

**cure-dent** [kyʀdɑ̃] *nm* toothpick

**curée** [kyʀe] *nf (fig)* scramble for the pickings

**cure-ongles** [kyʀɔ̃gl(ə)] *nm inv* nail cleaner

**cure-pipe** [kyʀpip] *nm* pipe cleaner

**curer** [kyʀe] *vt* to clean out; **se ~ les dents** to pick one's teeth

**curetage** [kyʀtaʒ] *nm (Méd)* curettage

**curieusement** [kyʀjøzmɑ̃] *adv* oddly

**curieux, -euse** [kyʀjø, -øz] *adj (étrange)* strange, curious; *(indiscret)* curious, inquisitive; *(intéressé)* inquiring, curious ▷ *nmpl (badauds)* onlookers, bystanders

**curiosité** [kyʀjozite] *nf* curiosity, inquisitiveness; *(objet)* curio(sity); *(site)* unusual feature *ou* sight

**curiste** [kyʀist(ə)] *nm/f* person taking the waters at a spa

**curriculum vitae** [kyʀikylɔmvite] *nm inv* curriculum vitae

**curry** [kyʀi] *nm* curry; **poulet au ~** curried chicken, chicken curry

**curseur** [kyʀsœʀ] *nm (Inform)* cursor; *(de règle)* slide; *(de fermeture-éclair)* slider

**cursif, -ive** [kyʀsif, -iv] *adj:* **écriture cursive** cursive script

**cursus** [kyʀsys] *nm* degree course

**curviligne** [kyʀviliɲ] *adj* curvilinear

**cutané, e** [kytane] *adj* cutaneous, skin *cpd*

**cuti-réaction** [kytireaksjɔ̃] *nf (Méd)* skin-test

**cuve** [kyv] *nf* vat; *(à mazout etc)* tank

**cuvée** [kyve] *nf* vintage

**cuvette** [kyvɛt] *nf (récipient)* bowl, basin; *(du lavabo)* (wash)basin; *(des w.-c.)* pan; *(Géo)* basin

**CV** *sigle m (Auto)* = **cheval vapeur**; *(Admin)* = **curriculum vitae**

**CVS** *sigle adj* (= *corrigées des variations saisonnières*) seasonally adjusted

**cx** *abr* (= *coefficient de pénétration dans l'air*) drag coefficient

**cyanure** [sjanyʀ] *nm* cyanide

**cybercafé** [sibɛʀkafe] *nm* cybercafé

**cyberculture** [sibɛʀkyltyʀ] *nf* cyberculture

**cyberespace** [sibɛʀɛspas] *nm* cyberspace

**cybernaute** [sibɛʀnot] *nm/f* Internet user

**cybernétique** [sibɛʀnetik] *nf* cybernetics *sg*

**cyclable** [siklabl(ə)] *adj:* **piste ~** cycle track

**cyclamen** [siklamɛn] *nm* cyclamen

**cycle** [sikl(ə)] *nm* cycle; *(Scol):* **premier/second ~** ≈ middle/upper school *(Brit)*, ≈ junior/senior high school *(US)*

**cyclique** [siklik] *adj* cyclic(al)

**cyclisme** [siklism(ə)] *nm* cycling

**cycliste** [siklist(ə)] *nm/f* cyclist ▷ *adj* cycle *cpd*; **coureur ~** racing cyclist

**cyclo-cross** [siklɔkʀɔs] *nm (Sport)* cyclo-cross; *(épreuve)* cyclo-cross race

**cyclomoteur** [siklɔmɔtœʀ] *nm* moped

**cyclomotoriste** [siklɔmɔtɔʀist(ə)] *nm/f* moped rider

**cyclone** [siklon] *nm* hurricane

**cyclotourisme** [siklɔtuʀism(ə)] *nm* (bi)cycle touring

**cygne** [siɲ] *nm* swan

**cylindre** [silɛ̃dʀ(ə)] *nm* cylinder; **moteur à 4 ~s en ligne** straight-4 engine

**cylindrée** [silɛ̃dʀe] *nf (Auto)* (cubic) capacity; **une (voiture de) grosse ~** a big-engined car

**cylindrique** [silɛ̃dʀik] *adj* cylindrical

**cymbale** [sɛ̃bal] *nf* cymbal

**cynique** [sinik] *adj* cynical

**cyniquement** [sinikmɑ̃] *adv* cynically

**cynisme** [sinism(ə)] *nm* cynicism

**cyprès** [sipʀɛ] *nm* cypress

**cypriote** [sipʀijɔt] *adj* Cypriot ▷ *nm/f:* **Cypriote** Cypriot

**cyrillique** [siʀilik] *adj* Cyrillic

**cystite** [sistit] *nf* cystitis

**cytise** [sitiz] *nm* laburnum

**cytologie** [sitɔlɔʒi] *nf* cytology

# Dd

**D, d** [de] *nm inv* D, d ▷ *abr*: **D** (*Météorologie*: = *dépression*) low, depression; **D comme Désiré** D for David (*Brit*) *ou* Dog (*US*); *voir* **système**

**d'** *prép, art voir* **de**

**Dacca** [daka] *n* Dacca

**dactylo** [daktilo] *nf* (*aussi*: **dactylographe**) typist; (*aussi*: **dactylographie**) typing, typewriting

**dactylographier** [daktilɔgʀafje] *vt* to type (out)

**dada** [dada] *nm* hobby-horse

**dadais** [dadɛ] *nm* ninny, lump

**dague** [dag] *nf* dagger

**dahlia** [dalja] *nm* dahlia

**dahoméen, ne** [daɔmeɛ̃, -ɛn] *adj* Dahomean

**Dahomey** [daɔme] *nm*: **le ~** Dahomey

**daigner** [deɲe] *vt* to deign

**daim** [dɛ̃] *nm* (*fallow*) deer *inv*; (*peau*) buckskin; (*imitation*) suede

**dais** [dɛ] *nm* (*tenture*) canopy

**Dakar** [dakaʀ] *n* Dakar

**dal.** *abr* (= *décalitre*) dal.

**dallage** [dalaʒ] *nm* paving

**dalle** [dal] *nf* slab; (*au sol*) paving stone, flag(stone); **que ~** nothing at all, damn all (*Brit*)

**daller** [dale] *vt* to pave

**dalmatien, ne** [dalmasjɛ̃, -ɛn] *nm/f* (*chien*) Dalmatian

**daltonien, ne** [daltɔnjɛ̃, -ɛn] *adj* colour-blind (*Brit*), color-blind (*US*)

**daltonisme** [daltɔnism(ə)] *nm* colour (*Brit*) *ou* color (*US*) blindness

**dam** [dam] *nm*: **au grand ~ de** much to the detriment (*ou* annoyance) of

**Damas** [dama] *n* Damascus

**damas** [dama] *nm* (*étoffe*) damask

**damassé, e** [damase] *adj* damask *cpd*

**dame** [dam] *nf* lady; (*Cartes, Échecs*) queen; **dames** *nfpl* (*jeu*) draughts *sg* (*Brit*), checkers *sg* (*US*); **les** (**toilettes des**) ~**s** the ladies' (toilets); ~ **de charité** benefactress; ~ **de compagnie** lady's companion

**dame-jeanne** [damʒan] (*pl* **dames-jeannes**) *nf* demijohn

**damer** [dame] *vt* to ram *ou* pack down; ~ **le pion à** (*fig*) to get the better of

**damier** [damje] *nm* draughts board (*Brit*), checkerboard (*US*); (*dessin*) check (pattern); **en ~** check

**damner** [dɑne] *vt* to damn

**dancing** [dɑ̃siŋ] *nm* dance hall

**dandiner** [dɑ̃dine]: **se dandiner** *vi* to sway about; (*en marchant*) to waddle along

**Danemark** [danmaʀk] *nm*: **le ~** Denmark

**danger** [dɑ̃ʒe] *nm* danger; **mettre en ~** to endanger, put in danger; **être en ~ de mort** to be in peril of one's life; **être hors de ~** to be out of danger

**dangereusement** [dɑ̃ʒʀøzmɑ̃] *adv* dangerously

**dangereux, -euse** [dɑ̃ʒʀø, -øz] *adj* dangerous

**danois, e** [danwa, -waz] *adj* Danish ▷ *nm* (*Ling*) Danish ▷ *nm/f*: **Danois, e** Dane

 **MOT-CLÉ**

**dans** [dɑ̃] *prép* **1** (*position*) in; (*à l'intérieur de*) inside; **c'est dans le tiroir/le salon** it's in the drawer/lounge; **dans la boîte** in *ou* inside the box; **marcher dans la ville/la rue** to walk about the town/along the street; **je l'ai lu dans le journal** I read it in the newspaper; **être dans les meilleurs** to be among *ou* one of the best

**2** (*direction*) into; **elle a couru dans le salon** she ran into the lounge

**3** (*provenance*) out of, from; **je l'ai pris dans le tiroir/salon** I took it out of *ou* from the drawer/lounge; **boire dans un verre** to drink out of *ou* from a glass

**4** (*temps*) in; **dans deux mois** in two months, in two months' time

**5** (*approximation*) about; **dans les 20 euros** about 20 euros

**dansant, e** [dɑ̃sɑ̃, -ɑ̃t] *adj*: **soirée ~e** evening of dancing; (*bal*) dinner dance

**danse** [dɑ̃s] *nf*: **la ~** dancing; (*classique*) (ballet) dancing; **une ~** a dance; ~ **du ventre** belly dancing

**danser** [dɑ̃se] *vi, vt* to dance

**danseur, -euse** [dɑ̃sœʀ, -øz] *nm/f* ballet dancer; (*au bal etc*) dancer; (: *cavalier*) partner; ~ **de claquettes** tap-dancer; **en danseuse** (*à vélo*) standing on the pedals

**Danube** [danyb] *nm*: **le ~** the Danube

**DAO** *sigle m* (= *dessin assisté par ordinateur*) CAD

**dard** [daʀ] *nm* sting (*organ*)

**darder** [daʀde] *vt* to shoot, send forth

**dare-dare** [daʀdaʀ] *adv* in double quick time

**Dar-es-Salaam, Dar-es-Salam** [daʀɛsalam] *n* Dar-es-Salaama

**darne** [daʀn] *nf* steak (*of fish*)

**darse** [daʀs(ə)] *nf* sheltered dock (*in a Mediterranean port*)

**dartre** [daʀtʀ(ə)] *nf* (*Méd*) sore

**datation** [datasjɔ̃] *nf* dating

**date** [dat] *nf* date; **faire ~** to mark a milestone; **de longue ~** *adj* longstanding; **~ de naissance** date of birth; **~ limite** deadline; (*d'un aliment: aussi*: **date limite de vente**) sell-by date

**dater** [date] *vt, vi* to date; **~ de** to date from, go back to; **à ~ de** (as) from

**dateur** [datœʀ] *nm* (*de montre*) date indicator; **timbre ~** date stamp

**datif** [datif] *nm* dative

**datte** [dat] *nf* date

**dattier** [datje] *nm* date palm

**daube** [dob] *nf*: **bœuf en ~** beef casserole

**dauphin** [dofɛ̃] *nm* (*Zool*) dolphin; (*du roi*) dauphin; (*fig*) heir apparent

**Dauphiné** [dofine] *nm*: **le ~** the Dauphiné

**dauphinois, e** [dofinwa, -waz] *adj* of *ou* from the Dauphiné

**daurade** [doʀad] *nf* sea bream

**davantage** [davɑ̃taʒ] *adv* more; (*plus longtemps*) longer; **~ de** more; **~ que** more than

**DB** *sigle f* (*Mil*) = **division blindée**

**DCA** *sigle f* (= *défense contre avions*) anti-aircraft defence

**DCT** *sigle m* (= *diphtérie coqueluche tétanos*) DPT

**DDASS** [das] *sigle f* (= *Direction départementale d'action sanitaire et sociale*) ≈ DWP (= *Department of Work and Pensions* (Brit)), ≈ SSA (= *Social Security Administration* (US))

**DDT** *sigle m* (= *dichloro-diphénol-trichloréthane*) DDT

🔵 **M O T - C L É**

**de, d'** (*de + le = du, de + les = des*) *prép* **1** (*appartenance*) of; **le toit de la maison** the roof of the house; **la voiture d'Elisabeth/de mes parents** Elizabeth's/my parents' car

**2** (*provenance*) from; **il vient de Londres** he comes from London; **de Londres à Paris** from London to Paris; **elle est sortie du cinéma** she came out of the cinema

**3** (*moyen*) with; **je l'ai fait de mes propres mains** I did it with my own two hands

**4** (*caractérisation, mesure*): **un mur de brique/bureau d'acajou** a brick wall/mahogany desk; **un billet de 10 euros** a 10 euro note; **une pièce de 2 m de large** *ou* **large de 2 m** a room 2 m wide, a 2m-wide room; **un bébé de 10 mois** a 10-month-old baby; **12 mois de crédit/travail** 12 months' credit/work; **elle est payée 20**

**euros de l'heure** she's paid 20 euros an hour *ou* per hour; **augmenter de 10 euros** to increase by 10 euros; **trois jours de libres** three free days, three days free; **un verre d'eau** a glass of water; **il mange de tout** he'll eat anything

**5** (*rapport*) from; **de quatre à six** from four to six

**6** (*de la part de*): **estimé de ses collègues** respected by his colleagues

**7** (*cause*): **mourir de faim** to die of hunger; **rouge de colère** red with fury

**8** (*vb + de + infin*) to; **il m'a dit de rester** he told me to stay

**9** (*en apposition*): **cet imbécile de Paul** that idiot Paul; **le terme de franglais** the term "franglais"

▷ *art* **1** (*phrases affirmatives*) some (*souvent omis*); **du vin, de l'eau, des pommes** (some) wine, (some) water, (some) apples; **des enfants sont venus** some children came; **pendant des mois** for months

**2** (*phrases interrogatives et négatives*) any; **a-t-il du vin?** has he got any wine?; **il n'a pas de pommes/d'enfants** he hasn't (got) any apples/children, he has no apples/children

**dé** [de] *nm* (*à jouer*) die *ou* dice; (*aussi*: **dé à coudre**) thimble; **dés** *nmpl* (*jeu*) (game of) dice; **un coup de dés** a throw of the dice; **couper en dés** (*Culin*) to dice

**DEA** *sigle m* (= *Diplôme d'études approfondies*) postgraduate diploma

**dealer** [dilœʀ] *nm* (*fam*) (drug) pusher

**déambulateur** [deɑ̃bylatœʀ] *nm* zimmer®

**déambuler** [deɑ̃byle] *vi* to stroll about

**déb.** *abr* = **débutant**; (*Comm*) = **à débattre**

**débâcle** [debɑkl(ə)] *nf* rout

**déballage** [debalaʒ] *nm* (*de marchandises*) display (*of loose goods*); (*fig: fam*) outpourings *pl*

**déballer** [debale] *vt* to unpack

**débandade** [debɑ̃dad] *nf* scattering; (*déroute*) rout

**débander** [debɑ̃de] *vt* to unbandage

**débaptiser** [debatize] *vt* (*rue*) to rename

**débarbouiller** [debaʀbuje] *vt* to wash; **se débarbouiller** *vi* to wash (one's face)

**débarcadère** [debaʀkadɛʀ] *nm* landing stage (*Brit*), wharf

**débardeur** [debaʀdœʀ] *nm* docker, stevedore; (*maillot*) slipover, tank top

**débarquement** [debaʀkəmɑ̃] *nm* unloading, landing; disembarkation; (*Mil*) landing; **le D~** the Normandy landings

**débarquer** [debaʀke] *vt* to unload, land ▷ *vi* to disembark; (*fig*) to turn up

**débarras** [debaʀa] *nm* lumber room; (*placard*) junk cupboard; (*remise*) outhouse; **bon ~!** good riddance!

**débarrasser** [debaʀase] *vt* to clear ▷ *vi* (*enlever le couvert*) to clear away; **~ qn de** (*vêtements, paquets*) to relieve sb of; (*habitude, ennemi*) to rid sb of; **~ qch de** (*fouillis etc*) to clear sth of; **se débarrasser**

**de** vt to get rid of; to rid o.s. of

**débat** [deba] vb voir **débattre** ▷ nm discussion, debate; **débats** nmpl (Pol) proceedings, debates

**débattre** [debatʀ(ə)] vt to discuss, debate; **se débattre** vi to struggle

**débauchage** [deboʃaʒ] nm (licenciement) laying off (of staff); (par un concurrent) poaching

**débauche** [deboʃ] nf debauchery; **une ~ de** (fig) a profusion of; (: de couleurs) a riot of

**débauché, e** [deboʃe] adj debauched ▷ nm/f profligate

**débaucher** [deboʃe] vt (licencier) to lay off, dismiss; (salarié d'une autre entreprise) to poach; (entraîner) to lead astray, debauch; (inciter à la grève) to incite

**débile** [debil] adj weak, feeble; (fam: idiot) dimwitted ▷ nm/f: **~ mental, e** mental defective

**débilitant, e** [debilitɑ̃, -ɑ̃t] adj debilitating

**débilité** [debilite] nf debility; (fam: idiotie) stupidity; **~ mentale** mental debility

**débiner** [debine]: **se débiner** vi to do a bunk (Brit), clear out

**débit** [debi] nm (d'un liquide, fleuve) (rate of) flow; (d'un magasin) turnover (of goods); (élocution) delivery; (bancaire) debit; **avoir un ~ de 10 euros** to be 10 euros in debit; **~ de boissons** drinking establishment; **~ de tabac** tobacconist's (shop) (Brit), tobacco ou smoke shop (US)

**débiter** [debite] vt (compte) to debit; (liquide, gaz) to yield, produce, give out; (couper: bois, viande) to cut up; (vendre) to retail; (péj: paroles etc) to come out with, churn out

**débiteur, -trice** [debitœʀ, -tʀis] nm/f debtor ▷ adj in debit; (compte) debit cpd

**déblai** [deblɛ] nm (nettoyage) clearing; **déblais** nmpl (terre) earth; (décombres) rubble

**déblaiement** [deblɛmɑ̃] nm clearing; **travaux de ~** earth moving sg

**déblatérer** [deblatere] vi: **~ contre** to go on about

**déblayer** [debleje] vt to clear; **~ le terrain** (fig) to clear the ground

**déblocage** [deblɔkaʒ] nm (des prix, cours) unfreezing

**débloquer** [deblɔke] vt (frein, fonds) to release; (prix) to unfreeze ▷ vi (fam) to talk rubbish

**débobiner** [debɔbine] vt to unwind

**déboires** [debwaʀ] nmpl setbacks

**déboisement** [debwazmɑ̃] nm deforestation

**déboiser** [debwaze] vt to clear of trees; (région) to deforest; **se déboiser** vi (colline, montagne) to become bare of trees

**déboîter** [debwate] vt (Auto) to pull out; **se ~ le genou** etc to dislocate one's knee etc

**débonnaire** [debɔnɛʀ] adj easy-going, good-natured

**débordant, e** [debɔʀdɑ̃, -ɑ̃t] adj (joie) unbounded; (activité) exuberant

**débordé, e** [debɔʀde] adj: **être ~ de** (travail, demandes) to be snowed under with

**débordement** [debɔʀdəmɑ̃] nm overflowing

**déborder** [debɔʀde] vi to overflow; (lait etc) to boil over ▷ vt (Mil, Sport) to outflank; **~ (de) qch** (dépasser) to extend beyond sth; **~ de** (joie, zèle) to be brimming over with ou bursting with

**débouché** [debuʃe] nm (pour vendre) outlet; (perspective d'emploi) opening; (sortie): **au ~ de la vallée** where the valley opens out (onto the plain)

**déboucher** [debuʃe] vt (évier, tuyau etc) to unblock; (bouteille) to uncork, open ▷ vi: **~ de** to emerge from, come out of; **~ sur** to come out onto; to open out onto; (fig) to arrive at, lead up to

**débouler** [debule] vi to go (ou come) tumbling down; (sans tomber) to come careering down ▷ vt: **~ l'escalier** to belt down the stairs

**déboulonner** [debulɔne] vt to dismantle; (fig: renvoyer) to dismiss; (: détruire le prestige de) to discredit

**débours** [debuʀ] nmpl outlay

**débourser** [debuʀse] vt to pay out, lay out

**déboussoler** [debusɔle] vt to disorientate, disorient

**debout** [dəbu] adv: **être ~** (personne) to be standing, stand; (: levé, éveillé) to be up (and about); (chose) to be upright; **être encore ~** (fig: en état) to be still going; to be still standing; to be still up; **mettre qn ~** to get sb to his feet; **mettre qch ~** to stand sth up; **se mettre ~** to get up (on one's feet); **se tenir ~** to stand; **~!** get up!; **cette histoire ne tient pas ~** this story doesn't hold water

**débouter** [debute] vt (Jur) to dismiss; **~ qn de sa demande** to dismiss sb's petition

**déboutonner** [debutɔne] vt to undo, unbutton; **se déboutonner** vi to come undone ou unbuttoned

**débraillé, e** [debʀaje] adj slovenly, untidy

**débrancher** [debʀɑ̃ʃe] vt (appareil électrique) to unplug; (téléphone, courant électrique) to disconnect, cut off

**débrayage** [debʀɛjaʒ] nm (Auto) clutch; (: action) disengaging the clutch; (grève) stoppage; **faire un double ~** to double-declutch

**débrayer** [debʀeje] vi (Auto) to declutch, disengage the clutch; (cesser le travail) to stop work

**débridé, e** [debʀide] adj unbridled, unrestrained

**débrider** [debʀide] vt (cheval) to unbridle; (Culin: volaille) to untruss

**débris** [debʀi] nm (fragment) fragment ▷ nmpl (déchets) pieces, debris sg; rubbish sg (Brit), garbage sg (US)

**débrouillard, e** [debʀujaʀ, -aʀd(ə)] adj smart, resourceful

**débrouillardise** [debʀujaʀdiz] nf smartness, resourcefulness

**débrouiller** [debʀuje] vt to disentangle, untangle; (fig) to sort out, unravel; **se débrouiller** vi to manage

**débroussailler** [debʀusaje] vt to clear (of

brushwood)

**débusquer** [debyske] vt to drive out (from cover)

**début** [deby] nm beginning, start; **débuts** nmpl beginnings; (de carrière) début sg; **faire ses ~s** to start out; **au ~** in ou at the beginning, at first; **au ~ de** at the beginning ou start of; **dès le ~** from the start

**débutant, e** [debytɑ̃, -ɑ̃t] nm/f beginner, novice

**débuter** [debyte] vi to begin, start; (faire ses débuts) to start out

**deçà** [dəsa]: **en ~ de** prép this side of; **en ~** adv on this side

**décacheter** [dekaʃte] vt to unseal, open

**décade** [dekad] nf (10 jours) (period of) ten days; (10 ans) decade

**décadence** [dekadɑ̃s] nf decadence; decline

**décadent, e** [dekadɑ̃, -ɑ̃t] adj decadent

**décaféiné, e** [dekafeine] adj decaffeinated, caffeine-free

**décalage** [dekalaʒ] nm move forward ou back; shift forward ou back; (écart) gap; (désaccord) discrepancy; **~ horaire** time difference (between time zones), time-lag

**décalaminer** [dekalamine] vt to decoke

**décalcification** [dekalsifikasjɔ̃] nf decalcification

**décalcifier** [dekalsifje]: **se décalcifier** vr to decalcify

**décalcomanie** [dekalkɔmani] nf transfer

**décaler** [dekale] vt (dans le temps: avancer) to bring forward; (: retarder) to put back; (changer de position) to shift forward ou back; **~ de 10 cm** to move forward ou back by 10 cm; **~ de deux heures** to bring ou move forward two hours; to put back two hours

**décalitre** [dekalitʀ(ə)] nm decalitre (Brit), decaliter (US)

**décalogue** [dekalɔg] nm Decalogue

**décalquer** [dekalke] vt to trace; (par pression) to transfer

**décamètre** [dekamɛtʀ(ə)] nm decametre (Brit), decameter (US)

**décamper** [dekɑ̃pe] vi to clear out ou off

**décan** [dekɑ̃] nm (Astrologie) decan

**décanter** [dekɑ̃te] vt to (allow to) settle (and decant); **se décanter** vi to settle

**décapage** [dekapaʒ] nm stripping; scouring; sanding

**décapant** [dekapɑ̃] nm acid solution; scouring agent; paint stripper

**décaper** [dekape] vt to strip; (avec abrasif) to scour; (avec papier de verre) to sand

**décapiter** [dekapite] vt to behead; (par accident) to decapitate; (fig) to cut the top off; (: organisation) to remove the top people from

**décapotable** [dekapɔtabl(ə)] adj convertible

**décapoter** [dekapɔte] vt to put down the top of

**décapsuler** [dekapsyle] vt to take the cap ou top off

**décapsuleur** [dekapsylœʀ] nm bottle-opener

**décarcasser** [dekaʀkase] vt: **se ~ pour qn/pour**

**faire qch** (fam) to slog one's guts out for sb/to do sth

**décathlon** [dekatlɔ̃] nm decathlon

**décati, e** [dekati] adj faded, aged

**décédé, e** [desede] adj deceased

**décéder** [desede] vi to die

**décelable** [des(ə)labl(ə)] adj discernible

**déceler** [desle] vt to discover, detect; (révéler) to indicate, reveal

**décélération** [deseleʀasjɔ̃] nf deceleration

**décélérer** [deseleʀe] vi to decelerate, slow down

**décembre** [desɑ̃bʀ(ə)] nm December; voir aussi **juillet**

**décemment** [desamɑ̃] adv decently

**décence** [desɑ̃s] nf decency

**décennal, e, -aux** [desenal, -o] adj (qui dure dix ans) having a term of ten years, ten-year; (qui revient tous les dix ans) ten-yearly

**décennie** [deseni] nf decade

**décent, e** [desɑ̃, -ɑ̃t] adj decent

**décentralisation** [desɑ̃tʀalizasjɔ̃] nf decentralization

**décentraliser** [desɑ̃tʀalize] vt to decentralize

**décentrer** [desɑ̃tʀe] vt to throw off centre; **se décentrer** vi to move off-centre

**déception** [desɛpsjɔ̃] nf disappointment

**décerner** [desɛʀne] vt to award

**décès** [desɛ] nm death, decease; **acte de ~** death certificate

**décevant, e** [desvɑ̃, -ɑ̃t] adj disappointing

**décevoir** [desvwaʀ] vt to disappoint

**déchaîné, e** [deʃene] adj unbridled, raging

**déchaînement** [deʃɛnmɑ̃] nm (de haine, violence) outbreak, outburst

**déchaîner** [deʃene] vt (passions, colère) to unleash; (rires etc) to give rise to, arouse; **se déchaîner** vi to be unleashed; (rires) to burst out; (se mettre en colère) to fly into a rage; **se ~ contre qn** to unleash one's fury on sb

**déchanter** [deʃɑ̃te] vi to become disillusioned

**décharge** [deʃaʀʒ(ə)] nf (dépôt d'ordures) rubbish tip ou dump; (électrique) electrical discharge; (salve) volley of shots; **à la ~ de** in defence of

**déchargement** [deʃaʀʒəmɑ̃] nm unloading

**décharger** [deʃaʀʒe] vt (marchandise, véhicule) to unload; (Élec) to discharge; (arme: neutraliser) to unload; (: faire feu) to discharge, fire; **~ qn de** (responsabilité) to relieve sb of, release sb from; **~ sa colère (sur)** to vent one's anger (on); **~ sa conscience** to unburden one's conscience; **se ~ dans** (se déverser) to flow into; **se ~ d'une affaire sur qn** to hand a matter over to sb

**décharné, e** [deʃaʀne] adj bony, emaciated, fleshless

**déchaussé, e** [deʃose] adj (dent) loose

**déchausser** [deʃose] vt (personne) to take the shoes off; (skis) to take off; **se déchausser** vi to take off one's shoes; (dent) to come ou work loose

**dèche** [dɛʃ] nf (fam): **être dans la ~** to be flat broke

**déchéance** [deʃeɑ̃s] nf (déclin) degeneration,

decay, decline; *(chute)* fall

**déchet** [deʃɛ] *nm (de bois, tissu etc)* scrap; *(perte: gén Comm)* wastage, waste; **déchets** *nmpl (ordures)* refuse *sg*, rubbish *sg (Brit)*, garbage *sg (US)*; **~s radioactifs** radioactive waste

**déchiffrage** [deʃifʀaʒ] *nm* sight-reading

**déchiffrer** [deʃifʀe] *vt* to decipher

**déchiqueté, e** [deʃikte] *adj* jagged(-edged), ragged

**déchiqueter** [deʃikte] *vt* to tear *ou* pull to pieces

**déchirant, e** [deʃiʀɑ̃, -ɑ̃t] *adj* heart-breaking, heart-rending

**déchiré, e** [deʃiʀe] *adj* torn; *(fig)* heart-broken

**déchirement** [deʃiʀmɑ̃] *nm (chagrin)* wrench, heartbreak; *(gén pl: conflit)* rift, split

**déchirer** [deʃiʀe] *vt* to tear, rip; *(mettre en morceaux)* to tear up; *(pour ouvrir)* to tear off; *(arracher)* to tear out; *(fig)* to tear apart; **se déchirer** *vi* to tear, rip; **se ~ un muscle/tendon** to tear a muscle/ tendon

**déchirure** [deʃiʀyʀ] *nf (accroc)* tear, rip; **~ musculaire** torn muscle

**déchoir** [deʃwaʀ] *vi (personne)* to lower o.s., demean o.s.; **~ de** to fall from

**déchu, e** [deʃy] *pp de* **déchoir** ▷ *adj* fallen; *(roi)* deposed

**décibel** [desibɛl] *nm* decibel

**décidé, e** [deside] *adj (personne, air)* determined; **c'est ~** it's decided; **être ~ à faire** to be determined to do

**décidément** [desidemɑ̃] *adv* undoubtedly; really

**décider** [deside] *vt*: **~ qch** to decide on sth; **~ de faire/que** to decide to do/that; **~ qn (à faire qch)** to persuade *ou* induce sb (to do sth); **~ de qch** to decide upon sth; *(chose)* to determine sth; **se décider** *vi (personne)* to decide, make up one's mind; *(problème, affaire)* to be resolved; **se ~ à qch** to decide on sth; **se ~ à faire** to decide *ou* make up one's mind to do; **se ~ pour qch** to decide on *ou* in favour of sth

**décideur** [desidœʀ] *nm* decision-maker

**décilitre** [desilitʀ(ə)] *nm* decilitre *(Brit)*, deciliter *(US)*

**décimal, e, -aux** [desimal, -o] *adj, nf* decimal

**décimalisation** [desimalizɑsjɔ̃] *nf* decimalization

**décimaliser** [desimalize] *vt* to decimalize

**décimer** [desime] *vt* to decimate

**décimètre** [desimɛtʀ(ə)] *nm* decimetre *(Brit)*, decimeter *(US)*; **double ~** (20 cm) ruler

**décisif, -ive** [desizif, -iv] *adj* decisive; *(qui l'emporte)*: **le facteur/l'argument ~** the deciding factor/argument

**décision** [desizjɔ̃] *nf* decision; *(fermeté)* decisiveness, decision; **prendre une ~** to make a decision; **prendre la ~ de faire** to take the decision to do; **emporter** *ou* **faire la ~** to be decisive

**déclamation** [deklamɑsjɔ̃] *nf* declamation; *(péj)* ranting, spouting

**déclamatoire** [deklamatwaʀ] *adj* declamatory

**déclamer** [deklame] *vt* to declaim; *(péj)* to spout ▷ *vi*: **~ contre** to rail against

**déclarable** [deklaʀabl(ə)] *adj (marchandise)* dutiable; *(revenus)* declarable

**déclaration** [deklaʀɑsjɔ̃] *nf* declaration; registration; *(discours: Pol etc)* statement; *(compte rendu)* report; **fausse ~** misrepresentation; **~ (d'amour)** declaration; **~ de décès** registration of death; **~ de guerre** declaration of war; **~ (d'impôts)** statement of income, tax declaration, ≈ tax return; **~ (de sinistre)** (insurance) claim; **~ de revenus** statement of income

**déclaré, e** [deklaʀe] *adj (juré)* avowed

**déclarer** [deklaʀe] *vt* to declare, announce; *(revenus, employés, marchandises)* to declare; *(décès, naissance)* to register; *(vol etc: à la police)* to report; **rien à ~** nothing to declare; **se déclarer** *vi (feu, maladie)* to break out; **~ la guerre** to declare war

**déclassé, e** [deklɑse] *adj* relegated, downgraded; *(matériel)* (to be) sold off

**déclassement** [deklɑsmɑ̃] *nm* relegation, downgrading; *(Rail etc)* change of class

**déclasser** [deklɑse] *vt* to relegate, downgrade; *(déranger: fiches, livres)* to get out of order

**déclenchement** [deklɑ̃ʃmɑ̃] *nm* release; setting off

**déclencher** [deklɑ̃ʃe] *vt (mécanisme etc)* to release; *(sonnerie)* to set off, activate; *(attaque, grève)* to launch; *(provoquer)* to trigger off; **se déclencher** *vi* to release itself; to go off

**déclencheur** [deklɑ̃ʃœʀ] *nm* release mechanism

**déclic** [deklik] *nm* trigger mechanism; *(bruit)* click

**déclin** [deklɛ̃] *nm* decline

**déclinaison** [deklinɛzɔ̃] *nf* declension

**décliner** [dekline] *vi* to decline ▷ *vt (invitation)* to decline, refuse; *(responsabilité)* to refuse to accept; *(nom, adresse)* to state; *(Ling)* to decline; **se décliner** *(Ling)* to decline

**déclivité** [deklivite] *nf* slope, incline; **en ~** sloping, on the incline

**décloisonner** [deklwazɔne] *vt* to decompartmentalize

**déclouer** [deklue] *vt* to unnail

**décocher** [dekɔʃe] *vt* to hurl; *(flèche, regard)* to shoot

**décoction** [dekɔksjɔ̃] *nf* decoction

**décodage** [dekɔdaʒ] *nm* deciphering, decoding

**décoder** [dekɔde] *vt* to decipher, decode

**décodeur** [dekɔdœʀ] *nm* decoder

**décoiffé, e** [dekwafe] *adj*: **elle est toute ~e** her hair is in a mess

**décoiffer** [dekwafe] *vt*: **~ qn** to disarrange *ou* mess up sb's hair; to take sb's hat off; **se décoiffer** *vi* to take off one's hat

**décoincer** [dekwɛ̃se] *vt* to unjam, loosen

**déçois** *etc* [deswa], **déçoive** *etc* [deswav] *vb voir* **décevoir**

**décolérer** [dekɔleʀe] *vi*: **il ne décolère pas** he's still angry, he hasn't calmed down

**décollage** [dekɔlaʒ] *nm* (*Aviat, Écon*) takeoff

**décollé, e** [dekɔle] *adj*: **oreilles ~es** sticking-out ears

**décollement** [dekɔlmɑ̃] *nm* (*Méd*): **~ de la rétine** retinal detachment

**décoller** [dekɔle] *vt* to unstick ▷ *vi* to take off; (*projet, entreprise*) to take off, get off the ground; **se décoller** *vi* to come unstuck

**décolleté, e** [dekɔlte] *adj* low-necked, low-cut; (*femme*) wearing a low-cut dress ▷ *nm* low neck(line); (*épaules*) (bare) neck and shoulders; (*plongeant*) cleavage

**décolleter** [dekɔlte] *vt* (*vêtement*) to give a low neckline to; (*Tech*) to cut

**décolonisation** [dekɔlɔnizasjɔ̃] *nf* decolonization

**décoloniser** [dekɔlɔnize] *vt* to decolonize

**décolorant** [dekɔlɔrɑ̃] *nm* decolorant, bleaching agent

**décoloration** [dekɔlɔrasjɔ̃] *nf*: **se faire faire une ~** (*chez le coiffeur*) to have one's hair bleached *ou* lightened

**décoloré, e** [dekɔlɔre] *adj* (*vêtement*) faded; (*cheveux*) bleached

**décolorer** [dekɔlɔre] *vt* (*tissu*) to fade; (*cheveux*) to bleach, lighten; **se décolorer** *vi* to fade

**décombres** [dekɔ̃br(ə)] *nmpl* rubble *sg*, debris *sg*

**décommander** [dekɔmɑ̃de] *vt* to cancel; (*invités*) to put off; **se décommander** *vi* to cancel, cry off

**décomposé, e** [dekɔ̃poze] *adj* (*pourri*) decomposed; (*visage*) haggard, distorted

**décomposer** [dekɔ̃poze] *vt* to break up; (*Chimie*) to decompose; (*Math*) to factorize; **se décomposer** *vi* to decompose

**décomposition** [dekɔ̃pozisjɔ̃] *nf* breaking up; decomposition; factorization; **en ~** (*organisme*) in a state of decay, decomposing

**décompresser** [dekɔ̃prese] *vi* (*fam: se détendre*) to unwind

**décompresseur** [dekɔ̃presœr] *nm* decompressor

**décompression** [dekɔ̃presjɔ̃] *nf* decompression

**décomprimer** [dekɔ̃prime] *vt* to decompress

**décompte** [dekɔ̃t] *nm* deduction; (*facture*) breakdown (of an account), detailed account

**décompter** [dekɔ̃te] *vt* to deduct

**déconcentration** [dekɔ̃sɑ̃trasjɔ̃] *nf* (*des industries etc*) dispersal; **~ des pouvoirs** devolution

**déconcentré, e** [dekɔ̃sɑ̃tre] *adj* (*sportif etc*) who has lost (his/her) concentration

**déconcentrer** [dekɔ̃sɑ̃tre] *vt* (*Admin*) to disperse; **se déconcentrer** *vi* to lose (one's) concentration

**déconcertant, e** [dekɔ̃sɛrtɑ̃, -ɑ̃t] *adj* disconcerting

**déconcerter** [dekɔ̃sɛrte] *vt* to disconcert, confound

**déconditionner** [dekɔ̃disjɔne] *vt*: **~ l'opinion américaine** to change the way the Americans have been forced to think

**déconfit, e** [dekɔ̃fi, -it] *adj* crestfallen, downcast

**déconfiture** [dekɔ̃fityr] *nf* collapse, ruin; (*morale*) defeat

**décongélation** [dekɔ̃ʒelɑsjɔ̃] *nf* defrosting, thawing

**décongeler** [dekɔ̃ʒle] *vt* to thaw (out)

**décongestionner** [dekɔ̃ʒɛstjɔne] *vt* (*Méd*) to decongest; (*rues*) to relieve congestion in

**déconnecter** [dekɔnɛkte] *vt* to disconnect

**déconner** [dekɔne] *vi* (*fam!: en parlant*) to talk (a load of) rubbish (*Brit*) *ou* garbage (*US*); (*: faire des bêtises*) to muck about; **sans ~** no kidding

**déconseiller** [dekɔ̃seje] *vt*: **~ qch (à qn)** to advise (sb) against sth; **~ à qn de faire** to advise sb against doing; **c'est déconseillé** it's not advised *ou* advisable

**déconsidérer** [dekɔ̃sidere] *vt* to discredit

**décontamination** [dekɔ̃taminasjɔ̃] *nf* decontamination

**décontaminer** [dekɔ̃tamine] *vt* to decontaminate

**décontenancer** [dekɔ̃tnɑ̃se] *vt* to disconcert, discountenance

**décontracté, e** [dekɔ̃trakte] *adj* relaxed

**décontracter** [dekɔ̃trakte] *vt*, **se décontracter** *vi* to relax

**décontraction** [dekɔ̃traksjɔ̃] *nf* relaxation

**déconvenue** [dekɔ̃vny] *nf* disappointment

**décor** [dekɔr] *nm* décor; (*paysage*) scenery; **décors** *nmpl* (*Théât*) scenery *sg*, decor *sg*; (*Ciné*) set *sg*; **changement de ~** (*fig*) change of scene; **entrer dans le ~** (*fig*) to run off the road; **en ~ naturel** (*Ciné*) on location

**décorateur, -trice** [dekɔratœr, -tris] *nm/f* (*interior*) decorator; (*Ciné*) set designer

**décoratif, -ive** [dekɔratif, -iv] *adj* decorative

**décoration** [dekɔrasjɔ̃] *nf* decoration

**décorer** [dekɔre] *vt* to decorate

**décortiqué, e** [dekɔrtike] *adj* shelled; hulled

**décortiquer** [dekɔrtike] *vt* to shell; (*riz*) to hull; (*fig*) to dissect

**décorum** [dekɔrɔm] *nm* decorum; etiquette

**décote** [dekɔt] *nf* tax relief

**découcher** [dekuʃe] *vi* to spend the night away

**découdre** [dekudr(ə)] *vt* (*vêtement, couture*) to unpick, take the stitching out of; (*bouton*) to take off; **se découdre** *vi* to come unstitched; (*bouton*) to come off; **en ~** (*fig*) to fight, do battle

**découler** [dekule] *vi*: **~ de** to ensue *ou* follow from

**découpage** [dekupaʒ] *nm* cutting up; carving; (*image*) cut-out (figure); **~ électoral** division into constituencies

**découper** [dekupe] *vt* (*papier, tissu etc*) to cut up; (*volaille, viande*) to carve; (*détacher: manche, article*) to cut out; **se ~ sur** (*ciel, fond*) to stand out against

**découplé, e** [dekuple] *adj*: **bien ~** well-built, well-proportioned

**découpure** [dekupyr] *nf*: **~s** (*morceaux*) cut-out bits; (*d'une côte, arête*) indentations, jagged outline *sg*

**décourageant, e** [dekuraʒɑ̃, ɑ̃t] *adj*
discouraging; (*personne, attitude*) discouraging,
negative

**découragement** [dekuraʒmɑ̃] *nm*
discouragement, despondency

**décourager** [dekuraʒe] *vt* to discourage,
dishearten; (*dissuader*) to discourage, put off; **se
décourager** *vi* to lose heart, become
discouraged; **~ qn de faire/de qch** to
discourage sb from doing/from sth, put sb off
doing/sth

**décousu, e** [dekuzy] *pp de* **découdre** ▷ *adj*
unstitched; (*fig*) disjointed, disconnected

**découvert, e** [dekuvɛʀ, -ɛʀt(ə)] *pp de* **découvrir**
▷ *adj* (*tête*) bare, uncovered; (*lieu*) open, exposed
▷ *nm* (*bancaire*) overdraft ▷ *nf* discovery; **à ~** *adv*
(*Mil*) exposed, without cover; (*fig*) openly ▷ *adj*
(*Comm*) overdrawn; **à visage ~** openly; **aller à la
~e** to go in search of

**découvrir** [dekuvʀiʀ] *vt* to discover; (*apercevoir*)
to see; (*enlever ce qui couvre ou protège*) to uncover;
(*montrer, dévoiler*) to reveal; **se découvrir** *vi* to
take off one's hat; (*se déshabiller*) to take
something off; (*au lit*) to uncover o.s.; (*ciel*) to
clear; **se ~ des talents** to find hidden talents
in o.s.

**décrasser** [dekrase] *vt* to clean

**décrêper** [dekrepe] *vt* (*cheveux*) to straighten

**décrépi, e** [dekrepi] *adj* peeling; with roughcast
rendering removed

**décrépit, e** [dekrepi, -it] *adj* decrepit

**décrépitude** [dekrepityd] *nf* decrepitude; decay

**decrescendo** [dekreʃɛndo] *nm* (*Mus*)
decrescendo; **aller ~** (*fig*) to decline, be on the
wane

**décret** [dekrɛ] *nm* decree

**décréter** [dekrete] *vt* to decree; (*ordonner*) to order

**décret-loi** [dekrɛlwa] *nm* statutory order

**décrié, e** [dekrije] *adj* disparaged

**décrire** [dekriʀ] *vt* to describe; (*courbe, cercle*) to
follow, describe

**décrisper** [dekrispe] *vt* to defuse

**décrit, e** [dekri, -it] *pp de* **décrire**

**décrivais** *etc* [dekrivɛ] *vb voir* **décrire**

**décrochage** [dekrɔʃaʒ] *nm*: **~ scolaire** (*Scol*)
= truancy

**décrochement** [dekrɔʃmɑ̃] *nm* (*d'un mur etc*)
recess

**décrocher** [dekrɔʃe] *vt* (*dépendre*) to take down;
(*téléphone*) to take off the hook; (: *pour répondre*): **~
(le téléphone)** to pick up *ou* lift the receiver;
(*fig: contrat etc*) to get, land ▷ *vi* to drop out; to
switch off; **se décrocher** *vi* (*tableau, rideau*) to
fall down

**décroîs** *etc* [dekrwa] *vb voir* **décroître**

**décroiser** [dekrwaze] *vt* (*bras*) to unfold; (*jambes*)
to uncross

**décroissant, e** [dekrwasɑ̃, -ɑ̃t] *vb voir* **décroître**
▷ *adj* decreasing, declining, diminishing; **par
ordre ~** in descending order

**décroître** [dekrwatr(ə)] *vi* to decrease,

decline diminish

**décrotter** [dekrɔte] *vt* (*chaussures*) to clean the
mud from; **se ~ le nez** to pick one's nose

**décru, e** [dekry] *pp de* **décroître**

**décrue** [dekry] *nf* drop in level (of the waters)

**décrypter** [dekripte] *vt* to decipher

**déçu, e** [desy] *pp de* **décevoir** ▷ *adj* disappointed

**déculotter** [dekylɔte] *vt*: **~ qn** to take off *ou*
down sb's trousers; **se déculotter** *vi* to take off
*ou* down one's trousers

**déculpabiliser** [dekylpabilize] *vt* (*personne*) to
relieve of guilt; (*chose*) to decriminalize

**décuple** [dekypl(ə)] *nm*: **le ~ de** ten times; **au ~**
tenfold

**décupler** [dekyple] *vt, vi* to increase tenfold

**déçut** *etc* [desy] *vb voir* **décevoir**

**dédaignable** [dedɛɲabl(ə)] *adj*: **pas ~** not to be
despised

**dédaigner** [dedɛɲe] *vt* to despise, scorn;
(*négliger*) to disregard, spurn; **~ de faire** to
consider it beneath one to do, not deign to do

**dédaigneusement** [dedɛɲøzmɑ̃] *adv*
scornfully, disdainfully

**dédaigneux, -euse** [dedɛɲø, -øz] *adj* scornful,
disdainful

**dédain** [dedɛ̃] *nm* scorn, disdain

**dédale** [dedal] *nm* maze

**dedans** [dədɑ̃] *adv* inside; (*pas en plein air*)
indoors, inside ▷ *nm* inside; **au ~** on the inside;
inside; **en ~** (*vers l'intérieur*) inwards; *voir aussi* **là**

**dédicace** [dedikas] *nf* (*imprimée*) dedication;
(*manuscrite, sur une photo etc*) inscription

**dédicacer** [dedikase] *vt*: **~ (à qn)** to sign (for sb),
autograph (for sb), inscribe (to sb)

**dédié, e** [dedje] *adj*: **ordinateur ~** dedicated
computer

**dédier** [dedje] *vt* to dedicate

**dédire** [dediʀ]: **se dédire** *vi* to go back on one's
word; (*se rétracter*) to retract, recant

**dédit, e** [dedi, -it] *pp de* **dédire** ▷ *nm* (*Comm*)
forfeit, penalty

**dédommagement** [dedɔmaʒmɑ̃] *nm*
compensation

**dédommager** [dedɔmaʒe] *vt*: **~ qn (de)** to
compensate sb (for); (*fig*) to repay sb (for)

**dédouaner** [dedwane] *vt* to clear through
customs

**dédoublement** [dedubləmɑ̃] *nm* splitting;
(*Psych*): **~ de la personnalité** split *ou* dual
personality

**dédoubler** [deduble] *vt* (*classe, effectifs*) to split
(into two); (*couverture etc*) to unfold; (*manteau*) to
remove the lining of; **~ un train/les trains** to
run a relief train/additional trains; **se
dédoubler** *vi* (*Psych*) to have a split personality

**dédramatiser** [dedramatize] *vt* (*situation*) to
defuse; (*événement*) to play down

**déductible** [dedyktibl(ə)] *adj* deductible

**déduction** [dedyksjɔ̃] *nf* (*d'argent*) deduction;
(*raisonnement*) deduction, inference

**déduire** [deduiʀ] *vt*: **~ qch (de)** (*ôter*) to deduct
sth (from); (*conclure*) to deduce *ou* infer sth (from)

**d**

**déesse** [dees] nf goddess

**DEFA** sigle m (= Diplôme d'État relatif aux fonctions d'animation) diploma for senior youth leaders

**défaillance** [defajɑ̃s] nf (syncope) blackout; (fatigue) (sudden) weakness no pl; (technique) fault, failure; (morale etc) weakness; **~ cardiaque** heart failure

**défaillant, e** [defajɑ̃, -ɑ̃t] adj defective; (Jur: témoin) defaulting

**défaillir** [defajiʀ] vi to faint; to feel faint; (mémoire etc) to fail

**défaire** [defɛʀ] vt (installation, échafaudage) to take down, dismantle; (paquet etc, nœud, vêtement) to undo; (bagages) to unpack; (ouvrage) to undo, unpick; (cheveux) to take out; **se défaire** vi to come undone; **se ~ de** vt (se débarrasser de) to get rid of; (se séparer de) to part with; **~ le lit** (pour changer les draps) to strip the bed; (pour se coucher) to turn back the bedclothes

**défait, e** [defɛ, -ɛt] pp de **défaire** ▷ adj (visage) haggard, ravaged ▷ nf defeat

**défaites** [defɛt] vb voir **défaire**

**défaitisme** [defetism(ə)] nm defeatism

**défaitiste** [defetist(ə)] adj, nm/f defeatist

**défalcation** [defalkɑsjɔ̃] nf deduction

**défalquer** [defalke] vt to deduct

**défasse** etc [defas] vb voir **défaire**

**défausser** [defose] vt to get rid of; **se défausser** vi (Cartes) to discard

**défaut** [defo] nm (moral) fault, failing, defect; (d'étoffe, métal) fault, flaw, defect; (manque, carence): **~ de** lack of; shortage of; (Inform) bug; **~ de la cuirasse** (fig) chink in the armour (Brit) ou armor (US); **en ~** at fault; in the wrong; **faire ~** (manquer) to be lacking; **à ~** adv failing that; **à ~ de** for lack ou want of; **par ~** (Jur) in his (ou her etc) absence

**défaveur** [defavœʀ] nf disfavour (Brit), disfavor (US)

**défavorable** [defavɔʀabl(ə)] adj unfavourable (Brit), unfavorable (US)

**défavoriser** [defavɔʀize] vt to put at a disadvantage

**défectif, -ive** [defɛktif, -iv] adj: **verbe ~** defective verb

**défection** [defɛksjɔ̃] nf defection, failure to give support ou assistance; failure to appear; **faire ~** (d'un parti etc) to withdraw one's support, leave

**défectueux, -euse** [defɛktɥø, -øz] adj faulty, defective

**défectuosité** [defɛktɥozite] nf defectiveness no pl; (défaut) defect, fault

**défendable** [defɑ̃dabl(ə)] adj defensible

**défendeur, -eresse** [defɑ̃dœʀ, -dʀɛs] nm/f (Jur) defendant

**défendre** [defɑ̃dʀ(ə)] vt to defend; (interdire) to forbid; **~ à qn qch/de faire** to forbid sb sth/to do; **il est défendu de cracher** spitting (is) prohibited ou is not allowed; **c'est défendu** it is forbidden; **se défendre** vi to defend o.s.; **il se défend** (fig) he can hold his own; **ça se défend**

(fig) it holds together; **se ~ de/contre** (se protéger) to protect o.s. from/against; **se ~ de** (se garder de) to refrain from; (nier): **se ~ de vouloir** to deny wanting

**défenestrer** [defənɛstʀe] vt to throw out of the window

**défense** [defɑ̃s] nf defence (Brit), defense (US); (d'éléphant etc) tusk; **ministre de la ~** Minister of Defence (Brit), Defence Secretary; **la ~ nationale** defence, the defence of the realm (Brit); **la ~ contre avions** anti-aircraft defence; **"~ de fumer/cracher"** "no smoking/spitting", "smoking/spitting prohibited"; **prendre la ~ de qn** to stand up for sb; **~ des consommateurs** consumerism

**défenseur** [defɑ̃sœʀ] nm defender; (Jur) counsel for the defence

**défensif, -ive** [defɑ̃sif, -iv] adj, nf defensive; **être sur la défensive** to be on the defensive

**déféquer** [defeke] vi to defecate

**déferai** etc [defʀe] vb voir **défaire**

**déférence** [defeʀɑ̃s] nf deference

**déférent, e** [defeʀɑ̃, -ɑ̃t] adj (poli) deferential, deferent

**déférer** [defeʀe] vt (Jur) to refer; **~ à** vt (requête, décision) to defer to; **~ qn à la justice** to hand sb over to justice

**déferlant, e** [defɛʀlɑ̃, -ɑ̃t] adj: **vague ~e** breaker

**déferlement** [defɛʀləmɑ̃] nm breaking; surge

**déferler** [defɛʀle] vi (vagues) to break; (fig) to surge

**défi** [defi] nm (provocation) challenge; (bravade) defiance; **mettre qn au ~ de faire qch** to challenge sb to do sth; **relever un ~** to take up ou accept a challenge

**défiance** [defjɑ̃s] nf mistrust, distrust

**déficeler** [defisle] vt (paquet) to undo, untie

**déficience** [defisjɑ̃s] nf deficiency

**déficient, e** [defisjɑ̃, -ɑ̃t] adj deficient

**déficit** [defisit] nm (Comm) deficit; (Psych etc: manque) defect; **~ budgétaire** budget deficit; **être en ~** to be in deficit

**déficitaire** [defisitɛʀ] adj (année, récolte) bad; **entreprise/budget ~** business/budget in deficit

**défier** [defje] vt (provoquer) to challenge; (fig) to defy, brave; **se ~ de** (se méfier de) to distrust, mistrust; **~ qn de faire** to challenge ou defy sb to do; **~ qn à** to challenge sb to; **~ toute comparaison/concurrence** to be incomparable/unbeatable

**défigurer** [defigyʀe] vt to disfigure; (boutons etc) to mar ou spoil (the looks of); (fig: œuvre) to mutilate, deface

**défilé** [defile] nm (Géo) (narrow) gorge ou pass; (soldats) parade; (manifestants) procession, march; **un ~ de** (voitures, visiteurs etc) a stream of

**défiler** [defile] vi (troupes) to march past; (sportifs) to parade; (manifestants) to march; (visiteurs) to pour, stream; **se défiler** vi (se dérober) to slip away, sneak off; **faire ~** (bande, film) to put on; (Inform) to scroll

**défini, e** [defini] *adj* definite
**définir** [definiʀ] *vt* to define
**définissable** [definisabl(ə)] *adj* definable
**définitif, -ive** [definitif, -iv] *adj* (*final*) final,
definitive; (*pour longtemps*) permanent,
definitive; (*sans appel*) final, definite ▷ *nf:* **en
définitive** eventually; (*somme toute*) when all is
said and done
**définition** [definisjɔ̃] *nf* definition; (*de mots
croisés*) clue; (*TV*) (picture) resolution
**définitivement** [definitivmã] *adv* definitively;
permanently; definitely
**défit** *etc* [defi] *vb voir* **défaire**
**déflagration** [deflagʀasjɔ̃] *nf* explosion
**déflation** [deflasjɔ̃] *nf* deflation
**déflationniste** [deflasjɔnist(ə)] *adj*
deflationist, deflationary
**déflecteur** [deflektœʀ] *nm* (*Auto*) quarterlight
(*Brit*), deflector (*US*)
**déflorer** [deflɔʀe] *vt* (*jeune fille*) to deflower; (*fig*)
to spoil the charm of
**défoncé, e** [defɔ̃se] *adj* smashed in; broken
down; (*route*) full of potholes ▷ *nm/f* addict
**défoncer** [defɔ̃se] *vt* (*caisse*) to stave in; (*porte*) to
smash in *ou* down; (*lit, fauteuil*) to burst (the
springs of); (*terrain, route*) to rip *ou* plough up; **se
défoncer** *vi* (*se donner à fond*) to give it all one's
got
**défont** [defɔ̃] *vb voir* **défaire**
**déformant, e** [defɔʀmã, -ãt] *adj:* **glace ~e** *ou*
**miroir ~** distorting mirror
**déformation** [defɔʀmasjɔ̃] *nf* loss of shape;
deformation; distortion; **~ professionnelle**
conditioning by one's job
**déformer** [defɔʀme] *vt* to put out of shape;
(*corps*) to deform; (*pensée, fait*) to distort; **se
déformer** *vi* to lose its shape
**défoulement** [defulmã] *nm* release of tension;
unwinding
**défouler** [defule]: **se défouler** *vi* (*Psych*) to work
off one's tensions, release one's pent-up
feelings; (*gén*) to unwind, let off steam
**défraîchi, e** [defʀeʃi] *adj* faded; (*article à vendre*)
shop-soiled
**défraîchir** [defʀeʃiʀ]: **se défraîchir** *vi* to fade; to
become shop-soiled
**défrayer** [defʀeje] *vt:* **~ qn** to pay sb's expenses;
**~ la chronique** to be in the news; **~ la
conversation** to be the main topic of
conversation
**défrichement** [defʀiʃmã] *nm* clearance
**défricher** [defʀiʃe] *vt* to clear (for cultivation)
**défriser** [defʀize] *vt* (*cheveux*) to straighten; (*fig*)
to annoy
**défroisser** [defʀwase] *vt* to smooth out
**défroque** [defʀɔk] *nf* cast-off
**défroqué** [defʀɔke] *nm* former monk (*ou* priest)
**défroquer** [defʀɔke] *vi* (*aussi:* **se défroquer**) to
give up the cloth, renounce one's vows
**défunt, e** [defœ̃, -œ̃t] *adj:* **son ~ père** his late
father ▷ *nm/f* deceased
**dégagé, e** [degaʒe] *adj* clear; (*ton, air*) casual,

jaunty
**dégagement** [degaʒmã] *nm* emission; freeing;
clearing; (*espace libre*) clearing; passage;
clearance; (*Football*) clearance; **voie de ~** slip
road; **itinéraire de ~** alternative route (*to relieve
traffic congestion*)
**dégager** [degaʒe] *vt* (*exhaler*) to give off, emit;
(*délivrer*) to free, extricate; (*Mil: troupes*) to relieve;
(*désencombrer*) to clear; (*isoler, mettre en valeur*) to
bring out; (*crédits*) to release; **se dégager** *vi*
(*odeur*) to emanate, be given off; (*passage, ciel*) to
clear; **~ qn de** (*engagement, parole etc*) to release *ou*
free sb from; **se ~ de** (*fig: engagement etc*) to get
out of; (*: promesse*) to go back on
**dégaine** [degɛn] *nf* awkward way of walking
**dégainer** [degene] *vt* to draw
**dégarni, e** [degaʀni] *adj* bald
**dégarnir** [degaʀniʀ] *vt* (*vider*) to empty, clear; **se
dégarnir** *vi* to empty; to be cleaned out *ou*
cleared; (*tempes, crâne*) to go bald
**dégâts** [degɑ] *nmpl* damage *sg;* **faire des ~** to
damage
**dégauchir** [degoʃiʀ] *vt* (*Tech*) to surface
**dégazer** [degaze] *vi* (*pétrolier*) to clean its tanks
**dégel** [deʒɛl] *nm* thaw; (*fig: des prix etc*)
unfreezing
**dégeler** [deʒle] *vt* to thaw (out); (*fig*) to unfreeze
▷ *vi* to thaw (out); **se dégeler** *vi* (*fig*) to thaw out
**dégénéré, e** [deʒeneʀe] *adj, nm/f* degenerate
**dégénérer** [deʒeneʀe] *vi* to degenerate; (*empirer*)
to go from bad to worse; (*devenir*) **~ en** to
degenerate into
**dégénérescence** [deʒeneʀesãs] *nf*
degeneration
**dégingandé, e** [deʒɛ̃gãde] *adj* gangling, lanky
**dégivrage** [deʒivʀaʒ] *nm* defrosting; de-icing
**dégivrer** [deʒivʀe] *vt* (*frigo*) to defrost; (*vitres*) to
de-ice
**dégivreur** [deʒivʀœʀ] *nm* defroster; de-icer
**déglinguer** [deglɛ̃ge] *vt* to bust
**déglutir** [deglytiʀ] *vt, vi* to swallow
**déglutition** [deglytisjɔ̃] *nf* swallowing
**dégonflé, e** [degɔ̃fle] *adj* (*pneu*) flat; (*fam*)
chicken ▷ *nm/f* (*fam*) chicken
**dégonfler** [degɔ̃fle] *vt* (*pneu, ballon*) to let down,
deflate ▷ *vi* (*désenfler*) to go down; **se dégonfler**
*vi* (*fam*) to chicken out
**dégorger** [degɔʀʒe] *vi* (*Culin*): **faire ~** to leave to
sweat; (*aussi:* **se dégorger**: *rivière*): **~ dans** to flow
into ▷ *vt* to disgorge
**dégoter** [degɔte] *vt* (*fam*) to dig up, find
**dégouliner** [deguline] *vi* to trickle, drip; **~ de** to
be dripping with
**dégoupiller** [degupije] *vt* (*grenade*) to take the
pin out of
**dégourdi, e** [deguʀdi] *adj* smart, resourceful
**dégourdir** [deguʀdiʀ] *vt* to warm (up); **se ~ (les
jambes)** to stretch one's legs
**dégoût** [degu] *nm* disgust, distaste
**dégoûtant, e** [degutã, -ãt] *adj* disgusting
**dégoûté, e** [degute] *adj* disgusted; **~ de** sick of
**dégoûter** [degute] *vt* to disgust; **cela me**

**d**

**dégoûte** I find this disgusting *ou* revolting; ~ **qn de qch** to put sb off sth; **se ~ de** to get *ou* become sick of

**dégoutter** [degute] *vi* to drip; **~ de** to be dripping with

**dégradant, e** [degʀadɑ̃, -ɑ̃t] *adj* degrading

**dégradation** [degʀadɑsjɔ̃] *nf* reduction in rank; defacement; degradation, debasement; deterioration; (*aussi:* **dégradations**: *dégâts*) damage *no pl*

**dégradé, e** [degʀade] *adj* (*couleur*) shaded off; (*teintes*) faded; (*cheveux*) layered ▷ *nm* (*Peinture*) gradation

**dégrader** [degʀade] *vt* (*Mil*: *officier*) to degrade; (*abîmer*) to damage, deface; (*avilir*) to degrade, debase; **se dégrader** *vi* (*relations, situation*) to deteriorate

**dégrafer** [degʀafe] *vt* to unclip, unhook, unfasten

**dégraissage** [degʀɛsaʒ] *nm* (*Écon*) cutbacks *pl*; **~ et nettoyage à sec** dry cleaning

**dégraissant** [degʀɛsɑ̃] *nm* spot remover

**dégraisser** [degʀese] *vt* (*soupe*) to skim; (*vêtement*) to take the grease marks out of; (*Écon*) to cut back; (: *entreprise*) to slim down

**degré** [dəgʀe] *nm* degree; (*d'escalier*) step; **brûlure au 1er/2ème ~** 1st/2nd degree burn; **équation du 1er/2ème ~** linear/quadratic equation; **le premier ~** (*Scol*) primary level; **alcool à 90 ~s** surgical spirit; **vin de 10 ~s 10°** wine (*on Gay-Lussac scale*); **par ~(s)** *adv* by degrees, gradually

**dégressif, -ive** [degʀesif, -iv] *adj* on a decreasing scale, degressive; **tarif ~** decreasing rate of charge

**dégrèvement** [degʀɛvmɑ̃] *nm* tax relief

**dégrever** [degʀəve] *vt* to grant tax relief to; to reduce the tax burden on

**dégriffé, e** [degʀife] *adj* sold without the designer's label; **voyage ~** discount holiday

**dégringolade** [degʀɛ̃gɔlad] *nf* tumble; (*fig*) collapse

**dégringoler** [degʀɛ̃gɔle] *vi* to tumble (down); (*fig*: *prix, monnaie etc*) to collapse

**dégriser** [degʀize] *vt* to sober up

**dégrossir** [degʀosiʀ] *vt* (*bois*) to trim; (*fig*) to work out roughly; (: *personne*) to knock the rough edges off

**déguenillé, e** [degnije] *adj* ragged, tattered

**déguerpir** [degɛʀpiʀ] *vi* to clear off

**dégueulasse** [degœlas] *adj* (*fam*) disgusting

**dégueuler** [degœle] *vi* (*fam*) to puke, throw up

**déguisé, e** [degize] *adj* disguised; dressed up; **~ en** disguised (*ou* dressed up) as

**déguisement** [degizmɑ̃] *nm* disguise; (*habits*: *pour s'amuser*) dressing-up clothes; (: *pour tromper*) disguise

**déguiser** [degize] *vt* to disguise; **se déguiser (en)** *vi* (*se costumer*) to dress up (as); (*pour tromper*) to disguise o.s. (as)

**dégustation** [degystɑsjɔ̃] *nf* tasting; sampling; savouring (*Brit*), savoring (*US*); (*séance*): **~ de vin(s)** wine-tasting

**déguster** [degyste] *vt* (*vins*) to taste; (*fromages etc*) to sample; (*savourer*) to enjoy, savour (*Brit*), savor (*US*)

**déhancher** [deɑ̃ʃe]: **se déhancher** *vi* to sway one's hips; to lean (one's weight) on one hip

**dehors** [dəɔʀ] *adv* outside; (*en plein air*) outdoors, outside ▷ *nm* outside ▷ *nmpl* (*apparences*) appearances, exterior *sg*; **mettre** *ou* **jeter ~** to throw out; **au ~** outside; (*en apparence*) outwardly; **au ~ de** outside; **de ~** from outside; **en ~** outside; outwards; **en ~ de** apart from

**déifier** [deifje] *vt* to deify

**déjà** [deʒa] *adv* already; (*auparavant*) before, already; **as-tu ~ été en France?** have you been to France before?; **c'est ~ pas mal** that's not too bad (at all); **c'est ~ quelque chose** (at least) it's better than nothing; **quel nom, ~?** what was the name again?

**déjanter** [deʒɑ̃te]: **se déjanter** *vi* (*pneu*) to come off the rim

**déjà-vu** [deʒavy] *nm*: **c'est du ~** there's nothing new in that

**déjeté, e** [deʒte] *adj* lop-sided, crooked

**déjeuner** [deʒœne] *vi* to (have) lunch; (*le matin*) to have breakfast ▷ *nm* lunch; (*petit déjeuner*) breakfast; **~ d'affaires** business lunch

**déjouer** [deʒwe] *vt* to elude, to foil, thwart

**déjuger** [deʒyʒe]: **se déjuger** *vi* to go back on one's opinion

**delà** [dəla] *adv*: **par ~, en ~ (de), au ~ (de)** beyond

**délabré, e** [delabʀe] *adj* dilapidated, broken-down

**délabrement** [delabʀəmɑ̃] *nm* decay, dilapidation

**délabrer** [delabʀe]: **se délabrer** *vi* to fall into decay, become dilapidated

**délacer** [delase] *vt* to unlace, undo

**délai** [delɛ] *nm* (*attente*) waiting period; (*sursis*) extension (of time); (*temps accordé*: *aussi:* **délais**) time limit; **sans ~** without delay; **à bref ~** shortly, very soon; at short notice; **dans les ~s** within the time limit; **un ~ de 30 jours** a period of 30 days; **comptez un ~ de livraison de 10 jours** allow 10 days for delivery

**délaissé, e** [delese] *adj* abandoned, deserted; neglected

**délaisser** [delese] *vt* (*abandonner*) to abandon, desert; (*négliger*) to neglect

**délassant, e** [delasɑ̃, -ɑ̃t] *adj* relaxing

**délassement** [delasmɑ̃] *nm* relaxation

**délasser** [delase] *vt* (*reposer*) to relax; (*divertir*) to divert, entertain; **se délasser** *vi* to relax

**délateur, -trice** [delatœʀ, -tʀis] *nm/f* informer

**délation** [delasjɔ̃] *nf* denouncement, informing

**délavé, e** [delave] *adj* faded

**délayage** [delejaʒ] *nm* mixing; thinning down

**délayer** [deleje] *vt* (*Culin*) to mix (with water *etc*); (*peinture*) to thin down; (*fig*) to pad out, spin out

**delco®** [dɛlko] *nm* (*Auto*) distributor; **tête de delco** distributor cap

**délectation** [delɛktasjɔ̃] *nf* delight

**délecter** [delɛkte]: **se délecter** vi: **se ~ de** to revel ou delight in

**délégation** [delegɑsjɔ̃] nf delegation; **~ de pouvoir** delegation of power

**délégué, e** [delege] adj delegated ▷ nm/f delegate; representative; **ministre ~ à** minister with special responsibility for

**déléguer** [delege] vt to delegate

**délestage** [delɛstaʒ] nm: **itinéraire de ~** alternative route (to relieve traffic congestion)

**délester** [delɛste] vt (navire) to unballast; **~ une route** to relieve traffic congestion on a road by diverting traffic

**Delhi** [deli] n Delhi

**délibérant, e** [deliberɑ̃, -ɑ̃t] adj: **assemblée ~e** deliberative assembly

**délibératif, -ive** [deliberatif, -iv] adj: **avoir voix délibérative** to have voting rights

**délibération** [deliberɑsjɔ̃] nf deliberation

**délibéré, e** [delibere] adj (conscient) deliberate; (déterminé) determined, resolute; **de propos ~** (à dessein, exprès) intentionally

**délibérément** [deliberemɑ̃] adv deliberately; (résolument) resolutely

**délibérer** [delibere] vi to deliberate

**délicat, e** [delika, -at] adj delicate; (plein de tact) tactful; (attentionné) thoughtful; (exigeant) fussy, particular; **procédés peu ~s** unscrupulous methods

**délicatement** [delikatmɑ̃] adv delicately; (avec douceur) gently

**délicatesse** [delikatɛs] nf delicacy; tactfulness; thoughtfulness; **délicatesses** nfpl attentions, consideration sg

**délice** [delis] nm delight

**délicieusement** [delisjøzmɑ̃] adv deliciously; delightfully

**délicieux, -euse** [delisjø, -øz] adj (au goût) delicious; (sensation, impression) delightful

**délictueux, -euse** [deliktɥø, -øz] adj criminal

**délié, e** [delje] adj nimble, agile; (mince) slender, fine ▷ nm: **les ~s** the upstrokes (in handwriting)

**délier** [delje] vt to untie; **~ qn de** (serment etc) to free ou release sb from

**délimitation** [delimitɑsjɔ̃] nf delimitation

**délimiter** [delimite] vt to delimit

**délinquance** [delɛ̃kɑ̃s] nf criminality; **~ juvénile** juvenile delinquency

**délinquant, e** [delɛ̃kɑ̃, -ɑ̃t] adj, nm/f delinquent

**déliquescence** [delikesɑ̃s] nf: **en ~** in a state of decay

**déliquescent, e** [delikesɑ̃, -ɑ̃t] adj decaying

**délirant, e** [delirɑ̃, -ɑ̃t] adj (Méd: fièvre) delirious; (imagination) frenzied; (fam: déraisonnable) crazy

**délire** [delir] nm (fièvre) delirium; (fig) frenzy; (: folie) lunacy

**délirer** [delire] vi to be delirious; (fig) to be raving

**délit** [deli] nm (criminal) offence; **~ de droit commun** violation of common law; **~ de fuite** failure to stop after an accident; **~ d'initiés** insider dealing ou trading; **~ de presse**

violation of the press laws

**délivrance** [delivrɑ̃s] nf freeing, release; (sentiment) relief

**délivrer** [delivre] vt (prisonnier) to (set) free, release; (passeport, certificat) to issue; **~ qn de** (ennemis) to set sb free from, deliver ou free sb from; (fig) to rid sb of

**délocalisation** [delɔkalizɑsjɔ̃] nf relocation

**délocaliser** [delɔkalize] vt (entreprise, emplois) relocate

**déloger** [delɔʒe] vt (locataire) to turn out; (objet coincé, ennemi) to dislodge

**déloyal, e, -aux** [delwajal, -o] adj (personne, conduite) disloyal; (procédé) unfair

**Delphes** [dɛlf] n Delphi

**delta** [delta] nm (Géo) delta

**deltaplane®** [dɛltaplan] nm hang-glider

**déluge** [delyʒ] nm (biblique) Flood, Deluge; (grosse pluie) downpour, deluge; (grand nombre): **~ de** flood of

**déluré, e** [delyre] adj smart, resourceful; (péj) forward, pert

**démagnétiser** [demaɲetize] vt to demagnetize

**démagogie** [demagɔʒi] nf demagogy

**démagogique** [demagɔʒik] adj demagogic, popularity-seeking; (Pol) vote-catching

**démagogue** [demagɔg] adj demagogic ▷ nm demagogue

**démaillé, e** [demaje] adj (bas) laddered (Brit), with a run (ou runs)

**demain** [dəmɛ̃] adv tomorrow; **~ matin/soir** tomorrow morning/evening; **~ midi** tomorrow at midday; **à ~!** see you tomorrow!

**demande** [dəmɑ̃d] nf (requête) request; (revendication) demand; (Admin, formulaire) application; (Écon): **la ~** demand; **"~s d'emploi"** "situations wanted"; **à la ~ générale** by popular request; **~ en mariage** (marriage) proposal; **faire sa ~ (en mariage)** to propose (marriage); **~ de naturalisation** application for naturalization; **~ de poste** job application

**demandé, e** [dəmɑ̃de] adj (article etc): **très ~** (very) much in demand

**demander** [dəmɑ̃de] vt to ask for; (question: date, heure, chemin) to ask; (requérir, nécessiter) to require, demand; **~ qch à qn** to ask sb for sth, ask sb sth; **ils demandent deux secrétaires et un ingénieur** they're looking for two secretaries and an engineer; **~ la main de qn** to ask for sb's hand (in marriage); **~ pardon à qn** to apologize to sb; **~ à ou de voir/faire** to ask to see/ask if one can do; **~ à qn de faire** to ask sb to do; **~ que/pourquoi** to ask that/why; **se ~ si/pourquoi** etc to wonder if/why etc; (emploi pronominal réfléchi) to ask o.s. if/why etc; **on vous demande au téléphone** you're wanted on the phone, there's someone for you on the phone; **il ne demande que ça** that's all he wants; **je ne demande pas mieux** I'm asking nothing more; **il ne demande qu'à faire** all he wants is to do

**demandeur, -euse** [dəmɑ̃dœr, -øz] nm/f: **~**

**d'emploi** job-seeker
**démangeaison** [demɑʒɛzɔ̃] nf itching
**démanger** [demɑʒe] vi to itch; **la main me démange** my hand is itching; **l'envie** ou **ça me démange de faire** I'm itching to do
**démantèlement** [demɑ̃tɛlmɑ̃] nm breaking up
**démanteler** [demɑ̃tle] vt to break up; to demolish
**démaquillant** [demakijɑ̃] nm make-up remover
**démaquiller** [demakije] vt: **se démaquiller** to remove one's make-up
**démarcage** [demaʀkaʒ] nm = **démarquage**
**démarcation** [demaʀkɑsjɔ̃] nf demarcation
**démarchage** [demaʀʃaʒ] nm (Comm) door-to-door selling
**démarche** [demaʀʃ(ə)] nf (allure) gait, walk; (intervention) step; approach; (fig: intellectuelle) thought processes pl; approach; **faire** ou **entreprendre des ~s** to take action; **faire des ~s auprès de qn** to approach sb
**démarcheur, -euse** [demaʀʃœʀ, -øz] nm/f (Comm) door-to-door salesman/woman; (Pol etc) canvasser
**démarquage** [demaʀkaʒ] nm marking down
**démarque** [demaʀk(ə)] nf (Comm: d'un article) mark-down
**démarqué, e** [demaʀke] adj (Football) unmarked; (Comm) reduced; **prix ~s** marked-down prices
**démarquer** [demaʀke] vt (prix) to mark down; (joueur) to stop marking; **se démarquer** vi (Sport) to shake off one's marker
**démarrage** [demaʀaʒ] nm starting no pl, start; **~ en côte** hill start
**démarrer** [demaʀe] vt to start up ▷ vi (conducteur) to start (up); (véhicule) to move off; (travaux, affaire) to get moving; (coureur: accélérer) to pull away
**démarreur** [demaʀœʀ] nm (Auto) starter
**démasquer** [demaske] vt to unmask; **se démasquer** to unmask; (fig) to drop one's mask
**démâter** [demɑte] vt to dismast ▷ vi to be dismasted
**démêlant, e** [demelɑ̃, -ɑ̃t] adj: **baume ~, crème ~e** (hair) conditioner
**démêler** [demele] vt to untangle, disentangle
**démêlés** [demele] nmpl problems
**démembrement** [demɑ̃bʀəmɑ̃] nm dismemberment
**démembrer** [demɑ̃bʀe] vt to dismember
**déménagement** [demenaʒmɑ̃] nm (du point de vue du locataire etc) move; (: du déménageur) removal (Brit), moving (US); **entreprise/ camion de ~** removal (Brit) ou moving (US) firm/van
**déménager** [demenaʒe] vt (meubles) to (re)move ▷ vi to move (house)
**déménageur** [demenaʒœʀ] nm removal man (Brit), (furniture) mover (US); (entrepreneur) furniture remover
**démence** [demɑ̃s] nf madness, insanity; (Méd)

dementia
**démener** [demne]: **se démener** vi to thrash about; (fig) to exert o.s.
**dément, e** [demɑ̃, -ɑ̃t] vb voir **démentir** ▷ adj (fou) mad (Brit), crazy; (fam) brilliant, fantastic
**démenti** [demɑ̃ti] nm refutation
**démentiel, le** [demɑ̃sjɛl] adj insane
**démentir** [demɑ̃tiʀ] vt (nouvelle, témoin) to refute; (faits etc) to belie, refute; **~ que** to deny that; **ne pas se ~** not to fail, keep up
**démerder** [demɛʀde]: **se démerder** vi (fam!) to bloody well manage for o.s.
**démériter** [demeʀite] vi: **~ auprès de qn** to come down in sb's esteem
**démesure** [deməzyʀ] nf immoderation, immoderateness
**démesuré, e** [deməzyʀe] adj immoderate, disproportionate
**démesurément** [deməzyʀemɑ̃] adv disproportionately
**démettre** [demɛtʀ(ə)] vt: **~ qn de** (fonction, poste) to dismiss sb from; **se ~ (de ses fonctions)** to resign (from) one's duties; **se ~ l'épaule** etc to dislocate one's shoulder etc
**demeurant** [dəmœʀɑ̃]: **au ~** adv for all that
**demeure** [dəmœʀ] nf residence; **dernière ~** (fig) last resting place; **mettre qn en ~ de faire** to enjoin ou order sb to do; **à ~** adv permanently
**demeuré, e** [dəmœʀe] adj backward ▷ nm/f backward person
**demeurer** [dəmœʀe] vi (habiter) to live; (séjourner) to stay; (rester) to remain; **en ~ là** (personne) to leave it at that; (: choses) to be left at that
**demi, e** [dəmi] adj: **et ~, trois heures/ bouteilles et ~es** three and a half hours/ bottles, three hours/bottles and a half ▷ nm (bière: = 0.25 litre) ≈ half-pint; (Football) half-back; **il est 2 heures et ~e** it's half past 2; **il est midi et ~** it's half past 12; **~ de mêlée/d'ouverture** (Rugby) scrum/fly half; **à ~** adv half-; **ouvrir à ~** to half-open; **faire les choses à ~** to do things by halves; **à la ~e** (heure) on the half-hour
**demi...** [dəmi] préfixe half-, semi..., demi-
**demi-bas** [dəmiba] nm inv (chaussette) knee-sock
**demi-bouteille** [dəmibutɛj] nf half-bottle
**demi-cercle** [dəmisɛʀkl(ə)] nm semicircle; **en ~** adj semicircular ▷ adv in a semicircle
**demi-douzaine** [dəmiduzɛn] nf half-dozen, half a dozen
**demi-finale** [dəmifinal] nf semifinal
**demi-finaliste** [dəmifinalist(ə)] nm/f semifinalist
**demi-fond** [dəmifɔ̃] nm (Sport) medium-distance running
**demi-frère** [dəmifʀɛʀ] nm half-brother
**demi-gros** [dəmigʀo] nm inv wholesale trade
**demi-heure** [dəmijœʀ] nf: **une ~** a half-hour, half an hour
**demi-jour** [dəmiʒuʀ] nm half-light
**demi-journée** [dəmiʒuʀne] nf half-day, half a day

**démilitariser** [demilitaʀize] vt to demilitarize
**demi-litre** [dəmilitʀ(ə)] nm half-litre (Brit), half-liter (US), half a litre ou liter
**demi-livre** [dəmilivʀ(ə)] nf half-pound, half a pound
**demi-longueur** [dəmilɔ̃gœʀ] nf (Sport) half-length, half a length
**demi-lune** [dəmilyn]: **en ~** adj inv semicircular
**demi-mal** [dəmimal] nm: **il n'y a que ~** there's not much harm done
**demi-mesure** [dəmimzyʀ] nf half-measure
**demi-mot** [dəmimo]: **à ~** adv without having to spell things out
**déminer** [demine] vt to clear of mines
**démineur** [deminœʀ] nm bomb disposal expert
**demi-pension** [dəmipɑ̃sjɔ̃] nf half-board; **être en ~** (Scol) to take school meals
**demi-pensionnaire** [dəmipɑ̃sjɔnɛʀ] nm/f (Scol) half-boarder
**demi-place** [dəmiplas] nf half-price; (Transports) half-fare
**démis, e** [demi, -iz] pp de **démettre** ▷ adj (épaule etc) dislocated
**demi-saison** [dəmisɛzɔ̃] nf: **vêtements de ~** spring ou autumn clothing
**demi-sel** [dəmisɛl] adj inv slightly salted
**demi-sœur** [dəmisœʀ] nf half-sister
**demi-sommeil** [dəmisɔmɛj] nm doze
**demi-soupir** [dəmisupiʀ] nm (Mus) quaver (Brit) ou eighth note (US) rest
**démission** [demisjɔ̃] nf resignation; **donner sa ~** to give ou hand in one's notice, hand in one's resignation
**démissionnaire** [demisjɔnɛʀ] adj outgoing ▷ nm/f person resigning
**démissionner** [demisjɔne] vi (de son poste) to resign, give ou hand in one's notice
**demi-tarif** [dəmitaʀif] nm half-price; (Transports) half-fare
**demi-ton** [dəmitɔ̃] nm (Mus) semitone
**demi-tour** [dəmituʀ] nm about-turn; **faire un ~** (Mil etc) to make an about-turn; **faire ~** to turn (and go) back; (Auto) to do a U-turn
**démobilisation** [demɔbilizasjɔ̃] nf demobilization; (fig) demotivation, demoralization
**démobiliser** [demɔbilize] vt to demobilize; (fig) to demotivate, demoralize
**démocrate** [demɔkʀat] adj democratic ▷ nm/f democrat
**démocrate-chrétien, ne** [demɔkʀatkʀetjɛ̃, -ɛn] nm/f Christian Democrat
**démocratie** [demɔkʀasi] nf democracy; **~ populaire/libérale** people's/liberal democracy
**démocratique** [demɔkʀatik] adj democratic
**démocratiquement** [demɔkʀatikmɑ̃] adv democratically
**démocratisation** [demɔkʀatizasjɔ̃] nf democratization
**démocratiser** [demɔkʀatize] vt to democratize
**démodé, e** [demɔde] adj old-fashioned
**démoder** [demɔde]: **se démoder** vi to go out of fashion

**démographe** [demɔgʀaf] nm/f demographer
**démographie** [demɔgʀafi] nf demography
**démographique** [demɔgʀafik] adj demographic; **poussée ~** increase in population
**demoiselle** [dəmwazɛl] nf (jeune fille) young lady; (célibataire) single lady, maiden lady; **~ d'honneur** bridesmaid
**démolir** [demɔliʀ] vt to demolish; (fig: personne) to do for
**démolisseur** [demɔlisœʀ] nm demolition worker
**démolition** [demɔlisjɔ̃] nf demolition
**démon** [demɔ̃] nm demon, fiend; evil spirit; (enfant turbulent) devil, demon; **le ~ du jeu/des femmes** a mania for gambling/women; **le D~** the Devil
**démonétiser** [demɔnetize] vt to demonetize
**démoniaque** [demɔnjak] adj fiendish
**démonstrateur, -trice** [demɔ̃stʀatœʀ, -tʀis] nm/f demonstrator
**démonstratif, -ive** [demɔ̃stʀatif, -iv] adj, nm (aussi Ling) demonstrative
**démonstration** [demɔ̃stʀasjɔ̃] nf demonstration; (aérienne, navale) display
**démontable** [demɔ̃tabl(ə)] adj folding
**démontage** [demɔ̃taʒ] nm dismantling
**démonté, e** [demɔ̃te] adj (fig) raging, wild
**démonte-pneu** [demɔ̃tǝpnø] nm tyre lever (Brit), tire iron (US)
**démonter** [demɔ̃te] vt (machine etc) to take down, dismantle; (pneu, porte) to take off; (cavalier) to throw, unseat; (fig: personne) to disconcert; **se démonter** vi (personne) to lose countenance
**démontrable** [demɔ̃tʀabl(ə)] adj demonstrable
**démontrer** [demɔ̃tʀe] vt to demonstrate, show
**démoralisant, e** [demɔʀalizɑ̃, -ɑ̃t] adj demoralizing
**démoralisateur, -trice** [demɔʀalizatœʀ, -tʀis] adj demoralizing
**démoraliser** [demɔʀalize] vt to demoralize
**démordre** [demɔʀdʀ] vi (aussi: **ne pas démordre de**) to refuse to give up, stick to
**démouler** [demule] vt (gâteau) to turn out
**démultiplication** [demyltiplikasjɔ̃] nf reduction; reduction ratio
**démuni, e** [demyni] adj (sans argent) impoverished; **~ de** without, lacking in
**démunir** [demyniʀ] vt: **~ qn de** to deprive sb of; **se ~ de** to part with, give up
**démuseler** [demyzle] vt to unmuzzle
**démystifier** [demistifje] vt to demystify
**démythifier** [demitifje] vt to demythologize
**dénatalité** [denatalite] nf fall in the birth rate
**dénationalisation** [denasjɔnalizasjɔ̃] nf denationalization
**dénationaliser** [denasjɔnalize] vt to denationalize
**dénaturé, e** [denatyʀe] adj (alcool) denaturized; (goûts) unnatural

d

**dénaturer** [denatyRe] vt (*goût*) to alter (completely); (*pensée, fait*) to distort, misrepresent

**dénégations** [denegɑsjɔ̃] nfpl denials

**déneigement** [denɛʒmɑ̃] nm snow clearance

**déneiger** [deneʒe] vt to clear snow from

**déni** [deni] nm: ~ **(de justice)** denial of justice

**déniaiser** [denjeze] vt: ~ **qn** to teach sb about life

**dénicher** [deniʃe] vt to unearth

**dénicotinisé, e** [denikɔtinize] adj nicotine-free

**denier** [dənje] nm (*monnaie*) formerly, *a coin of small value*; (*de bas*) denier; ~ **du culte** contribution to parish upkeep; **~s publics** public money; **de ses (propres) ~s** out of one's own pocket

**dénier** [denje] vt to deny; ~ **qch à qn** to deny sb sth

**dénigrement** [denigRəmɑ̃] nm denigration; **campagne de ~** smear campaign

**dénigrer** [denigRe] vt to denigrate, run down

**dénivelé, e** [denivle] adj (*chaussée*) on a lower level ▷ nm difference in height

**déniveler** [denivle] vt to make uneven; to put on a lower level

**dénivellation** [denivɛlɑsjɔ̃] nf, **dénivellement** [denivɛlmɑ̃] ▷ nm difference in level; (*pente*) ramp; (*creux*) dip

**dénombrer** [denɔ̃bRe] vt (*compter*) to count; (*énumérer*) to enumerate, list

**dénominateur** [denɔminatœR] nm denominator; ~ **commun** common denominator

**dénomination** [denɔminɑsjɔ̃] nf designation, appellation

**dénommé, e** [denɔme] adj: **le ~ Dupont** the man by the name of Dupont

**dénommer** [denɔme] vt to name

**dénoncer** [denɔ̃se] vt to denounce; **se dénoncer** vi to give o.s. up, come forward

**dénonciation** [denɔ̃sjɑsjɔ̃] nf denunciation

**dénoter** [denɔte] vt to denote

**dénouement** [denumɑ̃] nm outcome, conclusion; (*Théât*) dénouement

**dénouer** [denwe] vt to unknot, undo

**dénoyauter** [denwajote] vt to stone; **appareil à ~** stoner

**dénoyauteur** [denwajotœR] nm stoner

**denrée** [dɑ̃Re] nf commodity; (*aussi*: **denrée alimentaire**) food(stuff)

**dense** [dɑ̃s] adj dense

**densité** [dɑ̃site] nf denseness; (*Physique*) density

**dent** [dɑ̃] nf tooth; **avoir/garder une ~ contre qn** to have/hold a grudge against sb; **se mettre qch sous la ~** to eat sth; **être sur les ~s** to be on one's last legs; **faire ses ~s** to teethe, cut (one's) teeth; **en ~s de scie** serrated; (*irrégulier*) jagged; **avoir les ~s longues** (*fig*) to be ruthlessly ambitious; ~ **de lait/sagesse** milk/wisdom tooth

**dentaire** [dɑ̃tɛR] adj dental; **cabinet ~** dental surgery; **école ~** dental school

**denté, e** [dɑ̃te] adj: **roue ~e** cog wheel

**dentelé, e** [dɑ̃tle] adj jagged, indented

**dentelle** [dɑ̃tɛl] nf lace no pl

**dentelure** [dɑ̃tlyR] nf (*aussi*: **dentelures**) jagged outline

**dentier** [dɑ̃tje] nm denture

**dentifrice** [dɑ̃tifRis] adj, nm: **(pâte) ~** toothpaste; **eau ~** mouthwash

**dentiste** [dɑ̃tist(ə)] nm/f dentist

**dentition** [dɑ̃tisjɔ̃] nf teeth pl, dentition

**dénucléariser** [denykleaRize] vt to make nuclear-free

**dénudé, e** [denyde] adj bare

**dénuder** [denyde] vt to bare; **se dénuder** (*personne*) to strip

**dénué, e** [denɥe] adj: ~ **de** lacking in; (*intérêt*) devoid of

**dénuement** [denymɑ̃] nm destitution

**dénutrition** [denytRisjɔ̃] nf undernourishment

**déodorant** [deɔdɔRɑ̃] nm deodorant

**déodoriser** [deɔdɔRize] vt to deodorize

**déontologie** [deɔ̃tɔlɔʒi] nf code of ethics; (*professionnelle*) (professional) code of practice

**dép.** abr (= *département*) dept; (= *départ*) dep.

**dépannage** [depanaʒ] nm: **service/camion de ~** (*Auto*) breakdown service/truck

**dépanner** [depane] vt (*voiture, télévision*) to fix, repair; (*fig*) to bail out, help out

**dépanneur** [depanœR] nm (*Auto*) breakdown mechanic; (*TV*) television engineer

**dépanneuse** [depanøz] nf breakdown lorry (*Brit*), tow truck (*US*)

**dépareillé, e** [depaReje] adj (*collection, service*) incomplete; (*gant, volume, objet*) odd

**déparer** [depaRe] vt to spoil, mar

**départ** [depaR] nm leaving no pl, departure; (*Sport*) start; (*sur un horaire*) departure; **à son ~** when he left; **au ~** (*au début*) initially, at the start; **courrier au ~** outgoing mail

**départager** [depaRtaʒe] vt to decide between

**département** [depaRtəmɑ̃] nm department; *see note*

○ **DÉPARTEMENTS**
○
○ France is divided into 96 administrative
○ units called *départements*. These local
○ government divisions are headed by a state-
○ appointed 'préfet', and administered by an
○ elected 'Conseil général'. *Départements* are
○ usually named after prominent
○ geographical features such as rivers or
○ mountain ranges.

**départemental, e, -aux** [depaRtəmɑtal, -o] adj departmental

**départementaliser** [depaRtəmɑ̃talize] vt to devolve authority to

**départir** [depaRtiR]: **se ~ de** vt to abandon, depart from

**dépassé, e** [depɑse] adj superseded, outmoded; (*fig*) out of one's depth

**dépassement** [depɑsmɑ̃] nm (*Auto*)

overtaking *no pl*

**dépasser** [depɑse] *vt* (*véhicule, concurrent*) to overtake; (*endroit*) to pass, go past; (*somme, limite*) to exceed; (*fig: en beauté etc*) to surpass, outshine; (*être en saillie sur*) to jut out above (*ou* in front of); (*dérouter*): **cela me dépasse** it's beyond me ▷ *vi* (*Auto*) to overtake; (*jupon*) to show; **se dépasser** *vi* to excel o.s.

**dépassionner** [depasjɔne] *vt* (*débat etc*) to take the heat out of

**dépaver** [depave] *vt* to remove the cobblestones from

**dépaysé, e** [depeize] *adj* disorientated

**dépaysement** [depeizmɑ̃] *nm* disorientation; change of scenery

**dépayser** [depeize] *vt* (*désorienter*) to disorientate; (*changer agréablement*) to provide with a change of scenery.

**dépecer** [depəse] *vt* (*boucher*) to joint, cut up; (*animal*) to dismember

**dépêche** [depɛʃ] *nf* dispatch; ~ **(télégraphique)** telegram, wire

**dépêcher** [depeʃe] *vt* to dispatch; **se dépêcher** *vi* to hurry; **se ~ de faire qch** to hasten to do sth, hurry (in order) to do sth

**dépeindre** [depɛ̃dʀ(ə)] *vt* to depict

**dépénalisation** [depenalizasjɔ̃] *nf* decriminalization

**dépendance** [depɑ̃dɑ̃s] *nf* (*interdépendance*) dependence *no pl*, dependency; (*bâtiment*) outbuilding

**dépendant, e** [depɑ̃dɑ̃, -ɑ̃t] *vb voir* **dépendre** ▷ *adj* (*financièrement*) dependent

**dépendre** [depɑ̃dʀ(ə)] *vt* (*tableau*) to take down; ~ **de** *vt* to depend on, to be dependent on; (*appartenir*) to belong to; **ça dépend** it depends

**dépens** [depɑ̃] *nmpl*: **aux ~ de** at the expense of

**dépense** [depɑ̃s] *nf* spending *no pl*, expense, expenditure *no pl*; (*fig*) consumption; (: *de temps, de forces*) expenditure; **pousser qn à la ~** to make sb incur an expense; ~ **physique** (physical) exertion; **~s de fonctionnement** revenue expenditure; **~s d'investissement** capital expenditure; **~s publiques** public expenditure

**dépenser** [depɑ̃se] *vt* to spend; (*gaz, eau*) to use; (*fig*) to expend, use up; **se dépenser** *vi* (*se fatiguer*) to exert o.s.

**dépensier, -ière** [depɑ̃sje, -jɛʀ] *adj*: **il est ~** he's a spendthrift

**déperdition** [depɛʀdisjɔ̃] *nf* loss

**dépérir** [depeʀiʀ] *vi* (*personne*) to waste away; (*plante*) to wither

**dépersonnaliser** [depɛʀsɔnalize] *vt* to depersonalize

**dépêtrer** [depetʀe] *vt*: **se ~ de** (*situation*) to extricate o.s. from

**dépeuplé, e** [depœple] *adj* depopulated

**dépeuplement** [depœpləmɑ̃] *nm* depopulation

**dépeupler** [depœple] *vt* to depopulate; **se dépeupler** *vi* to be depopulated

**déphasage** [defɑzaʒ] *nm* (*fig*) being out of touch

**déphasé, e** [defɑze] *adj* (*Élec*) out of phase; (*fig*) out of touch

**déphaser** [defɑze] *vt* (*fig*) to put out of touch

**dépilation** [depilasjɔ̃] *nf* hair loss; hair removal

**dépilatoire** [depilatwaʀ] *adj* depilatory, hair-removing

**dépiler** [depile] *vt* (*épiler*) to depilate, remove hair from

**dépistage** [depistaʒ] *nm* (*Méd*) screening

**dépister** [depiste] *vt* to detect; (*Méd*) to screen; (*voleur*) to track down; (*poursuivants*) to throw off the scent

**dépit** [depi] *nm* vexation, frustration; **en ~ de** *prép* in spite of; **en ~ du bon sens** contrary to all good sense

**dépité, e** [depite] *adj* vexed, frustrated

**dépiter** [depite] *vt* to vex, frustrate

**déplacé, e** [deplase] *adj* (*propos*) out of place, uncalled-for; **personne ~e** displaced person

**déplacement** [deplasmɑ̃] *nm* moving; shifting; transfer; (*voyage*) trip, travelling *no pl* (Brit), traveling *no pl* (US); **en ~** away (on a trip); ~ **d'air** displacement of air; ~ **de vertèbre** slipped disc

**déplacer** [deplase] *vt* (*table, voiture*) to move, shift; (*employé*) to transfer, move; **se déplacer** *vi* (*objet*) to move; (*organe*) to become displaced; (*personne: bouger*) to move, walk; (: *voyager*) to travel ▷ *vt* (*vertèbre etc*) to displace

**déplaire** [deplɛʀ] *vi*: **ceci me déplaît** I don't like this, I dislike this; **il cherche à nous ~** he's trying to displease us *ou* be disagreeable to us; **se ~ quelque part** to dislike it *ou* be unhappy somewhere

**déplaisant, e** [deplɛzɑ̃, -ɑ̃t] *vb voir* **déplaire** ▷ *adj* disagreeable, unpleasant

**déplaisir** [deplɛziʀ] *nm* displeasure, annoyance

**déplaît** [deplɛ] *vb voir* **déplaire**

**dépliant** [deplijɑ̃] *nm* leaflet

**déplier** [deplije] *vt* to unfold; **se déplier** *vi* (*parachute*) to open

**déplisser** [deplise] *vt* to smooth out

**déploiement** [deplwamɑ̃] *nm* (*voir déployer*) deployment; display

**déplomber** [deplɔ̃be] *vt* (*caisse, compteur*) to break (open) the seal of; (*Inform*) to hack into

**déplorable** [deplɔʀabl(ə)] *adj* deplorable; lamentable

**déplorer** [deplɔʀe] *vt* (*regretter*) to deplore; (*pleurer sur*) to lament

**déployer** [deplwaje] *vt* to open out, spread; (*Mil*) to deploy; (*montrer*) to display, exhibit

**déplu** [deply] *pp de* **déplaire**

**dépointer** [depwɛ̃te] *vi* to clock out

**dépoli, e** [depɔli] *adj*: **verre ~** frosted glass

**dépolitiser** [depɔlitize] *vt* to depoliticize

**dépopulation** [depɔpylasjɔ̃] *nf* depopulation

**déportation** [depɔʀtasjɔ̃] *nf* deportation

**déporté, e** [depɔʀte] *nm/f* deportee; (*1939–45*) concentration camp prisoner

**déporter** [depɔʀte] *vt* (*Pol*) to deport; (*dévier*) to carry off course; **se déporter** *vi* (*voiture*) to swerve

**déposant, e** [depozã, -ãt] nm/f (épargnant) depositor

**dépose** [depoz] nf taking out; taking down

**déposé, e** [depoze] adj registered; voir aussi **marque**

**déposer** [depoze] vt (gén: mettre, poser) to lay down, put down, set down; (à la banque, à la consigne) to deposit; (caution) to put down; (passager) to drop (off), set down; (démonter: serrure, moteur) to take out; (: rideau) to take down; (roi) to depose; (Admin: faire enregistrer) to file; to register ▷ vi to form a sediment ou deposit; (Jur): ~ (**contre**) to testify ou give evidence (against); **se déposer** vi to settle; ~ **son bilan** (Comm) to go into (voluntary) liquidation

**dépositaire** [depozitɛʀ] nm/f (Jur) depository; (Comm) agent; ~ **agréé** authorized agent

**déposition** [depozisjɔ̃] nf (Jur) deposition

**déposséder** [deposede] vt to dispossess

**dépôt** [depo] nm (à la banque, sédiment) deposit; (entrepôt, réserve) warehouse, store; (gare) depot; (prison) cells pl; ~ **d'ordures** rubbish (Brit) ou garbage (US) dump, tip (Brit); ~ **de bilan** (voluntary) liquidation; ~ **légal** registration of copyright

**dépoter** [depote] vt (plante) to take from the pot, transplant

**dépotoir** [depotwaʀ] nm dumping ground, rubbish (Brit) ou garbage (US) dump; ~ **nucléaire** nuclear (waste) dump

**dépouille** [depuj] nf (d'animal) skin, hide; (humaine): ~ (**mortelle**) mortal remains pl

**dépouillé, e** [depuje] adj (fig) bare, bald; ~ **de** stripped of; lacking in

**dépouillement** [depujmã] nm (de scrutin) count, counting no pl

**dépouiller** [depuje] vt (animal) to skin; (spolier) to deprive of one's possessions; (documents) to go through, peruse; ~ **qn/qch de** to strip sb/sth of; ~ **le scrutin** to count the votes

**dépourvu, e** [depuʀvy] adj: ~ **de** lacking in, without; **au** ~ adv: **prendre qn au** ~ to catch sb unawares

**dépoussiérer** [depusjeʀe] vt to remove dust from

**dépravation** [depʀavasjɔ̃] nf depravity

**dépravé, e** [depʀave] adj depraved

**dépraver** [depʀave] vt to deprave

**dépréciation** [depʀesjɑsjɔ̃] nf depreciation

**déprécier** [depʀesje] vt to reduce the value of; **se déprécier** vi to depreciate

**déprédations** [depʀedɑsjɔ̃] nfpl damage sg

**dépressif, -ive** [depʀesif, -iv] adj depressive

**dépression** [depʀesjɔ̃] nf depression; ~ (**nerveuse**) (nervous) breakdown

**déprimant, e** [depʀimã, -ãt] adj depressing

**déprime** [depʀim] nf (fam): **la** ~ depression

**déprimé, e** [depʀime] adj (découragé) depressed

**déprimer** [depʀime] vt to depress

**déprogrammer** [depʀɔgʀame] vt (supprimer) to cancel

**DEPS** sigle (= dernier entré premier sorti) LIFO (= last in first out)

**dépt** abr (= département) dept

**dépuceler** [depysle] vt (fam) to take the virginity of

MOT-CLÉ

**depuis** [dəpɥi] prép 1 (point de départ dans le temps) since; **il habite Paris depuis 1983/l'an dernier** he has been living in Paris since 1983/ last year; **depuis quand?** since when?; **depuis quand le connaissez-vous?** how long have you known him?; **depuis lors** since then

2 (temps écoulé) for; **il habite Paris depuis cinq ans** he has been living in Paris for five years; **je le connais depuis trois ans** I've known him for three years; **depuis combien de temps êtes-vous ici?** how long have you been here?

3 (lieu): **il a plu depuis Metz** it's been raining since Metz; **elle a téléphoné depuis Valence** she rang from Valence

4 (quantité, rang) from; **depuis les plus petits jusqu'aux plus grands** from the youngest to the oldest

▷ adv (temps) since (then); **je ne lui ai pas parlé depuis** I haven't spoken to him since (then); **depuis que** conj (ever) since; **depuis qu'il m'a dit ça** (ever) since he said that to me

**dépuratif, -ive** [depyʀatif, -iv] adj depurative, purgative

**députation** [depytasjɔ̃] nf deputation; (fonction) position of deputy, ≈ parliamentary seat (Brit), ≈ seat in Congress (US)

**député, e** [depyte] nm/f (Pol) deputy, ≈ Member of Parliament (Brit), ≈ Congressman/woman (US)

**députer** [depyte] vt to delegate; ~ **qn auprès de** to send sb (as a representative) to

**déracinement** [deʀasinmã] nm (gén) uprooting; (d'un préjugé) eradication

**déraciner** [deʀasine] vt to uproot

**déraillement** [deʀajmã] nm derailment

**dérailler** [deʀaje] vi (train) to be derailed, go off ou jump the rails; (fam) to be completely off the track; **faire** ~ to derail

**dérailleur** [deʀajœʀ] nm (de vélo) dérailleur gears pl

**déraison** [deʀezɔ̃] nf unreasonableness

**déraisonnable** [deʀezɔnabl(ə)] adj unreasonable

**déraisonner** [deʀezɔne] vi to talk nonsense, rave

**dérangement** [deʀãʒmã] nm (gêne, déplacement) trouble; (gastrique etc) disorder; (mécanique) breakdown; **en** ~ (téléphone) out of order

**déranger** [deʀãʒe] vt (personne) to trouble, bother, disturb; (projets) to disrupt, upset; (objets, vêtements) to disarrange; **se déranger** to put o.s. out; (se déplacer) (take the trouble to) come (ou go) out; **est-ce que cela vous dérange si ...?** do you mind if ...?; **ça te**

**dérangerait de faire ...?** would you mind doing ...?; **ne vous dérangez pas** don't go to any trouble; don't disturb yourself

**dérapage** [deʀapaʒ] *nm* skid, skidding *no pl*; going out of control

**déraper** [deʀape] *vi* (*voiture*) to skid; (*personne, semelles, couteau*) to slip; (*fig: économie etc*) to go out of control

**dératé, e** [deʀate] *nm/f*: **courir comme un ~** to run like the clappers

**dératiser** [deʀatize] *vt* to rid of rats

**déréglé, e** [deʀegle] *adj* (*mœurs*) dissolute

**dérèglement** [deʀɛɡləmɑ̃] *nm* upsetting *no pl*, upset

**déréglementation** [deʀɛɡləmɑ̃tasjɔ̃] *nf* deregulation

**dérégler** [deʀegle] *vt* (*mécanisme*) to put out of order, cause to break down; (*estomac*) to upset; **se dérégler** *vi* to break down, go wrong

**dérider** [deʀide] *vt*, **se dérider** *vi* to cheer up

**dérision** [deʀizjɔ̃] *nf* derision; **tourner en ~** to deride; **par ~** in mockery

**dérisoire** [deʀizwaʀ] *adj* derisory

**dérivatif** [deʀivatif] *nm* distraction

**dérivation** [deʀivasjɔ̃] *nf* derivation; diversion

**dérive** [deʀiv] *nf* (*de dériveur*) centre-board; **aller à la ~** (*Navig, fig*) to drift; **~ des continents** (*Géo*) continental drift

**dérivé, e** [deʀive] *adj* derived ▷ *nm* (*Ling*) derivative; (*Tech*) by-product ▷ *nf* (*Math*) derivative

**dériver** [deʀive] *vt* (*Math*) to derive; (*cours d'eau etc*) to divert ▷ *vi* (*bateau*) to drift; **~ de** to derive from

**dériveur** [deʀivœʀ] *nm* sailing dinghy

**dermatite** [dɛʀmatit] *nf* dermatitis

**dermato** [dɛʀmato] *nm/f* (*fam*: = *dermatologue*) dermatologist

**dermatologie** [dɛʀmatɔlɔʒi] *nf* dermatology

**dermatologue** [dɛʀmatɔlɔɡ] *nm/f* dermatologist

**dermatose** [dɛʀmatoz] *nf* dermatosis

**dermite** [dɛʀmit] *nf* = **dermatite**

**dernier, -ière** [dɛʀnje, -jɛʀ] *adj* (*dans le temps, l'espace*) last; (*le plus récent: gén avant n*) latest, last; (*final, ultime: effort*) final; (*échelon, grade*) top, highest ▷ *nm* (*étage*) top floor; **lundi/le mois ~** last Monday/month; **du ~ chic** extremely smart; **le ~ cri** the last word (in fashion); **les ~s honneurs** the last tribute; **le ~ soupir, rendre le ~ soupir** to breathe one's last; **en ~** *adv* last; **ce ~, cette dernière** the latter

**dernièrement** [dɛʀnjɛʀmɑ̃] *adv* recently

**dernier-né, dernière-née** [dɛʀnje, dɛʀnjɛʀne] *nm/f* (*enfant*) last-born

**dérobade** [deʀɔbad] *nf* side-stepping *no pl*

**dérobé, e** [deʀɔbe] *adj* (*porte*) secret, hidden; **à la ~e** surreptitiously

**dérober** [deʀɔbe] *vt* to steal; (*cacher*): **~ qch à (la vue de) qn** to conceal *ou* hide sth from sb('s view); **se dérober** *vi* (*s'esquiver*) to slip away; (*fig*) to shy away; **se ~ sous** (*s'effondrer*) to give way

beneath; **se ~ à** (*justice, regards*) to hide from; (*obligation*) to shirk

**dérogation** [deʀɔɡasjɔ̃] *nf* (special) dispensation

**déroger** [deʀɔʒe]: **~ à** *vt* to go against, depart from

**dérouiller** [deʀuje] *vt*: **se ~ les jambes** to stretch one's legs

**déroulement** [deʀulmɑ̃] *nm* (*d'une opération etc*) progress

**dérouler** [deʀule] *vt* (*ficelle*) to unwind; (*papier*) to unroll; **se dérouler** *vi* to unwind; to unroll, come unrolled; (*avoir lieu*) to take place; (*se passer*) to go

**déroutant, e** [deʀutɑ̃, -ɑ̃t] *adj* disconcerting

**déroute** [deʀut] *nf* (*Mil*) rout; (*fig*) total collapse; **mettre en ~** to rout; **en ~** routed

**dérouter** [deʀute] *vt* (*avion, train*) to reroute, divert; (*étonner*) to disconcert, throw (out)

**derrick** [deʀik] *nm* derrick (*over oil well*)

**derrière** [dɛʀjɛʀ] *adv, prép* behind ▷ *nm* (*d'une maison*) back; (*postérieur*) behind, bottom; **les pattes de ~** the back legs, the hind legs; **par ~** from behind; (*fig*) in an underhand way, behind one's back

**derviche** [dɛʀviʃ] *nm* dervish

**DES** *sigle m* (= *diplôme d'études supérieures*) university post-graduate degree

**des** [de] *art voir* **de**

**dès** [de] *prép* from; **~ que** *conj* as soon as; **~ à présent** here and now; **~ son retour** as soon as he was (*ou* is) back; **~ réception** upon receipt; **~ lors** *adv* from then on; **~ lors que** *conj* from the moment (that)

**désabusé, e** [dezabyze] *adj* disillusioned

**désaccord** [dezakɔʀ] *nm* disagreement

**désaccordé, e** [dezakɔʀde] *adj* (*Mus*) out of tune

**désacraliser** [desakʀalize] *vt* to deconsecrate; (*fig: profession, institution*) to take the mystique out of

**désaffecté, e** [dezafɛkte] *adj* disused

**désaffection** [dezafɛksjɔ̃] *nf*: **~ pour** estrangement from

**désagréable** [dezagʀeable(ə)] *adj* unpleasant, disagreeable

**désagréablement** [dezagʀeabləmɑ̃] *adv* disagreeably, unpleasantly

**désagrégation** [dezagʀegasjɔ̃] *nf* disintegration

**désagréger** [dezagʀeʒe]: **se désagréger** *vi* to disintegrate, break up

**désagrément** [dezagʀemɑ̃] *nm* annoyance, trouble *no pl*

**désaltérant, e** [dezalteʀɑ̃, -ɑ̃t] *adj* thirst-quenching

**désaltérer** [dezalteʀe] *vt*: **se désaltérer** to quench one's thirst; **ça désaltère** it's thirst-quenching, it quenches your thirst

**désamorcer** [dezamɔʀse] *vt* to remove the primer from; (*fig*) to defuse; (: *prévenir*) to forestall

**désappointé, e** [dezapwɛ̃te] *adj* disappointed

**désapprobateur, -trice** [dezapRɔbatœR, -tRis] adj disapproving

**désapprobation** [dezapRɔbasjɔ̃] nf disapproval

**désapprouver** [dezapRuve] vt to disapprove of

**désarçonner** [dezaRsɔne] vt to unseat, throw; (fig) to throw, nonplus (Brit), disconcert

**désargenté, e** [dezaRʒɑ̃te] adj impoverished

**désarmant, e** [dezaRmɑ̃, -ɑ̃t] adj disarming

**désarmé, e** [dezaRme] adj (fig) disarmed

**désarmement** [dezaRməmɑ̃] nm disarmament

**désarmer** [dezaRme] vt (Mil, aussi fig) to disarm; (Navig) to lay up; (fusil) to unload; (: mettre le cran de sûreté) to put the safety catch on ▷ vi (pays) to disarm; (haine) to wane; (personne) to give up

**désarroi** [dezaRwa] nm helplessness, disarray

**désarticulé, e** [dezaRtikyle] adj (pantin, corps) dislocated

**désarticuler** [dezaRtikyle] vt: **se désarticuler** to contort (o.s.)

**désassorti, e** [dezasɔRti] adj non-matching, unmatched; (magasin, marchand) sold out

**désastre** [dezastR(ə)] nm disaster

**désastreux, -euse** [dezastRø, -øz] adj disastrous

**désavantage** [dezavɑ̃taʒ] nm disadvantage; (inconvénient) drawback, disadvantage

**désavantager** [dezavɑ̃taʒe] vt to put at a disadvantage

**désavantageux, -euse** [dezavɑ̃taʒø, -øz] adj unfavourable, disadvantageous

**désaveu** [dezavø] nm repudiation; (déni) disclaimer

**désavouer** [dezavwe] vt to disown, repudiate, disclaim

**désaxé, e** [dezakse] adj (fig) unbalanced

**désaxer** [dezakse] vt (roue) to put out of true; (personne) to throw off balance

**desceller** [desele] vt (pierre) to pull free

**descendance** [desɑ̃dɑ̃s] nf (famille) descendants pl, issue; (origine) descent

**descendant, e** [desɑ̃dɑ̃, -ɑ̃t] vb voir **descendre** ▷ nm/f descendant

**descendeur, -euse** [desɑ̃dœR, -øz] nm/f (Sport) downhiller

**descendre** [desɑ̃dR(ə)] vt (escalier, montagne) to go (ou come) down; (valise, paquet) to take ou get down; (étagère etc) to lower; (fam: abattre) to shoot down; (: boire) to knock back ▷ vi to go (ou come) down; (passager: s'arrêter) to get out, alight; (niveau, température) to go ou come down, fall, drop; (marée) to go out; **~ à pied/en voiture** to walk/drive down, go down on foot/by car; **~ de** (famille) to be descended from; **~ du train** to get out of ou off the train; **~ d'un arbre** to climb down from a tree; **~ de cheval** to dismount, get off one's horse; **~ à l'hôtel** to stay at a hotel; **~ dans la rue** (manifester) to take to the streets; **~ en ville** to go into town, go down town

**descente** [desɑ̃t] nf descent, going down; (chemin) way down; (Ski) downhill (race); **au milieu de la ~** halfway down; **freinez dans les ~s** use the brakes going downhill; **~ de lit** bedside rug; **~ (de police)** (police) raid

**descriptif, -ive** [dɛskRiptif, -iv] adj descriptive ▷ nm explanatory leaflet

**description** [dɛskRipsjɔ̃] nf description

**désembourber** [dezɑ̃buRbe] vt to pull out of the mud

**désembourgeoiser** [dezɑ̃buRʒwaze] vt: **~ qn** to get sb out of his (ou her) middle-class attitudes

**désembuer** [dezɑ̃bɥe] vt to demist

**désemparé, e** [dezɑ̃paRe] adj bewildered, distraught; (bateau, avion) crippled

**désemparer** [dezɑ̃paRe] vi: **sans ~** without stopping

**désemplir** [dezɑ̃pliR] vi: **ne pas ~** to be always full

**désenchanté, e** [dezɑ̃ʃɑ̃te] adj disenchanted, disillusioned

**désenchantement** [dezɑ̃ʃɑ̃tmɑ̃] nm disenchantment, disillusion

**désenclaver** [dezɑ̃klave] vt to open up

**désencombrer** [dezɑ̃kɔ̃bRe] vt to clear

**désenfler** [dezɑ̃fle] vi to become less swollen

**désengagement** [dezɑ̃gaʒmɑ̃] nm (Pol) disengagement

**désensabler** [dezɑ̃sable] vt to pull out of the sand

**désensibiliser** [desɑ̃sibilize] vt (Méd) to desensitize

**désenvenimer** [dezɑ̃vnime] vt (plaie) to remove the poison from; (fig) to take the sting out of

**désépaissir** [dezepesiR] vt to thin (out)

**déséquilibre** [dezekilibR(ə)] nm (position): **être en ~** to be unsteady; (fig: des forces, du budget) imbalance; (Psych) unbalance

**déséquilibré, e** [dezekilibRe] nm/f (Psych) unbalanced person

**déséquilibrer** [dezekilibRe] vt to throw off balance

**désert, e** [dezɛR, -ɛRt(ə)] adj deserted ▷ nm desert

**déserter** [dezɛRte] vi, vt to desert

**déserteur** [dezɛRtœR] nm deserter

**désertion** [dezɛRsjɔ̃] nf desertion

**désertique** [dezɛRtik] adj desert cpd; (inculte) barren, empty

**désescalade** [dezeskalad] nf (Mil) de-escalation

**désespérant, e** [dezɛspeRɑ̃, -ɑ̃t] adj hopeless, despairing

**désespéré, e** [dezɛspeRe] adj desperate; (regard) despairing; **état ~** (Méd) hopeless condition

**désespérément** [dezɛspeRemɑ̃] adv desperately

**désespérer** [dezɛspeRe] vt to drive to despair ▷ vi, **se désespérer** vi to despair; **~ de** to despair of

**désespoir** [dezɛspwaR] nm despair; **être ou faire le ~ de qn** to be the despair of sb; **en ~ de cause** in desperation

**déshabillé, e** [dezabije] adj undressed ▷ nm négligée

**déshabiller** [dezabije] vt to undress; **se déshabiller** vi to undress (o.s.)

**déshabituer** [dezabitɥe] vt: **se ~ de** to get out of

the habit of

**désherbant** [dezɛʀbɑ̃] nm weed-killer

**désherber** [dezɛʀbe] vt to weed

**déshérité, e** [dezeʀite] adj disinherited ▷ nm/f: **les ~s** (*pauvres*) the underprivileged, the deprived

**déshériter** [dezeʀite] vt to disinherit

**déshonneur** [dezɔnœʀ] nm dishonour (*Brit*), dishonor (*US*), disgrace

**déshonorer** [dezɔnɔʀe] vt to dishonour (*Brit*), dishonor (*US*), bring disgrace upon; **se déshonorer** vi to bring dishono(u)r on o.s.

**déshumaniser** [dezymanize] vt to dehumanize

**déshydratation** [dezidʀatasjɔ̃] nf dehydration

**déshydraté, e** [dezidʀate] adj dehydrated

**déshydrater** [dezidʀate] vt to dehydrate

**desiderata** [dezideʀata] nmpl requirements

**design** [dizajn] adj (*mobilier*) designer cpd ▷ nm (industrial) design

**désignation** [deziɲasjɔ̃] nf naming, appointment; (*signe, mot*) name, designation

**designer** [dizajnɛʀ] nm designer

**désigner** [deziɲe] vt (*montrer*) to point out, indicate; (*dénommer*) to denote, refer to; (*nommer: candidat etc*) to name, appoint

**désillusion** [dezilyzjɔ̃] nf disillusion(ment)

**désillusionner** [dezilyzjɔne] vt to disillusion

**désincarné, e** [dezɛ̃kaʀne] adj disembodied

**désinence** [dezinɑ̃s] nf ending, inflexion

**désinfectant, e** [dezɛ̃fɛktɑ̃, -ɑ̃t] adj, nm disinfectant

**désinfecter** [dezɛ̃fɛkte] vt to disinfect

**désinfection** [dezɛ̃fɛksjɔ̃] nf disinfection

**désinformation** [dezɛ̃fɔʀmasjɔ̃] nf disinformation

**désintégration** [dezɛ̃tegʀasjɔ̃] nf disintegration

**désintégrer** [dezɛ̃tegʀe] vt to break up; **se désintégrer** vi to disintegrate

**désintéressé, e** [dezɛ̃teʀese] adj (*généreux, bénévole*) disinterested, unselfish

**désintéressement** [dezɛ̃teʀesmɑ̃] nm (*générosité*) disinterestedness

**désintéresser** [dezɛ̃teʀese] vt: **se désintéresser (de)** to lose interest (in)

**désintérêt** [dezɛ̃teʀɛ] nm (*indifférence*) disinterest

**désintoxication** [dezɛ̃tɔksikasjɔ̃] nf treatment for alcoholism (*ou* drug addiction); **faire une cure de ~** to have *ou* undergo treatment for alcoholism (*ou* drug addiction)

**désintoxiquer** [dezɛ̃tɔksike] vt to treat for alcoholism (*ou* drug addiction)

**désinvolte** [dezɛ̃vɔlt(ə)] adj casual, off-hand

**désinvolture** [dezɛ̃vɔltyʀ] nf casualness

**désir** [deziʀ] nm wish; (*fort, sensuel*) desire

**désirable** [deziʀabl(ə)] adj desirable

**désirer** [deziʀe] vt to want, wish for; (*sexuellement*) to desire; **je désire ...** (*formule de politesse*) I would like ...; **il désire que tu l'aides** he would like *ou* he wants you to help him; **~ faire** to want *ou* wish to do; **ça laisse à ~** it

leaves something to be desired

**désireux, -euse** [deziʀø, -øz] adj: **~ de faire** anxious to do

**désistement** [dezistəmɑ̃] nm withdrawal

**désister** [deziste]: **se désister** vi to stand down, withdraw

**désobéir** [dezɔbeiʀ] vi: **~ (à qn/qch)** to disobey (sb/sth)

**désobéissance** [dezɔbeisɑ̃s] nf disobedience

**désobéissant, e** [dezɔbeisɑ̃, -ɑ̃t] adj disobedient

**désobligeant, e** [dezɔbliʒɑ̃, -ɑ̃t] adj disagreeable, unpleasant

**désobliger** [dezɔbliʒe] vt to offend

**désodorisant** [dezɔdɔʀizɑ̃] nm air freshener, deodorizer

**désodoriser** [dezɔdɔʀize] vt to deodorize

**désœuvré, e** [dezœvʀe] adj idle

**désœuvrement** [dezœvʀəmɑ̃] nm idleness

**désolant, e** [dezɔlɑ̃, -ɑ̃t] adj distressing

**désolation** [dezɔlasjɔ̃] nf (*affliction*) distress, grief; (*d'un paysage etc*) desolation, devastation

**désolé, e** [dezɔle] adj (*paysage*) desolate; **je suis ~** I'm sorry

**désoler** [dezɔle] vt to distress, grieve; **se désoler** vi to be upset

**désolidariser** [desɔlidaʀize] vt: **se ~ de** *ou* **d'avec** to dissociate o.s. from

**désopilant, e** [dezɔpilɑ̃, -ɑ̃t] adj screamingly funny, hilarious

**désordonné, e** [dezɔʀdɔne] adj untidy, disorderly

**désordre** [dezɔʀdʀ(ə)] nm disorder(liness), untidiness; (*anarchie*) disorder; **désordres** nmpl (*Pol*) disturbances, disorder sg; **en ~** in a mess, untidy

**désorganiser** [dezɔʀganize] vt to disorganize

**désorienté, e** [dezɔʀjɑ̃te] adj disorientated; (*fig*) bewildered

**désorienter** [dezɔʀjɑ̃te] vt (*fig*) to confuse

**désormais** [dezɔʀmɛ] adv in future, from now on

**désosser** [dezɔse] vt to bone

**despote** [dɛspɔt] nm despot; (*fig*) tyrant

**despotique** [dɛspɔtik] adj despotic

**despotisme** [dɛspɔtism(ə)] nm despotism

**desquamer** [dɛskwame]: **se desquamer** vi to flake off

**desquels, desquelles** [dekɛl] prép + pron voir **lequel**

**DESS** sigle m (= Diplôme d'études supérieures spécialisées) post-graduate diploma

**dessaisir** [deseziʀ] vt: **~ un tribunal d'une affaire** to remove a case from a court; **se ~ de** vt to give up, part with

**dessaler** [desale] vt (*eau de mer*) to desalinate; (*Culin: morue etc*) to soak; (*fig fam: délurer*): **~ qn** to teach sb a thing or two ▷ vi (*voilier*) to capsize

**Desse** abr = **duchesse**

**desséché, e** [deseʃe] adj dried up

**dessèchement** [desɛʃmɑ̃] nm drying out; dryness; hardness

**dessécher** [deseʃe] vt (*terre, plante*) to dry out,

d

parch; (*peau*) to dry out; (*volontairement: aliments etc*) to dry, dehydrate; (*fig: cœur*) to harden; **se dessécher** *vi* to dry out; (*peau, lèvres*) to go dry

**dessein** [desẽ] *nm* design; **dans le ~ de** with the intention of; **à ~** intentionally, deliberately

**desseller** [desele] *vt* to unsaddle

**desserrer** [deseʀe] *vt* to loosen; (*frein*) to release; (*poing, dents*) to unclench; (*objets alignés*) to space out; **ne pas ~ les dents** not to open one's mouth

**dessert** [deseʀ] *vb voir* **desservir** ▷ *nm* dessert, pudding

**desserte** [deseʀt(ə)] *nf* (*table*) side table; (*transport*): **la ~ du village est assurée par autocar** there is a coach service to the village; **chemin** *ou* **voie de ~** service road

**desservir** [deseʀviʀ] *vt* (*ville, quartier*) to serve; (: *voie de communication*) to lead into; (*vicaire: paroisse*) to serve; (*nuire à: personne*) to do a disservice to; (*débarrasser*): **~ (la table)** to clear the table

**dessiller** [desije] *vt* (*fig*): **~ les yeux à qn** to open sb's eyes

**dessin** [desẽ] *nm* (*œuvre, art*) drawing; (*motif*) pattern, design; (*contour*) (out)line; **le ~ industriel** draughtsmanship (*Brit*), draftsmanship (*US*); **~ animé** cartoon (film); **~ humoristique** cartoon

**dessinateur, -trice** [desinatœʀ, -tʀis] *nm/f* drawer; (*de bandes dessinées*) cartoonist; (*industriel*) draughtsman (*Brit*), draftsman (*US*); **dessinatrice de mode** fashion designer

**dessiner** [desine] *vt* to draw; (*concevoir: carrosserie, maison*) to design; (*robe: taille*) to show off; **se dessiner** *vi* (*forme*) to be outlined; (*fig: solution*) to emerge

**dessoûler** [desule] *vt, vi* to sober up

**dessous** [dəsu] *adv* underneath, beneath ▷ *nm* underside; (*étage inférieur*): **les voisins du ~** the downstairs neighbours ▷ *nmpl* (*sous-vêtements*) underwear *sg*; (*fig*) hidden aspects; **en ~** underneath; below; (*fig: en catimini*) slyly, on the sly; **par ~** underneath; below; **de ~ le lit** from under the bed; **au-~** *adv* below; **au-~ de** *prép* below; (*peu digne de*) beneath; **au-~ de tout** the (absolute) limit; **avoir le ~** to get the worst of it

**dessous-de-bouteille** [dəsudbutɛj] *nm* bottle mat

**dessous-de-plat** [dəsudpla] *nm inv* tablemat

**dessous-de-table** [dəsudtabl(ə)] *nm* (*fig*) bribe, under-the-counter payment

**dessus** [dəsy] *adv* on top; (*collé, écrit*) on it ▷ *nm* top; (*étage supérieur*): **les voisins/l'appartement du ~** the upstairs neighbours/flat; **en ~** above; **par ~** *adv* over it ▷ *prép* over; **au-~** above; **au-~ de** above; **avoir/prendre le ~** to have/get the upper hand; **reprendre le ~** to get over it; **bras ~ bras dessous** arm in arm; **sens ~ dessous** upside down; *voir* **ci-; là-**

**dessus-de-lit** [dəsydli] *nm inv* bedspread

**déstabiliser** [destabilize] *vt* (*Pol*) to destabilize

**destin** [destẽ] *nm* fate; (*avenir*) destiny

**destinataire** [destinatɛʀ] *nm/f* (*Postes*) addressee; (*d'un colis*) consignee; (*d'un mandat*) payee; **aux risques et périls du ~** at owner's risk

**destination** [destinasjɔ̃] *nf* (*lieu*) destination; (*usage*) purpose; **à ~ de** (*avion etc*) bound for; (*voyageur*) bound for, travelling to

**destinée** [destine] *nf* fate; (*existence, avenir*) destiny

**destiner** [destine] *vt*: **~ qn à** (*poste, sort*) to destine sb for; **~ qn/qch à** (*prédestiner*) to mark sb/sth out for; **~ qch à** (*envisager d'affecter*) to intend to use sth for; **~ qch à qn** (*envisager de donner*) to intend to give sth to sb, intend sb to have sth; (*adresser*) to intend sth for sb; **se ~ à l'enseignement** to intend to become a teacher; **être destiné à** (*sort*) to be destined to + *verbe*; (*usage*) to be intended *ou* meant for; (*sort*) to be in store for

**destituer** [destitɥe] *vt* to depose; **~ qn de ses fonctions** to relieve sb of his duties

**destitution** [destitysjɔ̃] *nf* deposition

**destructeur, -trice** [destʀyktœʀ, -tʀis] *adj* destructive

**destructif, -ive** [destʀyktif, -iv] *adj* destructive

**destruction** [destʀyksjɔ̃] *nf* destruction

**déstructuré, e** [destʀyktyʀe] *adj*: **vêtements ~s** casual clothes

**déstructurer** [destʀyktyʀe] *vt* to break down, take to pieces

**désuet, -ète** [desɥɛ, -ɛt] *adj* outdated, outmoded

**désuétude** [desɥetyd] *nf*: **tomber en ~** to fall into disuse, become obsolete

**désuni, e** [dezyni] *adj* divided, disunited

**désunion** [dezynjɔ̃] *nf* disunity

**désunir** [dezyniʀ] *vt* to disunite; **se désunir** *vi* (*athlète*) to get out of one's stride

**détachable** [detaʃabl(ə)] *adj* (*coupon etc*) tear-off *cpd*; (*capuche etc*) detachable

**détachant** [detaʃɑ̃] *nm* stain remover

**détaché, e** [detaʃe] *adj* (*fig*) detached ▷ *nm/f* (*représentant*) person on secondment (*Brit*) *ou* a posting

**détachement** [detaʃmɑ̃] *nm* detachment; (*fonctionnaire, employé*): **être en ~** to be on secondment (*Brit*) *ou* a posting

**détacher** [detaʃe] *vt* (*enlever*) to detach, remove; (*délier*) to untie; (*Admin*): **~ qn (auprès de** *ou* **à)** to send sb on secondment (to) (*Brit*), post sb (to); (*Mil*) to detail; (*vêtement: nettoyer*) to remove the stains from; **se détacher** *vi* (*tomber*) to come off; to come out; (*se défaire*) to come undone; (*Sport*) to pull *ou* break away; (*se délier: chien, prisonnier*) to break loose; **se ~ sur** to stand out against; **se ~ de** (*se désintéresser*) to grow away from

**détail** [detaj] *nm* detail; (*Comm*): **le ~** retail; **prix de ~** retail price; **au ~** *adv* (*Comm*) retail; (: *individuellement*) separately; **donner le ~ de** to give a detailed account of; (*compte*) to give a breakdown of; **en ~** in detail

**détaillant, e** [detajɑ̃, -ɑ̃t] *nm/f* retailer

**détaillé, e** [detaje] *adj* (*récit*) detailed
**détailler** [detaje] *vt* (*Comm*) to sell retail; to sell separately; (*expliquer*) to explain in detail; to detail; (*examiner*) to look over, examine
**détaler** [detale] *vi* (*lapin*) to scamper off; (*fam: personne*) to make off, scarper (*fam*)
**détartrant** [detartrɑ̃] *nm* descaling agent (*Brit*), scale remover
**détartrer** [detartre] *vt* to descale; (*dents*) to scale
**détaxe** [detaks(ə)] *nf* (*réduction*) reduction in tax; (*suppression*) removal of tax; (*remboursement*) tax refund
**détaxer** [detakse] *vt* (*réduire*) to reduce the tax on; (*ôter*) to remove the tax on
**détecter** [detɛkte] *vt* to detect
**détecteur** [detɛktœr] *nm* detector, sensor; **~ de mensonges** lie detector; **~ (de mines)** mine detector
**détection** [detɛksjɔ̃] *nf* detection
**détective** [detɛktiv] *nm* detective; **~ (privé)** private detective *ou* investigator
**déteindre** [detɛ̃dr(ə)] *vi* to fade; (*fig*): **~ sur** to rub off on
**déteint, e** [detɛ̃, -ɛ̃t] *pp de* **déteindre**
**dételer** [detle] *vt* to unharness; (*voiture, wagon*) to unhitch ▷ *vi* (*fig: s'arrêter*) to leave off (working)
**détendeur** [detɑ̃dœr] *nm* (*de bouteille à gaz*) regulator
**détendre** [detɑ̃dr(ə)] *vt* (*fil*) to slacken, loosen; (*personne, atmosphère*) to relax; (*: situation*) to relieve; **se détendre** *vi* to lose its tension; to relax
**détendu, e** [detɑ̃dy] *adj* relaxed
**détenir** [detnir] *vt* (*fortune, objet, secret*) to be in possession of; (*prisonnier*) to detain; (*record*) to hold; **~ le pouvoir** to be in power
**détente** [detɑ̃t] *nf* relaxation; (*Pol*) détente; (*d'une arme*) trigger; (*d'un athlète qui saute*) spring
**détenteur, -trice** [detɑ̃tœr, -tris] *nm/f* holder
**détention** [detɑ̃sjɔ̃] *nf* (*voir détenir*) possession; detention; holding; **~ préventive** (pre-trial) custody
**détenu, e** [detny] *pp de* **détenir** ▷ *nm/f* prisoner
**détergent** [detɛrʒɑ̃] *nm* detergent
**détérioration** [deterjɔrasjɔ̃] *nf* damaging; deterioration
**détériorer** [deterjɔre] *vt* to damage; **se détériorer** *vi* to deteriorate
**déterminant, e** [detɛrminɑ̃, -ɑ̃t] *adj*: **un facteur ~** a determining factor ▷ *nm* (*Ling*) determiner
**détermination** [detɛrminasjɔ̃] *nf* determining; (*résolution*) decision; (*fermeté*) determination
**déterminé, e** [detɛrmine] *adj* (*résolu*) determined; (*précis*) specific, definite
**déterminer** [detɛrmine] *vt* (*fixer*) to determine; (*décider*): **~ qn à faire** to decide sb to do; **se ~ à faire** to make up one's mind to do
**déterminisme** [detɛrminism(ə)] *nm* determinism

**déterré, e** [detere] *nm/f*: **avoir une mine de ~** to look like death warmed up (*Brit*) *ou* warmed over (*US*)
**déterrer** [detere] *vt* to dig up
**détersif, -ive** [detɛrsif, -iv] *adj, nm* detergent
**détestable** [detɛstabl(ə)] *adj* foul, detestable
**détester** [detɛste] *vt* to hate, detest
**détiendrai** [detjɛ̃dre], **détiens** *etc* [detjɛ̃] *vb voir* **détenir**
**détonant, e** [detɔnɑ̃, -ɑ̃t] *adj*: **mélange ~** explosive mixture
**détonateur** [detɔnatœr] *nm* detonator
**détonation** [detɔnasjɔ̃] *nf* detonation, bang, report (of a gun)
**détoner** [detɔne] *vi* to detonate, explode
**détonner** [detɔne] *vi* (*Mus*) to go out of tune; (*fig*) to clash
**détordre** [detɔrdr(ə)] *vt* to untwist, unwind
**détour** [detur] *nm* detour; (*tournant*) bend, curve; (*fig: subterfuge*) roundabout means; **sans ~** (*fig*) plainly
**détourné, e** [deturne] *adj* (*sentier, chemin, moyen*) roundabout
**détournement** [deturnəmɑ̃] *nm* diversion, rerouting; **~ d'avion** hijacking; **~ (de fonds)** embezzlement *ou* misappropriation (of funds); **~ de mineur** corruption of a minor
**détourner** [deturne] *vt* to divert; (*avion*) to divert, reroute; (*: par la force*) to hijack; (*yeux, tête*) to turn away; (*de l'argent*) to embezzle, misappropriate; **se détourner** to turn away; **~ la conversation** to change the subject; **~ qn de son devoir** to divert sb from his duty; **~ l'attention (de qn)** to distract *ou* divert (sb's) attention
**détracteur, -trice** [detraktœr, -tris] *nm/f* disparager, critic
**détraqué, e** [detrake] *adj* (*machine, santé*) broken-down ▷ *nm/f* (*fam*): **c'est un ~** he's unhinged
**détraquer** [detrake] *vt* to put out of order; (*estomac*) to upset; **se détraquer** *vi* to go wrong
**détrempe** [detrɑ̃p] *nf* (*Art*) tempera
**détrempé, e** [detrɑ̃pe] *adj* (*sol*) sodden, waterlogged
**détremper** [detrɑ̃pe] *vt* (*peinture*) to water down
**détresse** [detrɛs] *nf* distress; **en ~** (*avion etc*) in distress; **appel/signal de ~** distress call/signal
**détriment** [detrimɑ̃] *nm*: **au ~ de** to the detriment of
**détritus** [detritys] *nmpl* rubbish *sg*, refuse *sg*, garbage *sg* (*US*)
**détroit** [detrwa] *nm* strait; **le ~ de Bering** *ou* **Behring** the Bering Strait; **le ~ de Gibraltar** the Straits of Gibraltar; **le ~ du Bosphore** the Bosphorus; **le ~ de Magellan** the Strait of Magellan, the Magellan Strait
**détromper** [detrɔ̃pe] *vt* to disabuse; **se détromper** *vi*: **détrompez-vous** don't believe it
**détrôner** [detrone] *vt* to dethrone, depose; (*fig*) to oust, dethrone
**détrousser** [detruse] *vt* to rob

**d**

**détruire** [detrɥiʀ] vt to destroy; (fig: santé, réputation) to ruin; (documents) to shred
**détruit, e** [detrɥi, -it] pp de **détruire**
**dette** [dɛt] nf debt; ~ **publique** ou **de l'État** national debt
**DEUG** [døg] sigle m = **Diplôme d'études universitaires générales**; see note

⬤ **DEUG**
⬤
⬤ French students sit their DEUG ('diplôme
⬤ d'études universitaires générales') after two
⬤ years at university. They can then choose to
⬤ leave university altogether, or go on to study
⬤ for their 'licence'. The certificate specifies
⬤ the student's major subject and may be
⬤ awarded with distinction.

**deuil** [dœj] nm (perte) bereavement; (période) mourning; (chagrin) grief; **porter le ~** to wear mourning; **prendre le/être en ~** to go into/be in mourning
**DEUST** [dœst] sigle m = **Diplôme d'études universitaires scientifiques et techniques**
**deux** [dø] num two; **les ~** both; **ses ~ mains** both his hands, his two hands; **à ~ pas** a short distance away; **tous les ~ mois** every two months, every other month; **~ points** colon sg
**deuxième** [døzjɛm] num second
**deuxièmement** [døzjɛmmɑ̃] adv secondly, in the second place
**deux-pièces** [døpjɛs] nm inv (tailleur) two-piece (suit); (de bain) two-piece (swimsuit); (appartement) two-roomed flat (Brit) ou apartment (US)
**deux-roues** [døʀu] nm two-wheeled vehicle
**deux-temps** [døtɑ̃] adj two-stroke
**devais**etc [dəvɛ] vb voir **devoir**
**dévaler** [devale] vt to hurtle down
**dévaliser** [devalize] vt to rob, burgle
**dévalorisant, e** [devalɔʀizɑ̃, -ɑ̃t] adj depreciatory
**dévalorisation** [devalɔʀizɑsjɔ̃] nf depreciation
**dévaloriser** [devalɔʀize] vt to reduce the value of; **se dévaloriser** vi to depreciate
**dévaluation** [devalɥasjɔ̃] nf depreciation; (Écon: mesure) devaluation
**dévaluer** [devalɥe] vt, **se dévaluer** vi to devalue
**devancer** [dəvɑ̃se] vt to be ahead of; (distancer) to get ahead of; (arriver avant) to arrive before; (prévenir) to anticipate; **~ l'appel** (Mil) to enlist before call-up
**devancier, -ière** [dəvɑ̃sje, -jɛʀ] nm/f precursor
**devant** [dəvɑ̃] vb voir **devoir** ▷ adv in front; (à distance: en avant) ahead ▷ prép in front of; ahead of; (avec mouvement: passer) past; (fig) before, in front of; (: face à) faced with, in the face of; (: vu) in view of ▷ nm front; **prendre les ~s** to make the first move; **de ~** (roue, porte) front; **les pattes de ~** the front legs, the forelegs; **par ~** (boutonner) at the front; (entrer) the front way; **par-~ notaire** in the presence of a notary; **aller**

**au-~ de qn** to go out to meet sb; **aller au-~ de** (désirs de qn) to anticipate; **aller au-~ des ennuis** ou **difficultés** to be asking for trouble
**devanture** [dəvɑ̃tyʀ] nf (façade) (shop) front; (étalage) display; (shop) window
**dévastateur, -trice** [devastatœʀ, -tʀis] adj devastating
**dévastation** [devastɑsjɔ̃] nf devastation
**dévaster** [devaste] vt to devastate
**déveine** [devɛn] nf rotten luck no pl
**développement** [devlɔpmɑ̃] nm development
**développer** [devlɔpe] vt, **se développer** vi to develop
**devenir** [dəvniʀ] vi to become; **~ instituteur** to become a teacher; **que sont-ils devenus?** what has become of them?
**devenu, e** [dəvny] pp de **devenir**
**dévergondé, e** [devɛʀgɔ̃de] adj wild, shameless
**dévergonder** [devɛʀgɔ̃de] vt, **se dévergonder** vi to get into bad ways
**déverrouiller** [deveʀuje] vt to unbolt
**devers** [dəvɛʀ] adv: **par ~ soi** to oneself
**déverser** [devɛʀse] vt (liquide) to pour (out); (ordures) to tip (out); **se ~ dans** (fleuve, mer) to flow into
**déversoir** [devɛʀswaʀ] nm overflow
**dévêtir** [devetiʀ] vt, **se dévêtir** vi to undress
**devez** [dəve] vb voir **devoir**
**déviation** [devjɑsjɔ̃] nf deviation; (Auto) diversion (Brit), detour (US); **~ de la colonne (vertébrale)** curvature of the spine
**dévider** [devide] vt to unwind
**dévidoir** [devidwaʀ] nm reel
**deviendrai** [dəvjɛ̃dʀe], **deviens**etc [dəvjɛ̃] vb voir **devenir**
**dévier** [devje] vt (fleuve, circulation) to divert; (coup) to deflect ▷ vi to veer (off course); **(faire) ~** (projectile) to deflect; (véhicule) to push off course
**devin** [dəvɛ̃] nm soothsayer, seer
**deviner** [dəvine] vt to guess; (prévoir) to foretell, foresee; (apercevoir) to distinguish
**devinette** [dəvinɛt] nf riddle
**devint**etc [dəvɛ̃] vb voir **devenir**
**devis** [dəvi] nm estimate, quotation; **~ descriptif/estimatif** detailed/preliminary estimate
**dévisager** [devizaʒe] vt to stare at
**devise** [dəviz] nf (formule) motto, watchword; (Écon: monnaie) currency; **devises** nfpl (argent) currency sg
**deviser** [dəvize] vi to converse
**dévisser** [devise] vt to unscrew, undo; **se dévisser** vi to come unscrewed
**de visu** [devizy] adv: **se rendre compte de qch ~** to see sth for o.s.
**dévitaliser** [devitalize] vt (dent) to remove the nerve from
**dévoiler** [devwale] vt to unveil
**devoir** [dəvwaʀ] nm duty; (Scol) piece of homework, homework no pl; (: en classe) exercise ▷ vt (argent, respect): **~ qch (à qn)** to owe (sb) sth;

(*suivi de l'infinitif: obligation*): **il doit le faire** he has to do it, he must do it; (: *fatalité*): **cela devait arriver un jour** it was bound to happen; (: *intention*): **il doit partir demain** he is (due) to leave tomorrow; (: *probabilité*): **il doit être tard** it must be late; **se faire un ~ de faire qch** to make it one's duty to do sth; **~s de vacances** homework set for the holidays; **se ~ de faire qch** to be duty bound to do sth; **je devrais faire** I ought to *ou* should do; **tu n'aurais pas dû** you ought not to have *ou* shouldn't have; **comme il se doit** (*comme il faut*) as is right and proper

**dévolu, e** [devoly] *adj*: **~ à** allotted to ▷ *nm*: **jeter son ~ sur** to fix one's choice on

**devons** [dəvɔ̃] *vb voir* **devoir**

**dévorant, e** [devɔʀɑ̃, -ɑ̃t] *adj* (*faim, passion*) raging

**dévorer** [devɔʀe] *vt* to devour; (*feu, soucis*) to consume; **~ qn/qch des yeux** *ou* **du regard** (*fig*) to eye sb/sth intently; (: *convoitise*) to eye sb/sth greedily

**dévot, e** [devo, -ɔt] *adj* devout, pious ▷ *nm/f* devout person; **un faux ~** a falsely pious person

**dévotion** [devosjɔ̃] *nf* devoutness; **être à la ~ de qn** to be totally devoted to sb; **avoir une ~ pour qn** to worship sb

**dévoué, e** [devwe] *adj* devoted

**dévouement** [devumɑ̃] *nm* devotion, dedication

**dévouer** [devwe]: **se dévouer** *vi* (*se sacrifier*): **se ~ (pour)** to sacrifice o.s. (for); (*se consacrer*): **se ~ à** to devote *ou* dedicate o.s. to

**dévoyé, e** [devwaje] *adj* delinquent

**dévoyer** [devwaje] *vt* to lead astray; **se dévoyer** *vi* to go off the rails; **~ l'opinion publique** to influence public opinion

**devraie**tc [dəvʀe] *vb voir* **devoir**

**dextérité** [dɛksteʀite] *nf* skill, dexterity

**dézipper** [dezipe] *vt* (*Inform*) to unzip

**dfc** *abr* (= *désire faire connaissance*) *in personal column of newspaper*

**DG** *sigle m* = **directeur général**

**dg.** *abr* (= *décigramme*) dg.

**DGE** *sigle f* (= *Dotation globale d'équipement*) *state contribution to local government budget*

**DGSE** *sigle f* (= *Direction générale de la sécurité extérieure*) ≈ MI6 (*Brit*), ≈ CIA (*US*)

**diabète** [djabɛt] *nm* diabetes *sg*

**diabétique** [djabetik] *nm/f* diabetic

**diable** [djabl(ə)] *nm* devil; **une musique du ~** an unholy racket; **il fait une chaleur du ~** it's fiendishly hot; **avoir le ~ au corps** to be the very devil

**diablement** [djabləmɑ̃] *adv* fiendishly

**diableries** [djabləʀi] *nfpl* (*d'enfant*) devilment *sg*, mischief *sg*

**diablesse** [djablɛs] *nf* (*petite fille*) little devil

**diablotin** [djablɔtɛ̃] *nm* imp; (*pétard*) cracker

**diabolique** [djabɔlik] *adj* diabolical

**diabolo** [djabɔlo] *nm* (*jeu*) diabolo; (*boisson*) lemonade and fruit cordial; **~-(menthe)** lemonade and mint cordial

**diacre** [djakʀ(ə)] *nm* deacon

**diadème** [djadɛm] *nm* diadem

**diagnostic** [djagnɔstik] *nm* diagnosis *sg*

**diagnostiquer** [djagnɔstike] *vt* to diagnose

**diagonal, e, -aux** [djagɔnal, -o] *adj, nf* diagonal; **en ~e** diagonally; **lire en ~e** (*fig*) to skim through

**diagramme** [djagʀam] *nm* chart, graph

**dialecte** [djalɛkt(ə)] *nm* dialect

**dialectique** [djalɛktik] *adj* dialectic(al)

**dialogue** [djalɔg] *nm* dialogue; **~ de sourds** dialogue of the deaf

**dialoguer** [djalɔge] *vi* to converse; (*Pol*) to have a dialogue

**dialoguiste** [djalɔgist(ə)] *nm/f* dialogue writer

**dialyse** [djaliz] *nf* dialysis

**diamant** [djamɑ̃] *nm* diamond

**diamantaire** [djamɑ̃tɛʀ] *nm* diamond dealer

**diamétralement** [djametʀalmɑ̃] *adv* diametrically; **~ opposés** (*opinions*) diametrically opposed

**diamètre** [djametʀ(ə)] *nm* diameter

**diapason** [djapazɔ̃] *nm* tuning fork; (*fig*): **être/se mettre au ~ (de)** to be/get in tune (with)

**diaphane** [djafan] *adj* diaphanous

**diaphragme** [djafʀagm(ə)] *nm* (*Anat, Photo*) diaphragm; (*contraceptif*) diaphragm, cap; **ouverture du ~** (*Photo*) aperture

**diapo** [djapo], **diapositive** [djapozitiv] *nf* transparency, slide

**diaporama** [djapɔʀama] *nm* slide show

**diapré, e** [djapʀe] *adj* many-coloured (*Brit*), many-colored (*US*)

**diarrhée** [djaʀe] *nf* diarrhoea (*Brit*), diarrhea (*US*)

**diatribe** [djatʀib] *nf* diatribe

**dichotomie** [dikɔtɔmi] *nf* dichotomy

**Dictaphone** [diktafɔn] *nm* Dictaphone®

**dictateur** [diktatœʀ] *nm* dictator

**dictatorial, e, -aux** [diktatɔʀjal, -o] *adj* dictatorial

**dictature** [diktatyʀ] *nf* dictatorship

**dictée** [dikte] *nf* dictation; **prendre sous ~** to take down (*sth dictated*)

**dicter** [dikte] *vt* to dictate

**diction** [diksjɔ̃] *nf* diction, delivery; **cours de ~** speech production lesson(s)

**dictionnaire** [diksjɔnɛʀ] *nm* dictionary; **~ géographique** gazetteer

**dicton** [diktɔ̃] *nm* saying, dictum

**didacticiel** [didaktisjɛl] *nm* educational software

**didactique** [didaktik] *adj* didactic

**dièse** [djɛz] *nm* (*Mus*) sharp

**diesel** [djezɛl] *nm, adj inv* diesel

**diète** [djɛt] *nf* diet; **être à la ~** to be on a diet

**diététicien, ne** [djetetisjɛ̃, -ɛn] *nm/f* dietician

**diététique** [djetetik] *nf* dietetics *sg* ▷ *adj*: **magasin ~** health food shop (*Brit*) *ou* store (*US*)

**dieu, x** [djø] *nm* god; **D~** God; **le bon D~** the good Lord; **mon D~!** good heavens!

**diffamant, e** [difamɑ̃, -ɑ̃t] *adj* slanderous, defamatory; libellous
**diffamation** [difamɑsjɔ̃] *nf* slander; (*écrite*) libel; **attaquer qn en ~** to sue sb for slander (*ou* libel)
**diffamatoire** [difamatwaʀ] *adj* slanderous, defamatory; libellous
**diffamer** [difame] *vt* to slander, defame; to libel
**différé** [difeʀe] *adj* (*Inform*): **traitement ~** batch processing; **crédit ~** deferred credit ▷ *nm* (*TV*): **en ~** (pre-)recorded
**différemment** [difeʀamɑ̃] *adv* differently
**différence** [difeʀɑ̃s] *nf* difference; **à la ~ de** unlike
**différenciation** [difeʀɑ̃sjɑsjɔ̃] *nf* differentiation
**différencier** [difeʀɑ̃sje] *vt* to differentiate; **se différencier** *vi* (*organisme*) to become differentiated; **se ~ de** to differentiate o.s. from; (*être différent*) to differ from
**différend** [difeʀɑ̃] *nm* difference (of opinion), disagreement
**différent, e** [difeʀɑ̃, -ɑ̃t] *adj*: **~ (de)** different (from); **~s objets** different *ou* various objects; **à ~es reprises** on various occasions
**différentiel, le** [difeʀɑ̃sjɛl] *adj, nm* differential
**différer** [difeʀe] *vt* to postpone, put off ▷ *vi*: **~ (de)** to differ (from); **~ de faire** (*tarder*) to delay doing
**difficile** [difisil] *adj* difficult; (*exigeant*) hard to please, difficult (to please); **faire le** *ou* **la ~** to be hard to please, be difficult
**difficilement** [difisilmɑ̃] *adv* (*marcher, s'expliquer etc*) with difficulty; **~ lisible/compréhensible** difficult *ou* hard to read/understand
**difficulté** [difikylte] *nf* difficulty; **en ~** (*bateau, alpiniste*) in trouble *ou* difficulties; **avoir de la ~ à faire** to have difficulty (in) doing
**difforme** [difɔʀm(ə)] *adj* deformed, misshapen
**difformité** [difɔʀmite] *nf* deformity
**diffracter** [difʀakte] *vt* to diffract
**diffus, e** [dify, -yz] *adj* diffuse
**diffuser** [difyze] *vt* (*chaleur, bruit, lumière*) to diffuse; (*émission, musique*) to broadcast; (*nouvelle, idée*) to circulate; (*Comm: livres, journaux*) to distribute
**diffuseur** [difyzœʀ] *nm* diffuser; distributor
**diffusion** [difyzjɔ̃] *nf* diffusion, broadcast(ing); circulation; distribution
**digérer** [diʒeʀe] *vt* (*personne*) to digest; (: *machine*) to process; (*fig: accepter*) to stomach, put up with
**digeste** [diʒɛst(ə)] *adj* easily digestible
**digestible** [diʒɛstibl(ə)] *adj* digestible
**digestif, -ive** [diʒɛstif, -iv] *adj* digestive ▷ *nm* (after-dinner) liqueur
**digestion** [diʒɛstjɔ̃] *nf* digestion
**digit** [didʒit] *nm*: **~ binaire** binary digit
**digital, e, -aux** [diʒital, -o] *adj* digital
**digitale** [diʒital] *nf* digitalis, foxglove
**digne** [diɲ] *adj* dignified; **~ de** worthy of; **~ de foi** trustworthy
**dignitaire** [diɲiteʀ] *nm* dignitary

**dignité** [diɲite] *nf* dignity
**digression** [digʀesjɔ̃] *nf* digression
**digue** [dig] *nf* dike, dyke; (*pour protéger la côte*) sea wall
**dijonnais, e** [diʒɔnɛ, -ez] *adj* of *ou* from Dijon ▷ *nm/f*: **Dijonnais, e** inhabitant *ou* native of Dijon
**diktat** [diktat] *nm* diktat
**dilapidation** [dilapidɑsjɔ̃] *nf* (*voir vb*) squandering; embezzlement, misappropriation
**dilapider** [dilapide] *vt* to squander, waste; (*détourner: biens, fonds publics*) to embezzle, misappropriate
**dilater** [dilate] *vt* to dilate; (*gaz, métal*) to cause to expand; (*ballon*) to distend; **se dilater** *vi* to expand
**dilemme** [dilɛm] *nm* dilemma
**dilettante** [diletɑ̃t] *nm/f* dilettante; **en ~** in a dilettantish way
**dilettantisme** [diletɑ̃tism(ə)] *nm* dilettant(e)ism
**diligence** [diliʒɑ̃s] *nf* stagecoach, diligence; (*empressement*) despatch; **faire ~** to make haste
**diligent, e** [diliʒɑ̃, -ɑ̃t] *adj* prompt and efficient; diligent
**diluant** [dilɥɑ̃] *nm* thinner(s)
**diluer** [dilɥe] *vt* to dilute
**dilution** [dilysjɔ̃] *nf* dilution
**diluvien, ne** [dilyvjɛ̃, -ɛn] *adj*: **pluie ~ne** torrential rain
**dimanche** [dimɑ̃ʃ] *nm* Sunday; **le ~ des Rameaux/de Pâques** Palm/Easter Sunday; *voir aussi* **lundi**
**dîme** [dim] *nf* tithe
**dimension** [dimɑ̃sjɔ̃] *nf* (*grandeur*) size; (*gén pl: cotes, Math: de l'espace*) dimension
**diminué, e** [diminɥe] *adj* (*personne: physiquement*) run-down; (: *mentalement*) less alert
**diminuer** [diminɥe] *vt* to reduce, decrease; (*ardeur etc*) to lessen; (*personne: physiquement*) to undermine; (*dénigrer*) to belittle ▷ *vi* to decrease, diminish
**diminutif** [diminytif] *nm* (*Ling*) diminutive; (*surnom*) pet name
**diminution** [diminysjɔ̃] *nf* decreasing, diminishing
**dînatoire** [dinatwaʀ] *adj*: **goûter ~** = high tea (*Brit*); **apéritif ~** = evening buffet
**dinde** [dɛ̃d] *nf* turkey; (*femme stupide*) goose
**dindon** [dɛ̃dɔ̃] *nm* turkey
**dindonneau, x** [dɛ̃dɔno] *nm* turkey poult
**dîner** [dine] *nm* dinner ▷ *vi* to have dinner; **~ d'affaires/de famille** business/family dinner
**dînette** [dinɛt] *nf* (*jeu*): **jouer à la ~** to play at tea parties
**dingue** [dɛ̃g] *adj* (*fam*) crazy
**dinosaure** [dinozɔʀ] *nm* dinosaur
**diocèse** [djɔsɛz] *nm* diocese
**diode** [djɔd] *nf* diode
**diphasé, e** [difaze] *adj* (*Élec*) two-phase
**diphtérie** [difteʀi] *nf* diphtheria
**diphtongue** [diftɔ̃g] *nf* diphthong

**diplomate** [diplɔmat] *adj* diplomatic ▷ *nm*
diplomat; (*fig: personne habile*) diplomatist;
(*Culin: gâteau*) dessert made of sponge cake, candied
fruit and custard, ≈ trifle (Brit)
**diplomatie** [diplɔmasi] *nf* diplomacy
**diplomatique** [diplɔmatik] *adj* diplomatic
**diplôme** [diplom] *nm* diploma certificate;
(*examen*) (diploma) examination
**diplômé, e** [diplome] *adj* qualified
**dire** [diʁ] *nm*: **au ~ de** according to; **leurs ~s**
what they say ▷ *vt* to say; (*secret, mensonge*) to
tell; **~ dis pardon/merci** say sorry/thank you;
**~ qch à qn** to tell sb sth; **~ à qn qu'il fasse** *ou* **de
faire** to tell sb to do; **~ que** to say that; **on dit
que** they say that; **comme on dit** as they say;
**on dirait que** it looks (*ou* sounds *etc*) as though;
**on dirait du vin** you'd *ou* one would think it
was wine; **que dites-vous de** (*penser*) what do
you think of; **si cela lui dit** if he feels like it, if
he fancies it; **cela ne me dit rien** that doesn't
appeal to me; **à vrai ~** truth to tell; **pour ainsi
~** so to speak; **cela va sans ~** that goes without
saying; **dis donc!, dites donc!** (*pour attirer
l'attention*) hey!; (*au fait*) by the way; **et ~ que ...**
and to think that ...; **ceci** *ou* **cela dit** that being
said; (*à ces mots*) whereupon; **c'est dit, voilà
qui est dit** so that's settled; **il n'y a pas à ~**
there's no getting away from it; **c'est ~ si ...**
that just shows that ...; **c'est beaucoup/peu ~**
that's saying a lot/not saying much; **se dire** *vi*
(*à soi-même*) to say to oneself; (*se prétendre*): **se ~
malade** *etc* to say (that) one is ill *etc*; **ça se dit ...
en anglais** that is ... in English; **cela ne se dit
pas comme ça** you don't say it like that; **se ~
au revoir** to say goodbye (to each other)
**direct, e** [diʁɛkt] *adj* direct ▷ *nm* (*train*) through
train; **en ~** (*émission*) live; **train/bus ~** express
train/bus
**directement** [diʁɛktəmɑ̃] *adv* directly
**directeur, -trice** [diʁɛktœʁ, -tʁis] *nm/f*
(*d'entreprise*) director; (*de service*) manager/eress;
(*d'école*) head(teacher) (Brit), principal (US);
**comité ~** management *ou* steering committee;
**~ général** general manager; **~ de thèse** ≈ PhD
supervisor
**direction** [diʁɛksjɔ̃] *nf* management;
conducting; supervision; (*Auto*) steering; (*sens*)
direction; **sous la ~ de** (*Mus*) conducted by; **en ~
de** (*avion, train, bateau*) for; **"toutes ~s"** (*Auto*) "all
routes"
**directive** [diʁɛktiv] *nf* directive, instruction
**directorial, e, -aux** [diʁɛktɔʁjal, -o] *adj* (*bureau*)
director's; manager's; head teacher's
**directrice** [diʁɛktʁis] *adj f, nf voir* **directeur**
**dirent** [diʁ] *vb voir* **dire**
**dirigeable** [diʁiʒabl(ə)] *adj, nm*: (**ballon**) ~
dirigible
**dirigeant, e** [diʁiʒɑ̃, -ɑ̃t] *adj* managerial;
(*classes*) ruling ▷ *nm/f* (*d'un parti etc*) leader;
(*d'entreprise*) manager, member of the
management

**diriger** [diʁiʒe] *vt* (*entreprise*) to manage, run;
(*véhicule*) to steer; (*orchestre*) to conduct;
(*recherches, travaux*) to supervise, be in charge of;
(*braquer: regard, arme*): **~ sur** to point *ou* level *ou*
aim at; (*fig: critiques*): **~ contre** to aim at; **se
diriger** *vi* (*s'orienter*) to find one's way; **se ~ vers**
*ou* **sur** to make *ou* head for
**dirigisme** [diʁiʒism(ə)] *nm* (*Écon*) state
intervention, interventionism
**dirigiste** [diʁiʒist(ə)] *adj* interventionist
**dis** [di], **disais** *etc* [dizɛ] *vb voir* **dire**
**discal, e, -aux** [diskal, -o] *adj* (*Méd*): **hernie ~e**
slipped disc
**discernement** [disɛʁnəmɑ̃] *nm* discernment,
judgment
**discerner** [disɛʁne] *vt* to discern, make out
**disciple** [disipl(ə)] *nm/f* disciple
**disciplinaire** [disiplinɛʁ] *adj* disciplinary
**discipline** [disiplin] *nf* discipline
**discipliné, e** [disipline] *adj* (well-)disciplined
**discipliner** [disipline] *vt* to discipline; (*cheveux*)
to control
**discobole** [diskɔbɔl] *nm/f* discus thrower
**discographie** [diskɔgʁafi] *nf* discography
**discontinu, e** [diskɔ̃tiny] *adj* intermittent;
(*bande: sur la route*) broken
**discontinuer** [diskɔ̃tinɥe] *vi*: **sans ~** without
stopping, without a break
**disconvenir** [diskɔ̃vniʁ] *vi*: **ne pas ~ de qch/
que** not to deny sth/that
**discophile** [diskɔfil] *nm/f* record enthusiast
**discordance** [diskɔʁdɑ̃s] *nf* discordance;
conflict
**discordant, e** [diskɔʁdɑ̃, -ɑ̃t] *adj* discordant;
conflicting
**discorde** [diskɔʁd(ə)] *nf* discord, dissension
**discothèque** [diskɔtɛk] *nf* (*disques*) record
collection; (: *dans une bibliothèque*): **~ (de prêt)**
record library; (*boîte de nuit*) disco(thèque)
**discourais** *etc* [diskuʁɛ] *vb voir* **discourir**
**discourir** [diskuʁiʁ] *vi* to discourse, hold forth
**discours** [diskuʁ] *vb voir* **discourir** ▷ *nm* speech;
**~ direct/indirect** (*Ling*) direct/indirect *ou*
reported speech
**discourtois, e** [diskuʁtwa, waz] *adj*
discourteous
**discrédit** [diskʁedi] *nm*: **jeter le ~ sur** to
discredit
**discréditer** [diskʁedite] *vt* to discredit
**discret, -ète** [diskʁɛ, -ɛt] *adj* discreet; (*fig:
musique, style*) unobtrusive; (: *endroit*) quiet
**discrètement** [diskʁɛtmɑ̃] *adv* discreetly
**discrétion** [diskʁesjɔ̃] *nf* discretion; **à la ~ de
qn** at sb's discretion, in sb's hands; **à ~** (*boisson
etc*) unlimited, as much as one wants
**discrétionnaire** [diskʁesjɔnɛʁ] *adj*
discretionary
**discrimination** [diskʁiminasjɔ̃] *nf*
discrimination; **sans ~** indiscriminately
**discriminatoire** [diskʁiminatwaʁ] *adj*
discriminatory
**disculper** [diskylpe] *vt* to exonerate

**d**

**discussion** [diskysjɔ̃] nf discussion
**discutable** [diskytabl(ə)] adj (contestable)
doubtful; (à débattre) debatable
**discuté, e** [diskyte] adj controversial
**discuter** [diskyte] vt (contester) to question,
dispute; (débattre: prix) to discuss ▷ vi to talk;
(ergoter) to argue; ~ **de** to discuss
**dise**etc [diz] vb voir **dire**
**disert, e** [dizɛR, -ɛRt(ə)] adj loquacious
**disette** [dizɛt] nf food shortage
**diseuse** [dizøz] nf: ~ **de bonne aventure**
fortune-teller
**disgrâce** [disgRɑs] nf disgrace; **être en** ~ to be
in disgrace
**disgracié, e** [disgRasje] adj (en disgrâce) disgraced
**disgracieux, -euse** [disgRasjø, -øz] adj
ungainly, awkward
**disjoindre** [disʒwɛ̃dR(ə)] vt to take apart; **se**
**disjoindre** vi to come apart
**disjoint, e** [disʒwɛ̃, -wɛt] pp de **disjoindre** ▷ adj
loose
**disjoncteur** [disʒɔ̃ktœR] nm (Élec) circuit
breaker
**dislocation** [dislɔkɑsjɔ̃] nf dislocation
**disloquer** [dislɔke] vt (membre) to dislocate;
(chaise) to dismantle; (troupe) to disperse; **se**
**disloquer** vi (parti, empire) to break up; **se** ~
**l'épaule** to dislocate one's shoulder
**disons**etc [dizɔ̃] vb voir **dire**
**disparaître** [disparetR(ə)] vi to disappear; (à la
vue) to vanish, disappear; to be hidden ou
concealed; (être manquant) to go missing,
disappear; (se perdre: traditions etc) to die out;
(personne: mourir) to die; **faire** ~ (objet, tache, trace)
to remove; (personne) to get rid of
**disparate** [disparat] adj disparate; (couleurs) ill-
assorted
**disparité** [disparite] nf disparity
**disparition** [disparisjɔ̃] nf disappearance
**disparu, e** [dispary] pp de **disparaître** ▷ nm/f
missing person; (défunt) departed; **être porté** ~
to be reported missing
**dispendieux, -euse** [dispɑ̃djø, -øz] adj
extravagant, expensive
**dispensaire** [dispɑ̃sɛR] nm community clinic
**dispense** [dispɑ̃s] nf exemption; (permission)
special permission; ~ **d'âge** special exemption
from age limit
**dispenser** [dispɑ̃se] vt (donner) to lavish, bestow;
(exempter): ~ **qn de** to exempt sb from; **se** ~ **de** vt
to avoid, get out of
**disperser** [dispɛRse] vt to scatter; (fig: son
attention) to dissipate; **se disperser** vi to scatter;
(fig) to dissipate one's efforts
**dispersion** [dispɛRsjɔ̃] nf scattering; (des efforts)
dissipation
**disponibilité** [disponibilite] nf availability;
(Admin): **être en** ~ to be on leave of absence;
**disponibilités** nfpl (Comm) liquid assets
**disponible** [disponibl(ə)] adj available
**dispos** [dispo] adj m: **(frais et)** ~ fresh (as a
daisy)

**disposé, e** [dispoze] adj (d'une certaine manière)
arranged, laid-out; **bien/mal** ~ (humeur) in a
good/bad mood; **bien/mal** ~ **pour** ou **envers qn**
well/badly disposed towards sb; ~ **à** (prêt à)
willing ou prepared to
**disposer** [dispoze] vt (arranger, placer) to arrange;
(inciter): ~ **qn à qch/faire qch** to dispose ou
incline sb towards sth/to do sth ▷ vi: **vous**
**pouvez** ~ you may leave; ~ **de** vt to have (at
one's disposal); **se** ~ **à faire** to prepare to do, be
about to do
**dispositif** [dispozitif] nm device; (fig) system,
plan of action; set-up; (d'un texte de loi) operative
part; ~ **de sûreté** safety device
**disposition** [dispozisjɔ̃] nf (arrangement)
arrangement, layout; (humeur) mood; (tendance)
tendency; **dispositions** nfpl (mesures) steps,
measures; (préparatifs) arrangements; (de loi,
testament) provisions; (aptitudes) bent sg,
aptitude sg; **à la** ~ **de qn** at sb's disposal
**disproportion** [dispRopɔRsjɔ̃] nf disproportion
**disproportionné, e** [dispRopɔRsjone] adj
disproportionate, out of all proportion
**dispute** [dispyt] nf quarrel, argument
**disputer** [dispyte] vt (match) to play; (combat) to
fight; (course) to run; **se disputer** vi to quarrel,
have a quarrel; (match, combat, course) to take
place; ~ **qch à qn** to fight with sb for ou over sth
**disquaire** [diskɛR] nm/f record dealer
**disqualification** [diskalifikɑsjɔ̃] nf
disqualification
**disqualifier** [diskalifje] vt to disqualify; **se**
**disqualifier** vi to bring discredit on o.s.
**disque** [disk(ə)] nm (Mus) record; (Inform) disk,
disc; (forme, pièce) disc; (Sport) discus; ~ **compact**
compact disc; ~ **compact interactif** CD-I®; ~
**dur** hard disk; ~ **d'embrayage** (Auto) clutch
plate; ~ **laser** compact disc; ~ **de**
**stationnement** parking disc; ~ **système**
system disk
**disquette** [diskɛt] nf diskette, floppy (disk)
**dissection** [disɛksjɔ̃] nf dissection
**dissemblable** [disɑ̃blabl(ə)] adj dissimilar
**dissemblance** [disɑ̃blɑ̃s] nf dissimilarity,
difference
**dissémination** [diseminɑsjɔ̃] nf (voir vb)
scattering; dispersal; (des armes) proliferation
**disséminer** [disemine] vt to scatter; (troupes: sur
un territoire) to disperse
**dissension** [disɑ̃sjɔ̃] nf dissension; **dissensions**
nfpl dissension
**disséquer** [diseke] vt to dissect
**dissertation** [disɛRtɑsjɔ̃] nf (Scol) essay
**disserter** [disɛRte] vi: ~ **sur** to discourse upon
**dissidence** [disidɑ̃s] nf (concept) dissidence;
**rejoindre la** ~ to join the dissidents
**dissident, e** [disidɑ̃, -ɑ̃t] adj, nm/f dissident
**dissimilitude** [disimilityd] nf dissimilarity
**dissimulateur, -trice** [disimyltœR, -tRis] adj
dissembling ▷ nm/f dissembler
**dissimulation** [disimylɑsjɔ̃] nf concealing;
(duplicité) dissimulation; ~ **de bénéfices/de**

**revenus** concealment of profits/income
**dissimulé, e** [disimyle] *adj (personne: secret)*
  secretive; *(: fourbe, hypocrite)* deceitful
**dissimuler** [disimyle] *vt* to conceal; **se**
  **dissimuler** *vi* to conceal o.s.; to be concealed
**dissipation** [disipɑsjɔ̃] *nf* squandering;
  unruliness; *(débauche)* dissipation
**dissipé, e** [disipe] *adj (indiscipliné)* unruly
**dissiper** [disipe] *vt* to dissipate; *(fortune)* to
  squander, fritter away; **se dissiper** *vi (brouillard)*
  to clear, disperse; *(doutes)* to disappear, melt
  away; *(élève)* to become undisciplined *ou* unruly
**dissociable** [disɔsjabl(ə)] *adj* separable
**dissocier** [disɔsje] *vt* to dissociate; **se dissocier**
  *vi (éléments, groupe)* to break up, split up; **se ~ de**
  *(groupe, point de vue)* to dissociate o.s. from
**dissolu, e** [disɔly] *adj* dissolute
**dissoluble** [disɔlybl(ə)] *adj (Pol: assemblée)*
  dissolvable
**dissolution** [disɔlysjɔ̃] *nf* dissolving; *(Pol, Jur)*
  dissolution
**dissolvant, e** [disɔlvɑ̃, -ɑ̃t] *vb voir* **dissoudre**
  ▷ *nm (Chimie)* solvent; **~ (gras)** nail polish
  remover
**dissonant, e** [disɔnɑ̃, -ɑ̃t] *adj* discordant
**dissoudre** [disudʀ(ə)] *vt*, **se dissoudre** *vi* to
  dissolve
**dissous, -oute** [disu, -ut] *pp de* **dissoudre**
**dissuader** [disɥade] *vt*: **~ qn de faire/de qch** to
  dissuade sb from doing/from sth
**dissuasif, -ive** [disɥazif, iv] *adj* dissuasive
**dissuasion** [disɥazjɔ̃] *nf* dissuasion; **force de ~**
  deterrent power
**distance** [distɑ̃s] *nf* distance; *(fig: écart)* gap; **à ~**
  at *ou* from a distance; *(mettre en marche,*
  *commander)* by remote control; **(situé) à ~**
  *(Inform)* remote; **tenir qn à ~** to keep sb at a
  distance; **se tenir à ~** to keep one's distance; **à**
  **une ~ de 10 km, à 10 km de** ~ 10 km away, at a
  distance of 10 km; **à deux ans de ~** with a gap
  of two years; **prendre ses ~s** to space out;
  **garder ses ~s** to keep one's distance; **tenir la ~**
  *(Sport)* to cover the distance, last the course; **~**
  **focale** *(Photo)* focal length
**distancer** [distɑ̃se] *vt* to outdistance, leave
  behind
**distancier** [distɑ̃sje]: **se distancier** *vi* to
  distance o.s.
**distant, e** [distɑ̃, -ɑ̃t] *adj (réservé)* distant, aloof;
  *(éloigné)* distant, far away; **~ de** *(lieu)* far away *ou*
  a long way from; **~ de 5 km (d'un lieu)** 5 km
  away (from a place)
**distendre** [distɑ̃dʀ(ə)] *vt*, **se distendre** *vi* to
  distend
**distillation** [distilɑsjɔ̃] *nf* distillation, distilling
**distillé, e** [distile] *adj*: **eau ~e** distilled water
**distiller** [distile] *vt* to distil; *(fig)* to exude; to
  elaborate
**distillerie** [distilʀi] *nf* distillery
**distinct, e** [distɛ̃(kt), distɛ̃kt(ə)] *adj* distinct
**distinctement** [distɛ̃ktəmɑ̃] *adv* distinctly
**distinctif, -ive** [distɛ̃ktif, -iv] *adj* distinctive

**distinction** [distɛ̃ksjɔ̃] *nf* distinction
**distingué, e** [distɛ̃ge] *adj* distinguished
**distinguer** [distɛ̃ge] *vt* to distinguish; **se**
  **distinguer** *vi (s'illustrer)* to distinguish o.s.;
  *(différer)*: **se ~ (de)** to distinguish o.s. *ou* be
  distinguished (from)
**distinguo** [distɛ̃go] *nm* distinction
**distorsion** [distɔʀsjɔ̃] *nf (gén)* distortion; *(fig:*
  *déséquilibre)* disparity, imbalance
**distraction** [distʀaksjɔ̃] *nf (manque d'attention)*
  absent-mindedness; *(oubli)* lapse (in
  concentration *ou* attention); *(détente)* diversion,
  recreation; *(passe-temps)* distraction,
  entertainment
**distraire** [distʀɛʀ] *vt (déranger)* to distract;
  *(divertir)* to entertain, divert; *(détourner: somme*
  *d'argent)* to divert, misappropriate; **se distraire**
  *vi* to amuse *ou* enjoy o.s.
**distrait, e** [distʀɛ, -ɛt] *pp de* **distraire** ▷ *adj*
  absent-minded
**distraitement** [distʀɛtmɑ̃] *adv* absent-
  mindedly
**distrayant, e** [distʀɛjɑ̃, -ɑ̃t] *vb voir* **distraire**
  ▷ *adj* entertaining
**distribuer** [distʀibɥe] *vt* to distribute; to hand
  out; *(Cartes)* to deal (out); *(courrier)* to deliver
**distributeur** [distʀibytœʀ] *nm (Auto, Comm)*
  distributor; *(automatique)* (vending) machine; **~**
  **de billets** *(Rail)* ticket machine; *(Banque)* cash
  dispenser
**distribution** [distʀibysjɔ̃] *nf* distribution;
  *(postale)* delivery; *(choix d'acteurs)* casting;
  **circuits de ~** *(Comm)* distribution network; **~**
  **des prix** *(Scol)* prize giving
**district** [distʀik(t)] *nm* district
**dit, e** [di, dit] *pp de* **dire** ▷ *adj (fixé)*: **le jour ~** the
  arranged day; *(surnommé)*: **X, ~ Pierrot** X,
  known as *ou* called Pierrot
**dites** [dit] *vb voir* **dire**
**dithyrambique** [ditiʀɑ̃bik] *adj* eulogistic
**DIU** *sigle m* (= *dispositif intra-utérin*) IUD
**diurétique** [djyʀetik] *adj, nm* diuretic
**diurne** [djyʀn(ə)] *adj* diurnal, daytime *cpd*
**divagations** [divagɑsjɔ̃] *nfpl* ramblings;
  ravings
**divaguer** [divage] *vi* to ramble; *(malade)* to rave
**divan** [divɑ̃] *nm* divan
**divan-lit** [divɑ̃li] *nm* divan (bed)
**divergence** [divɛʀʒɑ̃s] *nf* divergence; **des ~s**
  **d'opinion au sein de ...** differences of opinion
  within ...
**divergent, e** [divɛʀʒɑ̃, -ɑ̃t] *adj* divergent
**diverger** [divɛʀʒe] *vi* to diverge
**divers, e** [divɛʀ, -ɛʀs(ə)] *adj (varié)* diverse,
  varied; *(différent)* different, various; **(frais) ~**
  *(Comm)* sundries, miscellaneous (expenses);
  **"~"** *(rubrique)* "miscellaneous"
**diversement** [divɛʀsəmɑ̃] *adv* in various *ou*
  diverse ways
**diversification** [divɛʀsifikɑsjɔ̃] *nf*
  diversification
**diversifier** [divɛʀsifje] *vt*, **se diversifier** *vi* to

**d**

diversify

**diversion** [divɛʀsjɔ̃] *nf* diversion; **faire** ~ to create a diversion

**diversité** [divɛʀsite] *nf* diversity, variety

**divertir** [divɛʀtiʀ] *vt* to amuse, entertain; **se divertir** *vi* to amuse *ou* enjoy o.s.

**divertissant, e** [divɛʀtisɑ̃, -ɑ̃t] *adj* entertaining

**divertissement** [divɛʀtismɑ̃] *nm* entertainment; (*Mus*) divertimento, divertissement

**dividende** [dividɑ̃d] *nm* (*Math, Comm*) dividend

**divin, e** [divɛ̃, -in] *adj* divine; (*fig: excellent*) heavenly, divine

**divinateur, -trice** [divinatœʀ, -tʀis] *adj* perspicacious

**divinatoire** [divinatwaʀ] *adj* (*art, science*) divinatory; **baguette** ~ divining rod

**diviniser** [divinize] *vt* to deify

**divinité** [divinite] *nf* divinity

**divisé, e** [divize] *adj* divided

**diviser** [divize] *vt* (*gén, Math*) to divide; (*morceler, subdiviser*) to divide (up), split (up); **se** ~ **en** to divide into; ~ **par** to divide by

**diviseur** [divizœʀ] *nm* (*Math*) divisor

**divisible** [divizibl(ə)] *adj* divisible

**division** [divizjɔ̃] *nf* (*gén*) division; ~ **du travail** (*Écon*) division of labour

**divisionnaire** [divizjɔnɛʀ] *adj*: **commissaire** ~ ≈ chief superintendent (*Brit*), ≈ police chief (*US*)

**divorce** [divɔʀs(ə)] *nm* divorce

**divorcé, e** [divɔʀse] *nm/f* divorcee

**divorcer** [divɔʀse] *vi* to get a divorce, get divorced; ~ **de** *ou* **d'avec qn** to divorce sb

**divulgation** [divylgɑsjɔ̃] *nf* disclosure

**divulguer** [divylge] *vt* to divulge, disclose

**dix** [di, dis, diz] *num* ten

**dix-huit** [dizɥit] *num* eighteen

**dix-huitième** [dizɥitjɛm] *num* eighteenth

**dixième** [dizjɛm] *num* tenth

**dix-neuf** [diznœf] *num* nineteen

**dix-neuvième** [diznœvjɛm] *num* nineteenth

**dix-sept** [disɛt] *num* seventeen

**dix-septième** [disɛtjɛm] *num* seventeenth

**dizaine** [dizɛn] *nf* (10) ten; (*environ 10*): **une** ~ **(de)** about ten, ten or so

**Djakarta** [dʒakaʀta] *n* Djakarta

**Djibouti** [dʒibuti] *n* Djibouti

**dl** *abr* (= *décilitre*) dl

**DM** *abr* (= *Deutschmark*) DM

**dm.** *abr* (= *décimètre*) dm.

**do** [do] *nm* (*note*) C; (*en chantant la gamme*) do(h)

**docile** [dɔsil] *adj* docile

**docilement** [dɔsilmɑ̃] *adv* docilely

**docilité** [dɔsilite] *nf* docility

**dock** [dɔk] *nm* dock; (*hangar, bâtiment*) warehouse

**docker** [dɔkɛʀ] *nm* docker

**docte** [dɔkt(ə)] *adj* (*péj*) learned

**docteur, e** [dɔktœʀ] *nm/f* doctor; ~ **en médecine** doctor of medicine

**doctoral, e, -aux** [dɔktɔʀal, -o] *adj* pompous, bombastic

**doctorat** [dɔktɔʀa] *nm*: ~ **(d'Université)** ≈ doctorate; ~ **d'État** ≈ PhD; ~ **de troisième cycle** ≈ doctorate

**doctoresse** [dɔktɔʀɛs] *nf* lady doctor

**doctrinaire** [dɔktʀinɛʀ] *adj* doctrinaire; (*sentencieux*) pompous, sententious

**doctrinal, e, -aux** [dɔktʀinal, o] *adj* doctrinal

**doctrine** [dɔktʀin] *nf* doctrine

**document** [dɔkymɑ̃] *nm* document

**documentaire** [dɔkymɑ̃tɛʀ] *adj, nm* documentary

**documentaliste** [dɔkymɑ̃talist(ə)] *nm/f* archivist; (*Presse, TV*) researcher

**documentation** [dɔkymɑ̃tɑsjɔ̃] *nf* documentation, literature; (*Presse, TV: service*) research

**documenté, e** [dɔkymɑ̃te] *adj* well-informed, well-documented; well-researched

**documenter** [dɔkymɑ̃te] *vt*: **se** ~ **(sur)** to gather information *ou* material (on *ou* about)

**Dodécanèse** [dɔdekanɛz] *nm* Dodecanese (Islands)

**dodeliner** [dɔdline] *vi*: ~ **de la tête** to nod one's head gently

**dodo** [dɔdo] *nm*: **aller faire** ~ to go to beddy-byes

**dodu, e** [dɔdy] *adj* plump

**dogmatique** [dɔgmatik] *adj* dogmatic

**dogmatisme** [dɔgmatism(ə)] *nm* dogmatism

**dogme** [dɔgm(ə)] *nm* dogma

**dogue** [dɔg] *nm* mastiff

**doigt** [dwa] *nm* finger; **à deux ~s de** within an ace (*Brit*) *ou* an inch of; **un** ~ **de lait/whisky** a drop of milk/whisky; **désigner** *ou* **montrer du** ~ to point at; **au** ~ **et à l'œil** to the letter; **connaître qch sur le bout du** ~ to know sth backwards; **mettre le** ~ **sur la plaie** (*fig*) to find the sensitive spot; ~ **de pied** toe

**doigté** [dwate] *nm* (*Mus*) fingering; (*fig: habileté*) diplomacy, tact

**doigtier** [dwatje] *nm* fingerstall

**dois** *etc* [dwa] *vb voir* **devoir**

**doit** *etc* [dwa] *vb voir* **devoir**

**doive** *etc* [dwav] *vb voir* **devoir**

**doléances** [dɔleɑ̃s] *nfpl* complaints; (*réclamations*) grievances

**dolent, e** [dɔlɑ̃, -ɑ̃t] *adj* doleful, mournful

**dollar** [dɔlaʀ] *nm* dollar

**dolmen** [dɔlmɛn] *nm* dolmen

**DOM** [dɔm] *sigle m ou mpl* = **Département(s) d'outre-mer**

**domaine** [dɔmɛn] *nm* estate, property; (*fig*) domain, field; **tomber dans le** ~ **public** (*livre etc*) to be out of copyright; **dans tous les ~s** in all areas

**domanial, e, -aux** [dɔmanjal, -o] *adj* national, state *cpd*

**dôme** [dom] *nm* dome

**domestication** [dɔmɛstikɑsjɔ̃] *nf* (*voir domestiquer*) domestication; harnessing

**domesticité** [dɔmɛstisite] *nf* (*domestic*) staff

**domestique** [dɔmɛstik] *adj* domestic ▷ *nm/f* servant, domestic

**domestiquer** [dɔmɛstike] *vt* to domesticate; (*vent, marées*) to harness

**domicile** [dɔmisil] *nm* home, place of residence; **à ~** at home; **élire ~ à** to take up residence in; **sans ~ fixe** of no fixed abode; **~ conjugal** marital home; **~ légal** domicile

**domicilié, e** [dɔmisilje] *adj*: **être ~ à** to have one's home in *ou* at

**dominant, e** [dɔminã, -ãt] *adj* dominant; (*plus important*) predominant ▷ *nf* (*caractéristique*) dominant characteristic; (*couleur*) dominant colour

**dominateur, -trice** [dɔminatœʀ, -tʀis] *adj* dominating; (*qui aime à dominer*) domineering

**domination** [dɔminasjɔ̃] *nf* domination

**dominer** [dɔmine] *vt* to dominate; (*passions etc*) to control, master; (*surpasser*) to outclass, surpass; (*surplomber*) to tower above, dominate ▷ *vi* to be in the dominant position; **se dominer** *vi* to control o.s.

**dominicain, e** [dɔminikɛ̃, -ɛn] *adj* Dominican

**dominical, e, -aux** [dɔminikal, -o] *adj* Sunday *cpd*, dominical

**Dominique** [dɔminik] *nf*: **la ~** Dominica

**domino** [dɔmino] *nm* domino; **dominos** *nmpl* (*jeu*) dominoes *sg*

**dommage** [dɔmaʒ] *nm* (*préjudice*) harm, injury; (*dégâts, pertes*) damage *no pl*; **c'est ~ de faire/que** it's a shame *ou* pity to do/that; **quel ~!** what a pity *ou* shame!; **~s corporels** physical injury

**dommages-intérêts** [dɔmaʒ(əz)ɛ̃teʀɛ] *nmpl* damages

**dompter** [dɔ̃te] *vt* to tame

**dompteur, -euse** [dɔ̃tœʀ, -øz] *nm/f* trainer; (*de lion*) lion tamer

**DOM-ROM** [dɔmʀɔm], **DOM-TOM** [dɔmtɔm] *sigle m ou mpl* (= *Département(s) et Régions/Territoire(s) d'outre-mer*) French overseas departments and regions; *see note*

> ⦾ **DOM-TOM, ROM ET COM**
>
> ⦾ There are four "Départements d'outre-mer"
> ⦾ or DOMs: Guadeloupe, Martinique, La
> ⦾ Réunion and French Guyana. They are run
> ⦾ in the same way as metropolitan
> ⦾ "départements" and their inhabitants are
> ⦾ French citizens. In administrative terms
> ⦾ they are also "Régions", and in this regard
> ⦾ are also referred to as "ROM" (Régions
> ⦾ d'outre-mer"). The term "DOM-TOM" is still
> ⦾ commonly used, but the term "Territoire
> ⦾ d'outre-mer" has been superseded by that of
> ⦾ "Collectivité d'outre-mer" (COM). The COMs
> ⦾ include French Polynesia, Wallis-and-
> ⦾ Futuna, New Caledonia and polar
> ⦾ territories. They are independent, but each
> ⦾ is supervised by a representative of the
> ⦾ French government.

**don** [dɔ̃] *nm* (*cadeau*) gift; (*charité*) donation; (*aptitude*) gift, talent; **avoir des ~s pour** to have a gift *ou* talent for; **faire ~ de** to make a gift of; **~ en argent** cash donation

**donateur, -trice** [dɔnatœʀ, -tʀis] *nm/f* donor

**donation** [dɔnasjɔ̃] *nf* donation

**donc** [dɔ̃k] *conj* therefore, so; (*après une digression*) so, then; (*intensif*): **voilà ~ la solution** so there's the solution; **je disais ~ que ...** as I was saying, ...; **venez ~ dîner à la maison** do come for dinner; **allons ~!** come now!; **faites ~** go ahead

**donjon** [dɔ̃ʒɔ̃] *nm* keep

**don Juan** [dɔ̃ʒɥɑ̃] *nm* Don Juan

**donnant, e** [dɔnɑ̃, -ɑ̃t] *adj*: **~, ~** fair's fair

**donne** [dɔn] *nf* (*Cartes*): **il y a mauvaise** *ou* **fausse ~** there's been a misdeal

**donné, e** [dɔne] *adj* (*convenu*) given; (*pas cher*) very cheap ▷ *nf* (*Math, Inform, gén*) datum; **c'est ~ it's a gift; **étant ~ ...** given ...

**données** [dɔne] *nfpl* data

**donner** [dɔne] *vt* to give; (*vieux habits etc*) to give away; (*spectacle*) to put on; (*film*) to show; **~ qch à qn** to give sb sth, give sth to sb; **~ sur** (*fenêtre, chambre*) to look (out) onto; **~ dans** (*piège etc*) to fall into; **faire ~ l'infanterie** (*Mil*) to send in the infantry; **~ l'heure à qn** to tell sb the time; **~ le ton** (*fig*) to set the tone; **~ à penser/entendre que ...** to make one think/give one to understand that ...; **se ~ à fond** (à son travail) to give one's all (to one's work); **se ~ du mal** *ou* **de la peine (pour faire qch)** to go to a lot of trouble (to do sth); **s'en ~ à cœur joie** (*fam*) to have a great time (of it)

**donneur, -euse** [dɔnœʀ, -øz] *nm/f* (*Méd*) donor; (*Cartes*) dealer; **~ de sang** blood donor

🔵 **MOT-CLÉ**

**dont** [dɔ̃] *pron relatif* **1** (*appartenance: objets*) whose, of which; (: *êtres animés*) whose; **la maison dont le toit est rouge** the house the roof of which is red, the house whose roof is red; **l'homme dont je connais la sœur** the man whose sister I know

**2** (*parmi lesquel(le)s*): **deux livres, dont l'un est ...** two books, one of which is ...; **il y avait plusieurs personnes, dont Gabrielle** there were several people, among them Gabrielle; **10 blessés, dont 2 grièvement** 10 injured, 2 of them seriously

**3** (*complément d'adjectif, de verbe*): **le fils dont il est si fier** the son he's so proud of; **ce dont je parle** what I'm talking about; **la façon dont il l'a fait** the way (in which) he did it

**donzelle** [dɔ̃zɛl] *nf* (*péj*) young madam

**dopage** [dɔpaʒ] *nm* doping

**dopant** [dɔpɑ̃] *nm* dope

**doper** [dɔpe] *vt* to dope; **se doper** *vi* to take dope

**doping** [dɔpiŋ] *nm* doping; (*excitant*) dope

**dorade** [dɔʀad] *nf* = **daurade**

**doré, e** [dɔʀe] *adj* golden; (*avec dorure*) gilt, gilded

**dorénavant** [dɔʀenavɑ̃] *adv* from now on, henceforth

**dorer** [dɔʀe] vt (cadre) to gild; **(faire)** ~ (Culin) to brown; (: gâteau) to glaze; **se ~ au soleil** to sunbathe; ~ **la pilule à qn** to sugar the pill for sb

**dorloter** [dɔʀlɔte] vt to pamper, cosset (Brit); **se faire** ~ to be pampered ou cosseted

**dormant, e** [dɔʀmɑ̃, -ɑ̃t] adj: **eau ~e** still water

**dorme**etc [dɔʀm(ə)] vb voir **dormir**

**dormeur, -euse** [dɔʀmœʀ, -øz] nm/f sleeper

**dormir** [dɔʀmiʀ] vi to sleep; (être endormi) to be asleep; ~ **à poings fermés** to sleep very soundly

**dorsal, e, -aux** [dɔʀsal, -o] adj dorsal; voir **rouleau**

**dortoir** [dɔʀtwaʀ] nm dormitory

**dorure** [dɔʀyʀ] nf gilding

**doryphore** [dɔʀifɔʀ] nm Colorado beetle

**dos** [do] nm back; (de livre) spine; **"voir au ~"** "see over"; **robe décolletée dans le ~** low-backed dress; **de ~** from the back, from behind; ~ **à** ~ back to back; **sur le** ~ on one's back; **à ~ de chameau** riding on a camel; **avoir bon** ~ to be a good excuse; **se mettre qn à ~** to turn sb against one

**dosage** [doza3] nm mixture

**dos-d'âne** [dodɑn] nm humpback; **pont en dos-d'âne** humpbacked bridge

**dose** [doz] nf (Méd) dose; **forcer la ~** (fig) to overstep the mark

**doser** [doze] vt to measure out; (mélanger) to mix in the correct proportions; (fig) to expend in the right amounts ou proportions; to strike a balance between

**doseur** [dozœʀ] nm measure; **bouchon ~** measuring cap

**dossard** [dosaʀ] nm number (worn by competitor)

**dossier** [dosje] nm (renseignements, fichier) file; (enveloppe) folder, file; (de chaise) back; (Presse) feature; **le ~ social/monétaire** (fig) the social/financial question; ~ **suspendu** suspension file

**dot** [dɔt] nf dowry

**dotation** [dɔtasjɔ̃] nf block grant; endowment

**doté, e** [dɔte] adj: ~ **de** equipped with

**doter** [dɔte] vt: ~ **qn/qch de** to equip sb/sth with

**douairière** [dwɛʀjɛʀ] nf dowager

**douane** [dwan] nf (poste, bureau) customs pl; (taxes) (customs) duty; **passer la ~** to go through customs; **en ~** (marchandises, entrepôt) bonded

**douanier, -ière** [dwanje, -jɛʀ] adj customs cpd ▷ nm customs officer

**doublage** [dubla3] nm (Ciné) dubbing

**double** [dubl(ə)] adj, adv double ▷ nm (2 fois plus): **le ~ (de)** twice as much (ou many) (as), double the amount (ou number) (of); (autre exemplaire) duplicate, copy; (sosie) double; (Tennis) doubles sg; **voir ~** to see double; **en ~ (exemplaire)** in duplicate; **faire ~ emploi** to be redundant; **à ~ sens** with a double meaning; **à ~ tranchant** two-edged; ~ **carburateur** twin carburettor; **à ~s commandes** dual-control; ~ **messieurs/mixte** men's/mixed doubles sg; ~ **toit** (de tente)

**fly sheet**; ~ **vue** second sight

**doublé, e** [duble] adj (vêtement): ~ **(de)** lined (with)

**double-cliquer** [dubl(ə)klike] vi (Inform) to double-click

**doublement** [dubləmɑ̃] nm doubling; twofold increase ▷ adv doubly; (pour deux raisons) in two ways, on two counts

**doubler** [duble] vt (multiplier par 2) to double; (vêtement) to line; (dépasser) to overtake, pass; (film) to dub; (acteur) to stand in for ▷ vi to double, increase twofold; **se ~ de** to be coupled with; ~ **(la classe)** (Scol) to repeat a year; ~ **un cap** (Navig) to round a cape; (fig) to get over a hurdle

**doublure** [dublyʀ] nf lining; (Ciné) stand-in

**douce** [dus] adj f voir **doux**

**douceâtre** [dusɑtʀ(ə)] adj sickly sweet

**doucement** [dusmɑ̃] adv gently; (à voix basse) softly; (lentement) slowly

**doucereux, -euse** [dusʀø, -øz] adj (péj) sugary

**douceur** [dusœʀ] nf softness; sweetness; mildness; gentleness; **douceurs** nfpl (friandises) sweets (Brit), candy sg (US); **en ~** gently

**douche** [duʃ] nf shower; **douches** nfpl shower room sg; **prendre une ~** to have ou take a shower; ~ **écossaise** (fig): ~ **froide** (fig) let-down

**doucher** [duʃe] vt: ~ **qn** to give sb a shower; (mouiller) to drench sb; (fig) to give sb a telling-off; **se doucher** vi to have ou take a shower

**doudoune** [dudun] nf padded jacket; (fam) boob

**doué, e** [dwe] adj gifted, talented; ~ **de** endowed with; **être ~ pour** to have a gift for

**douille** [duj] nf (Élec) socket; (de projectile) case

**douillet, te** [dujɛ, -et] adj cosy; (péj) soft

**douleur** [dulœʀ] nf pain; (chagrin) grief, distress; **ressentir des ~s** to feel pain; **il a eu la ~ de perdre son père** he suffered the grief of losing his father

**douloureux, -euse** [duluʀø, -øz] adj painful

**doute** [dut] nm doubt; **sans ~** adv no doubt; (probablement) probably; **sans nul** ou **aucun ~** without (a) doubt; **hors de ~** beyond doubt; **nul ~ que** there's no doubt that; **mettre en ~** to call into question; **mettre en ~ que** to question whether

**douter** [dute] vt to doubt; ~ **de** vt (allié) to doubt, have (one's) doubts about; (résultat) to be doubtful of; ~ **que** to doubt whether ou if; **j'en doute** I have my doubts; **se ~ de qch/que** to suspect sth/that; **je m'en doutais** I suspected as much; **il ne se doutait de rien** he didn't suspect a thing

**douteux, -euse** [dutø, -øz] adj (incertain) doubtful; (discutable) dubious, questionable; (péj) dubious-looking

**douve** [duv] nf (de château) moat; (de tonneau) stave

**Douvres** [duvʀ(ə)] n Dover

**doux, douce** [du, dus] adj (lisse, moelleux, pas vif: couleur, non calcaire: eau) soft; (sucré, agréable) sweet; (peu fort: moutarde etc, clément: climat) mild;

(*pas brusque*) gentle; **en douce** (*partir etc*) on the quiet

**douzaine** [duzɛn] *nf* (12) dozen; (*environ* 12): **une ~ (de)** a dozen or so, twelve or so

**douze** [duz] *num* twelve; **les D~** (*membres de la CEE*) the Twelve

**douzième** [duzjɛm] *num* twelfth

**doyen, ne** [dwajɛ̃, -ɛn] *nm/f* (*en âge, ancienneté*) most senior member; (*de faculté*) dean

**DPLG** *sigle* (= *diplômé par le gouvernement*) *extra certificate for architects, engineers etc*

**Dr** *abr* (= *docteur*) Dr

**dr.** *abr* (= *droit(e)*) R, r

**draconien, ne** [drakɔnjɛ̃, -ɛn] *adj* draconian, stringent

**dragage** [draɡaʒ] *nm* dredging

**dragée** [draʒe] *nf* sugared almond; (*Méd*) (sugar-coated) pill

**dragéifié, e** [draʒeifje] *adj* (*Méd*) sugar-coated

**dragon** [draɡɔ̃] *nm* dragon

**drague** [draɡ] *nf* (*filet*) dragnet; (*bateau*) dredger

**draguer** [draɡe] *vt* (*rivière: pour nettoyer*) to dredge; (*: pour trouver qch*) to drag; (*fam*) to try and pick up, chat up (*Brit*) ▷ *vi* (*fam*) to try and pick sb up, chat sb up (*Brit*)

**dragueur** [draɡœr] *nm* (*aussi:* **dragueur de mines**) minesweeper; (*fam*): **quel ~!** he's a great one for picking up girls!

**drain** [drɛ̃] *nm* (*Méd*) drain

**drainage** [drɛnaʒ] *nm* drainage

**drainer** [drɛne] *vt* to drain; (*fig: visiteurs, région*) to drain off

**dramatique** [dramatik] *adj* dramatic; (*tragique*) tragic ▷ *nf* (*TV*) (television) drama

**dramatisation** [dramatizasjɔ̃] *nf* dramatization

**dramatiser** [dramatize] *vt* to dramatize

**dramaturge** [dramatyrʒ(ə)] *nm* dramatist, playwright

**drame** [dram] *nm* (*Théât*) drama; (*catastrophe*) drama, tragedy; **~ familial** family drama

**drap** [dra] *nm* (*de lit*) sheet; (*tissu*) woollen fabric; **~ de plage** beach towel

**drapé** [drape] *nm* (*d'un vêtement*) hang

**drapeau, x** [drapo] *nm* flag; **sous les ~x** with the colours (*Brit*) *ou* colors (*US*), in the army

**draper** [drape] *vt* to drape; (*robe, jupe*) to arrange

**draperies** [drapri] *nfpl* hangings

**drap-housse** [draus] (*pl* **draps-housses**) *nm* fitted sheet

**drapier** [drapje] *nm* (*woollen*) cloth manufacturer; (*marchand*) clothier

**drastique** [drastik] *adj* drastic

**dressage** [drɛsaʒ] *nm* training

**dresser** [drɛse] *vt* (*mettre vertical, monter: tente*) to put up, erect; (*fig: liste, bilan, contrat*) to draw up; (*animal*) to train; **se dresser** *vi* (*falaise, obstacle*) to stand; (*avec grandeur, menace*) to tower (up); (*personne*) to draw o.s. up; **~ l'oreille** to prick up one's ears; **~ la table** to set *ou* lay the table; **~ qn contre qn d'autre** to set sb against sb else; **~ un procès-verbal** *ou* **une contravention à qn**

to book sb

**dresseur, -euse** [drɛsœr, -øz] *nm/f* trainer

**dressoir** [drɛswar] *nm* dresser

**dribbler** [drible] *vt, vi* (*Sport*) to dribble

**drille** [drij] *nm*: **joyeux ~** cheerful sort

**drogue** [drɔɡ] *nf* drug; **la ~** drugs *pl*; **~ dure/douce** hard/soft drugs *pl*

**drogué, e** [drɔɡe] *nm/f* drug addict

**droguer** [drɔɡe] *vt* (*victime*) to drug; (*malade*) to give drugs to; **se droguer** *vi* (*aux stupéfiants*) to take drugs; (*péj: de médicaments*) to dose o.s. up

**droguerie** [drɔɡri] *nf* ≈ hardware shop (*Brit*) *ou* store (*US*)

**droguiste** [drɔɡist(ə)] *nm* ≈ keeper (*ou* owner) of a hardware shop *ou* store

**droit, e** [drwa, drwat] *adj* (*non courbe*) straight; (*vertical*) upright, straight; (*fig: loyal, franc*) upright, straight(forward); (*opposé à gauche*) right, right-hand ▷ *adv* straight ▷ *nm* (*prérogative, Boxe*) right; (*taxe*) duty, tax; (*: d'inscription*) fee; (*lois, branche*): **le ~** law ▷ *nf* (*Pol*) right (wing); (*ligne*) straight line; **~ au but** *ou* **au fait/cœur** straight to the point/heart; **avoir le ~ de** to be allowed to; **avoir ~ à** to be entitled to; **être en ~ de** to have a *ou* the right to; **faire ~ à** to grant, accede to; **être dans son ~** to be within one's rights; **à bon ~** (*justement*) with good reason; **de quel ~?** by what right?; **à qui de ~** to whom it may concern; **à ~e** on the right; (*direction*) (to the) right; **à ~e de** to the right of; **de ~e, sur ~e** on your right; (*Pol*) right-wing; **~ d'auteur** copyright; **avoir ~ de cité (dans)** (*fig*) to belong (to); **~ coutumier** common law; **~ de regard** right of access *ou* inspection; **~ de réponse** right to reply; **~ de visite** (right of) access; **~ de vote** (right to) vote; **~s d'auteur** royalties; **~s de douane** customs duties; **~s de l'homme** human rights; **~s d'inscription** enrolment *ou* registration fees

**droitement** [drwatmɑ̃] *adv* (*agir*) uprightly

**droitier, -ière** [drwatje, -jɛr] *nm/f* right-handed person

**droiture** [drwatyr] *nf* uprightness, straightness

**drôle** [drol] *adj* (*amusant*) funny, amusing; (*bizarre*) funny, peculiar; **un ~ de ...** (*bizarre*) a strange *ou* funny ...; (*intensif*) an incredible ..., a terrific ...

**drôlement** [drolmɑ̃] *adv* funnily; peculiarly; (*très*) terribly, awfully; **il fait ~ froid** it's awfully cold

**drôlerie** [drolri] *nf* funniness; funny thing

**dromadaire** [drɔmadɛr] *nm* dromedary

**dru, e** [dry] *adj* (*cheveux*) thick, bushy; (*pluie*) heavy ▷ *adv* (*pousser*) thickly; (*tomber*) heavily

**drugstore** [drœɡstɔr] *nm* drugstore

**druide** [drɥid] *nm* Druid

**ds** *abr* = **dans**

**DST** *sigle f* (= *Direction de la surveillance du territoire*) *internal security service*, ≈ MI5 (*Brit*)

**DT** *sigle m* (= *diphtérie tétanos*) *vaccine*

**DTCP** *sigle m* (= *diphtérie tétanos coqueluche polio*) *vaccine*

**DTP** *sigle m* (= *diphtérie tétanos polio*) *vaccine*

**DTTAB** *sigle m* (= *diphtérie tétanos typhoïde A et B*) *vaccine*

**du** [dy] *art voir* **de**

**dû, due** [dy] *pp de* **devoir** ▷ *adj* (*somme*) owing, owed; (: *venant à échéance*) due; (*causé par*): **dû à** due to ▷ *nm* due; (*somme*) **dues** *pl*

**dualisme** [dɥalism(ə)] *nm* dualism

**Dubaï, Dubay** [dybaj] *n* Dubai

**dubitatif, -ive** [dybitatif, -iv] *adj* doubtful, dubious

**Dublin** [dyblɛ̃] *n* Dublin

**duc** [dyk] *nm* duke

**duché** [dyʃe] *nm* dukedom, duchy

**duchesse** [dyʃɛs] *nf* duchess

**duel** [dɥɛl] *nm* duel

**duettiste** [dɥetist(ə)] *nm/f* duettist

**duffel-coat** [dœfœlkot] *nm* duffel coat

**dûment** [dymɑ̃] *adv* duly

**dumping** [dœmpiŋ] *nm* dumping

**dune** [dyn] *nf* dune

**Dunkerque** [dœ̃kɛʀk] *n* Dunkirk

**duo** [dɥo] *nm* (*Mus*) duet; (*fig*: *couple*) duo, pair

**dupe** [dyp] *nf* dupe ▷ *adj*: (**ne pas**) **être ~ de** (not) to be taken in by

**duper** [dype] *vt* to dupe, deceive

**duperie** [dypʀi] *nf* deception, dupery

**duplex** [dyplɛks] *nm* (*appartement*) split-level apartment, duplex; (*TV*): **émission en ~** link-up

**duplicata** [dyplikata] *nm* duplicate

**duplicateur** [dyplikatœʀ] *nm* duplicator; **~ à alcool** spirit duplicator

**duplicité** [dyplisite] *nf* duplicity

**duquel** [dykɛl] *prép + pron voir* **lequel**

**dur, e** [dyʀ] *adj* (*pierre, siège, travail, problème*) hard; (*lumière, voix, climat*) harsh; (*sévère*) hard, harsh; (*cruel*) hard(-hearted); (*porte, col*) stiff; (*viande*) tough ▷ *adv* hard ▷ *nf*: **à la ~e** rough; **mener la vie ~e à qn** to give sb a hard time; **~ d'oreille** hard of hearing

**durabilité** [dyʀabilite] *nf* durability

**durable** [dyʀabl(ə)] *adj* lasting

**durablement** [dyʀabləmɑ̃] *adv* for the long term

**durant** [dyʀɑ̃] *prép* (*au cours de*) during; (*pendant*) for; **~ des mois, des mois ~** for months

**durcir** [dyʀsiʀ] *vt, vi*, **se durcir** *vi* to harden

**durcissement** [dyʀsismɑ̃] *nm* hardening

**durée** [dyʀe] *nf* length; (*d'une pile etc*) life; (*déroulement: des opérations etc*) duration; **pour une ~ illimitée** for an unlimited length of time; **de courte ~** (*séjour, répit*) brief, short-term; **de longue ~** (*effet*) long-term; **pile de longue ~** long-life battery

**durement** [dyʀmɑ̃] *adv* harshly

**durent** [dyʀ] *vb voir* **devoir**

**durer** [dyʀe] *vi* to last

**dureté** [dyʀte] *nf* (*voir dur*) hardness; harshness; stiffness; toughness

**durillon** [dyʀijɔ̃] *nm* callus

**durit®** [dyʀit] *nf* (*car radiator*) hose

**DUT** *sigle m* = **Diplôme universitaire de technologie**

**dut** *etc* [dy] *vb voir* **devoir**

**duvet** [dyvɛ] *nm* down; (*sac de couchage en*) ~ down-filled sleeping bag

**duveteux, -euse** [dyvtø, -øz] *adj* downy

**DVD** *sigle m* (= *digital versatile disc*) DVD

**dynamique** [dinamik] *adj* dynamic

**dynamiser** [dinamize] *vt* to pep up, enliven; (*équipe, service*) to inject some dynamism into

**dynamisme** [dinamism(ə)] *nm* dynamism

**dynamite** [dinamit] *nf* dynamite

**dynamiter** [dinamite] *vt* to (blow up with) dynamite

**dynamo** [dinamo] *nf* dynamo

**dynastie** [dinasti] *nf* dynasty

**dysenterie** [disɑ̃tʀi] *nf* dysentery

**dyslexie** [dislɛksi] *nf* dyslexia, word blindness

**dyslexique** [dislɛksik] *adj* dyslexic

**dyspepsie** [dispɛpsi] *nf* dyspepsia

# Ee

**E, e** [ə] *nm inv* E, e ▷ *abr* (= Est) E; **E comme Eugène** E for Edward (*Brit*) *ou* Easy (*US*)

**EAO** *sigle m* (= *enseignement assisté par ordinateur*) CAL (= *computer-aided learning*)

**EAU** *sigle mpl* (= *Émirats arabes unis*) UAE (= *United Arab Emirates*)

**eau, x** [o] *nf* water ▷ *nfpl* waters; **prendre l'~** (*chaussure etc*) to leak, let in water; **prendre les ~x** to take the waters; **faire ~** to leak; **tomber à l'~** (*fig*) to fall through; **à l'~ de rose** slushy, sentimental; **~ bénite** holy water; **~ de Cologne** eau de Cologne; **~ courante** running water; **~ distillée** distilled water; **~ douce** fresh water; **~ de Javel** bleach; **~ lourde** heavy water; **~ minérale** mineral water; **~ oxygénée** hydrogen peroxide; **~ plate** still water; **~ de pluie** rainwater; **~ salée** salt water; **~ de toilette** toilet water; **~x ménagères** dirty water (*from washing up etc*); **~x territoriales** territorial waters; **~x usées** liquid waste

**eau-de-vie** [odvi] (*pl* **eaux-de-vie**) *nf* brandy

**eau-forte** [ofɔʀt(ə)] (*pl* **eaux-fortes**) *nf* etching

**ébahi, e** [ebai] *adj* dumbfounded, flabbergasted

**ébahir** [ebaiʀ] *vt* to astonish, astound

**ébats** [eba] *vb voir* **ébattre** ▷ *nmpl* frolics, gambols

**ébattre** [ebatʀ(ə)]: **s'ébattre** *vi* to frolic

**ébauche** [eboʃ] *nf* (rough) outline, sketch

**ébaucher** [eboʃe] *vt* to sketch out, outline; (*fig*): **~ un sourire/geste** to give a hint of a smile/make a slight gesture; **s'ébaucher** *vi* to take shape

**ébène** [ebɛn] *nf* ebony

**ébéniste** [ebenist(ə)] *nm* cabinetmaker

**ébénisterie** [ebenistʀi] *nf* cabinetmaking; (*bâti*) cabinetwork

**éberlué, e** [ebɛʀlɥe] *adj* astounded, flabbergasted

**éblouir** [ebluiʀ] *vt* to dazzle

**éblouissant, e** [ebluisɑ̃, -ɑ̃t] *adj* dazzling

**éblouissement** [ebluismɑ̃] *nm* dazzle; (*faiblesse*) dizzy turn

**ébonite** [ebɔnit] *nf* vulcanite

**éborgner** [ebɔʀɲe] *vt*: **~ qn** to blind sb in one eye

**éboueur** [ebwœʀ] *nm* dustman (*Brit*), garbage man (*US*)

**ébouillanter** [ebujɑ̃te] *vt* to scald; (*Culin*) to blanch; **s'ébouillanter** *vi* to scald o.s

**éboulement** [ebulmɑ̃] *nm* falling rocks *pl*, rock fall; (*amas*) heap of boulders *etc*

**ébouler** [ebule]: **s'ébouler** *vi* to crumble, collapse

**éboulis** [ebuli] *nmpl* fallen rocks

**ébouriffé, e** [ebuʀife] *adj* tousled, ruffled

**ébouriffer** [ebuʀife] *vt* to tousle, ruffle

**ébranlement** [ebʀɑ̃lmɑ̃] *nm* shaking

**ébranler** [ebʀɑ̃le] *vt* to shake; (*rendre instable: mur, santé*) to weaken; **s'ébranler** *vi* (*partir*) to move off

**ébrécher** [ebʀeʃe] *vt* to chip

**ébriété** [ebʀijete] *nf*: **en état d'~** in a state of intoxication

**ébrouer** [ebʀue]: **s'ébrouer** *vi* (*souffler*) to snort; (*s'agiter*) to shake o.s.

**ébruiter** [ebʀɥite] *vt*, **s'ébruiter** *vi* to spread

**ébullition** [ebylisjɔ̃] *nf* boiling point; **en ~** boiling; (*fig*) in an uproar

**écaille** [ekaj] *nf* (*de poisson*) scale; (*de coquillage*) shell; (*matière*) tortoiseshell; (*de roc etc*) flake

**écaillé, e** [ekaje] *adj* (*peinture*) flaking

**écailler** [ekaje] *vt* (*poisson*) to scale; (*huître*) to open; **s'écailler** *vi* to flake *ou* peel (off)

**écarlate** [ekaʀlat] *adj* scarlet

**écarquiller** [ekaʀkije] *vt*: **~ les yeux** to stare wide-eyed

**écart** [ekaʀ] *nm* gap; (*embardée*) swerve; (*saut*) sideways leap; (*fig*) departure, deviation; **à l'~** *adv* out of the way; **à l'~ de** *prép* away from; (*fig*) out of; **faire le grand ~** (*Danse, Gymnastique*) to do the splits; **~ de conduite** misdemeanour

**écarté, e** [ekaʀte] *adj* (*lieu*) out-of-the-way, remote; (*ouvert*): **les jambes ~es** legs apart; **les bras ~s** arms outstretched

**écarteler** [ekaʀtəle] *vt* to quarter; (*fig*) to tear

**écartement** [ekaʀtəmɑ̃] *nm* space, gap; (*Rail*) gauge

**écarter** [ekaʀte] *vt* (*séparer*) to move apart, separate; (*éloigner*) to push back, move away; (*ouvrir: bras, jambes*) to spread, open; (*: rideau*) to draw (back); (*éliminer: candidat, possibilité*) to dismiss; (*Cartes*) to discard; **s'écarter** *vi* to part; (*personne*) to move away; **s'~ de** to wander from

**ecchymose** [ekimoz] *nf* bruise
**ecclésiastique** [eklezjastik] *adj* ecclesiastical
▷ *nm* ecclesiastic
**écervelé, e** [esɛʀvəle] *adj* scatterbrained, featherbrained
**ECG** *sigle m* (= *électrocardiogramme*) ECG
**échafaud** [eʃafo] *nm* scaffold
**échafaudage** [eʃafodaʒ] *nm* scaffolding; (*fig*) heap, pile
**échafauder** [eʃafode] *vt* (*plan*) to construct
**échalas** [eʃala] *nm* stake, pole; (*personne*) beanpole
**échalote** [eʃalɔt] *nf* shallot
**échancré, e** [eʃɑ̃kʀe] *adj* (*robe, corsage*) low-necked; (*côte*) indented
**échancrure** [eʃɑ̃kʀyʀ] *nf* (*de robe*) scoop neckline; (*de côte, arête rocheuse*) indentation
**échange** [eʃɑ̃ʒ] *nm* exchange; **en ~** in exchange; **en ~ de** in exchange *ou* return for; **libre ~** free trade; **~ de lettres/politesses/vues** exchange of letters/civilities/views; **~s commerciaux** trade; **~s culturels** cultural exchanges
**échangeable** [eʃɑ̃ʒabl(ə)] *adj* exchangeable
**échanger** [eʃɑ̃ʒe] *vt*: **~ qch (contre)** to exchange sth (for)
**échangeur** [eʃɑ̃ʒœʀ] *nm* (*Auto*) interchange
**échantillon** [eʃɑ̃tijɔ̃] *nm* sample
**échantillonnage** [eʃɑ̃tijɔnaʒ] *nm* selection of samples
**échappatoire** [eʃapatwaʀ] *nf* way out
**échappée** [eʃape] *nf* (*vue*) vista; (*Cyclisme*) breakaway
**échappement** [eʃapmɑ̃] *nm* (*Auto*) exhaust; **~ libre** cutout
**échapper** [eʃape]: **~ à** *vt* (*gardien*) to escape (from); (*punition, péril*) to escape; **~ à qn** (*détail, sens*) to escape sb; (*objet qu'on tient: aussi*: **échapper des mains de qn**) to slip out of sb's hands; **laisser ~** to let fall; (*cri etc*) to let out; **s'échapper** *vi* to escape; **l'~ belle** to have a narrow escape
**écharde** [eʃaʀd(ə)] *nf* splinter (of wood)
**écharpe** [eʃaʀp(ə)] *nf* scarf; (*de maire*) sash; (*Méd*) sling; **prendre en ~** (*dans une collision*) to hit sideways on
**écharper** [eʃaʀpe] *vt* to tear to pieces
**échasse** [eʃas] *nf* stilt
**échassier** [eʃasje] *nm* wader
**échauder** [eʃode] *vt*: **se faire ~** (*fig*) to get one's fingers burnt
**échauffement** [eʃofmɑ̃] *nm* overheating; (*Sport*) warm-up
**échauffer** [eʃofe] *vt* (*métal, moteur*) to overheat; (*fig: exciter*) to fire, excite; **s'échauffer** *vi* (*Sport*) to warm up; (*discussion*) to become heated
**échauffourée** [eʃofuʀe] *nf* clash, brawl; (*Mil*) skirmish
**échéance** [eʃeɑ̃s] *nf* (*d'un paiement: date*) settlement date; (: *somme due*) financial commitment(s); (*fig*) deadline; **à brève/longue ~** *adj* short-/long-term ▷ *adv* in the short/long term

**échéancier** [eʃeɑ̃sje] *nm* schedule
**échéant** [eʃeɑ̃]: **le cas ~** *adv* if the case arises
**échec** [eʃɛk] *nm* failure; (*Échecs*): **~ et mat/au roi** checkmate/check; **échecs** *nmpl* (*jeu*) chess *sg*; **mettre en ~** to put in check; **tenir en ~** to hold in check; **faire ~ à** to foil, thwart
**échelle** [eʃɛl] *nf* ladder; (*fig, d'une carte*) scale; **à l'~ de** on the scale of; **sur une grande/petite ~** on a large/small scale; **faire la courte ~ à qn** to give sb a leg up; **~ de corde** rope ladder
**échelon** [eʃlɔ̃] *nm* (*d'échelle*) rung; (*Admin*) grade
**échelonner** [eʃlɔne] *vt* to space out, spread out; (**versement**) **échelonné** (*payment*) by instalments
**écheveau, x** [eʃvo] *nm* skein, hank
**échevelé, e** [eʃəvle] *adj* tousled, dishevelled; (*fig*) wild, frenzied
**échine** [eʃin] *nf* backbone, spine
**échiner** [eʃine]: **s'échiner** *vi* (*se fatiguer*) to work o.s. to the bone
**échiquier** [eʃikje] *nm* chessboard
**écho** [eko] *nm* echo; **échos** *nmpl* (*potins*) gossip *sg*, rumours; (*Presse: rubrique*) "news in brief"; **rester sans ~** (*suggestion etc*) to come to nothing; **se faire l'~ de** to repeat, spread about
**échographie** [ekɔgʀafi] *nf* ultrasound (scan)
**échoir** [eʃwaʀ] *vi* (*dette*) to fall due; (*délais*) to expire; **~ à** *vt* to fall to
**échoppe** [eʃɔp] *nf* stall, booth
**échouer** [eʃwe] *vi* to fail; (*débris etc: sur la plage*) to be washed up; (*aboutir: personne dans un café etc*) to arrive ▷ *vt* (*bateau*) to ground; **s'échouer** *vi* to run aground
**échu, e** [eʃy] *pp de* **échoir** ▷ *adj* due, mature
**échut** *etc* [eʃy] *vb voir* **échoir**
**éclabousser** [eklabuse] *vt* to splash; (*fig*) to tarnish
**éclaboussure** [eklabusyʀ] *nf* splash; (*fig*) stain
**éclair** [eklɛʀ] *nm* (*d'orage*) flash of lightning, lightning *no pl*; (*Photo: de flash*) flash; (*fig*) flash, spark; (*gâteau*) éclair
**éclairage** [eklɛʀaʒ] *nm* lighting
**éclairagiste** [eklɛʀaʒist(ə)] *nm/f* lighting engineer
**éclaircie** [eklɛʀsi] *nf* bright *ou* sunny interval
**éclaircir** [eklɛʀsiʀ] *vt* to lighten; (*fig*) to clear up, clarify; (*Culin*) to thin (down); **s'éclaircir** *vi* (*ciel*) to brighten up, clear; (*cheveux*) to go thin; (*situation etc*) to become clearer; **s'~ la voix** to clear one's throat
**éclaircissement** [eklɛʀsismɑ̃] *nm* clearing up, clarification
**éclairer** [eklɛʀe] *vt* (*lieu*) to light (up); (*personne: avec une lampe de poche etc*) to light the way for; (*fig: instruire*) to enlighten; (: *rendre compréhensible*) to shed light on ▷ *vi*: **~ mal/bien** to give a poor/good light; **s'éclairer** *vi* (*phare, rue*) to light up; (*situation etc*) to become clearer; **s'~ à la bougie/l'électricité** to use candlelight/have electric lighting
**éclaireur, -euse** [eklɛʀœʀ, -øz] *nm/f* (*scout*) (boy) scout/(girl) guide ▷ *nm* (*Mil*) scout; **partir en ~**

to go off to reconnoitre

**éclat** [ekla] *nm* (*de bombe, de verre*) fragment; (*du soleil, d'une couleur etc*) brightness, brilliance; (*d'une cérémonie*) splendour; (*scandale*): **faire un ~** to cause a commotion; **action d'~** outstanding action; **voler en ~s** to shatter; **des ~s de verre** broken glass; flying glass; **~ de rire** burst *ou* roar of laughter; **~ de voix** shout

**éclatant, e** [eklatã, -ãt] *adj* brilliant, bright; (*succès*) resounding; (*revanche*) devastating

**éclater** [eklate] *vi* (*pneu*) to burst; (*bombe*) to explode; (*guerre, épidémie*) to break out; (*groupe, parti*) to break up; **~ de rire/en sanglots** to burst out laughing/sobbing

**éclectique** [eklɛktik] *adj* eclectic

**éclipse** [eklips(ə)] *nf* eclipse

**éclipser** [eklipse] *vt* to eclipse; **s'éclipser** *vi* to slip away

**éclopé, e** [eklope] *adj* lame

**éclore** [eklɔʀ] *vi* (*œuf*) to hatch; (*fleur*) to open (out)

**éclosion** [eklozjɔ̃] *nf* blossoming

**écluse** [eklyz] *nf* lock

**éclusier** [eklyzje] *nm* lock keeper

**éco-** [eko] *préfixe* eco-

**écœurant, e** [ekœʀɑ̃, -ãt] *adj* sickening; (*gâteau etc*) sickly

**écœurement** [ekœʀmɑ̃] *nm* disgust

**écœurer** [ekœʀe] *vt*: **~ qn** to make sb feel sick; (*fig: démoraliser*) to disgust sb

**école** [ekɔl] *nf* school; **aller à l'~** to go to school; **faire ~** to collect a following; **les grandes ~s** *prestige university-level colleges with competitive entrance examinations*; **~ maternelle** nursery school; *see note*; **~ primaire** primary (*Brit*) *ou* grade (*US*) school; **~ secondaire** secondary (*Brit*) *ou* high (*US*) school; **~ privée/publique/élémentaire** private/state/elementary school; **~ de dessin/danse/musique** art/dancing/music school; **~ hôtelière** catering college; **~ normale (d'instituteurs) (ENI)** *primary school teachers' training college*; **~ normale supérieure (ENS)** *grande école for training secondary school teachers*; **~ de secrétariat** secretarial college

○ **ÉCOLE MATERNELLE**
○
○ Nursery school (kindergarten) (*l'école*
○ *maternelle*) is publicly funded in France and,
○ though not compulsory, is attended by most
○ children between the ages of three and six.
○ Statutory education begins with primary
○ (grade) school (*l'école primaire*) and is attended
○ by children between the ages of six and 10 or
○ 11.

**écolier, -ière** [ekɔlje, -jɛʀ] *nm/f* schoolboy/girl

**écolo** [ekɔlo] *nm/f* (*fam*) ecologist ▷ *adj* ecological

**écologie** [ekɔlɔʒi] *nf* ecology; (*sujet scolaire*) environmental studies *pl*

**écologique** [ekɔlɔʒik] *adj* ecological; environmental

**écologiste** [ekɔlɔʒist(ə)] *nm/f* ecologist; environmentalist

**éconduire** [ekɔ̃dɥiʀ] *vt* to dismiss

**économat** [ekɔnɔma] *nm* (*fonction*) bursarship (*Brit*), treasurership (*US*); (*bureau*) bursar's office (*Brit*), treasury (*US*)

**économe** [ekɔnɔm] *adj* thrifty ▷ *nm/f* (*de lycée etc*) bursar (*Brit*), treasurer (*US*)

**économétrie** [ekɔnɔmetʀi] *nf* econometrics *sg*

**économie** [ekɔnɔmi] *nf* (*vertu*) economy, thrift; (*gain: d'argent, de temps etc*) saving; (*science*) economics *sg*; (*situation économique*) economy; **économies** *nfpl* (*pécule*) savings; **faire des ~s** to save up; **une ~ de temps/d'argent** a saving in time/of money; **~ dirigée** planned economy; **~ de marché** market economy

**économique** [ekɔnɔmik] *adj* (*avantageux*) economical; (*Écon*) economic

**économiquement** [ekɔnɔmikmɑ̃] *adv* economically; **les ~ faibles** (*Admin*) the low-paid, people on low incomes

**économiser** [ekɔnɔmize] *vt, vi* to save

**économiseur** [ekɔnɔmizœʀ] *nm*: **~ d'écran** (*Inform*) screen saver

**économiste** [ekɔnɔmist(ə)] *nm/f* economist

**écoper** [ekɔpe] *vi* to bale out; (*fig*) to cop it; **~ (de)** *vt* to get

**écorce** [ekɔʀs(ə)] *nf* bark; (*de fruit*) peel

**écorcer** [ekɔʀse] *vt* to bark

**écorché, e** [ekɔʀʃe] *adj*: **~ vif** flayed alive ▷ *nm* cut-away drawing

**écorcher** [ekɔʀʃe] *vt* (*animal*) to skin; (*égratigner*) to graze; **~ une langue** to speak a language brokenly; **s'~ le genou** *etc* to scrape *ou* graze one's knee *etc*

**écorchure** [ekɔʀʃyʀ] *nf* graze

**écorner** [ekɔʀne] *vt* (*taureau*) to dehorn; (*livre*) to make dog-eared

**écossais, e** [ekɔse, -ez] *adj* Scottish, Scots; (*whisky, confiture*) Scotch; (*écharpe, tissu*) tartan ▷ *nm* (*Ling*) Scots; (: *gaélique*) Gaelic; (*tissu*) tartan (cloth) ▷ *nm/f*: **Écossais, e** Scot, Scotsman/woman; **les É~** the Scots

**Écosse** [ekɔs] *nf*: **l'~** Scotland

**écosser** [ekɔse] *vt* to shell

**écosystème** [ekɔsistɛm] *nm* ecosystem

**écot** [eko] *nm*: **payer son ~** to pay one's share

**écoulement** [ekulmɑ̃] *nm* (*de faux billets*) circulation; (*de stock*) selling

**écouler** [ekule] *vt* to dispose of; **s'écouler** *vi* (*eau*) to flow (out); (*foule*) to drift away; (*jours, temps*) to pass (by)

**écourter** [ekuʀte] *vt* to curtail, cut short

**écoute** [ekut] *nf* (*Navig: cordage*) sheet; (*Radio, TV*): **temps d'~** (listening *ou* viewing) time; **heure de grande ~** peak listening *ou* viewing time; **prendre l'~** to tune in; **rester à l'~ (de)** to stay tuned in (to); **~s téléphoniques** phone tapping *sg*

**écouter** [ekute] *vt* to listen to

**écouteur** [ekutœʀ] *nm* (*Tél*) (additional)

environmental

**e**

141

earpiece; **écouteurs** nmpl (Radio) headphones, headset sg

**écoutille** [ekutij] nf hatch

**écr.** abr = **écrire**

**écrabouiller** [ekʀabuje] vt to squash, crush

**écran** [ekʀɑ̃] nm screen; (Inform) screen, VDU; ~ **de fumée/d'eau** curtain of smoke/water; **porter à l'~** (Ciné) to adapt for the screen; **le petit** ~ television, the small screen

**écrasant, e** [ekʀɑzɑ̃, -ɑ̃t] adj overwhelming

**écraser** [ekʀɑze] vt to crush; (piéton) to run over; (Inform) to overwrite; **se faire** ~ to be run over; **écrase(-toi)!** shut up!; **s'~ (au sol)** to crash; **s'~ contre** to crash into

**écrémé, e** [ekʀeme] adj (lait) skimmed

**écrémer** [ekʀeme] vt to skim

**écrevisse** [ekʀəvis] nf crayfish inv

**écrier** [ekʀije]: **s'écrier** vi to exclaim

**écrin** [ekʀɛ̃] nm case, box

**écrire** [ekʀiʀ] vt, vi to write ▷ vi: **ça s'écrit comment?** how is it spelt?; ~ **à qn que** to write and tell sb that; **s'écrire** vi to write to one another

**écrit, e** [ekʀi, -it] pp de **écrire** ▷ adj: **bien/mal** ~ well/badly written ▷ nm document; (examen) written paper; **par** ~ in writing

**écriteau, x** [ekʀito] nm notice, sign

**écritoire** [ekʀitwaʀ] nf writing case

**écriture** [ekʀityʀ] nf writing; (Comm) entry; **écritures** nfpl (Comm) accounts, books; **l'É~ (sainte), les É~s** the Scriptures

**écrivain** [ekʀivɛ̃] nm writer

**écrivais** etc [ekʀive] vb voir **écrire**

**écrou** [ekʀu] nm nut

**écrouer** [ekʀue] vt to imprison; (provisoirement) to remand in custody

**écroulé, e** [ekʀule] adj (de fatigue) exhausted; (par un malheur) overwhelmed; ~ **(de rire)** in stitches

**écroulement** [ekʀulmɑ̃] nm collapse

**écrouler** [ekʀule]: **s'écrouler** vi to collapse

**écru, e** [ekʀy] adj (toile) raw, unbleached; (couleur) off-white, écru

**écu** [eky] nm (bouclier) shield; (monnaie: ancienne) crown; (: de la CEE) ecu

**écueil** [ekœj] nm reef; (fig) pitfall; stumbling block

**écuelle** [ekɥɛl] nf bowl

**éculé, e** [ekyle] adj (chaussure) down-at-heel; (fig: péj) hackneyed

**écume** [ekym] nf foam; (Culin) scum; ~ **de mer** meerschaum

**écumer** [ekyme] vt (Culin) to skim; (fig) to plunder ▷ vi (mer) to foam; (fig) to boil with rage

**écumoire** [ekymwaʀ] nf skimmer

**écureuil** [ekyʀœj] nm squirrel

**écurie** [ekyʀi] nf stable

**écusson** [ekysɔ̃] nm badge

**écuyer, -ère** [ekɥije, -ɛʀ] nm/f rider

**eczéma** [ɛgzema] nm eczema

**éd.** abr = **édition**

**édam** [edam] nm (fromage) edam

**edelweiss** [edɛlvajs] nm inv edelweiss

**éden** [edɛn] nm Eden

**édenté, e** [edɑ̃te] adj toothless

**EDF** sigle f (= Électricité de France) national electricity company

**édifiant, e** [edifjɑ̃, -ɑ̃t] adj edifying

**édification** [edifikɑsjɔ̃] nf (d'un bâtiment) building, erection

**édifice** [edifis] nm building, edifice

**édifier** [edifje] vt to build, erect; (fig) to edify

**édiles** [edil] nmpl city fathers

**Édimbourg** [edɛ̃buʀ] n Edinburgh

**édit** [edi] nm edict

**édit.** abr = **éditeur**

**éditer** [edite] vt (publier) to publish; (: disque) to produce; (préparer: texte, Inform) to edit

**éditeur, -trice** [editœʀ, -tʀis] nm/f publisher; editor; ~ **de textes** (Inform) text editor

**édition** [edisjɔ̃] nf editing no pl; (série d'exemplaires) edition; (industrie du livre): l'~ publishing; ~ **sur écran** (Inform) screen editing

**édito** [edito] nm (fam: éditorial) editorial, leader

**éditorial, -aux** [editɔʀjal, -o] nm editorial, leader

**éditorialiste** [editɔʀjalist(ə)] nm/f editorial ou leader writer

**édredon** [edʀədɔ̃] nm eiderdown, comforter (US)

**éducateur, -trice** [edykatœʀ, -tʀis] nm/f teacher; ~ **spécialisé** specialist teacher

**éducatif, -ive** [edykatif, -iv] adj educational

**éducation** [edykɑsjɔ̃] nf education; (familiale) upbringing; (manières) (good) manners pl; **bonne/mauvaise** ~ good/bad upbringing; **sans** ~ bad-mannered, ill-bred; **l'É~ (nationale)** ≈ the Department for Education; ~ **permanente** continuing education; ~ **physique** physical education

**édulcorant** [edylkɔʀɑ̃] nm sweetener

**édulcorer** [edylkɔʀe] vt to sweeten; (fig) to tone down

**éduquer** [edyke] vt to educate; (élever) to bring up; (faculté) to train; **bien/mal éduqué** well/ badly brought up

**EEG** sigle m (= électroencéphalogramme) EEG

**effacé, e** [efase] adj (fig) retiring, unassuming

**effacer** [efase] vt to erase, rub out; (bande magnétique) to erase; (Inform: fichier, fiche) to delete; **s'effacer** vi (inscription etc) to wear off; (pour laisser passer) to step aside; ~ **le ventre** to pull one's stomach in

**effarant, e** [efaʀɑ̃, -ɑ̃t] adj alarming

**effaré, e** [efaʀe] adj alarmed

**effarement** [efaʀmɑ̃] nm alarm

**effarer** [efaʀe] vt to alarm

**effarouchement** [efaʀuʃmɑ̃] nm alarm

**effaroucher** [efaʀuʃe] vt to frighten ou scare away; (personne) to alarm

**effectif, -ive** [efɛktif, -iv] adj real; effective ▷ nm (Mil) strength; (Scol) total number of pupils, size; ~**s** numbers, strength sg; (Comm) manpower sg; **réduire l'~ de** to downsize

**effectivement** [efɛktivmɑ̃] adv effectively;

(*réellement*) actually, really; (*en effet*) indeed

**effectuer** [efɛktɥe] *vt* (*opération, mission*) to carry out; (*déplacement, trajet*) to make, complete; (*mouvement*) to execute, make; **s'effectuer** *vi* to be carried out

**efféminé, e** [efemine] *adj* effeminate

**effervescence** [efɛʀvesɑ̃s] *nf* (*fig*): **en ~** in a turmoil

**effervescent, e** [efɛʀvesɑ̃, -ɑ̃t] *adj* (*cachet, boisson*) effervescent; (*fig*) agitated, in a turmoil

**effet** [efɛ] *nm* (*résultat, artifice*) effect; (*impression*) impression; (*Comm*) bill; (*Jur: d'une loi, d'un jugement*): **avec ~ rétroactif** applied retrospectively; **effets** *nmpl* (*vêtements etc*) things; **~ de style/couleur/lumière** stylistic/colour/lighting effect; **~s de voix** dramatic effects with one's voice; **faire de l'~** (*médicament, menace*) to have an effect, be effective; **sous l'~ de** under the effect of; **donner de l'~ à une balle** (*Tennis*) to put some spin on a ball; **à cet ~** to that end; **en ~** *adv* indeed; **~ (de commerce)** bill of exchange; **~ de serre** greenhouse effect; **~s spéciaux** (*Ciné*) special effects

**effeuiller** [efœje] *vt* to remove the leaves (*ou* petals) from

**efficace** [efikas] *adj* (*personne*) efficient; (*action, médicament*) effective

**efficacité** [efikasite] *nf* efficiency; effectiveness

**effigie** [efiʒi] *nf* effigy; **brûler qn en ~** to burn an effigy of sb

**effilé, e** [efile] *adj* slender; (*pointe*) sharp; (*carrosserie*) streamlined

**effiler** [efile] *vt* (*cheveux*) to thin (out); (*tissu*) to fray

**effilocher** [efilɔʃe] : **s'effilocher** *vi* to fray

**efflanqué, e** [eflɑ̃ke] *adj* emaciated

**effleurement** [eflœʀmɑ̃] *nm*: **touche à ~** touch-sensitive control *ou* key

**effleurer** [eflœʀe] *vt* to brush (against); (*sujet*) to touch upon; (*idée, pensée*): **~ qn** to cross sb's mind

**effluves** [eflyv] *nmpl* exhalation(s)

**effondré, e** [efɔ̃dʀe] *adj* (*abattu: par un malheur, échec*) overwhelmed

**effondrement** [efɔ̃dʀəmɑ̃] *nm* collapse

**effondrer** [efɔ̃dʀe] : **s'effondrer** *vi* to collapse

**efforcer** [efɔʀse] : **s'efforcer de** *vt*: **s' ~ de faire** to try hard to do

**effort** [efɔʀ] *nm* effort; **faire un ~** to make an effort; **faire tous ses ~s** to try one's hardest; **faire l'~ de ...** to make the effort to ...; **sans ~** *adj* effortless ▷ *adv* effortlessly; **~ de mémoire** attempt to remember; **~ de volonté** effort of will

**effraction** [efʀaksjɔ̃] *nf* breaking-in; **s'introduire par ~ dans** to break into

**effrangé, e** [efʀɑ̃ʒe] *adj* fringed; (*effiloché*) frayed

**effrayant, e** [efʀɛjɑ̃, -ɑ̃t] *adj* frightening, fearsome; (*sens affaibli*) dreadful

**effrayer** [efʀeje] *vt* to frighten, scare; (*rebuter*) to put off; **s'effrayer (de)** *vi* to be frightened *ou* scared (by)

**effréné, e** [efʀene] *adj* wild

**effritement** [efʀitmɑ̃] *nm* crumbling; erosion; slackening off

**effriter** [efʀite] : **s'effriter** *vi* to crumble; (*monnaie*) to be eroded; (*valeurs*) to slacken off

**effroi** [efʀwa] *nm* terror, dread *no pl*

**effronté, e** [efʀɔ̃te] *adj* insolent

**effrontément** [efʀɔ̃temɑ̃] *adv* insolently

**effronterie** [efʀɔ̃tʀi] *nf* insolence

**effroyable** [efʀwajabl(ə)] *adj* horrifying, appalling

**effusion** [efyzjɔ̃] *nf* effusion; **sans ~ de sang** without bloodshed

**égailler** [egaje] : **s'égailler** *vi* to scatter, disperse

**égal, e, -aux** [egal, -o] *adj* (*identique, ayant les mêmes droits*) equal; (*plan: surface*) even, level; (*constant: vitesse*) steady; (*équitable*) even ▷ *nm/f* equal; **être ~ à** (*prix, nombre*) to be equal to; **ça m'est ~** it's all the same to me, it doesn't matter to me, I don't mind; **c'est ~, ...** all the same, ...; **sans ~** matchless, unequalled; **à l'~ de** (*comme*) just like; **d'~ à ~** as equals

**également** [egalmɑ̃] *adv* equally; evenly; steadily; (*aussi*) too, as well

**égaler** [egale] *vt* to equal

**égalisateur, -trice** [egalizatœʀ, -tʀis] *adj* (*Sport*): **but ~** equalizing goal, equalizer

**égalisation** [egalizasjɔ̃] *nf* (*Sport*) equalization

**égaliser** [egalize] *vt* (*sol, salaires*) to level (out); (*chances*) to equalize ▷ *vi* (*Sport*) to equalize

**égalitaire** [egalitɛʀ] *adj* egalitarian

**égalitarisme** [egalitaʀism(ə)] *nm* egalitarianism

**égalité** [egalite] *nf* equality; evenness; steadiness; (*Math*) identity; **être à ~ (de points)** to be level; **~ de droits** equality of rights; **~ d'humeur** evenness of temper

**égard** [egaʀ] *nm*: **~s** *nmpl* consideration *sg*; **à cet ~** in this respect; **à certains ~s/tous ~s** in certain respects/all respects; **eu ~ à** in view of; **par ~ pour** out of consideration for; **sans ~ pour** without regard for; **à l'~ de** *prép* towards; (*en ce qui concerne*) concerning, as regards

**égaré, e** [egaʀe] *adj* lost

**égarement** [egaʀmɑ̃] *nm* distraction; aberration

**égarer** [egaʀe] *vt* (*objet*) to mislay; (*moralement*) to lead astray; **s'égarer** *vi* to get lost, lose one's way; (*objet*) to go astray; (*fig: dans une discussion*) to wander

**égayer** [egeje] *vt* (*personne*) to amuse; (: *remonter*) to cheer up; (*récit, endroit*) to brighten up, liven up

**Égée** [eʒe] *adj*: **la mer ~** the Aegean (Sea)

**égéen, ne** [eʒeɛ̃, -ɛn] *adj* Aegean

**égérie** [eʒeʀi] *nf*: **l'~ de qn/qch** the brains behind sb/sth

**égide** [eʒid] *nf*: **sous l'~ de** under the aegis of

**églantier** [eglɑ̃tje] *nm* wild *ou* dog rose(-bush)

**églantine** [eglɑ̃tin] *nf* wild *ou* dog rose

**églefin** [egləfɛ̃] *nm* haddock

**église** [egliz] *nf* church
**égocentrique** [egɔsɑ̃tʀik] *adj* egocentric, self-centred
**égocentrisme** [egɔsɑ̃tʀism(ə)] *nm* egocentricity
**égoïne** [egɔin] *nf* handsaw
**égoïsme** [egɔism(ə)] *nm* selfishness, egoism
**égoïste** [egɔist(ə)] *adj* selfish, egoistic ▷ *nm/f* egoist
**égoïstement** [egɔistəmɑ̃] *adv* selfishly
**égorger** [egɔʀʒe] *vt* to cut the throat of
**égosiller** [egozije]: **s'égosiller** *vi* to shout o.s. hoarse
**égotisme** [egɔtism(ə)] *nm* egotism, egoism
**égout** [egu] *nm* sewer; **eaux d'~** sewage
**égoutier** [egutje] *nm* sewer worker
**égoutter** [egute] *vt* (*linge*) to wring out; (*vaisselle, fromage*) to drain ▷ *vi*, **s'égoutter** *vi* to drip
**égouttoir** [egutwaʀ] *nm* draining board; (*mobile*) draining rack
**égratigner** [egʀatiɲe] *vt* to scratch; **s'égratigner** *vi* to scratch o.s.
**égratignure** [egʀatiɲyʀ] *nf* scratch
**égrener** [egʀəne] *vt*: ~ **une grappe**, ~ **des raisins** to pick grapes off a bunch; **s'égrener** *vi* (*fig: heures etc*) to pass by; (: *notes*) to chime out
**égrillard, e** [egʀijaʀ, -aʀd(ə)] *adj* ribald, bawdy
**Égypte** [eʒipt] *nf*: **l'~** Egypt
**égyptien, ne** [eʒipsjɛ̃, -ɛn] *adj* Egyptian ▷ *nm/f*: **Égyptien, ne** Egyptian
**égyptologue** [eʒiptɔlɔg] *nm/f* Egyptologist
**eh** [e] *excl* hey!; **eh bien** well
**éhonté, e** [eɔte] *adj* shameless, brazen (*Brit*)
**éjaculation** [eʒakylasjɔ̃] *nf* ejaculation
**éjaculer** [eʒakyle] *vi* to ejaculate
**éjectable** [eʒɛktabl(ə)] *adj*: **siège** ~ ejector seat
**éjecter** [eʒɛkte] *vt* (*Tech*) to eject; (*fam*) to kick *ou* chuck out
**éjection** [eʒɛksjɔ̃] *nf* ejection
**élaboration** [elabɔʀasjɔ̃] *nf* elaboration
**élaboré, e** [elabɔʀe] *adj* (*complexe*) elaborate
**élaborer** [elabɔʀe] *vt* to elaborate; (*projet, stratégie*) to work out; (*rapport*) to draft
**élagage** [elagaʒ] *nm* pruning
**élaguer** [elage] *vt* to prune
**élan** [elɑ̃] *nm* (*Zool*) elk, moose; (*Sport: avant le saut*) run up; (*de véhicule*) momentum; (*fig: de tendresse etc*) surge; **prendre son ~/de l'~** to take a run up/gather speed; **perdre son ~** to lose one's momentum
**élancé, e** [elɑ̃se] *adj* slender
**élancement** [elɑ̃smɑ̃] *nm* shooting pain
**élancer** [elɑ̃se]: **s'élancer** *vi* to dash, hurl o.s.; (*fig: arbre, clocher*) to soar (upwards)
**élargir** [elaʀʒiʀ] *vt* to widen; (*vêtement*) to let out; (*Jur*) to release; **s'élargir** *vi* to widen; (*vêtement*) to stretch
**élargissement** [elaʀʒismɑ̃] *nm* widening; letting out
**élasticité** [elastisite] *nf* (*aussi Écon*) elasticity; ~ **de l'offre/de la demande** flexibility of supply/demand

**élastique** [elastik] *adj* elastic ▷ *nm* (*de bureau*) rubber band; (*pour la couture*) elastic *no pl*
**élastomère** [elastɔmɛʀ] *nm* elastomer
**Elbe** [ɛlb] *nf*: **l'île d'~** (the Island of) Elba; (*fleuve*): **l'~** the Elbe
**eldorado** [ɛldɔʀado] *nm* Eldorado
**électeur, -trice** [elɛktœʀ, -tʀis] *nm/f* elector, voter
**électif, -ive** [elɛktif, -iv] *adj* elective
**élection** [elɛksjɔ̃] *nf* election; **élections** *nfpl* (*Pol*) election(s); **sa terre/patrie d'~** the land/country of one's choice; ~ **partielle** ≈ by-election; ~**s législatives/présidentielles** general/presidential election *sg*; *see note*

⬤ **ÉLECTIONS LÉGISLATIVES**
⬤
⬤ *Élections législatives* are held in France every
⬤ five years to elect "députés" to the
⬤ "Assemblée nationale". The president is
⬤ chosen in the "élection présidentielle",
⬤ which also comes round every five years.
⬤ Voting is by direct universal suffrage and is
⬤ divided into two rounds. The ballots always
⬤ take place on a Sunday.

**électoral, e, -aux** [elɛktɔʀal, -o] *adj* electoral, election *cpd*
**électoralisme** [elɛktɔʀalism(ə)] *nm* electioneering
**électorat** [elɛktɔʀa] *nm* electorate
**électricien, ne** [elɛktʀisjɛ̃, -ɛn] *nm/f* electrician
**électricité** [elɛktʀisite] *nf* electricity; **allumer/éteindre l'~** to put on/off the light; ~ **statique** static electricity
**électrification** [elɛktʀifikasjɔ̃] *nf* (*Rail*) electrification; (*d'un village etc*) laying on of electricity
**électrifier** [elɛktʀifje] *vt* (*Rail*) to electrify
**électrique** [elɛktʀik] *adj* electric(al)
**électriser** [elɛktʀize] *vt* to electrify
**électro...** [elɛktʀo] *préfixe* electro...
**électro-aimant** [elɛktʀoɛmɑ̃] *nm* electromagnet
**électrocardiogramme** [elɛktʀokaʀdjɔgʀam] *nm* electrocardiogram
**électrocardiographe** [elɛktʀokaʀdjɔgʀaf] *nm* electrocardiograph
**électrochoc** [elɛktʀoʃɔk] *nm* electric shock treatment
**électrocuter** [elɛktʀokyte] *vt* to electrocute
**électrocution** [elɛktʀokysjɔ̃] *nf* electrocution
**électrode** [elɛktʀɔd] *nf* electrode
**électro-encéphalogramme** [elɛktʀoɑ̃sefalɔgʀam] *nm* electroencephalogram
**électrogène** [elɛktʀoʒɛn] *adj*: **groupe ~** generating set
**électrolyse** [elɛktʀɔliz] *nf* electrolysis *sg*
**électromagnétique** [elɛktʀomaɲetik] *adj* electromagnetic
**électroménager** [elɛktʀomenaʒe] *adj*:

**appareils ~s** domestic (electrical) appliances
▷ *nm*: **l'~** household appliances
**électron** [elɛktrɔ̃] *nm* electron
**électronicien, ne** [elɛktrɔnisjɛ̃, -ɛn] *nm/f*
electronics (Brit) *ou* electrical (US) engineer
**électronique** [elɛktrɔnik] *adj* electronic ▷ *nf*
(*science*) electronics *sg*
**électronucléaire** [elɛktrɔnykleɛʀ] *adj* nuclear
power *cpd* ▷ *nm*: **l'~** nuclear power
**électrophone** [elɛktrɔfɔn] *nm* record player
**électrostatique** [elɛktrɔstatik] *adj*
electrostatic ▷ *nf* electrostatics *sg*
**élégamment** [elegamɑ̃] *adv* elegantly
**élégance** [elegɑ̃s] *nf* elegance
**élégant, e** [elegɑ̃, -ɑ̃t] *adj* elegant; (*solution*)
neat, elegant; (*attitude, procédé*) courteous,
civilized
**élément** [elemɑ̃] *nm* element; (*pièce*)
component, part; **éléments** *nmpl* elements
**élémentaire** [elemɑ̃tɛʀ] *adj* elementary;
(*Chimie*) elemental
**éléphant** [elefɑ̃] *nm* elephant; **~ de mer**
elephant seal
**éléphanteau, x** [elefɑ̃to] *nm* baby elephant
**éléphantesque** [elefɑ̃tɛsk(ə)] *adj* elephantine
**élevage** [ɛlvaʒ] *nm* breeding; (*de bovins*) cattle
breeding *ou* rearing; (*ferme*) cattle farm
**élévateur** [elevatœʀ] *nm* elevator
**élévation** [elevasjɔ̃] *nf* (*gén*) elevation; (*voir*
*élever*) raising; (*voir s'élever*) rise
**élevé, e** [ɛlve] *adj* (*prix, sommet*) high; (*fig: noble*)
elevated; **bien/mal ~** well-/ill-mannered
**élève** [elɛv] *nm/f* pupil; **~ infirmière** student
nurse
**élever** [ɛlve] *vt* (*enfant*) to bring up, raise; (*bétail,*
*volaille*) to breed; (*abeilles*) to keep; (*hausser: taux,*
*niveau*) to raise; (*fig: âme, esprit*) to elevate; (*édifier:*
*monument*) to put up, erect; **s'élever** *vi* (*avion,*
*alpiniste*) to go up; (*niveau, température, aussi: cri etc*)
to rise; (*survenir: difficultés*) to arise; **s'~ à** (*frais,*
*dégâts*) to amount to, add up to; **s'~ contre** to
rise up against; **~ une protestation/critique**
to raise a protest/make a criticism; **~ qn au**
**rang de** to raise *ou* elevate sb to the rank of; **~**
**un nombre au carré/au cube** to square/cube a
number
**éleveur, -euse** [ɛlvœʀ, -øz] *nm/f* stock breeder
**elfe** [ɛlf(ə)] *nm* elf
**élidé, e** [elide] *adj* elided
**élider** [elide] *vt* to elide
**éligibilité** [eliʒibilite] *nf* eligibility
**éligible** [eliʒibl(ə)] *adj* eligible
**élimé, e** [elime] *adj* worn (thin), threadbare
**élimination** [eliminasjɔ̃] *nf* elimination
**éliminatoire** [eliminatwaʀ] *adj* eliminatory;
(*Sport*) disqualifying ▷ *nf* (*Sport*) heat
**éliminer** [elimine] *vt* to eliminate
**élire** [eliʀ] *vt* to elect; **~ domicile à** to take up
residence in *ou* at
**élision** [elizjɔ̃] *nf* elision
**élite** [elit] *nf* elite; **tireur d'~** crack rifleman;
**chercheur d'~** top-notch researcher

**élitisme** [elitism(ə)] *nm* elitism
**élitiste** [elitist(ə)] *adj* elitist
**élixir** [eliksiʀ] *nm* elixir
**elle** [ɛl] *pron* (*sujet*) she; (: *chose*) it; (*complément*)
her; it; **~s** (*sujet*) they; (*complément*) them;
**~-même** herself; itself; **~s-mêmes** themselves;
*voir* **il**
**ellipse** [elips(ə)] *nf* ellipse; (*Ling*) ellipsis *sg*
**elliptique** [eliptik] *adj* elliptical
**élocution** [elɔkysjɔ̃] *nf* delivery; **défaut d'~**
speech impediment
**éloge** [elɔʒ] *nm* praise *gen no pl*; **faire l'~ de** to
praise
**élogieusement** [elɔʒjøzmɑ̃] *adv* very
favourably
**élogieux, -euse** [elɔʒjø, -øz] *adj* laudatory, full
of praise
**éloigné, e** [elwaɲe] *adj* distant, far-off
**éloignement** [elwaɲmɑ̃] *nm* removal; putting
off; estrangement; (*fig: distance*) distance
**éloigner** [elwaɲe] *vt* (*objet*): **~ qch (de)** to move
*ou* take sth away (from); (*personne*): **~ qn (de)** to
take sb away *ou* remove sb (from); (*échéance*) to
put off, postpone; (*soupçons, danger*) to ward off;
**s'éloigner (de)** *vi* (*personne*) to go away (from);
(*véhicule*) to move away (from); (*affectivement*) to
become estranged (from)
**élongation** [elɔ̃gasjɔ̃] *nf* strained muscle
**éloquence** [elɔkɑ̃s] *nf* eloquence
**éloquent, e** [elɔkɑ̃, -ɑ̃t] *adj* eloquent
**élu, e** [ely] *pp de* **élire** ▷ *nm/f* (*Pol*) elected
representative
**élucider** [elyside] *vt* to elucidate
**élucubrations** [elykybʀasjɔ̃] *nfpl* wild
imaginings
**éluder** [elyde] *vt* to evade
**élus etc** [ely] *vb voir* **élire**
**élusif, -ive** [elyzif, -iv] *adj* elusive
**Élysée** [elize] *nm*: (**le palais de**) **l'~** the Élysée
palace; *see note*; **les Champs ~s** the Champs
Élysées

**émacié, e** [emasje] *adj* emaciated
**émail, -aux** [emaj, -o] *nm* enamel
**e-mail** [imɛl] *nm* email; **envoyer qch par ~** to
email sth
**émaillé, e** [emaje] *adj* enamelled; (*fig*): **~ de**
dotted with
**émailler** [emaje] *vt* to enamel
**émanation** [emanasjɔ̃] *nf* emanation
**émancipation** [emɑ̃sipasjɔ̃] *nf* emancipation

**émancipé, e** [emãsipe] *adj* emancipated

**émanciper** [emãsipe] *vt* to emancipate; **s'émanciper** (*fig*) to become emancipated *ou* liberated

**émaner** [emane]: ~ **de** *vt* to emanate from; (*Admin*) to proceed from

**émarger** [emaʀʒe] *vt* to sign; ~ **de 1000 euros à un budget** to receive 1000 euros out of a budget

**émasculer** [emaskyle] *vt* to emasculate

**emballage** [ãbalaʒ] *nm* wrapping; packing; (*papier*) wrapping; (*carton*) packaging

**emballer** [ãbale] *vt* to wrap (up); (*dans un carton*) to pack (up); (*fig: fam*) to thrill (to bits); **s'emballer** *vi* (*moteur*) to race; (*cheval*) to bolt; (*fig: personne*) to get carried away

**emballeur, -euse** [ãbalœʀ, -øz] *nm/f* packer

**embarcadère** [ãbaʀkadɛʀ] *nm* landing stage (*Brit*), pier

**embarcation** [ãbaʀkasjõ] *nf* (small) boat, (small) craft *inv*

**embardée** [ãbaʀde] *nf* swerve; **faire une** ~ to swerve

**embargo** [ãbaʀgo] *nm* embargo; **mettre l'**~ **sur** to put an embargo on, embargo

**embarquement** [ãbaʀkəmã] *nm* embarkation; loading; boarding

**embarquer** [ãbaʀke] *vt* (*personne*) to embark; (*marchandise*) to load; (*fam*) to cart off; (: *arrêter*) to nick ▷ *vi* (*passager*) to board; (*Navig*) to ship water; **s'embarquer** *vi* to board; **s'**~ **dans** (*affaire, aventure*) to embark upon

**embarras** [ãbaʀa] *nm* (*obstacle*) hindrance; (*confusion*) embarrassment; (*ennuis*): **être dans l'**~ to be in a predicament *ou* an awkward position; (*gêne financière*) to be in difficulties; ~ **gastrique** stomach upset

**embarrassant, e** [ãbaʀasã, -ãt] *adj* cumbersome; embarrassing; awkward

**embarrassé, e** [ãbaʀase] *adj* (*encombré*) encumbered; (*gêné*) embarrassed; (*explications etc*) awkward

**embarrasser** [ãbaʀase] *vt* (*encombrer*) to clutter (up); (*gêner*) to hinder, hamper; (*fig*) to cause embarrassment to; to put in an awkward position; **s'embarrasser de** *vi* to burden o.s. with

**embauche** [ãboʃ] *nf* hiring; **bureau d'**~ labour office

**embaucher** [ãboʃe] *vt* to take on, hire; **s'embaucher comme** *vi* to get (o.s.) a job as

**embauchoir** [ãboʃwaʀ] *nm* shoetree

**embaumer** [ãbome] *vt* to embalm; (*parfumer*) to fill with its fragrance; ~ **la lavande** to be fragrant with (the scent of) lavender

**embellie** [ãbeli] *nf* bright spell, brighter period

**embellir** [ãbeliʀ] *vt* to make more attractive; (*une histoire*) to embellish ▷ *vi* to grow lovelier *ou* more attractive

**embellissement** [ãbelismã] *nm* embellishment

**embêtant, e** [ãbɛtã, -ãt] *adj* annoying

**embêtement** [ãbɛtmã] *nm* problem, difficulty; **embêtements** *nmpl* trouble *sg*

**embêter** [ãbete] *vt* to bother; **s'embêter** *vi* (*s'ennuyer*) to be bored; **ça m'embête** it bothers me; **il ne s'embête pas!** (*ironique*) he does all right for himself!

**emblée** [ãble]: **d'**~ *adv* straightaway

**emblème** [ãblɛm] *nm* emblem

**embobiner** [ãbɔbine] *vt* (*enjôler*): ~ **qn** to get round sb

**emboîtable** [ãbwatabl(ə)] *adj* interlocking

**emboîter** [ãbwate] *vt* to fit together; **s'emboîter dans** to fit into; **s'**~ (**l'un dans l'autre**) to fit together; ~ **le pas à qn** to follow in sb's footsteps

**embolie** [ãbɔli] *nf* embolism

**embonpoint** [ãbõpwẽ] *nm* stoutness (*Brit*), corpulence; **prendre de l'**~ to grow stout (*Brit*) *ou* corpulent

**embouché, e** [ãbuʃe] *adj*: **mal** ~ foul-mouthed

**embouchure** [ãbuʃyʀ] *nf* (*Géo*) mouth; (*Mus*) mouthpiece

**embourber** [ãbuʀbe]: **s'embourber** *vi* to get stuck in the mud; (*fig*): **s'**~ **dans** to sink into

**embourgeoiser** [ãbuʀʒwaze]: **s'embourgeoiser** *vi* to adopt a middle-class outlook

**embout** [ãbu] *nm* (*de canne*) tip; (*de tuyau*) nozzle

**embouteillage** [ãbutejaʒ] *nm* traffic jam, (traffic) holdup (*Brit*)

**embouteiller** [ãbuteje] *vt* (*véhicules etc*) to block

**emboutir** [ãbutiʀ] *vt* (*Tech*) to stamp; (*heurter*) to crash into, ram

**embranchement** [ãbʀãʃmã] *nm* (*routier*) junction; (*classification*) branch

**embrancher** [ãbʀãʃe] *vt* (*tuyaux*) to join; ~ **qch sur** to join sth to

**embraser** [ãbʀaze]: **s'embraser** *vi* to flare up

**embrassade** [ãbʀasad] *nf* (*gén pl*) hugging and kissing *no pl*

**embrasse** [ãbʀas] *nf* (*de rideau*) tie-back, loop

**embrasser** [ãbʀase] *vt* to kiss; (*sujet, période*) to embrace, encompass; (*carrière*) to embark on; (*métier*) to go in for, take up; ~ **du regard** to take in (*with eyes*); **s'embrasser** *vi* to kiss (each other)

**embrasure** [ãbʀazyʀ] *nf*: **dans l'**~ **de la porte** in the door(way)

**embrayage** [ãbʀɛjaʒ] *nm* clutch

**embrayer** [ãbʀeje] *vi* (*Auto*) to let in the clutch ▷ *vt* (*fig: affaire*) to set in motion; ~ **sur qch** to begin on sth

**embrigader** [ãbʀigade] *vt* to recruit

**embrocher** [ãbʀɔʃe] *vt* to (put on a) spit (*ou* skewer)

**embrouillamini** [ãbʀujamini] *nm* (*fam*) muddle

**embrouillé, e** [ãbʀuje] *adj* (*affaire*) confused, muddled

**embrouiller** [ãbʀuje] *vt* (*fils*) to tangle (up); (*fiches, idées, personne*) to muddle up; **s'embrouiller** *vi* to get in a muddle

**embroussaillé, e** [ãbʀusaje] *adj* overgrown,

scrubby; (cheveux) bushy, shaggy

**embruns** [ɑ̃bʀœ̃] nmpl sea spray sg

**embryologie** [ɑ̃bʀijɔlɔʒi] nf embryology

**embryon** [ɑ̃bʀijɔ̃] nm embryo

**embryonnaire** [ɑ̃bʀijɔnɛʀ] adj embryonic

**embûches** [ɑ̃byʃ] nfpl pitfalls, traps

**embué, e** [ɑ̃bɥe] adj misted up; **yeux ~s de larmes** eyes misty with tears

**embuscade** [ɑ̃byskad] nf ambush; **tendre une ~ à** to lay an ambush for

**embusqué, e** [ɑ̃byske] adj in ambush ▷ nm (péj) shirker, skiver (Brit)

**embusquer** [ɑ̃byske]: **s'embusquer** vi to take up position (for an ambush)

**émêché, e** [emeʃe] adj tipsy, merry

**émeraude** [ɛmʀod] nf emerald ▷ adj inv emerald-green

**émergence** [emɛʀʒɑ̃s] nf (fig) emergence

**émerger** [emɛʀʒe] vi to emerge; (faire saillie, aussi fig) to stand out

**émeri** [emʀi] nm: **toile** ou **papier ~** emery paper

**émérite** [emeʀit] adj highly skilled

**émerveillement** [emɛʀvɛjmɑ̃] nm wonderment

**émerveiller** [emɛʀveje] vt to fill with wonder; **s'émerveiller de** vi to marvel at

**émet** etc [emɛ] vb voir **émettre**

**émétique** [emetik] nm emetic

**émetteur, -trice** [emetœʀ, -tʀis] adj transmitting; (poste) **(poste)** ~ transmitter

**émetteur-récepteur** [emetœʀʀesɛptœʀ] (pl **émetteurs-récepteurs**) nm transceiver

**émettre** [emɛtʀ(ə)] vt (son, lumière) to give out, emit; (message etc: Radio) to transmit; (billet, timbre, emprunt, chèque) to issue; (hypothèse, avis) to voice, put forward; (vœu) to express ▷ vi: **~ sur ondes courtes** to broadcast on short wave

**émeus** etc [emø] vb voir **émouvoir**

**émeute** [emøt] nf riot

**émeutier, -ière** [emøtje, -jɛʀ] nm/f rioter

**émeuve** etc [emœv] vb voir **émouvoir**

**émietter** [emjete] vt (pain, terre) to crumble; (fig) to split up, disperse; **s'émietter** vi (pain, terre) to crumble

**émigrant, e** [emigʀɑ̃, -ɑ̃t] nm/f emigrant

**émigration** [emigʀasjɔ̃] nf emigration

**émigré, e** [emigʀe] nm/f expatriate

**émigrer** [emigʀe] vi to emigrate

**émincer** [emɛ̃se] vt (Culin) to slice thinly

**éminemment** [eminamɑ̃] adv eminently

**éminence** [eminɑ̃s] nf distinction; (colline) knoll, hill; **Son É~** His Eminence; **~ grise** éminence grise

**éminent, e** [eminɑ̃, -ɑ̃t] adj distinguished

**émir** [emiʀ] nm emir

**émirat** [emiʀa] nm emirate; **les É~s arabes unis (EAU)** the United Arab Emirates (UAE)

**émis, e** [emi, -iz] pp de **émettre**

**émissaire** [emisɛʀ] nm emissary

**émission** [emisjɔ̃] nf (voir émettre) emission; transmission; issue; (Radio, TV) programme, broadcast

**émit** etc [emi] vb voir **émettre**

**emmagasinage** [ɑ̃magazinaʒ] nm storage; storing away

**emmagasiner** [ɑ̃magazine] vt to (put into) store; (fig) to store up

**emmailloter** [ɑ̃majɔte] vt to wrap up

**emmanchure** [ɑ̃mɑ̃ʃyʀ] nf armhole

**emmêlement** [ɑ̃mɛlmɑ̃] nm (état) tangle

**emmêler** [ɑ̃mele] vt to tangle (up); (fig) to muddle up; **s'emmêler** vi to get into a tangle

**emménagement** [ɑ̃menaʒmɑ̃] nm settling in

**emménager** [ɑ̃menaʒe] vi to move in; **~ dans** to move into

**emmener** [ɑ̃mne] vt to take (with one); (comme otage, capture) to take away; **~ qn au concert** to take sb to a concert

**emmental, emmenthal** [emɛtal] nm (fromage) Emmenthal

**emmerder** [ɑ̃mɛʀde] (fam!) vt to bug, bother; **s'emmerder** vi (s'ennuyer) to be bored stiff; **je t'emmerde!** to hell with you!

**emmitoufler** [ɑ̃mitufle] vt to wrap up (warmly); **s'emmitoufler** to wrap (o.s.) up (warmly)

**emmurer** [ɑ̃myʀe] vt to wall up, immure

**émoi** [emwa] nm (agitation, effervescence) commotion; (trouble) agitation; **en ~** (sens) excited, stirred

**émollient, e** [emɔljɑ̃, -ɑ̃t] adj (Méd) emollient

**émoluments** [emɔlymɑ̃] nmpl remuneration sg, fee sg

**émonder** [emɔ̃de] vt (arbre etc) to prune; (amande etc) to blanch

**émoticone** [emɔticon] nm (Inform) smiley

**émotif, -ive** [emɔtif, -iv] adj emotional

**émotion** [emosjɔ̃] nf emotion; **avoir des ~s** (fig) to get a fright; **donner des ~s à** to give a fright to; **sans ~** without emotion, coldly

**émotionnant, e** [emosjɔnɑ̃, -ɑ̃t] adj upsetting

**émotionnel, le** [emosjɔnɛl] adj emotional

**émotionner** [emosjɔne] vt to upset

**émoulu, e** [emuly] adj: **frais ~ de** fresh from, just out of

**émoussé, e** [emuse] adj blunt

**émousser** [emuse] vt to blunt; (fig) to dull

**émoustiller** [emustije] vt to titillate, arouse

**émouvant, e** [emuvɑ̃, -ɑ̃t] adj moving

**émouvoir** [emuvwaʀ] vt (troubler) to stir, affect; (toucher, attendrir) to move; (indigner) to rouse; (effrayer) to disturb, worry; **s'émouvoir** vi to be affected; to be moved; to be roused; to be disturbed ou worried

**empailler** [ɑ̃paje] vt to stuff

**empailleur, -euse** [ɑ̃pajœʀ, -øz] nm/f (d'animaux) taxidermist

**empaler** [ɑ̃pale] vt to impale

**empaquetage** [ɑ̃paktaʒ] nm packing, packaging

**empaqueter** [ɑ̃pakte] vt to pack up

**emparer** [ɑ̃paʀe]: **s'emparer de** vt (objet) to seize, grab; (comme otage, Mil) to seize; (peur etc) to take hold of

**empâter** [ãpate]: **s'empâter** vi to thicken out

**empattement** [ãpatmã] nm (Auto) wheelbase; (Typo) serif

**empêché, e** [ãpeʃe] adj detained

**empêchement** [ãpeʃmã] nm (unexpected) obstacle, hitch

**empêcher** [ãpeʃe] vt to prevent; ~ **qn de faire** to prevent ou stop sb (from) doing; ~ **que qch (n')arrive/qn (ne) fasse** to prevent sth from happening/sb from doing; **il n'empêche que** nevertheless, be that as it may; **il n'a pas pu s'~ de rire** he couldn't help laughing

**empêcheur** [ãpeʃœR] nm: ~ **de danser en rond** spoilsport, killjoy (Brit)

**empeigne** [ãpɛɲ] nf upper (of shoe)

**empennage** [ãpɛnaʒ] nm (Aviat) tailplane

**empereur** [ãpRœR] nm emperor

**empesé, e** [ãpəze] adj (fig) stiff, starchy

**empeser** [ãpəze] vt to starch

**empester** [ãpeste] vt (lieu) to stink out ▷ vi to stink, reek; ~ **le tabac/le vin** to stink ou reek of tobacco/wine

**empêtrer** [ãpetRe] vt: **s'empêtrer dans** (fils etc, aussi fig) to get tangled up in

**emphase** [ãfɑz] nf pomposity, bombast; **avec ~** pompously

**emphatique** [ãfatik] adj emphatic

**empiècement** [ãpjɛsmã] nm (Couture) yoke

**empierrer** [ãpjeRe] vt (route) to metal

**empiéter** [ãpjete]: ~ **sur** vt to encroach upon

**empiffrer** [ãpifRe]: **s'empiffrer** vi (péj) to stuff o.s.

**empiler** [ãpile] vt to pile (up), stack (up); **s'empiler** vi to pile up

**empire** [ãpiR] nm empire; (fig) influence; **style E~** Empire style; **sous l'~ de** in the grip of

**empirer** [ãpiRe] vi to worsen, deteriorate

**empirique** [ãpiRik] adj empirical

**empirisme** [ãpiRism(ə)] nm empiricism

**emplacement** [ãplasmã] nm site; **sur l'~ de** on the site of

**emplâtre** [ãplɑtR(ə)] nm plaster; (fam) twit

**emplette** [ãplet] nf: **faire l'~ de** to purchase; **emplettes** shopping sg; **faire des ~s** to go shopping

**emplir** [ãpliR] vt to fill; **s'emplir (de)** vi to fill (with)

**emploi** [ãplwa] nm use; (Comm, Écon): **l'~** employment; (poste) job, situation; **d'~ facile** easy to use; **le plein ~** full employment; **~ du temps** timetable, schedule

**emploie** etc [ãplwa] vb voir **employer**

**employé, e** [ãplwaje] nm/f employee; ~ **de bureau/banque** office/bank employee ou clerk; ~ **de maison** domestic (servant)

**employer** [ãplwaje] vt (outil, moyen, méthode, mot) to use; (ouvrier, main-d'œuvre) to employ; **s'~ à qch/à faire** to apply ou devote o.s. to sth/to doing

**employeur, -euse** [ãplwajœR, -øz] nm/f employer

**empocher** [ãpoʃe] vt to pocket

**empoignade** [ãpwaɲad] nf row, set-to

**empoigne** [ãpwaɲ] nf: **foire d'~** free-for-all

**empoigner** [ãpwaɲe] vt to grab; **s'empoigner** vi (fig) to have a row ou set-to

**empois** [ãpwa] nm starch

**empoisonnement** [ãpwazɔnmã] nm poisoning; (fam: ennui) annoyance, irritation

**empoisonner** [ãpwazɔne] vt to poison; (empester: air, pièce) to stink out; (fam): ~ **qn** to drive sb mad; **s'empoisonner** vi to poison o.s.: ~ **l'atmosphère** (aussi fig) to poison the atmosphere; (aussi: **il nous empoisonne l'existence**) he's the bane of our life

**empoissonner** [ãpwasɔne] vt (étang, rivière) to stock with fish

**emporté, e** [ãpɔRte] adj (personne, caractère) fiery

**emportement** [ãpɔRtəmã] nm fit of rage, anger no pl

**emporte-pièce** [ãpɔRtəpjɛs] nm inv (Tech) punch; **à l'~** adj (fig) incisive

**emporter** [ãpɔRte] vt to take (with one); (en dérobant ou enlevant, emmener: blessés, voyageurs) to take away; (entraîner) to carry away ou along; (arracher) to tear off; (rivière, vent) to carry away; (Mil: position) to take; (avantage, approbation) to win; **s'emporter** vi (de colère) to fly into a rage, lose one's temper; **la maladie qui l'a emporté** the illness which caused his death; **l'~** to gain victory; **l'~ (sur)** to get the upper hand (of); (méthode etc) to prevail (over); **boissons à ~** takeaway drinks

**empoté, e** [ãpɔte] adj (maladroit) clumsy

**empourpré, e** [ãpuRpRe] adj crimson

**empreint, e** [ãpRɛ̃, -ɛ̃t] adj: ~ **de** marked with; tinged with ▷ nf (de pied, main) print; (fig) stamp, mark; **~e (digitale)** fingerprint; **~e écologique** carbon footprint

**empressé, e** [ãpRese] adj attentive; (péj) overanxious to please, overattentive

**empressement** [ãpRɛsmã] nm eagerness

**empresser** [ãpRese]: **s'empresser** vi: **s'~ auprès de qn** to surround sb with attentions; **s'~ de faire** to hasten to do

**emprise** [ãpRiz] nf hold, ascendancy; **sous l'~ de** under the influence of

**emprisonnement** [ãpRizɔnmã] nm imprisonment

**emprisonner** [ãpRizɔne] vt to imprison, jail

**emprunt** [ãpRœ̃] nm borrowing no pl, loan (from debtor's point of view); (Ling etc) borrowing; **nom d'~** assumed name; ~ **d'État** government ou state loan; ~ **public à 5%** 5% public loan

**emprunté, e** [ãpRœ̃te] adj (fig) ill-at-ease, awkward

**emprunter** [ãpRœ̃te] vt to borrow; (itinéraire) to take, follow; (style, manière) to adopt, assume

**emprunteur, -euse** [ãpRœ̃tœR, -øz] nm/f borrower

**empuantir** [ãpɥãtiR] vt to stink out

**EMT** sigle f (= éducation manuelle et technique) handwork as a school subject

**ému, e** [emy] *pp de* **émouvoir** ▷ *adj* excited; touched; moved

**émulation** [emylɑsjɔ̃] *nf* emulation

**émule** [emyl] *nm/f* imitator

**émulsion** [emylsjɔ̃] *nf* emulsion; *(cosmétique)* (water-based) lotion

**émut**etc [emy] *vb voir* **émouvoir**

**EN** *sigle f* = **Éducation nationale**; *voir* **éducation**

 **MOT-CLÉ**

**en** [ɑ̃] *prép* **1** *(endroit, pays)* in; *(direction)* to; **habiter en France/ville** to live in France/town; **aller en France/ville** to go to France/town
**2** *(moment, temps)* in; **en été/juin** in summer/June; **en 3 jours/20 ans** in 3 days/20 years
**3** *(moyen)* by; **en avion/taxi** by plane/taxi
**4** *(composition)* made of; **c'est en verre/coton/laine** it's (made of) glass/cotton/wool; **en métal/plastique** made of metal/plastic; **un collier en argent** a silver necklace; **en deux volumes/une pièce** in two volumes/one piece
**5** *(description, état)*: **une femme (habillée) en rouge** a woman (dressed) in red; **peindre qch en rouge** to paint sth red; **en T/étoile** T-/star-shaped; **en chemise/chaussettes** in one's shirt sleeves/socks; **en soldat** as a soldier; **en civil** in civilian clothes; **cassé en plusieurs morceaux** broken into several pieces; **en réparation** being repaired, under repair; **en vacances** on holiday; **en bonne santé** healthy, in good health; **en deuil** in mourning; **le même en plus grand** the same but *ou* only bigger
**6** *(avec gérondif)* while; on; **en dormant** while sleeping, as one sleeps; **en sortant** on going out, as he *etc* went out; **sortir en courant** to run out; **en apprenant la nouvelle, il s'est évanoui** he fainted at the news *ou* when he heard the news
**7** *(matière)*: **fort en math** good at maths; **expert en** expert in
**8** *(conformité)*: **en tant que** as; **en bon politicien, il ...** good politician that he is, he ..., like a good *ou* true politician, he ...; **je te parle en ami** I'm talking to you as a friend ▷ *pron* **1** *(indéfini)*: **j'en ai/veux** I have/want some; **en as-tu?** have you got any?; **il n'y en a pas** there isn't *ou* aren't any; **je n'en veux pas** I don't want any; **j'en ai deux** I've got two; **combien y en a-t-il?** how many (of them) are there?; **j'en ai assez** I've got enough (of it *ou* them); *(j'en ai marre)* I've had enough; **où en étais-je?** where was I?
**2** *(provenance)* from there; **j'en viens** I've come from there
**3** *(cause)*: **il en est malade/perd le sommeil** he is ill/can't sleep because of it
**4** *(de la part de)*: **elle en est aimée** she is loved by him *(ou* them *etc)*
**5** *(complément de nom, d'adjectif, de verbe)*: **j'en connais les dangers** I know its *ou* the dangers;

**j'en suis fier/ai besoin** I am proud of it/need it; **il en est ainsi** *ou* **de même pour moi** it's the same for me, same here

**ENA** [ena] *sigle f* (= *École nationale d'administration*) *grande école for training civil servants*

**énarque** [enaʁk(ə)] *nm/f* former ENA student

**encablure** [ɑ̃kablyʁ] *nf (Navig)* cable's length

**encadrement** [ɑ̃kadʁəmɑ̃] *nm* framing; training; *(de porte)* frame; **~ du crédit** credit restrictions

**encadrer** [ɑ̃kadʁe] *vt (tableau, image)* to frame; *(fig: entourer)* to surround; *(personnel, soldats etc)* to train; *(Comm: crédit)* to restrict

**encadreur** [ɑ̃kadʁœʁ] *nm* (picture) framer

**encaisse** [ɑ̃kɛs] *nf* cash in hand; **~ or/métallique** gold/gold and silver reserves

**encaissé, e** [ɑ̃kese] *adj (vallée)* steep-sided; *(rivière)* with steep banks

**encaisser** [ɑ̃kese] *vt (chèque)* to cash; *(argent)* to collect; *(fig: coup, défaite)* to take

**encaisseur** [ɑ̃kɛsœʁ] *nm* collector *(of debts etc)*

**encan** [ɑ̃kɑ̃]: **à l'~** *adv* by auction

**encanailler** [ɑ̃kanaje]: **s'encanailler** *vi* to become vulgar *ou* common; to mix with the riff-raff

**encart** [ɑ̃kaʁ] *nm* insert; **~ publicitaire** publicity insert

**encarter** [ɑ̃kaʁte] *vt* to insert

**en-cas** [ɑ̃kɑ] *nm inv* snack

**encastrable** [ɑ̃kastʁabl(ə)] *adj (four, élément)* that can be built in

**encastré, e** [ɑ̃kastʁe] *adj (four, baignoire)* built-in

**encastrer** [ɑ̃kastʁe] *vt*: **~ qch dans** *(mur)* to embed sth in(to); *(boîtier)* to fit sth into; **s'encastrer dans** *vi* to fit into; *(heurter)* to crash into

**encaustique** [ɑ̃kostik] *nf* polish, wax

**encaustiquer** [ɑ̃kostike] *vt* to polish, wax

**enceinte** [ɑ̃sɛ̃t] *adj f*: **~ (de six mois)** (six months) pregnant ▷ *nf (mur)* wall; *(espace)* enclosure; **~ (acoustique)** speaker

**encens** [ɑ̃sɑ̃] *nm* incense

**encenser** [ɑ̃sɑ̃se] *vt* to (in)cense; *(fig)* to praise to the skies

**encensoir** [ɑ̃sɑ̃swaʁ] *nm* thurible *(Brit)*, censer

**encéphalogramme** [ɑ̃sefalɔgʁam] *nm* encephalogram

**encercler** [ɑ̃sɛʁkle] *vt* to surround

**enchaîné** [ɑ̃ʃene] *nm (Ciné)* link shot

**enchaînement** [ɑ̃ʃɛnmɑ̃] *nm (fig)* linking

**enchaîner** [ɑ̃ʃene] *vt* to chain up; *(mouvements, séquences)* to link (together) ▷ *vi* to carry on

**enchanté, e** [ɑ̃ʃɑ̃te] *adj (ravi)* delighted; *(ensorcelé)* enchanted; **~ (de faire votre connaissance)** pleased to meet you, how do you do?

**enchantement** [ɑ̃ʃɑ̃tmɑ̃] *nm* delight; *(magie)* enchantment; **comme par ~** as if by magic

**enchanter** [ɑ̃ʃɑ̃te] *vt* to delight

**enchanteur, -teresse** [ɑ̃ʃɑ̃tœʁ, -tʁɛs] *adj* enchanting

**enchâsser** [ɑ̃ʃase] *vt*: ~ **qch (dans)** to set sth (in)
**enchère** [ɑ̃ʃɛʀ] *nf* bid; **faire une** ~ to (make a) bid; **mettre/vendre aux ~s** to put up for (sale by)/sell by auction; **les ~s montent** the bids are rising; **faire monter les ~s** (*fig*) to raise the bidding
**enchérir** [ɑ̃ʃeʀiʀ] *vi*: ~ **sur qn** (*aux enchères, aussi fig*) to outbid sb
**enchérisseur, -euse** [ɑ̃ʃeʀisœʀ, -øz] *nm/f* bidder
**enchevêtrement** [ɑ̃ʃvetʀəmɑ̃] *nm* tangle
**enchevêtrer** [ɑ̃ʃvetʀe] *vt* to tangle (up)
**enclave** [ɑ̃klav] *nf* enclave
**enclaver** [ɑ̃klave] *vt* to enclose, hem in
**enclencher** [ɑ̃klɑ̃ʃe] *vt* (*mécanisme*) to engage; (*fig: affaire*) to set in motion; **s'enclencher** *vi* to engage
**enclin, e** [ɑ̃klɛ̃, -in] *adj*: ~ **à qch/à faire** inclined *ou* prone to sth/to do
**enclore** [ɑ̃klɔʀ] *vt* to enclose
**enclos** [ɑ̃klo] *nm* enclosure; (*clôture*) fence
**enclume** [ɑ̃klym] *nf* anvil
**encoche** [ɑ̃kɔʃ] *nf* notch
**encoder** [ɑ̃kɔde] *vt* to encode
**encodeur** [ɑ̃kɔdœʀ] *nm* encoder
**encoignure** [ɑ̃kɔɲyʀ] *nf* corner
**encoller** [ɑ̃kɔle] *vt* to paste
**encolure** [ɑ̃kɔlyʀ] *nf* (*tour de cou*) collar size; (*col, cou*) neck
**encombrant, e** [ɑ̃kɔ̃bʀɑ̃, -ɑ̃t] *adj* cumbersome, bulky
**encombre** [ɑ̃kɔ̃bʀ(ə)]: **sans ~** *adv* without mishap *ou* incident
**encombré, e** [ɑ̃kɔ̃bʀe] *adj* (*pièce, passage*) cluttered; (*lignes téléphoniques*) engaged; (*marché*) saturated
**encombrement** [ɑ̃kɔ̃bʀəmɑ̃] *nm* (*d'un lieu*) cluttering (up); (*d'un objet: dimensions*) bulk
**encombrer** [ɑ̃kɔ̃bʀe] *vt* to clutter (up); (*gêner*) to hamper; **s'encombrer de** *vi* (*bagages etc*) to load *ou* burden o.s. with; ~ **le passage** to block *ou* obstruct the way
**encontre** [ɑ̃kɔ̃tʀ(ə)]: **à l'~ de** *prép* against, counter to
**encorbellement** [ɑ̃kɔʀbɛlmɑ̃] *nm*: **fenêtre en ~** oriel window
**encorder** [ɑ̃kɔʀde] *vt*: **s'encorder** (*Alpinisme*) to rope up

🔵 **MOT-CLÉ**

**encore** [ɑ̃kɔʀ] *adv* **1** (*continuation*) still; **il y travaille encore** he's still working on it; **pas encore** not yet
**2** (*de nouveau*) again; **j'irai encore demain** I'll go again tomorrow; **encore une fois** (once) again; **encore un effort** one last effort; **encore deux jours** two more days
**3** (*intensif*) even, still; **encore plus fort/mieux** even louder/better, louder/better still; **hier encore** even yesterday; **non seulement ..., mais encore ...** not only ..., but also ...; **encore!** (*insatisfaction*) not again!; **quoi encore?** what now?
**4** (*restriction*) even so *ou* then, only; **encore pourrais-je le faire si ...** even so, I might be able to do it if ...; **si encore** if only; **encore que** *conj* although

**encourageant, e** [ɑ̃kuʀaʒɑ̃, -ɑ̃t] *adj* encouraging
**encouragement** [ɑ̃kuʀaʒmɑ̃] *nm* encouragement; (*récompense*) incentive
**encourager** [ɑ̃kuʀaʒe] *vt* to encourage; ~ **qn à faire qch** to encourage sb to do sth
**encourir** [ɑ̃kuʀiʀ] *vt* to incur
**encrasser** [ɑ̃kʀase] *vt* to foul up; (*Auto etc*) to soot up
**encre** [ɑ̃kʀ(ə)] *nf* ink; ~ **de Chine** Indian ink; ~ **indélébile** indelible ink; ~ **sympathique** invisible ink
**encrer** [ɑ̃kʀe] *vt* to ink
**encreur** [ɑ̃kʀœʀ] *adj m*: **rouleau ~** inking roller
**encrier** [ɑ̃kʀije] *nm* inkwell
**encroûter** [ɑ̃kʀute]: **s'encroûter** *vi* (*fig*) to get into a rut, get set in one's ways
**encyclique** [ɑ̃siklik] *nf* encyclical
**encyclopédie** [ɑ̃siklɔpedi] *nf* encyclopaedia (Brit), encyclopedia (US)
**encyclopédique** [ɑ̃siklɔpedik] *adj* encyclopaedic (Brit), encyclopedic (US)
**endémique** [ɑ̃demik] *adj* endemic
**endetté, e** [ɑ̃dete] *adj* in debt; (*fig*): **très ~ envers qn** deeply indebted to sb
**endettement** [ɑ̃dɛtmɑ̃] *nm* debts *pl*
**endetter** [ɑ̃dete] *vt*, **s'endetter** *vi* to get into debt
**endeuiller** [ɑ̃dœje] *vt* to plunge into mourning; **manifestation endeuillée par** event over which a tragic shadow was cast by
**endiablé, e** [ɑ̃djable] *adj* furious; (*enfant*) boisterous
**endiguer** [ɑ̃dige] *vt* to dyke (up); (*fig*) to check, hold back
**endimanché, e** [ɑ̃dimɑ̃ʃe] *adj* in one's Sunday best
**endimancher** [ɑ̃dimɑ̃ʃe] *vt*: **s'endimancher** to put on one's Sunday best; **avoir l'air endimanché** to be all done up to the nines (*fam*)
**endive** [ɑ̃div] *nf* chicory *no pl*
**endocrine** [ɑ̃dɔkʀin] *adj f*: **glande ~** endocrine (gland)
**endoctrinement** [ɑ̃dɔktʀinmɑ̃] *nm* indoctrination
**endoctriner** [ɑ̃dɔktʀine] *vt* to indoctrinate
**endolori, e** [ɑ̃dɔlɔʀi] *adj* painful
**endommager** [ɑ̃dɔmaʒe] *vt* to damage
**endormant, e** [ɑ̃dɔʀmɑ̃, -ɑ̃t] *adj* dull, boring
**endormi, e** [ɑ̃dɔʀmi] *pp de* **endormir** ▷ *adj* (*personne*) asleep; (*fig: indolent, lent*) sluggish; (*engourdi: main, pied*) numb
**endormir** [ɑ̃dɔʀmiʀ] *vt* to put to sleep; (*chaleur etc*) to send to sleep; (*Méd: dent, nerf*) to anaesthetize; (*fig: soupçons*) to allay; **s'endormir**

*vi* to fall asleep, go to sleep

**endoscope** [ɑ̃dɔskɔp] *nm* (*Méd*) endoscope

**endoscopie** [ɑ̃dɔskɔpi] *nf* endoscopy

**endosser** [ɑ̃dose] *vt* (*responsabilité*) to take, shoulder; (*chèque*) to endorse; (*uniforme, tenue*) to put on, don

**endroit** [ɑ̃dʀwa] *nm* place; (*localité*): **les gens de l'~** the local people; (*opposé à l'envers*) right side; **à cet ~** in this place; **à l'~** right side out; the right way up; (*vêtement*) the right way out; **à l'~ de** *prép* regarding, with regard to; **par ~s** in places

**enduire** [ɑ̃dɥiʀ] *vt* to coat; **~ qch de** to coat sth with

**enduit, e** [ɑ̃dɥi, -it] *pp de* **enduire** ▷ *nm* coating

**endurance** [ɑ̃dyʀɑ̃s] *nf* endurance

**endurant, e** [ɑ̃dyʀɑ̃, -ɑ̃t] *adj* tough, hardy

**endurcir** [ɑ̃dyʀsiʀ] *vt* (*physiquement*) to toughen; (*moralement*) to harden; **s'endurcir** *vi* to become tougher; to become hardened

**endurer** [ɑ̃dyʀe] *vt* to endure, bear

**énergétique** [enɛʀʒetik] *adj* (*ressources etc*) energy *cpd*; (*aliment*) energizing

**énergie** [enɛʀʒi] *nf* (*Physique*) energy; (*Tech*) power; (*fig: physique*) energy; (*: morale*) vigour, spirit; **~ éolienne/solaire** wind/solar power

**énergique** [enɛʀʒik] *adj* energetic; vigorous; (*mesures*) drastic, stringent

**énergiquement** [enɛʀʒikmɑ̃] *adv* energetically; drastically

**énergisant, e** [enɛʀʒizɑ̃, -ɑ̃t] *adj* energizing

**énergumène** [enɛʀgymɛn] *nm* rowdy character *ou* customer

**énervant, e** [enɛʀvɑ̃, -ɑ̃t] *adj* irritating

**énervé, e** [enɛʀve] *adj* nervy, on edge; (*agacé*) irritated

**énervement** [enɛʀvəmɑ̃] *nm* nerviness; irritation

**énerver** [enɛʀve] *vt* to irritate, annoy; **s'énerver** *vi* to get excited, get worked up

**enfance** [ɑ̃fɑ̃s] *nf* (*âge*) childhood; (*fig*) infancy; (*enfants*) children *pl*; **c'est l'~ de l'art** it's child's play; **petite ~** infancy; **souvenir/ami d'~** childhood memory/friend; **retomber en ~** to lapse into one's second childhood

**enfant** [ɑ̃fɑ̃] *nm/f* child; **~ adoptif/naturel** adopted/natural child; **bon ~** *adj* good-natured, easy-going; **~ de chœur** *nm* (*Rel*) altar boy; **~ prodige** child prodigy; **~ unique** only child

**enfanter** [ɑ̃fɑ̃te] *vi* to give birth ▷ *vt* to give birth to

**enfantillage** [ɑ̃fɑ̃tijaʒ] *nm* (*péj*) childish behaviour *no pl*

**enfantin, e** [ɑ̃fɑ̃tɛ̃, -in] *adj* childlike; (*péj*) childish; (*langage*) child *cpd*

**enfer** [ɑ̃fɛʀ] *nm* hell; **allure/bruit d'~** horrendous speed/noise

**enfermer** [ɑ̃fɛʀme] *vt* to shut up; (*à clef, interner*) to lock up; **s'enfermer** to shut o.s. away; **s'~ à clé** to lock o.s. in; **s'~ dans la solitude/le mutisme** to retreat into solitude/silence

**enferrer** [ɑ̃feʀe]: **s'enferrer** *vi*: **s'~ dans** to tangle o.s. up in

**enfiévré, e** [ɑ̃fjevʀe] *adj* (*fig*) feverish

**enfilade** [ɑ̃filad] *nf*: **une ~ de** a series *ou* line of; **prendre des rues en ~** to cross directly from one street into the next

**enfiler** [ɑ̃file] *vt* (*vêtement*): **~ qch** to slip sth on, slip into sth; (*insérer*): **~ qch dans** to stick sth into; (*rue, couloir*) to take; (*perles*) to string; (*aiguille*) to thread; **s'enfiler dans** *vi* to disappear into

**enfin** [ɑ̃fɛ̃] *adv* at last; (*en énumérant*) lastly; (*de restriction, résignation*) still; (*eh bien*) well; (*pour conclure*) in a word

**enflammé, e** [ɑ̃flame] *adj* (*torche, allumette*) burning; (*Méd: plaie*) inflamed; (*fig: nature, discours, déclaration*) fiery

**enflammer** [ɑ̃flame] *vt* to set fire to; (*Méd*) to inflame; **s'enflammer** *vi* to catch fire; to become inflamed

**enflé, e** [ɑ̃fle] *adj* swollen; (*péj: style*) bombastic, turgid

**enfler** [ɑ̃fle] *vi* to swell (up); **s'enfler** *vi* to swell

**enflure** [ɑ̃flyʀ] *nf* swelling

**enfoncé, e** [ɑ̃fɔ̃se] *adj* staved-in, smashed-in; (*yeux*) deep-set

**enfoncement** [ɑ̃fɔ̃smɑ̃] *nm* (*recoin*) nook

**enfoncer** [ɑ̃fɔ̃se] *vt* (*clou*) to drive in; (*faire pénétrer*): **~ qch dans** to push (*ou* drive) sth into; (*forcer: porte*) to break open; (*: plancher*) to cause to cave in; (*défoncer: côtes etc*) to smash; (*fam: surpasser*) to lick, beat (hollow) ▷ *vi* (*dans la vase etc*) to sink in; (*sol, surface porteuse*) to give way; **s'enfoncer** *vi* to sink; **s'~ dans** to sink into; (*forêt, ville*) to disappear into; **~ un chapeau sur la tête** to cram *ou* jam a hat on one's head; **~ qn dans la dette** to drag sb into debt

**enfouir** [ɑ̃fwiʀ] *vt* (*dans le sol*) to bury; (*dans un tiroir etc*) to tuck away; **s'enfouir dans/sous** to bury o.s. in/under

**enfourcher** [ɑ̃fuʀʃe] *vt* to mount; **~ son dada** (*fig*) to get on one's hobby-horse

**enfourner** [ɑ̃fuʀne] *vt* to put in the oven; (*poterie*) to put in the kiln; **~ qch dans** to shove *ou* stuff sth into; **s'enfourner dans** (*personne*) to dive into

**enfreignais** *etc* [ɑ̃fʀɛɲɛ] *vb voir* **enfreindre**

**enfreindre** [ɑ̃fʀɛ̃dʀ(ə)] *vt* to infringe, break

**enfuir** [ɑ̃fɥiʀ]: **s'enfuir** *vi* to run away *ou* off

**enfumer** [ɑ̃fyme] *vt* to smoke out

**enfuyais** *etc* [ɑ̃fɥijɛ] *vb voir* **enfuir**

**engagé, e** [ɑ̃gaʒe] *adj* (*littérature etc*) engagé, committed

**engageant, e** [ɑ̃gaʒɑ̃, -ɑ̃t] *adj* attractive, appealing

**engagement** [ɑ̃gaʒmɑ̃] *nm* taking on, engaging; starting; investing; (*promesse*) commitment; (*Mil: combat*) engagement; (*: recrutement*) enlistment; (*Sport*) entry; **prendre l'~ de faire** to undertake to do; **sans ~** (*Comm*) without obligation

**engager** [ɑ̃gaʒe] *vt* (*embaucher*) to take on,

engage; (*commencer*) to start; (*lier*) to bind, commit; (*impliquer, entraîner*) to involve; (*investir*) to invest, lay out; (*faire intervenir*) to engage; (*Sport: concurrents, chevaux*) to enter; (*inciter*): ~ **qn à faire** to urge sb to do; (*faire pénétrer*): ~ **qch dans** to insert sth into; ~ **qn à qch** to urge sth on sb; **s'engager** *vi* to get taken on; (*Mil*) to enlist; (*promettre, politiquement*) to commit o.s.; (*débuter*) to start (up); **s'~ à faire** to undertake to do; **s'~ dans** (*rue, passage*) to enter, turn into; (*s'emboîter*) to engage *ou* fit into; (*fig: affaire, discussion*) to enter into, embark on

**engazonner** [ɑ̃gazɔne] *vt* to turf

**engeance** [ɑ̃ʒɑ̃s] *nf* mob

**engelures** [ɑ̃ʒlyʀ] *nfpl* chilblains

**engendrer** [ɑ̃ʒɑ̃dʀe] *vt* to father; (*fig*) to create, breed

**engin** [ɑ̃ʒɛ̃] *nm* machine instrument; vehicle; (*péj*) gadget; (*Aviat: avion*) aircraft *inv*; (: *missile*) missile; ~ **blindé** armoured vehicle; ~ **(explosif)** (explosive) device; ~**s (spéciaux)** missiles

**englober** [ɑ̃glɔbe] *vt* to include

**engloutir** [ɑ̃glutiʀ] *vt* to swallow up; (*fig: dépenses*) to devour; **s'engloutir** *vi* to be engulfed

**englué, e** [ɑ̃glye] *adj* sticky

**engoncé, e** [ɑ̃gɔ̃se] *adj*: ~ **dans** cramped in

**engorgement** [ɑ̃gɔʀʒəmɑ̃] *nm* blocking; (*Méd*) engorgement

**engorger** [ɑ̃gɔʀʒe] *vt* to obstruct, block; **s'engorger** *vi* to become blocked

**engouement** [ɑ̃gumɑ̃] *nm* (sudden) passion

**engouffrer** [ɑ̃gufʀe] *vt* to swallow up, devour; **s'engouffrer dans** to rush into

**engourdi, e** [ɑ̃guʀdi] *adj* numb

**engourdir** [ɑ̃guʀdiʀ] *vt* to numb; (*fig*) to dull, blunt; **s'engourdir** *vi* to go numb

**engrais** [ɑ̃gʀɛ] *nm* manure; ~ **(chimique)** (chemical) fertilizer; ~ **organique/inorganique** organic/inorganic fertilizer

**engraisser** [ɑ̃gʀese] *vt* to fatten (up); (*terre: fertiliser*) to fertilize ▷ *vi* (*péj*) to get fat(ter)

**engranger** [ɑ̃gʀɑ̃ʒe] *vt* (*foin*) to bring in; (*fig*) to store away

**engrenage** [ɑ̃gʀənaʒ] *nm* gears *pl*, gearing; (*fig*) chain

**engueuler** [ɑ̃gœle] *vt* (*fam*) to bawl at *ou* out

**enguirlander** [ɑ̃giʀlɑ̃de] *vt* (*fam*) to give sb a bawling out, bawl at

**enhardir** [ɑ̃aʀdiʀ]: **s'enhardir** *vi* to grow bolder

**ENI** [eni] *sigle f* = **école normale (d'instituteurs)**

**énième** [enjɛm] *adj* = **nième**

**énigmatique** [enigmatik] *adj* enigmatic

**énigmatiquement** [enigmatikmɑ̃] *adv* enigmatically

**énigme** [enigm(ə)] *nf* riddle

**enivrant, e** [ɑ̃nivʀɑ̃, -ɑ̃t] *adj* intoxicating

**enivrer** [ɑ̃nivʀe] *vt*: **s'enivrer** to get drunk; **s'~ de** (*fig*) to become intoxicated with

**enjambée** [ɑ̃ʒɑ̃be] *nf* stride; **d'une ~** with one stride

**enjamber** [ɑ̃ʒɑ̃be] *vt* to stride over; (*pont etc*) to span, straddle

**enjeu, x** [ɑ̃ʒø] *nm* stakes *pl*

**enjoindre** [ɑ̃ʒwɛ̃dʀ(ə)] *vt*: ~ **à qn de faire** to enjoin *ou* order sb to do

**enjôler** [ɑ̃ʒole] *vt* to coax, wheedle

**enjôleur, -euse** [ɑ̃ʒolœʀ, -øz] *adj* (*sourire, paroles*) winning

**enjolivement** [ɑ̃ʒɔlivmɑ̃] *nm* embellishment

**enjoliver** [ɑ̃ʒɔlive] *vt* to embellish

**enjoliveur** [ɑ̃ʒɔlivœʀ] *nm* (*Auto*) hub cap

**enjoué, e** [ɑ̃ʒwe] *adj* playful

**enlacer** [ɑ̃lase] *vt* (*étreindre*) to embrace, hug; (*lianes*) to wind round, entwine

**enlaidir** [ɑ̃lediʀ] *vt* to make ugly ▷ *vi* to become ugly

**enlevé, e** [ɑ̃lve] *adj* (*morceau de musique*) played brightly

**enlèvement** [ɑ̃lɛvmɑ̃] *nm* removal; (*rapt*) abduction, kidnapping; **l'~ des ordures ménagères** refuse collection

**enlever** [ɑ̃lve] *vt* (*ôter: gén*) to remove; (: *vêtement, lunettes*) to take off; (: *Méd: organe*) to remove; (*emporter: ordures etc*) to collect, take away; (*kidnapper*) to abduct, kidnap; (*obtenir: prix, contrat*) to win; (*Mil: position*) to take; (*morceau de piano etc*) to execute with spirit *ou* brio; (*prendre*): ~ **qch à qn** to take sth (away) from sb; **s'enlever** *vi* (*tache*) to come out *ou* off; **la maladie qui nous l'a enlevé** (*euphémisme*) the illness which took him from us

**enliser** [ɑ̃lize]: **s'enliser** *vi* to sink, get stuck; (*dialogue etc*) to get bogged down

**enluminure** [ɑ̃lyminyʀ] *nf* illumination

**ENM** *sigle f* (= *École nationale de la magistrature*) grande école for law students

**enneigé, e** [ɑ̃neʒe] *adj* snowy; (*col*) snowed-up; (*maison*) snowed-in

**enneigement** [ɑ̃nɛʒmɑ̃] *nm* depth of snow, snowfall; **bulletin d'~** snow report

**ennemi, e** [ɛnmi] *adj* hostile; (*Mil*) enemy *cpd* ▷ *nm/f* enemy; **être ~ de** to be strongly averse *ou* opposed to

**ennième** [ɛnjɛm] *adj* = **nième**

**ennoblir** [ɑ̃nɔbliʀ] *vt* to ennoble

**ennui** [ɑ̃nɥi] *nm* (*lassitude*) boredom; (*difficulté*) trouble *no pl*; **avoir des ~s** to have problems; **s'attirer des ~s** to cause problems for o.s.

**ennuie etc** [ɑ̃nɥi] *vb voir* **ennuyer**

**ennuyé, e** [ɑ̃nɥije] *adj* (*air, personne*) preoccupied, worried

**ennuyer** [ɑ̃nɥije] *vt* to bother; (*lasser*) to bore; **s'ennuyer** *vi* to be bored; (*s'ennuyer de: regretter*) to miss; **si cela ne vous ennuie pas** if it's no trouble to you

**ennuyeux, -euse** [ɑ̃nɥijø, -øz] *adj* boring, tedious; (*agaçant*) annoying

**énoncé** [enɔ̃se] *nm* terms *pl*; wording; (*Ling*) utterance

**énoncer** [enɔ̃se] *vt* to say, express; (*conditions*) to set out, lay down, state

**énonciation** [enɔ̃sjɑsjɔ̃] *nf* statement

**enorgueillir** [ɑ̃nɔʀgœjiʀ]: **s'enorgueillir de** *vt* to pride o.s. on; to boast

**énorme** [enɔʀm(ə)] *adj* enormous, huge

**énormément** [enɔʀmemɑ̃] *adv* enormously, tremendously; ~ **de neige/gens** an enormous amount of snow/number of people

**énormité** [enɔʀmite] *nf* enormity, hugeness; (*propos*) outrageous remark

**en part.** *abr* (= *en particulier*) esp.

**enquérir** [ɑ̃keʀiʀ]: **s'enquérir de** *vt* to inquire about

**enquête** [ɑ̃kɛt] *nf* (*de journaliste, de police*) investigation; (*judiciaire, administrative*) inquiry; (*sondage d'opinion*) survey

**enquêter** [ɑ̃kete] *vi* to investigate; to hold an inquiry; (*faire un sondage*): ~ **(sur)** to do a survey (on), carry out an opinion poll (on)

**enquêteur, -euse** *ou* **-trice** [ɑ̃kɛtœʀ, -øz, -tʀis] *nm/f* officer in charge of an investigation; person conducting a survey; pollster

**enquiers, enquière** *etc* [ɑ̃kjɛʀ] *vb voir* **enquérir**

**enquiquiner** [ɑ̃kikine] *vt* to rile, irritate

**enquis, e** [ɑ̃ki, -iz] *pp de* **enquérir**

**enraciné, e** [ɑ̃ʀasine] *adj* deep-rooted

**enragé, e** [ɑ̃ʀaʒe] *adj* (*Méd*) rabid, with rabies; (*furieux*) furiously angry; (*fig*) fanatical; ~ **de** wild about

**enrageant, e** [ɑ̃ʀaʒɑ̃, -ɑ̃t] *adj* infuriating

**enrager** [ɑ̃ʀaʒe] *vi* to be furious, be in a rage; **faire** ~ **qn** to make sb wild with anger

**enrayer** [ɑ̃ʀeje] *vt* to check, stop; **s'enrayer** *vi* (*arme à feu*) to jam

**enrégimenter** [ɑ̃ʀeʒimɑ̃te] *vt* (*péj*) to enlist

**enregistrement** [ɑ̃ʀʒistʀəmɑ̃] *nm* recording; (*Admin*) registration; ~ **des bagages** (*à l'aéroport*) baggage check-in; ~ **magnétique** tape-recording

**enregistrer** [ɑ̃ʀʒistʀe] *vt* (*Mus*) to record; (*Inform*) to save; (*remarquer, noter*) to note, record; (*Comm: commande*) to note, enter; (*fig: mémoriser*) to make a mental note of; (*Admin*) to register; (*aussi:* **faire enregistrer**: *bagages: par train*) to register; (: *à l'aéroport*) to check in

**enregistreur, -euse** [ɑ̃ʀʒistʀœʀ, -øz] *adj* (*machine*) recording *cpd* ▷ *nm* (*appareil*): ~ **de vol** (*Aviat*) flight recorder

**enrhumé, e** [ɑ̃ʀyme] *adj*: **il est** ~ he has a cold

**enrhumer** [ɑ̃ʀyme]: **s'enrhumer** *vi* to catch a cold

**enrichir** [ɑ̃ʀiʃiʀ] *vt* to make rich(er); (*fig*) to enrich; **s'enrichir** *vi* to get rich(er)

**enrichissant, e** [ɑ̃ʀiʃisɑ̃, -ɑ̃t] *adj* instructive

**enrichissement** [ɑ̃ʀiʃismɑ̃] *nm* enrichment

**enrober** [ɑ̃ʀɔbe] *vt*: ~ **qch de** to coat sth with; (*fig*) to wrap sth up in

**enrôlement** [ɑ̃ʀolmɑ̃] *nm* enlistment

**enrôler** [ɑ̃ʀole] *vt* to enlist; **s'enrôler (dans)** *vi* to enlist (in)

**enroué, e** [ɑ̃ʀwe] *adj* hoarse

**enrouer** [ɑ̃ʀwe]: **s'enrouer** *vi* to go hoarse

**enrouler** [ɑ̃ʀule] *vt* (*fil, corde*) to wind (up); **s'enrouler** to coil up; ~ **qch autour de** to wind sth (a)round

**enrouleur, -euse** [ɑ̃ʀulœʀ, -øz] *adj* (*Tech*) winding ▷ *nm voir* **ceinture**

**enrubanné, e** [ɑ̃ʀybane] *adj* trimmed with ribbon

**ENS** *sigle f* = **école normale supérieure**

**ensabler** [ɑ̃sable] *vt* (*port, canal*) to silt up, sand up; (*embarcation*) to strand (on a sandbank); **s'ensabler** *vi* to silt up; to get stranded

**ensacher** [ɑ̃saʃe] *vt* to pack into bags

**ENSAM** *sigle f* (= *École nationale supérieure des arts et métiers*) *grande école for engineering students*

**ensanglanté, e** [ɑ̃sɑ̃glɑ̃te] *adj* covered with blood

**enseignant, e** [ɑ̃sɛɲɑ̃, -ɑ̃t] *adj* teaching ▷ *nm/f* teacher

**enseigne** [ɑ̃sɛɲ] *nf* sign ▷ *nm*: ~ **de vaisseau** lieutenant; **à telle** ~ **que** so much so that; **être logés à la même** ~ (*fig*) to be in the same boat; ~ **lumineuse** neon sign

**enseignement** [ɑ̃sɛɲmɑ̃] *nm* teaching; ~ **ménager** home economics; ~ **primaire** primary (*Brit*) *ou* grade school (*US*) education; ~ **secondaire** secondary (*Brit*) *ou* high school (*US*) education

**enseigner** [ɑ̃seɲe] *vt, vi* to teach; ~ **qch à qn/à qn que** to teach sb sth/sb that

**ensemble** [ɑ̃sɑ̃bl(ə)] *adv* together ▷ *nm* (*assemblage, Math*) set; (*totalité*): **l'** ~ **du/de la** the whole *ou* entire; (*vêtement féminin*) ensemble, suit; (*unité, harmonie*) unity; (*résidentiel*) housing development; **aller** ~ to go together; **impression/idée d'** ~ overall *ou* general impression/idea; **dans l'** ~ (*en gros*) on the whole; **dans son** ~ overall, in general; ~ **vocal/musical** vocal/musical ensemble

**ensemblier** [ɑ̃sɑ̃blije] *nm* interior designer

**ensemencer** [ɑ̃smɑ̃se] *vt* to sow

**enserrer** [ɑ̃seʀe] *vt* to hug (tightly)

**ENSET** [ɑ̃sɛt] *sigle f* (= *École normale supérieure de l'enseignement technique*) *grande école for training technical teachers*

**ensevelir** [ɑ̃səvliʀ] *vt* to bury

**ensilage** [ɑ̃silaʒ] *nm* (*aliment*) silage

**ensoleillé, e** [ɑ̃sɔleje] *adj* sunny

**ensoleillement** [ɑ̃sɔlɛjmɑ̃] *nm* period *ou* hours *pl* of sunshine

**ensommeillé, e** [ɑ̃sɔmeje] *adj* sleepy, drowsy

**ensorceler** [ɑ̃sɔʀsəle] *vt* to enchant, bewitch

**ensuite** [ɑ̃sɥit] *adv* then, next; (*plus tard*) afterwards, later; ~ **de quoi** after which

**ensuivre** [ɑ̃sɥivʀ(ə)]: **s'ensuivre** *vi* to follow, ensue; **il s'ensuit que ...** it follows that ...; **et tout ce qui s'ensuit** and all that goes with it

**entaché, e** [ɑ̃taʃe] *adj*: ~ **de** marred by; ~ **de nullité** null and void

**entacher** [ɑ̃taʃe] *vt* to soil

**entaille** [ɑ̃taj] *nf* (*encoche*) notch; (*blessure*) cut; **se faire une** ~ to cut o.s.

**entailler** [ɑ̃taje] *vt* to notch; to cut; **s'** ~ **le doigt** to cut one's finger

**entamer** [ɑ̃tame] *vt* to start; (*hostilités, pourparlers*) to open; (*fig: altérer*) to make a dent in; to damage

**entartrer** [ɑ̃taʀtʀe]: **s'entartrer** vi to fur up; (dents) to become covered with plaque

**entassement** [ɑ̃tasmɑ̃] nm (tas) pile, heap

**entasser** [ɑ̃tase] vt (empiler) to pile up, heap up; (tenir à l'étroit) to cram together; **s'entasser** vi to pile up; to cram; **s'~ dans** to cram into

**entendement** [ɑ̃tɑ̃dmɑ̃] nm understanding

**entendre** [ɑ̃tɑ̃dʀ(ə)] vt to hear; (comprendre) to understand; (vouloir dire) to mean; (vouloir): **~ être obéi/que** to intend ou mean to be obeyed/ that; **j'ai entendu dire que** I've heard (it said) that; **je suis heureux de vous l'~ dire** I'm pleased to hear you say it; **~ parler de** to hear of; **laisser ~ que, donner à ~ que** to let it be understood that; **~ raison** to see sense, listen to reason; **qu'est-ce qu'il ne faut pas ~**! whatever next!; **j'ai mal entendu** I didn't catch what was said; **je vous entends très mal** I can hardly hear you; **s'entendre** vi (sympathiser) to get on; (se mettre d'accord) to agree; **s'~ à qch/à faire** (être compétent) to be good at sth/doing; **ça s'entend** (est audible) it's audible; **je m'entends** I mean; **entendons-nous!** let's be clear what we mean

**entendu, e** [ɑ̃tɑ̃dy] pp de **entendre** ▷ adj (réglé) agreed; (au courant: air) knowing; **étant ~ que** since (it's understood ou agreed that); **(c'est) ~** all right, agreed; **c'est ~** (concession) all right, granted; **bien ~** of course

**entente** [ɑ̃tɑ̃t] nf (entre amis, pays) understanding, harmony; (accord, traité) agreement, understanding; **à double ~** (sens) with a double meaning

**entériner** [ɑ̃teʀine] vt to ratify, confirm

**entérite** [ɑ̃teʀit] nf enteritis no pl

**enterrement** [ɑ̃tɛʀmɑ̃] nm burying; (cérémonie) funeral, burial; (cortège funèbre) funeral procession

**enterrer** [ɑ̃teʀe] vt to bury

**entêtant, e** [ɑ̃tɛtɑ̃, -ɑ̃t] adj heady

**en-tête** [ɑ̃tɛt] nm heading; (de papier à lettres) letterhead; **papier à ~** headed notepaper

**entêté, e** [ɑ̃tete] adj stubborn

**entêtement** [ɑ̃tɛtmɑ̃] nm stubbornness

**entêter** [ɑ̃tete]: **s'entêter** vi: **s'~ (à faire)** to persist (in doing)

**enthousiasmant, e** [ɑ̃tuzjasmɑ̃, -ɑ̃t] adj exciting

**enthousiasme** [ɑ̃tuzjasm(ə)] nm enthusiasm; **avec ~** enthusiastically

**enthousiasmé, e** [ɑ̃tuzjasme] adj filled with enthusiasm

**enthousiasmer** [ɑ̃tuzjasme] vt to fill with enthusiasm; **s'~ (pour qch)** to get enthusiastic (about sth)

**enthousiaste** [ɑ̃tuzjast(ə)] adj enthusiastic

**enticher** [ɑ̃tiʃe]: **s'enticher de** vt to become infatuated with

**entier, -ière** [ɑ̃tje, -jɛʀ] adj (non entamé, en totalité) whole; (total, complet) complete; (fig: caractère) unbending, averse to compromise ▷ nm (Math)

whole; **en ~** totally; in its entirety; **se donner tout ~ à qch** to devote o.s. completely to sth; **lait ~** full-cream milk; **pain ~** wholemeal bread; **nombre ~** whole number

**entièrement** [ɑ̃tjɛʀmɑ̃] adv entirely, completely, wholly

**entité** [ɑ̃tite] nf entity

**entomologie** [ɑ̃tɔmɔlɔʒi] nf entomology

**entonner** [ɑ̃tɔne] vt (chanson) to strike up

**entonnoir** [ɑ̃tɔnwaʀ] nm (ustensile) funnel; (trou) shell-hole, crater

**entorse** [ɑ̃tɔʀs(ə)] nf (Méd) sprain; (fig): **~ à la loi/au règlement** infringement of the law/ rule; **se faire une ~ à la cheville/au poignet** to sprain one's ankle/wrist

**entortiller** [ɑ̃tɔʀtije] vt (envelopper): **~ qch dans/ avec** to wrap sth in/with; (enrouler): **~ qch autour de** to twist ou wind sth (a)round; (fam): **~ qn** to get (a)round sb; (: duper) to hoodwink sb (Brit), trick sb; **s'entortiller dans** vi (draps) to roll o.s. up in; (fig: réponses) to get tangled up in

**entourage** [ɑ̃tuʀaʒ] nm circle; family (circle); (d'une vedette etc) entourage; (ce qui enclôt) surround

**entouré, e** [ɑ̃tuʀe] adj (recherché, admiré) popular; **~ de** surrounded by

**entourer** [ɑ̃tuʀe] vt to surround; (apporter son soutien à) to rally round; **~ de** to surround with; (trait) to encircle with; **s'entourer de** vi to surround o.s. with; **s'~ de précautions** to take all possible precautions

**entouloupette** [ɑ̃tuʀlupɛt] nf mean trick

**entournures** [ɑ̃tuʀnyʀ] nfpl: **gêné aux ~** in financial difficulties; (fig) a bit awkward

**entracte** [ɑ̃tʀakt(ə)] nm interval

**entraide** [ɑ̃tʀɛd] nf mutual aid ou assistance

**entraider** [ɑ̃tʀede]: **s'entraider** vi to help each other

**entrailles** [ɑ̃tʀaj] nfpl entrails; (humaines) bowels

**entrain** [ɑ̃tʀɛ̃] nm spirit; **avec ~** (répondre, travailler) energetically; **faire qch sans ~** to do sth half-heartedly ou without enthusiasm

**entraînant, e** [ɑ̃tʀɛnɑ̃, -ɑ̃t] adj (musique) stirring, rousing

**entraînement** [ɑ̃tʀɛnmɑ̃] nm training; (Tech): **~ à chaîne/galet** chain/wheel drive; **manquer d'~** to be unfit; **~ par ergots/friction** (Inform) tractor/friction feed

**entraîner** [ɑ̃tʀene] vt (tirer: wagons) to pull; (charrier) to carry ou drag along; (Tech) to drive; (emmener: personne) to take (off); (mener à l'assaut, influencer) to lead; (Sport) to train; (impliquer) to entail; (causer) to lead to, bring about; **~ qn à faire** (inciter) to lead sb to do; **s'entraîner** vi (Sport) to train; **s'~ à qch/à faire** to train o.s. for sth/to do

**entraîneur** [ɑ̃tʀɛnœʀ] nm (Sport) coach, trainer; (Hippisme) trainer

**entraîneuse** [ɑ̃tʀɛnøz] nf (de bar) hostess

**entrapercevoir** [ɑ̃tʀapɛʀsəvwaʀ] vt to catch a glimpse of

**entrave** [ɑ̃tʀav] nf hindrance
**entraver** [ɑ̃tʀave] vt (*circulation*) to hold up; (*action, progrès*) to hinder, hamper
**entre** [ɑ̃tʀ(ə)] *prép* between; (*parmi*) among(st); **l'un d'~ eux/nous** one of them/us; **le meilleur d'~ eux/nous** the best of them/us; **ils préfèrent rester ~ eux** they prefer to keep to themselves; **~ autres (choses)** among other things; **~ nous, ...** between ourselves ..., between you and me ...; **ils se battent ~ eux** they are fighting among(st) themselves
**entrebâillé, e** [ɑ̃tʀəbaje] *adj* half-open, ajar
**entrebâillement** [ɑ̃tʀəbajmɑ̃] nm: **dans l'~ (de la porte)** in the half-open door
**entrebâiller** [ɑ̃tʀəbaje] vt to half open
**entrechat** [ɑ̃tʀəʃa] nm leap
**entrechoquer** [ɑ̃tʀəʃɔke]: **s'entrechoquer** vi to knock ou bang together
**entrecôte** [ɑ̃tʀəkot] nf entrecôte ou rib steak
**entrecoupé, e** [ɑ̃tʀəkupe] *adj* (*paroles, voix*) broken
**entrecouper** [ɑ̃tʀəkupe] vt: **~ qch de** to intersperse sth with; **~ un récit/voyage de** to interrupt a story/journey with; **s'entrecouper** vi (*traits, lignes*) to cut across each other
**entrecroiser** [ɑ̃tʀəkʀwaze] vt, **s'entrecroiser** vi to intertwine
**entrée** [ɑ̃tʀe] nf entrance; (*accès: au cinéma etc*) admission; (*billet*) (admission) ticket; (*Culin*) first course; (*Comm: de marchandises*) entry; (*Inform*) entry, input; **entrées** nfpl: **avoir ses ~s chez** ou **auprès de** to be a welcome visitor to; **d'~** *adv* from the outset; **erreur d'~** input error; **"~ interdite"** "no admittance ou entry"; **~ des artistes** stage door; **~ en matière** introduction; **~ principale** main entrance; **~ en scène** entrance; **~ de service** service entrance
**entrefaites** [ɑ̃tʀəfɛt]: **sur ces ~** *adv* at this juncture
**entrefilet** [ɑ̃tʀəfilɛ] nm (*article*) paragraph, short report
**entregent** [ɑ̃tʀəʒɑ̃] nm: **avoir de l'~** to have an easy manner
**entrejambes** [ɑ̃tʀəʒɑ̃b] nm inv crotch
**entrelacement** [ɑ̃tʀəlasmɑ̃] nm: **un ~ de ...** a network of ...
**entrelacer** [ɑ̃tʀəlase] vt, **s'entrelacer** vi to intertwine
**entrelarder** [ɑ̃tʀəlaʀde] vt to lard; (*fig*): **entrelardé de** interspersed with
**entremêler** [ɑ̃tʀəmele] vt: **~ qch de** to (inter)mingle sth with
**entremets** [ɑ̃tʀəmɛ] nm (cream) dessert
**entremetteur, -euse** [ɑ̃tʀəmɛtœʀ, -øz] nm/f go-between
**entremettre** [ɑ̃tʀəmɛtʀ(ə)]: **s'entremettre** vi to intervene
**entremise** [ɑ̃tʀəmiz] nf intervention; **par l'~ de** through
**entrepont** [ɑ̃tʀəpɔ̃] nm steerage; **dans l'~** in steerage

**entreposer** [ɑ̃tʀəpoze] vt to store, put into storage
**entrepôt** [ɑ̃tʀəpo] nm warehouse
**entreprenant, e** [ɑ̃tʀəpʀənɑ̃, -ɑ̃t] vb voir **entreprendre** ▷ *adj* (*actif*) enterprising; (*trop galant*) forward
**entreprendre** [ɑ̃tʀəpʀɑ̃dʀ(ə)] vt (*se lancer dans*) to undertake; (*commencer*) to begin ou start (upon); (*personne*) to buttonhole; **~ qn sur un sujet** to tackle sb on a subject; **~ de faire** to undertake to do
**entrepreneur** [ɑ̃tʀəpʀənœʀ] nm: **~ (en bâtiment)** (building) contractor; **~ de pompes funèbres** funeral director, undertaker
**entreprenne** etc [ɑ̃tʀəpʀɛn] vb voir **entreprendre**
**entrepris, e** [ɑ̃tʀəpʀi, -iz] pp de **entreprendre** ▷ nf (*société*) firm, business; (*action*) undertaking, venture
**entrer** [ɑ̃tʀe] vi to go (ou come) in, enter ▷ vt (*Inform*) to input, enter; **(faire) ~ qch dans** to get sth into; **~ dans** (*gén*) to enter; (*pièce*) to go (ou come) into, enter; (*club*) to join; (*heurter*) to run into; (*partager: vues, craintes de qn*) to share; (*être une composante de*) to go into; (*faire partie de*) to form part of; **~ au couvent** to enter a convent; **~ à l'hôpital** to go into hospital; **~ dans le système** (*Inform*) to log in; **~ en fureur** to become angry; **~ en ébullition** to start to boil; **~ en scène** to come on stage; **laisser ~ qn/qch** to let sb/sth in; **faire ~** (*visiteur*) to show in
**entresol** [ɑ̃tʀəsɔl] nm entresol, mezzanine
**entre-temps** [ɑ̃tʀətɑ̃] *adv* meanwhile, (in the) meantime
**entretenir** [ɑ̃tʀətniʀ] vt to maintain; (*amitié*) to keep alive; (*famille, maîtresse*) to support, keep; **~ qn (de)** to speak to sb (about); **s'entretenir (de)** to converse (about); **~ qn dans l'erreur** to let sb remain in ignorance
**entretenu, e** [ɑ̃tʀətny] pp de **entretenir** ▷ *adj* (*femme*) kept; **bien/mal ~** (*maison, jardin*) well/badly kept
**entretien** [ɑ̃tʀətjɛ̃] nm maintenance; (*discussion*) discussion, talk; (*audience*) interview; **frais d'~** maintenance charges
**entretiendrai** [ɑ̃tʀətjɛ̃dʀe], **entretiens** etc [ɑ̃tʀətjɛ̃] vb voir **entretenir**
**entretuer** [ɑ̃tʀətɥe]: **s'entretuer** vi to kill one another
**entreverrai** [ɑ̃tʀəvɛʀe], **entrevit** etc [ɑ̃tʀəvi] vb voir **entrevoir**
**entrevoir** [ɑ̃tʀəvwaʀ] vt (*à peine*) to make out; (*brièvement*) to catch a glimpse of
**entrevu, e** [ɑ̃tʀəvy] pp de **entrevoir** ▷ nf meeting; (*audience*) interview
**entrouvert, e** [ɑ̃tʀuvɛʀ, -ɛʀt(ə)] pp de **entrouvrir** ▷ *adj* half-open
**entrouvrir** [ɑ̃tʀuvʀiʀ] vt, **s'entrouvrir** vi to half open
**énumération** [enymeʀasjɔ̃] nf enumeration
**énumérer** [enymeʀe] vt to list, enumerate
**envahir** [ɑ̃vaiʀ] vt to invade; (*inquiétude, peur*) to

155

come over

**envahissant, e** [ãvaisã, -ãt] *adj* (*péj: personne*) interfering, intrusive

**envahissement** [ãvaismã] *nm* invasion

**envahisseur** [ãvaisœʀ] *nm* (*Mil*) invader

**envasement** [ãnvazmã] *nm* silting up

**envaser** [ãvaze]: **s'envaser** *vi* to get bogged down (in the mud)

**enveloppe** [ãvlɔp] *nf* (*de lettre*) envelope; (*Tech*) casing; outer layer; **mettre sous ~** to put in an envelope; **~ autocollante** self-seal envelope; **~ budgétaire** budget; **~ à fenêtre** window envelope

**envelopper** [ãvlɔpe] *vt* to wrap; (*fig*) to envelop, shroud; **s'~ dans un châle/une couverture** to wrap o.s. in a shawl/blanket

**envenimer** [ãvnime] *vt* to aggravate; **s'envenimer** *vi* (*plaie*) to fester; (*situation, relations*) to worsen

**envergure** [ãvɛʀgyʀ] *nf* (*d'un oiseau, avion*) wingspan; (*fig: étendue*) scope; (*: valeur*) calibre

**enverrai** *etc* [ãvɛʀe] *vb voir* **envoyer**

**envers** [ãvɛʀ] *prép* towards, to ▷ *nm* other side; (*d'une étoffe*) wrong side; **à l'~** upside down; back to front; (*vêtement*) inside out; **~ et contre tous** *ou* **tout** against all opposition

**enviable** [ãvjabl(ə)] *adj* enviable; **peu ~** unenviable

**envie** [ãvi] *nf* (*sentiment*) envy; (*souhait*) desire, wish; (*tache sur la peau*) birthmark; (*filet de peau*) hangnail; **avoir ~ de** to feel like; (*désir plus fort*) to want; **avoir ~ de faire** to feel like doing; to want to do; **avoir ~ que** to wish that; **donner à qn l'~ de faire** to make sb want to do; **ça lui fait ~** he would like that

**envier** [ãvje] *vt* to envy; **~ qch à qn** to envy sb sth; **n'avoir rien à ~ à** to have no cause to be envious of

**envieux, -euse** [ãvjø, -øz] *adj* envious

**environ** [ãviʀɔ̃] *adv*: **~ 3 h/2 km, 3 h/2km ~** (around) about 3 o'clock/2 km, 3 o'clock/2 km or so

**environnant, e** [ãviʀɔnã, -ãt] *adj* surrounding

**environnement** [ãviʀɔnmã] *nm* environment

**environnementaliste** [ãviʀɔnmãtalist(ə)] *nm/f* environmentalist

**environner** [ãviʀɔne] *vt* to surround

**environs** [ãviʀɔ̃] *nmpl* surroundings; **aux ~ de** around

**envisageable** [ãvizaʒabl(ə)] *adj* conceivable

**envisager** [ãvizaʒe] *vt* (*examiner, considérer*) to view, contemplate; (*avoir en vue*) to envisage; **~ de faire** to consider doing

**envoi** [ãvwa] *nm* sending; (*paquet*) parcel, consignment; **~ contre remboursement** (*Comm*) cash on delivery

**envoie** *etc* [ãvwa] *vb voir* **envoyer**

**envol** [ãvɔl] *nm* takeoff

**envolée** [ãvɔle] *nf* (*fig*) flight

**envoler** [ãvɔle]: **s'envoler** *vi* (*oiseau*) to fly away *ou* off; (*avion*) to take off; (*papier, feuille*) to blow away; (*fig*) to vanish (into thin air)

**envoûtant, e** [ãvutã, -ãt] *adj* enchanting

**envoûtement** [ãvutmã] *nm* bewitchment

**envoûter** [ãvute] *vt* to bewitch

**envoyé, e** [ãvwaje] *nm/f* (*Pol*) envoy; (*Presse*) correspondent ▷ *adj*: **bien ~** (*remarque, réponse*) well-aimed

**envoyer** [ãvwaje] *vt* to send; (*lancer*) to hurl, throw; **~ une gifle/un sourire à qn** to aim a blow/flash a smile at sb; **~ les couleurs** to run up the colours; **~ chercher** to send for; **~ par le fond** (*bateau*) to send to the bottom

**envoyeur, -euse** [ãvwajœʀ, -øz] *nm/f* sender

**enzyme** [ãzim] *nf ou m* enzyme

**éolien, ne** [eɔljɛ̃, -ɛn] *adj* wind *cpd* ▷ *nf* wind turbine; **pompe ~ne** windpump

**EOR** *sigle m* (= *élève officier de réserve*) ≈ military cadet

**éosine** [eɔzin] *nf* eosin (*antiseptic used in France to treat skin ailments*)

**épagneul, e** [epaɲœl] *nm/f* spaniel

**épais, se** [epɛ, -ɛs] *adj* thick

**épaisseur** [epɛsœʀ] *nf* thickness

**épaissir** [epesiʀ] *vt*, **s'épaissir** *vi* to thicken

**épaississement** [epesismã] *nm* thickening

**épanchement** [epãʃmã] *nm*: **un ~ de synovie** water on the knee; **épanchements** *nmpl* (*fig*) (sentimental) outpourings

**épancher** [epãʃe] *vt* to give vent to; **s'épancher** *vi* to open one's heart; (*liquide*) to pour out

**épandage** [epãdaʒ] *nm* manure spreading

**épanoui, e** [epanwi] *adj* (*éclos, ouvert, développé*) blooming; (*radieux*) radiant

**épanouir** [epanwiʀ]: **s'épanouir** *vi* (*fleur*) to bloom, open out; (*visage*) to light up; (*fig: se développer*) to blossom (out); (*: mentalement*) to open up

**épanouissement** [epanwismã] *nm* blossoming; opening up

**épargnant, e** [epaʀɲã, -ãt] *nm/f* saver, investor

**épargne** [epaʀɲ(ə)] *nf* saving; **l'~-logement** property investment

**épargner** [epaʀɲe] *vt* to save; (*ne pas tuer ou endommager*) to spare ▷ *vi* to save; **~ qch à qn** to spare sb sth

**éparpillement** [epaʀpijmã] *nm* (*de papier*) scattering; (*des efforts*) dissipation

**éparpiller** [epaʀpije] *vt* to scatter; (*pour répartir*) to disperse; (*fig: efforts*) to dissipate; **s'éparpiller** *vi* to scatter; (*fig*) to dissipate one's efforts

**épars, e** [epaʀ, -aʀs(ə)] *adj* (*maisons*) scattered; (*cheveux*) sparse

**épatant, e** [epatã, -ãt] *adj* (*fam*) super, splendid

**épaté, e** [epate] *adj*: **nez ~** flat nose (with wide nostrils)

**épater** [epate] *vt* to amaze; (*impressionner*) to impress

**épaule** [epol] *nf* shoulder

**épaulé-jeté** [epoleʒəte] *nm* (*pl* **épaulés-jetés**) *nm* (*Sport*) clean-and-jerk

**épaulement** [epolmã] *nm* escarpment; (*mur*) retaining wall

**épauler** [epole] *vt* (*aider*) to back up, support;

(*arme*) to raise (to one's shoulder) ▷ *vi* to (take) aim

**épaulette** [epolεt] *nf* (*Mil*, *d'un veston*) epaulette; (*de combinaison*) shoulder strap

**épave** [epav] *nf* wreck

**épée** [epe] *nf* sword

**épeler** [eple] *vt* to spell

**éperdu, e** [epεrdy] *adj* (*personne*) overcome; (*sentiment*) passionate; (*fuite*) frantic

**éperdument** [epεrdymã] *adv* (*aimer*) wildly; (*espérer*) fervently

**éperlan** [epεrlã] *nm* (*Zool*) smelt

**éperon** [eprɔ̃] *nm* spur

**éperonner** [eprɔne] *vt* to spur (on); (*navire*) to ram

**épervier** [epεrvje] *nm* (*Zool*) sparrowhawk; (*Pêche*) casting net

**éphèbe** [efεb] *nm* beautiful young man

**éphémère** [efemεr] *adj* ephemeral, fleeting

**éphéméride** [efemerid] *nf* block *ou* tear-off calendar

**épi** [epi] *nm* (*de blé, d'orge*) ear; **~ de cheveux** tuft of hair; **stationnement/se garer en ~** parking/to park at an angle to the kerb

**épice** [epis] *nf* spice

**épicé, e** [epise] *adj* highly spiced, spicy; (*fig*) spicy

**épicéa** [episea] *nm* spruce

**épicentre** [episãtr(ə)] *nm* epicentre

**épicer** [epise] *vt* to spice; (*fig*) to add spice to

**épicerie** [episri] *nf* (*magasin*) grocer's shop; (*denrées*) groceries *pl*; **~ fine** delicatessen (shop)

**épicier, -ière** [episje, -jεr] *nm/f* grocer

**épicurien, ne** [epikyrjε̃, -εn] *adj* epicurean

**épidémie** [epidemi] *nf* epidemic

**épidémique** [epidemik] *adj* epidemic

**épiderme** [epidεrm(ə)] *nm* skin, epidermis

**épidermique** [epidεrmik] *adj* skin *cpd*, epidermic

**épier** [epje] *vt* to spy on, watch closely; (*occasion*) to look out for

**épieu, x** [epjø] *nm* (hunting-)spear

**épigramme** [epigram] *nf* epigram

**épigraphe** [epigraf] *nf* epigraph

**épilation** [epilasjɔ̃] *nf* removal of unwanted hair

**épilatoire** [epilatwar] *adj* depilatory, hair-removing

**épilepsie** [epilεpsi] *nf* epilepsy

**épileptique** [epilεptik] *adj*, *nm/f* epileptic

**épiler** [epile] *vt* (*jambes*) to remove the hair from; (*sourcils*) to pluck; **s'~ les jambes** to remove the hair from one's legs; **s'~ les sourcils** to pluck one's eyebrows; **se faire ~** to get unwanted hair removed; **crème à ~** hair-removing *ou* depilatory cream; **pince à ~** eyebrow tweezers

**épilogue** [epilɔg] *nm* (*fig*) conclusion, dénouement

**épiloguer** [epilɔge] *vi*: **~ sur** to hold forth on

**épinards** [epinar] *nmpl* spinach *sg*

**épine** [epin] *nf* thorn, prickle; (*d'oursin etc*) spine, prickle; **~ dorsale** backbone

**épineux, -euse** [epinø, -øz] *adj* thorny, prickly

**épinglage** [epε̃glaʒ] *nm* pinning

**épingle** [epε̃gl(ə)] *nf* pin; **tirer son ~ du jeu** to play one's game well; **tiré à quatre ~s** well turned-out; **monter qch en ~** to build sth up, make a thing of sth (*fam*); **~ à chapeau** hatpin; **~ à cheveux** hairpin; **virage en ~ à cheveux** hairpin bend; **~ de cravate** tie pin; **~ de nourrice** *ou* **de sûreté** *ou* **double** safety pin, nappy (*Brit*) *ou* diaper (*US*) pin

**épingler** [epε̃gle] *vt* (*badge, décoration*): **~ qch sur** to pin sth on(to); (*Couture: tissu, robe*) to pin together; (*fam*) to catch, nick

**épinière** [epinjεr] *adj f voir* **moelle**

**Épiphanie** [epifani] *nf* Epiphany

**épique** [epik] *adj* epic

**épiscopal, e, -aux** [episkɔpal, -o] *adj* episcopal

**épiscopat** [episkɔpa] *nm* bishopric, episcopate

**épisiotomie** [epizjɔtɔmi] *nf* (*Méd*) episiotomy

**épisode** [epizɔd] *nm* episode; **film/roman à ~s** serialized film/novel, serial

**épisodique** [epizɔdik] *adj* occasional

**épisodiquement** [epizɔdikmã] *adv* occasionally

**épissure** [episyr] *nf* splice

**épistémologie** [epistemɔlɔʒi] *nf* epistemology

**épistolaire** [epistɔlεr] *adj* epistolary; **être en relations ~s avec qn** to correspond with sb

**épitaphe** [epitaf] *nf* epitaph

**épithète** [epitεt] *nf* (*nom, surnom*) epithet; **adjectif ~** attributive adjective

**épître** [epitr(ə)] *nf* epistle

**éploré, e** [eplɔre] *adj* in tears, tearful

**épluchage** [eplyʃaʒ] *nm* peeling; (*de dossier etc*) careful reading *ou* analysis

**épluche-légumes** [eplyʃlegym] *nm inv* potato peeler

**éplucher** [eplyʃe] *vt* (*fruit, légumes*) to peel; (*comptes, dossier*) to go over with a fine-tooth comb

**éplucheur** [eplyʃœr] *nm* (automatic) peeler

**épluchures** [eplyʃyr] *nfpl* peelings

**épointer** [epwε̃te] *vt* to blunt

**éponge** [epɔ̃ʒ] *nf* sponge; **passer l'~ (sur)** (*fig*) to let bygones be bygones (with regard to); **jeter l'~** (*fig*) to throw in the towel; **~ métallique** scourer

**éponger** [epɔ̃ʒe] *vt* (*liquide*) to mop *ou* sponge up; (*surface*) to sponge; (*fig: déficit*) to soak up, absorb; **s'~ le front** to mop one's brow

**épopée** [epɔpe] *nf* epic

**époque** [epɔk] *nf* (*de l'histoire*) age, era; (*de l'année, la vie*) time; **d'~** *adj* (*meuble*) period *cpd*; **à cette ~** at this (*ou* that) time *ou* period; **faire ~** to make history

**épouiller** [epuje] *vt* to pick lice off; (*avec un produit*) to delouse

**époumoner** [epumɔne]: **s'époumoner** *vi* to shout (*ou* sing) o.s. hoarse

**épouse** [epuz] *nf* wife

**épouser** [epuze] *vt* to marry; (*fig: idées*) to espouse; (: *forme*) to fit

**époussetage** [epustaʒ] *nm* dusting

**épousseter** [epuste] *vt* to dust

**époustouflant, e** [epustuflɑ̃, -ɑ̃t] *adj* staggering, mind-boggling

**époustoufler** [epustufle] *vt* to flabbergast, astound

**épouvantable** [epuvɑ̃tabl(ə)] *adj* appalling, dreadful

**épouvantablement** [epuvɑ̃tabləmɑ̃] *adj* terribly, dreadfully

**épouvantail** [epuvɑ̃taj] *nm* (*à moineaux*) scarecrow; (*fig*) bog(e)y; bugbear

**épouvante** [epuvɑ̃t] *nf* terror; **film d'~** horror film

**épouvanter** [epuvɑ̃te] *vt* to terrify

**époux** [epu] *nm* husband ▷ *nmpl*: **les ~** the (married) couple, the husband and wife

**éprendre** [eprɑ̃dR(ə)]: **s'éprendre de** *vt* to fall in love with

**épreuve** [eprœv] *nf* (*d'examen*) test; (*malheur, difficulté*) trial, ordeal; (*Photo*) print; (*Typo*) proof; (*Sport*) event; **à l'~ des balles/du feu** (*vêtement*) bulletproof/fireproof; **à toute ~** unfailing; **mettre à l'~** to put to the test; **~ de force** trial of strength; (*fig*) showdown; **~ de résistance** test of resistance; **~ de sélection** (*Sport*) heat

**épris, e** [epRi, -iz] *vb voir* **éprendre** ▷ *adj*: **~ de** in love with

**éprouvant, e** [epRuvɑ̃, -ɑ̃t] *adj* trying

**éprouvé, e** [epRuve] *adj* tested, proven

**éprouver** [epRuve] *vt* (*tester*) to test; (*mettre à l'épreuve*) to put to the test; (*marquer, faire souffrir*) to afflict, distress; (*ressentir*) to experience

**éprouvette** [epRuvɛt] *nf* test tube

**EPS** *sigle f* (= *Éducation physique et sportive*) ≈ PE

**épuisant, e** [epɥizɑ̃, -ɑ̃t] *adj* exhausting

**épuisé, e** [epɥize] *adj* exhausted; (*livre*) out of print

**épuisement** [epɥizmɑ̃] *nm* exhaustion; **jusqu'à ~ des stocks** while stocks last

**épuiser** [epɥize] *vt* (*fatiguer*) to exhaust, wear *ou* tire out; (*stock, sujet*) to exhaust; **s'épuiser** *vi* to wear *ou* tire o.s. out, exhaust o.s.; (*stock*) to run out

**épuisette** [epɥizɛt] *nf* landing net; shrimping net

**épuration** [epyRasjɔ̃] *nf* purification; purging; refinement

**épure** [epyR] *nf* working drawing

**épurer** [epyRe] *vt* (*liquide*) to purify; (*parti, administration*) to purge; (*langue, texte*) to refine

**équarrir** [ekaRiR] *vt* (*pierre, arbre*) to square (off); (*animal*) to quarter

**équateur** [ekwatœR] *nm* equator; **(la république de) l'É~** Ecuador

**équation** [ekwasjɔ̃] *nf* equation; **mettre en ~** to equate; **~ du premier/second degré** simple/ quadratic equation

**équatorial, e, -aux** [ekwatɔRjal, -o] *adj* equatorial

**équatorien, ne** [ekwatɔRjɛ̃, -ɛn] *adj* Ecuadorian ▷ *nm/f*: **Équatorien, ne** Ecuadorian

**équerre** [ekɛR] *nf* (*à dessin*) (set) square; (*pour fixer*) brace; **en ~** at right angles; **à l'~, d'~** straight; **double ~** T-square

**équestre** [ekɛstR(ə)] *adj* equestrian

**équeuter** [ekøte] *vt* (*Culin*) to remove the stalk(s) from

**équidé** [ekide] *nm* (*Zool*) member of the horse family

**équidistance** [ekɥidistɑ̃s] *nf*: **à ~ (de)** equidistant (from)

**équidistant, e** [ekɥidistɑ̃, -ɑ̃t] *adj*: **~ (de)** equidistant (from)

**équilatéral, e, -aux** [ekɥilateRal, -o] *adj* equilateral

**équilibrage** [ekilibRaʒ] *nm* (*Auto*): **~ des roues** wheel balancing

**équilibre** [ekilibR(ə)] *nm* balance; (*d'une balance*) equilibrium; **~ budgétaire** balanced budget; **garder/perdre l'~** to keep/lose one's balance; **être en ~** to be balanced; **mettre en ~** to make steady; **avoir le sens de l'~** to be well-balanced

**équilibré, e** [ekilibRe] *adj* (*fig*) well-balanced, stable

**équilibrer** [ekilibRe] *vt* to balance; **s'équilibrer** *vi* (*poids*) to balance; (*fig: défauts etc*) to balance each other out

**équilibriste** [ekilibRist(ə)] *nm/f* tightrope walker

**équinoxe** [ekinɔks] *nm* equinox

**équipage** [ekipaʒ] *nm* crew; **en grand ~** in great array

**équipe** [ekip] *nf* team; (*bande: parfois péj*) bunch; **travailler par ~s** to work in shifts; **travailler en ~** to work as a team; **faire ~ avec** to team up with; **~ de chercheurs** research team; **~ de secours** *ou* **de sauvetage** rescue team

**équipé, e** [ekipe] *adj* (*cuisine etc*) equipped, fitted(-out) ▷ *nf* escapade

**équipement** [ekipmɑ̃] *nm* equipment; **équipements** *nmpl* amenities, facilities; installations; **biens/dépenses d'~** capital goods/expenditure; **ministère de l'É~** department of public works; **~s sportifs/ collectifs** sports/community facilities *ou* resources

**équiper** [ekipe] *vt* to equip; (*voiture, cuisine*) to equip, fit out; **~ qn/qch de** to equip sb/sth with; **s'équiper** *vi* (*sportif*) to equip o.s., kit o.s. out

**équipier, -ière** [ekipje, -jɛR] *nm/f* team member

**équitable** [ekitabl(ə)] *adj* fair

**équitablement** [ekitabləmɑ̃] *adv* fairly, equitably

**équitation** [ekitasjɔ̃] *nf* (horse-)riding; **faire de l'~** to go (horse-)riding

**équité** [ekite] *nf* equity

**équivaille** *etc* [ekivaj] *vb voir* **équivaloir**

**équivalence** [ekivalɑ̃s] *nf* equivalence

**équivalent, e** [ekivalɑ̃, -ɑ̃t] *adj, nm* equivalent

**équivaloir** [ekivalwaR]: **~ à** *vt* to be equivalent to; (*représenter*) to amount to

**équivaut** *etc* [ekivo] *vb voir* **équivaloir**

**équivoque** [ekivɔk] *adj* equivocal, ambiguous;

*(louche)* dubious ▷ *nf* ambiguity

**érable** [eʀabl(ə)] *nm* maple

**éradication** [eʀadikɑsjɔ̃] *nf* eradication

**éradiquer** [eʀadike] *vt* to eradicate

**érafler** [eʀɑfle] *vt* to scratch; **s'~ la main/les jambes** to scrape *ou* scratch one's hand/legs

**éraflure** [eʀɑflyʀ] *nf* scratch

**éraillé, e** [eʀɑje] *adj (voix)* rasping, hoarse

**ère** [eʀ] *nf* era; **en l'an 1050 de notre ~** in the year 1050 A.D.

**érection** [eʀɛksjɔ̃] *nf* erection

**éreintant, e** [eʀɛ̃tɑ̃, -ɑ̃t] *adj* exhausting

**éreinté, e** [eʀɛ̃te] *adj* exhausted

**éreintement** [eʀɛ̃tmɑ̃] *nm* exhaustion

**éreinter** [eʀɛ̃te] *vt* to exhaust, wear out; *(fig: critiquer)* to slate; **s'~ (à faire qch/à qch)** to wear o.s. out (doing sth/with sth)

**ergonomie** [ɛʀɡɔnɔmi] *nf* ergonomics *sg*

**ergonomique** [ɛʀɡɔnɔmik] *adj* ergonomic

**ergot** [ɛʀɡo] *nm (de coq)* spur; *(Tech)* lug

**ergoter** [ɛʀɡɔte] *vi* to split hairs, argue over details

**ergoteur, -euse** [ɛʀɡɔtœʀ, -øz] *nm/f* hairsplitter

**ériger** [eʀiʒe] *vt (monument)* to erect; **~ qch en principe/loi** to make sth a principle/law; **s'~ en critique (de)** to set o.s. up as a critic (of)

**ermitage** [ɛʀmitaʒ] *nm* retreat

**ermite** [ɛʀmit] *nm* hermit

**éroder** [eʀɔde] *vt* to erode

**érogène** [eʀɔʒɛn] *adj* erogenous

**érosion** [eʀozjɔ̃] *nf* erosion

**érotique** [eʀɔtik] *adj* erotic

**érotiquement** [eʀɔtikmɑ̃] *adv* erotically

**érotisme** [eʀɔtism(ə)] *nm* eroticism

**errance** [eʀɑ̃s] *nf* wandering

**errant, e** [eʀɑ̃, -ɑ̃t] *adj*: **un chien ~** a stray dog

**erratum** [eʀatɔm, -a] *(pl* **errata)** *nm* erratum

**errements** [eʀmɑ̃] *nmpl* misguided ways

**errer** [eʀe] *vi* to wander

**erreur** [eʀœʀ] *nf* mistake, error; *(Inform)* error; *(morale):* **~s** *nfpl* errors; **être dans l'~** to be wrong; **induire qn en ~** to mislead sb; **par ~** by mistake; **sauf ~** unless I'm mistaken; **faire ~** to be mistaken; **~ de date** mistake in the date; **~ de fait** error of fact; **~ d'impression** *(Typo)* misprint; **~ judiciaire** miscarriage of justice; **~ de jugement** error of judgment; **~ matérielle** *ou* **d'écriture** clerical error; **~ tactique** tactical error

**erroné, e** [eʀɔne] *adj* wrong, erroneous

**ersatz** [ɛʀzats] *nm* substitute, ersatz; **~ de café** coffee substitute

**éructer** [eʀykte] *vi* to belch

**érudit, e** [eʀydi, -it] *adj* erudite, learned ▷ *nm/f* scholar

**érudition** [eʀydisjɔ̃] *nf* erudition, scholarship

**éruptif, -ive** [eʀyptif, -iv] *adj* eruptive

**éruption** [eʀypsjɔ̃] *nf* eruption; *(cutanée)* outbreak; *(: boutons)* rash; *(fig: de joie, colère, folie)* outburst

**E/S** *abr (= entrée/sortie)* I/O *(= in/out)*

**es** [ɛ] *vb voir* **être**

**ès** [ɛs] *prép*: **licencié ès lettres/sciences** ≈ Bachelor of Arts/Science; **docteur ès lettres** ≈ doctor of philosophy, ≈ PhD

**esbroufe** [ɛsbʀuf] *nf*: **faire de l'~** to have people on

**escabeau, x** [ɛskabo] *nm (tabouret)* stool; *(échelle)* stepladder

**escadre** [ɛskadʀ(ə)] *nf (Navig)* squadron; *(Aviat)* wing

**escadrille** [ɛskadʀij] *nf (Aviat)* flight

**escadron** [ɛskadʀɔ̃] *nm* squadron

**escalade** [ɛskalad] *nf* climbing *no pl*; *(Pol etc)* escalation

**escalader** [ɛskalade] *vt* to climb, scale

**escalator** [ɛskalatɔʀ] *nm* escalator

**escale** [ɛskal] *nf (Navig)* call; *(: port)* port of call; *(Aviat)* stop(over); **faire ~ à** to put in at, call in at; to stop over at; **~ technique** *(Aviat)* refuelling stop

**escalier** [ɛskalje] *nm* stairs *pl*; **dans l'~** *ou* **les ~s** on the stairs; **descendre l'~** *ou* **les ~s** to go downstairs; **~ mécanique** *ou* **roulant** escalator; **~ de secours** fire escape; **~ de service** backstairs; **~ à vis** *ou* **en colimaçon** spiral staircase

**escalope** [ɛskalɔp] *nf* escalope

**escamotable** [ɛskamɔtabl(ə)] *adj (train d'atterrissage, antenne)* retractable; *(table, lit)* foldaway

**escamoter** [ɛskamɔte] *vt (esquiver)* to get round, evade; *(faire disparaître)* to conjure away; *(dérober: portefeuille etc)* to snatch; *(train d'atterrissage)* to retract; *(mots)* to miss out

**escapade** [ɛskapad] *nf*: **faire une ~** to go on a jaunt; *(s'enfuir)* to run away *ou* off

**escarbille** [ɛskaʀbij] *nf* bit of grit

**escarcelle** [ɛskaʀsɛl] *nf*: **faire tomber dans l'~** *(argent)* to bring in

**escargot** [ɛskaʀɡo] *nm* snail

**escarmouche** [ɛskaʀmuʃ] *nf (Mil)* skirmish; *(fig: propos hostiles)* angry exchange

**escarpé, e** [ɛskaʀpe] *adj* steep

**escarpement** [ɛskaʀpəmɑ̃] *nm* steep slope

**escarpin** [ɛskaʀpɛ̃] *nm* flat(-heeled) shoe

**escarre** [ɛskaʀ] *nf* bedsore

**Escaut** [ɛsko] *nm*: **l'~** the Scheldt

**escient** [esjɑ̃] *nm*: **à bon ~** advisedly

**esclaffer** [ɛsklafe]: **s'esclaffer** *vi* to guffaw

**esclandre** [ɛsklɑ̃dʀ(ə)] *nm* scene, fracas

**esclavage** [ɛsklavaʒ] *nm* slavery

**esclavagiste** [ɛsklavaʒist(ə)] *adj* pro-slavery ▷ *nm/f* supporter of slavery

**esclave** [ɛsklav] *nm/f* slave; **être ~ de** *(fig)* to be a slave of

**escogriffe** [ɛskɔɡʀif] *nm (péj)* beanpole

**escompte** [ɛskɔ̃t] *nm* discount

**escompter** [ɛskɔ̃te] *vt (Comm)* to discount; *(espérer)* to expect, reckon upon; **~ que** to reckon *ou* expect that

**escorte** [ɛskɔʀt(ə)] *nf* escort; **faire ~ à** to escort

**escorter** [ɛskɔʀte] *vt* to escort

**escorteur** [ɛskɔʀtœʀ] *nm (Navig)* escort (ship)

e

**escouade** [ɛskwad] nf squad; (fig: groupe de personnes) group

**escrime** [ɛskRim] nf fencing; **faire de l'~** to fence

**escrimer** [ɛskRime]: **s'escrimer** vi: **s'~ à faire** to wear o.s. out doing

**escrimeur, -euse** [ɛskRimœR, -øz] nm/f fencer

**escroc** [ɛskRo] nm swindler, con-man

**escroquer** [ɛskRɔke] vt: **~ qn (de qch)/qch à qn** to swindle sb (out of sth)/sth out of sb

**escroquerie** [ɛskRɔkRi] nf swindle

**ésotérique** [ezɔteRik] adj esoteric

**espace** [ɛspas] nm space; **~ publicitaire** advertising space; **~ vital** living space

**espacé, e** [ɛspase] adj spaced out

**espacement** [ɛspasmɑ̃] nm: **~ proportionnel** proportional spacing (on printer)

**espacer** [ɛspase] vt to space out; **s'espacer** vi (visites etc) to become less frequent

**espadon** [ɛspadɔ̃] nm swordfish inv

**espadrille** [ɛspadRij] nf rope-soled sandal

**Espagne** [ɛspaɲ(ə)] nf: **l'~** Spain

**espagnol, e** [ɛspaɲɔl] adj Spanish ▷ nm (Ling) Spanish ▷ nm/f: **Espagnol, e** Spaniard

**espagnolette** [ɛspaɲɔlɛt] nf (window) catch; **fermé à l'~** resting on the catch

**espalier** [ɛspalje] nm (arbre fruitier) espalier

**espèce** [ɛspɛs] nf (Bio, Bot, Zool) species inv; (gén: sorte) sort, kind, type; (péj): **~ de maladroit/de brute!** you clumsy oaf/you brute!; **espèces** nfpl (Comm) cash sg; (Rel) species; **de toute ~** of all kinds ou sorts; **en l'~** adv in the case in point; **payer en ~s** to pay (in) cash; **cas d'~** individual case; **l'~ humaine** humankind

**espérance** [ɛspeRɑ̃s] nf hope; **~ de vie** life expectancy

**espéranto** [ɛspeRɑ̃to] nm Esperanto

**espérer** [ɛspeRe] vt to hope for; **j'espère (bien)** I hope so; **~ que/faire** to hope that/to do; **~ en** to trust in

**espiègle** [ɛspjɛgl(ə)] adj mischievous

**espièglerie** [ɛspjɛgləRi] nf mischievousness; (tour, farce) piece of mischief, prank

**espion, ne** [ɛspjɔ̃, -ɔn] nm/f spy; **avion ~** spy plane

**espionnage** [ɛspjɔnaʒ] nm espionage, spying; **film/roman d'~** spy film/novel

**espionner** [ɛspjɔne] vt to spy (up)on

**esplanade** [ɛsplanad] nf esplanade

**espoir** [ɛspwaR] nm hope; **l'~ de qch/de faire qch** the hope of sth/of doing sth; **avoir bon ~ que ...** to have high hopes that ...; **garder l'~ que ...** to remain hopeful that ...; **un ~ de la boxe/du ski** one of boxing's/skiing's hopefuls, one of the hopes of boxing/skiing; **sans ~** adj hopeless

**esprit** [ɛspRi] nm (pensée, intellect) mind; (humour, ironie) wit; (mentalité, d'une loi etc, fantôme etc) spirit; **l'~ d'équipe/de compétition** team/competitive spirit; **faire de l'~** to try to be witty; **reprendre ses ~s** to come to; **perdre l'~** to lose one's mind; **avoir bon/mauvais ~** to be

of a good/bad disposition; **avoir l'~ à faire qch** to have a mind to do sth; **avoir l'~ critique** to be critical; **~ de contradiction** contrariness; **~ de corps** esprit de corps; **~ de famille** family loyalty; **l'~ malin** (le diable) the Evil One; **~s chagrins** fault-finders

**esquif** [ɛskif] nm skiff

**esquimau, de, -x** [ɛskimo, -od] adj Eskimo ▷ nm (Ling) Eskimo; (glace): **E~®** ice lolly (Brit), popsicle (US) ▷ nm/f: **Esquimau, de** Eskimo; **chien ~** husky

**esquinter** [ɛskɛ̃te] vt (fam) to mess up; **s'esquinter** vi: **s'~ à faire qch** to knock o.s. out doing sth

**esquisse** [ɛskis] nf sketch; **l'~ d'un sourire/changement** a hint of a smile/of change

**esquisser** [ɛskise] vt to sketch; **s'esquisser** vi (amélioration) to begin to be detectable; **~ un sourire** to give a hint of a smile

**esquive** [ɛskiv] nf (Boxe) dodging; (fig) sidestepping

**esquiver** [ɛskive] vt to dodge; **s'esquiver** vi to slip away

**essai** [ɛsɛ] nm trying; (tentative) attempt, try; (Rugby) try; (Littérature) essay; **essais** nmpl (Auto) trials; **à l'~** on a trial basis; **~ gratuit** (Comm) free trial

**essaim** [ɛsɛ̃] nm swarm

**essaimer** [eseme] vi to swarm; (fig) to spread, expand

**essayage** [esɛjaʒ] nm (d'un vêtement) trying on, fitting; **salon d'~** fitting room; **cabine d'~** fitting room (cubicle)

**essayer** [eseje] vt (gén) to try; (vêtement, chaussures) to try (on); (restaurant, méthode, voiture) to try (out) ▷ vi to try; **~ de faire** to try ou attempt to do; **s'~ à faire** to try one's hand at doing; **essayez un peu!** (menace) just you try!

**essayeur, -euse** [esɛjœR, -øz] nm/f (chez un tailleur etc) fitter

**essayiste** [esejist(ə)] nm/f essayist

**ESSEC** [ɛsɛk] sigle f (= École supérieure des sciences économiques et sociales) grande école for management and business studies

**essence** [esɑ̃s] nf (de voiture) petrol (Brit), gas(oline) (US); (extrait de plante, Philosophie) essence; (espèce: d'arbre) species inv; **prendre de l'~** to get (some) petrol ou gas; **par ~** (essentiellement) essentially; **~ de citron/rose** lemon/rose oil; **~ sans plomb** unleaded petrol; **~ de térébenthine** turpentine

**essentiel, le** [esɑ̃sjɛl] adj essential ▷ nm: **l'~ d'un discours/d'une œuvre** the essence of a speech/work of art; **emporter l'~** to take the essentials; **c'est l'~** (ce qui importe) that's the main thing; **l'~ de** (la majeure partie) the main part of

**essentiellement** [esɑ̃sjɛlmɑ̃] adv essentially

**esseulé, e** [esœle] adj forlorn

**essieu, x** [esjø] nm axle

**essor** [esɔR] nm (de l'économie etc) rapid expansion; **prendre son ~** (oiseau) to fly off

**essorage** [esɔʀaʒ] *nm* wringing out; spin-drying; spinning; shaking

**essorer** [esɔʀe] *vt* (*en tordant*) to wring (out); (*par la force centrifuge*) to spin-dry; (*salade*) to spin; (: *en secouant*) to shake dry

**essoreuse** [esɔʀøz] *nf* mangle, wringer; (*à tambour*) spin-dryer

**essoufflé, e** [esufle] *adj* out of breath, breathless

**essouffler** [esufle] *vt* to make breathless; **s'essouffler** *vi* to get out of breath; (*fig: économie*) to run out of steam

**essuie***etc* [esɥi] *vb voir* **essuyer**

**essuie-glace** [esɥiglas] *nm* windscreen (*Brit*) *ou* windshield (*US*) wiper

**essuie-mains** [esɥimɛ̃] *nm inv* hand towel

**essuierai***etc* [esɥiʀe] *vb voir* **essuyer**

**essuie-tout** [esɥitu] *nm inv* kitchen paper

**essuyer** [esɥije] *vt* to wipe; (*fig: subir*) to suffer; **s'essuyer**(*après le bain*) to dry o.s.; ~ **la vaisselle** to dry up, dry the dishes

**est** [ɛ] *vb voir* **être** ⊳ *nm* [ɛst]: **l'~** the east ⊳ *adj inv* east; (*région*) east(ern); **à l'~** in the east; (*direction*) to the east, east(wards); **à l'~ de** (to the) east of; **les pays de l'E~** the eastern countries

**estafette** [ɛstafɛt] *nf* (*Mil*) dispatch rider

**estafilade** [ɛstafilad] *nf* gash, slash

**est-allemand, e** [ɛstalmã, -ãd] *adj* East German

**estaminet** [ɛstaminɛ] *nm* tavern

**estampe** [ɛstãp] *nf* print, engraving

**estamper** [ɛstãpe] *vt* (*monnaies etc*) to stamp; (*fam: escroquer*) to swindle

**estampille** [ɛstãpij] *nf* stamp

**est-ce que** [ɛskə] *adv*: ~ **c'est cher/c'était bon?** is it expensive/was it good?; **quand est-ce qu'il part?** when does he leave?, when is he leaving?; **où est-ce qu'il va?** where's he going?; *voir aussi* **que**

**este** [ɛst(ə)] *adj* Estonian ⊳ *nm/f*: **Este**Estonian

**esthète** [ɛstɛt] *nm/f* aesthete

**esthéticienne** [ɛstetisjɛn] *nf* beautician

**esthétique** [ɛstetik] *adj* (*sens, jugement*) aesthetic; (*beau*) attractive, aesthetically pleasing ⊳ *nf* aesthetics *sg*; **l'~ industrielle** industrial design

**esthétiquement** [ɛstetikmã] *adv* aesthetically

**estimable** [ɛstimabl(ə)] *adj* respected

**estimatif, -ive** [ɛstimatif, -iv] *adj* estimated

**estimation** [ɛstimasjɔ̃] *nf* valuation; assessment; **d'après mes ~s** according to my calculations

**estime** [ɛstim] *nf* esteem, regard; **avoir de l'~ pour qn** to think highly of sb

**estimer** [ɛstime] *vt* (*respecter*) to esteem, hold in high regard; (*expertiser*) to value; (*évaluer*) to assess, estimate; (*penser*): ~ **que/être** to consider that/o.s. to be; **s'estimer satisfait/ heureux** *vi* to feel satisfied/happy; **j'estime la distance à 10 km** I reckon the distance to be 10 km

**estival, e, -aux** [ɛstival, -o] *adj* summer *cpd*;

**station ~e** (summer) holiday resort

**estivant, e** [ɛstivã, -ãt] *nm/f* (summer) holiday-maker

**estoc** [ɛstɔk] *nm*: **frapper d'~ et de taille** to cut and thrust

**estocade** [ɛstɔkad] *nf* death-blow

**estomac** [ɛstɔma] *nm* stomach; **avoir mal à l'~** to have stomach ache; **avoir l'~ creux** to have an empty stomach

**estomaqué, e** [ɛstɔmake] *adj* flabbergasted

**estompe** [ɛstɔ̃p] *nf* stump; (*dessin*) stump drawing

**estompé, e** [ɛstɔ̃pe] *adj* blurred

**estomper** [ɛstɔ̃pe] *vt* (*Art*) to shade off; (*fig*) to blur, dim; **s'estomper** *vi* (*sentiments*) to soften; (*contour*) to become blurred

**Estonie** [ɛstɔni] *nf*: **l'~** Estonia

**estonien, ne** [ɛstɔnjɛ̃, -ɛn] *adj* Estonian ⊳ *nm* (*Ling*) Estonian ⊳ *nm/f*: **Estonien, ne**Estonian

**estrade** [ɛstʀad] *nf* platform, rostrum

**estragon** [ɛstʀagɔ̃] *nm* tarragon

**estropié, e** [ɛstʀɔpje] *nm/f* cripple

**estropier** [ɛstʀɔpje] *vt* to cripple, maim; (*fig*) to twist, distort

**estuaire** [ɛstɥɛʀ] *nm* estuary

**estudiantin, e** [ɛstydjãtɛ̃, -in] *adj* student *cpd*

**esturgeon** [ɛstyʀʒɔ̃] *nm* sturgeon

**et** [e] *conj* and; **et lui?** what about him?; **et alors?, et (puis) après?** so what?; (*ensuite*) and then?

**ét.** *abr* = **étage**

**ETA** [eta] *sigle m* (*Pol*) ETA

**étable** [etabl(ə)] *nf* cowshed

**établi, e** [etabli] *adj* established ⊳ *nm* (work)bench

**établir** [etabliʀ] *vt* (*papiers d'identité, facture*) to make out; (*liste, programme*) to draw up; (*gouvernement, artisan etc: aider à s'installer*) to set up, establish; (*entreprise, atelier, camp*) to set up; (*réputation, usage, fait, culpabilité, relations*) to establish; (*Sport: record*) to set; **s'établir** *vi* (*se faire: entente etc*) to be established; **s'~ (à son compte)** to set up in business; **s'~ à/près de** to settle in/near

**établissement** [etablismã] *nm* making out; drawing up; setting up, establishing; (*entreprise, institution*) establishment; ~ **de crédit** credit institution; ~ **hospitalier** hospital complex; ~ **industriel** industrial plant, factory; ~ **scolaire** school, educational establishment

**étage** [etaʒ] *nm* (*d'immeuble*) storey (*Brit*), story (*US*), floor; (*de fusée*) stage; (*Géo: de culture, végétation*) level; **au 2ème ~** on the 2nd (*Brit*) *ou* 3rd (*US*) floor; **à l'~** upstairs; **maison à deux ~s** two-storey *ou* -story house; **de bas ~** *adj* low-born; (*médiocre*) inferior

**étager** [etaʒe] *vt* (*cultures*) to lay out in tiers; **s'étager** *vi* (*prix*) to range; (*zones, cultures*) to lie on different levels

**étagère** [etaʒɛʀ] *nf* (*rayon*) shelf; (*meuble*) shelves *pl*, set of shelves

**étai** [etɛ] *nm* stay, prop

**étain** [etɛ̃] *nm* tin; (*Orfèvrerie*) pewter *no pl*
**étais** *etc* [etɛ] *vb voir* **être**
**étal** [etal] *nm* stall
**étalage** [etalaʒ] *nm* display; (*vitrine*) display window; **faire ~ de** to show off, parade
**étalagiste** [etalaʒist(ə)] *nm/f* window-dresser
**étale** [etal] *adj* (*mer*) slack
**étalement** [etalmɑ̃] *nm* spreading; (*échelonnement*) staggering
**étaler** [etale] *vt* (*carte, nappe*) to spread (out); (*peinture, liquide*) to spread; (*échelonner: paiements, dates, vacances*) to spread, stagger; (*exposer: marchandises*) to display; (*richesses, connaissances*) to parade; **s'étaler** *vi* (*liquide*) to spread out; (*fam*) to come a cropper (*Brit*), fall flat on one's face; **s' ~ sur** (*paiements etc*) to be spread over
**étalon** [etalɔ̃] *nm* (*mesure*) standard; (*cheval*) stallion; **l' ~ -or** the gold standard
**étalonner** [etalɔne] *vt* to calibrate
**étamer** [etame] *vt* (*casserole*) to tin(plate); (*glace*) to silver
**étamine** [etamin] *nf* (*Bot*) stamen; (*tissu*) butter muslin
**étanche** [etɑ̃ʃ] *adj* (*récipient, aussi fig*) watertight; (*montre, vêtement*) waterproof; **~ à l'air** airtight
**étanchéité** [etɑ̃ʃeite] *nf* watertightness; airtightness
**étancher** [etɑ̃ʃe] *vt* (*liquide*) to stop (flowing); **~ sa soif** to quench *ou* slake one's thirst
**étançon** [etɑ̃sɔ̃] *nm* (*Tech*) prop
**étançonner** [etɑ̃sɔne] *vt* to prop up
**étang** [etɑ̃] *nm* pond
**étant** [etɑ̃] *vb voir* **être**; **donné**
**étape** [etap] *nf* stage; (*lieu d'arrivée*) stopping place; (*Cyclisme*) staging point; **faire ~ à** to stop off at; **brûler les ~s** (*fig*) to cut corners
**état** [eta] *nm* (*Pol, condition*) state; (*d'un article d'occasion etc*) condition, state; (*liste*) inventory, statement; (*condition: professionnelle*) profession, trade; (*: sociale*) status; **en bon/mauvais ~** in good/poor condition; **en ~ (de marche)** in (working) order; **remettre en ~** to repair; **hors d'~** out of order; **être en ~/hors d'~ de faire** to be in a state/in no fit state to do; **en tout ~ de cause** in any event; **être dans tous ses ~s** to be in a state; **faire ~ de** (*alléguer*) to put forward; **en ~ d'arrestation** under arrest; **~ de grâce** (*Rel*) state of grace; (*fig*) honeymoon period; **en ~ de grâce** (*fig*) inspired; **en ~ d'ivresse** under the influence of drink; **~ de choses** (*situation*) state of affairs; **~ civil** civil status; (*bureau*) registry office (*Brit*); **~ d'esprit** frame of mind; **~ des lieux** inventory of fixtures; **~ de santé** state of health; **~ de siège/d'urgence** state of siege/emergency; **~ de veille** (*Psych*) waking state; **~s d'âme** moods; **les É~s barbaresques** the Barbary States; **les É~s du Golfe** the Gulf States; **~s de service** service record *sg*
**étatique** [etatik] *adj* state *cpd*, State *cpd*
**étatisation** [etatizasjɔ̃] *nf* nationalization
**étatiser** [etatize] *vt* to bring under state control
**étatisme** [etatism(ə)] *nm* state control

**étatiste** [etatist(ə)] *adj* (*doctrine etc*) of state control ▷ *nm/f* partisan of state control
**état-major** [etamaʒɔʀ] (*pl* **états-majors**) *nm* (*Mil*) staff; (*d'un parti etc*) top advisers *pl*; (*d'une entreprise*) top management
**État-providence** [etapʀɔvidɑ̃s] *nm* welfare state
**États-Unis** [etazyni] *nmpl*: **les ~ (d'Amérique)** the United States (of America)
**étau, x** [eto] *nm* vice (*Brit*), vise (*US*)
**étayer** [eteje] *vt* to prop *ou* shore up; (*fig*) to back up
**et cætera, et cetera** [ɛtseteʀa], **etc.** *adv* et cetera, and so on, etc
**été** [ete] *pp de* **être** ▷ *nm* summer; **en ~** in summer
**éteignais** *etc* [etɛɲɛ] *vb voir* **éteindre**
**éteignoir** [etɛɲwaʀ] *nm* (*candle*) snuffer; (*péj*) killjoy, wet blanket
**éteindre** [etɛ̃dʀ(ə)] *vt* (*lampe, lumière, radio, chauffage*) to turn *ou* switch off; (*cigarette, incendie, bougie*) to put out, extinguish; (*Jur: dette*) to extinguish; **s'éteindre** *vi* to go off; to go out; (*mourir*) to pass away
**éteint, e** [etɛ̃, -ɛ̃t] *pp de* **éteindre** ▷ *adj* (*fig*) lacklustre, dull; (*volcan*) extinct; **tous feux ~s** (*Auto: rouler*) without lights
**étendard** [etɑ̃daʀ] *nm* standard
**étendre** [etɑ̃dʀ(ə)] *vt* (*appliquer: pâte, liquide*) to spread; (*déployer: carte etc*) to spread out; (*sur un fil: lessive, linge*) to hang up *ou* out; (*bras, jambes, par terre: blessé*) to stretch out; (*diluer*) to dilute, thin; (*fig: agrandir*) to extend; (*fam: adversaire*) to floor; **s'étendre** *vi* (*augmenter, se propager*) to spread; (*terrain, forêt etc*): **s' ~ jusqu'à/de ...** à to stretch as far as/from ... to; **s' ~ (sur)** (*s'allonger*) to stretch out (upon); (*se coucher*) to lie down (on); (*fig: expliquer*) to elaborate *ou* enlarge (upon)
**étendu, e** [etɑ̃dy] *adj* extensive ▷ *nf* (*d'eau, de sable*) stretch, expanse; (*importance*) extent
**éternel, le** [etɛʀnɛl] *adj* eternal; **les neiges ~les** perpetual snow
**éternellement** [etɛʀnɛlmɑ̃] *adv* eternally
**éterniser** [etɛʀnize]: **s'éterniser** *vi* to last for ages; (*personne*) to stay for ages
**éternité** [etɛʀnite] *nf* eternity; **il y a** *ou* **ça fait une ~ que** it's ages since; **de toute ~** from time immemorial
**éternuement** [etɛʀnymɑ̃] *nm* sneeze
**éternuer** [etɛʀnɥe] *vi* to sneeze
**êtes** [ɛt] *vb voir* **être**
**étêter** [etete] *vt* (*arbre*) to poll(ard); (*clou, poisson*) to cut the head off
**éther** [etɛʀ] *nm* ether
**éthéré, e** [etere] *adj* ethereal
**Éthiopie** [etjɔpi] *nf*: **l' ~** Ethiopia
**éthiopien, ne** [etjɔpjɛ̃, -ɛn] *adj* Ethiopian
**éthique** [etik] *adj* ethical ▷ *nf* ethics *sg*
**ethnie** [ɛtni] *nf* ethnic group
**ethnique** [ɛtnik] *adj* ethnic
**ethnographe** [ɛtnɔgʀaf] *nm/f* ethnographer
**ethnographie** [ɛtnɔgʀafi] *nf* ethnography

**ethnographique** [ɛtnɔgʀafik] *adj* ethnographic(al)

**ethnologie** [ɛtnɔlɔʒi] *nf* ethnology

**ethnologique** [ɛtnɔlɔʒik] *adj* ethnological

**ethnologue** [ɛtnɔlɔg] *nm/f* ethnologist

**éthylique** [etilik] *adj* alcoholic

**éthylisme** [etilism(ə)] *nm* alcoholism

**étiage** [etjaʒ] *nm* low water

**étiez** [etje] *vb voir* **être**

**étincelant, e** [etɛ̃slɑ̃, -ɑ̃t] *adj* sparkling

**étinceler** [etɛ̃sle] *vi* to sparkle

**étincelle** [etɛ̃sɛl] *nf* spark

**étioler** [etjɔle]: **s'étioler** *vi* to wilt

**étions** [etjɔ̃] *vb voir* **être**

**étique** [etik] *adj* skinny, bony

**étiquetage** [etiktaʒ] *nm* labelling

**étiqueter** [etikte] *vt* to label

**étiquette** [etikɛt] *vb voir* **étiqueter** ▷ *nf* label; (*protocole*): **l'~** etiquette

**étirer** [etiʀe] *vt* to stretch; (*ressort*) to stretch out; **s'étirer** *vi* (*personne*) to stretch; (*convoi, route*): **s'~ sur** to stretch out over

**étoffe** [etɔf] *nf* material, fabric; **avoir l'~ d'un chef** *etc* to be cut out to be a leader *etc*; **avoir de l'~** to be a forceful personality

**étoffer** [etɔfe] *vt* to flesh out; **s'étoffer** *vi* to fill out

**étoile** [etwal] *nf* star ▷ *adj*: **danseuse** *ou* **danseur ~** leading dancer; **la bonne/mauvaise ~ de qn** sb's lucky/unlucky star; **à la belle ~** (out) in the open; **~ filante** shooting star; **~ de mer** starfish; **~ polaire** pole star

**étoilé, e** [etwale] *adj* starry

**étole** [etɔl] *nf* stole

**étonnamment** [etɔnamɑ̃] *adv* amazingly

**étonnant, e** [etɔnɑ̃, -ɑ̃t] *adj* surprising

**étonné, e** [etɔne] *adj* surprised

**étonnement** [etɔnmɑ̃] *nm* surprise; **à mon grand ~ ...** to my great surprise *ou* amazement ...

**étonner** [etɔne] *vt* to surprise; **s'étonner que/ de** to be surprised that/at; **cela m'~ait (que)** (*j'en doute*) I'd be (very) surprised (if)

**étouffant, e** [etufɑ̃, -ɑ̃t] *adj* stifling

**étouffé, e** [etufe] *adj* (*asphyxié*) suffocated; (*assourdi: cris, rires*) smothered ▷ *nf*: **à l'~e** (*Culin: poisson, légumes*) steamed; (*: viande*) braised

**étouffement** [etufmɑ̃] *nm* suffocation

**étouffer** [etufe] *vt* to suffocate; (*bruit*) to muffle; (*scandale*) to hush up ▷ *vi* to suffocate; (*avoir trop chaud, aussi fig*) to feel stifled; **s'étouffer** *vi* (*en mangeant etc*) to choke

**étouffoir** [etufwaʀ] *nm* (*Mus*) damper

**étourderie** [etuʀdəʀi] *nf* heedlessness *no pl*; thoughtless blunder; **faute d'~** careless mistake

**étourdi, e** [etuʀdi] *adj* (*distrait*) scatterbrained, heedless

**étourdiment** [etuʀdimɑ̃] *adv* rashly

**étourdir** [etuʀdiʀ] *vt* (*assommer*) to stun, daze; (*griser*) to make dizzy *ou* giddy

**étourdissant, e** [etuʀdisɑ̃, -ɑ̃t] *adj* staggering

**étourdissement** [etuʀdismɑ̃] *nm* dizzy spell

**étourneau, x** [etuʀno] *nm* starling

**étrange** [etʀɑ̃ʒ] *adj* strange

**étrangement** [etʀɑ̃ʒmɑ̃] *adv* strangely

**étranger, -ère** [etʀɑ̃ʒe, -ɛʀ] *adj* foreign; (*pas de la famille, non familier*) strange ▷ *nm/f* foreigner; stranger ▷ *nm*: **l'~** foreign countries; **à l'~** abroad; **de l'~** from abroad; **~ à** (*mal connu*) unfamiliar to; (*sans rapport*) irrelevant to

**étrangeté** [etʀɑ̃ʒte] *nf* strangeness

**étranglé, e** [etʀɑ̃gle] *adj*: **d'une voix ~e** in a strangled voice

**étranglement** [etʀɑ̃gləmɑ̃] *nm* (*d'une vallée etc*) constriction, narrow passage

**étrangler** [etʀɑ̃gle] *vt* to strangle; (*fig: presse, libertés*) to stifle; **s'étrangler** *vi* (*en mangeant etc*) to choke; (*se resserrer*) to make a bottleneck

**étrave** [etʀav] *nf* stem

 **MOT-CLÉ**

**être** [ɛtʀ(ə)] *nm* being; **être humain** human being

▷ *vb copule* **1** (*état, description*) to be; **il est instituteur** he is *ou* he's a teacher; **vous êtes grand/intelligent/fatigué** you are *ou* you're tall/clever/tired

**2** (*+à: appartenir*) to be; **le livre est à Paul** the book is Paul's *ou* belongs to Paul; **c'est à moi/ eux** it is *ou* it's mine/theirs

**3** (*+de: provenance*): **il est de Paris** he is from Paris; (*appartenance*;): **il est des nôtres** he is one of us

**4** (*date*): **nous sommes le 10 janvier** it's the 10th of January (today)

▷ *vi* to be; **je ne serai pas ici demain** I won't be here tomorrow

▷ *vb aux* **1** to have; to be; **être arrivé/allé** to have arrived/gone; **il est parti** he has left, he has gone

**2** (*forme passive*) to be; **être fait par** to be made by; **il a été promu** he has been promoted

**3** (*+à +inf: obligation, but*): **c'est à réparer** it needs repairing; **c'est à essayer** it should be tried; **il est à espérer que ...** it is *ou* it's to be hoped that ...

▷ *vb impers* **1**: **il est** (*avec adjectif*) it is; **il est impossible de le faire** it's impossible to do it

**2** (*heure, date*): **il est 10 heures** it is *ou* it's 10 o'clock

**3** (*emphatique*): **c'est moi** it's me; **c'est à lui de le faire** it's up to him to do it; *voir aussi* **est-ce que; n'est-ce pas; c'est-à-dire; ce**

**étreindre** [etʀɛ̃dʀ(ə)] *vt* to clutch, grip; (*amoureusement, amicalement*) to embrace; **s'étreindre** to embrace

**étreinte** [etʀɛ̃t] *nf* clutch, grip; embrace; **resserrer son ~ autour de** (*fig*) to tighten one's grip on *ou* around

**étrenner** [etʀene] *vt* to use (*ou* wear) for the first time

**étrennes** [etʀɛn] *nfpl* *(cadeaux)* New Year's present; *(gratifications)* ≈ Christmas box *sg*, ≈ Christmas bonus

**étrier** [etʀije] *nm* stirrup

**étriller** [etʀije] *vt* *(cheval)* to curry; *(fam: battre)* to slaughter *(fig)*

**étriper** [etʀipe] *vt* to gut; *(fam)*: **~ qn** to tear sb's guts out

**étriqué, e** [etʀike] *adj* skimpy

**étroit, e** [etʀwa, -wat] *adj* narrow; *(vêtement)* tight; *(fig: serré)* close, tight; **à l'~** cramped; **~ d'esprit** narrow-minded

**étroitement** [etʀwatmã] *adv* closely

**étroitesse** [etʀwatɛs] *nf* narrowness; **~ d'esprit** narrow-mindedness

**étrusque** [etʀysk(ə)] *adj* Etruscan

**étude** [etyd] *nf* studying; *(ouvrage, rapport, Mus)* study; *(de notaire: bureau)* office; *(: charge)* practice; *(Scol: salle de travail)* study room; **études** *nfpl* *(Scol)* studies; **être à l'~** *(projet etc)* to be under consideration; **faire des ~s (de droit/médecine)** to study (law/medicine); **~s secondaires/supérieures** secondary/higher education; **~ de cas** case study; **~ de faisabilité** feasibility study; **~ de marché** *(Écon)* market research

**étudiant, e** [etydjã, -ãt] *adj, nm/f* student

**étudié, e** [etydje] *adj* *(démarche)* studied; *(système)* carefully designed; *(prix)* keen

**étudier** [etydje] *vt, vi* to study

**étui** [etɥi] *nm* case

**étuve** [etyv] *nf* steamroom; *(appareil)* sterilizer

**étuvée** [etyve]: **à l'~** *adv* braised

**étymologie** [etimɔlɔʒi] *nf* etymology

**étymologique** [etimɔlɔʒik] *adj* etymological

**eu, eue** [y] *pp de* **avoir**

**EU** *sigle mpl* (= États-Unis) US

**EUA** *sigle mpl* (= États-Unis d'Amérique) USA

**eucalyptus** [økaliptys] *nm* eucalyptus

**Eucharistie** [økaʀisti] *nf*: **l'~** the Eucharist, the Lord's Supper

**eucharistique** [økaʀistik] *adj* eucharistic

**euclidien, ne** [øklidjɛ̃, -ɛn] *adj* Euclidian

**eugénique** [øʒenik] *adj* eugenic ▷ *nf* eugenics *sg*

**eugénisme** [øʒenism(ə)] *nm* eugenics *sg*

**euh** [ø] *excl* er

**eunuque** [ønyk] *nm* eunuch

**euphémique** [øfemik] *adj* euphemistic

**euphémisme** [øfemism(ə)] *nm* euphemism

**euphonie** [øfɔni] *nf* euphony

**euphorbe** [øfɔʀb(ə)] *nf* *(Bot)* spurge

**euphorie** [øfɔʀi] *nf* euphoria

**euphorique** [øfɔʀik] *adj* euphoric

**euphorisant, e** [øfɔʀizã, -ãt] *adj* exhilarating

**eurafricain, e** [øʀafʀikɛ̃, -ɛn] *adj* Eurafrican

**eurasiatique** [øʀazjatik] *adj* Eurasiatic

**Eurasie** [øʀazi] *nf*: **l'~** Eurasia

**eurasien, ne** [øʀazjɛ̃, -ɛn] *adj* Eurasian

**EURATOM** [øʀatɔm] *sigle f* Euratom

**eurent** [yʀ(ə)] *vb voir* **avoir**

**euro** [øʀo] *nm* euro

**euro-** [øʀo] *préfixe* Euro-

**eurocrate** [øʀɔkʀat] *nm/f* *(péj)* Eurocrat

**eurodevise** [øʀɔdəviz] *nf* Eurocurrency

**eurodollar** [øʀodɔlaʀ] *nm* Eurodollar

**Euroland** [øʀɔlãd] *nm* Euroland

**euromonnaie** [øʀɔmɔnɛ] *nf* Eurocurrency

**Europe** [øʀɔp] *nf*: **l'~** Europe; **l'~ centrale** Central Europe; **l'~ verte** European agriculture

**européanisation** [øʀɔpeanizasjɔ̃] *nf* Europeanization

**européaniser** [øʀɔpeanize] *vt* to Europeanize

**européen, ne** [øʀɔpeɛ̃, -ɛn] *adj* European ▷ *nm/f*: **Européen, ne** European

**eurosceptique** [øʀosɛptik] *nm/f* Eurosceptic

**Eurovision** [øʀovizjɔ̃] *nf* Eurovision; **émission en ~** Eurovision broadcast

**eus** *etc* [y] *vb voir* **avoir**

**euthanasie** [øtanazi] *nf* euthanasia

**eux** [ø] *pron* *(sujet)* they; *(objet)* them; **~, ils ont fait ...** THEY did ...

**évacuation** [evakɥasjɔ̃] *nf* evacuation

**évacué, e** [evakɥe] *nm/f* evacuee

**évacuer** [evakɥe] *vt* *(salle, région)* to evacuate, clear; *(occupants, population)* to evacuate; *(toxine etc)* to evacuate, discharge

**évadé, e** [evade] *adj* escaped ▷ *nm/f* escapee

**évader** [evade]: **s'évader** *vi* to escape

**évaluation** [evalɥasjɔ̃] *nf* assessment, evaluation

**évaluer** [evalɥe] *vt* to assess, evaluate

**évanescent, e** [evanesã, -ãt] *adj* evanescent

**évangélique** [evãʒelik] *adj* evangelical

**évangélisation** [evãʒelizasjɔ̃] *nf* evangelization

**évangéliser** [evãʒelize] *vt* to evangelize

**évangéliste** [evãʒelist(ə)] *nm* evangelist

**évangile** [evãʒil] *nm* gospel; *(texte de la Bible)*: **É~** Gospel; **ce n'est pas l'É~** *(fig)* it's not gospel

**évanoui, e** [evanwi] *adj* in a faint; **tomber ~** to faint

**évanouir** [evanwiʀ]: **s'évanouir** *vi* to faint, pass out; *(disparaître)* to vanish, disappear

**évanouissement** [evanwismã] *nm* *(syncope)* fainting fit; *(Méd)* loss of consciousness

**évaporation** [evapɔʀasjɔ̃] *nf* evaporation

**évaporé, e** [evapɔʀe] *adj* giddy, scatterbrained

**évaporer** [evapɔʀe]: **s'évaporer** *vi* to evaporate

**évasé, e** [evaze] *adj* *(jupe etc)* flared

**évaser** [evaze] *vt* *(tuyau)* to widen, open out; *(jupe, pantalon)* to flare; **s'évaser** *vi* to widen, open out

**évasif, -ive** [evazif, -iv] *adj* evasive

**évasion** [evazjɔ̃] *nf* escape; **littérature d'~** escapist literature; **~ des capitaux** *(Écon)* flight of capital; **~ fiscale** tax avoidance

**évasivement** [evazivmã] *adv* evasively

**évêché** [eveʃe] *nm* *(fonction)* bishopric; *(palais)* bishop's palace

**éveil** [evɛj] *nm* awakening; **être en ~** to be alert; **mettre qn en ~, donner l'~ à qn** to arouse sb's suspicions; **activités d'~** early-learning activities

**éveillé, e** [eveje] *adj* awake; (*vif*) alert, sharp
**éveiller** [eveje] *vt* to (a)waken; **s'éveiller** *vi* to
(a)waken; (*fig*) to be aroused
**événement** [evɛnmã] *nm* event
**éventail** [evãtaj] *nm* fan; (*choix*) range; **en ~**
fanned out; fan-shaped
**éventaire** [evãtɛʀ] *nm* stall, stand
**éventé, e** [evãte] *adj* (*parfum, vin*) stale
**éventer** [evãte] *vt* (*secret, complot*) to uncover;
(*avec un éventail*) to fan; **s'éventer** *vi* (*parfum, vin*)
to go stale
**éventrer** [evãtʀe] *vt* to disembowel; (*fig*) to tear
*ou* rip open
**éventualité** [evãtɥalite] *nf* eventuality;
possibility; **dans l'~ de** in the event of; **parer à**
**toute ~** to guard against all eventualities
**éventuel, le** [evãtɥɛl] *adj* possible
**éventuellement** [evãtɥɛlmã] *adv* possibly
**évêque** [evɛk] *nm* bishop
**Everest** [ɛvʀɛst] *nm*: **(mont) ~** (Mount) Everest
**évertuer** [evɛʀtɥe]: **s'évertuer** *vi*: **s'~ à faire** to
try very hard to do
**éviction** [eviksjõ] *nf* ousting, supplanting; (*de
locataire*) eviction
**évidemment** [evidamã] *adv* obviously
**évidence** [evidãs] *nf* obviousness; (*fait*) obvious
fact; **se rendre à l'~** to bow before the evidence;
**nier l'~** to deny the evidence; **à l'~** evidently;
**de toute ~** quite obviously *ou* evidently; **en ~**
conspicuous; **mettre en ~** to bring to the fore
**évident, e** [evidã, -ãt] *adj* obvious, evident; **ce**
**n'est pas ~** (*cela pose des problèmes*) it's not (all
that) straightforward, it's not as simple as all
that
**évider** [evide] *vt* to scoop out
**évier** [evje] *nm* (kitchen) sink
**évincer** [evɛ̃se] *vt* to oust, supplant
**évitable** [evitabl(ə)] *adj* avoidable
**évitement** [evitmã] *nm*: **place d'~** (*Auto*)
passing place
**éviter** [evite] *vt* to avoid; **~ de faire/que qch ne**
**se passe** to avoid doing/sth happening; **~ qch à**
**qn** to spare sb sth
**évocateur, -trice** [evɔkatœʀ, -tʀis] *adj*
evocative, suggestive
**évocation** [evɔkasjõ] *nf* evocation
**évolué, e** [evɔlɥe] *adj* advanced; (*personne*)
broad-minded
**évoluer** [evɔlɥe] *vi* (*enfant, maladie*) to develop;
(*situation, moralement*) to evolve, develop; (*aller et
venir: danseur etc*) to move about, circle
**évolutif, -ive** [evɔlytif, -iv] *adj* evolving
**évolution** [evɔlysjõ] *nf* development; evolution;
**évolutions** *nfpl* movements
**évolutionnisme** [evɔlysjɔnism(ə)] *nm*
evolutionism
**évoquer** [evɔke] *vt* to call to mind, evoke;
(*mentionner*) to mention
**ex.** *abr* (= *exemple*) ex.
**ex-** [ɛks] *préfixe* ex-
**exacerbé, e** [ɛgzasɛʀbe] *adj* (*orgueil, sensibilité*)
exaggerated

**exacerber** [ɛgzasɛʀbe] *vt* to exacerbate
**exact, e** [ɛgzakt] *adj* (*précis*) exact, accurate,
precise; (*correct*) correct; (*ponctuel*) punctual;
**l'heure ~e** the right *ou* exact time
**exactement** [ɛgzaktəmã] *adv* exactly,
accurately, precisely; correctly; (*c'est cela même*)
exactly
**exaction** [ɛgzaksjõ] *nf* (*d'argent*) exaction; (*gén pl*:
*actes de violence*) abuse(s)
**exactitude** [ɛgzaktityd] *nf* exactitude,
accurateness, precision
**ex aequo** [ɛgzeko] *adj* equally placed; **classé**
**1er ~** placed equal first
**exagération** [ɛgzaʒeʀasjõ] *nf* exaggeration
**exagéré, e** [ɛgzaʒeʀe] *adj* (*prix etc*) excessive
**exagérément** [ɛgzaʒeʀemã] *adv* excessively
**exagérer** [ɛgzaʒeʀe] *vt* to exaggerate ▷ *vi*
(*abuser*) to go too far; (*dépasser les bornes*) to
overstep the mark; **s'exagérer qch** to exaggerate sth
**exaltant, e** [ɛgzaltã, -ãt] *adj* exhilarating
**exaltation** [ɛgzaltasjõ] *nf* exaltation
**exalté, e** [ɛgzalte] *adj* (over)excited ▷ *nm/f* (*péj*)
fanatic
**exalter** [ɛgzalte] *vt* (*enthousiasmer*) to excite,
elate; (*glorifier*) to exalt
**examen** [ɛgzamɛ̃] *nm* examination; (*Scol*)
exam, examination; **à l'~** (*dossier, projet*) under
consideration; (*Comm*) on approval; **~ blanc**
mock exam(ination); **~ de la vue** sight test
**examinateur, -trice** [ɛgzaminatœʀ, -tʀis] *nm/f*
examiner
**examiner** [ɛgzamine] *vt* to examine
**exaspérant, e** [ɛgzaspeʀã, -ãt] *adj* exasperating
**exaspération** [ɛgzaspeʀasjõ] *nf* exasperation
**exaspéré, e** [ɛgzaspeʀe] *adj* exasperated
**exaspérer** [ɛgzaspeʀe] *vt* to exasperate;
(*aggraver*) to exacerbate
**exaucer** [ɛgzose] *vt* (*vœu*) to grant, fulfil; **~ qn** to
grant sb's wishes
**ex cathedra** [ɛkskatedʀa] *adj, adv* ex cathedra
**excavateur** [ɛkskavatœʀ] *nm* excavator,
mechanical digger
**excavation** [ɛkskavasjõ] *nf* excavation
**excavatrice** [ɛkskavatʀis] *nf* = **excavateur**
**excédent** [ɛksedã] *nm* surplus; **en ~** surplus;
**payer 60 euros d'~** (*de bagages*) to pay 60 euros
excess baggage; **~ de bagages** excess baggage;
**~ commercial** trade surplus
**excédentaire** [ɛksedãtɛʀ] *adj* surplus, excess
**excéder** [ɛksede] *vt* (*dépasser*) to exceed; (*agacer*)
to exasperate; **excédé de fatigue** exhausted;
**excédé de travail** worn out with work
**excellence** [ɛksɛlãs] *nf* excellence; (*titre*)
Excellency; **par ~** par excellence
**excellent, e** [ɛksɛlã, -ãt] *adj* excellent
**exceller** [ɛksele] *vi*: **~ (dans)** to excel (in)
**excentricité** [ɛksãtʀisite] *nf* eccentricity
**excentrique** [ɛksãtʀik] *adj* eccentric; (*quartier*)
outlying ▷ *nm/f* eccentric
**excentriquement** [ɛksãtʀikmã] *adv*
eccentrically

165

**excepté, e** [ɛksɛpte] *adj, prép*: **les élèves ~s, ~ les élèves** except for *ou* apart from the pupils; **~ si/ quand** except if/when; **~ que** except that

**excepter** [ɛksɛpte] *vt* to except

**exception** [ɛksɛpsjɔ̃] *nf* exception; **faire ~** to be an exception; **faire une ~** to make an exception; **sans ~** without exception; **à l'~ de** except for, with the exception of; **d'~** *(mesure, loi)* special, exceptional

**exceptionnel, le** [ɛksɛpsjɔnɛl] *adj* exceptional; *(prix)* special

**exceptionnellement** [ɛksɛpsjɔnɛlmɑ̃] *adv* exceptionally; *(par exception)* by way of an exception, on this occasion

**excès** [ɛksɛ] *nm* surplus ▷ *nmpl* excesses; **à l'~** *(méticuleux, généreux)* to excess; **avec ~** to excess; **sans ~** in moderation; **tomber dans l'inverse** to go to the opposite extreme; **~ de langage** immoderate language; **~ de pouvoir** abuse of power; **~ de vitesse** speeding *no pl*, exceeding the speed limit; **~ de zèle** overzealousness *no pl*

**excessif, -ive** [ɛksesif, -iv] *adj* excessive

**excessivement** [ɛksesivmɑ̃] *adv* *(trop: cher)* excessively, inordinately; *(très: riche, laid)* extremely, incredibly; **manger/boire ~** to eat/drink to excess

**exciper** [ɛksipe] : **~ de** *vt* to plead

**excipient** [ɛksipjɑ̃] *nm* *(Méd)* inert base, excipient

**exciser** [ɛksize] *vt* *(Méd)* to excise

**excision** [ɛksizjɔ̃] *nf* *(Méd)* excision; *(rituelle)* circumcision

**excitant, e** [ɛksitɑ̃, -ɑ̃t] *adj* exciting ▷ *nm* stimulant

**excitation** [ɛksitasjɔ̃] *nf* *(état)* excitement

**excité, e** [ɛksite] *adj* excited

**exciter** [ɛksite] *vt* to excite; *(café etc)* to stimulate; **s'exciter** *vi* to get excited; **~ qn à** *(révolte etc)* to incite sb to

**exclamation** [ɛksklamasjɔ̃] *nf* exclamation

**exclamer** [ɛksklame]: **s'exclamer** *vi* to exclaim

**exclu, e** [ɛkskly] *pp de* **exclure** ▷ *adj*: **il est/n'est pas ~ que ...** it's out of the question/not impossible that ...; **ce n'est pas ~** it's not impossible, I don't rule that out

**exclure** [ɛksklyʀ] *vt* *(faire sortir)* to expel; *(ne pas compter)* to exclude, leave out; *(rendre impossible)* to exclude, rule out

**exclusif, -ive** [ɛksklyzif, -iv] *adj* exclusive; **avec la mission exclusive/dans le but ~ de ...** with the sole mission/aim of ...; **agent ~** sole agent

**exclusion** [ɛksklyzjɔ̃] *nf* expulsion; **à l'~ de** with the exclusion *ou* exception of

**exclusivement** [ɛksklyzivmɑ̃] *adv* exclusively

**exclusivité** [ɛksklyzivite] *nf* exclusiveness; *(Comm)* exclusive rights *pl*; **passer en ~** *(film)* to go on general release

**excommunier** [ɛkskɔmynje] *vt* to excommunicate

**excréments** [ɛkskʀemɑ̃] *nmpl* excrement *sg*, faeces

**excréter** [ɛkskʀete] *vt* to excrete

**excroissance** [ɛkskʀwasɑ̃s] *nf* excrescence, outgrowth

**excursion** [ɛkskyʀsjɔ̃] *nf* *(en autocar)* excursion, trip; *(à pied)* walk, hike; **faire une ~** to go on an excursion *ou* a trip; to go on a walk *ou* hike

**excursionniste** [ɛkskyʀsjɔnist(ə)] *nm/f* tripper; hiker

**excusable** [ɛkskyzabl(ə)] *adj* excusable

**excuse** [ɛkskyz] *nf* excuse; **excuses** *nfpl* apology *sg*, apologies; **faire des ~s** to apologize; **faire ses ~s** to offer one's apologies; **mot d'~** *(Scol)* note from one's parent(s) *(to explain absence etc)*; **lettre d'~s** letter of apology

**excuser** [ɛkskyze] *vt* to excuse; **~ qn de qch** *(dispenser)* to excuse sb from sth; **s'excuser (de)** to apologize (for); **"excusez-moi"** "I'm sorry"; *(pour attirer l'attention)* "excuse me"; **se faire ~** to ask to be excused

**exécrable** [ɛgzekʀabl(ə)] *adj* atrocious

**exécrer** [ɛgzekʀe] *vt* to loathe, abhor

**exécutant, e** [ɛgzekytɑ̃, -ɑ̃t] *nm/f* performer

**exécuter** [ɛgzekyte] *vt* *(prisonnier)* to execute; *(tâche etc)* to execute, carry out; *(Mus: jouer)* to perform, execute; *(Inform)* to run; **s'exécuter** *vi* to comply

**exécuteur, -trice** [ɛgzekytœʀ, -tʀis] *nm/f* *(testamentaire)* executor ▷ *nm* *(bourreau)* executioner

**exécutif, -ive** [ɛgzekytif, -iv] *adj, nm* *(Pol)* executive

**exécution** [ɛgzekysjɔ̃] *nf* execution; carrying out; **mettre à ~** to carry out

**exécutoire** [ɛgzekytwaʀ] *adj* *(Jur)* (legally) binding

**exégèse** [ɛgzeʒɛz] *nf* exegesis

**exégète** [ɛgzeʒɛt] *nm* exegete

**exemplaire** [ɛgzɑ̃plɛʀ] *adj* exemplary ▷ *nm* copy

**exemple** [ɛgzɑ̃pl(ə)] *nm* example; **par ~** for instance, for example; *(valeur intensive)* really!; **sans ~** *(bêtise, gourmandise etc)* unparalleled; **donner l'~** to set an example; **prendre ~ sur** to take as a model; **à l'~ de** just like; **pour l'~** *(punir)* as an example

**exempt, e** [ɛgzɑ̃, -ɑ̃t] *adj*: **~ de** *(dispensé de)* exempt from; *(sans)* free from; **~ de taxes** tax-free

**exempter** [ɛgzɑ̃te] *vt*: **~ de** to exempt from

**exercé, e** [ɛgzɛʀse] *adj* trained

**exercer** [ɛgzɛʀse] *vt* *(pratiquer)* to exercise, practise; *(faire usage de: prérogative)* to exercise; *(effectuer: influence, contrôle, pression)* to exert; *(former)* to exercise, train ▷ *vi* *(médecin)* to be in practice; **s'exercer** *(sportif, musicien)* to practise; *(se faire sentir: pression etc)*: **s'~ (sur ou contre)** to be exerted (on); **s'~ à faire qch** to train o.s. to do sth

**exercice** [ɛgzɛʀsis] *nm* practice; exercising; *(tâche, travail)* exercise; *(Comm, Admin: période)* accounting period; **l'~** *(sportive etc)* exercise; *(Mil)* drill; **en ~** *(juge)* in office; *(médecin)* practising; **dans l'~ de ses fonctions** in the discharge of his duties; **~s d'assouplissement** limbering-up (exercises)

**exergue** [ɛgzɛrg(ə)] *nm*: **mettre en ~** *(inscription)* to inscribe; **porter en ~** to be inscribed with

**exhalaison** [ɛgzalɛzɔ̃] *nf* exhalation

**exhaler** [ɛgzale] *vt (parfum)* to exhale; *(souffle, son, soupir)* to utter, breathe; **s'exhaler** *vi* to rise (up)

**exhausser** [ɛgzose] *vt* to raise (up)

**exhausteur** [ɛgzostœr] *nm* extractor fan

**exhaustif, -ive** [ɛgzostif, -iv] *adj* exhaustive

**exhiber** [ɛgzibe] *vt (montrer: papiers, certificat)* to present, produce; *(péj)* to display, flaunt; **s'exhiber** *(personne)* to parade; *(exhibitionniste)* to expose o.s.

**exhibitionnisme** [ɛgzibisjɔnism(ə)] *nm* exhibitionism

**exhibitionniste** [ɛgzibisjɔnist(ə)] *nm/f* exhibitionist

**exhortation** [ɛgzɔrtasjɔ̃] *nf* exhortation

**exhorter** [ɛgzɔrte] *vt*: **~ qn à faire** to urge sb to do

**exhumer** [ɛgzyme] *vt* to exhume

**exigeant, e** [ɛgziʒɑ̃, -ɑ̃t] *adj* demanding; *(péj)* hard to please

**exigence** [ɛgziʒɑ̃s] *nf* demand, requirement

**exiger** [ɛgziʒe] *vt* to demand, require

**exigible** [ɛgziʒibl(ə)] *adj (Comm, Jur)* payable

**exigu, ë** [ɛgzigy] *adj* cramped, tiny

**exigüité** [ɛgzigɥite] *nf (d'un lieu)* cramped nature

**exil** [ɛgzil] *nm* exile; **en ~** in exile

**exilé, e** [ɛgzile] *nm/f* exile

**exiler** [ɛgzile] *vt* to exile; **s'exiler** to go into exile

**existant, e** [ɛgzistɑ̃, -ɑ̃t] *adj (actuel, présent)* existing

**existence** [ɛgzistɑ̃s] *nf* existence; **dans l'~** in life

**existentialisme** [ɛgzistɑ̃sjalism(ə)] *nm* existentialism

**existentiel, le** [ɛgzistɑ̃sjɛl] *adj* existential

**exister** [ɛgziste] *vi* to exist; **il existe un/des** there is a/are (some)

**exode** [ɛgzɔd] *nm* exodus

**exonération** [ɛgzɔnerasjɔ̃] *nf* exemption

**exonéré, e** [ɛgzɔnere] *adj*: **~ de TVA** zero-rated (for VAT)

**exonérer** [ɛgzɔnere] *vt*: **~ de** to exempt from

**exorbitant, e** [ɛgzɔrbitɑ̃, -ɑ̃t] *adj* exorbitant

**exorbité, e** [ɛgzɔrbite] *adj*: **yeux ~s** bulging eyes

**exorciser** [ɛgzɔrsize] *vt* to exorcize

**exorde** [ɛgzɔrd(ə)] *nm* introduction

**exotique** [ɛgzɔtik] *adj* exotic

**exotisme** [ɛgzɔtism(ə)] *nm* exoticism

**expansif, -ive** [ɛkspɑ̃sif, -iv] *adj* expansive, communicative

**expansion** [ɛkspɑ̃sjɔ̃] *nf* expansion

**expansionniste** [ɛkspɑ̃sjɔnist(ə)] *adj* expansionist

**expansivité** [ɛkspɑ̃sivite] *nf* expansiveness

**expatrié, e** [ɛkspatrije] *nm/f* expatriate

**expatrier** [ɛkspatrije] *vt (argent)* to take *ou* send

out of the country; **s'expatrier** to leave one's country

**expectative** [ɛkspɛktativ] *nf*: **être dans l'~** to be waiting to see

**expectorant, e** [ɛkspɛktɔrɑ̃, -ɑ̃t] *adj*: **sirop ~** expectorant (syrup)

**expectorer** [ɛkspɛktɔre] *vi* to expectorate

**expédient** [ɛkspedjɑ̃] *nm (parfois péj)* expedient; **vivre d'~s** to live by one's wits

**expédier** [ɛkspedje] *vt (lettre, paquet)* to send; *(troupes, renfort)* to dispatch; *(péj: travail etc)* to dispose of, dispatch

**expéditeur, -trice** [ɛkspeditœr, -tris] *nm/f (Postes)* sender

**expéditif, -ive** [ɛkspeditif, -iv] *adj* quick, expeditious

**expédition** [ɛkspedisjɔ̃] *nf* sending; *(scientifique, sportive, Mil)* expedition; **~ punitive** punitive raid

**expéditionnaire** [ɛkspedisjɔnɛr] *adj*: **corps ~** *(Mil)* task force

**expérience** [ɛksperjɑ̃s] *nf (de la vie, des choses)* experience; *(scientifique)* experiment; **avoir de l'~** to have experience, be experienced; **avoir l'~ de** to have experience of; **faire l'~ de qch** to experience sth; **~ de chimie/d'électricité** chemical/electrical experiment

**expérimental, e, -aux** [ɛksperimɑ̃tal, -o] *adj* experimental

**expérimentalement** [ɛksperimɑ̃talmɑ̃] *adv* experimentally

**expérimenté, e** [ɛksperimɑ̃te] *adj* experienced

**expérimenter** [ɛksperimɑ̃te] *vt (machine, technique)* to test out, experiment with

**expert, e** [ɛkspɛr, -ɛrt(ə)] *adj*: **~ en** expert in ▷ *nm (spécialiste)* expert; **~ en assurances** insurance valuer

**expert-comptable** [ɛkspɛrkɔ̃tabl(ə)] *(pl* **experts-comptables**) *nm* ≈ chartered *(Brit) ou* certified public *(US)* accountant

**expertise** [ɛkspɛrtiz] *nf* valuation; assessment; valuer's *(ou assessor's)* report; *(Jur)* (forensic) examination

**expertiser** [ɛkspɛrtize] *vt (objet de valeur)* to value; *(voiture accidentée etc)* to assess damage to

**expier** [ɛkspje] *vt* to expiate, atone for

**expiration** [ɛkspirasjɔ̃] *nf* expiry *(Brit)*, expiration; breathing out *no pl*

**expirer** [ɛkspire] *vi (prendre fin, littéraire: mourir)* to expire; *(respirer)* to breathe out

**explétif, -ive** [ɛkspletif, -iv] *adj (Ling)* expletive

**explicable** [ɛksplikabl(ə)] *adj*: **pas ~** inexplicable

**explicatif, -ive** [ɛksplikatif, -iv] *adj (mot, texte, note)* explanatory

**explication** [ɛksplikasjɔ̃] *nf* explanation; *(discussion)* discussion; **~ de texte** *(Scol)* critical analysis (of a text)

**explicite** [ɛksplisit] *adj* explicit

**explicitement** [ɛksplisitmɑ̃] *adv* explicitly

**expliciter** [ɛksplisite] *vt* to make explicit

**expliquer** [ɛksplike] *vt* to explain; **~ (à qn)**

**e**

**comment/que** to point out *ou* explain (to sb) how/that; **s'expliquer**(*se faire comprendre: personne*) to explain o.s.; (*discuter*) to discuss things; (*se disputer*) to have it out; (*comprendre*): **je m'explique son retard/absence** I understand his lateness/absence; **son erreur s'explique** one can understand his mistake

**exploit** [ɛksplwa] *nm* exploit, feat

**exploitable** [ɛskplwatabl(ə)] *adj* (*gisement etc*) that can be exploited; ~ **par une machine** machine-readable

**exploitant** [ɛksplwatɑ̃] *nm* farmer

**exploitation** [ɛksplwatɑsjɔ̃] *nf* exploitation; running; (*entreprise*): ~ **agricole** farming concern

**exploiter** [ɛksplwate] *vt* to exploit; (*entreprise, ferme*) to run, operate

**exploiteur, -euse** [ɛksplwatœr, -øz] *nm/f* (*péj*) exploiter

**explorateur, -trice** [ɛksplɔratœr, -tris] *nm/f* explorer

**exploration** [ɛksplɔrɑsjɔ̃] *nf* exploration

**explorer** [ɛksplɔre] *vt* to explore

**exploser** [ɛksploze] *vi* to explode, blow up; (*engin explosif*) to go off; (*fig: joie, colère*) to burst out, explode; (: *personne: de colère*) to explode, flare up; **faire** ~ (*bombe*) to explode, detonate; (*bâtiment, véhicule*) to blow up

**explosif, -ive** [ɛksplozif, -iv] *adj, nm* explosive

**explosion** [ɛksplozjɔ̃] *nf* explosion; ~ **de joie/colère** outburst of joy/rage; ~ **démographique** population explosion

**exponentiel, le** [ɛkspɔnɑ̃sjɛl] *adj* exponential

**exportateur, -trice** [ɛkspɔrtatœr, -tris] *adj* exporting ▷ *nm* exporter

**exportation** [ɛkspɔrtɑsjɔ̃] *nf* export

**exporter** [ɛkspɔrte] *vt* to export

**exposant** [ɛkspozɑ̃] *nm* exhibitor; (*Math*) exponent

**exposé, e** [ɛkspoze] *nm* (*écrit*) exposé; (*oral*) talk ▷ *adj*: ~ **au sud** facing south, with a southern aspect; **bien** ~ well situated; **très** ~ very exposed

**exposer** [ɛkspoze] *vt* (*montrer: marchandise*) to display; (: *peinture*) to exhibit, show; (*parler de: problème, situation*) to explain, expose, set out; (*mettre en danger, orienter: maison etc*) to expose; ~ **qn/qch à** to expose sb/sth to; ~ **sa vie** to risk one's life; **s'exposer à**(*soleil, danger*) to expose o.s. to; (*critiques, punition*) to lay o.s. open to

**exposition** [ɛkspozisjɔ̃] *nf* (*voir exposer*) displaying; exhibiting; explanation, exposition; exposure; (*voir exposé*) aspect, situation; (*manifestation*) exhibition; (*Photo*) exposure; (*introduction*) exposition

**exprès¹** [ɛksprɛ] *adv* (*délibérément*) on purpose; (*spécialement*) specially; **faire** ~ **de faire qch** to do sth on purpose

**exprès², -esse** [ɛksprɛs] *adj* (*ordre, défense*) express, formal ▷ *adj inv, adv* (*Postes*) express; **envoyer qch en** ~ to send sth express

**express** [ɛksprɛs] *adj, nm*: (**café**) ~ espresso;

(**train**) ~ fast train

**expressément** [ɛksprɛsemɑ̃] *adv* expressly, specifically

**expressif, -ive** [ɛksprɛsif, -iv] *adj* expressive

**expression** [ɛksprɛsjɔ̃] *nf* expression; **réduit à sa plus simple** ~ reduced to its simplest terms; **liberté/moyens d'**~ freedom/means of expression; ~ **toute faite** set phrase

**expressionnisme** [ɛksprɛsjɔnism(ə)] *nm* expressionism

**expressivité** [ɛksprɛsivite] *nf* expressiveness

**exprimer** [ɛksprime] *vt* (*sentiment, idée*) to express; (*faire sortir: jus, liquide*) to press out; **s'exprimer** *vi* (*personne*) to express o.s.

**expropriation** [ɛksprɔprijasjɔ̃] *nf* expropriation; **frapper d'**~ to put a compulsory purchase order on

**exproprier** [ɛksprɔprije] *vt* to buy up (*ou* buy the property of) by compulsory purchase, expropriate

**expulser** [ɛkspylse] *vt* (*d'une salle, d'un groupe*) to expel; (*locataire*) to evict; (*Football*) to send off

**expulsion** [ɛkspylsjɔ̃] *nf* expulsion; eviction; sending off

**expurger** [ɛkspyrʒe] *vt* to expurgate, bowdlerize

**exquis, e** [ɛkski, -iz] *adj* (*gâteau, parfum, élégance*) exquisite; (*personne, temps*) delightful

**exsangue** [ɛksɑ̃g] *adj* bloodless, drained of blood

**exsuder** [ɛksyde] *vt* to exude

**extase** [ɛkstaz] *nf* ecstasy; **être en** ~ to be in raptures

**extasier** [ɛkstazje]: **s'extasier** *vi*: **s'**~ **sur** to go into raptures over

**extatique** [ɛkstatik] *adj* ecstatic

**extenseur** [ɛkstɑ̃sœr] *nm* (*Sport*) chest expander

**extensible** [ɛkstɑ̃sibl(ə)] *adj* extensible

**extensif, -ive** [ɛkstɑ̃sif, -iv] *adj* extensive

**extension** [ɛkstɑ̃sjɔ̃] *nf* (*d'un muscle, ressort*) stretching; (*Méd*): **à l'**~ in traction; (*fig*) extension; expansion

**exténuant, e** [ɛkstenyɑ̃, -ɑ̃t] *adj* exhausting

**exténuer** [ɛkstenye] *vt* to exhaust

**extérieur, e** [ɛksterjœr] *adj* (*de dehors: porte, mur etc*) outer, outside; (: *commerce, politique*) foreign; (: *influences, pressions*) external; (*au dehors: escalier, w.-c.*) outside; (*apparent: calme, gaieté etc*) outer ▷ *nm* (*d'une maison, d'un récipient etc*) outside, exterior; (*d'une personne: apparence*) exterior; (*d'un pays, d'un groupe social*): **l'**~ the outside world; **à l'**~ (*dehors*) outside; (*fig: à l'étranger*) abroad

**extérieurement** [ɛksterjœrmɑ̃] *adv* (*de dehors*) on the outside; (*en apparence*) on the surface

**extérioriser** [ɛksterjɔrize] *vt* to exteriorize

**extermination** [ɛkstɛrminɑsjɔ̃] *nf* extermination, wiping out

**exterminer** [ɛkstɛrmine] *vt* to exterminate, wipe out

**externat** [ɛkstɛrna] *nm* day school

**externe** [ɛkstɛrn(ə)] *adj* external, outer ▷ *nm/f* (*Méd*) non-resident medical student, extern

(US); (Scol) day pupil

**extincteur** [ɛkstɛ̃ktœR] nm (fire) extinguisher

**extinction** [ɛkstɛ̃ksjɔ̃] nf extinction; (Jur: d'une dette) extinguishment; ~ **de voix** (Méd) loss of voice

**extirper** [ɛkstiRpe] vt (tumeur) to extirpate; (plante) to root out, pull up; (préjugés) to eradicate

**extorquer** [ɛkstɔRke] vt (de l'argent, un renseignement): ~ **qch à qn** to extort sth from sb

**extorsion** [ɛkstɔRsjɔ̃] nf: ~ **de fonds** extortion of money

**extra** [ɛkstRa] adj inv first-rate; (marchandises) top-quality ▷ nm inv extra help ▷ préfixe extra(-)

**extraction** [ɛkstRaksjɔ̃] nf extraction

**extrader** [ɛkstRade] vt to extradite

**extradition** [ɛkstRadisjɔ̃] nf extradition

**extra-fin, e** [ɛkstRafɛ̃, -in] adj extra-fine

**extra-fort, e** [ɛkstRafɔR] adj extra strong

**extraire** [ɛkstRER] vt to extract

**extrait, e** [ɛkstRɛ, -ɛt] pp de **extraire** ▷ nm (de plante) extract; (de film, livre) extract, excerpt; ~ **de naissance** birth certificate

**extra-lucide** [ɛkstRalysid] adj: **voyante ~** clairvoyant

**extraordinaire** [ɛkstRaɔRdinɛR] adj extraordinary; (Pol, Admin) special; **ambassadeur ~** ambassador extraordinary; **assemblée ~** extraordinary meeting; **par ~** by some unlikely chance

**extraordinairement** [ɛkstRaɔRdinɛRmɑ̃] adv extraordinarily

**extrapoler** [ɛkstRapole] vt, vi to extrapolate

**extra-sensoriel, le** [ɛkstRasɑ̃sɔRjɛl] adj extrasensory

**extra-terrestre** [ɛkstRatɛRɛstR(ə)] nm/f

extraterrestrial

**extra-utérin, e** [ɛkstRayteRɛ̃, -in] adj extrauterine

**extravagance** [ɛkstRavagɑ̃s] nf extravagance no pl; extravagant behaviour no pl

**extravagant, e** [ɛkstRavagɑ̃, -ɑ̃t] adj (personne, attitude) extravagant; (idée) wild

**extraverti, e** [ɛkstRavɛRti] adj extrovert

**extrayais** etc [ɛkstRɛjɛ] vb voir **extraire**

**extrême** [ɛkstRɛm] adj, nm extreme; (intensif): **d'une ~ simplicité/brutalité** extremely simple/brutal; **d'un ~ à l'autre** from one extreme to another; **à l'~** in the extreme; **à l'~ rigueur** in the absolute extreme

**extrêmement** [ɛkstRɛmmɑ̃] adv extremely

**extrême-onction** [ɛkstRɛmɔ̃ksjɔ̃] (pl **extrêmes-onctions**) nf (Rel) last rites pl, Extreme Unction

**Extrême-Orient** [ɛkstRɛmɔRjɑ̃] nm: **l'~** the Far East

**extrême-oriental, e, -aux** [ɛkstRɛmɔRjɑ̃tal, -o] adj Far Eastern

**extrémisme** [ɛkstRemism(ə)] nm extremism

**extrémiste** [ɛkstRemist(ə)] adj, nm/f extremist

**extrémité** [ɛkstRemite] nf (bout) end; (situation) straits pl, plight; (geste désespéré) extreme action; **extrémités** nfpl (pieds et mains) extremities; **à la dernière ~** (à l'agonie) on the point of death

**extroverti, e** [ɛkstRɔvɛRti] adj = **extraverti**

**exubérance** [ɛgzybeRɑ̃s] nf exuberance

**exubérant, e** [ɛgzybeRɑ̃, -ɑ̃t] adj exuberant

**exulter** [ɛgzylte] vi to exult

**exutoire** [ɛgzytwaR] nm outlet, release

**ex-voto** [ɛksvɔto] nm inv ex-voto

**eye-liner** [ajlajnœR] nm eyeliner

e

# Ff

**F, f** [εf] *nm inv* F, f ▷ *abr* = **féminin**; (= *franc*) fr.;
(= *Fahrenheit*) F; (= *frère*) Br(o).; (= *femme*) W;
(*appartement*): **un F2/F3** a 2-/3-roomed flat (*Brit*)
*ou* apartment (*US*); **F comme François** F for
Frederick (*Brit*) *ou* Fox (*US*)

**fa** [fa] *nm inv* (*Mus*) F; (*en chantant la gamme*) fa

**fable** [fabl(ə)] *nf* fable; (*mensonge*) story, tale

**fabricant** [fabrikɑ̃] *nm* manufacturer, maker

**fabrication** [fabrikasjɔ̃] *nf* manufacture,
making

**fabrique** [fabrik] *nf* factory

**fabriquer** [fabrike] *vt* to make; (*industriellement*)
to manufacture, make; (*construire: voiture*) to
manufacture, build; (: *maison*) to build; (*fig:
inventer: histoire, alibi*) to make up; (*fam*): **qu'est-
ce qu'il fabrique?** what is he up to?; **~ en série**
to mass-produce

**fabulateur, -trice** [fabylatœr, -tris] *nm/f:* **c'est
un ~** he fantasizes, he makes up stories

**fabulation** [fabylasjɔ̃] *nf* (*Psych*) fantasizing

**fabuleusement** [fabyløzmɑ̃] *adv* fabulously,
fantastically

**fabuleux, -euse** [fabylø, -øz] *adj* fabulous,
fantastic

**fac** [fak] *abr f* (*fam*: = *faculté*) Uni (*Brit: fam*)
= college (*US*)

**façade** [fasad] *nf* front, façade; (*fig*) façade

**face** [fas] *nf* face; (*fig: aspect*) side ▷ *adj*: **le côté ~**
heads; **perdre/sauver la ~** to lose/save face;
**regarder qn en ~** to look sb in the face; **la
maison/le trottoir d'en ~** the house/pavement
opposite; **en ~ de** *prép* opposite; (*fig*) in front of;
**de ~** *adv* from the front; face on; **~ à** *prép*
facing; (*fig*) faced with, in the face of; **faire ~ à**
to face; **faire ~ à la demande** (*Comm*) to meet
the demand; **~ à ~** *adv* facing each other ▷ *nm
inv* encounter

**face-à-main** [fasamɛ̃] (*pl* **faces-à-main**) *nm*
lorgnette

**facéties** [fasesi] *nfpl* jokes, pranks

**facétieux, -euse** [fasesjø, -øz] *adj* mischievous

**facette** [fasɛt] *nf* facet

**fâché, e** [faʃe] *adj* angry; (*désolé*) sorry

**fâcher** [faʃe] *vt* to anger; **se fâcher** *vi* to get
angry; **se ~ avec** (*se brouiller*) to fall out with

**fâcherie** [faʃri] *nf* quarrel

**fâcheusement** [faʃøzmɑ̃] *adv* unpleasantly;
(*impressionné etc*) badly; **avoir ~ tendance à** to
have an irritating tendency to

**fâcheux, -euse** [faʃø, -øz] *adj* unfortunate,
regrettable

**facho** [faʃo] *adj, nm/f* (*fam*: = *fasciste*) fascist

**facial, e, -aux** [fasjal, -o] *adj* facial

**faciès** [fasjɛs] *nm* (*visage*) features *pl*

**facile** [fasil] *adj* easy; (*accommodant*) easy-going

**facilement** [fasilmɑ̃] *adv* easily

**facilité** [fasilite] *nf* easiness; (*disposition, don*)
aptitude; (*moyen, occasion, possibilité*): **il a la ~ de
rencontrer les gens** he has every opportunity
to meet people; **facilités** *nfpl* facilities; (*Comm*)
terms; **~s de crédit** credit terms; **~s de
paiement** easy terms

**faciliter** [fasilite] *vt* to make easier

**façon** [fasɔ̃] *nf* (*manière*) way; (*d'une robe etc*)
making-up; cut; (: *main-d'œuvre*) labour (*Brit*),
labor (*US*); (*imitation*): **châle ~ cachemire**
cashmere-style shawl; **façons** *nfpl* (*péj*) fuss *sg*;
**faire des ~s** (*péj: être affecté*) to be affected; (: *faire
des histoires*) to make a fuss; **de quelle ~?** (in)
what way?; **sans ~** *adv* without fuss ▷ *adj*
unaffected; **d'une autre ~** in another way; **en
aucune ~** in no way; **de ~ à** so as to; **de ~ à ce
que, de (telle) ~ que** so that; **de toute ~**
anyway, in any case; **(c'est une) ~ de parler** it's
a way of putting it; **travail à ~** tailoring

**façonner** [fasɔne] *vt* (*fabriquer*) to manufacture;
(*travailler: matière*) to shape, fashion; (*fig*) to
mould, shape

**fac-similé** [faksimile] *nm* facsimile

**facteur, -trice** [faktœr, -tris] *nm/f* postman/
woman (*Brit*), mailman/woman (*US*) ▷ *nm*
(*Math, gén*) factor; **~ d'orgues** organ builder; **~
de pianos** piano maker; **~ rhésus** rhesus factor

**factice** [faktis] *adj* artificial

**faction** [faksjɔ̃] *nf* (*groupe*) faction; (*Mil*) guard *ou*
sentry (duty); watch; **en ~** on guard; standing
watch

**factionnaire** [faksjɔnɛr] *nm* guard, sentry

**factoriel, le** [faktɔrjɛl] *adj, nf* factorial

**factotum** [faktɔtɔm] *nm* odd-job man,
dogsbody (*Brit*)

**factuel, le** [faktɥɛl] *adj* factual

**facturation** [faktyʀasjɔ̃] nf invoicing; (bureau) invoicing (office)

**facture** [faktyʀ] nf (à payer: gén) bill; (: Comm) invoice; (d'un artisan, artiste) technique, workmanship

**facturer** [faktyʀe] vt to invoice

**facturier, -ière** [faktyʀje, -jɛʀ] nm/f invoice clerk

**facultatif, -ive** [fakyltatif, -iv] adj optional; (arrêt de bus) request cpd

**faculté** [fakylte] nf (intellectuelle, d'université) faculty; (pouvoir, possibilité) power

**fadaises** [fadɛz] nfpl twaddle sg

**fade** [fad] adj insipid

**fading** [fadiŋ] nm (Radio) fading

**fagot** [fago] nm (de bois) bundle of sticks

**fagoté, e** [fagote] adj (fam): **drôlement ~** oddly dressed

**faible** [fɛbl(ə)] adj weak; (voix, lumière, vent) faint; (élève, copie) poor; (rendement, intensité, revenu etc) low ▷ nm weak point; (pour quelqu'un) weakness, soft spot; **~ d'esprit** feeble-minded

**faiblement** [fɛbləmã] adv weakly; (peu: éclairer etc) faintly

**faiblesse** [fɛblɛs] nf weakness

**faiblir** [febliʀ] vi to weaken; (lumière) to dim; (vent) to drop

**faïence** [fajãs] nf earthenware no pl; (objet) piece of earthenware

**faignant, e** [fɛɲã, -ãt] nm/f = **fainéant, e**

**faille** [faj] vb voir **falloir** ▷ nf (Géo) fault; (fig) flaw, weakness

**failli, e** [faji] adj, nm/f bankrupt

**faillible** [fajibl(ə)] adj fallible

**faillir** [fajiʀ] vi: **j'ai failli tomber/lui dire** I almost ou nearly fell/told him; **~ à une promesse/un engagement** to break a promise/an agreement

**faillite** [fajit] nf bankruptcy; (échec: d'une politique etc) collapse; **être en ~** to be bankrupt; **faire ~** to go bankrupt

**faim** [fɛ̃] nf hunger; (fig): **~ d'amour/de richesse** hunger ou yearning for love/wealth; **avoir ~** to be hungry; **rester sur sa ~** (aussi fig) to be left wanting more

**fainéant, e** [fɛneã, -ãt] nm/f idler, loafer

**fainéantise** [feneãtiz] nf idleness, laziness

 MOT-CLÉ

**faire** [fɛʀ] vt 1 (fabriquer, être l'auteur de) to make; (produire) to produce; (construire: maison, bateau) to build; **faire du vin/une offre/un film** to make wine/an offer/a film; **faire du bruit** to make a noise

2 (effectuer: travail, opération) to do; **que faites-vous?** (quel métier etc) what do you do?; (quelle activité: au moment de la question) what are you doing?; **que faire?** what are we going to do?, what can be done (about it)?; **faire la lessive/le ménage** to do the washing/the housework

3 (études) to do; (sport, musique) to play; **faire du droit/du français** to do law/French; **faire du rugby/piano** to play rugby/the piano; **faire du cheval/du ski** to go riding/skiing

4 (visiter): **faire les magasins** to go shopping; **faire l'Europe** to tour ou do Europe

5 (simuler): **faire le malade/l'ignorant** to act the invalid/the fool

6 (transformer, avoir un effet sur): **faire de qn un frustré/avocat** to make sb frustrated/a lawyer; **ça ne me fait rien** (m'est égal) I don't care ou mind; (me laisse froid) it has no effect on me; **ça ne fait rien** it doesn't matter; **faire que** (impliquer) to mean that

7 (calculs, prix, mesures): **deux et deux font quatre** two and two are ou make four; **ça fait 10 m/15 euros** it's 10 m/15 euros; **je vous le fais 10 euros** I'll let you have it for 10 euros

8 (vb+de): **qu'a-t-il fait de sa valise/de sa sœur?** what has he done with his case/his sister?

9: **ne faire que: il ne fait que critiquer** (sans cesse) all he (ever) does is criticize; (seulement) he's only criticizing

10 (dire) to say; **vraiment? fit-il** really? he said

11 (maladie) to have; **faire du diabète/de la tension** to have diabetes sg/high blood pressure

▷ vi 1 (agir, s'y prendre) to act, do; **il faut faire vite** we (ou you etc) must act quickly; **comment a-t-il fait pour?** how did he manage to?; **faites comme chez vous** make yourself at home; **je n'ai pas pu faire autrement** there was nothing else I could do

2 (paraître) to look; **faire vieux/démodé** to look old/old-fashioned; **ça fait bien** it looks good; **tu fais jeune dans cette robe** that dress makes you look young(er)

3 (remplaçant un autre verbe) to do; **ne le casse pas comme je l'ai fait** don't break it as I did; **je peux le voir? — faites!** can I see it? — please do!; **remets-le en place — je viens de le faire** put it back in its place — I just have (done)

▷ vb impers 1: **il fait beau** etc the weather is fine etc; voir aussi **jour; froid** etc

2 (temps écoulé, durée): **ça fait deux ans qu'il est parti** it's two years since he left; **ça fait deux ans qu'il y est** he's been there for two years

▷ vb aux 1: **faire** (+infinitif: action directe) to make; **faire tomber/bouger qch** to make sth fall/move; **faire démarrer un moteur/chauffer de l'eau** to start up an engine/heat some water; **cela fait dormir** it makes you sleep; **faire travailler les enfants** to make the children work ou get the children to work; **il m'a fait traverser la rue** he helped me to cross the road

2 (indirectement, par un intermédiaire): **faire réparer qch** to get ou have sth repaired; **faire punir les enfants** to have the children punished; **il m'a fait ouvrir la porte** he got me to open the door

**se faire** vi 1 (vin, fromage) to mature

2: **cela se fait beaucoup/ne se fait pas** it's

done a lot/not done

**3** (+*nom ou pron*): **se faire une jupe** to make o.s. a skirt; **se faire des amis** to make friends; **se faire du souci** to worry; **se faire des illusions** to delude o.s.; **se faire beaucoup d'argent** to make a lot of money; **il ne s'en fait pas** he doesn't worry

**4** (+*adj*: *devenir*): **se faire vieux** to be getting old; (*délibérément*): **se faire beau** to do o.s. up

**5**: **se faire à** (*s'habituer*) to get used to; **je n'arrive pas à me faire à la nourriture/au climat** I can't get used to the food/climate

**6** (+*infinitif*): **se faire examiner la vue/opérer** to have one's eyes tested/have an operation; **se faire couper les cheveux** to get one's hair cut; **il va se faire tuer/punir** he's going to get himself killed/get (himself) punished; **il s'est fait aider** he got somebody to help him; **il s'est fait aider par Simon** he got Simon to help him; **se faire faire un vêtement** to get a garment made for o.s.

**7** (*impersonnel*): **comment se fait-il/faisait-il que?** how is it/was it that?; **il peut se faire que nous utilisions ...** it's possible that we could use ...

**faire-part** [fɛʀpaʀ] *nm inv* announcement (*of birth, marriage etc*)

**fair-play** [fɛʀplɛ] *adj inv* fair play

**fais** [fɛ] *vb voir* **faire**

**faisabilité** [fəzabilite] *nf* feasibility

**faisable** [fəzabl(ə)] *adj* feasible

**faisais***etc* [fəzɛ] *vb voir* **faire**

**faisan, e** [fəzɑ̃, -an] *nm/f* pheasant

**faisandé, e** [fəzɑ̃de] *adj* high (*bad*); (*fig péj*) corrupt, decadent

**faisceau, x** [fɛso] *nm* (*de lumière etc*) beam; (*de branches etc*) bundle

**faiseur, -euse** [fəzœʀ, -øz] *nm/f* (*gén: péj*): **~ de** maker of ▷ *nm* (bespoke) tailor; **~ d'embarras** fusspot; **~ de projets** schemer

**faisons***etc* [fəzɔ̃] *vb voir* **faire**

**faisselle** [fɛsɛl] *nf* cheese strainer

**fait¹** [fɛ] *vb voir* **faire** ▷ *nm* (*événement*) event, occurrence; (*réalité, donnée*) fact; **le ~ que/de manger** the fact that/of eating; **être le ~ de** (*causé par*) to be the work of; **être au ~ (de)** to be informed (of); **mettre qn au ~** to inform sb, put sb in the picture; **au ~** (*à propos*) by the way; **en venir au ~** to get to the point; **de ~** *adj* (*opposé à: de droit*) de facto ▷ *adv* in fact; **du ~ de ceci/qu'il a menti** because of *ou* on account of this/his having lied; **de ce ~** therefore, for this reason; **en ~** in fact; **en ~ de repas** by way of a meal; **prendre ~ et cause pour qn** to support sb, side with sb; **prendre qn sur le ~** to catch sb in the act; **dire à qn son ~** to give sb a piece of one's mind; **hauts ~s** (*exploits*) exploits; **~ d'armes** feat of arms; **~ divers** (short) news item; **les ~s et gestes de qn** sb's actions *ou* doings

**fait², e** [fɛ, fɛt] *pp de* **faire** ▷ *adj* (*mûr: fromage,*

*melon*) ripe; (*maquillé: yeux*) made-up; (*vernis: ongles*) painted, polished; **un homme ~** a grown man; **tout(e) ~(e)** (*préparé à l'avance*) ready-made; **c'en est ~ de notre tranquillité** that's the end of our peace; **c'est bien ~ (pour lui** *ou* **eux** *etc*) it serves him (*ou* them *etc*) right

**faîte** [fɛt] *nm* top; (*fig*) pinnacle, height

**faites** [fɛt] *vb voir* **faire**

**faîtière** [fɛtjɛʀ] *nf* (*de tente*) ridge pole

**faitout** [fɛtu] *nm* stewpot

**fakir** [fakiʀ] *nm* (*Théât*) wizard

**falaise** [falɛz] *nf* cliff

**falbalas** [falbala] *nmpl* fripperies, frills

**fallacieux, -euse** [falasjø, -øz] *adj* (*raisonnement*) fallacious; (*apparences*) deceptive; (*espoir*) illusory

**falloir** [falwaʀ] *vb impers*: **il faut faire les lits** we (*ou* you *etc*) have to *ou* must make the beds; **il faut que je fasse les lits** I have to *ou* must make the beds; **il a fallu qu'il parte** he had to leave; **il faudrait qu'elle rentre** she ought to go home; **il va ~ 10 euros** we'll (*ou* I'll *etc*) need 10 euros; **il doit ~ du temps** that must take time; **il vous faut tourner à gauche après l'église** you have to turn left past the church; **nous avons ce qu'il (nous) faut** we have what we need; **il faut qu'il ait oublié** he must have forgotten; **il a fallu qu'il l'apprenne** he would have to hear about it; **il ne fallait pas** (*pour remercier*) you shouldn't have (done); **faut le faire!** (it) takes some doing! ▷ *vi*: **s'en falloir: il s'en est fallu de 10 euros/5 minutes** we (*ou* they *etc*) were 10 euros short/5 minutes late (*ou* early); **il s'en faut de beaucoup qu'il soit ...** he is far from being ...; **il s'en est fallu de peu que cela n'arrive** it very nearly happened; **ou peu s'en faut** or just about, or as good as; **comme il faut** *adj* proper ▷ *adv* properly

**fallu** [faly] *pp de* **falloir**

**falot, e** [falo, -ɔt] *adj* dreary, colourless (*Brit*), colorless (*US*) ▷ *nm* lantern

**falsification** [falsifikasjɔ̃] *nf* falsification

**falsifier** [falsifje] *vt* to falsify

**famé, e** [fame] *adj*: **mal ~** disreputable, of ill repute

**famélique** [famelik] *adj* half-starved

**fameux, -euse** [famø, -øz] *adj* (*illustre: parfois péj*) famous; (*bon: repas, plat etc*) first-rate, first-class; (*intensif*): **un ~ problème** *etc* a real problem *etc*; **pas ~** not great, not much good

**familial, e, -aux** [familjal, -o] *adj* family *cpd* ▷ *nf* (*Auto*) family estate car (*Brit*), station wagon (*US*)

**familiariser** [familjaʀize] *vt*: **~ qn avec** to familiarize sb with; **se ~ avec** to familiarize o.s. with

**familiarité** [familjaʀite] *nf* familiarity; informality; **familiarités** *nfpl* familiarities; **~ avec** (*sujet, science*) familiarity with

**familier, -ière** [familje, -jɛʀ] *adj* (*connu, impertinent*) familiar; (*dénotant une certaine intimité*) informal, friendly; (*Ling*) informal, colloquial ▷ *nm* regular (visitor)

**familièrement** [familjɛʀmɑ̃] *adv* *(sans façon: s'entretenir)* informally; *(cavalièrement)* familiarly

**famille** [famij] *nf* family; **il a de la ~ à Paris** he has relatives in Paris

**famine** [famin] *nf* famine

**fan** [fan] *nm/f* fan

**fana** [fana] *adj, nm/f* *(fam)* = **fanatique**

**fanal, -aux** [fanal, -o] *nm* beacon; lantern

**fanatique** [fanatik] *adj:* **~ (de)** fanatical (about) ▷ *nm/f* fanatic

**fanatisme** [fanatism(ə)] *nm* fanaticism

**fane** [fan] *nf* top

**fané, e** [fane] *adj* faded

**faner** [fane]: **se faner** *vi* to fade

**faneur, -euse** [fanœʀ, -øz] *nm/f* haymaker ▷ *nf* *(Tech)* tedder

**fanfare** [fɑ̃faʀ] *nf* *(orchestre)* brass band; *(musique)* fanfare; **en ~** *(avec bruit)* noisily

**fanfaron, ne** [fɑ̃faʀɔ̃, -ɔn] *nm/f* braggart

**fanfaronnades** [fɑ̃faʀɔnad] *nfpl* bragging *no pl*

**fanfreluches** [fɑ̃fʀəlyʃ] *nfpl* trimming *no pl*

**fange** [fɑ̃ʒ] *nf* mire

**fanion** [fanjɔ̃] *nm* pennant

**fanon** [fanɔ̃] *nm* *(de baleine)* plate of baleen; *(repli de peau)* dewlap, wattle

**fantaisie** [fɑ̃tezi] *nf* *(spontanéité)* fancy, imagination; *(caprice)* whim; extravagance; *(Mus)* fantasia ▷ *adj:* **bijou (de) ~** (piece of) costume jewellery (Brit) *ou* jewelry (US); **pain (de) ~** fancy bread

**fantaisiste** [fɑ̃tezist(ə)] *adj* *(péj)* unorthodox, eccentric ▷ *nm/f* *(de music-hall)* variety artist *ou* entertainer

**fantasmagorique** [fɑ̃tasmagɔʀik] *adj* phantasmagorical

**fantasme** [fɑ̃tasm(ə)] *nm* fantasy

**fantasmer** [fɑ̃tasme] *vi* to fantasize

**fantasque** [fɑ̃task(ə)] *adj* whimsical, capricious; fantastic

**fantassin** [fɑ̃tasɛ̃] *nm* infantryman

**fantastique** [fɑ̃tastik] *adj* fantastic

**fantoche** [fɑ̃tɔʃ] *nm* *(péj)* puppet

**fantomatique** [fɑ̃tɔmatik] *adj* ghostly

**fantôme** [fɑ̃tom] *nm* ghost, phantom

**FAO** *sigle f* (= Food and Agricultural Organization) FAO

**faon** [fɑ̃] *nm* fawn (deer)

**FAQ** *abr f* (= foire aux questions) FAQ *pl* (= frequently asked questions)

**faramineux, -euse** [faʀaminø, -øz] *adj* *(fam)* fantastic

**farandole** [faʀɑ̃dɔl] *nf* farandole

**farce** [faʀs(ə)] *nf* *(viande)* stuffing; *(blague)* (practical) joke; *(Théât)* farce; **faire une ~ à qn** to play a (practical) joke on sb; **~s et attrapes** jokes and novelties

**farceur, -euse** [faʀsœʀ, -øz] *nm/f* practical joker; *(fumiste)* clown

**farci, e** [faʀsi] *adj* *(Culin)* stuffed

**farcir** [faʀsiʀ] *vt* *(viande)* to stuff; *(fig):* **~ qch de** to stuff sth with; **se farcir** *(fam):* **je me suis farci la vaisselle** I've got stuck *ou* landed with the washing-up

**fard** [faʀ] *nm* make-up; **~ à joues** blusher

**fardeau, x** [faʀdo] *nm* burden

**farder** [faʀde] *vt* to make up; *(vérité)* to disguise; **se farder** to make o.s. up

**farfelu, e** [faʀfəly] *adj* wacky *(fam)*, hare-brained

**farfouiller** [faʀfuje] *vi* *(péj)* to rummage around

**fariboles** [faʀibɔl] *nfpl* nonsense *no pl*

**farine** [faʀin] *nf* flour; **~ de blé** wheatflour; **~ de maïs** cornflour (Brit), cornstarch (US); **~ lactée** *(pour bouillie)* baby cereal

**fariner** [faʀine] *vt* to flour

**farineux, -euse** [faʀinø, -øz] *adj* *(sauce, pomme)* floury ▷ *nmpl* *(aliments)* starchy foods

**farniente** [faʀnjɛnte] *nm* idleness

**farouche** [faʀuʃ] *adj* shy, timid; *(sauvage)* savage, wild; *(violent)* fierce

**farouchement** [faʀuʃmɑ̃] *adv* fiercely

**fart** [faʀ(t)] *nm* (ski) wax

**farter** [faʀte] *vt* to wax

**fascicule** [fasikyl] *nm* volume

**fascinant, e** [fasinɑ̃, -ɑ̃t] *adj* fascinating

**fascination** [fasinasjɔ̃] *nf* fascination

**fasciner** [fasine] *vt* to fascinate

**fascisant, e** [faʃizɑ̃, -ɑ̃t] *adj* fascistic

**fascisme** [faʃism(ə)] *nm* fascism

**fasciste** [faʃist(ə)] *adj, nm/f* fascist

**fasse** *etc* [fas] *vb voir* **faire**

**faste** [fast(ə)] *nm* splendour (Brit), splendor (US) ▷ *adj:* **c'est un jour ~** it's his *(ou* our *etc)* lucky day

**fastidieux, -euse** [fastidjø, -øz] *adj* tedious, tiresome

**fastueux, -euse** [fastɥø, -øz] *adj* sumptuous, luxurious

**fat** [fa] *adj m* conceited, smug

**fatal, e** [fatal] *adj* fatal; *(inévitable)* inevitable

**fatalement** [fatalmɑ̃] *adv* inevitably

**fatalisme** [fatalism(ə)] *nm* fatalism

**fataliste** [fatalist(ə)] *adj* fatalistic

**fatalité** [fatalite] *nf* *(destin)* fate; *(coïncidence)* fateful coincidence; *(caractère inévitable)* inevitability

**fatidique** [fatidik] *adj* fateful

**fatigant, e** [fatigɑ̃, -ɑ̃t] *adj* tiring; *(agaçant)* tiresome

**fatigue** [fatig] *nf* tiredness, fatigue; *(détérioration)* fatigue; **les ~s du voyage** the wear and tear of the journey

**fatigué, e** [fatige] *adj* tired

**fatiguer** [fatige] *vt* to tire, make tired; *(Tech)* to put a strain on, strain; *(fig: importuner)* to wear out ▷ *vi* *(moteur)* to labour (Brit), labor (US), strain; **se fatiguer** *vi* to get tired; to tire o.s. (out); **se ~ à faire qch** to tire o.s. out doing sth

**fatras** [fatʀa] *nm* jumble, hotchpotch

**fatuité** [fatɥite] *nf* conceitedness, smugness

**faubourg** [fobuʀ] *nm* suburb

**faubourien, ne** [fobuʀjɛ̃, -ɛn] *adj* *(accent)* working-class

**fauché, e** [foʃe] *adj* *(fam)* broke

**f**

173

**faucher** [foʃe] *vt* (*herbe*) to cut; (*champs, blés*) to reap; (*fig*) to cut down; to mow down; (*fam: voler*) to pinch, nick

**faucheur, -euse** [foʃœʀ, -øz] *nm/f* reaper, mower

**faucille** [fosij] *nf* sickle

**faucon** [fokɔ̃] *nm* falcon, hawk

**faudra** *etc* [fodʀa] *vb voir* **falloir**

**faufil** [fofil] *nm* (*Couture*) tacking thread

**faufilage** [fofilaʒ] *nm* (*Couture*) tacking

**faufiler** [fofile] *vt* to tack, baste; **se faufiler** *vi*: **se ~ dans** to edge one's way into; **se ~ parmi/entre** to thread one's way among/between

**faune** [fon] *nf* (*Zool*) wildlife, fauna; (*fig péj*) set, crowd ▷ *nm* faun; **~ marine** marine (animal) life

**faussaire** [fosɛʀ] *nm/f* forger

**fausse** [fos] *adj f voir* **faux**

**faussement** [fosmɑ̃] *adv* (*accuser*) wrongly, wrongfully; (*croire*) falsely, erroneously

**fausser** [fose] *vt* (*objet*) to bend, buckle; (*fig*) to distort; **~ compagnie à qn** to give sb the slip

**fausset** [fosɛ] *nm*: **voix de ~** falsetto voice

**fausseté** [foste] *nf* wrongness; falseness

**faut** [fo] *vb voir* **falloir**

**faute** [fot] *nf* (*erreur*) mistake, error; (*péché, manquement*) misdemeanour; (*Football etc*) offence; (*Tennis*) fault; (*responsabilité*): **par la ~ de** through the fault of, because of; **c'est de sa/ma ~** it's his/my fault; **être en ~** to be in the wrong; **prendre qn en ~** to catch sb out; **~ de** (*temps, argent*) for *ou* through lack of; **~ de mieux** for want of anything *ou* something better; **sans ~** *adv* without fail; **~ de frappe** typing error; **~ d'inattention** careless mistake; **~ d'orthographe** spelling mistake; **~ professionnelle** professional misconduct *no pl*

**fauteuil** [fotœj] *nm* armchair; **~ à bascule** rocking chair; **~ club** (big) easy chair; **~ d'orchestre** seat in the front stalls (*Brit*) *ou* the orchestra (*US*); **~ roulant** wheelchair

**fauteur** [fotœʀ] *nm*: **~ de troubles** trouble-maker

**fautif, -ive** [fotif, -iv] *adj* (*incorrect*) incorrect, inaccurate; (*responsable*) at fault, in the wrong; (*coupable*) guilty ▷ *nm/f* culprit

**fauve** [fov] *nm* wildcat; (*peintre*) Fauve ▷ *adj* (*couleur*) fawn

**fauvette** [fovɛt] *nf* warbler

**fauvisme** [fovism(ə)] *nm* (*Art*) Fauvism

**faux**[1] [fo] *nf* scythe

**faux**[2]**, fausse** [fo, fos] *adj* (*inexact*) wrong; (*piano, voix*) out of tune; (*falsifié*) fake, forged; (*sournois, postiche*) false ▷ *adv* (*Mus*) out of tune ▷ *nm* (*copie*) fake, forgery; (*opposé au vrai*): **le ~** falsehood; **le ~ numéro/la fausse clé** the wrong number/key; **faire fausse route** to go the wrong way; **faire ~ bond à qn** to let sb down; **~ ami** (*Ling*) faux ami; **~ col** detachable collar; **~ départ** (*Sport, fig*) false start; **~ frais** *nmpl* extras, incidental expenses; **~ frère** (*fig péj*) false friend; **~ mouvement** awkward movement; **~ nez** false nose; **~ nom** assumed name; **~ pas** tripping *no pl*; (*fig*) faux pas; **~ témoignage** (*délit*) perjury; **fausse alerte** false alarm; **fausse clé** skeleton key; **fausse couche** (*Méd*) miscarriage; **fausse joie** vain joy; **fausse note** wrong note

**faux-filet** [fofilɛ] *nm* sirloin

**faux-fuyant** [fofɥijɑ̃] *nm* equivocation

**faux-monnayeur** [fomɔnɛjœʀ] *nm* counterfeiter, forger

**faux-semblant** [fosɑ̃blɑ̃] *nm* pretence (*Brit*), pretense (*US*)

**faux-sens** [fosɑ̃s] *nm* mistranslation

**faveur** [favœʀ] *nf* favour (*Brit*), favor (*US*); **traitement de ~** preferential treatment; **à la ~ de** under cover of; (*grâce à*) thanks to; **en ~ de** in favo(u)r of

**favorable** [favɔʀabl(ə)] *adj* favo(u)rable

**favori, te** [favɔʀi, -it] *adj, nm/f* favo(u)rite

**favoris** [favɔʀi] *nmpl* (*barbe*) sideboards (*Brit*), sideburns

**favoriser** [favɔʀize] *vt* to favour (*Brit*), favor (*US*)

**favoritisme** [favɔʀitism(ə)] *nm* (*péj*) favo(u)ritism

**fax** [faks] *nm* fax

**faxer** *vt* to fax

**fayot** [fajo] *nm* (*fam*) crawler

**FB** *abr* (= *franc belge*) BF, FB

**FBI** *sigle m* FBI

**FC** *sigle m* (= *Football Club*) FC

**fébrile** [febʀil] *adj* feverish, febrile; **capitaux ~s** (*Écon*) hot money

**fébrilement** [febʀilmɑ̃] *adv* feverishly

**fécal, e, -aux** [fekal, -o] *adj voir* **matière**

**fécond, e** [fekɔ̃, -ɔ̃d] *adj* fertile

**fécondation** [fekɔ̃dasjɔ̃] *nf* fertilization

**féconder** [fekɔ̃de] *vt* to fertilize

**fécondité** [fekɔ̃dite] *nf* fertility

**fécule** [fekyl] *nf* potato flour

**féculent** [fekylɑ̃] *nm* starchy food

**fédéral, e, -aux** [fedeʀal, -o] *adj* federal

**fédéralisme** [fedeʀalism(ə)] *nm* federalism

**fédéraliste** [fedeʀalist(ə)] *adj* federalist

**fédération** [fedeʀasjɔ̃] *nf* federation; **la F~ française de football** the French football association

**fée** [fe] *nf* fairy

**féerie** [feʀi] *nf* enchantment

**féerique** [feʀik] *adj* magical, fairytale *cpd*

**feignant, e** [fɛɲɑ̃, -ɑ̃t] *nm/f* = **fainéant, e**

**feindre** [fɛ̃dʀ(ə)] *vt* to feign ▷ *vi* to dissemble; **~ de faire** to pretend to do

**feint, e** [fɛ̃, fɛ̃t] *pp de* **feindre** ▷ *adj* feigned ▷ *nf* (*Sport: escrime*) feint; (: *Football, Rugby*) dummy (*Brit*), fake (*US*); (*fam: ruse*) sham

**feinter** [fɛ̃te] *vi* (*Sport: escrime*) to feint; (: *Football, Rugby*) to dummy (*Brit*), fake (*US*) ▷ *vt* (*fam: tromper*) to fool

**fêlé, e** [fele] *adj* (*aussi fig*) cracked

**fêler** [fele] *vt* to crack

**félicitations** [felisitasjɔ̃] *nfpl* congratulations

**félicité** [felisite] *nf* bliss

**féliciter** [felisite] *vt*: ~ **qn (de)** to congratulate sb
(on)
**félin, e** [felɛ̃, -in] *adj* feline ▷ *nm* (big) cat
**félon, ne** [felɔ̃, -ɔn] *adj* perfidious, treacherous
**félonie** [feloni] *nf* treachery
**fêlure** [felyʀ] *nf* crack
**femelle** [fəmɛl] *adj* (*aussi Élec, Tech*) female ▷ *nf*
female
**féminin, e** [feminɛ̃, -in] *adj* feminine; (*sexe*)
female; (*équipe, vêtements etc*) women's; (*parfois
péj: homme*) effeminate ▷ *nm* (Ling) feminine
**féminiser** [feminize] *vt* to feminize; (*rendre
efféminé*) to make effeminate; **se féminiser** *vi*:
**cette profession se féminise** this profession
is attracting more women
**féminisme** [feminism(ə)] *nm* feminism
**féministe** [feminist(ə)] *adj, nf* feminist
**féminité** [feminite] *nf* femininity
**femme** [fam] *nf* woman; (*épouse*) wife; **être
très ~** to be very much a woman; **devenir ~** to
attain womanhood; **~ d'affaires**
businesswoman; **~ de chambre** chambermaid;
**~ fatale** femme fatale; **~ au foyer** housewife; **~
d'intérieur** (real) homemaker; **~ de ménage**
domestic help, cleaning lady; **~ du monde**
society woman; **~-objet** sex object; **~ de tête**
determined, intellectual woman
**fémoral, e, -aux** [femɔʀal, -o] *adj* femoral
**fémur** [femyʀ] *nm* femur, thighbone
**FEN** [fɛn] *sigle f* (= *Fédération de l'Éducation nationale*)
teachers' trades union
**fenaison** [fənɛzɔ̃] *nf* haymaking
**fendillé, e** [fɑ̃dije] *adj* (*terre etc*) crazed
**fendre** [fɑ̃dʀ(ə)] *vt* (*couper en deux*) to split;
(*fissurer*) to crack; (*fig: traverser*) to cut through; to
push one's way through; **se fendre** *vi* to crack
**fendu, e** [fɑ̃dy] *adj* (*sol, mur*) cracked; (*jupe*) slit
**fenêtre** [fənɛtʀ(ə)] *nf* window; **~ à guillotine**
sash window
**fennec** [fenɛk] *nm* fennec
**fenouil** [fənuj] *nm* fennel
**fente** [fɑ̃t] *nf* slit; (*fissure*) crack
**féodal, e, -aux** [feɔdal, -o] *adj* feudal
**féodalisme** [feɔdalism(ə)] *nm* feudalism
**féodalité** [feɔdalite] *nf* feudalism
**fer** [fɛʀ] *nm* iron; (*de cheval*) shoe; **fers** *nmpl*
(*Méd*) forceps; **mettre aux ~s** (*enchaîner*) to put
in chains; **au ~ rouge** with a red-hot iron;
**santé/main de ~** iron constitution/hand; **~ à
cheval** horseshoe; **en ~ à cheval** (*fig*)
horseshoe-shaped; **~ forgé** wrought iron; **~ à
friser** curling tongs; **~ de lance** spearhead;
**~ (à repasser)** iron; **~ à souder** soldering iron
**ferai** *etc* [fəʀe] *vb voir* **faire**
**fer-blanc** [fɛʀblɑ̃] *nm* tin(plate)
**ferblanterie** [fɛʀblɑ̃tʀi] *nf* tinplate making;
(*produit*) tinware
**ferblantier** [fɛʀblɑ̃tje] *nm* tinsmith
**férié, e** [feʀje] *adj*: **jour ~** public holiday
**ferions** *etc* [fəʀjɔ̃] *vb voir* **faire**
**férir** [feʀiʀ]: **sans coup ~** *adv* without meeting
any opposition

**fermage** [fɛʀmaʒ] *nm* tenant farming
**ferme** [fɛʀm(ə)] *adj* firm ▷ *adv* (*travailler etc*)
hard; (*discuter*) ardently ▷ *nf* (*exploitation*) farm;
(*maison*) farmhouse; **tenir ~** to stand firm
**fermé, e** [fɛʀme] *adj* closed, shut; (*gaz, eau etc*)
off; (*fig: personne*) uncommunicative; (: *milieu*)
exclusive
**fermement** [fɛʀməmɑ̃] *adv* firmly
**ferment** [fɛʀmɑ̃] *nm* ferment
**fermentation** [fɛʀmɑ̃tasjɔ̃] *nf* fermentation
**fermenter** [fɛʀmɑ̃te] *vi* to ferment
**fermer** [fɛʀme] *vt* to close, shut; (*cesser
l'exploitation de*) to close down, shut down; (*eau,
lumière, électricité, robinet*) to put off, turn off;
(*aéroport, route*) to close ▷ *vi* to close, shut; to
close down, shut down; **se fermer** *vi* (*yeux*) to
close, shut; (*fleur, blessure*) to close up; **~ à clef** to
lock; **~ au verrou** to bolt; **~ les yeux (sur qch)**
(*fig*) to close one's eyes (to sth); **se ~ à** (*pitié,
amour*) to close one's heart *ou* mind to
**fermeté** [fɛʀməte] *nf* firmness
**fermette** [fɛʀmɛt] *nf* farmhouse
**fermeture** [fɛʀmətyʀ] *nf* closing; shutting;
closing *ou* shutting down; putting *ou* turning
off; (*dispositif*) catch; fastening, fastener; **heure
de ~** (*Comm*) closing time; **jour de ~** (*Comm*) day
on which the shop (*etc*) is closed; **~ éclair®** *ou* **à
glissière** zip (fastener) (*Brit*), zipper; *voir* **fermer**
**fermier, -ière** [fɛʀmje, -jɛʀ] *nm/f* farmer ▷ *nf*
(*femme de fermier*) farmer's wife ▷ *adj*: **beurre/
cidre ~** farm butter/cider
**fermoir** [fɛʀmwaʀ] *nm* clasp
**féroce** [feʀɔs] *adj* ferocious, fierce
**férocement** [feʀɔsmɑ̃] *adv* ferociously
**férocité** [feʀɔsite] *nf* ferocity, ferociousness
**ferons** *etc* [fəʀɔ̃] *vb voir* **faire**
**ferraille** [feʀaj] *nf* scrap iron; **mettre à la ~** to
scrap; **bruit de ~** clanking
**ferrailler** [feʀaje] *vi* to clank
**ferrailleur** [feʀajœʀ] *nm* scrap merchant
**ferrant** [feʀɑ̃] *adj m voir* **maréchal-ferrant**
**ferré, e** [feʀe] *adj* (*chaussure*) hobnailed; (*canne*)
steel-tipped; **~ sur** (*fam: savant*) well up on
**ferrer** [feʀe] *vt* (*cheval*) to shoe; (*chaussure*) to nail;
(*canne*) to tip; (*poisson*) to strike
**ferreux, -euse** [feʀø, -øz] *adj* ferrous
**ferronnerie** [feʀɔnʀi] *nf* ironwork; **~ d'art**
wrought iron work
**ferronnier** [feʀɔnje] *nm* craftsman in wrought
iron; (*marchand*) ironware merchant
**ferroviaire** [feʀɔvjɛʀ] *adj* rail *cpd*, railway *cpd*
(*Brit*), railroad *cpd* (US)
**ferrugineux, -euse** [feʀyʒinø, -øz] *adj*
ferruginous
**ferrure** [feʀyʀ] *nf* (ornamental) hinge
**ferry** [feʀe], **ferry-boat** [feʀebot] *nm* ferry
**fertile** [fɛʀtil] *adj* fertile; **~ en incidents**
eventful, packed with incidents
**fertilisant** [fɛʀtilizɑ̃] *nm* fertilizer
**fertilisation** [fɛʀtilizasjɔ̃] *nf* fertilization
**fertiliser** [fɛʀtilize] *vt* to fertilize
**fertilité** [fɛʀtilite] *nf* fertility

**f**

**féru, e** [feʁy] *adj:* ~ **de** with a keen interest in
**férule** [feʁyl] *nf:* **être sous la ~ de qn** to be
under sb's (iron) rule
**fervent, e** [fɛʁvɑ̃, -ɑ̃t] *adj* fervent
**ferveur** [fɛʁvœʁ] *nf* fervour (*Brit*), fervor (*US*)
**fesse** [fɛs] *nf* buttock; **les ~s** the bottom *sg*, the
buttocks
**fessée** [fese] *nf* spanking
**fessier** [fesje] *nm* (*fam*) behind
**festin** [fɛstɛ̃] *nm* feast
**festival** [fɛstival] *nm* festival
**festivalier** [fɛstivalje] *nm* festival-goer
**festivités** [fɛstivite] *nfpl* festivities,
merrymaking *sg*
**feston** [fɛstɔ̃] *nm* (*Archit*) festoon; (*Couture*)
scallop
**festoyer** [fɛstwaje] *vi* to feast
**fêtard** [fɛtaʁ] *nm* (*péj*) high liver, merrymaker
**fête** [fɛt] *nf* (*religieuse*) feast; (*publique*) holiday;
(*en famille etc*) celebration; (*kermesse*) fête, fair,
festival; (*du nom*) feast day, name day; **faire la ~**
to live it up; **faire ~ à qn** to give sb a warm
welcome; **se faire une ~ de** to look forward to;
to enjoy; **ça va être sa ~!** (*fam*) he's going to get
it!; **jour de ~** holiday; **les ~s (de fin d'année)**
the festive season; **la salle/le comité des ~s**
the village hall/festival committee; **la ~ des
Mères/Pères** Mother's/Father's Day; **~ de
charité** charity fair *ou* fête; **~ foraine** (fun)fair;
**la ~ de la musique;** *see note;* **~ mobile** movable
feast (day); **la F~ Nationale** the national
holiday

**Fête-Dieu** [fɛtdjø] *nf:* **la ~** Corpus Christi
**fêter** [fete] *vt* to celebrate; (*personne*) to have a
celebration for
**fétiche** [fetiʃ] *nm* fetish; **animal ~, objet ~**
mascot
**fétichisme** [fetiʃism(ə)] *nm* fetishism
**fétichiste** [fetiʃist(ə)] *adj* fetishist
**fétide** [fetid] *adj* fetid
**fétu** [fety] *nm:* ~ **de paille** wisp of straw
**feu¹** [fø] *adj inv:* ~ **son père** his late father
**feu², x** [fø] *nm* (*gén*) fire; (*signal lumineux*) light;
(*de cuisinière*) ring; (*sensation de brûlure*) burning
(sensation); **feux** *nmpl* fire *sg*; (*Auto*) (traffic)
lights; **tous ~x éteints** (*Navig, Auto*) without
lights; **au ~!** (*incendie*) fire!; **à ~ doux/vif** over a
slow/brisk heat; **à petit ~** (*Culin*) over a gentle
heat; (*fig*) slowly; **faire ~** to fire; **ne pas faire
long ~** (*fig*) not to last long; **commander le ~**
(*Mil*) to give the order to (open) fire; **tué au ~**
(*Mil*) killed in action; **mettre à ~** (*fusée*) to fire
off; **pris entre deux ~x** caught in the crossfire;

**en ~** on fire; **être tout ~ tout flamme (pour)**
(*passion*) to be aflame with passion (for);
(*enthousiasme*) to be fired with enthusiasm (for);
**prendre ~** to catch fire; **mettre le ~ à** to set fire
to, set on fire; **faire du ~** to make a fire; **avez-
vous du ~?** (*pour cigarette*) have you (got) a light?;
**~ rouge/vert/orange** (*Auto*) red/green/amber
(*Brit*) *ou* yellow (*US*) light; **donner le ~ vert à
qch/qn** (*fig*) to give sth/sb the go-ahead *ou* green
light; **~ arrière** (*Auto*) rear light; **~ d'artifice**
firework; (*spectacle*) fireworks *pl*; **~ de camp**
campfire; **~ de cheminée** chimney fire; **~ de
joie** bonfire; **~ de paille** (*fig*) flash in the pan;
**~x de brouillard** (*Auto*) fog lights *ou* lamps; **~x
de croisement** (*Auto*) dipped (*Brit*) *ou* dimmed
(*US*) headlights; **~x de position** (*Auto*)
sidelights; **~x de route** (*Auto*) headlights (on
full (*Brit*) *ou* high (*US*) beam); **~x de
stationnement** parking lights
**feuillage** [fœjaʒ] *nm* foliage, leaves *pl*
**feuille** [fœj] *nf* (*d'arbre*) leaf; **~ (de papier)** sheet
(of paper); **rendre ~ blanche** (*Scol*) to give in a
blank paper; **~ d'or/de métal** gold/metal leaf;
**~ de chou** (*péj: journal*) rag; **~ d'impôts** tax form;
**~ de maladie** medical expenses claim form; **~
morte** dead leaf; **~ de paye** pay slip; **~ de
présence** attendance sheet; **~ de température**
temperature chart; **~ de vigne** (*Bot*) vine leaf;
(*sur statue*) fig leaf; **~ volante** loose sheet
**feuillet** [fœjɛ] *nm* leaf, page
**feuilletage** [fœjtaʒ] *nm* (*aspect feuilleté*) flakiness
**feuilleté, e** [fœjte] *adj* (*Culin*) flaky; (*verre*)
laminated
**feuilleter** [fœjte] *vt* (*livre*) to leaf through
**feuilleton** [fœjtɔ̃] *nm* serial
**feuillette** *etc* [fœjɛt] *vb voir* **feuilleter**
**feuillu, e** [fœjy] *adj* leafy ▷ *nm* broad-leaved tree
**feulement** [følmɑ̃] *nm* growl
**feutre** [føtʁ(ə)] *nm* felt; (*chapeau*) felt hat; (*stylo*)
felt-tip(ped pen)
**feutré, e** [føtʁe] *adj* feltlike; (*pas, voix*) muffled
**feutrer** [føtʁe] *vt* to felt; (*fig: bruits*) to muffle
▷ *vi*, **se feutrer** *vi* (*tissu*) to felt
**feutrine** [føtʁin] *nf* (lightweight) felt
**fève** [fɛv] *nf* broad bean; (*dans la galette des Rois*)
charm (*hidden in cake eaten on Twelfth Night*)
**février** [fevʁije] *nm* February; *voir aussi* **juillet**
**fez** [fɛz] *nm* fez
**FF** *abr* (= *franc français*) FF
**FFA** *sigle fpl* (= *Forces françaises en Allemagne*) French
forces in Germany
**FFF** *abr* = **Fédération française de football**
**FFI** *sigle fpl* = **Forces françaises de l'intérieur
(1942–45)** ▷ *sigle m* member of the FFI
**FFL** *sigle fpl* (= *Forces françaises libres*) Free French
Army
**Fg** *abr* = **faubourg**
**FGA** *sigle m* (= *Fonds de garantie automobile*) fund
financed through insurance premiums, to compensate
victims of uninsured losses
**FGEN** *sigle f* (= *Fédération générale de l'éducation
nationale*) teachers' trade union

**fi** [fi] *excl*: **faire fi de** to snap one's fingers at
**fiabilité** [fjabilite] *nf* reliability
**fiable** [fjabl(ə)] *adj* reliable
**fiacre** [fjakʀ(ə)] *nm* (hackney) cab *ou* carriage
**fiançailles** [fjɑ̃saj] *nfpl* engagement *sg*
**fiancé, e** [fjɑ̃se] *nm/f* fiancé (fiancée) ▷ *adj*: **être**
~ **(à)** to be engaged (to)
**fiancer** [fjɑ̃se]: **se fiancer** *vi*: **se ~ (avec)** to
become engaged (to)
**fiasco** [fjasko] *nm* fiasco
**fibranne** [fibʀan] *nf* bonded fibre *ou* fiber (US)
**fibre** [fibʀ(ə)] *nf* fibre, fiber (US); **avoir la ~
paternelle/militaire** to be a born father/
soldier; **~ optique** optical fibre *ou* fiber; **~ de
verre** fibreglass (Brit), fiberglass (US), glass
fibre *ou* fiber
**fibreux, -euse** [fibʀø, -øz] *adj* fibrous; (viande)
stringy
**fibrome** [fibʀom] *nm* (Méd) fibroma
**ficelage** [fisla3] *nm* tying (up)
**ficelé, e** [fisle] *adj* (fam): **être mal ~** (habillé) to be
badly got up; **bien/mal ~** (conçu: roman, projet)
well/badly put together
**ficeler** [fisle] *vt* to tie up
**ficelle** [fisɛl] *nf* string *no pl*; (morceau) piece *ou*
length of string; (pain) stick of French bread;
**ficelles** *nfpl* (fig) strings; **tirer sur la ~** (fig) to go
too far
**fiche** [fiʃ] *nf* (carte) (index) card; (formulaire) form;
(Élec) plug; **~ de paye** pay slip; **~ signalétique**
(Police) identification card; **~ technique** data
sheet, specification *ou* spec sheet
**ficher** [fiʃe] *vt* (dans un fichier) to file; (: Police) to
put on file; (fam) to do; (: donner) to give;
(: mettre) to stick *ou* shove; (planter): **~ qch dans**
to stick *ou* drive sth into; **~ qn à la porte** (fam) to
chuck sb out; **fiche(-moi) le camp** (fam) clear
off; **fiche-moi la paix** (fam) leave me alone; **se
~ dans** (s'enfoncer) to get stuck in, embed itself
in; **se ~ de** (fam) to make fun of; not to care
about
**fichier** [fiʃje] *nm* (gén, Inform) file; (à cartes) card
index; **~ actif** *ou* **en cours d'utilisation** (Inform)
active file; **~ d'adresses** mailing list; **~
d'archives** (Inform) archive file
**fichu, e** [fiʃy] *pp de* **ficher** (fam) ▷ *adj* (fam: fini,
inutilisable) bust, done for; (: intensif) wretched,
darned ▷ *nm* (foulard) (head)scarf; **être ~ de** to
be capable of; **mal ~** feeling lousy; useless;
**bien ~** great
**fictif, -ive** [fiktif, -iv] *adj* fictitious
**fiction** [fiksjɔ̃] *nf* fiction; (fait imaginé) invention
**fictivement** [fiktivmɑ̃] *adv* fictitiously
**fidèle** [fidɛl] *adj*: **~ (à)** faithful (to) ▷ *nm/f* (Rel):
**les ~s** the faithful; (à l'église) the congregation
**fidèlement** [fidɛlmɑ̃] *adv* faithfully
**fidélité** [fidelite] *nf* faithfulness
**Fidji** [fidʒi] *nfpl*: **(les îles) ~** Fiji
**fiduciaire** [fidysjɛʀ] *adj* fiduciary; **héritier ~**
heir, trustee; **monnaie ~** flat money
**fief** [fjɛf] *nm* fief; (fig) preserve; stronghold
**fieffé, e** [fjefe] *adj* (ivrogne, menteur) arrant, out-
and-out

**fiel** [fjɛl] *nm* gall
**fiente** [fjɑ̃t] *nf* (bird) droppings *pl*
**fier¹** [fje]: **se ~ à** *vt* to trust
**fier², fière** [fjɛʀ] *adj* proud; **~ de** proud of; **avoir
fière allure** to cut a fine figure
**fièrement** [fjɛʀmɑ̃] *adv* proudly
**fierté** [fjɛʀte] *nf* pride
**fièvre** [fjɛvʀ(ə)] *nf* fever; **avoir de la ~/39 de ~** to
have a high temperature/a temperature of 39°
C; **~ typhoïde** typhoid fever
**fiévreusement** [fjevʀøzmɑ̃] *adv* (fig) feverishly
**fiévreux, -euse** [fjevʀø, -øz] *adj* feverish
**FIFA** [fifa] *sigle f* (= Fédération internationale de
Football association) FIFA
**fifre** [fifʀ(ə)] *nm* fife; (personne) fife-player
**fig** *abr* (= figure) fig
**figé, e** [fiʒe] *adj* (manières) stiff; (société) rigid;
(sourire) set
**figer** [fiʒe] *vt* to congeal; (fig: personne) to freeze,
root to the spot; **se figer** *vi* to congeal; to freeze;
(institutions etc) to become set, stop evolving
**fignoler** [fiɲɔle] *vt* to put the finishing
touches to
**figue** [fig] *nf* fig
**figuier** [figje] *nm* fig tree
**figurant, e** [figyʀɑ̃, -ɑ̃t] *nm/f* (Théât) walk-on;
(Ciné) extra
**figuratif, -ive** [figyʀatif, -iv] *adj*
representational, figurative
**figuration** [figyʀasjɔ̃] *nf* walk-on parts *pl*;
extras *pl*
**figure** [figyʀ] *nf* (visage) face; (image, tracé, forme,
personnage) figure; (illustration) picture, diagram;
**faire ~ de** to look like; **faire bonne ~** to put up a
good show; **faire triste ~** to be a sorry sight; **~
de rhétorique** figure of speech
**figuré, e** [figyʀe] *adj* (sens) figurative
**figurer** [figyʀe] *vi* to appear ▷ *vt* to represent;
**se ~ que** to imagine that; **figurez-vous que ...**
would you believe that ...?
**figurine** [figyʀin] *nf* figurine
**fil** [fil] *nm* (brin, fig: d'une histoire) thread; (du
téléphone) cable, wire; (textile de lin) linen; (d'un
couteau: tranchant) edge; **au ~ des années** with
the passing of the years; **au ~ de l'eau** with the
stream *ou* current; **de ~ en aiguille** one thing
leading to another; **ne tenir qu'à un ~** (vie,
réussite etc) to hang by a thread; **donner du ~ à
retordre à qn** to make life difficult for sb;
**donner/recevoir un coup de ~** to make/get a
phone call; **~ à coudre** (sewing) thread *ou* yarn;
**~ dentaire** dental floss; **~ électrique** electric
wire; **~ de fer** wire; **~ de fer barbelé** barbed
wire; **~ à pêche** fishing line; **~ à plomb** plumb
line; **~ à souder** soldering wire
**filament** [filamɑ̃] *nm* (Élec) filament; (de liquide)
trickle, thread
**filandreux, -euse** [filɑ̃dʀø, -øz] *adj* stringy
**filant, e** [filɑ̃, -ɑ̃t] *adj*: **étoile ~e** shooting star
**filasse** [filas] *adj inv* white blond
**filature** [filatyʀ] *nf* (fabrique) mill; (policière)

**f**

shadowing *no pl*; tailing *no pl*; **prendre qn en ~** to shadow *ou* tail sb

**file** [fil] *nf* line; **~ (d'attente)** queue (*Brit*), line (*US*); **prendre la ~** to join the (end of the) queue *ou* line; **prendre la ~ de droite** (*Auto*) to move into the right-hand lane; **se mettre en ~** to form a line; (*Auto*) to get into lane; **stationner en double ~** (*Auto*) to double-park; **à la ~** *adv* (*d'affilée*) in succession; (*à la suite*) one after another; **à la** *ou* **en ~ indienne** in single file

**filer** [file] *vt* (*tissu, toile, verre*) to spin; (*dérouler: câble etc*) to pay ou let out; (*prendre en filature*) to shadow, tail; (*fam: donner*): **~ qch à qn** to slip sb sth ▷ *vi* (*bas, maille, liquide, pâte*) to run; (*aller vite*) to fly past *ou* by; (*fam: partir*) to make off; **~ à l'anglaise** to take French leave; **~ doux** to behave o.s., toe the line; **~ un mauvais coton** to be in a bad way

**filet** [file] *nm* net; (*Culin*) fillet; (*d'eau, de sang*) trickle; **tendre un ~** (*police*) to set a trap; **~ (à bagages)** (*Rail*) luggage rack; **~ (à provisions)** string bag

**filetage** [filta3] *nm* threading; thread

**fileter** [filte] *vt* to thread

**filial, e, -aux** [filjal, -o] *adj* filial ▷ *nf* (*Comm*) subsidiary; affiliate

**filiation** [filjasjɔ̃] *nf* filiation

**filière** [filjɛʀ] *nf*: **passer par la ~** to go through the (administrative) channels; **suivre la ~** to work one's way up (through the hierarchy)

**filiforme** [filifɔʀm(ə)] *adj* spindly; threadlike

**filigrane** [filigʀan] *nm* (*d'un billet, timbre*) watermark; **en ~** (*fig*) showing just beneath the surface

**filin** [filɛ̃] *nm* (*Navig*) rope

**fille** [fij] *nf* girl; (*opposé à fils*) daughter; **vieille ~** old maid; **~ de joie** prostitute; **~ de salle** waitress

**fille-mère** [fijmɛʀ] (*pl* **filles-mères**) *nf* unmarried mother

**fillette** [fijɛt] *nf* (little) girl

**filleul, e** [fijœl] *nm/f* godchild, godson (goddaughter)

**film** [film] *nm* (*pour photo*) (roll of) film; (*œuvre*) film, picture, movie; (*couche*) film; **~ muet/parlant** silent/talking picture *ou* movie; **~ alimentaire** clingfilm; **~ d'amour/d'animation/d'horreur** romantic/animated/horror film; **~ comique** comedy; **~ policier** thriller

**filmer** [filme] *vt* to film

**filon** [filɔ̃] *nm* vein, lode; (*fig*) lucrative line, money-spinner

**filou** [filu] *nm* (*escroc*) swindler

**fils** [fis] *nm* son; **~ de famille** moneyed young man; **~ à papa** (*péj*) daddy's boy

**filtrage** [filtʀa3] *nm* filtering

**filtrant, e** [filtʀɑ̃, -ɑ̃t] *adj* (*huile solaire etc*) filtering

**filtre** [filtʀ(ə)] *nm* filter; **"~ ou sans ~?"** (*cigarettes*) "tipped or plain?"; **~ à air** air filter

**filtrer** [filtʀe] *vt* to filter; (*fig: candidats, visiteurs*) to screen ▷ *vi* to filter (through)

**fin¹** [fɛ̃] *nf* end; **fins** *nfpl* (*but*) ends; **à (la) ~ mai, ~ mai** at the end of May; **en ~ de semaine** at the end of the week; **prendre ~** to come to an end; **toucher à sa ~** to be drawing to a close; **mettre ~ à** to put an end to; **mener à bonne ~** to bring to a successful conclusion; **à cette ~** to this end; **à toutes ~s utiles** for your information; **à la ~** in the end, eventually; **sans ~** *adj* endless ▷ *adv* endlessly; **~ de non-recevoir** (*Jur, Admin*) objection; **~ de section** (*de ligne d'autobus*) stage

**fin², e** [fɛ̃, fin] *adj* (*papier, couche, fil*) thin; (*cheveux, poudre, pointe, visage*) fine; (*taille*) neat, slim; (*esprit, remarque*) subtle; shrewd ▷ *adv* (*moudre, couper*) finely ▷ *nm*: **vouloir jouer au plus ~ (avec qn)** to try to outsmart sb ▷ *nf* (*alcool*) liqueur brandy; **c'est ~!** (*ironique*) how clever!; **~ prêt/soûl** quite ready/drunk; **un ~ gourmet** a gourmet; **un ~ tireur** a crack shot; **avoir la vue/l'ouïe ~e** to have sharp eyes/ears, have keen eyesight/hearing; **or/linge/vin ~** fine gold/linen/wine; **le ~ fond de** the very depths of; **le ~ mot de** the real story behind; **la ~e fleur de** the flower of; **une ~e mouche** (*fig*) a sly customer; **~es herbes** mixed herbs

**final, e** [final] *adj, nf* final ▷ *nm* (*Mus*) finale; **quarts de ~e** quarter finals; **8èmes/16èmes de ~e** 2nd/1st round (*in 5 round knock-out competition*)

**finalement** [finalmɑ̃] *adv* finally, in the end; (*après tout*) after all

**finaliste** [finalist(ə)] *nm/f* finalist

**finalité** [finalite] *nf* (*but*) aim, goal; (*fonction*) purpose

**finance** [finɑ̃s] *nf* finance; **finances** *nfpl* (*situation financière*) finances; (*activités financières*) finance *sg*; **moyennant ~** for a fee *ou* consideration

**financement** [finɑ̃smɑ̃] *nm* financing

**financer** [finɑ̃se] *vt* to finance

**financier, -ière** [finɑ̃sje, -jɛʀ] *adj* financial ▷ *nm* financier

**financièrement** [finɑ̃sjɛʀmɑ̃] *adv* financially

**finasser** [finase] *vi* (*péj*) to wheel and deal

**finaud, e** [fino, -od] *adj* wily

**fine** [fin] *adj f, nf voir* **fin, e**

**finement** [finmɑ̃] *adv* thinly; finely; neatly, slimly; subtly; shrewdly

**finesse** [finɛs] *nf* thinness; fineness; neatness, slimness; subtlety; shrewdness; **finesses** *nfpl* (*subtilités*) niceties; finer points

**fini, e** [fini] *adj* finished; (*Math*) finite; (*intensif*): **un menteur ~** a liar through and through ▷ *nm* (*d'un objet manufacturé*) finish

**finir** [finiʀ] *vt* to finish ▷ *vi* to finish, end; **~ quelque part** to end *ou* finish up somewhere; **~ de faire** to finish doing; (*cesser*) to stop doing; **~ par faire** to end *ou* finish up doing; **il finit par m'agacer** he's beginning to get on my nerves; **~ en pointe/tragédie** to end in a point/in tragedy; **en ~ avec** to be *ou* have done with; **à n'en plus ~** (*route, discussions*) never-ending; **il**

**va mal** ~ he will come to a bad end; **c'est bientôt fini?** *(reproche)* have you quite finished?

**finish** [finiʃ] *nm (Sport)* finish

**finissage** [finisaʒ] *nm* finishing

**finisseur, -euse** [finisœʀ, -øz] *nm/f (Sport)* strong finisher

**finition** [finisjɔ̃] *nf* finishing; finish

**finlandais, e** [fɛ̃lɑ̃dɛ, -ɛz] *adj* Finnish ▷ *nm/f:* **Finlandais, e** Finn

**Finlande** [fɛ̃lɑ̃d] *nf:* **la** ~ Finland

**finnois, e** [finwa, -waz] *adj* Finnish ▷ *nm (Ling)* Finnish

**fiole** [fjɔl] *nf* phial

**fiord** [fjɔʀ(d)] *nm* = **fjord**

**fioriture** [fjɔʀityʀ] *nf* embellishment, flourish

**fioul** [fjul] *nm* fuel oil

**firent** [fiʀ] *vb voir* **faire**

**firmament** [fiʀmamɑ̃] *nm* firmament, skies *pl*

**firme** [fiʀm(ə)] *nf* firm

**fis** [fi] *vb voir* **faire**

**fisc** [fisk] *nm* tax authorities *pl*, ≈ Inland Revenue *(Brit)*, ≈ Internal Revenue Service (US)

**fiscal, e, -aux** [fiskal, -o] *adj* tax *cpd*, fiscal

**fiscaliser** [fiskalize] *vt* to subject to tax

**fiscaliste** [fiskalist(ə)] *nm/f* tax specialist

**fiscalité** [fiskalite] *nf* tax system; *(charges)* taxation

**fissible** [fisibl(ə)] *adj* fissile

**fission** [fisjɔ̃] *nf* fission

**fissure** [fisyʀ] *nf* crack

**fissurer** [fisyʀe] *vt,* **se fissurer** *vi* to crack

**fiston** [fistɔ̃] *nm (fam)* son, lad

**fit** [fi] *vb voir* **faire**

**FIV** *sigle f (= fécondation in vitro)* IVF

**fixage** [fiksaʒ] *nm (Photo)* fixing

**fixateur** [fiksatœʀ] *nm (Photo)* fixer; *(pour cheveux)* hair cream

**fixatif** [fiksatif] *nm* fixative

**fixation** [fiksasjɔ̃] *nf* fixing; fastening; setting; *(de ski)* binding; *(Psych)* fixation

**fixe** [fiks(ə)] *adj* fixed; *(emploi)* steady, regular ▷ *nm (salaire)* basic salary; **à heure** ~ at a set time; **menu à prix** ~ set menu

**fixé, e** [fikse] *adj (heure, jour)* appointed; **être** ~ **(sur)** to have made up one's mind (about); to know for certain (about)

**fixement** [fiksəmɑ̃] *adv* fixedly, steadily

**fixer** [fikse] *vt (attacher):* ~ **qch (à/sur)** to fix *ou* fasten sth (to/onto); *(déterminer)* to fix, set; *(Chimie, Photo)* to fix; *(poser son regard sur)* to look hard at, stare at; **se fixer** *(s'établir)* to settle down; ~ **son choix sur qch** to decide on sth; **se** ~ **sur** *(attention)* to focus on

**fixité** [fiksite] *nf* fixedness

**fjord** [fjɔʀ(d)] *nm* fjord, fiord

**fl.** *abr (= fleuve)* r, R; *(= florin)* fl

**flacon** [flakɔ̃] *nm* bottle

**flagada** [flagada] *adj inv (fam: fatigué)* shattered

**flagellation** [flaʒelasjɔ̃] *nf* flogging

**flageller** [flaʒele] *vt* to flog, scourge

**flageoler** [flaʒɔle] *vi* to have knees like jelly

**flageolet** [flaʒɔlɛ] *nm (Mus)* flageolet; *(Culin)* dwarf kidney bean

**flagornerie** [flagɔʀnəʀi] *nf* toadying, fawning

**flagorneur, -euse** [flagɔʀnœʀ, -øz] *nm/f* toady, fawner

**flagrant, e** [flagʀɑ̃, -ɑ̃t] *adj* flagrant, blatant; **en** ~ **délit** in the act, in flagrante delicto

**flair** [flɛʀ] *nm* sense of smell; *(fig)* intuition

**flairer** [fleʀe] *vt (humer)* to sniff (at); *(détecter)* to scent

**flamand, e** [flamɑ̃, -ɑ̃d] *adj* Flemish ▷ *nm (Ling)* Flemish ▷ *nm/f:* **Flamand, e** Fleming; **les F-s** the Flemish

**flamant** [flamɑ̃] *nm* flamingo

**flambant** [flɑ̃bɑ̃] *adv:* ~ **neuf** brand new

**flambé, e** [flɑ̃be] *adj (Culin)* flambé ▷ *nf* blaze; *(fig)* flaring-up, explosion

**flambeau, x** [flɑ̃bo] *nm (flaming)* torch; **se passer le** ~ *(fig)* to hand down the *(ou* a) tradition

**flambée** [flɑ̃be] *nf (feu)* blaze; *(Comm):* ~ **des prix** (sudden) shooting up of prices

**flamber** [flɑ̃be] *vi* to blaze (up) ▷ *vt (poulet)* to singe; *(aiguille)* to sterilize

**flambeur, -euse** [flɑ̃bœʀ, -øz] *nm/f* big-time gambler

**flamboyant, e** [flɑ̃bwajɑ̃, -ɑ̃t] *adj* blazing; flaming

**flamboyer** [flɑ̃bwaje] *vi* to blaze (up); *(fig)* to flame

**flamenco** [flamɛnko] *nm* flamenco

**flamingant, e** [flamɛ̃gɑ̃, -ɑ̃t] *adj* Flemish-speaking ▷ *nm/f:* **Flamingant, e** Flemish speaker; *(Pol)* Flemish nationalist

**flamme** [flam] *nf* flame; *(fig)* fire, fervour; **en ~s** on fire, ablaze

**flammèche** [flamɛʃ] *nf* (flying) spark

**flammerole** [flamʀɔl] *nf* will-o'-the-wisp

**flan** [flɑ̃] *nm (Culin)* custard tart *ou* pie

**flanc** [flɑ̃] *nm* side; *(Mil)* flank; **à** ~ **de colline** on the hillside; **prêter le** ~ **à** *(fig)* to lay o.s. open to

**flancher** [flɑ̃ʃe] *vi (cesser de fonctionner)* to fail, pack up; *(armée)* to quit

**Flandre** [flɑ̃dʀ(ə)] *nf:* **la** ~ *(aussi:* **les Flandres)** Flanders

**flanelle** [flanɛl] *nf* flannel

**flâner** [flɑne] *vi* to stroll

**flânerie** [flɑnʀi] *nf* stroll

**flâneur, -euse** [flɑnœʀ, -øz] *adj* idle ▷ *nm/f* stroller

**flanquer** [flɑ̃ke] *vt* to flank; *(fam: jeter):* ~ **par terre/à la porte** to fling to the ground/chuck out; (: *donner):* ~ **la frousse à qn** to put the wind up sb, give sb an awful fright

**flapi, e** [flapi] *adj* dog-tired

**flaque** [flak] *nf (d'eau)* puddle; *(d'huile, de sang etc)* pool

**flash** [flaʃ] *(pl* **-es)** *nm (Photo)* flash; ~ **(d'information)** newsflash

**flasque** [flask(ə)] *adj* flabby ▷ *nf (flacon)* flask

**flatter** [flate] *vt* to flatter; *(caresser)* to stroke; **se** ~ **de qch** to pride o.s. on sth

**flatterie** [flatʀi] *nf* flattery

f

**flatteur, -euse** [flatœR, -øz] *adj* flattering ▷ *nm/f* flatterer

**flatulence** [flatylãs], **flatuosité** [flatɥozite] *nf* (*Méd*) flatulence, wind

**FLB** *abr* (= *franco long du bord*) FAS ▷ *sigle m* (*Pol*) = **Front de libération de la Bretagne**

**FLC** *sigle m* = **Front de libération de la Corse**

**fléau, x** [fleo] *nm* scourge, curse; (*de balance*) beam; (*pour le blé*) flail

**fléchage** [fleʃaʒ] *nm* (*d'un itinéraire*) signposting

**flèche** [flɛʃ] *nf* arrow; (*de clocher*) spire; (*de grue*) jib; (*trait d'esprit, critique*) shaft; **monter en ~** (*fig*) to soar, rocket; **partir en ~** (*fig*) to be off like a shot; **à ~ variable** (*avion*) swing-wing *cpd*

**flécher** [fleʃe] *vt* to arrow, mark with arrows

**fléchette** [fleʃɛt] *nf* dart; **fléchettes** *nfpl* (*jeu*) darts *sg*

**fléchir** [fleʃiR] *vt* (*corps, genou*) to bend; (*fig*) to sway, weaken ▷ *vi* (*poutre*) to sag, bend; (*fig*) to weaken, flag; (: *baisser: prix*) to fall off

**fléchissement** [fleʃismã] *nm* bending; sagging; flagging; (*de l'économie*) dullness

**flegmatique** [flɛgmatik] *adj* phlegmatic

**flegme** [flɛgm(ə)] *nm* composure

**flemmard, e** [flemaR, -aRd(ə)] *nm/f* lazybones *sg*, loafer

**flemme** [flɛm] *nf* (*fam*): **j'ai la ~ de le faire** I can't be bothered

**flétan** [fletã] *nm* (*Zool*) halibut

**flétrir** [fletRiR] *vt* to wither; (*stigmatiser*) to condemn (in the most severe terms); **se flétrir** *vi* to wither

**fleur** [flœR] *nf* flower; (*d'un arbre*) blossom; **être en ~** (*arbre*) to be in blossom; **tissu à ~s** flowered *ou* flowery fabric; **la (fine) ~ de** (*fig*) the flower of; **être ~ bleue** to be soppy *ou* sentimental; **à ~ de terre** just above the ground; **faire une ~ à qn** to do sb a favour (*Brit*) *ou* favor (*US*); **~ de lis** fleur-de-lis

**fleurer** [flœRe] *vt*: **~ la lavande** to have the scent of lavender

**fleuret** [flœRɛ] *nm* (*arme*) foil; (*sport*) fencing

**fleurette** [flœRɛt] *nf*: **conter ~ à qn** to whisper sweet nothings to sb

**fleuri, e** [flœRi] *adj* in flower *ou* bloom; surrounded by flowers; (*fig: style*) flowery; (: *teint*) glowing

**fleurir** [flœRiR] *vi* (*rose*) to flower; (*arbre*) to blossom; (*fig*) to flourish ▷ *vt* (*tombe*) to put flowers on; (*chambre*) to decorate with flowers

**fleuriste** [flœRist(ə)] *nm/f* florist

**fleuron** [flœRɔ̃] *nm* jewel (*fig*)

**fleuve** [flœv] *nm* river; **roman-~** saga; **discours-~** interminable speech

**flexibilité** [flɛksibilite] *nf* flexibility

**flexible** [flɛksibl(ə)] *adj* flexible

**flexion** [flɛksjɔ̃] *nf* flexing, bending; (*Ling*) inflection

**flibustier** [flibystje] *nm* buccaneer

**flic** [flik] *nm* (*fam: péj*) cop

**flingue** [flɛ̃g] *nm* (*fam*) shooter

**flipper** *nm* [flipœR] pinball (machine) ▷ *vi*

[flipe] (*fam: être déprimé*) to feel down, be on a downer; (: *être exalté*) to freak out

**flirt** [flœRt] *nm* flirting; (*personne*) boyfriend, girlfriend

**flirter** [flœRte] *vi* to flirt

**FLN** *sigle m* = **Front de libération nationale** (during the Algerian war)

**FLNKS** *sigle m* (= *Front de libération nationale kanak et socialiste*) political movement in New Caledonia

**flocon** [flɔkɔ̃] *nm* flake; (*de laine etc: boulette*) flock; **~s d'avoine** oat flakes, porridge oats

**floconneux, -euse** [flɔkɔnø, -øz] *adj* fluffy, fleecy

**flonflons** [flɔ̃flɔ̃] *nmpl* blare *sg*

**flopée** [flɔpe] *nf*: **une ~ de** loads of

**floraison** [flɔRɛzɔ̃] *nf* flowering; blossoming; flourishing; *voir* **fleurir**

**floral, e, -aux** [flɔRal, -o] *adj* floral, flower *cpd*

**floralies** [flɔRali] *nfpl* flower show *sg*

**flore** [flɔR] *nf* flora

**Florence** [flɔRãs] *n* (*ville*) Florence

**florentin, e** [flɔRãtɛ̃, -in] *adj* Florentine

**floriculture** [flɔRikyltyR] *nf* flower-growing

**florissant, e** [flɔRisã, -ãt] *vb voir* **fleurir** ▷ *adj* flourishing; (*santé, teint, mine*) blooming

**flot** [flo] *nm* flood, stream; (*marée*) flood tide; **flots** *nmpl* (*de la mer*) waves; **être à ~** (*Navig*) to be afloat; (*fig*) to be on an even keel; **à ~s** (*couler*) in torrents; **entrer à ~s** to stream *ou* pour in

**flottage** [flɔtaʒ] *nm* (*du bois*) floating

**flottaison** [flɔtɛzɔ̃] *nf*: **ligne de ~** waterline

**flottant, e** [flɔtã, -ãt] *adj* (*vêtement*) loose(-fitting); (*cours, barème*) floating

**flotte** [flɔt] *nf* (*Navig*) fleet; (*fam*) water; rain

**flottement** [flɔtmã] *nm* (*fig*) wavering, hesitation; (*Écon*) floating

**flotter** [flɔte] *vi* to float; (*nuage, odeur*) to drift; (*drapeau*) to fly; (*vêtements*) to hang loose ▷ *vb impers* (*fam: pleuvoir*): **il flotte** it's raining ▷ *vt* to float; **faire ~** to float

**flotteur** [flɔtœR] *nm* float

**flottille** [flɔtij] *nf* flotilla

**flou, e** [flu] *adj* fuzzy, blurred; (*fig*) woolly (*Brit*), vague; (*non ajusté: robe*) loose(-fitting)

**flouer** [flue] *vt* to swindle

**FLQ** *abr* (= *franco long du quai*) FAQ

**fluctuant, e** [flyktɥã, -ãt] *adj* (*prix, cours*) fluctuating; (*opinions*) changing

**fluctuation** [flyktɥasjɔ̃] *nf* fluctuation

**fluctuer** [flyktɥe] *vi* to fluctuate

**fluet, te** [flyɛ, -ɛt] *adj* thin, slight; (*voix*) thin

**fluide** [flyid] *adj* fluid; (*circulation etc*) flowing freely ▷ *nm* fluid; (*force*) (mysterious) power

**fluidifier** [flyidifje] *vt* to make fluid

**fluidité** [flyidite] *nf* fluidity; free flow

**fluor** [flyɔR] *nm* fluorine

**fluoré, e** [flyɔRe] *adj* fluoridated

**fluorescent, e** [flyɔRɛsã, -ãt] *adj* fluorescent

**flûte** [flyt] *nf* (*aussi*: **flûte traversière**) flute; (*verre*) flute glass; (*pain*) long loaf; **petite ~** piccolo; **~! drat it!**; **~ (à bec)** recorder; **~ de Pan** panpipes *pl*

**flûtiste** [flytist(ə)] *nm/f* flautist, flute player

**fluvial, e, -aux** [flyvjal, -o] *adj* river *cpd*, fluvial

**flux** [fly] *nm* incoming tide; (*écoulement*) flow; **le ~ et le re~** the ebb and flow

**fluxion** [flyksjɔ̃] *nf*: **~ de poitrine** pneumonia

**FM** *sigle f* (= *frequency modulation*) FM

**Fme** *abr* (= *femme*) W

**FMI** *sigle m* (= *Fonds monétaire international*) IMF

**FN** *sigle m* (= *Front national*) ≈ NF (= *National Front*)

**FNAC** [fnak] *sigle f* (= *Fédération nationale des achats des cadres*) chain of discount shops (hi-fi, photo etc)

**FNSEA** *sigle f* (= *Fédération nationale des syndicats d'exploitants agricoles*) farmers' union

**FO** *sigle f* (= *Force ouvrière*) trades union

**foc** [fɔk] *nm* jib

**focal, e, -aux** [fɔkal, -o] *adj* focal ▷ *nf* focal length

**focaliser** [fɔkalize] *vt* to focus

**foehn** [føn] *nm* foehn, föhn

**fœtal, e, -aux** [fetal, -o] *adj* fetal, foetal (*Brit*)

**fœtus** [fetys] *nm* fetus, foetus (*Brit*)

**foi** [fwa] *nf* faith; **sous la ~ du serment** under *ou* on oath; **ajouter ~ à** to lend credence to; **faire ~ (prouver)** to be evidence; **digne de ~** reliable; **sur la ~ de** on the word *ou* strength of; **être de bonne/mauvaise ~** to be in good faith/ not to be in good faith; **ma ~!** well!

**foie** [fwa] *nm* liver; **~ gras** foie gras

**foin** [fwɛ̃] *nm* hay; **faire les ~s** to make hay; **faire du ~ (fam)** to kick up a row

**foire** [fwaʀ] *nf* fair; (*fête foraine*) (fun) fair; (*fig: désordre, confusion*) bear garden; **~ aux questions** (*Internet*) frequently asked questions; **faire la ~** to whoop it up; **~ (exposition)** trade fair

**fois** [fwa] *nf* time; **une/deux ~** once/twice; **trois/vingt ~** three/twenty times; **deux ~ deux** twice two; **deux/quatre ~ plus grand (que)** twice/four times as big (as); **une ~ (passé)** once; (*futur*) sometime; **une (bonne) ~ pour toutes** once and for all; **encore une ~** again, once more; **il était une ~** once upon a time; **une ~ que c'est fait** once it's done; **une ~ parti** once he (*ou* I etc) had left; **des ~ (parfois)** sometimes; **si des ~ ... (fam)** if ever ...; **non mais des ~! (fam)** (now) look here!; **à la ~ (ensemble)** (all) at once; **à la ~ grand et beau** both tall and handsome

**foison** [fwazɔ̃] *nf*: **une ~ de** an abundance of; **à ~** *adv* in plenty

**foisonnant, e** [fwazɔnɑ̃, -ɑ̃t] *adj* teeming

**foisonnement** [fwazɔnmɑ̃] *nm* profusion, abundance

**foisonner** [fwazɔne] *vi* to abound; **~ en** *ou* **de** to abound in

**fol** [fɔl] *adj m voir* **fou**

**folâtre** [fɔlɑtʀ(ə)] *adj* playful

**folâtrer** [fɔlɑtʀe] *vi* to frolic (about)

**folichon, ne** [fɔliʃɔ̃, -ɔn] *adj*: **ça n'a rien de ~** it's not a lot of fun

**folie** [fɔli] *nf* (*d'une décision, d'un acte*) madness, folly; (*état*) madness, insanity; (*acte*) folly; **la ~ des grandeurs** delusions of grandeur; **faire des ~s (en dépenses)** to be extravagant

**folklore** [fɔlklɔʀ] *nm* folklore

**folklorique** [fɔlklɔʀik] *adj* folk *cpd*; (*fam*) weird

**folle** [fɔl] *adj f, nf voir* **fou**

**follement** [fɔlmɑ̃] *adv* (*très*) madly, wildly

**follet** [fɔlɛ] *adj m*: **feu ~** will-o'-the-wisp

**fomentateur, -trice** [fɔmɑ̃tatœʀ, -tʀis] *nm/f* agitator

**fomenter** [fɔmɑ̃te] *vt* to stir up, foment

**foncé, e** [fɔ̃se] *adj* dark; **bleu ~** dark blue

**foncer** [fɔ̃se] *vt* to make darker; (*Culin: moule etc*) to line ▷ *vi* to go darker; (*fam: aller vite*) to tear *ou* belt along; **~ sur** to charge at

**fonceur, -euse** [fɔ̃sœʀ, -øz] *nm/f* whizz kid

**foncier, -ière** [fɔ̃sje, -jɛʀ] *adj* (*honnêteté etc*) basic, fundamental; (*malhonnêteté*) deep-rooted; (*Comm*) real estate *cpd*

**foncièrement** [fɔ̃sjɛʀmɑ̃] *adv* basically; (*absolument*) thoroughly

**fonction** [fɔ̃ksjɔ̃] *nf* (*rôle, Math, Ling*) function; (*emploi, poste*) post, position; **fonctions** *nfpl* (*professionnelles*) duties; **entrer en ~s** to take up one's post *ou* duties; to take up office; **voiture de ~** company car; **être ~ de** (*dépendre de*) to depend on; **en ~ de** (*par rapport à*) according to; **faire ~ de** to serve as; **la ~ publique** the state *ou* civil (*Brit*) service

**fonctionnaire** [fɔ̃ksjɔnɛʀ] *nm/f* state employee *ou* official; (*dans l'administration*) ≈ civil servant (*Brit*)

**fonctionnariser** [fɔ̃ksjɔnaʀize] *vt* (*Admin: personne*) to give the status of a state employee to

**fonctionnel, le** [fɔ̃ksjɔnɛl] *adj* functional

**fonctionnellement** [fɔ̃ksjɔnɛlmɑ̃] *adv* functionally

**fonctionnement** [fɔ̃ksjɔnmɑ̃] *nm* working; functioning; operation

**fonctionner** [fɔ̃ksjɔne] *vi* to work, function; (*entreprise*) to operate, function; **faire ~** to work, operate

**fond** [fɔ̃] *nm voir aussi* **fonds**; (*d'un récipient, trou*) bottom; (*d'une salle, scène*) back; (*d'un tableau, décor*) background; (*opposé à la forme*) content; (*petite quantité*): **un ~ de verre** a drop; (*Sport*): **le ~** long distance (running); **course/épreuve de ~** long-distance race/trial; **au ~ de** at the bottom of; at the back of; **aller au ~ des choses** to get to the root of things; **le ~ de sa pensée** his (*ou* her) true thoughts *ou* feelings; **sans ~** *adj* bottomless; **envoyer par le ~** (*Navig: couler*) to sink, scuttle; **à ~** *adv* (*connaître, soutenir*) thoroughly; (*appuyer, visser*) right down *ou* home; **à ~ (de train)** *adv* (*fam*) full tilt; **dans le ~, au ~** *adv* (*en somme*) basically, really; **de ~ en comble** *adv* from top to bottom; **~ sonore** background noise; background music; **~ de teint** foundation

**fondamental, e, -aux** [fɔ̃damɑ̃tal, -o] *adj* fundamental

**fondamentalement** [fɔ̃damɑ̃talmɑ̃] *adv* fundamentally

**fondamentalisme** [fɔ̃damɑ̃talism(ə)] *nm* fundamentalism

**fondamentaliste** [fɔ̃damɑ̃talist(ə)] *adj, nm/f* fundamentalist

**fondant, e** [fɔ̃dɑ̃, -ɑ̃t] *adj* (*neige*) melting; (*poire*) that melts in the mouth; (*chocolat*) fondant

**fondateur, -trice** [fɔ̃datœʀ, -tʀis] *nm/f* founder; **membre ~** founder (*Brit*) *ou* founding (*US*) member

**fondation** [fɔ̃dasjɔ̃] *nf* founding; (*établissement*) foundation; **fondations** *nfpl* (*d'une maison*) foundations; **travail de ~** foundation works *pl*

**fondé, e** [fɔ̃de] *adj* (*accusation etc*) well-founded ▷ *nm*: **~ de pouvoir** authorized representative; **mal ~** unfounded; **être ~ à croire** to have grounds for believing *ou* good reason to believe

**fondement** [fɔ̃dmɑ̃] *nm* (*derrière*) behind; **fondements** *nmpl* foundations; **sans ~** *adj* (*rumeur etc*) groundless, unfounded

**fonder** [fɔ̃de] *vt* to found; (*fig*): **~ qch sur** to base sth on; **se ~ sur** (*personne*) to base o.s. on; **~ un foyer** (*se marier*) to set up home

**fonderie** [fɔ̃dʀi] *nf* smelting works *sg*

**fondeur, -euse** [fɔ̃dœʀ, -øz] *nm/f* (*skieur*) long-distance skier ▷ *nm*: (**ouvrier**) **~** caster

**fondre** [fɔ̃dʀ(ə)] *vt* to melt; (*dans l'eau: sucre, sel*) to dissolve; (*fig: mélanger*) to merge, blend ▷ *vi* to melt; to dissolve; (*fig*) to melt away; (*se précipiter*): **~ sur** to swoop down on; **se fondre** *vi* (*se combiner, se confondre*) to merge into each other; to dissolve; **~ en larmes** to dissolve into tears

**fondrière** [fɔ̃dʀijɛʀ] *nf* rut

**fonds** [fɔ̃] *nm* (*de bibliothèque*) collection; (*Comm*): **~ (de commerce)** business; (*fig*): **~ de probité** *etc* fund of integrity *etc* ▷ *nmpl* (*argent*) funds; **à ~ perdus** *adv* with little or no hope of getting the money back; **être en ~** to be in funds; **mise de ~** investment, (capital) outlay; **F~ monétaire international (FMI)** International Monetary Fund (IMF); **~ de roulement** *nm* float

**fondu, e** [fɔ̃dy] *adj* (*beurre, neige*) melted; (*métal*) molten ▷ *nm* (*Ciné*): **~ (enchaîné)** dissolve ▷ *nf* (*Culin*) fondue

**fongicide** [fɔ̃ʒisid] *nm* fungicide

**font** [fɔ̃] *vb voir* **faire**

**fontaine** [fɔ̃tɛn] *nf* fountain; (*source*) spring

**fontanelle** [fɔ̃tanɛl] *nf* fontanelle

**fonte** [fɔ̃t] *nf* melting; (*métal*) cast iron; **la ~ des neiges** the (spring) thaw

**fonts baptismaux** [fɔ̃batismo] *nmpl* (baptismal) font *sg*

**foot** [fut], **football** [futbol] *nm* football, soccer

**footballeur, -euse** [futbolœʀ, -øz] *nm/f* footballer (*Brit*), football *ou* soccer player

**footing** [futiŋ] *nm* jogging; **faire du ~** to go jogging

**for** [fɔʀ] *nm*: **dans** *ou* **en son ~ intérieur** in one's heart of hearts

**forage** [fɔʀaʒ] *nm* drilling, boring

**forain, e** [fɔʀɛ̃, -ɛn] *adj* fairground *cpd* ▷ *nm* (*marchand*) stallholder; (*acteur etc*) fairground entertainer

**forban** [fɔʀbɑ̃] *nm* (*pirate*) pirate; (*escroc*) crook

**forçat** [fɔʀsa] *nm* convict

**force** [fɔʀs(ə)] *nf* strength; (*puissance: surnaturelle etc*) power; (*Physique, Mécanique*) force; **forces** *nfpl* (*physiques*) strength *sg*; (*Mil*) forces; (*effectifs*): **d'importantes ~s de police** large contingents of police; **avoir de la ~** to be strong; **être à bout de ~** to have no strength left; **à la ~ du poignet** (*fig*) by the sweat of one's brow; **à ~ de faire** by dint of doing; **arriver en ~** (*nombreux*) to arrive in force; **cas de ~ majeure** case of absolute necessity; (*Assurances*) act of God; **~ de la nature** natural force; **de ~** *adv* forcibly, by force; **de toutes mes/ses ~s** with all my/his strength; **par la ~** using force; **par la ~ des choses/d'habitude** by force of circumstances/habit; **à toute ~** (*absolument*) at all costs; **faire ~ de rames/voiles** to ply the oars/cram on sail; **être de ~ à faire** to be up to doing; **de première ~** first class; (*Assurances*) **~ armée** (*les troupes*) the army; **~ d'âme** fortitude; **~ de frappe** strike force; **~ d'inertie** force of inertia; **la ~ publique** the authorities responsible for public order; **~s d'intervention** (*Mil, Police*) peace-keeping force *sg*; **les ~s de l'ordre** the police

**forcé, e** [fɔʀse] *adj* forced; (*bain*) unintended; (*inévitable*): **c'est ~!** it's inevitable!, it HAS to be!

**forcément** [fɔʀsemɑ̃] *adv* necessarily, inevitably; (*bien sûr*) of course

**forcené, e** [fɔʀsəne] *adj* frenzied ▷ *nm/f* maniac

**forceps** [fɔʀsɛps] *nm* forceps *pl*

**forcer** [fɔʀse] *vt* (*contraindre*): **~ qn à faire** to force sb to do; (*porte, serrure, plante*) to force; (*moteur, voix*) to strain ▷ *vi* (*Sport*) to overtax o.s.; **se ~ à faire qch** to force o.s. to do sth; **~ la dose/l'allure** to overdo it/increase the pace; **~ l'attention/le respect** to command attention/respect; **~ la consigne** to bypass orders

**forcing** [fɔʀsiŋ] *nm* (*Sport*): **faire le ~** to pile on the pressure

**forcir** [fɔʀsiʀ] *vi* (*grossir*) to broaden out; (*vent*) to freshen

**forclore** [fɔʀklɔʀ] *vt* (*Jur: personne*) to debar

**forclusion** [fɔʀklyzjɔ̃] *nf* (*Jur*) debarment

**forer** [fɔʀe] *vt* to drill, bore

**forestier, -ière** [fɔʀɛstje, -jɛʀ] *adj* forest *cpd*

**foret** [fɔʀɛ] *nm* drill

**forêt** [fɔʀɛ] *nf* forest; **Office National des F~s** (*Admin*) ≈ Forestry Commission (*Brit*), ≈ National Forest Service (*US*); **la F~ Noire** the Black Forest

**foreuse** [fɔʀøz] *nf* (*electric*) drill

**forfait** [fɔʀfɛ] *nm* (*Comm*) fixed *ou* set price; all-in deal *ou* price; (*crime*) infamy; **déclarer ~** to withdraw; **gagner par ~** to win by a walkover; **travailler à ~** to work for a lump sum

**forfaitaire** [fɔʀfɛtɛʀ] *adj* set; inclusive

**forfait-vacances** [fɔʀfɛvakɑ̃s] (*pl* **forfaits-vacances**) *nm* package holiday

**forfanterie** [fɔʀfɑ̃tʀi] *nf* boastfulness *no pl*

**forge** [fɔʀʒ(ə)] *nf* forge, smithy

**forgé, e** [fɔʀʒe] *adj*: **~ de toutes pièces** (*histoire*) completely fabricated

**forger** [fɔʀʒe] vt to forge; (fig: personnalité) to form; (: prétexte) to contrive, make up
**forgeron** [fɔʀʒəʀɔ̃] nm (black)smith
**formaliser** [fɔʀmalize]: **se formaliser** vi: **se ~ (de)** to take offence (at)
**formalisme** [fɔʀmalism(ə)] nm formality
**formalité** [fɔʀmalite] nf formality
**format** [fɔʀma] nm size; **petit ~** small size; (Photo) 35 mm (film)
**formater** [fɔʀmate] vt (disque) to format; **non formaté** unformatted
**formateur, -trice** [fɔʀmatœʀ, -tʀis] adj formative
**formation** [fɔʀmasjɔ̃] nf forming; (éducation) training; (Mus) group; (Mil, Aviat, Géo) formation; **la ~ permanente** ou **continue** continuing education; **la ~ professionnelle** vocational training
**forme** [fɔʀm(ə)] nf (gén) form; (d'un objet) shape, form; **formes** nfpl (bonnes manières) proprieties; (d'une femme) figure sg; **en ~ de poire** pear-shaped, in the shape of a pear; **sous ~ de** in the form of; in the guise of; **sous ~ de cachets** in the form of tablets; **être en (bonne** ou **pleine) ~**, **avoir la ~** (Sport etc) to be on form; **en bonne et due ~** in due form; **pour la ~** for the sake of form; **sans autre ~ de procès** (fig) without further ado; **prendre ~** to take shape
**formel, le** [fɔʀmɛl] adj (preuve, décision) definite, positive; (logique) formal
**formellement** [fɔʀmɛlmɑ̃] adv (interdit) strictly
**former** [fɔʀme] vt (gén) to form; (éduquer: soldat, ingénieur etc) to train; **se former** to form; to train
**formidable** [fɔʀmidabl(ə)] adj tremendous
**formidablement** [fɔʀmidabləmɑ̃] adv tremendously
**formol** [fɔʀmɔl] nm formalin, formol
**formosan, e** [fɔʀmozɑ̃, -an] adj Formosan
**Formose** [fɔʀmoz] nm Formosa
**formulaire** [fɔʀmylɛʀ] nm forma
**formulation** [fɔʀmylasjɔ̃] nf formulation; expression; voir **formuler**
**formule** [fɔʀmyl] nf (gén) formula; (formulaire) form; **selon la ~ consacrée** as one says; **~ de politesse** polite phrase; (en fin de lettre) letter ending
**formuler** [fɔʀmyle] vt (émettre: réponse, vœux) to formulate; (expliciter: sa pensée) to express
**forniquer** [fɔʀnike] vi to fornicate
**fort, e** [fɔʀ, fɔʀt(ə)] adj strong; (intensité, rendement) high, great; (corpulent) large; (doué): **être ~ (en)** to be good (at) ▷ adv (serrer, frapper) hard; (sonner) loud(ly); (beaucoup) greatly, very much; (très) very ▷ nm (édifice) fort; (point fort) strong point, forte; (gén pl: personne, pays): **le ~**, **les ~s** the strong; **c'est un peu ~!** it's a bit much!; **à plus ~e raison** even more so, all the more reason; **avoir ~ à faire avec qn** to have a hard job with sb; **se faire ~ de faire** to claim one can do; **~ bien/peu** very well/few; **au plus ~ de** (au milieu de) in the thick of, at the height of; **~e tête** rebel

**fortement** [fɔʀtəmɑ̃] adv strongly; (s'intéresser) deeply
**forteresse** [fɔʀtəʀɛs] nf fortress
**fortifiant** [fɔʀtifjɑ̃] nm tonic
**fortifications** [fɔʀtifikasjɔ̃] nfpl fortifications
**fortifier** [fɔʀtifje] vt to strengthen, fortify; (Mil) to fortify; **se fortifier** vi (personne, santé) to grow stronger
**fortin** [fɔʀtɛ̃] nm (small) fort
**fortiori** [fɔʀtjɔʀi]: **à ~** adv all the more so
**FORTRAN** [fɔʀtʀɑ̃] nm FORTRAN
**fortuit, e** [fɔʀtɥi, -it] adj fortuitous, chance cpd
**fortuitement** [fɔʀtɥitmɑ̃] adv fortuitously
**fortune** [fɔʀtyn] nf fortune; **faire ~** to make one's fortune; **de ~** adj makeshift; (compagnon) chance cpd
**fortuné, e** [fɔʀtyne] adj wealthy, well-off
**forum** [fɔʀɔm] nm forum
**fosse** [fos] nf (grand trou) pit; (tombe) grave; **la ~ aux lions/ours** the lions' den/bear pit; **~ commune** common ou communal grave; **~ (d'orchestre)** (orchestra) pit; **~ à purin** cesspit; **~ septique** septic tank; **~s nasales** nasal fossae
**fossé** [fose] nm ditch; (fig) gulf, gap
**fossette** [fosɛt] nf dimple
**fossile** [fosil] nm fossil ▷ adj fossilized, fossil cpd
**fossilisé, e** [fosilize] adj fossilized
**fossoyeur** [foswajœʀ] nm gravedigger
**fou, fol, folle** [fu, fɔl] adj mad, crazy; (déréglé etc) wild, erratic; (mèche) stray; (herbe) wild; (fam: extrême, très grand) terrific, tremendous ▷ nm/f madman/woman ▷ nm (du roi) jester, fool; (Échecs) bishop; **~ à lier**, **~ furieux (folle furieuse)** raving mad; **être ~ de** to be mad ou crazy about; (chagrin, joie, colère) to be wild with; **faire le ~** to play ou act the fool; **avoir le ~ rire** to have the giggles
**foucade** [fukad] nf caprice
**foudre** [fudʀ(ə)] nf lightning; **foudres** nfpl (fig: colère) wrath sg
**foudroyant, e** [fudʀwajɑ̃, -ɑ̃t] adj devastating; (maladie, poison) violent
**foudroyer** [fudʀwaje] vt to strike down; **~ qn du regard** to look daggers at sb; **il a été foudroyé** he was struck by lightning
**fouet** [fwɛ] nm whip; (Culin) whisk; **de plein ~** adv head on
**fouettement** [fwɛtmɑ̃] nm lashing no pl
**fouetter** [fwete] vt to whip; to whisk
**fougasse** [fugas] nf type of flat pastry
**fougère** [fuʒɛʀ] nf fern
**fougue** [fug] nf ardour (Brit), ardor (US), spirit
**fougueusement** [fugøzmɑ̃] adv ardently
**fougueux, -euse** [fugø, -øz] adj fiery, ardent
**fouille** [fuj] nf search; **fouilles** nfpl (archéologiques) excavations; **passer à la ~** to be searched
**fouillé, e** [fuje] adj detailed
**fouiller** [fuje] vt to search; (creuser) to dig; (: archéologue) to excavate; (approfondir: étude etc) to go into ▷ vi (archéologue) to excavate; **~ dans/parmi** to rummage in/among

**fouillis** [fuji] *nm* jumble, muddle
**fouine** [fwin] *nf* stone marten
**fouiner** [fwine] *vi* (*péj*): ~ **dans** to nose around *ou* about in
**fouineur, -euse** [fwinœR, -øz] *adj* nosey ⊳ *nm/f* nosey parker, snooper
**fouir** [fwiR] *vt* to dig
**fouisseur, -euse** [fwisœR, -øz] *adj* burrowing
**foulage** [fula3] *nm* pressing
**foulante** [fulɑ̃t] *adj f*: **pompe** ~ force pump
**foulard** [fulaR] *nm* scarf
**foule** [ful] *nf* crowd; **une** ~ **de** masses of; **venir en** ~ to come in droves
**foulée** [fule] *nf* stride; **dans la** ~ **de** on the heels of
**fouler** [fule] *vt* to press; (*sol*) to tread upon; **se fouler** *vi* (*fam*) to overexert o.s.; **se** ~ **la cheville** to sprain one's ankle; ~ **aux pieds** to trample underfoot
**foulure** [fulyR] *nf* sprain
**four** [fuR] *nm* oven; (*de potier*) kiln; (*Théât: échec*) flop; **allant au** ~ ovenproof
**fourbe** [fuRb(ə)] *adj* deceitful
**fourberie** [fuRbəRi] *nf* deceit
**fourbi** [fuRbi] *nm* (*fam*) gear, junk
**fourbir** [fuRbiR] *vt*: ~ **ses armes** (*fig*) to get ready for the fray
**fourbu, e** [fuRby] *adj* exhausted
**fourche** [fuRʃ(ə)] *nf* pitchfork; (*de bicyclette*) fork
**fourcher** [fuRʃe] *vi*: **ma langue a fourché** it was a slip of the tongue
**fourchette** [fuRʃet] *nf* fork; (*Statistique*) bracket, margin
**fourchu, e** [fuRʃy] *adj* split; (*arbre etc*) forked
**fourgon** [fuRgɔ̃] *nm* van; (*Rail*) wag(g)on; ~ **mortuaire** hearse
**fourgonnette** [fuRgɔnɛt] *nf* (delivery) van
**fourmi** [fuRmi] *nf* ant; **avoir des** ~**s** (*fig*) to have pins and needles
**fourmilière** [fuRmiljɛR] *nf* ant-hill; (*fig*) hive of activity
**fourmillement** [fuRmijmɑ̃] *nm* (*démangeaison*) pins and needles *pl*; (*grouillement*) swarming *no pl*
**fourmiller** [fuRmije] *vi* to swarm; ~ **de** to be teeming with, be swarming with
**fournaise** [fuRnɛz] *nf* blaze; (*fig*) furnace, oven
**fourneau, x** [fuRno] *nm* stove
**fournée** [fuRne] *nf* batch
**fourni, e** [fuRni] *adj* (*barbe, cheveux*) thick; (*magasin*): **bien** ~ (**en**) well stocked (with)
**fournil** [fuRni] *nm* bakehouse
**fournir** [fuRniR] *vt* to supply; (*preuve, exemple*) to provide, supply; (*effort*) to put in; ~ **qch à qn** to supply sth to sb, supply *ou* provide sb with sth; ~ **qn en** (*Comm*) to supply sb with; **se** ~ **chez** to shop at
**fournisseur, -euse** [fuRnisœR, -øz] *nm/f* supplier; (*Internet*): ~ **d'accès à Internet** (Internet) service provider
**fourniture** [fuRnityR] *nf* supply(ing); **fournitures** *nfpl* supplies; ~**s de bureau** office

supplies, stationery; ~**s scolaires** school stationery
**fourrage** [fuRa3] *nm* fodder
**fourrager**[1] [fuRa3e] *vi*: ~ **dans/parmi** to rummage through/among
**fourrager**[2], **-ère** [fuRa3e, -ɛR] *adj* fodder *cpd* ⊳ *nf* (*Mil*) fourragère
**fourré, e** [fuRe] *adj* (*bonbon, chocolat*) filled; (*manteau, botte*) fur-lined ⊳ *nm* thicket
**fourreau, x** [fuRo] *nm* sheath; (*de parapluie*) cover; **robe** ~ figure-hugging dress
**fourrer** [fuRe] *vt* (*fam*): ~ **qch dans** to stick *ou* shove sth into; **se** ~ **dans/sous** to get into/ under; **se** ~ **dans** (*une mauvaise situation*) to land o.s. into
**fourre-tout** [fuRtu] *nm inv* (*sac*) holdall; (*péj*) junk room (*ou* cupboard); (*fig*) rag-bag
**fourreur** [fuRœR] *nm* furrier
**fourrière** [fuRjɛR] *nf* pound
**fourrure** [fuRyR] *nf* fur; (*sur l'animal*) coat; **manteau/col de** ~ fur coat/collar
**fourvoyer** [fuRvwaje]: **se fourvoyer** *vi* to go astray, stray; **se** ~ **dans** to stray into
**foutre** [futR(ə)] *vt* (*fam!*) = **ficher⚓**; (*fam*)
**foutu, e** [futy] *adj* (*fam!*) = **fichu**
**foyer** [fwaje] *nm* (*de cheminée*) hearth; (*fig*) seat, centre; (*famille*) family; (*domicile*) home; (*local de réunion*) (social) club; (*résidence*) hostel; (*salon*) foyer; (*Optique, Photo*) focus; **lunettes à double** ~ bi-focal glasses
**FP** *sigle f* (= *franchise postale*) *exemption from postage*
**FPA** *sigle f* (= *Formation professionnelle pour adultes*) adult education
**FPLP** *sigle m* (= *Front populaire de la libération de la Palestine*) PFLP (= *Popular Front for the Liberation of Palestine*)
**fracas** [fRaka] *nm* din; crash
**fracassant, e** [fRakasɑ̃, -ɑ̃t] *adj* sensational, staggering
**fracasser** [fRakase] *vt* to smash; **se fracasser contre** *ou* **sur** to crash against
**fraction** [fRaksjɔ̃] *nf* fraction
**fractionnement** [fRaksjɔnmɑ̃] *nm* division
**fractionner** [fRaksjɔne] *vt* to divide (up), split (up)
**fracture** [fRaktyR] *nf* fracture; ~ **du crâne** fractured skull; ~ **de la jambe** broken leg
**fracturer** [fRaktyRe] *vt* (*coffre, serrure*) to break open; (*os, membre*) to fracture
**fragile** [fRa3il] *adj* fragile, delicate; (*fig*) frail
**fragiliser** [fRa3ilize] *vt* to weaken, make fragile
**fragilité** [fRa3ilite] *nf* fragility
**fragment** [fRagmɑ̃] *nm* (*d'un objet*) fragment, piece; (*d'un texte*) passage, extract
**fragmentaire** [fRagmɑ̃tɛR] *adj* sketchy
**fragmenter** [fRagmɑ̃te] *vt* to split up
**frai** [fRɛ] *nm* spawn; (*ponte*) spawning
**fraîche** [fRɛʃ] *adj f voir* **frais**
**fraîchement** [fRɛʃmɑ̃] *adv* (*sans enthousiasme*) coolly; (*récemment*) freshly, newly
**fraîcheur** [fRɛʃœR] *nf* coolness; freshness; *voir* **frais**

**fraîchir** [fʀeʃiʀ] *vi* to get cooler; *(vent)* to freshen
**frais, fraîche** [fʀe, fʀeʃ] *adj (air, eau, accueil)* cool; *(petit pois, œufs, nouvelles, couleur, troupes)* fresh; **le voilà ~!** he's in a (right) mess! ▷ *adv (récemment)* newly, fresh(ly); **il fait ~** it's cool; **servir ~** chill before serving, serve chilled ▷ *nm*: **mettre au ~** to put in a cool place; **prendre le ~** to take a breath of cool air ▷ *nmpl (débours)* expenses; *(Comm)* costs; charges; **faire des ~** to spend; to go to a lot of expense; **faire les ~ de** to bear the brunt of; **faire les ~ de la conversation** *(parler)* to do most of the talking; *(en être le sujet)* to be the topic of conversation; **il en a été pour ses ~** he could have spared himself the trouble; **rentrer dans ses ~** to recover one's expenses; **~ de déplacement** travel(ling) expenses; **~ d'entretien** upkeep; **~ généraux** overheads; **~ de scolarité** school fees, tuition *(US)*
**fraise** [fʀez] *nf* strawberry; *(Tech)* countersink (bit); *(de dentiste)* drill; **~ des bois** wild strawberry
**fraiser** [fʀeze] *vt* to countersink; *(Culin: pâte)* to knead
**fraiseuse** [fʀezøz] *nf (Tech)* milling machine
**fraisier** [fʀezje] *nm* strawberry plant
**framboise** [fʀɑ̃bwaz] *nf* raspberry
**framboisier** [fʀɑ̃bwazje] *nm* raspberry bush
**franc, franche** [fʀɑ̃, fʀɑ̃ʃ] *adj (personne)* frank, straightforward; *(visage)* open; *(net: refus, couleur)* clear; *(: coupure)* clean; *(intensif)* downright; *(exempt)*: **~ de port** free; *(boutique)* duty-free ▷ *adv*: **parler ~** to be frank *ou* candid ▷ *nm* franc
**français, e** [fʀɑ̃se, -ez] *adj* French ▷ *nm (Ling)* French ▷ *nm/f*: **Français, e** Frenchman/woman; **les F~** the French
**franc-comtois, e** *(mpl* **francs-comtois)** [fʀɑ̃kɔ̃twa, -waz] *adj ou* from (the) Franche-Comté
**France** [fʀɑ̃s] *nf*: **la ~** France; **en ~** in France; **~ 2, ~ 3** *public-sector television channels; see note*

**⊚ FRANCE TÉLÉVISION**

⊚ *France 2* and *France 3* are public-sector
⊚ television channels. France 2 is a national
⊚ general interest and entertainment
⊚ channel; France 3 provides regional news
⊚ and information as well as programmes for
⊚ the national network.

**Francfort** [fʀɑ̃kfɔʀ] *n* Frankfurt
**franche** [fʀɑ̃ʃ] *adj f voir* **franc**
**Franche-Comté** [fʀɑ̃ʃkɔ̃te] *nf* Franche-Comté
**franchement** [fʀɑ̃ʃmɑ̃] *adv* frankly; clearly; *(tout à fait)* downright ▷ *excl* well, really!; *voir* **franc**
**franchir** [fʀɑ̃ʃiʀ] *vt (obstacle)* to clear, get over; *(seuil, ligne, rivière)* to cross; *(distance)* to cover
**franchisage** [fʀɑ̃ʃizaʒ] *nm (Comm)* franchising
**franchise** [fʀɑ̃ʃiz] *nf* frankness; *(douanière, d'impôt)* exemption; *(Assurances)* excess; *(Comm)*

franchise; **~ de bagages** baggage allowance
**franchissable** [fʀɑ̃ʃisabl(ə)] *adj (obstacle)* surmountable
**francilien, ne** [fʀɑ̃siljɛ̃, -ɛn] *adj* of *ou* from the Île-de-France region ▷ *nm/f*: **Francilien, ne** person from the Île-de-France region
**franciscain, e** [fʀɑ̃siskɛ̃, -ɛn] *adj* Franciscan
**franciser** [fʀɑ̃size] *vt* to gallicize, Frenchify
**franc-jeu** [fʀɑ̃ʒø] *nm*: **jouer ~** to play fair
**franc-maçon** [fʀɑ̃masɔ̃] *(pl* **francs-maçons)** *nm* Freemason
**franc-maçonnerie** [fʀɑ̃masɔnʀi] *nf* Freemasonry
**franco** [fʀɑ̃ko] *adv (Comm)*: **~ (de port)** postage paid
**franco...** [fʀɑ̃ko] *préfixe* franco-
**franco-canadien** [fʀɑ̃kokanadjɛ̃] *nm (Ling)* Canadian French
**francophile** [fʀɑ̃kɔfil] *adj* Francophile
**francophobe** [fʀɑ̃kɔfɔb] *adj* Francophobe
**francophone** [fʀɑ̃kɔfɔn] *adj* French-speaking ▷ *nm/f* French speaker
**francophonie** [fʀɑ̃kɔfɔni] *nf* French-speaking communities *pl*
**franco-québécois** [fʀɑ̃kokebekwa] *nm (Ling)* Quebec French
**franc-parler** [fʀɑ̃paʀle] *nm inv* outspokenness
**franc-tireur** [fʀɑ̃tiʀœʀ] *nm (Mil)* irregular; *(fig)* freelance
**frange** [fʀɑ̃ʒ] *nf* fringe; *(cheveux)* fringe *(Brit)*, bangs *(US)*
**frangé, e** [fʀɑ̃ʒe] *adj (tapis, nappe)*: **~ de** trimmed with
**frangin** [fʀɑ̃ʒɛ̃] *nm (fam)* brother
**frangine** [fʀɑ̃ʒin] *nf (fam)* sis, sister
**frangipane** [fʀɑ̃ʒipan] *nf* almond paste
**franglais** [fʀɑ̃ɡlɛ] *nm* Franglais
**franquette** [fʀɑ̃ket]: **à la bonne ~** *adv* without any fuss
**frappant, e** [fʀapɑ̃, -ɑ̃t] *adj* striking
**frappe** [fʀap] *nf (d'une dactylo, pianiste, machine à écrire)* touch; *(Boxe)* punch; *(péj)* hood, thug
**frappé, e** [fʀape] *adj (Culin)* iced; **~ de panique** panic-stricken; **~ de stupeur** thunderstruck, dumbfounded
**frapper** [fʀape] *vt* to hit, strike; *(étonner)* to strike; *(monnaie)* to strike, stamp; **se frapper** *vi (s'inquiéter)* to get worked up; **~ à la porte** to knock at the door; **~ dans ses mains** to clap one's hands; **~ du poing sur** to bang one's fist on; **~ un grand coup** *(fig)* to strike a blow
**frasques** [fʀask(ə)] *nfpl* escapades; **faire des ~** to get up to mischief
**fraternel, le** [fʀatɛʀnɛl] *adj* brotherly, fraternal
**fraternellement** [fʀatɛʀnɛlmɑ̃] *adv* in a brotherly way
**fraterniser** [fʀatɛʀnize] *vi* to fraternize
**fraternité** [fʀatɛʀnite] *nf* brotherhood
**fratricide** [fʀatʀisid] *adj* fratricidal
**fraude** [fʀod] *nf* fraud; *(Scol)* cheating; **passer qch en ~** to smuggle sth in *(ou* out); **~ fiscale** tax evasion

## frauder | friterie

**frauder** [fʀode] *vi*, *vt* to cheat; **~ le fisc** to evade paying tax(es)

**fraudeur, -euse** [fʀodœʀ, -øz] *nm/f* person guilty of fraud; *(candidat)* candidate who cheats; *(au fisc)* tax evader

**frauduleusement** [fʀodyløzmɑ̃] *adv* fraudulently

**frauduleux, -euse** [fʀodylø, -øz] *adj* fraudulent

**frayer** [fʀeje] *vt* to open up, clear ▷ *vi* to spawn; *(fréquenter)*: **~ avec** to mix *ou* associate with; **se ~ un passage dans** to clear o.s. a path through, force one's way through

**frayeur** [fʀejœʀ] *nf* fright

**fredaines** [fʀəden] *nfpl* mischief *sg*, escapades

**fredonner** [fʀədɔne] *vt* to hum

**freezer** [fʀizœʀ] *nm* freezing compartment

**frégate** [fʀegat] *nf* frigate

**frein** [fʀɛ̃] *nm* brake; **mettre un ~ à** *(fig)* to put a brake on, check; **sans ~** *(sans limites)* unchecked; **~ à main** handbrake; **~ moteur** engine braking; **~s à disques** disc brakes; **~s à tambour** drum brakes

**freinage** [fʀɛnaʒ] *nm* braking; **distance de ~** braking distance; **traces de ~** tyre *(Brit) ou* tire *(US)* marks

**freiner** [fʀene] *vi* to brake ▷ *vt* *(progrès etc)* to check

**frelaté, e** [fʀəlate] *adj* adulterated; *(fig)* tainted

**frêle** [fʀɛl] *adj* frail, fragile

**frelon** [fʀəlɔ̃] *nm* hornet

**freluquet** [fʀəlyke] *nm* *(péj)* whippersnapper

**frémir** [fʀemiʀ] *vi* *(de froid, de peur)* to tremble, shiver; *(de joie)* to quiver; *(eau)* to (begin to) bubble

**frémissement** [fʀemismɑ̃] *nm* shiver; quiver; bubbling *no pl*

**frêne** [fʀɛn] *nm* ash (tree)

**frénésie** [fʀenezi] *nf* frenzy

**frénétique** [fʀenetik] *adj* frenzied, frenetic

**frénétiquement** [fʀenetikmɑ̃] *adv* frenetically

**fréon®** [fʀeɔ̃] *nm* Freon®

**fréquemment** [fʀekamɑ̃] *adv* frequently

**fréquence** [fʀekɑ̃s] *nf* frequency

**fréquent, e** [fʀekɑ̃, -ɑ̃t] *adj* frequent

**fréquentable** [fʀekɑ̃tabl(ə)] *adj*: **il est peu ~** he's not the type one can associate oneself with

**fréquentation** [fʀekɑ̃tasjɔ̃] *nf* frequenting; seeing; **fréquentations** *nfpl* company *sg*

**fréquenté, e** [fʀekɑ̃te] *adj*: **très ~** (very) busy; **mal ~** patronized by disreputable elements

**fréquenter** [fʀekɑ̃te] *vt* *(lieu)* to frequent; *(personne)* to see; **se fréquenter** to see a lot of each other

**frère** [fʀɛʀ] *nm* brother ▷ *adj*: **partis/pays ~s** sister parties/countries

**fresque** [fʀɛsk(ə)] *nf* *(Art)* fresco

**fret** [fʀɛ] *nm* freight

**fréter** [fʀete] *vt* to charter

**frétiller** [fʀetije] *vi* to wriggle; to quiver; **~ de la queue** to wag its tail

**fretin** [fʀətɛ̃] *nm*: **le menu ~** the small fry

**freudien, ne** [fʀødjɛ̃, -ɛn] *adj* Freudian

**freux** [fʀø] *nm* *(Zool)* rook

**friable** [fʀijabl(ə)] *adj* crumbly

**friand, e** [fʀijɑ̃, -ɑ̃d] *adj*: **~ de** very fond of ▷ *nm* *(Culin)* small minced-meat *(Brit) ou* ground-meat *(US)* pie; *(: sucré)* small almond cake

**friandise** [fʀijɑ̃diz] *nf* sweet

**fric** [fʀik] *nm* *(fam)* cash, bread

**fricassée** [fʀikase] *nf* fricassee

**fric-frac** [fʀikfʀak] *nm* break-in

**friche** [fʀiʃ]: **en ~** *adj*, *adv* (lying) fallow

**friction** [fʀiksjɔ̃] *nf* *(massage)* rub, rub-down; *(chez le coiffeur)* scalp massage; *(Tech, fig)* friction

**frictionner** [fʀiksjɔne] *vt* to rub (down); to massage

**frigidaire®** [fʀiʒidɛʀ] *nm* refrigerator

**frigide** [fʀiʒid] *adj* frigid

**frigidité** [fʀiʒidite] *nf* frigidity

**frigo** [fʀigo] *nm* (= *frigidaire*) fridge

**frigorifier** [fʀigɔʀifje] *vt* to refrigerate; *(fig: personne)* to freeze

**frigorifique** [fʀigɔʀifik] *adj* refrigerating

**frileusement** [fʀiløzmɑ̃] *adv* with a shiver

**frileux, -euse** [fʀilø, -øz] *adj* sensitive to (the) cold; *(fig)* overcautious

**frimas** [fʀima] *nmpl* wintry weather *sg*

**frime** [fʀim] *nf* *(fam)*: **c'est de la ~** it's all put on; **pour la ~** just for show

**frimer** [fʀime] *vi* to put on an act

**frimeur, -euse** [fʀimœʀ, -øz] *nm/f* poser

**frimousse** [fʀimus] *nf* (sweet) little face

**fringale** [fʀɛ̃gal] *nf*: **avoir la ~** to be ravenous

**fringant, e** [fʀɛ̃gɑ̃, -ɑ̃t] *adj* dashing

**fringues** [fʀɛ̃g] *nfpl* *(fam)* clothes, gear *no pl*

**fripé, e** [fʀipe] *adj* crumpled

**friperie** [fʀipʀi] *nf* *(commerce)* secondhand clothes shop; *(vêtements)* secondhand clothes

**fripes** [fʀip] *nfpl* secondhand clothes

**fripier, -ière** [fʀipje, -jɛʀ] *nm/f* secondhand clothes dealer

**fripon, ne** [fʀipɔ̃, -ɔn] *adj* roguish, mischievous ▷ *nm/f* rascal, rogue

**fripouille** [fʀipuj] *nf* scoundrel

**frire** [fʀiʀ] *vt* *(aussi:* **faire frire***)* ▷ *vi* to fry

**Frisbee®** [fʀizbi] *nm* Frisbee®

**frise** [fʀiz] *nf* frieze

**frisé, e** [fʀize] *adj* curly, curly-haired ▷ *nf*: **(chicorée) ~e** curly endive

**friser** [fʀize] *vt* to curl; *(fig: surface)* to skim, graze; *(: mort)* to come within a hair's breadth of; *(: hérésie)* to verge on ▷ *vi* *(cheveux)* to curl; *(personne)* to have curly hair; **se faire ~** to have one's hair curled

**frisette** [fʀizɛt] *nf* little curl

**frisotter** [fʀizɔte] *vi* *(cheveux)* to curl tightly

**frisquet** [fʀiskɛ] *adj m* chilly

**frisson** [fʀisɔ̃], **frissonnement** [fʀisɔnmɑ̃] *nm* shudder, shiver; quiver

**frissonner** [fʀisɔne] *vi* *(personne)* to shudder, shiver; *(feuilles)* to quiver

**frit, e** [fʀi, fʀit] *pp de* **frire** ▷ *adj* fried ▷ *nf*: **(pommes) ~es** chips *(Brit)*, French fries

**friterie** [fʀitʀi] *nf* ≈ chip shop *(Brit)*,

≈ hamburger stand (US)

**friteuse** [fʀitøz] nf chip pan (Brit), deep (fat) fryer

**friture** [fʀityʀ] nf (huile) (deep) fat; (plat): ~ **(de poissons)** fried fish; (Radio) crackle, crackling no pl; **fritures** nfpl (aliments frits) fried food sg

**frivole** [fʀivɔl] adj frivolous

**frivolité** [fʀivɔlite] nf frivolity

**froc** [fʀɔk] nm (Rel) habit; (fam: pantalon) trousers pl, pants pl

**froid, e** [fʀwa, fʀwad] adj cold ▷ nm cold; (absence de sympathie) coolness no pl; **il fait** ~ it's cold; **avoir** ~ to be cold; **prendre** ~ to catch a chill ou cold; **à** ~ adv (démarrer) (from) cold; **(pendant) les grands** ~**s** (in) the depths of winter, (during) the cold season; **jeter un** ~ (fig) to cast a chill; **être en** ~ **avec** to be on bad terms with; **battre** ~ **à qn** to give sb the cold shoulder

**froidement** [fʀwadmã] adv (accueillir) coldly; (décider) coolly

**froideur** [fʀwadœʀ] nf coolness no pl

**froisser** [fʀwase] vt to crumple (up), crease; (fig) to hurt, offend; **se froisser** vi to crumple, crease; to take offence (Brit) ou offense (US); **se** ~ **un muscle** to strain a muscle

**frôlement** [fʀolmã] nm (contact) light touch

**frôler** [fʀole] vt to brush against; (projectile) to skim past; (fig) to come within a hair's breadth of, come very close to

**fromage** [fʀɔmaʒ] nm cheese; ~ **blanc** soft white cheese; ~ **de tête** pork brawn

**fromager, -ère** [fʀɔmaʒe, -ɛʀ] nm/f cheese merchant ▷ adj (industrie) cheese cpd

**fromagerie** [fʀɔmaʒʀi] nf cheese dairy

**froment** [fʀɔmã] nm wheat

**fronce** [fʀɔ̃s] nf (de tissu) gather

**froncement** [fʀɔ̃smã] nm: ~ **de sourcils** frown

**froncer** [fʀɔ̃se] vt to gather; ~ **les sourcils** to frown

**frondaisons** [fʀɔ̃dɛzɔ̃] nfpl foliage sg

**fronde** [fʀɔ̃d] nf sling; (fig) rebellion, rebelliousness

**frondeur, -euse** [fʀɔ̃dœʀ, -øz] adj rebellious

**front** [fʀɔ̃] nm forehead, brow; (Mil, Météorologie, Pol) front; **avoir le** ~ **de faire** to have the effrontery to do; **de** ~ adv (se heurter) head-on; (rouler) together (2 or 3 abreast); (simultanément) at once; **faire** ~ **à** to face up to; ~ **de mer** (sea) front

**frontal, e, -aux** [fʀɔ̃tal, -o] adj frontal

**frontalier, -ière** [fʀɔ̃talje, -jɛʀ] adj border cpd, frontier cpd ▷ nm/f: **(travailleurs)** ~**s** workers who cross the border to go to work, commuters from across the border

**frontière** [fʀɔ̃tjɛʀ] nf (Géo, Pol) frontier, border; (fig) frontier, boundary

**frontispice** [fʀɔ̃tispis] nm frontispiece

**fronton** [fʀɔ̃tɔ̃] nm pediment; (de pelote basque) (front) wall

**frottement** [fʀɔtmã] nm rubbing, scraping; **frottements** nmpl (fig: difficultés) friction sg

**frotter** [fʀɔte] vi to rub, scrape ▷ vt to rub; (pour nettoyer) to rub (up); (: avec une brosse) to scrub; ~ **une allumette** to strike a match; **se** ~ **à qn** to cross swords with sb; **se** ~ **à qch** to come up against sth; **se** ~ **les mains** (fig) to rub one's hands (gleefully)

**frottis** [fʀɔti] nm (Méd) smear

**frottoir** [fʀɔtwaʀ] nm (d'allumettes) friction strip; (pour encaustiquer) (long-handled) brush

**frou-frou** [fʀufʀu] (pl **frous-frous**) nm rustle

**frousse** [fʀus] nf (fam: peur): **avoir la** ~ to be in a blue funk

**fructifier** [fʀyktifje] vi to yield a profit; **faire** ~ to turn to good account

**fructueux, -euse** [fʀyktɥø, -øz] adj fruitful; profitable

**frugal, e, -aux** [fʀygal, -o] adj frugal

**frugalement** [fʀygalmã] adv frugally

**frugalité** [fʀygalite] nf frugality

**fruit** [fʀɥi] nm fruit gen no pl; ~**s de mer** (Culin) seafood(s); ~**s secs** dried fruit sg

**fruité, e** [fʀɥite] adj (vin) fruity

**fruiterie** [fʀɥitʀi] nf (boutique) greengrocer's (Brit), fruit (and vegetable) store (US)

**fruitier, -ière** [fʀɥitje, -jɛʀ] adj: **arbre** ~ fruit tree ▷ nm/f fruiterer (Brit), fruit merchant (US)

**fruste** [fʀyst(ə)] adj unpolished, uncultivated

**frustrant, e** [fʀystʀã, -ãt] adj frustrating

**frustration** [fʀystʀasjɔ̃] nf frustration

**frustré, e** [fʀystʀe] adj frustrated

**frustrer** [fʀystʀe] vt to frustrate; (priver): ~ **qn de qch** to deprive sb of sth

**FS** abr (= franc suisse) FS, SF

**FSE** sigle m (= foyer socio-éducatif) community home

**FTP** sigle mpl (= Francs-tireurs et partisans) Communist Resistance in 1940–45

**fuchsia** [fyʃja] nm fuchsia

**fuel** [fjul], **fuel-oil** [fjulɔjl] nm fuel oil; (pour chauffer) heating oil

**fugace** [fygas] adj fleeting

**fugitif, -ive** [fyʒitif, -iv] adj (lueur, amour) fleeting; (prisonnier etc) runaway ▷ nm/f fugitive, runaway

**fugue** [fyg] nf (d'un enfant) running away no pl; (Mus) fugue; **faire une** ~ to run away, abscond

**fuir** [fɥiʀ] vt to flee from; (éviter) to shun ▷ vi to run away; (gaz, robinet) to leak

**fuite** [fɥit] nf flight; (écoulement) leak, leakage; (divulgation) leak; **être en** ~ to be on the run; **mettre en** ~ to put to flight; **prendre la** ~ to take flight

**fulgurant, e** [fylgyʀã, -ãt] adj lightning cpd, dazzling

**fulminant, e** [fylminã, -ãt] adj (lettre, regard) furious; ~ **de colère** raging with anger

**fulminer** [fylmine] vi: ~ **(contre)** to thunder forth (against)

**fumant, e** [fymã, -ãt] adj smoking; (liquide) steaming; **un coup** ~ (fam) a master stroke

**fumé, e** [fyme] adj (Culin) smoked; (verre) tinted ▷ nf smoke; **partir en** ~**e** to go up in smoke

**fume-cigarette** [fymsigaʀɛt] nm inv cigarette

holder

**fumer** [fyme] vi to smoke; (liquide) to steam ▷ vt to smoke; (terre, champ) to manure

**fumerie** [fymʀi] nf: ~ **d'opium** opium den

**fumerolles** [fymʀɔl] nfpl gas and smoke (from volcano)

**fûmes** [fym] vb voir **être**

**fumet** [fymɛ] nm aroma

**fumeur, -euse** [fymœʀ, -øz] nm/f smoker; **(compartiment)** ~**s** smoking compartment

**fumeux, -euse** [fymø, -øz] adj (péj) woolly (Brit), hazy

**fumier** [fymje] nm manure

**fumigation** [fymigɑsjɔ̃] nf fumigation

**fumigène** [fymiʒɛn] adj smoke cpd

**fumiste** [fymist(ə)] nm (ramoneur) chimney sweep ▷ nm/f (péj: paresseux) shirker; (charlatan) phoney

**fumisterie** [fymistəʀi] nf (péj) fraud, con

**fumoir** [fymwaʀ] nm smoking room

**funambule** [fynɑ̃byl] nm tightrope walker

**funèbre** [fynɛbʀ(ə)] adj funeral cpd; (fig) doleful; funereal

**funérailles** [fyneʀɑj] nfpl funeral sg

**funéraire** [fyneʀɛʀ] adj funeral cpd, funerary

**funeste** [fynɛst(ə)] adj disastrous; deathly

**funiculaire** [fynikylɛʀ] nm funicular (railway)

**FUNU** [fyny] sigle f (= Force d'urgence des Nations unies) UNEF (= United Nations Emergency Forces)

**fur** [fyʀ]: **au ~ et à mesure** adv as one goes along; **au ~ et à mesure que** as; **au ~ et à mesure de leur progression** as they advance (ou advanced)

**furax** [fyʀaks] adj inv (fam) livid

**furent** [fyʀ] vb voir **être**

**furet** [fyʀɛ] nm ferret

**fureter** [fyʀte] vi (péj) to nose about

**fureur** [fyʀœʀ] nf fury; (passion): ~ **de** passion for; **faire** ~ to be all the rage

**furibard, e** [fyʀibaʀ, -aʀd(ə)] adj (fam) livid, absolutely furious

**furibond, e** [fyʀibɔ̃, -ɔ̃d] adj livid, absolutely furious

**furie** [fyʀi] nf fury; (femme) shrew, vixen; **en ~** (mer) raging

**furieusement** [fyʀjøzmɑ̃] adv furiously

**furieux, -euse** [fyʀjø, -øz] adj furious

**furoncle** [fyʀɔ̃kl(ə)] nm boil

**furtif, -ive** [fyʀtif, -iv] adj furtive

**furtivement** [fyʀtivmɑ̃] adv furtively

**fus** [fy] vb voir **être**

**fusain** [fyzɛ̃] nm (Bot) spindle-tree; (Art) charcoal

**fuseau, x** [fyzo] nm (pantalon) (ski-)pants pl; (pour filer) spindle; **en ~** (jambes) tapering; (colonne) bulging; ~ **horaire** time zone

**fusée** [fyze] nf rocket; ~ **éclairante** flare

**fuselage** [fyzlaʒ] nm fuselage

**fuselé, e** [fyzle] adj slender; (galbé) tapering

**fuser** [fyze] vi (rires etc) to burst forth

**fusible** [fyzibl(ə)] nm (Élec: fil) fuse wire; (: fiche) fuse

**fusil** [fyzi] nm (de guerre, à canon rayé) rifle, gun; (de chasse, à canon lisse) shotgun, gun; ~ **à deux coups** double-barrelled rifle ou shotgun; ~ **sous-marin** spear-gun

**fusilier** [fyzilje] nm (Mil) rifleman

**fusillade** [fyzijad] nf gunfire no pl, shooting no pl; (combat) gun battle

**fusiller** [fyzije] vt to shoot; ~ **qn du regard** to look daggers at sb

**fusil-mitrailleur** [fyzimitʀajœʀ] (pl **fusils-mitrailleurs**) nm machine gun

**fusion** [fyzjɔ̃] nf fusion, melting; (fig) merging; (Comm) merger; **en ~** (métal, roches) molten

**fusionnement** [fyzjɔnmɑ̃] nm merger

**fusionner** [fyzjɔne] vi to merge

**fustiger** [fystiʒe] vt to denounce

**fut** [fy] vb voir **être**

**fût** [fy] vb voir **être** ▷ nm (tonneau) barrel, cask; (de canon) stock; (d'arbre) bole, trunk; (de colonne) shaft

**futaie** [fytɛ] nf forest, plantation

**futé, e** [fyte] adj crafty

**fûtes** [fyt] vb voir **être**

**futile** [fytil] adj (inutile) futile; (frivole) frivolous

**futilement** [fytilmɑ̃] adv frivolously

**futilité** [fytilite] nf futility; frivolousness; (chose futile) futile pursuit (ou thing etc)

**futon** [fytɔ̃] nm futon

**futur, e** [fytyʀ] adj, nm future; **son ~ époux** her husband-to-be; **au ~** (Ling) in the future

**futuriste** [fytyʀist(ə)] adj futuristic

**futurologie** [fytyʀɔlɔʒi] nf futurology

**fuyant, e** [fɥijɑ̃, -ɑ̃t] vb voir **fuir** ▷ adj (regard etc) evasive; (lignes etc) receding; (perspective) vanishing

**fuyard, e** [fɥijaʀ, -aʀd(ə)] nm/f runaway

**fuyons** etc [fɥijɔ̃] vb voir **fuir**

# Gg

**G, g** [ʒe] *nm inv* G, g ▷ *abr* (= *gramme*) g; (= *gauche*)
L, l; **G comme Gaston** G for George; **le G8** (*Pol*)
the G8 nations, the Group of Eight

**gabardine** [gabaʀdin] *nf* gabardine

**gabarit** [gabaʀi] *nm* (*fig: dimension, taille*) size;
(: *valeur*) calibre; (*Tech*) template; **du même ~**
(*fig*) of the same type, of that ilk

**gabegie** [gabʒi] *nf* (*péj*) chaos

**Gabon** [gabɔ̃] *nm*: **le ~** Gabon

**gabonais, e** [gabɔnɛ, -ɛz] *adj* Gabonese

**gâcher** [gaʃe] *vt* (*gâter*) to spoil, ruin; (*gaspiller*) to
waste; (*plâtre*) to temper; (*mortier*) to mix

**gâchette** [gaʃɛt] *nf* trigger

**gâchis** [gaʃi] *nm* (*désordre*) mess; (*gaspillage*)
waste *no pl*

**gadget** [gadʒɛt] *nm* thingumajig; (*nouveauté*)
gimmick

**gadin** [gadɛ̃] *nm* (*fam*): **prendre un ~** to come a
cropper (*Brit*)

**gadoue** [gadu] *nf* sludge

**gaélique** [gaelik] *adj* Gaelic ▷ *nm* (*Ling*) Gaelic

**gaffe** [gaf] *nf* (*instrument*) boat hook; (*fam: erreur*)
blunder; **faire ~** (*fam*) to watch out

**gaffer** [gafe] *vi* to blunder

**gaffeur, -euse** [gafœʀ, -øz] *nm/f* blunderer

**gag** [gag] *nm* gag

**gaga** [gaga] *adj* (*fam*) gaga

**gage** [gaʒ] *nm* (*dans un jeu*) forfeit; (*fig: de fidélité*)
token; **gages** *nmpl* (*salaire*) wages; (*garantie*)
guarantee *sg*; **mettre en ~** to pawn; **laisser en**
**~** to leave as security

**gager** [gaʒe] *vt*: **~ que** to bet *ou* wager that

**gageure** [gaʒyʀ] *nf*: **c'est une ~** it's attempting
the impossible

**gagnant, e** [gaɲɑ̃, -ɑ̃t] *adj*: **billet/numéro ~**
winning ticket/number ▷ *adv*: **jouer ~** (*aux*
*courses*) to be bound to win ▷ *nm/f* winner

**gagne-pain** [gaɲpɛ̃] *nm inv* job

**gagne-petit** [gaɲpəti] *nm inv* low wage earner

**gagner** [gaɲe] *vt* (*concours, procès, pari*) to win;
(*somme d'argent, revenu*) to earn; (*aller vers, atteindre*)
to reach; (*s'emparer de*) to overcome; (*envahir*) to
spread to; (*se concilier*): **~ qn** to win sb over ▷ *vi*
to win; (*fig*) to gain; **~ du temps/de la place** to
gain time/save space; **~ sa vie** to earn one's
living; **~ du terrain** (*aussi fig*) to gain ground; **~**

**qn de vitesse** to outstrip sb; (*aussi fig*): **~ à faire**
(*s'en trouver bien*) to be better off doing; **il y gagne**
it's in his interest, it's to his advantage

**gagneur** [gaɲœʀ] *nm* winner

**gai, e** [ge] *adj* cheerful; (*livre, pièce de théâtre*)
light-hearted; (*un peu ivre*) merry

**gaiement** [gemɑ̃] *adv* cheerfully

**gaieté** [gete] *nf* cheerfulness; **gaietés** *nfpl*
(*souvent ironique*) delights; **de ~ de cœur** with a
light heart

**gaillard, e** [gajaʀ, -aʀd(ə)] *adj* (*robuste*) sprightly;
(*grivois*) bawdy, ribald ▷ *nm/f* (*strapping*) fellow/
wench

**gaillardement** [gajaʀdəmɑ̃] *adv* cheerfully

**gain** [gɛ̃] *nm* (*revenu*) earnings *pl*; (*bénéfice: gén pl*)
profits *pl*; (*au jeu: gén pl*) winnings *pl*; (*fig: de*
*temps, place*) saving; (: *avantage*) benefit; (: *lucre*)
gain; **avoir ~ de cause** to win the case; (*fig*) to
be proved right; **obtenir ~ de cause** (*fig*) to win
out

**gaine** [gɛn] *nf* (*corset*) girdle; (*fourreau*) sheath;
(*de fil électrique etc*) outer covering

**gaine-culotte** [gɛnkylɔt] (*pl* **gaines-culottes**) *nf*
pantie girdle

**gainer** [gene] *vt* to cover

**gala** [gala] *nm* official reception; **soirée de ~**
gala evening

**galamment** [galamɑ̃] *adv* courteously

**galant, e** [galɑ̃, -ɑ̃t] *adj* (*courtois*) courteous,
gentlemanly; (*entreprenant*) flirtatious, gallant;
(*aventure, poésie*) amorous; **en ~e compagnie**
(*homme*) with a lady friend; (*femme*) with a
gentleman friend

**galanterie** [galɑ̃tʀi] *nf* gallantry

**galantine** [galɑ̃tin] *nf* galantine

**Galapagos** [galapagɔs] *nfpl*: **les (îles) ~** the
Galapagos Islands

**galaxie** [galaksi] *nf* galaxy

**galbe** [galb(ə)] *nm* curve(s); shapeliness

**galbé, e** [galbe] *adj* (*jambes*) (well-)rounded;
**bien ~** shapely

**gale** [gal] *nf* (*Méd*) scabies *sg*; (*de chien*) mange

**galéjade** [galeʒad] *nf* tall story

**galère** [galɛʀ] *nf* galley

**galérer** [galere] *vi* (*fam*) to work hard, slave
(away)

**galerie** [galʀi] *nf* gallery; (*Théât*) circle; (*de voiture*) roof rack; (*fig: spectateurs*) audience; ~ **marchande** shopping mall; ~ **de peinture** (private) art gallery

**galérien** [galeʀjɛ̃] *nm* galley slave

**galet** [galɛ] *nm* pebble; (*Tech*) wheel; **galets** *nmpl* pebbles, shingle *sg*

**galette** [galɛt] *nf* (*gâteau*) flat pastry cake; (*crêpe*) savoury pancake; **la ~ des Rois** *cake traditionally eaten on Twelfth Night*

**galeux, -euse** [galø, -øz] *adj*: **un chien ~** a mangy dog

**Galice** [galis] *nf*: **la ~** Galicia (*in Spain*)

**Galicie** [galisi] *nf*: **la ~** Galicia; (*in Central Europe*)

**galiléen, ne** [galileɛ̃, -ɛn] *adj* Galilean

**galimatias** [galimatja] *nm* (*péj*) gibberish

**galipette** [galipɛt] *nf*: **faire des ~s** to turn somersaults

**Galles** [gal] *nfpl*: **le pays de ~** Wales

**gallicisme** [galisism(ə)] *nm* French idiom; (*tournure fautive*) gallicism

**gallois, e** [galwa, -waz] *adj* Welsh ▷ *nm* (*Ling*) Welsh ▷ *nm/f*: **Gallois, e** Welshman(-woman)

**gallo-romain, e** [galoʀɔmɛ̃, -ɛn] *adj* Gallo-Roman

**galoche** [galɔʃ] *nf* clog

**galon** [galɔ̃] *nm* (*Mil*) stripe; (*décoratif*) piece of braid; **prendre du ~** to be promoted

**galop** [galo] *nm* gallop; **au ~** at a gallop; ~ **d'essai** (*fig*) trial run

**galopade** [galɔpad] *nf* stampede

**galopant, e** [galɔpɑ̃, -ɑ̃t] *adj*: **inflation ~e** galloping inflation; **démographie ~e** exploding population

**galoper** [galɔpe] *vi* to gallop

**galopin** [galɔpɛ̃] *nm* urchin, ragamuffin

**galvaniser** [galvanize] *vt* to galvanize

**galvaudé, e** [galvode] *adj* (*expression*) hackneyed; (*mot*) clichéd

**galvauder** [galvode] *vt* to debase

**gambade** [gɑ̃bad] *nf*: **faire des ~s** to skip *ou* frisk about

**gambader** [gɑ̃bade] *vi* to skip *ou* frisk about

**gamberger** [gɑ̃bɛʀʒe] (*fam*) *vi* to (have a) think ▷ *vt* to dream up

**Gambie** [gɑ̃bi] *nf*: **la ~** (*pays*) Gambia; (*fleuve*) the Gambia

**gamelle** [gamɛl] *nf* mess tin; billy can; (*fam*): **ramasser une ~** to fall flat on one's face

**gamin, e** [gamɛ̃, -in] *nm/f* kid ▷ *adj* mischievous, playful

**gaminerie** [gaminʀi] *nf* mischievousness, playfulness

**gamme** [gam] *nf* (*Mus*) scale; (*fig*) range

**gammé, e** [game] *adj*: **croix ~e** swastika

**Gand** [gɑ̃] *n* Ghent

**Gange** [gɑ̃ʒ] *nm*: **le ~** the Ganges

**gang** [gɑ̃g] *nm* gang

**ganglion** [gɑ̃glijɔ̃] *nm* ganglion; (*lymphatique*) gland; **avoir des ~s** to have swollen glands

**gangrène** [gɑ̃gʀɛn] *nf* gangrene; (*fig*) corruption; corrupting influence

**gangster** [gɑ̃gstɛʀ] *nm* gangster

**gangstérisme** [gɑ̃gsteʀism(ə)] *nm* gangsterism

**gangue** [gɑ̃g] *nf* coating

**ganse** [gɑ̃s] *nf* braid

**gant** [gɑ̃] *nm* glove; **prendre des ~s** (*fig*) to handle the situation with kid gloves; **relever le ~** (*fig*) to take up the gauntlet; ~ **de crin** massage glove; ~ **de toilette** (face) flannel (*Brit*), face cloth; **~s de boxe** boxing gloves; **~s de caoutchouc** rubber gloves

**ganté, e** [gɑ̃te] *adj*: ~ **de blanc** wearing white gloves

**ganterie** [gɑ̃tʀi] *nf* glove trade; (*magasin*) glove shop

**garage** [gaʀaʒ] *nm* garage; ~ **à vélos** bicycle shed

**garagiste** [gaʀaʒist(ə)] *nm/f* (*propriétaire*) garage owner; (*mécanicien*) garage mechanic

**garant, e** [gaʀɑ̃, -ɑ̃t] *nm/f* guarantor ▷ *nm* guarantee; **se porter ~ de** to vouch for; to be answerable for

**garantie** [gaʀɑ̃ti] *nf* guarantee, warranty; (*gage*) security, surety; **(bon de) ~** guarantee *ou* warranty slip; ~ **de bonne exécution** performance bond

**garantir** [gaʀɑ̃tiʀ] *vt* to guarantee; (*protéger*): ~ **de** to protect from; **je vous garantis que** I can assure you that; **garanti pure laine/2 ans** guaranteed pure wool/for 2 years

**garce** [gaʀs(ə)] *nf* (*péj*) bitch

**garçon** [gaʀsɔ̃] *nm* boy; (*célibataire*) bachelor; (*jeune homme*) boy, lad; (*aussi*: **garçon de café**) waiter; ~ **boucher/coiffeur** butcher's/hairdresser's assistant; ~ **de courses** messenger; ~ **d'écurie** stable lad; ~ **manqué** tomboy

**garçonnet** [gaʀsɔnɛ] *nm* small boy

**garçonnière** [gaʀsɔnjɛʀ] *nf* bachelor flat

**garde** [gaʀd(ə)] *nm* (*de prisonnier*) guard; (*de domaine etc*) warden; (*soldat, sentinelle*) guardsman ▷ *nf* guarding; looking after; (*soldats, Boxe, Escrime*) guard; (*faction*) watch; (*d'une arme*) hilt; (*Typo: aussi*: **page** *ou* **feuille de garde**) flyleaf; (: *collée*) endpaper; **de ~** *adj, adv* on duty; **monter la ~** to stand guard; **être sur ses ~s** to be on one's guard; **mettre en ~** to warn; **mise en ~** warning; **prendre ~ (à)** to be careful (of); **avoir la ~ des enfants** (*après divorce*) to have custody of the children; ~ **champêtre** *nm* rural policeman; ~ **du corps** *nm* bodyguard; ~ **d'enfants** *nf* child minder; ~ **forestier** *nm* forest warden; ~ **mobile** *nm, nf* mobile guard; ~ **des Sceaux** *nm* ≈ Lord Chancellor (*Brit*), ≈ Attorney General (*US*); ~ **à vue** *nf* (*Jur*) ≈ police custody

**garde-à-vous** [gaʀdavu] *nm inv*: **être/se mettre au ~** to be at/stand to attention; ~ **(fixe)!** (*Mil*) attention!

**garde-barrière** [gaʀdəbaʀjɛʀ] (*pl* **gardes-barrière(s)**) *nm/f* level-crossing keeper

**garde-boue** [gaʀdəbu] *nm inv* mudguard

**garde-chasse** [gaʀdəʃas] (*pl* **gardes-chasse(s)**)

*nm* gamekeeper

**garde-côte** [gaʀdəkot] *nm* (*vaisseau*) coastguard boat

**garde-feu** [gaʀdəfø] *nm inv* fender

**garde-fou** [gaʀdəfu] *nm* railing, parapet

**garde-malade** [gaʀdəmalad] (*pl* **gardes-malade(s)**) *nf* home nurse

**garde-manger** [gaʀdmɑ̃ʒe] *nm inv* (*boîte*) meat safe; (*placard*) pantry, larder

**garde-meuble** [gaʀdəmœbl(ə)] *nm* furniture depository

**garde-pêche** [gaʀdəpɛʃ] *nm inv* (*personne*) water bailiff; (*navire*) fisheries protection ship

**garder** [gaʀde] *vt* (*conserver*) to keep; (: *sur soi*: *vêtement, chapeau*) to keep on; (*surveiller*: *enfants*) to look after; (: *immeuble, lieu, prisonnier*) to guard; **se garder** *vi* (*aliment*: *se conserver*) to keep; **se ~ de faire** to be careful not to do; **~ le lit/la chambre** to stay in bed/indoors; **~ le silence** to keep silent *ou* quiet; **~ la ligne** to keep one's figure; **~ à vue** to keep in custody; **pêche/chasse gardée** private fishing/hunting (ground)

**garderie** [gaʀdəʀi] *nf* day nursery, crèche

**garde-robe** [gaʀdəʀɔb] *nf* wardrobe

**gardeur, -euse** [gaʀdœʀ, -øz] *nm/f* (*de vaches*) cowherd; (*de chèvres*) goatherd

**gardian** [gaʀdjɑ̃] *nm* cowboy (*in the Camargue*)

**gardien, ne** [gaʀdjɛ̃, -ɛn] *nm/f* (*garde*) guard; (*de prison*) warder; (*de domaine, réserve*) warden; (*de musée etc*) attendant; (*de phare, cimetière*) keeper; (*d'immeuble*) caretaker; (*fig*) guardian; **~ de but** goalkeeper; **~ de nuit** night watchman; **~ de la paix** policeman

**gardiennage** [gaʀdjɛnaʒ] *nm* (*emploi*) caretaking; **société de ~** security firm

**gardon** [gaʀdɔ̃] *nm* roach

**gare** [gaʀ] *nf* (*railway*) station, train station (*US*) ▷ *excl*: **~ à ...** mind ...!, watch out for ...!; **~ à ne pas ...** mind you don't ...; **~ à toi!** watch out!; **sans crier ~** without warning; **~ maritime** harbour station; **~ routière** coach (*Brit*) *ou* bus station; (*de camions*) haulage (*Brit*) *ou* trucking (*US*) depot; **~ de triage** marshalling yard

**garenne** [gaʀɛn] *nf voir* **lapin**

**garer** [gaʀe] *vt* to park; **se garer** *vi* to park; (*pour laisser passer*) to draw into the side

**gargantuesque** [gaʀgɑ̃tɥɛsk(ə)] *adj* gargantuan

**gargariser** [gaʀgaʀize]: **se gargariser** *vi* to gargle; **se ~ de** (*fig*) to revel in

**gargarisme** [gaʀgaʀism(ə)] *nm* gargling *no pl*; (*produit*) gargle

**gargote** [gaʀgɔt] *nf* cheap restaurant, greasy spoon (*fam*)

**gargouille** [gaʀguj] *nf* gargoyle

**gargouillement** [gaʀgujmɑ̃] *nm* = **gargouillis**

**gargouiller** [gaʀguje] *vi* (*estomac*) to rumble; (*eau*) to gurgle

**gargouillis** [gaʀguji] *nm* (*gén pl*: *voir vb*) rumbling; gurgling

**garnement** [gaʀnəmɑ̃] *nm* rascal, scallywag

**garni, e** [gaʀni] *adj* (*plat*) served with vegetables (*and chips, pasta or rice*) ▷ *nm* (*appartement*) furnished accommodation *no pl* (*Brit*) *ou* accommodations *pl* (*US*)

**garnir** [gaʀniʀ] *vt* to decorate; (*remplir*) to fill; (*recouvrir*) to cover; **se garnir** *vi* (*pièce, salle*) to fill up; **~ qch de** (*orner*) to decorate sth with; to trim sth with; (*approvisionner*) to fill *ou* stock sth with; (*protéger*) to fit sth with; (*Culin*) to garnish sth with

**garnison** [gaʀnizɔ̃] *nf* garrison

**garniture** [gaʀnityʀ] *nf* (*Culin*: *légumes*) vegetables *pl*; (: *persil etc*) garnish; (: *farce*) filling; (*décoration*) trimming; (*protection*) fittings *pl*; **~ de cheminée** mantelpiece ornaments *pl*; **~ de frein** (*Auto*) brake lining; **~ intérieure** (*Auto*) interior trim; **~ périodique** sanitary towel (*Brit*) *ou* napkin (*US*)

**garrigue** [gaʀig] *nf* scrubland

**garrot** [gaʀo] *nm* (*Méd*) tourniquet; (*torture*) garrotte

**garrotter** [gaʀote] *vt* to tie up; (*fig*) to muzzle

**gars** [gɑ] *nm* lad; (*type*) guy

**Gascogne** [gaskɔɲ] *nf*: **la ~** Gascony

**gascon, ne** [gaskɔ̃, -ɔn] *adj* Gascon ▷ *nm*: **G~** (*hâbleur*) braggart

**gas-oil** [gazɔjl] *nm* diesel oil

**gaspillage** [gaspijaʒ] *nm* waste

**gaspiller** [gaspije] *vt* to waste

**gaspilleur, -euse** [gaspijœʀ, -øz] *adj* wasteful

**gastrique** [gastʀik] *adj* gastric, stomach *cpd*

**gastro-entérite** [gastʀoɑ̃teʀit] *nf* (*Méd*) gastro-enteritis

**gastro-intestinal, e, -aux** [gastʀoɛ̃tɛstinal, -o] *adj* gastrointestinal

**gastronome** [gastʀɔnɔm] *nm/f* gourmet

**gastronomie** [gastʀɔnɔmi] *nf* gastronomy

**gastronomique** [gastʀɔnɔmik] *adj*: **menu ~** gourmet menu

**gâteau, x** [gɑto] *nm* cake ▷ *adj inv* (*fam*: *trop indulgent*): **papa-/maman-~** doting father/mother; **~ d'anniversaire** birthday cake; **~ de riz** rice pudding; **~ sec** biscuit

**gâter** [gɑte] *vt* to spoil; **se gâter** *vi* (*dent, fruit*) to go bad; (*temps, situation*) to change for the worse

**gâterie** [gɑtʀi] *nf* little treat

**gâteux, -euse** [gɑtø, -øz] *adj* senile

**gâtisme** [gɑtism(ə)] *nm* senility

**GATT** [gat] *sigle m* (= *General Agreement on Tariffs and Trade*) GATT

**gauche** [goʃ] *adj* left, left-hand; (*maladroit*) awkward, clumsy ▷ *nf* (*Pol*) left (wing); (*Boxe*) left; **à ~** on the left; (*direction*) (to the) left; **à ~ de** (on *ou* to the) left of; **à la ~ de** to the left of; **sur votre ~** on your left; **de ~** (*Pol*) left-wing

**gauchement** [goʃmɑ̃] *adv* awkwardly, clumsily

**gaucher, -ère** [goʃe, -ɛʀ] *adj* left-handed

**gaucherie** [goʃʀi] *nf* awkwardness, clumsiness

**gauchir** [goʃiʀ] *vt* (*planche, objet*) to warp; (*fig*: *fait, idée*) to distort

**gauchisant, e** [goʃizɑ̃, -ɑ̃t] *adj* with left-wing tendencies

191

**gauchisme** [goʃism(ə)] *nm* leftism

**gauchiste** [goʃist(ə)] *adj, nm/f* leftist

**gaufre** [gofʀ(ə)] *nf* (*pâtisserie*) waffle; (*de cire*) honeycomb

**gaufrer** [gofʀe] *vt* (*papier*) to emboss; (*tissu*) to goffer

**gaufrette** [gofʀɛt] *nf* wafer

**gaufrier** [gofʀije] *nm* (*moule*) waffle iron

**Gaule** [gol] *nf*: **la ~** Gaul

**gaule** [gol] *nf* (*perche*) (long) pole; (*canne à pêche*) fishing rod

**gauler** [gole] *vt* (*arbre*) to beat (*using a long pole to bring down fruit*); (*fruits*) to beat down (*with a pole*)

**gaullisme** [golism(ə)] *nm* Gaullism

**gaulliste** [golist(ə)] *adj, nm/f* Gaullist

**gaulois, e** [golwa, -waz] *adj* Gallic; (*grivois*) bawdy ▷ *nm/f*: **Gaulois, e** Gaul

**gauloiserie** [golwazʀi] *nf* bawdiness

**gausser** [gose]: **se ~ de** *vt* to deride

**gaver** [gave] *vt* to force-feed; (*fig*): **~ de** to cram with, fill up with; (*personne*): **se ~ de** to stuff o.s. with

**gay** [gɛ] *adj, nm* (*fam*) gay

**gaz** [gaz] *nm inv* gas; **mettre les ~** (*Auto*) to put one's foot down; **chambre/masque à ~** gas chamber/mask; **~ en bouteille** bottled gas; **~ butane** Calor gas® (*Brit*), butane gas; **~ carbonique** carbon dioxide; **~ hilarant** laughing gas; **~ lacrymogène** tear gas; **~ naturel** natural gas; **~ de ville** town gas (*Brit*), manufactured domestic gas

**gaze** [gaz] *nf* gauze

**gazéifié, e** [gazeifje] *adj* carbonated, aerated

**gazelle** [gazɛl] *nf* gazelle

**gazer** [gaze] *vt* to gas ▷ *vi* (*fam*) to be going *ou* working well

**gazette** [gazɛt] *nf* news sheet

**gazeux, -euse** [gazø, -øz] *adj* gaseous; (*eau*) sparkling; (*boisson*) fizzy

**gazoduc** [gazɔdyk] *nm* gas pipeline

**gazole** [gazɔl] *nm* = **gas-oil**

**gazomètre** [gazɔmɛtʀ(ə)] *nm* gasometer

**gazon** [gazɔ̃] *nm* (*herbe*) turf, grass; (*pelouse*) lawn

**gazonner** [gazɔne] *vt* (*terrain*) to grass over

**gazouillement** [gazujmɑ̃] *nm* (*voir vb*) chirping; babbling

**gazouiller** [gazuje] *vi* (*oiseau*) to chirp; (*enfant*) to babble

**gazouillis** [gazuji] *nmpl* chirp *sg*

**GB** *sigle f* (= *Grande Bretagne*) GB

**gd** *abr* (= *grand*) L

**GDF** *sigle m* (= *Gaz de France*) national gas company

**geai** [ʒɛ] *nm* jay

**géant, e** [ʒeɑ̃, -ɑ̃t] *adj* gigantic, giant; (*Comm*) giant-size ▷ *nm/f* giant

**geignement** [ʒɛɲmɑ̃] *nm* groaning, moaning

**geindre** [ʒɛ̃dʀ(ə)] *vi* to groan, moan

**gel** [ʒɛl] *nm* frost; (*de l'eau*) freezing; (*fig: des salaires, prix*) freeze; freezing; (*produit de beauté*) gel; **~ douche** shower gel

**gélatine** [ʒelatin] *nf* gelatine

**gélatineux, -euse** [ʒelatinø, -øz] *adj* jelly-like, gelatinous

**gelé, e** [ʒəle] *adj* frozen ▷ *nf* jelly; (*gel*) frost; **~ blanche** hoarfrost, white frost

**geler** [ʒəle] *vt, vi* to freeze; **il gèle** it's freezing

**gélule** [ʒelyl] *nf* capsule

**gelures** [ʒəlyʀ] *nfpl* frostbite *sg*

**Gémeaux** [ʒemo] *nmpl*: **les ~** Gemini, the Twins; **être des ~** to be Gemini

**gémir** [ʒemiʀ] *vi* to groan, moan

**gémissement** [ʒemismɑ̃] *nm* groan, moan

**gemme** [ʒɛm] *nf* gem(stone)

**gémonies** [ʒemɔni] *nfpl*: **vouer qn aux ~** to subject sb to public scorn

**gén.** *abr* (= *généralement*) gen.

**gênant, e** [ʒɛnɑ̃, -ɑ̃t] *adj* (*objet*) awkward, in the way; (*histoire, personne*) embarrassing

**gencive** [ʒɑ̃siv] *nf* gum

**gendarme** [ʒɑ̃daʀm(ə)] *nm* gendarme

**gendarmer** [ʒɑ̃daʀme]: **se gendarmer** *vi* to kick up a fuss

**gendarmerie** [ʒɑ̃daʀməʀi] *nf* military police force in countryside and small towns; their police station or barracks

**gendre** [ʒɑ̃dʀ(ə)] *nm* son-in-law

**gène** [ʒɛn] *nm* (*Bio*) gene

**gêne** [ʒɛn] *nf* (*à respirer, bouger*) discomfort, difficulty; (*dérangement*) bother, trouble; (*manque d'argent*) financial difficulties *pl ou* straits *pl*; (*confusion*) embarrassment; **sans ~** *adj* inconsiderate

**gêné, e** [ʒene] *adj* embarrassed; (*dépourvu d'argent*) short (of money)

**généalogie** [ʒenealɔʒi] *nf* genealogy

**généalogique** [ʒenealɔʒik] *adj* genealogical

**gêner** [ʒene] *vt* (*incommoder*) to bother; (*encombrer*) to hamper; (*bloquer le passage*) to be in the way of; (*déranger*) to bother; (*embarrasser*): **~ qn** to make sb feel ill-at-ease; **se gêner** to put o.s. out; **ne vous gênez pas!** (*ironique*) go right ahead!, don't mind me!; **je vais me ~!** (*ironique*) why should I care?

**général, e, -aux** [ʒeneʀal, -o] *adj, nm* general ▷ *nf*: (**répétition**) **~e** final dress rehearsal; **en ~** usually, in general; **à la satisfaction ~e** to everyone's satisfaction

**généralement** [ʒeneʀalmɑ̃] *adv* generally

**généralisable** [ʒeneʀalizabl(ə)] *adj* generally applicable

**généralisation** [ʒeneʀalizasjɔ̃] *nf* generalization

**généraliser** [ʒeneʀalize] *vt, vi* to generalize; **se généraliser** *vi* to become widespread

**généraliste** [ʒeneʀalist(ə)] *nm/f* (*Méd*) general practitioner, GP

**généralité** [ʒeneʀalite] *nf*: **la ~ des ...** the majority of ...; **généralités** *nfpl* generalities; (*introduction*) general points

**générateur, -trice** [ʒeneʀatœʀ, -tʀis] *adj*: **~ de** which causes *ou* brings about ▷ *nf* (*Élec*) generator

**génération** [ʒeneʀasjɔ̃] *nf* generation

**généreusement** [ʒeneʀøzmã] *adv* generously
**généreux, -euse** [ʒeneʀø, -øz] *adj* generous
**générique** [ʒeneʀik] *adj* generic ▷ *nm* (*Ciné, TV*) credits *pl*, credit titles *pl*
**générosité** [ʒeneʀozite] *nf* generosity
**Gênes** [ʒɛn] *n* Genoa
**genèse** [ʒənɛz] *nf* genesis
**genêt** [ʒənɛ] *nm* (*Bot*) broom *no pl*
**généticien, ne** [ʒenetisjɛ̃, -ɛn] *nm/f* geneticist
**génétique** [ʒenetik] *adj* genetic ▷ *nf* genetics *sg*
**génétiquement** [ʒenetikmã] *adv* genetically
**gêneur, -euse** [ʒɛnœʀ, -øz] *nm/f* (*personne qui gêne*) obstacle; (*importun*) intruder
**Genève** [ʒənɛv] *n* Geneva
**genevois, e** [ʒənəvwa, -waz] *adj* Genevan
**genévrier** [ʒənevʀije] *nm* juniper
**génial, e, -aux** [ʒenjal, -o] *adj* of genius; (*fam*) fantastic, brilliant
**génie** [ʒeni] *nm* genius; (*Mil*): **le ~** ≈ the Engineers *pl*; **avoir du ~** to have genius; **~ civil** civil engineering; **~ génétique** genetic engineering
**genièvre** [ʒənjɛvʀ(ə)] *nm* (*Bot*) juniper (tree); (*boisson*) Dutch gin; **grain de ~** juniper berry
**génisse** [ʒenis] *nf* heifer; **foie de ~** ox liver
**génital, e, -aux** [ʒenital, -o] *adj* genital
**génitif** [ʒenitif] *nm* genitive
**génocide** [ʒenɔsid] *nm* genocide
**génois, e** [ʒenwa, -waz] *adj* Genoese ▷ *nf* (*gâteau*) ≈ sponge cake
**genou, x** [ʒnu] *nm* knee; **à ~x** on one's knees; **se mettre à ~x** to kneel down
**genouillère** [ʒənujɛʀ] *nf* (*Sport*) kneepad
**genre** [ʒɑ̃ʀ] *nm* (*espèce, sorte*) kind, type, sort; (*allure*) manner; (*Ling*) gender; (*Art*) genre; (*Zool etc*) genus; **se donner du ~** to give o.s. airs; **avoir bon ~** to have style; **avoir mauvais ~** to be ill-mannered
**gens** [ʒɑ̃] *nmpl* (*f in some phrases*) people *pl*; **les ~ d'Église** the clergy; **les ~ du monde** society people; **~ de maison** domestics
**gentiane** [ʒɑ̃sjan] *nf* gentian
**gentil, le** [ʒɑ̃ti, -ij] *adj* kind; (*enfant: sage*) good; (*sympa: endroit etc*) nice; **c'est très ~ à vous** it's very kind *ou* good *ou* nice of you
**gentilhommière** [ʒɑ̃tijɔmjɛʀ] *nf* (small) manor house *ou* country seat
**gentillesse** [ʒɑ̃tijɛs] *nf* kindness
**gentillet, te** [ʒɑ̃tijɛ, -ɛt] *adj* nice little
**gentiment** [ʒɑ̃timɑ̃] *adv* kindly
**génuflexion** [ʒenyflɛksjɔ̃] *nf* genuflexion
**géo** *abr* (= *géographie*) geography
**géodésique** [ʒeɔdezik] *adj* geodesic
**géographe** [ʒeɔgʀaf] *nm/f* geographer
**géographie** [ʒeɔgʀafi] *nf* geography
**géographique** [ʒeɔgʀafik] *adj* geographical
**geôlier** [ʒolje] *nm* jailer
**géologie** [ʒeɔlɔʒi] *nf* geology
**géologique** [ʒeɔlɔʒik] *adj* geological
**géologiquement** [ʒeɔlɔʒikmã] *adv* geologically
**géologue** [ʒeɔlɔg] *nm/f* geologist
**géomètre** [ʒeɔmɛtʀ(ə)] *nm*: (**arpenteur-**)~

(land) surveyor
**géométrie** [ʒeɔmetʀi] *nf* geometry; **à ~ variable** (*Aviat*) swing-wing
**géométrique** [ʒeɔmetʀik] *adj* geometric
**géophysique** [ʒeɔfizik] *nf* geophysics *sg*
**géopolitique** [ʒeɔpɔlitik] *nf* geopolitics *sg*
**Géorgie** [ʒeɔʀʒi] *nf*: **la ~** (*URSS, USA*) Georgia; **la ~ du Sud** South Georgia
**géorgien, ne** [ʒeɔʀʒjɛ̃, -ɛn] *adj* Georgian
**géostationnaire** [ʒeɔstasjɔnɛʀ] *adj* geostationary
**géothermique** [ʒeɔtɛʀmik] *adj*: **énergie ~** geothermal energy
**gérance** [ʒeʀɑ̃s] *nf* management; **mettre en ~** to appoint a manager for; **prendre en ~** to take over (the management of)
**géranium** [ʒeʀanjɔm] *nm* geranium
**gérant, e** [ʒeʀɑ̃, -ɑ̃t] *nm/f* manager/manageress; **~ d'immeuble** managing agent
**gerbe** [ʒɛʀb(ə)] *nf* (*de fleurs, d'eau*) spray; (*de blé*) sheaf; (*fig*) shower, burst
**gercé, e** [ʒɛʀse] *adj* chapped
**gercer** [ʒɛʀse] *vi*, **se gercer** *vi* to chap
**gerçure** [ʒɛʀsyʀ] *nf* crack
**gérer** [ʒeʀe] *vt* to manage
**gériatrie** [ʒeʀjatʀi] *nf* geriatrics *sg*
**gériatrique** [ʒeʀjatʀik] *adj* geriatric
**germain, e** [ʒɛʀmɛ̃, -ɛn] *adj*: **cousin ~** first cousin
**germanique** [ʒɛʀmanik] *adj* Germanic
**germaniste** [ʒɛʀmanist(ə)] *nm/f* German scholar
**germe** [ʒɛʀm(ə)] *nm* germ
**germer** [ʒɛʀme] *vi* to sprout; (*semence, aussi fig*) to germinate
**gérondif** [ʒeʀɔ̃dif] *nm* gerund; (*en latin*) gerundive
**gérontologie** [ʒeʀɔ̃tɔlɔʒi] *nf* gerontology
**gérontologue** [ʒeʀɔ̃tɔlɔg] *nm/f* gerontologist
**gésier** [ʒezje] *nm* gizzard
**gésir** [ʒeziʀ] *vi* to be lying (down); *voir aussi* **ci-gît**
**gestation** [ʒɛstasjɔ̃] *nf* gestation
**geste** [ʒɛst(ə)] *nm* gesture; move; motion; **il fit un ~ de la main pour m'appeler** he signed to me to come over, he waved me over; **ne faites pas un ~** (*ne bougez pas*) don't move
**gesticuler** [ʒɛstikyle] *vi* to gesticulate
**gestion** [ʒɛstjɔ̃] *nf* management; **~ des disques** (*Inform*) housekeeping; **~ de fichier(s)** (*Inform*) file management
**gestionnaire** [ʒɛstjɔnɛʀ] *nm/f* administrator; **~ de fichiers** (*Inform*) file manager
**geyser** [ʒezɛʀ] *nm* geyser
**Ghana** [gana] *nm*: **le ~** Ghana
**ghetto** [geto] *nm* ghetto
**gibecière** [ʒibsjɛʀ] *nf* (*de chasseur*) gamebag; (*sac en bandoulière*) shoulder bag
**gibelotte** [ʒiblɔt] *nf* rabbit fricassee in white wine
**gibet** [ʒibɛ] *nm* gallows *pl*
**gibier** [ʒibje] *nm* (*animaux*) game; (*fig*) prey
**giboulée** [ʒibule] *nf* sudden shower
**giboyeux, -euse** [ʒibwajø, -øz] *adj* well-stocked

**g**

with game

**Gibraltar** [ʒibʀaltaʀ] *nm* Gibraltar

**gibus** [ʒibys] *nm* opera hat

**giclée** [ʒikle] *nf* spurt, squirt

**gicler** [ʒikle] *vi* to spurt, squirt

**gicleur** [ʒiklœʀ] *nm* (Auto) jet

**GIE** *sigle m* = **groupement d'intérêt économique**

**gifle** [ʒifl(ə)] *nf* slap (in the face)

**gifler** [ʒifle] *vt* to slap (in the face)

**gigantesque** [ʒigɑ̃tɛsk(ə)] *adj* gigantic

**gigantisme** [ʒigɑ̃tism(ə)] *nm* (Méd) gigantism; (des mégalopoles) vastness

**gigaoctet** [ʒigaɔktɛ] *nm* gigabyte

**GIGN** *sigle m* (= Groupe d'intervention de la gendarmerie nationale) special crack force of the gendarmerie, ≈ SAS (Brit)

**gigogne** [ʒigɔɲ] *adj*: **lits ~s** truckle (Brit) *ou* trundle (US) beds; **tables/poupées ~s** nest of tables/dolls

**gigolo** [ʒigolo] *nm* gigolo

**gigot** [ʒigo] *nm* leg (of mutton *ou* lamb)

**gigoter** [ʒigɔte] *vi* to wriggle (about)

**gilet** [ʒilɛ] *nm* waistcoat; (pull) cardigan; (de corps) vest; **~ pare-balles** bulletproof jacket; **~ de sauvetage** life jacket

**gin** [dʒin] *nm* gin

**gingembre** [ʒɛ̃ʒɑ̃bʀ(ə)] *nm* ginger

**gingivite** [ʒɛ̃ʒivit] *nf* inflammation of the gums, gingivitis

**ginseng** [ʒinsɛŋ] *nm* ginseng

**girafe** [ʒiʀaf] *nf* giraffe

**giratoire** [ʒiʀatwaʀ] *adj*: **sens ~** roundabout

**girofle** [ʒiʀɔfl(ə)] *nm*: **clou de ~** clove

**giroflée** [ʒiʀɔfle] *nf* wallflower

**girolle** [ʒiʀɔl] *nf* chanterelle

**giron** [ʒiʀɔ̃] *nm* (genoux) lap; (fig: sein) bosom

**Gironde** [ʒiʀɔ̃d] *nf*: **la ~** the Gironde

**girophare** [ʒiʀɔfaʀ] *nm* revolving (flashing) light

**girouette** [ʒiʀwɛt] *nf* weather vane *ou* cock

**gis** [ʒi], **gisais** *etc* [ʒizɛ] *vb voir* **gésir**

**gisement** [ʒizmɑ̃] *nm* deposit

**gît** [ʒi] *vb voir* **gésir**

**gitan, e** [ʒitɑ̃, -an] *nm/f* gipsy

**gîte** [ʒit] *nm* home; shelter; (du lièvre) form; **~ (rural)** (country) holiday cottage *ou* apartment

**gîter** [ʒite] *vi* (Navig) to list

**givrage** [ʒivʀaʒ] *nm* icing

**givrant, e** [ʒivʀɑ̃, -ɑ̃t] *adj*: **brouillard ~** freezing fog

**givre** [ʒivʀ(ə)] *nm* (hoar)frost

**givré, e** [ʒivʀe] *adj*: **citron ~/orange ~e** lemon/orange sorbet (served in fruit skin)

**glabre** [glabʀ(ə)] *adj* hairless; (menton) clean-shaven

**glaçage** [glasaʒ] *nm* (au sucre) icing; (au blanc d'œuf, de la viande) glazing

**glace** [glas] *nf* ice; (crème glacée) ice cream; (verre) sheet of glass; (miroir) mirror; (de voiture) window; **glaces** *nfpl* (Géo) ice sheets, ice *sg*; **de ~** (fig: accueil, visage) frosty, icy; **rester de ~** to remain unmoved

**glacé, e** [glase] *adj* icy; (boisson) iced

**glacer** [glase] *vt* to freeze; (boisson) to chill, ice; (gâteau) to ice (Brit), frost (US); (papier, tissu) to glaze; (fig): **~ qn** to chill sb; (fig) to make sb's blood run cold

**glaciaire** [glasjɛʀ] *adj* (période) ice *cpd*; (relief) glacial

**glacial, e** [glasjal] *adj* icy

**glacier** [glasje] *nm* (Géo) glacier; (marchand) ice-cream maker

**glacière** [glasjɛʀ] *nf* icebox

**glaçon** [glasɔ̃] *nm* icicle; (pour boisson) ice cube

**gladiateur** [gladjatœʀ] *nm* gladiator

**glaïeul** [glajœl] *nm* gladiola

**glaire** [glɛʀ] *nf* (Méd) phlegm *no pl*

**glaise** [glɛz] *nf* clay

**glaive** [glɛv] *nm* two-edged sword

**gland** [glɑ̃] *nm* (de chêne) acorn; (décoration) tassel; (Anat) glans

**glande** [glɑ̃d] *nf* gland

**glander** [glɑ̃de] *vi* (fam) to fart around (Brit) (!), screw around (US) (!)

**glaner** [glane] *vt, vi* to glean

**glapir** [glapiʀ] *vi* to yelp

**glapissement** [glapismɑ̃] *nm* yelping

**glas** [glɑ] *nm* knell, toll

**glauque** [glok] *adj* dull blue-green

**glissade** [glisad] *nf* (par jeu) slide; (chute) slip; (dérapage) skid; **faire des ~s** to slide

**glissant, e** [glisɑ̃, -ɑ̃t] *adj* slippery

**glisse** [glis] *nf*: **sports de ~** sports involving sliding or gliding (eg skiing, surfing, windsurfing)

**glissement** [glismɑ̃] *nm* sliding; (fig) shift; **~ de terrain** landslide

**glisser** [glise] *vi* (avancer) to glide *ou* slide along; (coulisser, tomber) to slide; (déraper) to slip; (être glissant) to be slippery ▷ *vt*: **~ qch sous/dans/à** to slip sth under/into/to; **~ sur** (fig: détail etc) to skate over; **se ~ dans/entre** to slip into/between

**glissière** [glisjɛʀ] *nf* slide channel; **à ~** (porte, fenêtre) sliding; **~ de sécurité** (Auto) crash barrier

**glissoire** [gliswaʀ] *nf* slide

**global, e, -aux** [glɔbal, -o] *adj* overall

**globalement** [glɔbalmɑ̃] *adv* taken as a whole

**globe** [glɔb] *nm* globe; **sous ~** under glass; **~ oculaire** eyeball; **le ~ terrestre** the globe

**globe-trotter** [glɔbtʀɔtœʀ] *nm* globe-trotter

**globule** [glɔbyl] *nm* (du sang): **~ blanc/rouge** white/red corpuscle

**globuleux, -euse** [glɔbylø, -øz] *adj*: **yeux ~** protruding eyes

**gloire** [glwaʀ] *nf* glory; (mérite) distinction, credit; (personne) celebrity

**glorieux, -euse** [glɔʀjø, -øz] *adj* glorious

**glorifier** [glɔʀifje] *vt* to glorify, extol; **se ~ de** to glory in

**gloriole** [glɔʀjɔl] *nf* vainglory

**glose** [gloz] *nf* gloss

**glossaire** [glɔsɛʀ] *nm* glossary

**glotte** [glɔt] *nf* (Anat) glottis

**glouglouter** [gluglute] *vi* to gurgle

**gloussement** [glusmã] nm (de poule) cluck; (rire) chuckle
**glousser** [gluse] vi to cluck; (rire) to chuckle
**glouton, ne** [glutɔ̃, -ɔn] adj gluttonous, greedy
**gloutonnerie** [glutɔnʀi] nf gluttony
**glu** [gly] nf birdlime
**gluant, e** [glyã, -ãt] adj sticky, gummy
**glucide** [glysid] nm carbohydrate
**glucose** [glykoz] nm glucose
**gluten** [glytɛn] nm gluten
**glycérine** [gliseʀin] nf glycerine
**glycine** [glisin] nf wisteria
**GMT** sigle adj (= Greenwich Mean Time) GMT
**gnangnan** [nãnã] adj inv (fam: livre, film) soppy
**GNL** sigle m (= gaz naturel liquéfié) LNG (= liquefied natural gas)
**gnôle** [njol] nf (fam) booze no pl; **un petit verre de ~** a drop of the hard stuff
**gnome** [gnom] nm gnome
**gnon** [nɔ̃] nm (fam: coup de poing) bash; (: marque) dent
**GO** sigle fpl (= grandes ondes) LW ▷ sigle m (= gentil organisateur) title given to leaders on Club Méditerranée holidays; extended to refer to easy-going leader of any group
**Go** abr (= gigaoctet) GB
**go** [go]: **tout de go** adv straight out
**goal** [gol] nm goalkeeper
**gobelet** [gɔblɛ] nm (en métal) tumbler; (en plastique) beaker; (à dés) cup
**gober** [gɔbe] vt to swallow
**goberger** [gɔbɛʀʒe]: **se goberger** vi to cosset o.s.
**Gobi** [gɔbi] n: **désert de ~** Gobi Desert
**godasse** [gɔdas] nf (fam) shoe
**godet** [gɔdɛ] nm pot; (Couture) unpressed pleat
**godiller** [gɔdije] vi (Navig) to scull; (Ski) to wedeln
**goéland** [gɔelã] nm (sea)gull
**goélette** [gɔelɛt] nf schooner
**goémon** [gɔemɔ̃] nm wrack
**gogo** [gɔgo] nm (péj) mug, sucker; **à ~** adv galore
**goguenard, e** [gɔgnaʀ, -aʀd(ə)] adj mocking
**goguette** [gɔgɛt] nf: **en ~** on the binge
**goinfre** [gwɛ̃fʀ(ə)] nm glutton
**goinfrer** [gwɛ̃fʀe]: **se goinfrer** vi to make a pig of o.s.; **se ~ de** to guzzle
**goitre** [gwatʀ(ə)] nm goitre
**golf** [gɔlf] nm (jeu) golf; (terrain) golf course; **~ miniature** crazy ou miniature golf
**golfe** [gɔlf(ə)] nm gulf; bay; **le ~ d'Aden** the Gulf of Aden; **le ~ de Gascogne** the Bay of Biscay; **le ~ du Lion** the Gulf of Lions; **le ~ Persique** the Persian Gulf
**golfeur, -euse** [gɔlfœʀ, -øz] nm/f golfer
**gominé, e** [gɔmine] adj slicked down
**gomme** [gɔm] nf (à effacer) rubber (Brit), eraser; (résine) gum; **boule** ou **pastille de ~** throat pastille
**gommé, e** [gɔme] adj: **papier ~** gummed paper
**gommer** [gɔme] vt (effacer) to rub out (Brit), erase; (enduire de gomme) to gum
**gond** [gɔ̃] nm hinge; **sortir de ses ~s** (fig) to fly off the handle

**gondole** [gɔ̃dɔl] nf gondola; (pour l'étalage) shelves pl, gondola
**gondoler** [gɔ̃dɔle]: **se gondoler** vi to warp, buckle; (fam: rire) to hoot with laughter; to be in stitches
**gondolier** [gɔ̃dɔlje] nm gondolier
**gonflable** [gɔ̃flabl(ə)] adj inflatable
**gonflage** [gɔ̃flaʒ] nm inflating, blowing up
**gonflé, e** [gɔ̃fle] adj swollen; (ventre) bloated; (fam: culotté): **être ~** to have a nerve
**gonflement** [gɔ̃fləmã] nm inflation; (Méd) swelling
**gonfler** [gɔ̃fle] vt (pneu, ballon) to inflate, blow up; (nombre, importance) to inflate ▷ vi (pied etc) to swell (up); (Culin: pâte) to rise
**gonfleur** [gɔ̃flœʀ] nm air pump
**gong** [gɔ̃g] nm gong
**gonzesse** [gɔ̃zɛs] nf (fam) chick, bird (Brit)
**goret** [gɔʀɛ] nm piglet
**gorge** [gɔʀʒ(ə)] nf (Anat) throat; (poitrine) breast; (Géo) gorge; (rainure) groove; **avoir mal à la ~** to have a sore throat; **avoir la ~ serrée** to have a lump in one's throat
**gorgé, e** [gɔʀʒe] adj: **~ de** filled with; (eau) saturated with ▷ nf mouthful; sip; gulp; **boire à petites/grandes ~es** to take little sips/big gulps
**gorille** [gɔʀij] nm gorilla; (fam) bodyguard
**gosier** [gozje] nm throat
**gosse** [gɔs] nm/f kid
**gothique** [gɔtik] adj gothic
**gouache** [gwaʃ] nf gouache
**gouaille** [gwaj] nf street wit, cocky humour (Brit) ou humor (US)
**goudron** [gudʀɔ̃] nm (asphalte) tar(mac) (Brit), asphalt; (du tabac) tar
**goudronner** [gudʀɔne] vt to tar(mac) (Brit), asphalt
**gouffre** [gufʀ(ə)] nm abyss, gulf
**goujat** [guʒa] nm boor
**goujon** [guʒɔ̃] nm gudgeon
**goulée** [gule] nf gulp
**goulet** [gulɛ] nm bottleneck
**goulot** [gulo] nm neck; **boire au ~** to drink from the bottle
**goulu, e** [guly] adj greedy
**goulûment** [gulymã] adv greedily
**goupille** [gupij] nf (metal) pin
**goupiller** [gupije] vt to pin (together)
**goupillon** [gupijɔ̃] nm (Rel) sprinkler; (brosse) bottle brush; **le ~** (fig) the cloth, the clergy
**gourd, e** [guʀ, guʀd(ə)] adj numb (with cold); (fam) oafish
**gourde** [guʀd(ə)] nf (récipient) flask; (fam) (clumsy) clot ou oaf
**gourdin** [guʀdɛ̃] nm club, bludgeon
**gourer** [guʀe] (fam): **se gourer** vi to boob
**gourmand, e** [guʀmã, -ãd] adj greedy
**gourmandise** [guʀmãdiz] nf greed; (bonbon) sweet (Brit), piece of candy (US)
**gourmet** [guʀmɛ] nm epicure
**gourmette** [guʀmɛt] nf chain bracelet
**gourou** [guʀu] nm guru

**g**

195

**gousse** [gus] nf (de vanille etc) pod; ~ **d'ail** clove of garlic

**gousset** [gusɛ] nm (de gilet) fob

**goût** [gu] nm taste; (fig: appréciation) taste, liking; **le (bon)** ~ good taste; **de bon** ~ in good taste, tasteful; **de mauvais** ~ in bad taste, tasteless; **avoir bon/mauvais** ~ (aliment) to taste nice/nasty; (personne) to have good/bad taste; **avoir du/manquer de** ~ to have/lack taste; **avoir du** ~ **pour** to have a liking for; **prendre** ~ **à** to develop a taste ou a liking for

**goûter** [gute] vt (essayer) to taste; (apprécier) to enjoy ▷ vi to have (afternoon) tea ▷ nm (afternoon) tea; ~ **à** to taste, sample; ~ **de** to have a taste of; ~ **d'enfants/d'anniversaire** children's tea/birthday party

**goutte** [gut] nf drop; (Méd) gout; (alcool) nip (Brit), tot (Brit), drop (US); **gouttes** nfpl (Méd) drops; ~ **à** ~ adv a drop at a time; **tomber** ~ **à** ~ to drip

**goutte-à-goutte** [gutagut] nm inv (Méd) drip; **alimenter au** ~ to drip-feed

**gouttelette** [gutlɛt] nf droplet

**goutter** [gute] vi to drip

**gouttière** [gutjɛʀ] nf gutter

**gouvernail** [guvɛʀnaj] nm rudder; (barre) helm, tiller

**gouvernant, e** [guvɛʀnɑ̃, -ɑ̃t] adj ruling cpd ▷ nf housekeeper; (d'un enfant) governess

**gouverne** [guvɛʀn(ə)] nf: **pour sa** ~ for his guidance

**gouvernement** [guvɛʀnəmɑ̃] nm government

**gouvernemental, e, -aux** [guvɛʀnəmɑ̃tal, -o] adj (politique) government cpd; (journal, parti) pro-government

**gouverner** [guvɛʀne] vt to govern; (diriger) to steer; (fig) to control

**gouverneur** [guvɛʀnœʀ] nm governor; (Mil) commanding officer

**goyave** [gɔjav] nf guava

**GPL** sigle m (= gaz de pétrole liquéfié) LPG (= liquefied petroleum gas)

**GQG** sigle m (= grand quartier général) GHQ

**grabataire** [gʀabatɛʀ] adj bedridden ▷ nm/f bedridden invalid

**grâce** [gʀɑs] nf grace; (faveur) favour; (Jur) pardon; **grâces** nfpl (Rel) grace sg; **de bonne/mauvaise** ~ with (a) good/bad grace; **dans les bonnes** ~**s de qn** in favour with sb; **faire** ~ **à qn de qch** to spare sb sth; **rendre** ~(**s**) **à** to give thanks to; **demander** ~ to beg for mercy; **droit de** ~ right of reprieve; **recours en** ~ plea for pardon; ~ **à** prép thanks to

**gracier** [gʀasje] vt to pardon

**gracieusement** [gʀasjøzmɑ̃] adv graciously, kindly; (gratuitement) freely; (avec grâce) gracefully

**gracieux, -euse** [gʀasjø, -øz] adj (charmant, élégant) graceful; (aimable) gracious, kind; **à titre** ~ free of charge

**gracile** [gʀasil] adj slender

**gradation** [gʀadasjɔ̃] nf gradation

**grade** [gʀad] nm (Mil) rank; (Scol) degree; **monter en** ~ to be promoted

**gradé** [gʀade] nm (Mil) officer

**gradin** [gʀadɛ̃] nm (dans un théâtre) tier; (de stade) step; **gradins** nmpl (de stade) terracing no pl (Brit), standing area; **en** ~**s** terraced

**graduation** [gʀadɥasjɔ̃] nf graduation

**gradué, e** [gʀadɥe] adj (exercices) graded (for difficulty); (thermomètre, verre) graduated

**graduel, le** [gʀadɥɛl] adj gradual; progressive

**graduer** [gʀadɥe] vt (effort etc) to increase gradually; (règle, verre) to graduate

**graffiti** [gʀafiti] nmpl graffiti

**grain** [gʀɛ̃] nm (gén) grain; (de chapelet) bead; (Navig) squall; (averse) heavy shower; (fig: petite quantité): **un** ~ **de** a touch of; ~ **de beauté** beauty spot; ~ **de café** coffee bean; ~ **de poivre** peppercorn; ~ **de poussière** speck of dust; ~ **de raisin** grape

**graine** [gʀɛn] nf seed; **mauvaise** ~ (mauvais sujet) bad lot; **une** ~ **de voyou** a hooligan in the making

**graineterie** [gʀɛntʀi] nf seed merchant's (shop)

**grainetier, -ière** [gʀɛntje, -jɛʀ] nm/f seed merchant

**graissage** [gʀɛsaʒ] nm lubrication, greasing

**graisse** [gʀɛs] nf fat; (lubrifiant) grease; ~ **saturée** saturated fat

**graisser** [gʀɛse] vt to lubricate, grease; (tacher) to make greasy

**graisseux, -euse** [gʀɛsø, -øz] adj greasy; (Anat) fatty

**grammaire** [gʀamɛʀ] nf grammar

**grammatical, e, -aux** [gʀamatikal, -o] adj grammatical

**gramme** [gʀam] nm gramme

**grand, e** [gʀɑ̃, gʀɑ̃d] adj (haut) tall; (gros, vaste, large) big, large; (long) long; (sens abstraits) great ▷ adv: ~ **ouvert** wide open; **un** ~ **buveur** a heavy drinker; **un** ~ **homme** a great man; **son** ~ **frère** his big ou older brother; **avoir** ~ **besoin de** to be in dire ou desperate need of; **il est** ~ **temps de** it's high time to; **il est assez** ~ **pour** he's big ou old enough to; **voir** ~ to think big; **en** ~ on a large scale; **au** ~ **air** in the open (air); **les** ~**s blessés/brûlés** the severely injured/burned; **de** ~ **matin** at the crack of dawn; ~ **écart** splits pl; ~ **ensemble** housing scheme; ~ **jour** broad daylight; ~ **livre** (Comm) ledger; ~ **magasin** department store; ~ **malade** very sick person; ~ **public** general public; ~**e personne** grown-up; ~**e surface** hypermarket, superstore; ~**es écoles** prestige university-level colleges with competitive entrance examinations; see note; ~**es lignes** (Rail) main lines; ~**es vacances** summer holidays

● GRANDES ÉCOLES
●
● The grandes écoles are highly-respected
● institutes of higher education which train
● students for specific careers. Students who

have spent two years after the "baccalauréat" in the "classes préparatoires" are recruited by competitive entry examination. The prestigious *grandes écoles* have a strong corporate identity and tend to furnish France with its intellectual, administrative and political élite.

**grand-angle** [gʀɑ̃tɑ̃gl(ə)] (*pl* **grands-angles**) *nm* (*Photo*) wide-angle lens
**grand-angulaire** [gʀɑ̃tɑ̃gylɛʀ] (*pl* **grands-angulaires**) *nm* (*Photo*) wide-angle lens
**grand-chose** [gʀɑ̃ʃoz] *nm/f inv*: **pas ~** not much
**Grande-Bretagne** [gʀɑ̃dbʀətaɲ] *nf*: **la ~** (Great) Britain; **en ~** in (Great) Britain
**grandement** [gʀɑ̃dmɑ̃] *adv* (*tout à fait*) greatly; (*largement*) easily; (*généreusement*) lavishly
**grandeur** [gʀɑ̃dœʀ] *nf* (*dimension*) size; (*fig: ampleur, importance*) magnitude; (: *gloire, puissance*) greatness; **~ nature** *adj* life-size
**grand-guignolesque** [gʀɑ̃giɲɔlɛsk(ə)] *adj* gruesome
**grandiloquent, e** [gʀɑ̃dilɔkɑ̃, -ɑ̃t] *adj* bombastic, grandiloquent
**grandiose** [gʀɑ̃djoz] *adj* (*paysage, spectacle*) imposing
**grandir** [gʀɑ̃diʀ] *vi* (*enfant, arbre*) to grow; (*bruit, hostilité*) to increase, grow ▷ *vt*: **~ qn** (*vêtement, chaussure*) to make sb look taller; (*fig*) to make sb grow in stature
**grandissant, e** [gʀɑ̃disɑ̃, -ɑ̃t] *adj* growing
**grand-mère** [gʀɑ̃mɛʀ] (*pl* **grand(s)-mères**) *nf* grandmother
**grand-messe** [gʀɑ̃mɛs] *nf* high mass
**grand-oncle** [gʀɑ̃tɔ̃kl(ə), gʀɑ̃zɔ̃kl(ə)] (*pl* **grands-oncles**) *nm* great-uncle
**grand-peine** [gʀɑ̃pɛn]: **à ~** *adv* with (great) difficulty
**grand-père** [gʀɑ̃pɛʀ] (*pl* **grands-pères**) *nm* grandfather
**grand-route** [gʀɑ̃ʀut] *nf* main road
**grand-rue** [gʀɑ̃ʀy] *nf* high street
**grands-parents** [gʀɑ̃paʀɑ̃] *nmpl* grandparents
**grand-tante** [gʀɑ̃tɑ̃t] (*pl* **grand(s)-tantes**) *nf* great-aunt
**grand-voile** [gʀɑ̃vwal] *nf* mainsail
**grange** [gʀɑ̃ʒ] *nf* barn
**granit, granite** [gʀanit] *nm* granite
**granitique** [gʀanitik] *adj* granite; (*terrain*) granitic
**granule** [gʀanyl] *nm* small pill
**granulé** [gʀanyle] *nm* granule
**granuleux, -euse** [gʀanylø, -øz] *adj* granular
**graphe** [gʀaf] *nm* graph
**graphie** [gʀafi] *nf* written form
**graphique** [gʀafik] *adj* graphic ▷ *nm* graph
**graphisme** [gʀafism(ə)] *nm* graphic arts *pl*; graphics *sg*; (*écriture*) handwriting
**graphiste** [gʀafist(ə)] *nm/f* graphic designer
**graphologie** [gʀafɔlɔʒi] *nf* graphology
**graphologue** [gʀafɔlɔg] *nm/f* graphologist
**grappe** [gʀap] *nf* cluster; **~ de raisin** bunch of grapes
**grappiller** [gʀapije] *vt* to glean
**grappin** [gʀapɛ̃] *nm* grapnel; **mettre le ~ sur** (*fig*) to get one's claws on
**gras, se** [gʀa, gʀas] *adj* (*viande, soupe*) fatty; (*personne*) fat; (*surface, main, cheveux*) greasy; (*terre*) sticky; (*toux*) loose, phlegmy; (*rire*) throaty; (*plaisanterie*) coarse; (*crayon*) soft-lead; (*Typo*) bold ▷ *nm* (*Culin*) fat; **faire la ~se matinée** to have a lie-in (*Brit*), sleep late; **matière ~se** fat (*content*)
**gras-double** [gʀadubl(ə)] *nm* (*Culin*) tripe
**grassement** [gʀasmɑ̃] *adv* (*généreusement*): **~ payé** handsomely paid; (*grossièrement: rire*) coarsely
**grassouillet, te** [gʀasujɛ, -ɛt] *adj* podgy, plump
**gratifiant, e** [gʀatifjɑ̃, -ɑ̃t] *adj* gratifying, rewarding
**gratification** [gʀatifikasjɔ̃] *nf* bonus
**gratifier** [gʀatifje] *vt*: **~ qn de** to favour (*Brit*) *ou* favor (*US*) sb with; to reward sb with; (*sourire etc*) to favo(u)r sb with
**gratin** [gʀatɛ̃] *nm* (*Culin*) cheese- (*ou* crumb-)topped dish; (: *croûte*) topping; **au ~** au gratin; **tout le ~ parisien** all the best people of Paris
**gratiné** [gʀatine] *adj* (*Culin*) au gratin; (*fam*) hellish ▷ *nf* (*soupe*) onion soup au gratin
**gratis** [gʀatis] *adv, adj* free
**gratitude** [gʀatityd] *nf* gratitude
**gratte-ciel** [gʀatsjɛl] *nm inv* skyscraper
**grattement** [gʀatmɑ̃] *nm* (*bruit*) scratching (*noise*)
**gratte-papier** [gʀatpapje] *nm inv* (*péj*) penpusher
**gratter** [gʀate] *vt* (*frotter*) to scrape; (*enlever*) to scrape off; (*bras, bouton*) to scratch; **se gratter** to scratch o.s.
**grattoir** [gʀatwaʀ] *nm* scraper
**gratuit, e** [gʀatɥi, -ɥit] *adj* (*entrée*) free; (*billet*) free, complimentary; (*fig*) gratuitous
**gratuité** [gʀatɥite] *nf* being free (of charge); gratuitousness
**gratuitement** [gʀatɥitmɑ̃] *adv* (*sans payer*) free; (*sans preuve, motif*) gratuitously
**gravats** [gʀava] *nmpl* rubble *sg*
**grave** [gʀav] *adj* (*dangereux: maladie, accident*) serious, bad; (*sérieux: sujet, problème*) serious, grave; (*personne, air*) grave, solemn; (*voix, son*) deep, low-pitched ▷ *nm* (*Mus*) low register; **ce n'est pas ~!** it's all right, don't worry; **blessé ~** seriously injured person
**graveleux, -euse** [gʀavlø, -øz] *adj* (*terre*) gravelly; (*fruit*) gritty; (*contes, propos*) smutty
**gravement** [gʀavmɑ̃] *adv* seriously; badly; gravely
**graver** [gʀave] *vt* (*plaque, nom*) to engrave; (*CD, DVD*) to burn; (*fig*): **~ qch dans son esprit/sa mémoire** to etch sth in one's mind/memory
**graveur** [gʀavœʀ] *nm* engraver; **~ de CD/DVD** CD/DVD burner *or* writer
**gravier** [gʀavje] *nm* (loose) gravel *no pl*
**gravillons** [gʀavijɔ̃] *nmpl* gravel *sg*, loose

**g**

chippings *ou* gravel

**gravir** [gRaviR] *vt* to climb (up)

**gravitation** [gRavitasjɔ̃] *nf* gravitation

**gravité** [gRavite] *nf* (*voir grave*) seriousness; gravity; (*Physique*) gravity

**graviter** [gRavite] *vi*: ~ **autour de** to revolve around

**gravure** [gRavyR] *nf* engraving; (*reproduction*) print; plate

**gré** [gRe] *nm*: **à son** ~ *adj* to his liking ▷ *adv* as he pleases; **au** ~ **de** according to, following; **contre le** ~ **de qn** against sb's will; **de son (plein)** ~ of one's own free will; **de** ~ **ou de force** whether one likes it or not; **de bon** ~ willingly; **bon** ~ **mal** ~ like it or not; willy-nilly; **de** ~ **à** ~ (*Comm*) by mutual agreement; **savoir (bien)** ~ **à qn de qch** to be (most) grateful to sb for sth

**grec, grecque** [gREk] *adj* Greek; (*classique: vase etc*) Grecian ▷ *nm* (*Ling*) Greek ▷ *nm/f*: **Grec, Grecque** Greek

**Grèce** [gREs] *nf*: **la** ~ Greece

**gredin, e** [gRədɛ̃, -in] *nm/f* rogue, rascal

**gréement** [gRemɑ̃] *nm* rigging

**greffe** [gREf] *nf* graft; transplant ▷ *nm* (*Jur*) office

**greffer** [gRefe] *vt* (*Bot, Méd: tissu*) to graft; (*Méd: organe*) to transplant

**greffier** [gRefje] *nm* clerk of the court

**grégaire** [gRegER] *adj* gregarious

**grège** [gRE3] *adj*: **soie** ~ raw silk

**grêle** [gREl] *adj* (*very*) thin ▷ *nf* hail

**grêlé, e** [gRele] *adj* pockmarked

**grêler** [gRele] *vb impers*: **il grêle** it's hailing ▷ *vt*: **la région a été grêlée** the region was damaged by hail

**grêlon** [gRelɔ̃] *nm* hailstone

**grelot** [gRəlo] *nm* little bell

**grelottant, e** [gRəlɔtɑ̃, -ɑ̃t] *adj* shivering, shivery

**grelotter** [gRəlɔte] *vi* (*trembler*) to shiver

**Grenade** [gRənad] *n* Granada ▷ *nf* (*île*) Grenada

**grenade** [gRənad] *nf* (*explosive*) grenade; (*Bot*) pomegranate; ~ **lacrymogène** teargas grenade

**grenadier** [gRənadje] *nm* (*Mil*) grenadier; (*Bot*) pomegranate tree

**grenadine** [gRənadin] *nf* grenadine

**grenat** [gRəna] *adj inv* dark red

**grenier** [gRənje] *nm* (*de maison*) attic; (*de ferme*) loft

**grenouille** [gRənuj] *nf* frog

**grenouillère** [gRənujER] *nf* (*de bébé*) leggings; (: *combinaison*) sleepsuit

**grenu, e** [gRəny] *adj* grainy, grained

**grès** [gRE] *nm* (*roche*) sandstone; (*poterie*) stoneware

**grésil** [gRezi] *nm* (fine) hail

**grésillement** [gRezijmɑ̃] *nm* sizzling; crackling

**grésiller** [gRezije] *vi* to sizzle; (*Radio*) to crackle

**grève** [gREv] *nf* (*d'ouvriers*) strike; (*plage*) shore; **se mettre en/faire** ~ to go on/be on strike; ~ **bouchon** partial strike (*in key areas of a company*);

~ **de la faim** hunger strike; ~ **perlée** go-slow (*Brit*), slowdown (*US*); ~ **sauvage** wildcat strike; ~ **de solidarité** sympathy strike; ~ **surprise** lightning strike; ~ **sur le tas** sit down strike; ~ **tournante** strike by rota; ~ **du zèle** work-to-rule (*Brit*), slowdown (*US*)

**grever** [gRəve] *vt* (*budget, économie*) to put a strain on; **grevé d'impôts** crippled by taxes; **grevé d'hypothèques** heavily mortgaged

**gréviste** [gRevist(ə)] *nm/f* striker

**gribouillage** [gRibuja3] *nm* scribble, scrawl

**gribouiller** [gRibuje] *vt* to scribble, scrawl ▷ *vi* to doodle

**gribouillis** [gRibuji] *nm* (*dessin*) doodle; (*action*) doodling *no pl*; (*écriture*) scribble

**grief** [gRijɛf] *nm* grievance; **faire** ~ **à qn de** to reproach sb for

**grièvement** [gRijɛvmɑ̃] *adv* seriously

**griffe** [gRif] *nf* claw; (*fig*) signature; (: *d'un couturier, parfumeur*) label, signature

**griffé, e** [gRife] *adj* designer(-label) *cpd*

**griffer** [gRife] *vt* to scratch

**griffon** [gRifɔ̃] *nm* (*chien*) griffon

**griffonnage** [gRifɔna3] *nm* scribble

**griffonner** [gRifɔne] *vt* to scribble

**griffure** [gRifyR] *nf* scratch

**grignoter** [gRiɲɔte] *vt, vi* to nibble

**gril** [gRil] *nm* steak *ou* grill pan

**grillade** [gRijad] *nf* grill

**grillage** [gRija3] *nm* (*treillis*) wire netting; (*clôture*) wire fencing

**grillager** [gRija3e] *vt* (*objet*) to put wire netting on; (*périmètre, jardin*) to put wire fencing around

**grille** [gRij] *nf* (*portail*) (metal) gate; (*clôture*) railings *pl*; (*d'égout*) (metal) grate; (*fig*) grid

**grille-pain** [gRijpɛ̃] *nm inv* toaster

**griller** [gRije] *vt* (*aussi*: **faire griller**: *pain*) to toast; (: *viande*) to grill (*Brit*), broil (*US*); (: *café*) to roast; (*fig: ampoule etc*) to burn out, blow; ~ **un feu rouge** to jump the lights (*Brit*), run a stoplight (*US*) ▷ *vi* (*brûler*) to be roasting

**grillon** [gRijɔ̃] *nm* (*Zool*) cricket

**grimace** [gRimas] *nf* grimace; (*pour faire rire*): **faire des** ~**s** to pull *ou* make faces

**grimacer** [gRimase] *vi* to grimace

**grimacier, -ière** [gRimasje, -jER] *adj*: **c'est un enfant** ~ that child is always pulling faces

**grimer** [gRime] *vt* to make up

**grimoire** [gRimwaR] *nm* (*illisible*) unreadable scribble; (*livre de magie*) book of magic spells

**grimpant, e** [gRɛ̃pɑ̃, -ɑ̃t] *adj*: **plante** ~**e** climbing plant, climber

**grimper** [gRɛ̃pe] *vi, vt* to climb ▷ *nm*: **le** ~ (*Sport*) rope-climbing; ~ **à/sur** to climb (up)/climb onto

**grimpeur, -euse** [gRɛ̃pœR, -øz] *nm/f* climber

**grinçant, e** [gRɛ̃sɑ̃, -ɑ̃t] *adj* grating

**grincement** [gRɛ̃smɑ̃] *nm* grating (noise); creaking (noise)

**grincer** [gRɛ̃se] *vi* (*porte, roue*) to grate; (*plancher*) to creak; ~ **des dents** to grind one's teeth

**grincheux, -euse** [gRɛ̃ʃø, -øz] *adj* grumpy

**gringalet** [gʀɛ̃galɛ] *adj m* puny ▷ *nm* weakling
**griotte** [gʀijɔt] *nf* Morello cherry
**grippal, e, -aux** [gʀipal, -o] *adj (état)* flu-like
**grippe** [gʀip] *nf* flu, influenza; **avoir la ~** to have (the) flu; **prendre qn/qch en ~** *(fig)* to take a sudden dislike to sb/sth; **~ aviaire** bird flu; **~ porcine** swine flu
**grippé, e** [gʀipe] *adj*: **être ~** to have (the) flu; *(moteur)* to have seized up *(Brit) ou* jammed
**gripper** [gʀipe] *vt, vi* to jam
**grippe-sou** [gʀipsu] *nm/f* penny pincher
**gris, e** [gʀi, gʀiz] *adj* grey *(Brit),* gray *(US); (ivre)* tipsy ▷ *nm (couleur)* grey *(Brit),* gray *(US);* **il fait ~** it's a dull *ou* grey day; **faire ~e mine** to look miserable *ou* morose; **faire ~e mine à qn** to give sb a cool reception
**grisaille** [gʀizaj] *nf* greyness *(Brit),* grayness *(US),* dullness
**grisant, e** [gʀizɑ̃, -ɑ̃t] *adj* intoxicating, exhilarating
**grisâtre** [gʀizɑtʀ(ə)] *adj* greyish *(Brit),* grayish *(US)*
**griser** [gʀize] *vt* to intoxicate; **se ~ de** *(fig)* to become intoxicated with
**griserie** [gʀizʀi] *nf* intoxication
**grisonnant, e** [gʀizɔnɑ̃, -ɑ̃t] *adj* greying *(Brit),* graying *(US)*
**grisonner** [gʀizɔne] *vi* to be going grey *(Brit) ou* gray *(US)*
**Grisons** [gʀizɔ̃] *nmpl*: **les ~** Graubünden
**grisou** [gʀizu] *nm* firedamp
**gris-vert** [gʀivɛʀ] *adj* grey-green
**grive** [gʀiv] *nf (Zool)* thrush
**grivois, e** [gʀivwa, -waz] *adj* saucy
**grivoiserie** [gʀivwazʀi] *nf* sauciness
**Groenland** [gʀɔɛnlɑ̃d] *nm*: **le ~** Greenland
**grog** [gʀɔg] *nm* grog
**groggy** [gʀɔgi] *adj inv* dazed
**grogne** [gʀɔɲ] *nf* grumble
**grognement** [gʀɔɲmɑ̃] *nm* grunt; growl
**grogner** [gʀɔɲe] *vi* to growl; *(fig)* to grumble
**grognon, ne** [gʀɔɲɔ̃, -ɔn] *adj* grumpy, grouchy
**groin** [gʀwɛ̃] *nm* snout
**grommeler** [gʀɔmle] *vi* to mutter to o.s.
**grondement** [gʀɔ̃dmɑ̃] *nm* rumble; growl
**gronder** [gʀɔ̃de] *vi (canon, moteur, tonnerre)* to rumble; *(animal)* to growl; *(fig: révolte)* to be brewing ▷ *vt* to scold
**groom** [gʀum] *nm* page, bellhop *(US)*
**gros, se** [gʀo, gʀos] *adj* big, large; *(obèse)* fat; *(problème, quantité)* great; *(travaux, dégâts)* extensive; *(large: trait, fil)* thick, heavy ▷ *adv*: **risquer/gagner ~** to risk/win a lot ▷ *nm (Comm)*: **le ~** the wholesale business; **écrire ~** to write in big letters; **prix de ~** wholesale price; **par ~ temps/~se mer** in rough weather/heavy seas; **le ~ de** the main body of; *(du travail etc)* the bulk of; **en avoir ~ sur le cœur** to be upset; **en ~** roughly; *(Comm)* wholesale; **~ lot** jackpot; **~ mot** coarse word, vulgarity; **~ œuvre** shell (of building); **~ plan** *(Photo)* close-up; **~ porteur** wide-bodied aircraft, jumbo (jet); **~ sel** cooking

salt; **~ titre** headline; **~se caisse** big drum
**groseille** [gʀozɛj] *nf*: **~ (rouge)/(blanche)** red/white currant; **~ à maquereau** gooseberry
**groseillier** [gʀozeje] *nm* red *ou* white currant bush; gooseberry bush
**grosse** [gʀos] *adj f voir* **gros** ▷ *nf (Comm)* gross
**grossesse** [gʀosɛs] *nf* pregnancy; **~ nerveuse** phantom pregnancy
**grosseur** [gʀosœʀ] *nf* size; fatness; *(tumeur)* lump
**grossier, -ière** [gʀosje, -jɛʀ] *adj* coarse; *(travail)* rough; crude; *(évident: erreur)* gross
**grossièrement** [gʀosjɛʀmɑ̃] *adv* coarsely; roughly; crudely; *(en gros)* roughly
**grossièreté** [gʀosjɛʀte] *nf* coarseness; rudeness
**grossir** [gʀosiʀ] *vi (personne)* to put on weight; *(fig)* to grow, get bigger; *(rivière)* to swell ▷ *vt* to increase; *(exagérer)* to exaggerate; *(au microscope)* to magnify, enlarge; *(vêtement)*: **~ qn** to make sb look fatter
**grossissant, e** [gʀosisɑ̃, -ɑ̃t] *adj* magnifying, enlarging
**grossissement** [gʀosismɑ̃] *nm (optique)* magnification
**grossiste** [gʀosist(ə)] *nm/f* wholesaler
**grosso modo** [gʀosomɔdo] *adv* roughly
**grotesque** [gʀɔtɛsk(ə)] *adj* grotesque
**grotte** [gʀɔt] *nf* cave
**grouiller** [gʀuje] *vi (foule)* to mill about; *(fourmis)* to swarm about; **~ de** to be swarming with
**groupe** [gʀup] *nm* group; **cabinet de ~** group practice; **médecine de ~** group practice; **~ électrogène** generator; **~ de parole** support group; **~ de pression** pressure group; **~ sanguin** blood group; **~ scolaire** school complex
**groupement** [gʀupmɑ̃] *nm* grouping; *(groupe)* group; **~ d'intérêt économique (GIE)** ≈ trade association
**grouper** [gʀupe] *vt* to group; *(ressources, moyens)* to pool; **se grouper** to get together
**groupuscule** [gʀupyskyl] *nm* clique
**gruau** [gʀyo] *nm*: **pain de ~** wheaten bread
**grue** [gʀy] *nf* crane; **faire le pied de ~** *(fam)* to hang around (waiting), kick one's heels *(Brit)*
**gruger** [gʀyʒe] *vt* to cheat, dupe
**grumeaux** [gʀymo] *nmpl (Culin)* lumps
**grumeleux, -euse** [gʀymlø, -øz] *adj (sauce etc)* lumpy; *(peau etc)* bumpy
**grutier** [gʀytje] *nm* crane driver
**gruyère** [gʀyjɛʀ] *nm* gruyère *(Brit) ou* Swiss cheese
**Guadeloupe** [gwadlup] *nf*: **la ~** Guadeloupe
**guadeloupéen, ne** [gwadlupeɛ̃, -ɛn] *adj* Guadelupian
**Guatémala** [gwatemala] *nm*: **le ~** Guatemala
**guatémalien, ne** [gwatemaljɛ̃, -ɛn] *adj* Guatemalan
**guatémaltèque** [gwatemaltɛk] *adj* Guatemalan
**gué** [ge] *nm* ford; **passer à ~** to ford
**guenilles** [gənij] *nfpl* rags

**g**

**guenon** [gənɔ̃] *nf* female monkey
**guépard** [gepaʀ] *nm* cheetah
**guêpe** [gɛp] *nf* wasp
**guêpier** [gepje] *nm* (*fig*) trap
**guère** [gɛʀ] *adv* (*avec adjectif, adverbe*): **ne ... ~**
hardly; (*avec verbe*): **ne ... ~** (*tournure négative*)
much; hardly ever; (very) long; **il n'y a ~ que/**
**de** there's hardly anybody (*ou* anything) but/
hardly any
**guéridon** [geʀidɔ̃] *nm* pedestal table
**guérilla** [geʀija] *nf* guerrilla warfare
**guérillero** [geʀijeʀo] *nm* guerrilla
**guérir** [geʀiʀ] *vt* (*personne, maladie*) to cure;
(*membre, plaie*) to heal ▷ *vi* (*personne*) to recover, be
cured; (*plaie, chagrin*) to heal; **~ de** to be cured of,
recover from; **~ qn de** to cure sb of
**guérison** [geʀizɔ̃] *nf* curing; healing; recovery
**guérissable** [geʀisabl(ə)] *adj* curable
**guérisseur, -euse** [geʀisœʀ, -øz] *nm/f* healer
**guérite** [geʀit] *nf* (*Mil*) sentry box; (*sur un*
*chantier*) (workman's) hut
**Guernesey** [gɛʀnəzɛ] *nf* Guernsey
**guernesiais, e** [gɛʀnəzjɛ, -ɛz] *adj* of *ou* from
Guernsey
**guerre** [gɛʀ] *nf* war; (*méthode*): **~ atomique/de**
**tranchées** atomic/trench warfare *no pl*; **en ~** at
war; **faire la ~ à** to wage war against; **de ~**
**lasse** (*fig*) tired of fighting *ou* resisting; **de**
**bonne ~** fair and square; **~ civile/mondiale**
civil/world war; **~ froide/sainte** cold/holy war;
**~ d'usure** war of attrition
**guerrier, -ière** [geʀje, -jɛʀ] *adj* warlike ▷ *nm/f*
warrior
**guerroyer** [gɛʀwaje] *vi* to wage war
**guet** [gɛ] *nm*: **faire le ~** to be on the watch *ou*
look-out
**guet-apens** [gɛtapɑ̃] (*pl* **guets-apens**) *nm*
ambush
**guêtre** [gɛtʀ(ə)] *nf* gaiter
**guetter** [gete] *vt* (*épier*) to watch (intently);
(*attendre*) to watch (out) for; (: *pour surprendre*) to
be lying in wait for
**guetteur** [getœʀ] *nm* look-out
**gueule** [gœl] *nf* mouth; (*fam: visage*) mug;
(: *bouche*) gob (!), mouth; **ta ~!** (*fam*) shut up!; **~**
**de bois** (*fam*) hangover
**gueule-de-loup** [gœldəlu] (*pl* **gueules-de-loup**)
*nf* snapdragon
**gueuler** [gœle] *vi* (*fam*) to bawl
**gueuleton** [gœltɔ̃] *nm* (*fam*) blowout (*Brit*), big
meal
**gueux** [gø] *nm* beggar; (*coquin*) rogue
**gui** [gi] *nm* mistletoe
**guibole** [gibɔl] *nf* (*fam*) leg
**guichet** [giʃɛ] *nm* (*de bureau, banque*) counter,
window; (*d'une porte*) wicket, hatch; **les ~s** (*à la*
*gare, au théâtre*) the ticket office; **jouer à ~s**
**fermés** to play to a full house
**guichetier, -ière** [giʃtje, -jɛʀ] *nm/f* counter clerk
**guide** [gid] *nm* guide; (*livre*) guide(book) ▷ *nf*

(*fille scout*) (girl) guide (*Brit*), girl scout (*US*);
**guides** *nfpl* (*d'un cheval*) reins
**guider** [gide] *vt* to guide
**guidon** [gidɔ̃] *nm* handlebars *pl*
**guigne** [giɲ] *nf* (*fam*): **avoir la ~** to be jinxed
**guignol** [giɲɔl] *nm* ≈ Punch and Judy show; (*fig*)
clown
**guillemets** [gijmɛ] *nmpl*: **entre ~** in inverted
commas *ou* quotation marks; **~ de répétition**
ditto marks
**guilleret, te** [gijʀɛ, -ɛt] *adj* perky, bright
**guillotine** [gijɔtin] *nf* guillotine
**guillotiner** [gijɔtine] *vt* to guillotine
**guimauve** [gimov] *nf* (*Bot*) marshmallow; (*fig*)
sentimentality, sloppiness
**guimbarde** [gɛ̃baʀd(ə)] *nf* old banger (*Brit*),
jalopy
**guindé, e** [gɛ̃de] *adj* stiff, starchy
**Guinée** [gine] *nf*: **la (République de) ~** (the
Republic of) Guinea; **la ~ équatoriale**
Equatorial Guinea
**Guinée-Bissau** [ginebiso] *nf*: **la ~** Guinea-
Bissau
**guinéen, ne** [gineɛ̃, -ɛn] *adj* Guinean
**guingois** [gɛ̃gwa]: **de ~** *adv* askew
**guinguette** [gɛ̃gɛt] *nf* open-air café *ou* dance hall
**guirlande** [giʀlɑ̃d] *nf* garland; (*de papier*) paper
chain; **~ lumineuse** lights *pl*, fairy lights *pl*
(*Brit*); **~ de Noël** tinsel *no pl*
**guise** [giz] *nf*: **à votre ~** as you wish *ou* please;
**en ~ de** by way of
**guitare** [gitaʀ] *nf* guitar
**guitariste** [gitaʀist(ə)] *nm/f* guitarist, guitar
player
**gustatif, -ive** [gystatif, -iv] *adj* gustatory; *voir*
**papille**
**guttural, e, -aux** [gytyʀal, -o] *adj* guttural
**guyanais, e** [gɥijanɛ, -ɛz] *adj* Guyanese,
Guyanan; (*français*) Guianese, Guianan
**Guyane** [gɥijan] *nf*: **la ~** Guyana; **la ~**
**(française)** (French) Guiana
**gvt** *abr* (= *gouvernement*) govt
**gym** [ʒim] *nf* (*exercices*) gym
**gymkhana** [ʒimkana] *nm* rally; **~**
**motocycliste** (motorbike) scramble (*Brit*),
motocross
**gymnase** [ʒimnɑz] *nm* gym(nasium)
**gymnaste** [ʒimnast(ə)] *nm/f* gymnast
**gymnastique** [ʒimnastik] *nf* gymnastics *sg*; (*au*
*réveil etc*) keep-fit exercises *pl*; **~ corrective**
remedial gymnastics
**gynécologie** [ʒinekɔlɔʒi] *nf* gynaecology (*Brit*),
gynecology (*US*)
**gynécologique** [ʒinekɔlɔʒik] *adj*
gynaecological (*Brit*), gynecological (*US*)
**gynécologue** [ʒinekɔlɔg] *nm/f* gynaecologist
(*Brit*), gynecologist (*US*)
**gypse** [ʒips(ə)] *nm* gypsum
**gyrophare** [ʒiʀofaʀ] *nm* (*sur une voiture*) revolving
(flashing) light

# Hh

**H, h** [aʃ] *nm inv* H, h ▷ *abr* (= *homme*) M;
(= *hydrogène*) H = **heure**; **à l'heure H** at zero
hour; **bombe H** H bomb; **H comme Henri** H
for Harry (*Brit*) *ou* How (*US*)

**ha.** *abr* (= *hectare*) ha.

**hab.** *abr* = **habitant**

**habile** [abil] *adj* skilful; (*malin*) clever

**habilement** [abilmɑ̃] *adv* skilfully; cleverly

**habileté** [abilte] *nf* skill, skilfulness; cleverness

**habilité, e** [abilite] *adj*: ~ **à faire** entitled to do,
empowered to do

**habiliter** [abilite] *vt* to empower, entitle

**habillage** [abijaʒ] *nm* dressing

**habillé, e** [abije] *adj* dressed; (*chic*) dressy;
(*Tech*): ~ **de** covered with; encased in

**habillement** [abijmɑ̃] *nm* clothes *pl*; (*profession*)
clothing industry

**habiller** [abije] *vt* to dress; (*fournir en vêtements*) to
clothe; **s'habiller** to dress (o.s.); (*se déguiser,
mettre des vêtements chic*) to dress up; **s'~ de/en** to
dress in/dress up as; **s'~ chez/à** to buy one's
clothes from/at

**habilleuse** [abijøz] *nf* (*Ciné, Théât*) dresser

**habit** [abi] *nm* outfit; **habits** *nmpl* (*vêtements*)
clothes; ~ (**de soirée**) tails *pl*; evening dress;
**prendre l'~** (*Rel: entrer en religion*) to enter (holy)
orders

**habitable** [abitabl(ə)] *adj* (in)habitable

**habitacle** [abitakl(ə)] *nm* cockpit; (*Auto*)
passenger cell

**habitant, e** [abitɑ̃, -ɑ̃t] *nm/f* inhabitant; (*d'une
maison*) occupant, occupier; **loger chez l'~** to
stay with the locals

**habitat** [abita] *nm* housing conditions *pl*; (*Bot,
Zool*) habitat

**habitation** [abitasjɔ̃] *nf* living; (*demeure*)
residence, home; (*maison*) house; ~**s à loyer
modéré (HLM)** low-rent, state-owned housing,
= council housing *sg* (*Brit*), = public housing
units (*US*)

**habité, e** [abite] *adj* inhabited; lived in

**habiter** [abite] *vt* to live in; (*sentiment*) to dwell
in ▷ *vi*: ~ **à/dans** to live in *ou* at/in; ~ **chez** *ou*
**avec qn** to live with sb; ~ **16 rue Montmartre**
to live at number 16 rue Montmartre; ~ **rue
Montmartre** to live in rue Montmartre

**habitude** [abityd] *nf* habit; **avoir l'~ de faire** to
be in the habit of doing; **avoir l'~ des enfants**
to be used to children; **prendre l'~ de faire qch**
to get into the habit of doing sth; **perdre une ~**
to get out of a habit; **d'~** usually; **comme d'~** as
usual; **par ~** out of habit

**habitué, e** [abitɥe] *adj*: **être ~ à** to be used *ou*
accustomed to ▷ *nm/f* regular visitor; (*client*)
regular (customer)

**habituel, le** [abitɥɛl] *adj* usual

**habituellement** [abitɥɛlmɑ̃] *adv* usually

**habituer** [abitɥe] *vt*: ~ **qn à** to get sb used to;
**s'habituer à** to get used to

**'hâbleur, -euse** ['ɑblœʀ, -øz] *adj* boastful

**'hache** ['aʃ] *nf* axe

**'haché, e** ['aʃe] *adj* minced (*Brit*), ground (*US*);
(*persil*) chopped; (*fig*) jerky

**'hache-légumes** ['aʃlegym] *nm inv* vegetable
chopper

**'hacher** ['aʃe] *vt* (*viande*) to mince (*Brit*), grind
(*US*); (*persil*) to chop; ~ **menu** to mince *ou* grind
finely; to chop finely

**'hachette** ['aʃɛt] *nf* hatchet

**'hache-viande** ['aʃvjɑ̃d] *nm inv* (meat) mincer
(*Brit*) *ou* grinder (*US*); (*couteau*) (meat) cleaver

**'hachis** ['aʃi] *nm* mince *no pl* (*Brit*), hamburger
meat (*US*); ~ **de viande** minced (*Brit*) *ou* ground
(*US*) meat

**'hachisch** ['aʃiʃ] *nm* hashish

**'hachoir** ['aʃwaʀ] *nm* chopper; (meat) mincer
(*Brit*) *ou* grinder (*US*); (*planche*) chopping board

**'hachurer** ['aʃyʀe] *vt* to hatch

**'hachures** ['aʃyʀ] *nfpl* hatching *sg*

**'hagard, e** ['agaʀ, -aʀd(ə)] *adj* wild, distraught

**'haie** ['ɛ] *nf* hedge; (*Sport*) hurdle; (*fig: rang*) line,
row; **200 m ~s** 200 m hurdles; ~ **d'honneur**
guard of honour

**'haillons** ['ajɔ̃] *nmpl* rags

**'haine** ['ɛn] *nf* hatred

**'haineux, -euse** ['ɛnø, -øz] *adj* full of hatred

**'haïr** ['aiʀ] *vt* to detest, hate; **se 'haïr** to hate
each other

**'hais** ['ɛ], **'haïs** *etc* ['ai] *vb voir* **'haïr**

**'haïssable** ['aisabl(ə)] *adj* detestable

**Haïti** [aiti] *n* Haiti

**haïtien, ne** [aisjɛ̃, -ɛn] *adj* Haitian

**'halage** ['alaʒ] *nm*: **chemin de** ~ towpath
**'hâle** ['ɑl] *nm* (sun)tan
**'hâlé, e** ['ɑle] *adj* (sun)tanned, sunburnt
**haleine** [alɛn] *nf* breath; **perdre** ~ to get out of
breath; **à perdre** ~ until one is gasping for
breath; **avoir mauvaise** ~ to have bad breath;
**reprendre** ~ to get one's breath back; **hors d'**~
out of breath; **tenir en** ~ to hold spellbound;
(*en attente*) to keep in suspense; **de longue** ~ *adj*
long-term
**'haler** ['ale] *vt* to haul in; (*remorquer*) to tow
**'haleter** ['alte] *vi* to pant
**'hall** ['ol] *nm* hall
**hallali** [alali] *nm* kill
**'halle** ['al] *nf* (covered) market; **'halles** *nfpl*
central food market *sg*
**'hallebarde** ['albaʀd] *nf* halberd; **il pleut des ~s**
(*fam*) it's bucketing down
**hallucinant, e** [alysinɑ̃, -ɑ̃t] *adj* staggering
**hallucination** [alysinɑsjɔ̃] *nf* hallucination
**hallucinatoire** [alysinatwaʀ] *adj* hallucinatory
**halluciné, e** [alysine] *nm/f* person suffering
from hallucinations; (*fou*) (raving) lunatic
**hallucinogène** [a(l)lysinɔʒɛn] *adj*
hallucinogenic ▷ *nm* hallucinogen
**'halo** ['alo] *nm* halo
**halogène** [alɔʒɛn] *nm*: **lampe (à)** ~ halogen
lamp
**'halte** ['alt(ə)] *nf* stop, break; (*escale*) stopping
place; (*Rail*) halt ▷ *excl* stop!; **faire** ~ to stop
**'halte-garderie** ['altgaʀdəʀi] (*pl* **'haltes-
garderies**) *nf* crèche
**haltère** [altɛʀ] *nm* (*à boules, disques*) dumbbell,
barbell; (**poids et**) ~**s** weightlifting
**haltérophile** [alteʀɔfil] *nm/f* weightlifter
**haltérophilie** [alteʀɔfili] *nf* weightlifting
**'hamac** ['amak] *nm* hammock
**'Hambourg** ['ɑ̃buʀ] *n* Hamburg
**'hamburger** ['ɑ̃buʀɡœʀ] *nm* hamburger
**'hameau, x** ['amo] *nm* hamlet
**hameçon** [amsɔ̃] *nm* (fish) hook
**'hampe** ['ɑ̃p] *nf* (*de drapeau etc*) pole; (*de lance*)
shaft
**'hamster** ['amstɛʀ] *nm* hamster
**'hanche** ['ɑ̃ʃ] *nf* hip
**'hand-ball** ['ɑ̃dbal] *nm* handball
**'handballeur, -euse** ['ɑ̃dbalœʀ, -øz] *nm/f*
handball player
**'handicap** ['ɑ̃dikap] *nm* handicap
**'handicapé, e** ['ɑ̃dikape] *adj* handicapped ▷ *nm/
f* physically (*ou* mentally) handicapped person;
~ **moteur** spastic
**'handicaper** ['ɑ̃dikape] *vt* to handicap
**'hangar** ['ɑ̃ɡaʀ] *nm* shed; (*Aviat*) hangar
**'hanneton** ['antɔ̃] *nm* cockchafer
**'Hanovre** ['anɔvʀ(ə)] *n* Hanover
**'hanter** ['ɑ̃te] *vt* to haunt
**'hantise** ['ɑ̃tiz] *nf* obsessive fear
**'happer** ['ape] *vt* to snatch; (*train etc*) to hit
**'harangue** ['aʀɑ̃ɡ] *nf* harangue
**'haranguer** ['aʀɑ̃ɡe] *vt* to harangue
**'haras** ['aʀɑ] *nm* stud farm

**'harassant, e** ['aʀasɑ̃, -ɑ̃t] *adj* exhausting
**'harcèlement** ['aʀsɛlmɑ̃] *nm* harassment; ~
**sexuel** sexual harassment
**'harceler** ['aʀsəle] *vt* (*Mil, Chasse*) to harass,
harry; (*importuner*) to plague
**'hardes** ['aʀd(ə)] *nfpl* rags
**'hardi, e** ['aʀdi] *adj* bold, daring
**'hardiesse** ['aʀdjɛs] *nf* audacity; **avoir la** ~ **de** to
have the audacity *ou* effrontery to
**harem** ['aʀɛm] *nm* harem
**hareng** ['aʀɑ̃] *nm* herring
**'hargne** ['aʀɲ(ə)] *nf* aggressivity, aggressiveness
**'hargneusement** ['aʀɲøzmɑ̃] *adv* belligerently,
aggressively
**'hargneux, -euse** ['aʀɲø, -øz] *adj* (*propos,
personne*) belligerent, aggressive; (*chien*) fierce
**'haricot** ['aʀiko] *nm* bean; ~ **blanc/rouge**
haricot/kidney bean; ~ **vert** French (*Brit*) *ou*
green bean
**harmonica** [aʀmɔnika] *nm* mouth organ
**harmonie** [aʀmɔni] *nf* harmony
**harmonieux, -euse** [aʀmɔnjø, -øz] *adj*
harmonious
**harmonique** [aʀmɔnik] *adj, nm ou f* harmonic
**harmoniser** [aʀmɔnize] *vt* to harmonize;
**s'harmoniser** (*couleurs, teintes*) to go well
together
**harmonium** [aʀmɔnjɔm] *nm* harmonium
**'harnaché, e** ['aʀnaʃe] *adj* (*fig*) rigged out
**'harnachement** ['aʀnaʃmɑ̃] *nm* (*habillement*) rig-
out; (*équipement*) harness, equipment
**'harnacher** ['aʀnaʃe] *vt* to harness
**'harnais** ['aʀnɛ] *nm* harness
**'haro** ['aʀo] *nm*: **crier** ~ **sur qn/qch** to inveigh
against sb/sth
**'harpe** ['aʀp(ə)] *nf* harp
**'harpie** ['aʀpi] *nf* harpy
**'harpiste** ['aʀpist(ə)] *nm/f* harpist
**'harpon** ['aʀpɔ̃] *nm* harpoon
**'harponner** ['aʀpone] *vt* to harpoon; (*fam*) to
collar
**'hasard** ['azaʀ] *nm*: **le** ~ chance, fate; **un** ~ a
coincidence; (*aubaine, chance*) a stroke of luck;
**au** ~ (*sans but*) aimlessly; (*à l'aveuglette*) at
random, haphazardly; **par** ~ by chance;
**comme par** ~ as if by chance; **à tout** ~ on the
off chance; (*en cas de besoin*) just in case
**'hasarder** ['azaʀde] *vt* (*mot*) to venture; (*fortune*)
to risk; **se** ~ **à faire** to risk doing, venture to do
**'hasardeux, -euse** ['azaʀdø, -øz] *adj* hazardous,
risky; (*hypothèse*) rash
**'haschisch** ['aʃiʃ] *nm* hashish
**'hâte** ['ɑt] *nf* haste; **à la** ~ hurriedly, hastily; **en**
~ posthaste, with all possible speed; **avoir** ~ **de**
to be eager *ou* anxious to
**'hâter** ['ɑte] *vt* to hasten; **se 'hâter** to hurry; **se**
~ **de** to hurry *ou* hasten to
**'hâtif, -ive** ['ɑtif, -iv] *adj* (*travail*) hurried;
(*décision*) hasty; (*légume*) early
**'hâtivement** ['ɑtivmɑ̃] *adv* hurriedly; hastily
**'hauban** ['obɑ̃] *nm* (*Navig*) shroud
**'hausse** ['os] *nf* rise, increase; (*de fusil*) backsight

adjuster; **à la ~** upwards; **en ~** rising

**'hausser** ['ose] *vt* to raise; **~ les épaules** to shrug (one's shoulders); **se ~ sur la pointe des pieds** to stand (up) on tiptoe *ou* tippy-toe (*US*)

**'haut, e** ['o, 'ot] *adj* high; (*grand*) tall; (*son, voix*) high(-pitched) ▷ *adv* high ▷ *nm* top (part); **de 3 m de ~, ~ de 3 m** 3 m high, 3 m in height; **en ~e montagne** high up in the mountains; **en ~ lieu** in high places; **à ~e voix, (tout) ~** aloud, out loud; **des ~s et des bas** ups and downs; **du ~ de** from the top of; **tomber de ~** to fall from a height; (*fig*) to have one's hopes dashed; **dire qch bien ~** to say sth plainly; **prendre qch de (très) ~** to react haughtily to sth; **traiter qn de ~** to treat sb with disdain; **de ~ en bas** from top to bottom; downwards; **~ en couleur** (*chose*) highly coloured; (*personne*): **un personnage ~ en couleur** a colourful character; **plus ~** higher up, further up; (*dans un texte*) above; (*parler*) louder; **en ~** up above; at (*ou* to) the top; (*dans une maison*) upstairs; **en ~ de** at the top of; **~ les mains!** hands up!, stick 'em up!; **la ~e couture/coiffure** haute couture/coiffure; **~ débit** (*Inform*) broadband; **~e fidélité** hi-fi, high fidelity; **la ~e finance** high finance; **~e trahison** high treason

**'hautain, e** ['otɛ̃, -ɛn] *adj* (*personne, regard*) haughty

**'hautbois** ['obwa] *nm* oboe

**'hautboïste** ['oboist(ə)] *nm/f* oboist

**'haut-de-forme** ['odfɔʀm(ə)] (*pl* **'hauts-de-forme**) *nm* top hat

**'haute-contre** ['otkɔ̃tʀ(ə)] (*pl* **'hautes-contre**) *nf* counter-tenor

**'hautement** ['otmã] *adv* (*ouvertement*) openly; (*supérieurement*): **~ qualifié** highly qualified

**'hauteur** ['otœʀ] *nf* height; (*Géo*) height, hill; (*fig*) loftiness; haughtiness; **à ~ de** up to (the level of); **à ~ des yeux** at eye level; **à la ~ de** (*sur la même ligne*) level with; by; (*fig*) equal to; **à la ~** (*fig*) up to it, equal to the task

**'Haute-Volta** ['otvɔlta] *nf*: **la ~** Upper Volta

**'haut-fond** ['ofɔ̃] (*pl* **'hauts-fonds**) *nm* shallow

**'haut-fourneau** ['ofuʀno] (*pl* **'hauts-fourneaux**) *nm* blast *ou* smelting furnace

**'haut-le-cœur** ['olkœʀ] *nm inv* retch, heave

**'haut-le-corps** ['olkɔʀ] *nm inv* start, jump

**'haut-parleur** ['opaʀlœʀ] (*pl* **-s**) *nm* (loud)speaker

**'hauturier, -ière** ['otyʀje, -jɛʀ] *adj* (*Navig*) deep-sea

**'havanais, e** ['avanɛ, -ɛz] *adj* of *ou* from Havana

**'Havane** ['avan] *nf*: **la ~** Havana ▷ *nm*: **'havane** (*cigare*) Havana

**'hâve** ['av] *adj* gaunt

**'havrais, e** ['avʀɛ, -ɛz] *adj* of *ou* from Le Havre

**'havre** ['avʀ(ə)] *nm* haven

**'havresac** ['avʀəsak] *nm* haversack

**Hawaï** [awai] *n* Hawaii; **les îles ~** the Hawaiian Islands

**hawaïen, ne** [awajɛ̃, -ɛn] *adj* Hawaiian ▷ *nm* (*Ling*) Hawaiian

**'Haye** ['ɛ] *n*: **la ~** the Hague

**'hayon** ['ɛjɔ̃] *nm* tailgate

**HCR** *sigle m* (= *Haut-Commissariat des Nations unies pour les réfugiés*) UNHCR

**hdb.** *abr* (= *heures de bureau*) o.h. = **office hours**

**'hé** ['e] *excl* hey!

**hebdo** [ɛbdo] *nm* (*fam*) weekly

**hebdomadaire** [ɛbdɔmadɛʀ] *adj, nm* weekly

**hébergement** [ebɛʀʒəmã] *nm* accommodation, lodging; taking in

**héberger** [ebɛʀʒe] *vt* to accommodate, lodge; (*réfugiés*) to take in

**hébergeur** [ebɛʀʒœʀ] *nm* (*Internet*) host

**hébété, e** [ebete] *adj* dazed

**hébétude** [ebetyd] *nf* stupor

**hébraïque** [ebʀaik] *adj* Hebrew, Hebraic

**hébreu, x** [ebʀø] *adj m, nm* Hebrew

**Hébrides** [ebʀid] *nf*: **les ~** the Hebrides

**HEC** *sigle fpl* (= *École des hautes études commerciales*) *grande école for management and business studies*

**hécatombe** [ekatɔ̃b] *nf* slaughter

**hectare** [ɛktaʀ] *nm* hectare, 10,000 square metres

**hecto...** [ɛkto] *préfixe* hecto...

**hectolitre** [ɛktɔlitʀ(ə)] *nm* hectolitre

**hédoniste** [edɔnist(ə)] *adj* hedonistic

**hégémonie** [eʒemɔni] *nf* hegemony

**'hein** ['ɛ̃] *excl* eh?; (*sollicitant l'approbation*): **tu m'approuves, ~?** so I did the right thing then?; **Paul est venu, ~?** Paul came, did he?; **que fais-tu, ~?** hey! what are you doing?

**'hélas** ['elas] *excl* alas! ▷ *adv* unfortunately

**'héler** [ele] *vt* to hail

**hélice** [elis] *nf* propeller

**hélicoïdal, e, -aux** [elikɔidal, -o] *adj* helical; helicoid

**hélicoptère** [elikɔptɛʀ] *nm* helicopter

**héliogravure** [eljɔgʀavyʀ] *nf* heliogravure

**héliomarin, e** [eljɔmaʀɛ̃, -in] *adj*: **centre ~** *centre offering sea and sun therapy*

**héliotrope** [eljɔtʀɔp] *nm* (*Bot*) heliotrope

**héliport** [elipɔʀ] *nm* heliport

**héliporté, e** [elipɔʀte] *adj* transported by helicopter

**hélium** [eljɔm] *nm* helium

**hellénique** [elenik] *adj* Hellenic

**hellénisant, e** [elenizɑ̃, -ɑ̃t], **helléniste** [elenist(ə)] *nm/f* hellenist

**Helsinki** [ɛlzinki] *n* Helsinki

**helvète** [ɛlvɛt] *adj* Helvetian ▷ *nm/f*: **Helvète** Helvetian

**Helvétie** [ɛlvesi] *nf*: **la ~** Helvetia

**helvétique** [ɛlvetik] *adj* Swiss

**hématologie** [ematɔlɔʒi] *nf* (*Méd*) haematology.

**hématome** [ematom] *nm* haematoma

**hémicycle** [emisikl(ə)] *nm* semicircle; (*Pol*): **l'~** the benches (in French parliament)

**hémiplégie** [emipleʒi] *nf* paralysis of one side, hemiplegia

**hémisphère** [emisfɛʀ] *nf*: **~ nord/sud** northern/southern hemisphere

**hémisphérique** [emisfeʀik] *adj* hemispherical

**hémoglobine** [emɔglɔbin] *nf* haemoglobin
(*Brit*), hemoglobin (*US*)
**hémophile** [emɔfil] *adj* haemophiliac (*Brit*),
hemophiliac (*US*)
**hémophilie** [emɔfili] *nf* haemophilia (*Brit*),
hemophilia (*US*)
**hémorragie** [emɔraʒi] *nf* bleeding *no pl*,
haemorrhage (*Brit*), hemorrhage (*US*); ~
**cérébrale** cerebral haemorrhage; ~ **interne**
internal bleeding *ou* haemorrhage
**hémorroïdes** [emɔrɔid] *nfpl* piles,
haemorrhoids (*Brit*), hemorrhoids (*US*)
**hémostatique** [emɔstatik] *adj* haemostatic
(*Brit*), hemostatic (*US*)
**'henné** ['ene] *nm* henna
**'hennir** ['enir] *vi* to neigh, whinny
**'hennissement** ['enismɑ̃] *nm* neighing,
whinnying
**'hep** ['ɛp] *excl* hey!
**hépatite** [epatit] *nf* hepatitis, liver infection
**héraldique** [eraldik] *adj* heraldry
**herbacé, e** [ɛrbase] *adj* herbaceous
**herbage** [ɛrbaʒ] *nm* pasture
**herbe** [ɛrb(ə)] *nf* grass; (*Culin, Méd*) herb; **en ~**
unripe; (*fig*) budding; **touffe/brin d'~** clump/
blade of grass
**herbeux, -euse** [ɛrbø, -øz] *adj* grassy
**herbicide** [ɛrbisid] *nm* weed-killer
**herbier** [ɛrbje] *nm* herbarium
**herbivore** [ɛrbivɔr] *nm* herbivore
**herboriser** [ɛrbɔrize] *vi* to collect plants
**herboriste** [ɛrbɔrist(ə)] *nm/f* herbalist
**herboristerie** [ɛrbɔristri] *nf* (*magasin*)
herbalist's shop; (*commerce*) herb trade
**herculéen, ne** [ɛrkyleɛ̃, -ɛn] *adj* (*fig*) herculean
**'hère** ['ɛr] *nm*: **pauvre ~** poor wretch
**héréditaire** [erediter] *adj* hereditary
**hérédité** [eredite] *nf* heredity
**hérésie** [erezi] *nf* heresy
**hérétique** [eretik] *nm/f* heretic
**'hérissé, e** ['erise] *adj* bristling; ~ **de** spiked
with; (*fig*) bristling with
**'hérisser** ['erise] *vt*: ~ **qn** (*fig*) to ruffle sb; **se**
**'hérisser** *vi* to bristle, bristle up
**'hérisson** ['erisɔ̃] *nm* hedgehog
**héritage** [eritaʒ] *nm* inheritance; (*fig*) heritage;
(: *legs*) legacy; **faire un (petit) ~** to come into (a
little) money
**hériter** [erite] *vi*: ~ **de qch (de qn)** to inherit sth
(from sb); ~ **de qn** to inherit sb's property
**héritier, -ière** [eritje, -jɛr] *nm/f* heir/heiress
**hermaphrodite** [ɛrmafrɔdit] *adj* (*Bot, Zool*)
hermaphrodite
**hermétique** [ɛrmetik] *adj* (à l'*air*) airtight; (à
l'*eau*) watertight; (*fig: écrivain, style*) abstruse;
(: *visage*) impenetrable
**hermétiquement** [ɛrmetikmɑ̃] *adv*
hermetically
**hermine** [ɛrmin] *nf* ermine
**'hernie** ['ɛrni] *nf* hernia
**héroïne** [erɔin] *nf* heroine; (*drogue*) heroin
**héroïnomane** [erɔinɔman] *nm/f* heroin addict

**héroïque** [erɔik] *adj* heroic
**héroïquement** [erɔikmɑ̃] *adv* heroically
**héroïsme** [erɔism(ə)] *nm* heroism
**'héron** ['erɔ̃] *nm* heron
**'héros** ['ero] *nm* hero
**herpès** [ɛrpɛs] *nm* herpes
**'herse** ['ɛrs(ə)] *nf* harrow; (*de château*) portcullis
**hertz** [ɛrts] *nm* (*Élec*) hertz
**hertzien, ne** [ɛrtsjɛ̃, -ɛn] *adj* (*Élec*) Hertzian
**hésitant, e** [ezitɑ̃, -ɑ̃t] *adj* hesitant
**hésitation** [ezitɑsjɔ̃] *nf* hesitation
**hésiter** [ezite] *vi*: ~ **(à faire)** to hesitate (to do); ~
**sur qch** to hesitate over sth
**hétéro** [etero] *adj inv* (*hétérosexuel(le)*) hetero
**hétéroclite** [eterɔklit] *adj* heterogeneous;
(*objets*) sundry
**hétérogène** [eterɔʒɛn] *adj* heterogeneous
**hétérosexuel, le** [eterɔsekɥɛl] *adj* heterosexual
**'hêtre** ['ɛtr(ə)] *nm* beech
**heure** [œr] *nf* hour; (*Scol*) period; (*moment,
moment fixé*) time; **c'est l'~** it's time; **pourriez-
vous me donner l'~, s'il vous plaît?** could you
tell me the time, please?; **quelle ~ est-il?** what
time is it?; **2 ~s (du matin)** 2 o'clock (in the
morning); **à la bonne ~!** (*parfois ironique*)
splendid!; **être à l'~** to be on time; (*montre*) to be
right; **le bus passe à l'~** the bus runs on the
hour; **mettre à l'~** to set right; **sur l'~** at once;
**pour l'~** for the time being; **d'~ en ~** from one
hour to the next; (*régulièrement*) hourly; **d'une ~**
**à l'autre** from hour to hour; **de bonne ~** early;
**deux ~s de marche/travail** two hours'
walking/work; **une ~ d'arrêt** an hour's break
*ou* stop; ~ **d'été** summer time (*Brit*), daylight
saving time (*US*); ~ **de pointe** rush hour; **~s de**
**bureau** office hours; **~s supplémentaires**
overtime *sg*
**heureusement** [œrøzmɑ̃] *adv* (*par bonheur*)
fortunately, luckily; ~ **que** ... it's a good job that
..., fortunately ...
**heureux, -euse** [œrø, -øz] *adj* happy; (*chanceux*)
lucky, fortunate; (*judicieux*) felicitous, fortunate;
**être ~ de qch** to be pleased *ou* happy about sth;
**être ~ de faire/que** to be pleased *ou* happy to
do/that; **s'estimer ~ de qch/que** to consider
o.s. fortunate with sth/that; **encore ~ que** ...
just as well that ...
**'heurt** ['œr] *nm* (*choc*) collision; **'heurts** *nmpl*
(*fig*) clashes
**'heurté, e** ['œrte] *adj* (*fig*) jerky, uneven;
(: *couleurs*) clashing
**'heurter** ['œrte] *vt* (*mur*) to strike, hit; (*personne*)
to collide with; (*fig*) to go against, upset; **se**
**'heurter** (*couleurs, tons*) to clash; **se ~ à** to collide
with; (*fig*) to come up against; ~ **qn de front** to
clash head-on with sb
**'heurtoir** ['œrtwar] *nm* door knocker
**hévéa** [evea] *nm* rubber tree

**hexagonal, e, -aux** [ɛgzagɔnal, -o] *adj*
hexagonal; *(français)* French *(see note at hexagone)*
**hexagone** [ɛgzagon] *nm* hexagon; *(la France)*
France *(because of its roughly hexagonal shape)*
**HF** *sigle f* (= *haute fréquence*) HF
**hiatus** [jatys] *nm* hiatus
**hibernation** [ibɛRnɑsjɔ̃] *nf* hibernation
**hiberner** [ibɛRne] *vi* to hibernate
**hibiscus** [ibiskys] *nm* hibiscus
**'hibou, x** ['ibu] *nm* owl
**'hic** ['ik] *nm* (*fam*) snag
**'hideusement** ['idøzmɑ̃] *adv* hideously
**'hideux, -euse** ['idø, -øz] *adj* hideous
**hier** [jɛR] *adv* yesterday; **~ matin/soir/midi**
yesterday morning/evening/at midday; **toute**
**la journée d'~** all day yesterday; **toute la**
**matinée d'~** all yesterday morning
**'hiérarchie** ['jeRaRʃi] *nf* hierarchy
**'hiérarchique** ['jeRaRʃik] *adj* hierarchic
**'hiérarchiquement** ['jeRaRʃikmɑ̃] *adv*
hierarchically
**'hiérarchiser** ['jeRaRʃize] *vt* to organize into a
hierarchy
**'hiéroglyphe** ['jeRɔglif] *nm* hieroglyphic
**'hiéroglyphique** ['jeRɔglifik] *adj* hieroglyphic
**'hi-fi** ['ifi] *nf inv* hi-fi
**hilarant, e** [ilaRɑ̃, -ɑ̃t] *adj* hilarious
**hilare** [ilaR] *adj* mirthful
**hilarité** [ilaRite] *nf* hilarity, mirth
**Himalaya** [imalaja] *nm*: **l'~** the Himalayas *pl*
**himalayen, ne** [imalajɛ̃, -ɛn] *adj* Himalayan
**hindou, e** [ɛ̃du] *adj, nm/f* Hindu; *(Indien)* Indian
**hindouisme** [ɛ̃duism(ə)] *nm* Hinduism
**Hindoustan** [ɛ̃dustɑ̃] *nm*: **l'~** Hindustan
**'hippie** ['ipi] *nm/f* hippy
**hippique** [ipik] *adj* equestrian, horse *cpd*
**hippisme** [ipism(ə)] *nm* (horse-)riding
**hippocampe** [ipɔkɑ̃p] *nm* sea horse
**hippodrome** [ipɔdRom] *nm* racecourse
**hippophagique** [ipɔfaʒik] *adj*: **boucherie ~**
horse butcher's
**hippopotame** [ipɔpɔtam] *nm* hippopotamus
**hirondelle** [iRɔ̃dɛl] *nf* swallow
**hirsute** [iRsyt] *adj* (*personne*) hairy; (*barbe*)
shaggy; (*tête*) tousled
**hispanique** [ispanik] *adj* Hispanic
**hispanisant, e** [ispanizɑ̃, -ɑ̃t], **hispaniste**
[ispanist(ə)] *nm/f* Hispanist
**hispano-américain, e** [ispanɔameRikɛ̃, -ɛn] *adj*
Spanish-American
**hispano-arabe** [ispanɔaRab] *adj* Hispano-
Moresque
**'hisser** ['ise] *vt* to hoist, haul up; **se 'hisser sur**
to haul o.s. up onto
**histoire** [istwaR] *nf* (*science, événements*) history;
(*anecdote, récit, mensonge*) story; (*affaire*) business
*no pl*; (*chichis: gén pl*) fuss *no pl*; **histoires** *nfpl*
(*ennuis*) trouble *sg*; **l'~ de France** French history,
the history of France; **l'~ sainte** biblical
history; **~ géo** humanities *pl*; **une ~ de** (*fig*) a
question of
**histologie** [istɔlɔʒi] *nf* histology

**historien, ne** [istɔRjɛ̃, -ɛn] *nm/f* historian
**historique** [istɔRik] *adj* historical; (*important*)
historic ▷ *nm* (*exposé, récit*): **faire l'~ de** to give
the background to
**historiquement** [istɔRikmɑ̃] *adv* historically
**'hit-parade** ['itpaRad] *nm*: **le ~** the charts
**HIV** *sigle m* (= *human immunodeficiency virus*) HIV
**hiver** [ivɛR] *nm* winter; **en ~** in winter
**hivernal, e, -aux** [ivɛRnal, -o] *adj* (*de l'hiver*)
winter *cpd*; (*comme en hiver*) wintry
**hivernant, e** [ivɛRnɑ̃, -ɑ̃t] *nm/f* winter holiday-
maker
**hiverner** [ivɛRne] *vi* to winter
**HLM** *sigle m ou f* (= *habitations à loyer modéré*) low-
rent, state-owned housing; **un(e) ~** ≈ a council flat
(*ou* house) (Brit), ≈ a public housing unit (US)
**Hme** *abr* (= *homme*) M
**HO** *abr* (= *hors œuvre*) labour not included (*on*
*invoices*)
**'hobby** ['ɔbi] *nm* hobby
**'hochement** ['ɔʃmɑ̃] *nm*: **~ de tête** nod; shake of
the head
**'hocher** ['ɔʃe] *vt*: **~ la tête** to nod; (*signe négatif ou*
*dubitatif*) to shake one's head
**'hochet** ['ɔʃɛ] *nm* rattle
**'hockey** ['ɔkɛ] *nm*: **~ (sur glace/gazon)** (ice/
field) hockey
**'hockeyeur, -euse** ['ɔkɛjœR, -øz] *nm/f* hockey
player
**'holà** ['ɔla] *nm*: **mettre le ~ à qch** to put a stop to
sth
**'holding** ['ɔldiŋ] *nm* holding company
**'hold-up** ['ɔldœp] *nm inv* hold-up
**'hollandais, e** ['ɔlɑ̃dɛ, -ɛz] *adj* Dutch ▷ *nm* (*Ling*)
Dutch ▷ *nm/f*: **'Hollandais, e** Dutchman/
woman; **les 'Hollandais** the Dutch
**'Hollande** ['ɔlɑ̃d] *nf*: **la ~** Holland ▷ *nm*:
**'hollande** (*fromage*) Dutch cheese
**holocauste** [ɔlɔkost(ə)] *nm* holocaust
**hologramme** [ɔlɔgRam] *nm* hologram
**'homard** ['ɔmaR] *nm* lobster
**homéopathe** [ɔmeɔpat] *n* homoeopath
**homéopathie** [ɔmeɔpati] *nf* homoeopathy
**homéopathique** [ɔmeɔpatik] *adj* homoeopathic
**homérique** [ɔmeRik] *adj* Homeric
**homicide** [ɔmisid] *nm* murder ▷ *nm/f*
murderer/eress; **~ involontaire** manslaughter
**hommage** [ɔmaʒ] *nm* tribute; **hommages** *nmpl*:
**présenter ses ~s** to pay one's respects; **rendre**
**~ à** to pay tribute *ou* homage to; **en ~ de** as a
token of; **faire ~ de qch à qn** to present sb with
sth
**homme** [ɔm] *nm* man; (*espèce humaine*): **l'~** man,
mankind; **~ des cavernes** caveman; **~ d'Église** churchman,
clergyman; **~ d'État** statesman; **~ de loi**
lawyer; **~ de main** hired man; **~ de paille**
stooge; **~ politique** politician; **l'~ de la rue** the
man in the street; **~ à tout faire** odd-job man
**homme-grenouille** [ɔmgRənuj] (*pl* **hommes-**
**grenouilles**) *nm* frogman
**homme-orchestre** [ɔmɔRkɛstR(ə)] (*pl* **hommes-**

**orchestres)** nm one-man band
**homme-sandwich** [ɔmsɑ̃dwitʃ] (pl **hommes-sandwichs**) nm sandwich (board) man
**homo** [ɔmo] adj, nm/f = **homosexuel**
**homogène** [ɔmɔʒɛn] adj homogeneous
**homogénéisé, e** [ɔmɔʒeneize] adj: **lait ~** homogenized milk
**homogénéité** [ɔmɔʒeneite] nf homogeneity
**homologation** [ɔmɔlɔgɑsjɔ̃] nf ratification; official recognition
**homologue** [ɔmɔlɔg] nm/f counterpart, opposite number
**homologué, e** [ɔmɔlɔge] adj (Sport) officially recognized, ratified; (tarif) authorized
**homologuer** [ɔmɔlɔge] vt (Jur) to ratify; (Sport) to recognize officially, ratify
**homonyme** [ɔmɔnim] nm (Ling) homonym; (d'une personne) namesake
**homosexualité** [ɔmɔsɛksɥalite] nf homosexuality
**homosexuel, le** [ɔmɔsɛksɥɛl] adj homosexual
'**Honduras** ['ɔ̃dyʀas] nm: **le ~** Honduras
'**hondurien, ne** ['ɔ̃dyʀjɛ̃, -ɛn] adj Honduran
'**Hong-Kong** ['ɔ̃gkɔ̃g] n Hong Kong
'**hongre** ['ɔ̃gʀ(ə)] adj (cheval) gelded ▷ nm gelding
'**Hongrie** ['ɔ̃gʀi] nf: **la ~** Hungary
'**hongrois, e** ['ɔ̃gʀwa, -waz] adj Hungarian ▷ nm (Ling) Hungarian ▷ nm/f: '**Hongrois, e** Hungarian
**honnête** [ɔnɛt] adj (intègre) honest; (juste, satisfaisant) fair
**honnêtement** [ɔnɛtmɑ̃] adv honestly
**honnêteté** [ɔnɛtte] nf honesty
**honneur** [ɔnœʀ] nm honour; (mérite): **l'~ lui revient** the credit is his; **à qui ai-je l'~?** to whom have I the pleasure of speaking?; **"j'ai l'~ de ..."** "I have the honour of ..."; **en l'~ de** (personne) in honour of; (événement) on the occasion of; **faire ~ à** (engagements) to honour; (famille, professeur) to be a credit to; (fig: repas etc) to do justice to; **être à l'~** to be in the place of honour; **être en ~** to be in favour; **membre d'~** honorary member; **table d'~** top table
**Honolulu** [ɔnɔlyly] n Honolulu
**honorable** [ɔnɔʀabl(ə)] adj worthy, honourable; (suffisant) decent
**honorablement** [ɔnɔʀabləmɑ̃] adv honourably, decently
**honoraire** [ɔnɔʀɛʀ] adj honorary; **honoraires** nmpl fees; **professeur ~** professor emeritus
**honorer** [ɔnɔʀe] vt to honour; (estimer) to hold in high regard; (faire honneur à) to do credit to; **~ qn de** to honour sb with; **s'honorer de** to pride o.s. upon
**honorifique** [ɔnɔʀifik] adj honorary
'**honte** ['ɔ̃t] nf shame; **avoir ~ de** to be ashamed of; **faire ~ à qn** to make sb (feel) ashamed
'**honteusement** ['ɔ̃tøzmɑ̃] adv shamefully
'**honteux, -euse** ['ɔ̃tø, -øz] adj ashamed; (conduite, acte) shameful, disgraceful

**hôpital, -aux** [ɔpital, -o] nm hospital
'**hoquet** ['ɔkɛ] nm hiccough; **avoir le ~** to have (the) hiccoughs
'**hoqueter** ['ɔkte] vi to hiccough
**horaire** [ɔʀɛʀ] adj hourly ▷ nm timetable, schedule; **horaires** nmpl (heures de travail) hours; **~ flexible** ou **mobile** ou **à la carte** ou **souple** flex(i)time
'**horde** ['ɔʀd(ə)] nf horde
'**horions** ['ɔʀjɔ̃] nmpl blows
**horizon** [ɔʀizɔ̃] nm horizon; (paysage) landscape, view; **sur l'~** on the skyline ou horizon
**horizontal, e, -aux** [ɔʀizɔ̃tal, -o] adj horizontal ▷ nf: **à l'~e** on the horizontal
**horizontalement** [ɔʀizɔ̃talmɑ̃] adv horizontally
**horloge** [ɔʀlɔʒ] nf clock; **l'~ parlante** the speaking clock; **~ normande** grandfather clock; **~ physiologique** biological clock
**horloger, -ère** [ɔʀlɔʒe, -ɛʀ] nm/f watchmaker; clockmaker
**horlogerie** [ɔʀlɔʒʀi] nf watchmaking; watchmaker's (shop); clockmaker's (shop); **pièces d'~** watch parts ou components
'**hormis** ['ɔʀmi] prép save
**hormonal, e, -aux** [ɔʀmɔnal, -o] adj hormonal
**hormone** [ɔʀmɔn] nf hormone
**horodaté, e** [ɔʀɔdate] adj (ticket) time- and date-stamped; (stationnement) pay and display
**horodateur, -trice** [ɔʀɔdatœʀ, -tʀis] adj (appareil) for stamping the time and date ▷ nm/f (parking) ticket machine
**horoscope** [ɔʀɔskɔp] nm horoscope
**horreur** [ɔʀœʀ] nf horror; **avoir ~ de** to loathe, detest; **quelle ~!** how awful!; **cela me fait ~** I find that awful
**horrible** [ɔʀibl(ə)] adj horrible
**horriblement** [ɔʀibləmɑ̃] adv horribly
**horrifiant, e** [ɔʀifjɑ̃, -ɑ̃t] adj horrifying
**horrifier** [ɔʀifje] vt to horrify
**horrifique** [ɔʀifik] adj horrific
**horripilant, e** [ɔʀipilɑ̃, -ɑ̃t] adj exasperating
**horripiler** [ɔʀipile] vt to exasperate
'**hors** ['ɔʀ] prép except (for); **~ de** out of; **~ ligne** (Inform) off line; **~ pair** outstanding; **~ de propos** inopportune; **~ série** (sur mesure) made-to-order; (exceptionnel) exceptional; **~ service (HS)**, **~ d'usage** out of service; **être ~ de soi** to be beside o.s.
'**hors-bord** ['ɔʀbɔʀ] nm inv outboard motor; (canot) speedboat (with outboard motor)
'**hors-concours** ['ɔʀkɔ̃kuʀ] adj inv ineligible to compete; (fig) in a class of one's own
'**hors-d'œuvre** ['ɔʀdœvʀ(ə)] nm inv hors d'œuvre
'**hors-jeu** ['ɔʀʒø] nm inv being offside no pl
'**hors-la-loi** ['ɔʀlalwa] nm inv outlaw
'**hors-piste, 'hors-pistes** ['ɔʀpist] nm inv (Ski) cross-country
**hors-taxe** [ɔʀtaks] adj (sur une facture, prix) excluding VAT; (boutique, marchandises) duty-free
'**hors-texte** ['ɔʀtɛkst(ə)] nm inv plate

**hortensia** [ɔʀtɑ̃sja] *nm* hydrangea
**horticole** [ɔʀtikɔl] *adj* horticultural
**horticulteur, -trice** [ɔʀtikyltœʀ, -tʀis] *nm/f* horticulturalist (*Brit*), horticulturist (*US*)
**horticulture** [ɔʀtikyltyʀ] *nf* horticulture
**hospice** [ɔspis] *nm* (*de vieillards*) home; (*asile*) hospice
**hospitalier, -ière** [ɔspitalje, -jɛʀ] *adj* (*accueillant*) hospitable; (*Méd: service, centre*) hospital *cpd*
**hospitalisation** [ɔspitalizɑsjɔ̃] *nf* hospitalization
**hospitaliser** [ɔspitalize] *vt* to take (*ou* send) to hospital, hospitalize
**hospitalité** [ɔspitalite] *nf* hospitality
**hospitalo-universitaire** [ɔspitaloynivɛʀsitɛʀ] *adj*: **centre ~ (CHU)** ≈ (teaching) hospital
**hostie** [ɔsti] *nf* host; (*Rel*)
**hostile** [ɔstil] *adj* hostile
**hostilité** [ɔstilite] *nf* hostility; **hostilités** *nfpl* hostilities
**hôte** [ot] *nm* (*maître de maison*) host; (*client*) patron; (*fig*) inhabitant, occupant ▷ *nm/f* (*invité*) guest; **~ payant** paying guest
**hôtel** [otɛl] *nm* hotel; **aller à l'~** to stay in a hotel; **~ (particulier)** (private) mansion; **~ de ville** town hall
**hôtelier, -ière** [otəlje, -jɛʀ] *adj* hotel *cpd* ▷ *nm/f* hotelier, hotel-keeper
**hôtellerie** [otɛlʀi] *nf* (*profession*) hotel business; (*auberge*) inn
**hôtesse** [otɛs] *nf* hostess; **~ de l'air** flight attendant; **~ (d'accueil)** receptionist
**'hotte** ['ɔt] *nf* (*panier*) basket (*carried on the back*); (*de cheminée*) hood; **~ aspirante** cooker hood
**'houblon** ['ublɔ̃] *nm* (*Bot*) hop; (*pour la bière*) hops *pl*
**'houe** ['u] *nf* hoe
**'houille** ['uj] *nf* coal; **~ blanche** hydroelectric power
**'houiller, -ère** ['uje, -ɛʀ] *adj* coal *cpd*; (*terrain*) coal-bearing ▷ *nf* coal mine
**'houle** ['ul] *nf* swell
**'houlette** ['ulɛt] *nf*: **sous la ~ de** under the guidance of
**'houleux, -euse** ['ulø, -øz] *adj* heavy, swelling; (*fig*) stormy, turbulent
**'houppe** ['up], **'houppette** ['upɛt] *nf* powder puff; (*cheveux*) tuft
**'hourra** ['uʀa] *nm* cheer ▷ *excl* hurrah!
**'houspiller** ['uspije] *vt* to scold
**'housse** ['us] *nf* cover; (*pour protéger provisoirement*) dust cover; (*pour recouvrir à neuf*) loose *ou* stretch cover; **~ (penderie)** hanging wardrobe
**'houx** ['u] *nm* holly
**hovercraft** [ovœʀkʀaft] *nm* hovercraft
**HS** *abr* = **hors service**
**HT** *abr* = **hors taxe**
**'hublot** ['yblo] *nm* porthole
**'huche** ['yʃ] *nf*: **~ à pain** bread bin
**'huées** ['ɥe] *nfpl* boos
**'huer** ['ɥe] *vt* to boo; (*hibou, chouette*) to hoot
**huile** [ɥil] *nf* oil; (*Art*) oil painting; (*fam*) bigwig;

**mer d'~** (*très calme*) glassy sea, sea of glass; **faire tache d'~** (*fig*) to spread; **~ d'arachide** groundnut oil; **~ essentielle** essential oil; **~ de foie de morue** cod-liver oil; **~ de ricin** castor oil; **~ solaire** suntan oil; **~ de table** salad oil
**huiler** [ɥile] *vt* to oil
**huilerie** [ɥilʀi] *nf* (*usine*) oil-works
**huileux, -euse** [ɥilø, -øz] *adj* oily
**huilier** [ɥilje] *nm* (oil and vinegar) cruet
**huis** [ɥi] *nm*: **à ~ clos** in camera
**huissier** [ɥisje] *nm* usher; (*Jur*) ≈ bailiff
**'huit** ['ɥi(t)] *num* eight; **samedi en ~** a week on Saturday; **dans ~ jours** in a week('s time)
**'huitaine** ['ɥitɛn] *nf*: **une ~ de** about eight, eight or so; **une ~ de jours** a week or so
**'huitante** ['ɥitɑ̃t] *num* (*Suisse*) eighty
**'huitième** ['ɥitjɛm] *num* eighth
**huître** [ɥitʀ(ə)] *nf* oyster
**'hululement** ['ylylmɑ̃] *nm* hooting
**'hululer** ['ylyle] *vi* to hoot
**humain, e** [ymɛ̃, -ɛn] *adj* human; (*compatissant*) humane ▷ *nm* human (being)
**humainement** [ymɛnmɑ̃] *adv* humanly; humanely
**humanisation** [ymanizɑsjɑ̃] *nf* humanization
**humaniser** [ymanize] *vt* to humanize
**humaniste** [ymanist(ə)] *nm/f* (*Ling*) classicist; humanist
**humanitaire** [ymanitɛʀ] *adj* humanitarian
**humanitarisme** [ymanitaʀism(ə)] *nm* humanitarianism
**humanité** [ymanite] *nf* humanity
**humanoïde** [ymanɔid] *nm/f* humanoid
**humble** [œ̃bl(ə)] *adj* humble
**humblement** [œ̃bləmɑ̃] *adv* humbly
**humecter** [ymɛkte] *vt* to dampen; **s'~ les lèvres** to moisten one's lips
**'humer** ['yme] *vt* to inhale; (*pour sentir*) to smell
**humérus** [ymeʀys] *nm* (*Anat*) humerus
**humeur** [ymœʀ] *nf* mood; (*tempérament*) temper; (*irritation*) bad temper; **de bonne/mauvaise ~** in a good/bad mood; **être d'~ à faire qch** to be in the mood for doing sth
**humide** [ymid] *adj* (*linge*) damp; (*main, yeux*) moist; (*climat, chaleur*) humid; (*saison, route*) wet
**humidificateur** [ymidifikatœʀ] *nm* humidifier
**humidifier** [ymidifje] *vt* to humidify
**humidité** [ymidite] *nf* humidity; dampness; **traces d'~** traces of moisture *ou* damp
**humiliant, e** [ymiljɑ̃, -ɑ̃t] *adj* humiliating
**humiliation** [ymiljɑsjɔ̃] *nf* humiliation
**humilier** [ymilje] *vt* to humiliate; **s'~ devant qn** to humble o.s. before sb
**humilité** [ymilite] *nf* humility
**humoriste** [ymɔʀist(ə)] *nm/f* humorist
**humoristique** [ymɔʀistik] *adj* humorous; humoristic
**humour** [ymuʀ] *nm* humour; **avoir de l'~** to have a sense of humour; **~ noir** sick humour
**humus** [ymys] *nm* humus
**'huppé, e** ['ype] *adj* crested; (*fam*) posh
**'hurlement** ['yʀləmɑ̃] *nm* howling *no pl*, howl;

**h**

yelling *no pl*, yell

**'hurler** ['yʀle] *vi* to howl, yell; *(fig: vent)* to howl; *(: couleurs etc)* to clash; ~ **à la mort** *(chien)* to bay at the moon

**hurluberlu** [yʀlybɛʀly] *nm (péj)* crank ▷ *adj* cranky

**'hutte** ['yt] *nf* hut

**hybride** [ibʀid] *adj* hybrid

**hydratant, e** [idʀatɑ̃, -ɑ̃t] *adj (crème)* moisturizing

**hydrate** [idʀat] *nm*: ~**s de carbone** carbohydrates

**hydrater** [idʀate] *vt* to hydrate

**hydraulique** [idʀolik] *adj* hydraulic

**hydravion** [idʀavjɔ̃] *nm* seaplane, hydroplane

**hydro...** [idʀo] *préfixe* hydro...

**hydrocarbure** [idʀokaʀbyʀ] *nm* hydrocarbon

**hydrocution** [idʀokysjɔ̃] *nf* immersion syncope

**hydro-électrique** [idʀoelɛktʀik] *adj* hydroelectric

**hydrogène** [idʀoʒɛn] *nm* hydrogen

**hydroglisseur** [idʀoglisœʀ] *nm* hydroplane

**hydrographie** [idʀogʀafi] *nf (fleuves)* hydrography

**hydrophile** [idʀofil] *adj voir* **coton**

**hyène** [jɛn] *nf* hyena

**hygiène** [iʒjɛn] *nf* hygiene; ~ **intime** personal hygiene

**hygiénique** [iʒenik] *adj* hygienic

**hymne** [imn(ə)] *nm* hymn; ~ **national** national anthem

**hyper...** [ipɛʀ] *préfixe* hyper...

**hyperlien** [ipɛʀljɛ̃] *nm (Inform)* hyperlink

**hypermarché** [ipɛʀmaʀʃe] *nm* hypermarket

**hypermétrope** [ipɛʀmetʀop] *adj* long-sighted

**hypernerveux, -euse** [ipɛʀnɛʀvø, -øz] *adj* highly-strung

**hypersensible** [ipɛʀsɑ̃sibl(ə)] *adj* hypersensitive

**hypertendu, e** [ipɛʀtɑ̃dy] *adj* having high blood pressure, hypertensive

**hypertension** [ipɛʀtɑ̃sjɔ̃] *nf* high blood pressure, hypertension

**hypertexte** [ipɛʀtɛkst] *nm (Inform)* hypertext

**hypertrophié, e** [ipɛʀtʀofje] *adj* hypertrophic

**hypnose** [ipnoz] *nf* hypnosis

**hypnotique** [ipnotik] *adj* hypnotic

**hypnotiser** [ipnotize] *vt* to hypnotize

**hypnotiseur** [ipnotizœʀ] *nm* hypnotist

**hypnotisme** [ipnotism(ə)] *nm* hypnotism

**hypocondriaque** [ipokɔ̃dʀijak] *adj* hypochondriac

**hypocrisie** [ipokʀizi] *nf* hypocrisy

**hypocrite** [ipokʀit] *adj* hypocritical ▷ *nm/f* hypocrite

**hypocritement** [ipokʀitmɑ̃] *adv* hypocritically

**hypotendu, e** [ipotɑ̃dy] *adj* having low blood pressure, hypotensive

**hypotension** [ipotɑ̃sjɔ̃] *nf* low blood pressure, hypotension

**hypoténuse** [ipotenyz] *nf* hypotenuse

**hypothécaire** [ipotekɛʀ] *adj* mortgage; **garantie/prêt** ~ mortgage security/loan

**hypothèque** [ipotɛk] *nf* mortgage

**hypothéquer** [ipoteke] *vt* to mortgage

**hypothermie** [ipotɛʀmi] *nf* hypothermia

**hypothèse** [ipotɛz] *nf* hypothesis; **dans l'** ~ **où** assuming that

**hypothétique** [ipotetik] *adj* hypothetical

**hypothétiquement** [ipotetikmɑ̃] *adv* hypothetically

**hystérectomie** [isteʀɛktomi] *nf* hysterectomy

**hystérie** [isteʀi] *nf* hysteria; ~ **collective** mass hysteria

**hystérique** [isteʀik] *adj* hysterical

**Hz** *abr* (= *Hertz*) Hz

# I i

**I, i** [i] *nm inv* I, i; **I comme Irma** I for Isaac (*Brit*) *ou* Item (*US*)

**IAC** *sigle f* (= *insémination artificielle entre conjoints*) AIH

**IAD** *sigle f* (= *insémination artificielle par donneur extérieur*) AID

**ibère** [ibɛʀ] *adj* Iberian ▷ *nm/f*: **Ibère** Iberian

**ibérique** [ibeʀik] *adj*: **la péninsule ~** the Iberian peninsula

**ibid.** [ibid] *abr* (= *ibidem*) ibid., ib.

**iceberg** [isbɛʀg] *nm* iceberg

**ici** [isi] *adv* here; **jusqu'~** as far as this; (*temporel*) until now; **d'~ là** by then; (*en attendant*) in the meantime; **d'~ peu** before long

**icône** [ikon] *nf* (*aussi Inform*) icon

**iconoclaste** [ikɔnɔklast(ə)] *nm/f* iconoclast

**iconographie** [ikɔnɔgʀafi] *nf* iconography; (*illustrations*) (collection of) illustrations

**id.** [id] *abr* (=*idem*) id.

**idéal, e, -aux** [ideal, -o] *adj* ideal ▷ *nm* ideal; (*système de valeurs*) ideals *pl*

**idéalement** [idealmɑ̃] *adv* ideally

**idéalisation** [idealizasjɔ̃] *nf* idealization

**idéaliser** [idealize] *vt* to idealize

**idéalisme** [idealism(ə)] *nm* idealism

**idéaliste** [idealist(ə)] *adj* idealistic ▷ *nm/f* idealist

**idée** [ide] *nf* idea; (*illusion*): **se faire des ~s** to imagine things, get ideas into one's head; **avoir dans l'~ que** to have an idea that; **mon ~, c'est que ...** I suggest that ..., I think that ...; **à l'~ de/que** at the idea of/that, at the thought of/ that; **je n'ai pas la moindre ~** I haven't the faintest idea; **avoir ~ que** to have an idea that; **avoir des ~s larges/étroites** to be broad-/ narrow-minded; **venir à l'~ de qn** to occur to sb; **en voilà des ~s!** the very idea!; **~ fixe** idée fixe, obsession; **~s noires** black *ou* dark thoughts; **~s reçues** accepted ideas *ou* wisdom

**identifiable** [idɑ̃tifjabl(ə)] *adj* identifiable

**identifiant** [idɑ̃tifjɑ̃] *nm* (*Inform*) login

**identification** [idɑ̃tifikasjɔ̃] *nf* identification

**identifier** [idɑ̃tifje] *vt* to identify; **~ qch/qn à** to identify sth/sb with; **s'~ avec** *ou* **à qn/qch** (*héros etc*) to identify with sb/sth

**identique** [idɑ̃tik] *adj*: **~ (à)** identical (to)

**identité** [idɑ̃tite] *nf* identity; **~ judiciaire** (*Police*) ≈ Criminal Records Office

**idéogramme** [ideogʀam] *nm* ideogram

**idéologie** [ideɔlɔʒi] *nf* ideology

**idéologique** [ideɔlɔʒik] *adj* ideological

**idiomatique** [idjɔmatik] *adj*: **expression ~** idiom, idiomatic expression

**idiome** [idjom] *nm* (*Ling*) idiom

**idiot, e** [idjo, idjɔt] *adj* idiotic ▷ *nm/f* idiot

**idiotie** [idjɔsi] *nf* idiocy; (*propos*) idiotic remark

**idiotisme** [idjɔtism(ə)] *nm* idiom, idiomatic phrase

**idoine** [idwan] *adj* fitting

**idolâtrer** [idɔlatʀe] *vt* to idolize

**idolâtrie** [idɔlatʀi] *nf* idolatry

**idole** [idɔl] *nf* idol

**idylle** [idil] *nf* idyll

**idyllique** [idilik] *adj* idyllic

**if** [if] *nm* yew

**IFOP** [ifɔp] *sigle m* (= *Institut français d'opinion publique*) French market research institute

**IGH** *sigle m* = **immeuble de grande hauteur**

**igloo** [iglu] *nm* igloo

**IGN** *sigle m* = **Institut géographique national**

**ignare** [iɲaʀ] *adj* ignorant

**ignifuge** [iɲifyʒ] *adj* fireproofing ▷ *nm* fireproofing (substance)

**ignifuger** [iɲifyʒe] *vt* to fireproof

**ignoble** [iɲɔbl(ə)] *adj* vile

**ignominie** [iɲɔmini] *nf* ignominy; (*acte*) ignominious *ou* base act

**ignominieux, -euse** [iɲɔminjø, øz] *adj* ignominious

**ignorance** [iɲɔʀɑ̃s] *nf* ignorance; **dans l'~ de** in ignorance of, ignorant of

**ignorant, e** [iɲɔʀɑ̃, -ɑ̃t] *adj* ignorant ▷ *nm/f*: **faire l'~** to pretend one doesn't know; **~ de** ignorant of, not aware of; **~ en** ignorant of, knowing nothing of

**ignoré, e** [iɲɔʀe] *adj* unknown

**ignorer** [iɲɔʀe] *vt* (*ne pas connaître*) not to know, be unaware *ou* ignorant of; (*être sans expérience de: plaisir, guerre etc*) not to know about, have no experience of; (*bouder: personne*) to ignore; **j'ignore comment/si** I do not know how/if; **~ que** to be unaware that, not to know that; **je**

**n'ignore pas que ...** I'm not forgetting that ..., I'm not unaware that ...; **je l'ignore** I don't know

**IGPN** sigle f (= Inspection générale de la police nationale) police disciplinary body

**IGS** sigle f (= Inspection générale des services) police disciplinary body for Paris

**iguane** [igwan] nm iguana

**il** [il] pron he; (animal, chose, en tournure impersonnelle) it; NB: en anglais les navires et les pays sont en général assimilés aux femelles, et les bébés aux choses, si le sexe n'est pas spécifié; **ils** they; **il neige** it's snowing; voir aussi **avoir**

**île** [il] nf island; **les Î-s** the West Indies; **l'~ de Beauté** Corsica; **l'~ Maurice** Mauritius; **les ~s anglo-normandes** the Channel Islands; **les ~s Britanniques** the British Isles; **les ~s Cocos** ou **Keeling** the Cocos ou Keeling Islands; **les ~s Cook** the Cook Islands; **les ~s Scilly** the Scilly Isles, the Scillies; **les ~s Shetland** the Shetland Islands, Shetland; **les ~s Sorlingues**; = **les îles Scilly**; **les ~s Vierges** the Virgin Islands

**iliaque** [iljak] adj (Anat): **os/artère ~** iliac bone/artery

**illégal, e, -aux** [ilegal, -o] adj illegal, unlawful (Admin)

**illégalement** [ilegalmã] adv illegally

**illégalité** [ilegalite] nf illegality; unlawfulness; **être dans l'~** to be outside the law

**illégitime** [ileʒitim] adj illegitimate; (optimisme, sévérité) unjustified, unwarranted

**illégitimement** [ileʒitimmã] adv illegitimately

**illégitimité** [ileʒitimite] nf illegitimacy; **gouverner dans l'~** to rule illegally

**illettré, e** [iletʀe] adj, nm/f illiterate

**illicite** [ilisit] adj illicit

**illicitement** [ilisitmã] adv illicitly

**illico** [iliko] adv (fam) pronto

**illimité, e** [ilimite] adj (immense) boundless, unlimited; (congé, durée) indefinite, unlimited

**illisible** [ilizibl(ə)] adj illegible; (roman) unreadable

**illisiblement** [ilizibləmã] adv illegibly

**illogique** [iloʒik] adj illogical

**illogisme** [iloʒism(ə)] nm illogicality

**illumination** [ilyminasjɔ̃] nf illumination, floodlighting; (inspiration) flash of inspiration; **illuminations** nfpl illuminations, lights

**illuminé, e** [ilymine] adj lit up; illuminated, floodlit ▷ nm/f (fig: péj) crank

**illuminer** [ilymine] vt to light up; (monument, rue: pour une fête) to illuminate, floodlight; **s'illuminer** vi to light up

**illusion** [ilyzjɔ̃] nf illusion; **se faire des ~s** to delude o.s.; **faire ~** to delude ou fool people; **~ d'optique** optical illusion

**illusionner** [ilyzjɔne] vt to delude; **s'~ (sur qn/qch)** to delude o.s. (about sb/sth)

**illusionnisme** [ilyzjɔnism(ə)] nm conjuring

**illusionniste** [ilyzjɔnist(ə)] nm/f conjuror

**illusoire** [ilyzwaʀ] adj illusory, illusive

**illustrateur** [ilystʀatœʀ] nm illustrator

**illustratif, -ive** [ilystʀatif, -iv] adj illustrative

**illustration** [ilystʀasjɔ̃] nf illustration; (d'un ouvrage: photos) illustrations pl

**illustre** [ilystʀ(ə)] adj illustrious, renowned

**illustré, e** [ilystʀe] adj illustrated ▷ nm illustrated magazine; (pour enfants) comic

**illustrer** [ilystʀe] vt to illustrate; **s'illustrer** to become famous, win fame

**îlot** [ilo] nm small island, islet; (de maisons) block; (petite zone): **un ~ de verdure** an island of greenery, a patch of green

**ils** [il] pron voir **il**

**image** [imaʒ] nf (gén) picture; (comparaison, ressemblance, Optique) image; **~ de** picture ou image of; **~ d'Épinal** (social) stereotype; **~ de marque** brand image; (d'une personne) (public) image; (d'une entreprise) corporate image; **~ pieuse** holy picture

**imagé, e** [imaʒe] adj full of imagery

**imaginable** [imaʒinabl(ə)] adj imaginable; **difficilement ~** hard to imagine

**imaginaire** [imaʒinɛʀ] adj imaginary

**imaginatif, -ive** [imaʒinatif, -iv] adj imaginative

**imagination** [imaʒinasjɔ̃] nf imagination; (chimère) fancy, imagining; **avoir de l'~** to be imaginative, have a good imagination

**imaginer** [imaʒine] vt to imagine; (croire): **qu'allez-vous ~ là?** what on earth are you thinking of?; (inventer: expédient, mesure) to devise, think up; **s'imaginer** vt (se figurer: scène etc) to imagine, picture; **s'~ à 60 ans** to picture ou imagine o.s. at 60; **s'~ que** to imagine that; **s'~ pouvoir faire qch** to think one can do sth; **j'imagine qu'il a voulu plaisanter** I suppose he was joking; **~ de faire** (se mettre dans l'idée de) to dream up the idea of doing

**imbattable** [ɛ̃batabl(ə)] adj unbeatable

**imbécile** [ɛ̃besil] adj idiotic ▷ nm/f idiot; (Méd) imbecile

**imbécillité** [ɛ̃besilite] nf idiocy; imbecility; idiotic action (ou remark etc)

**imberbe** [ɛ̃bɛʀb(ə)] adj beardless

**imbiber** [ɛ̃bibe] vt: **~ qch de** to moisten ou wet sth with; **s'imbiber de** to become saturated with; **imbibé(e) d'eau** (chaussures, étoffe) saturated; (terre) waterlogged

**imbriqué, e** [ɛ̃bʀike] adj overlapping

**imbriquer** [ɛ̃bʀike]: **s'imbriquer** vi to overlap (each other); (fig) to become interlinked ou interwoven

**imbroglio** [ɛ̃bʀɔljo] nm imbroglio

**imbu, e** [ɛ̃by] adj: **~ de** full of; **~ de soi-même/sa supériorité** full of oneself/one's superiority

**imbuvable** [ɛ̃byvabl(ə)] adj undrinkable

**imitable** [imitabl(ə)] adj imitable; **facilement ~** easily imitated

**imitateur, -trice** [imitatœʀ, -tʀis] nm/f (gén) imitator; (Music-Hall: d'une personnalité) impersonator

**imitation** [imitasjɔ̃] nf imitation; impersonation; **sac ~ cuir** bag in imitation ou

simulated leather; **à l'~ de** in imitation of
**imiter** [imite] vt to imitate; (personne) to imitate,
impersonate; (contrefaire: signature, document) to
forge, copy; (ressembler à) to look like; **il se leva
et je l'imitai** he got up and I did likewise
**imm.** abr = **immeuble**
**immaculé, e** [imakyle] adj spotless,
immaculate; **l'I~e Conception** (Rel) the
Immaculate Conception
**immanent, e** [imanɑ̃, -ɑ̃t] adj immanent
**immangeable** [ɛ̃mɑ̃ʒabl(ə)] adj inedible,
uneatable
**immanquable** [ɛ̃mɑ̃kabl(ə)] adj (cible)
impossible to miss; (fatal, inévitable) bound to
happen, inevitable
**immanquablement** [ɛ̃mɑ̃kabləmɑ̃] adv
inevitably
**immatériel, le** [imateʀjɛl] adj ethereal;
(Philosophie) immaterial
**immatriculation** [imatʀikylasjɔ̃] nf
registration
**immatriculer** [imatʀikyle] vt to register; **faire/
se faire ~** to register; **voiture immatriculée
dans la Seine** car with a Seine registration
(number)
**immature** [imatyʀ] adj immature
**immaturité** [imatyʀite] nf immaturity
**immédiat, e** [imedja, -at] adj immediate ▷ nm:
**dans l'~** for the time being; **dans le voisinage
~ de** in the immediate vicinity of
**immédiatement** [imedjatmɑ̃] adv
immediately
**immémorial, e, -aux** [imemɔʀjal, -o] adj
ancient, age-old
**immense** [imɑ̃s] adj immense
**immensément** [imɑ̃semɑ̃] adv immensely
**immensité** [imɑ̃site] nf immensity
**immerger** [imɛʀʒe] vt to immerse, submerge;
(câble etc) to lay under water; (déchets) to dump
at sea; **s'immerger** vi (sous-marin) to dive,
submerge
**immérité, e** [imeʀite] adj undeserved
**immersion** [imɛʀsjɔ̃] nf immersion
**immettable** [ɛ̃metabl(ə)] adj unwearable
**immeuble** [imœbl(ə)] nm building ▷ adj (Jur)
immovable, real; **~ locatif** block of rented flats
(Brit), rental building (US); **~ de rapport**
investment property
**immigrant, e** [imigʀɑ̃, -ɑ̃t] nm/f immigrant
**immigration** [imigʀasjɔ̃] nf immigration
**immigré, e** [imigʀe] nm/f immigrant
**immigrer** [imigʀe] vi to immigrate
**imminence** [iminɑ̃s] nf imminence
**imminent, e** [iminɑ̃, -ɑ̃t] adj imminent,
impending
**immiscer** [imise]: **s'immiscer** vi: **s'~ dans** to
interfere in ou with
**immixtion** [imiksjɔ̃] nf interference
**immobile** [imɔbil] adj still, motionless; (pièce de
machine) fixed; (fig) unchanging; **rester/se
tenir ~** to stay/keep still
**immobilier, -ière** [imɔbilje, -jɛR] adj property

cpd, in real property ▷ nm: **l'~** the property ou
the real estate business
**immobilisation** [imɔbilizasjɔ̃] nf
immobilization; **immobilisations** nfpl (Jur)
fixed assets
**immobiliser** [imɔbilize] vt (gén) to immobilize;
(circulation, véhicule, affaires) to bring to a
standstill; **s'immobiliser** (personne) to stand
still; (machine, véhicule) to come to a halt ou a
standstill
**immobilisme** [imɔbilism(ə)] nm strong
resistance ou opposition to change
**immobilité** [imɔbilite] nf immobility
**immodéré, e** [imɔdeʀe] adj immoderate,
inordinate
**immodérément** [imɔdeʀemɑ̃] adv
immoderately
**immoler** [imɔle] vt to sacrifice
**immonde** [imɔ̃d] adj foul; (sale: ruelle, taudis)
squalid
**immondices** [imɔ̃dis] nfpl (ordures) refuse sg;
(saletés) filth sg
**immoral, e, -aux** [imɔʀal, -o] adj immoral
**immoralisme** [imɔʀalism(ə)] nm immoralism
**immoralité** [imɔʀalite] nf immorality
**immortaliser** [imɔʀtalize] vt to immortalize
**immortel, le** [imɔʀtɛl] adj immortal ▷ nf (Bot)
everlasting (flower)
**immuable** [imɥabl(ə)] adj (inébranlable)
immutable; (qui ne change pas) unchanging;
(personne): **~ dans ses convictions** immoveable
(in one's convictions)
**immunisation** [imynizasjɔ̃] nf immunization
**immunisé, e** [im(m)ynize] adj: **~ contre**
immune to
**immuniser** [imynize] vt (Méd) to immunize; **~
qn contre** to immunize sb against; (fig) to
make sb immune to
**immunitaire** [imynitɛR] adj immune
**immunité** [imynite] nf immunity; **~
diplomatique** diplomatic immunity; **~
parlementaire** parliamentary privilege
**immunologie** [imynɔlɔʒi] nf immunology
**immutabilité** [imytabilite] nf immutability
**impact** [ɛ̃pakt] nm impact; **point d'~** point of
impact
**impair, e** [ɛ̃pɛʀ] adj odd ▷ nm faux pas, blunder;
**numéros ~s** odd numbers
**impalpable** [ɛ̃palpabl(ə)] adj impalpable
**impaludation** [ɛ̃palydasjɔ̃] nf inoculation
against malaria
**imparable** [ɛ̃paʀabl(ə)] adj unstoppable
**impardonnable** [ɛ̃paʀdɔnabl(ə)] adj
unpardonable, unforgivable; **vous êtes ~
d'avoir fait cela** it's unforgivable of you to
have done that
**imparfait, e** [ɛ̃paʀfɛ, -ɛt] adj imperfect ▷ nm
(Ling) imperfect (tense)
**imparfaitement** [ɛ̃paʀfɛtmɑ̃] adv imperfectly
**impartial, e, -aux** [ɛ̃paʀsjal, -o] adj impartial,
unbiased
**impartialité** [ɛ̃paʀsjalite] nf impartiality

**impartir** [ɛ̃paʀtiʀ] *vt*: ~ **qch à qn** to assign sth to sb; *(dons)* to bestow sth upon sb; **dans les délais impartis** in the time allowed

**impasse** [ɛ̃pɑs] *nf* dead-end, cul-de-sac; *(fig)* deadlock; **être dans l'**~ *(négociations)* to have reached deadlock; ~ **budgétaire** budget deficit

**impassibilité** [ɛ̃pasibilite] *nf* impassiveness

**impassible** [ɛ̃pasibl(ə)] *adj* impassive

**impassiblement** [ɛ̃pasibləmɑ̃] *adv* impassively

**impatiemment** [ɛ̃pasjamɑ̃] *adv* impatiently

**impatience** [ɛ̃pasjɑ̃s] *nf* impatience

**impatient, e** [ɛ̃pasjɑ̃, -ɑ̃t] *adj* impatient; ~ **de faire qch** keen *ou* impatient to do sth

**impatienter** [ɛ̃pasjɑ̃te] *vt* to irritate, annoy; **s'impatienter** *vi* to get impatient; **s'**~ **de/contre** to lose patience at/with, grow impatient at/with

**impayable** [ɛ̃pejabl(ə)] *adj (drôle)* priceless

**impayé, e** [ɛ̃peje] *adj* unpaid, outstanding

**impeccable** [ɛ̃pekabl(ə)] *adj* faultless, impeccable; *(propre)* spotlessly clean; *(chic)* impeccably dressed; *(fam)* smashing

**impeccablement** [ɛ̃pekabləmɑ̃] *adv* impeccably

**impénétrable** [ɛ̃penetʀabl(ə)] *adj* impenetrable

**impénitent, e** [ɛ̃penitɑ̃, -ɑ̃t] *adj* unrepentant

**impensable** [ɛ̃pɑ̃sabl(ə)] *adj* unthinkable, unbelievable

**imper** [ɛ̃pɛʀ] *nm (imperméable)* mac

**impératif, -ive** [ɛ̃peʀatif, -iv] *adj* imperative; *(Jur)* mandatory ▷ *nm (Ling)* imperative; **impératifs** *nmpl* requirements; demands

**impérativement** [ɛ̃peʀativmɑ̃] *adv* imperatively

**impératrice** [ɛ̃peʀatʀis] *nf* empress

**imperceptible** [ɛ̃pɛʀsɛptibl(ə)] *adj* imperceptible

**imperceptiblement** [ɛ̃pɛʀsɛptibləmɑ̃] *adv* imperceptibly

**imperdable** [ɛ̃pɛʀdabl(ə)] *adj* that cannot be lost

**imperfectible** [ɛ̃pɛʀfɛktibl(ə)] *adj* which cannot be perfected

**imperfection** [ɛ̃pɛʀfɛksjɔ̃] *nf* imperfection

**impérial, e, -aux** [ɛ̃peʀjal, -o] *adj* imperial ▷ *nf* upper deck; **autobus à -e** double-decker bus

**impérialisme** [ɛ̃peʀjalism(ə)] *nm* imperialism

**impérialiste** [ɛ̃peʀjalist(ə)] *adj* imperialist

**impérieusement** [ɛ̃peʀjøzmɑ̃] *adv*: **avoir** ~ **besoin de qch** to have urgent need of sth

**impérieux, -euse** [ɛ̃peʀjø, -øz] *adj (caractère, ton)* imperious; *(obligation, besoin)* pressing, urgent

**impérissable** [ɛ̃peʀisabl(ə)] *adj* undying, imperishable

**imperméabilisation** [ɛ̃pɛʀmeabilizasjɔ̃] *nf* waterproofing

**imperméabiliser** [ɛ̃pɛʀmeabilize] *vt* to waterproof

**imperméable** [ɛ̃pɛʀmeabl(ə)] *adj* waterproof; *(Géo)* impermeable; *(fig)*: ~ **à** impervious to ▷ *nm* raincoat; ~ **à l'air** airtight

**impersonnel, le** [ɛ̃pɛʀsɔnɛl] *adj* impersonal

**impertinemment** [ɛ̃pɛʀtinamɑ̃] *adv* impertinently

**impertinence** [ɛ̃pɛʀtinɑ̃s] *nf* impertinence

**impertinent, e** [ɛ̃pɛʀtinɑ̃, -ɑ̃t] *adj* impertinent

**imperturbable** [ɛ̃pɛʀtyʀbabl(ə)] *adj (personne)* imperturbable; *(sang-froid)* unshakeable; **rester** ~ to remain unruffled

**imperturbablement** [ɛ̃pɛʀtyʀbabləmɑ̃] *adv* imperturbably; unshakeably

**impétrant, e** [ɛ̃petʀɑ̃, -ɑ̃t] *nm/f (Jur)* applicant

**impétueux, -euse** [ɛ̃petɥø, -øz] *adj* fiery

**impétuosité** [ɛ̃petɥozite] *nf* fieriness

**impie** [ɛ̃pi] *adj* impious, ungodly

**impiété** [ɛ̃pjete] *nf* impiety

**impitoyable** [ɛ̃pitwajabl(ə)] *adj* pitiless, merciless

**impitoyablement** [ɛ̃pitwajabləmɑ̃] *adv* mercilessly

**implacable** [ɛ̃plakabl(ə)] *adj* implacable

**implacablement** [ɛ̃plakabləmɑ̃] *adv* implacably

**implant** [ɛ̃plɑ̃] *nm (Méd)* implant

**implantation** [ɛ̃plɑ̃tasjɔ̃] *nf* establishment; settling; implantation

**implanter** [ɛ̃plɑ̃te] *vt (usine, industrie, usage)* to establish; *(colons etc)* to settle; *(idée, préjugé)* to implant; **s'implanter dans** *vi* to be established in; to settle in; to become implanted in

**implémenter** [ɛ̃plemɑ̃te] *vt (aussi Inform)* to implement

**implication** [ɛ̃plikasjɔ̃] *nf* implication

**implicite** [ɛ̃plisit] *adj* implicit

**implicitement** [ɛ̃plisitmɑ̃] *adv* implicitly

**impliquer** [ɛ̃plike] *vt* to imply; ~ **qn (dans)** to implicate sb (in)

**implorant, e** [ɛ̃plɔʀɑ̃, -ɑ̃t] *adj* imploring

**implorer** [ɛ̃plɔʀe] *vt* to implore

**imploser** [ɛ̃plɔze] *vi* to implode

**implosion** [ɛ̃plozjɔ̃] *nf* implosion

**impoli, e** [ɛ̃pɔli] *adj* impolite, rude

**impoliment** [ɛ̃pɔlimɑ̃] *adv* impolitely

**impolitesse** [ɛ̃pɔlitɛs] *nf* impoliteness, rudeness; *(propos)* impolite *ou* rude remark

**impondérable** [ɛ̃pɔ̃deʀabl(ə)] *nm* imponderable

**impopulaire** [ɛ̃pɔpylɛʀ] *adj* unpopular

**impopularité** [ɛ̃pɔpylaʀite] *nf* unpopularity

**importable** [ɛ̃pɔʀtabl(ə)] *adj (Comm: marchandise)* importable; *(vêtement: immettable)* unwearable

**importance** [ɛ̃pɔʀtɑ̃s] *nf* importance; **avoir de l'**~ to be important; **sans** ~ unimportant; **d'**~ important, considerable; **quelle** ~? what does it matter?

**important, e** [ɛ̃pɔʀtɑ̃, -ɑ̃t] *adj* important; *(en quantité)* considerable, sizeable; *(: gamme, dégâts)* extensive; *(péj: airs, ton)* self-important ▷ *nm*: **l'**~ the important thing

**importateur, -trice** [ɛ̃pɔʀtatœʀ, -tʀis] *adj* importing ▷ *nm/f* importer; **pays** ~ **de blé** wheat-importing country

**importation** [ɛ̃pɔʀtasjɔ̃] *nf* import; introduction; *(produit)* import

**importer** [ɛ̃pɔʀte] *vt (Comm)* to import;

(*maladies, plantes*) to introduce ▷ *vi* (*être important*) to matter; **~ à qn** to matter to sb; **il importe de** it is important to; **il importe qu'il fasse** he must do, it is important that he should do; **peu m'importe** I don't mind, I don't care; **peu importe** it doesn't matter; **peu importe (que)** it doesn't matter (if); **peu importe le prix** never mind the price; *voir aussi* **n'importe**
**import-export** [ɛ̃pɔʀɛkspɔʀ] *nm* import-export business
**importun, e** [ɛ̃pɔʀtœ̃, -yn] *adj* irksome, importunate; (*arrivée, visite*) inopportune, ill-timed ▷ *nm* intruder
**importuner** [ɛ̃pɔʀtyne] *vt* to bother
**imposable** [ɛ̃pozabl(ə)] *adj* taxable
**imposant, e** [ɛ̃pozɑ̃, -ɑ̃t] *adj* imposing
**imposé, e** [ɛ̃poze] *adj* (*soumis à l'impôt*) taxed; (*Gym etc: figures*) set
**imposer** [ɛ̃poze] *vt* (*taxer*) to tax; (*Rel*): **~ les mains** to lay on hands; **~ qch à qn** to impose sth on sb; **s'imposer** *vi* (*être nécessaire*) to be imperative; (*montrer sa proéminence*) to stand out, emerge; (*artiste: se faire connaître*) to win recognition, come to the fore; **en ~** to be imposing; **en ~ à** to impress; **ça s'impose** it's essential, it's vital
**imposition** [ɛ̃pozisjɔ̃] *nf* (*Admin*) taxation
**impossibilité** [ɛ̃posibilite] *nf* impossibility; **être dans l'~ de faire** to be unable to do, find it impossible to do
**impossible** [ɛ̃posibl(ə)] *adj* impossible ▷ *nm*: **l'~** the impossible; **~ à faire** impossible to do; **il m'est ~ de le faire** it is impossible for me to do it, I can't possibly do it; **faire l'~ (pour que)** to do one's utmost (so that); **si, par ~ ...** if, by some miracle ...
**imposteur** [ɛ̃pɔstœʀ] *nm* impostor
**imposture** [ɛ̃pɔstyʀ] *nf* imposture, deception
**impôt** [ɛ̃po] *nm* tax; (*taxes*) taxation, taxes *pl*; **impôts** *nmpl* (*contributions*) (income) tax *sg*; **payer 1000 euros d'~s** to pay 1,000 euros in tax; **~ direct/indirect** direct/indirect tax; **~ sur le chiffre d'affaires** tax on turnover; **~ foncier** land tax; **~ sur la fortune** wealth tax; **~ sur les plus-values** capital gains tax; **~ sur le revenu** income tax; **~ sur le RPP** personal income tax; **~ sur les sociétés** tax on companies; **~s locaux** rates, local taxes (*US*), ≈ council tax (*Brit*)
**impotence** [ɛ̃pɔtɑ̃s] *nf* disability
**impotent, e** [ɛ̃pɔtɑ̃, -ɑ̃t] *adj* disabled
**impraticable** [ɛ̃pʀatikabl(ə)] *adj* (*projet*) impracticable, unworkable; (*piste*) impassable
**imprécation** [ɛ̃pʀekasjɔ̃] *nf* imprecation
**imprécis, e** [ɛ̃pʀesi, -iz] *adj* (*contours, souvenir*) imprecise, vague; (*tir*) inaccurate, imprecise
**imprécision** [ɛ̃pʀesizjɔ̃] *nf* imprecision
**imprégner** [ɛ̃pʀeɲe] *vt* (*tissu, tampon*): **~ (de)** to soak *ou* impregnate (with); (*lieu, air*): **~ (de)** to fill (with); (*amertume, ironie*) to pervade; **s'imprégner de** *vi* to become impregnated with; to be filled with; (*fig*) to absorb
**imprenable** [ɛ̃pʀənabl(ə)] *adj* (*forteresse*)

impregnable; **vue ~** unimpeded outlook
**impresario** [ɛ̃pʀesaʀjo] *nm* manager, impresario
**impression** [ɛ̃pʀesjɔ̃] *nf* impression; (*d'un ouvrage, tissu*) printing; (*Photo*) exposure; **faire bonne ~** to make a good impression; **donner une ~ de/l'~ que** to give the impression of/that; **avoir l'~ de/que** to have the impression of/that; **faire ~** to make an impression; **~s de voyage** impressions of one's journey
**impressionnable** [ɛ̃pʀesjɔnabl(ə)] *adj* impressionable
**impressionnant, e** [ɛ̃pʀesjɔnɑ̃, -ɑ̃t] *adj* impressive; upsetting
**impressionner** [ɛ̃pʀesjɔne] *vt* (*frapper*) to impress; (*troubler*) to upset; (*Photo*) to expose
**impressionnisme** [ɛ̃pʀesjɔnism(ə)] *nm* impressionism
**impressionniste** [ɛ̃pʀesjɔnist(ə)] *adj, nm/f* impressionist
**imprévisible** [ɛ̃pʀevizibl(ə)] *adj* unforeseeable; (*réaction, personne*) unpredictable
**imprévoyance** [ɛ̃pʀevwajɑ̃s] *nf* lack of foresight
**imprévoyant, e** [ɛ̃pʀevwajɑ̃, -ɑ̃t] *adj* lacking in foresight; (*en matière d'argent*) improvident
**imprévu, e** [ɛ̃pʀevy] *adj* unforeseen, unexpected ▷ *nm* unexpected incident; **l'~** the unexpected; **en cas d'~** if anything unexpected happens; **sauf ~** barring anything unexpected
**imprimante** [ɛ̃pʀimɑ̃t] *nf* (*Inform*) printer; **~ à bulle d'encre** bubblejet printer; **~ à jet d'encre** ink-jet printer; **~ à laser** laser printer; **~ (ligne par) ligne** line printer; **~ à marguerite** daisy-wheel printer
**imprimé** [ɛ̃pʀime] *nm* (*formulaire*) printed form; (*Postes*) printed matter *no pl*; (*tissu*) printed fabric; **un ~ à fleurs/pois** (*tissu*) a floral/polka-dot print
**imprimer** [ɛ̃pʀime] *vt* to print; (*Inform*) to print (out); (*apposer: visa, cachet*) to stamp; (*empreinte etc*) to imprint; (*publier*) to publish; (*communiquer: mouvement, impulsion*) to impart, transmit
**imprimerie** [ɛ̃pʀimʀi] *nf* printing; (*établissement*) printing works *sg*; (*atelier*) printing house, printery
**imprimeur** [ɛ̃pʀimœʀ] *nm* printer; **~-éditeur/-libraire** printer and publisher/bookseller
**improbable** [ɛ̃pʀɔbabl(ə)] *adj* unlikely, improbable
**improductif, -ive** [ɛ̃pʀɔdyktif, -iv] *adj* unproductive
**impromptu, e** [ɛ̃pʀɔ̃pty] *adj* impromptu; (*départ*) sudden
**imprononçable** [ɛ̃pʀɔnɔ̃sabl(ə)] *adj* unpronounceable
**impropre** [ɛ̃pʀɔpʀ(ə)] *adj* inappropriate; **~ à** unsuitable for
**improprement** [ɛ̃pʀɔpʀəmɑ̃] *adv* improperly
**impropriété** [ɛ̃pʀɔpʀijete] *nf*: **~ (de langage)** incorrect usage *no pl*
**improvisation** [ɛ̃pʀɔvizasjɔ̃] *nf* improvization

213

**improvisé, e** [ɛ̃pʀɔvize] *adj* makeshift, improvized; (*jeu etc*) scratch, improvized; **avec des moyens ~s** using whatever comes to hand

**improviser** [ɛ̃pʀɔvize] *vt, vi* to improvize; **s'improviser** (*secours, réunion*) to be improvized; **s'~ cuisinier** to (decide to) act as cook; **~ qn cuisinier** to get sb to act as cook

**improviste** [ɛ̃pʀɔvist(ə)]: **à l'~** *adv* unexpectedly, without warning

**imprudemment** [ɛ̃pʀydamɑ̃] *adv* carelessly; unwisely, imprudently

**imprudence** [ɛ̃pʀydɑ̃s] *nf* carelessness *no pl*; imprudence *no pl*; act of carelessness; (:) foolish *ou* unwise action

**imprudent, e** [ɛ̃pʀydɑ̃, -ɑ̃t] *adj* (*conducteur, geste, action*) careless; (*remarque*) unwise, imprudent; (*projet*) foolhardy

**impubère** [ɛ̃pybɛʀ] *adj* below the age of puberty

**impubliable** [ɛ̃pyblijabl(ə)] *adj* unpublishable

**impudemment** [ɛ̃pydamɑ̃] *adv* impudently

**impudence** [ɛ̃pydɑ̃s] *nf* impudence

**impudent, e** [ɛ̃pydɑ̃, -ɑ̃t] *adj* impudent

**impudeur** [ɛ̃pydœʀ] *nf* shamelessness

**impudique** [ɛ̃pydik] *adj* shameless

**impuissance** [ɛ̃pɥisɑ̃s] *nf* helplessness; ineffectualness; impotence

**impuissant, e** [ɛ̃pɥisɑ̃, -ɑ̃t] *adj* helpless; (*sans effet*) ineffectual; (*sexuellement*) impotent ▷ *nm* impotent man; **~ à faire qch** powerless to do sth

**impulsif, -ive** [ɛ̃pylsif, -iv] *adj* impulsive

**impulsion** [ɛ̃pylsjɔ̃] *nf* (*Élec, instinct*) impulse; (*élan, influence*) impetus

**impulsivement** [ɛ̃pylsivmɑ̃] *adv* impulsively

**impulsivité** [ɛ̃pylsivite] *nf* impulsiveness

**impunément** [ɛ̃pynemɑ̃] *adv* with impunity

**impuni, e** [ɛ̃pyni] *adj* unpunished

**impunité** [ɛ̃pynite] *nf* impunity

**impur, e** [ɛ̃pyʀ] *adj* impure

**impureté** [ɛ̃pyʀte] *nf* impurity

**imputable** [ɛ̃pytabl(ə)] *adj* (*attribuable*): **~ à** imputable to, ascribable to; (*Comm: somme*): **~ sur** chargeable to

**imputation** [ɛ̃pytasjɔ̃] *nf* imputation, charge

**imputer** [ɛ̃pyte] *vt* (*attribuer*): **~ qch à** to ascribe *ou* impute sth to; (*Comm*): **~ qch à** *ou* **sur** to charge sth to

**imputrescible** [ɛ̃pytʀesibl(ə)] *adj* rotproof

**in** [in] *adj inv* in, trendy

**INA** [ina] *sigle m* (= *Institut national de l'audio-visuel*) library of television archives

**inabordable** [inabɔʀdabl(ə)] *adj* (*lieu*) inaccessible; (*cher*) prohibitive

**inaccentué, e** [inaksɑ̃tɥe] *adj* (*Ling*) unstressed

**inacceptable** [inaksɛptabl(ə)] *adj* unacceptable

**inaccessible** [inaksesibl(ə)] *adj* inaccessible; (*objectif*) unattainable; (*insensible*): **~ à** impervious to

**inaccoutumé, e** [inakutyme] *adj* unaccustomed

**inachevé, e** [inaʃve] *adj* unfinished

**inactif, -ive** [inaktif, -iv] *adj* inactive, idle

**inaction** [inaksjɔ̃] *nf* inactivity

**inactivité** [inaktivite] *nf* (*Admin*): **en ~** out of active service

**inadaptation** [inadaptasjɔ̃] *nf* (*Psych*) maladjustment

**inadapté, e** [inadapte] *adj* (*Psych: adulte, enfant*) maladjusted ▷ *nm/f* (*péj: adulte: asocial*) misfit; **~ à** not adapted to, unsuited to

**inadéquat, e** [inadekwa, wat] *adj* inadequate

**inadéquation** [inadekwasjɔ̃] *nf* inadequacy

**inadmissible** [inadmisibl(ə)] *adj* inadmissible

**inadvertance** [inadvɛʀtɑ̃s]: **par ~** *adv* inadvertently

**inaliénable** [inaljenabl(ə)] *adj* inalienable

**inaltérable** [inalteʀabl(ə)] *adj* (*matière*) stable; (*fig*) unchanging; **~ à** unaffected by; **couleur ~ (au lavage/à la lumière)** fast colour/fade-resistant colour

**inamovible** [inamɔvibl(ə)] *adj* fixed; (*Jur*) irremovable

**inanimé, e** [inanime] *adj* (*matière*) inanimate; (*évanoui*) unconscious; (*sans vie*) lifeless

**inanité** [inanite] *nf* futility

**inanition** [inanisjɔ̃] *nf*: **tomber d'~** to faint with hunger (and exhaustion)

**inaperçu, e** [inapɛʀsy] *adj*: **passer ~** to go unnoticed

**inappétence** [inapetɑ̃s] *nf* lack of appetite

**inapplicable** [inaplikabl(ə)] *adj* inapplicable

**inapplication** [inaplikɑsjɔ̃] *nf* lack of application

**inappliqué, e** [inaplike] *adj* lacking in application

**inappréciable** [inapʀesjabl(ə)] *adj* (*service*) invaluable; (*différence, nuance*) inappreciable

**inapte** [inapt(ə)] *adj*: **~ à** incapable of; (*Mil*) unfit for

**inaptitude** [inaptityd] *nf* inaptitude; unfitness

**inarticulé, e** [inaʀtikyle] *adj* inarticulate

**inassimilable** [inasimilabl(ə)] *adj* that cannot be assimilated

**inassouvi, e** [inasuvi] *adj* unsatisfied, unfulfilled

**inattaquable** [inatakabl(ə)] *adj* (*Mil*) unassailable; (*texte, preuve*) irrefutable

**inattendu, e** [inatɑ̃dy] *adj* unexpected ▷ *nm*: **l'~** the unexpected

**inattentif, -ive** [inatɑ̃tif, -iv] *adj* inattentive; **~ à** (*dangers, détails*) heedless of

**inattention** [inatɑ̃sjɔ̃] *nf* inattention; (*inadvertance*): **une minute d'~** a minute of inattention, a minute's carelessness; **par ~** inadvertently; **faute d'~** careless mistake

**inaudible** [inodibl(ə)] *adj* inaudible

**inaugural, e, -aux** [inɔgyʀal, -o] *adj* (*cérémonie*) inaugural, opening; (*vol, voyage*) maiden

**inauguration** [inɔgyʀasjɔ̃] *nf* unveiling; opening; **discours/cérémonie d'~** inaugural speech/ceremony

**inaugurer** [inɔgyʀe] *vt* (*monument*) to unveil; (*exposition, usine*) to open; (*fig*) to inaugurate

**inauthenticité** [inotɑ̃tisite] *nf* inauthenticity

**inavouable** [inavwabl(ə)] *adj* undisclosable; (*honteux*) shameful

**inavoué, e** [inavwe] *adj* unavowed

**INC** *sigle m* (= *Institut national de la consommation*) consumer research organization

**inca** [ɛ̃ka] *adj inv* Inca ▷ *nm/f*: **Inca** Inca

**incalculable** [ɛ̃kalkylabl(ə)] *adj* incalculable; **un nombre ~ de** countless numbers of

**incandescence** [ɛ̃kãdesãs] *nf* incandescence; **en ~** incandescent, white-hot; **porter à ~** to heat white-hot; **lampe/manchon à ~** incandescent lamp/(gas) mantle

**incandescent, e** [ɛ̃kãdesã, -ãt] *adj* incandescent, white-hot

**incantation** [ɛ̃kãtasjɔ̃] *nf* incantation

**incantatoire** [ɛ̃kãtatwaʀ] *adj*: **formule ~** incantation

**incapable** [ɛ̃kapabl(ə)] *adj* incapable; **~ de faire** incapable of doing; (*empêché*) unable to do

**incapacitant, e** [ɛ̃kapasitã, -ãt] *adj* (*Mil*) incapacitating

**incapacité** [ɛ̃kapasite] *nf* incapability; (*Jur*) incapacity; **être dans l'~ de faire** to be unable to do; **~ permanente/de travail** permanent/industrial disablement; **~ électorale** ineligibility to vote

**incarcération** [ɛ̃kaʀseʀasjɔ̃] *nf* incarceration

**incarcérer** [ɛ̃kaʀseʀe] *vt* to incarcerate

**incarnat, e** [ɛ̃kaʀna, -at] *adj* (*rosy*) pink

**incarnation** [ɛ̃kaʀnasjɔ̃] *nf* incarnation

**incarné, e** [ɛ̃kaʀne] *adj* incarnate; (*ongle*) ingrown

**incarner** [ɛ̃kaʀne] *vt* to embody, personify; (*Théât*) to play; (*Rel*) to incarnate; **s'incarner dans** *vi* (*Rel*) to be incarnate in

**incartade** [ɛ̃kaʀtad] *nf* prank, escapade

**incassable** [ɛ̃kasabl(ə)] *adj* unbreakable

**incendiaire** [ɛ̃sãdjɛʀ] *adj* incendiary; (*fig: discours*) inflammatory ▷ *nm/f* fire-raiser, arsonist

**incendie** [ɛ̃sãdi] *nm* fire; **~ criminel** arson *no pl*; **~ de forêt** forest fire

**incendier** [ɛ̃sãdje] *vt* (*mettre le feu à*) to set fire to, set alight; (*brûler complètement*) to burn down

**incertain, e** [ɛ̃sɛʀtɛ̃, -ɛn] *adj* uncertain; (*temps*) uncertain, unsettled; (*imprécis: contours*) indistinct, blurred

**incertitude** [ɛ̃sɛʀtityd] *nf* uncertainty

**incessamment** [ɛ̃sɛsamã] *adv* very shortly

**incessant, e** [ɛ̃sɛsã, -ãt] *adj* incessant, unceasing

**incessible** [ɛ̃sesibl(ə)] *adj* (*Jur*) non-transferable

**inceste** [ɛ̃sɛst(ə)] *nm* incest

**incestueux, -euse** [ɛ̃sɛstɥø, -øz] *adj* incestuous

**inchangé, e** [ɛ̃ʃãʒe] *adj* unchanged, unaltered

**inchantable** [ɛ̃ʃãtabl(ə)] *adj* unsingable

**inchauffable** [ɛ̃ʃofabl(ə)] *adj* impossible to heat

**incidemment** [ɛ̃sidamã] *adv* in passing

**incidence** [ɛ̃sidãs] *nf* (*effet, influence*) effect; (*Physique*) incidence

**incident** [ɛ̃sidã] *nm* incident; **~ de frontière** border incident; **~ de parcours** minor hitch *ou*

setback; **~ technique** technical difficulties *pl*, technical hitch

**incinérateur** [ɛ̃sineʀatœʀ] *nm* incinerator

**incinération** [ɛ̃sineʀasjɔ̃] *nf* (*d'ordures*) incineration; (*crémation*) cremation

**incinérer** [ɛ̃sineʀe] *vt* (*ordures*) to incinerate; (*mort*) to cremate

**incise** [ɛ̃siz] *nf* (*Ling*) interpolated clause

**inciser** [ɛ̃size] *vt* to make an incision in; (*abcès*) to lance

**incisif, -ive** [ɛ̃sizif, -iv] *adj* incisive, cutting ▷ *nf* incisor

**incision** [ɛ̃sizjɔ̃] *nf* incision; (*d'un abcès*) lancing

**incitation** [ɛ̃sitasjɔ̃] *nf* (*encouragement*) incentive; (*provocation*) incitement

**inciter** [ɛ̃site] *vt*: **~ qn à (faire) qch** to prompt *ou* encourage sb to do sth; (*à la révolte etc*) to incite sb to do sth

**incivil, e** [ɛ̃sivil] *adj* uncivil

**incivilité** [ɛ̃sivilite] *nf* (*grossièreté*) incivility; **incivilités** *nfpl* antisocial behaviour *sg*

**inclinable** [ɛ̃klinabl(ə)] *adj* (*dossier etc*) tilting; **siège à dossier ~** reclining seat

**inclinaison** [ɛ̃klinɛzɔ̃] *nf* (*déclivité: d'une route etc*) incline; (: *d'un toit*) slope; (*état penché: d'un mur*) lean; (: *de la tête*) tilt; (: *d'un navire*) list

**inclination** [ɛ̃klinasjɔ̃] *nf* (*penchant*) inclination, tendency; **montrer de l'~ pour les sciences** *etc* to show an inclination for the sciences *etc*; **~s égoïstes/altruistes** egoistic/altruistic tendencies; **~ de (la) tête** nod (of the head); **~ (de buste)** bow

**incliner** [ɛ̃kline] *vt* (*bouteille*) to tilt; (*tête*) to incline; (*inciter*): **~ qn à qch/à faire** to encourage sb towards sth/to do ▷ *vi*: **~ à qch/à faire** (*tendre à, pencher pour*) to incline towards sth/doing, tend towards sth/to do; **s'incliner** *vi* (*route*) to slope; (*toit*) to be sloping; **s'~ (devant)** to bow (before)

**inclure** [ɛ̃klyʀ] *vt* to include; (*joindre à un envoi*) to enclose; **jusqu'au 10 mars inclus** until 10th March inclusive

**inclus, e** [ɛ̃kly, -yz] *pp* **de inclure** ▷ *adj* (*joint à un envoi*) enclosed; (*compris: frais, dépense*) included; (*Math: ensemble*): **~ dans** included in; **jusqu'au troisième chapitre ~** up to and including the third chapter

**inclusion** [ɛ̃klyzjɔ̃] *nf* (*voir inclure*) inclusion; enclosing

**inclusivement** [ɛ̃klyzivmã] *adv* inclusively

**inclut** [ɛ̃kly] *vb voir* **inclure**

**incoercible** [ɛ̃kɔɛʀsibl(ə)] *adj* uncontrollable

**incognito** [ɛ̃kɔnito] *adv* incognito ▷ *nm*: **garder l'~** to remain incognito

**incohérence** [ɛ̃kɔeʀãs] *nf* inconsistency; incoherence

**incohérent, e** [ɛ̃kɔeʀã, -ãt] *adj* inconsistent; incoherent

**incollable** [ɛ̃kɔlabl(ə)] *adj* (*riz*) that does not stick; (*fam: personne*): **il est ~** he's got all the answers

**incolore** [ɛ̃kɔlɔʀ] *adj* colourless

**incomber** [ɛ̃kɔ̃be]: ~ **à** vt (devoirs, responsabilité) to rest ou be incumbent upon; (: frais, travail) to be the responsibility of

**incombustible** [ɛ̃kɔ̃bystibl(ə)] adj incombustible

**incommensurable** [ɛ̃kɔmɑ̃syRabl(ə)] adj immeasurable

**incommodant, e** [ɛ̃kɔmɔdɑ̃, -ɑ̃t] adj (bruit) annoying; (chaleur) uncomfortable

**incommode** [ɛ̃kɔmɔd] adj inconvenient; (posture, siège) uncomfortable

**incommodément** [ɛ̃kɔmɔdemɑ̃] adv (installé, assis) uncomfortably; (logé, situé) inconveniently

**incommoder** [ɛ̃kɔmɔde] vt: ~ **qn** to bother ou inconvenience sb; (embarrasser) to make sb feel uncomfortable ou ill at ease

**incommodité** [ɛ̃kɔmɔdite] nf inconvenience

**incommunicable** [ɛ̃kɔmynikabl(ə)] adj (Jur: droits, privilèges) non-transferable; (pensée) incommunicable

**incomparable** [ɛ̃kɔ̃paRabl(ə)] adj not comparable; (inégalable) incomparable, matchless

**incomparablement** [ɛ̃kɔ̃paRabləmɑ̃] adv incomparably

**incompatibilité** [ɛ̃kɔ̃patibilite] nf incompatibility; ~ **d'humeur** (mutual) incompatibility

**incompatible** [ɛ̃kɔ̃patibl(ə)] adj incompatible

**incompétence** [ɛ̃kɔ̃petɑ̃s] nf lack of expertise; incompetence

**incompétent, e** [ɛ̃kɔ̃petɑ̃, -ɑ̃t] adj (ignorant) inexpert; (incapable) incompetent, not competent

**incomplet, -ète** [ɛ̃kɔ̃plɛ, -ɛt] adj incomplete

**incomplètement** [ɛ̃kɔ̃plɛtmɑ̃] adv not completely, incompletely

**incompréhensible** [ɛ̃kɔ̃pReɑ̃sibl(ə)] adj incomprehensible

**incompréhensif, -ive** [ɛ̃kɔ̃pReɑ̃sif, -iv] adj lacking in understanding, unsympathetic

**incompréhension** [ɛ̃kɔ̃pReɑ̃sjɔ̃] nf lack of understanding

**incompressible** [ɛ̃kɔ̃pResibl(ə)] adj (Physique) incompressible; (fig: dépenses) that cannot be reduced; (Jur: peine) irreducible

**incompris, e** [ɛ̃kɔ̃pRi, -iz] adj misunderstood

**inconcevable** [ɛ̃kɔ̃svabl(ə)] adj (conduite etc) inconceivable; (mystère) incredible

**inconciliable** [ɛ̃kɔ̃siljabl(ə)] adj irreconcilable

**inconditionnel, le** [ɛ̃kɔ̃disjɔnɛl] adj unconditional; (partisan) unquestioning ▷ nm/f (partisan) unquestioning supporter

**inconditionnellement** [ɛ̃kɔ̃disjɔnɛlmɑ̃] adv unconditionally

**inconduite** [ɛ̃kɔ̃dɥit] nf bad ou unsuitable behaviour no pl

**inconfort** [ɛ̃kɔ̃fɔR] nm lack of comfort, discomfort

**inconfortable** [ɛ̃kɔ̃fɔRtabl(ə)] adj uncomfortable

**inconfortablement** [ɛ̃kɔ̃fɔRtabləmɑ̃] adv uncomfortably

**incongru, e** [ɛ̃kɔ̃gRy] adj unseemly; (remarque) ill-chosen, incongruous

**incongruité** [ɛ̃kɔ̃gRyite] nf unseemliness; incongruity; (parole incongrue) ill-chosen remark

**inconnu, e** [ɛ̃kɔny] adj unknown; (sentiment, plaisir) new, strange ▷ nm/f stranger; unknown person (ou artist etc) ▷ nm: **l'~** the unknown ▷ nf (Math) unknown; (fig) unknown factor

**inconsciemment** [ɛ̃kɔ̃sjamɑ̃] adv unconsciously

**inconscience** [ɛ̃kɔ̃sjɑ̃s] nf unconsciousness; recklessness

**inconscient, e** [ɛ̃kɔ̃sjɑ̃, -ɑ̃t] adj unconscious; (irréfléchi) reckless ▷ nm (Psych): **l'~** the subconscious, the unconscious; ~ **de** unaware of

**inconséquence** [ɛ̃kɔ̃sekɑ̃s] nf inconsistency; thoughtlessness; (action, parole) thoughtless thing to do (ou say)

**inconséquent, e** [ɛ̃kɔ̃sekɑ̃, -ɑ̃t] adj (illogique) inconsistent; (irréfléchi) thoughtless

**inconsidéré, e** [ɛ̃kɔ̃sideRe] adj ill-considered

**inconsidérément** [ɛ̃kɔ̃sideRemɑ̃] adv thoughtlessly

**inconsistant, e** [ɛ̃kɔ̃sistɑ̃, -ɑ̃t] adj flimsy, weak; (crème etc) runny

**inconsolable** [ɛ̃kɔ̃sɔlabl(ə)] adj inconsolable

**inconstance** [ɛ̃kɔ̃stɑ̃s] nf inconstancy, fickleness

**inconstant, e** [ɛ̃kɔ̃stɑ̃, -ɑ̃t] adj inconstant, fickle

**inconstitutionnel, le** [ɛ̃kɔ̃stitysjɔnɛl] adj unconstitutional

**incontestable** [ɛ̃kɔ̃tɛstabl(ə)] adj unquestionable, indisputable

**incontestablement** [ɛ̃kɔ̃tɛstabləmɑ̃] adv unquestionably, indisputably

**incontesté, e** [ɛ̃kɔ̃tɛste] adj undisputed

**incontinence** [ɛ̃kɔ̃tinɑ̃s] nf (Méd) incontinence

**incontinent, e** [ɛ̃kɔ̃tinɑ̃, -ɑ̃t] adj (Méd) incontinent ▷ adv (tout de suite) forthwith

**incontournable** [ɛ̃kɔ̃tuRnabl(ə)] adj unavoidable

**incontrôlable** [ɛ̃kɔ̃tRolabl(ə)] adj unverifiable

**incontrôlé, e** [ɛ̃kɔ̃tRole] adj uncontrolled

**inconvenance** [ɛ̃kɔ̃vnɑ̃s] nf (parole, action) impropriety

**inconvenant, e** [ɛ̃kɔ̃vnɑ̃, -ɑ̃t] adj unseemly, improper

**inconvénient** [ɛ̃kɔ̃venjɑ̃] nm (d'une situation, d'un projet) disadvantage, drawback; (d'un remède, changement etc) risk, inconvenience; **si vous n'y voyez pas d'~** if you have no objections; **y a-t-il un ~ à ...?** (risque) isn't there a risk in ...?; (objection) is there any objection to ...?

**inconvertible** [ɛ̃kɔ̃vɛRtibl(ə)] adj inconvertible

**incorporation** [ɛ̃kɔRpɔRasjɔ̃] nf (Mil) call-up

**incorporé, e** [ɛ̃kɔRpɔRe] adj (micro etc) built-in

**incorporel, le** [ɛ̃kɔRpɔRɛl] adj (Jur): **biens ~s** intangible property

**incorporer** [ɛ̃kɔRpɔRe] vt: ~ **(à)** to mix in (with); (paragraphe etc): ~ **(dans)** to incorporate (in);

(*territoire, immigrants*): ~ (**dans**) to incorporate (into); (*Mil: appeler*) to recruit, call up; (: *affecter*): ~ **qn dans** to enlist sb into

**incorrect, e** [ɛ̃kɔʀɛkt] *adj* (*impropre, inconvenant*) improper; (*défectueux*) faulty; (*inexact*) incorrect; (*impoli*) impolite; (*déloyal*) underhand

**incorrectement** [ɛ̃kɔʀɛktəmɑ̃] *adv* improperly; faultily; incorrectly; impolitely; in an underhand way

**incorrection** [ɛ̃kɔʀɛksjɔ̃] *nf* impropriety; incorrectness; underhand nature; (*terme impropre*) impropriety; (*action, remarque*) improper behaviour (*ou* remark)

**incorrigible** [ɛ̃kɔʀiʒibl(ə)] *adj* incorrigible

**incorruptible** [ɛ̃kɔʀyptibl(ə)] *adj* incorruptible

**incrédibilité** [ɛ̃kʀedibilite] *nf* incredibility

**incrédule** [ɛ̃kʀedyl] *adj* incredulous; (*Rel*) unbelieving

**incrédulité** [ɛ̃kʀedylite] *nf* incredulity; **avec ~** incredulously

**increvable** [ɛ̃kʀəvabl(ə)] *adj* (*pneu*) puncture-proof; (*fam*) tireless

**incriminer** [ɛ̃kʀimine] *vt* (*personne*) to incriminate; (*action, conduite*) to bring under attack; (*bonne foi, honnêteté*) to call into question; **livre/article incriminé** offending book/article

**incrochetable** [ɛ̃kʀɔʃtabl(ə)] *adj* (*serrure*) that can't be picked, burglarproof

**incroyable** [ɛ̃kʀwajabl(ə)] *adj* incredible, unbelievable

**incroyablement** [ɛ̃kʀwajabləmɑ̃] *adv* incredibly, unbelievably

**incroyant, e** [ɛ̃kʀwajɑ̃, -ɑ̃t] *nm/f* non-believer

**incrustation** [ɛ̃kʀystasjɔ̃] *nf* inlaying *no pl*; inlay; (*dans une chaudière etc*) fur *no pl*, scale *no pl*

**incruster** [ɛ̃kʀyste] *vt* (*Art*): ~ **qch dans/qch de** to inlay sth into/sth with; (*radiateur etc*) to coat with scale *ou* fur; **s'incruster** *vi* (*invité*) to take root; (*radiateur etc*) to become coated with scale *ou* fur; **s' ~ dans** (*corps étranger, caillou*) to become embedded in

**incubateur** [ɛ̃kybatœʀ] *nm* incubator

**incubation** [ɛ̃kybasjɔ̃] *nf* incubation

**inculpation** [ɛ̃kylpasjɔ̃] *nf* charging *no pl*; charge; **sous l' ~ de** on a charge of

**inculpé, e** [ɛ̃kylpe] *nm/f* accused

**inculper** [ɛ̃kylpe] *vt*: ~ (**de**) to charge (with)

**inculquer** [ɛ̃kylke] *vt*: ~ **qch à** to inculcate sth in, instil sth into

**inculte** [ɛ̃kylt(ə)] *adj* uncultivated; (*esprit, peuple*) uncultured; (*barbe*) unkempt

**incultivable** [ɛ̃kyltivabl(ə)] *adj* (*terrain*) unworkable

**inculture** [ɛ̃kyltyʀ] *nf* lack of education

**incurable** [ɛ̃kyʀabl(ə)] *adj* incurable

**incurie** [ɛ̃kyʀi] *nf* carelessness

**incursion** [ɛ̃kyʀsjɔ̃] *nf* incursion, foray

**incurvé, e** [ɛ̃kyʀve] *adj* curved

**incurver** [ɛ̃kyʀve] *vt* (*barre de fer*) to bend into a curve; **s'incurver** *vi* (*planche, route*) to bend

**Inde** [ɛ̃d] *nf*: **l'~** India

**indécemment** [ɛ̃desamɑ̃] *adv* indecently

**indécence** [ɛ̃desɑ̃s] *nf* indecency; (*propos, acte*) indecent remark (*ou* act *etc*)

**indécent, e** [ɛ̃desɑ̃, -ɑ̃t] *adj* indecent

**indéchiffrable** [ɛ̃deʃifʀabl(ə)] *adj* indecipherable

**indéchirable** [ɛ̃deʃiʀabl(ə)] *adj* tear-proof

**indécis, e** [ɛ̃desi, -iz] *adj* indecisive; (*perplexe*) undecided

**indécision** [ɛ̃desizjɔ̃] *nf* indecision, indecisiveness

**indéclinable** [ɛ̃deklinabl(ə)] *adj* (*Ling: mot*) indeclinable

**indécomposable** [ɛ̃dekɔ̃pozabl(ə)] *adj* that cannot be broken down

**indécrottable** [ɛ̃dekʀɔtabl(ə)] *adj* (*fam*) hopeless

**indéfectible** [ɛ̃defɛktibl(ə)] *adj* (*attachement*) indestructible

**indéfendable** [ɛ̃defɑ̃dabl(ə)] *adj* indefensible

**indéfini, e** [ɛ̃defini] *adj* (*imprécis, incertain*) undefined; (*illimité, Ling*) indefinite

**indéfiniment** [ɛ̃definimɑ̃] *adv* indefinitely

**indéfinissable** [ɛ̃definisabl(ə)] *adj* indefinable

**indéformable** [ɛ̃defɔʀmabl(ə)] *adj* that keeps its shape

**indélébile** [ɛ̃delebil] *adj* indelible

**indélicat, e** [ɛ̃delika, -at] *adj* tactless; (*malhonnête*) dishonest

**indélicatesse** [ɛ̃delikatɛs] *nf* tactlessness; dishonesty

**indémaillable** [ɛ̃demɑjabl(ə))] *adj* run-resist

**indemne** [ɛ̃dɛmn(ə)] *adj* unharmed

**indemnisable** [ɛ̃dɛmnizabl(ə)] *adj* entitled to compensation

**indemnisation** [ɛ̃dɛmnizasjɔ̃] *nf* (*somme*) indemnity, compensation

**indemniser** [ɛ̃dɛmnize] *vt*: ~ **qn (de)** to compensate sb (for); **se faire ~** to get compensation

**indemnité** [ɛ̃dɛmnite] *nf* (*dédommagement*) compensation *no pl*; (*allocation*) allowance; ~ **de licenciement** redundancy payment; ~ **de logement** housing allowance; ~ **parlementaire** ≈ MP's (*Brit*) *ou* Congressman's (*US*) salary

**indémontable** [ɛ̃demɔ̃tabl(ə)] *adj* (*meuble etc*) that cannot be dismantled, in one piece

**indéniable** [ɛ̃denjabl(ə)] *adj* undeniable, indisputable

**indéniablement** [ɛ̃denjabləmɑ̃] *adv* undeniably

**indépendamment** [ɛ̃depɑ̃damɑ̃] *adv* independently; ~ **de** independently of; (*abstraction faite de*) irrespective of; (*en plus de*) over and above

**indépendance** [ɛ̃depɑ̃dɑ̃s] *nf* independence; ~ **matérielle** financial independence

**indépendant, e** [ɛ̃depɑ̃dɑ̃, -ɑ̃t] *adj* independent; ~ **de** independent of; **chambre ~e** room with private entrance; **travailleur ~** self-employed worker

**indépendantiste** [ɛ̃depɑ̃dɑ̃tist(ə)] *adj, nm/f* separatist

217

**indéracinable** [ɛ̃deʀasinabl(ə)] *adj (fig: croyance etc)* ineradicable

**indéréglable** [ɛ̃deʀeglabl(ə)] *adj* which will not break down

**indescriptible** [ɛ̃dɛskʀiptibl(ə)] *adj* indescribable

**indésirable** [ɛ̃deziʀabl(ə)] *adj* undesirable

**indestructible** [ɛ̃dɛstʀyktibl(ə)] *adj* indestructible; *(marque, impression)* indelible

**indéterminable** [ɛ̃detɛʀminabl(ə)] *adj* indeterminable

**indétermination** [ɛ̃detɛʀminasjɔ̃] *nf* indecision, indecisiveness

**indéterminé, e** [ɛ̃detɛʀmine] *adj* unspecified; indeterminate; indeterminable

**index** [ɛ̃dɛks] *nm (doigt)* index finger; *(d'un livre etc)* index; **mettre à l'~** to blacklist

**indexation** [ɛ̃dɛksasjɔ̃] *nf* indexing

**indexé, e** [ɛ̃dɛkse] *adj (Écon)*: **~ (sur)** index-linked (to)

**indexer** [ɛ̃dɛkse] *vt (salaire, emprunt)*: **~ (sur)** to index (on)

**indicateur** [ɛ̃dikatœʀ] *nm (Police)* informer; *(livre)* guide; *(: liste)* directory; *(Tech)* gauge; indicator; *(Écon)* indicator ▷ *adj*: **poteau ~** signpost; **tableau ~** indicator (board); **~ des chemins de fer** railway timetable; **~ de direction** *(Auto)* indicator; **~ immobilier** property gazette; **~ de niveau** level, gauge; **~ de pression** pressure gauge; **~ de rues** street directory; **~ de vitesse** speedometer

**indicatif, -ive** [ɛ̃dikatif, -iv] *adj*: **à titre ~** for (your) information ▷ *nm (Ling)* indicative; *(d'une émission)* theme *ou* signature tune; *(Tél)* dialling code; **~ d'appel** *(Radio)* call sign

**indication** [ɛ̃dikasjɔ̃] *nf* indication; *(renseignement)* information *no pl*; **indications** *nfpl (directives)* instructions; **~ d'origine** *(Comm)* place of origin

**indice** [ɛ̃dis] *nm (marque, signe)* indication, sign; *(Police: lors d'une enquête)* clue; *(Jur: présomption)* piece of evidence; *(Science, Écon, Tech)* index; *(Admin)* grading; rating; **~ du coût de la vie** cost-of-living index; **~ inférieur** subscript; **~ d'octane** octane rating; **~ des prix** price index; **~ de traitement** salary grading

**indicible** [ɛ̃disibl(ə)] *adj* inexpressible

**indien, ne** [ɛ̃djɛ̃, -ɛn] *adj* Indian ▷ *nm/f*: **Indien, ne** *(d'Amérique)* Native American; *(d'Inde)* Indian

**indifféremment** [ɛ̃difeʀamɑ̃] *adv (sans distinction)* equally; indiscriminately

**indifférence** [ɛ̃difeʀɑ̃s] *nf* indifference

**indifférencié, e** [ɛ̃difeʀɑ̃sje] *adj* undifferentiated

**indifférent, e** [ɛ̃difeʀɑ̃, -ɑ̃t] *adj (peu intéressé)* indifferent; **~ à** *(insensible à)* indifferent to, unconcerned about; *(peu intéressant pour)* indifferent to; immaterial to; **ça m'est ~ (que ...)** it doesn't matter to me (whether ...)

**indifférer** [ɛ̃difeʀe] *vt*: **cela m'indiffère** I'm indifferent about it

**indigence** [ɛ̃diʒɑ̃s] *nf* poverty; **être dans l'~** to be destitute

**indigène** [ɛ̃diʒɛn] *adj* native, indigenous; *(de la région)* local ▷ *nm/f* native

**indigent, e** [ɛ̃diʒɑ̃, -ɑ̃t] *adj* destitute, poverty-stricken; *(fig)* poor

**indigeste** [ɛ̃diʒɛst(ə)] *adj* indigestible

**indigestion** [ɛ̃diʒɛstjɔ̃] *nf* indigestion *no pl*; **avoir une ~** to have indigestion

**indignation** [ɛ̃diɲasjɔ̃] *nf* indignation; **avec ~** indignantly

**indigne** [ɛ̃diɲ] *adj*: **~ (de)** unworthy (of)

**indigné, e** [ɛ̃diɲe] *adj* indignant

**indignement** [ɛ̃diɲmɑ̃] *adv* shamefully

**indigner** [ɛ̃diɲe] *vt* to make indignant; **s'indigner (de/contre)** *vi* to be *(ou* become) indignant (at)

**indignité** [ɛ̃diɲite] *nf* unworthiness *no pl*; *(acte)* shameful act

**indigo** [ɛ̃digo] *nm* indigo

**indiqué, e** [ɛ̃dike] *adj (date, lieu)* given, appointed; *(adéquat)* appropriate, suitable; *(conseillé)* advisable; *(remède, traitement)* appropriate

**indiquer** [ɛ̃dike] *vt (désigner)*: **~ qch/qn à qn** to point sth/sb out to sb; *(pendule, aiguille)* to show; *(étiquette, plan)* to show, indicate; *(faire connaître: médecin, lieu)*: **~ qch/qn à qn** to tell sb of sth/sb; *(renseigner sur)* to point out, tell; *(déterminer: date, lieu)* to give, state; *(dénoter)* to indicate, point to; **~ du doigt** to point out; **~ de la main** to indicate with one's hand; **~ du regard** to glance towards *ou* in the direction of; **pourriez-vous m'~ les toilettes/l'heure?** could you direct me to the toilets/tell me the time?

**indirect, e** [ɛ̃diʀɛkt] *adj* indirect

**indirectement** [ɛ̃diʀɛktəmɑ̃] *adv* indirectly; *(apprendre)* in a roundabout way

**indiscernable** [ɛ̃disɛʀnabl(ə)] *adj* undiscernable

**indiscipline** [ɛ̃disiplin] *nf* lack of discipline

**indiscipliné, e** [ɛ̃disipline] *adj* undisciplined; *(fig)* unmanageable

**indiscret, -ète** [ɛ̃diskʀɛ, -ɛt] *adj* indiscreet

**indiscrétion** [ɛ̃diskʀesjɔ̃] *nf* indiscretion; **sans ~, ...** without wishing to be indiscreet, ...

**indiscutable** [ɛ̃diskytabl(ə)] *adj* indisputable

**indiscutablement** [ɛ̃diskytabləmɑ̃] *adv* indisputably

**indiscuté, e** [ɛ̃diskyte] *adj (incontesté: droit, chef)* undisputed

**indispensable** [ɛ̃dispɑ̃sabl(ə)] *adj* indispensable, essential; **~ à qn/pour faire qch** essential for sb/to do sth

**indisponibilité** [ɛ̃disponibilite] *nf* unavailability

**indisponible** [ɛ̃dispɔnibl(ə)] *adj* unavailable

**indisposé, e** [ɛ̃dispoze] *adj* indisposed, unwell

**indisposer** [ɛ̃dispoze] *vt (incommoder)* to upset; *(déplaire à)* to antagonize

**indisposition** [ɛ̃dispozisjɔ̃] *nf (slight)* illness, indisposition

**indissociable** [ɛ̃disɔsjabl(ə)] *adj* indissociable
**indissoluble** [ɛ̃disɔlybl(ə)] *adj* indissoluble
**indissolublement** [ɛ̃disɔlyblǝmā] *adv*
indissolubly
**indistinct, e** [ɛ̃distɛ̃, -ɛ̃kt(ə)] *adj* indistinct
**indistinctement** [ɛ̃distɛ̃ktǝmā] *adv (voir,
prononcer)* indistinctly; *(sans distinction)* without
distinction, indiscriminately
**individu** [ɛ̃dividy] *nm* individual
**individualiser** [ɛ̃dividɥalize] *vt* to
individualize; *(personnaliser)* to tailor to
individual requirements; **s'individualiser** *vi* to
develop one's own identity
**individualisme** [ɛ̃dividɥalism(ə)] *nm*
individualism
**individualiste** [ɛ̃dividɥalist(ə)] *nm/f*
individualist
**individualité** [ɛ̃dividɥalite] *nf* individuality
**individuel, le** [ɛ̃dividɥɛl] *adj (gén)* individual;
*(opinion, livret, contrôle, avantages)* personal;
**chambre ~le** single room; **maison ~le**
detached house; **propriété ~le** personal *ou*
private property
**individuellement** [ɛ̃dividɥelmā] *adv*
individually
**indivis, e** [ɛ̃divi, -iz] *adj (Jur: bien, succession)*
indivisible; *(: cohéritiers, propriétaires)* joint
**indivisible** [ɛ̃divizibl(ə)] *adj* indivisible
**Indochine** [ɛ̃dɔʃin] *nf*: **l'~** Indochina
**indochinois, e** [ɛ̃dɔʃinwa, -waz] *adj*
Indochinese
**indocile** [ɛ̃dɔsil] *adj* unruly
**indo-européen, ne** [ɛ̃dɔøʁɔpeɛ̃, -ɛn] *adj* Indo-
European ▷ *nm (Ling)* Indo-European
**indolence** [ɛ̃dɔlās] *nf* indolence
**indolent, e** [ɛ̃dɔlā, -āt] *adj* indolent
**indolore** [ɛ̃dɔlɔʁ] *adj* painless
**indomptable** [ɛ̃dɔ̃tabl(ə)] *adj* untameable; *(fig)*
invincible, indomitable
**indompté, e** [ɛ̃dɔ̃te] *adj (cheval)* unbroken
**Indonésie** [ɛ̃donezi] *nf*: **l'~** Indonesia
**indonésien, ne** [ɛ̃dɔnezjɛ̃, -ɛn] *adj* Indonesian
▷ *nm/f*: **Indonésien, ne** Indonesian
**indu, e** [ɛ̃dy] *adj*: **à des heures ~es** at an
ungodly hour
**indubitable** [ɛ̃dybitabl(ə)] *adj* indubitable
**indubitablement** [ɛ̃dybitablǝmā] *adv*
indubitably
**induction** [ɛ̃dyksjɔ̃] *nf* induction
**induire** [ɛ̃dɥiʁ] *vt*: **~ qch de** to induce sth from;
**~ qn en erreur** to lead sb astray, mislead sb
**indulgence** [ɛ̃dylʒās] *nf* indulgence; leniency;
**avec ~** indulgently; leniently
**indulgent, e** [ɛ̃dylʒā, -āt] *adj (parent, regard)*
indulgent; *(juge, examinateur)* lenient
**indûment** [ɛ̃dymā] *adv* without due cause;
*(illégitimement)* wrongfully
**industrialisation** [ɛ̃dystʁijalizasjɔ̃] *nf*
industrialization
**industrialisé, e** [ɛ̃dystʁijalize] *adj*
industrialized
**industrialiser** [ɛ̃dystʁijalize] *vt* to

**industrialize; s'industrialiser** *vi* to become
industrialized
**industrie** [ɛ̃dystʁi] *nf* industry; **~ automobile/
textile** car/textile industry; **~ du spectacle**
entertainment business
**industriel, le** [ɛ̃dystʁijɛl] *adj* industrial; *(produit
industriellement: pain etc)* mass-produced, factory-
produced ▷ *nm* industrialist; *(fabricant)*
manufacturer
**industriellement** [ɛ̃dystʁijɛlmā] *adv*
industrially
**industrieux, -euse** [ɛ̃dystʁijø, -øz] *adj*
industrious
**inébranlable** [inebʁālabl(ə)] *adj (masse, colonne)*
solid; *(personne, certitude, foi)* steadfast,
unwavering
**inédit, e** [inedi, -it] *adj (correspondance etc)*
(hitherto) unpublished; *(spectacle, moyen)* novel,
original
**ineffable** [inefabl(ə)] *adj* inexpressible,
ineffable
**ineffaçable** [inefasabl(ə)] *adj* indelible
**inefficace** [inefikas] *adj (remède, moyen)*
ineffective; *(machine, employé)* inefficient
**inefficacité** [inefikasite] *nf* ineffectiveness;
inefficiency
**inégal, e, -aux** [inegal, -o] *adj* unequal;
*(irrégulier)* uneven
**inégalable** [inegalabl(e)] *adj* matchless
**inégalé, e** [inegale] *adj* unmatched, unequalled
**inégalement** [inegalmā] *adv* unequally
**inégalité** [inegalite] *nf* inequality; unevenness
*no pl*; **~ de deux hauteurs** difference *ou*
disparity between two heights; **~s de terrain**
uneven ground
**inélégance** [inelegās] *nf* inelegance
**inélégant, e** [inelegā, -āt] *adj* inelegant;
*(indélicat)* discourteous
**inéligible** [ineliʒibl(ə)] *adj* ineligible
**inéluctable** [inelyktabl(ə)] *adj* inescapable
**inéluctablement** [inelyktablǝmā] *adv*
inescapably
**inemployable** [ināplwajabl(ə)] *adj* unusable
**inemployé, e** [ināplwaje] *adj* unused
**inénarrable** [inenaʁabl(ə)] *adj* hilarious
**inepte** [inɛpt(ə)] *adj* inept
**ineptie** [inɛpsi] *nf* ineptitude; *(propos)*
nonsense *no pl*
**inépuisable** [inepɥizabl(ə)] *adj* inexhaustible
**inéquitable** [inekitabl(ə)] *adj* inequitable
**inerte** [inɛʁt(ə)] *adj* lifeless; *(apathique)* passive,
inert; *(Physique, Chimie)* inert
**inertie** [inɛʁsi] *nf* inertia
**inescompté, e** [inɛskɔ̃te] *adj* unexpected,
unhoped-for
**inespéré, e** [inɛspeʁe] *adj* unhoped-for,
unexpected
**inesthétique** [inɛstetik] *adj* unsightly
**inestimable** [inɛstimabl(e)] *adj* priceless; *(fig:
bienfait)* invaluable
**inévitable** [inevitabl(ə)] *adj* unavoidable; *(fatal,
habituel)* inevitable

i

**inévitablement** [inevitabləmɑ̃] adv inevitably
**inexact, e** [inɛgzakt] adj inaccurate, inexact; (non ponctuel) unpunctual
**inexactement** [inɛgzaktəmɑ̃] adv inaccurately
**inexactitude** [inɛgzaktityd] nf inaccuracy
**inexcusable** [inɛkskyzabl(ə)] adj inexcusable, unforgivable
**inexécutable** [inɛgzekytabl(ə)] adj impracticable, unworkable; (Mus) unplayable
**inexistant, e** [inɛgzistɑ̃, -ɑ̃t] adj non-existent
**inexorable** [inɛgzɔrabl(ə)] adj inexorable; (personne: dur): ~ (à) unmoved (by)
**inexorablement** [inɛgzɔrabləmɑ̃] adv inexorably
**inexpérience** [inɛkspeʀjɑ̃s] nf inexperience, lack of experience
**inexpérimenté, e** [inɛkspeʀimɑ̃te] adj inexperienced; (arme, procédé) untested
**inexplicable** [inɛksplikabl(ə)] adj inexplicable
**inexplicablement** [inɛksplikabləmɑ̃] adv inexplicably
**inexpliqué, e** [inɛksplike] adj unexplained
**inexploitable** [inɛksplwatabl(ə)] adj (gisement, richesse) unexploitable; (données, renseignements) unusable
**inexploité, e** [inɛksplwate] adj unexploited, untapped
**inexploré, e** [inɛksplɔre] adj unexplored
**inexpressif, -ive** [inɛkspresif, -iv] adj inexpressive; (regard etc) expressionless
**inexpressivité** [inɛkspresivite] nf expressionlessness
**inexprimable** [inɛksprimabl(ə)] adj inexpressible
**inexprimé, e** [inɛksprime] adj unspoken, unexpressed
**inexpugnable** [inɛkspygnabl(ə)] adj impregnable
**inextensible** [inɛkstɑ̃sibl(ə)] adj (tissu) non-stretch
**in extenso** [inɛkstɛ̃so] adv in full
**inextinguible** [inɛkstɛ̃gibl(ə)] adj (soif) unquenchable; (rire) uncontrollable
**in extremis** [inɛkstremis] adv at the last minute ▷ adj last-minute; (testament) death bed cpd
**inextricable** [inɛkstrikabl(ə)] adj inextricable
**inextricablement** [inɛkstrikabləmɑ̃] adv inextricably
**infaillibilité** [ɛ̃fajibilite] nf infallibility
**infaillible** [ɛ̃fajibl(ə)] adj infallible; (instinct) infallible, unerring
**infailliblement** [ɛ̃fajibləmɑ̃] adv (certainement) without fail
**infaisable** [ɛ̃fəzabl(ə)] adj (travail etc) impossible, impractical
**infamant, e** [ɛ̃famɑ̃, -ɑ̃t] adj libellous, defamatory
**infâme** [ɛ̃fɑm] adj vile
**infamie** [ɛ̃fami] nf infamy
**infanterie** [ɛ̃fɑ̃tri] nf infantry
**infanticide** [ɛ̃fɑ̃tisid] nm/f child-murderer, murderess ▷ nm (meurtre) infanticide

**infantile** [ɛ̃fɑ̃til] adj (Méd) infantile, child cpd; (péj: ton, réaction) infantile, childish
**infantilisme** [ɛ̃fɑ̃tilism(ə)] nm infantilism
**infarctus** [ɛ̃farktys] nm: ~ **(du myocarde)** coronary (thrombosis)
**infatigable** [ɛ̃fatigabl(ə)] adj tireless, indefatigable
**infatigablement** [ɛ̃fatigabləmɑ̃] adv tirelessly, indefatigably
**infatué, e** [ɛ̃fatɥe] adj conceited; ~ **de** full of
**infécond, e** [ɛ̃fekɔ̃, -ɔ̃d] adj infertile, barren
**infect, e** [ɛ̃fɛkt] adj vile, foul; (repas, vin) revolting, foul
**infecter** [ɛ̃fɛkte] vt (atmosphère, eau) to contaminate; (Méd) to infect; **s'infecter** vi to become infected ou septic
**infectieux, -euse** [ɛ̃fɛksjø, -øz] adj infectious
**infection** [ɛ̃fɛksjɔ̃] nf infection
**inféoder** [ɛ̃feode] vt: **s'inféoder à** to pledge allegiance to
**inférer** [ɛ̃fere] vt: ~ **qch de** to infer sth from
**inférieur, e** [ɛ̃feʀjœʀ] adj lower; (en qualité, intelligence) inferior ▷ nm/f inferior; ~ **à** (somme, quantité) less ou smaller than; (moins bon que) inferior to; (tâche: pas à la hauteur de) unequal to
**infériorité** [ɛ̃feʀjɔʀite] nf inferiority; ~ **en nombre** inferiority in numbers
**infernal, e, -aux** [ɛ̃fɛrnal, -o] adj (chaleur, rythme) infernal; (méchanceté, complot) diabolical
**infester** [ɛ̃fɛste] vt to infest; **infesté de moustiques** infested with mosquitoes, mosquito-ridden
**infidèle** [ɛ̃fidɛl] adj unfaithful; (Rel) infidel
**infidélité** [ɛ̃fidelite] nf unfaithfulness no pl
**infiltration** [ɛ̃filtrɑsjɔ̃] nf infiltration
**infiltrer** [ɛ̃filtre]: **s'infiltrer** vi: s'~ **dans** to penetrate into; (liquide) to seep into; (fig: noyauter) to infiltrate
**infime** [ɛ̃fim] adj minute, tiny; (inférieur) lowly
**infini, e** [ɛ̃fini] adj infinite ▷ nm infinity; **à l'~** (Math) to infinity; (discourir) ad infinitum, endlessly; (agrandir, varier) infinitely; (à perte de vue) endlessly (into the distance)
**infiniment** [ɛ̃finimɑ̃] adv infinitely; ~ **grand/ petit** (Math) infinitely great/infinitesimal
**infinité** [ɛ̃finite] nf: **une ~ de** an infinite number of
**infinitésimal, e, -aux** [ɛ̃finitezimal, -o] adj infinitesimal
**infinitif, -ive** [ɛ̃finitif, -iv] adj, nm infinitive
**infirme** [ɛ̃firm(ə)] adj disabled ▷ nm/f disabled person; ~ **de guerre** war cripple; ~ **du travail** industrially disabled person
**infirmer** [ɛ̃firme] vt to invalidate
**infirmerie** [ɛ̃firməri] nf sick bay
**infirmier, -ière** [ɛ̃firmje, -jɛr] nm/f nurse ▷ adj: **élève** ~ student nurse; **infirmière chef** sister; **infirmière diplômée** registered nurse; **infirmière visiteuse** visiting nurse, ≈ district nurse (Brit)
**infirmité** [ɛ̃firmite] nf disability

**inflammable** [ɛ̃flamabl(ə)] *adj* (in)flammable
**inflammation** [ɛ̃flamɑsjɔ̃] *nf* inflammation
**inflammatoire** [ɛ̃flamatwaʀ] *adj* (*Méd*)
inflammatory
**inflation** [ɛ̃flɑsjɔ̃] *nf* inflation; **~ rampante/
galopante** creeping/galloping inflation
**inflationniste** [ɛ̃flɑsjɔnist(ə)] *adj* inflationist
**infléchir** [ɛ̃fleʃiʀ] *vt* (*fig: politique*) to reorientate,
redirect; **s'infléchir** *vi* (*poutre, tringle*) to bend,
sag
**inflexibilité** [ɛ̃flɛksibilite] *nf* inflexibility
**inflexible** [ɛ̃flɛksibl(ə)] *adj* inflexible
**inflexion** [ɛ̃flɛksjɔ̃] *nf* inflexion; **~ de la tête**
slight nod (of the head)
**infliger** [ɛ̃fliʒe] *vt*: **~ qch (à qn)** to inflict sth (on
sb); (*amende, sanction*) to impose sth (on sb)
**influençable** [ɛ̃flyɑ̃sabl(ə)] *adj* easily influenced
**influence** [ɛ̃flyɑ̃s] *nf* influence; (*d'un médicament*)
effect
**influencer** [ɛ̃flyɑ̃se] *vt* to influence
**influent, e** [ɛ̃flyɑ̃, -ɑ̃t] *adj* influential
**influer** [ɛ̃flye]: **~ sur** *vt* to have an influence
upon
**influx** [ɛ̃fly] *nm*: **~ nerveux** (nervous) impulse
**infobulle** [ɛ̃fobyl] *nf* (*Inform*) help bubble
**infographie** [ɛ̃fɔgʀafi] *nf* computer graphics *sg*
**informateur, -trice** [ɛ̃fɔʀmatœʀ, -tʀis] *nm/f*
informant
**informaticien, ne** [ɛ̃fɔʀmatisjɛ̃, -ɛn] *nm/f*
computer scientist
**informatif, -ive** [ɛ̃fɔʀmatif, -iv] *adj* informative
**information** [ɛ̃fɔʀmɑsjɔ̃] *nf* (*renseignement*) piece
of information; (*Presse, TV: nouvelle*) item of
news; (*diffusion de renseignements, Inform*)
information; (*Jur*) inquiry, investigation;
**informations** *nfpl* (TV) news *sg*; **voyage d'~**
fact-finding trip; **agence d'~** news agency;
**journal d'~** quality (*Brit*) *ou* serious newspaper
**informatique** [ɛ̃fɔʀmatik] *nf* (*technique*) data
processing; (*science*) computer science ▷ *adj*
computer *cpd*
**informatisation** [ɛ̃fɔʀmatizɑsjɔ̃] *nf*
computerization
**informatiser** [ɛ̃fɔʀmatize] *vt* to computerize
**informe** [ɛ̃fɔʀm(ə)] *adj* shapeless
**informé, e** [ɛ̃fɔʀme] *adj*: **jusqu'à plus ample ~**
until further information is available
**informel, le** [ɛ̃fɔʀmɛl] *adj* informal
**informer** [ɛ̃fɔʀme] *vt*: **~ qn (de)** to inform sb (of)
▷ *vi* (*Jur*): **~ contre qn/sur qch** to initiate
inquiries about sb/sth; **s'informer (sur)** to
inform o.s. (about); **s'~ (de qch/si)** to inquire *ou*
find out (about sth/whether *ou* if)
**informulé, e** [ɛ̃fɔʀmyle] *adj* unformulated
**infortune** [ɛ̃fɔʀtyn] *nf* misfortune
**infos** [ɛ̃fo] *nfpl* (= *informations*) news
**infraction** [ɛ̃fʀaksjɔ̃] *nf* offence; **~ à** violation *ou*
breach of; **être en ~** to be in breach of the law
**infranchissable** [ɛ̃fʀɑ̃ʃisabl(ə)] *adj* impassable;
(*fig*) insuperable
**infrarouge** [ɛ̃fʀaʀuʒ] *adj, nm* infrared
**infrason** [ɛ̃fʀasɔ̃] *nm* infrasonic vibration

**infrastructure** [ɛ̃fʀastʀyktyʀ] *nf* (*d'une route etc*)
substructure; (*Aviat, Mil*) ground installations
*pl*; (*touristique etc*) facilities *pl*
**infréquentable** [ɛ̃fʀekɑ̃tabl(ə)] *adj* not to be
associated with
**infroissable** [ɛ̃fʀwasabl(ə)] *adj* crease-resistant
**infructueux, -euse** [ɛ̃fʀyktɥø, -øz] *adj* fruitless,
unfruitful
**infus, e** [ɛ̃fy, -yz] *adj*: **avoir la science ~e** to have
innate knowledge
**infuser** [ɛ̃fyze] *vt* (*aussi*: **faire infuser**: *thé*) to
brew; (: *tisane*) to infuse ▷ *vi* to brew; to infuse;
**laisser ~** (to leave) to brew
**infusion** [ɛ̃fyzjɔ̃] *nf* (*tisane*) infusion, herb tea
**ingambe** [ɛ̃gɑ̃b] *adj* spry, nimble
**ingénier** [ɛ̃ʒenje]: **s'ingénier** *vi*: **s'~ à faire** to
strive to do
**ingénierie** [ɛ̃ʒeniʀi] *nf* engineering
**ingénieur** [ɛ̃ʒenjœʀ] *nm* engineer; **~
agronome/chimiste** agricultural/chemical
engineer; **~ conseil** consulting engineer; **~ du
son** sound engineer
**ingénieusement** [ɛ̃ʒenjøzmɑ̃] *adv* ingeniously
**ingénieux, -euse** [ɛ̃ʒenjø, -øz] *adj* ingenious,
clever
**ingéniosité** [ɛ̃ʒenjozite] *nf* ingenuity
**ingénu, e** [ɛ̃ʒeny] *adj* ingenuous, artless ▷ *nf*
(*Théât*) ingénue
**ingénuité** [ɛ̃ʒenɥite] *nf* ingenuousness
**ingénument** [ɛ̃ʒenymɑ̃] *adv* ingenuously
**ingérence** [ɛ̃ʒeʀɑ̃s] *nf* interference
**ingérer** [ɛ̃ʒeʀe]: **s'ingérer** *vi*: **s'~ dans** to
interfere in
**ingouvernable** [ɛ̃guvɛʀnabl(ə)] *adj*
ungovernable
**ingrat, e** [ɛ̃gʀa, -at] *adj* (*personne*) ungrateful;
(*sol*) poor; (*travail, sujet*) arid, thankless; (*visage*)
unprepossessing
**ingratitude** [ɛ̃gʀatityd] *nf* ingratitude
**ingrédient** [ɛ̃gʀedjɑ̃] *nm* ingredient
**inguérissable** [ɛ̃geʀisabl(ə)] *adj* incurable
**ingurgiter** [ɛ̃gyʀʒite] *vt* to swallow; **faire ~ qch
à qn** to make sb swallow sth; (*fig: connaissances*)
to force sth into sb
**inhabile** [inabil] *adj* clumsy; (*fig*) inept
**inhabitable** [inabitabl(ə)] *adj* uninhabitable
**inhabité, e** [inabite] *adj* (*régions*) uninhabited;
(*maison*) unoccupied
**inhabituel, le** [inabitɥɛl] *adj* unusual
**inhalateur** [inalatœʀ] *nm* inhaler; **~ d'oxygène**
oxygen mask
**inhalation** [inalɑsjɔ̃] *nf* (*Méd*) inhalation; **faire
des ~s** to use an inhalation bath
**inhaler** [inale] *vt* to inhale
**inhérent, e** [ineʀɑ̃, -ɑ̃t] *adj*: **~ à** inherent in
**inhiber** [inibe] *vt* to inhibit
**inhibition** [inibisjɔ̃] *nf* inhibition
**inhospitalier, -ière** [inɔspitalje, -jɛʀ] *adj*
inhospitable
**inhumain, e** [inymɛ̃, -ɛn] *adj* inhuman
**inhumation** [inymɑsjɔ̃] *nf* interment, burial
**inhumer** [inyme] *vt* to inter, bury

**inimaginable** [inimaʒinabl(ə)] *adj*
unimaginable
**inimitable** [inimitabl(ə)] *adj* inimitable
**inimitié** [inimitje] *nf* enmity
**ininflammable** [inɛ̃flamabl(ə)] *adj* non-
flammable
**inintelligent, e** [inɛ̃teliʒɑ̃, -ɑ̃t] *adj* unintelligent
**inintelligible** [inɛ̃teliʒibl(ə)] *adj* unintelligible
**inintelligiblement** [inɛ̃teliʒibləmɑ̃] *adv*
unintelligibly
**inintéressant, e** [inɛ̃teʀɛsɑ̃, -ɑ̃t] *adj*
uninteresting
**ininterrompu, e** [inɛ̃teʀɔ̃py] *adj* (*file, série*)
unbroken; (*flot, vacarme*) uninterrupted, non-
stop; (*effort*) unremitting, continuous
**iniquité** [inikite] *nf* iniquity
**initial, e, -aux** [inisjal, -o] *adj, nf* initial;
**initiales** *nfpl* initials
**initialement** [inisjalmɑ̃] *adv* initially
**initialiser** [inisjalize] *vt* to initialize
**initiateur, -trice** [inisjatœʀ, -tʀis] *nm/f*
initiator; (*d'une mode, technique*) innovator,
pioneer
**initiation** [inisjasjɔ̃] *nf* initiation
**initiatique** [inisjatik] *adj* (*rites, épreuves*)
initiatory
**initiative** [inisjativ] *nf* initiative; **prendre l'~
de qch/de faire** to take the initiative for sth/of
doing; **avoir de l'~** to have initiative, show
enterprise; **esprit/qualités d'~** spirit/qualities
of initiative; **à** *ou* **sur l'~ de qn** on sb's
initiative; **de sa propre ~** on one's own
initiative
**initié, e** [inisje] *adj* initiated ▷ *nm/f* initiate
**initier** [inisje] *vt* to initiate; **~ qn à** to initiate sb
into; (*faire découvrir: art, jeu*) to introduce sb to;
**s'initier à** *vi* (*métier, profession, technique*) to
become initiated into
**injectable** [ɛ̃ʒɛktabl(ə)] *adj* injectable
**injecté, e** [ɛ̃ʒɛkte] *adj*: **yeux ~s de sang**
bloodshot eyes
**injecter** [ɛ̃ʒɛkte] *vt* to inject
**injection** [ɛ̃ʒɛksjɔ̃] *nf* injection; **à ~** (*Auto*) fuel
injection *cpd*
**injonction** [ɛ̃ʒɔ̃ksjɔ̃] *nf* injunction, order; **~ de
payer** (*Jur*) order to pay
**injouable** [ɛ̃ʒwabl(ə)] *adj* unplayable
**injure** [ɛ̃ʒyʀ] *nf* insult, abuse *no pl*
**injurier** [ɛ̃ʒyʀje] *vt* to insult, abuse
**injurieux, -euse** [ɛ̃ʒyʀjø, -øz] *adj* abusive,
insulting
**injuste** [ɛ̃ʒyst(ə)] *adj* unjust, unfair
**injustement** [ɛ̃ʒystəmɑ̃] *adv* unjustly, unfairly
**injustice** [ɛ̃ʒystis] *nf* injustice
**injustifiable** [ɛ̃ʒystifjabl(ə)] *adj* unjustifiable
**injustifié, e** [ɛ̃ʒystifje] *adj* unjustified,
unwarranted
**inlassable** [ɛ̃lasabl(ə)] *adj* tireless,
indefatigable
**inlassablement** [ɛ̃lasabləmɑ̃] *adv* tirelessly
**inné, e** [ine] *adj* innate, inborn
**innocemment** [inɔsamɑ̃] *adv* innocently

**innocence** [inɔsɑ̃s] *nf* innocence
**innocent, e** [inɔsɑ̃, -ɑ̃t] *adj* innocent ▷ *nm/f*
innocent person; **faire l'~** to play *ou* come the
innocent
**innocenter** [inɔsɑ̃te] *vt* to clear, prove innocent
**innocuité** [inɔkɥite] *nf* innocuousness
**innombrable** [inɔ̃bʀabl(ə)] *adj* innumerable
**innommable** [inɔmabl(ə)] *adj* unspeakable
**innovateur, -trice** [inɔvatœʀ, -tʀis] *adj*
innovatory
**innovation** [inɔvasjɔ̃] *nf* innovation
**innover** [inɔve] *vi*: **~ en matière d'art** to break
new ground in the field of art
**inobservance** [inɔpsɛʀvɑ̃s] *nf* non-observance
**inobservation** [inɔpsɛʀvasjɔ̃] *nf* non-
observation, inobservance
**inoccupé, e** [inɔkype] *adj* unoccupied
**inoculer** [inɔkyle] *vt*: **~ qch à qn** (*volontairement*)
to inoculate sb with sth; (*accidentellement*) to
infect sb with sth; **~ qn contre** to inoculate sb
against
**inodore** [inɔdɔʀ] *adj* (*gaz*) odourless; (*fleur*)
scentless
**inoffensif, -ive** [inɔfɑ̃sif, -iv] *adj* harmless,
innocuous
**inondable** [inɔ̃dabl(ə)] *adj* (*zone etc*) liable to
flooding
**inondation** [inɔ̃dasjɔ̃] *nf* flooding *no pl*; (*torrent,
eau*) flood
**inonder** [inɔ̃de] *vt* to flood; (*fig*) to inundate,
overrun; **~ de** (*fig*) to flood *ou* swamp with
**inopérable** [inɔpeʀabl(ə)] *adj* inoperable
**inopérant, e** [inɔpeʀɑ̃, -ɑ̃t] *adj* inoperative,
ineffective
**inopiné, e** [inɔpine] *adj* unexpected, sudden
**inopinément** [inɔpinemɑ̃] *adv* unexpectedly
**inopportun, e** [inɔpɔʀtœ̃, -yn] *adj* ill-timed,
untimely; inappropriate; (*moment*) inopportune
**inorganisation** [inɔʀganizasjɔ̃] *nf* lack of
organization
**inorganisé, e** [inɔʀganize] *adj* (*travailleurs*) non-
organized
**inoubliable** [inublijabl(ə)] *adj* unforgettable
**inouï, e** [inwi] *adj* unheard-of, extraordinary
**inox** [inɔks] *adj, nm* (= *inoxydable*) stainless (steel)
**inoxydable** [inɔksidabl(ə)] *adj* stainless;
(*couverts*) stainless steel *cpd*
**inqualifiable** [ɛ̃kalifjabl(ə)] *adj* unspeakable
**inquiet, -ète** [ɛ̃kjɛ, -ɛt] *adj* (*par nature*) anxious;
(*momentanément*) worried; **~ de qch/au sujet de
qn** worried about sth/sb
**inquiétant, e** [ɛ̃kjetɑ̃, -ɑ̃t] *adj* worrying,
disturbing
**inquiéter** [ɛ̃kjete] *vt* to worry, disturb; (*harceler*)
to harass; **s'inquiéter** to worry, become
anxious; **s'~ de** to worry about; (*s'enquérir de*) to
inquire about
**inquiétude** [ɛ̃kjetyd] *nf* anxiety; **donner de l'~**
*ou* **des ~s à** to worry; **avoir de l'~** *ou* **des ~s au
sujet de** to feel anxious *ou* worried about
**inquisiteur, -trice** [ɛ̃kizitœʀ, -tʀis] *adj* (*regards,
questions*) inquisitive, prying

**inquisition** [ɛ̃kizisjɔ̃] *nf* inquisition
**INRA** [inʀa] *sigle m* = **Institut national de la recherche agronomique**
**inracontable** [ɛ̃ʀakɔ̃tabl(ə)] *adj (trop osé)* unrepeatable; *(trop compliqué):* **l'histoire est ~** the story is too complicated to relate
**insaisissable** [ɛ̃sezisabl(ə)] *adj* elusive
**insalubre** [ɛ̃salybʀ(ə)] *adj* unhealthy, insalubrious
**insalubrité** [ɛ̃salybʀite] *nf* unhealthiness, insalubrity
**insanité** [ɛ̃sanite] *nf* madness *no pl*, insanity *no pl*
**insatiable** [ɛ̃sasjabl(ə)] *adj* insatiable
**insatisfaction** [ɛ̃satisfaksjɔ̃] *nf* dissatisfaction
**insatisfait, e** [ɛ̃satisfɛ, -ɛt] *adj (non comblé)* unsatisfied; *(: passion, envie)* unfulfilled; *(mécontent)* dissatisfied
**inscription** [ɛ̃skʀipsjɔ̃] *nf (sur un mur, écriteau etc)* inscription; *(à une institution: voir s'inscrire)* enrolment; registration
**inscrire** [ɛ̃skʀiʀ] *vt (marquer: sur son calepin etc)* to note *ou* write down; *(: sur un mur, une affiche etc)* to write; *(: dans la pierre, le métal)* to inscribe; *(mettre: sur une liste, un budget etc)* to put down; *(enrôler: soldat)* to enlist; **~ qn à** *(club, école etc)* to enrol sb at; **s'inscrire** *vi (pour une excursion etc)* to put one's name down; **s'~ (à)** *(club, parti)* to join; *(université)* to register *ou* enrol (at); *(examen, concours)* to register *ou* enter (for); **s'~ dans** *(se situer: négociations etc)* to come within the scope of; **s'~ en faux contre** to deny (strongly); *(Jur)* to challenge
**inscrit, e** [ɛ̃skʀi, it] *pp de* **inscrire** ▷ *adj (étudiant, électeur etc)* registered
**insécable** [ɛ̃sekabl(ə)] *adj (Inform)* indivisible; **espace ~** hard space
**insecte** [ɛ̃sɛkt(ə)] *nm* insect
**insecticide** [ɛ̃sɛktisid] *nm* insecticide
**insécurité** [ɛ̃sekyʀite] *nf* insecurity, lack of security
**INSEE** [inse] *sigle m (= Institut national de la statistique et des études économiques)* national institute of statistical and economic information
**insémination** [ɛ̃seminasjɔ̃] *nf* insemination
**insensé, e** [ɛ̃sɑ̃se] *adj* insane, mad
**insensibiliser** [ɛ̃sɑ̃sibilize] *vt* to anaesthetize; *(à une allergie)* to desensitize; **~ à qch** *(fig)* to cause to become insensitive to sth
**insensibilité** [ɛ̃sɑ̃sibilite] *nf* insensitivity
**insensible** [ɛ̃sɑ̃sibl(ə)] *adj (nerf, membre)* numb; *(dur, indifférent)* insensitive; *(imperceptible)* imperceptible
**insensiblement** [ɛ̃sɑ̃sibləmɑ̃] *adv (doucement, peu à peu)* imperceptibly
**inséparable** [ɛ̃separabl(ə)] *adj:* **~ (de)** inseparable (from) ▷ *nmpl:* **~s** *(oiseaux)* lovebirds
**insérer** [ɛ̃seʀe] *vt* to insert; **s'~ dans** to fit into; *(fig)* to come within
**INSERM** [ɛ̃sɛʀm] *sigle m (= Institut national de la santé et de la recherche médicale)* national institute for medical research

**insert** [ɛ̃sɛʀ] *nm* enclosed fireplace burning solid fuel
**insertion** [ɛ̃sɛʀsjɔ̃] *nf (d'une personne)* integration
**insidieusement** [ɛ̃sidjøzmɑ̃] *adv* insidiously
**insidieux, -euse** [ɛ̃sidjø, -øz] *adj* insidious
**insigne** [ɛ̃siɲ] *nm (d'un parti, club)* badge ▷ *adj* distinguished; **insignes** *nmpl (d'une fonction)* insignia *pl*
**insignifiant, e** [ɛ̃siɲifjɑ̃, -ɑ̃t] *adj* insignificant; *(somme, affaire, détail)* trivial, insignificant
**insinuant, e** [ɛ̃sinɥɑ̃, -ɑ̃t] *adj* ingratiating
**insinuation** [ɛ̃sinɥasjɔ̃] *nf* innuendo, insinuation
**insinuer** [ɛ̃sinɥe] *vt* to insinuate, imply; **s'insinuer dans** *vi* to seep into; *(fig)* to worm one's way into, creep into
**insipide** [ɛ̃sipid] *adj* insipid
**insistance** [ɛ̃sistɑ̃s] *nf* insistence; **avec ~** insistently
**insistant, e** [ɛ̃sistɑ̃, -ɑ̃t] *adj* insistent
**insister** [ɛ̃siste] *vi* to insist; *(s'obstiner)* to keep on; **~ sur** *(détail, note)* to stress; **~ pour qch/ pour faire qch** to be insistent about sth/about doing sth
**insociable** [ɛ̃sɔsjabl(ə)] *adj* unsociable
**insolation** [ɛ̃sɔlasjɔ̃] *nf (Méd)* sunstroke *no pl*; *(ensoleillement)* period of sunshine
**insolence** [ɛ̃sɔlɑ̃s] *nf* insolence *no pl*; **avec ~** insolently
**insolent, e** [ɛ̃sɔlɑ̃, -ɑ̃t] *adj* insolent
**insolite** [ɛ̃sɔlit] *adj* strange, unusual
**insoluble** [ɛ̃sɔlybl(ə)] *adj* insoluble
**insolvable** [ɛ̃sɔlvabl(ə)] *adj* insolvent
**insomniaque** [ɛ̃sɔmnjak] *adj, nm/f* insomniac
**insomnie** [ɛ̃sɔmni] *nf* insomnia *no pl*, sleeplessness *no pl*; **avoir des ~s** to suffer from insomnia
**insondable** [ɛ̃sɔ̃dabl(ə)] *adj* unfathomable
**insonore** [ɛ̃sɔnɔʀ] *adj* soundproof
**insonorisation** [ɛ̃sɔnɔʀizasjɔ̃] *nf* soundproofing
**insonoriser** [ɛ̃sɔnɔʀize] *vt* to soundproof
**insouciance** [ɛ̃susjɑ̃s] *nf* carefree attitude; heedless attitude
**insouciant, e** [ɛ̃susjɑ̃, -ɑ̃t] *adj* carefree; *(imprévoyant)* heedless
**insoumis, e** [ɛ̃sumi, -iz] *adj (caractère, enfant)* rebellious, refractory; *(contrée, tribu)* unsubdued; *(Mil: soldat)* absent without leave ▷ *nm (Mil: soldat)* absentee
**insoumission** [ɛ̃sumisjɔ̃] *nf* rebelliousness; *(Mil)* absence without leave
**insoupçonnable** [ɛ̃supsɔnabl(ə)] *adj* above suspicion
**insoupçonné, e** [ɛ̃supsɔne] *adj* unsuspected
**insoutenable** [ɛ̃sutnabl(ə)] *adj (argument)* untenable; *(chaleur)* unbearable
**inspecter** [ɛ̃spɛkte] *vt* to inspect
**inspecteur, -trice** [ɛ̃spɛktœʀ, -tʀis] *nm/f* inspector; *(des assurances)* assessor; **~ d'Académie** (regional) director of education; **~ (de l'enseignement) primaire** primary school inspector; **~ des finances** ≈ tax inspector *(Brit)*,

≈ Internal Revenue Service agent (US); ~ **(de police)** (police) inspector

**inspection** [ɛspɛksjɔ̃] *nf* inspection

**inspirateur, -trice** [ɛspiʀatœʀ, -tʀis] *nm/f* (*instigateur*) instigator; (*animateur*) inspirer

**inspiration** [ɛspiʀɑsjɔ̃] *nf* inspiration; breathing in *no pl*; (*idée*) flash of inspiration, brainwave; **sous l'~ de** prompted by

**inspiré, e** [ɛspiʀe] *adj*: **être bien/mal ~ de faire qch** to be well-advised/ill-advised to do sth

**inspirer** [ɛspiʀe] *vt* (*gén*) to inspire ▷ *vi* (*aspirer*) to breathe in; **s'inspirer de** (*artiste*) to draw one's inspiration from; (*tableau*) to be inspired by; ~ **qch à qn** (*œuvre, projet, action*) to inspire sb with sth; (*dégoût, crainte, horreur*) to fill sb with sth; **ça ne m'inspire pas** I'm not keen on the idea

**instabilité** [ɛstabilite] *nf* instability

**instable** [ɛstabl(ə)] *adj* (*meuble, équilibre*) unsteady; (*population, temps*) unsettled; (*paix, régime, caractère*) unstable

**installateur** [ɛstalatœʀ] *nm* fitter

**installation** [ɛstalɑsjɔ̃] *nf* installation; putting in *ou* up; fitting out; settling in; (*appareils etc*) fittings *pl*, installations *pl*; **installations** *nfpl* installations; (*industrielles*) plant *sg*; (*de loisirs*) facilities

**installé, e** [ɛstale] *adj*: **bien/mal ~** well/poorly equipped; (*personne*) well/not very well set up *ou* organized

**installer** [ɛstale] *vt* (*loger*): ~ **qn** to get sb settled, install sb; (*asseoir, coucher*) to settle (down); (*placer*) to put, place; (*meuble*) to put in; (*rideau, étagère, tente*) to put up; (*gaz, électricité etc*) to put in, install; (*appartement*) to fit out; (*aménager*): ~ **une salle de bains dans une pièce** to fit out a room with a bathroom suite; **s'installer** *vi* (*s'établir: artisan, dentiste etc*) to set o.s. up; (*se loger*): **s'~ à l'hôtel/chez qn** to move into a hotel/in with sb; (*emménager*) to settle in; (*sur un siège, à un emplacement*) to settle (down); (*fig: maladie, grève*) to take a firm hold *ou* grip

**instamment** [ɛstamɑ̃] *adv* urgently

**instance** [ɛstɑ̃s] *nf* (*Jur: procédure*) (legal) proceedings *pl*; (*Admin: autorité*) authority; **instances** *nfpl* (*prières*) entreaties; **affaire en ~** matter pending; **courrier en ~** mail ready for posting; **être en ~ de divorce** to be awaiting a divorce; **train en ~ de départ** train on the point of departure; **tribunal de première ~** court of first instance; **en seconde ~** on appeal

**instant** [ɛstɑ̃] *nm* moment, instant; **dans un ~** in a moment; **à l'~** this instant; **je l'ai vu à l'~** I've just this minute seen him, I saw him a moment ago; **à l'~ (même) où** at the (very) moment that *ou* when, (just) as; **à chaque ~, à tout ~** at any moment; constantly; **pour l'~** for the moment, for the time being; **par ~s** at times; **de tous les ~s** perpetual; **dès l'~ où** *ou* **que ...** from the moment when ..., since that moment when ...

**instantané, e** [ɛstɑ̃tane] *adj* (*lait, café*) instant;

(*explosion, mort*) instantaneous ▷ *nm* snapshot

**instantanément** [ɛstɑ̃tanemɑ̃] *adv* instantaneously

**instar** [ɛstaʀ]: **à l'~ de** *prép* following the example of, like

**instaurer** [ɛstɔʀe] *vt* to institute; **s'instaurer** *vi* to set o.s. up; (*collaboration etc*) to be established

**instigateur, -trice** [ɛstigatœʀ, -tʀis] *nm/f* instigator

**instigation** [ɛstigɑsjɔ̃] *nf*: **à l'~ de qn** at sb's instigation

**instiller** [ɛstile] *vt* to instil, apply

**instinct** [ɛstɛ̃] *nm* instinct; **d'~** (*spontanément*) instinctively; ~ **grégaire** herd instinct; ~ **de conservation** instinct of self-preservation

**instinctif, -ive** [ɛstɛ̃ktif, -iv] *adj* instinctive

**instinctivement** [ɛstɛ̃ktivmɑ̃] *adv* instinctively

**instit** [ɛstit] (*fam*) *nm/f* (primary school) teacher

**instituer** [ɛstitɥe] *vt* to institute, set up; **s'~ défenseur d'une cause** to set o.s up as defender of a cause

**institut** [ɛstity] *nm* institute; ~ **de beauté** beauty salon; ~ **médico-légal** mortuary; **I~ universitaire de technologie (IUT)** technical college

**instituteur, -trice** [ɛstitytœʀ, -tʀis] *nm/f* (primary (*Brit*) *ou* grade (*US*) school) teacher

**institution** [ɛstitysjɔ̃] *nf* institution; (*collège*) private school

**institutionnaliser** [ɛstitysjɔnalize] *vt* to institutionalize

**instructeur, -trice** [ɛstʀyktœʀ, -tʀis] *adj* (*Mil*): **sergent ~** drill sergeant; (*Jur*): **juge ~** examining (*Brit*) *ou* committing (*US*) magistrate ▷ *nm/f* instructor

**instructif, -ive** [ɛstʀyktif, -iv] *adj* instructive

**instruction** [ɛstʀyksjɔ̃] *nf* (*enseignement, savoir*) education; (*Jur*) (preliminary) investigation and hearing; (*directive*) instruction; (*Admin: document*) directive; **instructions** *nfpl* instructions; (*mode d'emploi*) directions, instructions; ~ **civique** civics *sg*; ~ **primaire/publique** primary/public education; ~ **religieuse** religious education; ~ **professionnelle** vocational training

**instruire** [ɛstʀɥiʀ] *vt* (*élèves*) to teach; (*recrues*) to train; (*Jur: affaire*) to conduct the investigation for; **s'instruire** to educate o.s.; **s'~ auprès de qn de qch** (*s'informer*) to find sth out from sb; ~ **qn de qch** (*informer*) to inform *ou* advise sb of sth; ~ **contre qn** (*Jur*) to investigate sb

**instruit, e** [ɛstʀɥi, -it] *pp de* **instruire** ▷ *adj* educated

**instrument** [ɛstʀymɑ̃] *nm* instrument; ~ **à cordes/vent** stringed/wind instrument; ~ **de mesure** measuring instrument; ~ **de musique** musical instrument; ~ **de travail** (working) tool

**instrumental, e, -aux** [ɛstʀymɑ̃tal, -o] *adj* instrumental

**instrumentation** [ɛstʀymɑ̃tɑsjɔ̃] *nf* instrumentation

**instrumentiste** [ɛ̃stʀymɑ̃tist(ə)] nm/f
instrumentalist

**insu** [ɛ̃sy] nm: **à l'~ de qn** without sb knowing

**insubmersible** [ɛ̃sybmɛʀsibl(ə)] adj unsinkable

**insubordination** [ɛ̃sybɔʀdinasjɔ̃] nf
rebelliousness; (Mil) insubordination

**insubordonné, e** [ɛ̃sybɔʀdɔne] adj
insubordinate

**insuccès** [ɛ̃syksɛ] nm failure

**insuffisamment** [ɛ̃syfizamɑ̃] adv insufficiently

**insuffisance** [ɛ̃syfizɑ̃s] nf insufficiency;
inadequacy; **insuffisances** nfpl (lacunes)
inadequacies; **~ cardiaque** cardiac
insufficiency no pl; **~ hépatique** liver deficiency

**insuffisant, e** [ɛ̃syfizɑ̃, -ɑ̃t] adj insufficient;
(élève, travail) inadequate

**insuffler** [ɛ̃syfle] vt: **~ qch dans** to blow sth into;
**~ qch à qn** to inspire sb with sth

**insulaire** [ɛ̃sylɛʀ] adj island cpd; (attitude)
insular

**insularité** [ɛ̃sylaʀite] nf insularity

**insuline** [ɛ̃sylin] nf insulin

**insultant, e** [ɛ̃syltɑ̃, -ɑ̃t] adj insulting

**insulte** [ɛ̃sylt(ə)] nf insult

**insulter** [ɛ̃sylte] vt to insult

**insupportable** [ɛ̃sypɔʀtabl(ə)] adj unbearable

**insurgé, e** [ɛ̃syʀʒe] adj, nm/f insurgent, rebel

**insurger** [ɛ̃syʀʒe]: **s'insurger** vi: **s'~ (contre)** to
rise up ou rebel (against)

**insurmontable** [ɛ̃syʀmɔ̃tabl(ə)] adj (difficulté)
insuperable; (aversion) unconquerable

**insurpassable** [ɛ̃syʀpasabl(ə)] adj
unsurpassable, unsurpassed

**insurrection** [ɛ̃syʀɛksjɔ̃] nf insurrection, revolt

**insurrectionnel, le** [ɛ̃syʀɛksjɔnɛl] adj
insurrectionary

**intact, e** [ɛ̃takt] adj intact

**intangible** [ɛ̃tɑ̃ʒibl(ə)] adj intangible; (principe)
inviolable

**intarissable** [ɛ̃taʀisabl(ə)] adj inexhaustible

**intégral, e, -aux** [ɛ̃tegʀal, -o] adj complete ▷ nf
(Math) integral; (œuvres complètes) complete
works

**intégralement** [ɛ̃tegʀalmɑ̃] adv in full, fully

**intégralité** [ɛ̃tegʀalite] nf (d'une somme, d'un
revenu) whole (ou full) amount; **dans son ~** in its
entirety

**intégrant, e** [ɛ̃tegʀɑ̃, -ɑ̃t] adj: **faire partie ~e de**
to be an integral part of, be part and parcel of

**intégration** [ɛ̃tegʀasjɔ̃] nf integration

**intégrationniste** [ɛ̃tegʀasjɔnist(ə)] adj, nm/f
integrationist

**intégré, e** [ɛ̃tegʀe] adj: **circuit ~** integrated
circuit

**intègre** [ɛ̃tegʀ(ə)] adj perfectly honest, upright

**intégrer** [ɛ̃tegʀe] vt: **~ qch à** ou **dans** to
integrate sth into; **s'~ à** ou **dans** to become
integrated into

**intégrisme** [ɛ̃tegʀism(ə)] nm fundamentalism

**intégriste** [ɛ̃tegʀist(ə)] adj, nm/f
fundamentalist

**intégrité** [ɛ̃tegʀite] nf integrity

**intellect** [ɛ̃telɛkt] nm intellect

**intellectuel, le** [ɛ̃telɛktɥɛl] adj, nm/f
intellectual; (péj) highbrow

**intellectuellement** [ɛ̃telɛktɥɛlmɑ̃] adv
intellectually

**intelligemment** [ɛ̃teliʒamɑ̃] adv intelligently

**intelligence** [ɛ̃teliʒɑ̃s] nf intelligence;
(compréhension): **l'~ de** the understanding of;
(complicité): **regard d'~** glance of complicity,
meaningful ou knowing look; (accord): **vivre en
bonne ~ avec qn** to be on good terms with sb;
**intelligences** nfpl (Mil, fig) secret contacts; **être
d'~** to have an understanding; **~ artificielle**
artificial intelligence (A.I.)

**intelligent, e** [ɛ̃teliʒɑ̃, -ɑ̃t] adj intelligent;
(capable): **~ en affaires** competent in business

**intelligentsia** [ɛ̃telidʒɛnsja] nf intelligentsia

**intelligible** [ɛ̃teliʒibl(ə)] adj intelligible

**intello** [ɛ̃telo] adj, nm/f (fam) highbrow

**intempérance** [ɛ̃tɑ̃peʀɑ̃s] nf overindulgence no
pl; intemperance no pl

**intempérant, e** [ɛ̃tɑ̃peʀɑ̃, -ɑ̃t] adj
overindulgent; (moralement) intemperate

**intempéries** [ɛ̃tɑ̃peʀi] nfpl bad weather sg

**intempestif, -ive** [ɛ̃tɑ̃pɛstif, -iv] adj untimely

**intenable** [ɛ̃tnabl(ə)] adj unbearable

**intendance** [ɛ̃tɑ̃dɑ̃s] nf (Mil) supply corps;
(: bureau) supplies office; (Scol) bursar's office

**intendant, e** [ɛ̃tɑ̃dɑ̃, -ɑ̃t] nm/f (Mil)
quartermaster; (Scol) bursar; (d'une propriété)
steward

**intense** [ɛ̃tɑ̃s] adj intense

**intensément** [ɛ̃tɑ̃semɑ̃] adv intensely

**intensif, -ive** [ɛ̃tɑ̃sif, -iv] adj intensive; **cours ~**
crash course; **~ en main-d'œuvre** labour-
intensive; **~ en capital** capital-intensive

**intensification** [ɛ̃tɑ̃sifikasjɔ̃] nf intensification

**intensifier** [ɛ̃tɑ̃sifje] vt, **s'intensifier** vi to
intensify

**intensité** [ɛ̃tɑ̃site] nf intensity

**intensivement** [ɛ̃tɑ̃sivmɑ̃] adv intensively

**intenter** [ɛ̃tɑ̃te] vt: **~ un procès contre** ou **à qn**
to start proceedings against sb

**intention** [ɛ̃tɑ̃sjɔ̃] nf intention; (Jur) intent;
**avoir l'~ de faire** to intend to do, have the
intention of doing; **dans l'~ de faire qch** with
a view to doing sth; **à l'~ de** prép for;
(renseignement) for the benefit ou information of;
(film, ouvrage) aimed at; **à cette ~** with this aim
in view; **sans ~** unintentionally; **faire qch
sans mauvaise ~** to do sth without ill intent;
**agir dans une bonne ~** to act with good
intentions

**intentionné, e** [ɛ̃tɑ̃sjɔne] adj: **bien ~** well-
meaning ou -intentioned; **mal ~** ill-
intentioned

**intentionnel, le** [ɛ̃tɑ̃sjɔnɛl] adj intentional,
deliberate

**intentionnellement** [ɛ̃tɑ̃sjɔnɛlmɑ̃] adv
intentionally, deliberately

**inter** [ɛ̃tɛʀ] nm (Tél: interurbain) long-distance
call service; (Sport): **~ gauche/droit** inside-

left/-right

**interactif, -ive** [ɛ̃tɛʀaktif, -iv] *adj (aussi Inform)* interactive

**interaction** [ɛ̃tɛʀaksjɔ̃] *nf* interaction

**interbancaire** [ɛ̃tɛʀbɑ̃kɛʀ] *adj* interbank

**intercalaire** [ɛ̃tɛʀkalɛʀ] *adj, nm:* **(feuillet)** ~ insert; **(fiche)** ~ divider

**intercaler** [ɛ̃tɛʀkale] *vt* to insert; **s'intercaler entre** *vi* to come in between; to slip in between

**intercéder** [ɛ̃tɛʀsede] *vi:* ~ **(pour qn)** to intercede (on behalf of sb)

**intercepter** [ɛ̃tɛʀsɛpte] *vt* to intercept; *(lumière, chaleur)* to cut off

**intercepteur** [ɛ̃tɛʀsɛptœʀ] *nm (Aviat)* interceptor

**interception** [ɛ̃tɛʀsɛpsjɔ̃] *nf* interception; **avion d'**~ interceptor

**intercession** [ɛ̃tɛʀsesjɔ̃] *nf* intercession

**interchangeable** [ɛ̃tɛʀʃɑ̃ʒabl(ə)] *adj* interchangeable

**interclasse** [ɛ̃tɛʀklɑs] *nm (Scol)* break (between classes)

**interclubs** [ɛ̃tɛʀklœb] *adj inv* interclub

**intercommunal, e, -aux** [ɛ̃tɛʀkɔmynal, -o] *adj* intervillage, intercommunity

**intercommunautaire** [ɛ̃tɛʀkɔmynotɛʀ] *adj* intercommunity

**intercontinental, e, -aux** [ɛ̃tɛʀkɔ̃tinɑtal, -o] *adj* intercontinental

**intercostal, e, -aux** [ɛ̃tɛʀkɔstal, -o] *adj* intercostal, between the ribs

**interdépartemental, e, -aux** [ɛ̃tɛʀdepaʀtəmɑ̃tal, -o] *adj* interdepartmental

**interdépendance** [ɛ̃tɛʀdepɑ̃dɑ̃s] *nf* interdependence

**interdépendant, e** [ɛ̃tɛʀdepɑ̃dɑ̃, -ɑ̃t] *adj* interdependent

**interdiction** [ɛ̃tɛʀdiksjɔ̃] *nf* ban; ~ **de faire qch** ban on doing sth; ~ **de séjour** *(Jur)* order banning ex-prisoner from frequenting specified places

**interdire** [ɛ̃tɛʀdiʀ] *vt* to forbid; *(Admin: stationnement, meeting, passage)* to ban, prohibit; *(: journal, livre)* to ban; ~ **qch à qn** to forbid sb sth; ~ **à qn de faire** to forbid sb to do, prohibit sb from doing; *(empêchement)* to prevent *ou* preclude sb from doing; **s'interdire qch** *vi* *(éviter)* to refrain *ou* abstain from sth; *(se refuser)*: **il s'interdit d'y penser** he doesn't allow himself to think about it

**interdisciplinaire** [ɛ̃tɛʀdisiplinɛʀ] *adj* interdisciplinary

**interdit, e** [ɛ̃tɛʀdi, -it] *pp de* **interdire** ▷ *adj* *(stupéfait)* taken aback; *(défendu)* forbidden, prohibited ▷ *nm* interdict, prohibition; **film** ~ **aux moins de 18/13 ans** ≈ 18-/PG-rated film; **sens** ~ one way; **stationnement** ~ no parking; ~ **de chéquier** having cheque book facilities suspended; ~ **de séjour** subject to an "interdiction de séjour"

**intéressant, e** [ɛ̃teʀesɑ̃, -ɑ̃t] *adj* interesting; **faire l'**~ to draw attention to o.s.

**intéressé, e** [ɛ̃teʀese] *adj (parties)* involved,

concerned; *(amitié, motifs)* self-interested ▷ *nm:* **l'**~ the interested party; **les** ~**s** those concerned *ou* involved

**intéressement** [ɛ̃teʀesmɑ̃] *nm (Comm)* profit-sharing

**intéresser** [ɛ̃teʀese] *vt* to interest; *(toucher)* to be of interest *ou* concern to; *(Admin: concerner)* to affect, concern; *(Comm: travailleur)* to give a share in the profits to; *(: partenaire)* to interest (in the business); **s'intéresser à** *vi* to take an interest in, be interested in; ~ **qn à qch** to get sb interested in sth

**intérêt** [ɛ̃teʀɛ] *nm (aussi Comm)* interest; *(égoïsme)* self-interest; **porter de l'**~ **à qn** to take an interest in sb; **agir par** ~ to act out of self-interest; **avoir des** ~**s dans** *(Comm)* to have a financial interest *ou* a stake in; **avoir** ~ **à faire** to do well to do; **il y a** ~ **à …** it would be a good thing to …; ~ **composé** compound interest

**interface** [ɛ̃tɛʀfas] *nf (Inform)* interface

**interférence** [ɛ̃tɛʀfeʀɑ̃s] *nf* interference

**interférer** [ɛ̃tɛʀfeʀe] *vi:* ~ **(avec)** to interfere (with)

**intergouvernemental, e, -aux** [ɛ̃tɛʀguvɛʀnəmɑ̃tal, -o] *adj* intergovernmental

**intérieur, e** [ɛ̃teʀjœʀ] *adj (mur, escalier, poche)* inside; *(commerce, politique)* domestic; *(cour, calme, vie)* inner; *(navigation)* inland ▷ *nm (d'une maison, d'un récipient etc)* inside; *(d'un pays, aussi: décor, mobilier)* interior; *(Pol)* **l'I**~ (the Department of) the Interior, ≈ the Home Office *(Brit)*; **à l'**~ **(de)** inside; *(fig)* within; **de l'**~ *(fig)* from the inside; **en** ~ *(Ciné)* in the studio; **vêtement d'**~ indoor garment

**intérieurement** [ɛ̃teʀjœʀmɑ̃] *adv* inwardly

**intérim** [ɛ̃teʀim] *nm (période)* interim period; *(travail)* temping; **agence d'**~ temping agency; **assurer l'**~ **(de)** to deputize (for); **président par** ~ interim president; **travailler en** ~ to temp

**intérimaire** [ɛ̃teʀimɛʀ] *adj* temporary, interim ▷ *nm/f (secrétaire etc)* temporary, temp *(Brit)*; *(suppléant)* deputy

**intérioriser** [ɛ̃teʀjɔʀize] *vt* to internalize

**interjection** [ɛ̃tɛʀʒɛksjɔ̃] *nf* interjection

**interjeter** [ɛ̃tɛʀʒəte] *vt (Jur):* ~ **appel** to lodge an appeal

**interligne** [ɛ̃tɛʀliɲ] *nm* inter-line space ▷ *nf (Typo)* lead, leading; **simple/double** ~ single/double spacing

**interlocuteur, -trice** [ɛ̃tɛʀlɔkytœʀ, -tʀis] *nm/f* speaker; *(Pol):* ~ **valable** valid representative; **son** ~ the person he *ou* she was speaking to

**interlope** [ɛ̃tɛʀlɔp] *adj (illicit; (milieu, bar)* shady

**interloquer** [ɛ̃tɛʀlɔke] *vt* to take aback

**interlude** [ɛ̃tɛʀlyd] *nm* interlude

**intermède** [ɛ̃tɛʀmɛd] *nm* interlude

**intermédiaire** [ɛ̃tɛʀmedjɛʀ] *adj* intermediate; middle; half-way ▷ *nm/f* intermediary; *(Comm)* middleman; **sans** ~ directly; **par l'**~ **de** through

**interminable** [ɛ̃tɛʀminabl(ə)] *adj* never-ending

**interminablement** [ɛ̃tɛʀminabləmɑ̃] *adv* interminably

**interministériel, le** [ɛ̃tɛʀministeʀjɛl] *adj*: **comité ~** interdepartmental committee

**intermittence** [ɛ̃tɛʀmitɑ̃s] *nf*: **par ~** intermittently, sporadically

**intermittent, e** [ɛ̃tɛʀmitɑ̃, -ɑ̃t] *adj* intermittent, sporadic

**internat** [ɛ̃tɛʀna] *nm* (*Scol*) boarding school

**international, e, -aux** [ɛ̃tɛʀnasjɔnal, -o] *adj, nm/f* international

**internationalisation** [ɛ̃tɛʀnasjɔnalizɑsjɔ̃] *nf* internationalization

**internationaliser** [ɛ̃tɛʀnasjɔnalize] *vt* to internationalize

**internationalisme** [ɛ̃tɛʀnasjɔnalism(ə)] *nm* internationalism

**internaute** [ɛ̃tɛʀnot] *nm/f* Internet user

**interne** [ɛ̃tɛʀn(ə)] *adj* internal ▷ *nm/f* (*Scol*) boarder; (*Méd*) houseman (*Brit*), intern (*US*)

**internement** [ɛ̃tɛʀnəmɑ̃] *nm* (*Pol*) internment; (*Méd*) confinement

**interner** [ɛ̃tɛʀne] *vt* (*Pol*) to intern; (*Méd*) to confine to a mental institution

**Internet** [ɛ̃tɛʀnɛt] *nm*: **l'~** the Internet

**interparlementaire** [ɛ̃tɛʀparləmɑ̃tɛʀ] *adj* interparliamentary

**interpellation** [ɛ̃tɛʀpelɑsjɔ̃] *nf* interpellation; (*Pol*) question

**interpeller** [ɛ̃tɛʀpele] *vt* (*appeler*) to call out to; (*apostropher*) to shout at; (*Police*) to take in for questioning; (*Pol*) to question; **s'interpeller** *vi* to exchange insults

**interphone** [ɛ̃tɛʀfɔn] *nm* intercom

**interplanétaire** [ɛ̃tɛʀplanetɛʀ] *adj* interplanetary

**Interpol** [ɛ̃tɛʀpɔl] *sigle m* Interpol

**interpoler** [ɛ̃tɛʀpɔle] *vt* to interpolate

**interposer** [ɛ̃tɛʀpoze] *vt* to interpose; **s'interposer** *vi* to intervene; **par personnes interposées** through a third party

**interprétariat** [ɛ̃tɛʀpretarja] *nm* interpreting

**interprétation** [ɛ̃tɛʀpretɑsjɔ̃] *nf* interpretation

**interprète** [ɛ̃tɛʀpʀɛt] *nm/f* interpreter; (*porte-parole*) spokesman

**interpréter** [ɛ̃tɛʀpʀete] *vt* to interpret

**interprofessionnel, le** [ɛ̃tɛʀpʀofesjɔnɛl] *adj* interprofessional

**interrogateur, -trice** [ɛ̃tɛʀɔgatœʀ, -tʀis] *adj* questioning, inquiring ▷ *nm/f* (*Scol*) (oral) examiner

**interrogatif, -ive** [ɛ̃tɛʀɔgatif, -iv] *adj* (*Ling*) interrogative

**interrogation** [ɛ̃tɛʀɔgɑsjɔ̃] *nf* question; (*Scol*) (written *ou* oral) test

**interrogatoire** [ɛ̃tɛʀɔgatwaʀ] *nm* (*Police*) questioning *no pl*; (*Jur*) cross-examination, interrogation

**interroger** [ɛ̃tɛʀɔʒe] *vt* to question; (*Inform*) to search; (*Scol*: *candidat*) to test; **~ qn (sur qch)** to question sb (about sth); **~ qn du regard** to look questioningly at sb, give sb a questioning look; **s'~ sur qch** to ask o.s. about sth, ponder (about) sth

**interrompre** [ɛ̃tɛʀɔ̃pʀ(ə)] *vt* (*gén*) to interrupt; (*travail, voyage*) to break off, interrupt; **s'interrompre** *vi* to break off

**interrupteur** [ɛ̃tɛʀyptœʀ] *nm* switch

**interruption** [ɛ̃tɛʀypsjɔ̃] *nf* interruption; **sans ~** without a break; **~ de grossesse** termination of pregnancy; **~ volontaire de grossesse** voluntary termination of pregnancy, abortion

**interscolaire** [ɛ̃tɛʀskɔlɛʀ] *adj* interschool(s)

**intersection** [ɛ̃tɛʀsɛksjɔ̃] *nf* intersection

**intersidéral, e, -aux** [ɛ̃tɛʀsideʀal, -o] *adj* interstellar

**interstice** [ɛ̃tɛʀstis] *nm* crack, slit

**intersyndical, e, -aux** [ɛ̃tɛʀsɛ̃dikal, -o] *adj* interunion

**interurbain** [ɛ̃tɛʀyʀbɛ̃] (*Tél*) *nm* long-distance call service ▷ *adj* long-distance

**intervalle** [ɛ̃tɛʀval] *nm* (*espace*) space; (*de temps*) interval; **dans l'~** in the meantime; **à deux mois d'~** after a space of two months; **à ~s rapprochés** at close intervals; **par ~s** at intervals

**intervenant, e** [ɛ̃tɛʀvənɑ̃, -ɑ̃t] *vb voir* **intervenir** ▷ *nm/f* speaker (*at conference*)

**intervenir** [ɛ̃tɛʀvəniʀ] *vi* (*gén*) to intervene; (*survenir*) to take place; (*faire une conférence*) to give a talk *ou* lecture; **~ auprès de/en faveur de qn** to intervene with/on behalf of sb; **la police a dû ~** police had to step in *ou* intervene; **les médecins ont dû ~** the doctors had to operate

**intervention** [ɛ̃tɛʀvɑ̃sjɔ̃] *nf* intervention; (*conférence*) talk, paper; **~ (chirurgicale)** operation

**interventionnisme** [ɛ̃tɛʀvɑ̃sjɔnism(ə)] *nm* interventionism

**interventionniste** [ɛ̃tɛʀvɑ̃sjɔnist(ə)] *adj* interventionist

**intervenu, e** [ɛ̃tɛʀv(ə)ny] *pp de* **intervenir**

**intervertible** [ɛ̃tɛʀvɛʀtibl(ə)] *adj* interchangeable

**intervertir** [ɛ̃tɛʀvɛʀtiʀ] *vt* to invert (the order of), reverse

**interviendrai** [ɛ̃tɛʀvjɛ̃dʀe], **interviens** *etc* [ɛ̃tɛʀvjɛ̃] *vb voir* **intervenir**

**interview** [ɛ̃tɛʀvju] *nf* interview

**interviewer** [ɛ̃tɛʀvjuve] *vt* to interview ▷ *nm* [ɛ̃tɛʀvjuvœʀ] (*journaliste*) interviewer

**intervins** *etc* [ɛ̃tɛʀvɛ̃] *vb voir* **intervenir**

**intestat** [ɛ̃tɛsta] *adj* (*Jur*): **décéder ~** to die intestate

**intestin, e** [ɛ̃tɛstɛ̃, -in] *adj* internal ▷ *nm* intestine; **~ grêle** small intestine

**intestinal, e, -aux** [ɛ̃tɛstinal, -o] *adj* intestinal

**intime** [ɛ̃tim] *adj* intimate; (*vie, journal*) private; (*convictions*) inmost; (*dîner, cérémonie*) held among friends, quiet ▷ *nm/f* close friend

**intimement** [ɛ̃timmɑ̃] *adv* (*profondément*) deeply, firmly; (*étroitement*) intimately

**intimer** [ɛ̃time] *vt* (*Jur*) to notify; **~ à qn l'ordre de faire** to order sb to do

**intimidant, e** [ɛ̃timidɑ̃, -ɑ̃t] *adj* intimidating
**intimidation** [ɛ̃timidɑsjɔ̃] *nf* intimidation;
**manœuvres d'~** (*action*) acts of intimidation;
(*stratégie*) intimidatory tactics
**intimider** [ɛ̃timide] *vt* to intimidate
**intimité** [ɛ̃timite] *nf* intimacy; (*vie privée*)
privacy; private life; **dans l'~** in private; (*sans
formalités*) with only a few friends, quietly
**intitulé** [ɛ̃tityle] *nm* title
**intituler** [ɛ̃tityle] *vt*: **comment a-t-il intitulé
son livre?** what title did he give his book?;
**s'intituler** *vi* to be entitled; (*personne*) to call o.s.
**intolérable** [ɛ̃tɔleʀabl(ə)] *adj* intolerable
**intolérance** [ɛ̃tɔleʀɑ̃s] *nf* intolerance; **~ aux
antibiotiques** intolerance to antibiotics
**intolérant, e** [ɛ̃tɔleʀɑ̃, -ɑ̃t] *adj* intolerant
**intonation** [ɛ̃tɔnasjɔ̃] *nf* intonation
**intouchable** [ɛ̃tuʃabl(ə)] *adj* (*fig*) above the law,
sacrosanct; (*Rel*) untouchable
**intox** [ɛ̃tɔks] (*fam*) *nf* brainwashing
**intoxication** [ɛ̃tɔksikasjɔ̃] *nf* poisoning *no pl*;
(*toxicomanie*) drug addiction; (*fig*) brainwashing;
**~ alimentaire** food poisoning
**intoxiqué, e** [ɛ̃tɔksike] *nm/f* addict
**intoxiquer** [ɛ̃tɔksike] *vt* to poison; (*fig*) to
brainwash; **s'intoxiquer** to poison o.s.
**intradermique** [ɛ̃tʀadɛʀmik] *adj, nf*:
**(injection) ~** intradermal *ou* intracutaneous
injection
**intraduisible** [ɛ̃tʀadɥizibl(ə)] *adj*
untranslatable; (*fig*) inexpressible
**intraitable** [ɛ̃tʀɛtabl(ə)] *adj* inflexible,
uncompromising
**intramusculaire** [ɛ̃tʀamyskylɛʀ] *adj, nf*:
**(injection) ~** intramuscular injection
**intranet** [ɛ̃tʀanɛt] *nm* intranet
**intransigeance** [ɛ̃tʀɑ̃ziʒɑ̃s] *nf* intransigence
**intransigeant, e** [ɛ̃tʀɑ̃ziʒɑ̃, -ɑ̃t] *adj*
intransigent; (*morale, passion*) uncompromising
**intransitif, -ive** [ɛ̃tʀɑ̃zitif, -iv] *adj* (*Ling*)
intransitive
**intransportable** [ɛ̃tʀɑ̃spɔʀtabl(ə)] *adj* (*blessé*)
unable to travel
**intraveineux, -euse** [ɛ̃tʀavɛno, -øz] *adj*
intravenous
**intrépide** [ɛ̃tʀepid] *adj* dauntless, intrepid
**intrépidité** [ɛ̃tʀepidite] *nf* dauntlessness
**intrigant, e** [ɛ̃tʀigɑ̃, -ɑ̃t] *nm/f* schemer
**intrigue** [ɛ̃tʀig] *nf* intrigue; (*scénario*) plot
**intriguer** [ɛ̃tʀige] *vi* to scheme ▷ *vt* to puzzle,
intrigue
**intrinsèque** [ɛ̃tʀɛ̃sɛk] *adj* intrinsic
**introductif, -ive** [ɛ̃tʀɔdyktif, -iv] *adj*
introductory
**introduction** [ɛ̃tʀɔdyksjɔ̃] *nf* introduction;
**paroles/chapitre d'~** introductory words/
chapter; **lettre/mot d'~** letter/note of
introduction
**introduire** [ɛ̃tʀɔdɥiʀ] *vt* to introduce; (*visiteur*)
to show in; (*aiguille, clef*): **~ qch dans** to insert *ou*
introduce sth into; (*personne*): **~ à qch** to
introduce to sth; (: *présenter*): **~ qn à qn/dans un**

**club** to introduce sb to sb/to a club; **s'introduire**
*vi* (*techniques, usages*) to be introduced; **s'~ dans**
to gain entry into; to get o.s. accepted into; (*eau,
fumée*) to get into; **~ au clavier** to key in
**introduit, e** [ɛ̃tʀɔdɥi, -it] *pp de* **introduire** ▷ *adj*:
**bien ~** (*personne*) well-received
**introniser** [ɛ̃tʀɔnize] *vt* to enthrone
**introspection** [ɛ̃tʀɔspɛksjɔ̃] *nf* introspection
**introuvable** [ɛ̃tʀuvabl(ə)] *adj* which cannot be
found; (*Comm*) unobtainable
**introverti, e** [ɛ̃tʀɔvɛʀti] *nm/f* introvert
**intrus, e** [ɛ̃tʀy, -yz] *nm/f* intruder
**intrusion** [ɛ̃tʀyzjɔ̃] *nf* intrusion; (*ingérence*)
interference
**intuitif, -ive** [ɛ̃tɥitif, -iv] *adj* intuitive
**intuition** [ɛ̃tɥisjɔ̃] *nf* intuition; **avoir une ~** to
have a feeling; **avoir l'~ de qch** to have an
intuition of sth; **avoir de l'~** to have intuition
**intuitivement** [ɛ̃tɥitivmɑ̃] *adv* intuitively
**inusable** [inyzabl(ə)] *adj* hard-wearing
**inusité, e** [inyzite] *adj* rarely used
**inutile** [inytil] *adj* useless; (*superflu*)
unnecessary
**inutilement** [inytilmɑ̃] *adv* needlessly
**inutilisable** [inytilizabl(ə)] *adj* unusable
**inutilisé, e** [inytilize] *adj* unused
**inutilité** [inytilite] *nf* uselessness
**invaincu, e** [ɛ̃vɛ̃ky] *adj* unbeaten; (*armée, peuple*)
unconquered
**invalide** [ɛ̃valid] *adj* disabled ▷ *nm/f*: **~ de
guerre** disabled ex-serviceman; **~ du travail**
industrially disabled person
**invalider** [ɛ̃valide] *vt* to invalidate
**invalidité** [ɛ̃validite] *nf* disability
**invariable** [ɛ̃vaʀjabl(ə)] *adj* invariable
**invariablement** [ɛ̃vaʀjabləmɑ̃] *adv* invariably
**invasion** [ɛ̃vazjɔ̃] *nf* invasion
**invective** [ɛ̃vɛktiv] *nf* invective
**invectiver** [ɛ̃vɛktive] *vt* to hurl abuse at ▷ *vi*: **~
contre** to rail against
**invendable** [ɛ̃vɑ̃dabl(ə)] *adj* unsaleable,
unmarketable
**invendu, e** [ɛ̃vɑ̃dy] *adj* unsold ▷ *nm* return;
**invendus** *nmpl* unsold goods
**inventaire** [ɛ̃vɑ̃tɛʀ] *nm* inventory; (*Comm: liste*)
stocklist; (: *opération*) stocktaking *no pl*; (*fig*)
survey; **faire un ~** to make an inventory;
(*Comm*) to take stock; **faire *ou* procéder à l'~** to
take stock
**inventer** [ɛ̃vɑ̃te] *vt* to invent; (*subterfuge*) to
devise, invent; (*histoire, excuse*) to make up,
invent; **~ de faire** to hit on the idea of doing
**inventeur, -trice** [ɛ̃vɑ̃tœʀ, -tʀis] *nm/f* inventor
**inventif, -ive** [ɛ̃vɑ̃tif, -iv] *adj* inventive
**invention** [ɛ̃vɑ̃sjɔ̃] *nf* invention; (*imagination,
inspiration*) inventiveness
**inventivité** [ɛ̃vɑ̃tivite] *nf* inventiveness
**inventorier** [ɛ̃vɑ̃tɔʀje] *vt* to make an inventory
of
**invérifiable** [ɛ̃veʀifjabl(ə)] *adj* unverifiable
**inverse** [ɛ̃vɛʀs(ə)] *adj* (*ordre*) reverse; (*sens*)
opposite; (*rapport*) inverse ▷ *nm* reverse; inverse;

**en proportion ~** in inverse proportion; **dans le sens ~ des aiguilles d'une montre** anticlockwise; **en sens ~** in (ou from) the opposite direction; **à l'~** conversely

**inversement** [ɛ̃vɛʀsəmɑ̃] adv conversely

**inverser** [ɛ̃vɛʀse] vt to reverse, invert; (Élec) to reverse

**inversion** [ɛ̃vɛʀsjɔ̃] nf reversal; inversion

**invertébré, e** [ɛ̃vɛʀtebʀe] adj, nm invertebrate

**inverti, e** [ɛ̃vɛʀti] nm/f homosexual

**investigation** [ɛ̃vɛstigɑsjɔ̃] nf investigation, inquiry

**investir** [ɛ̃vɛstiʀ] vt to invest; **s'investir** vi (Psych) to involve o.s.; **~ qn de** to vest ou invest sb with

**investissement** [ɛ̃vɛstismɑ̃] nm investment; (Psych) involvement

**investisseur** [ɛ̃vɛstisœʀ] nm investor

**investiture** [ɛ̃vɛstityʀ] nf investiture; (à une élection) nomination

**invétéré, e** [ɛ̃veteʀe] adj (habitude) ingrained; (bavard, buveur) inveterate

**invincible** [ɛ̃vɛ̃sibl(ə)] adj invincible, unconquerable

**invinciblement** [ɛ̃vɛ̃sibləmɑ̃] adv (fig) invincibly

**inviolabilité** [ɛ̃vjɔlabilite] nf: **~ parlementaire** parliamentary immunity

**inviolable** [ɛ̃vjɔlabl(ə)] adj inviolable

**invisible** [ɛ̃vizibl(ə)] adj invisible; (fig: personne) not available

**invitation** [ɛ̃vitɑsjɔ̃] nf invitation; **à/sur l'~ de qn** at/on sb's invitation; **carte/lettre d'~** invitation card/letter

**invite** [ɛ̃vit] nf invitation

**invité, e** [ɛ̃vite] nm/f guest

**inviter** [ɛ̃vite] vt to invite; **~ qn à faire qch** to invite sb to do sth; (chose) to induce ou tempt sb to do sth

**invivable** [ɛ̃vivabl(ə)] adj unbearable, impossible

**involontaire** [ɛ̃vɔlɔ̃tɛʀ] adj (mouvement) involuntary; (insulte) unintentional; (complice) unwitting

**involontairement** [ɛ̃vɔlɔ̃tɛʀmɑ̃] adv involuntarily

**invoquer** [ɛ̃vɔke] vt (Dieu, muse) to call upon, invoke; (prétexte) to put forward (as an excuse); (témoignage) to call upon; (loi, texte) to refer to; **~ la clémence de qn** to beg sb ou appeal to sb for clemency

**invraisemblable** [ɛ̃vʀɛsɑ̃blabl(ə)] adj unlikely, improbable; (bizarre) incredible

**invraisemblance** [ɛ̃vʀɛsɑ̃blɑ̃s] nf unlikelihood no pl, improbability

**invulnérable** [ɛ̃vylneʀabl(ə)] adj invulnerable

**iode** [jɔd] nm iodine

**iodé, e** [jɔde] adj iodized

**ion** [jɔ̃] nm ion

**ionique** [jɔnik] adj (Archit) Ionic; (Science) ionic

**ioniseur** [jɔnizœʀ] nm ionizer

**iota** [jɔta] nm: **sans changer un ~** without changing one iota ou the tiniest bit

**IPC** sigle m (= Indice des prix à la consommation) CPI

**iPod**® [aipɔd] nm iPod®

**IR.** abr = **infrarouge**

**IRA** sigle f (= Irish Republican Army) IRA

**irai** etc [iʀe] vb voir **aller**

**Irak** [iʀak] nm: **l'~** Iraq ou Irak

**irakien, ne** [iʀakjɛ̃, -ɛn] adj Iraqi ▷ nm/f: **Irakien, ne** Iraqi

**Iran** [iʀɑ̃] nm: **l'~** Iran

**iranien, ne** [iʀanjɛ̃, -ɛn] adj Iranian ▷ nm (Ling) Iranian ▷ nm/f: **Iranien, ne** Iranian

**Iraq** [iʀak] nm = **Irak**

**iraquien, ne** [iʀakjɛ̃, -ɛn] adj, nm/f = **irakien, ne**

**irascible** [iʀasibl(ə)] adj short-tempered, irascible

**irions** etc [iʀjɔ̃] vb voir **aller**

**iris** [iʀis] nm iris

**irisé, e** [iʀize] adj iridescent

**irlandais, e** [iʀlɑ̃dɛ, -ɛz] adj, nm (Ling) Irish ▷ nm/f: **Irlandais, e** Irishman/woman; **les I~** the Irish

**Irlande** [iʀlɑ̃d] nf: **l'~** (pays) Ireland; (état) the Irish Republic, the Republic of Ireland, Eire; **~ du Nord** Northern Ireland, Ulster; **~ du Sud** Southern Ireland, Irish Republic, Eire; **la mer d'~** the Irish Sea

**ironie** [iʀɔni] nf irony

**ironique** [iʀɔnik] adj ironical

**ironiquement** [iʀɔnikmɑ̃] adv ironically

**ironiser** [iʀɔnize] vi to be ironical

**irons** etc [iʀɔ̃] vb voir **aller**

**IRPP** sigle m (= impôt sur le revenu des personnes physiques) income tax

**irradiation** [iʀadjɑsjɔ̃] nf irradiation

**irradier** [iʀadje] vi to radiate ▷ vt to irradiate

**irraisonné, e** [iʀɛzɔne] adj irrational, unreasoned

**irrationnel, le** [iʀasjɔnɛl] adj irrational

**irrattrapable** [iʀatʀapabl(ə)] adj (retard) that cannot be made up; (bévue) that cannot be made good

**irréalisable** [iʀealizabl(ə)] adj unrealizable; (projet) impracticable

**irréalisme** [iʀealism(ə)] nm lack of realism

**irréaliste** [iʀealist(ə)] adj unrealistic

**irréalité** [iʀealite] nf unreality

**irrecevable** [iʀsəvabl(ə)] adj unacceptable

**irréconciliable** [iʀekɔ̃siljabl(ə)] adj irreconcilable

**irrécouvrable** [iʀekuvʀabl(ə)] adj irrecoverable

**irrécupérable** [iʀekypeʀabl(ə)] adj unreclaimable, beyond repair; (personne) beyond redemption ou recall

**irrécusable** [iʀekyzabl(ə)] adj (témoignage) unimpeachable; (preuve) incontestable, indisputable

**irréductible** [iʀedyktibl(ə)] adj indomitable, implacable; (Math: fraction, équation) irreducible

**irréductiblement** [iʀedyktibləmɑ̃] adv implacably

**irréel, le** [iʀeɛl] adj unreal

**irréfléchi, e** [iʀefleʃi] adj thoughtless

**irréfutable** [iʀefytabl(ə)] adj irrefutable

229

**irréfutablement** [iʀefytabləmɑ̃] *adv*
irrefutably
**irrégularité** [iʀegylaʀite] *nf* irregularity;
unevenness *no pl*
**irrégulier, -ière** [iʀegylje, -jɛʀ] *adj* irregular;
(*surface, rythme, écriture*) uneven, irregular; (*élève,
athlète*) erratic
**irrégulièrement** [iʀegyljɛʀmɑ̃] *adv* irregularly
**irrémédiable** [iʀemedjabl(ə)] *adj* irreparable
**irrémédiablement** [iʀemedjabləmɑ̃] *adv*
irreparably
**irremplaçable** [iʀɑ̃plasabl(ə)] *adj* irreplaceable
**irréparable** [iʀepaʀabl(ə)] *adj* beyond repair,
irreparable; (*fig*) irreparable
**irrépréhensible** [iʀepʀeɑ̃sibl(ə)] *adj*
irreproachable
**irrépressible** [iʀepʀesibl(ə)] *adj* irrepressible
**irréprochable** [iʀepʀɔʃabl(ə)] *adj*
irreproachable, beyond reproach; (*tenue, toilette*)
impeccable
**irrésistible** [iʀezistibl(ə)] *adj* irresistible;
(*preuve, logique*) compelling
**irrésistiblement** [iʀezistibləmɑ̃] *adv*
irresistibly
**irrésolu, e** [iʀezɔly] *adj* irresolute
**irrésolution** [iʀezɔlysjɔ̃] *nf* irresoluteness
**irrespectueux, -euse** [iʀɛspɛktɥø, -øz] *adj*
disrespectful
**irrespirable** [iʀɛspiʀabl(ə)] *adj* unbreathable;
(*fig*) oppressive, stifling
**irresponsabilité** [iʀɛspɔ̃sabilite] *nf*
irresponsibility
**irresponsable** [iʀɛspɔ̃sabl(ə)] *adj* irresponsible
**irrévérencieux, -euse** [iʀeveʀɑ̃sjø, -øz] *adj*
irreverent
**irréversible** [iʀevɛʀsibl(ə)] *adj* irreversible
**irréversiblement** [iʀevɛʀsibləmɑ̃] *adv*
irreversibly
**irrévocable** [iʀevɔkabl(ə)] *adj* irrevocable
**irrévocablement** [iʀevɔkabləmɑ̃] *adv*
irrevocably
**irrigation** [iʀigasjɔ̃] *nf* irrigation
**irriguer** [iʀige] *vt* to irrigate
**irritabilité** [iʀitabilite] *nf* irritability
**irritable** [iʀitabl(ə)] *adj* irritable
**irritant, e** [iʀitɑ̃, -ɑ̃t] *adj* irritating; (*Méd*)
irritant
**irritation** [iʀitasjɔ̃] *nf* irritation
**irrité, e** [iʀite] *adj* irritated
**irriter** [iʀite] *vt* (*agacer*) to irritate, annoy; (*Méd:
enflammer*) to irritate; **s'~ contre qn/de qch** to
get annoyed *ou* irritated with sb/at sth
**irruption** [iʀypsjɔ̃] *nf* irruption *no pl*; **faire ~
dans** to burst into
**ISBN** *sigle m* (= *International Standard Book Number*)
ISBN
**ISF** *sigle m* (= *impôt de solidarité sur la fortune*) wealth tax
**Islam** [islam] *nm* Islam
**islamique** [islamik] *adj* Islamic
**islamiste** [islamist(ə)] *adj, nm/f* Islamic
**islandais, e** [islɑ̃dɛ, -ɛz] *adj* Icelandic ▷ *nm* (*Ling*)
Icelandic ▷ *nm/f*: **I~, e** Icelander

**Islande** [islɑ̃d] *nf*: **l'~** Iceland
**ISMH** *sigle m* = **Inventaire supplémentaire des
monuments historiques**; **monument inscrit
à l'~** = listed building
**isocèle** [izɔsɛl] *adj* isoceles
**isolant, e** [izɔlɑ̃, -ɑ̃t] *adj* insulating; (*insonorisant*)
soundproofing ▷ *nm* insulator
**isolateur** [izɔlatœʀ] *nm* (*Élec*) insulator
**isolation** [izɔlasjɔ̃] *nf* insulation; **~
acoustique/thermique** sound/thermal
insulation
**isolationnisme** [izɔlasjɔnism(ə)] *nm*
isolationism
**isolé, e** [izɔle] *adj* isolated; (*Élec*) insulated
**isolement** [izɔlmɑ̃] *nm* isolation; solitary
confinement
**isolément** [izɔlemɑ̃] *adv* in isolation
**isoler** [izɔle] *vt* to isolate; (*prisonnier*) to put in
solitary confinement; (*ville*) to cut off, isolate;
(*Élec*) to insulate
**isoloir** [izɔlwaʀ] *nm* polling booth
**isorel®** [izɔʀɛl] *nm* hardboard
**isotherme** [izɔtɛʀm(ə)] *adj* (*camion*) refrigerated
**Israël** [isʀaɛl] *nm*: **l'~** Israel
**israélien, ne** [isʀaeljɛ̃, -ɛn] *adj* Israeli ▷ *nm/f*:
**Israélien, ne** Israeli
**israélite** [isʀaelit] *adj* Jewish; (*dans l'Ancien
Testament*) Israelite ▷ *nm/f*: **Israélite** Jew/Jewess;
Israelite
**issu, e** [isy] *adj*: **~ de** descended from; (*fig*)
stemming from ▷ *nf* (*ouverture, sortie*) exit;
(*solution*) way out, solution; (*dénouement*)
outcome; **à l'~e de** at the conclusion *ou* close of;
**rue sans ~e** dead end, no through road (*Brit*), no
outlet (*US*); **~e de secours** emergency exit
**Istamboul, Istanbul** [istabul] *n* Istanbul
**isthme** [ism(ə)] *nm* isthmus
**Italie** [itali] *nf*: **l'~** Italy
**italien, ne** [italjɛ̃, -ɛn] *adj* Italian ▷ *nm* (*Ling*)
Italian ▷ *nm/f*: **Italien, ne** Italian
**italique** [italik] *nm*: **en ~(s)** in italics
**item** [itɛm] *nm* item; (*question*) question, test
**itinéraire** [itineʀɛʀ] *nm* itinerary, route
**itinérant, e** [itineʀɑ̃, -ɑ̃t] *adj* itinerant,
travelling
**ITP** *sigle m* (= *ingénieur des travaux publics*) civil
engineer
**IUT** *sigle m* = **Institut universitaire de
technologie**
**IVG** *sigle f* (= *interruption volontaire de grossesse*)
abortion
**ivoire** [ivwaʀ] *nm* ivory
**ivoirien, ne** [ivwaʀjɛ̃, -ɛn] *adj* of *ou* from the
Ivory Coast
**ivraie** [ivʀɛ] *nf*: **séparer le bon grain de l'~** (*fig*)
to separate the wheat from the chaff
**ivre** [ivʀ(ə)] *adj* drunk; **~ de** (*colère*) wild with;
(*bonheur*) drunk *ou* intoxicated with; **~ mort**
dead drunk
**ivresse** [ivʀɛs] *nf* drunkenness; (*euphorie*)
intoxication
**ivrogne** [ivʀɔɲ] *nm/f* drunkard

# Jj

**J, j** [ʒi] *nm inv* J, j ▷ *abr* = **jour**; **jour J** D-day;
(= *Joule*) J; **J comme Joseph** J for Jack (*Brit*) *ou* Jig
(US)

**j'** [ʒ] *pron voir* **je**

**jabot** [ʒabo] *nm* (*Zool*) crop; (*de vêtement*) jabot

**jacasser** [ʒakase] *vi* to chatter

**jachère** [ʒaʃɛʀ] *nf*: (**être**) **en ~** (to lie) fallow

**jacinthe** [ʒasɛ̃t] *nf* hyacinth; **~ des bois**
bluebell

**jack** [dʒak] *nm* jack plug

**jacquard** [ʒakaʀ] *adj inv* Fair Isle

**jacquerie** [ʒakʀi] *nf* riot

**jade** [ʒad] *nm* jade

**jadis** [ʒadis] *adv* in times past, formerly

**jaguar** [ʒagwaʀ] *nm* (*Zool*) jaguar

**jaillir** [ʒajiʀ] *vi* (*liquide*) to spurt out, gush out;
(*lumière*) to flood out; (*fig*) to rear up; to burst out

**jaillissement** [ʒajismɑ̃] *nm* spurt, gush

**jais** [ʒɛ] *nm* jet; (**d'un noir**) **de ~** jet-black

**jalon** [ʒalɔ̃] *nm* range pole; (*fig*) milestone;
**poser des ~s** (*fig*) to pave the way

**jalonner** [ʒalɔne] *vt* to mark out; (*fig*) to mark,
punctuate

**jalousement** [ʒaluzmɑ̃] *adv* jealously

**jalouser** [ʒaluze] *vt* to be jealous of

**jalousie** [ʒaluzi] *nf* jealousy; (*store*) (venetian)
blind

**jaloux, -ouse** [ʒalu, -uz] *adj* jealous; **être ~ de
qn/qch** to be jealous of sb/sth

**jamaïquain, e** [ʒamaikɛ̃, -ɛn] *adj* Jamaican

**Jamaïque** [ʒamaik] *nf*: **la ~** Jamaica

**jamais** [ʒamɛ] *adv* never; (*sans négation*) ever;
**ne ... ~** never; **~ de la vie!** never!; **si ~ ...** if ever ...;
**à (tout) ~, pour ~** for ever, for ever and ever

**jambage** [ʒɑ̃baʒ] *nm* (*de lettre*) downstroke; (*de
porte*) jamb

**jambe** [ʒɑ̃b] *nf* leg; **à toutes ~s** as fast as one's
legs can carry one

**jambières** [ʒɑ̃bjɛʀ] *nfpl* legwarmers; (*Sport*) shin
pads

**jambon** [ʒɑ̃bɔ̃] *nm* ham

**jambonneau, x** [ʒɑ̃bɔno] *nm* knuckle of ham

**jante** [ʒɑ̃t] *nf* (wheel) rim

**janvier** [ʒɑ̃vje] *nm* January; *voir aussi* **juillet**

**Japon** [ʒapɔ̃] *nm*: **le ~** Japan

**japonais, e** [ʒapɔnɛ, -ɛz] *adj* Japanese ▷ *nm*
(*Ling*) Japanese ▷ *nm/f*: **Japonais, e** Japanese

**japonaiserie** [ʒapɔnɛzʀi] *nf* (*bibelot*) Japanese
curio

**jappement** [ʒapmɑ̃] *nm* yap, yelp

**japper** [ʒape] *vi* to yap, yelp

**jaquette** [ʒakɛt] *nf* (*de cérémonie*) morning coat;
(*de femme*) jacket; (*de livre*) dust cover, (dust)
jacket

**jardin** [ʒaʀdɛ̃] *nm* garden; **~ d'acclimatation**
zoological gardens *pl*; **~ botanique** botanical
gardens *pl*; **~ d'enfants** nursery school; **~
potager** vegetable garden; **~ public** (public)
park, public gardens *pl*; **~s suspendus** hanging
gardens; **~ zoologique** zoological gardens

**jardinage** [ʒaʀdinaʒ] *nm* gardening

**jardiner** [ʒaʀdine] *vi* to garden, do some
gardening

**jardinet** [ʒaʀdinɛ] *nm* little garden

**jardinier, -ière** [ʒaʀdinje, -jɛʀ] *nm/f* gardener
▷ *nf* (*de fenêtre*) window box; **jardinière
d'enfants** nursery school teacher; **jardinière
(de légumes)** (*Culin*) mixed vegetables

**jargon** [ʒaʀgɔ̃] *nm* (*charabia*) gibberish;
(*publicitaire, scientifique etc*) jargon

**jarre** [ʒaʀ] *nf* (earthenware) jar

**jarret** [ʒaʀɛ] *nm* back of knee; (*Culin*) knuckle,
shin

**jarretelle** [ʒaʀtɛl] *nf* suspender (*Brit*), garter (US)

**jarretière** [ʒaʀtjɛʀ] *nf* garter

**jars** [ʒaʀ] *nm* (*Zool*) gander

**jaser** [ʒaze] *vi* to chatter, prattle; (*indiscrètement*)
to gossip

**jasmin** [ʒasmɛ̃] *nm* jasmine

**jaspe** [ʒasp(ə)] *nm* jasper

**jaspé, e** [ʒaspe] *adj* marbled, mottled

**jatte** [ʒat] *nf* basin, bowl

**jauge** [ʒoʒ] *nf* (*capacité*) capacity, tonnage;
(*instrument*) gauge; **~ (de niveau) d'huile**
dipstick

**jauger** [ʒoʒe] *vt* to gauge the capacity of; (*fig*) to
size up; **~ 3 000 tonneaux** to measure 3,000
tons

**jaunâtre** [ʒonɑtʀ(ə)] *adj* (*couleur, teint*) yellowish

**jaune** [ʒon] *adj, nm* yellow ▷ *nm/f* Asiatic; (*briseur
de grève*) blackleg ▷ *adv* (*fam*): **rire ~** to laugh on
the other side of one's face; **~ d'œuf** (egg) yolk

**jaunir** [ʒoniʀ] *vi, vt* to turn yellow
**jaunisse** [ʒonis] *nf* jaundice
**Java** [ʒava] *nf* Java
**java** [ʒava] *nf (fam)*: **faire la ~** to live it up, have a real party
**javanais, e** [ʒavanɛ, -ɛz] *adj* Javanese
**Javel** [ʒavɛl] *nf voir* **eau**
**javelliser** [ʒavelize] *vt (eau)* to chlorinate
**javelot** [ʒavlo] *nm* javelin; *(Sport)*: **faire du ~** to throw the javelin
**jazz** [dʒaz] *nm* jazz
**J.-C.** *abr* = **Jésus-Christ**
**je, j'** [ʒ(ə)] *pron* I
**jean** [dʒin] *nm* jeans *pl*
**jeannette** [ʒanɛt] *nf (planchette)* sleeve board; *(petite fille scout)* Brownie
**jeep®** [(d)ʒip] *nf (Auto)* Jeep®
**jérémiades** [ʒeʀemjad] *nfpl* moaning *sg*
**jerrycan** [ʒeʀikan] *nm* jerry can
**Jersey** [ʒɛʀzɛ] *nf* Jersey
**jersey** [ʒɛʀzɛ] *nm* jersey; *(Tricot)*: **pointe de ~** stocking stitch
**jersiais, e** [ʒɛʀzjɛ, -ɛz] *adj* Jersey *cpd*, of *ou* from Jersey
**Jérusalem** [ʒeʀyzalɛm] *n* Jerusalem
**jésuite** [ʒezɥit] *nm* Jesuit
**Jésus-Christ** [ʒezykʀi(st)] *n* Jesus Christ; **600 avant/après ~** *ou* **J.-C.** 600 B.C./A.D.
**jet¹** [ʒɛ] *nm (lancer)* throwing *no pl*, throw; *(jaillissement)* jet; spurt; *(de tuyau)* nozzle; *(fig)*: **premier ~** *(ébauche)* rough outline; **arroser au ~** to hose; **d'un (seul) ~** *(d'un seul coup)* at *(ou* in) one go; **du premier ~** at the first attempt *ou* shot; **~ d'eau** spray; *(fontaine)* fountain
**jet²** [dʒɛt] *nm (avion)* jet
**jetable** [ʒətabl(ə)] *adj* disposable
**jeté** [ʒəte] *nm (Tricot)*: **un ~** make one; **~ de table** (table) runner; **~ de lit** bedspread
**jetée** [ʒəte] *nf* jetty; pier
**jeter** [ʒəte] *vt (gén)* to throw; *(se défaire de)* to throw away *ou* out; *(son, lueur etc)* to give out; **~ qch à qn** to throw sth to sb; *(de façon agressive)* to throw sth at sb; *(Navig)*: **~ l'ancre** to cast anchor; **~ un coup d'œil (à)** to take a look (at); **~ les bras en avant/la tête en arrière** to throw one's arms forward/one's head back(ward); **~ l'effroi parmi** to spread fear among; **~ un sort à qn** to cast a spell on sb; **~ qn dans la misère** to reduce sb to poverty; **~ qn dehors/en prison** to throw sb out/into prison; **~ l'éponge** *(fig)* to throw in the towel; **~ des fleurs à qn** *(fig)* to say lovely things to sb; **~ la pierre à qn** *(accuser, blâmer)* to accuse sb; **se ~ sur** to throw o.s. onto; **se ~ dans** *(fleuve)* to flow into; **se ~ par la fenêtre** to throw o.s. out of the window; **se ~ à l'eau** *(fig)* to take the plunge
**jeton** [ʒətɔ̃] *nm (au jeu)* counter; *(de téléphone)* token; **~s de présence** (director's) fees
**jette** *etc* [ʒɛt] *vb voir* **jeter**
**jeu, x** [ʒø] *nm (divertissement, Tech: d'une pièce)* play; *(défini par des règles, Tennis: partie, Football etc: façon de jouer)* game; *(Théât etc)* acting; *(fonctionnement*

working, interplay; *(série d'objets, jouet)* set; *(Cartes)* hand; *(au casino)*: **le ~** gambling; **cacher son ~** *(fig)* to keep one's cards hidden, conceal one's hand; **c'est un ~ d'enfant!** *(fig)* it's child's play!; **en ~** at stake; at work; *(Football)* in play; **remettre en ~** to throw in; **entrer/mettre en ~** to come/bring into play; **par ~** *(pour s'amuser)* for fun; **d'entrée de ~** *(tout de suite, dès le début)* from the outset; **entrer dans le ~/le ~ de qn** *(fig)* to play the game/sb's game; **jouer gros ~** to play for high stakes; **se piquer/se prendre au ~** to get excited over/get caught up in the game; **~ d'arcade** video game; **~ de boules** game of bowls; *(endroit)* bowling pitch; *(boules)* set of bowls; **~ de cartes** card game; *(paquet)* pack of cards; **~ de construction** building set; **~ d'échecs** chess set; **~ d'écritures** *(Comm)* paper transaction; **~ électronique** electronic game; **~ de hasard** game of chance; **~ de mots** pun; **le ~ de l'oie** snakes and ladders *sg*; **~ d'orgue(s)** organ stop; **~ de patience** puzzle; **~ de physionomie** facial expressions *pl*; **~ de société** parlour game; **~ télévisé** television game; **~ vidéo** computer game; **~x de lumière** lighting effects; **J-x olympiques (JO)** Olympic Games
**jeu-concours** [ʒøkɔ̃kuʀ] *(pl* **jeux-concours**) *nm* competition
**jeudi** [ʒødi] *nm* Thursday; **~ saint** Maundy Thursday; *voir aussi* **lundi**
**jeun** [ʒœ̃]: **à ~** *adv* on an empty stomach
**jeune** [ʒœn] *adj* young ▷ *adv*: **faire/s'habiller ~** to look/dress young; **les ~s** young people, the young; **~ fille** *nf* girl; **~ homme** *nm* young man; **~ loup** *nm (Pol, Écon)* young go-getter; **~ premier** leading man; **~s gens** *nmpl* young people; **~s mariés** *nmpl* newly weds
**jeûne** [ʒøn] *nm* fast
**jeûner** [ʒøne] *vt* to fast, go without food
**jeunesse** [ʒœnɛs] *nf* youth; *(aspect)* youthfulness; *(jeunes)* young people *pl*, youth
**jf** *sigle f* = **jeune fille**
**jh** *sigle m* = **jeune homme**
**JI** *sigle m* = **juge d'instruction**
**jiu-jitsu** [ʒyʒitsy] *nm inv (Sport)* jujitsu
**JMF** *sigle f* (= *Jeunesses musicales de France)* association to promote music among the young
**JO** *sigle m* = **Journal officiel** ▷ *sigle mpl* = **Jeux olympiques**
**joaillerie** [ʒɔajʀi] *nf* jewel trade; jewellery *(Brit)*, jewelry *(US)*
**joaillier, -ière** [ʒɔaje, -jɛʀ] *nm/f* jeweller *(Brit)*, jeweler *(US)*
**job** [dʒɔb] *nm* job
**jobard** [ʒɔbaʀ] *nm (péj)* sucker, mug
**jockey** [ʒɔkɛ] *nm* jockey
**jodler** [ʒɔdle] *vi* to yodel
**jogging** [dʒɔgiŋ] *nm* tracksuit *(Brit)*, sweatsuit *(US)*; **faire du ~** to jog, go jogging
**joie** [ʒwa] *nf* joy
**joignais** *etc* [ʒwaɲɛ] *vb voir* **joindre**
**joindre** [ʒwɛ̃dʀ(ə)] *vt* to join; **~ qch à** *(à une lettre)*

to enclose sth with; (à un mail) to attach sth to; (contacter) to contact, get in touch with; **~ les mains/talons** to put one's hands/heels together; **~ les deux bouts** (fig: du mois) to make ends meet; **se joindre** (mains etc) to come together; **se ~ à qn** to join sb; **se ~ à qch** to join in sth

**joint, e** [ʒwɛ̃, -ɛ̃t] pp de **joindre** ▷ adj: **~ (à)** (lettre, paquet) attached (to), enclosed (with); **pièce ~e** (de lettre) enclosure; (de mail) attachment ▷ nm joint; (ligne) join; (de ciment etc) pointing no pl; **chercher/trouver le ~** (fig) to look for/come up with the answer; **~ de cardan** cardan joint; **~ de culasse** cylinder head gasket; **~ de robinet** washer; **~ universel** universal joint

**jointure** [ʒwɛ̃tyʀ] nf (Anat: articulation) joint; (Tech: assemblage) joint; (: ligne) join

**joker** [ʒɔkɛʀ] nm (Cartes) joker; (Inform): **(caractère) ~** wild card

**joli, e** [ʒɔli] adj pretty, attractive; **une ~e somme/situation** a nice little sum/situation; **un ~ gâchis** etc a nice mess etc; **c'est du ~!** that's very nice!; **tout ça, c'est bien ~ mais ...** that's all very well but ...

**joliment** [ʒɔlimɑ̃] adv prettily, attractively; (fam: très) pretty

**jonc** [ʒɔ̃] nm (bul)rush; (bague, bracelet) band

**joncher** [ʒɔ̃ʃe] vt (choses) to be strewed on; **jonché de** strewn with

**jonction** [ʒɔ̃ksjɔ̃] nf joining; **(point de) ~** (de routes) junction; (de fleuves) confluence; **opérer une ~** (Mil etc) to rendez-vous

**jongler** [ʒɔ̃gle] vi to juggle; (fig): **~ avec** to juggle with, play with

**jongleur, -euse** [ʒɔ̃glœʀ, -øz] nm/f juggler

**jonquille** [ʒɔ̃kij] nf daffodil

**Jordanie** [ʒɔʀdani] nf: **la ~** Jordan

**jordanien, ne** [ʒɔʀdanjɛ̃, -ɛn] adj Jordanian ▷ nm/f: **Jordanien, ne** Jordanian

**jouable** [ʒwabl(ə)] adj playable

**joue** [ʒu] nf cheek; **mettre en ~** to take aim at

**jouer** [ʒwe] vt (partie, carte, coup, Mus: morceau) to play; (somme d'argent, réputation) to stake, wager; (pièce, rôle) to perform; (film) to show; (simuler: sentiment) to affect, feign ▷ vi to play; (Théât, Ciné) to act, perform; (bois, porte: se voiler) to warp; (clef, pièce: avoir du jeu) to be loose; (entrer ou être en jeu) to come into play, come into it; **~ sur** (miser) to gamble on; **~ de** (Mus) to play; **~ du couteau/des coudes** to use knives/one's elbows; **~ à** (jeu, sport, roulette) to play; **~ au héros** to act ou play the hero; **~ avec** (risquer) to gamble with; **se ~ de** (difficultés) to make light of; **se ~ de qn** to deceive ou dupe sb; **~ un tour à qn** to play a trick on sb; **~ la comédie** (fig) to put on an act, put it on; **~ aux courses** to back horses, bet on horses; **~ à la baisse/hausse** (Bourse) to play for a fall/rise; **~ serré** to play a close game; **~ de malchance** to be dogged with ill-luck; **~ sur les mots** to play with words; **à toi/nous de ~** it's your/our go ou turn

**jouet** [ʒwɛ] nm toy; **être le ~ de** (illusion etc) to be

the victim of

**joueur, -euse** [ʒwœʀ, -øz] nm/f player ▷ adj (enfant, chat) playful; **être beau/mauvais ~** to be a good/bad loser

**jouffu, e** [ʒufly] adj chubby(-cheeked)

**joug** [ʒu] nm yoke

**jouir** [ʒwiʀ]: **~ de** vt to enjoy

**jouissance** [ʒwisɑ̃s] nf pleasure; (Jur) use

**jouisseur, -euse** [ʒwisœʀ, -øz] nm/f sensualist

**joujou** [ʒuʒu] nm (fam) toy

**jour** [ʒuʀ] nm day; (opposé à la nuit) day, daytime; (clarté) daylight; (fig: aspect): **sous un ~ favorable/nouveau** in a favourable/new light; (ouverture) opening; (Couture) openwork no pl; **au ~ le ~** from day to day; **de nos ~s** these days, nowadays; **tous les ~s** every day; **de ~ en ~** day by day; **d'un ~ à l'autre** from one day to the next; **du ~ au lendemain** overnight; **il fait ~** it's daylight; **en plein ~** in broad daylight; **au ~** in daylight; **au petit ~** at daybreak; **au grand ~** (fig) in the open; **mettre au ~** to uncover, disclose; **être à ~** to be up to date; **mettre à ~** to bring up to date, update; **mise à ~** updating; **donner le ~ à** to give birth to; **voir le ~** to be born; **se faire ~** (fig) to become clear; **~ férié** public holiday; **le ~ J** D-day; **~ ouvrable** working day

**Jourdain** [ʒuʀdɛ̃] nm: **le ~** the (River) Jordan

**journal, -aux** [ʒuʀnal, -o] nm (news)paper; (personnel) journal, diary; **~ de bord** log; **~ de mode** fashion magazine; **le J~ officiel (de la République française) (JO)** bulletin giving details of laws and official announcements; **parlé/télévisé** radio/television news sg

**journalier, -ière** [ʒuʀnalje, -jɛʀ] adj daily; (banal) everyday ▷ nm day labourer

**journalisme** [ʒuʀnalism(ə)] nm journalism

**journaliste** [ʒuʀnalist(ə)] nm/f journalist

**journalistique** [ʒuʀnalistik] adj journalistic

**journée** [ʒuʀne] nf day; **la ~ continue** the 9 to 5 working day (with short lunch break)

**journellement** [ʒuʀnɛlmɑ̃] adv (tous les jours) daily; (souvent) every day

**joute** [ʒut] nf (tournoi) duel; (verbale) duel, battle of words

**jouvence** [ʒuvɑ̃s] nf: **bain de ~** rejuvenating experience

**jouxter** [ʒukste] vt to adjoin

**jovial** [ʒɔvjal] adj jovial, jolly

**jovialité** [ʒɔvjalite] nf joviality

**joyau, x** [ʒwajo] nm gem, jewel

**joyeusement** [ʒwajøzmɑ̃] adv joyfully, gladly

**joyeux, -euse** [ʒwajø, -øz] adj joyful, merry; **~ Noël!** Merry ou Happy Christmas!; **joyeuses Pâques!** Happy Easter!; **~ anniversaire!** many happy returns!

**JT** sigle m = **journal télévisé**

**jubilation** [ʒybilɑsjɔ̃] nf jubilation

**jubilé** [ʒybile] nm jubilee

**jubiler** [ʒybile] vi to be jubilant, exult

**jucher** [ʒyʃe] vt: **~ qch sur** to perch sth (up)on ▷ vi (oiseau): **~ sur** to perch (up)on; **se ~ sur** to perch o.s. (up)on

**judaïque** [ʒydaik] *adj (loi)* Judaic; *(religion)* Jewish

**judaïsme** [ʒydaism(ə)] *nm* Judaism

**judas** [ʒyda] *nm (trou)* spy-hole

**Judée** [ʒyde] *nf:* **la** ~ Jud(a)ea

**judéo-** [ʒydeɔ] *préfixe* Judeo-

**judéo-allemand, e** [ʒydeɔalmɑ̃, -ɑ̃d] *adj, nm* Yiddish

**judéo-chrétien, ne** [ʒydeɔkretjɛ̃, -ɛn] *adj* Judeo-Christian

**judiciaire** [ʒydisjɛʀ] *adj* judicial

**judicieusement** [ʒydisjøzmɑ̃] *adv* judiciously

**judicieux, -euse** [ʒydisjø, -øz] *adj* judicious

**judo** [ʒydo] *nm* judo

**judoka** [ʒydɔka] *nm/f* judoka

**juge** [ʒyʒ] *nm* judge; ~ **d'instruction** examining *(Brit) ou* committing *(US)* magistrate; ~ **de paix** justice of the peace; ~ **de touche** linesman

**jugé** [ʒyʒe] *nm:* **au** ~ *adv* by guesswork

**jugement** [ʒyʒmɑ̃] *nm* judgment; *(Jur: au pénal)* sentence; (: *au civil*) decision; ~ **de valeur** value judgment

**jugeote** [ʒyʒɔt] *nf (fam)* gumption

**juger** [ʒyʒe] *vt* to judge ⊳ *nm:* **au** ~ by guesswork; ~ **qn/qch satisfaisant** to consider sb/sth (to be) satisfactory; ~ **que** to think *ou* consider that; ~ **bon de faire** to consider it a good idea to do, see fit to do; ~ **de** *vt* to judge; **jugez de ma surprise** imagine my surprise

**jugulaire** [ʒygylɛʀ] *adj* jugular ⊳ *nf (Mil)* chinstrap

**juguler** [ʒygyle] *vt (maladie)* to halt; *(révolte)* to suppress; *(inflation etc)* to control, curb

**juif, -ive** [ʒɥif, -iv] *adj* Jewish ⊳ *nm/f:* **Juif, ive** Jew/Jewess *ou* Jewish woman

**juillet** [ʒɥijɛ] *nm* July; **le premier** ~ the first of July *(Brit)*, July first *(US)*; **le deux/onze** ~ the second/eleventh of July, July second/eleventh; **il est venu le 5** ~ he came on 5th July *ou* July 5th; **en** ~ in July; **début/fin** ~ at the beginning/end of July; *see note*

● **LE 14 JUILLET**

● *Le 14 juillet* is a national holiday in France and
● commemorates the storming of the Bastille
● during the French Revolution. Throughout
● the country there are celebrations, which
● feature parades, music, dancing and
● firework displays. In Paris a military parade
● along the Champs-Élysées is attended by
● the President.

**juin** [ʒɥɛ̃] *nm* June; *voir aussi* **juillet**

**juive** [ʒwiv] *adj, nf voir* **juif**

**jumeau, -elle, -x** [ʒymo, -ɛl] *adj, nm/f* twin; **maisons jumelles** semidetached houses

**jumelage** [ʒymlaʒ] *nm* twinning

**jumeler** [ʒymle] *vt* to twin; **roues jumelées** double wheels; **billets de loterie jumelés** double series lottery tickets; **pari jumelé** double bet

**jumelle** [ʒymɛl] *adj f, nf voir* **jumeau** ⊳ *vb voir* **jumeler**

**jumelles** [ʒymɛl] *nfpl* binoculars

**jument** [ʒymɑ̃] *nf* mare

**jungle** [ʒɔ̃gl(ə)] *nf* jungle

**junior** [ʒynjɔʀ] *adj* junior

**junte** [ʒœ̃t] *nf* junta

**jupe** [ʒyp] *nf* skirt

**jupe-culotte** [ʒypkylɔt] *(pl* **jupes-culottes**) *nf* divided skirt, culotte(s)

**jupette** [ʒypɛt] *nf* short skirt

**jupon** [ʒypɔ̃] *nm* waist slip *ou* petticoat

**Jura** [ʒyʀa] *nm:* **le** ~ the Jura (Mountains)

**jurassien, ne** [ʒyʀasjɛ̃, -ɛn] *adj* of *ou* from the Jura Mountains

**juré, e** [ʒyʀe] *nm/f* juror ⊳ *adj:* **ennemi** ~ sworn *ou* avowed enemy

**jurer** [ʒyʀe] *vt (obéissance etc)* to swear, vow ⊳ *vi (dire des jurons)* to swear, curse; *(dissoner)*: ~ **(avec)** to clash (with); *(s'engager)*: ~ **de faire/que** to swear *ou* vow to do/that; *(affirmer)*: ~ **que** to swear *ou* vouch that; ~ **de qch** *(s'en porter garant)* to swear to sth; **ils ne jurent que par lui** they swear by him; **je vous jure!** honestly!

**juridiction** [ʒyʀidiksjɔ̃] *nf* jurisdiction; *(tribunal, tribunaux)* court(s) of law

**juridique** [ʒyʀidik] *adj* legal

**juridiquement** [ʒyʀidikmɑ̃] *adv (devant la justice)* juridically; *(du point de vue du droit)* legally

**jurisconsulte** [ʒyʀikɔ̃sylt(ə)] *nm* jurisconsult

**jurisprudence** [ʒyʀispʀydɑ̃s] *nf (Jur: décisions)* (legal) precedents; *(principes juridiques)* jurisprudence; **faire** ~ *(faire autorité)* to set a precedent

**juriste** [ʒyʀist(ə)] *nm/f* jurist; lawyer

**juron** [ʒyʀɔ̃] *nm* curse, swearword

**jury** [ʒyʀi] *nm (Jur)* jury; *(Scol)* board (of examiners), jury

**jus** [ʒy] *nm* juice; *(de viande)* gravy, (meat) juice; ~ **de fruits** fruit juice; ~ **de raisin/tomates** grape/tomato juice

**jusant** [ʒyzɑ̃] *nm* ebb (tide)

**jusqu'au-boutiste** [ʒyskobutist(ə)] *nm/f* extremist, hardliner

**jusque** [ʒysk(ə)]: **jusqu'à** *prép (endroit)* as far as, (up) to; *(moment)* until, till; *(limite)* up to; ~ **sur/dans** up to, as far as; *(y compris)* even on/in; ~ **vers** until about; **jusqu'à ce que** *conj* until; ~ **là** *(temps)* until then; *(espace)* up to there; **jusqu'ici** *(temps)* until now; *(espace)* up to here; **jusqu'à présent** until now, so far

**justaucorps** [ʒystokɔʀ] *nm inv (Danse, Sport)* leotard

**juste** [ʒyst(ə)] *adj (équitable)* just, fair; *(légitime)* just, justified; *(exact, vrai)* right; *(étroit, insuffisant)* tight ⊳ *adv* right; tight; *(chanter)* in tune; *(seulement)* just; ~ **assez/au-dessus** just enough/above; **pouvoir tout** ~ **faire** to be only just able to do; **au** ~ exactly, actually; **comme de** ~ of course, naturally; **le** ~ **milieu** the happy medium; **à ~ titre** rightfully

**justement** [ʒystəmɑ̃] *adv* rightly; justly; (*précisément*): **c'est ~ ce qu'il fallait faire** that's just *ou* precisely what needed doing

**justesse** [ʒystɛs] *nf* (*précision*) accuracy; (*d'une remarque*) aptness; (*d'une opinion*) soundness; **de ~** just, by a narrow margin

**justice** [ʒystis] *nf* (*équité*) fairness, justice; (*Admin*) justice; **rendre la ~** to dispense justice; **traduire en ~** to bring before the courts; **obtenir ~** to obtain justice; **rendre ~ à qn** to do sb justice; **se faire ~** to take the law into one's own hands; (*se suicider*) to take one's life

**justiciable** [ʒystisjabl(ə)] *adj*: **~ de** (*Jur*) answerable to

**justicier, -ière** [ʒystisje, -jɛʀ] *nm/f* judge, righter of wrongs

**justifiable** [ʒystifjabl(ə)] *adj* justifiable

**justificatif, -ive** [ʒystifikatif, -iv] *adj* (*document etc*) supporting ▷ *nm* supporting proof

**justification** [ʒystifikɑsjɔ̃] *nf* justification

**justifier** [ʒystifje] *vt* to justify; **~ de** *vt* to prove; **non justifié** unjustified; **justifié à droite/ gauche** ranged right/left

**jute** [ʒyt] *nm* jute

**juteux, -euse** [ʒytø, -øz] *adj* juicy

**juvénile** [ʒyvenil] *adj* young, youthful

**juxtaposer** [ʒykstapoze] *vt* to juxtapose

**juxtaposition** [ʒykstapozisjɔ̃] *nf* juxtaposition

**j**

# Kk

**K, k** [kɑ] *nm inv* K, k ▷ *abr* (= *kilo*) kg; **K comme Kléber** K for King

**K 7** [kasɛt] *nf* cassette

**Kaboul, Kabul** [kabul] *n* Kabul

**kabyle** [kabil] *adj* Kabyle ▷ *nm* (*Ling*) Kabyle ▷ *nm/f:* **Kabyle** Kabyle

**Kabylie** [kabili] *nf:* **la ~** Kabylia

**kafkaïen, ne** [kafkajɛ̃, -ɛn] *adj* Kafkaesque

**kaki** [kaki] *adj inv* khaki

**Kalahari** [kalaaʀi] *n:* **désert de ~** Kalahari Desert

**kaléidoscope** [kaleidɔskɔp] *nm* kaleidoscope

**Kampala** [kɑ̃pala] *n* Kampala

**Kampuchéa** [kɑ̃putʃea] *nm:* **le ~ (démocratique)** (the People's Republic of) Kampuchea

**kangourou** [kɑ̃guʀu] *nm* kangaroo

**kaolin** [kaɔlɛ̃] *nm* kaolin

**kapok** [kapɔk] *nm* kapok

**karaoke** [kaʀaoke] *nm* karaoke

**karaté** [kaʀate] *nm* karate

**kart** [kaʀt] *nm* go-cart

**karting** [kaʀtiŋ] *nm* go-carting, karting

**kascher** [kaʃɛʀ] *adj inv* kosher

**kayak** [kajak] *nm* kayak

**Kazakhstan** [kaʒakstɑ̃] *nm* Kazakhstan

**Kenya** [kenja] *nm:* **le ~** Kenya

**kenyan, e** [kenjɑ̃, -an] *adj* Kenyan ▷ *nm/f:* **Kenyan, e** Kenyan

**képi** [kepi] *nm* kepi

**Kerguelen** [kɛʀgelɛn] *nfpl:* **les (îles) ~** Kerguelen

**kermesse** [kɛʀmɛs] *nf* bazaar, (charity) fête; village fair

**kérosène** [keʀozɛn] *nm* jet fuel; rocket fuel

**kg** *abr* (= *kilogramme*) kg

**KGB** *sigle m* KGB

**khmer, -ère** [kmɛʀ] *adj* Khmer ▷ *nm* (*Ling*) Khmer

**khôl** [kol] *nm* khol

**kibboutz** [kibuts] *nm* kibbutz

**kidnapper** [kidnape] *vt* to kidnap

**kidnappeur, -euse** [kidnapœʀ, -øz] *nm/f* kidnapper

**kidnapping** [kidnapiŋ] *nm* kidnapping

**Kilimandjaro** [kilimɑ̃dʒaʀo] *nm:* **le ~** Mount Kilimanjaro

**kilo** [kilo] *nm* kilo

**kilogramme** [kilɔgʀam] *nm* kilogramme (*Brit*), kilogram (*US*)

**kilométrage** [kilɔmetʀaʒ] *nm* number of kilometres travelled, ≈ mileage

**kilomètre** [kilɔmɛtʀ(ə)] *nm* kilometre (*Brit*), kilometer (*US*); **~s-heure** kilometres per hour

**kilométrique** [kilɔmetʀik] *adj* (*distance*) in kilometres; **compteur ~** ≈ mileage indicator

**kilooctet** [kilɔɔktɛ] *nm* kilobyte

**kilowatt** [kilɔwat] *nm* kilowatt

**kinésithérapeute** [kineziteʀapøt] *nm/f* physiotherapist

**kinésithérapie** [kineziteʀapi] *nf* physiotherapy

**kiosque** [kjɔsk(ə)] *nm* kiosk, stall; (*Tél etc*) *telephone and/or videotext information service;* **~ à journaux** newspaper kiosk

**kir** [kiʀ] *nm* kir (*white wine with blackcurrant liqueur*)

**Kirghizistan** [kiʀgizistɑ̃] *nm* Kirghizia

**kirsch** [kiʀʃ] *nm* kirsch

**kit** [kit] *nm* kit; **~ piéton** *ou* **mains libres** hands-free kit; **en ~** in kit form

**kitchenette** [kitʃ(ə)nɛt] *nf* kitchenette

**kiwi** [kiwi] *nm* (*Zool*) kiwi; (*Bot*) kiwi (fruit)

**klaxon** [klaksɔn] *nm* horn

**klaxonner** [klaksɔne] *vi, vt* to hoot (*Brit*), honk (one's horn) (*US*)

**kleptomane** [klɛptɔman] *nm/f* kleptomaniac

**km** *abr* (= *kilomètre*) km

**km/h** *abr* = **kilomètres/heure**

**knock-out** [nɔkawt] *nm* knock-out

**Ko** *abr* (*Inform:* = *kilooctet*) kB

**K.-O.** [kao] *adj inv* (knocked) out, out for the count

**koala** [kɔala] *nm* koala (bear)

**kolkhoze** [kɔlkoz] *nm* kolkhoz

**Kosovo** [kɔsɔvo] *nm:* **le ~** Kosovo

**Koweit** [kɔwɛt] *nm:* **le ~** Kuwait, Koweit

**koweitien, ne** [kɔwetjɛ̃, -ɛn] *adj* Kuwaiti ▷ *nm/f:* **Koweitien, ne** Kuwaiti

**krach** [kʀak] *nm* (*Écon*) crash

**kraft** [kʀaft] *nm* brown *ou* kraft paper

**Kremlin** [kʀɛmlɛ̃] *nm:* **le ~** the Kremlin

**Kuala Lumpur** [kwalalympuʀ] *n* Kuala

Lumpur
**kurde** [kyʀd(ə)] *adj* Kurdish ▷ *nm (Ling)* Kurdish
▷ *nm/f*: **Kurde** Kurd
**Kurdistan** [kyʀdistɑ̃] *nm*: **le** ~ Kurdistan
**Kuweit** [kɔwɛt] *nm* = **Koweit**

**kW** *abr* (= *kilowatt*) kW
**k-way**® [kawɛ] *nm* (lightweight nylon) cagoule
**kW/h** *abr* (= *kilowatt/heure*) kW/h
**kyrielle** [kiʀjɛl] *nf*: **une** ~ **de** a stream of
**kyste** [kist(ə)] *nm* cyst

k

# Ll

**L, l** [ɛl] *nm inv* L, l ▷ *abr* (= *litre*) l; (*Scol*): **L ès L**
= **Licence ès Lettres**; **L en D** = **Licence en Droit**;
**L comme Louis** L for Lucy (*Brit*) *ou* Love (*US*)

**l'** [l] *art déf voir* **le**

**la** [la] *art déf, pron voir* **le** ▷ *nm* (*Mus*) A; (*en chantant
la gamme*) la

**là** [la] *adv voir aussi* **-ci; celui** there; (*ici*) here; (*dans
le temps*) then; **est-ce que Catherine est là?** is
Catherine there (*ou* here)?; **c'est là que** this is
where; **là où** where; **de là** (*fig*) hence; **par là**
(*fig*) by that; **tout est là** (*fig*) that's what it's all
about

**là-bas** [laba] *adv* there

**label** [label] *nm* stamp, seal

**labeur** [labœR] *nm* toil *no pl*, toiling *no pl*

**labo** [labo] *nm* (= *laboratoire*) lab

**laborantin, e** [labɔRãtɛ̃, -in] *nm/f* laboratory
assistant

**laboratoire** [labɔRatwaR] *nm* laboratory; **~ de
langues/d'analyses** language/(medical)
analysis laboratory

**laborieusement** [labɔRjøzmã] *adv* laboriously

**laborieux, -euse** [labɔRjø, -øz] *adj* (*tâche*)
laborious; **classes laborieuses** working
classes

**labour** [labuR] *nm* ploughing *no pl* (*Brit*),
plowing *no pl* (*US*); **labours** *nmpl* (*champs*)
ploughed fields; **cheval de ~** plough- *ou* cart-
horse; **bœuf de ~** ox

**labourage** [labuRaʒ] *nm* ploughing (*Brit*),
plowing (*US*)

**labourer** [labuRe] *vt* to plough (*Brit*), plow (*US*);
(*fig*) to make deep gashes *ou* furrows in

**laboureur** [labuRœR] *nm* ploughman (*Brit*),
plowman (*US*)

**labrador** [labRadɔR] *nm* (*chien*) labrador; (*Géo*):
**le L~** Labrador

**labyrinthe** [labiRɛ̃t] *nm* labyrinth, maze

**lac** [lak] *nm* lake; **le ~ Léman** Lake Geneva; **les
Grands L~s** the Great Lakes; *voir aussi* **lacs**

**lacer** [lase] *vt* to lace *ou* do up

**lacérer** [laseRe] *vt* to tear to shreds

**lacet** [lasɛ] *nm* (*de chaussure*) lace; (*de route*) sharp
bend; (*piège*) snare; **chaussures à ~s** lace-up *ou*
lacing shoes

**lâche** [lɑʃ] *adj* (*poltron*) cowardly; (*desserré*) loose,
slack; (*morale, mœurs*) lax ▷ *nm/f* coward

**lâchement** [lɑʃmã] *adv* (*par peur*) like a coward;
(*par bassesse*) despicably

**lâcher** [lɑʃe] *nm* (*de ballons, oiseaux*) release ▷ *vt* to
let go of; (*ce qui tombe, abandonner*) to drop; (*oiseau,
animal: libérer*) to release, set free; (*fig: mot,
remarque*) to let slip, come out with; (*Sport:
distancer*) to leave behind ▷ *vi* (*fil, amarres*) to
break, give way; (*freins*) to fail; **~ les amarres**
(*Navig*) to cast off (the moorings); **~ prise** to let
go

**lâcheté** [lɑʃte] *nf* cowardice; (*bassesse*) lowness

**lacis** [lasi] *nm* (*de ruelles*) maze

**laconique** [lakɔnik] *adj* laconic

**laconiquement** [lakɔnikmã] *adv* laconically

**lacrymal, e, aux** [lakRimal, -o] *adj* (*canal, glande*)
tear *cpd*

**lacrymogène** [lakRimɔʒɛn] *adj*: **grenade/gaz ~**
tear gas grenade/tear gas

**lacs** [la] *nm* (*piège*) snare

**lactation** [laktasjɔ̃] *nf* lactation

**lacté, e** [lakte] *adj* milk *cpd*

**lactique** [laktik] *adj*: **acide/ferment ~** lactic
acid/ferment

**lactose** [laktoz] *nm* lactose, milk sugar

**lacune** [lakyn] *nf* gap

**lacustre** [lakystR(ə)] *adj* lake *cpd*, lakeside *cpd*

**lad** [lad] *nm* stable-lad

**là-dedans** [ladədã] *adv* inside (there), in it; (*fig*)
in that

**là-dehors** [ladəɔR] *adv* out there

**là-derrière** [ladɛRjɛR] *adv* behind there; (*fig*)
behind that

**là-dessous** [ladsu] *adv* underneath, under
there; (*fig*) behind that

**là-dessus** [ladsy] *adv* on there; (*fig*) at that
point; (: *à ce sujet*) about that

**là-devant** [ladvã] *adv* there (in front)

**ladite** [ladit] *adj voir* **ledit**

**ladre** [ladR(ə)] *adj* miserly

**lagon** [lagɔ̃] *nm* lagoon

**Lagos** [lagɔs] *n* Lagos

**lagune** [lagyn] *nf* lagoon

**là-haut** [lao] *adv* up there

**laïc** [laik] *adj, nm/f* = **laïque**

**laïciser** [laisize] *vt* to secularize

laïcité [laisite] nf secularity, secularism

laid, e [lɛ, lɛd] adj ugly; (fig: acte) mean, cheap

laideron [lɛdRɔ̃] nm ugly girl

laideur [lɛdœR] nf ugliness no pl; meanness no pl

laie [lɛ] nf wild sow

lainage [lɛnaʒ] nm woollen garment; (étoffe) woollen material

laine [lɛn] nf wool; ~ **peignée** worsted (wool); ~ **à tricoter** knitting wool; ~ **de verre** glass wool; ~ **vierge** new wool

laineux, -euse [lɛnø, -øz] adj woolly

lainier, -ière [lenje, -jɛR] adj (industrie etc) woollen

laïque [laik] adj lay, civil; (Scol) state cpd (as opposed to private and Roman Catholic) ▷ nm/f layman(-woman)

laisse [lɛs] nf (de chien) lead, leash; **tenir en ~** to keep on a lead ou leash

laissé-pour-compte, laissée-, laissés-[lesepuRkɔ̃t] adj (Comm) unsold; (: refusé) returned ▷ nm/f (fig) reject; **les laissés-pour-compte de la reprise économique** those who are left out of the economic upturn

laisser [lese] vt to leave ▷ vb aux: ~ **qn faire** to let sb do; **se ~ exploiter** to let o.s. be exploited; **se ~ aller** to let o.s. go; ~ **qn tranquille** to let ou leave sb alone; **laisse-toi faire** let me (ou him) do it; **rien ne laisse penser que ...** there is no reason to think that ...; **cela ne laisse pas de surprendre** nonetheless it is surprising

laisser-aller [leseale] nm carelessness, slovenliness

laisser-faire [lesefeR] nm laissez-faire

laissez-passer [lesepase] nm inv pass

lait [lɛ] nm milk; **frère/sœur de ~** foster brother/sister; ~ **écrémé/concentré/condensé** skimmed/condensed/evaporated milk; ~ **en poudre** powdered milk, milk powder; ~ **de chèvre/vache** goat's/cow's milk; ~ **maternel** mother's milk; ~ **démaquillant/de beauté** cleansing/beauty lotion

laitage [lɛtaʒ] nm milk product

laiterie [lɛtRi] nf dairy

laiteux, -euse [lɛtø, -øz] adj milky

laitier, -ière [letje, -jɛR] adj dairy ▷ nm/f milkman (dairywoman)

laiton [lɛtɔ̃] nm brass

laitue [lety] nf lettuce

laïus [lajys] nm (péj) spiel

lama [lama] nm llama

lambeau, x [lãbo] nm scrap; **en ~x** in tatters, tattered

lambin, e [lãbɛ̃, -in] adj (péj) slow

lambiner [lãbine] vi (péj) to dawdle

lambris [lãbRi] nm panelling no pl

lambrissé, e [lãbRise] adj panelled

lame [lam] nf blade; (vague) wave; (lamelle) strip; ~ **de fond** ground swell no pl; ~ **de rasoir** razor blade

lamé [lame] nm lamé

lamelle [lamɛl] nf (lame) small blade; (morceau) sliver; (de champignon) gill; **couper en ~s** to slice thinly

lamentable [lamãtabl(ə)] adj (déplorable) appalling; (pitoyable) pitiful

lamentablement [lamãtabləmã] adv (échouer) miserably; (se conduire) appallingly

lamentation [lamãtasjɔ̃] nf wailing no pl, lamentation; moaning no pl

lamenter [lamãte]: **se lamenter** vi: ~ **(sur)** to moan (over)

laminage [laminaʒ] nm lamination

laminer [lamine] vt to laminate; (fig: écraser) to wipe out

laminoir [laminwaR] nm rolling mill; **passer au ~** (fig) to go (ou put) through the mill

lampadaire [lãpadɛR] nm (de salon) standard lamp; (dans la rue) street lamp

lampe [lãp(ə)] nf lamp; (Tech) valve; ~ **à alcool** spirit lamp; ~ **à bronzer** sunlamp; ~ **de poche** torch (Brit), flashlight (US); ~ **à souder** blowlamp; ~ **témoin** warning light

lampée [lãpe] nf gulp, swig

lampe-tempête [lãptãpɛt] (pl lampes-tempête) nf storm lantern

lampion [lãpjɔ̃] nm Chinese lantern

lampiste [lãpist(ə)] nm light (maintenance) man; (fig) underling

lamproie [lãpRwa] nf lamprey

lance [lãs] nf spear; ~ **d'arrosage** garden hose; ~ **à eau** water hose; ~ **d'incendie** fire hose

lancée [lãse] nf: **être/continuer sur sa ~** to be under way/keep going

lance-flammes [lãsflam] nm inv flamethrower

lance-fusées [lãsfyze] nm inv rocket launcher

lance-grenades [lãsgRənad] nm inv grenade launcher

lancement [lãsmã] nm launching no pl, launch; **offre de ~** introductory offer

lance-missiles [lãsmisil] nm inv missile launcher

lance-pierres [lãspjɛR] nm inv catapult

lancer [lãse] nm (Sport) throwing no pl, throw; (Pêche) rod and reel fishing ▷ vt to throw; (émettre, projeter) to throw out, send out; (produit, fusée, bateau, artiste) to launch; (injure) to hurl, fling; (proclamation, mandat d'arrêt) to issue; (emprunt) to float; (moteur) to send roaring away; ~ **qch à qn** to throw sth to sb; (de façon agressive) to throw sth at sb; ~ **un cri** ou **un appel** to shout ou call out; **se lancer** vi (prendre de l'élan) to build up speed; (se précipiter): **se ~ sur** ou **contre** to rush at; **se ~ dans** (discussion) to launch into; (aventure) to embark on; (les affaires, la politique) to go into; ~ **du poids** nm putting the shot

lance-roquettes [lãsRɔkɛt] nm inv rocket launcher

lance-torpilles [lãstɔRpij] nm inv torpedo tube

lanceur, -euse [lãsœR, -øz] nm/f bowler; (Baseball) pitcher ▷ nm (Espace) launcher

lancinant, e [lãsinã, -ãt] adj (regrets etc) haunting; (douleur) shooting

lanciner [lãsine] vi to throb; (fig) to nag

239

**landais, e** [lɑ̃dɛ, -ɛz] adj of ou from the Landes
**landau** [lɑ̃do] nm pram (Brit), baby carriage (US)
**lande** [lɑ̃d] nf moor
**Landes** [lɑ̃d] nfpl: **les** ~ the Landes
**langage** [lɑ̃gaʒ] nm language; ~ **d'assemblage** (Inform) assembly language; ~ **du corps** body language; ~ **évolué/machine** (Inform) high-level/machine language; ~ **de programmation** (Inform) programming language
**lange** [lɑ̃ʒ] nm flannel blanket; **langes** nmpl swaddling clothes
**langer** [lɑ̃ʒe] vt to change (the nappy (Brit) ou diaper (US) of); **table à** ~ changing table
**langoureusement** [lɑ̃guRøzmɑ̃] adv languorously
**langoureux, -euse** [lɑ̃guRø, -øz] adj languorous
**langouste** [lɑ̃gust(ə)] nf crayfish inv
**langoustine** [lɑ̃gustin] nf Dublin Bay prawn
**langue** [lɑ̃g] nf (Anat, Culin) tongue; (Ling) language; (bande): ~ **de terre** spit of land; **tirer la** ~ (**à**) to stick out one's tongue (at); **donner sa** ~ **au chat** to give up, give in; **de** ~ **française** French-speaking; ~ **de bois** officialese; ~ **maternelle** native language, mother tongue; ~ **verte** slang; ~ **vivante** modern language
**langue-de-chat** [lɑ̃gdəʃa] nf finger biscuit
**languedocien, ne** [lɑ̃gdɔsjɛ̃, -ɛn] adj of ou from the Languedoc
**languette** [lɑ̃gɛt] nf tongue
**langueur** [lɑ̃gœR] nf languidness
**languir** [lɑ̃giR] vi to languish; (conversation) to flag; **se languir** vi to be languishing; **faire** ~ **qn** to keep sb waiting
**languissant, e** [lɑ̃gisɑ̃, -ɑ̃t] adj languid
**lanière** [lanjɛR] nf (de fouet) lash; (de valise, bretelle) strap
**lanoline** [lanɔlin] nf lanolin
**lanterne** [lɑ̃tɛRn(ə)] nf (portable) lantern; (électrique) light, lamp; (de voiture) (side)light; ~ **rouge** (fig) tail-ender; ~ **vénitienne** Chinese lantern
**lanterneau, x** [lɑ̃tɛRno] nm skylight
**lanterner** [lɑ̃tɛRne] vi: **faire** ~ **qn** to keep sb hanging around
**Laos** [laɔs] nm: **le** ~ Laos
**laotien, ne** [laɔsjɛ̃, -ɛn] adj Laotian
**lapalissade** [lapalisad] nf statement of the obvious
**La Paz** [lapaz] n La Paz
**laper** [lape] vt to lap up
**lapereau, x** [lapRo] nm young rabbit
**lapidaire** [lapidɛR] adj stone cpd; (fig) terse
**lapider** [lapide] vt to stone
**lapin** [lapɛ̃] nm rabbit; (fourrure) cony; **coup du** ~ rabbit punch; **poser un** ~ **à qn** to stand sb up; ~ **de garenne** wild rabbit
**lapis** [lapis], **lapis-lazuli** [lapislazyli] nm inv lapis lazuli
**lapon, e** [lapɔ̃, -ɔn] adj Lapp, Lappish ▷ nm (Ling)

Lapp, Lappish ▷ nm/f: **Lapon, e** Lapp, Laplander
**Laponie** [lapɔni] nf: **la** ~ Lapland
**laps** [laps] nm: ~ **de temps** space of time, time no pl
**lapsus** [lapsys] nm slip
**laquais** [lakɛ] nm lackey
**laque** [lak] nf lacquer; (brute) shellac; (pour cheveux) hair spray ▷ nm lacquer; piece of lacquer ware
**laqué, e** [lake] adj lacquered
**laquelle** [lakɛl] pron voir **lequel**
**larbin** [laRbɛ̃] nm (péj) flunkey
**larcin** [laRsɛ̃] nm theft
**lard** [laR] nm (graisse) fat; (bacon) (streaky) bacon
**larder** [laRde] vt (Culin) to lard
**lardon** [laRdɔ̃] nm (Culin) piece of chopped bacon; (fam: enfant) kid
**large** [laRʒ(ə)] adj wide; broad; (fig) generous ▷ adv: **calculer/voir** ~ to allow extra/think big ▷ nm (largeur): **5 m de** ~ 5 m wide ou in width; (mer): **le** ~ the open sea; **en** ~ adv sideways; **au** ~ **de** off; ~ **d'esprit** broad-minded; **ne pas en mener** ~ to have one's heart in one's boots
**largement** [laRʒəmɑ̃] adv widely; (de loin) greatly; (amplement, au minimum) easily; (sans compter: donner etc) generously
**largesse** [laRʒɛs] nf generosity; **largesses** nfpl liberalities
**largeur** [laRʒœR] nf (qu'on mesure) width; (impression visuelle) wideness, width; breadth; broadness
**larguer** [laRge] vt to drop; (fam: se débarrasser de) to get rid of; ~ **les amarres** to cast off (the moorings)
**larme** [laRm(ə)] nf tear; (fig): **une** ~ **de** a drop of; **en** ~s in tears; **pleurer à chaudes** ~s to cry one's eyes out, cry bitterly
**larmoyant, e** [laRmwajɑ̃, -ɑ̃t] adj tearful
**larmoyer** [laRmwaje] vi (yeux) to water; (se plaindre) to whimper
**larron** [laRɔ̃] nm thief
**larve** [laRv(ə)] nf (Zool) larva; (fig) worm
**larvé, e** [laRve] adj (fig) latent
**laryngite** [laRɛ̃ʒit] nf laryngitis
**laryngologiste** [laRɛ̃gɔlɔʒist(ə)] nm/f throat specialist
**larynx** [laRɛ̃ks] nm larynx
**las, lasse** [lɑ, lɑs] adj weary
**lasagne** [lazaɲ] nf lasagne
**lascar** [laskaR] nm character; (malin) rogue
**lascif, -ive** [lasif, -iv] adj lascivious
**laser** [lazɛR] nm: (**rayon**) ~ laser (beam); **chaîne** ou **platine** ~ compact disc (player); **disque** ~ compact disc
**lassant, e** [lasɑ̃, -ɑ̃t] adj tiresome, wearisome
**lasse** [lɑs] adj f voir **las**
**lasser** [lase] vt to weary, tire; **se** ~ **de** to grow weary ou tired of
**lassitude** [lasityd] nf lassitude, weariness
**lasso** [laso] nm lasso; **prendre au** ~ to lasso
**latent, e** [latɑ̃, -ɑ̃t] adj latent

**latéral, e, aux** [lateʀal, -o] adj side cpd, lateral
**latéralement** [lateʀalmɑ̃] adv edgeways; (arriver, souffler) from the side
**latex** [latɛks] nm inv latex
**latin, e** [latɛ̃, -in] adj Latin ▷ nm (Ling) Latin ▷ nm/f: **Latin, e** Latin; **j'y perds mon ~** it's all Greek to me
**latiniste** [latinist(ə)] nm/f Latin scholar (ou student)
**latino-américain, e** [latinɔameʀikɛ̃, -ɛn] adj Latin-American
**latitude** [latityd] nf latitude; (fig): **avoir la ~ de faire** to be left free ou be at liberty to do; **à 48° de ~ Nord** at latitude 48° North; **sous toutes les ~s** (fig) world-wide, throughout the world
**latrines** [latʀin] nfpl latrines
**latte** [lat] nf lath, slat; (de plancher) board
**lattis** [lati] nm lathwork
**laudanum** [lodanɔm] nm laudanum
**laudatif, -ive** [lodatif, -iv] adj laudatory
**lauréat, e** [lɔʀea, -at] nm/f winner
**laurier** [lɔʀje] nm (Bot) laurel; (Culin) bay leaves pl; **lauriers** nmpl (fig) laurels
**laurier-rose** [lɔʀjeʀoz] (pl **lauriers-roses**) nm oleander
**laurier-tin** [lɔʀjetɛ̃] (pl **lauriers-tins**) nm laurustinus
**lavable** [lavabl(ə)] adj washable
**lavabo** [lavabo] nm washbasin; **lavabos** nmpl toilet sg
**lavage** [lavaʒ] nm washing no pl, wash; **~ d'estomac/d'intestin** stomach/intestinal wash; **~ de cerveau** brainwashing no pl
**lavande** [lavɑ̃d] nf lavender
**lavandière** [lavɑ̃djɛʀ] nf washerwoman
**lave** [lav] nf lava no pl
**lave-glace** [lavglas] nm (Auto) windscreen (Brit) ou windshield (US) washer
**lave-linge** [lavlɛ̃ʒ] nm inv washing machine
**lavement** [lavmɑ̃] nm (Méd) enema
**laver** [lave] vt to wash; (tache) to wash off; (fig: affront) to avenge; **se laver** to have a wash, wash; **se ~ les mains/dents** to wash one's hands/clean one's teeth; **~ la vaisselle/le linge** to wash the dishes/clothes; **~ qn de** (accusation) to clear sb of
**laverie** [lavʀi] nf: **~ (automatique)** launderette
**lavette** [lavɛt] nf (chiffon) dish cloth; (brosse) dish mop; (fam: homme) wimp, drip
**laveur, -euse** [lavœʀ, -øz] nm/f cleaner
**lave-vaisselle** [lavvɛsɛl] nm inv dishwasher
**lavis** [lavi] nm (technique) washing; (dessin) wash drawing
**lavoir** [lavwaʀ] nm wash house; (bac) washtub
**laxatif, -ive** [laksatif, -iv] adj, nm laxative
**laxisme** [laksism(ə)] nm laxity
**laxiste** [laksist(ə)] adj lax
**layette** [lɛjɛt] nf layette
**layon** [lɛjɔ̃] nm trail
**lazaret** [lazaʀɛ] nm quarantine area
**lazzi** [ladzi] nm gibe

**LCR** sigle f (= Ligue communiste révolutionnaire) political party

◯ MOT-CLÉ

**le, l', la** [l(ə)] (pl **les**) art déf **1** the; **le livre/la pomme/l'arbre** the book/the apple/the tree; **les étudiants** the students
**2** (noms abstraits): **le courage/l'amour/la jeunesse** courage/love/youth
**3** (indiquant la possession): **se casser la jambe** etc to break one's leg etc; **levez la main** put your hand up; **avoir les yeux gris/le nez rouge** to have grey eyes/a red nose
**4** (temps): **le matin/soir** in the morning/evening; mornings/evenings; **le jeudi** etc (d'habitude) on Thursdays etc; (ce jeudi-là etc) on (the) Thursday; **nous venons le 3 décembre** (parlé) we're coming on the 3rd of December ou on December the 3rd; (écrit) we're coming on (on) 3rd ou 3 December
**5** (distribution, évaluation) a, an; **trois euros le mètre/kilo** three euros a ou per metre/kilo; **le tiers/quart de** a third/quarter of
▷ pron **1** (personne: mâle) him; (: femelle) her; (: pluriel) them; **je le/la/les vois** I can see him/her/them
**2** (animal, chose: singulier) it; (: pluriel) them; **je le (ou la) vois** I can see it; **je les vois** I can see them
**3** (remplaçant une phrase): **je ne le savais pas** I didn't know (about it); **il était riche et ne l'est plus** he was once rich but no longer is

**lé** [le] nm (de tissu) width; (de papier peint) strip, length
**leader** [lidœʀ] nm leader
**leadership** [lidœʀʃip] nm (Pol) leadership
**leasing** [liziŋ] nm leasing
**lèche-bottes** [lɛʃbɔt] nm inv bootlicker
**lèchefrite** [lɛʃfʀit] nf dripping pan ou tray
**lécher** [leʃe] vt to lick; (laper: lait, eau) to lick ou lap up; (finir, polir) to over-refine; **~ les vitrines** to go window-shopping; **se ~ les doigts/lèvres** to lick one's fingers/lips
**lèche-vitrines** [lɛʃvitʀin] nm inv: **faire du ~** to go window-shopping
**leçon** [ləsɔ̃] nf lesson; **faire la ~** to teach; **faire la ~ à** (fig) to give a lecture to; **~s de conduite** driving lessons; **~s particulières** private lessons ou tuition sg (Brit)
**lecteur, -trice** [lɛktœʀ, -tʀis] nm/f reader; (d'université) (foreign language) assistant (Brit), (foreign) teaching assistant (US) ▷ nm (Tech): **~ de cassettes** cassette player; **~ de CD/DVD** (Inform: d'ordinateur) CD/DVD drive; (de salon) CD/DVD player; **~ MP3** MP3 player
**lectorat** [lɛktɔʀa] nm (foreign language ou teaching) assistantship
**lecture** [lɛktyʀ] nf reading
**LED** [lɛd] sigle f (= light emitting diode) LED
**ledit** [lədi], **ladite** [ladit] (mpl **lesdits** [ledi]) (fpl

241

**lesdites** [ledit]) *adj* the aforesaid
**légal, e, -aux** [legal, -o] *adj* legal
**légalement** [legalmɑ̃] *adv* legally
**légalisation** [legalizɑsjɔ̃] *nf* legalization
**légaliser** [legalize] *vt* to legalize
**légalité** [legalite] *nf* legality, lawfulness; **être
dans/sortir de la** ~ to be within/step outside
the law
**légat** [lega] *nm* (*Rel*) legate
**légataire** [legatɛʀ] *nm* legatee
**légendaire** [leʒɑ̃dɛʀ] *adj* legendary
**légende** [leʒɑ̃d] *nf* (*mythe*) legend; (*de carte, plan*)
key, legend; (*de dessin*) caption
**léger, -ère** [leʒe, -ɛʀ] *adj* light; (*bruit, retard*)
slight; (*boisson, parfum*) weak; (*couche, étoffe*) thin;
(*superficiel*) thoughtless; (*volage*) free and easy;
flighty; (*peu sérieux*) lightweight; **blessé** ~
slightly injured person; **à la légère** *adv* (*parler,
agir*) rashly, thoughtlessly
**légèrement** [leʒɛʀmɑ̃] *adv* lightly;
thoughtlessly, rashly; ~ **plus grand** slightly
bigger
**légèreté** [leʒɛʀte] *nf* lightness; thoughtlessness
**légiférer** [leʒifeʀe] *vi* to legislate
**légion** [leʒjɔ̃] *nf* legion; **la L- étrangère** the
Foreign Legion; **la L- d'honneur** the Legion of
Honour; *see note*

⬤ **LÉGION D'HONNEUR**
⬤
⬤ Created by Napoleon in 1802 to reward
⬤ services to the French nation, the *Légion
⬤ d'honneur* is a prestigious group of men and
⬤ women headed by the President of the
⬤ Republic, "the Grand Maître". Members
⬤ receive a nominal tax-free payment each
⬤ year.

**légionnaire** [leʒjɔnɛʀ] *nm* (*Mil*) legionnaire; (*de
la Légion d'honneur*) holder of the Legion of
Honour
**législateur** [leʒislatœʀ] *nm* legislator,
lawmaker
**législatif, -ive** [leʒislatif, -iv] *adj* legislative;
**législatives** *nfpl* general election *sg*
**législation** [leʒislɑsjɔ̃] *nf* legislation
**législature** [leʒislatyʀ] *nf* legislature; (*période*)
term (of office)
**légiste** [leʒist(ə)] *nm* jurist ▷ *adj:* **médecin** ~
forensic scientist (*Brit*), medical examiner (*US*)
**légitime** [leʒitim] *adj* (*Jur*) lawful, legitimate;
(*enfant*) legitimate; (*fig*) rightful, legitimate; **en
état de** ~ **défense** in self-defence
**légitimement** [leʒitimmɑ̃] *adv* lawfully;
legitimately; rightfully
**légitimer** [leʒitime] *vt* (*enfant*) to legitimize;
(*justifier: conduite etc*) to justify
**légitimité** [leʒitimite] *nf* (*Jur*) legitimacy
**legs** [lɛg] *nm* legacy
**léguer** [lege] *vt:* ~ **qch à qn** (*Jur*) to bequeath sth
to sb; (*fig*) to hand sth down *ou* pass sth on to sb
**légume** [legym] *nm* vegetable; ~**s verts** green

vegetables; ~**s secs** pulses
**légumier** [legymje] *nm* vegetable dish
**leitmotiv** [lejtmɔtiv] *nm* leitmotiv, leitmotif
**Léman** [lemɑ̃] *nm voir* **lac**
**lendemain** [lɑ̃dmɛ̃] *nm:* **le** ~ the next *ou*
following day; **le** ~ **matin/soir** the next *ou*
following morning/evening; **le** ~ **de** the day
after; **au** ~ **de** in the days following; in the
wake of; **penser au** ~ to think of the future;
**sans** ~ short-lived; **de beaux** ~**s** bright
prospects; **des** ~**s qui chantent** a rosy future
**lénifiant, e** [lenifjɑ̃, -ɑ̃t] *adj* soothing
**léniniste** [leninist(ə)] *adj, nm/f* Leninist
**lent, e** [lɑ̃, lɑ̃t] *adj* slow
**lente** [lɑ̃t] *nf* nit
**lentement** [lɑ̃tmɑ̃] *adv* slowly
**lenteur** [lɑ̃tœʀ] *nf* slowness *no pl*; **lenteurs** *nfpl*
(*actions, décisions lentes*) slowness *sg*
**lentille** [lɑ̃tij] *nf* (*Optique*) lens *sg*; (*Bot*) lentil; ~
**d'eau** duckweed; ~**s de contact** contact lenses
**léonin, e** [leonɛ̃, -in] *adj* (*fig: contrat etc*) one-sided
**léopard** [leɔpaʀ] *nm* leopard
**LEP** [lɛp] *sigle m* (= *lycée d'enseignement professionnel*)
*secondary school for vocational training, pre-1986*
**lèpre** [lɛpʀ(ə)] *nf* leprosy
**lépreux, -euse** [lepʀø, -øz] *nm/f* leper ▷ *adj* (*fig*)
flaking, peeling

◯ **MOT-CLÉ**

**lequel, laquelle** [ləkɛl, lakɛl] (*mpl* **lesquels**, *fpl*
**lesquelles**) (*à + lequel = **auquel**, de + lequel =
**duquel***) *pron* **1** (*interrogatif*) which, which one
**2** (*relatif: personne: sujet*) who; (: *objet, après
préposition*) whom; (: *sujet: possessif*) whose; (: *chose*)
which; **je l'ai proposé au directeur, lequel
est d'accord** I suggested it to the director, who
agrees; **la femme à laquelle j'ai acheté mon
chien** the woman from whom I bought my dog;
**le pont sur lequel nous sommes passés** the
bridge (over) which we crossed; **un homme
sur la compétence duquel on peut compter**
a man whose competence one can count on
▷ *adj:* **auquel cas** in which case

**les** [le] *art déf, pron voir* **le**
**lesbienne** [lɛsbjɛn] *nf* lesbian
**lesdits** [ledi], **lesdites** [ledit] *adj voir* **ledit**
**lèse-majesté** [lɛzmaʒɛste] *nf inv:* **crime de** ~
crime of lese-majesty
**léser** [leze] *vt* to wrong; (*Méd*) to injure
**lésiner** [lezine] *vt:* ~ (**sur**) to skimp (on)
**lésion** [lezjɔ̃] *nf* lesion, damage *no pl*; ~**s
cérébrales** brain damage
**Lesotho** [lezoto] *nm:* **le** ~ Lesotho
**lesquels, lesquelles** [lekɛl] *pron voir* **lequel**
**lessivable** [lesivabl(ə)] *adj* washable
**lessive** [lesiv] *nf* (*poudre*) washing powder; (*linge*)
washing *no pl*, wash; (*opération*) washing *no pl*;
**faire la** ~ to do the washing
**lessivé, e** [lesive] *adj* (*fam*) washed out
**lessiver** [lesive] *vt* to wash

**lessiveuse** [lesivøz] *nf* (*récipient*) washtub
**lessiviel** [lesivjɛl] *adj* detergent
**lest** [lɛst] *nm* ballast; **jeter** *ou* **lâcher du ~** (*fig*) to make concessions
**leste** [lɛst(ə)] *adj* (*personne, mouvement*) sprightly, nimble; (*désinvolte: manières*) offhand; (*osé: plaisanterie*) risqué
**lestement** [lɛstəmɑ̃] *adv* nimbly
**lester** [lɛste] *vt* to ballast
**letchi** [lɛtʃi] *nm* = **litchi**
**léthargie** [letaʀʒi] *nf* lethargy
**léthargique** [letaʀʒik] *adj* lethargic
**letton, ne** [lɛtɔ̃, -ɔn] *adj* Latvian, Lett
**Lettonie** [lɛtɔni] *nf*: **la ~** Latvia
**lettre** [lɛtʀ(ə)] *nf* letter; **lettres** *nfpl* (*étude, culture*) literature *sg*; (*Scol*) arts (subjects); **à la ~** (*au sens propre*) literally; (*ponctuellement*) to the letter; **en ~s majuscules** *ou* **capitales** in capital letters, in capitals; **en toutes ~s** in words, in full; **~ de change** bill of exchange; **~ piégée** letter bomb; **~ de voiture (aérienne)** (air) waybill, (air) bill of lading; **~s de noblesse** pedigree
**lettré, e** [letʀe] *adj* well-read, scholarly
**lettre-transfert** [lɛtʀətʀɑ̃sfɛʀ] (*pl* **lettres-transferts**) *nf* (pressure) transfer
**leu** [lø] *nm voir* **queue**
**leucémie** [løsemi] *nf* leukaemia

🅞 MOT-CLÉ

**leur** [lœʀ] *adj poss* their; **leur maison** their house; **leurs amis** their friends; **à leur approche** as they came near; **à leur vue** at the sight of them
▷ *pron* **1** (*objet indirect*) (to) them; **je leur ai dit la vérité** I told them the truth; **je le leur ai donné** I gave it to them, I gave it them
**2** (*possessif*): **le (la) leur, les leurs** theirs

**leurre** [lœʀ] *nm* (*appât*) lure; (*fig*) delusion; (*: piège*) snare
**leurrer** [lœʀe] *vt* to delude, deceive
**leurs** [lœʀ] *adj voir* **leur**
**levain** [ləvɛ̃] *nm* leaven; **sans ~** unleavened
**levant, e** [ləvɑ̃, -ɑ̃t] *adj*: **soleil ~** rising sun ▷ *nm*: **le L~** the Levant; **au soleil ~** at sunrise
**levantin, e** [ləvɑ̃tɛ̃, -in] *adj* Levantine ▷ *nm/f*: **Levantin, e** Levantine
**levé, e** [ləve] *adj*: **être ~** to be up ▷ *nm*: **~ de terrain** land survey; **à mains ~es** (*vote*) by a show of hands; **au pied ~** at a moment's notice
**levée** [ləve] *nf* (*Postes*) collection; (*Cartes*) trick; **~ de boucliers** general outcry; **~ du corps** *collection of the body from house of the deceased, before funeral*; **~ d'écrou** release from custody; **~ de terre** levee; **~ de troupes** levy
**lever** [ləve] *vt* (*vitre, bras etc*) to raise; (*soulever de terre, supprimer: interdiction, siège*) to lift; (*: difficulté*) to remove; (*séance*) to close; (*impôts, armée*) to levy; (*Chasse: lièvre*) to start; (*: perdrix*) to flush;

(*fam: fille*) to pick up ▷ *vi* (*Culin*) to rise ▷ *nm*: **au ~** on getting up; **se lever** *vi* to get up; (*soleil*) to rise; (*jour*) to break; (*brouillard*) to lift; **levez-vous!, lève-toi!** stand up!, get up!; **ça va se ~** the weather will clear; **~ du jour** daybreak; **~ du rideau** (*Théât*) curtain; **~ de rideau** (*pièce*) curtain raiser; **~ de soleil** sunrise
**lève-tard** [lɛvtaʀ] *nm/f inv* late riser
**lève-tôt** [lɛvto] *nm/f inv* early riser, early bird
**levier** [ləvje] *nm* lever; **faire ~ sur** to lever up (*ou* off); **~ de changement de vitesse** gear lever
**lévitation** [levitɑsjɔ̃] *nf* levitation
**levraut** [ləvʀo] *nm* (*Zool*) leveret
**lèvre** [lɛvʀ(ə)] *nf* lip; **lèvres** *nfpl* (*d'une plaie*) edges; **petites/grandes ~s** labia minora/majora; **du bout des ~s** half-heartedly
**lévrier** [levʀije] *nm* greyhound
**levure** [ləvyʀ] *nf* yeast; **~ chimique** baking powder
**lexical, e, -aux** [lɛksikal, -o] *adj* lexical
**lexicographe** [lɛksikɔgʀaf] *nm/f* lexicographer
**lexicographie** [lɛksikɔgʀafi] *nf* lexicography, dictionary writing
**lexicologie** [lɛksikɔlɔʒi] *nf* lexicology
**lexique** [lɛksik] *nm* vocabulary, lexicon; (*glossaire*) vocabulary
**lézard** [lezaʀ] *nm* lizard; (*peau*) lizard skin
**lézarde** [lezaʀd(ə)] *nf* crack
**lézarder** [lezaʀde]: **se lézarder** *vi* to crack
**liaison** [ljezɔ̃] *nf* (*rapport*) connection, link; (*Rail, Aviat etc*) link; (*relation: d'amitié*) friendship; (*: d'affaires*) relationship; (*: amoureuse*) affair; (*Culin, Phonétique*) liaison; **entrer/être en ~ avec** to get/be in contact with; **~ radio** radio contact; **~ (de transmission de données)** (*Inform*) data link
**liane** [ljan] *nf* creeper
**liant, e** [ljɑ̃, -ɑ̃t] *adj* sociable
**liasse** [ljas] *nf* wad, bundle
**Liban** [libɑ̃] *nm*: **le ~** (the) Lebanon
**libanais, e** [libanɛ, -ɛz] *adj* Lebanese ▷ *nm/f*: **Libanais, e** Lebanese
**libations** [libɑsjɔ̃] *nfpl* libations
**libelle** [libɛl] *nm* lampoon
**libellé** [libele] *nm* wording
**libeller** [libele] *vt* (*chèque, mandat*): **~ (au nom de)** to make out (to); (*lettre*) to word
**libellule** [libelyl] *nf* dragonfly
**libéral, e, -aux** [libeʀal, -o] *adj, nm/f* liberal; **les professions ~es** the professions
**libéralement** [libeʀalmɑ̃] *adv* liberally
**libéralisation** [libeʀalizɑsjɔ̃] *nf* liberalization; **~ du commerce** easing of trade restrictions
**libéraliser** [libeʀalize] *vt* to liberalize
**libéralisme** [libeʀalism(ə)] *nm* liberalism
**libéralité** [libeʀalite] *nf* liberality *no pl*, generosity *no pl*
**libérateur, -trice** [libeʀatœʀ, -tʀis] *adj* liberating ▷ *nm/f* liberator
**libération** [libeʀɑsjɔ̃] *nf* liberation, freeing; release; discharge; **~ conditionnelle** release on

parole

**libéré, e** [libeʀe] *adj* liberated; ~ **de** freed from; **être** ~ **sous caution/sur parole** to be released on bail/on parole

**libérer** [libeʀe] *vt* (*délivrer*) to free, liberate; (: *moralement, Psych*) to liberate; (*relâcher: prisonnier*) to release; (: *soldat*) to discharge; (*dégager: gaz, cran d'arrêt*) to release; (*Écon: échanges commerciaux*) to ease restrictions on; **se libérer** (*de rendez-vous*) to try and be free, get out of previous engagements; ~ **qn de** (*liens, dette*) to free sb from; (*promesse*) to release sb from

**Libéria** [libeʀja] *nm*: **le** ~ Liberia

**libérien, ne** [libeʀjɛ̃, -ɛn] *adj* Liberian ▷ *nm/f*: **Libérien, ne** Liberian

**libéro** [libeʀo] *nm* (*Football*) sweeper

**libertaire** [libeʀtɛʀ] *adj* libertarian

**liberté** [libeʀte] *nf* freedom; (*loisir*) free time; **libertés** *nfpl* (*privautés*) liberties; **mettre/être en** ~ to set/be free; **en** ~ **provisoire/surveillée/ conditionnelle** on bail/probation/parole; ~ **d'association** right of association; ~ **de conscience** freedom of conscience; ~ **du culte** freedom of worship; ~ **d'esprit** independence of mind; ~ **d'opinion** freedom of thought; ~ **de la presse** freedom of the press; ~ **de réunion** right to hold meetings; ~ **syndicale** union rights *pl*; ~**s individuelles** personal freedom *sg*; ~**s publiques** civil rights

**libertin, e** [libeʀtɛ̃, -in] *adj* libertine, licentious

**libertinage** [libeʀtinaʒ] *nm* licentiousness

**libidineux, -euse** [libidinø, -øz] *adj* lustful

**libido** [libido] *nf* libido

**libraire** [libʀɛʀ] *nm/f* bookseller

**libraire-éditeur** [libʀɛʀeditœʀ] (*pl* **libraires- éditeurs**) *nm* publisher and bookseller

**librairie** [libʀɛʀi] *nf* bookshop

**librairie-papeterie** [libʀɛʀipapetʀi] (*pl* **librairies-papeteries**) *nf* bookseller's and stationer's

**libre** [libʀ(ə)] *adj* free; (*route*) clear; (*place etc*) vacant, free; (*fig: propos, manières*) open; (*Scol*) private and Roman Catholic (*as opposed to* "*laïque*"); **de** ~ (*place*) free; ~ **de qch/de faire** free from sth/to do; **vente** ~ (*Comm*) unrestricted sale; ~ **arbitre** free will; ~ **concurrence** free-market economy; ~ **entreprise** free enterprise

**libre-échange** [libʀeʃɑ̃ʒ] *nm* free trade

**librement** [libʀəmɑ̃] *adv* freely

**libre-penseur, -euse** [libʀəpɑ̃sœʀ, -øz] *nm/f* free thinker

**libre-service** [libʀəsɛʀvis] *nm inv* (*magasin*) self-service store; (*restaurant*) self-service restaurant

**librettiste** [libʀetist(ə)] *nm/f* librettist

**Libye** [libi] *nf*: **la** ~ Libya

**libyen, ne** [libjɛ̃, -ɛn] *adj* Libyan ▷ *nm/f*: **Libyen, ne** Libyan

**lice** [lis] *nf*: **entrer en** ~ (*fig*) to enter the lists

**licence** [lisɑ̃s] *nf* (*permis*) permit; (*diplôme*) (first) degree; *see note*; (*liberté*) liberty; (*poétique, orthographique*) licence (Brit), license (US); (*des mœurs*) licentiousness; ~ **ès lettres/en droit** arts/law degree

◉ **LICENCE**
◉
◉ After the "DEUG", French university
◉ students undertake a third year of study to
◉ complete their *licence*. This is roughly
◉ equivalent to a bachelor's degree in Britain.

**licencié, e** [lisɑ̃sje] *nm/f* (*Scol*): ~ **ès lettres/en droit** ≈ Bachelor of Arts/Law, arts/law graduate; (*Sport*) permit-holder

**licenciement** [lisɑ̃simɑ̃] *nm* dismissal; redundancy; laying off *no pl*

**licencier** [lisɑ̃sje] *vt* (*renvoyer*) to dismiss; (*débaucher*) to make redundant; to lay off

**licencieux, -euse** [lisɑ̃sjø, -øz] *adj* licentious

**lichen** [likɛn] *nm* lichen

**licite** [lisit] *adj* lawful

**licorne** [likɔʀn(ə)] *nf* unicorn

**licou** [liku] *nm* halter

**lie** [li] *nf* dregs *pl*, sediment

**lié, e** [lje] *adj*: **très** ~ **avec** (*fig*) very friendly with *ou* close to; ~ **par** (*serment, promesse*) bound by; **avoir partie** ~**e** (**avec qn**) to be involved (with sb)

**Liechtenstein** [liʃtɛnʃtajn] *nm*: **le** ~ Liechtenstein

**lie-de-vin** [lidvɛ̃] *adj inv* wine(-coloured)

**liège** [ljɛʒ] *nm* cork

**liégeois, e** [ljeʒwa, -waz] *adj* of *ou* from Liège ▷ *nm/f*: **Liégeois, e** inhabitant *ou* native of Liège; **café/chocolat** ~ *coffee/chocolate ice cream topped with whipped cream*

**lien** [ljɛ̃] *nm* (*corde, fig: affectif, culturel*) bond; (*rapport*) link, connection; (*analogie*) link; ~ **de parenté** family tie

**lier** [lje] *vt* (*attacher*) to tie up; (*joindre*) to link up; (*fig: unir, engager*) to bind; (*Culin*) to thicken; ~ **qch à** (*attacher*) to tie sth to; (*associer*) to link sth to; ~ **conversation (avec)** to strike up a conversation (with); **se lier avec** to make friends with

**lierre** [ljɛʀ] *nm* ivy

**liesse** [ljɛs] *nf*: **être en** ~ to be jubilant

**lieu, x** [ljø] *nm* place; **lieux** *nmpl* (*locaux*) premises; (*endroit: d'un accident etc*) scene *sg*; **en** ~ **sûr** in a safe place; **en haut** ~ in high places; **vider** *ou* **quitter les** ~**x** to leave the premises; **arriver/être sur les** ~**x** to arrive/be on the scene; **en premier** ~ in the first place; **en dernier** ~ lastly; **avoir** ~ to take place; **avoir** ~ **de faire** to have grounds *ou* good reason for doing; **tenir** ~ **de** to take the place of; (*servir de*) to serve as; **donner** ~ **à** to give rise to, give cause for; **au** ~ **de** instead of; **au** ~ **qu'il y aille** instead of him going; ~ **commun** commonplace; ~ **géométrique** locus; ~ **de naissance** place of birth

**lieu-dit** [ljødi] (*pl* **lieux-dits**) *nm* locality

**lieue** [ljø] *nf* league

**lieutenant** [ljøtnɑ̃] nm lieutenant; ~ **de vaisseau** (Navig) lieutenant

**lieutenant-colonel** [ljøtnɑ̃kɔlɔnɛl] (pl **lieutenants-colonels**) nm (armée de terre) lieutenant colonel; (armée de l'air) wing commander (Brit), lieutenant colonel (US)

**lièvre** [ljɛvʀ(ə)] nm hare; (coureur) pacemaker; **lever un ~** (fig) to bring up a prickly subject

**liftier, -ière** [liftje, -jɛʀ] nm,f lift (Brit) ou elevator (US) attendant

**lifting** [liftiŋ] nm face lift

**ligament** [ligamɑ̃] nm ligament

**ligature** [ligatyʀ] nf ligature

**lige** [liʒ] adj: **homme ~** (péj) henchman

**ligne** [liɲ] nf (gén) line; (Transports: liaison) service; (: trajet) route; (silhouette): **garder la ~** to keep one's figure; **en ~** (Inform) on line; **en ~ droite** as the crow flies; **"à la ~"** "new paragraph"; **entrer en ~ de compte** to be taken into account; to come into it; **~ de but/médiane** goal/halfway line; **~ d'arrivée/de départ** finishing/starting line; **~ de conduite** course of action; **~ directrice** guiding line; **~ fixe** (Tél) fixed line (phone); **~ d'horizon** skyline; **~ de mire** line of sight; **~ de touche** touchline

**ligné, e** [liɲe] adj: **papier ~** ruled paper ▷ nf (race, famille) line, lineage; (postérité) descendants pl

**ligneux, -euse** [liɲø, -øz] adj ligneous, woody

**lignite** [liɲit] nm lignite

**ligoter** [ligɔte] vt to tie up

**ligue** [lig] nf league

**liguer** [lige]: **se liguer** vi to form a league; **se ~ contre** (fig) to combine against

**lilas** [lila] nm lilac

**lillois, e** [lilwa, -waz] adj of ou from Lille

**Lima** [lima] n Lima

**limace** [limas] nf slug

**limaille** [limaj] nf: **~ de fer** iron filings pl

**limande** [limɑ̃d] nf dab

**limande-sole** [limɑ̃dsɔl] nf lemon sole

**limbes** [lɛ̃b] nmpl limbo sg; **être dans les ~** (fig: projet etc) to be up in the air

**lime** [lim] nf (Tech) file; (Bot) lime; **~ à ongles** nail file

**limer** [lime] vt (bois, métal) to file (down); (ongles) to file; (fig: prix) to pare down

**limier** [limje] nm (Zool) bloodhound; (détective) sleuth

**liminaire** [liminɛʀ] adj (propos) introductory

**limitatif, -ive** [limitatif, -iv] adj restrictive

**limitation** [limitasjɔ̃] nf limitation, restriction; **sans ~ de temps** with no time limit; **~ des naissances** birth control; **~ de vitesse** speed limit

**limite** [limit] nf (de terrain) boundary; (partie ou point extrême) limit; **dans la ~ de** within the limits of; **à la ~** (au pire) if the worst comes (ou came) to the worst; **sans ~s** (bêtise, richesse, pouvoir) limitless, boundless; **vitesse/charge ~** maximum speed/load; **cas ~** borderline case; **date ~** deadline; **date ~ de vente/**

**consommation** sell-by/best-before date; **prix ~** upper price limit; **~ d'âge** maximum age, age limit

**limiter** [limite] vt (restreindre) to limit, restrict; (délimiter) to border, form the boundary of; **se ~ (à qch/à faire)** (personne) to limit ou confine o.s. (to sth/to doing sth); **se ~ à** (chose) to be limited to

**limitrophe** [limitʀɔf] adj border cpd; **~ de** bordering on

**limogeage** [limɔʒaʒ] nm dismissal

**limoger** [limɔʒe] vt to dismiss

**limon** [limɔ̃] nm silt

**limonade** [limɔnad] nf lemonade (Brit), (lemon) soda (US)

**limonadier, -ière** [limɔnadje, -jɛʀ] nm/f (commerçant) café owner; (fabricant de limonade) soft drinks manufacturer

**limoneux, -euse** [limɔnø, -øz] adj muddy

**limousin, e** [limuzɛ̃, -in] adj of ou from Limousin ▷ nm (région): **le L~** the Limousin ▷ nf limousine

**limpide** [lɛ̃pid] adj limpid

**lin** [lɛ̃] nm (Bot) flax; (tissu, toile) linen

**linceul** [lɛ̃sœl] nm shroud

**linéaire** [lineɛʀ] adj linear ▷ nm: **~ (de vente)** shelves pl

**linéament** [lineamɑ̃] nm outline

**linge** [lɛ̃ʒ] nm (serviettes etc) linen; (pièce de tissu) cloth; (aussi: **linge de corps**) underwear; (aussi: **linge de toilette**) towel; (lessive) washing; **~ sale** dirty linen

**lingère** [lɛ̃ʒɛʀ] nf linen maid

**lingerie** [lɛ̃ʒʀi] nf lingerie, underwear

**lingot** [lɛ̃go] nm ingot

**linguiste** [lɛ̃gɥist(ə)] nm/f linguist

**linguistique** [lɛ̃gɥistik] adj linguistic ▷ nf linguistics sg

**lino** [lino], **linoléum** [linɔleɔm] nm lino(leum)

**linotte** [linɔt] nf: **tête de ~** bird brain

**linteau, x** [lɛ̃to] nm lintel

**lion, ne** [ljɔ̃, ljɔn] nm/f lion (lioness); (signe): **le L~** Leo, the Lion; **être du L~** to be Leo; **~ de mer** sea lion

**lionceau, x** [ljɔ̃so] nm lion cub

**liposuccion** [liposyksjɔ̃] nf liposuction

**lippu, e** [lipy] adj thick-lipped

**liquéfier** [likefje] vt to liquefy; **se liquéfier** vi (gaz etc) to liquefy; (fig: personne) to succumb

**liqueur** [likœʀ] nf liqueur

**liquidateur, -trice** [likidatœʀ, -tʀis] nm/f (Jur) receiver; **~ judiciaire** official liquidator

**liquidation** [likidasjɔ̃] nf liquidation; (Comm) clearance (sale); **~ judiciaire** compulsory liquidation

**liquide** [likid] adj liquid ▷ nm liquid; (Comm): **en ~** in ready money ou cash

**liquider** [likide] vt (société, biens, témoin gênant) to liquidate; (compte, problème) to settle; (Comm: articles) to clear, sell off

**liquidités** [likidite] nfpl (Comm) liquid assets

**liquoreux, -euse** [likɔʀø, -øz] adj syrupy

245

**lire** [liʀ] *nf* (*monnaie*) lira ▷ *vt, vi* to read; ~ **qch à qn** to read sth (out) to sb
**lis** *vb* [li] *voir* **lire** ▷ *nm* [lis] = **lys**
**lisais** *etc* [lize] *vb voir* **lire**
**Lisbonne** [lizbɔn] *n* Lisbon
**lise** *etc* [liz] *vb voir* **lire**
**liseré** [lizʀe] *nm* border, edging
**liseron** [lizʀɔ̃] *nm* bindweed
**liseuse** [lizøz] *nf* book-cover; (*veste*) bed jacket
**lisible** [lizibl(ə)] *adj* legible; (*digne d'être lu*) readable
**lisiblement** [lizibləmɑ̃] *adv* legibly
**lisière** [lizjɛʀ] *nf* (*de forêt*) edge; (*de tissu*) selvage
**lisons** [lizɔ̃] *vb voir* **lire**
**lisse** [lis] *adj* smooth
**lisser** [lise] *vt* to smooth
**lisseur** [lisœʀ] *nm* straighteners *pl*
**listage** [lista3] *nm* (*Inform*) listing
**liste** [list(ə)] *nf* list; (*Inform*) listing; **faire la ~ de** to list, make out a list of; ~ **d'attente** waiting list; ~ **civile** civil list; ~ **électorale** electoral roll; ~ **de mariage** wedding (present) list; ~ **noire** hit list
**lister** [liste] *vt* to list
**listéria** [listeʀja] *nf* listeria
**listing** [listiŋ] *nm* (*Inform*) listing; **qualité ~** draft quality
**lit** [li] *nm* (*gén*) bed; **faire son ~** to make one's bed; **aller/se mettre au ~** to go to/get into bed; **chambre avec un grand ~** room with a double bed; **prendre le ~** to take to one's bed; **d'un premier ~** (*Jur*) of a first marriage; ~ **de camp** camp bed (*Brit*), cot (*US*); ~ **d'enfant** cot (*Brit*), crib (*US*)
**litanie** [litani] *nf* litany
**lit-cage** [lika3] (*pl* **lits-cages**) *nm* folding bed
**litchi** [litʃi] *nm* lychee
**literie** [litʀi] *nf* bedding; (*linge*) bedding, bedclothes *pl*
**litho** [lito], **lithographie** [litɔgʀafi] *nf* litho(graphy); (*épreuve*) litho(graph)
**litière** [litjɛʀ] *nf* litter
**litige** [liti3] *nm* dispute; **en ~** in contention
**litigieux, -euse** [liti3jø, -øz] *adj* litigious, contentious
**litote** [litɔt] *nf* understatement
**litre** [litʀ(ə)] *nm* litre; (*récipient*) litre measure
**littéraire** [liteʀɛʀ] *adj* literary
**littéral, e, -aux** [liteʀal, -o] *adj* literal
**littéralement** [liteʀalmɑ̃] *adv* literally
**littérature** [liteʀatyʀ] *nf* literature
**littoral, e, -aux** [litɔʀal, -o] *adj* coastal ▷ *nm* coast
**Lituanie** [lituani] *nf*: **la ~** Lithuania
**lituanien, ne** [lituanjɛ̃, -ɛn] *adj* Lithuanian ▷ *nm* (*Ling*) Lithuanian ▷ *nm/f*: **Lituanien, ne** Lithuanian
**liturgie** [lityʀ3i] *nf* liturgy
**liturgique** [lityʀ3ik] *adj* liturgical
**livide** [livid] *adj* livid, pallid
**living** [liviŋ], **living-room** [liviŋʀum] *nm* living room

**livrable** [livʀabl(ə)] *adj* (*Comm*) that can be delivered
**livraison** [livʀɛzɔ̃] *nf* delivery; ~ **à domicile** home delivery (service)
**livre** [livʀ(ə)] *nm* book; (*imprimerie etc*): **le ~** the book industry ▷ *nf* (*poids, monnaie*) pound; **traduire qch à ~ ouvert** to translate sth off the cuff *ou* at sight; ~ **blanc** official report (*on war, natural disaster etc, prepared by independent body*); ~ **de bord** (*Navig*) logbook; ~ **de comptes** account(s) book; ~ **de cuisine** cookery book (*Brit*), cookbook; ~ **de messe** mass *ou* prayer book; ~ **d'or** visitors' book; ~ **de poche** paperback (*small and cheap*); ~ **sterling** pound sterling; ~ **verte** green pound
**livré, e** [livʀe] *nf* livery ▷ *adj*: ~ **à** (*l'anarchie etc*) given over to; ~ **à soi-même** left to oneself *ou* one's own devices
**livrer** [livʀe] *vt* (*Comm*) to deliver; (*otage, coupable*) to hand over; (*secret, information*) to give away; **se ~ à** (*se confier*) to confide in; (*se rendre*) to give o.s. up to; (*s'abandonner à: débauche etc*) to give o.s. up *ou* over to; (*faire: pratiques, actes*) to indulge in; (*travail*) to be engaged in, engage in; (*: sport*) to practise; (*: enquête*) to carry out; ~ **bataille** to give battle
**livresque** [livʀɛsk(ə)] *adj* (*péj*) bookish
**livret** [livʀɛ] *nm* booklet; (*d'opéra*) libretto; ~ **de caisse d'épargne** (savings) bank-book; ~ **de famille** (official) family record book; ~ **scolaire** (school) report book
**livreur, -euse** [livʀœʀ, -øz] *nm/f* delivery boy *ou* man/girl *ou* woman
**LO** *sigle f* (= **Lutte ouvrière**) *political party*
**lob** [lɔb] *nm* lob
**lobe** [lɔb] *nm*: ~ **de l'oreille** ear lobe
**lober** [lɔbe] *vt* to lob
**local, e, -aux** [lɔkal, -o] *adj* local ▷ *nm* (*salle*) premises *pl* ▷ *nmpl* premises
**localement** [lɔkalmɑ̃] *adv* locally
**localisé, e** [lɔkalize] *adj* localized
**localiser** [lɔkalize] *vt* (*repérer*) to locate, place; (*limiter*) to localize, confine
**localité** [lɔkalite] *nf* locality
**locataire** [lɔkatɛʀ] *nm/f* tenant; (*de chambre*) lodger
**locatif, -ive** [lɔkatif, -iv] *adj* (*charges, réparations*) incumbent upon the tenant; (*valeur*) rental; (*immeuble*) with rented flats, used as a letting *ou* rental (*US*) concern
**location** [lɔkasjɔ̃] *nf* (*par le locataire*) renting; (*par l'usager: de voiture etc*) hiring (*Brit*), renting (*US*); (*par le propriétaire*) renting out, letting; hiring out (*Brit*); (*de billets, places*) booking; (*bureau*) booking office; "~ **de voitures**" "car hire (*Brit*) *ou* rental (*US*)"
**location-vente** [lɔkasjɔ̃vɑ̃t] *nf* form of hire purchase (*Brit*) *ou* installment plan (*US*)
**lock-out** [lɔkawt] *nm inv* lockout
**locomoteur, -trice** [lɔkɔmɔtœʀ, -tʀis] *adj, nf* locomotive
**locomotion** [lɔkɔmosjɔ̃] *nf* locomotion

**locomotive** [lɔkɔmɔtiv] *nf* locomotive, engine; (*fig*) pacesetter, pacemaker

**locuteur, -trice** [lɔkytœʀ, -tʀis] *nm/f* (*Ling*) speaker

**locution** [lɔkysjɔ̃] *nf* phrase

**loden** [lɔdɛn] *nm* loden

**lofer** [lɔfe] *vi* (*Navig*) to luff

**logarithme** [lɔgaʀitm(ə)] *nm* logarithm

**loge** [lɔʒ] *nf* (*Théât: d'artiste*) dressing room; (: *de spectateurs*) box; (*de concierge, franc-maçon*) lodge

**logeable** [lɔʒabl(ə)] *adj* habitable; (*spacieux*) roomy

**logement** [lɔʒmɑ̃] *nm* flat (*Brit*), apartment (*US*); accommodation *no pl* (*Brit*), accommodations *pl* (*US*); **le ~** housing; **chercher un ~** to look for a flat *ou* apartment, look for accommodation(s); **construire des ~s bon marché** to build cheap housing *sg*; **crise du ~** housing shortage; **~ de fonction** (*Admin*) company flat *ou* apartment, accommodation(s) provided with one's job

**loger** [lɔʒe] *vt* to accommodate ▷ *vi* to live; **se loger: trouver à se ~** to find accommodation; **se ~ dans** (*balle, flèche*) to lodge itself in

**logeur, -euse** [lɔʒœʀ, -øz] *nm/f* landlord (landlady)

**loggia** [lɔdʒja] *nf* loggia

**logiciel** [lɔʒisjɛl] *nm* (*Inform*) piece of software

**logicien, ne** [lɔʒisjɛ̃, -ɛn] *nm/f* logician

**logique** [lɔʒik] *adj* logical ▷ *nf* logic; **c'est ~** it stands to reason

**logiquement** [lɔʒikmɑ̃] *adv* logically

**logis** [lɔʒi] *nm* home; abode, dwelling

**logisticien, ne** [lɔʒistisjɛ̃, -ɛn] *nm/f* logistician

**logistique** [lɔʒistik] *nf* logistics *sg* ▷ *adj* logistic

**logo** [lɔgo], **logotype** [lɔgotip] *nm* logo

**loi** [lwa] *nf* law; **faire la ~** to lay down the law; **les ~s de la mode** (*fig*) the dictates of fashion; **proposition de ~** (private member's) bill; **projet de ~** (government) bill

**loi-cadre** [lwakadʀ(ə)] (*pl* **lois-cadres**) *nf* (*Pol*) blueprint law

**loin** [lwɛ̃] *adv* far; (*dans le temps: futur*) a long way off; (: *passé*) a long time ago; **plus ~** further; **moins ~ (que)** not as far (as); **~ de** far from; **~ d'ici** a long way from here; **pas ~ de 100 euros** not far off 100 euros; **au ~** far off; **de ~** far from a distance; (*fig: de beaucoup*) by far; **il vient de ~** he's come a long way; he comes from a long way away; **de ~ en ~** here and there; (*de temps en temps*) (every) now and then; **~ de là** (*au contraire*) far from it

**lointain, e** [lwɛ̃tɛ̃, -ɛn] *adj* faraway, distant; (*dans le futur, passé*) distant, far-off; (*cause, parent*) remote, distant ▷ *nm*: **dans le ~** in the distance

**loi-programme** [lwapʀɔgʀam] (*pl* **lois-programmes**) *nf* (*Pol*) act providing framework for government programme

**loir** [lwaʀ] *nm* dormouse

**Loire** [lwaʀ] *nf*: **la ~** the Loire

**loisible** [lwazibl(ə)] *adj*: **il vous est ~ de ...** you are free to ...

**loisir** [lwaziʀ] *nm*: **heures de ~** spare time;

**loisirs** *nmpl* leisure *sg*; (*activités*) leisure activities; **avoir le ~ de faire** to have the time *ou* opportunity to do; **(tout) à ~** (*en prenant son temps*) at leisure; (*autant qu'on le désire*) at one's pleasure

**lombaire** [lɔ̃bɛʀ] *adj* lumbar

**lombalgie** [lɔ̃balʒi] *nf* back pain

**londonien, ne** [lɔ̃dɔnjɛ̃, -ɛn] *adj* London *cpd*, of London ▷ *nm/f*: **Londonien, ne** Londoner

**Londres** [lɔ̃dʀ(ə)] *n* London

**long, longue** [lɔ̃, lɔ̃g] *adj* long ▷ *adv*: **en savoir ~** to know a great deal ▷ *nm*: **de 3 m de ~** 3 m long, 3 m in length ▷ *nf*: **à la longue** in the end; **faire ~ feu** to fizzle out; **ne pas faire ~ feu** not to last long; **au ~ cours** (*Navig*) ocean *cpd*, ocean-going; **de longue date** *adj* long-standing; **longue durée** *adj* long-term; **de longue haleine** *adj* long-term; **être ~ à faire** to take a long time to do; **en ~** *adv* lengthwise, lengthways; **(tout) le ~ de** (all) along; **tout au ~ de** (*année, vie*) throughout; **de ~ en large** (*marcher*) to and fro, up and down; **en ~ et en large** (*fig*) in every detail

**longanimité** [lɔ̃ganimite] *nf* forbearance

**long-courrier** [lɔ̃kuʀje] *nm* (*Aviat*) long-haul aircraft

**longe** [lɔ̃ʒ] *nf* (*corde: pour attacher*) tether; (*pour mener*) lead; (*Culin*) loin

**longer** [lɔ̃ʒe] *vt* to go (*ou* walk *ou* drive) along(side); (*mur, route*) to border

**longévité** [lɔ̃ʒevite] *nf* longevity

**longiligne** [lɔ̃ʒiliɲ] *adj* long-limbed

**longitude** [lɔ̃ʒityd] *nf* longitude; **à 45° de ~ ouest** at 45°longitude west

**longitudinal, e, -aux** [lɔ̃ʒitydinal, -o] *adj* longitudinal, lengthways; (*entaille, vallée*) running lengthways

**longtemps** [lɔ̃tɑ̃] *adv* (for) a long time, (for) long; **ça ne va pas durer ~** it won't last long; **avant ~** before long; **pour/pendant ~** for a long time; **je n'en ai pas pour ~** I shan't be long; **mettre ~ à faire** to take a long time to do; **il en a pour ~** he'll be a long time; **il y a ~ que je travaille** I have been working (for) a long time; **il n'y a pas ~ que je l'ai rencontré** it's not long since I met him

**longue** [lɔ̃g] *adj f voir* **long**

**longuement** [lɔ̃gmɑ̃] *adv* (*longtemps: parler, regarder*) for a long time; (*en détail: expliquer, raconter*) at length

**longueur** [lɔ̃gœʀ] *nf* length; **longueurs** *nfpl* (*fig: d'un film etc*) tedious parts; **sur une ~ de 10 km** for *ou* over 10 km; **en ~** *adv* lengthwise, lengthways; **tirer en ~** to drag on; **à ~ de journée** all day long; **d'une ~** (*gagner*) by a length; **~ d'onde** wavelength

**longue-vue** [lɔ̃gvy] *nf* telescope

**look** [luk] (*fam*) *nm* look, image

**looping** [lupiŋ] *nm* (*Aviat*): **faire des ~s** to loop the loop

**lopin** [lɔpɛ̃] *nm*: **~ de terre** patch of land

**loquace** [lɔkas] *adj* talkative, loquacious

**loque** [lɔk] nf (personne) wreck; **loques** nfpl (habits) rags; **être** ou **tomber en ~s** to be in rags

**loquet** [lɔkɛ] nm latch

**lorgner** [lɔʀɲe] vt to eye; (convoiter) to have one's eye on

**lorgnette** [lɔʀɲɛt] nf opera glasses pl

**lorgnon** [lɔʀɲɔ̃] nm (face-à-main) lorgnette; (pince-nez) pince-nez

**loriot** [lɔʀjo] nm (golden) oriole

**lorrain, e** [lɔʀɛ̃, -ɛn] adj of ou from Lorraine; **quiche ~e** quiche

**lors** [lɔʀ]: **~ de** prép (au moment de) at the time of; (pendant) during; **~ même que** even though

**lorsque** [lɔʀsk(ə)] conj when, as

**losange** [lɔzɑ̃ʒ] nm diamond; (Géom) lozenge; **en ~** diamond-shaped

**lot** [lo] nm (part) share; (de loterie) prize; (fig: destin) fate, lot; (Comm, Inform) batch; **~ de consolation** consolation prize

**loterie** [lɔtʀi] nf lottery; (tombola) raffle; **L~ nationale** French national lottery

**loti, e** [lɔti] adj: **bien/mal ~** well-/badly off, lucky/unlucky

**lotion** [losjɔ̃] nf lotion; **~ après rasage** after-shave (lotion); **~ capillaire** hair lotion

**lotir** [lɔtiʀ] vt (terrain: diviser) to divide into plots; (: vendre) to sell by lots

**lotissement** [lɔtismɑ̃] nm (groupe de maisons, d'immeubles) housing development; (parcelle) (building) plot, lot

**loto** [lɔto] nm lotto

**lotte** [lɔt] nf (Zool: de rivière) burbot; (: de mer) monkfish

**louable** [lwabl(ə)] adj (appartement, garage) rentable; (action, personne) praiseworthy, commendable

**louage** [lwaʒ] nm: **voiture de ~** hired (Brit) ou rented (US) car; (à louer) hire (Brit) ou rental (US) car

**louange** [lwɑ̃ʒ] nf: **à la ~ de** in praise of; **louanges** nfpl praise sg

**loubar, loubard** [lubaʀ] nm (fam) lout

**louche** [luʃ] adj shady, dubious ▷ nf ladle

**loucher** [luʃe] vi to squint; (fig): **~ sur** to have one's (beady) eye on

**louer** [lwe] vt (maison: propriétaire) to let, rent (out); (: locataire) to rent; (voiture etc) to hire out (Brit), rent (out); to hire (Brit), rent; (réserver) to book; (faire l'éloge de) to praise; "**à ~**" "to let" (Brit), "for rent" (US); **~ qn de** to praise sb for; **se ~ de** to congratulate o.s. on

**loufoque** [lufɔk] adj (fam) crazy, zany

**loukoum** [lukum] nm Turkish delight

**loulou** [lulu] nm (chien) spitz; **~ de Poméranie** Pomeranian (dog)

**loup** [lu] nm wolf; (poisson) bass; (masque) (eye) mask; **jeune ~** young go-getter; **~ de mer** (marin) old seadog

**loupe** [lup] nf magnifying glass; **~ de noyer** burr walnut; **à la ~** (fig) in minute detail

**louper** [lupe] vt (fam: manquer) to miss; (: gâcher) to mess up, bungle

**lourd, e** [luʀ, luʀd(ə)] adj heavy; (chaleur, temps) sultry; (fig: personne, style) heavy-handed ▷ adv: **peser ~** to be heavy; **~ de** (menaces) charged with; (conséquences) fraught with; **artillerie/industrie ~e** heavy artillery/industry

**lourdaud, e** [luʀdo, -od] adj oafish

**lourdement** [luʀdəmɑ̃] adv heavily; **se tromper ~** to make a big mistake

**lourdeur** [luʀdœʀ] nf heaviness; **~ d'estomac** indigestion no pl

**loustic** [lustik] nm (fam péj) joker

**loutre** [lutʀ(ə)] nf otter; (fourrure) otter skin

**louve** [luv] nf she-wolf

**louveteau, x** [luvto] nm (Zool) wolf-cub; (scout) cub (scout)

**louvoyer** [luvwaje] vi (Navig) to tack; (fig) to hedge, evade the issue

**lover** [lɔve]: **se lover** vi to coil up

**loyal, e, -aux** [lwajal, -o] adj (fidèle) loyal, faithful; (fair-play) fair

**loyalement** [lwajalmɑ̃] adv loyally, faithfully; fairly

**loyalisme** [lwajalism(ə)] nm loyalty

**loyauté** [lwajote] nf loyalty, faithfulness; fairness

**loyer** [lwaje] nm rent; **~ de l'argent** interest rate

**LP** sigle m (= lycée professionnel) secondary school for vocational training

**LPO** sigle f (= Ligue pour la protection des oiseaux) bird protection society

**LSD** sigle m (= Lyserg Säure Diäthylamid) LSD

**lu, e** [ly] pp de **lire**

**lubie** [lybi] nf whim, craze

**lubricité** [lybʀisite] nf lust

**lubrifiant** [lybʀifjɑ̃] nm lubricant

**lubrifier** [lybʀifje] vt to lubricate

**lubrique** [lybʀik] adj lecherous

**lucarne** [lykaʀn(ə)] nf skylight

**lucide** [lysid] adj (conscient) lucid, conscious; (perspicace) clear-headed

**lucidité** [lysidite] nf lucidity

**luciole** [lysjɔl] nf firefly

**lucratif, -ive** [lykʀatif, -iv] adj lucrative; profitable; **à but non ~** non profit-making

**ludique** [lydik] adj play cpd, playing

**ludothèque** [lydɔtɛk] nf toy library

**luette** [lɥɛt] nf uvula

**lueur** [lɥœʀ] nf (chatoyante) glimmer no pl; (métallique, mouillée) gleam no pl; (rougeoyante) glow no pl; (pâle) (faint) light; (fig) spark; (: d'espérance) glimmer, gleam

**luge** [lyʒ] nf sledge (Brit), sled (US); **faire de la ~** to sledge (Brit), sled (US), toboggan

**lugubre** [lygybʀ(ə)] adj gloomy; dismal

⊙ **MOT-CLÉ**

**lui** [lɥi] pp de **luire**
▷ pron **1** (objet indirect: mâle) (to) him; (: femelle) (to) her; (: chose, animal) (to) it; **je lui ai parlé** I have spoken to him (ou to her); **il lui a offert**

**un cadeau** he gave him (*ou* her) a present; **je le lui ai donné** I gave it to him (*ou* her)
**2** (*après préposition, comparatif: personne*) him; (: *chose, animal*) it; **elle est contente de lui** she is pleased with him; **je la connais mieux que lui** I know her better than he does; **cette voiture est à lui** this car belongs to him, this is HIS car
**3** (*sujet, forme emphatique*) he; **lui, il est à Paris** HE is in Paris; **c'est lui qui l'a fait** HE did it

**lui-même** [lɥimɛm] *pron* (*personne*) himself; (*chose*) itself
**luire** [lɥiʀ] *vi* (*gén*) to shine, gleam; (*surface mouillée*) to glisten; (*reflets chauds, cuivrés*) to glow
**luisant, e** [lɥizɑ̃, -ɑ̃t] *vb voir* **luire** ▷ *adj* shining, gleaming
**lumbago** [lɔ̃bago] *nm* lumbago
**lumière** [lymjɛʀ] *nf* light; **lumières** *nfpl* (*d'une personne*) knowledge *sg*, wisdom *sg*; **à la ~ de** by the light of; (*fig: événements*) in the light of; **fais de la ~** let's have some light, give us some light; **faire (toute) la ~ sur** (*fig*) to clarify (completely); **mettre en ~** (*fig*) to highlight; **~ du jour/soleil** day/sunlight
**luminaire** [lyminɛʀ] *nm* lamp, light
**lumineux, -euse** [lyminø, -øz] *adj* (*émettant de la lumière*) luminous; (*éclairé*) illuminated; (*ciel, journée, couleur*) bright; (*relatif à la lumière: rayon etc*) of light, light *cpd*; (*fig: regard*) radiant
**luminosité** [lyminɔzite] *nf* (*Tech*) luminosity
**lump** [lœp] *nm*: **œufs de ~** lump-fish roe
**lunaire** [lynɛʀ] *adj* lunar, moon *cpd*
**lunatique** [lynatik] *adj* whimsical, temperamental
**lunch** [lœntʃ] *nm* (*réception*) buffet lunch
**lundi** [lœdi] *nm* Monday; **on est ~** it's Monday; **le ~ 20 août** Monday 20th August; **il est venu ~** he came on Monday; **le(s) ~(s)** on Mondays; **à ~!** see you (on) Monday!; **~ de Pâques** Easter Monday; **~ de Pentecôte** Whit Monday (*Brit*)
**lune** [lyn] *nf* moon; **pleine/nouvelle ~** full/new moon; **être dans la ~** (*distrait*) to have one's head in the clouds; **~ de miel** honeymoon
**luné, e** [lyne] *adj*: **bien/mal ~** in a good/bad mood
**lunette** [lynɛt] *nf*: **~s** *nfpl* glasses, spectacles; (*protectrices*) goggles; **~ d'approche** telescope; **~ arrière** (*Auto*) rear window; **~s noires** dark glasses; **~s de soleil** sunglasses
**lurent** [lyʀ] *vb voir* **lire**
**lurette** [lyʀɛt] *nf*: **il y a belle ~** ages ago
**luron, ne** [lyʀɔ̃, -ɔn] *nm/f* lad/lass; **joyeux** *ou* **gai ~** gay dog
**lus** *etc* [ly] *vb voir* **lire**
**lustre** [lystʀ(ə)] *nm* (*de plafond*) chandelier; (*fig: éclat*) lustre
**lustrer** [lystʀe] *vt*: **~ qch** (*faire briller*) to make sth shine; (*user*) to make sth shiny
**lut** [ly] *vb voir* **lire**
**luth** [lyt] *nm* lute
**luthier** [lytje] *nm* (*stringed-*)instrument maker

**lutin** [lytɛ̃] *nm* imp, goblin
**lutrin** [lytʀɛ̃] *nm* lectern
**lutte** [lyt] *nf* (*conflit*) struggle; (*Sport*): **la ~** wrestling; **de haute ~** after a hard-fought struggle; **~ des classes** class struggle; **~ libre** (*Sport*) all-in wrestling
**lutter** [lyte] *vi* to fight, struggle; (*Sport*) to wrestle
**lutteur, -euse** [lytœʀ, -øz] *nm/f* (*Sport*) wrestler; (*fig*) battler, fighter
**luxation** [lyksasjɔ̃] *nf* dislocation
**luxe** [lyks(ə)] *nm* luxury; **un ~ de** (*détails, précautions*) a wealth of; **de ~** *adj* luxury *cpd*
**Luxembourg** [lyksɑ̃buʀ] *nm*: **le ~** Luxembourg
**luxembourgeois, e** [lyksɑ̃buʀʒwa, -waz] *adj* of *ou* from Luxembourg ▷ *nm/f*: **Luxembourgeois, e** inhabitant *ou* native of Luxembourg
**luxer** [lykse] *vt*: **se ~ l'épaule** to dislocate one's shoulder
**luxueusement** [lyksɥøzmɑ̃] *adv* luxuriously
**luxueux, -euse** [lyksɥø, -øz] *adj* luxurious
**luxure** [lyksyʀ] *nf* lust
**luxuriant, e** [lyksyʀjɑ̃, -ɑ̃t] *adj* luxuriant, lush
**luzerne** [lyzɛʀn(ə)] *nf* lucerne, alfalfa
**lycée** [lise] *nm* (state) secondary (*Brit*) *ou* high (*US*) school; **~ technique** technical secondary *ou* high school; *see note*

● **LYCÉE**

French pupils spend the last three years of their secondary education at a *lycée*, where they sit their "baccalauréat" before leaving school or going on to higher education. There are various types of *lycée*, including the "lycées d'enseignement technologique", providing technical courses, and "lycées d'enseignement professionnel", providing vocational courses. Some *lycées*, particularly those with a wide catchment area or those which run specialist courses, have boarding facilities.

**lycéen, ne** [liseɛ̃, -ɛn] *nm/f* secondary school pupil
**Lycra®** [likʀa] *nm* Lycra®
**lymphatique** [lɛ̃fatik] *adj* (*fig*) lethargic, sluggish
**lymphe** [lɛ̃f] *nf* lymph
**lyncher** [lɛ̃ʃe] *vt* to lynch
**lynx** [lɛ̃ks] *nm* lynx
**Lyon** [ljɔ̃] *n* Lyons
**lyonnais, e** [ljɔnɛ, -ɛz] *adj* of *ou* from Lyons; (*Culin*) Lyonnaise
**lyophilisé, e** [ljɔfilize] *adj* freeze-dried
**lyre** [liʀ] *nf* lyre
**lyrique** [liʀik] *adj* lyrical; (*Opéra*) lyric; **artiste ~** opera singer; **comédie ~** comic opera; **théâtre ~** opera house (*for light opera*)
**lyrisme** [liʀism(ə)] *nm* lyricism
**lys** [lis] *nm* lily

# Mm

**M, m** [ɛm] *nm inv* M, m ▷ *abr* = **majeur**;
**masculin**; **mètre**; **Monsieur**; (= *million*) M; **M
comme Marcel** M for Mike

**m'** [m] *pron voir* **me**

**MA** *sigle m* = **maître auxiliaire**

**ma** [ma] *adj poss voir* **mon**

**maboul, e** [mabul] *adj* (*fam*) loony

**macabre** [makɑbʀ(ə)] *adj* macabre, gruesome

**macadam** [makadam] *nm* tarmac (*Brit*), asphalt

**macaron** [makaʀɔ̃] *nm* (*gâteau*) macaroon;
(*insigne*) (round) badge

**macaroni** [makaʀɔni] *nm*, **macaronis** *nmpl*
macaroni *sg*; **~(s) au gratin** macaroni cheese
(*Brit*), macaroni and cheese (*US*)

**Macédoine** [masedwan] *nf* Macedonia

**macédoine** [masedwan] *nf*: **~ de fruits** fruit
salad; **~ de légumes** mixed vegetables *pl*

**macérer** [maseʀe] *vi, vt* to macerate

**mâchefer** [maʃfɛʀ] *nm* clinker, cinders *pl*

**mâcher** [mɑʃe] *vt* to chew; **ne pas ~ ses mots**
not to mince one's words; **~ le travail à qn** (*fig*)
to spoon-feed sb, do half sb's work for him

**machiavélique** [makjavelik] *adj* Machiavellian

**machin** [maʃɛ̃] *nm* (*fam*) thingamajig, thing;
(*personne*): **M~** what's-his-name

**machinal, e, -aux** [maʃinal, -o] *adj* mechanical,
automatic

**machinalement** [maʃinalmɑ̃] *adv*
mechanically, automatically

**machination** [maʃinɑsjɔ̃] *nf* scheming, frame-
up

**machine** [maʃin] *nf* machine; (*locomotive; de
navire etc*) engine; (*fig: rouages*) machinery; (*fam:
personne*): **M~** what's-her-name; **faire ~ arrière**
(*Navig*) to go astern; (*fig*) to back-pedal; **~ à
laver/coudre/tricoter** washing/sewing/
knitting machine; **~ à écrire** typewriter; **~ à
sous** fruit machine; **~ à vapeur** steam engine

**machine-outil** [maʃinuti] (*pl* **machines-outils**)
*nf* machine tool

**machinerie** [maʃinʀi] *nf* machinery, plant;
(*d'un navire*) engine room

**machinisme** [maʃinism(ə)] *nm* mechanization

**machiniste** [maʃinist(ə)] *nm* (*Théât*) scene
shifter; (*de bus, métro*) driver

**macho** [matʃo] (*fam*) *nm* male chauvinist

**mâchoire** [mɑʃwaʀ] *nf* jaw; **~ de frein** brake
shoe

**mâchonner** [mɑʃɔne] *vt* to chew (at)

**maçon** [masɔ̃] *nm* bricklayer; (*constructeur*)
builder

**mâcon** [mɑkɔ̃] *nm* Mâcon wine

**maçonner** [masɔne] *vt* (*revêtir*) to face, render
(with cement); (*boucher*) to brick up

**maçonnerie** [masɔnʀi] *nf* (*murs: de brique*)
brickwork; (: *de pierre*) masonry, stonework;
(*activité*) bricklaying; building; **~ de béton**
concrete

**maçonnique** [masɔnik] *adj* masonic

**macramé** [makʀame] *nm* macramé

**macrobiotique** [makʀɔbjɔtik] *adj* macrobiotic

**macrocosme** [makʀɔkɔsm(ə)] *nm* macrocosm

**macro-économie** [makʀɔekɔnɔmi] *nf*
macroeconomics *sg*

**maculer** [makyle] *vt* to stain; (*Typo*) to mackle

**Madagascar** [madagaskaʀ] *nf* Madagascar

**Madame** [madam] (*pl* **Mesdames** [medam]) *nf*:
**~ X** Mrs X; **occupez-vous de ~/Monsieur/
Mademoiselle** please serve this lady/
gentleman/(young) lady; **bonjour ~/
Monsieur/Mademoiselle** good morning; (*ton
déférent*) good morning Madam/Sir/Madam; (*le
nom est connu*) good morning Mrs X/Mr X/Miss X;
**~/Monsieur/Mademoiselle!** (*pour appeler*)
excuse me!; (*ton déférent*) Madam/Sir/Miss!; **~/
Monsieur/Mademoiselle** (*sur lettre*) Dear
Madam/Sir/Madam; **chère ~/cher Monsieur/
chère Mademoiselle** Dear Mrs X/Mr X/Miss X;
**~ la Directrice** the director; the manageress;
the head teacher; **Mesdames** Ladies

**Madeleine** [madlɛn]: **îles de la ~** *nfpl* Magdalen
Islands

**madeleine** [madlɛn] *nf* madeleine, ≈ sponge
finger cake

**Mademoiselle** [madmwazɛl] (*pl*
**Mesdemoiselles** [medmwazɛl]) *nf* Miss; *voir
aussi* **Madame**

**Madère** [madɛʀ] *nf* Madeira ▷ *nm*: **madère**
Madeira (wine)

**madone** [madɔn] *nf* Madonna

**madré, e** [madʀe] *adj* crafty, wily

**Madrid** [madʀid] *n* Madrid

**madrier** [madʀije] nm beam
**madrigal, -aux** [madʀigal, -o] nm madrigal
**madrilène** [madʀilɛn] adj of ou from Madrid
**maestria** [maɛstʀija] nf (masterly) skill
**maestro** [maɛstʀo] nm maestro
**mafia, maffia** [mafja] nf Maf(f)ia
**magasin** [magazɛ̃] nm (boutique) shop; (entrepôt) warehouse; (d'arme, appareil-photo) magazine; **en ~** (Comm) in stock; **faire les ~s** to go (a)round the shops, do the shops; **~ d'alimentation** grocer's (shop) (Brit), grocery store (US)
**magasinier** [magazinje] nm warehouseman
**magazine** [magazin] nm magazine
**mage** [maʒ] nm: **les Rois M~s** the Magi, the (Three) Wise Men
**Maghreb** [magʀɛb] nm: **le ~** the Maghreb, North(-West) Africa
**maghrébin, e** [magʀebɛ̃, -in] adj of ou from the Maghreb ▷ nm/f: **Maghrébin, e** North African, Maghrebi
**magicien, ne** [maʒisjɛ̃, -ɛn] nm/f magician
**magie** [maʒi] nf magic; **~ noire** black magic
**magique** [maʒik] adj (occulte) magic; (fig) magical
**magistral, e, -aux** [maʒistʀal, -o] adj (œuvre, adresse) masterly; (ton) authoritative; (gifle etc) sound, resounding; (ex cathedra): **enseignement ~** lecturing, lectures pl; **cours ~** lecture
**magistrat** [maʒistʀa] nm magistrate
**magistrature** [maʒistʀatyʀ] nf magistracy, magistrature; **~ assise** judges pl, bench; **~ debout** state prosecutors pl
**magma** [magma] nm (Géo) magma; (fig) jumble
**magnanime** [maɲanim] adj magnanimous
**magnanimité** [maɲanimite] nf magnanimity
**magnat** [magna] nm tycoon, magnate
**magner** [maɲe]: **se magner** vi (fam) to get a move on
**magnésie** [maɲezi] nf magnesia
**magnésium** [maɲezjɔm] nm magnesium
**magnétique** [maɲetik] adj magnetic
**magnétiser** [maɲetize] vt to magnetize; (fig) to mesmerize, hypnotize
**magnétiseur, -euse** [maɲetizœʀ, -øz] nm/f hypnotist
**magnétisme** [maɲetism(ə)] nm magnetism
**magnéto** [maɲeto] nm (à cassette) cassette deck; (magnétophone) tape recorder
**magnétophone** [maɲetɔfɔn] nm tape recorder; **~ à cassettes** cassette recorder
**magnétoscope** [maɲetɔskɔp] nm: **~ (à cassette)** video (recorder)
**magnificence** [maɲifisɑ̃s] nf (faste) magnificence, splendour (Brit), splendor (US); (générosité) munificence, lavishness
**magnifier** [maɲifje] vt (glorifier) to glorify; (idéaliser) to idealize
**magnifique** [maɲifik] adj magnificent
**magnifiquement** [maɲifikmɑ̃] adv magnificently
**magnolia** [maɲɔlja] nm magnolia

**magnum** [magnɔm] nm magnum
**magot** [mago] nm (argent) pile (of money); (économies) nest egg
**magouille** [maguj] nf (fam) scheming
**magret** [magʀɛ] nm: **~ de canard** duck breast
**mahométan, e** [maɔmetɑ̃, -an] adj Mohammedan, Mahometan
**mai** [mɛ] nm May; see note; voir aussi **juillet**

◉ **LE PREMIER MAI**

◉
◉ *Le premier mai* is a public holiday in France
◉ and commemorates the trades union
◉ demonstrations in the United States in 1886
◉ when workers demanded the right to an
◉ eight-hour working day. Sprigs of lily of the
◉ valley are traditionally exchanged. *Le 8 mai* is
◉ also a public holiday and commemorates
◉ the surrender of the German army to
◉ Eisenhower on 7 May, 1945. It is marked by
◉ parades of ex-servicemen and ex-
◉ servicewomen in most towns. The social
◉ upheavals of May and June 1968, with their
◉ student demonstrations, workers' strikes
◉ and general rioting, are usually referred to
◉ as "les événements de mai 68". De Gaulle's
◉ Government survived, but reforms in
◉ education and a move towards
◉ decentralization ensued.

**m**

**maigre** [mɛgʀ(ə)] adj (very) thin, skinny; (viande) lean; (fromage) low-fat; (végétation) thin, sparse; (fig) poor, meagre, skimpy ▷ adv: **faire ~** not to eat meat; **jours ~s** days of abstinence, fish days
**maigrelet, te** [mɛgʀəlɛ, -ɛt] adj skinny, scrawny
**maigreur** [mɛgʀœʀ] nf thinness
**maigrichon, ne** [megʀiʃɔ̃, -ɔn] adj = **maigrelet, te**
**maigrir** [megʀiʀ] vi to get thinner, lose weight ▷ vt: **~ qn** (vêtement) to make sb look slim(mer)
**mail** [mɛl] nm email
**mailing** [meliŋ] nm direct mail no pl; **un ~** a mailshot
**maille** [maj] nf (boucle) stitch; (ouverture) hole (in the mesh); **avoir ~ à partir avec qn** to have a brush with sb; **~ à l'endroit/à l'envers** knit one/purl one; (boucle) plain/purl stitch
**maillechort** [majʃɔʀ] nm nickel silver
**maillet** [majɛ] nm mallet
**maillon** [majɔ̃] nm link
**maillot** [majo] nm (aussi: **maillot de corps**) vest; (de danseur) leotard; (de sportif) jersey; **~ de bain** bathing costume (Brit), swimsuit; (d'homme) bathing trunks pl; **~ deux pièces** two-piece swimsuit, bikini; **~ jaune** yellow jersey
**main** [mɛ̃] nf hand; **la ~ dans la ~** hand in hand; **à deux ~s** with both hands; **à une ~** with one hand; **à la ~** (tenir, avoir) in one's hand; (faire, tricoter etc) by hand; **se donner la ~** to hold hands; **donner ou tendre la ~ à qn** to hold out one's hand to sb; **se serrer la ~** to shake hands;

**serrer la ~ à qn** to shake hands with sb; **sous la ~** to ou at hand; **haut les ~s!** hands up!; **à ~ levée** (Art) freehand; **à ~s levées** (voter) with a show of hands; **attaque à ~ armée** armed attack; **à ~ droite/gauche** to the right/left; **à remettre en ~s propres** to be delivered personally; **de première ~** (renseignement) first-hand; (Comm: voiture etc) with only one previous owner; **faire ~ basse sur** to help o.s. to; **mettre la dernière ~ à** to put the finishing touches to; **mettre la ~ à la pâte** (fig) to lend a hand; **avoir/passer la ~** (Cartes) to lead/hand over the lead; **s'en laver les ~s** (fig) to wash one's hands of it; **se faire/perdre la ~** to get one's hand in/lose one's touch; **avoir qch bien en ~** to have got the hang of sth; **en un tour de ~** (fig) in the twinkling of an eye; **~ courante** handrail

**mainate** [mɛnat] nm myna(h) bird

**main-d'œuvre** [mɛ̃dœvʀ(ə)] nf manpower, labour (Brit), labor (US)

**main-forte** [mɛ̃fɔʀt(ə)] nf: **prêter ~ à qn** to come to sb's assistance

**mainmise** [mɛ̃miz] nf seizure; (fig): **avoir la ~ sur** to have a grip ou stranglehold on

**mains-libres** [mɛ̃libʀ] adj inv (téléphone, kit) hands-free

**maint, e** [mɛ̃, mɛ̃t] adj many a; **~s** many; **à ~es reprises** time and (time) again

**maintenance** [mɛ̃tnɑ̃s] nf maintenance, servicing

**maintenant** [mɛ̃tnɑ̃] adv now; (actuellement) nowadays

**maintenir** [mɛ̃tniʀ] vt (retenir, soutenir) to support; (contenir: foule etc) to keep in check, hold back; (conserver) to maintain, uphold; (affirmer) to maintain; **se maintenir** vi (paix, temps) to hold; (préjugé) to persist; (malade) to remain stable

**maintien** [mɛ̃tjɛ̃] nm maintaining, upholding; (attitude) bearing; **~ de l'ordre** maintenance of law and order

**maintiendrai** [mɛ̃tjɛ̃dʀe], **maintiens** etc [mɛ̃tjɛ̃] vb voir **maintenir**

**maire** [mɛʀ] nm mayor

**mairie** [meʀi] nf (endroit) town hall; (administration) town council

**mais** [mɛ] conj but; **~ non!** of course not!; **~ enfin** but after all; (indignation) look here!; **~ encore?** is that all?

**maïs** [mais] nm maize (Brit), corn (US)

**maison** [mɛzɔ̃] nf (bâtiment) house; (chez-soi) home; (Comm) firm; (famille): **ami de la ~** friend of the family ▷ adj inv (Culin) home-made; (: au restaurant) made by the chef; (Comm) in-house, own; (fam) first-rate; **à la ~** at home; (direction) home; **~ d'arrêt** (short-stay) prison; **~ centrale** prison; **~ close** brothel; **~ de correction** = remand home (Brit), = reformatory (US); **~ de la culture** = arts centre; **~ des jeunes** = youth club; **~ mère** parent company; **~ de passe** = **maison close**; **~ de repos** convalescent home; **~ de retraite** old people's home; **~ de santé**

mental home

**Maison-Blanche** [mɛzɔ̃blɑ̃ʃ] nf: **la ~** the White House

**maisonnée** [mɛzɔne] nf household, family

**maisonnette** [mɛzɔnɛt] nf small house

**maître, -esse** [mɛtʀ(ə), mɛtʀɛs] nm/f master (mistress); (Scol) teacher, schoolmaster(-mistress) ▷ nm (peintre etc) master; (titre): **M~ (Mᵉ)** Maître, term of address for lawyers etc ▷ nf (amante) mistress ▷ adj (principal, essentiel) main; **maison de ~** family seat; **être ~ de** (soi-même, situation) to be in control of; **se rendre ~ de** (pays, ville) to gain control of; (situation, incendie) to bring under control; **être passé ~ dans l'art de** to be a (past) master in the art of; **une maîtresse femme** a forceful woman; **~ d'armes** fencing master; **~ auxiliaire (MA)** (Scol) temporary teacher; **~ chanteur** blackmailer; **~ de chapelle** choirmaster; **~ de conférences** = senior lecturer (Brit), = assistant professor (US); **~/maîtresse d'école** teacher, schoolmaster/-mistress; **~ d'hôtel** (domestique) butler; (d'hôtel) head waiter; **~ de maison** host; **~ nageur** lifeguard; **~ d'œuvre** (Constr) project manager; **~ d'ouvrage** (Constr) client; **~ queux** chef; **maîtresse de maison** hostess; (ménagère) housewife

**maître-assistant, e** [mɛtʀasistɑ̃, -ɑ̃t] (pl **maîtres-assistants, es**) nm/f = lecturer

**maîtrise** [mɛtʀiz] nf (aussi: **maîtrise de soi**) self-control; (habileté) skill, mastery; (suprématie) mastery, command; (diplôme) = master's degree; see note; (chefs d'équipe) supervisory staff

---

🅜 **MAÎTRISE**
🅜
🅜
🅜 The maîtrise is a French degree which is
🅜 awarded to university students if they
🅜 successfully complete two more years' study
🅜 after the "DEUG". Students wishing to go on
🅜 to do research or to take the "agrégation"
🅜 must hold a maîtrise.

---

**maîtriser** [mɛtʀize] vt (cheval, incendie) to (bring under) control; (sujet) to master; (émotion) to control; **se maîtriser** to control o.s.

**majesté** [maʒɛste] nf majesty

**majestueux, -euse** [maʒɛstɥø, -øz] adj majestic

**majeur, e** [maʒœʀ] adj (important) major; (Jur) of age; (fig) adult ▷ nm/f (Jur) person who has come of age ou attained his (ou her) majority ▷ nm (doigt) middle finger; **en ~e partie** for the most part; **la ~e partie de** the major part of

**major** [maʒɔʀ] nm adjutant; (Scol): **~ de la promotion** first in one's year

**majoration** [maʒɔʀasjɔ̃] nf increase

**majordome** [maʒɔʀdɔm] nm major-domo

**majorer** [maʒɔʀe] vt to increase

**majorette** [maʒɔʀɛt] nf majorette

**majoritaire** [maʒɔʀitɛʀ] adj majority cpd;

**système/scrutin ~** majority system/ballot
**majorité** [maʒɔʀite] *nf* (*gén*) majority; (*parti*) party in power; **en ~** (*composé etc*) mainly
**Majorque** [maʒɔʀk(ə)] *nf* Majorca
**majuscule** [maʒyskyl] *adj, nf*: (**lettre**) **~** capital (letter)
**mal, maux** [mal, mo] *nm* (*opposé au bien*) evil; (*tort, dommage*) harm; (*douleur physique*) pain, ache; (*maladie*) illness, sickness *no pl*; (*difficulté, peine*) trouble; (*souffrance morale*) pain ▷ *adv* badly ▷ *adj*: **c'est ~ (de faire)** it's bad *ou* wrong (to do); **être ~** to be uncomfortable; **être ~ avec qn** to be on bad terms with sb; **être au plus ~** (*malade*) to be very bad; (*brouillé*) to be at daggers drawn; **il comprend ~** he has difficulty in understanding; **il a ~ compris** he misunderstood; **~ tourner** to go wrong; **dire/penser du ~ de** to speak/think ill of; **ne vouloir de ~ à personne** to wish nobody any ill; **il n'a rien fait de ~** he has done nothing wrong; **avoir du ~ à faire qch** to have trouble doing sth; **se donner du ~ pour faire qch** to go to a lot of trouble to do sth; **ne voir aucun ~ à** to see no harm in, see nothing wrong in; **craignant ~ faire** fearing he *etc* was doing the wrong thing; **sans penser** *ou* **songer à ~** without meaning any harm; **faire du ~ à qn** to hurt sb; to harm sb; **se faire ~** to hurt o.s.; **se faire ~ au pied** to hurt one's foot; **ça fait ~** it hurts; **j'ai ~ (ici)** it hurts (here); **j'ai ~ au dos** my back aches, I've got a pain in my back; **avoir ~ à la tête/à la gorge** to have a headache/a sore throat; **avoir ~ aux dents/à l'oreille** to have toothache/earache; **avoir le ~ de l'air** to be airsick; **avoir le ~ du pays** to be homesick; **~ de mer** seasickness; **~ de la route** carsickness; **~ en point** *adj inv* in a bad state; **maux de ventre** stomach ache *sg*; *voir aussi* **cœur**
**malabar** [malabaʀ] *nm* (*fam*) muscle man
**malade** [malad] *adj* ill, sick; (*poitrine, jambe*) bad; (*plante*) diseased; (*fig: entreprise, monde*) ailing ▷ *nm/f* invalid, sick person; (*à l'hôpital etc*) patient; **tomber ~** to fall ill; **être ~ du cœur** to have heart trouble *ou* a bad heart; **grand ~** seriously ill person; **~ mental** mentally sick *ou* ill person
**maladie** [maladi] *nf* (*spécifique*) disease, illness; (*mauvaise santé*) illness, sickness; (*fig: manie*) mania; **être rongé par la ~** to be wasting away (through illness); **~ d'Alzheimer** Alzheimer's disease; **~ de peau** skin disease
**maladif, -ive** [maladif, -iv] *adj* sickly; (*curiosité, besoin*) pathological
**maladresse** [maladʀɛs] *nf* clumsiness *no pl*; (*gaffe*) blunder
**maladroit, e** [maladʀwa, -wat] *adj* clumsy
**maladroitement** [maladʀwatmã] *adv* clumsily
**mal-aimé, e** [maleme] *nm/f* unpopular person; (*de la scène politique, de la société*) persona non grata
**malais, e** [malɛ, -ɛz] *adj* Malay, Malayan ▷ *nm* (*Ling*) Malay ▷ *nm/f*: **Malais, e** Malay, Malayan
**malaise** [malɛz] *nm* (*Méd*) feeling of faintness;

feeling of discomfort; (*fig*) uneasiness, malaise; **avoir un ~** to feel faint *ou* dizzy
**malaisé, e** [maleze] *adj* difficult
**Malaisie** [malezi] *nf*: **la ~** Malaya, West Malaysia; **la péninsule de ~** the Malay Peninsula
**malappris, e** [malapʀi, -iz] *nm/f* ill-mannered *ou* boorish person
**malaria** [malaʀja] *nf* malaria
**malavisé, e** [malavize] *adj* ill-advised, unwise
**Malawi** [malawi] *nm*: **le ~** Malawi
**malaxer** [malakse] *vt* (*pétrir*) to knead; (*mêler*) to mix
**Malaysia** [malɛzja] *nf*: **la ~** Malaysia
**malbouffe** [malbuf] *nf* (*fam*): **la ~** junk food
**malchance** [malʃɑ̃s] *nf* misfortune, ill luck *no pl*; **par ~** unfortunately; **quelle ~!** what bad luck!
**malchanceux, -euse** [malʃɑ̃sø, -øz] *adj* unlucky
**malcommode** [malkɔmɔd] *adj* impractical, inconvenient
**Maldives** [maldiv] *nfpl*: **les ~** the Maldive Islands
**maldonne** [maldɔn] *nf* (*Cartes*) misdeal; **il y a ~** (*fig*) there's been a misunderstanding
**mâle** [mɑl] *adj* (*Élec, Tech*) male; (*viril: voix, traits*) manly ▷ *nm* male
**malédiction** [malediksjɔ̃] *nf* curse
**maléfice** [malefis] *nm* evil spell
**maléfique** [malefik] *adj* evil, baleful
**malencontreusement** [malɑ̃kɔ̃tʀøzmɑ̃] *adv* (*arriver*) at the wrong moment; (*rappeler, mentionner*) inopportunely
**malencontreux, -euse** [malɑ̃kɔ̃tʀø, -øz] *adj* unfortunate, untoward
**malentendant, e** [malɑ̃tɑ̃dɑ̃, -ɑ̃t] *nm/f*: **les ~s** the hard of hearing
**malentendu** [malɑ̃tɑ̃dy] *nm* misunderstanding
**malfaçon** [malfasɔ̃] *nf* fault
**malfaisant, e** [malfəzɑ̃, -ɑ̃t] *adj* evil, harmful
**malfaiteur** [malfɛtœʀ] *nm* lawbreaker, criminal; (*voleur*) thief
**malfamé, e** [malfame] *adj* disreputable, of ill repute
**malfrat** [malfʀa] *nm* villain, crook
**malgache** [malgaʃ] *adj* Malagasy, Madagascan ▷ *nm* (*Ling*) Malagasy ▷ *nm/f*: **Malgache** Malagasy, Madagascan
**malgré** [malgʀe] *prép* in spite of, despite; **~ tout** *adv* in spite of everything
**malhabile** [malabil] *adj* clumsy
**malheur** [malœʀ] *nm* (*situation*) adversity, misfortune; (*événement*) misfortune; (*: plus fort*) disaster, tragedy; **par ~** unfortunately; **quel ~!** what a shame *ou* pity!; **faire un ~** (*fam: un éclat*) to do something desperate; (*: avoir du succès*) to be a smash hit
**malheureusement** [malœʀøzmɑ̃] *adv* unfortunately
**malheureux, -euse** [malœʀø, -øz] *adj* (*triste*) unhappy, miserable; (*infortuné, regrettable*) unfortunate; (*malchanceux*) unlucky; (*insignifiant*) wretched ▷ *nm/f* (*infortuné, misérable*) poor soul; (*indigent, miséreux*) unfortunate

m

creature; **les ~** the destitute; **avoir la main malheureuse** (au jeu) to be unlucky; (tout casser) to be ham-fisted

**malhonnête** [malɔnɛt] adj dishonest

**malhonnêtement** [malɔnɛtmɑ̃] adv dishonestly

**malhonnêteté** [malɔnɛtte] nf dishonesty; rudeness no pl

**Mali** [mali] nm: **le ~** Mali

**malice** [malis] nf mischievousness; (méchanceté): **par ~** out of malice ou spite; **sans ~** guileless

**malicieusement** [malisjøzmɑ̃] adv mischievously

**malicieux, -euse** [malisjø, -øz] adj mischievous

**malien, ne** [maljɛ̃, -ɛn] adj Malian

**malignité** [maliɲite] nf (d'une tumeur, d'un mal) malignancy

**malin, -igne** [malɛ̃, -iɲ] adj (futé: f gén: **maline**) smart, shrewd; (: sourire) knowing; (Méd, influence) malignant; **faire le ~** to show off; **éprouver un ~ plaisir à** to take malicious pleasure in

**malingre** [malɛ̃gʀ(ə)] adj puny

**malintentionné, e** [malɛ̃tɑ̃sjɔne] adj ill-intentioned, malicious

**malle** [mal] nf trunk; (Auto): **~ (arrière)** boot (Brit), trunk (US)

**malléable** [maleabl(ə)] adj malleable

**malle-poste** [malpɔst(ə)] (pl **malles-poste**) nf mail coach

**mallette** [malɛt] nf (valise) (small) suitcase; (aussi: **mallette de voyage**) overnight case; (pour documents) attaché case

**malmener** [malməne] vt to manhandle; (fig) to give a rough ride to

**malnutrition** [malnytʀisjɔ̃] nf malnutrition

**malodorant, e** [malɔdɔʀɑ̃, -ɑ̃t] adj foul-smelling

**malotru** [malɔtʀy] nm lout, boor

**Malouines** [malwin] nfpl: **les ~** the Falklands, the Falkland Islands

**malpoli, e** [malpɔli] nm/f rude individual

**malpropre** [malpʀɔpʀ(ə)] adj (personne, vêtement) dirty; (travail) slovenly; (histoire, plaisanterie) unsavoury (Brit), unsavory (US), smutty; (malhonnête) dishonest

**malpropreté** [malpʀɔpʀəte] nf dirtiness

**malsain, e** [malsɛ̃, -ɛn] adj unhealthy

**malséant, e** [malseɑ̃, -ɑ̃t] adj unseemly, unbecoming

**malsonnant, e** [malsɔnɑ̃, -ɑ̃t] adj offensive

**malt** [malt] nm malt; **pur ~** (whisky) malt (whisky)

**maltais, e** [maltɛ, -ɛz] adj Maltese

**Malte** [malt(ə)] nf Malta

**malté, e** [malte] adj (lait etc) malted

**maltraiter** [maltʀete] vt (brutaliser) to manhandle, ill-treat; (critiquer, éreinter) to slate (Brit), roast

**malus** [malys] nm (Assurances) car insurance weighting, penalty

**malveillance** [malvɛjɑ̃s] nf (animosité) ill will; (intention de nuire) malevolence; (Jur) malicious intent no pl

**malveillant, e** [malvɛjɑ̃, -ɑ̃t] adj malevolent, malicious

**malvenu, e** [malvəny] adj: **être ~ de** ou **à faire qch** not to be in a position to do sth

**malversation** [malvɛʀsasjɔ̃] nf embezzlement, misappropriation (of funds)

**mal-vivre** [malvivʀ] nm inv malaise

**maman** [mamɑ̃] nf mum(my) (Brit), mom (US)

**mamelle** [mamɛl] nf teat

**mamelon** [mamlɔ̃] nm (Anat) nipple; (colline) knoll, hillock

**mamie** [mami] nf (fam) granny

**mammifère** [mamifɛʀ] nm mammal

**mammouth** [mamut] nm mammoth

**manager** [manadʒɛʀ] nm (Sport) manager; (Comm): **~ commercial** commercial director

**manche** [mɑ̃ʃ] nf (de vêtement) sleeve; (d'un jeu, tournoi) round; (Géo): **la M~** the (English) Channel ▷ nm (d'outil, casserole) handle; (de pelle, pioche etc) shaft; (de violon, guitare) neck; (fam) clumsy oaf; **faire la ~** to pass the hat; **~ à air** nf (Aviat) wind-sock; **~ à balai** nm broomstick; (Aviat, Inform) joystick

**manchette** [mɑ̃ʃɛt] nf (de chemise) cuff; (coup) forearm blow; (titre) headline

**manchon** [mɑ̃ʃɔ̃] nm (de fourrure) muff; **~ à incandescence** incandescent (gas) mantle

**manchot** [mɑ̃ʃo] nm one-armed man; armless man; (Zool) penguin

**mandarine** [mɑ̃daʀin] nf mandarin (orange), tangerine

**mandat** [mɑ̃da] nm (postal) postal ou money order; (d'un député etc) mandate; (procuration) power of attorney, proxy; (Police) warrant; **~ d'amener** summons sg; **~ d'arrêt** warrant for arrest; **~ de dépôt** committal order; **~ de perquisition** (Police) search warrant

**mandataire** [mɑ̃datɛʀ] nm/f (représentant, délégué) representative; (Jur) proxy

**mandat-carte** [mɑ̃dakaʀt(ə)] (pl **mandats-cartes**) nm money order (in postcard form)

**mandater** [mɑ̃date] vt (personne) to appoint; (Pol: député) to elect

**mandat-lettre** [mɑ̃datɛtʀ(ə)] (pl **mandats-lettres**) nm money order (with space for correspondence)

**mandchou, e** [mɑ̃tʃu] adj Manchu, Manchurian ▷ nm (Ling) Manchu ▷ nm/f: **Mandchou, e** Manchu

**Mandchourie** [mɑ̃tʃuʀi] nf: **la ~** Manchuria

**mander** [mɑ̃de] vt to summon

**mandibule** [mɑ̃dibyl] nf mandible

**mandoline** [mɑ̃dɔlin] nf mandolin(e)

**manège** [manɛʒ] nm riding school; (à la foire) roundabout (Brit), merry-go-round; (fig) game, ploy; **faire un tour de ~** to go for a ride on a ou the roundabout etc; **~ (de chevaux de bois)** roundabout (Brit), merry-go-round

**manette** [manɛt] nf lever, tap; **~ de jeu** (Inform)

joystick

**manganèse** [mɑ̃ganɛz] nm manganese

**mangeable** [mɑ̃ʒabl(ə)] adj edible, eatable

**mangeaille** [mɑ̃ʒaj] nf (péj) grub

**mangeoire** [mɑ̃ʒwaʀ] nf trough, manger

**manger** [mɑ̃ʒe] vt to eat; (ronger: rouille etc) to eat into ou away; (utiliser, consommer) to eat up ▷ vi to eat

**mange-tout** [mɑ̃ʒtu] nm inv mange-tout

**mangeur, -euse** [mɑ̃ʒœʀ, -øz] nm/f eater

**mangouste** [mɑ̃gust(ə)] nf mongoose

**mangue** [mɑ̃g] nf mango

**maniabilité** [manjabilite] nf (d'un outil) handiness; (d'un véhicule, voilier) manoeuvrability

**maniable** [manjabl(ə)] adj (outil) handy; (voiture, voilier) easy to handle; manoeuvrable (Brit), maneuverable (US); (fig: personne) easily influenced, manipulable

**maniaque** [manjak] adj (pointilleux, méticuleux) finicky, fussy; (atteint de manie) suffering from a mania ▷ nm/f maniac

**manie** [mani] nf mania; (tic) odd habit

**maniement** [manimɑ̃] nm handling; ~ d'armes arms drill

**manier** [manje] vt to handle; **se manier** vi (fam) to get a move on

**maniéré, e** [manjeʀe] adj affected

**manière** [manjɛʀ] nf (façon) way, manner; (genre, style) style; **manières** nfpl (attitude) manners; (chichis) fuss sg; **de ~ à** so as to; **de telle ~ que** in such a way that; **de cette ~** in this way ou manner; **d'une ~ générale** generally speaking, as a general rule; **de toute ~** in any case; **d'une certaine ~** in a (certain) way; **faire des ~s** to put on airs; **employer la ~ forte** to use strong-arm tactics

**manif** [manif] nf (manifestation) demo

**manifestant, e** [manifɛstɑ̃, -ɑ̃t] nm/f demonstrator

**manifestation** [manifɛstasjɔ̃] nf (de joie, mécontentement) expression, demonstration; (symptôme) outward sign; (fête etc) event; (Pol) demonstration

**manifeste** [manifɛst(ə)] adj obvious, evident ▷ nm manifesto

**manifestement** [manifɛstəmɑ̃] adv obviously

**manifester** [manifɛste] vt (volonté, intentions) to show, indicate; (joie, peur) to express, show ▷ vi (Pol) to demonstrate; **se manifester** vi (émotion) to show ou express itself; (difficultés) to arise; (symptômes) to appear; (témoin etc) to come forward

**manigance** [manigɑ̃s] nf scheme

**manigancer** [manigɑ̃se] vt to plot, devise

**Manille** [manij] n Manila

**manioc** [manjɔk] nm cassava, manioc

**manipulateur, -trice** [manipylatœʀ, -tʀis] nm/f (technicien) technician, operator; (prestidigitateur) conjurer; (péj) manipulator

**manipulation** [manipylasjɔ̃] nf handling; manipulation

**manipuler** [manipyle] vt to handle; (fig) to manipulate

**manivelle** [manivɛl] nf crank

**manne** [man] nf (Rel) manna; (fig) godsend

**mannequin** [mankɛ̃] nm (Couture) dummy; (Mode) model

**manœuvrable** [manœvʀabl(ə)] adj (bateau, véhicule) manoeuvrable (Brit), maneuverable (US)

**manœuvre** [manœvʀ(ə)] nf (gén) manoeuvre (Brit), maneuver (US) ▷ nm (ouvrier) labourer (Brit), laborer (US)

**manœuvrer** [manœvʀe] vt to manoeuvre (Brit), maneuver (US); (levier, machine) to operate; (personne) to manipulate ▷ vi to manoeuvre ou maneuver

**manoir** [manwaʀ] nm manor ou country house

**manomètre** [manɔmɛtʀ(ə)] nm gauge, manometer

**manquant, e** [mɑ̃kɑ̃, -ɑ̃t] adj missing

**manque** [mɑ̃k] nm (insuffisance): ~ **de** lack of; (vide) emptiness, gap; (Méd) withdrawal; **manques** nmpl (lacunes) faults, defects; **par ~ de** for want of; ~ **à gagner** loss of profit ou earnings

**manqué** [mɑ̃ke] adj failed; **garçon ~** tomboy

**manquement** [mɑ̃kmɑ̃] nm: ~ **à** (discipline, règle) breach of

**manquer** [mɑ̃ke] vi (faire défaut) to be lacking; (être absent) to be missing; (échouer) to fail ▷ vt to miss ▷ vb impers: **il (nous) manque encore 10 euros** we are still 10 euros short; **il manque des pages (au livre)** there are some pages missing ou some pages are missing (from the book); **l'argent qui leur manque** the money they need ou are short of; **le pied/la voix lui manqua** he missed his footing/his voice failed him; ~ **à qn** (absent etc): **il/cela me manque** I miss him/that; ~ **à** vt (règles etc) to be in breach of, fail to observe; ~ **de** vt to lack; (Comm) to be out of (stock of); **ne pas ~ de faire: il n'a pas manqué de le dire** he certainly said it; ~ **(de) faire: il a manqué (de) se tuer** he very nearly got killed; **il ne manquerait plus qu'il fasse** all we need now is for him to do it; **je n'y manquerai pas** leave it to me, I'll definitely do it

**mansarde** [mɑ̃saʀd(ə)] nf attic

**mansardé, e** [mɑ̃saʀde] adj attic cpd

**mansuétude** [mɑ̃sɥetyd] nf leniency

**mante** [mɑ̃t] nf: ~ **religieuse** praying mantis

**manteau, x** [mɑ̃to] nm coat; ~ **de cheminée** mantelpiece; **sous le ~** (fig) under cover

**mantille** [mɑ̃tij] nf mantilla

**manucure** [manykyʀ] nf manicurist

**manuel, le** [manɥɛl] adj manual ▷ nm/f manually gifted pupil (as opposed to intellectually gifted) ▷ nm (ouvrage) manual, handbook

**manuellement** [manɥɛlmɑ̃] adv manually

**manufacture** [manyfaktyʀ] nf (établissement) factory; (fabrication) manufacture

**manufacturé, e** [manyfaktyʀe] adj manufactured

**m**

**manufacturier, -ière** [manyfaktyʀje, -jɛʀ] *nm/f* factory owner

**manuscrit, e** [manyskʀi, -it] *adj* handwritten ▷ *nm* manuscript

**manutention** [manytɑ̃sjɔ̃] *nf* (*Comm*) handling; (*local*) storehouse

**manutentionnaire** [manytɑ̃sjɔnɛʀ] *nm/f* warehouseman(-woman), packer

**manutentionner** [manytɑ̃sjɔne] *vt* to handle

**mappemonde** [mapmɔ̃d] *nf* (*plane*) map of the world; (*sphère*) globe

**maquereau, x** [makʀo] *nm* mackerel *inv*; (*fam: proxénète*) pimp

**maquerelle** [makʀɛl] *nf* (*fam*) madam

**maquette** [makɛt] *nf* (*d'un décor, bâtiment, véhicule*) (scale) model; (*Typo*) mockup; (: *d'une page illustrée, affiche*) paste-up; (: *prêt à la reproduction*) artwork

**maquignon** [makiɲɔ̃] *nm* horse-dealer

**maquillage** [makijaʒ] *nm* making up; faking; (*produits*) make-up

**maquiller** [makije] *vt* (*personne, visage*) to make up; (*truquer: passeport, statistique*) to fake; (: *voiture volée*) to do over (*respray etc*); **se maquiller** to make o.s. up

**maquilleur, -euse** [makijœʀ, -øz] *nm/f* make-up artist

**maquis** [maki] *nm* (*Géo*) scrub; (*fig*) tangle; (*Mil*) maquis, underground fighting *no pl*

**maquisard, e** [makizaʀ, -aʀd(ə)] *nm/f* maquis, member of the Resistance

**marabout** [maʀabu] *nm* (*Zool*) marabou(t)

**maraîcher, -ère** [maʀeʃe, maʀɛʃɛʀ] *adj*: **cultures maraîchères** market gardening *sg* ▷ *nm/f* market gardener

**marais** [maʀɛ] *nm* marsh, swamp; **~ salant** saltworks

**marasme** [maʀasm(ə)] *nm* (*Pol, Écon*) stagnation, sluggishness; (*accablement*) dejection, depression

**marathon** [maʀatɔ̃] *nm* marathon

**marâtre** [maʀɑtʀ(ə)] *nf* cruel mother

**maraude** [maʀod] *nf* pilfering, thieving (*of poultry, crops*); (*dans un verger*) scrumping; (*vagabondage*) prowling; **en ~** on the prowl; (*taxi*) cruising

**maraudeur, -euse** [maʀodœʀ, -øz] *nm/f* marauder; prowler

**marbre** [maʀbʀ(ə)] *nm* (*pierre, statue*) marble; (*d'une table, commode*) marble top; (*Typo*) stone, bed; **rester de ~** to remain stonily indifferent

**marbrer** [maʀbʀe] *vt* to mottle, blotch; (*Tech: papier*) to marble

**marbrerie** [maʀbʀaʀi] *nf* (*atelier*) marble mason's workshop; (*industrie*) marble industry

**marbrures** [maʀbʀyʀ] *nfpl* blotches *pl*; (*Tech*) marbling *sg*

**marc** [maʀ] *nm* (*de raisin, pommes*) marc; **~ de café** coffee grounds *pl ou* dregs *pl*

**marcassin** [maʀkasɛ̃] *nm* young wild boar

**marchand, e** [maʀʃɑ̃, -ɑ̃d] *nm/f* shopkeeper, tradesman(-woman); (*au marché*) stallholder;

(*spécifique*): **~ de cycles/tapis** bicycle/carpet dealer; **~ de charbon/vins** coal/wine merchant ▷ *adj*: **prix/valeur ~(e)** market price/value; **qualité ~e** standard quality; **~ en gros/au détail** wholesaler/retailer; **~ de biens** real estate agent; **~ de canons** (*péj*) arms dealer; **~ de couleurs** ironmonger (*Brit*), hardware dealer (*US*); **~/e de fruits** fruiterer (*Brit*), fruit seller (*US*); **~/e de journaux** newsagent; **~/e de légumes** greengrocer (*Brit*), produce dealer (*US*); **~/e de poisson** fishmonger (*Brit*), fish seller (*US*); **~/e de(s) quatre-saisons** costermonger (*Brit*), street vendor (selling fresh fruit and vegetables); **~ de sable** (*fig*) sandman; **~ de tableaux** art dealer

**marchandage** [maʀʃɑ̃daʒ] *nm* bargaining; (*péj: électoral*) bargaining, manoeuvring

**marchander** [maʀʃɑ̃de] *vt* (*article*) to bargain *ou* haggle over; (*éloges*) to be sparing with ▷ *vi* to bargain, haggle

**marchandisage** [maʀʃɑ̃dizaʒ] *nm* merchandizing

**marchandise** [maʀʃɑ̃diz] *nf* goods *pl*, merchandise *no pl*

**marche** [maʀʃ(ə)] *nf* (*d'escalier*) step; (*activité*) walking; (*promenade, trajet, allure*) walk; (*démarche*) walk, gait; (*Mil etc, Mus*) march; (*fonctionnement*) running; (*progression*) progress; course; **à une heure de ~** an hour's walk (away); **ouvrir/fermer la ~** to lead the way/ bring up the rear; **dans le sens de la ~** (*Rail*) facing the engine; **en ~** (*monter etc*) while the vehicle is moving *ou* in motion; **mettre en ~** to start; **remettre qch en ~** to set *ou* start sth going again; **se mettre en ~** (*personne*) to get moving; (*machine*) to start; **~ arrière** (*Auto*) reverse (gear); **faire ~ arrière** (*Auto*) to reverse; (*fig*) to backtrack, back-pedal; **~ à suivre** (correct) procedure; (*sur notice*) (step by step) instructions *pl*

**marché** [maʀʃe] *nm* (*lieu, Comm, Écon*) market; (*ville*) trading centre; (*transaction*) bargain, deal; **par-dessus le ~** into the bargain; **faire son ~** to do one's shopping; **mettre le ~ en main à qn** to tell sb to take it or leave it; **~ au comptant** (*Bourse*) spot market; **~ aux fleurs** flower market; **~ noir** black market; **faire du ~ noir** to buy and sell on the black market; **~ aux puces** flea market; **~ à terme** (*Bourse*) forward market; **~ du travail** labour market

**marchepied** [maʀʃəpje] *nm* (*Rail*) step; (*Auto*) running board; (*fig*) stepping stone

**marcher** [maʀʃe] *vi* to walk; (*Mil*) to march; (*aller: voiture, train, affaires*) to go; (*prospérer*) to go well; (*fonctionner*) to work, run; (*fam*) to go along, agree; (: *croire naïvement*) to be taken in; **~ sur** to walk on; (*mettre le pied sur*) to step on *ou* in; (*Mil*) to march upon; **~ dans** (*herbe etc*) to walk in *ou* on; (*flaque*) to step in; **faire ~ qn** (*pour rire*) to pull sb's leg; (*pour tromper*) to lead sb up the garden path

**marcheur, -euse** [maʀʃœʀ, -øz] *nm/f* walker

**mardi** [maʀdi] *nm* Tuesday; **M~ gras** Shrove Tuesday; *voir aussi* **lundi**

**mare** [maʀ] *nf* pond; **~ de sang** pool of blood

**marécage** [maʀekaʒ] *nm* marsh, swamp

**marécageux, -euse** [maʀekaʒø, -øz] *adj* marshy, swampy

**maréchal, -aux** [maʀeʃal, -o] *nm* marshal; **~ des logis** (*Mil*) sergeant

**maréchal-ferrant** [maʀeʃalfɛʀɑ̃, maʀeʃo-] (*pl* **maréchaux-ferrants**) *nm* blacksmith

**maréchaussée** [maʀeʃose] *nf* (*humoristique*: *gendarmes*) constabulary (*Brit*), police

**marée** [maʀe] *nf* tide; (*poissons*) fresh (sea) fish; **~ haute/basse** high/low tide; **~ montante/descendante** rising/ebb tide; **~ noire** oil slick

**marelle** [maʀɛl] *nf*: (**jouer à**) **la ~** (to play) hopscotch

**marémotrice** [maʀemɔtʀis] *adj f* tidal

**mareyeur, -euse** [maʀejœʀ, -øz] *nm/f* wholesale (sea) fish merchant

**margarine** [maʀgaʀin] *nf* margarine

**marge** [maʀʒ(ə)] *nf* margin; **en ~** in the margin; **en ~ de** (*fig*) on the fringe of; (*en dehors de*) cut off from; (*qui se rapporte à*) connected with; **~ bénéficiaire** profit margin, mark-up; **~ de sécurité** safety margin

**margelle** [maʀʒɛl] *nf* coping

**margeur** [maʀʒœʀ] *nm* margin stop

**marginal, e, -aux** [maʀʒinal, -o] *adj* marginal ▷ *nm/f* dropout

**marguerite** [maʀgəʀit] *nf* marguerite, (oxeye) daisy

**marguillier** [maʀgije] *nm* churchwarden

**mari** [maʀi] *nm* husband

**mariage** [maʀjaʒ] *nm* (*union, état, fig*) marriage; (*noce*) wedding; **~ civil/religieux** registry office (*Brit*) *ou* civil/church wedding; **un ~ de raison/d'amour** a marriage of convenience/a love match; **~ blanc** unconsummated marriage; **~ en blanc** white wedding

**marié, e** [maʀje] *adj* married ▷ *nm/f* (bride)groom/bride; **les ~s** the bride and groom; **les (jeunes) ~s** the newly-weds

**marier** [maʀje] *vt* to marry; (*fig*) to blend; **se ~ (avec)** to marry, get married (to); (*fig*) to blend (with)

**marijuana** [maʀiʒwana] *nf* marijuana

**marin, e** [maʀɛ̃, -in] *adj* sea *cpd*, marine ▷ *nm* sailor ▷ *nf* navy; (*Art*) seascape; (*couleur*) navy (blue); **avoir le pied ~** to be a good sailor; (*garder son équilibre*) to have one's sea legs; **~e de guerre** navy; **~e marchande** merchant navy; **~e à voiles** sailing ships *pl*

**marina** [maʀina] *nf* marina

**marinade** [maʀinad] *nf* marinade

**marine** [maʀin] *adj f, nf voir* **marin** ▷ *adj inv* navy (blue) ▷ *nm* (*Mil*) marine

**mariner** [maʀine] *vi, vt* to marinate, marinade

**marinier** [maʀinje] *nm* bargee

**marinière** [maʀinjɛʀ] *nf* (*blouse*) smock ▷ *adj inv*: **moules ~** (*Culin*) mussels in white wine

**marionnette** [maʀjɔnɛt] *nf* puppet

**marital, e, -aux** [maʀital, -o] *adj*: **autorisation ~e** husband's permission

**maritalement** [maʀitalmɑ̃] *adv*: **vivre ~** to live together (as husband and wife)

**maritime** [maʀitim] *adj* sea *cpd*, maritime; (*ville*) coastal, seaside; (*droit*) shipping, maritime

**marjolaine** [maʀʒɔlɛn] *nf* marjoram

**marketing** [maʀkətiŋ] *nm* (*Comm*) marketing

**marmaille** [maʀmaj] *nf* (*péj*) (gang of) brats *pl*

**marmelade** [maʀməlad] *nf* (*compote*) stewed fruit, compote; **~ d'oranges** (orange) marmalade; **en ~** (*fig*) crushed (to a pulp)

**marmite** [maʀmit] *nf* (cooking-)pot

**marmiton** [maʀmitɔ̃] *nm* kitchen boy

**marmonner** [maʀmɔne] *vt, vi* to mumble, mutter

**marmot** [maʀmo] *nm* (*fam*) brat

**marmotte** [maʀmɔt] *nf* marmot

**marmotter** [maʀmɔte] *vt* (*prière*) to mumble, mutter

**marne** [maʀn(ə)] *nf* (*Géo*) marl

**Maroc** [maʀɔk] *nm*: **le ~** Morocco

**marocain, e** [maʀɔkɛ̃, -ɛn] *adj* Moroccan ▷ *nm/f*: **Marocain, e** Moroccan

**maroquin** [maʀɔkɛ̃] *nm* (*peau*) morocco (leather); (*fig*) (minister's) portfolio

**maroquinerie** [maʀɔkinʀi] *nf* (*industrie*) leather craft; (*commerce*) leather shop; (*articles*) fine leather goods *pl*

**maroquinier** [maʀɔkinje] *nm* (*fabricant*) leather craftsman; (*marchand*) leather dealer

**marotte** [maʀɔt] *nf* fad

**marquant, e** [maʀkɑ̃, -ɑ̃t] *adj* outstanding

**marque** [maʀk(ə)] *nf* mark; (*Sport, Jeu*) score; (*Comm*: *de produits*) brand, make; (: *de disques*) label; (*insigne*: *d'une fonction*) badge; (*fig*): **~ d'affection** token of affection; **~ de joie** sign of joy; **à vos ~s!** (*Sport*) on your marks!; **de ~** *adj* (*Comm*) brand-name *cpd*; proprietary; (*fig*) high-class; (: *personnage, hôte*) distinguished; **produit de ~** quality product; **~ déposée** registered trademark; **~ de fabrique** trademark

**marqué, e** [maʀke] *adj* marked

**marquer** [maʀke] *vt* to mark; (*inscrire*) to write down; (*bétail*) to brand; (*Sport*: *but etc*) to score; (: *joueur*) to mark; (*accentuer*: *taille etc*) to emphasize; (*manifester*: *refus, intérêt*) to show ▷ *vi* (*événement, personnalité*) to stand out, be outstanding; (*Sport*) to score; **~ qn de son influence/empreinte** to have an influence/leave its impression on sb; **~ un temps d'arrêt** to pause momentarily; **~ le pas** (*fig*) to mark time; **il a marqué ce jour-là d'une pierre blanche** that was a red-letter day for him; **~ les points** (*tenir la marque*) to keep the score

**marqueté, e** [maʀkəte] *adj* inlaid

**marqueterie** [maʀkətʀi] *nf* inlaid work, marquetry

**marqueur, -euse** [maʀkœʀ, -øz] *nm/f* (*Sport*: *de but*) scorer ▷ *nm* (*crayon feutre*) marker pen

**marquis, e** [maʀki, -iz] *nm/f* marquis *ou* marquess (marchioness) ▷ *nf* (*auvent*) glass

**m**

canopy *ou* awning

**Marquises** [maʀkiz] *nfpl*: **les (îles)** ~ the Marquesas Islands

**marraine** [maʀɛn] *nf* godmother; *(d'un navire, d'une rose etc)* namer

**Marrakech** [maʀakɛʃ] *n* Marrakech *ou* Marrakesh

**marrant, e** [maʀɑ̃, -ɑ̃t] *adj (fam)* funny

**marre** [maʀ] *adv (fam)*: **en avoir ~ de** to be fed up with

**marrer** [maʀe]: **se marrer** *vi (fam)* to have a (good) laugh

**marron, ne** [maʀɔ̃, -ɔn] *nm (fruit)* chestnut ▷ *adj inv* brown ▷ *adj (péj)* crooked; *(: faux)* bogus; **~s glacés** marrons glacés

**marronnier** [maʀɔnje] *nm* chestnut (tree)

**Mars** [maʀs] *nm ou f* Mars

**mars** [maʀs] *nm* March; *voir aussi* **juillet**

**marseillais, e** [maʀsɛjɛ, -ɛz] *adj* of *ou* from Marseilles ▷ *nf*: **la M~e** *the French national anthem; see note*

**Marseille** [maʀsɛj] *n* Marseilles

**marsouin** [maʀswɛ̃] *nm* porpoise

**marsupiaux** [maʀsypjo] *nmpl* marsupials

**marteau, x** [maʀto] *nm* hammer; *(de porte)* knocker; **~ pneumatique** pneumatic drill

**marteau-pilon** [maʀtopilɔ̃] *(pl* **marteaux-pilons)** *nm* power hammer

**marteau-piqueur** [maʀtopikœʀ] *(pl* **marteaux-piqueurs)** *nm* pneumatic drill

**martel** [maʀtɛl] *nm*: **se mettre ~ en tête** to worry o.s.

**martèlement** [maʀtɛlmɑ̃] *nm* hammering

**marteler** [maʀtəle] *vt* to hammer; *(mots, phrases)* to rap out

**martial, e, -aux** [maʀsjal, -o] *adj* martial; **cour ~e** court-martial

**martien, ne** [maʀsjɛ̃, -ɛn] *adj* Martian, of *ou* from Mars

**martinet** [maʀtinɛ] *nm (fouet)* small whip; *(Zool)* swift

**martingale** [maʀtɛ̃gal] *nf (Couture)* half-belt; *(Jeu)* winning formula

**martiniquais, e** [maʀtinikɛ, -ɛz] *adj* of *ou* from Martinique

**Martinique** [maʀtinik] *nf*: **la ~** Martinique

**martin-pêcheur** *(pl* **martins-pêcheurs)** [maʀtɛ̃pɛʃœʀ] *nm* kingfisher

**martre** [maʀtʀ(ə)] *nf* marten; **~ zibeline** sable

**martyr, e** [maʀtiʀ] *nm/f* martyr ▷ *adj* martyred;

**enfants ~s** battered children

**martyre** [maʀtiʀ] *nm* martyrdom; *(fig: sens affaibli)* agony, torture; **souffrir le ~** to suffer agonies

**martyriser** [maʀtiʀize] *vt (Rel)* to martyr; *(fig)* to bully; *(: enfant)* to batter

**mas** [ma(s)] *nm* traditional house or farm in Provence

**mascara** [maskaʀa] *nm* mascara

**mascarade** [maskaʀad] *nf* masquerade

**mascotte** [maskɔt] *nf* mascot

**masculin, e** [maskylɛ̃, -in] *adj* masculine; *(sexe, population)* male; *(équipe, vêtements)* men's; *(viril)* manly ▷ *nm* masculine

**masochisme** [mazɔʃism(ə)] *nm* masochism

**masochiste** [mazɔʃist(ə)] *adj* masochistic ▷ *nm/f* masochist

**masque** [mask(ə)] *nm* mask; **~ de beauté** face pack; **~ à gaz** gas mask; **~ de plongée** diving mask

**masqué, e** [maske] *adj* masked

**masquer** [maske] *vt (cacher: porte, goût)* to hide, conceal; *(dissimuler: vérité, projet)* to mask, obscure

**massacrant, e** [masakʀɑ̃, -ɑ̃t] *adj*: **humeur ~e** foul temper

**massacre** [masakʀ(ə)] *nm* massacre, slaughter; **jeu de ~** *(fig)* wholesale slaughter

**massacrer** [masakʀe] *vt* to massacre, slaughter; *(fig: adversaire)* to slaughter; *(: texte etc)* to murder

**massage** [masaʒ] *nm* massage

**masse** [mas] *nf* mass; *(péj)*: **la ~** the masses *pl*; *(Élec)* earth; *(maillet)* sledgehammer; **masses** *nfpl* masses; **une ~ de, des ~s de** *(fam)* masses *ou* loads of; **en ~** *adv (en bloc)* in bulk; *(en foule)* en masse ▷ *adj (exécutions, production)* mass *cpd*; **~ monétaire** *(Écon)* money supply; **~ salariale** *(Comm)* wage(s) bill

**massepain** [maspɛ̃] *nm* marzipan

**masser** [mase] *vt (assembler)* to gather; *(pétrir)* to massage; **se masser** *vi* to gather

**masseur, -euse** [masœʀ, -øz] *nm/f (personne)* masseur(-euse) ▷ *nm (appareil)* massager

**massicot** [masiko] *nm (Typo)* guillotine

**massif, -ive** [masif, -iv] *adj (porte)* solid, massive; *(visage)* heavy, large; *(bois, or)* solid; *(dose)* massive; *(déportations etc)* mass *cpd* ▷ *nm (montagneux)* massif; *(de fleurs)* clump, bank

**massivement** [masivmɑ̃] *adv (répondre)* en masse; *(administrer, injecter)* in massive doses

**massue** [masy] *nf* club, bludgeon ▷ *adj inv*: **argument ~** sledgehammer argument

**mastectomie** [mastɛktɔmi] *nf* mastectomy

**mastic** [mastik] *nm (pour vitres)* putty; *(pour fentes)* filler

**masticage** [mastikaʒ] *nm (d'une fente)* filling; *(d'une vitre)* puttying

**mastication** [mastikɑsjɔ̃] *nf* chewing, mastication

**mastiquer** [mastike] *vt (aliment)* to chew, masticate; *(fente)* to fill; *(vitre)* to putty

**mastoc** [mastɔk] *adj inv* hefty

**mastodonte** [mastɔdɔ̃t] *nm* monster *(fig)*

**masturbation** [mastyʀbɑsjɔ̃] *nf* masturbation
**masturber** [mastyʀbe] *vt:* **se masturber** to masturbate
**m'as-tu-vu** [matyvy] *nm/f inv* show-off
**masure** [mazyʀ] *nf* tumbledown cottage
**mat, e** [mat] *adj (couleur, métal)* mat(t); *(bruit, son)* dull ▷ *adj inv (Échecs):* **être ~** to be checkmate
**mât** [mɑ] *nm (Navig)* mast; *(poteau)* pole, post
**matamore** [matamɔʀ] *nm* braggart, blusterer
**match** [matʃ] *nm* match; **~ nul** draw, tie *(US)*; **faire ~ nul** to draw *(Brit)*, tie *(US)*; **~ aller** first leg; **~ retour** second leg, return match
**matelas** [matla] *nm* mattress; **~ pneumatique** air bed *ou* mattress; **~ à ressorts** spring *ou* interior-sprung mattress
**matelassé, e** [matlase] *adj* padded; *(tissu)* quilted
**matelasser** [matlase] *vt* to pad
**matelot** [matlo] *nm* sailor, seaman
**mater** [mate] *vt (personne)* to bring to heel, subdue; *(révolte)* to put down; *(fam)* to watch, look at
**matérialisation** [mateʀjalizɑsjɔ̃] *nf* materialization
**matérialiser** [mateʀjalize] *vt:* **se matérialiser** *vi* to materialize
**matérialisme** [mateʀjalism(ə)] *nm* materialism
**matérialiste** [mateʀjalist(ə)] *adj* materialistic ▷ *nm/f* materialist
**matériau, x** [mateʀjo] *nm* material; **matériaux** *nmpl* material(s); **~x de construction** building materials
**matériel, le** [mateʀjɛl] *adj* material; *(organisation, aide, obstacle)* practical; *(fig: péj: personne)* materialistic ▷ *nm* equipment *no pl*; *(de camping etc)* gear *no pl*; *(Inform)* hardware; **il n'a pas le temps ~ de le faire** he doesn't have the time (needed) to do it; **~ d'exploitation** *(Comm)* plant; **~ roulant** rolling stock
**matériellement** [mateʀjɛlmɑ̃] *adv (financièrement)* materially; **~ à l'aise** comfortably off; **je n'en ai ~ pas le temps** I simply do not have the time
**maternel, le** [matɛʀnɛl] *adj (amour, geste)* motherly, maternal; *(grand-père, oncle)* maternal ▷ *nf (aussi:* **école maternelle)** (state) nursery school
**materner** [matɛʀne] *vt (personne)* to mother
**maternisé, e** [matɛʀnize] *adj:* **lait ~** (infant) formula
**maternité** [matɛʀnite] *nf (établissement)* maternity hospital; *(état de mère)* motherhood, maternity; *(grossesse)* pregnancy
**math** [mat] *nfpl* maths *(Brit)*, math *(US)*
**mathématicien, ne** [matematisjɛ̃, -ɛn] *nm/f* mathematician
**mathématique** [matematik] *adj* mathematical
**mathématiques** [matematik] *nfpl* mathematics *sg*
**matheux, -euse** [matø, -øz] *nm/f (fam)* maths *(Brit) ou* math *(US)* student; *(fort en math)* mathematical genius

**maths** [mat] *nfpl* maths *(Brit)*, math *(US)*
**matière** [matjɛʀ] *nf (Physique)* matter; *(Comm, Tech)* material; matter *no pl*; *(fig: d'un livre etc)* subject matter; *(Scol)* subject; **en ~ de** as regards; **donner ~ à** to give cause to; **~ plastique** plastic; **~s fécales** faeces; **~s grasses** fat (content) *sg*; **~s premières** raw materials
**MATIF** [matif] *sigle m (= Marché à terme des instruments financiers) body which regulates the activities of the French Stock Exchange*
**Matignon** [matiɲɔ̃] *nm:* **(l'hôtel) ~** the French Prime Minister's residence; *see note*

⊚ **HÔTEL MATIGNON**
⊚
⊚ The *hôtel Matignon* is the Paris office and
⊚ residence of the French Prime Minister. By
⊚ extension, the term "Matignon" is often
⊚ used to refer to the Prime Minister and his
⊚ or her staff.

**matin** [matɛ̃] *nm, adv* morning; **le ~** *(pendant le matin)* in the morning; **demain ~** tomorrow morning; **le lendemain ~** (the) next morning; **du ~ au soir** from morning till night; **une heure du ~** one o'clock in the morning; **de grand** *ou* **bon ~** early in the morning
**matinal, e, -aux** [matinal, -o] *adj (toilette, gymnastique)* morning *cpd; (de bonne heure)* early; **être ~** *(personne)* to be up early; *(: habituellement)* to be an early riser
**matinée** [matine] *nf* morning; *(spectacle)* matinée, afternoon performance
**matois, e** [matwa, -waz] *adj* wily
**matou** [matu] *nm* tom(cat)
**matraquage** [matʀakaʒ] *nm* beating up; **~ publicitaire** plug, plugging
**matraque** [matʀak] *nf (de malfaiteur)* cosh *(Brit)*, club; *(de policier)* truncheon *(Brit)*, billy *(US)*
**matraquer** [matʀake] *vt* to beat up (with a truncheon *ou* billy); to cosh *(Brit)*, club; *(fig: touristes etc)* to rip off; *(: disque)* to plug
**matriarcal, e, -aux** [matʀijaʀkal, -o] *adj* matriarchal
**matrice** [matʀis] *nf (Anat)* womb; *(Tech)* mould; *(Math etc)* matrix
**matricule** [matʀikyl] *nf (aussi:* **registre matricule)** roll, register ▷ *nm (aussi:* **numéro matricule:** *Mil)* regimental number; *(: Admin)* reference number
**matrimonial, e, -aux** [matʀimɔnjal, -o] *adj* marital, marriage *cpd*
**matrone** [matʀɔn] *nf* matron
**mâture** [mɑtyʀ] *nf* masts *pl*
**maturité** [matyʀite] *nf* maturity; *(d'un fruit)* ripeness, maturity
**maudire** [modiʀ] *vt* to curse
**maudit, e** [modi, -it] *adj (fam: satané)* blasted, confounded
**maugréer** [mogʀee] *vi* to grumble
**mauresque** [mɔʀɛsk(ə)] *adj* Moorish
**Maurice** [mɔʀis] *nf:* **(l'île) ~** Mauritius

**m**

**mauricien, ne** [mɔʀisjɛ̃, -ɛn] adj Mauritian
**Mauritanie** [mɔʀitani] nf: **la ~** Mauritania
**mauritanien, ne** [mɔʀitanjɛ̃, -ɛn] adj
Mauritanian
**mausolée** [mozɔle] nm mausoleum
**maussade** [mosad] adj (air, personne) sullen; (ciel,
temps) dismal
**mauvais, e** [mɔvɛ, -ɛz] adj bad; (méchant,
malveillant) malicious, spiteful; (faux): **le ~
numéro** the wrong number ▷ nm: **le ~** the bad
side ▷ adv: **il fait ~** the weather is bad; **sentir ~**
to have a nasty smell, smell bad ou nasty; **la
mer est ~e** the sea is rough; **~ coucheur**
awkward customer; **~ coup** (fig) criminal
venture; **~ garçon** tough; **~ pas** tight spot; **~
plaisant** hoaxer; **~ traitements** ill treatment
sg; **~e herbe** weed; **~e langue** gossip,
scandalmonger (Brit); **~e passe** difficult
situation; (période) bad patch; **~e tête** rebellious
ou headstrong customer
**mauve** [mov] adj (couleur) mauve ▷ nf (Bot)
mallow
**mauviette** [movjɛt] nf (péj) weakling
**maux** [mo] nmpl voir **mal**
**max.** abr (= maximum) max
**maximal, e, -aux** [maksimal, -o] adj maximal
**maxime** [maksim] nf maxim
**maximum** [maksimɔm] adj, nm maximum;
**atteindre un/son ~** to reach a/his peak; **au ~**
adv (le plus possible) to the full; as much as one
can; (tout au plus) at the (very) most ou maximum
**Mayence** [majãs] n Mainz
**mayonnaise** [majɔnɛz] nf mayonnaise
**Mayotte** [majɔt] nf Mayotte
**mazout** [mazut] nm (fuel) oil; **chaudière/
poêle à ~** oil-fired boiler/stove
**mazouté, e** [mazute] adj oil-polluted
**MDM** sigle mpl (= Médecins du Monde) medical
association for aid to Third World countries
**Mᵉ** abr = **Maître**
**me, m'** [m(ə)] pron me; (réfléchi) myself
**méandres** [meãdʀ(ə)] nmpl meanderings
**mec** [mɛk] nm (fam) guy, bloke (Brit)
**mécanicien, ne** [mekanisjɛ̃, -ɛn] nm/f
mechanic; (Rail) (train ou engine) driver; **~
navigant** ou **de bord** (Aviat) flight engineer
**mécanique** [mekanik] adj mechanical ▷ nf
(science) mechanics sg; (technologie) mechanical
engineering; (mécanisme) mechanism;
engineering; works pl; **ennui ~** engine trouble
no pl; **s'y connaître en ~** to be mechanically
minded; **~ hydraulique** hydraulics sg; **~
ondulatoire** wave mechanics sg
**mécaniquement** [mekanikmã] adv
mechanically
**mécanisation** [mekanizɑsjɔ̃] nf mechanization
**mécaniser** [mekanize] vt to mechanize
**mécanisme** [mekanism(ə)] nm mechanism; **~
des taux de change** exchange rate mechanism
**mécano** [mekano] nm (fam) mechanic
**mécène** [mesɛn] nm patron
**méchamment** [meʃamã] adv nastily,

maliciously; spitefully; viciously
**méchanceté** [meʃãste] nf (d'une personne, d'une
parole) nastiness, maliciousness, spitefulness;
(parole, action) nasty ou spiteful ou malicious
remark (ou action)
**méchant, e** [meʃã, -ãt] adj nasty, malicious,
spiteful; (enfant: pas sage) naughty; (animal)
vicious; (avant le nom: péjorative) nasty
**mèche** [mɛʃ] nf (de lampe, bougie) wick; (d'un
explosif) fuse; (Méd) pack, dressing; (de vilebrequin,
perceuse) bit; (de dentiste) drill; (de fouet) lash; (de
cheveux) lock; **se faire faire des ~s** (chez le coiffeur)
to have one's hair streaked, have highlights
put in one's hair; **vendre la ~** to give the game
away; **de ~ avec** in league with
**méchoui** [meʃwi] nm whole sheep barbecue
**mécompte** [mekɔ̃t] nm (erreur) miscalculation;
(déception) disappointment
**méconnais** etc [mekɔnɛ] vb voir **méconnaître**
**méconnaissable** [mekɔnɛsabl(ə)] adj
unrecognizable
**méconnaissais** etc [mekɔnɛsɛ] vb voir
**méconnaître**
**méconnaissance** [mekɔnɛsãs] nf ignorance
**méconnaître** [mekɔnɛtʀ(ə)] vt (ignorer) to be
unaware of; (mésestimer) to misjudge
**méconnu, e** [mekɔny] pp de **méconnaître** ▷ adj
(génie etc) unrecognized
**mécontent, e** [mekɔ̃tã, -ãt] adj: **~ (de)**
(insatisfait) discontented ou dissatisfied ou
displeased (with); (contrarié) annoyed (at) ▷ nm/f
malcontent, dissatisfied person
**mécontentement** [mekɔ̃tãtmã] nm
dissatisfaction, discontent, displeasure;
annoyance
**mécontenter** [mekɔ̃tãte] vt to displease
**Mecque** [mɛk] nf: **la ~** Mecca
**mécréant, e** [mekʀeã, -ãt] adj (peuple) infidel;
(personne) atheistic
**méd.** abr = **médecin**
**médaille** [medaj] nf medal
**médaillé, e** [medaje] nm/f (Sport) medal-holder
**médaillon** [medajɔ̃] nm (portrait) medallion;
(bijou) locket; (Culin) médaillon; **en ~** adj (carte
etc) inset
**médecin** [medsɛ̃] nm doctor; **~ du bord** (Navig)
ship's doctor; **~ généraliste** general
practitioner, GP; **~ légiste** forensic scientist
(Brit), medical examiner (US); **~ traitant** family
doctor, GP
**médecine** [medsin] nf medicine; **~ générale**
general medicine; **~ infantile** paediatrics sg
(Brit), pediatrics sg (US); **~ légale** forensic
medicine; **~ préventive** preventive medicine;
**~ du travail** occupational ou industrial
medicine; **~s parallèles** ou **douces** alternative
medicine
**MEDEF** [medɛf] sigle m (= Mouvement des entreprises
de France) French employers' confederation
**médian, e** [medjã, -an] adj median
**médias** [medja] nmpl: **les ~** the media
**médiateur, -trice** [medjatœʀ, -tʀis] nm/f voir

**médiation** mediator; arbitrator

**médiathèque** [medjatɛk] *nf* media library

**médiation** [medjɑsjɔ̃] *nf* mediation; (*dans conflit social etc*) arbitration

**médiatique** [medjatik] *adj* media *cpd*

**médiatisé, e** [medjatize] *adj* reported in the media; **ce procès a été très ~** (*péj*) this trial was turned into a media event

**médiator** [medjatɔʀ] *nm* plectrum

**médical, e, -aux** [medikal, -o] *adj* medical; **visiteur** *ou* **délégué ~** medical rep *ou* representative

**médicalement** [medikalmɑ̃] *adv* medically

**médicament** [medikamɑ̃] *nm* medicine, drug

**médicamenteux, -euse** [medikamɑ̃tø, -øz] *adj* medicinal

**médication** [medikɑsjɔ̃] *nf* medication

**médicinal, e, -aux** [medisinal, -o] *adj* medicinal

**médico-légal, e, -aux** [medikɔlegal, -o] *adj* forensic

**médico-social, e, -aux** [medikɔsɔsjal, -o] *adj*: **assistance ~e** medical and social assistance

**médiéval, e, -aux** [medjeval, -o] *adj* medieval

**médiocre** [medjɔkʀ(ə)] *adj* mediocre, poor

**médiocrité** [medjɔkʀite] *nf* mediocrity

**médire** [mediʀ] *vi*: **~ de** to speak ill of

**médisance** [medizɑ̃s] *nf* scandalmongering *no pl* (Brit), mud-slinging *no pl*; (*propos*) piece of scandal *ou* malicious gossip

**médisant, e** [medizɑ̃, -ɑ̃t] *vb voir* **médire** ▷ *adj* slanderous, malicious

**médit, e** [medi, -it] *pp de* **médire**

**méditatif, -ive** [meditatif, -iv] *adj* thoughtful

**méditation** [meditɑsjɔ̃] *nf* meditation

**méditer** [medite] *vt* (*approfondir*) to meditate on, ponder (over); (*combiner*) to meditate ▷ *vi* to meditate; **~ de faire** to contemplate doing, plan to do

**Méditerranée** [mediteʀane] *nf*: **la (mer) ~** the Mediterranean (Sea)

**méditerranéen, ne** [mediteʀaneɛ̃, -ɛn] *adj* Mediterranean ▷ *nm/f*: **Méditerranéen, ne** Mediterranean

**médium** [medjɔm] *nm* medium (*spiritualist*)

**médius** [medjys] *nm* middle finger

**méduse** [medyz] *nf* jellyfish

**méduser** [medyze] *vt* to dumbfound

**meeting** [mitiŋ] *nm* (Pol, Sport) rally, meeting; **~ d'aviation** air show

**méfait** [mefɛ] *nm* (*faute*) misdemeanour, wrongdoing; **méfaits** *nmpl* (*ravages*) ravages

**méfiance** [mefjɑ̃s] *nf* mistrust, distrust

**méfiant, e** [mefjɑ̃, -ɑ̃t] *adj* mistrustful, distrustful

**méfier** [mefje]: **se méfier** *vi* to be wary; (*faire attention*) to be careful; **se ~ de** *vt* to mistrust, distrust, be wary of; to be careful about

**mégalomane** [megalɔman] *adj* megalomaniac

**mégalomanie** [megalɔmani] *nf* megalomania

**mégalopole** [megalɔpɔl] *nf* megalopolis

**méga-octet** [megaɔktɛ] *nm* megabyte

**mégarde** [megaʀd(ə)] *nf*: **par ~** accidentally;

(*par erreur*) by mistake

**mégatonne** [megatɔn] *nf* megaton

**mégère** [meʒɛʀ] *nf* (*péj: femme*) shrew

**mégot** [mego] *nm* cigarette end *ou* butt

**mégoter** [megɔte] *vi* to nitpick

**meilleur, e** [mɛjœʀ] *adj, adv* better; (*valeur superlative*) best ▷ *nm*: **le ~** (*celui qui ...*) the best (one); (*ce qui ...*) the best ▷ *nf*: **la ~e** the best (one); **le ~ des deux** the better of the two; **de ~e heure** earlier; **~ marché** cheaper

**méjuger** [meʒyʒe] *vt* to misjudge

**mél** [mɛl] *nm* email

**mélancolie** [melɑ̃kɔli] *nf* melancholy, gloom

**mélancolique** [melɑ̃kɔlik] *adj* melancholy, gloomy

**mélange** [melɑ̃ʒ] *nm* (*opération*) mixing; blending; (*résultat*) mixture; blend; **sans ~** unadulterated

**mélanger** [melɑ̃ʒe] *vt* (*substances*) to mix; (*vins, couleurs*) to blend; (*mettre en désordre, confondre*) to mix up, muddle (up); **se mélanger** (*liquides, couleurs*) to blend, mix

**mélanine** [melanin] *nf* melanin

**mélasse** [melas] *nf* treacle, molasses *sg*

**mêlée** [mele] *nf* (*bataille, cohue*) mêlée, scramble; (*lutte, conflit*) tussle, scuffle; (*Rugby*) scrum(mage)

**mêler** [mele] *vt* (*substances, odeurs, races*) to mix; (*embrouiller*) to muddle (up), mix up; **se mêler** to mix; (*se joindre, s'allier*) to mingle; **se ~ à** (*personne*) to join; to mix with; (*: odeurs etc*) to mingle with; **se ~ de** (*personne*) to meddle with, interfere in; **mêle-toi de tes affaires!** mind your own business!; **~ à** *ou* **avec** *ou* **de** to mix with; to mingle with; **~ qn à** (*affaire*) to get sb mixed up *ou* involved in

**mélo** [melo] *nm adj* = **mélodrame**; **mélodramatique**

**mélodie** [melɔdi] *nf* melody

**mélodieux, -euse** [melɔdjø, -øz] *adj* melodious, tuneful

**mélodique** [melɔdik] *adj* melodic

**mélodramatique** [melɔdʀamatik] *adj* melodramatic

**mélodrame** [melɔdʀam] *nm* melodrama

**mélomane** [melɔman] *nm/f* music lover

**melon** [məlɔ̃] *nm* (Bot) (honeydew) melon; (*aussi*: **chapeau melon**) bowler (hat); **~ d'eau** watermelon

**mélopée** [melɔpe] *nf* monotonous chant

**membrane** [mɑ̃bʀan] *nf* membrane

**membre** [mɑ̃bʀ(ə)] *nm* (Anat) limb; (*personne, pays, élément*) member ▷ *adj* member; **être ~ de** to be a member of; **~ (viril)** (male) organ

**mémé** [meme] *nf* (*fam*) granny; (*: vieille femme*) old dear

**⊙ MOT-CLÉ**

**même** [mɛm] *adj* **1** (*avant le nom*) same; **en même temps** at the same time; **ils ont les mêmes goûts** they have the same *ou* similar

**m**

tastes

**2** (*après le nom: renforcement*): **il est la loyauté même** he is loyalty itself; **ce sont ses paroles/celles-là même** they are his very words/the very ones

▷ *pron*: **le (la) même** the same one

▷ *adv* **1** (*renforcement*): **il n'a même pas pleuré** he didn't even cry; **même lui l'a dit** even HE said it; **ici même** at this very place; **même si** even if

**2**: **à même**: **à même la bouteille** straight from the bottle; **à même la peau** next to the skin; **être à même de faire** to be in a position to do, be able to do; **mettre qn à même de faire** to enable sb to do

**3**: **de même** likewise; **faire de même** to do likewise *ou* the same; **lui de même** so does (*ou* did *ou* is) he; **de même que** just as; **il en va de même pour** the same goes for

**mémento** [memēto] *nm* (*agenda*) appointments diary; (*ouvrage*) summary

**mémo** [memo] (*fam*) *nm* memo

**mémoire** [memwaʀ] *nf* memory ▷ *nm* (*Admin, Jur*) memorandum; (*Scol*) dissertation, paper; **avoir la ~ des visages/chiffres** to have a (good) memory for faces/figures; **n'avoir aucune ~** to have a terrible memory; **avoir de la ~** to have a good memory; **à la ~ de** to the *ou* in memory of; **pour ~** *adv* for the record; **de ~** *adv* from memory; **de ~ d'homme** in living memory; **mettre en ~** (*Inform*) to store; **~ morte** ROM; **~ vive** RAM

**mémoires** [memwaʀ] *nmpl* memoirs

**mémorable** [memɔʀabl(ə)] *adj* memorable

**mémorandum** [memɔʀãdɔm] *nm* memorandum; (*carnet*) notebook

**mémorial, -aux** [memɔʀjal, -o] *nm* memorial

**mémoriser** [memɔʀize] *vt* to memorize; (*Inform*) to store

**menaçant, e** [mənasã, -ãt] *adj* threatening, menacing

**menace** [mənas] *nf* threat; **~ en l'air** empty threat

**menacer** [mənase] *vt* to threaten; **~ qn de qch/de faire qch** to threaten sb with sth/to do sth

**ménage** [menaʒ] *nm* (*travail*) housekeeping, housework; (*couple*) (married) couple; (*famille, Admin*) household; **faire le ~** to do the housework; **faire des ~s** to work as a cleaner (*in private homes*); **monter son ~** to set up house; **se mettre en ~ (avec)** to set up house (with); **heureux en ~** happily married; **faire bon ~ avec** to get on well with; **~ de poupée** doll's kitchen set; **~ à trois** love triangle

**ménagement** [menaʒmã] *nm* care and attention; **ménagements** *nmpl* (*égards*) consideration *sg*, attention *sg*

**ménager¹** [menaʒe] *vt* (*traiter avec mesure*) to handle with tact; to treat considerately; (*utiliser*) to use with care; (: *avec économie*) to use sparingly; (*prendre soin de*) to take (great) care of,

look after; (*organiser*) to arrange; (*installer*) to put in; to make; **se ménager** to look after o.s.; **~ qch à qn** (*réserver*) to have sth in store for sb

**ménager², -ère** [menaʒe, -ɛʀ] *adj* household *cpd*, domestic ▷ *nf* (*femme*) housewife; (*couverts*) canteen (of cutlery)

**ménagerie** [menaʒʀi] *nf* menagerie

**mendiant, e** [mãdjã, -ãt] *nm/f* beggar

**mendicité** [mãdisite] *nf* begging

**mendier** [mãdje] *vi* to beg ▷ *vt* to beg (for); (*fig: éloges, compliments*) to fish for

**menées** [məne] *nfpl* intrigues, manœuvres (*Brit*), maneuvers (*US*); (*Comm*) activities

**mener** [məne] *vt* to lead; (*enquête*) to conduct; (*affaires*) to manage, conduct, run ▷ *vi*: **~ (à la marque)** to lead, be in the lead; **~ à/dans** (*emmener*) to take to/into; **~ qch à bonne fin** *ou* **à terme** *ou* **à bien** to see sth through (to a successful conclusion), complete sth successfully

**meneur, -euse** [mənœʀ, -øz] *nm/f* leader; (*péj: agitateur*) ringleader; **~ d'hommes** born leader; **~ de jeu** host, quizmaster (*Brit*)

**menhir** [meniʀ] *nm* standing stone

**méningite** [menēʒit] *nf* meningitis *no pl*

**ménisque** [menisk] *nm* (*Anat*) meniscus

**ménopause** [menɔpoz] *nf* menopause

**menotte** [mənɔt] *nf* (*langage enfantin*) handie; **menottes** *nfpl* handcuffs; **passer les ~s à** to handcuff

**mens** [mã] *vb voir* **mentir**

**mensonge** [mãsɔ̃ʒ] *nm*: **le ~** lying *no pl*; **un ~** a lie

**mensonger, -ère** [mãsɔ̃ʒe, -ɛʀ] *adj* false

**menstruation** [mãstʀɥasjɔ̃] *nf* menstruation

**menstruel, le** [mãstʀɥɛl] *adj* menstrual

**mensualiser** [mãsɥalize] *vt* to pay monthly

**mensualité** [mãsɥalite] *nf* (*somme payée*) monthly payment; (*somme perçue*) monthly salary

**mensuel, le** [mãsɥɛl] *adj* monthly ▷ *nm/f* (*employé*) employee paid monthly ▷ *nm* (*Presse*) monthly

**mensuellement** [mãsɥɛlmã] *adv* monthly

**mensurations** [mãsyʀasjɔ̃] *nfpl* measurements

**mentais** *etc* [mãtɛ] *vb voir* **mentir**

**mental, e, -aux** [mãtal, -o] *adj* mental

**mentalement** [mãtalmã] *adv* in one's head, mentally

**mentalité** [mãtalite] *nf* mentality

**menteur, -euse** [mãtœʀ, -øz] *nm/f* liar

**menthe** [mãt] *nf* mint; **~ (à l'eau)** peppermint cordial

**mentholé, e** [mãtɔle] *adj* menthol *cpd*, mentholated

**mention** [mãsjɔ̃] *nf* (*note*) note, comment; (*Scol*): **~ (très) bien/passable** (very) good/satisfactory pass; **faire ~ de** to mention; **"rayer la ~ inutile"** "delete as appropriate"

**mentionner** [mãsjɔne] *vt* to mention

**mentir** [mãtiʀ] *vi* to lie

**menton** [mãtɔ̃] *nm* chin

**mentonnière** [mɑ̃tɔnjɛʀ] *nf* chin strap
**menu, e** [məny] *adj (mince)* thin; *(petit)* tiny; *(frais, difficulté)* minor ▷ *adv (couper, hacher)* very fine ▷ *nm* menu; **par le ~** *(raconter)* in minute detail; **~ touristique** popular *ou* tourist menu; **~e monnaie** small change
**menuet** [mənɥɛ] *nm* minuet
**menuiserie** [mənɥizʀi] *nf (travail)* joinery, carpentry; *(d'amateur)* woodwork; *(local)* joiner's workshop; *(ouvrages)* woodwork *no pl*
**menuisier** [mənɥizje] *nm* joiner, carpenter
**méprendre** [mepʀɑ̃dʀ(ə)]: **se méprendre** *vi*: **se méprendre sur** to be mistaken about
**mépris, e** [mepʀi, -iz] *pp de* **méprendre** ▷ *nm (dédain)* contempt, scorn; *(indifférence)*: **le ~ de** contempt *ou* disregard for; **au ~ de** regardless of, in defiance of
**méprisable** [mepʀizabl(ə)] *adj* contemptible, despicable
**méprisant, e** [mepʀizɑ̃, -ɑ̃t] *adj* contemptuous, scornful
**méprise** [mepʀiz] *nf* mistake, error; *(malentendu)* misunderstanding
**mépriser** [mepʀize] *vt* to scorn, despise; *(gloire, danger)* to scorn, spurn
**mer** [mɛʀ] *nf* sea; *(marée)* tide; **~ fermée** inland sea; **en ~** at sea; **prendre la ~** to put out to sea; **en haute** *ou* **pleine ~** off shore, on the open sea; **la ~ Adriatique** the Adriatic (Sea); **la ~ des Antilles** *ou* **des Caraïbes** the Caribbean (Sea); **la ~ Baltique** the Baltic (Sea); **la ~ Caspienne** the Caspian Sea; **la ~ de Corail** the Coral Sea; **la ~ Égée** the Aegean (Sea); **la ~ Ionienne** the Ionian Sea; **la ~ Morte** the Dead Sea; **la ~ Noire** the Black Sea; **la ~ du Nord** the North Sea; **la ~ Rouge** the Red Sea; **la ~ des Sargasses** the Sargasso Sea; **les ~s du Sud** the South Seas; **la ~ Tyrrhénienne** the Tyrrhenian Sea
**mercantile** [mɛʀkɑ̃til] *adj (péj)* mercenary
**mercantilisme** [mɛʀkɑ̃tilism(ə)] *nm (esprit mercantile)* mercenary attitude
**mercenaire** [mɛʀsənɛʀ] *nm* mercenary
**mercerie** [mɛʀsəʀi] *nf (Couture)* haberdashery *(Brit)*, notions *pl (US)*; *(boutique)* haberdasher's *(shop) (Brit)*, notions store *(US)*
**merci** [mɛʀsi] *excl* thank you ▷ *nf*: **à la ~ de qn/qch** at sb's mercy/the mercy of sth; **~ beaucoup** thank you very much; **~ de** *ou* **pour** thank you for; **sans ~** *adj* merciless ▷ *adv* mercilessly
**mercier, -ière** [mɛʀsje, -jɛʀ] *nm/f* haberdasher
**mercredi** [mɛʀkʀədi] *nm* Wednesday; **~ des Cendres** Ash Wednesday; *voir aussi* **lundi**
**mercure** [mɛʀkyʀ] *nm* mercury
**merde** [mɛʀd(ə)] *(fam!)* *nf* shit (!) ▷ *excl* (bloody) hell (!)
**merdeux, -euse** [mɛʀdø, -øz] *nm/f (fam!)* little bugger *(Brit)* (!), little devil
**mère** [mɛʀ] *nf* mother ▷ *adj inv* mother *cpd*; **~ célibataire** single parent, unmarried mother
**merguez** [mɛʀgɛz] *nf* spicy North African sausage
**méridien** [meʀidjɛ̃] *nm* meridian
**méridional, e, -aux** [meʀidjɔnal, -o] *adj*

southern; *(du midi de la France)* Southern (French) ▷ *nm/f* Southerner
**meringue** [məʀɛ̃g] *nf* meringue
**mérinos** [meʀinos] *nm* merino
**merisier** [məʀizje] *nm* wild cherry (tree)
**méritant, e** [meʀitɑ̃, -ɑ̃t] *adj* deserving
**mérite** [meʀit] *nm* merit; **le ~ (de ceci) lui revient** the credit (for this) is his
**mériter** [meʀite] *vt* to deserve; **~ de réussir** to deserve to succeed; **il mérite qu'on fasse ...** he deserves people to do ...
**méritocratie** [meʀitɔkʀasi] *nf* meritocracy
**méritoire** [meʀitwaʀ] *adj* praiseworthy, commendable
**merlan** [mɛʀlɑ̃] *nm* whiting
**merle** [mɛʀl(ə)] *nm* blackbird
**mérou** [meʀu] *nm* grouper *(fish)*
**merveille** [mɛʀvɛj] *nf* marvel, wonder; **faire ~** *ou* **des ~s** to work wonders; **à ~** perfectly, wonderfully
**merveilleux, -euse** [mɛʀvejø, -øz] *adj* marvellous, wonderful
**mes** [me] *adj poss voir* **mon**
**mésalliance** [mezaljɑ̃s] *nf* misalliance, mismatch
**mésallier** [mezalje]: **se mésallier** *vi* to marry beneath (*ou* above) o.s.
**mésange** [mezɑ̃ʒ] *nf* tit(mouse); **~ bleue** bluetit
**mésaventure** [mezavɑ̃tyʀ] *nf* misadventure, misfortune
**Mesdames** [medam] *nfpl voir* **Madame**
**Mesdemoiselles** [medmwazɛl] *nfpl voir* **Mademoiselle**
**mésentente** [mezɑ̃tɑ̃t] *nf* dissension, disagreement
**mésestimer** [mezɛstime] *vt* to underestimate, underrate
**Mésopotamie** [mezɔpɔtami] *nf*: **la ~** Mesopotamia
**mesquin, e** [mɛskɛ̃, -in] *adj* mean, petty
**mesquinerie** [mɛskinʀi] *nf* meanness *no pl*, pettiness *no pl*
**mess** [mɛs] *nm* mess
**message** [mesaʒ] *nm* message; **~ d'erreur** *(Inform)* error message; **~ électronique** *(Inform)* email; **~ publicitaire** ad, advertisement; **~ téléphoné** telegram dictated by telephone
**messager, -ère** [mesaʒe, -ɛʀ] *nm/f* messenger
**messagerie** [mesaʒʀi] *nf*: **~ électronique** electronic mail, email; **~ instantanée** instant messaging, IM; **~ rose** lonely hearts and contact service on videotext; **~s aériennes/maritimes** air freight/shipping service *sg*; **~s de presse** press distribution service; **~ vocale** voice mail
**messe** [mɛs] *nf* mass; **aller à la ~** to go to mass; **~ de minuit** midnight mass; **faire des ~s basses** *(fig, péj)* to mutter
**messie** [mesi] *nm*: **le M~** the Messiah
**Messieurs** [mesjø] *nmpl voir* **Monsieur**
**mesure** [məzyʀ] *nf (évaluation, dimension)* measurement; *(étalon, récipient, contenu)* measure; *(Mus: cadence)* time, tempo; *(: division)*

**m**

bar; (*retenue*) moderation; (*disposition*) measure, step; **unité/système de ~** unit/system of measurement; **sur ~** (*costume*) made-to-measure; (*fig*) personally adapted; **à la ~ de** (*fig*: *personne*) worthy of; (*chambre etc*) on the same scale as; **dans la ~ où** insofar as, inasmuch as; **dans une certaine ~** to some *ou* a certain extent; **à ~ que** as; **en ~** (*Mus*) in time *ou* tempo; **être en ~ de** to be in a position to; **dépasser la ~** (*fig*) to overstep the mark

**mesuré, e** [məzyʀe] *adj* (*ton, effort*) measured; (*personne*) restrained

**mesurer** [məzyʀe] *vt* to measure; (*juger*) to weigh up, assess; (*limiter*) to limit, ration; (*modérer*) to moderate; (*proportionner*): **~ qch à** to match sth to, gear sth to; **se ~ avec** to have a confrontation with; to tackle; **il mesure 1 m 80** he's 1 m 80 tall

**met** [mɛ] *vb voir* **mettre**

**métabolisme** [metabɔlism(ə)] *nm* metabolism

**métairie** [meteʀi] *nf* smallholding

**métal, -aux** [metal, -o] *nm* metal

**métalangage** [metalɑ̃gaʒ] *nm* metalanguage

**métallique** [metalik] *adj* metallic

**métallisé, e** [metalize] *adj* metallic

**métallurgie** [metalyʀʒi] *nf* metallurgy

**métallurgique** [metalyʀʒik] *adj* steel *cpd*, metal *cpd*

**métallurgiste** [metalyʀʒist(ə)] *nm/f* (*ouvrier*) steel *ou* metal worker; (*industriel*) metallurgist

**métamorphose** [metamɔʀfoz] *nf* metamorphosis

**métamorphoser** [metamɔʀfoze] *vt* to transform

**métaphore** [metafɔʀ] *nf* metaphor

**métaphorique** [metafɔʀik] *adj* metaphorical, figurative

**métaphoriquement** [metafɔʀikmɑ̃] *adv* metaphorically

**métaphysique** [metafizik] *nf* metaphysics *sg* ▷ *adj* metaphysical

**métapsychique** [metapsiʃik] *adj* psychic, parapsychological

**métayer, -ère** [meteje, metɛjeʀ] *nm/f* (tenant) farmer

**météo** [meteo] *nf* (*bulletin*) (weather) forecast; (*service*) ≈ Met Office (*Brit*), ≈ National Weather Service (*US*)

**météore** [meteɔʀ] *nm* meteor

**météorite** [meteɔʀit] *nm ou f* meteorite

**météorologie** [meteɔʀɔlɔʒi] *nf* (*étude*) meteorology; (*service*) ≈ Meteorological Office (*Brit*), ≈ National Weather Service (*US*)

**météorologique** [meteɔʀɔlɔʒik] *adj* meteorological, weather *cpd*

**météorologue** [meteɔʀɔlɔg] *nm*, **météorologiste** [meteɔʀɔlɔʒist(ə)] *nm/f* meteorologist, weather forecaster

**métèque** [metɛk] *nm* (*péj*) wop (!)

**méthane** [metan] *nm* methane

**méthanier** [metanje] *nm* (*bateau*) (liquefied) gas carrier *ou* tanker

**méthode** [metɔd] *nf* method; (*livre, ouvrage*) manual, tutor

**méthodique** [metɔdik] *adj* methodical

**méthodiquement** [metɔdikmɑ̃] *adv* methodically

**méthodiste** [metɔdist(ə)] *adj, nm/f* (*Rel*) Methodist

**méthylène** [metilɛn] *nm*: **bleu de ~** *nm* methylene blue

**méticuleux, -euse** [metikylø, -øz] *adj* meticulous

**métier** [metje] *nm* (*profession: gén*) job; (: *manuel*) trade; (: *artisanal*) craft; (*technique, expérience*) (acquired) skill *ou* technique; (*aussi*: **métier à tisser**) (weaving) loom; **être du ~** to be in the trade *ou* profession

**métis, se** [metis] *adj, nm/f* half-caste, half-breed

**métisser** [metise] *vt* to cross(breed)

**métrage** [metʀaʒ] *nm* (*de tissu*) length; (*Ciné*) footage, length; **long/moyen/court ~** feature *ou* full-length/medium-length/short film

**mètre** [mɛtʀ(ə)] *nm* metre (*Brit*), meter (*US*); (*règle*) (metre *ou* meter) rule; (*ruban*) tape measure; **~ carré/cube** square/cubic metre *ou* meter

**métrer** [metʀe] *vt* (*Tech*) to measure (in metres *ou* meters); (*Constr*) to survey

**métreur, -euse** [metʀœʀ, -øz] *nm/f*: **~ (vérificateur), métreuse (vérificatrice)** (quantity) surveyor

**métrique** [metʀik] *adj* metric ▷ *nf* metrics *sg*

**métro** [metʀo] *nm* underground (*Brit*), subway (*US*)

**métronome** [metʀɔnɔm] *nm* metronome

**métropole** [metʀɔpɔl] *nf* (*capitale*) metropolis; (*pays*) home country

**métropolitain, e** [metʀɔpɔlitɛ̃, -ɛn] *adj* metropolitan

**mets** [mɛ] *nm* dish ▷ *vb voir* **mettre**

**mettable** [mɛtabl(ə)] *adj* fit to be worn, decent

**metteur** [metœʀ] *nm*: **~ en scène** (*Théât*) producer; (*Ciné*) director; **~ en ondes** (*Radio*) producer

Ⓞ **MOT-CLÉ**

**mettre** [mɛtʀ(ə)] *vt* **1** (*placer*) to put; **mettre en bouteille/en sac** to bottle/put in bags *ou* sacks; **mettre qch à la poste** to post sth (*Brit*), mail sth (*US*); **mettre en examen (pour)** to charge (with) (*Brit*), indict (for) (*US*); **mettre une note gaie/amusante** to inject a cheerful/an amusing note; **mettre qn debout/assis** to help sb up *ou* to their feet/help sb to sit down

**2** (*vêtements: revêtir*) to put on; (: *porter*) to wear; **mets ton gilet** put your cardigan on; **je ne mets plus mon manteau** I no longer wear my coat

**3** (*faire fonctionner: chauffage, électricité*) to put on; (: *réveil, minuteur*) to set; (*installer: gaz, eau*) to put in, lay on; **mettre en marche** to start up

**4** (*consacrer*): **mettre du temps/deux heures à**

**faire qch** to take time/two hours to do sth; **y mettre du sien** to pull one's weight

**5** (*noter, écrire*) to say, put (down); **qu'est-ce qu'il a mis sur la carte?** what did he say *ou* write on the card?; **mettez au pluriel ...** put ... into the plural

**6** (*supposer*): **mettons que ...** let's suppose *ou* say that ...

**7** (*faire*+*vb*): **faire mettre le gaz/l'électricité** to have gas/electricity put in *ou* installed

**se mettre** *vi* **1** (*se placer*): **vous pouvez vous mettre là** you can sit (*ou* stand) there; **où ça se met?** where does it go?; **se mettre au lit** to get into bed; **se mettre au piano** to sit down at the piano; **se mettre à l'eau** to get into the water; **se mettre de l'encre sur les doigts** to get ink on one's fingers

**2** (*s'habiller*): **se mettre en maillot de bain** to get into *ou* put on a swimsuit; **n'avoir rien à se mettre** to have nothing to wear

**3** (*dans rapports*): **se mettre bien/mal avec qn** to get on the right/wrong side of sb; **se mettre qn à dos** to get on sb's bad side; **se mettre avec qn** (*prendre parti*) to side with sb; (*faire équipe*) to team up with sb; (*en ménage*) to move in with sb

**4**: **se mettre à** to begin, start; **se mettre à faire** to begin *ou* start doing *ou* to do; **se mettre au piano** to start learning the piano; **se mettre au régime** to go on a diet; **se mettre au travail/à l'étude** to get down to work/one's studies; **il est temps de s'y mettre** it's time we got down to it *ou* got on with it

**meublant, e** [mœblɑ̃, -ɑ̃t] *adj* (*tissus etc*) effective (in the room)

**meuble** [mœbl(ə)] *nm* (*objet*) piece of furniture; (*ameublement*) furniture *no pl* ▷ *adj* (*terre*) loose, friable; (*Jur*): **biens ~s** movables

**meublé** [mœble] *nm* (*pièce*) furnished room; (*appartement*) furnished flat (*Brit*) *ou* apartment (US)

**meubler** [mœble] *vt* to furnish; (*fig*): **~ qch (de)** to fill sth (with); **se meubler** to furnish one's house

**meuf** [mœf] *nf* (*fam*) woman

**meugler** [møgle] *vi* to low, moo

**meule** [møl] *nf* (*à broyer*) millstone; (*à aiguiser*) grindstone; (*à polir*) buff wheel; (*de foin, blé*) stack; (*de fromage*) round

**meunerie** [mønʀi] *nf* (*industrie*) flour trade; (*métier*) milling

**meunier, -ière** [mønje, -jɛʀ] *nm* miller ▷ *nf* miller's wife ▷ *adj f* (*Culin*) meunière

**meurs** *etc* [mœʀ] *vb voir* **mourir**

**meurtre** [mœʀtʀ(ə)] *nm* murder

**meurtrier, -ière** [mœʀtʀije, -jɛʀ] *adj* (*arme, épidémie, combat*) deadly; (*accident*) fatal; (*carrefour, route*) lethal; (*fureur, instincts*) murderous ▷ *nm/f* murderer(-ess) ▷ *nf* (*ouverture*) loophole

**meurtrir** [mœʀtʀiʀ] *vt* to bruise; (*fig*) to wound

**meurtrissure** [mœʀtʀisyʀ] *nf* bruise; (*fig*) scar

**meus** *etc* [mœ] *vb voir* **mouvoir**

**Meuse** [mœz] *nf*: **la ~** the Meuse

**meute** [møt] *nf* pack

**meuve** *etc* [mœv] *vb voir* **mouvoir**

**mévente** [mevɑ̃t] *nf* slump (in sales)

**mexicain, e** [mɛksikɛ̃, -ɛn] *adj* Mexican ▷ *nm/f*: **Mexicain, e** Mexican

**Mexico** [mɛksiko] *n* Mexico City

**Mexique** [mɛksik] *nm*: **le ~** Mexico

**mezzanine** [mɛdzanin] *nf* mezzanine (floor)

**MF** *sigle mpl* = **millions de francs** ▷ *sigle f* (*Radio*: = *modulation de fréquence*) FM

**Mgr** *abr* = **Monseigneur**

**mi** [mi] *nm* (*Mus*) E; (*en chantant la gamme*) mi

**mi...** [mi] *préfixe* half(-), mid-; **à la mi-janvier** in mid-January; **mi-bureau, mi-chambre** half office, half bedroom; **à mi-jambes/-corps** (up *ou* down) to the knees/waist; **à mi-hauteur/-pente** halfway up (*ou* down)/up (*ou* down) the hill

**miaou** [mjau] *nm* miaow

**miaulement** [mjolmɑ̃] *nm* (*cri*) miaow; (*continu*) miaowing *no pl*

**miauler** [mjole] *vi* to miaow

**mi-bas** [miba] *nm inv* knee-length sock

**mica** [mika] *nm* mica

**mi-carême** [mikaʀɛm] *nf*: **la ~** the third Thursday in Lent

**miche** [miʃ] *nf* round *ou* cob loaf

**mi-chemin** [miʃmɛ̃]: **à ~** *adv* halfway, midway

**mi-clos, e** [miklo, -kloz] *adj* half-closed

**micmac** [mikmak] *nm* (*péj*) carry-on

**mi-côte** [mikot]: **à ~** *adv* halfway up (*ou* down) the hill

**mi-course** [mikuʀs]: **à ~** *adv* halfway through the race

**micro** [mikʀo] *nm* mike, microphone; **~ cravate** lapel mike

**microbe** [mikʀɔb] *nm* germ, microbe

**microbiologie** [mikʀɔbjɔlɔʒi] *nf* microbiology

**microchirurgie** [mikʀoʃiʀyʀʒi] *nf* microsurgery

**microclimat** [mikʀoklima] *nm* microclimate

**microcosme** [mikʀokɔsm(ə)] *nm* microcosm

**micro-édition** [mikʀoedisjɔ̃] *nf* desk-top publishing

**micro-électronique** [mikʀoelɛktʀonik] *nf* microelectronics *sg*

**microfiche** [mikʀɔfiʃ] *nf* microfiche

**microfilm** [mikʀɔfilm] *nm* microfilm

**micro-onde** [mikʀɔɔ̃d] *nf*: **four à ~s** microwave oven

**micro-ordinateur** [mikʀɔɔʀdinatœʀ] *nm* microcomputer

**micro-organisme** [mikʀoɔʀganism(ə)] *nm* micro-organism

**microphone** [mikʀɔfɔn] *nm* microphone

**microplaquette** [mikʀɔplakɛt] *nf* microchip

**microprocesseur** [mikʀɔpʀɔsɛsœʀ] *nm* microprocessor

**microscope** [mikʀɔskɔp] *nm* microscope; **au ~** under *ou* through the microscope

**microscopique** [mikʀɔskɔpik] *adj* microscopic

**microsillon** [mikʀɔsijɔ̃] *nm* long-playing record

**m**

**MIDEM** [midɛm] *sigle m* (= *Marché international du disque et de l'édition musicale*) music industry trade fair
**midi** [midi] *nm* (*milieu du jour*) midday, noon; (*moment du déjeuner*) lunchtime; (*sud*) south; (: *de la France*): **le M~** the South (of France), the Midi; **à ~** at 12 (o'clock) *ou* midday *ou* noon; **tous les ~s** every lunchtime; **le repas de ~** lunch; **en plein ~** (right) in the middle of the day; (*sud*) facing south
**midinette** [midinɛt] *nf* silly young townie
**mie** [mi] *nf* inside (of the loaf)
**miel** [mjɛl] *nm* honey; **être tout ~** (*fig*) to be all sweetness and light
**mielleux, -euse** [mjɛlø, -øz] *adj* (*péj*) sugary, honeyed
**mien, ne** [mjɛ̃, mjɛn] *adj, pron*: **le (la) ~(ne)**, **les ~s** mine; **les ~s** (*ma famille*) my family
**miette** [mjɛt] *nf* (*de pain, gâteau*) crumb; (*fig: de la conversation etc*) scrap; **en ~s** (*fig*) in pieces *ou* bits

**⊙ MOT-CLÉ**

**mieux** [mjø] *adv* **1** (*d'une meilleure façon*): **mieux (que)** better (than); **elle travaille/mange mieux** she works/eats better; **aimer mieux** to prefer; **j'attendais mieux de vous** I expected better of you; **elle va mieux** she is better; **de mieux en mieux** better and better
**2** (*de la meilleure façon*) best; **ce que je sais le mieux** what I know best; **les livres les mieux faits** the best made books
**3** (*intensif*): **vous feriez mieux de faire ...** you would be better to do ...; **crier à qui mieux mieux** to try to shout each other down
▷ *adj* **1** (*plus à l'aise, en meilleure forme*) better; **se sentir mieux** to feel better
**2** (*plus satisfaisant*) better; **c'est mieux ainsi** it's better like this; **c'est le mieux des deux** it's the better of the two; **le/la mieux, les mieux** the best; **demandez-lui, c'est le mieux** ask him, it's the best thing
**3** (*plus joli*) better-looking; (*plus gentil*) nicer; **il est mieux que son frère** (*plus beau*) he's better-looking than his brother; (*plus gentil*) he's nicer than his brother; **il est mieux sans moustache** he looks better without a moustache
**4**: **au mieux** at best; **au mieux avec** on the best of terms with; **pour le mieux** for the best; **qui mieux est** even better, better still
▷ *nm* **1** (*progrès*) improvement
**2**: **de mon/ton mieux** as best I/you can (*ou* could); **faire de son mieux** to do one's best; **du mieux qu'il peut** the best he can; **faute de mieux** for lack *ou* want of anything better, failing anything better

**mieux-être** [mjøzɛtʀ(ə)] *nm* greater well-being; (*financier*) improved standard of living
**mièvre** [mjɛvʀ(ə)] *adj* sickly sentimental
**mignon, ne** [miɲɔ̃, -ɔn] *adj* sweet, cute
**migraine** [migʀɛn] *nf* headache; migraine

**migrant, e** [migʀɑ̃, -ɑ̃t] *adj, nm/f* migrant
**migrateur, -trice** [migʀatœʀ, -tʀis] *adj* migratory
**migration** [migʀasjɔ̃] *nf* migration
**mijaurée** [miʒɔʀe] *nf* pretentious (young) madam
**mijoter** [miʒɔte] *vt* to simmer; (*préparer avec soin*) to cook lovingly; (*affaire, projet*) to plot, cook up
▷ *vi* to simmer
**mil** [mil] *num* = **mille**
**Milan** [milɑ̃] *n* Milan
**milanais, e** [milanɛ, -ɛz] *adj* Milanese
**mildiou** [mildju] *nm* mildew
**milice** [milis] *nf* militia
**milicien, ne** [milisjɛ̃, -ɛn] *nm/f* militiaman(-woman)
**milieu, x** [miljø] *nm* (*centre*) middle; (*fig*) middle course *ou* way; (*aussi*: **juste milieu**) happy medium; (*Bio, Géo*) environment; (*entourage social*) milieu; (*familial*) background; circle; (*pègre*): **le ~** the underworld; **au ~ de** in the middle of; **au beau** *ou* **en plein ~ (de)** right in the middle (of); **~ de terrain** (*Football*: *joueur*) midfield player; (: *joueurs*) midfield
**militaire** [militɛʀ] *adj* military ▷ *nm* serviceman; **service ~** military service
**militant, e** [militɑ̃, -ɑ̃t] *adj, nm/f* militant
**militantisme** [militɑ̃tism(ə)] *nm* militancy
**militariser** [militaʀize] *vt* to militarize
**militarisme** [militaʀism(ə)] *nm* (*péj*) militarism
**militer** [milite] *vi* to be a militant; **~ pour/ contre** to militate in favour of/against
**milk-shake** [milkʃɛk] *nm* milk shake
**mille** [mil] *num* a *ou* one thousand ▷ *nm* (*mesure*): **~ (marin)** nautical mile; **mettre dans le ~** to hit the bull's-eye; (*fig*) to be bang on (target)
**millefeuille** [milfœj] *nm* cream *ou* vanilla slice
**millénaire** [milenɛʀ] *nm* millennium ▷ *adj* thousand-year-old; (*fig*) ancient
**mille-pattes** [milpat] *nm inv* centipede
**millésime** [milezim] *nm* year
**millésimé, e** [milezime] *adj* vintage *cpd*
**millet** [mijɛ] *nm* millet
**milliard** [miljaʀ] *nm* milliard, thousand million (*Brit*), billion (*US*)
**milliardaire** [miljaʀdɛʀ] *nm/f* multimillionaire (*Brit*), billionaire (*US*)
**millième** [miljɛm] *num* thousandth
**millier** [milje] *nm* thousand; **un ~ (de)** a thousand or so, about a thousand; **par ~s** in (their) thousands, by the thousand
**milligramme** [miligʀam] *nm* milligramme (*Brit*), milligram (*US*)
**millimétré, e** [milimetʀe] *adj*: **papier ~** graph paper
**millimètre** [milimetʀ(ə)] *nm* millimetre (*Brit*), millimeter (*US*)
**million** [miljɔ̃] *nm* million; **deux ~s de** two million; **riche à ~s** worth millions
**millionième** [miljɔnjɛm] *num* millionth
**millionnaire** [miljɔnɛʀ] *nm/f* millionaire
**mi-lourd** [miluʀ] *adj m, nm* light heavyweight

**mime** [mim] *nm/f (acteur)* mime(r); *(imitateur)* mimic ▷ *nm (art)* mime, miming

**mimer** [mime] *vt* to mime; *(singer)* to mimic, take off

**mimétisme** [mimetism(ə)] *nm (Bio)* mimicry

**mimique** [mimik] *nf (funny)* face; *(signes)* gesticulations *pl*, sign language *no pl*

**mimosa** [mimoza] *nm* mimosa

**mi-moyen** [mimwajɛ̃] *adj m, nm* welterweight

**MIN** *sigle m (= Marché d'intérêt national) wholesale market for fruit, vegetables and agricultural produce*

**min.** *abr (= minimum)* min

**minable** [minabl(ə)] *adj (personne)* shabby (-looking); *(travail)* pathetic

**minaret** [minaʀɛ] *nm* minaret

**minauder** [minode] *vi* to mince, simper

**minauderies** [minodʀi] *nfpl* simpering *sg*

**mince** [mɛ̃s] *adj* thin; *(personne, taille)* slim; *(fig: profit, connaissances)* slight, small; *(: prétexte)* weak ▷ *excl:* **~ (alors)!** darn it!

**minceur** [mɛ̃sœʀ] *nf* thinness slimness, slenderness

**mincir** [mɛ̃siʀ] *vi* to get slimmer *ou* thinner

**mine** [min] *nf (physionomie)* expression, look; *(extérieur)* exterior, appearance; *(de crayon)* lead; *(gisement, exploitation, explosif)* mine; **mines** *nfpl (péj)* simpering airs; **les M~s** *(Admin)* the national mining and geological service, the government vehicle testing department; **avoir bonne ~** *(personne)* to look well; *(ironique)* to look an utter idiot; **avoir mauvaise ~** to look unwell; **faire ~ de faire** to make a pretence of doing; **ne pas payer de ~** to be not much to look at; **~ de rien** *adv* with a casual air; although you wouldn't think so; **~ de charbon** coal mine; **~ à ciel ouvert** opencast *(Brit) ou* open-air *(US)* mine

**miner** [mine] *vt (saper)* to undermine, erode; *(Mil)* to mine

**minerai** [minʀɛ] *nm* ore

**minéral, e, -aux** [mineʀal, -o] *adj* mineral; *(Chimie)* inorganic ▷ *nm* mineral

**minéralier** [mineʀalje] *nm (bateau)* ore tanker

**minéralisé, e** [mineʀalize] *adj* mineralized

**minéralogie** [mineʀalɔʒi] *nf* mineralogy

**minéralogique** [mineʀalɔʒik] *adj* mineralogical; **plaque ~** number *(Brit) ou* license *(US)* plate; **numéro ~** registration *(Brit) ou* license *(US)* number

**minet, te** [minɛ, -ɛt] *nm/f (chat)* pussy-cat; *(péj)* young trendy

**mineur, e** [minœʀ] *adj* minor ▷ *nm/f (Jur)* minor ▷ *nm (travailleur)* miner; *(Mil)* sapper; **~ de fond** face worker

**miniature** [minjatyʀ] *adj, nf* miniature

**miniaturisation** [minjatyʀizasjɔ̃] *nf* miniaturization

**miniaturiser** [minjatyʀize] *vt* to miniaturize

**minibus** [minibys] *nm* minibus

**mini-cassette** [minikasɛt] *nf* cassette (recorder)

**minichaîne** [miniʃɛn] *nf* mini system

**minier, -ière** [minje, -jɛʀ] *adj* mining

**mini-jupe** [miniʒyp] *nf* mini-skirt

**minimal, e, -aux** [minimal, -o] *adj* minimum

**minimaliste** [minimalist(ə)] *adj (Art)* minimalist

**minime** [minim] *adj* minor, minimal ▷ *nm/f (Sport)* junior

**minimiser** [minimize] *vt* to minimize; *(fig)* to play down

**minimum** [minimɔm] *adj, nm* minimum; **au ~** at the very least; **~ vital** *(salaire)* living wage; *(niveau de vie)* subsistence level

**mini-ordinateur** [miniɔʀdinatœʀ] *nm* minicomputer

**ministère** [ministɛʀ] *nm (cabinet)* government; *(département)* ministry *(Brit)*, department; *(Rel)* ministry; **~ public** *(Jur)* Prosecution, State Prosecutor

**ministériel, le** [ministeʀjɛl] *adj* government *cpd*; ministerial, departmental; *(partisan)* pro-government

**ministrable** [ministʀabl(ə)] *adj (Pol):* **il est ~** he's a potential minister

**ministre** [ministʀ(ə)] *nm* minister *(Brit)*, secretary; *(Rel)* minister; **~ d'État** senior minister *ou* secretary

**Minitel®** [minitɛl] *nm* videotext terminal and service

**minium** [minjɔm] *nm* red lead paint

**minois** [minwa] *nm* little face

**minorer** [minɔʀe] *vt* to cut, reduce

**minoritaire** [minɔʀitɛʀ] *adj* minority *cpd*

**minorité** [minɔʀite] *nf* minority; **être en ~** to be in the *ou* a minority; **mettre en ~** *(Pol)* to defeat

**Minorque** [minɔʀk] *nf* Minorca

**minorquin, e** [minɔʀkɛ̃, -in] *adj* Minorcan

**minoterie** [minɔtʀi] *nf* flour-mill

**minuit** [minɥi] *nm* midnight

**minuscule** [minyskyl] *adj* minute, tiny ▷ *nf:* **(lettre) ~** small letter

**minutage** [minytaʒ] *nm* timing

**minute** [minyt] *nf* minute; *(Jur: original)* minute, draft ▷ *excl* just a minute!, hang on!; **à la ~** *(présent)* (just) this instant; *(passé)* there and then; **entrecôte** *ou* **steak ~** minute steak

**minuter** [minyte] *vt* to time

**minuterie** [minytʀi] *nf* time switch

**minuteur** [minytœʀ] *nm* timer

**minutie** [minysi] *nf* meticulousness; minute detail; **avec ~** meticulously; in minute detail

**minutieusement** [minysjøzmɑ̃] *adv (organiser, travailler)* meticulously; *(examiner)* minutely

**minutieux, -euse** [minysjø, -øz] *adj (personne)* meticulous; *(inspection)* minutely detailed; *(travail)* requiring painstaking attention to detail

**mioche** [mjɔʃ] *nm (fam)* nipper, brat

**mirabelle** [miʀabɛl] *nf (fruit)* (cherry) plum; *(eau-de-vie)* plum brandy

**miracle** [miʀakl(ə)] *nm* miracle

**miraculé, e** [miʀakyle] *adj* who has been miraculously cured *(ou* rescued)

**miraculeux, -euse** [miʀakylø, -øz] *adj*

**m**

miraculous

**mirador** [miradɔʀ] nm (Mil) watchtower

**mirage** [miraʒ] nm mirage

**mire** [miʀ] nf (d'un fusil) sight; (TV) test card; **point de ~** target; (fig) focal point; **ligne de ~** line of sight

**mirent** [miʀ] vb voir **mettre**

**mirer** [miʀe] vt (œufs) to candle; **se mirer** vi: **se ~ dans** (personne) to gaze at one's reflection in; (: chose) to be mirrored in

**mirifique** [miʀifik] adj wonderful

**mirobolant, e** [miʀɔbɔlɑ̃, -ɑ̃t] adj fantastic

**miroir** [miʀwaʀ] nm mirror

**miroiter** [miʀwate] vi to sparkle, shimmer; **faire ~ qch à qn** to paint sth in glowing colours for sb, dangle sth in front of sb's eyes

**miroiterie** [miʀwatʀi] nf (usine) mirror factory; (magasin) mirror dealer's (shop)

**Mis** abr = **marquis**

**mis, e** [mi, miz] pp de **mettre** ▷ adj (couvert, table) set, laid; (personne): **bien ~** well dressed ▷ nf (argent: au jeu) stake; (tenue) clothing; attire; **être de ~e** to be acceptable ou in season; **~e en bouteilles** bottling; **~e en examen** charging, indictment; **~e à feu** blast-off; **~e de fonds** capital outlay; **~e à jour** (Inform) update; **~e à mort** kill; **~e à pied** (d'un employé) suspension; lay-off; **~e sur pied** (d'une affaire, entreprise) setting up; **~e en plis** set; **~e au point** (Photo) focusing; (fig) clarification; **~e à prix** reserve (Brit) ou upset price; **~e en scène** production

**misaine** [mizɛn] nf: **mât de ~** foremast

**misanthrope** [mizɑ̃tʀɔp] nm/f misanthropist

**Mise** abr = **marquise**

**mise** [miz] adj f, pf voir **mis**

**miser** [mize] vt (enjeu) to stake, bet; **~ sur** vt (cheval, numéro) to bet on; (fig) to bank ou count on

**misérable** [mizeʀabl(ə)] adj (lamentable, malheureux) pitiful, wretched; (pauvre) poverty-stricken; (insignifiant, mesquin) miserable ▷ nm/f wretch; (miséreux) poor wretch

**misère** [mizɛʀ] nf (pauvreté) (extreme) poverty, destitution; **misères** nfpl (malheurs) woes, miseries; (ennuis) little troubles; **être dans la ~** to be destitute ou poverty-stricken; **salaire de ~** starvation wage; **faire des ~s à qn** to torment sb; **~ noire** utter destitution, abject poverty

**miséreux, -euse** [mizeʀø, -øz] adj poverty-stricken ▷ nm/f down-and-out

**miséricorde** [mizeʀikɔʀd(ə)] nf mercy, forgiveness

**miséricordieux, -euse** [mizeʀikɔʀdjø, -øz] adj merciful, forgiving

**misogyne** [mizɔʒin] adj misogynous ▷ nm/f misogynist

**missel** [misɛl] nm missal

**missile** [misil] nm missile

**mission** [misjɔ̃] nf mission; **partir en ~** (Admin, Pol) to go on an assignment

**missionnaire** [misjɔnɛʀ] nm/f missionary

**missive** [misiv] nf missive

**mistral** [mistʀal] nm mistral (wind)

**mit** [mi] vb voir **mettre**

**mitaine** [mitɛn] nf mitt(en)

**mite** [mit] nf clothes moth

**mité, e** [mite] adj moth-eaten

**mi-temps** [mitɑ̃] nf inv (Sport: période) half; (: pause) half-time; **à ~** adj, adv part-time

**miteux, -euse** [mitø, -øz] adj seedy, shabby

**mitigé, e** [mitiʒe] adj (conviction, ardeur) lukewarm; (sentiments) mixed

**mitonner** [mitɔne] vt (préparer) to cook with loving care; (fig) to cook up quietly

**mitoyen, ne** [mitwajɛ̃, -ɛn] adj common, party cpd; **maisons ~nes** semi-detached houses; (plus de deux) terraced (Brit) ou row (US) houses

**mitraille** [mitʀaj] nf (balles de fonte) grapeshot; (décharge d'obus) shellfire

**mitrailler** [mitʀaje] vt to machine-gun; (fig: photographier) to snap away at; **~ qn de** to pelt ou bombard sb with

**mitraillette** [mitʀajɛt] nf submachine gun

**mitrailleur** [mitʀajœʀ] nm machine gunner ▷ adj m: **fusil ~** machine gun

**mitrailleuse** [mitʀajøz] nf machine gun

**mitre** [mitʀ(ə)] nf mitre

**mitron** [mitʀɔ̃] nm baker's boy

**mi-voix** [mivwa]: **à ~** adv in a low ou hushed voice

**mixage** [miksaʒ] nm (Ciné) (sound) mixing

**mixer, mixeur** [miksœʀ] nm (Culin) (food) mixer

**mixité** [miksite] nf (Scol) coeducation

**mixte** [mikst(ə)] adj (gén) mixed; (Scol) mixed, coeducational; **à usage ~** dual-purpose; **cuisinière ~** combined gas and electric cooker; **équipe ~** combined team

**mixture** [mikstyʀ] nf mixture; (fig) concoction

**MJC** sigle f (= maison des jeunes et de la culture) community arts centre and youth club

**ml** abr (= millilitre) ml

**MLF** sigle m (= Mouvement de libération de la femme) Women's Movement

**Mlle** (pl **-s**) abr = **Mademoiselle**

**MM** abr = **Messieurs**; voir **Monsieur**

**Mme** (pl **-s**) abr = **Madame**

**MMS** sigle m (= Multimedia messaging service) MMS

**mn.** abr (= minute) min

**mnémotechnique** [mnemɔtɛknik] adj mnemonic

**MNS** sigle m (= maître nageur sauveteur) ≈ lifeguard

**MO** sigle f (= main-d'œuvre) labour costs (on invoices)

**Mo** abr = **méga-octet; métro**

**mobile** [mɔbil] adj mobile; (amovible) loose, removable; (pièce de machine) moving; (élément de meuble etc) movable ▷ nm (motif) motive; (œuvre d'art) mobile; (Physique) moving object ou body; **(téléphone) ~** mobile (phone) (Brit), cell (phone) (US)

**mobilier, -ière** [mɔbilje, -jɛʀ] adj (Jur) personal ▷ nm (meubles) furniture; **valeurs mobilières** transferable securities; **vente mobilière** sale of personal property ou chattels

**mobilisation** [mɔbilizasjɔ̃] *nf* mobilization
**mobiliser** [mɔbilize] *vt* (*Mil, gén*) to mobilize
**mobilité** [mɔbilite] *nf* mobility
**mobylette®** [mɔbilɛt] *nf* moped
**mocassin** [mɔkasɛ̃] *nm* moccasin
**moche** [mɔʃ] *adj* (*fam: laid*) ugly; (: *mauvais, méprisable*) rotten
**modalité** [mɔdalite] *nf* form, mode; **modalités** *nfpl* (*d'un accord etc*) clauses, terms; **~s de paiement** methods of payment
**mode** [mɔd] *nf* fashion; (*commerce*) fashion trade *ou* industry ▷ *nm* (*manière*) form, mode, method; (*Ling*) mood; (*Inform, Mus*) mode; **travailler dans la ~** to be in the fashion business; **à la ~** fashionable, in fashion; **~ dialogué** (*Inform*) interactive *ou* conversational mode; **~ d'emploi** directions *pl* (for use); **~ de vie** way of life
**modelage** [mɔdlaʒ] *nm* modelling
**modelé** [mɔdle] *nm* (*Géo*) relief; (*du corps etc*) contours *pl*
**modèle** [mɔdɛl] *adj* model ▷ *nm* model; (*qui pose: de peintre*) sitter; (*type*) type; (*gabarit, patron*) pattern; **~ courant** *ou* **de série** (*Comm*) production model; **~ déposé** registered design; **~ réduit** small-scale model
**modeler** [mɔdle] *vt* (*Art*) to model, mould; (*vêtement, érosion*) to mould, shape; **~ qch sur/d'après** to model sth on
**modélisation** [mɔdelizasjɔ̃] *nf* (*Math*) modelling
**modéliste** [mɔdelist(ə)] *nm/f* (*Couture*) designer; (*de modèles réduits*) model maker
**modem** [mɔdɛm] *nm* (*Inform*) modem
**modérateur, -trice** [mɔderatœr, -tris] *adj* moderating ▷ *nm/f* moderator
**modération** [mɔderasjɔ̃] *nf* moderation; **~ de peine** reduction of sentence
**modéré, e** [mɔdere] *adj, nm/f* moderate
**modérément** [mɔderemɑ̃] *adv* moderately, in moderation
**modérer** [mɔdere] *vt* to moderate; **se modérer** *vi* to restrain o.s
**moderne** [mɔdɛrn(ə)] *adj* modern ▷ *nm* (*Art*) modern style; (*ameublement*) modern furniture
**modernisation** [mɔdɛrnizasjɔ̃] *nf* modernization
**moderniser** [mɔdɛrnize] *vt* to modernize
**modernisme** [mɔdɛrnism(ə)] *nm* modernism
**modernité** [mɔdɛrnite] *nf* modernity
**modeste** [mɔdɛst(ə)] *adj* modest; (*origine*) humble, lowly
**modestement** [mɔdɛstəmɑ̃] *adv* modestly
**modestie** [mɔdɛsti] *nf* modesty; **fausse ~** false modesty
**modicité** [mɔdisite] *nf*: **la ~ des prix** *etc* the low prices *etc*
**modificatif, -ive** [mɔdifikatif, -iv] *adj* modifying
**modification** [mɔdifikasjɔ̃] *nf* modification
**modifier** [mɔdifje] *vt* to modify, alter; (*Ling*) to modify; **se modifier** *vi* to alter

**modique** [mɔdik] *adj* (*salaire, somme*) modest
**modiste** [mɔdist(ə)] *nf* milliner
**modulaire** [mɔdylɛr] *adj* modular
**modulation** [mɔdylasjɔ̃] *nf* modulation; **~ de fréquence (FM** *ou* **MF)** frequency modulation (FM)
**module** [mɔdyl] *nm* module
**moduler** [mɔdyle] *vt* to modulate; (*air*) to warble
**moelle** [mwal] *nf* marrow; (*fig*) pith, core; **~ épinière** spinal chord
**moelleux, -euse** [mwalø, -øz] *adj* soft; (*au goût, à l'ouïe*) mellow; (*gracieux, souple*) smooth
**moellon** [mwalɔ̃] *nm* rubble stone
**mœurs** [mœr] *nfpl* (*conduite*) morals; (*manières*) manners; (*pratiques sociales*) habits; (*mode de vie*) life style *sg*; (*d'une espèce animale*) behaviour *sg* (*Brit*), behavior *sg* (*US*); **femme de mauvaises ~** loose woman; **passer dans les ~** to become the custom; **contraire aux bonnes ~** contrary to proprieties
**mohair** [mɔɛr] *nm* mohair
**moi** [mwa] *pron* me; (*emphatique*): **~, je ...** for my part, I ..., I myself ... ▷ *nm inv* (*Psych*) ego, self; **à ~!** (*à l'aide*) help (me)!
**moignon** [mwaɲɔ̃] *nm* stump
**moi-même** [mwamɛm] *pron* myself; (*emphatique*) I myself
**moindre** [mwɛ̃dr(ə)] *adj* lesser; lower; **le (la) ~, les ~s** the least; the slightest; **le (la) ~ de** the least of; **c'est la ~ des choses** it's nothing at all
**moindrement** [mwɛ̃drəmɑ̃] *adv*: **pas le ~** not in the least
**moine** [mwan] *nm* monk, friar
**moineau, x** [mwano] *nm* sparrow

**MOT-CLÉ**

**moins** [mwɛ̃] *adv* **1** (*comparatif*): **moins (que)** less (than); **moins grand que** less tall than, not as tall as; **il a trois ans de moins que moi** he's three years younger than me; **il est moins intelligent que moi** he's not as clever as me, he's less clever than me; **moins je travaille, mieux je me porte** the less I work, the better I feel
**2** (*superlatif*): **le moins** (the) least; **c'est ce que j'aime le moins** it's what I like (the) least; **le(la) moins doué(e)** the least gifted; **au moins, du moins** at least; **pour le moins** at the very least
**3**: **moins de** (*quantité*) less (than); (*nombre*) fewer (than); **moins de sable/d'eau** less sand/water; **moins de livres/gens** fewer books/people; **moins de deux ans** less than two years; **moins de midi** not yet midday
**4**: **de moins, en moins: 100 euros/3 jours de moins** 100 euros/3 days less; **trois livres en moins** three books fewer; three books too few; **de l'argent en moins** less money; **le soleil en moins** but for the sun, minus the sun; **de moins en moins** less and less; **en moins de**

**deux** in a flash *ou* a trice
**5**: **à moins de, à moins que** unless; **à moins de faire** unless we do (*ou* he does *etc*); **à moins que tu ne fasses** unless you do; **à moins d'un accident** barring any accident
▷ *prép*: **quatre moins deux** four minus two; **dix heures moins cinq** five to ten; **il fait moins cinq** it's five (degrees) below (freezing), it's minus five; **il est moins cinq** it's five to
▷ *nm* (*signe*) minus sign

**moins-value** [mwɛvaly] *nf* (*Écon, Comm*) depreciation
**moire** [mwaʀ] *nf* moiré
**moiré, e** [mwaʀe] *adj* (*tissu, papier*) moiré, watered; (*reflets*) shimmering
**mois** [mwa] *nm* month; (*salaire, somme dû*) (monthly) pay *ou* salary; **treizième ~, double ~** extra month's salary
**moïse** [mɔiz] *nm* Moses basket
**moisi, e** [mwazi] *adj* mouldy (*Brit*), moldy (*US*), mildewed ▷ *nm* mould, mold, mildew; **odeur de ~** musty smell
**moisir** [mwaziʀ] *vi* to go mouldy (*Brit*) *ou* moldy (*US*), (*fig*) to rot; (*personne*) to hang about ▷ *vt* to make mouldy *ou* moldy
**moisissure** [mwazisyʀ] *nf* mould *no pl* (*Brit*), mold *no pl* (*US*)
**moisson** [mwasɔ̃] *nf* harvest; (*époque*) harvest (time); (*fig*): **faire une ~ de** to gather a wealth of
**moissonner** [mwasɔne] *vt* to harvest, reap; (*fig*) to collect
**moissonneur, -euse** [mwasɔnœʀ, -øz] *nm/f* harvester, reaper ▷ *nf* (*machine*) harvester
**moissonneuse-batteuse** [mwasɔnøzbatøz] (*pl* **moissonneuses-batteuses**) *nf* combine harvester
**moite** [mwat] *adj* (*peau, mains*) sweaty, sticky; (*atmosphère*) muggy
**moitié** [mwatje] *nf* half; (*épouse*): **sa ~** his better half; **la ~** half; **la ~ de** half (of), half the amount (*ou* number) of; **la ~ du temps/des gens** half the time/the people; **à la ~ de** halfway through; **~ moins grand** half as tall; **~ plus long** half as long again, longer by half; **à ~** half (*avant le verbe*), half- (*avant l'adjectif*); **à ~ prix** (at) half price, half-price; **de ~** by half; **~ ~** half-and-half
**moka** [mɔka] *nm* (*café*) mocha coffee; (*gâteau*) mocha cake
**mol** [mɔl] *adj m voir* **mou**
**molaire** [mɔlɛʀ] *nf* molar
**moldave** [mɔldav] *adj* Moldavian
**Moldavie** [mɔldavi] *nf*: **la ~** Moldavia
**môle** [mol] *nm* jetty
**moléculaire** [mɔlekylɛʀ] *adj* molecular
**molécule** [mɔlekyl] *nf* molecule
**moleskine** [mɔlɛskin] *nf* imitation leather
**molester** [mɔlɛste] *vt* to manhandle, maul (about)
**molette** [mɔlɛt] *nf* toothed *ou* cutting wheel
**mollasse** [mɔlas] *adj* (*péj: sans énergie*) sluggish;

(*: flasque*) flabby
**molle** [mɔl] *adj f voir* **mou**
**mollement** [mɔlmã] *adv* softly; (*péj*) sluggishly; (*protester*) feebly
**mollesse** [mɔlɛs] *nf* (*voir mou*) softness; flabbiness; limpness; sluggishness; feebleness
**mollet** [mɔlɛ] *nm* calf ▷ *adj m*: **œuf ~** soft-boiled egg
**molletière** [mɔltjɛʀ] *adj f*: **bande ~** puttee
**molleton** [mɔltɔ̃] *nm* (*Textiles*) felt
**molletonné, e** [mɔltɔne] *adj* (*gants etc*) fleece-lined
**mollir** [mɔliʀ] *vi* (*jambes*) to give way; (*Navig: vent*) to drop, die down; (*fig: personne*) to relent; (*: courage*) to fail, flag
**mollusque** [mɔlysk(ə)] *nm* (*Zool*) mollusc; (*fig: personne*) lazy lump
**molosse** [mɔlɔs] *nm* big ferocious dog
**môme** [mom] *nm/f* (*fam: enfant*) brat; (*: fille*) bird (*Brit*), chick
**moment** [mɔmã] *nm* moment; (*occasion*): **profiter du ~** to take (advantage of) the opportunity; **ce n'est pas le ~** this is not the right time; **à un certain ~** at some point; **à un ~ donné** at a certain point; **à quel ~?** when exactly?; **au même ~** at the same time; (*instant*) at the same moment; **pour un bon ~** for a good while; **pour le ~** for the moment, for the time being; **au ~ de** at the time of; **au ~ où** as; at a time when; **à tout ~** at any time *ou* moment; (*continuellement*) constantly, continually; **en ce ~** at the moment; (*aujourd'hui*) at present; **sur le ~** at the time; **par ~s** now and then, at times; **d'un ~ à l'autre** any time (now); **du ~ où** *ou* **que** seeing that, since; **n'avoir pas un ~ à soi** not to have a minute to oneself
**momentané, e** [mɔmãtane] *adj* temporary, momentary
**momentanément** [mɔmãtanemã] *adv* for a moment, for a while
**momie** [mɔmi] *nf* mummy
**mon** [mɔ̃], **ma** [ma] (*pl* **mes** [me]) *adj poss* my
**monacal, e, -aux** [mɔnakal, -o] *adj* monastic
**Monaco** [mɔnako] *nm*: **le ~** Monaco
**monarchie** [mɔnaʀʃi] *nf* monarchy
**monarchiste** [mɔnaʀʃist(ə)] *adj, nm/f* monarchist
**monarque** [mɔnaʀk(ə)] *nm* monarch
**monastère** [mɔnastɛʀ] *nm* monastery
**monastique** [mɔnastik] *adj* monastic
**monceau, x** [mɔ̃so] *nm* heap
**mondain, e** [mɔ̃dɛ̃, -ɛn] *adj* (*soirée, vie*) society *cpd*; (*obligations*) social; (*peintre, écrivain*) fashionable; (*personne*) society *cpd* ▷ *nm/f* society man/woman, socialite ▷ *nf*: **la Mondaine, la police ~e** ≈ the vice squad
**mondanités** [mɔ̃danite] *nfpl* (*vie mondaine*) society life *sg*; (*paroles*) (society) small talk *sg*; (*Presse*) (society) gossip column *sg*
**monde** [mɔ̃d] *nm* world; (*personnes mondaines*): **le ~** (high) society; (*milieu*): **être du même ~** to move in the same circles; (*gens*): **il y a du ~**

(*beaucoup de gens*) there are a lot of people; (*quelques personnes*) there are some people; **y a-t-il du ~ dans le salon?** is there anybody in the lounge?; **beaucoup/peu de ~** many/few people; **le meilleur** *etc* **du ~** the best *etc* in the world; **mettre au ~** to bring into the world; **pas le moins du ~** not in the least; **se faire un ~ de qch** to make a great deal of fuss about sth; **tour du ~** round-the-world trip; **homme/femme du ~** society man/woman

**mondial, e, -aux** [mɔ̃djal, -o] *adj* (*population*) world *cpd*; (*influence*) world-wide

**mondialement** [mɔ̃djalmɑ̃] *adv* throughout the world

**mondialisation** [mɔ̃djalizasjɔ̃] *nf* (*d'une technique*) global application; (*d'un conflit*) global spread

**mondovision** [mɔ̃dɔvizjɔ̃] *nf* (world coverage by) satellite television

**monégasque** [mɔnegask(ə)] *adj* Monegasque, of *ou* from Monaco ▷ *nm/f*: **Monégasque** Monegasque

**monétaire** [mɔnetɛʀ] *adj* monetary

**monétarisme** [mɔnetaʀism(ə)] *nm* monetarism

**monétique** [mɔnetik] *nf* electronic money

**mongol, e** [mɔ̃gɔl] *adj* Mongol, Mongolian ▷ *nm* (*Ling*) Mongolian ▷ *nm/f*: **Mongol, e** (*Méd*) Mongol, Mongoloid; (*de la Mongolie*) Mongolian

**Mongolie** [mɔ̃gɔli] *nf*: **la ~** Mongolia

**mongolien, ne** [mɔ̃gɔljɛ̃, -ɛn] *adj, nm/f* mongol

**mongolisme** [mɔ̃gɔlism(ə)] *nm* mongolism, Down's syndrome

**moniteur, -trice** [mɔnitœʀ, -tʀis] *nm/f* (*Sport*) instructor (instructress); (*de colonie de vacances*) supervisor ▷ *nm* (*écran*) monitor; **~ cardiaque** cardiac monitor; **~ d'auto-école** driving instructor

**monitorage** [mɔnitɔʀaʒ] *nm* monitoring

**monitorat** [mɔnitɔʀa] *nm* (*formation*) instructor's training (course); (*fonction*) instructorship

**monnaie** [mɔnɛ] *nf* (*pièce*) coin; (*Écon: gén: moyen d'échange*) currency; (*petites pièces*): **avoir de la ~** to have (some) change; **faire de la ~** to get (some) change; **avoir/faire la ~ de 20 euros** to have change of/get change for 20 euros; **faire** *ou* **donner à qn la ~ de 20 euros** to give sb change for 20 euros, change 20 euros for sb; **rendre à qn la ~ (sur 20 euros)** to give sb the change (from *ou* out of 20 euros); **servir de ~ d'échange** (*fig*) to be used as a bargaining counter *ou* as bargaining counters; **payer en ~ de singe** to fob (sb) off with empty promises; **c'est ~ courante** it's a common occurrence; **~ légale** legal tender

**monnayable** [mɔnɛjabl(ə)] *adj* (*vendable*) convertible into cash; **mes services sont ~s** my services are worth money

**monnayer** [mɔnɛje] *vt* to convert into cash; (*talent*) to capitalize on

**monnayeur** [mɔnɛjœʀ] *nm voir* **faux**

**mono** [mɔno] *nf* (*monophonie*) mono ▷ *nm* (*monoski*) monoski

**monochrome** [mɔnɔkʀom] *adj* monochrome

**monocle** [mɔnɔkl(ə)] *nm* monocle, eyeglass

**monocoque** [mɔnɔkɔk] *adj* (*voiture*) monocoque ▷ *nm* (*voilier*) monohull

**monocorde** [mɔnɔkɔʀd(ə)] *adj* monotonous

**monoculture** [mɔnɔkyltyʀ] *nf* single-crop farming, monoculture

**monogamie** [mɔnɔgami] *nf* monogamy

**monogramme** [mɔnɔgʀam] *nm* monogram

**monokini** [mɔnɔkini] *nm* one-piece bikini, bikini pants *pl*

**monolingue** [mɔnɔlɛ̃g] *adj* monolingual

**monolithique** [mɔnɔlitik] *adj* (*lit, fig*) monolithic

**monologue** [mɔnɔlɔg] *nm* monologue, soliloquy; **~ intérieur** stream of consciousness

**monologuer** [mɔnɔlɔge] *vi* to soliloquize

**monôme** [mɔnom] *nm* (*Math*) monomial; (*d'étudiants*) students' rag procession

**monoparental, e, -aux** [mɔnɔpaʀɑ̃tal, -o] *adj*: **famille ~e** single-parent *ou* one-parent family

**monophasé, e** [mɔnɔfaze] *adj* single-phase *cpd*

**monophonie** [mɔnɔfɔni] *nf* monophony

**monoplace** [mɔnɔplas] *adj, nm, nf* single-seater, one-seater

**monoplan** [mɔnɔplɑ̃] *nm* monoplane

**monopole** [mɔnɔpɔl] *nm* monopoly

**monopolisation** [mɔnɔpɔlizasjɔ̃] *nf* monopolization

**monopoliser** [mɔnɔpɔlize] *vt* to monopolize

**monorail** [mɔnɔʀaj] *nm* monorail; monorail train

**monoski** [mɔnɔski] *nm* monoski

**monosyllabe** [mɔnɔsilab] *nm* monosyllable, word of one syllable

**monosyllabique** [mɔnɔsilabik] *adj* monosyllabic

**monotone** [mɔnɔtɔn] *adj* monotonous

**monotonie** [mɔnɔtɔni] *nf* monotony

**monseigneur** [mɔ̃sɛɲœʀ] *nm* (*archevêque, évêque*) Your (*ou* His) Grace; (*cardinal*) Your (*ou* His) Eminence; **M~ Thomas** Bishop Thomas; Cardinal Thomas

**Monsieur** [məsjø] (*pl* **Messieurs** [mesjø]) *nm* (*titre*) Mr; (*homme quelconque*): **un/le monsieur** a/the gentleman; *voir aussi* **Madame**

**monstre** [mɔ̃stʀ(ə)] *nm* monster ▷ *adj* (*fam: effet, publicité*) massive; **un travail ~** a fantastic amount of work; an enormous job; **~ sacré** superstar

**monstrueux, -euse** [mɔ̃stʀyø, -øz] *adj* monstrous

**monstruosité** [mɔ̃stʀyozite] *nf* monstrosity

**mont** [mɔ̃] *nm*: **par ~s et par vaux** up hill and down dale; **le M~ Blanc** Mont Blanc; **~ de Vénus** mons veneris

**montage** [mɔ̃taʒ] *nm* putting up; (*d'un bijou*) mounting, setting; (*d'une machine etc*) assembly; (*Photo*) photomontage; (*Ciné*) editing; **~ sonore** sound editing

**m**

**montagnard, e** [mɔ̃taɲaʀ, -aʀd(ə)] *adj*
mountain *cpd* ▷ *nm/f* mountain-dweller
**montagne** [mɔ̃taɲ] *nf* (*cime*) mountain; (*région*):
**la ~** the mountains *pl*; **la haute ~** the high
mountains; **les ~s Rocheuses** the Rocky
Mountains, the Rockies; **~s russes** big dipper
*sg*, switchback *sg*
**montagneux, -euse** [mɔ̃taɲø, -øz] *adj*
mountainous; hilly
**montant, e** [mɔ̃tɑ̃, -ɑ̃t] *adj* (*mouvement, marée*)
rising; (*chemin*) uphill; (*robe, corsage*) high-
necked ▷ *nm* (*somme, total*) (sum) total, (total)
amount; (*de fenêtre*) upright; (*de lit*) post
**mont-de-piété** [mɔ̃dpjete] (*pl* **monts-de-piété**)
*nm* pawnshop
**monte** [mɔ̃t] *nf* (*accouplement*): **la ~** stud; (*d'un
jockey*) seat
**monté, e** [mɔ̃te] *adj*: **être ~ contre qn** to be
angry with sb; (*fourni, équipé*): **~ en** equipped
with
**monte-charge** [mɔ̃tʃaʀʒ(ə)] *nm inv* goods lift,
hoist
**montée** [mɔ̃te] *nf* rising, rise; (*escalade*) ascent,
climb; (*chemin*) way up; (*côte*) hill; **au milieu de
la ~** halfway up; **le moteur chauffe dans les
~s** the engine overheats going uphill
**Monténégro** [mɔ̃tenegʀo] *nm*: **le ~** Montenegro
**monte-plats** [mɔ̃tpla] *nm inv* service lift
**monter** [mɔ̃te] *vt* (*escalier, côte*) to go (*ou* come)
up; (*valise, paquet*) to take (*ou* bring) up; (*cheval*)
to mount; (*femelle*) to cover, serve; (*tente,
échafaudage*) to put up; (*machine*) to assemble;
(*bijou*) to mount, set; (*Couture*) to sew on;
(*: manche*) to set in; (*Ciné*) to edit; (*Théât*) to put
on, stage; (*société, coup etc*) to set up; (*fournir,
équiper*) to equip ▷ *vi* to go (*ou* come) up; (*avion,
voiture*) to climb, go up; (*chemin, niveau,
température, voix, prix*) to go up, rise; (*brouillard,
bruit*) to rise, come up; (*passager*) to get on; (*à
cheval*): **~ bien/mal** to ride well/badly; **~ à
cheval/bicyclette** to get on *ou* mount a horse/
bicycle; (*faire du cheval etc*) to ride (a horse), to
(ride a) bicycle; **~ à pied/en voiture** to walk/
drive up, go up on foot/by car; **~ dans le train/
l'avion** to get into the train/plane, board the
train/plane; **~ sur** to climb up onto; **~ sur** *ou* **à
un arbre/une échelle** to climb (up) a tree/
ladder; **~ à bord** to (get on) board; **~ à la tête de
qn** to go to sb's head; **~ sur les planches** to go
on the stage; **~ en grade** to be promoted; **se
monter** (*s'équiper*) to equip o.s., get kitted out
(*Brit*); **se ~ à** (*frais etc*) to add up to, come to; **~ qn
contre qn** to set sb against sb; **~ la tête à qn** to
give sb ideas
**monteur, -euse** [mɔ̃tœʀ, -øz] *nm/f* (*Tech*) fitter;
(*Ciné*) (film) editor
**montgolfière** [mɔ̃gɔlfjɛʀ] *nf* hot-air balloon
**monticule** [mɔ̃tikyl] *nm* mound
**montmartrois, e** [mɔ̃martʀwa, -waz] *adj* of *ou*
from Montmartre
**montre** [mɔ̃tʀ(ə)] *nf* watch; (*ostentation*): **pour
la ~** for show; **~ en main** exactly, to the minute;

**faire ~ de** to show, display; **contre la ~** (*Sport*)
against the clock; **~ de plongée** diver's watch
**montréalais, e** [mɔ̃ʀeale, -ɛz] *adj* of *ou* from
Montreal ▷ *nm/f*: **Montréalais, e** Montrealer
**montre-bracelet** [mɔ̃tʀəbʀaslɛ] (*pl* **montres-
bracelets**) *nf* wrist watch
**montrer** [mɔ̃tʀe] *vt* to show; **se montrer** to
appear; **~ qch à qn** to show sb sth; **~ qch du
doigt** to point to sth, point one's finger at sth;
**se ~ intelligent** to prove (to be) intelligent
**montreur, -euse** [mɔ̃tʀœʀ, -øz] *nm/f*: **~ de
marionnettes** puppeteer
**monture** [mɔ̃tyʀ] *nf* (*bête*) mount; (*d'une bague*)
setting; (*de lunettes*) frame
**monument** [mɔnymɑ̃] *nm* monument; **~ aux
morts** war memorial
**monumental, e, -aux** [mɔnymɑ̃tal, -o] *adj*
monumental
**moquer** [mɔke]: **se ~ de** *vt* to make fun of,
laugh at; (*fam: se désintéresser de*) not to care
about; (*tromper*): **se ~ de qn** to take sb for a ride
**moquerie** [mɔkʀi] *nf* mockery *no pl*
**moquette** [mɔkɛt] *nf* fitted carpet, wall-to-wall
carpeting *no pl*
**moquetter** [mɔkete] *vt* to carpet
**moqueur, -euse** [mɔkœʀ, -øz] *adj* mocking
**moral, e, -aux** [mɔʀal, -o] *adj* moral ▷ *nm*
morale ▷ *nf* (*conduite*) morals *pl* (*règles*), moral
code, ethic; (*valeurs*) moral standards *pl*,
morality; (*science*) ethics *sg*, moral philosophy;
(*conclusion: d'une fable etc*) moral; **au ~, sur le
plan ~** morally; **avoir le ~ à zéro** to be really
down; **faire la ~ à** to lecture, preach at
**moralement** [mɔʀalmɑ̃] *adv* morally
**moralisateur, -trice** [mɔʀalizatœʀ, -tʀis] *adj*
moralizing, sanctimonious ▷ *nm/f* moralizer
**moraliser** [mɔʀalize] *vt* (*sermonner*) to lecture,
preach at
**moraliste** [mɔʀalist(ə)] *nm/f* moralist ▷ *adj*
moralistic
**moralité** [mɔʀalite] *nf* (*d'une action, attitude*)
morality; (*conduite*) morals *pl*; (*conclusion,
enseignement*) moral
**moratoire** [mɔʀatwaʀ] *adj m*: **intérêts ~s** (*Écon*)
interest on arrears
**morbide** [mɔʀbid] *adj* morbid
**morceau, x** [mɔʀso] *nm* piece, bit; (*d'une œuvre*)
passage, extract; (*Mus*) piece; (*Culin: de viande*)
cut; **mettre en ~x** to pull to pieces *ou* bits
**morceler** [mɔʀsəle] *vt* to break up, divide up
**morcellement** [mɔʀsɛlmɑ̃] *nm* breaking up
**mordant, e** [mɔʀdɑ̃, -ɑ̃t] *adj* scathing, cutting;
(*froid*) biting ▷ *nm* (*dynamisme, énergie*) spirit;
(*fougue*) bite, punch
**mordicus** [mɔʀdikys] *adv* (*fam*) obstinately,
stubbornly
**mordiller** [mɔʀdije] *vt* to nibble at, chew at
**mordoré, e** [mɔʀdɔʀe] *adj* lustrous bronze
**mordre** [mɔʀdʀ(ə)] *vt* to bite; (*lime, vis*) to bite
into ▷ *vi* (*poisson*) to bite; **~ dans** to bite into; **~
sur** (*fig*) to go over into, overlap into; **~ à qch**
(*comprendre, aimer*) to take to; **~ à l'hameçon** to

bite, rise to the bait

**mordu, e** [mɔʀdy] *pp de* **mordre** ▷ *adj (amoureux)* smitten ▷ *nm/f*: **un ~ du jazz/de la voile** a jazz/ sailing fanatic *ou* buff

**morfondre** [mɔʀfɔ̃dʀ(ə)]: **se morfondre** *vi* to mope

**morgue** [mɔʀg(ə)] *nf (arrogance)* haughtiness; *(lieu: de la police)* morgue; *(: à l'hôpital)* mortuary

**moribond, e** [mɔʀibɔ̃, -ɔ̃d] *adj* dying, moribund

**morille** [mɔʀij] *nf* morel *(mushroom)*

**mormon, e** [mɔʀmɔ̃, -ɔn] *adj, nm/f* Mormon

**morne** [mɔʀn(ə)] *adj (personne, visage)* glum, gloomy; *(temps, vie)* dismal, dreary

**morose** [mɔʀoz] *adj* sullen, morose; *(marché)* sluggish

**morphine** [mɔʀfin] *nf* morphine

**morphinomane** [mɔʀfinɔman] *nm/f* morphine addict

**morphologie** [mɔʀfɔlɔʒi] *nf* morphology

**morphologique** [mɔʀfɔlɔʒik] *adj* morphological

**mors** [mɔʀ] *nm* bit

**morse** [mɔʀs(ə)] *nm (Zool)* walrus; *(Tél)* Morse (code)

**morsure** [mɔʀsyʀ] *nf* bite

**mort¹** [mɔʀ] *nf* death; **se donner la ~** to take one's own life; **de ~** *(silence, pâleur)* deathly; **blessé à ~** fatally wounded *ou* injured; **à la vie, à la ~** for better, for worse; **~ clinique** brain death; **~ subite du nourrisson, ~ au berceau** cot death

**mort²** [mɔʀ, mɔʀt(ə)] *pp de* **mourir** ▷ *adj* dead ▷ *nm/f (défunt)* dead man/woman; *(victime)*: **il y a eu plusieurs ~s** several people were killed, there were several killed ▷ *nm (Cartes)* dummy; **~ ou vif** dead or alive; **~ de peur/fatigue** frightened to death/dead tired; **~s et blessés** casualties; **faire le ~** to play dead; *(fig)* to lie low

**mortadelle** [mɔʀtadɛl] *nf* mortadella

**mortalité** [mɔʀtalite] *nf* mortality, death rate

**mort-aux-rats** [mɔʀtoʀa] *nf inv* rat poison

**mortel, le** [mɔʀtɛl] *adj (poison etc)* deadly, lethal; *(accident, blessure)* fatal; *(Rel: danger, frayeur)* mortal; *(fig: froid)* deathly; *(: ennui, soirée)* deadly *(boring)* ▷ *nm/f* mortal

**mortellement** [mɔʀtɛlmɑ̃] *adv (blessé etc)* fatally, mortally; *(pâle etc)* deathly; *(fig: ennuyeux etc)* deadly

**morte-saison** [mɔʀtəsɛzɔ̃] *(pl* **mortes-saisons)** *nf* slack *ou* off season

**mortier** [mɔʀtje] *nm (gén)* mortar

**mortifier** [mɔʀtifje] *vt* to mortify

**mort-né, e** [mɔʀne] *adj (enfant)* stillborn; *(fig)* abortive

**mortuaire** [mɔʀtɥɛʀ] *adj* funeral *cpd*; **avis ~s** death announcements, intimations; **chapelle ~** mortuary chapel; **couronne ~** *(funeral)* wreath; **domicile ~** house of the deceased; **drap ~** pall

**morue** [mɔʀy] *nf (Zool)* cod *inv*; *(Culin: salée)* salt-cod

**morvandeau, -elle, x** [mɔʀvɑ̃do, -ɛl] *adj* of *ou*

from the Morvan region

**morveux, -euse** [mɔʀvø, -øz] *adj (fam)* snotty-nosed

**mosaïque** [mɔzaik] *nf (Art)* mosaic; *(fig)* patchwork

**Moscou** [mɔsku] *n* Moscow

**moscovite** [mɔskɔvit] *adj ou* from Moscow, Moscow *cpd* ▷ *nm/f*: **Moscovite** Muscovite

**mosquée** [mɔske] *nf* mosque

**mot** [mo] *nm* word; *(message)* line, note; *(bon mot etc)* saying; **le ~ de la fin** the last word; **~ à ~** *adj, adv* word for word; **~ pour ~** word for word, verbatim; **sur** *ou* **à ces ~s** with these words; **en un ~** in a word; **à ~s couverts** in veiled terms; **prendre qn au ~** to take sb at his word; **se donner le ~** to send the word round; **avoir son ~ à dire** to have a say; **~ d'ordre** watchword; **~ de passe** password; **~s croisés** crossword (puzzle) *sg*

**motard** [mɔtaʀ] *nm (policier)* motorcycle cop

**motel** [mɔtɛl] *nm* motel

**moteur, -trice** [mɔtœʀ, -tʀis] *adj (Anat, Physiol)* motor; *(Tech)* driving; *(Auto)*: **à 4 roues motrices** 4-wheel drive ▷ *nm* engine, motor; *(fig)* mover, mainspring; **à ~** power-driven, motor *cpd*; **~ à deux temps** two-stroke engine; **~ à explosion** internal combustion engine; **~ à réaction** jet engine; **~ de recherche** search engine; **~ thermique** heat engine

**motif** [mɔtif] *nm (cause)* motive; *(décoratif)* design, pattern, motif; *(d'un tableau)* subject, motif; *(Mus)* figure, motif; **motifs** *nmpl (Jur)* grounds *pl*; **sans ~** *adj* groundless

**motion** [mɔsjɔ̃] *nf* motion; **~ de censure** motion of censure, vote of no confidence

**motivation** [mɔtivasjɔ̃] *nf* motivation

**motivé, e** [mɔtive] *adj (acte)* justified; *(personne)* motivated

**motiver** [mɔtive] *vt (justifier)* to justify, account for; *(Admin, Jur, Psych)* to motivate

**moto** [mɔto] *nf (motor)bike*; **~ verte** *ou* **de trial** trail *(Brit) ou* dirt *(US)* bike

**moto-cross** [mɔtokʀɔs] *nm* motocross

**motoculteur** [mɔtokyltœʀ] *nm (motorized)* cultivator

**motocyclette** [mɔtosiklɛt] *nf* motorbike, motorcycle

**motocyclisme** [mɔtosiklism(ə)] *nm* motorcycle racing

**motocycliste** [mɔtosiklist(ə)] *nm/f* motorcyclist

**motoneige** [mɔtonɛʒ] *nf* snow bike

**motorisé, e** [mɔtoʀize] *adj (troupe)* motorized; *(personne)* having one's own transport

**motrice** [mɔtʀis] *adj f voir* **moteur**

**motte** [mɔt] *nf*: **~ de terre** lump of earth, clod (of earth); **~ de gazon** turf, sod; **~ de beurre** lump of butter

**motus** [mɔtys] *excl*: **~ (et bouche cousue)!** mum's the word!

**mou, mol, molle** [mu, mɔl] *adj* soft; *(péj: visage,*

m

*traits*) flabby; (: *geste*) limp; (: *personne*) sluggish; (: *résistance, protestations*) feeble ▷ *nm* (*homme mou*) wimp; (*abats*) lights *pl*, lungs *pl*; (*de la corde*): **avoir du ~** to be slack; **donner du ~** to slacken, loosen; **avoir les jambes molles** to be weak at the knees

**mouchard, e** [muʃaʀ, -aʀd(ə)] *nm/f* (*péj*: *Scol*) sneak; (: *Police*) stool pigeon, grass (*Brit*) ▷ *nm* (*appareil*) control device; (: *de camion*) tachograph

**mouche** [muʃ] *nf* fly; (*Escrime*) button; (*de taffetas*) patch; **prendre la ~** to go into a huff; **faire ~** to score a bull's-eye

**moucher** [muʃe] *vt* (*enfant*) to blow the nose of; (*chandelle*) to snuff (out); **se moucher** to blow one's nose

**moucheron** [muʃʀɔ̃] *nm* midge

**moucheté, e** [muʃte] *adj* (*cheval*) dappled; (*laine*) flecked; (*Escrime*) buttoned

**mouchoir** [muʃwaʀ] *nm* handkerchief, hanky; **~ en papier** tissue, paper hanky

**moudre** [mudʀ(ə)] *vt* to grind

**moue** [mu] *nf* pout; **faire la ~** to pout; (*fig*) to pull a face

**mouette** [mwɛt] *nf* (sea)gull

**moufette, mouffette** [mufɛt] *nf* skunk

**moufle** [mufl(ə)] *nf* (*gant*) mitt(en); (*Tech*) pulley block

**mouflon** [muflɔ̃] *nm* mouf(f)lon

**mouillage** [muja3] *nm* (*Navig*: *lieu*) anchorage, moorings *pl*

**mouillé, e** [muje] *adj* wet

**mouiller** [muje] *vt* (*humecter*) to wet, moisten; (*tremper*): **~ qn/qch** to make sb/sth wet; (*Culin*: *ragoût*) to add stock *ou* wine to; (*couper, diluer*) to water down; (*mine etc*) to lay ▷ *vi* (*Navig*) to lie *ou* be at anchor; **se mouiller** to get wet; (*fam*) to commit o.s.; to get (o.s.) involved; **~ l'ancre** to drop *ou* cast anchor

**mouillette** [mujɛt] *nf* (*bread*) finger

**mouillure** [mujyʀ] *nf* wet *no pl*; (*tache*) wet patch

**moulage** [mula3] *nm* moulding (*Brit*), molding (US); casting; (*objet*) cast

**moulais** *etc* [mulɛ] *vb voir* **moudre**

**moulant, e** [mulɑ̃, -ɑ̃t] *adj* figure-hugging

**moule** [mul] *vb voir* **moudre** ▷ *nf* (*mollusque*) mussel ▷ *nm* (*creux, Culin*) mould (*Brit*), mold (US); (*modèle plein*) cast; **~ à gâteau** *nm* cake tin (*Brit*) *ou* pan (US); **~ à gaufre** *nm* waffle iron; **~ à tarte** *nm* pie *ou* flan dish

**moulent** [mul] *vb voir* **moudre**; **mouler**

**mouler** [mule] *vt* (*brique*) to mould (*Brit*), mold (US); (*statue*) to cast; (*visage, bas-relief*) to make a cast of; (*lettre*) to shape with care; (*vêtement*) to hug, fit closely round; **~ qch sur** (*fig*) to model sth on

**moulin** [mulɛ̃] *nm* mill; (*fam*) engine; **~ à café** coffee mill; **~ à eau** watermill; **~ à légumes** (vegetable) shredder; **~ à paroles** (*fig*) chatterbox; **~ à poivre** pepper mill; **~ à prières** prayer wheel; **~ à vent** windmill

**mouliner** [muline] *vt* to shred

**moulinet** [mulinɛ] *nm* (*de treuil*) winch; (*de canne*

*à pêche*) reel; (*mouvement*): **faire des ~s avec qch** to whirl sth around

**moulinette®** [mulinɛt] *nf* (vegetable) shredder

**moulons** *etc* [mulɔ̃] *vb voir* **moudre**

**moulu, e** [muly] *pp de* **moudre** ▷ *adj* (*café*) ground

**moulure** [mulyʀ] *nf* (*ornement*) moulding (*Brit*), molding (US)

**mourant, e** [muʀɑ̃, -ɑ̃t] *vb voir* **mourir** ▷ *adj* dying ▷ *nm/f* dying man/woman

**mourir** [muʀiʀ] *vi* to die; (*civilisation*) to die out; **~ assassiné** to be murdered; **~ de froid/faim/ vieillesse** to die of exposure/hunger/old age; **~ de faim/d'ennui** (*fig*) to be starving/be bored to death; **~ d'envie de faire** to be dying to do; **s'ennuyer à ~** to be bored to death

**mousquetaire** [muskətɛʀ] *nm* musketeer

**mousqueton** [muskətɔ̃] *nm* (*fusil*) carbine; (*anneau*) snap-link, karabiner

**moussant, e** [musɑ̃, -ɑ̃t] *adj* foaming; **bain ~** foam *ou* bubble bath, bath foam

**mousse** [mus] *nf* (*Bot*) moss; (*écume: sur eau, bière*) froth, foam; (: *shampooing*) lather; (*de champagne*) bubbles *pl*; (*Culin*) mousse; (*en caoutchouc etc*) foam ▷ *nm* (*Navig*) ship's boy; **bain de ~** bubble bath; **bas ~** stretch stockings; **balle ~** rubber ball; **~ carbonique** (fire-fighting) foam; **~ de nylon** nylon foam; (*tissu*) stretch nylon; **~ à raser** shaving foam

**mousseline** [muslin] *nf* (*Textiles*) muslin; chiffon; **pommes ~** (*Culin*) creamed potatoes

**mousser** [muse] *vi* to foam; to lather

**mousseux, -euse** [musø, -øz] *adj* (*chocolat*) frothy; (*eau*) foamy, frothy; (*vin*) sparkling ▷ *nm*: **(vin) ~** sparkling wine

**mousson** [musɔ̃] *nf* monsoon

**moussu, e** [musy] *adj* mossy

**moustache** [mustaʃ] *nf* moustache; **moustaches** *nfpl* (*d'animal*) whiskers *pl*

**moustachu, e** [mustaʃy] *adj* wearing a moustache

**moustiquaire** [mustikɛʀ] *nf* (*rideau*) mosquito net; (*chassis*) mosquito screen

**moustique** [mustik] *nm* mosquito

**moutarde** [mutaʀd(ə)] *nf* mustard ▷ *adj inv* mustard(-coloured)

**moutardier** [mutaʀdje] *nm* mustard jar

**mouton** [mutɔ̃] *nm* (*Zool, péj*) sheep *inv*; (*peau*) sheepskin; (*Culin*) mutton

**mouture** [mutyʀ] *nf* grinding; (*péj*) rehash

**mouvant, e** [muvɑ̃, -ɑ̃t] *adj* unsettled; changing; shifting

**mouvement** [muvmɑ̃] *nm* (*gen, aussi: mécanisme*) movement; (*ligne courbe*) contours *pl*; (*fig: tumulte, agitation*) activity, bustle; (: *impulsion*) impulse; reaction; (*geste*) gesture; (*Mus: rythme*) tempo; **en ~** in motion; on the move; **mettre qch en ~** to set sth in motion, set sth going; **~ d'humeur** fit *ou* burst of temper; **~ d'opinion** trend of (public) opinion; **le ~ perpétuel** perpetual motion

**mouvementé, e** [muvmɑ̃te] *adj* (*vie, poursuite*)

eventful; (*réunion*) turbulent

**mouvoir** [muvwaʀ] *vt* (*levier, membre*) to move; (*machine*) to drive; **se mouvoir** to move

**moyen, ne** [mwajɛ̃, -ɛn] *adj* average; (*tailles, prix*) medium; (*de grandeur moyenne*) medium-sized ▷ *nm* (*façon*) means *sg*, way ▷ *nf* average; (*Statistique*) mean; (*Scol: à l'examen*) pass mark; (*Auto*) average speed; **moyens** *nmpl* (*capacités*) means; **au ~ de** by means of; **y a-t-il ~ de ...?** is it possible to ...?, can one ...?; **par quel ~?** how?, which way?, by which means?; **par tous les ~s** by every means, every possible way; **avec les ~s du bord** (*fig*) with what's available *ou* what comes to hand; **employer les grands ~s** to resort to drastic measures; **par ses propres ~s** all by oneself; **en ~ne** on (an) average; **faire la ~ne** to work out the average; **~ de locomotion/d'expression** means of transport/expression; **~ âge** Middle Ages; **~ de transport** means of transport; **~ne** average age; **~ne entreprise** (*Comm*) medium-sized firm

**moyenâgeux, -euse** [mwajɛnaʒø, -øz] *adj* medieval

**moyen-courrier** [mwajɛ̃kuʀje] *nm* (*Aviat*) medium-haul aircraft

**moyennant** [mwajɛnɑ̃] *prép* (*somme*) for; (*service, conditions*) in return for; (*travail, effort*) with

**moyennement** [mwajɛnmɑ̃] *adv* fairly, moderately; (*faire*) fairly *ou* moderately well

**Moyen-Orient** [mwajɛnɔʀjɑ̃] *nm*: **le ~** the Middle East

**moyeu, x** [mwajø] *nm* hub

**mozambicain, e** [mɔzɑ̃bikɛ̃, -ɛn] *adj* Mozambican

**Mozambique** [mɔzɑ̃bik] *nm*: **le ~** Mozambique

**MRAP** *sigle m* = **Mouvement contre le racisme et pour l'amitié entre les peuples**

**MRG** *sigle m* (= *Mouvement des radicaux de gauche*) *political party*

**ms** *abr* (= *manuscrit*) MS., ms

**MSF** *sigle mpl* = **Médecins sans frontières**

**MST** *sigle f* (= *maladie sexuellement transmissible*) STD (= *sexually transmitted disease*)

**mû, mue** [my] *pp de* **mouvoir**

**mucosité** [mykozite] *nf* mucus *no pl*

**mucus** [mykys] *nm* mucus *no pl*

**mue** [my] *pp de* **mouvoir** ▷ *nf* moulting (*Brit*), molting (*US*); sloughing; breaking of the voice

**muer** [mɥe] *vi* (*oiseau, mammifère*) to moult (*Brit*), molt (*US*); (*serpent*) to slough (its skin); (*jeune garçon*): **il mue** his voice is breaking; **se ~ en** to transform into

**muet, te** [mɥɛ, -ɛt] *adj* dumb; (*fig*): **~ d'admiration** *etc* speechless with admiration *etc*; (*joie, douleur, Ciné*) silent; (*Ling: lettre*) silent, mute; (*carte*) blank ▷ *nm/f* mute ▷ *nm*: **le ~** (*Ciné*) the silent cinema *ou* (*esp US*) movies

**mufle** [myfl(ə)] *nm* muzzle; (*goujat*) boor ▷ *adj* boorish

**mugir** [myʒiʀ] *vi* (*bœuf*) to bellow; (*vache*) to low, moo; (*fig*) to howl

**mugissement** [myʒismɑ̃] *nm* (*voir mugir*) bellowing; lowing, mooing; howling

**muguet** [mygɛ] *nm* (*Bot*) lily of the valley; (*Méd*) thrush

**mulâtre, tresse** [mylɑtʀ(ə), -tʀɛs] *nm/f* mulatto

**mule** [myl] *nf* (*Zool*) (she-)mule

**mules** [myl] *nfpl* (*pantoufles*) mules

**mulet** [mylɛ] *nm* (*Zool*) (he-)mule; (*poisson*) mullet

**muletier, -ière** [myltje, -jɛʀ] *adj*: **sentier *ou* chemin ~** mule track

**mulot** [mylo] *nm* fieldmouse

**multicolore** [myltikɔlɔʀ] *adj* multicoloured (*Brit*), multicolored (*US*)

**multicoque** [myltikɔk] *nm* multihull

**multidisciplinaire** [myltidisiplinɛʀ] *adj* multidisciplinary

**multiforme** [myltifɔʀm(ə)] *adj* many-sided

**multilatéral, e, -aux** [myltilateʀal, -o] *adj* multilateral

**multimilliardaire** [myltimiljaʀdɛʀ], **multimillionnaire** [myltimiljɔnɛʀ] *adj, nm/f* multimillionaire

**multinational, e, -aux** [myltinasjɔnal, -o] *adj, nf* multinational

**multiple** [myltipl(ə)] *adj* multiple, numerous; (*varié*) many, manifold ▷ *nm* (*Math*) multiple

**multiplex** [myltiplɛks] *nm* (*Radio*) live link-up

**multiplicateur** [myltiplikatœʀ] *nm* multiplier

**multiplication** [myltiplikasjɔ̃] *nf* multiplication

**multiplicité** [myltiplisite] *nf* multiplicity

**multiplier** [myltiplije] *vt* to multiply; **se multiplier** *vi* to multiply; (*fig: personne*) to be everywhere at once

**multiprogrammation** [myltipʀɔgʀamasjɔ̃] *nf* (*Inform*) multiprogramming

**multipropriété** [myltipʀɔpʀijete] *nf* timesharing *no pl*

**multirisque** [myltiʀisk] *adj*: **assurance ~** multiple-risk insurance

**multisalles** [myltisal] *adj*: (**cinéma**) **~** multiplex (cinema)

**multitraitement** [myltitʀɛtmɑ̃] *nm* (*Inform*) multiprocessing

**multitude** [myltityd] *nf* multitude; mass; **une ~ de** a vast number of, a multitude of

**Munich** [mynik] *n* Munich

**munichois, e** [mynikwa, -waz] *adj* of *ou* from Munich

**municipal, e, -aux** [mynisipal, -o] *adj* municipal; town *cpd*

**municipalité** [mynisipalite] *nf* (*corps municipal*) town council, corporation; (*commune*) town, municipality

**munificence** [mynifisɑ̃s] *nf* munificence

**munir** [myniʀ] *vt*: **~ qn/qch de** to equip sb/sth with; **se ~ de** to provide o.s. with

**munitions** [mynisjɔ̃] *nfpl* ammunition *sg*

**muqueuse** [mykøz] *nf* mucous membrane

**mur** [myʀ] *nm* wall; (*fig*) stone *ou* brick wall;

**m**

**faire le ~** (*interne, soldat*) to jump the wall; **~ du son** sound barrier

**mûr, e** [myʀ] *adj* ripe; (*personne*) mature ▷ *nf* (*de la ronce*) blackberry; (*du mûrier*) mulberry

**muraille** [myʀaj] *nf* (high) wall

**mural, e, -aux** [myʀal, -o] *adj* wall *cpd* ▷ *nm* (*Art*) mural

**mûre** [myʀ] *nf voir* **mûr**

**mûrement** [myʀmã] *adv*: **ayant ~ réfléchi** having given the matter much thought

**murène** [myʀɛn] *nf* moray (eel)

**murer** [myʀe] *vt* (*enclos*) to wall (in); (*porte, issue*) to wall up; (*personne*) to wall up *ou* in

**muret** [myʀɛ] *nm* low wall

**mûrier** [myʀje] *nm* mulberry tree; (*ronce*) blackberry bush

**mûrir** [myʀiʀ] *vi* (*fruit, blé*) to ripen; (*abcès, furoncle*) to come to a head; (*fig: idée, personne*) to mature; (*projet*) to develop ▷ *vt* (*fruit, blé*) to ripen; (*personne*) to (make) mature; (*pensée, projet*) to nurture

**murmure** [myʀmyʀ] *nm* murmur; **murmures** *nmpl* (*plaintes*) murmurings, mutterings

**murmurer** [myʀmyʀe] *vi* to murmur; (*se plaindre*) to mutter, grumble

**mus** *etc* [my] *vb voir* **mouvoir**

**musaraigne** [myzaʀɛɲ] *nf* shrew

**musarder** [myzaʀde] *vi* to idle (about); (*en marchant*) to dawdle (along)

**musc** [mysk] *nm* musk

**muscade** [myskad] *nf* (*aussi*: **noix muscade**) nutmeg

**muscat** [myska] *nm* (*raisin*) muscat grape; (*vin*) muscatel (wine)

**muscle** [myskl(ə)] *nm* muscle

**musclé, e** [myskle] *adj* (*personne, corps*) muscular; (*fig: politique, régime etc*) strong-arm *cpd*

**muscler** [myskle] *vt* to develop the muscles of

**musculaire** [myskylɛʀ] *adj* muscular

**musculation** [myskylasjõ] *nf*: **exercices de ~** muscle-developing exercises

**musculature** [myskylatyʀ] *nf* muscle structure, muscles *pl*, musculature

**muse** [myz] *nf* muse

**museau, x** [myzo] *nm* muzzle

**musée** [myze] *nm* museum; (*de peinture*) art gallery

**museler** [myzle] *vt* to muzzle

**muselière** [myzəljɛʀ] *nf* muzzle

**musette** [myzɛt] *nf* (*sac*) lunch bag ▷ *adj inv* (*orchestre etc*) accordion *cpd*

**muséum** [myzeɔm] *nm* museum

**musical, e, -aux** [myzikal, -o] *adj* musical

**music-hall** [myzikol] *nm* variety theatre; (*genre*) variety

**musicien, ne** [myzisjɛ̃, -ɛn] *adj* musical ▷ *nm/f* musician

**musique** [myzik] *nf* music; (*fanfare*) band; **faire de la ~** to make music; (*jouer d'un instrument*) to play an instrument; **~ de chambre** chamber

music; **~ de fond** background music

**musqué, e** [myske] *adj* musky

**must** [mœst] *nm* must

**musulman, e** [myzylmã, -an] *adj, nm/f* Moslem, Muslim

**mutant, e** [mytã, -ãt] *nm/f* mutant

**mutation** [mytasjõ] *nf* (*Admin*) transfer; (*Bio*) mutation

**muter** [myte] *vt* (*Admin*) to transfer

**mutilation** [mytilasjõ] *nf* mutilation

**mutilé, e** [mytile] *nm/f* disabled person (*through loss of limbs*); **~ de guerre** disabled ex-serviceman; **grand ~** severely disabled person

**mutiler** [mytile] *vt* to mutilate, maim; (*fig*) to mutilate, deface

**mutin, e** [mytɛ̃, -in] *adj* (*enfant, air, ton*) mischievous, impish ▷ *nm/f* (*Mil, Navig*) mutineer

**mutiner** [mytine]: **se mutiner** *vi* to mutiny

**mutinerie** [mytinʀi] *nf* mutiny

**mutisme** [mytism(ə)] *nm* silence

**mutualiste** [mytɥalist(ə)] *adj*: **société ~** mutual benefit society, ≈ Friendly Society

**mutualité** [mytɥalite] *nf* (*assurance*) mutual (benefit) insurance scheme

**mutuel, le** [mytɥɛl] *adj* mutual ▷ *nf* mutual benefit society

**mutuellement** [mytɥɛlmã] *adv* each other, one another

**Myanmar** [mjanmaʀ] *nm* Myanmar

**myocarde** [mjɔkaʀd(ə)] *nm voir* **infarctus**

**myope** [mjɔp] *adj* short-sighted

**myopie** [mjɔpi] *nf* short-sightedness, myopia

**myosotis** [mjɔzɔtis] *nm* forget-me-not

**myriade** [miʀjad] *nf* myriad

**myrtille** [miʀtij] *nf* bilberry (*Brit*), blueberry (*US*), whortleberry

**mystère** [mistɛʀ] *nm* mystery

**mystérieusement** [misteʀjøzmã] *adv* mysteriously

**mystérieux, -euse** [misteʀjø, -øz] *adj* mysterious

**mysticisme** [mistisism(ə)] *nm* mysticism

**mystificateur, -trice** [mistifikatœʀ, -tʀis] *nm/f* hoaxer, practical joker

**mystification** [mistifikasjõ] *nf* (*tromperie, mensonge*) hoax; (*mythe*) mystification

**mystifier** [mistifje] *vt* to fool, take in; (*tromper*) to mystify

**mystique** [mistik] *adj* mystic, mystical ▷ *nm/f* mystic

**mythe** [mit] *nm* myth

**mythifier** [mitifje] *vt* to turn into a myth, mythologize

**mythique** [mitik] *adj* mythical

**mythologie** [mitɔlɔʒi] *nf* mythology

**mythologique** [mitɔlɔʒik] *adj* mythological

**mythomane** [mitɔman] *adj, nm/f* mythomaniac

# Nn

**N, n** [ɛn] *nm inv* N, n ▷ *abr* (= *nord*) N; **N comme Nicolas** N for Nelly (*Brit*) *ou* Nan (*US*)
**n'** [n] *adv voir* **ne**
**nabot** [nabo] *nm* dwarf
**nacelle** [nasɛl] *nf* (*de ballon*) basket
**nacre** [nakʀ(ə)] *nf* mother-of-pearl
**nacré, e** [nakʀe] *adj* pearly
**nage** [naʒ] *nf* swimming; (*manière*) style of swimming, stroke; **traverser/s'éloigner à la ~** to swim across/away; **en ~** bathed in perspiration; **~ indienne** sidestroke; **~ libre** freestyle; **~ papillon** butterfly
**nageoire** [naʒwaʀ] *nf* fin
**nager** [naʒe] *vi* to swim; (*fig: ne rien comprendre*) to be all at sea; **~ dans** to be swimming in; (*vêtements*) to be lost in; **~ dans le bonheur** to be overjoyed
**nageur, -euse** [naʒœʀ, -øz] *nm/f* swimmer
**naguère** [nagɛʀ] *adv* (*il y a peu de temps*) not long ago; (*autrefois*) formerly
**naïf, -ïve** [naif, naiv] *adj* naïve
**nain, e** [nɛ̃, nɛn] *adj*, *nm/f* dwarf
**Nairobi** [naiʀɔbi] *n* Nairobi
**nais** [nɛ], **naissais** *etc* [nɛsɛ] *vb voir* **naître**
**naissance** [nɛsɑ̃s] *nf* birth; **donner ~ à** to give birth to; (*fig*) to give rise to; **prendre ~** to originate; **aveugle de ~** born blind; **Français de ~** French by birth; **à la ~ des cheveux** at the roots of the hair; **lieu de ~** place of birth
**naissant, e** [nɛsɑ̃, -ɑ̃t] *vb voir* **naître** ▷ *adj* budding, incipient; (*jour*) dawning
**naît** [nɛ] *vb voir* **naître**
**naître** [nɛtʀ(ə)] *vi* to be born; (*conflit, complications*): **~ de** to arise from, be born out of; **~ à** (*amour, poésie*) to awaken to; **je suis né en 1960** I was born in 1960; **il naît plus de filles que de garçons** there are more girls born than boys; **faire ~** (*fig*) to give rise to, arouse
**naïvement** [naivmɑ̃] *adv* naïvely
**naïveté** [naivte] *nf* naivety
**nana** [nana] *nf* (*fam: fille*) bird (*Brit*), chick
**nantais, e** [nɑ̃tɛ, -ɛz] *adj* of *ou* from Nantes
**nantir** [nɑ̃tiʀ] *vt*: **~ qn de** to provide sb with; **les nantis** (*péj*) the well-to-do
**napalm** [napalm] *nm* napalm
**naphtaline** [naftalin] *nf*: **boules de ~** mothballs

**Naples** [napl(ə)] *n* Naples
**napolitain, e** [napɔlitɛ̃, -ɛn] *adj* Neapolitan; **tranche ~e** Neapolitan ice cream
**nappe** [nap] *nf* tablecloth; (*fig*) sheet; layer; **~ de mazout** oil slick; **~ (phréatique)** water table
**napper** [nape] *vt*: **~ qch de** to coat sth with
**napperon** [napʀɔ̃] *nm* table-mat; **~ individuel** place mat
**naquis** *etc* [naki] *vb voir* **naître**
**narcisse** [naʀsis] *nm* narcissus
**narcissique** [naʀsisik] *adj* narcissistic
**narcissisme** [naʀsisism(ə)] *nm* narcissism
**narcodollars** [naʀkodɔlaʀ] *nmpl* drug money *no pl*
**narcotique** [naʀkɔtik] *adj*, *nm* narcotic
**narguer** [naʀge] *vt* to taunt
**narine** [naʀin] *nf* nostril
**narquois, e** [naʀkwa, -waz] *adj* derisive, mocking
**narrateur, -trice** [naʀatœʀ, -tʀis] *nm/f* narrator
**narration** [naʀasjɔ̃] *nf* narration, narrative; (*Scol*) essay
**narrer** [naʀe] *vt* to tell the story of, recount
**NASA** [nasa] *sigle f* (= National Aeronautics and Space Administration) NASA
**nasal, e, -aux** [nazal, -o] *adj* nasal
**naseau, x** [nazo] *nm* nostril
**nasillard, e** [nazijaʀ, -aʀd(ə)] *adj* nasal
**nasiller** [nazije] *vi* to speak with a (nasal) twang
**nasse** [nas] *nf* fish-trap
**natal, e** [natal] *adj* native
**nataliste** [natalist(ə)] *adj* supporting a rising birth rate
**natalité** [natalite] *nf* birth rate
**natation** [natasjɔ̃] *nf* swimming; **faire de la ~** to go swimming (*regularly*)
**natif, -ive** [natif, -iv] *adj* native
**nation** [nɑsjɔ̃] *nf* nation; **les N~s unies (NU)** the United Nations (UN)
**national, e, -aux** [nasjɔnal, -o] *adj* national ▷ *nf*: **(route) ~e** ≈ A road (*Brit*), ≈ state highway (*US*); **obsèques ~es** state funeral
**nationalisation** [nasjɔnalizasjɔ̃] *nf* nationalization
**nationaliser** [nasjɔnalize] *vt* to nationalize
**nationalisme** [nasjɔnalism(ə)] *nm* nationalism
**nationaliste** [nasjɔnalist(ə)] *adj*, *nm/f* nationalist

**n**

**nationalité** [nasjɔnalite] *nf* nationality; **de ~
française** of French nationality
**natte** [nat] *nf* (*tapis*) mat; (*cheveux*) plait
**natter** [nate] *vt* (*cheveux*) to plait
**naturalisation** [natyʀalizɑsjɔ̃] *nf*
naturalization
**naturaliser** [natyʀalize] *vt* to naturalize;
(*empailler*) to stuff
**naturaliste** [natyʀalist(ə)] *nm/f* naturalist;
(*empailleur*) taxidermist
**nature** [natyʀ] *nf* nature ▷ *adj, adv* (*Culin*) plain,
without seasoning or sweetening; (*café, thé:
sans lait*) black; (: *sans sucre*) without sugar;
**payer en ~** to pay in kind; **peint d'après ~**
painted from life; **être de ~ à faire qch** (*propre
à*) to be the sort of thing (*ou* person) to do sth; **~
morte** still-life
**naturel, le** [natyʀɛl] *adj* natural ▷ *nm*
naturalness; (*caractère*) disposition, nature;
(*autochtone*) native; (*aussi:* **au naturel**: *Culin*) in
water; in its own juices
**naturellement** [natyʀɛlmɑ̃] *adv* naturally; (*bien
sûr*) of course
**naturisme** [natyʀism(ə)] *nm* naturism
**naturiste** [natyʀist(ə)] *nm/f* naturist
**naufrage** [nofʀaʒ] *nm* (ship)wreck; (*fig*) wreck;
**faire ~** to be shipwrecked
**naufragé, e** [nofʀaʒe] *nm/f* shipwreck victim,
castaway
**nauséabond, e** [nozeabɔ̃, -ɔ̃d] *adj* foul, nauseous
**nausée** [noze] *nf* nausea; **avoir la ~** to feel sick;
**avoir des ~s** to have waves of nausea, feel
nauseous *ou* sick
**nautique** [notik] *adj* nautical, water *cpd*; **sports
~s** water sports
**nautisme** [notism(ə)] *nm* water sports *pl*
**naval, e** [naval] *adj* naval
**navarrais, e** [navaʀɛ, -ɛz] *adj* Navarrese
**navet** [navɛ] *nm* turnip; (*péj*) third-rate film
**navette** [navɛt] *nf* shuttle; (*en car etc*) shuttle
(service); **faire la ~ (entre)** to go to and fro
(between), shuttle (between); **~ spatiale** space
shuttle
**navigabilité** [navigabilite] *nf* (*d'un navire*)
seaworthiness; (*d'un avion*) airworthiness
**navigable** [navigabl(ə)] *adj* navigable
**navigant, e** [navigɑ̃, -ɑ̃t] *adj* (*Aviat: personnel*)
flying ▷ *nm/f:* **les ~s** the flying staff *ou* personnel
**navigateur** [navigatœʀ] *nm* (*Navig*) seafarer,
sailor; (*Aviat*) navigator; (*Inform*) browser
**navigation** [navigɑsjɔ̃] *nf* navigation, sailing;
(*Comm*) shipping; **compagnie de ~** shipping
company; **~ spatiale** space navigation
**naviguer** [navige] *vi* to navigate, sail
**navire** [naviʀ] *nm* ship; **~ de guerre** warship; **~
marchand** merchantman
**navire-citerne** [naviʀsitɛʀn(ə)] (*pl* **navires-
citernes**) *nm* tanker
**navire-hôpital** [naviʀɔpital, -to] (*pl* **navires-
hôpitaux**) *nm* hospital ship
**navrant, e** [navʀɑ̃, -ɑ̃t] *adj* (*affligeant*) upsetting;
(*consternant*) annoying

**navrer** [navʀe] *vt* to upset, distress; **je suis
navré (de/de faire/que)** I'm so sorry (for/for
doing/that)
**NB** *abr* (= *nota bene*) NB
**nbr.** *abr* = **nombreux**
**nbses** *abr* = **nombreuses**
**ND** *sigle f* = **Notre Dame**
**NDA** *sigle f* = **note de l'auteur**
**NDE** *sigle f* = **note de l'éditeur**
**NDLR** *sigle f* = **note de la rédaction**
**NDT** *sigle f* = **note du traducteur**
**ne, n'** [n(ə)] *adv voir* **pas; plus; jamais** *etc*;
(*explétif*) *non traduit*
**né, e** [ne] *pp de* **naître**; **né en 1960** born in 1960;
**née Scott** née Scott; **né(e) de ... et de ...** son/
daughter of ... and of ...; **né d'une mère
française** having a French mother; **né pour
commander** born to lead ▷ *adj:* **un comédien
né** a born comedian
**néanmoins** [neɑ̃mwɛ̃] *adv* nevertheless, yet
**néant** [neɑ̃] *nm* nothingness; **réduire à ~** to
bring to nought; (*espoir*) to dash
**nébuleux, -euse** [nebylø, -øz] *adj* (*ciel*) cloudy;
(*fig*) nebulous ▷ *nf* (*Astronomie*) nebula
**nébuliser** [nebylize] *vt* (*liquide*) to spray
**nébulosité** [nebylozite] *nf* cloud cover; **~
variable** cloudy in places
**nécessaire** [nesesɛʀ] *adj* necessary ▷ *nm*
necessary; (*sac*) kit; **faire le ~** to do the
necessary; **n'emporter que le strict ~** to take
only what is strictly necessary; **~ de couture**
sewing kit; **~ de toilette** toilet bag; **~ de
voyage** overnight bag
**nécessairement** [nesesɛʀmɑ̃] *adv* necessarily
**nécessité** [nesesite] *nf* necessity; **se trouver
dans la ~ de faire qch** to find it necessary to do
sth; **par ~** out of necessity
**nécessiter** [nesesite] *vt* to require
**nécessiteux, -euse** [nesesitø, -øz] *adj* needy
**nec plus ultra** [nɛkplysyltʀa] *nm:* **le ~ de** the
last word in
**nécrologie** [nekʀɔlɔʒi] *nf* obituary
**nécrologique** [nekʀɔlɔʒik] *adj:* **article ~**
obituary; **rubrique ~** obituary column
**nécromancie** [nekʀɔmɑ̃si] *nf* necromancy
**nécrose** [nekʀoz] *nf* necrosis
**nectar** [nɛktaʀ] *nm* nectar
**nectarine** [nɛktaʀin] *nf* nectarine
**néerlandais, e** [neɛʀlɑ̃dɛ, -ɛz] *adj* Dutch, of the
Netherlands ▷ *nm* (*Ling*) Dutch ▷ *nm/f:*
**Néerlandais, e** Dutchman/woman; **les N~** the
Dutch
**nef** [nɛf] *nf* (*d'église*) nave
**néfaste** [nefast(ə)] *adj* baneful; ill-fated
**négatif, -ive** [negatif, iv] *adj* negative ▷ *nm*
(*Photo*) negative
**négation** [negɑsjɔ̃] *nf* denial; (*Ling*) negation
**négativement** [negativmɑ̃] *adv:* **répondre ~** to
give a negative response
**négligé, e** [negliʒe] *adj* (*en désordre*) slovenly ▷ *nm*
(*tenue*) negligee
**négligeable** [negliʒabl(ə)] *adj* insignificant,

negligible

**négligemment** [negliʒamã] *adv* carelessly

**négligence** [negliʒãs] *nf* carelessness *no pl*; *(faute)* careless omission

**négligent, e** [negliʒã, -ãt] *adj* careless; *(Jur etc)* negligent

**négliger** [negliʒe] *vt (épouse, jardin)* to neglect; *(tenue)* to be careless about; *(avis, précautions)* to disregard, overlook; ~ **de faire** to fail to do, not bother to do; **se négliger** to neglect o.s

**négoce** [negɔs] *nm* trade

**négociable** [negɔsjabl(ə)] *adj* negotiable

**négociant** [negɔsjã] *nm* merchant

**négociateur** [negɔsjatœʀ] *nm* negotiator

**négociation** [negɔsjasjɔ̃] *nf* negotiation; **~s collectives** collective bargaining *sg*

**négocier** [negɔsje] *vi, vt* to negotiate

**nègre** [nɛgʀ(ə)] *nm (péj)* Negro; *(péj: écrivain)* ghost writer ▷ *adj (péj)* Negro

**négresse** [negʀɛs] *nf (péj)* Negress

**négrier** [negʀije] *nm (fig)* slave driver

**neige** [nɛʒ] *nf* snow; **battre les œufs en ~** *(Culin)* to whip *ou* beat the egg whites until stiff; **~ carbonique** dry ice; **~ fondue** *(par terre)* slush; *(qui tombe)* sleet; **~ poudreuse** powdery snow

**neiger** [neʒe] *vi* to snow

**neigeux, -euse** [nɛʒø, -øz] *adj* snowy, snow-covered

**nénuphar** [nenyfaʀ] *nm* water-lily

**néo-calédonien, ne** [neɔkaledɔnjɛ̃, -ɛn] *adj* New Caledonian ▷ *nm/f:* **Néo-calédonien, ne** native of New Caledonia

**néocapitalisme** [neokapitalism(ə)] *nm* neocapitalism

**néo-colonialisme** [neokɔlɔnjalism(ə)] *nm* neocolonialism

**néologisme** [neɔlɔʒism(ə)] *nm* neologism

**néon** [neɔ̃] *nm* neon

**néo-natal, e** [neɔnatal] *adj* neonatal

**néophyte** [neɔfit] *nm/f* novice

**néo-zélandais, e** [neɔzelɑ̃dɛ, -ɛz] *adj* New Zealand *cpd* ▷ *nm/f:* **Néo-zélandais, e** New Zealander

**Népal** [nepal] *nm:* **le ~** Nepal

**népalais, e** [nepalɛ, -ɛz] *adj* Nepalese, Nepali ▷ *nm (Ling)* Nepalese, Nepali ▷ *nm/f:* **Népalais, e** Nepalese, Nepali

**néphrétique** [nefʀetik] *adj (Méd: colique)* nephritic

**néphrite** [nefʀit] *nf (Méd)* nephritis

**népotisme** [nepɔtism(ə)] *nm* nepotism

**nerf** [nɛʀ] *nm* nerve; *(fig)* spirit; *(: forces)* stamina; **nerfs** *nmpl* nerves; **être** *ou* **vivre sur les ~s** to live on one's nerves; **être à bout de ~s** to be at the end of one's tether; **passer ses ~s sur qn** to take it out on sb

**nerveusement** [nɛʀvøzmã] *adv* nervously

**nerveux, -euse** [nɛʀvø, -øz] *adj* nervous; *(cheval)* highly-strung; *(voiture)* nippy, responsive; *(tendineux)* sinewy

**nervosité** [nɛʀvozite] *nf* nervousness; *(émotivité)* excitability

**nervure** [nɛʀvyʀ] *nf (de feuille)* vein; *(Archit, Tech)* rib

**n'est-ce pas** [nɛspɑ] *adv* isn't it?, won't you? *etc (selon le verbe qui précède)*; **c'est bon, n'est-ce pas?** it's good, isn't it?; **il a peur, n'est-ce pas?** he's afraid, isn't he?; **n'est-ce pas que c'est bon?** don't you think it's good?; **lui, n'est-ce pas, il peut se le permettre** he, of course, can afford to do that, can't he?

**net, nette** [nɛt] *adj (sans équivoque, distinct)* clear; *(photo)* sharp; *(évident)* definite; *(propre)* neat, clean; *(Comm: prix, salaire, poids)* net ▷ *adv (refuser)* flatly ▷ *nm:* **mettre au ~** to copy out; **s'arrêter ~** to stop dead; **la lame a cassé ~** the blade snapped clean through; **faire place nette** to make a clean sweep; **~ d'impôt** tax free

**Net** [nɛt] *nm (Internet):* **le ~** the Net

**netiquette** [nɛtikɛt] *nf* netiquette

**nettement** [nɛtmã] *adv (distinctement)* clearly; *(évidemment)* definitely; *(avec comparatif, superlatif):* **~ mieux** definitely *ou* clearly better

**netteté** [nɛtte] *nf* clearness

**nettoie** *etc* [nɛtwa] *vb voir* **nettoyer**

**nettoiement** [netwamã] *nm (Admin)* cleaning; **service du ~** refuse collection

**nettoierai** *etc* [nɛtwaʀe] *vb voir* **nettoyer**

**nettoyage** [nɛtwajaʒ] *nm* cleaning; **~ à sec** dry cleaning

**nettoyant** [netwajã] *nm (produit)* cleaning agent

**nettoyer** [nɛtwaje] *vt* to clean; *(fig)* to clean out

**neuf¹** [nœf] *num* nine

**neuf², neuve** [nœf, nœv] *adj* new ▷ *nm:* **repeindre à ~** to redecorate; **remettre à ~** to do up (as good as new), refurbish; **n'acheter que du ~** to buy everything new; **quoi de ~?** what's new?

**neurasthénique** [nøʀastenik] *adj* neurasthenic

**neurochirurgie** [nøʀoʃiʀyʀʒi] *nf* neurosurgery

**neurochirurgien** [nøʀoʃiʀyʀʒjɛ̃] *nm* neurosurgeon

**neuroleptique** [nøʀɔlɛptik] *adj* neuroleptic

**neurologie** [nøʀɔlɔʒi] *nf* neurology

**neurologique** [nøʀɔlɔʒik] *adj* neurological

**neurologue** [nøʀɔlɔg] *nm/f* neurologist

**neurone** [nøʀɔn] *nm* neuron(e)

**neuropsychiatre** [nøʀopsikjatʀ(ə)] *nm/f* neuropsychiatrist

**neutralisation** [nøtʀalizasjɔ̃] *nf* neutralization

**neutraliser** [nøtʀalize] *vt* to neutralize

**neutralisme** [nøtʀalism(ə)] *nm* neutralism

**neutralité** [nøtʀalite] *nf* neutrality

**neutre** [nøtʀ(ə)] *adj, nm (Ling)* neutral

**neutron** [nøtʀɔ̃] *nm* neutron

**neuve** [nœv] *adj f voir* **neuf**

**neuvième** [nœvjɛm] *num* ninth

**neveu, x** [nəvø] *nm* nephew

**névralgie** [nevʀalʒi] *nf* neuralgia

**névralgique** [nevʀalʒik] *adj (fig: sensible)* sensitive; **centre ~** nerve centre

**névrite** [nevʀit] *nf* neuritis

**névrose** [nevʀoz] *nf* neurosis

**névrosé, e** [nevʀoze] *adj, nm/f* neurotic

**névrotique** [nevʀɔtik] *adj* neurotic

**n**

**New York** [njujɔRk] *n* New York
**new-yorkais, e** [njujɔRkɛ,-ɛz] *adj* of *ou* from
New York, New York *cpd* ▷ *nm/f:* **New-Yorkais, e**
New Yorker
**nez** [ne] *nm* nose; **rire au ~ de qn** to laugh in
sb's face; **avoir du ~** to have flair; **avoir le ~ fin**
to have foresight; **~ à ~ avec** face to face with; **à**
**vue de ~** roughly
**NF** *sigle mpl* = **nouveaux francs** ▷ *sigle f* (*Industrie:*
= *norme française*) industrial standard
**ni** [ni] *conj:* **ni l'un ni l'autre ne sont** *ou* **n'est**
neither one nor the other is; **il n'a rien dit ni**
**fait** he hasn't said or done anything
**Niagara** [njagaRa] *nm:* **les chutes du ~** the
Niagara Falls
**niais, e** [njɛ,-ɛz] *adj* silly, thick
**niaiserie** [njɛzRi] *nf* gullibility; (*action, propos,*
*futilité*) silliness
**Nicaragua** [nikaRagwa] *nm:* **le ~** Nicaragua
**nicaraguayen, ne** [nikaRagwajɛ̃,-ɛn] *adj*
Nicaraguan ▷ *nm/f:* **Nicaraguayen, ne**
Nicaraguan
**Nice** [nis] *n* Nice
**niche** [niʃ] *nf* (*du chien*) kennel; (*de mur*) recess,
niche; (*farce*) trick
**nichée** [niʃe] *nf* brood, nest
**nicher** [niʃe] *vi* to nest; **se ~ dans** (*personne: se*
*blottir*) to snuggle into; (: *se cacher*) to hide in;
(*objet*) to lodge itself in
**nichon** [niʃɔ̃] *nm* (*fam*) boob, tit
**nickel** [nikɛl] *nm* nickel
**niçois, e** [niswa, -waz] *adj* of *ou* from Nice;
(*Culin*) Nicoise
**nicotine** [nikɔtin] *nf* nicotine
**nid** [ni] *nm* nest; (*fig: repaire etc*) den, lair; **~**
**d'abeilles** (*Couture, Textile*) honeycomb stitch; **~**
**de poule** pothole
**nièce** [njɛs] *nf* niece
**nième** [ɛnjɛm] *adj:* **la ~ fois** the nth *ou*
umpteenth time
**nier** [nje] *vt* to deny
**nigaud, e** [nigo, -od] *nm/f* booby, fool
**Niger** [niʒɛR] *nm:* **le ~** Niger; (*fleuve*) the Niger
**Nigéria** [niʒeRja] *nm ou f* Nigeria
**nigérian, e** [niʒeRjɑ̃, -an] *adj* Nigerian ▷ *nm/f:*
**Nigérian, e** Nigerian
**nigérien, ne** [niʒeRjɛ̃,-ɛn] *adj* of *ou* from Niger
**night-club** [najtklœb] *nm* nightclub
**nihilisme** [niilism(ə)] *nm* nihilism
**nihiliste** [niilist(ə)] *adj* nihilist, nihilistic
**Nil** [nil] *nm:* **le ~** the Nile
**n'importe** [nɛ̃pɔRt(ə)] *adv:* **n'importe!** no
matter!; **n'importe qui/quoi/où** anybody/
anything/anywhere; **n'importe quoi!** (*fam:*
*désapprobation*) what rubbish!; **n'importe**
**quand** any time; **n'importe quel/quelle** any;
**n'importe lequel/laquelle** any (one);
**n'importe comment** (*sans soin*) carelessly;
**n'importe comment, il part ce soir** he's
leaving tonight in any case
**nippes** [nip] *nfpl* (*fam*) togs
**nippon, e** *ou* **ne** [nipɔ̃, -ɔn] *adj* Japanese

**nique** [nik] *nf:* **faire la ~ à** to thumb one's nose
at (*fig*)
**nitouche** [nituʃ] *nf* (*péj*): **c'est une sainte ~** she
looks as if butter wouldn't melt in her mouth
**nitrate** [nitRat] *nm* nitrate
**nitrique** [nitRik] *adj:* **acide ~** nitric acid
**nitroglycérine** [nitRɔgliseRin] *nf*
nitroglycerin(e)
**niveau, x** [nivo] *nm* level; (*des élèves, études*)
standard; **au ~ de** at the level of; (*personne*) on a
level with; **de ~ (avec)** level (with); **le ~ de la**
**mer** sea level; **~ (à bulle)** spirit level; **~ (d'eau)**
water level; **~ de vie** standard of living
**niveler** [nivle] *vt* to level
**niveleuse** [nivløz] *nf* (*Tech*) grader
**nivellement** [nivɛlmɑ̃] *nm* levelling
**nivernais, e** [nivɛRnɛ, -ɛz] *adj* of *ou* from Nevers
(and region) ▷ *nm/f:* **Nivernais, e** inhabitant *ou*
native of Nevers (and region)
**NL** *sigle f* = **nouvelle lune**
**NN** *abr* (= *nouvelle norme*) revised standard of hotel
classification
**n°** *abr* (*numéro*) no
**nobiliaire** [nɔbiljɛR] *adj f voir* **particule**
**noble** [nɔbl(ə)] *adj* noble; (*de qualité: métal etc*)
precious ▷ *nm/f* noble(man/-woman)
**noblesse** [nɔblɛs] *nf* (*classe sociale*) nobility;
(*d'une action etc*) nobleness
**noce** [nɔs] *nf* wedding; (*gens*) wedding party (*ou*
guests *pl*); **il l'a épousée en secondes ~s** she
was his second wife; **faire la ~** (*fam*) to go on a
binge; **~s d'or/d'argent/de diamant** golden/
silver/diamond wedding
**noceur** [nɔsœR] *nm* (*fam*): **c'est un sacré ~** he's
a real party animal
**nocif, -ive** [nɔsif, -iv] *adj* harmful, noxious
**noctambule** [nɔktɑ̃byl] *nm* night-bird
**nocturne** [nɔktyRn(ə)] *adj* nocturnal ▷ *nf* (*Sport*)
floodlit fixture; (*d'un magasin*) late opening
**Noël** [nɔɛl] *nm* Christmas; **la (fête de) ~**
Christmas time
**nœud** [nø] *nm* (*de corde, du bois, Navig*) knot;
(*ruban*) bow; (*fig: liens*) bond, tie; (: *d'une question*)
crux; (*Théât etc*) **le ~ de l'action** the web of
events; **~ coulant** noose; **~ gordien** Gordian
knot; **~ papillon** bow tie
**noie** *etc* [nwa] *vb voir* **noyer**
**noir, e** [nwaR] *adj* black; (*obscur, sombre*) dark
▷ *nm/f* black man/woman ▷ *nm:* **dans le ~** in
the dark ▷ *nf* (*Mus*) crotchet (Brit), quarter note
(US); **il fait ~** it is dark; **au ~** *adv* (*acheter, vendre*)
on the black market; **travail au ~**
moonlighting
**noirâtre** [nwaRɑtR(ə)] *adj* (*teinte*) blackish
**noirceur** [nwaRsœR] *nf* blackness; darkness
**noircir** [nwaRsiR] *vt, vi* to blacken
**noise** [nwaz] *nf:* **chercher ~ à** to try and pick a
quarrel with
**noisetier** [nwaztje] *nm* hazel (tree)
**noisette** [nwazɛt] *nf* hazelnut; (*morceau: de*
*beurre etc*) small knob ▷ *adj* (*yeux*) hazel
**noix** [nwa] *nf* walnut; (*fam*) twit; (*Culin*): **une ~**

**de beurre** a knob of butter; **à la ~** (fam) worthless; **~ de cajou** cashew nut; **~ de coco** coconut; **~ muscade** nutmeg; **~ de veau** (Culin) round fillet of veal

**nom** [nɔ̃] nm name; (Ling) noun; **connaître qn de ~** to know sb by name; **au ~ de** in the name of; **~ d'une pipe** ou **d'un chien!** (fam) for goodness' sake!; **~ de Dieu!** (fam!) bloody hell! (Brit), my God!; **~ commun/propre** common/proper noun; **~ composé** (Ling) compound noun; **~ déposé** trade name; **~ d'emprunt** assumed name; **~ de famille** surname; **~ de fichier** file name; **~ de jeune fille** maiden name

**nomade** [nɔmad] adj nomadic ▷ nm/f nomad

**nombre** [nɔ̃bʀ(ə)] nm number; **venir en ~** to come in large numbers; **depuis ~ d'années** for many years; **ils sont au ~ de trois** there are three of them; **au ~ de mes amis** among my friends; **sans ~** countless; **(bon) ~ de** (beaucoup, plusieurs) a (large) number of; **~ premier/entier** prime/whole number

**nombreux, -euse** [nɔ̃bʀø, -øz] adj many, numerous; (avec nom sg: foule etc) large; **peu ~** few; small; **de ~ cas** many cases

**nombril** [nɔ̃bʀi] nm navel

**nomenclature** [nɔmɑ̃klatyʀ] nf wordlist; list of items

**nominal, e, -aux** [nɔminal, -o] adj nominal; (appel, liste) of names

**nominatif, -ive** [nɔminatif, -iv] nm (Ling) nominative ▷ adj: **liste nominative** list of names; **carte nominative** calling card; **titre ~** registered name

**nomination** [nɔminasjɔ̃] nf nomination

**nommément** [nɔmemɑ̃] adv (désigner) by name

**nommer** [nɔme] vt (baptiser) to name, give a name to; (qualifier) to call; (mentionner) to name, give the name of; (élire) to appoint, nominate; **se nommer: il se nomme Pascal** his name's Pascal, he's called Pascal

**non** [nɔ̃] adv (réponse) no; (suivi d'un adjectif, adverbe) not; **Paul est venu, ~?** Paul came, didn't he?; **répondre** ou **dire que ~** to say no; **~ pas que** not that; **~ plus: moi ~ plus** neither do I, I don't either; **je préférerais que ~** I would prefer not; **il se trouve que ~** perhaps not; **je pense que ~** I don't think so; **~ mais!** well really!; **~ mais des fois!** you must be joking!; **~ alcoolisé** non-alcoholic; **~ loin/seulement** not far/only

**nonagénaire** [nɔnaʒenɛʀ] nm/f nonagenarian

**non-agression** [nɔnagʀesjɔ̃] nf: **pacte de ~** non-aggression pact

**nonante** [nɔnɑ̃t] num (Belgique, Suisse) ninety

**non-assistance** [nɔnasistɑ̃s] nf (Jur): **~ à personne en danger** failure to render assistance to a person in danger

**nonce** [nɔ̃s] nm (Rel) nuncio

**nonchalamment** [nɔ̃ʃalamɑ̃] adv nonchalantly

**nonchalance** [nɔ̃ʃalɑ̃s] nf nonchalance, casualness

**nonchalant, e** [nɔ̃ʃalɑ̃, -ɑ̃t] adj nonchalant, casual

**non-conformisme** [nɔ̃kɔ̃fɔʀmism(ə)] nm nonconformism

**non-conformiste** [nɔ̃kɔ̃fɔʀmist(ə)] adj, nm/f non-conformist

**non-conformité** [nɔ̃kɔ̃fɔʀmite] nf nonconformity

**non-croyant, e** [nɔ̃kʀwajɑ̃, -ɑ̃t] nm/f (Rel) non-believer

**non-engagé, e** [nɔnɑ̃gaʒe] adj non-aligned

**non-fumeur** [nɔ̃fymœʀ] nm non-smoker

**non-ingérence** [nɔnɛ̃ʒeʀɑ̃s] nf non-interference

**non-initié, e** [nɔninisje] nm/f lay person; **les ~s** the uninitiated

**non-inscrit, e** [nɔnɛ̃skʀi, -it] nm/f (Pol: député) independent

**non-intervention** [nɔnɛ̃tɛʀvɑ̃sjɔ̃] nf non-intervention

**non-lieu** [nɔ̃ljø] nm: **il y a eu ~** the case was dismissed

**nonne** [nɔn] nf nun

**nonobstant** [nɔnɔpstɑ̃] prép notwithstanding

**non-paiement** [nɔ̃pɛmɑ̃] nm non-payment

**non-prolifération** [nɔ̃pʀɔlifeʀasjɔ̃] nf non-proliferation

**non-résident** [nɔ̃ʀezidɑ̃] nm (Écon) non-resident

**non-retour** [nɔ̃ʀətuʀ] nm: **point de ~** point of no return

**non-sens** [nɔ̃sɑ̃s] nm absurdity

**non-spécialiste** [nɔ̃spesjalist(ə)] nm/f non-specialist

**non-stop** [nɔnstɔp] adj inv nonstop

**non-syndiqué, e** [nɔ̃sɛ̃dike] nm/f non-union member

**non-violence** [nɔ̃vjɔlɑ̃s] nf nonviolence

**non-violent, e** [nɔ̃vjɔlɑ̃, -ɑ̃t] adj non-violent

**nord** [nɔʀ] nm North ▷ adj northern; north; **au ~** (situation) in the north; (direction) to the north; **au ~ de** north of, to the north of; **perdre le ~** to lose one's way (fig)

**nord-africain, e** [nɔʀafʀikɛ̃, -ɛn] adj North-African ▷ nm/f: **Nord-Africain, e** North African

**nord-américain, e** [nɔʀameʀikɛ̃, -ɛn] adj North American ▷ nm/f: **Nord-Américain, e** North American

**nord-coréen, ne** [nɔʀkɔʀeɛ̃, -ɛn] adj North Korean ▷ nm/f: **Nord-Coréen, ne** North Korean

**nord-est** [nɔʀɛst] nm North-East

**nordique** [nɔʀdik] adj (pays, race) Nordic; (langues) Scandinavian, Nordic ▷ nm/f: **Nordique** Scandinavian

**nord-ouest** [nɔʀwɛst] nm North-West

**nord-vietnamien, ne** [nɔʀvjɛtnamjɛ̃, -ɛn] adj North Vietnamese ▷ nm/f: **Nord-Vietnamien, ne** North Vietnamese

**normal, e, -aux** [nɔʀmal, -o] adj normal ▷ nf: **la ~e** the norm, the average

**normalement** [nɔʀmalmɑ̃] adv (en général) normally; (comme prévu): **~, il le fera demain** he should be doing it tomorrow, he's supposed to do it tomorrow

**normalien, ne** [nɔʀmaljɛ̃, -ɛn] *nm/f student of* École normale supérieure

**normalisation** [nɔʀmalizasjɔ̃] *nf* standardization; normalization

**normaliser** [nɔʀmalize] *vt* (*Comm, Tech*) to standardize; (*Pol*) to normalize

**normand, e** [nɔʀmɑ̃, -ɑ̃d] *adj* (*de Normandie*) Norman ▷ *nm/f:* **Normand, e** (*de Normandie*) Norman

**Normandie** [nɔʀmɑ̃di] *nf:* **la ~** Normandy

**norme** [nɔʀm(ə)] *nf* norm; (*Tech*) standard

**Norvège** [nɔʀvɛʒ] *nf:* **la ~** Norway

**norvégien, ne** [nɔʀveʒjɛ̃, -ɛn] *adj* Norwegian ▷ *nm* (*Ling*) Norwegian ▷ *nm/f:* **Norvégien, ne** Norwegian

**nos** [no] *adj poss voir* **notre**

**nostalgie** [nɔstalʒi] *nf* nostalgia

**nostalgique** [nɔstalʒik] *adj* nostalgic

**notable** [nɔtabl(ə)] *adj* notable, noteworthy; (*marqué*) noticeable, marked ▷ *nm* prominent citizen

**notablement** [nɔtabləmɑ̃] *adv* notably; (*sensiblement*) noticeably

**notaire** [nɔtɛʀ] *nm* notary; solicitor

**notamment** [nɔtamɑ̃] *adv* in particular, among others

**notariat** [nɔtaʀja] *nm* profession of notary (*ou* solicitor)

**notarié, e** [nɔtaʀje] *adj:* **acte ~** deed drawn up by a notary (*ou* solicitor)

**notation** [nɔtasjɔ̃] *nf* notation

**note** [nɔt] *nf* (*écrite, Mus*) note; (*Scol*) mark (*Brit*), grade; (*facture*) bill; **prendre des ~s** to take notes; **prendre ~ de** to note; (*par écrit*) to note, write down; **dans la ~** exactly right; **forcer la ~** to exaggerate; **une ~ de tristesse/de gaieté** a sad/happy note; **~ de service** memorandum

**noté, e** [nɔte] *adj:* **être bien/mal ~** (*employé etc*) to have a good/bad record

**noter** [nɔte] *vt* (*écrire*) to write down, note; (*remarquer*) to note, notice; (*Scol, Admin: donner une appréciation*) to mark, give a grade to; **notez bien que …** (please) note that …

**notice** [nɔtis] *nf* summary, short article; (*brochure*): **~ explicative** explanatory leaflet, instruction booklet

**notification** [nɔtifikasjɔ̃] *nf* notification

**notifier** [nɔtifje] *vt:* **~ qch à qn** to notify sb of sth, notify sth to sb

**notion** [nɔsjɔ̃] *nf* notion, idea; **notions** *nfpl* (*rudiments*) rudiments

**notoire** [nɔtwaʀ] *adj* widely known; (*en mal*) notorious; **le fait est ~** the fact is common knowledge

**notoriété** [nɔtɔʀjete] *nf:* **c'est de ~ publique** it's common knowledge

**notre, nos** [nɔtʀ(ə), no] *adj poss* our

**nôtre** [notʀ(ə)] *adj* ours ▷ *pron:* **le/la ~** ours; **les ~s** ours; (*alliés etc*) our own people; **soyez des ~s** join us

**nouba** [nuba] *nf* (*fam*): **faire la ~** to live it up

**nouer** [nwe] *vt* to tie, knot; (*fig: alliance etc*) to

strike up; **~ la conversation** to start a conversation; **se nouer** *vi:* **c'est là où l'intrigue se noue** it's at that point that the strands of the plot come together; **ma gorge se noua** a lump came to my throat

**noueux, -euse** [nwø, -øz] *adj* gnarled

**nougat** [nuga] *nm* nougat

**nougatine** [nugatin] *nf kind of nougat*

**nouille** [nuj] *nf* (*fam*) noodle (*Brit*), fathead; **nouilles** *nfpl* (*pâtes*) noodles; pasta *sg*

**nounou** [nunu] *nf* nanny

**nounours** [nunuʀs] *nm* teddy (bear)

**nourri, e** [nuʀi] *adj* (*feu etc*) sustained

**nourrice** [nuʀis] *nf* ≈ baby-minder; (*autrefois*) wet-nurse

**nourrir** [nuʀiʀ] *vt* to feed; (*fig: espoir*) to harbour, nurse; **logé nourri** with board and lodging; **~ au sein** to breast-feed; **se ~ de légumes** to live on vegetables

**nourrissant, e** [nuʀisɑ̃, -ɑ̃t] *adj* nourishing, nutritious

**nourrisson** [nuʀisɔ̃] *nm* (unweaned) infant

**nourriture** [nuʀityʀ] *nf* food

**nous** [nu] *pron* (*sujet*) we; (*objet*) us

**nous-mêmes** [numɛm] *pron* ourselves

**nouveau, nouvel, -elle, x** [nuvo, -ɛl] *adj* new; (*original*) novel ▷ *nm/f* new pupil (*ou* employee) ▷ *nm:* **il y a du ~** there's something new ▷ *nf* (piece of) news *sg*; (*Littérature*) short story; **nouvelles** *nfpl* (*Presse, TV*) news; **de ~, à ~** again; **je suis sans nouvelles de lui** I haven't heard from him; **Nouvel An** New Year; **~ venu, nouvelle venue** newcomer; **~x mariés** newly-weds; **nouvelle vague** new wave

**nouveau-né, e** [nuvone] *nm/f* newborn (baby)

**nouveauté** [nuvote] *nf* novelty; (*chose nouvelle*) innovation, something new; (*Comm*) new film (*ou* book *ou* creation *etc*)

**nouvel** *adj m*, **nouvelle** *adj f, nf* [nuvɛl] *voir* **nouveau**

**Nouvelle-Angleterre** [nuvɛlɑ̃glətɛʀ] *nf:* **la ~** New England

**Nouvelle-Calédonie** [nuvɛlkaledɔni] *nf:* **la ~** New Caledonia

**Nouvelle-Écosse** [nuvɛlekɔs] *nf:* **la ~** Nova Scotia

**Nouvelle-Galles du Sud** [nuvɛlgaldysyd] *nf:* **la ~** New South Wales

**Nouvelle-Guinée** [nuvɛlgine] *nf:* **la ~** New Guinea

**nouvellement** [nuvɛlmɑ̃] *adv* (*arrivé etc*) recently, newly

**Nouvelle-Orléans** [nuvɛlɔʀleɑ̃] *nf:* **la ~** New Orleans

**Nouvelles-Hébrides** [nuvɛlsebʀid] *nfpl:* **les ~** the New Hebrides

**Nouvelle-Zélande** [nuvɛlzelɑ̃d] *nf:* **la ~** New Zealand

**nouvelliste** [nuvelist(ə)] *nm/f* editor *ou* writer of short stories

**novateur, -trice** [nɔvatœʀ, -tʀis] *adj* innovative ▷ *nm/f* innovator

**novembre** [nɔvɑ̃bʀ(ə)] *nm* November; *see note*; *voir aussi* **juillet**

> **◉ LE 11 NOVEMBRE**
>
> ◉ *Le 11 novembre* is a public holiday in France
> ◉ and commemorates the signing of the
> ◉ armistice, near Compiègne, at the end of the
> ◉ First World War.

**novice** [nɔvis] *adj* inexperienced ▷ *nm/f* novice
**noviciat** [nɔvisja] *nm* (*Rel*) noviciate
**noyade** [nwajad] *nf* drowning *no pl*
**noyau, x** [nwajo] *nm* (*de fruit*) stone; (*Bio, Physique*) nucleus; (*Élec, Géo, fig: centre*) core; (*fig: d'artistes etc*) group; (*: de résistants etc*) cell
**noyautage** [nwajotaʒ] *nm* (*Pol*) infiltration
**noyauter** [nwajote] *vt* (*Pol*) to infiltrate
**noyé, e** [nwaje] *nm/f* drowning (*ou* drowned) man/woman ▷ *adj* (*fig: dépassé*) out of one's depth
**noyer** [nwaje] *nm* walnut (tree); (*bois*) walnut ▷ *vt* to drown; (*fig*) to flood; to submerge; (*Auto: moteur*) to flood; **se noyer** to be drowned, drown; (*suicide*) to drown o.s.; **~ son chagrin** to drown one's sorrows; **~ le poisson** to duck the issue
**NSP** *sigle m* (*Rel*) = **Notre Saint Père**; (*dans les sondages*: = *ne sais pas*) don't know
**NT** *sigle m* (= *Nouveau Testament*) NT
**NU** *sigle fpl* (= *Nations unies*) UN
**nu, e** [ny] *adj* naked; (*membres*) naked, bare; (*chambre, fil, plaine*) bare ▷ *nm* (*Art*) nude; **le nu intégral** total nudity; **se mettre nu** to strip; **mettre à nu** to bare
**nuage** [nɥaʒ] *nm* cloud; **être dans les ~s** (*distrait*) to have one's head in the clouds; **~ de lait** drop of milk
**nuageux, -euse** [nɥaʒø, -øz] *adj* cloudy
**nuance** [nɥɑ̃s] *nf* (*de couleur, sens*) shade; **il y a une ~ (entre)** there's a slight difference (between); **une ~ de tristesse** a tinge of sadness
**nuancé, e** [nɥɑ̃se] *adj* (*opinion*) finely-shaded, subtly differing; **être ~ dans ses opinions** to have finely-shaded opinions
**nuancer** [nɥɑ̃se] *vt* (*pensée, opinion*) to qualify
**nubile** [nybil] *adj* nubile
**nucléaire** [nykleɛʀ] *adj* nuclear ▷ *nm* nuclear power
**nudisme** [nydism(ə)] *nm* nudism
**nudiste** [nydist(ə)] *adj, nm/f* nudist
**nudité** [nydite] *nf voir* **nu** nudity, nakedness; bareness
**nuée** [nɥe] *nf*: **une ~ de** a cloud *ou* host *ou* swarm of
**nues** [ny] *nfpl*: **tomber des ~** to be taken aback; **porter qn aux ~** to praise sb to the skies
**nui** [nɥi] *pp de* **nuire**
**nuire** [nɥiʀ] *vi* to be harmful; **~ à** to harm, do damage to
**nuisance** [nɥizɑ̃s] *nf* nuisance; **nuisances** *nfpl*

pollution *sg*
**nuisible** [nɥizibl(ə)] *adj* harmful; (**animal**) ~ pest
**nuisis** *etc* [nɥizi] *vb voir* **nuire**
**nuit** [nɥi] *nf* night; **payer sa ~** to pay for one's overnight accommodation; **il fait ~** it's dark; **cette ~** (*hier*) last night; (*aujourd'hui*) tonight; **de ~** (*vol, service*) night *cpd*; **~ blanche** sleepless night; **~ de noces** wedding night; **~ de Noël** Christmas Eve
**nuitamment** [nɥitamɑ̃] *adv* by night
**nuitées** [nɥite] *nfpl* overnight stays, beds occupied (*in statistics*)
**nul, nulle** [nyl] *adj* (*aucun*) no; (*minime*) nil, non-existent; (*non valable*) null; (*péj*) useless, hopeless ▷ *pron* none, no one; **résultat ~**, **match ~** draw; **nulle part** *adv* nowhere
**nullement** [nylmɑ̃] *adv* by no means
**nullité** [nylite] *nf* nullity; (*péj*) hopelessness; (*: personne*) hopeless individual, nonentity
**numéraire** [nymeʀɛʀ] *nm* cash; metal currency
**numéral, e, -aux** [nymeral, -o] *adj* numeral
**numérateur** [nymeratœʀ] *nm* numerator
**numération** [nymeʀasjɔ̃] *nf*: **~ décimale/binaire** decimal/binary notation; **~ globulaire** blood count
**numérique** [nymeʀik] *adj* numerical; (*Inform*) digital
**numériquement** [nymeʀikmɑ̃] *adv* numerically; (*Inform*) digitally
**numériser** [nymeʀize] *vt* (*Inform*) to digitize
**numéro** [nymeʀo] *nm* number; (*spectacle*) act, turn; **faire** *ou* **composer un ~** to dial a number; **~ d'identification personnel** personal identification number (PIN); **~ d'immatriculation** *ou* **minéralogique** *ou* **de police** registration (*Brit*) *ou* license (*US*) number; **~ de téléphone** (tele)phone number; **~ vert** ≈ Freefone® number (*Brit*), ≈ toll-free number (*US*)
**numérotage** [nymeʀotaʒ] *nm* numbering
**numérotation** [nymeʀotasjɔ̃] *nf* numeration
**numéroter** [nymeʀote] *vt* to number
**numerus clausus** [nymeʀysklozys] *nm inv* restriction *ou* limitation of numbers
**numismate** [nymismat] *nm/f* numismatist, coin collector
**nu-pieds** [nypje] *nm inv* sandal ▷ *adj inv* barefoot
**nuptial, e, -aux** [nypsjal, -o] *adj* nuptial; wedding *cpd*
**nuptialité** [nypsjalite] *nf*: **taux de ~** marriage rate
**nuque** [nyk] *nf* nape of the neck
**nu-tête** [nytɛt] *adj inv* bareheaded
**nutritif, -ive** [nytʀitif, -iv] *adj* nutritional; (*aliment*) nutritious, nourishing
**nutrition** [nytʀisjɔ̃] *nf* nutrition
**nutritionnel, le** [nytʀisjɔnɛl] *adj* nutritional
**nutritionniste** [nytʀisjɔnist(ə)] *nm/f* nutritionist
**nylon** [nilɔ̃] *nm* nylon
**nymphomane** [nɛ̃fɔman] *adj, nf* nymphomaniac

**n**

# Oo

**O, o** [o] *nm inv* O, o ▷ *abr* (= *ouest*) W; **O comme Oscar** O for Oliver (*Brit*) *ou* Oboe (*US*)

**OAS** *sigle f* (= *Organisation de l'armée secrète*) *organization opposed to Algerian independence* (1961–63)

**oasis** [ɔazis] *nf ou m* oasis

**obédience** [ɔbedjɑ̃s] *nf* allegiance

**obéir** [ɔbeiʀ] *vi* to obey; **~ à** to obey; (*moteur, véhicule*) to respond to

**obéissance** [ɔbeisɑ̃s] *nf* obedience

**obéissant, e** [ɔbeisɑ̃, -ɑ̃t] *adj* obedient

**obélisque** [ɔbelisk(ə)] *nm* obelisk

**obèse** [ɔbɛz] *adj* obese

**obésité** [ɔbezite] *nf* obesity

**objecter** [ɔbʒɛkte] *vt* (*prétexter*) to plead, put forward as an excuse; **~ qch à** (*argument*) to put forward sth against; **~ (à qn) que** to object (to sb) that

**objecteur** [ɔbʒɛktœʀ] *nm*: **~ de conscience** conscientious objector

**objectif, -ive** [ɔbʒɛktif, -iv] *adj* objective ▷ *nm* (*Optique, Photo*) lens *sg*; (*Mil: fig*) objective; **~ grand angulaire/à focale variable** wide-angle/zoom lens

**objection** [ɔbʒɛksjɔ̃] *nf* objection; **~ de conscience** conscientious objection

**objectivement** [ɔbʒɛktivmɑ̃] *adv* objectively

**objectivité** [ɔbʒɛktivite] *nf* objectivity

**objet** [ɔbʒɛ] *nm* (*chose*) object; (*d'une discussion, recherche*) subject; **être** *ou* **faire l'~ de** (*discussion*) to be the subject of; (*soins*) to be given *ou* shown; **sans ~** *adj* purposeless; (*sans fondement*) groundless; **~ d'art** objet d'art; **~s personnels** personal items; **~s de toilette** toiletries; **~s trouvés** lost property *sg* (*Brit*), lost-and-found *sg* (*US*); **~s de valeur** valuables

**obligataire** [ɔbligatɛʀ] *adj* bond *cpd* ▷ *nm/f* bondholder, debenture holder

**obligation** [ɔbligasjɔ̃] *nf* obligation; (*gén pl: devoir*) duty; (*Comm*) bond, debenture; **sans ~ d'achat** with no obligation (to buy); **être dans l'~ de faire** to be obliged to do; **avoir l'~ de faire** to be under an obligation to do; **~s familiales** family obligations *ou* responsibilities; **~s militaires** military obligations *ou* duties

**obligatoire** [ɔbligatwaʀ] *adj* compulsory, obligatory

**obligatoirement** [ɔbligatwaʀmɑ̃] *adv* compulsorily; (*fatalement*) necessarily

**obligé, e** [ɔbliʒe] *adj* (*redevable*): **être très ~ à qn** to be most obliged to sb; (*contraint*): **je suis (bien) ~ (de le faire)** I have to (do it); (*nécessaire: conséquence*) necessary; **c'est ~!** it's inevitable!

**obligeamment** [ɔbliʒamɑ̃] *adv* obligingly

**obligeance** [ɔbliʒɑ̃s] *nf*: **avoir l'~ de** to be kind *ou* good enough to

**obligeant, e** [ɔbliʒɑ̃, -ɑ̃t] *adj* obliging; kind

**obliger** [ɔbliʒe] *vt* (*contraindre*): **~ qn à faire** to force *ou* oblige sb to do; (*Jur: engager*) to bind; (*rendre service à*) to oblige

**oblique** [ɔblik] *adj* oblique; **regard ~** sidelong glance; **en ~** *adv* diagonally

**obliquer** [ɔblike] *vi*: **~ vers** to turn off towards

**oblitération** [ɔbliteʀasjɔ̃] *nf* cancelling *no pl*, cancellation; obstruction

**oblitérer** [ɔbliteʀe] *vt* (*timbre-poste*) to cancel; (*Méd: canal, vaisseau*) to obstruct

**oblong, oblongue** [ɔblɔ̃, ɔblɔ̃g] *adj* oblong

**obnubiler** [ɔbnybile] *vt* to obsess

**obole** [ɔbɔl] *nf* offering

**obscène** [ɔpsɛn] *adj* obscene

**obscénité** [ɔpsenite] *nf* obscenity

**obscur, e** [ɔpskyʀ] *adj* (*sombre*) dark; (*fig: raisons*) obscure; (: *sentiment, malaise*) vague; (: *personne, vie*) humble, lowly

**obscurcir** [ɔpskyʀsiʀ] *vt* to darken; (*fig*) to obscure; **s'obscurcir** *vi* to grow dark

**obscurité** [ɔpskyʀite] *nf* darkness; **dans l'~** in the dark, in darkness; (*anonymat, médiocrité*) in obscurity

**obsédant, e** [ɔpsedɑ̃, -ɑ̃t] *adj* obsessive

**obsédé, e** [ɔpsede] *nm/f* fanatic; **~(e) sexuel(le)** sex maniac

**obséder** [ɔpsede] *vt* to obsess, haunt

**obsèques** [ɔpsɛk] *nfpl* funeral *sg*

**obséquieux, -euse** [ɔpsekjø, -øz] *adj* obsequious

**observance** [ɔpsɛʀvɑ̃s] *nf* observance

**observateur, -trice** [ɔpsɛʀvatœʀ, -tʀis] *adj* observant, perceptive ▷ *nm/f* observer

**observation** [ɔpsɛʀvasjɔ̃] *nf* observation; (*d'un règlement etc*) observance; (*commentaire*) observation, remark; (*reproche*) reproof; **en ~** (*Méd*) under observation

**observatoire** [ɔpsɛʀvatwaʀ] *nm* observatory; (*lieu élevé*) observation post, vantage point

**observer** [ɔpsɛʀve] *vt* (*regarder*) to observe, watch; (*examiner*) to examine; (*scientifiquement*, *aussi: règlement, jeûne etc*) to observe; (*surveiller*) to watch; (*remarquer*) to observe, notice; **faire ~ qch à qn** (*dire*) to point out sth to sb; **s'observer** *vi* (*se surveiller*) to keep a check on o.s.

**obsession** [ɔpsesjɔ̃] *nf* obsession; **avoir l'~ de** to have an obsession with

**obsessionnel, le** [ɔpsesjɔnɛl] *adj* obsessive

**obsolescent, e** [ɔpsɔlesã, -ãt] *adj* obsolescent

**obstacle** [ɔpstakl(ə)] *nm* obstacle; (*Équitation*) jump, hurdle; **faire ~ à** (*lumière*) to block out; (*projet*) to hinder, put obstacles in the path of; **~s antichars** tank defences

**obstétricien, ne** [ɔpstetʀisjɛ̃, -ɛn] *nm/f* obstetrician

**obstétrique** [ɔpstetʀik] *nf* obstetrics *sg*

**obstination** [ɔpstinasjɔ̃] *nf* obstinacy

**obstiné, e** [ɔpstine] *adj* obstinate

**obstinément** [ɔpstinemã] *adv* obstinately

**obstiner** [ɔpstine]: **s'obstiner** *vi* to insist, dig one's heels in; **s'~ à faire** to persist (obstinately) in doing; **s'~ sur qch** to keep working at sth, labour away at sth

**obstruction** [ɔpstʀyksjɔ̃] *nf* obstruction, blockage; (*Sport*) obstruction; **faire de l'~** (*fig*) to be obstructive

**obstruer** [ɔpstʀye] *vt* to block, obstruct; **s'obstruer** *vi* to become blocked

**obtempérer** [ɔptãpeʀe] *vi* to obey; **~ à** to obey, comply with

**obtenir** [ɔptəniʀ] *vt* to obtain, get; (*total*) to arrive at, reach; (*résultat*) to achieve, obtain; **~ de pouvoir faire** to obtain permission to do; **~ qch à qn** to obtain sth for sb; **~ de qn qu'il fasse** to get sb to agree to do(ing)

**obtention** [ɔptɑ̃sjɔ̃] *nf* obtaining

**obtenu, e** [ɔpt(ə)ny] *pp de* **obtenir**

**obtiendrai** [ɔptjɛ̃dʀe], **obtiens** [ɔptjɛ̃], **obtint** *etc* [ɔptɛ̃] *vb voir* **obtenir**

**obturateur** [ɔptyʀatœʀ] *nm* (*Photo*) shutter; **~ à rideau** focal plane shutter

**obturation** [ɔptyʀasjɔ̃] *nf* closing (up); **~ (dentaire)** filling; **vitesse d'~** (*Photo*) shutter speed

**obturer** [ɔptyʀe] *vt* to close (up); (*dent*) to fill

**obtus, e** [ɔpty, -yz] *adj* obtuse

**obus** [ɔby] *nm* shell; **~ explosif** high-explosive shell; **~ incendiaire** incendiary device, fire bomb

**obvier** [ɔbvje]: **~ à** *vt* to obviate

**OC** *sigle fpl* (= *ondes courtes*) SW

**occasion** [ɔkazjɔ̃] *nf* (*aubaine, possibilité*) opportunity; (*circonstance*) occasion; (*Comm*: *article non neuf*) secondhand buy; (: *acquisition avantageuse*) bargain; **à plusieurs ~s** on several occasions; **à la première ~** at the first *ou* earliest opportunity; **avoir l'~ de faire** to have

the opportunity to do; **être l'~ de** to occasion, give rise to; **à l'~** *adv* sometimes, on occasions; (*un jour*) some time; **à l'~ de** on the occasion of; **d'~** *adj, adv* secondhand

**occasionnel, le** [ɔkazjɔnɛl] *adj* (*fortuit*) chance *cpd*; (*non régulier*) occasional; (: *travail*) casual

**occasionnellement** [ɔkazjɔnɛlmã] *adv* occasionally, from time to time

**occasionner** [ɔkazjɔne] *vt* to cause, bring about; **~ qch à qn** to cause sb sth

**occident** [ɔksidã] *nm*: **l'O~** the West

**occidental, e, -aux** [ɔksidãtal, -o] *adj* western; (*Pol*) Western ▷ *nm/f* Westerner

**occidentaliser** [ɔksidãtalize] *vt* (*coutumes*, *mœurs*) to westernize

**occiput** [ɔksipyt] *nm* back of the head, occiput

**occire** [ɔksiʀ] *vt* to slay

**occitan, e** [ɔksitã, -an] *adj* of the langue d'oc, of Provençal French

**occlusion** [ɔklyzjɔ̃] *nf*: **~ intestinale** obstruction of the bowel

**occulte** [ɔkylt(ə)] *adj* occult, supernatural

**occulter** [ɔkylte] *vt* (*fig*) to overshadow

**occupant, e** [ɔkypã, -ãt] *adj* occupying ▷ *nm/f* (*d'un appartement*) occupier, occupant; (*d'un véhicule*) occupant ▷ *nm* (*Mil*) occupying forces *pl*; (*Pol: d'usine etc*) occupier

**occupation** [ɔkypasjɔ̃] *nf* occupation; **l'O~** the Occupation (of France)

**occupationnel, le** [ɔkypasjɔnɛl] *adj*: **thérapie ~le** occupational therapy

**occupé, e** [ɔkype] *adj* (*Mil, Pol*) occupied; (*personne: affairé, pris*) busy; (*esprit: absorbé*) occupied; (*place, sièges*) taken; (*toilettes, ligne*) engaged

**occuper** [ɔkype] *vt* to occupy; (*poste, fonction*) to hold; (*main-d'œuvre*) to employ; **s'~ (à qch)** to occupy o.s. ou keep o.s. busy (with sth); **s'~ de** (*être responsable de*) to be in charge of; (*se charger de: affaire*) to take charge of, deal with; (: *clients etc*) to attend to; (*s'intéresser à, pratiquer: politique etc*) to be involved in; **ça occupe trop de place** it takes up too much room

**occurrence** [ɔkyʀãs] *nf*: **en l'~** in this case

**OCDE** *sigle f* (= *Organisation de coopération et de développement économique*) OECD

**océan** [ɔseã] *nm* ocean; **l'~ Indien** the Indian Ocean

**Océanie** [ɔseani] *nf*: **l'~** Oceania, South Sea Islands

**océanique** [ɔseanik] *adj* oceanic

**océanographe** [ɔseanɔgʀaf] *nm/f* oceanographer

**océanographie** [ɔseanɔgʀafi] *nf* oceanography

**océanologie** [ɔseanɔlɔʒi] *nf* oceanology

**ocelot** [ɔslo] *nm* (*Zool*) ocelot; (*fourrure*) ocelot fur

**ocre** [ɔkʀ(ə)] *adj inv* ochre

**octane** [ɔktan] *nm* octane

**octante** [ɔktãt] *num* (*Belgique, Suisse*) eighty

**octave** [ɔktav] *nf* octave

**octet** [ɔktɛ] *nm* byte

**octobre** [ɔktɔbʀ(ə)] *nm* October; *voir aussi* **juillet**

**o**

**octogénaire** [ɔktɔʒenɛR] *adj, nm/f* octogenarian
**octogonal, e, -aux** [ɔktɔgɔnal, -o] *adj* octagonal
**octogone** [ɔktɔgɔn] *nm* octagon
**octroi** [ɔktRwa] *nm* granting
**octroyer** [ɔktRwaje] *vt*: ~ **qch à qn** to grant sth
to sb, grant sb sth
**oculaire** [ɔkylɛR] *adj* ocular, eye *cpd* ▷ *nm* (*de microscope*) eyepiece
**oculiste** [ɔkylist(ə)] *nm/f* eye specialist, oculist
**ode** [ɔd] *nf* ode
**odeur** [ɔdœR] *nf* smell
**odieusement** [ɔdjøzmɑ̃] *adv* odiously
**odieux, -euse** [ɔdjø, -øz] *adj* odious, hateful
**odontologie** [ɔdɔ̃tɔlɔʒi] *nf* odontology
**odorant, e** [ɔdɔRɑ̃, -ɑ̃t] *adj* sweet-smelling, fragrant
**odorat** [ɔdɔRa] *nm* (sense of) smell; **avoir l'~ fin**
to have a keen sense of smell
**odoriférant, e** [ɔdɔRiferɑ̃, -ɑ̃t] *adj* sweet-smelling, fragrant
**odyssée** [ɔdise] *nf* odyssey
**OEA** *sigle f* (= *Organisation des États américains*) OAS
**œcuménique** [ekymenik] *adj* ecumenical
**œdème** [edɛm] *nm* oedema (Brit), edema (US)
**œil** [œj] (*pl* **yeux** [jø]) *nm* eye; **avoir un ~ poché**
*ou* **au beurre noir** to have a black eye; **à l'~** (*fam*)
for free; **à l'~ nu** with the naked eye; **tenir qn à**
**l'~** to keep an eye *ou* a watch on sb; **avoir l'~ à** to
keep an eye on; **faire de l'~ à qn** to make eyes at
sb; **voir qch d'un bon/mauvais ~** to view sth
in a favourable/an unfavourable light; **à l'~ vif**
with a lively expression; **à mes/ses yeux** in
my/his eyes; **de ses propres yeux** with his
own eyes; **fermer les yeux (sur)** (*fig*) to turn a
blind eye (to); **les yeux fermés** (*aussi fig*) with
one's eyes shut; **fermer l'~** to get a moment's
sleep; ~ **pour ~, dent pour dent** an eye for an
eye, a tooth for a tooth; **pour les beaux yeux**
**de qn** (*fig*) for love of sb; ~ **de verre** glass eye
**œil-de-bœuf** [œjdəbœf] (*pl* **œils-de-bœuf**) *nm*
bull's-eye (window)
**œillade** [œjad] *nf*: **lancer une ~ à qn** to wink
at sb, give sb a wink; **faire des ~s à** to make
eyes at
**œillères** [œjɛR] *nfpl* blinkers (Brit), blinders (US);
**avoir des ~** (*fig*) to be blinkered, wear blinders
**œillet** [œjɛ] *nm* (Bot) carnation; (*trou*) eyelet
**œnologue** [enɔlɔg] *nm/f* wine expert
**œsophage** [ezɔfaʒ] *nm* oesophagus (Brit),
esophagus (US)
**œstrogène** [estRɔʒɛn] *adj* oestrogen (Brit),
estrogen (US)
**œuf** [œf] *nm* egg; **étouffer dans l'~** to nip in the
bud; ~ **à la coque/dur/mollet** boiled/hard-boiled/soft-boiled egg; ~ **au plat/poché** fried/
poached egg; ~**s brouillés** scrambled eggs; ~
**de Pâques** Easter egg; ~ **à repriser** darning egg
**œuvre** [œvR(ə)] *nf* (*tâche*) task, undertaking;
(*ouvrage achevé, livre, tableau etc*) work; (*ensemble de la production artistique*) works *pl*; (*organisation charitable*) charity ▷ *nm* (*d'un artiste*) works *pl*;
(Constr): **le gros ~** the shell; **œuvres** *nfpl* (*actes*)

deeds, works; **être/se mettre à l'~** to be at/get
(down) to work; **mettre en ~** (*moyens*) to make
use of; (*plan, loi, projet etc*) to implement; ~ **d'art**
work of art; **bonnes ~s** good works *ou* deeds; ~**s**
**de bienfaisance** charitable works
**OFCE** *sigle m* (= *Observatoire français des conjonctures économiques*) economic research institute
**offensant, e** [ɔfɑ̃sɑ̃, -ɑ̃t] *adj* offensive, insulting
**offense** [ɔfɑ̃s] *nf* (*affront*) insult; (Rel: *péché*)
transgression, trespass
**offenser** [ɔfɑ̃se] *vt* to offend, hurt; (*principes,
Dieu*) to offend against; **s'offenser de** *vi* to take
offence (Brit) *ou* offense (US) at
**offensif, -ive** [ɔfɑ̃sif, -iv] *adj* (*armes, guerre*)
offensive ▷ *nf* offensive; (*fig: du froid, de l'hiver*)
onslaught; **passer à l'offensive** to go into the
attack *ou* offensive
**offert, e** [ɔfɛR, -ɛRt] *pp de* **offrir**
**offertoire** [ɔfɛRtwaR] *nm* offertory
**office** [ɔfis] *nm* (*charge*) office; (*agence*) bureau,
agency; (Rel) service ▷ *nm ou f* (*pièce*) pantry;
**faire ~ de** to act as; to do duty as; **d'~** *adv*
automatically; **bons ~s** (Pol) good offices; ~ **du**
**tourisme** tourist bureau
**officialiser** [ɔfisjalize] *vt* to make official
**officiel, le** [ɔfisjɛl] *adj, nm/f* official
**officiellement** [ɔfisjɛlmɑ̃] *adv* officially
**officier** [ɔfisje] *nm* officer ▷ *vi* (Rel) to officiate;
~ **de l'état-civil** registrar; ~ **ministériel**
member of the legal profession; ~ **de police**
≈ police officer
**officieusement** [ɔfisjøzmɑ̃] *adv* unofficially
**officieux, -euse** [ɔfisjø, -øz] *adj* unofficial
**officinal, e, -aux** [ɔfisinal, -o] *adj*: **plantes ~es**
medicinal plants
**officine** [ɔfisin] *nf* (*de pharmacie*) dispensary;
(Admin: *pharmacie*) pharmacy; (*gén péj: bureau*)
agency, office
**offrais** *etc* [ɔfRɛ] *vb voir* **offrir**
**offrande** [ɔfRɑ̃d] *nf* offering
**offrant** [ɔfRɑ̃] *nm*: **au plus ~** to the highest
bidder
**offre** [ɔfR(ə)] *vb voir* **offrir** ▷ *nf* offer; (*aux enchères*)
bid; (Admin: *soumission*) tender; (Écon): **l'~**
supply; ~ **d'emploi** job advertised; **"~s**
**d'emploi"** "situations vacant"; ~ **publique**
**d'achat (OPA)** takeover bid; ~**s de service** offer
of service
**offrir** [ɔfRiR] *vt*: ~ (**à qn**) to offer (to sb); (*faire
cadeau*) to give to (sb); **s'offrir** *vi* (*se présenter:
occasion, paysage*) to present itself ▷ *vt* (*se payer:
vacances, voiture*) to treat o.s. to; ~ (**à qn**) **de faire**
**qch** to offer to do sth (for sb); ~ **à boire à qn** to
offer sb a drink; **s'~ à faire qch** to offer *ou*
volunteer to do sth; **s'~ comme guide/en**
**otage** to offer one's services as (a) guide/offer
o.s. as (a) hostage; **s'~ aux regards** (*personne*) to
expose o.s. to the public gaze
**offset** [ɔfsɛt] *nm* offset (printing)
**offusquer** [ɔfyske] *vt* to offend; **s'offusquer de**
to take offence (Brit) *ou* offense (US) at, be
offended by

**ogive** [ɔʒiv] *nf* (*Archit*) diagonal rib; (*d'obus, de missile*) nose cone; **voûte en ~** rib vault; **arc en ~** lancet arch; **~ nucléaire** nuclear warhead

**OGM** *sigle m* GMO

**ogre** [ɔgʀ(ə)] *nm* ogre

**oh** [o] *excl* oh!; **oh la la!** oh (dear)!; **pousser des oh! et des ah!** to gasp with admiration

**oie** [wa] *nf* (*Zool*) goose; **~ blanche** (*fig*) young innocent

**oignon** [ɔɲɔ̃] *nm* (*Culin*) onion; (*de tulipe etc: bulbe*) bulb; (*Méd*) bunion; **ce ne sont pas tes ~s** (*fam*) that's none of your business

**oindre** [wɛ̃dʀ(ə)] *vt* to anoint

**oiseau, x** [wazo] *nm* bird; **~ de proie** bird of prey

**oiseau-mouche** [wazomuʃ] (*pl* **oiseaux-mouches**) *nm* hummingbird

**oiseleur** [wazlœʀ] *nm* bird-catcher

**oiselier, -ière** [wazəlje, -jɛʀ] *nm/f* bird-seller

**oisellerie** [wazɛlʀi] *nf* bird shop

**oiseux, -euse** [wazø, -øz] *adj* pointless, idle; (*sans valeur, importance*) trivial

**oisif, -ive** [wazif, -iv] *adj* idle ▷ *nm/f* (*péj*) man/lady of leisure

**oisillon** [wazijɔ̃] *nm* little *ou* baby bird

**oisiveté** [wazivte] *nf* idleness

**OIT** *sigle f* (= *Organisation internationale du travail*) ILO

**OK** [okɛ] *excl* OK!, all right!

**OL** *sigle fpl* (= *ondes longues*) LW

**oléagineux, -euse** [ɔleaʒinø, -øz] *adj* oleaginous, oil-producing

**oléiculture** [ɔleikyltyʀ] *nm* olive growing

**oléoduc** [ɔleɔdyk] *nm* (oil) pipeline

**olfactif, -ive** [ɔlfaktif, -iv] *adj* olfactory

**olibrius** [ɔlibʀijys] *nm* oddball

**oligarchie** [ɔligaʀʃi] *nf* oligarchy

**oligo-élément** [ɔligoelemɑ̃] *nm* trace element

**oligopole** [ɔligɔpɔl] *nm* oligopoly

**olivâtre** [ɔlivɑtʀ(ə)] *adj* olive-greenish; (*teint*) sallow

**olive** [ɔliv] *nf* (*Bot*) olive ▷ *adj inv* olive-green

**oliveraie** [ɔlivʀɛ] *nf* olive grove

**olivier** [ɔlivje] *nm* olive (tree); (*bois*) olive (wood)

**olographe** [ɔlɔgʀaf] *adj*: **testament ~** will written, dated and signed by the testator

**OLP** *sigle f* (= *Organisation de libération de la Palestine*) PLO

**olympiade** [ɔlɛ̃pjad] *nf* (*période*) Olympiad; **les ~s** (*jeux*) the Olympiad *sg*

**olympien, ne** [ɔlɛ̃pjɛ̃, -ɛn] *adj* Olympian, of Olympian aloofness

**olympique** [ɔlɛ̃pik] *adj* Olympic

**OM** *sigle fpl* (= *ondes moyennes*) MW

**Oman** [ɔman] *nm*: **l'~, le sultanat d'~** (the Sultanate of) Oman

**ombilical, e, -aux** [ɔ̃bilikal, -o] *adj* umbilical

**ombrage** [ɔ̃bʀaʒ] *nm* (*ombre*) (leafy) shade; (*fig*): **prendre ~ de** to take umbrage at; **faire** *ou* **porter ~ à qn** to offend sb

**ombragé, e** [ɔ̃bʀaʒe] *adj* shaded, shady

**ombrageux, -euse** [ɔ̃bʀaʒø, -øz] *adj* (*cheval*) skittish, nervous; (*personne*) touchy, easily offended

**ombre** [ɔ̃bʀ(ə)] *nf* (*espace non ensoleillé*) shade; (*ombre portée, tache*) shadow; **à l'~** in the shade; (*fam: en prison*) behind bars; **à l'~ de** in the shade of; (*tout près de, fig*) in the shadow of; **tu me fais de l'~** you're in my light; **ça nous donne de l'~** it gives us (some) shade; **il n'y a pas l'~ d'un doute** there's not the shadow of a doubt; **dans l'~** in the shade; **vivre dans l'~** (*fig*) to live in obscurity; **laisser dans l'~** (*fig*) to leave in the dark; **~ à paupières** eye shadow; **~ portée** shadow; **~s chinoises** (*spectacle*) shadow show *sg*

**ombrelle** [ɔ̃bʀɛl] *nf* parasol, sunshade

**ombrer** [ɔ̃bʀe] *vt* to shade

**OMC** *sigle f* (= *organisation mondiale du commerce*) WTO

**omelette** [ɔmlɛt] *nf* omelette; **~ baveuse** runny omelette; **~ au fromage/au jambon** cheese/ham omelette; **~ aux herbes** omelette with herbs; **~ norvégienne** baked Alaska

**omettre** [ɔmɛtʀ(ə)] *vt* to omit, leave out; **~ de faire** to fail *ou* omit to do

**omis, e** [ɔmi, -iz] *pp de* **omettre**

**omission** [ɔmisjɔ̃] *nf* omission

**omnibus** [ɔmnibys] *nm* slow *ou* stopping train

**omnipotent, e** [ɔmnipotɑ̃, -ɑ̃t] *adj* omnipotent

**omnipraticien, ne** [ɔmnipratisjɛ̃, -ɛn] *nm/f* (*Méd*) general practitioner

**omniprésent, e** [ɔmnipʀezɑ̃, -ɑ̃t] *adj* omnipresent

**omniscient, e** [ɔmnisjɑ̃, -ɑ̃t] *adj* omniscient

**omnisports** [ɔmnispɔʀ] *adj inv* (*club*) general sports *cpd*; (*salle*) multi-purpose *cpd*; (*terrain*) all-purpose *cpd*

**omnium** [ɔmnjɔm] *nm* (*Comm*) corporation; (*Cyclisme*) omnium; (*Courses*) open handicap

**omnivore** [ɔmnivɔʀ] *adj* omnivorous

**omoplate** [ɔmɔplat] *nf* shoulder blade

**OMS** *sigle f* (= *Organisation mondiale de la santé*) WHO

🔵 **MOT-CLÉ**

**on** [ɔ̃] *pron* **1** (*indéterminé*) you, one; **on peut le faire ainsi** you *ou* one can do it like this, it can be done like this; **on dit que ...** they say that ..., it is said that ..

**2** (*quelqu'un*): **on les a attaqués** they were attacked; **on vous demande au téléphone** there's a phone call for you, you're wanted on the phone; **on frappe à la porte** someone's knocking at the door

**3** (*nous*) we; **on va y aller demain** we're going tomorrow

**4** (*les gens*) they; **autrefois, on croyait ...** they used to believe ..

**5**: **on ne peut plus** *adv*: **on ne peut plus stupide** as stupid as can be

**once** [ɔ̃s] *nf*: **une ~ de** an ounce of

287

**oncle** [ɔ̃kl(ə)] *nm* uncle
**onction** [ɔ̃ksjɔ̃] *nf voir* **extrême-onction**
**onctueux, -euse** [ɔ̃ktɥø, -øz] *adj* creamy,
smooth; *(fig)* smooth, unctuous
**onde** [ɔ̃d] *nf (Physique)* wave; **sur l'~** on the
waters; **sur les ~s** on the radio; **mettre en ~s**
to produce for the radio; **~ de choc** shock wave;
**~s courtes (OC)** short wave *sg*; **petites ~s (PO)**,
**~s moyennes (OM)** medium wave *sg*; **grandes
~s (GO)**, **~s longues (OL)** long wave *sg*; **~s
sonores** sound waves
**ondée** [ɔ̃de] *nf* shower
**on-dit** [ɔ̃di] *nm inv* rumour
**ondoyer** [ɔ̃dwaje] *vi* to ripple, wave ▷ *vt (Rel)* to
baptize *(in an emergency)*
**ondulant, e** [ɔ̃dylɑ̃, -ɑ̃t] *adj (démarche)* swaying;
*(ligne)* undulating
**ondulation** [ɔ̃dylɑsjɔ̃] *nf* undulation; wave
**ondulé, e** [ɔ̃dyle] *adj* undulating; wavy
**onduler** [ɔ̃dyle] *vi* to undulate; *(cheveux)* to wave
**onéreux, -euse** [ɔneʀø, -øz] *adj* costly; **à titre ~**
in return for payment
**ONF** *sigle m* (= *Office national des forêts*) ≈ Forestry
Commission *(Brit)*, ≈ National Forest Service
*(US)*
**ONG** *sigle f* (= *organisation non-gouvernementale*) NGO
**ongle** [ɔ̃gl(ə)] *nm (Anat)* nail; **manger** *ou* **ronger
ses ~s** to bite one's nails; **se faire les ~s** to do
one's nails
**onglet** [ɔ̃glɛ] *nm (rainure)* (thumbnail) groove;
*(bande de papier)* tab
**onguent** [ɔ̃gɑ̃] *nm* ointment
**onirique** [ɔniʀik] *adj* dreamlike, dream *cpd*
**onirisme** [ɔniʀism(ə)] *nm* dreams *pl*
**onomatopée** [ɔnɔmatɔpe] *nf* onomatopoeia
**ont** [ɔ̃] *vb voir* **avoir**
**ontarien, ne** [ɔ̃taʀjɛ̃, -ɛn] *adj* Ontarian
**ONU** [ɔny] *sigle f* (= *Organisation des Nations unies*)
UN(O)
**onusien, ne** [ɔnyzjɛ̃, -ɛn] *adj* of the UN(O), of
the United Nations (Organization)
**onyx** [ɔniks] *nm* onyx
**onze** [ɔ̃z] *num* eleven
**onzième** [ɔ̃zjɛm] *num* eleventh
**op** [ɔp] *nf (opération)*: **salle d'op** (operating)
theatre
**OPA** *sigle f* = **offre publique d'achat**
**opacité** [ɔpasite] *nf* opaqueness
**opale** [ɔpal] *nf* opal
**opalescent, e** [ɔpalesɑ̃, -ɑ̃t] *adj* opalescent
**opalin, e** [ɔpalɛ̃, -in] *adj*, *nf* opaline
**opaque** [ɔpak] *adj (vitre, verre)* opaque; *(brouillard,
nuit)* impenetrable
**OPE** *sigle f* (= *offre publique d'échange*) take-over bid
*where bidder offers shares in his company in exchange for
shares in target company*
**OPEP** [ɔpɛp] *sigle f* (= *Organisation des pays
exportateurs de pétrole*) OPEC
**opéra** [ɔpeʀa] *nm* opera; *(édifice)* opera house
**opérable** [ɔpeʀabl(ə)] *adj* operable
**opéra-comique** [ɔpeʀakɔmik] *(pl* **opéras-
comiques)** *nm* light opera, opéra comique

**opérant, e** [ɔpeʀɑ̃, -ɑ̃t] *adj (mesure)* effective
**opérateur, -trice** [ɔpeʀatœʀ, -tʀis] *nm/f*
operator; **~ (de prise de vues)** cameraman
**opération** [ɔpeʀasjɔ̃] *nf* operation; *(Comm)*
dealing; **salle/table d'~** operating theatre/
table; **~ de sauvetage** rescue operation; **~ à
cœur ouvert** open-heart surgery *no pl*
**opérationnel, le** [ɔpeʀasjɔnel] *adj* operational
**opératoire** [ɔpeʀatwaʀ] *adj (manœuvre, méthode)*
operating; *(choc etc)* post-operative
**opéré, e** [ɔpeʀe] *nm/f* post-operative patient
**opérer** [ɔpeʀe] *vt (Méd)* to operate on; *(faire,
exécuter)* to carry out, make ▷ *vi (remède: faire effet)*
to act, work; *(procéder)* to proceed; *(Méd)* to
operate; **s'opérer** *vi (avoir lieu)* to occur, take
place; **se faire ~** to have an operation; **se faire
~ des amygdales/du cœur** to have one's tonsils
out/have a heart operation
**opérette** [ɔpeʀet] *nf* operetta, light opera
**ophtalmique** [ɔftalmik] *adj* ophthalmic
**ophtalmologie** [ɔftalmɔlɔʒi] *nf* ophthalmology
**ophtalmologue** [ɔftalmɔlɔg] *nm/f*
ophthalmologist
**opiacé, e** [ɔpjase] *adj* opiate
**opiner** [ɔpine] *vi*: **~ de la tête** to nod assent ▷ *vt*:
**~ à** to consent to
**opiniâtre** [ɔpinjɑtʀ(ə)] *adj* stubborn
**opiniâtreté** [ɔpinjɑtʀəte] *nf* stubbornness
**opinion** [ɔpinjɔ̃] *nf* opinion; **l'~ (publique)**
public opinion; **avoir bonne/mauvaise ~ de** to
have a high/low opinion of
**opiomane** [ɔpjɔman] *nm/f* opium addict
**opium** [ɔpjɔm] *nm* opium
**OPJ** *sigle m* (= *officier de police judiciaire*) ≈ DC
(= *Detective Constable*)
**opportun, e** [ɔpɔʀtœ̃, -yn] *adj* timely,
opportune; **en temps ~** at the appropriate time
**opportunément** [ɔpɔʀtynemɑ̃] *adv*
opportunely
**opportunisme** [ɔpɔʀtynism(ə)] *nm*
opportunism
**opportuniste** [ɔpɔʀtynist(ə)] *adj*, *nm/f*
opportunist
**opportunité** [ɔpɔʀtynite] *nf* timeliness,
opportuneness
**opposant, e** [ɔpozɑ̃, -ɑ̃t] *adj* opposing ▷ *nm/f*
opponent
**opposé, e** [ɔpoze] *adj (direction, rive)* opposite;
*(faction)* opposing; *(couleurs)* contrasting;
*(opinions, intérêts)* conflicting; *(contre)*: **~ à**
opposed to, against ▷ *nm*: **l'~** the other *ou*
opposite side *(ou* direction); *(contraire)* the
opposite; **être ~ à** to be opposed to; **à l'~** *(fig)* on
the other hand; **à l'~ de** on the other *ou*
opposite side from; *(fig)* contrary to, unlike
**opposer** [ɔpoze] *vt (meubles, objets)* to place
opposite each other; *(personnes, armées, équipes)* to
oppose; *(couleurs, termes, tons)* to contrast;
*(comparer: livres, avantages)* to contrast; **~ qch à**
*(comme obstacle, défense)* to set sth against; *(comme
objection)* to put sth forward against; *(en
contraste)* to set sth opposite; to match sth with;

**s'opposer** vi (sens réciproque) to conflict; to clash; to face each other; to contrast; **s'~ à** (interdire, empêcher) to oppose; (tenir tête à) to rebel against; **sa religion s'y oppose** it's against his religion; **s'~ à ce que qn fasse** to be opposed to sb's doing

**opposition** [ɔpozisjɔ̃] nf opposition; **par ~** in contrast; **par ~ à** as opposed to, in contrast with; **entrer en ~ avec** to come into conflict with; **être en ~ avec** (idées, conduite) to be at variance with; **faire ~ à un chèque** to stop a cheque

**oppressant, e** [ɔpresɑ̃, -ɑ̃t] adj oppressive

**oppresser** [ɔprese] vt to oppress; **se sentir oppressé** to feel breathless

**oppresseur** [ɔpresœr] nm oppressor

**oppressif, -ive** [ɔpresif, -iv] adj oppressive

**oppression** [ɔpresjɔ̃] nf oppression; (malaise) feeling of suffocation

**opprimer** [ɔprime] vt (asservir: peuple, faibles) to oppress; (étouffer: liberté, opinion) to suppress, stifle; (chaleur etc) to suffocate, oppress

**opprobre** [ɔprɔbr(ə)] nm disgrace

**opter** [ɔpte] vi: **~ pour** to opt for; **~ entre** to choose between

**opticien, ne** [ɔptisjɛ̃, -ɛn] nm/f optician

**optimal, e, -aux** [ɔptimal, -o] adj optimal

**optimisation** [ɔptimizasjɔ̃] nf optimization

**optimiser** [ɔptimize] vt to optimize

**optimisme** [ɔptimism(ə)] nm optimism

**optimiste** [ɔptimist(ə)] adj optimistic ▷ nm/f optimist

**optimum** [ɔptimɔm] adj, nm optimum

**option** [ɔpsjɔ̃] nf option; (Auto: supplément) optional extra; **matière à ~** (Scol) optional subject (Brit), elective (US); **prendre une ~ sur** to take (out) an option on; **~ par défaut** (Inform) default (option)

**optionnel, le** [ɔpsjɔnɛl] adj optional

**optique** [ɔptik] adj (nerf) optic; (verres) optical ▷ nf (Photo: lentilles etc) optics pl; (science, industrie) optics sg; (fig: manière de voir) perspective

**opulence** [ɔpylɑ̃s] nf wealth, opulence

**opulent, e** [ɔpylɑ̃, -ɑ̃t] adj wealthy, opulent; (formes, poitrine) ample, generous

**OPV** sigle f (= offre publique de vente) public offer of sale

**or** [ɔr] nm gold ▷ conj now, but; **d'or** (fig) golden; **en or** gold cpd; (occasion) golden; **un mari/ enfant en or** a treasure; **une affaire en or** (achat) a real bargain; (commerce) a gold mine; **plaqué or** gold-plated; **or noir** black gold

**oracle** [ɔrakl(ə)] nm oracle

**orage** [ɔraʒ] nm (thunder)storm

**orageux, -euse** [ɔraʒø, -øz] adj stormy

**oraison** [ɔrɛzɔ̃] nf orison, prayer; **~ funèbre** funeral oration

**oral, e, -aux** [ɔral, -o] adj (déposition, promesse) oral, verbal; (Méd): **par voie ~e** by mouth, orally ▷ nm (Scol) oral

**oralement** [ɔralmɑ̃] adv orally

**orange** [ɔrɑ̃ʒ] adj inv, nf orange; **~ sanguine** blood orange; **~ pressée** freshly-squeezed orange juice

**orangé, e** [ɔrɑ̃ʒe] adj orangey, orange-coloured

**orangeade** [ɔrɑ̃ʒad] nf orangeade

**oranger** [ɔrɑ̃ʒe] nm orange tree

**orangeraie** [ɔrɑ̃ʒrɛ] nf orange grove

**orangerie** [ɔrɑ̃ʒri] nf orangery

**orang-outan, orang-outang** [ɔrɑ̃utɑ̃] nm orang-utan

**orateur** [ɔratœr] nm speaker; orator

**oratoire** [ɔratwar] nm (lieu, chapelle) oratory; (au bord du chemin) wayside shrine ▷ adj oratorical

**oratorio** [ɔratɔrjo] nm oratorio

**orbital, e, -aux** [ɔrbital, -o] adj orbital; **station ~e** space station

**orbite** [ɔrbit] nf (Anat) (eye-)socket; (Physique) orbit; **mettre sur ~** to put into orbit; (fig) to launch; **dans l'~ de** (fig) within the sphere of influence of

**Orcades** [ɔrkad] nfpl: **les ~** the Orkneys, the Orkney Islands

**orchestral, e, -aux** [ɔrkɛstral, -o] adj orchestral

**orchestrateur, -trice** [ɔrkɛstratœr, -tris] nm/f orchestrator

**orchestration** [ɔrkɛstrasjɔ̃] nf orchestration

**orchestre** [ɔrkɛstr(ə)] nm orchestra; (de jazz, danse) band; (places) stalls pl (Brit), orchestra (US)

**orchestrer** [ɔrkɛstre] vt (Mus) to orchestrate; (fig) to mount, stage-manage

**orchidée** [ɔrkide] nf orchid

**ordinaire** [ɔrdinɛr] adj ordinary; (coutumier: maladresse etc) usual; (de tous les jours) everyday; (modèle, qualité) standard ▷ nm ordinary; (menus) everyday fare ▷ nf (essence) ≈ two-star (petrol) (Brit), ≈ regular (gas) (US); **d'~** usually, normally; **à l'~** usually, ordinarily

**ordinairement** [ɔrdinɛrmɑ̃] adv ordinarily, usually

**ordinal, e, -aux** [ɔrdinal, -o] adj ordinal

**ordinateur** [ɔrdinatœr] nm computer; **mettre sur ~** to computerize, put on computer; **~ de bureau** desktop computer; **~ individuel** ou **personnel** personal computer; **~ portable** laptop (computer)

**ordination** [ɔrdinasjɔ̃] nf ordination

**ordonnance** [ɔrdɔnɑ̃s] nf organization; (groupement, disposition) layout; (Méd) prescription; (Jur) order; (Mil) orderly, batman (Brit); **d'~** (Mil) regulation cpd; **officier d'~** aide-de-camp

**ordonnateur, -trice** [ɔrdɔnatœr, -tris] nm/f (d'une cérémonie, fête) organizer; **~ des pompes funèbres** funeral director

**ordonné, e** [ɔrdɔne] adj tidy, orderly; (Math) ordered ▷ nf (Math) Y-axis, ordinate

**ordonner** [ɔrdɔne] vt (agencer) to organize, arrange; (: meubles, appartement) to lay out, arrange; (donner un ordre): **~ à qn de faire** to order sb to do; (Math) to (arrange in) order; (Rel) to ordain; (Méd) to prescribe; (Jur) to order; **s'ordonner** vi (faits) to organize themselves

**ordre** [ɔʀdʀ(ə)] *nm* (*gén*) order; (*propreté et soin*) orderliness, tidiness; (*association professionnelle, honorifique*) association; (*Comm*): **à l'~ de** payable to; (*nature*): **d'~ pratique** of a practical nature; **ordres** *nmpl* (*Rel*) holy orders; **avoir de l'~** to be tidy *ou* orderly; **mettre en ~** to tidy (up), put in order; **mettre bon ~ à** to put to rights, sort out; **procéder par ~** to take things one at a time; **être aux ~s de qn/sous les ~s de qn** to be at sb's disposal/under sb's command; **rappeler qn à l'~** to call sb to order; **jusqu'à nouvel ~** until further notice; **dans le même ~ d'idées** in this connection; **par ~ d'entrée en scène** in order of appearance; **un ~ de grandeur** some idea of the size (*ou* amount); **de premier ~** first-rate; **~ de grève** strike call; **~ du jour** (*d'une réunion*) agenda; (*Mil*) order of the day; **à l'~ du jour** on the agenda; (*fig*) topical; (*Mil: citer*) in dispatches; **~ de mission** (*Mil*) orders *pl*; **~ public** law and order; **~ de route** marching orders *pl*

**ordure** [ɔʀdyʀ] *nf* filth *no pl*; (*propos, écrit*) obscenity, (piece of) filth; **ordures** *nfpl* (*balayures, déchets*) rubbish *sg*, refuse *sg*; **~s ménagères** household refuse

**ordurier, -ière** [ɔʀdyʀje, -jɛʀ] *adj* lewd, filthy

**oreille** [ɔʀɛj] *nf* (*Anat*) ear; (*de marmite, tasse*) handle; (*Tech: d'un écrou*) wing; **avoir de l'~** to have a good ear (for music); **avoir l'~ fine** to have good *ou* sharp ears; **l'~ basse** crestfallen, dejected; **se faire tirer l'~** to take a lot of persuading; **dire qch à l'~ de qn** to have a word in sb's ear (about sth)

**oreiller** [ɔʀeje] *nm* pillow

**oreillette** [ɔʀɛjɛt] *nf* (*Anat*) auricle

**oreillons** [ɔʀejɔ̃] *nmpl* mumps *sg*

**ores** [ɔʀ]: **d'~ et déjà** *adv* already

**orfèvre** [ɔʀfɛvʀ(ə)] *nm* goldsmith; silversmith

**orfèvrerie** [ɔʀfɛvʀəʀi] *nf* (*art, métier*) goldsmith's (*ou* silversmith's) trade; (*ouvrage*) (silver *ou* gold) plate

**orfraie** [ɔʀfʀɛ] *nm* white-tailed eagle; **pousser des cris d'~** to yell at the top of one's voice

**organe** [ɔʀgan] *nm* organ; (*véhicule, instrument*) instrument; (*voix*) voice; (*porte-parole*) representative, mouthpiece; **~s de commande** (*Tech*) controls; **~s de transmission** (*Tech*) transmission system *sg*

**organigramme** [ɔʀganigʀam] *nm* (*hiérarchique, structure*) organization chart; (*des opérations*) flow chart

**organique** [ɔʀganik] *adj* organic

**organisateur, -trice** [ɔʀganizatœʀ, -tʀis] *nm/f* organizer

**organisation** [ɔʀganizasjɔ̃] *nf* organization; **O~ des Nations unies (ONU)** United Nations (Organization) (UN, UNO); **O~ mondiale de la santé (OMS)** World Health Organization (WHO); **O~ du traité de l'Atlantique Nord (OTAN)** North Atlantic Treaty Organization (NATO)

**organisationnel, le** [ɔʀganizasjɔnɛl] *adj* organizational

**organiser** [ɔʀganize] *vt* to organize; (*mettre sur pied: service etc*) to set up; **s'organiser** *vi* to get organized

**organisme** [ɔʀganism(ə)] *nm* (*Bio*) organism; (*corps humain*) body; (*Admin, Pol etc*) body, organism

**organiste** [ɔʀganist(ə)] *nm/f* organist

**orgasme** [ɔʀgasm(ə)] *nm* orgasm, climax

**orge** [ɔʀʒ(ə)] *nf* barley

**orgeat** [ɔʀʒa] *nm*: **sirop d'~** barley water

**orgelet** [ɔʀʒəlɛ] *nm* sty(e)

**orgie** [ɔʀʒi] *nf* orgy

**orgue** [ɔʀg(ə)] *nm* organ; **orgues** *nfpl* organ *sg*; **~ de Barbarie** barrel *ou* street organ

**orgueil** [ɔʀgœj] *nm* pride

**orgueilleux, -euse** [ɔʀgœjø, -øz] *adj* proud

**Orient** [ɔʀjɑ̃] *nm*: **l'~** the East, the Orient

**orientable** [ɔʀjɑ̃tabl(ə)] *adj* (*phare, lampe etc*) adjustable

**oriental, e, -aux** [ɔʀjɑ̃tal, -o] *adj* oriental, eastern; (*frontière*) eastern ▷ *nm/f*: **Oriental, e** Oriental

**orientation** [ɔʀjɑ̃tasjɔ̃] *nf* positioning; adjustment; orientation; direction; (*d'une maison etc*) aspect; (*d'un journal*) leanings *pl*; **avoir le sens de l'~** to have a (good) sense of direction; **course d'~** orienteering exercise; **~ professionnelle** careers advice *ou* guidance; (*service*) careers advisory service

**orienté, e** [ɔʀjɑ̃te] *adj* (*fig: article, journal*) slanted; **bien/mal ~** (*appartement*) well/badly positioned; **~ au sud** facing south, with a southern aspect

**orienter** [ɔʀjɑ̃te] *vt* (*situer*) to position; (*placer, disposer: pièce mobile*) to adjust, position; (*tourner*) to direct, turn; (*voyageur, touriste, recherches*) to direct; (*fig: élève*) to orientate; **s'orienter** *vi* (*se repérer*) to find one's bearings; **s'~ vers** (*fig*) to turn towards

**orienteur, -euse** [ɔʀjɑ̃tœʀ, -øz] *nm/f* (*Scol*) careers adviser

**orifice** [ɔʀifis] *nm* opening, orifice

**oriflamme** [ɔʀiflam] *nf* banner, standard

**origan** [ɔʀigɑ̃] *nm* oregano

**originaire** [ɔʀiʒinɛʀ] *adj* original; **être ~ de** (*pays, lieu*) to be a native of; (*provenir de*) to originate from; to be native to

**original, e, -aux** [ɔʀiʒinal, -o] *adj* original; (*bizarre*) eccentric ▷ *nm/f* (*fam: excentrique*) eccentric; (: *fantaisiste*) joker ▷ *nm* (*document etc, Art*) original; (*dactylographie*) top copy

**originalité** [ɔʀiʒinalite] *nf* (*d'un nouveau modèle*) originality *no pl*; (*excentricité, bizarrerie*) eccentricity

**origine** [ɔʀiʒin] *nf* origin; (*d'un message, appel téléphonique*) source; (*d'une révolution, réussite*) root; **origines** *nfpl* (*d'une personne*) origins; **d'~** of origin; (*pneus etc*) original; (*bureau postal*) dispatching; **d'~ française** of French origin; **dès l'~** at *ou* from the outset; **à l'~** originally; **avoir son ~ dans** to have its origins in, originate in

**originel, le** [ɔriʒinɛl] *adj* original

**originellement** [ɔriʒinɛlmɑ̃] *adv* (*à l'origine*)
originally; (*dès l'origine*) from the beginning

**oripeaux** [ɔripo] *nmpl* rags

**ORL** *sigle f* (= *oto-rhino-laryngologie*) ENT ▷ *sigle m/f*
(= *oto-rhino-laryngologiste*) ENT specialist; **être en
~** (*malade*) to be in the ENT hospital *ou*
department

**orme** [ɔrm(ə)] *nm* elm

**orné, e** [ɔrne] *adj* ornate; **~ de** adorned *ou*
decorated with

**ornement** [ɔrnəmɑ̃] *nm* ornament; (*fig*)
embellishment, adornment; **~s sacerdotaux**
vestments

**ornemental, e, -aux** [ɔrnəmɑ̃tal, -o] *adj*
ornamental

**ornementer** [ɔrnəmɑ̃te] *vt* to ornament

**orner** [ɔrne] *vt* to decorate, adorn; **~ qch de** to
decorate sth with

**ornière** [ɔrnjɛr] *nf* rut; (*fig*): **sortir de l'~**
(*routine*) to get out of the rut; (*impasse*) to get out
of a spot

**ornithologie** [ɔrnitɔlɔʒi] *nf* ornithology

**ornithologue** [ɔrnitɔlɔg] *nm/f* ornithologist; **~
amateur** birdwatcher

**orphelin, e** [ɔrfəlɛ̃, -in] *adj* orphan(ed) ▷ *nm/f*
orphan; **~ de père/mère** fatherless/motherless

**orphelinat** [ɔrfəlina] *nm* orphanage

**ORSEC** [ɔrsɛk] *sigle f* = **Organisation des
secours**; **le plan ~** *disaster contingency plan*

**ORSECRAD** [ɔrsɛkrad] *sigle m* = **ORSEC en cas
d'accident nucléaire**

**orteil** [ɔrtɛj] *nm* toe; **gros ~** big toe

**ORTF** *sigle m* (= *Office de radio-diffusion télévision
française*) (*former*) French broadcasting corporation

**orthodontiste** [ɔrtɔdɔ̃tist(ə)] *nm/f*
orthodontist

**orthodoxe** [ɔrtɔdɔks(ə)] *adj* orthodox

**orthodoxie** [ɔrtɔdɔksi] *nf* orthodoxy

**orthogénie** [ɔrtɔʒeni] *nf* family planning

**orthographe** [ɔrtɔgraf] *nf* spelling

**orthographier** [ɔrtɔgrafje] *vt* to spell; **mal
orthographié** misspelt

**orthopédie** [ɔrtɔpedi] *nf* orthopaedics *sg* (*Brit*),
orthopedics *sg* (*US*)

**orthopédique** [ɔrtɔpedik] *adj* orthopaedic
(*Brit*), orthopedic (*US*)

**orthopédiste** [ɔrtɔpedist(ə)] *nm/f* orthopaedic
(*Brit*) *ou* orthopedic (*US*) specialist

**orthophonie** [ɔrtɔfɔni] *nf* (*Méd*) speech
therapy; (*Ling*) correct pronunciation

**orthophoniste** [ɔrtɔfɔnist(ə)] *nm/f* speech
therapist

**ortie** [ɔrti] *nf* (stinging) nettle; **~ blanche**
white dead-nettle

**OS** *sigle m* = **ouvrier spécialisé**

**os** [ɔs] *nm* bone; **sans os** (*Boucherie*) off the bone,
boned; **os à moelle** marrowbone

**oscillation** [ɔsilasjɔ̃] *nf* oscillation; **oscillations**
*nfpl* (*fig*) fluctuations

**osciller** [ɔsile] *vi* (*pendule*) to swing; (*au vent etc*)
to rock; (*Tech*) to oscillate; (*fig*): **~ entre** to

waver *ou* fluctuate between

**osé, e** [oze] *adj* daring, bold

**oseille** [ozɛj] *nf* sorrel

**oser** [oze] *vi, vt* to dare; **~ faire** to dare (to) do

**osier** [ozje] *nm* (*Bot*) willow; **d'~, en ~**
wicker(work) *cpd*

**Oslo** [ɔslo] *n* Oslo

**osmose** [ɔsmoz] *nf* osmosis

**ossature** [ɔsatyr] *nf* (*Anat: squelette*) frame,
skeletal structure; (: *du visage*) bone structure;
(*fig*) framework

**osselet** [ɔslɛ] *nm* (*Anat*) ossicle; **jouer aux ~s** to
play jacks

**ossements** [ɔsmɑ̃] *nmpl* bones

**osseux, -euse** [ɔsø, -øz] *adj* bony; (*tissu, maladie,
greffe*) bone *cpd*

**ossifier** [ɔsifje]: **s'ossifier** *vi* to ossify

**ossuaire** [ɔsɥɛr] *nm* ossuary

**Ostende** [ɔstɑ̃d] *n* Ostend

**ostensible** [ɔstɑ̃sibl(ə)] *adj* conspicuous

**ostensiblement** [ɔstɑ̃sibləmɑ̃] *adv*
conspicuously

**ostensoir** [ɔstɑ̃swar] *nm* monstrance

**ostentation** [ɔstɑ̃tasjɔ̃] *nf* ostentation; **faire ~
de** to parade, make a display of

**ostentatoire** [ɔstɑ̃tatwar] *adj* ostentatious

**ostracisme** [ɔstrasism(ə)] *nm* ostracism;
**frapper d'~** to ostracize

**ostréicole** [ɔstreikɔl] *adj* oyster *cpd*

**ostréiculture** [ɔstreikyltyr] *nf* oyster-farming

**otage** [ɔtaʒ] *nm* hostage; **prendre qn comme ~**
to take sb hostage

**OTAN** [ɔtɑ̃] *sigle f* (= *Organisation du traité de
l'Atlantique Nord*) NATO

**otarie** [ɔtari] *nf* sea-lion

**ôter** [ote] *vt* to remove; (*soustraire*) to take away;
**~ qch à qn** to take sth (away) from sb; **~ qch de**
to remove sth from; **six ôté de dix égale
quatre** six from ten equals *ou* is four

**otite** [ɔtit] *nf* ear infection

**oto-rhino** [ɔtɔrino(-)], **oto-rhino-
laryngologiste** *nm/f* ear, nose and throat
specialist

**ottomane** [ɔtɔman] *nf* ottoman

**ou** [u] *conj* or; **ou ... ou** either ... or; **ou bien** or
(else)

**MOT-CLÉ**

**où** [u] *pron relatif* **1** (*position, situation*) where, that
(*souvent omis*); **la chambre où il était** the room
(that) he was in, the room where he was; **la
ville où je l'ai rencontré** the town where I met
him; **la pièce d'où il est sorti** the room he
came out of; **le village d'où je viens** the village
I come from; **les villes par où il est passé** the
towns he went through

**2** (*temps, état*) that (*souvent omis*); **le jour où il est
parti** the day (that) he left; **au prix où c'est** at
the price it is

▷ *adv* **1** (*interrogation*) where; **où est-il/va-t-il?**
where is he/is he going?; **par où?** which way?;

**d'où vient que ...?** how come ...?
**2** (position) where; **je sais où il est** I know
where he is; **où que l'on aille** wherever you go

**OUA** sigle f (= Organisation de l'unité africaine) OAU
(= Organization of African Unity)
**ouais** [wɛ] excl yeah
**ouate** [wat] nf cotton wool (Brit), cotton (US);
(bourre) padding, wadding; ~ **(hydrophile)**
cotton wool (Brit), (absorbent) cotton (US)
**ouaté, e** [wate] adj cotton-wool; (doublé)
padded; (fig: atmosphère) cocoon-like; (: pas, bruit)
muffled
**oubli** [ubli] nm (acte): **l'~ de** forgetting;
(étourderie) forgetfulness no pl; (négligence)
omission, oversight; (absence de souvenirs)
oblivion; ~ **de soi** self-effacement, self-
negation
**oublier** [ublije] vt (gén) to forget; (ne pas voir:
erreurs etc) to miss; (ne pas mettre: virgule, nom) to
leave out, forget; (laisser quelque part: chapeau etc)
to leave behind; **s'oublier** vi to forget o.s.;
(enfant, animal) to have an accident (euphemism); ~
**l'heure** to forget (about) the time
**oubliettes** [ublijɛt] nfpl dungeon sg; **(jeter) aux**
~ (fig) (to put) completely out of mind
**oublieux, -euse** [ublijø, -øz] adj forgetful
**oued** [wɛd] nm wadi
**ouest** [wɛst] nm west ▷ adj inv west; (région)
western; **à l'~** in the west, (to the) west,
westwards; **à l'~ de** (to the) west of; **vent d'~**
westerly wind
**ouest-allemand, e** [wɛstalmɑ̃, -ɑ̃d] adj West
German
**ouf** [uf] excl phew!
**Ouganda** [ugɑ̃da] nm: **l'~** Uganda
**ougandais, e** [ugɑ̃dɛ, -ɛz] adj Ugandan
**oui** [wi] adv yes; **répondre (par)** ~ to answer
yes; **mais ~, bien sûr** yes, of course; **je pense
que** ~ I think so; **pour un** ~ **ou pour un non** for
no apparent reason
**ouï-dire** [widiʀ]: **par** ~ adv by hearsay
**ouïe** [wi] nf hearing; **ouïes** nfpl (de poisson) gills;
(de violon) sound-hole sg
**ouïr** [wiʀ] vt to hear; **avoir ouï dire que** to have
heard it said that
**ouistiti** [wistiti] nm marmoset
**ouragan** [uʀagɑ̃] nm hurricane; (fig) storm
**Oural** [uʀal] nm: **l'~** (fleuve) the Ural; (aussi: **les
monts Oural**) the Urals, the Ural Mountains
**ourdir** [uʀdiʀ] vt (complot) to hatch
**ourdou** [uʀdu] adj inv Urdu ▷ nm (Ling) Urdu
**ourlé, e** [uʀle] adj hemmed; (fig) rimmed
**ourler** [uʀle] vt to hem
**ourlet** [uʀlɛ] nm hem; (de l'oreille) rim; **faire un
~ à** to hem
**ours** [uʀs] nm bear; ~ **brun/blanc** brown/polar
bear; ~ **marin** fur seal; ~ **mal léché** uncouth
fellow; ~ **(en peluche)** teddy (bear)
**ourse** [uʀs(ə)] nf (Zool) she-bear; **la Grande/
Petite O~** the Great/Little Bear, Ursa Major/
Minor

**oursin** [uʀsɛ̃] nm sea urchin
**ourson** [uʀsɔ̃] nm (bear-)cub
**ouste** [ust(ə)] excl hop it!
**outil** [uti] nm tool
**outillage** [utijaʒ] nm set of tools; (d'atelier)
equipment no pl
**outiller** [utije] vt (ouvrier, usine) to equip
**outrage** [utʀaʒ] nm insult; **faire subir les
derniers ~s à** (femme) to ravish; ~ **aux bonnes
mœurs** (Jur) outrage to public decency; ~ **à
magistrat** (Jur) contempt of court; ~ **à la
pudeur** (Jur) indecent behaviour no pl
**outragé, e** [utʀaʒe] adj offended; outraged
**outrageant, e** [utʀaʒɑ̃, -ɑ̃t] adj offensive
**outrager** [utʀaʒe] vt to offend gravely; (fig:
contrevenir à) to outrage, insult
**outrageusement** [utʀaʒøzmɑ̃] adv
outrageously
**outrance** [utʀɑ̃s] nf excessiveness no pl, excess;
**à** ~ adv excessively, to excess
**outrancier, -ière** [utʀɑ̃sje, -jɛʀ] adj extreme
**outre** [utʀ(ə)] nf goatskin, water skin ▷ prép
besides ▷ adv: **passer** ~ to carry on regardless;
**passer** ~ **à** to disregard, take no notice of; **en** ~
besides, moreover; ~ **que** apart from the fact
that; ~ **mesure** immoderately; unduly
**outré, e** [utʀe] adj (flatterie, éloge) excessive,
exaggerated; (indigné, scandalisé) outraged
**outre-Atlantique** [utʀatlɑ̃tik] adv across the
Atlantic
**outrecuidance** [utʀəkɥidɑ̃s] nf
presumptuousness no pl
**outre-Manche** [utʀəmɑ̃ʃ] adv across the
Channel
**outremer** [utʀəmɛʀ] adj inv ultramarine
**outre-mer** [utʀəmɛʀ] adv overseas; **d'~**
overseas
**outrepasser** [utʀəpase] vt to go beyond, exceed
**outrer** [utʀe] vt (pensée, attitude) to exaggerate;
(indigner: personne) to outrage
**outre-Rhin** [utʀəʀɛ̃] adv across the Rhine, in
Germany
**outsider** [awtsajdœʀ] nm outsider
**ouvert, e** [uvɛʀ, -ɛʀt(ə)] pp de **ouvrir** ▷ adj open;
(robinet, gaz etc) on; **à bras ~s** with open arms
**ouvertement** [uvɛʀtəmɑ̃] adv openly
**ouverture** [uvɛʀtyʀ] nf opening; (Mus)
overture; (Pol): **l'~** the widening of the political
spectrum; (Photo): ~ **(du diaphragme)**
aperture; **ouvertures** nfpl (propositions)
overtures; ~ **d'esprit** open-mindedness;
**heures d'~** (Comm) opening hours; **jours d'~**
(Comm) days of opening
**ouvrable** [uvʀabl(ə)] adj: **jour** ~ working day,
weekday; **heures ~s** business hours
**ouvrage** [uvʀaʒ] nm (tâche, de tricot etc, Mil) work
no pl; (objet: Couture, Art) (piece of) work; (texte,
livre) work; **panier** ou **corbeille à** ~ work basket;
~ **d'art** (Génie Civil) bridge or tunnel etc
**ouvragé, e** [uvʀaʒe] adj finely embroidered (ou
worked ou carved)
**ouvrant, e** [uvʀɑ̃, -ɑ̃t] vb voir **ouvrir** ▷ adj: **toit** ~

sunroof

**ouvré, e** [uvʀe] *adj* finely-worked; **jour ~** working day

**ouvre-boîte, ouvre-boîtes** [uvʀəbwat] *nm inv* tin (Brit) *ou* can opener

**ouvre-bouteille, ouvre-bouteilles** [uvʀəbutɛj] *nm inv* bottle-opener

**ouvreuse** [uvʀøz] *nf* usherette

**ouvrier, -ière** [uvʀije, -jɛʀ] *nm/f* worker ▷ *nf* (Zool) worker (bee) ▷ *adj* working-class; (problèmes, conflit) industrial, labour *cpd* (Brit), labor *cpd* (US); (revendications) workers'; **classe ouvrière** working class; **~ agricole** farmworker; **~ qualifié** skilled worker; **~ spécialisé (OS)** semiskilled worker; **~ d'usine** factory worker

**ouvrir** [uvʀiʀ] *vt* (gén) to open; (brèche, passage) to open up; (commencer l'exploitation de, créer) to open (up); (eau, électricité, chauffage, robinet) to turn on; (Méd: abcès) to open up, cut open ▷ *vi* to open; to open up; (Cartes): **~ à trèfle** to open in clubs; **s'ouvrir** *vi* to open; **s'~ à** (art etc) to open one's mind to; **s'~ à qn (de qch)** to open one's heart to sb (about sth); **s'~ les veines** to slash *ou* cut one's wrists; **~ sur** to open onto; **~ l'appétit à qn** to whet sb's appetite; **~ des horizons** to open up new horizons; **~ l'esprit** to broaden one's horizons; **~ une session** (Inform) to log in

**ouvroir** [uvʀwaʀ] *nm* workroom, sewing room

**ovaire** [ɔvɛʀ] *nm* ovary

**ovale** [ɔval] *adj* oval

**ovation** [ɔvasjɔ̃] *nf* ovation

**ovationner** [ɔvasjɔne] *vt*: **~ qn** to give sb an ovation

**ovin, e** [ɔvɛ̃, -in] *adj* ovine

**OVNI** [ɔvni] *sigle m* (= objet volant non identifié) UFO

**ovoïde** [ɔvɔid] *adj* egg-shaped

**ovulation** [ɔvylɑsjɔ̃] *nf* (Physiol) ovulation

**ovule** [ɔvyl] *nm* (Physiol) ovum; (Méd) pessary

**oxfordien, ne** [ɔksfɔʀdjɛ̃, -ɛn] *adj* Oxonian ▷ *nm/f*: **Oxfordien, ne** Oxonian

**oxydable** [ɔksidabl(ə)] *adj* liable to rust

**oxyde** [ɔksid] *nm* oxide; **~ de carbone** carbon monoxide

**oxyder** [ɔkside]: **s'oxyder** *vi* to become oxidized

**oxygéné, e** [ɔksiʒene] *adj*: **eau ~e** hydrogen peroxide; **cheveux ~s** bleached hair

**oxygène** [ɔksiʒɛn] *nm* oxygen; (fig): **cure d'~** fresh air cure

**ozone** [ozɔn] *nm* ozone; **trou dans la couche d'~** hole in the ozone layer

**o**

# Pp

**P, p** [pe] *nm inv* P, p ▷ *abr* (= *Père*) Fr; (= *page*) p; **P comme Pierre** P for Peter
**PA** *sigle fpl* = **petites annonces**
**PAC** *sigle f* (= *Politique agricole commune*) CAP
**pacage** [pakaʒ] *nm* grazing, pasture
**pacemaker** [pɛsmɛkœʀ] *nm* pacemaker
**pachyderme** [paʃidɛʀm(ə)] *nm* pachyderm; elephant
**pacificateur, -trice** [pasifikatœʀ, -tʀis] *adj* pacificatory
**pacification** [pasifikɑsjɔ̃] *nf* pacification
**pacifier** [pasifje] *vt* to pacify
**pacifique** [pasifik] *adj* (*personne*) peaceable; (*intentions, coexistence*) peaceful ▷ *nm*: **le P~, l'océan P~** the Pacific (Ocean)
**pacifiquement** [pasifikmɑ̃] *adv* peaceably; peacefully
**pacifisme** [pasifism(ə)] *nm* pacifism
**pacifiste** [pasifist(ə)] *nm/f* pacifist
**pack** [pak] *nm* pack
**pacotille** [pakɔtij] *nf* (*péj*) cheap goods *pl*; **de ~** cheap
**PACS** [paks] *sigle m* (= *pacte civil de solidarité*) ≈ civil partnership
**pacser** [pakse]: **se pacser** *vi* ≈ to form a civil partnership
**pacte** [pakt(ə)] *nm* pact, treaty
**pactiser** [paktize] *vi*: **~ avec** to come to terms with
**pactole** [paktɔl] *nm* gold mine (*fig*)
**paddock** [padɔk] *nm* paddock
**Padoue** [padu] *n* Padua
**PAF** *sigle f* (= *Police de l'air et des frontières*) police authority responsible for civil aviation, border control *etc* ▷ *sigle m* (= *paysage audiovisuel français*) French broadcasting scene
**pagaie** [pagɛ] *nf* paddle
**pagaille** [pagaj] *nf* mess, shambles *sg*; **il y en a en ~** there are loads *ou* heaps of them
**paganisme** [paganism(ə)] *nm* paganism
**pagayer** [pageje] *vi* to paddle
**page** [paʒ] *nf* page; (*passage: d'un roman*) passage ▷ *nm* page (boy); **mettre en ~s** to make up (into pages); **mise en ~** layout; **à la ~** (*fig*) up-to-date; **~ d'accueil** (*Inform*) home page; **~ blanche** blank page; **~ de garde** endpaper; **~ Web** (*Inform*) web page
**page-écran** [paʒekʀɑ̃] (*pl* **pages-écrans**) *nf* (*Inform*) screen page
**pagination** [paʒinɑsjɔ̃] *nf* pagination
**paginer** [paʒine] *vt* to paginate
**pagne** [paɲ] *nm* loincloth
**pagode** [pagɔd] *nf* pagoda
**paie** [pɛ] *nf* = **paye**
**paiement** [pemɑ̃] *nm* = **payement**
**païen, ne** [pajɛ̃, -ɛn] *adj, nm/f* pagan, heathen
**paillard, e** [pajaʀ, -aʀd(ə)] *adj* bawdy
**paillasse** [pajas] *nf* (*matelas*) straw mattress; (*d'un évier*) draining board
**paillasson** [pajasɔ̃] *nm* doormat
**paille** [paj] *nf* straw; (*défaut*) flaw; **être sur la ~** to be ruined; **~ de fer** steel wool
**paillé, e** [paje] *adj* with a straw seat
**pailleté, e** [pajte] *adj* sequined
**paillette** [pajɛt] *nf* speck, flake; **paillettes** *nfpl* (*décoratives*) sequins, spangles; **lessive en ~s** soapflakes *pl*
**pain** [pɛ̃] *nm* (*substance*) bread; (*unité*) loaf (of bread); (*morceau*): **~ de cire** *etc* bar of wax *etc*; (*Culin*): **~ de poisson/légumes** fish/vegetable loaf; **petit ~** (bread) roll; **~ bis/complet** brown/wholemeal (*Brit*) *ou* wholewheat (*US*) bread; **~ de campagne** farmhouse bread; **~ d'épice** ≈ gingerbread; **~ grillé** toast; **~ de mie** sandwich loaf; **~ perdu** French toast; **~ de seigle** rye bread; **~ de sucre** sugar loaf
**pair, e** [pɛʀ] *adj* (*nombre*) even ▷ *nm* peer; **aller de ~ (avec)** to go hand in hand *ou* together (with); **au ~** (*Finance*) at par; **valeur au ~** par value; **jeune fille au ~** au pair
**paire** [pɛʀ] *nf* pair; **une ~ de lunettes/tenailles** a pair of glasses/pincers; **faire la ~: les deux font la ~** they are two of a kind
**pais** [pɛ] *vb voir* **paître**
**paisible** [pezibl(ə)] *adj* peaceful, quiet
**paisiblement** [peziblǝmɑ̃] *adv* peacefully, quietly
**paître** [pɛtʀ(ə)] *vi* to graze
**paix** [pɛ] *nf* peace; (*fig*) peacefulness, peace; **faire la ~ avec** to make peace with; **avoir la ~** to have peace (and quiet)
**Pakistan** [pakistɑ̃] *nm*: **le ~** Pakistan

**pakistanais, e** [pakistanɛ, -ɛz] *adj* Pakistani
**PAL** *sigle m* (= *Phase Alternation Line*) PAL
**palabrer** [palabʀe] *vi* to argue endlessly
**palabres** [palabʀ(ə)] *nfpl ou mpl* endless
discussions
**palace** [palas] *nm* luxury hotel
**palais** [palɛ] *nm* palace; (*Anat*) palate; **le P~
Bourbon** *the seat of the French National Assembly;* **le
P~ de l'Élysée** the Élysée Palace; **~ des
expositions** exhibition centre; **le P~ de
Justice** the Law Courts *pl*
**palan** [palɑ̃] *nm* hoist
**pale** [pal] *nf* (*d'hélice*) blade; (*de roue*) paddle
**pâle** [pɑl] *adj* pale; (*fig*): **une ~ imitation** a pale
imitation; **bleu ~** pale blue; **~ de colère** white
*ou* pale with anger
**palefrenier** [palfʀənje] *nm* groom (*for horses*)
**paléontologie** [paleɔ̃tɔlɔʒi] *nf* paleontology
**paléontologiste** [paleɔ̃tɔlɔʒist(ə)],
**paléontologue** [paleɔ̃tɔlɔg] *nm/f*
paleontologist
**Palerme** [palɛʀm(ə)] *n* Palermo
**Palestine** [palɛstin] *nf*: **la ~** Palestine
**palestinien, ne** [palɛstinjɛ̃, -ɛn] *adj* Palestinian
▷ *nm/f*: **Palestinien, ne** Palestinian
**palet** [palɛ] *nm* disc; (*Hockey*) puck
**paletot** [palto] *nm* (short) coat
**palette** [palɛt] *nf* palette; (*de produits*) range
**palétuvier** [paletyvje] *nm* mangrove
**pâleur** [pɑlœʀ] *nf* paleness
**palier** [palje] *nm* (*d'escalier*) landing; (*fig*) level,
plateau; (: *phase stable*) levelling (*Brit*) *ou* leveling
(*US*) off, new level; (*Tech*) bearing; **nos voisins
de ~** our neighbo(u)rs across the landing (*Brit*)
*ou* the hall (*US*); **en ~** at one level; **par ~s** in stages
**palière** [paljɛʀ] *adj f* landing *cpd*
**pâlir** [paliʀ] *vi* to turn *ou* go pale; (*couleur*) to
fade; **faire ~ qn** (*de jalousie*) to make sb green
(with envy)
**palissade** [palisad] *nf* fence
**palissandre** [palisɑ̃dʀ(ə)] *nm* rosewood
**palliatif** [paljatif] *nm* palliative; (*expédient*)
stopgap measure
**pallier** [palje] *vt*: **~ à** *vt* to offset, make up for
**palmarès** [palmaʀɛs] *nm* record (of
achievements); (*Scol*) prize list; (*Sport*) list of
winners
**palme** [palm(ə)] *nf* (*Bot*) palm leaf; (*symbole*)
palm; (*de plongeur*) flipper; **~s (académiques)**
*decoration for services to education*
**palmé, e** [palme] *adj* (*pattes*) webbed
**palmeraie** [palməʀɛ] *nf* palm grove
**palmier** [palmje] *nm* palm tree
**palmipède** [palmipɛd] *nm* palmiped,
webfooted bird
**palois, e** [palwa, -waz] *adj* of *ou* from Pau ▷ *nm/f*:
**Palois, e** inhabitant *ou* native of Pau
**palombe** [palɔ̃b] *nf* woodpigeon, ringdove
**pâlot, te** [pɑlo, -ɔt] *adj* pale, peaky
**palourde** [paluʀd(ə)] *nf* clam
**palpable** [palpabl(ə)] *adj* tangible, palpable
**palper** [palpe] *vt* to feel, finger

**palpitant, e** [palpitɑ̃, -ɑ̃t] *adj* thrilling, gripping
**palpitation** [palpitasjɔ̃] *nf* palpitation
**palpiter** [palpite] *vi* (*cœur, pouls*) to beat; (: *plus
fort*) to pound, throb; (*narines, chair*) to quiver
**paludisme** [palydism(ə)] *nm* malaria
**palustre** [palystʀ(ə)] *adj* (*coquillage etc*) marsh
*cpd*; (*fièvre*) malarial
**pâmer** [pɑme]: **se pâmer** *vi* to swoon; (*fig*): **se ~
devant** to go into raptures over
**pâmoison** [pɑmwazɔ̃] *nf*: **tomber en ~** to
swoon
**pampa** [pɑ̃pa] *nf* pampas *pl*
**pamphlet** [pɑ̃flɛ] *nm* lampoon, satirical tract
**pamphlétaire** [pɑ̃fletɛʀ] *nm/f* lampoonist
**pamplemousse** [pɑ̃pləmus] *nm* grapefruit
**pan** [pɑ̃] *nm* section, piece; (*côté: d'un prisme, d'une
tour*) side, face ▷ *excl* bang!; **~ de chemise** shirt
tail; **~ de mur** section of wall
**panacée** [panase] *nf* panacea
**panachage** [panaʃaʒ] *nm* blend, mix; (*Pol*) *voting
for candidates from different parties instead of for the set
list of one party*
**panache** [panaʃ] *nm* plume; (*fig*) spirit, panache
**panaché, e** [panaʃe] *adj*: **œillet ~** variegated
carnation; **glace ~e** mixed ice cream; **salade ~e**
mixed salad; **bière ~e** shandy
**panais** [panɛ] *nm* parsnip
**Panama** [panama] *nm*: **le ~** Panama
**panaméen, ne** [panameɛ̃, -ɛn] *adj* Panamanian
▷ *nm/f*: **Panaméen, ne** Panamanian
**panaris** [panaʀi] *nm* whitlow
**pancarte** [pɑ̃kaʀt(ə)] *nf* sign, notice; (*dans un
défilé*) placard
**pancréas** [pɑ̃kʀeas] *nm* pancreas
**panda** [pɑ̃da] *nm* panda
**pandémie** [pɑ̃demi] *nf* pandemic
**pané, e** [pane] *adj* fried in breadcrumbs
**panégyrique** [paneʒiʀik] *nm*: **faire le ~ de qn**
to extol sb's merits *ou* virtues
**panier** [panje] *nm* basket; (*à diapositives*)
magazine; **mettre au ~** to chuck away; **~ de
crabes: c'est un ~ de crabes** (*fig*) they're
constantly at one another's throats; **~ percé**
(*fig*) spendthrift; **~ à provisions** shopping
basket; **~ à salade** (*Culin*) salad shaker; (*Police*)
paddy wagon, police van
**panier-repas** [panjeʀ(ə)pɑ] (*pl* **paniers-repas**)
*nm* packed lunch
**panification** [panifikasjɔ̃] *nf* bread-making
**panique** [panik] *adj* panicky ▷ *nf* panic
**paniquer** [panike] *vi* to panic
**panne** [pan] *nf* (*d'un mécanisme, moteur*)
breakdown; **être/tomber en ~** to have broken
down/break down; **être en ~ d'essence** *ou* **en
sèche** to have run out of petrol (*Brit*) *ou* gas (*US*);
**mettre en ~** (*Navig*) to bring to; **~ d'électricité**
*ou* **de courant** power *ou* electrical failure
**panneau, x** [pano] *nm* (*écriteau*) sign, notice; (*de
boiserie, de tapisserie etc*) panel; **tomber dans le ~**
(*fig*) to walk into the trap; **~ d'affichage** notice
(*Brit*) *ou* bulletin (*US*) board; **~ électoral** board
for election poster; **~ indicateur** signpost; **~**

295

**publicitaire** hoarding (*Brit*), billboard (*US*); ~ **de signalisation** roadsign; ~ **solaire** solar panel

**panonceau, x** [panɔso] *nm* (*de magasin etc*) sign; (*de médecin etc*) plaque

**panoplie** [panɔpli] *nf* (*jouet*) outfit; (*d'armes*) display; (*fig*) array

**panorama** [panɔrama] *nm* (*vue*) all-round view, panorama; (*peinture*) panorama; (*fig: étude complète*) complete overview

**panoramique** [panɔramik] *adj* panoramic; (*carrosserie*) with panoramic windows ▷ *nm* (*Ciné, TV*) panoramic shot

**panse** [pɑs] *nf* paunch

**pansement** [pɑsmɑ] *nm* dressing, bandage; ~ **adhésif** sticking plaster (*Brit*), bandaid® (*US*)

**panser** [pɑse] *vt* (*plaie*) to dress, bandage; (*bras*) to put a dressing on, bandage; (*cheval*) to groom

**pantacourt** [pɑtakur] *nm* cropped trousers *pl*

**pantalon** [pɑtalɔ] *nm* trousers *pl* (*Brit*), pants *pl* (*US*), pair of trousers *ou* pants; ~ **de ski** ski pants *pl*

**pantalonnade** [pɑtalɔnad] *nf* slapstick (comedy)

**pantelant, e** [pɑtlɑ, -ɑt] *adj* gasping for breath, panting

**panthère** [pɑtɛr] *nf* panther

**pantin** [pɑtɛ] *nm* (*jouet*) jumping jack; (*péj: personne*) puppet

**pantois** [pɑtwa] *adj m*: **rester** ~ to be flabbergasted

**pantomime** [pɑtɔmim] *nf* mime; (*pièce*) mime show; (*péj*) fuss, carry-on

**pantouflard, e** [pɑtuflar, -ard(ə)] *adj* (*péj*) stay-at-home

**pantoufle** [pɑtufl(ə)] *nf* slipper

**panure** [panyr] *nf* breadcrumbs *pl*

**PAO** *sigle f* (= *publication assistée par ordinateur*) DTP

**paon** [pɑ] *nm* peacock

**papa** [papa] *nm* dad(dy)

**papauté** [papote] *nf* papacy

**papaye** [papaj] *nf* pawpaw

**pape** [pap] *nm* pope

**paperasse** [papras] *nf* (*péj*) bumf *no pl*, papers *pl*; forms *pl*

**paperasserie** [paprasri] *nf* (*péj*) red tape *no pl*; paperwork *no pl*

**papeterie** [papetri] *nf* (*fabrication du papier*) paper-making (industry); (*usine*) paper mill; (*magasin*) stationer's (shop (*Brit*)); (*articles*) stationery

**papetier, -ière** [paptje, -jɛr] *nm/f* paper-maker; stationer

**papetier-libraire** [paptjɛlibrɛr] (*pl* **papetiers-libraires**) *nm* bookseller and stationer

**papi** [papi] *nm* (*fam*) granddad

**papier** [papje] *nm* paper; (*feuille*) sheet *ou* piece of paper; (*article*) article; (*écrit officiel*) document; **papiers** *nmpl* (*aussi*: **papiers d'identité**) (identity) papers; **sur le** ~ (*théoriquement*) on paper; **noircir du** ~ to write page after page; ~ **couché/glacé** art/glazed paper; ~

**(d')aluminium** aluminium (*Brit*) *ou* aluminum (*US*) foil, tinfoil; ~ **d'Arménie** incense paper; ~ **bible** India *ou* bible paper; ~ **de brouillon** rough *ou* scrap paper; ~ **bulle** manil(l)a paper; ~ **buvard** blotting paper; ~ **calque** tracing paper; ~ **carbone** carbon paper; ~ **collant** Sellotape® (*Brit*), Scotch tape® (*US*), sticky tape; ~ **en continu** continuous stationery; ~ **à dessin** drawing paper; ~ **d'emballage** wrapping paper; ~ **gommé** gummed paper; ~ **hygiénique** toilet paper; ~ **journal** newsprint; (*pour emballer*) newspaper; ~ **à lettres** writing paper, notepaper; ~ **mâché** papier-mâché; ~ **machine** typing paper; ~ **peint** wallpaper; ~ **pelure** India paper; ~ **à pliage accordéon** fanfold paper; ~ **de soie** tissue paper; ~ **thermique** thermal paper; ~ **de tournesol** litmus paper; ~ **de verre** sandpaper

**papier-filtre** [papjefiltr(ə)] (*pl* **papiers-filtres**) *nm* filter paper

**papier-monnaie** [papjemɔnɛ] (*pl* **papiers-monnaies**) *nm* paper money

**papille** [papij] *nf*: **~s gustatives** taste buds

**papillon** [papijɔ] *nm* butterfly; (*fam: contravention*) (parking) ticket; (*Tech: écrou*) wing *ou* butterfly nut; ~ **de nuit** moth

**papillonner** [papijɔne] *vi* to flit from one thing (*ou* person) to another

**papillote** [papijɔt] *nf* (*pour cheveux*) curlpaper; (*de gigot*) (paper) frill

**papilloter** [papijɔte] *vi* (*yeux*) to blink; (*paupières*) to flutter; (*lumière*) to flicker

**papotage** [papɔtaʒ] *nm* chitchat

**papoter** [papɔte] *vi* to chatter

**papou, e** [papu] *adj* Papuan

**Papouasie-Nouvelle-Guinée** [papwazinuvɛlgine] *nf*: **la** ~ Papua-New-Guinea

**paprika** [paprika] *nm* paprika

**papyrus** [papirys] *nm* papyrus

**pâque** [pɑk] *nf*: **la** ~ Passover; *voir aussi* **Pâques**

**paquebot** [pakbo] *nm* liner

**pâquerette** [pɑkrɛt] *nf* daisy

**Pâques** [pɑk] *nm, nfpl*: **faire ses** ~ to do one's Easter duties; **l'île de** ~ Easter Island

**paquet** [pakɛ] *nm* packet; (*colis*) parcel; (*ballot*) bundle; (*dans négociations*) package (deal); (*fig: tas*): ~ **de** pile *ou* heap of; **paquets** *nmpl* (*bagages*) bags; **mettre le** ~ (*fam*) to give one's all; ~ **de mer** big wave

**paquetage** [paktaʒ] *nm* (*Mil*) kit, pack

**paquet-cadeau** [pakɛkado] (*pl* **paquets-cadeaux**) *nm* gift-wrapped parcel

**par** [par] *prép* by; **finir** *etc* ~ to end *etc* with; ~ **amour** out of love; **passer ~ Lyon/la côte** to go via *ou* through Lyons/along by the coast; ~ **la fenêtre** (*jeter, regarder*) out of the window; **trois ~ jour/personne** three a *ou* per day/head; **deux ~ deux** two at a time; (*marcher etc*) in twos; ~ **où?** which way?; ~ **ici** this way; (*dans le coin*) here; ~**-ci**, ~**-là** here and there

**para** [para] *nm* (*parachutiste*) para

**parabole** [parabɔl] *nf* (*Rel*) parable; (*Géom*)

parabola
**parabolique** [paʀabɔlik] *adj* parabolic;
**antenne ~** satellite dish
**parachever** [paʀaʃve] *vt* to perfect
**parachutage** [paʀaʃytaʒ] *nm* (*de soldats, vivres*)
parachuting-in; **nous sommes contre le ~**
**d'un candidat parisien dans notre**
**circonscription** (*Pol, fig*) we are against a
Parisian candidate being landed on us
**parachute** [paʀaʃyt] *nm* parachute
**parachuter** [paʀaʃyte] *vt* (*soldat etc*) to
parachute; (*fig*) to pitchfork; **il a été**
**parachuté à la tête de l'entreprise** he was
brought in from outside as head of the
company
**parachutisme** [paʀaʃytism(ə)] *nm* parachuting
**parachutiste** [paʀaʃytist(ə)] *nm/f* parachutist;
(*Mil*) paratrooper
**parade** [paʀad] *nf* (*spectacle, défilé*) parade;
(*Escrime, Boxe*) parry; (*ostentation*): **faire ~ de** to
display, show off; (*défense, riposte*): **trouver la ~**
**à une attaque** to find the answer to an attack;
**de ~** *adj* ceremonial; (*superficiel*) superficial,
outward
**parader** [paʀade] *vi* to swagger (around), show
off
**paradis** [paʀadi] *nm* heaven, paradise; **P~**
**terrestre** (*Rel*) Garden of Eden; (*fig*) heaven on
earth
**paradisiaque** [paʀadizjak] *adj* heavenly, divine
**paradoxal, e, -aux** [paʀadɔksal, -o] *adj*
paradoxical
**paradoxalement** [paʀadɔksalmɑ̃] *adv*
paradoxically
**paradoxe** [paʀadɔks(ə)] *nm* paradox
**parafe** [paʀaf] *nm*, **parafer** [paʀafe] ▷ *vt* =
**paraphe; parapher**
**paraffine** [paʀafin] *nf* paraffin; paraffin wax
**paraffiné, e** [paʀafine] *adj*: **papier ~** wax(ed)
paper
**parafoudre** [paʀafudʀ(ə)] *nm* (*Élec*) lightning
conductor
**parages** [paʀaʒ] *nmpl* (*Navig*) waters; **dans les ~**
**(de)** in the area *ou* vicinity (of)
**paragraphe** [paʀagʀaf] *nm* paragraph
**Paraguay** [paʀagwɛ] *nm*: **le ~** Paraguay
**paraguayen, ne** [paʀagwajɛ̃, -ɛn] *adj*
Paraguayan ▷ *nm/f*: **Paraguayen, ne**
Paraguayan
**paraître** [paʀɛtʀ(ə)] *vb copule* to seem, look,
appear ▷ *vi* to appear; (*être visible*) to show;
(*Presse, Édition*) to be published, come out,
appear; (*briller*) to show off; **laisser ~ qch** to let
(sth) show ▷ *vb impers*: **il paraît que** it seems *ou*
appears that; **il me paraît que** it seems to me
that; **il paraît absurde de** it seems absurd to;
**il ne paraît pas son âge** he doesn't look his
age; **~ en justice** to appear before the court(s);
**~ en scène/en public/à l'écran** to appear on
stage/in public/on the screen
**parallèle** [paʀalɛl] *adj* parallel; (*police, marché*)
unofficial; (*société, énergie*) alternative ▷ *nm*

(*comparaison*): **faire un ~ entre** to draw a
parallel between; (*Géo*) parallel ▷ *nf* parallel
(line); **en ~** in parallel; **mettre en ~** (*choses*
*opposées*) to compare; (*choses semblables*) to
parallel
**parallèlement** [paʀalɛlmɑ̃] *adv* in parallel; (*fig*:
*en même temps*) at the same time
**parallélépipède** [paʀalelepipɛd] *nm*
parallelepiped
**parallélisme** [paʀalelism(ə)] *nm* parallelism;
(*Auto*) wheel alignment
**parallélogramme** [paʀalelɔgʀam] *nm*
parallelogram
**paralyser** [paʀalize] *vt* to paralyze
**paralysie** [paʀalizi] *nf* paralysis
**paralytique** [paʀalitik] *adj, nm/f* paralytic
**paramédical, e, -aux** [paʀamedikal, -o] *adj*
paramedical
**paramètre** [paʀamɛtʀ(ə)] *nm* parameter
**paramilitaire** [paʀamilitɛʀ] *adj* paramilitary
**paranoïa** [paʀanɔja] *nf* paranoia
**paranoïaque** [paʀanɔjak] *nm/f* paranoiac
**paranormal, e, -aux** [paʀanɔʀmal, -o] *adj*
paranormal
**parapet** [paʀapɛ] *nm* parapet
**paraphe** [paʀaf] *nm* (*trait*) flourish; (*signature*)
initials *pl*; signature
**parapher** [paʀafe] *vt* to initial; to sign
**paraphrase** [paʀafʀɑz] *nf* paraphrase
**paraphraser** [paʀafʀɑze] *vt* to paraphrase
**paraplégie** [paʀapleʒi] *nf* paraplegia
**paraplégique** [paʀapleʒik] *adj, nm/f* paraplegic
**parapluie** [paʀaplɥi] *nm* umbrella; **~ atomique**
*ou* **nucléaire** nuclear umbrella; **~ pliant**
telescopic umbrella
**parapsychique** [paʀapsiʃik] *adj*
parapsychological
**parapsychologie** [paʀapsikɔlɔʒi] *nf*
parapsychology
**parapublic, -ique** [paʀapyblik] *adj* partly state-
controlled
**parascolaire** [paʀaskɔlɛʀ] *adj* extracurricular
**parasitaire** [paʀazitɛʀ] *adj* parasitic(al)
**parasite** [paʀazit] *nm* parasite ▷ *adj* (*Bot, Bio*)
parasitic(al); **parasites** *nmpl* (*Tél*)
interference *sg*
**parasitisme** [paʀazitism(ə)] *nm* parasitism
**parasol** [paʀasɔl] *nm* parasol, sunshade
**paratonnerre** [paʀatɔnɛʀ] *nm* lightning
conductor
**paravent** [paʀavɑ̃] *nm* folding screen; (*fig*)
screen
**parc** [paʀk] *nm* (public) park, gardens *pl*; (*de*
*château etc*) grounds *pl*; (*pour le bétail*) pen,
enclosure; (*d'enfant*) playpen; (*Mil: entrepôt*)
depot; (*ensemble d'unités*) stock; (*de voitures etc*)
fleet; **~ d'attractions** amusement park; **~**
**automobile** (*d'un pays*) number of cars on the
roads; **~ à huîtres** oyster bed; **~ à thème** theme
park; **~ national** national park; **~ naturel**
nature reserve; **~ de stationnement** car park;
**~ zoologique** zoological gardens *pl*

**p**

**parcelle** [paʀsɛl] *nf* fragment, scrap; *(de terrain)* plot, parcel

**parcelliser** [paʀselize] *vt* to divide *ou* split up

**parce que** [paʀsk(ə)] *conj* because

**parchemin** [paʀʃəmɛ̃] *nm* parchment

**parcheminé, e** [paʀʃəmine] *adj* wrinkled; *(papier)* with a parchment finish

**parcimonie** [paʀsimɔni] *nf* parsimony, parsimoniousness

**parcimonieux, -euse** [paʀsimɔnjø, -øz] *adj* parsimonious, miserly

**parcmètre** [paʀkmɛtʀ(ə)], **parcomètre** [paʀkɔmɛtʀ(ə)] *nm* parking meter

**parcotrain** [paʀkɔtʀɛ̃] *nm* station car park *(Brit) ou* parking lot *(US)*, park-and-ride car park *(Brit)*

**parcourir** [paʀkuʀiʀ] *vt (trajet, distance)* to cover; *(article, livre)* to skim *ou* glance through; *(lieu)* to go all over, travel up and down; *(frisson, vibration)* to run through; ~ **des yeux** to run one's eye over

**parcours** [paʀkuʀ] *vb voir* **parcourir** ▷ *nm (trajet)* journey; *(itinéraire)* route; *(Sport: terrain)* course; *(: tour)* round; run; lap; ~ **du combattant** assault course

**parcouru, e** [paʀkuʀy] *pp de* **parcourir**

**par-delà** [paʀdəla] *prép* beyond

**par-dessous** [paʀdəsu] *prép, adv* under(neath)

**pardessus** [paʀdəsy] *nm* overcoat

**par-dessus** [paʀdəsy] *prép* over (the top of) ▷ *adv* over (the top); ~ **le marché** on top of it all

**par-devant** [paʀdəvɑ̃] *prép* in the presence of, before ▷ *adv* at the front; round the front

**pardon** [paʀdɔ̃] *nm* forgiveness *no pl* ▷ *excl (excuses)* (I'm) sorry; *(pour interpeller etc)* excuse me; *(demander de répéter)* (I beg your) pardon? *(Brit)*, pardon me? *(US)*

**pardonnable** [paʀdɔnabl(ə)] *adj* forgivable, excusable

**pardonner** [paʀdɔne] *vt* to forgive; ~ **qch à qn** to forgive sb for sth; **qui ne pardonne pas** *(maladie, erreur)* fatal

**paré, e** [paʀe] *adj* ready, prepared

**pare-balles** [paʀbal] *adj inv* bulletproof

**pare-boue** [paʀbu] *nm inv* mudflap

**pare-brise** [paʀbʀiz] *nm inv* windscreen *(Brit)*, windshield *(US)*

**pare-chocs** [paʀʃɔk] *nm inv* bumper *(Brit)*, fender *(US)*

**pare-étincelles** [paʀetɛ̃sɛl] *nm inv* fireguard

**pare-feu** [paʀfø] *nm inv* firebreak ▷ *adj inv*: **portes** ~ fire (resistant) doors

**pareil, le** [paʀɛj] *adj (identique)* the same, alike; *(similaire)* similar; *(tel)*: **un courage/livre** ~ such courage/a book, courage/a book like this; **de** ~**s livres** such books ▷ *adv*: **habillés** ~ dressed the same (way), dressed alike; **faire** ~ to do the same (thing); **j'en veux un** ~ I'd like one just like it; **rien de** ~ no *(ou* any) such thing, nothing *(ou* anything) like it; **ses** ~**s** one's fellow men; one's peers; **ne pas avoir son (sa)** ~**(le)** to be second to none; ~ **à** the same as; similar to; **sans** ~ unparalleled, unequalled;

**c'est du** ~ **au même** it comes to the same thing, it's six (of one) and half-a-dozen (of the other); **en** ~ **cas** in such a case; **rendre la** ~**le à qn** to pay sb back in his own coin

**pareillement** [paʀɛjmɑ̃] *adv* the same, alike; in such a way; *(également)* likewise

**parement** [paʀmɑ̃] *nm (Constr: revers d'un col, d'une manche)* facing; *(Rel)*: ~ **d'autel** antependium

**parent, e** [paʀɑ̃, -ɑ̃t] *nm/f*: **un/une** ~**/e** a relative *ou* relation ▷ *adj*: **être** ~ **de** to be related to; **parents** *nmpl (père et mère)* parents; *(famille, proches)* relatives, relations; ~ **unique** lone parent; ~**s par alliance** relatives *ou* relations by marriage; ~**s en ligne directe** blood relations

**parental, e, -aux** [paʀɑ̃tal, -o] *adj* parental

**parenté** [paʀɑ̃te] *nf (lien)* relationship; *(personnes)* relatives *pl*, relations *pl*

**parenthèse** [paʀɑ̃tɛz] *nf (ponctuation)* bracket, parenthesis; *(Math)* bracket; *(digression)* parenthesis, digression; **ouvrir/fermer la** ~ to open/close brackets; **entre** ~**s** in brackets; *(fig)* incidentally

**parer** [paʀe] *vt* to adorn; *(Culin)* to dress, trim; *(éviter)* to ward off; ~ **à** *(danger)* to ward off; *(inconvénient)* to deal with; **se** ~ **de** *(fig: qualité, titre)* to assume; ~ **à toute éventualité** to be ready for every eventuality; ~ **au plus pressé** to attend to what's most urgent

**pare-soleil** [paʀsɔlɛj] *nm inv* sun visor

**paresse** [paʀɛs] *nf* laziness

**paresser** [paʀese] *vi* to laze around

**paresseusement** [paʀɛsøzmɑ̃] *adv* lazily; sluggishly

**paresseux, -euse** [paʀɛsø, -øz] *adj* lazy; *(fig)* slow, sluggish ▷ *nm (Zool)* sloth

**parfaire** [paʀfɛʀ] *vt* to perfect, complete

**parfait, e** [paʀfɛ, -ɛt] *pp de* **parfaire** ▷ *adj* perfect ▷ *nm (Ling)* perfect (tense); *(Culin)* parfait ▷ *excl* fine, excellent

**parfaitement** [paʀfɛtmɑ̃] *adv* perfectly ▷ *excl* (most) certainly

**parfaites** [paʀfɛt], **parfasse** [paʀfas], **parferai** *etc* [paʀfʀe] *vb voir* **parfaire**

**parfois** [paʀfwa] *adv* sometimes

**parfum** [paʀfœ̃] *nm (produit)* perfume, scent; *(odeur: de fleur)* scent, fragrance; *(: de tabac, vin)* aroma; *(goût: de glace, milk-shake)* flavour *(Brit)*, flavor *(US)*

**parfumé, e** [paʀfyme] *adj (fleur, fruit)* fragrant; *(papier à lettres etc)* scented; *(femme)* wearing perfume *ou* scent, perfumed; *(aromatisé)*: ~ **au café** coffee-flavoured *(Brit) ou* -flavored *(US)*

**parfumer** [paʀfyme] *vt (odeur, bouquet)* to perfume; *(mouchoir)* to put scent *ou* perfume on; *(crème, gâteau)* to flavour *(Brit)*, flavor *(US)*; **se parfumer** to put on (some) perfume *ou* scent; *(d'habitude)* to use perfume *ou* scent

**parfumerie** [paʀfymʀi] *nf (commerce)* perfumery; *(produits)* perfumes *pl*; *(boutique)* perfume shop *(Brit) ou* store *(US)*

**pari** [paʀi] *nm* bet, wager; *(Sport)* bet; ~ **mutuel urbain (PMU)** *system of betting on horses*

**paria** [paʀja] *nm* outcast

**parier** [paʀje] *vt* to bet; **j'aurais parié que si/ non** I'd have said he (*ou* you *etc*) would/wouldn't

**parieur** [paʀjœʀ] *nm* (*turfiste etc*) punter

**Paris** [paʀi] *n* Paris

**parisien, ne** [paʀizjɛ̃, -ɛn] *adj* Parisian; (*Géo, Admin*) Paris *cpd* ▷ *nm/f*: **Parisien, ne** Parisian

**paritaire** [paʀitɛʀ] *adj*: **commission** ~ joint commission

**parité** [paʀite] *nf* parity; ~ **de change** (*Écon*) exchange parity

**parjure** [paʀʒyʀ] *nm* (*faux serment*) false oath, perjury; (*violation de serment*) breach of oath, perjury ▷ *nm/f* perjurer

**parjurer** [paʀʒyʀe]: **se parjurer** *vi* to perjure o.s

**parka** [paʀka] *nf* parka

**parking** [paʀkiŋ] *nm* (*lieu*) car park (*Brit*), parking lot (*US*)

**parlant, e** [paʀlɑ̃, -ɑ̃t] *adj* (*fig*) graphic, vivid; (*: comparaison, preuve*) eloquent; (*Ciné*) talking ▷ *adv*: **généralement** ~ generally speaking

**parlé, e** [paʀle] *adj*: **langue ~e** spoken language

**parlement** [paʀləmɑ̃] *nm* parliament; **le P~ européen** the European Parliament

**parlementaire** [paʀləmɑ̃tɛʀ] *adj* parliamentary ▷ *nm/f* (*député*) ≈ Member of Parliament (*Brit*) *ou* Congress (*US*); parliamentarian; (*négociateur*) negotiator, mediator

**parlementarisme** [paʀləmɑ̃taʀism(ə)] *nm* parliamentary government

**parlementer** [paʀləmɑ̃te] *vi* (*ennemis*) to negotiate, parley; (*s'entretenir, discuter*) to argue at length, have lengthy talks

**parler** [paʀle] *nm* speech; dialect ▷ *vi* to speak, talk; (*avouer*) to talk; ~ **(à qn) de** to talk *ou* speak (to sb) about; ~ **pour qn** (*intercéder*) to speak for sb; ~ **en l'air** to say the first thing that comes into one's head; ~ **le/en français** to speak French/in French; ~ **affaires** to talk business; ~ **en dormant/du nez** to talk in one's sleep/ through one's nose; **sans** ~ **de** (*fig*) not to mention, to say nothing of; **tu parles!** you must be joking!; **n'en parlons plus!** let's forget it!

**parleur** [paʀlœʀ] *nm*: **beau** ~ fine talker

**parloir** [paʀlwaʀ] *nm* (*d'une prison, d'un hôpital*) visiting room; (*Rel*) parlour (*Brit*), parlor (*US*)

**parlote** [paʀlɔt] *nf* chitchat

**Parme** [paʀm(ə)] *n* Parma

**parme** [paʀm(ə)] *adj* violet (blue)

**parmesan** [paʀməzɑ̃] *nm* Parmesan (cheese)

**parmi** [paʀmi] *prép* among(st)

**parodie** [paʀɔdi] *nf* parody

**parodier** [paʀɔdje] *vt* (*œuvre, auteur*) to parody

**paroi** [paʀwa] *nf* wall; (*cloison*) partition; ~ **rocheuse** rock face

**paroisse** [paʀwas] *nf* parish

**paroissial, e, -aux** [paʀwasjal, -o] *adj* parish *cpd*

**paroissien, ne** [paʀwasjɛ̃, -ɛn] *nm/f* parishioner ▷ *nm* prayer book

**parole** [paʀɔl] *nf* (*faculté*): **la** ~ speech; (*mot,*

*promesse*) word; (*Rel*): **la bonne** ~ the word of God; **paroles** *nfpl* (*Mus*) words, lyrics; **tenir** ~ to keep one's word; **avoir la** ~ to have the floor; **n'avoir qu'une** ~ to be true to one's word; **donner la** ~ **à qn** to hand over to sb; **prendre la** ~ to speak; **demander la** ~ to ask for permission to speak; **perdre la** ~ to lose the power of speech; (*fig*) to lose one's tongue; **je le crois sur** ~ I'll take his word for it, I'll take him at his word; **temps de** ~ (*TV, Radio etc*) discussion time; **ma** ~! my word!, good heavens!; ~ **d'honneur** word of honour (*Brit*) *ou* honor (*US*)

**parolier, -ière** [paʀɔlje, -jɛʀ] *nm/f* lyricist; (*Opéra*) librettist

**paroxysme** [paʀɔksism(ə)] *nm* height, paroxysm

**parpaing** [paʀpɛ̃] *nm* bond-stone, parpen

**parquer** [paʀke] *vt* (*voiture, matériel*) to park; (*bestiaux*) to pen (in *ou* up); (*prisonniers*) to pack in

**parquet** [paʀkɛ] *nm* (*parquet*) floor; (*Jur: bureau*) public prosecutor's office; **le** ~ **(général)** (*magistrats*) ≈ the Bench

**parqueter** [paʀkəte] *vt* to lay a parquet floor in

**parrain** [paʀɛ̃] *nm* godfather; (*d'un navire*) namer; (*d'un nouvel adhérent*) sponsor, proposer

**parrainage** [paʀɛnaʒ] *nm* sponsorship

**parrainer** [paʀɛne] *vt* (*nouvel adhérent*) to sponsor, propose; (*entreprise*) to promote, sponsor

**parricide** [paʀisid] *nm, nf* parricide

**pars** [paʀ] *vb voir* **partir**

**parsemer** [paʀsəme] *vt* (*feuilles, papiers*) to be scattered over; ~ **qch de** to scatter sth with

**parsi, e** [paʀsi] *adj* Parsee

**part** [paʀ] *vb voir* **partir** ▷ *nf* (*qui revient à qn*) share; (*fraction, partie*) part; (*de gâteau, fromage*) portion; (*Finance*) (non-voting) share; **prendre** ~ **à** (*débat etc*) to take part in; (*soucis, douleur de qn*) to share in; **faire** ~ **de qch à qn** to announce sth to sb, inform sb of sth; **pour ma** ~ as for me, as far as I'm concerned; **à** ~ **entière** *adj* full; **de la** ~ **de** (*au nom de*) on behalf of; (*donné par*) from; **c'est de la** ~ **de qui?** (*au téléphone*) who's calling *ou* speaking (please)?; **de toute(s)** ~**(s)** from all sides *ou* quarters; **de** ~ **et d'autre** on both sides, on either side; **de** ~ **en** ~ right through; **d'une** ~ **... d'autre** ~ on the one hand ... on the other hand; **nulle/autre/quelque** ~ nowhere/ elsewhere/somewhere; **à** ~ *adv* separately; (*de côté*) aside ▷ *prép* apart from, except for ▷ *adj* exceptional, special; **pour une large** *ou* **bonne** ~ to a great extent; **prendre qch en bonne/ mauvaise** ~ to take sth well/badly; **faire la** ~ **des choses** to make allowances; **faire la** ~ **du feu** (*fig*) to cut one's losses; **faire la** ~ **(trop) belle à qn** to give sb more than his (*ou* her) share

**part.** *abr* = **particulier**

**partage** [paʀtaʒ] *nm voir* **partager** sharing (out) *no pl*, share-out; sharing; dividing up; (*Pol: de suffrages*) share; **recevoir qch en** ~ to receive sth as one's share (*ou* lot); **sans** ~ undivided

**partagé, e** [paʀtaʒe] *adj* (*opinions etc*) divided; (*amour*) shared; **être ~ entre** to be shared between; **être ~ sur** to be divided about

**partager** [paʀtaʒe] *vt* to share; (*distribuer, répartir*) to share (out); (*morceler, diviser*) to divide (up); **se partager** *vt* (*héritage etc*) to share between themselves (*ou* ourselves *etc*)

**partance** [paʀtɑ̃s]: **en ~** *adv* outbound, due to leave; **en ~ pour** (bound) for

**partant, e** [paʀtɑ̃, -ɑ̃t] *vb voir* **partir** ▷ *adj*: **être ~ pour qch** (*d'accord pour*) to be quite ready for sth ▷ *nm* (*Sport*) starter; (*Hippisme*) runner

**partenaire** [paʀtənɛʀ] *nm/f* partner; **~s sociaux** management and workforce

**parterre** [paʀtɛʀ] *nm* (*de fleurs*) (flower) bed, border; (*Théât*) stalls *pl*

**parti** [paʀti] *nm* (*Pol*) party; (*décision*) course of action; (*personne à marier*) match; **tirer ~ de** to take advantage of, turn to good account; **prendre le ~ de faire** to make up one's mind to do, resolve to do; **prendre le ~ de qn** to stand up for sb, side with sb; **prendre ~ (pour/contre)** to take sides *ou* a stand (for/against); **prendre son ~ de** to come to terms with; **~ pris** bias

**partial, e, -aux** [paʀsjal, -o] *adj* biased, partial

**partialement** [paʀsjalmɑ̃] *adv* in a biased way

**partialité** [paʀsjalite] *nf* bias, partiality

**participant, e** [paʀtisipɑ̃, -ɑ̃t] *nm/f* participant; (*à un concours*) entrant; (*d'une société*) member

**participation** [paʀtisipasjɔ̃] *nf* participation; sharing; (*Comm*) interest; **la ~ aux bénéfices** profit-sharing; **la ~ ouvrière** worker participation; **"avec la ~ de ..."** "featuring ..."

**participe** [paʀtisip] *nm* participle; **~ passé/présent** past/present participle

**participer** [paʀtisipe]: **~ à** *vt* (*course, réunion*) to take part in; (*profits etc*) to share in; (*frais etc*) to contribute to; (*entreprise: financièrement*) to cooperate in; (*chagrin, succès de qn*) to share (in); **~ de** *vt* to partake of.

**particulariser** [paʀtikylaʀize] *vt*: **se particulariser** to mark o.s. (*ou* itself) out

**particularisme** [paʀtikylaʀism(ə)] *nm* sense of identity

**particularité** [paʀtikylaʀite] *nf* particularity; (*distinctive*) characteristic, feature

**particule** [paʀtikyl] *nf* particle; **~ (nobiliaire)** nobiliary particle

**particulier, -ière** [paʀtikylje, -jɛʀ] *adj* (*personnel, privé*) private; (*spécial*) special, particular; (*caractéristique*) characteristic, distinctive; (*spécifique*) particular ▷ *nm* (*individu: Admin*) private individual; **"~ vend ..."** (*Comm*) "for sale privately ...", "for sale by owner ..." (*US*); **~ à** peculiar to; **en ~** *adv* (*surtout*) in particular, particularly; (*à part*) separately; (*en privé*) in private

**particulièrement** [paʀtikyljɛʀmɑ̃] *adv* particularly

**partie** [paʀti] *nf* (*gén*) part; (*profession, spécialité*) field, subject; (*Jur etc: protagonistes*) party; (*de*

cartes, tennis etc*) game; (*fig: lutte, combat*) struggle, fight; **une ~ de campagne/de pêche** an outing in the country/a fishing party *ou* trip; **en ~** *adv* partly, in part; **faire ~ de** to belong to; (*chose*) to be part of; **prendre qn à ~** to take sb to task; (*malmener*) to set on sb; **en grande ~** largely, in the main; **ce n'est que ~ remise** it will be for another time *ou* the next time; **avoir ~ liée avec qn** to be in league with sb; **~ civile** (*Jur*) party claiming damages in a criminal case

**partiel, le** [paʀsjɛl] *adj* partial ▷ *nm* (*Scol*) class exam

**partiellement** [paʀsjɛlmɑ̃] *adv* partially, partly

**partir** [paʀtiʀ] *vi* (*gén*) to go; (*quitter*) to go, leave; (*s'éloigner*) to go (*ou* drive *etc*) away *ou* off; (*moteur*) to start; (*pétard*) to go off; (*bouchon*) to come out; (*bouton*) to come off; **~ de** (*lieu: quitter*) to leave; (*: commencer à*) to start from; (*date*) to run *ou* start from; **~ pour/à** (*lieu, pays etc*) to leave for/go off to; **à ~ de** from

**partisan, e** [paʀtizɑ̃, -an] *nm/f* partisan; (*d'un parti, régime etc*) supporter ▷ *adj* (*lutte, querelle*) partisan, one-sided; **être ~ de qch/faire** to be in favour (*Brit*) *ou* favor (*US*) of sth/doing

**partitif, -ive** [paʀtitif, -iv] *adj*: **article ~** partitive article

**partition** [paʀtisjɔ̃] *nf* (*Mus*) score

**partout** [paʀtu] *adv* everywhere; **~ où il allait** everywhere *ou* wherever he went; **trente ~** (*Tennis*) thirty all

**paru** [paʀy] *pp de* **paraître**

**parure** [paʀyʀ] *nf* (*bijoux etc*) finery *no pl*; jewellery *no pl* (*Brit*), jewelry *no pl* (*US*); (*assortiment*) set

**parus** *etc* [paʀy] *vb voir* **paraître**

**parution** [paʀysjɔ̃] *nf* publication, appearance

**parvenir** [paʀvəniʀ]: **~ à** *vt* (*atteindre*) to reach; (*obtenir, arriver à*) to attain; (*réussir*) **~ à faire** to manage to do, succeed in doing; **faire ~ qch à qn** to have sth sent to sb

**parvenu, e** [paʀvəny] *pp de* **parvenir** ▷ *nm/f* (*péj*) parvenu, upstart

**parviendrai** [paʀvjẽdʀe], **parviens** *etc* [paʀvjẽ] *vb voir* **parvenir**

**parvis** [paʀvi] *nm* square (*in front of a church*)

---

**Ⓞ MOT-CLÉ**

**pas¹** [pɑ] *adv* **1** (*en corrélation avec ne, non etc*) not; **il ne pleure pas** (*habituellement*) he does not *ou* doesn't cry; (*maintenant*) he's not *ou* isn't crying; **je ne mange pas de viande** I don't *ou* do not eat meat; **il n'a pas pleuré/ne pleurera pas** he did not *ou* didn't/will not *ou* won't cry; **ils n'ont pas de voiture/d'enfants** they haven't got a car/any children, they have no car/children; **il m'a dit de ne pas le faire** he told me not to do it; **non pas que ...** not that ...

**2** (*employé sans ne etc*): **pas moi** not me, not I, I don't (*ou* can't *etc*); **elle travaille, (mais) lui pas** *ou* **pas lui** she works but he doesn't *ou* does not; **une pomme pas mûre** an apple which isn't ripe; **pas plus tard qu'hier** only yesterday; **pas du tout** not at all; **pas de sucre, merci** no sugar, thanks; **ceci est à vous ou pas?** is this yours or not?, is this yours or isn't it?

**3**: **pas mal** (*joli: personne, maison*) not bad; **pas mal fait** not badly done *ou* made; **comment ça va? — pas mal** how are things? — not bad; **pas mal de** quite a lot of

**pas²** [pɑ] *nm* (*allure, mesure*) pace; (*démarche*) tread; (*enjambée, Danse, fig: étape*) step; (*bruit*) (*foot*)step; (*trace*) footprint; (*allure*) pace; (*d'un cheval*) walk; (*mesure*) pace; (*Tech: de vis, d'écrou*) thread; **~ à ~** step by step; **au ~** at a walking pace; **de ce ~** (*à l'instant même*) straightaway, at once; **marcher à grands ~** to stride along; **mettre qn au ~** to bring sb to heel; **au ~ de gymnastique/de course** at a jog trot/at a run; **à ~ de loup** stealthily; **faire les cent ~** to pace up and down; **faire les premiers ~** to make the first move; **retourner** *ou* **revenir sur ses ~** to retrace one's steps; **se tirer d'un mauvais ~** to get o.s. out of a tight spot; **sur le ~ de la porte** on the doorstep; **le ~ de Calais** (*détroit*) the Straits *pl* of Dover; **~ de porte** (*fig*) key money

**pascal, e, -aux** [paskal, -o] *adj* Easter *cpd*

**passable** [pɑsabl(ə)] *adj* passable, tolerable

**passablement** [pɑsabləmɑ̃] *adv* (*pas trop mal*) reasonably well; (*beaucoup*) quite a lot

**passade** [pɑsad] *nf* passing fancy, whim

**passage** [pɑsaʒ] *nm* (*fait de passer*) *voir* **passer**; (*lieu, prix de la traversée, extrait de livre etc*) passage; (*chemin*) way; (*itinéraire*): **sur le ~ du cortège** along the route of the procession; **"laissez/ n'obstruez pas le ~"** "keep clear/do not obstruct"; **au ~** (*en passant*) as I (*ou* he etc) went by; **de ~** (*touristes*) passing through; (*amants etc*) casual; **~ clouté** pedestrian crossing; **"~ interdit"** "no entry"; **~ à niveau** level (Brit) *ou* grade (US) crossing; **"~ protégé"** *right of way over secondary road(s) on your right*; **~ souterrain** subway (Brit), underpass; **~ à tabac** beating-up; **~ à vide** (*fig*) bad patch

**passager, -ère** [pɑsaʒe, -ɛʀ] *adj* passing; (*hôte*) short-stay *cpd*; (*oiseau*) migratory ▷ *nm/f* passenger; **~ clandestin** stowaway

**passagèrement** [pɑsaʒɛʀmɑ̃] *adv* temporarily, for a short time

**passant, e** [pɑsɑ̃, -ɑ̃t] *adj* (*rue, endroit*) busy ▷ *nm/f* passer-by ▷ *nm* (*pour ceinture etc*) loop; **en ~**: **remarquer qch en ~** to notice sth in passing

**passation** [pɑsɑsjɔ̃] *nf* (*Jur: d'un acte*) signing; **~ des pouvoirs** transfer *ou* handover of power

**passe** [pɑs] *nf* (*Sport, magnétique*) pass; (*Navig*) channel ▷ *nm* (*passe-partout*) master *ou* skeleton key; **être en ~ de faire** to be on the way to doing; **être dans une mauvaise ~** (*fig*) to be going through a bad patch; **être dans une bonne ~** (*fig*) to be in a healthy situation; **~ d'armes** (*fig*) heated exchange

**passé, e** [pɑse] *adj* (*événement, temps*) past; (*couleur, tapisserie*) faded; (*précédent*): **dimanche ~** last Sunday ▷ *prép* after ▷ *nm* past; (*Ling*) past (tense); **il est ~ midi** *ou* **midi ~** it's gone (Brit) *ou* past twelve; **~ de mode** out of fashion; **~ composé** perfect (tense); **~ simple** past historic

**passe-droit** [pɑsdʀwa] *nm* special privilege

**passéiste** [pɑseist(ə)] *adj* backward-looking

**passementerie** [pɑsmɑ̃tʀi] *nf* trimmings *pl*

**passe-montagne** [pɑsmɔ̃taɲ] *nm* balaclava

**passe-partout** [pɑspaʀtu] *nm inv* master *ou* skeleton key ▷ *adj inv* all-purpose

**passe-passe** [pɑspɑs] *nm*: **tour de ~** trick, sleight of hand *no pl*

**passe-plat** [pɑspla] *nm* serving hatch

**passeport** [pɑspɔʀ] *nm* passport

**passer** [pɑse] *vi* (*se rendre, aller*) to go; (*voiture, piétons: défiler*) to pass (by), go by; (*faire une halte rapide: facteur, laitier etc*) to come, call; (: *pour rendre visite*) to call *ou* drop in; (*courant, air, lumière, franchir un obstacle etc*) to get through; (*accusé, projet de loi*): **~ devant** to come before; (*film, émission*) to be on; (*temps, jours*) to pass, go by; (*liquide, café*) to go through; (*être digéré, avalé*) to go down; (*couleur, papier*) to fade; (*mode*) to die out; (*douleur*) to pass, go away; (*Cartes*) to pass; (*Scol*) to go up (to the next class); (*devenir*): **~ président** to be appointed *ou* become president ▷ *vt* (*frontière, rivière etc*) to cross; (*douane*) to go through; (*examen*) to sit, take; (*visite médicale etc*) to have; (*journée, temps*) to spend; (*donner*): **~ qch à qn** to pass sth to sb; to give sb sth; (*transmettre*): **~ qch à qn** to pass sth on to sb; (*enfiler: vêtement, mettre*): **(faire) ~ qch dans/par** to get sth into/through; (*café*) to pour the water on; (*thé, soupe*) to strain; (*film, pièce*) to show, put on; (*disque*) to play, put on; (*marché, accord*) to agree on; (*tolérer*): **~ qch à qn** to let sb get away with sth; **se passer** *vi* (*avoir lieu: scène, action*) to take place; (*se dérouler: entretien etc*) to go; (*arriver*): **que s'est-il passé?** what happened?; (*s'écouler: semaine etc*) to pass, go by; **se ~ de** *vt* to go *ou* do without; **se ~ les mains sous l'eau/de l'eau sur le visage** to put one's hands under the tap/run water over one's face; **en passant** in passing; **~ par** to go through; **passez devant/par ici** go in front/ this way; **~ sur** *vt* (*faute, détail inutile*) to pass over; **~ dans les mœurs/l'usage** to become the custom/normal usage; **~ avant qch/qn** (*fig*) to come before sth/sb; **laisser ~** (*air, lumière, personne*) to let through; (*occasion*) to let slip, miss; (*erreur*) to overlook; **faire ~** (*message*) to get over *ou* across; **faire ~ à qn le goût de qch** to cure sb of his (*ou* her) taste for sth; **~ à la radio/ fouille** to be X-rayed/searched; **~ à la radio/ télévision** to be on the radio/on television; **~ à table** to sit down to eat; **~ au salon** to go through to *ou* into the sitting room; **~ à l'opposition** to go over to the opposition; **~ aux aveux** to confess, make a confession; **~ à l'action** to go into action; **~ pour riche** to be taken for a rich man; **il passait pour avoir** he was said to have; **faire ~ qn/qch pour** to make sb/sth out to be; **passe encore de le penser, mais de le dire!** it's one thing to think it, but to say it!; **passons!** let's say no more (about it); **et j'en passe!** and that's not all!; **~ en seconde, ~ la seconde** (Auto) to change into second; **~ qch en fraude** to smuggle sth in (ou out); **la main par la portière** to stick one's hand out of the door; **~ le balai/l'aspirateur** to sweep up/hoover; **~ commande/la parole à qn** to hand over to sb; **je vous passe M. X** (je vous mets en communication avec lui) I'm putting you through to Mr X; (je lui passe l'appareil) here is Mr X, I'll hand you over to Mr X; **~ prendre** to (come and) collect

**passereau, x** [pasʀo] nm sparrow
**passerelle** [pasʀɛl] nf footbridge; (de navire, avion) gangway; (Navig): **~ (de commandement)** bridge
**passe-temps** [pastɑ̃] nm inv pastime
**passette** [pasɛt] nf (tea-)strainer
**passeur, -euse** [pasœʀ, -øz] nm/f smuggler
**passible** [pasibl(ə)] adj: **~ de** liable to
**passif, -ive** [pasif, -iv] adj passive ▷ nm (Ling) passive; (Comm) liabilities pl
**passion** [pasjɔ̃] nf passion; **avoir la ~ de** to have a passion for; **fruit de la ~** passion fruit
**passionnant, e** [pasjɔnɑ̃, -ɑ̃t] adj fascinating
**passionné, e** [pasjɔne] adj (personne, tempérament) passionate; (description) impassioned ▷ nm/f: **c'est un ~ d'échecs** he's a chess fanatic; **être ~ de** ou **pour qch** to have a passion for sth
**passionnel, le** [pasjɔnɛl] adj of passion
**passionnément** [pasjɔnemɑ̃] adv passionately
**passionner** [pasjɔne] vt (personne) to fascinate, grip; (débat, discussion) to inflame; **se ~ pour** to take an avid interest in; to have a passion for
**passivement** [pasivmɑ̃] adv passively
**passivité** [pasivite] nf passivity, passiveness
**passoire** [paswaʀ] nf sieve; (à légumes) colander; (à thé) strainer
**pastel** [pastɛl] nm, adj inv (Art) pastel
**pastèque** [pastɛk] nf watermelon
**pasteur** [pastœʀ] nm (protestant) minister, pastor
**pasteurisation** [pastœʀizasjɔ̃] nf pasteurization
**pasteurisé, e** [pastœʀize] adj pasteurized
**pasteuriser** [pastœʀize] vt to pasteurize
**pastiche** [pastiʃ] nm pastiche
**pastille** [pastij] nf (à sucer) lozenge, pastille; (de papier etc) (small) disc; **~s pour la toux** cough drops ou lozenges
**pastis** [pastis] nm anise-flavoured alcoholic drink
**pastoral, e, -aux** [pastɔʀal, -o] adj pastoral
**patagon, ne** [patagɔ̃, -ɔn] adj Patagonian
**Patagonie** [patagɔni] nf: **la ~** Patagonia
**patate** [patat] nf spud; **~ douce** sweet potato
**pataud, e** [pato, -od] adj lumbering
**patauger** [patoʒe] vi (pour s'amuser) to splash

about; (avec effort) to wade about; (fig) to flounder; **~ dans** (en marchant) to wade through
**patch** [patʃ] nm nicotine patch
**patchouli** [patʃuli] nm patchouli
**patchwork** [patʃwœʀk] nm patchwork
**pâte** [pɑt] nf (à tarte) pastry; (à pain) dough; (à frire) batter; (substance molle) paste; cream; **pâtes** nfpl (macaroni etc) pasta sg; **fromage à ~ dure/molle** hard/soft cheese; **~ d'amandes** almond paste; **~ brisée** shortcrust (Brit) ou pie crust (US) pastry; **~ à choux/feuilletée** choux/puff ou flaky (Brit) pastry; **~ de fruits** crystallized fruit no pl; **~ à modeler** modelling clay, Plasticine® (Brit); **~ à papier** paper pulp
**pâté** [pɑte] nm (charcuterie: terrine) pâté; (tache) ink blot; (de sable) sandpie; **~ (en croûte)** = meat pie; **~ de foie** liver pâté; **~ de maisons** block (of houses)
**pâtée** [pɑte] nf mash, feed
**patelin** [patlɛ̃] nm little place
**patente** [patɑ̃t] nf (Comm) trading licence (Brit) ou license (US)
**patenté, e** [patɑ̃te] adj (Comm) licensed; (fig: attitré) registered, (officially) recognized
**patère** [patɛʀ] nf (coat-)peg
**paternalisme** [patɛʀnalism(ə)] nm paternalism
**paternaliste** [patɛʀnalist(ə)] adj paternalistic
**paternel, le** [patɛʀnɛl] adj (amour, soins) fatherly; (ligne, autorité) paternal
**paternité** [patɛʀnite] nf paternity, fatherhood
**pâteux, -euse** [pɑtø, -øz] adj thick; pasty; **avoir la bouche** ou **langue pâteuse** to have a furred (Brit) ou coated tongue
**pathétique** [patetik] adj pathetic, moving
**pathologie** [patɔlɔʒi] nf pathology
**pathologique** [patɔlɔʒik] adj pathological
**patibulaire** [patibylɛʀ] adj sinister
**patiemment** [pasjamɑ̃] adv patiently
**patience** [pasjɑ̃s] nf patience; **être à bout de ~** to have run out of patience; **perdre/prendre ~** to lose (one's)/have patience
**patient, e** [pasjɑ̃, -ɑ̃t] adj, nm/f patient
**patienter** [pasjɑ̃te] vi to wait
**patin** [patɛ̃] nm skate; (sport) skating; (de traîneau, luge) runner; (pièce de tissu) cloth pad (used as slippers to protect polished floor); **~ (de frein)** brake block; **~s (à glace)** (ice) skates; **~s à roulettes** roller skates
**patinage** [patinaʒ] nm skating; **~ artistique/de vitesse** figure/speed skating
**patine** [patin] nf sheen
**patiner** [patine] vi to skate; (embrayage) to slip; (roue, voiture) to spin; **se patiner** vi (meuble, cuir) to acquire a sheen, become polished
**patineur, -euse** [patinœʀ, -øz] nm/f skater
**patinoire** [patinwaʀ] nf skating rink, (ice) rink
**patio** [patjo] nm patio
**pâtir** [pɑtiʀ]: **~ de** vt to suffer because of
**pâtisserie** [pɑtisʀi] nf (boutique) cake shop; (métier) confectionery; (à la maison) pastry- ou cake-making, baking; **pâtisseries** nfpl (gâteaux)

pastries, cakes

**pâtissier, -ière** [patisje, -jɛʀ] nm/f pastrycook; confectioner

**patois** [patwa] nm dialect, patois

**patraque** [patʀak] (fam) adj peaky, off-colour

**patriarche** [patʀijaʀʃ(ə)] nm patriarch

**patrie** [patʀi] nf homeland

**patrimoine** [patʀimwan] nm inheritance, patrimony; (culture) heritage; ~ **génétique** ou **héréditaire** genetic inheritance

**patriote** [patʀijɔt] adj patriotic ▷ nm/f patriot

**patriotique** [patʀijɔtik] adj patriotic

**patriotisme** [patʀijɔtism(ə)] nm patriotism

**patron, ne** [patʀɔ̃, -ɔn] nm/f (chef) boss, manager(-ess); (propriétaire) owner, proprietor(-tress); (employeur) employer; (Méd) = senior consultant; (Rel) patron saint ▷ nm (Couture) pattern; ~ **de thèse** supervisor (of postgraduate thesis)

**patronage** [patʀɔnaʒ] nm patronage; (organisation, club) (parish) youth club; (parish) children's club

**patronal, e, -aux** [patʀɔnal, -o] adj (syndicat, intérêts) employers'

**patronat** [patʀɔna] nm employers pl

**patronner** [patʀɔne] vt to sponsor, support

**patronnesse** [patʀɔnɛs] adj f: **dame** ~ patroness

**patronyme** [patʀɔnim] nm name

**patronymique** [patʀɔnimik] adj: **nom** ~ patronymic (name)

**patrouille** [patʀuj] nf patrol

**patrouiller** [patʀuje] vi to patrol, be on patrol

**patrouilleur** [patʀujœʀ] nm (Aviat) scout (plane); (Navig) patrol boat

**patte** [pat] nf (jambe) leg; (pied: de chien, chat) paw; (: d'oiseau) foot; (languette) strap; (: de poche) flap; (favoris): ~**s (de lapin)** (short) sideburns; **à ~s d'éléphant** adj (pantalon) flared; ~**s de mouche** (fig) spidery scrawl sg; ~**s d'oie** (fig) crow's feet

**pattemouille** [patmuj] nf damp cloth (for ironing)

**pâturage** [patyʀaʒ] nm pasture

**pâture** [patyʀ] nf food

**paume** [pom] nf palm

**paumé, e** [pome] nm/f (fam) drop-out

**paumer** [pome] vt (fam) to lose

**paupérisation** [popeʀizasjɔ̃] nf pauperization

**paupérisme** [popeʀism(ə)] nm pauperism

**paupière** [popjɛʀ] nf eyelid

**paupiette** [popjɛt] nf: ~ **s de veau** veal olives

**pause** [poz] nf (arrêt) break; (en parlant, Mus) pause; ~ **de midi** lunch break

**pause-café** [pozkafe] (pl **pauses-café**) nf coffee-break

**pauvre** [povʀ(ə)] adj poor ▷ nm/f poor man/ woman; **les ~s** the poor; ~ **en calcium** low in calcium

**pauvrement** [povʀəmã] adv poorly

**pauvreté** [povʀəte] nf (état) poverty; **pauvreté énergétique** fuel poverty

**pavage** [pavaʒ] nm paving; cobbles pl

**pavaner** [pavane]: **se pavaner** vi to strut about

**pavé, e** [pave] adj (cour) paved; (rue) cobbled ▷ nm (bloc) paving stone; cobblestone; (pavage) paving; (bifteck) slab of steak; (fam: livre) hefty tome; **être sur le** ~ (sans domicile) to be on the streets; (sans emploi) to be out of a job; ~ **numérique** (Inform) keypad

**pavillon** [pavijɔ̃] nm (de banlieue) small (detached) house; (kiosque) lodge; pavilion; (d'hôpital) ward; (Mus: de cor etc) bell; (Anat: de l'oreille) pavilion, pinna; (Navig) flag; ~ **de complaisance** flag of convenience

**pavoiser** [pavwaze] vt to deck with flags ▷ vi to put out flags; (fig) to rejoice, exult

**pavot** [pavo] nm poppy

**payable** [pɛjabl(ə)] adj payable

**payant, e** [pɛjã, -ãt] adj (spectateurs etc) paying; (billet) that you pay for, to be paid for; (fig: entreprise) profitable; **c'est** ~ you have to pay, there is a charge

**paye** [pɛj] nf pay, wages pl

**payement** [pɛjmã] nm payment

**payer** [peje] vt (créancier, employé, loyer) to pay; (achat, réparations, fig: faute) to pay for ▷ vi to pay; (métier) to pay, be well-paid; (effort, tactique etc) to pay off; **être bien/mal payé** to be well/badly paid; **il me l'a fait ~ 10 euros** he charged me 10 euros for it; ~ **qn de** (ses efforts, peines) to reward sb for; ~ **qch à qn** to buy sth for sb, buy sb sth; **ils nous ont payé le voyage** they paid for our trip; ~ **de sa personne** to give of oneself; ~ **d'audace** to act with great daring; ~ **cher qch** to pay dear(ly) for sth; **cela ne paie pas de mine** it doesn't look much; **se** ~ **qch** to buy o.s. sth; **se** ~ **de mots** to shoot one's mouth off; **se** ~ **la tête de qn** to take the mickey out of sb (Brit), make a fool of sb; (duper) to take sb for a ride

**payeur, -euse** [pɛjœʀ, -øz] adj (organisme, bureau) payments cpd ▷ nm/f payer

**pays** [pei] nm (territoire, habitants) country, land; (région) region; (village) village; **du** ~ adj local; **le ~ de Galles** Wales

**paysage** [peizaʒ] nm landscape

**paysager, -ère** [peizaʒe, -ɛʀ] adj (jardin, parc) landscaped

**paysagiste** [peizaʒist(ə)] nm/f (de jardin) landscape gardener; (Art) landscapist, landscape painter

**paysan, ne** [peizã, -an] nm/f countryman/- woman; farmer; (péj) peasant ▷ adj country cpd, farming, farmers'

**paysannat** [peizana] nm peasantry

**Pays-Bas** [peiba] nmpl: **les ~** the Netherlands

**PC** sigle m (Pol) = **parti communiste**; (Inform: = personal computer) PC; (= prêt conventionné) type of loan for house purchase; (Constr) = **permis de construire**; (Mil) = **poste de commandement**

**pcc** abr (= pour copie conforme) c.c

**Pce** abr = **prince**

**Pcesse** abr = **princesse**

**PCV** abr = **percevoir**; voir **communication**

**PDA** sigle m (= personal digital assistant) PDA

**p de p** abr = **pas de porte**

**PDG** *sigle m* = **président directeur général**
**p.-ê.** *abr* = **peut-être**
**PEA** *sigle m* (= *plan d'épargne en actions*) *building society savings plan*
**péage** [peaʒ] *nm* toll; (*endroit*) tollgate; **pont à ~** toll bridge
**peau, x** [po] *nf* skin; (*cuir*): **gants de ~** leather gloves; **être bien/mal dans sa ~** to be at ease/odds with oneself; **se mettre dans la ~ de qn** to put o.s. in sb's place *ou* shoes; **faire ~ neuve** (*se renouveler*) to change one's image; **~ de chamois** (*chiffon*) chamois leather, shammy; **~ d'orange** orange peel
**peaufiner** [pofine] *vt* to polish (up)
**Peau-Rouge** [poRuʒ] *nm/f* Red Indian, red skin
**peccadille** [pekadij] *nf* trifle, peccadillo
**péché** [peʃe] *nm* sin; **~ mignon** weakness
**pêche** [pɛʃ] *nf* (*sport, activité*) fishing; (*poissons pêchés*) catch; (*fruit*) peach; **aller à la ~** to go fishing; **avoir la ~** (*fam*) to be on (top) form; **~ à la ligne** (*en rivière*) angling; **~ sous-marine** deep-sea fishing
**pêche-abricot** [peʃabRiko] (*pl* **pêches-abricots**) *nf* yellow peach
**pécher** [peʃe] *vi* (*Rel*) to sin; (*fig: personne*) to err; (*: chose*) to be flawed; **~ contre la bienséance** to break the rules of good behaviour
**pêcher** [peʃe] *nm* peach tree ▷ *vi* to go fishing; (*en rivière*) to go angling ▷ *vt* (*attraper*) to catch, land; (*chercher*) to fish for; **~ au chalut** to trawl
**pécheur, -eresse** [peʃœR, peʃRɛs] *nm/f* sinner
**pêcheur** [peʃœR] *nm voir* **pêcher** fisherman; angler; **~ de perles** pearl diver
**pectine** [pɛktin] *nf* pectin
**pectoral, e, -aux** [pɛktɔRal, -o] *adj* (*Anat*) pectoral; (*sirop*) throat *cpd*, cough *cpd* ▷ *nmpl* pectoral muscles
**pécule** [pekyl] *nm* savings *pl*, nest egg; (*d'un détenu*) earnings *pl* (*paid on release*)
**pécuniaire** [pekynjɛR] *adj* financial
**pédagogie** [pedagɔʒi] *nf* educational methods *pl*, pedagogy
**pédagogique** [pedagɔʒik] *adj* educational; **formation ~** teacher training
**pédagogue** [pedagɔg] *nm/f* teacher, education(al)ist
**pédale** [pedal] *nf* pedal; **mettre la ~ douce** to soft-pedal
**pédaler** [pedale] *vi* to pedal
**pédalier** [pedalje] *nm* pedal and gear mechanism
**pédalo** [pedalo] *nm* pedalo, pedal-boat
**pédant, e** [pedɑ̃, -ɑ̃t] *adj* (*péj*) pedantic ▷ *nm/f* pedant
**pédantisme** [pedɑ̃tism(ə)] *nm* pedantry
**pédéraste** [pederast(ə)] *nm* homosexual, pederast
**pédérastie** [pederasti] *nf* homosexuality, pederasty
**pédestre** [pedɛstR(ə)] *adj*: **tourisme ~** hiking; **randonnée ~** (*activité*) rambling; (*excursion*) ramble

**pédiatre** [pedjatR(ə)] *nm/f* paediatrician (*Brit*), pediatrician *ou* pediatrist (*US*), child specialist
**pédiatrie** [pedjatRi] *nf* paediatrics *sg* (*Brit*), pediatrics *sg* (*US*)
**pédicure** [pedikyR] *nm/f* chiropodist
**pedigree** [pedigRe] *nm* pedigree
**peeling** [piliŋ] *nm* exfoliation treatment
**PEEP** *sigle f* = **Fédération des parents d'élèves de l'enseignement public**
**pègre** [pɛgR(ə)] *nf* underworld
**peignais** *etc* [peɲɛ] *vb voir* **peindre**
**peigne** [pɛɲ] *vb voir* **peindre**; **peigner** ▷ *nm* comb
**peigné, e** [peɲe] *adj*: **laine ~e** wool worsted; combed wool
**peigner** [peɲe] *vt* to comb (the hair of); **se peigner** to comb one's hair
**peignez** *etc* [peɲe] *vb voir* **peindre**
**peignoir** [peɲwaR] *nm* dressing gown; **~ de bain** bathrobe; **~ de plage** beach robe
**peignons** [peɲɔ̃] *vb voir* **peindre**
**peinard, e** [penaR, -aRd(ə)] *adj* (*emploi*) cushy (*Brit*), easy; (*personne*): **on est ~ ici** we're left in peace here
**peindre** [pɛ̃dR(ə)] *vt* to paint; (*fig*) to portray, depict
**peine** [pɛn] *nf* (*affliction*) sorrow, sadness *no pl*; (*mal, effort*) trouble *no pl*, effort; (*difficulté*) difficulty; (*punition, châtiment*) punishment; (*Jur*) sentence; **faire de la ~ à qn** to distress *ou* upset sb; **prendre la ~ de faire** to go to the trouble of doing; **se donner de la ~** to make an effort; **ce n'est pas la ~ de faire** there's no point in doing, it's not worth doing; **ce n'est pas la ~ que vous fassiez** there's no point (in) you doing; **avoir de la ~ à faire** to have difficulty doing; **donnez-vous** *ou* **veuillez-vous donner la ~ d'entrer** please do come in; **c'est ~ perdue** it's a waste of time (and effort); **à ~** *adv* scarcely, hardly, barely; **à ~ ... que** hardly ... than; **c'est à ~ si ...** it's (*ou* it was) a job to ...; **sous ~: sous ~ d'être puni** for fear of being punished; **défense d'afficher sous ~ d'amende** billposters will be fined; **~ capitale** capital punishment; **~ de mort** death sentence *ou* penalty
**peiner** [pene] *vi* to work hard; to struggle; (*moteur, voiture*) to labour (*Brit*), labor (*US*) ▷ *vt* to grieve, sadden
**peint, e** [pɛ̃, pɛ̃t] *pp de* **peindre**
**peintre** [pɛ̃tR(ə)] *nm* painter; **~ en bâtiment** house painter, painter and decorator; **~ d'enseignes** signwriter
**peinture** [pɛ̃tyR] *nf* painting; (*couche de couleur, couleur*) paint; (*surfaces peintes: aussi:* **peintures**) paintwork; **je ne peux pas le voir en ~** I can't stand the sight of him; **~ mate/brillante** matt/gloss paint; **"~ fraîche"** "wet paint"
**péjoratif, -ive** [peʒɔRatif, -iv] *adj* pejorative, derogatory
**Pékin** [pekɛ̃] *n* Peking
**pékinois, e** [pekinwa, -waz] *adj* Pekin(g)ese ▷ *nm* (*chien*) peke, pekin(g)ese; (*Ling*) Mandarin,

Pekin(g)ese ⊳ nm/f: **Pékinois, e** Pekin(g)ese
**PEL** sigle m (= plan d'épargne logement) savings scheme
   providing lower-interest mortgages
**pelade** [pəlad] nf alopecia
**pelage** [pəlaʒ] nm coat, fur
**pelé, e** [pəle] adj (chien) hairless; (vêtement)
   threadbare; (terrain) bare
**pêle-mêle** [pɛlmɛl] adv higgledy-piggledy
**peler** [pəle] vt, vi to peel
**pèlerin** [pɛlʀɛ̃] nm pilgrim
**pèlerinage** [pɛlʀinaʒ] nm (voyage) pilgrimage;
   (lieu) place of pilgrimage, shrine
**pèlerine** [pɛlʀin] nf cape
**pélican** [pelikɑ̃] nm pelican
**pelisse** [pəlis] nf fur-lined cloak
**pelle** [pɛl] nf shovel; (d'enfant, de terrassier) spade;
   **~ à gâteau** cake slice; **~ mécanique**
   mechanical digger
**pelletée** [pɛlte] nf shovelful; spadeful
**pelleter** [pɛlte] vt to shovel (up)
**pelleteuse** [pɛltøz] nf mechanical digger,
   excavator
**pelletier** [pɛltje] nm furrier
**pellicule** [pelikyl] nf film; **pellicules** nfpl (Méd)
   dandruff sg
**Péloponnèse** [pelɔpɔnɛz] nm: **le ~** the
   Peloponnese
**pelote** [pəlɔt] nf (de fil, laine) ball; (d'épingles) pin
   cushion; **~ basque** pelota
**peloter** [pəlɔte] vt (fam) to feel (up); **se peloter**
   vi to pet
**peloton** [pəlɔtɔ̃] nm (groupe: de personnes) group;
   (: de pompiers, gendarmes) squad; (: Sport) pack; (de
   laine) ball; **~ d'exécution** firing squad
**pelotonner** [pəlɔtɔne]: **se pelotonner** vi to curl
   (o.s.) up
**pelouse** [pəluz] nf lawn; (Hippisme) spectating area
   inside racetrack
**peluche** [pəlyʃ] nf (bit of) fluff; **animal en ~** soft
   toy, fluffy animal
**pelucher** [p(ə)lyʃe] vi to become fluffy, fluff up
**pelucheux, -euse** [p(ə)lyʃø, -øz] adj fluffy
**pelure** [pəlyʀ] nf peeling, peel no pl; **~ d'oignon**
   onion skin
**pénal, e, -aux** [penal, -o] adj penal
**pénalisation** [penalizasjɔ̃] nf (Sport) sanction,
   penalty
**pénaliser** [penalize] vt to penalize
**pénalité** [penalite] nf penalty
**penalty, ies** [penalti, -z] nm (Sport) penalty
   (kick)
**pénard, e** [penaʀ, -aʀd(ə)] adj = **peinard**
**pénates** [penat] nmpl: **regagner ses ~** to return
   to the bosom of one's family
**penaud, e** [pəno, -od] adj sheepish, contrite
**penchant** [pɑ̃ʃɑ̃] nm: **un ~ à faire/à qch** a
   tendency to do/to sth; **un ~ pour qch** a liking
   ou fondness for sth
**penché, e** [pɑ̃ʃe] adj slanting
**pencher** [pɑ̃ʃe] vi to tilt, lean over ⊳ vt to tilt; **se
   pencher** vi to lean over; (se baisser) to bend
   down; **se ~ sur** to bend over; (fig: problème) to

look into; **se ~ au dehors** to lean out; **~ pour** to
   be inclined to favour (Brit) ou favor (US)
**pendable** [pɑ̃dabl(ə)] adj: **tour ~** rotten trick;
   **c'est un cas ~!** he (ou she) deserves to be shot!
**pendaison** [pɑ̃dɛzɔ̃] nf hanging
**pendant, e** [pɑ̃dɑ̃, -ɑ̃t] adj hanging (out);
   (Admin, Jur) pending ⊳ nm counterpart;
   matching piece ⊳ prép during; **faire ~ à** to
   match; to be the counterpart of; **~ que** while;
   **~s d'oreilles** drop ou pendant earrings
**pendeloque** [pɑ̃dlɔk] nf pendant
**pendentif** [pɑ̃dɑ̃tif] nm pendant
**penderie** [pɑ̃dʀi] nf wardrobe; (placard) walk-in
   cupboard
**pendiller** [pɑ̃dije] vi to flap (about)
**pendre** [pɑ̃dʀ(ə)] vt, vi to hang; **se ~ (à)** (se
   suicider) to hang o.s. (on); **~ à** to hang (down)
   from; **~ qch à** (mur) to hang sth (up) on; (plafond)
   to hang sth (up) from; **se ~ à** (se suspendre) to
   hang from
**pendu, e** [pɑ̃dy] pp de **pendre** ⊳ nm/f hanged
   man (ou woman)
**pendulaire** [pɑ̃dylɛʀ] adj pendular, of a
   pendulum
**pendule** [pɑ̃dyl] nf clock ⊳ nm pendulum
**pendulette** [pɑ̃dylɛt] nf small clock
**pêne** [pɛn] nm bolt
**pénétrant, e** [penetʀɑ̃, -ɑ̃t] adj (air, froid) biting;
   (pluie) that soaks right through you; (fig: odeur)
   noticeable; (œil, regard) piercing; (clairvoyant,
   perspicace) perceptive ⊳ nf (route) expressway
**pénétration** [penetʀasjɔ̃] nf (fig: d'idées etc)
   penetration; (perspicacité) perception
**pénétré, e** [penetʀe] adj (air, ton) earnest; **être ~
   de soi-même/son importance** to be full of
   oneself/one's own importance
**pénétrer** [penetʀe] vi to come ou get in ⊳ vt to
   penetrate; **~ dans** to enter; (froid, projectile) to
   penetrate; (: air, eau) to come into, get into;
   (mystère, secret) to fathom; **se ~ de qch** to get sth
   firmly set in one's mind
**pénible** [penibl(ə)] adj (astreignant) hard;
   (affligeant) painful; (personne, caractère) tiresome;
   **il m'est ~ de ...** I'm sorry to ...
**péniblement** [peniblǝmɑ̃] adv with difficulty
**péniche** [peniʃ] nf barge; **~ de débarquement**
   landing craft inv
**pénicilline** [penisilin] nf penicillin
**péninsulaire** [penɛ̃sylɛʀ] adj peninsular
**péninsule** [penɛ̃syl] nf peninsula
**pénis** [penis] nm penis
**pénitence** [penitɑ̃s] nf (repentir) penitence;
   (peine) penance; (punition, châtiment)
   punishment; **mettre un enfant en ~ =** to
   make a child stand in the corner; **faire ~** to do a
   penance
**pénitencier** [penitɑ̃sje] nm prison, penitentiary
   (US)
**pénitent, e** [penitɑ̃, -ɑ̃t] adj penitent
**pénitentiaire** [penitɑ̃sjɛʀ] adj prison cpd,
   penitentiary (US)
**pénombre** [penɔ̃bʀ(ə)] nf half-light

**p**

**pensable** [pãsabl(ə)] *adj*: **ce n'est pas** ~ it's unthinkable

**pensant, e** [pãsã, -ãt] *adj*: **bien** ~ right-thinking

**pense-bête** [pãsbɛt] *nm* aide-mémoire, mnemonic device

**pensée** [pãse] *nf* thought; (*démarche, doctrine*) thinking *no pl*; (*Bot*) pansy; **se représenter qch par la** ~ to conjure up a mental picture of sth; **en** ~ in one's mind

**penser** [pãse] *vi* to think ▷ *vt* to think; (*concevoir: problème, machine*) to think out; ~ **à** to think of; (*songer à: ami, vacances*) to think of ou about; (*réfléchir à: problème, offre*): ~ **à qch** to think about sth, think sth over; ~ **à faire qch** to think of doing sth; ~ **faire qch** to be thinking of doing sth, intend to do sth; **faire** ~ **à** to remind one of; **n'y pensons plus** let's forget it; **vous n'y pensez pas!** don't let it bother you!; **sans** ~ **à mal** without meaning any harm; **je le pense aussi** I think so too; **je pense que oui/non** I think so/don't think so

**penseur** [pãsœR] *nm* thinker; **libre** ~ freethinker

**pensif, -ive** [pãsif, -iv] *adj* pensive, thoughtful

**pension** [pãsjɔ̃] *nf* (*allocation*) pension; (*prix du logement*) board and lodging, bed and board; (*maison particulière*) boarding house; (*hôtel*) guesthouse, hotel; (*école*) boarding school; **prendre** ~ **chez** to take board and lodging at; **prendre qn en** ~ to take sb (in) as a lodger; **mettre en** ~ to send to boarding school; ~ **alimentaire** (*d'étudiant*) living allowance; (*de divorcée*) maintenance allowance; alimony; ~ **complète** full board; ~ **de famille** boarding house, guesthouse; ~ **de guerre/d'invalidité** war/disablement pension

**pensionnaire** [pãsjɔnɛR] *nm/f* boarder; guest

**pensionnat** [pãsjɔna] *nm* boarding school

**pensionné, e** [pãsjɔne] *nm/f* pensioner

**pensivement** [pãsivmã] *adv* pensively, thoughtfully

**pensum** [pɛ̃sɔm] *nm* (*Scol*) punishment exercise; (*fig*) chore

**pentagone** [pɛ̃tagɔn] *nm* pentagon; **le P**~ the Pentagon

**pentathlon** [pɛ̃tatlɔ̃] *nm* pentathlon

**pente** [pãt] *nf* slope; **en** ~ *adj* sloping

**Pentecôte** [pãtkot] *nf*: **la** ~ Whitsun (*Brit*), Pentecost; (*dimanche*) Whitsunday (*Brit*); **lundi de** ~ Whit Monday (*Brit*)

**pénurie** [penyRi] *nf* shortage; ~ **de maind'œuvre** undermanning

**PEP** [pɛp] *sigle m* (= *plan d'épargne populaire*) individual savings plan

**pépé** [pepe] *nm* (*fam*) grandad

**pépère** [pepɛR] *adj* (*fam*) cushy; (*fam*) quiet ▷ *nm* (*fam*) grandad

**pépier** [pepje] *vi* to chirp, tweet

**pépin** [pepɛ̃] *nm* (*Bot: graine*) pip; (*fam: ennui*) snag, hitch; (*: parapluie*) brolly (*Brit*), umbrella

**pépinière** [pepinjɛR] *nf* nursery; (*fig*) nest, breeding-ground

**pépiniériste** [pepinjeRist(ə)] *nm* nurseryman

**pépite** [pepit] *nf* nugget

**PEPS** *abr* (= *premier entré premier sorti*) first in first out

**PER** [pɛR] *sigle m* (= *plan d'épargne retraite*) type of personal pension plan

**perçant, e** [pɛRsã, -ãt] *adj* (*vue, regard, yeux*) sharp, keen; (*cri, voix*) piercing, shrill

**percée** [pɛRse] *nf* (*trouée*) opening; (*Mil, Comm: fig*) breakthrough; (*Sport*) break

**perce-neige** [pɛRsənɛʒ] *nm ou f inv* snowdrop

**perce-oreille** [pɛRsɔRɛj] *nm* earwig

**percepteur** [pɛRsɛptœR] *nm* tax collector

**perceptible** [pɛRsɛptibl(ə)] *adj* (*son, différence*) perceptible; (*impôt*) payable, collectable

**perception** [pɛRsɛpsjɔ̃] *nf* perception; (*d'impôts etc*) collection; (*bureau*) tax (collector's) office

**percer** [pɛRse] *vt* to pierce; (*ouverture etc*) to make; (*mystère, énigme*) to penetrate ▷ *vi* to come through; (*réussir*) to break through; ~ **une dent** to cut a tooth

**perceuse** [pɛRsøz] *nf* drill; ~ **à percussion** hammer drill

**percevable** [pɛRsəvabl(ə)] *adj* collectable, payable

**percevoir** [pɛRsəvwaR] *vt* (*distinguer*) to perceive, detect; (*taxe, impôt*) to collect; (*revenu, indemnité*) to receive

**perche** [pɛRʃ(ə)] *nf* (*Zool*) perch; (*bâton*) pole; ~ **à son** (*sound*) boom

**percher** [pɛRʃe] *vt*: ~ **qch sur** to perch sth on ▷ *vi*, **se percher** *vi* (*oiseau*) to perch

**perchiste** [pɛRʃist(ə)] *nm/f* (*Sport*) pole vaulter; (*TV etc*) boom operator

**perchoir** [pɛRʃwaR] *nm* perch; (*fig*) presidency of the French National Assembly

**perclus, e** [pɛRkly, -yz] *adj*: ~ **de** (*rhumatismes*) crippled with

**perçois** *etc* [pɛRswa] *vb voir* **percevoir**

**percolateur** [pɛRkɔlatœR] *nm* percolator

**perçu, e** [pɛRsy] *pp de* **percevoir**

**percussion** [pɛRkysjɔ̃] *nf* percussion

**percussionniste** [pɛRkysjɔnist(ə)] *nm/f* percussionist

**percutant, e** [pɛRkytã, -ãt] *adj* (*article etc*) resounding, forceful

**percuter** [pɛRkyte] *vt* to strike; (*véhicule*) to crash into ▷ *vi*: ~ **contre** to crash into

**percuteur** [pɛRkytœR] *nm* firing pin, hammer

**perdant, e** [pɛRdã, -ãt] *nm/f* loser ▷ *adj* losing

**perdition** [pɛRdisjɔ̃] *nf* (*morale*) ruin; **en** ~ (*Navig*) in distress; **lieu de** ~ den of vice

**perdre** [pɛRdR(ə)] *vt* to lose; (*gaspiller: temps, argent*) to waste; (*: occasion*) to waste, miss; (*personne: moralement etc*) to ruin ▷ *vi* to lose; (*sur une vente etc*) to lose out; (*récipient*) to leak; **se perdre** *vi* (*s'égarer*) to get lost, lose one's way; (*fig: se gâter*) to go to waste; (*disparaître*) to disappear, vanish; **il ne perd rien pour attendre** it can wait, it'll keep

**perdreau, x** [pɛRdRo] *nm* (*young*) partridge

**perdrix** [pɛRdRi] *nf* partridge

**perdu, e** [pɛʀdy] *pp de* **perdre** ▷ *adj* (*enfant, cause, objet*) lost; (*isolé*) out-of-the-way; (*Comm: emballage*) non-returnable; (*récolte etc*) ruined; (*malade*): **il est ~** there's no hope left for him; **à vos moments ~s** in your spare time

**père** [pɛʀ] *nm* father; **pères** *nmpl* (*ancêtres*) forefathers; **de ~ en fils** from father to son; **~ de famille** father; family man; **mon ~** (*Rel*) Father; **le ~ Noël** Father Christmas

**pérégrinations** [peʀegʀinasjɔ̃] *nfpl* travels

**péremption** [peʀɑ̃psjɔ̃] *nf*: **date de ~** expiry date

**péremptoire** [peʀɑ̃ptwaʀ] *adj* peremptory

**pérennité** [peʀenite] *nf* durability, lasting quality

**péréquation** [peʀekwasjɔ̃] *nf* (*des salaires*) realignment; (*des prix, impôts*) equalization

**perfectible** [pɛʀfɛktibl(ə)] *adj* perfectible

**perfection** [pɛʀfɛksjɔ̃] *nf* perfection; **à la ~** *adv* to perfection

**perfectionné, e** [pɛʀfɛksjɔne] *adj* sophisticated

**perfectionnement** [pɛʀfɛksjɔnmɑ̃] *nm* improvement

**perfectionner** [pɛʀfɛksjɔne] *vt* to improve, perfect; **se ~ en anglais** to improve one's English

**perfectionniste** [pɛʀfɛksjɔnist(ə)] *nm/f* perfectionist

**perfide** [pɛʀfid] *adj* perfidious, treacherous

**perfidie** [pɛʀfidi] *nf* treachery

**perforant, e** [pɛʀfɔʀɑ̃, -ɑ̃t] *adj* (*balle*) armour-piercing (*Brit*), armor-piercing (*US*)

**perforateur, -trice** [pɛʀfɔʀatœʀ, -tʀis] *nm/f* punch-card operator ▷ *nm* (*perceuse*) borer; drill ▷ *nf* (*perceuse*) borer; drill; (*pour cartes*) card-punch; (*de bureau*) punch

**perforation** [pɛʀfɔʀasjɔ̃] *nf* perforation; punching; (*trou*) hole

**perforatrice** [pɛʀfɔʀatʀis] *nf voir* **perforateur**

**perforé, e** [pɛʀfɔʀe] *adj*: **bande ~** punched tape; **carte ~** punch card

**perforer** [pɛʀfɔʀe] *vt* to perforate, punch a hole *ou* holes in; (*ticket, bande, carte*) to punch

**perforeuse** [pɛʀfɔʀøz] *nf* (*machine*) (card) punch; (*personne*) card punch operator

**performance** [pɛʀfɔʀmɑ̃s] *nf* performance

**performant, e** [pɛʀfɔʀmɑ̃, -ɑ̃t] *adj* (*Écon: produit, entreprise*) high-return *cpd*; (*Tech: appareil, machine*) high-performance *cpd*

**perfusion** [pɛʀfyzjɔ̃] *nf* perfusion; **faire une ~ à qn** to put sb on a drip

**péricliter** [peʀiklite] *vi* to go downhill

**péridurale** [peʀidyʀal] *nf* epidural

**périgourdin, e** [peʀiguʀdɛ̃, -in] *adj* of *ou* from the Périgord

**péril** [peʀil] *nm* peril; **au ~ de sa vie** at the risk of his life; **à ses risques et ~s** at his (*ou* her) own risk

**périlleux, -euse** [peʀijø, -øz] *adj* perilous

**périmé, e** [peʀime] *adj* (out)dated; (*Admin*) out-of-date, expired

**périmètre** [peʀimɛtʀ(ə)] *nm* perimeter

**périnatal, e** [peʀinatal] *adj* perinatal

**période** [peʀjɔd] *nf* period

**périodique** [peʀjɔdik] *adj* (*phases*) periodic; (*publication*) periodical; (*Math: fraction*) recurring ▷ *nm* periodical; **garniture** *ou* **serviette ~** sanitary towel (*Brit*) *ou* napkin (*US*)

**périodiquement** [peʀjɔdikmɑ̃] *adv* periodically

**péripéties** [peʀipesi] *nfpl* events, episodes

**périphérie** [peʀifeʀi] *nf* periphery; (*d'une ville*) outskirts *pl*

**périphérique** [peʀifeʀik] *adj* (*quartiers*) outlying; (*Anat, Tech*) peripheral; (*station de radio*) operating from a neighbouring country ▷ *nm* (*Inform*) peripheral; (*Auto*): (**boulevard**) **~** ring road (*Brit*), beltway (*US*)

**périphrase** [peʀifʀaz] *nf* circumlocution

**périple** [peʀipl(ə)] *nm* journey

**périr** [peʀiʀ] *vi* to die, perish

**périscolaire** [peʀiskɔlɛʀ] *adj* extracurricular

**périscope** [peʀiskɔp] *nm* periscope

**périssable** [peʀisabl(ə)] *adj* perishable

**péristyle** [peʀistil] *nm* peristyle

**péritonite** [peʀitɔnit] *nf* peritonitis

**perle** [pɛʀl(ə)] *nf* pearl; (*de plastique, métal, sueur*) bead; (*personne, chose*) gem, treasure; (*erreur*) gem, howler

**perlé, e** [pɛʀle] *adj* (*rire*) rippling, tinkling; (*travail*) exquisite; (*orge*) pearl *cpd*; **grève ~e** go-slow, selective strike (action)

**perler** [pɛʀle] *vi* to form in droplets

**perlier, -ière** [pɛʀlje, -jɛʀ] *adj* pearl *cpd*

**permanence** [pɛʀmanɑ̃s] *nf* permanence; (*local*) (duty) office, strike headquarters; (*service des urgences*) emergency service; (*Scol*) study room; **assurer une ~** (*service public, bureaux*) to operate *ou* maintain a basic service; **être de ~** to be on call *ou* duty; **en ~** *adv* (*toujours*) permanently; (*continûment*) continuously

**permanent, e** [pɛʀmanɑ̃, -ɑ̃t] *adj* permanent; (*spectacle*) continuous; (*armée, comité*) standing ▷ *nf* perm ▷ *nm/f* (*d'un syndicat, parti*) paid official

**perméable** [pɛʀmeabl(ə)] *adj* (*terrain*) permeable; **~ à** (*fig*) receptive *ou* open to

**permettre** [pɛʀmɛtʀ(ə)] *vt* to allow, permit; **~ à qn de faire/qch** to allow sb to do/sth; **se ~ de faire qch** to take the liberty of doing sth; **permettez!** excuse me!

**permis, e** [pɛʀmi, -iz] *pp de* **permettre** ▷ *nm* permit, licence (*Brit*), license (*US*); **~ de chasse** hunting permit; **~ (de conduire)** (driving) licence (*Brit*), driver's license (*US*); **~ de construire** planning permission (*Brit*), building permit (*US*); **~ d'inhumer** burial certificate; **~ poids lourds** = HGV (driving) licence (*Brit*), = class E driver's license (*US*); **~ de séjour** residence permit; **~ de travail** work permit

**permissif, -ive** [pɛʀmisif, -iv] *adj* permissive

**permission** [pɛʀmisjɔ̃] *nf* permission; (*Mil*) leave; (: *papier*) pass; **en ~** on leave; **avoir la ~ de faire** to have permission to do, be allowed to do

**permissionnaire** [pɛʀmisjɔnɛʀ] *nm* soldier on leave

p

**permutable** [pɛʀmytabl(ə)] *adj* which can be changed *ou* switched around

**permuter** [pɛʀmyte] *vt* to change around, permutate ▷ *vi* to change, swap

**pernicieux, -euse** [pɛʀnisjø, -øz] *adj* pernicious

**péroné** [peʀɔne] *nm* fibula

**pérorer** [peʀɔʀe] *vi* to hold forth

**Pérou** [peʀu] *nm*: **le ~** Peru

**perpendiculaire** [pɛʀpɑ̃dikylɛʀ] *adj, nf* perpendicular

**perpendiculairement** [pɛʀpɑ̃dikylɛʀmɑ̃] *adv* perpendicularly

**perpète** [pɛʀpɛt] *nf*: **à ~** *(fam: loin)* miles away; *(: longtemps)* forever

**perpétrer** [pɛʀpetʀe] *vt* to perpetrate

**perpétuel, le** [pɛʀpetɥɛl] *adj* perpetual; *(Admin etc)* permanent; for life

**perpétuellement** [pɛʀpetɥɛlmɑ̃] *adv* perpetually, constantly

**perpétuer** [pɛʀpetɥe] *vt* to perpetuate; **se perpétuer** *(usage, injustice)* to be perpetuated; *(espèces)* to survive

**perpétuité** [pɛʀpetɥite] *nf*: **à ~** *adj, adv* for life; **être condamné à ~** to be sentenced to life imprisonment, receive a life sentence

**perplexe** [pɛʀplɛks(ə)] *adj* perplexed, puzzled

**perplexité** [pɛʀplɛksite] *nf* perplexity

**perquisition** [pɛʀkizisjɔ̃] *nf* (police) search

**perquisitionner** [pɛʀkizisjɔne] *vi* to carry out a search

**perron** [peʀɔ̃] *nm* steps *pl (in front of mansion etc)*

**perroquet** [peʀɔkɛ] *nm* parrot

**perruche** [peʀyʃ] *nf* budgerigar *(Brit)*, budgie *(Brit)*, parakeet *(US)*

**perruque** [peʀyk] *nf* wig

**persan, e** [pɛʀsɑ̃, -an] *adj* Persian ▷ *nm (Ling)* Persian

**perse** [pɛʀs(ə)] *adj* Persian ▷ *nm (Ling)* Persian ▷ *nm/f*: **Perse** Persian ▷ *nf*: **la P~** Persia

**persécuter** [pɛʀsekyte] *vt* to persecute

**persécution** [pɛʀsekysjɔ̃] *nf* persecution

**persévérance** [pɛʀseveʀɑ̃s] *nf* perseverance

**persévérant, e** [pɛʀseveʀɑ̃, -ɑ̃t] *adj* persevering

**persévérer** [pɛʀseveʀe] *vi* to persevere; **~ à croire que** to continue to believe that

**persiennes** [pɛʀsjɛn] *nfpl* (slatted) shutters

**persiflage** [pɛʀsiflaʒ] *nm* mockery *no pl*

**persifleur, -euse** [pɛʀsiflœʀ, -øz] *adj* mocking

**persil** [pɛʀsi] *nm* parsley

**persillé, e** [pɛʀsije] *adj* (sprinkled) with parsley; *(fromage)* veined; *(viande)* marbled, with fat running through

**Persique** [pɛʀsik] *adj*: **le golfe ~** the (Persian) Gulf

**persistance** [pɛʀsistɑ̃s] *nf* persistence

**persistant, e** [pɛʀsistɑ̃, -ɑ̃t] *adj* persistent; *(feuilles)* evergreen; **à feuillage ~** evergreen

**persister** [pɛʀsiste] *vi* to persist; **~ à faire qch** to persist in doing sth

**personnage** [pɛʀsɔnaʒ] *nm (notable)* personality; figure; *(individu)* character, individual; *(Théât)* character; *(Peinture)* figure

**personnaliser** [pɛʀsɔnalize] *vt* to personalize; *(appartement)* to give a personal touch to

**personnalité** [pɛʀsɔnalite] *nf* personality; *(personnage)* prominent figure

**personne** [pɛʀsɔn] *nf* person ▷ *pron* nobody, no one; *(quelqu'un)* anybody, anyone; **personnes** *nfpl* people *pl*; **il n'y a ~** there's nobody in *ou* there, there isn't anybody in *ou* there; **10 euros par ~** 10 euros per person *ou* a head; **en ~** personally, in person; **~ âgée** elderly person; **~ à charge** *(Jur)* dependent; **~ morale** *ou* **civile** *(Jur)* legal entity

**personnel, le** [pɛʀsɔnɛl] *adj* personal; *(égoïste: personne)* selfish, self-centred; *(idée, opinion)*: **j'ai des idées ~les à ce sujet** I have my own ideas about that ▷ *nm* personnel, staff; **service du ~** personnel department

**personnellement** [pɛʀsɔnɛlmɑ̃] *adv* personally

**personnification** [pɛʀsɔnifikasjɔ̃] *nf* personification; **c'est la ~ de la cruauté** he's cruelty personified

**personnifier** [pɛʀsɔnifje] *vt* to personify; to typify; **c'est l'honnêteté personnifiée** he *(ou* she *etc)* is honesty personified

**perspective** [pɛʀspɛktiv] *nf (Art)* perspective; *(vue, coup d'œil)* view; *(point de vue)* viewpoint, angle; *(chose escomptée, envisagée)* prospect; **en ~** in prospect

**perspicace** [pɛʀspikas] *adj* clear-sighted, gifted with *ou* showing) insight

**perspicacité** [pɛʀspikasite] *nf* insight, perspicacity

**persuader** [pɛʀsɥade] *vt*: **~ qn (de/de faire)** to persuade sb (of/to do); **j'en suis persuadé** I'm quite sure *ou* convinced (of it)

**persuasif, -ive** [pɛʀsɥazif, -iv] *adj* persuasive

**persuasion** [pɛʀsɥazjɔ̃] *nf* persuasion

**perte** [pɛʀt(ə)] *nf* loss; *(de temps)* waste; *(fig: morale)* ruin; **pertes** *nfpl* losses; **à ~** *(Comm)* at a loss; **à ~ de vue** as far as the eye can *(ou* could) see; *(fig)* interminably; **en pure ~** for absolutely nothing; **courir à sa ~** to be on the road to ruin; **être en ~ de vitesse** *(fig)* to be losing momentum; **avec ~ et fracas** forcibly; **~ de chaleur** heat loss; **~ sèche** dead loss; **~s blanches** (vaginal) discharge *sg*

**pertinemment** [pɛʀtinamɑ̃] *adv* to the point; *(savoir)* perfectly well, full well

**pertinence** [pɛʀtinɑ̃s] *nf* pertinence, relevance; discernment

**pertinent, e** [pɛʀtinɑ̃, -ɑ̃t] *adj (remarque)* apt, pertinent, relevant; *(analyse)* discerning, judicious

**perturbateur, -trice** [pɛʀtyʀbatœʀ, -tʀis] *adj* disruptive

**perturbation** [pɛʀtyʀbasjɔ̃] *nf (dans un service public)* disruption; *(agitation, trouble)* perturbation; **~ (atmosphérique)** atmospheric disturbance

**perturber** [pɛʀtyʀbe] *vt* to disrupt; *(Psych)* to perturb, disturb

**péruvien, ne** [peʀyvjɛ̃, -ɛn] *adj* Peruvian ▷ *nm/f*:

**Péruvien, ne** Peruvian

**pervenche** [pɛʀvɑ̃ʃ] *nf* periwinkle; *(fam)* traffic warden *(Brit)*, meter maid *(US)*

**pervers, e** [pɛʀvɛʀ, -ɛʀs(ə)] *adj* perverted, depraved; *(malfaisant)* perverse

**perversion** [pɛʀvɛʀsjɔ̃] *nf* perversion

**perversité** [pɛʀvɛʀsite] *nf* depravity; perversity

**perverti, e** [pɛʀvɛʀti] *nm/f* pervert

**pervertir** [pɛʀvɛʀtiʀ] *vt* to pervert

**pesage** [pəzaʒ] *nm* weighing; *(Hippisme: action)* weigh-in; *(: salle)* weighing room; *(: enceinte)* enclosure

**pesamment** [pəzamɑ̃] *adv* heavily

**pesant, e** [pəzɑ̃, -ɑ̃t] *adj* heavy; *(fig)* burdensome ▷ *nm*: **valoir son ~ de** to be worth one's weight in

**pesanteur** [pəzɑ̃tœʀ] *nf* gravity

**pèse-bébé** [pɛzbebe] *nm* (baby) scales *pl*

**pesée** [pəze] *nf* weighing; *(Boxe)* weigh-in; *(pression)* pressure

**pèse-lettre** [pɛzlɛtʀ(ə)] *nm* letter scales *pl*

**pèse-personne** [pɛzpɛʀsɔn] *nm* (bathroom) scales *pl*

**peser** [pəze] *vt* to weigh; *(considérer, comparer)* to weigh up ▷ *vi* to be heavy; *(fig)* to carry weight; **~ sur** *(levier, bouton)* to press, push; *(fig: accabler)* to lie heavy on; *(: influencer)* to influence; **~ à qn** to weigh heavy on sb

**pessaire** [pɛsɛʀ] *nm* pessary

**pessimisme** [pesimism(ə)] *nm* pessimism

**pessimiste** [pesimist(ə)] *adj* pessimistic ▷ *nm/f* pessimist

**peste** [pɛst(ə)] *nf* plague; *(fig)* pest, nuisance

**pester** [pɛste] *vi*: **~ contre** to curse

**pesticide** [pɛstisid] *nm* pesticide

**pestiféré, e** [pɛstifeʀe] *nm/f* plague victim

**pestilentiel, le** [pɛstilɑ̃sjɛl] *adj* foul

**pet** [pɛ] *nm (fam!)* fart *(!)*

**pétale** [petal] *nm* petal

**pétanque** [petɑ̃k] *nf type of bowls; see note*

⬤ **PÉTANQUE**
⬤
⬤
⬤ *Pétanque* is a version of the game of "boules",
⬤ played on a variety of hard surfaces.
⬤ Standing with their feet together, players
⬤ throw steel bowls at a wooden jack. *Pétanque*
⬤ originated in the South of France and is still
⬤ very much associated with that area.

**pétarade** [petaʀad] *nf* backfiring *no pl*

**pétarader** [petaʀade] *vi* to backfire

**pétard** [petaʀ] *nm (feu d'artifice)* banger *(Brit)*, firecracker; *(de cotillon)* cracker; *(Rail)* detonator

**pet-de-nonne** [pɛdnɔn] *(pl* **pets-de-nonne)** *nm* ≈ choux bun

**péter** [pete] *vi (fam: casser, sauter)* to burst; to bust; *(fam!)* to fart *(!)*

**pète-sec** [pɛtsɛk] *adj inv* abrupt, sharp (-tongued)

**pétillant, e** [petijɑ̃, -ɑ̃t] *adj* sparkling

**pétiller** [petije] *vi (flamme, bois)* to crackle; *(mousse, champagne)* to bubble; *(pierre, métal)* to glisten; *(yeux)* to sparkle; *(fig)*: **~ d'esprit** to sparkle with wit

**petit, e** [pəti, -it] *adj (gén)* small; *(main, objet, colline, en âge: enfant)* small, little; *(mince, fin: personne, taille, pluie)* slight; *(voyage)* short, little; *(bruit etc)* faint, slight; *(mesquin)* mean; *(peu important)* minor ▷ *nm/f (petit enfant)* little one, child; **petits** *nmpl (d'un animal)* young *pl*; **faire des ~s** to have kittens *(ou* puppies *etc)*; **en ~** in miniature; **mon ~** son; little one; **ma ~e** dear; little one; **pauvre ~** poor little thing; **la classe des ~s** the infant class; **pour ~s et grands** for children and adults; **les tout-~s** the little ones, the tiny tots; **~ à ~** bit by bit, gradually; **~(e) ami/e** boyfriend/girlfriend; **les ~es annonces** the small ads; **~ déjeuner** breakfast; **~ doigt** little finger; **le ~ écran** the small screen; **~ four** petit four; **~ pain** (bread) roll; **~e monnaie** small change; **~e vérole** smallpox; **~s pois** petit pois *pl*, garden peas; **~es gens** people of modest means

**petit-beurre** [pətibœʀ] *(pl* **petits-beurre)** *nm* sweet butter biscuit *(Brit)* ou cookie *(US)*

**petit-bourgeois, petite-bourgeoise** [pətibuʀʒwa, pətitbuʀʒwaz] *(pl* **petit(e)s-bourgeois(es))** *adj (péj)* petit-bourgeois, middle-class

**petite-fille** [pətitfij] *(pl* **petites-filles)** *nf* granddaughter

**petitement** [pətitmɑ̃] *adv* poorly; meanly; **être logé ~** to be in cramped accommodation

**petitesse** [pətitɛs] *nf* smallness; *(d'un salaire, de revenus)* modestness; *(mesquinerie)* meanness

**petit-fils** [pətifis] *(pl* **petits-fils)** *nm* grandson

**pétition** [petisjɔ̃] *nf* petition; **faire signer une ~** to get up a petition

**pétitionnaire** [petisjɔnɛʀ] *nm/f* petitioner

**pétitionner** [petisjɔne] *vi* to petition

**petit-lait** [pətilɛ] *(pl* **petits-laits)** *nm* whey *no pl*

**petit-nègre** [pətinɛgʀ(ə)] *nm (péj)* pidgin French

**petits-enfants** [pətizɑ̃fɑ̃] *nmpl* grandchildren

**petit-suisse** [pətisɥis] *(pl* **petits-suisses)** *nm* small individual pot of cream cheese

**pétoche** [petɔʃ] *nf (fam)*: **avoir la ~** to be scared out of one's wits

**pétri, e** [petʀi] *adj*: **~ d'orgueil** filled with pride

**pétrifier** [petʀifje] *vt* to petrify; *(fig)* to paralyze, transfix

**pétrin** [petʀɛ̃] *nm* kneading-trough; *(fig)*: **dans le ~** in a jam *ou* fix

**pétrir** [petʀiʀ] *vt* to knead

**pétrochimie** [petʀɔʃimi] *nf* petrochemistry

**pétrochimique** [petʀɔʃimik] *adj* petrochemical

**pétrodollar** [petʀɔdɔlaʀ] *nm* petrodollar

**pétrole** [petʀɔl] *nm* oil; *(aussi:* **pétrole lampant)** paraffin *(Brit)*, kerosene *(US)*

**pétrolier, -ière** [petʀɔlje, -jɛʀ] *adj* oil *cpd*; *(pays)* oil-producing ▷ *nm (navire)* oil tanker; *(financier)* oilman; *(technicien)* petroleum engineer

**pétrolifère** [petʀɔlifɛʀ] *adj* oil(-bearing)

**P et T** *sigle fpl* = **postes et télécommunications**

**pétulant, e** [petylɑ̃, -ɑ̃t] *adj* exuberant

⬤ MOT-CLÉ

**peu** [pø] *adv* **1** (*modifiant verbe, adjectif, adverbe*): **il boit peu** he doesn't drink (very) much; **il est peu bavard** he's not very talkative; **peu avant/après** shortly before/afterwards; **pour peu qu'il fasse** if he should do, if by any chance he does
**2** (*modifiant nom*): **peu de: peu de gens/d'arbres** few *ou* not (very) many people/trees; **il a peu d'espoir** he hasn't (got) much hope, he has little hope; **pour peu de temps** for (only) a short while; **à peu de frais** for very little cost
**3: peu à peu** little by little; **à peu près** just about, more or less; **à peu près 10 kg/10 euros** approximately 10 kg/10 euros
▷ *nm* **1: le peu de gens qui** the few people who; **le peu de sable qui** what little sand, the little sand which
**2: un peu** a little; **un petit peu** a little bit; **un peu d'espoir** a little hope; **elle est un peu bavarde** she's rather talkative; **un peu plus/moins de** slightly more/less (*ou* fewer) than; **pour un peu il ..., un peu plus et il ...** he very nearly *ou* all but ...; **essayez un peu!** have a go!, just try it!
▷ *pron*: **peu le savent** few know (it); **avant** *ou* **sous peu** shortly, before long; **depuis peu** for a short *ou* little while; (*au passé*) a short *ou* little while ago; **de peu** (only) just; **c'est peu de chose** it's nothing; **il est de peu mon cadet** he's just a little *ou* bit younger than me

**peuplade** [pœplad] *nf* (*horde, tribu*) tribe, people
**peuple** [pœpl(ə)] *nm* people; (*masse*): **un ~ de vacanciers** a crowd of holiday-makers; **il y a du ~** there are a lot of people
**peuplé, e** [pœple] *adj*: **très/peu ~** densely/sparsely populated
**peupler** [pœple] *vt* (*pays, région*) to populate; (*étang*) to stock; (*hommes, poissons*) to inhabit; (*fig: imagination, rêves*) to fill; **se peupler** *vi* (*ville, région*) to become populated; (*fig: s'animer*) to fill (up), be filled
**peuplier** [pøplije] *nm* poplar (tree)
**peur** [pœʀ] *nf* fear; **avoir ~ (de/de faire/que)** to be frightened *ou* afraid (of/of doing/that); **prendre ~** to take fright; **faire ~ à** to frighten; **de ~ de/que** for fear of/that; **j'ai ~ qu'il ne soit trop tard** I'm afraid it might be too late; **j'ai ~ qu'il (ne) vienne (pas)** I'm afraid he may (not) come
**peureux, -euse** [pœʀø, -øz] *adj* fearful, timorous
**peut** [pø] *vb voir* **pouvoir**
**peut-être** [pøtɛtʀ(ə)] *adv* perhaps, maybe; **~ que** perhaps, maybe; **~ bien qu'il fera/est** he may well do/be
**peuvent** [pœv], **peux** *etc* [pø] *vb voir* **pouvoir**
**p. ex.** *abr* (= *par exemple*) e.g.

**phalange** [falɑ̃ʒ] *nf* (*Anat*) phalanx; (*Mil: fig*) phalanx
**phallique** [falik] *adj* phallic
**phallocrate** [falɔkʀat] *nm* male chauvinist
**phallocratie** [falɔkʀasi] *nf* male chauvinism
**phallus** [falys] *nm* phallus
**pharaon** [faʀaɔ̃] *nm* Pharaoh
**phare** [faʀ] *nm* (*en mer*) lighthouse; (*d'aéroport*) beacon; (*de véhicule*) headlight, headlamp (*Brit*)
▷ *adj*: **produit ~** leading product; **se mettre en ~s, mettre ses ~s** to put on one's headlights; **~s de recul** reversing (*Brit*) *ou* back-up (*US*) lights
**pharmaceutique** [faʀmasøtik] *adj* pharmaceutic(al)
**pharmacie** [faʀmasi] *nf* (*science*) pharmacology; (*magasin*) chemist's (*Brit*), pharmacy; (*officine*) dispensary; (*produits*) pharmaceuticals *pl*; (*armoire*) medicine chest *ou* cupboard, first-aid cupboard
**pharmacien, ne** [faʀmasjɛ̃, -ɛn] *nm/f* pharmacist, chemist (*Brit*)
**pharmacologie** [faʀmakɔlɔʒi] *nf* pharmacology
**pharyngite** [faʀɛ̃ʒit] *nf* pharyngitis *no pl*
**pharynx** [faʀɛ̃ks] *nm* pharynx
**phase** [faz] *nf* phase
**phénoménal, e, -aux** [fenɔmenal, -o] *adj* phenomenal
**phénomène** [fenɔmɛn] *nm* phenomenon; (*monstre*) freak
**philanthrope** [filɑ̃tʀɔp] *nm/f* philanthropist
**philanthropie** [filɑ̃tʀɔpi] *nf* philanthropy
**philanthropique** [filɑ̃tʀɔpik] *adj* philanthropic
**philatélie** [filateli] *nf* philately, stamp collecting
**philatélique** [filatelik] *adj* philatelic
**philatéliste** [filatelist(ə)] *nm/f* philatelist, stamp collector
**philharmonique** [filaʀmɔnik] *adj* philharmonic
**philippin, e** [filipɛ̃, -in] *adj* Filipino
**Philippines** [filipin] *nfpl*: **les ~** the Philippines
**philistin** [filistɛ̃] *nm* philistine
**philo** [filo] *nf* (*fam*: = *philosophie*) philosophy
**philosophe** [filɔzɔf] *nm/f* philosopher ▷ *adj* philosophical
**philosopher** [filɔzɔfe] *vi* to philosophize
**philosophie** [filɔzɔfi] *nf* philosophy
**philosophique** [filɔzɔfik] *adj* philosophical
**philosophiquement** [filɔzɔfikmɑ̃] *adv* philosophically
**philtre** [filtʀ(ə)] *nm* philtre, love potion
**phlébite** [flebit] *nf* phlebitis
**phlébologue** [flebɔlɔg] *nm/f* vein specialist
**phobie** [fɔbi] *nf* phobia
**phonétique** [fɔnetik] *adj* phonetic ▷ *nf* phonetics *sg*
**phonétiquement** [fɔnetikmɑ̃] *adv* phonetically
**phonographe** [fɔnɔgʀaf] *nm* (wind-up) gramophone
**phoque** [fɔk] *nm* seal; (*fourrure*) sealskin

**phosphate** [fɔsfat] *nm* phosphate
**phosphaté, e** [fɔsfate] *adj* phosphate-enriched
**phosphore** [fɔsfɔʀ] *nm* phosphorus
**phosphoré, e** [fɔsfɔʀe] *adj* phosphorous
**phosphorescent, e** [fɔsfɔʀesɑ̃, -ɑ̃t] *adj*
luminous
**phosphorique** [fɔsfɔʀik] *adj*: **acide ~**
phosphoric acid
**photo** [fɔto] *nf* (*photographie*) photo ▷ *adj*:
**appareil/pellicule ~** camera/film; **en ~** in *ou* on
a photo; **prendre en ~** to take a photo of;
**aimer la/faire de la ~** to like taking/take
photos; **~ en couleurs** colour photo; **~**
**d'identité** passport photo
**photo...** [fɔtɔ] *préfixe* photo...
**photocopie** [fɔtɔkɔpi] *nf* (*procédé*)
photocopying; (*document*) photocopy
**photocopier** [fɔtɔkɔpje] *vt* to photocopy
**photocopieur** [fɔtɔkɔpjœʀ] *nm*,
**photocopieuse** [fɔtɔkɔpjøz] *nf* (photo)copier
**photo-électrique** [fɔtɔelɛktʀik] *adj* photoelectric
**photo-finish** [fɔtɔfiniʃ] (*pl* **photos-finish**) *nf*
(*appareil*) photo finish camera; (*photo*) photo
finish picture; **il y a eu ~ pour la troisième**
**place** there was a photo finish for third place
**photogénique** [fɔtɔʒenik] *adj* photogenic
**photographe** [fɔtɔɡʀaf] *nm/f* photographer
**photographie** [fɔtɔɡʀafi] *nf* (*procédé, technique*)
photography; (*cliché*) photograph; **faire de la ~**
to do photography as a hobby; (*comme métier*) to
be a photographer
**photographier** [fɔtɔɡʀafje] *vt* to photograph,
take
**photographique** [fɔtɔɡʀafik] *adj*
photographic
**photogravure** [fɔtɔɡʀavyʀ] *nf* photoengraving
**photomaton®** [fɔtɔmatɔ̃] *nm* photo-booth,
photomat
**photomontage** [fɔtɔmɔ̃taʒ] *nm* photomontage
**photophone** [fɔtɔfɔn] *nm* camera phone
**photo-robot** [fɔtɔʀɔbo] *nf* Identikit® (picture)
**photosensible** [fɔtɔsɑ̃sibl(ə)] *adj*
photosensitive
**photostat** [fɔtɔsta] *nm* photostat
**phrase** [fʀɑz] *nf* (*Ling*) sentence; (*propos, Mus*)
phrase; **phrases** *nfpl* (*péj*) flowery language *sg*
**phraséologie** [fʀazeɔlɔʒi] *nf* phraseology;
(*rhétorique*) flowery language
**phraseur, -euse** [fʀazœʀ, -øz] *nm/f*: **c'est un ~**
he uses such flowery language
**phrygien, ne** [fʀiʒjɛ̃, -ɛn] *adj*: **bonnet ~**
Phrygian cap
**phtisie** [ftizi] *nf* consumption
**phylloxéra** [filɔkseʀa] *nm* phylloxera
**physicien, ne** [fizisjɛ̃, -ɛn] *nm/f* physicist
**physiologie** [fizjɔlɔʒi] *nf* physiology
**physiologique** [fizjɔlɔʒik] *adj* physiological
**physiologiquement** [fizjɔlɔʒikmɑ̃] *adv*
physiologically
**physionomie** [fizjɔnɔmi] *nf* face; (*d'un paysage*
*etc*) physiognomy

**physionomiste** [fizjɔnɔmist(ə)] *nm/f* good
judge of faces; person who has a good memory
for faces
**physiothérapie** [fizjɔteʀapi] *nf* natural
medicine, alternative medicine
**physique** [fizik] *adj* physical ▷ *nm* physique
▷ *nf* physics *sg*; **au ~** physically
**physiquement** [fizikmɑ̃] *adv* physically
**phytothérapie** [fitɔteʀapi] *nf* herbal medicine
**p.i.** *abr* = **par intérim**; *voir* **intérim**
**piaffer** [pjafe] *vi* to stamp
**piaillement** [pjɑjmɑ̃] *nm* squawking *no pl*
**piailler** [pjɑje] *vi* to squawk
**pianiste** [pjanist(ə)] *nm/f* pianist
**piano** [pjano] *nm* piano; **~ à queue** grand piano
**pianoter** [pjanɔte] *vi* to tinkle away (at the
piano); (*tapoter*): **~ sur** to drum one's fingers on
**piaule** [pjol] *nf* (*fam*) pad
**piauler** [pjole] *vi* (*enfant*) to whimper; (*oiseau*) to
cheep
**PIB** *sigle m* (= *produit intérieur brut*) GDP
**pic** [pik] *nm* (*instrument*) pick(axe); (*montagne*)
peak; (*Zool*) woodpecker; **à ~** *adv* vertically; (*fig*)
just at the right time; **couler à ~** (*bateau*) to go
straight down; **~ à glace** ice pick
**picard, e** [pikaʀ, -aʀd(ə)] *adj* of *ou* from Picardy
**Picardie** [pikaʀdi] *nf*: **la ~** Picardy
**picaresque** [pikaʀɛsk(ə)] *adj* picaresque
**piccolo** [pikɔlo] *nm* piccolo
**pichenette** [piʃnɛt] *nf* flick
**pichet** [piʃɛ] *nm* jug
**pickpocket** [pikpɔkɛt] *nm* pickpocket
**pick-up** [pikœp] *nm inv* record player
**picorer** [pikɔʀe] *vt* to peck
**picot** [piko] *nm* sprocket; **entraînement par**
**roue à ~s** sprocket feed
**picotement** [pikɔtmɑ̃] *nm* smarting *no pl*,
prickling *no pl*
**picoter** [pikɔte] *vt* (*oiseau*) to peck ▷ *vi* (*irriter*) to
smart, prickle
**pictural, e, -aux** [piktyʀal, -o] *adj* pictorial
**pie** [pi] *nf* magpie; (*fig*) chatterbox ▷ *adj inv*:
**cheval ~** piebald; **vache ~** black and white cow
**pièce** [pjɛs] *nf* (*d'un logement*) room; (*Théât*) play;
(*de mécanisme, machine*) part; (*de monnaie*) coin;
(*Couture*) patch; (*document*) document; (*de drap,*
*fragment, d'une collection*) piece; (*de bétail*) head;
**mettre en ~s** to smash to pieces; **deux euros ~**
two euros each; **vendre à la ~** to sell separately
*ou* individually; **travailler/payer à la ~** to do
piecework/pay piece rate; **de toutes ~s: c'est**
**inventé de toutes ~s** it's a complete
fabrication; **un maillot une ~** a one-piece
swimsuit; **un deux-~s cuisine** a two-room(ed)
flat (*Brit*) *ou* apartment (*US*) with kitchen; **tout**
**d'une ~** (*personne: franc*) blunt; (: *sans souplesse*)
inflexible; **~ à conviction** exhibit; **~ d'eau**
ornamental lake *ou* pond; **~ d'identité: avez-**
**vous une ~ d'identité?** have you got any
(means of) identification?; **~ jointe** (*Inform*)
attachment; **~ montée** tiered cake; **~ de**
**rechange** spare (part); **~ de résistance** pièce de

résistance; (*plat*) main dish; **~s détachées** spares, (spare) parts; **en ~s détachées** (*à monter*) in kit form; **~s justificatives** supporting documents

**pied** [pje] *nm* foot; (*de verre*) stem; (*de table*) leg; (*de lampe*) base; (*plante*) plant; **~s nus** barefoot; **à ~ on** foot; **à ~ sec** without getting one's feet wet; **à ~ d'œuvre** ready to start (work); **au ~ de la lettre** literally; **au ~ levé** at a moment's notice; **de ~ en cap** from head to foot; **en ~** (*portrait*) full-length; **avoir ~** to be able to touch the bottom, not to be out of one's depth; **avoir le ~ marin** to be a good sailor; **perdre ~** to lose one's footing; (*fig*) to get out of one's depth; **sur ~** (*Agr*) on the stalk, uncut; (*debout, rétabli*) up and about; **mettre sur ~** (*entreprise*) to set up; **mettre à ~** to suspend; to lay off; **mettre qn au ~ du mur** to get sb with his (*ou* her) back to the wall; **sur le ~ de guerre** ready for action; **sur un ~ d'égalité** on an equal footing; **sur ~ d'intervention** on stand-by; **faire du ~ à qn** (*prévenir*) to give sb a (warning) kick; (*galamment*) to play footsie with sb; **mettre les ~s quelque part** to set foot somewhere; **faire des ~s et des mains** (*fig*) to move heaven and earth, pull out all the stops; **c'est le ~!** (*fam*) it's terrific!; **se lever du bon ~/du ~ gauche** to get out of bed on the right/wrong side; **~ de lit** footboard; **~ de nez: faire un ~ de nez à** to thumb one's nose at; **~ de vigne** vine

**pied-à-terre** [pjetatɛʀ] *nm inv* pied-à-terre

**pied-bot** [pjebo] (*pl* **pieds-bots**) *nm* person with a club foot

**pied-de-biche** [pjedbiʃ] (*pl* **pieds-de-biche**) *nm* claw; (*Couture*) presser foot

**pied-de-poule** [pjedpul] *adj inv* hound's-tooth

**piédestal, -aux** [pjedɛstal, -o] *nm* pedestal

**pied-noir** [pjenwaʀ] (*pl* **pieds-noirs**) *nm* Algerian-born Frenchman

**piège** [pjɛʒ] *nm* trap; **prendre au ~** to trap

**piéger** [pjeʒe] *vt* (*animal, fig*) to trap; (*avec une bombe*) to booby-trap; **lettre/voiture piégée** letter-/car-bomb

**piercing** [pjɛʀsiŋ] *nm* piercing

**pierraille** [pjɛʀaj] *nf* loose stones *pl*

**pierre** [pjɛʀ] *nf* stone; **première ~** (*d'un édifice*) foundation stone; **mur de ~s sèches** drystone wall; **faire d'une ~ deux coups** to kill two birds with one stone; **~ à briquet** flint; **~ fine** semiprecious stone; **~ ponce** pumice stone; **~ de taille** freestone *no pl*; **~ tombale** tombstone, gravestone; **~ de touche** touchstone

**pierreries** [pjɛʀʀi] *nfpl* gems, precious stones

**pierreux, -euse** [pjɛʀø, -øz] *adj* stony

**piété** [pjete] *nf* piety

**piétinement** [pjetinmɑ̃] *nm* stamping *no pl*

**piétiner** [pjetine] *vi* (*trépigner*) to stamp (one's foot); (*marquer le pas*) to stand about; (*fig*) to be at a standstill ▷ *vt* to trample on

**piéton, ne** [pjetɔ̃, -ɔn] *nm/f* pedestrian ▷ *adj* pedestrian *cpd*

**piétonnier, -ière** [pjetɔnje, -jɛʀ] *adj* pedestrian *cpd*

**piètre** [pjɛtʀ(ə)] *adj* poor, mediocre

**pieu, x** [pjø] *nm* (*piquet*) post; (*pointu*) stake; (*fam: lit*) bed

**pieusement** [pjøzmɑ̃] *adv* piously

**pieuvre** [pjœvʀ(ə)] *nf* octopus

**pieux, -euse** [pjø, -øz] *adj* pious

**pif** [pif] *nm* (*fam*) conk (*Brit*), beak; **au ~ = au pifomètre**

**piffer** [pife] *vt* (*fam*): **je ne peux pas le ~** I can't stand him

**pifomètre** [pifɔmɛtʀ(ə)] *nm* (*fam*): **choisir** *etc* **au ~** to follow one's nose when choosing *etc*

**pige** [piʒ] *nf* piecework rate

**pigeon** [piʒɔ̃] *nm* pigeon; **~ voyageur** homing pigeon

**pigeonnant, e** [piʒɔnɑ̃, -ɑ̃t] *adj* full, well-developed

**pigeonneau, x** [piʒɔno] *nm* young pigeon

**pigeonnier** [piʒɔnje] *nm* pigeon loft, dovecot(e)

**piger** [piʒe] *vi* (*fam*) to get it ▷ *vt* (*fam*) to get, understand

**pigiste** [piʒist(ə)] *nm/f* (*typographe*) typesetter on piecework; (*journaliste*) freelance journalist (*paid by the line*)

**pigment** [pigmɑ̃] *nm* pigment

**pignon** [piɲɔ̃] *nm* (*de mur*) gable; (*d'engrenage*) cog(wheel), gearwheel; (*graine*) pine kernel; **avoir ~ sur rue** (*fig*) to have a prosperous business

**pile** [pil] *nf* (*tas, pilier*) pile; (*Élec*) battery ▷ *adj*: **le côté ~** tails ▷ *adv* (*net, brusquement*) dead; (*à temps, à point nommé*) just at the right time; **à deux heures ~** at two on the dot; **jouer à ~ ou face** to toss up (for it); **~ ou face?** heads or tails?

**piler** [pile] *vt* to crush, pound

**pileux, -euse** [pilø, -øz] *adj*: **système ~** (body) hair

**pilier** [pilje] *nm* (*colonne, support*) pillar; (*personne*) mainstay; (*Rugby*) prop (forward)

**pillage** [pijaʒ] *nm* pillaging, plundering, looting

**pillard, e** [pijaʀ, -aʀd(ə)] *nm/f* looter; plunderer

**piller** [pije] *vt* to pillage, plunder, loot

**pilleur, -euse** [pijœʀ, -øz] *nm/f* looter

**pilon** [pilɔ̃] *nm* (*instrument*) pestle; (*de volaille*) drumstick; **mettre un livre au ~** to pulp a book

**pilonner** [pilɔne] *vt* to pound

**pilori** [pilɔʀi] *nm*: **mettre** *ou* **clouer au ~** to pillory

**pilotage** [pilɔtaʒ] *nm* piloting; flying; **~ automatique** automatic piloting; **~ sans visibilité** blind flying

**pilote** [pilɔt] *nm* pilot; (*de char, voiture*) driver ▷ *adj* pilot *cpd*; **usine/ferme ~** experimental factory/farm; **~ de chasse/d'essai/de ligne** fighter/test/airline pilot; **~ de course** racing driver

**piloter** [pilɔte] *vt* (*navire*) to pilot; (*avion*) to fly; (*automobile*) to drive; (*fig*): **~ qn** to guide sb round

**pilotis** [pilɔti] *nm* pile; stilt

**pilule** [pilyl] *nf* pill; **prendre la ~** to be on the

pill; **~ du lendemain** morning-after pill

**pimbêche** [pɛ̃bɛʃ] *nf (péj)* stuck-up girl

**piment** [pimɑ̃] *nm (Bot)* pepper, capsicum; *(fig)* spice, piquancy; **~ rouge** *(Culin)* chilli

**pimenté, e** [pimɑ̃te] *adj* hot and spicy

**pimenter** [pimɑ̃te] *vt (plat)* to season (with peppers *ou* chillis); *(fig)* to add *ou* give spice to

**pimpant, e** [pɛ̃pɑ̃, -ɑ̃t] *adj* spruce

**pin** [pɛ̃] *nm* pine (tree); *(bois)* pine(wood)

**pinacle** [pinakl(ə)] *nm*: **porter qn au ~** *(fig)* to praise sb to the skies

**pinard** [pinaʀ] *nm (fam)* (cheap) wine, plonk (Brit)

**pince** [pɛ̃s] *nf (outil)* pliers *pl*; *(de homard, crabe)* pincer, claw; *(Couture: pli)* dart; **~ à sucre/glace** sugar/ice tongs *pl*; **~ à épiler** tweezers *pl*; **~ à linge** clothes peg (Brit) *ou* pin (US); **~ universelle** (universal) pliers *pl*; **~s de cycliste** bicycle clips

**pincé, e** [pɛ̃se] *adj (air)* stiff; *(mince: bouche)* pinched ▷ *nf*: **une ~e de** a pinch of

**pinceau, x** [pɛ̃so] *nm* (paint)brush

**pincement** [pɛ̃smɑ̃] *nm*: **~ au cœur** twinge of regret

**pince-monseigneur** [pɛ̃smɔ̃sɛɲœʀ] *(pl* **pinces-monseigneur)** *nf* crowbar

**pince-nez** [pɛ̃sne] *nm inv* pince-nez

**pincer** [pɛ̃se] *vt* to pinch; *(Mus: cordes)* to pluck; *(Couture)* to dart, put darts in; *(fam)* to nab; **se ~ le doigt** to squeeze *ou* nip one's finger; **se ~ le nez** to hold one's nose

**pince-sans-rire** [pɛ̃ssɑ̃ʀiʀ] *adj inv* deadpan

**pincettes** [pɛ̃sɛt] *nfpl* tweezers; *(pour le feu)* (fire) tongs

**pinçon** [pɛ̃sɔ̃] *nm* pinch mark

**pinède** [pinɛd] *nf* pinewood, pine forest

**pingouin** [pɛ̃gwɛ̃] *nm* penguin

**ping-pong** [piŋpɔ̃g] *nm* table tennis

**pingre** [pɛ̃gʀ(ə)] *adj* niggardly

**pinson** [pɛ̃sɔ̃] *nm* chaffinch

**pintade** [pɛ̃tad] *nf* guinea-fowl

**pin up** [pinœp] *nf inv* pin-up (girl)

**pioche** [pjɔʃ] *nf* pickaxe

**piocher** [pjɔʃe] *vt* to dig up (with a pickaxe); *(fam)* to swot (Brit) *ou* grind (US) at; **~ dans** to dig into

**piolet** [pjɔlɛ] *nm* ice axe

**pion, ne** [pjɔ̃, pjɔn] *nm/f (Scol: péj)* student paid to supervise schoolchildren ▷ *nm (Échecs)* pawn; *(Dames)* piece, draught (Brit), checker (US)

**pionnier** [pjɔnje] *nm* pioneer

**pipe** [pip] *nf* pipe; **fumer la** *ou* **une ~** to smoke a pipe; **~ de bruyère** briar pipe

**pipeau, x** [pipo] *nm* (reed-)pipe

**pipe-line** [piplin] *nm* pipeline

**piper** [pipe] *vt (dé)* to load; *(carte)* to mark; **sans ~ mot** *(fam)* without a squeak; **les dés sont pipés** *(fig)* the dice are loaded

**pipette** [pipɛt] *nf* pipette

**pipi** [pipi] *nm (fam)*: **faire ~** to have a wee

**piquant, e** [pikɑ̃, -ɑ̃t] *adj (barbe, rosier etc)* prickly; *(saveur, sauce)* hot, pungent; *(fig: description, style)* racy; *(: mordant, caustique)* biting ▷ *nm (épine)* thorn, prickle; *(de hérisson)* quill, spine; *(fig)* spiciness, spice

**pique** [pik] *nf (arme)* pike; *(fig)*: **envoyer** *ou* **lancer des ~s à qn** to make cutting remarks to sb ▷ *nm (Cartes: couleur)* spades *pl*; *(: carte)* spade

**piqué, e** [pike] *adj (Couture)* (machine-)stitched; quilted; *(livre, glace)* mildewed; *(vin)* sour; *(Mus: note)* staccato; *(fam: personne)* nuts ▷ *nm (Aviat)* dive; *(Textiles)* piqué

**pique-assiette** [pikasjɛt] *nm/f inv (péj)* scrounger, sponger

**pique-fleurs** [pikflœʀ] *nm inv* flower holder

**pique-nique** [piknik] *nm* picnic

**pique-niquer** [piknike] *vi* to (have a) picnic

**pique-niqueur, -euse** [piknikœʀ, -øz] *nm/f* picnicker

**piquer** [pike] *vt (percer)* to prick; *(Méd)* to give an injection to; *(: animal blessé etc)* to put to sleep; *(insecte, fumée, ortie)* to sting; *(: poivre)* to burn; *(: froid)* to bite; *(Couture)* to machine (stitch); *(intérêt etc)* to rouse; *(fam: prendre)* to pick up; *(: voler)* to pinch; *(: arrêter)* to nab; *(planter)*: **~ qch dans** to stick sth into; *(fixer)*: **~ qch à** *ou* **sur** to pin sth onto ▷ *vi (oiseau, avion)* to go into a dive; *(saveur)* to be pungent; to be sour; **se piquer** *(avec une aiguille)* to prick o.s.; *(se faire une piqûre)* to inject o.s.; *(se vexer)* to get annoyed; **se ~ de faire** to pride o.s. on doing; **~ sur** to swoop down on; to head straight for; **~ du nez** *(avion)* to go into a nose-dive; **~ une tête** *(plonger)* to dive headfirst; **~ un galop/un cent mètres** to break into a gallop/put on a sprint; **~ une crise** to throw a fit; **~ au vif** *(fig)* to sting

**piquet** [pikɛ] *nm (pieu)* post, stake; *(de tente)* peg; **mettre un élève au ~** to make a pupil stand in the corner; **~ de grève** (strike) picket; **~ d'incendie** fire-fighting squad

**piqueté, e** [pikte] *adj*: **~ de** dotted with

**piquette** [pikɛt] *nf (fam)* cheap wine, plonk (Brit)

**piqûre** [pikyʀ] *nf (d'épingle)* prick; *(d'ortie)* sting; *(de moustique)* bite; *(Méd)* injection, shot (US); *(Couture)* (straight) stitch; straight stitching; *(de ver)* hole; *(tache)* (spot of) mildew; **faire une ~ à qn** to give sb an injection

**piranha** [piʀana] *nm* piranha

**piratage** [piʀataʒ] *nm (Inform)* piracy

**pirate** [piʀat] *adj* pirate *cpd* ▷ *nm* pirate; *(fig: escroc)* crook, shark; *(Inform)* hacker; **~ de l'air** hijacker

**pirater** [piʀate] *vi (Inform)* to hack ▷ *vt (Inform)* to hack into

**piraterie** [piʀatʀi] *nf* (act of) piracy; **~ aérienne** hijacking

**pire** [piʀ] *adj (comparatif)* worse; *(superlatif)*: **le (la) ~ ...** the worst ... ▷ *nm*: **le ~ (de)** the worst (of)

**Pirée** [piʀe] *n* Piraeus

**pirogue** [piʀɔg] *nf* dugout (canoe)

**pirouette** [piʀwɛt] *nf* pirouette; *(fig: volte-face)* about-turn

**pis** [pi] *nm (de vache)* udder; *(pire)*: **le ~** the worst

▷ *adj, adv* worse; **qui ~ est** what is worse; **au ~ aller** if the worst comes to the worst, at worst

**pis-aller** [pizale] *nm inv* stopgap

**pisciculture** [pisikyltyʀ] *nf* fish farming

**piscine** [pisin] *nf* (swimming) pool; **~ couverte** indoor (swimming) pool

**Pise** [piz] *n* Pisa

**pissenlit** [pisɑ̃li] *nm* dandelion

**pisser** [pise] *vi (fam!)* to pee

**pissotière** [pisɔtjɛʀ] *nf (fam)* public urinal

**pistache** [pistaʃ] *nf* pistachio (nut)

**pistard** [pistaʀ] *nm (Cyclisme)* track cyclist

**piste** [pist(ə)] *nf (d'un animal, sentier)* track, trail; *(indice)* lead; *(de stade, de magnétophone: de cirque)* ring; *(de danse)* floor; *(de patinage)* rink; *(de ski)* run; *(Aviat)* runway; **~ cavalière** bridle path; **~ cyclable** cycle track, bikeway *(US)*; **~ sonore** sound track

**pister** [piste] *vt* to track, trail

**pisteur** [pistœʀ] *nm (Ski)* member of the ski patrol

**pistil** [pistil] *nm* pistil

**pistolet** [pistɔlɛ] *nm (arme)* pistol, gun; *(à peinture)* spray gun; **~ à bouchon/air comprimé** popgun/airgun; **~ à eau** water pistol

**pistolet-mitrailleur** [pistɔlɛmitʀajœʀ] *(pl* **pistolets-mitrailleurs)** *nm* submachine gun

**piston** [pistɔ̃] *nm (Tech)* piston; *(Mus)* valve; *(fig: appui)* string-pulling

**pistonner** [pistɔne] *vt (candidat)* to pull strings for

**pitance** [pitɑ̃s] *nf (péj)* (means of) sustenance

**piteusement** [pitøzmɑ̃] *adv (échouer)* miserably

**piteux, -euse** [pitø, -øz] *adj* pitiful, sorry *(avant le nom)*; **en ~ état** in a sorry state

**pitié** [pitje] *nf* pity; **sans ~** *adj* pitiless, merciless; **faire ~** to inspire pity; **il me fait ~** I pity him, I feel sorry for him; **avoir ~ de** *(compassion)* to pity, feel sorry for; *(merci)* to have pity *ou* mercy on; **par ~!** for pity's sake!

**piton** [pitɔ̃] *nm (clou)* peg, bolt; **~ rocheux** rocky outcrop

**pitoyable** [pitwajabl(ə)] *adj* pitiful

**pitre** [pitʀ(ə)] *nm* clown

**pitrerie** [pitʀəʀi] *nf* tomfoolery *no pl*

**pittoresque** [pitɔʀɛsk(ə)] *adj* picturesque; *(expression, détail)* colourful *(Brit)*, colorful *(US)*

**pivert** [pivɛʀ] *nm* green woodpecker

**pivoine** [pivwan] *nf* peony

**pivot** [pivo] *nm* pivot; *(d'une dent)* post

**pivoter** [pivɔte] *vi (fauteuil)* to swivel; *(porte)* to revolve; **~ sur ses talons** to swing round

**pixel** [piksɛl] *nm* pixel

**pizza** [pidza] *nf* pizza

**PJ** *sigle f* = **police judiciaire** ▷ *sigle fpl* (= *pièces jointes)* encl

**PL** *sigle m (Auto)* = **poids lourd**

**Pl.** *abr* = **place**

**placage** [plakaʒ] *nm (bois)* veneer

**placard** [plakaʀ] *nm (armoire)* cupboard; *(affiche)* poster, notice; *(Typo)* galley; **~ publicitaire** display advertisement

**placarder** [plakaʀde] *vt (affiche)* to put up; *(mur)* to stick posters on

**place** [plas] *nf (emplacement, situation, classement)* place; *(de ville, village)* square; *(Écon)*: **~ financière/boursière** money/stock market; *(espace libre)* room, space; *(de parking)* space; *(siège: de train, cinéma, voiture)* seat; *(prix: au cinéma etc)* price; (: *dans un bus, taxi)* fare; *(emploi)* job; **en ~** *(mettre)* in its place; **de ~ en ~, par ~s** here and there, in places; **sur ~** on the spot; **faire ~ à** to give way to; **faire de la ~ à** to make room for; **ça prend de la ~** it takes up a lot of room *ou* space; **prendre ~** to take one's place; **remettre qn à sa ~** to put sb in his *(ou* her) place; **ne pas rester** *ou* **tenir en ~** to be always on the go; **à la ~ de** in place of, instead of; **une quatre ~s** *(Auto)* a four-seater; **il y a 20 ~s assises/debout** there are 20 seats/there is standing room for 20; **~ forte** fortified town; **~ d'honneur** place *(ou* seat) of honour *(Brit)* ou honor *(US)*

**placé, e** [plase] *adj (Hippisme)* placed; **haut ~** *(fig)* high-ranking; **être bien/mal ~** to be well/ badly placed; *(spectateur)* to have a good/bad seat; **être bien/mal ~ pour faire** to be in/not to be in a position to do

**placebo** [plasebo] *nm* placebo

**placement** [plasmɑ̃] *nm* placing; *(Finance)* investment; **agence** *ou* **bureau de ~** employment agency

**placenta** [plasɑ̃ta] *nm* placenta

**placer** [plase] *vt* to place, put; *(convive, spectateur)* to seat; *(capital, argent)* to place, invest; *(dans la conversation)* to put *ou* get in; **~ qn chez** to get sb a job at *(ou* with); **se ~ au premier rang** to go and stand *(ou* sit) in the first row

**placide** [plasid] *adj* placid

**placidité** [plasidite] *nf* placidity

**placier, -ière** [plasje, -jɛʀ] *nm/f* commercial rep(resentative), salesman/woman

**Placoplâtre®** [plakoplatʀ] *nm* plasterboard

**plafond** [plafɔ̃] *nm* ceiling

**plafonner** [plafɔne] *vt (pièce)* to put a ceiling (up) in ▷ *vi* to reach one's *(ou* a) ceiling

**plafonnier** [plafɔnje] *nm* ceiling light; *(Auto)* interior light

**plage** [plaʒ] *nf* beach; *(station)* (seaside) resort; *(fig)* band, bracket; *(de disque)* track, band; **~ arrière** *(Auto)* parcel *ou* back shelf

**plagiaire** [plaʒjɛʀ] *nm/f* plagiarist

**plagiat** [plaʒja] *nm* plagiarism

**plagier** [plaʒje] *vt* to plagiarize

**plagiste** [plaʒist(ə)] *nm/f* beach attendant

**plaid** [plɛd] *nm (tartan)* car rug, lap robe *(US)*

**plaidant, e** [plɛdɑ̃, -ɑ̃t] *adj* litigant

**plaider** [plede] *vi (avocat)* to plead; *(plaignant)* to go to court, litigate ▷ *vt* to plead; **~ pour** *(fig)* to speak for

**plaideur, -euse** [plɛdœʀ, -øz] *nm/f* litigant

**plaidoirie** [pledwaʀi] *nf (Jur)* speech for the defence *(Brit)* ou defense *(US)*

**plaidoyer** [pledwaje] *nm (Jur)* speech for the defence *(Brit)* ou defense *(US)*; *(fig)* plea

**plaie** [plɛ] *nf* wound
**plaignant, e** [plɛɲɑ̃, -ɑ̃t] *vb voir* **plaindre** ▷ *nm/f* plaintiff
**plaindre** [plɛ̃dʀ(ə)] *vt* to pity, feel sorry for; **se plaindre** *vi* (*gémir*) to moan; (*protester, rouspéter*): **se ~ (à qn) (de)** to complain (to sb) (about); (*souffrir*): **se ~ de** to complain of
**plaine** [plɛn] *nf* plain
**plain-pied** [plɛ̃pje]: **de ~** *adv* at street-level; (*fig*) straight; **de ~ (avec)** on the same level (as)
**plaint, e** [plɛ̃, -ɛ̃t] *pp de* **plaindre** ▷ *nf* (*gémissement*) moan, groan; (*doléance*) complaint; **porter ~e** to lodge a complaint
**plaintif, -ive** [plɛ̃tif, -iv] *adj* plaintive
**plaire** [plɛʀ] *vi* to be a success, be successful; to please; **~ à: cela me plaît** I like it; **essayer de ~ à qn** (*en étant serviable etc*) to try and please sb; **elle plaît aux hommes** she's a success with men, men like her; **se ~ quelque part** to like being somewhere, like it somewhere; **se ~ à faire** to take pleasure in doing; **ce qu'il vous plaira** what(ever) you like *ou* wish; **s'il vous/te plaît** please
**plaisamment** [plɛzamɑ̃] *adv* pleasantly
**plaisance** [plɛzɑ̃s] *nf* (*aussi*: **navigation de plaisance**) (pleasure) sailing, yachting
**plaisancier** [plɛzɑ̃sje] *nm* amateur sailor, yachting enthusiast
**plaisant, e** [plɛzɑ̃, -ɑ̃t] *adj* pleasant; (*histoire, anecdote*) amusing
**plaisanter** [plɛzɑ̃te] *vi* to joke ▷ *vt* (*personne*) to tease, make fun of; **pour ~** for a joke; **on ne plaisante pas avec cela** that's no joking matter; **tu plaisantes!** you're joking *ou* kidding!
**plaisanterie** [plɛzɑ̃tʀi] *nf* joke; joking *no pl*
**plaisantin** [plɛzɑ̃tɛ̃] *nm* joker; (*fumiste*) fly-by-night
**plaise** *etc* [plɛz] *vb voir* **plaire**
**plaisir** [pleziʀ] *nm* pleasure; **faire ~ à qn** (*délibérément*) to be nice to sb, please sb; (*cadeau, nouvelle etc*): **ceci me fait ~** I'm delighted *ou* very pleased with this; **prendre ~ à/à faire** to take pleasure in/in doing; **j'ai le ~ de ...** it is with great pleasure that I ...; **M. et Mme X ont le ~ de vous faire part de ...** M. and Mme X are pleased to announce ...; **se faire un ~ de faire qch** to be (only too) pleased to do sth; **faites-moi le ~ de ...** would you mind ..., would you be kind enough to ...; **à ~** freely; for the sake of it; **au ~ (de vous revoir)** (I hope to) see you again; **pour le** *ou* **pour son** *ou* **par ~** for pleasure
**plaît** [plɛ] *vb voir* **plaire**
**plan, e** [plɑ̃, -an] *adj* flat ▷ *nm* plan; (*Géom*) plane; (*fig*) level, plane; (*Ciné*) shot; **au premier/second ~** in the foreground/middle distance; **à l'arrière ~** in the background; **mettre qch au premier ~** (*fig*) to consider sth to be of primary importance; **sur le ~ sexuel** sexually, as far as sex is concerned; **laisser/rester en ~** to abandon/be abandoned; **~ d'action** plan of action; **~ directeur** (*Écon*)

master plan; **~ d'eau** lake; pond; **~ de travail** work-top, work surface; **~ de vol** (*Aviat*) flight plan
**planche** [plɑ̃ʃ] *nf* (*pièce de bois*) plank, (wooden) board; (*illustration*) plate; (*de salades, radis, poireaux*) bed; (*d'un plongeoir*) (diving) board; **les ~s** (*Théât*) the boards; **en ~s** *adj* wooden; **faire la ~** (*dans l'eau*) to float on one's back; **avoir du pain sur la ~** to have one's work cut out; **~ à découper** chopping board; **~ à dessin** drawing board; **~ à pain** breadboard; **~ à repasser** ironing board; **~ (à roulettes)** (*planche*) skateboard; (*sport*) skateboarding; **~ de salut** (*fig*) sheet anchor; **~ à voile** (*planche*) windsurfer, sailboard; (*sport*) windsurfing
**plancher** [plɑ̃ʃe] *nm* floor; (*planches*) floorboards *pl*; (*fig*) minimum level ▷ *vi* to work hard
**planchiste** [plɑ̃ʃist(ə)] *nm/f* windsurfer
**plancton** [plɑ̃ktɔ̃] *nm* plankton
**planer** [plane] *vi* (*oiseau, avion*) to glide; (*fumée, vapeur*) to float, hover; (*drogué*) to be (on a) high; **~ sur** (*fig*) to hang over; to hover above
**planétaire** [planetɛʀ] *adj* planetary
**planétarium** [planetaʀjɔm] *nm* planetarium
**planète** [planɛt] *nf* planet
**planeur** [planœʀ] *nm* glider
**planification** [planifikasjɔ̃] *nf* (economic) planning
**planifier** [planifje] *vt* to plan
**planisphère** [planisfɛʀ] *nm* planisphere
**planning** [planiŋ] *nm* programme (*Brit*), program (*US*), schedule; **~ familial** family planning
**planque** [plɑ̃k] *nf* (*fam: combine, filon*) cushy (*Brit*) *ou* easy number; (: *cachette*) hideout
**planquer** [plɑ̃ke] *vt* (*fam*) to hide (away), stash away; **se planquer** to hide
**plant** [plɑ̃] *nm* seedling, young plant
**plantage** [plɑ̃taʒ] *nm* (*d'ordinateur*) crash
**plantaire** [plɑ̃tɛʀ] *adj voir* **voûte**
**plantation** [plɑ̃tasjɔ̃] *nf* planting; (*de fleurs, légumes*) bed; (*exploitation*) plantation
**plante** [plɑ̃t] *nf* plant; **~ d'appartement** house *ou* pot plant; **~ du pied** sole (of the foot); **~ verte** house plant
**planter** [plɑ̃te] *vt* (*plante*) to plant; (*enfoncer*) to hammer *ou* drive in; (*tente*) to put up, pitch; (*drapeau, échelle, décors*) to put up; (*fam: mettre*) to dump; (: *abandonner*): **~ là** to ditch; **se planter** *vi* (*fam: se tromper*) to get it wrong; (*ordinateur*) to crash; **~ qch dans** to hammer *ou* drive sth into; to stick sth into; **se ~ dans** to sink into; to get stuck in; **se ~ devant** to plant o.s. in front of
**planteur** [plɑ̃tœʀ] *nm* planter
**planton** [plɑ̃tɔ̃] *nm* orderly
**plantureux, -euse** [plɑ̃tyʀø, -øz] *adj* (*repas*) copious, lavish; (*femme*) buxom
**plaquage** [plakaʒ] *nm* (*Rugby*) tackle
**plaque** [plak] *nf* plate; (*de verre*) sheet; (*de verglas, d'eczéma*) patch; (*dentaire*) plaque; (*avec inscription*) plaque; **~ (minéralogique** *ou* **de police** *ou* **d'immatriculation)** number (*Brit*) *ou* license

**p**

(US) plate; **~ de beurre** slab of butter; **~ chauffante** hotplate; **~ de chocolat** bar of chocolate; **~ de cuisson** hob; **~ d'identité** identity disc; **~ tournante** (*fig*) centre (*Brit*), center (*US*)

**plaqué, e** [plake] *adj*: **~ or/argent** gold-/silver-plated ▷ *nm*: **~ or/argent** gold/silver plate; **~ acajou** with a mahogany veneer

**plaquer** [plake] *vt* (*bijou*) to plate; (*bois*) to veneer; (*aplatir*): **~ qch sur/contre** to make sth stick *ou* cling to; (*Rugby*) to bring down; (*fam*: *laisser tomber*) to drop, ditch; **se ~ contre** to flatten o.s. against; **~ qn contre** to pin sb to

**plaquette** [plakɛt] *nf* tablet; (*de chocolat*) bar; (*de beurre*) slab, packet; (*livre*) small volume; (*Méd*: *de pilules, gélules*) pack, packet; **~ de frein** (*Auto*) brake pad

**plasma** [plasma] *nm* plasma

**plastic** [plastik] *nm* plastic explosive

**plastifié, e** [plastifje] *adj* plastic-coated

**plastifier** [plastifje] *vt* (*document, photo*) to laminate

**plastiquage** [plastikaʒ] *nm* bombing, bomb attack

**plastique** [plastik] *adj* plastic ▷ *nm* plastic ▷ *nf* plastic arts *pl*; (*d'une statue*) modelling

**plastiquer** [plastike] *vt* to blow up

**plastiqueur** [plastikœʀ] *nm* terrorist (*planting a plastic bomb*)

**plastron** [plastʀɔ̃] *nm* shirt front

**plastronner** [plastʀɔne] *vi* to swagger

**plat, e** [pla, -at] *adj* flat; (*fade*: *vin*) flat-tasting, insipid; (*personne, livre*) dull ▷ *nm* (*récipient, Culin*) dish; (*d'un repas*): **le premier ~** the first course; (*partie plate*): **le ~ de la main** the flat of the hand; (: *d'une route*) flat (part); **à ~ ventre** *adv* face down; (*tomber*) flat on one's face; **à ~** *adj* (*pneu, batterie*) flat; (*fam*: *fatigué*) dead beat, tired out; **~ cuisiné** pre-cooked meal (*ou* dish); **~ du jour** dish of the day; **~ principal** *ou* **de résistance** main course; **~s préparés** convenience food(s)

**platane** [platan] *nm* plane tree

**plateau, x** [plato] *nm* (*support*) tray; (*d'une table*) top; (*d'une balance*) pan; (*Géo*) plateau; (*de tourne-disques*) turntable; (*Ciné*) set; (*TV*): **nous avons deux journalistes sur le ~ ce soir** we have two journalists with us tonight; **~ à fromages** cheeseboard

**plateau-repas** [platoʀəpa] (*pl* **plateaux-repas**) *nm* tray meal, TV dinner (*US*)

**plate-bande** [platbɑ̃d] (*pl* **plates-bandes**) *nf* flower bed

**platée** [plate] *nf* dish(ful)

**plate-forme** [platfɔʀm(ə)] (*pl* **plates-formes**) *nf* platform; **~ de forage/pétrolière** drilling/oil rig

**platine** [platin] *nm* platinum ▷ *nf* (*d'un tourne-disque*) turntable; **~ disque/cassette** record/cassette deck; **~ laser** *ou* **compact-disc** compact disc (player)

**platitude** [platityd] *nf* platitude

**platonique** [platɔnik] *adj* platonic

**plâtras** [platʀa] *nm* rubble *no pl*

**plâtre** [platʀ(ə)] *nm* (*matériau*) plaster; (*statue*) plaster statue; (*Méd*) (plaster) cast; **plâtres** *nmpl* plasterwork *sg*; **avoir un bras dans le ~** to have an arm in plaster

**plâtrer** [platʀe] *vt* to plaster; (*Méd*) to set *ou* put in a (plaster) cast

**plâtrier** [platʀije] *nm* plasterer

**plausible** [plozibl(ə)] *adj* plausible

**play-back** [plɛbak] *nm* miming

**play-boy** [plɛbɔj] *nm* playboy

**plébiscite** [plebisit] *nm* plebiscite

**plébisciter** [plebisite] *vt* (*approuver*) to give overwhelming support to; (*élire*) to elect by an overwhelming majority

**plectre** [plɛktʀ(ə)] *nm* plectrum

**plein, e** [plɛ̃, -ɛn] *adj* full; (*porte, roue*) solid; (*chienne, jument*) big (with young) ▷ *nm*: **faire le ~ (d'essence)** to fill up (with petrol (*Brit*) *ou* gas (*US*)) ▷ *prép*: **avoir de l'argent ~ les poches** to have loads of money; **~ de** full of; **avoir les mains ~es** to have one's hands full; **à ~es mains** (*ramasser*) in handfuls; (*empoigner*) firmly; **à ~ régime** at maximum revs; (*fig*) at full speed; **à ~ temps** full-time; **en ~ air** in the open air; **jeux en ~ air** outdoor games; **en ~ mer** on the open sea; **en ~ soleil** in direct sunlight; **en ~e nuit/rue** in the middle of the night/street; **en ~ milieu** right in the middle; **en ~ jour** in broad daylight; **les ~s** the downstrokes (*in handwriting*); **faire le ~ des voix** to get the maximum number of votes possible; **en ~ sur** right on; **en avoir ~ le dos** (*fam*) to have had it up to here

**pleinement** [plɛnmɑ̃] *adv* fully; to the full

**plein-emploi** [plɛnɑ̃plwa] *nm* full employment

**plénière** [plenjɛʀ] *adj f*: **assemblée ~** plenary assembly

**plénipotentiaire** [plenipɔtɑ̃sjɛʀ] *nm* plenipotentiary

**plénitude** [plenityd] *nf* fullness

**pléthore** [pletɔʀ] *nf*: **~ de** overabundance *ou* plethora of

**pléthorique** [pletɔʀik] *adj* (*classes*) overcrowded; (*documentation*) excessive

**pleurer** [plœʀe] *vi* to cry; (*yeux*) to water ▷ *vt* to mourn (for); **~ sur** *vt* to lament (over), bemoan; **~ de rire** to laugh till one cries

**pleurésie** [plœʀezi] *nf* pleurisy

**pleureuse** [plœʀøz] *nf* professional mourner

**pleurnicher** [plœʀniʃe] *vi* to snivel, whine

**pleurs** [plœʀ] *nmpl*: **en ~** in tears

**pleut** [plø] *vb voir* **pleuvoir**

**pleutre** [pløtʀ(ə)] *adj* cowardly

**pleuvait** *etc* [pløvɛ] *vb voir* **pleuvoir**

**pleuviner** [pløvine] *vb impers* to drizzle

**pleuvoir** [pløvwaʀ] *vb impers* to rain ▷ *vi* (*fig*): **~ (sur)** to shower down (upon), be showered upon; **il pleut** it's raining; **il pleut des cordes** *ou* **à verse** *ou* **à torrents** it's pouring (down), it's raining cats and dogs

**pleuvra** etc [pløvʀa] vb voir **pleuvoir**

**plexiglas**® [plɛksiglɑs] nm Plexiglas® (US)

**pli** [pli] nm fold; (de jupe) pleat; (de pantalon) crease; (aussi: **faux pli**) crease; (enveloppe) envelope; (lettre) letter; (Cartes) trick; **prendre le ~ de faire** to get into the habit of doing; **ça ne fait pas un ~!** don't you worry!; ~ **d'aisance** inverted pleat

**pliable** [plijabl(ə)] adj pliable, flexible

**pliage** [plijaʒ] nm folding; (Art) origami

**pliant, e** [plijɑ̃, -ɑ̃t] adj folding ▷ nm folding stool, campstool

**plier** [plije] vt to fold; (pour ranger) to fold up; (table pliante) to fold down; (genou, bras) to bend ▷ vi to bend; (fig) to yield; **se ~ à** to submit to; ~ **bagages** (fig) to pack up (and go)

**plinthe** [plɛ̃t] nf skirting board

**plissé, e** [plise] adj (jupe, robe) pleated; (peau) wrinkled; (Géo) folded ▷ nm (Couture) pleats pl

**plissement** [plismɑ̃] nm (Géo) fold

**plisser** [plise] vt (chiffonner: papier, étoffe) to crease; (rider: front) to furrow, wrinkle; (: bouche) to pucker; (jupe) to put pleats in; **se plisser** vi (vêtement, étoffe) to crease

**pliure** [plijyʀ] nf (du bras, genou) bend; (d'un ourlet) fold

**plomb** [plɔ̃] nm (métal) lead; (d'une cartouche) (lead) shot; (Pêche) sinker; (sceau) (lead) seal; (Élec) fuse; **de ~** (soleil) blazing; **sans ~** (essence) unleaded; **sommeil de ~** heavy ou very deep sleep; **mettre à ~** to plumb

**plombage** [plɔ̃baʒ] nm (de dent) filling

**plomber** [plɔ̃be] vt (canne, ligne) to weight (with lead); (colis, wagon) to put a lead seal on; (Tech: mur) to plumb; (dent) to fill (Brit), stop (US); (Inform) to protect

**plomberie** [plɔ̃bʀi] nf plumbing

**plombier** [plɔ̃bje] nm plumber

**plonge** [plɔ̃ʒ] nf: **faire la ~** to be a washer-up (Brit) ou dishwasher (person)

**plongeant, e** [plɔ̃ʒɑ̃, -ɑ̃t] adj (vue) from above; (tir, décolleté) plunging

**plongée** [plɔ̃ʒe] nf (Sport) diving no pl; (: sans scaphandre) skin diving; (de sous-marin) submersion, dive; **en ~** (sous-marin) submerged; (prise de vue) high angle

**plongeoir** [plɔ̃ʒwaʀ] nm diving board

**plongeon** [plɔ̃ʒɔ̃] nm dive

**plonger** [plɔ̃ʒe] vi to dive ▷ vt: ~ **qch dans** to plunge sth into; ~ **dans un sommeil profond** to sink straight into a deep sleep; ~ **qn dans l'embarras** to throw sb into a state of confusion

**plongeur, -euse** [plɔ̃ʒœʀ, -øz] nm/f diver; (de café) washer-up (Brit), dishwasher (person)

**plot** [plo] nm (Élec) contact

**ploutocratie** [plutɔkʀasi] nf plutocracy

**ploutocratique** [plutɔkʀatik] adj plutocratic

**ployer** [plwaje] vt to bend ▷ vi to bend; (plancher) to sag

**plu** [ply] pp de **plaire**; **pleuvoir**

**pluie** [plɥi] nf rain; (averse, ondée) **une ~ brève** a shower; (fig): ~ **de** shower of; **une ~ fine** fine rain; **retomber en ~** to shower down; **sous la ~** in the rain

**plumage** [plymaʒ] nm plumage no pl, feathers pl

**plume** [plym] nf feather; (pour écrire) (pen) nib; (fig) pen; **dessin à la ~** pen and ink drawing

**plumeau, x** [plymo] nm feather duster

**plumer** [plyme] vt to pluck

**plumet** [plymɛ] nm plume

**plumier** [plymje] nm pencil box

**plupart** [plypaʀ]: **la ~** pron the majority, most (of them); **la ~ des** most, the majority of; **la ~ du temps/d'entre nous** most of the time/of us; **pour la ~** adv for the most part, mostly

**pluralisme** [plyʀalism(ə)] nm pluralism

**pluralité** [plyʀalite] nf plurality

**pluridisciplinaire** [plyʀidisiplinɛʀ] adj multidisciplinary

**pluriel** [plyʀjɛl] nm plural; **au ~** in the plural

**plus¹** [ply] vb voir **plaire**

 **MOT-CLÉ**

**plus²** [ply] adv **1** (forme négative): **ne ... plus** no more, no longer; **je n'ai plus d'argent** I've got no more money ou no money left; **il ne travaille plus** he's no longer working, he doesn't work any more

**2** [ply, plyz] (+voyelle: comparatif) more, ...+er; (superlatif): **le plus** the most, the ...+est; **plus grand/intelligent (que)** bigger/more intelligent (than); **le plus grand/intelligent** the biggest/most intelligent; **tout au plus** at the very most

**3** [plys] (davantage) more; **il travaille plus (que)** he works more (than); **plus il travaille, plus il est heureux** the more he works, the happier he is; **plus de pain** more bread; **plus de 10 personnes/trois heures/quatre kilos** more than ou over 10 people/three hours/four kilos; **trois heures de plus que** three hours more than; **plus de minuit** after ou past midnight; **de plus** what's more, moreover; **il a trois ans de plus que moi** he's three years older than me; **trois kilos en plus** three kilos more; **en plus de** in addition to; **de plus en plus** more and more; **en plus de cela ...** what is more ...; **plus ou moins** more or less; **ni plus ni moins** no more, no less; **sans plus** (but) no more than that, (but) that's all; **qui plus est** what is more ▷ prép [plys]: **quatre plus deux** four plus two

**plusieurs** [plyzjœʀ] adj, pron several; **ils sont ~** there are several of them

**plus-que-parfait** [plyskəpaʀfɛ] nm pluperfect, past perfect

**plus-value** [plyvaly] nf (d'un bien) appreciation; (bénéfice) capital gain; (budgétaire) surplus

**plut** [ply] vb voir **plaire**; **pleuvoir**

**plutonium** [plytɔnjɔm] nm plutonium

**plutôt** [plyto] adv rather; **je ferais ~ ceci** I'd rather ou sooner do this; **fais ~ comme ça** try

**P**

317

this way instead; ~ **que (de) faire** rather than *ou* instead of doing

**pluvial, e, -aux** [plyvjal, -o] *adj (eaux)* rain *cpd*

**pluvieux, -euse** [plyvjø, -øz] *adj* rainy, wet

**pluviosité** [plyvjɔzite] *nf* rainfall

**PM** *sigle f* = **Police militaire**

**p.m.** *abr (= pour mémoire)* for the record

**PME** *sigle fpl* = **petites et moyennes entreprises**

**PMI** *sigle fpl* = **petites et moyennes industries**
  ▷ *sigle f* = **protection maternelle et infantile**

**PMU** *sigle m* = **pari mutuel urbain**; *(café)* betting agency; *see note*

⬤ **PMU**
⬤
⬤ The PMU ("pari mutuel urbain") is a
⬤ Government-regulated network of betting
⬤ counters run from bars displaying the PMU
⬤ sign. Punters buy fixed-price tickets
⬤ predicting winners or finishing positions in
⬤ horse races. The traditional bet is the
⬤ "tiercé", a triple bet, although other
⬤ multiple bets ("quarté" and so on) are
⬤ becoming increasingly popular.

**PNB** *sigle m (= produit national brut)* GNP

**pneu** [pnø] *nm (de roue)* tyre (Brit), tire (US); *(message)* letter sent by pneumatic tube

**pneumatique** [pnømatik] *adj* pneumatic; *(gonflable)* inflatable ▷ *nm* tyre (Brit), tire (US)

**pneumonie** [pnømɔni] *nf* pneumonia

**PO** *sigle fpl (= petites ondes)* MW

**po** [po] *abr voir* **science**

**p.o.** *abr (= par ordre)* p.p. *(on letters etc)*

**Pô** [po] *nm:* **le Pô** the Po

**poche** [pɔʃ] *nf* pocket; *(déformation):* **faire une/des ~(s)** to bag; *(sous les yeux)* bag, pouch; *(Zool)* pouch ▷ *nm (livre de poche)* (pocket-size) paperback; **de ~** pocket *cpd;* **en être de sa ~** to be out of pocket; **c'est dans la ~** it's in the bag

**poché, e** [pɔʃe] *adj:* **œuf ~** poached egg; **œil ~** black eye

**pocher** [pɔʃe] *vt (Culin)* to poach; *(Art)* to sketch ▷ *vi (vêtement)* to bag

**poche-revolver** [pɔʃʀəvɔlvɛʀ] *(pl* **poches-revolver)** *nf* hip pocket

**pochette** [pɔʃɛt] *nf (de timbres)* wallet, envelope; *(d'aiguilles etc)* case; *(sac: de femme)* clutch bag, purse; *(: d'homme)* bag; *(sur veston)* breast pocket; *(mouchoir)* breast pocket handkerchief; **~ d'allumettes** book of matches; **~ de disque** record sleeve; **~ surprise** lucky bag

**pochoir** [pɔʃwaʀ] *nm (Art: cache)* stencil; *(: tampon)* transfer

**podcast** [pɔdkast] *nm (Inform)* podcast

**podcaster** [pɔdkaste] *vi (Inform)* to podcast

**podium** [pɔdjɔm] *nm* podium

**poêle** [pwɑl] *nm* stove ▷ *nf:* **~ (à frire)** frying pan

**poêlon** [pwɑlɔ̃] *nm* casserole

**poème** [pɔɛm] *nm* poem

**poésie** [pɔezi] *nf (poème)* poem; *(art):* **la ~** poetry

**poète** [pɔɛt] *nm* poet; *(fig)* dreamer ▷ *adj* poetic

**poétique** [pɔetik] *adj* poetic

**pognon** [pɔɲɔ̃] *nm (fam: argent)* dough

**poids** [pwa] *nm* weight; *(Sport)* shot; **vendre au ~** to sell by weight; **de ~** *adj (argument etc)* weighty; **prendre du ~** to put on weight; **faire le ~** *(fig)* to measure up; **~ plume/mouche/coq/moyen** *(Boxe)* feather/fly/bantam/middleweight; **~ et haltères** weight lifting *sg;* **~ lourd** *(Boxe)* heavyweight; *(camion: aussi:* **PL)** (big) lorry (Brit), truck (US); *(: Admin)* large goods vehicle (Brit), truck (US); **~ mort** dead weight; **~ utile** net weight

**poignant, e** [pwaɲɑ̃, -ɑ̃t] *adj* poignant, harrowing

**poignard** [pwaɲaʀ] *nm* dagger

**poignarder** [pwaɲaʀde] *vt* to stab, knife

**poigne** [pwaɲ] *nf* grip; *(fig)* firm-handedness; **à ~** firm-handed

**poignée** [pwaɲe] *nf (de sel etc, fig)* handful; *(de couvercle, porte)* handle; **~ de main** handshake

**poignet** [pwaɲɛ] *nm (Anat)* wrist; *(de chemise)* cuff

**poil** [pwal] *nm (Anat)* hair; *(de pinceau, brosse)* bristle; *(de tapis, tissu)* strand; *(pelage)* coat; *(ensemble des poils):* **avoir du ~ sur la poitrine** to have hair(s) on one's chest, have a hairy chest; **à ~** *adj (fam)* starkers; **au ~** *adj (fam)* hunky-dory; **de tout ~** of all kinds; **être de bon/mauvais ~** to be in a good/bad mood; **~ à gratter** itching powder

**poilu, e** [pwaly] *adj* hairy

**poinçon** [pwɛ̃sɔ̃] *nm* awl; bodkin; *(marque)* hallmark

**poinçonner** [pwɛ̃sɔne] *vt (marchandise)* to stamp; *(bijou etc)* to hallmark; *(billet, ticket)* to clip, punch

**poinçonneuse** [pwɛ̃sɔnøz] *nf (outil)* punch

**poindre** [pwɛ̃dʀ(ə)] *vi (fleur)* to come up; *(aube)* to break; *(jour)* to dawn

**poing** [pwɛ̃] *nm* fist; **dormir à ~s fermés** to sleep soundly

**point** [pwɛ̃] *vb voir* **poindre** ▷ *nm (marque, signe)* dot; *(: de ponctuation)* full stop, period (US); *(moment, de score etc, fig: question)* point; *(endroit)* spot; *(Couture, Tricot)* stitch ▷ *adv* = **pas; ne ... ~** not (at all); **faire le ~** *(Navig)* to take a bearing; *(fig)* to take stock (of the situation); **faire le ~ sur** to review; **en tout ~** in every respect; **sur le ~ de faire** (just) about to do; **au ~ que, à tel ~ que** so much so that; **mettre au ~** *(mécanisme, procédé)* to develop; *(appareil photo)* to focus; *(affaire)* to settle; **à ~** *(Culin)* just right; *(: viande)* medium; **à ~ (nommé)** just at the right time; **~ de croix/tige/chaînette** *(Couture)* cross/stem/chain stitch; **~ mousse/jersey** *(Tricot)* garter/stocking stitch; **~ de départ/d'arrivée/d'arrêt** departure/arrival/stopping point; **~ chaud** *(Mil, Pol)* hot spot; **~ de chute** landing place; *(fig)* stopping-off point; **~ (de côté)** stitch *(pain);* **~ culminant** summit; *(fig)* height, climax; **~ d'eau** spring, water point; **~ d'exclamation**

exclamation mark; ~ **faible** weak spot; ~ **final** full stop, period (US); ~ **d'interrogation** question mark; ~ **mort** (Finance) break-even point; **au** ~ **mort** (Auto) in neutral; (affaire, entreprise) at a standstill; ~ **noir** (sur le visage) blackhead; (Auto) accident black spot; ~ **de non-retour** point of no return; ~ **de repère** landmark; (dans le temps) point of reference; ~ **de vente** retail outlet; ~ **de vue** viewpoint; (fig: opinion) point of view; **du** ~ **de vue de** from the point of view of; ~**s cardinaux** points of the compass, cardinal points; ~**s de suspension** suspension points

**pointage** [pwɛtaʒ] nm ticking off; checking in

**pointe** [pwɛt] nf point; (de la côte) headland; (allusion) dig; sally; (fig): **une** ~ **d'ail/d'accent** a touch ou hint of garlic/of an accent; **pointes** nfpl (Danse) points, point shoes; **être à la** ~ **de** (fig) to be in the forefront of; **faire** ou **pousser une** ~ **jusqu'à ...** to press on as far as ...; **sur la** ~ **des pieds** on tiptoe; **en** ~ adv (tailler) into a point ▷ adj pointed, tapered; **de** ~ adj (technique etc) leading; (vitesse) maximum, top; **heures/jours de** ~ peak hours/days; **faire du 180 en** ~ (Auto) to have a top ou maximum speed of 180; **faire des** ~**s** (Danse) to dance on points; ~ **d'asperge** asparagus tip; ~ **de courant** surge (of current); ~ **de vitesse** burst of speed

**pointer** [pwɛte] vt (cocher) to tick off; (employés etc) to check in; (diriger: canon, longue-vue, doigt): ~ **vers qch** to point at sth; (Mus: note) to dot ▷ vi (employé) to clock in ou on; (pousses) to come through; (jour) to break; ~ **les oreilles** (chien) to prick up its ears

**pointeur, -euse** [pwɛtœʀ, -øz] nm/f time-keeper ▷ nf timeclock ▷ nm (Inform) cursor

**pointillé** [pwɛtije] nm (trait) dotted line; (Art) stippling no pl

**pointilleux, -euse** [pwɛtijø, -øz] adj particular, pernickety

**pointu, e** [pwɛty] adj pointed; (clou) sharp; (voix) shrill; (analyse) precise

**pointure** [pwɛtyʀ] nf size

**point-virgule** [pwɛviʀgyl] (pl **points-virgules**) nm semi-colon

**poire** [pwaʀ] nf pear; (fam: péj) mug; ~ **électrique** (pear-shaped) switch; ~ **à injections** syringe

**poireau, x** [pwaʀo] nm leek

**poireauter** [pwaʀote] vi (fam) to hang about (waiting)

**poirier** [pwaʀje] nm pear tree; (Sport): **faire le** ~ to do a headstand

**pois** [pwa] nm (Bot) pea; (sur une étoffe) dot, spot; **à** ~ (cravate etc) spotted, polka-dot cpd; ~ **chiche** chickpea; ~ **de senteur** sweet pea; ~ **cassés** split peas

**poison** [pwazɔ̃] nm poison

**poisse** [pwas] nf rotten luck

**poisser** [pwase] vt to make sticky

**poisseux, -euse** [pwasø, -øz] adj sticky

**poisson** [pwasɔ̃] nm fish gen inv; **les P~s** (signe) Pisces, the Fish; **être des P~s** to be Pisces; **pêcher** ou **prendre du** ~ ou **des** ~**s** to fish; ~ **d'avril** April fool; (blague) April fool's day trick; see note; ~ **rouge** goldfish

● **POISSON D'AVRIL**

● The traditional April Fools' Day prank in
● France involves attaching a cut-out paper
● fish, known as a "poisson d'avril", to the
● back of one's victim, without being caught.

**poisson-chat** [pwasɔ̃ʃa] (pl **poissons-chats**) nm catfish

**poissonnerie** [pwasɔnʀi] nf fishmonger's (Brit), fish store (US)

**poissonneux, -euse** [pwasɔnø, -øz] adj abounding in fish

**poissonnier, -ière** [pwasɔnje, -jɛʀ] nm/f fishmonger (Brit), fish merchant (US) ▷ nf (ustensile) fish kettle

**poisson-scie** [pwasɔ̃si] (pl **poissons-scies**) nm sawfish

**poitevin, e** [pwatvɛ̃, -in] adj (région) of ou from Poitou; (ville) of ou from Poitiers

**poitrail** [pwatʀaj] nm (d'un cheval etc) breast

**poitrine** [pwatʀin] nf (Anat) chest; (seins) bust, bosom; (Culin) breast; ~ **de bœuf** brisket

**poivre** [pwavʀ(ə)] nm pepper; ~ **en grains/moulu** whole/ground pepper; ~ **de cayenne** cayenne (pepper); ~ **et sel** adj (cheveux) pepper-and-salt

**poivré, e** [pwavʀe] adj peppery

**poivrer** [pwavʀe] vt to pepper

**poivrier** [pwavʀije] nm (Bot) pepper plant

**poivrière** [pwavʀijɛʀ] nf pepperpot, pepper shaker (US)

**poivron** [pwavʀɔ̃] nm pepper, capsicum; ~ **vert/rouge** green/red pepper

**poix** [pwa] nf pitch (tar)

**poker** [pɔkɛʀ] nm: **le** ~ poker; **partie de** ~ (fig) gamble; ~ **d'as** four aces

**polaire** [pɔlɛʀ] adj polar

**polar** [pɔlaʀ] (fam) nm detective novel

**polarisation** [pɔlaʀizasjɔ̃] nf (Physique, Élec) polarization; (fig) focusing

**polariser** [pɔlaʀize] vt to polarize; (fig: attirer) to attract; (: réunir, concentrer) to focus; **être polarisé sur** (personne) to be completely bound up with ou absorbed by

**pôle** [pol] nm (Géo, Élec) pole; **le** ~ **Nord/Sud** the North/South Pole; ~ **d'attraction** (fig) centre of attraction

**polémique** [pɔlemik] adj controversial, polemic(al) ▷ nf controversy

**polémiquer** [pɔlemike] vi to be involved in controversy

**polémiste** [pɔlemist(ə)] nm/f polemist, polemicist

**poli, e** [pɔli] adj polite; (lisse) smooth; polished

**police** [pɔlis] nf police; (discipline): **assurer la** ~ **de** ou **dans** to keep order in; **peine de simple** ~

*sentence given by a magistrates' or police court*; ~
**(d'assurance)** (insurance) policy; ~ **(de
caractères)** (*Typo, Inform*) font, typeface; ~
**judiciaire (PJ)** ≈ Criminal Investigation
Department (CID) (*Brit*), ≈ Federal Bureau of
Investigation (FBI) (*US*); ~ **des mœurs** ≈ vice
squad; ~ **secours** ≈ emergency services *pl*

**polichinelle** [pɔliʃinɛl] *nm* Punch; (*péj*) buffoon;
**secret de ~** open secret

**policier, -ière** [pɔlisje, -jɛR] *adj* police *cpd* ▷ *nm*
policeman; (*aussi*: **roman policier**) detective
novel

**policlinique** [pɔliklinik] *nf* ≈ outpatients *sg*
(clinic)

**poliment** [pɔlimɑ̃] *adv* politely

**polio** [pɔljo] *nf* (*aussi*: **poliomyélite**) polio ▷ *nm/f*
(*aussi*: **poliomyélitique**) polio patient *ou* case

**poliomyélite** [pɔljɔmjelit] *nf* poliomyelitis

**poliomyélitique** [pɔljɔmjelitik] *nm/f* polio
patient *ou* case

**polir** [pɔliR] *vt* to polish

**polisson, ne** [pɔlisɔ̃, -ɔn] *adj* naughty

**politesse** [pɔlitɛs] *nf* politeness; **politesses** *nfpl*
(exchange of) courtesies; **rendre une ~ à qn** to
return sb's favour (*Brit*) *ou* favor (*US*)

**politicard** [pɔlitikaR] *nm* (*péj*) politico, political
schemer

**politicien, ne** [pɔlitisjɛ̃, -ɛn] *adj* political ▷ *nm/f*
politician

**politique** [pɔlitik] *adj* political ▷ *nf* (*science,
activité*) politics *sg*; (*principes, tactique*) policy,
policies *pl* ▷ *nm* (*politicien*) politician; ~
**étrangère/intérieure** foreign/domestic policy

**politique-fiction** [pɔlitikfiksjɔ̃] *nf* political
fiction

**politiquement** [pɔlitikmɑ̃] *adv* politically

**politisation** [pɔlitizasjɔ̃] *nf* politicization

**politiser** [pɔlitize] *vt* to politicize; ~ **qn** to make
sb politically aware

**pollen** [pɔlɛn] *nm* pollen

**polluant, e** [pɔlɥɑ̃, -ɑ̃t] *adj* polluting ▷ *nm*
polluting agent, pollutant

**polluer** [pɔlɥe] *vt* to pollute

**pollueur, -euse** [pɔlɥœR, -øz] *nm/f* polluter

**pollution** [pɔlysjɔ̃] *nf* pollution

**polo** [pɔlo] *nm* (*sport*) polo; (*tricot*) polo shirt

**Pologne** [pɔlɔɲ] *nf*: **la ~** Poland

**polonais, e** [pɔlɔnɛ, -ɛz] *adj* Polish ▷ *nm* (*Ling*)
Polish ▷ *nm/f*: **Polonais, e** Pole

**poltron, ne** [pɔltRɔ̃, -ɔn] *adj* cowardly

**poly...** [pɔli] *préfixe* poly...

**polyamide** [pɔliamid] *nf* polyamide

**polychrome** [pɔlikRom] *adj* polychrome,
polychromatic

**polyclinique** [pɔliklinik] *nf* (private) clinic
(*treating different illnesses*)

**polycopie** [pɔlikɔpi] *nf* (*procédé*) duplicating;
(*reproduction*) duplicated copy

**polycopié, e** [pɔlikɔpje] *adj* duplicated ▷ *nm*
handout, duplicated notes *pl*

**polycopier** [pɔlikɔpje] *vt* to duplicate

**polyculture** [pɔlikyltyR] *nf* mixed farming

**polyester** [pɔliɛstɛR] *nm* polyester

**polyéthylène** [pɔlietilɛn] *nm* polyethylene

**polygame** [pɔligam] *adj* polygamous

**polygamie** [pɔligami] *nf* polygamy

**polyglotte** [pɔliglɔt] *adj* polyglot

**polygone** [pɔligɔn] *nm* polygon

**Polynésie** [pɔlinezi] *nf*: **la ~** Polynesia; **la ~
française** French Polynesia

**polynésien, ne** [pɔlinezjɛ̃, -ɛn] *adj* Polynesian

**polynôme** [pɔlinom] *nm* polynomial

**polype** [pɔlip] *nm* polyp

**polystyrène** [pɔlistiRɛn] *nm* polystyrene

**polytechnicien, ne** [pɔlitɛknisjɛ̃, -ɛn] *nm/f*
student or former student of the École polytechnique

**Polytechnique** [pɔlitɛknik] *nf*: **(École) ~**
prestigious military academy producing high-ranking
officers and engineers

**polyvalent, e** [pɔlivalɑ̃, -ɑ̃t] *adj* (*vaccin*)
polyvalent; (*personne*) versatile; (*salle*) multi-
purpose ▷ *nm* ≈ tax inspector

**pomélo** [pɔmelo] *nm* pomelo, grapefruit

**pommade** [pɔmad] *nf* ointment, cream

**pomme** [pɔm] *nf* (*Bot*) apple; (*boule décorative*)
knob; (*pomme de terre*): **steak ~s (frites)** steak
and chips (*Brit*) *ou* (French) fries (*US*); **tomber
dans les ~s** (*fam*) to pass out; ~ **d'Adam** Adam's
apple; **~s allumettes** French fries (*thin-cut*); ~
**d'arrosoir** (sprinkler) rose; ~ **de pin** pine *ou* fir
cone; ~ **de terre** potato; **~s vapeur** boiled
potatoes

**pommé, e** [pɔme] *adj* (*chou etc*) firm

**pommeau, x** [pɔmo] *nm* (*boule*) knob; (*de selle*)
pommel

**pommelé, e** [pɔmle] *adj*: **gris ~** dapple grey

**pommette** [pɔmɛt] *nf* cheekbone

**pommier** [pɔmje] *nm* apple tree

**pompe** [pɔ̃p] *nf* pump; (*faste*) pomp (and
ceremony); ~ **à eau/essence** water/petrol
pump; ~ **à huile** oil pump; ~ **à incendie** fire
engine (*apparatus*); **~s funèbres** undertaker's *sg*,
funeral parlour *sg* (*Brit*), mortician's *sg* (*US*)

**Pompéi** [pɔ̃pei] *n* Pompeii

**pompéien, ne** [pɔ̃pejɛ̃, -ɛn] *adj* Pompeiian

**pomper** [pɔ̃pe] *vt* to pump; (*évacuer*) to pump
out; (*aspirer*) to pump up; (*absorber*) to soak up
▷ *vi* to pump

**pompeusement** [pɔ̃pøzmɑ̃] *adv* pompously

**pompeux, -euse** [pɔ̃pø, -øz] *adj* pompous

**pompier** [pɔ̃pje] *nm* fireman ▷ *adj m* (*style*)
pretentious, pompous

**pompiste** [pɔ̃pist(ə)] *nm/f* petrol (*Brit*) *ou* gas (*US*)
pump attendant

**pompon** [pɔ̃pɔ̃] *nm* pompom, bobble

**pomponner** [pɔ̃pɔne] *vt* to titivate (*Brit*),
dress up

**ponce** [pɔ̃s] *nf*: **pierre ~** pumice stone

**poncer** [pɔ̃se] *vt* to sand (down)

**ponceuse** [pɔ̃søz] *nf* sander

**poncif** [pɔ̃sif] *nm* cliché

**ponction** [pɔ̃ksjɔ̃] *nf* (*d'argent etc*) withdrawal;
~ **lombaire** lumbar puncture

**ponctualité** [pɔ̃ktɥalite] *nf* punctuality

**ponctuation** [pɔ̃ktɥasjɔ̃] *nf* punctuation
**ponctuel, le** [pɔ̃ktɥɛl] *adj* (*à l'heure, Tech*) punctual; (*fig: opération etc*) one-off, single; (*scrupuleux*) punctilious, meticulous
**ponctuellement** [pɔ̃ktɥɛlmɑ̃] *adv* punctually; punctiliously, meticulously
**ponctuer** [pɔ̃ktɥe] *vt* to punctuate; (*Mus*) to phrase
**pondéré, e** [pɔ̃deʀe] *adj* level-headed, composed
**pondérer** [pɔ̃deʀe] *vt* to balance
**pondeuse** [pɔ̃døz] *nf* layer, laying hen
**pondre** [pɔ̃dʀ(ə)] *vt* to lay; (*fig*) to produce ▷ *vi* to lay
**poney** [pɔnɛ] *nm* pony
**pongiste** [pɔ̃ʒist(ə)] *nm/f* table tennis player
**pont** [pɔ̃] *nm* bridge; (*Auto*): ~ **arrière/avant** rear/front axle; (*Navig*) deck; **faire le** ~ to take the extra day off; *see note*; **faire un** ~ **d'or à qn** to offer sb a fortune to take a job; ~ **aérien** airlift; ~ **basculant** bascule bridge; ~ **d'envol** flight deck; ~ **élévateur** hydraulic ramp; ~ **de graissage** ramp (*in garage*); ~ **à péage** tollbridge; ~ **roulant** travelling crane; ~ **suspendu** suspension bridge; ~ **tournant** swing bridge; **P-s et Chaussées** highways department

> ● FAIRE LE PONT
> ●
> ● The expression "faire le pont" refers to the
> ● practice of taking a Monday or Friday off to
> ● make a long weekend if a public holiday
> ● falls on a Tuesday or Thursday. The French
> ● commonly take an extra day off work to give
> ● four consecutive days' holiday at
> ● "l'Ascension", "le 14 juillet" and le "15 août".

**ponte** [pɔ̃t] *nf* laying; (*œufs pondus*) clutch ▷ *nm* (*fam*) big shot
**pontife** [pɔ̃tif] *nm* pontiff
**pontifier** [pɔ̃tifje] *vi* to pontificate
**pont-levis** [pɔ̃lvi] (*pl* **ponts-levis**) *nm* drawbridge
**ponton** [pɔ̃tɔ̃] *nm* pontoon (*on water*)
**pop** [pɔp] *adj inv* pop ▷ *nm*: **le** ~ pop (music)
**pop-corn** [pɔpkɔʀn] *nm* popcorn
**popeline** [pɔplin] *nf* poplin
**populace** [pɔpylas] *nf* (*péj*) rabble
**populaire** [pɔpylɛʀ] *adj* popular; (*manifestation*) mass *cpd*, of the people; (*milieux, clientèle*) working-class; (*Ling: mot etc*) used by the lower classes (of society)
**populariser** [pɔpylaʀize] *vt* to popularize
**popularité** [pɔpylaʀite] *nf* popularity
**population** [pɔpylasjɔ̃] *nf* population; ~ **active/agricole** working/farming population
**populeux, -euse** [pɔpylø, -øz] *adj* densely populated
**porc** [pɔʀ] *nm* (*Zool*) pig; (*Culin*) pork; (*peau*) pigskin
**porcelaine** [pɔʀsəlɛn] *nf* (*substance*) porcelain, china; (*objet*) piece of china(ware)

**porcelet** [pɔʀsəlɛ] *nm* piglet
**porc-épic** [pɔʀkepik] (*pl* **porcs-épics**) *nm* porcupine
**porche** [pɔʀʃ(ə)] *nm* porch
**porcher, -ère** [pɔʀʃe, -ɛʀ] *nm/f* pig-keeper
**porcherie** [pɔʀʃəʀi] *nf* pigsty
**porcin, e** [pɔʀsɛ̃, -in] *adj* (*race*) porcine; (*élevage*) pig *cpd*; (*fig*) piglike
**pore** [pɔʀ] *nm* pore
**poreux, -euse** [pɔʀø, -øz] *adj* porous
**porno** [pɔʀno] *adj* porno ▷ *nm* porn
**pornographie** [pɔʀnɔgʀafi] *nf* pornography
**pornographique** [pɔʀnɔgʀafik] *adj* pornographic
**port** [pɔʀ] *nm* (*Navig*) harbour (*Brit*), harbor (*US*), port; (*ville, Inform*) port; (*de l'uniforme etc*) wearing; (*pour lettre*) postage; (*pour colis, aussi: posture*) carriage; ~ **de commerce/de pêche** commercial/fishing port; **arriver à bon** ~ to arrive safe and sound; ~ **d'arme** (*Jur*) carrying of a firearm; ~ **d'attache** (*Navig*) port of registry; (*fig*) home base; ~ **d'escale** port of call; ~ **franc** free port
**portable** [pɔʀtabl(ə)] *adj* (*vêtement*) wearable; (*portatif*) portable; (*téléphone*) mobile (*Brit*), cell (*US*) ▷ *nm* (*Inform*) laptop (computer); (*téléphone*) mobile (phone) (*Brit*), cell (phone) (*US*)
**portail** [pɔʀtaj] *nm* gate; (*de cathédrale*) portal
**portant, e** [pɔʀtɑ̃, -ɑ̃t] *adj* (*murs*) structural, supporting; (*roues*) running; **bien/mal** ~ in good/poor health
**portatif, -ive** [pɔʀtatif, -iv] *adj* portable
**porte** [pɔʀt(ə)] *nf* door; (*de ville, forteresse, Ski*) gate; **mettre à la** ~ to throw out; **prendre la** ~ to leave, go away; **à ma/sa** ~ (*tout près*) on my/his (*ou* her) doorstep; ~ **d'embarquement** (*Aviat*) (departure) gate; ~ **d'entrée** front door; ~ **à** ~ *nm* door-to-door selling; ~ **de secours** emergency exit; ~ **de service** service entrance
**porté, e** [pɔʀte] *adj*: **être** ~ **à faire qch** to be apt to do sth, tend to do sth; **être** ~ **sur qch** to be partial to sth
**porte-à-faux** [pɔʀtafo] *nm*: **en** ~ cantilevered; (*fig*) in an awkward position
**porte-aiguilles** [pɔʀtegɥij] *nm inv* needle case
**porte-avions** [pɔʀtavjɔ̃] *nm inv* aircraft carrier
**porte-bagages** [pɔʀtbagaʒ] *nm inv* luggage rack (*ou* basket *etc*)
**porte-bébé** [pɔʀtbebe] *nm* baby sling *ou* carrier
**porte-bonheur** [pɔʀtbɔnœʀ] *nm inv* lucky charm
**porte-bouteilles** [pɔʀtbutɛj] *nm inv* bottle carrier; (*à casiers*) wine rack
**porte-cartes** [pɔʀtəkaʀt(ə)] *nm inv* (*de cartes d'identité*) card holder; (*de cartes géographiques*) map wallet
**porte-cigarettes** [pɔʀtsigaʀɛt] *nm inv* cigarette case
**porte-clefs** [pɔʀtəkle] *nm inv* key ring
**porte-conteneurs** [pɔʀtəkɔ̃tnœʀ] *nm inv* container ship
**porte-couteau, x** [pɔʀtkuto] *nm* knife rest

**P**

**porte-crayon** [pɔʀtkʀɛjɔ̃] *nm* pencil holder
**porte-documents** [pɔʀtdɔkymɑ̃] *nm inv*
attaché *ou* document case
**porte-drapeau, x** [pɔʀtdʀapo] *nm* standard
bearer
**portée** [pɔʀte] *nf* (*d'une arme*) range; (*fig:*
*importance*) impact, import; (: *capacités*) scope,
capability; (*de chatte etc*) litter; (*Mus*) stave, staff;
**à/hors de ~ (de)** within/out of reach (of); **à ~ de**
**(la) main** within (arm's) reach; **à ~ de voix**
within earshot; **à la ~ de qn** (*fig*) at sb's level,
within sb's capabilities; **à la ~ de toutes les**
**bourses** to suit every pocket, within everyone's
means
**portefaix** [pɔʀtəfɛ] *nm inv* porter
**porte-fenêtre** [pɔʀtfənɛtʀ(ə)] (*pl* **portes-**
**fenêtres**) *nf* French window
**portefeuille** [pɔʀtəfœj] *nm* wallet; (*Pol, Bourse*)
portfolio; **faire un lit en ~** to make an apple-
pie bed
**porte-jarretelles** [pɔʀtʒaʀtɛl] *nm inv* suspender
belt (*Brit*), garter belt (*US*)
**porte-jupe** [pɔʀtəʒyp] *nm* skirt hanger
**portemanteau, x** [pɔʀtmɑ̃to] *nm* coat rack
**porte-mine** [pɔʀtəmin] *nm* propelling (*Brit*) *ou*
mechanical (*US*) pencil
**porte-monnaie** [pɔʀtmɔnɛ] *nm inv* purse
**porte-parapluies** [pɔʀtpaʀaplɥi] *nm inv*
umbrella stand
**porte-parole** [pɔʀtpaʀɔl] *nm inv* spokesperson
**porte-plume** [pɔʀtəplym] *nm inv* penholder
**porter** [pɔʀte] *vt* (*charge ou sac etc, aussi: fœtus*) to
carry; (*sur soi: vêtement, barbe, bague*) to wear; (*fig:*
*responsabilité etc*) to bear, carry; (*inscription, marque,*
*titre, patronyme: arbre: fruits, fleurs*) to bear;
(*jugement*) to pass; (*apporter*): **~ qch quelque**
**part/à qn** to take sth somewhere/to sb;
(*inscrire*): **~ qch sur** to put sth down on; to enter
sth in ▷ *vi* (*voix, regard, canon*) to carry; (*coup,*
*argument*) to hit home; **se porter** *vi* (*se sentir*): **se**
**~ bien/mal** to be well/unwell; (*aller*): **se ~ vers**
to go towards; **~ sur** (*peser*) to rest on; (*accent*) to
fall on; (*conférence etc*) to concern; (*heurter*) to
strike; **être porté à faire** to be apt *ou* inclined
to do; **elle portait le nom de Rosalie** she was
called Rosalie; **~ qn au pouvoir** to bring sb to
power; **~ bonheur à qn** to bring sb luck; **~ qn à**
**croire** to lead sb to believe; **~ son âge** to look
one's age; **~ un toast** to drink a toast; **~ de**
**l'argent au crédit d'un compte** to credit an
account with some money; **se ~ partie civile** *to*
*associate in a court action with the public prosecutor;* **se**
**~ garant de qch** to guarantee sth, vouch for
sth; **se ~ candidat à la députation** ≈ to stand
for Parliament (*Brit*), ≈ run for Congress (*US*); **se**
**faire ~ malade** to report sick; **~ la main à son**
**chapeau** to raise one's hand to one's hat; **~ son**
**effort sur** to direct one's efforts towards; **~ un**
**fait à la connaissance de qn** to bring a fact to
sb's attention *ou* notice
**porte-savon** [pɔʀtsavɔ̃] *nm* soap dish
**porte-serviettes** [pɔʀtsɛʀvjɛt] *nm inv* towel rail

**portes-ouvertes** [pɔʀtuvɛʀt(ə)] *adj inv:*
**journée ~** open day
**porteur, -euse** [pɔʀtœʀ, -øz] *adj* (*Comm*) strong,
promising; (*nouvelle, chèque etc*): **être ~ de** to be
the bearer of ▷ *nm/f* (*de messages*) bearer ▷ *nm* (*de*
*bagages*) porter; (*Comm: de chèque*) bearer;
(: *d'actions*) holder; (**avion**) **gros ~** wide-bodied
aircraft, jumbo (jet)
**porte-voix** [pɔʀtəvwa] *nm inv* megaphone,
loudhailer (*Brit*)
**portier** [pɔʀtje] *nm* doorman,
commissionaire (*Brit*)
**portière** [pɔʀtjɛʀ] *nf* door
**portillon** [pɔʀtijɔ̃] *nm* gate
**portion** [pɔʀsjɔ̃] *nf* (*part*) portion, share; (*partie*)
portion, section
**portique** [pɔʀtik] *nm* (*Sport*) crossbar; (*Archit*)
portico; (*Rail*) gantry
**porto** [pɔʀto] *nm* port (wine)
**portoricain, e** [pɔʀtɔʀikɛ̃, -ɛn] *adj* Puerto Rican
**Porto Rico** [pɔʀtɔʀiko] *nf* Puerto Rico
**portrait** [pɔʀtʀɛ] *nm* portrait; (*photographie*)
photograph; (*fig*): **elle est le ~ de sa mère** she's
the image of her mother
**portraitiste** [pɔʀtʀɛtist(ə)] *nm/f* portrait
painter
**portrait-robot** [pɔʀtʀɛʀɔbo] *nm* Identikit® *ou*
Photo-fit ® (*Brit*) picture
**portuaire** [pɔʀtɥɛʀ] *adj* port *cpd*, harbour *cpd*
(*Brit*), harbor *cpd* (*US*)
**portugais, e** [pɔʀtygɛ, -ɛz] *adj* Portuguese ▷ *nm*
(*Ling*) Portuguese ▷ *nm/f:* **Portugais, e**
Portuguese
**Portugal** [pɔʀtygal] *nm:* **le ~** Portugal
**POS** *sigle m* (= *plan d'occupation des sols*) zoning
ordinances *ou* regulations
**pose** [poz] *nf* (*de moquette*) laying; (*de rideaux,*
*papier peint*) hanging; (*attitude, d'un modèle*) pose;
(*Photo*) exposure
**posé, e** [poze] *adj* calm, unruffled
**posément** [pozemɑ̃] *adv* calmly
**posemètre** [pozmɛtʀ(ə)] *nm* exposure meter
**poser** [poze] *vt* (*déposer*): **~ qch (sur)/qn à** to put
sth down (on)/drop sb at; (*placer*): **~ qch sur/**
**quelque part** to put sth on/somewhere;
(*installer: moquette, carrelage*) to lay; (*rideaux, papier*
*peint*) to hang; (*Math: chiffre*) to put (down);
(*question*) to ask; (*principe, conditions*) to lay *ou* set
down; (*problème*) to formulate; (*difficulté*) to
pose; (*personne: mettre en valeur*) to give standing
to ▷ *vi* (*modèle*) to pose; to sit; **se poser** (*oiseau,*
*avion*) to land; (*question*) to arise; **se ~ en** to pass
o.s off as, pose as; **~ son** *ou* **un regard sur qn/**
**qch** to turn one's gaze on sb/sth; **~ sa**
**candidature** to apply; (*Pol*) to put o.s. up for
election
**poseur, -euse** [pozœʀ, -øz] *nm/f* (*péj*) show-off,
poseur; **~ de parquets/carrelages** floor/tile
layer
**positif, -ive** [pozitif, -iv] *adj* positive
**position** [pozisjɔ̃] *nf* position; **prendre ~** (*fig*) to
take a stand

**positionner** [pozisjɔne] *vt* to position; *(compte en banque)* to calculate the balance of

**positivement** [pozitivmɑ̃] *adv* positively

**posologie** [pozɔlɔʒi] *nf* directions *pl* for use, dosage

**possédant, e** [posedɑ̃, -ɑ̃t] *adj (classe)* wealthy ▷ *nm/f:* **les ~s** the haves, the wealthy

**possédé, e** [posede] *nm/f* person possessed

**posséder** [posede] *vt* to own, possess; *(qualité, talent)* to have, possess; *(bien connaître: métier, langue)* to have mastered, have a thorough knowledge of; *(sexuellement, aussi: suj: colère)* to possess; *(fam: duper)* to take in

**possesseur** [posesœʀ] *nm* owner

**possessif, -ive** [posesif, -iv] *adj, nm (Ling)* possessive

**possession** [posesjɔ̃] *nf* ownership *no pl*; possession; *(aussi:* **être/entrer en possession de qch)** to be in/take possession of sth

**possibilité** [posibilite] *nf* possibility; **possibilités** *nfpl (moyens)* means; *(potentiel)* potential *sg;* **avoir la ~ de faire** to be in a position to do; to have the opportunity to do

**possible** [posibl(ə)] *adj* possible; *(projet, entreprise)* feasible ▷ *nm:* **faire son ~** to do all one can, do one's utmost; **(ce n'est) pas ~!** impossible!; **le plus/moins de livres ~** as many/few books as possible; **dès que ~** as soon as possible; **gentil** *etc* **au ~** as nice *etc* as it is possible to be

**postal, e, -aux** [postal, -o] *adj* postal, post office *cpd;* **sac ~** mailbag, postbag

**postdater** [postdate] *vt* to postdate

**poste** [post(ə)] *nf (service)* post, postal service; *(administration, bureau)* post office ▷ *nm (fonction, Mil)* post; *(Tél)* extension; *(de radio etc)* set; *(de budget)* item; **postes** *nfpl* post office; **P~s télécommunications et télédiffusion (PTT)** *postal and telecommunications service;* **agent** *ou* **employé des ~s** post office worker; **mettre à la ~ to post; ~ de commandement (PC)** *nm (Mil etc)* headquarters; **~ de contrôle** *nm* checkpoint; **~ de douane** *nm* customs post; **~ émetteur** *nm* transmitting set; **~ d'essence** *nm* filling station; **~ d'incendie** *nm* fire point; **~ de péage** *nm* tollgate; **~ de pilotage** *nm* cockpit; **~ (de police)** *nm* police station; **~ de radio** *nm* radio set; **~ restante (PR)** *nf* poste restante *(Brit)*, general delivery *(US)*; **~ de secours** *nm* first-aid post; **~ de télévision** *nm* television set; **~ de travail** *nm* work station

**poster** *vt* [poste] to post ▷ *nm* [postɛʀ] poster; **se poster** to position o.s

**postérieur, e** [posteʀjœʀ] *adj (date)* later; *(partie)* back ▷ *nm (fam)* behind

**postérieurement** [posteʀjœʀmɑ̃] *adv* later, subsequently; **~ à** after

**posteriori** [posteʀjɔʀi]: **a ~** *adv* with hindsight, a posteriori

**postérité** [posteʀite] *nf* posterity

**postface** [postfas] *nf* appendix

**posthume** [postym] *adj* posthumous

**postiche** [postiʃ] *adj* false ▷ *nm* hairpiece

**postier, -ière** [postje, -jɛʀ] *nm/f* post office worker

**postillon** [postijɔ̃] *nm:* **envoyer des ~s** to splutter

**postillonner** [postijone] *vi* to splutter

**post-natal, e** [postnatal] *adj* postnatal

**postopératoire** [postopeʀatwaʀ] *adj* postoperative

**postscolaire** [postskɔlɛʀ] *adj* further, continuing

**post-scriptum** [postskʀiptɔm] *nm inv* postscript

**postsynchronisation** [postsɛ̃kʀɔnizasjɔ̃] *nf* dubbing

**postsynchroniser** [postsɛ̃kʀɔnize] *vt* to dub

**postulant, e** [postylɑ̃, -ɑ̃t] *nm/f (candidat)* applicant; *(Rel)* postulant

**postulat** [postyla] *nm* postulate

**postuler** [postyle] *vt (emploi)* to apply for, put in for

**posture** [postyʀ] *nf* posture, position; *(fig)* position

**pot** [po] *nm* jar, pot; *(en plastique, carton)* carton; *(en métal)* tin; *(fam):* **avoir du ~** to be lucky; **boire** *ou* **prendre un ~** *(fam)* to have a drink; **découvrir le ~ aux roses** to find out what's been going on; **~ catalytique** catalytic converter; **~ (de chambre)** (chamber)pot; **~ d'échappement** exhaust pipe; **~ de fleurs** plant pot, flowerpot; *(plante)* pot plant; **~ à tabac** tobacco jar

**potable** [potabl(ə)] *adj (fig: boisson)* drinkable; *(: travail, devoir)* decent; **eau (non) ~** (not) drinking water

**potache** [potaʃ] *nm* schoolboy

**potage** [potaʒ] *nm* soup

**potager, -ère** [potaʒe, -ɛʀ] *adj (plante)* edible, vegetable *cpd;* **(jardin) ~** kitchen *ou* vegetable garden

**potasse** [potas] *nf* potassium hydroxide; *(engrais)* potash

**potasser** [potase] *vt (fam)* to swot up *(Brit)*, cram

**potassium** [potasjɔm] *nm* potassium

**pot-au-feu** [potofø] *nm inv (beef)* stew; *(viande)* stewing beef ▷ *adj (fam: personne)* stay-at-home

**pot-de-vin** [podvɛ̃] *(pl* **pots-de-vin)** *nm* bribe

**pote** [pot] *nm (fam)* mate *(Brit)*, pal

**poteau, x** [poto] *nm* post; **~ de départ/arrivée** starting/finishing post; **~ (d'exécution)** execution post, stake; **~ indicateur** signpost; **~ télégraphique** telegraph pole; **~x (de but)** goal-posts

**potée** [pote] *nf* hotpot *(of pork and cabbage)*

**potelé, e** [potle] *adj* plump, chubby

**potence** [potɑ̃s] *nf* gallows *sg;* **en ~** T-shaped

**potentat** [potɑ̃ta] *nm* potentate; *(fig: péj)* despot

**potentiel, le** [potɑ̃sjɛl] *adj, nm* potential

**potentiellement** [potɑ̃sjɛlmɑ̃] *adv* potentially

**poterie** [potʀi] *nf (fabrication)* pottery; *(objet)* piece of pottery

**potiche** [potiʃ] *nf* large vase

**potier** [potje] *nm* potter

**potins** [potɛ̃] *nmpl* gossip *sg*

**p**

## potion | pousse-café

**potion** [posjɔ̃] nf potion
**potiron** [pɔtiRɔ̃] nm pumpkin
**pot-pourri** [popuRi] (pl **pots-pourris**) nm (Mus) medley
**pou, x** [pu] nm louse
**pouah** [pwa] excl ugh!, yuk!
**poubelle** [pubɛl] nf (dust)bin
**pouce** [pus] nm thumb; **se tourner** ou **se rouler les ~s** (fig) to twiddle one's thumbs; **manger sur le ~** to eat on the run, snatch something to eat
**poudre** [pudR(ə)] nf powder; (fard) (face) powder; (explosif) gunpowder; **en ~**: **café en ~** instant coffee; **savon en ~** soap powder; **lait en ~** dried ou powdered milk; **~ à canon** gunpowder; **~ à éternuer** sneezing powder; **~ à récurer** scouring powder; **~ de riz** face powder
**poudrer** [pudRe] vt to powder
**poudreux, -euse** [pudRø, -øz] adj dusty; (neige) powdery, powder cpd
**poudrier** [pudRije] nm (powder) compact
**poudrière** [pudRijɛR] nf powder magazine; (fig) powder keg
**pouf** [puf] nm pouffe
**pouffer** [pufe] vi: **~ (de rire)** to snigger; to giggle
**pouffiasse** [pufjas] nf (fam) fat cow; (prostituée) tart
**pouilleux, -euse** [pujø, -øz] adj flea-ridden; (fig) seedy
**poulailler** [pulaje] nm henhouse; (Théât): **le ~** the gods sg
**poulain** [pulɛ̃] nm foal; (fig) protégé
**poularde** [pulaRd(ə)] nf fatted chicken
**poule** [pul] nf (Zool) hen; (Culin) (boiling) fowl; (Sport) (round-robin) tournament; (Rugby) group; (fam) bird (Brit), chick, broad (US); (prostituée) tart; **~ d'eau** moorhen; **~ mouillée** coward; **~ pondeuse** laying hen, layer; **~ au riz** chicken and rice
**poulet** [pulɛ] nm chicken; (fam) cop
**poulette** [pulɛt] nf (jeune poule) pullet
**pouliche** [puliʃ] nf filly
**poulie** [puli] nf pulley
**poulpe** [pulp(ə)] nm octopus
**pouls** [pu] nm pulse; (Anat): **prendre le ~ de qn** to take sb's pulse
**poumon** [pumɔ̃] nm lung; **~ d'acier** ou **artificiel** iron ou artificial lung
**poupe** [pup] nf stern; **en ~** astern
**poupée** [pupe] nf doll; **jouer à la ~** to play with one's doll (ou dolls); **de ~** (très petit): **jardin de ~** doll's garden, pocket-handkerchief-sized garden
**poupin, e** [pupɛ̃, -in] adj chubby
**poupon** [pupɔ̃] nm babe-in-arms
**pouponner** [pupɔne] vi to fuss (around)
**pouponnière** [pupɔnjɛR] nf crèche, day nursery
**pour** [puR] prép for ▷ nm: **le ~ et le contre** the pros and cons; **~ faire** (so as) to do, in order to do; **~ avoir fait** for having done; **~ que** so that, in order that; **~ moi** (à mon avis, pour ma part) for my part, personally; **~ riche qu'il soit** rich

though he may be; **~ 20 euros d'essence** 20 euros' worth of petrol; **~ cent** per cent; **~ ce qui est de** as for; **y être ~ quelque chose** to have something to do with it
**pourboire** [puRbwaR] nm tip
**pourcentage** [puRsɑ̃taʒ] nm percentage; **travailler au ~** to work on commission
**pourchasser** [puRʃase] vt to pursue
**pourfendeur** [puRfɑ̃dœR] nm sworn opponent
**pourfendre** [puRfɑ̃dR(ə)] vt to assail
**pourlécher** [puRleʃe]: **se pourlécher** vi to lick one's lips
**pourparlers** [puRpaRle] nmpl talks, negotiations; **être en ~ avec** to be having talks with
**pourpre** [puRpR(ə)] adj crimson
**pourquoi** [puRkwa] adv, conj why ▷ nm inv: **le ~ (de)** the reason (for)
**pourrai** etc [puRe] vb voir **pouvoir**
**pourri, e** [puRi] adj rotten; (roche, pierre) crumbling; (temps, climat) filthy, foul ▷ nm: **sentir le ~** to smell rotten
**pourriel** [puRjel] nm (Inform) spam
**pourrir** [puRiR] vi to rot; (fruit) to go rotten ou bad; (fig: situation) to deteriorate ▷ vt to rot; (fig: corrompre: personne) to corrupt; (: gâter: enfant) to spoil thoroughly
**pourrissement** [puRismɑ̃] nm deterioration
**pourriture** [puRityR] nf rot
**pourrons** etc [puRɔ̃] vb voir **pouvoir**
**poursuis** etc [puRsɥi] vb voir **poursuivre**
**poursuite** [puRsɥit] nf pursuit, chase; **poursuites** nfpl (Jur) legal proceedings; **(course) ~** track race; (fig) chase
**poursuivant, e** [puRsɥivɑ̃, -ɑ̃t] nm/f pursuer; (Jur) plaintiff
**poursuivre** [puRsɥivR(ə)] vt to pursue, chase (after); (relancer) to hound, harry; (obséder) to haunt; (Jur) to bring proceedings against, prosecute; (: au civil) to sue; (but) to strive towards; (voyage, études) to carry on with, continue ▷ vi to carry on, go on; **se poursuivre** vi to go on, continue
**pourtant** [puRtɑ̃] adv yet; **mais ~** but nevertheless, but even so; **c'est ~ facile** (and) yet it's easy
**pourtour** [puRtuR] nm perimeter
**pourvoi** [puRvwa] nm appeal
**pourvoir** [puRvwaR] nm (Comm) supply ▷ vt: **~ qch/qn de** to equip sth/sb with ▷ vi: **~ à** to provide for; (emploi) to fill; **se pourvoir** vi (Jur): **se ~ en cassation** to take one's case to the Court of Appeal
**pourvoyeur, -euse** [puRvwajœR, -øz] nm/f supplier
**pourvu, e** [puRvy] pp de **pourvoir** ▷ adj: **~ de** equipped with; **~ que** conj (si) provided that, so long as; (espérons que) let's hope (that)
**pousse** [pus] nf growth; (bourgeon) shoot
**poussé, e** [puse] adj sophisticated, advanced; (moteur) souped-up
**pousse-café** [puskafe] nm inv (after-dinner)

liqueur

**poussée** [puse] *nf* thrust; (*coup*) push; (*Méd*) eruption; (*fig*) upsurge

**pousse-pousse** [puspus] *nm inv* rickshaw

**pousser** [puse] *vt* to push; (*acculer*) to drive sb to do sth; (*moteur, voiture*) to drive hard; (*émettre: cri etc*) to give; (*stimuler*) to urge on; to drive hard; (*poursuivre*) to carry on; (*inciter*): ~ **qn à faire qch** to urge *ou* press sb to do sth ▷ *vi* to push; (*croître*) to grow; (*aller*): ~ **plus loin** to push on a bit further; **se pousser** *vi* to move over; **faire** ~ (*plante*) to grow; ~ **le dévouement** *etc* **jusqu'à ...** to take devotion *etc* as far as ...

**poussette** [puset] *nf* (*voiture d'enfant*) pushchair (*Brit*), stroller (*US*)

**poussette-canne** [pusɛtkan] (*pl* **poussettes-cannes**) *nf* baby buggy (*Brit*), (folding) stroller (*US*)

**poussier** [pusje] *nm* coaldust

**poussière** [pusjɛʀ] *nf* dust; (*grain*) speck of dust; **et des ~s** (*fig*) and a bit; ~ **de charbon** coaldust

**poussiéreux, -euse** [pusjeʀø, -øz] *adj* dusty

**poussif, -ive** [pusif, -iv] *adj* wheezy, wheezing

**poussin** [pusɛ̃] *nm* chick

**poussoir** [puswaʀ] *nm* button

**poutre** [putʀ(ə)] *nf* beam; (*en fer, ciment armé*) girder; ~**s apparentes** exposed beams

**poutrelle** [putʀɛl] *nf* (*petite poutre*) small beam; (*barre d'acier*) girder

Ⓞ **MOT-CLÉ**

**pouvoir** [puvwaʀ] *nm* power; (*Pol: dirigeants*): **le pouvoir** those in power; **les pouvoirs publics** the authorities; **avoir pouvoir de faire** (*autorisation*) to have (the) authority to do; (*droit*) to have the right to do; **pouvoir absolu** absolute power; **pouvoir absorbant** absorbency; **pouvoir d'achat** purchasing power; **pouvoir calorifique** calorific value
▷ *vb semi-aux* **1** (*être en état de*) can, be able to; **je ne peux pas le réparer** I can't *ou* I am not able to repair it; **déçu de ne pas pouvoir le faire** disappointed not to be able to do it
**2** (*avoir la permission*) can, may, be allowed to; **vous pouvez aller au cinéma** you can *ou* may go to the pictures
**3** (*probabilité, hypothèse*) may, might, could; **il a pu avoir un accident** he may *ou* might *ou* could have had an accident; **il aurait pu le dire!** he might *ou* could have said (so)!
**4** (*expressions*): **tu ne peux pas savoir!** you have no idea!; **tu peux le dire!** you can say that again!
▷ *vb impers* may, might, could; **il peut arriver que** it may *ou* might *ou* could happen that; **il pourrait pleuvoir** it might rain
▷ *vt* **1** can, be able to; **j'ai fait tout ce que j'ai pu** I did all I could; **je n'en peux plus** (*épuisé*) I'm exhausted; (*à bout*) I can't take any more
**2** (*vb + adj ou adv comparatif*): **je me porte on ne peut mieux** I'm absolutely fine, I couldn't be

better; **elle est on ne peut plus gentille** she couldn't be nicer, she's as nice as can be
**se pouvoir** *vi*: **il se peut que** it may *ou* might be that; **cela se pourrait** that's quite possible

**PP** *sigle f* (= *préventive de la pellagre: vitamine*) niacin
▷ *abr* (= *pages*) pp

**p.p.** *abr* (= *par procuration*) p.p.

**p.p.c.m.** *sigle m* (*Math:* = *plus petit commun multiple*) LCM (= *lowest common multiple*)

**PQ** *sigle f* (*Canada:* = *province de Québec*) PQ

**PR** *sigle f* = **parti républicain** ▷ *sigle f* = **poste restante**

**pr** *abr* = **pour**

**pragmatique** [pʀagmatik] *adj* pragmatic

**pragmatisme** [pʀagmatism(ə)] *nm* pragmatism

**Prague** [pʀag] *n* Prague

**prairie** [pʀeʀi] *nf* meadow

**praline** [pʀalin] *nf* (*bonbon*) sugared almond; (*au chocolat*) praline

**praliné, e** [pʀaline] *adj* (*amande*) sugared; (*chocolat, glace*) praline cpd

**praticable** [pʀatikabl(ə)] *adj* (*route etc*) passable, practicable; (*projet*) practicable

**praticien, ne** [pʀatisjɛ̃, -ɛn] *nm/f* practitioner

**pratiquant, e** [pʀatikɑ̃, -ɑ̃t] *adj* practising (*Brit*), practicing (*US*)

**pratique** [pʀatik] *nf* practice ▷ *adj* practical; (*commode: horaire etc*) convenient; (: *outil*) handy, useful; **dans la** ~ in (actual) practice; **mettre en** ~ to put into practice

**pratiquement** [pʀatikmɑ̃] *adv* (*dans la pratique*) in practice; (*pour ainsi dire*) practically, virtually

**pratiquer** [pʀatike] *vt* to practise (*Brit*), practice (*US*); (*Sport etc*) to go in for, play; (*appliquer: méthode, théorie*) to apply; (*intervention, opération*) to carry out; (*ouverture, abri*) to make ▷ *vi* (*Rel*) to be a churchgoer

**pré** [pʀe] *nm* meadow

**préados** [pʀeado] *nmpl* pre-teens

**préalable** [pʀealabl(ə)] *adj* preliminary; **condition** ~ (**de**) precondition (for), prerequisite (for); **sans avis** ~ without prior *ou* previous notice; **au** ~ first, beforehand

**préalablement** [pʀealabləmɑ̃] *adv* first, beforehand

**Préalpes** [pʀealp(ə)] *nfpl*: **les** ~ the Pre-Alps

**préalpin, e** [pʀealpɛ̃, -in] *adj* of the Pre-Alps

**préambule** [pʀeɑ̃byl] *nm* preamble; (*fig*) prelude; **sans** ~ straight away

**préau, x** [pʀeo] *nm* (*d'une cour d'école*) covered playground; (*d'un monastère, d'une prison*) inner courtyard

**préavis** [pʀeavi] *nm* notice; ~ **de congé** notice; **communication avec** ~ (*Tél*) personal *ou* person-to-person call

**prébende** [pʀebɑ̃d] *nf* (*péj*) remuneration

**précaire** [pʀekɛʀ] *adj* precarious

**précaution** [pʀekosjɔ̃] *nf* precaution; **avec** ~ cautiously; **prendre des** *ou* **ses** ~**s** to take precautions; **par** ~ as a precaution; **pour plus**

**de** ~ to be on the safe side; **~s oratoires** carefully phrased remarks

**précautionneux, -euse** [pʀekosjønø, -øz] adj cautious, careful

**précédemment** [pʀesedamã] adv before, previously

**précédent, e** [pʀesedã, -ãt] adj previous ▷ nm precedent; **sans** ~ unprecedented; **le jour** ~ the day before, the previous day

**précéder** [pʀesede] vt to precede; (marcher ou rouler devant) to be in front of; (arriver avant) to get ahead of

**précepte** [pʀesɛpt(ə)] nm precept

**précepteur, -trice** [pʀesɛptœʀ, -tʀis] nm/f (private) tutor

**préchauffer** [pʀeʃofe] vt to preheat

**prêcher** [pʀeʃe] vt, vi to preach

**prêcheur, -euse** [pʀeʃœʀ, -øz] adj moralizing ▷ nm/f (Rel) preacher; (fig) moralizer

**précieusement** [pʀesjøzmã] adv (avec soin) carefully; (avec préciosité) preciously

**précieux, -euse** [pʀesjø, -øz] adj precious; (collaborateur, conseils) invaluable; (style, écrivain) précieux, precious

**préciosité** [pʀesjozite] nf preciosity, preciousness

**précipice** [pʀesipis] nm drop, chasm; (fig) abyss; **au bord du** ~ at the edge of the precipice

**précipitamment** [pʀesipitamã] adv hurriedly, hastily

**précipitation** [pʀesipitasjõ] nf (hâte) haste; **~s (atmosphériques)** precipitation sg

**précipité, e** [pʀesipite] adj (respiration) fast; (pas) hurried; (départ) hasty

**précipiter** [pʀesipite] vt (faire tomber): ~ **qn/qch du haut de** to throw ou hurl sb/sth off ou from; (hâter: marche) to quicken; (: départ) to hasten; **se précipiter** vi (événements) to move faster; (respiration) to speed up; **se** ~ **sur/vers** to rush at/towards; **se** ~ **au-devant de qn** to throw o.s. before sb

**précis, e** [pʀesi, -iz] adj precise; (tir, mesures) accurate, precise ▷ nm handbook

**précisément** [pʀesizemã] adv precisely; **ma vie n'est pas** ~ **distrayante** my life is not exactly entertaining

**préciser** [pʀesize] vt (expliquer) to be more specific about, clarify; (spécifier) to state, specify; **se préciser** vi to become clear(er)

**précision** [pʀesizjõ] nf precision; accuracy; (détail) point ou detail (made clear or to be clarified); **précisions** nfpl further details

**précoce** [pʀekɔs] adj early; (enfant) precocious; (calvitie) premature

**précocité** [pʀekɔsite] nf earliness; precociousness

**préconçu, e** [pʀekõsy] adj preconceived

**préconiser** [pʀekɔnize] vt to advocate

**précuit, e** [pʀekɥi, -it] adj precooked

**précurseur** [pʀekyʀsœʀ] adj m precursory ▷ nm forerunner, precursor

**prédateur** [pʀedatœʀ] nm predator

**prédécesseur** [pʀedesesœʀ] nm predecessor

**prédécoupé, e** [pʀedekupe] adj pre-cut

**prédestiner** [pʀedɛstine] vt: ~ **qn à qch/à faire** to predestine sb for sth/to do

**prédicateur** [pʀedikatœʀ] nm preacher

**prédiction** [pʀediksjõ] nf prediction

**prédilection** [pʀedilɛksjõ] nf: **avoir une** ~ **pour** to be partial to; **de** ~ favourite (Brit), favorite (US)

**prédire** [pʀediʀ] vt to predict

**prédisposer** [pʀedispoze] vt: ~ **qn à qch/à faire** to predispose sb to sth/to do

**prédisposition** [pʀedispozisjõ] nf predisposition

**prédit, e** [pʀedi, -it] pp de **prédire**

**prédominance** [pʀedɔminãs] nf predominance

**prédominant, e** [pʀedɔminã, -ãt] adj predominant; prevailing

**prédominer** [pʀedɔmine] vi to predominate; (avis) to prevail

**pré-électoral, e, -aux** [pʀeelɛktɔʀal, -o] adj pre-election cpd

**pré-emballé, e** [pʀeãbale] adj pre-packed

**prééminent, e** [pʀeeminã, -ãt] adj pre-eminent

**préemption** [pʀeãpsjõ] nf: **droit de** ~ (Jur) pre-emptive right

**pré-encollé, e** [pʀeãkɔle] adj pre-pasted

**préétabli, e** [pʀeetabli] adj pre-established

**préexistant, e** [pʀeɛgzistã, -ãt] adj pre-existing

**préfabriqué, e** [pʀefabʀike] adj prefabricated; (péj: sourire) artificial ▷ nm prefabricated material

**préface** [pʀefas] nf preface

**préfacer** [pʀefase] vt to write a preface for

**préfectoral, e, -aux** [pʀefɛktɔʀal, -o] adj prefectoral

**préfecture** [pʀefɛktyʀ] nf prefecture; see note; ~ **de police** police headquarters

---

○ **PRÉFECTURE**
○
○ The préfecture is the administrative
○ headquarters of the "département". The
○ "préfet", a senior civil servant appointed by
○ the government, is responsible for putting
○ government policy into practice. France's 22
○ regions, each comprising a number of
○ "départements", also have a "préfet de
○ région".

---

**préférable** [pʀefeʀabl(ə)] adj preferable

**préféré, e** [pʀefeʀe] adj, nm/f favourite (Brit), favorite (US)

**préférence** [pʀefeʀãs] nf preference; **de** ~ preferably; **de** ou **par** ~ **à** in preference to, rather than; **donner la** ~ **à qn** to give preference to sb; **par ordre de** ~ in order of preference; **obtenir la** ~ **sur** to have preference over

**préférentiel, le** [pʀefeʀãsjɛl] adj preferential

**préférer** [pʀefeʀe] vt: ~ **qn/qch (à)** to prefer sb/sth (to), like sb/sth better (than); ~ **faire** to prefer to do; **je préférerais du thé** I would rather have tea, I'd prefer tea

**préfet** [pʀefɛ] *nm* prefect; **~ de police** ≈ Chief Constable (*Brit*), ≈ Police Commissioner (*US*)

**préfigurer** [pʀefiɡyʀe] *vt* to prefigure

**préfixe** [pʀefiks(ə)] *nm* prefix

**préhistoire** [pʀeistwaʀ] *nf* prehistory

**préhistorique** [pʀeistɔʀik] *adj* prehistoric

**préjudice** [pʀeʒydis] *nm* (*matériel*) loss; (*moral*) harm *no pl*; **porter ~ à** to harm, be detrimental to; **au ~ de** at the expense of

**préjudiciable** [pʀeʒydisjabl(ə)] *adj*: **~ à** prejudicial *ou* harmful to

**préjugé** [pʀeʒyʒe] *nm* prejudice; **avoir un ~ contre** to be prejudiced against; **bénéficier d'un ~ favorable** to be viewed favourably

**préjuger** [pʀeʒyʒe]: **~ de** *vt* to prejudge

**prélasser** [pʀelɑse]: **se prélasser** *vi* to lounge

**prélat** [pʀela] *nm* prelate

**prélavage** [pʀelavaʒ] *nm* pre-wash

**prélèvement** [pʀelɛvmɑ̃] *nm* deduction; withdrawal; **faire un ~ de sang** to take a blood sample

**prélever** [pʀelve] *vt* (*échantillon*) to take; **~ (sur)** (*argent*) to deduct (from); (: *sur son compte*) to withdraw (from)

**préliminaire** [pʀeliminɛʀ] *adj* preliminary; **préliminaires** *nmpl* preliminaries; (*négociations*) preliminary talks

**prélude** [pʀelyd] *nm* prelude; (*avant le concert*) warm-up

**prématuré, e** [pʀematyʀe] *adj* premature; (*retraite*) early ▷ *nm* premature baby

**prématurément** [pʀematyʀemɑ̃] *adv* prematurely

**préméditation** [pʀemeditɑsjɔ̃] *nf*: **avec ~** *adj* premeditated ▷ *adv* with intent

**préméditer** [pʀemedite] *vt* to premeditate, plan

**prémices** [pʀemis] *nfpl* beginnings

**premier, -ière** [pʀəmje, -jɛʀ] *adj* first; (*branche, marche, grade*) bottom; (*fig: fondamental*) basic; prime; (*en importance*) first, foremost ▷ *nm* (*premier étage*) first (*Brit*) *ou* second (*US*) floor ▷ *nf* (*Auto*) first (gear); (*Rail, Aviat etc*) first class; (*Scol: classe*) penultimate school year (*age 16–17*); (*Théât*) first night; (*Ciné*) première; (*Escrime*) first; **au ~ abord** at first sight; **au** *ou* **du ~ coup** at the first attempt *ou* go; **de ~ ordre** first-class, first-rate; **de première qualité, de ~ choix** best *ou* top quality; **de première importance** of the highest importance; **de première nécessité** absolutely essential; **le ~ venu** the first person to come along; **jeune ~** leading man; **le ~ de l'an** New Year's Day; **enfant du ~ lit** child of a first marriage; **en ~ lieu** in the first place; **~ âge** (*d'un enfant*) the first three months (of life); **P~ Ministre** Prime Minister

**premièrement** [pʀəmjɛʀmɑ̃] *adv* firstly

**première-née** [pʀəmjɛʀne] (*pl* **premières-nées**) *nf* first-born

**premier-né** [pʀəmjene] (*pl* **premiers-nés**) *nm* first-born

**prémisse** [pʀemis] *nf* premise

**prémolaire** [pʀemɔlɛʀ] *nf* premolar

**prémonition** [pʀemɔnisjɔ̃] *nf* premonition

**prémonitoire** [pʀemɔnitwaʀ] *adj* premonitory

**prémunir** [pʀemyniʀ]: **se prémunir** *vi*: **se ~ contre** to protect o.s. from, guard against

**prenant, e** [pʀənɑ̃, -ɑ̃t] *vb voir* **prendre** ▷ *adj* absorbing, engrossing

**prénatal, e** [pʀenatal] *adj* (*Méd*) antenatal; (*allocation*) maternity *cpd*

**prendre** [pʀɑ̃dʀ(ə)] *vt* to take; (*aller chercher*) to get, fetch; (*se procurer*) to get; (*réserver: place*) to book; (*acquérir: du poids, de la valeur*) to put on, gain; (*malfaiteur, poisson*) to catch; (*passager*) to pick up; (*personnel, aussi: couleur, goût*) to take on; (*locataire*) to take in; (*traiter: enfant, problème*) to handle; (*voix, ton*) to put on; (*prélever: pourcentage, argent*) to take off; (*ôter*): **~ qch à** to take sth from; (*coincer*): **se ~ les doigts dans** to get one's fingers caught in ▷ *vi* (*liquide, ciment*) to set; (*greffe, vaccin*) to take; (*mensonge*) to be successful; (*feu: foyer*) to go; (: *incendie*) to start; (*allumette*) to light; (*se diriger*): **~ à gauche** to turn (to the) left; **~ son origine** *ou* **sa source** (*mot, rivière*) to have its source; **~ qn pour** to take sb for; **se ~ pour** to think one is; **~ sur soi de faire qch** to take it upon o.s. to do sth; **~ qn en sympathie/horreur** to get to like/loathe sb; **à tout ~** all things considered; **s'en ~ à** (*agresser*) to set about; (*passer sa colère sur*) to take it out on; (*critiquer*) to attack; (*remettre en question*) to challenge; **se ~ d'amitié/d'affection pour** to befriend/become fond of; **s'y ~** (*procéder*) to set about it; **s'y ~ à l'avance** to see to it in advance; **s'y ~ à deux fois** to try twice, make two attempts

**preneur** [pʀənœʀ] *nm*: **être ~** to be willing to buy; **trouver ~** to find a buyer

**preniez** [pʀənje] *vb voir* **prendre**

**prenne** *etc* [pʀɛn] *vb voir* **prendre**

**prénom** [pʀenɔ̃] *nm* first name

**prénommer** [pʀenɔme] *vt*: **elle se prénomme Claude** her (first) name is Claude

**prénuptial, e, -aux** [pʀenypsjal, -o] *adj* premarital

**préoccupant, e** [pʀeɔkypɑ̃, -ɑ̃t] *adj* worrying

**préoccupation** [pʀeɔkypɑsjɔ̃] *nf* (*souci*) concern; (*idée fixe*) preoccupation

**préoccupé, e** [pʀeɔkype] *adj* concerned; preoccupied

**préoccuper** [pʀeɔkype] *vt* (*tourmenter, tracasser*) to concern; (*absorber, obséder*) to preoccupy; **se ~ de qch** to be concerned about sth; to show concern about sth

**préparateur, -trice** [pʀepaʀatœʀ, -tʀis] *nm/f* assistant

**préparatifs** [pʀepaʀatif] *nmpl* preparations

**préparation** [pʀepaʀɑsjɔ̃] *nf* preparation; (*Scol*) piece of homework

**préparatoire** [pʀepaʀatwaʀ] *adj* preparatory

**préparer** [pʀepaʀe] *vt* to prepare; (*café, repas*) to

make; (*examen*) to prepare for; (*voyage, entreprise*) to plan; **se préparer** *vi* (*orage, tragédie*) to brew, be in the air; **se ~ (à qch/à faire)** to prepare (o.s.) *ou* get ready (for sth/to do); **~ qch à qn** (*surprise etc*) to have sth in store for sb; **~ qn à qch** (*nouvelle etc*) to prepare sb for sth

**prépondérance** [pʀepɔ̃deʀɑ̃s] *nf*: **~ (sur)** predominance (over)

**prépondérant, e** [pʀepɔ̃deʀɑ̃, -ɑ̃t] *adj* major, dominating; **voix ~e** casting vote

**préposé, e** [pʀepoze] *adj*: **~ à** in charge of ▷ *nm/f* (*gén: employé*) employee; (*Admin: facteur*) postman/woman (*Brit*), mailman/woman (*US*); (*de la douane etc*) official; (*de vestiaire*) attendant

**préposer** [pʀepoze] *vt*: **~ qn à qch** to appoint sb to sth

**préposition** [pʀepozisjɔ̃] *nf* preposition

**prérentrée** [pʀeʀɑ̃tʀe] *nf* in-service training period before start of school term

**préretraite** [pʀeʀətʀɛt] *nf* early retirement

**prérogative** [pʀeʀɔgativ] *nf* prerogative

**près** [pʀɛ] *adv* near, close; **~ de** *prép* near (to), close to; (*environ*) nearly, almost; **~ d'ici** near here; **de ~** *adv* closely; **à cinq kg ~** to within about five kg; **à cela ~ que** apart from the fact that; **je ne suis pas ~ de lui pardonner** I'm nowhere near ready to forgive him; **on n'est pas à un jour ~** one day (either way) won't make any difference, we're not going to quibble over the odd day

**présage** [pʀezaʒ] *nm* omen

**présager** [pʀezaʒe] *vt* (*prévoir*) to foresee; (*annoncer*) to portend

**pré-salé** [pʀesale] (*pl* **prés-salés**) *nm* (*Culin*) salt-meadow lamb

**presbyte** [pʀɛsbit] *adj* long-sighted (*Brit*), far-sighted (*US*)

**presbytère** [pʀɛsbitɛʀ] *nm* presbytery

**presbytérien, ne** [pʀɛsbiteʀjɛ̃, -ɛn] *adj, nm/f* Presbyterian

**presbytie** [pʀɛsbisi] *nf* long-sightedness (*Brit*), far-sightedness (*US*)

**prescience** [pʀesjɑ̃s] *nf* prescience, foresight

**préscolaire** [pʀeskɔlɛʀ] *adj* preschool *cpd*

**prescription** [pʀɛskʀipsjɔ̃] *nf* (*instruction*) order, instruction; (*Méd, Jur*) prescription

**prescrire** [pʀɛskʀiʀ] *vt* to prescribe; **se prescrire** *vi* (*Jur*) to lapse

**prescrit, e** [pʀɛskʀi, -it] *pp de* **prescrire** ▷ *adj* (*date etc*) stipulated

**préséance** [pʀeseɑ̃s] *nf* precedence *no pl*

**présélection** [pʀeselɛksjɔ̃] *nf* (*de candidats*) short-listing; **effectuer une ~** to draw up a shortlist

**présélectionner** [pʀeselɛksjɔne] *vt* to preselect; (*dispositif*) to preset; (*candidats*) to make an initial selection from among, short-list (*Brit*)

**présence** [pʀezɑ̃s] *nf* presence; (*au bureau etc*) attendance; **en ~** face to face; **en ~ de** in (the) presence of; (*fig*) in the face of; **faire acte de ~** to put in a token appearance; **~ d'esprit** presence of mind

**présent, e** [pʀezɑ̃, -ɑ̃t] *adj, nm* present; (*Admin, Comm*): **la ~e lettre/loi** this letter/law ▷ *nm/f*: **les ~s** (*personnes*) those present ▷ *nf* (*Comm: lettre*): **la ~e** this letter; **à ~** now, at present; **dès à ~** here and now; **jusqu'à ~** up till now, until now; **à ~ que** now that

**présentable** [pʀezɑ̃tabl(ə)] *adj* presentable

**présentateur, -trice** [pʀezɑ̃tatœʀ, -tʀis] *nm/f* presenter

**présentation** [pʀezɑ̃tasjɔ̃] *nf* presentation; introduction; (*allure*) appearance

**présenter** [pʀezɑ̃te] *vt* to present; (*invité, candidat*) to introduce; (*félicitations, condoléances*) to offer; (*montrer: billet, pièce d'identité*) to show, produce; (*faire inscrire: candidat*) to put forward; (*soumettre*) to submit ▷ *vi*: **~ mal/bien** to have an unattractive/a pleasing appearance; **se présenter** *vi* (*sur convocation*) to report, come; (*se faire connaître*) to come forward; (*à une élection*) to stand; (*occasion*) to arise; **se ~ à un examen** to sit an exam; **se ~ bien/mal** to look good/not too good

**présentoir** [pʀezɑ̃twaʀ] *nm* (*étagère*) display shelf; (*vitrine*) showcase; (*étal*) display stand

**préservatif** [pʀezɛʀvatif] *nm* condom, sheath

**préservation** [pʀezɛʀvasjɔ̃] *nf* protection, preservation

**préserver** [pʀezɛʀve] *vt*: **~ de** (*protéger*) to protect from; (*sauver*) to save from

**présidence** [pʀezidɑ̃s] *nf* presidency; chairmanship

**président** [pʀezidɑ̃] *nm* (*Pol*) president; (*d'une assemblée, Comm*) chairman; **~ directeur général (PDG)** chairman and managing director (*Brit*), chairman and president (*US*); **~ du jury** (*Jur*) foreman of the jury; (*d'examen*) chief examiner

**présidente** [pʀezidɑ̃t] *nf* president; (*femme du président*) president's wife; (*d'une réunion*) chairwoman

**présidentiable** [pʀezidɑ̃sjabl(ə)] *adj, nm/f* potential president

**présidentiel, le** [pʀezidɑ̃sjɛl] *adj* presidential; **présidentielles** *nfpl* presidential election(s)

**présider** [pʀezide] *vt* to preside over; (*dîner*) to be the guest of honour (*Brit*) *ou* honor (*US*) at; **~ à** *vt* to direct; to govern

**présomption** [pʀezɔ̃psjɔ̃] *nf* presumption

**présomptueux, -euse** [pʀezɔ̃ptɥø, -øz] *adj* presumptuous

**presque** [pʀɛsk(ə)] *adv* almost, nearly; **~ rien** hardly anything; **~ pas** hardly (at all); **~ pas de** hardly any; **personne, ou ~** next to nobody, hardly anyone; **la ~ totalité (de)** almost *ou* nearly all

**presqu'île** [pʀɛskil] *nf* peninsula

**pressant, e** [pʀesɑ̃, -ɑ̃t] *adj* urgent; (*personne*) insistent; **se faire ~** to become insistent

**presse** [pʀɛs] *nf* press; (*affluence*): **heures de ~** busy times; **sous ~** gone to press; **mettre sous ~** to send to press; **avoir une bonne/mauvaise ~** to have a good/bad press; **~ féminine**

women's magazines *pl*; ~ **d'information** quality newspapers *pl*

**pressé, e** [pʀese] *adj* in a hurry; *(air)* hurried; *(besogne)* urgent ▷ *nm*: **aller au plus** ~ to see to first things first; **être ~ de faire qch** to be in a hurry to do sth; **orange ~e** freshly squeezed orange juice

**presse-citron** [pʀɛssitʀɔ̃] *nm inv* lemon squeezer

**presse-fruits** [pʀɛsfʀɥi] *nm inv* lemon squeezer

**pressentiment** [pʀesɑ̃timɑ̃] *nm* foreboding, premonition

**pressentir** [pʀesɑ̃tiʀ] *vt* to sense; *(prendre contact avec)* to approach

**presse-papiers** [pʀɛspapje] *nm inv* paperweight

**presse-purée** [pʀɛspyʀe] *nm inv* potato masher

**presser** [pʀese] *vt* (fruit, éponge) to squeeze; *(interrupteur, bouton)* to press, push; *(allure, affaire)* to speed up; *(débiteur etc)* to press; *(inciter):* ~ **qn de faire** to urge ou press sb to do ▷ *vi* to be urgent; **se presser** *(se hâter)* to hurry (up); *(se grouper)* to crowd; **rien ne presse** there's no hurry; **se ~ contre qn** to squeeze up against sb; ~ **le pas** to quicken one's step; ~ **qn entre ses bras** to squeeze sb tight

**pressing** [pʀesiŋ] *nm* (repassage) steam-pressing; *(magasin)* dry-cleaner's

**pression** [pʀesjɔ̃] *nf* pressure; *(bouton)* press stud (Brit), snap fastener; **faire ~ sur** to put pressure on; **sous ~** pressurized, under pressure; *(fig)* keyed up; ~ **artérielle** blood pressure

**pressoir** [pʀeswaʀ] *nm* (wine ou oil etc) press

**pressurer** [pʀesyʀe] *vt* (fig) to squeeze

**pressurisé, e** [pʀesyʀize] *adj* pressurized

**prestance** [pʀɛstɑ̃s] *nf* presence, imposing bearing

**prestataire** [pʀɛstatɛʀ] *nm/f* person receiving benefits; *(Comm):* ~ **de services** provider of services

**prestation** [pʀɛstasjɔ̃] *nf* (allocation) benefit; *(d'une assurance)* cover no pl; *(d'une entreprise)* service provided; *(d'un joueur, artiste)* performance; ~ **de serment** taking the oath; ~ **de service** provision of a service; ~**s familiales** ≈ child benefit

**preste** [pʀɛst(ə)] *adj* nimble

**prestement** [pʀɛstəmɑ̃] *adv* nimbly

**prestidigitateur, -trice** [pʀɛstidiʒitatœʀ, -tʀis] *nm/f* conjurer

**prestidigitation** [pʀɛstidiʒitasjɔ̃] *nf* conjuring

**prestige** [pʀɛstiʒ] *nm* prestige

**prestigieux, -euse** [pʀɛstiʒjø, -øz] *adj* prestigious

**présumer** [pʀezyme] *vt*: ~ **que** to presume ou assume that; ~ **de** to overrate; ~ **qn coupable** to presume sb guilty

**présupposé** [pʀesypoze] *nm* presupposition

**présupposer** [pʀesypoze] *vt* to presuppose

**présupposition** [pʀesypozisjɔ̃] *nf* presupposition

**présure** [pʀezyʀ] *nf* rennet

**prêt, e** [pʀɛ, pʀɛt] *adj* ready ▷ *nm* lending no pl; *(somme prêtée)* loan; ~ **à faire** ready to do; ~ **à tout** ready for anything; ~ **sur gages** pawnbroking no pl

**prêt-à-porter** [pʀɛtapɔʀte] *(pl* **prêts-à-porter)** *nm* ready-to-wear ou off-the-peg (Brit) clothes *pl*

**prétendant** [pʀetɑ̃dɑ̃] *nm* pretender; *(d'une femme)* suitor

**prétendre** [pʀetɑ̃dʀ(ə)] *vt* (affirmer): ~ **que** to claim that; *(avoir l'intention de):* ~ **faire qch** to mean ou intend to do sth; ~ **à** *vt* (droit, titre) to lay claim to

**prétendu, e** [pʀetɑ̃dy] *adj* (supposé) so-called

**prétendument** [pʀetɑ̃dymɑ̃] *adv* allegedly

**prête-nom** [pʀɛtnɔ̃] *nm* (péj) figurehead; *(Comm etc)* dummy

**prétentieux, -euse** [pʀetɑ̃sjø, -øz] *adj* pretentious

**prétention** [pʀetɑ̃sjɔ̃] *nf* pretentiousness; *(exigence, ambition)* claim; **sans ~** unpretentious

**prêter** [pʀete] *vt* (livres, argent): ~ **qch (à)** to lend sth (to); *(supposer):* ~ **à qn** (caractère, propos) to attribute to sb ▷ *vi*: **se prêter** *(tissu, cuir)* to give; ~ **à** *(commentaires etc)* to be open to, give rise to; **se ~ à** to lend o.s. (ou itself) to; *(manigances etc)* to go along with; ~ **assistance à** to give help to; ~ **attention** to pay attention; ~ **serment** to take the oath; ~ **l'oreille** to listen

**prêteur, -euse** [pʀetœʀ, -øz] *nm/f* moneylender; ~ **sur gages** pawnbroker

**prétexte** [pʀetɛkst(ə)] *nm* pretext, excuse; **sous aucun ~** on no account; **sous (le) ~ que/de** on the pretext that/of

**prétexter** [pʀetɛkste] *vt* to give as a pretext ou an excuse

**prêtre** [pʀetʀ(ə)] *nm* priest

**prêtre-ouvrier** [pʀetʀuvʀije] *(pl* **prêtres-ouvriers)** *nm* worker-priest

**prêtrise** [pʀetʀiz] *nf* priesthood

**preuve** [pʀœv] *nf* proof; *(indice)* proof, evidence no pl; **jusqu'à ~ du contraire** until proved otherwise; **faire ~ de** to show; **faire ses ~s** to prove o.s. (ou itself); ~ **matérielle** material evidence

**prévaloir** [pʀevalwaʀ] *vi* to prevail; **se ~ de** *vt* to take advantage of; *(tirer vanité de)* to pride o.s. on

**prévarication** [pʀevaʀikasjɔ̃] *nf* maladministration

**prévaut** *etc* [pʀevo] *vb voir* **prévaloir**

**prévenances** [pʀevnɑ̃s] *nfpl* thoughtfulness *sg*, kindness *sg*

**prévenant, e** [pʀevnɑ̃, -ɑ̃t] *adj* thoughtful, kind

**prévenir** [pʀevniʀ] *vt* (éviter) to avoid, prevent; *(anticiper)* to anticipate; ~ **qn (de)** *(avertir)* to warn sb (about); *(informer)* to tell ou inform sb (about); ~ **qn contre** *(influencer)* to prejudice sb against

**préventif, -ive** [pʀevɑ̃tif, -iv] *adj* preventive

**prévention** [pʀevɑ̃sjɔ̃] *nf* prevention; *(préjugé)* prejudice; *(Jur)* custody, detention; ~ **routière** road safety

**prévenu, e** [pʀevny] *nm/f* (*Jur*) defendant, accused

**prévisible** [pʀevizibl(ə)] *adj* foreseeable

**prévision** [pʀevizjɔ̃] *nf*: **~s** predictions; (*météorologiques, économiques*) forecast *sg*; **en ~ de** in anticipation of; **~s météorologiques** *ou* **du temps** weather forecast *sg*

**prévisionnel, le** [pʀevizjɔnɛl] *adj* concerned with future requirements

**prévit** *etc* [pʀevi] *vb voir* **prévoir**

**prévoir** [pʀevwaʀ] *vt* (*deviner*) to foresee; (*s'attendre à*) to expect, reckon on; (*prévenir*) to anticipate; (*organiser*) to plan; (*préparer, réserver*) to allow; **prévu pour quatre personnes** designed for four people; **prévu pour 10 h** scheduled for 10 o'clock

**prévoyance** [pʀevwajɑ̃s] *nf* foresight; **société/caisse de ~** provident society/contingency fund

**prévoyant, e** [pʀevwajɑ̃, -ɑ̃t] *vb voir* **prévoir** ▷ *adj* gifted with (*ou* showing) foresight, far-sighted

**prévu, e** [pʀevy] *pp de* **prévoir**

**prier** [pʀije] *vi* to pray ▷ *vt* (*Dieu*) to pray to; (*implorer*) to beg; (*demander*): **~ qn de faire** to ask sb to do; (*inviter*): **~ qn à dîner** to invite sb to dinner; **se faire ~** to need coaxing *ou* persuading; **je vous en prie** (*allez-y*) please do; (*de rien*) don't mention it; **je vous prie de faire** please (would you) do

**prière** [pʀijɛʀ] *nf* prayer; (*demande instante*) plea, entreaty; **"~ de faire ..."** "please do ..."

**primaire** [pʀimɛʀ] *adj* primary; (*péj: personne*) simple-minded; (*: idées*) simplistic ▷ *nm* (*Scol*) primary education

**primauté** [pʀimote] *nf* (*fig*) primacy

**prime** [pʀim] *nf* (*bonification*) bonus; (*subside*) allowance; (*Comm: cadeau*) free gift; (*Assurances, Bourse*) premium ▷ *adj*: **de ~ abord** at first glance; **~ de risque** danger money *no pl*; **~ de transport** travel allowance

**primer** [pʀime] *vt* (*l'emporter sur*) to prevail over; (*récompenser*) to award a prize to ▷ *vi* to dominate, prevail

**primesautier, -ière** [pʀimsotje, -jɛʀ] *adj* impulsive

**primeur** [pʀimœʀ] *nf*: **avoir la ~ de** to be the first to hear (*ou* see *etc*); **primeurs** *nfpl* (*fruits, légumes*) early fruits and vegetables; **marchand de ~** greengrocer (*Brit*), produce dealer (*US*)

**primevère** [pʀimvɛʀ] *nf* primrose

**primitif, -ive** [pʀimitif, -iv] *adj* primitive; (*originel*) original ▷ *nm/f* primitive

**primo** [pʀimo] *adv* first (of all), firstly

**primordial, e, -aux** [pʀimɔʀdjal, -o] *adj* essential, primordial

**prince** [pʀɛ̃s] *nm* prince; **~ charmant** Prince Charming; **~ de Galles** *nm inv* (*tissu*) check cloth; **~ héritier** crown prince

**princesse** [pʀɛ̃sɛs] *nf* princess

**princier, -ière** [pʀɛ̃sje, -jɛʀ] *adj* princely

**principal, e, -aux** [pʀɛ̃sipal, -o] *adj* principal, main ▷ *nm* (*Scol*) head (teacher) (*Brit*), principal

(*US*); (*essentiel*) main thing ▷ *nf* (*Ling*): (**proposition**) **~e** main clause

**principalement** [pʀɛ̃sipalmɑ̃] *adv* principally, mainly

**principauté** [pʀɛ̃sipote] *nf* principality

**principe** [pʀɛ̃sip] *nm* principle; **partir du ~ que** to work on the principle *ou* assumption that; **pour le ~** on principle, for the sake of it; **de ~** *adj* (*hostilité*) automatic; (*accord*) in principle; **par ~** on principle; **en ~** (*habituellement*) as a rule; (*théoriquement*) in principle

**printanier, -ière** [pʀɛ̃tanje, -jɛʀ] *adj* spring, spring-like

**printemps** [pʀɛ̃tɑ̃] *nm* spring; **au ~** in spring

**priori** [pʀijɔʀi]: **a ~** *adv* at first glance, initially; a priori

**prioritaire** [pʀijɔʀitɛʀ] *adj* having priority; (*Auto*) having right of way; (*Inform*) foreground

**priorité** [pʀijɔʀite] *nf* (*Auto*): **avoir la ~ (sur)** to have right of way (over); **~ à droite** right of way to vehicles coming from the right; **en ~** as a (matter of) priority

**pris, e** [pʀi, pʀiz] *pp de* **prendre** ▷ *adj* (*place*) taken; (*billets*) sold; (*journée, mains*) full; (*personne*) busy; (*crème, ciment*) set; (*Méd: enflammé*): **avoir le nez/la gorge ~(e)** to have a stuffy nose/a bad throat; (*saisi*): **être ~ de peur/de fatigue** to be stricken with fear/overcome with fatigue

**prise** [pʀiz] *nf* (*d'une ville*) capture; (*Pêche, Chasse*) catch; (*de judo ou catch, point d'appui ou pour empoigner*) hold; (*Élec: fiche*) plug; (*: femelle*) socket; (*: au mur*) point; **en ~** (*Auto*) in gear; **être aux ~s avec** to be grappling with; to be battling with; **lâcher ~** to let go; **donner ~ à** (*fig*) to give rise to; **avoir ~ sur qn** to have a hold over sb; **~ en charge** (*taxe*) pick-up charge; (*par la sécurité sociale*) undertaking to reimburse costs; **~ de contact** initial meeting, first contact; **~ de courant** power point; **~ d'eau** water (supply) point; tap; **~ multiple** adaptor; **~ d'otages** hostage-taking; **~ à partie** (*Jur*) action against a judge; **~ de sang** blood test; **~ de son** sound recording; **~ de tabac** pinch of snuff; **~ de terre** earth; **~ de vue** (*photo*) shot; (*action*): **~ de vue(s)** filming, shooting

**priser** [pʀize] *vt* (*tabac, héroïne*) to take; (*estimer*) to prize, value ▷ *vi* to take snuff

**prisme** [pʀism(ə)] *nm* prism

**prison** [pʀizɔ̃] *nf* prison; **aller/être en ~** to go to/be in prison *ou* jail; **faire de la ~** to serve time; **être condamné à cinq ans de ~** to be sentenced to five years' imprisonment *ou* five years in prison

**prisonnier, -ière** [pʀizɔnje, -jɛʀ] *nm/f* prisoner ▷ *adj* captive; **faire qn ~** to take sb prisoner

**prit** [pʀi] *vb voir* **prendre**

**privatif, -ive** [pʀivatif, -iv] *adj* (*jardin etc*) private; (*peine*) which deprives one of one's liberties

**privations** [pʀivasjɔ̃] *nfpl* privations, hardships

**privatisation** [pʀivatizasjɔ̃] *nf* privatization

**privatiser** [pʀivatize] *vt* to privatize

**privautés** [pʀivote] *nfpl* liberties
**privé, e** [pʀive] *adj* private; (*dépourvu*): ~ **de**
  without, lacking; **en** ~, **dans le** ~ in private
**priver** [pʀive] *vt*: ~ **qn de** to deprive sb of; **se** ~
  **de** to go *ou* do without; **ne pas se** ~ **de faire** not
  to refrain from doing
**privilège** [pʀivilɛʒ] *nm* privilege
**privilégié, e** [pʀivileʒje] *adj* privileged
**privilégier** [pʀivileʒje] *vt* to favour (*Brit*), favor
  (*US*)
**prix** [pʀi] *nm* (*valeur*) price; (*récompense, Scol*)
  prize; **mettre à** ~ to set a reserve (*Brit*) *ou* an
  upset (*US*) price on; **au** ~ **fort** at a very high
  price; **acheter qch à** ~ **d'or** to pay a (small)
  fortune for sth; **hors de** ~ exorbitantly priced;
  **à aucun** ~ not at any price; **à tout** ~ at all costs;
  **grand** ~ (*Sport*) Grand Prix; ~ **d'achat/de vente/**
  **de revient** purchasing/selling/cost price; ~
  **conseillé** manufacturer's recommended price
  (MRP)
**pro** [pʀo] *nm* (= *professionnel*) pro
**probabilité** [pʀobabilite] *nf* probability; **selon**
  **toute** ~ in all probability
**probable** [pʀobabl(ə)] *adj* likely, probable
**probablement** [pʀobabləmã] *adv* probably
**probant, e** [pʀobã, -ãt] *adj* convincing
**probatoire** [pʀobatwaʀ] *adj* (*examen, test*)
  preliminary; (*stage*) probationary, trial *cpd*
**probité** [pʀobite] *nf* integrity, probity
**problématique** [pʀoblematik] *adj*
  problematic(al) ▷ *nf* problematics *sg*; (*problème*)
  problem
**problème** [pʀoblɛm] *nm* problem
**procédé** [pʀosede] *nm* (*méthode*) process;
  (*comportement*) behaviour *no pl* (*Brit*), behavior *no*
  *pl* (*US*)
**procéder** [pʀosede] *vi* to proceed; to behave; ~ **à**
  *vt* to carry out
**procédure** [pʀosedyʀ] *nf* (*Admin, Jur*) procedure
**procès** [pʀosɛ] *nm* (*Jur*) trial; (: *poursuites*)
  proceedings *pl*; **être en** ~ **avec** to be involved in
  a lawsuit with; **faire le** ~ **de qn/qch** (*fig*) to put
  sb/sth on trial; **sans autre forme de** ~ without
  further ado
**processeur** [pʀosesœʀ] *nm* processor
**procession** [pʀosesjõ] *nf* procession
**processus** [pʀosesys] *nm* process
**procès-verbal, -aux** [pʀosɛveʀbal, -o] *nm*
  (*constat*) statement; (*aussi*: **PV**): **avoir un** ~ to get
  a parking ticket; to be booked; (*de réunion*)
  minutes *pl*
**prochain, e** [pʀoʃɛ̃, -ɛn] *adj* next; (*proche*)
  impending; near ▷ *nm* fellow man; **la ~e fois/**
  **semaine ~e** next time/week; **à la ~e!** (*fam*): **à la**
  **~e fois** see you!, till the next time!; **un** ~ **jour**
  (some day) soon
**prochainement** [pʀoʃɛnmã] *adv* soon, shortly
**proche** [pʀoʃ] *adj* nearby; (*dans le temps*)
  imminent; close at hand; (*parent, ami*) close;
  **proches** *nmpl* (*parents*) close relatives, next of
  kin; (*amis*): **l'un de ses ~s** one of those close to
  him (*ou* her); **être** ~ (**de**) to be near, be close to);

**de** ~ **en** ~ gradually
**Proche-Orient** [pʀoʃoʀjã] *nm*: **le** ~ the Near East
**proclamation** [pʀoklamasjõ] *nf* proclamation
**proclamer** [pʀoklame] *vt* to proclaim; (*résultat*
  *d'un examen*) to announce
**procréer** [pʀokʀee] *vt* to procreate
**procuration** [pʀokyʀasjõ] *nf* proxy; power of
  attorney; **voter par** ~ to vote by proxy
**procurer** [pʀokyʀe] *vt* (*fournir*): ~ **qch à qn** to get
  *ou* obtain sth for sb; (*causer: plaisir etc*): ~ **qch à**
  **qn** to bring *ou* give sb sth; **se procurer** *vt* to get
**procureur** [pʀokyʀœʀ] *nm* public prosecutor; ~
  **général** public prosecutor (*in appeal court*)
**prodigalité** [pʀodigalite] *nf* (*générosité*)
  generosity; (*extravagance*) extravagance,
  wastefulness
**prodige** [pʀodiʒ] *nm* (*miracle, merveille*) marvel,
  wonder; (*personne*) prodigy
**prodigieusement** [pʀodiʒjøzmã] *adv*
  tremendously
**prodigieux, -euse** [pʀodiʒjø, -øz] *adj*
  prodigious; phenomenal
**prodigue** [pʀodig] *adj* (*généreux*) generous;
  (*dépensier*) extravagant, wasteful; **fils** ~ prodigal
  son
**prodiguer** [pʀodige] *vt* (*argent, biens*) to be lavish
  with; (*soins, attentions*): ~ **qch à qn** to lavish sth
  on sb
**producteur, -trice** [pʀodyktœʀ, -tʀis] *adj*: ~ **de**
  **blé** wheat-producing; (*Ciné*): **société**
  **productrice** film *ou* movie company ▷ *nm/f*
  producer
**productif, -ive** [pʀodyktif, -iv] *adj* productive
**production** [pʀodyksjõ] *nf* (*gén*) production;
  (*rendement*) output; (*produits*) products *pl*, goods
  *pl*; (*œuvres*): **la** ~ **dramatique du XVIIe siècle**
  the plays of the 17th century
**productivité** [pʀodyktivite] *nf* productivity
**produire** [pʀodɥiʀ] *vt, vi* to produce; **se**
  **produire** *vi* (*acteur*) to perform, appear;
  (*événement*) to happen, occur
**produit, e** [pʀodɥi, -it] *pp de* **produire** ▷ *nm* (*gén*)
  product; ~ **d'entretien** cleaning product; ~
  **national brut (PNB)** gross national product
  (GNP); ~ **net** net profit; ~ **pour la vaisselle**
  washing-up (*Brit*) *ou* dish-washing (*US*) liquid;
  ~ **des ventes** income from sales; **~s agricoles**
  farm produce *sg*; **~s alimentaires** foodstuffs;
  **~s de beauté** beauty products, cosmetics
**proéminent, e** [pʀoeminã, -ãt] *adj* prominent
**prof** [pʀof] *nm* (*fam*: = *professeur*) teacher;
  professor; lecturer
**prof.** [pʀof] *abr* = **professeur; professionnel**
**profane** [pʀofan] *adj* (*Rel*) secular; (*ignorant, non*
  *initié*) uninitiated ▷ *nm/f* layman
**profaner** [pʀofane] *vt* to desecrate; (*fig*:
  *sentiment*) to defile; (: *talent*) to debase
**proférer** [pʀofeʀe] *vt* to utter
**professer** [pʀofese] *vt* to profess
**professeur, e** [pʀofesœʀ] *nm/f* teacher; (*titulaire*
  *d'une chaire*) professor; ~ **(de faculté)**
  (university) lecturer

**P**

**profession** [pʀɔfɛsjɔ̃] nf (libérale) profession; (gén) occupation; **faire ~ de** (opinion, religion) to profess; **de ~** by profession; **"sans ~"** "unemployed"; (femme mariée) "housewife"

**professionnel, le** [pʀɔfɛsjɔnɛl] adj professional ▷ nm/f professional; (ouvrier qualifié) skilled worker

**professoral, e, -aux** [pʀɔfesɔʀal, -o] adj professorial; **le corps ~** the teaching profession

**professorat** [pʀɔfesɔʀa] nm: **le ~** the teaching profession

**profil** [pʀɔfil] nm profile; (d'une voiture) line, contour; **de ~** in profile

**profilé, e** [pʀɔfile] adj shaped; (aile etc) streamlined

**profiler** [pʀɔfile] vt to streamline; **se profiler** vi (arbre, tour) to stand out, be silhouetted

**profit** [pʀɔfi] nm (avantage) benefit, advantage; (Comm, Finance) profit; **au ~ de** in aid of; **tirer** ou **retirer ~ de** to profit from; **mettre à ~** to take advantage of; to turn to good account; **~s et pertes** (Comm) profit and loss(es)

**profitable** [pʀɔfitabl(ə)] adj beneficial; profitable

**profiter** [pʀɔfite] vi: **~ de** to take advantage of; to make the most of; **~ de ce que** ... to take advantage of the fact that ...; **~ à** to be of benefit to, benefit; to be profitable to

**profiteur, -euse** [pʀɔfitœʀ, -øz] nm/f (péj) profiteer

**profond, e** [pʀɔfɔ̃, -ɔ̃d] adj deep; (méditation, mépris) profound; **peu ~** (eau, vallée, puits) shallow; (coupure) superficial; **au plus ~ de** in the depths of, at the (very) bottom of; **la France ~e** the heartlands of France

**profondément** [pʀɔfɔ̃demɑ̃] adv deeply; profoundly

**profondeur** [pʀɔfɔ̃dœʀ] nf depth

**profusément** [pʀɔfyzemɑ̃] adv profusely

**profusion** [pʀɔfyzjɔ̃] nf profusion; **à ~** in plenty

**progéniture** [pʀɔʒenityʀ] nf offspring inv

**progiciel** [pʀɔʒisjɛl] nm (Inform) (software) package; **~ d'application** applications package, applications software no pl

**progouvernemental, e, -aux** [pʀɔguvɛʀnəmɑ̃tal, -o] adj pro-government cpd

**programmable** [pʀɔgʀamabl(ə)] adj programmable

**programmateur, -trice** [pʀɔgʀamatœʀ, -tʀis] nm/f (Ciné, TV) programme (Brit) ou program (US) planner ▷ nm (de machine à laver etc) timer

**programmation** [pʀɔgʀamasjɔ̃] nf programming

**programme** [pʀɔgʀam] nm programme (Brit), program (US); (TV, Radio) program(me)s pl; (Scol) syllabus, curriculum; (Inform) program; **au ~ de ce soir** (TV) among tonight's program(me)s

**programmé, e** [pʀɔgʀame] adj: **enseignement ~** programmed learning

**programmer** [pʀɔgʀame] vt (TV, Radio) to put on, show; (organiser, prévoir) to schedule; (Inform) to program

**programmeur, -euse** [pʀɔgʀamœʀ, -øz] nm/f (computer) programmer

**progrès** [pʀɔgʀɛ] nm progress no pl; **faire des/ être en ~** to make/be making progress

**progresser** [pʀɔgʀese] vi to progress; (troupes etc) to make headway ou progress

**progressif, -ive** [pʀɔgʀesif, -iv] adj progressive

**progression** [pʀɔgʀesjɔ̃] nf progression; (d'une troupe etc) advance, progress

**progressiste** [pʀɔgʀesist(ə)] adj progressive

**progressivement** [pʀɔgʀesivmɑ̃] adv progressively

**prohiber** [pʀɔibe] vt to prohibit, ban

**prohibitif, -ive** [pʀɔibitif, -iv] adj prohibitive

**prohibition** [pʀɔibisjɔ̃] nf ban, prohibition; (Hist) Prohibition

**proie** [pʀwa] nf prey no pl; **être la ~ de** to fall prey to; **être en ~ à** (doutes, sentiment) to be prey to; (douleur, mal) to be suffering

**projecteur** [pʀɔʒɛktœʀ] nm projector; (de théâtre, cirque) spotlight

**projectile** [pʀɔʒɛktil] nm missile; (d'arme) projectile, bullet (ou shell etc)

**projection** [pʀɔʒɛksjɔ̃] nf projection; showing; **conférence avec ~s** lecture with slides (ou a film)

**projectionniste** [pʀɔʒɛksjɔnist(ə)] nm/f (Ciné) projectionist

**projet** [pʀɔʒɛ] nm plan; (ébauche) draft; **faire des ~s** to make plans; **~ de loi** bill

**projeter** [pʀɔʒte] vt (envisager) to plan; (film, photos) to project; (passer) to show; (ombre, lueur) to throw, cast, project; (jeter) to throw up (ou off ou out); **~ de faire qch** to plan to do sth

**prolétaire** [pʀɔletɛʀ] adj, nm/f proletarian

**prolétariat** [pʀɔletaʀja] nm proletariat

**prolétarien, -ne** [pʀɔletaʀjɛ̃, -ɛn] adj proletarian

**prolifération** [pʀɔlifeʀasjɔ̃] nf proliferation

**proliférer** [pʀɔlifeʀe] vi to proliferate

**prolifique** [pʀɔlifik] adj prolific

**prolixe** [pʀɔliks(ə)] adj verbose

**prolo** [pʀɔlo] nm/f (fam: = prolétaire) prole (péj)

**prologue** [pʀɔlɔg] nm prologue

**prolongateur** [pʀɔlɔ̃gatœʀ] nm (Élec) extension cable

**prolongation** [pʀɔlɔ̃gasjɔ̃] nf prolongation; extension; **prolongations** nfpl (Football) extra time sg

**prolongement** [pʀɔlɔ̃ʒmɑ̃] nm extension; **prolongements** nmpl (fig) repercussions, effects; **dans le ~ de** running on from

**prolonger** [pʀɔlɔ̃ʒe] vt (débat, séjour) to prolong; (délai, billet, rue) to extend; (chose) to be a continuation ou an extension of; **se prolonger** vi to go on

**promenade** [pʀɔmnad] nf walk (ou drive ou ride); **faire une ~** to go for a walk; **une ~ (à pied)/en voiture/à vélo** a walk/drive/(bicycle) ride

**promener** [pʀɔmne] vt (personne, chien) to take out for a walk; (fig) to carry around; to trail round; *(doigts, regard)*: ~ **qch sur** to run sth over; **se promener** *vi (à pied)* to go for *(ou* be out for) a walk; *(en voiture)* to go for *(ou* be out for) a drive; *(fig)*: **se ~ sur** to wander over

**promeneur, -euse** [pʀɔmnœʀ, -øz] *nm/f* walker, stroller

**promenoir** [pʀɔmənwaʀ] *nm* gallery, (covered) walkway

**promesse** [pʀɔmɛs] *nf* promise; ~ **d'achat** commitment to buy

**prometteur, -euse** [pʀɔmɛtœʀ, -øz] *adj* promising

**promettre** [pʀɔmɛtʀ(ə)] *vt* to promise ▷ *vi (récolte, arbre)* to look promising; *(enfant, musicien)* to be promising; **se ~ de faire** to resolve *ou* mean to do; ~ **à qn de faire** to promise sb that one will do

**promeus** *etc* [pʀɔmø] *vb voir* **promouvoir**

**promis, e** [pʀɔmi, -iz] *pp de* **promettre** ▷ *adj*: **être ~ à qch** *(destiné)* to be destined for sth

**promiscuité** [pʀɔmiskɥite] *nf* crowding; lack of privacy

**promit** [pʀɔmi] *vb voir* **promettre**

**promontoire** [pʀɔmɔ̃twaʀ] *nm* headland

**promoteur, -trice** [pʀɔmɔtœʀ, -tʀis] *nm/f (instigateur)* instigator, promoter; ~ **(immobilier)** property developer *(Brit)*, real estate promoter *(US)*

**promotion** [pʀɔmɔsjɔ̃] *nf (avancement)* promotion; *(Scol)* year *(Brit)*, class; **en ~** *(Comm)* on promotion, on (special) offer

**promotionnel, le** [pʀɔmɔsjɔnɛl] *adj (article)* on promotion, on (special) offer; *(vente)* promotional

**promouvoir** [pʀɔmuvwaʀ] *vt* to promote

**prompt, e** [pʀɔ̃, pʀɔ̃t] *adj* swift, rapid; *(intervention, changement)* sudden; ~ **à faire qch** quick to do sth

**promptement** [pʀɔ̃ptəmɑ̃] *adv* swiftly

**prompteur**® [pʀɔ̃tœʀ] *nm* Autocue® *(Brit)*, Teleprompter® *(US)*

**promptitude** [pʀɔ̃tityd] *nf* swiftness, rapidity

**promu, e** [pʀɔmy] *pp de* **promouvoir**

**promulguer** [pʀɔmylge] *vt* to promulgate

**prôner** [pʀone] *vt (louer)* to laud, extol; *(préconiser)* to advocate, commend

**pronom** [pʀɔnɔ̃] *nm* pronoun

**pronominal, e, -aux** [pʀɔnɔminal, -o] *adj* pronominal; *(verbe)* reflexive, pronominal

**prononcé, e** [pʀɔnɔ̃se] *adj* pronounced, marked

**prononcer** [pʀɔnɔ̃se] *vt (son, mot, jugement)* to pronounce; *(dire)* to utter; *(allocution)* to deliver ▷ *vi (Jur)* to deliver *ou* give a verdict; ~ **bien/mal** to have good/poor pronunciation; **se prononcer** *vi* to reach a decision, give a verdict; **se ~ sur** to give an opinion on; **se ~ contre** to come down against; **ça se prononce comment?** how do you pronounce this?

**prononciation** [pʀɔnɔ̃sjasjɔ̃] *nf* pronunciation

**pronostic** [pʀɔnɔstik] *nm (Méd)* prognosis; *(fig: aussi:* **pronostics**) forecast

**pronostiquer** [pʀɔnɔstike] *vt (Méd)* to

prognosticate; *(annoncer, prévoir)* to forecast, foretell

**pronostiqueur, -euse** [pʀɔnɔstikœʀ, -øz] *nm/f* forecaster

**propagande** [pʀɔpagɑ̃d] *nf* propaganda; **faire de la ~ pour qch** to plug *ou* push sth

**propagandiste** [pʀɔpagɑ̃dist(ə)] *nm/f* propagandist

**propagation** [pʀɔpagasjɔ̃] *nf* propagation

**propager** [pʀɔpaʒe] *vt* to spread; **se propager** *vi* to spread; *(Physique)* to be propagated

**propane** [pʀɔpan] *nm* propane

**propension** [pʀɔpɑ̃sjɔ̃] *nf*: ~ **à (faire) qch** propensity to (do) sth

**prophète** [pʀɔfɛt], **prophétesse** [pʀɔfetɛs] *nm/f* prophet(ess)

**prophétie** [pʀɔfesi] *nf* prophecy

**prophétique** [pʀɔfetik] *adj* prophetic

**prophétiser** [pʀɔfetize] *vt* to prophesy

**prophylactique** [pʀɔfilaktik] *adj* prophylactic

**propice** [pʀɔpis] *adj* favourable *(Brit)*, favorable *(US)*

**proportion** [pʀɔpɔʀsjɔ̃] *nf* proportion; **il n'y a aucune ~ entre le prix demandé et le prix réel** the asking price bears no relation to the real price; **à ~ de** proportionally to, in proportion to; **en ~ (de)** in proportion (to); **hors de ~** out of proportion; **toute(s) ~(s) gardée(s)** making due allowance(s)

**proportionné, e** [pʀɔpɔʀsjɔne] *adj*: **bien ~** well-proportioned; ~ **à** proportionate to

**proportionnel, le** [pʀɔpɔʀsjɔnɛl] *adj* proportional; ~ **à** proportional to ▷ *nf* proportional representation

**proportionnellement** [pʀɔpɔʀsjɔnɛlmɑ̃] *adv* proportionally, proportionately

**proportionner** [pʀɔpɔʀsjɔne] *vt*: ~ **qch à** to proportion *ou* adjust sth to

**propos** [pʀɔpo] *nm (paroles)* talk *no pl*, remark; *(intention, but)* intention, aim; *(sujet)*: **à quel ~?** what about?; **à ~ de** about, regarding; **à tout ~** for no reason at all; **à ce ~** on that subject, in this connection; **à ~** *adv* by the way; *(opportunément)* (just) at the right moment; **hors de ~, mal à ~** *adv* at the wrong moment

**proposer** [pʀɔpoze] *vt (suggérer)*: ~ **qch (à qn)/de faire** to suggest sth (to sb)/doing, propose sth (to sb)/(to) do; *(offrir)*: ~ **qch à qn/de faire** to offer sb sth/to do; *(candidat)* to nominate, put forward; *(loi, motion)* to propose; **se ~ (pour faire)** to offer one's services (to do); **se ~ de faire** to intend *ou* propose to do

**proposition** [pʀɔpozisjɔ̃] *nf* suggestion; proposal; offer; *(Ling)* clause; **sur la ~ de** at the suggestion of; ~ **de loi** private bill

**propre** [pʀɔpʀ(ə)] *adj* clean; *(net)* neat, tidy; *(qui ne salit pas: chien, chat)* house-trained; *(: enfant)* toilet-trained; *(fig: honnête)* honest; *(possessif)* own; *(sens)* literal; *(particulier)*: ~ **à** peculiar to, characteristic of; *(approprié)*: ~ **à** suitable *ou* appropriate for; *(de nature à)*: ~ **à faire** likely to do, that will do ▷ *nm*: **recopier au ~** to make a

fair copy of; *(particularité)*: **le ~ de** the
peculiarity of, the distinctive feature of; **au ~**
*(Ling)* literally; **appartenir à qn en ~** to belong
to sb (exclusively); **~ à rien** *nm/f (péj)* good-for-
nothing

**proprement** [pʀɔpʀəmɑ̃] *adv* cleanly; neatly,
tidily; **à ~ parler** strictly speaking; **le village ~
dit** the actual village, the village itself

**propret, te** [pʀɔpʀɛ, -ɛt] *adj* neat and tidy, spick-
and-span

**propreté** [pʀɔpʀəte] *nf* cleanliness, cleanness;
neatness, tidiness

**propriétaire** [pʀɔpʀijetɛʀ] *nm/f* owner; *(d'hôtel
etc)* proprietor(-tress), owner; *(pour le locataire)*
landlord(-lady); **~ (immobilier)** house-owner;
householder; **~ récoltant** grower; **~ (terrien)**
landowner

**propriété** [pʀɔpʀijete] *nf (droit)* ownership;
*(objet, immeuble etc)* property *gen no pl; (villa)*
residence, property; *(terres)* property *gen no pl,*
land *gen no pl; (qualité, Chimie, Math)* property;
*(correction)* appropriateness, suitability; **~
artistique et littéraire** artistic and literary
copyright; **~ industrielle** patent rights *pl*

**propulser** [pʀɔpylse] *vt (missile)* to propel;
*(projeter)* to hurl, fling

**propulsion** [pʀɔpylsjɔ̃] *nf* propulsion

**prorata** [pʀɔʀata] *nm inv:* **au ~ de** in proportion
to, on the basis of

**prorogation** [pʀɔʀɔgasjɔ̃] *nf* deferment;
extension; adjournment

**proroger** [pʀɔʀɔʒe] *vt* to put back, defer;
*(prolonger)* to extend; *(assemblée)* to adjourn,
prorogue

**prosaïque** [pʀɔzaik] *adj* mundane, prosaic

**proscription** [pʀɔskʀipsjɔ̃] *nf* banishment;
*(interdiction)* banning; prohibition

**proscrire** [pʀɔskʀiʀ] *vt (bannir)* to banish;
*(interdire)* to ban, prohibit

**prose** [pʀoz] *nf* prose *(style)*

**prosélyte** [pʀɔzelit] *nm/f* proselyte, convert

**prospecter** [pʀɔspɛkte] *vt* to prospect; *(Comm)*
to canvass

**prospecteur-placier** [pʀɔspɛktœʀplasje] *(pl
**prospecteurs-placiers**) nm* placement officer

**prospectif, -ive** [pʀɔspɛktif, -iv] *adj* prospective

**prospectus** [pʀɔspɛktys] *nm (feuille)* leaflet;
*(dépliant)* brochure, leaflet

**prospère** [pʀɔspɛʀ] *adj* prosperous; *(santé,
entreprise)* thriving, flourishing

**prospérer** [pʀɔspeʀe] *vi* to thrive

**prospérité** [pʀɔspeʀite] *nf* prosperity

**prostate** [pʀɔstat] *nf* prostate (gland)

**prosterner** [pʀɔstɛʀne]: **se prosterner** *vi* to
bow low, prostrate o.s

**prostituée** [pʀɔstitɥe] *nf* prostitute

**prostitution** [pʀɔstitysjɔ̃] *nf* prostitution

**prostré, e** [pʀɔstʀe] *adj* prostrate

**protagoniste** [pʀɔtagɔnist(ə)] *nm* protagonist

**protecteur, -trice** [pʀɔtɛktœʀ, -tʀis] *adj*
protective; *(air, ton: péj)* patronizing ▷ *nm/f
(défenseur)* protector; *(des arts)* patron

**protection** [pʀɔtɛksjɔ̃] *nf* protection; *(d'un
personnage influent: aide)* patronage; **écran de ~**
protective screen; **~ civile** state-financed civilian
rescue service; **~ maternelle et infantile (PMI)**
social service concerned with child welfare

**protectionnisme** [pʀɔtɛksjɔnism(ə)] *nm*
protectionism

**protectionniste** [pʀɔtɛksjɔnist(ə)] *adj*
protectionist

**protégé, e** [pʀɔteʒe] *nm/f* protégé(e)

**protège-cahier** [pʀɔtɛʒkaje] *nm* exercise book
cover

**protéger** [pʀɔteʒe] *vt* to protect; *(aider, patronner:
personne, arts)* to be a patron of; *(: carrière)* to
further; **se ~ de/contre** to protect o.s. from

**protège-slip** [pʀɔtɛʒslip] *nm* panty liner

**protéine** [pʀɔtein] *nf* protein

**protestant, e** [pʀɔtɛstɑ̃, -ɑ̃t] *adj, nm/f* Protestant

**protestantisme** [pʀɔtɛstɑ̃tism(ə)] *nm*
Protestantism

**protestataire** [pʀɔtɛstatɛʀ] *nm/f* protestor

**protestation** [pʀɔtɛstasjɔ̃] *nf (plainte)* protest;
*(déclaration)* protestation, profession

**protester** [pʀɔtɛste] *vi:* **~ (contre)** to protest
(against *ou* about); **~ de** *(son innocence, sa loyauté)*
to protest

**prothèse** [pʀɔtɛz] *nf* artificial limb, prosthesis;
**~ dentaire** *(appareil)* denture; *(science)* dental
engineering

**protocolaire** [pʀɔtɔkɔlɛʀ] *adj* formal; *(questions,
règles)* of protocol

**protocole** [pʀɔtɔkɔl] *nm* protocol; *(fig)*
etiquette; **~ d'accord** draft treaty; **~ opératoire**
*(Méd)* operating procedure

**prototype** [pʀɔtɔtip] *nm* prototype

**protubérance** [pʀɔtybeʀɑ̃s] *nf* bulge,
protuberance

**protubérant, e** [pʀɔtybeʀɑ̃, -ɑ̃t] *adj* protruding,
bulging, protuberant

**proue** [pʀu] *nf* bow(s *pl*), prow

**prouesse** [pʀuɛs] *nf* feat

**prouver** [pʀuve] *vt* to prove

**provenance** [pʀɔvnɑ̃s] *nf* origin; *(de mot,
coutume)* source; **avion en ~ de** plane (arriving)
from

**provençal, e, -aux** [pʀɔvɑ̃sal, -o] *adj* Provençal
▷ *nm (Ling)* Provençal

**Provence** [pʀɔvɑ̃s] *nf:* **la ~** Provence

**provenir** [pʀɔvniʀ]: **~ de** *vt* to come from;
*(résulter de)* to be due to, be the result of

**proverbe** [pʀɔvɛʀb(ə)] *nm* proverb

**proverbial, e, -aux** [pʀɔvɛʀbjal, -o] *adj*
proverbial

**providence** [pʀɔvidɑ̃s] *nf:* **la ~** providence

**providentiel, le** [pʀɔvidɑ̃sjɛl] *adj* providential

**province** [pʀɔvɛ̃s] *nf* province

**provincial, e, -aux** [pʀɔvɛ̃sjal, -o] *adj, nm/f*
provincial

**proviseur** [pʀɔvizœʀ] *nm* ≈ head (teacher) *(Brit)*,
≈ principal *(US)*

**provision** [pʀɔvizjɔ̃] *nf (réserve)* stock, supply;
*(avance: à un avocat, avoué)* retainer, retaining fee;

(*Comm*) funds *pl* (in account); reserve;
**provisions** *nfpl* (*vivres*) provisions, food *no pl*;
**faire ~ de** to stock up with; **placard** *ou* **armoire**
**à ~s** food cupboard
**provisoire** [pʀɔvizwaʀ] *adj* temporary; (*Jur*)
provisional; **mise en liberté ~** release on bail
**provisoirement** [pʀɔvizwaʀmɑ̃] *adv*
temporarily, for the time being
**provocant, e** [pʀɔvɔkɑ̃, -ɑ̃t] *adj* provocative
**provocateur, -trice** [pʀɔvɔkatœʀ, -tʀis] *adj*
provocative ▷ *nm* (*meneur*) agitator
**provocation** [pʀɔvɔkasjɔ̃] *nf* provocation
**provoquer** [pʀɔvɔke] *vt* (*défier*) to provoke;
(*causer*) to cause, bring about; (: *curiosité*) to
arouse, give rise to; (: *aveux*) to prompt, elicit;
(*inciter*): **~ qn à** to incite sb to
**prox.** *abr* = **proximité**
**proxénète** [pʀɔksenɛt] *nm* procurer
**proxénétisme** [pʀɔksenetism(ə)] *nm* procuring
**proximité** [pʀɔksimite] *nf* nearness, closeness,
proximity; (*dans le temps*) imminence, closeness;
**à ~** near *ou* close by; **à ~ de** near (to), close to
**prude** [pʀyd] *adj* prudish
**prudemment** [pʀydamɑ̃] *adv* (*voir prudent*)
carefully; cautiously; prudently; wisely, sensibly
**prudence** [pʀydɑ̃s] *nf* carefulness; caution;
prudence; **avec ~** carefully; cautiously; wisely;
**par (mesure de) ~** as a precaution
**prudent, e** [pʀydɑ̃, -ɑ̃t] *adj* (*pas téméraire*) careful,
cautious, prudent; (: *en général*) safety-
conscious; (*sage, conseillé*) wise, sensible; (*réservé*)
cautious; **ce n'est pas ~** it's risky; it's not
sensible; **soyez ~** take care, be careful
**prune** [pʀyn] *nf* plum
**pruneau, x** [pʀyno] *nm* prune
**prunelle** [pʀynɛl] *nf* pupil; (*œil*) eye; (*Bot*) sloe;
(*eau de vie*) sloe gin
**prunier** [pʀynje] *nm* plum tree
**Prusse** [pʀys] *nf*: **la ~** Prussia
**PS** *sigle m* = **parti socialiste**; (= *post-scriptum*) PS
**psalmodier** [psalmɔdje] *vt* to chant; (*fig*) to
drone out
**psaume** [psom] *nm* psalm
**pseudonyme** [psødɔnim] *nm* (*gén*) fictitious
name; (*d'écrivain*) pseudonym, pen name; (*de
comédien*) stage name
**PSIG** *sigle m* (= *Peloton de surveillance et d'intervention
de gendarmerie*) *type of police commando squad*
**PSU** *sigle m* = **parti socialiste unifié**
**psy** [psi] *nm/f* (*fam*: = *psychiatre, psychologue*) shrink
**psychanalyse** [psikanaliz] *nf* psychoanalysis
**psychanalyser** [psikanalize] *vt* to
psychoanalyze; **se faire ~** to undergo
(psycho)analysis
**psychanalyste** [psikanalist(ə)] *nm/f*
psychoanalyst
**psychanalytique** [psikanalitik] *adj*
psychoanalytical
**psychédélique** [psikedelik] *adj* psychedelic
**psychiatre** [psikjatʀ(ə)] *nm/f* psychiatrist
**psychiatrie** [psikjatʀi] *nf* psychiatry
**psychiatrique** [psikjatʀik] *adj* psychiatric;

(*hôpital*) mental, psychiatric
**psychique** [psiʃik] *adj* psychological
**psychisme** [psiʃism(ə)] *nm* psyche
**psychologie** [psikɔlɔʒi] *nf* psychology
**psychologique** [psikɔlɔʒik] *adj* psychological
**psychologiquement** [psikɔlɔʒikmɑ̃] *adv*
psychologically
**psychologue** [psikɔlɔg] *nm/f* psychologist;
**être ~** (*fig*) to be a good psychologist
**psychomoteur, -trice** [psikɔmɔtœʀ, -tʀis] *adj*
psychomotor
**psychopathe** [psikɔpat] *nm/f* psychopath
**psychopédagogie** [psikɔpedagɔʒi] *nf*
educational psychology
**psychose** [psikoz] *nf* (*Méd*) psychosis; (*obsession,
idée fixe*) obsessive fear
**psychosomatique** [psikɔsɔmatik] *adj*
psychosomatic
**psychothérapie** [psikɔteʀapi] *nf*
psychotherapy
**psychotique** [psikɔtik] *adj* psychotic
**PTCA** *sigle m* = **poids total en charge autorisé**
**Pte** *abr* = **Porte**
**pte** *abr* (= *pointe*) pt
**PTMA** *sigle m* (= *poids total maximum autorisé*)
maximum loaded weight
**PTT** *sigle fpl* = **poste**
**pu** [py] *pp de* **pouvoir**
**puanteur** [pɥɑ̃tœʀ] *nf* stink, stench
**pub** [pyb] *nf* (*fam*) = **publicité**; **la ~** advertising
**pubère** [pybɛʀ] *adj* pubescent
**puberté** [pybɛʀte] *nf* puberty
**pubis** [pybis] *nm* (*bas-ventre*) pubes *pl*; (*os*) pubis
**public, -ique** [pyblik] *adj* public; (*école,
instruction*) state *cpd*; (*scrutin*) open ▷ *nm* public;
(*assistance*) audience; **en ~** in public; **le grand ~**
the general public
**publication** [pyblikɑsjɔ̃] *nf* publication
**publiciste** [pyblisist(ə)] *nm/f* adman
**publicitaire** [pyblisitɛʀ] *adj* advertising *cpd*;
(*film, voiture*) publicity *cpd*; (*vente*) promotional
▷ *nm* adman; **rédacteur ~** copywriter
**publicité** [pyblisite] *nf* (*méthode, profession*)
advertising; (*annonce*) advertisement;
(*révélations*) publicity
**publier** [pyblije] *vt* to publish; (*nouvelle*) to
publicize, make public
**publipostage** [pyblipɔstaʒ] *nm* mailshot,
(mass) mailing
**publique** [pyblik] *adj f voir* **public**
**publiquement** [pyblikmɑ̃] *adv* publicly
**puce** [pys] *nf* flea; (*Inform*) chip; (**marché aux)
~s** flea market *sg*; **mettre la ~ à l'oreille de qn**
to give sb something to think about
**puceau, x** [pyso] *adj m*: **être ~** to be a virgin
**pucelle** [pysɛl] *adj f*: **être ~** to be a virgin
**puceron** [pysʀɔ̃] *nm* aphid
**pudeur** [pydœʀ] *nf* modesty
**pudibond, e** [pydibɔ̃, -ɔ̃d] *adj* prudish
**pudique** [pydik] *adj* (*chaste*) modest; (*discret*)
discreet
**pudiquement** [pydikmɑ̃] *adv* modestly

**puer** [pɥe] (*péj*) *vi* to stink ▷ *vt* to stink of, reek of
**puéricultrice** [pɥeʀikyltʀis] *nf* ≈ nursery nurse
**puériculture** [pɥeʀikyltyʀ] *nf* infant care
**puéril, e** [pɥeʀil] *adj* childish
**puérilement** [pɥeʀilmɑ̃] *adv* childishly
**puérilité** [pɥeʀilite] *nf* childishness; (*acte, idée*) childish thing
**pugilat** [pyʒila] *nm* (fist) fight
**puis** [pɥi] *vb voir* **pouvoir** ▷ *adv* (*ensuite*) then; (*dans une énumération*) next; (*en outre*): **et ~** and (then); **et ~ (après** *ou* **quoi)?** so (what)?
**puisard** [pɥizaʀ] *nm* (*égout*) cesspool
**puiser** [pɥize] *vt*: **~ (dans)** to draw (from); **~ dans qch** to dip into sth
**puisque** [pɥisk(ə)] *conj* since; (*valeur intensive*): **~ je te le dis!** I'm telling you!
**puissamment** [pɥisamɑ̃] *adv* powerfully
**puissance** [pɥisɑ̃s] *nf* power; **en ~** *adj* potential; **deux (à la) ~ cinq** two to the power (of) five
**puissant, e** [pɥisɑ̃, -ɑ̃t] *adj* powerful
**puisse** *etc* [pɥis] *vb voir* **pouvoir**
**puits** [pɥi] *nm* well; **~ artésien** artesian well; **~ de mine** mine shaft; **~ de science** fount of knowledge
**pull** [pyl], **pull-over** [pylɔvœʀ] *nm* sweater, jumper (*Brit*)
**pulluler** [pylyle] *vi* to swarm; (*fig: erreurs*) to abound, proliferate
**pulmonaire** [pylmɔnɛʀ] *adj* lung *cpd*; (*artère*) pulmonary
**pulpe** [pylp(ə)] *nf* pulp
**pulsation** [pylsasjɔ̃] *nf* (*Méd*) beat
**pulsé** [pylse] *adj m*: **chauffage à air ~** warm air heating
**pulsion** [pylsjɔ̃] *nf* (*Psych*) drive, urge
**pulvérisateur** [pylveʀizatœʀ] *nm* spray
**pulvérisation** [pylveʀizasjɔ̃] *nf* spraying
**pulvériser** [pylveʀize] *vt* (*solide*) to pulverize; (*liquide*) to spray; (*fig: anéantir: adversaire*) to pulverize; (: *record*) to smash, shatter; (: *argument*) to demolish
**puma** [pyma] *nm* puma, cougar
**punaise** [pynɛz] *nf* (*Zool*) bug; (*clou*) drawing pin (*Brit*), thumb tack (*US*)
**punch** [pɔ̃ʃ] *nm* (*boisson*) punch [pœnʃ] (*Boxe*) punching ability; (*fig*) punch
**punching-ball** [pœnʃiŋbol] *nm* punchball
**punir** [pyniʀ] *vt* to punish; **~ qn de qch** to punish sb for sth
**punitif, -ive** [pynitif, -iv] *adj* punitive
**punition** [pynisjɔ̃] *nf* punishment
**pupille** [pypij] *nf* (*Anat*) pupil ▷ *nm/f* (*enfant*) ward; **~ de l'État** child in care; **~ de la Nation** war orphan
**pupitre** [pypitʀ(ə)] *nm* (*Scol*) desk; (*Rel*) lectern; (*de chef d'orchestre*) rostrum; **~ de commande** control panel

**pur, e** [pyʀ] *adj* pure; (*vin*) undiluted; (*whisky*) neat; (*intentions*) honourable (*Brit*), honorable (*US*) ▷ *nm* (*personne*) hard-liner; **en ~e perte** fruitlessly, to no avail
**purée** [pyʀe] *nf*: **~ (de pommes de terre)** ≈ mashed potatoes *pl*; **~ de marrons** chestnut purée; **~ de pois** (*fig*) peasoup(er)
**purement** [pyʀmɑ̃] *adv* purely
**pureté** [pyʀte] *nf* purity
**purgatif** [pyʀɡatif] *nm* purgative, purge
**purgatoire** [pyʀɡatwaʀ] *nm* purgatory
**purge** [pyʀʒ(ə)] *nf* (*Pol*) purge; (*Méd*) purging *no pl*; purge
**purger** [pyʀʒe] *vt* (*radiateur*) to flush (out), drain; (*circuit hydraulique*) to bleed; (*Méd, Pol*) to purge; (*Jur: peine*) to serve
**purification** [pyʀifikasjɔ̃] *nf* (*de l'eau*) purification; **~ ethnique** ethnic cleansing
**purifier** [pyʀifje] *vt* to purify; (*Tech: métal*) to refine
**purin** [pyʀɛ̃] *nm* liquid manure
**puriste** [pyʀist(ə)] *nm/f* purist
**puritain, e** [pyʀitɛ̃, -ɛn] *adj, nm/f* Puritan
**puritanisme** [pyʀitanism(ə)] *nm* Puritanism
**pur-sang** [pyʀsɑ̃] *nm inv* thoroughbred, purebred
**purulent, e** [pyʀylɑ̃, -ɑ̃t] *adj* purulent
**pus** [py] *vb voir* **pouvoir** ▷ *nm* pus
**pusillanime** [pyzilanim] *adj* fainthearted
**pustule** [pystyl] *nf* pustule
**putain** [pytɛ̃] *nf* (*fam!*) whore (!); **ce/cette ~ de ...** this bloody (*Brit*) *ou* goddamn (*US*) ... (!)
**putois** [pytwa] *nm* polecat; **crier comme un ~** to yell one's head off
**putréfaction** [pytʀefaksjɔ̃] *nf* putrefaction
**putréfier** [pytʀefje] *vt*, **se putréfier** *vi* to putrefy, rot
**putride** [pytʀid] *adj* putrid
**putsch** [putʃ] *nm* (*Pol*) putsch
**puzzle** [pœzl(ə)] *nm* jigsaw (puzzle)
**PV** *sigle m* = **procès-verbal**
**PVC** *sigle f* (= *polychlorure de vinyle*) PVC
**PVD** *sigle mpl* (= *pays en voie de développement*) developing countries
**Px** *abr* = **prix**
**pygmée** [piɡme] *nm* pygmy
**pyjama** [piʒama] *nm* pyjamas *pl*, pair of pyjamas
**pylône** [pilon] *nm* pylon
**pyramide** [piʀamid] *nf* pyramid
**pyrénéen, ne** [piʀeneɛ̃, -ɛn] *adj* Pyrenean
**Pyrénées** [piʀene] *nfpl*: **les ~** the Pyrenees
**pyrex®** [piʀɛks] *nm* Pyrex®
**pyrogravure** [piʀɔɡʀavyʀ] *nf* poker-work
**pyromane** [piʀɔman] *nm/f* arsonist
**python** [pitɔ̃] *nm* python

# Qq

**Q, q** [ky] *nm inv* Q, q ▷ *abr* (= *quintal*) q; **Q comme Quintal** Q for Queen
**Qatar** [katar] *nm*: **le** ~ Qatar
**QCM** *sigle m* (= *questionnaire à choix multiples*) multiple-choice test
**QG** *sigle m* (= *quartier général*) HQ
**QHS** *sigle m* (= *quartier de haute sécurité*) high-security wing *ou* prison
**QI** *sigle m* (= *quotient intellectuel*) IQ
**qqch.** *abr* (= *quelque chose*) sth
**qqe** *abr* = **quelque**
**qqes** *abr* = **quelques**
**qqn** *abr* (= *quelqu'un*) sb, s.o.
**quadra** [k(w)adra] (*fam*) *nm/f* (= *quadragénaire*) person in his (*ou* her) forties; **les ~s** forty somethings (*fam*)
**quadragénaire** [kadraʒenɛr] *nm/f* (*de quarante ans*) forty-year-old; (*de quarante à cinquante ans*) man/woman in his/her forties
**quadrangulaire** [kwadrɑ̃gylɛr] *adj* quadrangular
**quadrature** [kwadratyr] *nf*: **c'est la ~ du cercle** it's like trying to square the circle
**quadrichromie** [kwadrikrɔmi] *nf* four-colour (*Brit*) *ou* -color (*US*) printing
**quadrilatère** [k(w)adrilatɛr] *nm* (*Géom, Mil*) quadrilateral; (*terrain*) four-sided area
**quadrillage** [kadrijaʒ] *nm* (*lignes etc*) square pattern, criss-cross pattern
**quadrillé, e** [kadrije] *adj* (*papier*) squared
**quadriller** [kadrije] *vt* (*papier*) to mark out in squares; (*Police: ville, région etc*) to keep under tight control, be positioned throughout
**quadrimoteur** [k(w)adrimɔtœr] *nm* four-engined plane
**quadripartite** [kwadripartit] *adj* (*entre pays*) four-power; (*entre partis*) four-party
**quadriphonie** [kadrifɔni] *nf* quadraphony
**quadriréacteur** [k(w)adrireaktœr] *nm* four-engined jet
**quadrupède** [k(w)adrypɛd] *nm* quadruped
**quadruple** [k(w)adrypl(ə)] *nm*: **le ~ de** four times as much as
**quadrupler** [k(w)adryple] *vt, vi* to quadruple, increase fourfold
**quadruplés, -ées** [k(w)adryple] *nm/fpl* quadruplets, quads

**quai** [ke] *nm* (*de port*) quay; (*de gare*) platform; (*de cours d'eau, canal*) embankment; **être à ~** (*navire*) to be alongside; (*train*) to be in the station; **le Q~ d'Orsay** offices of the French Ministry for Foreign Affairs; **le Q~ des Orfèvres** central police headquarters
**qualifiable** [kalifjabl(ə)] *adj*: **ce n'est pas ~** it defies description
**qualificatif, -ive** [kalifikatif, -iv] *adj* (*Ling*) qualifying ▷ *nm* (*terme*) term; (*Ling*) qualifier
**qualification** [kalifikɑsjɔ̃] *nf* qualification
**qualifié, e** [kalifje] *adj* qualified; (*main d'œuvre*) skilled
**qualifier** [kalifje] *vt* to qualify; (*appeler*): ~ **qch/qn de** to describe sth/sb as; **se qualifier** *vi* (*Sport*) to qualify; **être qualifié pour** to be qualified for
**qualitatif, -ive** [kalitatif, -iv] *adj* qualitative
**qualité** [kalite] *nf* quality; (*titre, fonction*) position; **en ~ de** in one's capacity as; **ès ~s** in an official capacity; **avoir ~ pour** to have authority to; **de ~** *adj* quality *cpd*; **rapport ~-prix** value (for money)
**quand** [kɑ̃] *conj, adv* when; ~ **je serai riche** when I'm rich; ~ **même** (*cependant, pourtant*) nevertheless; (*tout de même*) all the same; really; ~ **bien même** even though
**quant** [kɑ̃]: ~ **à** *prép* (*pour ce qui est de*) as for, as to; (*au sujet de*) regarding
**quant-à-soi** [kɑ̃taswa] *nm*: **rester sur son ~** to remain aloof
**quantième** [kɑ̃tjɛm] *nm* date, day (of the month)
**quantifiable** [kɑ̃tifjabl(ə)] *adj* quantifiable
**quantifier** [kɑ̃tifje] *vt* to quantify
**quantitatif, -ive** [kɑ̃titatif, -iv] *adj* quantitative
**quantitativement** [kɑ̃titativmɑ̃] *adv* quantitatively
**quantité** [kɑ̃tite] *nf* quantity, amount; (*Science*) quantity; (*grand nombre*): **une** *ou* **des ~(s) de** a great deal of; a lot of; **en grande** *ou* **en large** quantities; **en ~s industrielles** in vast amounts; **du travail en ~** a great deal of work; ~ **de** many
**quarantaine** [karɑ̃tɛn] *nf* (*isolement*)

*q*

quarantine; (*âge*): **avoir la ~** to be around forty; (*nombre*): **une ~ (de)** forty or so, about forty; **mettre en ~** to put into quarantine; (*fig*) to send to Coventry (*Brit*), ostracize

**quarante** [kaʀɑ̃t] *num* forty

**quarantième** [kaʀɑ̃tjɛm] *num* fortieth

**quark** [kwaʀk] *nm* quark

**quart** [kaʀ] *nm* (*fraction*) quarter; (*surveillance*) watch; (*partie*): **un ~ de poulet/fromage** a chicken quarter/a quarter of a cheese; **un ~ de beurre** a quarter kilo of butter, ≈ a half pound of butter; **un ~ de vin** a quarter litre of wine; **une livre un ~** *ou* **et ~** one and a quarter pounds; **le ~ de** a quarter of; **~ d'heure** quarter of an hour; **deux heures et** *ou* **un ~** (a) quarter past two, (a) quarter after two (*US*); **il est le ~** it's (a) quarter past *ou* after (*US*); **une heure moins le ~** (a) quarter to one, (a) quarter of one (*US*); **il est moins le ~** it's (a) quarter to; **être de/prendre le ~** to keep/take the watch; **~ de tour** quarter turn; **au ~ de tour** (*fig*) straight off; **~s de finale** (*Sport*) quarter finals

**quarté** [kaʀte] *nm* (*Courses*) system of forecast betting giving first four horses

**quarteron** [kaʀtəʀɔ̃] *nm* (*péj*) small bunch, handful

**quartette** [kwaʀtɛt] *nm* quartet(te)

**quartier** [kaʀtje] *nm* (*de ville*) district, area; (*de bœuf, de la lune*) quarter; (*de fruit, fromage*) piece; **quartiers** *nmpl* (*Mil, Blason*) quarters; **cinéma/ salle de ~** local cinema/hall; **avoir ~ libre** to be free; (*Mil*) to have leave from barracks; **ne pas faire de ~** to spare no one, give no quarter; **~ commerçant/résidentiel** shopping/ residential area; **~ général (QG)** headquarters (HQ)

**quartier-maître** [kaʀtjemɛtʀ(ə)] *nm* ≈ leading seaman

**quartz** [kwaʀts] *nm* quartz

**quasi** [kazi] *adv* almost, nearly ▷ *préfixe*: **~- certitude** near certainty

**quasiment** [kazimɑ̃] *adv* almost, very nearly

**quaternaire** [kwatɛʀnɛʀ] *adj* (*Géo*) Quaternary

**quatorze** [katɔʀz(ə)] *num* fourteen

**quatorzième** [katɔʀzjɛm] *num* fourteenth

**quatrain** [katʀɛ̃] *nm* quatrain

**quatre** [katʀ(ə)] *num* four; **à ~ pattes** on all fours; **tiré à ~ épingles** dressed up to the nines; **faire les ~ cent coups** to be a bit wild; **se mettre en ~ pour qn** to go out of one's way for sb; **~ à ~** (*monter, descendre*) four at a time; **à ~ mains** (*jouer*) four-handed

**quatre-vingt-dix** [katʀəvɛ̃dis] *num* ninety

**quatre-vingts** [katʀəvɛ̃] *num* eighty

**quatre-vingt-un** *num* eighty-one

**quatrième** [katʀijɛm] *num* fourth

**quatuor** [kwatɥɔʀ] *nm* quartet(te)

**MOT-CLÉ**

**que** [kə] *conj* **1** (*introduisant complétive*) that; **il sait que tu es là** he knows (that) you're here; **je**

**veux que tu acceptes** I want you to accept; **il a dit que oui** he said he would (*ou* it was *etc*)

**2** (*reprise d'autres conjonctions*): **quand il rentrera et qu'il aura mangé** when he gets back and (when) he has eaten; **si vous y allez ou que vous ...** if you go there or if you ...

**3** (*en tête de phrase: hypothèse, souhait etc*): **qu'il le veuille ou non** whether he likes it or not; **qu'il fasse ce qu'il voudra!** let him do as he pleases!

**4** (*but*): **tenez-le qu'il ne tombe pas** hold it so (that) it doesn't fall

**5** (*après comparatif*) than; as; *voir aussi* **plus; aussi; autant** *etc*

**6** (*seulement*): **ne ... que** only; **il ne boit que de l'eau** he only drinks water

**7** (*temps*): **elle venait à peine de sortir qu'il se mit à pleuvoir** she had just gone out when it started to rain, no sooner had she gone out than it started to rain; **il y a quatre ans qu'il est parti** it is four years since he left, he left four years ago

▷ *adv* (*exclamation*): **qu'il** *ou* **qu'est-ce qu'il est bête/court vite!** he's so silly!/he runs so fast!; **que de livres!** what a lot of books!

▷ *pron* **1** (*relatif: personne*) whom; (: *chose*) that, which; **l'homme que je vois** the man (whom) I see; **le livre que tu vois** the book (that *ou* which) you see; **un jour que j'étais ...** a day when I was ..

**2** (*interrogatif*) what; **que fais-tu?, qu'est-ce que tu fais?** what are you doing?; **qu'est-ce que c'est?** what is it?, what's that?; **que faire?** what can we do?; **que préfères-tu, celui-ci ou celui-là?** which (one) do you prefer, this one or that one?

**Québec** [kebɛk] *n* (*ville*) Quebec ▷ *nm*: **le ~** Quebec (Province)

**québécois, e** [kebekwa, -waz] *adj* Quebec *cpd* ▷ *nm* (*Ling*) Quebec French ▷ *nm/f*: **Québécois, e** Quebecois, Quebec(k)er

**MOT-CLÉ**

**quel, quelle** [kɛl] *adj* **1** (*interrogatif: personne*) who; (: *chose*) what; which; **quel est cet homme?** who is this man?; **quel est ce livre?** what is this book?; **quel livre/homme?** what book/man?; (*parmi un certain choix*) which book/ man?; **quels acteurs préférez-vous?** which actors do you prefer?; **dans quels pays êtes-vous allé?** which *ou* what countries did you go to?

**2** (*exclamatif*): **quelle surprise/coïncidence!** what a surprise/coincidence!

**3**: **quel(le) que soit le coupable** whoever is guilty; **quel que soit votre avis** whatever your opinion (may be)

**quelconque** [kɛlkɔ̃k] *adj* (*médiocre*) indifferent, poor; (*sans attrait*) ordinary, plain; (*indéfini*): **un ami/prétexte ~** some friend/pretext or other;

**un livre ~ suffira** any book will do; **pour une raison ~** for some reason (or other)

 MOT-CLÉ

**quelque** [kɛlkə] *adj* **1** some; a few; *(tournure interrogative)* any; **quelque espoir** some hope; **il a quelques amis** he has a few *ou* some friends; **a-t-il quelques amis?** has he any friends?; **les quelques livres qui** the few books which; **20 kg et quelque(s)** a bit over 20 kg; **il habite à quelque distance d'ici** he lives some distance *ou* way (away) from here

**2**: **quelque ... que** whatever, whichever; **quelque livre qu'il choisisse** whatever *(ou* whichever) book he chooses; **par quelque temps qu'il fasse** whatever the weather

**3**: **quelque chose** something; *(tournure interrogative)* anything; **quelque chose d'autre** something else; anything else; **y être pour quelque chose** to have something to do with it; **faire quelque chose à qn** to have an effect on sb, do something to sb; **quelque part** somewhere; anywhere; **en quelque sorte** as it were

▷ *adv* **1** *(environ)*: **quelque 100 mètres** some 100 metres

**2**: **quelque peu** rather, somewhat

**quelquefois** [kɛlkəfwa] *adv* sometimes
**quelques-uns, --unes** [kɛlkəzœ̃, -yn] *pron* some, a few; **~ des lecteurs** some of the readers
**quelqu'un** [kɛlkœ̃] *pron* someone, somebody; *(tournure interrogative ou négative+)* anyone *ou* anybody; **quelqu'un d'autre** someone *ou* somebody else; anybody else
**quémander** [kemɑ̃de] *vt* to beg for
**qu'en dira-t-on** [kɑ̃diratɔ̃] *nm inv*: **le qu'en dira-t-on** gossip, what people say
**quenelle** [kənɛl] *nf* quenelle
**quenouille** [kənuj] *nf* distaff
**querelle** [kərɛl] *nf* quarrel; **chercher ~ à qn** to pick a quarrel with sb
**quereller** [kərele]: **se quereller** *vi* to quarrel
**querelleur, -euse** [kərɛlœr, -øz] *adj* quarrelsome
**qu'est-ce que** [kɛskə] *voir* **que**
**qu'est-ce qui** [kɛski] *voir* **qui**
**question** [kɛstjɔ̃] *nf* (*gén*) question; *(fig)* matter; issue; **il a été ~ de** we *(ou* they) spoke about; **il est ~ de les emprisonner** there's talk of them being jailed; **c'est une ~ de temps** it's a matter *ou* question of time; **de quoi est-il ~?** what is it about?; **il n'en est pas ~** there's no question of it; **en ~** in question; **hors de ~** out of the question; **je ne me suis jamais posé la ~** I've never thought about it; **(re)mettre en ~** *(autorité, science)* to question; **poser la ~ de confiance** *(Pol)* to ask for a vote of confidence; **~ piège** *(d'apparence facile)* trick question; *(pour nuire)* loaded question; **~ subsidiaire** tiebreaker
**questionnaire** [kɛstjɔnɛr] *nm* questionnaire

**questionner** [kɛstjɔne] *vt* to question
**quête** [kɛt] *nf* (*collecte*) collection; *(recherche)* quest, search; **faire la ~** *(à l'église)* to take the collection; *(artiste)* to pass the hat round; **se mettre en ~ de qch** to go in search of sth
**quêter** [kete] *vi* *(à l'église)* to take the collection; *(dans la rue)* to collect money (for charity) ▷ *vt* to seek
**quetsche** [kwɛtʃ(ə)] *nf* damson
**queue** [kø] *nf* tail; *(fig: du classement)* bottom; *(: de poêle)* handle; *(: de fruit, feuille)* stalk; *(: de train, colonne, file)* rear; *(file: de personnes)* queue *(Brit)*, line *(US)*; **en ~ (de train)** at the rear of the train); **faire la ~** to queue (up) *(Brit)*, line up *(US)*; **se mettre à la ~** to join the queue *ou* line; **histoire sans ~ ni tête** cock and bull story; **à la ~ leu leu** in single file; *(fig)* one after the other; **~ de cheval** ponytail; **~ de poisson: faire une ~ de poisson à qn** *(Auto)* to cut in front of sb; **finir en ~ de poisson** *(film)* to come to an abrupt end
**queue-de-pie** [kødpi] *(pl* **queues-de-pie**) *nf* (*habit*) tails *pl*, tail coat
**queux** [kø] *adj m voir* **maître**
**qui** [ki] *pron (personne)* who; *(avec préposition)* whom; *(chose, animal)* which, that; *(interrogatif indirect: sujet)*: **je me demande ~ est là?** I wonder who is there?; *(: objet)*: **elle ne sait à ~ se plaindre** she doesn't know who to complain to *ou* to whom to complain; **qu'est-ce ~ est sur la table?** what is on the table?; **à ~ est ce sac?** whose bag is this?; **à ~ parlais-tu?** who were you talking to?, to whom were you talking?; **chez ~ allez-vous?** whose house are you going to?; **amenez ~ vous voulez** bring who(ever) you like; **~ est-ce ~ ...?** who?; **~ est-ce que ...?** who?; whom?; **~ que ce soit** whoever it may be
**quiche** [kiʃ] *nf* quiche; **~ lorraine** quiche Lorraine
**quiconque** [kikɔ̃k] *pron (celui qui)* whoever, anyone who; *(n'importe qui, personne)* anyone, anybody
**quidam** [kɥidam] *nm (hum)* fellow
**quiétude** [kjetyd] *nf (d'un lieu)* quiet, tranquillity; *(d'une personne)* peace (of mind), serenity; **en toute ~** in complete peace; *(mentale)* with complete peace of mind
**quignon** [kiɲɔ̃] *nm*: **~ de pain** *(croûton)* crust of bread; *(morceau)* hunk of bread
**quille** [kij] *nf* ninepin, skittle *(Brit)*; *(Navig: d'un bateau)* keel; **(jeu de) ~s** ninepins *sg*, skittles *sg (Brit)*
**quincaillerie** [kɛ̃kajri] *nf (ustensiles, métier)* hardware, ironmongery *(Brit)*; *(magasin)* hardware shop *ou* store *(US)*, ironmonger's *(Brit)*
**quincaillier, -ière** [kɛ̃kaje, -jɛr] *nm/f* hardware dealer, ironmonger *(Brit)*
**quinconce** [kɛ̃kɔ̃s] *nm*: **en ~** in staggered rows
**quinine** [kinin] *nf* quinine
**quinqua** [kɛ̃ka] *(fam) nm/f (= quinquagénaire)* person in his *(ou* her) fifties; **les ~s** fifty somethings *(fam)*

**quinquagénaire** [kɛ̃kaʒenɛʀ] *nm/f* (*de cinquante ans*) fifty-year old; (*de cinquante à soixante ans*) man/woman in his/her fifties

**quinquennal, e, -aux** [kɛ̃kenal, -o] *adj* five-year, quinquennial

**quinquennat** [kɛ̃kena] *nm* five year term of office (*of French President*)

**quintal, -aux** [kɛ̃tal, -o] *nm* quintal (*100 kg*)

**quinte** [kɛ̃t] *nf*: ~ **(de toux)** coughing fit

**quintessence** [kɛ̃tesɑ̃s] *nf* quintessence, very essence

**quintette** [kɛ̃tɛt] *nm* quintet(te)

**quintuple** [kɛ̃typl(ə)] *nm*: **le ~ de** five times as much as

**quintupler** [kɛ̃typle] *vt, vi* to increase fivefold

**quintuplés, -ées** [kɛ̃typle] *nm/fpl* quintuplets, quins

**quinzaine** [kɛ̃zɛn] *nf*: **une ~ (de)** about fifteen, fifteen or so; **une ~ (de jours)** (*deux semaines*) a fortnight (*Brit*), two weeks; ~ **publicitaire** *ou* **commerciale** (two-week) sale

**quinze** [kɛ̃z] *num* fifteen; **demain en ~** a fortnight (*Brit*) *ou* two weeks tomorrow; **dans ~ jours** in a fortnight('s time) (*Brit*), in two weeks(' time)

**quinzième** [kɛ̃zjɛm] *num* fifteenth

**quiproquo** [kipʀoko] *nm* (*méprise sur une personne*) mistake; (*malentendu sur un sujet*) misunderstanding; (*Théât*) (case of) mistaken identity

**Quito** [kito] *n* Quito

**quittance** [kitɑ̃s] *nf* (*reçu*) receipt; (*facture*) bill

**quitte** [kit] *adj*: **être ~ envers qn** to be no longer in sb's debt; (*fig*) to be quits with sb; **être ~ de** (*obligation*) to be clear of; **en être ~ à bon compte** to have got off lightly; ~ **à faire** even if it means doing; ~ **ou double** (*jeu*) double or quits; (*fig*): **c'est du ~ ou double** it's a big risk

**quitter** [kite] *vt* to leave; (*espoir, illusion*) to give up; (*vêtement*) to take off; **se quitter** (*couples, interlocuteurs*) to part; **ne quittez pas** (*au téléphone*) hold the line; **ne pas ~ qn d'une semelle** to stick to sb like glue

**quitus** [kitys] *nm* final discharge; **donner ~ à** to discharge

**qui-vive** [kiviv] *nm inv*: **être sur le ~** to be on the alert

**quoi** [kwa] *pron* (*interrogatif*) what; ~ **de neuf** *ou* **de nouveau?** what's new *ou* the news?; **as-tu de ~ écrire?** have you anything to write with?; **il n'a pas de ~ se l'acheter** he can't afford it, he hasn't got the money to buy it; **il y a de ~ être fier** that's something to be proud of; **"il n'y a pas de ~"** "(please) don't mention it", "not at all"; ~ **qu'il arrive** whatever happens; ~ **qu'il en soit** be that as it may; ~ **que ce soit** anything at all; **en ~ puis-je vous aider?** how can I help you?; **à ~ bon?** what's the use *ou* point?; **et puis ~ encore!** what(ever) next!; ~ **faire?** what's to be done?; **sans ~** (*ou sinon*) otherwise

**quoique** [kwak(ə)] *conj* (al)though

**quolibet** [kɔlibɛ] *nm* gibe, jeer

**quorum** [kɔʀɔm] *nm* quorum

**quota** [kwɔta] *nm* quota

**quote-part** [kɔtpaʀ] *nf* share

**quotidien, ne** [kɔtidjɛ̃, -ɛn] *adj* (*journalier*) daily; (*banal*) ordinary, everyday ▷ *nm* (*journal*) daily (paper); (*vie quotidienne*) daily life, day-to-day existence; **les grands ~s** the big (national) dailies

**quotidiennement** [kɔtidjɛnmɑ̃] *adv* daily, every day

**quotient** [kɔsjɑ̃] *nm* (*Math*) quotient; ~ **intellectuel (QI)** intelligence quotient (IQ)

**quotité** [kɔtite] *nf* (*Finance*) quota

# Rr

**R, r** [ɛʀ] *nm inv* R, r ▷ *abr* = **route**; **rue**; **R comme Raoul** R for Robert (*Brit*) *ou* Roger (*US*)
**rab** [ʀab] (*fam*), **rabiot** [ʀabjo] *nm* extra, more
**rabâcher** [ʀabɑʃe] *vi* to harp on ▷ *vt* keep on repeating
**rabais** [ʀabɛ] *nm* reduction, discount; **au ~** at a reduction *ou* discount
**rabaisser** [ʀabese] *vt* (*rabattre*) to reduce; (*dénigrer*) to belittle
**rabane** [ʀaban] *nf* raffia (matting)
**Rabat** [ʀaba(t)] *n* Rabat
**rabat** [ʀaba] *vb voir* **rabattre** ▷ *nm* flap
**rabat-joie** [ʀabaʒwa] *nm/f inv* killjoy (*Brit*), spoilsport
**rabatteur, -euse** [ʀabatœʀ, -øz] *nm/f* (*de gibier*) beater; (*péj*) tout
**rabattre** [ʀabatʀ(ə)] *vt* (*couvercle, siège*) to pull down; (*col*) to turn down; (*couture*) to stitch down; (*gibier*) to drive; (*somme d'un prix*) to deduct, take off; (*orgueil, prétentions*) to humble; (*Tricot*) to decrease; **se rabattre** *vi* (*bords, couvercle*) to fall shut; (*véhicule, coureur*) to cut in; **se ~ sur** (*accepter*) to fall back on
**rabattu, e** [ʀabaty] *pp de* **rabattre** ▷ *adj* turned down
**rabbin** [ʀabɛ̃] *nm* rabbi
**rabique** [ʀabik] *adj* rabies *cpd*
**râble** [ʀɑbl(ə)] *nm* back; (*Culin*) saddle
**râblé, e** [ʀɑble] *adj* broad-backed, stocky
**rabot** [ʀabo] *nm* plane
**raboter** [ʀabɔte] *vt* to plane (down)
**raboteux, -euse** [ʀabɔtø, -øz] *adj* uneven, rough
**rabougri, e** [ʀabugʀi] *adj* stunted
**rabrouer** [ʀabʀue] *vt* to snub, rebuff
**racaille** [ʀakɑj] *nf* (*péj*) rabble, riffraff
**raccommodage** [ʀakɔmɔdaʒ] *nm* mending *no pl*, repairing *no pl*; darning *no pl*
**raccommoder** [ʀakɔmɔde] *vt* to mend, repair; (*chaussette etc*) to darn; (*fam: réconcilier: amis, ménage*) to bring together again; **se ~ (avec)** (*fam*) to patch it up (with)
**raccompagner** [ʀakɔ̃paɲe] *vt* to take *ou* see back
**raccord** [ʀakɔʀ] *nm* link; **~ de maçonnerie** pointing *no pl*; **~ de peinture** join; touch-up

**raccordement** [ʀakɔʀdəmɑ̃] *nm* joining up; connection
**raccorder** [ʀakɔʀde] *vt* to join (up), link up; (*pont etc*) to connect, link; **se ~ à** to join up with; (*fig: se rattacher à*) to tie in with; **~ au réseau du téléphone** to connect to the telephone service
**raccourci** [ʀakuʀsi] *nm* short cut; **en ~** in brief
**raccourcir** [ʀakuʀsiʀ] *vt* to shorten ▷ *vi* (*vêtement*) to shrink
**raccroc** [ʀakʀo]: **par ~** *adv* by chance
**raccrocher** [ʀakʀoʃe] *vt* (*tableau, vêtement*) to hang back up; (*récepteur*) to put down; (*fig: affaire*) to save ▷ *vi* (*Tél*) to hang up, ring off; **se ~ à** *vt* to cling to, hang on to; **ne raccrochez pas** (*Tél*) hold on, don't hang up
**race** [ʀas] *nf* race; (*d'animaux, fig: espèce*) breed; (*ascendance, origine*) stock, race; **de ~** *adj* purebred, pedigree
**racé, e** [ʀase] *adj* thoroughbred
**rachat** [ʀaʃa] *nm* buying; buying back; redemption; atonement
**racheter** [ʀaʃte] *vt* (*article perdu*) to buy another; (*davantage*): **~ du lait/trois œufs** to buy more milk/another three eggs *ou* three more eggs; (*après avoir vendu*) to buy back; (*d'occasion*) to buy; (*Comm: part, firme*) to buy up; (*: pension, rente*) to redeem; (*Rel: pécheur*) to redeem; (*: péché*) to atone for, expiate; (*mauvaise conduite, oubli, défaut*) to make up for; **se racheter** (*Rel*) to redeem o.s.; (*gén*) to make amends, make up for it
**rachitique** [ʀaʃitik] *adj* suffering from rickets; (*fig*) scraggy, scrawny
**rachitisme** [ʀaʃitism(ə)] *nm* rickets *sg*
**racial, e, -aux** [ʀasjal, -o] *adj* racial
**racine** [ʀasin] *nf* root; (*fig: attache*) roots *pl*; **~ carrée/cubique** square/cube root; **prendre ~** (*fig*) to take root; to put down roots
**racisme** [ʀasism(ə)] *nm* racism, racialism
**raciste** [ʀasist(ə)] *adj, nm/f* racist, racialist
**racket** [ʀakɛt] *nm* racketeering *no pl*
**racketteur** [ʀakɛtœʀ] *nm* racketeer
**raclée** [ʀɑkle] *nf* (*fam*) hiding, thrashing
**raclement** [ʀɑkləmɑ̃] *nm* (*bruit*) scraping (noise)
**racler** [ʀɑkle] *vt* (*os, plat*) to scrape; (*tache, boue*) to scrape off; (*fig: instrument*) to scrape on; (*chose: frotter contre*) to scrape (against)

r

**raclette** [ʀaklɛt] *nf* (*Culin*) raclette (*Swiss cheese dish*)

**racloir** [ʀaklwaʀ] *nm* (*outil*) scraper

**racolage** [ʀakɔlaʒ] *nm* soliciting; touting

**racoler** [ʀakɔle] *vt* (*attirer: prostituée*) to solicit; (*: parti, marchand*) to tout for; (*attraper*) to pick up

**racoleur, -euse** [ʀakɔlœʀ, -øz] *adj* (*péj*) cheap and alluring ▷ *nm* (*péj: de clients etc*) tout ▷ *nf* streetwalker

**racontars** [ʀakɔtaʀ] *nmpl* stories, gossip *sg*

**raconter** [ʀakɔte] *vt*: ~ (**à qn**) (*décrire*) to relate (to sb), tell (sb) about; (*dire*) to tell (sb)

**racorni, e** [ʀakɔʀni] *adj* hard(ened)

**racornir** [ʀakɔʀniʀ] *vt* to harden

**radar** [ʀadaʀ] *nm* radar; **système** ~ radar system; **écran** ~ radar screen

**rade** [ʀad] *nf* (*natural*) harbour; **en** ~ **de Toulon** in Toulon harbour; **rester en** ~ (*fig*) to be left stranded

**radeau, x** [ʀado] *nm* raft; ~ **de sauvetage** life raft

**radial, e, -aux** [ʀadjal, -o] *adj* radial

**radiant, e** [ʀadjɑ̃, -ɑ̃t] *adj* radiant

**radiateur** [ʀadjatœʀ] *nm* radiator, heater; (*Auto*) radiator; ~ **électrique/à gaz** electric/gas heater *ou* fire

**radiation** [ʀadjɑsjɔ̃] *nf* (*d'un nom etc*) striking off *no pl*; (*Physique*) radiation

**radical, e, -aux** [ʀadikal, -o] *adj* radical ▷ *nm* (*Ling*) stem; (*Math*) root sign; (*Pol*) radical

**radicalement** [ʀadikalmɑ̃] *adv* radically, completely

**radicaliser** [ʀadikalize] *vt* (*durcir: opinions etc*) to harden; **se radicaliser** *vi* (*mouvement etc*) to become more radical

**radicalisme** [ʀadikalism(ə)] *nm* (*Pol*) radicalism

**radier** [ʀadje] *vt* to strike off

**radiesthésie** [ʀadjɛstezi] *nf* divination (by radiation)

**radiesthésiste** [ʀadjɛstezist(ə)] *nm/f* diviner

**radieux, -euse** [ʀadjø, -øz] *adj* (*visage, personne*) radiant; (*journée, soleil*) brilliant, glorious

**radin, e** [ʀadɛ̃, -in] *adj* (*fam*) stingy

**radio** [ʀadjo] *nf* radio; (*Méd*) X-ray ▷ *nm* (*personne*) radio operator; **à la** ~ on the radio; **avoir la** ~ to have a radio; **passer à la** ~ to be on the radio; **se faire faire une** ~/**une** ~ **des poumons** to have an X-ray/a chest X-ray

**radio...** [ʀadjo] *préfixe* radio...

**radioactif, -ive** [ʀadjɔaktif, -iv] *adj* radioactive

**radioactivité** [ʀadjɔaktivite] *nf* radioactivity

**radioamateur** [ʀadjɔamatœʀ] *nm* (radio) ham

**radiobalise** [ʀadjɔbaliz] *nf* radio beacon

**radiocassette** [ʀadjɔkasɛt] *nf* cassette radio

**radiodiffuser** [ʀadjɔdifyze] *vt* to broadcast

**radiodiffusion** [ʀadjɔdifyzjɔ̃] *nf* (radio) broadcasting

**radioélectrique** [ʀadjɔelɛktʀik] *adj* radio *cpd*

**radiographie** [ʀadjɔgʀafi] *nf* radiography; (*photo*) X-ray photograph, radiograph

**radiographier** [ʀadjɔgʀafje] *vt* to X-ray; **se faire** ~ to have an X-ray

**radioguidage** [ʀadjɔgidaʒ] *nm* (*Navig, Aviat*) radio control; (*Auto*) (broadcast of) traffic information

**radioguider** [ʀadjɔgide] *vt* (*Navig, Aviat*) to guide by radio, control by radio

**radiologie** [ʀadjɔlɔʒi] *nf* radiology

**radiologique** [ʀadjɔlɔʒik] *adj* radiological

**radiologue** [ʀadjɔlɔg] *nm/f* radiologist

**radiophonique** [ʀadjɔfɔnik] *adj*: **programme/émission/jeu** ~ radio programme/broadcast/game

**radio-réveil** [ʀadjɔʀevɛj] *nm* clock radio

**radioscopie** [ʀadjɔskɔpi] *nf* radioscopy

**radio-taxi** [ʀadjɔtaksi] *nm* radiotaxi

**radiotélescope** [ʀadjɔtelɛskɔp] *nm* radiotelescope

**radiotélévisé, e** [ʀadjɔtelevize] *adj* broadcast on radio and television

**radiothérapie** [ʀadjɔteʀapi] *nf* radiotherapy

**radis** [ʀadi] *nm* radish; ~ **noir** horseradish *no pl*

**radium** [ʀadjɔm] *nm* radium

**radoter** [ʀadɔte] *vi* to ramble on

**radoub** [ʀadu] *nm*: **bassin** *ou* **cale de** ~ dry dock

**radouber** [ʀadube] *vt* to repair, refit

**radoucir** [ʀadusiʀ]: **se radoucir** *vi* (*se réchauffer*) to become milder; (*se calmer*) to calm down; to soften

**radoucissement** [ʀadusismɑ̃] *nm* milder period, better weather

**rafale** [ʀafal] *nf* (*vent*) gust (of wind); (*de balles, d'applaudissements*) burst; ~ **de mitrailleuse** burst of machine-gun fire

**raffermir** [ʀafɛʀmiʀ] *vt*, **se raffermir** *vi* (*tissus, muscle*) to firm up; (*fig*) to strengthen

**raffermissement** [ʀafɛʀmismɑ̃] *nm* (*fig*) strengthening

**raffinage** [ʀafinaʒ] *nm* refining

**raffiné, e** [ʀafine] *adj* refined

**raffinement** [ʀafinmɑ̃] *nm* refinement

**raffiner** [ʀafine] *vt* to refine

**raffinerie** [ʀafinʀi] *nf* refinery

**raffoler** [ʀafɔle]: ~ **de** *vt* to be very keen on

**raffut** [ʀafy] *nm* (*fam*) row, racket

**rafiot** [ʀafjo] *nm* tub

**rafistoler** [ʀafistɔle] *vt* (*fam*) to patch up

**rafle** [ʀafl(ə)] *nf* (*de police*) roundup, raid

**rafler** [ʀafle] *vt* (*fam*) to swipe, nick

**rafraîchir** [ʀafʀeʃiʀ] *vt* (*atmosphère, température*) to cool (down); (*aussi*: **mettre à rafraîchir**) to chill; (*air, eau*) to freshen up; (*: boisson*) to refresh; (*fig: rénover*) to brighten up ▷ *vi*: **mettre du vin/une boisson à** ~ to chill wine/a drink; **se rafraîchir** to grow cooler; to freshen up; (*personne: en buvant etc*) to refresh o.s.; ~ **la mémoire à qn** to refresh sb's memory

**rafraîchissant, e** [ʀafʀeʃisɑ̃, -ɑ̃t] *adj* refreshing

**rafraîchissement** [ʀafʀeʃismɑ̃] *nm* cooling; (*boisson*) cool drink; **rafraîchissements** *nmpl* (*boissons, fruits etc*) refreshments

**ragaillardir** [ʀagajaʀdiʀ] *vt* (*fam*) to perk *ou* buck up

**rage** [ʀaʒ] *nf* (*Méd*): **la** ~ rabies; (*fureur*) rage, fury; **faire ~** to rage; **~ de dents** (raging) toothache

**rager** [Raʒe] vi to fume (with rage); **faire ~ qn** to enrage sb, get sb mad

**rageur, -euse** [RaʒœR, -øz] adj snarling; ill-tempered

**raglan** [Raglɑ̃] adj inv raglan

**ragot** [Rago] nm (fam) malicious gossip no pl

**ragoût** [Ragu] nm (plat) stew

**ragoûtant, e** [Ragutɑ̃, -ɑ̃t] adj: **peu ~** unpalatable

**rai** [RE] nm: **un ~ de soleil/lumière** a shaft of sunlight/light

**raid** [REd] nm (Mil) raid; (attaque aérienne) air raid; (Sport) long-distance trek

**raide** [REd] adj (tendu) taut, tight; (escarpé) steep; (droit: cheveux) straight; (ankylosé, dur, guindé) stiff; (fam: cher) steep, stiff; (: sans argent) flat broke; (osé, licencieux) daring ▷ adv (en pente) steeply; **~ mort** stone dead

**raideur** [REdœR] nf steepness; stiffness

**raidir** [RediR] vt (muscles) to stiffen; (câble) to pull taut, tighten; **se raidir** vi to stiffen; to become taut; (personne: se crisper) to tense up; (: devenir intransigeant) to harden

**raidissement** [Redismɑ̃] nm stiffening; tightening; hardening

**raie** [RE] nf (Zool) skate, ray; (rayure) stripe; (des cheveux) parting

**raifort** [RefɔR] nm horseradish

**rail** [Raj] nm (barre d'acier) rail; (chemins de fer) railways pl (Brit), railroads pl (US); (la voie ferrée) the rails, the track sg; **par ~** by rail; **~ conducteur** live ou conductor rail

**railler** [Raje] vt to scoff at, jeer at

**raillerie** [RajRi] nf mockery

**railleur, -euse** [RajœR, -øz] adj mocking

**rainurage** [RenyRaʒ] nm (Auto) uneven road surface

**rainure** [RenyR] nf groove; slot

**rais** [RE] nm inv = **rai**

**raisin** [Rezɛ̃] nm (aussi: **raisins**) grapes pl; (variété): **~ blanc/noir** white (ou green)/black grape; **~ muscat** muscat grape; **~s secs** raisins

**raison** [Rezɔ̃] nf reason; **avoir ~** to be right; **donner ~ à qn** (personne) to agree with sb; (fait) to prove sb right; **avoir ~ de qn/qch** to get the better of sb/sth; **se faire une ~** to learn to live with it; **perdre la ~** to become insane; (fig) to take leave of one's senses; **recouvrer la ~** to come to one's senses; **ramener qn à la ~** to make sb see sense; **demander ~ à qn de** (affront etc) to demand satisfaction from sb for; **entendre ~** to listen to reason, see reason; **plus que de ~** too much, more than is reasonable; **~ de plus** all the more reason; **à plus forte ~** all the more so; **en ~ de** (à cause de) because of; (à proportion de) in proportion to; **à ~ de** at the rate of; **~ d'État** reason of state; **~ d'être** raison d'être; **~ sociale** corporate name

**raisonnable** [Rezɔnabl(ə)] adj reasonable, sensible

**raisonnablement** [Rezɔnabləmɑ̃] adv reasonably

**raisonné, e** [Rezɔne] adj reasoned

**raisonnement** [Rezɔnmɑ̃] nm reasoning; arguing; argument

**raisonner** [Rezɔne] vi (penser) to reason; (argumenter, discuter) to argue ▷ vt (personne) to reason with; (attitude: justifier) to reason out; **se raisonner** to reason with oneself

**raisonneur, -euse** [RezɔnœR, -øz] adj (péj) quibbling

**rajeunir** [RaʒœniR] vt (coiffure, robe): **~ qn** to make sb look younger; (cure etc) to rejuvenate; (fig: rafraîchir) to brighten up; (: moderniser) to give a new look to; (: en recrutant) to inject new blood into ▷ vi (personne) to become (ou look) younger; (entreprise, quartier) to be modernized

**rajout** [Raʒu] nm addition

**rajouter** [Raʒute] vt (commentaire) to add; **~ du sel/un œuf** to add some more salt/another egg; **~ que** to add that; **en ~** to lay it on thick

**rajustement** [Raʒystəmɑ̃] nm adjustment

**rajuster** [Raʒyste] vt (vêtement) to straighten, tidy; (salaires) to adjust; (machine) to readjust; **se rajuster** to tidy ou straighten o.s. up

**râle** [Ral] nm groan; **~ d'agonie** death rattle

**ralenti** [Ralɑ̃ti] nm: **au ~** (Ciné) in slow motion; (fig) at a slower pace; **tourner au ~** (Auto) to tick over, idle

**ralentir** [RalɑtiR] vt, vi, **se ralentir** vi to slow down

**ralentissement** [Ralɑ̃tismɑ̃] nm slowing down

**râler** [Rale] vi to groan; (fam) to grouse, moan (and groan)

**ralliement** [Ralimɑ̃] nm (rassemblement) rallying; (adhésion: à une cause, une opinion) winning over; **point/signe de ~** rallying point/sign

**rallier** [Ralje] vt (rassembler) to rally; (rejoindre) to rejoin; (gagner à sa cause) to win over; **se ~ à** (avis) to come over ou round to

**rallonge** [Ralɔ̃ʒ] nf (de table) (extra) leaf; (argent etc) extra no pl; (Élec) extension (cable ou flex); (fig: de crédit etc) extension

**rallonger** [Ralɔ̃ʒe] vt to lengthen

**rallumer** [Ralyme] vt to light up again, relight; (fig) to revive; **se rallumer** vi (lumière) to come on again

**rallye** [Rali] nm rally; (Pol) march

**ramages** [Ramaʒ] nmpl (dessin) leaf pattern sg; (chants) songs

**ramassage** [Ramasaʒ] nm: **~ scolaire** school bus service

**ramassé, e** [Ramase] adj (trapu) squat, stocky; (concis: expression etc) compact

**ramasse-miettes** [Ramasmjet] nm inv table-tidy

**ramasser** [Ramase] vt (objet tombé ou par terre: fam) to pick up; (recueillir) to collect; (récolter) to gather; (: pommes de terre) to lift; **se ramasser** vi (sur soi-même) to huddle up; to crouch

**ramasseur, -euse** [RamasœR, -øz] nm/f: **~ de balles** ballboy/girl

343

**ramassis** [ʀamɑsi] *nm* (*péj: de gens*) bunch; (: *de choses*) jumble

**rambarde** [ʀɑ̃baʀd(ə)] *nf* guardrail

**rame** [ʀam] *nf* (*aviron*) oar; (*de métro*) train; (*de papier*) ream; ~ **de haricots** bean support; **faire force de ~s** to row hard

**rameau, x** [ʀamo] *nm* (small) branch; (*fig*) branch; **les R~x** (*Rel*) Palm Sunday *sg*

**ramener** [ʀamne] *vt* to bring back; (*reconduire*) to take back; (*rabattre: couverture, visière*): ~ **qch sur** to pull sth back over; ~ **qch à** (*réduire à, Math*) to reduce sth to; ~ **qn à la vie/raison** to bring sb back to life/bring sb to his (*ou* her) senses; **se ramener** *vi* (*fam*) to roll *ou* turn up; **se ~ à** (*se réduire à*) to come *ou* boil down to

**ramequin** [ʀamkɛ̃] *nm* ramekin

**ramer** [ʀame] *vi* to row

**rameur, -euse** [ʀamœʀ, -øz] *nm/f* rower

**rameuter** [ʀamøte] *vt* to gather together

**ramier** [ʀamje] *nm*: (**pigeon**) ~ woodpigeon

**ramification** [ʀamifikasjɔ̃] *nf* ramification

**ramifier** [ʀamifje]: **se ramifier** *vi* (*tige, secte, réseau*): **se ~ (en)** to branch out (into); (*veines, nerfs*) to ramify

**ramolli, e** [ʀamɔli] *adj* soft

**ramollir** [ʀamɔliʀ] *vt* to soften; **se ramollir** *vi* (*os, tissus*) to get (*ou* go) soft; (*beurre, asphalte*) to soften

**ramonage** [ʀamɔnaʒ] *nm* (chimney-)sweeping

**ramoner** [ʀamɔne] *vt* (*cheminée*) to sweep; (*pipe*) to clean

**ramoneur** [ʀamɔnœʀ] *nm* (chimney) sweep

**rampe** [ʀɑ̃p] *nf* (*d'escalier*) banister(s *pl*); (*dans un garage, d'un terrain*) ramp; (*Théât*): **la ~** the footlights *pl*; (*lampes: lumineuse, de balisage*) floodlights *pl*; **passer la ~** (*toucher le public*) to get across to the audience; ~ **de lancement** launching pad

**ramper** [ʀɑ̃pe] *vi* (*reptile, animal*) to crawl; (*plante*) to creep

**rancard** [ʀɑ̃kaʀ] *nm* (*fam*) date; tip

**rancart** [ʀɑ̃kaʀ] *nm*: **mettre au ~** (*article, projet*) to scrap; (*personne*) to put on the scrapheap

**rance** [ʀɑ̃s] *adj* rancid

**rancir** [ʀɑ̃siʀ] *vi* to go off, go rancid

**rancœur** [ʀɑ̃kœʀ] *nf* rancour (*Brit*), rancor (*US*), resentment

**rançon** [ʀɑ̃sɔ̃] *nf* ransom; (*fig*): **la ~ du succès** *etc* the price of success *etc*

**rançonner** [ʀɑ̃sɔne] *vt* to hold to ransom

**rancune** [ʀɑ̃kyn] *nf* grudge, rancour (*Brit*), rancor (*US*); **garder ~ à qn (de qch)** to bear sb a grudge (for sth); **sans ~!** no hard feelings!

**rancunier, -ière** [ʀɑ̃kynje, -jɛʀ] *adj* vindictive, spiteful

**randonnée** [ʀɑ̃dɔne] *nf* ride; (*à pied*) walk, ramble; hike, hiking *no pl*

**randonneur, -euse** [ʀɑ̃dɔnœʀ, -øz] *nm/f* hiker

**rang** [ʀɑ̃] *nm* (*rangée*) row; (*de perles*) row, string, rope; (*grade, condition sociale, classement*) rank; **rangs** *nmpl* (*Mil*) ranks; **se mettre en ~s/sur un ~** to get into *ou* form rows/a line; **sur trois**

~**s** (lined up) three deep; **se mettre en ~s par quatre** to form fours *ou* rows of four; **se mettre sur les ~s** (*fig*) to get into the running; **au premier ~** in the first row; (*fig*) ranking first; **rentrer dans le ~** to get into line; **au ~ de** (*au nombre de*) among (the ranks of); **avoir ~ de** to hold the rank of

**rangé, e** [ʀɑ̃ʒe] *adj* (*sérieux*) orderly, steady

**rangée** [ʀɑ̃ʒe] *nf* row

**rangement** [ʀɑ̃ʒmɑ̃] *nm* tidying-up, putting-away; **faire des ~s** to tidy up

**ranger** [ʀɑ̃ʒe] *vt* (*classer, grouper*) to order, arrange; (*mettre à sa place*) to put away; (*voiture dans la rue*) to park; (*mettre de l'ordre dans*) to tidy up; (*arranger, disposer: en cercle etc*) to arrange; (*fig: classer*): ~ **qn/qch parmi** to rank sb/sth among; **se ranger** *vi* (*se placer, se disposer: autour d'une table etc*) to take one's place, sit round; (*véhicule, conducteur: s'écarter*) to pull over; (: *s'arrêter*) to pull in; (*piéton*) to step aside; (*s'assagir*) to settle down; **se ~ à** (*avis*) to come round to, fall in with

**ranimer** [ʀanime] *vt* (*personne évanouie*) to bring round; (*revigorer: forces, courage*) to restore; (*réconforter: troupes etc*) to kindle new life in; (*douleur, souvenir*) to revive; (*feu*) to rekindle

**rap** [ʀap] *nm* rap (music)

**rapace** [ʀapas] *nm* bird of prey ▷ *adj* (*péj*) rapacious, grasping; ~ **diurne/nocturne** diurnal/nocturnal bird of prey

**rapatrié, e** [ʀapatʀije] *nm/f* repatriate (*esp French North African settler*)

**rapatriement** [ʀapatʀimɑ̃] *nm* repatriation

**rapatrier** [ʀapatʀije] *vt* to repatriate; (*capitaux*) to bring (back) into the country

**râpe** [ʀɑp] *nf* (*Culin*) grater; (*à bois*) rasp

**râpé, e** [ʀɑpe] *adj* (*tissu*) threadbare; (*Culin*) grated

**râper** [ʀɑpe] *vt* (*Culin*) to grate; (*gratter, râcler*) to rasp

**rapetasser** [ʀaptase] *vt* (*fam*) to patch up

**rapetisser** [ʀaptise] *vt*: ~ **qch** to shorten sth; to make sth look smaller ▷ *vi*, **se rapetisser** *vi* to shrink

**râpeux, -euse** [ʀɑpø, -øz] *adj* rough

**raphia** [ʀafja] *nm* raffia

**rapide** [ʀapid] *adj* fast; (*prompt*) quick; (*intelligence*) quick ▷ *nm* express (train); (*de cours d'eau*) rapid

**rapidement** [ʀapidmɑ̃] *adv* fast; quickly

**rapidité** [ʀapidite] *nf* speed; quickness

**rapiécer** [ʀapjese] *vt* to patch

**rappel** [ʀapɛl] *nm* (*d'un ambassadeur, Mil*) recall; (*Théât*) curtain call; (*Méd: vaccination*) booster; (*Admin: de salaire*) back pay *no pl*; (*d'une aventure, d'un nom*) reminder; (*de limitation de vitesse: sur écriteau*) speed limit sign (*reminder*); (*Tech*) return; (*Navig*) sitting out; (*Alpinisme: aussi*: **rappel de corde**) abseiling *no pl*, roping down *no pl*; abseil; ~ **à l'ordre** call to order

**rappeler** [ʀaple] *vt* (*pour faire revenir, retéléphoner*) to call back; (*ambassadeur, Mil*) to recall; (*acteur*) to call back (onto the stage); (*faire se souvenir*): ~

**qch à qn** to remind sb of sth; **se rappeler** *vt* (*se souvenir de*) to remember, recall; ~ **qn à la vie** to bring sb back to life; ~ **qn à la décence** to recall sb to a sense of decency; **ça rappelle la Provence** it's reminiscent of Provence, it reminds you of Provence; **se ~ que...** to remember that...

**rappelle** *etc* [Rapɛl] *vb voir* **rappeler**

**rappliquer** [Raplike] *vi* (*fam*) to turn up

**rapport** [RapɔR] *nm* (*compte rendu*) report; (*profit*) yield, return; revenue; (*lien, analogie*) relationship; (*corrélation*) connection; (*proportion: Math, Tech*) ratio; **rapports** *nmpl* (*entre personnes, pays*) relations; **avoir ~ à** to have something to do with, concern; **être en ~ avec** (*idée de corrélation*) to be related to; **être/se mettre en ~ avec qn** to be/get in touch with sb; **par ~ à** (*comparé à*) in relation to; (*à propos de*) with regard to; **sous le ~ de** from the point of view of; **sous tous (les) ~s** in all respects; **~s (sexuels)** (sexual) intercourse *sg*; ~ **qualité-prix** value (for money)

**rapporté, e** [RapɔRte] *adj*: **pièce ~e** (*Couture*) patch

**rapporter** [RapɔRte] *vt* (*rendre, ramener*) to bring back; (*apporter davantage*) to bring more; (*Couture*) to sew on; (*investissement*) to yield; (: *activité*) to bring in; (*relater*) to report; (*Jur: annuler*) to revoke ▷ *vi* (*investissement*) to give a good return *ou* yield; (*activité*) to be very profitable; (*péj: moucharder*) to tell; ~ **qch à** (*fig: rattacher*) to relate sth to; **se ~ à** (*correspondre à*) to relate to; **s'en ~ à** to rely on

**rapporteur, -euse** [RapɔRtœR, -øz] *nm/f* (*de procès, commission*) reporter; (*péj*) telltale ▷ *nm* (*Géom*) protractor

**rapproché, e** [RapRoʃe] *adj* (*proche*) near, close at hand; **~s** (*l'un de l'autre*) at close intervals

**rapprochement** [RapRoʃmɑ̃] *nm* (*réconciliation: de nations, familles*) reconciliation; (*analogie, rapport*) parallel

**rapprocher** [RapRoʃe] *vt* (*chaise d'une table*): ~ **qch (de)** to bring sth closer (to); (*deux objets*) to bring closer together; (*réunir*) to bring together; (*comparer*) to establish a parallel between; **se rapprocher** *vi* to draw closer *ou* nearer; (*fig: familles, pays*) to come together; to come closer together; **se ~ de** to come closer to; (*présenter une analogie avec*) to be close to

**rapt** [Rapt] *nm* abduction

**raquette** [Rakɛt] *nf* (*de tennis*) racket; (*de ping-pong*) bat; (*à neige*) snowshoe

**rare** [RɑR] *adj* rare; (*main-d'œuvre, denrées*) scarce; (*cheveux, herbe*) sparse; **il est ~ que** it's rare that, it's unusual that; **se faire ~** to become scarce; (*fig: personne*) to make oneself scarce

**raréfaction** [RaRefaksjɔ̃] *nf* scarcity; (*de l'air*) rarefaction

**raréfier** [RaRefje]: **se raréfier** *vi* to grow scarce; (*air*) to rarefy

**rarement** [RaRmɑ̃] *adv* rarely, seldom

**rareté** [RaRte] *nf voir* **rare** rarity; scarcity

**rarissime** [RaRisim] *adj* extremely rare

**RAS** *abr* = **rien à signaler**

**ras, e** [Rɑ, Rɑz] *adj* (*tête, cheveux*) close-cropped; (*poil, herbe*) short; (*mesure, cuillère*) level ▷ *adv* short; **faire table ~e** to make a clean sweep; **en ~e campagne** in open country; **à ~ bords** to the brim; **au ~ de** level with; **en avoir ~ le bol** (*fam*) to be fed up; ~ **du cou** *adj* (*pull, robe*) crew-neck

**rasade** [Razad] *nf* glassful

**rasant, e** [Razɑ̃, ɑ̃t] *adj* (*Mil: balle, tir*) grazing; (*fam*) boring

**rascasse** [Raskas] *nf* (*Zool*) scorpion fish

**rasé, e** [Raze] *adj*: ~ **de frais** freshly shaven; ~ **de près** close-shaven

**rase-mottes** [Razmɔt] *nm inv*: **faire du ~** to hedgehop; **vol en ~** hedgehopping

**raser** [Raze] *vt* (*barbe, cheveux*) to shave off; (*menton, personne*) to shave; (*fam: ennuyer*) to bore; (*démolir*) to raze (to the ground); (*frôler*) to graze, skim; **se raser** to shave; (*fam*) to be bored (to tears)

**rasoir** [RazwaR] *nm* razor; ~ **électrique** electric shaver *ou* razor; ~ **mécanique** *ou* **de sûreté** safety razor

**rassasier** [Rasazje] *vt* to satisfy; **être rassasié** (*dégoûté*) to be sated; to have had more than enough

**rassemblement** [Rasɑ̃bləmɑ̃] *nm* (*groupe*) gathering; (*Pol*) union; association; (*Mil*): **le ~** parade

**rassembler** [Rasɑ̃ble] *vt* (*réunir*) to assemble, gather; (*regrouper, amasser*) to gather together, collect; **se rassembler** *vi* to gather; ~ **ses idées/ses esprits/son courage** to collect one's thoughts/gather one's wits/screw up one's courage

**rasseoir** [RaswaR]: **se rasseoir** *vi* to sit down again

**rassir** [Rasir] *vi* to go stale

**rassis, e** [Rasi, -iz] *adj* (*pain*) stale

**rassurant, e** [Rasyrɑ̃, -ɑ̃t] *adj* (*nouvelles etc*) reassuring

**rassuré, e** [Rasyre] *adj*: **ne pas être très ~** to be rather ill at ease

**rassurer** [Rasyre] *vt* to reassure; **se rassurer** to be reassured; **rassure-toi** don't worry

**rat** [Ra] *nm* rat; ~ **d'hôtel** hotel thief; ~ **musqué** muskrat

**ratatiné, e** [Ratatine] *adj* shrivelled (up), wrinkled

**ratatiner** [Ratatine] *vt* to shrivel; (*peau*) to wrinkle; **se ratatiner** *vi* to shrivel; to become wrinkled

**ratatouille** [Ratatuj] *nf* (*Culin*) ratatouille

**rate** [Rat] *nf* female rat; (*Anat*) spleen

**raté, e** [Rate] *adj* (*tentative*) unsuccessful, failed ▷ *nm/f* failure ▷ *nm* misfiring *no pl*

**râteau, x** [Rato] *nm* rake

**râtelier** [Ratəlje] *nm* rack; (*fam*) false teeth *pl*

**rater** [Rate] *vi* (*ne pas partir: coup de feu*) to fail to go off; (*affaire, projet etc*) to go wrong, fail ▷ *vt* (*cible, train, occasion*) to miss; (*démonstration, plat*) to

r

spoil; (*examen*) to fail; ~ **son coup** to fail, not to bring it off

**raticide** [ʀatisid] *nm* rat poison

**ratification** [ʀatifikɑsjɔ̃] *nf* ratification

**ratifier** [ʀatifje] *vt* to ratify

**ratio** [ʀasjo] *nm* ratio

**ration** [ʀɑsjɔ̃] *nf* ration; (*fig*) share; ~ **alimentaire** food intake

**rationalisation** [ʀasjɔnalizɑsjɔ̃] *nf* rationalization

**rationaliser** [ʀasjɔnalize] *vt* to rationalize

**rationnel, le** [ʀasjɔnɛl] *adj* rational

**rationnellement** [ʀasjɔnɛlmɑ̃] *adv* rationally

**rationnement** [ʀasjɔnmɑ̃] *nm* rationing; **ticket de ~ ration** coupon

**rationner** [ʀasjɔne] *vt* to ration; (*personne*) to put on rations; **se rationner** to ration o.s.

**ratisser** [ʀatise] *vt* (*allée*) to rake; (*feuilles*) to rake up; (*armée, police*) to comb; ~ **large** to cast one's net wide

**raton** [ʀatɔ̃] *nm*: ~ **laveur** raccoon

**RATP** *sigle f* (= *Régie autonome des transports parisiens*) *Paris transport authority*

**rattacher** [ʀataʃe] *vt* (*animal, cheveux*) to tie up again; (*incorporer: Admin etc*): ~ **qch à** to join sth to, unite sth with; (*fig: relier*): ~ **qch à** to link sth with, relate sth to; (: *lier*): ~ **qn à** to bind *ou* tie sb to; **se ~ à** (*fig: avoir un lien avec*) to be linked (*ou* connected) with

**rattrapage** [ʀatʀapaʒ] *nm* (*Scol*) remedial classes *pl*; (*Écon*) catching up

**rattraper** [ʀatʀape] *vt* (*fugitif*) to recapture; (*retenir, empêcher de tomber*) to catch (hold of); (*atteindre, rejoindre*) to catch up with; (*réparer: erreur*) to make up for; **se rattraper** *vi* (*regagner: du temps*) to make up for lost time; (: *de l'argent etc*) to make good one's losses; (*réparer une gaffe etc*) to make up for it; **se ~ (à)** (*se raccrocher*) to stop o.s. falling (by catching hold of); ~ **son retard/le temps perdu** to make up (for) lost time

**rature** [ʀatyʀ] *nf* deletion, erasure

**raturer** [ʀatyʀe] *vt* to cross out, delete, erase

**rauque** [ʀok] *adj* raucous; hoarse

**ravagé, e** [ʀavaʒe] *adj* (*visage*) harrowed

**ravager** [ʀavaʒe] *vt* to devastate, ravage

**ravages** [ʀavaʒ] *nmpl* ravages; **faire des ~** to wreak havoc; (*fig: séducteur*) to break hearts

**ravalement** [ʀavalmɑ̃] *nm* restoration

**ravaler** [ʀavale] *vt* (*mur, façade*) to restore; (*déprécier*) to lower; (*avaler de nouveau*) to swallow again; ~ **sa colère/son dégoût** to stifle one's anger/swallow one's distaste

**ravauder** [ʀavode] *vt* to repair, mend

**rave** [ʀav] *nf* (*Bot*) rape

**ravi, e** [ʀavi] *adj* delighted; **être ~ de/que** to be delighted with/that

**ravier** [ʀavje] *nm* hors d'œuvre dish

**ravigote** [ʀavigɔt] *adj*: **sauce ~** *oil and vinegar dressing with shallots*

**ravigoter** [ʀavigɔte] *vt* (*fam*) to buck up

**ravin** [ʀavɛ̃] *nm* gully, ravine

**raviner** [ʀavine] *vt* to furrow, gully

**ravioli** [ʀavjɔli] *nmpl* ravioli *sg*

**ravir** [ʀaviʀ] *vt* (*enchanter*) to delight; (*enlever*): ~ **qch à qn** to rob sb of sth; **à ~** *adv* delightfully, beautifully; **être beau à ~** to be ravishingly beautiful

**raviser** [ʀavize]: **se raviser** *vi* to change one's mind

**ravissant, e** [ʀavisɑ̃, -ɑ̃t] *adj* delightful

**ravissement** [ʀavismɑ̃] *nm* (*enchantement, délice*) rapture

**ravisseur, -euse** [ʀavisœʀ, -øz] *nm/f* abductor, kidnapper

**ravitaillement** [ʀavitajmɑ̃] *nm* resupplying; refuelling; (*provisions*) supplies *pl*; **aller au ~** to go for fresh supplies; ~ **en vol** (*Aviat*) in-flight refuelling

**ravitailler** [ʀavitaje] *vt* to resupply; (*véhicule*) to refuel; **se ravitailler** *vi* to get fresh supplies

**raviver** [ʀavive] *vt* (*feu*) to rekindle, revive; (*douleur*) to revive; (*couleurs*) to brighten up

**ravoir** [ʀavwaʀ] *vt* to get back

**rayé, e** [ʀeje] *adj* (*à rayures*) striped; (*éraflé*) scratched

**rayer** [ʀeje] *vt* (*érafler*) to scratch; (*barrer*) to cross *ou* score out; (*d'une liste: radier*) to cross *ou* strike off

**rayon** [ʀɛjɔ̃] *nm* (*de soleil etc*) ray; (*Géom*) radius; (*de roue*) spoke; (*étagère*) shelf; (*de grand magasin*) department; (*fig: domaine*) responsibility, concern; (*de ruche*) (honey)comb; **dans un ~ de** within a radius of; **rayons** *nmpl* (*radiothérapie*) radiation; ~ **d'action** range; ~ **de braquage** (*Auto*) turning circle; ~ **laser** laser beam; ~ **de soleil** sunbeam, ray of sunlight *ou* sunshine; **~s X** X-rays

**rayonnage** [ʀɛjɔnaʒ] *nm* set of shelves

**rayonnant, e** [ʀɛjɔnɑ̃, -ɑ̃t] *adj* radiant

**rayonne** [ʀɛjɔn] *nf* rayon

**rayonnement** [ʀɛjɔnmɑ̃] *nm* radiation; (*fig: éclat*) radiance; (: *influence*) influence

**rayonner** [ʀɛjɔne] *vi* (*chaleur, énergie*) to radiate; (*fig: émotion*) to shine forth; (: *visage*) to be radiant; (*avenues, axes*) to radiate; (*touriste*) to go touring (*from one base*)

**rayure** [ʀejyʀ] *nf* (*motif*) stripe; (*éraflure*) scratch; (*rainure, d'un fusil*) groove; **à ~s** striped

**raz-de-marée** [ʀɑdmaʀe] *nm inv* tidal wave

**razzia** [ʀazja] *nf* raid, foray

**RBE** *sigle m* (= *revenu brut d'exploitation*) gross profit (*of a farm*)

**R-D** *sigle f* (= *Recherche-Développement*) R & D

**RDA** *sigle f* (= *République démocratique allemande*) GDR

**rdc** *abr* = **rez-de-chaussée**

**ré** [ʀe] *nm* (*Mus*) D; (*en chantant la gamme*) re

**réabonnement** [ʀeabɔnmɑ̃] *nm* renewal of subscription

**réabonner** [ʀeabɔne] *vt*: ~ **qn à** to renew sb's subscription to; **se ~ (à)** to renew one's subscription (to)

**réac** [ʀeak] *adj, nm/f* (*fam*: = *réactionnaire*)

reactionary

**réacteur** [ʀeaktœʀ] *nm* jet engine; ~ **nucléaire** nuclear reactor

**réactif** [ʀeaktif] *nm* reagent

**réaction** [ʀeaksjɔ̃] *nf* reaction; **par** ~ jet-propelled; **avion/moteur à** ~ jet (plane)/jet engine; ~ **en chaîne** chain reaction

**réactionnaire** [ʀeaksjɔnɛʀ] *adj, nm/f* reactionary

**réactualiser** [ʀeaktɥalize] *vt* to update, bring up to date

**réadaptation** [ʀeadaptasjɔ̃] *nf* readjustment; rehabilitation

**réadapter** [ʀeadapte] *vt* to readjust; (*Méd*) to rehabilitate; **se** ~ **(à)** to readjust (to)

**réaffirmer** [ʀeafiʀme] *vt* to reaffirm, reassert

**réagir** [ʀeaʒiʀ] *vi* to react

**réajuster** [ʀeaʒyste] *vt* = **rajuster**

**réalisable** [ʀealizabl(ə)] *adj* (*projet, plan*) feasible; (*Comm: valeur*) realizable

**réalisateur, -trice** [ʀealizatœʀ, -tʀis] *nm/f* (*TV, Ciné*) director

**réalisation** [ʀealizasjɔ̃] *nf* carrying out; realization; fulfilment; achievement; production; (*œuvre*) production, work; (*création*) creation

**réaliser** [ʀealize] *vt* (*projet, opération*) to carry out, realize; (*rêve, souhait*) to realize, fulfil; (*exploit*) to achieve; (*achat, vente*) to make; (*film*) to produce; (*se rendre compte de, Comm: bien, capital*) to realize; **se réaliser** *vi* to be realized

**réalisme** [ʀealism(ə)] *nm* realism

**réaliste** [ʀealist(ə)] *adj* realistic; (*peintre, roman*) realist ▷ *nm/f* realist

**réalité** [ʀealite] *nf* reality; **en** ~ in (actual) fact; **dans la** ~ in reality; ~ **virtuelle** virtual reality

**réanimation** [ʀeanimasjɔ̃] *nf* resuscitation; **service de** ~ intensive care unit

**réanimer** [ʀeanime] *vt* (*Méd*) to resuscitate

**réapparaître** [ʀeapaʀɛtʀ(ə)] *vi* to reappear

**réapparition** [ʀeapaʀisjɔ̃] *nf* reappearance

**réapprovisionner** [ʀeapʀovizjɔne] *vt* (*magasin*) to restock; **se** ~ **(en)** to restock (with)

**réarmement** [ʀeaʀməmɑ̃] *nm* rearmament

**réarmer** [ʀeaʀme] *vt* (*arme*) to reload ▷ *vi* (*état*) to rearm

**réassortiment** [ʀeasɔʀtimɑ̃] *nm* (*Comm*) restocking

**réassortir** [ʀeasɔʀtiʀ] *vt* to match up

**réassurance** [ʀeasyʀɑ̃s] *nf* reinsurance

**réassurer** [ʀeasyʀe] *vt* to reinsure

**rebaptiser** [ʀəbatize] *vt* (*rue*) to rename

**rébarbatif, -ive** [ʀebaʀbatif, -iv] *adj* forbidding; (*style*) off-putting (*Brit*), crabbed

**rebattre** [ʀəbatʀ(ə)] *vt*: ~ **les oreilles à qn de qch** to keep harping on to sb about sth

**rebattu, e** [ʀəbaty] *pp de* **rebattre** ▷ *adj* hackneyed

**rebelle** [ʀəbɛl] *nm/f* rebel ▷ *adj* (*troupes*) rebel; (*enfant*) rebellious; (*mèche etc*) unruly; ~ **à qch** unamenable to sth; ~ **à faire** unwilling to do

**rebeller** [ʀəbele]: **se rebeller** *vi* to rebel

**rébellion** [ʀebeljɔ̃] *nf* rebellion; (*rebelles*) rebel forces *pl*

**rebiffer** [ʀəbife]: **se rebiffer** *vr* to fight back

**reboisement** [ʀəbwazmɑ̃] *nm* reafforestation

**reboiser** [ʀəbwaze] *vt* to replant with trees, reafforest

**rebond** [ʀəbɔ̃] *nm* (*voir rebondir*) bounce; rebound

**rebondi, e** [ʀəbɔ̃di] *adj* (*ventre*) rounded; (*joues*) chubby, well-rounded

**rebondir** [ʀəbɔ̃diʀ] *vi* (*ballon: au sol*) to bounce; (: *contre un mur*) to rebound; (*fig: procès, action, conversation*) to get moving again, be suddenly revived

**rebondissement** [ʀəbɔ̃dismɑ̃] *nm* new development

**rebord** [ʀəbɔʀ] *nm* edge

**reboucher** [ʀəbuʃe] *vt* (*flacon*) to put the stopper (*ou* top) back on, recork; (*trou*) to stop up

**rebours** [ʀəbuʀ]: **à** ~ *adv* the wrong way

**rebouteux, -euse** [ʀəbutø, -øz] *nm/f* (*péj*) bonesetter

**reboutonner** [ʀəbutɔne] *vt* (*vêtement*) to button up (again)

**rebrousse-poil** [ʀəbʀuspwal]: **à** ~ *adv* the wrong way

**rebrousser** [ʀəbʀuse] *vt* (*cheveux, poils*) to brush back, brush up; ~ **chemin** to turn back

**rebuffade** [ʀəbyfad] *nf* rebuff

**rébus** [ʀebys] *nm inv* (*jeu d'esprit*) rebus; (*fig*) puzzle

**rebut** [ʀəby] *nm*: **mettre au** ~ to scrap, discard

**rebutant, e** [ʀəbytɑ̃, -ɑ̃t] *adj* (*travail, démarche*) off-putting, disagreeable

**rebuter** [ʀəbyte] *vt* to put off

**récalcitrant, e** [ʀekalsitʀɑ̃, -ɑ̃t] *adj* refractory, recalcitrant

**recaler** [ʀəkale] *vt* (*Scol*) to fail

**récapitulatif, -ive** [ʀekapitylatif, -iv] *adj* (*liste, tableau*) summary *cpd*, that sums up

**récapituler** [ʀekapityle] *vt* to recapitulate; (*résumer*) to sum up

**recel** [ʀəsɛl] *nm* receiving (stolen goods)

**receler** [ʀəsəle] *vt* (*produit d'un vol*) to receive; (*malfaiteur*) to harbour; (*fig*) to conceal

**receleur, -euse** [ʀəsəlœʀ, -øz] *nm/f* receiver

**récemment** [ʀesamɑ̃] *adv* recently

**recensement** [ʀəsɑ̃smɑ̃] *nm* census; inventory

**recenser** [ʀəsɑ̃se] *vt* (*population*) to take a census of; (*inventorier*) to make an inventory of; (*dénombrer*) to list

**récent, e** [ʀesɑ̃, -ɑ̃t] *adj* recent

**récépissé** [ʀesepise] *nm* receipt

**réceptacle** [ʀesɛptakl(ə)] *nm* (*où les choses aboutissent*) recipient; (*où les choses sont stockées*) repository; (*Bot*) receptacle

**récepteur, -trice** [ʀesɛptœʀ, -tʀis] *adj* receiving ▷ *nm* receiver; ~ **(de radio)** radio set *ou* receiver

**réceptif, -ive** [ʀesɛptif, -iv] *adj*: ~ **(à)** receptive (to)

**réception** [ʀesɛpsjɔ̃] *nf* receiving *no pl*; (*d'une marchandise, commande*) receipt; (*accueil*) reception, welcome; (*bureau*) reception (desk);

**r**

(*réunion mondaine*) reception, party; (*pièces*) reception rooms *pl*; (*Sport: après un saut*) landing; (*du ballon*) catching *no pl*; **jour/heures de** ~ day/hours for receiving visitors (*ou* students *etc*)

**réceptionner** [ʀɛsɛpsjɔne] *vt* (*Comm*) to take delivery of; (*Sport: ballon*) to catch (and control)

**réceptionniste** [ʀɛsɛpsjɔnist(ə)] *nm/f* receptionist

**réceptivité** [ʀɛsɛptivite] *nf* (*à une influence*) receptiveness; (*à une maladie*) susceptibility

**récessif, -ive** [ʀɛsesif, -iv] *adj* (*Biol*) recessive

**récession** [ʀɛsesjɔ̃] *nf* recession

**recette** [ʀəsɛt] *nf* (*Culin*) recipe; (*fig*) formula, recipe; (*Comm*) takings *pl*; (*Admin: bureau*) tax *ou* revenue office; **recettes** *nfpl* (*Comm: rentrées*) receipts; **faire** ~ (*spectacle, exposition*) to be a winner

**receveur, -euse** [ʀəsvœʀ, -øz] *nm/f* (*des contributions*) tax collector; (*des postes*) postmaster/mistress; (*d'autobus*) conductor/conductress; (*Méd: de sang, organe*) recipient

**recevoir** [ʀəsvwaʀ] *vt* to receive; (*lettre, prime*) to receive, get; (*client, patient, représentant*) to see; (*jour, soleil: pièce*) to get; (*Scol: candidat*) to pass ▷ *vi* to receive visitors; to give parties; to see patients *etc*; **se recevoir** *vi* (*athlète*) to land; ~ **qn à dîner** to invite sb to dinner; **il reçoit de huit à 10** he's at home from eight to 10, he will see visitors from eight to 10; (*docteur, dentiste etc*) he sees patients from eight to 10; **être reçu** (*à un examen*) to pass; **être bien/mal reçu** to be well/badly received

**rechange** [ʀəʃɑ̃ʒ]: **de** ~ *adj* (*pièces, roue*) spare; (*fig: solution*) alternative; **des vêtements de** ~ a change of clothes

**rechaper** [ʀəʃape] *vt* to remould (*Brit*), remold (*US*), retread

**réchapper** [ʀeʃape]: ~ **de** *ou* **à** *vt* (*accident, maladie*) to come through; **va-t-il en** ~? is he going to get over it?, is he going to come through (it)?

**recharge** [ʀəʃaʀʒ(ə)] *nf* refill

**rechargeable** [ʀəʃaʀʒabl(ə)] *adj* refillable; rechargeable

**recharger** [ʀəʃaʀʒe] *vt* (*camion, fusil, appareil photo*) to reload; (*briquet, stylo*) to refill; (*batterie*) to recharge

**réchaud** [ʀeʃo] *nm* (portable) stove, plate-warmer

**réchauffé** [ʀeʃofe] *nm* (*nourriture*) reheated food; (*fig*) stale news (*ou* joke *etc*)

**réchauffement** [ʀeʃofmɑ̃] *nm* warming (up); **le** ~ **de la planète** global warming

**réchauffer** [ʀeʃofe] *vt* (*plat*) to reheat; (*mains, personne*) to warm; **se réchauffer** *vi* to get warmer; **se** ~ **les doigts** to warm (up) one's fingers

**rêche** [ʀɛʃ] *adj* rough

**recherche** [ʀəʃɛʀʃ(ə)] *nf* (*action*): **la** ~ **de** the search for; (*raffinement*) affectedness, studied elegance; (*scientifique etc*): **la** ~ research; **recherches** *nfpl* (*de la police*) investigations;

(*scientifiques*) research *sg*; **être/se mettre à la** ~ **de** to be/go in search of

**recherché, e** [ʀəʃɛʀʃe] *adj* (*rare, demandé*) much sought-after; (*entouré: acteur, femme*) in demand; (*raffiné*) studied, affected

**rechercher** [ʀəʃɛʀʃe] *vt* (*objet égaré, personne*) to look for, search for; (*témoins, coupable, main-d'œuvre*) to look for; (*causes d'un phénomène, nouveau procédé*) to try to find; (*bonheur etc, l'amitié de qn*) to seek; **"~ et remplacer"** (*Inform*) "find and replace"

**rechigner** [ʀəʃiɲe] *vi*: ~ **(à)** to balk (at)

**rechute** [ʀəʃyt] *nf* (*Méd*) relapse; (*dans le péché, le vice*) lapse; **faire une** ~ to have a relapse

**rechuter** [ʀəʃyte] *vi* (*Méd*) to relapse

**récidive** [ʀesidiv] *nf* (*Jur*) second (*ou* subsequent) offence; (*fig*) repetition; (*Méd*) recurrence

**récidiver** [ʀesidive] *vi* to commit a second (*ou* subsequent) offence; (*fig*) to do it again

**récidiviste** [ʀesidivist(ə)] *nm/f* second (*ou* habitual) offender, recidivist

**récif** [ʀesif] *nm* reef

**récipiendaire** [ʀesipjɑ̃dɛʀ] *nm* recipient (of diploma etc); (*d'une société*) newly elected member

**récipient** [ʀesipjɑ̃] *nm* container

**réciproque** [ʀesipʀɔk] *adj* reciprocal ▷ *nf*: **la** ~ (*l'inverse*) the converse

**réciproquement** [ʀesipʀɔkmɑ̃] *adv* reciprocally; **et** ~ and vice versa

**récit** [ʀesi] *nm* (*action de narrer*) telling; (*conte, histoire*) story

**récital** [ʀesital] *nm* recital

**récitant, e** [ʀesitɑ̃, -ɑ̃t] *nm/f* narrator

**récitation** [ʀesitasjɔ̃] *nf* recitation

**réciter** [ʀesite] *vt* to recite

**réclamation** [ʀeklamasjɔ̃] *nf* complaint; **réclamations** *nfpl* (*bureau*) complaints department *sg*

**réclame** [ʀeklam] *nf*: **la** ~ advertising; **une** ~ an ad(vertisement), an advert (*Brit*); **faire de la** ~ **(pour qch/qn)** to advertise (sth/sb); **article en** ~ special offer

**réclamer** [ʀeklame] *vt* (*aide, nourriture etc*) to ask for; (*revendiquer: dû, part, indemnité*) to claim, demand; (*nécessiter*) to demand, require ▷ *vi* to complain; **se** ~ **de** to give as one's authority; to claim filiation with

**reclassement** [ʀəklasmɑ̃] *nm* reclassifying; regrading; rehabilitation

**reclasser** [ʀəklase] *vt* (*fiches, dossiers*) to reclassify; (*fig: fonctionnaire etc*) to regrade; (: *ouvrier licencié*) to place, rehabilitate

**reclus, e** [ʀəkly, -yz] *nm/f* recluse

**réclusion** [ʀeklyzjɔ̃] *nf* imprisonment; ~ **à perpétuité** life imprisonment

**recoiffer** [ʀəkwafe] *vt*: ~ **un enfant** to do a child's hair again; **se recoiffer** to do one's hair again

**recoin** [ʀəkwɛ̃] *nm* nook, corner; (*fig*) hidden recess

**reçois** *etc* [ʀəswa] *vb voir* **recevoir**

**reçoive** *etc* [ʀəswav] *vb voir* **recevoir**

**recoller** [Rəkɔle] vt (enveloppe) to stick back down
**récolte** [Rekɔlt(ə)] nf harvesting, gathering; (produits) harvest, crop; (fig) crop, collection; (: d'observations) findings
**récolter** [Rekɔlte] vt to harvest, gather (in); (fig) to get
**recommandable** [Rəkɔmɑ̃dabl(ə)] adj commendable; **peu** ~ not very commendable
**recommandation** [Rəkɔmɑ̃dasjɔ̃] nf recommendation
**recommandé** [Rəkɔmɑ̃de] nm (méthode etc) recommended; (Postes): **en** ~ by registered mail
**recommander** [Rəkɔmɑ̃de] vt to recommend; (qualités etc) to commend; (Postes) to register; ~ **qch à qn** to recommend sth to sb; ~ **à qn de faire** to recommend sb to do; ~ **qn auprès de qn** ou **à qn** to recommend sb to sb; **il est recommandé de faire ...** it is recommended that one does ...; **se** ~ **à qn** to commend o.s. to sb; **se** ~ **de qn** to give sb's name as a reference
**recommencer** [Rəkɔmɑ̃se] vt (reprendre: lutte, séance) to resume, start again; (refaire: travail, explications) to start afresh, start (over) again; (récidiver: erreur) to make again ▷ vi to start again; (récidiver) to do it again; ~ **à faire** to start doing again; **ne recommence pas!** don't do that again!
**récompense** [Rekɔ̃pɑ̃s] nf reward; (prix) award; **recevoir qch en** ~ to get sth as a reward, be rewarded with sth
**récompenser** [Rekɔ̃pɑ̃se] vt: ~ **qn (de** ou **pour)** to reward sb (for)
**réconciliation** [Rekɔ̃siljasjɔ̃] nf reconciliation
**réconcilier** [Rekɔ̃silje] vt to reconcile; ~ **qn avec qn** to reconcile sb with sb; ~ **qn avec qch** to reconcile sb to sth; **se réconcilier (avec)** to be reconciled (with)
**reconductible** [Rəkɔ̃dyktibl(ə)] adj (Jur: contrat, bail) renewable
**reconduction** [Rəkɔ̃dyksjɔ̃] nf renewal; (Pol: d'une politique) continuation
**reconduire** [Rəkɔ̃dɥiʀ] vt (raccompagner) to take ou see back; (: à la porte) to show out; (: à son domicile) to see home, take home; (Jur, Pol: renouveler) to renew
**réconfort** [Rekɔ̃fɔʀ] nm comfort
**réconfortant, e** [Rekɔ̃fɔʀtɑ̃, -ɑ̃t] adj (idée, paroles) comforting; (boisson) fortifying
**réconforter** [Rekɔ̃fɔʀte] vt (consoler) to comfort; (revigorer) to fortify
**reconnais** etc [R(ə)kɔnɛ] vb voir **reconnaître**
**reconnaissable** [Rəkɔnɛsabl(ə)] adj recognizable
**reconnaissance** [Rəkɔnɛsɑ̃s] nf recognition; acknowledgement; (gratitude) gratitude, gratefulness; (Mil) reconnaissance, recce; **en** ~ (Mil) on reconnaissance; ~ **de dette** acknowledgement of a debt, IOU
**reconnaissant, e** [Rəkɔnɛsɑ̃, -ɑ̃t] vb voir **reconnaître** ▷ adj grateful; **je vous serais** ~ **de bien vouloir** I should be most grateful if you would (kindly)

**reconnaître** [Rəkɔnɛtʀ(ə)] vt to recognize; (Mil: lieu) to reconnoitre; (Jur: enfant, dette, droit) to acknowledge; ~ **que** to admit ou acknowledge that; ~ **qn/qch à** (l'identifier grâce à) to recognize sb/sth by; ~ **à qn: je lui reconnais certaines qualités** I recognize certain qualities in him; **se** ~ **quelque part** (s'y retrouver) to find one's way around (a place)
**reconnu, e** [R(ə)kɔny] pp de **reconnaître** ▷ adj (indiscuté, connu) recognized
**reconquérir** [Rəkɔ̃keʀiʀ] vt to reconquer, recapture; (sa dignité etc) to recover
**reconquête** [Rəkɔ̃kɛt] nf recapture; recovery
**reconsidérer** [Rəkɔ̃sideʀe] vt to reconsider
**reconstituant, e** [Rəkɔ̃stitɥɑ̃, -ɑ̃t] adj (régime) strength-building ▷ nm tonic, pick-me-up
**reconstituer** [Rəkɔ̃stitɥe] vt (monument ancien) to recreate, build a replica of; (fresque, vase brisé) to piece together, reconstitute; (événement, accident) to reconstruct; (fortune, patrimoine) to rebuild; (Bio: tissus etc) to regenerate
**reconstitution** [Rəkɔ̃stitysjɔ̃] nf (d'un accident etc) reconstruction
**reconstruction** [Rəkɔ̃stʀyksjɔ̃] nf rebuilding, reconstruction
**reconstruire** [Rəkɔ̃stʀɥiʀ] vt to rebuild, reconstruct
**reconversion** [Rəkɔ̃vɛʀsjɔ̃] nf (du personnel) redeployment
**reconvertir** [Rəkɔ̃vɛʀtiʀ] vt (usine) to reconvert; (personnel, troupes etc) to redeploy; **se** ~ **dans** (un métier, une branche) to move into, be redeployed into
**recopier** [Rəkɔpje] vt (transcrire) to copy out again, write out again; (mettre au propre: devoir) to make a clean ou fair copy of
**record** [Rəkɔʀ] nm, adj record; ~ **du monde** world record
**recoucher** [Rəkuʃe] vt (enfant) to put back to bed
**recoudre** [Rəkudʀ(ə)] vt (bouton) to sew back on; (plaie, incision) to sew (back) up, stitch up
**recoupement** [Rəkupmɑ̃] nm: **faire un** ~ ou **des** ~**s** to cross-check; **par** ~ by cross-checking
**recouper** [Rəkupe] vt (tranche) to cut again; (vêtement) to recut ▷ vi (Cartes) to cut again; **se recouper** vi (témoignages) to tie ou match up
**recourais** etc [Rəkuʀɛ] vb voir **recourir**
**recourbé, e** [Rəkuʀbe] adj curved; hooked; bent
**recourber** [Rəkuʀbe] vt (branche, tige de métal) to bend
**recourir** [Rəkuʀiʀ] vi (courir de nouveau) to run again; (refaire une course) to race again; ~ **à** vt (ami, agence) to turn ou appeal to; (force, ruse, emprunt) to resort to, have recourse to
**recours** [Rəkuʀ] vb voir **recourir** ▷ nm (Jur) appeal; **avoir** ~ **à**; = **recourir à**; **dernier** ~ as a last resort; **sans** ~ final; with no way out; ~ **en grâce** plea for clemency (ou pardon)
**recouru, e** [Rəkuʀy] pp de **recourir**
**recousu, e** [Rəkuzy] pp de **recoudre**
**recouvert, e** [Rəkuvɛʀ, -ɛʀt(ə)] pp de **recouvrir**
**recouvrable** [Rəkuvʀabl(ə)] adj (somme)

r

recoverable

**recouvrais** etc [RəkuvRɛ] vb voir **recouvrer**; **recouvrir**

**recouvrement** [RəkuvRəmɑ̃] nm recovery

**recouvrer** [RəkuvRe] vt (vue, santé etc) to recover, regain; (impôts) to collect; (créance) to recover

**recouvrir** [RəkuvRiR] vt (couvrir à nouveau) to recover; (couvrir entièrement: aussi fig) to cover; (cacher, masquer) to conceal, hide; **se recouvrir** (se superposer) to overlap

**recracher** [RəkRaʃe] vt to spit out

**récréatif, -ive** [RekReatif, -iv] adj of entertainment; recreational

**récréation** [RekReɑsjɔ̃] nf recreation, entertainment; (Scol) break

**recréer** [RəkRee] vt to recreate

**récrier** [RekRije]: **se récrier** vi to exclaim

**récriminations** [RekRiminɑsjɔ̃] nfpl remonstrations, complaints

**récriminer** [Rekrimine] vi: ~ **contre qn/qch** to remonstrate against sb/sth

**recroqueviller** [RəkRɔkvije]: **se recroqueviller** vi (feuilles) to curl ou shrivel up; (personne) to huddle up

**recru, e** [RəkRy] adj: ~ **de fatigue** exhausted ▷ nf recruit

**recrudescence** [RəkRydesɑ̃s] nf fresh outbreak

**recrutement** [RəkRytmɑ̃] nm recruiting, recruitment

**recruter** [RəkRyte] vt to recruit

**rectal, e, -aux** [Rɛktal, -o] adj: **par voie ~e** rectally

**rectangle** [Rɛktɑ̃gl(ə)] nm rectangle

**rectangulaire** [Rɛktɑ̃gylɛR] adj rectangular

**recteur** [RɛktœR] nm ≈ (regional) director of education (Brit), ≈ state superintendent of education (US)

**rectificatif, -ive** [Rɛktifikatif, -iv] adj corrected ▷ nm correction

**rectification** [Rɛktifikɑsjɔ̃] nf correction

**rectifier** [Rɛktifje] vt (tracé, virage) to straighten; (calcul, adresse) to correct; (erreur, faute) to rectify, put right

**rectiligne** [Rɛktiliɲ] adj straight; (Géom) rectilinear

**rectitude** [Rɛktityd] nf rectitude, uprightness

**recto** [Rɛkto] nm front (of a sheet of paper)

**rectorat** [RɛktɔRa] nm (fonction) position of recteur; (bureau) recteur's office; voir aussi **recteur**

**rectum** [Rɛktɔm] nm rectum

**reçu, e** [Rəsy] pp de **recevoir** ▷ adj (admis, consacré) accepted ▷ nm (Comm) receipt

**recueil** [Rəkœj] nm collection

**recueillement** [Rəkœjmɑ̃] nm meditation, contemplation

**recueilli, e** [Rəkœji] adj contemplative

**recueillir** [RəkœjiR] vt to collect; (voix, suffrages) to win; (accueillir: réfugiés, chat) to take in; **se recueillir** vi to gather one's thoughts; to meditate

**recuire** [RəkɥiR] vi: **faire ~** to recook

**recul** [Rəkyl] nm retreat; recession; decline;

(d'arme à feu) recoil, kick; **avoir un mouvement de** ~ to recoil, start back; **prendre du** ~ to stand back; **avec le** ~ with the passing of time, in retrospect

**reculade** [Rəkylad] nf (péj) climb-down

**reculé, e** [Rəkyle] adj remote

**reculer** [Rəkyle] vi to move back, back away; (Auto) to reverse, back (up); (fig: civilisation, épidémie) to (be on the) decline; (: se dérober) to shrink back ▷ vt to move back; to reverse, back (up); (fig: possibilités, limites) to extend; (: date, décision) to postpone; ~ **devant** (danger, difficulté) to shrink from; ~ **pour mieux sauter** (fig) to postpone the evil day

**reculons** [Rəkylɔ̃]: **à** ~ adv backwards

**récupérable** [Rekyperabl(ə)] adj (créance) recoverable; (heures) which can be made up; (ferraille) salvageable

**récupération** [RekypeRɑsjɔ̃] nf (de métaux etc) salvage, reprocessing; (Pol) bringing into line

**récupérer** [RekypeRe] vt (rentrer en possession de) to recover, get back; (: forces) to recover; (déchets etc) to salvage (for reprocessing); (remplacer: journée, heures de travail) to make up; (délinquant etc) to rehabilitate; (Pol) to bring into line ▷ vi to recover

**récurer** [RekyRe] vt to scour; **poudre à** ~ scouring powder

**reçus** etc [Rəsy] vb voir **recevoir**

**récusable** [Rekyzabl(ə)] adj (témoin) challengeable; (témoignage) impugnable

**récuser** [Rekyze] vt to challenge; **se récuser** to decline to give an opinion

**recyclage** [Rəsiklaʒ] nm reorientation; retraining; recycling; **cours de** ~ retraining course

**recycler** [Rəsikle] vt (Scol) to reorientate; (employés) to retrain; (matériau) to recycle; **se recycler** to retrain; to go on a retraining course

**rédacteur, -trice** [RedaktœR, -tRis] nm/f (journaliste) writer; subeditor; (d'ouvrage de référence) editor, compiler; ~ **en chef** chief editor; ~ **publicitaire** copywriter

**rédaction** [Redaksjɔ̃] nf writing; (rédacteurs) editorial staff; (bureau) editorial office(s); (Scol: devoir) essay, composition

**reddition** [Redisjɔ̃] nf surrender

**redéfinir** [RədefiniR] vt to redefine

**redemander** [Rədmɑ̃de] vt (renseignement) to ask again for; (nourriture): ~ **de** to ask for more (ou another); (objet prêté): ~ **qch** to ask for sth back

**redémarrer** [RədemaRe] vi (véhicule) to start again, get going again; (fig: industrie etc) to get going again

**rédemption** [Redɑ̃psjɔ̃] nf redemption

**redéploiement** [Rədeplwamɑ̃] nm redeployment

**redescendre** [Rədesɑ̃dR(ə)] vi (à nouveau) to go back down; (après la montée) to go down (again) ▷ vt (pente etc) to go down

**redevable** [Rədvabl(ə)] adj: **être ~ de qch à qn** (somme) to owe sb sth; (fig) to be indebted to sb for sth

**redevance** [ʀədvɑ̃s] *nf* (*Tél*) rental charge; (TV) licence (*Brit*) *ou* license (*US*) fee

**redevenir** [ʀədvəniʀ] *vi* to become again

**rédhibitoire** [ʀedibitwaʀ] *adj*: **vice ~** (*Jur*) latent *defect in merchandise that renders the sales contract void*; (*fig*: *défaut*) crippling

**rediffuser** [ʀədifyze] *vt* (*Radio, TV*) to repeat, broadcast again

**rediffusion** [ʀədifyzjɔ̃] *nf* repeat (programme)

**rédiger** [ʀediʒe] *vt* to write; (*contrat*) to draw up

**redire** [ʀədiʀ] *vt* to repeat; **trouver à ~ à** to find fault with

**redistribuer** [ʀədistʀibɥe] *vt* (*cartes etc*) to deal again; (*richesses, tâches, revenus*) to redistribute

**redite** [ʀədit] *nf* (needless) repetition

**redondance** [ʀədɔ̃dɑ̃s] *nf* redundancy

**redonner** [ʀədɔne] *vt* (*restituer*) to give back, return; (*du courage, des forces*) to restore

**redoublé, e** [ʀəduble] *adj*: **à coups ~s** even harder, twice as hard

**redoubler** [ʀəduble] *vi* (*tempête, violence*) to intensify, get even stronger *ou* fiercer *etc*; (*Scol*) to repeat a year ▷ *vt* (*Scol: classe*) to repeat; (*Ling: lettre*) to double; **le vent redouble de violence** the wind is blowing twice as hard

**redoutable** [ʀədutabl(ə)] *adj* formidable, fearsome

**redouter** [ʀədute] *vt* to fear; (*appréhender*) to dread; **~ de faire** to dread doing

**redoux** [ʀədu] *nm* milder spell

**redressement** [ʀədʀɛsmɑ̃] *nm* (*de l'économie etc*) putting right; **maison de ~** reformatory; **~ fiscal** repayment of back taxes

**redresser** [ʀədʀese] *vt* (*arbre, mât*) to set upright, right; (*pièce tordue*) to straighten out; (*Aviat, Auto*) to straighten up; (*situation, économie*) to put right; **se redresser** *vi* (*objet penché*) to right itself; to straighten up; (*personne*) to sit (*ou* stand) up; to sit (*ou* stand) up straight; (*fig: pays, situation*) to recover; **~ (les roues)** (*Auto*) to straighten up

**redresseur** [ʀədʀɛsœʀ] *nm*: **~ de torts** righter of wrongs

**réducteur, -trice** [ʀedyktœʀ, -tʀis] *adj* simplistic

**réduction** [ʀedyksjɔ̃] *nf* reduction; **en ~** *adv* in miniature, scaled-down

**réduire** [ʀedɥiʀ] *vt* (*gén, Culin, Math*) to reduce; (*prix, dépenses*) to cut, reduce; (*carte*) to scale down, reduce; (*Méd: fracture*) to set; **~ qn/qch à** to reduce sb/sth to; **se ~ à** (*revenir à*) to boil down to; **se ~ en** (*se transformer en*) to be reduced to; **en être réduit à** to be reduced to

**réduit, e** [ʀedɥi, -it] *pp de* **réduire** ▷ *adj* (*prix, tarif, échelle*) reduced; (*mécanisme*) scaled-down; (*vitesse*) reduced ▷ *nm* tiny room; recess

**rééditer** [ʀeedite] *vt* to republish

**réédition** [ʀeedisjɔ̃] *nf* new edition

**rééducation** [ʀeedykasjɔ̃] *nf* (*d'un membre*) re-education; (*de délinquants, d'un blessé*) rehabilitation; **~ de la parole** speech therapy;

**centre de ~** physiotherapy *ou* physical therapy (*US*) centre

**rééduquer** [ʀeedyke] *vt* to reeducate; to rehabilitate

**réel, le** [ʀeɛl] *adj* real ▷ *nm*: **le ~** reality

**réélection** [ʀeelɛksjɔ̃] *nf* re-election

**rééligible** [ʀeeliʒibl(ə)] *adj* re-eligible

**réélire** [ʀeeliʀ] *vt* to re-elect

**réellement** [ʀeelmɑ̃] *adv* really

**réembaucher** [ʀeɑ̃boʃe] *vt* to take on again

**réemploi** [ʀeɑ̃plwa] *nm* = **remploi**

**réemployer** [ʀeɑ̃plwaje] *vt* (*méthode, produit*) to re-use; (*argent*) to reinvest; (*personnel, employé*) to re-employ

**rééquilibrer** [ʀeekilibʀe] *vt* (*budget*) to balance (again)

**réescompte** [ʀeeskɔ̃t] *nm* rediscount

**réessayer** [ʀeeseje] *vt* to try on again

**réévaluation** [ʀeevalɥasjɔ̃] *nf* revaluation

**réévaluer** [ʀeevalɥe] *vt* to revalue

**réexaminer** [ʀeɛgzamine] *vt* to re-examine

**réexpédier** [ʀeɛkspedje] *vt* (*à l'envoyeur*) to return, send back; (*au destinataire*) to send on, forward

**réexporter** [ʀeɛkspɔʀte] *vt* to re-export

**réf.** *abr* = **référence(s)**; **V/~.** Your ref

**refaire** [ʀəfɛʀ] *vt* (*faire de nouveau, recommencer*) to do again; (*réparer, restaurer*) to do up; **se refaire** *vi* (*en argent*) to make up one's losses; **se ~ une santé** to recuperate; **se ~ à qch** (*se réhabituer à*) to get used to sth again

**refasse** *etc* [ʀəfas] *vb voir* **refaire**

**réfection** [ʀefɛksjɔ̃] *nf* repair; **en ~** under repair

**réfectoire** [ʀefɛktwaʀ] *nm* refectory

**referai** *etc* [ʀ(ə)fʀe] *vb voir* **refaire**

**référé** [ʀefeʀe] *nm* (*Jur*) emergency interim proceedings *ou* ruling

**référence** [ʀefeʀɑ̃s] *nf* reference; **références** *nfpl* (*recommandations*) reference *sg*; **faire ~ à** to refer to; **ouvrage de ~** reference work; **ce n'est pas une ~** (*fig*) that's no recommendation

**référendum** [ʀefeʀɑ̃dɔm] *nm* referendum

**référer** [ʀefeʀe]: **se ~ à** *vt* to refer to; **en ~ à qn** to refer the matter to sb

**refermer** [ʀəfɛʀme] *vt* to close again, shut again

**refiler** [ʀəfile] *vt* (*fam*): **~ qch à qn** to palm (*Brit*) *ou* fob sth off on sb; to pass sth on to sb

**refit** *etc* [ʀəfi] *vb voir* **refaire**

**réfléchi, e** [ʀefleʃi] *adj* (*caractère*) thoughtful; (*action*) well-thought-out; (*Ling*) reflexive

**réfléchir** [ʀefleʃiʀ] *vt* to reflect ▷ *vi* to think; **~ à** *ou* **sur** to think about; **c'est tout réfléchi** my mind's made up

**réflecteur** [ʀeflɛktœʀ] *nm* (*Auto*) reflector

**reflet** [ʀəflɛ] *nm* reflection; (*sur l'eau etc*) sheen *no pl*, glint; **reflets** *nmpl* gleam *sg*

**refléter** [ʀəflete] *vt* to reflect; **se refléter** *vi* to be reflected

**réflex** [ʀeflɛks] *adj inv* (*Photo*) reflex

**réflexe** [ʀeflɛks(ə)] *adj, nm* reflex; **~ conditionné** conditioned reflex

**réflexion** [ʀeflɛksjɔ̃] *nf* (*de la lumière etc, pensée*) reflection; (*fait de penser*) thought; (*remarque*) remark; **réflexions** *nfpl* (*méditations*) thought *sg*, reflection *sg*; **sans ~** without thinking; **~ faite, à la ~** après réflexion, on reflection; **délai de ~** cooling-off period; **groupe de ~** think tank

**réflexologie** [ʀeflɛksɔlɔʒi] *nf* reflexology

**refluer** [ʀəflye] *vi* to flow back; (*foule*) to surge back

**reflux** [ʀəfly] *nm* (*de la mer*) ebb; (*fig*) backward surge

**refondre** [ʀəfɔ̃dʀ(ə)] *vt* (*texte*) to recast

**refont** [ʀ(ə)fɔ̃] *vb voir* **refaire**

**reformater** [ʀəfɔʀmate] *vt* to reformat

**réformateur, -trice** [ʀefɔʀmatœʀ, -tʀis] *nm/f* reformer ⊳ *adj* (*mesures*) reforming

**Réformation** [ʀefɔʀmɑsjɔ̃] *nf*: **la ~** the Reformation

**réforme** [ʀefɔʀm(ə)] *nf* reform; (*Mil*) declaration of unfitness for service; discharge (*on health grounds*); (*Rel*): **la R~** the Reformation

**réformé, e** [ʀefɔʀme] *adj, nm/f* (*Rel*) Protestant

**reformer** [ʀəfɔʀme] *vt*, **se reformer** *vi* to reform; **~ les rangs** (*Mil*) to fall in again

**réformer** [ʀefɔʀme] *vt* to reform; (*Mil: recrue*) to declare unfit for service; (*: soldat*) to discharge, invalid out; (*matériel*) to scrap

**réformisme** [ʀefɔʀmism(ə)] *nm* reformism, policy of reform

**réformiste** [ʀefɔʀmist(ə)] *adj, nm/f* (*Pol*) reformist

**refoulé, e** [ʀəfule] *adj* (*Psych*) repressed

**refoulement** [ʀəfulmɑ̃] *nm* (*d'une armée*) driving back; (*Psych*) repression

**refouler** [ʀəfule] *vt* (*envahisseurs*) to drive back, repulse; (*liquide*) to force back; (*fig*) to suppress; (*Psych*) to repress

**réfractaire** [ʀefʀaktɛʀ] *adj* (*minerai*) refractory; (*brique*) fire *cpd*; (*maladie*) which is resistant to treatment; (*prêtre*) non-juring; **soldat ~** draft evader; **être ~ à** to resist

**réfracter** [ʀefʀakte] *vt* to refract

**réfraction** [ʀefʀaksjɔ̃] *nf* refraction

**refrain** [ʀəfʀɛ̃] *nm* (*Mus*) refrain, chorus; (*air, fig*) tune

**refréner, réfréner** [ʀəfʀene, ʀefʀene] *vt* to curb, check

**réfrigérant, e** [ʀefʀiʒeʀɑ̃, -ɑ̃t] *adj* refrigerant, cooling

**réfrigérateur** [ʀefʀiʒeʀatœʀ] *nm* refrigerator; **~-congélateur** fridge-freezer

**réfrigération** [ʀefʀiʒeʀasjɔ̃] *nf* refrigeration

**réfrigéré, e** [ʀefʀiʒeʀe] *adj* (*camion, wagon*) refrigerated

**réfrigérer** [ʀefʀiʒeʀe] *vt* to refrigerate; (*fam: glacer: aussi fig*) to cool

**refroidir** [ʀəfʀwadiʀ] *vt* to cool; (*fig*) to have a cooling effect on ⊳ *vi* to cool (down); **se refroidir** *vi* (*prendre froid*) to catch a chill; (*temps*) to get cooler *ou* colder; (*fig*) to cool (off)

**refroidissement** [ʀəfʀwadismɑ̃] *nm* cooling; (*grippe etc*) chill

**refuge** [ʀəfyʒ] *nm* refuge; (*pour piétons*) (traffic) island; **demander ~ à qn** to ask sb for refuge

**réfugié, e** [ʀefyʒje] *adj, nm/f* refugee

**réfugier** [ʀefyʒje]: **se réfugier** *vi* to take refuge

**refus** [ʀəfy] *nm* refusal; **ce n'est pas de ~** I won't say no, it's very welcome

**refuser** [ʀəfyze] *vt* to refuse; (*Scol: candidat*) to fail ⊳ *vi* to refuse; **~ qch à qn/de faire** to refuse sb sth/to do; **~ du monde** to have to turn people away; **se ~ à qch** *ou* **à faire qch** to refuse to do sth; **il ne se refuse rien** he doesn't stint himself; **se ~ à qn** to refuse sb

**réfutable** [ʀefytabl(ə)] *adj* refutable

**réfuter** [ʀefyte] *vt* to refute

**regagner** [ʀəgaɲe] *vt* (*argent, faveur*) to win back; (*lieu*) to get back to; **~ le temps perdu** to make up for lost time; **~ du terrain** to regain ground

**regain** [ʀəgɛ̃] *nm* (*herbe*) second crop of hay; (*renouveau*): **~ de qch** renewed sth

**régal** [ʀegal] *nm* treat; **un ~ pour les yeux** a pleasure *ou* delight to look at

**régalade** [ʀegalad] *adv*: **à la ~** from the bottle (held away from the lips)

**régaler** [ʀegale] *vt*: **~ qn** to treat sb to a delicious meal; **~ qn de** to treat sb to; **se régaler** *vi* to have a delicious meal; (*fig*) to enjoy o.s

**regard** [ʀəgaʀ] *nm* (*coup d'œil*) look, glance; (*expression*) look (in one's eye); **parcourir/ menacer du ~** to cast an eye over/look threateningly at; **au ~ de** (*loi, morale*) from the point of view of; **en ~** (*vis à vis*) opposite; **en ~ de** in comparison with

**regardant, e** [ʀəgaʀdɑ̃, -ɑ̃t] *adj*: **très/peu ~ (sur)** quite fussy/very free (about); (*économe*) very tight-fisted/quite generous (with)

**regarder** [ʀəgaʀde] *vt* (*examiner, observer, lire*) to look at; (*film, télévision, match*) to watch; (*envisager: situation, avenir*) to view; (*considérer: son intérêt etc*) to be concerned with; (*être orienté vers*): **~ (vers)** to face; (*concerner*) to concern ⊳ *vi* to look; **~ à** *vt* (*dépense, qualité, détails*) to be fussy with *ou* over; **~ à faire** to hesitate to do; **dépenser sans ~** to spend freely; **~ qn/qch comme** to regard sb/sth as; **~ (qch) dans le dictionnaire** to look (sth up) in the dictionary; **~ par la fenêtre** to look out of the window; **cela me regarde** it concerns me, it's my business

**régate** [ʀegat], **régates** *nf(pl)* regatta

**régénérer** [ʀeʒeneʀe] *vt* to regenerate; (*fig*) to revive

**régent** [ʀeʒɑ̃] *nm* regent

**régenter** [ʀeʒɑ̃te] *vt* to rule over; to dictate to

**régie** [ʀeʒi] *nf* (*Comm, Industrie*) state-owned company; (*Théât, Ciné*) production; (*Radio, TV*) control room; **la ~ de l'État** state control

**regimber** [ʀəʒɛ̃be] *vi* to balk, jib

**régime** [ʀeʒim] *nm* (*Pol Géo*) régime; (*Admin: carcéral, fiscal etc*) system; (*Méd*) diet; (*Tech*) (engine) speed; (*fig*) rate, pace; (*de bananes, dattes*) bunch; **se mettre au/suivre un ~** to go on/be on a diet; **~ sans sel** salt-free diet; **à bas/**

**haut** ~ (*Auto*) at low/high revs; **à plein** ~ flat out, at full speed; ~ **matrimonial** marriage settlement

**régiment** [ʀeʒimɑ̃] *nm* (*Mil*: *unité*) regiment; (*fig*: *fam*): **un** ~ **de** an army of; **un copain de** ~ a pal from military service *ou* (one's) army days

**région** [ʀeʒjɔ̃] *nf* region; **la** ~ **parisienne** the Paris area

**régional, e, -aux** [ʀeʒjɔnal, -o] *adj* regional

**régionalisation** [ʀeʒjɔnalizasjɔ̃] *nf* regionalization

**régionalisme** [ʀeʒjɔnalism(ə)] *nm* regionalism

**régir** [ʀeʒiʀ] *vt* to govern

**régisseur** [ʀeʒisœʀ] *nm* (*d'un domaine*) steward; (*Ciné, TV*) assistant director; (*Théât*) stage manager

**registre** [ʀəʒistʀ(ə)] *nm* (*livre*) register; logbook; ledger; (*Mus, Ling*) register; (*d'orgue*) stop; ~ **de comptabilité** ledger; ~ **de l'état civil** register of births, marriages and deaths

**réglable** [ʀeglabl(ə)] *adj* (*siège, flamme etc*) adjustable; (*achat*) payable

**réglage** [ʀeglaʒ] *nm* (*d'une machine*) adjustment; (*d'un moteur*) tuning

**réglé, e** [ʀegle] *adj* well-ordered; stable, steady; (*papier*) ruled; (*arrangé*) settled

**règle** [ʀɛgl(ə)] *nf* (*instrument*) ruler; (*loi, prescription*) rule; **règles** *nfpl* (*Physiol*) period *sg*; **avoir pour** ~ **de** to make it a rule that *ou* to; **en** ~ (*papiers d'identité*) in order; **être/se mettre en** ~ to be/put o.s. straight with the authorities; **en** ~ **générale** as a (general) rule; **être la** ~ to be the rule; **être de** ~ to be usual; ~ **à calcul** slide rule; ~ **de trois** (*Math*) rule of three

**règlement** [ʀɛgləmɑ̃] *nm* settling; (*paiement*) settlement; (*arrêté*) regulation; (*règles, statuts*) regulations *pl*, rules *pl*; ~ **à la commande** cash with order; ~ **de compte(s)** settling of scores; ~ **en espèces/par chèque** payment in cash/by cheque; ~ **intérieur** (*Scol*) school rules *pl*; (*Admin*) by-laws *pl*; ~ **judiciaire** compulsory liquidation

**réglementaire** [ʀɛgləmɑ̃tɛʀ] *adj* conforming to the regulations; (*tenue, uniforme*) regulation *cpd*

**réglementation** [ʀɛgləmɑ̃tasjɔ̃] *nf* regulation, control; (*règlements*) regulations *pl*

**réglementer** [ʀɛgləmɑ̃te] *vt* to regulate, control

**régler** [ʀegle] *vt* (*mécanisme, machine*) to regulate, adjust; (*moteur*) to tune; (*thermostat etc*) to set, adjust; (*emploi du temps etc*) to organize, plan; (*question, conflit, facture, dette*) to settle; (*fournisseur*) to settle up with, pay; (*papier*) to rule; ~ **qch sur** to model sth on; ~ **son compte** to sort sb out, settle sb; ~ **un compte** to settle a score with sb

**réglisse** [ʀeglis] *nf ou m* liquorice; **bâton de** ~ liquorice stick

**règne** [ʀɛɲ] *nm* (*d'un roi etc, fig*) reign; (*Bio*): **le** ~ **végétal/animal** the vegetable/animal kingdom

**régner** [ʀeɲe] *vi* (*roi*) to rule, reign; (*fig*) to reign

**regonfler** [ʀ(ə)gɔ̃fle] *vt* (*ballon, pneu*) to reinflate, blow up again

**regorger** [ʀəgɔʀʒe] *vi* to overflow; ~ **de** to overflow with, be bursting with

**régresser** [ʀegʀese] *vi* (*phénomène*) to decline; (*enfant, malade*) to regress

**régressif, -ive** [ʀegʀesif, -iv] *adj* regressive

**régression** [ʀegʀesjɔ̃] *nf* decline; regression; **être en** ~ to be on the decline

**regret** [ʀəgʀɛ] *nm* regret; **à** ~ with regret; **avec** ~ regretfully; **être au** ~ **de devoir/ne pas pouvoir faire** to regret to have to/that one is unable to do; **j'ai le** ~ **de vous informer que** ... I regret to inform you that ...

**regrettable** [ʀəgʀɛtabl(ə)] *adj* regrettable

**regretter** [ʀəgʀete] *vt* to regret; (*personne*) to miss; ~ **d'avoir fait** to regret doing; ~ **que** to regret that, be sorry that; **non, je regrette** no, I'm sorry

**regroupement** [ʀ(ə)gʀupmɑ̃] *nm* grouping together; (*groupe*) group

**regrouper** [ʀəgʀupe] *vt* (*grouper*) to group together; (*contenir*) to include, comprise; **se regrouper** *vi* to gather (together)

**régularisation** [ʀegylaʀizasjɔ̃] *nf* (*de papiers, passeport*) putting in order; (*de sa situation: par le mariage*) regularization; (*d'un mécanisme*) regulation

**régulariser** [ʀegylaʀize] *vt* (*fonctionnement, trafic*) to regulate; (*passeport, papiers*) to put in order; (*sa situation*) to straighten out, regularize

**régularité** [ʀegylaʀite] *nf* regularity

**régulateur, -trice** [ʀegylatœʀ, -tʀis] *adj* regulating ▷ *nm* (*Tech*): ~ **de vitesse/de température** speed/temperature regulator

**régulation** [ʀegylasjɔ̃] *nf* (*du trafic*) regulation; ~ **des naissances** birth control

**régulier, -ière** [ʀegylje, -jɛʀ] *adj* (*gén*) regular; (*vitesse, qualité*) steady; (*répartition, pression*) even; (*Transports: ligne, service*) scheduled, regular; (*légal, réglementaire*) lawful, in order; (*fam: correct*) straight, on the level

**régulièrement** [ʀegyljɛʀmɑ̃] *adv* regularly; steadily; evenly; normally

**régurgiter** [ʀegyʀʒite] *vt* to regurgitate

**réhabiliter** [ʀeabilite] *vt* to rehabilitate; (*fig*) to restore to favour (*Brit*) *ou* favor (*US*)

**réhabituer** [ʀeabitɥe] *vt*: **se** ~ **à qch/à faire qch** to get used to sth again/to doing sth again

**rehausser** [ʀəose] *vt* to heighten, raise; (*fig*) to set off, enhance

**réimporter** [ʀeɛ̃pɔʀte] *vt* to reimport

**réimposer** [ʀeɛ̃poze] *vt* (*Finance*) to reimpose; to tax again

**réimpression** [ʀeɛ̃pʀesjɔ̃] *nf* reprinting; (*ouvrage*) reprint

**réimprimer** [ʀeɛ̃pʀime] *vt* to reprint

**Reims** [ʀɛ̃s] *n* Rheims

**rein** [ʀɛ̃] *nm* kidney; **reins** *nmpl* (*dos*) back *sg*; **avoir mal aux** ~**s** to have backache; ~ **artificiel** kidney machine

**réincarnation** [ʀeɛ̃kaʀnasjɔ̃] *nf* reincarnation

**réincarner** [ʀeɛ̃kaʀne]: **se réincarner** *vr* to be reincarnated

r

**reine** [ʀɛn] *nf* queen
**reine-claude** [ʀɛnklod] *nf* greengage
**reinette** [ʀɛnɛt] *nf* rennet, pippin
**réinitialisation** [ʀeinisjalizasjɔ̃] *nf* (*Inform*) reset
**réinscriptible** [ʀeɛ̃skʀiptibl] *adj* (*CD, DVD*) rewritable
**réinsérer** [ʀeɛ̃seʀe] *vt* (*délinquant, handicapé etc*) to rehabilitate
**réinsertion** [ʀeɛ̃sɛʀsjɔ̃] *nf* rehabilitation
**réintégrer** [ʀeɛ̃tegʀe] *vt* (*lieu*) to return to; (*fonctionnaire*) to reinstate
**réitérer** [ʀeiteʀe] *vt* to repeat, reiterate
**rejaillir** [ʀəʒajiʀ] *vi* to splash up; ~ **sur** to splash up onto; (*fig*) to rebound on; to fall upon
**rejet** [ʀəʒɛ] *nm* (*action, aussi Méd*) rejection; (*Poésie*) enjambement, rejet; (*Bot*) shoot
**rejeter** [ʀəʒte] *vt* (*relancer*) to throw back; (*vomir*) to bring *ou* throw up; (*écarter*) to reject; (*déverser*) to throw out, discharge; (*reporter*): ~ **un mot à la fin d'une phrase** to transpose a word to the end of a sentence; **se ~ sur qch** (*accepter faute de mieux*) to fall back on sth; ~ **la tête/les épaules en arrière** to throw one's head/pull one's shoulders back; ~ **la responsabilité de qch sur qn** to lay the responsibility for sth at sb's door
**rejeton** [ʀəʒtɔ̃] *nm* offspring
**rejette** *etc* [ʀ(ə)ʒɛt] *vb voir* **rejeter**
**rejoignais** *etc* [ʀ(ə)ʒwaɲɛ] *vb voir* **rejoindre**
**rejoindre** [ʀəʒwɛ̃dʀ(ə)] *vt* (*famille, régiment*) to rejoin, return to; (*lieu*) to get (back) to; (*route etc*) to meet, join; (*rattraper*) to catch up (with); **se rejoindre** *vi* to meet; **je te rejoins au café** I'll see *ou* meet you at the café
**réjoui, e** [ʀeʒwi] *adj* joyous
**réjouir** [ʀeʒwiʀ] *vt* to delight; **se réjouir** *vi* to be delighted; **se ~ de qch/de faire** to be delighted about sth/to do; **se ~ que** to be delighted that
**réjouissances** [ʀeʒwisɑ̃s] *nfpl* (*joie*) rejoicing *sg*; (*fête*) festivities, merry-making *sg*
**réjouissant, e** [ʀeʒwisɑ̃, -ɑ̃t] *adj* heartening, delightful
**relâche** [ʀəlaʃ]: **faire ~** *vi* (*navire*) to put into port; (*Ciné*) to be closed; **c'est le jour de ~** (*Ciné*) it's closed today; **sans ~** *adv* without respite *ou* a break
**relâché, e** [ʀəlaʃe] *adj* loose, lax
**relâchement** [ʀəlaʃmɑ̃] *nm* (*d'un prisonnier*) release; (*de la discipline, musculaire*) relaxation
**relâcher** [ʀəlaʃe] *vt* (*ressort, prisonnier*) to release; (*étreinte, cordes*) to loosen; (*discipline*) to relax ▷ *vi* (*Navig*) to put into port; **se relâcher** *vi* to loosen; (*discipline*) to become slack *ou* lax; (*élève etc*) to slacken off
**relais** [ʀəlɛ] *nm* (*Sport*): (**course de**) ~ relay (race); (*Radio, TV*) relay; (*intermédiaire*) go-between; **équipe de** ~ (*Sport*) relay team; **prendre le ~ (de**) to take over (from); ~ **de poste** post house, coaching inn; ~ **routier** ≈ transport café (*Brit*), ≈ truck stop (*US*)
**relance** [ʀəlɑ̃s] *nf* boosting, revival; (*Écon*)

reflation
**relancer** [ʀəlɑ̃se] *vt* (*balle*) to throw back (again); (*moteur*) to restart; (*fig*) to boost, revive; (*personne*): ~ **qn** to pester sb; to get on to sb again
**relater** [ʀəlate] *vt* to relate, recount
**relatif, -ive** [ʀəlatif, -iv] *adj* relative
**relation** [ʀəlɑsjɔ̃] *nf* (*récit*) account, report; (*rapport*) relation(ship); **relations** *nfpl* (*rapports*) relations; relationship; (*connaissances*) connections; **être/entrer en ~(s) avec** to be in contact *ou* be dealing/get in contact with; **mettre qn en ~(s) avec** to put sb in touch with; ~**s internationales** international relations; ~**s publiques** public relations; ~**s (sexuelles)** sexual relations, (sexual) intercourse *sg*
**relativement** [ʀəlativmɑ̃] *adv* relatively; ~ **à** in relation to
**relativiser** [ʀəlativize] *vt* to see in relation to; to put into context
**relativité** [ʀəlativite] *nf* relativity
**relax** [ʀəlaks] *adj inv*, **relaxe** [ʀəlaks(ə)] ▷ *adj* relaxed, informal, casual; easy-going; (**fauteuil-**)~ *nm* reclining chair
**relaxant, e** [ʀəlaksɑ̃, -ɑ̃t] *adj* (*cure, médicament*) relaxant; (*ambiance*) relaxing
**relaxation** [ʀ(ə)laksasjɔ̃] *nf* relaxation
**relaxer** [ʀəlakse] *vt* to relax; (*Jur*) to discharge; **se relaxer** *vi* to relax
**relayer** [ʀəleje] *vt* (*collaborateur, coureur etc*) to relieve, take over from; (*Radio, TV*) to relay; **se relayer** (*dans une activité*) to take it in turns
**relecture** [ʀ(ə)lɛktyʀ] *nf* rereading
**relégation** [ʀəlegɑsjɔ̃] *nf* (*Sport*) relegation
**reléguer** [ʀəlege] *vt* to relegate; ~ **au second plan** to push into the background
**relent** [ʀəlɑ̃], **relents** *nm(pl)* stench *sg*
**relevé, e** [ʀəlve] *adj* (*bord de chapeau*) turned-up; (*manches*) rolled-up; (*fig: style*) elevated; (*: sauce*) highly-seasoned ▷ *nm* (*lecture*) reading; (*de cotes*) plotting; (*liste*) statement; list; (*facture*) account; ~ **de compte** bank statement; ~ **d'identité bancaire (RIB)** (bank) account number
**relève** [ʀəlɛv] *nf* relief; (*équipe*) relief team (*ou* troops *pl*); **prendre la** ~ to take over
**relèvement** [ʀəlɛvmɑ̃] *nm* (*d'un taux, niveau*) raising
**relever** [ʀəlve] *vt* (*statue, meuble*) to stand up again; (*personne tombée*) to help up; (*vitre, plafond, niveau de vie*) to raise; (*pays, économie, entreprise*) to put back on its feet; (*col*) to turn up; (*style, conversation*) to elevate; (*plat, sauce*) to season; (*sentinelle, équipe*) to relieve; (*souligner: fautes, points*) to pick out; (*constater: traces etc*) to find, pick up; (*répliquer à: remarque*) to react to, reply to; (*: défi*) to accept, take up; (*noter: adresse etc*) to take down, note; (*: plan*) to sketch; (*: cotes etc*) to plot; (*compteur*) to read; (*ramasser: cahiers, copies*) to collect, take in ▷ *vi* (*jupe, bord*) to ride up; ~ **de** *vt* (*maladie*) to be recovering from; (*être du ressort de*) to be a matter for; (*Admin: dépendre de*) to come under; (*fig*) to pertain to; **se relever** *vi* (*se*

*remettre debout*) to get up; (*fig*): **se ~ (de)** to recover (from); **~ qn de** (*vœux*) to release sb from; (*fonctions*) to relieve sb of; **~ la tête** to look up; to hold up one's head

**relief** [ʀəljɛf] *nm* relief; (*de pneu*) tread pattern; **reliefs** *nmpl* (*restes*) remains; **en ~** in relief; (*photographie*) three-dimensional; **mettre en ~** (*fig*) to bring out, highlight

**relier** [ʀəlje] *vt* to link up; (*livre*) to bind; **~ qch à** to link sth to; **livre relié cuir** leather-bound book

**relieur, -euse** [ʀəljœʀ, -øz] *nm/f* (book)binder

**religieusement** [ʀ(ə)liʒjøzmɑ̃] *adv* religiously; (*enterré, mariés*) in church; **vivre ~** to lead a religious life

**religieux, -euse** [ʀəliʒjø, -øz] *adj* religious ▷ *nm* monk ▷ *nf* nun; (*gâteau*) cream bun

**religion** [ʀəliʒjɔ̃] *nf* religion; (*piété, dévotion*) faith; **entrer en ~** to take one's vows

**reliquaire** [ʀəlikɛʀ] *nm* reliquary

**reliquat** [ʀəlika] *nm* (*d'une somme*) balance; (*Jur: de succession*) residue

**relique** [ʀəlik] *nf* relic

**relire** [ʀəliʀ] *vt* (*à nouveau*) to reread, read again; (*vérifier*) to read over; **se relire** to read through what one has written

**reliure** [ʀəljyʀ] *nf* binding; (*art, métier*): **la ~** book-binding

**reloger** [ʀ(ə)lɔʒe] *vt* (*locataires, sinistrés*) to rehouse

**relooker** [ʀəluke] *vt*: **~ qn** to give sb a makeover

**relu, e** [ʀəly] *pp de* **relire**

**reluire** [ʀəlɥiʀ] *vi* to gleam

**reluisant, e** [ʀəlɥizɑ̃, -ɑ̃t] *vb voir* **reluire** ▷ *adj* gleaming; **peu ~** (*fig*) unattractive; unsavoury (*Brit*), unsavory (*US*)

**reluquer** [ʀ(ə)lyke] *vt* (*fam*) to eye (up), ogle

**remâcher** [ʀəmɑʃe] *vt* to chew *ou* ruminate over

**remailler** [ʀəmaje] *vt* (*tricot*) to darn; (*filet*) to mend

**remaniement** [ʀəmanimɑ̃] *nm*: **~ ministériel** Cabinet reshuffle

**remanier** [ʀəmanje] *vt* to reshape, recast; (*Pol*) to reshuffle

**remarier** [ʀ(ə)maʀje]: **se remarier** *vi* to remarry, get married again

**remarquable** [ʀəmaʀkabl(ə)] *adj* remarkable

**remarquablement** [ʀ(ə)maʀkabləmɑ̃] *adv* remarkably

**remarque** [ʀəmaʀk(ə)] *nf* remark; (*écrite*) note

**remarquer** [ʀəmaʀke] *vt* (*voir*) to notice; (*dire*): **~ que** to remark that; **se ~** to be noticeable; **se faire ~** to draw attention to o.s.; **faire ~ (à qn) que** to point out (to sb) that; **faire ~ qch (à qn)** to point sth out (to sb); **remarquez, ...** mark you, ..., mind you, ...

**remballer** [ʀɑ̃bale] *vt* to wrap up (again); (*dans un carton*) to pack up (again)

**rembarrer** [ʀɑ̃baʀe] *vt*: **~ qn** (*repousser*) to rebuff sb; (*remettre à sa place*) to put sb in his (*ou* her) place

**remblai** [ʀɑ̃blɛ] *nm* embankment

**remblayer** [ʀɑ̃bleje] *vt* to bank up; (*fossé*) to fill in

**rembobiner** [ʀɑ̃bɔbine] *vt* to rewind

**rembourrage** [ʀɑ̃buʀaʒ] *nm* stuffing; padding

**rembourré, e** [ʀɑ̃buʀe] *adj* padded

**rembourrer** [ʀɑ̃buʀe] *vt* to stuff; (*dossier, vêtement, souliers*) to pad

**remboursable** [ʀɑ̃buʀsabl(ə)] *adj* repayable

**remboursement** [ʀɑ̃buʀsəmɑ̃] *nm* repayment; **envoi contre ~** cash on delivery

**rembourser** [ʀɑ̃buʀse] *vt* to pay back, repay

**rembrunir** [ʀɑ̃bʀyniʀ]: **se rembrunir** *vi* to grow sombre (*Brit*) *ou* somber (*US*)

**remède** [ʀəmɛd] *nm* (*médicament*) medicine; (*traitement, fig*) remedy, cure; **trouver un ~ à** (*Méd, fig*) to find a cure for

**remédier** [ʀəmedje]: **~ à** *vt* to remedy

**remembrement** [ʀəmɑ̃bʀəmɑ̃] *nm* (*Agr*) regrouping of lands

**remémorer** [ʀəmemɔʀe]: **se remémorer** *vt* to recall, recollect

**remerciements** [ʀəmɛʀsimɑ̃] *nmpl* thanks; **(avec) tous mes ~** (with) grateful *ou* many thanks

**remercier** [ʀəmɛʀsje] *vt* to thank; (*congédier*) to dismiss; **~ qn de/d'avoir fait** to thank sb for/for having done; **non, je vous remercie** no thank you

**remettre** [ʀəmɛtʀ(ə)] *vt* (*vêtement*): **~ qch** to put sth back on, put sth on again; (*replacer*): **~ qch quelque part** to put sth back somewhere; (*ajouter*): **~ du sel/un sucre** to add more salt/ another lump of sugar; (*rétablir: personne*): **~ qn** to set sb back on his (*ou* her) feet; (*rendre, restituer*): **~ qch à qn** to give sth back to sb, return sth to sb; (*donner, confier: paquet, argent*): **~ qch à qn** to hand sth over to sb, deliver sth to sb; (*prix, décoration*): **~ qch à qn** to present sb with sth; (*ajourner*): **~ qch (à)** to postpone sth *ou* put sth off (until); **se remettre** *vi* to get better, recover; **se ~ de** to recover from, get over; **s'en ~ à** to leave it (up) to; **se ~ à faire/qch** to start doing/sth again; **~ un moteur/une machine en marche** to get an engine/a machine going again; **~ en état/en ordre** to repair/sort out; **~ en cause/question** to challenge/question again; **~ sa démission** to hand in one's notice; **~ qch à neuf** to make sth as good as new; **~ qn à sa place** (*fig*) to put sb in his (*ou* her) place

**réminiscence** [ʀeminisɑ̃s] *nf* reminiscence

**remis, e** [ʀəmi, -iz] *pp de* **remettre** ▷ *nf* delivery; presentation; (*rabais*) discount; (*local*) shed; **~ en marche/en ordre** starting up again/sorting out; **~ en cause/question** calling into question/challenging; **~ de fonds** remittance; **~ en jeu** (*Football*) throw-in; **~ à neuf** restoration; **~ de peine** remission of sentence

**remiser** [ʀəmize] *vt* to put away

**rémission** [ʀemisjɔ̃]: **sans ~** *adj* irremediable *adv* unremittingly

**remodeler** [ʀəmɔdle] *vt* to remodel; (*fig: restructurer*) to restructure

**355**

**rémois, e** [ʀemwa, -waz] *adj ou* from Rheims
▷ *nm/f*: **Rémois, e** inhabitant *ou* native of Rheims
**remontant** [ʀəmɔ̃tɑ̃] *nm* tonic, pick-me-up
**remontée** [ʀəmɔ̃te] *nf* rising; ascent; **~s mécaniques** (*Ski*) ski lifts, ski tows
**remonte-pente** [ʀəmɔ̃tpɑ̃t] *nm* ski lift, (ski) tow
**remonter** [ʀəmɔ̃te] *vi* (*à nouveau*) to go back up; (*à cheval*) to remount; (*après une descente*) to go up (again); (*en voiture*) to get back in; (*jupe*) to ride up ▷ *vt* (*pente*) to go up; (*fleuve*) to sail (*ou* swim *etc*) up; up; (*manches, pantalon*) to roll up; (*col*) to turn up; (*niveau, limite*) to raise; (*fig: personne*) to buck up; (*moteur, meuble*) to put back together, reassemble; (*garde-robe etc*) to renew, replenish; (*montre, mécanisme*) to wind up; **~ le moral à qn** to raise sb's spirits; **~ à** (*dater de*) to date *ou* go back to; **~ en voiture** to get back into the car
**remontoir** [ʀəmɔ̃twaʀ] *nm* winding mechanism, winder
**remontrance** [ʀəmɔ̃tʀɑ̃s] *nf* reproof, reprimand
**remontrer** [ʀəmɔ̃tʀe] *vt* (*montrer de nouveau*): **~ qch (à qn)** to show sth again (to sb); (*fig*): **en ~ à** to prove one's superiority over
**remords** [ʀəmɔʀ] *nm* remorse *no pl*; **avoir des ~** to feel remorse, be conscience-stricken
**remorque** [ʀəmɔʀk(ə)] *nf* trailer; **prendre/être en ~** to tow/be on tow; **être à la ~** (*fig*) to tag along (behind)
**remorquer** [ʀəmɔʀke] *vt* to tow
**remorqueur** [ʀəmɔʀkœʀ] *nm* tug(boat)
**rémoulade** [ʀemulad] *nf* dressing with mustard and herbs
**rémouleur** [ʀemulœʀ] *nm* (knife- *ou* scissor-) grinder
**remous** [ʀəmu] *nm* (*d'un navire*) (back)wash *no pl*; (*de rivière*) swirl, eddy *pl*; (*fig*) stir *sg*
**rempailler** [ʀɑ̃paje] *vt* to reseat (*with straw*)
**rempart** [ʀɑ̃paʀ] *nm* rampart; **faire à qn un ~ de son corps** to shield sb with one's (own) body
**remparts** [ʀɑ̃paʀ] *nmpl* walls, ramparts
**rempiler** [ʀɑ̃pile] *vt* (*dossiers, livres etc*) to pile up again ▷ *vi* (*Mil: fam*) to join up again
**remplaçant, e** [ʀɑ̃plasɑ̃, -ɑ̃t] *nm/f* replacement, substitute, stand-in; (*Théât*) understudy; (*Scol*) supply (*Brit*) *ou* substitute (*US*) teacher
**remplacement** [ʀɑ̃plasmɑ̃] *nm* replacement; (*job*) replacement work *no pl*; (*suppléance: Scol*) supply (*Brit*) *ou* substitute (*US*) teacher; **assurer le ~ de qn** (*remplaçant*) to stand in *ou* substitute for sb; **faire des ~s** (*professeur*) to do supply *ou* substitute teaching; (*médecin*) to do locum work
**remplacer** [ʀɑ̃place] *vt* to replace; (*prendre temporairement la place de*) to stand in for; (*tenir lieu de*) to take the place of, act as a substitute for; **~ qch/qn par** to replace sth/sb with
**rempli, e** [ʀɑ̃pli] *adj* (*emploi du temps*) full, busy; **~ de** full of, filled with
**remplir** [ʀɑ̃pliʀ] *vt* to fill (up); (*questionnaire*) to fill out *ou* up; (*obligations, fonction, condition*) to fulfil; **se remplir** *vi* to fill up; **~ qch de** to fill

sth with
**remplissage** [ʀɑ̃plisaʒ] *nm* (*fig: péj*) padding
**remploi** [ʀɑ̃plwa] *nm* re-use
**rempocher** [ʀɑ̃pɔʃe] *vt* to put back into one's pocket
**remporter** [ʀɑ̃pɔʀte] *vt* (*marchandise*) to take away; (*fig*) to win, achieve
**rempoter** [ʀɑ̃pɔte] *vt* to repot
**remuant, e** [ʀəmɥɑ̃, -ɑ̃t] *adj* restless
**remue-ménage** [ʀəmymenaʒ] *nm inv* commotion
**remuer** [ʀəmɥe] *vt* to move; (*café, sauce*) to stir ▷ *vi* to move; (*fig: opposants*) to show signs of unrest; **se remuer** *vi* to move; (*se démener*) to stir o.s.; (*fam*) to get a move on
**rémunérateur, -trice** [ʀemyneʀatœʀ, -tʀis] *adj* remunerative, lucrative
**rémunération** [ʀemyneʀasjɔ̃] *nf* remuneration
**rémunérer** [ʀemyneʀe] *vt* to remunerate, pay
**renâcler** [ʀənɑkle] *vi* to snort; (*fig*) to grumble, balk
**renaissance** [ʀənɛsɑ̃s] *nf* rebirth, revival; **la R~** the Renaissance
**renaître** [ʀənɛtʀ(ə)] *vi* to be revived; **~ à la vie** to take on a new lease of life; **~ à l'espoir** to find fresh hope
**rénal, e, -aux** [ʀenal, -o] *adj* renal, kidney *cpd*
**renard** [ʀənaʀ] *nm* fox
**renardeau** [ʀənaʀdo] *nm* fox cub
**rencard** [ʀɑ̃kaʀ] *nm* = **rancard**
**rencart** [ʀɑ̃kaʀ] *nm* = **rancart**
**renchérir** [ʀɑ̃ʃeʀiʀ] *vi* to become more expensive; (*fig*): **~ (sur)** to add something (to)
**renchérissement** [ʀɑ̃ʃeʀismɑ̃] *nm* increase (in the cost *ou* price of)
**rencontre** [ʀɑ̃kɔ̃tʀ(ə)] *nf* (*de cours d'eau*) confluence; (*de véhicules*) collision; (*entrevue, congrès, match etc*) meeting; (*imprévue*) encounter; **faire la ~ de qn** to meet sb; **aller à la ~ de qn** to go and meet sb; **amours de ~** casual love affairs
**rencontrer** [ʀɑ̃kɔ̃tʀe] *vt* to meet; (*mot, expression*) to come across; (*difficultés*) to meet with; **se rencontrer** to meet; (*véhicules*) to collide
**rendement** [ʀɑ̃dmɑ̃] *nm* (*d'un travailleur, d'une machine*) output; (*d'une culture*) yield; (*d'un investissement*) return; **à plein ~** at full capacity
**rendez-vous** [ʀɑ̃devu] *nm* (*rencontre*) appointment; (: *d'amoureux*) date; (*lieu*) meeting place; **donner ~ à qn** to arrange to meet sb; **recevoir sur ~** to have an appointment system; **fixer un ~ à qn** to give sb an appointment; **avoir/prendre ~ (avec)** to have/make an appointment (with); **prendre ~ chez le médecin** to make an appointment with the doctor; **~ spatial** *ou* **orbital** docking (in space)
**rendormir** [ʀɑ̃dɔʀmiʀ]: **se rendormir** *vr* to go back to sleep
**rendre** [ʀɑ̃dʀ(ə)] *vt* (*livre, argent etc*) to give back, return; (*otages, visite, politesse, Jur: verdict*) to return; (*honneurs*) to pay; (*sang, aliments*) to bring up; (*sons: instrument*) to produce, make; (*exprimer, traduire*) to render; (*jugement*) to pronounce,

render; (faire devenir): **~ qn célèbre/qch possible** to make sb famous/sth possible; **se rendre** vi (capituler) to surrender, give o.s. up; (aller): **se ~ quelque part** to go somewhere; **se ~ à** (arguments etc) to bow to; (ordres) to comply with; **se ~ compte de qch** to realize sth; **~ la vue/la santé à qn** to restore sb's sight/health; **~ la liberté à qn** to set sb free; **~ la monnaie à qn** to give change; **se ~ insupportable/malade** to become unbearable/make o.s. ill

**rendu, e** [ʀɑ̃dy] pp de **rendre** ▷ adj (fatigué) exhausted

**renégat, e** [ʀɛnega, -at] nm/f renegade

**renégocier** [ʀənegɔsje] vt to renegociate

**rênes** [ʀɛn] nfpl reins

**renfermé, e** [ʀɑ̃fɛʀme] adj (fig) withdrawn ▷ nm: **sentir le ~** to smell stuffy

**renfermer** [ʀɑ̃fɛʀme] vt to contain; **se renfermer (sur soi-même)** to withdraw into o.s

**renfiler** [ʀɑ̃file] vt (collier) to rethread; (pull) to slip on

**renflé, e** [ʀɑ̃fle] adj bulging, bulbous

**renflement** [ʀɑ̃fləmɑ̃] nm bulge

**renflouer** [ʀɑ̃flue] vt to refloat; (fig) to set back on its (ou his/her etc) feet (again)

**renfoncement** [ʀɑ̃fɔ̃smɑ̃] nm recess

**renforcer** [ʀɑ̃fɔʀse] vt to reinforce; **~ qn dans ses opinions** to confirm sb's opinion

**renfort** [ʀɑ̃fɔʀ]: **~s** nmpl reinforcements; **en ~** as a back-up; **à grand ~ de** with a great deal of

**renfrogné, e** [ʀɑ̃fʀɔɲe] adj sullen, scowling

**renfrogner** [ʀɑ̃fʀɔɲe]: **se renfrogner** vi to scowl

**rengager** [ʀɑ̃gaʒe] vt (personnel) to take on again; **se rengager** (Mil) to re-enlist

**rengaine** [ʀɑ̃gɛn] nf (péj) old tune

**rengainer** [ʀɑ̃gene] vt (revolver) to put back in its holster; (épée) to sheathe; (fam: compliment, discours) to save, withhold

**rengorger** [ʀɑ̃gɔʀʒe]: **se rengorger** vi (fig) to puff o.s. up

**renier** [ʀənje] vt (parents) to disown, repudiate; (engagements) to go back on; (foi) to renounce

**renifler** [ʀənifle] vi to sniff ▷ vt (tabac) to sniff up; (odeur) to sniff

**rennais, e** [ʀɛnɛ, -ɛz] adj of ou from Rennes ▷ nm/f: **Rennais, e** inhabitant ou native of Rennes

**renne** [ʀɛn] nm reindeer inv

**renom** [ʀənɔ̃] nm reputation; (célébrité) renown; **vin de grand ~** highly renowned wine

**renommé, e** [ʀ(ə)nɔme] adj celebrated, renowned ▷ nf fame

**renoncement** [ʀənɔ̃smɑ̃] nm abnegation, renunciation

**renoncer** [ʀənɔ̃se] vi: **~ à** vt to give up; **~ à faire** to give up the idea of doing; **j'y renonce!** I give up!

**renouer** [ʀənwe] vt (cravate etc) to retie; (fig: conversation, liaison) to renew, resume; **~ avec** (tradition) to revive; (habitude) to take up again; **~ avec qn** to take up with sb again

**renouveau, x** [ʀənuvo] nm revival; **~ de succès** renewed success

**renouvelable** [ʀ(ə)nuvlabl(ə)] adj (contrat, bail, énergie) renewable; (expérience) which can be renewed

**renouveler** [ʀənuvle] vt to renew; (exploit, méfait) to repeat; **se renouveler** vi (incident) to recur, happen again, be repeated; (cellules etc) to be renewed ou replaced; (artiste, écrivain) to try something new

**renouvellement** [ʀ(ə)nuvɛlmɑ̃] nm renewal; recurrence

**rénovation** [ʀenɔvasjɔ̃] nf renovation; restoration; reform(ing); redevelopment

**rénover** [ʀenɔve] vt (immeuble) to renovate, do up; (meuble) to restore; (enseignement) to reform; (quartier) to redevelop

**renseignement** [ʀɑ̃sɛɲmɑ̃] nm information no pl, piece of information; (Mil) intelligence no pl; **prendre des ~s sur** to make inquiries about, ask for information about; **(guichet des) ~s** information desk; **(service des) ~s** (Tél) directory inquiries (Brit), information (US); **service de ~s** (Mil) intelligence service; **les ~s généraux** ≈ the secret police

**renseigner** [ʀɑ̃seɲe] vt: **~ qn (sur)** to give information to sb (about); **se renseigner** vi to ask for information, make inquiries

**rentabiliser** [ʀɑ̃tabilize] vt (capitaux, production) to make profitable

**rentabilité** [ʀɑ̃tabilite] nf profitability; cost-effectiveness; (d'un investissement) return; **seuil de ~** break-even point

**rentable** [ʀɑ̃tabl(ə)] adj profitable; cost-effective

**rente** [ʀɑ̃t] nf income; (pension) pension; (titre) government stock ou bond; **~ viagère** life annuity

**rentier, -ière** [ʀɑ̃tje, -jɛʀ] nm/f person of private ou independent means

**rentrée** [ʀɑ̃tʀe] nf: **~ (d'argent)** cash no pl coming in; **la ~ (des classes ou scolaire)** the start of the new school year; **la ~ (parlementaire)** the reopening ou reassembly of parliament; **faire sa ~** (artiste, acteur) to make a comeback

**rentrer** [ʀɑ̃tʀe] vi (entrer de nouveau) to go (ou come) back in; (entrer) to go (ou come) in; (revenir chez soi) to go (ou come) (back) home; (air, clou: pénétrer) to go in; (revenu, argent) to come in ▷ vt (foins) to bring in; (véhicule) to put away; (chemise dans pantalon etc) to tuck in; (griffes) to draw in; (train d'atterrissage) to raise; (fig: larmes, colère etc) to hold back; **~ le ventre** to pull in one's stomach; **~ dans** to go (ou come) back into; to go (ou come) into; (famille, patrie) to go back ou return to; (heurter) to crash into; (appartenir à) to be included in; (: catégorie etc) to fall into; **~ dans l'ordre** to get back to normal; **~ dans ses frais** to recover one's expenses (ou initial outlay)

**renverrai** etc [ʀɑ̃vɛʀe] vb voir **renvoyer**

**renversant, e** [ʀɑ̃vɛʀsɑ̃, -ɑ̃t] adj amazing, astounding

**renverse** [ʀɑ̃vɛʀs(ə)]: **à la ~** adv backwards

**r**

**renversé, e** [ʀɑ̃vɛʀse] *adj* *(écriture)* backhand; *(image)* reversed; *(stupéfait)* staggered

**renversement** [ʀɑ̃vɛʀsəmɑ̃] *nm* *(d'un régime, des traditions)* overthrow; **~ de la situation** reversal of the situation

**renverser** [ʀɑ̃vɛʀse] *vt* *(faire tomber: chaise, verre)* to knock over, overturn; *(piéton)* to knock down; *(liquide, contenu)* to spill, upset; *(retourner: verre, image)* to turn upside down, invert; *(: ordre des mots etc)* to reverse; *(fig: gouvernement etc)* to overthrow; *(stupéfier)* to bowl over, stagger; **se renverser** *vi* to fall over; to overturn; to spill; **se ~ (en arrière)** to lean back; **~ la tête/le corps (en arrière)** to tip one's head back/throw oneself back; **~ la vapeur** *(fig)* to change course

**renvoi** [ʀɑ̃vwa] *nm* dismissal; return; reflection; postponement; *(référence)* cross-reference; *(éructation)* belch

**renvoyer** [ʀɑ̃vwaje] *vt* to send back; *(congédier)* to dismiss; *(Tennis)* to return; *(lumière)* to reflect; *(son)* to echo; *(ajourner)*: **~ qch (à)** to postpone sth (until); **~ qch à qn** *(rendre)* to return sth to sb; **~ qn à** *(fig)* to refer sb to

**réorganisation** [ʀeɔʀganizasjɔ̃] *nf* reorganization

**réorganiser** [ʀeɔʀganize] *vt* to reorganize

**réorienter** [ʀeɔʀjɑ̃te] *vt* to reorient(ate), redirect

**réouverture** [ʀeuvɛʀtyʀ] *nf* reopening

**repaire** [ʀəpɛʀ] *nm* den

**repaître** [ʀəpɛtʀ(ə)] *vt* to feast; to feed; **se ~ de** *vt* *(animal)* to feed on; *(fig)* to wallow in; revel in

**répandre** [ʀepɑ̃dʀ(ə)] *vt* *(renverser)* to spill; *(étaler, diffuser)* to spread; *(lumière)* to shed; *(chaleur, odeur)* to give off; **se répandre** *vi* to spill; to spread; **se ~ en** *(injures etc)* to pour out

**répandu, e** [ʀepɑ̃dy] *pp de* **répandre** ▷ *adj* *(opinion, usage)* widespread

**réparable** [ʀepaʀabl(ə)] *adj* *(montre etc)* repairable; *(perte etc)* which can be made up for

**reparaître** [ʀəpaʀɛtʀ(ə)] *vi* to reappear

**réparateur, -trice** [ʀepaʀatœʀ, -tʀis] *nm/f* repairer

**réparation** [ʀepaʀasjɔ̃] *nf* repairing *no pl*, repair; **en ~** *(machine etc)* under repair; **demander à qn ~ de** *(offense etc)* to ask sb to make amends for

**réparer** [ʀepaʀe] *vt* to repair; *(fig: offense)* to make up for, atone for; *(: oubli, erreur)* to put right

**reparler** [ʀəpaʀle] *vi*: **~ de qn/qch** to talk about sb/sth again; **~ à qn** to speak to sb again

**repars** *etc* [ʀəpaʀ] *vb voir* **repartir**

**repartie** [ʀəpaʀti] *nf* retort; **avoir de la ~** to be quick at repartee

**repartir** [ʀəpaʀtiʀ] *vi* to set off again; to leave again; *(fig)* to get going again, pick up again; **~ à zéro** to start from scratch (again)

**répartir** [ʀepaʀtiʀ] *vt* *(pour attribuer)* to share out; *(pour disperser, disposer)* to divide up; *(poids, chaleur)* to distribute; *(étaler: dans le temps)*: **~ sur** to spread over; *(classer, diviser)*: **~ en** to divide into,

split up into; **se répartir** *vt* *(travail, rôles)* to share out between themselves

**répartition** [ʀepaʀtisjɔ̃] *nf* sharing out; dividing up; distribution

**repas** [ʀəpɑ] *nm* meal; **à l'heure des ~** at mealtimes

**repassage** [ʀəpɑsaʒ] *nm* ironing

**repasser** [ʀəpɑse] *vi* to come *(ou* go) back ▷ *vt* *(vêtement, tissu)* to iron; *(examen)* to retake, resit; *(film)* to show again; *(lame)* to sharpen; *(leçon, rôle: revoir)* to go over (again); *(plat, pain)*: **~ qch à qn** to pass sth back to sb

**repasseuse** [ʀəpɑsøz] *nf* *(machine)* ironing machine

**repayer** [ʀəpeje] *vt* to pay again

**repêchage** [ʀəpɛʃaʒ] *nm* *(Scol)*: **question de ~** question to give candidates a second chance

**repêcher** [ʀəpɛʃe] *vt* *(noyé)* to recover the body of, fish out; *(fam: candidat)* to pass *(by inflating marks)*; to give a second chance to

**repeindre** [ʀəpɛ̃dʀ(ə)] *vt* to repaint

**repentir** [ʀəpɑ̃tiʀ] *nm* repentance; **se repentir** *vi*: **se ~ (de)** to repent (of)

**répercussions** [ʀepɛʀkysjɔ̃] *nfpl* repercussions

**répercuter** [ʀepɛʀkyte] *vt* *(réfléchir, renvoyer: son, voix)* to reflect; *(faire transmettre: consignes, charges etc)* to pass on; **se répercuter** *vi* *(bruit)* to reverberate; *(fig)*: **se ~ sur** to have repercussions on

**repère** [ʀəpɛʀ] *nm* mark; *(monument etc)* landmark; **(point de) ~** point of reference

**repérer** [ʀəpeʀe] *vt* *(erreur, connaissance)* to spot; *(abri, ennemi)* to locate; **se repérer** *vi* to get one's bearings; **se faire ~** to be spotted

**répertoire** [ʀepɛʀtwaʀ] *nm* *(liste)* (alphabetical) list; *(carnet)* index notebook; *(Inform)* directory; *(de carnet)* thumb index; *(indicateur)* directory, index; *(d'un théâtre, artiste)* repertoire

**répertorier** [ʀepɛʀtɔʀje] *vt* to itemize, list

**répéter** [ʀepete] *vt* to repeat; *(préparer: leçon)* ▷ *aussi vi* to learn, go over; *(Théât)* to rehearse; **se répéter** *(redire)* to repeat o.s.; *(se reproduire)* to be repeated, recur

**répéteur** [ʀepetœʀ] *nm* *(Tél)* repeater

**répétitif, -ive** [ʀepetitif, -iv] *adj* repetitive

**répétition** [ʀepetisjɔ̃] *nf* repetition; *(Théât)* rehearsal; **répétitions** *nfpl* *(leçons)* private coaching *sg*; **armes à ~** repeater weapons; **~ générale** final dress rehearsal

**repeupler** [ʀəpœple] *vt* to repopulate; *(forêt, rivière)* to restock

**repiquage** [ʀəpikaʒ] *nm* pricking out, planting out; re-recording

**repiquer** [ʀəpike] *vt* *(plants)* to prick out, plant out; *(enregistrement)* to re-record

**répit** [ʀepi] *nm* respite; **sans ~** without letting up

**replacer** [ʀəplase] *vt* to replace, put back

**replanter** [ʀəplɑ̃te] *vt* to replant

**replat** [ʀəpla] *nm* ledge

**replâtrer** [ʀəplɑtʀe] *vt* *(mur)* to replaster

**replet, -ète** [ʀəplɛ, -ɛt] *adj* chubby, fat

**repli** [Rəpli] *nm (d'une étoffe)* fold; *(Mil, fig)* withdrawal

**replier** [Rəplije] *vt (rabattre)* to fold down *ou* over; **se replier** *vi (armée)* to withdraw, fall back; **se ~ sur soi-même** to withdraw into oneself

**réplique** [Replik] *nf (repartie, fig)* reply; *(objection)* retort; *(Théât)* line; *(copie)* replica; **donner la ~ à** to play opposite; **sans ~** *adj* no-nonsense; irrefutable

**répliquer** [Replike] *vi* to reply; *(avec impertinence)* to answer back; *(riposter)* to retaliate

**replonger** [Rəplɔ̃ʒe] *vt*: **~ qch dans** to plunge sth back into; **se ~ dans** *(journal etc)* to immerse o.s. in again

**répondant, e** [Repɔ̃dɑ̃, -ɑ̃t] *nm/f (garant)* guarantor, surety

**répondeur** [Repɔ̃dœR] *nm* answering machine

**répondre** [Repɔ̃dR(ə)] *vi* to answer, reply; *(freins, mécanisme)* to respond; **~ à** *vt* to reply to, answer; *(avec impertinence)*: **~ à qn** to answer sb back; *(invitation, convocation)* to reply to; *(affection, salut)* to return; *(provocation: mécanisme etc)* to respond to; *(correspondre à: besoin)* to answer; *(: conditions)* to meet; *(: description)* to match; **~ que** to answer *ou* reply that; **~ de** to answer for

**réponse** [Repɔ̃s] *nf* answer, reply; **avec ~ payée** *(Postes)* reply-paid, post-paid (US); **avoir ~ à tout** to have an answer for everything; **en ~ à** in reply to; **carte-/bulletin-~** reply card/slip

**report** [RəpɔR] *nm* postponement; transfer; **~ d'incorporation** *(Mil)* deferment

**reportage** [RəpɔRtaʒ] *nm (bref)* report; *(écrit: documentaire)* story; article; *(en direct)* commentary; *(genre, activité)*: **le ~** reporting

**reporter** *nm* [RəpɔRtɛR] reporter ▷ *vt* [RəpɔRte] *(total)*: **~ qch sur** to carry sth forward *ou* over to; *(ajourner)*: **~ qch (à)** to postpone sth (until); *(transférer)*: **~ qch sur** to transfer sth to; **se ~ à** *(époque)* to think back to; *(document)* to refer to

**repos** [Rəpo] *nm* rest; *(fig)* peace (and quiet); *(mental)* peace of mind; *(Mil)*: **~!** (stand) at ease!; **en ~** at rest; **au ~** at rest; *(soldat)* at ease; **de tout ~** safe

**reposant, e** [R(ə)pozɑ̃, -ɑ̃t] *adj* restful; *(sommeil)* refreshing

**repose** [Rəpoz] *nf* refitting

**reposé, e** [Rəpoze] *adj* fresh, rested; **à tête ~e** in a leisurely way, taking time to think

**repose-pied** [Rəpozpje] *nm inv* footrest

**reposer** [Rəpoze] *vt (verre, livre)* to put down; *(rideaux, carreaux)* to put back; *(délasser)* to rest; *(problème)* to reformulate ▷ *vi (liquide, pâte)* to settle, rest; *(personne)*: **ici repose ...** here lies ...; **~ sur** to be built on; *(fig)* to rest on; **se reposer** *vi* to rest; **se ~ sur qn** to rely on sb

**repoussant, e** [Rəpusɑ̃, -ɑ̃t] *adj* repulsive

**repoussé, e** [Rəpuse] *adj (cuir)* embossed (by hand)

**repousser** [Rəpuse] *vi* to grow again ▷ *vt* to repel, repulse; *(offre)* to turn down, reject; *(tiroir, personne)* to push back; *(différer)* to put back

**répréhensible** [RepReɑ̃sibl(ə)] *adj* reprehensible

**reprendre** [RəpRɑ̃dR(ə)] *vt (prisonnier, ville)* to recapture; *(objet prêté, donné)* to take back; *(chercher)*: **je viendrai te ~ à 4 h** I'll come and fetch you *ou* I'll come back for you at 4; *(se resservir de)*: **~ du pain/un œuf** to take *(ou* eat) more bread/another egg; *(Comm: article usagé)* to take back; to take in part exchange; *(firme, entreprise)* to take over; *(travail, promenade)* to resume; *(emprunter: argument, idée)* to take up, use; *(refaire: article etc)* to go over again; *(jupe etc)* to alter; *(émission, pièce)* to put on again; *(réprimander)* to tell off; *(corriger)* to correct ▷ *vi (classes, pluie)* to start (up) again; *(activités, travaux, combats)* to resume, start (up) again; *(affaires, industrie)* to pick up; *(dire)*: **reprit-il** he went on; **se reprendre** *(se ressaisir)* to recover, pull o.s. together; **s'y ~** to make another attempt; **~ des forces** to recover one's strength; **~ courage** to take new heart; **~ ses habitudes/ sa liberté** to get back into one's old habits/ regain one's freedom; **~ la route** to resume one's journey, set off again; **~ connaissance** to come to, regain consciousness; **~ haleine** *ou* **son souffle** to get one's breath back; **~ la parole** to speak again

**repreneur** [RəpRənœR] *nm* company fixer *ou* doctor

**reprenne** *etc* [RəpRɛn] *vb voir* **reprendre**

**représailles** [RəpRezɑj] *nfpl* reprisals, retaliation *sg*

**représentant, e** [RəpRezɑ̃tɑ̃, -ɑ̃t] *nm/f* representative

**représentatif, -ive** [RəpRezɑ̃tatif, -iv] *adj* representative

**représentation** [RəpRezɑ̃tasjɔ̃] *nf* representation; performing; *(symbole, image)* representation; *(spectacle)* performance; *(Comm)*: **la ~** commercial travelling; sales representation; **frais de ~** *(d'un diplomate)* entertainment allowance

**représenter** [RəpRezɑ̃te] *vt* to represent; *(donner: pièce, opéra)* to perform; **se représenter** *vt (se figurer)* to imagine; to visualize ▷ *vi*: **se ~ à** *(Pol)* to stand *ou* run again at; *(Scol)* to resit

**répressif, -ive** [Represif, -iv] *adj* repressive

**répression** [Represjɔ̃] *nf voir* **réprimer** suppression; repression; *(Pol)*: **la ~** repression; **mesures de ~** repressive measures

**réprimande** [Reprimɑ̃d] *nf* reprimand, rebuke

**réprimander** [Reprimɑ̃de] *vt* to reprimand, rebuke

**réprimer** [Reprime] *vt (émotions)* to suppress; *(peuple etc)* to repress

**repris, e** [Rəpri, -iz] *pp de* **reprendre** ▷ *nm*: **~ de justice** ex-prisoner, ex-convict

**reprise** [RəpRiz] *nf (recommencement)* resumption; *(économique)* recovery; *(TV)* repeat; *(Ciné)* rerun; *(Boxe etc)* round; *(Auto)* acceleration *no pl*; *(Comm)* trade-in, part exchange; *(de location)* sum asked for any extras or improvements made to the property; *(raccommodage)* darn; mend; **la ~ des hostilités** the resumption of hostilities; **à**

**plusieurs ~s** on several occasions, several times

**repriser** [ʀəpʀize] *vt* to darn; to mend; **aiguille/ coton à ~** darning needle/thread

**réprobateur, -trice** [ʀepʀɔbatœʀ, -tʀis] *adj* reproving

**réprobation** [ʀepʀɔbɑsjɔ̃] *nf* reprobation

**reproche** [ʀəpʀɔʃ] *nm (remontrance)* reproach; **ton/air de ~** reproachful tone/look; **faire des ~s à qn** to reproach sb; **faire ~ à qn de qch** to reproach sb for sth; **sans ~(s)** beyond *ou* above reproach

**reprocher** [ʀəpʀɔʃe] *vt*: **~ qch à qn** to reproach *ou* blame sb for sth; **~ qch à** *(machine, théorie)* to have sth against; **se ~ qch/d'avoir fait qch** to blame o.s for sth/for doing sth

**reproducteur, -trice** [ʀəpʀɔdyktœʀ, -tʀis] *adj* reproductive

**reproduction** [ʀəpʀɔdyksjɔ̃] *nf* reproduction; **~ interdite** all rights (of reproduction) reserved

**reproduire** [ʀəpʀɔdɥiʀ] *vt* to reproduce; **se reproduire** *vi (Bio)* to reproduce; *(recommencer)* to recur, re-occur

**reprographie** [ʀəpʀɔgʀafi] *nf* (photo)copying

**réprouvé, e** [ʀepʀuve] *nm/f* reprobate

**réprouver** [ʀepʀuve] *vt* to reprove

**reptation** [ʀɛptɑsjɔ̃] *nf* crawling

**reptile** [ʀɛptil] *nm* reptile

**repu, e** [ʀəpy] *pp de* **repaître** ▷ *adj* satisfied, sated

**républicain, e** [ʀepyblikɛ̃, -ɛn] *adj, nm/f* republican

**république** [ʀepyblik] *nf* republic; **R~ arabe du Yémen** Yemen Arab Republic; **R~ Centrafricaine** Central African Republic; **R~ de Corée** South Korea; **R~ dominicaine** Dominican Republic; **R~ d'Irlande** Irish Republic, Eire; **R~ populaire de Chine** People's Republic of China; **R~ populaire démocratique de Corée** Democratic People's Republic of Korea; **R~ populaire du Yémen** People's Democratic Republic of Yemen

**répudier** [ʀepydje] *vt (femme)* to repudiate; *(doctrine)* to renounce

**répugnance** [ʀepyɲɑ̃s] *nf* repugnance, loathing; **avoir** *ou* **éprouver de la ~ pour** *(médicament, comportement, travail etc)* to have an aversion to; **avoir** *ou* **éprouver de la ~ à faire qch** to be reluctant to do sth

**répugnant, e** [ʀepyɲɑ̃, -ɑ̃t] *adj* repulsive, loathsome

**répugner** [ʀepyɲe]: **~ à** *vt*: **~ à qn** to repel *ou* disgust sb; **~ à faire** to be loath *ou* reluctant to do

**répulsion** [ʀepylsjɔ̃] *nf* repulsion

**réputation** [ʀepytɑsjɔ̃] *nf* reputation; **avoir la ~ d'être ...** to have a reputation for being ...; **connaître qn/qch de ~** to know sb/sth by repute; **de ~ mondiale** world-renowned

**réputé, e** [ʀepyte] *adj* renowned; **être ~ pour** to have a reputation for, be renowned for

**requérir** [ʀəkeʀiʀ] *vt (nécessiter)* to require, call

for; *(au nom de la loi)* to call upon; *(Jur: peine)* to call for, demand

**requête** [ʀəkɛt] *nf* request, petition; *(Jur)* petition

**requiem** [ʀekɥijɛm] *nm* requiem

**requiers** *etc* [ʀəkjɛʀ] *vb voir* **requérir**

**requin** [ʀəkɛ̃] *nm* shark

**requinquer** [ʀəkɛ̃ke] *vt* to set up, pep up

**requis, e** [ʀəki, -iz] *pp de* **requérir** ▷ *adj* required

**réquisition** [ʀekizisjɔ̃] *nf* requisition

**réquisitionner** [ʀekizisjɔne] *vt* to requisition

**réquisitoire** [ʀekizitwaʀ] *nm (Jur)* closing speech for the prosecution; *(fig)*: **~ contre** indictment of

**RER** *sigle m* (= *Réseau express régional*) Greater Paris high speed train service

**rescapé, e** [ʀɛskape] *nm/f* survivor

**rescousse** [ʀɛskus] *nf*: **aller à la ~ qn** to go to sb's aid *ou* rescue; **appeler qn à la ~** to call on sb for help

**réseau, x** [ʀezo] *nm* network

**réséda** [ʀezeda] *nm (Bot)* reseda, mignonette

**réservation** [ʀezɛʀvɑsjɔ̃] *nf* reservation; booking

**réserve** [ʀezɛʀv(ə)] *nf (retenue)* reserve; *(entrepôt)* storeroom; *(restriction, aussi: d'Indiens)* reservation; *(de pêche, chasse)* preserve; *(restrictions)*: **faire des ~s** to have reservations; **officier de ~** reserve officer; **sous toutes ~s** with all reserve; *(dire)* with reservations; **sous ~ de** subject to; **sans ~** *adv* unreservedly; **en ~** in reserve; **de ~** *(provisions etc)* in reserve

**réservé, e** [ʀezɛʀve] *adj (discret)* reserved; *(chasse, pêche)* private; **~ à** *ou* **pour** reserved for

**réserver** [ʀezɛʀve] *vt (gén)* to reserve; *(chambre, billet etc)* to book, reserve; *(mettre de côté, garder)*: **~ qch pour** *ou* **à** to keep *ou* save sth for; **~ qch à qn** to reserve (*ou* book) sth for sb; *(fig: destiner)* to have sth in store for sb; **se ~ le droit de faire** to reserve the right to do

**réserviste** [ʀezɛʀvist(ə)] *nm* reservist

**réservoir** [ʀezɛʀvwaʀ] *nm* tank

**résidence** [ʀezidɑ̃s] *nf* residence; **~ principale/ secondaire** main/second home; **~ universitaire** hall of residence; **(en) ~ surveillée** (under) house arrest

**résident, e** [ʀezidɑ̃, -ɑ̃t] *nm/f (ressortissant)* foreign resident; *(d'un immeuble)* resident ▷ *adj* *(Inform)* resident

**résidentiel, le** [ʀezidɑ̃sjɛl] *adj* residential

**résider** [ʀezide] *vi*: **~ à** *ou* **dans** *ou* **en** to reside in; **~ dans** *(fig)* to lie in

**résidu** [ʀezidy] *nm* residue *no pl*

**résiduel, le** [ʀezidɥɛl] *adj* residual

**résignation** [ʀeziɲɑsjɔ̃] *nf* resignation

**résigné, e** [ʀeziɲe] *adj* resigned

**résigner** [ʀeziɲe] *vt* to relinquish, resign; **se résigner** *vi*: **se ~ (à qch/à faire)** to resign o.s. (to sth/to doing)

**résiliable** [ʀeziljabl(ə)] *adj* which can be terminated

**résilier** [ʀezilje] *vt* to terminate

**résille** [ʀezij] *nf* (hair)net

**résine** [ʀezin] *nf* resin

**résiné, e** [ʀezine] *adj*: **vin ~** retsina

**résineux, -euse** [ʀezinø, -øz] *adj* resinous ▷ *nm* coniferous tree

**résistance** [ʀezistɑ̃s] *nf* resistance; (*de réchaud, bouilloire: fil*) element

**résistant, e** [ʀezistɑ̃, -ɑ̃t] *adj* (*personne*) robust, tough; (*matériau*) strong, hard-wearing ▷ *nm/f* (*patriote*) Resistance worker *ou* fighter

**résister** [ʀeziste] *vi* to resist; **~ à** *vt* (*assaut, tentation*) to resist; (*effort, souffrance*) to withstand; (*matériau, plante*) to stand up to, withstand; (*personne: désobéir à*) to stand up to, oppose

**résolu, e** [ʀezɔly] *pp de* **résoudre** ▷ *adj* (*ferme*) resolute; **être ~ à qch/faire** to be set upon sth/ doing

**résolument** [ʀezɔlymɑ̃] *adv* resolutely, steadfastly; **~ contre qch** firmly against sth

**résolution** [ʀezɔlysjɔ̃] *nf* solving; (*fermeté, décision, Inform*) resolution; **prendre la ~ de** to make a resolution to

**résolvais** *etc* [ʀezɔlvε] *vb voir* **résoudre**

**résonance** [ʀezɔnɑ̃s] *nf* resonance

**résonner** [ʀezɔne] *vi* (*cloche, pas*) to reverberate, resound; (*salle*) to be resonant; **~ de** to resound with

**résorber** [ʀezɔʀbe]: **se résorber** *vi* (*Méd*) to be resorbed; (*fig*) to be absorbed

**résoudre** [ʀezudʀ(ə)] *vt* to solve; **~ qn à faire qch** to get sb to make up his (*ou* her) mind to do sth; **~ de faire** to resolve to do; **se ~ à faire** to bring o.s. to do

**respect** [ʀεspε] *nm* respect; **tenir en ~** to keep at bay

**respectabilité** [ʀεspεktabilite] *nf* respectability

**respectable** [ʀεspεktabl(ə)] *adj* respectable

**respecter** [ʀεspεkte] *vt* to respect; **faire ~** to enforce; **le lexicographe qui se respecte** (*fig*) any self-respecting lexicographer

**respectif, -ive** [ʀεspεktif, -iv] *adj* respective

**respectivement** [ʀεspεktivmɑ̃] *adv* respectively

**respectueusement** [ʀεspεktɥøzmɑ̃] *adv* respectfully

**respectueux, -euse** [ʀεspεktɥø, -øz] *adj* respectful; **~ de** respectful of

**respirable** [ʀεspiʀabl(ə)] *adj*: **peu ~** unbreathable

**respiration** [ʀεspiʀasjɔ̃] *nf* breathing *no pl*; **faire une ~ complète** to breathe in and out; **retenir sa ~** to hold one's breath; **~ artificielle** artificial respiration

**respiratoire** [ʀεspiʀatwaʀ] *adj* respiratory

**respirer** [ʀεspiʀe] *vi* to breathe; (*fig: se reposer*) to get one's breath, have a break; (: *être soulagé*) to breathe again ▷ *vt* to breathe (in), inhale; (*manifester: santé, calme etc*) to exude

**resplendir** [ʀεsplɑ̃diʀ] *vi* to shine; (*fig*): **~ (de)** to be radiant (with)

**resplendissant, e** [ʀεsplɑ̃disɑ̃, -ɑ̃t] *adj* radiant

**responsabilité** [ʀεspɔ̃sabilite] *nf* responsibility; (*légale*) liability; **refuser la ~ de** to deny responsibility (*ou* liability) for; **prendre ses ~s** to assume responsibility for one's actions; **~ civile** civil liability; **~ pénale/ morale/collective** criminal/moral/collective responsibility

**responsable** [ʀεspɔ̃sabl(ə)] *adj* responsible ▷ *nm/f* (*du ravitaillement etc*) person in charge; (*de parti, syndicat*) official; **~ de** responsible for; (*légalement: de dégâts etc*) liable for; (*chargé de*) in charge of, responsible for

**resquiller** [ʀεskije] *vi* (*au cinéma, au stade*) to get in on the sly; (*dans le train*) to fiddle a free ride

**resquilleur, -euse** [ʀεskijœʀ, -øz] *nm/f* (*qui n'est pas invité*) gatecrasher; (*qui ne paie pas*) fare dodger

**ressac** [ʀəsak] *nm* backwash

**ressaisir** [ʀəseziʀ]: **se ressaisir** *vi* to regain one's self-control; (*équipe sportive*) to rally

**ressasser** [ʀəsase] *vt* (*remâcher*) to keep turning over; (*redire*) to keep trotting out

**ressemblance** [ʀəsɑ̃blɑ̃s] *nf* (*visuelle*) resemblance, similarity, likeness; (: *Art*) likeness; (*analogie, trait commun*) similarity

**ressemblant, e** [ʀəsɑ̃blɑ̃, -ɑ̃t] *adj* (*portrait*) lifelike, true to life

**ressembler** [ʀəsɑ̃ble]: **~ à** *vt* to be like, resemble; (*visuellement*) to look like; **se ressembler** *vi* to be (*ou* look) alike

**ressemeler** [ʀəsɑ̃mle] *vt* to (re)sole

**ressens** *etc* [ʀ(ə)sɑ̃] *vb voir* **ressentir**

**ressentiment** [ʀəsɑ̃timɑ̃] *nm* resentment

**ressentir** [ʀəsɑ̃tiʀ] *vt* to feel; **se ~ de** to feel (*ou* show) the effects of

**resserre** [ʀəsεʀ] *nf* shed

**resserrement** [ʀ(ə)sεʀmɑ̃] *nm* narrowing; strengthening; (*goulet*) narrow part

**resserrer** [ʀəsεʀe] *vt* (*pores*) to close; (*nœud, boulon*) to tighten (up); (*fig: liens*) to strengthen; **se resserrer** *vi* (*route, vallée*) to narrow; (*liens*) to strengthen; **se ~ (autour de)** to draw closer (around), to close in (on)

**ressers** *etc* [ʀ(ə)sεʀ] *vb voir* **resservir**

**resservir** [ʀəsεʀviʀ] *vi* to do *ou* serve again ▷ *vt*: **~ qch (à qn)** to serve sth up again (to sb); **~ de qch (à qn)** to give (sb) a second helping of sth; **~ qn (d'un plat)** to give sb a second helping (of a dish); **se ~ de** (*plat*) to take a second helping of; (*outil etc*) to use again

**ressort** [ʀəsɔʀ] *vb voir* **ressortir** ▷ *nm* (*pièce*) spring; (*force morale*) spirit; (*recours*): **en dernier ~** as a last resort; (*compétence*): **être du ~ de** to fall within the competence of

**ressortir** [ʀəsɔʀtiʀ] *vi* to go (*ou* come) out (again); (*contraster*) to stand out; **~ de** (*résulter de*): **il ressort de ceci que** it emerges from this that; **~ à** (*Jur*) to come under the jurisdiction of; (*Admin*) to be the concern of; **faire ~** (*fig: souligner*) to bring out

**ressortissant, e** [ʀəsɔʀtisɑ̃, -ɑ̃t] *nm/f* national

**ressouder** [ʀəsude] *vt* to solder together again

**ressource** [ʀəsuʀs(ə)] *nf*: **avoir la ~ de** to have

**r**

the possibility of; **ressources** *nfpl* resources; *(fig)* possibilities; **leur seule ~ était de** the only course open to them was to; **~s d'énergie** energy resources

**ressusciter** [ʀesysite] *vt* to resuscitate, restore to life; *(fig)* to revive, bring back ▷ *vi* to rise (from the dead); *(fig: pays)* to come back to life

**restant, e** [ʀɛstɑ̃, -ɑ̃t] *adj* remaining ▷ *nm*: **le ~ (de)** the remainder (of); **un ~ de** *(de trop)* some leftover; *(fig: vestige)* a remnant *ou* last trace of

**restaurant** [ʀɛstoʀɑ̃] *nm* restaurant; **manger au ~** to eat out; **~ d'entreprise** staff canteen *ou* cafeteria (US); **~ universitaire (RU)** university refectory *ou* cafeteria (US)

**restaurateur, -trice** [ʀɛstoʀatœʀ, -tʀis] *nm/f* restaurant owner, restaurateur; *(de tableaux)* restorer

**restauration** [ʀɛstoʀasjɔ̃] *nf* restoration; *(hôtellerie)* catering; **~ rapide** fast food

**restaurer** [ʀɛstoʀe] *vt* to restore; **se restaurer** *vi* to have something to eat

**restauroute** [ʀɛstoʀut] *nm* = **restoroute**

**reste** [ʀɛst(ə)] *nm (restant)*: **le ~ (de)** the rest (of); *(de trop)*: **un ~ (de)** some leftover; *(vestige)*: **un ~ de** a remnant *ou* last trace of; *(Math)* remainder; **restes** *nmpl* leftovers; *(d'une cité etc, dépouille mortelle)* remains; **avoir du temps de ~** to have time to spare; **ne voulant pas être en ~** not wishing to be outdone; **partir sans attendre** *ou* **demander son ~** *(fig)* to leave without waiting to hear more; **du ~, au ~** *adv* besides, moreover; **pour le ~, quant au ~** *adv* as for the rest

**rester** [ʀɛste] *vi (dans un lieu, un état, une position)* to stay, remain; *(subsister)* to remain, be left; *(durer)* to last, live on ▷ *vb impers*: **il reste du pain/ deux œufs** there's some bread/there are two eggs left (over); **il reste du temps/10 minutes** there's some time/there are 10 minutes left; **il me reste assez de temps** I have enough time left; **voilà tout ce qui (me) reste** that's all I've got left; **ce qui reste à faire** what remains to be done; **ce qui me reste à faire** what remains for me to do; **(il) reste à savoir/établir si ...** it remains to be seen/established if *ou* whether ...; **il n'en reste pas moins que ...** the fact remains that ..., it's nevertheless a fact that ...; **en ~ à** *(stade, menaces)* to go no further than, only go as far as; **restons-en là** let's leave it at that; **~ sur une impression** to retain an impression; **y ~:** **il a failli y ~** he nearly met his end

**restituer** [ʀɛstitɥe] *vt (objet, somme)*: **~ qch (à qn)** to return *ou* restore sth (to sb); *(énergie)* to release; *(son)* to reproduce

**restitution** [ʀɛstitysjɔ̃] *nf* restoration

**restoroute** [ʀɛstoʀut] *nm* motorway (Brit) *ou* highway (US) restaurant

**restreindre** [ʀɛstʀɛ̃dʀ(ə)] *vt* to restrict, limit; **se restreindre** *(dans ses dépenses etc)* to cut down; *(champ de recherches)* to narrow

**restreint, e** [ʀɛstʀɛ̃, -ɛ̃t] *pp de* **restreindre** ▷ *adj* restricted, limited

**restrictif, -ive** [ʀɛstʀiktif, -iv] *adj* restrictive, limiting

**restriction** [ʀɛstʀiksjɔ̃] *nf* restriction; *(condition)* qualification; **restrictions** *nfpl (mentales)* reservations; **sans ~** *adv* unreservedly

**restructuration** [ʀəstʀyktyʀasjɔ̃] *nf* restructuring

**restructurer** [ʀəstʀyktyʀe] *vt* to restructure

**résultante** [ʀezyltɑ̃t] *nf (conséquence)* result, consequence

**résultat** [ʀezylta] *nm* result; *(conséquence)* outcome *no pl*, result; *(d'élection etc)* results *pl*; **résultats** *nmpl (d'une enquête)* findings; **~s sportifs** sports results

**résulter** [ʀezylte]: **~ de** *vt* to result from, be the result of; **il résulte de ceci que ...** the result of this is that ...

**résumé** [ʀezyme] *nm* summary, résumé; **faire le ~ de** to summarize; **en ~** *adv* in brief; *(pour conclure)* to sum up

**résumer** [ʀezyme] *vt (texte)* to summarize; *(récapituler)* to sum up; *(fig)* to epitomize, typify; **se résumer** *vi (personne)* to sum up (one's ideas); **se ~ à** to come down to

**resurgir** [ʀəsyʀʒiʀ] *vi* to reappear, re-emerge

**résurrection** [ʀezyʀɛksjɔ̃] *nf* resurrection; *(fig)* revival

**rétablir** [ʀetabliʀ] *vt* to restore, re-establish; *(personne: traitement)*: **~ qn** to restore sb to health, help sb recover; *(Admin)*: **~ qn dans son emploi/ses droits** to reinstate sb in his post/ restore sb's rights; **se rétablir** *vi (guérir)* to recover; *(silence, calme)* to return, be restored; *(Gym etc)*: **se ~ (sur)** to pull o.s. up (onto)

**rétablissement** [ʀetablismɑ̃] *nm* restoring; recovery; pull-up

**rétamer** [ʀetame] *vt* to re-coat, re-tin

**rétameur** [ʀetamœʀ] *nm* tinker

**retaper** [ʀətape] *vt (maison, voiture etc)* to do up; *(fam: revigorer)* to buck up; *(redactylographier)* to retype

**retard** [ʀətaʀ] *nm (d'une personne attendue)* lateness *no pl*; *(sur l'horaire, un programme, une échéance)* delay; *(fig: scolaire, mental etc)* backwardness; **être en ~** *(pays)* to be backward; *(dans paiement, travail)* to be behind; **en ~ (de deux heures)** (two hours) late; **avoir un ~ de deux km** *(Sport)* to be two km behind; **rattraper son ~** to catch up; **avoir du ~** to be late; *(sur un programme)* to be behind (schedule); **prendre du ~** *(train, avion)* to be delayed; *(montre)* to lose (time); **sans ~** *adv* without delay; **~ à l'allumage** *(Auto)* retarded spark; **~ scolaire** backwardness at school

**retardataire** [ʀətaʀdatɛʀ] *adj* late; *(enfant, idées)* backward ▷ *nm/f* latecomer; backward child

**retardé, e** [ʀətaʀde] *adj* backward

**retardement** [ʀətaʀdəmɑ̃]: **à ~** *adj* delayed action *cpd*; **bombe à ~** time bomb

**retarder** [ʀətaʀde] *vt (sur un horaire)*: **~ qn (d'une heure)** to delay sb (an hour); *(sur un programme)*: **~ qn (de trois mois)** to set sb back *ou* delay sb (three months); (*départ, date*): ~ qch (de deux jours) to put sth back (two days), delay sth (for *ou* by two days); (*horloge*) to put back ▷ *vi* (*montre*) to be slow; (: *habituellement*) to lose (time); **je retarde (d'une heure)** I'm (an hour) slow

**retendre** [Rətɑ̃dR(ə)] *vt* (*câble etc*) to stretch again; (*Mus: cordes*) to retighten

**retenir** [RətniR] *vt* (*garder, retarder*) to keep, detain; (*maintenir: objet qui glisse, fig: colère, larmes, rire*) to hold back; (: *objet suspendu*) to hold; (: *chaleur, odeur*) to retain; (*fig: empêcher d'agir*): ~ qn (de faire) to hold sb back (from doing); (*se rappeler*) to retain; (*réserver*) to reserve; (*accepter*) to accept; (*prélever*): ~ qch (sur) to deduct sth (from); se retenir (*euphémisme*) to hold on; (*se raccrocher*): se ~ à to hold onto; (*se contenir*): se ~ de faire to restrain o.s. from doing; ~ son souffle *ou* haleine to hold one's breath; ~ qn à dîner to ask sb to stay for dinner; je pose trois et je retiens deux put down three and carry two

**rétention** [Retɑ̃sjɔ̃] *nf*: ~ d'urine urine retention

**retentir** [Rətɑ̃tiR] *vi* to ring out; (*salle*): ~ de to ring *ou* resound with; ~ sur *vt* (*fig*) to have an effect upon

**retentissant, e** [Rətɑ̃tisɑ̃, -ɑ̃t] *adj* resounding; (*fig*) impact-making

**retentissement** [Rətɑ̃tismɑ̃] *nm* (*retombées*) repercussions *pl*; effect, impact

**retenu, e** [Rətny] *pp de* **retenir** ▷ *adj* (*place*) reserved; (*personne: empêché*) held up; (*propos: contenu, discret*) restrained ▷ *nf* (*prélèvement*) deduction; (*Math*) number to carry over; (*Scol*) detention; (*modération*) (self-)restraint; (*réserve*) reserve, reticence; (*Auto*) tailback

**réticence** [Retisɑ̃s] *nf* reticence *no pl*, reluctance *no pl*; **sans** ~ without hesitation

**réticent, e** [Retisɑ̃, -ɑ̃t] *adj* reticent, reluctant

**retiendrai** [Rətjɛ̃dRe], **retiens** *etc* [Rətjɛ̃] *vb voir* **retenir**

**rétif, -ive** [Retif, -iv] *adj* restive

**rétine** [Retin] *nf* retina

**retint** *etc* [Rətɛ̃] *vb voir* **retenir**

**retiré, e** [Rətire] *adj* (*solitaire*) secluded; (*éloigné*) remote

**retirer** [Rətire] *vt* to withdraw; (*vêtement, lunettes*) to take off, remove; (*enlever*): ~ qch à qn to take sth from sb; (*extraire*): ~ qn/qch de to take sb away from/sth out of, remove sb/sth from; (*reprendre: bagages, billets*) to collect, pick up; ~ des avantages de to derive advantages from; se retirer *vi* (*partir, reculer*) to withdraw; (*prendre sa retraite*) to retire; se ~ de to withdraw from; to retire from

**retombées** [Rətɔ̃be] *nfpl* (*radioactives*) fallout *sg*; (*fig*) fallout; spin-offs

**retomber** [Rətɔ̃be] *vi* (*à nouveau*) to fall again; (*rechuter*): ~ malade/dans l'erreur to fall ill again/fall back into error; (*atterrir: après un saut etc*) to land; (*tomber, redescendre*) to fall back; (*pendre*) to fall, hang (down); (*échoir*): ~ sur qn to

fall on sb

**retordre** [RətɔRdR(ə)] *vt*: **donner du fil à ~ à qn** to make life difficult for sb

**rétorquer** [RetɔRke] *vt*: ~ (à qn) que to retort (to sb) that

**retors, e** [RətɔR, -ɔRs(ə)] *adj* wily

**rétorsion** [RetɔRsjɔ̃] *nf*: **mesures de** ~ reprisals

**retouche** [Rətuʃ] *nf* touching up *no pl*; alteration; **faire une** ~ *ou* **des ~s** to touch up

**retoucher** [Rətuʃe] *vt* (*photographie, tableau*) to touch up; (*texte, vêtement*) to alter

**retour** [RətuR] *nm* return; **au** ~ (*en arrivant*) when we (*ou* they *etc*) get (*ou* got) back; (*en route*) on the way back; **pendant le** ~ on the way *ou* journey back; **à mon/ton** ~ on my/your return; **au** ~ **de** on the return of; **être de** ~ (**de**) to be back (from); **de ~ à .../chez moi** back at .../back home; **en** ~ *adv* in return; **par ~ du courrier** by return of post; **par un juste** ~ **des choses** by a favourable twist of fate; **match** ~ return match; ~ **en arrière** (*Ciné*) flashback; (*mesure*) backward step; ~ **de bâton** kickback; ~ **de chariot** carriage return; ~ **à l'envoyeur** (*Postes*) return to sender; ~ **de flamme** backfire; ~ **(automatique) à la ligne** (*Inform*) wordwrap; ~ **de manivelle** (*fig*) backfire; ~ **offensif** renewed attack; ~ **aux sources** (*fig*) return to basics

**retournement** [RətuRnəmɑ̃] *nm* (*d'une personne: revirement*) turning (round); ~ **de la situation** reversal of the situation

**retourner** [RətuRne] *vt* (*dans l'autre sens: matelas, crêpe*) to turn (over); (: *caisse*) to turn upside down; (: *sac, vêtement*) to turn inside out; (*fig: argument*) to turn back; (*en remuant: terre, sol, foin*) to turn over; (*émouvoir: personne*) to shake; (*renvoyer, restituer*): ~ qch à qn to return sth to sb ▷ *vi* (*aller, revenir*): ~ **quelque part/à** to go back *ou* return somewhere/to; ~ **à** (*état, activité*) to return to, go back to; se retourner *vi* to turn over; (*tourner la tête*) to turn round; **s'en** ~ to go back; se retourner contre (*fig*) to turn against; **savoir de quoi il retourne** to know what it is all about; ~ **sa veste** (*fig*) to turn one's coat; ~ **en arrière** *ou* **sur ses pas** to turn back, retrace one's steps; ~ **aux sources** to go back to basics

**retracer** [RətRase] *vt* to relate, recount

**rétracter** [RetRakte] *vt*, **se rétracter** *vi* to retract

**retraduire** [RətRaduiR] *vt* to translate again; (*dans la langue de départ*) to translate back

**retrait** [RətRɛ] *nm voir* **retirer** withdrawal; collection; *voir* **se retirer** withdrawal; (*rétrécissement*) shrinkage; **en** ~ *adj* set back; **écrire en** ~ to indent; ~ **du permis (de conduire)** disqualification from driving (*Brit*), revocation of driver's license (*US*)

**retraite** [RətRɛt] *nf* (*d'une armée, Rel, refuge*) retreat; (*d'un employé*) retirement; (*revenu*) (retirement) pension; **être/mettre à la** ~ to be retired/pension off *ou* retire; **prendre sa** ~ to retire; ~ **anticipée** early retirement; ~ **aux flambeaux** torchlight tattoo

**retraité, e** [ʀətʀete] adj retired ▷ nm/f (old age) pensioner

**retraitement** [ʀətʀɛtmã] nm reprocessing

**retraiter** [ʀətʀɛte] vt to reprocess

**retranchement** [ʀətʀãʃmã] nm entrenchment; **poursuivre qn dans ses derniers ~s** to drive sb into a corner

**retrancher** [ʀətʀãʃe] vt (passage, détails) to take out, remove; (nombre, somme): **~ qch de** to take ou deduct sth from; (couper) to cut off; **se ~ derrière/dans** to entrench o.s. behind/in; (fig) to take refuge behind/in

**retranscrire** [ʀətʀãskʀiʀ] vt to retranscribe

**retransmettre** [ʀətʀãsmɛtʀ(ə)] vt (Radio) to broadcast, relay; (TV) to show

**retransmission** [ʀətʀãsmisjõ] nf broadcast; showing

**retravailler** [ʀətʀavaje] vi to start work again ▷ vt to work on again

**retraverser** [ʀətʀavɛʀse] vt (dans l'autre sens) to cross back over

**rétréci, e** [ʀetʀesi] adj (idées, esprit) narrow

**rétrécir** [ʀetʀesiʀ] vt (vêtement) to take in ▷ vi to shrink; **se rétrécir** vi to narrow

**rétrécissement** [ʀetʀesismã] nm narrowing

**retremper** [ʀətʀãpe] vt: **se ~ dans** (fig) to reimmerse o.s. in

**rétribuer** [ʀetʀibɥe] vt (travail) to pay for; (personne) to pay

**rétribution** [ʀetʀibysjõ] nf payment

**rétro** [ʀetʀo] adj inv old-style ▷ nm (rétroviseur) (rear-view) mirror; **la mode ~** the nostalgia vogue

**rétroactif, -ive** [ʀetʀoaktif, -iv] adj retroactive

**rétrocéder** [ʀetʀosede] vt to retrocede

**rétrocession** [ʀetʀosesjõ] nf retrocession

**rétrofusée** [ʀetʀofyze] nf retrorocket

**rétrograde** [ʀetʀogʀad] adj reactionary, backward-looking

**rétrograder** [ʀetʀogʀade] vi (élève) to fall back; (économie) to regress; (Auto) to change down

**rétroprojecteur** [ʀetʀopʀɔʒɛktœʀ] nm overhead projector

**rétrospectif, -ive** [ʀetʀospɛktif, -iv] adj, nf retrospective

**rétrospectivement** [ʀetʀospɛktivmã] adv in retrospect

**retroussé, e** [ʀətʀuse] adj: **nez ~** turned-up nose

**retrousser** [ʀətʀuse] vt to roll up; (fig: nez) to wrinkle; (: lèvres) to curl

**retrouvailles** [ʀətʀuvaj] nfpl reunion sg

**retrouver** [ʀətʀuve] vt (fugitif, objet perdu) to find; (occasion) to find again; (calme, santé) to regain; (reconnaître: expression, style) to recognize; (revoir) to see again; (rejoindre) to meet (again), join; **se retrouver** vi to meet; (s'orienter) to find one's way; **se ~ quelque part** to find o.s. somewhere; to end up somewhere; **se ~ seul/sans argent** to find o.s. alone/with no money; **se ~ dans** (calculs, dossiers, désordre) to make sense of; **s'y ~** (rentrer dans ses frais) to break even

**rétroviseur** [ʀetʀovizœʀ] nm (rear-view) mirror

**réunifier** [ʀeynifje] vt to reunify

**Réunion** [ʀeynjõ] nf: **la ~, l'île de la ~** Réunion

**réunion** [ʀeynjõ] nf bringing together; joining; (séance) meeting

**réunionnais, e** [ʀeynjɔnɛ, -ɛz] adj of ou from Réunion

**réunir** [ʀeyniʀ] vt (convoquer) to call together; (rassembler) to gather together; (cumuler) to combine; (rapprocher) to bring together (again), reunite; (rattacher) to join (together); **se réunir** vi (se rencontrer) to meet; (s'allier) to unite

**réussi, e** [ʀeysi] adj successful

**réussir** [ʀeysiʀ] vi to succeed, be successful; (à un examen) to pass; (plante, culture) to thrive, do well ▷ vt to make a success of; to bring off; **~ à faire** to succeed in doing; **~ à qn** to go right for sb; (aliment) to agree with sb; **le travail/le mariage lui réussit** work/married life agrees with him

**réussite** [ʀeysit] nf success; (Cartes) patience

**réutiliser** [ʀeytilize] vt to re-use

**revaloir** [ʀəvalwaʀ] vt: **je vous revaudrai cela** I'll repay you some day; (en mal) I'll pay you back for this

**revalorisation** [ʀəvalɔʀizasjõ] nf revaluation; raising

**revaloriser** [ʀəvalɔʀize] vt (monnaie) to revalue; (salaires, pensions) to raise the level of; (institution, tradition) to reassert the value of

**revanche** [ʀəvãʃ] nf revenge; **prendre sa ~ (sur)** to take one's revenge (on); **en ~** (par contre) on the other hand; (en compensation) in return

**rêvasser** [ʀɛvase] vi to daydream

**rêve** [ʀɛv] nm dream; (activité psychique): **le ~** dreaming; **paysage/silence de ~** dreamlike landscape/silence; **~ éveillé** daydreaming no pl, daydream

**rêvé, e** [ʀɛve] adj (endroit, mari etc) ideal

**revêche** [ʀəvɛʃ] adj surly, sour-tempered

**réveil** [ʀevɛj] nm (d'un dormeur) waking up no pl; (fig) awakening; (pendule) alarm (clock); **au ~** when I (ou you etc) wake (ou woke) up, on waking (up); **sonner le ~** (Mil) to sound the reveille

**réveille-matin** [ʀevɛjmatɛ̃] nm inv alarm clock

**réveiller** [ʀevɛje] vt (personne) to wake up; (fig) to awaken, revive; **se réveiller** vi to wake up; (fig) to be revived, reawaken

**réveillon** [ʀevɛjõ] nm Christmas Eve; (de la Saint-Sylvestre) New Year's Eve; Christmas Eve (ou New Year's Eve) party ou dinner

**réveillonner** [ʀevɛjɔne] vi to celebrate Christmas Eve (ou New Year's Eve)

**révélateur, -trice** [ʀevelatœʀ, -tʀis] adj: **~ (de qch)** revealing (sth) ▷ nm (Photo) developer

**révélation** [ʀevelasjõ] nf revelation

**révéler** [ʀevele] vt (gén) to reveal; (divulguer) to disclose, reveal; (dénoter) to reveal, show; (faire connaître au public): **~ qn/qch** to make sb/sth widely known, bring sb/sth to the public's notice; **se révéler** vi to be revealed, reveal itself; **se ~ facile/faux** to prove (to be) easy/false; **se ~ cruel/un allié sûr** to show o.s. to be cruel/a trustworthy ally

**revenant, e** [ʀəvnã, -ãt] *nm/f* ghost

**revendeur, -euse** [ʀəvãdœʀ, -øz] *nm/f* (*détaillant*) retailer; (*d'occasions*) secondhand dealer

**revendicatif, -ive** [ʀəvãdikatif, -iv] *adj* (*mouvement*) protest *cpd*

**revendication** [ʀəvãdikasjɔ̃] *nf* claim, demand; **journée de ~** day of action (in support of one's claims)

**revendiquer** [ʀəvãdike] *vt* to claim, demand; (*responsabilité*) to claim ▷ *vi* to agitate in favour of one's claims

**revendre** [ʀəvãdʀ(ə)] *vt* (*d'occasion*) to resell; (*détailler*) to sell; (*vendre davantage de*): **~ du sucre/un foulard/deux bagues** to sell more sugar/another scarf/another two rings; **à ~** *adv* (*en abondance*) to spare

**revenir** [ʀəvniʀ] *vi* to come back; (*Culin*): **faire ~** to brown; (*coûter*): **~ cher/à 100 euros (à qn)** to cost (sb) a lot/100 euros; **~ à** (*études, projet*) to return to, go back to; (*équivaloir à*) to amount to; **~ à qn** (*rumeur, nouvelle*) to get back to sb, reach sb's ears; (*part, honneur*) to go to sb, be sb's; (*souvenir, nom*) to come back to sb; **~ de** (*fig: maladie, étonnement*) to recover from; **~ sur** (*question, sujet*) to go back over; (*engagement*) to go back on; **~ à la charge** to return to the attack; **~ à soi** to come round; **n'en pas ~: je n'en reviens** I can't get over it; **~ sur ses pas** to retrace one's steps; **cela revient à dire que/au même** it amounts to saying that/to the same thing; **~ de loin** (*fig*) to have been at death's door

**revente** [ʀəvãt] *nf* resale

**revenu, e** [ʀəvny] *pp de* **revenir** ▷ *nm* income; (*de l'État*) revenue; (*d'un capital*) yield; **revenus** *nmpl* income *sg*; **~ national brut** gross national income

**rêver** [ʀeve] *vi, vt* to dream; (*rêvasser*) to (day)dream; **~ de** (*voir en rêve*) to dream of *ou* about; **~ de qch/de faire** to dream of sth/of doing; **~ à** to dream of

**réverbération** [ʀeveʀbeʀasjɔ̃] *nf* reflection

**réverbère** [ʀeveʀbɛʀ] *nm* street lamp *ou* light

**réverbérer** [ʀeveʀbeʀe] *vt* to reflect

**reverdir** [ʀəvɛʀdiʀ] *vi* (*arbre etc*) to turn green again

**révérence** [ʀeveʀãs] *nf* (*vénération*) reverence; (*salut: d'homme*) bow; (: *de femme*) curtsey

**révérencieux, -euse** [ʀeveʀãsjø, -øz] *adj* reverent

**révérend, e** [ʀeveʀã, -ãd] *adj*: **le ~ père Pascal** the Reverend Father Pascal

**révérer** [ʀeveʀe] *vt* to revere

**rêverie** [ʀɛvʀi] *nf* daydreaming *no pl*, daydream

**reverrai** *etc* [ʀəvɛʀe] *vb voir* **revoir**

**revers** [ʀəvɛʀ] *nm* (*de feuille, main*) back; (*d'étoffe*) wrong side; (*de pièce, médaille*) back, reverse; (*Tennis, Ping-Pong*) backhand; (*de veston*) lapel; (*de*

*pantalon*) turn-up; (*fig: échec*) setback; **~ de fortune** reverse of fortune; **d'un ~ de main** with the back of one's hand; **le ~ de la médaille** (*fig*) the other side of the coin; **prendre à ~** (*Mil*) to take from the rear

**reverser** [ʀəvɛʀse] *vt* (*reporter: somme etc*): **~ sur** to put back into; (*liquide*): **~ (dans)** to pour some more (into)

**réversible** [ʀevɛʀsibl(ə)] *adj* reversible

**revêtement** [ʀəvɛtmã] *nm* (*de paroi*) facing; (*des sols*) flooring; (*de chaussée*) surface; (*de tuyau etc: enduit*) coating

**revêtir** [ʀəvetiʀ] *vt* (*habit*) to don, put on; (*fig*) to take on; **~ qn de** to dress sb in; (*fig*) to endow *ou* invest sb with; **~ qch de** to cover sth with; (*fig*) to cloak sth in; **~ d'un visa** to append a visa to

**rêveur, -euse** [ʀɛvœʀ, -øz] *adj* dreamy ▷ *nm/f* dreamer

**reviendrai** *etc* [ʀəvjɛ̃dʀe] *vb voir* **revenir**

**revienne** *etc* [ʀəvjɛn] *vb voir* **revenir**

**revient** [ʀəvjɛ̃] *vb voir* **revenir** ▷ *nm*: **prix de ~** cost price

**revigorer** [ʀəvigɔʀe] *vt* to invigorate, revive, buck up

**revint** *etc* [ʀəvɛ̃] *vb voir* **revenir**

**revirement** [ʀəviʀmã] *nm* change of mind; (*d'une situation*) reversal

**revis** *etc* [ʀəvi] *vb voir* **revoir**

**révisable** [ʀevizabl(ə)] *adj* (*procès, taux etc*) reviewable, subject to review

**réviser** [ʀevize] *vt* (*texte, Scol: matière*) to revise; (*comptes*) to audit; (*machine, installation, moteur*) to overhaul, service; (*Jur: procès*) to review

**révision** [ʀevizjɔ̃] *nf* revision; auditing *no pl*; overhaul, servicing *no pl*; review; **conseil de ~** (*Mil*) recruiting board; **faire ses ~s** (*Scol*) to do one's revision (*Brit*), revise (*Brit*), review (*US*); **la ~ des 10 000 km** (*Auto*) the 10,000 km service

**révisionnisme** [ʀevizjɔnism(ə)] *nm* revisionism

**revisser** [ʀəvise] *vt* to screw back again

**revit** [ʀəvi] *vb voir* **revoir**

**revitaliser** [ʀəvitalize] *vt* to revitalize

**revivifier** [ʀəvivifje] *vt* to revitalize

**revivre** [ʀəvivʀ(ə)] *vi* (*reprendre des forces*) to come alive again; (*traditions*) to be revived ▷ *vt* (*épreuve, moment*) to relive; **faire ~** (*mode, institution, usage*) to bring back to life

**révocable** [ʀevɔkabl(ə)] *adj* (*délégué*) dismissible; (*contrat*) revocable

**révocation** [ʀevɔkasjɔ̃] *nf* dismissal; revocation

**revoir** [ʀəvwaʀ] *vt* to see again; (*réviser*) to revise (*Brit*), review (*US*) ▷ *nm*: **au ~** goodbye; **dire au ~ à qn** to say goodbye to sb; **se revoir** (*amis*) to meet (again), see each other again

**révoltant, e** [ʀevɔltã, -ãt] *adj* revolting

**révolte** [ʀevɔlt(ə)] *nf* rebellion, revolt

**révolter** [ʀevɔlte] *vt* to revolt, outrage; **se révolter** *vi*: **se ~ (contre)** to rebel (against); **se ~ (à)** to be outraged (by)

**révolu, e** [ʀevɔly] *adj* past; (*Admin*): **âgé de 18 ans ~s** over 18 years of age; **après trois ans ~s**

r

when three full years have passed

**révolution** [ʀevɔlysjɔ̃] *nf* revolution; **être en ~** (*pays etc*) to be in revolt; **la ~ industrielle** the industrial revolution

**révolutionnaire** [ʀevɔlysjɔnɛʀ] *adj, nm/f* revolutionary

**révolutionner** [ʀevɔlysjɔne] *vt* to revolutionize; (*fig*) to stir up

**revolver** [ʀevɔlvɛʀ] *nm* gun; (*à barillet*) revolver

**révoquer** [ʀevɔke] *vt* (*fonctionnaire*) to dismiss, remove from office; (*arrêt, contrat*) to revoke

**revoyais** *etc* [ʀəvwajɛ] *vb voir* **revoir**

**revu, e** [ʀəvy] *pp de* **revoir** ▷ *nf* (*inventaire, examen*) review; (*Mil: défilé*) review, march past; (*: inspection*) inspection, review; (*périodique*) review, magazine; (*pièce satirique*) revue; (*de music-hall*) variety show; **passer en ~** to review, inspect; (*fig*) to review; **~ de (la) presse** press review

**révulsé, e** [ʀevylse] *adj* (*yeux*) rolled upwards; (*visage*) contorted

**Reykjavik** [ʀekjavik] *n* Reykjavik

**rez-de-chaussée** [ʀedʃose] *nm inv* ground floor

**rez-de-jardin** [ʀedʒaʀdɛ̃] *nm inv* garden level

**RF** *sigle f* = **République française**

**RFA** *sigle f* (= *République fédérale d'Allemagne*) FRG

**RFO** *sigle f* (= *Radio-Télévision Française d'Outre-mer*) French overseas broadcasting service

**RG** *sigle mpl* (= *renseignements généraux*) security section of the police force

**rhabiller** [ʀabije] *vt*: **se rhabiller** to get dressed again, put one's clothes on again

**rhapsodie** [ʀapsɔdi] *nf* rhapsody

**rhéostat** [ʀeɔsta] *nm* rheostat

**rhésus** [ʀezys] *adj, nm* rhesus; **~ positif/négatif** rhesus positive/negative

**rhétorique** [ʀetɔʀik] *nf* rhetoric ▷ *adj* rhetorical

**Rhin** [ʀɛ̃] *nm*: **le ~** the Rhine

**rhinite** [ʀinit] *nf* rhinitis

**rhinocéros** [ʀinɔseʀɔs] *nm* rhinoceros

**rhinopharyngite** [ʀinɔfaʀɛ̃ʒit] *nf* throat infection

**rhodanien, ne** [ʀɔdanjɛ̃, -ɛn] *adj* Rhône *cpd*, of the Rhône

**Rhodes** [ʀɔd] *n*: (**l'île de) ~** (the island of) Rhodes

**Rhodésie** [ʀɔdezi] *nf*: **la ~** Rhodesia

**rhodésien, ne** [ʀɔdezjɛ̃, -ɛn] *adj* Rhodesian

**rhododendron** [ʀɔdɔdɛ̃dʀɔ̃] *nm* rhododendron

**Rhône** [ʀon] *nm*: **le ~** the Rhône

**rhubarbe** [ʀybaʀb(ə)] *nf* rhubarb

**rhum** [ʀɔm] *nm* rum

**rhumatisant, e** [ʀymatizɑ̃, -ɑ̃t] *adj, nm/f* rheumatic

**rhumatismal, e, -aux** [ʀymatismal, -o] *adj* rheumatic

**rhumatisme** [ʀymatism(ə)] *nm* rheumatism *no pl*

**rhumatologie** [ʀymatɔlɔʒi] *nf* rheumatology

**rhumatologue** [ʀymatɔlɔg] *nm/f* rheumatologist

**rhume** [ʀym] *nm* cold; **~ de cerveau** head cold;

**le ~ des foins** hay fever

**rhumerie** [ʀɔmʀi] *nf* (*distillerie*) rum distillery

**RI** *sigle m* (*Mil*) = **régiment d'infanterie**

**ri** [ʀi] *pp de* **rire**

**riant, e** [ʀjɑ̃, -ɑ̃t] *vb voir* **rire** ▷ *adj* smiling, cheerful; (*campagne, paysage*) pleasant

**RIB** *sigle m* = **relevé d'identité bancaire**

**ribambelle** [ʀibɑ̃bɛl] *nf*: **une ~** a herd *ou* swarm of

**ricain, e** [ʀikɛ̃, -ɛn] *adj* (*fam*) Yank, Yankee

**ricanement** [ʀikanmɑ̃] *nm* snigger; giggle

**ricaner** [ʀikane] *vi* (*avec méchanceté*) to snigger; (*bêtement, avec gêne*) to giggle

**riche** [ʀiʃ] *adj* (*gén*) rich; (*personne, pays*) rich, wealthy; **~ en** rich in; **~ de** full of; rich in

**richement** [ʀiʃmɑ̃] *adv* richly

**richesse** [ʀiʃɛs] *nf* wealth; (*fig*) richness; **richesses** *nfpl* wealth *sg*; treasures; **~ en vitamines** high vitamin content

**richissime** [ʀiʃisim] *adj* extremely rich *ou* wealthy

**ricin** [ʀisɛ̃] *nm*: **huile de ~** castor oil

**ricocher** [ʀikɔʃe] *vi*: **~ (sur)** to rebound (off); (*sur l'eau*) to bounce (on *ou* off); **faire ~** (*galet*) to skim

**ricochet** [ʀikɔʃɛ] *nm* rebound; bounce; **faire ~** to rebound, bounce; (*fig*) to rebound; **faire des ~s** to skip stones; **par ~** *adv* on the rebound; (*fig*) as an indirect result

**rictus** [ʀiktys] *nm* grin, (snarling) grimace

**ride** [ʀid] *nf* wrinkle; (*fig*) ripple

**ridé, e** [ʀide] *adj* wrinkled

**rideau, x** [ʀido] *nm* curtain; **tirer/ouvrir les ~x** to draw/open the curtains; **~ de fer** metal shutter; (*Pol*): **le ~ de fer** the Iron Curtain

**ridelle** [ʀidɛl] *nf* slatted side (*of truck*)

**rider** [ʀide] *vt* to wrinkle; (*fig*) to ripple, ruffle the surface of; **se rider** *vi* to become wrinkled

**ridicule** [ʀidikyl] *adj* ridiculous ▷ *nm* ridiculousness *no pl*; **le ~** ridicule; (*travers: gén pl*) absurdities *pl*; **tourner en ~** to ridicule

**ridiculement** [ʀidikylmɑ̃] *adv* ridiculously

**ridiculiser** [ʀidikylize] *vt* to ridicule; **se ridiculiser** to make a fool of o.s

**ridule** [ʀidyl] *nf* (*euph: ride*) little wrinkle

**rie** *etc* [ʀi] *vb voir* **rire**

○ **MOT-CLÉ**

**rien** [ʀjɛ̃] *pron* **1**: (**ne**) **... rien** nothing; (*tournure négative*) anything; **qu'est-ce que vous avez?** — **rien** what have you got? — nothing; **il n'a rien dit/fait** he said/did nothing, he hasn't said/ done anything; **il n'a rien** (*n'est pas blessé*) he's all right; **ça ne fait rien** it doesn't matter; **il n'y est pour rien** he's got nothing to do with it

**2** (*quelque chose*): **a-t-il jamais rien fait pour nous?** has he ever done anything for us?

**3**: **rien de**: **rien d'intéressant** nothing interesting; **rien d'autre** nothing else; **rien du tout** nothing at all; **il n'a rien d'un champion** he's no champion, there's nothing of the champion about him

**4: rien que** just, only; nothing but; **rien que pour lui faire plaisir** only *ou* just to please him; **rien que la vérité** nothing but the truth; **rien que cela** that alone
▷ *excl*: **de rien!** not at all!, don't mention it!; **il n'en est rien!** nothing of the sort!; **rien à faire!** it's no good!, it's no use!
▷ *nm*: **un petit rien** (*cadeau*) a little something; **des riens** trivia *pl*; **un rien de** a hint of; **en un rien de temps** in no time at all; **avoir peur d'un rien** to be frightened of the slightest thing

**rieur, -euse** [ʀjœʀ, -øz] *adj* cheerful
**rigide** [ʀiʒid] *adj* stiff; (*fig*) rigid; (*moralement*) strict
**rigidité** [ʀiʒidite] *nf* stiffness; **la ~ cadavérique** rigor mortis
**rigolade** [ʀigɔlad] *nf*: **la ~** fun; (*fig*): **c'est de la ~** it's a big farce; (*c'est facile*) it's a cinch
**rigole** [ʀigɔl] *nf* (*conduit*) channel; (*filet d'eau*) rivulet
**rigoler** [ʀigɔle] *vi* (*rire*) to laugh; (*s'amuser*) to have (some) fun; (*plaisanter*) to be joking *ou* kidding
**rigolo, ote** [ʀigɔlo, -ɔt] *adj* (*fam*) funny ▷ *nm/f* comic; (*péj*) fraud, phoney
**rigorisme** [ʀigɔʀism(ə)] *nm* (moral) rigorism
**rigoriste** [ʀigɔʀist(ə)] *adj* rigorist
**rigoureusement** [ʀiguʀøzmɑ̃] *adv* rigorously; **~ vrai/interdit** strictly true/forbidden
**rigoureux, -euse** [ʀiguʀø, -øz] *adj* (*morale*) rigorous, strict; (*personne*) stern, strict; (*climat, châtiment*) rigorous, harsh, severe; (*interdiction, neutralité*) strict; (*preuves, analyse, méthode*) rigorous
**rigueur** [ʀigœʀ] *nf* rigour (*Brit*), rigor (*US*); strictness; harshness; **"tenue de soirée de ~"** "evening dress (to be worn)"; **être de ~** to be the usual thing, be the rule; **à la ~** at a pinch; possibly; **tenir ~ à qn de qch** to hold sth against sb
**riions** *etc* [ʀijɔ̃] *vb voir* **rire**
**rillettes** [ʀijɛt] *nfpl* ≈ potted meat *sg*
**rime** [ʀim] *nf* rhyme; **n'avoir ni ~ ni raison** to have neither rhyme nor reason
**rimer** [ʀime] *vi*: **~ (avec)** to rhyme (with); **ne ~ à rien** not to make sense
**Rimmel**® [ʀimɛl] *nm* mascara
**rinçage** [ʀɛ̃saʒ] *nm* rinsing (out); (*opération*) rinse
**rince-doigts** [ʀɛ̃sdwa] *nm inv* finger-bowl
**rincer** [ʀɛ̃se] *vt* to rinse; (*récipient*) to rinse out; **se ~ la bouche** to rinse one's mouth out
**ring** [ʀiŋ] *nm* (boxing) ring; **monter sur le ~** (*aussi fig*) to enter the ring; (: *faire carrière de boxeur*) to take up boxing
**ringard, e** [ʀɛ̃gaʀ, -aʀd(ə)] *adj* (*péj*) old-fashioned
**Rio de Janeiro** [ʀiodʒaneʀ(o)] *n* Rio de Janeiro
**rions** [ʀiɔ̃] *vb voir* **rire**
**ripaille** [ʀipaj] *nf*: **faire ~** to feast
**riper** [ʀipe] *vi* to slip, slide

**ripoliné, e** [ʀipɔline] *adj* enamel-painted
**riposte** [ʀipɔst(ə)] *nf* retort, riposte; (*fig*) counter-attack, reprisal
**riposter** [ʀipɔste] *vi* to retaliate ▷ *vt*: **~ que** to retort that; **~ à** *vt* to counter; to reply to
**ripper** [ʀipe] *vt* (*Inform*) to rip
**rire** [ʀiʀ] *vi* to laugh; (*se divertir*) to have fun; (*plaisanter*) to joke ▷ *nm* laugh; **le ~** laughter; **~ de** *vt* to laugh at; **se ~ de** to make light of; **tu veux ~!** you must be joking!; **~ aux éclats/aux larmes** to roar with laughter/laugh until one cries; **~ jaune** to force oneself to laugh; **~ sous cape** to laugh up one's sleeve; **~ au nez de qn** to laugh in sb's face; **pour ~** (*pas sérieusement*) for a joke *ou* a laugh
**ris** [ʀi] *vb voir* **rire** ▷ *nm*: **~ de veau** (calf) sweetbread
**risée** [ʀize] *nf*: **être la ~ de** to be the laughing stock of
**risette** [ʀizɛt] *nf*: **faire ~ (à)** to give a nice little smile (to)
**risible** [ʀizibl(ə)] *adj* laughable, ridiculous
**risque** [ʀisk(ə)] *nm* risk; **l'attrait du ~** the lure of danger; **prendre des ~s** to take risks; **à ses ~s et périls** at his own risk; **au ~ de** at the risk of; **~ d'incendie** fire risk; **~ calculé** calculated risk
**risqué, e** [ʀiske] *adj* risky; (*plaisanterie*) risqué, daring
**risquer** [ʀiske] *vt* to risk; (*allusion, question*) to venture, hazard; **tu risques qu'on te renvoie** you risk being dismissed; **ça ne risque rien** it's quite safe; **~ de: il risque de se tuer** he could get *ou* risks getting himself killed; **il a risqué de se tuer** he almost got himself killed; **ce qui risque de se produire** what might *ou* could well happen; **il ne risque pas de recommencer** there's no chance of him doing that again; **se risquer dans** (*s'aventurer*) to venture into; **se risquer à faire** (*tenter*) to dare to do; **~ le tout pour le tout** to risk the lot
**risque-tout** [ʀiskətu] *nm/f inv* daredevil
**rissoler** [ʀisɔle] *vi, vt*: **(faire) ~** to brown
**ristourne** [ʀistuʀn(ə)] *nf* rebate; discount
**rit** *etc* [ʀi] *vb voir* **rire**
**rite** [ʀit] *nm* rite; (*fig*) ritual
**ritournelle** [ʀituʀnɛl] *nf* (*fig*) tune; **c'est toujours la même ~** (*fam*) it's always the same old story
**rituel, le** [ʀitɥɛl] *adj, nm* ritual
**rituellement** [ʀitɥɛlmɑ̃] *adv* religiously
**riv.** *abr* (= *rivière*) R
**rivage** [ʀivaʒ] *nm* shore
**rival, e, -aux** [ʀival, -o] *adj, nm/f* rival; **sans ~** *adj* unrivalled
**rivaliser** [ʀivalize] *vi*: **~ avec** to rival, vie with; (*être comparable*) to hold its own against, compare with; **~ avec qn de** (*élégance etc*) to vie with *ou* rival sb in
**rivalité** [ʀivalite] *nf* rivalry
**rive** [ʀiv] *nf* shore; (*de fleuve*) bank
**river** [ʀive] *vt* (*clou, pointe*) to clinch; (*plaques*) to

**r**

367

rivet together; **être rivé sur/à** to be riveted
on/to
**riverain, e** [ʀivʀɛ̃, -ɛn] *adj* riverside *cpd*; lakeside
*cpd*; roadside *cpd* ▷ *nm/f* riverside (*ou* lakeside)
resident; local *ou* roadside resident
**rivet** [ʀivɛ] *nm* rivet
**riveter** [ʀivte] *vt* to rivet (together)
**Riviera** [ʀivjeʀa] *nf*: **la ~ (italienne)** the Italian
Riviera
**rivière** [ʀivjɛʀ] *nf* river; **~ de diamants**
diamond rivière
**rixe** [ʀiks(ə)] *nf* brawl, scuffle
**Riyad** [ʀijad] *n* Riyadh
**riz** [ʀi] *nm* rice; **~ au lait** ≈ rice pudding
**rizière** [ʀizjɛʀ] *nf* paddy field
**RMC** *sigle f* = **Radio Monte Carlo**
**RMI** *sigle m* (= *revenu minimum d'insertion*) ≈ income
support (*Brit*), ≈ welfare (*US*)
**RN** *sigle f* = **route nationale**
**robe** [ʀɔb] *nf* dress; (*de juge, d'ecclésiastique*) robe;
(*de professeur*) gown; (*pelage*) coat; **~ de soirée/de
mariée** evening/wedding dress; **~ de baptême**
christening robe; **~ de chambre** dressing
gown; **~ de grossesse** maternity dress
**robinet** [ʀɔbinɛ] *nm* tap, faucet (*US*); **~ du gaz**
gas tap; **~ mélangeur** mixer tap
**robinetterie** [ʀɔbinɛtʀi] *nf* taps *pl*, plumbing
**roboratif, -ive** [ʀɔbɔʀatif, -iv] *adj* bracing,
invigorating
**robot** [ʀɔbo] *nm* robot; **~ de cuisine** food
processor
**robotique** [ʀɔbɔtik] *nf* robotics *sg*
**robotiser** [ʀɔbɔtize] *vt* (*personne, travailleur*) to
turn into a robot; (*monde, vie*) to automate
**robuste** [ʀɔbyst(ə)] *adj* robust, sturdy
**robustesse** [ʀɔbystɛs] *nf* robustness, sturdiness
**roc** [ʀɔk] *nm* rock
**rocade** [ʀɔkad] *nf* (*Auto*) bypass
**rocaille** [ʀɔkaj] *nf* (*pierres*) loose stones *pl*;
(*terrain*) rocky *ou* stony ground; (*jardin*) rockery,
rock garden ▷ *adj* (*style*) rocaille
**rocailleux, -euse** [ʀɔkajø, -øz] *adj* rocky, stony;
(*voix*) harsh
**rocambolesque** [ʀɔkãbɔlɛsk(ə)] *adj* fantastic,
incredible
**roche** [ʀɔʃ] *nf* rock
**rocher** [ʀɔʃe] *nm* rock; (*Anat*) petrosal bone
**rochet** [ʀɔʃɛ] *nm*: **roue à ~** ratchet wheel
**rocheux, -euse** [ʀɔʃø, -øz] *adj* rocky; **les
(montagnes) Rocheuses** the Rockies, the
Rocky Mountains
**rock** [ʀɔk], **rock and roll** [ʀɔkɛnʀɔl] *nm*
(*musique*) rock(-'n'-roll); (*danse*) rock
**rocker** [ʀɔkœʀ] *nm* (*chanteur*) rock musician;
(*adepte*) rock fan
**rocking-chair** [ʀɔkiŋ(t)ʃɛʀ] *nm* rocking chair
**rococo** [ʀɔkɔko] *nm* rococo ▷ *adj* rococo
**rodage** [ʀɔdaʒ] *nm* running in (*Brit*), breaking
in (*US*); **en ~** (*Auto*) running *ou* breaking in
**rodé, e** [ʀɔde] *adj* run in (*Brit*), broken in (*US*);
(*personne*): **~ à qch** having got the hang of sth
**rodéo** [ʀɔdeo] *nm* rodeo

**roder** [ʀɔde] *vt* (*moteur, voiture*) to run in (*Brit*),
break in (*US*); **~ un spectacle** to iron out the
initial problems of a show
**rôder** [ʀode] *vi* to roam *ou* wander about; (*de
façon suspecte*) to lurk (about *ou* around)
**rôdeur, -euse** [ʀodœʀ, -øz] *nm/f* prowler
**rodomontades** [ʀɔdɔmɔ̃tad] *nfpl* bragging *sg*;
sabre rattling *sg*
**rogatoire** [ʀɔgatwaʀ] *adj*: **commission ~** letters
rogatory
**rogne** [ʀɔɲ] *nf*: **être en ~** to be mad *ou* in a
temper; **se mettre en ~** to get mad *ou* in a
temper
**rogner** [ʀɔɲe] *vt* to trim; (*fig*) to whittle down; **~
sur** (*fig*) to cut down *ou* back on
**rognons** [ʀɔɲɔ̃] *nmpl* kidneys
**rognures** [ʀɔɲyʀ] *nfpl* trimmings
**rogue** [ʀɔg] *adj* arrogant
**roi** [ʀwa] *nm* king; **les R~s mages** the Three
Wise Men, the Magi; **le jour** *ou* **la fête des R~s**,
**les R~s** Twelfth Night; *see note*

  ◉ **FÊTE DES ROIS**
  ◉
  ◉ The '*fête des Rois*' is celebrated on 6 January.
  ◉ Figurines representing the Three Wise Men
  ◉ are traditionally added to the Christmas
  ◉ crib ('crèche') and people eat 'galette des
  ◉ Rois', a flat cake in which a porcelain charm
  ◉ ('la fève') is hidden. Whoever finds the
  ◉ charm is king or queen for the day and can
  ◉ choose a partner.

**roitelet** [ʀwatlɛ] *nm* wren; (*péj*) kinglet
**rôle** [ʀol] *nm* role; (*contribution*) part
**rollers** [ʀɔlœʀ] *nmpl* Rollerblades®
**rollmops** [ʀɔlmɔps] *nm* rollmop
**romain, e** [ʀɔmɛ̃, -ɛn] *adj* Roman ▷ *nm/f*:
**Romain, e** Roman ▷ *nf* (*Culin*) cos (lettuce)
**roman, e** [ʀɔmã, -an] *adj* (*Archit*) Romanesque;
(*Ling*) Romance *cpd*, Romanic ▷ *nm* novel; **~
d'amour** love story; **~ d'espionnage** spy novel *ou*
story; **~ noir** thriller; **~ policier** detective novel
**romance** [ʀɔmãs] *nf* ballad
**romancer** [ʀɔmãse] *vt* to romanticize
**romanche** [ʀɔmãʃ] *nm* Romansh
**romancier, -ière** [ʀɔmãsje, -jɛʀ] *nm/f* novelist
**romand, e** [ʀɔmã, -ãd] *adj* of *ou* from French-
speaking Switzerland ▷ *nm/f*: **Romand, e**
French-speaking Swiss
**romanesque** [ʀɔmanɛsk(ə)] *adj* (*fantastique*)
fantastic; storybook *cpd*; (*sentimental*) romantic;
(*Littérature*) novelistic
**roman-feuilleton** [ʀɔmãfœjtɔ̃] (*pl* **romans-
feuilletons**) *nm* serialized novel
**roman-fleuve** [ʀɔmãflœv] (*pl* **romans-fleuves**)
*nm* saga, roman-fleuve
**romanichel, le** [ʀɔmaniʃɛl] *nm/f* gipsy
**roman-photo** [ʀɔmãfɔto] (*pl* **romans-photos**)
*nm* (*romantic*) picture story
**romantique** [ʀɔmãtik] *adj* romantic
**romantisme** [ʀɔmãtism(ə)] *nm* romanticism

**romarin** [ʀɔmaʀɛ̃] *nm* rosemary
**rombière** [ʀɔ̃bjɛʀ] *nf (péj)* old bag
**Rome** [ʀɔm] *n* Rome
**rompre** [ʀɔ̃pʀ(ə)] *vt* to break; *(entretien, fiançailles)* to break off ▷ *vi (fiancés)* to break it off; **se rompre** *vi* to break; *(Méd)* to burst, rupture; **se ~ les os** *ou* **le cou** to break one's neck; **~ avec** to break with; **à tout ~** *adv* wildly; **applaudir à tout ~** to bring down the house, applaud wildly; **~ la glace** *(fig)* to break the ice; **rompez (les rangs)!** *(Mil)* dismiss!, fall out!
**rompu, e** [ʀɔ̃py] *pp de* **rompre** ▷ *adj (fourbu)* exhausted, worn out; **~ à** with wide experience of; inured to
**romsteck** [ʀɔ̃mstɛk] *nm* rump steak *no pl*
**ronce** [ʀɔ̃s] *nf (Bot)* bramble branch; *(Menuiserie)*: **~ de noyer** burr walnut; **ronces** *nfpl* brambles, thorns
**ronchonner** [ʀɔ̃ʃɔne] *vi (fam)* to grouse, grouch
**rond, e** [ʀɔ̃, ʀɔ̃d] *adj* round; *(joues, mollets)* well-rounded; *(fam: ivre)* tight; *(sincère, décidé)*: **être ~ en affaires** to be on the level in business, do an honest deal ▷ *nm (cercle)* ring; *(fam: sou)*: **je n'ai plus un ~** I haven't a penny left ▷ *nf (gén: de surveillance)* rounds *pl*, patrol; *(danse)* round (dance); *(Mus)* semibreve *(Brit)*, whole note *(US)* ▷ *adv*: **tourner ~** *(moteur)* to run smoothly; **ça ne tourne pas ~** *(fig)* there's something not quite right about it; **pour faire un compte ~** to make (it) a round figure, to round (it) off; **avoir le dos ~** to be round-shouldered; **en ~** *(s'asseoir, danser)* in a ring; **à la ~e** *(alentour)*: **à 10 km à la ~e** for 10 km round; *(à chacun son tour)*: **passer qch à la ~e** to pass sth (a)round; **faire des ~s de jambe** to bow and scrape; **~ de serviette** napkin ring
**rond-de-cuir** [ʀɔ̃dkɥiʀ] *(pl* **ronds-de-cuir)** *nm (péj)* penpusher
**rondelet, te** [ʀɔ̃dlɛ, -ɛt] *adj* plump; *(fig: somme)* tidy; *(: bourse)* well-lined, fat
**rondelle** [ʀɔ̃dɛl] *nf (Tech)* washer; *(tranche)* slice, round
**rondement** [ʀɔ̃dmɑ̃] *adv (avec décision)* briskly; *(loyalement)* frankly
**rondeur** [ʀɔ̃dœʀ] *nf (d'un bras, des formes)* plumpness; *(bonhomie)* friendly straightforwardness; **rondeurs** *nfpl (d'une femme)* curves
**rondin** [ʀɔ̃dɛ̃] *nm* log
**rond-point** [ʀɔ̃pwɛ̃] *(pl* **ronds-points)** *nm* roundabout *(Brit)*, traffic circle *(US)*
**ronflant, e** [ʀɔ̃flɑ̃, -ɑ̃t] *adj (péj)* high-flown, grand
**ronflement** [ʀɔ̃fləmɑ̃] *nm* snore, snoring *no pl*
**ronfler** [ʀɔ̃fle] *vi* to snore; *(moteur, poêle)* to hum; *(: plus fort)* to roar
**ronger** [ʀɔ̃ʒe] *vt* to gnaw (at); *(vers, rouille)* to eat into; **~ son frein** to champ (at) the bit; *(fig)*: **se ~ de souci, se ~ les sangs** to worry o.s. sick, fret; **se ~ les ongles** to bite one's nails
**rongeur, -euse** [ʀɔ̃ʒœʀ, -øz] *nm/f* rodent
**ronronnement** [ʀɔ̃ʀɔnmɑ̃] *nm* purring; *(bruit)* purr

**ronronner** [ʀɔ̃ʀɔne] *vi* to purr
**roque** [ʀɔk] *nm (Échecs)* castling
**roquefort** [ʀɔkfɔʀ] *nm* Roquefort
**roquer** [ʀɔke] *vi* to castle
**roquet** [ʀɔkɛ] *nm* nasty little lap-dog
**roquette** [ʀɔkɛt] *nf* rocket; **~ antichar** antitank rocket
**rosace** [ʀozas] *nf (vitrail)* rose window, rosace; *(motif: de plafond etc)* rose
**rosaire** [ʀozɛʀ] *nm* rosary
**rosbif** [ʀɔsbif] *nm*: **du ~** roasting beef; *(cuit)* roast beef; **un ~** a joint of (roasting) beef
**rose** [ʀoz] *nf* rose; *(vitrail)* rose window ▷ *adj* pink; **~ bonbon** *adj inv* candy pink; **~ des vents** compass card
**rosé, e** [ʀoze] *adj* pinkish; *(vin)* **~ rosé** (wine)
**roseau, x** [ʀozo] *nm* reed
**rosée** [ʀoze] *adj f voir* **rosé** ▷ *nf*: **goutte de ~** dewdrop
**roseraie** [ʀozʀɛ] *nf* rose garden; *(plantation)* rose nursery
**rosette** [ʀozɛt] *nf* rosette *(gen of the Légion d'honneur)*
**rosier** [ʀozje] *nm* rosebush, rose tree
**rosir** [ʀoziʀ] *vi* to go pink
**rosse** [ʀɔs] *nf (péj: cheval)* nag ▷ *adj* nasty, vicious
**rosser** [ʀɔse] *vt (fam)* to thrash
**rossignol** [ʀɔsiɲɔl] *nm (Zool)* nightingale; *(crochet)* picklock
**rot** [ʀo] *nm* belch; *(de bébé)* burp
**rotatif, -ive** [ʀɔtatif, -iv] *adj* rotary ▷ *nf* rotary press
**rotation** [ʀɔtasjɔ̃] *nf* rotation; *(fig)* rotation, swap-around; *(renouvellement)* turnover; **par ~** on a rota *(Brit)* ou rotation *(US)* basis; **~ des cultures** crop rotation; **~ des stocks** stock turnover
**rotatoire** [ʀɔtatwaʀ] *adj*: **mouvement ~** rotary movement
**roter** [ʀɔte] *vi (fam)* to burp, belch
**rôti** [ʀoti] *nm*: **du ~** roasting meat; *(cuit)* roast meat; **un ~ de bœuf/porc** a joint of (roasting) beef/pork
**rotin** [ʀɔtɛ̃] *nm* rattan (cane); **fauteuil en ~** cane (arm)chair
**rôtir** [ʀotiʀ] *vt (aussi:* **faire rôtir)** to roast ▷ *vi* to roast; **se ~ au soleil** to bask in the sun
**rôtisserie** [ʀotisʀi] *nf (restaurant)* steakhouse; *(comptoir, magasin)* roast meat counter *(ou shop)*
**rôtissoire** [ʀotiswaʀ] *nf (roasting)* spit
**rotonde** [ʀɔtɔ̃d] *nf (Archit)* rotunda; *(Rail)* engine shed
**rotondité** [ʀɔtɔ̃dite] *nf* roundness
**rotor** [ʀɔtɔʀ] *nm* rotor
**Rotterdam** [ʀɔtɛʀdam] *n* Rotterdam
**rotule** [ʀɔtyl] *nf* kneecap, patella
**roturier, -ière** [ʀɔtyʀje, -jɛʀ] *nm/f* commoner
**rouage** [ʀwaʒ] *nm* cog(wheel), gearwheel; *(de montre)* part; *(fig)* cog; **rouages** *nmpl (fig)* internal structure *sg*
**Rouanda** [ʀwɑ̃da] *nm*: **le ~** Rwanda

**roubaisien, ne** [Rubεzjε̃, -εn] adj of ou from Roubaix

**roublard, e** [RublaR, -aRd(ə)] adj (péj) crafty, wily

**rouble** [Rubl(ə)] nm rouble

**roucoulement** [Rukulmɑ̃] nm (de pigeons, fig) coo, cooing

**roucouler** [Rukule] vi to coo; (fig: péj) to warble; (: amoureux) to bill and coo

**roue** [Ru] nf wheel; **faire la ~** (paon) to spread ou fan its tail; (Gym) to do a cartwheel; **descendre en ~ libre** to freewheel ou coast down; **pousser à la ~** to put one's shoulder to the wheel; **grande ~** (à la foire) big wheel; **~ à aubes** paddle wheel; **~ dentée** cogwheel; **~ de secours** spare wheel

**roué, e** [Rwe] adj wily

**rouennais, e** [Rwanε, -εz] adj of ou from Rouen

**rouer** [Rwe] vt: **~ qn de coups** to give sb a thrashing

**rouet** [Rwε] nm spinning wheel

**rouge** [Ruʒ] adj, nm/f red ▷ nm red; (fard) rouge; **(vin) ~** red wine; **passer au ~** (signal) to go red; (automobiliste) to go through a red light; **porter au ~** (métal) to bring to red heat; **sur la liste ~** (Tél) ex-directory (Brit), unlisted (US); **~ de honte/colère** red with shame/anger; **se fâcher tout/voir ~** to blow one's top/see red; **~ (à lèvres)** lipstick

**rougeâtre** [RuʒɑtR(ə)] adj reddish

**rougeaud, e** [Ruʒo, -od] adj (teint) red; (personne) red-faced

**rouge-gorge** [RuʒgɔRʒ(ə)] nm robin (redbreast)

**rougeoiement** [Ruʒwamɑ̃] nm reddish glow

**rougeole** [Ruʒɔl] nf measles sg

**rougeoyant, e** [Ruʒwajɑ̃, -ɑ̃t] adj (ciel, braises) glowing; (aube, reflets) glowing red

**rougeoyer** [Ruʒwaje] vi to glow red

**rouget** [Ruʒε] nm mullet

**rougeur** [Ruʒœʀ] nf redness; (du visage) red face; **rougeurs** nfpl (Méd) red blotches

**rougir** [RuʒiR] vi (de honte, timidité) to blush, flush; (de plaisir, colère) to flush; (fraise, tomate) to go ou turn red; (ciel) to redden

**rouille** [Ruj] adj inv rust-coloured, rusty ▷ nf rust; (Culin) spicy (Provençal) sauce served with fish dishes

**rouillé, e** [Ruje] adj rusty

**rouiller** [Ruje] vt to rust ▷ vi to rust, go rusty; **se rouiller** vi to rust; (fig: mentalement) to become rusty; (: physiquement) to grow stiff

**roulade** [Rulad] nf (Gym) roll; (Culin) rolled meat no pl; (Mus) roulade, run

**roulage** [Rulaʒ] nm (transport) haulage

**roulant, e** [Rulɑ̃, -ɑ̃t] adj (meuble) on wheels; (surface, trottoir) moving; **matériel ~** (Rail) rolling stock; **personnel ~** (Rail) train crews pl

**roulé, e** [Rule] adj: **bien ~e** (fam: femme) shapely, curvy

**rouleau, x** [Rulo] nm (de papier, tissu, pièces de monnaie, Sport) roll; (de machine à écrire) roller, platen; (à mise en plis, à peinture, vague) roller; **être au bout du ~** (fig) to be at the end of the line; **~ compresseur** steamroller; **~ à pâtisserie** rolling pin; **~ de pellicule** roll of film

**roulé-boulé** [Rulebule] (pl **roulés-boulés**) (Sport) roll

**roulement** [Rulmɑ̃] nm (bruit) rumbling no pl, rumble; (rotation) rotation; turnover; (: de capitaux) circulation; **par ~** on a rota (Brit) ou rotation (US) basis; **~ (à billes)** ball bearings pl; **~ de tambour** drum roll; **~ d'yeux** roll(ing) of the eyes

**rouler** [Rule] vt to roll; (papier, tapis) to roll up; (Culin: pâte) to roll out; (fam) to do, con ▷ vi (bille, boule) to roll; (voiture, train) to go, run; (automobiliste) to drive; (cycliste) to ride; (bateau) to roll; (tonnerre) to rumble, roll; (dégringoler): **~ en bas de** to roll down; **~ sur** (conversation) to turn on; **se ~ dans** (boue) to roll in; (couverture) to roll o.s. (up) in; **~ dans la farine** (fam) to con; **~ les épaules/hanches** to sway one's shoulders/wiggle one's hips; **~ les "r"** to roll one's r's; **~ sur l'or** to be rolling in money, be rolling in it; **~ (sa bosse)** to go places

**roulette** [Rulεt] nf (de table, fauteuil) castor; (de pâtissier) pastry wheel; (jeu): **la ~** roulette; **à ~s** on castors; **la ~ russe** Russian roulette

**roulis** [Ruli] nm roll(ing)

**roulotte** [Rulɔt] nf caravan

**roumain, e** [Rumε̃, -εn] adj Rumanian, Romanian ▷ nm (Ling) Rumanian, Romanian ▷ nm/f: **Roumain, e** Rumanian, Romanian

**Roumanie** [Rumani] nf: **la ~** Rumania, Romania

**roupiller** [Rupije] vi (fam) to sleep

**rouquin, e** [Rukε̃, -in] nm/f (péj) redhead

**rouspéter** [Ruspete] vi (fam) to moan, grouse

**rousse** [Rus] adj f voir **roux**

**rousseur** [Rusœr] nf: **tache de ~** freckle

**roussi** [Rusi] nm: **ça sent le ~** there's a smell of burning; (fig) I can smell trouble

**roussir** [RusiR] vt to scorch ▷ vi (feuilles) to go ou turn brown; (Culin): **faire ~** to brown

**routage** [Rutaʒ] nm (collective) mailing

**routard, e** [RutaR, -aRd(ə)] nm/f traveller

**route** [Rut] nf road; (fig: chemin) way; (itinéraire, parcours) route; (fig: voie) road, path; **par (la) ~** by road; **il y a trois heures de ~** it's a three-hour ride ou journey; **en ~** adv on the way; **en ~!** let's go!; **en cours de ~** en route; **mettre en ~** to start up; **se mettre en ~** to set off; **faire ~ vers** to head towards; **faire fausse ~** (fig) to be on the wrong track; **~ nationale (RN)** ≈ A-road (Brit), ≈ state highway (US)

**routier, -ière** [Rutje, -jεR] adj road cpd ▷ nm (camionneur) (long-distance) lorry (Brit) ou truck driver; (restaurant) ≈ transport café (Brit), ≈ truck stop (US); (scout) ≈ rover; (cycliste) road racer ▷ nf (voiture) touring car; **vieux ~** old stager; **carte routière** road map

**routine** [Rutin] nf routine; **visite/contrôle de ~** routine visit/check

**routinier, -ière** [Rutinje, -jεR] adj (péj: travail) humdrum, routine; (: personne) addicted to routine

**rouvert, e** [ʀuvɛʀ, -ɛʀt(ə)] pp de **rouvrir**
**rouvrir** [ʀuvʀiʀ] vt, vi to reopen, open again; **se rouvrir** vi (blessure) to open up again
**roux, rousse** [ʀu, ʀus] adj red; (personne) red-haired ▷ nm/f redhead ▷ nm (Culin) roux
**royal, e, -aux** [ʀwajal, -o] adj royal; (fig) fit for a king, princely; blissful; thorough
**royalement** [ʀwajalmã] adv royally
**royaliste** [ʀwajalist(ə)] adj, nm/f royalist
**royaume** [ʀwajom] nm kingdom; (fig) realm; **le ~ des cieux** the kingdom of heaven
**Royaume-Uni** [ʀwajomyni] nm: **le ~** the United Kingdom
**royauté** [ʀwajote] nf (dignité) kingship; (régime) monarchy
**RP** sigle f (= recette principale) ≈ main post office = **région parisienne** ▷ sigle fpl (= relations publiques) PR
**RPR** sigle m (= Rassemblement pour la République) political party
**R.S.V.P.** abr (= répondez s'il vous plaît) R.S.V.P
**RTB** sigle f = **Radio-Télévision belge**
**Rte** abr = **route**
**RTL** sigle f = **Radio-Télévision Luxembourg**
**RU** [ʀy] sigle m = **restaurant universitaire**
**ruade** [ʀɥad] nf kick
**Ruanda** [ʀwɑ̃da] nm: **le ~** Rwanda
**ruban** [ʀybɑ̃] nm (gén) ribbon; (pour ourlet, couture) binding; (de téléscripteur etc) tape; (d'acier) strip; **~ adhésif** adhesive tape; **~ carbone** carbon ribbon
**rubéole** [ʀybeɔl] nf German measles sg, rubella
**rubicond, e** [ʀybikɔ̃, -ɔ̃d] adj rubicund, ruddy
**rubis** [ʀybi] nm ruby; (Horlogerie) jewel; **payer ~ sur l'ongle** to pay cash on the nail
**rubrique** [ʀybʀik] nf (titre, catégorie) heading, rubric; (Presse: article) column
**ruche** [ʀyʃ] nf hive
**rucher** [ʀyʃe] nm apiary
**rude** [ʀyd] adj (barbe, toile) rough; (métier, tâche) hard, tough; (climat) severe, harsh; (bourru) harsh, rough; (fruste) rugged, tough; (fam) jolly good; **être mis à ~ épreuve** to be put through the mill
**rudement** [ʀydmã] adv (tomber, frapper) hard; (traiter, reprocher) harshly; (fam: très) terribly; (: beaucoup) terribly hard
**rudesse** [ʀydɛs] nf roughness; toughness; severity; harshness
**rudimentaire** [ʀydimɑ̃tɛʀ] adj rudimentary, basic
**rudiments** [ʀydimɑ̃] nmpl rudiments; basic knowledge sg; basic principles
**rudoyer** [ʀydwaje] vt to treat harshly
**rue** [ʀy] nf street; **être/jeter qn à la ~** to be on the streets/throw sb out onto the street
**ruée** [ʀɥe] nf rush; **la ~ vers l'or** the gold rush
**ruelle** [ʀɥɛl] nf alley(way)
**ruer** [ʀɥe] vi (cheval) to kick out; **se ruer** vi: **se ~ sur** to pounce on; **se ~ vers/dans/hors de** to rush ou dash towards/into/out of; **~ dans les brancards** to become rebellious

**rugby** [ʀygbi] nm rugby (football); **~ à treize/quinze** rugby league/union
**rugir** [ʀyʒiʀ] vi to roar
**rugissement** [ʀyʒismɑ̃] nm roar, roaring no pl
**rugosité** [ʀygozite] nf roughness; (aspérité) rough patch
**rugueux, -euse** [ʀygø, -øz] adj rough
**ruine** [ʀɥin] nf ruin; **ruines** nfpl ruins; **tomber en ~** to fall into ruin(s)
**ruiner** [ʀɥine] vt to ruin
**ruineux, -euse** [ʀɥinø, -øz] adj terribly expensive to buy (ou run), ruinous; extravagant
**ruisseau, x** [ʀɥiso] nm stream, brook; (caniveau) gutter; (fig): **~x de larmes/sang** floods of tears/streams of blood
**ruisselant, e** [ʀɥislɑ̃, -ɑ̃t] adj streaming
**ruisseler** [ʀɥisle] vi to stream; **~ (d'eau)** to be streaming (with water); **~ de lumière** to stream with light
**ruissellement** [ʀɥisɛlmɑ̃] nm streaming; **~ de lumière** stream of light
**rumeur** [ʀymœʀ] nf (bruit confus) rumbling; hubbub no pl; (protestation) murmur(ing); (nouvelle) rumour (Brit), rumor (US)
**ruminer** [ʀymine] vt (herbe) to ruminate; (fig) to ruminate on ou over, chew over ▷ vi (vache) to chew the cud, ruminate
**rumsteck** [ʀɔ̃mstɛk] nm = **romsteck**
**rupestre** [ʀypɛstʀ(ə)] adj (plante) rock cpd; (art) wall cpd
**rupture** [ʀyptyʀ] nf (de câble, digue) breaking; (de tendon) rupture, tearing; (de négociations etc) breakdown; (de contrat) breach; (séparation, désunion) break-up, split; **en ~ de ban** at odds with authority; **en ~ de stock** (Comm) out of stock
**rural, e, -aux** [ʀyʀal, -o] adj rural, country cpd ▷ nmpl: **les ruraux** country people
**ruse** [ʀyz] nf: **la ~** cunning, craftiness; trickery; **une ~** a trick, a ruse; **par ~** by trickery
**rusé, e** [ʀyze] adj cunning, crafty
**russe** [ʀys] adj Russian ▷ nm (Ling) Russian ▷ nm/f: **Russe** Russian
**Russie** [ʀysi] nf: **la ~** Russia; **la ~ blanche** White Russia; **la ~ soviétique** Soviet Russia
**rustine** [ʀystin] nf repair patch (for bicycle inner tube)
**rustique** [ʀystik] adj rustic; (plante) hardy
**rustre** [ʀystʀ(ə)] nm boor
**rut** [ʀyt] nm: **être en ~** (animal domestique) to be in ou on heat; (animal sauvage) to be rutting
**rutabaga** [ʀytabaga] nm swede
**rutilant, e** [ʀytilɑ̃, -ɑ̃t] adj gleaming
**RV** sigle m = **rendez-vous**
**Rwanda** [ʀwɑ̃da] nm: **le ~** Rwanda
**rythme** [ʀitm(ə)] nm rhythm; (vitesse) rate; (: de la vie) pace, tempo; **au ~ de 10 par jour** at the rate of 10 a day
**rythmé, e** [ʀitme] adj rhythmic(al)
**rythmer** [ʀitme] vt to give rhythm to
**rythmique** [ʀitmik] adj rhythmic(al) ▷ nf rhythmics sg

r

# Ss

**S, s** [ɛs] *nm inv* S, s ▷ *abr* (= *sud*) S; (= *seconde*) sec;
(= *siècle*) c., century; **S comme Suzanne** S for
Sugar

**s'** [s] *pron voir* **se**

**s/** *abr* = **sur**

**SA** *sigle f* = **société anonyme**; (= *Son Altesse*) HH

**sa** [sa] *adj possessif voir* **son**

**sabbatique** [sabatik] *adj*: **année ~** sabbatical
year

**sable** [sabl(ə)] *nm* sand; **~s mouvants**
quicksand(s)

**sablé** [sable] *adj* (*allée*) sandy ▷ *nm* shortbread
biscuit; **pâte ~e** (*Culin*) shortbread dough

**sabler** [sable] *vt* to sand; (*contre le verglas*) to grit;
**~ le champagne** to drink champagne

**sableux, -euse** [sablø, -øz] *adj* sandy

**sablier** [sablije] *nm* hourglass; (*de cuisine*) egg
timer

**sablière** [sablijɛʀ] *nf* sand quarry

**sablonneux, -euse** [sablɔnø, -øz] *adj* sandy

**saborder** [sabɔʀde] *vt* (*navire*) to scuttle; (*fig*) to
wind up, shut down

**sabot** [sabo] *nm* clog; (*de cheval, bœuf*) hoof; **~ (de
Denver)** (wheel) clamp; **~ de frein** brake shoe

**sabotage** [sabɔtaʒ] *nm* sabotage

**saboter** [sabɔte] *vt* (*travail, morceau de musique*) to
botch, make a mess of; (*machine, installation,
négociation etc*) to sabotage

**saboteur, -euse** [sabɔtœʀ, -øz] *nm/f* saboteur

**sabre** [sabʀ(ə)] *nm* sabre; **le ~** (*fig*) the sword, the
army

**sabrer** [sabʀe] *vt* to cut down

**sac** [sak] *nm* bag; (*à charbon etc*) sack; (*pillage*)
sack(ing); **mettre à ~** to sack; **~ à provisions/
de voyage** shopping/travelling bag; **~ de
couchage** sleeping bag; **~ à dos** rucksack; **~ à
main** handbag; **~ de plage** beach bag

**saccade** [sakad] *nf* jerk; **par ~s** jerkily;
haltingly

**saccadé, e** [sakade] *adj* jerky

**saccage** [sakaʒ] *nm* havoc

**saccager** [sakaʒe] *vt* (*piller*) to sack, lay waste;
(*dévaster*) to create havoc in, wreck

**saccharine** [sakaʀin] *nf* saccharin(e)

**saccharose** [sakaʀoz] *nm* sucrose

**SACEM** [sasɛm] *sigle f* (= *Société des auteurs,
compositeurs et éditeurs de musique*) body responsible for
collecting and distributing royalties

**sacerdoce** [sasɛʀdɔs] *nm* priesthood; (*fig*)
calling, vocation

**sacerdotal, e, -aux** [sasɛʀdɔtal, -o] *adj* priestly,
sacerdotal

**sachant** *etc* [saʃɑ̃] *vb voir* **savoir**

**sache** *etc* [saʃ] *vb voir* **savoir**

**sachet** [saʃɛ] *nm* (small) bag; (*de lavande, poudre,
shampooing*) sachet; **thé en ~s** tea bags; **~ de thé**
tea bag

**sacoche** [sakɔʃ] *nf* (*gén*) bag; (*de bicyclette*)
saddlebag; (*du facteur*) (post)bag; (*d'outils*)
toolbag

**sacquer** [sake] *vt* (*fam: candidat, employé*) to sack;
(: *réprimander, mal noter*) to plough

**sacraliser** [sakʀalize] *vt* to make sacred

**sacre** [sakʀ(ə)] *nm* coronation; consecration

**sacré, e** [sakʀe] *adj* sacred; (*fam: satané*) blasted;
(: *fameux*): **un ~ ...** a heck of a ...; (*Anat*) sacral

**sacrement** [sakʀəmɑ̃] *nm* sacrament; **les
derniers ~s** the last rites

**sacrer** [sakʀe] *vt* (*roi*) to crown; (*évêque*) to
consecrate ▷ *vi* to curse, swear

**sacrifice** [sakʀifis] *nm* sacrifice; **faire le ~ de** to
sacrifice

**sacrificiel, le** [sakʀifisjɛl] *adj* sacrificial

**sacrifier** [sakʀifje] *vt* to sacrifice; **~ à** *vt* to
conform to; **se sacrifier** to sacrifice o.s;
**articles sacrifiés** (*Comm*) items sold at rock-
bottom *ou* give-away prices

**sacrilège** [sakʀilɛʒ] *nm* sacrilege ▷ *adj*
sacrilegious

**sacristain** [sakʀistɛ̃] *nm* sexton; sacristan

**sacristie** [sakʀisti] *nf* sacristy; (*culte protestant*)
vestry

**sacro-saint, e** [sakʀosɛ̃, -ɛ̃t] *adj* sacrosanct

**sadique** [sadik] *adj* sadistic ▷ *nm/f* sadist

**sadisme** [sadism(ə)] *nm* sadism

**sadomasochisme** [sadɔmazoʃism(ə)] *nm*
sadomasochism

**sadomasochiste** [sadɔmazoʃist(ə)] *nm/f*
sadomasochist

**safari** [safaʀi] *nm* safari; **faire un ~** to go on
safari

**safari-photo** [safaʀifoto] *nm* photographic

safari

**SAFER** [safɛR] *sigle f* (= *Société d'aménagement foncier et d'établissement rural*) *organization with the right to buy land in order to retain it for agricultural use*

**safran** [safRɑ̃] *nm* saffron

**saga** [saga] *nf* saga

**sagace** [sagas] *adj* sagacious, shrewd

**sagacité** [sagasite] *nf* sagacity, shrewdness

**sagaie** [sagɛ] *nf* assegai

**sage** [saʒ] *adj* wise; (*enfant*) good ▷ *nm* wise man; sage

**sage-femme** [saʒfam] *nf* midwife

**sagement** [saʒmɑ̃] *adv* (*raisonnablement*) wisely, sensibly; (*tranquillement*) quietly

**sagesse** [saʒɛs] *nf* wisdom

**Sagittaire** [saʒitɛR] *nm*: **le ~** Sagittarius, the Archer; **être du ~** to be Sagittarius

**Sahara** [saaRa] *nm*: **le ~** the Sahara (Desert); **le ~ occidental** (*pays*) Western Sahara

**saharien, ne** [saaRjɛ̃, -ɛn] *adj* Saharan ▷ *nf* safari jacket

**Sahel** [saɛl] *nm*: **le ~** the Sahel

**sahélien, ne** [saeljɛ̃, -ɛn] *adj* Sahelian

**saignant, e** [sɛɲɑ̃, -ɑ̃t] *adj* (*viande*) rare; (*blessure, plaie*) bleeding

**saignée** [seɲe] *nf* (*Méd*) bleeding *no pl*, bloodletting *no pl*; (*Anat*) **la ~ du bras** the bend of the arm; (*fig: Mil*) heavy losses *pl*; (*: prélèvement*) savage cut

**saignement** [sɛɲmɑ̃] *nm* bleeding; **~ de nez** nosebleed

**saigner** [seɲe] *vi* to bleed ▷ *vt* to bleed; (*animal*) to bleed to death; **~ qn à blanc** (*fig*) to bleed sb white; **~ du nez** to have a nosebleed

**Saigon** [sajgɔ̃] *n* Saigon

**saillant, e** [sajɑ̃, -ɑ̃t] *adj* (*pommettes, menton*) prominent; (*corniche etc*) projecting; (*fig*) salient, outstanding

**saillie** [saji] *nf* (*sur un mur etc*) projection; (*trait d'esprit*) witticism; (*accouplement*) covering, serving; **faire ~** to project, stick out; **en ~, formant ~** projecting, overhanging

**saillir** [sajiR] *vi* to project, stick out; (*veine, muscle*) to bulge ▷ *vt* (*Élevage*) to cover, serve

**sain, e** [sɛ̃, sɛn] *adj* healthy; (*dents, constitution*) healthy, sound; (*lectures*) wholesome; **~ et sauf** safe and sound, unharmed; **~ d'esprit** sound in mind, sane

**saindoux** [sɛ̃du] *nm* lard

**sainement** [sɛnmɑ̃] *adv* (*vivre*) healthily; (*raisonner*) soundly

**saint, e** [sɛ̃, sɛ̃t] *adj* holy; (*fig*) saintly ▷ *nm/f* saint; **la S~e Vierge** the Blessed Virgin

**saint-bernard** [sɛ̃bɛRnaR] *nm inv* (*chien*) St Bernard

**Sainte-Hélène** [sɛ̃telɛn] *nf* St Helena

**Sainte-Lucie** [sɛ̃tlysi] *nf* Saint Lucia

**Saint-Esprit** [sɛ̃tɛspRi] *nm*: **le ~** the Holy Spirit *ou* Ghost

**sainteté** [sɛ̃te] *nf* holiness; saintliness

**Saint-Laurent** [sɛ̃lɔRɑ̃] *nm*: **le ~** the St Lawrence

**Saint-Marin** [sɛ̃maRɛ̃] *nm*: **le ~** San Marino

**Saint-Père** [sɛ̃pɛR] *nm*: **le ~** the Holy Father, the Pontiff

**Saint-Pierre** [sɛ̃pjɛR] *nm* Saint Peter; (*église*) Saint Peter's

**Saint-Pierre-et-Miquelon** [sɛ̃pjɛRemiklɔ̃] *nm* Saint Pierre and Miquelon

**Saint-Siège** [sɛ̃sjɛʒ] *nm*: **le ~** the Holy See

**Saint-Sylvestre** [sɛ̃silvɛstR(ə)] *nf*: **la ~** New Year's Eve

**Saint-Thomas** [sɛ̃tɔma] *nf* Saint Thomas

**Saint-Vincent et les Grenadines** [sɛ̃vɛ̃sɑ̃elegRənadin] *nm* St Vincent and the Grenadines

**sais** *etc* [sɛ] *vb voir* **savoir**

**saisie** [sezi] *nf* seizure; **à la ~** (*texte*) being keyed; **~ (de données)** (*data*) capture

**saisine** [sezin] *nf* (*Jur*) *submission of a case to the court*

**saisir** [seziR] *vt* to take hold of, grab; (*fig: occasion*) to seize; (*comprendre*) to grasp; (*entendre*) to get, catch; (*émotions*) to take hold of, come over; (*Inform*) to capture, keyboard; (*Culin*) to fry quickly; (*Jur: biens, publication*) to seize; (*: juridiction*): **~ un tribunal d'une affaire** to submit *ou* refer a case to a court; **se ~ de** *vt* to seize; **être saisi** (*frappé de*) to be overcome

**saisissant, e** [sezisɑ̃, -ɑ̃t] *adj* startling, striking; (*froid*) biting

**saisissement** [sezismɑ̃] *nm*: **muet/figé de ~** speechless/frozen with emotion

**saison** [sɛzɔ̃] *nf* season; **la belle/mauvaise ~** the summer/winter months; **être de ~** to be in season; **en/hors ~** in/out of season; **haute/basse/morte ~** high/low/slack season; **la ~ des pluies/des amours** the rainy/mating season

**saisonnier, -ière** [sɛzɔnje, -jɛR] *adj* seasonal ▷ *nm* (*travailleur*) seasonal worker; (*vacancier*) seasonal holidaymaker

**sait** [sɛ] *vb voir* **savoir**

**salace** [salas] *adj* salacious

**salade** [salad] *nf* (*Bot*) lettuce *etc* (*generic term*); (*Culin*) (green) salad; (*fam*) tangle, muddle; **salades** *nfpl* (*fam*): **raconter des ~s** to tell tales (*fam*); **haricots en ~** bean salad; **~ de concombres** cucumber salad; **~ de fruits** fruit salad; **~ niçoise** salade niçoise; **~ russe** Russian salad; **~ de tomates** tomato salad; **~ verte** green salad

**saladier** [saladje] *nm* (salad) bowl

**salaire** [salɛR] *nm* (*annuel, mensuel*) salary; (*hebdomadaire, journalier*) pay, wages *pl*; (*fig*) reward; **~ de base** basic salary (*ou* wage); **~ de misère** starvation wage; **~ minimum interprofessionnel de croissance (SMIC)** *index-linked guaranteed minimum wage*

**salaison** [salɛzɔ̃] *nf* salting; **salaisons** *nfpl* salt meat *sg*

**salamandre** [salamɑ̃dR(ə)] *nf* salamander

**salami** [salami] *nm* salami *no pl*, salami sausage

**salant** [salɑ̃] *adj m*: **marais ~** salt pan

**salarial, e, -aux** [salaRjal, -o] *adj* salary *cpd*, wage(s) *cpd*

373

**salariat** [salaʀja] *nm* salaried staff
**salarié, e** [salaʀje] *adj* salaried; wage-earning
▷ *nm/f* salaried employee; wage-earner
**salaud** [salo] *nm* (*fam!*) sod (*!*), bastard (*!*)
**sale** [sal] *adj* dirty; (*fig: avant le nom*) nasty
**salé, e** [sale] *adj* (*liquide, saveur*) salty; (*Culin*)
salted, salt *cpd*; (*fig*) spicy, juicy; (: *note, facture*)
steep, stiff ▷ *nm* (*porc salé*) salt pork; **petit ~**
≈ boiling bacon
**salement** [salmɑ̃] *adv* (*manger etc*) dirtily,
messily
**saler** [sale] *vt* to salt
**saleté** [salte] *nf* (*état*) dirtiness; (*crasse*) dirt,
filth; (*tache etc*) dirt *no pl*, something dirty, dirty
mark; (*fig: tour*) filthy trick; (: *chose sans valeur*)
rubbish *no pl*; (: *obscénité*) filth *no pl*; (: *microbe etc*)
bug; **vivre dans la ~** to live in squalor
**salière** [saljɛʀ] *nf* saltcellar
**saligaud** [saligo] *nm* (*fam!*) bastard (*!*), sod (*!*)
**salin, e** [salɛ̃, -in] *adj* saline ▷ *nf* saltworks *sg*
**salinité** [salinite] *nf* salinity, salt-content
**salir** [saliʀ] *vt* to (make) dirty; (*fig*) to soil the
reputation of; **se salir** to get dirty
**salissant, e** [salisɑ̃, -ɑ̃t] *adj* (*tissu*) which shows
the dirt; (*métier*) dirty, messy
**salissure** [salisyʀ] *nf* dirt *no pl*; (*tache*) dirty
mark
**salive** [saliv] *nf* saliva
**saliver** [salive] *vi* to salivate
**salle** [sal] *nf* room; (*d'hôpital*) ward; (*de restaurant*)
dining room; (*d'un cinéma*) auditorium; (: *public*)
audience; **faire ~ comble** to have a full house;
**~ d'armes** (*pour l'escrime*) arms room; **~
d'attente** waiting room; **~ de bain(s)**
bathroom; **~ de bal** ballroom; **~ de cinéma**
cinema; **~ de classe** classroom; **~ commune**
(*d'hôpital*) ward; **~ de concert** concert hall; **~ de
consultation** consulting room (*Brit*), office
(*US*); **~ de danse** dance hall; **~ de douches**
shower-room; **~ d'eau** shower-room; **~
d'embarquement** (*à l'aéroport*) departure
lounge; **~ d'exposition** showroom; **~ de jeux**
games room; playroom; **~ des machines**
engine room; **~ à manger** dining room;
(*mobilier*) dining room suite; **~ obscure** cinema
(*Brit*), movie theater (*US*); **~ d'opération**
(*d'hôpital*) operating theatre; **~ des professeurs**
staffroom; **~ de projection** film theatre; **~ de
séjour** living room; **~ de spectacle** theatre;
cinema; **~ des ventes** saleroom
**salmonellose** [salmɔneloz] *nf* (*Méd*) salmonella
poisoning
**Salomon** [salɔmɔ̃]: **les îles ~** the Solomon
Islands
**salon** [salɔ̃] *nm* lounge, sitting room; (*mobilier*)
lounge suite; (*exposition*) exhibition, show;
(*mondain, littéraire*) salon; **~ de coiffure**
hairdressing salon; **~ de discussion** (*Inform*)
chatroom; **~ de thé** tearoom
**salopard** [salɔpaʀ] *nm* (*fam!*) bastard (*!*)
**salope** [salɔp] *nf* (*fam!*) bitch (*!*)
**saloper** [salɔpe] *vt* (*fam!*) to muck up, mess up

**saloperie** [salɔpʀi] *nf* (*fam!*) filth *no pl*; dirty
trick, rubbish *no pl*
**salopette** [salɔpɛt] *nf* dungarees *pl*; (*d'ouvrier*)
overall(s)
**salpêtre** [salpɛtʀ(ə)] *nm* saltpetre
**salsifis** [salsifi] *nm* salsify, oyster plant
**SALT** [salt] *sigle* (= *Strategic Arms Limitation Talks ou
Treaty*) SALT
**saltimbanque** [saltɛ̃bɑ̃k] *nm/f* (*travelling*)
acrobat
**salubre** [salybʀ(ə)] *adj* healthy, salubrious
**salubrité** [salybʀite] *nf* healthiness, salubrity;
**~ publique** public health
**saluer** [salɥe] *vt* (*pour dire bonjour, fig*) to greet;
(*pour dire au revoir*) to take one's leave; (*Mil*) to
salute
**salut** [saly] *nm* (*sauvegarde*) safety; (*Rel*)
salvation; (*geste*) wave; (*parole*) greeting; (*Mil*)
salute ▷ *excl* (*fam: pour dire bonjour*) hi (there);
(: *pour dire au revoir*) see you!, bye!
**salutaire** [salytɛʀ] *adj* (*remède*) beneficial;
(*conseils*) salutary
**salutations** [salytɑsjɔ̃] *nfpl* greetings; **recevez
mes ~ distinguées** *ou* **respectueuses** yours
faithfully
**salutiste** [salytist(ə)] *nm/f* Salvationist
**Salvador** [salvadɔʀ] *nm*: **le ~** El Salvador
**salve** [salv(ə)] *nf* salvo; volley of shots; **~
d'applaudissements** burst of applause
**Samarie** [samaʀi] *nf*: **la ~** Samaria
**samaritain** [samaʀitɛ̃] *nm*: **le bon S~** the Good
Samaritan
**samedi** [samdi] *nm* Saturday; *voir aussi* **lundi**
**Samoa** [samɔa] *nfpl*: **les (îles) ~** Samoa, the
Samoa Islands
**SAMU** [samy] *sigle m* (= *service d'assistance médicale
d'urgence*) ≈ ambulance (service) (*Brit*),
≈ paramedics (*US*)
**sanatorium** [sanatɔʀjɔm] *nm* sanatorium
**sanctifier** [sɑ̃ktifje] *vt* to sanctify
**sanction** [sɑ̃ksjɔ̃] *nf* sanction; (*fig*) penalty;
**prendre des ~s contre** to impose sanctions on
**sanctionner** [sɑ̃ksjɔne] *vt* (*loi, usage*) to
sanction; (*punir*) to punish
**sanctuaire** [sɑ̃ktɥɛʀ] *nm* sanctuary
**sandale** [sɑ̃dal] *nf* sandal; **~s à lanières** strappy
sandals
**sandalette** [sɑ̃dalɛt] *nf* sandal
**sandwich** [sɑ̃dwitʃ] *nm* sandwich; **pris en ~**
sandwiched
**sang** [sɑ̃] *nm* blood; **en ~** covered in blood;
**jusqu'au ~** (*mordre, pincer*) till the blood comes;
**se faire du mauvais ~** to fret, get in a state
**sang-froid** [sɑ̃fʀwa] *nm* calm, sangfroid;
**garder/perdre/reprendre son ~** to keep/lose/
regain one's cool; **de ~** in cold blood
**sanglant, e** [sɑ̃glɑ̃, -ɑ̃t] *adj* bloody, covered in
blood; (*combat*) bloody; (*fig: reproche, affront*) cruel
**sangle** [sɑ̃gl(ə)] *nf* strap; **sangles** *nfpl* (*pour lit etc*)
webbing *sg*
**sangler** [sɑ̃gle] *vt* to strap up; (*animal*) to girth
**sanglier** [sɑ̃glije] *nm* (wild) boar

**sanglot** [sɑ̃glo] nm sob
**sangloter** [sɑ̃glɔte] vi to sob
**sangsue** [sɑ̃sy] nf leech
**sanguin, e** [sɑ̃gɛ̃, -in] adj blood cpd; (fig) fiery
  ▷ nf blood orange; (Art) red pencil drawing
**sanguinaire** [sɑ̃ginɛʀ] adj (animal, personne)
  bloodthirsty; (lutte) bloody
**sanguinolent, e** [sɑ̃ginɔlɑ̃, -ɑ̃t] adj streaked
  with blood
**Sanisette**® [sanizɛt] nf coin-operated public
  lavatory
**sanitaire** [sanitɛʀ] adj health cpd; **sanitaires**
  nmpl (salle de bain et w.-c.) bathroom sg;
  **installation/appareil** ~ bathroom plumbing/
  appliance
**sans** [sɑ̃] prép without; ~ **qu'il s'en aperçoive**
  without him ou his noticing; ~ **scrupules**
  unscrupulous; ~ **manches** sleeveless
**sans-abri** [sɑ̃zabʀi] nmpl homeless
**sans-emploi** [sɑ̃zɑ̃plwa] nmpl jobless
**sans-façon** [sɑ̃fasɔ̃] adj inv fuss-free; free and
  easy
**sans-gêne** [sɑ̃ʒɛn] adj inv inconsiderate ▷ nm inv
  (attitude) lack of consideration
**sans-logis** [sɑ̃lɔʒi] nmpl homeless
**sans-souci** [sɑ̃susi] adj inv carefree
**sans-travail** [sɑ̃tʀavaj] nmpl unemployed,
  jobless
**santal** [sɑ̃tal] nm sandal(wood)
**santé** [sɑ̃te] nf health; **avoir une ~ de fer** to be
  bursting with health; **être en bonne ~** to be in
  good health, be healthy; **boire à la ~ de qn** to
  drink (to) sb's health; **"à la ~ de"** "here's to"; **à
  ta** ou **votre ~!** cheers!; **service de ~** (dans un port
  etc) quarantine service; **la ~ publique** public
  health
**Santiago** [sɑ̃tjago], **Santiago du Chili**
  [sɑ̃tjagodyʃili] n Santiago (de Chile)
**santon** [sɑ̃tɔ̃] nm ornamental figure at a Christmas
  crib
**saoudien, ne** [saudjɛ̃, -ɛn] adj Saudi (Arabian)
  ▷ nm/f: **Saoudien, ne** Saudi (Arabian)
**saoul, e** [su, sul] adj = **soûl, e**
**sape** [sap] nf: **travail de** ~ (Mil) sap; (fig)
  insidious undermining process ou work; **sapes**
  nfpl (fam) gear sg, togs
**saper** [sape] vt to undermine, sap; **se saper** vi
  (fam) to dress
**sapeur** [sapœʀ] nm sapper
**sapeur-pompier** [sapœʀpɔ̃pje] nm fireman
**saphir** [safiʀ] nm sapphire; (d'électrophone)
  needle, sapphire
**sapin** [sapɛ̃] nm fir (tree); (bois) fir; ~ **de Noël**
  Christmas tree
**sapinière** [sapinjɛʀ] nf fir plantation ou forest
**SAR** sigle f (= Son Altesse Royale) HRH
**sarabande** [saʀabɑ̃d] nf saraband; (fig)
  hullabaloo; whirl
**sarbacane** [saʀbakan] nf blowpipe, blowgun;
  (jouet) peashooter
**sarcasme** [saʀkasm(ə)] nm sarcasm no pl;
  (propos) piece of sarcasm

**sarcastique** [saʀkastik] adj sarcastic
**sarcastiquement** [saʀkastikmɑ̃] adv
  sarcastically
**sarclage** [saʀklaʒ] nm weeding
**sarcler** [saʀkle] vt to weed
**sarcloir** [saʀklwaʀ] nm (weeding) hoe, spud
**sarcophage** [saʀkɔfaʒ] nm sarcophagus
**Sardaigne** [saʀdɛɲ] nf: **la** ~ Sardinia
**sarde** [saʀd(ə)] adj Sardinian
**sardine** [saʀdin] nf sardine; **~s à l'huile**
  sardines in oil
**sardinerie** [saʀdinʀi] nf sardine cannery
**sardinier, -ière** [saʀdinje, -jɛʀ] adj (pêche,
  industrie) sardine cpd ▷ nm (bateau) sardine boat
**sardonique** [saʀdɔnik] adj sardonic
**sari** [saʀi] nm sari
**SARL** [saʀl] sigle f = **société à responsabilité
  limitée**
**sarment** [saʀmɑ̃] nm: ~ **(de vigne)** vine shoot
**sarrasin** [saʀazɛ̃] nm buckwheat
**sarrau** [saʀo] nm smock
**Sarre** [saʀ] nf: **la** ~ the Saar
**sarriette** [saʀjɛt] nf savory
**sarrois, e** [saʀwa, -waz] adj Saar cpd ▷ nm/f:
  **Sarrois, e** inhabitant ou native of the Saar
**sas** [sas] nm (de sous-marin, d'engin spatial) airlock;
  (d'écluse) lock
**satané, e** [satane] adj (fam) confounded
**satanique** [satanik] adj satanic, fiendish
**satelliser** [satelize] vt (fusée) to put into orbit;
  (fig: pays) to make into a satellite
**satellite** [satelit] nm satellite; **pays** ~ satellite
  country
**satellite-espion** [satelitɛspjɔ̃] (pl **satellites-
  espions**) nm spy satellite
**satellite-observatoire** [satelitɔpsɛʀvatwaʀ]
  (pl **satellites-observatoires**) nm observation
  satellite
**satellite-relais** [satelitʀəlɛ] (pl **satellites-relais**)
  nm (TV) relay satellite
**satiété** [sasjete] nf: **à** ~ adv to satiety ou satiation;
  (répéter) ad nauseam
**satin** [satɛ̃] nm satin
**satiné, e** [satine] adj satiny; (peau) satin-
  smooth
**satinette** [satinɛt] nf satinet, sateen
**satire** [satiʀ] nf satire; **faire la** ~ to satirize
**satirique** [satiʀik] adj satirical
**satiriser** [satiʀize] vt to satirize
**satiriste** [satiʀist(ə)] nm/f satirist
**satisfaction** [satisfaksjɔ̃] nf satisfaction; **à ma
  grande** ~ to my great satisfaction; **obtenir** ~ to
  obtain ou get satisfaction; **donner** ~ **(à)** to give
  satisfaction (to)
**satisfaire** [satisfɛʀ] vt to satisfy; **se satisfaire
  de** to be satisfied ou content with; ~ **à** vt
  (engagement) to fulfil; (revendications, conditions) to
  satisfy, meet
**satisfaisant, e** [satisfəzɑ̃, -ɑ̃t] vb voir **satisfaire**
  ▷ adj satisfactory; (qui fait plaisir) satisfying
**satisfait, e** [satisfɛ, -ɛt] pp de **satisfaire** ▷ adj
  satisfied; ~ **de** happy ou satisfied with

**S**

**satisfasse** [satisfas], **satisferai** etc [satisfʀe] vb
voir **satisfaire**
**saturation** [satyʀɑsjɔ̃] nf saturation; **arriver à**
~ to reach saturation point
**saturer** [satyʀe] vt to saturate; ~ **qn/qch de** to
saturate sb/sth with
**saturnisme** [satyʀnism(ə)] nm (Méd) lead
poisoning
**satyre** [satiʀ] nm satyr; (péj) lecher
**sauce** [sos] nf sauce; (avec un rôti) gravy; **en** ~ in a
sauce; ~ **blanche** white sauce; ~ **chasseur**
sauce chasseur; ~ **tomate** tomato sauce
**saucer** [sose] vt (assiette) to soak up the sauce
from
**saucière** [sosjeʀ] nf sauceboat; gravy boat
**saucisse** [sosis] nf sausage
**saucisson** [sosisɔ̃] nm (slicing) sausage; ~ **à l'ail**
garlic sausage
**saucissonner** [sosisɔne] vt to cut up, slice ▷ vi
to picnic
**sauf¹** [sof] prép except; ~ **si** (à moins que) unless; ~
**avis contraire** unless you hear to the contrary;
~ **empêchement** barring (any) problems; ~
**erreur** if I'm not mistaken; ~ **imprévu** unless
anything unforeseen arises, barring accidents
**sauf², sauve** [sof, sov] adj unharmed, unhurt;
(fig: honneur) intact, saved; **laisser la vie sauve**
**à qn** to spare sb's life
**sauf-conduit** [sofkɔ̃dɥi] nm safe-conduct
**sauge** [soʒ] nf sage
**saugrenu, e** [sogʀəny] adj preposterous,
ludicrous
**saule** [sol] nm willow (tree); ~ **pleureur**
weeping willow
**saumâtre** [somɑtʀ(ə)] adj briny; (désagréable:
plaisanterie) unsavoury (Brit), unsavory (US)
**saumon** [somɔ̃] nm salmon inv ▷ adj inv salmon
(pink)
**saumoné, e** [somɔne] adj: **truite** ~e salmon
trout
**saumure** [somyʀ] nf brine
**sauna** [sona] nm sauna
**saupoudrer** [sopudʀe] vt: ~ **qch de** to sprinkle
sth with
**saupoudreuse** [sopudʀøz] nf dredger
**saur** [sɔʀ] adj m: **hareng** ~ smoked ou red
herring, kipper
**saurai** etc [sɔʀe] vb voir **savoir**
**saut** [so] nm jump; (discipline sportive) jumping;
**faire un** ~ to (make a) jump ou leap; **faire un** ~
**chez qn** to pop over to sb's (place); **au** ~ **du lit**
on getting out of bed; ~ **en hauteur/longueur**
high/long jump; ~ **à la corde** skipping; ~ **de**
**page/ligne** (Inform) page/line break; ~ **en**
**parachute** parachuting no pl; ~ **à la perche**
pole vaulting; ~ **à l'élastique** bungee jumping;
~ **périlleux** somersault
**saute** [sot] nf: ~ **de vent/température** sudden
change of wind direction/in the temperature;
**avoir des** ~**s d'humeur** to have sudden
changes of mood
**sauté, e** [sote] adj (Culin) sauté ▷ nm: ~ **de veau**
sauté of veal
**saute-mouton** [sotmutɔ̃] nm: **jouer à** ~ to play
leapfrog
**sauter** [sote] vi to jump, leap; (exploser) to blow
up, explode; (: fusibles) to blow; (se rompre) to
snap, burst; (se détacher) to pop out (ou off) ▷ vt
to jump (over), leap (over); (fig: omettre) to skip,
miss (out); **faire** ~ to blow up; to burst open;
(Culin) to sauté; ~ **à pieds joints/à cloche-pied**
to make a standing jump/to hop; ~ **en**
**parachute** to make a parachute jump; ~ **à la**
**corde** to skip; ~ **de joie** to jump for joy; ~ **de**
**colère** to be hopping with rage ou hopping
mad; ~ **au cou de qn** to fly into sb's arms; ~ **aux**
**yeux** to be quite obvious; ~ **au plafond** (fig) to
hit the roof
**sauterelle** [sotʀel] nf grasshopper
**sauterie** [sotʀi] nf party, hop
**sauteur, -euse** [sotœʀ, -øz] nm/f (athlète)
jumper ▷ nf (casserole) shallow pan, frying pan;
~ **à la perche** pole vaulter; ~ **à skis** skijumper
**sautillement** [sotijmɑ̃] nm hopping; skipping
**sautiller** [sotije] vi to hop; to skip
**sautoir** [sotwaʀ] nm chain; (Sport: emplacement)
jumping pit; ~ **(de perles)** string of pearls
**sauvage** [sovaʒ] adj (gén) wild; (peuplade) savage;
(farouche) unsociable; (barbare) wild, savage; (non
officiel) unauthorized, unofficial ▷ nm/f savage;
(timide) unsociable type, recluse
**sauvagement** [sovaʒmɑ̃] adv savagely
**sauvageon, ne** [sovaʒɔ̃, -ɔn] nm/f little savage
**sauvagerie** [sovaʒʀi] nf wildness; savagery;
unsociability
**sauve** [sov] adj f voir **sauf**
**sauvegarde** [sovgaʀd(ə)] nf safeguard; **sous la**
~ **de** under the protection of; **disquette/**
**fichier de** ~ (Inform) backup disk/file
**sauvegarder** [sovgaʀde] vt to safeguard;
(Inform: enregistrer) to save; (: copier) to back up
**sauve-qui-peut** [sovkipø] nm inv stampede,
mad rush ▷ excl run for your life!
**sauver** [sove] vt to save; (porter secours à) to
rescue; (récupérer) to salvage, rescue; **se sauver**
vi (s'enfuir) to run away; (fam: partir) to be off; ~
**qn de** to save sb from; ~ **la vie à qn** to save sb's
life; ~ **les apparences** to keep up appearances
**sauvetage** [sovtaʒ] nm rescue; ~ **en montagne**
mountain rescue; **ceinture de** ~ lifebelt (Brit),
life preserver (US); **brassière** ou **gilet de** ~
lifejacket (Brit), life preserver (US)
**sauveteur** [sovtœʀ] nm rescuer
**sauvette** [sovet]: **à la** ~ adv (vendre) without
authorization; (se marier etc) hastily, hurriedly;
**vente à la** ~ (unauthorized) street trading,
(street) peddling
**sauveur** [sovœʀ] nm saviour (Brit), savior (US)
**SAV** sigle m = **service après-vente**
**savais** etc [save] vb voir **savoir**
**savamment** [savamɑ̃] adv (avec érudition)
learnedly; (habilement) skilfully, cleverly
**savane** [savan] nf savannah
**savant, e** [savɑ̃, -ɑ̃t] adj scholarly, learned; (calé)

clever ▷ *nm* scientist; **animal** ~ performing animal

**savate** [savat] *nf* worn-out shoe; (*Sport*) French boxing

**saveur** [savœʀ] *nf* flavour (*Brit*), flavor (*US*); (*fig*) savour (*Brit*), savor (*US*)

**Savoie** [savwa] *nf*: **la** ~ Savoy

**savoir** [savwaʀ] *vt* to know; (*être capable de*): **il sait nager** he knows how to swim, he can swim ▷ *nm* knowledge; **se savoir** (*être connu*) to be known; **se savoir malade/incurable** to know that one is ill/incurably ill; **il est petit: tu ne peux pas ~!** you won't believe how small he is!; **vous n'êtes pas sans ~ que** you are not *ou* will not be unaware of the fact that; **je crois ~ que ...** I believe that ..., I think I know that ...; **je n'en sais rien** I (really) don't know; **à ~ (que)** that is, namely; **faire ~ qch à qn** to inform sb about sth, let sb know sth; **pas que je sache** not as far as I know; **sans le ~** *adv* unknowingly, unwittingly; **en ~ long** to know a lot

**savoir-faire** [savwaʀfɛʀ] *nm inv* savoir-faire, know-how

**savoir-vivre** [savwaʀvivʀ(ə)] *nm inv*: **le** ~ savoir-faire, good manners *pl*

**savon** [savɔ̃] *nm* (*produit*) soap; (*morceau*) bar *ou* tablet of soap; (*fam*): **passer un ~ à qn** to give sb a good dressing-down

**savonner** [savɔne] *vt* to soap

**savonnerie** [savɔnʀi] *nf* soap factory

**savonnette** [savɔnɛt] *nf* bar *ou* tablet of soap

**savonneux, -euse** [savɔnø, -øz] *adj* soapy

**savons** [savɔ̃] *vb voir* **savoir**

**savourer** [savuʀe] *vt* to savour (*Brit*), savor (*US*)

**savoureux, -euse** [savuʀø, -øz] *adj* tasty; (*fig*) spicy, juicy

**savoyard, e** [savwajaʀ, -aʀd(ə)] *adj* Savoyard

**Saxe** [saks(ə)] *nf*: **la** ~ Saxony

**saxo** [saksɔ], **saxophone** [saksɔfɔn] *nm* sax(ophone)

**saxophoniste** [saksɔfɔnist(ə)] *nm/f* saxophonist, sax(ophone) player

**saynète** [sɛnɛt] *nf* playlet

**SBB** *sigle f* (= *Schweizerische Bundesbahn*) *Swiss federal railways*

**sbire** [sbiʀ] *nm* (*péj*) henchman

**sc.** *abr* = **scène**

**s/c** *abr* (= *sous couvert de*) ≈ c/o

**scabreux, -euse** [skabʀø, -øz] *adj* risky; (*indécent*) improper, shocking

**scalpel** [skalpɛl] *nm* scalpel

**scalper** [skalpe] *vt* to scalp

**scampi** [skãpi] *nmpl* scampi

**scandale** [skãdal] *nm* scandal; (*tapage*): **faire du** ~ to make a scene, create a disturbance; **faire** ~ to scandalize people; **au grand** ~ **de ...** to the great indignation of ...

**scandaleusement** [skãdaløzmã] *adv* scandalously, outrageously

**scandaleux, -euse** [skãdalø, -øz] *adj* scandalous, outrageous

**scandaliser** [skãdalize] *vt* to scandalize; **se** ~ **(de)** to be scandalized (by)

**scander** [skãde] *vt* (*vers*) to scan; (*mots, syllabes*) to stress separately; (*slogans*) to chant

**scandinave** [skãdinav] *adj* Scandinavian ▷ *nm/f*: **Scandinave** Scandinavian

**Scandinavie** [skãdinavi] *nf*: **la** ~ Scandinavia

**scanner** [skanɛʀ] *nm* (*Méd*) scanner

**scanographie** [skanɔgʀafi] *nf* (*Méd*) scanning; (*image*) scan

**scaphandre** [skafãdʀ(ə)] *nm* (*de plongeur*) diving suit; (*de cosmonaute*) spacesuit; ~ **autonome** aqualung

**scaphandrier** [skafãdʀije] *nm* diver

**scarabée** [skaʀabe] *nm* beetle

**scarlatine** [skaʀlatin] *nf* scarlet fever

**scarole** [skaʀɔl] *nf* endive

**scatologique** [skatɔlɔʒik] *adj* scatological, lavatorial

**sceau, x** [so] *nm* seal; (*fig*) stamp, mark; **sous le** ~ **du secret** under the seal of secrecy

**scélérat, e** [seleʀa, -at] *nm/f* villain, blackguard ▷ *adj* villainous, blackguardly

**sceller** [sele] *vt* to seal

**scellés** [sele] *nmpl* seals

**scénario** [senaʀjo] *nm* (*Ciné*) screenplay, script; (: *idée, plan*) scenario; (*fig*) pattern; scenario

**scénariste** [senaʀist(ə)] *nm/f* scriptwriter

**scène** [sɛn] *nf* (*gén*) scene; (*estrade, fig: théâtre*) stage; **entrer en** ~ to come on stage; **mettre en** ~ (*Théât*) to stage; (*Ciné*) to direct; (*fig*) to present, introduce; **sur le devant de la** ~ (*en pleine actualité*) in the forefront; **porter à la** ~ to adapt for the stage; **faire une** ~ **(à qn)** to make a scene (with sb); ~ **de ménage** domestic fight *ou* scene

**scénique** [senik] *adj* (*effets*) theatrical; (*art*) scenic

**scepticisme** [sɛptisism(ə)] *nm* scepticism

**sceptique** [sɛptik] *adj* sceptical ▷ *nm/f* sceptic

**sceptre** [sɛptʀ(ə)] *nm* sceptre

**schéma** [ʃema] *nm* (*diagramme*) diagram, sketch; (*fig*) outline

**schématique** [ʃematik] *adj* diagrammatic(al), schematic; (*fig*) oversimplified

**schématiquement** [ʃematikmã] *adv* schematically, diagrammatically

**schématisation** [ʃematizasjɔ̃] *nf* schematization; oversimplification

**schématiser** [ʃematize] *vt* to schematize; to (over)simplify

**schismatique** [ʃismatik] *adj* schismatic

**schisme** [ʃism(ə)] *nm* schism; rift, split

**schiste** [ʃist(ə)] *nm* schist

**schizophrène** [skizɔfʀɛn] *nm/f* schizophrenic

**schizophrénie** [skizɔfʀeni] *nf* schizophrenia

**sciatique** [sjatik] *adj*: **nerf** ~ sciatic nerve ▷ *nf* sciatica

**scie** [si] *nf* saw; (*fam: rengaine*) catch-tune; (: *personne*) bore; ~ **à bois** wood saw; ~ **circulaire** circular saw; ~ **à découper** fretsaw; ~ **à métaux** hacksaw; ~ **sauteuse** jigsaw

**S**

**sciemment** [sjamɑ̃] adv knowingly, wittingly
**science** [sjɑ̃s] nf science; (savoir) knowledge; (savoir-faire) art, skill; **~s économiques** economics; **~s humaines/sociales** social sciences; **~s naturelles** natural science sg, biology sg; **~s po** political studies
**science-fiction** [sjɑ̃sfiksjɔ̃] nf science fiction
**scientifique** [sjɑ̃tifik] adj scientific ▷ nm/f (savant) scientist; (étudiant) science student
**scientifiquement** [sjɑ̃tifikmɑ̃] adv scientifically
**scier** [sje] vt to saw; (retrancher) to saw off
**scierie** [siʀi] nf sawmill
**scieur** [sjœʀ] nm: **~ de long** pit sawyer
**Scilly** [sili]: **les îles ~** the Scilly Isles, the Scillies, the Isles of Scilly
**scinder** [sɛ̃de] vt, **se scinder** vi to split (up)
**scintillant, e** [sɛ̃tijɑ̃, -ɑ̃t] adj sparkling
**scintillement** [sɛ̃tijmɑ̃] nm sparkling no pl
**scintiller** [sɛ̃tije] vi to sparkle
**scission** [sisjɔ̃] nf split
**sciure** [sjyʀ] nf: **~ (de bois)** sawdust
**sclérose** [skleʀoz] nf sclerosis; (fig) ossification; **~ en plaques (SEP)** multiple sclerosis (MS)
**sclérosé, e** [skleʀoze] adj sclerosed, sclerotic; ossified
**scléroser** [skleʀoze]: **se scléroser** vi to become sclerosed; (fig) to become ossified
**scolaire** [skɔlɛʀ] adj school cpd; (péj) schoolish; **l'année ~** the school year; (à l'université) the academic year; **en âge ~** of school age
**scolarisation** [skɔlaʀizɑsjɔ̃] nf (d'un enfant) schooling; **la ~ d'une région** the provision of schooling in a region; **le taux de ~** the proportion of children in full-time education
**scolariser** [skɔlaʀize] vt to provide with schooling (ou schools)
**scolarité** [skɔlaʀite] nf schooling; **frais de ~** school fees (Brit), tuition (US)
**scolastique** [skɔlastik] adj (péj) scholastic
**scoliose** [skɔljoz] nf curvature of the spine, scoliosis
**scoop** [skup] nm (Presse) scoop, exclusive
**scooter** [skutœʀ] nm (motor) scooter
**scorbut** [skɔʀbyt] nm scurvy
**score** [skɔʀ] nm score; (électoral etc) result
**scories** [skɔʀi] nfpl scoria pl
**scorpion** [skɔʀpjɔ̃] nm (signe): **le S~** Scorpio, the Scorpion; **être du S~** to be Scorpio
**scotch** [skɔtʃ] nm (whisky) scotch, whisky; (adhésif) Sellotape® (Brit), Scotch tape® (US)
**scotcher** [skɔtʃe] vt to sellotape® (Brit), scotchtape® (US)
**scout, e** [skut] adj, nm scout
**scoutisme** [skutism(ə)] nm (boy) scout movement; (activités) scouting
**scribe** [skʀib] nm scribe; (péj) penpusher
**scribouillard** [skʀibujaʀ] nm penpusher
**script** [skʀipt(ə)] nm printing; (Ciné) (shooting) script
**scripte** [skʀipt(ə)] nf continuity girl
**script-girl** [skʀiptgœʀl] nf continuity girl

**scriptural, e, -aux** [skʀiptyʀal, -o] adj: **monnaie ~e** bank money
**scrupule** [skʀypyl] nm scruple; **être sans ~s** to be unscrupulous; **se faire un ~ de qch** to have scruples ou qualms about doing sth
**scrupuleusement** [skʀypyløzmɑ̃] adv scrupulously
**scrupuleux, -euse** [skʀypylø, -øz] adj scrupulous
**scrutateur, -trice** [skʀytatœʀ, -tʀis] adj searching ▷ nm/f scrutineer
**scruter** [skʀyte] vt to search, scrutinize; (l'obscurité) to peer into; (motifs, comportement) to examine, scrutinize
**scrutin** [skʀytɛ̃] nm (vote) ballot; (ensemble des opérations) poll; **~ proportionnel/majoritaire** election on a proportional/majority basis; **~ à deux tours** poll with two ballots ou rounds; **~ de liste** list system
**sculpter** [skylte] vt to sculpt; (érosion) to carve
**sculpteur** [skyltœʀ] nm sculptor
**sculptural, e, -aux** [skyltyʀal, -o] adj sculptural; (fig) statuesque
**sculpture** [skyltyʀ] nf sculpture; **~ sur bois** wood carving
**sdb.** abr = **salle de bain**
**SDF** sigle m (= sans domicile fixe) homeless person; **les ~** the homeless
**SDN** sigle f (= Société des Nations) League of Nations
**SE** sigle f (= Son Excellence) HE

○ **MOT-CLÉ**

**se, s'** [s(ə)] pron **1** (emploi réfléchi) oneself; (: masc) himself; (: fém) herself; (: sujet non humain) itself; (: pl) themselves; **se voir comme l'on est** to see o.s. as one is
**2** (réciproque) one another, each other; **ils s'aiment** they love one another ou each other
**3** (passif): **cela se répare facilement** it is easily repaired
**4** (possessif): **se casser la jambe/laver les mains** to break one's leg/wash one's hands

**séance** [seɑ̃s] nf (d'assemblée, récréative) meeting, session; (de tribunal) sitting, session; (musicale, Ciné, Théât) performance; **ouvrir/lever la ~** to open/close the meeting; **~ tenante** forthwith
**séant, e** [seɑ̃, -ɑ̃t] adj seemly, fitting ▷ nm posterior
**seau, x** [so] nm bucket, pail; **~ à glace** ice bucket
**sébum** [sebɔm] nm sebum
**sec, sèche** [sɛk, sɛʃ] adj dry; (raisins, figues) dried; (cœur, personne: insensible) hard, cold; (maigre, décharné) spare, lean; (réponse, ton) sharp, curt; (démarrage) sharp, sudden ▷ nm: **tenir au ~** to keep in a dry place ▷ adv hard; (démarrer) sharply; **boire ~** to be a heavy drinker; **je le bois ~** I drink it straight ou neat; **à pied ~** without getting one's feet wet; **à ~** adj dried up; (à court d'argent) broke
**SECAM** [sekam] sigle m (= procédé séquentiel à

*mémoire*) SECAM

**sécante** [sekɑ̃t] *nf* secant

**sécateur** [sekatœʀ] *nm* secateurs *pl* (*Brit*), shears *pl*, pair of secateurs *ou* shears

**sécession** [sesesjɔ̃] *nf*: **faire ~** to secede; **la guerre de S~** the American Civil War

**séchage** [seʃaʒ] *nm* drying; (*de bois*) seasoning

**sèche** [sɛʃ] *adj f voir* **sec** ▷ *nf* (*fam*) cigarette, fag (*Brit*)

**sèche-cheveux** [sɛʃʃəvø] *nm inv* hair-drier

**sèche-linge** [sɛʃlɛ̃ʒ] *nm inv* drying cabinet

**sèche-mains** [sɛʃmɛ̃] *nm inv* hand drier

**sèchement** [sɛʃmɑ̃] *adv* (*frapper etc*) sharply; (*répliquer etc*) drily, sharply

**sécher** [seʃe] *vt* to dry; (*dessécher: peau, blé*) to dry (out); (: *étang*) to dry up; (*bois*) to season; (*fam: classe, cours*) to skip, miss ▷ *vi* to dry; to dry out; to dry up; (*fam: candidat*) to be stumped; **se sécher** (*après le bain*) to dry o.s.

**sécheresse** [seʃʀɛs] *nf* dryness; (*absence de pluie*) drought

**séchoir** [seʃwaʀ] *nm* drier

**second, e** [səgɔ̃, -ɔ̃d] *adj* second ▷ *nm* (*assistant*) second in command; (*étage*) second floor (*Brit*), third floor (*US*); (*Navig*) first mate ▷ *nf* second; (*Scol*) ≈ fifth form (*Brit*), ≈ tenth grade (*US*); **en ~** (*en second rang*) in second place; **voyager en ~e** to travel second-class; **doué de ~e vue** having (the gift of) second sight; **trouver son ~ souffle** (*Sport, fig*) to get one's second wind; **être dans un état ~** to be in a daze (*ou* trance); **de ~e main** second-hand

**secondaire** [səgɔ̃dɛʀ] *adj* secondary

**seconder** [səgɔ̃de] *vt* to assist; (*favoriser*) to back

**secouer** [səkwe] *vt* to shake; (*passagers*) to rock; (*traumatiser*) to shake (up); **se secouer** (*chien*) to shake itself; (*fam: se démener*) to shake o.s. up; **~ la poussière d'un tapis** to shake the dust off a carpet; **~ la tête** to shake one's head

**secourable** [səkuʀabl(ə)] *adj* helpful

**secourir** [səkuʀiʀ] *vt* (*aller sauver*) to (go and) rescue; (*prodiguer des soins à*) to help, assist; (*venir en aide à*) to assist, aid

**secourisme** [səkuʀism(ə)] *nm* (*premiers soins*) first aid; (*sauvetage*) life saving

**secouriste** [səkuʀist(ə)] *nm/f* first-aid worker

**secourons** *etc* [səkuʀɔ̃] *vb voir* **secourir**

**secours** [səkuʀ] *vb voir* **secourir** ▷ *nm* help, aid, assistance ▷ *nmpl* aid *sg*; **cela lui a été d'un grand ~** this was a great help to him; **au ~!** help!; **appeler au ~** to shout *ou* call for help; **appeler qn à son ~** to call sb to one's assistance; **porter ~ à qn** to give sb assistance, help sb; **les premiers ~** first aid *sg*; **le ~ en montagne** mountain rescue

**secouru, e** [səkuʀy] *pp de* **secourir**

**secousse** [səkus] *nf* jolt, bump; (*électrique*) shock; (*fig: psychologique*) jolt, shock; **~ sismique** *ou* **tellurique** earth tremor

**secret, -ète** [səkʀɛ, -ɛt] *adj* secret; (*fig: renfermé*) reticent, reserved ▷ *nm* secret; (*discrétion absolue*): **le ~** secrecy; **en ~** in secret, secretly; **au ~** in solitary confinement; **~ de fabrication** trade secret; **~ professionnel** professional secrecy

**secrétaire** [səkʀetɛʀ] *nm/f* secretary ▷ *nm* (*meuble*) writing desk, secretaire; **~ d'ambassade** embassy secretary; **~ de direction** private *ou* personal secretary; **~ d'État** ≈ junior minister; **~ général (SG)** Secretary-General; (*Comm*) company secretary; **~ de mairie** town clerk; **~ médicale** medical secretary; **~ de rédaction** sub-editor

**secrétariat** [s(ə)kʀetaʀja] *nm* (*profession*) secretarial work; (*bureau: d'entreprise, d'école*) (secretary's) office; (: *d'organisation internationale*) secretariat; (*Pol etc: fonction*) secretaryship, office of Secretary

**secrètement** [səkʀɛtmɑ̃] *adv* secretly

**sécréter** [sekʀete] *vt* to secrete

**sécrétion** [sekʀesjɔ̃] *nf* secretion

**sectaire** [sɛktɛʀ] *adj* sectarian, bigoted

**sectarisme** [sɛktaʀism(ə)] *nm* sectarianism

**secte** [sɛkt(ə)] *nf* sect

**secteur** [sɛktœʀ] *nm* sector; (*Admin*) district; (*Élec*): **branché sur le ~** plugged into the mains (supply); **fonctionne sur pile et ~** battery or mains operated; **le ~ privé/public** (*Écon*) the private/public sector; **le ~ primaire/tertiaire** the primary/tertiary sector

**section** [sɛksjɔ̃] *nf* section; (*de parcours d'autobus*) fare stage; (*Mil: unité*) platoon; **~ rythmique** rhythm section

**sectionner** [sɛksjɔne] *vt* to sever; **se sectionner** *vi* to be severed

**sectionneur** [sɛksjɔnœʀ] *nm* (*Élec*) isolation switch

**sectoriel, le** [sɛktɔʀjɛl] *adj* sector-based

**sectorisation** [sɛktɔʀizasjɔ̃] *nf* division into sectors

**sectoriser** [sɛktɔʀize] *vt* to divide into sectors

**sécu** [seky] *nf* (*fam: = sécurité sociale*) ≈ dole (*Brit*), ≈ Welfare (*US*)

**séculaire** [sekylɛʀ] *adj* secular; (*très vieux*) age-old

**séculariser** [sekylaʀize] *vt* to secularize

**séculier, -ière** [sekylje, -jɛʀ] *adj* secular

**sécurisant, e** [sekyʀizɑ̃, -ɑ̃t] *adj* secure, giving a sense of security

**sécuriser** [sekyʀize] *vt* to give a sense of security to

**sécurité** [sekyʀite] *nf* security; (*absence de danger*) safety; **impression de ~** sense of security; **la ~ internationale** international security; **système de ~** security (*ou* safety) system; **être en ~** to be safe; **la ~ de l'emploi** job security; **la ~ routière** road safety; **la ~ sociale** ≈ (the) Social Security (*Brit*), ≈ (the) Welfare (*US*)

**sédatif, -ive** [sedatif, -iv] *adj, nm* sedative

**sédentaire** [sedɑ̃tɛʀ] *adj* sedentary

**sédiment** [sedimɑ̃] *nm* sediment; **sédiments** *nmpl* (*alluvions*) sediment *sg*

**sédimentaire** [sedimɑ̃tɛʀ] *adj* sedimentary

**sédimentation** [sedimɑ̃tasjɔ̃] *nf*

**S**

379

sedimentation

**séditieux, -euse** [sedisjø, -øz] *adj* insurgent; seditious

**sédition** [sedisjɔ̃] *nf* insurrection; sedition

**séducteur, -trice** [sedyktœr, -tris] *adj* seductive ▷ *nm/f* seducer (seductress)

**séduction** [sedyksjɔ̃] *nf* seduction; *(charme, attrait)* appeal, charm

**séduire** [sedɥir] *vt* to charm; *(femme: abuser de)* to seduce; *(chose)* to appeal to

**séduisant, e** [sedɥizɑ̃, -ɑ̃t] *vb voir* **séduire** ▷ *adj (femme)* seductive; *(homme, offre)* very attractive

**séduit, e** [sedɥi, -it] *pp de* **séduire**

**segment** [sɛgmɑ̃] *nm* segment; *(Auto)*: ~ **(de piston)** piston ring; ~ **de frein** brake shoe

**segmenter** [sɛgmɑ̃te] *vt,* **se segmenter** *vi* to segment

**ségrégation** [segregasjɔ̃] *nf* segregation

**ségrégationnisme** [segregasjɔnism(ə)] *nm* segregationism

**ségrégationniste** [segregasjɔnist(ə)] *adj* segregationist

**seiche** [sɛʃ] *nf* cuttlefish

**séide** [seid] *nm (péj)* henchman

**seigle** [sɛɡl(ə)] *nm* rye

**seigneur** [sɛɲœr] *nm* lord; **le S~** the Lord

**seigneurial, e, -aux** [sɛɲœrjal, -o] *adj* lordly, stately

**sein** [sɛ̃] *nm* breast; *(entrailles)* womb; **au ~ de** *prép (équipe, institution)* within; *(flots, bonheur)* in the midst of; **donner le ~ à** *(bébé)* to feed (at the breast); to breast-feed; **nourrir au ~** to breast-feed

**Seine** [sɛn] *nf*: **la ~** the Seine

**séisme** [seism(ə)] *nm* earthquake

**séismique** *etc* [seismik] *voir* **sismique** *etc*

**SEITA** [seita] *sigle f* = **Société d'exploitation industrielle des tabacs et allumettes**

**seize** [sɛz] *num* sixteen

**seizième** [sɛzjɛm] *num* sixteenth

**séjour** [seʒur] *nm* stay; *(pièce)* living room

**séjourner** [seʒurne] *vi* to stay

**sel** [sɛl] *nm* salt; *(fig)* wit; spice; ~ **de cuisine/de table** cooking/table salt; ~ **gemme** rock salt; ~**s de bain** bathsalts

**sélect, e** [selɛkt] *adj* select

**sélectif, -ive** [selɛktif, -iv] *adj* selective

**sélection** [selɛksjɔ̃] *nf* selection; **faire/opérer une ~ parmi** to make a selection from among; **épreuve de ~** *(Sport)* trial (for selection); ~ **naturelle** natural selection; ~ **professionnelle** professional recruitment

**sélectionné, e** [selɛksjɔne] *adj (joueur)* selected; *(produit)* specially selected

**sélectionner** [selɛksjɔne] *vt* to select

**sélectionneur, -euse** [selɛksjɔnœr, -øz] *nm/f* selector

**sélectivement** [selɛktivmɑ̃] *adv* selectively

**sélectivité** [selɛktivite] *nf* selectivity

**self** [sɛlf] *nm (fam)* self-service

**self-service** [sɛlfsɛrvis] *adj* self-service ▷ *nm* self-service (restaurant); *(magasin)* self-service

shop

**selle** [sɛl] *nf* saddle; **selles** *nfpl (Méd)* stools; **aller à la ~** *(Méd)* to have a bowel movement; **se mettre en ~** to mount, get into the saddle

**seller** [sele] *vt* to saddle

**sellette** [sɛlɛt] *nf*: **être sur la ~** to be on the carpet *(fig)*

**sellier** [selje] *nm* saddler

**selon** [səlɔ̃] *prép* according to; *(en se conformant à)* in accordance with; ~ **moi** as I see it; ~ **que** according to, depending on whether

**SEm** *sigle f* (= *Son Éminence*) HE

**semailles** [səmaj] *nfpl* sowing *sg*

**semaine** [səmɛn] *nf* week; *(salaire)* week's wages *ou* pay, weekly wages *ou* pay; **en ~** during the week, on weekdays; **à la petite ~** from day to day; **la ~ sainte** Holy Week

**semainier** [səmenje] *nm (bracelet)* bracelet made up of seven bands; *(calendrier)* desk diary; *(meuble)* chest of (seven) drawers

**sémantique** [semɑ̃tik] *adj* semantic ▷ *nf* semantics *sg*

**sémaphore** [semafɔr] *nm (Rail)* semaphore signal

**semblable** [sɑ̃blabl(ə)] *adj* similar; *(de ce genre)*: **de ~s mésaventures** such mishaps ▷ *nm* fellow creature *ou* man; ~ **à** similar to, like

**semblant** [sɑ̃blɑ̃] *nm*: **un ~ de vérité** a semblance of truth; **faire ~ (de faire)** to pretend (to do)

**sembler** [sɑ̃ble] *vb copule* to seem ▷ *vb impers*: **il semble (bien) que/inutile de** it (really) seems *ou* appears that/useless to; **il me semble (bien) que** it (really) seems to me that, I (really) think that; **il me semble le connaître** I think *ou* I've a feeling I know him; ~ **être** to seem to be; **comme bon lui semble** as he sees fit; **me semble-t-il, à ce qu'il me semble** it seems to me, to my mind

**semelle** [səmɛl] *nf* sole; *(intérieure)* insole, inner sole; **battre la ~** to stamp one's feet (to keep them warm); *(fig)* to hang around (waiting); ~**s compensées** platform soles

**semence** [səmɑ̃s] *nf (graine)* seed; *(clou)* tack

**semer** [səme] *vt* to sow; *(fig: éparpiller)* to scatter; *(confusion)* to spread; *(: poursuivants)* to lose, shake off; ~ **la discorde parmi** to sow discord among; **semé de** *(difficultés)* riddled with

**semestre** [səmɛstr(ə)] *nm* half-year; *(Scol)* semester

**semestriel, le** [səmɛstrijɛl] *adj* half-yearly; semestral

**semeur, -euse** [səmœr, -øz] *nm/f* sower

**semi-automatique** [səmiɔtɔmatik] *adj* semiautomatic

**semiconducteur** [səmikɔ̃dyktœr] *nm (Inform)* semiconductor

**semi-conserve** [səmikɔ̃sɛrv(ə)] *nf* semi-perishable foodstuff

**semi-fini** [səmifini] *adj m (produit)* semi-finished

**semi-liberté** [səmilibɛrte] *nf (Jur)* partial release from prison *(in order to follow a profession or*

*undergo medical treatment)*
**sémillant, e** [semijɑ̃, -ɑ̃t] *adj* vivacious; dashing
**séminaire** [seminɛʀ] *nm* seminar; (*Rel*) seminary
**séminariste** [seminaʀist(ə)] *nm* seminarist
**sémiologie** [semjɔlɔʒi] *nf* semiology
**semi-public, -ique** [səmipyblik] *adj* (*Jur*) semipublic
**semi-remorque** [səmiʀəmɔʀk(ə)] *nf* trailer ▷ *nm* articulated lorry (*Brit*), semi(trailer) (*US*)
**semis** [səmi] *nm* (*terrain*) seedbed, seed plot; (*plante*) seedling
**sémite** [semit] *adj* Semitic
**sémitique** [semitik] *adj* Semitic
**semoir** [səmwaʀ] *nm* seed-bag; seeder
**semonce** [səmɔ̃s] *nf*: **un coup de ~** a shot across the bows
**semoule** [səmul] *nf* semolina; **~ de riz** ground rice
**sempiternel, le** [sɛ̃pitɛʀnɛl] *adj* eternal, never-ending
**sénat** [sena] *nm* senate; *see note*

**sénateur** [senatœʀ] *nm* senator
**sénatorial, e, -aux** [senatɔʀjal, -o] *adj* senatorial, Senate *cpd*
**Sénégal** [senegal] *nm*: **le ~** Senegal
**sénégalais, e** [senegale, -ɛz] *adj* Senegalese
**sénevé** [sɛnve] *nm* (*Bot*) mustard; (*graine*) mustard seed
**sénile** [senil] *adj* senile
**sénilité** [senilite] *nf* senility
**senior** [senjɔʀ] *nm/f* (*Sport*) senior
**sens** [sɑ̃] *vb voir* **sentir** ▷ *nm* [sɑ̃s] (*Physiol, instinct*) sense; (*signification*) meaning, sense; (*direction*) direction, way ▷ *nmpl* (*sensualité*) senses; **reprendre ses ~** to regain consciousness; **avoir le ~ des affaires/de la mesure** to have business sense/a sense of moderation; **ça n'a pas de ~** that doesn't make (any) sense; **en dépit du bon ~** contrary to all good sense; **tomber sous le ~** to stand to reason, be perfectly obvious; **en un ~, dans un ~** in a way; **en ce ~ que** in the sense that; **à mon ~** to my mind; **dans le ~ des aiguilles d'une montre** clockwise; **dans le ~ de la longueur/largeur** lengthways/widthways; **dans le mauvais ~** the wrong way; in the wrong direction; **bon ~** good sense; **~ commun** common sense; **~**

**dessus dessous** upside down; **~ interdit, ~ unique** one-way street
**sensass** [sɑ̃sas] *adj* (*fam*) fantastic
**sensation** [sɑ̃sasjɔ̃] *nf* sensation; **faire ~** to cause a sensation, create a stir; **à ~** (*péj*) sensational
**sensationnel, le** [sɑ̃sasjɔnɛl] *adj* sensational
**sensé, e** [sɑ̃se] *adj* sensible
**sensibilisation** [sɑ̃sibilizasjɔ̃] *nf* consciousness-raising; **une campagne de ~ de l'opinion** a campaign to raise public awareness
**sensibiliser** [sɑ̃sibilize] *vt* to sensitize; **~ qn (à)** to make sb sensitive (to)
**sensibilité** [sɑ̃sibilite] *nf* sensitivity; (*affectivité, émotivité*) sensitivity, sensibility
**sensible** [sɑ̃sibl(ə)] *adj* sensitive; (*aux sens*) perceptible; (*appréciable: différence, progrès*) appreciable, noticeable; (*quartier*) problem *cpd*; **~ à** sensitive to
**sensiblement** [sɑ̃sibləmɑ̃] *adv* (*notablement*) appreciably, noticeably; (*à peu près*) **ils ont ~ le même poids** they weigh approximately the same
**sensiblerie** [sɑ̃sibləri] *nf* sentimentality; squeamishness
**sensitif, -ive** [sɑ̃sitif, -iv] *adj* (*nerf*) sensory; (*personne*) oversensitive
**sensoriel, le** [sɑ̃sɔʀjɛl] *adj* sensory, sensorial
**sensualité** [sɑ̃sɥalite] *nf* sensuality, sensuousness
**sensuel, le** [sɑ̃sɥɛl] *adj* sensual; sensuous
**sent** [sɑ̃] *vb voir* **sentir**
**sente** [sɑ̃t] *nf* path
**sentence** [sɑ̃tɑ̃s] *nf* (*jugement*) sentence; (*adage*) maxim
**sentencieusement** [sɑ̃tɑ̃sjøzmɑ̃] *adv* sententiously
**sentencieux, -euse** [sɑ̃tɑ̃sjø, -øz] *adj* sententious
**senteur** [sɑ̃tœʀ] *nf* scent, perfume
**senti, e** [sɑ̃ti] *adj*: **bien ~** (*mots etc*) well-chosen
**sentier** [sɑ̃tje] *nm* path
**sentiment** [sɑ̃timɑ̃] *nm* feeling; (*conscience, impression*): **avoir le ~ de/que** to be aware of/ have the feeling that; **recevez mes ~s respectueux** yours faithfully; **faire du ~** (*péj*) to be sentimental; **si vous me prenez par les ~s** if you appeal to my feelings
**sentimental, e, -aux** [sɑ̃timɑ̃tal, -o] *adj* sentimental; (*vie, aventure*) love *cpd*
**sentimentalisme** [sɑ̃timɑ̃talism(ə)] *nm* sentimentalism
**sentimentalité** [sɑ̃timɑ̃talite] *nf* sentimentality
**sentinelle** [sɑ̃tinɛl] *nf* sentry; **en ~** standing guard; (*soldat: en faction*) on sentry duty
**sentir** [sɑ̃tiʀ] *vt* (*par l'odorat*) to smell; (*par le goût*) to taste; (*au toucher, fig*) to feel; (*répandre une odeur de*) to smell of; (: *ressemblance*) to smell like; (*avoir la saveur de*) to taste of; to taste like; (*fig: dénoter, annoncer*) to be indicative of; to smack of; to

**S**

foreshadow ▷ *vi* to smell; ~ **mauvais** to smell bad; **se ~ bien** to feel good; **se ~ mal** (*être indisposé*) to feel unwell *ou* ill; **se ~ le courage/la force de faire** to feel brave/strong enough to do; **ne plus se ~ de joie** to be beside o.s. with joy; **il ne peut pas le ~** (*fam*) he can't stand him

**seoir** [swaʀ]: **~ à** *vt* to become, befit; **comme il (leur) sied** as it is fitting (to them)

**Séoul** [seul] *n* Seoul

**SEP** *sigle f* (= *sclérose en plaques*) MS

**séparation** [separasjɔ̃] *nf* separation; (*cloison*) division, partition; **~ de biens** division of property (*in marriage settlement*); **~ de corps** legal separation

**séparatisme** [separatism(ə)] *nm* separatism

**séparatiste** [separatist(ə)] *adj, nm/f* (*Pol*) separatist

**séparé, e** [separe] *adj* (*appartements, pouvoirs*) separate; (*époux*) separated; **~ de** separate from; separated from

**séparément** [separemã] *adv* separately

**séparer** [separe] *vt* (*gén*) to separate; (*divergences etc*) to divide; to drive apart; (: *différences, obstacles*) to stand between; (*détacher*): **~ qch de** to pull sth (off) from; (*dissocier*) to distinguish between; (*diviser*) **~ qch par** to divide sth (up) with; **~ une pièce en deux** to divide a room into two; **se séparer** (*époux*) to separate, part; (*prendre congé: amis etc*) to part, leave each other; (*adversaires*) to separate; (*se diviser: route, tige etc*) to divide; (*se détacher*): **se ~ (de)** to split off (from); to come off; **se ~ de** (*époux*) to separate *ou* part from; (*employé, objet personnel*) to part with

**sépia** [sepja] *nf* sepia

**sept** [sɛt] *num* seven

**septante** [sɛptɑ̃t] *num* (*Belgique, Suisse*) seventy

**septembre** [sɛptɑ̃bʀ(ə)] *nm* September; *voir aussi* **juillet**

**septennal, e, -aux** [sɛptenal, -o] *adj* seven-year; (*festival*) seven-year, septennial

**septennat** [sɛptena] *nm* seven-year term (of office)

**septentrional, e, -aux** [sɛptɑ̃tʀijɔnal, -o] *adj* northern

**septicémie** [sɛptisemi] *nf* blood poisoning, septicaemia

**septième** [sɛtjɛm] *num* seventh; **être au ~ ciel** to be on cloud nine

**septique** [sɛptik] *adj*: **fosse ~** septic tank

**septuagénaire** [sɛptɥaʒenɛʀ] *adj, nm/f* septuagenarian

**sépulcral, e, -aux** [sepylkʀal, -o] *adj* (*voix*) sepulchral

**sépulcre** [sepylkʀ(ə)] *nm* sepulchre

**sépulture** [sepyltyʀ] *nf* burial; (*tombeau*) burial place, grave

**séquelles** [sekɛl] *nfpl* after-effects; (*fig*) aftermath *sg*; consequences

**séquence** [sekɑ̃s] *nf* sequence

**séquentiel, le** [sekɑ̃sjɛl] *adj* sequential

**séquestration** [sekɛstʀasjɔ̃] *nf* illegal confinement; impounding

**séquestre** [sekɛstʀ(ə)] *nm* impoundment; **mettre sous ~** to impound

**séquestrer** [sekɛstʀe] *vt* (*personne*) to confine illegally; (*biens*) to impound

**serai** *etc* [səʀe] *vb voir* **être**

**sérail** [seʀaj] *nm* seraglio; harem; **rentrer au ~** to return to the fold

**serbe** [sɛʀb(ə)] *adj* Serbian ▷ *nm* (*Ling*) Serbian ▷ *nm/f*: **Serbe** Serb

**Serbie** [sɛʀbi] *nf*: **la ~** Serbia

**serbo-croate** [sɛʀbɔkʀɔat] *adj* Serbo-Croat, Serbo-Croatian ▷ *nm* (*Ling*) Serbo-Croat

**serein, e** [səʀɛ̃, -ɛn] *adj* serene; (*jugement*) dispassionate

**sereinement** [səʀɛnmɑ̃] *adv* serenely

**sérénade** [seʀenad] *nf* serenade; (*fam*) hullabaloo

**sérénité** [seʀenite] *nf* serenity

**serez** [səʀe] *vb voir* **être**

**serf, serve** [sɛʀ, sɛʀv(ə)] *nm/f* serf

**serfouette** [sɛʀfwɛt] *nf* weeding hoe

**serge** [sɛʀʒ(ə)] *nf* serge

**sergent** [sɛʀʒɑ̃] *nm* sergeant

**sergent-chef** [sɛʀʒɑ̃ʃɛf] *nm* staff sergeant

**sergent-major** [sɛʀʒɑ̃maʒɔʀ] *nm* = quartermaster sergeant

**sériciculture** [seʀisikyltyʀ] *nf* silkworm breeding, sericulture

**série** [seʀi] *nf* (*de questions, d'accidents, TV*) series *inv*; (*de clés, casseroles, outils*) set; (*catégorie: Sport*) rank; class; **en ~** in quick succession; (*Comm*) mass *cpd*; **de ~** *adj* standard; **hors ~** (*Comm*) custom-built; (*fig*) outstanding; **imprimante ~** (*Inform*) serial printer; **soldes de fin de ~s** end of line special offers; **~ noire** *nm* (*crime*) thriller ▷ *nf* (*suite de malheurs*) run of bad luck

**sérier** [seʀje] *vt* to classify, sort out

**sérieusement** [seʀjøzmɑ̃] *adv* seriously; reliably; responsibly; **il parle ~** he's serious, he means it; **~?** are you serious?, do you mean it?

**sérieux, -euse** [seʀjø, -øz] *adj* serious; (*élève, employé*) reliable, responsible; (*client, maison*) reliable, dependable; (*offre, proposition*) genuine, serious; (*grave, sévère*) serious, solemn; (*maladie, situation*) serious, grave; (*important*) considerable ▷ *nm* seriousness; reliability; **ce n'est pas ~** (*raisonnable*) that's not on; **garder son ~** to keep a straight face; **manquer de ~** not to be very responsible (*ou* reliable); **prendre qch/qn au ~** to take sth/sb seriously

**sérigraphie** [seʀigʀafi] *nf* silk screen printing

**serin** [səʀɛ̃] *nm* canary

**seriner** [səʀine] *vt*: **~ qch à qn** to drum sth into sb

**seringue** [səʀɛ̃g] *nf* syringe

**serions** *etc* [səʀjɔ̃] *vb voir* **être**

**serment** [sɛʀmɑ̃] *nm* (*juré*) oath; (*promesse*) pledge, vow; **prêter ~** to take the *ou* an oath; **faire le ~ de** to take a vow to, swear to; **sous ~** on *ou* under oath

**sermon** [sɛʀmɔ̃] *nm* sermon; (*péj*) sermon, lecture

**sermonner** [sɛʁmɔne] vt to lecture

**SERNAM** [sɛʁnam] sigle m (= Service national de messageries) rail delivery service

**sérologie** [seʁɔlɔʒi] nf serology

**séronégatif, -ive** [seʁonegatif, -iv] adj HIV negative

**séropositif, -ive** [seʁopozitif, -iv] adj HIV positive

**serpe** [sɛʁp(ə)] nf billhook

**serpent** [sɛʁpɑ̃] nm snake; ~ **à sonnettes** rattlesnake; ~ **monétaire (européen)** (European) monetary snake

**serpenter** [sɛʁpɑ̃te] vi to wind

**serpentin** [sɛʁpɑ̃tɛ̃] nm (tube) coil; (ruban) streamer

**serpillière** [sɛʁpijɛʁ] nf floorcloth

**serrage** [seʁaʒ] nm tightening; **collier de ~** clamp

**serre** [sɛʁ] nf (Agr) greenhouse; ~ **chaude** hothouse; ~ **froide** unheated greenhouse

**serré, e** [seʁe] adj (tissu) closely woven; (réseau) dense; (écriture) close; (habits) tight; (fig: lutte, match) tight, close-fought; (passagers etc) (tightly) packed; (café) strong ▷ adv: **jouer ~** to play it close, play a close game; **écrire ~** to write a cramped hand; **avoir la gorge ~e** to have a lump in one's throat

**serre-livres** [sɛʁlivʁ(ə)] nm inv book ends pl

**serrement** [sɛʁmɑ̃] nm: ~ **de main** handshake; ~ **de cœur** pang of anguish

**serrer** [seʁe] vt (tenir) to grip ou hold tight; (comprimer, coincer) to squeeze; (poings, mâchoires) to clench; (vêtement) to be too tight for; to fit tightly; (rapprocher) to close up, move closer together; (ceinture, nœud, frein, vis) to tighten ▷ vi: ~ **à droite** to keep to the right; to move into the right-hand lane; **se serrer** (se rapprocher) to squeeze up; **se ~ contre qn** to huddle up to sb; **se ~ les coudes** to stick together, back one another up; **se ~ la ceinture** to tighten one's belt; ~ **la main à qn** to shake sb's hand; ~ **qn dans ses bras** to hug sb, clasp sb in one's arms; ~ **la gorge à qn** (chagrin) to bring a lump to sb's throat; ~ **les dents** to clench ou grit one's teeth; ~ **qn de près** to follow close behind sb; ~ **le trottoir** to hug the kerb; ~ **sa droite** to keep well to the right; ~ **la vis à qn** to crack down harder on sb; ~ **les rangs** to close ranks

**serres** [sɛʁ] nfpl (griffes) claws, talons

**serre-tête** [sɛʁtɛt] nm inv (bandeau) headband; (bonnet) skullcap

**serrure** [seʁyʁ] nf lock

**serrurerie** [seʁyʁʁi] nf (métier) locksmith's trade; (ferronnerie) ironwork; ~ **d'art** ornamental ironwork

**serrurier** [seʁyʁje] nm locksmith

**sers, sert** [sɛʁ] vb voir **servir**

**sertir** [sɛʁtiʁ] vt (pierre) to set; (pièces métalliques) to crimp

**sérum** [seʁɔm] nm serum; ~ **antivenimeux** snakebite serum; ~ **sanguin** (blood) serum

**servage** [sɛʁvaʒ] nm serfdom

**servant** [sɛʁvɑ̃] nm server

**servante** [sɛʁvɑ̃t] nf (maid)servant

**serve** [sɛʁv] nf voir **serf** ▷ vb voir **servir**

**serveur, -euse** [sɛʁvœʁ, -øz] nm/f waiter (waitress) ▷ nm (Inform) server ▷ adj: **centre ~** (Inform) service centre

**servi, e** [sɛʁvi] adj: **être bien ~** to get a large helping (ou helpings); **vous êtes ~?** are you being served?

**serviable** [sɛʁvjabl(ə)] adj obliging, willing to help

**service** [sɛʁvis] nm (gén) service; (série de repas): **premier ~** first sitting; (pourboire) service (charge); (assortiment de vaisselle) set, service; (linge de table) set; (bureau: de la vente etc) department, section; (travail): **pendant le ~** on duty; **services** nmpl (travail, Écon) services, inclusive/exclusive of service; **faire le ~** to serve; **être en ~ chez qn** (domestique) to be in sb's service; **être au ~ de** (patron, patrie) to be in the service of; **être au ~ de qn** (collaborateur, voiture) to be at sb's service; **porte de ~** tradesman's entrance; **rendre ~ à** to help; **il aime rendre ~** he likes to help; **rendre un ~ à qn** to do sb a favour; **heures de ~** hours of duty; **être de ~** to be on duty; **reprendre du ~** to get back into action; **avoir 25 ans de ~** to have completed 25 years' service; **être/mettre en ~** to be in/put into service ou operation; **hors ~** not in use; out of order; ~ **à thé/café** tea/coffee set ou service; ~ **après-vente (SAV)** after-sales service; **en ~ commandé** on an official assignment; ~ **funèbre** funeral service; ~ **militaire** military service; see note; ~ **d'ordre** police (ou stewards) in charge of maintaining order; ~**s publics** public services, (public) utilities; ~**s secrets** secret service sg; ~**s sociaux** social services

🔹 **SERVICE MILITAIRE**

🔹 Until 1997, French men over the age of 18 who were passed as fit, and who were not in full-time higher education, were required to do ten months' "service militaire". Conscientious objectors were required to do two years' community service. Since 1997, military service has been suspended in France. However, all sixteen-year-olds, both male and female, are required to register for a compulsory one-day training course, the "JAPD" ("journée d'appel de préparation à la défense"), which covers basic information on the principles and organization of defence in France, and also advises on career opportunities in the military and in the voluntary sector. Young people must attend the training day before their eighteenth birthday.

**serviette** [sɛʁvjɛt] nf (de table) (table) napkin, serviette; (de toilette) towel; (porte-documents) briefcase; ~ **éponge** terry towel; ~ **hygiénique** sanitary towel

**servile** [sɛʀvil] *adj* servile

**servir** [sɛʀviʀ] *vt* (*gén*) to serve; (*dîneur: au restaurant*) to wait on; (*client: au magasin*) to serve, attend to; (*fig: aider*): ~ **qn** to aid sb; to serve sb's interests; to stand sb in good stead; (*Comm: rente*) to pay ▷ *vi* (*Tennis*) to serve; (*Cartes*) to deal; (*être militaire*) to serve; ~ **qch à qn** to serve sb with sth, help sb to sth; **qu'est-ce que je vous sers?** what can I get you?; **se servir** (*prendre d'un plat*) to help o.s.; (*s'approvisionner*): **se ~ chez** to shop at; **se ~ de** (*plat*) to help o.s. to; (*voiture, outil, relations*) to use; ~ **à qn** (*diplôme, livre*) to be of use to sb; **ça m'a servi pour faire** it was useful to me when I did; I used it to do; ~ **à qch/à faire** (*outil etc*) to be used for sth/for doing; **ça peut** ~ it may come in handy; **à quoi cela sert-il (de faire)?** what's the use (of doing)?; **cela ne sert à rien** it's no use; ~ **(à qn) de ...** to serve as ... (for sb); ~ **à dîner (à qn)** to serve dinner (to sb)

**serviteur** [sɛʀvitœʀ] *nm* servant

**servitude** [sɛʀvityd] *nf* servitude; (*fig*) constraint; (*Jur*) easement

**servofrein** [sɛʀvɔfʀɛ̃] *nm* servo(-assisted) brake

**servomécanisme** [sɛʀvɔmekanism(ə)] *nm* servo system

**ses** [se] *adj possessif voir* **son**

**sésame** [sezam] *nm* (*Bot*) sesame; (*graine*) sesame seed

**session** [sesjɔ̃] *nf* session

**set** [sɛt] *nm* set; (*napperon*) placemat; ~ **de table** set of placemats

**seuil** [sœj] *nm* doorstep; (*fig*) threshold; **sur le ~ de la maison** in the doorway of his house, on his doorstep; **au ~ de** (*fig*) on the threshold ou brink ou edge of; ~ **de rentabilité** (*Comm*) breakeven point

**seul, e** [sœl] *adj* (*sans compagnie*) alone; (*avec nuance affective: isolé*) lonely; (*unique*): **un ~ livre** only one book, a single book; **le ~ livre** the only book; ~ **ce livre, ce livre ~** this book alone, only this book; **d'un ~ coup** (*soudainement*) all at once; (*à la fois*) at one blow ▷ *adv* (*vivre*) alone, on one's own; **parler tout** ~ to talk to oneself; **faire qch (tout)** ~ to do sth (all) on one's own ou (all) by oneself ▷ *nm, nf*: **il en reste un(e) ~(e)** there's only one left; **pas un(e) ~(e)** not a single; **à lui (tout)** ~ single-handed, on his own; ~ **à** ~ in private

**seulement** [sœlmɑ̃] *adv* (*pas davantage*): ~ **cinq, cinq** ~ only five; (*exclusivement*): ~ **eux** only them, them alone; (*pas avant*): ~ **hier/à 10h** only yesterday/at 10 o'clock; (*mais, toutefois*): **il consent,** ~ **il demande des garanties** he agrees, only he wants guarantees; **non** ~ **... mais aussi** ou **encore** not only ... but also

**sève** [sɛv] *nf* sap

**sévère** [sevɛʀ] *adj* severe

**sévèrement** [sevɛʀmɑ̃] *adv* severely

**sévérité** [sevɛʀite] *nf* severity

**sévices** [sevis] *nmpl* (*physical*) cruelty *sg*, ill treatment *sg*

**Séville** [sevil] *n* Seville

**sévir** [seviʀ] *vi* (*punir*) to use harsh measures, crack down; (*fléau*) to rage, be rampant; ~ **contre** (*abus*) to deal ruthlessly with, crack down on

**sevrage** [səvʀaʒ] *nm* weaning; deprivation; (*d'un toxicomane*) withdrawal

**sevrer** [səvʀe] *vt* to wean; (*fig*): ~ **qn de** to deprive sb of

**sexagénaire** [sɛgzaʒenɛʀ] *adj, nm/f* sexagenarian

**SExc** *sigle f* (= *Son Excellence*) HE

**sexe** [sɛks(ə)] *nm* sex; (*organe mâle*) member

**sexisme** [sɛksism(ə)] *nm* sexism

**sexiste** [sɛksist(ə)] *adj, nm* sexist

**sexologie** [sɛksɔlɔʒi] *nf* sexology

**sexologue** [sɛksɔlɔg] *nm/f* sexologist, sex specialist

**sextant** [sɛkstɑ̃] *nm* sextant

**sexualité** [sɛksɥalite] *nf* sexuality

**sexué, e** [sɛksɥe] *adj* sexual

**sexuel, le** [sɛksɥɛl] *adj* sexual; **acte ~** sex act

**sexuellement** [sɛksɥɛlmɑ̃] *adv* sexually

**seyait** [sejɛ] *vb voir* **seoir**

**seyant, e** [sejɑ̃, -ɑ̃t] *vb voir* **seoir** ▷ *adj* becoming

**Seychelles** [seʃɛl] *nfpl*: **les ~** the Seychelles

**SG** *sigle m* = **secrétaire général**

**SGEN** *sigle m* (= *Syndicat général de l'éducation nationale*) trades union

**shaker** [ʃɛkœʀ] *nm* (*cocktail*) shaker

**shampooiner** [ʃɑ̃pwine] *vt* to shampoo

**shampooineur, -euse** [ʃɑ̃pwinœʀ, -øz] *nm/f* (*personne*) junior (*who does the shampooing*)

**shampooing** [ʃɑ̃pwɛ̃] *nm* shampoo; **se faire un** ~ to shampoo one's hair; ~ **colorant** (colour) rinse; ~ **traitant** medicated shampoo

**Shetland** [ʃɛtlɑ̃d] *n*: **les îles ~** the Shetland Islands, Shetland

**shoot** [ʃut] *nm* (*Football*) shot

**shooter** [ʃute] *vi* (*Football*) to shoot; **se shooter** (*drogué*) to mainline

**shopping** [ʃɔpiŋ] *nm*: **faire du** ~ to go shopping

**short** [ʃɔʀt] *nm* (pair of) shorts *pl*

**SI** *sigle m* = **syndicat d'initiative**

MOT-CLÉ

**si** [si] *nm* (*Mus*) B; (*en chantant la gamme*) ti ▷ *adv* **1** (*oui*) yes; **"Paul n'est pas venu" — "si!"** "Paul hasn't come" — "Yes he has!"; **je vous assure que si** I assure you he did/she is *etc* **2** (*tellement*) so; **si gentil/rapidement** so kind/ fast; (*tant et*) **si bien que** so much so that; **si rapide qu'il soit** however fast he may be ▷ *conj* if; **si tu veux** if you want; **je me demande si** I wonder if *ou* whether; **si j'étais toi** if I were you; **si seulement** if only; **si ce n'est que** apart from; **une des plus belles, si**

**ce n'est la plus belle** one of the most beautiful, if not THE most beautiful; **s'il est aimable, eux par contre ...** while ou whereas he's nice, they (on the other hand) ...

**siamois, e** [sjamwa, -waz] adj Siamese; **frères/ sœurs ~(es)** Siamese twins
**Sibérie** [siberi] nf: **la ~** Siberia
**sibérien, ne** [siberjɛ̃, -ɛn] adj Siberian ▷ nm/f: **Sibérien, ne** Siberian
**sibyllin, e** [sibilɛ̃, -in] adj sibylline
**SICAV** [sikav] sigle f (= société d'investissement à capital variable) open-ended investment trust, share in such a trust
**Sicile** [sisil] nf: **la ~** Sicily
**sicilien, ne** [sisiljɛ̃, -ɛn] adj Sicilian
**sida** [sida] nm (= syndrome immuno-déficitaire acquis) AIDS sg
**sidéral, e, -aux** [sideral, -o] adj sideral
**sidérant, e** [siderɑ̃, -ɑ̃t] adj staggering
**sidéré, e** [sidere] adj staggered
**sidérurgie** [sideryrʒi] nf steel industry
**sidérurgique** [sideryrʒik] adj steel cpd
**sidérurgiste** [sideryrʒist(ə)] nm/f steel worker
**siècle** [sjɛkl(ə)] nm century; (époque): **le ~ des lumières/de l'atome** the age of enlightenment/atomic age; (Rel): **le ~** the world
**sied** [sje] vb voir **seoir**
**siège** [sjɛʒ] nm seat; (d'entreprise) head office; (d'organisation) headquarters pl; (Mil) siege; **lever le ~** to raise the siege; **mettre le ~ devant** to besiege; **présentation par le ~** (Méd) breech presentation; **~ avant/arrière** (Auto) front/back seat; **~ baquet** bucket seat; **~ social** registered office
**siéger** [sjeʒe] vi (assemblée, tribunal) to sit; (résider, se trouver) to lie, be located
**sien, ne** [sjɛ̃, sjɛn] pron: **le(la) ~(ne), les ~s(-nes)**; his; hers; (d'une chose) its; **y mettre du ~** to pull one's weight; **faire des ~nes** (fam) to be up to one's (usual) tricks; **les ~s** (sa famille) one's family
**siérait** etc [sjerɛ] vb voir **seoir**
**Sierra Leone** [sjɛraleone] nf: **la ~** Sierra Leone
**sieste** [sjɛst(ə)] nf (afternoon) snooze ou nap, siesta; **faire la ~** to have a snooze ou nap
**sieur** [sjœr] nm: **le ~ Thomas** Mr Thomas; (en plaisantant) Master Thomas
**sifflant, e** [siflɑ̃, -ɑ̃t] adj (bruit) whistling; (toux) wheezing; **(consonne) ~e** sibilant
**sifflement** [sifləmɑ̃] nm whistle, whistling no pl; wheezing no pl; hissing no pl
**siffler** [sifle] vi (gén) to whistle; (avec un sifflet) to blow (on) one's whistle; (en respirant) to wheeze; (serpent, vapeur) to hiss ▷ vt (chanson) to whistle; (chien etc) to whistle for; (fille) to whistle at; (pièce, orateur) to hiss, boo; (faute) to blow one's whistle at; (fin du match, départ) to blow one's whistle for; (fam: verre, bouteille) to guzzle, knock back (Brit)

**sifflet** [siflɛ] nm whistle; **sifflets** nmpl (de mécontentement) whistles, boos; **coup de ~** whistle
**siffloter** [siflɔte] vi, vt to whistle
**sigle** [sigl(ə)] nm acronym, (set of) initials pl
**signal, -aux** [sinal, -o] nm (signe convenu, appareil) signal; (indice, écriteau) sign; **donner le ~ de** to give the signal for; **~ d'alarme** alarm signal; **~ d'alerte/de détresse** warning/distress signal; **~ horaire** time signal; **~ optique/sonore** warning light/sound; visual/acoustic signal; **signaux (lumineux)** (Auto) traffic signals; **signaux routiers** road signs; (lumineux) traffic lights
**signalement** [sinalmɑ̃] nm description, particulars pl
**signaler** [sinale] vt to indicate; to announce; to report; (être l'indice de) to indicate; (faire remarquer): **~ qch à qn/à qn que** to point out sth to sb/to sb that; (appeler l'attention sur): **~ qn à la police** to bring sb to the notice of the police; **se ~ par** to distinguish o.s. by; **se ~ à l'attention de qn** to attract sb's attention
**signalétique** [sinaletik] adj: **fiche ~** identification sheet
**signalisation** [sinalizasjɔ̃] nf signalling, signposting; signals pl; roadsigns pl; **panneau de ~** roadsign
**signaliser** [sinalize] vt to put up roadsigns on; to put signals on
**signataire** [sinatɛr] nm/f signatory
**signature** [sinatyr] nf signature; (action) signing
**signe** [sin] nm sign; (Typo) mark; **ne pas donner ~ de vie** to give no sign of life; **c'est bon ~** it's a good sign; **c'est ~ que** it's a sign that; **faire un ~ de la main/tête** to give a sign with one's hand/shake one's head; **faire ~ à qn** (fig) to get in touch with sb; **faire ~ à qn d'entrer** to motion (to) sb to come in; **en ~ de** as a sign ou mark of; **le ~ de la croix** the sign of the Cross; **~ de ponctuation** punctuation mark; **~ du zodiaque** sign of the zodiac; **~s particuliers** distinguishing marks
**signer** [sine] vt to sign; **se signer** vi to cross o.s
**signet** [sinɛ] nm bookmark
**significatif, -ive** [sinifikatif, -iv] adj significant
**signification** [sinifikasjɔ̃] nf meaning
**signifier** [sinifje] vt (vouloir dire) to mean, signify; (faire connaître): **~ qch (à qn)** to make sth known (to sb); (Jur): **~ qch à qn** to serve notice of sth on sb
**silence** [silɑ̃s] nm silence; (Mus) rest; **garder le ~ (sur qch)** to keep silent (about sth), say nothing (about sth); **passer sous ~** to pass over (in silence); **réduire au ~** to silence
**silencieusement** [silɑ̃sjøzmɑ̃] adv silently
**silencieux, -euse** [silɑ̃sjø, -øz] adj quiet, silent ▷ nm silencer (Brit), muffler (US)
**silex** [silɛks] nm flint
**silhouette** [silwɛt] nf outline, silhouette;

**S**

385

(*lignes, contour*) outline; (*figure*) figure

**silice** [silis] *nf* silica

**siliceux, -euse** [silisø, -øz] *adj* (*terrain*) chalky

**silicium** [silisjɔm] *nm* silicon; **plaquette de ~** silicon chip

**silicone** [silikɔn] *nf* silicone

**silicose** [silikoz] *nf* silicosis, dust disease

**sillage** [sijaʒ] *nm* wake; (*fig*) trail; **dans le ~ de** (*fig*) in the wake of

**sillon** [sijɔ̃] *nm* (*d'un champ*) furrow; (*de disque*) groove

**sillonner** [sijɔne] *vt* (*creuser*) to furrow; (*traverser*) to cross, criss-cross

**silo** [silo] *nm* silo

**simagrées** [simagʀe] *nfpl* fuss *sg*; airs and graces

**simiesque** [simjɛsk(ə)] *adj* monkey-like, ape-like

**similaire** [similɛʀ] *adj* similar

**similarité** [similaʀite] *nf* similarity

**simili** [simili] *nm* imitation; (*Typo*) half-tone ▷ *nf* half-tone engraving

**simili...** [simili] *préfixe* imitation *cpd*, artificial

**similicuir** [similikɥiʀ] *nm* imitation leather

**similigravure** [similigʀavyʀ] *nf* half-tone engraving

**similitude** [similityd] *nf* similarity

**simple** [sɛ̃pl(ə)] *adj* (*gén*) simple; (*non multiple*) single; **simples** *nmpl* (*Méd*) medicinal plants; **~ messieurs** *nm* (*Tennis*) men's singles *sg*; **un ~ particulier** an ordinary citizen; **une ~ formalité** a mere formality; **cela varie du ~ au double** it can double, it can double the price *etc*; **dans le plus ~ appareil** in one's birthday suit; **~ course** *adj* single; **~ d'esprit** *nm/f* simpleton; **~ soldat** private

**simplement** [sɛ̃pləmɑ̃] *adv* simply

**simplet, te** [sɛ̃plɛ, -ɛt] *adj* (*personne*) simple-minded

**simplicité** [sɛ̃plisite] *nf* simplicity; **en toute ~** quite simply

**simplification** [sɛ̃plifikasjɔ̃] *nf* simplification

**simplifier** [sɛ̃plifje] *vt* to simplify

**simpliste** [sɛ̃plist(ə)] *adj* simplistic

**simulacre** [simylakʀ(ə)] *nm* enactment; (*péj*): **un ~ de** a pretence of, a sham

**simulateur, -trice** [simylatœʀ, -tʀis] *nm/f* shammer, pretender; (*qui se prétend malade*) malingerer ▷ *nm*: **~ de vol** flight simulator

**simulation** [simylasjɔ̃] *nf* shamming, simulation; malingering

**simuler** [simyle] *vt* to sham, simulate

**simultané, e** [simyltane] *adj* simultaneous

**simultanéité** [simyltaneite] *nf* simultaneity

**simultanément** [simyltanemɑ̃] *adv* simultaneously

**Sinaï** [sinai] *nm*: **le ~** Sinai

**sinapisme** [sinapism(ə)] *nm* (*Méd*) mustard poultice

**sincère** [sɛ̃sɛʀ] *adj* sincere; genuine; heartfelt; **mes ~s condoléances** my deepest sympathy

**sincèrement** [sɛ̃sɛʀmɑ̃] *adv* sincerely; genuinely

**sincérité** [sɛ̃seʀite] *nf* sincerity; **en toute ~** in all sincerity

**sinécure** [sinekyʀ] *nf* sinecure

**sine die** [sinedje] *adv* sine die, indefinitely

**sine qua non** [sinekwanɔn] *adj*: **condition ~** indispensable condition

**Singapour** [sɛ̃gapuʀ] *nm*: **le ~** Singapore

**singe** [sɛ̃ʒ] *nm* monkey; (*de grande taille*) ape

**singer** [sɛ̃ʒe] *vt* to ape, mimic

**singeries** [sɛ̃ʒʀi] *nfpl* antics; (*simagrées*) airs and graces

**singulariser** [sɛ̃gylaʀize] *vt* to mark out; **se singulariser** to call attention to o.s.

**singularité** [sɛ̃gylaʀite] *nf* peculiarity

**singulier, -ière** [sɛ̃gylje, -jɛʀ] *adj* remarkable, singular; (*Ling*) singular ▷ *nm* singular

**singulièrement** [sɛ̃gyljɛʀmɑ̃] *adv* singularly, remarkably

**sinistre** [sinistʀ(ə)] *adj* sinister; (*intensif*): **un ~ imbécile** an incredible idiot ▷ *nm* (*incendie*) blaze; (*catastrophe*) disaster; (*Assurances*) damage (*giving rise to a claim*)

**sinistré, e** [sinistʀe] *adj* disaster-stricken ▷ *nm/f* disaster victim

**sinistrose** [sinistʀoz] *nf* pessimism

**sino...** [sino] *préfixe*: **sino-indien** Sino-Indian, Chinese-Indian

**sinon** [sinɔ̃] *conj* (*autrement, sans quoi*) otherwise, or else; (*sauf*) except, other than; (*si ce n'est*) if not

**sinueux, -euse** [sinɥø, -øz] *adj* winding; (*fig*) tortuous

**sinuosités** [sinɥozite] *nfpl* winding *sg*, curves

**sinus** [sinys] *nm* (*Anat*) sinus; (*Géom*) sine

**sinusite** [sinyzit] *nf* sinusitis, sinus infection

**sinusoïdal, e, -aux** [sinyzɔidal, -o] *adj* sinusoidal

**sinusoïde** [sinyzɔid] *nf* sinusoid

**sionisme** [sjɔnism(ə)] *nm* Zionism

**sioniste** [sjɔnist(ə)] *adj*, *nm/f* Zionist

**siphon** [sifɔ̃] *nm* (*tube, d'eau gazeuse*) siphon; (*d'évier etc*) U-bend

**siphonner** [sifɔne] *vt* to siphon

**sire** [siʀ] *nm* (*titre*): **S~** Sire; **un triste ~** an unsavoury individual

**sirène** [siʀɛn] *nf* siren; **~ d'alarme** fire alarm; (*pendant la guerre*) air-raid siren

**sirop** [siʀo] *nm* (*à diluer: de fruit etc*) syrup, cordial (*Brit*); (*boisson*) fruit drink; (*pharmaceutique*) syrup, mixture; **~ de menthe** mint syrup *ou* cordial; **~ contre la toux** cough syrup *ou* mixture

**siroter** [siʀɔte] *vt* to sip

**sirupeux, -euse** [siʀypø, -øz] *adj* syrupy

**sis, e** [si, siz] *adj*: **~ rue de la Paix** located in the rue de la Paix

**sisal** [sizal] *nm* (*Bot*) sisal

**sismique** [sismik] *adj* seismic

**sismographe** [sismɔgʀaf] *nm* seismograph

**sismologie** [sismɔlɔʒi] *nf* seismology

**site** [sit] *nm* (*paysage, environnement*) setting;

(*d'une ville etc: emplacement*) site; ~ **(pittoresque)** beauty spot; **~s touristiques** places of interest; **~s naturels/historiques** natural/historic sites; ~ **web** (*Inform*) website

**sitôt** [sito] *adv*: ~ **parti** as soon as he *etc* had left; ~ **après** straight after; **pas de** ~ not for a long time; ~ **(après) que** as soon as

**situation** [sitɥasjɔ̃] *nf* (*gén*) situation; (*d'un édifice, d'une ville*) situation, position; (*emplacement*) location; **être en** ~ **de faire qch** to be in a position to do sth; ~ **de famille** marital status

**situé, e** [sitɥe] *adj*: **bien** ~ well situated, in a good location; ~ **à/près de** situated at/near

**situer** [sitɥe] *vt* to site, situate; (*en pensée*) to set, place; **se situer** *vi*: **se** ~ **à/près de** to be situated at/near

**SIVOM** [sivɔm] *sigle m* (= *Syndicat intercommunal à vocation multiple*) association of "communes"

**six** [sis] *num* six

**sixième** [sizjɛm] *num* sixth; **en** ~ (*Scol: classe*) first form (*Brit*), sixth grade (*US*)

**skaï®** [skaj] *nm* ≈ Leatherette®

**skate** [skɛt], **skate-board** [skɛtbɔʀd] *nm* (*sport*) skateboarding; (*planche*) skateboard

**sketch** [skɛtʃ] *nm* (*variety*) sketch

**ski** [ski] *nm* (*objet*) ski; (*sport*) skiing; **faire du** ~ to ski; ~ **alpin** Alpine skiing; ~ **court** short ski; ~ **évolutif** short ski method; ~ **de fond** cross-country skiing; ~ **nautique** water-skiing; ~ **de piste** downhill skiing; ~ **de randonnée** cross-country skiing

**ski-bob** [skibɔb] *nm* skibob

**skier** [skje] *vi* to ski

**skieur, -euse** [skjœʀ, -øz] *nm/f* skier

**skif, skiff** [skif] *nm* skiff

**slalom** [slalɔm] *nm* slalom; **faire du** ~ **entre** to slalom between

**slalomer** [slalɔme] *vi* (*entre des obstacles*) to weave in and out; (*Ski*) to slalom

**slalomeur, -euse** [slalɔmœʀ, -øz] *nm/f* (*Ski*) slalom skier

**slave** [slav] *adj* Slav(onic), Slavic ▷ *nm* (*Ling*) Slavonic ▷ *nm/f*: **Slave** Slav

**slip** [slip] *nm* (*sous-vêtement*) underpants *pl*, pants *pl* (*Brit*), briefs *pl*; (*de bain: d'homme*) (bathing *ou* swimming) trunks *pl*; (: *du bikini*) (bikini) briefs *pl ou* bottoms *pl*

**slogan** [slɔgɑ̃] *nm* slogan

**slovaque** [slɔvak] *adj* Slovak ▷ *nm* (*Ling*) Slovak ▷ *nm/f*: **Slovaque** Slovak

**Slovaquie** [slɔvaki] *nf*: **la** ~ Slovakia

**slovène** [slɔvɛn] *adj* Slovene ▷ *nm* (*Ling*) Slovene ▷ *nm/f*: **Slovène** Slovene

**Slovénie** [slɔveni] *nf*: **la** ~ Slovenia

**slow** [slo] *nm* (*danse*) slow number

**SM** *sigle f* (= *Sa Majesté*) HM

**SMAG** [smag] *sigle m* = **salaire minimum agricole garanti**

**smasher** [smaʃe] *vi* to smash the ball ▷ *vt* (*balle*) to smash

**SMIC** [smik] *sigle m* = **salaire minimum**

**interprofessionnel de croissance**; *see note*

● **SMIC**
●
● In France, the *SMIC* ("salaire minimum
● interprofessionnel de croissance") is the
● minimum hourly rate which workers over
● the age of 18 must legally be paid. It is index-
● linked and is raised each time the cost of
● living rises by 2 per cent.

**smicard, e** [smikaʀ, -aʀd(ə)] *nm/f* minimum wage earner

**smocks** [smɔk] *nmpl* (*Couture*) smocking *no pl*

**smoking** [smɔkiŋ] *nm* dinner *ou* evening suit

**SMS** *sigle m* = **short message service**; (*message*) text (message)

**SMUR** [smyʀ] *sigle m* (= *service médical d'urgence et de réanimation*) specialist mobile emergency unit

**snack** [snak] *nm* snack bar

**SNC** *abr* = **service non compris**

**SNCB** *sigle f* (= *Société nationale des chemins de fer belges*) Belgian railways

**SNCF** *sigle f* (= *Société nationale des chemins de fer français*) French railways

**SNES** [snɛs] *sigle m* (= *Syndicat national de l'enseignement secondaire*) secondary teachers' union

**SNE-sup** [ɛsɛnəsyp] *sigle m* (= *Syndicat national de l'enseignement supérieur*) university teachers' union

**SNJ** *sigle m* (= *Syndicat national des journalistes*) journalists' union

**snob** [snɔb] *adj* snobbish ▷ *nm/f* snob

**snober** [snɔbe] *vt*: ~ **qn** to give sb the cold shoulder, treat sb with disdain

**snobinard, e** [snɔbinaʀ, -aʀd(ə)] *nm/f* snooty *ou* stuck-up person

**snobisme** [snɔbism(ə)] *nm* snobbery

**SNSM** *sigle f* (= *Société nationale de sauvetage en mer*) national sea-rescue association

**s.o.** *abr* (= *sans objet*) no longer applicable

**sobre** [sɔbʀ(ə)] *adj* temperate, abstemious; (*élégance, style*) restrained, sober; ~ **de** (*gestes, compliments*) sparing of

**sobrement** [sɔbʀəmɑ̃] *adv* in moderation, abstemiously; soberly

**sobriété** [sɔbʀijete] *nf* temperance, abstemiousness; sobriety

**sobriquet** [sɔbʀikɛ] *nm* nickname

**soc** [sɔk] *nm* ploughshare

**sociabilité** [sɔsjabilite] *nf* sociability

**sociable** [sɔsjabl(ə)] *adj* sociable

**social, e, -aux** [sɔsjal, -o] *adj* social

**socialisant, e** [sɔsjalizɑ̃, -ɑ̃t] *adj* with socialist tendencies

**socialisation** [sɔsjalizɑsjɔ̃] *nf* socialisation

**socialiser** [sɔsjalize] *vt* to socialize

**socialisme** [sɔsjalism(ə)] *nm* socialism

**socialiste** [sɔsjalist(ə)] *adj, nm/f* socialist

**sociétaire** [sɔsjetɛʀ] *nm/f* member

**société** [sɔsjete] *nf* society; (*d'abeilles, de fourmis*) colony; (*sportive*) club; (*Comm*) company; **la bonne** ~ polite society; **se plaire dans la** ~ **de**

**S**

to enjoy the society of; **l'archipel de la S~** the Society Islands; **la ~ d'abondance/de consommation** the affluent/consumer society; **~ par actions** joint stock company; **~ anonyme (SA)** = limited company (Ltd) (Brit), = incorporated company (Inc.) (US); **~ d'investissement à capital variable (SICAV)** = investment trust (Brit), = mutual fund (US); **~ à responsabilité limitée (SARL)** type of limited liability company (with non-negotiable shares); **~ savante** learned society; **~ de services** service company

**socioculturel, le** [sɔsjokyltyʀɛl] adj sociocultural

**socio-économique** [sɔsjoekɔnɔmik] adj socioeconomic

**socio-éducatif, --ive** [sɔsjoedykatif, -iv] adj socioeducational

**sociolinguistique** [sɔsjolɛ̃ɡɥistik] adj sociolinguistic

**sociologie** [sɔsjɔlɔʒi] nf sociology

**sociologique** [sɔsjɔlɔʒik] adj sociological

**sociologue** [sɔsjɔlɔg] nm/f sociologist

**socio-professionnel, le** [sɔsjoprɔfesjɔnɛl] adj socioprofessional

**socle** [sɔkl(ə)] nm (de colonne, statue) plinth, pedestal; (de lampe) base

**socquette** [sɔkɛt] nf ankle sock

**soda** [sɔda] nm (boisson) fizzy drink, soda (US)

**sodium** [sɔdjɔm] nm sodium

**sodomie** [sɔdɔmi] nf sodomy; buggery

**sodomiser** [sɔdɔmize] vt to sodomize; to bugger

**sœur** [sœʀ] nf sister; (religieuse) nun, sister; **~ Élisabeth** (Rel) Sister Elizabeth; **~ de lait** foster sister

**sofa** [sɔfa] nm sofa

**Sofia** [sɔfja] n Sofia

**SOFRES** [sɔfʀɛs] sigle f (= Société française d'enquête par sondage) company which conducts opinion polls

**soi** [swa] pron oneself; **cela va de ~** that ou it goes without saying, it stands to reason

**soi-disant** [swadizã] adj inv so-called ▷ adv supposedly

**soie** [swa] nf silk; (de porc, sanglier: poil) bristle

**soient** [swa] vb voir **être**

**soierie** [swaʀi] nf (industrie) silk trade; (tissu) silk

**soif** [swaf] nf thirst; (fig): **~ de** thirst ou craving for; **avoir ~** to be thirsty; **donner ~ à qn** to make sb thirsty

**soigné, e** [swaɲe] adj (tenue) well-groomed, neat; (travail) careful, meticulous; (fam) whopping; stiff

**soigner** [swaɲe] vt (malade, maladie: docteur) to treat; (: infirmière, mère) to nurse, look after; (blessé) to tend; (travail, détails) to take care over; (jardin, chevelure, invités) to look after

**soigneur** [swaɲœʀ] nm (Cyclisme, Football) trainer; (Boxe) second

**soigneusement** [swaɲøzmã] adv carefully

**soigneux, -euse** [swaɲø, -øz] adj (propre) tidy, neat; (méticuleux) painstaking, careful; **~ de** careful with

**soi-même** [swamɛm] pron oneself

**soin** [swɛ̃] nm (application) care; (propreté, ordre) tidiness, neatness; (responsabilité): **le ~ de qch** the care of sth; **soins** nmpl (à un malade, blessé) treatment sg, medical attention sg; (attentions, prévenance) care and attention sg; (hygiène) care sg; **~s de la chevelure/de beauté** hair/beauty care; **~s du corps/ménage** care of one's body/the home; **avoir** ou **prendre ~ de** to take care of, look after; **avoir** ou **prendre ~ de faire** to take care to do; **faire qch avec (grand) ~** to do sth (very) carefully; **sans ~** adj careless; untidy; **les premiers ~s** first aid sg; **aux bons ~s de** c/o, care of; **être aux petits ~s pour qn** to wait on sb hand and foot, see to sb's every need; **confier qn aux ~s de qn** to hand sb over to sb's care

**soir** [swaʀ] nm, adv evening; **le ~** in the evening(s); **ce ~** this evening, tonight; **à ce ~!** see you this evening (ou tonight)!; **la veille au ~** the previous evening; **sept/dix heures du ~** seven in the evening/ten at night; **le repas/journal du ~** the evening meal/newspaper; **dimanche ~** Sunday evening; **hier ~** yesterday evening; **demain ~** tomorrow evening, tomorrow night

**soirée** [swaʀe] nf evening; (réception) party; **donner en ~** (film, pièce) to give an evening performance of

**soit** [swa] vb voir **être** ▷ conj (à savoir) namely, to wit; (ou): **soit ... ~** either ... or ▷ adv so be it, very well; **~ un triangle ABC** let ABC be a triangle; **~ que ... ~ que** ou **ou que** whether ... or whether

**soixantaine** [swasãtɛn] nf: **une ~ (de)** sixty or so, about sixty; **avoir la ~** to be around sixty

**soixante** [swasãt] num sixty

**soixante-dix** [swasãtdis] num seventy

**soixante-dixième** [swasãtdizjɛm] num seventieth

**soixante-huitard, e** [swazãtɥitaʀ, -aʀd(ə)] adj relating to the demonstrations of May 1968 ▷ nm/f participant in the demonstrations of May 1968

**soixantième** [swasãtjɛm] num sixtieth

**soja** [sɔʒa] nm soya; (graines) soya beans pl; **germes de ~** beansprouts

**sol** [sɔl] nm ground; (de logement) floor; (revêtement) flooring no pl; (territoire, Agr, Géo) soil; (Mus) G; (: en chantant la gamme) so(h)

**solaire** [sɔlɛʀ] adj solar, sun cpd

**solarium** [sɔlaʀjɔm] nm solarium

**soldat** [sɔlda] nm soldier; **S~ inconnu** Unknown Warrior ou Soldier; **~ de plomb** tin ou toy soldier

**solde** [sɔld(ə)] nf pay ▷ nm (Comm) balance; **soldes** nmpl ou nfpl (Comm) sales; (articles) sale goods; **à la ~ de qn** (péj) in sb's pay; **~ créditeur/débiteur** credit/debit balance; **~ à payer** balance outstanding; **en ~** at sale price; **aux ~s** at the sales

**solder** [sɔlde] vt (compte) to settle; (marchandise) to sell at sale price, sell off; **se ~ par** (fig) to end in; **article soldé (à) 10 euros** item reduced to 10 euros

**soldeur, -euse** [sɔldœʀ, -øz] *nm/f* (*Comm*) discounter

**sole** [sɔl] *nf* sole *inv* (*fish*)

**soleil** [sɔlɛj] *nm* sun; (*lumière*) sun(light); (*temps ensoleillé*) sun(shine); (*feu d'artifice*) Catherine wheel; (*d'acrobate*) grand circle; (*Bot*) sunflower; **il y a** *ou* **il fait du ~** it's sunny; **au ~** in the sun; **en plein ~** in full sun; **le ~ levant/couchant** the rising/setting sun; **le ~ de minuit** the midnight sun

**solennel, le** [sɔlanɛl] *adj* solemn; ceremonial

**solennellement** [sɔlanɛlmɑ̃] *adv* solemnly

**solennité** [sɔlanite] *nf* (*d'une fête*) solemnity; **solennités** *nfpl* (*formalités*) formalities

**solénoïde** [sɔlenɔid] *nm* (*Élec*) solenoid

**solfège** [sɔlfɛʒ] *nm* rudiments *pl* of music; (*exercices*) ear training *no pl*

**solfier** [sɔlfje] *vt*: **~ un morceau** to sing a piece using the sol-fa

**soli** [sɔli] *nmpl de* **solo**

**solidaire** [sɔlidɛʀ] *adj* (*personnes*) who stand together, who show solidarity; (*pièces mécaniques*) interdependent; (*Jur: engagement*) binding on all parties; (*: débiteurs*) jointly liable; **être ~ de** (*collègues*) to stand by; (*mécanisme*) to be bound up with, be dependent on

**solidairement** [sɔlidɛʀmɑ̃] *adv* jointly

**solidariser** [sɔlidaʀize]: **se ~ avec** *vt* to show solidarity with

**solidarité** [sɔlidaʀite] *nf* (*entre personnes*) solidarity; (*de mécanisme, phénomènes*) interdependence; **par ~ (avec)** (*cesser le travail etc*) in sympathy (with)

**solide** [sɔlid] *adj* solid; (*mur, maison, meuble*) solid, sturdy; (*connaissances, argument*) sound; (*personne*) robust, sturdy; (*estomac*) strong ▷ *nm* solid; **avoir les reins ~s** (*fig*) to be in a good financial position; to have sound financial backing

**solidement** [sɔlidmɑ̃] *adv* solidly; (*fermement*) firmly

**solidifier** [sɔlidifje] *vt*, **se solidifier** *vi* to solidify

**solidité** [sɔlidite] *nf* solidity; sturdiness

**soliloque** [sɔlilɔk] *nm* soliloquy

**soliste** [sɔlist(ə)] *nm/f* soloist

**solitaire** [sɔlitɛʀ] *adj* (*sans compagnie*) solitary, lonely; (*isolé*) solitary, isolated, lone; (*lieu*) lonely ▷ *nm/f* recluse; loner ▷ *nm* (*diamant, jeu*) solitaire

**solitude** [sɔlityd] *nf* loneliness; (*paix*) solitude

**solive** [sɔliv] *nf* joist

**sollicitations** [sɔlisitasjɔ̃] *nfpl* (*requêtes*) entreaties, appeals; (*attractions*) enticements; (*Tech*) stress *sg*

**solliciter** [sɔlisite] *vt* (*personne*) to appeal to; (*emploi, faveur*) to seek; (*moteur*) to prompt; (*occupations, attractions etc*): **~ qn** to appeal to sb's curiosity *etc*; to entice sb; to make demands on sb's time; **~ qn de faire** to appeal to sb *ou* request sb to do

**sollicitude** [sɔlisityd] *nf* concern

**solo** [sɔlo] *nm* (*pl* **soli** [sɔli]) (*Mus*) solo

**sol-sol** [sɔlsɔl] *adj inv* surface-to-surface

**solstice** [sɔlstis] *nm* solstice; **~ d'hiver/d'été** winter/summer solstice

**solubilisé, e** [sɔlybilize] *adj* soluble

**solubilité** [sɔlybilite] *nf* solubility

**soluble** [sɔlybl(ə)] *adj* (*sucre, cachet*) soluble; (*problème etc*) soluble, solvable

**soluté** [sɔlyte] *nm* solution

**solution** [sɔlysjɔ̃] *nf* solution; **~ de continuité** gap, break; **~ de facilité** easy way out

**solutionner** [sɔlysjɔne] *vt* to solve, find a solution for

**solvabilité** [sɔlvabilite] *nf* solvency

**solvable** [sɔlvabl(ə)] *adj* solvent

**solvant** [sɔlvɑ̃] *nm* solvent

**Somalie** [sɔmali] *nf*: **la ~** Somalia

**somalien, ne** [sɔmaljɛ̃, -ɛn] *adj* Somalian

**somatique** [sɔmatik] *adj* somatic

**sombre** [sɔ̃bʀ(ə)] *adj* dark; (*fig*) sombre, gloomy; (*sinistre*) awful, dreadful

**sombrer** [sɔ̃bʀe] *vi* (*bateau*) to sink, go down; **~ corps et biens** to go down with all hands; **~ dans** (*misère, désespoir*) to sink into

**sommaire** [sɔmɛʀ] *adj* (*simple*) basic; (*expéditif*) summary ▷ *nm* summary; **faire le ~ de** to make a summary of, summarize; **exécution ~** summary execution

**sommairement** [sɔmɛʀmɑ̃] *adv* basically; summarily

**sommation** [sɔmɑsjɔ̃] *nf* (*Jur*) summons *sg*; (*avant de faire feu*) warning

**somme** [sɔm] *nf* (*Math*) sum; (*fig*) amount; (*argent*) sum, amount ▷ *nm*: **faire un ~** to have a (short) nap; **faire la ~ de** to add up; **en ~, ~ toute** all in all

**sommeil** [sɔmɛj] *nm* sleep; **avoir ~** to be sleepy; **avoir le ~ léger** to be a light sleeper; **en ~** (*fig*) dormant

**sommeiller** [sɔmeje] *vi* to doze; (*fig*) to lie dormant

**sommelier** [sɔməlje] *nm* wine waiter

**sommer** [sɔme] *vt*: **~ qn de faire** to command *ou* order sb to do; (*Jur*) to summon sb to do

**sommes** [sɔm] *vb voir* **être**; *voir aussi* **somme**

**sommet** [sɔmɛ] *nm* top; (*d'une montagne*) summit, top; (*fig: de la perfection, gloire*) height; (*Géom: d'angle*) vertex; (*conférence*) summit (conference)

**sommier** [sɔmje] *nm* bed base, bedspring (US); (*Admin: registre*) register; **~ à ressorts** (interior sprung) divan base (*Brit*), box spring (US); **~ à lattes** slatted bed base

**sommité** [sɔmite] *nf* prominent person, leading light

**somnambule** [sɔmnɑbyl] *nm/f* sleepwalker

**somnambulisme** [sɔmnɑbylism(ə)] *nm* sleepwalking

**somnifère** [sɔmnifɛʀ] *nm* sleeping drug; (*comprimé*) sleeping pill *ou* tablet

**somnolence** [sɔmnɔlɑ̃s] *nf* drowsiness

**somnolent, e** [sɔmnɔlɑ̃, -ɑ̃t] *adj* sleepy, drowsy

**S**

**somnoler** [sɔmnɔle] *vi* to doze
**somptuaire** [sɔ̃ptɥɛR] *adj:* **lois ~s** sumptuary laws; **dépenses ~s** extravagant expenditure *sg*
**somptueusement** [sɔ̃ptɥøzmɑ̃] *adv* sumptuously
**somptueux, -euse** [sɔ̃ptɥø, -øz] *adj* sumptuous; *(cadeau)* lavish
**somptuosité** [sɔ̃ptɥozite] *nf* sumptuousness; *(d'un cadeau)* lavishness
**son¹** [sɔ̃], **sa** [sa] *(pl* **ses** [se]) *adj possessif (antécédent humain mâle)* his; (: *femelle)* her; (: *valeur indéfinie)* one's, his (her); (: *non humain)* its; *voir* **il**
**son²** [sɔ̃] *nm* sound; *(de blé etc)* bran; **~ et lumière** *adj inv* son et lumière
**sonar** [sɔnaR] *nm (Navig)* sonar
**sonate** [sɔnat] *nf* sonata
**sondage** [sɔ̃daʒ] *nm (de terrain)* boring, drilling; *(de mer, atmosphère)* sounding; probe; *(enquête)* survey, sounding out of opinion; **~ (d'opinion)** (opinion) poll
**sonde** [sɔ̃d] *nf (Navig)* lead *ou* sounding line; *(Météorologie)* sonde; *(Méd)* probe; catheter; *(d'alimentation)* feeding tube; *(Tech)* borer, driller; *(de forage, sondage)* drill; *(pour fouiller etc)* probe; **~ à avalanche** pole *(for probing snow and locating victims)*; **~ spatiale** probe
**sonder** [sɔ̃de] *vt (Navig)* to sound; *(atmosphère, plaie, bagages etc)* to probe; *(Tech)* to bore, drill; *(fig: personne)* to sound out; (: *opinion)* to probe; **~ le terrain** *(fig)* to see how the land lies
**songe** [sɔ̃ʒ] *nm* dream
**songer** [sɔ̃ʒe] *vi* to dream; **~ à** *(rêver à)* to muse over, think over; *(penser à)* to think of; *(envisager)* to contemplate, think of, consider; **~ que** to consider that; to think that
**songerie** [sɔ̃ʒʀi] *nf* reverie
**songeur, -euse** [sɔ̃ʒœR, -øz] *adj* pensive; **ça me laisse ~** that makes me wonder
**sonnailles** [sɔnaj] *nfpl* jingle of bells
**sonnant, e** [sɔnɑ̃, -ɑ̃t] *adj:* **en espèces ~es et trébuchantes** in coin of the realm; **à huit heures ~es** on the stroke of eight
**sonné, e** [sɔne] *adj (fam)* cracked; *(passé):* **il est midi ~** it's gone twelve; **il a quarante ans bien ~s** he's well into his forties
**sonner** [sɔne] *vi (retentir)* to ring; *(donner une impression)* to sound ▷ *vt (cloche)* to ring; *(glas, tocsin)* to sound; *(portier, infirmière)* to ring for; *(messe)* to ring the bell for; *(fam: choc, coup)* to knock out; **~ du clairon** to sound the bugle; **~ bien/mal/creux** to sound good/bad/hollow; **~ faux** *(instrument)* to sound out of tune; *(rire)* to ring false; **~ les heures** to strike the hours; **minuit vient de ~** midnight has just struck; **~ chez qn** to ring sb's doorbell, ring at sb's door
**sonnerie** [sɔnʀi] *nf (son)* ringing; *(sonnette)* bell; *(mécanisme d'horloge)* striking mechanism; *(de téléphone portable)* ringtone; **~ d'alarme** alarm bell; **~ de clairon** bugle call
**sonnet** [sɔnɛ] *nm* sonnet
**sonnette** [sɔnɛt] *nf* bell; **~ d'alarme** alarm bell;

**~ de nuit** night-bell
**sono** [sɔno] *nf (= sonorisation)* PA (system); *(d'une discothèque)* sound system
**sonore** [sɔnɔR] *adj (voix)* sonorous, ringing; *(salle, métal)* resonant; *(ondes, film, signal)* sound *cpd*; *(Ling)* voiced; **effets ~s** sound effects
**sonorisation** [sɔnɔʀizasjɔ̃] *nf (installations)* public address system; *(d'une discothèque)* sound system
**sonoriser** [sɔnɔʀize] *vt (film, spectacle)* to add the sound track to; *(salle)* to fit with a public address system
**sonorité** [sɔnɔʀite] *nf (de piano, violon)* tone; *(de voix, mot)* sonority; *(d'une salle)* resonance; acoustics *pl*
**sonothèque** [sɔnɔtɛk] *nf* sound library
**sont** [sɔ̃] *vb voir* **être**
**sophisme** [sɔfism(ə)] *nm* sophism
**sophiste** [sɔfist(ə)] *nm/f* sophist
**sophistication** [sɔfistikasjɔ̃] *nf* sophistication
**sophistiqué, e** [sɔfistike] *adj* sophisticated
**soporifique** [sɔpɔʀifik] *adj* soporific
**soprano** [sɔpʀano] *nm/f* soprano
**sorbet** [sɔʀbɛ] *nm* water ice, sorbet
**sorbetière** [sɔʀbətjɛR] *nf* ice-cream maker
**sorbier** [sɔʀbje] *nm* service tree
**sorcellerie** [sɔʀsɛlʀi] *nf* witchcraft *no pl*, sorcery *no pl*
**sorcier, -ière** [sɔʀsje, -jɛR] *nm/f* sorcerer (witch *ou* sorceress) ▷ *adj:* **ce n'est pas ~** *(fam)* it's as easy as pie
**sordide** [sɔʀdid] *adj* sordid; squalid
**Sorlingues** [sɔʀlɛ̃g] *nfpl:* **les (îles) ~** the Scilly Isles, the Isles of Scilly, the Scillies
**sornettes** [sɔʀnɛt] *nfpl* twaddle *sg*
**sort** [sɔʀ] *vb voir* **sortir** ▷ *nm (fortune, destinée)* fate; *(condition, situation)* lot; *(magique):* **jeter un ~** to cast a spell; **un coup du ~** a blow dealt by fate; **le ~ en est jeté** the die is cast; **tirer au ~** to draw lots; **tirer qch au ~** to draw lots for sth
**sortable** [sɔʀtabl(ə)] *adj:* **il n'est pas ~** you can't take him anywhere
**sortant, e** [sɔʀtɑ̃, -ɑ̃t] *vb voir* **sortir** ▷ *adj (numéro)* which comes up *(in a draw etc)*; *(député, président)* outgoing
**sorte** [sɔʀt(ə)] *vb voir* **sortir** ▷ *nf* sort, kind; **une ~ de** a sort of; **de la ~** *adv* in that way; **en quelque ~** in a way; **de ~ à** so as to, in order to; **de (telle) ~ que, en ~ que** *(de manière que)* so that; *(si bien que)* so much so that; **faire en ~ que** to see to it that
**sortie** [sɔʀti] *nf (issue)* way out, exit; *(Mil)* sortie; *(fig: verbale)* outburst; sally; (: *parole incongrue)* odd remark; *(d'un gaz, de l'eau)* outlet; *(promenade)* outing; *(le soir: au restaurant etc)* night out; *(de produits)* export; *(de capitaux)* outflow; *(Comm: somme):* **~s** items of expenditure; outgoings; *(Inform)* output; *(d'imprimante)* printout; **à sa ~** as he went out *ou* left; **à la ~ de l'école/l'usine** *(moment)* after school/work; when school/the factory comes out; *(lieu)* at the school/factory gates; **à la ~ de ce nouveau modèle** when this

new model comes (ou came) out, when they bring (ou brought) out this new model; **~ de bain** (*vêtement*) bathrobe; **"~ de camions"** "vehicle exit"; **~ papier** hard copy; **~ de secours** emergency exit

**sortilège** [sɔʀtilɛʒ] *nm* (magic) spell

**sortir** [sɔʀtiʀ] *vi* (*gén*) to come out; (*partir, se promener, aller au spectacle etc*) to go out; (*bourgeon, plante, numéro gagnant*) to come up ▷ *vt* (*gén*) to take out; (*produit, ouvrage, modèle*) to bring out; (*boniments, incongruités*) to come out with; (*Inform*) to output; (: *sur papier*) to print out; (*fam: expulser*) to throw out ▷ *nm*: **au ~ de l'hiver/l'enfance** as winter/childhood nears its end; **~ qch de** to take sth out of; **~ qn d'embarras** to get sb out of trouble; **~ de** (*gén*) to leave; (*endroit*) to go (ou come) out of, leave; (*rainure etc*) to come out of; (*maladie*) to get over; (*époque*) to get through; (*cadre, compétence*) to be outside; (*provenir de: famille etc*) to come from; **~ de table** to leave the table; **~ du système** (*Inform*) to log out; **~ de ses gonds** (*fig*) to fly off the handle; **se ~ de** (*affaire, situation*) to get out of; **s'en ~** (*malade*) to pull through; (*d'une difficulté etc*) to come through all right; to get through, be able to manage

**SOS** *sigle m* mayday, SOS

**sosie** [sɔzi] *nm* double

**sot, sotte** [so, sɔt] *adj* silly, foolish ▷ *nm/f* fool

**sottement** [sɔtmɑ̃] *adv* foolishly

**sottise** [sɔtiz] *nf* silliness *no pl*, foolishness *no pl*; (*propos, acte*) silly ou foolish thing (to do ou say)

**sou** [su] *nm*: **près de ses ~s** tight-fisted; **sans le ~ penniless**; **~ à ~** penny by penny; **pas un ~ de bon sens** not a scrap ou an ounce of good sense; **de quatre ~s** worthless

**souahéli, e** [swaeli] *adj* Swahili ▷ *nm* (*Ling*) Swahili

**soubassement** [subɑsmɑ̃] *nm* base

**soubresaut** [subʀəso] *nm* (*de peur etc*) start; (*cahot: d'un véhicule*) jolt

**soubrette** [subʀɛt] *nf* soubrette, maidservant

**souche** [suʃ] *nf* (*d'arbre*) stump; (*de carnet*) counterfoil (*Brit*), stub; **dormir comme une ~** to sleep like a log; **de vieille ~** of old stock

**souci** [susi] *nm* (*inquiétude*) worry; (*préoccupation*) concern; (*Bot*) marigold; **se faire du ~** to worry; **avoir (le) ~ de** to have concern for; **par ~ de** for the sake of, out of concern for

**soucier** [susje]: **se ~ de** *vt* to care about

**soucieux, -euse** [susjø, -øz] *adj* concerned, worried; **~ de** concerned about; **peu ~ de/que** caring little about/whether

**soucoupe** [sukup] *nf* saucer; **~ volante** flying saucer

**soudain, e** [sudɛ̃, -ɛn] *adj* (*douleur, mort*) sudden ▷ *adv* suddenly, all of a sudden

**soudainement** [sudɛnmɑ̃] *adv* suddenly

**soudaineté** [sudɛnte] *nf* suddenness

**Soudan** [sudɑ̃] *nm*: **le ~** the Sudan

**soudanais, e** [sudanɛ, -ɛz] *adj* Sudanese

**soude** [sud] *nf* soda

**soudé, e** [sude] *adj* (*fig: pétales, organes*) joined

(together)

**souder** [sude] *vt* (*avec fil à souder*) to solder; (*par soudure autogène*) to weld; (*fig*) to bind ou knit together; to fuse (together); **se souder** *vi* (*os*) to knit (together)

**soudeur, -euse** [sudœʀ, -øz] *nm/f* (*ouvrier*) welder

**soudoyer** [sudwaje] *vt* (*péj*) to bribe, buy over

**soudure** [sudyʀ] *nf* soldering; welding; (*joint*) soldered joint; weld; **faire la ~** (*Comm*) to fill a gap; (*fig: assurer une transition*) to bridge the gap

**souffert, e** [sufɛʀ, -ɛʀt(ə)] *pp de* **souffrir**

**soufflage** [suflaʒ] *nm* (*du verre*) glass-blowing

**souffle** [sufl(ə)] *nm* (*en expirant*) breath; (*en soufflant*) puff, blow; (*respiration*) breathing; (*d'explosion, de ventilateur*) blast; (*du vent*) blowing; (*fig*) inspiration; **retenir son ~** to hold one's breath; **avoir du/manquer de ~** to have a lot of puff/be short of breath; **être à bout de ~** to be out of breath; **avoir le ~ court** to be short-winded; **un ~ d'air** ou **de vent** a breath of air, a puff of wind; **~ au cœur** (*Méd*) heart murmur

**soufflé, e** [sufle] *adj* (*Culin*) souffléd; (*fam: ahuri, stupéfié*) staggered ▷ *nm* (*Culin*) soufflé

**souffler** [sufle] *vi* (*gén*) to blow; (*haleter*) to puff (and blow) ▷ *vt* (*feu, bougie*) to blow out; (*chasser: poussière etc*) to blow away; (*Tech: verre*) to blow; (*explosion*) to destroy (with its blast); (*dire*): **~ qch à qn** to whisper sth to sb; (*fam: voler*): **~ qch à qn** to pinch sth from sb; **~ son rôle à qn** to prompt sb; **ne pas ~ mot** not to breathe a word; **laisser ~ qn** (*fig*) to give sb a breather

**soufflet** [sufle] *nm* (*instrument*) bellows *pl*; (*entre wagons*) vestibule; (*Couture*) gusset; (*gifle*) slap (in the face)

**souffleur, -euse** [suflœʀ, -øz] *nm/f* (*Théât*) prompter; (*Tech*) glass-blower

**souffrance** [sufʀɑ̃s] *nf* suffering; **en ~** (*marchandise*) awaiting delivery; (*affaire*) pending

**souffrant, e** [sufʀɑ̃, -ɑ̃t] *adj* unwell

**souffre-douleur** [sufʀədulœʀ] *nm inv* whipping boy (*Brit*), butt, underdog

**souffreteux, -euse** [sufʀətø, -øz] *adj* sickly

**souffrir** [sufʀiʀ] *vi* to suffer; (*éprouver des douleurs*) to be in pain ▷ *vt* to suffer, endure; (*supporter*) to bear, stand; (*admettre: exception etc*) to allow ou admit of; **~ de** (*maladie, froid*) to suffer from; **~ des dents** to have trouble with one's teeth; **ne pas pouvoir ~ qch/que ...** not to be able to endure ou bear sth/that ...; **faire ~ qn** (*personne*) to make sb suffer; (: *dents, blessure etc*) to hurt sb

**soufre** [sufʀ(ə)] *nm* sulphur (*Brit*), sulfur (*US*)

**soufrer** [sufʀe] *vt* (*vignes*) to treat with sulphur ou sulfur

**souhait** [swɛ] *nm* wish; **tous nos ~s de** good wishes ou our best wishes for; **riche** *etc* **à ~** as rich *etc* as one could wish; **à vos ~s!** bless you!

**souhaitable** [swɛtabl(ə)] *adj* desirable

**souhaiter** [swete] *vt* to wish for; **~ le bonjour à qn** to bid sb good day; **~ la bonne année à qn** to wish sb a happy New Year; **il est à ~ que** it is to

**S**

391

be hoped that

**souiller** [suje] vt to dirty, soil; (fig) to sully, tarnish

**souillure** [sujyʀ] nf stain

**soûl, e** [su, sul] adj drunk; (fig): **~ de musique/ plaisirs** drunk with music/pleasure ▷ nm: **tout son ~** to one's heart's content

**soulagement** [sulaʒmɑ̃] nm relief

**soulager** [sulaʒe] vt to relieve; **~ qn de** to relieve sb of

**soûler** [sule] vt: **~ qn** to get sb drunk; (boisson) to make sb drunk; (fig) to make sb's head spin ou reel; **se soûler** to get drunk; **se ~ de** (fig) to intoxicate o.s with

**soûlerie** [sulʀi] nf (péj) drunken binge

**soulèvement** [sulɛvmɑ̃] nm uprising; (Géo) upthrust

**soulever** [sulve] vt to lift; (vagues, poussière) to send up; (peuple) to stir up (to revolt); (enthousiasme) to arouse; (question, débat, protestations, difficultés) to raise; **se soulever** vi (peuple) to rise up; (personne couchée) to lift o.s. up; (couvercle etc) to lift; **cela me soulève le cœur** it makes me feel sick

**soulier** [sulje] nm shoe; **~s bas** low-heeled shoes; **~s plats/à talons** flat/heeled shoes

**souligner** [suliɲe] vt to underline; (fig) to emphasize, stress

**soumettre** [sumɛtʀ(ə)] vt (pays) to subject, subjugate; (rebelles) to put down, subdue; **~ qn/ qch à** to subject sb/sth to; **~ qch à qn** (projet etc) to submit sth to sb; **se ~ (à)** (se rendre, obéir) to submit (to); **se ~ à** (formalités etc) to submit to; (régime etc) to submit o.s. to

**soumis, e** [sumi, -iz] pp de **soumettre** ▷ adj submissive; **revenus ~ à l'impôt** taxable income

**soumission** [sumisjɔ̃] nf (voir se soumettre) submission; (docilité) submissiveness; (Comm) tender

**soumissionner** [sumisjɔne] vt (Comm: travaux) to bid for, tender for

**soupape** [supap] nf valve; **~ de sûreté** safety valve

**soupçon** [supsɔ̃] nm suspicion; (petite quantité): **un ~ de** a hint ou touch of; **avoir ~ de** to suspect; **au dessus de tout ~** above (all) suspicion

**soupçonner** [supsɔne] vt to suspect; **~ qn de qch/d'être** to suspect sb of sth/of being

**soupçonneux, -euse** [supsɔnø, -øz] adj suspicious

**soupe** [sup] nf soup; **~ au lait** adj inv quick-tempered; **~ à l'oignon/de poisson** onion/fish soup; **~ populaire** soup kitchen

**soupente** [supɑ̃t] nf (mansarde) attic; (placard) cupboard (Brit) ou closet (US) under the stairs

**souper** [supe] vi to have supper ▷ nm supper; **avoir soupé de** (fam) to be sick and tired of

**soupeser** [supəze] vt to weigh in one's hand(s), feel the weight of; (fig) to weigh up

**soupière** [supjɛʀ] nf (soup) tureen

**soupir** [supiʀ] nm sigh; (Mus) crotchet rest (Brit),

quarter note rest (US); **rendre le dernier ~** to breathe one's last

**soupirail, -aux** [supiʀaj, -o] nm (small) basement window

**soupirant** [supiʀɑ̃] nm (péj) suitor, wooer

**soupirer** [supiʀe] vi to sigh; **~ après qch** to yearn for sth

**souple** [supl(ə)] adj supple; (col) soft; (fig: règlement, caractère) flexible; (: démarche, taille) lithe, supple

**souplesse** [suplɛs] nf suppleness; flexibility

**source** [suʀs(ə)] nf (point d'eau) spring; (d'un cours d'eau, fig) source; **prendre sa ~ à/dans** (cours d'eau) to have its source at/in; **tenir qch de bonne ~/de ~ sûre** to have sth on good authority/from a reliable source; **~ thermale/ d'eau minérale** hot ou thermal/mineral spring

**sourcier, -ière** [suʀsje, -jɛʀ] nm water diviner

**sourcil** [suʀsij] nm (eye)brow

**sourcilière** [suʀsiljɛʀ] adj f voir **arcade**

**sourciller** [suʀsije] vi: **sans ~** without turning a hair ou batting an eyelid

**sourcilleux, -euse** [suʀsijø, -øz] adj (hautain, sévère) haughty, supercilious; (pointilleux) finicky, pernickety

**sourd, e** [suʀ, suʀd(ə)] adj deaf; (bruit, voix) muffled; (couleur) muted; (douleur) dull; (lutte) silent, hidden; (Ling) voiceless ▷ nm/f deaf person; **être ~ à** to be deaf to

**sourdement** [suʀdəmɑ̃] adv (avec un bruit sourd) dully; (secrètement) silently

**sourdine** [suʀdin] nf (Mus) mute; **en ~** adv softly, quietly; **mettre une ~ à** (fig) to tone down

**sourd-muet, sourde-muette** [suʀmyɛ, suʀdmyɛt] adj deaf-and-dumb ▷ nm/f deaf-mute

**sourdre** [suʀdʀ(ə)] vi (eau) to spring up; (fig) to rise

**souriant, e** [suʀjɑ̃, -ɑ̃t] vb voir **sourire** ▷ adj cheerful

**souricière** [suʀisjɛʀ] nf mousetrap; (fig) trap

**sourie** etc [suʀi] vb voir **sourire**

**sourire** [suʀiʀ] nm smile ▷ vi to smile; **~ à qn** to smile at sb; (fig) to appeal to sb; (: chance) to smile on sb; **faire un ~ à qn** to give sb a smile; **garder le ~** to keep smiling

**souris** [suʀi] nf (aussi Inform) mouse

**sournois, e** [suʀnwa, -waz] adj deceitful, underhand

**sournoisement** [suʀnwazmɑ̃] adv deceitfully

**sournoiserie** [suʀnwazʀi] nf deceitfulness, underhandedness

**sous** [su] prép (gén) under; **~ la pluie/le soleil** in the rain/sunshine; **~ mes yeux** before my eyes; **~ terre** adj, adv underground; **~ vide** adj, adv vacuum-packed; **~ l'influence/l'action de** under the influence of/by the action of; **~ antibiotiques/perfusion** on antibiotics/a drip; **~ cet angle/ce rapport** from this angle/ in this respect; **~ peu** adv shortly, before long

**sous...** [su, suz + vowel] préfixe sub-; under...

**sous-alimentation** [suzalimãtasjɔ̃] nf undernourishment

**sous-alimenté, e** [suzalimãte] adj undernourished

**sous-bois** [subwa] nm inv undergrowth

**sous-catégorie** [sukategɔʀi] nf subcategory

**sous-chef** [suʃɛf] nm deputy chief, second in command; **~ de bureau** deputy head clerk

**sous-comité** [sukɔmite] nm subcommittee

**sous-commission** [sukɔmisjɔ̃] nf subcommittee

**sous-continent** [sukɔ̃tinã] nm subcontinent

**sous-couche** [sukuʃ] nf (de peinture) undercoat

**souscripteur, -trice** [suskʀiptœʀ, -tʀis] nm/f subscriber

**souscription** [suskʀipsjɔ̃] nf subscription; **offert en ~** available on subscription

**souscrire** [suskʀiʀ]: **~ à** vt to subscribe to

**sous-cutané, e** [sukytane] adj subcutaneous

**sous-développé, e** [sudevlɔpe] adj underdeveloped

**sous-développement** [sudevlɔpmã] nm underdevelopment

**sous-directeur, -trice** [sudiʀɛktœʀ, -tʀis] nm/f assistant manager/manageress, submanager/manageress

**sous-emploi** [suzãplwa] nm underemployment

**sous-employé, e** [suzãplwaje] adj underemployed

**sous-ensemble** [suzãsãbl(ə)] nm subset

**sous-entendre** [suzãtãdʀ(ə)] vt to imply, infer

**sous-entendu, e** [suzãtãdy] adj implied; (Ling) understood ▷ nm innuendo, insinuation

**sous-équipé, e** [suzekipe] adj under-equipped; **~ en infrastructures industrielles** (Écon: pays, région) with an insufficient industrial infrastructure

**sous-estimer** [suzɛstime] vt to underestimate

**sous-exploiter** [suzɛksplwate] vt to underexploit

**sous-exposer** [suzɛkspoze] vt to underexpose

**sous-fifre** [sufifʀ(ə)] nm (péj) underling

**sous-groupe** [sugʀup] nm subgroup

**sous-homme** [suzɔm] nm sub-human

**sous-jacent, e** [suʒasã, -ãt] adj underlying

**sous-lieutenant** [suljøtnã] nm sub-lieutenant

**sous-locataire** [sulɔkatɛʀ] nm/f subtenant

**sous-location** [sulɔkasjɔ̃] nf subletting

**sous-louer** [sulwe] vt to sublet

**sous-main** [sumɛ̃] nm inv desk blotter; **en ~** adv secretly

**sous-marin, e** [sumaʀɛ̃, -in] adj (flore, volcan) submarine; (navigation, pêche, explosif) underwater ▷ nm submarine

**sous-médicalisé, e** [sumedikalize] adj lacking adequate medical care

**sous-nappe** [sunap] nf undercloth

**sous-officier** [suzɔfisje] nm = non-commissioned officer (NCO)

**sous-ordre** [suzɔʀdʀ(ə)] nm subordinate; **créancier en ~** creditor's creditor

**sous-payé, e** [supeje] adj underpaid

**sous-préfecture** [supʀefɛktyʀ] nf sub-prefecture

**sous-préfet** [supʀefɛ] nm sub-prefect

**sous-production** [supʀɔdyksjɔ̃] nf underproduction

**sous-produit** [supʀɔdɥi] nm by-product; (fig: péj) pale imitation

**sous-programme** [supʀɔgʀam] nm (Inform) subroutine

**sous-pull** [supul] nm thin poloneck sweater

**sous-secrétaire** [susəkʀetɛʀ] nm: **~ d'État** Under-Secretary of State

**soussigné, e** [susiɲe] adj: **je ~** I the undersigned

**sous-sol** [susɔl] nm basement; (Géo) subsoil

**sous-tasse** [sutas] nf saucer

**sous-tendre** [sutãdʀ(ə)] vt to underlie

**sous-titre** [sutitʀ(ə)] nm subtitle

**sous-titré, e** [sutitʀe] adj with subtitles

**soustraction** [sustʀaksjɔ̃] nf subtraction

**soustraire** [sustʀɛʀ] vt to subtract, take away; (dérober): **~ qch à qn** to remove sth from sb; **~ qn à** (danger) to shield sb from; **se ~ à** (autorité, obligation, devoir) to elude, escape from

**sous-traitance** [sutʀɛtãs(ə)] nf subcontracting

**sous-traitant** [sutʀɛtã] nm subcontractor

**sous-traiter** [sutʀɛte] vt, vi to subcontract

**soustrayais** etc [sustʀɛje] vb voir **soustraire**

**sous-verre** [suvɛʀ] nm inv glass mount

**sous-vêtement** [suvɛtmã] nm undergarment, item of underwear; **sous-vêtements** nmpl underwear sg

**soutane** [sutan] nf cassock, soutane

**soute** [sut] nf hold; **~ à bagages** baggage hold

**soutenable** [sutnabl(ə)] adj (opinion) tenable, defensible

**soutenance** [sutnãs] nf: **~ de thèse** = viva (voce)

**soutènement** [sutɛnmã] nm: **mur de ~** retaining wall

**souteneur** [sutnœʀ] nm procurer

**soutenir** [sutniʀ] vt to support; (assaut, choc, regard) to stand up to, withstand; (intérêt, effort) to keep up; (assurer): **~ que** to maintain that; **se soutenir** (dans l'eau etc) to hold o.s. up; (être soutenable: point de vue) to be tenable; (s'aider mutuellement) to stand by each other; **~ la comparaison avec** to bear ou stand comparison with; **~ le regard de qn** to be able to look sb in the face

**soutenu, e** [sutny] pp de **soutenir** ▷ adj (efforts) sustained, unflagging; (style) elevated; (couleur) strong

**souterrain, e** [sutɛʀɛ̃, -ɛn] adj underground; (fig) subterranean ▷ nm underground passage

**soutien** [sutjɛ̃] nm support; **apporter son ~ à** to lend one's support to; **~ de famille** breadwinner

**soutiendrai** etc [sutjɛ̃dʀe] vb voir **soutenir**

**soutien-gorge** [sutjɛ̃gɔʀʒ(ə)] (pl **soutiens-gorge**) nm bra; (de maillot de bain) top

**soutiens** [sutjɛ̃], **soutint** etc [sutɛ̃] vb voir **soutenir**

**soutirer** [sutiʀe] vt: **~ qch à qn** to squeeze ou get

393

sth out of sb

**souvenance** [suvnɑ̃s] *nf*: **avoir ~ de** to recollect

**souvenir** [suvniʀ] *nm* (*réminiscence*) memory; (*cadeau*) souvenir, keepsake; (*de voyage*) souvenir ▷ *vb*: **se ~ de** *vt* to remember; **se ~ que** to remember that; **garder le ~ de** to retain the memory of; **en ~ de** in memory *ou* remembrance of; **avec mes affectueux/ meilleurs ~s**, ... with love from, .../regards, ...

**souvent** [suvɑ̃] *adv* often; **peu ~** seldom, infrequently; **le plus ~** more often than not, most often

**souvenu, e** [suvəny] *pp de* **se souvenir**

**souverain, e** [suvʀɛ̃, -ɛn] *adj* sovereign; (*fig: mépris*) supreme ▷ *nm/f* sovereign, monarch

**souverainement** [suvʀɛnmɑ̃] *adv* (*sans appel*) with sovereign power; (*extrêmement*) supremely, intensely

**souveraineté** [suvʀɛnte] *nf* sovereignty

**souviendrai** [suvjɛ̃dʀe], **souviens** [suvjɛ̃], **souvint** *etc* [suvɛ̃] *vb voir* **se souvenir**

**soviétique** [sɔvjetik] *adj* Soviet ▷ *nm/f*: **Soviétique** Soviet citizen

**soviétologue** [sɔvjetɔlɔg] *nm/f* Kremlinologist

**soyeux, -euse** [swajø, -øz] *adj* silky

**soyez** *etc* [swaje] *vb voir* **être**

**soyons** *etc* [swajɔ̃] *vb voir* **être**

**SPA** *sigle f* (= *Société protectrice des animaux*) ≈ RSPCA (Brit), ≈ SPCA (US)

**spacieux, -euse** [spasjø, -øz] *adj* spacious; roomy

**spaciosité** [spasjɔzite] *nf* spaciousness

**spaghettis** [spageti] *nmpl* spaghetti *sg*

**sparadrap** [spaʀadʀa] *nm* adhesive *ou* sticking (Brit) plaster, bandaid® (US)

**Sparte** [spaʀt(ə)] *nf* Sparta

**spartiate** [spaʀsjat] *adj* Spartan; **spartiates** *nfpl* (*sandales*) Roman sandals

**spasme** [spazm(ə)] *nm* spasm

**spasmodique** [spazmɔdik] *adj* spasmodic

**spatial, e, -aux** [spasjal, -o] *adj* (*Aviat*) space *cpd*; (*Psych*) spatial

**spatule** [spatyl] *nf* (*ustensile*) slice; spatula; (*bout*) tip

**speaker, ine** [spikœʀ, -kʀin] *nm/f* announcer

**spécial, e, -aux** [spesjal, -o] *adj* special; (*bizarre*) peculiar

**spécialement** [spesjalmɑ̃] *adv* especially, particularly; (*tout exprès*) specially; **pas ~** not particularly

**spécialisation** [spesjalizasjɔ̃] *nf* specialization

**spécialisé, e** [spesjalize] *adj* specialised; **ordinateur ~** dedicated computer

**spécialiser** [spesjalize]: **se spécialiser** *vi* to specialize

**spécialiste** [spesjalist(ə)] *nm/f* specialist

**spécialité** [spesjalite] *nf* speciality; (*Scol*) special field; **~ pharmaceutique** patent medicine

**spécieux, -euse** [spesjø, -øz] *adj* specious

**spécification** [spesifikasjɔ̃] *nf* specification

**spécificité** [spesifisite] *nf* specificity

**spécifier** [spesifje] *vt* to specify, state

**spécifique** [spesifik] *adj* specific

**spécifiquement** [spesifikmɑ̃] *adv* (*typiquement*) typically; (*tout exprès*) specifically

**spécimen** [spesimɛn] *nm* specimen; (*revue etc*) specimen *ou* sample copy

**spectacle** [spɛktakl(ə)] *nm* (*tableau, scène*) sight; (*représentation*) show; (*industrie*) show business, entertainment; **se donner en ~** (*péj*) to make a spectacle *ou* an exhibition of o.s; **pièce/revue à grand ~** spectacular (play/revue); **au ~ de ...** at the sight of ...

**spectaculaire** [spɛktakylɛʀ] *adj* spectacular

**spectateur, -trice** [spɛktatœʀ, -tʀis] *nm/f* (*Ciné etc*) member of the audience; (*Sport*) spectator; (*d'un événement*) onlooker, witness

**spectre** [spɛktʀ(ə)] *nm* (*fantôme, fig*) spectre; (*Physique*) spectrum; **~ solaire** solar spectrum

**spéculateur, -trice** [spekylatœʀ, -tʀis] *nm/f* speculator

**spéculatif, -ive** [spekylatif, -iv] *adj* speculative

**spéculation** [spekylasjɔ̃] *nf* speculation

**spéculer** [spekyle] *vi* to speculate; **~ sur** (*Comm*) to speculate in; (*réfléchir*) to speculate on; (*tabler sur*) to bank *ou* rely on

**spéléologie** [speleɔlɔʒi] *nf* (*étude*) speleology; (*activité*) potholing

**spéléologue** [speleɔlɔg] *nm/f* speleologist; potholer

**spermatozoïde** [spɛʀmatozɔid] *nm* sperm, spermatozoon

**sperme** [spɛʀm(ə)] *nm* semen, sperm

**spermicide** [spɛʀmisid] *adj, nm* spermicide

**sphère** [sfɛʀ] *nf* sphere

**sphérique** [sfeʀik] *adj* spherical

**sphincter** [sfɛ̃ktɛʀ] *nm* sphincter

**sphinx** [sfɛ̃ks] *nm inv* sphinx; (*Zool*) hawkmoth

**spiral, -aux** [spiʀal, -o] *nm* hairspring

**spirale** [spiʀal] *nf* spiral; **en ~** in spiral; (*d'une spirale*) whorl

**spire** [spiʀ] *nf* (*d'une spirale*) turn; (*d'une coquille*) whorl

**spiritisme** [spiʀitism(ə)] *nm* spiritualism, spiritism

**spirituel, le** [spiʀitɥɛl] *adj* spiritual; (*fin, piquant*) witty; **musique ~le** sacred music; **concert ~** concert of sacred music

**spirituellement** [spiʀitɥɛlmɑ̃] *adv* spiritually; wittily

**spiritueux** [spiʀitɥø] *nm* spirit

**splendeur** [splɑ̃dœʀ] *nf* splendour (Brit), splendor (US)

**splendide** [splɑ̃did] *adj* splendid, magnificent

**spolier** [spɔlje] *vt*: **~ qn (de)** to despoil sb (of)

**spongieux, -euse** [spɔ̃ʒjø, -øz] *adj* spongy

**sponsor** [spɔ̃sɔʀ] *nm* sponsor

**sponsoriser** [spɔ̃sɔʀize] *vt* to sponsor

**spontané, e** [spɔ̃tane] *adj* spontaneous

**spontanéité** [spɔ̃taneite] *nf* spontaneity

**spontanément** [spɔ̃tanemɑ̃] *adv* spontaneously

**sporadique** [spɔʀadik] *adj* sporadic

**sporadiquement** [spɔʀadikmɑ̃] *adv*

sporadically

**sport** [spɔʀ] *nm* sport ▷ *adj inv* (*vêtement*) casual; (*fair-play*) sporting; **faire du** ~ to do sport; ~ **individuel/d'équipe** individual/team sport; ~ **de combat** combative sport; **~s d'hiver** winter sports

**sportif, -ive** [spɔʀtif, -iv] *adj* (*journal, association, épreuve*) sports *cpd*; (*allure, démarche*) athletic; (*attitude, esprit*) sporting; **les résultats ~s** the sports results

**sportivement** [spɔʀtivmɑ̃] *adv* sportingly

**sportivité** [spɔʀtivite] *nf* sportsmanship

**spot** [spɔt] *nm* (*lampe*) spot(light); (*annonce*): ~ **(publicitaire)** commercial (break)

**spray** [spʀɛ] *nm* spray, aerosol

**sprint** [spʀint] *nm* sprint; **piquer un** ~ to put on a (final) spurt

**sprinter** *nm* [spʀintœʀ] sprinter ▷ *vi* [spʀinte] to sprint

**squale** [skwal] *nm* (*type of*) shark

**square** [skwaʀ] *nm* public garden(s)

**squash** [skwaʃ] *nm* squash

**squat** [skwat] *nm* (*lieu*) squat

**squatter** *nm* [skwatœʀ] squatter ▷ *vt* [skwate] to squat

**squelette** [skəlɛt] *nm* skeleton

**squelettique** [skəletik] *adj* scrawny; (*fig*) skimpy

**SRAS** *sigle m* (= *syndrome respiratoire aigu sévère*) SARS

**Sri Lanka** [sʀilɑ̃ka] *nm* Sri Lanka

**sri-lankais, e** [sʀilɑ̃kɛ, -ɛz] *adj* Sri-Lankan

**SS** *sigle f* = **sécurité sociale**; (= *Sa Sainteté*) HH

**ss** *abr* = **sous**

**SSR** *sigle f* (= *Société suisse romande*) *the Swiss French-language broadcasting company*

**St, Ste** *abr* (= *Saint(e)*) St

**stabilisateur, -trice** [stabilizatœʀ, -tʀis] *adj* stabilizing ▷ *nm* stabilizer; (*d'un véhicule*) anti-roll device; (*d'un avion*) tailplane

**stabiliser** [stabilize] *vt* to stabilize; (*terrain*) to consolidate

**stabilité** [stabilite] *nf* stability

**stable** [stabl(ə)] *adj* stable, steady

**stade** [stad] *nm* (*Sport*) stadium; (*phase, niveau*) stage

**stadier** [stadje] *nm* steward (*working in a stadium*), stage

**stage** [staʒ] *nm* training period; training course; (*d'avocat stagiaire*) articles *pl*; ~ **en entreprise** work experience placement

**stagiaire** [staʒjɛʀ] *nm/f, adj* trainee (*cpd*)

**stagnant, e** [stagnɑ̃, -ɑ̃t] *adj* stagnant

**stagnation** [stagnasjɔ̃] *nf* stagnation

**stagner** [stagne] *vi* to stagnate

**stalactite** [stalaktit] *nf* stalactite

**stalagmite** [stalagmit] *nf* stalagmite

**stalle** [stal] *nf* stall, box

**stand** [stɑ̃d] *nm* (*d'exposition*) stand; (*de foire*) stall; ~ **de tir** (*à la foire, Sport*) shooting range; ~ **de ravitaillement** pit

**standard** [stɑ̃daʀ] *adj inv* standard ▷ *nm* (*type,*

*norme*) standard; (*téléphonique*) switchboard

**standardisation** [stɑ̃daʀdizasjɔ̃] *nf* standardization

**standardiser** [stɑ̃daʀdize] *vt* to standardize

**standardiste** [stɑ̃daʀdist(ə)] *nm/f* switchboard operator

**standing** [stɑ̃diŋ] *nm* standing; **immeuble de grand** ~ block of luxury flats (*Brit*), condo(minium) (*US*)

**star** [staʀ] *nf* star

**starlette** [staʀlɛt] *nf* starlet

**starter** [staʀtɛʀ] *nm* (*Auto*) choke; (*Sport: personne*) starter; **mettre le** ~ to pull out the choke

**station** [stasjɔ̃] *nf* station; (*de bus*) stop; (*de villégiature*) resort; (*posture*): **la** ~ **debout** standing, an upright posture; ~ **balnéaire** seaside resort; ~ **de graissage** lubrication bay; ~ **de lavage** carwash; ~ **de ski** ski resort; ~ **de sports d'hiver** winter sports resort; ~ **de taxis** taxi rank (*Brit*) *ou* stand (*US*); ~ **thermale** thermal spa; ~ **de travail** workstation

**stationnaire** [stasjɔnɛʀ] *adj* stationary

**stationnement** [stasjɔnmɑ̃] *nm* parking; **zone de** ~ **interdit** no parking area; ~ **alterné** parking on alternate sides

**stationner** [stasjɔne] *vi* to park

**station-service** [stasjɔ̃sɛʀvis] *nf* service station

**statique** [statik] *adj* static

**statisticien, ne** [statistisjɛ̃, -ɛn] *nm/f* statistician

**statistique** [statistik] *nf* (*science*) statistics *sg*; (*rapport, étude*) statistic ▷ *adj* statistical; **statistiques** *nfpl* (*données*) statistics *pl*

**statistiquement** [statistikmɑ̃] *adv* statistically

**statue** [staty] *nf* statue

**statuer** [statɥe] *vi*: ~ **sur** to rule on, give a ruling on

**statuette** [statɥɛt] *nf* statuette

**statu quo** [statykwo] *nm* status quo

**stature** [statyʀ] *nf* stature; **de haute** ~ of great stature

**statut** [staty] *nm* status; **statuts** *nmpl* (*Jur, Admin*) statutes

**statutaire** [statytɛʀ] *adj* statutory

**Sté** *abr* (= *société*) soc

**steak** [stɛk] *nm* steak

**stèle** [stɛl] *nf* stela, stele

**stellaire** [stelɛʀ] *adj* stellar

**stencil** [stɛnsil] *nm* stencil

**sténo** [steno] *nm/f* (*aussi*: **sténographe**) shorthand typist (*Brit*), stenographer (*US*) ▷ *nf* (*aussi*: **sténographie**) shorthand; **prendre en** ~ to take down in shorthand

**sténodactylo** [stenodaktilo] *nm/f* shorthand typist (*Brit*), stenographer (*US*)

**sténodactylographie** [stenodaktilografi] *nf* shorthand typing (*Brit*), stenography (*US*)

**sténographe** [stenograf] *nm/f* shorthand typist (*Brit*), stenographer (*US*)

**sténographie** [stenografi] *nf* shorthand; **prendre en** ~ to take down in shorthand

**sténographier** [stenɔgʀafje] vt to take down in shorthand

**sténographique** [stenɔgʀafik] adj shorthand cpd

**stentor** [stɑ̃tɔʀ] nm: **voix de** ~ stentorian voice

**step®** [stɛp] nm step aerobics sg®, step Reebok®

**stéphanois, e** [stefanwa, -waz] adj of ou from Saint-Étienne

**steppe** [stɛp] nf steppe

**stère** [stɛʀ] nm stere

**stéréo** nf (aussi: **stéréophonie**) stereo; **émission en** ~ stereo broadcast ▷ adj (aussi: **stéréophonique**) stereo

**stéréophonie** [steʀeɔfɔni] nf stereo(phony); **émission en** ~ stereo broadcast

**stéréophonique** [steʀeɔfɔnik] adj stereo(phonic)

**stéréoscope** [steʀeɔskɔp] nm stereoscope

**stéréoscopique** [steʀeɔskɔpik] adj stereoscopic

**stéréotype** [steʀeɔtip] nm stereotype

**stéréotypé, e** [steʀeɔtipe] adj stereotyped

**stérile** [steʀil] adj sterile; (terre) barren; (fig) fruitless, futile

**stérilement** [steʀilmɑ̃] adv fruitlessly

**stérilet** [steʀilɛ] nm coil, loop

**stérilisateur** [steʀilizatœʀ] nm sterilizer

**stérilisation** [steʀilizasjɔ̃] nf sterilization

**stériliser** [steʀilize] vt to sterilize

**stérilité** [steʀilite] nf sterility

**sternum** [stɛʀnɔm] nm breastbone, sternum

**stéthoscope** [stetɔskɔp] nm stethoscope

**stick** [stik] nm stick

**stigmates** [stigmat] nmpl scars, marks; (Rel) stigmata pl

**stigmatiser** [stigmatize] vt to denounce, stigmatize

**stimulant, e** [stimylɑ̃, -ɑ̃t] adj stimulating ▷ nm (Méd) stimulant; (fig) stimulus, incentive

**stimulateur** [stimylatœʀ] nm: ~ **cardiaque** pacemaker

**stimulation** [stimylɑsjɔ̃] nf stimulation

**stimuler** [stimyle] vt to stimulate

**stimulus** [stimylys] nm (pl **stimuli** [stimyli]) stimulus

**stipulation** [stipylɑsjɔ̃] nf stipulation

**stipuler** [stipyle] vt to stipulate, specify

**stock** [stɔk] nm stock; **en** ~ in stock

**stockage** [stɔkaʒ] nm stocking; storage

**stocker** [stɔke] vt to stock; (déchets) to store

**Stockholm** [stɔkɔlm] n Stockholm

**stockiste** [stɔkist(ə)] nm stockist

**stoïcisme** [stɔisism(ə)] nm stoicism

**stoïque** [stɔik] adj stoic, stoical

**stoïquement** [stɔikmɑ̃] adv stoically

**stomacal, e, -aux** [stɔmakal, -o] adj gastric, stomach cpd

**stomatologie** [stɔmatɔlɔʒi] nf stomatology

**stomatologue** [stɔmatɔlɔg] nm/f stomatologist

**stop** [stɔp] nm (Auto: écriteau) stop sign; (: signal) brake-light; (dans un télégramme) stop ▷ excl stop!

**stoppage** [stɔpaʒ] nm invisible mending

**stopper** [stɔpe] vt to stop, halt; (Couture) to mend ▷ vi to stop, halt

**store** [stɔʀ] nm blind; (de magasin) shade, awning

**strabisme** [stʀabism(ə)] nm squint(ing)

**strangulation** [stʀɑ̃gylɑsjɔ̃] nf strangulation

**strapontin** [stʀapɔ̃tɛ̃] nm jump ou foldaway seat

**Strasbourg** [stʀazbuʀ] n Strasbourg

**strass** [stʀas] nm paste, strass

**stratagème** [stʀataʒɛm] nm stratagem

**strate** [stʀat] nf (Géo) stratum, layer

**stratège** [stʀatɛʒ] nm strategist

**stratégie** [stʀateʒi] nf strategy

**stratégique** [stʀateʒik] adj strategic

**stratégiquement** [stʀateʒikmɑ̃] adv strategically

**stratifié, e** [stʀatifje] adj (Géo) stratified; (Tech) laminated

**stratosphère** [stʀatɔsfɛʀ] nf stratosphere

**stress** [stʀɛs] nm inv stress

**stressant, e** [stʀɛsɑ̃, -ɑ̃t] adj stressful

**stresser** [stʀɛse] vt to stress, cause stress in

**strict, e** [stʀikt(ə)] adj strict; (tenue, décor) severe, plain; **son droit le plus** ~ his most basic right; **dans la plus ~e intimité** strictly in private; **le** ~ **nécessaire/minimum** the bare essentials/minimum

**strictement** [stʀiktəmɑ̃] adv strictly; plainly

**strident, e** [stʀidɑ̃, -ɑ̃t] adj shrill, strident

**stridulations** [stʀidylɑsjɔ̃] nfpl stridulations, chirrings

**strie** [stʀi] nf streak; (Anat, Géo) stria

**strier** [stʀije] vt to streak; to striate

**strip-tease** [stʀiptiz] nm striptease

**strip-teaseuse** [stʀiptizøz] nf stripper, striptease artist

**striures** [stʀijyʀ] nfpl streaking sg

**strophe** [stʀɔf] nf verse, stanza

**structure** [stʀyktyʀ] nf structure; **~s d'accueil/touristiques** reception/tourist facilities

**structurer** [stʀyktyʀe] vt to structure

**strychnine** [stʀiknin] nf strychnine

**stuc** [styk] nm stucco

**studieusement** [stydjøzmɑ̃] adv studiously

**studieux, -euse** [stydjø, -øz] adj (élève) studious; (vacances) study cpd

**studio** [stydjo] nm (logement) studio flat (Brit) ou apartment (US); (d'artiste, TV etc) studio

**stupéfaction** [stypefaksjɔ̃] nf stupefaction, astonishment

**stupéfait, e** [stypefɛ, -ɛt] adj astonished

**stupéfiant, e** [stypefjɑ̃, -ɑ̃t] adj stunning, astonishing ▷ nm (Méd) drug, narcotic

**stupéfier** [stypefje] vt to stupefy; (étonner) to stun, astonish

**stupeur** [stypœʀ] nf (inertie, insensibilité) stupor; (étonnement) astonishment, amazement

**stupide** [stypid] adj stupid; (hébété) stunned

**stupidement** [stypidmɑ̃] adv stupidly

**stupidité** [stypidite] nf stupidity no pl; (propos, action) stupid thing (to say ou do)

**stups** [styp] *nmpl* = **stupéfiants**; **brigade des ~** narcotics bureau *ou* squad

**style** [stil] *nm* style; **meuble/robe de ~** piece of period furniture/period dress; **~ de vie** lifestyle

**stylé, e** [stile] *adj* well-trained

**stylet** [stilɛ] *nm* (*poignard*) stiletto; (*Chirurgie*) stylet

**stylisé, e** [stilize] *adj* stylized

**styliste** [stilist(ə)] *nm/f* designer; stylist

**stylistique** [stilistik] *nf* stylistics *sg* ▷ *adj* stylistic

**stylo** [stilo] *nm*: **~ (à encre)** (fountain) pen; **~ (à) bille** ballpoint pen

**stylo-feutre** [stilɔføtʀ(ə)] *nm* felt-tip pen

**su, e** [sy] *pp de* **savoir** ▷ *nm*: **au su de** with the knowledge of

**suaire** [sɥɛʀ] *nm* shroud

**suant, e** [sɥɑ̃, -ɑ̃t] *adj* sweaty

**suave** [sɥav] *adj* (*odeur*) sweet; (*voix*) suave, smooth; (*coloris*) soft, mellow

**subalterne** [sybaltɛʀn(ə)] *adj* (*employé, officier*) junior; (*rôle*) subordinate, subsidiary ▷ *nm/f* subordinate, inferior

**subconscient** [sypkɔ̃sjɑ̃] *nm* subconscious

**subdiviser** [sybdivize] *vt* to subdivide

**subdivision** [sybdivizjɔ̃] *nf* subdivision

**subir** [sybiʀ] *vt* (*affront, dégâts, mauvais traitements*) to suffer; (*influence, charme*) to be under, be subjected to; (*traitement, opération, châtiment*) to undergo; (*personne*) to suffer, be subjected to

**subit, e** [sybi, -it] *adj* sudden

**subitement** [sybitmɑ̃] *adv* suddenly, all of a sudden

**subjectif, -ive** [sybʒɛktif, -iv] *adj* subjective

**subjectivement** [sybʒɛktivmɑ̃] *adv* subjectively

**subjectivité** [sybʒɛktivite] *nf* subjectivity

**subjonctif** [sybʒɔ̃ktif] *nm* subjunctive

**subjuguer** [sybʒyge] *vt* to subjugate

**sublime** [syblim] *adj* sublime

**sublimer** [syblime] *vt* to sublimate

**submergé, e** [sybmɛʀʒe] *adj* submerged; (*fig*): **~ de** snowed under with; overwhelmed with

**submerger** [sybmɛʀʒe] *vt* to submerge; (*foule*) to engulf; (*fig*) to overwhelm

**submersible** [sybmɛʀsibl(ə)] *nm* submarine

**subordination** [sybɔʀdinasjɔ̃] *nf* subordination

**subordonné, e** [sybɔʀdɔne] *adj, nm/f* subordinate; **~ à** (*personne*) subordinate to; (*résultats etc*) subject to, depending on

**subordonner** [sybɔʀdɔne] *vt*: **~ qn/qch à** to subordinate sb/sth to

**subornation** [sybɔʀnasjɔ̃] *nf* bribing

**suborner** [sybɔʀne] *vt* to bribe

**subrepticement** [sybʀɛptismɑ̃] *adv* surreptitiously

**subroger** [sybʀɔʒe] *vt* (*Jur*) to subrogate

**subside** [sypsid] *nm* grant

**subsidiaire** [sypsidjɛʀ] *adj* subsidiary; **question ~** deciding question

**subsistance** [sybzistɑ̃s] *nf* subsistence; **pourvoir à la ~ de qn** to keep sb, provide for sb's subsistence *ou* keep

**subsister** [sybziste] *vi* (*rester*) to remain, subsist; (*vivre*) to live; (*survivre*) to live on

**subsonique** [sybsɔnik] *adj* subsonic

**substance** [sypstɑ̃s] *nf* substance; **en ~** in substance

**substantiel, le** [sypstɑ̃sjɛl] *adj* substantial

**substantif** [sypstɑ̃tif] *nm* noun, substantive

**substantiver** [sypstɑ̃tive] *vt* to nominalize

**substituer** [sypstitɥe] *vt*: **~ qn/qch à** to substitute sb/sth for; **se ~ à qn** (*représenter*) to substitute for sb; (*évincer*) to substitute o.s. for sb

**substitut** [sypstity] *nm* (*Jur*) deputy public prosecutor; (*succédané*) substitute

**substitution** [sypstitysjɔ̃] *nf* substitution

**subterfuge** [syptɛʀfyʒ] *nm* subterfuge

**subtil, e** [syptil] *adj* subtle

**subtilement** [syptilmɑ̃] *adv* subtly

**subtiliser** [syptilize] *vt*: **~ qch (à qn)** to spirit sth away (from sb)

**subtilité** [syptilite] *nf* subtlety

**subtropical, e, -aux** [sybtʀɔpikal, -o] *adj* subtropical

**suburbain, e** [sybyʀbɛ̃, -ɛn] *adj* suburban

**subvenir** [sybvəniʀ]: **~ à** *vt* to meet

**subvention** [sybvɑ̃sjɔ̃] *nf* subsidy, grant

**subventionner** [sybvɑ̃sjɔne] *vt* to subsidize

**subversif, -ive** [sybvɛʀsif, -iv] *adj* subversive

**subversion** [sybvɛʀsjɔ̃] *nf* subversion

**suc** [syk] *nm* (*Bot*) sap; (*de viande, fruit*) juice; **~s gastriques** gastric juices

**succédané** [syksedane] *nm* substitute

**succéder** [syksede]: **~ à** *vt* (*directeur, roi etc*) to succeed; (*venir après: dans une série*) to follow, succeed; **se succéder** *vi* (*accidents, années*) to follow one another

**succès** [syksɛ] *nm* success; **avec ~** successfully; **sans ~** unsuccessfully; **avoir du ~** to be a success, be successful; **à ~** successful; **livre à ~** bestseller; **~ de librairie** bestseller; **~ (féminins)** conquests

**successeur** [syksesœʀ] *nm* successor

**successif, -ive** [syksesif, -iv] *adj* successive

**succession** [syksesjɔ̃] *nf* (*série, Pol*) succession; (*Jur: patrimoine*) estate, inheritance; **prendre la ~ de** (*directeur*) to succeed, take over from; (*entreprise*) to take over

**successivement** [syksesivmɑ̃] *adv* successively

**succinct, e** [syksɛ̃, -ɛ̃t] *adj* succinct

**succinctement** [syksɛ̃tmɑ̃] *adv* succinctly

**succion** [syksjɔ̃] *nf*: **bruit de ~** sucking noise

**succomber** [sykɔ̃be] *vi* to die, succumb; (*fig*): **~ à** to give way to, succumb to

**succulent, e** [sykylɑ̃, -ɑ̃t] *adj* succulent

**succursale** [sykyʀsal] *nf* branch; **magasin à ~s multiples** chain *ou* multiple store

**sucer** [syse] *vt* to suck

**sucette** [sysɛt] *nf* (*bonbon*) lollipop; (*de bébé*) dummy (*Brit*), comforter, pacifier (*US*)

**suçoter** [sysɔte] *vt* to suck

**sucre** [sykʀ(ə)] *nm* (*substance*) sugar; (*morceau*) lump of sugar, sugar lump *ou* cube; **~ de canne/**

**S**

**betterave** cane/beet sugar; ~ **en morceaux/ cristallisé/en poudre** lump *ou* cube/ granulated/caster sugar; ~ **glace** icing sugar; ~ **d'orge** barley sugar

**sucré, e** [sykʀe] *adj* (*produit alimentaire*) sweetened; (*au goût*) sweet; (*péj*) sugary, honeyed

**sucrer** [sykʀe] *vt* (*thé, café*) to sweeten, put sugar in; ~ **qn** to put sugar in sb's tea (*ou* coffee *etc*); **se sucrer** to help o.s. to sugar, have some sugar; (*fam*) to line one's pocket(s)

**sucrerie** [sykʀəʀi] *nf* (*usine*) sugar refinery; **sucreries** *nfpl* (*bonbons*) sweets, sweet things

**sucrier, -ière** [sykʀije, -jɛʀ] *adj* (*industrie*) sugar *cpd*; (*région*) sugar-producing ▷ *nm* (*fabricant*) sugar producer; (*récipient*) sugar bowl *ou* basin

**sud** [syd] *nm*: **le** ~ the south ▷ *adj inv* south; (*côte*) south, southern; **au** ~ (*situation*) in the south; (*direction*) to the south; **au** ~ **de** (to the) south of

**sud-africain, e** [sydafʀikɛ̃, -ɛn] *adj* South African ▷ *nm/f*: **Sud-Africain, e** South African

**sud-américain, e** [sydameʀikɛ̃, -ɛn] *adj* South American ▷ *nm/f*: **Sud-Américain, e** South American

**sudation** [sydasjɔ̃] *nf* sweating, sudation

**sud-coréen, ne** [sydkɔʀeɛ̃, -ɛn] *adj* South Korean ▷ *nm/f*: **Sud-Coréen, ne** South Korean

**sud-est** [sydɛst] *nm, adj inv* south-east

**sud-ouest** [sydwɛst] *nm, adj inv* south-west

**sud-vietnamien, ne** [sydvjɛtnamjɛ̃, -ɛn] *adj* South Vietnamese ▷ *nm/f*: **Sud-Vietnamien, ne** South Vietnamese

**Suède** [sɥɛd] *nf*: **la** ~ Sweden

**suédois, e** [sɥedwa, -waz] *adj* Swedish ▷ *nm* (*Ling*) Swedish ▷ *nm/f*: **Suédois, e** Swede

**suer** [sɥe] *vi* to sweat; (*suinter*) to ooze ▷ *vt* (*fig*) to exude; ~ **à grosses gouttes** to sweat profusely

**sueur** [sɥœʀ] *nf* sweat; **en** ~ sweating, in a sweat; **avoir des ~s froides** to be in a cold sweat

**suffire** [syfiʀ] *vi* (*être assez*): ~ (**à qn/pour qch/ pour faire**) to be enough *ou* sufficient (for sb/ for sth/to do); (*satisfaire*): **cela lui suffit** he's content with this, this is enough for him; **se suffire** *vi* to be self-sufficient; **cela suffit pour les irriter/qu'ils se fâchent** it's enough to annoy them/for them to get angry; **il suffit d'une négligence/qu'on oublie pour que** ... it only takes one act of carelessness/one only needs to forget for ...; **ça suffit!** that's enough!, that'll do!

**suffisamment** [syfizamɑ̃] *adv* sufficiently, enough; ~ **de** sufficient, enough

**suffisance** [syfizɑ̃s] *nf* (*vanité*) self-importance, bumptiousness; (*quantité*): **en** ~ in plenty

**suffisant, e** [syfizɑ̃, -ɑ̃t] *adj* (*temps, ressources*) sufficient; (*résultats*) satisfactory; (*vaniteux*) self-important, bumptious

**suffisons** *etc* [syfizɔ̃] *vb voir* **suffire**

**suffixe** [syfiks(ə)] *nm* suffix

**suffocant, e** [syfɔkɑ̃, -ɑ̃t] *adj* (*étouffant*)

suffocating; (*stupéfiant*) staggering

**suffocation** [syfɔkasjɔ̃] *nf* suffocation

**suffoquer** [syfɔke] *vt* to choke, suffocate; (*stupéfier*) to stagger, astound ▷ *vi* to choke, suffocate; ~ **de colère/d'indignation** to choke with anger/indignation

**suffrage** [syfʀaʒ] *nm* (*Pol: voix*) vote; (*: méthode*): ~ **universel/direct/indirect** universal/direct/ indirect suffrage; (*du public etc*) approval *no pl*; ~**s exprimés** valid votes

**suggérer** [sygʒeʀe] *vt* to suggest; ~ **que/de faire** to suggest that/doing

**suggestif, -ive** [sygʒɛstif, -iv] *adj* suggestive

**suggestion** [sygʒɛstjɔ̃] *nf* suggestion

**suggestivité** [sygʒɛstivite] *nf* suggestiveness, suggestive nature

**suicidaire** [sɥisidɛʀ] *adj* suicidal

**suicide** [sɥisid] *nm* suicide ▷ *adj*: **opération** ~ suicide mission

**suicidé, e** [sɥiside] *nm/f* suicide

**suicider** [sɥiside]: **se suicider** *vi* to commit suicide

**suie** [sɥi] *nf* soot

**suif** [sɥif] *nm* tallow

**suinter** [sɥɛ̃te] *vi* to ooze

**suis** [sɥi] *vb voir* **être**; **suivre**

**suisse** [sɥis] *adj* Swiss ▷ *nm* (*bedeau*) ≈ verger ▷ *nm/f*: **Suisse** Swiss *pl inv* ▷ *nf*: **la S~** Switzerland; **la S~ romande/allemande** French-speaking/German-speaking Switzerland; ~ **romand** Swiss French

**suisse-allemand, e** [sɥisalmɑ̃, -ɑ̃d] *adj, nm/f* Swiss German

**Suissesse** [sɥisɛs] *nf* Swiss (woman *ou* girl)

**suit** [sɥi] *vb voir* **suivre**

**suite** [sɥit] *nf* (*continuation: d'énumération etc*) rest, remainder; (*: de feuilleton*) continuation; (*: second film etc sur le même thème*) sequel; (*série: de maisons, succès*): **une** ~ **de** a series *ou* succession of; (*Math*) series *sg*; (*conséquence*) result; (*ordre, liaison logique*) coherence; (*appartement, Mus*) suite; (*escorte*) retinue, suite; **suites** *nfpl* (*d'une maladie etc*) effects; **prendre la** ~ **de** (*directeur etc*) to succeed, take over from; **donner** ~ **à** (*requête, projet*) to follow up; **faire** ~ **à** to follow; (**faisant**) ~ **à votre lettre du** further to your letter of the; **sans** ~ *adj* incoherent, disjointed ▷ *adv* incoherently, disjointedly; **de** ~ *adv* (*d'affilée*) in succession; (*immédiatement*) at once; **par la** ~ afterwards, subsequently; **à la** ~ *adv* one after the other; **à la** ~ **de** (*derrière*) behind; (*en conséquence de*) following; **par** ~ **de** owing to, as a result of; **avoir de la** ~ **dans les idées** to show great singleness of purpose; **attendre la ~ des événements** to (wait and see) what happens

**suivant, e** [sɥivɑ̃, -ɑ̃t] *vb voir* **suivre** ▷ *adj* next, following; (*ci-après*): **l'exercice** ~ the following exercise ▷ *prép* (*selon*) according to; ~ **que** according to whether; **au ~!** next!

**suive** *etc* [sɥiv] *vb voir* **suivre**

**suiveur** [sɥivœʀ] *nm* (*Cyclisme*) (official) follower; (*péj*) (camp) follower

**suivi, e** [sɥivi] *pp de* **suivre** ▷ *adj* (*régulier*)
regular; (*Comm: article*) in general production;
(*cohérent*) consistent; coherent ▷ *nm* follow-up;
**très/peu ~** (*cours*) well-/poorly-attended; (*mode*)
widely/not widely adopted; (*feuilleton etc*)
widely/not widely followed
**suivre** [sɥivʀ(ə)] *vt* (*gén*) to follow; (*Scol: cours*) to
attend; (: *leçon*) to follow, attend to; (: *programme*)
to keep up with; (*Comm: article*) to continue to
stock ▷ *vi* to follow; (*élève: écouter*) to attend, pay
attention; (: *assimiler le programme*) to keep up,
follow; **se suivre** (*accidents, personnes, voitures etc*)
to follow one after the other; (*raisonnement*) to be
coherent; **~ des yeux** to follow with one's eyes;
**faire ~** (*lettre*) to forward; **~ son cours** (*enquête
etc*) to run *ou* take its course; **"à ~"** "to be
continued"
**sujet, te** [syʒɛ, -ɛt] *adj:* **être ~ à** (*accidents*) to be
prone to; (*vertige etc*) to be liable *ou* subject to
▷ *nm/f* (*d'un souverain*) subject ▷ *nm* subject; **un ~
de dispute/discorde/mécontentement** a
cause for argument/dissension/dissatisfaction;
**c'est à quel ~?** what is it about?; **avoir ~ de se
plaindre** to have cause for complaint; **au ~ de**
*prép* about; **~ à caution** *adj* questionable; **~ de
conversation** topic *ou* subject of conversation;
**~ d'examen** (*Scol*) examination question;
examination paper; **~ d'expérience** (*Bio etc*)
experimental subject
**sujétion** [syʒesjɔ̃] *nf* subjection; (*fig*)
constraint
**sulfater** [sylfate] *vt* to spray with copper
sulphate
**sulfureux, -euse** [sylfyʀø, -øz] *adj* sulphurous
(*Brit*), sulfurous (*US*)
**sulfurique** [sylfyʀik] *adj:* **acide ~** sulphuric (*Brit*)
*ou* sulfuric (*US*) acid
**sulfurisé, e** [sylfyʀize] *adj:* **papier ~** greaseproof
(*Brit*) *ou* wax (*US*) paper
**Sumatra** [symatʀa] *nf* Sumatra
**summum** [sɔmɔm] *nm:* **le ~ de** the height of
**super** [sypɛʀ] *adj inv* great, fantastic ▷ *nm*
(= *supercarburant*) ≈ 4-star (*Brit*), ≈ premium (*US*)
**superbe** [sypɛʀb(ə)] *adj* magnificent, superb
▷ *nf* arrogance
**superbement** [sypɛʀbəmã] *adv* superbly
**supercarburant** [sypɛʀkaʀbyʀã] *nm* ≈ 4-star
petrol (*Brit*), ≈ premium gas (*US*)
**supercherie** [sypɛʀʃəʀi] *nf* trick, trickery *no pl*;
(*fraude*) fraud
**supérette** [sypɛʀɛt] *nf* minimarket
**superfétatoire** [sypɛʀfetatwaʀ] *adj*
superfluous
**superficie** [sypɛʀfisi] *nf* (*surface*) area; (*fig*)
surface
**superficiel, le** [sypɛʀfisjɛl] *adj* superficial
**superficiellement** [sypɛʀfisjɛlmã] *adv*
superficially
**superflu, e** [sypɛʀfly] *adj* superfluous ▷ *nm:* **le ~**
the superfluous
**superforme** [sypɛʀfɔʀm(ə)] *nf* (*fam*) top form,
excellent shape

**super-grand** [sypɛʀgʀã] *nm* superpower
**super-huit** [sypɛʀɥit] *adj:* **camera/film ~**
super-eight camera/film
**supérieur, e** [sypeʀjœʀ] *adj* (*lèvre, étages, classes*)
upper; (*plus élevé: température, niveau*): **~ (à)** higher
(than); (*meilleur: qualité, produit*): **~ (à)** superior
(to); (*excellent, hautain*) superior ▷ *nm/f* superior;
**Mère ~e** Mother Superior; **à l'étage ~** on the
next floor up; **~ en nombre** superior in number
**supérieurement** [sypeʀjœʀmã] *adv*
exceptionally well; (*avec adjectif*) exceptionally
**supériorité** [sypeʀjɔʀite] *nf* superiority
**superlatif** [sypɛʀlatif] *nm* superlative
**supermarché** [sypɛʀmaʀʃe] *nm* supermarket
**supernova** [sypɛʀnɔva] *nf* supernova
**superposable** [sypɛʀpozabl(ə)] *adj* (*figures*) that
may be superimposed; (*lits*) stackable
**superposer** [sypɛʀpoze] *vt* to superpose;
(*meubles, caisses*) to stack; (*faire chevaucher*) to
superimpose; **se superposer** (*images, souvenirs*)
to be superimposed; **lits superposés** bunk
beds
**superposition** [sypɛʀpozisjɔ̃] *nf* superposition;
superimposition
**superpréfet** [sypɛʀpʀefɛ] *nm* prefect in charge of a
region
**superproduction** [sypɛʀpʀɔdyksjɔ̃] *nf* (*film*)
spectacular
**superpuissance** [sypɛʀpɥisãs] *nf* superpower
**supersonique** [sypɛʀsɔnik] *adj* supersonic
**superstitieux, -euse** [sypɛʀstisjø, -øz] *adj*
superstitious
**superstition** [sypɛʀstisjɔ̃] *nf* superstition
**superstructure** [sypɛʀstʀyktyʀ] *nf*
superstructure
**supertanker** [sypɛʀtãkœʀ] *nm* supertanker
**superviser** [sypɛʀvize] *vt* to supervise
**supervision** [sypɛʀvizjɔ̃] *nf* supervision
**suppl.** *abr =* **supplément**
**supplanter** [syplãte] *vt* to supplant
**suppléance** [sypleãs] *nf* (*poste*) supply post (*Brit*),
substitute teacher's post (*US*)
**suppléant, e** [sypleã, -ãt] *adj* (*juge, fonctionnaire*)
deputy *cpd*; (*professeur*) supply *cpd* (*Brit*),
substitute *cpd* (*US*) ▷ *nm/f* deputy; supply *ou*
substitute teacher; **médecin ~** locum
**suppléer** [syplee] *vt* (*ajouter: mot manquant etc*) to
supply, provide; (*compenser: lacune*) to fill in;
(: *défaut*) to make up for; (*remplacer: professeur*) to
stand in for; (: *juge*) to deputize for; **~ à** *vt* to
make up for; to substitute for
**supplément** [syplemã] *nm* supplement; **un ~
de travail** extra *ou* additional work; **un ~ de
frites** an extra portion of chips *etc*; **un ~ de
10 euros** a supplement of 10 euros, an extra *ou*
additional 10 euros; **ceci est en ~** (*au menu etc*)
this is extra, there is an extra charge for this; **~
d'information** additional information
**supplémentaire** [syplemãtɛʀ] *adj* additional,
further; (*train, bus*) relief *cpd*, extra
**supplétif, -ive** [sypletif, -iv] *adj* (*Mil*) auxiliary
**suppliant, e** [syplijã, -ãt] *adj* imploring

**supplication** [syplikɑsjɔ̃] nf (Rel) supplication; **supplications** nfpl (adjurations) pleas, entreaties
**supplice** [syplis] nm (peine corporelle) torture no pl; form of torture; (douleur physique, morale) torture, agony; **être au ~** to be in agony
**supplier** [syplije] vt to implore, beseech
**supplique** [syplik] nf petition
**support** [sypɔʀ] nm support; (pour livre, outils) stand; **~ audio-visuel** audio-visual aid; **~ publicitaire** advertising medium
**supportable** [sypɔʀtabl(ə)] adj (douleur, température) bearable; (procédé, conduite) tolerable
**supporter** nm [sypɔʀtɛʀ] supporter, fan ▷ vt [sypɔʀte] (poids, poussée, Sport: concurrent, équipe) to support; (conséquences, épreuve) to bear, endure; (défauts, personne) to tolerate, put up with; (chose: chaleur etc) to withstand; (personne: chaleur, vin) to take
**supposé, e** [sypoze] adj (nombre) estimated; (auteur) supposed
**supposer** [sypoze] vt to suppose; (impliquer) to presuppose; **en supposant** ou **à ~ que** supposing (that)
**supposition** [sypozisjɔ̃] nf supposition
**suppositoire** [sypozitwaʀ] nm suppository
**suppôt** [sypo] nm (péj) henchman
**suppression** [sypʀesjɔ̃] nf (voir supprimer) removal; deletion; cancellation; suppression
**supprimer** [sypʀime] vt (cloison, cause, anxiété) to remove; (clause, mot) to delete; (congés, service d'autobus etc) to cancel; (publication, article) to suppress; (emplois, privilèges, témoin gênant) to do away with; **~ qch à qn** to deprive sb of sth
**suppurer** [sypyʀe] vi to suppurate
**supputations** [sypytɑsjɔ̃] nfpl calculations, reckonings
**supputer** [sypyte] vt to calculate, reckon
**supranational, e, -aux** [sypʀanasjɔnal, -o] adj supranational
**suprématie** [sypʀemasi] nf supremacy
**suprême** [sypʀɛm] adj supreme
**suprêmement** [sypʀɛmmɑ̃] adv supremely

⭕ **MOT-CLÉ**

**sur¹** [syʀ] prép **1** (position) on; (pardessus) over; (au-dessus) above; **pose-le sur la table** put it on the table; **je n'ai pas d'argent sur moi** I haven't any money on me
**2** (direction) towards; **en allant sur Paris** going towards Paris; **sur votre droite** on ou to your right
**3** (à propos de) on, about; **un livre/une conférence sur Balzac** a book/lecture on ou about Balzac
**4** (proportion, mesures) out of; by; **un sur 10** one in 10; (Scol) one out of 10; **sur 20, deux sont venus** out of 20, two came; **4 m sur 2** 4 m by 2; **avoir accident sur accident** to have one accident after another
**5** (cause): **sur sa recommandation** on ou at his recommendation; **sur son invitation** at his invitation
**6**: **sur ce** adv whereupon; **sur ce, il faut que je vous quitte** and now I must leave you

**sur², e** [syʀ] adj sour
**sûr, e** [syʀ] adj sure, certain; (digne de confiance) reliable; (sans danger) safe; **peu ~** unreliable; **~ de qch** sure ou certain of sth; **être ~ de qn** to be sure of sb; **~ et certain** absolutely certain; **~ de soi** self-assured, self-confident; **le plus ~ est de** the safest thing is to
**surabondance** [syʀabɔ̃dɑ̃s] nf overabundance
**surabondant, e** [syʀabɔ̃dɑ̃, -ɑ̃t] adj overabundant
**surabonder** [syʀabɔ̃de] vi to be overabundant; **~ de** to abound with, have an overabundance of
**suractivité** [syʀaktivite] nf hyperactivity
**suraigu, ë** [syʀegy] adj very shrill
**surajouter** [syʀaʒute] vt: **~ qch à** to add sth to
**suralimentation** [syʀalimɑ̃tɑsjɔ̃] nf overfeeding; (Tech: d'un moteur) supercharging
**suralimenté, e** [syʀalimɑ̃te] adj (personne) overfed; (moteur) supercharged
**suranné, e** [syʀane] adj outdated, outmoded
**surarmement** [syʀaʀməmɑ̃] nm (excess) stockpiling of arms (ou weapons)
**surbaissé, e** [syʀbese] adj lowered, low
**surcapacité** [syʀkapasite] nf overcapacity
**surcharge** [syʀʃaʀʒ(ə)] nf (de passagers, marchandises) excess load; (de détails, d'ornements) overabundance, excess; (correction) alteration; (Postes) surcharge; **prendre des passagers en ~** to take on excess ou extra passengers; **~ de bagages** excess luggage; **~ de travail** extra work
**surchargé, e** [syʀʃaʀʒe] adj (décoration, style) over-elaborate, overfussy; (voiture, emploi du temps) overloaded
**surcharger** [syʀʃaʀʒe] vt to overload; (timbre-poste) to surcharge; (décoration) to overdo
**surchauffe** [syʀʃof] nf overheating
**surchauffé, e** [syʀʃofe] adj overheated; (fig: imagination) overactive
**surchoix** [syʀʃwa] adj inv top-quality
**surclasser** [syʀklase] vt to outclass
**surconsommation** [syʀkɔ̃sɔmɑsjɔ̃] nf (Écon) overconsumption
**surcoté, e** [syʀkɔte] adj overpriced
**surcouper** [syʀkupe] vt to overtrump
**surcroît** [syʀkʀwa] nm: **~ de qch** additional sth; **par** ou **de ~** moreover; **en ~** in addition
**surdi-mutité** [syʀdimytite] nf: **atteint de ~** deaf and dumb
**surdité** [syʀdite] nf deafness; **atteint de ~ totale** profoundly deaf
**surdoué, e** [syʀdwe] adj gifted
**sureau, x** [syʀo] nm elder (tree)
**sureffectif** [syʀefɛktif] nm overmanning
**surélever** [syʀelve] vt to raise, heighten
**sûrement** [syʀmɑ̃] adv reliably; safely, securely; (certainement) certainly; **~ pas** certainly not

**suremploi** [syrɑ̃plwa] nm (Écon) overemployment

**surenchère** [syrɑ̃ʃɛr] nf (aux enchères) higher bid; (sur prix fixe) overbid; (fig) overstatement; outbidding tactics pl; ~ **de violence** build-up of violence; ~ **électorale** political (ou electoral) one-upmanship

**surenchérir** [syrɑ̃ʃerir] vi to bid higher; to raise one's bid; (fig) to try and outbid each other

**surendettement** [syrɑ̃dɛtmɑ̃] nm excessive debt

**surent** [syr] vb voir **savoir**

**surentraîné, e** [syrɑ̃trene] adj overtrained

**suréquipé, e** [syrekipe] adj overequipped

**surestimer** [syrɛstime] vt (tableau) to overvalue; (possibilité, personne) to overestimate

**sûreté** [syrte] nf (voir sûr) reliability; safety; (Jur) guaranty; surety; **mettre en** ~ to put in a safe place; **pour plus de** ~ as an extra precaution; to be on the safe side; **la** ~ **de l'État** State security; **la S~ (nationale)** division of the Ministère de l'Intérieur heading all police forces except the gendarmerie and the Paris préfecture de police

**surexcité, e** [syrɛksite] adj overexcited

**surexciter** [syrɛksite] vt (personne) to overexcite; **cela surexcite ma curiosité** it really rouses my curiosity

**surexploiter** [syrɛksplwate] vt to overexploit

**surexposer** [syrɛkspoze] vt to overexpose

**surf** [sœrf] nm surfing; **faire du** ~ to go surfing

**surface** [syrfas] nf surface; (superficie) surface area; **faire** ~ to surface; **en** ~ adv near the surface; (fig) superficially; **la pièce fait 100 m²** **de** ~ the room has a surface area of 100m²; ~ **de** **réparation** (Sport) penalty area; ~ **porteuse** ou **de sustentation** (Aviat) aerofoil

**surfait, e** [syrfɛ, -ɛt] adj overrated

**surfer** [sœrfe] vi to surf; ~ **sur Internet** to surf the Internet

**surfeur, -euse** [sœrf r, -øz] nm/f surfer

**surfiler** [syrfile] vt (Couture) to oversew

**surfin, e** [syrfɛ̃, -in] adj superfine

**surgélateur** [syrʒelatœr] nm deep freeze

**surgélation** [syrʒelasjɔ̃] nf deep-freezing

**surgelé, e** [syrʒəle] adj (deep-)frozen

**surgeler** [syrʒəle] vt to (deep-)freeze

**surgir** [syrʒir] vi (personne, véhicule) to appear suddenly; (jaillir) to shoot up; (montagne etc) to rise up, loom up; (fig: problème, conflit) to arise

**surhomme** [syrɔm] nm superman

**surhumain, e** [syrymɛ̃, -ɛn] adj superhuman

**surimposer** [syrɛ̃poze] vt to overtax

**surimpression** [syrɛ̃presjɔ̃] nf (Photo) double exposure; **en** ~ superimposed

**surimprimer** [syrɛ̃prime] vt to overstrike, overprint

**Surinam** [syrinam] nm: **le** ~ Surinam

**surinfection** [syrɛ̃fɛksjɔ̃] nf (Méd) secondary infection

**surjet** [syrʒɛ] nm (Couture) overcast seam

**sur-le-champ** [syrləʃɑ̃] adv immediately

**surlendemain** [syrlɑ̃dmɛ̃] nm: **le** ~ (**soir**) two days later (in the evening); **le** ~ **de** two days after

**surligneur** [syrliɲœr] nm (feutre) highlighter (pen)

**surmenage** [syrmənaʒ] nm overwork; **le** ~ **intellectuel** mental fatigue

**surmené, e** [syrməne] adj overworked

**surmener** [syrməne] vt, **se surmener** vi to overwork

**surmonter** [syrmɔ̃te] vt (coupole etc) to surmount, top; (vaincre) to overcome, surmount

**surmultiplié, e** [syrmyltiplije] adj, nf: (**vitesse**) ~**e** overdrive

**surnager** [syrnaʒe] vi to float

**surnaturel, le** [syrnatyrɛl] adj, nm supernatural

**surnom** [syrnɔ̃] nm nickname

**surnombre** [syrnɔ̃br(ə)] nm: **être en** ~ to be too many (ou one too many)

**surnommer** [syrnɔme] vt to nickname

**surnuméraire** [syrnymerɛr] nm/f supernumerary

**suroît** [syrwa] nm sou'wester

**surpasser** [syrpase] vt to surpass; **se surpasser** vi to surpass o.s., excel o.s.

**surpayer** [syrpeje] vt (personne) to overpay; (article etc) to pay too much for

**surpeuplé, e** [syrpœple] adj overpopulated

**surpeuplement** [syrpœpləmɑ̃] nm overpopulation

**surpiquer** [syrpike] vt (Couture) to overstitch

**surpiqûre** [syrpikyr] nf (Couture) overstitching

**surplace** [syrplas] nm: **faire du** ~ to mark time

**surplis** [syrpli] nm surplice

**surplomb** [syrplɔ̃] nm overhang; **en** ~ overhanging

**surplomber** [syrplɔ̃be] vi to be overhanging ▷ vt to overhang; (dominer) to tower above

**surplus** [syrply] nm (Comm) surplus; (reste): ~ **de** **bois** wood left over; **au** ~ moreover; ~ **américains** American army surplus sg

**surpopulation** [syrpɔpylasjɔ̃] nf overpopulation

**surprenant, e** [syrprənɑ̃, -ɑ̃t] vb voir **surprendre** ▷ adj amazing

**surprendre** [syrprɑ̃dr(ə)] vt (étonner, prendre à l'improviste) to amaze, surprise; (secret) to discover; (tomber sur: intrus etc) to catch; (fig) to detect; to chance ou happen upon; (clin d'œil) to intercept; (conversation) to overhear; (orage, nuit etc) to catch out, take by surprise; ~ **la** **vigilance/bonne foi de qn** to catch sb out/ betray sb's good faith; **se** ~ **à faire** to catch ou find o.s. doing

**surprime** [syrprim] nf additional premium

**surpris, e** [syrpri, -iz] pp de **surprendre** ▷ adj: ~ (**de/que**) amazed ou surprised (at/that)

**surprise** [syrpriz] nf surprise; **faire une** ~ **à qn** to give sb a surprise; **voyage sans** ~**s** uneventful journey; **par** ~ adv by surprise

**surprise-partie** [syrprizparti] nf party

**surprit** [syrpri] vb voir **surprendre**

**surproduction** [syʀpʀɔdyksjɔ̃] *nf* overproduction

**surréaliste** [syʀʀealist(ə)] *adj, nm/f* surrealist

**sursaut** [syʀso] *nm* start, jump; ~ **de** (*énergie, indignation*) sudden fit *ou* burst of; **en** ~ *adv* with a start

**sursauter** [syʀsote] *vi* to (give a) start, jump

**surseoir** [syʀswaʀ]: ~ **à** *vt* to defer; (*Jur*) to stay

**sursis** [syʀsi] *nm* (*Jur: gén*) suspended sentence; (*à l'exécution capitale, aussi fig*) reprieve; (*Mil*): ~ (**d'appel** *ou* **d'incorporation**) deferment; **condamné à cinq mois (de prison) avec** ~ given a five-month suspended (prison) sentence

**sursitaire** [syʀsiteʀ] *nm* (*Mil*) deferred conscript

**sursois** [syʀswa], **sursoyais** *etc* [syʀswaje] *vb voir* **surseoir**

**surtaxe** [syʀtaks(ə)] *nf* surcharge

**surtension** [syʀtɑ̃sjɔ̃] *nf* (*Élec*) overvoltage

**surtout** [syʀtu] *adv* (*avant tout, d'abord*) above all; (*spécialement, particulièrement*) especially; **il aime le sport,** ~ **le football** he likes sport, especially football; **cet été, il a** ~ **fait de la pêche** this summer he went fishing more than anything (else); ~ **pas d'histoires!** no fuss now!; ~, **ne dites rien!** whatever you do – don't say anything!; ~ **pas!** certainly not, indeed not!; ~ **que ...** especially as ...

**survécu, e** [syʀveky] *pp de* **survivre**

**surveillance** [syʀvεjɑ̃s] *nf* watch; (*Police, Mil*) surveillance; **sous** ~ **médicale** under medical supervision; **la** ~ **du territoire** internal security; *voir aussi* **DST**

**surveillant, e** [syʀvεjɑ̃, -ɑ̃t] *nm/f* (*de prison*) warder; (*Scol*) monitor; (*de travaux*) supervisor, overseer

**surveiller** [syʀveje] *vt* (*enfant, élèves, bagages*) to watch, keep an eye on; (*malade*) to watch over; (*prisonnier, suspect*) to keep (a) watch on; (*territoire, bâtiment*) to (keep) watch over; (*travaux, cuisson*) to supervise; (*Scol: examen*) to invigilate; **se surveiller** to keep a check *ou* watch on o.s.; ~ **son langage/sa ligne** to watch one's language/figure

**survenir** [syʀvəniʀ] *vi* (*incident, retards*) to occur, arise; (*événement*) to take place; (*personne*) to appear, arrive

**survenu, e** [syʀv(ə)ny] *pp de* **survenir**

**survêt** [syʀvεt], **survêtement** [syʀvεtmɑ̃] *nm* tracksuit (*Brit*), sweat suit (*US*)

**survie** [syʀvi] *nf* survival; (*Rel*) afterlife; **équipement de** ~ survival equipment; **une** ~ **de quelques mois** a few more months of life

**surviens** [syʀvjɛ̃], **survint** *etc* [syʀvɛ̃] *vb voir* **survenir**

**survit** *etc* [syʀvi] *vb voir* **survivre**

**survitrage** [syʀvitʀaʒ] *nm* double-glazing

**survivance** [syʀvivɑ̃s] *nf* relic

**survivant, e** [syʀvivɑ̃, -ɑ̃t] *vb voir* **survivre** ▷ *nm/f* survivor

**survivre** [syʀvivʀ(ə)] *vi* to survive; ~ **à** *vt* (*accident etc*) to survive; (*personne*) to outlive; **la**

---

**victime a peu de chance de** ~ the victim has little hope of survival

**survol** [syʀvɔl] *nm* flying over

**survoler** [syʀvɔle] *vt* to fly over; (*fig: livre*) to skim through; (: *question, problèmes*) to skim over

**survolté, e** [syʀvɔlte] *adj* (*Élec*) stepped up, boosted; (*fig*) worked up

**sus** [sy(s)]: **en** ~ **de** *prép* in addition to, over and above; **en** ~ *adv* in addition; ~ **à** *excl*: ~ **au tyran!** at the tyrant! *vb* [sy] *voir* **savoir**

**susceptibilité** [sysεptibilite] *nf* sensitivity *no pl*

**susceptible** [sysεptibl(ə)] *adj* touchy, sensitive; ~ **d'amélioration** *ou* **d'être amélioré** that can be improved, open to improvement; ~ **de faire** (*capacité*) able to do; (*probabilité*) liable to do

**susciter** [sysite] *vt* (*admiration*) to arouse; (*obstacles, ennuis*): ~ (**à qn**) to create (for sb)

**susdit, e** [sysdi, -dit] *adj* foresaid

**susmentionné, e** [sysmɑ̃sjɔne] *adj* above-mentioned

**susnommé, e** [sysnɔme] *adj* above-named

**suspect, e** [syspε(kt), -εkt(ə)] *adj* suspicious; (*témoignage, opinions, vin etc*) suspect ▷ *nm/f* suspect; **peu** ~ **de** most unlikely to be suspected of

**suspecter** [syspεkte] *vt* to suspect; (*honnêteté de qn*) to question, have one's suspicions about; ~ **qn d'être/d'avoir fait qch** to suspect sb of being/having done sth

**suspendre** [syspɑ̃dʀ(ə)] *vt* (*accrocher: vêtement*): ~ **qch (à)** to hang sth up (on); (*fixer: lustre etc*): ~ **qch à** to hang sth from; (*interrompre, démettre*) to suspend; (*remettre*) to defer; **se** ~ **à** to hang from

**suspendu, e** [syspɑ̃dy] *pp de* **suspendre** ▷ *adj* (*accroché*): ~ **à** hanging on (*ou* from); (*perché*): **au-dessus de** suspended over; (*Auto*): **bien/mal** ~ with good/poor suspension; **être** ~ **aux lèvres de qn** to hang upon sb's every word

**suspens** [syspɑ̃]: **en** ~ *adv* (*affaire*) in abeyance; **tenir en** ~ to keep in suspense

**suspense** [syspɑ̃s] *nm* suspense

**suspension** [syspɑ̃sjɔ̃] *nf* suspension; deferment; (*Auto*) suspension; (*lustre*) pendant light fitting; **en** ~ in suspension, suspended; ~ **d'audience** adjournment

**suspicieux, -euse** [syspisjø, -øz] *adj* suspicious

**suspicion** [syspisjɔ̃] *nf* suspicion

**sustentation** [systɑ̃tasjɔ̃] *nf* (*Aviat*) lift; **base** *ou* **polygone de** ~ support polygon

**sustenter** [systɑ̃te]: **se sustenter** *vi* to take sustenance

**susurrer** [sysyʀe] *vt* to whisper

**sut** [sy] *vb voir* **savoir**

**suture** [sytyʀ] *nf*: **point de** ~ stitch

**suturer** [sytyʀe] *vt* to stitch up, suture

**suzeraineté** [syzʀεnte] *nf* suzerainty

**svelte** [svεlt(ə)] *adj* slender, svelte

**SVP** *sigle* (= *s'il vous plaît*) please

**Swaziland** [swazilɑ̃d] *nm*: **le** ~ Swaziland

**sweat** [swit] *nm* (*fam*) sweatshirt

**sweat-shirt** [switʃœʀt] (*pl* **-s**) *nm* sweatshirt

**syllabe** [silab] *nf* syllable

**sylphide** [silfid] *nf* (*fig*): **sa taille de** ~ her sylph-like figure

**sylvestre** [silvɛstʀ(ə)] *adj*: **pin** ~ Scots pine, Scotch fir

**sylvicole** [silvikɔl] *adj* forestry *cpd*

**sylviculteur** [silvikyltœʀ] *nm* forester

**sylviculture** [silvikyltyʀ] *nf* forestry, sylviculture

**symbole** [sɛ̃bɔl] *nm* symbol

**symbolique** [sɛ̃bɔlik] *adj* symbolic; (*geste, offrande*) token *cpd*; (*salaire, dommages-intérêts*) nominal

**symboliquement** [sɛ̃bɔlikmɑ̃] *adv* symbolically

**symboliser** [sɛ̃bɔlize] *vt* to symbolize

**symétrie** [simetʀi] *nf* symmetry

**symétrique** [simetʀik] *adj* symmetrical

**symétriquement** [simetʀikmɑ̃] *adv* symmetrically

**sympa** [sɛ̃pa] *adj inv* (= *sympathique*) nice; friendly; good

**sympathie** [sɛ̃pati] *nf* (*inclination*) liking; (*affinité*) fellow feeling; (*condoléances*) sympathy; **accueillir avec** ~ (*projet*) to receive favourably; **avoir de la** ~ **pour qn** to like sb, have a liking for sb; **témoignages de** ~ expressions of sympathy; **croyez à toute ma** ~ you have my deepest sympathy

**sympathique** [sɛ̃patik] *adj* (*personne, figure*) nice, friendly, likeable; (*geste*) friendly; (*livre*) good; (*déjeuner*) nice; (*réunion, endroit*) pleasant, nice

**sympathisant, e** [sɛ̃patizɑ̃, -ɑ̃t] *nm/f* sympathizer

**sympathiser** [sɛ̃patize] *vi* (*voisins etc: s'entendre*) to get on (*Brit*) *ou* along (*US*) (well); (: *se fréquenter*) to socialize, see each other; ~ **avec** to get on *ou* along (well) with, to see, socialize with

**symphonie** [sɛ̃fɔni] *nf* symphony

**symphonique** [sɛ̃fɔnik] *adj* (*orchestre, concert*) symphony *cpd*; (*musique*) symphonic

**symposium** [sɛ̃pozjɔm] *nm* symposium

**symptomatique** [sɛ̃ptɔmatik] *adj* symptomatic

**symptôme** [sɛ̃ptom] *nm* symptom

**synagogue** [sinagɔg] *nf* synagogue

**synchrone** [sɛ̃kʀɔn] *adj* synchronous

**synchronique** [sɛ̃kʀɔnik] *adj*: **tableau** ~ synchronic table of events

**synchronisation** [sɛ̃kʀɔnizasjɔ̃] *nf* synchronization; (*Auto*): ~ **des vitesses** synchromesh

**synchronisé, e** [sɛ̃kʀɔnize] *adj* synchronized

**synchroniser** [sɛ̃kʀɔnize] *vt* to synchronize

**syncope** [sɛ̃kɔp] *nf* (*Méd*) blackout; (*Mus*) syncopation; **tomber en** ~ to faint, pass out

**syncopé, e** [sɛ̃kɔpe] *adj* syncopated

**syndic** [sɛ̃dik] *nm* managing agent

**syndical, e, -aux** [sɛ̃dikal, -o] *adj* (trade-)union *cpd*; **centrale** ~**e** group of affiliated trade unions

**syndicalisme** [sɛ̃dikalism(ə)] *nm* (*mouvement*) trade unionism; (*activités*) union(ist) activities *pl*

**syndicaliste** [sɛ̃dikalist(ə)] *nm/f* trade unionist

**syndicat** [sɛ̃dika] *nm* (*d'ouvriers, employés*) (trade(s)) union; (*autre association d'intérêts*) union, association; ~ **d'initiative** (**SI**) tourist office *ou* bureau; ~ **patronal** employers' syndicate, federation of employers; ~ **de propriétaires** association of property owners

**syndiqué, e** [sɛ̃dike] *adj* belonging to a (trade) union; **non** ~ non-union

**syndiquer** [sɛ̃dike]: **se syndiquer** *vi* to form a trade union; (*adhérer*) to join a trade union

**syndrome** [sɛ̃dʀom] *nm* syndrome; ~ **prémenstruel** premenstrual syndrome (PMS)

**synergie** [sinɛʀʒi] *nf* synergy

**synode** [sinɔd] *nm* synod

**synonyme** [sinɔnim] *adj* synonymous ▷ *nm* synonym; ~ **de** synonymous with

**synopsis** [sinɔpsis] *nm ou nf* synopsis

**synoptique** [sinɔptik] *adj*: **tableau** ~ synoptic table

**synovie** [sinɔvi] *nf* synovia; **épanchement de** ~ water on the knee

**syntaxe** [sɛ̃taks(ə)] *nf* syntax

**synthèse** [sɛ̃tɛz] *nf* synthesis; **faire la** ~ **de** to synthesize

**synthétique** [sɛ̃tetik] *adj* synthetic

**synthétiser** [sɛ̃tetize] *vt* to synthesize

**synthétiseur** [sɛ̃tetizœʀ] *nm* (*Mus*) synthesizer

**syphilis** [sifilis] *nf* syphilis

**Syrie** [siʀi] *nf*: **la** ~ Syria

**syrien, ne** [siʀjɛ̃, -ɛn] *adj* Syrian ▷ *nm/f*: **Syrien, ne** Syrian

**systématique** [sistematik] *adj* systematic

**systématiquement** [sistematikmɑ̃] *adv* systematically

**systématiser** [sistematize] *vt* to systematize

**système** [sistɛm] *nm* system; **le** ~ **D** resourcefulness; ~ **décimal** decimal system; ~ **expert** expert system; ~ **d'exploitation** (*Inform*) operating system; ~ **immunitaire** immune system; ~ **métrique** metric system; ~ **solaire** solar system

**S**

**T, t** [te] *nm inv* T, t ▷ *abr* (= *tonne*) t; **T comme Thérèse** T for Tommy

**t'** [t(ə)] *pron voir* **te**

**ta** [ta] *adj poss voir* **ton**

**tabac** [taba] *nm* tobacco; (*aussi:* **débit** *ou* **bureau de tabac**) tobacconist's (shop) ▷ *adj inv:* **(couleur)** ~ buff, tobacco *cpd;* **passer qn à** ~ to beat sb up; **faire un** ~ (*fam*) to be a big hit; ~ **blond/brun** light/dark tobacco; ~ **gris** shag; ~ **à priser** snuff

**tabagie** [tabaʒi] *nf* smoke den

**tabagisme** [tabaʒism(ə)] *nm* nicotine addiction; ~ **passif** passive smoking

**tabasser** [tabase] *vt* to beat up

**tabatière** [tabatjɛʀ] *nf* snuffbox

**tabernacle** [tabɛʀnakl(ə)] *nm* tabernacle

**table** [tabl(ə)] *nf* table; **avoir une bonne** ~ to keep a good table; **à** ~! dinner *etc* is ready!; **se mettre à** ~ to sit down to eat; (*fig: fam*) to come clean; **mettre** *ou* **dresser/desservir la** ~ to lay *ou* set/clear the table; **faire** ~ **rase de** to make a clean sweep of; ~ **de basse** coffee table; ~ **de cuisson** (*à l'électricité*) hotplate; (*au gaz*) gas ring; ~ **d'écoute** wire-tapping set; ~ **d'harmonie** sounding board; ~ **d'hôte** set menu; ~ **de lecture** turntable; ~ **des matières** (table of) contents *pl;* ~ **de multiplication** multiplication table; ~ **des négociations** negotiating table; ~ **de nuit** *ou* **de chevet** bedside table; ~ **ronde** (*débat*) round table; ~ **roulante** (tea) trolley; ~ **de toilette** washstand; ~ **traçante** (*Inform*) plotter

**tableau, x** [tablo] *nm* (*Art*) painting; (*reproduction, fig*) picture; (*panneau*) board; (*schéma*) table, chart; ~ **d'affichage** notice board; ~ **de bord** dashboard; (*Aviat*) instrument panel; ~ **de chasse** tally; ~ **de contrôle** console, control panel; ~ **de maître** masterpiece; ~ **noir** blackboard

**tablée** [table] *nf* (*personnes*) table

**tabler** [table] *vi:* ~ **sur** to count *ou* bank on

**tablette** [tablet] *nf* (*planche*) shelf; ~ **de chocolat** bar of chocolate

**tableur** [tablœʀ] *nm* (*Inform*) spreadsheet

**tablier** [tablije] *nm* apron; (*de pont*) roadway; (*de cheminée*) (flue-)shutter

**tabou, e** [tabu] *adj, nm* taboo

**tabouret** [tabuʀɛ] *nm* stool

**tabulateur** [tabylatœʀ] *nm* (*Tech*) tabulator

**tac** [tak] *nm:* **du** ~ **au** ~ tit for tat

**tache** [taʃ] *nf* (*saleté*) stain, mark; (*Art: de couleur, lumière*) spot; splash, patch; **faire** ~ **d'huile** to spread, gain ground; ~ **de rousseur** *ou* **de son** freckle; ~ **de vin** (*sur la peau*) strawberry mark

**tâche** [taʃ] *nf* task; **travailler à la** ~ to do piecework

**tacher** [taʃe] *vt* to stain, mark; (*fig*) to sully, stain; **se tacher** *vi* (*fruits*) to become marked

**tâcher** [taʃe] *vi:* ~ **de faire** to try to do, endeavour (*Brit*) *ou* endeavor (*US*) to do

**tâcheron** [taʃʀɔ̃] *nm* (*fig*) drudge

**tacheté, e** [taʃte] *adj:* ~ **de** speckled *ou* spotted with

**tachisme** [taʃism(ə)] *nm* (*Peinture*) tachisme

**tachygraphe** [takigʀaf] *nm* tachograph

**tachymètre** [takimɛtʀ(ə)] *nm* tachometer

**tacite** [tasit] *adj* tacit

**tacitement** [tasitmɑ̃] *adv* tacitly

**taciturne** [tasityʀn(ə)] *adj* taciturn

**tacot** [tako] *nm* (*péj: voiture*) banger (*Brit*), clunker (*US*)

**tact** [takt] *nm* tact; **avoir du** ~ to be tactful, have tact

**tacticien, ne** [taktisjɛ̃, -ɛn] *nm/f* tactician

**tactile** [taktil] *adj* tactile

**tactique** [taktik] *adj* tactical ▷ *nf* (*technique*) tactics *nsg;* (*plan*) tactic

**Tadjikistan** [tadʒikistɑ̃] *nm* Tajikistan

**taffetas** [tafta] *nm* taffeta

**Tage** [taʒ] *nm:* **le** ~ the (river) Tagus

**Tahiti** [taiti] *nf* Tahiti

**tahitien, ne** [taisjɛ̃, -ɛn] *adj* Tahitian

**taie** [tɛ] *nf:* ~ **(d'oreiller)** pillowslip, pillowcase

**tailler** [tajade] *vt* to gash

**taille** [taj] *nf* cutting; pruning; (*milieu du corps*) waist; (*hauteur*) height; (*grandeur*) size; **de** ~ **à faire** capable of doing; **de** ~ *adj* sizeable; **quelle** ~ **faites- vous?** what size are you?

**taillé, e** [taje] *adj* (*moustache, ongles, arbre*) trimmed; ~ **pour** (*fait pour, apte à*) cut out for; tailor-made for; ~ **en pointe** sharpened to a point

**taille-crayon, taille-crayons** [tɑjkRɛjɔ̃] *nm inv* pencil sharpener

**tailler** [tɑje] *vt* (*pierre, diamant*) to cut; (*arbre, plante*) to prune; (*vêtement*) to cut out; (*crayon*) to sharpen; **se tailler** *vt* (*ongles, barbe*) to trim, cut; (*fig: réputation*) to gain, win ▷ *vi* (*fam: s'enfuir*) to beat it; **~ dans** (*chair, bois*) to cut into; **~ grand/petit** to be on the large/small side

**tailleur** [tɑjœR] *nm* (*couturier*) tailor; (*vêtement*) suit, costume; **en ~** (*assis*) cross-legged; **~ de diamants** diamond-cutter

**taillis** [tɑji] *nm* copse

**tain** [tɛ̃] *nm* silvering; **glace sans ~** two-way mirror

**taire** [tɛR] *vt* to keep to o.s., conceal ▷ *vi*: **faire ~ qn** to make sb be quiet; (*fig*) to silence sb; **se taire** *vi* (*s'arrêter de parler*) to fall silent, stop talking; (*ne pas parler*) to be silent *ou* quiet; (*s'abstenir de s'exprimer*) to keep quiet; (*bruit, voix*) to disappear; **tais-toi!, taisez-vous!** be quiet!

**Taiwan** [tajwan] *nf* Taiwan

**talc** [talk] *nm* talc, talcum powder

**talé, e** [tale] *adj* (*fruit*) bruised

**talent** [talɑ̃] *nm* talent; **avoir du ~** to be talented, have talent

**talentueux, -euse** [talɑ̃tɥø, -øz] *adj* talented

**talion** [taljɔ̃] *nm*: **la loi du ~** an eye for an eye

**talisman** [talismɑ̃] *nm* talisman

**talkie-walkie** [tɔkiwɔki] *nm* walkie-talkie

**taloche** [talɔʃ] *nf* (*fam: claque*) slap; (*Tech*) plaster float

**talon** [talɔ̃] *nm* heel; (*de chèque, billet*) stub, counterfoil (*Brit*); **~s plats/aiguilles** flat/stiletto heels; **être sur les ~s de qn** to be on sb's heels; **tourner les ~s** to turn on one's heel; **montrer les ~s** (*fig*) to show a clean pair of heels

**talonner** [talɔne] *vt* to follow hard behind; (*fig*) to hound; (*Rugby*) to heel

**talonnette** [talɔnɛt] *nf* (*de chaussure*) heelpiece; (*de pantalon*) stirrup

**talquer** [talke] *vt* to put talc(um powder) on

**talus** [taly] *nm* embankment; **~ de remblai/déblai** embankment/excavation slope

**tamarin** [tamaRɛ̃] *nm* (*Bot*) tamarind

**tambour** [tɑ̃buR] *nm* (*Mus, also Tech*) drum; (*musicien*) drummer; (*porte*) revolving door(s *pl*); **sans ~ ni trompette** unobtrusively

**tambourin** [tɑ̃buRɛ̃] *nm* tambourine

**tambouriner** [tɑ̃buRine] *vi*: **~ contre** to drum against *ou* on

**tambour-major** [tɑ̃buRmaʒɔR] (*pl* **tambours-majors**) *nm* drum major

**tamis** [tami] *nm* sieve

**Tamise** [tamiz] *nf*: **la ~** the Thames

**tamisé, e** [tamize] *adj* (*fig*) subdued, soft

**tamiser** [tamize] *vt* to sieve, sift

**tampon** [tɑ̃pɔ̃] *nm* (*de coton, d'ouate*) pad; (*aussi*: **tampon hygiénique** *ou* **périodique**) tampon; (*amortisseur, Inform: aussi*: **mémoire tampon**) buffer; (*bouchon*) plug, stopper; (*cachet, timbre*) stamp; (*Chimie*) buffer; **~ encreur** inking pad; **~ (à récurer)** scouring pad

**tamponné, e** [tɑ̃pɔne] *adj*: **solution ~e** buffer solution

**tamponner** [tɑ̃pɔne] *vt* (*timbres*) to stamp; (*heurter*) to crash *ou* ram into; (*essuyer*) to mop up; **se tamponner** (*voitures*) to crash (into each other)

**tamponneuse** [tɑ̃pɔnøz] *adj f*: **autos ~s** dodgems, bumper cars

**tam-tam** [tamtam] *nm* tomtom

**tancer** [tɑ̃se] *vt* to scold

**tanche** [tɑ̃ʃ] *nf* tench

**tandem** [tɑ̃dɛm] *nm* tandem; (*fig*) duo, pair

**tandis** [tɑ̃di]: **~ que** *conj* while

**tangage** [tɑ̃gaʒ] *nm* pitching (and tossing)

**tangent, e** [tɑ̃ʒɑ̃, -ɑ̃t] *adj* (*Math*): **~ à** tangential to; (*fam: de justesse*) close ▷ *nf* (*Math*) tangent

**Tanger** [tɑ̃ʒe] *n* Tangier

**tango** [tɑ̃go] *nm* (*Mus*) tango ▷ *adj inv* (*couleur*) dark orange

**tanguer** [tɑ̃ge] *vi* to pitch (and toss)

**tanière** [tanjɛR] *nf* lair, den

**tanin** [tanɛ̃] *nm* tannin

**tank** [tɑ̃k] *nm* tank

**tanker** [tɑ̃kɛR] *nm* tanker

**tankini** [tɑ̃kini] *nm* tankini

**tanné, e** [tane] *adj* weather-beaten

**tanner** [tane] *vt* to tan

**tannerie** [tanRi] *nf* tannery

**tanneur** [tanœR] *nm* tanner

**tant** [tɑ̃] *adv* so much; **~ de** (*sable, eau*) so much; (*gens, livres*) so many; **~ que** *conj* as long as; **~ que** (*comparatif*) as much as; **~ mieux** that's great; so much the better; **~ mieux pour lui** good for him; **~ pis** too bad; **un ~ soit peu** (*un peu*) a little bit; (*même un peu*) (even) remotely; **~ bien que mal** as well as can be expected; **~ s'en faut** far from it, not by a long way

**tante** [tɑ̃t] *nf* aunt

**tantinet** [tɑ̃tinɛ]: **un ~** *adv* a tiny bit

**tantôt** [tɑ̃to] *adv* (*parfois*): **~ ... ~** now ... now; (*cet après-midi*) this afternoon

**Tanzanie** [tɑ̃zani] *nf*: **la ~** Tanzania

**tanzanien, ne** [tɑ̃zanjɛ̃, -ɛn] *adj* Tanzanian

**TAO** *sigle f* (= *traduction assistée par ordinateur*) MAT (= *machine-aided translation*)

**taon** [tɑ̃] *nm* horsefly, gadfly

**tapage** [tapaʒ] *nm* uproar, din; (*fig*) fuss, row; **~ nocturne** (*Jur*) disturbance of the peace (*at night*)

**tapageur, -euse** [tapaʒœR, -øz] *adj* (*bruyant: enfants etc*) noisy; (*toilette*) loud, flashy; (*publicité*) obtrusive

**tape** [tap] *nf* slap

**tape-à-l'œil** [tapalœj] *adj inv* flashy, showy

**taper** [tape] *vt* (*personne*) to clout; (*porte*) to bang, slam; (*dactylographier*) to type (out); (*Inform*) to key(board); (*fam: emprunter*): **~ qn de 10 euros** to touch sb for 10 euros, cadge 10 euros off sb ▷ *vi* (*soleil*) to beat down; **se taper** *vt* (*fam: travail*) to get landed with; (: *boire, manger*) to down; **~ sur qn** to thump sb; (*fig*) to run sb down; **~ sur qch**

**t**

405

(*clou etc*) to hit sth; (*table etc*) to bang on sth; ~ **à** (*porte etc*) to knock on; ~ **dans** (*se servir*) to dig into; ~ **des mains/pieds** to clap one's hands/ stamp one's feet; ~ **(à la machine)** to type

**tapi, e** [tapi] *adj*: ~ **dans/derrière** (*blotti*) crouching *ou* cowering in/behind; (*caché*) hidden away in/behind

**tapinois** [tapinwa]: **en** ~ *adv* stealthily

**tapioca** [tapjɔka] *nm* tapioca

**tapir** [tapiʀ]: **se tapir** *vi* to hide away

**tapis** [tapi] *nm* carpet; (*de table*) cloth; **mettre sur le** ~ (*fig*) to bring up for discussion; **aller au** ~ (*Boxe*) to go down; **envoyer au** ~ (*Boxe*) to floor; ~ **roulant** conveyor belt; ~ **de sol** (*de tente*) groundsheet; ~ **de souris** (*Inform*) mouse mat

**tapis-brosse** [tapibʀɔs] *nm* doormat

**tapisser** [tapise] *vt* (*avec du papier peint*) to paper; (*recouvrir*): ~ **qch (de)** to cover sth (with)

**tapisserie** [tapisʀi] *nf* (*tenture, broderie*) tapestry; (: *travail*) tapestry-making; (: *ouvrage*) tapestry work; (*papier peint*) wallpaper; (*fig*): **faire** ~ to sit out, be a wallflower

**tapissier, -ière** [tapisje, -jɛʀ] *nm/f*: ~-**décorateur** upholsterer and decorator

**tapoter** [tapɔte] *vt* to pat, tap

**taquet** [takɛ] *nm* (*cale*) wedge; (*cheville*) peg

**taquin, e** [takɛ̃, -in] *adj* teasing

**taquiner** [takine] *vt* to tease

**taquinerie** [takinʀi] *nf* teasing *no pl*

**tarabiscoté, e** [taʀabiskɔte] *adj* over-ornate, fussy

**tarabuster** [taʀabyste] *vt* to bother, worry

**tarama** [taʀama] *nm* (*Culin*) taramasalata

**tarauder** [taʀode] *vt* (*Tech*) to tap; to thread; (*fig*) to pierce

**tard** [taʀ] *adv* late; **au plus** ~ at the latest; **plus** ~ later (on) ▷ *nm*: **sur le** ~ (*à une heure avancée*) late in the day; (*vers la fin de la vie*) late in life

**tarder** [taʀde] *vi* (*chose*) to be a long time coming; (*personne*): ~ **à faire** to delay doing; **il me tarde d'être** I am longing to be; **sans (plus)** ~ without (further) delay

**tardif, -ive** [taʀdif, -iv] *adj* (*heure, repas, fruit*) late; (*talent, goût*) late in developing

**tardivement** [taʀdivmɑ̃] *adv* late

**tare** [taʀ] *nf* (*Comm*) tare; (*fig*) defect; blemish

**taré, e** [taʀe] *nm/f* cretin

**targette** [taʀʒɛt] *nf* (*verrou*) bolt

**targuer** [taʀge]: **se** ~ **de** *vt* to boast about

**tarif** [taʀif] *nm* (*liste*) price list, tariff (*Brit*); (*barème*) rate, rates *pl*, tariff (*Brit*); (: *de taxis etc*) fares *pl*; **voyager à plein** ~**/à** ~ **réduit** to travel at full/reduced fare

**tarifaire** [taʀifɛʀ] *adj* (*voir tarif*) relating to price lists *etc*

**tarifé, e** [taʀife] *adj*: ~ **10 euros** priced at 10 euros

**tarifer** [taʀife] *vt* to fix the price *ou* rate for

**tarification** [taʀifikasjɔ̃] *nf* fixing of a price scale

**tarir** [taʀiʀ] *vi* to dry up, run dry ▷ *vt* to dry up

**tarot** [taʀo], **tarots** *nm(pl)* tarot cards

**tartare** [taʀtaʀ] *adj* (*Culin*) tartar(e)

**tarte** [taʀt(ə)] *nf* tart; ~ **aux pommes/à la crème** apple/custard tart

**tartelette** [taʀtəlɛt] *nf* tartlet

**tartine** [taʀtin] *nf* slice of bread (and butter (*ou* jam)); ~ **de miel** slice of bread and honey; ~ **beurrée** slice of bread and butter

**tartiner** [taʀtine] *vt* to spread; **fromage à** ~ cheese spread

**tartre** [taʀtʀ(ə)] *nm* (*des dents*) tartar; (*de chaudière*) fur, scale

**tas** [tɑ] *nm* heap, pile; (*fig*): **un** ~ **de** heaps of, lots of; **en** ~ in a heap *ou* pile; **dans le** ~ (*fig*) in the crowd; among them; **formé sur le** ~ trained on the job

**Tasmanie** [tasmani] *nf*: **la** ~ Tasmania

**tasmanien, ne** [tasmanjɛ̃, -ɛn] *adj* Tasmanian

**tasse** [tɑs] *nf* cup; **boire la** ~ (*en se baignant*) to swallow a mouthful; ~ **à café/thé** coffee/ teacup

**tassé, e** [tɑse] *adj*: **bien** ~ (*café etc*) strong

**tasseau, x** [tɑso] *nm* length of wood

**tassement** [tɑsmɑ̃] *nm* (*de vertèbres*) compression; (*Écon, Pol: ralentissement*) fall-off, slowdown; (*Bourse*) dullness

**tasser** [tɑse] *vt* (*terre, neige*) to pack down; (*entasser*): ~ **qch dans** to cram sth into; **se tasser** *vi* (*terrain*) to settle; (*personne: avec l'âge*) to shrink; (*fig*) to sort itself out, settle down

**tâter** [tɑte] *vt* to feel; (*fig*) to sound out; ~ **de** (*prison etc*) to have a taste of; **se tâter** (*hésiter*) to be in two minds; ~ **le terrain** (*fig*) to test the ground

**tatillon, ne** [tatijɔ̃, -ɔn] *adj* pernickety

**tâtonnement** [tɑtɔnmɑ̃] *nm*: **par** ~**s** (*fig*) by trial and error

**tâtonner** [tɑtɔne] *vi* to grope one's way along; (*fig*) to grope around (in the dark)

**tâtons** [tɑtɔ̃]: **à** ~ *adv*: **chercher/avancer à** ~ to grope around for/grope one's way forward

**tatouage** [tatwaʒ] *nm* tattooing; (*dessin*) tattoo

**tatouer** [tatwe] *vt* to tattoo

**taudis** [todi] *nm* hovel, slum

**taule** [tol] *nf* (*fam*) nick (*Brit*), jail

**taupe** [top] *nf* mole; (*peau*) moleskin

**taupinière** [topinjɛʀ] *nf* molehill

**taureau, x** [tɔʀo] *nm* bull; (*signe*): **le T~** Taurus, the Bull; **être du T~** to be Taurus

**taurillon** [tɔʀijɔ̃] *nm* bull-calf

**tauromachie** [tɔʀɔmaʃi] *nf* bullfighting

**taux** [to] *nm* rate; (*d'alcool*) level; ~ **d'escompte** discount rate; ~ **d'intérêt** interest rate; ~ **de mortalité** mortality rate

**tavelé, e** [tavle] *adj* marked

**taverne** [tavɛʀn(ə)] *nf* inn, tavern

**taxable** [taksabl(ə)] *adj* taxable

**taxation** [taksɑsjɔ̃] *nf* taxation; (*Tél*) charges *pl*

**taxe** [taks(ə)] *nf* tax; (*douanière*) duty; **toutes** ~**s comprises (TTC)** inclusive of tax; ~ **de base** (*Tél*) unit charge; ~ **de séjour** tourist tax; ~ **à** *ou* **sur la valeur ajoutée (TVA)** value added tax (VAT)

**taxer** [takse] *vt* (*personne*) to tax; (*produit*) to put a

tax on, tax; **~ qn de qch** *(qualifier)* to call sb sth;
*(accuser)* to accuse sb of sth, tax sb with sth
**taxi** [taksi] *nm* taxi
**taxidermie** [taksidɛʀmi] *nf* taxidermy
**taxidermiste** [taksidɛʀmist(ə)] *nm/f*
taxidermist
**taximètre** [taksimɛtʀ(ə)] *nm* (taxi)meter
**taxiphone** [taksifɔn] *nm* pay phone
**TB** *abr* = **très bien, très bon**
**tbe** *abr* (= *très bon état*) VGC, vgc
**TCF** *sigle m* (= *Touring Club de France*) ≈ AA *ou* RAC
(*Brit*), ≈ AAA (*US*)
**Tchad** [tʃad] *nm*: **le ~** Chad
**tchadien, ne** [tʃadjɛ̃, -ɛn] *adj* Chad(ian), of *ou*
from Chad
**tchao** [tʃao] *excl* (*fam*) bye(-bye)!
**tchécoslovaque** [tʃekɔslɔvak] *adj*
Czechoslovak(ian) ▷ *nm/f*: **Tchécoslovaque**
Czechoslovak(ian)
**Tchécoslovaquie** [tʃekɔslɔvaki] *nf*: **la ~**
Czechoslovakia
**tchèque** [tʃɛk] *adj* Czech ▷ *nm* (*Ling*) Czech
▷ *nm/f*: **Tchèque** Czech; **la République ~** the
Czech Republic
**Tchétchénie** [tʃetʃeni] *nf*: **la ~** Chechnya
**TCS** *sigle m* (= *Touring Club de Suisse*) ≈ AA *ou* RAC
(*Brit*), ≈ AAA (*US*)
**TD** *sigle mpl* = **travaux dirigés**
**te, t'** [t(ə)] *pron* you; (*réfléchi*) yourself
**té** [te] *nm* T-square
**technicien, ne** [tɛknisjɛ̃, -ɛn] *nm/f* technician
**technicité** [tɛknisite] *nf* technical nature
**technico-commercial, e, -aux**
[tɛknikokɔmɛʀsjal, -o] *adj*: **agent ~** sales
technician
**technique** [tɛknik] *adj* technical ▷ *nf*
technique
**techniquement** [tɛknikmɑ̃] *adv* technically
**techno** [tɛkno] *nf* (*fam: Mus*): **la (musique) ~**
techno (music); (*fam*) = **technologie**
**technocrate** [tɛknɔkʀat] *nm/f* technocrat
**technocratie** [tɛknɔkʀasi] *nf* technocracy
**technologie** [tɛknɔlɔʒi] *nf* technology
**technologique** [tɛknɔlɔʒik] *adj* technological
**technologue** [tɛknɔlɔg] *nm/f* technologist
**teck** [tɛk] *nm* teak
**teckel** [tekɛl] *nm* dachshund
**tee-shirt** [tiʃœrt] *nm* T-shirt, tee-shirt
**Téhéran** [teeʀɑ̃] *n* Teheran
**teigne** [tɛɲ] *vb voir* **teindre** ▷ *nf* (*Zool*) moth;
(*Méd*) ringworm
**teigneux, -euse** [tɛɲø, -øz] *adj* (*péj*) nasty,
scabby
**teindre** [tɛ̃dʀ(ə)] *vt* to dye; **se ~ (les cheveux)** to
dye one's hair
**teint, e** [tɛ̃, tɛ̃t] *pp de* **teindre** ▷ *adj* dyed ▷ *nm* (*du
visage: permanent*) complexion, colouring (*Brit*),
coloring (*US*); (*momentané*) colour (*Brit*), color
(*US*) ▷ *nf* shade, colour, color; (*fig: petite dose*):
**une ~e de** a hint of; **grand ~** *adj inv* colourfast;
**bon ~** *adj inv* (*couleur*) fast; (*tissu*) colourfast;
(*personne*) staunch, firm

**teinté, e** [tɛ̃te] *adj* (*verres*) tinted; (*bois*) stained; **~
acajou** mahogany-stained; **~ de** (*fig*) tinged
with
**teinter** [tɛ̃te] *vt* to tint; (*bois*) to stain; (*fig: d'ironie
etc*) to tinge
**teinture** [tɛ̃tyʀ] *nf* dyeing; (*substance*) dye;
(*Méd*): **~ d'iode** tincture of iodine
**teinturerie** [tɛ̃tyʀʀi] *nf* dry cleaner's
**teinturier, -ière** [tɛ̃tyʀje, -jɛʀ] *nm/f* dry cleaner
**tel, telle** [tɛl] *adj* (*pareil*) such; (*indéfini*) such-
and-such a, a given; (*comme*): **~ un/des ...** like a/
like ...; (*intensif*): **un ~/de ~s ...** such (a)/such ...;
**rien de ~** nothing like it, no such thing; **~ que**
*conj* like, such as; **~ quel** as it is *ou* stands (*ou*
was *etc*)
**tél.** *abr* = **téléphone**
**Tel Aviv** [tɛlaviv] *n* Tel Aviv
**télé** [tele] *nf* (*télévision*) TV, telly (*Brit*); **à la ~** on TV
*ou* telly
**télébenne** [telebɛn] *nm, nf* telecabine, gondola
**télécabine** [telekabin] *nm, nf* telecabine,
gondola
**télécarte** [telekaʀt(ə)] *nf* phonecard
**téléchargeable** [teleʃaʀʒabl] *adj* downloadable
**téléchargement** [teleʃaʀʒemɑ̃] *nm* (*action*)
downloading; (*fichier*) download
**télécharger** [teleʃaʀʒe] *vt* (*Inform*) to download
**TELECOM** [telekɔm] *abr* (= *Télécommunications*)
≈ Telecom.
**télécommande** [telekɔmɑ̃d] *nf* remote control
**télécommander** [telekɔmɑ̃de] *vt* to operate by
remote control, radio-control
**télécommunications** [telekɔmynikasjɔ̃] *nfpl*
telecommunications
**télécopie** [telekɔpi] *nf* fax, telefax
**télécopieur** [telekɔpjœʀ] *nm* fax (machine)
**télédétection** [teledetɛksjɔ̃] *nf* remote sensing
**télédiffuser** [teledifyze] *vt* to broadcast (on
television)
**télédiffusion** [teledifyzjɔ̃] *nf* television
broadcasting
**télédistribution** [teledistʀibysjɔ̃] *nf* cable TV
**téléenseignement** [teleɑ̃sɛɲmɑ̃] *nm* distance
teaching (*ou* learning)
**téléférique** [telefeʀik] *nm* = **téléphérique**
**téléfilm** [telefilm] *nm* film made for TV, TV film
**télégramme** [telegʀam] *nm* telegram
**télégraphe** [telegʀaf] *nm* telegraph
**télégraphie** [telegʀafi] *nf* telegraphy
**télégraphier** [telegʀafje] *vt* to telegraph, cable
**télégraphique** [telegʀafik] *adj* telegraph *cpd*,
telegraphic; (*fig*) telegraphic
**télégraphiste** [telegʀafist(ə)] *nm/f* telegraphist
**téléguider** [telegide] *vt* to operate by remote
control, radio-control
**téléinformatique** [teleɛ̃fɔʀmatik] *nf* remote
access computing
**téléjournal, -aux** [teleʒuʀnal, -o] *nm* television
news magazine programme
**télématique** [telematik] *nf* telematics *nsg* ▷ *adj*
telematic
**téléobjectif** [teleɔbʒɛktif] *nm* telephoto lens *nsg*

**téléopérateur, trice** [teleɔpeʀatœʀ, tʀis] *nm/f* call-centre operator

**télépathie** [telepati] *nf* telepathy

**téléphérique** [telefeʀik] *nm* cable-car

**téléphone** [telefɔn] *nm* telephone; **avoir le** ~ to be on the (tele)phone; **au** ~ on the phone; ~ **arabe** bush telegraph; ~ **à carte** cardphone; ~ **avec appareil photo** cameraphone; ~ **mobile** *ou* **portable** mobile (phone) (*Brit*), cell (phone) (*US*); ~ **rouge** hotline; ~ **sans fil** cordless (tele)phone

**téléphoner** [telefɔne] *vt* to telephone ▷ *vi* to telephone; to make a phone call; ~ **à** to phone up, ring up, call up

**téléphonie** [telefɔni] *nf* telephony

**téléphonique** [telefɔnik] *adj* telephone *cpd*, phone *cpd*; **cabine** ~ call box (*Brit*), (tele)phone box (*Brit*) *ou* booth; **conversation/appel** ~ (tele)phone conversation/call

**téléphoniste** [telefɔnist(ə)] *nm/f* telephonist, telephone operator; (*d'entreprise*) switchboard operator

**téléport** [telepɔʀ] *nm* teleport

**téléprospection** [telepʀɔspɛksjɔ̃] *nf* telesales

**téléréalité** [teleʀealite] *nf* reality TV

**télescopage** [telɛskɔpaʒ] *nm* crash

**télescope** [telɛskɔp] *nm* telescope

**télescoper** [telɛskɔpe] *vt* to smash up; **se télescoper** (*véhicules*) to collide, crash into each other

**télescopique** [telɛskɔpik] *adj* telescopic

**téléscripteur** [teleskʀiptœʀ] *nm* teleprinter

**télésiège** [telesjɛʒ] *nm* chairlift

**téléski** [teleski] *nm* ski-tow; ~ **à archets** T-bar tow; ~ **à perche** button lift

**téléspectateur, -trice** [telespɛktatœʀ, -tʀis] *nm/f* (television) viewer

**télétexte®** [teletɛkst] *nm* Teletext®

**téléthon** [teletɔ̃] *nm* telethon

**télétransmission** [teletʀɑ̃smisjɔ̃] *nf* remote transmission

**télétype** [teletip] *nm* teleprinter

**télévente** [televɑ̃t] *nf* telesales

**téléviser** [televize] *vt* to televise

**téléviseur** [televizœʀ] *nm* television set

**télévision** [televizjɔ̃] *nf* television; **(poste de)** ~ television (set); **avoir la** ~ to have a television; **à la** ~ on television; ~ **par câble/satellite** cable/satellite television

**télex** [telɛks] *nm* telex

**télexer** [telɛkse] *vt* to telex

**télexiste** [telɛksist(ə)] *nm/f* telex operator

**telle** [tɛl] *adj f voir* **tel**

**tellement** [tɛlmɑ̃] *adv* (*tant*) so much; (*si*) so; ~ **plus grand (que)** so much bigger (than); ~ **de** (*sable, eau*) so much; (*gens, livres*) so many; **il s'est endormi** ~ **il était fatigué** he was so tired (that) he fell asleep; **pas** ~ not really; **pas** ~ **fort/lentement** not (all) that strong/slowly; **il ne mange pas** ~ he doesn't eat (all that) much

**tellurique** [telyʀik] *adj*: **secousse** ~ earth tremor

**téméraire** [temeʀɛʀ] *adj* reckless, rash

**témérité** [temeʀite] *nf* recklessness, rashness

**témoignage** [temwaɲaʒ] *nm* (*Jur: déclaration*) testimony *no pl*, evidence *no pl*; (: *faits*) evidence *no pl*; (*gén: rapport, récit*) account; (*fig: d'affection etc*) token, mark; expression

**témoigner** [temwaɲe] *vt* (*manifester: intérêt, gratitude*) to show ▷ *vi* (*Jur*) to testify, give evidence; ~ **que** to testify that; (*fig: démontrer*) to reveal that, testify to the fact that; ~ **de** *vt* (*confirmer*) to bear witness to, testify to

**témoin** [temwɛ̃] *nm* witness; (*fig*) testimony; (*Sport*) baton; (*Constr*) telltale ▷ *adj* control *cpd*, test *cpd*; ~ **le fait que** ... (as) witness the fact that ...; **appartement**-~ show flat (*Brit*), model apartment (*US*); **être** ~ **de** (*voir*) to witness; **prendre à** ~ to call to witness; ~ **à charge** witness for the prosecution; ~ **de connexion** (*Inform*) cookie; **T~ de Jehovah** Jehovah's Witness; ~ **de moralité** character reference; ~ **oculaire** eyewitness

**tempe** [tɑ̃p] *nf* (*Anat*) temple

**tempérament** [tɑ̃peʀamɑ̃] *nm* temperament, disposition; (*santé*) constitution; **à** ~ (*vente*) on deferred (payment) terms; (*achat*) by instalments, hire purchase *cpd*; **avoir du** ~ to be hot-blooded

**tempérance** [tɑ̃peʀɑ̃s] *nf* temperance; **société de** ~ temperance society

**tempérant, e** [tɑ̃peʀɑ̃, -ɑ̃t] *adj* temperate

**température** [tɑ̃peʀatyʀ] *nf* temperature; **prendre la** ~ **de** to take the temperature of; (*fig*) to gauge the feeling of; **avoir** *ou* **faire de la** ~ to be running *ou* have a temperature

**tempéré, e** [tɑ̃peʀe] *adj* temperate

**tempérer** [tɑ̃peʀe] *vt* to temper

**tempête** [tɑ̃pɛt] *nf* storm; ~ **de sable/neige** sand/snowstorm; **vent de** ~ gale

**tempêter** [tɑ̃pete] *vi* to rant and rave

**temple** [tɑ̃pl(ə)] *nm* temple; (*protestant*) church

**tempo** [tɛmpo] *nm* tempo

**temporaire** [tɑ̃pɔʀɛʀ] *adj* temporary

**temporairement** [tɑ̃pɔʀɛʀmɑ̃] *adv* temporarily

**temporel, le** [tɑ̃pɔʀɛl] *adj* temporal

**temporisateur, -trice** [tɑ̃pɔʀizatœʀ, -tʀis] *adj* temporizing, delaying

**temporisation** [tɑ̃pɔʀizɑsjɔ̃] *nf* temporizing, playing for time

**temporiser** [tɑ̃pɔʀize] *vi* to temporize, play for time

**temps** [tɑ̃] *nm* (*atmosphérique*) weather; (*durée*) time; (*époque*) time, times *pl*; (*Ling*) tense; (*Mus*) beat; (*Tech*) stroke; **les** ~ **changent/sont durs** times are changing/hard; **il fait beau/ mauvais** ~ the weather is fine/bad; **avoir le** ~/ **tout le** ~/**juste le** ~ to have time/plenty of time/ just enough time; **avoir fait son** ~ (*fig*) to have had its (*ou* his *etc*) day; **en** ~ **de paix/guerre** in peacetime/wartime; **en** ~ **utile** *ou* **voulu** in due time *ou* course; **de** ~ **en** ~, **de** ~ **à autre** from time to time, now and again; **en même** ~ at the same time; **à** ~ (*partir, arriver*) in time; **à plein/ mi-**~ *adv, adj* full-/part-time; **à** ~ **partiel** *adv, adj*

part-time; **dans le ~** at one time; **de tout ~**
always; **du ~ que** at the time when, in the days
when; **dans le** *ou* **du** *ou* **au ~ où** at the time
when; **pendant ce ~** in the meantime; **~**
**d'accès** (*Inform*) access time; **~ d'arrêt** pause,
halt; **~ mort** (*Sport*) stoppage (time); (*Comm*)
slack period; **~ partagé** (*Inform*) time-sharing; **~**
**réel** (*Inform*) real time

**tenable** [tənabl(ə)] *adj* bearable

**tenace** [tənas] *adj* tenacious, persistent

**ténacité** [tenasite] *nf* tenacity, persistence

**tenailler** [tənɑje] *vt* (*fig*) to torment, torture

**tenailles** [tənɑj] *nfpl* pincers

**tenais** *etc* [t(ə)nε] *vb voir* **tenir**

**tenancier, -ière** [tənɑ̃sje, -jεʀ] *nm/f* (*d'hôtel, de*
*bistro*) manager (manageress)

**tenant, e** [tənɑ̃, -ɑ̃t] *adj f voir* **séance** ▷ *nm/f*
(*Sport*): **~ du titre** title-holder ▷ *nm*: **d'un seul ~**
in one piece; **les ~s et les aboutissants** (*fig*) the
ins and outs

**tendance** [tɑ̃dɑ̃s] *nf* (*opinions*) leanings *pl*,
sympathies *pl*; (*inclination*) tendency; (*évolution*)
trend; **~ à la hausse/baisse** upward/downward
trend; **avoir ~ à** to have a tendency to, tend to

**tendancieux, -euse** [tɑ̃dɑ̃sjø, -øz] *adj*
tendentious

**tendeur** [tɑ̃dœʀ] *nm* (*de vélo*) chain-adjuster; (*de*
*câble*) wire-strainer; (*de tente*) runner; (*attache*)
elastic strap

**tendinite** [tɑ̃dinit] *nf* tendinitis, tendonitis

**tendon** [tɑ̃dɔ̃] *nm* tendon, sinew; **~ d'Achille**
Achilles' tendon

**tendre** [tɑ̃dʀ(ə)] *adj* (*viande, légumes*) tender; (*bois,*
*roche, couleur*) soft; (*affectueux*) tender, loving ▷ *vt*
(*élastique, peau*) to stretch, draw tight; (*muscle*) to
tense; (*donner*): **~ qch à qn** to hold sth out to sb;
to offer sb sth; (*fig: piège*) to set, lay; (*tapisserie*):
**tendu de soie** hung with silk, with silk
hangings; **se tendre** *vi* (*corde*) to tighten;
(*relations*) to become strained; **~ à qch/à faire** to
tend towards sth/to do; **~ l'oreille** to prick up
one's ears; **~ la main/le bras** to hold out one's
hand/stretch out one's arm; **~ la perche à qn**
(*fig*) to throw sb a line

**tendrement** [tɑ̃dʀəmɑ̃] *adv* tenderly, lovingly

**tendresse** [tɑ̃dʀεs] *nf* tenderness; **tendresses**
*nfpl* (*caresses etc*) tenderness *no pl*, caresses

**tendu, e** [tɑ̃dy] *pp de* **tendre** ▷ *adj* tight; tensed;
strained

**ténèbres** [tenεbʀ(ə)] *nfpl* darkness *nsg*

**ténébreux, -euse** [tenebʀø, -øz] *adj* obscure,
mysterious; (*personne*) saturnine

**Ténérife** [teneʀif] *nf* Tenerife

**teneur** [tənœʀ] *nf* content, substance; (*d'une*
*lettre*) terms *pl*, content; **~ en cuivre** copper
content

**ténia** [tenja] *nm* tapeworm

**tenir** [təniʀ] *vt* to hold; (*magasin, hôtel*) to run;
(*promesse*) to keep ▷ *vi* to hold; (*neige, gel*) to last;
(*survivre*) to survive; **se tenir** *vi* (*avoir lieu*) to be
held, take place; (*être: personne*) to stand; **se ~**
**droit** to stand up (*ou* sit up) straight; **bien se ~**

to behave well; **se ~ à qch** to hold on to sth;
**s'en ~ à qch** to confine o.s. to sth; to stick to sth;
**~ à** *vt* to be attached to, care about (*ou* for); (*avoir*
*pour cause*) to be due to, stem from; **~ à faire** to
want to do, be keen to do; **~ à ce que qn fasse**
**qch** to be anxious that sb should do sth; **~ de** *vt*
to partake of; (*ressembler à*) to take after; **ça ne**
**tient qu'à lui** it is entirely up to him; **~ qn**
**pour** to take sb for; **~ qch de qn** (*histoire*) to have
heard *ou* learnt sth from sb; (*qualité, défaut*) to
have inherited *ou* got sth from sb; **~ les**
**comptes** to keep the books; **~ un rôle** to play a
part; **~ de la place** to take up space *ou* room; **~**
**l'alcool** to be able to hold a drink; **~ le coup** to
hold out; **~ bon** to stand *ou* hold fast; **~ trois**
**jours/deux mois** (*résister*) to hold out *ou* last
three days/two months; **~ au chaud/à l'abri** to
keep hot/under shelter *ou* cover; **~ prêt** to have
ready; **~ sa langue** (*fig*) to hold one's tongue;
**tiens** (*ou* **tenez**), **voilà le stylo** there's the pen!;
**tiens, Alain!** look, here's Alain!; **tiens?**
(*surprise*) really?; **tiens-toi bien!** (*pour informer*)
brace yourself!, take a deep breath!

**tennis** [tenis] *nm* tennis; (*aussi*: **court de tennis**)
tennis court ▷ *nmpl ou fpl* (*aussi*: **chaussures de**
**tennis**) tennis *ou* gym shoes; **~ de table** table
tennis

**tennisman** [tenisman] *nm* tennis player

**ténor** [tenɔʀ] *nm* tenor

**tension** [tɑ̃sjɔ̃] *nf* tension; (*fig: des relations, de la*
*situation*) tension; (: *concentration, effort*) strain;
(*Méd*) blood pressure; **faire** *ou* **avoir de la ~** to
have high blood pressure; **~ nerveuse/raciale**
nervous/racial tension

**tentaculaire** [tɑ̃takylεʀ] *adj* (*fig*) sprawling

**tentacule** [tɑ̃takyl] *nm* tentacle

**tentant, e** [tɑ̃tɑ̃, -ɑ̃t] *adj* tempting

**tentateur, -trice** [tɑ̃tatœʀ, -tʀis] *adj* tempting
▷ *nm* (*Rel*) tempter

**tentation** [tɑ̃tasjɔ̃] *nf* temptation

**tentative** [tɑ̃tativ] *nf* attempt, bid; **~ d'évasion**
escape bid; **~ de suicide** suicide attempt

**tente** [tɑ̃t] *nf* tent; **~ à oxygène** oxygen tent

**tenter** [tɑ̃te] *vt* (*éprouver, attirer*) to tempt;
(*essayer*): **~ qch/de faire** to attempt *ou* try sth/to
do; **être tenté de** to be tempted to; **~ sa chance**
to try one's luck

**tenture** [tɑ̃tyʀ] *nf* hanging

**tenu, e** [təny] *pp de* **tenir** ▷ *adj* (*maison, comptes*):
**bien ~** well-kept; (*obligé*): **~ de faire** under an
obligation to do ▷ *nf* (*action de tenir*) running;
keeping; holding; (*vêtements*) clothes *pl*, gear;
(*allure*) dress *no pl*, appearance; (*comportement*)
manners *pl*, behaviour (*Brit*), behavior (*US*);
**être en ~e** to be dressed (up); **se mettre en ~e**
to dress (up); **en grande ~e** in full dress; **en**
**petite ~e** scantily dressed *ou* clad; **avoir de la**
**~e** to have good manners; (*journal*) to have a
high standard; **~e de combat** combat gear *ou*
dress; **~e de pompier** fireman's uniform; **~e**
**de route** (*Auto*) road-holding; **~e de soirée**
evening dress; **~e de sport/voyage** sports/

**t**

travelling clothes *pl ou* gear *no pl*

**ténu, e** [teny] *adj (indice, nuance)* tenuous, subtle; *(fil, objet)* fine; *(voix)* thin

**TER** *abr m* (= *Train Régional Express) local train*

**ter** [tɛʀ] *adj:* **16** ~16b *ou* B

**térébenthine** [teʀebɑ̃tin] *nf:* **(essence de)** ~ (oil of) turpentine

**tergal**® [tɛʀgal] *nm* Terylene®

**tergiversations** [tɛʀʒivɛʀsɑsjɔ̃] *nfpl* shilly-shallying *no pl*

**tergiverser** [tɛʀʒivɛʀse] *vi* to shilly-shally

**terme** [tɛʀm(ə)] *nm* term; *(fin)* end; **être en bons/mauvais ~s avec qn** to be on good/bad terms with sb; **vente/achat à ~** *(Comm)* forward sale/purchase; **au ~ de** at the end of; **en d'autres ~s** in other words; **moyen ~** *(solution intermédiaire)* middle course; **à court/long ~** *adj* short-/long-term *ou* -range ▷ *adv* in the short/long term; **à ~** *adj (Méd)* full-term ▷ *adv* sooner or later, eventually; *(Méd)* at term; **avant ~** *(Méd)* ▷ *adj* premature ▷ *adv* prematurely; **mettre un ~ à** to put an end *ou* a stop to; **toucher à son ~** to be nearing its end

**terminaison** [tɛʀminɛzɔ̃] *nf (Ling)* ending

**terminal, e, -aux** [tɛʀminal, -o] *adj (partie, phase)* final; *(Méd)* terminal ▷ *nm* terminal ▷ *nf (Scol)* ≈ sixth form *ou* final year *(Brit)*, ≈ twelfth grade *(US)*

**terminer** [tɛʀmine] *vt* to end; *(travail, repas)* to finish; **se terminer** *vi* to end; **se ~ par** to end with

**terminologie** [tɛʀminɔlɔʒi] *nf* terminology

**terminus** [tɛʀminys] *nm* terminus; **~!** all change!

**termite** [tɛʀmit] *nm* termite, white ant

**termitière** [tɛʀmitjɛʀ] *nf* ant-hill

**ternaire** [tɛʀnɛʀ] *adj* compound

**terne** [tɛʀn(ə)] *adj* dull

**ternir** [tɛʀniʀ] *vt* to dull; *(fig)* to sully, tarnish; **se ternir** *vi* to become dull

**terrain** [tɛʀɛ̃] *nm (sol, fig)* ground; *(Comm)* land *no pl*, plot (of land); *(: à bâtir)* site; **sur le ~** *(fig)* on the field; **~ de football/rugby** football/rugby pitch *(Brit) ou* field *(US)*; **~ d'atterrissage** landing strip; **~ d'aviation** airfield; **~ de camping** campsite; **un ~ d'entente** an area of agreement; **~ de golf** golf course; **~ de jeu** playground; *(Sport)* games field; **~ de sport** sports ground; **~ vague** waste ground *no pl*

**terrasse** [tɛʀas] *nf* terrace; *(de café)* pavement area, terrasse; **à la ~** *(café)* outside

**terrassement** [tɛʀasmɑ̃] *nm* earth-moving, earthworks *pl*; embankment

**terrasser** [tɛʀase] *vt (adversaire)* to floor, bring down; *(maladie etc)* to lay low

**terrassier** [tɛʀasje] *nm* navvy, roadworker

**terre** [tɛʀ] *nf (gén, aussi Élec)* earth; *(substance)* soil, earth; *(opposé à mer)* land *no pl*; *(contrée)* land; **terres** *nfpl (terrains)* lands, land *nsg*; **travail de la ~** work on the land; **en ~** *(pipe, poterie)* clay *cpd*; **mettre en ~** *(plante etc)* to plant; *(personne: enterrer)* to bury; **à ou par ~** *(mettre, être)* on the ground *(ou* floor); *(jeter, tomber)* to the ground,

down; **~ à ~** *adj inv* down-to-earth, matter-of-fact; **la T~ Adélie** Adélie Coast *ou* Land; **~ de bruyère** (heath-)peat; **~ cuite** earthenware; terracotta; **la ~ ferme** dry land, terra firma; **la T~ de Feu** Tierra del Fuego; **~ glaise** clay; **la T~ promise** the Promised Land; **la T~ Sainte** the Holy Land

**terreau** [tɛʀo] *nm* compost

**Terre-Neuve** [tɛʀnœv] *nf:* **la ~** *(aussi:* **l'île de Terre-Neuve)** Newfoundland

**terre-plein** [tɛʀplɛ̃] *nm* platform

**terrer** [tɛʀe]: **se terrer** *vi* to hide away; to go to ground

**terrestre** [tɛʀɛstʀ(ə)] *adj (surface)* earth's, of the earth; *(Bot, Zool, Mil)* land *cpd*; *(Rel)* earthly, worldly

**terreur** [tɛʀœʀ] *nf* terror *no pl*, fear

**terreux, -euse** [tɛʀø, -øz] *adj* muddy; *(goût)* earthy

**terrible** [tɛʀibl(ə)] *adj* terrible, dreadful; *(fam: fantastique)* terrific

**terriblement** [tɛʀibləmɑ̃] *adv (très)* terribly, awfully

**terrien, ne** [tɛʀjɛ̃, -ɛn] *adj:* **propriétaire ~** landowner ▷ *nm/f* countryman/woman, man/woman of the soil; *(non martien etc)* earthling; *(non marin)* landsman

**terrier** [tɛʀje] *nm* burrow, hole; *(chien)* terrier

**terrifiant, e** [tɛʀifjɑ̃, -ɑ̃t] *adj (effrayant)* terrifying; *(extraordinaire)* terrible, awful

**terrifier** [tɛʀifje] *vt* to terrify

**terril** [tɛʀil] *nm* slag heap

**terrine** [tɛʀin] *nf (récipient)* terrine; *(Culin)* pâté

**territoire** [tɛʀitwaʀ] *nm* territory; **T~ des Afars et des Issas** French Territory of Afars and Issas

**territorial, e, -aux** [tɛʀitɔʀjal, -o] *adj* territorial; **eaux ~es** territorial waters; **armée ~e** regional defence force, ≈ Territorial Army *(Brit)*; **collectivités ~es** local and regional authorities

**terroir** [tɛʀwaʀ] *nm (Agr)* soil; *(région)* region; **accent du ~** country *ou* rural accent

**terroriser** [tɛʀɔʀize] *vt* to terrorize

**terrorisme** [tɛʀɔʀism(ə)] *nm* terrorism

**terroriste** [tɛʀɔʀist(ə)] *nm/f* terrorist

**tertiaire** [tɛʀsjɛʀ] *adj* tertiary ▷ *nm (Écon)* tertiary sector, service industries *pl*

**tertiarisation** [tɛʀsjaʀizasjɔ̃] *nf* expansion or development of the service sector

**tertre** [tɛʀtʀ(ə)] *nm* hillock, mound

**tes** [te] *adj poss voir* **ton**

**tesson** [tesɔ̃] *nm:* **~ de bouteille** piece of broken bottle

**test** [tɛst] *nm* test; **~ de grossesse** pregnancy test

**testament** [tɛstamɑ̃] *nm (Jur)* will; *(fig)* legacy; *(Rel):* **T~** Testament; **faire son ~** to make one's will

**testamentaire** [tɛstamɑ̃tɛʀ] *adj* of a will

**tester** [tɛste] *vt* to test

**testicule** [tɛstikyl] *nm* testicle

**tétanie** [tetani] *nf* tetany

**tétanos** [tetanos] *nm* tetanus

**tétard** [tetar] *nm* tadpole

**tête** [tɛt] *nf* head; (*cheveux*) hair *no pl*; (*visage*) face; (*longueur*): **gagner d'une (courte)** ~ to win by a (short) head; (*Football*) header; **de** ~ *adj* (*wagon etc*) front *cpd*; (*concurrent*) leading ▷ *adv* (*calculer*) in one's head, mentally; **par** ~ (*par personne*) per head; **se mettre en** ~ **que** to get it into one's head that; **se mettre en** ~ **de faire** to take it into one's head to do; **prendre la** ~ **de qch** to take the lead in sth; **perdre la** ~ (*fig*: *s'affoler*) to lose one's head; (: *devenir fou*) to go off one's head; **ça ne va pas, la** ~? (*fam*) are you crazy?; **tenir** ~ **à qn** to stand up to *ou* defy sb; **la** ~ **en bas** with one's head down; **la** ~ **la première** (*tomber*) head-first; **la** ~ **basse** hanging one's head; **avoir la** ~ **dure** (*fig*) to be thickheaded; **faire une** ~ (*Football*) to head the ball; **faire la** ~ (*fig*) to sulk; **en** ~ (*Sport*) in the lead; at the front *ou* head; **de la** ~ **aux pieds** from head to toe; ~ **d'affiche** (*Théât etc*) top of the bill; ~ **de bétail** head *inv* of cattle; ~ **brûlée** desperado; ~ **chercheuse** homing device; ~ **d'enregistrement** recording head; ~ **d'impression** printhead; ~ **de lecture** (playback) head; ~ **de ligne** (*Transports*) start of the line; ~ **de liste** (*Pol*) chief candidate; ~ **de mort** skull and crossbones; ~ **de pont** (*Mil*) bridge- *ou* beachhead; ~ **de série** (*Tennis*) seeded player, seed; ~ **de Turc** (*fig*) whipping boy (*Brit*), butt; ~ **de veau** (*Culin*) calf's head

**tête-à-queue** [tɛtakø] *nm inv*: **faire un** ~ to spin round

**tête-à-tête** [tɛtatɛt] *nm inv* tête-à-tête; (*service*) breakfast set for two; **en** ~ in private, alone together

**tête-bêche** [tɛtbɛʃ] *adv* head to tail

**tétée** [tete] *nf* (*action*) sucking; (*repas*) feed

**téter** [tete] *vt*: ~ **(sa mère)** to suck at one's mother's breast, feed

**tétine** [tetin] *nf* teat; (*sucette*) dummy (*Brit*), pacifier (*US*)

**téton** [tetɔ̃] *nm* breast

**têtu, e** [tety] *adj* stubborn, pigheaded

**texte** [tɛkst(ə)] *nm* text; (*Scol*: *d'un devoir*) subject, topic; **apprendre son** ~ (*Théât*) to learn one's lines; **un** ~ **de loi** the wording of a law

**textile** [tɛkstil] *adj* textile *cpd* ▷ *nm* textile; (*industrie*) textile industry

**Texto®** [tɛksto] *nm* text (message)

**texto** [tɛksto] (*fam*) *adj* word for word

**textuel, le** [tɛkstɥɛl] *adj* literal, word for word

**textuellement** [tɛkstɥɛlmɑ̃] *adv* literally

**texture** [tɛkstyʀ] *nf* texture; (*fig*: *d'un texte, livre*) feel

**TF1** *sigle f* (= *Télévision française 1*) TV channel

**TG** *sigle f* = **Trésorerie générale**

**TGI** *sigle m* = **tribunal de grande instance**

**TGV** *sigle m* = **train à grande vitesse**

**thaï, e** [tai] *adj* Thai ▷ *nm* (*Ling*) Thai

**thaïlandais, e** [tailɑ̃dɛ, -ɛz] *adj* Thai

**Thaïlande** [tailɑ̃d] *nf*: **la** ~ Thailand

**thalassothérapie** [talasɔteʀapi] *nf* sea-water therapy

**thé** [te] *nm* tea; (*réunion*) tea party; **prendre le** ~ to have tea; ~ **au lait/citron** tea with milk/lemon

**théâtral, e, -aux** [teatʀal, -o] *adj* theatrical

**théâtre** [teatʀ(ə)] *nm* theatre; (*techniques, genre*) drama, theatre; (*activité*) stage, theatre; (*œuvres*) plays *pl*, dramatic works *pl*; (*fig*: *lieu*): **le** ~ **de** the scene of; (*péj*) histrionics *pl*, playacting; **faire du** ~ (*en professionnel*) to be on the stage; (*en amateur*) to do some acting; ~ **filmé** filmed stage productions *pl*

**thébain, e** [tebɛ̃, -ɛn] *adj* Theban

**Thèbes** [tɛb] *n* Thebes

**théière** [tejɛʀ] *nf* teapot

**théine** [tein] *nf* theine

**théisme** [teism(ə)] *nm* theism

**thématique** [tematik] *adj* thematic

**thème** [tɛm] *nm* theme; (*Scol*: *traduction*) prose (composition); ~ **astral** birth chart

**théocratie** [teɔkʀasi] *nf* theocracy

**théologie** [teɔlɔʒi] *nf* theology

**théologien, ne** [teɔlɔʒjɛ̃, -ɛn] *nm* theologian

**théologique** [teɔlɔʒik] *adj* theological

**théorème** [teɔʀɛm] *nm* theorem

**théoricien, ne** [teɔʀisjɛ̃, -ɛn] *nm/f* theoretician, theorist

**théorie** [teɔʀi] *nf* theory; **en** ~ in theory

**théorique** [teɔʀik] *adj* theoretical

**théoriquement** [teɔʀikmɑ̃] *adv* theoretically

**théoriser** [teɔʀize] *vi* to theorize

**thérapeutique** [teʀapøtik] *adj* therapeutic ▷ *nf* (*Méd*: *branche*) therapeutics *nsg*; (: *traitement*) therapy

**thérapie** [teʀapi] *nf* therapy; ~ **de groupe** group therapy

**thermal, e, -aux** [tɛʀmal, -o] *adj* thermal; **station** ~**e** spa; **cure** ~**e** water cure

**thermes** [tɛʀm(ə)] *nmpl* thermal baths; (*romains*) thermae *pl*

**thermique** [tɛʀmik] *adj* (*énergie*) thermic; (*unité*) thermal

**thermodynamique** [tɛʀmɔdinamik] *nf* thermodynamics *nsg*

**thermoélectrique** [tɛʀmoelɛktʀik] *adj* thermoelectric

**thermomètre** [tɛʀmɔmɛtʀ(ə)] *nm* thermometer

**thermonucléaire** [tɛʀmɔnykleɛʀ] *adj* thermonuclear

**thermos®** [tɛʀmos] *nm ou nf*: **(bouteille)** **thermos** vacuum *ou* Thermos® flask (*Brit*) *ou* bottle (*US*)

**thermostat** [tɛʀmɔsta] *nm* thermostat

**thésauriser** [tezɔʀize] *vi* to hoard money

**thèse** [tɛz] *nf* thesis

**Thessalie** [tesali] *nf*: **la** ~ Thessaly

**thibaude** [tibod] *nf* carpet underlay

**thon** [tɔ̃] *nm* tuna (fish)

**thonier** [tɔnje] *nm* tuna boat

**thoracique** [tɔʀasik] *adj* thoracic

**t**

**thorax** [tɔʀaks] *nm* thorax
**thrombose** [tʀɔ̃boz] *nf* thrombosis
**thym** [tɛ̃] *nm* thyme
**thyroïde** [tiʀɔid] *nf* thyroid (gland)
**TI** *sigle m* = **tribunal d'instance**
**tiare** [tjaʀ] *nf* tiara
**Tibet** [tibɛ] *nm*: **le ~** Tibet
**tibétain, e** [tibetɛ̃, -ɛn] *adj* Tibetan
**tibia** [tibja] *nm* shin; (*os*) shinbone, tibia
**Tibre** [tibʀ(ə)] *nm*: **le ~** the Tiber
**TIC** *sigle fpl* (= *technologies de l'information et de la communication*) ICT *sg*
**tic** [tik] *nm* tic, (nervous) twitch; (*de langage etc*) mannerism
**ticket** [tikɛ] *nm* ticket; **~ de caisse** till receipt; **~ modérateur** *patient's contribution towards medical costs*; **~ de quai** platform ticket; **~ repas** luncheon voucher
**tic-tac** [tiktak] *nm inv* tick-tock
**tictaquer** [tiktake] *vi* to tick (away)
**tiède** [tjɛd] *adj* (*bière etc*) lukewarm; (*thé, café etc*) tepid; (*bain, accueil, sentiment*) lukewarm; (*vent, air*) mild, warm ▷ *adv*: **boire ~** to drink things lukewarm
**tièdement** [tjɛdmã] *adv* coolly, half-heartedly
**tiédeur** [tjedœʀ] *nf* lukewarmness; (*du vent, de l'air*) mildness
**tiédir** [tjediʀ] *vi* (*se réchauffer*) to grow warmer; (*refroidir*) to cool
**tien, tienne** [tjɛ̃, tjɛn] *pron*: **le ~ (la ~ne), les ~s (~nes)** yours; **à la ~ne!** cheers!
**tiendrai** *etc* [tjɛ̃dʀe] *vb voir* **tenir**
**tienne** [tjɛn] *vb voir* **tenir** ▷ *pron voir* **tien**
**tiens** [tjɛ̃] *vb, excl voir* **tenir**
**tierce** [tjɛʀs(ə)] *adj f, nf voir* **tiers**
**tiercé** [tjɛʀse] *nm* *system of forecast betting giving first three horses*
**tiers, tierce** [tjɛʀ, tjɛʀs(ə)] *adj* third ▷ *nm* (*Jur*) third party; (*fraction*) third ▷ *nf* (*Mus*) third; (*Cartes*) tierce; **une tierce personne** a third party; **assurance au ~** third-party insurance; **le ~ monde** the third world; **~ payant** *direct payment by insurers of medical expenses*; **~ provisionnel** *interim payment of tax*
**tifs** [tif] (*fam*) *nmpl* hair
**TIG** *sigle m* = **travail d'intérêt général**
**tige** [tiʒ] *nf* stem; (*baguette*) rod
**tignasse** [tiɲas] *nf* (*péj*) shock *ou* mop of hair
**Tigre** [tigʀ(ə)] *nm*: **le ~** the Tigris
**tigre** [tigʀ(ə)] *nm* tiger
**tigré, e** [tigʀe] *adj* (*rayé*) striped; (*tacheté*) spotted
**tigresse** [tigʀɛs] *nf* tigress
**tilleul** [tijœl] *nm* lime (tree), linden (tree); (*boisson*) lime(-blossom) tea
**tilt** [tilt(ə)] *nm*: **faire ~** (*fig: échouer*) to miss the target; (: *inspirer*) to ring a bell
**timbale** [tɛ̃bal] *nf* (metal) tumbler; **timbales** *nfpl* (*Mus*) timpani, kettledrums
**timbrage** [tɛ̃bʀaʒ] *nm*: **dispensé de ~** post(age) paid
**timbre** [tɛ̃bʀ(ə)] *nm* (*tampon*) stamp; (*aussi*: **timbre-poste**) (postage) stamp; (*cachet de la poste*) postmark; (*sonnette*) bell; (*Mus: de voix, instrument*) timbre, tone; **~ anti-tabac** nicotine patch; **~ dateur** date stamp
**timbré, e** [tɛ̃bʀe] *adj* (*enveloppe*) stamped; (*voix*) resonant; (*fam: fou*) cracked, nuts
**timbrer** [tɛ̃bʀe] *vt* to stamp
**timide** [timid] *adj* (*emprunté*) shy, timid; (*timoré*) timid, timorous
**timidement** [timidmã] *adv* shyly; timidly
**timidité** [timidite] *nf* shyness; timidity
**timonerie** [timɔnʀi] *nf* wheelhouse
**timonier** [timɔnje] *nm* helmsman
**timoré, e** [timɔʀe] *adj* timorous
**tint** *etc* [tɛ̃] *vb voir* **tenir**
**tintamarre** [tɛ̃tamaʀ] *nm* din, uproar
**tintement** [tɛ̃tmã] *nm* ringing, chiming; **~s d'oreilles** ringing in the ears
**tinter** [tɛ̃te] *vi* to ring, chime; (*argent, clés*) to jingle
**Tipp-Ex®** [tipɛks] *nm* Tipp-Ex®
**tique** [tik] *nf* tick (*insect*)
**tiquer** [tike] *vi* (*personne*) to make a face
**TIR** *sigle mpl* (= *Transports internationaux routiers*) TIR
**tir** [tiʀ] *nm* (*sport*) shooting; (*fait ou manière de tirer*) firing *no pl*; (*Football*) shot; (*stand*) shooting gallery; **~ d'obus/de mitraillette** shell/machine gun fire; **~ à l'arc** archery; **~ de barrage** barrage fire; **~ au fusil** (rifle) shooting; **~ au pigeon** (*d'argile*) clay pigeon shooting
**tirade** [tiʀad] *nf* tirade
**tirage** [tiʀaʒ] *nm* (*action*) printing; (*Photo*) print; (*Inform*) printout; (*de journal*) circulation; (*de livre*) (print-)run; edition; (*de cheminée*) draught (*Brit*), draft (*US*); (*de loterie*) draw; (*fig: désaccord*) friction; **~ au sort** drawing lots
**tiraillement** [tiʀajmã] *nm* (*douleur*) sharp pain; (*fig: doutes*) agony *no pl* of indecision; (*conflits*) friction *no pl*
**tirailler** [tiʀaje] *vt* to pull at, tug at; (*fig*) to gnaw at ▷ *vi* to fire at random
**tirailleur** [tiʀajœʀ] *nm* skirmisher
**tirant** [tiʀã] *nm*: **~ d'eau** draught (*Brit*), draft (*US*)
**tire** [tiʀ] *nf*: **vol à la ~** pickpocketing
**tiré** [tiʀe] *adj* (*visage, traits*) drawn ▷ *nm* (*Comm*) drawee; **~ par les cheveux** far-fetched; **~ à part** off-print
**tire-au-flanc** [tiʀoflã] *nm inv* (*péj*) skiver
**tire-bouchon** [tiʀbuʃɔ̃] *nm* corkscrew
**tire-bouchonner** [tiʀbuʃɔne] *vt* to twirl
**tire-d'aile** [tiʀdɛl]: **à tire-d'aile** *adv* swiftly
**tire-fesses** [tiʀfɛs] *nm inv* ski-tow
**tire-lait** [tiʀlɛ] *nm inv* breast-pump
**tire-larigot** [tiʀlaʀigo]: **à ~** *adv* as much as one likes, to one's heart's content
**tirelire** [tiʀliʀ] *nf* moneybox
**tirer** [tiʀe] *vt* (*gén*) to pull; (*extraire*): **~ qch de** to take *ou* pull sth out of; to get sth out of; to extract sth from; (*tracer: ligne, trait*) to draw, trace; (*fermer: volet, porte, trappe*) to pull to, close; (: *rideau*) to draw; (*choisir: carte, conclusion, aussi*

Comm: *chèque*) to draw; (*en faisant feu*: *balle, coup*) to fire; (: *animal*) to shoot; (*journal, livre, photo*) to print; (*Football*: *corner etc*) to take ▷ vi (*faire feu*) to fire; (*faire du tir, Football*) to shoot; (*cheminée*) to draw; **se tirer** vi (*fam*) to push off; (*aussi*: **s'en tirer**) to pull through; ~ **sur** (*corde, poignée*) to pull on *ou* at; (*faire feu sur*) to shoot *ou* fire at; (*pipe*) to draw on; (*fig*: *avoisiner*) to verge *ou* border on; ~ **six mètres** (*Navig*) to draw six metres of water; ~ **son nom de** to take *ou* get its name from; ~ **la langue** to stick out one's tongue; ~ **qn de** (*embarras etc*) to help *ou* get sb out of; ~ **à l'arc/la carabine** to shoot with a bow and arrow/with a rifle; ~ **en longueur** to drag on; ~ **à sa fin** to be drawing to an end; ~ **les cartes** to read *ou* tell the cards

**tiret** [tiʀɛ] *nm* dash; (*en fin de ligne*) hyphen
**tireur** [tiʀœʀ] *nm* gunman; (*Comm*) drawer; **bon ~** good shot; ~ **d'élite** marksman; ~ **de cartes** fortuneteller
**tiroir** [tiʀwaʀ] *nm* drawer
**tiroir-caisse** [tiʀwaʀkɛs] *nm* till
**tisane** [tizan] *nf* herb tea
**tison** [tizɔ̃] *nm* brand
**tisonner** [tizɔne] *vt* to poke
**tisonnier** [tizɔnje] *nm* poker
**tissage** [tisaʒ] *nm* weaving *no pl*
**tisser** [tise] *vt* to weave
**tisserand, e** [tisʀɑ̃, -ɑ̃d] *nm/f* weaver
**tissu¹** [tisy] *nm* fabric, material, cloth *no pl*; (*fig*) fabric; (*Anat, Bio*) tissue; ~ **de mensonges** web of lies
**tissu², e** [tisy] *adj*: ~ **de** woven through with
**tissu-éponge** [tisyepɔ̃ʒ] *nm* (terry) towelling *no pl*
**titane** [titan] *nm* titanium
**titanesque** [titanɛsk(ə)] *adj* titanic
**titiller** [titile] *vt* to titillate
**titrage** [titʀaʒ] *nm* (*d'un film*) titling; (*d'un alcool*) determination of alcohol content
**titre** [titʀ(ə)] *nm* (*gén*) title; (*de journal*) headline; (*diplôme*) qualification; (*Comm*) security; (*Chimie*) titre; **en ~** (*champion, responsable*) official, recognized; **à juste ~** with just cause, rightly; **à quel ~?** on what grounds?; **à aucun ~** on no account; **au même ~ (que)** in the same way (as); **au ~ de la coopération** *etc* in the name of cooperation *etc*; **à ~ d'exemple** as an *ou* by way of an example; **à ~ exceptionnel** exceptionally; **à ~ d'information** for (your) information; **à ~ gracieux** free of charge; **à ~ d'essai** on a trial basis; **à ~ privé** in a private capacity; ~ **courant** running head; ~ **de propriété** title deed; ~ **de transport** ticket
**titré, e** [titʀe] *adj* (*livre, film*) entitled; (*personne*) titled
**titrer** [titʀe] *vt* (*Chimie*) to titrate; to assay; (*Presse*) to run as a headline; (*vin*): ~ **10°** to be 10° proof
**titubant, e** [titybɑ̃, -ɑ̃t] *adj* staggering, reeling
**tituber** [titybe] *vi* to stagger *ou* reel (along)
**titulaire** [titylɛʀ] *adj* (*Admin*) appointed, with

tenure ▷ *nm* (*Admin*) incumbent; **être ~ de** to hold
**titularisation** [titylaʀizasjɔ̃] *nf* granting of tenure
**titulariser** [titylaʀize] *vt* to give tenure to
**TNP** *sigle m* = **Théâtre national populaire**
**TNT** *sigle m* (= *Trinitrotoluène*) TNT ▷ *sigle f* (= *Télévision numérique terrestre*) digital television
**toast** [tost] *nm* slice *ou* piece of toast; (*de bienvenue*) (welcoming) toast; **porter un ~ à qn** to propose *ou* drink a toast to sb
**toboggan** [tɔbɔgɑ̃] *nm* toboggan; (*jeu*) slide; (*Auto*) flyover (*Brit*), overpass (*US*); ~ **de secours** (*Aviat*) escape chute
**toc** [tɔk] *nm*: **en ~** imitation *cpd*
**tocsin** [tɔksɛ̃] *nm* alarm (bell)
**toge** [tɔʒ] *nf* toga; (*de juge*) gown
**Togo** [tɔgo] *nm*: **le ~** Togo
**togolais, e** [tɔgɔlɛ, -ɛz] *adj* Togolese
**tohu-bohu** [tɔybɔy] *nm* (*désordre*) confusion; (*tumulte*) commotion
**toi** [twa] *pron* you; ~, **tu l'as fait?** did YOU do it?
**toile** [twal] *nf* (*matériau*) cloth *no pl*; (*bâche*) piece of canvas; (*tableau*) canvas; **grosse ~** canvas; **tisser sa ~** (*araignée*) to spin its web; ~ **d'araignée** spider's web; (*au plafond etc*: *à enlever*) cobweb; ~ **cirée** oilcloth; ~ **émeri** emery cloth; ~ **de fond** (*fig*) backdrop; ~ **de jute** hessian; ~ **de lin** linen; ~ **de tente** canvas
**toilettage** [twalɛtaʒ] *nm* grooming *no pl*; (*d'un texte*) tidying up
**toilette** [twalɛt] *nf* wash; (*s'habiller et se préparer*) getting ready, washing and dressing; (*habits*) outfit; dress *no pl*; **toilettes** *nfpl* toilet *nsg*; **les ~s des dames/messieurs** the ladies'/gents' (toilets) (*Brit*), the ladies'/men's (rest)room (*US*); **faire sa ~** to have a wash, get washed; **faire la ~ de** (*animal*) to groom; (*voiture etc*) to clean, wash; (*texte*) to tidy up; **articles de ~** toiletries; ~ **intime** personal hygiene
**toi-même** [twamɛm] *pron* yourself
**toise** [twaz] *nf*: **passer à la ~** to have one's height measured
**toiser** [twaze] *vt* to eye up and down
**toison** [twazɔ̃] *nf* (*de mouton*) fleece; (*cheveux*) mane
**toit** [twa] *nm* roof; ~ **ouvrant** sun roof
**toiture** [twatyʀ] *nf* roof
**Tokyo** [tɔkjo] *n* Tokyo
**tôle** [tol] *nf* sheet metal *no pl*; (*plaque*) steel (*ou* iron) sheet; **tôles** *nfpl* (*carrosserie*) bodywork *nsg* (*Brit*), body *nsg*; panels; ~ **d'acier** sheet steel *no pl*; ~ **ondulée** corrugated iron
**Tolède** [tɔlɛd] *n* Toledo
**tolérable** [tɔleʀabl(ə)] *adj* tolerable, bearable
**tolérance** [tɔleʀɑ̃s] *nf* tolerance; (*hors taxe*) allowance
**tolérant, e** [tɔleʀɑ̃, -ɑ̃t] *adj* tolerant
**tolérer** [tɔleʀe] *vt* to tolerate; (*Admin*: *hors taxe etc*) to allow
**tôlerie** [tolʀi] *nf* sheet metal manufacture; (*atelier*) sheet metal workshop; (*ensemble des tôles*)

**t**

413

panels *pl*

**tollé** [tɔle] *nm*: **un ~ (de protestations)** a general outcry

**TOM** [tɔm] *sigle nm(pl)* = **territoire(s) d'outre-mer**

**tomate** [tɔmat] *nf* tomato

**tombal, e** [tɔbal] *adj*: **pierre ~e** tombstone, gravestone

**tombant, e** [tɔbā, -āt] *adj* (*fig*) drooping, sloping

**tombe** [tɔb] *nf* (*sépulture*) grave; (*avec monument*) tomb

**tombeau, x** [tɔbo] *nm* tomb; **à ~ ouvert** at breakneck speed

**tombée** [tɔbe] *nf*: **à la ~ du jour** *ou* **de la nuit** at the close of day, at nightfall

**tomber** [tɔbe] *vi* to fall ▷ *vt*: **~ la veste** to slip off one's jacket; **laisser ~** to drop; **~ sur** *vt* (*rencontrer*) to come across; (*attaquer*) to set about; **~ de fatigue/sommeil** to drop from exhaustion/be falling asleep on one's feet; **~ à l'eau** (*fig: projet etc*) to fall through; **~ en panne** to break down; **~ juste** (*opération, calcul*) to come out right; **~ en ruine** to fall into ruins; **ça tombe bien/mal** (*fig*) that's come at the right/wrong time; **il est bien/mal tombé** (*fig*) he's been lucky/unlucky

**tombereau, x** [tɔbro] *nm* tipcart

**tombeur** [tɔbœʀ] *nm* (*péj*) Casanova

**tombola** [tɔbɔla] *nf* tombola

**Tombouctou** [tɔbuktu] *n* Timbuktu

**tome** [tɔm] *nm* volume

**tommette** [tɔmɛt] *nf* hexagonal floor tile

**ton¹, ta** (*pl* **tes**) [tɔ̃, ta, te] *adj poss* your

**ton²** [tɔ̃] *nm* (*gén*) tone; (*Mus*) key; (*couleur*) shade, tone; (*de la voix: hauteur*) pitch; **donner le ~** to set the tone; **élever** *ou* **hausser le ~** to raise one's voice; **de bon ~** in good taste; **si vous le prenez sur ce ~** if you're going to take it like that; **~ sur ~** in matching shades

**tonal, e** [tɔnal] *adj* tonal

**tonalité** [tɔnalite] *nf* (*au téléphone*) dialling tone; (*Mus*) tonality; (: *ton*) key; (*fig*) tone

**tondeuse** [tɔdøz] *nf* (*à gazon*) (lawn)mower; (*du coiffeur*) clippers *pl*; (*pour la tonte*) shears *pl*

**tondre** [tɔdʀ(ə)] *vt* (*pelouse, herbe*) to mow; (*haie*) to cut, clip; (*mouton, toison*) to shear; (*cheveux*) to crop

**tondu, e** [tɔdy] *pp de* **tondre** ▷ *adj* (*cheveux*) cropped; (*mouton, crâne*) shorn

**Tonga** [tɔga]: **les îles ~** Tonga

**tongs** [tɔg] *nfpl* flip-flops (*Brit*), thongs (*US*)

**tonicité** [tɔnisite] *nf* (*Méd: des tissus*) tone; (*fig: de l'air, la mer*) bracing effect

**tonifiant, e** [tɔnifjā, -āt] *adj* invigorating, revivifying

**tonifier** [tɔnifje] *vt* (*air, eau*) to invigorate; (*peau, organisme*) to tone up

**tonique** [tɔnik] *adj* fortifying; (*personne*) dynamic ▷ *nm, nf* tonic

**tonitruant, e** [tɔnitʀyā, -āt] *adj*: **voix ~e** thundering voice

**Tonkin** [tɔkɛ̃] *nm*: **le ~** Tonkin, Tongking

**tonkinois, e** [tɔkinwa, -waz] *adj* Tonkinese

**tonnage** [tɔnaʒ] *nm* tonnage

**tonnant, e** [tɔnā, -āt] *adj* thunderous

**tonne** [tɔn] *nf* metric ton, tonne

**tonneau, x** [tɔno] *nm* (*à vin, cidre*) barrel; (*Navig*) ton; **faire des ~x** (*voiture, avion*) to roll over

**tonnelet** [tɔnlɛ] *nm* keg

**tonnelier** [tɔnəlje] *nm* cooper

**tonnelle** [tɔnɛl] *nf* bower, arbour (*Brit*), arbor (*US*)

**tonner** [tɔne] *vi* to thunder; (*parler avec véhémence*): **~ contre qn/qch** to inveigh against sb/sth; **il tonne** it is thundering, there's some thunder

**tonnerre** [tɔnɛʀ] *nm* thunder; **coup de ~** (*fig*) thunderbolt, bolt from the blue; **un ~ d'applaudissements** thundering applause; **du ~** *adj* (*fam*) terrific

**tonsure** [tɔsyʀ] *nf* bald patch; (*de moine*) tonsure

**tonte** [tɔt] *nf* shearing

**tonton** [tɔtɔ̃] *nm* uncle

**tonus** [tɔnys] *nm* (*des muscles*) tone; (*d'une personne*) dynamism

**top** [tɔp] *nm*: **au troisième ~** at the third stroke ▷ *adj*: **~ secret** top secret ▷ *excl* go!

**topaze** [tɔpaz] *nf* topaz

**toper** [tɔpe] *vi*: **tope-/topez-là** it's a deal!, you're on!

**topinambour** [tɔpinābuʀ] *nm* Jerusalem artichoke

**topo** [tɔpo] *nm* (*discours, exposé*) talk; (*fam*) spiel

**topographie** [tɔpɔgʀafi] *nf* topography

**topographique** [tɔpɔgʀafik] *adj* topographical

**toponymie** [tɔpɔnimi] *nf* study of place names, toponymy

**toquade** [tɔkad] *nf* fad, craze

**toque** [tɔk] *nf* (*de fourrure*) fur hat; **~ de jockey/juge** jockey's/judge's cap; **~ de cuisinier** chef's hat

**toqué, e** [tɔke] *adj* (*fam*) touched, cracked

**torche** [tɔʀʃ(ə)] *nf* torch; **se mettre en ~** (*parachute*) to candle

**torcher** [tɔʀʃe] *vt* (*fam*) to wipe

**torchère** [tɔʀʃɛʀ] *nf* flare

**torchon** [tɔʀʃɔ̃] *nm* cloth, duster; (*à vaisselle*) tea towel *ou* cloth

**tordre** [tɔʀdʀ(ə)] *vt* (*chiffon*) to wring; (*barre, fig: visage*) to twist; **se tordre** *vi* (*barre*) to bend; (*roue*) to twist, buckle; (*ver, serpent*) to writhe; **se ~ le pied/bras** to twist one's foot/arm; **se ~ de douleur/rire** to writhe in pain/be doubled up with laughter

**tordu, e** [tɔʀdy] *pp de* **tordre** ▷ *adj* (*fig*) warped, twisted

**torero** [tɔʀeʀo] *nm* bullfighter

**tornade** [tɔʀnad] *nf* tornado

**toron** [tɔʀɔ̃] *nm* strand (of rope)

**Toronto** [tɔʀɔto] *n* Toronto

**torontois, e** [tɔʀɔtwa, -waz] *adj* Torontonian ▷ *nm/f*: **Torontois, e** Torontonian

**torpeur** [tɔʀpœʀ] *nf* torpor, drowsiness

**torpille** [tɔʀpij] *nf* torpedo

**torpiller** [tɔʀpije] *vt* to torpedo
**torpilleur** [tɔʀpijœʀ] *nm* torpedo boat
**torréfaction** [tɔʀefaksjɔ̃] *nf* roasting
**torréfier** [tɔʀefje] *vt* to roast
**torrent** [tɔʀɑ̃] *nm* torrent, mountain stream;
 (*fig*) **un ~ de** a torrent *ou* flood of; **il pleut à ~s**
 the rain is lashing down
**torrentiel, le** [tɔʀɑ̃sjɛl] *adj* torrential
**torride** [tɔʀid] *adj* torrid
**tors, torse** *ou* **torte** [tɔʀ, tɔʀs(ə) ᴿouʰtɔʀt(ə)] *adj*
 twisted
**torsade** [tɔʀsad] *nf* twist; (*Archit*) cable
 moulding (*Brit*) *ou* molding (*US*)
**torsader** [tɔʀsade] *vt* to twist
**torse** [tɔʀs(ə)] *nm* torso; (*poitrine*) chest
**torsion** [tɔʀsjɔ̃] *nf* (*action*) twisting; (*Tech*,
 *Physique*) torsion
**tort** [tɔʀ] *nm* (*défaut*) fault; (*préjudice*) wrong *no pl*;
 **torts** *nmpl* (*Jur*) fault *nsg*; **avoir ~** to be wrong;
 **être dans son ~** to be in the wrong; **donner ~ à**
 **qn** to lay the blame on sb; (*fig*) to prove sb
 wrong; **causer du ~ à** to harm; to be harmful *ou*
 detrimental to; **en ~** in the wrong, at fault; **à ~**
 wrongly; **à ~ ou à raison** rightly or wrongly; **à ~**
 **et à travers** wildly
**torte** [tɔʀt(ə)] *adj f voir* **tors**
**torticolis** [tɔʀtikɔli] *nm* stiff neck
**tortiller** [tɔʀtije] *vt* (*corde, mouchoir*) to twist;
 (*doigts*) to twiddle; **se tortiller** *vi* to wriggle,
 squirm
**tortionnaire** [tɔʀsjɔnɛʀ] *nm* torturer
**tortue** [tɔʀty] *nf* tortoise; (*fig*) slowcoach (*Brit*),
 slowpoke (*US*)
**tortueux, -euse** [tɔʀtɥø, -øz] *adj* (*rue*) twisting;
 (*fig*) tortuous
**torture** [tɔʀtyʀ] *nf* torture
**torturer** [tɔʀtyʀe] *vt* to torture; (*fig*) to torment
**torve** [tɔʀv(ə)] *adj:* **regard ~** menacing *ou* grim
 look
**toscan, e** [tɔskɑ̃, -an] *adj* Tuscan
**Toscane** [tɔskan] *nf:* **la ~** Tuscany
**tôt** [to] *adv* early; **~ ou tard** sooner or later; **si ~**
 so early; (*déjà*) so soon; **au plus ~** at the earliest,
 as soon as possible; **plus ~** earlier; **il eut ~ fait**
 **de faire ...** he soon did ...
**total, e, -aux** [tɔtal, -o] *adj, nm* total; **au ~** in
 total *ou* all; (*fig*) all in all; **faire le ~** to work out
 the total
**totalement** [tɔtalmɑ̃] *adv* totally, completely
**totalisateur** [tɔtalizatœʀ] *nm* adding machine
**totaliser** [tɔtalize] *vt* to total (up)
**totalitaire** [tɔtalitɛʀ] *adj* totalitarian
**totalitarisme** [tɔtalitaʀism(ə)] *nm*
 totalitarianism
**totalité** [tɔtalite] *nf:* **la ~ de: la ~ des élèves** all
 (of) the pupils; **la ~ de la population/classe**
 the whole population/class; **en ~** entirely
**totem** [tɔtɛm] *nm* totem
**toubib** [tubib] *nm* (*fam*) doctor
**touchant, e** [tuʃɑ̃, -ɑ̃t] *adj* touching
**touche** [tuʃ] *nf* (*de piano, de machine à écrire*) key;
 (*de violon*) fingerboard; (*de télécommande etc*) key,

button; (*Peinture etc*) stroke, touch; (*fig: de couleur,
nostalgie*) touch, hint; (*Rugby*) line-out; (*Football:
aussi:* **remise en touche**) throw-in; (*aussi:* **ligne
de touche**) touch-line; (*Escrime*) hit; **en ~** in (*ou*
into) touch; **avoir une drôle de ~** to look a
sight; **~ de commande/de fonction/de retour**
(*Inform*) control/function/return key; **~ à**
**effleurement** *ou* **sensitive** touch-sensitive
control *ou* key
**touche-à-tout** [tuʃatu] *nm inv* (*péj: gén: enfant*)
meddler; (: *fig: inventeur etc*) dabbler
**toucher** [tuʃe] *nm* touch ▷ *vt* to touch; (*palper*) to
feel; (*atteindre: d'un coup de feu etc*) to hit; (*affecter*)
to touch, affect; (*concerner*) to concern, affect;
(*contacter*) to reach, contact; (*recevoir: récompense*)
to receive, get; (: *salaire*) to draw, get; (*chèque*) to
cash; (*aborder: problème, sujet*) to touch on; **au ~** to
the touch; by the feel; **se toucher** (*être en contact*)
to touch; **~ à** to touch; (*modifier*) to touch,
tamper *ou* meddle with; (*traiter de, concerner*) to
have to do with, concern; **je vais lui en ~ un**
**mot** I'll have a word with him about it; **~ au**
**but** (*fig*) to near one's goal; **~ à sa fin** to be
drawing to a close
**touffe** [tuf] *nf* tuft
**touffu, e** [tufy] *adj* thick, dense; (*fig*) complex,
involved
**toujours** [tuʒuʀ] *adv* always; (*encore*) still;
(*constamment*) forever; **depuis ~** always; **essaie**
**~** (you can) try anyway; **pour ~** forever; **~ est-il**
**que** the fact remains that; **~ plus** more and
more
**toulonnais, e** [tulɔnɛ, -ɛz] *adj* of *ou* from Toulon
**toulousain, e** [tuluzɛ̃, -ɛn] *adj* of *ou* from
Toulouse
**toupet** [tupɛ] *nm* quiff (*Brit*), tuft; (*fam*) nerve,
cheek (*Brit*)
**toupie** [tupi] *nf* (spinning) top
**tour** [tuʀ] *nf* tower; (*immeuble*) high-rise block
(*Brit*) *ou* building (*US*), tower block (*Brit*); (*Échecs*)
castle, rook ▷ *nm* (*excursion: à pied*) stroll, walk;
(: *en voiture etc*) run, ride; (: *plus long*) trip; (*Sport:
aussi:* **tour de piste**) lap; (*d'être servi ou de jouer etc*,
*tournure, de vis ou clef*) turn; (*de roue etc*) revolution;
(*circonférence*): **de 3 m de ~** 3 m round, with a
circumference *ou* girth of 3 m; (*Pol: aussi:* **tour de
scrutin**) ballot; (*ruse, de prestidigitation, de cartes*)
trick; (*de potier*) wheel; (*à bois, métaux*) lathe;
**faire le ~ de** to go (a)round; (*à pied*) to walk
(a)round; (*fig*) to review; **faire le ~ de l'Europe**
to tour Europe; **faire un ~** to go for a walk; (*en
voiture etc*) to go for a ride; **faire 2 ~s** to go
(a)round twice; (*hélice etc*) to turn *ou* revolve
twice; **fermer à double ~** *vi* to double-lock the
door; **c'est au ~ de Renée** it's Renée's turn; **à ~**
**de rôle, ~ à ~** in turn; **à ~ de bras** with all one's
strength; (*fig*) non-stop, relentlessly; **~ de**
**taille/tête** waist/head measurement; **~ de**
**chant** song recital; **~ de contrôle** *nf* control
tower; **le T~ de France** the Tour de France; *see
note*; **~ de garde** spell of duty; **~ d'horizon** (*fig*)
general survey; **~ de lit** valance; **~ de main**

**t**

dexterity, knack; **en un ~ de main** (as) quick as a flash; **~ de passe-passe** trick, sleight of hand; **~ de reins** sprained back

### ● TOUR DE FRANCE

The *Tour de France* is an annual road race for professional cyclists. It takes about three weeks to complete and is divided into daily stages, or "étapes" of approximately 175km (110 miles) over terrain of varying levels of difficulty. The leading cyclist wears a yellow jersey, the "maillot jaune". The route varies; it is not usually confined to France but always ends in Paris. In addition, there are a number of time trials.

**tourangeau, elle, x** [tuʀɑ̃ʒo, -ɛl] *adj* (*de la région*) of *ou* from Touraine; (*de la ville*) of *ou* from Tours
**tourbe** [tuʀb(ə)] *nf* peat
**tourbière** [tuʀbjɛʀ] *nf* peat-bog
**tourbillon** [tuʀbijɔ̃] *nm* whirlwind; (*d'eau*) whirlpool; (*fig*) whirl, swirl
**tourbillonner** [tuʀbijɔne] *vi* to whirl, swirl; (*objet, personne*) to whirl *ou* twirl round
**tourelle** [tuʀɛl] *nf* turret
**tourisme** [tuʀism(ə)] *nm* tourism; **agence de ~** tourist agency; **avion/voiture de ~** private plane/car; **faire du ~** to do some sightseeing, go touring
**touriste** [tuʀist(ə)] *nm/f* tourist
**touristique** [tuʀistik] *adj* tourist *cpd*; (*région*) touristic (*péj*), with tourist appeal
**tourment** [tuʀmɑ̃] *nm* torment
**tourmente** [tuʀmɑ̃t] *nf* storm
**tourmenté, e** [tuʀmɑ̃te] *adj* tormented, tortured; (*mer, période*) turbulent
**tourmenter** [tuʀmɑ̃te] *vt* to torment; **se tourmenter** *vi* to fret, worry o.s.
**tournage** [tuʀnaʒ] *nm* (*d'un film*) shooting
**tournant, e** [tuʀnɑ̃, -ɑ̃t] *adj* (*feu, scène*) revolving; (*chemin*) winding; (*escalier*) spiral *cpd*; (*mouvement*) circling ▷ *nm* (*de route*) bend (*Brit*), curve (*US*); (*fig*) turning point; *voir* **plaque; grève**
**tourné, e** [tuʀne] *adj* (*lait, vin*) sour, off; (*Menuiserie: bois*) turned; (*fig: compliment*) well-phrased; **bien ~** (*femme*) shapely; **mal ~** (*lettre*) badly expressed; **avoir l'esprit mal ~** to have a dirty mind
**tournebroche** [tuʀnəbʀɔʃ] *nm* roasting spit
**tourne-disque** [tuʀnədisk(ə)] *nm* record player
**tournedos** [tuʀnədo] *nm* tournedos
**tournée** [tuʀne] *nf* (*du facteur etc*) round; (*d'artiste, politicien*) tour; (*au café*) round (of drinks); **faire la ~ de** to go (a)round
**tournemain** [tuʀnəmɛ̃]: **en un ~** *adv* in a flash
**tourner** [tuʀne] *vt* to turn; (*sauce, mélange*) to stir; (*contourner*) to get (a)round; (*Ciné*) to shoot; to make ▷ *vi* to turn; (*moteur*) to run; (*compteur*) to tick away; (*lait etc*) to turn (sour); (*fig: chance, vie*) to turn out; **se tourner** *vi* to turn (a)round;

**se ~ vers** to turn to; to turn towards; **bien ~** to turn out well; **~ autour de** to go (a)round; (*planète*) to revolve (a)round; (*péj*) to hang (a)round; **~ autour du pot** (*fig*) to go (a)round in circles; **~ à/en** to turn into; **~ en ridicule** to turn to ridicule; **~ le dos à** (*mouvement*) to turn one's back on; (*position*) to have one's back to; **~ court** to come to a sudden end; **se ~ les pouces** to twiddle one's thumbs; **~ la tête** to look away; **~ la tête à qn** (*fig*) to go to sb's head; **~ de l'œil** to pass out; **~ la page** (*fig*) to turn the page
**tournesol** [tuʀnəsɔl] *nm* sunflower
**tourneur** [tuʀnœʀ] *nm* turner; lathe-operator
**tournevis** [tuʀnəvis] *nm* screwdriver
**tourniquer** [tuʀnike] *vi* to go (a)round in circles
**tourniquet** [tuʀnikɛ] *nm* (*pour arroser*) sprinkler; (*portillon*) turnstile; (*présentoir*) revolving stand, spinner; (*Chirurgie*) tourniquet
**tournis** [tuʀni] *nm*: **avoir/donner le ~** to feel/make dizzy
**tournoi** [tuʀnwa] *nm* tournament
**tournoyer** [tuʀnwaje] *vi* (*oiseau*) to wheel (a)round; (*fumée*) to swirl (a)round
**tournure** [tuʀnyʀ] *nf* (*Ling: syntaxe*) turn of phrase; form; (: *d'une phrase*) phrasing; (*évolution*): **la ~ de qch** the way sth is developing; (*aspect*): **la ~ de** the look of; **la ~ des événements** the turn of events; **prendre ~** to take shape
**tour-opérateur** [tuʀɔpeʀatœʀ] *nm* tour operator
**tourte** [tuʀt(ə)] *nf* pie
**tourteau, x** [tuʀto] *nm* (*Agr*) oilcake, cattle-cake; (*Zool*) edible crab
**tourtereaux** [tuʀtəʀo] *nmpl* lovebirds
**tourterelle** [tuʀtəʀɛl] *nf* turtledove
**tourtière** [tuʀtjɛʀ] *nf* pie dish *ou* plate
**tous** [tu] *adj* [tus] ▷ *pron voir* **tout**
**Toussaint** [tusɛ̃] *nf*: **la ~** All Saints' Day
**tousser** [tuse] *vi* to cough
**toussoter** [tusɔte] *vi* to have a slight cough; (*pour avertir*) to give a slight cough

### ◯ MOT-CLÉ

**tout, e** [tu, tut] (*mpl* **tous**, *fpl* **toutes**) *adj* **1** (*avec article singulier*) all; **tout le lait** all the milk; **toute la nuit** all night, the whole night; **tout le livre** the whole book; **tout un pain** a whole loaf; **tout le temps** all the time, the whole time; **c'est tout le contraire** it's quite the opposite; **c'est toute une affaire** *ou* **histoire** it's quite a business, it's a whole rigmarole
**2** (*avec article pluriel*) every; all; **tous les livres** all the books; **toutes les nuits** every night; **toutes les fois** every time; **toutes les trois/deux semaines** every third/other *ou* second week, every three/two weeks; **tous les deux** both *ou* each of us (*ou* them *ou* you); **toutes les trois** all three of us (*ou* them *ou* you)

**3** *(sans article)*: **à tout âge** at any age; **pour toute nourriture, il avait …** his only food was …; **de tous côtés, de toutes parts** from everywhere, from every side
▷ *pron* everything, all; **il a tout fait** he's done everything; **je les vois tous** I can see them all *ou* all of them; **nous y sommes tous allés** all of us went, we all went; **en tout** in all; **en tout et pour tout** all in all; **tout ce qu'il sait** all he knows; **c'était tout ce qu'il y a de chic** it was the last word *ou* the ultimate in chic
▷ *nm* whole; **le tout** all of it (*ou* them); **le tout est de …** the main thing is to …; **pas du tout** not at all; **elle a tout d'une mère/d'une intrigante** she's a real *ou* true mother/schemer; **du tout au tout** utterly
▷ *adv* **1** *(très, complètement)* very; **tout près** *ou* **à côté** very near; **le tout premier** the very first; **tout seul** all alone; **il était tout rouge** he was really *ou* all red; **parler tout bas** to speak very quietly; **le livre tout entier** the whole book; **tout en haut** right at the top; **tout droit** straight ahead
**2**: **tout en** while; **tout en travaillant** while working, as he *etc* works
**3**: **tout d'abord** first of all; **tout à coup** suddenly; **tout à fait** absolutely; **tout à fait!** exactly!; **tout à l'heure** a short while ago; *(futur)* in a short while, shortly; **à tout à l'heure!** see you later!; **il répondit tout court que non** he just answered no (and that was all); **tout de même** all the same; **tout le monde** everybody; **tout ou rien** all or nothing; **tout simplement** quite simply; **tout de suite** immediately, straight away

**tout-à-l'égout** [tutalegu] *nm inv* mains drainage
**toutefois** [tutfwa] *adv* however
**toutou** [tutu] *nm (fam)* doggie
**tout-petit** [tup(ə)ti] *nm* toddler
**tout-puissant, toute-puissante** [tupҷisɑ̃, tutpҷisɑ̃t] *adj* all-powerful, omnipotent
**tout-venant** [tuvnɑ̃] *nm*: **le ~** everyday stuff
**toux** [tu] *nf* cough
**toxémie** [tɔksemi] *nf* toxaemia *(Brit)*, toxemia *(US)*
**toxicité** [tɔksisite] *nf* toxicity
**toxicologie** [tɔksikɔlɔʒi] *nf* toxicology
**toxicomane** [tɔksikɔman] *nm/f* drug addict
**toxicomanie** [tɔksikɔmani] *nf* drug addiction
**toxine** [tɔksin] *nf* toxin
**toxique** [tɔksik] *adj* toxic, poisonous
**toxoplasmose** [tɔksoplasmoz] *nf* toxoplasmosis
**TP** *sigle mpl* = **travaux pratiques**; **travaux publics**
▷ *sigle m* = **trésor public**
**TPG** *sigle m* = **Trésorier-payeur général**
**tps** *abr* = **temps**
**trac** [tRak] *nm* nerves *pl*; *(Théât)* stage fright; **avoir le ~** to get an attack of nerves; to have

stage fright; **tout à ~** all of a sudden
**traçant, e** [tRasɑ̃, -ɑ̃t] *adj*: **table ~e** *(Inform)* (graph) plotter
**tracas** [tRaka] *nm* bother *no pl*, worry *no pl*
**tracasser** [tRakase] *vt* to worry, bother; *(harceler)* to harass; **se tracasser** *vi* to worry o.s., fret
**tracasserie** [tRakasRi] *nf* annoyance *no pl*; harassment *no pl*
**tracassier, -ière** [tRakasje, -jɛR] *adj* irksome
**trace** [tRas] *nf (empreintes)* tracks *pl*; *(marques, aussi fig)* mark; *(restes, vestige)* trace; *(indice)* sign; *(aussi:* **suivre à la trace**) to track; **~s de pas** footprints
**tracé** [tRase] *nm (contour)* line; *(plan)* layout
**tracer** [tRase] *vt* to draw; *(mot)* to trace; *(piste)* to open up; *(fig: chemin)* to show
**traceur** [tRasœR] *nm (Inform)* plotter
**trachée** [tRaʃe], **trachée-artère** [tRaʃeaRtɛR] *nf* windpipe, trachea
**trachéite** [tRakeit] *nf* tracheitis
**tract** [tRakt] *nm* tract, pamphlet; *(publicitaire)* handout
**tractations** [tRaktɑsjɔ̃] *nfpl* dealings, bargaining *nsg*
**tracter** [tRakte] *vt* to tow
**tracteur** [tRaktœR] *nm* tractor
**traction** [tRaksjɔ̃] *nf* traction; *(Gym)* pull-up; **~ avant/arrière** front-wheel/rear-wheel drive; **~ électrique** electric(al) traction *ou* haulage
**trad.** *abr (= traduit)* translated; *(= traduction)* translation; *(= traducteur)* translator
**tradition** [tRadisjɔ̃] *nf* tradition
**traditionalisme** [tRadisjɔnalism(ə)] *nm* traditionalism
**traditionaliste** [tRadisjɔnalist(ə)] *adj, nm/f* traditionalist
**traditionnel, le** [tRadisjɔnɛl] *adj* traditional
**traditionnellement** [tRadisjɔnɛlmɑ̃] *adv* traditionally
**traducteur, -trice** [tRadyktœR, -tRis] *nm/f* translator
**traduction** [tRadyksjɔ̃] *nf* translation
**traduire** [tRadҷiR] *vt* to translate; *(exprimer)* to render, convey; **se ~ par** to find expression in; **~ en français** to translate into French; **~ en justice** to bring before the courts
**traduis** *etc* [tRadҷi] *vb voir* **traduire**
**traduisible** [tRadҷizibl(ə)] *adj* translatable
**traduit, e** [tRadҷi, -it] *pp de* **traduire**
**trafic** [tRafik] *nm* traffic; **~ d'armes** arms dealing; **~ de drogue** drug peddling
**trafiquant, e** [tRafikɑ̃, -ɑ̃t] *nm/f* trafficker; dealer
**trafiquer** [tRafike] *vt (péj)* to doctor, tamper with ▷ *vi* to traffic, be engaged in trafficking
**tragédie** [tRaʒedi] *nf* tragedy
**tragédien, ne** [tRaʒedjɛ̃, -ɛn] *nm/f* tragedian/tragedienne
**tragi-comique** [tRaʒikɔmik] *adj* tragi-comic
**tragique** [tRaʒik] *adj* tragic ▷ *nm*: **prendre qch au ~** to make a tragedy out of sth

**t**

**tragiquement** [tʀaʒikmɑ̃] *adv* tragically
**trahir** [tʀaiʀ] *vt* to betray; *(fig)* to give away,
reveal; **se trahir** to betray o.s., give o.s. away
**trahison** [tʀaizɔ̃] *nf* betrayal; *(Jur)* treason
**traie** *etc* [tʀɛ] *vb voir* **traire**
**train** [tʀɛ̃] *nm (Rail)* train; *(allure)* pace; *(fig:
ensemble)* set; **être en ~ de faire qch** to be doing
sth; **mettre qch en ~** to get sth under way; **se
mettre en ~** *(commencer)* to get started; *(faire de la
gymnastique)* to warm up; **se sentir en ~** to feel
in good form; **aller bon ~** to make good
progress; **~ avant/arrière** front-wheel/rear-
wheel axle unit; **~ à grande vitesse (TGV)**
high-speed train; **~ d'atterrissage**
undercarriage; **~ autos-couchettes** car-
sleeper train; **~ électrique** *(jouet)* (electric)
train set; **~ de pneus** set of tyres *ou* tires; **~ de
vie** style of living
**traînailler** [tʀɛnɑje] *vi* = **traînasser**
**traînant, e** [tʀɛnɑ̃, -ɑ̃t] *adj (voix, ton)* drawling
**traînard, e** [tʀɛnaʀ, -aʀd(ə)] *nm/f (péj)*
slowcoach *(Brit)*, slowpoke *(US)*
**traînasser** [tʀɛnase] *vi* to dawdle
**traîne** [tʀɛn] *nf (de robe)* train; **être à la ~** to be in
tow; *(en arrière)* to lag behind; *(en désordre)* to be
lying around
**traîneau, x** [tʀɛno] *nm* sleigh, sledge
**traînée** [tʀɛne] *nf* streak, trail; *(péj)* slut
**traîner** [tʀene] *vt (remorque)* to pull; *(enfant, chien)*
to drag *ou* trail along; *(maladie)*: **il traîne un
rhume depuis l'hiver** he has a cold which has
been dragging on since winter ▷ *vi (être en
désordre)* to lie around; *(marcher lentement)* to
dawdle (along); *(vagabonder)* to hang about; *(agir
lentement)* to idle about; *(durer)* to drag on; **se
traîner** *vi (ramper)* to crawl along; *(marcher avec
difficulté)* to drag o.s. along; *(durer)* to drag on; **se
~ par terre** to crawl (on the ground); **~ qn au
cinéma** to drag sb to the cinema; **~ les pieds** to
drag one's feet; **~ par terre** to trail on the
ground; **~ en longueur** to drag out
**training** [tʀɛniŋ] *nm (pull)* tracksuit top;
*(chaussure)* trainer *(Brit)*, sneaker *(US)*
**train-train** [tʀɛ̃tʀɛ̃] *nm* humdrum routine
**traire** [tʀɛʀ] *vt* to milk
**trait, e** [tʀɛ, -ɛt] *pp de* **traire** ▷ *nm (ligne)* line; *(de
dessin)* stroke; *(caractéristique)* feature, trait;
*(flèche)* dart, arrow; shaft; **traits** *nmpl (du visage)*
features; **d'un ~** *(boire)* in one gulp; **de ~** *adj
(animal)* draught *(Brit)*, draft *(US)*; **avoir ~ à** to
concern; **~ pour ~** line for line; **~ de caractère**
characteristic, trait; **~ d'esprit** flash of wit; **~
de génie** brainwave; **~ d'union** hyphen; *(fig)*
link
**traitable** [tʀɛtabl(ə)] *adj (personne)*
accommodating; *(sujet)* manageable
**traitant, e** [tʀɛtɑ̃, -ɑ̃t] *adj*: **votre médecin ~**
your usual *ou* family doctor; **shampooing ~**
medicated shampoo; **crème ~e** conditioning
cream, conditioner
**traite** [tʀɛt] *nf (Comm)* draft; *(Agr)* milking;

*(trajet)* stretch; **d'une (seule) ~** without
stopping (once); **la ~ des noirs** the slave trade;
**la ~ des blanches** the white slave trade
**traité** [tʀɛte] *nm* treaty
**traitement** [tʀɛtmɑ̃] *nm* treatment; processing;
*(salaire)* salary; **suivre un ~** to undergo
treatment; **mauvais ~** ill-treatment; **~ de
données** *ou* **de l'information** *(Inform)* data
processing; **~ hormono-supplétif** hormone
replacement therapy; **~ par lots** *(Inform)* batch
processing; **~ de texte** *(Inform)* word processing
**traiter** [tʀete] *vt (gén)* to treat; *(Tech: matériaux)* to
process, treat; *(Inform)* to process; *(affaire)* to deal
with, handle; *(qualifier)*: **~ qn d'idiot** to call sb a
fool ▷ *vi* to deal; **~ de** *vt* to deal with; **bien/mal
~** to treat well/ill-treat
**traiteur** [tʀɛtœʀ] *nm* caterer
**traître, -esse** [tʀɛtʀ(ə), -tʀɛs] *adj (dangereux)*
treacherous ▷ *nm* traitor; **prendre qn en ~** to
make an insidious attack on sb
**traîtrise** [tʀetʀiz] *nf* treachery
**trajectoire** [tʀaʒɛktwaʀ] *nf* trajectory, path
**trajet** [tʀaʒɛ] *nm* journey; *(itinéraire)* route; *(fig)*
path, course
**tralala** [tʀalala] *nm (péj)* fuss
**tram** [tʀam] *nm* tram *(Brit)*, streetcar *(US)*
**trame** [tʀam] *nf (de tissu)* weft; *(fig)* framework;
texture; *(Typo)* screen
**tramer** [tʀame] *vt* to plot, hatch
**trampoline** [tʀɑ̃pɔlin], **trampolino** [tʀɑ̃pɔlino]
*nm* trampoline; *(Sport)* trampolining
**tramway** [tʀamwɛ] *nm* tram(way); *(voiture)*
tram(car) *(Brit)*, streetcar *(US)*
**tranchant, e** [tʀɑ̃ʃɑ̃, -ɑ̃t] *adj* sharp; *(fig: personne)*
peremptory; *(: couleurs)* striking ▷ *nm (d'un
couteau)* cutting edge; *(de la main)* edge; **à double
~** *(argument, procédé)* double-edged
**tranche** [tʀɑ̃ʃ] *nf (morceau)* slice; *(arête)* edge;
*(partie)* section; *(série)* block; *(d'impôts, revenus etc)*
bracket; *(loterie)* issue; **~ d'âge** age bracket; **~
(de silicium)** wafer
**tranché, e** [tʀɑ̃ʃe] *adj (couleurs)* distinct, sharply
contrasted; *(opinions)* clear-cut, definite ▷ *nf*
trench
**trancher** [tʀɑ̃ʃe] *vt* to cut, sever; *(fig: résoudre)* to
settle ▷ *vi* to be decisive; *(entre deux choses)* to
settle the argument; **~ avec** to contrast sharply
with
**tranchet** [tʀɑ̃ʃɛ] *nm* knife
**tranchoir** [tʀɑ̃ʃwaʀ] *nm* chopper
**tranquille** [tʀɑ̃kil] *adj* calm, quiet; *(enfant, élève)*
quiet; *(rassuré)* easy in one's mind, with one's
mind at rest; **se tenir ~** *(enfant)* to be quiet;
**avoir la conscience ~** to have an easy
conscience; **laisse-moi/laisse-ça ~** leave me/it
alone
**tranquillement** [tʀɑ̃kilmɑ̃] *adv* calmly
**tranquillisant, e** [tʀɑ̃kilizɑ̃, -ɑ̃t] *adj (nouvelle)*
reassuring ▷ *nm* tranquillizer
**tranquilliser** [tʀɑ̃kilize] *vt* to reassure; **se
tranquilliser** to calm (o.s.) down
**tranquillité** [tʀɑ̃kilite] *nf* quietness, peace (and

quiet); **en toute** ~ with complete peace of mind; ~ **d'esprit** peace of mind

**transaction** [tʀɑ̃zaksjɔ̃] *nf (Comm)* transaction, deal

**transafricain, e** [tʀɑ̃safʀikɛ̃, -ɛn] *adj* transafrican

**transalpin, e** [tʀɑ̃zalpɛ̃, -in] *adj* transalpine

**transaméricain, e** [tʀɑ̃zameʀikɛ̃, -ɛn] *adj* transamerican

**transat** [tʀɑ̃zat] *nm* deckchair ▷ *nf* = **course transatlantique**

**transatlantique** [tʀɑ̃zatlɑ̃tik] *adj* transatlantic ▷ *nm* transatlantic liner

**transborder** [tʀɑ̃sbɔʀde] *vt* to tran(s)ship

**transcendant, e** [tʀɑ̃sɑ̃dɑ̃, -ɑ̃t] *adj (Philosophie, Math)* transcendental; *(supérieur)* transcendent

**transcodeur** [tʀɑ̃skɔdœʀ] *nm* compiler

**transcontinental, e, -aux** [tʀɑ̃skɔ̃tinɑtal, -o] *adj* transcontinental

**transcription** [tʀɑ̃skʀipsjɔ̃] *nf* transcription

**transcrire** [tʀɑ̃skʀiʀ] *vt* to transcribe

**transe** [tʀɑ̃s] *nf*: **entrer en** ~ to go into a trance; **transes** *nfpl* agony *nsg*

**transférable** [tʀɑ̃sfeʀabl(ə)] *adj* transferable

**transfèrement** [tʀɑ̃sfɛʀmɑ̃] *nm* transfer

**transférer** [tʀɑ̃sfeʀe] *vt* to transfer

**transfert** [tʀɑ̃sfɛʀ] *nm* transfer

**transfiguration** [tʀɑ̃sfigyʀasjɔ̃] *nf* transformation, transfiguration

**transfigurer** [tʀɑ̃sfigyʀe] *vt* to transform

**transfo** [tʀɑ̃sfo] *nm* (= *transformateur*) transformer

**transformable** [tʀɑ̃sfɔʀmabl(ə)] *adj* convertible

**transformateur** [tʀɑ̃sfɔʀmatœʀ] *nm* transformer

**transformation** [tʀɑ̃sfɔʀmasjɔ̃] *nf* transformation; *(Rugby)* conversion; **industries de** ~ processing industries

**transformer** [tʀɑ̃sfɔʀme] *vt* to transform, alter *("alter" implique un changement moins radical); (matière première, appartement, Rugby)* to convert; ~ **en** to transform into; to turn into; to convert into; **se transformer** *vi* to be transformed; to alter

**transfuge** [tʀɑ̃sfyʒ] *nm* renegade

**transfuser** [tʀɑ̃sfyze] *vt* to transfuse

**transfusion** [tʀɑ̃sfyzjɔ̃] *nf*: ~ **sanguine** blood transfusion

**transgénique** [tʀɑ̃sʒenik] *adj* transgenic

**transgresser** [tʀɑ̃sgʀese] *vt* to contravene, disobey

**transhumance** [tʀɑ̃zymɑ̃s] *nf* transhumance, seasonal move to new pastures

**transi, e** [tʀɑ̃zi] *adj* numb (with cold), chilled to the bone

**transiger** [tʀɑ̃ziʒe] *vi* to compromise, come to an agreement; ~ **sur** *ou* **avec qch** to compromise on sth

**transistor** [tʀɑ̃zistɔʀ] *nm* transistor

**transistorisé, e** [tʀɑ̃zistɔʀize] *adj* transistorized

**transit** [tʀɑ̃zit] *nm* transit; **de** ~ transit *cpd*; **en** ~ in transit

**transitaire** [tʀɑ̃zitɛʀ] *nm/f* forwarding agent

**transiter** [tʀɑ̃zite] *vi* to pass in transit

**transitif, -ive** [tʀɑ̃zitif, -iv] *adj* transitive

**transition** [tʀɑ̃zisjɔ̃] *nf* transition; **de** ~ transitional

**transitoire** [tʀɑ̃zitwaʀ] *adj (mesure, gouvernement)* transitional, provisional; *(fugitif)* transient

**translucide** [tʀɑ̃slysid] *adj* translucent

**transmet** *etc* [tʀɑ̃smɛ] *vb voir* **transmettre**

**transmettais** *etc* [tʀɑ̃smɛtɛ] *vb voir* **transmettre**

**transmetteur** [tʀɑ̃smɛtœʀ] *nm* transmitter

**transmettre** [tʀɑ̃smɛtʀ(ə)] *vt (passer):* ~ **qch à qn** to pass sth on to sb; *(Tech, Tél, Méd)* to transmit; *(TV, Radio: retransmettre)* to broadcast

**transmis, e** [tʀɑ̃smi, -iz] *pp de* **transmettre**

**transmissible** [tʀɑ̃smisibl(ə)] *adj* transmissible

**transmission** [tʀɑ̃smisjɔ̃] *nf* transmission, passing on; *(Auto)* transmission; **transmissions** *nfpl* ≈ signals corps *nsg*; ~ **de données** *(Inform)* data transmission; ~ **de pensée** thought transmission

**transocéanien, ne** [tʀɑ̃zɔseanjɛ̃, -ɛn] **transocéanique** [tʀɑ̃zɔseanik] *adj* transoceanic

**transparaître** [tʀɑ̃spaʀɛtʀ(ə)] *vi* to show (through)

**transparence** [tʀɑ̃spaʀɑ̃s] *nf* transparence; **par** ~ *(regarder)* against the light; *(voir)* showing through

**transparent, e** [tʀɑ̃spaʀɑ̃, -ɑ̃t] *adj* transparent

**transpercer** [tʀɑ̃spɛʀse] *vt* to go through, pierce

**transpiration** [tʀɑ̃spiʀasjɔ̃] *nf* perspiration

**transpirer** [tʀɑ̃spiʀe] *vi* to perspire; *(information, nouvelle)* to come to light

**transplant** [tʀɑ̃splɑ̃] *nm* transplant

**transplantation** [tʀɑ̃splɑ̃tɑsjɔ̃] *nf* transplant

**transplanter** [tʀɑ̃splɑ̃te] *vt (Méd, Bot)* to transplant; *(personne)* to uproot, move

**transport** [tʀɑ̃spɔʀ] *nm* transport; *(émotions):* ~ **de colère** fit of rage; ~ **de joie** transport of delight; ~ **de voyageurs/marchandises** passenger/goods transportation; ~**s en commun** public transport *nsg*; ~**s routiers** haulage *(Brit)*, trucking *(US)*

**transportable** [tʀɑ̃spɔʀtabl(ə)] *adj (marchandises)* transportable; *(malade)* fit (enough) to be moved

**transporter** [tʀɑ̃spɔʀte] *vt* to carry, move; *(Comm)* to transport, convey; *(fig):* ~ **qn (de joie)** to send sb into raptures; **se** ~ **quelque part** *(fig)* to let one's imagination carry one away (somewhere)

**transporteur** [tʀɑ̃spɔʀtœʀ] *nm* haulage contractor *(Brit)*, trucker *(US)*

**transposer** [tʀɑ̃spoze] *vt* to transpose

**transposition** [tʀɑ̃spozisjɔ̃] *nf* transposition

**transrhénan, e** [tʀɑ̃sʀenɑ̃, -an] *adj* transrhenane

**transsaharien, ne** [tʀɑ̃ssaaʀjɛ̃, -ɛn] *adj* trans-Saharan

**transsexuel, le** [tʀɑ̃ssɛksɥɛl] *adj, nm/f* transsexual

**transsibérien, ne** [tʀɑ̃ssibeʀjɛ̃, -ɛn] *adj* trans-Siberian

**transvaser** [tʀɑ̃svaze] *vt* to decant

**transversal, e, -aux** [tʀɑ̃svɛʀsal, -o] *adj* transverse, cross(-); *(route etc)* cross-country; *(mur, chemin, rue)* running at right angles; *(Auto)*: **axe ~** main cross-country road *(Brit) ou* highway *(US)*

**transversalement** [tʀɑ̃svɛʀsalmɑ̃] *adv* crosswise

**trapèze** [tʀapɛz] *nm (Géom)* trapezium; *(au cirque)* trapeze

**trapéziste** [tʀapezist(ə)] *nm/f* trapeze artist

**trappe** [tʀap] *nf (de cave, grenier)* trap door; *(piège)* trap

**trappeur** [tʀapœʀ] *nm* trapper, fur trader

**trapu, e** [tʀapy] *adj* squat, stocky

**traquenard** [tʀaknaʀ] *nm* trap

**traquer** [tʀake] *vt* to track down; *(harceler)* to hound

**traumatisant, e** [tʀomatizɑ̃, -ɑ̃t] *adj* traumatic

**traumatiser** [tʀomatize] *vt* to traumatize

**traumatisme** [tʀomatism(ə)] *nm* traumatism

**traumatologie** [tʀomatɔlɔʒi] *nf* branch of medicine concerned with accidents

**travail, -aux** [tʀavaj, -o] *nm (gén)* work; *(tâche, métier)* work *no pl*, job; *(Écon, Méd)* labour *(Brit)*, labor *(US)*; *(Inform)* job ▷ *nmpl (de réparation, agricoles etc)* work *nsg*; *(sur route)* roadworks; *(de construction)* building (work) *nsg*; **être/entrer en ~** *(Méd)* to be in/go into labour; **être sans ~** *(employé)* to be out of work, be unemployed; **~ d'intérêt général (TIG)** ≈ community service; **~ (au) noir** moonlighting; **~ posté** shiftwork; **travaux des champs** farmwork *nsg*; **travaux dirigés (TD)** *(Scol)* supervised practical work *nsg*; **travaux forcés** hard labour *nsg*; **travaux manuels** *(Scol)* handicrafts; **travaux ménagers** housework *nsg*; **travaux pratiques (TP)** *(gén)* practical work; *(en laboratoire)* lab work *(Brit)*, lab *(US)*; **travaux publics (TP)** ≈ public works *nsg*

**travaillé, e** [tʀavaje] *adj (style)* polished

**travailler** [tʀavaje] *vi* to work; *(bois)* to warp ▷ *vt (bois, métal)* to work; *(pâte)* to knead; *(objet d'art, discipline, fig: influencer)* to work on; **cela le travaille** it is on his mind; **~ la terre** to work the land; **~ son piano** to do one's piano practice; **~ à** to work on; *(fig: contribuer à)* to work towards; **~ à faire** to endeavour *(Brit) ou* endeavor *(US)* to do

**travailleur, -euse** [tʀavajœʀ, -øz] *adj* hardworking ▷ *nm/f* worker; **~ de force** labourer *(Brit)*, laborer *(US)*; **~ intellectuel** non-manual worker; **~ social** social worker; **travailleuse familiale** home help

**travailliste** [tʀavajist(ə)] *adj* ≈ Labour *cpd* ▷ *nm/f* member of the Labour party

**travée** [tʀave] *nf* row; *(Archit)* bay; span

**traveller's** [tʀavlœʀs], **traveller's chèque**

[tʀavlœʀsʃɛk] *nm* traveller's cheque

**travelling** [tʀavliŋ] *nm (chariot)* dolly; *(technique)* tracking; **~ optique** zoom shots *pl*

**travelo** [tʀavlo] *nm (fam)* (drag) queen

**travers** [tʀavɛʀ] *nm* fault, failing; **en ~ (de)** across; **au ~ (de)** through; **de ~** *adj* askew ▷ *adv* sideways; *(fig)* the wrong way; **à ~** through; **regarder de ~** *(fig)* to look askance at

**traverse** [tʀavɛʀs(ə)] *nf (de voie ferrée)* sleeper; **chemin de ~** shortcut

**traversée** [tʀavɛʀse] *nf* crossing

**traverser** [tʀavɛʀse] *vt (gén)* to cross; *(ville, tunnel, aussi: percer, fig)* to go through; *(ligne, trait)* to run across

**traversin** [tʀavɛʀsɛ̃] *nm* bolster

**travesti** [tʀavɛsti] *nm (costume)* fancy dress; *(artiste de cabaret)* female impersonator, drag artist; *(comme mode de vie)* transvestite

**travestir** [tʀavɛstiʀ] *vt (vérité)* to misrepresent; **se travestir** *(se costumer)* to dress up; *(artiste)* to put on drag; *(Psych)* to dress as a woman

**trayais** *etc* [tʀɛjɛ] *vb voir* **traire**

**trayeuse** [tʀɛjøz] *nf* milking machine

**trébucher** [tʀebyʃe] *vi*: **~ (sur)** to stumble (over), trip (over)

**trèfle** [tʀɛfl(ə)] *nm (Bot)* clover; *(Cartes: couleur)* clubs *pl*; *(: carte)* club; **~ à quatre feuilles** four-leaf clover

**treillage** [tʀɛjaʒ] *nm* lattice work

**treille** [tʀɛj] *nf (tonnelle)* vine arbour *(Brit) ou* arbor *(US)*; *(vigne)* climbing vine

**treillis** [tʀɛji] *nm (métallique)* wire-mesh; *(toile)* canvas; *(Mil: tenue)* combat uniform; *(pantalon)* combat trousers *pl*

**treize** [tʀɛz] *num* thirteen

**treizième** [tʀɛzjɛm] *num* thirteenth; *see note*

● **TREIZIÈME MOIS**
●
● The *treizième mois* is an end-of-year bonus
● roughly corresponding to one month's
● salary. For many employees it is a standard
● part of their salary package.

**tréma** [tʀema] *nm* diaeresis

**tremblant, e** [tʀɑ̃blɑ̃, -ɑ̃t] *adj* trembling, shaking

**tremble** [tʀɑ̃bl(ə)] *nm (Bot)* aspen

**tremblé, e** [tʀɑ̃ble] *adj* shaky

**tremblement** [tʀɑ̃bləmɑ̃] *nm* trembling *no pl*, shaking *no pl*, shivering *no pl*; **~ de terre** earthquake

**trembler** [tʀɑ̃ble] *vi* to tremble, shake; **~ de** *(froid, fièvre)* to shiver *ou* tremble with; *(peur)* to shake *ou* tremble with; **~ pour qn** to fear for sb

**tremblotant, e** [tʀɑ̃blɔtɑ̃, -ɑ̃t] *adj* trembling

**trembloter** [tʀɑ̃blɔte] *vi* to tremble *ou* shake slightly

**trémolo** [tʀemɔlo] *nm (d'un instrument)* tremolo; *(de la voix)* quaver

**trémousser** [tʀemuse]: **se trémousser** *vi* to jig about, wriggle about

**trempe** [tʀɑ̃p] *nf (fig)*: **de cette/sa** ~ of this/his calibre *(Brit) ou* caliber *(US)*

**trempé, e** [tʀɑ̃pe] *adj* soaking (wet), drenched; *(Tech)*: **acier** ~ tempered steel

**tremper** [tʀɑ̃pe] *vt* to soak, drench; *(aussi*: **faire tremper, mettre à tremper**) to soak; *(plonger)*: ~ **qch dans** to dip sth in(to) ▷ *vi* to soak; *(fig)*: ~ **dans** to be involved *ou* have a hand in; **se tremper** *vi* to have a quick dip; **se faire** ~ to get soaked *ou* drenched

**trempette** [tʀɑ̃pɛt] *nf*: **faire** ~ to go paddling

**tremplin** [tʀɑ̃plɛ̃] *nm* springboard; *(Ski)* ski jump

**trentaine** [tʀɑ̃tɛn] *nf (âge)*: **avoir la** ~ to be around thirty; **une** ~ **(de)** thirty or so, about thirty

**trente** [tʀɑ̃t] *num* thirty; **voir** ~-**six chandelles** *(fig)* to see stars; **être/se mettre sur son** ~ **et un** to be/get dressed to kill; ~-**trois tours** *nm* long-playing record, LP

**trentième** [tʀɑ̃tjɛm] *num* thirtieth

**trépanation** [tʀepanasjɔ̃] *nf* trepan

**trépaner** [tʀepane] *vt* to trepan, trephine

**trépasser** [tʀepase] *vi* to pass away

**trépidant, e** [tʀepidɑ̃, -ɑ̃t] *adj (fig: rythme)* pulsating; *(: vie)* hectic

**trépidation** [tʀepidasjɔ̃] *nf (d'une machine, d'un moteur)* vibration; *(fig: de la vie)* whirl

**trépider** [tʀepide] *vi* to vibrate

**trépied** [tʀepje] *nm (d'appareil)* tripod; *(meuble)* trivet

**trépignement** [tʀepiɲmɑ̃] *nm* stamping (of feet)

**trépigner** [tʀepiɲe] *vi* to stamp (one's feet)

**très** [tʀɛ] *adv* very; ~ **beau/bien** very beautiful/well; ~ **critiqué** much criticized; ~ **industrialisé** highly industrialized; **j'ai** ~ **faim** I'm very hungry

**trésor** [tʀezɔʀ] *nm* treasure; *(Admin)* finances *pl*; *(d'une organisation)* funds *pl*; ~ **(public) (TP)** public revenue; *(service)* public revenue office

**trésorerie** [tʀezɔʀʀi] *nf (fonds)* funds *pl*; *(gestion)* accounts *pl*; *(bureaux)* accounts department; *(poste)* treasurership; **difficultés de** ~ cash problems, shortage of cash *ou* funds; ~ **générale (TG)** *local government finance office*

**trésorier, -ière** [tʀezɔʀje, -jɛʀ] *nm/f* treasurer

**Trésorier-payeur** [tʀezɔʀjepejœʀ] *nm*: ~ **général (TPG)** paymaster

**tressaillement** [tʀesajmɑ̃] *nm* shiver, shudder; quiver

**tressaillir** [tʀesajiʀ] *vi (de peur etc)* to shiver, shudder; *(de joie)* to quiver

**tressauter** [tʀesote] *vi* to start, jump

**tresse** [tʀɛs] *nf (de cheveux)* braid, plait; *(cordon, galon)* braid

**tresser** [tʀese] *vt (cheveux)* to braid, plait; *(fil, jonc)* to plait; *(corbeille)* to weave; *(corde)* to twist

**tréteau, x** [tʀeto] *nm* trestle; **les** ~**x** *(fig: Théât)* the boards

**treuil** [tʀœj] *nm* winch

**trêve** [tʀɛv] *nf (Mil, Pol)* truce; *(fig)* respite; **sans** ~ unremittingly; ~ **de** ... enough of this ...; **les États de la T**~ the Trucial States

**tri** [tʀi] *nm (voir trier)* sorting (out) *no pl*; selection; screening; *(Inform)* sort; *(Postes: action)* sorting; *(: bureau)* sorting office

**triage** [tʀijaʒ] *nm (Rail)* shunting; *(gare)* marshalling yard

**trial** [tʀijal] *nm (Sport)* scrambling

**triangle** [tʀijɑ̃gl(ə)] *nm* triangle; ~ **isocèle/ équilatéral** isosceles/equilateral triangle; ~ **rectangle** right-angled triangle

**triangulaire** [tʀijɑ̃gylɛʀ] *adj* triangular

**triathlon** [tʀi(j)atlɔ̃] *nm* triathlon

**tribal, e, -aux** [tʀibal, -o] *adj* tribal

**tribord** [tʀibɔʀ] *nm*: **à** ~ to starboard, on the starboard side

**tribu** [tʀiby] *nf* tribe

**tribulations** [tʀibylɑsjɔ̃] *nfpl* tribulations, trials

**tribunal, -aux** [tʀibynal, -o] *nm (Jur)* court; *(Mil)* tribunal; ~ **de police/pour enfants** police/ juvenile court; ~ **d'instance (TI)** ≈ magistrates' court (Brit), ≈ district court (US); ~ **de grande instance (TGI)** ≈ High Court (Brit), ≈ Supreme Court (US)

**tribune** [tʀibyn] *nf (estrade)* platform, rostrum; *(débat)* forum; *(d'église, de tribunal)* gallery; *(de stade)* stand; ~ **libre** *(Presse)* opinion column

**tribut** [tʀiby] *nm* tribute

**tributaire** [tʀibytɛʀ] *adj*: **être** ~ **de** to be dependent on; *(Géo)* to be a tributary of

**tricentenaire** [tʀisɑ̃tnɛʀ] *nm* tercentenary, tricentennial

**tricher** [tʀiʃe] *vi* to cheat

**tricherie** [tʀiʃʀi] *nf* cheating *no pl*

**tricheur, -euse** [tʀiʃœʀ, -øz] *nm/f* cheat

**trichromie** [tʀikʀɔmi] *nf* three-colour (Brit) *ou* - color (US) printing

**tricolore** [tʀikɔlɔʀ] *adj* three-coloured (Brit), three-colored (US); *(français: drapeau)* red, white and blue; *(: équipe etc)* French

**tricot** [tʀiko] *nm (technique, ouvrage)* knitting *no pl*; *(tissu)* knitted fabric; *(vêtement)* jersey, sweater; ~ **de corps** vest (Brit), undershirt (US)

**tricoter** [tʀikɔte] *vt* to knit; **machine/aiguille à** ~ knitting machine/needle (Brit) *ou* pin (US)

**trictrac** [tʀiktʀak] *nm* backgammon

**tricycle** [tʀisikl(ə)] *nm* tricycle

**tridimensionnel, le** [tʀidimɑ̃sjɔnɛl] *adj* three-dimensional

**triennal, e, -aux** [tʀienal, -o] *adj (prix, foire, élection)* three-yearly; *(charge, mandat, plan)* three-year

**trier** [tʀije] *vt (classer)* to sort (out); *(choisir)* to select; *(visiteurs)* to sort; *(Postes, Inform)* to sort

**trieur, -euse** [tʀijœʀ, -øz] *nm/f* sorter

**trigonométrie** [tʀigɔnɔmetʀi] *nf* trigonometry

**trigonométrique** [tʀigɔnɔmetʀik] *adj* trigonometric

**trilingue** [tʀilɛ̃g] *adj* trilingual

**trilogie** [tʀilɔʒi] *nf* trilogy

**trimaran** [tʀimaʀɑ̃] *nm* trimaran

**trimbaler** [tʀɛ̃bale] *vt* to cart around, trail

along

**trimer** [tʀime] vi to slave away

**trimestre** [tʀimɛstʀ(ə)] nm (Scol) term; (Comm) quarter

**trimestriel, le** [tʀimɛstʀijɛl] adj quarterly; (Scol) end-of-term

**trimoteur** [tʀimɔtœʀ] nm three-engined aircraft

**tringle** [tʀɛ̃gl(ə)] nf rod

**Trinité** [tʀinite] nf Trinity

**Trinité et Tobago** [tʀiniteetɔbago] nf Trinidad and Tobago

**trinquer** [tʀɛ̃ke] vi to clink glasses; (fam) to cop it; ~ **à qch/la santé de qn** to drink to sth/sb

**trio** [tʀijo] nm trio

**triolet** [tʀijɔlɛ] nm (Mus) triplet

**triomphal, e, -aux** [tʀijɔ̃fal, -o] adj triumphant, triumphal

**triomphalement** [tʀijɔ̃falmɑ̃] adv triumphantly

**triomphant, e** [tʀijɔ̃fɑ̃, -ɑ̃t] adj triumphant

**triomphateur, -trice** [tʀijɔ̃fatœʀ, -tʀis] nm/f (triumphant) victor

**triomphe** [tʀijɔ̃f] nm triumph; **être reçu/ porté en ~** to be given a triumphant welcome/ be carried shoulder-high in triumph

**triompher** [tʀijɔ̃fe] vi to triumph; ~ **de** to triumph over, overcome

**triparti, e** [tʀipaʀti] adj (aussi: **tripartite**: réunion, assemblée) tripartite, three-party

**triperie** [tʀipʀi] nf tripe shop

**tripes** [tʀip] nfpl (Culin) tripe nsg; (fam) guts

**triplace** [tʀiplas] adj three-seater cpd

**triple** [tʀipl(ə)] adj (à trois éléments) triple; (trois fois plus grand) treble ▷ nm: **le ~ (de)** (comparaison) three times as much (as); **en ~ exemplaire** in triplicate; ~ **saut** (Sport) triple jump

**triplé** [tʀiple] nm hat-trick (Brit), triple success

**triplement** [tʀipləmɑ̃] adv (à un degré triple) three times over; (de trois façons) in three ways; (pour trois raisons) on three counts ▷ nm trebling, threefold increase

**tripler** [tʀiple] vi, vt to triple, treble, increase threefold

**triplés, -ées** [tʀiple] nm/fpl triplets

**Tripoli** [tʀipɔli] n Tripoli

**triporteur** [tʀipɔʀtœʀ] nm delivery tricycle

**tripot** [tʀipo] nm (péj) dive

**tripotage** [tʀipɔtaʒ] nm (péj) jiggery-pokery

**tripoter** [tʀipɔte] vt to fiddle with, finger ▷ vi (fam) to rummage about

**trique** [tʀik] nf cudgel

**trisannuel, le** [tʀizanɥɛl] adj triennial

**trisomie** [tʀizɔmi] nf Down's syndrome

**triste** [tʀist(ə)] adj sad; (péj): ~ **personnage/ affaire** sorry individual/affair; **c'est pas ~!** (fam) it's something else!

**tristement** [tʀistəmɑ̃] adv sadly

**tristesse** [tʀistɛs] nf sadness

**triton** [tʀitɔ̃] nm triton

**triturer** [tʀityʀe] vt (pâte) to knead; (objets) to manipulate

**trivial, e, -aux** [tʀivjal, -o] adj coarse, crude; (commun) mundane

**trivialité** [tʀivjalite] nf coarseness, crudeness; mundaneness

**troc** [tʀɔk] nm (Écon) barter; (transaction) exchange, swap

**troène** [tʀɔɛn] nm privet

**troglodyte** [tʀɔglɔdit] nm/f cave dweller, troglodyte

**trognon** [tʀɔɲɔ̃] nm (de fruit) core; (de légume) stalk

**trois** [tʀwa] num three

**trois-huit** [tʀwaɥit] nmpl: **faire les ~** to work eight-hour shifts (round the clock)

**troisième** [tʀwazjɛm] num third; **le ~ âge** the years of retirement

**troisièmement** [tʀwazjɛmmɑ̃] adv thirdly

**trois quarts** [tʀwakaʀ] nmpl: **les ~ de** three-quarters of

**trolleybus** [tʀɔlɛbys] nm trolley bus

**trombe** [tʀɔ̃b] nf waterspout; **des ~s d'eau** a downpour; **en ~** (arriver, passer) like a whirlwind

**trombone** [tʀɔ̃bɔn] nm (Mus) trombone; (de bureau) paper clip; ~ **à coulisse** slide trombone

**tromboniste** [tʀɔ̃bɔnist(ə)] nm/f trombonist

**trompe** [tʀɔ̃p] nf (d'éléphant) trunk; (Mus) trumpet, horn; ~ **d'Eustache** Eustachian tube; ~**s utérines** Fallopian tubes

**trompe-l'œil** [tʀɔ̃plœj] nm: **en trompe-l'œil** in trompe-l'œil style

**tromper** [tʀɔ̃pe] vt to deceive; (fig: espoir, attente) to disappoint; (vigilance, poursuivants) to elude; **se tromper** vi to make a mistake, be mistaken; **se tromper de voiture/jour** to take the wrong car/ get the day wrong; **se ~ de 3 cm/20 euros** to be out by 3 cm/20 euros

**tromperie** [tʀɔ̃pʀi] nf deception, trickery no pl

**trompette** [tʀɔ̃pɛt] nf trumpet; **en ~** (nez) turned-up

**trompettiste** [tʀɔ̃petist(ə)] nm/f trumpet player

**trompeur, -euse** [tʀɔ̃pœʀ, -øz] adj deceptive, misleading

**tronc** [tʀɔ̃] nm (Bot, Anat) trunk; (d'église) collection box; ~ **d'arbre** tree trunk; ~ **commun** (Scol) common-core syllabus; ~ **de cône** truncated cone

**tronche** [tʀɔ̃ʃ] nf (fam) mug, face

**tronçon** [tʀɔ̃sɔ̃] nm section

**tronçonner** [tʀɔ̃sɔne] vt (arbre) to saw up; (pierre) to cut up

**tronçonneuse** [tʀɔ̃sɔnøz] nf chain saw

**trône** [tʀon] nm throne; **monter sur le ~** to ascend the throne

**trôner** [tʀone] vi (fig) to have (ou take) pride of place (Brit), have the place of honour (Brit) ou honor (US)

**tronquer** [tʀɔ̃ke] vt to truncate; (fig) to curtail

**trop** [tʀo] adv too; (avec verbe) too much; (aussi: **trop nombreux**) too many; (aussi: **trop souvent**) too often; ~ **peu (nombreux)** too few; ~ **longtemps** (for) too long; ~ **de** (nombre) too many; (*quantité*) too much; **de ~, en ~: des livres en ~** a few books too many, a few extra books; **du lait en ~** too much milk; **trois livres/cinq euros de ~** three books too many/ five euros too much

**trophée** [tʀɔfe] *nm* trophy

**tropical, e, -aux** [tʀɔpikal, -o] *adj* tropical

**tropique** [tʀɔpik] *nm* tropic; **tropiques** *nmpl* tropics; **~ du Cancer/Capricorne** Tropic of Cancer/Capricorn

**trop-plein** [tʀɔplɛ̃] *nm* (*tuyau*) overflow *ou* outlet (pipe); (*liquide*) overflow

**troquer** [tʀɔke] *vt*: **~ qch contre** to barter *ou* trade sth for; (*fig*) to swap sth for

**trot** [tʀo] *nm* trot; **aller au ~** to trot along; **partir au ~** to set off at a trot

**trotter** [tʀɔte] *vi* to trot; (*fig*) to scamper along (*ou* about)

**trotteuse** [tʀɔtøz] *nf* (*de montre*) second hand

**trottiner** [tʀɔtine] *vi* (*fig*) to scamper along (*ou* about)

**trottinette** [tʀɔtinɛt] *nf* (child's) scooter

**trottoir** [tʀɔtwaʀ] *nm* pavement (*Brit*), sidewalk (*US*); **faire le ~** (*péj*) to walk the streets; **~ roulant** moving pavement (*Brit*) *ou* walkway

**trou** [tʀu] *nm* hole; (*fig*) gap; (*Comm*) deficit; **~ d'aération** (air) vent; **~ d'air** air pocket; **~ de mémoire** blank, lapse of memory; **~ noir** black hole; **~ de la serrure** keyhole

**troublant, e** [tʀublɑ̃, -ɑ̃t] *adj* disturbing

**trouble** [tʀubl(ə)] *adj* (*liquide*) cloudy; (*image, mémoire*) indistinct, hazy; (*affaire*) shady, murky ▷ *adv* indistinctly ▷ *nm* (*désarroi*) distress, agitation; (*émoi sensuel*) turmoil, agitation; (*embarras*) confusion; (*zizanie*) unrest, discord; **troubles** *nmpl* (*Pol*) disturbances, troubles, unrest *nsg*; (*Méd*) trouble *nsg*, disorders; **~s de la personnalité** personality problems; **~s de la vision** eye trouble

**trouble-fête** [tʀubləfɛt] *nm/f inv* spoilsport

**troubler** [tʀuble] *vt* (*embarrasser*) to confuse, disconcert; (*émouvoir*) to agitate; to disturb; to perturb; (*perturber: ordre etc*) to disrupt, disturb; (*liquide*) to make cloudy; **se troubler** *vi* (*personne*) to become flustered *ou* confused; **~ l'ordre public** to cause a breach of the peace

**troué, e** [tʀue] *adj* with a hole (*ou* holes) in it ▷ *nf* gap; (*Mil*) breach

**trouer** [tʀue] *vt* to make a hole (*ou* holes) in; (*fig*) to pierce

**trouille** [tʀuj] *nf* (*fam*): **avoir la ~** to be scared stiff, be scared out of one's wits

**troupe** [tʀup] *nf* (*Mil*) troop; (*groupe*) troop, group; **la ~** (*Mil: l'armée*) the army; (*: les simples soldats*) the troops *pl*; **~ (de théâtre)** (theatrical) company; **~s de choc** shock troops

**troupeau, x** [tʀupo] *nm* (*de moutons*) flock; (*de vaches*) herd

**trousse** [tʀus] *nf* case, kit; (*d'écolier*) pencil case; (*de docteur*) instrument case; **aux ~s de** (*fig*) on the heels *ou* tail of; **~ à outils** toolkit; **~ de toilette** toilet *ou* sponge (*Brit*) bag

**trousseau, x** [tʀuso] *nm* (*de mariée*) trousseau; **~ de clefs** bunch of keys

**trouvaille** [tʀuvaj] *nf* find; (*fig: idée, expression etc*) brainwave

**trouvé, e** [tʀuve] *adj*: **tout ~** ready-made

**trouver** [tʀuve] *vt* to find; (*rendre visite*): **aller/ venir ~ qn** to go/come and see sb; **je trouve que** I find *ou* think that; **~ à boire/critiquer** to find something to drink/criticize; **~ asile/ refuge** to find refuge/shelter; **se trouver** *vi* (*être*) to be; (*être soudain*) to find o.s.; **se ~ être/ avoir** to happen to be/have; **il se trouve que** it happens that, it turns out that; **se ~ bien** to feel well; **se ~ mal** to pass out

**truand** [tʀyɑ̃] *nm* villain, crook

**truander** [tʀyɑ̃de] *vi* (*fam*) to cheat, do

**trublion** [tʀyblijɔ̃] *nm* troublemaker

**truc** [tʀyk] *nm* (*astuce*) way, device; (*de cinéma, prestidigitateur*) trick effect; (*chose*) thing; (*machin*) thingumajig, whatsit (*Brit*); **avoir le ~** to have the knack; **c'est pas son** (*ou* **mon** *etc*) **~** (*fam*) it's not really his (*ou* my *etc*) thing

**truchement** [tʀyʃmɑ̃] *nm*: **par le ~ de qn** through (the intervention of) sb

**trucider** [tʀyside] *vt* (*fam*) to do in, bump off

**truculence** [tʀykylɑ̃s] *nf* colourfulness (*Brit*), colorfulness (*US*)

**truculent, e** [tʀykylɑ̃, -ɑ̃t] *adj* colourful (*Brit*), colorful (*US*)

**truelle** [tʀyɛl] *nf* trowel

**truffe** [tʀyf] *nf* truffle; (*nez*) nose

**truffé, e** [tʀyfe] *adj*: **~ de** (*fig*) peppered with; (*fautes*) riddled with; (*pièges*) bristling with

**truffer** [tʀyfe] *vt* (*Culin*) to garnish with truffles; **truffé de** (*fig: citations*) peppered with; (*: pièges*) bristling with

**truie** [tʀɥi] *nf* sow

**truite** [tʀɥit] *nf* trout *inv*

**truquage** [tʀyka3] *nm* fixing; (*Ciné*) special effects *pl*

**truquer** [tʀyke] *vt* (*élections, serrure, dés*) to fix; (*Ciné*) to use special effects in

**trust** [tʀœst] *nm* (*Comm*) trust

**truster** [tʀœste] *vt* (*Comm*) to monopolize

**ts** *abr* = **tous**

**tsar** [dzaʀ] *nm* tsar

**tsé-tsé** [tsetse] *nf*: **mouche ~** tsetse fly

**TSF** *sigle f* (= *télégraphie sans fil*) wireless

**tsigane** [tsigan] *adj, nm/f* = **tzigane**

**TSVP** *abr* (= *tournez s'il vous plaît*) PTO

**tt** *abr* = **tout**

**TT, TTA** *sigle m* (= *transit temporaire (autorisé)*) vehicle registration for cars etc bought in France for export tax-free by non-residents

**TTC** *abr* = **toutes taxes comprises**

**ttes** *abr* = **toutes**

**TU** *sigle m* = **temps universel**

**tu¹** [ty] *pron* you ▷ *nm*: **employer le tu** to use the "tu" form

**tu², e** [ty] *pp de* **taire**

**tuant, e** [tɥɑ̃, -ɑ̃t] *adj* (*épuisant*) killing; (*énervant*) infuriating

t

423

**tuba** [tyba] *nm (Mus)* tuba; *(Sport)* snorkel
**tubage** [tybaʒ] *nm (Méd)* intubation
**tube** [tyb] *nm* tube; *(de canalisation, métallique etc)* pipe; *(chanson, disque)* hit song *ou* record; ~ **digestif** alimentary canal, digestive tract; ~ **à essai** test tube
**tuberculeux, -euse** [tybɛʀkylø, -øz] *adj* tubercular ▷ *nm/f* tuberculosis *ou* TB patient
**tuberculose** [tybɛʀkyloz] *nf* tuberculosis, TB
**tubulaire** [tybylɛʀ] *adj* tubular
**tubulure** [tybylyʀ] *nf* pipe; piping *no pl*; *(Auto):* ~ **d'échappement/d'admission** exhaust/inlet manifold
**TUC** [tyk] *sigle m* (= *travail d'utilité collective*) community work scheme for the young unemployed
**tuciste** [tysist(ə)] *nm/f* young person on a community work scheme
**tué, e** [tɥe] *nm/f:* **cinq ~s** five killed *ou* dead
**tue-mouche** [tymuʃ] *adj:* **papier ~(s)** flypaper
**tuer** [tɥe] *vt* to kill; **se tuer** *(se suicider)* to kill o.s.; *(dans un accident)* to be killed; **se ~ au travail** *(fig)* to work o.s. to death
**tuerie** [tyʀi] *nf* slaughter *no pl*, massacre
**tue-tête** [tytɛt]: **à ~** *adv* at the top of one's voice
**tueur** [tɥœʀ] *nm* killer; ~ **à gages** hired killer
**tuile** [tɥil] *nf* tile; *(fam)* spot of bad luck, blow
**tulipe** [tylip] *nf* tulip
**tulle** [tyl] *nm* tulle
**tuméfié, e** [tymefje] *adj* puffy, swollen
**tumeur** [tymœʀ] *nf* growth, tumour *(Brit)*, tumor *(US)*
**tumulte** [tymylt(ə)] *nm* commotion, hubbub
**tumultueux, -euse** [tymyltɥø, -øz] *adj* stormy, turbulent
**tuner** [tynɛʀ] *nm* tuner
**tungstène** [tœ̃kstɛn] *nm* tungsten
**tunique** [tynik] *nf* tunic; *(de femme)* smock, tunic
**Tunis** [tynis] *n* Tunis
**Tunisie** [tynizi] *nf:* **la ~** Tunisia
**tunisien, ne** [tynizjɛ̃, -ɛn] *adj* Tunisian ▷ *nm/f:* **Tunisien, ne** Tunisian
**tunisois, e** [tynizwa, -waz] *adj* of *ou* from Tunis
**tunnel** [tynɛl] *nm* tunnel; **le ~ sous la Manche** the Channel Tunnel, the Chunnel
**TUP** *sigle m* (= *titre universel de paiement*) ≈ payment slip
**turban** [tyʀbɑ̃] *nm* turban
**turbin** [tyʀbɛ̃] *nm (fam)* work *no pl*
**turbine** [tyʀbin] *nf* turbine
**turbo** [tyʀbo] *nm* turbo; **un moteur ~** a turbo(-charged) engine
**turbomoteur** [tyʀbɔmɔtœʀ] *nm* turbo(-boosted) engine
**turbopropulseur** [tyʀbɔpʀɔpylsœʀ] *nm* turboprop
**turboréacteur** [tyʀbɔʀeaktœʀ] *nm* turbojet
**turbot** [tyʀbo] *nm* turbot
**turbotrain** [tyʀbɔtʀɛ̃] *nm* turbotrain
**turbulences** [tyʀbylɑ̃s] *nfpl (Aviat)* turbulence *sg*
**turbulent, e** [tyʀbylɑ̃, -ɑ̃t] *adj* boisterous, unruly
**turc, turque** [tyʀk(ə)] *adj* Turkish; *(w.-c.)*

seatless ▷ *nm (Ling)* Turkish ▷ *nm/f:* **Turc, Turque** Turk/Turkish woman; **à la turque** *adv (assis)* cross-legged
**turf** [tyʀf] *nm* racing
**turfiste** [tyʀfist(ə)] *nm/f* racegoer
**Turks et Caïques** [tyʀkekaik], **Turks et Caicos** [tyʀkekaikɔs] *nfpl* Turks and Caicos Islands
**turpitude** [tyʀpityd] *nf* base act, baseness *no pl*
**turque** [tyʀk(ə)] *adj f, nf voir* **turc**
**Turquie** [tyʀki] *nf:* **la ~** Turkey
**turquoise** [tyʀkwaz] *nf, adj inv* turquoise
**tus** *etc* [ty] *vb voir* **taire**
**tut** *etc* [ty] *vb voir* **taire**
**tutelle** [tytɛl] *nf (Jur)* guardianship; *(Pol)* trusteeship; **sous la ~ de** *(fig)* under the supervision of
**tuteur, -trice** [tytœʀ, -tʀis] *nm/f (Jur)* guardian; *(de plante)* stake, support
**tutoiement** [tytwamɑ̃] *nm* use of familiar "tu" form
**tutoyer** [tytwaje] *vt:* ~ **qn** to address sb as "tu"
**tutti quanti** [tutikwɑ̃ti] *nmpl:* **et ~** and all the rest (of them)
**tutu** [tyty] *nm (Danse)* tutu
**tuyau, x** [tɥijo] *nm* pipe; *(flexible)* tube; *(fam: conseil)* tip; (: *mise au courant*) gen *no pl*; ~ **d'arrosage** hosepipe; ~ **d'échappement** exhaust pipe; ~ **d'incendie** fire hose
**tuyauté, e** [tɥijote] *adj* fluted
**tuyauterie** [tɥijotʀi] *nf* piping *no pl*
**tuyère** [tɥijɛʀ] *nf* nozzle
**TV** [teve] *nf* TV, telly *(Brit)*
**TVA** *sigle f* (= *taxe à*) *ou sur la valeur ajoutée*, VAT
**TVHD** *abr f* (= *télévision haute-définition*) HDTV
**tweed** [twid] *nm* tweed
**tympan** [tɛ̃pɑ̃] *nm (Anat)* eardrum
**type** [tip] *nm* type; *(personne, chose: représentant)* classic example, epitome; *(fam)* chap, guy ▷ *adj* typical, standard; **avoir le ~ nordique** to be Nordic-looking
**typé, e** [tipe] *adj* ethnic *(euph)*
**typhoïde** [tifɔid] *nf* typhoid (fever)
**typhon** [tifɔ̃] *nm* typhoon
**typhus** [tifys] *nm* typhus (fever)
**typique** [tipik] *adj* typical
**typiquement** [tipikmɑ̃] *adv* typically
**typographe** [tipɔgʀaf] *nm/f* typographer
**typographie** [tipɔgʀafi] *nf* typography; *(procédé)* letterpress (printing)
**typographique** [tipɔgʀafik] *adj* typographical; letterpress *cpd*
**typologie** [tipɔlɔʒi] *nf* typology
**tyran** [tiʀɑ̃] *nm* tyrant
**tyrannie** [tiʀani] *nf* tyranny
**tyrannique** [tiʀanik] *adj* tyrannical
**tyranniser** [tiʀanize] *vt* to tyrannize
**Tyrol** [tiʀɔl] *nm:* **le ~** the Tyrol
**tyrolien, ne** [tiʀɔljɛ̃, -ɛn] *adj* Tyrolean
**tzar** [dzaʀ] *nm* = **tsar**
**tzigane** [dzigan] *adj* gipsy, tzigane ▷ *nm/f* (Hungarian) gipsy, Tzigane

# Uu

**U, u** [y] *nm inv* U, u; **U comme Ursule** U for Uncle
**ubiquité** [ybikɥite] *nf*: **avoir le don d'~** to be
everywhere at once, be ubiquitous
**UDF** *sigle f* (= *Union pour la démocratie française*)
political party
**UE** *sigle f* (= *Union européenne*) EU
**UEFA** [yefa] *sigle f* (= *Union of European Football
Associations*) UEFA
**UEM** *sigle f* (= *Union économique et monétaire*) EMU
**UER** *sigle f* (= *unité d'enseignement et de recherche*) old
title of UFR; (= *Union européenne de radiodiffusion*)
EBU (= *European Broadcasting Union*)
**UFC** *sigle f* (= *Union fédérale des consommateurs*)
national consumer group
**UFR** *sigle f* (= *unité de formation et de recherche*)
≈ university department
**UHF** *sigle f* (= *ultra-haute fréquence*) UHF
**UHT** *sigle* (= *ultra-haute température*) UHT
**UIT** *sigle f* (= *Union internationale des
télécommunications*) ITU (= *International
Telecommunications Union*)
**Ukraine** [ykrɛn] *nf*: **l'~** the Ukraine
**ukrainien, ne** [ykrɛnjɛ̃, -ɛn] *adj* Ukrainian ▷ *nm*
(*Ling*) Ukrainian ▷ *nm/f*: **Ukrainien, ne**
Ukrainian
**ulcère** [ylsɛʀ] *nm* ulcer; **~ à l'estomac** stomach
ulcer
**ulcérer** [ylseʀe] *vt* (*Méd*) to ulcerate; (*fig*) to
sicken, appal
**ulcéreux, -euse** [ylseʀø, -øz] *adj* (*plaie, lésion*)
ulcerous; (*membre*) ulcerated
**ULM** *sigle m* (= *ultra léger motorisé*) microlight
**ultérieur, e** [ylteʀjœʀ] *adj* later, subsequent;
**remis à une date ~e** postponed to a later date
**ultérieurement** [ylteʀjœʀmɑ̃] *adv* later
**ultimatum** [yltimatɔm] *nm* ultimatum
**ultime** [yltim] *adj* final
**ultra...** [yltʀa] *préfixe* ultra...
**ultramoderne** [yltʀamɔdɛʀn(ə)] *adj* ultra-
modern
**ultra-rapide** [yltʀaʀapid] *adj* ultra-fast
**ultra-sensible** [yltʀasɑ̃sibl(ə)] *adj* (*Photo*) high-
speed
**ultrason, ultra-son** [yltʀasɔ̃] *nm* ultrasound *no
pl*; **ultra(-)sons** *nmpl* ultrasonics
**ultraviolet, ultra-violet, te** [yltʀavjɔlɛ, -ɛt] *adj*

ultraviolet ▷ *nm*: **les ultra(-)violets** ultraviolet
rays
**ululer** [ylyle] *vi* = **hululer**
**UME** *sigle f* (= *Union monétaire européenne*) EMU
**UMP** *sigle f* (= *Union pour un mouvement populaire*)
political party

 **MOT-CLÉ**

**un, une** [œ̃, yn] *art indéf* a; (*devant voyelle*) an; **un
garçon/vieillard** a boy/an old man; **une fille** a
girl
▷ *pron* one; **l'un des meilleurs** one of the best;
**l'un ..., l'autre** (the) one ..., the other; **les
uns ..., les autres** some ..., others; **l'un et
l'autre** both (of them); **l'un ou l'autre** either
(of them); **l'un l'autre, les uns les autres**
each other, one another; **pas un seul** not a
single one; **un par un** one by one
▷ *num* one; **une pomme seulement** one apple
only
▷ *nf*: **la une** (*Presse*) the front page

**unanime** [ynanim] *adj* unanimous; **ils sont ~s
(à penser que)** they are unanimous (in
thinking that)
**unanimement** [ynanimmɑ̃] *adv* (*par tous*)
unanimously; (*d'un commun accord*) with one
accord
**unanimité** [ynanimite] *nf* unanimity; **à l'~**
unanimously; **faire l'~** to be approved
unanimously
**UNEF** [ynɛf] *sigle f* = **Union nationale des
étudiants de France**
**UNESCO** [ynɛsko] *sigle f* (= *United Nations
Educational, Scientific and Cultural Organization*)
UNESCO
**Unetelle** [yntɛl] *nf voir* **Untel**
**UNI** *sigle f* = **Union nationale interuniversitaire**
**uni, e** [yni] *adj* (*ton, tissu*) plain; (*surface*) smooth,
even; (*famille*) close(-knit); (*pays*) united
**UNICEF** [ynisɛf] *sigle m ou f* (= *United Nations
International Children's Emergency Fund*) UNICEF
**unidirectionnel, le** [ynidiʀɛksjɔnɛl] *adj*
unidirectional, one-way
**unième** [ynjɛm] *num*: **vingt/trente et ~**

**u**

twenty-/thirty-first; **cent ~** (one) hundred and
first
**unificateur, -trice** [ynifikatœʀ, -tʀis] *adj*
unifying
**unification** [ynifikɑsjɔ̃] *nf* uniting; unification;
standardization
**unifier** [ynifje] *vt* to unite, unify; (*systèmes*) to
standardize, unify; **s'unifier** *vi* to become
united
**uniforme** [ynifɔʀm(ə)] *adj* (*mouvement*) regular,
uniform; (*surface, ton*) even; (*objets, maisons*)
uniform; (*fig: vie, conduite*) unchanging ▷ *nm*
uniform; **être sous l'~** (*Mil*) to be serving
**uniformément** [ynifɔʀmemɑ̃] *adv* uniformly
**uniformisation** [ynifɔʀmizɑsjɔ̃] *nf*
standardization
**uniformiser** [ynifɔʀmize] *vt* to make uniform;
(*systèmes*) to standardize
**uniformité** [ynifɔʀmite] *nf* regularity;
uniformity; evenness
**unijambiste** [yniʒɑ̃bist(ə)] *nm/f* one-legged
man/woman
**unilatéral, e, -aux** [ynilateʀal, -o] *adj*
unilateral; **stationnement ~** parking on one
side only
**unilatéralement** [ynilateʀalmɑ̃] *adv*
unilaterally
**uninominal, e, -aux** [yninɔminal, -o] *adj*
uncontested
**union** [ynjɔ̃] *nf* union; **~ conjugale** union of
marriage; **~ de consommateurs** consumers'
association; **~ libre** free love; **l'U~ des
Républiques socialistes soviétiques (URSS)**
the Union of Soviet Socialist Republics (USSR);
**l'U~ soviétique** the Soviet Union
**unique** [ynik] *adj* (*seul*) only; (*le même*): **un prix/
système ~** a single price/system; (*exceptionnel*)
unique; **ménage à salaire ~** one-salary family;
**route à voie ~** single-lane road; **fils/fille ~** only
son/daughter, only child; **~ en France** the only
one of its kind in France
**uniquement** [ynikmɑ̃] *adv* only, solely; (*juste*)
only, merely
**unir** [yniʀ] *vt* (*nations*) to unite; (*éléments, couleurs*)
to combine; (*en mariage*) to unite, join together;
**~ qch à** to unite sth with; to combine sth with;
**s'unir** *vi* to unite; (*en mariage*) to be joined
together; **s'~ à** *ou* **avec** to unite with
**unisexe** [yniseks] *adj* unisex
**unisson** [ynisɔ̃] *nf* **à l'~** *adv* in unison
**unitaire** [yniteʀ] *adj* unitary; (*Pol*) unitarian;
**prix ~** unit price
**unité** [ynite] *nf* (*harmonie, cohésion*) unity; (*Comm,
Mil, de mesure, Math*) unit; **~ centrale** central
processing unit; **~ de valeur** (university)
course, credit
**univers** [yniveʀ] *nm* universe
**universalisation** [yniveʀsalizɑsjɔ̃] *nf*
universalization
**universaliser** [yniveʀsalize] *vt* to universalize
**universalité** [yniveʀsalite] *nf* universality
**universel, le** [yniveʀsel] *adj* universal; (*esprit*)

all-embracing
**universellement** [yniveʀselmɑ̃] *adv*
universally
**universitaire** [yniveʀsiteʀ] *adj* university *cpd*;
(*diplôme, études*) academic, university *cpd* ▷ *nm/f*
academic
**université** [yniveʀsite] *nf* university
**univoque** [ynivɔk] *adj* unambiguous; (*Math*)
one-to-one
**UNR** *sigle f* (= *Union pour la nouvelle république*) former
political party
**UNSS** *sigle f* = **Union nationale du sport scolaire**
**Untel, Unetelle** [œ̃tel, yntel] *nm/f*: **Monsieur ~**
Mr so-and-so
**uranium** [yʀanjɔm] *nm* uranium
**urbain, e** [yʀbɛ̃, -en] *adj* urban, city *cpd*, town
*cpd*; (*poli*) urbane
**urbanisation** [yʀbanizɑsjɔ̃] *nf* urbanization
**urbaniser** [yʀbanize] *vt* to urbanize
**urbanisme** [yʀbanism(ə)] *nm* town planning
**urbaniste** [yʀbanist(ə)] *nm/f* town planner
**urbanité** [yʀbanite] *nf* urbanity
**urée** [yʀe] *nf* urea
**urémie** [yʀemi] *nf* uraemia (*Brit*), uremia (*US*)
**urgence** [yʀʒɑ̃s] *nf* urgency; (*Méd etc*)
emergency; **d'~** *adj* emergency *cpd* ▷ *adv* as a
matter of urgency; **en cas d'~** in case of
emergency; **service des ~s** emergency service
**urgent, e** [yʀʒɑ̃, -ɑ̃t] *adj* urgent
**urinaire** [yʀineʀ] *adj* urinary
**urinal, -aux** [yʀinal, -o] *nm* (bed) urinal
**urine** [yʀin] *nf* urine
**uriner** [yʀine] *vi* to urinate
**urinoir** [yʀinwaʀ] *nm* (public) urinal
**urne** [yʀn(ə)] *nf* (*électorale*) ballot box; (*vase*) urn;
**aller aux ~s** (*voter*) to go to the polls
**urologie** [yʀɔlɔʒi] *nf* urology
**URSS** [*parfois* : yʀs] *sigle f* (= *Union des Républiques
Socialistes Soviétiques*) USSR
**URSSAF** [yʀsaf] *sigle f* (= *Union pour le recouvrement
de la sécurité sociale et des allocations familiales*)
administrative body responsible for social security funds
and payments
**urticaire** [yʀtikeʀ] *nf* nettle rash, urticaria
**Uruguay** [yʀygwe] *nm*: **l'~** Uruguay
**uruguayen, ne** [yʀygwajɛ̃, -en] *adj* Uruguayan
▷ *nm/f*: **Uruguayen, ne** Uruguayan
**us** [ys] *nmpl*: **us et coutumes** (habits and)
customs
**USA** *sigle mpl* (= *United States of America*) USA
**usage** [yzaʒ] *nm* (*emploi, utilisation*) use; (*coutume*)
custom; (*éducation*) (good) manners *pl*, (good)
breeding; (*Ling*): **l'~** usage; **faire ~ de** (*pouvoir,
droit*) to exercise; **avoir l'~ de** to have the use of;
**à l'~** *adv* with use; **à l'~ de** (*pour*) for (use of); **en
~** in use; **hors d'~** out of service; **à ~ interne** to
be taken; **à ~ externe** for external use only
**usagé, e** [yzaʒe] *adj* (*usé*) worn; (*d'occasion*) used
**usager, -ère** [yzaʒe, -eʀ] *nm/f* user
**usé, e** [yze] *adj* worn (down *ou* out *ou* away);
ruined; (*banal*) hackneyed
**user** [yze] *vt* (*outil*) to wear down; (*vêtement*) to

wear out; (*matière*) to wear away; (*consommer: charbon etc*) to use; (*fig: santé*) to ruin; (*: personne*) to wear out; **s'user** *vi* to wear; to wear out; (*fig*) to decline; **s'~ à la tâche** to wear o.s. out with work; **~ de** *vt* (*moyen, procédé*) to use, employ; (*droit*) to exercise

**usine** [yzin] *nf* factory; **~ atomique** nuclear power plant; **~ à gaz** gasworks *sg*; **~ marémotrice** tidal power station

**usiner** [yzine] *vt* (*Tech*) to machine; (*fabriquer*) to manufacture

**usité, e** [yzite] *adj* in common use, common; **peu ~** rarely used

**ustensile** [ystɑ̃sil] *nm* implement; **~ de cuisine** kitchen utensil

**usuel, le** [yzɥɛl] *adj* everyday, common

**usufruit** [yzyfʀɥi] *nm* usufruct

**usuraire** [yzyʀɛʀ] *adj* usurious

**usure** [yzyʀ] *nf* wear; worn state; (*de l'usurier*) usury; **avoir qn à l'~** to wear sb down; **~ normale** fair wear and tear

**usurier, -ière** [yzyʀje, -jɛʀ] *nm/f* usurer

**usurpateur, -trice** [yzyʀpatœʀ, -tʀis] *nm/f* usurper

**usurpation** [yzyʀpasjɔ̃] *nf* usurpation

**usurper** [yzyʀpe] *vt* to usurp

**ut** [yt] *nm* (*Mus*) C

**UTA** *sigle f* = **Union des transporteurs aériens**

**utérin, e** [yteʀɛ̃, -in] *adj* uterine

**utérus** [yteʀys] *nm* uterus, womb

**utile** [ytil] *adj* useful; **~ à qn/qch** of use to sb/sth

**utilement** [ytilmɑ̃] *adv* usefully

**utilisable** [ytilizabl(ə)] *adj* usable

**utilisateur, -trice** [ytilizatœʀ, -tʀis] *nm/f* user

**utilisation** [ytilizasjɔ̃] *nf* use

**utiliser** [ytilize] *vt* to use

**utilitaire** [ytilitɛʀ] *adj* utilitarian; (*objets*) practical ▷ *nm* (*Inform*) utility

**utilité** [ytilite] *nf* usefulness *no pl*; use; **jouer les ~s** (*Théât*) to play bit parts; **reconnu d'~ publique** state-approved; **c'est d'une grande ~** it's extremely useful; **il n'y a aucune ~ à ...** there's no use in ...

**utopie** [ytɔpi] *nf* (*idée, conception*) utopian idea *ou* view; (*société etc idéale*) utopia

**utopique** [ytɔpik] *adj* utopian

**utopiste** [ytɔpist(ə)] *nm/f* utopian

**UV** *sigle f* (*Scol*) = **unité de valeur** ▷ *sigle mpl* (= *ultra-violets*) UV

**uvule** [yvyl] *nf* uvula

**u**

# Vv

**V, v** [ve] *nm inv* V, v ▷ *abr* (= *voir, verset*) v = **vers**;
(*de poésie*) l.; (: *en direction de*) toward(s); **V
comme Victor** V for Victor; **en V** V-shaped;
**encolure en V** V-neck; **décolleté en V**
plunging neckline

**va** [va] *vb voir* **aller**

**vacance** [vakɑ̃s] *nf* (*Admin*) vacancy; **vacances**
*nfpl* holiday(s) *pl* (*Brit*), vacation *sg* (*US*); **les
grandes ~s** the summer holidays *ou* vacation;
**prendre des/ses ~s** to take a holiday *ou*
vacation/one's holiday(s) *ou* vacation; **aller en
~s** to go on holiday *ou* vacation

**vacancier, -ière** [vakɑ̃sje, -jɛʀ] *nm/f*
holidaymaker (*Brit*), vacationer (*US*)

**vacant, e** [vakɑ̃, -ɑ̃t] *adj* vacant

**vacarme** [vakaʀm(ə)] *nm* row, din

**vacataire** [vakatɛʀ] *nm/f* temporary
(employee); (*enseignement*) supply (*Brit*) *ou*
substitute (*US*) teacher; (*Université*) part-time
temporary lecturer

**vaccin** [vaksɛ̃] *nm* vaccine; (*opération*)
vaccination

**vaccination** [vaksinɑsjɔ̃] *nf* vaccination

**vacciner** [vaksine] *vt* to vaccinate; (*fig*) to make
immune; **être vacciné** (*fig*) to be immune

**vache** [vaʃ] *nf* (*Zool*) cow; (*cuir*) cowhide ▷ *adj*
(*fam*) rotten, mean; **~ à eau** (*canvas*) water bag;
**(manger de la) ~ enragée** (to go through) hard
times; **~ à lait** (*péj*) mug, sucker; **~ laitière**
dairy cow; **période des ~s maigres** lean times
*pl*, lean period

**vachement** [vaʃmɑ̃] *adv* (*fam*) damned, really

**vacher, -ère** [vaʃe, -ɛʀ] *nm/f* cowherd

**vacherie** [vaʃʀi] *nf* (*fam*) meanness *no pl*; (*action*)
dirty trick; (*propos*) nasty remark

**vacherin** [vaʃʀɛ̃] *nm* (*fromage*) vacherin cheese;
(*gâteau*): **~ glacé** vacherin (*type of cream gâteau*)

**vachette** [vaʃɛt] *nf* calfskin

**vacillant, e** [vasijɑ̃, -ɑ̃t] *adj* wobbly; flickering;
failing, faltering

**vaciller** [vasije] *vi* to sway, wobble; (*bougie,
lumière*) to flicker; (*fig*) to be failing, falter; **~
dans ses réponses** to falter in one's replies; **~
dans ses résolutions** to waver in one's
resolutions

**vacuité** [vakɥite] *nf* emptiness, vacuity

**vade-mecum** [vademekɔm] *nm inv* pocketbook

**vadrouille** [vadʀuj] *nf*: **être/partir en ~** to be
on/go for a wander

**vadrouiller** [vadʀuje] *vi* to wander around *ou*
about

**va-et-vient** [vaevjɛ̃] *nm inv* (*de pièce mobile*) to and
fro (*ou* up and down) movement; (*de personnes,
véhicules*) comings and goings *pl*, to-ings and
fro-ings *pl*; (*Élec*) two-way switch

**vagabond, e** [vagabɔ̃, -ɔ̃d] *adj* wandering;
(*imagination*) roaming, roving ▷ *nm* (*rôdeur*)
tramp, vagrant; (*voyageur*) wanderer

**vagabondage** [vagabɔ̃daʒ] *nm* roaming,
wandering; (*Jur*) vagrancy

**vagabonder** [vagabɔ̃de] *vi* to roam, wander

**vagin** [vaʒɛ̃] *nm* vagina

**vaginal, e, -aux** [vaʒinal, -o] *adj* vaginal

**vagissement** [vaʒismɑ̃] *nm* cry (*of newborn baby*)

**vague** [vag] *nf* wave ▷ *adj* vague; (*regard*)
faraway; (*manteau, robe*) loose(-fitting);
(*quelconque*): **un ~ bureau/cousin** some office/
cousin or other ▷ *nm*: **être dans le ~** to be
rather in the dark; **rester dans le ~** to keep
things rather vague; **regarder dans le ~** to
gaze into space; **~ à l'âme** *nm* vague
melancholy; **~ d'assaut** *nf* (*Mil*) wave of
assault; **~ de chaleur** *nf* heatwave; **~ de fond**
*nf* ground swell; **~ de froid** *nf* cold spell

**vaguelette** [vaglɛt] *nf* ripple

**vaguement** [vagmɑ̃] *adv* vaguely

**vaillamment** [vajamɑ̃] *adv* bravely, gallantly

**vaillant, e** [vajɑ̃, -ɑ̃t] *adj* (*courageux*) brave,
gallant; (*robuste*) vigorous, hale and hearty;
**n'avoir plus un sou ~** to be penniless

**vaille** [vaj] *vb voir* **valoir**

**vain, e** [vɛ̃, vɛn] *adj* vain; **en ~** *adv* in vain

**vaincre** [vɛ̃kʀ(ə)] *vt* to defeat; (*fig*) to conquer,
overcome

**vaincu, e** [vɛ̃ky] *pp de* **vaincre** ▷ *nm/f* defeated
party

**vainement** [vɛnmɑ̃] *adv* vainly

**vainquais** *etc* [vɛ̃kɛ] *vb voir* **vaincre**

**vainqueur** [vɛ̃kœʀ] *nm* victor; (*Sport*) winner
▷ *adj m* victorious

**vais** [vɛ] *vb voir* **aller**

**vaisseau, x** [veso] *nm* (*Anat*) vessel; (*Navig*) ship,

vessel; **~ spatial** spaceship
**vaisselier** [vɛsəlje] *nm* dresser
**vaisselle** [vɛsɛl] *nf* (*service*) crockery; (*plats etc à laver*) (dirty) dishes *pl*; **faire la ~** to do the washing-up (*Brit*) *ou* the dishes
**val** (*pl* **vaux** *ou* **vals**) [val, vo] *nmpl* valley
**valable** [valabl(ə)] *adj* valid; (*acceptable*) decent, worthwhile
**valablement** [valabləmɑ̃] *adv* legitimately; (*de façon satisfaisante*) satisfactorily
**Valence** [valɑ̃s] *n* (*en Espagne*) Valencia; (*en France*) Valence
**valent** *etc* [val] *vb voir* **valoir**
**valet** [valɛ] *nm* valet; (*péj*) lackey; (*Cartes*) jack, knave (*Brit*); **~ de chambre** manservant, valet; **~ de ferme** farmhand; **~ de pied** footman
**valeur** [valœʀ] *nf* (*gén*) value; (*mérite*) worth, merit; (*Comm: titre*) security; **mettre en ~** (*bien*) to exploit; (*terrain, région*) to develop; (*fig*) to highlight; to show off to advantage; **avoir de la ~** to be valuable; **prendre de la ~** to go up *ou* gain in value; **sans ~** worthless; **~ absolue** absolute value; **~ d'échange** exchange value; **~ nominale** face value; **~s mobilières** transferable securities
**valeureux, -euse** [valœʀø, -øz] *adj* valorous
**validation** [validɑsjɔ̃] *nf* validation
**valide** [valid] *adj* (*en bonne santé*) fit, well; (*indemne*) able-bodied, fit; (*valable*) valid
**valider** [valide] *vt* to validate
**validité** [validite] *nf* validity
**valions** *etc* [valjɔ̃] *vb voir* **valoir**
**valise** [valiz] *nf* (suit)case; **faire sa ~** to pack one's (suit)case; **la ~ (diplomatique)** the diplomatic bag
**vallée** [vale] *nf* valley
**vallon** [valɔ̃] *nm* small valley
**vallonné, e** [valɔne] *adj* undulating
**vallonnement** [valɔnmɑ̃] *nm* undulation
**valoir** [valwaʀ] *vi* (*être valable*) to hold, apply ▷ *vt* (*prix, valeur, effort*) to be worth; (*causer*): **~ qch à qn** to earn sb sth; **se valoir** to be of equal merit; (*péj*) to be two of a kind; **faire ~** (*droits, prérogatives*) to assert; (*domaine, capitaux*) to exploit; **faire ~ que** to point out that; **se faire ~** to make the most of o.s.; **à ~ on** account; **à ~ sur** to be deducted from; (*fig*) to backtrack, backpedal; **cela ne me dit rien qui vaille** I don't like the look of it at all; **ce climat ne me vaut rien** this climate doesn't suit me; **~ la peine** to be worth the trouble, be worth it; **~ mieux: il vaut mieux se taire** it's better to say nothing; **il vaut mieux que je fasse/comme ceci** it's better if I do/like this; **ça ne vaut rien** it's worthless; **que vaut ce candidat?** how good is this applicant?
**valorisation** [valɔʀizasjɔ̃] *nf* (*economic*) development; increased standing
**valoriser** [valɔʀize] *vt* (*Écon*) to develop (the economy of); (*produit*) to increase the value of; (*Psych*) to increase the standing of; (*fig*) to highlight, bring out

**valse** [vals(ə)] *nf* waltz; **c'est la ~ des étiquettes** the prices don't stay the same from one moment to the next
**valser** [valse] *vi* to waltz; (*fig*): **aller ~** to go flying
**valu, e** [valy] *pp de* **valoir**
**valve** [valv(ə)] *nf* valve
**vamp** [vɑ̃p] *nf* vamp
**vampire** [vɑ̃piʀ] *nm* vampire
**van** [vɑ̃] *nm* horse box (*Brit*) *ou* trailer (*US*)
**vandale** [vɑ̃dal] *nm/f* vandal
**vandalisme** [vɑ̃dalism(ə)] *nm* vandalism
**vanille** [vanij] *nf* vanilla; **glace à la ~** vanilla ice cream
**vanillé, e** [vanije] *adj* vanilla *cpd*
**vanité** [vanite] *nf* vanity
**vaniteux, -euse** [vanitø, -øz] *adj* vain, conceited
**vanity-case** [vaniti(e)kɛz] *nm* vanity case
**vanne** [van] *nf* gate; (*fam: remarque*) dig, (nasty) crack; **lancer une ~ à qn** to have a go at sb (*Brit*), knock sb
**vanneau, x** [vano] *nm* lapwing
**vanner** [vane] *vt* to winnow
**vannerie** [vanʀi] *nf* basketwork
**vantail, -aux** [vɑ̃taj, -o] *nm* door, leaf
**vantard, e** [vɑ̃taʀ, -aʀd(ə)] *adj* boastful
**vantardise** [vɑ̃taʀdiz] *nf* boastfulness *no pl*; boast
**vanter** [vɑ̃te] *vt* to speak highly of, vaunt; **se vanter** *vi* to boast, brag; **se ~ de** to pride o.s. on; (*péj*) to boast of
**va-nu-pieds** [vanypje] *nm/f inv* tramp, beggar
**vapeur** [vapœʀ] *nf* steam; (*émanation*) vapour (*Brit*), vapor (*US*), fumes *pl*; (*brouillard, buée*) haze; **vapeurs** *nfpl* (*bouffées*) vapours, vapors; **à ~** steam-powered, steam *cpd*; **à toute ~** full steam ahead; (*fig*) at full tilt; **renverser la ~** to reverse engines; (*fig*) to backtrack, backpedal; **cuit à la ~** steamed
**vapocuiseur** [vapɔkɥizœʀ] *nm* pressure cooker
**vaporeux, -euse** [vapɔʀø, -øz] *adj* (*flou*) hazy, misty; (*léger*) filmy, gossamer *cpd*
**vaporisateur** [vapɔʀizatœʀ] *nm* spray
**vaporiser** [vapɔʀize] *vt* (*Chimie*) to vaporize; (*parfum etc*) to spray
**vaquer** [vake] *vi* (*Admin*) to be on vacation; **~ à ses occupations** to attend to one's affairs, go about one's business
**varappe** [vaʀap] *nf* rock climbing
**varappeur, -euse** [vaʀapœʀ, -øz] *nm/f* (rock) climber
**varech** [vaʀɛk] *nm* wrack, varec
**vareuse** [vaʀøz] *nf* (*blouson*) pea jacket; (*d'uniforme*) tunic
**variable** [vaʀjabl(ə)] *adj* variable; (*temps, humeur*) changeable; (*Tech: à plusieurs positions etc*) adaptable; (*Ling*) inflectional; (*divers: résultats*) varied, various ▷ *nf* (*Inform, Math*) variable
**variante** [vaʀjɑ̃t] *nf* variant
**variation** [vaʀjasjɔ̃] *nf* variation; changing *no pl*, change; (*Mus*) variation

**V**

429

**varice** [vaʀis] *nf* varicose vein
**varicelle** [vaʀisɛl] *nf* chickenpox
**varié, e** [vaʀje] *adj* varied; (*divers*) various; **hors-d'œuvre ~s** selection of hors d'œuvres
**varier** [vaʀje] *vi* to vary; (*temps, humeur*) to change ▷ *vt* to vary
**variété** [vaʀjete] *nf* variety; **spectacle de ~s** variety show
**variole** [vaʀjɔl] *nf* smallpox
**variqueux, -euse** [vaʀikø, -øz] *adj* varicose
**Varsovie** [vaʀsɔvi] *n* Warsaw
**vas** [va] *vb voir* **aller**; **~-y!** [vazi] go on!
**vasculaire** [vaskylɛʀ] *adj* vascular
**vase** [vaz] *nm* vase ▷ *nf* silt, mud; **en ~ clos** in isolation; **~ de nuit** chamberpot; **~s communicants** communicating vessels
**vasectomie** [vazɛktɔmi] *nf* vasectomy
**vaseline** [vazlin] *nf* Vaseline®
**vaseux, -euse** [vazø, -øz] *adj* silty, muddy; (*fig: confus*) woolly, hazy; (: *fatigué*) peaky; (: *étourdi*) woozy
**vasistas** [vazistɑs] *nm* fanlight
**vasque** [vask(ə)] *nf* (*bassin*) basin; (*coupe*) bowl
**vassal, e, -aux** [vasal, -o] *nm/f* vassal
**vaste** [vast(ə)] *adj* vast, immense
**Vatican** [vatikɑ̃] *nm*: **le ~** the Vatican
**vaticiner** [vatisine] *vi* (*péj*) to make pompous predictions
**va-tout** [vatu] *nm*: **jouer son ~** to stake one's all
**vaudeville** [vodvil] *nm* vaudeville, light comedy
**vaudrai** *etc* [vodʀe] *vb voir* **valoir**
**vau-l'eau** [volo]: **à vau-l'eau** *adv* with the current; **s'en aller à vau-l'eau** (*fig: projets*) to be adrift
**vaurien, ne** [voʀjɛ̃, -ɛn] *nm/f* good-for-nothing, guttersnipe
**vaut** [vo] *vb voir* **valoir**
**vautour** [votuʀ] *nm* vulture
**vautrer** [votʀe]: **se vautrer** *vi*: **se ~ dans** to wallow in; **se ~ sur** to sprawl on
**vaux** [vo] *pl de* **val** ▷ *vb voir* **valoir**
**va-vite** [vavit]: **à la ~** *adv* in a rush
**vd** *abr* = **vend**
**VDQS** *sigle m* (= *vin délimité de qualité supérieure*) label guaranteeing quality of wine
**vds** *abr* = **vends**
**veau, x** [vo] *nm* (*Zool*) calf; (*Culin*) veal; (*peau*) calfskin; **tuer le ~ gras** to kill the fatted calf
**vecteur** [vɛktœʀ] *nm* vector; (*Mil, Bio*) carrier
**vécu, e** [veky] *pp de* **vivre** ▷ *adj* real(-life)
**vedettariat** [vədɛtaʀja] *nm* stardom; (*attitude*) acting like a star
**vedette** [vədɛt] *nf* (*artiste etc*) star; (*canot*) patrol boat; launch; **avoir la ~** to top the bill, get star billing; **mettre qn en ~** (*Ciné etc*) to give sb the starring role; (*fig*) to push sb into the limelight; **voler la ~ à qn** to steal the show from sb
**végétal, e, -aux** [veʒetal, -o] *adj* vegetable ▷ *nm* vegetable, plant
**végétalien, ne** [veʒetaljɛ̃, -ɛn] *adj, nm/f* vegan
**végétalisme** [veʒetalism(ə)] *nm* veganism
**végétarien, ne** [veʒetaʀjɛ̃, -ɛn] *adj, nm/f* vegetarian

**végétarisme** [veʒetaʀism(ə)] *nm* vegetarianism
**végétatif, -ive** [veʒetatif, -iv] *adj*: **une vie ~ive** a vegetable existence
**végétation** [veʒetɑsjɔ̃] *nf* vegetation; **végétations** *nfpl* (*Méd*) adenoids
**végéter** [veʒete] *vi* (*fig*) to vegetate
**véhémence** [veemɑ̃s] *nf* vehemence
**véhément, e** [veemɑ̃, -ɑ̃t] *adj* vehement
**véhicule** [veikyl] *nm* vehicle; **~ utilitaire** commercial vehicle
**véhiculer** [veikyle] *vt* (*personnes, marchandises*) to transport, convey; (*fig: idées, substances*) to convey, serve as a vehicle for
**veille** [vɛj] *nf* (*garde*) watch; (*Psych*) wakefulness; (*jour*): **la ~** the day before, the previous day; **la ~ au soir** the previous evening; **la ~ de** the day before; **à la ~ de** on the eve of; **l'état de ~** the waking state
**veillée** [veje] *nf* (*soirée*) evening; (*réunion*) evening gathering; **~ d'armes** night before combat; (*fig*) vigil; **~ (mortuaire)** watch
**veiller** [veje] *vi* (*rester debout*) to stay up; (*ne pas dormir*) to be awake; (*être de garde*) to be on watch; (*être vigilant*) to be watchful ▷ *vt* (*malade, mort*) to watch over, sit up with; **~ à** *vt* to attend to, see to; **~ à ce que** to make sure that, see to it that; **~ sur** *vt* to keep a watch *ou* an eye on
**veilleur** [vɛjœʀ] *nm*: **~ de nuit** night watchman
**veilleuse** [vɛjøz] *nf* (*lampe*) night light; (*Auto*) sidelight; (*flamme*) pilot light; **en ~** *adj* (*lampe*) dimmed; (*fig: affaire*) shelved, set aside
**veinard, e** [vɛnaʀ, -aʀd(ə)] *nm/f* (*fam*) lucky devil
**veine** [vɛn] *nf* (*Anat, du bois etc*) vein; (*filon*) vein, seam; (*fam: chance*): **avoir de la ~** to be lucky; (*inspiration*) inspiration
**veiné, e** [vene] *adj* veined; (*bois*) grained
**veineux, -euse** [venø, -øz] *adj* venous
**Velcro®** [vɛlkʀo] *nm* Velcro®
**vêler** [vele] *vi* to calve
**vélin** [velɛ̃] *nm*: **(papier) ~** vellum (paper)
**véliplanchiste** [veliplɑ̃ʃist(ə)] *nm/f* windsurfer
**velléitaire** [veleitɛʀ] *adj* irresolute, indecisive
**velléités** [veleite] *nfpl* vague impulses
**vélo** [velo] *nm* bike, cycle; **faire du ~** to go cycling
**véloce** [velɔs] *adj* swift
**vélocité** [velɔsite] *nf* (*Mus*) nimbleness, swiftness; (*vitesse*) velocity
**vélodrome** [velɔdʀom] *nm* velodrome
**vélomoteur** [velɔmɔtœʀ] *nm* moped
**véloski** [veloski] *nm* skibob
**velours** [vəluʀ] *nm* velvet; **~ côtelé** corduroy
**velouté, e** [vəlute] *adj* (*au toucher*) velvety; (*à la vue*) soft, mellow; (*au goût*) smooth, mellow ▷ *nm*: **~ d'asperges/de tomates** cream of asparagus/tomato soup
**velouteux, -euse** [vəlutø, -øz] *adj* velvety
**velu, e** [vəly] *adj* hairy
**venais** *etc* [vəne] *vb voir* **venir**
**venaison** [vənɛzɔ̃] *nf* venison

**vénal, e, -aux** [venal, -o] *adj* venal

**vénalité** [venalite] *nf* venality

**venant** [vənɑ̃]: **à tout ~** *adv* to all and sundry

**vendable** [vɑ̃dabl(ə)] *adj* saleable, marketable

**vendange** [vɑ̃dɑ̃ʒ] *nf* (*opération, période: aussi:* **vendanges**) grape harvest; (*raisins*) grape crop, grapes *pl*

**vendanger** [vɑ̃dɑ̃ʒe] *vi* to harvest the grapes

**vendangeur, -euse** [vɑ̃dɑ̃ʒœʀ, -øz] *nm/f* grape-picker

**vendéen, ne** [vɑ̃deɛ̃, -ɛn] *adj* of *ou* from the Vendée

**vendeur, -euse** [vɑ̃dœʀ, -øz] *nm/f* (*de magasin*) shop *ou* sales assistant (*Brit*), sales clerk (*US*); (*Comm*) salesman/woman ▷ *nm* (*Jur*) vendor, seller; **~ de journaux** newspaper seller

**vendre** [vɑ̃dʀ(ə)] *vt* to sell; **~ qch à qn** to sell sb sth; **cela se vend à la douzaine** these are sold by the dozen; **"à ~"** "for sale"

**vendredi** [vɑ̃dʀədi] *nm* Friday; **V~ saint** Good Friday; *voir aussi* **lundi**

**vendu, e** [vɑ̃dy] *pp de* **vendre** ▷ *adj* (*péj*) corrupt

**venelle** [vənɛl] *nf* alley

**vénéneux, -euse** [venenø, -øz] *adj* poisonous

**vénérable** [veneʀabl(ə)] *adj* venerable

**vénération** [veneʀasjɔ̃] *nf* veneration

**vénérer** [veneʀe] *vt* to venerate

**vénerie** [vɛnʀi] *nf* hunting

**vénérien, ne** [veneʀjɛ̃, -ɛn] *adj* venereal

**Venezuela** [venezɥela] *nm*: **le ~** Venezuela

**vénézuélien, ne** [venezɥeljɛ̃, -ɛn] *adj* Venezuelan ▷ *nm/f*: **Vénézuélien, ne** Venezuelan

**vengeance** [vɑ̃ʒɑ̃s] *nf* vengeance *no pl*, revenge *no pl*; (*acte*) act of vengeance *ou* revenge

**venger** [vɑ̃ʒe] *vt* to avenge; **se venger** *vi* to avenge o.s.; (*par rancune*) to take revenge; **se ~ de qch** to avenge o.s. for sth; to take one's revenge for sth; **se ~ de qn** to take revenge on sb; **se ~ sur** to wreak vengeance upon; to take revenge on *ou* through; to take it out on

**vengeur, -eresse** [vɑ̃ʒœʀ, -ʒʀɛs] *adj* vengeful ▷ *nm/f* avenger

**véniel, le** [venjɛl] *adj* venial

**venimeux, -euse** [vənimø, -øz] *adj* poisonous, venomous; (*fig: haineux*) venomous, vicious

**venin** [vənɛ̃] *nm* venom, poison; (*fig*) venom

**venir** [vəniʀ] *vi* to come; **~ de** to come from; **~ de faire: je viens d'y aller/de le voir** I've just been there/seen him; **s'il vient à pleuvoir** if it should rain, if it happens to rain; **en ~ à faire:** **j'en viens à croire que** I am coming to believe that; **où veux-tu en ~?** what are you getting at?; **il en est venu à mendier** he has been reduced to begging; **en ~ aux mains** to come to blows; **les années/générations à ~** the years/generations to come; **il me vient une idée** an idea has just occurred to me; **il me vient des soupçons** I'm beginning to be suspicious; **je te vois ~** I know what you're after; **faire ~** (*docteur, plombier*) to call (out); **d'où vient que ...?** how is it that ...?; **~ au monde** to come into the world

**Venise** [vəniz] *n* Venice

**vénitien, ne** [venisjɛ̃, -ɛn] *adj* Venetian

**vent** [vɑ̃] *nm* wind; **il y a du ~** it's windy; **c'est du ~** it's all hot air; **au ~** to windward; **sous le ~** to leeward; **avoir le ~ debout/arrière** to head into the wind/have the wind astern; **dans le ~** (*fam*) trendy; **prendre le ~** (*fig*) to see which way the wind blows; **avoir ~ de** to get wind of; **contre ~s et marées** come hell or high water

**vente** [vɑ̃t] *nf* sale; **la ~** (*activité*) selling; (*secteur*) sales *pl*; **mettre en ~** to put on sale; (*objets personnels*) to put up for sale; **~ de charité** jumble (*Brit*) *ou* rummage (*US*) sale; **~ par correspondance (VPC)** mail-order selling; **~ aux enchères** auction sale

**venté, e** [vɑ̃te] *adj* windswept, windy

**venter** [vɑ̃te] *vb impers*: **il vente** the wind is blowing

**venteux, -euse** [vɑ̃tø, -øz] *adj* windswept, windy

**ventilateur** [vɑ̃tilatœʀ] *nm* fan

**ventilation** [vɑ̃tilasjɔ̃] *nf* ventilation

**ventiler** [vɑ̃tile] *vt* to ventilate; (*total, statistiques*) to break down

**ventouse** [vɑ̃tuz] *nf* (*ampoule*) cupping glass; (*de caoutchouc*) suction pad; (*Zool*) sucker

**ventre** [vɑ̃tʀ(ə)] *nm* (*Anat*) stomach; (*fig*) belly; **prendre du ~** to be getting a paunch; **avoir mal au ~** to have (a) stomach ache

**ventricule** [vɑ̃tʀikyl] *nm* ventricle

**ventriloque** [vɑ̃tʀilɔk] *nm/f* ventriloquist

**ventripotent, e** [vɑ̃tʀipɔtɑ̃, -ɑ̃t] *adj* potbellied

**ventru, e** [vɑ̃tʀy] *adj* potbellied

**venu, e** [vəny] *pp de* **venir** ▷ *adj*: **être mal ~ à** *ou* **de faire** to have no grounds for doing, be in no position to do; **mal ~** ill-timed, unwelcome; **bien ~** timely, welcome ▷ *nf* coming

**vêpres** [vɛpʀ(ə)] *nfpl* vespers

**ver** [vɛʀ] *nm* worm; (*des fruits etc*) maggot; (*du bois*) woodworm *no pl*; **~ blanc** May beetle grub; **~ luisant** glow-worm; **~ à soie** silkworm; **~ solitaire** tapeworm; **~ de terre** earthworm

**véracité** [veʀasite] *nf* veracity

**véranda** [veʀɑ̃da] *nf* veranda(h)

**verbal, e, -aux** [vɛʀbal, -o] *adj* verbal

**verbalement** [vɛʀbalmɑ̃] *adv* verbally

**verbaliser** [vɛʀbalize] *vi* (*Police*) to book *ou* report an offender; (*Psych*) to verbalize

**verbe** [vɛʀb(ə)] *nm* (*Ling*) verb; (*voix*): **avoir le ~ sonore** to have a sonorous tone (of voice); (*expression*): **la magie du ~** the magic of language *ou* the word; (*Rel*): **le V~** the Word

**verbeux, -euse** [vɛʀbø, -øz] *adj* verbose, wordy

**verbiage** [vɛʀbjaʒ] *nm* verbiage

**verbosité** [vɛʀbozite] *nf* verbosity

**verdâtre** [vɛʀdɑtʀ(ə)] *adj* greenish

**verdeur** [vɛʀdœʀ] *nf* (*vigueur*) vigour (*Brit*), vigor (*US*), vitality; (*crudité*) forthrightness; (*défaut de maturité*) tartness, sharpness

**verdict** [vɛʀdik(t)] *nm* verdict

**verdir** [vɛʀdiʀ] *vi, vt* to turn green

**verdoyant, e** [vɛʀdwajɑ̃, -ɑ̃t] *adj* green, verdant

**verdure** [vɛʀdyʀ] *nf* (*arbres, feuillages*) greenery;

(*légumes verts*) green vegetables *pl*, greens *pl*
**véreux, -euse** [veʀø, -øz] *adj* worm-eaten;
(*malhonnête*) shady, corrupt
**verge** [vɛʀʒ(ə)] *nf* (*Anat*) penis; (*baguette*) stick,
cane
**verger** [vɛʀʒe] *nm* orchard
**vergeture** [vɛʀʒətyʀ] *nf gén pl* stretch mark
**verglacé, e** [vɛʀglase] *adj* icy, iced-over
**verglas** [vɛʀgla] *nm* (black) ice
**vergogne** [vɛʀgɔɲ]: **sans ~** *adv* shamelessly
**véridique** [veʀidik] *adj* truthful
**vérificateur, -trice** [veʀifikatœʀ, -tʀis] *nm/f*
controller, checker ▷ *nf* (*machine*) verifier; **~ des
comptes** (*Finance*) auditor
**vérification** [veʀifikasjɔ̃] *nf* checking *no pl*,
check; **~ d'identité** identity check
**vérifier** [veʀifje] *vt* to check; (*corroborer*) to
confirm, bear out; **se vérifier** *vi* to be
confirmed *ou* verified
**vérin** [veʀɛ̃] *nm* jack
**véritable** [veʀitabl(ə)] *adj* real; (*ami, amour*) true;
**un ~ désastre** an absolute disaster
**véritablement** [veʀitabləmɑ̃] *adv* (*effectivement*)
really; (*absolument*) absolutely
**vérité** [veʀite] *nf* truth; (*d'un portrait*)
lifelikeness; (*sincérité*) truthfulness, sincerity;
**en ~, à la ~** to tell the truth
**verlan** [vɛʀlɑ̃] *nm* (back) slang; *see note*

⬤ **VERLAN**
⬤
⬤ Verlan is a form of slang popularized in the
⬤ 1950's. It consists of inverting a word's
⬤ syllables, the term *verlan* itself coming from
⬤ "l'envers" ("à l'envers" = back to front).
⬤ Typical examples are "féca" ("café"), "ripou"
⬤ ("pourri"), "meuf" ("femme"), and "beur"
⬤ ("Arabe").

**vermeil, le** [vɛʀmej] *adj* bright red, ruby red
▷ *nm* (*substance*) vermeil
**vermicelles** [vɛʀmisɛl] *nmpl* vermicelli *sg*
**vermifuge** [vɛʀmifyʒ] *nm*: **poudre ~** worm
powder
**vermillon** [vɛʀmijɔ̃] *adj inv* vermilion, scarlet
**vermine** [vɛʀmin] *nf* vermin *pl*
**vermoulu, e** [vɛʀmuly] *adj* worm-eaten, with
woodworm
**vermout, vermouth** [vɛʀmut] *nm* vermouth
**verni, e** [vɛʀni] *adj* varnished; glazed; (*fam*)
lucky; **cuir ~** patent leather; **souliers ~s** patent
(leather) shoes
**vernir** [vɛʀniʀ] *vt* (*bois, tableau, ongles*) to varnish;
(*poterie*) to glaze
**vernis** [vɛʀni] *nm* (*enduit*) varnish; glaze; (*fig*)
veneer; **~ à ongles** nail varnish (*Brit*) *ou* polish
**vernissage** [vɛʀnisaʒ] *nm* varnishing; glazing;
(*d'une exposition*) preview
**vernisser** [vɛʀnise] *vt* to glaze
**vérole** [veʀɔl] *nf* (*variole*) smallpox; (*fam: syphilis*)
pox
**Vérone** [veʀɔn] *n* Verona

**verrai** *etc* [veʀe] *vb voir* **voir**
**verre** [vɛʀ] *nm* glass; (*de lunettes*) lens *sg*; **verres**
*nmpl* (*lunettes*) glasses; **boire ou prendre un ~** to
have a drink; **~ à vin/à liqueur** wine/liqueur
glass; **~ à dents** tooth mug; **~ dépoli** frosted
glass; **~ de lampe** lamp glass *ou* chimney; **~ de
montre** watch glass; **~ à pied** stemmed glass;
**~s de contact** contact lenses; **~s fumés** tinted
lenses
**verrerie** [vɛʀʀi] *nf* (*fabrique*) glassworks *sg*;
(*activité*) glass-making, glass-working; (*objets*)
glassware
**verrier** [vɛʀje] *nm* glass-blower
**verrière** [vɛʀjɛʀ] *nf* (*grand vitrage*) window; (*toit
vitré*) glass roof
**verrons** *etc* [vɛʀɔ̃] *vb voir* **voir**
**verroterie** [vɛʀɔtʀi] *nf* glass beads *pl*, glass
jewellery (*Brit*) *ou* jewelry (*US*)
**verrou** [vɛʀu] *nm* (*targette*) bolt; (*fig*)
constriction; **mettre le ~** to bolt the door;
**mettre qn sous les ~s** to put sb behind bars
**verrouillage** [vɛʀujaʒ] *nm* (*dispositif*) locking
mechanism; (*Auto*): **~ central ou centralisé**
central locking
**verrouiller** [vɛʀuje] *vt* to bolt; to lock; (*Mil:
brèche*) to close
**verrue** [vɛʀy] *nf* wart; (*plantaire*) verruca; (*fig*)
eyesore
**vers** [vɛʀ] *nm* line ▷ *nmpl* (*poésie*) verse *sg* ▷ *prép*
(*en direction de*) toward(s); (*près de*) around
(about); (*temporel*) about, around
**versant** [vɛʀsɑ̃] *nm* slopes *pl*, side
**versatile** [vɛʀsatil] *adj* fickle, changeable
**verse** [vɛʀs(ə)]: **à ~** *adv*: **il pleut à ~** it's pouring
(with rain)
**versé, e** [vɛʀse] *adj*: **être ~ dans** (*science*) to be
(well-)versed in
**Verseau** [vɛʀso] *nm*: **le ~** Aquarius, the water-
carrier; **être du ~** to be Aquarius
**versement** [vɛʀsəmɑ̃] *nm* payment; (*sur un
compte*) deposit, remittance; **en trois ~s** in
three instalments
**verser** [vɛʀse] *vt* (*liquide, grains*) to pour; (*larmes,
sang*) to shed; (*argent*) to pay; (*soldat: affecter*): **~
qn dans** to assign sb to ▷ *vi* (*véhicule*) to
overturn; (*fig*): **~ dans** to lapse into; **~ à un
compte** to pay into an account
**verset** [vɛʀsɛ] *nm* verse; versicle
**verseur** [vɛʀsœʀ] *adj m voir* **bec; bouchon**
**versification** [vɛʀsifikasjɔ̃] *nf* versification
**versifier** [vɛʀsifje] *vt* to put into verse ▷ *vi* to
versify, write verse
**version** [vɛʀsjɔ̃] *nf* version; (*Scol*) translation
(*into the mother tongue*); **film en ~ originale** film
in the original language
**verso** [vɛʀso] *nm* back; **voir au ~** see over(leaf)
**vert, e** [vɛʀ, vɛʀt(ə)] *adj* green; (*vin*) young;
(*vigoureux*) sprightly; (*cru*) forthright ▷ *nm*
green; **dire des ~es (et des pas mûres)** to say
some pretty spicy things; **il en a vu des ~es**
he's seen a thing or two; **~ bouteille** *adj inv*
bottle-green; **~ d'eau** *adj inv* sea-green; **~**

**pomme** adj inv apple-green

**vert-de-gris** [vɛʀdəgʀi] nm verdigris ▷ adj inv grey(ish)-green

**vertébral, e, aux** [vɛʀtebʀal, -o] adj back cpd; voir **colonne**

**vertébré, e** [vɛʀtebʀe] adj, nm vertebrate

**vertèbre** [vɛʀtɛbʀ(ə)] nf vertebra

**vertement** [vɛʀtəmɑ̃] adv (réprimander) sharply

**vertical, e, -aux** [vɛʀtikal, -o] adj, nf vertical; **à la ~e** adv vertically

**verticalement** [vɛʀtikalmɑ̃] adv vertically

**verticalité** [vɛʀtikalite] nf verticalness, verticality

**vertige** [vɛʀtiʒ] nm (peur du vide) vertigo; (étourdissement) dizzy spell; (fig) fever; **ça me donne le ~** it makes me dizzy; (fig) it makes my head spin ou reel

**vertigineux, -euse** [vɛʀtiʒinø, -øz] adj (hausse, vitesse) breathtaking; (altitude, gorge) breathtakingly high (ou deep)

**vertu** [vɛʀty] nf virtue; **une ~** a saint, a paragon of virtue; **avoir la ~ de faire** to have the virtue of doing; **en ~ de** prép in accordance with

**vertueusement** [vɛʀtɥøzmɑ̃] adv virtuously

**vertueux, -euse** [vɛʀtɥø, -øz] adj virtuous

**verve** [vɛʀv(ə)] nf witty eloquence; **être en ~** to be in brilliant form

**verveine** [vɛʀvɛn] nf (Bot) verbena, vervain; (infusion) verbena tea

**vésicule** [vezikyl] nf vesicle; **~ biliaire** gall-bladder

**vespasienne** [vɛspazjɛn] nf urinal

**vespéral, e, -aux** [vɛspeʀal, -o] adj vespertine, evening cpd

**vessie** [vesi] nf bladder

**veste** [vɛst(ə)] nf jacket; **~ droite/croisée** single-/double-breasted jacket; **retourner sa ~** (fig) to change one's colours

**vestiaire** [vɛstjɛʀ] nm (au théâtre etc) cloakroom; (de stade etc) changing-room (Brit), locker-room (US); (métallique): (**armoire**) **~** locker

**vestibule** [vɛstibyl] nm hall

**vestige** [vɛstiʒ] nm (objet) relic; (fragment) trace; (fig) remnant, vestige; **vestiges** nmpl (d'une ville) remains; (d'une civilisation, du passé) remnants, relics

**vestimentaire** [vɛstimɑ̃tɛʀ] adj (dépenses) clothing; (détail) of dress; (élégance) sartorial

**veston** [vɛstɔ̃] nm jacket

**Vésuve** [vezyv] nm: **le ~** Vesuvius

**vêtais** etc [vɛtɛ] vb voir **vêtir**

**vêtement** [vɛtmɑ̃] nm garment, item of clothing; (Comm): **le ~** the clothing industry; **vêtements** nmpl clothes; **~s de sport** sportswear sg, sports clothes

**vétéran** [veteʀɑ̃] nm veteran

**vétérinaire** [veteʀinɛʀ] adj veterinary ▷ nm/f vet, veterinary surgeon (Brit), veterinarian (US)

**vétille** [vetij] nf trifle, triviality

**vétilleux, -euse** [vetijø, -øz] adj punctilious

**vêtir** [vetiʀ] vt to clothe, dress; **se vêtir** to dress (o.s.)

**vêtit** etc [veti] vb voir **vêtir**

**vétiver** [vetivɛʀ] nm (Bot) vetiver

**veto** [veto] nm veto; **droit de ~** right of veto; **mettre** ou **opposer un ~ à** to veto

**vêtu, e** [vɛty] pp de **vêtir** ▷ adj: **~ de** dressed in, wearing; **chaudement ~** warmly dressed

**vétuste** [vetyst(ə)] adj ancient, timeworn

**vétusté** [vetyste] nf age, delapidation

**veuf, veuve** [vœf, v v] adj widowed ▷ nm widower ▷ nf widow

**veuille** [vœj], **veuillez** etc [vœje] vb voir **vouloir**

**veule** [vøl] adj spineless

**veulent** etc [vœl] vb voir **vouloir**

**veulerie** [vølʀi] nf spinelessness

**veut** [vø] vb voir **vouloir**

**veuvage** [vœvaʒ] nm widowhood

**veuve** [vœv] adj f, nf voir **veuf**

**veux** [vø] vb voir **vouloir**

**vexant, e** [vɛksɑ̃, -ɑ̃t] adj (contrariant) annoying; (blessant) upsetting

**vexations** [vɛksasjɔ̃] nfpl humiliations

**vexatoire** [vɛksatwaʀ] adj: **mesures ~s** harassment sg

**vexer** [vɛkse] vt to hurt, upset; **se vexer** vi to be hurt, get upset

**VF** sigle f (Ciné) = **version française**

**VHF** sigle f (= Very High Frequency) VHF

**via** [vja] prép via

**viabiliser** [vjabilize] vt to provide with services (water etc)

**viabilité** [vjabilite] nf viability; (d'un chemin) practicability

**viable** [vjabl(ə)] adj viable

**viaduc** [vjadyk] nm viaduct

**viager, -ère** [vjaʒe, -ɛʀ] adj: **rente viagère** life annuity ▷ nm: **mettre en ~** to sell in return for a life annuity

**viande** [vjɑ̃d] nf meat

**viatique** [vjatik] nm (Rel) viaticum; (fig) provisions pl ou money for the journey

**vibrant, e** [vibʀɑ̃, -ɑ̃t] adj vibrating; (voix) vibrant; (émouvant) emotive

**vibraphone** [vibʀafɔn] nm vibraphone, vibes pl

**vibraphoniste** [vibʀafɔnist(ə)] nm/f vibraphone player

**vibration** [vibʀasjɔ̃] nf vibration

**vibratoire** [vibʀatwaʀ] adj vibratory

**vibrer** [vibʀe] vi to vibrate; (son, voix) to be vibrant; (fig) to be stirred; **faire ~** to (cause to) vibrate; to stir, thrill

**vibromasseur** [vibʀɔmasœʀ] nm vibrator

**vicaire** [vikɛʀ] nm curate

**vice...** [vis] préfixe vice-

**vice** [vis] nm vice; (défaut) fault; **~ caché** (Comm) latent ou inherent defect; **~ de forme** legal flaw ou irregularity

**vice-consul** [viskɔ̃syl] nm vice-consul

**vice-présidence** [vispʀezidɑ̃s] nf (d'un pays) vice-presidency; (d'une société) vice-presidency, vice-chairmanship (Brit)

**vice-président, e** [vispʀezidɑ̃, -ɑ̃t] nm/f vice-president; vice-chairman

**V**

433

**vice-roi** [visʀwa] *nm* viceroy
**vice-versa** [viseveʀsa] *adv* vice versa
**vichy** [viʃi] *nm* (*toile*) gingham; (*eau*) Vichy
water; **carottes V~** boiled carrots
**vichyssois, e** [viʃiswa, -waz] *adj* *ou* from
Vichy, Vichy *cpd* ▷ *nf* (*soupe*) vichyssoise (soup),
*cream of leek and potato soup* ▷ *nm/f*: **Vichyssois, e**
native *ou* inhabitant of Vichy
**vicié, e** [visje] *adj* (*air*) polluted, tainted; (*Jur*)
invalidated
**vicier** [visje] *vt* (*Jur*) to invalidate
**vicieux, -euse** [visjø, -øz] *adj* (*pervers*)
dirty(-minded); (*méchant*) nasty; (*fautif*)
incorrect, wrong
**vicinal, e, -aux** [visinal, -o] *adj*: **chemin ~**
byroad, byway
**vicissitudes** [visisityd] *nfpl* (trials and)
tribulations
**vicomte** [vikɔ̃t] *nm* viscount
**vicomtesse** [vikɔ̃tɛs] *nf* viscountess
**victime** [viktim] *nf* victim; (*d'accident*) casualty;
**être (la) ~ de** to be the victim of; **être ~ d'une
attaque/d'un accident** to suffer a stroke/be
involved in an accident
**victoire** [viktwaʀ] *nf* victory
**victorieusement** [viktɔʀjøzmɑ̃] *adv*
triumphantly, victoriously
**victorieux, -euse** [viktɔʀjø, -øz] *adj* victorious;
(*sourire, attitude*) triumphant
**victuailles** [viktɥaj] *nfpl* provisions
**vidange** [vidɑ̃ʒ] *nf* (*d'un fossé, réservoir*) emptying;
(*Auto*) oil change; (*de lavabo: bonde*) waste outlet;
**vidanges** *nfpl* (*matières*) sewage *sg*; **faire la ~**
(*Auto*) to change the oil, do an oil change;
**tuyau de ~** drainage pipe
**vidanger** [vidɑ̃ʒe] *vt* to empty; **faire ~ la
voiture** to have the oil changed in one's car
**vide** [vid] *adj* empty ▷ *nm* (*Physique*) vacuum;
(*espace*) (empty) space, gap; (*sous soi: dans une
falaise etc*) drop; (*futilité, néant*) void; **~ de** empty
of; (*de sens etc*) devoid of; **sous ~** *adv* in a
vacuum; **emballé sous ~** vacuum-packed;
**regarder dans le ~** to stare into space; **avoir
peur du ~** to be afraid of heights; **parler dans
le ~** to waste one's breath; **faire le ~** (*dans son
esprit*) to make one's mind go blank; **faire le ~
autour de qn** to isolate sb; **à ~** *adv* (*sans
occupants*) empty; (*sans charge*) unladen; (*Tech*)
without gripping *ou* being in gear
**vidé, e** [vide] *adj* (*épuisé*) done in, all in
**vidéo** [video] *nf, adj inv* video; **~ inverse** reverse
video
**vidéocassette** [videokasɛt] *nf* video cassette
**vidéoclip** [videoklip] *nm* music video
**vidéoclub** [videoklœb] *nm* video club
**vidéoconférence** [videokɔ̃feʀɑ̃s] *nf* videoconference
**vidéodisque** [videodisk] *nm* videodisc
**vide-ordures** [vidɔʀdyʀ] *nm inv* (rubbish) chute
**vidéotex®** [videotɛks] *nm* teletext
**vidéothèque** [videotɛk] *nf* video library
**vide-poches** [vidpɔʃ] *nm inv* tidy; (*Auto*) glove
compartment

**vide-pomme** [vidpɔm] *nm inv* apple-corer
**vider** [vide] *vt* to empty; (*Culin: volaille, poisson*) to
gut, clean out; (*régler: querelle*) to settle; (*fatiguer*)
to wear out; (*fam: expulser*) to throw out, chuck
out; **se vider** *vi* to empty; **~ les lieux** to quit *ou*
vacate the premises
**videur** [vidœʀ] *nm* (*de boîte de nuit*) bouncer
**vie** [vi] *nf* life; **être en ~** to be alive; **sans ~**
lifeless; **à ~** for life; **membre à ~** life member;
**dans la ~ courante** in everyday life; **avoir la ~
dure** to have nine lives; to die hard; **mener la ~
dure à qn** to make life a misery for sb
**vieil** [vjɛj] *adj m voir* **vieux**
**vieillard** [vjɛjaʀ] *nm* old man; **les ~s** old people,
the elderly
**vieille** [vjɛj] *adj f, nf voir* **vieux**
**vieilleries** [vjɛjʀi] *nfpl* old things *ou* stuff *sg*
**vieillesse** [vjɛjɛs] *nf* old age; (*vieillards*): **la ~** the
old *pl*, the elderly *pl*
**vieilli, e** [vjeji] *adj* (*marqué par l'âge*) aged; (*suranné*)
dated
**vieillir** [vjejiʀ] *vi* (*prendre de l'âge*) to grow old;
(*population, vin*) to age; (*doctrine, auteur*) to become
dated ▷ *vt* to age; **il a beaucoup vieilli** he has
aged a lot; **se vieillir** to make o.s. older
**vieillissement** [vjejismɑ̃] *nm* growing old;
ageing
**vieillot, te** [vjɛjo, -ɔt] *adj* antiquated, quaint
**vielle** [vjɛl] *nf* hurdy-gurdy
**viendrai** *etc* [vjɛ̃dʀe] *vb voir* **venir**
**Vienne** [vjɛn] *n* (*en Autriche*) Vienna
**vienne** [vjɛn], **viens** *etc* [vjɛ̃] *vb voir* **venir**
**viennois, e** [vjɛnwa, -waz] *adj* Viennese
**viens** [vjɛ̃] *vb voir* **venir**
**vierge** [vjɛʀʒ(ə)] *adj* virgin; (*film*) blank; (*page*)
clean, blank; (*jeune fille*): **être ~** to be a virgin
▷ *nf* virgin; (*signe*): **la V~** Virgo, the Virgin; **être
de la V~** to be Virgo; **~ de** (*sans*) free from,
unsullied by
**Viêtnam, Vietnam** [vjɛtnam] *nm*: **le ~**
Vietnam; **le ~ du Nord/du Sud** North/South
Vietnam
**vietnamien, ne** [vjɛtnamjɛ̃, -ɛn] *adj*
Vietnamese ▷ *nm* (*Ling*) Vietnamese ▷ *nm/f*:
**Vietnamien, ne** Vietnamese; **V~, ne du Nord/
Sud** North/South Vietnamese
**vieux, vieil, vieille** [vjø, vjɛj] *adj* old ▷ *nm/f* old
man/woman ▷ *nmpl*: **les ~** the old, old people;
(*fam: parents*) the old folk *ou* ones; **un petit ~** a
little old man; **mon ~/ma vieille** (*fam*) old man/
girl; **pauvre ~** poor old soul; **prendre un coup
de ~** to put years on; **se faire ~** to make o.s. look
older; **un ~ de la vieille** one of the old brigade;
**~ garçon** *nm* bachelor; **~ jeu** *adj inv* old-
fashioned; **~ rose** *adj inv* old rose; **vieil or** *adj
inv* old gold; **vieille fille** *nf* spinster
**vif, vive** [vif, viv] *adj* (*animé*) lively; (*alerte*) sharp,
quick; (*brusque*) sharp, brusque; (*aigu*) sharp;
(*lumière, couleur*) brilliant; (*air*) crisp; (*vent,
émotion*) keen; (*froid*) bitter; (*fort: regret, déception*)
great, deep; (*vivant*): **brûlé ~** burnt alive; **eau
vive** running water; **de vive voix** personally;

**piquer qn au** ~ to cut sb to the quick; **tailler dans le** ~ to cut into the living flesh; **à** ~ (plaie) open; **avoir les nerfs à** ~ to be on edge; **sur le** ~ (Art) from life; **entrer dans le** ~ **du sujet** to get to the very heart of the matter

**vif-argent** [vifaʀʒɑ̃] nm inv quicksilver

**vigie** [viʒi] nf (matelot) look-out; (poste) look-out post, crow's nest

**vigilance** [viʒilɑ̃s] nf vigilance

**vigilant, e** [viʒilɑ̃, -ɑ̃t] adj vigilant

**vigile** [viʒil] nm (veilleur de nuit) (night) watchman; (police privée) vigilante

**vigne** [viɲ] nf (plante) vine; (plantation) vineyard; ~ **vierge** Virginia creeper

**vigneron** [viɲʀɔ̃] nm wine grower

**vignette** [viɲɛt] nf (motif) vignette; (de marque) manufacturer's label ou seal; (petite illustration) (small) illustration; (Admin) ≈ (road) tax disc (Brit), ≈ license plate sticker (US); (: sur médicament) price label (on medicines for reimbursement by Social Security)

**vignoble** [viɲɔbl(ə)] nm (plantation) vineyard; (vignes d'une région) vineyards pl

**vigoureusement** [viguʀøzmɑ̃] adv vigorously

**vigoureux, -euse** [viguʀø, -øz] adj vigorous, robust

**vigueur** [vigœʀ] nf vigour (Brit), vigor (US); **être/entrer en** ~ to be in/come into force; **en** ~ current

**vil, e** [vil] adj vile, base; **à** ~ **prix** at a very low price

**vilain, e** [vilɛ̃, -ɛn] adj (laid) ugly; (affaire, blessure) nasty; (pas sage: enfant) naughty ▷ nm (paysan) villein, villain; **ça va tourner au** ~ things are going to turn nasty; ~ **mot** bad word

**vilainement** [vilɛnmɑ̃] adv badly

**vilebrequin** [vilbʀəkɛ̃] nm (outil) (bit-)brace; (Auto) crankshaft

**vilenie** [vilni] nf vileness no pl, baseness no pl

**vilipender** [vilipɑ̃de] vt to revile, vilify

**villa** [vila] nf (detached) house

**village** [vilaʒ] nm village; ~ **de toile** tent village; ~ **de vacances** holiday village

**villageois, e** [vilaʒwa, -waz] adj village cpd ▷ nm/f villager

**ville** [vil] nf town; (importante) city; (administration): **la** ~ ≈ the Corporation, ≈ the (town) council; **aller en** ~ to go to town; **habiter en** ~ to live in town; ~ **jumelée** twin town; ~ **nouvelle** new town

**ville-champignon** [vilʃɑ̃piɲɔ̃] (pl **villes-champignons**) nf boom town

**ville-dortoir** [vildɔʀtwaʀ] (pl **villes-dortoirs**) nf dormitory town

**villégiature** [vileʒjatyʀ] nf (séjour) holiday; (lieu) (holiday) resort

**vin** [vɛ̃] nm wine; **avoir le** ~ **gai/triste** to get happy/miserable after a few drinks; ~ **blanc/rosé/rouge** white/rosé/red wine; ~ **d'honneur** reception; (with wine and snacks); ~ **de messe** altar wine; ~ **ordinaire** ou **de table** table wine; ~ **de pays** local wine; voir aussi **AOC**; **VDQS**

**vinaigre** [vinɛgʀ(ə)] nm vinegar; **tourner au** ~ (fig) to turn sour; ~ **de vin/d'alcool** wine/spirit vinegar

**vinaigrette** [vinɛgʀɛt] nf vinaigrette, French dressing

**vinaigrier** [vinɛgʀije] nm (fabricant) vinegar-maker; (flacon) vinegar cruet ou bottle

**vinasse** [vinas] nf (péj) cheap wine, plonk (Brit)

**vindicatif, -ive** [vɛ̃dikatif, -iv] adj vindictive

**vindicte** [vɛ̃dikt(ə)] nf: **désigner qn à la** ~ **publique** to expose sb to public condemnation

**vineux, -euse** [vinø, -øz] adj win(e)y

**vingt** [vɛ̃, vɛ̃t] (+ voyelle following 2nd pron) num twenty; ~-**quatre heures sur** ~-**quatre** twenty-four hours a day, round the clock

**vingtaine** [vɛ̃tɛn] nf: **une** ~ **(de)** around twenty, twenty or so

**vingtième** [vɛ̃tjɛm] num twentieth

**vinicole** [vinikɔl] adj (production) wine cpd; (région) wine-growing

**vinification** [vinifikasjɔ̃] nf wine-making, wine production; (des sucres) vinification

**vins** etc [vɛ̃] vb voir **venir**

**vinyle** [vinil] nm vinyl

**viol** [vjɔl] nm (d'une femme) rape; (d'un lieu sacré) violation

**violacé, e** [vjɔlase] adj purplish, mauvish

**violation** [vjɔlasjɔ̃] nf desecration; violation; (d'un droit) breach

**violemment** [vjɔlamɑ̃] adv violently

**violence** [vjɔlɑ̃s] nf violence; **violences** nfpl acts of violence; **faire** ~ **à qn** to do violence to sb; **se faire** ~ to force o.s

**violent, e** [vjɔlɑ̃, -ɑ̃t] adj violent; (remède) drastic; (besoin, désir) intense, urgent

**violenter** [vjɔlɑ̃te] vt to assault (sexually)

**violer** [vjɔle] vt (femme) to rape; (sépulture) to desecrate, violate; (loi, traité) to violate

**violet, te** [vjɔlɛ, -ɛt] adj, nm purple, mauve ▷ nf (fleur) violet

**violeur** [vjɔlœʀ] nm rapist

**violine** [vjɔlin] nf deep purple

**violon** [vjɔlɔ̃] nm violin; (dans la musique folklorique etc) fiddle; (fam: prison) lock-up; **premier** ~ first violin; ~ **d'Ingres** (artistic) hobby

**violoncelle** [vjɔlɔ̃sɛl] nm cello

**violoncelliste** [vjɔlɔ̃selist(ə)] nm/f cellist

**violoniste** [vjɔlɔnist(ə)] nm/f violinist, violin-player; (folklorique etc) fiddler

**VIP** sigle m (= Very Important Person) VIP

**vipère** [vipɛʀ] nf viper, adder

**virage** [viʀaʒ] nm (d'un véhicule) turn; (d'une route, piste) bend; (Chimie) change in colour (Brit) ou color (US); (de cuti-réaction) positive reaction; (Photo) toning; (fig: Pol) about-turn; **prendre un** ~ to go into a bend, take a bend; ~ **sans visibilité** blind bend

**viral, e, -aux** [viʀal, -o] adj viral

**virée** [viʀe] nf (courte) run; (: à pied) walk; (longue) trip; hike, walking tour

**virement** [viʀmɑ̃] nm (Comm) transfer; ~ **bancaire** (bank) credit transfer, ≈ (bank) giro transfer (*Brit*); **~ postal** Post office credit transfer, ≈ Girobank® transfer (*Brit*)

**virent** [viʀ] *vb voir* **voir**

**virer** [viʀe] *vt* (*Comm*): **~ qch (sur)** to transfer sth (into); (*Photo*) to tone; (*fam: renvoyer*) to sack, boot out ▷ *vi* to turn; (*Chimie*) to change colour (*Brit*) *ou* color (*US*); (*cuti-réaction*) to come up positive; (*Photo*) to tone; **~ au bleu** to turn blue; **~ de bord** to tack; (*fig*) to change tack; **~ sur l'aile** to bank

**virevolte** [viʀvɔlt(ə)] *nf* twirl; (*d'avis, d'opinion*) about-turn

**virevolter** [viʀvɔlte] *vi* to twirl around

**virginal, e, -aux** [viʀʒinal, -o] *adj* virginal

**virginité** [viʀʒinite] *nf* virginity; (*fig*) purity

**virgule** [viʀgyl] *nf* comma; (*Math*) point; **quatre ~ deux** four point two; **~ flottante** floating decimal

**viril, e** [viʀil] *adj* (*propre à l'homme*) masculine; (*énergique, courageux*) manly, virile

**viriliser** [viʀilize] *vt* to make (more) manly *ou* masculine

**virilité** [viʀilite] *nf* (*attributs masculins*) masculinity; (*fermeté, courage*) manliness; (*sexuelle*) virility

**virologie** [viʀɔlɔʒi] *nf* virology

**virtualité** [viʀtɥalite] *nf* virtuality; potentiality

**virtuel, le** [viʀtɥɛl] *adj* potential; (*théorique*) virtual

**virtuellement** [viʀtɥɛlmɑ̃] *adj* potentially; (*presque*) virtually

**virtuose** [viʀtɥoz] *nm/f* (*Mus*) virtuoso; (*gén*) master

**virtuosité** [viʀtɥozite] *nf* virtuosity; masterliness, masterful skills *pl*

**virulence** [viʀylɑ̃s] *nf* virulence

**virulent, e** [viʀylɑ̃, -ɑ̃t] *adj* virulent

**virus** [viʀys] *nm* virus

**vis** [vi] *voir* **voir**; **vivre** ▷ *nf* [vis] screw; **~ à tête plate/ronde** flat-headed/round-headed screw; **~ platinées** (*Auto*) (contact) points; **~ sans fin** worm, endless screw

**visa** [viza] *nm* (*sceau*) stamp; (*validation de passeport*) visa; **~ de censure** (censor's) certificate

**visage** [vizaʒ] *nm* face; **à ~ découvert** (*franchement*) openly

**visagiste** [vizaʒist(ə)] *nm/f* beautician

**vis-à-vis** [vizavi] *adv* face to face ▷ *nm* person opposite; house *etc* opposite; **~ de** *prép* opposite; (*fig*) towards, vis-à-vis; **en ~** facing *ou* opposite each other; **sans ~** (*immeuble*) with an open outlook

**viscéral, e, -aux** [viseʀal, -o] *adj* (*fig*) deepseated, deep-rooted

**viscères** [viseʀ] *nmpl* intestines, entrails

**viscose** [viskoz] *nf* viscose

**viscosité** [viskozite] *nf* viscosity

**visée** [vize] *nf* (*avec une arme*) aiming; (*Arpentage*) sighting; **visées** *nfpl* (*intentions*) designs; **avoir des ~s sur qn/qch** to have designs on sb/sth

**viser** [vize] *vi* to aim ▷ *vt* to aim at; (*concerner*) to

be aimed *ou* directed at; (*apposer un visa sur*) to stamp, visa; **~ à qch/faire** to aim at sth/at doing *ou* to do

**viseur** [vizœʀ] *nm* (*d'arme*) sights *pl*; (*Photo*) viewfinder

**visibilité** [vizibilite] *nf* visibility; **sans ~** (*pilotage, virage*) blind *cpd*

**visible** [vizibl(ə)] *adj* visible; (*disponible*): **est-il ~?** can he see me?, will he see visitors?

**visiblement** [vizibləmɑ̃] *adv* visibly, obviously

**visière** [vizjeʀ] *nf* (*de casquette*) peak; (*qui s'attache*) eyeshade

**vision** [vizjɔ̃] *nf* vision; (*sens*) (eye)sight, vision; (*fait de voir*): **la ~ de** the sight of; **première ~** (*Ciné*) first showing

**visionnaire** [vizjɔneʀ] *adj, nm/f* visionary

**visionner** [vizjɔne] *vt* to view

**visionneuse** [vizjɔnøz] *nf* viewer

**visiophone** [vizjɔfɔn] *nm* videophone

**visite** [vizit] *nf* visit; (*visiteur*) visitor; (*touristique: d'un musée etc*) tour; (*Comm: de représentant*) call; (*expertise, d'inspection*) inspection; (*médicale, à domicile*) visit, call; **la ~** (*Méd*) medical examination; (*Mil: d'entrée*) medicals *pl*; (: *quotidienne*) sick parade; **faire une ~ à qn** to call on sb, pay sb a visit; **rendre ~ à qn** to visit sb, pay sb a visit; **être en ~ (chez qn)** to be visiting (sb); **heures de ~** (*hôpital, prison*) visiting hours; **le droit de ~** (*Jur: aux enfants*) right of access, access; **~ de douane** customs inspection *ou* examination; **~ guidée** guided tour

**visiter** [vizite] *vt* to visit; (*musée, ville*) to visit, go round

**visiteur, -euse** [vizitœʀ, -øz] *nm/f* visitor; **~ des douanes** customs inspector; **~ médical** medical rep(resentative); **~ de prison** prison visitor

**vison** [vizɔ̃] *nm* mink

**visqueux, -euse** [viskø, -øz] *adj* viscous; (*péj*) gooey; (: *manières*) slimy

**visser** [vise] *vt*: **~ qch** (*fixer, serrer*) to screw sth on

**visu** [vizy]: **de ~** *adv* with one's own eyes

**visualisation** [vizɥalizasjɔ̃] *nf* (*Inform*) display; **écran de ~** visual display unit (VDU)

**visualiser** [vizɥalize] *vt* to visualize; (*Inform*) to display, bring up on screen

**visuel, le** [vizɥɛl] *adj* visual

**visuellement** [vizɥɛlmɑ̃] *adv* visually

**vit** [vi] *vb voir* **vivre**; **voir**

**vital, e, -aux** [vital, -o] *adj* vital

**vitalité** [vitalite] *nf* vitality

**vitamine** [vitamin] *nf* vitamin

**vitaminé, e** [vitamine] *adj* with (added) vitamins

**vitaminique** [vitaminik] *adj* vitamin *cpd*

**vite** [vit] *adv* (*rapidement*) quickly, fast; (*sans délai*) quickly; soon; **faire ~** (*agir rapidement*) to act fast; (*se dépêcher*) to be quick; **ce sera ~ fini** this will soon be finished; **viens ~** come quick(ly)

**vitesse** [vites] *nf* speed; (*Auto: dispositif*) gear; **faire de la ~** to drive fast *ou* at speed; **prendre qn de ~** to outstrip sb, get ahead of sb; **prendre**

**de la ~** to pick up *ou* gather speed; **à toute ~** at full *ou* top speed; **en perte de ~** *(avion)* losing lift; *(fig)* losing momentum; **changer de ~** *(Auto)* to change gear; **~ acquise** momentum; **~ de croisière** cruising speed; **~ de pointe** top speed; **~ du son** speed of sound

**viticole** [vitikɔl] *adj (industrie)* wine *cpd; (région)* wine-growing

**viticulteur** [vitikyltœʀ] *nm* wine grower

**viticulture** [vitikyltyʀ] *nf* wine growing

**vitrage** [vitʀaʒ] *nm (cloison)* glass partition; *(toit)* glass roof; *(rideau)* net curtain

**vitrail, -aux** [vitʀaj, -o] *nm* stained-glass window

**vitre** [vitʀ(ə)] *nf* (window) pane; *(de portière, voiture)* window

**vitré, e** [vitʀe] *adj* glass *cpd*

**vitrer** [vitʀe] *vt* to glaze

**vitreux, -euse** [vitʀø, -øz] *adj* vitreous; *(terne)* glassy

**vitrier** [vitʀije] *nm* glazier

**vitrifier** [vitʀifje] *vt* to vitrify; *(parquet)* to glaze

**vitrine** [vitʀin] *nf (devanture)* (shop) window; *(étalage)* display; *(petite armoire)* display cabinet; **en ~** in the window, on display; **~ publicitaire** display case, showcase

**vitriol** [vitʀijɔl] *nm* vitriol; **au ~** *(fig)* vitriolic

**vitupérations** [vitypeʀasjɔ̃] *nfpl* invective *sg*

**vitupérer** [vitypeʀe] *vi* to rant and rave; **~ contre** to rail against

**vivable** [vivabl(ə)] *adj (personne)* livable-with; *(endroit)* fit to live in

**vivace** *adj* [vivas] *(arbre, plante)* hardy; *(fig)* enduring ▷ *adv* [vivatʃe] *(Mus)* vivace

**vivacité** [vivasite] *nf (voir vif)* liveliness, vivacity; sharpness; brilliance

**vivant, e** [vivɑ̃, -ɑ̃t] *vb voir* **vivre** ▷ *adj (qui vit)* living, alive; *(animé)* lively; *(preuve, exemple)* living; *(langue)* modern ▷ *nm:* **du ~ de qn** in sb's lifetime; **les ~s et les morts** the living and the dead

**vivarium** [vivaʀjɔm] *nm* vivarium

**vivats** [viva] *nmpl* cheers

**vive** [viv] *adj f voir* **vif** ▷ *vb voir* **vivre** ▷ *excl:* **~ le roi!** long live the king!; **~ les vacances!** hurrah for the holidays!

**vivement** [vivmɑ̃] *adv* vivaciously; sharply ▷ *excl:* **~ les vacances!** I can't wait for the holidays!, roll on the holidays!

**viveur** [vivœʀ] *nm (péj)* high liver, pleasure-seeker

**vivier** [vivje] *nm (au restaurant etc)* fish tank; *(étang)* fishpond

**vivifiant, e** [vivifjɑ̃, -ɑ̃t] *adj* invigorating

**vivifier** [vivifje] *vt* to invigorate; *(fig: souvenirs, sentiments)* to liven up, enliven

**vivions** [vivjɔ̃] *vb voir* **vivre**

**vivipare** [vivipaʀ] *adj* viviparous

**vivisection** [viviseksjɔ̃] *nf* vivisection

**vivoter** [vivɔte] *vi (personne)* to scrape a living, get by; *(fig: affaire etc)* to struggle along

**vivre** [vivʀ(ə)] *vi, vt* to live ▷ *nm:* **le ~ et le logement** board and lodging; **vivres** *nmpl* provisions, food supplies; **il vit encore** he is still alive; **se laisser ~** to take life as it comes; **ne plus ~** *(être anxieux)* to live on one's nerves; **il a vécu** *(eu une vie aventureuse)* he has seen life; **ce régime a vécu** this regime has had its day; **être facile à ~** to be easy to get on with; **faire ~ qn** *(pourvoir à sa subsistance)* to provide (a living) for sb; **~ mal** *(chichement)* to have a meagre existence; **~ de** *(salaire etc)* to live on

**vivrier, -ière** [vivʀije, -jɛʀ] *adj* food-producing *cpd*

**vlan** [vlɑ̃] *excl* wham!, bang!

**VO** *sigle f (Ciné)* = **version originale**; **voir un film en VO** to see a film in its original language

**v° ** *abr* = **verso**

**vocable** [vɔkabl(ə)] *nm* term

**vocabulaire** [vɔkabylɛʀ] *nm* vocabulary

**vocal, e, -aux** [vɔkal, -o] *adj* vocal

**vocalique** [vɔkalik] *adj* vocalic, vowel *cpd*

**vocalise** [vɔkaliz] *nf* singing exercise

**vocaliser** [vɔkalize] *vi (Ling)* to vocalize; *(Mus)* to do one's singing exercises

**vocation** [vɔkasjɔ̃] *nf* vocation, calling; **avoir la ~** to have a vocation

**vociférations** [vɔsifeʀasjɔ̃] *nfpl* cries of rage, screams

**vociférer** [vɔsifeʀe] *vi, vt* to scream

**vodka** [vɔdka] *nf* vodka

**vœu, x** [vø] *nm* wish; *(à Dieu)* vow; **faire ~ de** to take a vow of; **avec tous nos ~x** with every good wish *ou* our best wishes; **meilleurs ~x** best wishes; *(sur une carte)* "Season's Greetings"; **~x de bonheur** best wishes for your future happiness; **~x de bonne année** best wishes for the New Year

**vogue** [vɔg] *nf* fashion, vogue; **en ~** in fashion, in vogue

**voguer** [vɔge] *vi* to sail

**voici** [vwasi] *prép (pour introduire, désigner)* here is; *(+ sg)* here are; *(+ pl):* **et ~ que ...** and now it *(ou* he) ...; **il est parti ~ trois ans** he left three years ago; **~ une semaine que je l'ai vue** it's a week since I've seen her; **me ~** here I am; *voir aussi* **voilà**

**voie** [vwa] *vb voir* **voir** ▷ *nf* way; *(Rail)* track, line; *(Auto)* lane; **par ~ buccale** *ou* **orale** orally; **par ~ rectale** rectally; **suivre la ~ hiérarchique** to go through official channels; **ouvrir/montrer la ~** to open up/show the way; **être en bonne ~** to be shaping *ou* going well; **mettre qn sur la ~** to put sb on the right track; **être en ~ d'achèvement/de rénovation** to be nearing completion/in the process of renovation; **à ~ étroite** narrow-gauge; **à ~ unique** single-track; **route à deux/trois ~s** two-/three-lane road; **par la ~ aérienne/maritime** by air/sea; **~ d'eau** *(Navig)* leak; **~ express** expressway; **~ de fait** *(Jur)* assault (and battery); **~ ferrée** track; railway line *(Brit)*, railroad *(US)*; **par ~ ferrée** by rail, by railroad; **~ de garage** *(Rail)* siding; **la ~ lactée** the Milky Way; **~ navigable** waterway;

**~ prioritaire** (*Auto*) road with right of way; **~ privée** private road; **la ~ publique** the public highway

**voilà** [vwala] *prép* (*en désignant*) there is; (+*sg*) there are; (+*pl*): **les ~ voici** here ou there they are; **en ~** ou **voici un** here's one, there's one; **~** ou **voici deux ans** two years ago; **~** ou **voici deux ans que** it's two years since; **et ~!** there we are!; **~ tout** that's all; **"~** ou **voici"** (*en offrant etc*) "there ou here you are"

**voilage** [vwalaʒ] *nm* (*rideau*) net curtain; (*tissu*) net

**voile** [vwal] *nm* veil; (*tissu léger*) net ▷ *nf* sail; (*sport*) sailing; **prendre le ~** to take the veil; **mettre à la ~** to make way under sail; **~ du palais** *nm* soft palate, velum; **~ au poumon** *nm* shadow on the lung

**voiler** [vwale] *vt* to veil; (*Photo*) to fog; (*fausser: roue*) to buckle; (: *bois*) to warp; **se voiler** *vi* (*lune, regard*) to mist over; (*ciel*) to grow hazy; (*voix*) to become husky; (*roue, disque*) to buckle; (*planche*) to warp; **se ~ la face** to hide one's face

**voilette** [vwalɛt] *nf* (*hat*) veil

**voilier** [vwalje] *nm* sailing ship; (*de plaisance*) sailing boat

**voilure** [vwalyʀ] *nf* (*de voilier*) sails *pl*; (*d'avion*) aerofoils *pl* (*Brit*), airfoils *pl* (*US*); (*de parachute*) canopy

**voir** [vwaʀ] *vi, vt* to see; **se voir**: **se ~ critiquer/transformer** to be criticized/transformed; **cela se voit** (*cela arrive*) it happens; (*c'est visible*) that's obvious, it shows; **~ à faire qch** to see to it that sth is done; **~ loin** (*fig*) to be far-sighted; **~ venir** (*fig*) to wait and see; **faire ~ qch à qn** to show sb sth; **en faire ~ à qn** (*fig*) to give sb a hard time; **ne pas pouvoir ~ qn** (*fig*) not to be able to stand sb; **regardez ~** just look; **montrez ~** show (me); **dites ~** tell me; **voyons!** let's see now; (*indignation etc*) come (along) now!; **c'est à ~!** we'll see!; **c'est ce qu'on va ~!** we'll see about that!; **avoir quelque chose à ~ avec** to have something to do with; **ça n'a rien à ~ avec lui** that has nothing to do with him

**voire** [vwaʀ] *adv* indeed; nay; or even

**voirie** [vwaʀi] *nf* highway maintenance; (*administration*) highways department; (*enlèvement des ordures*) refuse (*Brit*) ou garbage (*US*) collection

**vois** [vwa] *vb voir* **voir**

**voisin, e** [vwazɛ̃, -in] *adj* (*proche*) neighbouring (*Brit*), neighboring (*US*); (*contigu*) next; (*ressemblant*) connected ▷ *nm/f* neighbo(u)r; (*de table, de dortoir etc*) person next to me (*ou* him *etc*); **~ de palier** neighbo(u)r across the landing (*Brit*) *ou* hall (*US*)

**voisinage** [vwazinaʒ] *nm* (*proximité*) proximity; (*environs*) vicinity; (*quartier, voisins*) neighbourhood (*Brit*), neighborhood (*US*); **relations de bon ~** neighbo(u)rly terms

**voisiner** [vwazine] *vi*: **~ avec** to be side by side with

**voit** [vwa] *vb voir* **voir**

**voiture** [vwatyʀ] *nf* car; (*wagon*) coach, carriage; **en ~!** all aboard!; **~ à bras** handcart; **~ d'enfant** pram (*Brit*), baby carriage (*US*); **~ d'infirme** invalid carriage; **~ de sport** sports car

**voiture-lit** [vwatyʀli] (*pl* **voitures-lits**) *nf* sleeper

**voiture-restaurant** [vwatyʀʀɛstɔʀɑ̃] (*pl* **voitures-restaurants**) *nf* dining car

**voix** [vwa] *nf* voice; (*Pol*) vote; **~ de la conscience/raison** the voice of conscience/reason; **à haute ~** aloud; **à ~ basse** in a low voice; **faire la grosse ~** to speak gruffly; **avoir de la ~** to have a good voice; **rester sans ~** to be speechless; **~ de basse/ténor** *etc* bass/tenor *etc* voice; **à deux/quatre ~** (*Mus*) in two/four parts; **avoir ~ au chapitre** to have a say in the matter; **mettre aux ~** to put to the vote; **~ off** voice-over

**vol** [vɔl] *nm* (*mode de locomotion*) flying; (*trajet, voyage, groupe d'oiseaux*) flight; (*mode d'appropriation*) theft, stealing; (*larcin*) theft; **à ~ d'oiseau** as the crow flies; **au ~: attraper qch au ~** to catch sth as it flies past; **saisir une remarque au ~** to pick up a passing remark; **prendre son ~** to take flight; **de haut ~** (*fig*) of the highest order; **en ~** in flight; **~ avec effraction** breaking and entering *no pl*, breaking; **~ à l'étalage** shoplifting *no pl*; **~ libre** hang-gliding; **~ à main armée** armed robbery; **~ de nuit** night flight; **~ plané** (*Aviat*) glide, gliding *no pl*; **~ à la tire** pickpocketing *no pl*; **~ à voile** gliding

**vol.** *abr* (= *volume*) vol

**volage** [vɔlaʒ] *adj* fickle

**volaille** [vɔlaj] *nf* (*oiseaux*) poultry *pl*; (*viande*) poultry *no pl*; (*oiseau*) fowl

**volailler** [vɔlaje] *nm* poulterer

**volant, e** [vɔlɑ̃, -ɑ̃t] *adj voir* **feuille** *etc* ▷ *nm* (*d'automobile*) (steering) wheel; (*de commande*) wheel; (*objet lancé*) shuttlecock; (*jeu*) battledore and shuttlecock; (*bande de tissu*) flounce; (*feuillet détachable*) tear-off portion; **le personnel ~, les ~s** (*Aviat*) the flight staff; **~ de sécurité** (*fig*) reserve, margin, safeguard

**volatil, e** [vɔlatil] *adj* volatile

**volatile** [vɔlatil] *nm* (*volaille*) bird; (*tout oiseau*) winged creature

**volatiliser** [vɔlatilize]: **se volatiliser** *vi* (*Chimie*) to volatilize; (*fig*) to vanish into thin air

**vol-au-vent** [vɔlovɑ̃] *nm inv* vol-au-vent

**volcan** [vɔlkɑ̃] *nm* volcano; (*fig: personne*) hothead

**volcanique** [vɔlkanik] *adj* volcanic; (*fig: tempérament*) volatile

**volcanologie** [vɔlkanɔlɔʒi] *nf* vulcanology

**volcanologue** [vɔlkanɔlɔg] *nm/f* vulcanologist

**volée** [vɔle] *nf* (*groupe d'oiseaux*) flight, flock; (*Tennis*) volley; **~ de coups/de flèches** volley of blows/arrows; **à la ~: rattraper à la ~** to catch in midair; **lancer à la ~** to fling about; **semer à la ~** to (sow) broadcast; **à toute ~** (*sonner les cloches*) vigorously; (*lancer un projectile*) with full force; **de haute ~** (*fig*) of the highest order

**voler** [vɔle] vi (avion, oiseau, fig) to fly; (voleur) to steal ▷ vt (objet) to steal; (personne) to rob; ~ **en éclats** to smash to smithereens; ~ **de ses propres ailes** (fig) to stand on one's own two feet; ~ **au vent** to fly in the wind; ~ **qch à qn** to steal sth from sb

**volet** [vɔlɛ] nm (de fenêtre) shutter; (Aviat) flap; (de feuillet, document) section; (fig: d'un plan) facet; **trié sur le** ~ hand-picked

**voleter** [vɔlte] vi to flutter (about)

**voleur, -euse** [vɔlœʀ, -øz] nm/f thief ▷ adj thieving; **"au ~!"** "stop thief!"

**volière** [vɔljɛʀ] nf aviary

**volley** [vɔlɛ], **volley-ball** [vɔlɛbol] nm volleyball

**volleyeur, -euse** [vɔlɛjœʀ, -øz] nm/f volleyball player

**volontaire** [vɔlɔ̃tɛʀ] adj (acte, activité) voluntary; (délibéré) deliberate; (caractère, personne: décidé) self-willed ▷ nm/f volunteer

**volontairement** [vɔlɔ̃tɛʀmɑ̃] adv voluntarily; deliberately

**volontariat** [vɔlɔ̃taʀja] nm voluntary service

**volontarisme** [vɔlɔ̃taʀism(ə)] nm voluntarism

**volontariste** [vɔlɔ̃taʀist(ə)] adj, nm/f voluntarist

**volonté** [vɔlɔ̃te] nf (faculté de vouloir) will; (énergie, fermeté) will(power); (souhait, désir) wish; **se servir/boire à** ~ to take/drink as much as one likes; **bonne** ~ goodwill, willingness; **mauvaise** ~ lack of goodwill, unwillingness

**volontiers** [vɔlɔ̃tje] adv (de bonne grâce) willingly; (avec plaisir) willingly, gladly; (habituellement, souvent) readily, willingly; **"~"** "with pleasure", "I'd be glad to"

**volt** [vɔlt] nm volt

**voltage** [vɔltaʒ] nm voltage

**volte-face** [vɔltəfas] nf inv about-turn; (fig) about-turn, U-turn; **faire** ~ to do an about-turn; to do a U-turn

**voltige** [vɔltiʒ] nf (Équitation) trick riding; (au cirque) acrobatics sg; (Aviat) (aerial) acrobatics sg; **numéro de haute** ~ acrobatic act

**voltiger** [vɔltiʒe] vi to flutter (about)

**voltigeur** [vɔltiʒœʀ] nm (au cirque) acrobat; (Mil) light infantryman

**voltmètre** [vɔltmɛtʀ(ə)] nm voltmeter

**volubile** [vɔlybil] adj voluble

**volubilis** [vɔlybilis] nm convolvulus

**volume** [vɔlym] nm volume; (Géom: solide) solid

**volumineux, -euse** [vɔlyminø, -øz] adj voluminous, bulky

**volupté** [vɔlypte] nf sensual delight ou pleasure

**voluptueusement** [vɔlyptɥøzmɑ̃] adv voluptuously

**voluptueux, -euse** [vɔlyptɥø, -øz] adj voluptuous

**volute** [vɔlyt] nf (Archit) volute; ~ **de fumée** curl of smoke

**vomi** [vɔmi] nm vomit

**vomir** [vɔmiʀ] vi to vomit, be sick ▷ vt to vomit, bring up; (fig) to belch out, spew out; (exécrer) to loathe, abhor

**vomissements** [vɔmismɑ̃] nmpl (action) vomiting no pl; **des** ~ vomit sg

**vomissure** [vɔmisyʀ] nf vomit no pl

**vomitif** [vɔmitif] nm emetic

**vont** [vɔ̃] vb voir **aller**

**vorace** [vɔʀas] adj voracious

**voracement** [vɔʀasmɑ̃] adv voraciously

**voracité** [vɔʀasite] nf voracity

**vos** [vo] adj poss voir **votre**

**Vosges** [voʒ] nfpl: **les** ~ the Vosges

**vosgien, ne** [voʒjɛ̃, -ɛn] adj of ou from the Vosges ▷ nm/f inhabitant ou native of the Vosges

**VOST** sigle f (Ciné: = version originale sous-titrée) subtitled version

**votant, e** [vɔtɑ̃, -ɑ̃t] nm/f voter

**vote** [vɔt] nm vote; ~ **par correspondance/procuration** postal/proxy vote; ~ **à main levée** vote by show of hands; ~ **secret**, ~ **à bulletins secrets** secret ballot

**voter** [vɔte] vi to vote ▷ vt (loi, décision) to vote for

**votre** [vɔtʀ(ə)] (pl **vos** [vo]) adj poss your

**vôtre** [votʀ(ə)] pron: **le** ~, **la** ~, **les** ~**s** yours; **les** ~**s** (fig) your family ou folks; **à la** ~ (toast) your (good) health!

**voudrai** etc [vudʀe] vb voir **vouloir**

**voué, e** [vwe] adj: ~ **à** doomed to, destined for

**vouer** [vwe] vt: ~ **qch à** (Dieu/un saint) to dedicate sth to; ~ **sa vie/son temps à** (étude, cause etc) to devote one's life/time to; ~ **une haine/amitié éternelle à qn** to vow undying hatred/friendship to sb

(V) MOT-CLÉ

**vouloir** [vulwaʀ] nm: **le bon vouloir de qn** sb's goodwill; sb's pleasure
▷ vt **1** (exiger, désirer) to want; **vouloir faire/que qn fasse** to want to do/sb to do; **voulez-vous du thé?** would you like ou do you want some tea?; **vouloir qch à qn** to wish sth for sb; **que me veut-il?** what does he want with me?; **que veux-tu que je te dise?** what do you want me to say?; **sans le vouloir** (involontairement) without meaning to, unintentionally; **je voudrais ceci/faire** I would ou I'd like this/to do; **le hasard a voulu que ...** as fate would have it, ...; **la tradition veut que ...** tradition demands that ...; **... qui se veut moderne ...** which purports to be modern
**2** (consentir): **je veux bien** (bonne volonté) I'll be happy to; (concession) fair enough, that's fine; **oui, si on veut** (en quelque sorte) yes, if you like; **comme tu veux** as you wish; (en quelque sorte) if you like; **veuillez attendre** please wait; **veuillez agréer ...** (formule épistolaire) yours faithfully
**3**: **en vouloir** (être ambitieux) to be out to win; **en vouloir à qn** to bear sb a grudge; **je lui en veux d'avoir fait ça** I resent his having done that; **s'en vouloir (de)** to be annoyed with o.s. (for);

V

439

**il en veut à mon argent** he's after my money
**4**: **vouloir de** to want; **la compagnie ne veut
plus de lui** the firm doesn't want him any
more; **elle ne veut pas de son aide** she doesn't
want his help
**5**: **vouloir dire** to mean

**voulu, e** [vuly] *pp de* **vouloir** ▷ *adj (requis)*
required, requisite; *(délibéré)* deliberate,
intentional
**voulus** *etc* [vuly] *vb voir* **vouloir**
**vous** [vu] *pron* you; *(objet indirect)* (to) you;
*(réfléchi)* yourself; *(réciproque)* each other ▷ *nm*:
**employer le ~** *(vouvoyer)* to use the "vous" form;
**~-même** yourself; **~-mêmes** yourselves
**voûte** [vut] *nf* vault; **la ~ céleste** the vault of
heaven; **~ du palais** *(Anat)* roof of the mouth; **~
plantaire** arch (of the foot)
**voûté, e** [vute] *adj* vaulted, arched; *(dos,
personne)* bent, stooped
**voûter** [vute] *vt (Archit)* to arch, vault; **se voûter**
*vi (dos, personne)* to become stooped
**vouvoiement** [vuvwamã] *nm* use of formal
"vous" form
**vouvoyer** [vuvwaje] *vt*: **~ qn** to address sb as
"vous"
**voyage** [vwajaʒ] *nm* journey, trip; *(fait de
voyager)*: **le ~** travel(ling); **partir/être en ~** to go
off/be away on a journey *ou* trip; **faire un ~** to
go on *ou* make a trip *ou* journey; **faire bon ~** to
have a good journey; **les gens du ~** travelling
people; **~ d'agrément/d'affaires** pleasure/
business trip; **~ de noces** honeymoon; **~
organisé** package tour
**voyager** [vwajaʒe] *vi* to travel
**voyageur, -euse** [vwajaʒœʀ, -øz] *nm/f* traveller;
*(passager)* passenger ▷ *adj (tempérament)*
nomadic, wayfaring; **~ (de commerce)**
commercial traveller
**voyagiste** [vwajaʒist(ə)] *nm* tour operator
**voyais** *etc* [vwajɛ] *vb voir* **voir**
**voyance** [vwajãs] *nf* clairvoyance
**voyant, e** [vwajã, -ãt] *adj (couleur)* loud, gaudy
▷ *nm/f (personne qui voit)* sighted person ▷ *nm
(signal)* (warning) light ▷ *nf* clairvoyant
**voyelle** [vwajɛl] *nf* vowel
**voyeur, -euse** [vwajœʀ, -øz] *nm/f* voyeur;
peeping Tom
**voyeurisme** [vwajœʀism(ə)] *nm* voyeurism
**voyons** *etc* [vwajɔ̃] *vb voir* **voir**
**voyou** [vwaju] *nm* lout, hoodlum; *(enfant)*
guttersnipe
**VPC** *sigle f (= vente par correspondance)* mail order
selling
**vrac** [vʀak]: **en ~** *adv* higgledy-piggledy; *(Comm)*
in bulk
**vrai, e** [vʀɛ] *adj (véridique: récit, faits)* true; *(non
factice, authentique)* real ▷ *nm*: **le ~** the truth; **à ~
dire** to tell the truth; **il est ~ que** it is true that;
**être dans le ~** to be right
**vraiment** [vʀɛmã] *adv* really

**vraisemblable** [vʀɛsãblabl(ə)] *adj (plausible)*
likely, plausible; *(probable)* likely, probable
**vraisemblablement** [vʀɛsãblabləmã] *adv* in all
likelihood, very likely
**vraisemblance** [vʀɛsãblãs] *nf* likelihood,
plausibility; *(romanesque)* verisimilitude; **selon
toute ~** in all likelihood
**vraquier** [vʀakje] *nm* freighter
**vrille** [vʀij] *nf (de plante)* tendril; *(outil)* gimlet;
*(spirale)* spiral; *(Aviat)* spin
**vriller** [vʀije] *vt* to bore into, pierce
**vrombir** [vʀɔ̃biʀ] *vi* to hum
**vrombissant, e** [vʀɔ̃bisã, -ãt] *adj* humming
**vrombissement** [vʀɔ̃bismã] *nm* hum(ming)
**VRP** *sigle m (= voyageur, représentant, placier)* (sales)
rep
**VTT** *sigle m (= vélo tout-terrain)* mountain bike
**vu¹** [vy] *prép (en raison de)* in view of; **vu que** in
view of the fact that
**vu², e¹** [vy] *pp de* **voir** ▷ *adj*: **bien/mal vu**
*(personne)* well/poorly thought of; *(conduite)*
good/bad form ▷ *nm*: **au vu et au su de tous**
openly and publicly; **ni vu ni connu** what the
eye doesn't see ...!, no one will be any the wiser;
**c'est tout vu** it's a foregone conclusion
**vue²** [vy] *nf (fait de voir)*: **la ~ de** the sight of; *(sens,
faculté)* (eye)sight; *(panorama, image, photo)* view;
*(spectacle)* sight; **vues** *nfpl (idées)* views; *(dessein)*
designs; **perdre la ~** to lose one's (eye)sight;
**perdre de ~** to lose sight of; **à la ~ de tous** in
full view of everybody; **hors de ~** out of sight; **à
première ~** at first sight; **connaître de ~** to
know by sight; **à ~ (Comm)** at sight; **tirer à ~** to
shoot on sight; **à ~ d'œil** *adv* visibly; *(à première
vue)* at a quick glance; **avoir ~ sur** to have a view
of; **en ~ (visible)** in sight; *(Comm)* in the public
eye; **avoir qch en ~ (intentions)** to have one's
sights on sth; **en ~ de faire** with the intention
of doing, with a view to doing; **~ d'ensemble**
overall view; **~ de l'esprit** theoretical view
**vulcanisation** [vylkanizasjɔ̃] *nf* vulcanization
**vulcaniser** [vylkanize] *vt* to vulcanize
**vulcanologie** [vylkanɔlɔʒi] *nf* = **volcanologie**
**vulcanologue** [vylkanɔlɔg] *nm/f* =
**volcanologue**
**vulgaire** [vylgɛʀ] *adj (grossier)* vulgar, coarse;
*(trivial)* commonplace, mundane; *(péj:
quelconque)*: **de ~s touristes/chaises de cuisine**
common tourists/kitchen chairs; *(Bot, Zool: non
latin)* common
**vulgairement** [vylgɛʀmã] *adv* vulgarly,
coarsely; *(communément)* commonly
**vulgariser** [vylgaʀize] *vt* to popularize
**vulgarité** [vylgaʀite] *nf* vulgarity, coarseness
**vulnérabilité** [vylneʀabilite] *nf* vulnerability
**vulnérable** [vylneʀabl(ə)] *adj* vulnerable
**vulve** [vylv(ə)] *nf* vulva
**Vve** *abr* = **veuve**
**VVF** *sigle m (= village vacances famille)* state-subsidized
holiday village
**vx** *abr* = **vieux**

# Ww

**W, w** [dubləve] *nm inv* W, w ▷ *abr* (= *watt*) W; **W comme William** W for William

**wagon** [vagɔ̃] *nm* (*de voyageurs*) carriage; (*de marchandises*) truck, wagon

**wagon-citerne** [vagɔ̃sitɛʀn(ə)] (*pl* **wagons-citernes**) *nm* tanker

**wagon-lit** [vagɔ̃li] (*pl* **wagons-lits**) *nm* sleeper, sleeping car

**wagonnet** [vagɔnɛ] *nm* small truck

**wagon-poste** [vagɔ̃pɔst(ə)] (*pl* **wagons-postes**) *nm* mail van

**wagon-restaurant** [vagɔ̃ʀɛstɔʀɑ̃] (*pl* **wagons-restaurants**) *nm* restaurant *ou* dining car

**Walkman**® [wɔkman] *nm* Walkman®, personal stereo

**Wallis et Futuna** [walisefytyna]: **les îles ~** the Wallis and Futuna Islands

**wallon, ne** [walɔ̃, -ɔn] *adj* Walloon ▷ *nm* (*Ling*) Walloon ▷ *nm/f*: **Wallon, ne** Walloon

**Wallonie** [walɔni] *nf*: **la ~** French-speaking (part of) Belgium

**water-polo** [watɛʀpɔlo] *nm* water polo

**waters** [watɛʀ] *nmpl* toilet *sg*, loo *sg* (*Brit*)

**watt** [wat] *nm* watt

**WC** [vese] *nmpl* toilet *sg*, lavatory *sg*

**Web** [wɛb] *nm inv*: **le ~** the (World Wide) Web

**webcam** [wɛbkam] *nf* webcam

**webmaster** [-mastœʀ], **webmestre** [-mɛstʀ] *nm/f* webmaster

**week-end** [wikɛnd] *nm* weekend

**western** [wɛstɛʀn] *nm* western

**Westphalie** [vɛsfali] *nf*: **la ~** Westphalia

**whisky** [wiski] (*pl* **whiskies**) *nm* whisky

**white-spirit** [wajtspiʀit] *nm* white spirit

**widget** [widʒɛt] *nm* (*Inform*) widget

**wifi, Wi-Fi** [wifi] *nm inv* (= *wireless fidelity*) wifi, Wi-Fi

**wok** [wɔk] *nm* wok

**WWW** *sigle m*: **World Wide Web** WWW

X

# Xx

**X, x** [iks] *nm inv* X, x ▷ *sigle m* = **(École) polytechnique**; **plainte contre X** (*Jur*) action against person or persons unknown; **X comme Xavier** X for Xmas

**xénophobe** [gzenɔfɔb] *adj* xenophobic ▷ *nm/f* xenophobe

**xénophobie** [gzenɔfɔbi] *nf* xenophobia

**xérès** [gzeʀɛs] *nm* sherry

**xylographie** [ksilɔgʀafi] *nf* xylography; (*image*) xylograph

**xylophone** [ksilɔfɔn] *nm* xylophone

# Yy

**Y, y** [igʀɛk] *nm inv* Y, y; **Y comme Yvonne** Y for Yellow (Brit) *ou* Yoke (US)

**y** [i] *adv* (*à cet endroit*) there; (*dessus*) on it (*ou* them); (*dedans*) in it (*ou* them) ▷ *pron* (*about ou on ou of*) it (*vérifier la syntaxe du verbe employé*); **j'y pense** I'm thinking about it; *voir aussi* **aller; avoir**

**yacht** [jɔt] *nm* yacht

**yaourt** [jauʀt] *nm* yoghurt

**yaourtière** [jauʀtjɛʀ] *nf* yoghurt-maker

**Yémen** [jemɛn] *nm*: **le ~** Yemen

**yéménite** [jemenit] *adj* Yemeni

**yeux** [jø] *nmpl de* **œil**

**yoga** [jɔga] *nm* yoga

**yoghourt** [jɔguʀt] *nm* = **yaourt**

**yole** [jɔl] *nf* skiff

**yougoslave** [jugɔslav] *adj* Yugoslav(ian) ▷ *nm/f*: **Yougoslave** Yugoslav(ian)

**Yougoslavie** [jugɔslavi] *nf*: **la ~** Yugoslavia

**youyou** [juju] *nm* dinghy

**yo-yo** [jojo] *nm inv* yo-yo

**yucca** [juka] *nm* yucca (tree *ou* plant)

# Zz

**Z, z** [zɛd] *nm inv* Z, z; **Z comme Zoé** Z for Zebra
**ZAC** [zak] *sigle f* (= *zone d'aménagement concerté*) urban development zone
**ZAD** [zad] *sigle f* (= *zone d'aménagement différé*) future development zone
**Zaïre** [zaiʀ] *nm*: **le ~** Zaïre
**zaïrois, e** [zaiʀwa, -waz] *adj* Zairian
**Zambèze** [zɑ̃bɛz] *nm* **le ~** the Zambezi
**Zambie** [zɑ̃bi] *nf*: **la ~** Zambia
**zambien, ne** [zɑ̃bjɛ̃, -ɛn] *adj* Zambian
**zapper** [zape] *vi* to zap
**zapping** [zapiŋ] *nm*: **faire du ~** to flick through the channels
**zébré, e** [zebʀe] *adj* striped, streaked
**zèbre** [zɛbʀ(ə)] *nm* (*Zool*) zebra
**zébrure** [zebʀyʀ] *nf* stripe, streak
**zélateur, -trice** [zelatœʀ, -tʀis] *nm/f* partisan, zealot
**zélé, e** [zele] *adj* zealous
**zèle** [zɛl] *nm* diligence, assiduousness; **faire du ~** (*péj*) to be over-zealous
**zénith** [zenit] *nm* zenith
**ZEP** [zɛp] *sigle f* (= *zone d'éducation prioritaire*) area targeted for special help in education
**zéro** [zeʀo] *nm* zero, nought (*Brit*); **au-dessous de ~** below zero (Centigrade), below freezing; **partir de ~** to start from scratch; **réduire à ~** to reduce to nothing; **trois (buts) à ~** three (goals to) nil
**zeste** [zɛst(ə)] *nm* peel, zest; **un ~ de citron** a piece of lemon peel
**zézaiement** [zezɛmɑ̃] *nm* lisp
**zézayer** [zezeje] *vi* to have a lisp
**ZI** *sigle f* = **zone industrielle**
**zibeline** [ziblin] *nf* sable
**ZIF** [zif] *sigle f* (= *zone d'intervention foncière*) intervention zone
**zigouiller** [ziguje] *vt* (*fam*) to do in

**zigzag** [zigzag] *nm* zigzag
**zigzaguer** [zigzage] *vi* to zigzag (along)
**Zimbabwe** [zimbabwe] *nm*: **le ~** Zimbabwe
**zimbabwéen, ne** [zimbabweɛ̃, -ɛn] *adj* Zimbabwean
**zinc** [zɛ̃g] *nm* (*Chimie*) zinc; (*comptoir*) bar, counter
**zinguer** [zɛ̃ge] *vt* to cover with zinc
**zipper** [zipe] *vt* (*Inform*) to zip
**zircon** [ziʀkɔ̃] *nm* zircon
**zizanie** [zizani] *nf*: **semer la ~** to stir up ill-feeling
**zizi** [zizi] *nm* (*fam*) willy (*Brit*), peter (*US*)
**zodiacal, e, -aux** [zɔdjakal, -o] *adj* (*signe*) of the zodiac
**zodiaque** [zɔdjak] *nm* zodiac
**zona** [zona] *nm* shingles *sg*
**zonage** [zonaʒ] *nm* (*Admin*) zoning
**zonard, e** [zonaʀ, -aʀd] *nm/f* (*fam*) (young) hooligan *ou* thug
**zone** [zon] *nf* zone, area; (*quartiers*): **la ~** the slum belt; **de seconde ~** (*fig*) second-rate; **~ d'action** (*Mil*) sphere of activity; **~ bleue** ≈ restricted parking area; **~ d'extension** *ou* **d'urbanisation** urban development area; **~ franche** free zone; **~ industrielle (ZI)** industrial estate; **~ piétonne** pedestrian precinct; **~ résidentielle** residential area; **~ tampon** buffer zone
**zoner** [zone] *vi* (*fam*) to hang around
**zoo** [zoo] *nm* zoo
**zoologie** [zɔɔlɔʒi] *nf* zoology
**zoologique** [zɔɔlɔʒik] *adj* zoological
**zoologiste** [zɔɔlɔʒist(ə)] *nm/f* zoologist
**zoom** [zum] *nm* (*Photo*) zoom (lens)
**ZUP** [zyp] *sigle f* = **zone à urbaniser en priorité**; = **ZAC**
**Zurich** [zyʀik] *n* Zürich
**zut** [zyt] *excl* dash (it)! (*Brit*), nuts! (*US*)

# Aa

**A, aˡ** [eɪ] *n* (*letter*) A, a *m*; (*Scol: mark*) A; (*Mus*) la *m*; **A for Andrew, A for Able** (*US*) A comme Anatole; **A shares** *npl* (*Brit Stock Exchange*) actions *fpl* prioritaires

**◯ KEYWORD**

**a²** [eɪ, ə] (*before vowel and silent h* **an**) *indef art* **1** un(e); **a book** un livre; **an apple** une pomme; **she's a doctor** elle est médecin
**2** (*instead of the number "one"*) un(e); **a year ago** il y a un an; **a hundred/thousand** *etc* **pounds** cent/mille *etc* livres
**3** (*in expressing ratios, prices etc*): **three a day/week** trois par jour/semaine; **10 km an hour** 10 km à l'heure; **£5 a person** 5£ par personne; **30p a kilo** 30p le kilo

**a.** *abbr* = **acre**
**A2** *n* (*Brit: Scol*) deuxième partie de l'examen équivalent au baccalauréat
**A.A.** *n abbr* (*Brit*: = *Automobile Association*) ≈ ACF *m*; (*US*: = *Associate in/of Arts*) diplôme universitaire; (= *Alcoholics Anonymous*) AA; (= *anti-aircraft*) AA
**A.A.A.** *n abbr* (= *American Automobile Association*) ≈ ACF *m*; (*Brit*) = **Amateur Athletics Association**
**A & R** *n abbr* (*Mus*) = **artists and repertoire**; **~ man** découvreur *m* de talent
**AAUP** *n abbr* (= *American Association of University Professors*) syndicat universitaire
**AB** *abbr* (*Brit*) = **able-bodied seaman**; (*Canada*) = **Alberta**
**aback** [ə'bæk] *adv*: **to be taken ~** être déconcenancé(e)
**abacus** (*pl* **abaci**) ['æbəkəs, -saɪ] *n* boulier *m*
**abandon** [ə'bændən] *vt* abandonner ▷ *n* abandon *m*; **to ~ ship** évacuer le navire
**abandoned** [ə'bændənd] *adj* (*child, house etc*) abandonné(e); (*unrestrained*) sans retenue
**abase** [ə'beɪs] *vt*: **to ~ o.s. (so far as to do)** s'abaisser (à faire)
**abashed** [ə'bæʃt] *adj* confus(e), embarrassé(e)
**abate** [ə'beɪt] *vi* s'apaiser, se calmer
**abatement** [ə'beɪtmənt] *n*: **noise ~** lutte *f* contre le bruit
**abattoir** ['æbətwɑːʳ] *n* (*Brit*) abattoir *m*

**abbey** ['æbɪ] *n* abbaye *f*
**abbot** ['æbət] *n* père supérieur
**abbreviate** [ə'briːvɪeɪt] *vt* abréger
**abbreviation** [əbriːvɪ'eɪʃən] *n* abréviation *f*
**ABC** *n abbr* (= *American Broadcasting Company*) chaîne de télévision
**abdicate** ['æbdɪkeɪt] *vt, vi* abdiquer
**abdication** [æbdɪ'keɪʃən] *n* abdication *f*
**abdomen** ['æbdəmən] *n* abdomen *m*
**abdominal** [æb'dɔmɪnl] *adj* abdominal(e)
**abduct** [æb'dʌkt] *vt* enlever
**abduction** [æb'dʌkʃən] *n* enlèvement *m*
**Aberdonian** [æbə'dəunɪən] *adj* d'Aberdeen ▷ *n* habitant(e) d'Aberdeen, natif(-ive) d'Aberdeen
**aberration** [æbə'reɪʃən] *n* anomalie *f*; **in a moment of mental ~** dans un moment d'égarement
**abet** [ə'bɛt] *vt see* **aid**
**abeyance** [ə'beɪəns] *n*: **in ~** (*law*) en désuétude; (*matter*) en suspens
**abhor** [əb'hɔːʳ] *vt* abhorrer, exécrer
**abhorrent** [əb'hɔrənt] *adj* odieux(-euse), exécrable
**abide** [ə'baɪd] *vt* souffrir, supporter; **I can't ~ it/him** je ne le supporte pas
▷ **abide by** *vt fus* observer, respecter
**abiding** [ə'baɪdɪŋ] *adj* (*memory etc*) durable
**ability** [ə'bɪlɪtɪ] *n* compétence *f*; capacité *f*; (*skill*) talent *m*; **to the best of my ~** de mon mieux
**abject** ['æbdʒɛkt] *adj* (*poverty*) sordide; (*coward*) méprisable; **an ~ apology** les excuses les plus plates
**ablaze** [ə'bleɪz] *adj* en feu, en flammes; **~ with light** resplendissant de lumière
**able** ['eɪbl] *adj* compétent(e); **to be ~ to do sth** pouvoir faire qch, être capable de faire qch
**able-bodied** ['eɪbl'bɔdɪd] *adj* robuste; **~ seaman** (*Brit*) matelot breveté
**ably** ['eɪblɪ] *adv* avec compétence *or* talent, habilement
**ABM** *n abbr* = **anti-ballistic missile**
**abnormal** [æb'nɔːməl] *adj* anormal(e)
**abnormality** [æbnɔː'mælɪtɪ] *n* (*condition*) caractère anormal; (*instance*) anomalie *f*
**aboard** [ə'bɔːd] *adv* à bord ▷ *prep* à bord de; (*train*) dans

**abode** [ə'bəud] *n* (*old*) demeure *f*; (*Law*): **of no fixed ~** sans domicile fixe
**abolish** [ə'bɒlɪʃ] *vt* abolir
**abolition** [æbə'lɪʃən] *n* abolition *f*
**abominable** [ə'bɒmɪnəbl] *adj* abominable
**aborigine** [æbə'rɪdʒɪnɪ] *n* aborigène *m/f*
**abort** [ə'bɔ:t] *vt* (*Med*) faire avorter; (*Comput, fig*) abandonner
**abortion** [ə'bɔ:ʃən] *n* avortement *m*; **to have an ~** se faire avorter
**abortionist** [ə'bɔ:ʃənɪst] *n* avorteur(-euse)
**abortive** [ə'bɔ:tɪv] *adj* manqué(e)
**abound** [ə'baund] *vi* abonder; **to ~ in** abonder en, regorger de

KEYWORD

**about** [ə'baut] *adv* **1** (*approximately*) environ, à peu près; **about a hundred/thousand** *etc* environ cent/mille *etc*, une centaine (de)/un millier (de) *etc*; **it takes about 10 hours** ça prend environ *or* à peu près 10 heures; **at about 2 o'clock** vers 2 heures; **I've just about finished** j'ai presque fini
**2** (*referring to place*) çà et là, de-ci de-là; **to run about** courir çà et là; **to walk about** se promener, aller et venir; **is Paul about?** (*Brit*) est-ce que Paul est là?; **it's about here** c'est par ici, c'est dans les parages; **they left all their things lying about** ils ont laissé traîner toutes leurs affaires
**3**: **to be about to do sth** être sur le point de faire qch; **I'm not about to do all that for nothing** (*inf*) je ne vais quand même pas faire tout ça pour rien
**4** (*opposite*): **it's the other way about** (*Brit*) c'est l'inverse
▷ *prep* **1** (*relating to*) au sujet de, à propos de; **a book about London** un livre sur Londres; **what is it about?** de quoi s'agit-il?; **we talked about it** nous en avons parlé; **do something about it!** faites quelque chose!; **what** *or* **how about doing this?** et si nous faisions ceci?
**2** (*referring to place*) dans; **to walk about the town** se promener dans la ville

**above** [ə'bʌv] *adv* au-dessus ▷ *prep* au-dessus de; (*more than*) plus de; **mentioned ~** mentionné ci-dessus; **costing ~ £10** coûtant plus de 10 livres; **~ all** par-dessus tout, surtout
**aboveboard** [ə'bʌv'bɔ:d] *adj* franc (franche), loyal(e); honnête
**abrasion** [ə'breɪʒən] *n* frottement *m*; (*on skin*) écorchure *f*
**abrasive** [ə'breɪzɪv] *adj* abrasif(-ive); (*fig*) caustique, agressif(-ive)
**abreast** [ə'brest] *adv* de front; **to keep ~ of** se tenir au courant de
**abridge** [ə'brɪdʒ] *vt* abréger
**abroad** [ə'brɔ:d] *adv* à l'étranger; **there is a rumour ~ that ...** (*fig*) le bruit court que ...
**abrupt** [ə'brʌpt] *adj* (*steep, blunt*) abrupt(e);

(*sudden, gruff*) brusque
**abruptly** [ə'brʌptlɪ] *adv* (*speak, end*) brusquement
**abscess** ['æbsɪs] *n* abcès *m*
**abscond** [əb'skɒnd] *vi* disparaître, s'enfuir
**absence** ['æbsəns] *n* absence *f*; **in the ~ of** (*person*) en l'absence de; (*thing*) faute de
**absent** ['æbsənt] *adj* absent(e); **~ without leave (AWOL)** (*Mil*) en absence irrégulière
**absentee** [æbsən'ti:] *n* absent(e)
**absenteeism** [æbsən'ti:ɪzəm] *n* absentéisme *m*
**absent-minded** ['æbsənt'maɪndɪd] *adj* distrait(e)
**absent-mindedness** ['æbsənt'maɪndɪdnɪs] *n* distraction *f*
**absolute** ['æbsəlu:t] *adj* absolu(e)
**absolutely** [æbsə'lu:tlɪ] *adv* absolument
**absolve** [əb'zɒlv] *vt*: **to ~ sb (from)** (*sin etc*) absoudre qn (de); **to ~ sb from** (*oath*) délier qn de
**absorb** [əb'zɔ:b] *vt* absorber; **to be ~ed in a book** être plongé(e) dans un livre
**absorbent** [əb'zɔ:bənt] *adj* absorbant(e)
**absorbent cotton** [əb'zɔ:bənt-] *n* (*US*) coton *m* hydrophile
**absorbing** [əb'zɔ:bɪŋ] *adj* absorbant(e); (*book, film etc*) captivant(e)
**absorption** [əb'sɔ:pʃən] *n* absorption *f*
**abstain** [əb'steɪn] *vi*: **to ~ (from)** s'abstenir (de)
**abstemious** [əb'sti:mɪəs] *adj* sobre, frugal(e)
**abstention** [əb'stenʃən] *n* abstention *f*
**abstinence** ['æbstɪnəns] *n* abstinence *f*
**abstract** ['æbstrækt] *adj* abstrait(e) ▷ *n* (*summary*) résumé *m* ▷ *vt* [æb'strækt] extraire
**absurd** [əb'sə:d] *adj* absurde
**absurdity** [əb'sə:dɪtɪ] *n* absurdité *f*
**ABTA** ['æbtə] *n abbr* = **Association of British Travel Agents**
**Abu Dhabi** ['æbu:'dɑ:bɪ] *n* Ab(o)u Dhabî *m*
**abundance** [ə'bʌndəns] *n* abondance *f*
**abundant** [ə'bʌndənt] *adj* abondant(e)
**abuse** *n* [ə'bju:s] (*insults*) insultes *fpl*, injures *fpl*; (*ill-treatment*) mauvais traitements *mpl*; (*of power etc*) abus *m* ▷ *vt* [ə'bju:z] (*insult*) insulter; (*ill-treat*) malmener; (*power etc*) abuser de; **to be open to ~** se prêter à des abus
**abusive** [ə'bju:sɪv] *adj* grossier(-ière), injurieux(-euse)
**abysmal** [ə'bɪzməl] *adj* exécrable; (*ignorance etc*) sans bornes
**abyss** [ə'bɪs] *n* abîme *m*, gouffre *m*
**AC** *n abbr* (*US*) = **athletic club**
**a/c** *abbr* (*Banking etc*) = **account**; **account current**
**academic** [ækə'demɪk] *adj* universitaire; (*person: scholarly*) intellectuel(-le); (*pej: issue*) oiseux(-euse), purement théorique ▷ *n* universitaire *m/f*; **~ freedom** liberté *f* académique
**academic year** *n* (*University*) année *f* universitaire; (*Scol*) année scolaire
**academy** [ə'kædəmɪ] *n* (*learned body*) académie *f*; (*school*) collège *m*; **military/naval ~** école militaire/navale; **~ of music** conservatoire *m*

**ACAS** ['eɪkæs] *n abbr* (Brit: = Advisory, Conciliation and Arbitration Service) organisme de conciliation et d'arbitrage des conflits du travail

**accede** [æk'siːd] *vi*: **to ~ to** (request, throne) accéder à

**accelerate** [æk'sɛləreɪt] *vt, vi* accélérer

**acceleration** [æksɛlə'reɪʃən] *n* accélération *f*

**accelerator** [æk'sɛləreɪtəʳ] *n* (Brit) accélérateur *m*

**accent** ['æksɛnt] *n* accent *m*

**accentuate** [æk'sɛntjueɪt] *vt* (syllable) accentuer; (need, difference etc) souligner

**accept** [ək'sɛpt] *vt* accepter

**acceptable** [ək'sɛptəbl] *adj* acceptable

**acceptance** [ək'sɛptəns] *n* acceptation *f*; **to meet with general ~** être favorablement accueilli par tous

**access** ['æksɛs] *n* accès *m* ▷ *vt* (Comput) accéder à; **to have ~ to** (information, library etc) avoir accès à, pouvoir utiliser or consulter; (person) avoir accès auprès de; **the burglars gained ~ through a window** les cambrioleurs sont entrés par une fenêtre

**accessible** [æk'sɛsəbl] *adj* accessible

**accession** [æk'sɛʃən] *n* accession *f*; (of king) avènement *m*; (to library) acquisition *f*

**accessory** [æk'sɛsərɪ] *n* accessoire *m*; **toilet accessories** (Brit) articles *mpl* de toilette; **~ to** (Law) accessoire à

**access road** *n* voie *f* d'accès; (to motorway) bretelle *f* de raccordement

**access time** *n* (Comput) temps *m* d'accès

**accident** ['æksɪdənt] *n* accident *m*; (chance) hasard *m*; **to meet with** or **to have an ~** avoir un accident; **I've had an ~** j'ai eu un accident; **~s at work** accidents du travail; **by ~** (by chance) par hasard; (not deliberately) accidentellement

**accidental** [æksɪ'dɛntl] *adj* accidentel(le)

**accidentally** [æksɪ'dɛntəlɪ] *adv* accidentellement

**Accident and Emergency Department** *n* (Brit) service *m* des urgences

**accident insurance** *n* assurance *f* accident

**accident-prone** ['æksɪdənt'prəun] *adj* sujet(te) aux accidents

**acclaim** [ə'kleɪm] *vt* acclamer ▷ *n* acclamations *fpl*

**acclamation** [æklə'meɪʃən] *n* (approval) acclamation *f*; (applause) ovation *f*

**acclimatize** [ə'klaɪmətaɪz] (US), **acclimate** [ə'klaɪmət] *vt*: **to become ~d** s'acclimater

**accolade** ['ækəleɪd] *n* accolade *f*; (fig) marque *f* d'honneur

**accommodate** [ə'kɔmədeɪt] *vt* loger, recevoir; (oblige, help) obliger; (car etc) contenir; (adapt): **to ~ one's plans to** adapter ses projets à

**accommodating** [ə'kɔmədeɪtɪŋ] *adj* obligeant(e), arrangeant(e)

**accommodation**, (US) **accommodations** [əkɔmə'deɪʃən(z)] *n(pl)* logement *m*; **he's found ~** il a trouvé à se loger; **"~ to let"** (Brit) "appartement or studio etc à louer"; **they have**

**~ for 500** ils peuvent recevoir 500 personnes, il y a de la place pour 500 personnes; **the hall has seating ~ for 600** (Brit) la salle contient 600 places assises

**accompaniment** [ə'kʌmpənɪmənt] *n* accompagnement *m*

**accompanist** [ə'kʌmpənɪst] *n* accompagnateur(-trice)

**accompany** [ə'kʌmpənɪ] *vt* accompagner

**accomplice** [ə'kʌmplɪs] *n* complice *m/f*

**accomplish** [ə'kʌmplɪʃ] *vt* accomplir

**accomplished** [ə'kʌmplɪʃt] *adj* accompli(e)

**accomplishment** [ə'kʌmplɪʃmənt] *n* (skill: gen pl) talent *m*; (completion) accomplissement *m*; (achievement) réussite *f*

**accord** [ə'kɔːd] *n* accord *m* ▷ *vt* accorder; **of his own ~** de son plein gré; **with one ~** d'un commun accord

**accordance** [ə'kɔːdəns] *n*: **in ~ with** conformément à

**according** [ə'kɔːdɪŋ]: **~ to** (prep) selon; **~ to plan** comme prévu

**accordingly** [ə'kɔːdɪŋlɪ] *adv* (appropriately) en conséquence; (as a result) par conséquent

**accordion** [ə'kɔːdɪən] *n* accordéon *m*

**accost** [ə'kɔst] *vt* accoster, aborder

**account** [ə'kaunt] *n* (Comm) compte *m*; (report) compte rendu, récit *m*; **accounts** *npl* (Comm: records) comptabilité *f*, comptes; **"~ payee only"** (Brit) "chèque non endossable"; **to keep an ~ of** noter; **to bring sb to ~ for sth/for having done sth** amener qn à rendre compte de qch/ d'avoir fait qch; **by all ~s** au dire de tous; **of little ~** de peu d'importance; **of no ~** sans importance; **on ~** en acompte; **to buy sth on ~** acheter qch à crédit; **on no ~** en aucun cas; **on ~ of** à cause de; **to take into ~**, **take ~ of** tenir compte de

▷ **account for** *vt fus* (explain) expliquer, rendre compte de; (represent) représenter; **all the children were ~ed for** aucun enfant ne manquait; **four people are still not ~ed for** on n'a pas toujours pas retrouvé quatre personnes

**accountability** [əkauntə'bɪlɪtɪ] *n* responsabilité *f*; (financial, political) transparence *f*

**accountable** [ə'kauntəbl] *adj*: **~ (for/to)** responsable (de/devant)

**accountancy** [ə'kauntənsɪ] *n* comptabilité *f*

**accountant** [ə'kauntənt] *n* comptable *m/f*

**accounting** [ə'kauntɪŋ] *n* comptabilité *f*

**accounting period** *n* exercice financier, période *f* comptable

**account number** *n* numéro *m* de compte

**account payable** *n* compte *m* fournisseurs

**account receivable** *n* compte *m* clients

**accredited** [ə'krɛdɪtɪd] *adj* (person) accrédité(e)

**accretion** [ə'kriːʃən] *n* accroissement *m*

**accrue** [ə'kruː] *vi* s'accroître; (mount up) s'accumuler; **to ~ to** s'ajouter à; **~d interest** intérêt couru

**accumulate** [ə'kjuːmjuleɪt] *vt* accumuler,

447

amasser ▷ *vi* s'accumuler, s'amasser
**accumulation** [əkjuːmjuˈleɪʃən] *n*
accumulation *f*
**accuracy** [ˈækjʊrəsɪ] *n* exactitude *f*, précision *f*
**accurate** [ˈækjʊrɪt] *adj* exact(e), précis(e);
(*device*) précis
**accurately** [ˈækjʊrɪtlɪ] *adv* avec précision
**accusation** [ækjuːˈzeɪʃən] *n* accusation *f*
**accusative** [əˈkjuːzətɪv] *n* (*Ling*) accusatif *m*
**accuse** [əˈkjuːz] *vt*: **to ~ sb (of sth)** accuser qn
(de qch)
**accused** [əˈkjuːzd] *n* (*Law*) accusé(e)
**accuser** [əˈkjuːzəʳ] *n* accusateur(-trice)
**accustom** [əˈkʌstəm] *vt* accoutumer, habituer;
**to ~ o.s. to sth** s'habituer à qch
**accustomed** [əˈkʌstəmd] *adj* (*usual*)
habituel(le); **~ to** habitué(e) *or* accoutumé(e) à
**AC/DC** *abbr* = **alternating current/direct
current**
**ACE** [eɪs] *n abbr* = **American Council on
Education**
**ace** [eɪs] *n* as *m*; **within an ~ of** (*Brit*) à deux
doigts *or* un cheveu de
**acerbic** [əˈsəːbɪk] *adj* (*also fig*) acerbe
**acetate** [ˈæsɪteɪt] *n* acétate *m*
**ache** [eɪk] *n* mal *m*, douleur *f* ▷ *vi* (*be sore*) faire
mal, être douloureux(-euse); (*yearn*): **to ~ to do
sth** mourir d'envie de faire qch; **I've got
stomach ~** *or* (*US*) **a stomach ~** j'ai mal à
l'estomac; **my head ~s** j'ai mal à la tête; **I'm
aching all over** j'ai mal partout
**achieve** [əˈtʃiːv] *vt* (*aim*) atteindre; (*victory,
success*) remporter, obtenir; (*task*) accomplir
**achievement** [əˈtʃiːvmənt] *n* exploit *m*, réussite
*f*; (*of aims*) réalisation *f*
**Achilles heel** [əˈkɪliːz-] *n* talon *m* d'Achille
**acid** [ˈæsɪd] *adj*, *n* acide (*m*)
**acidity** [əˈsɪdɪtɪ] *n* acidité *f*
**acid rain** *n* pluies *fpl* acides
**acid test** *n* (*fig*) épreuve décisive
**acknowledge** [əkˈnɒlɪdʒ] *vt* (*also*: **acknowledge
receipt of**) accuser réception de; (*fact*)
reconnaître
**acknowledgement** [əkˈnɒlɪdʒmənt] *n* (*of letter*)
accusé *m* de réception; **acknowledgements** (*in
book*) remerciements *mpl*
**ACLU** *n abbr* (= *American Civil Liberties Union*) ligue *des
droits de l'homme*
**acme** [ˈækmɪ] *n* point culminant
**acne** [ˈæknɪ] *n* acné *m*
**acorn** [ˈeɪkɔːn] *n* gland *m*
**acoustic** [əˈkuːstɪk] *adj* acoustique
**acoustics** [əˈkuːstɪks] *n*, *npl* acoustique *f*
**acquaint** [əˈkweɪnt] *vt*: **to ~ sb with sth** mettre
qn au courant de qch; **to be ~ed with** (*person*)
connaître; (*fact*) savoir
**acquaintance** [əˈkweɪntəns] *n* connaissance *f*;
**to make sb's ~** faire la connaissance de qn
**acquiesce** [ækwɪˈɛs] *vi* (*agree*): **to ~ (in)**
acquiescer (à)
**acquire** [əˈkwaɪəʳ] *vt* acquérir
**acquired** [əˈkwaɪəd] *adj* acquis(e); **an ~ taste** un

goût acquis
**acquisition** [ækwɪˈzɪʃən] *n* acquisition *f*
**acquisitive** [əˈkwɪzɪtɪv] *adj* qui a l'instinct de
possession *or* le goût de la propriété
**acquit** [əˈkwɪt] *vt* acquitter; **to ~ o.s. well** s'en
tirer très honorablement
**acquittal** [əˈkwɪtl] *n* acquittement *m*
**acre** [ˈeɪkəʳ] *n* acre *f* (= 4047 *m*²)
**acreage** [ˈeɪkərɪdʒ] *n* superficie *f*
**acrid** [ˈækrɪd] *adj* (*smell*) âcre; (*fig*) mordant(e)
**acrimonious** [ækrɪˈməʊnɪəs] *adj*
acrimonieux(-euse), aigre
**acrobat** [ˈækrəbæt] *n* acrobate *m/f*
**acrobatic** [ækrəˈbætɪk] *adj* acrobatique
**acrobatics** [ækrəˈbætɪks] *n*, *npl* acrobatie *f*
**acronym** [ˈækrənɪm] *n* acronyme *m*
**Acropolis** [əˈkrɒpəlɪs] *n*: **the ~** l'Acropole *f*
**across** [əˈkrɒs] *prep* (*on the other side*) de l'autre
côté de; (*crosswise*) en travers de ▷ *adv* de l'autre
côté; en travers; **to walk ~ (the road)** traverser
(la route); **to run/swim ~** traverser en courant/
à la nage; **to take sb ~ the road** faire traverser
la route à qn; **a road ~ the wood** une route qui
traverse le bois; **the lake is 12 km ~** le lac fait 12
km de large; **~ from** en face de; **to get sth ~ (to
sb)** faire comprendre qch (à qn)
**acrylic** [əˈkrɪlɪk] *adj*, *n* acrylique (*m*)
**ACT** *n abbr* (= *American College Test*) *examen de fin
d'études secondaires*
**act** [ækt] *n* acte *m*, action *f*; (*Theat: part of play*)
acte; (: *of performer*) numéro *m*; (*Law*) loi *f* ▷ *vi*
agir; (*Theat*) jouer; (*pretend*) jouer la comédie
▷ *vt* (*role*) jouer, tenir; **~ of God** (*Law*)
catastrophe naturelle; **to catch sb in the ~**
prendre qn sur le fait *or* en flagrant délit; **it's
only an ~** c'est du cinéma; **to ~ Hamlet** (*Brit*)
tenir *or* jouer le rôle d'Hamlet; **to ~ as** servir de;
**it ~s as a deterrent** cela a un effet dissuasif;
**~ing in my capacity as chairman, I ...** en ma
qualité de président, je ...
 ▶ **act on** *vt*: **to ~ on sth** agir sur la base de qch
 ▶ **act out** *vt* (*event*) raconter en mimant;
 (*fantasies*) réaliser
 ▶ **act up** (*inf*) *vi* (*person*) se conduire mal; (*knee,
 back, injury*) jouer des tours; (*machine*) être
 capricieux(-ieuse)
**acting** [ˈæktɪŋ] *adj* suppléant(e), par intérim ▷ *n*
(*of actor*) jeu *m*; (*activity*): **to do some ~** faire du
théâtre (*or* du cinéma); **he is the ~ manager** il
remplace (provisoirement) le directeur
**action** [ˈækʃən] *n* action *f*; (*Mil*) combat(s) *m(pl)*;
(*Law*) procès *m*, action en justice ▷ *vt* (*Comm*)
mettre en œuvre; **to bring an ~ against sb**
(*Law*) poursuivre qn en justice, intenter un
procès contre qn; **killed in ~** (*Mil*) tué au champ
d'honneur; **out of ~** hors de combat; (*machine
etc*) hors d'usage; **to take ~** agir, prendre des
mesures; **to put a plan into ~** mettre un projet
à exécution
**action replay** *n* (*Brit TV*) ralenti *m*
**activate** [ˈæktɪveɪt] *vt* (*mechanism*) actionner,
faire fonctionner; (*Chem, Physics*) activer

**active** ['æktɪv] *adj* actif(-ive); *(volcano)* en activité; **to play an ~ part in** jouer un rôle actif dans

**active duty** *n* (*US Mil*) campagne *f*

**actively** ['æktɪvlɪ] *adv* activement; *(discourage)* vivement

**active partner** *n* (*Comm*) associé(e) *m/f*

**active service** *n* (*Brit Mil*) campagne *f*

**activist** ['æktɪvɪst] *n* activiste *m/f*

**activity** [æk'tɪvɪtɪ] *n* activité *f*

**activity holiday** *n* vacances actives

**actor** ['æktər] *n* acteur *m*

**actress** ['æktrɪs] *n* actrice *f*

**actual** ['æktjuəl] *adj* réel(le), véritable; *(emphatic use)* lui-même (elle-même)

**actually** ['æktjuəlɪ] *adv* réellement, véritablement; *(in fact)* en fait

**actuary** ['æktjuərɪ] *n* actuaire *m*

**actuate** ['æktjueɪt] *vt* déclencher, actionner

**acuity** [ə'kju:ɪtɪ] *n* acuité *f*

**acumen** ['ækjumən] *n* perspicacité *f*; **business ~** sens *m* des affaires

**acupuncture** ['ækjupʌŋktʃər] *n* acuponcture *f*

**acute** [ə'kju:t] *adj* aigu(ë); *(mind, observer)* pénétrant(e)

**A.D.** *adv abbr* (= *Anno Domini*) ap. J.-C. ▷ *n abbr* (*US Mil*) = **active duty**

**ad** [æd] *n abbr* = **advertisement**

**adamant** ['ædəmənt] *adj* inflexible

**Adam's apple** ['ædəmz-] *n* pomme *f* d'Adam

**adapt** [ə'dæpt] *vt* adapter ▷ *vi*: **to ~ (to)** s'adapter (à)

**adaptability** [ədæptə'bɪlɪtɪ] *n* faculté *f* d'adaptation

**adaptable** [ə'dæptəbl] *adj* (*device*) adaptable; *(person)* qui s'adapte facilement

**adaptation** [ædæp'teɪʃən] *n* adaptation *f*

**adapter, adaptor** [ə'dæptər] *n* (*Elec*) adaptateur *m*; *(for several plugs)* prise *f* multiple

**ADC** *n abbr* (*Mil*) = **aide-de-camp**; (*US*: = *Aid to Dependent Children*) aide pour enfants assistés

**add** [æd] *vt* ajouter; *(figures: also*: **to add up**) additionner ▷ *vi*: **to ~ to** *(increase)* ajouter à, accroître ▷ *n* (*Internet*) **thanks for the ~** merci pour l'ajout

▶ **add on** *vt* ajouter ▷ *vi* (*fig*): **it doesn't ~ up** cela ne rime à rien

▶ **add up to** *vt fus* (*Math*) s'élever à; (*fig: mean*) signifier; **it doesn't ~ up to much** ça n'est pas grand'chose

**adder** ['ædər] *n* vipère *f*

**addict** ['ædɪkt] *n* toxicomane *m/f*; (*fig*) fanatique *m/f*; **heroin ~** héroïnomane *m/f*; **drug ~** drogué(e) *m/f*

**addicted** [ə'dɪktɪd] *adj*: **to be ~ to** (*drink, drugs*) être adonné(e) à; (*fig: football etc*) être un(e) fanatique de

**addiction** [ə'dɪkʃən] *n* (*Med*) dépendance *f*

**addictive** [ə'dɪktɪv] *adj* qui crée une dépendance

**adding machine** ['ædɪŋ-] *n* machine *f* à calculer

**Addis Ababa** ['ædɪs'æbəbə] *n* Addis Abeba, Addis Ababa

**addition** [ə'dɪʃən] *n* (*adding up*) addition *f*; (*thing added*) ajout *m*; **in ~** de plus, de surcroît; **in ~ to** en plus de

**additional** [ə'dɪʃənl] *adj* supplémentaire

**additive** ['ædɪtɪv] *n* additif *m*

**address** [ə'drɛs] *n* adresse *f*; (*talk*) discours *m*, allocution *f* ▷ *vt* adresser; (*speak to*) s'adresser à; **my ~ is …** mon adresse, c'est …; **form of ~** titre *m*; **what form of ~ do you use for …?** comment s'adresse-t-on à …?; **to ~** (*o.s. to*) sth (*problem, issue*) aborder qch; **absolute/relative ~** (*Comput*) adresse absolue/relative

**address book** *n* carnet *m* d'adresses

**addressee** [ædrɛ'si:] *n* destinataire *m/f*

**Aden** ['eɪdən] *n*: **Gulf of ~** Golfe *m* d'Aden

**adenoids** ['ædɪnɔɪdz] *npl* végétations *fpl*

**adept** ['ædɛpt] *adj*: **~ at** expert(e) à *or* en

**adequate** ['ædɪkwɪt] *adj* (*enough*) suffisant(e); *(satisfactory)* satisfaisant(e); **to feel ~ to the task** se sentir à la hauteur de la tâche

**adequately** ['ædɪkwɪtlɪ] *adv* de façon adéquate

**adhere** [əd'hɪər] *vi*: **to ~ to** adhérer à; (*fig: rule, decision*) se tenir à

**adhesion** [əd'hi:ʒən] *n* adhésion *f*

**adhesive** [əd'hi:zɪv] *adj* adhésif(-ive) ▷ *n* adhésif *m*

**adhesive tape** *n* (*Brit*) ruban *m* adhésif; (*US Med*) sparadrap *m*

**ad hoc** [æd'hɔk] *adj* (*decision*) de circonstance; (*committee*) ad hoc

**ad infinitum** ['ædɪnfɪ'naɪtəm] *adv* à l'infini

**adjacent** [ə'dʒeɪsənt] *adj* adjacent(e), contigu(ë); **~ to** adjacent à

**adjective** ['ædʒɛktɪv] *n* adjectif *m*

**adjoin** [ə'dʒɔɪn] *vt* jouxter

**adjoining** [ə'dʒɔɪnɪŋ] *adj* voisin(e), adjacent(e), attenant(e) ▷ *prep* voisin de, adjacent à

**adjourn** [ə'dʒɜ:n] *vt* ajourner ▷ *vi* suspendre la séance; lever la séance; clore la session; (*go*) se retirer; **to ~ a meeting till the following week** reporter une réunion à la semaine suivante; **they ~ed to the pub** (*Brit inf*) ils ont filé au pub

**adjournment** [ə'dʒɜ:nmənt] *n* (*period*) ajournement *m*

**Adjt** *abbr* (*Mil*: = *adjutant*) Adj

**adjudicate** [ə'dʒu:dɪkeɪt] *vt* (*contest*) juger; (*claim*) statuer (sur) ▷ *vi* se prononcer

**adjudication** [ədʒu:dɪ'keɪʃən] *n* (*Law*) jugement *m*

**adjust** [ə'dʒʌst] *vt* (*machine*) ajuster, régler; (*prices, wages*) rajuster ▷ *vi*: **to ~ (to)** s'adapter (à)

**adjustable** [ə'dʒʌstəbl] *adj* réglable

**adjuster** [ə'dʒʌstər] *n see* **loss**

**adjustment** [ə'dʒʌstmənt] *n* (*of machine*) ajustage *m*, réglage *m*; (*of prices, wages*) rajustement *m*; (*of person*) adaptation *f*

**adjutant** ['ædʒətənt] *n* adjudant *m*

**ad-lib** [æd'lɪb] *vt, vi* improviser ▷ *n* improvisation *f* ▷ *adv*: **ad lib** à volonté, à discrétion

**adman** ['ædmæn] (*irreg*) *n* (*inf*) publicitaire *m*

**admin** ['ædmɪn] *n abbr* (*inf*) = **administration**

**administer** [əd'mɪnɪstər] *vt* administrer; (*justice*) rendre

**administration** [ədmɪnɪs'treɪʃən] *n*
(*management*) administration *f*; (*government*)
gouvernement *m*

**administrative** [əd'mɪnɪstrətɪv] *adj*
administratif(-ive)

**administrator** [əd'mɪnɪstreɪtə<sup>r</sup>] *n*
administrateur(-trice)

**admirable** ['ædmərəbl] *adj* admirable

**admiral** ['ædmərəl] *n* amiral *m*

**Admiralty** ['ædmərəltɪ] *n* (*Brit: also*: **Admiralty
Board**) ministère *m* de la Marine

**admiration** [ædmə'reɪʃən] *n* admiration *f*

**admire** [əd'maɪə<sup>r</sup>] *vt* admirer

**admirer** [əd'maɪərə<sup>r</sup>] *n* (*fan*) admirateur(-trice)

**admiring** [əd'maɪərɪŋ] *adj* admiratif(-ive)

**admissible** [əd'mɪsəbl] *adj* acceptable,
admissible; (*evidence*) recevable

**admission** [əd'mɪʃən] *n* admission *f*; (*to
exhibition, night club etc*) entrée *f*; (*confession*) aveu
*m*; **"~ free"**, **"free ~"** "entrée libre"; **by his own
~** de son propre aveu

**admission charge** *n* droits *mpl* d'admission

**admit** [əd'mɪt] *vt* laisser entrer; admettre;
(*agree*) reconnaître, admettre; (*crime*)
reconnaître avoir commis; **"children not
~ted"** "entrée interdite aux enfants"; **this
ticket ~s two** ce billet est valable pour deux
personnes; **I must ~ that ...** je dois admettre *or*
reconnaître que ...
  ▸ **admit of** *vt fus* admettre, permettre
  ▸ **admit to** *vt fus* reconnaître, avouer

**admittance** [əd'mɪtəns] *n* admission *f*, (droit *m*
d')entrée *f*; **"no ~"** "défense d'entrer"

**admittedly** [əd'mɪtɪdlɪ] *adv* il faut en convenir

**admonish** [əd'mɒnɪʃ] *vt* donner un
avertissement à; réprimander

**ad nauseam** [æd'nɔːsɪæm] *adv* à satiété

**ado** [ə'duː] *n*: **without (any) more ~** sans plus
de cérémonies

**adolescence** [ædəu'lɛsns] *n* adolescence *f*

**adolescent** [ædəu'lɛsnt] *adj, n* adolescent(e)

**adopt** [ə'dɒpt] *vt* adopter

**adopted** [ə'dɒptɪd] *adj* adoptif(-ive), adopté(e)

**adoption** [ə'dɒpʃən] *n* adoption *f*

**adore** [ə'dɔː<sup>r</sup>] *vt* adorer

**adoring** [ə'dɔːrɪŋ] *adj*: **his ~ wife** sa femme qui
est en adoration devant lui

**adoringly** [ə'dɔːrɪŋlɪ] *adv* avec adoration

**adorn** [ə'dɔːn] *vt* orner

**adornment** [ə'dɔːnmənt] *n* ornement *m*

**ADP** *n abbr* = **automatic data processing**

**adrenalin** [ə'drɛnəlɪn] *n* adrénaline *f*; **to get
the ~ going** faire monter le taux d'adrénaline

**Adriatic** [eɪdrɪ'ætɪk]

**Adriatic Sea** *n*: **the Adriatic (Sea)** la mer
Adriatique, l'Adriatique *f*

**adrift** [ə'drɪft] *adv* à la dérive; **to come ~** (*boat*)
aller à la dérive; (*wire, rope, fastening etc*) se défaire

**adroit** [ə'drɔɪt] *adj* adroit(e), habile

**ADSL** *n abbr* (*asymmetric digital subscriber line*)
ADSL *m*

**ADT** *abbr* (*US: = Atlantic Daylight Time*) heure d'été de

New York

**adult** ['ædʌlt] *n* adulte *m/f* ▸ *adj* (*grown-up*)
adulte; (*for adults*) pour adultes

**adult education** *n* éducation *f* des adultes

**adulterate** [ə'dʌltəreɪt] *vt* frelater, falsifier

**adulterer** [ə'dʌltərə<sup>r</sup>] *n* homme *m* adultère

**adulteress** [ə'dʌltərɪs] *n* femme *f* adultère

**adultery** [ə'dʌltərɪ] *n* adultère *m*

**adulthood** ['ædʌlthud] *n* âge *m* adulte

**advance** [əd'vɑːns] *n* avance *f* ▸ *vt* avancer ▸ *vi*
s'avancer; **in ~** en avance, d'avance; **to make
~s to sb** (*gen*) faire des propositions à qn;
(*amorously*) faire des avances à qn; **~ booking**
location *f*; **~ notice**, **~ warning** préavis *m*;
(*verbal*) avertissement *m*; **do I need to book in
~?** est-ce qu'il faut réserver à l'avance?

**advanced** [əd'vɑːnst] *adj* avancé(e); (*Scol: studies*)
supérieur(e); **~ in years** d'un âge avancé

**advancement** [əd'vɑːnsmənt] *n* avancement *m*

**advantage** [əd'vɑːntɪdʒ] *n* (*also Tennis*) avantage
*m*; **to take ~ of** (*person*) exploiter; (*opportunity*)
profiter de; **it's to our ~** c'est notre intérêt; **it's
to our ~ to ...** nous avons intérêt à ...

**advantageous** [ædvən'teɪdʒəs] *adj*
avantageux(-euse)

**advent** ['ædvənt] *n* avènement *m*, venue *f*; **A~**
(*Rel*) avent *m*

**Advent calendar** *n* calendrier *m* de l'avent

**adventure** [əd'vɛntʃə<sup>r</sup>] *n* aventure *f*

**adventure playground** *n* aire *f* de jeux

**adventurous** [əd'vɛntʃərəs] *adj*
aventureux(-euse)

**adverb** ['ædvəːb] *n* adverbe *m*

**adversary** ['ædvəsərɪ] *n* adversaire *m/f*

**adverse** ['ædvəːs] *adj* adverse; (*effect*)
négatif(-ive); (*weather, publicity*) mauvais(e);
(*wind*) contraire; **~ to** hostile à; **in ~
circumstances** dans l'adversité

**adversity** [əd'vəːsɪtɪ] *n* adversité *f*

**advert** ['ædvəːt] *n abbr* (*Brit*) = **advertisement**

**advertise** ['ædvətaɪz] *vi* faire de la publicité *or*
de la réclame; (*in classified ads etc*) mettre une
annonce ▸ *vt* faire de la publicité *or* de la
réclame pour; (*in classified ads etc*) mettre une
annonce pour vendre; **to ~ for** (*staff*) recruter
par (voie d')annonce

**advertisement** [əd'vəːtɪsmənt] *n* publicité *f*,
réclame *f*; (*in classified ads etc*) annonce *f*

**advertiser** ['ædvətaɪzə<sup>r</sup>] *n* annonceur *m*

**advertising** ['ædvətaɪzɪŋ] *n* publicité *f*

**advertising agency** *n* agence *f* de publicité

**advertising campaign** *n* campagne *f* de
publicité

**advice** [əd'vaɪs] *n* conseils *mpl*; (*notification*) avis
*m*; **a piece of ~** un conseil; **to ask (sb) for ~**
demander conseil (à qn); **to take legal ~**
consulter un avocat

**advice note** *n* (*Brit*) avis *m* d'expédition

**advisable** [əd'vaɪzəbl] *adj* recommandable,
indiqué(e)

**advise** [əd'vaɪz] *vt* conseiller; **to ~ sb of sth**
aviser *or* informer qn de qch; **to ~ against sth/**

doing sth déconseiller qch/conseiller de ne pas faire qch; **you would be well/ill ~d to go** vous feriez mieux d'y aller/de ne pas y aller, vous auriez intérêt à y aller/à ne pas y aller

**advisedly** [əd'vaɪzɪdlɪ] *adv (deliberately)* délibérément

**adviser, advisor** [əd'vaɪzəʳ] *n* conseiller(-ère)

**advisory** [əd'vaɪzərɪ] *adj* consultatif(-ive); **in an ~ capacity** à titre consultatif

**advocate** *n* ['ædvəkɪt] *(lawyer)* avocat (plaidant); *(upholder)* défenseur *m*, avocat(e) ▷ *vt* ['ædvəkeɪt] recommander, prôner; **to be an ~ of** être partisan(e) de

**advt.** *abbr* = **advertisement**

**AEA** *n abbr (Brit: = Atomic Energy Authority)* ≈ AEN *f* (*= Agence pour l'énergie nucléaire*)

**AEC** *n abbr (US: = Atomic Energy Commission)* CEA *m* (*= Commissariat à l'énergie atomique*)

**AEEU** *n abbr (Brit: = Amalgamated Engineering and Electrical Union)* syndicat de techniciens et d'électriciens

**Aegean** [iː'dʒiːən] *n, adj:* **the ~ (Sea)** la mer Égée, l'Égée *f*

**aegis** ['iːdʒɪs] *n:* **under the ~ of** sous l'égide de

**aeon** ['iːən] *n* éternité *f*

**aerial** ['ɛərɪəl] *n* antenne *f* ▷ *adj* aérien(ne)

**aerobatics** ['ɛərəu'bætɪks] *npl* acrobaties aériennes

**aerobics** [ɛə'rəubɪks] *n* aérobic *m*

**aerodrome** ['ɛərədrəum] *n (Brit)* aérodrome *m*

**aerodynamic** ['ɛərəudaɪ'næmɪk] *adj* aérodynamique

**aeronautics** [ɛərə'nɔːtɪks] *n* aéronautique *f*

**aeroplane** ['ɛərəpleɪn] *n (Brit)* avion *m*

**aerosol** ['ɛərəsɔl] *n* aérosol *m*

**aerospace industry** ['ɛərəuspeɪs-] *n* (industrie) aérospatiale *f*

**aesthetic** [ɪs'θɛtɪk] *adj* esthétique

**afar** [ə'faːʳ] *adv:* **from ~** de loin

**AFB** *n abbr (US)* = **Air Force Base**

**AFDC** *n abbr (US: = Aid to Families with Dependent Children)* aide pour enfants assistés

**affable** ['æfəbl] *adj* affable

**affair** [ə'fɛəʳ] *n* affaire *f; (also:* **love affair**) liaison *f*; aventure *f;* **affairs** *(business)* affaires

**affect** [ə'fɛkt] *vt* affecter; *(subj: disease)* atteindre

**affectation** [æfɛk'teɪʃən] *n* affectation *f*

**affected** [ə'fɛktɪd] *adj* affecté(e)

**affection** [ə'fɛkʃən] *n* affection *f*

**affectionate** [ə'fɛkʃənɪt] *adj* affectueux(-euse)

**affectionately** [ə'fɛkʃənɪtlɪ] *adv* affectueusement

**affidavit** [æfɪ'deɪvɪt] *n (Law)* déclaration écrite sous serment

**affiliated** [ə'fɪlɪeɪtɪd] *adj* affilié(e); **~ company** filiale *f*

**affinity** [ə'fɪnɪtɪ] *n* affinité *f*

**affirm** [ə'fəːm] *vt* affirmer

**affirmation** [æfə'meɪʃən] *n* affirmation *f*, assertion *f*

**affirmative** [ə'fəːmətɪv] *adj* affirmatif(-ive) ▷ *n:* **in the ~** dans *or* par l'affirmative

**affix** [ə'fɪks] *vt* apposer, ajouter

**afflict** [ə'flɪkt] *vt* affliger

**affliction** [ə'flɪkʃən] *n* affliction *f*

**affluence** ['æfluəns] *n* aisance *f*, opulence *f*

**affluent** ['æfluənt] *adj* opulent(e); *(person, family, surroundings)* aisé(e), riche; **the ~ society** la société d'abondance

**afford** [ə'fɔːd] *vt (goods etc)* avoir les moyens d'acheter *or* d'entretenir; *(behaviour)* se permettre; *(provide)* fournir, procurer; **can we ~ a car?** avons-nous de quoi acheter *or* les moyens d'acheter une voiture?; **I can't ~ the time** je n'ai vraiment pas le temps

**affordable** [ə'fɔːdəbl] *adj* abordable

**affray** [ə'freɪ] *n (Brit Law)* échauffourée *f*, rixe *f*

**affront** [ə'frʌnt] *n* affront *m*

**affronted** [ə'frʌntɪd] *adj* insulté(e)

**Afghan** ['æfgæn] *adj* afghan(e) ▷ *n* Afghan(e)

**Afghanistan** [æf'gænɪstæn] *n* Afghanistan *m*

**afield** [ə'fiːld] *adv:* **far ~** loin

**AFL-CIO** *n abbr (= American Federation of Labor and Congress of Industrial Organizations)* confédération syndicale

**afloat** [ə'fləut] *adj* à flot ▷ *adv:* **to stay ~** surnager; **to keep/get a business ~** maintenir à flot/lancer une affaire

**afoot** [ə'fut] *adv:* **there is something ~** il se prépare quelque chose

**aforementioned** [ə'fɔːmɛnʃənd] *adj*, **aforesaid** [ə'fɔːsɛd] ▷ *adj* susdit(e), susmentionné(e)

**afraid** [ə'freɪd] *adj* effrayé(e); **to be ~ of** *or* **to** avoir peur de; **I am ~ that** je crains que + *sub;* **I'm ~ so/not** oui/non, malheureusement

**afresh** [ə'frɛʃ] *adv* de nouveau

**Africa** ['æfrɪkə] *n* Afrique *f*

**African** ['æfrɪkən] *adj* africain(e) ▷ *n* Africain(e)

**African-American** ['æfrɪkənə'mɛrɪkən] *adj* afro-américain(e) ▷ *n* Afro-Américain(e)

**Afrikaans** [æfrɪ'kɑːns] *n* afrikaans *m*

**Afrikaner** [æfrɪ'kɑːnəʳ] *n* Afrikaner *m/f*

**Afro-American** ['æfrəuə'mɛrɪkən] *adj* afro-américain(e)

**AFT** *n abbr (= American Federation of Teachers)* syndicat enseignant

**aft** [ɑːft] *adv* à l'arrière, vers l'arrière

**after** ['ɑːftəʳ] *prep, adv* après ▷ *conj* après que, après avoir *or* être + *pp;* **~ dinner** après (le) dîner; **the day ~ tomorrow** après-demain; **it's quarter ~ two** (US) il est deux heures et quart; **~ having done/~ he left** après avoir fait/ après son départ; **to name sb ~ sb** donner à qn le nom de qn; **to ask ~ sb** demander des nouvelles de qn; **what/who are you ~?** que/qui cherchez-vous?; **the police are ~ him** la police est à ses trousses; **~ you!** après vous!; **~ all** après tout

**afterbirth** ['ɑːftəbəːθ] *n* placenta *m*

**aftercare** ['ɑːftəkɛəʳ] *n (Brit Med)* post-cure *f*

**after-effects** ['ɑːftərɪfɛkts] *npl (of disaster, radiation, drink etc)* répercussions *fpl; (of illness)* séquelles *fpl*, suites *fpl*

**afterlife** ['ɑːftəlaɪf] *n* vie future

**aftermath** ['ɑːftəmɑːθ] *n* conséquences *fpl;* **in the ~ of** dans les mois *or* années *etc* qui

suivirent, au lendemain de
**afternoon** [ˈɑːftəˈnuːn] n après-midi m or f;
**good ~!** bonjour!; (goodbye) au revoir!
**afters** [ˈɑːftəz] n (Brit inf: dessert) dessert m
**after-sales service** [ɑːftəˈseɪlz-] n service m
après-vente, SAV m
**after-shave** [ˈɑːftəʃeɪv], **after-shave lotion** n
lotion f après-rasage
**aftershock** [ˈɑːftəʃɒk] n réplique f (sismique)
**aftersun** [ˈɑːftəsʌn], **aftersun cream,
aftersun lotion** n après-soleil m inv
**aftertaste** [ˈɑːftəteɪst] n arrière-goût m
**afterthought** [ˈɑːftəθɔːt] n: **I had an ~** il m'est
venu une idée après coup
**afterwards** [ˈɑːftəwədz], (US) **afterward**
[ˈɑːftəwəd] adv après
**again** [əˈgɛn] adv de nouveau, encore (une fois);
**to do sth ~** refaire qch; **not ... ~** ne ... plus; **~
and ~** à plusieurs reprises; **he's opened it ~** il
l'a rouvert, il l'a de nouveau or l'a encore ouvert;
**now and ~** de temps à autre
**against** [əˈgɛnst] prep contre; (compared to) par
rapport à; **~ a blue background** sur un fond
bleu; **(as) ~** (Brit) contre
**age** [eɪdʒ] n âge m ▷ vt, vi vieillir; **what ~ is he?**
quel âge a-t-il?; **he is 20 years of ~** il a 20 ans;
**under ~** mineur(e); **to come of ~** atteindre sa
majorité; **it's been ~s since I saw you** ça fait
une éternité que je ne t'ai pas vu
**aged** [ˈeɪdʒd] adj âgé(e); **~ 10** âgé de 10 ans; **the ~**
[ˈeɪdʒɪd] ▷ npl les personnes âgées
**age group** n tranche f d'âge; **the 40 to 50 ~** la
tranche d'âge des 40 à 50 ans
**ageing** [ˈeɪdʒɪŋ] adj vieillissant(e)
**ageless** [ˈeɪdʒlɪs] adj sans âge
**age limit** n limite f d'âge
**agency** [ˈeɪdʒənsɪ] n agence f; **through or by
the ~ of** par l'entremise or l'action de
**agenda** [əˈdʒɛndə] n ordre m du jour; **on the ~** à
l'ordre du jour
**agent** [ˈeɪdʒənt] n agent m; (firm)
concessionnaire m
**aggravate** [ˈægrəveɪt] vt (situation) aggraver;
(annoy) exaspérer, agacer
**aggravation** [ægrəˈveɪʃən] n agacements mpl
**aggregate** [ˈægrɪgɪt] n ensemble m, total m; **on
~** (Sport) au total des points
**aggression** [əˈgrɛʃən] n agression f
**aggressive** [əˈgrɛsɪv] adj agressif(-ive)
**aggressiveness** [əˈgrɛsɪvnɪs] n agressivité f
**aggressor** [əˈgrɛsər] n agresseur m
**aggrieved** [əˈgriːvd] adj chagriné(e), affligé(e)
**aggro** [ˈægrəu] n (inf: physical) grabuge m;
(: hassle) embêtements mpl
**aghast** [əˈgɑːst] adj consterné(e), atterré(e)
**agile** [ˈædʒaɪl] adj agile
**agility** [əˈdʒɪlɪtɪ] n agilité f, souplesse f
**agitate** [ˈædʒɪteɪt] vt rendre inquiet(-ète) or
agité(e) ▷ vi faire de l'agitation (politique); **to ~
for** faire campagne pour
**agitator** [ˈædʒɪteɪtər] n agitateur(-trice)
(politique)

**AGM** n abbr (= annual general meeting) AG f
**ago** [əˈgəu] adv: **two days ~** il y a deux jours; **not
long ~** il n'y a pas longtemps; **as long ~ as 1960**
déjà en 1960; **how long ~?** il y a combien de
temps (de cela)?
**agog** [əˈgɒg] adj: **(all) ~** en émoi
**agonize** [ˈægənaɪz] vi: **he ~d over the problem**
ce problème lui a causé bien du tourment
**agonizing** [ˈægənaɪzɪŋ] adj angoissant(e); (cry)
déchirant(e)
**agony** [ˈægənɪ] n (pain) douleur f atroce; (distress)
angoisse f; **to be in ~** souffrir le martyre
**agony aunt** n (Brit inf) journaliste qui tient la rubrique
du courrier du cœur
**agony column** n courrier m du cœur
**agree** [əˈgriː] vt (price) convenir de ▷ vi: **to ~ with**
(person) être d'accord avec; (statements etc)
concorder avec; (Ling) s'accorder avec; **to ~ to
do** accepter de or consentir à faire; **to ~ to sth**
consentir à qch; **to ~ that** (admit) convenir or
reconnaître que; **it was ~d that ...** il a été
convenu que ...; **they ~ on this** ils sont d'accord
sur ce point; **they ~d on going/a price** ils se
mirent d'accord pour y aller/sur un prix; **garlic
doesn't ~ with me** je ne supporte pas l'ail
**agreeable** [əˈgriːəbl] adj (pleasant) agréable;
(willing) consentant(e), d'accord; **are you ~ to
this?** est-ce que vous êtes d'accord?
**agreed** [əˈgriːd] adj (time, place) convenu(e); **to
be ~** être d'accord
**agreement** [əˈgriːmənt] n accord m; **in ~**
d'accord; **by mutual ~** d'un commun accord
**agricultural** [ægrɪˈkʌltʃərəl] adj agricole
**agriculture** [ˈægrɪkʌltʃər] n agriculture f
**aground** [əˈgraund] adv: **to run ~** s'échouer
**ahead** [əˈhɛd] adv en avant; devant; **go right ~**
**straight ~** (direction) allez tout droit; **go ~!**
(permission) allez-y!; **~ of** devant; (fig: schedule etc)
en avance sur; **~ of time** en avance; **they were
(right) ~ of us** ils nous précédaient (de peu), ils
étaient (juste) devant nous
**AI** n abbr = **Amnesty International**; (Comput) =
**artificial intelligence**
**AIB** n abbr (Brit: = Accident Investigation Bureau)
commission d'enquête sur les accidents
**AID** n abbr (= artificial insemination by donor) IAD f;
(US: = Agency for International Development) agence
pour le développement international
**aid** [eɪd] n aide f; (device) appareil m ▷ vt aider;
**with the ~ of** avec l'aide de; **in ~ of** en faveur
de; **to ~ and abet** (Law) se faire le complice de
**aide** [eɪd] n (person) assistant(e)
**AIDS** [eɪdz] n abbr (= acquired immune (or
immuno-)deficiency syndrome) SIDA m
**AIH** n abbr (= artificial insemination by husband) IAC f
**ailing** [ˈeɪlɪŋ] adj (person) souffreteux(euse);
(economy) malade
**ailment** [ˈeɪlmənt] n affection f
**aim** [eɪm] vt: **to ~ sth (at)** (gun, camera) braquer or
pointer qch (sur); (missile) lancer qch (à or contre
or en direction de); (remark, blow) destiner or
adresser qch (à) ▷ vi (also: **to take aim**) viser ▷ n

*(objective)* but *m*; *(skill)*: **his ~ is bad** il vise mal;
**to ~ at** viser; *(fig)* viser (à); avoir pour but *or*
ambition; **to ~ to do** avoir l'intention de faire
**aimless** ['eɪmlɪs] *adj* sans but
**aimlessly** ['eɪmlɪslɪ] *adv* sans but
**ain't** [eɪnt] *(inf)* = **am not; aren't; isn't**
**air** [ɛəʳ] *n* air *m* ▷ *vt* aérer; *(idea, grievance, views)*
mettre sur le tapis; *(knowledge)* faire étalage de
▷ *cpd (currents, attack etc)* aérien(ne); **to throw**
**sth into the ~** *(ball etc)* jeter qch en l'air; **by ~**
par avion; **to be on the ~** *(Radio, TV: programme)*
être diffusé(e); *(: station)* émettre
**airbag** ['ɛəbæg] *n* airbag *m*
**air base** *n* base aérienne
**airbed** ['ɛəbɛd] *n (Brit)* matelas *m* pneumatique
**airborne** ['ɛəbɔːn] *adj (plane)* en vol; *(troops)*
aeroporté(e); *(particles)* dans l'air; **as soon as**
**the plane was ~** dès que l'avion eut décollé
**air cargo** *n* fret aérien
**air-conditioned** ['ɛəkən'dɪʃənd] *adj*
climatisé(e), à air conditionné
**air conditioning** [-kən'dɪʃnɪŋ] *n* climatisation *f*
**air-cooled** ['ɛəku:ld] *adj* à refroidissement à air
**aircraft** ['ɛəkrɑːft] *n inv* avion *m*
**aircraft carrier** *n* porte-avions *m inv*
**air cushion** *n* coussin *m* d'air
**airdrome** ['ɛədrəum] *n (US)* aérodrome *m*
**airfield** ['ɛəfiːld] *n* terrain *m* d'aviation
**Air Force** *n* Armée *f* de l'air
**air freight** *n* fret aérien
**air freshener** [-'frɛʃnəʳ] *n* désodorisant *m*
**airgun** ['ɛəgʌn] *n* fusil *m* à air comprimé
**air hostess** *n (Brit)* hôtesse *f* de l'air
**airily** ['ɛərɪlɪ] *adv* d'un air dégagé
**airing** ['ɛərɪŋ] *n*: **to give an ~ to** aérer; *(fig: ideas,*
*views etc)* mettre sur le tapis
**airing cupboard** *n (Brit)* placard qui contient la
*chaudière et dans lequel on met le linge à sécher*
**air letter** *n (Brit)* aérogramme *m*
**airlift** ['ɛəlɪft] *n* pont aérien
**airline** ['ɛəlaɪn] *n* ligne aérienne, compagnie
aérienne
**airliner** ['ɛəlaɪnəʳ] *n* avion *m* de ligne
**airlock** ['ɛəlɔk] *n* sas *m*
**airmail** ['ɛəmeɪl] *n*: **by ~** par avion
**air mattress** *n* matelas *m* pneumatique
**air mile** *n* air mile *m*
**airplane** ['ɛəpleɪn] *n (US)* avion *m*
**air pocket** *n* trou *m* d'air
**airport** ['ɛəpɔːt] *n* aéroport *m*
**air raid** *n* attaque aérienne
**air rifle** *n* carabine *f* à air comprimé
**airsick** ['ɛəsɪk] *adj*: **to be ~** avoir le mal de l'air
**airspace** ['ɛəspeɪs] *n* espace *m* aérien
**airspeed** ['ɛəspiːd] *n* vitesse relative
**airstrip** ['ɛəstrɪp] *n* terrain *m* d'atterrissage
**air terminal** *n* aérogare *f*
**airtight** ['ɛətaɪt] *adj* hermétique
**air time** *n (Radio, TV)* temps *m* d'antenne
**air traffic control** *n* contrôle *m* de la navigation
aérienne
**air-traffic controller** *n* aiguilleur *m* du ciel

**airway** ['ɛəweɪ] *n (Aviat)* voie aérienne; **airways**
*(Anat)* voies aériennes
**airy** ['ɛərɪ] *adj* bien aéré(e); *(manners)* dégagé(e)
**aisle** [aɪl] *n (of church: central)* allée *f* centrale;
*(: side)* nef *f* latérale, bas-côté *m*; *(in theatre,*
*supermarket)* allée; *(on plane)* couloir *m*
**aisle seat** *n* place *f* côté couloir
**ajar** [ə'dʒɑːʳ] *adj* entrouvert(e)
**AK** *abbr (US)* = **Alaska**
**aka** *abbr (= also known as)* alias
**akin** [ə'kɪn] *adj*: **~ to** semblable à, du même
ordre que
**AL** *abbr (US)* = **Alabama**
**ALA** *n abbr* = **American Library Association**
**Ala.** *abbr (US)* = **Alabama**
**à la carte** [ælæ'kɑːt] *adv* à la carte
**alacrity** [ə'lækrɪtɪ] *n*: **with ~** avec
empressement, promptement
**alarm** [ə'lɑːm] *n* alarme *f* ▷ *vt* alarmer
**alarm call** *n* coup *m* de fil pour réveiller; **could I**
**have an ~ at 7 am, please?** pouvez-vous me
réveiller à 7 heures, s'il vous plaît?
**alarm clock** *n* réveille-matin *m inv*, réveil *m*
**alarmed** [ə'lɑːmd] *adj (frightened)* alarmé(e);
*(protected by an alarm)* protégé(e) par un système
d'alarme; **to become ~** prendre peur
**alarming** [ə'lɑːmɪŋ] *adj* alarmant(e)
**alarmingly** [ə'lɑːmɪŋlɪ] *adv* d'une manière
alarmante; **~ close** dangereusement proche; **~**
**quickly** à une vitesse inquiétante
**alarmist** [ə'lɑːmɪst] *n* alarmiste *m/f*
**alas** [ə'læs] *excl* hélas
**Alas.** *abbr (US)* = **Alaska**
**Alaska** [ə'læskə] *n* Alaska *m*
**Albania** [æl'beɪnɪə] *n* Albanie *f*
**Albanian** [æl'beɪnɪən] *adj* albanais(e) ▷ *n*
Albanais(e); *(Ling)* albanais *m*
**albatross** ['ælbətrɔs] *n* albatros *m*
**albeit** [ɔːl'biːɪt] *conj* bien que + *sub*, encore que +
*sub*
**album** ['ælbəm] *n* album *m*
**albumen** ['ælbjumɪn] *n* albumine *f*; *(of egg)*
albumen *m*
**alchemy** ['ælkɪmɪ] *n* alchimie *f*
**alcohol** ['ælkəhɔl] *n* alcool *m*
**alcohol-free** ['ælkəhɔlfriː] *adj* sans alcool
**alcoholic** [ælkə'hɔlɪk] *adj, n* alcoolique *(m/f)*
**alcoholism** ['ælkəhɔlɪzəm] *n* alcoolisme *m*
**alcove** ['ælkəuv] *n* alcôve *f*
**Ald.** *abbr* = **alderman**
**alderman** ['ɔːldəmən] *n* conseiller municipal
*(en Angleterre)*
**ale** [eɪl] *n* bière *f*
**alert** [ə'ləːt] *adj* alerte, vif (vive); *(watchful)*
vigilant(e) ▷ *n* alerte *f* ▷ *vt* alerter; **to ~ sb (to**
**sth)** attirer l'attention de qn (sur qch); **to ~ sb**
**to the dangers of sth** avertir qn des dangers de
qch; **on the ~** sur le qui-vive; *(Mil)* en état
d'alerte
**Aleutian Islands** [ə'luːʃən-] *npl* îles
Aléoutiennes
**A levels** *npl* = baccalauréat *msg*

a

**Alexandria** [ˌælɪgˈzɑːndrɪə] n Alexandrie
**alfresco** [ælˈfreskəu] adj, adv en plein air
**algebra** [ˈældʒɪbrə] n algèbre m
**Algeria** [ælˈdʒɪərɪə] n Algérie f
**Algerian** [ælˈdʒɪərɪən] adj algérien(ne) ▷ n Algérien(ne)
**Algiers** [ælˈdʒɪəz] n Alger
**algorithm** [ˈælgərɪðəm] n algorithme m
**alias** [ˈeɪlɪəs] adv alias ▷ n faux nom, nom d'emprunt
**alibi** [ˈælɪbaɪ] n alibi m
**alien** [ˈeɪlɪən] n (from abroad) étranger(-ère); (from outer space) extraterrestre ▷ adj: ~ (to) étranger(-ère) (à)
**alienate** [ˈeɪlɪəneɪt] vt aliéner; (subj: person) s'aliéner
**alienation** [eɪlɪəˈneɪʃən] n aliénation f
**alight** [əˈlaɪt] adj, adv en feu ▷ vi mettre pied à terre; (passenger) descendre; (bird) se poser
**align** [əˈlaɪn] vt aligner
**alignment** [əˈlaɪnmənt] n alignement m; **it's out of ~ (with)** ce n'est pas aligné (avec)
**alike** [əˈlaɪk] adj semblable, pareil(le) ▷ adv de même; **to look ~** se ressembler
**alimony** [ˈælɪmənɪ] n (payment) pension f alimentaire
**alive** [əˈlaɪv] adj vivant(e); (active) plein(e) de vie; **~ with** grouillant(e) de; **~ to** sensible à
**alkali** [ˈælkəlaɪ] n alcali m

🅞 KEYWORD

**all** [ɔːl] adj (singular) tout(e); (plural) tous (toutes); **all day** toute la journée; **all night** toute la nuit; **all men** tous les hommes; **all five** tous les cinq; **all the food** toute la nourriture; **all the books** tous les livres; **all the time** tout le temps; **all his life** toute sa vie
▷ pron 1 tout; **I ate it all, I ate all of it** j'ai tout mangé; **all of us went** nous y sommes tous allés; **all of the boys went** tous les garçons y sont allés; **is that all?** c'est tout?; (in shop) ce sera tout?
2 (in phrases): **above all** surtout, par-dessus tout; **after all** après tout; **at all: not at all** (in answer to question) pas du tout; (in answer to thanks) je vous en prie!; **I'm not at all tired** je ne suis pas du tout fatigué(e); **anything at all will do** n'importe quoi fera l'affaire; **all in all** tout bien considéré, en fin de compte
▷ adv: **all alone** tout(e) seul(e); **it's not as hard as all that** ce n'est pas si difficile que ça; **all the more/the better** d'autant plus/mieux; **all but** presque, pratiquement; **to be all in** (Brit inf) être complètement à plat; **the score is 2 all** le score est de 2 partout

**Allah** [ˈælə] n Allah m
**all-around** [ɔːləˈraund] adj (US) = **all-round**
**allay** [əˈleɪ] vt (fears) apaiser, calmer
**all clear** n (also fig) fin f d'alerte
**allegation** [ælɪˈgeɪʃən] n allégation f

**allege** [əˈlɛdʒ] vt alléguer, prétendre; **he is ~d to have said** il aurait dit
**alleged** [əˈlɛdʒd] adj prétendu(e)
**allegedly** [əˈlɛdʒɪdlɪ] adv à ce que l'on prétend, paraît-il
**allegiance** [əˈliːdʒəns] n fidélité f, obéissance f
**allegory** [ˈælɪgərɪ] n allégorie f
**all-embracing** [ˈɔːlɪmˈbreɪsɪŋ] adj universel(le)
**allergic** [əˈləːdʒɪk] adj: **~ to** allergique à; **I'm ~ to penicillin** je suis allergique à la pénicilline
**allergy** [ˈælədʒɪ] n allergie f
**alleviate** [əˈliːvɪeɪt] vt soulager, adoucir
**alley** [ˈælɪ] n ruelle f; (in garden) allée f
**alleyway** [ˈælɪweɪ] n ruelle f
**alliance** [əˈlaɪəns] n alliance f
**allied** [ˈælaɪd] adj allié(e)
**alligator** [ˈælɪgeɪtər] n alligator m
**all-important** [ˈɔːlɪmˈpɔːtənt] adj capital(e), crucial(e)
**all-in** [ˈɔːlɪn] adj, adv (Brit: charge) tout compris
**all-in wrestling** n (Brit) catch m
**alliteration** [əlɪtəˈreɪʃən] n allitération f
**all-night** [ˈɔːlˈnaɪt] adj ouvert(e) or qui dure toute la nuit
**allocate** [ˈæləkeɪt] vt (share out) répartir, distribuer; **to ~ sth to** (duties) assigner or attribuer qch à; (sum, time) allouer qch à; **to ~ sth for** affecter qch à
**allocation** [æləuˈkeɪʃən] n (see vb) répartition f; attribution f; allocation f; affectation f; (money) crédit(s) m(pl); somme(s) allouée(s)
**allot** [əˈlɔt] vt (share out) répartir, distribuer; **to ~ sth to** (time) allouer qch à; (duties) assigner qch à; **in the ~ted time** dans le temps imparti
**allotment** [əˈlɔtmənt] n (share) part f; (garden) lopin m de terre (loué à la municipalité)
**all-out** [ˈɔːlaut] adj (effort etc) total(e)
**allow** [əˈlau] vt (practice, behaviour) permettre, autoriser; (sum to spend etc) accorder, allouer; (sum, time estimated) compter, prévoir; (claim, goal) admettre; (concede): **to ~ that** convenir que; **to ~ sb to do** permettre à qn de faire, autoriser qn à faire; **he is ~ed to ...** on lui permet de ...; **smoking is not ~ed** il est interdit de fumer; **we must ~ three days for the journey** il faut compter trois jours pour le voyage
▷ **allow for** vt fus tenir compte de
**allowance** [əˈlauəns] n (money received) allocation f; (: from parent etc) subside m; (: for expenses) indemnité f; (US: pocket money) argent m de poche; (Tax) somme f déductible du revenu imposable, abattement m; **to make ~s for** (person) essayer de comprendre; (thing) tenir compte de
**alloy** [ˈælɔɪ] n alliage m
**all right** adv (feel, work) bien; (as answer) d'accord
**all-round** [ˈɔːlˈraund] adj compétent(e) dans tous les domaines; (athlete etc) complet(-ète)
**all-rounder** [ɔːlˈraundər] n (Brit): **to be a good ~** être doué(e) en tout
**allspice** [ˈɔːlspaɪs] n poivre m de la Jamaïque
**all-time** [ˈɔːlˈtaɪm] adj (record) sans précédent,

absolu(e)

**allude** [ə'lu:d] *vi:* **to ~ to** faire allusion à

**alluring** [ə'ljuərɪŋ] *adj* séduisant(e), alléchant(e)

**allusion** [ə'lu:ʒən] *n* allusion *f*

**alluvium** [ə'lu:vɪəm] *n* alluvions *fpl*

**ally** ['ælaɪ] *n* allié *m* ▷ *vt* [ə'laɪ]: **to ~ o.s. with** s'allier avec

**almighty** [ɔ:l'maɪtɪ] *adj* tout(e)-puissant(e); *(tremendous)* énorme

**almond** ['ɑ:mənd] *n* amande *f*

**almost** ['ɔ:lməʊst] *adv* presque; **he ~ fell** il a failli tomber

**alms** [ɑ:mz] *n* aumône(s) *f(pl)*

**aloft** [ə'lɔft] *adv* en haut, en l'air; *(Naut)* dans la mâture

**alone** [ə'ləʊn] *adj, adv* seul(e); **to leave sb ~** laisser qn tranquille; **to leave sth ~** ne pas toucher à qch; **let ~ ...** sans parler de ...; encore moins ...

**along** [ə'lɔŋ] *prep* le long de ▷ *adv:* **is he coming ~ with us?** vient-il avec nous?; **he was hopping/limping ~** il venait or avançait en sautillant/boitant; **~ with** avec, en plus de; *(person)* en compagnie de; **all ~** *(all the time)* depuis le début

**alongside** [ə'lɔŋ'saɪd] *prep (along)* le long de; *(beside)* à côté de ▷ *adv* bord à bord; côte à côte; **we brought our boat ~** *(of a pier, shore etc)* nous avons accosté

**aloof** [ə'lu:f] *adj* distant(e) ▷ *adv* à distance, à l'écart; **to stand ~** se tenir à l'écart or à distance

**aloofness** [ə'lu:fnɪs] *n* réserve (hautaine), attitude distante

**aloud** [ə'laud] *adv* à haute voix

**alphabet** ['ælfəbɛt] *n* alphabet *m*

**alphabetical** [ælfə'bɛtɪkl] *adj* alphabétique; **in ~ order** par ordre alphabétique

**alphanumeric** [ælfənju:'mɛrɪk] *adj* alphanumérique

**alpine** ['ælpaɪn] *adj* alpin(e), alpestre; **~ hut** cabane *f or* refuge *m* de montagne; **~ pasture** pâturage *m* (de montagne); **~ skiing** ski alpin

**Alps** [ælps] *npl:* **the ~** les Alpes *fpl*

**already** [ɔ:l'rɛdɪ] *adv* déjà

**alright** ['ɔ:l'raɪt] *adv (Brit)* = **all right**

**Alsace** [æl'sæs] *n* Alsace *f*

**Alsatian** [æl'seɪʃən] *adj* alsacien(ne), d'Alsace ▷ *n* Alsacien(ne); *(Brit: dog)* berger allemand

**also** ['ɔ:lsəʊ] *adv* aussi

**Alta.** *abbr (Canada)* = **Alberta**

**altar** ['ɔltə'] *n* autel *m*

**alter** ['ɔltə'] *vt, vi* changer

**alteration** [ɔltə'reɪʃən] *n* changement *m*, modification *f*; **alterations** *npl (Sewing)* retouches *fpl*; *(Archit)* modifications *fpl*; **timetable subject to ~** horaires sujets à modifications

**altercation** [ɔltə'keɪʃən] *n* altercation *f*

**alternate** *adj* [ɔl'tə:nɪt] alterné(e), alternant(e), alternatif(-ive); *(US)* = **alternative** ▷ *vi* ['ɔltə:neɪt] alterner; **to ~ with** alterner avec; **on**

**~ days** un jour sur deux, tous les deux jours

**alternately** [ɔl'tə:nɪtlɪ] *adv* alternativement, en alternant

**alternating** ['ɔltə:neɪtɪŋ] *adj (current)* alternatif(-ive)

**alternative** [ɔl'tə:nətɪv] *adj (solution, plan)* autre, de remplacement; *(energy)* doux (douce); *(lifestyle)* parallèle ▷ *n (choice)* alternative *f*; *(other possibility)* autre possibilité *f*; **~ medicine** médecine alternative, médecine douce

**alternatively** [ɔl'tə:nətɪvlɪ] *adv:* **~ one could ...** une autre *or* l'autre solution serait de ...

**alternative medicine** *n* médecines *fpl* parallèles *or* douces

**alternator** ['ɔltə:neɪtə'] *n (Aut)* alternateur *m*

**although** [ɔ:l'ðəʊ] *conj* bien que + *sub*

**altitude** ['æltɪtju:d] *n* altitude *f*

**alto** ['æltəʊ] *n (female)* contralto *m*; *(male)* haute-contre *f*

**altogether** [ɔ:ltə'gɛðə'] *adv* entièrement, tout à fait; *(on the whole)* tout compte fait; *(in all)* en tout; **how much is that ~?** ça fait combien en tout?

**altruism** ['æltruɪzəm] *n* altruisme *m*

**altruistic** [æltru'ɪstɪk] *adj* altruiste

**aluminium** [ælju'mɪnɪəm] *(US)*, **aluminum** [ə'lu:mɪnəm] *n* aluminium *m*

**alumna** *(pl* **-e)** [ə'lʌmnə, -ni:] *n (US Scol)* ancienne élève; *(University)* ancienne étudiante

**alumnus** *(pl* **alumni)** [ə'lʌmnəs, -naɪ] *n (US Scol)* ancien élève; *(University)* ancien étudiant

**always** ['ɔ:lweɪz] *adv* toujours

**Alzheimer's** ['æltshaɪməz], **Alzheimer's disease** *n* maladie *f* d'Alzheimer

**AM** *abbr* = **amplitude modulation** ▷ *n abbr* (= *Assembly Member)* député *m* au Parlement gallois

**am** [æm] *vb see* **be**

**a.m.** *adv abbr* (= *ante meridiem)* du matin

**AMA** *n abbr* = **American Medical Association**

**amalgam** [ə'mælgəm] *n* amalgame *m*

**amalgamate** [ə'mælgəmeɪt] *vt, vi* fusionner

**amalgamation** [əmælgə'meɪʃən] *n* fusion *f*; *(Comm)* fusionnement *m*

**amass** [ə'mæs] *vt* amasser

**amateur** ['æmətə'] *n* amateur *m* ▷ *adj (Sport)* amateur *inv*; **~ dramatics** le théâtre amateur

**amateurish** ['æmətərɪʃ] *adj (pej)* d'amateur, un peu amateur

**amaze** [ə'meɪz] *vt* stupéfier; **to be ~d (at)** être stupéfait(e) (de)

**amazed** [ə'meɪzd] *adj* stupéfait(e)

**amazement** [ə'meɪzmənt] *n* surprise *f*, étonnement *m*

**amazing** [ə'meɪzɪŋ] *adj* étonnant(e), incroyable; *(bargain, offer)* exceptionnel(le)

**amazingly** [ə'meɪzɪŋlɪ] *adv* incroyablement

**Amazon** ['æməzən] *n (Geo, Mythology)* Amazone *f* ▷ *cpd* amazonien(ne), de l'Amazone; **the ~ basin** le bassin de l'Amazone; **the ~ jungle** la forêt amazonienne

**Amazonian** [æmə'zəʊnɪən] *adj* amazonien(ne)

**ambassador** [æm'bæsədəʳ] n ambassadeur m
**amber** ['æmbəʳ] n ambre m; **at ~** (Brit Aut) à l'orange
**ambidextrous** [æmbɪ'dɛkstrəs] adj ambidextre
**ambience** ['æmbɪəns] n ambiance f
**ambiguity** [æmbɪ'gjuɪtɪ] n ambiguïté f
**ambiguous** [æm'bɪgjuəs] adj ambigu(ë)
**ambition** [æm'bɪʃən] n ambition f
**ambitious** [æm'bɪʃəs] adj ambitieux(-euse)
**ambivalent** [æm'bɪvələnt] adj (attitude) ambivalent(e)
**amble** ['æmbl] vi (also: **to amble along**) aller d'un pas tranquille
**ambulance** ['æmbjuləns] n ambulance f; **call an ~!** appelez une ambulance!
**ambush** ['æmbuʃ] n embuscade f ▷ vt tendre une embuscade à
**ameba** [ə'mi:bə] n (US) = **amoeba**
**ameliorate** [ə'mi:lɪəreɪt] vt améliorer
**amen** ['ɑ:'mɛn] excl amen
**amenable** [ə'mi:nəbl] adj: **~ to** (advice etc) disposé(e) à écouter or suivre; **~ to the law** responsable devant la loi
**amend** [ə'mɛnd] vt (law) amender; (text) corriger; (habits) réformer ▷ vi s'amender, se corriger; **to make ~s** réparer ses torts, faire amende honorable
**amendment** [ə'mɛndmənt] n (to law) amendement m; (to text) correction f
**amenities** [ə'mi:nɪtɪz] npl aménagements mpl, équipements mpl
**amenity** [ə'mi:nɪtɪ] n charme m, agrément m
**America** [ə'mɛrɪkə] n Amérique f
**American** [ə'mɛrɪkən] adj américain(e) ▷ n Américain(e)
**American football** n (Brit) football m américain
**americanize** [ə'mɛrɪkənaɪz] vt américaniser
**amethyst** ['æmɪθɪst] n améthyste f
**Amex** ['æmɛks] n abbr = **American Stock Exchange**
**amiable** ['eɪmɪəbl] adj aimable, affable
**amicable** ['æmɪkəbl] adj amical(e); (Law) à l'amiable
**amicably** ['æmɪkəblɪ] adv amicalement
**amid** [ə'mɪd], **amidst** [ə'mɪdst] prep parmi, au milieu de
**amiss** [ə'mɪs] adj, adv: **there's something ~** il y a quelque chose qui ne va pas or qui cloche; **to take sth ~** prendre qch mal or de travers
**ammo** ['æməu] n abbr (inf) = **ammunition**
**ammonia** [ə'məunɪə] n (gas) ammoniac m; (liquid) ammoniaque f
**ammunition** [æmju'nɪʃən] n munitions fpl; (fig) arguments mpl
**ammunition dump** n dépôt m de munitions
**amnesia** [æm'ni:zɪə] n amnésie f
**amnesty** ['æmnɪstɪ] n amnistie f; **to grant an ~ to** accorder une amnistie à
**Amnesty International** n Amnesty International
**amoeba**, (US) **ameba** [ə'mi:bə] n amibe f
**amok** [ə'mɔk] adv: **to run ~** être pris(e) d'un accès de folie furieuse

**among** [ə'mʌŋ], **amongst** [ə'mʌŋst] prep parmi, entre
**amoral** [æ'mɔrəl] adj amoral(e)
**amorous** ['æmərəs] adj amoureux(-euse)
**amorphous** [ə'mɔ:fəs] adj amorphe
**amortization** [əmɔ:taɪ'zeɪʃən] n (Comm) amortissement m
**amount** [ə'maunt] n (sum of money) somme f; (total) montant m; (quantity) quantité f; nombre m ▷ vi: **~ to** (total) s'élever à; (be same as) équivaloir à, revenir à; **this ~s to a refusal** cela équivaut à un refus; **the total ~** (of money) le montant total
**amp** ['æmp], **ampère** ['æmpɛəʳ] n ampère m; **a 13 ~ plug** une fiche de 13 A
**ampersand** ['æmpəsænd] n signe &, "et" commercial
**amphetamine** [æm'fɛtəmi:n] n amphétamine f
**amphibian** [æm'fɪbɪən] n batracien m
**amphibious** [æm'fɪbɪəs] adj amphibie
**amphitheatre**, (US) **amphitheater** ['æmfɪθɪətəʳ] n amphithéâtre m
**ample** ['æmpl] adj ample, spacieux(-euse); (enough): **this is ~** c'est largement suffisant; **to have ~ time/room** avoir bien assez de temps/place, avoir largement le temps/la place
**amplifier** ['æmplɪfaɪəʳ] n amplificateur m
**amplify** ['æmplɪfaɪ] vt amplifier
**amply** ['æmplɪ] adv amplement, largement
**ampoule**, (US) **ampule** ['æmpu:l] n (Med) ampoule f
**amputate** ['æmpjuteɪt] vt amputer
**amputee** [æmpju'ti:] n amputé(e)
**Amsterdam** ['æmstədæm] n Amsterdam
**amt** abbr = **amount**
**Amtrak** ['æmtræk] (US) n société mixte de transports ferroviaires interurbains pour voyageurs
**amuck** [ə'mʌk] adv = **amok**
**amuse** [ə'mju:z] vt amuser; **to ~ o.s. with sth/by doing sth** se divertir avec qch/à faire qch; **to be ~d at** être amusé par; **he was not ~d** il n'a pas apprécié
**amusement** [ə'mju:zmənt] n amusement m; (pastime) distraction f
**amusement arcade** n salle f de jeu
**amusement park** n parc m d'attractions
**amusing** [ə'mju:zɪŋ] adj amusant(e), divertissant(e)
**an** [æn, ən, n] indef art see **a**
**ANA** n abbr = **American Newspaper Association; American Nurses Association**
**anachronism** [ə'nækrənɪzəm] n anachronisme m
**anaemia**, (US) **anemia** [ə'ni:mɪə] n anémie f
**anaemic**, (US) **anemic** [ə'ni:mɪk] adj anémique
**anaesthetic**, (US) **anesthetic** [ænɪs'θɛtɪk] adj, n anesthésique m; **under the ~** sous anesthésie; **local/general ~** anesthésie locale/générale
**anaesthetist** [æ'ni:sθɪtɪst] n anesthésiste m/f
**anagram** ['ænəgræm] n anagramme m
**anal** ['eɪnl] adj anal(e)

**analgesic** [ænæl'dʒiːsɪk] *adj, n* analgésique (*m*)
**analogous** [ə'næləgəs] *adj*: ~ (**to** *or* **with**) analogue (à)
**analogue, analog** ['ænələg] *adj* (*watch, computer*) analogique
**analogy** [ə'nælədʒɪ] *n* analogie *f*; **to draw an ~ between** établir une analogie entre
**analyse**, (*US*) **analyze** ['ænəlaɪz] *vt* analyser
**analysis** (*pl* **analyses**) [ə'næləsɪs, -siːz] *n* analyse *f*; **in the last ~** en dernière analyse
**analyst** ['ænəlɪst] *n* (*political analyst etc*) analyste *m/f*; (*US*) psychanalyste *m/f*
**analytic** [ænə'lɪtɪk], **analytical** [ænə'lɪtɪkəl] *adj* analytique
**analyze** ['ænəlaɪz] *vt* (*US*) = **analyse**
**anarchic** [æ'nɑːkɪk] *adj* anarchique
**anarchist** ['ænəkɪst] *adj, n* anarchiste (*m/f*)
**anarchy** ['ænəkɪ] *n* anarchie *f*
**anathema** [ə'næθɪmə] *n*: **it is ~ to him** il a cela en abomination
**anatomical** [ænə'tɒmɪkəl] *adj* anatomique
**anatomy** [ə'nætəmɪ] *n* anatomie *f*
**ANC** *n abbr* (= *African National Congress*) ANC *m*
**ancestor** ['ænsɪstə<sup>r</sup>] *n* ancêtre *m*, aïeul *m*
**ancestral** [æn'sɛstrəl] *adj* ancestral(e)
**ancestry** ['ænsɪstrɪ] *n* ancêtres *mpl*; ascendance *f*
**anchor** ['æŋkə<sup>r</sup>] *n* ancre *f* ▷ *vi* (*also*: **to drop anchor**) jeter l'ancre, mouiller ▷ *vt* mettre à l'ancre; (*fig*): **to ~ sth to** fixer qch à; **to weigh ~** lever l'ancre
**anchorage** ['æŋkərɪdʒ] *n* mouillage *m*, ancrage *m*
**anchor man, anchor woman** (*irreg*) *n* (TV, Radio) présentateur(-trice)
**anchovy** ['æntʃəvɪ] *n* anchois *m*
**ancient** ['eɪnʃənt] *adj* ancien(ne), antique; (*person*) d'un âge vénérable; (*car*) antédiluvien(ne); **~ monument** monument *m* historique
**ancillary** [æn'sɪlərɪ] *adj* auxiliaire
**and** [ænd] *conj* et; **~ so on** et ainsi de suite; **try ~ come** tâchez de venir; **come ~ sit here** venez vous asseoir ici; **he talked ~ talked** il a parlé pendant des heures; **better ~ better** de mieux en mieux; **more ~ more** de plus en plus
**Andes** ['ændiːz] *npl*: **the ~** les Andes *fpl*
**Andorra** [æn'dɔːrə] *n* (principauté *f* d')Andorre *f*
**anecdote** ['ænɪkdəut] *n* anecdote *f*
**anemia** *etc* [ə'niːmɪə] *n* (*US*) = **anaemia** *etc*
**anemic** [ə'niːmɪk] *adj* = **anaemic**
**anemone** [ə'nɛmənɪ] *n* (*Bot*) anémone *f*; **sea ~** anémone de mer
**anesthesiologist** [ænɪsθiːzɪ'ɔlədʒɪst] *n* (*US*) anesthésiste *m/f*
**anesthetic** [ænɪs'θɛtɪk] *n, adj* (*US*) = **anaesthetic**
**anesthetist** [æ'niːsθɪtɪst] *n* = **anaesthetist**
**anew** [ə'njuː] *adv* à nouveau
**angel** ['eɪndʒəl] *n* ange *m*
**angel dust** *n* poussière *f* d'ange
**anger** ['æŋgə<sup>r</sup>] *n* colère *f* ▷ *vt* mettre en colère,

irriter
**angina** [æn'dʒaɪnə] *n* angine *f* de poitrine
**angle** ['æŋgl] *n* angle *m* ▷ *vi*: **to ~ for** (*trout*) pêcher; (*compliments*) chercher, quêter; **from their ~** de leur point de vue
**angler** ['æŋglə<sup>r</sup>] *n* pêcheur(-euse) à la ligne
**Anglican** ['æŋglɪkən] *adj, n* anglican(e)
**anglicize** ['æŋglɪsaɪz] *vt* angliciser
**angling** ['æŋglɪŋ] *n* pêche *f* à la ligne
**Anglo-** ['æŋgləu] *prefix* anglo(-)
**Anglo-French** ['æŋgləu'frɛntʃ] *adj* anglo-français(e)
**Anglo-Saxon** ['æŋgləu'sæksən] *adj, n* anglo-saxon(ne)
**Angola** [æŋ'gəulə] *n* Angola *m*
**Angolan** [æŋ'gəulən] *adj* angolais(e) ▷ *n* Angolais(e)
**angrily** ['æŋgrɪlɪ] *adv* avec colère
**angry** ['æŋgrɪ] *adj* en colère, furieux(-euse); (*wound*) enflammé(e); **to be ~ with sb/at sth** être furieux contre qn/de qch; **to get ~** se fâcher, se mettre en colère; **to make sb ~** mettre qn en colère
**anguish** ['æŋgwɪʃ] *n* angoisse *f*
**anguished** ['æŋgwɪʃt] *adj* (*mentally*) angoissé(e); (*physically*) plein(e) de souffrance
**angular** ['æŋgjulə<sup>r</sup>] *adj* anguleux(-euse)
**animal** ['ænɪməl] *n* animal *m* ▷ *adj* animal(e)
**animal rights** *npl* droits *mpl* de l'animal
**animate** *vt* ['ænɪmeɪt] animer ▷ *adj* ['ænɪmɪt] animé(e), vivant(e)
**animated** ['ænɪmeɪtɪd] *adj* animé(e)
**animation** [ænɪ'meɪʃən] *n* (*of person*) entrain *m*; (*of street, Cine*) animation *f*
**animosity** [ænɪ'mɔsɪtɪ] *n* animosité *f*
**aniseed** ['ænɪsiːd] *n* anis *m*
**Ankara** ['æŋkərə] *n* Ankara
**ankle** ['æŋkl] *n* cheville *f*
**ankle socks** *npl* socquettes *fpl*
**annex** ['ænɛks] *n* (*Brit: also*: **annexe**) annexe *f* ▷ *vt* [ə'nɛks] annexer
**annexation** [ænɛks'eɪʃən] *n* annexion *f*
**annihilate** [ə'naɪəleɪt] *vt* annihiler, anéantir
**annihilation** [ənaɪə'leɪʃən] *n* anéantissement *m*
**anniversary** [ænɪ'vəːsərɪ] *n* anniversaire *m*
**anniversary dinner** *n* dîner commémoratif *or* anniversaire
**annotate** ['ænəuteɪt] *vt* annoter
**announce** [ə'nauns] *vt* annoncer; (*birth, death*) faire part de; **he ~d that he wasn't going** il a déclaré qu'il n'irait pas
**announcement** [ə'naunsmənt] *n* annonce *f*; (*for births etc: in newspaper*) avis *m* de faire-part; (: *letter, card*) faire-part *m*; **I'd like to make an ~** j'ai une communication à faire
**announcer** [ə'naunsə<sup>r</sup>] *n* (Radio, TV: between programmes) speaker(ine); (: *in a programme*) présentateur(-trice)
**annoy** [ə'nɔɪ] *vt* agacer, ennuyer, contrarier; **to be ~ed (at sth/with sb)** être en colère *or* irrité (contre qch/qn); **don't get ~ed!** ne vous fâchez pas!

**a**

457

**annoyance** [ə'nɔɪəns] n mécontentement m, contrariété f

**annoying** [ə'nɔɪɪŋ] adj agaçant(e), contrariant(e)

**annual** ['ænjuəl] adj annuel(le) ▷ n (Bot) plante annuelle; (book) album m

**annual general meeting** n (Brit) assemblée générale annuelle

**annually** ['ænjuəlɪ] adv annuellement

**annual report** n rapport annuel

**annuity** [ə'njuːɪtɪ] n rente f; **life** ~ rente viagère

**annul** [ə'nʌl] vt annuler; (law) abroger

**annulment** [ə'nʌlmənt] n (see vb) annulation f; abrogation f

**annum** ['ænəm] n see **per**

**Annunciation** [ənʌnsɪ'eɪʃən] n Annonciation f

**anode** ['ænəud] n anode f

**anoint** [ə'nɔɪnt] vt oindre

**anomalous** [ə'nɔmələs] adj anormal(e)

**anomaly** [ə'nɔmælɪ] n anomalie f

**anon.** [ə'nɔn] abbr = **anonymous**

**anonymity** [ænə'nɪmɪtɪ] n anonymat m

**anonymous** [ə'nɔnɪməs] adj anonyme; **to remain** ~ garder l'anonymat

**anorak** ['ænəræk] n anorak m

**anorexia** [ænə'rɛksɪə] n (also: **anorexia nervosa**) anorexie f

**anorexic** [ænə'rɛksɪk] adj, n anorexique (m/f)

**another** [ə'nʌðər] adj: ~ **book** (one more) un autre livre, encore un livre, un livre de plus; (a different one) un autre livre ▷ pron un(e) autre, encore un(e), un(e) de plus; ~ **drink?** encore un verre?; **in** ~ **five years** dans cinq ans; see also **one**

**ANSI** ['ænsɪ] n abbr (= American National Standards Institution) ANSI m (= Institut américain de normalisation)

**answer** ['ɑːnsər] n réponse f; (to problem) solution f ▷ vi répondre ▷ vt répondre à; (problem) résoudre; (prayer) exaucer; **in** ~ **to your letter** suite à or en réponse à votre lettre; **to** ~ **the phone** répondre (au téléphone); **to** ~ **the bell** or **the door** aller or venir ouvrir (la porte)
▸ **answer back** vi répondre, répliquer
▸ **answer for** vt fus répondre de, se porter garant de; (crime, one's actions) répondre de
▸ **answer to** vt fus (description) répondre or correspondre à

**answerable** ['ɑːnsərəbl] adj: ~ (**to sb/for sth**) responsable (devant qn/de qch); **I am** ~ **to no-one** je n'ai de comptes à rendre à personne

**answering machine** ['ɑːnsərɪŋ-] n répondeur m

**answerphone** ['ɑːnsərfəun] n (esp Brit) répondeur m (téléphonique)

**ant** [ænt] n fourmi f

**ANTA** n abbr = **American National Theater and Academy**

**antagonism** [æn'tægənɪzəm] n antagonisme m

**antagonist** [æn'tægənɪst] n antagoniste m/f, adversaire m/f

**antagonistic** [æntægə'nɪstɪk] adj (attitude, feelings) hostile

**antagonize** [æn'tægənaɪz] vt éveiller l'hostilité de, contrarier

**Antarctic** [ænt'ɑːktɪk] adj antarctique, austral(e) ▷ n: **the** ~ l'Antarctique m

**Antarctica** [ænt'ɑːktɪkə] n Antarctique m, Terres Australes

**Antarctic Circle** n cercle m Antarctique

**Antarctic Ocean** n océan m Antarctique or Austral

**ante** ['æntɪ] n: **to up the** ~ faire monter les enjeux

**ante...** ['æntɪ] prefix anté..., anti..., pré...

**anteater** ['ænti:tər] n fourmilier m, tamanoir m

**antecedent** [æntɪ'siːdənt] n antécédent m

**antechamber** ['æntɪtʃeɪmbər] n antichambre f

**antelope** ['æntɪləup] n antilope f

**antenatal** ['æntɪ'neɪtl] adj prénatal(e)

**antenatal clinic** n service m de consultation prénatale

**antenna** (pl **-e**) [æn'tɛnə, -niː] n antenne f

**anthem** ['ænθəm] n motet m; **national** ~ hymne national

**ant-hill** ['ænthɪl] n fourmilière f

**anthology** [æn'θɔlədʒɪ] n anthologie f

**anthrax** ['ænθræks] n anthrax m

**anthropologist** [ænθrə'pɔlədʒɪst] n anthropologue m/f

**anthropology** [ænθrə'pɔlədʒɪ] n anthropologie f

**anti** ['æntɪ] prefix anti-

**anti-aircraft** ['æntɪ'ɛəkrɑːft] adj antiaérien(ne)

**anti-aircraft defence** n défense f contre avions, DCA f

**antiballistic** ['æntɪbə'lɪstɪk] adj antibalistique

**antibiotic** ['æntɪbaɪ'ɔtɪk] adj, n antibiotique m

**antibody** ['æntɪbɔdɪ] n anticorps m

**anticipate** [æn'tɪsɪpeɪt] vt s'attendre à, prévoir; (wishes, request) aller au devant de, devancer; **this is worse than I** ~**d** c'est pire que je ne pensais; **as** ~**d** comme prévu

**anticipation** [æntɪsɪ'peɪʃən] n attente f; **thanking you in** ~ en vous remerciant d'avance, avec mes remerciements anticipés

**anticlimax** ['æntɪ'klaɪmæks] n déception f

**anticlockwise** ['æntɪ'klɔkwaɪz] (Brit) adv dans le sens inverse des aiguilles d'une montre

**antics** ['æntɪks] npl singeries fpl

**anticyclone** ['æntɪ'saɪkləun] n anticyclone m

**antidepressant** ['æntɪdɪ'prɛsnt] n antidépresseur m

**antidote** ['æntɪdəut] n antidote m, contrepoison m

**antifreeze** ['æntɪfriːz] n antigel m

**anti-globalization** [æntɪgləubəlaɪ'zeɪʃən] n antimondialisation f

**antihistamine** [æntɪ'hɪstəmɪn] n antihistaminique m

**Antilles** [æn'tɪliːz] npl: **the** ~ les Antilles fpl

**antipathy** [æn'tɪpəθɪ] n antipathie f

**antiperspirant** [æntɪ'pəːspɪrənt] n déodorant m

**Antipodean** [æntɪpə'diːən] adj australien(ne) et néozélandais(e), d'Australie et de Nouvelle-Zélande

**Antipodes** [æn'tɪpədiːz] npl: **the** ~ l'Australie f

et la Nouvelle-Zélande

**antiquarian** [æntɪ'kwɛərɪən] *adj*: ~ **bookshop** librairie *f* d'ouvrages anciens ▷ *n* expert *m* en objets *or* livres anciens; amateur *m* d'antiquités

**antiquated** ['æntɪkweɪtɪd] *adj* vieilli(e), suranné(e), vieillot(te)

**antique** [æn'tiːk] *n* (*ornament*) objet *m* d'art ancien; (*furniture*) meuble ancien ▷ *adj* ancien(ne); (*pre-mediaeval*) antique

**antique dealer** *n* antiquaire *m/f*

**antique shop** *n* magasin *m* d'antiquités

**antiquity** [æn'tɪkwɪtɪ] *n* antiquité *f*

**anti-Semitic** ['æntɪsɪ'mɪtɪk] *adj* antisémite

**anti-Semitism** ['æntɪ'semɪtɪzəm] *n* antisémitisme *m*

**antiseptic** [æntɪ'septɪk] *adj*, *n* antiseptique (*m*)

**antisocial** ['æntɪ'səuʃəl] *adj* (*unfriendly*) peu liant(e), insociable; (*against society*) antisocial(e)

**antitank** [æntɪ'tæŋk] *adj* antichar

**antithesis** (*pl* **antitheses**) [æn'tɪθɪsɪs, -siːz] *n* antithèse *f*

**antitrust** [æntɪ'trʌst] *adj*: ~ **legislation** loi *f* anti-trust

**antiviral** [æntɪ'vaɪərəl] *adj* (*Med*) antiviral

**antivirus** [æntɪ'vaɪərəs] *adj* antivirus *inv*; ~ **software** (logiciel *m*) antivírus *m*

**antlers** ['æntləz] *npl* bois *mpl*, ramure *f*

**Antwerp** ['æntwəːp] *n* Anvers

**anus** ['eɪnəs] *n* anus *m*

**anvil** ['ænvɪl] *n* enclume *f*

**anxiety** [æŋ'zaɪətɪ] *n* anxiété *f*; (*keenness*): ~ **to do** grand désir *or* impatience *f* de faire

**anxious** ['æŋkʃəs] *adj* (très) inquiet(-ète); (*always worried*) anxieux(-euse); (*worrying*) angoissant(e); (*keen*): ~ **to do/that** qui tient beaucoup à faire/à ce que + *sub*; impatient(e) de faire/que + *sub*; **I'm very ~ about you** je me fais beaucoup de souci pour toi

**anxiously** ['æŋkʃəslɪ] *adv* anxieusement

⚪ **KEYWORD**

**any** ['enɪ] *adj* **1** (*in questions etc: singular*) du, de l', de la; (: *plural*) des; **do you have any butter/ children/ink?** avez-vous du beurre/des enfants/de l'encre?

**2** (*with negative*) de, d'; **I don't have any money/ books** je n'ai pas d'argent/de livres; **without any difficulty** sans la moindre difficulté

**3** (*no matter which*) n'importe quel(le); (*each and every*) tout(e), chaque; **choose any book you like** vous pouvez choisir n'importe quel livre; **any teacher you ask will tell you** n'importe quel professeur vous le dira

**4** (*in phrases*): **in any case** de toute façon; **any day now** d'un jour à l'autre; **at any moment** à tout moment, d'un instant à l'autre; **at any rate** en tout cas; **at any time** n'importe quand; **he might come (at) any time** il pourrait venir n'importe quand; **come (at) any time** venez quand vous voulez

▷ *pron* **1** (*in questions etc*) en; **have you got any?**

est-ce que vous en avez?; **can any of you sing?** est-ce que parmi vous il y en a qui savent chanter?

**2** (*with negative*) en; **I don't have any (of them)** je n'en ai pas, je n'en ai aucun

**3** (*no matter which one(s)*) n'importe lequel (*or* laquelle); (*anybody*) n'importe qui; **take any of those books (you like)** vous pouvez prendre n'importe lequel de ces livres

▷ *adv* **1** (*in questions etc*): **do you want any more soup/sandwiches?** voulez-vous encore de la soupe/des sandwichs?; **are you feeling any better?** est-ce que vous vous sentez mieux?

**2** (*with negative*): **I can't hear him any more** je ne l'entends plus; **don't wait any longer** n'attendez pas plus longtemps

**anybody** ['enɪbɔdɪ] *pron* n'importe qui; (*in interrogative sentences*) quelqu'un; (*in negative sentences*): **I don't see** ~ je ne vois personne; **if ~ should phone ...** si quelqu'un téléphone ...

**anyhow** ['enɪhau] *adv* quoi qu'il en soit; (*haphazardly*) n'importe comment; **she leaves things just** ~ elle laisse tout traîner; **I shall go** ~ j'irai de toute façon

**anyone** ['enɪwʌn] *pron* = **anybody**

**anyplace** ['enɪpleɪs] *adv* (*US*) = **anywhere**

**anything** ['enɪθɪŋ] *pron* (*no matter what*) n'importe quoi; (*in questions*) quelque chose; (*with negative*) ne ... rien; **I don't want** ~ je ne veux rien; **can you see** ~? tu vois quelque chose?; **if ~ happens to me ...** s'il m'arrive quoi que ce soit ...; **you can say** ~ **you like** vous pouvez dire ce que vous voulez; ~ **will do** n'importe quoi fera l'affaire; **he'll eat** ~ il mange de tout; ~ **else?** (*in shop*) avec ceci?; **it can cost** ~ **between £15 and £20** (*Brit*) ça peut coûter dans les 15 à 20 livres

**anytime** ['enɪtaɪm] *adv* (*at any moment*) d'un moment à l'autre; (*whenever*) n'importe quand

**anyway** ['enɪweɪ] *adv* de toute façon; ~, **I couldn't come even if I wanted to** de toute façon, je ne pouvais pas venir même si je le voulais; **I shall go** ~ j'irai quand même; **why are you phoning,** ~? au fait, pourquoi tu me téléphones?

**anywhere** ['enɪwɛəʳ] *adv* n'importe où; (*in interrogative sentences*) quelque part; (*in negative sentences*): **I can't see him** ~ je ne le vois nulle part; **can you see him** ~? tu le vois quelque part?; **put the books down** ~ pose les livres n'importe où; ~ **in the world** (*no matter where*) n'importe où dans le monde

**Anzac** ['ænzæk] *n abbr* (= *Australia-New Zealand Army Corps*) soldat du corps ANZAC

**Anzac Day** *n* voir article

⬤ **ANZAC DAY**
⬤
⬤ *Anzac Day* est le 25 avril, jour férié en
⬤ Australie et en Nouvelle-Zélande
⬤ commémorant le débarquement des soldats

● du corps "ANZAC" à Gallipoli en 1915,
● pendant la Première Guerre mondiale. Ce
● fut la plus célèbre des campagnes du corps
● "ANZAC".

**apart** [ə'pɑːt] adv (to one side) à part; de côté; à l'écart; (separately) séparément; **to take/pull** ~ démonter; **10 miles/a long way** ~ à 10 miles; très éloignés l'un de l'autre; **they are living** ~ ils sont séparés; ~ **from** (prep) à part, excepté

**apartheid** [ə'pɑːteɪt] n apartheid m

**apartment** [ə'pɑːtmənt] n (US) appartement m, logement m; (room) chambre f

**apartment building** n (US) immeuble m; maison divisée en appartements

**apathetic** [æpə'θɛtɪk] adj apathique, indifférent(e)

**apathy** ['æpəθɪ] n apathie f, indifférence f

**APB** n abbr (US: = all points bulletin) expression de la police signifiant "découvrir et appréhender le suspect"

**ape** [eɪp] n (grand) singe ▷ vt singer

**Apennines** ['æpənaɪnz] npl: **the** ~ les Apennins mpl

**aperitif** [ə'pɛrɪtɪf] n apéritif m

**aperture** ['æpətʃjuəʳ] n orifice m, ouverture f; (Phot) ouverture (du diaphragme)

**APEX** ['eɪpɛks] n abbr (Aviat: = advance purchase excursion) APEX m

**apex** ['eɪpɛks] n sommet m

**aphid** ['eɪfɪd] n puceron m

**aphrodisiac** [æfrəu'dɪzɪæk] adj, n aphrodisiaque (m)

**API** n abbr = **American Press Institute**

**apiece** [ə'piːs] adv (for each person) chacun(e), par tête; (for each item) chacun(e), la pièce

**aplomb** [ə'plɔm] n sang-froid m, assurance f

**APO** n abbr (US: = Army Post Office) service postal de l'armée

**apocalypse** [ə'pɔkəlɪps] n apocalypse f

**apolitical** [eɪpə'lɪtɪkl] adj apolitique

**apologetic** [əpɔlə'dʒɛtɪk] adj (tone, letter) d'excuse; **to be very** ~ **about** s'excuser vivement de

**apologetically** [əpɔlə'dʒɛtɪkəlɪ] adv (say) en s'excusant

**apologize** [ə'pɔlədʒaɪz] vi: **to** ~ **(for sth to sb)** s'excuser (de qch auprès de qn), présenter des excuses (à qn pour qch)

**apology** [ə'pɔlədʒɪ] n excuses fpl; **to send one's apologies** envoyer une lettre or un mot d'excuse, s'excuser (de ne pas pouvoir venir); **please accept my apologies** vous voudrez bien m'excuser

**apoplectic** [æpə'plɛktɪk] adj (Med) apoplectique; (inf): ~ **with rage** fou (folle) de rage

**apoplexy** ['æpəplɛksɪ] n apoplexie f

**apostle** [ə'pɔsl] n apôtre m

**apostrophe** [ə'pɔstrəfɪ] n apostrophe f

**app** n abbr (Comput) = application

**appal**, (US) **appall** [ə'pɔːl] vt consterner, atterrer; horrifier

**Appalachian Mountains** [æpə'leɪʃən-] npl: **the** ~ les (monts mpl) Appalaches mpl

**appalling** [ə'pɔːlɪŋ] adj épouvantable; (stupidity) consternant(e); **she's an** ~ **cook** c'est une très mauvaise cuisinière

**apparatus** [æpə'reɪtəs] n appareil m, dispositif m; (in gymnasium) agrès mpl

**apparel** [ə'pærl] n (US) habillement m, confection f

**apparent** [ə'pærənt] adj apparent(e); **it is** ~ **that** il est évident que

**apparently** [ə'pærəntlɪ] adv apparemment

**apparition** [æpə'rɪʃən] n apparition f

**appeal** [ə'piːl] vi (Law) faire or interjeter appel ▷ n (Law) appel m; (request) appel; prière f; (charm) attrait m, charme m; **to** ~ **for** demander (instamment); implorer; **to** ~ **to** (beg) faire appel à; (be attractive) plaire à; **to** ~ **to sb for mercy** implorer la pitié de qn, prier or adjurer qn d'avoir pitié; **it doesn't** ~ **to me** cela ne m'attire pas; **right of** ~ droit m de recours

**appealing** [ə'piːlɪŋ] adj (attractive) attrayant(e); (touching) attendrissant(e)

**appear** [ə'pɪəʳ] vi apparaître, se montrer; (Law) comparaître; (publication) paraître, sortir, être publié(e); (seem) paraître, sembler; **it would** ~ **that** il semble que; **to** ~ **in Hamlet** jouer dans Hamlet; **to** ~ **on TV** passer à la télé

**appearance** [ə'pɪərəns] n apparition f; parution f; (look, aspect) apparence f, aspect m; **to put in** or **make an** ~ faire acte de présence; (Theat): **by order of** ~ par ordre d'entrée en scène; **to keep up** ~**s** sauver les apparences; **to all** ~**s** selon toute apparence

**appease** [ə'piːz] vt apaiser, calmer

**appeasement** [ə'piːzmənt] n (Pol) apaisement m

**append** [ə'pɛnd] vt (Comput) ajouter (à la fin d'un fichier)

**appendage** [ə'pɛndɪdʒ] n appendice m

**appendices** [ə'pɛndɪsiːz] npl of **appendix**

**appendicitis** [əpɛndɪ'saɪtɪs] n appendicite f

**appendix** (pl **appendices**) [ə'pɛndɪks, -siːz] n appendice m; **to have one's** ~ **out** se faire opérer de l'appendicite

**appetite** ['æpɪtaɪt] n appétit m; **that walk has given me an** ~ cette promenade m'a ouvert l'appétit

**appetizer** ['æpɪtaɪzəʳ] n (food) amuse-gueule m; (drink) apéritif m

**appetizing** ['æpɪtaɪzɪŋ] adj appétissant(e)

**applaud** [ə'plɔːd] vt, vi applaudir

**applause** [ə'plɔːz] n applaudissements mpl

**apple** ['æpl] n pomme f; (also: **apple tree**) pommier m; **it's the** ~ **of my eye** j'y tiens comme à la prunelle de mes yeux

**apple pie** n tarte f aux pommes

**apple turnover** n chausson m aux pommes

**appliance** [ə'plaɪəns] n appareil m; **electrical** ~**s** l'électroménager m

**applicable** [ə'plɪkəbl] adj applicable; **the law is** ~ **from January** la loi entre en vigueur au mois de janvier; **to be** ~ **to** (relevant) valoir pour

**applicant** ['æplɪkənt] *n*: ~ **(for)** (*Admin: for benefit etc*) demandeur(-euse) (de); (*for post*) candidat(e) (à)

**application** [æplɪ'keɪʃən] *n* application *f*; (*for a job, a grant etc*) demande *f*; candidature *f*; (*Comput*) (logiciel *m*) applicatif *m*; **on** ~ sur demande

**application form** *n* formulaire *m* de demande

**application program** *n* (*Comput*) (logiciel *m*) applicatif *m*

**applications package** *n* (*Comput*) progiciel *m* d'application

**applied** [ə'plaɪd] *adj* appliqué(e); ~ **arts** *npl* arts décoratifs

**apply** [ə'plaɪ] *vt*: **to** ~ **(to)** (*paint, ointment*) appliquer (sur); (*law, etc*) appliquer (à) ▷ *vi*: **to** ~ **to** (*ask*) s'adresser à; (*be suitable for, relevant to*) s'appliquer à, être valable pour; **to** ~ **(for)** (*permit, grant*) faire une demande (en vue d'obtenir); (*job*) poser sa candidature (pour), faire une demande d'emploi (concernant); **to** ~ **the brakes** actionner les freins, freiner; **to** ~ **o.s. to** s'appliquer à

**appoint** [ə'pɔɪnt] *vt* (*to post*) nommer, engager; (*date, place*) fixer, désigner

**appointee** [əpɔɪn'tiː] *n* personne nommée; candidat retenu

**appointment** [ə'pɔɪntmənt] *n* (*to post*) nomination *f*; (*job*) poste *m*; (*arrangement to meet*) rendez-vous *m*; **to have an** ~ avoir un rendez-vous; **to make an** ~ **(with)** prendre rendez-vous (avec); **I'd like to make an** ~ je voudrais prendre rendez-vous; **"~s (vacant)"** (*Press*) "offres d'emploi"; **by** ~ sur rendez-vous

**apportion** [ə'pɔːʃən] *vt* (*share out*) répartir, distribuer; **to** ~ **sth to sb** attribuer *or* assigner *or* allouer qch à qn

**appraisal** [ə'preɪzl] *n* évaluation *f*

**appraise** [ə'preɪz] *vt* (*value*) estimer; (*situation etc*) évaluer

**appreciable** [ə'priːʃəbl] *adj* appréciable

**appreciably** [ə'priːʃəblɪ] *adv* sensiblement, de façon appréciable

**appreciate** [ə'priːʃɪeɪt] *vt* (*like*) apprécier, faire cas de; (*be grateful for*) être reconnaissant(e) de; (*assess*) évaluer; (*be aware of*) comprendre, se rendre compte de ▷ *vi* (*Finance*) prendre de la valeur; **I** ~ **your help** je vous remercie pour votre aide

**appreciation** [əpriːʃɪ'eɪʃən] *n* appréciation *f*; (*gratitude*) reconnaissance *f*; (*Finance*) hausse *f*, valorisation *f*

**appreciative** [ə'priːʃɪətɪv] *adj* (*person*) sensible; (*comment*) élogieux(-euse)

**apprehend** [æprɪ'hɛnd] *vt* appréhender, arrêter; (*understand*) comprendre

**apprehension** [æprɪ'hɛnʃən] *n* appréhension *f*, inquiétude *f*

**apprehensive** [æprɪ'hɛnsɪv] *adj* inquiet(-ète), appréhensif(-ive)

**apprentice** [ə'prɛntɪs] *n* apprenti *m* ▷ *vt*: **to be ~d to** être en apprentissage chez

**apprenticeship** [ə'prɛntɪʃɪp] *n* apprentissage

*m*; **to serve one's** ~ faire son apprentissage

**appro.** ['æprəu] *abbr* (*Brit Comm: inf*) = **approval**

**approach** [ə'prəutʃ] *vi* approcher ▷ *vt* (*come near*) approcher de; (*ask, apply to*) s'adresser à; (*subject, passer-by*) aborder ▷ *n* approche *f*; accès *m*, abord *m*; démarche *f* (*auprès de qn*); démarche *f* (*intellectuelle*); **to** ~ **sb about sth** aller *or* venir voir qn pour qch

**approachable** [ə'prəutʃəbl] *adj* accessible

**approach road** *n* voie *f* d'accès

**approbation** [æprə'beɪʃən] *n* approbation *f*

**appropriate** *adj* [ə'prəuprɪɪt] (*tool etc*) qui convient, approprié(e); (*moment, remark*) opportun(e) ▷ *vt* [ə'prəuprɪeɪt] (*take*) s'approprier; (*allot*): **to** ~ **sth for** affecter qch à; ~ **for** *or* **to** approprié à; **it would not be** ~ **for me to comment** il ne me serait pas approprié de commenter

**appropriately** [ə'prəuprɪɪtlɪ] *adv* pertinemment, avec à-propos

**appropriation** [əprəuprɪ'eɪʃən] *n* dotation *f*, affectation *f*

**approval** [ə'pruːvəl] *n* approbation *f*; **to meet with sb's** ~ (*proposal etc*) recueillir l'assentiment de qn; **on** ~ (*Comm*) à l'examen

**approve** [ə'pruːv] *vt* approuver
▷ **approve of** *vt fus* (*thing*) approuver; (*person*): **they don't** ~ **of her** ils n'ont pas bonne opinion d'elle

**approved school** [ə'pruːvd-] *n* (*Brit*) centre *m* d'éducation surveillée

**approvingly** [ə'pruːvɪŋlɪ] *adv* d'un air approbateur

**approx.** *abbr* (= *approximately*) env

**approximate** [ə'prɒksɪmɪt] *adj* approximatif(-ive) ▷ *vt* [ə'prɒksɪmeɪt] se rapprocher de; être proche de

**approximately** [ə'prɒksɪmətlɪ] *adv* approximativement

**approximation** [əprɒksɪ'meɪʃən] *n* approximation *f*

**Apr.** *abbr* = **April**

**apr** *n abbr* (= *annual percentage rate*) taux (d'intérêt) annuel

**apricot** ['eɪprɪkɒt] *n* abricot *m*

**April** ['eɪprəl] *n* avril *m*; ~ **fool!** poisson d'avril!; *for phrases see also* **July**

**April Fools' Day** *n* le premier avril; *voir article*

> ⬤ **APRIL FOOLS' DAY**
> ⬤
> ⬤ *April Fools' Day* est le 1er avril, à l'occasion
> ⬤ duquel on fait des farces de toutes sortes. Les
> ⬤ victimes de ces farces sont les "April fools".
> ⬤ Traditionnellement, on n'est censé faire des
> ⬤ farces que jusqu'à midi.

**apron** ['eɪprən] *n* tablier *m*; (*Aviat*) aire *f* de stationnement

**apse** [æps] *n* (*Archit*) abside *f*

**APT** *n abbr* (*Brit*: = *advanced passenger train*) ≈ TGV *m*

**Apt.** *abbr* (= *apartment*) appt

**apt** [æpt] *adj* (*suitable*) approprié(e); (*able*): ~ **(at)** doué(e) (pour); apte (à); (*likely*): ~ **to do** susceptible de faire; ayant tendance à faire

**aptitude** ['æptɪtjuːd] *n* aptitude *f*

**aptitude test** *n* test *m* d'aptitude

**aptly** ['æptlɪ] *adv* (fort) à propos

**aqualung** ['ækwəlʌŋ] *n* scaphandre *m* autonome

**aquarium** [ə'kwɛərɪəm] *n* aquarium *m*

**Aquarius** [ə'kwɛərɪəs] *n* le Verseau; **to be ~** être du Verseau

**aquatic** [ə'kwætɪk] *adj* aquatique; (*sport*) nautique

**aqueduct** ['ækwɪdʌkt] *n* aqueduc *m*

**AR** *abbr* (*US*) = **Arkansas**

**ARA** *n abbr* (*Brit*) = **Associate of the Royal Academy**

**Arab** ['ærəb] *n* Arabe *m/f* ▷ *adj* arabe

**Arabia** [ə'reɪbɪə] *n* Arabie *f*

**Arabian** [ə'reɪbɪən] *adj* arabe

**Arabian Desert** *n* désert *m* d'Arabie

**Arabian Sea** *n* mer *f* d'Arabie

**Arabic** ['ærəbɪk] *adj, n* arabe (*m*)

**Arabic numerals** *npl* chiffres *mpl* arabes

**arable** ['ærəbl] *adj* arable

**ARAM** *n abbr* (*Brit*) = **Associate of the Royal Academy of Music**

**arbiter** ['aːbɪtəʳ] *n* arbitre *m*

**arbitrary** ['aːbɪtrərɪ] *adj* arbitraire

**arbitrate** ['aːbɪtreɪt] *vi* arbitrer; trancher

**arbitration** [aːbɪ'treɪʃən] *n* arbitrage *m*; **the dispute went to ~** le litige a été soumis à arbitrage

**arbitrator** ['aːbɪtreɪtəʳ] *n* arbitre *m*, médiateur(-trice)

**ARC** *n abbr* = **American Red Cross**

**arc** [aːk] *n* arc *m*

**arcade** [aː'keɪd] *n* arcade *f*; (*passage with shops*) passage *m*, galerie *f*; (*with games*) salle *f* de jeu

**arch** [aːtʃ] *n* arche *f*; (*of foot*) cambrure *f*, voûte *f* plantaire ▷ *vt* arquer, cambrer ▷ *adj* malicieux(-euse) ▷ *prefix*: ~(-) achevé(e); par excellence; **pointed ~** ogive *f*

**archaeological** [aːkɪə'lɔdʒɪkl] *adj* archéologique

**archaeologist** [aːkɪ'ɔlədʒɪst] *n* archéologue *m/f*

**archaeology**, (*US*) **archeology** [aːkɪ'ɔlədʒɪ] *n* archéologie *f*

**archaic** [aː'keɪɪk] *adj* archaïque

**archangel** ['aːkeɪndʒəl] *n* archange *m*

**archbishop** [aːtʃ'bɪʃəp] *n* archevêque *m*

**archenemy** ['aːtʃ'ɛnɪmɪ] *n* ennemi *m* de toujours *or* par excellence

**archeology** [aːkɪ'ɔlədʒɪ] (*US*) = **archaeology**

**archer** ['aːtʃəʳ] *n* archer *m*

**archery** ['aːtʃərɪ] *n* tir *m* à l'arc

**archetypal** ['aːkɪtaɪpəl] *adj* archétype

**archetype** ['aːkɪtaɪp] *n* prototype *m*, archétype *m*

**archipelago** [aːkɪ'pɛlɪgəu] *n* archipel *m*

**architect** ['aːkɪtɛkt] *n* architecte *m*

**architectural** [aːkɪ'tɛktʃərəl] *adj* architectural(e)

**architecture** ['aːkɪtɛktʃəʳ] *n* architecture *f*

**archive** ['aːkaɪv] *n* (*often pl*) archives *fpl*

**archive file** *n* (*Comput*) fichier *m* d'archives

**archives** ['aːkaɪvz] *npl* archives *fpl*

**archivist** ['aːkɪvɪst] *n* archiviste *m/f*

**archway** ['aːtʃweɪ] *n* voûte *f*, porche voûté *or* cintré

**ARCM** *n abbr* (*Brit*) = **Associate of the Royal College of Music**

**Arctic** ['aːktɪk] *adj* arctique ▷ *n*: **the ~** l'Arctique *m*

**Arctic Circle** *n* cercle *m* Arctique

**Arctic Ocean** *n* océan *m* Arctique

**ARD** *n abbr* (*US Med*) = **acute respiratory disease**

**ardent** ['aːdənt] *adj* fervent(e)

**ardour**, (*US*) **ardor** ['aːdəʳ] *n* ardeur *f*

**arduous** ['aːdjuəs] *adj* ardu(e)

**are** [aːʳ] *vb see* **be**

**area** ['ɛərɪə] *n* (*Geom*) superficie *f*; (*zone*) région *f*; (: *smaller*) secteur *m*; (*in room*) coin *m*; (*knowledge, research*) domaine *m*; **the London ~** la région Londonienne

**area code** (*US*) *n* (*Tel*) indicatif *m* de zone

**arena** [ə'riːnə] *n* arène *f*

**aren't** [aːnt] = **are not**

**Argentina** [aːdʒən'tiːnə] *n* Argentine *f*

**Argentinian** [aːdʒən'tɪnɪən] *adj* argentin(e) ▷ *n* Argentin(e)

**arguable** ['aːgjuəbl] *adj* discutable, contestable; **it is ~ whether** on peut se demander si

**arguably** ['aːgjuəblɪ] *adv*: **it is ~ ...** on peut soutenir que c'est ...

**argue** ['aːgjuː] *vi* (*quarrel*) se disputer; (*reason*) argumenter ▷ *vt* (*debate: case, matter*) débattre; **to ~ about sth (with sb)** se disputer (avec qn) au sujet de qch; **to ~ that** objecter *or* alléguer que, donner comme argument que

**argument** ['aːgjumənt] *n* (*quarrel*) dispute *f*, discussion *f*; (*reasons*) argument *m*; (*debate*) discussion, controverse *f*; **~ for/against** argument pour/contre

**argumentative** [aːgju'mɛntətɪv] *adj* ergoteur(-euse), raisonneur(-euse)

**aria** ['aːrɪə] *n* aria *f*

**ARIBA** [ə'riːbə] *n abbr* (*Brit*) = **Associate of the Royal Institute of British Architects**

**arid** ['ærɪd] *adj* aride

**aridity** [ə'rɪdɪtɪ] *n* aridité *f*

**Aries** ['ɛərɪz] *n* le Bélier; **to be ~** être du Bélier

**arise** (*pt* **arose**, *pp* **-n**) [ə'raɪz, ə'rəuz, ə'rɪzn] *vi* survenir, se présenter; **to ~ from** résulter de; **should the need ~** en cas de besoin

**aristocracy** [ærɪs'tɔkrəsɪ] *n* aristocratie *f*

**aristocrat** ['ærɪstəkræt] *n* aristocrate *m/f*

**aristocratic** [ærɪstə'krætɪk] *adj* aristocratique

**arithmetic** [ə'rɪθmətɪk] *n* arithmétique *f*

**arithmetical** [ærɪθ'mɛtɪkl] *adj* arithmétique

**Ariz.** *abbr* (*US*) = **Arizona**

**ark** [aːk] *n*: **Noah's A~** l'Arche *f* de Noé

**Ark.** *abbr* (*US*) = **Arkansas**

**arm** [ɑːm] *n* bras *m* ▷ *vt* armer; **arms** *npl*
(*weapons, Heraldry*) armes *fpl*; **~ in ~** bras dessus
bras dessous
**armaments** ['ɑːmənts] *npl* (*weapons*)
armement *m*
**armband** ['ɑːmbænd] *n* brassard *m*
**armchair** ['ɑːmtʃeəʳ] *n* fauteuil *m*
**armed** [ɑːmd] *adj* armé(e)
**armed forces** *npl*: **the ~** les forces armées
**armed robbery** *n* vol *m* à main armée
**Armenia** [ɑːˈmiːnɪə] *n* Arménie *f*
**Armenian** [ɑːˈmiːnɪən] *adj* arménien(ne) ▷ *n*
Arménien(ne); (*Ling*) arménien *m*
**armful** ['ɑːmful] *n* brassée *f*
**armistice** ['ɑːmɪstɪs] *n* armistice *m*
**armour**, (US) **armor** ['ɑːməʳ] *n* armure *f*; (*also*:
**armour-plating**) blindage *m*; (*Mil*: *tanks*)
blindés *mpl*
**armoured car**, (US) **armored car** ['ɑːməd-] *n*
véhicule blindé
**armoury**, (US) **armory** ['ɑːmərɪ] *n* arsenal *m*
**armpit** ['ɑːmpɪt] *n* aisselle *f*
**armrest** ['ɑːmrest] *n* accoudoir *m*
**arms control** *n* contrôle *m* des armements
**arms race** *n* course *f* aux armements
**army** ['ɑːmɪ] *n* armée *f*
**A road** *n* (*Brit*) ≈ route nationale
**aroma** [əˈrəumə] *n* arôme *m*
**aromatherapy** [ərəuməˈθerəpɪ] *n*
aromathérapie *f*
**aromatic** [ærəˈmætɪk] *adj* aromatique
**arose** [əˈrəuz] *pt of* **arise**
**around** [əˈraund] *adv* (tout) autour; (*nearby*)
dans les parages ▷ *prep* autour de; (*near*) près de;
(*fig*: *about*) environ; (*: date, time*) vers; **is he ~?** est-
il dans les parages or là?
**arousal** [əˈrauzəl] *n* (*sexual*) excitation sexuelle,
éveil *m*
**arouse** [əˈrauz] *vt* (*sleeper*) éveiller; (*curiosity,
passions*) éveiller, susciter; (*anger*) exciter
**arrange** [əˈreɪndʒ] *vt* arranger; (*programme*)
arrêter, convenir de ▷ *vi*: **we have ~d for a car
to pick you up** nous avons prévu qu'une
voiture vienne vous prendre; **it was ~d that ...**
il a été convenu que ..., il a été décidé que ...; **to
~ to do sth** prévoir de faire qch
**arrangement** [əˈreɪndʒmənt] *n* arrangement
*m*; **to come to an ~** (**with sb**) se mettre d'accord
(avec qn); **home deliveries by ~** livraison à
domicile sur demande; **arrangements** *npl*
(*plans etc*) arrangements *mpl*, dispositions *fpl*;
**I'll make ~s for you to be met** je vous enverrai
chercher
**arrant** ['ærənt] *adj*: **he's talking ~ nonsense** il
raconte vraiment n'importe quoi
**array** [əˈreɪ] *n* (*of objects*) déploiement *m*, étalage
*m*; (*Math, Comput*) tableau *m*
**arrears** [əˈrɪəz] *npl* arriéré *m*; **to be in ~ with
one's rent** devoir un arriéré de loyer, être en
retard pour le paiement de son loyer
**arrest** [əˈrest] *vt* arrêter; (*sb's attention*) retenir,
attirer ▷ *n* arrestation *f*; **under ~** en état

d'arrestation
**arresting** [əˈrestɪŋ] *adj* (*fig*: *beauty*) saisissant(e);
(*: charm, candour*) désarmant(e)
**arrival** [əˈraɪvl] *n* arrivée *f*; (*Comm*) arrivage *m*;
(*person*) arrivant(e); **new ~** nouveau venu/
nouvelle venue; (*baby*) nouveau-né(e)
**arrive** [əˈraɪv] *vi* arriver
▷ **arrive at** *vt fus* (*decision, solution*) parvenir à
**arrogance** ['ærəgəns] *n* arrogance *f*
**arrogant** ['ærəgənt] *adj* arrogant(e)
**arrow** ['ærəu] *n* flèche *f*
**arse** [ɑːs] *n* (*Brit inf!*) cul *m* (!)
**arsenal** ['ɑːsɪnl] *n* arsenal *m*
**arsenic** ['ɑːsnɪk] *n* arsenic *m*
**arson** ['ɑːsn] *n* incendie criminel
**art** [ɑːt] *n* art *m*; (*craft*) métier *m*; **work of ~**
œuvre *f* d'art; **Arts** *npl* (*Scol*) les lettres *fpl*
**art college** *n* école *f* des beaux-arts
**artefact** ['ɑːtɪfækt] *n* objet fabriqué
**arterial** [ɑːˈtɪərɪəl] *adj* (*Anat*) artériel(le); (*road
etc*) à grande circulation
**artery** ['ɑːtərɪ] *n* artère *f*
**artful** ['ɑːtful] *adj* rusé(e)
**art gallery** *n* musée *m* d'art; (*saleroom*) galerie *f*
de peinture
**arthritis** [ɑːˈθraɪtɪs] *n* arthrite *f*
**artichoke** ['ɑːtɪtʃəuk] *n* artichaut *m*; **Jerusalem
~** topinambour *m*
**article** ['ɑːtɪkl] *n* article *m*; (*Brit Law*: *training*):
**articles** *npl* ≈ stage *m*; **~s of clothing**
vêtements *mpl*
**articles of association** *npl* (*Comm*) statuts *mpl*
d'une société
**articulate** [*adj* ɑːˈtɪkjulɪt, *vb* ɑːˈtɪkjuleɪt] *adj*
(*person*) qui s'exprime clairement et aisément;
(*speech*) bien articulé(e), prononcé(e) clairement
▷ *vi* articuler, parler distinctement ▷ *vt*
articuler
**articulated lorry** [ɑːˈtɪkjuleɪtɪd-] *n* (*Brit*)
(camion *m*) semi-remorque *m*
**artifact** ['ɑːtɪfækt] *n* (US) objet fabriqué
**artifice** ['ɑːtɪfɪs] *n* ruse *f*
**artificial** [ɑːtɪˈfɪʃəl] *adj* artificiel(le)
**artificial insemination** [-ɪnsemɪˈneɪʃən] *n*
insémination artificielle
**artificial intelligence** *n* intelligence
artificielle
**artificial respiration** *n* respiration artificielle
**artillery** [ɑːˈtɪlərɪ] *n* artillerie *f*
**artisan** ['ɑːtɪzæn] *n* artisan(e)
**artist** ['ɑːtɪst] *n* artiste *m/f*
**artistic** [ɑːˈtɪstɪk] *adj* artistique
**artistry** ['ɑːtɪstrɪ] *n* art *m*, talent *m*
**artless** ['ɑːtlɪs] *adj* naïf (naïve), simple,
ingénu(e)
**arts** [ɑːts] *npl* (*Scol*) lettres *fpl*
**art school** *n* ≈ école *f* des beaux-arts
**artwork** ['ɑːtwəːk] *n* maquette *f* (*prête pour la
photogravure*)
**ARV** *n abbr* (= *American Revised Version*) traduction
américaine de la Bible
**AS** *n abbr* (*US Scol*: = *Associate in/of Science*) diplôme

universitaire ▷ abbr (US) = **American Samoa**

 KEYWORD

**as** [æz] conj **1** (time: moment) comme, alors que; à mesure que; (: duration) tandis que; **he came in as I was leaving** il est arrivé comme je partais; **as the years went by** à mesure que les années passaient; **as from tomorrow** à partir de demain

**2** (since, because) comme, puisque; **he left early as he had to be home by 10** comme il or puisqu'il devait être de retour avant 10h, il est parti de bonne heure

**3** (referring to manner, way) comme; **do as you wish** faites comme vous voudrez; **as she said** comme elle disait

▷ adv **1** (in comparisons): **as big as** aussi grand que; **twice as big as** deux fois plus grand que; **big as it is** si grand que ce soit; **much as I like them, I ...** je les aime bien, mais je ...; **as much** or **many as** autant que; **as much money/many books as** autant d'argent/de livres que; **as soon as** dès que

**2** (concerning): **as for** or **to that** quant à cela, pour ce qui est de cela

**3**: **as if** or **though** comme si; **he looked as if he was ill** il avait l'air d'être malade; see also **long**; **such**; **well**

▷ prep (in the capacity of) en tant que, en qualité de; **he works as a driver** il travaille comme chauffeur; **as chairman of the company, he ...** en tant que président de la société, il ...; **dressed up as a cowboy** déguisé en cowboy; **he gave me it as a present** il me l'a offert, il m'en a fait cadeau

**ASA** n abbr (= American Standards Association) association de normalisation
**a.s.a.p.** abbr = **as soon as possible**
**asbestos** [æz'bɛstəs] n asbeste m, amiante m
**ascend** [ə'sɛnd] vt gravir
**ascendancy** [ə'sɛndənsɪ] n ascendant m
**ascendant** [ə'sɛndənt] n: **to be in the ~** monter
**ascension** [ə'sɛnʃən] n: **the A~** (Rel) l'Ascension f
**Ascension Island** n île f de l'Ascension
**ascent** [ə'sɛnt] n (climb) ascension f
**ascertain** [æsə'teɪn] vt s'assurer de, vérifier; établir
**ascetic** [ə'sɛtɪk] adj ascétique
**asceticism** [ə'sɛtɪsɪzəm] n ascétisme m
**ASCII** ['æskiː] n abbr (= American Standard Code for Information Interchange) ASCII
**ascribe** [ə'skraɪb] vt: **to ~ sth to** attribuer qch à; (blame) imputer qch à
**ASCU** n abbr (US) = **Association of State Colleges and Universities**
**ASE** n abbr = **American Stock Exchange**
**ASH** [æʃ] n abbr (Brit: = Action on Smoking and Health) ligue anti-tabac
**ash** [æʃ] n (dust) cendre f; (also: **ash tree**) frêne m
**ashamed** [ə'feɪmd] adj honteux(-euse),

confus(e); **to be ~ of** avoir honte de; **to be ~ (of o.s.) for having done** avoir honte d'avoir fait
**ashen** ['æʃən] adj (pale) cendreux(-euse), blême
**ashore** [ə'ʃɔːʳ] adv à terre; **to go ~** aller à terre, débarquer
**ashtray** ['æʃtreɪ] n cendrier m
**Ash Wednesday** n mercredi m des Cendres
**Asia** ['eɪʃə] n Asie f
**Asia Minor** n Asie Mineure
**Asian** ['eɪʃən] n (from Asia) Asiatique m/f; (Brit: from Indian subcontinent) Indo-Pakistanais(-e) ▷ adj asiatique; indo-pakistanais(-e)
**Asiatic** [eɪsɪ'ætɪk] adj asiatique
**aside** [ə'saɪd] adv de côté; à l'écart ▷ n aparté m; **~ from** prep à part, excepté
**ask** [ɑːsk] vt demander; (invite) inviter; **to ~ sb sth/to do sth** demander à qn qch/de faire qch; **to ~ sb the time** demander l'heure à qn; **to ~ sb about sth** questionner qn au sujet de qch; se renseigner auprès de qn au sujet de qch; **to ~ about the price** s'informer du prix, se renseigner au sujet du prix; **to ~ (sb) a question** poser une question (à qn); **to ~ sb out to dinner** inviter qn au restaurant
▶ **ask after** vt fus demander des nouvelles de
▶ **ask for** vt fus demander; **it's just ~ing for trouble** or **for it** ce serait chercher des ennuis
**askance** [ə'skɑːns] adv: **to look ~ at sb** regarder qn de travers or d'un œil désapprobateur
**askew** [ə'skjuː] adv de travers, de guingois
**asking price** ['ɑːskɪŋ-] n prix demandé
**asleep** [ə'sliːp] adj endormi(e); **to be ~** dormir, être endormi; **to fall ~** s'endormir
**ASLEF** ['æzlɛf] n abbr (Brit: = Associated Society of Locomotive Engineers and Firemen) syndicat de cheminots
**AS level** n abbr (= Advanced Subsidiary level) première partie de l'examen équivalent au baccalauréat
**asp** [æsp] n aspic m
**asparagus** [əs'pærəgəs] n asperges fpl
**asparagus tips** npl pointes fpl d'asperges
**ASPCA** n abbr (= American Society for the Prevention of Cruelty to Animals) ≈ SPA f
**aspect** ['æspɛkt] n aspect m; (direction in which a building etc faces) orientation f, exposition f
**aspersions** [əs'pəːʃənz] npl: **to cast ~ on** dénigrer
**asphalt** ['æsfælt] n asphalte m
**asphyxiate** [æs'fɪksɪeɪt] vt asphyxier
**asphyxiation** [æsfɪksɪ'eɪʃən] n asphyxie f
**aspiration** [æspə'reɪʃən] n aspiration f
**aspire** [əs'paɪəʳ] vi: **to ~ to** aspirer à
**aspirin** ['æsprɪn] n aspirine f
**aspiring** [əs'paɪərɪŋ] adj (artist, writer) en herbe; (manager) potentiel(le)
**ass** [æs] n âne m; (inf) imbécile m/f; (US inf!) cul m (!)
**assail** [ə'seɪl] vt assaillir
**assailant** [ə'seɪlənt] n agresseur m; assaillant m
**assassin** [ə'sæsɪn] n assassin m
**assassinate** [ə'sæsɪneɪt] vt assassiner

**assassination** [əsæsɪˈneɪʃən] n assassinat m
**assault** [əˈsɔːlt] n (Mil) assaut m; (gen: attack) agression f; (Law): ~ **(and battery)** voies fpl de fait, coups mpl et blessures fpl ▷ vt attaquer; (sexually) violenter
**assemble** [əˈsɛmbl] vt assembler ▷ vi s'assembler, se rassembler
**assembly** [əˈsɛmblɪ] n (meeting) rassemblement m; (parliament) assemblée f; (construction) assemblage m
**assembly language** n (Comput) langage m d'assemblage
**assembly line** n chaîne f de montage
**assent** [əˈsɛnt] n assentiment m, consentement m ▷ vi: **to ~ (to sth)** donner son assentiment (à qch), consentir (à qch)
**assert** [əˈsəːt] vt affirmer, déclarer; établir; (authority) faire valoir; (innocence) protester de; **to ~ o.s.** s'imposer
**assertion** [əˈsəːʃən] n assertion f, affirmation f
**assertive** [əˈsəːtɪv] adj assuré(e); péremptoire
**assess** [əˈsɛs] vt évaluer, estimer; (tax, damages) établir or fixer le montant de; (property etc: for tax) calculer la valeur imposable de; (person) juger la valeur de
**assessment** [əˈsɛsmənt] n évaluation f, estimation f; (of tax) fixation f; (of property) calcul m de la valeur imposable; (judgment): ~ **(of)** jugement m or opinion f (sur)
**assessor** [əˈsɛsəʳ] n expert m (en matière d'impôt et d'assurance)
**asset** [ˈæsɛt] n avantage m, atout m; (person) atout; **assets** npl (Comm) capital m; avoir(s) m(pl); actif m
**asset-stripping** [ˈæsɛtˈstrɪpɪŋ] n (Comm) récupération f (et démantèlement m) d'une entreprise en difficulté
**assiduous** [əˈsɪdjuəs] adj assidu(e)
**assign** [əˈsaɪn] vt (date) fixer, arrêter; **to ~ sth to** (task) assigner qch à; (resources) affecter qch à; (cause, meaning) attribuer qch à
**assignment** [əˈsaɪnmənt] n (task) mission f; (homework) devoir m
**assimilate** [əˈsɪmɪleɪt] vt assimiler
**assimilation** [əsɪmɪˈleɪʃən] n assimilation f
**assist** [əˈsɪst] vt aider, assister; (injured person etc) secourir
**assistance** [əˈsɪstəns] n aide f, assistance f; secours mpl
**assistant** [əˈsɪstənt] n assistant(e), adjoint(e); (Brit: also: **shop assistant**) vendeur(-euse)
**assistant manager** n sous-directeur m
**assizes** [əˈsaɪzɪz] npl assises fpl
**associate** [adj, n əˈsəʊʃiːt, vb əˈsəʊʃɪeɪt] adj, n associé(e) ▷ vt associer ▷ vi: **to ~ with sb** fréquenter qn; ~ **director** directeur adjoint; ~**d company** société affiliée
**association** [əsəʊsɪˈeɪʃən] n association f; **in ~ with** en collaboration avec
**association football** n (Brit) football m
**assorted** [əˈsɔːtɪd] adj assorti(e); **in ~ sizes** en plusieurs tailles

**assortment** [əˈsɔːtmənt] n assortiment m; (of people) mélange m
**Asst.** abbr = **assistant**
**assuage** [əˈsweɪdʒ] vt (grief, pain) soulager; (thirst, appetite) assouvir
**assume** [əˈsjuːm] vt supposer; (responsibilities etc) assumer; (attitude, name) prendre, adopter
**assumed name** [əˈsjuːmd-] n nom m d'emprunt
**assumption** [əˈsʌmpʃən] n supposition f, hypothèse f; (of power) assomption f, prise f; **on the ~ that** dans l'hypothèse où; (on condition that) à condition que
**assurance** [əˈʃuərəns] n assurance f; **I can give you no ~s** je ne peux rien vous garantir
**assure** [əˈʃuəʳ] vt assurer
**assured** [əˈʃuəd] adj assuré(e)
**AST** abbr (US: = Atlantic Standard Time) heure d'hiver de New York
**asterisk** [ˈæstərɪsk] n astérisque m
**astern** [əˈstəːn] adv à l'arrière
**asteroid** [ˈæstərɔɪd] n astéroïde m
**asthma** [ˈæsmə] n asthme m
**asthmatic** [æsˈmætɪk] adj, n asthmatique m/f
**astigmatism** [əˈstɪgmətɪzəm] n astigmatisme m
**astir** [əˈstəːʳ] adv en émoi
**astonish** [əˈstɔnɪʃ] vt étonner, stupéfier
**astonished** [əˈstɔnɪʃd] adj étonné(e); **to be ~ at** être étonné(e) de
**astonishing** [əˈstɔnɪʃɪŋ] adj étonnant(e), stupéfiant(e); **I find it ~ that ...** je trouve incroyable que ... + sub
**astonishingly** [əˈstɔnɪʃɪŋlɪ] adv incroyablement
**astonishment** [əˈstɔnɪʃmənt] n (grand) étonnement m, stupéfaction f
**astound** [əˈstaund] vt stupéfier, sidérer
**astray** [əˈstreɪ] adv: **to go ~** s'égarer; (fig) quitter le droit chemin; **to lead ~** (morally) détourner du droit chemin; **to go ~ in one's calculations** faire fausse route dans ses calculs
**astride** [əˈstraɪd] adv à cheval ▷ prep à cheval sur
**astringent** [əsˈtrɪndʒənt] adj astringent(e) ▷ n astringent m
**astrologer** [əsˈtrɔlədʒəʳ] n astrologue m
**astrology** [əsˈtrɔlədʒɪ] n astrologie f
**astronaut** [ˈæstrənɔːt] n astronaute m/f
**astronomer** [əsˈtrɔnəməʳ] n astronome m
**astronomical** [æstrəˈnɔmɪkl] adj astronomique
**astronomy** [əsˈtrɔnəmɪ] n astronomie f
**astrophysics** [ˈæstrəuˈfɪzɪks] n astrophysique f
**astute** [əsˈtjuːt] adj astucieux(-euse), malin(-igne)
**asunder** [əˈsʌndəʳ] adv: **to tear ~** déchirer
**ASV** n abbr (= American Standard Version) traduction de la Bible
**asylum** [əˈsaɪləm] n asile m; **to seek political ~** demander l'asile politique
**asylum seeker** [-siːkəʳ] n demandeur(-euse) d'asile
**asymmetric** [eɪsɪˈmɛtrɪk], **asymmetrical**

[eɪsɪ'mɛtrɪkl] *adj* asymétrique

**O** KEYWORD

**at** [æt] *prep* **1** (*referring to position, direction*) à; **at the top** au sommet; **at home/school** à la maison *or* chez soi/à l'école; **at the baker's** à la boulangerie, chez le boulanger; **to look at sth** regarder qch
**2** (*referring to time*): **at 4 o'clock** à 4 heures; **at Christmas** à Noël; **at night** la nuit; **at times** par moments, parfois
**3** (*referring to rates, speed etc*) à; **at £1 a kilo** une livre le kilo; **two at a time** deux à la fois; **at 50 km/h** à 50 km/h; **at full speed** à toute vitesse
**4** (*referring to manner*): **at a stroke** d'un seul coup; **at peace** en paix
**5** (*referring to activity*): **to be at work** (*in the office etc*) être au travail; (*working*) travailler; **to play at cowboys** jouer aux cowboys; **to be good at sth** être bon en qch
**6** (*referring to cause*): **shocked/surprised/annoyed at sth** choqué par/étonné de/agacé par qch; **I went at his suggestion** j'y suis allé sur son conseil
**7** (@ *symbol*) arobase *f*

**ate** [eɪt] *pt of* **eat**
**atheism** ['eɪθɪɪzəm] *n* athéisme *m*
**atheist** ['eɪθɪɪst] *n* athée *m/f*
**Athenian** [ə'θiːnɪən] *adj* athénien(ne) ▷ *n* Athénien(ne)
**Athens** ['æθɪnz] *n* Athènes
**athlete** ['æθliːt] *n* athlète *m/f*
**athletic** [æθ'lɛtɪk] *adj* athlétique
**athletics** [æθ'lɛtɪks] *n* athlétisme *m*
**Atlantic** [ət'læntɪk] *adj* atlantique ▷ *n*: **the ~ (Ocean)** l'(océan *m*) Atlantique *m*
**atlas** ['ætləs] *n* atlas *m*
**Atlas Mountains** *npl*: **the ~** les monts *mpl* de l'Atlas, l'Atlas *m*
**A.T.M.** *n abbr* (= *Automated Telling Machine*) guichet *m* automatique
**atmosphere** ['ætməsfɪər] *n* (*air*) atmosphère *f*; (*fig: of place etc*) atmosphère, ambiance *f*
**atmospheric** [ætməs'fɛrɪk] *adj* atmosphérique
**atmospherics** [ætməs'fɛrɪks] *n* (*Radio*) parasites *mpl*
**atoll** ['ætɔl] *n* atoll *m*
**atom** ['ætəm] *n* atome *m*
**atom bomb** *n* bombe *f* atomique
**atomic** [ə'tɔmɪk] *adj* atomique
**atomic bomb** *n* bombe *f* atomique
**atomizer** ['ætəmaɪzər] *n* atomiseur *m*
**atone** [ə'təun] *vi*: **to ~ for** expier, racheter
**atonement** [ə'təunmənt] *n* expiation *f*
**ATP** *n abbr* (= *Association of Tennis Professionals*) ATP *f* (= *Association des tennismen professionnels*)
**atrocious** [ə'trəuʃəs] *adj* (*very bad*) atroce, exécrable
**atrocity** [ə'trɔsɪtɪ] *n* atrocité *f*
**atrophy** ['ætrəfɪ] *n* atrophie *f* ▷ *vt* atrophier ▷ *vi*

s'atrophier

**attach** [ə'tætʃ] *vt* (*gen*) attacher; (*document, letter, to email*) joindre; (*employee, troops*) affecter; **to be ~ed to sb/sth** (*to like*) être attaché à qn/qch; **the ~ed letter** la lettre ci-jointe
**attaché** [ə'tæʃeɪ] *n* attaché *m*
**attaché case** *n* mallette *f*, attaché-case *m*
**attachment** [ə'tætʃmənt] *n* (*tool*) accessoire *m*; (*Comput*) fichier *m* joint; (*love*): **~ (to)** affection *f* (pour), attachement *m* (à)
**attack** [ə'tæk] *vt* attaquer; (*task etc*) s'attaquer à ▷ *n* attaque *f*; **heart ~** crise *f* cardiaque
**attacker** [ə'tækər] *n* attaquant *m*; agresseur *m*
**attain** [ə'teɪn] *vt* (*also*: **to attain to**) parvenir à, atteindre; (*knowledge*) acquérir
**attainments** [ə'teɪnmənts] *npl* connaissances *fpl*, résultats *mpl*
**attempt** [ə'tɛmpt] *n* tentative *f* ▷ *vt* essayer, tenter; **~ed theft** *etc* (*Law*) tentative de vol *etc*; **to make an ~ on sb's life** attenter à la vie de qn; **he made no ~ to help** il n'a rien fait pour m'aider *or* l'aider *etc*
**attempted** [ə'tɛmptɪd] *adj*: **~ murder/suicide** tentative *f* de meurtre/suicide
**attend** [ə'tɛnd] *vt* (*course*) suivre; (*meeting, talk*) assister à; (*school, church*) aller à, fréquenter; (*patient*) soigner, s'occuper de; **to ~ (up)on** servir; être au service de
▷ **attend to** *vt fus* (*needs, affairs etc*) s'occuper de; (*customer*) s'occuper de, servir
**attendance** [ə'tɛndəns] *n* (*being present*) présence *f*; (*people present*) assistance *f*
**attendant** [ə'tɛndənt] *n* employé(e); gardien(ne) ▷ *adj* concomitant(e), qui accompagne *or* s'ensuit
**attention** [ə'tɛnʃən] *n* attention *f*; **attentions** attentions *fpl*, prévenances *fpl* ▷ *excl* (*Mil*) garde-à-vous!; **at ~** (*Mil*) au garde-à-vous; **for the ~ of** (*Admin*) à l'attention de; **it has come to my ~ that ...** je constate que ...
**attentive** [ə'tɛntɪv] *adj* attentif(-ive); (*kind*) prévenant(e)
**attentively** [ə'tɛntɪvlɪ] *adv* attentivement, avec attention
**attenuate** [ə'tɛnjueɪt] *vt* atténuer ▷ *vi* s'atténuer
**attest** [ə'tɛst] *vi*: **to ~ to** témoigner de attester (de)
**attic** ['ætɪk] *n* grenier *m*, combles *mpl*
**attire** [ə'taɪər] *n* habit *m*, atours *mpl*
**attitude** ['ætɪtjuːd] *n* (*behaviour*) attitude *f*, manière *f*; (*posture*) pose *f*, attitude; (*view*): **~ (to)** attitude (envers)
**attorney** [ə'təːnɪ] *n* (*US: lawyer*) avocat *m*; (*having proxy*) mandataire *m*; **power of ~** procuration *f*
**Attorney General** *n* (*Brit*) ≈ procureur général; (*US*) ≈ garde *m* des Sceaux, ministre *m* de la Justice
**attract** [ə'trækt] *vt* attirer
**attraction** [ə'trækʃən] *n* (*gen pl: pleasant things*) attraction *f*, attrait *m*; (*Physics*) attraction; (*fig: towards sb, sth*) attirance *f*

**attractive** [ə'træktɪv] *adj* séduisant(e), attrayant(e)
**attribute** ['ætrɪbjuːt] *n* attribut *m* ▷ *vt* [ə'trɪbjuːt]: **to ~ sth to** attribuer qch à
**attrition** [ə'trɪʃən] *n*: **war of ~** guerre *f* d'usure
**Atty. Gen.** *abbr* = **Attorney General**
**ATV** *n abbr* (= *all terrain vehicle*) véhicule *m* tout-terrain
**atypical** [eɪ'tɪpɪkl] *adj* atypique
**aubergine** ['əubəʒiːn] *n* aubergine *f*
**auburn** ['ɔːbən] *adj* auburn *inv*, châtain roux *inv*
**auction** ['ɔːkʃən] *n* (*also*: **sale by auction**) vente *f* aux enchères ▷ *vt* (*also*: **to sell by auction**) vendre aux enchères; (*also*: **to put up for auction**) mettre aux enchères
**auctioneer** [ɔːkʃə'nɪər] *n* commissaire-priseur *m*
**auction room** *n* salle *f* des ventes
**audacious** [ɔː'deɪʃəs] *adj* impudent(e); audacieux(-euse), intrépide
**audacity** [ɔː'dæsɪtɪ] *n* impudence *f*; audace *f*
**audible** ['ɔːdɪbl] *adj* audible
**audience** ['ɔːdɪəns] *n* (*people*) assistance *f*, public *m*; (*on radio*) auditeurs *mpl*; (*at theatre*) spectateurs *mpl*; (*interview*) audience *f*
**audiovisual** [ɔːdɪəu'vɪzjuəl] *adj* audio-visuel(le); **~ aids** supports *or* moyens audiovisuels
**audit** ['ɔːdɪt] *n* vérification *f* des comptes, apurement *m* ▷ *vt* vérifier, apurer
**audition** [ɔː'dɪʃən] *n* audition *f* ▷ *vi* auditionner
**auditor** ['ɔːdɪtər] *n* vérificateur *m* des comptes
**auditorium** [ɔːdɪ'tɔːrɪəm] *n* auditorium *m*, salle *f* de concert *or* de spectacle
**Aug.** *abbr* = **August**
**augment** [ɔːg'mɛnt] *vt*, *vi* augmenter
**augur** ['ɔːgər] *vt* (*be a sign of*) présager, annoncer ▷ *vi*: **it ~s well** c'est bon signe *or* de bon augure, cela s'annonce bien
**August** ['ɔːgəst] *n* août *m*; *for phrases see also* **July**
**august** [ɔː'gʌst] *adj* majestueux(-euse), imposant(e)
**aunt** [ɑːnt] *n* tante *f*
**auntie, aunty** ['ɑːntɪ] *n diminutive of* **aunt**
**au pair** ['əu'pɛər] *n* (*also*: **au pair girl**) jeune fille *f* au pair
**aura** ['ɔːrə] *n* atmosphère *f*; (*of person*) aura *f*
**auspices** ['ɔːspɪsɪz] *npl*: **under the ~ of** sous les auspices de
**auspicious** [ɔːs'pɪʃəs] *adj* de bon augure, propice
**austere** [ɔs'tɪər] *adj* austère
**austerity** [ɔs'tɛrɪtɪ] *n* austérité *f*
**Australasia** [ɔːstrə'leɪzɪə] *n* Australasie *f*
**Australia** [ɔs'treɪlɪə] *n* Australie *f*
**Australian** [ɔs'treɪlɪən] *adj* australien(ne) ▷ *n* Australien(ne)
**Austria** ['ɔstrɪə] *n* Autriche *f*
**Austrian** ['ɔstrɪən] *adj* autrichien(ne) ▷ *n* Autrichien(ne)
**AUT** *n abbr* (*Brit*: = *Association of University Teachers*) syndicat universitaire
**authentic** [ɔː'θɛntɪk] *adj* authentique

**authenticate** [ɔː'θɛntɪkeɪt] *vt* établir l'authenticité de
**authenticity** [ɔːθɛn'tɪsɪtɪ] *n* authenticité *f*
**author** ['ɔːθər] *n* auteur *m*
**authoritarian** [ɔːθɔrɪ'tɛərɪən] *adj* autoritaire
**authoritative** [ɔː'θɔrɪtətɪv] *adj* (*account*) digne de foi; (*study, treatise*) qui fait autorité; (*manner*) autoritaire
**authority** [ɔː'θɔrɪtɪ] *n* autorité *f*; (*permission*) autorisation (formelle); **the authorities** les autorités *fpl*, l'administration *f*; **to have ~ to do sth** être habilité à faire qch
**authorization** [ɔːθəraɪ'zeɪʃən] *n* autorisation *f*
**authorize** ['ɔːθəraɪz] *vt* autoriser
**authorized capital** ['ɔːθəraɪzd-] *n* (*Comm*) capital social
**authorship** ['ɔːθəʃɪp] *n* paternité *f* (*littéraire etc*)
**autistic** [ɔː'tɪstɪk] *adj* autistique
**auto** ['ɔːtəu] *n* (*US*) auto *f*, voiture *f*
**autobiography** [ɔːtəbaɪ'ɔgrəfɪ] *n* autobiographie *f*
**autocratic** [ɔːtə'krætɪk] *adj* autocratique
**autograph** ['ɔːtəgrɑːf] *n* autographe *m* ▷ *vt* signer, dédicacer
**autoimmune** [ɔːtəʊɪ'mjuːn] *adj* auto-immune
**automat** ['ɔːtəmæt] *n* (*vending machine*) distributeur *m* (automatique); (*US*: *place*) cafétéria *f* avec distributeurs automatiques
**automated** ['ɔːtəmeɪtɪd] *adj* automatisé(e)
**automatic** [ɔːtə'mætɪk] *adj* automatique ▷ *n* (*gun*) automatique *m*; (*washing machine*) lave-linge *m* automatique; (*car*) voiture *f* à transmission automatique
**automatically** [ɔːtə'mætɪklɪ] *adv* automatiquement
**automatic data processing** *n* traitement *m* automatique des données
**automation** [ɔːtə'meɪʃən] *n* automatisation *f*
**automaton** (*pl* **automata**) [ɔː'tɔmətən, -tə] *n* automate *m*
**automobile** ['ɔːtəməbiːl] *n* (*US*) automobile *f*
**autonomous** [ɔː'tɔnəməs] *adj* autonome
**autonomy** [ɔː'tɔnəmɪ] *n* autonomie *f*
**autopsy** ['ɔːtɔpsɪ] *n* autopsie *f*
**autumn** ['ɔːtəm] *n* automne *m*
**auxiliary** [ɔːg'zɪlɪərɪ] *adj*, *n* auxiliaire (*m/f*)
**AV** *n abbr* (= *Authorized Version*) traduction anglaise de la Bible ▷ *abbr* = **audiovisual**
**Av.** *abbr* (= *avenue*) Av
**avail** [ə'veɪl] *vt*: **to ~ o.s. of** user de; profiter de ▷ *n*: **to no ~** sans résultat, en vain, en pure perte
**availability** [əveɪlə'bɪlɪtɪ] *n* disponibilité *f*
**available** [ə'veɪləbl] *adj* disponible; **every ~ means** tous les moyens possibles *or* à sa (*or* notre *etc*) disposition; **is the manager ~?** est-ce que le directeur peut (me) recevoir?; (*on phone*) pourrais-je parler au directeur?; **to make sth ~ to sb** mettre qch à la disposition de qn
**avalanche** ['ævəlɑːnʃ] *n* avalanche *f*
**avant-garde** ['ævãɲ'gɑːd] *adj* d'avant-garde
**avaricious** [ævə'rɪʃəs] *adj* âpre au gain
**avdp.** *abbr* = **avoirdupois**

467

**Ave.** *abbr* = **avenue**
**avenge** [ə'vɛndʒ] *vt* venger
**avenue** ['ævənju:] *n* avenue *f*; *(fig)* moyen *m*
**average** ['ævərɪdʒ] *n* moyenne *f* ▷ *adj*
moyen(ne) ▷ *vt* (*a certain figure*) atteindre *or* faire
*etc* en moyenne; **on ~** en moyenne; **above/
below (the) ~** au-dessus/en-dessous de la
moyenne
  ▶ **average out** *vi*: **to ~ out at** représenter en
  moyenne, donner une moyenne de
**averse** [ə'və:s] *adj*: **to be ~ to sth/doing**
éprouver une forte répugnance envers qch/à
faire; **I wouldn't be ~ to a drink** un petit verre
ne serait pas de refus, je ne dirais pas non à un
petit verre
**aversion** [ə'və:ʃən] *n* aversion *f*, répugnance *f*
**avert** [ə'və:t] *vt* (*danger*) prévenir, écarter; (*one's
eyes*) détourner
**aviary** ['eɪvɪərɪ] *n* volière *f*
**aviation** [eɪvɪ'eɪʃən] *n* aviation *f*
**avid** ['ævɪd] *adj* avide
**avidly** ['ævɪdlɪ] *adv* avidement, avec avidité
**avocado** [ævə'kɑ:dəu] *n* (*Brit: also:* **avocado
pear**) avocat *m*
**avoid** [ə'vɔɪd] *vt* éviter
**avoidable** [ə'vɔɪdəbl] *adj* évitable
**avoidance** [ə'vɔɪdəns] *n* le fait d'éviter
**avowed** [ə'vaud] *adj* déclaré(e)
**AVP** *n abbr* (US) = **assistant vice-president**
**AWACS** ['eɪwæks] *n abbr* (= *airborne warning and
control system*) AWACS (*système aéroporté d'alerte et de
contrôle*)
**await** [ə'weɪt] *vt* attendre; **~ing attention/
delivery** (*Comm*) en souffrance; **long ~ed** tant
attendu(e)
**awake** [ə'weɪk] (*pt* **awoke**) [ə'wəuk] (*pp* **awoken**)
[ə'wəukən] *adj* éveillé(e); *(fig)* en éveil ▷ *vt*
éveiller ▷ *vi* s'éveiller; **~ to** conscient de; **to be
~ être** réveillé(e); **he was still ~** il ne dormait
pas encore
**awakening** [ə'weɪknɪŋ] *n* réveil *m*
**award** [ə'wɔ:d] *n* (*for bravery*) récompense *f*; (*prize*)
prix *m*; (*Law: damages*) dommages-intérêts *mpl*
▷ *vt* (*prize*) décerner; (*Law: damages*) accorder
**aware** [ə'wɛə'] *adj*: **~ of** (*conscious*) conscient(e)
de; (*informed*) au courant de; **to become ~ of/
that** prendre conscience de/que; se rendre
compte de/que; **politically/socially ~**
sensibilisé(e) aux *or* ayant pris conscience des
problèmes politiques/sociaux; **I am fully ~
that** je me rends parfaitement compte que
**awareness** [ə'wɛənɪs] *n* conscience *f*,
connaissance *f*; **to develop people's ~ (of)**
sensibiliser le public (à)
**awash** [ə'wɔʃ] *adj* recouvert(e) (d'eau); **~ with**
inondé(e) de
**away** [ə'weɪ] *adv* (au) loin; (*movement*): **she went
~** elle est partie ▷ *adj* (*not in, not here*) absent(e);
**far ~** (au) loin; **two kilometres ~** à (une

distance de) deux kilomètres, à deux
kilomètres de distance; **two hours ~ by car** à
deux heures de voiture *or* de route; **the holiday
was two weeks ~** il restait deux semaines
jusqu'aux vacances; **~ from** loin de; **he's ~ for
a week** il est parti (pour) une semaine; **he's ~
in Milan** il est (parti) à Milan; **to take sth ~
from sb** prendre qch à qn; **to take sth ~ from
sth** (*subtract*) ôter qch de qch; **to work/pedal ~**
travailler/pédaler à cœur joie; **to fade ~** (*colour*)
s'estomper; (*sound*) s'affaiblir
**away game** *n* (*Sport*) match *m* à l'extérieur
**awe** [ɔ:] *n* respect mêlé de crainte, effroi mêlé
d'admiration
**awe-inspiring** ['ɔ:ɪnspaɪərɪŋ], **awesome**
['ɔ:səm] *adj* impressionnant(e)
**awesome** ['ɔ:səm] (US) *adj* (*inf: excellent*)
génial(e)
**awestruck** ['ɔ:strʌk] *adj* frappé(e) d'effroi
**awful** ['ɔ:fəl] *adj* affreux(-euse); **an ~ lot of**
énormément de
**awfully** ['ɔ:fəlɪ] *adv* (*very*) terriblement,
vraiment
**awhile** [ə'waɪl] *adv* un moment, quelque temps
**awkward** ['ɔ:kwəd] *adj* (*clumsy*) gauche,
maladroit(e); (*inconvenient*) peu pratique;
(*embarrassing*) gênant; **I can't talk just now,
it's a bit ~** je ne peux pas parler tout de suite,
c'est un peu difficile
**awkwardness** ['ɔ:kwədnɪs] *n* (*embarrassment*)
gêne *f*
**awl** [ɔ:l] *n* alêne *f*
**awning** ['ɔ:nɪŋ] *n* (*of tent*) auvent *m*; (*of shop*)
store *m*; (*of hotel etc*) marquise *f* (de toile)
**awoke** [ə'wəuk] *pt of* **awake**
**awoken** [ə'wəukən] *pp of* **awake**
**AWOL** ['eɪwɔl] *abbr* (*Mil*) = **absent without leave**
**awry** [ə'raɪ] *adv, adj* de travers; **to go ~** mal
tourner
**axe**, (US) **ax** [æks] *n* hache *f* ▷ *vt* (*employee*)
renvoyer; (*project etc*) abandonner; (*jobs*)
supprimer; **to have an ~ to grind** (*fig*) prêcher
pour son saint
**axes** ['æksi:z] *npl of* **axis**
**axiom** ['æksɪəm] *n* axiome *m*
**axiomatic** [æksɪəu'mætɪk] *adj* axiomatique
**axis** (*pl* **axes**) ['æksɪs, -si:z] *n* axe *m*
**axle** ['æksl] *n* (*also:* **axle-tree**) essieu *m*
**ay, aye** [aɪ] *excl* (*yes*) oui ▷ *n*: **the ay(e)s** les oui
**AYH** *n abbr* = **American Youth Hostels**
**AZ** *abbr* (US) = **Arizona**
**azalea** [ə'zeɪlɪə] *n* azalée *f*
**Azerbaijan** [æzəbaɪ'dʒɑ:n] *n* Azerbaïdjan *m*
**Azerbaijani, Azeri** [æzəbaɪ'dʒɑ:nɪ, ə'zɛərɪ] *adj*
azerbaïdjanais(e) ▷ *n* Azerbaïdjanais(e)
**Azores** [ə'zɔ:z] *npl*: **the ~** les Açores *fpl*
**AZT** *n abbr* (= *azidothymidine*) AZT *f*
**Aztec** ['æztɛk] *adj* aztèque ▷ *n* Aztèque *m/f*
**azure** ['eɪʒə'] *adj* azuré(e)

# Bb

**B, b** [biː] *n* (*letter*) B, b *m*; (*Scol: mark*) B; (*Mus*): **B** si *m*; **B for Benjamin,** (US) **B for Baker** B comme Berthe; **B road** *n* (*Brit Aut*) route départementale

**b.** *abbr* = **born**

**B.A.** *abbr* = **British Academy**; (*Scol*) = **Bachelor of Arts**

**babble** ['bæbl] *vi* babiller ▷ *n* babillage *m*

**baboon** [bə'buːn] *n* babouin *m*

**baby** ['beɪbɪ] *n* bébé *m*

**baby carriage** *n* (US) voiture *f* d'enfant

**baby food** *n* aliments *mpl* pour bébé(s)

**baby grand** *n* (*also:* **baby grand piano**) (piano *m*) demi-queue *m*

**babyish** ['beɪbɪɪʃ] *adj* enfantin(e), de bébé

**baby-minder** ['beɪbɪmaɪndə<sup>r</sup>] *n* (*Brit*) gardienne *f* (d'enfants)

**baby-sit** ['beɪbɪsɪt] *vi* garder les enfants

**baby-sitter** ['beɪbɪsɪtə<sup>r</sup>] *n* baby-sitter *m/f*

**baby wipe** *n* lingette *f* (pour bébé)

**bachelor** ['bætʃələ<sup>r</sup>] *n* célibataire *m*; **B~ of Arts/Science (BA/BSc)** ≈ licencié(e) ès *or* en lettres/sciences; **B~ of Arts/Science degree (BA/BSc)** *n* ≈ licence *f* ès *or* en lettres/sciences; *voir article*

### ◉ BACHELOR'S DEGREE

◉
◉ Un *Bachelor's degree* est un diplôme accordé
◉ après trois ou quatre années d'université.
◉ Les *Bachelor's degrees* les plus courants sont le
◉ "BA" (Bachelor of Arts), le "BSc" (Bachelor of
◉ Science), le "BEd" (Bachelor of Education) et
◉ le "LLB" (Bachelor of Laws).

**bachelor party** *n* (US) enterrement *m* de vie de garçon

**back** [bæk] *n* (*of person, horse*) dos *m*; (*of hand*) dos, revers *m*; (*of house*) derrière *m*; (*of car, train*) arrière *m*; (*of chair*) dossier *m*; (*of page*) verso *m*; (*of crowd*): **can the people at the ~ hear me properly?** est-ce que les gens du fond peuvent m'entendre?; (*Football*) arrière *m*; **to have one's ~ to the wall** (*fig*) être au pied du mur; **to break the ~ of a job** (*Brit*) faire le gros d'un travail; **~ to front** à l'envers ▷ *vt* (*financially*) soutenir (financièrement); (*candidate: also:* **back up**)

soutenir, appuyer; (*horse: at races*) parier *or* miser sur; (*car*) (faire) reculer ▷ *vi* reculer; (*car etc*) faire marche arrière ▷ *adj* (*in compounds*) de derrière, à l'arrière; **~ seat/wheel** (*Aut*) siège *m*/roue *f* arrière *inv*; **~ payments/rent** arriéré *m* de paiements/loyer; **~ garden/room** jardin/pièce sur l'arrière; **to take a ~ seat** (*fig*) se contenter d'un second rôle, être relégué(e) au second plan ▷ *adv* (*not forward*) en arrière; (*returned*): **he's ~** il est rentré, il est de retour; **when will you be ~?** quand seras-tu de retour?; **he ran ~** il est revenu en courant; (*restitution*): **throw the ball ~** renvoie la balle; **can I have it ~?** puis-je le ravoir?, peux-tu me le rendre?; (*again*): **he called ~** il a rappelé

▶ **back down** *vi* rabattre de ses prétentions

▶ **back on to** *vt fus*: **the house ~s on to the golf course** la maison donne derrière sur le terrain de golf

▶ **back out** *vi* (*of promise*) se dédire

▶ **back up** *vt* (*person*) soutenir; (*Comput*) faire une copie de sauvegarde de

**backache** ['bækeɪk] *n* mal *m* au dos

**backbencher** [bæk'bentʃə<sup>r</sup>] (*Brit*) *n* membre du parlement sans portefeuille

**back benches** *npl* (*Brit*) *voir article*

### ◉ BACK BENCHES

◉
◉ Le terme *back benches* désigne les bancs les
◉ plus éloignés de l'allée centrale de la
◉ Chambre des communes. Les députés qui
◉ occupent ces bancs sont les "backbenchers"
◉ et ils n'ont pas de portefeuille ministériel.

**backbiting** ['bækbaɪtɪŋ] *n* médisance(s) *f(pl)*

**backbone** ['bækbəʊn] *n* colonne vertébrale, épine dorsale; **he's the ~ of the organization** c'est sur lui que repose l'organisation

**backchat** ['bæktʃæt] *n* (*Brit inf*) impertinences *fpl*

**backcloth** ['bækklɔθ] *n* (*Brit*) toile *f* de fond

**backcomb** ['bækkəʊm] *vt* (*Brit*) crêper

**backdate** [bæk'deɪt] *vt* (*letter*) antidater; **~d pay rise** augmentation *f* avec effet rétroactif

**back door** *n* porte *f* de derrière

**backdrop** ['bækdrɔp] *n* = **backcloth**

**backer** ['bækə<sup>r</sup>] n partisan m; (Comm)
commanditaire m
**backfire** [bæk'faɪə<sup>r</sup>] vi (Aut) pétarader; (plans)
mal tourner
**backgammon** ['bækgæmən] n trictrac m
**background** ['bækgraund] n arrière-plan m; (of
events) situation f, conjoncture f; (basic knowledge)
éléments mpl de base; (experience) formation f
▷ cpd (noise, music) de fond; ~ **reading** lecture(s)
générale(s) (sur un sujet); **family** ~ milieu
familial
**backhand** ['bækhænd] n (Tennis: also: **backhand
stroke**) revers m
**backhanded** ['bæk'hændɪd] adj (fig) déloyal(e);
équivoque
**backhander** ['bæk'hændə<sup>r</sup>] n (Brit: bribe) pot-de-
vin m
**backing** ['bækɪŋ] n (fig) soutien m, appui m;
(Comm) soutien (financier); (Mus)
accompagnement m
**backlash** ['bæklæʃ] n contre-coup m,
répercussion f
**backlog** ['bæklɔg] n: ~ **of work** travail m en
retard
**back number** n (of magazine etc) vieux numéro
**backpack** ['bækpæk] n sac m à dos
**backpacker** ['bækpækə<sup>r</sup>] n randonneur(-euse)
**back pain** n mal m de dos
**back pay** n rappel m de salaire
**backpedal** ['bækpɛdl] vi (fig) faire marche
arrière
**backseat driver** ['bæksi:t-] n passager qui donne
des conseils au conducteur
**backside** ['bæksaɪd] n (inf) derrière m,
postérieur m
**backslash** ['bækslæʃ] n barre oblique inversée
**backslide** ['bækslaɪd] vi retomber dans l'erreur
**backspace** ['bækspeɪs] vi (in typing) appuyer sur
la touche retour
**backstage** [bæk'steɪdʒ] adv dans les coulisses
**back-street** ['bækstri:t] adj (abortion)
clandestin(e); ~ **abortionist** avorteur(-euse)
(clandestin(e))
**backstroke** ['bækstrəuk] n dos crawlé
**backtrack** ['bæktræk] vi (fig) = **backpedal**
**backup** ['bækʌp] adj (train, plane)
supplémentaire, de réserve; (Comput) de
sauvegarde ▷ n (support) appui m, soutien m;
(Comput: also: **backup file**) sauvegarde f
**backward** ['bækwəd] adj (movement) en arrière;
(measure) rétrograde; (person, country) arriéré(e),
attardé(e); (shy) hésitant(e); ~ **and forward
movement** mouvement de va-et-vient
**backwards** ['bækwədz] adv (move, go) en arrière;
(read a list) à l'envers, à rebours; (fall) à la
renverse; (walk) à reculons; (in time) en arrière,
vers le passé; **to know sth** ~ or (US) ~ **and
forwards** (inf) connaître qch sur le bout des
doigts
**backwater** ['bækwɔ:tə<sup>r</sup>] n (fig) coin reculé; bled
perdu
**backyard** [bæk'jɑ:d] n arrière-cour f

**bacon** ['beɪkən] n bacon m, lard m
**bacteria** [bæk'tɪərɪə] npl bactéries fpl
**bacteriology** [bæktɪərɪ'ɔlədʒɪ] n bactériologie f
**bad** [bæd] adj mauvais(e); (child) vilain(e);
(mistake, accident) grave; (meat, food) gâté(e),
avarié(e); **his** ~ **leg** sa jambe malade; **to go** ~
(meat, food) se gâter; (milk) tourner; **to have a** ~
**time of it** traverser une mauvaise passe; **I feel**
~ **about it** (guilty) j'ai un peu mauvaise
conscience; ~ **debt** créance douteuse; **in** ~
**faith** de mauvaise foi
**baddie, baddy** ['bædɪ] n (inf: Cine etc)
méchant m
**bade** [bæd] pt of **bid**
**badge** [bædʒ] n insigne m; (of policeman) plaque
f; (stick-on, sew-on) badge m
**badger** ['bædʒə<sup>r</sup>] n blaireau m ▷ vt harceler
**badly** ['bædlɪ] adv (work, dress etc) mal; **to reflect**
~ **on sb** donner une mauvaise image de qn; ~
**wounded** grièvement blessé; **he needs it** ~ il
en a absolument besoin; **things are going** ~ les
choses vont mal; ~ **off** (adj, adv) dans la gêne
**bad-mannered** ['bæd'mænəd] adj mal élevé(e)
**badminton** ['bædmɪntən] n badminton m
**bad-mouth** ['bæd'mauθ] vt (US inf) débiner
**bad-tempered** ['bæd'tɛmpəd] adj (by nature)
ayant mauvais caractère; (on one occasion) de
mauvaise humeur
**baffle** ['bæfl] vt (puzzle) déconcerter
**baffling** ['bæflɪŋ] adj déroutant(e),
déconcertant(e)
**bag** [bæg] n sac m; (of hunter) gibecière f, chasse f
▷ vt (inf: take) empocher; s'approprier; (Tech)
mettre en sacs; ~**s of** (inf: lots of) des tas de; **to
pack one's** ~**s** faire ses valises or bagages; ~**s
under the eyes** poches fpl sous les yeux
**bagful** ['bægful] n plein sac
**baggage** ['bægɪdʒ] n bagages mpl
**baggage allowance** n franchise f de bagages
**baggage reclaim** n (at airport) livraison f des
bagages
**baggy** ['bægɪ] adj avachi(e), qui fait des poches
**Baghdad** [bæg'dæd] n Baghdâd, Bagdad
**bag lady** n (inf) clocharde f
**bagpipes** ['bægpaɪps] npl cornemuse f
**bag-snatcher** ['bægsnætʃə<sup>r</sup>] n (Brit) voleur m à
l'arraché
**bag-snatching** ['bægsnætʃɪŋ] n (Brit) vol m à
l'arraché
**Bahamas** [bə'hɑ:məz] npl: **the** ~ les Bahamas fpl
**Bahrain** [bɑː'reɪn] n Bahreïn m
**bail** [beɪl] n caution f ▷ vt (prisoner: also: **grant
bail to**) mettre en liberté sous caution; (boat:
also: **bail out**) écoper; **to be released on** ~ être
libéré(e) sous caution; see **bale**
▶ **bail out** vt (prisoner) payer la caution de
**bailiff** ['beɪlɪf] n huissier m
**bait** [beɪt] n appât m ▷ vt appâter; (fig: tease)
tourmenter
**bake** [beɪk] vt (faire) cuire au four ▷ vi (bread etc)
cuire (au four); (make cakes etc) faire de la
pâtisserie

**baked beans** [beɪkt-] *npl* haricots blancs à la sauce tomate

**baked potato** *n* pomme *f* de terre en robe des champs

**baker** ['beɪkə<sup>r</sup>] *n* boulanger *m*

**bakery** ['beɪkərɪ] *n* boulangerie *f*; boulangerie industrielle

**baking** ['beɪkɪŋ] *n* (*process*) cuisson *f*

**baking powder** *n* levure *f* (chimique)

**baking tin** *n* (*for cake*) moule *m* à gâteaux; (*for meat*) plat *m* pour le four

**baking tray** *n* plaque *f* à gâteaux

**balaclava** [bælə'klɑːvə] *n* (*also:* **balaclava helmet**) passe-montagne *m*

**balance** ['bæləns] *n* équilibre *m*; (*Comm: sum*) solde *m*; (*remainder*) reste *m*; (*scales*) balance *f* ▷ *vt* mettre *or* faire tenir en équilibre; (*pros and cons*) peser; (*budget*) équilibrer; (*account*) balancer; (*compensate*) compenser, contrebalancer; **~ of trade/payments** balance commerciale/des comptes *or* paiements; **~ carried forward** solde *m* à reporter; **~ brought forward** solde reporté; **to ~ the books** arrêter les comptes, dresser le bilan

**balanced** ['bælənst] *adj* (*personality, diet*) équilibré(e); (*report*) objectif(-ive)

**balance sheet** *n* bilan *m*

**balcony** ['bælkənɪ] *n* balcon *m*; **do you have a room with a ~?** avez-vous une chambre avec balcon?

**bald** [bɔːld] *adj* chauve; (*tyre*) lisse

**baldness** ['bɔːldnɪs] *n* calvitie *f*

**bale** [beɪl] *n* balle *f*, ballot *m*
  ▶ **bale out** *vi* (*of a plane*) sauter en parachute ▷ *vt* (*Naut: water, boat*) écoper

**Balearic Islands** [bælɪ'ærɪk-] *npl*: **the ~** les (îles *fpl*) Baléares *fpl*

**baleful** ['beɪlful] *adj* funeste, maléfique

**balk** [bɔːk] *vi*: **to ~ (at)** (*person*) regimber (contre); (*horse*) se dérober (devant)

**Balkan** ['bɔːlkən] *adj* balkanique ▷ *n*: **the ~s** les Balkans *mpl*

**ball** [bɔːl] *n* boule *f*; (*football*) ballon *m*; (*for tennis, golf*) balle *f*; (*dance*) bal *m*; **to play ~** jouer au ballon (*or* à la balle); (*fig*) coopérer; **to be on the ~** (*fig: competent*) être à la hauteur; (: *alert*) être éveillé(e), être vif (vive); **to start the ~ rolling** (*fig*) commencer; **the ~ is in their court** (*fig*) la balle est dans leur camp

**ballad** ['bæləd] *n* ballade *f*

**ballast** ['bæləst] *n* lest *m*

**ball bearings** *n* roulement *m* à billes

**ball cock** *n* robinet *m* à flotteur

**ballerina** [bælə'riːnə] *n* ballerine *f*

**ballet** ['bæleɪ] *n* ballet *m*; (*art*) danse *f* (classique)

**ballet dancer** *n* danseur(-euse) de ballet

**ballet shoe** *n* chausson *m* de danse

**ballistic** [bə'lɪstɪk] *adj* balistique

**ballistics** [bə'lɪstɪks] *n* balistique *f*

**balloon** [bə'luːn] *n* ballon *m*; (*in comic strip*) bulle *f* ▷ *vi* gonfler

**balloonist** [bə'luːnɪst] *n* aéronaute *m/f*

**ballot** ['bælət] *n* scrutin *m*

**ballot box** *n* urne (électorale)

**ballot paper** *n* bulletin *m* de vote

**ballpark** ['bɔːlpɑːk] *n* (*US*) stade *m* de base-ball

**ballpark figure** *n* (*inf*) chiffre approximatif

**ballpoint** ['bɔːlpɔɪnt], **ballpoint pen** *n* stylo *m* à bille

**ballroom** ['bɔːlrum] *n* salle *f* de bal

**balls** [bɔːlz] *npl* (*inf!*) couilles *fpl* (!)

**balm** [bɑːm] *n* baume *m*

**balmy** ['bɑːmɪ] *adj* (*breeze, air*) doux (douce); (*Brit inf*) = **barmy**

**BALPA** ['bælpə] *n abbr* (= *British Airline Pilots' Association*) *syndicat des pilotes de ligne*

**balsa** ['bɔːlsə], **balsa wood** *n* balsa *m*

**balsam** ['bɔːlsəm] *n* baume *m*

**Baltic** [bɔːltɪk] *adj, n*: **the ~ (Sea)** la (mer) Baltique

**balustrade** [bæləs'treɪd] *n* balustrade *f*

**bamboo** [bæm'buː] *n* bambou *m*

**bamboozle** [bæm'buːzl] *vt* (*inf*) embobiner

**ban** [bæn] *n* interdiction *f* ▷ *vt* interdire; **he was ~ned from driving** (*Brit*) on lui a retiré le permis (de conduire)

**banal** [bə'nɑːl] *adj* banal(e)

**banana** [bə'nɑːnə] *n* banane *f*

**band** [bænd] *n* bande *f*; (*at a dance*) orchestre *m*; (*Mil*) musique *f*, fanfare *f*
  ▶ **band together** *vi* se liguer

**bandage** ['bændɪdʒ] *n* bandage *m*, pansement *m* ▷ *vt* (*wound, leg*) mettre un pansement *or* un bandage sur; (*person*) mettre un pansement *or* un bandage à

**Band-Aid**® ['bændeɪd] *n* (*US*) pansement adhésif

**B. & B.** *n abbr* = **bed and breakfast**

**bandit** ['bændɪt] *n* bandit *m*

**bandstand** ['bændstænd] *n* kiosque *m* (à musique)

**bandwagon** ['bændwægən] *n*: **to jump on the ~** (*fig*) monter dans *or* prendre le train en marche

**bandy** ['bændɪ] *vt* (*jokes, insults*) échanger
  ▶ **bandy about** *vt* employer à tout bout de champ *or* à tort et à travers

**bandy-legged** ['bændɪ'lɛgɪd] *adj* aux jambes arquées

**bane** [beɪn] *n*: **it** (*or* **he** *etc*) **is the ~ of my life** c'est (*or* il est *etc*) le drame de ma vie

**bang** [bæŋ] *n* détonation *f*; (*of door*) claquement *m*; (*blow*) coup (violent) ▷ *vt* frapper (violemment); (*door*) claquer ▷ *vi* détoner; claquer ▷ *adv*: **to be ~ on time** (*Brit inf*) être à l'heure pile; **to ~ at the door** cogner à la porte; **to ~ into sth** se cogner contre qch

**banger** ['bæŋə<sup>r</sup>] *n* (*Brit: car: also:* **old banger**) (vieux) tacot; (*Brit inf: sausage*) saucisse *f*; (*firework*) pétard *m*

**Bangkok** [bæŋ'kɔk] *n* Bangkok

**Bangladesh** [bæŋglə'dɛʃ] *n* Bangladesh *m*

**Bangladeshi** [bæŋglə'dɛʃɪ] *adj* du Bangladesh ▷ *n* habitant(e) du Bangladesh

**bangle** ['bæŋgl] n bracelet m
**bangs** [bæŋz] npl (US: fringe) frange f
**banish** ['bænɪʃ] vt bannir
**banister** ['bænɪstə'] n, **banisters** ['bænɪstəz] npl rampe f (d'escalier)
**banjo** (pl **-es** or **-s**) ['bændʒəʊ] n banjo m
**bank** [bæŋk] n banque f; (of river, lake) bord m, rive f; (of earth) talus m, remblai m ▷ vi (Aviat) virer sur l'aile; (Comm): **they ~ with Pitt's** leur banque or banquier est Pitt's
▸ **bank on** vt fus miser or tabler sur
**bank account** n compte m en banque
**bank balance** n solde m bancaire
**bank card** (Brit) n carte f d'identité bancaire
**bank charges** npl (Brit) frais mpl de banque
**bank draft** n traite f bancaire
**banker** ['bæŋkə'] n banquier m; **~'s card** (Brit) carte f d'identité bancaire; **~'s order** (Brit) ordre m de virement
**bank giro** n paiement m par virement
**bank holiday** n (Brit) jour férié (où les banques sont fermées); voir article

◉ **BANK HOLIDAY**
◉
◉ Le terme bank holiday s'applique au
◉ Royaume-Uni aux jours fériés pendant
◉ lesquels banques et commerces sont fermés.
◉ Les principaux bank holidays à part Noël et
◉ Pâques se situent au mois de mai et fin août,
◉ et contrairement aux pays de tradition
◉ catholique, ne coïncident pas
◉ nécessairement avec une fête religieuse.

**banking** ['bæŋkɪŋ] n opérations fpl bancaires; profession f de banquier
**banking hours** npl heures fpl d'ouverture des banques
**bank loan** n prêt m bancaire
**bank manager** n directeur m d'agence (bancaire)
**banknote** ['bæŋknəʊt] n billet m de banque
**bank rate** n taux m de l'escompte
**bankrupt** ['bæŋkrʌpt] n failli(e) ▷ adj en faillite; **to go ~** faire faillite
**bankruptcy** ['bæŋkrʌptsɪ] n faillite f
**bank statement** n relevé m de compte
**banner** ['bænə'] n bannière f
**bannister** ['bænɪstə'] n, **bannisters** ['bænɪstəz] npl = **banister; banisters**
**banns** [bænz] npl bans mpl (de mariage)
**banquet** ['bæŋkwɪt] n banquet m, festin m
**bantam-weight** ['bæntəmweɪt] n poids m coq inv
**banter** ['bæntə'] n badinage m
**baptism** ['bæptɪzəm] n baptême m
**Baptist** ['bæptɪst] n baptiste m/f
**baptize** [bæp'taɪz] vt baptiser
**bar** [ba:'] n (pub) bar m; (counter) comptoir m, bar; (rod: of metal etc) barre f; (of window etc) barreau m; (of chocolate) tablette f, plaque f; (fig: obstacle) obstacle m; (prohibition) mesure f d'exclusion; (Mus) mesure f ▷ vt (road) barrer; (window) munir de barreaux; (person) exclure; (activity) interdire; **~ of soap** savonnette f; **behind ~s** (prisoner) derrière les barreaux; **the B~** (Law) le barreau; **~ none** sans exception
**Barbados** [ba:'beɪdɔs] n Barbade f
**barbaric** [ba:'bærɪk] adj barbare
**barbarous** ['ba:bərəs] adj barbare, cruel(le)
**barbecue** ['ba:bɪkju:] n barbecue m
**barbed wire** ['ba:bd-] n fil m de fer barbelé
**barber** ['ba:bə'] n coiffeur m (pour hommes)
**barber's** ['ba:bəz], **barber's shop**, (US) **barber shop** n salon m de coiffure (pour hommes); **to go to the barber's** aller chez le coiffeur
**barbiturate** [ba:'bɪtjʊrɪt] n barbiturique m
**Barcelona** [ba:sə'ləʊnə] n Barcelone
**bar chart** n diagramme m en bâtons
**bar code** n code m à barres, code-barre m
**bare** [bɛə'] adj nu(e) ▷ vt mettre à nu, dénuder; (teeth) montrer; **the ~ essentials** le strict nécessaire
**bareback** ['bɛəbæk] adv à cru, sans selle
**barefaced** ['bɛəfeɪst] adj impudent(e), effronté(e)
**barefoot** ['bɛəfut] adj, adv nu-pieds, (les) pieds nus
**bareheaded** [bɛə'hɛdɪd] adj, adv nu-tête, (la) tête nue
**barely** ['bɛəlɪ] adv à peine
**Barents Sea** ['bærənts-] n: **the ~** la mer de Barents
**bargain** ['ba:gɪn] n (transaction) marché m; (good buy) affaire f, occasion f ▷ vi (haggle) marchander; (negotiate) négocier, traiter; **into the ~** par-dessus le marché
▸ **bargain for** vt fus (inf): **he got more than he ~ed for!** il en a eu pour son argent!
**bargaining** ['ba:gənɪŋ] n marchandage m; négociations fpl
**bargaining position** n: **to be in a weak/strong ~** être en mauvaise/bonne position pour négocier
**barge** [ba:dʒ] n péniche f
▸ **barge in** vi (walk in) faire irruption; (interrupt talk) intervenir mal à propos
▸ **barge into** vt fus rentrer dans
**baritone** ['bærɪtəʊn] n baryton m
**barium meal** ['bɛərɪəm-] n (bouillie f de) sulfate m de baryum
**bark** [ba:k] n (of tree) écorce f; (of dog) aboiement m ▷ vi aboyer
**barley** ['ba:lɪ] n orge f
**barley sugar** n sucre m d'orge
**barmaid** ['ba:meɪd] n serveuse f (de bar), barmaid f
**barman** ['ba:mən] (irreg) n serveur m (de bar), barman m
**bar meal** n repas m de bistrot; **to go for a ~** aller manger au bistrot
**barmy** ['ba:mɪ] adj (Brit inf) timbré(e), cinglé(e)
**barn** [ba:n] n grange f
**barnacle** ['ba:nəkl] n anatife m, bernache f
**barn owl** n chouette-effraie f, chat-huant m

**barometer** [bə'rɔmɪtə<sup>r</sup>] n baromètre m
**baron** ['bærən] n baron m; **the press/oil ~s** les
magnats mpl or barons mpl de la presse/du
pétrole
**baroness** ['bærənɪs] n baronne f
**barrack** ['bærək] vt (Brit) chahuter
**barracking** ['bærəkɪŋ] n (Brit): **to give sb a ~**
chahuter qn
**barracks** ['bærəks] npl caserne f
**barrage** ['bærɑːʒ] n (Mil) tir m de barrage; (dam)
barrage m; (of criticism) feu m
**barrel** ['bærəl] n tonneau m; (of gun) canon m
**barrel organ** n orgue m de Barbarie
**barren** ['bærən] adj stérile; (hills) aride
**barrette** [bə'ret] (US) n barrette f
**barricade** [bærɪ'keɪd] n barricade f ▷ vt
barricader
**barrier** ['bærɪə<sup>r</sup>] n barrière f; (Brit: also: **crash
barrier**) rail m de sécurité
**barrier cream** n (Brit) crème protectrice
**barring** ['bɑːrɪŋ] prep sauf
**barrister** ['bærɪstə<sup>r</sup>] n (Brit) avocat (plaidant);
voir article

> **BARRISTER**
>
> En Angleterre, un barrister, que l'on appelle
> également "barrister-at-law", est un avocat
> qui représente ses clients devant la cour et
> plaide pour eux. Le client doit d'abord passer
> par l'intermédiaire d'un "solicitor". On
> obtient le diplôme de barrister après avoir fait
> des études dans l'une des "Inns of Court", les
> quatre écoles de droit londoniennes.

**barrow** ['bærəu] n (cart) charrette f à bras
**barstool** ['bɑːstuːl] n tabouret m de bar
**Bart.** abbr (Brit) = **baronet**
**bartender** ['bɑːtɛndə<sup>r</sup>] n (US) serveur m (de bar),
barman m
**barter** ['bɑːtə<sup>r</sup>] n échange m, troc m ▷ vt: **to ~ sth
for** échanger qch contre
**base** [beɪs] n base f ▷ vt (troops): **to be ~d at** être
basé(e) à; (opinion, belief): **to ~ sth on** baser or
fonder qch sur ▷ adj vil(e), bas(se); **coffee-~d** à
base de café; **a Paris-~d firm** une maison
opérant de Paris or dont le siège est à Paris; **I'm
~d in London** je suis basé(e) à Londres
**baseball** ['beɪsbɔːl] n base-ball m
**baseball cap** n casquette f de base-ball
**baseboard** ['beɪsbɔːd] n (US) plinthe f
**base camp** n camp m de base
**Basel** [bɑːl] n = **Basle**
**baseline** ['beɪslaɪn] n (Tennis) ligne f de fond
**basement** ['beɪsmənt] n sous-sol m
**base rate** n taux m de base
**bases** ['beɪsiːz] npl of **basis** ['beɪsɪs] ▷ npl of **base**
**bash** [bæʃ] vt (inf) frapper, cogner ▷ n: **I'll have a
~ (at it)** (Brit inf) je vais essayer un coup; **~ed in**
adj enfoncé(e), défoncé(e)
▶ **bash up** vt (inf: car) bousiller; (: Brit: person)
tabasser

**bashful** ['bæʃful] adj timide; modeste
**bashing** ['bæʃɪŋ] n (inf) raclée f; **Paki-~**
= ratonnade f; **queer-~** chasse f aux pédés
**BASIC** ['beɪsɪk] n (Comput) BASIC m
**basic** ['beɪsɪk] adj (precautions, rules) élémentaire;
(principles, research) fondamental(e); (vocabulary,
salary) de base; (minimal) réduit(e) au minimum,
rudimentaire
**basically** ['beɪsɪklɪ] adv (in fact) en fait;
(essentially) fondamentalement
**basic rate** n (of tax) première tranche
d'imposition
**basics** ['beɪsɪks] npl: **the ~** l'essentiel m
**basil** ['bæzl] n basilic m
**basin** ['beɪsn] n (vessel, also Geo) cuvette f, bassin
m; (Brit: for food) bol m; (: bigger) saladier m; (also:
**washbasin**) lavabo m
**basis** (pl **bases**) ['beɪsɪs, -siːz] n base f; **on a
part-time/trial ~** à temps partiel/à l'essai; **on
the ~ of what you've said** d'après or compte
tenu de ce que vous dites
**bask** [bɑːsk] vi: **to ~ in the sun** se chauffer au
soleil
**basket** ['bɑːskɪt] n corbeille f; (with handle)
panier m
**basketball** ['bɑːskɪtbɔːl] n basket-ball m
**basketball player** n basketteur(-euse)
**Basle** [bɑːl] n Bâle
**basmati rice** [bəz'mætɪ-] n riz m basmati
**Basque** [bæsk] adj basque ▷ n Basque m/f; **the ~
Country** le Pays basque
**bass** [beɪs] n (Mus) basse f
**bass clef** n clé f de fa
**bass drum** n grosse caisse f
**bassoon** [bə'suːn] n basson m
**bastard** ['bɑːstəd] n enfant naturel(le),
bâtard(e); (inf!) salaud m (!)
**baste** [beɪst] vt (Culin) arroser; (Sewing) bâtir,
faufiler
**bat** [bæt] n chauve-souris f; (for baseball etc) batte
f; (Brit: for table tennis) raquette f ▷ vt: **he didn't ~
an eyelid** il n'a pas sourcillé or bronché; **off
one's own ~** de sa propre initiative
**batch** [bætʃ] n (of bread) fournée f; (of papers)
liasse f; (of applicants, letters) paquet m; (of work)
monceau m; (of goods) lot m
**bated** ['beɪtɪd] adj: **with ~ breath** en retenant
son souffle
**bath** (pl **-s**) [bɑːθ, bɑːðz] n bain m; (bathtub)
baignoire f ▷ vt baigner, donner un bain à; **to
have a ~** prendre un bain; see also **baths**
**bathe** [beɪð] vi se baigner ▷ vt baigner; (wound
etc) laver
**bather** ['beɪðə<sup>r</sup>] n baigneur(-euse)
**bathing** ['beɪðɪŋ] n baignade f
**bathing cap** n bonnet m de bain
**bathing costume**, (US) **bathing suit** n
maillot m (de bain)
**bathmat** ['bɑːθmæt] n tapis m de bain
**bathrobe** ['bɑːθrəub] n peignoir m de bain
**bathroom** ['bɑːθrum] n salle f de bains
**baths** [bɑːðz] npl (Brit: also: **swimming baths**)

piscine f

**bath towel** n serviette f de bain

**bathtub** ['bɑ:θtʌb] n baignoire f

**batman** ['bætmən] (irreg) n (Brit Mil) ordonnance f

**baton** ['bætən] n bâton m; (Mus) baguette f; (club) matraque f

**battalion** [bə'tælıən] n bataillon m

**batten** ['bætn] n (Carpentry) latte f; (Naut: on sail) latte de voile

▶ **batten down** vt (Naut): **to ~ down the hatches** fermer les écoutilles

**batter** ['bætər] vt battre ▷ n pâte f à frire

**battered** ['bætəd] adj (hat, pan) cabossé(e); **~ wife/child** épouse/enfant maltraité(e) or martyr(e)

**battering ram** ['bætərıŋ-] n bélier m; (fig)

**battery** ['bætərı] n (for torch, radio) pile f; (Aut, Mil) batterie f

**battery charger** n chargeur m

**battery farming** n élevage m en batterie

**battle** ['bætl] n bataille f, combat m ▷ vi se battre, lutter; **that's half the ~** (fig) c'est déjà bien; **it's a** or **we're fighting a losing ~** (fig) c'est perdu d'avance, c'est peine perdue

**battle dress** n tenue f de campagne or d'assaut

**battlefield** ['bætlfi:ld] n champ m de bataille

**battlements** ['bætlmənts] npl remparts mpl

**battleship** ['bætlʃɪp] n cuirassé m

**batty** ['bætı] adj (inf: person) toqué(e); (: idea, behaviour) loufoque

**bauble** ['bɔ:bl] n babiole f

**baulk** [bɔ:lk] vi = **balk**

**bauxite** ['bɔ:ksaɪt] n bauxite f

**Bavaria** [bə'vɛərɪə] n Bavière f

**Bavarian** [bə'vɛərɪən] adj bavarois(e) ▷ n Bavarois(e)

**bawdy** ['bɔ:dı] adj paillard(e)

**bawl** [bɔ:l] vi hurler, brailler

**bay** [beɪ] n (of sea) baie f; (Brit: for parking) place f de stationnement; (: for loading) aire f de chargement; (horse) bai(e) m/f; **B~ of Biscay** golfe m de Gascogne; **to hold sb at ~** tenir qn à distance or en échec

**bay leaf** n laurier m

**bayonet** ['beɪənɪt] n baïonnette f

**bay tree** n laurier m

**bay window** n baie vitrée

**bazaar** [bə'zɑ:r] n (shop, market) bazar m; (sale) vente f de charité

**bazooka** [bə'zu:kə] n bazooka m

**BB** n abbr (Brit: = Boys' Brigade) mouvement de garçons

**BBB** n abbr (US: = Better Business Bureau) organisme de défense du consommateur

**BBC** n abbr (= British Broadcasting Corporation) office de la radiodiffusion et télévision britannique; voir article

◉ **BBC**
◉
◉ La BBC est un organisme centralisé dont les
◉ membres, nommés par l'État, gèrent les
◉ chaînes de télévision publiques (BBC1, qui

◉ présente des émissions d'intérêt général, et
◉ BBC2, qui est plutôt orientée vers les
◉ émissions plus culturelles, et les chaînes
◉ numériques) et les stations de radio
◉ publiques. Bien que non contrôlée par l'État,
◉ la BBC est responsable devant le
◉ "Parliament" quant au contenu des
◉ émissions qu'elle diffuse. Par ailleurs, la
◉ BBC offre un service mondial de diffusion
◉ d'émissions, en anglais et dans 43 autres
◉ langues, appelé "BBC World Service". La BBC
◉ est financée par la redevance télévision et
◉ par l'exportation d'émissions.

**B.C.** adv abbr (= before Christ) av. J.-C. ▷ abbr (Canada) = **British Columbia**

**BCG** n abbr (= Bacillus Calmette-Guérin) BCG m

**BD** n abbr (= Bachelor of Divinity) diplôme universitaire

**B/D** abbr = **bank draft**

**BDS** n abbr (= Bachelor of Dental Surgery) diplôme universitaire

**KEYWORD**

**be** [bi:] (pt **was, were**, pp **been**) aux vb **1** (with present participle: forming continuous tenses): **what are you doing?** que faites-vous?; **they're coming tomorrow** ils viennent demain; **I've been waiting for you for 2 hours** je t'attends depuis 2 heures

**2** (with pp: forming passives) être; **to be killed** être tué(e); **the box had been opened** la boîte avait été ouverte; **he was nowhere to be seen** on ne le voyait nulle part

**3** (in tag questions): **it was fun, wasn't it?** c'était drôle, n'est-ce pas?; **he's good-looking, isn't he?** il est beau, n'est-ce pas?; **she's back, is she?** elle est rentrée, n'est-ce pas or alors?

**4** (+to + infinitive): **the house is to be sold** (necessity) la maison doit être vendue; (future) la maison va être vendue; **he's not to open it** il ne doit pas l'ouvrir; **am I to understand that ...?** dois-je comprendre que ...?; **he was to have come yesterday** il devait venir hier

**5** (possibility, supposition): **if I were you, I ...** à votre place, je ..., si j'étais vous, je ...

▷ vb + complement **1** (gen) être; **I'm English** je suis anglais(e); **I'm tired** je suis fatigué(e); **I'm hot/cold** j'ai chaud/froid; **he's a doctor** il est médecin; **be careful/good/quiet!** faites attention/soyez sages/taisez-vous!; **2 and 2 are 4** 2 et 2 font 4

**2** (of health) aller; **how are you?** comment allez-vous?; **I'm better now** je vais mieux maintenant; **he's fine now** il va bien maintenant; **he's very ill** il est très malade

**3** (of age) avoir; **how old are you?** quel âge avez-vous?; **I'm sixteen (years old)** j'ai seize ans

**4** (cost) coûter; **how much was the meal?** combien a coûté le repas?; **that'll be £5, please** ça fera 5 livres, s'il vous plaît; **this shirt is £17** cette chemise coûte 17 livres

▷ vi **1** (exist, occur etc) être, exister; **the prettiest girl that ever was** la fille la plus jolie qui ait jamais existé; **is there a God?** y a-t-il un dieu?; **be that as it may** quoi qu'il en soit; **so be it** soit

**2** (referring to place) être, se trouver; **I won't be here tomorrow** je ne serai pas là demain; **Edinburgh is in Scotland** Édimbourg est or se trouve en Écosse

**3** (referring to movement) aller; **where have you been?** où êtes-vous allé(s)?

▷ impers vb **1** (referring to time) être; **it's 5 o'clock** il est 5 heures; **it's the 28th of April** c'est le 28 avril

**2** (referring to distance): **it's 10 km to the village** le village est à 10 km

**3** (referring to the weather) faire; **it's too hot/cold** il fait trop chaud/froid; **it's windy today** il y a du vent aujourd'hui

**4** (emphatic): **it's me/the postman** c'est moi/le facteur; **it was Maria who paid the bill** c'est Maria qui a payé la note

**B/E** abbr = **bill of exchange**

**beach** [biːtʃ] n plage f ▷ vt échouer

**beachcomber** ['biːtʃkəʊməʳ] n ramasseur m d'épaves; (fig) bon(-ne) m/f à rien

**beachwear** ['biːtʃwɛəʳ] n tenues fpl de plage

**beacon** ['biːkən] n (lighthouse) fanal m; (marker) balise f; (also: **radio beacon**) radiophare m

**bead** [biːd] n perle f; (of dew, sweat) goutte f; **beads** npl (necklace) collier m

**beady** ['biːdɪ] adj: **~ eyes** yeux mpl de fouine

**beagle** ['biːgl] n beagle m

**beak** [biːk] n bec m

**beaker** ['biːkəʳ] n gobelet m

**beam** [biːm] n (Archit) poutre f; (of light) rayon m; (Radio) faisceau m radio ▷ vi rayonner; **to drive on full** or **main** or (US) **high ~** rouler en pleins phares

**beaming** ['biːmɪŋ] adj (sun, smile) radieux(-euse)

**bean** [biːn] n haricot m; (of coffee) grain m

**beanpole** ['biːnpəʊl] n (inf) perche f

**beansprouts** ['biːnsprauts] npl pousses fpl or germes mpl de soja

**bear** [bɛəʳ] (pt **bore**, pp **borne**) [bɔːʳ, bɔːn] n ours m; (Stock Exchange) baissier m ▷ vt porter; (endure) supporter; (traces, signs) porter; (Comm: interest) rapporter ▷ vi: **to ~ right/left** obliquer à droite/gauche, se diriger vers la droite/gauche; **to ~ the responsibility of** assumer la responsabilité de; **to ~ comparison with** soutenir la comparaison avec; **I can't ~ him** je ne peux pas le supporter or souffrir; **to bring pressure to ~ on sb** faire pression sur qn
▶ **bear out** vt (theory, suspicion) confirmer
▶ **bear up** vi supporter, tenir le coup; **he bore up well** il a tenu le coup
▶ **bear with** vt fus (sb's moods, temper) supporter; **~ with me a minute** un moment, s'il vous plaît

**bearable** ['bɛərəbl] adj supportable

**beard** [bɪəd] n barbe f

**bearded** ['bɪədɪd] adj barbu(e)

**bearer** ['bɛərəʳ] n porteur m; (of passport etc) titulaire m/f

**bearing** ['bɛərɪŋ] n maintien m, allure f; (connection) rapport m; (Tech): **(ball) bearings** npl roulement m (à billes); **to take a ~** faire le point; **to find one's ~s** s'orienter

**beast** [biːst] n bête f; (inf: person) brute f

**beastly** ['biːstlɪ] adj infect(e)

**beat** [biːt] n battement m; (Mus) temps m, mesure f; (of policeman) ronde f ▷ vt, vi (pt -, pp -en) battre; **off the ~en track** hors des chemins or sentiers battus; **to ~ it** (inf) ficher le camp; **to ~ about the bush** tourner autour du pot; **that ~s everything!** c'est le comble!
▶ **beat down** vt (door) enfoncer; (price) faire baisser; (seller) faire descendre ▷ vi (rain) tambouriner; (sun) taper
▶ **beat off** vt repousser
▶ **beat up** vt (eggs) battre; (inf: person) tabasser

**beater** ['biːtəʳ] n (for eggs, cream) fouet m, batteur m

**beating** ['biːtɪŋ] n raclée f

**beat-up** ['biːt'ʌp] adj (inf) déglingué(e)

**beautician** [bjuːˈtɪʃən] n esthéticien(ne)

**beautiful** ['bjuːtɪful] adj beau (belle)

**beautifully** ['bjuːtɪflɪ] adv admirablement

**beautify** ['bjuːtɪfaɪ] vt embellir

**beauty** ['bjuːtɪ] n beauté f; **the ~ of it is that ...** le plus beau, c'est que ...

**beauty contest** n concours m de beauté

**beauty parlour**, (US) **beauty parlor** [-'pɑːləʳ] n institut m de beauté

**beauty queen** n reine f de beauté

**beauty salon** n institut m de beauté

**beauty sleep** n: **I need my ~** j'ai besoin de faire un gros dodo

**beauty spot** n (on skin) grain m de beauté; (Brit Tourism) site naturel (d'une grande beauté)

**beaver** ['biːvəʳ] n castor m

**becalmed** [bɪˈkɑːmd] adj immobilisé(e) par le calme plat

**became** [bɪˈkeɪm] pt of **become**

**because** [bɪˈkɔz] conj parce que; **~ of** (prep) à cause de

**beck** [bɛk] n: **to be at sb's ~ and call** être à l'entière disposition de qn

**beckon** ['bɛkən] vt (also: **beckon to**) faire signe (de venir) à

**become** [bɪˈkʌm] vi devenir; **to ~ fat/thin** grossir/maigrir; **to ~ angry** se mettre en colère; **it became known that** on apprit que; **what has ~ of him?** qu'est-il devenu?

**becoming** [bɪˈkʌmɪŋ] adj (behaviour) convenable, bienséant(e); (clothes) seyant(e)

**BECTU** ['bɛktu] n abbr (Brit) = **Broadcasting, Entertainment, Cinematographic and Theatre Union**

**BEd** n abbr (= Bachelor of Education) diplôme d'aptitude à l'enseignement

**bed** [bɛd] n lit m; (of flowers) parterre m; (of coal, clay) couche f; (of sea, lake) fond m; **to go to ~**

aller se coucher
▶ **bed down** vi se coucher
**bed and breakfast** n (terms) chambre et petit déjeuner; (place) ≈ chambre f d'hôte; voir article

⬤ **BED AND BREAKFAST**

⬤ Un bed and breakfast est une petite pension
⬤ dans une maison particulière ou une ferme
⬤ où l'on peut louer une chambre avec petit
⬤ déjeuner compris pour un prix modique par
⬤ rapport à ce que l'on paierait dans un hôtel.
⬤ Ces établissements sont communément
⬤ appelés "B & B", et sont signalés par une
⬤ pancarte dans le jardin ou au-dessus de la
⬤ porte.

**bedbug** ['bɛdbʌg] n punaise f
**bedclothes** ['bɛdkləuðz] npl couvertures fpl et draps mpl
**bedcover** ['bɛdkʌvəʳ] n couvre-lit m, dessus-de-lit m
**bedding** ['bɛdɪŋ] n literie f
**bedevil** [bɪ'dɛvl] vt (harass) harceler; **to be ~led by** être victime de
**bedfellow** ['bɛdfɛləu] n: **they are strange ~s** (fig) ça fait un drôle de mélange
**bedlam** ['bɛdləm] n chahut m, cirque m
**bed linen** n draps mpl de lit (et taies fpl d'oreillers), literie f
**bedpan** ['bɛdpæn] n bassin m (hygiénique)
**bedpost** ['bɛdpəust] n colonne f de lit
**bedraggled** [bɪ'drægld] adj dépenaillé(e), les vêtements en désordre
**bedridden** ['bɛdrɪdn] adj cloué(e) au lit
**bedrock** ['bɛdrɔk] n (fig) principes essentiels or de base, essentiel m; (Geo) roche f en place, socle m
**bedroom** ['bɛdrum] n chambre f (à coucher)
**Beds** abbr (Brit) = **Bedfordshire**
**bed settee** n canapé-lit m
**bedside** ['bɛdsaɪd] n: **at sb's ~** au chevet de qn ▷ cpd (book, lamp) de chevet
**bedside lamp** n lampe f de chevet
**bedside table** n table f de chevet
**bedsit** ['bɛdsɪt], **bedsitter** ['bɛdsɪtəʳ] n (Brit) chambre meublée, studio m
**bedspread** ['bɛdsprɛd] n couvre-lit m, dessus-de-lit m
**bedtime** ['bɛdtaɪm] n: **it's ~** c'est l'heure de se coucher
**bee** [biː] n abeille f; **to have a ~ in one's bonnet (about sth)** être obnubilé(e) (par qch)
**beech** [biːtʃ] n hêtre m
**beef** [biːf] n bœuf m; **roast ~** rosbif m
▶ **beef up** vt (inf: support) renforcer; (: essay) étoffer
**beefburger** ['biːfbəːgəʳ] n hamburger m
**beehive** ['biːhaɪv] n ruche f
**bee-keeping** ['biːkiːpɪŋ] n apiculture f
**beeline** ['biːlaɪn] n: **to make a ~ for** se diriger tout droit vers

**been** [biːn] pp of **be**
**beep** [biːp] n bip m
**beeper** ['biːpəʳ] n (pager) bip m
**beer** [bɪəʳ] n bière f
**beer belly** n (inf) bedaine f (de buveur de bière)
**beer can** n canette f de bière
**beer garden** n (Brit) jardin m d'un pub (où l'on peut emmener ses consommations)
**beet** [biːt] n (vegetable) betterave f; (US: also: **red beet**) betterave (potagère)
**beetle** ['biːtl] n scarabée m, coléoptère m
**beetroot** ['biːtruːt] n (Brit) betterave f
**befall** [bɪ'fɔːl] vi, vt (irreg: like **fall**) advenir (à)
**befit** [bɪ'fɪt] vt seoir à
**before** [bɪ'fɔːʳ] prep (of time) avant; (of space) devant ▷ conj avant que + sub; avant de ▷ adv avant; **~ going** avant de partir; **~ she goes** avant qu'elle (ne) parte; **the week ~** la semaine précédente or d'avant; **I've seen it ~** je l'ai déjà vu; **I've never seen it ~** c'est la première fois que je le vois
**beforehand** [bɪ'fɔːhænd] adv au préalable, à l'avance
**befriend** [bɪ'frɛnd] vt venir en aide à; traiter en ami
**befuddled** [bɪ'fʌdld] adj: **to be ~** avoir les idées brouillées
**beg** [bɛg] vi mendier ▷ vt mendier; (favour) quémander, solliciter; (forgiveness, mercy etc) demander; (entreat) supplier; **to ~ sb to do sth** supplier qn de faire qch; **I ~ your pardon** (apologising) excusez-moi; (: not hearing) pardon?; **that ~s the question of ...** cela soulève la question de ..., cela suppose réglée la question de ...; see also **pardon**
**began** [bɪ'gæn] pt of **begin**
**beggar** ['bɛgəʳ] n (also: **beggarman, beggarwoman**) mendiant(e)
**begin** [bɪ'gɪn] (pt **began**, pp **begun** [bɪ'gɪn, -'gæn, -'gʌn]) vt, vi commencer; **to ~ doing** or **to do sth** commencer à faire qch; **~ning (from) Monday** à partir de lundi; **I can't ~ to thank you** je ne saurais vous remercier; **to ~ with** d'abord, pour commencer
**beginner** [bɪ'gɪnəʳ] n débutant(e)
**beginning** [bɪ'gɪnɪŋ] n commencement m, début m; **right from the ~** dès le début
**begrudge** [bɪ'grʌdʒ] vt: **to ~ sb sth** envier qch à qn; donner qch à contrecœur or à regret à qn
**beguile** [bɪ'gaɪl] vt (enchant) enjôler
**beguiling** [bɪ'gaɪlɪŋ] adj (charming) séduisant(e), enchanteur(eresse)
**begun** [bɪ'gʌn] pp of **begin**
**behalf** [bɪ'hɑːf] n: **on ~ of**, (US) **in ~ of** (representing) de la part de; au nom de; (for benefit of) pour le compte de; **on my/his ~** de ma/sa part
**behave** [bɪ'heɪv] vi se conduire, se comporter; (well: also: **behave o.s.**) se conduire bien or comme il faut
**behaviour**, (US) **behavior** [bɪ'heɪvjəʳ] n comportement m, conduite f

**behead** [bɪ'hɛd] *vt* décapiter

**beheld** [bɪ'hɛld] *pt, pp of* **behold**

**behind** [bɪ'haɪnd] *prep* derrière; *(time)* en retard sur; *(supporting)*: **to be ~ sb** soutenir qn ▷ *adv* derrière; en retard ▷ *n* derrière *m*; **~ the scenes** dans les coulisses; **to leave sth ~** *(forget)* oublier de prendre qch; **to be ~ (schedule) with sth** être en retard dans qch

**behold** [bɪ'həʊld] *vt (irreg: like* **hold**) apercevoir, voir

**beige** [beɪʒ] *adj* beige

**Beijing** ['beɪ'dʒɪŋ] *n* Pékin

**being** ['biːɪŋ] *n* être *m*; **to come into ~** prendre naissance

**Beirut** [beɪ'ruːt] *n* Beyrouth

**Belarus** [bɛlə'rus] *n* Biélorussie *f*, Bélarus *m*

**Belarussian** [bɛlə'rʌʃən] *adj* biélorusse ▷ *n* Biélorusse *m/f*; *(Ling)* biélorusse *m*

**belated** [bɪ'leɪtɪd] *adj* tardif(-ive)

**belch** [bɛltʃ] *vi* avoir un renvoi, roter ▷ *vt (also:* **belch out**: *smoke etc)* vomir, cracher

**beleaguered** [bɪ'liːɡɪd] *adj (city)* assiégé(e); *(army)* cerné(e); *(fig)* sollicité(e) de toutes parts

**Belfast** ['bɛlfɑːst] *n* Belfast

**belfry** ['bɛlfrɪ] *n* beffroi *m*

**Belgian** ['bɛldʒən] *adj* belge, de Belgique ▷ *n* Belge *m/f*

**Belgium** ['bɛldʒəm] *n* Belgique *f*

**Belgrade** [bɛl'ɡreɪd] *n* Belgrade

**belie** [bɪ'laɪ] *vt* démentir; *(give false impression of)* occulter

**belief** [bɪ'liːf] *n (opinion)* conviction *f*; *(trust, faith)* foi *f*; *(acceptance as true)* croyance *f*; **it's beyond ~** c'est incroyable; **in the ~ that** dans l'idée que

**believable** [bɪ'liːvəbl] *adj* croyable

**believe** [bɪ'liːv] *vt, vi* croire, estimer; **to ~ in** *(God)* croire en; *(ghosts, method)* croire à; **I don't ~ in corporal punishment** je ne suis pas partisan des châtiments corporels; **he is ~d to be abroad** il serait à l'étranger

**believer** [bɪ'liːvər] *n (in idea, activity)* partisan(e); **~ in** partisan(e) de; *(Rel)* croyant(e)

**belittle** [bɪ'lɪtl] *vt* déprécier, rabaisser

**Belize** [bɛ'liːz] *n* Bélize *m*

**bell** [bɛl] *n* cloche *f*; *(small)* clochette *f*, grelot *m*; *(on door)* sonnette *f*; *(electric)* sonnerie *f*; **that rings a ~** *(fig)* cela me rappelle qch

**bell-bottoms** ['bɛlbɔtəmz] *npl* pantalon *m* à pattes d'éléphant

**bellboy** ['bɛlbɔɪ], *(US)* **bellhop** ['bɛlhɔp] *n* groom *m*, chasseur *m*

**belligerent** [bɪ'lɪdʒərənt] *adj (at war)* belligérant(e); *(fig)* agressif(-ive)

**bellow** ['bɛləʊ] *vi (bull)* meugler; *(person)* brailler ▷ *vt (orders)* hurler

**bellows** ['bɛləʊz] *npl* soufflet *m*

**bell pepper** *n (esp US)* poivron *m*

**bell push** *n (Brit)* bouton *m* de sonnette

**belly** ['bɛlɪ] *n* ventre *m*

**bellyache** ['bɛlɪeɪk] *(inf) n* colique *f* ▷ *vi* ronchonner

**belly button** *(inf) n* nombril *m*

**bellyful** ['bɛlɪful] *n (inf)*: **I've had a ~** j'en ai ras le bol

**belong** [bɪ'lɔŋ] *vi*: **to ~ to** appartenir à; *(club etc)* faire partie de; **this book ~s here** ce livre va ici, la place de ce livre est ici

**belongings** [bɪ'lɔŋɪŋz] *npl* affaires *fpl*, possessions *fpl*; **personal ~** effets personnels

**Belorussia** [bɛlə'rʌʃə] *n* Biélorussie *f*

**Belorussian** [bɛlə'rʌʃən] *adj, n* = **Belarussian**

**beloved** [bɪ'lʌvɪd] *adj* (bien-)aimé(e), chéri(e) ▷ *n* bien-aimé(e)

**below** [bɪ'ləʊ] *prep* sous, au-dessous de ▷ *adv* en dessous; en contre-bas; **see ~** voir plus bas *or* plus loin *or* ci-dessous; **temperatures ~ normal** températures inférieures à la normale

**belt** [bɛlt] *n* ceinture *f*; *(Tech)* courroie *f* ▷ *vt (thrash)* donner une raclée à ▷ *vi (Brit inf)* filer (à toutes jambes); **industrial ~** zone industrielle

▶ **belt out** *vt (song)* chanter à tue-tête *or* à pleins poumons

▶ **belt up** *vi (Brit inf)* la boucler

**beltway** ['bɛltweɪ] *n (US Aut)* route *f* de ceinture; (: *motorway)* périphérique *m*

**bemoan** [bɪ'məʊn] *vt* se lamenter sur

**bemused** [bɪ'mjuːzd] *adj* médusé(e)

**bench** [bɛntʃ] *n* banc *m*; *(in workshop)* établi *m*; **the B~** *(Law: judges)* la magistrature, la Cour

**bench mark** *n* repère *m*

**bend** [bɛnd] *(pt, pp* **bent** [bɛnt]) *vt* courber; *(leg, arm)* plier ▷ *vi* se courber ▷ *n (Brit: in road)* virage *m*, tournant *m*; *(in pipe, river)* coude *m*

▶ **bend down** *vi* se baisser

▶ **bend over** *vi* se pencher

**bends** [bɛndz] *npl (Med)* maladie *f* des caissons

**beneath** [bɪ'niːθ] *prep* sous, au-dessous de; *(unworthy of)* indigne de ▷ *adv* dessous, au-dessous, en bas

**benefactor** ['bɛnɪfæktər] *n* bienfaiteur *m*

**benefactress** ['bɛnɪfæktrɪs] *n* bienfaitrice *f*

**beneficial** [bɛnɪ'fɪʃəl] *adj*: **~ (to)** salutaire (pour), bénéfique (à)

**beneficiary** [bɛnɪ'fɪʃərɪ] *n (Law)* bénéficiaire *m/f*

**benefit** ['bɛnɪfɪt] *n* avantage *m*, profit *m*; *(allowance of money)* allocation *f* ▷ *vt* faire du bien à, profiter à ▷ *vi*: **he'll ~ from it** cela lui fera du bien, il y gagnera *or* s'en trouvera bien

**benefit performance** *n* représentation *f or* gala *m* de bienfaisance

**Benelux** ['bɛnɪlʌks] *n* Bénélux *m*

**benevolent** [bɪ'nɛvələnt] *adj* bienveillant(e)

**BEng** *n abbr (= Bachelor of Engineering)* diplôme universitaire

**benign** [bɪ'naɪn] *adj (person, smile)* bienveillant(e), affable; *(Med)* bénin(-igne)

**bent** [bɛnt] *pt, pp of* **bend** ▷ *n* inclination *f*, penchant *m* ▷ *adj (wire, pipe)* coudé(e); *(inf: dishonest)* véreux(-euse); **to be ~ on** être résolu(e) à

**bequeath** [bɪ'kwiːð] *vt* léguer

**bequest** [bɪ'kwɛst] *n* legs *m*

**bereaved** [bɪ'riːvd] *n*: **the ~** la famille du disparu ▷ *adj* endeuillé(e)

**bereavement** [bɪˈriːvmənt] n deuil m
**beret** [ˈbɛreɪ] n béret m
**Bering Sea** [ˈbeɪrɪŋ-] n: **the ~** la mer de Béring
**berk** [bəːk] n (Brit inf) andouille m/f
**Berks** abbr (Brit) = **Berkshire**
**Berlin** [bəːˈlɪn] n Berlin; **East/West ~** Berlin Est/Ouest
**berm** [bəːm] n (US Aut) accotement m
**Bermuda** [bəːˈmjuːdə] n Bermudes fpl
**Bermuda shorts** npl bermuda m
**Bern** [bəːn] n Berne
**berry** [ˈbɛrɪ] n baie f
**berserk** [bəˈsəːk] adj: **to go ~** être pris(e) d'une rage incontrôlable; se déchaîner
**berth** [bəːθ] n (bed) couchette f; (for ship) poste m d'amarrage, mouillage m ▷ vi (in harbour) venir à quai; (at anchor) mouiller; **to give sb a wide ~** (fig) éviter qn
**beseech** (pt, pp **besought**) [bɪˈsiːtʃ, -ˈsɔːt] vt implorer, supplier
**beset** (pt, pp **-**) [bɪˈsɛt] vt assaillir ▷ adj: **~ with** semé(e) de
**besetting** [bɪˈsɛtɪŋ] adj: **his ~ sin** son vice, son gros défaut
**beside** [bɪˈsaɪd] prep à côté de; (compared with) par rapport à; **that's ~ the point** ça n'a rien à voir; **to be ~ o.s. (with anger)** être hors de soi
**besides** [bɪˈsaɪdz] adv en outre, de plus ▷ prep en plus de; (except) excepté
**besiege** [bɪˈsiːdʒ] vt (town) assiéger; (fig) assaillir
**besotted** [bɪˈsɔtɪd] adj (Brit): **~ with** entiché(e) de
**besought** [bɪˈsɔːt] pt, pp of **beseech**
**bespectacled** [bɪˈspɛktɪkld] adj à lunettes
**bespoke** [bɪˈspəuk] adj (Brit: garment) fait(e) sur mesure; **~ tailor** tailleur m à façon
**best** [bɛst] adj meilleur(e) ▷ adv le mieux; **the ~ part of** (quantity) le plus clair de, la plus grande partie de; **at ~** au mieux; **to make the ~ of sth** s'accommoder de qch (du mieux que l'on peut); **to do one's ~** faire de son mieux; **to the ~ of my knowledge** pour autant que je sache; **to the ~ of my ability** du mieux que je pourrai; **he's not exactly patient at the ~ of times** il n'est jamais spécialement patient; **the ~ thing to do is ...** le mieux, c'est de ...
**best-before date** n date f de limite d'utilisation or de consommation
**best man** (irreg) n garçon m d'honneur
**bestow** [bɪˈstəu] vt accorder; (title) conférer
**bestseller** [ˈbɛstˈsɛləʳ] n best-seller m, succès m de librairie
**bet** [bɛt] n pari m ▷ vt, vi (pt, pp - or **-ted**) parier; **it's a safe ~** (fig) il y a de fortes chances; **to ~ sb sth** parier qch à qn
**Bethlehem** [ˈbɛθlɪhɛm] n Bethléem
**betray** [bɪˈtreɪ] vt trahir
**betrayal** [bɪˈtreɪəl] n trahison f
**better** [ˈbɛtəʳ] adj meilleur(e) ▷ adv mieux ▷ vt améliorer ▷ n: **to get the ~ of** triompher de, l'emporter sur; **a change for the ~** une amélioration; **I had ~ go** il faut que je m'en

aille; **you had ~ do it** vous feriez mieux de le faire; **he thought ~ of it** il s'est ravisé; **to get ~** (Med) aller mieux; (improve) s'améliorer; **that's ~!** c'est mieux!; **~ off** adj plus à l'aise financièrement; (fig): **you'd be ~ off this way** vous vous trouveriez mieux ainsi, ce serait mieux or plus pratique ainsi
**betting** [ˈbɛtɪŋ] n paris mpl
**betting shop** n (Brit) bureau m de paris
**between** [bɪˈtwiːn] prep entre ▷ adv au milieu, dans l'intervalle; **the road ~ here and London** la route d'ici à Londres; **we only had 5 ~ us** nous n'en avions que 5 en tout
**bevel** [ˈbɛvəl] n (also: **bevel edge**) biseau m
**beverage** [ˈbɛvərɪdʒ] n boisson f (gén sans alcool)
**bevy** [ˈbɛvɪ] n: **a ~ of** un essaim or une volée de
**bewail** [bɪˈweɪl] vt se lamenter sur
**beware** [bɪˈwɛəʳ] vt, vi: **to ~ (of)** prendre garde (à); **"~ of the dog"** "(attention) chien méchant"
**bewildered** [bɪˈwɪldəd] adj dérouté(e), ahuri(e)
**bewildering** [bɪˈwɪldrɪŋ] adj déroutant(e), ahurissant(e)
**bewitching** [bɪˈwɪtʃɪŋ] adj enchanteur(-teresse)
**beyond** [bɪˈjɔnd] prep (in space, time) au-delà de; (exceeding) au-dessus de ▷ adv au-delà; **~ doubt** hors de doute; **~ repair** irréparable
**b/f** abbr = **brought forward**
**BFPO** n abbr (= British Forces Post Office) service postal de l'armée
**bhp** n abbr (Aut: = brake horsepower) puissance f aux freins
**bi...** [baɪ] prefix bi...
**biannual** [baɪˈænjuəl] adj semestriel(le)
**bias** [ˈbaɪəs] n (prejudice) préjugé m, parti pris; (preference) prévention f
**biased, biassed** [ˈbaɪəst] adj partial(e), montrant un parti pris; **to be bias(s)ed against** avoir un préjugé contre
**biathlon** [baɪˈæθlən] n biathlon m
**bib** [bɪb] n bavoir m, bavette f
**Bible** [ˈbaɪbl] n Bible f
**bibliography** [bɪblɪˈɔɡrəfɪ] n bibliographie f
**bicarbonate of soda** [baɪˈkɑːbənɪt-] n bicarbonate m de soude
**bicentenary** [baɪsɛnˈtiːnərɪ] n, **bicentennial** [baɪsɛnˈtɛnɪəl] ▷ n bicentenaire m
**biceps** [ˈbaɪsɛps] n biceps m
**bicker** [ˈbɪkəʳ] vi se chamailler
**bicycle** [ˈbaɪsɪkl] n bicyclette f
**bicycle path** n, **bicycle track** n piste f cyclable
**bicycle pump** n pompe f à vélo
**bid** [bɪd] n offre f; (at auction) enchère f; (attempt) tentative f ▷ vi (pt, pp -) faire une enchère or offre ▷ vt (pt **bade**) [bæd] (pp **-den**) [ˈbɪdn] faire une enchère or offre de; **to ~ sb good day** souhaiter le bonjour à qn
**bidden** [ˈbɪdn] pp of **bid**
**bidder** [ˈbɪdəʳ] n: **the highest ~** le plus offrant
**bidding** [ˈbɪdɪŋ] n enchères fpl
**bide** [baɪd] vt: **to ~ one's time** attendre son heure

**bidet** ['bi:deɪ] n bidet m
**bidirectional** ['baɪdɪ'rɛkʃənl] adj
bidirectionnel(le)
**biennial** [baɪ'ɛnɪəl] adj biennal(e), bisannuel(le)
▷ n biennale f; (plant) plante bisannuelle
**bier** [bɪər] n bière f (cercueil)
**bifocals** [baɪ'fəuklz] npl lunettes fpl à double
foyer
**big** [bɪg] adj (in height: person, building, tree)
grand(e); (in bulk, amount: person, parcel, book)
gros(se); **to do things in a ~ way** faire les
choses en grand
**bigamy** ['bɪgəmɪ] n bigamie f
**big dipper** [-'dɪpər] n montagnes fpl russes
**big end** n (Aut) tête f de bielle
**biggish** ['bɪgɪʃ] adj (see big) assez grand(e), assez
gros(se)
**bigheaded** ['bɪg'hɛdɪd] adj prétentieux(-euse)
**big-hearted** ['bɪg'hɑ:tɪd] adj au grand cœur
**bigot** ['bɪgət] n fanatique m/f, sectaire m/f
**bigoted** ['bɪgətɪd] adj fanatique, sectaire
**bigotry** ['bɪgətrɪ] n fanatisme m, sectarisme m
**big toe** n gros orteil
**big top** n grand chapiteau
**big wheel** n (at fair) grande roue
**bigwig** ['bɪgwɪg] n (inf) grosse légume, huile f
**bike** [baɪk] n vélo m, bécane f
**bike lane** n piste f cyclable
**bikini** [bɪ'ki:nɪ] n bikini m
**bilateral** [baɪ'lætərl] adj bilatéral(e)
**bile** [baɪl] n bile f
**bilingual** [baɪ'lɪŋgwəl] adj bilingue
**bilious** ['bɪlɪəs] adj bilieux(-euse); (fig)
maussade, irritable
**bill** [bɪl] n note f, facture f; (in restaurant) addition
f, note f; (Pol) projet m de loi; (US: banknote) billet
m (de banque); (notice) affiche f; (of bird) bec m;
(Theat): **on the ~** à l'affiche ▷ vt (item) facturer;
(customer) remettre la facture à; **may I have the
~ please?** (est-ce que je peux avoir) l'addition,
s'il vous plaît?; **put it on my ~** mettez-le sur
mon compte; **"post no ~s"** "défense
d'afficher"; **to fit** or **fill the ~** (fig) faire
l'affaire; **~ of exchange** lettre f de change; **~ of
lading** connaissement m; **~ of sale** contrat m de
vente
**billboard** ['bɪlbɔ:d] (US) n panneau m
d'affichage
**billet** ['bɪlɪt] n cantonnement m (chez
l'habitant) ▷ vt (troops) cantonner
**billfold** ['bɪlfəuld] n (US) portefeuille m
**billiards** ['bɪljədz] n (jeu m de) billard m
**billion** ['bɪljən] n (Brit) billion m (million de
millions); (US) milliard m
**billow** ['bɪləu] n nuage m ▷ vi (smoke) s'élever en
nuage; (sail) se gonfler
**billy goat** ['bɪlɪgəut] n bouc m
**bimbo** ['bɪmbəu] n (inf) ravissante idiote f
**bin** [bɪn] n boîte f; (Brit: also: **dustbin, litter bin**)
poubelle f; (for coal) coffre m
**binary** ['baɪnərɪ] adj binaire
**bind** (pt, pp **bound**) [baɪnd, baund] vt attacher;

(book) relier; (oblige) obliger, contraindre ▷ n (inf:
nuisance) scie f
▶ **bind over** vt (Law) mettre en liberté
conditionnelle
▶ **bind up** vt (wound) panser; **to be bound up in**
(work, research etc) être complètement absorbé
par, être accroché par; **to be bound up with**
(person) être accroché à
**binder** ['baɪndər] n (file) classeur m
**binding** ['baɪndɪŋ] n (of book) reliure f ▷ adj
(contract) qui constitue une obligation
**binge** [bɪndʒ] n (inf): **to go on a ~** faire la
bringue
**bingo** ['bɪŋgəu] n sorte de jeu de loto pratiqué dans des
établissements publics
**bin liner** n sac m poubelle
**binoculars** [bɪ'nɔkjuləz] npl jumelles fpl
**biochemistry** [baɪə'kɛmɪstrɪ] n biochimie f
**biodegradable** ['baɪəudɪ'greɪdəbl] adj
biodégradable
**biodiversity** ['baɪəudaɪ'və:sɪtɪ] n biodiversité f
**biofuel** ['baɪəufjuəl] n combustible m
organique
**biographer** [baɪ'ɔgrəfər] n biographe m/f
**biographic** [baɪə'græfɪk], **biographical**
[baɪə'græfɪkl] adj biographique
**biography** [baɪ'ɔgrəfɪ] n biographie f
**biological** [baɪə'lɔdʒɪkl] adj biologique
**biological clock** n horloge f physiologique
**biologist** [baɪ'ɔlədʒɪst] n biologiste m/f
**biology** [baɪ'ɔlədʒɪ] n biologie f
**biometric** [baɪə'mɛtrɪk] adj biométrique
**biophysics** ['baɪəu'fɪzɪks] n biophysique f
**biopic** ['baɪəupɪk] n film m biographique
**biopsy** ['baɪɔpsɪ] n biopsie f
**biosphere** ['baɪəsfɪər] n biosphère f
**biotechnology** ['baɪəutɛk'nɔlədʒɪ] n
biotechnologie f
**birch** [bə:tʃ] n bouleau m
**bird** [bə:d] n oiseau m; (Brit inf: girl) nana f
**bird flu** n grippe f aviaire
**bird of prey** n oiseau m de proie
**bird's-eye view** ['bə:dzaɪ-] n vue f à vol d'oiseau;
(fig) vue d'ensemble or générale
**bird watcher** [-wɔtʃər] n ornithologue m/f
amateur
**birdwatching** ['bə:dwɔtʃɪŋ] n ornithologie f
(d'amateur)
**Biro®** ['baɪərəu] n stylo m à bille
**birth** [bə:θ] n naissance f; **to give ~ to** donner
naissance à, mettre au monde; (subj: animal)
mettre bas
**birth certificate** n acte m de naissance
**birth control** n (policy) limitation f des
naissances; (methods) méthode(s)
contraceptive(s)
**birthday** ['bə:θdeɪ] n anniversaire m ▷ cpd (cake,
card etc) d'anniversaire
**birthmark** ['bə:θmɑ:k] n envie f, tache f de vin
**birthplace** ['bə:θpleɪs] n lieu m de naissance
**birth rate** n (taux m de) natalité f
**Biscay** ['bɪskeɪ] n: **the Bay of ~** le golfe de

Gascogne

**biscuit** ['bɪskɪt] n (Brit) biscuit m; (US) petit pain au lait

**bisect** [baɪ'sɛkt] vt couper or diviser en deux

**bisexual** ['baɪ'sɛksjuəl] adj, n bisexuel(le)

**bishop** ['bɪʃəp] n évêque m; (Chess) fou m

**bistro** ['bi:strəu] n petit restaurant m, bistrot m

**bit** [bɪt] pt of **bite** ▷ n morceau m; (Comput) bit m, élément m binaire; (of tool) mèche f; (of horse) mors m; **a ~ of** un peu de; **a ~ mad/dangerous** un peu fou/risqué; **~ by ~** petit à petit; **to come to ~s** (break) tomber en morceaux, se déglinguer; **bring all your ~s and pieces** apporte toutes tes affaires; **to do one's ~** y mettre du sien

**bitch** [bɪtʃ] n (dog) chienne f; (inf!) salope f (!), garce f

**bite** [baɪt] vt, vi (pt **bit**, pp **bitten** [bɪt, 'bɪtn]) mordre; (insect) piquer ▷ n morsure f; (insect bite) piqûre f; (mouthful) bouchée f; **let's have a ~ (to eat)** mangeons un morceau; **to ~ one's nails** se ronger les ongles

**biting** ['baɪtɪŋ] adj mordant(e)

**bit part** n (Theat) petit rôle

**bitten** ['bɪtn] pp of **bite**

**bitter** ['bɪtəʳ] adj amer(-ère); (criticism) cinglant(e); (icy: weather, wind) glacial(e) ▷ n (Brit: beer) bière f (à forte teneur en houblon); **to the ~ end** jusqu'au bout

**bitterly** ['bɪtəlɪ] adv (complain, weep) amèrement; (oppose, criticise) durement, âprement; (jealous, disappointed) horriblement; **it's ~ cold** il fait un froid de loup

**bitterness** ['bɪtənɪs] n amertume f; goût amer

**bittersweet** ['bɪtəswi:t] adj aigre-doux (douce)

**bitty** ['bɪtɪ] adj (Brit inf) décousu(e)

**bitumen** ['bɪtjumɪn] n bitume m

**bivouac** ['bɪvuæk] n bivouac m

**bizarre** [bɪ'zɑːʳ] adj bizarre

**bk** abbr = **bank**; **book**

**BL** n abbr (= Bachelor of Law(s), Bachelor of Letters) diplôme universitaire; (US: = Bachelor of Literature) diplôme universitaire

**bl** abbr = **bill of lading**

**blab** [blæb] vi jaser, trop parler ▷ vt (also: **blab out**) laisser échapper, aller raconter

**black** [blæk] adj noir(e) ▷ n (colour) noir m; (person): **B~** noir(e) ▷ vt (shoes) cirer; (Brit Industry) boycotter; **to give sb a ~ eye** pocher l'œil à qn, faire un œil au beurre noir à qn; **there it is in ~ and white** (fig) c'est écrit noir sur blanc; **to be in the ~** (in credit) avoir un compte créditeur; **~ and blue** (bruised) couvert(e) de bleus

▷ **black out** vi (faint) s'évanouir

**black belt** n (Judo etc) ceinture noire; **he's a ~** il est ceinture noire

**blackberry** ['blækbərɪ] n mûre f

**blackbird** ['blækbəːd] n merle m

**blackboard** ['blækbɔːd] n tableau noir

**black box** n (Aviat) boîte noire

**black coffee** n café noir

**Black Country** n (Brit): **the ~** le Pays Noir (dans les Midlands)

**blackcurrant** ['blæk'kʌrənt] n cassis m

**black economy** n (Brit) travail m au noir

**blacken** ['blækn] vt noircir

**Black Forest** n: **the ~** la Forêt Noire

**blackhead** ['blækhɛd] n point noir

**black hole** n (Astronomy) trou noir

**black ice** n verglas m

**blackjack** ['blækdʒæk] n (Cards) vingt-et-un m; (US: truncheon) matraque f

**blackleg** ['blæklɛg] n (Brit) briseur m de grève, jaune m

**blacklist** ['blæklɪst] n liste noire ▷ vt mettre sur la liste noire

**blackmail** ['blækmeɪl] n chantage m ▷ vt faire chanter, soumettre au chantage

**blackmailer** ['blækmeɪləʳ] n maître-chanteur m

**black market** n marché noir

**blackout** ['blækaut] n panne f d'électricité; (in wartime) black-out m; (TV) interruption f d'émission; (fainting) syncope f

**black pepper** n poivre noir

**black pudding** n boudin m (noir)

**Black Sea** n: **the ~** la mer Noire

**black sheep** n brebis galeuse

**blacksmith** ['blæksmɪθ] n forgeron m

**black spot** n (Aut) point noir

**bladder** ['blædəʳ] n vessie f

**blade** [bleɪd] n lame f; (of oar) plat m; (of propeller) pale f; **a ~ of grass** un brin d'herbe

**blame** [bleɪm] n faute f, blâme m ▷ vt: **to ~ sb/sth for sth** attribuer à qn/qch la responsabilité de qch; reprocher qch à qn/qch; **who's to ~?** qui est le fautif or coupable or responsable?; **I'm not to ~** ce n'est pas ma faute

**blameless** ['bleɪmlɪs] adj irréprochable

**blanch** [blɑːntʃ] vi (person, face) blêmir ▷ vt (Culin) blanchir

**bland** [blænd] adj affable; (taste, food) doux (douce), fade

**blank** [blæŋk] adj blanc (blanche); (look) sans expression, dénué(e) d'expression ▷ n espace m vide, blanc m; (cartridge) cartouche f à blanc; **his mind was a ~** il avait la tête vide; **we drew a ~** (fig) nous n'avons abouti à rien

**blank cheque**, (US) **blank check** n chèque m en blanc; **to give sb a ~ to do ...** (fig) donner carte blanche à qn pour faire ...

**blanket** ['blæŋkɪt] n couverture f; (of snow, cloud) couche f ▷ adj (statement, agreement) global(e), de portée générale; **to give ~ cover** (insurance policy) couvrir tous les risques

**blare** [blɛəʳ] vi (brass band, horns, radio) beugler

**blasé** ['blɑːzeɪ] adj blasé(e)

**blasphemous** ['blæsfɪməs] adj (words) blasphématoire; (person) blasphémateur(-trice)

**blasphemy** ['blæsfɪmɪ] n blasphème m

**blast** [blɑːst] n explosion f; (shock wave) souffle m; (of air, steam) bouffée f ▷ vt faire sauter or exploser ▷ excl (Brit inf) zut!; **(at) full ~** (play music etc) à plein volume

▸ **blast off** vi (Space) décoller

**blast-off** ['blɑ:stɔf] n (Space) lancement m

**blatant** ['bleɪtənt] adj flagrant(e), criant(e)

**blatantly** ['bleɪtəntlɪ] adv (lie) ouvertement; **it's ~ obvious** c'est l'évidence même

**blaze** [bleɪz] n (fire) incendie m; (flames: of fire, sun etc) embrasement m; (: in hearth) flamme f, flambée f; (fig) flamboiement m ▷ vi (fire) flamber; (fig) flamboyer, resplendir ▷ vt: **to ~ a trail** (fig) montrer la voie; **in a ~ of publicity** à grand renfort de publicité

**blazer** ['bleɪzər] n blazer m

**bleach** [bli:tʃ] n (also: **household bleach**) eau f de Javel ▷ vt (linen) blanchir

**bleached** [bli:tʃt] adj (hair) oxygéné(e), décoloré(e)

**bleachers** ['bli:tʃəz] npl (US Sport) gradins mpl (en plein soleil)

**bleak** [bli:k] adj morne, désolé(e); (weather) triste, maussade; (smile) lugubre; (prospect, future) morose

**bleary-eyed** ['blɪərɪ'aɪd] adj aux yeux pleins de sommeil

**bleat** [bli:t] n bêlement m ▷ vi bêler

**bled** ['bled] pt, pp of **bleed**

**bleed** (pt, pp **bled**) [bli:d, bled] vt saigner; (brakes, radiator) purger ▷ vi saigner; **my nose is ~ing** je saigne du nez

**bleep** [bli:p] n (Radio, TV) top m; (of pocket device) bip m ▷ vi émettre des signaux ▷ vt (doctor etc) appeler (au moyen d'un bip)

**bleeper** ['bli:pər] n (of doctor etc) bip m

**blemish** ['blemɪʃ] n défaut m; (on reputation) tache f

**blend** [blend] n mélange m ▷ vt mélanger ▷ vi (colours etc: also: **blend in**) se mélanger, se fondre, s'allier

**blender** ['blendər] n (Culin) mixeur m

**bless** (pt, pp **-ed** or **blest**) [bles, blest] vt bénir; **to be ~ed with** avoir le bonheur de jouir de or d'avoir; **~ you!** (after sneeze) à tes souhaits!

**blessed** ['blesɪd] adj (Rel: holy) béni(e); (happy) bienheureux(-euse); **it rains every ~ day** il ne se passe pas de jour sans qu'il ne pleuve

**blessing** ['blesɪŋ] n bénédiction f; (godsend) bienfait m; **to count one's ~s** s'estimer heureux; **it was a ~ in disguise** c'est un bien pour un mal

**blew** [blu:] pt of **blow**

**blight** [blaɪt] n (of plants) rouille f ▷ vt (hopes etc) anéantir, briser

**blimey** ['blaɪmɪ] excl (Brit inf) mince alors!

**blind** [blaɪnd] adj aveugle ▷ n (for window) store m ▷ vt aveugler; **to turn a ~ eye (on or to)** fermer les yeux (sur); **the blind** npl les aveugles mpl

**blind alley** n impasse f

**blind corner** n (Brit) virage m sans visibilité

**blind date** n rendez-vous galant (avec un(e) inconnu(e))

**blindfold** ['blaɪndfəuld] n bandeau m ▷ adj, adv les yeux bandés ▷ vt bander les yeux à

**blindly** ['blaɪndlɪ] adv aveuglément

**blindness** ['blaɪndnɪs] n cécité f; (fig)

**blind spot** n (Aut etc) angle m aveugle; (fig) angle mort

**blink** [blɪŋk] vi cligner des yeux; (light) clignoter ▷ n: **the TV's on the ~** (inf) la télé ne va pas tarder à nous lâcher

**blinkers** ['blɪŋkəz] npl œillères fpl

**blinking** ['blɪŋkɪŋ] adj (Brit inf): **this ~ ...** ce fichu or sacré ...

**blip** [blɪp] n (on radar etc) spot m; (on graph) petite aberration; (fig) petite anomalie (passagère)

**bliss** [blɪs] n félicité f, bonheur m sans mélange

**blissful** ['blɪsful] adj (event, day) merveilleux(-euse); (smile) de bonheur; **a ~ sigh** un soupir d'aise; **in ~ ignorance** dans une ignorance béate

**blissfully** ['blɪsfulɪ] adv (smile) béatement; (happy) merveilleusement

**blister** ['blɪstər] n (on skin) ampoule f, cloque f; (on paintwork) boursouflure f ▷ vi (paint) se boursoufler, se cloquer

**BLit, BLitt** n abbr (= Bachelor of Literature) diplôme universitaire

**blithely** ['blaɪðlɪ] adv (unconcernedly) tranquillement; (joyfully) gaiement

**blithering** ['blɪðərɪŋ] adj (inf): **this ~ idiot** cet espèce d'idiot

**blitz** [blɪts] n bombardement (aérien); **to have a ~ on sth** (fig) s'attaquer à qch

**blizzard** ['blɪzəd] n blizzard m, tempête f de neige

**BLM** n abbr (US: = Bureau of Land Management) ≈ les domaines

**bloated** ['bləutɪd] adj (face) bouffi(e); (stomach, person) gonflé(e)

**blob** [blɔb] n (drop) goutte f; (stain, spot) tache f

**bloc** [blɔk] n (Pol) bloc m

**block** [blɔk] n bloc m; (in pipes) obstruction f; (toy) cube m; (of buildings) pâté m (de maisons) ▷ vt bloquer; (fig) faire obstacle à; (Comput) grouper; **the sink is ~ed** l'évier est bouché; **~ of flats** (Brit) immeuble (locatif); **3 ~s from here** à trois rues d'ici; **mental ~** blocage m; **~ and tackle** (Tech) palan m

▸ **block up** vt boucher

**blockade** [blɔ'keɪd] n blocus m ▷ vt faire le blocus de

**blockage** ['blɔkɪdʒ] n obstruction f

**block booking** n réservation f en bloc

**blockbuster** ['blɔkbʌstər] n (film, book) grand succès

**block capitals** npl majuscules fpl d'imprimerie

**blockhead** ['blɔkhed] n imbécile m/f

**block letters** npl majuscules fpl

**block release** n (Brit) congé m de formation

**block vote** n (Brit) vote m de délégation

**blog** [blɔg] n blog m, blogue m ▷ vi bloguer

**blogger** ['blɔgər] (inf) n (person) blogueur(-euse) m/f

**blogging** [blɔgɪŋ] n blogging m

**bloke** [bləuk] n (Brit inf) type m

**blond, blonde** [blɔnd] adj, n blond(e)

481

**blood** [blʌd] n sang m
**blood bank** n banque f du sang
**blood count** n numération f globulaire
**bloodcurdling** ['blʌdkə:dlɪŋ] adj à vous glacer le sang
**blood donor** n donneur(-euse) de sang
**blood group** n groupe sanguin
**bloodhound** ['blʌdhaund] n limier m
**bloodless** ['blʌdlɪs] adj (victory) sans effusion de sang; (pale) anémié(e)
**bloodletting** ['blʌdletɪŋ] n (Med) saignée f; (fig) effusion f de sang, représailles fpl
**blood poisoning** n empoisonnement m du sang
**blood pressure** n tension (artérielle); **to have high/low ~** faire de l'hypertension/l'hypotension
**bloodshed** ['blʌdʃɛd] n effusion f de sang, carnage m
**bloodshot** ['blʌdʃɒt] adj: **~ eyes** yeux injectés de sang
**blood sports** npl sports mpl sanguinaires
**bloodstained** ['blʌdsteɪnd] adj taché(e) de sang
**bloodstream** ['blʌdstri:m] n sang m, système sanguin
**blood test** n analyse f de sang
**bloodthirsty** ['blʌdθə:stɪ] adj sanguinaire
**blood transfusion** n transfusion f de sang
**blood type** n groupe sanguin
**blood vessel** n vaisseau sanguin
**bloody** ['blʌdɪ] adj sanglant(e); (Brit inf!): **this ~ ...** ce foutu ..., ce putain de ... (!) ▷ adv: **~ strong/good** (Brit: inf!) vachement or sacrément fort/bon
**bloody-minded** ['blʌdɪ'maɪndɪd] adj (Brit inf) contrariant(e), obstiné(e)
**bloom** [blu:m] n fleur f; (fig) épanouissement m ▷ vi être en fleur; (fig) s'épanouir; être florissant(e)
**blooming** ['blu:mɪŋ] adj (inf): **this ~ ...** ce fichu or sacré ...
**blossom** ['blɒsəm] n fleur(s) f(pl) ▷ vi être en fleurs; (fig) s'épanouir; **to ~ into** (fig) devenir
**blot** [blɒt] n tache f ▷ vt tacher; (ink) sécher; **to be a ~ on the landscape** gâcher le paysage; **to ~ one's copy book** (fig) faire un impair
▶ **blot out** vt (memories) effacer; (view) cacher, masquer; (nation, city) annihiler
**blotchy** ['blɒtʃɪ] adj (complexion) couvert(e) de marbrures
**blotting paper** ['blɒtɪŋ-] n buvard m
**blotto** ['blɒtəu] adj (inf) bourré(e)
**blouse** [blauz] n (feminine garment) chemisier m, corsage m
**blow** [bləu] (pt **blew**, pp **-n**) [blu:, bləun] n coup m ▷ vi souffler ▷ vt (glass) souffler; (instrument) jouer de; (fuse) faire sauter; **to ~ one's nose** se moucher; **to ~ a whistle** siffler; **to come to ~s** en venir aux coups
▶ **blow away** vi s'envoler ▷ vt chasser, faire s'envoler
▶ **blow down** vt faire tomber, renverser
▶ **blow off** vi s'envoler ▷ vt (hat) emporter;

(ship): **to ~ off course** faire dévier
▶ **blow out** vi (fire, flame) s'éteindre; (tyre) éclater; (fuse) sauter
▶ **blow over** vi s'apaiser
▶ **blow up** vi exploser, sauter ▷ vt faire sauter; (tyre) gonfler; (Phot) agrandir
**blow-dry** ['bləudraɪ] n (hairstyle) brushing m ▷ vt faire un brushing à
**blowlamp** ['bləulæmp] n (Brit) chalumeau m
**blown** [bləun] pp of **blow**
**blow-out** ['bləuaut] n (of tyre) éclatement m; (Brit: inf: big meal) gueuleton m
**blowtorch** ['bləutɔ:tʃ] n chalumeau m
**blowzy** ['blauzɪ] adj (Brit) peu soigné(e)
**BLS** n abbr (US) = **Bureau of Labor Statistics**
**blubber** ['blʌbər] n blanc m de baleine ▷ vi (pej) pleurer comme un veau
**bludgeon** ['blʌdʒən] n gourdin m, trique f
**blue** [blu:] adj bleu(e); (depressed) triste; **~ film/joke** film m/histoire f pornographique; **(only) once in a ~ moon** tous les trente-six du mois; **out of the ~** (fig) à l'improviste, sans qu'on s'y attende
**blue baby** n enfant bleu(e)
**bluebell** ['blu:bɛl] n jacinthe f des bois
**blueberry** ['blu:bərɪ] n myrtille f, airelle f
**bluebottle** ['blu:bɒtl] n mouche f à viande
**blue cheese** n (fromage) bleu m
**blue-chip** ['blu:tʃɪp] adj: **~ investment** investissement m de premier ordre
**blue-collar worker** ['blu:kɒlər-] n ouvrier(-ère) col bleu
**blue jeans** npl blue-jeans mpl
**blueprint** ['blu:prɪnt] n bleu m; (fig) projet m, plan directeur
**blues** [blu:z] npl: **the ~** (Mus) le blues; **to have the ~** (inf: feeling) avoir le cafard
**bluff** [blʌf] vi bluffer ▷ n bluff m; (cliff) promontoire m, falaise f ▷ adj (person) bourru(e), brusque; **to call sb's ~** mettre qn au défi d'exécuter ses menaces
**blunder** ['blʌndər] n gaffe f, bévue f ▷ vi faire une gaffe or une bévue; **to ~ into sb/sth** buter contre qn/qch
**blunt** [blʌnt] adj (knife) émoussé(e), peu tranchant(e); (pencil) mal taillé(e); (person) brusque, ne mâchant pas ses mots ▷ vt émousser; **~ instrument** (Law) instrument contondant
**bluntly** ['blʌntlɪ] adv carrément, sans prendre de gants
**bluntness** ['blʌntnɪs] n (of person) brusquerie f, franchise brutale
**blur** [blə:r] n (shape): **to become a ~** devenir flou ▷ vt brouiller, rendre flou(e)
**blurb** [blə:b] n (for book) texte m de présentation; (pej) baratin m
**blurred** [blə:d] adj flou(e)
**blurt** [blə:t]: **to ~ out** vt (reveal) lâcher; (say) balbutier, dire d'une voix entrecoupée
**blush** [blʌʃ] vi rougir ▷ n rougeur f
**blusher** ['blʌʃər] n rouge m à joues

**bluster** ['blʌstə$^r$] n paroles fpl en l'air; (boasting) fanfaronnades fpl; (threats) menaces fpl en l'air ▷ vi parler en l'air; fanfaronner

**blustering** ['blʌstərɪŋ] adj fanfaron(ne)

**blustery** ['blʌstərɪ] adj (weather) à bourrasques

**Blvd** abbr (= boulevard) Bd

**BM** n abbr = **British Museum**; (Scol: = Bachelor of Medicine) diplôme universitaire

**BMA** n abbr = **British Medical Association**

**BMJ** n abbr = **British Medical Journal**

**BMus** n abbr (= Bachelor of Music) diplôme universitaire

**BMX** n abbr (= bicycle motorcross) BMX m

**BO** n abbr (inf: = body odour) odeurs corporelles; (US) = **box office**

**boar** [bɔː$^r$] n sanglier m

**board** [bɔːd] n (wooden) planche f; (on wall) panneau m; (for chess etc) plateau m; (cardboard) carton m; (committee) conseil m, comité m; (in firm) conseil d'administration; (Naut, Aviat): on ~ à bord ▷ vt (ship) monter à bord de; (train) monter dans; **full ~** (Brit) pension complète; **half ~** (Brit) demi-pension f; **~ and lodging** (n) chambre f avec pension; **with ~ and lodging** logé nourri; **above ~** (fig) régulier(-ère); **across the ~** (fig: adv) systématiquement; (: adj) de portée générale; **to go by the ~** (hopes, principles) être abandonné(e); (be unimportant) compter pour rien, n'avoir aucune importance
  ▶ **board up** vt (door) condamner (au moyen de planches, de tôle)

**boarder** ['bɔːdə$^r$] n pensionnaire m/f; (Scol) interne m/f, pensionnaire

**board game** n jeu m de société

**boarding card** ['bɔːdɪŋ-] n (Aviat, Naut) carte f d'embarquement

**boarding house** ['bɔːdɪŋ-] n pension f

**boarding party** ['bɔːdɪŋ-] n section f d'abordage

**boarding pass** ['bɔːdɪŋ-] n (Brit) = **boarding card**

**boarding school** ['bɔːdɪŋ-] n internat m, pensionnat m

**board meeting** n réunion f du conseil d'administration

**board room** n salle f du conseil d'administration

**boardwalk** ['bɔːdwɔːk] n (US) cheminement m en planches

**boast** [bəust] vi: **to ~ (about or of)** se vanter (de) ▷ vt s'enorgueillir de ▷ n vantardise f; sujet m d'orgueil or de fierté

**boastful** ['bəustful] adj vantard(e)

**boastfulness** ['bəustfulnɪs] n vantardise f

**boat** [bəut] n bateau m; (small) canot m; barque f; **to go by ~** aller en bateau; **to be in the same ~** (fig) être logé à la même enseigne

**boater** ['bəutə$^r$] n (hat) canotier m

**boating** ['bəutɪŋ] n canotage m

**boat people** npl boat people mpl

**boatswain** ['bəusn] n maître m d'équipage

**bob** [bɔb] vi (boat, cork on water: also: **bob up and down**) danser, se balancer ▷ n (Brit inf) = **shilling**

▶ **bob up** vi surgir or apparaître brusquement

**bobbin** ['bɔbɪn] n bobine f; (of sewing machine) navette f

**bobby** ['bɔbɪ] n (Brit inf) ≈ agent m (de police)

**bobby pin** ['bɔbɪ-] n (US) pince f à cheveux

**bobsleigh** ['bɔbsleɪ] n bob m

**bode** [bəud] vi: **to ~ well/ill (for)** être de bon/mauvais augure (pour)

**bodice** ['bɔdɪs] n corsage m

**bodily** ['bɔdɪlɪ] adj corporel(le); (pain, comfort) physique; (needs) matériel(le) ▷ adv (carry, lift) dans ses bras

**body** ['bɔdɪ] n corps m; (of car) carrosserie f; (of plane) fuselage m; (also: **body stocking**) body m, justaucorps m; (fig: society) organe m, organisme m; (: quantity) ensemble m, masse f; (of wine) corps; **ruling ~** organe directeur; **in a ~** en masse, ensemble; (speak) comme un seul et même homme

**body blow** n (fig) coup dur, choc m

**body-building** ['bɔdɪbɪldɪŋ] n body-building m, culturisme m

**bodyguard** ['bɔdɪgɑːd] n garde m du corps

**body language** n langage m du corps

**body repairs** npl travaux mpl de carrosserie

**body search** n fouille f (corporelle); **to carry out a ~ on sb** fouiller qn; **to submit to** or **undergo a ~** se faire fouiller

**bodywork** ['bɔdɪwəːk] n carrosserie f

**boffin** ['bɔfɪn] n (Brit) savant m

**bog** [bɔg] n tourbière f ▷ vt: **to get ~ged down (in)** (fig) s'enliser (dans)

**boggle** ['bɔgl] vi: **the mind ~s** c'est incroyable, on en reste sidéré

**bogie** ['bəugɪ] n bogie m

**Bogotá** [bəugə'tɑː] n Bogotá

**bogus** ['bəugəs] adj bidon inv; fantôme

**Bohemia** [bəu'hiːmɪə] n Bohême f

**Bohemian** [bəu'hiːmɪən] adj bohémien(ne) ▷ n Bohémien(ne); (gipsy: also: **bohemian**) bohémien(ne)

**boil** [bɔɪl] vt (faire) bouillir ▷ vi bouillir ▷ n (Med) furoncle m; **to come to the** or (US) **a ~** bouillir; **to bring to the** or (US) **a ~** porter à ébullition
  ▶ **boil down** vi (fig): **to ~ down to** se réduire or ramener à
  ▶ **boil over** vi déborder

**boiled egg** n œuf m à la coque

**boiler** ['bɔɪlə$^r$] n chaudière f

**boiler suit** n (Brit) bleu m de travail, combinaison f

**boiling** ['bɔɪlɪŋ] adj: **I'm ~ (hot)** (inf) je crève de chaud

**boiling point** n point m d'ébullition

**boil-in-the-bag** [bɔɪlɪnðə'bæg] adj (rice etc) en sachet cuisson

**boisterous** ['bɔɪstərəs] adj bruyant(e), tapageur(-euse)

**bold** [bəuld] adj hardi(e), audacieux(-euse); (pej) effronté(e); (outline, colour) franc (franche), tranché(e), marqué(e)

483

**boldness** ['bəuldnıs] n hardiesse f, audace f; aplomb m, effronterie f
**bold type** n (Typ) caractères mpl gras
**Bolivia** [bə'lıvıə] n Bolivie f
**Bolivian** [bə'lıvıən] adj bolivien(ne) ▷ n Bolivien(ne)
**bollard** ['bɔləd] n (Naut) bitte f d'amarrage; (Brit Aut) borne lumineuse or de signalisation
**Bollywood** ['bɔlıwud] n Bollywood m
**bolshy** ['bɔlʃı] adj râleur(-euse); **to be in a ~ mood** être peu coopératif(-ive)
**bolster** ['bəulstər] n traversin m
  ▸ **bolster up** vt soutenir
**bolt** [bəult] n verrou m; (with nut) boulon m ▷ adv: **~ upright** droit(e) comme un piquet ▷ vt (door) verrouiller; (food) engloutir ▷ vi se sauver, filer (comme une flèche); **a ~ from the blue** (horse) s'emballer; (fig) un coup de tonnerre dans un ciel bleu
**bomb** [bɔm] n bombe f ▷ vt bombarder
**bombard** [bɔm'bɑːd] vt bombarder
**bombardment** [bɔm'bɑːdmənt] n bombardement m
**bombastic** [bɔm'bæstık] adj grandiloquent(e), pompeux(-euse)
**bomb disposal** n: **~ unit** section f de déminage; **~ expert** artificier m
**bomber** ['bɔmər] n caporal m d'artillerie; (Aviat) bombardier m; (terrorist) poseur m de bombes
**bombing** ['bɔmıŋ] n bombardement m
**bomb scare** n alerte f à la bombe
**bombshell** ['bɔmʃɛl] n obus m; (fig) bombe f
**bomb site** n zone f de bombardement
**bona fide** ['bəunə'faıdı] adj de bonne foi; (offer) sérieux(-euse)
**bonanza** [bə'nænzə] n filon m
**bond** [bɔnd] n lien m; (binding promise) engagement m, obligation f; (Finance) obligation; **bonds** npl (chains) chaînes fpl; **in ~** (of goods) en entrepôt
**bondage** ['bɔndıdʒ] n esclavage m
**bonded warehouse** ['bɔndıd-] n entrepôt m sous douanes
**bone** [bəun] n os m; (of fish) arête f ▷ vt désosser; ôter les arêtes de
**bone china** n porcelaine f tendre
**bone-dry** ['bəun'draı] adj absolument sec (sèche)
**bone idle** adj fainéant(e)
**bone marrow** n moelle osseuse
**boner** ['bəunər] n (US) gaffe f, bourde f
**bonfire** ['bɔnfaıər] n feu m (de joie); (for rubbish) feu
**bonk** [bɔŋk] (inf!) vt s'envoyer (!), sauter (!) ▷ vi s'envoyer en l'air (!)
**bonkers** ['bɔŋkəz] adj (Brit inf) cinglé(e), dingue
**Bonn** [bɔn] n Bonn
**bonnet** ['bɔnıt] n bonnet m; (Brit: of car) capot m
**bonny** [bɔnı] adj (Scottish) joli(e)
**bonus** ['bəunəs] n (money) prime f; (advantage) avantage m
**bony** ['bəunı] adj (arm, face: Med: tissue)

osseux(-euse); (thin: person) squelettique; (meat) plein(e) d'os; (fish) plein d'arêtes
**boo** [buː] excl hou!, peuh! ▷ vt huer ▷ n huée f
**boob** [buːb] n (inf: breast) nichon m; (: Brit: mistake) gaffe f
**booby prize** ['buːbı-] n timbale f (ironique)
**booby trap** ['buːbı-] n guet-apens m
**booby-trapped** ['buːbıtræpt] adj piégé(e)
**book** [buk] n livre m; (of stamps, tickets etc) carnet m; (Comm): **books** npl comptes mpl, comptabilité f ▷ vt (ticket) prendre; (seat, room) réserver; (driver) dresser un procès-verbal à; (football player) prendre le nom de, donner un carton à; **I ~ed a table in the name of ...** j'ai réservé une table au nom de ...; **to keep the ~s** tenir la comptabilité; **by the ~** à la lettre, selon les règles; **to throw the ~ at sb** passer un savon à qn
  ▸ **book in** vi (Brit: at hotel) prendre sa chambre
  ▸ **book up** vt réserver; **all seats are ~ed up** tout est pris, c'est complet
**bookable** ['bukəbl] adj: **seats are ~** on peut réserver ses places
**bookcase** ['bukkeıs] n bibliothèque f (meuble)
**book ends** npl serre-livres m inv
**booking** ['bukıŋ] n (Brit) réservation f; **I confirmed my ~ by fax/email** j'ai confirmé ma réservation par fax/e-mail
**booking office** n (Brit) bureau m de location
**book-keeping** ['buk'kiːpıŋ] n comptabilité f
**booklet** ['buklıt] n brochure f
**bookmaker** ['bukmeıkər] n bookmaker m
**bookmark** ['bukmɑːk] n (for book) marque-page m; (Comput) signet m
**bookseller** ['buksɛlər] n libraire m/f
**bookshelf** ['bukʃɛlf] n (single) étagère f (à livres); (bookcase) bibliothèque f; **bookshelves** rayons mpl (de bibliothèque)
**bookshop** ['bukʃɔp], **bookstore** n librairie f
**bookstall** ['bukstɔːl] n kiosque m à journaux
**book store** ['bukstɔːr] n = **bookshop**
**book token** n bon-cadeau m (pour un livre)
**book value** n valeur f comptable
**bookworm** ['bukwəːm] n dévoreur(-euse) de livres
**boom** [buːm] n (noise) grondement m; (in prices, population) forte augmentation; (busy period) boom m, vague f de prospérité ▷ vi gronder; prospérer
**boomerang** ['buːməræŋ] n boomerang m
**boom town** n ville f en plein essor
**boon** [buːn] n bénédiction f, grand avantage
**boorish** ['buərıʃ] adj grossier(-ère), rustre
**boost** [buːst] n stimulant m, remontant m ▷ vt stimuler; **to give a ~ to sb's spirits** or **to sb** remonter le moral à qn
**booster** ['buːstər] n (TV) amplificateur m (de signal); (Elec) survolteur m; (also: **booster rocket**) booster m; (Med: vaccine) rappel m
**booster seat** n (Aut: for children) siège m rehausseur
**boot** [buːt] n botte f; (for hiking) chaussure f (de

marche); (*ankle boot*) bottine *f*; (*Brit: of car*) coffre *m* ▷ *vt* (*Comput*) lancer, mettre en route; **to ~** (*in addition*) par-dessus le marché, en plus; **to give sb the ~** (*inf*) flanquer qn dehors, virer qn

**booth** [buːð] *n* (*at fair*) baraque (foraine); (*of telephone etc*) cabine *f*; (*also:* **voting booth**) isoloir *m*

**bootleg** [ˈbuːtleg] *adj* de contrebande; **~ record** enregistrement *m* pirate

**booty** [ˈbuːtɪ] *n* butin *m*

**booze** [buːz] (*inf*) *n* boissons *fpl* alcooliques, alcool *m* ▷ *vi* boire, picoler

**boozer** [ˈbuːzəʳ] *n* (*inf: person*): **he's a ~** il picole pas mal; (*Brit inf: pub*) pub *m*

**border** [ˈbɔːdəʳ] *n* bordure *f*; bord *m*; (*of a country*) frontière *f*; **the B~s** la région frontière entre l'Écosse et l'Angleterre

▶ **border on** *vt fus* être voisin(e) de, toucher à

**borderline** [ˈbɔːdəlaɪn] *n* (*fig*) ligne *f* de démarcation ▷ *adj*: **~ case** cas *m* limite

**bore** [bɔːʳ] *pt of* **bear** ▷ *vt* (*person*) ennuyer, raser; (*hole*) percer; (*well, tunnel*) creuser ▷ *n* (*person*) raseur(-euse); (*boring thing*) barbe *f*; (*of gun*) calibre *m*

**bored** [bɔːd] *adj*: **to be ~** s'ennuyer; **he's ~ to tears** *or* **to death** *or* **stiff** il s'ennuie à mourir

**boredom** [ˈbɔːdəm] *n* ennui *m*

**boring** [ˈbɔːrɪŋ] *adj* ennuyeux(-euse)

**born** [bɔːn] *adj*: **to be ~** naître; **I was ~ in 1960** je suis né en 1960; **~ blind** aveugle de naissance; **a ~ comedian** un comédien-né

**born-again** [bɔːnəˈgɛn] *adj*: **~ Christian** ≈ évangéliste *m/f*

**borne** [bɔːn] *pp of* **bear**

**Borneo** [ˈbɔːnɪəu] *n* Bornéo *f*

**borough** [ˈbʌrə] *n* municipalité *f*

**borrow** [ˈbɔrəu] *vt*: **to ~ sth (from sb)** emprunter qch (à qn); **may I ~ your car?** est-ce que je peux vous emprunter votre voiture?

**borrower** [ˈbɔrəuəʳ] *n* emprunteur(-euse)

**borrowing** [ˈbɔrəuɪŋ] *n* emprunt(s) *mpl*

**borstal** [ˈbɔːstl] *n* (*Brit*) ≈ maison *f* de correction

**Bosnia** [ˈbɔznɪə] *n* Bosnie *f*

**Bosnia-Herzegovina** [ˈbɔznɪə-hɛrzəˈgəuviːnə] *n*, **Bosnia-Hercegovina** Bosnie-Herzégovine *f*

**Bosnian** [ˈbɔznɪən] *adj* bosniaque, bosnien(ne) ▷ *n* Bosniaque *m/f*, Bosnien(ne)

**bosom** [ˈbuzəm] *n* poitrine *f*; (*fig*) sein *m*

**bosom friend** *n* ami(e) intime

**boss** [bɔs] *n* patron(ne) ▷ *vt* (*also:* **boss about, boss around**) mener à la baguette

**bossy** [ˈbɔsɪ] *adj* autoritaire

**bosun** [ˈbəusn] *n* maître *m* d'équipage

**botanical** [bəˈtænɪkl] *adj* botanique

**botanist** [ˈbɔtənɪst] *n* botaniste *m/f*

**botany** [ˈbɔtənɪ] *n* botanique *f*

**botch** [bɔtʃ] *vt* (*also:* **botch up**) saboter, bâcler

**both** [bəuθ] *adj* les deux, l'un(e) et l'autre ▷ *pron*: **~ (of them)** les deux, tous (toutes) (les) deux, l'un(e) et l'autre; **~ of us went, we ~ went** nous y sommes allés tous les deux ▷ *adv*: **~ A and B** A et B; **they sell ~ the fabric and the finished**

**curtains** ils vendent (et) le tissu et les rideaux (finis), ils vendent à la fois le tissu et les rideaux (finis)

**bother** [ˈbɔðəʳ] *vt* (*worry*) tracasser; (*needle, bait*) importuner, ennuyer; (*disturb*) déranger ▷ *vi* (*also:* **bother o.s.**) se tracasser, se faire du souci ▷ *n* (*trouble*) ennuis *mpl*; **it is a ~ to have to do** c'est vraiment ennuyeux d'avoir à faire ▷ *excl* zut!; **to ~ doing** prendre la peine de faire; **I'm sorry to ~ you** excusez-moi de vous déranger; **please don't ~** ne vous dérangez pas; **don't ~** ce n'est pas la peine; **it's no ~** aucun problème

**Botswana** [bɔtˈswɑːnə] *n* Botswana *m*

**bottle** [ˈbɔtl] *n* bouteille *f*; (*baby's*) biberon *m*; (*of perfume, medicine*) flacon *m* ▷ *vt* mettre en bouteille(s); **~ of wine/milk** bouteille de vin/lait; **wine/milk ~** bouteille à vin/lait

▶ **bottle up** *vt* refouler, contenir

**bottle bank** *n* conteneur *m* (de bouteilles)

**bottleneck** [ˈbɔtlnɛk] *n* (*in traffic*) bouchon *m*; (*in production*) goulet *m* d'étranglement

**bottle-opener** [ˈbɔtləupnəʳ] *n* ouvre-bouteille *m*

**bottom** [ˈbɔtəm] *n* (*of container, sea etc*) fond *m*; (*buttocks*) derrière *m*; (*of page, list*) bas *m*; (*of chair*) siège *m*; (*of mountain, tree, hill*) pied *m* ▷ *adj* (*shelf, step*) du bas; **to get to the ~ of sth** (*fig*) découvrir le fin fond de qch

**bottomless** [ˈbɔtəmlɪs] *adj* sans fond, insondable

**bottom line** *n*: **the ~ is that ...** l'essentiel, c'est que ...

**botulism** [ˈbɔtjulɪzəm] *n* botulisme *m*

**bough** [bau] *n* branche *f*, rameau *m*

**bought** [bɔːt] *pt, pp of* **buy**

**boulder** [ˈbəuldəʳ] *n* gros rocher (*gén lisse, arrondi*)

**bounce** [bauns] *vi* (*ball*) rebondir; (*cheque*) être refusé (*étant sans provision*); (*also:* **to bounce forward/out etc**) bondir, s'élancer ▷ *vt* faire rebondir ▷ *n* (*rebound*) rebond *m*; **he's got plenty of ~** (*fig*) il est plein d'entrain *or* d'allant

**bouncer** [ˈbaunsəʳ] *n* (*inf: at dance, club*) videur *m*

**bound** [baund] *pt, pp of* **bind** ▷ *n* (*gen pl*) limite *f*; (*leap*) bond *m* ▷ *vi* (*leap*) bondir ▷ *vt* (*limit*) borner ▷ *adj*: **to be ~ to do sth** (*obliged*) être obligé(e) *or* avoir obligation de faire qch; **he's ~ to fail** (*likely*) il est sûr d'échouer, son échec est inévitable *or* assuré; **~ by** (*law, regulation*) engagé(e) par; **~ for** à destination de; **out of ~s** dont l'accès est interdit

**boundary** [ˈbaundrɪ] *n* frontière *f*

**boundless** [ˈbaundlɪs] *adj* illimité(e), sans bornes

**bountiful** [ˈbauntɪful] *adj* (*person*) généreux(-euse); (*God*) bienfaiteur(-trice); (*supply*) ample

**bounty** [ˈbauntɪ] *n* (*generosity*) générosité *f*

**bouquet** [ˈbukeɪ] *n* bouquet *m*

**bourbon** [ˈbuəbən] *n* (*US: also:* **bourbon whiskey**) bourbon *m*

**bourgeois** [ˈbuəʒwɑː] *adj, n* bourgeois(e)

**bout** [baut] *n* période *f*; (*of malaria etc*) accès *m*,

485

crise f, attaque f; (Boxing etc) combat m, match m

**boutique** [buːˈtiːk] n boutique f

**bow¹** [bəu] n nœud m; (weapon) arc m; (Mus) archet m

**bow²** [bau] n (with body) révérence f, inclination f (du buste or corps); (Naut: also: **bows**) proue f ▷ vi faire une révérence, s'incliner; (yield): **to ~ to** or **before** s'incliner devant, se soumettre à; **to ~ to the inevitable** accepter l'inévitable or l'inéluctable

**bowels** [bauəlz] npl intestins mpl; (fig) entrailles fpl

**bowl** [bəul] n (for eating) bol m; (for washing) cuvette f; (ball) boule f; (of pipe) fourneau m ▷ vi (Cricket) lancer (la balle)
▶ **bowl over** vt (fig) renverser

**bow-legged** [ˈbəuˈlɛgɪd] adj aux jambes arquées

**bowler** [ˈbəuləʳ] n joueur m de boules; (Cricket) lanceur m (de la balle); (Brit: also: **bowler hat**) (chapeau m) melon m

**bowling** [ˈbəulɪŋ] n (game) jeu m de boules, jeu de quilles

**bowling alley** n bowling m

**bowling green** n terrain m de boules (gazonné et carré)

**bowls** [bəulz] n (jeu m de) boules fpl

**bow tie** [bəu-] n nœud m papillon

**box** [bɔks] n boîte f; (also: **cardboard box**) carton m; (crate) caisse f; (Theat) loge f ▷ vt mettre en boîte; (Sport) boxer avec ▷ vi boxer, faire de la boxe

**boxer** [ˈbɔksəʳ] n (person) boxeur m; (dog) boxer m

**boxer shorts** [ˈbɔksəʃɔːts] npl caleçon m

**boxing** [ˈbɔksɪŋ] n (sport) boxe f

**Boxing Day** n (Brit) le lendemain de Noël; voir article

**boxing gloves** npl gants mpl de boxe

**boxing ring** n ring m

**box number** n (for advertisements) numéro m d'annonce

**box office** n bureau m de location

**box room** n débarras m; chambrette f

**boy** [bɔɪ] n garçon m

**boy band** n boys band m

**boycott** [ˈbɔɪkɔt] n boycottage m ▷ vt boycotter

**boyfriend** [ˈbɔɪfrɛnd] n (petit) ami

**boyish** [ˈbɔɪɪʃ] adj d'enfant, de garçon; **to look ~** (man: appear youthful) faire jeune

**Bp** abbr = **bishop**

**BR** abbr = **British Rail**

**Br.** abbr (Rel) = **brother**

**bra** [brɑː] n soutien-gorge m

**brace** [breɪs] n (support) attache f, agrafe f; (Brit: also: **braces**: on teeth) appareil m (dentaire); (tool)

vilebrequin m; (Typ: also: **brace bracket**) accolade f ▷ vt (support) consolider, soutenir; **braces** npl (Brit: for trousers) bretelles fpl; **to ~ o.s.** (fig) se préparer mentalement

**bracelet** [ˈbreɪslɪt] n bracelet m

**bracing** [ˈbreɪsɪŋ] adj tonifiant(e), tonique

**bracken** [ˈbrækən] n fougère f

**bracket** [ˈbrækɪt] n (Tech) tasseau m, support m; (group) classe f, tranche f; (also: **brace bracket**) accolade f; (also: **round bracket**) parenthèse f; (also: **square bracket**) crochet m ▷ vt mettre entre parenthèses; (fig: also: **bracket together**) regrouper; **income ~** tranche f des revenus; **in ~s** entre parenthèses or crochets

**brackish** [ˈbrækɪʃ] adj (water) saumâtre

**brag** [bræg] vi se vanter

**braid** [breɪd] n (trimming) galon m; (of hair) tresse f, natte f

**Braille** [breɪl] n braille m

**brain** [breɪn] n cerveau m; **brains** npl (intellect, food) cervelle f; **he's got ~s** il est intelligent

**brainchild** [ˈbreɪntʃaɪld] n trouvaille (personnelle), invention f

**braindead** [ˈbreɪndɛd] adj (Med) dans un coma dépassé; (inf) demeuré(e)

**brainless** [ˈbreɪnlɪs] adj sans cervelle, stupide

**brainstorm** [ˈbreɪnstɔːm] n (fig) moment m d'égarement; (US: brainwave) idée f de génie

**brainwash** [ˈbreɪnwɔʃ] vt faire subir un lavage de cerveau à

**brainwave** [ˈbreɪnweɪv] n idée f de génie

**brainy** [ˈbreɪnɪ] adj intelligent(e), doué(e)

**braise** [breɪz] vt braiser

**brake** [breɪk] n frein m ▷ vt, vi freiner

**brake light** n feu m de stop

**brake pedal** n pédale f de frein

**bramble** [ˈbræmbl] n ronces fpl; (fruit) mûre f

**bran** [bræn] n son m

**branch** [brɑːntʃ] n branche f; (Comm) succursale f; (: of bank) agence f; (of association) section locale ▷ vi bifurquer
▶ **branch off** vi (road) bifurquer
▶ **branch out** vi diversifier ses activités; **to ~ out into** étendre ses activités à

**branch line** n (Rail) bifurcation f, embranchement m

**branch manager** n directeur(-trice) de succursale (or d'agence)

**brand** [brænd] n marque (commerciale) ▷ vt (cattle) marquer (au fer rouge); (fig: pej): **to ~ sb a communist** etc traiter or qualifier qn de communiste etc

**brandish** [ˈbrændɪʃ] vt brandir

**brand name** n nom m de marque

**brand-new** [ˈbrændˈnjuː] adj tout(e) neuf (neuve), flambant neuf (neuve)

**brandy** [ˈbrændɪ] n cognac m, fine f

**brash** [bræʃ] adj effronté(e)

**Brasilia** [brəˈzɪlɪə] n Brasilia

**brass** [brɑːs] n cuivre m (jaune), laiton m; **the ~** (Mus) les cuivres

**brass band** n fanfare f

**b**

**brass tacks** *npl*: **to get down to** ~ en venir au fait

**brat** [bræt] *n* (*pej*) mioche *m/f*, môme *m/f*

**bravado** [brə'vɑ:dəu] *n* bravade *f*

**brave** [breɪv] *adj* courageux(-euse), brave ▷ *n* guerrier indien ▷ *vt* braver, affronter

**bravery** ['breɪvərɪ] *n* bravoure *f*, courage *m*

**brawl** [brɔːl] *n* rixe *f*, bagarre *f* ▷ *vi* se bagarrer

**brawn** [brɔːn] *n* muscle *m*; (*meat*) fromage *m* de tête

**brawny** ['brɔːnɪ] *adj* musclé(e), costaud(e)

**bray** [breɪ] *n* braiement *m* ▷ *vi* braire

**brazen** ['breɪzn] *adj* impudent(e), effronté(e) ▷ *vt*: **to ~ it out** payer d'effronterie, crâner

**brazier** ['breɪzɪə'] *n* brasero *m*

**Brazil** [brə'zɪl] *n* Brésil *m*

**Brazilian** [brə'zɪljən] *adj* brésilien(ne) ▷ *n* Brésilien(ne)

**Brazil nut** *n* noix *f* du Brésil

**breach** [briːtʃ] *vt* ouvrir une brèche dans ▷ *n* (*gap*) brèche *f*; (*estrangement*) brouille *f*; (*breaking*): **~ of contract** rupture *f* de contrat; **~ of the peace** attentat *m* à l'ordre public; **~ of trust** abus *m* de confiance

**bread** [brɛd] *n* pain *m*; (*inf: money*) fric *m*; **~ and butter** (*n*) tartines (beurrées); (*fig*) subsistance *f*; **to earn one's daily ~** gagner son pain; **to know which side one's ~ is buttered (on)** savoir où est son avantage *or* intérêt

**breadbin** ['brɛdbɪn] *n* (*Brit*) boîte *f or* huche *f* à pain

**breadboard** ['brɛdbɔːd] *n* planche *f* à pain; (*Comput*) montage expérimental

**breadbox** ['brɛdbɔks] *n* (*US*) boîte *f or* huche *f* à pain

**breadcrumbs** ['brɛdkrʌmz] *npl* miettes *fpl* de pain; (*Culin*) chapelure *f*, panure *f*

**breadline** ['brɛdlaɪn] *n*: **to be on the ~** être sans le sou *or* dans l'indigence

**breadth** [brɛtθ] *n* largeur *f*

**breadwinner** ['brɛdwɪnə'] *n* soutien *m* de famille

**break** [breɪk] (*pt* **broke**, *pp* **broken** [brəuk, 'brəukən]) *vt* casser, briser; (*promise*) rompre; (*law*) violer ▷ *vi* se casser, se briser; (*weather*) tourner; (*storm*) éclater; (*day*) se lever ▷ *n* (*gap*) brèche *f*; (*fracture*) cassure *f*; (*rest*) interruption *f*, arrêt *m*; (*: short*) pause *f*; (*: at school*) récréation *f*; (*chance*) chance *f*, occasion *f* favorable; **to ~ one's leg** *etc* se casser la jambe *etc*; **to ~ a record** battre un record; **to ~ the news to sb** annoncer la nouvelle à qn; **to ~ with sb** rompre avec qn; **to ~ even** *vi* rentrer dans ses frais; **to ~ free** *or* **loose** *vi* se dégager, s'échapper; **to take a ~** (*few minutes*) faire une pause, s'arrêter cinq minutes; (*holiday*) prendre un peu de repos; **without a ~** sans interruption, sans arrêt

▶ **break down** *vt* (*door etc*) enfoncer; (*resistance*) venir à bout de; (*figures, data*) décomposer, analyser ▷ *vi* s'effondrer; (*Med*) faire une dépression (nerveuse); (*Aut*) tomber en panne; **my car has broken down** ma voiture est en panne

▶ **break in** *vt* (*horse etc*) dresser ▷ *vi* (*burglar*) entrer par effraction; (*interrupt*) interrompre

▶ **break into** *vt fus* (*house*) s'introduire *or* pénétrer par effraction dans

▶ **break off** *vi* (*speaker*) s'interrompre; (*branch*) se rompre ▷ *vt* (*talks, engagement*) rompre

▶ **break open** *vt* (*door etc*) forcer, fracturer

▶ **break out** *vi* éclater, se déclarer; (*prisoner*) s'évader; **to ~ out in spots** se couvrir de boutons

▶ **break through** *vi*: **the sun broke through** le soleil a fait son apparition ▷ *vt fus* (*defences, barrier*) franchir; (*crowd*) se frayer un passage à travers

▶ **break up** *vi* (*partnership*) cesser, prendre fin; (*marriage*) se briser; (*crowd, meeting*) se séparer; (*ship*) se disloquer; (*Scol: pupils*) être en vacances; (*line*) couper; **the line's** *or* **you're ~ing up** ça coupe ▷ *vt* fracasser, casser; (*fight etc*) interrompre, faire cesser; (*marriage*) désunir

**breakable** ['breɪkəbl] *adj* cassable, fragile ▷ *n*: **~s** objets *mpl* fragiles

**breakage** ['breɪkɪdʒ] *n* casse *f*; **to pay for ~s** payer la casse

**breakaway** ['breɪkəweɪ] *adj* (*group etc*) dissident(e)

**breakdown** ['breɪkdaun] *n* (*Aut*) panne *f*; (*in communications, marriage*) rupture *f*; (*Med: also*: **nervous breakdown**) dépression (nerveuse); (*of figures*) ventilation *f*, répartition *f*

**breakdown service** *n* (*Brit*) service *m* de dépannage

**breakdown truck**, (*US*) **breakdown van** *n* dépanneuse *f*

**breaker** ['breɪkə'] *n* brisant *m*

**breakeven** ['breɪk'iːvn] *cpd*: **~ chart** graphique *m* de rentabilité; **~ point** seuil *m* de rentabilité

**breakfast** ['brɛkfəst] *n* petit déjeuner *m*; **what time is ~?** le petit déjeuner est à quelle heure?

**breakfast cereal** *n* céréales *fpl*

**break-in** ['breɪkɪn] *n* cambriolage *m*

**breaking and entering** *n* (*Law*) effraction *f*

**breaking point** ['breɪkɪŋ-] *n* limites *fpl*

**breakthrough** ['breɪkθruː] *n* percée *f*

**break-up** ['breɪkʌp] *n* (*of partnership, marriage*) rupture *f*

**break-up value** *n* (*Comm*) valeur *f* de liquidation

**breakwater** ['breɪkwɔːtə'] *n* brise-lames *m inv*, digue *f*

**breast** [brɛst] *n* (*of woman*) sein *m*; (*chest*) poitrine *f*; (*of chicken, turkey*) blanc *m*

**breast-feed** ['brɛstfiːd] *vt, vi* (*irreg: like* **feed**) allaiter

**breast pocket** *n* poche *f* (de) poitrine

**breast-stroke** ['brɛststrəuk] *n* brasse *f*

**breath** [brɛθ] *n* haleine *f*, souffle *m*; **to go out for a ~ of air** sortir prendre l'air; **to take a deep ~** respirer à fond; **out of ~** à bout de souffle, essoufflé(e)

**breathalyse** ['brɛθəlaɪz] *vt* faire subir l'alcootest à

**Breathalyser®** ['brɛθəlaɪzəʳ] (*Brit*) *n* alcootest *m*
**breathe** [bri:ð] *vt, vi* respirer; **I won't ~ a word about it** je n'en soufflerai pas mot, je n'en dirai rien à personne
  ▶ **breathe in** *vi* inspirer ▷ *vt* aspirer
  ▶ **breathe out** *vt, vi* expirer
**breather** ['bri:ðəʳ] *n* moment *m* de repos *or* de répit
**breathing** ['bri:ðɪŋ] *n* respiration *f*
**breathing space** *n* (*fig*) (moment *m* de) répit *m*
**breathless** ['brɛθlɪs] *adj* essoufflé(e), haletant(e), oppressé(e); **~ with excitement** le souffle coupé par l'émotion
**breathtaking** ['brɛθteɪkɪŋ] *adj* stupéfiant(e), à vous couper le souffle
**breath test** *n* alcootest *m*
**bred** [brɛd] *pt, pp of* **breed**
**-bred** [brɛd] *suffix*: **well/ill~** bien/mal élevé(e)
**breed** [bri:d] (*pt, pp* **bred**) [brɛd] *vt* élever, faire l'élevage de; (*fig: hate, suspicion*) engendrer ▷ *vi* se reproduire ▷ *n* race *f*, variété *f*
**breeder** ['bri:dəʳ] *n* (*person*) éleveur *m*; (*Physics: also*: **breeder reactor**) (réacteur *m*) surrégénérateur *m*
**breeding** ['bri:dɪŋ] *n* reproduction *f*; élevage *m*; (*upbringing*) éducation *f*
**breeze** [bri:z] *n* brise *f*
**breeze-block** ['bri:zblɔk] *n* (*Brit*) parpaing *m*
**breezy** ['bri:zɪ] *adj* (*day, weather*) venteux(-euse); (*manner*) désinvolte; (*person*) jovial(e)
**Breton** ['brɛtən] *adj* breton(ne) ▷ *n* Breton(ne); (*Ling*) breton *m*
**brevity** ['brɛvɪtɪ] *n* brièveté *f*
**brew** [bru:] *vt* (*tea*) faire infuser; (*beer*) brasser; (*plot*) tramer, préparer ▷ *vi* (*tea*) infuser; (*beer*) fermenter; (*fig*) se préparer, couver
**brewer** ['bru:əʳ] *n* brasseur *m*
**brewery** ['bru:ərɪ] *n* brasserie *f* (*fabrique*)
**briar** ['braɪəʳ] *n* (*thorny bush*) ronces *fpl*; (*wild rose*) églantine *f*
**bribe** [braɪb] *n* pot-de-vin *m* ▷ *vt* acheter; soudoyer; **to ~ sb to do sth** soudoyer qn pour qu'il fasse qch
**bribery** ['braɪbərɪ] *n* corruption *f*
**bric-a-brac** ['brɪkəbræk] *n* bric-à-brac *m*
**brick** [brɪk] *n* brique *f*
**bricklayer** ['brɪkleɪəʳ] *n* maçon *m*
**brickwork** ['brɪkwə:k] *n* briquetage *m*, maçonnerie *f*
**brickworks** ['brɪkwə:ks] *n* briqueterie *f*
**bridal** ['braɪdl] *adj* nuptial(e); **~ party** noce *f*
**bride** [braɪd] *n* mariée *f*, épouse *f*
**bridegroom** ['braɪdgru:m] *n* marié *m*, époux *m*
**bridesmaid** ['braɪdzmeɪd] *n* demoiselle *f* d'honneur
**bridge** [brɪdʒ] *n* pont *m*; (*Naut*) passerelle *f* (de commandement); (*of nose*) arête *f*; (*Cards, Dentistry*) bridge *m* ▷ *vt* (*river*) construire un pont sur; (*gap*) combler
**bridging loan** ['brɪdʒɪŋ-] *n* (*Brit*) prêt *m* relais
**bridle** ['braɪdl] *n* bride *f* ▷ *vt* refréner, mettre la bride à; (*horse*) brider

**bridle path** *n* piste *or* allée cavalière
**brief** [bri:f] *adj* bref (brève) ▷ *n* (*Law*) dossier *m*, cause *f*; (*gen*) tâche *f* ▷ *vt* mettre au courant; (*Mil*) donner des instructions à; **briefs** *npl* slip *m*; **in ~ ...** (en) bref ...
**briefcase** ['bri:fkeɪs] *n* serviette *f*; porte-documents *m inv*
**briefing** ['bri:fɪŋ] *n* instructions *fpl*; (*Press*) briefing *m*
**briefly** ['bri:flɪ] *adv* brièvement; (*visit*) en coup de vent; **to glimpse ~** entrevoir
**briefness** ['bri:fnɪs] *n* brièveté *f*
**Brig.** *abbr* = **brigadier**
**brigade** [brɪˈgeɪd] *n* (*Mil*) brigade *f*
**brigadier** [brɪgəˈdɪəʳ] *n* brigadier général
**bright** [braɪt] *adj* brillant(e); (*room, weather*) clair(e); (*person: clever*) intelligent(e), doué(e); (*: cheerful*) gai(e); (*idea*) génial(e); (*colour*) vif (vive); **to look on the ~ side** regarder le bon côté des choses
**brighten** ['braɪtn] (*also*: **brighten up**) *vt* (*room*) éclaircir; égayer ▷ *vi* s'éclaircir; (*person*) retrouver un peu de sa gaieté
**brightly** ['braɪtlɪ] *adv* brillamment
**brill** [brɪl] *adj* (*Brit inf*) super *inv*
**brilliance** ['brɪljəns] *n* éclat *m*; (*fig: of person*) brio *m*
**brilliant** ['brɪljənt] *adj* brillant(e); (*light, sunshine*) éclatant(e); (*inf: great*) super
**brim** [brɪm] *n* bord *m*
**brimful** ['brɪm'ful] *adj* plein(e) à ras bord; (*fig*) débordant(e)
**brine** [braɪn] *n* eau salée; (*Culin*) saumure *f*
**bring** (*pt, pp* **brought**) [brɪŋ, brɔ:t] *vt* (*thing*) apporter; (*person*) amener; **to ~ sth to an end** mettre fin à qch; **I can't ~ myself to fire him** je ne peux me résoudre à le mettre à la porte
  ▶ **bring about** *vt* provoquer, entraîner
  ▶ **bring back** *vt* rapporter; (*person*) ramener
  ▶ **bring down** *vt* (*lower*) abaisser; (*shoot down*) abattre; (*government*) faire s'effondrer
  ▶ **bring forward** *vt* avancer; (*Book-Keeping*) reporter
  ▶ **bring in** *vt* (*person*) faire entrer; (*object*) rentrer; (*Pol: legislation*) introduire; (*Law: verdict*) rendre; (*produce: income*) rapporter
  ▶ **bring off** *vt* (*task, plan*) réussir, mener à bien; (*deal*) mener à bien
  ▶ **bring on** *vt* (*illness, attack*) provoquer; (*player, substitute*) amener
  ▶ **bring out** *vt* sortir; (*meaning*) faire ressortir, mettre en relief; (*new product, book*) sortir
  ▶ **bring round, bring to** *vt* (*unconscious person*) ranimer
  ▶ **bring up** *vt* élever; (*carry up*) monter; (*question*) soulever; (*food: vomit*) vomir, rendre
**brink** [brɪŋk] *n* bord *m*; **on the ~ of doing** sur le point de faire, à deux doigts de faire; **she was on the ~ of tears** elle était au bord des larmes
**brisk** [brɪsk] *adj* vif (vive); (*abrupt*) brusque; (*trade etc*) actif(-ive); **to go for a ~ walk** se promener d'un bon pas; **business is ~** les

affaires marchent (bien)
**bristle** ['brɪsl] *n* poil *m* ▷ *vi* se hérisser;
  **bristling with** hérissé(e) de
**bristly** ['brɪslɪ] *adj* (*beard, hair*) hérissé(e); **your chin's all ~** ton menton gratte
**Brit** [brɪt] *n abbr* (*inf:* = *British person*) Britannique *m/f*
**Britain** ['brɪtən] *n* (*also:* **Great Britain**) la Grande-Bretagne; **in ~** en Grande-Bretagne
**British** ['brɪtɪʃ] *adj* britannique ▷ *npl:* **the ~** les Britanniques *mpl*
**British Isles** *npl:* **the ~** les îles *fpl* Britanniques
**British Rail** *n* compagnie ferroviaire britannique, ≈ SNCF *f*
**British Summer Time** *n* heure *f* d'été britannique
**Briton** ['brɪtən] *n* Britannique *m/f*
**Brittany** ['brɪtənɪ] *n* Bretagne *f*
**brittle** ['brɪtl] *adj* cassant(e), fragile
**Bro.** *abbr* (*Rel*) = **brother**
**broach** [brəʊtʃ] *vt* (*subject*) aborder
**B road** *n* (*Brit*) ≈ route départementale
**broad** [brɔːd] *adj* large; (*distinction*) général(e); (*accent*) prononcé(e) ▷ *n* (*US inf*) nana *f*; **~ hint** allusion transparente; **in ~ daylight** en plein jour; **the ~ outlines** les grandes lignes
**broadband** ['brɔːdbænd] *n* transmission *f* à haut débit
**broad bean** *n* fève *f*
**broadcast** ['brɔːdkɑːst] (*pt, pp* **~**) *n* émission *f* ▷ *vt* (*Radio*) radiodiffuser; (*TV*) téléviser ▷ *vi* émettre
**broadcaster** ['brɔːdkɑːstəʳ] *n* personnalité *f* de la radio *or* de la télévision
**broadcasting** ['brɔːdkɑːstɪŋ] *n* radiodiffusion *f*; télévision *f*
**broadcasting station** *n* station *f* de radio (*or* de télévision)
**broaden** ['brɔːdn] *vt* élargir; **to ~ one's mind** élargir ses horizons ▷ *vi* s'élargir
**broadly** ['brɔːdlɪ] *adv* en gros, généralement
**broad-minded** ['brɔːd'maɪndɪd] *adj* large d'esprit
**broadsheet** ['brɔːdʃiːt] *n* (*Brit*) journal *m* grand format
**broccoli** ['brɔkəlɪ] *n* brocoli *m*
**brochure** ['brəʊʃjʊəʳ] *n* prospectus *m*, dépliant *m*
**brogue** ['brəʊg] *n* (*accent*) accent régional; (*shoe*) (*sorte de*) chaussure basse de cuir épais
**broil** [brɔɪl] (*US*) *vt* rôtir
**broke** [brəʊk] *pt of* **break** ▷ *adj* (*inf*) fauché(e); **to go ~** (*business*) faire faillite
**broken** ['brəʊkn] *pp of* **break** ▷ *adj* (*stick, leg etc*) cassé(e); (*machine: also:* **broken down**) fichu(e); (*promise, vow*) rompu(e); **a ~ marriage** un couple dissocié; **a ~ home** un foyer désuni; **in ~ French/English** dans un français/anglais approximatif *or* hésitant
**broken-down** ['brəʊkn'daʊn] *adj* (*car*) en panne; (*machine*) fichu(e); (*house*) en ruines
**broken-hearted** ['brəʊkn'hɑːtɪd] *adj* (ayant) le cœur brisé
**broker** ['brəʊkəʳ] *n* courtier *m*

**brokerage** ['brəʊkrɪdʒ] *n* courtage *m*
**brolly** ['brɔlɪ] *n* (*Brit inf*) pépin *m*, parapluie *m*
**bronchitis** [brɔŋ'kaɪtɪs] *n* bronchite *f*
**bronze** [brɔnz] *n* bronze *m*
**bronzed** ['brɔnzd] *adj* bronzé(e), hâlé(e)
**brooch** [brəʊtʃ] *n* broche *f*
**brood** [bruːd] *n* couvée *f* ▷ *vi* (*hen, storm*) couver; (*person*) méditer (sombrement), ruminer
**broody** ['bruːdɪ] *adj* (*fig*) taciturne, mélancolique
**brook** [brʊk] *n* ruisseau *m*
**broom** [brum] *n* balai *m*; (*Bot*) genêt *m*
**broomstick** ['brumstɪk] *n* manche *m* à balai
**Bros.** *abbr* (*Comm:* = *brothers*) Frères
**broth** [brɔθ] *n* bouillon *m* de viande et de légumes
**brothel** ['brɔθl] *n* maison close, bordel *m*
**brother** ['brʌðəʳ] *n* frère *m*
**brotherhood** ['brʌðəhud] *n* fraternité *f*
**brother-in-law** ['brʌðərɪn'lɔːʳ] *n* beau-frère *m*
**brotherly** ['brʌðəlɪ] *adj* fraternel(le)
**brought** [brɔːt] *pt, pp of* **bring**
**brow** [braʊ] *n* front *m*; (*rare: gen: eyebrow*) sourcil *m*; (*of hill*) sommet *m*
**browbeat** ['braʊbiːt] *vt* intimider, brusquer
**brown** [braʊn] *adj* brun(e), marron *inv*; (*hair*) châtain *inv*; (*tanned*) bronzé(e); (*rice, bread, flour*) complet(-ète) ▷ *n* (*colour*) brun *m*, marron *m* ▷ *vt* brunir; (*Culin*) faire dorer, faire roussir; **to go ~** (*person*) bronzer; (*leaves*) jaunir
**brown bread** *n* pain *m* bis
**Brownie** ['braʊnɪ] *n* jeannette *f* éclaireuse (cadette)
**brown paper** *n* papier *m* d'emballage, papier kraft
**brown rice** *n* riz *m* complet
**brown sugar** *n* cassonade *f*
**browse** [braʊz] *vi* (*in shop*) regarder (*sans acheter*); (*among books*) bouquiner, feuilleter les livres; (*animal*) paître; **to ~ through a book** feuilleter un livre
**browser** [braʊzəʳ] *n* (*Comput*) navigateur *m*
**bruise** [bruːz] *n* bleu *m*, ecchymose *f*, contusion *f* ▷ *vt* contusionner, meurtrir ▷ *vi* (*fruit*) se taler, se meurtrir; **to ~ one's arm** se faire un bleu au bras
**Brum** [brʌm] *n abbr*, **Brummagem** ['brʌmədʒəm] *n* (*inf*) Birmingham
**Brummie** ['brʌmɪ] *n* (*inf*) habitant(e) de Birmingham; natif(-ive) de Birmingham
**brunch** [brʌntʃ] *n* brunch *m*
**brunette** [bruː'nɛt] *n* (*femme*) brune
**brunt** [brʌnt] *n:* **the ~ of** (*attack, criticism etc*) le plus gros de
**brush** [brʌʃ] *n* brosse *f*; (*for painting*) pinceau *m*; (*for shaving*) blaireau *m*; (*quarrel*) accrochage *m*, prise *f* de bec ▷ *vt* brosser; (*also:* **brush past, brush against**) effleurer, frôler; **to have a ~ with sb** s'accrocher avec qn; **to have a ~ with the police** avoir maille à partir avec la police
  ▶ **brush aside** *vt* écarter, balayer
  ▶ **brush up** *vt* (*knowledge*) rafraîchir, réviser

**brushed** [brʌʃt] adj (Tech: steel, chrome etc) brossé(e); (nylon, denim etc) gratté(e)
**brush-off** ['brʌʃɔf] n (inf): **to give sb the ~** envoyer qn promener
**brushwood** ['brʌʃwud] n broussailles fpl, taillis m
**brusque** [bruːsk] adj (person, manner) brusque, cassant(e); (tone) sec (sèche), cassant(e)
**Brussels** ['brʌslz] n Bruxelles
**Brussels sprout** [-spraut] n chou m de Bruxelles
**brutal** ['bruːtl] adj brutal(e)
**brutality** [bruːˈtælɪtɪ] n brutalité f
**brutalize** ['bruːtəlaɪz] vt (harden) rendre brutal(e); (ill-treat) brutaliser
**brute** [bruːt] n brute f ▷ adj: **by ~ force** par la force
**brutish** ['bruːtɪʃ] adj grossier(-ère), brutal(e)
**BS** n abbr (US: = Bachelor of Science) diplôme universitaire
**bs** abbr = **bill of sale**
**BSA** n abbr = **Boy Scouts of America**
**B.Sc.** n abbr = **Bachelor of Science**
**BSE** n abbr (= bovine spongiform encephalopathy) ESB f, BSE f
**BSI** n abbr (= British Standards Institution) association de normalisation
**BST** abbr (= British Summer Time) heure f d'été
**Bt.** abbr (Brit) = **baronet**
**btu** n abbr (= British thermal unit) btu (= 1054,2 joules)
**bubble** ['bʌbl] n bulle f ▷ vi bouillonner, faire des bulles; (sparkle, fig) pétiller
**bubble bath** n bain moussant
**bubble gum** n chewing-gum m
**bubblejet printer** ['bʌbldʒɛt-] n imprimante f à bulle d'encre
**bubbly** ['bʌblɪ] adj (drink) pétillant(e); (person) plein(e) de vitalité ▷ n (inf) champ m
**Bucharest** [buːkəˈrɛst] n Bucarest
**buck** [bʌk] n mâle m (d'un lapin, lièvre, daim etc); (US inf) dollar m ▷ vi ruer, lancer une ruade; **to pass the ~ (to sb)** se décharger de la responsabilité (sur qn)
▶ **buck up** vi (cheer up) reprendre du poil de la bête, se remonter ▷ vt: **to ~ one's ideas up** se reprendre
**bucket** ['bʌkɪt] n seau m ▷ vi (Brit inf): **the rain is ~ing (down)** il pleut à verse
**Buckingham Palace** ['bʌkɪŋhəm-] n le palais de Buckingham; voir article

⬤ **BUCKINGHAM PALACE**
⬤
⬤ Buckingham Palace est la résidence officielle
⬤ londonienne du souverain britannique
⬤ depuis 1762. Construit en 1703, il fut à
⬤ l'origine le palais du duc de Buckingham. Il
⬤ a été partiellement reconstruit au début du
⬤ XXe siècle.

**buckle** ['bʌkl] n boucle f ▷ vt (belt etc) boucler, attacher ▷ vi (warp) tordre, gauchir; (: wheel) se voiler
▶ **buckle down** vi s'y mettre
**Bucks** [bʌks] abbr (Brit) = **Buckinghamshire**
**bud** [bʌd] n bourgeon m; (of flower) bouton m ▷ vi bourgeonner; (flower) éclore
**Buddha** ['budə] n Bouddha m
**Buddhism** ['budɪzəm] n bouddhisme m
**Buddhist** ['budɪst] adj bouddhiste ▷ n Bouddhiste m/f
**budding** ['bʌdɪŋ] adj (flower) en bouton; (poet etc) en herbe; (passion etc) naissant(e)
**buddy** ['bʌdɪ] n (US) copain m
**budge** [bʌdʒ] vt faire bouger ▷ vi bouger
**budgerigar** ['bʌdʒərɪgɑːʳ] n perruche f
**budget** ['bʌdʒɪt] n budget m ▷ vi: **to ~ for sth** inscrire qch au budget; **I'm on a tight ~** je dois faire attention à mon budget
**budgie** ['bʌdʒɪ] n = **budgerigar**
**Buenos Aires** ['bweɪnɔsˈaɪrɪz] n Buenos Aires
**buff** [bʌf] adj (couleur f) chamois m ▷ n (inf: enthusiast) mordu(e)
**buffalo** (pl - or -es) ['bʌfələu] n (Brit) buffle m; (US) bison m
**buffer** ['bʌfəʳ] n tampon m; (Comput) mémoire f tampon ▷ vi mettre en mémoire tampon
**buffering** ['bʌfərɪŋ] n (Comput) mise f en mémoire tampon
**buffer state** n état m tampon
**buffer zone** n zone f tampon
**buffet** n ['bufeɪ] (food Brit: bar) buffet m ▷ vt ['bʌfɪt] gifler, frapper; secouer, ébranler
**buffet car** n (Brit Rail) voiture-bar f
**buffet lunch** n lunch m
**buffoon** [bəˈfuːn] n buffon m, pitre m
**bug** [bʌg] n (bedbug etc) punaise f; (esp US: any insect) insecte m, bestiole f; (fig: germ) virus m, microbe m; (spy device) dispositif m d'écoute (électronique), micro clandestin; (Comput: of program) erreur f; (: of equipment) défaut m ▷ vt (room) poser des micros dans; (inf: annoy) embêter; **I've got the travel ~** (fig) j'ai le virus du voyage
**bugbear** ['bʌgbɛəʳ] n cauchemar m, bête noire
**bugger** ['bʌgəʳ] (inf!) n salaud m (!), connard m (!) ▷ vb: **~ off!** tire-toi! (!); **~ (it)!** merde! (!)
**buggy** ['bʌgɪ] n poussette f
**bugle** ['bjuːgl] n clairon m
**build** [bɪld] n (of person) carrure f, charpente f ▷ vt (pt, pp **built**) [bɪlt] construire, bâtir
▶ **build on** vt fus (fig) tirer parti de, partir de
▶ **build up** vt accumuler, amasser; (business) développer; (reputation) bâtir
**builder** ['bɪldəʳ] n entrepreneur m
**building** ['bɪldɪŋ] n (trade) construction f; (structure) bâtiment m, construction; (: residential, offices) immeuble m
**building contractor** n entrepreneur m (en bâtiment)
**building industry** n (industrie f du) bâtiment m
**building site** n chantier m (de construction)
**building society** n (Brit) société f de crédit

immobilier; *voir article*

**building trade** *n* = **building industry**
**build-up** ['bɪldʌp] *n* (*of gas etc*) accumulation *f*; (*publicity*): **to give sb/sth a good** ~ faire de la pub pour qn/qch
**built** [bɪlt] *pt, pp of* **build**
**built-in** ['bɪlt'ɪn] *adj* (*cupboard*) encastré(e); (*device*) incorporé(e); intégré(e)
**built-up** ['bɪlt'ʌp] *adj*: ~ **area** agglomération (urbaine); zone urbanisée
**bulb** [bʌlb] *n* (*Bot*) bulbe *m*, oignon *m*; (*Elec*) ampoule *f*
**bulbous** ['bʌlbəs] *adj* bulbeux(-euse)
**Bulgaria** [bʌl'gɛərɪə] *n* Bulgarie *f*
**Bulgarian** [bʌl'gɛərɪən] *adj* bulgare ▷ *n* Bulgare *m/f*; (*Ling*) bulgare *m*
**bulge** [bʌldʒ] *n* renflement *m*, gonflement *m*; (*in birth rate, sales*) brusque augmentation *f* ▷ *vi* faire saillie; présenter un renflement; (*pocket, file*): **to be bulging with** être plein(e) à craquer de
**bulimia** [bə'lɪmɪə] *n* boulimie *f*
**bulimic** [bju:'lɪmɪk] *adj, n* boulimique *m/f*
**bulk** [bʌlk] *n* masse *f*, volume *m*; **in** ~ (*Comm*) en gros, en vrac; **the** ~ **of** la plus grande *or* grosse partie de
**bulk buying** [-'baɪɪŋ] *n* achat *m* en gros
**bulk carrier** *n* cargo *m*
**bulkhead** ['bʌlkhɛd] *n* cloison *f* (étanche)
**bulky** ['bʌlkɪ] *adj* volumineux(-euse), encombrant(e)
**bull** [bul] *n* taureau *m*; (*male elephant, whale*) mâle *m*; (*Stock Exchange*) haussier *m*; (*Rel*) bulle *f*
**bulldog** ['buldɔg] *n* bouledogue *m*
**bulldoze** ['buldəuz] *vt* passer *or* raser au bulldozer; **I was ~d into doing it** (*fig: inf*) on m'a forcé la main
**bulldozer** ['buldəuzər] *n* bulldozer *m*
**bullet** ['bulɪt] *n* balle *f* (*de fusil etc*)
**bulletin** ['bulɪtɪn] *n* bulletin *m*, communiqué *m*; (*also*: **news bulletin**) (bulletin d')informations *fpl*
**bulletin board** *n* (*Comput*) messagerie *f* (électronique)
**bulletproof** ['bulɪtpru:f] *adj* à l'épreuve des balles; ~ **vest** gilet *m* pare-balles

**bullfight** ['bulfaɪt] *n* corrida *f*, course *f* de taureaux
**bullfighter** ['bulfaɪtər] *n* torero *m*
**bullfighting** ['bulfaɪtɪŋ] *n* tauromachie *f*
**bullion** ['buljən] *n* or *m or* argent *m* en lingots
**bullock** ['bulək] *n* bœuf *m*
**bullring** ['bulrɪŋ] *n* arène *f*
**bull's-eye** ['bulzaɪ] *n* centre *m* (*de la cible*)
**bullshit** ['bulʃɪt] (*inf!*) *n* connerie(s) *f(pl)* (!) ▷ *vt* raconter des conneries à (!) ▷ *vi* déconner (!)
**bully** ['bulɪ] *n* brute *f*, tyran *m* ▷ *vt* tyranniser, rudoyer; (*frighten*) intimider
**bullying** ['bulɪŋ] *n* brimades *fpl*
**bum** [bʌm] *n* (*inf: Brit: backside*) derrière *m*; (: *esp US: tramp*) vagabond(e), traîne-savates *m/f inv*; (: *idler*) glandeur *m*
▷ **bum around** *vi* (*inf*) vagabonder
**bumblebee** ['bʌmblbi:] *n* bourdon *m*
**bumf** [bʌmf] *n* (*inf: forms etc*) paperasses *fpl*
**bump** [bʌmp] *n* (*blow*) coup *m*, choc *m*; (*jolt*) cahot *m*; (*on road etc, on head*) bosse *f* ▷ *vt* heurter, cogner; (*car*) emboutir
▷ **bump along** *vi* avancer en cahotant
▷ **bump into** *vt fus* rentrer dans, tamponner; (*inf: meet*) tomber sur
**bumper** ['bʌmpər] *n* pare-chocs *m inv* ▷ *adj*: ~ **crop/harvest** récolte/moisson exceptionnelle
**bumper cars** *npl* (*US*) autos tamponneuses
**bumph** [bʌmf] *n* = **bumf**
**bumptious** ['bʌmpʃəs] *adj* suffisant(e), prétentieux(-euse)
**bumpy** ['bʌmpɪ] *adj* (*road*) cahoteux(-euse); **it was a ~ flight/ride** on a été secoués dans l'avion/la voiture
**bun** [bʌn] *n* (*cake*) petit gâteau; (*bread*) petit pain au lait; (*of hair*) chignon *m*
**bunch** [bʌntʃ] *n* (*of flowers*) bouquet *m*; (*of keys*) trousseau *m*; (*of bananas*) régime *m*; (*of people*) groupe *m*; **bunches** *npl* (*in hair*) couettes *fpl*; ~ **of grapes** grappe *f* de raisin
**bundle** ['bʌndl] *n* paquet *m* ▷ *vt* (*also*: **bundle up**) faire un paquet de; (*put*): **to ~ sth/sb into** fourrer *or* enfourner qch/qn dans
▷ **bundle off** *vt* (*person*) faire sortir (en toute hâte); expédier
▷ **bundle out** *vt* éjecter, sortir (sans ménagements)
**bun fight** *n* (*Brit inf*) réception *f*; (*tea party*) thé *m*
**bung** [bʌŋ] *n* bonde *f*, bouchon *m* ▷ *vt* (*Brit: throw: also*: **bung into**) flanquer; (*also*: **bung up**: *pipe, hole*) boucher; **my nose is ~ed up** j'ai le nez bouché
**bungalow** ['bʌŋgələu] *n* bungalow *m*
**bungee jumping** ['bʌndʒi:'dʒʌmpɪŋ] *n* saut *m* à l'élastique
**bungle** ['bʌŋgl] *vt* bâcler, gâcher
**bunion** ['bʌnjən] *n* oignon *m* (*au pied*)
**bunk** [bʌŋk] *n* couchette *f*; (*Brit inf*): **to do a ~** mettre les bouts *or* les voiles
▷ **bunk off** *vi* (*Brit inf: Scol*) sécher (les cours); **I'll ~ off at 3 o'clock this afternoon** je vais mettre les bouts *or* les voiles à 3 heures cet après-midi

**bunk beds** *npl* lits superposés
**bunker** ['bʌŋkəʳ] *n* (*coal store*) soute *f* à charbon; (*Mil, Golf*) bunker *m*
**bunny** ['bʌnɪ] *n* (*also:* **bunny rabbit**) lapin *m*
**bunny girl** *n* (*Brit*) hôtesse *de cabaret*
**bunny hill** *n* (*US Ski*) piste *f* pour débutants
**bunting** ['bʌntɪŋ] *n* pavoisement *m*, drapeaux *mpl*
**buoy** [bɔɪ] *n* bouée *f*
▶ **buoy up** *vt* faire flotter; (*fig*) soutenir, épauler
**buoyancy** ['bɔɪənsɪ] *n* (*of ship*) flottabilité *f*
**buoyant** ['bɔɪənt] *adj* (*ship*) flottable; (*carefree*) gai(e), plein(e) d'entrain; (*Comm: market, economy*) actif(-ive); (: *prices, currency*) soutenu(e)
**burden** ['bə:dn] *n* fardeau *m*, charge *f* ▷ *vt* charger; (*oppress*) accabler, surcharger; **to be a ~ to sb** être un fardeau pour qn
**bureau** (*pl* **-x**) ['bjuərəu, -z] *n* (*Brit: writing desk*) bureau *m*, secrétaire *m*; (*US: chest of drawers*) commode *f*; (*office*) bureau, office *m*
**bureaucracy** [bjuə'rɔkrəsɪ] *n* bureaucratie *f*
**bureaucrat** ['bjuərəkræt] *n* bureaucrate *m/f*, rond-de-cuir *m*
**bureaucratic** [bjuərə'krætɪk] *adj* bureaucratique
**bureau de change** [-də'ʃɑ̃ʒ] (*pl* **bureaux de change**) *n* bureau *m* de change
**bureaux** ['bjuərəuz] *npl of* **bureau**
**burgeon** ['bə:dʒən] *vi* (*fig*) être en expansion rapide
**burger** ['bə:gəʳ] *n* hamburger *m*
**burglar** ['bə:gləʳ] *n* cambrioleur *m*
**burglar alarm** *n* sonnerie *f* d'alarme
**burglarize** ['bə:gləraɪz] *vt* (*US*) cambrioler
**burglary** ['bə:glərɪ] *n* cambriolage *m*
**burgle** ['bə:gl] *vt* cambrioler
**Burgundy** ['bə:gəndɪ] *n* Bourgogne *f*
**burial** ['bɛrɪəl] *n* enterrement *m*
**burial ground** *n* cimetière *m*
**burly** ['bə:lɪ] *adj* de forte carrure, costaud(e)
**Burma** ['bə:mə] *n* Birmanie *f*; *see also* **Myanmar**
**Burmese** [bə:'mi:z] *adj* birman(e), de Birmanie ▷ *n* (*pl inv*) Birman(e); (*Ling*) birman *m*
**burn** [bə:n] *vt, vi* (*pt, pp* **-ed** *or* **-t**) [bə:nt] brûler ▷ *n* brûlure *f*; **the cigarette ~t a hole in her dress** la cigarette a fait un trou dans sa robe; **I've ~t myself!** je me suis brûlé(e)!
▶ **burn down** *vt* incendier, détruire par le feu
▶ **burn out** *vt* (*writer etc*): **to ~ o.s. out** s'user (à force de travailler)
**burner** ['bə:nəʳ] *n* brûleur *m*
**burning** ['bə:nɪŋ] *adj* (*building, forest*) en flammes; (*issue, question*) brûlant(e); (*ambition*) dévorant(e)
**burnish** ['bə:nɪʃ] *vt* polir
**Burns' Night** [bə:nz-] *n* fête écossaise à la mémoire du poète Robert Burns; *voir article*

● **BURNS' NIGHT**
●
● *Burns' Night* est une fête qui a lieu le 25
● janvier, à la mémoire du poète écossais
● Robert Burns (1759–1796), à l'occasion de
● laquelle les Écossais partout dans le monde
● organisent un souper, en général arrosé de
● whisky. Le plat principal est toujours le
● haggis, servi avec de la purée de pommes de
● terre et de la purée de rutabagas. On apporte
● le haggis à son des cornemuses et au cours
● du repas on lit des poèmes de Burns et on
● chante ses chansons.

**burnt** [bə:nt] *pt, pp of* **burn**
**burnt sugar** *n* (*Brit*) caramel *m*
**burp** [bə:p] (*inf*) *n* rot *m* ▷ *vi* roter
**burrow** ['bʌrəu] *n* terrier *m* ▷ *vt* creuser ▷ *vi* (*rabbit*) creuser un terrier; (*rummage*) fouiller
**bursar** ['bə:səʳ] *n* économe *m/f*; (*Brit: student*) boursier(-ère)
**bursary** ['bə:sərɪ] *n* (*Brit*) bourse *f* (d'études)
**burst** [bə:st] (*pt, pp* **-**) *vt* faire éclater; (*river: banks etc*) rompre ▷ *vi* éclater; (*tyre*) crever ▷ *n* explosion *f*; (*also:* **burst pipe**) fuite *f* (*due à une rupture*); **a ~ of enthusiasm/energy** un accès d'enthousiasme/d'énergie; **~ of laughter** éclat *m* de rire; **a ~ of applause** une salve d'applaudissement; **a ~ of gunfire** une rafale de tir; **a ~ of speed** une pointe de vitesse; **~ blood vessel** rupture *f* de vaisseau sanguin; **the river has ~ its banks** le cours d'eau est sorti de son lit; **to ~ into flames** s'enflammer soudainement; **to ~ out laughing** éclater de rire; **to ~ into tears** fondre en larmes; **to ~ open** (*vi*) s'ouvrir violemment *or* soudainement; **to be ~ing with** (*container*) être plein(e) (à craquer) de, regorger de; (*fig*) être débordant(e) de
▶ **burst into** *vt fus* (*room etc*) faire irruption dans
▶ **burst out of** *vt fus* sortir précipitamment de
**bury** ['bɛrɪ] *vt* enterrer; **to ~ one's face in one's hands** se couvrir le visage de ses mains; **to ~ one's head in the sand** (*fig*) pratiquer la politique de l'autruche; **to ~ the hatchet** (*fig*) enterrer la hache de guerre
**bus** (*pl* **-es**) [bʌs, 'bʌsɪz] *n* autobus *m*
**busboy** ['bʌsbɔɪ] *n* (*US*) aide-serveur *m*
**bus conductor** *n* receveur(-euse) *m/f* de bus
**bush** [buʃ] *n* buisson *m*; (*scrub land*) brousse *f*; **to beat about the ~** tourner autour du pot
**bushed** [buʃt] *adj* (*inf*) crevé(e), claqué(e)
**bushel** ['buʃl] *n* boisseau *m*
**bushfire** ['buʃfaɪəʳ] *n* feu *m* de brousse
**bushy** ['buʃɪ] *adj* broussailleux(-euse), touffu(e)
**busily** ['bɪzɪlɪ] *adv*: **to be ~ doing sth** s'affairer à faire qch
**business** ['bɪznɪs] *n* (*matter, firm*) affaire *f*; (*trading*) affaires *fpl*; (*job, duty*) travail *m*; **to be away on ~** être en déplacement d'affaires; **I'm here on ~** je suis là pour affaires; **he's in the insurance ~** il est dans les assurances; **to do ~ with sb** traiter avec qn; **it's none of my ~** cela ne me regarde pas, ce ne sont pas mes affaires; **he means ~** il ne plaisante pas, il est sérieux
**business address** *n* adresse professionnelle *or* au bureau

**business card** n carte f de visite (professionnelle)

**business class** n (on plane) classe f affaires

**businesslike** ['bɪznɪslaɪk] adj sérieux(-euse), efficace

**businessman** ['bɪznɪsmən] (irreg) n homme m d'affaires

**business trip** n voyage m d'affaires

**businesswoman** ['bɪznɪswumən] (irreg) n femme f d'affaires

**busker** ['bʌskər] n (Brit) artiste ambulant(e)

**bus lane** n (Brit) voie réservée aux autobus

**bus pass** n carte f de bus

**bus shelter** n abribus m

**bus station** n gare routière

**bus stop** n arrêt m d'autobus

**bust** [bʌst] n buste m; (measurement) tour m de poitrine ▷ adj (inf: broken) fichu(e), fini(e) ▷ vt (inf: Police: arrest) pincer; **to go ~** faire faillite

**bustle** ['bʌsl] n remue-ménage m, affairement m ▷ vi s'affairer, se démener

**bustling** ['bʌslɪŋ] adj (person) affairé(e); (town) très animé(e)

**bust-up** ['bʌstʌp] n (Brit inf) engueulade f

**busty** ['bʌstɪ] adj (inf) à la poitrine plantureuse

**busy** ['bɪzɪ] adj occupé(e); (shop, street) très fréquenté(e); (US: telephone, line) occupé ▷ vt: **to ~ o.s.** s'occuper; **he's a ~ man** (normally) c'est un homme très pris; (temporarily) il est très pris

**busybody** ['bɪzɪbɔdɪ] n mouche f du coche, âme f charitable

**busy signal** n (US) tonalité f occupé inv

**but** [bʌt] conj mais; **I'd love to come, but I'm busy** j'aimerais venir mais je suis occupé; **he's not English but French** il n'est pas anglais mais français; **but that's far too expensive!** mais c'est bien trop cher!

▷ prep (apart from, except) sauf, excepté; **nothing but** rien d'autre que; **we've had nothing but trouble** nous n'avons eu que des ennuis; **no-one but him can do it** lui seul peut le faire; **who but a lunatic would do such a thing?** qui sinon un fou ferait une chose pareille?; **but for you/your help** sans toi/ton aide; **anything but that** tout sauf or excepté ça, tout mais pas ça; **the last but one** (Brit) l'avant-dernier(-ère)

▷ adv (just, only) ne ... que; **she's but a child** elle n'est qu'une enfant; **had I but known** si seulement j'avais su; **I can but try** je peux toujours essayer; **all but finished** pratiquement terminé; **anything but finished** tout sauf fini, très loin d'être fini

**butane** ['bju:teɪn] n (also: **butane gas**) butane m

**butch** [butʃ] adj (inf: man) costaud, viril; (: woman) costaude, masculine

**butcher** ['butʃər] n boucher m ▷ vt massacrer; (cattle etc for meat) tuer

**butcher's** ['butʃəʳz], **butcher's shop** n boucherie f

**butler** ['bʌtlər] n maître m d'hôtel

**butt** [bʌt] n (cask) gros tonneau; (thick end) (gros) bout; (of gun) crosse f; (of cigarette) mégot m; (Brit fig: target) cible f ▷ vt donner un coup de tête à
▶ **butt in** vi (interrupt) interrompre

**butter** ['bʌtər] n beurre m ▷ vt beurrer

**buttercup** ['bʌtəkʌp] n bouton m d'or

**butter dish** n beurrier m

**butterfingers** ['bʌtəfɪŋgəz] n (inf) maladroit(e)

**butterfly** ['bʌtəflaɪ] n papillon m; (Swimming: also: **butterfly stroke**) brasse f papillon

**buttocks** ['bʌtəks] npl fesses fpl

**button** ['bʌtn] n bouton m; (US: badge) pin m ▷ vt (also: **button up**) boutonner ▷ vi se boutonner

**buttonhole** ['bʌtnhəul] n boutonnière f ▷ vt accrocher, arrêter, retenir

**buttress** ['bʌtrɪs] n contrefort m

**buxom** ['bʌksəm] adj aux formes avantageuses or épanouies, bien galbé(e)

**buy** [baɪ] (pt, pp bought [bɔ:t]) vt acheter; (Comm: company) (r)acheter ▷ n achat m; **that was a good/bad ~** c'était un bon/mauvais achat; **to ~ sb sth/sth from sb** acheter qch à qn; **to ~ sb a drink** offrir un verre or à boire à qn; **can I ~ you a drink?** je vous offre un verre?; **where can I ~ some postcards?** où est-ce que je peux acheter des cartes postales?
▶ **buy back** vt racheter
▶ **buy in** vt (Brit: goods) acheter, faire venir
▶ **buy into** vt fus (Brit Comm) acheter des actions de
▶ **buy off** vt (bribe) acheter
▶ **buy out** vt (partner) désintéresser; (business) racheter
▶ **buy up** vt acheter en bloc, rafler

**buyer** ['baɪəʳ] n acheteur(-euse) m/f; **~'s market** marché m favorable aux acheteurs

**buy-out** ['baɪaut] n (Comm) rachat m (d'entreprise)

**buzz** [bʌz] n bourdonnement m; (inf: phone call): **to give sb a ~** passer un coup de fil à qn ▷ vi bourdonner ▷ vt (call on intercom) appeler; (with buzzer) sonner; (Aviat: plane, building) raser; **my head is ~ing** j'ai la tête qui bourdonne
▶ **buzz off** vi (inf) s'en aller, ficher le camp

**buzzard** ['bʌzəd] n buse f

**buzzer** ['bʌzəʳ] n timbre m électrique

**buzz word** n (inf) mot m à la mode or dans le vent

**by** [baɪ] prep **1** (referring to cause, agent) par, de; **killed by lightning** tué par la foudre; **surrounded by a fence** entouré d'une barrière; **a painting by Picasso** un tableau de Picasso
**2** (referring to method, manner, means): **by bus/car** en autobus/voiture; **by train** le or en train; **to pay by cheque** payer par chèque; **by moonlight/candlelight** à la lueur de la lune/d'une bougie; **by saving hard, he ...** à force d'économiser, il ...

**3** (*via, through*) par; **we came by Dover** nous sommes venus par Douvres
**4** (*close to, past*) à côté de; **the house by the school** la maison à côté de l'école; **a holiday by the sea** des vacances au bord de la mer; **she sat by his bed** elle était assise à son chevet; **she went by me** elle est passée à côté de moi; **I go by the post office every day** je passe devant la poste tous les jours
**5** (*with time: not later than*) avant; (: *during*): **by daylight** à la lumière du jour; **by night** la nuit, de nuit; **by 4 o'clock** avant 4 heures; **by this time tomorrow** d'ici demain à la même heure; **by the time I got here it was too late** lorsque je suis arrivé il était déjà trop tard
**6** (*amount*) à; **by the kilo/metre** au kilo/au mètre; **paid by the hour** payé à l'heure; **to increase** *etc* **by the hour** augmenter *etc* d'heure en heure
**7** (*Math: measure*): **to divide/multiply by 3** diviser/multiplier par 3; **a room 3 metres by 4** une pièce de 3 mètres sur 4; **it's broader by a metre** c'est plus large d'un mètre; **the bullet missed him by inches** la balle est passée à quelques centimètres de lui; **one by one** un à un; **little by little** petit à petit, peu à peu
**8** (*according to*) d'après, selon; **it's 3 o'clock by my watch** il est 3 heures à ma montre; **it's all right by me** je n'ai rien contre

**9**: (**all**) **by oneself** *etc* tout(e) seul(e)
▷ *adv* **1** *see* **go**; **pass** *etc*
**2**: **by and by** un peu plus tard, bientôt; **by and large** dans l'ensemble

**bye** ['baɪ], **bye-bye** ['baɪ'baɪ] *excl* au revoir!, salut!
**bye-law** ['baɪlɔ:] *n* = **by-law**
**by-election** ['baɪɪlɛkʃən] *n* (*Brit*) élection (législative) partielle
**Byelorussia** [bjɛləu'rʌʃə] *n* Biélorussie *f*
**Byelorussian** [bjɛləu'rʌʃən] *adj, n* = **Belorussian**
**bygone** ['baɪgɔn] *adj* passé(e) ▷ *n*: **let ~s be ~s** passons l'éponge, oublions le passé
**by-law** ['baɪlɔ:] *n* arrêté municipal
**bypass** ['baɪpɑ:s] *n* rocade *f*; (*Med*) pontage *m*
▷ *vt* éviter
**by-product** ['baɪprɔdʌkt] *n* sous-produit *m*, dérivé *m*; (*fig*) conséquence *f* secondaire, retombée *f*
**byre** ['baɪəʳ] *n* (*Brit*) étable *f* (à vaches)
**bystander** ['baɪstændəʳ] *n* spectateur(-trice), badaud(e)
**byte** [baɪt] *n* (*Comput*) octet *m*
**byway** ['baɪweɪ] *n* chemin détourné
**byword** ['baɪwə:d] *n*: **to be a ~ for** être synonyme de (*fig*)
**by-your-leave** ['baɪjɔ:'li:v] *n*: **without so much as a ~** sans même demander la permission

# Cc

**C¹, c¹** [si:] n (letter) C, c m; (Scol: mark) C; (Mus): **C**
do m; **C for Charlie** C comme Célestin
**C²** abbr (= Celsius, centigrade) C
**c²** abbr (= century) s.; (= circa) v.; (US etc) = **cent(s)**
**CA** n abbr = **Central America**; (Brit) = **chartered
accountant** ▷ abbr (US) = **California**
**ca.** abbr (= circa) v
**c/a** abbr = **capital account; credit account;
current account**
**CAA** n abbr (Brit) = **Civil Aviation Authority**; (US:
= Civil Aeronautics Authority) direction de l'aviation
civile
**CAB** n abbr (Brit) = **Citizens' Advice Bureau**
**cab** [kæb] n taxi m; (of train, truck) cabine f; (horse-
drawn) fiacre m
**cabaret** ['kæbəreɪ] n attractions fpl; (show)
spectacle m de cabaret
**cabbage** ['kæbɪdʒ] n chou m
**cabbie, cabby** ['kæbɪ], **cab driver** n (inf) taxi m,
chauffeur m de taxi
**cabin** ['kæbɪn] n (house) cabane f, hutte f; (on ship)
cabine f; (on plane) compartiment m
**cabin crew** n (Aviat) équipage m
**cabin cruiser** n yacht m (à moteur)
**cabinet** ['kæbɪnɪt] n (Pol) cabinet m; (furniture)
petit meuble à tiroirs et rayons; (also: **display
cabinet**) vitrine f, petite armoire vitrée
**cabinet-maker** ['kæbɪnɪt'meɪkər] n ébéniste m
**cabinet minister** n ministre m (membre du
cabinet)
**cable** ['keɪbl] n câble m ▷ vt câbler, télégraphier
**cable car** ['keɪblkɑ:r] n téléphérique m
**cablegram** ['keɪblgræm] n câblogramme m
**cable railway** n (Brit) funiculaire m
**cable television** n télévision f par câble
**cache** [kæʃ] n cachette f; **a ~ of food** etc un dépôt
secret de provisions etc, une cachette contenant
des provisions etc
**cackle** ['kækl] vi caqueter
**cactus** (pl **cacti**) ['kæktəs, -taɪ] n cactus m
**CAD** n abbr (= computer-aided design) CAO f
**caddie** ['kædɪ] n caddie m
**cadet** [kə'dɛt] n (Mil) élève m officier; **police ~**
élève agent de police
**cadge** [kædʒ] vt (inf) se faire donner; **to ~ a
meal (off sb)** se faire inviter à manger (par qn)

**cadre** ['kædrɪ] n cadre m
**Caesarean**, (US) **Cesarean** [si:'zɛərɪən] adj: **~
(section)** césarienne f
**CAF** abbr (Brit: = cost and freight) C et F
**café** ['kæfeɪ] n ≈ café(-restaurant) m (sans alcool)
**cafeteria** [kæfɪ'tɪərɪə] n cafétéria f
**caffeine** ['kæfi:n] n caféine f
**cage** [keɪdʒ] n cage f ▷ vt mettre en cage
**cagey** ['keɪdʒɪ] adj (inf) réticent(e), méfiant(e)
**cagoule** [kə'gu:l] n K-way® m
**cahoots** [kə'hu:ts] n: **to be in ~ (with)** être de
mèche (avec)
**CAI** n abbr (= computer-aided instruction) EAO m
**Cairo** ['kaɪərəʊ] n le Caire
**cajole** [kə'dʒəʊl] vt couvrir de flatteries or de
gentillesses
**cake** [keɪk] n gâteau m; **~ of soap** savonnette f;
**it's a piece of ~** (inf) c'est un jeu d'enfant; **he
wants to have his ~ and eat it (too)** (fig) il veut
tout avoir
**caked** [keɪkt] adj: **~ with** raidi(e) par, couvert(e)
d'une croûte de
**cake shop** n pâtisserie f
**Cal.** abbr (US) = **California**
**calamitous** [kə'læmɪtəs] adj catastrophique,
désastreux(-euse)
**calamity** [kə'læmɪtɪ] n calamité f, désastre m
**calcium** ['kælsɪəm] n calcium m
**calculate** ['kælkjuleɪt] vt calculer; (estimate:
chances, effect) évaluer
 ▶ **calculate on** vt fus: **to ~ on sth/on doing sth**
compter sur qch/faire qch
**calculated** ['kælkjuleɪtɪd] adj (insult, action)
délibéré(e); **a ~ risk** un risque pris en toute
connaissance de cause
**calculating** ['kælkjuleɪtɪŋ] adj
calculateur(-trice)
**calculation** [kælkju'leɪʃən] n calcul m
**calculator** ['kælkjuleɪtər] n machine f à
calculer, calculatrice f
**calculus** ['kælkjuləs] n analyse f
(mathématique), calcul infinitésimal;
**integral/differential ~** calcul intégral/
différentiel
**calendar** ['kæləndər] n calendrier m
**calendar year** n année civile

**calf** (*pl* **calves**) [kɑːf, kɑːvz] *n* (*of cow*) veau *m*; (*of other animals*) petit *m*; (*also:* **calfskin**) veau *m*, vachette *f*; (*Anat*) mollet *m*

**caliber** ['kælɪbəʳ] *n* (*US*) = **calibre**

**calibrate** ['kælɪbreɪt] *vt* (*gun etc*) calibrer; (*scale of measuring instrument*) étalonner

**calibre,** (*US*) **caliber** ['kælɪbəʳ] *n* calibre *m*

**calico** ['kælɪkəu] *n* (*Brit*) calicot *m*; (*US*) indienne *f*

**Calif.** *abbr* (*US*) = **California**

**California** [kælɪˈfɔːnɪə] *n* Californie *f*

**calipers** ['kælɪpəz] *npl* (*US*) = **callipers**

**call** [kɔːl] *vt* (*gen, also Tel*) appeler; (*announce: flight*) annoncer; (*meeting*) convoquer; (*strike*) lancer ▷ *vi* appeler; (*visit: also:* **call in, call round**) passer ▷ *n* (*shout*) appel *m*, cri *m*; (*summons: for flight etc, fig: lure*) appel; (*visit*) visite *f*; (*also:* **telephone call**) coup *m* de téléphone; communication *f*; **to be on** ~ être de permanence; **to be ~ed** s'appeler; **she's ~ed Suzanne** elle s'appelle Suzanne; **who is ~ing?** (*Tel*) qui est à l'appareil?; **London ~ing** (*Radio*) ici Londres; **please give me a ~ at 7** appelez-moi à 7 heures; **to make a ~** téléphoner, passer un coup de fil; **can I make a ~ from here?** est-ce que je peux téléphoner d'ici?; **to pay a ~ on sb** rendre visite à qn, passer voir qn; **there's not much ~ for these items** ces articles ne sont pas très demandés

▶ **call at** *vt fus* (*ship*) faire escale à; (*train*) s'arrêter à

▶ **call back** *vi* (*return*) repasser; (*Tel*) rappeler ▷ *vt* (*Tel*) rappeler; **can you ~ back later?** pouvez-vous rappeler plus tard?

▶ **call for** *vt fus* (*demand*) demander; (*fetch*) passer prendre

▶ **call in** *vt* (*doctor, expert, police*) appeler, faire venir

▶ **call off** *vt* annuler; **the strike was ~ed off** l'ordre de grève a été rapporté

▶ **call on** *vt fus* (*visit*) rendre visite à, passer voir; (*request*): **to ~ on sb to do** inviter qn à faire

▶ **call out** *vi* pousser un cri *or* des cris ▷ *vt* (*doctor, police, troops*) appeler

▶ **call up** *vt* (*Mil*) appeler, mobiliser; (*Tel*) appeler

**call box** ['kɔːlbɔks] *n* (*Brit*) cabine *f* téléphonique

**call centre,** (*US*) **call center** *n* centre *m* d'appels

**caller** ['kɔːləʳ] *n* (*Tel*) personne *f* qui appelle; (*visitor*) visiteur *m*; **hold the line, ~!** (*Tel*) ne quittez pas, Monsieur (*or* Madame)!

**call girl** *n* call-girl *f*

**call-in** ['kɔːlɪn] *n* (*US Radio, TV*) programme *m* à ligne ouverte

**calling** ['kɔːlɪŋ] *n* vocation *f*; (*trade, occupation*) état *m*

**calling card** *n* (*US*) carte *f* de visite

**callipers,** (*US*) **calipers** ['kælɪpəz] *npl* (*Math*) compas *m*; (*Med*) appareil *m* orthopédique; gouttière *f*; étrier *m*

**callous** ['kæləs] *adj* dur(e), insensible

**callousness** ['kæləsnɪs] *n* dureté *f*, manque *m* de cœur, insensibilité *f*

**callow** ['kæləu] *adj* sans expérience (de la vie)

**calm** [kɑːm] *adj* calme ▷ *n* calme *m* ▷ *vt* calmer, apaiser

▶ **calm down** *vi* se calmer, s'apaiser ▷ *vt* calmer, apaiser

**calmly** ['kɑːmlɪ] *adv* calmement, avec calme

**calmness** ['kɑːmnɪs] *n* calme *m*

**Calor gas®** ['kælə-] *n* (*Brit*) butane *m*, butagaz® *m*

**calorie** ['kælərɪ] *n* calorie *f*; **low ~ product** produit *m* pauvre en calories

**calve** [kɑːv] *vi* vêler, mettre bas

**calves** [kɑːvz] *npl of* **calf**

**CAM** *n abbr* (= *computer-aided manufacturing*) FAO *f*

**camber** ['kæmbəʳ] *n* (*of road*) bombement *m*

**Cambodia** [kæmˈbəudɪə] *n* Cambodge *m*

**Cambodian** [kæmˈbəudɪən] *adj* cambodgien(ne) ▷ *n* Cambodgien(ne)

**Cambs** *abbr* (*Brit*) = **Cambridgeshire**

**camcorder** ['kæmkɔːdəʳ] *n* caméscope *m*

**came** [keɪm] *pt of* **come**

**camel** ['kæməl] *n* chameau *m*

**cameo** ['kæmɪəu] *n* camée *m*

**camera** ['kæmərə] *n* appareil-photo *m*; (*Cine, TV*) caméra *f*; **digital ~** appareil numérique; **in ~** à huis clos, en privé

**cameraman** ['kæmərəmæn] (*irreg*) *n* caméraman *m*

**camera phone** *n* téléphone *m* avec appareil photo

**Cameroon, Cameroun** [kæməˈruːn] *n* Cameroun *m*

**camouflage** ['kæməflɑːʒ] *n* camouflage *m* ▷ *vt* camoufler

**camp** [kæmp] *n* camp *m* ▷ *vi* camper ▷ *adj* (*man*) efféminé(e)

**campaign** [kæmˈpeɪn] *n* (*Mil, Pol*) campagne *f* ▷ *vi* (*also fig*) faire campagne; **to ~ for/against** militer pour/contre

**campaigner** [kæmˈpeɪnəʳ] *n*: **~ for** partisan(e) de; **~ against** opposant(e) à

**camp bed** ['kæmpˈbed] *n* (*Brit*) lit *m* de camp

**camper** ['kæmpəʳ] *n* campeur(-euse); (*vehicle*) camping-car *m*

**camping** ['kæmpɪŋ] *n* camping *m*; **to go ~** faire du camping

**camping gas®** *n* butane *m*

**campsite** ['kæmpsaɪt] *n* (*terrain m de*) camping *m*

**campus** ['kæmpəs] *n* campus *m*

**camshaft** ['kæmʃɑːft] *n* arbre *m* à came

**can¹** [kæn] *n* (*of milk, oil, water*) bidon *m*; (*tin*) boîte *f* (de conserve) ▷ *vt* mettre en conserve; **a ~ of beer** une canette de bière; **he had to carry the ~** (*Brit inf*) on lui a fait porter le chapeau; *see also* **keyword**

⬤ KEYWORD

**can²** [kæn] (*negative* **cannot, can't**, *conditional and pt* **could**) *aux vb* **1** (*be able to*) pouvoir; **you can do**

**it if you try** vous pouvez le faire si vous essayez; **I can't hear you** je ne t'entends pas

**2** (*know how to*) savoir; **I can swim/play tennis/drive** je sais nager/jouer au tennis/conduire; **can you speak French?** parlez-vous français?

**3** (*may*) pouvoir; **can I use your phone?** puis-je me servir de votre téléphone?

**4** (*expressing disbelief, puzzlement etc*): **it can't be true!** ce n'est pas possible!; **what CAN he want?** qu'est-ce qu'il peut bien vouloir?

**5** (*expressing possibility, suggestion etc*): **he could be in the library** il est peut-être dans la bibliothèque; **she could have been delayed** il se peut qu'elle ait été retardée; **they could have forgotten** ils ont pu oublier

**Canada** ['kænədə] *n* Canada *m*
**Canadian** [kə'neɪdɪən] *adj* canadien(ne) ▷ *n* Canadien(ne)
**canal** [kə'næl] *n* canal *m*
**canary** [kə'nɛərɪ] *n* canari *m*, serin *m*
**Canary Islands, Canaries** [kə'nɛərɪz] *npl*: **the ~** les (îles *fpl*) Canaries *fpl*
**Canberra** ['kænbərə] *n* Canberra
**cancel** ['kænsəl] *vt* annuler; (*train*) supprimer; (*party, appointment*) décommander; (*cross out*) barrer, rayer; (*stamp*) oblitérer; (*cheque*) faire opposition à; **I would like to ~ my booking** je voudrais annuler ma réservation
  ▶ **cancel out** *vt* annuler; **they ~ each other out** ils s'annulent
**cancellation** [kænsə'leɪʃən] *n* annulation *f*; suppression *f*; oblitération *f*; (*Tourism*) réservation annulée, client *etc* qui s'est décommandé
**Cancer** ['kænsər] *n* (*Astrology*) le Cancer; **to be ~** être du Cancer
**cancer** ['kænsər] *n* cancer *m*
**cancerous** ['kænsrəs] *adj* cancéreux(-euse)
**cancer patient** *n* cancéreux(-euse)
**cancer research** *n* recherche *f* contre le cancer
**C and F** *abbr* (*Brit*: = *cost and freight*) C et F
**candid** ['kændɪd] *adj* (très) franc (franche), sincère
**candidacy** ['kændɪdəsɪ] *n* candidature *f*
**candidate** ['kændɪdeɪt] *n* candidat(e)
**candidature** ['kændɪdətʃər] *n* (*Brit*) = **candidacy**
**candied** ['kændɪd] *adj* confit(e); **~ apple** (*US*) pomme caramélisée
**candle** ['kændl] *n* bougie *f*; (*of tallow*) chandelle *f*; (*in church*) cierge *m*
**candlelight** ['kændllaɪt] *n*: **by ~** à la lumière d'une bougie; (*dinner*) aux chandelles
**candlestick** ['kændlstɪk] *n* (*also*: **candle holder**) bougeoir *m*; (*bigger, ornate*) chandelier *m*
**candour**, (*US*) **candor** ['kændər] *n* (grande) franchise *or* sincérité
**C & W** *n abbr* = **country and western**
**candy** ['kændɪ] *n* sucre candi; (*US*) bonbon *m*
**candy bar** (*US*) *n* barre *f* chocolatée
**candyfloss** ['kændɪflɔs] *n* (*Brit*) barbe *f* à papa
**candy store** *n* (*US*) confiserie *f*

**cane** [keɪn] *n* canne *f*; (*for baskets, chairs etc*) rotin *m* ▷ *vt* (*Brit Scol*) administrer des coups de bâton à
**canine** ['keɪnaɪn] *adj* canin(e)
**canister** ['kænɪstər] *n* boîte *f* (*gén en métal*); (*of gas*) bombe *f*
**cannabis** ['kænəbɪs] *n* (*drug*) cannabis *m*; (*cannabis plant*) chanvre indien
**canned** ['kænd] *adj* (*food*) en boîte, en conserve; (*inf: music*) enregistré(e); (*Brit inf: drunk*) bourré(e); (*US inf: worker*) mis(e) à la porte
**cannibal** ['kænɪbəl] *n* cannibale *m/f*, anthropophage *m/f*
**cannibalism** ['kænɪbəlɪzəm] *n* cannibalisme *m*, anthropophagie *f*
**cannon** (*pl* - *or* -**s**) ['kænən] *n* (*gun*) canon *m*
**cannonball** ['kænənbɔːl] *n* boulet *m* de canon
**cannon fodder** *n* chair *f* à canon
**cannot** ['kænɔt] = **can not**
**canny** ['kænɪ] *adj* madré(e), finaud(e)
**canoe** [kə'nuː] *n* pirogue *f*; (*Sport*) canoë *m*
**canoeing** [kə'nuːɪŋ] *n* (*sport*) canoë *m*
**canoeist** [kə'nuːɪst] *n* canoéiste *m/f*
**canon** ['kænən] *n* (*clergyman*) chanoine *m*; (*standard*) canon *m*
**canonize** ['kænənaɪz] *vt* canoniser
**can-opener** [-'əupnər] *n* ouvre-boîte *m*
**canopy** ['kænəpɪ] *n* baldaquin *m*; dais *m*
**cant** [kænt] *n* jargon *m* ▷ *vt*, *vi* pencher
**can't** [kɑːnt] = **can not**
**Cantab.** *abbr* (*Brit*: = *cantabrigiensis*) *of Cambridge*
**cantankerous** [kæn'tæŋkərəs] *adj* querelleur(-euse), acariâtre
**canteen** [kæn'tiːn] *n* (*eating place*) cantine *f*; (*Brit: of cutlery*) ménagère *f*
**canter** ['kæntər] *n* petit galop ▷ *vi* aller au petit galop
**cantilever** ['kæntɪliːvər] *n* porte-à-faux *m inv*
**canvas** ['kænvəs] *n* (*gen*) toile *f*; **under ~** (*camping*) sous la tente; (*Naut*) toutes voiles dehors
**canvass** ['kænvəs] *vi* (*Pol*): **to ~ for** faire campagne pour ▷ *vt* (*Pol: district*) faire la tournée électorale dans; (: *person*) solliciter le suffrage de; (*Comm: district*) prospecter; (*citizens, opinions*) sonder
**canvasser** ['kænvəsər] *n* (*Pol*) agent électoral; (*Comm*) démarcheur *m*
**canvassing** ['kænvəsɪŋ] *n* (*Pol*) prospection électorale, démarchage électoral; (*Comm*) démarchage, prospection
**canyon** ['kænjən] *n* cañon *m*, gorge (profonde)
**CAP** *n abbr* (= *Common Agricultural Policy*) PAC *f*
**cap** [kæp] *n* casquette *f*; (*for swimming*) bonnet *m* de bain; (*of pen*) capuchon *m*; (*of bottle*) capsule *f*; (*Brit: contraceptive: also*: **Dutch cap**) diaphragme *m*; (*Football*) sélection *f* pour l'équipe nationale ▷ *vt* capsuler; (*outdo*) surpasser; (*put limit on*) plafonner; **~ped with** coiffé(e) de; **and to ~ it all, he ...** (*Brit*) pour couronner le tout, il ...
**capability** [keɪpə'bɪlɪtɪ] *n* aptitude *f*, capacité *f*
**capable** ['keɪpəbl] *adj* capable; **~ of** (*interpretation*

*etc*) susceptible de
**capacious** [kə'peɪʃəs] *adj* vaste
**capacity** [kə'pæsɪtɪ] *n* (*of container*) capacité *f*, contenance *f*; (*ability*) aptitude *f*; **filled to ~** plein(e); **in his ~ as** en sa qualité de; **in an advisory ~** à titre consultatif; **to work at full ~** travailler à plein rendement
**cape** [keɪp] *n* (*garment*) cape *f*; (*Geo*) cap *m*
**Cape of Good Hope** *n* cap *m* de Bonne Espérance
**caper** ['keɪpər] *n* (*Culin: gen pl*) câpre *f*; (*prank*) farce *f*
**Cape Town** *n* Le Cap
**capita** ['kæpɪtə] *see* **per capita**
**capital** ['kæpɪtl] *n* (*also:* **capital city**) capitale *f*; (*money*) capital *m*; (*also:* **capital letter**) majuscule *f*
**capital account** *n* balance *f* des capitaux; (*of country*) compte capital
**capital allowance** *n* provision *f* pour amortissement
**capital assets** *npl* immobilisations *fpl*
**capital expenditure** *n* dépenses *fpl* d'équipement
**capital gains tax** *n* impôt *m* sur les plus-values
**capital goods** *n* biens *mpl* d'équipement
**capital-intensive** ['kæpɪtlɪn'tɛnsɪv] *adj* à forte proportion de capitaux
**capitalism** ['kæpɪtəlɪzəm] *n* capitalisme *m*
**capitalist** ['kæpɪtəlɪst] *adj, n* capitaliste *m/f*
**capitalize** ['kæpɪtəlaɪz] *vt* (*provide with capital*) financer
▶ **capitalize on** *vt fus* (*fig*) profiter de
**capital punishment** *n* peine capitale
**capital transfer tax** *n* (*Brit*) impôt *m* sur le transfert de propriété
**Capitol** ['kæpɪtl] *n*: **the ~** le Capitole; *voir article*

⊙ **CAPITOL**
⊙
⊙ Le *Capitol* est le siège du "Congress", à
⊙ Washington. Il est situé sur Capitol Hill.

**capitulate** [kə'pɪtjuleɪt] *vi* capituler
**capitulation** [kəpɪtju'leɪʃən] *n* capitulation *f*
**capricious** [kə'prɪʃəs] *adj* capricieux(-euse), fantasque
**Capricorn** ['kæprɪkɔ:n] *n* le Capricorne; **to be ~** être du Capricorne
**caps** [kæps] *abbr* = **capital letters**
**capsize** [kæp'saɪz] *vt* faire chavirer ▷ *vi* chavirer
**capsule** ['kæpsju:l] *n* capsule *f*
**Capt.** *abbr* (= *captain*) Cne
**captain** ['kæptɪn] *n* capitaine *m* ▷ *vt* commander, être le capitaine de
**caption** ['kæpʃən] *n* légende *f*
**captivate** ['kæptɪveɪt] *vt* captiver, fasciner
**captive** ['kæptɪv] *adj, n* captif(-ive)
**captivity** [kæp'tɪvɪtɪ] *n* captivité *f*
**captor** ['kæptər] *n* (*unlawful*) ravisseur *m*; (*lawful*): **his ~s** les gens (*or* ceux *etc*) qui l'ont arrêté

**capture** ['kæptʃər] *vt* (*prisoner, animal*) capturer; (*town*) prendre; (*attention*) capter; (*Comput*) saisir ▷ *n* capture *f*; (*of data*) saisie *f* de données
**car** [kɑ:ʳ] *n* voiture *f*, auto *f*; (*US Rail*) wagon *m*, voiture; **by ~** en voiture
**carafe** [kə'ræf] *n* carafe *f*
**carafe wine** *n* (*in restaurant*) ≈ vin ouvert
**caramel** ['kærəməl] *n* caramel *m*
**carat** ['kærət] *n* carat *m*; **18 ~ gold** or *m* à 18 carats
**caravan** ['kærəvæn] *n* caravane *f*
**caravan site** *n* (*Brit*) camping *m* pour caravanes
**caraway** ['kærəweɪ] *n*: **~ seed** graine *f* de cumin, cumin *m*
**carbohydrate** [kɑ:bəu'haɪdreɪt] *n* hydrate *m* de carbone; (*food*) féculent *m*
**carbolic acid** [kɑ:'bɔlɪk-] *n* phénol *m*
**car bomb** *n* voiture piégée
**carbon** ['kɑ:bən] *n* carbone *m*
**carbonated** ['kɑ:bəneɪtɪd] *adj* (*drink*) gazeux(-euse)
**carbon copy** *n* carbone *m*
**carbon dioxide** [-daɪ'ɔksaɪd] *n* gaz *m* carbonique, dioxyde *m* de carbone
**carbon footprint** *n* empreinte *f* carbone
**carbon monoxide** [-mɔ'nɔksaɪd] *n* oxyde *m* de carbone
**carbon paper** *n* papier *m* carbone
**carbon ribbon** *n* ruban *m* carbone
**car boot sale** *n* *marché aux puces où des particuliers vendent des objets entreposés dans le coffre de leur voiture.*
**carburettor**, (*US*) **carburetor** [kɑ:bju'rɛtəʳ] *n* carburateur *m*
**carcass** ['kɑ:kəs] *n* carcasse *f*
**carcinogenic** [kɑ:sɪnə'dʒɛnɪk] *adj* cancérigène
**card** [kɑ:d] *n* carte *f*; (*material*) carton *m*; (*membership card*) carte d'adhérent; **to play ~s** jouer aux cartes
**cardamom** ['kɑ:dəməm] *n* cardamome *f*
**cardboard** ['kɑ:dbɔ:d] *n* carton *m*
**cardboard box** *n* (boîte *f* en) carton *m*
**cardboard city** *n* *endroit de la ville où dorment les SDF dans des boîtes en carton*
**card-carrying member** ['kɑ:dkærɪŋ-] *n* membre actif
**card game** *n* jeu *m* de cartes
**cardiac** ['kɑ:dɪæk] *adj* cardiaque
**cardigan** ['kɑ:dɪgən] *n* cardigan *m*
**cardinal** ['kɑ:dɪnl] *adj* cardinal(e); (*importance*) capital(e) ▷ *n* cardinal *m*
**card index** *n* fichier *m* (alphabétique)
**cardphone** ['kɑ:dfəun] *n* téléphone *m* à carte (magnétique)
**cardsharp** ['kɑ:dʃɑ:p] *n* tricheur(-euse) professionnel(le)
**card vote** *n* (*Brit*) vote *m* de délégués
**CARE** [keəʳ] *n abbr* (= *Cooperative for American Relief Everywhere*) association charitable
**care** [keəʳ] *n* soin *m*, attention *f*; (*worry*) souci *m* ▷ *vi*: **to ~ about** (*feel interest for*) se soucier de, s'intéresser à; (*person: love*) être attaché(e) à; **in sb's ~** à la garde de qn, confié à qn; **~ of** (*on letter*)

chez; **"with ~"** "fragile"; **to take ~ (to do)** faire attention (à faire); **to take ~ of** (vt) s'occuper de; **the child has been taken into ~** l'enfant a été placé en institution; **would you ~ to/for ...?** voulez-vous ...?; **I wouldn't ~ to do it** je n'aimerais pas le faire; **I don't ~** ça m'est bien égal, peu m'importe; **I couldn't ~ less** cela m'est complètement égal, je m'en fiche complètement

▶ **care for** vt fus s'occuper de; (like) aimer

**careen** [kə'riːn] vi (ship) donner de la bande ▷ vt caréner, mettre en carène

**career** [kə'rɪəʳ] n carrière f ▷ vi (also: **career along**) aller à toute allure

**career girl** n jeune fille f or femme f qui veut faire carrière

**careers officer** n conseiller(-ère) d'orientation (professionnelle)

**career woman** (irreg) n femme ambitieuse

**carefree** ['kɛəfriː] adj sans souci, insouciant(e)

**careful** ['kɛəful] adj soigneux(-euse); (cautious) prudent(e); **(be) ~!** (fais) attention!; **to be ~ with one's money** regarder à la dépense

**carefully** ['kɛəfəlɪ] adv avec soin, soigneusement; prudemment

**caregiver** ['kɛəgɪvəʳ] (US) n (professional) travailleur social; (unpaid) personne qui s'occupe d'un proche qui est malade

**careless** ['kɛəlɪs] adj négligent(e); (heedless) insouciant(e)

**carelessly** ['kɛəlɪslɪ] adv négligemment; avec insouciance

**carelessness** ['kɛəlɪsnɪs] n manque m de soin, négligence f; insouciance f

**carer** ['kɛərəʳ] n (professional) travailleur social; (unpaid) personne qui s'occupe d'un proche qui est malade

**caress** [kə'rɛs] n caresse f ▷ vt caresser

**caretaker** ['kɛəteɪkəʳ] n gardien(ne), concierge m/f

**caretaker government** n (Brit) gouvernement m intérimaire

**car-ferry** ['kɑːfɛrɪ] n (on sea) ferry(-boat) m; (on river) bac m

**cargo** (pl **-es**) ['kɑːgəu] n cargaison f, chargement m

**cargo boat** n cargo m

**cargo plane** n avion-cargo m

**car hire** n (Brit) location f de voitures

**Caribbean** [kærɪ'biːən] adj, n: **the ~ (Sea)** la mer des Antilles or des Caraïbes

**caricature** ['kærɪkətjuəʳ] n caricature f

**caring** ['kɛərɪŋ] adj (person) bienveillant(e); (society, organization) humanitaire

**carnage** ['kɑːnɪdʒ] n carnage m

**carnal** ['kɑːnl] adj charnel(le)

**carnation** [kɑː'neɪʃən] n œillet m

**carnival** ['kɑːnɪvl] n (public celebration) carnaval m; (US: funfair) fête foraine

**carnivorous** [kɑː'nɪvərəs] adj carnivore, carnassier(-ière)

**carol** ['kærəl] n: (**Christmas**) **~** chant m de Noël

**carouse** [kə'rauz] vi faire la bringue

**carousel** [kærə'sɛl] n (for luggage) carrousel m; (US) manège m

**carp** [kɑːp] n (fish) carpe f

▶ **carp at** vt fus critiquer

**car park** (Brit) n parking m, parc m de stationnement

**carpenter** ['kɑːpɪntəʳ] n charpentier m; (joiner) menuisier m

**carpentry** ['kɑːpɪntrɪ] n charpenterie f, métier m de charpentier; (woodwork: at school etc) menuiserie f

**carpet** ['kɑːpɪt] n tapis m ▷ vt recouvrir (d'un tapis); **fitted ~** (Brit) moquette f

**carpet bombing** n bombardement intensif

**carpet slippers** npl pantoufles fpl

**carpet sweeper** [-'swiːpəʳ] n balai m mécanique

**car phone** n téléphone m de voiture

**car rental** n (US) location f de voitures

**carriage** ['kærɪdʒ] n (Brit Rail) wagon m; (horse-drawn) voiture f; (of goods) transport m; (: cost) port m; (of typewriter) chariot m; (bearing) maintien m, port m; **~ forward** port dû; **~ free** franco de port; **~ paid** (en) port payé

**carriage return** n retour m à la ligne

**carriageway** ['kærɪdʒweɪ] n (Brit: part of road) chaussée f

**carrier** ['kærɪəʳ] n transporteur m, camionneur m; (company) entreprise f de transport; (Med) porteur(-euse); (Naut) porte-avions m inv

**carrier bag** n (Brit) sac m en papier or en plastique

**carrier pigeon** n pigeon voyageur

**carrion** ['kærɪən] n charogne f

**carrot** ['kærət] n carotte f

**carry** ['kærɪ] vt (subj: person) porter; (: vehicle) transporter; (a motion, bill) voter, adopter; (Math: figure) retenir; (Comm: interest) rapporter; (involve: responsibilities etc) comporter, impliquer; (Med: disease) être porteur de ▷ vi (sound) porter; **to get carried away** (fig) s'emballer, s'enthousiasmer; **this loan carries 10% interest** ce prêt est à 10% (d'intérêt)

▶ **carry forward** vt (gen, Book-Keeping) reporter

▶ **carry on** vi (continue) continuer; (inf: make a fuss) faire des histoires ▷ vt (conduct: business) diriger; (: conversation) entretenir; (continue: business, conversation) continuer; **to ~ on with sth/doing** continuer qch/à faire

▶ **carry out** vt (orders) exécuter; (investigation) effectuer; (idea, threat) mettre à exécution

**carrycot** ['kærɪkɔt] n (Brit) porte-bébé m

**carry-on** ['kærɪ'ɔn] n (inf: fuss) histoires fpl; (: annoying behaviour) cirque m, cinéma m

**cart** [kɑːt] n charrette f ▷ vt (inf) transporter

**carte blanche** ['kɑːt'blɔ̃ʃ] n: **to give sb ~** donner carte blanche à qn

**cartel** [kɑː'tɛl] n (Comm) cartel m

**cartilage** ['kɑːtɪlɪdʒ] n cartilage m

**cartographer** [kɑː'tɔgrəfəʳ] n cartographe m/f

**cartography** [kɑː'tɔgrəfɪ] n cartographie f

**carton** ['kɑːtən] n (box) carton m; (of yogurt) pot m (en carton); (of cigarettes) cartouche f

**cartoon** [kɑːˈtuːn] n (Press) dessin m (humoristique); (satirical) caricature f; (comic strip) bande dessinée; (Cine) dessin animé

**cartoonist** [kɑːˈtuːnɪst] n dessinateur(-trice) humoristique; caricaturiste m/f; auteur m de dessins animés; auteur de bandes dessinées

**cartridge** [ˈkɑːtrɪdʒ] n (for gun, pen) cartouche f; (for camera) chargeur m; (music tape) cassette f; (of record player) cellule f

**cartwheel** [ˈkɑːtwiːl] n roue f; **to turn a ~** faire la roue

**carve** [kɑːv] vt (meat: also: **carve up**) découper; (wood, stone) tailler, sculpter

**carving** [ˈkɑːvɪŋ] n (in wood etc) sculpture f

**carving knife** n couteau m à découper

**car wash** n station f de lavage (de voitures)

**Casablanca** [kæsəˈblæŋkə] n Casablanca

**cascade** [kæsˈkeɪd] n cascade f ▷ vi tomber en cascade

**case** [keɪs] n cas m; (Law) affaire f, procès m; (box) caisse f, boîte f; (for glasses) étui m; (Brit: also: **suitcase**) valise f; (Typ): **lower/upper ~** minuscule f/majuscule f; **to have a good ~** avoir de bons arguments; **there's a strong ~ for reform** il y aurait lieu d'engager une réforme; **in ~ of** en cas de; **in ~ he** au cas où il; **just in ~** à tout hasard; **in any ~** en tout cas, de toute façon

**case history** n (Med) dossier médical, antécédents médicaux

**case study** n étude f de cas

**cash** [kæʃ] n argent m; (Comm) (argent m) liquide m, numéraire m; liquidités fpl; (: in payment) argent comptant, espèces fpl ▷ vt encaisser; **to pay (in) ~** payer (en argent) comptant or en espèces; **~ with order/on delivery** (Comm) payable or paiement à la commande/livraison; **to be short of ~** être à court d'argent; **I haven't got any ~** je n'ai pas de liquide
  ▶ **cash in** vt (insurance policy etc) toucher
  ▶ **cash in on** vt fus profiter de

**cash account** n compte m caisse

**cash and carry** n libre-service m de gros, cash and carry m inv

**cashback** [ˈkæʃbæk] n (discount) remise f; (at supermarket etc) retrait m (à la caisse)

**cashbook** [ˈkæʃbʊk] n livre m de caisse

**cash box** n caisse f

**cash card** n carte f de retrait

**cash desk** n (Brit) caisse f

**cash discount** n escompte m de caisse (pour paiement au comptant), remise f au comptant

**cash dispenser** n distributeur m automatique de billets

**cashew** [kæˈʃuː] n (also: **cashew nut**) noix f de cajou

**cash flow** n cash-flow m, marge brute d'autofinancement

**cashier** [kæˈʃɪəʳ] n caissier(-ère) ▷ vt (Mil) destituer, casser

**cashmere** [ˈkæʃmɪəʳ] n cachemire m

**cash payment** n paiement comptant, versement m en espèces

**cash point** n distributeur m automatique de billets

**cash price** n prix comptant

**cash register** n caisse enregistreuse

**cash sale** n vente f au comptant

**casing** [ˈkeɪsɪŋ] n revêtement (protecteur), enveloppe (protectrice)

**casino** [kəˈsiːnəʊ] n casino m

**cask** [kɑːsk] n tonneau m

**casket** [ˈkɑːskɪt] n coffret m; (US: coffin) cercueil m

**Caspian Sea** [ˈkæspɪən-] n: **the ~** la mer Caspienne

**casserole** [ˈkæsərəʊl] n (pot) cocotte f; (food) ragoût m (en cocotte)

**cassette** [kæˈset] n cassette f

**cassette deck** n platine f cassette

**cassette player** n lecteur m de cassettes

**cassette recorder** n magnétophone m à cassettes

**cast** [kɑːst] (vb: pt, pp -) vt (throw) jeter; (shadow: lit) projeter; (: fig) jeter; (glance) jeter; (shed) perdre; se dépouiller de; (metal) couler, fondre ▷ n (Theat) distribution f; (mould) moule m; (also: **plaster cast**) plâtre m; **to ~ sb as Hamlet** attribuer à qn le rôle d'Hamlet; **to ~ one's vote** voter, exprimer son suffrage; **to ~ doubt on** jeter un doute sur
  ▶ **cast aside** vt (reject) rejeter
  ▶ **cast off** vi (Naut) larguer les amarres; (Knitting) arrêter les mailles ▷ vt (Knitting) arrêter
  ▶ **cast on** (Knitting) vt monter ▷ vi monter les mailles

**castanets** [kæstəˈnɛts] npl castagnettes fpl

**castaway** [ˈkɑːstəweɪ] n naufragé(e)

**caste** [kɑːst] n caste f, classe sociale

**caster sugar** [ˈkɑːstə-] n (Brit) sucre m semoule

**casting vote** [ˈkɑːstɪŋ-] n (Brit) voix prépondérante (pour départager)

**cast-iron** [ˈkɑːstaɪən] adj (lit) de or en fonte; (fig: will) de fer; (alibi) en béton

**cast iron** n fonte f

**castle** [ˈkɑːsl] n château m; (fortress) château-fort m; (Chess) tour f

**cast-offs** [ˈkɑːstɔfs] npl vêtements mpl dont on ne veut plus

**castor** [ˈkɑːstəʳ] n (wheel) roulette f

**castor oil** n huile f de ricin

**castrate** [kæsˈtreɪt] vt châtrer

**casual** [ˈkæʒjuːl] adj (by chance) de hasard, fait(e) au hasard, fortuit(e); (irregular: work etc) temporaire; (unconcerned) désinvolte; **~ wear** vêtements mpl sport inv

**casual labour** n main-d'œuvre f temporaire

**casually** [ˈkæʒjuːlɪ] adv avec désinvolture, négligemment; (by chance) fortuitement

**casualty** [ˈkæʒjuːltɪ] n accidenté(e), blessé(e); (dead) victime f, mort(e); (Brit: Med: department) urgences fpl; **heavy casualties** lourdes pertes

**casualty ward** n (Brit) service m des urgences

**cat** [kæt] n chat m
**catacombs** ['kætəku:mz] npl catacombes fpl
**Catalan** ['kætəlæn] adj catalan(e)
**catalogue**, (US) **catalog** ['kætəlɔg] n catalogue m ▷ vt cataloguer
**catalyst** ['kætəlɪst] n catalyseur m
**catalytic converter** [kætə'lɪtɪkkən'vɜːtə<sup>r</sup>] n pot m catalytique
**catapult** ['kætəpʌlt] n lance-pierres m inv, fronde f; (History) catapulte f
**cataract** ['kætərækt] n (also Med) cataracte f
**catarrh** [kə'tɑː<sup>r</sup>] n rhume m chronique, catarrhe f
**catastrophe** [kə'tæstrəfɪ] n catastrophe f
**catastrophic** [kætə'strɔfɪk] adj catastrophique
**catcall** ['kætkɔːl] n (at meeting etc) sifflet m
**catch** [kætʃ] (pt, pp **caught** [kɔːt]) vt (ball, train, thief, cold) attraper; (person: by surprise) prendre, surprendre; (understand) saisir; (get entangled) accrocher ▷ vi (fire) prendre; (get entangled) s'accrocher ▷ n (fish etc) prise f; (thief etc) capture f; (hidden problem) attrape f; (Tech) loquet m; cliquet m; **to ~ sb's attention** or **eye** attirer l'attention de qn; **to ~ fire** prendre feu; **to ~ sight of** apercevoir; **to play ~** jouer à chat; (with ball) jouer à attraper le ballon
  ▸ **catch on** vi (become popular) prendre; (understand): **to ~ on (to sth)** saisir (qch)
  ▸ **catch out** vt (Brit: fig: with trick question) prendre en défaut
  ▸ **catch up** vi (with work) se rattraper, combler son retard ▷ vt (also: **catch up with**) rattraper
**catch-22** ['kætʃtwentɪ'tu:] n: **it's a ~ situation** c'est (une situation) sans issue
**catching** ['kætʃɪŋ] adj (Med) contagieux(-euse)
**catchment area** ['kætʃmənt-] n (Brit Scol) aire f de recrutement; (Geo) bassin m hydrographique
**catch phrase** n slogan m, expression toute faite
**catchy** ['kætʃɪ] adj (tune) facile à retenir
**catechism** ['kætɪkɪzəm] n catéchisme m
**categoric** [kætɪ'gɔrɪk], **categorical** [kætɪ'gɔrɪkl] adj catégorique
**categorize** ['kætɪgəraɪz] vt classer par catégories
**category** ['kætɪgərɪ] n catégorie f
**cater** ['keɪtə<sup>r</sup>] vi: **to ~ for** (Brit: needs) satisfaire, pourvoir à; (: readers, consumers) s'adresser à, pourvoir aux besoins de; (Comm: parties etc) préparer des repas pour
**caterer** ['keɪtərə<sup>r</sup>] n traiteur m; fournisseur m
**catering** ['keɪtərɪŋ] n restauration f; approvisionnement m, ravitaillement m
**caterpillar** ['kætəpɪlə<sup>r</sup>] n chenille f ▷ cpd (vehicle) à chenille; **~ track** n chenille f
**cat flap** n chatière f
**cathedral** [kə'θiːdrəl] n cathédrale f
**cathode** ['kæθəud] n cathode f
**cathode ray tube** n tube m cathodique
**Catholic** ['kæθəlɪk] (Rel) adj catholique ▷ n catholique m/f
**catholic** ['kæθəlɪk] adj (wide-ranging) éclectique; universel(le); libéral(e)

**catsup** ['kætsəp] n (US) ketchup m
**cattle** ['kætl] npl bétail m, bestiaux mpl
**catty** ['kætɪ] adj méchant(e)
**catwalk** ['kætwɔːk] n passerelle f; (for models) podium m (de défilé de mode)
**Caucasian** [kɔː'keɪzɪən] adj, n caucasien(ne)
**Caucasus** ['kɔːkəsəs] n Caucase m
**caucus** ['kɔːkəs] n (US Pol) comité électoral (pour désigner des candidats); voir article; (Brit Pol: group) comité local (d'un parti politique)

○ **CAUCUS**
○
○ Un caucus aux États-Unis est une réunion
○ restreinte des principaux dirigeants d'un
○ parti politique, précédant souvent une
○ assemblée générale, dans le but de choisir
○ des candidats ou de définir une ligne
○ d'action. Par extension, ce terme désigne
○ également l'état-major d'un parti politique.

**caught** [kɔːt] pt, pp of **catch**
**cauliflower** ['kɔlɪflauə<sup>r</sup>] n chou-fleur m
**cause** [kɔːz] n cause f ▷ vt causer; **there is no ~ for concern** il n'y a pas lieu de s'inquiéter; **to ~ sth to be done** faire faire qch; **to ~ sb to do sth** faire faire qch à qn
**causeway** ['kɔːzweɪ] n chaussée (surélevée)
**caustic** ['kɔːstɪk] adj caustique
**caution** ['kɔːʃən] n prudence f; (warning) avertissement m ▷ vt avertir, donner un avertissement à
**cautious** ['kɔːʃəs] adj prudent(e)
**cautiously** ['kɔːʃəslɪ] adv prudemment, avec prudence
**cautiousness** ['kɔːʃəsnɪs] n prudence f
**cavalier** [kævə'lɪə<sup>r</sup>] adj cavalier(-ère), désinvolte ▷ n (knight) cavalier m
**cavalry** ['kævəlrɪ] n cavalerie f
**cave** [keɪv] n caverne f, grotte f ▷ vi: **to go caving** faire de la spéléo(logie)
  ▸ **cave in** vi (roof etc) s'effondrer
**caveman** ['keɪvmæn] (irreg) n homme m des cavernes
**cavern** ['kævən] n caverne f
**caviar, caviare** ['kævɪɑː<sup>r</sup>] n caviar m
**cavity** ['kævɪtɪ] n cavité f; (Med) carie f
**cavity wall insulation** n isolation f des murs creux
**cavort** [kə'vɔːt] vi cabrioler, faire des cabrioles
**cayenne** [keɪ'ɛn] n (also: **cayenne pepper**) poivre m de cayenne
**CB** n abbr (= Citizens' Band (Radio)) CB f; (Brit: = Companion of (the Order of) the Bath) titre honorifique
**CBC** n abbr (= Canadian Broadcasting Corporation) organisme de radiodiffusion
**CBE** n abbr (= Companion of (the Order of) the British Empire) titre honorifique
**CBI** n abbr (= Confederation of British Industry) ≈ MEDEF m (= Mouvement des entreprises de France)
**CBS** n abbr (US: = Columbia Broadcasting System) chaîne de télévision

**CC** *abbr* (*Brit*) = **county council**
**cc** *abbr* (= *cubic centimetre*) cm³; (*on letter etc*) = **carbon copy**
**CCA** *n abbr* (*US:* = *Circuit Court of Appeals*) cour d'appel itinérante
**CCTV** *n abbr* = **closed-circuit television**
**CCU** *n abbr* (*US:* = *coronary care unit*) unité *f* de soins cardiologiques
**CD** *n abbr* (= *compact disc*) CD *m*; (*Mil: Brit*) = **Civil Defence (Corps)**; (: *US*) = **Civil Defense** ▷ *abbr* (*Brit:* = *Corps Diplomatique*) CD
**CD burner** *n* graveur *m* de CD
**CDC** *n abbr* (*US:* = **center for disease control**
**CD player** *n* platine *f* laser
**Cdr.** *abbr* (= *commander*) Cdt
**CD-ROM** [si:di:'rɔm] *n abbr* (= *compact disc read-only memory*) CD-ROM *m inv*
**CDT** *abbr* (*US:* = *Central Daylight Time*) heure d'été du centre
**CDW** *n abbr* = **collision damage waiver**
**CD writer** *n* graveur *m* de CD
**cease** [si:s] *vt, vi* cesser
**ceasefire** ['si:sfaɪər] *n* cessez-le-feu *m*
**ceaseless** ['si:slɪs] *adj* incessant(e), continuel(le)
**CED** *n abbr* (*US*) = **Committee for Economic Development**
**cedar** ['si:dər] *n* cèdre *m*
**cede** [si:d] *vt* céder
**cedilla** [sɪ'dɪlə] *n* cédille *f*
**CEEB** *n abbr* (*US:* = *College Entrance Examination Board*) commission d'admission dans l'enseignement supérieur
**ceilidh** ['keɪlɪ] *n* bal *m* folklorique écossais *or* irlandais
**ceiling** ['si:lɪŋ] *n* (*also fig*) plafond *m*
**celebrate** ['sɛlɪbreɪt] *vt, vi* célébrer
**celebrated** ['sɛlɪbreɪtɪd] *adj* célèbre
**celebration** [sɛlɪ'breɪʃən] *n* célébration *f*
**celebrity** [sɪ'lɛbrɪtɪ] *n* célébrité *f*
**celeriac** [sə'lɛrɪæk] *n* céleri(-rave) *m*
**celery** ['sɛlərɪ] *n* céleri *m* (en branches)
**celestial** [sɪ'lɛstɪəl] *adj* céleste
**celibacy** ['sɛlɪbəsɪ] *n* célibat *m*
**cell** [sɛl] *n* (*gen*) cellule *f*; (*Elec*) élément *m* (*de pile*)
**cellar** ['sɛlər] *n* cave *f*
**'cellist** ['tʃɛlɪst] *n* violoncelliste *m/f*
**cello** ['tʃɛləu] *n* violoncelle *m*
**Cellophane®** ['sɛləfeɪn] *n* cellophane® *f*
**cellphone** ['sɛlfəun] *n* (téléphone *m*) portable *m*, mobile *m*
**cellular** ['sɛljulər] *adj* cellulaire
**cellulose** ['sɛljuləus] *n* cellulose *f*
**Celsius** ['sɛlsɪəs] *adj* Celsius *inv*
**Celt** [kɛlt, sɛlt] *n* Celte *m/f*
**Celtic** ['kɛltɪk, 'sɛltɪk] *adj* celte, celtique ▷ *n* (*Ling*) celtique *m*
**cement** [sə'mɛnt] *n* ciment *m* ▷ *vt* cimenter
**cement mixer** *n* bétonnière *f*
**cemetery** ['sɛmɪtrɪ] *n* cimetière *m*
**cenotaph** ['sɛnətɑ:f] *n* cénotaphe *m*
**censor** ['sɛnsər] *n* censeur *m* ▷ *vt* censurer

**censorship** ['sɛnsəʃɪp] *n* censure *f*
**censure** ['sɛnʃər] *vt* blâmer, critiquer
**census** ['sɛnsəs] *n* recensement *m*
**cent** [sɛnt] *n* (*unit of dollar, euro*) cent *m* (= *un centième du dollar, de l'euro*); *see also* **per**
**centenary** [sɛn'ti:nərɪ], (*US*) **centennial** [sɛn'tɛnɪəl] *n* centenaire *m*
**center** ['sɛntər] *n, vt* (*US*) = **centre** [sɛntɪ] *prefix*
**centigrade** ['sɛntɪgreɪd] *adj* centigrade
**centilitre**, (*US*) **centiliter** ['sɛntɪli:tər] *n* centilitre *m*
**centimetre**, (*US*) **centimeter** ['sɛntɪmi:tər] *n* centimètre *m*
**centipede** ['sɛntɪpi:d] *n* mille-pattes *m inv*
**central** ['sɛntrəl] *adj* central(e)
**Central African Republic** *n* République Centrafricaine
**Central America** *n* Amérique centrale
**central heating** *n* chauffage central
**centralize** ['sɛntrəlaɪz] *vt* centraliser
**central processing unit** *n* (*Comput*) unité centrale (de traitement)
**central reservation** *n* (*Brit Aut*) terre-plein central
**centre**, (*US*) **center** ['sɛntər] *n* centre *m* ▷ *vt* centrer; (*Phot*) cadrer; (*concentrate*): **to ~ (on)** centrer (sur)
**centrefold**, (*US*) **centerfold** ['sɛntəfəuld] *n* (*Press*) pages centrales détachables (*avec photo de pin up*)
**centre-forward** ['sɛntə'fɔ:wəd] *n* (*Sport*) avant-centre *m*
**centre-half** ['sɛntə'hɑ:f] *n* (*Sport*) demi-centre *m*
**centrepiece**, (*US*) **centerpiece** ['sɛntəpi:s] *n* milieu *m* de table; (*fig*) pièce maîtresse
**centre spread** *n* (*Brit*) publicité *f* en double page
**centre-stage** [sɛntə'steɪdʒ] *n*: **to take ~** occuper le centre de la scène
**centrifugal** [sɛn'trɪfjugl] *adj* centrifuge
**centrifuge** ['sɛntrɪfju:ʒ] *n* centrifugeuse *f*
**century** ['sɛntjurɪ] *n* siècle *m*; **in the twentieth ~** au vingtième siècle
**CEO** *n abbr* (*US*) = **chief executive officer**
**ceramic** [sɪ'ræmɪk] *adj* céramique
**cereal** ['si:rɪəl] *n* céréale *f*
**cerebral** ['sɛrɪbrəl] *adj* cérébral(e)
**ceremonial** [sɛrɪ'məunɪəl] *n* cérémonial *m*; (*rite*) rituel *m*
**ceremony** ['sɛrɪmənɪ] *n* cérémonie *f*; **to stand on ~** faire des façons
**cert** [sə:t] *n* (*Brit inf*): **it's a dead ~** ça ne fait pas un pli
**certain** ['sə:tən] *adj* certain(e); **to make ~ of** s'assurer de; **for ~** certainement, sûrement
**certainly** ['sə:tənlɪ] *adv* certainement
**certainty** ['sə:təntɪ] *n* certitude *f*
**certificate** [sə'tɪfɪkɪt] *n* certificat *m*
**certified letter** ['sə:tɪfaɪd-] *n* (*US*) lettre recommandée
**certified public accountant** ['sə:tɪfaɪd-] *n* (*US*) expert-comptable *m*
**certify** ['sə:tɪfaɪ] *vt* certifier; (*award diploma to*)

conférer un diplôme *etc* à; *(declare insane)*
déclarer malade mental(e) ▷ *vi:* **to ~ to** attester
**cervical** [ˈsəːvɪkl] *adj:* **~ cancer** cancer *m* du col
de l'utérus; **~ smear** frottis vaginal
**cervix** [ˈsəːvɪks] *n* col *m* de l'utérus
**Cesarean** [siːˈzɛərɪən] *adj,n (US)* = **Caesarean**
**cessation** [səˈseɪʃən] *n* cessation *f*, arrêt *m*
**cesspit** [ˈsɛspɪt] *n* fosse *f* d'aisance
**CET** *abbr (= Central European Time)* heure *d'Europe
centrale*
**Ceylon** [sɪˈlɔn] *n* Ceylan *m*
**cf.** *abbr (= compare)* cf., voir
**c/f** *abbr (Comm)* = **carried forward**
**CFC** *n abbr (= chlorofluorocarbon)* CFC *m*
**CG** *n abbr (US)* = **coastguard**
**cg** *abbr (= centigram)* cg
**CH** *n abbr (Brit: = Companion of Honour)* titre
*honorifique*
**ch** *abbr (Brit: = central heating)* cc
**ch.** *abbr (= chapter)* chap
**Chad** [tʃæd] *n* Tchad *m*
**chafe** [tʃeɪf] *vt* irriter, frotter contre ▷ *vi (fig):* **to
~ against** se rebiffer contre, regimber contre
**chaffinch** [ˈtʃæfɪntʃ] *n* pinson *m*
**chagrin** [ˈʃæɡrɪn] *n* contrariété *f*, déception *f*
**chain** [tʃeɪn] *n (gen)* chaîne *f* ▷ *vt (also:* **chain up)**
enchaîner, attacher (avec une chaîne)
**chain reaction** *n* réaction *f* en chaîne
**chain-smoke** [ˈtʃeɪnsməuk] *vi* fumer cigarette
sur cigarette
**chain store** *n* magasin *m* à succursales
multiples
**chair** [tʃɛəʳ] *n* chaise *f*; *(armchair)* fauteuil *m*; *(of
university)* chaire *f*; *(of meeting)* présidence *f* ▷ *vt
(meeting)* présider; **the ~** *(US: electric chair)* la
chaise électrique
**chairlift** [ˈtʃɛəlɪft] *n* télésiège *m*
**chairman** [ˈtʃɛəmən] *(irreg)* *n* président *m*
**chairperson** [ˈtʃɛəpəːsn] *(irreg)* *n* président(e)
**chairwoman** [ˈtʃɛəwumən] *n* présidente *f*
**chalet** [ˈʃæleɪ] *n* chalet *m*
**chalice** [ˈtʃælɪs] *n* calice *m*
**chalk** [tʃɔːk] *n* craie *f*
▷ **chalk up** *vt* écrire à la craie; *(fig: success etc)*
remporter
**challenge** [ˈtʃælɪndʒ] *n* défi *m* ▷ *vt* défier;
*(statement, right)* mettre en question, contester;
**to ~ sb to a fight/game** inviter qn à se battre/à
jouer *(sous forme d'un défi)*; **to ~ sb to do** mettre
qn au défi de faire
**challenger** [ˈtʃælɪndʒəʳ] *n (Sport)* challenger *m*
**challenging** [ˈtʃælɪndʒɪŋ] *adj (task, career)* qui
représente un défi *or* une gageure; *(tone, look)* de
défi, provocateur(-trice)
**chamber** [ˈtʃeɪmbəʳ] *n* chambre *f*; *(Brit Law: gen
pl)* cabinet *m*; **~ of commerce** chambre de
commerce
**chambermaid** [ˈtʃeɪmbəmeɪd] *n* femme *f* de
chambre
**chamber music** *n* musique *f* de chambre
**chamberpot** [ˈtʃeɪmbəpɔt] *n* pot *m* de chambre
**chameleon** [kəˈmiːlɪən] *n* caméléon *m*

**chamois** [ˈʃæmwɑː] *n* chamois *m*
**chamois leather** [ˈʃæmɪ-] *n* peau *f* de chamois
**champagne** [ʃæmˈpeɪn] *n* champagne *m*
**champers** [ˈʃæmpəz] *n (inf)* champ *m*
**champion** [ˈtʃæmpɪən] *n (also of cause)*
champion(ne) ▷ *vt* défendre
**championship** [ˈtʃæmpɪənʃɪp] *n*
championnat *m*
**chance** [tʃɑːns] *n (luck)* hasard *m*; *(opportunity)*
occasion *f*, possibilité *f*; *(hope, likelihood)* chance
*f*; *(risk)* risque *m* ▷ *vt (risk)* risquer; *(happen):* **to ~
to do** faire par hasard ▷ *adj* fortuit(e), de
hasard; **there is little ~ of his coming** il est
peu probable *or* il y a peu de chances qu'il
vienne; **to take a ~** prendre un risque; **it's the
~ of a lifetime** c'est une occasion unique; **by ~**
par hasard; **to ~ doing sth** se risquer à faire
qch; **to ~ it** risquer le coup, essayer
▷ **chance on, chance upon** *vt fus (person)* tomber
sur, rencontrer par hasard; *(thing)* trouver par
hasard
**chancel** [ˈtʃɑːnsəl] *n* chœur *m*
**chancellor** [ˈtʃɑːnsələʳ] *n* chancelier *m*
**Chancellor of the Exchequer** [-ɪksˈtʃɛkəʳ] *(Brit)*
*n* chancelier *m* de l'Échiquier
**chandelier** [ʃændəˈlɪəʳ] *n* lustre *m*
**change** [tʃeɪndʒ] *vt (alter, replace: Comm: money)*
changer; *(switch, substitute: hands, trains, clothes,
one's name etc)* changer de; *(transform):* **to ~ sb
into** changer *or* transformer qn en ▷ *vi (gen)*
changer; *(change clothes)* se changer; *(be
transformed):* **to ~ into** se changer *or* transformer
en ▷ *n* changement *m*; *(money)* monnaie *f*; **to ~
gear** *(Aut)* changer de vitesse; **to ~ one's mind**
changer d'avis; **she ~d into an old skirt** elle
(s'est changée et) a enfilé une vieille jupe; **a ~
of clothes** des vêtements de rechange; **for a ~**
pour changer; **small ~** petite monnaie; **to give
sb ~ for** *or* **of £10** faire à qn la monnaie de 10
livres; **do you have ~ for £10?** vous avez la
monnaie de 10 livres?; **where can I ~ some
money?** où est-ce que je peux changer de
l'argent?; **keep the ~!** gardez la monnaie!
▷ **change over** *vi (swap)* échanger; *(change:
drivers etc)* changer; *(change sides: players etc)*
changer de côté; **to ~ over from sth to sth**
passer de qch à qch
**changeable** [ˈtʃeɪndʒəbl] *adj (weather)* variable;
*(person)* d'humeur changeante
**change machine** *n* distributeur *m* de monnaie
**changeover** [ˈtʃeɪndʒəuvəʳ] *n (to new system)*
changement *m*, passage *m*
**changing** [ˈtʃeɪndʒɪŋ] *adj* changeant(e)
**changing room** *n (Brit: in shop)* salon *m*
d'essayage; *(: Sport)* vestiaire *m*
**channel** [ˈtʃænl] *n (TV)* chaîne *f*; *(waveband,
groove, fig: medium)* canal *m*; *(of river, sea)* chenal *m*
▷ *vt* canaliser; *(fig: interest, energies):* **to ~ into**
diriger vers; **through the usual ~s** en suivant
la filière habituelle; **green/red ~** *(Customs)*
couloir *m or* sortie *f* "rien à déclarer"/
"marchandises à déclarer"; **the (English) C~** la

Manche

**channel-hopping** ['tʃænl'hɔpɪŋ] n (TV) zapping m

**Channel Islands** npl: **the** ~ les îles fpl Anglo-Normandes

**Channel Tunnel** n: **the** ~ le tunnel sous la Manche

**chant** [tʃɑːnt] n chant m; mélopée f; (Rel) psalmodie f ▷ vt chanter, scander; psalmodier

**chaos** ['keɪɔs] n chaos m

**chaos theory** n théorie f du chaos

**chaotic** [keɪ'ɔtɪk] adj chaotique

**chap** [tʃæp] n (Brit inf: man) type m; (term of address): **old** ~ mon vieux ▷ vt (skin) gercer, crevasser

**chapel** ['tʃæpl] n chapelle f

**chaperon** ['ʃæpərəun] n chaperon m ▷ vt chaperonner

**chaplain** ['tʃæplɪn] n aumônier m

**chapped** [tʃæpt] adj (skin, lips) gercé(e)

**chapter** ['tʃæptəʳ] n chapitre m

**char** [tʃɑːʳ] vt (burn) carboniser ▷ vi (Brit: cleaner) faire des ménages ▷ n (Brit) = **charlady**

**character** ['kærɪktəʳ] n caractère m; (in novel, film) personnage m; (eccentric person) numéro m, phénomène m; **a person of good** ~ une personne bien

**character code** n (Comput) code m de caractère

**characteristic** ['kærɪktə'rɪstɪk] adj, n caractéristique (f)

**characterize** ['kærɪktəraɪz] vt caractériser; **to** ~ **(as)** définir (comme)

**charade** [ʃə'rɑːd] n charade f

**charcoal** ['tʃɑːkəul] n charbon m de bois; (Art) charbon

**charge** [tʃɑːdʒ] n (accusation) accusation f; (Law) inculpation f; (cost) prix (demandé); (of gun, battery, Mil: attack) charge f ▷ vt (gun, battery, Mil: enemy) charger; (customer, sum) faire payer ▷ vi (gen with: up, along etc) foncer; **charges** npl (costs) frais mpl; (Brit Tel): **to reverse the** ~**s** téléphoner en PCV; **bank/labour** ~**s** frais mpl de banque/main-d'œuvre; **is there a** ~? doit-on payer?; **there's no** ~ c'est gratuit, on ne fait pas payer; **extra** ~ supplément m; **to take** ~ **of** se charger de; **to be in** ~ **of** être responsable de, s'occuper de; **to** ~ **in/out** entrer/sortir en trombe; **to** ~ **down/up** dévaler/grimper à toute allure; **to** ~ **sb (with)** (Law) inculper qn (de); **to have** ~ **of sb** avoir la charge de qn; **they** ~**d us £10 for the meal** ils nous ont fait payer le repas 10 livres, ils nous ont compté 10 livres pour le repas; **how much do you** ~ **for this repair?** combien demandez-vous pour cette réparation?; **to** ~ **an expense (up) to sb** mettre une dépense sur le compte de qn; ~ **it to my account** facturez-le sur mon compte

**charge account** n compte m client

**charge card** n carte f de client (émise par un grand magasin)

**chargehand** ['tʃɑːdʒhænd] n (Brit) chef m d'équipe

**charger** ['tʃɑːdʒəʳ] n (also: **battery charger**) chargeur m; (old: warhorse) cheval m de bataille

**charismatic** [kærɪz'mætɪk] adj charismatique

**charitable** ['tʃærɪtəbl] adj charitable

**charity** ['tʃærɪtɪ] n charité f; (organization) institution f charitable or de bienfaisance, œuvre f (de charité)

**charity shop** n (Brit) boutique vendant des articles d'occasion au profit d'une organisation caritative

**charlady** ['tʃɑːleɪdɪ] n (Brit) femme f de ménage

**charm** [tʃɑːm] n charme m; (on bracelet) breloque f ▷ vt charmer, enchanter

**charm bracelet** n bracelet m à breloques

**charming** ['tʃɑːmɪŋ] adj charmant(e)

**chart** [tʃɑːt] n tableau m, diagramme m; graphique m; (map) carte marine; (weather chart) carte f du temps ▷ vt dresser or établir la carte de; (sales, progress) établir la courbe de; **charts** npl (Mus) hit-parade m; **to be in the** ~**s** (record, pop group) figurer au hit-parade

**charter** ['tʃɑːtəʳ] vt (plane) affréter ▷ n (document) charte f; **on** ~ (plane) affrété(e)

**chartered accountant** ['tʃɑːtəd-] n (Brit) expert-comptable m

**charter flight** n charter m

**charwoman** ['tʃɑːwumən] (irreg) n = **charlady**

**chase** [tʃeɪs] vt poursuivre, pourchasser; (also: **chase away**) chasser ▷ n poursuite f, chasse f
  ▶ **chase down** vt (US) = **chase up**
  ▶ **chase up** vt (Brit: person) relancer; (: information) rechercher

**chasm** ['kæzəm] n gouffre m, abîme m

**chassis** ['ʃæsɪ] n châssis m

**chastened** ['tʃeɪsnd] adj assagi(e), rappelé(e) à la raison

**chastening** ['tʃeɪsnɪŋ] adj qui fait réfléchir

**chastise** [tʃæs'taɪz] vt punir, châtier; corriger

**chastity** ['tʃæstɪtɪ] n chasteté f

**chat** [tʃæt] vi (also: **have a chat**) bavarder, causer; (on Internet) chatter ▷ n conversation f
  ▶ **chat up** vt (Brit inf: girl) baratiner

**chatline** ['tʃætlaɪn] n numéro téléphonique qui permet de bavarder avec plusieurs personnes en même temps

**chat room** n (Internet) salon m de discussion

**chat show** n (Brit) talk-show m

**chattel** ['tʃætl] n see **good**

**chatter** ['tʃætəʳ] vi (person) bavarder, papoter ▷ n bavardage m, papotage m; **my teeth are** ~**ing** je claque des dents

**chatterbox** ['tʃætəbɔks] n moulin m à paroles, babillard(e)

**chattering classes** ['tʃætərɪŋ-] npl: **the** ~ (inf, pej) les intellos mpl

**chatty** ['tʃætɪ] adj (style) familier(-ière); (person) enclin(e) à bavarder or au papotage

**chauffeur** ['ʃəufəʳ] n chauffeur m (de maître)

**chauvinism** ['ʃəuvɪnɪzəm] n (also: **male chauvinism**) phallocratie f, machisme m; (nationalism) chauvinisme m

**chauvinist** ['ʃəuvɪnɪst] n (also: **male chauvinist**) phallocrate m, macho m; (nationalist) chauvin(e)

**ChE** *abbr* = **chemical engineer**
**cheap** [tʃi:p] *adj* bon marché *inv*, pas cher
(chère); (*reduced: ticket*) à prix réduit; (: *fare*)
réduit(e); (*joke*) facile, d'un goût douteux; (*poor
quality*) à bon marché, de qualité médiocre ▷ *adv*
à bon marché, pour pas cher; **~er** *adj* moins
cher (chère); **can you recommend a ~ hotel/
restaurant, please?** pourriez-vous m'indiquer
un hôtel/restaurant bon marché?
**cheap day return** *n* billet *m* d'aller et retour
réduit (*valable pour la journée*)
**cheapen** ['tʃi:pn] *vt* rabaisser, déprécier
**cheaply** ['tʃi:plɪ] *adv* à bon marché, à bon
compte
**cheat** [tʃi:t] *vi* tricher; (*in exam*) copier ▷ *vt*
tromper, duper; (*rob*): **to ~ sb out of sth**
escroquer qch à qn ▷ *n* tricheur(-euse) *m/f*;
escroc *m*; (*trick*) duperie *f*, tromperie *f*
▸ **cheat on** *vt fus* tromper
**cheating** ['tʃi:tɪŋ] *n* tricherie *f*
**Chechnya** [tʃɪtʃˈnjɑ:] *n* Tchétchénie *f*
**check** [tʃɛk] *vt* vérifier; (*passport, ticket*) contrôler;
(*halt*) enrayer; (*restrain*) maîtriser ▷ *vi* (*official etc*)
se renseigner ▷ *n* vérification *f*; contrôle *m*;
(*curb*) frein *m*; (*Brit: bill*) addition *f*; (*US*) =
**cheque**; (*pattern: gen pl*) carreaux *mpl* ▷ *adj* (*also:*
**checked**: *pattern, cloth*) à carreaux; **to ~ with sb**
demander à qn; **to keep a ~ on sb/sth**
surveiller qn/qch
▸ **check in** *vi* (*in hotel*) remplir sa fiche (d'hôtel);
(*at airport*) se présenter à l'enregistrement ▷ *vt*
(*luggage*) (faire) enregistrer
▸ **check off** *vt* (*tick off*) cocher
▸ **check out** *vi* (*in hotel*) régler sa note ▷ *vt*
(*luggage*) retirer; (*investigate: story*) vérifier;
(*person*) prendre des renseignements sur
▸ **check up** *vi*: **to ~ up (on sth)** vérifier (qch); **to
~ up on sb** se renseigner sur le compte de qn
**checkbook** ['tʃɛkbuk] *n* (*US*) = **chequebook**
**checked** ['tʃɛkt] *adj* (*pattern, cloth*) à carreaux
**checkered** ['tʃɛkəd] *adj* (*US*) = **chequered**
**checkers** ['tʃɛkəz] *n* (*US*) jeu *m* de dames
**check guarantee card** *n* (*US*) carte *f* (d'identité)
bancaire
**check-in** ['tʃɛkin] *n* (*also:* **check-in desk**: *at airport*)
enregistrement *m*
**checking account** ['tʃɛkɪŋ-] *n* (*US*) compte
courant
**checklist** ['tʃɛklɪst] *n* liste *f* de contrôle
**checkmate** ['tʃɛkmeɪt] *n* échec et mat *m*
**checkout** ['tʃɛkaut] *n* (*in supermarket*) caisse *f*
**checkpoint** ['tʃɛkpɔɪnt] *n* contrôle *m*
**checkroom** ['tʃɛkru:m] (*US*) *n* consigne *f*
**checkup** ['tʃɛkʌp] *n* (*Med*) examen médical,
check-up *m*
**cheddar** ['tʃedər] *n* (*also:* **cheddar cheese**)
cheddar *m*
**cheek** [tʃi:k] *n* joue *f*; (*impudence*) toupet *m*, culot
*m*; **what a ~!** quel toupet!
**cheekbone** ['tʃi:kbəun] *n* pommette *f*
**cheeky** ['tʃi:kɪ] *adj* effronté(e), culotté(e)
**cheep** [tʃi:p] *n* (*of bird*) piaulement *m* ▷ *vi* piauler

**cheer** [tʃɪər] *vt* acclamer, applaudir; (*gladden*)
réjouir, réconforter ▷ *vi* applaudir ▷ *n* (*gen pl*)
acclamations *fpl*, applaudissements *mpl*; bravos
*mpl*, hourras *mpl*; **~s!** à la vôtre!
▸ **cheer on** *vt* encourager (par des cris *etc*)
▸ **cheer up** *vi* se dérider, reprendre courage ▷ *vt*
remonter le moral à *or* de, dérider, égayer
**cheerful** ['tʃɪəful] *adj* gai(e), joyeux(-euse)
**cheerfulness** ['tʃɪəfulnɪs] *n* gaieté *f*, bonne
humeur
**cheerio** [tʃɪərɪˈəu] *excl* (*Brit*) salut!, au revoir!
**cheerleader** ['tʃɪəli:dər] *n* membre d'un groupe de
majorettes qui chantent et dansent pour soutenir leur
équipe pendant les matchs de football américain
**cheerless** ['tʃɪəlɪs] *adj* sombre, triste
**cheese** [tʃi:z] *n* fromage *m*
**cheeseboard** ['tʃi:zbɔ:d] *n* plateau *m* à
fromages; (*with cheese on it*) plateau *m* de
fromages
**cheeseburger** ['tʃi:zbə:gər] *n* cheeseburger *m*
**cheesecake** ['tʃi:zkeɪk] *n* tarte *f* au fromage
**cheetah** ['tʃi:tə] *n* guépard *m*
**chef** [ʃef] *n* chef (cuisinier)
**chemical** ['kemɪkl] *adj* chimique ▷ *n* produit *m*
chimique
**chemist** ['kemɪst] *n* (*Brit: pharmacist*)
pharmacien(ne); (*scientist*) chimiste *m/f*
**chemistry** ['kemɪstrɪ] *n* chimie *f*
**chemist's** ['kemɪsts], **chemist's shop** *n* (*Brit*)
pharmacie *f*
**chemotherapy** [ki:məuˈθerəpɪ] *n*
chimiothérapie *f*
**cheque**, (*US*) **check** [tʃek] *n* chèque *m*; **to pay by
~** payer par chèque
**chequebook**, (*US*) **checkbook** ['tʃekbuk] *n*
chéquier *m*, carnet *m* de chèques
**cheque card** *n* (*Brit*) carte *f* (d'identité) bancaire
**chequered**, (*US*) **checkered** ['tʃekəd] *adj* (*fig*)
varié(e)
**cherish** ['tʃerɪʃ] *vt* chérir; (*hope etc*) entretenir
**cheroot** [ʃəˈru:t] *n* cigare *m* de Manille
**cherry** ['tʃerɪ] *n* cerise *f*; (*also:* **cherry tree**)
cerisier *m*
**Ches** *abbr* (*Brit*) = **Cheshire**
**chess** [tʃes] *n* échecs *mpl*
**chessboard** ['tʃesbɔ:d] *n* échiquier *m*
**chessman** ['tʃesmən] (*irreg*) *n* pièce *f* (de jeu
d'échecs)
**chessplayer** ['tʃespleɪər] *n* joueur(-euse)
d'échecs
**chest** [tʃest] *n* poitrine *f*; (*box*) coffre *m*, caisse *f*;
**to get sth off one's ~** (*inf*) vider son sac
**chest measurement** *n* tour *m* de poitrine
**chestnut** ['tʃesnʌt] *n* châtaigne *f*; (*also:*
**chestnut tree**) châtaignier *m*; (*colour*) châtain *m*
▷ *adj* (*hair*) châtain *inv*; (*horse*) alezan
**chest of drawers** *n* commode *f*
**chesty** ['tʃestɪ] *adj* (*cough*) de poitrine
**chew** [tʃu:] *vt* mâcher
**chewing gum** ['tʃu:ɪŋ-] *n* chewing-gum *m*
**chic** [ʃi:k] *adj* chic *inv*, élégant(e)
**chick** [tʃɪk] *n* poussin *m*; (*inf*) pépée *f*

**chicken** ['tʃɪkɪn] n poulet m; (inf: coward) poule mouillée
▶ **chicken out** vi (inf) se dégonfler
**chicken feed** n (fig) broutilles fpl, bagatelle f
**chickenpox** ['tʃɪkɪnpɔks] n varicelle f
**chickpea** ['tʃɪkpiː] n pois m chiche
**chicory** ['tʃɪkərɪ] n chicorée f; (salad) endive f
**chide** [tʃaɪd] vt réprimander, gronder
**chief** [tʃiːf] n chef m ▷ adj principal(e); **C~ of Staff** (Mil) chef d'État-major
**chief constable** n (Brit) ≈ préfet m de police
**chief executive**, (US) **chief executive officer** n directeur(-trice) général(e)
**chiefly** ['tʃiːflɪ] adv principalement, surtout
**chilblain** ['tʃɪlbleɪn] n engelure f
**child** (pl **children**) [tʃaɪld, 'tʃɪldrən] n enfant m/f
**child abuse** n maltraitance f d'enfants; (sexual) abus mpl sexuels sur des enfants
**child benefit** n (Brit) ≈ allocations familiales
**childbirth** ['tʃaɪldbɜːθ] n accouchement m
**childcare** ['tʃaɪldkɛəʳ] n (for working parents) garde f des enfants (pour les parents qui travaillent)
**childhood** ['tʃaɪldhud] n enfance f
**childish** ['tʃaɪldɪʃ] adj puéril(e), enfantin(e)
**childless** ['tʃaɪldlɪs] adj sans enfants
**childlike** ['tʃaɪldlaɪk] adj innocent(e), pur(e)
**child minder** n (Brit) garde f d'enfants
**child prodigy** n enfant m/f prodige
**children** ['tʃɪldrən] npl of **child**
**children's home** ['tʃɪldrənz-] n ≈ foyer m d'accueil (pour enfants)
**Chile** ['tʃɪlɪ] n Chili m
**Chilean** ['tʃɪlɪən] adj chilien(ne) ▷ n Chilien(ne)
**chill** [tʃɪl] n (of water) froid m; (of air) fraîcheur f; (Med) refroidissement m, coup m de froid ▷ adj froid(e), glacial(e) ▷ vt (person) faire frissonner; refroidir; (Culin) mettre au frais, rafraîchir; **"serve ~ed"** "à servir frais"
▶ **chill out** vi (inf: esp US) se relaxer
**chilli, chili** ['tʃɪlɪ] n piment m (rouge)
**chilling** ['tʃɪlɪŋ] adj (wind) frais (fraîche), froid(e); (look, smile) glacé(e); (thought) qui donne le frisson
**chilly** ['tʃɪlɪ] adj froid(e), glacé(e); (sensitive to cold) frileux(-euse); **to feel ~** avoir froid
**chime** [tʃaɪm] n carillon m ▷ vi carillonner, sonner
**chimney** ['tʃɪmnɪ] n cheminée f
**chimney sweep** n ramoneur m
**chimpanzee** [tʃɪmpæn'ziː] n chimpanzé m
**chin** [tʃɪn] n menton m
**China** ['tʃaɪnə] n Chine f
**china** ['tʃaɪnə] n (material) porcelaine f; (crockery) (vaisselle f en) porcelaine
**Chinese** [tʃaɪ'niːz] adj chinois(e) ▷ n (pl inv) Chinois(e); (Ling) chinois m
**chink** [tʃɪŋk] n (opening) fente f, fissure f; (noise) tintement m
**chinwag** ['tʃɪnwæg] n (Brit inf): **to have a ~** tailler une bavette
**chip** [tʃɪp] n (gen pl: Culin: Brit) frite f; (: US: also: **potato chip**) chip m; (of wood) copeau m; (of glass, stone) éclat m; (also: **microchip**) puce f; (in gambling) fiche f ▷ vt (cup, plate) ébrécher; **when the ~s are down** (fig) au moment critique
▶ **chip in** vi (inf) mettre son grain de sel
**chip and PIN** n carte f à puce; **chip and PIN machine** machine f à carte (à puce)
**chipboard** ['tʃɪpbɔːd] n aggloméré m, panneau m de particules
**chipmunk** ['tʃɪpmʌŋk] n suisse m (animal)
**chippings** ['tʃɪpɪŋz] npl: **loose ~** gravillons mpl
**chip shop** n (Brit) friterie f; voir article

---

◉ **CHIP SHOP**
◉
◉ Un chip shop, que l'on appelle également un
◉ "fish-and-chip shop", est un magasin où
◉ l'on vend des plats à emporter. Les chip shops
◉ sont d'ailleurs à l'origine des "takeaways".
◉ On y achète en particulier du poisson frit et
◉ des frites, mais on y trouve également des
◉ plats traditionnels britanniques ("steak
◉ pies", saucisses, etc). Tous les plats étaient à
◉ l'origine emballés dans du papier journal.
◉ Dans certains de ces magasins, on peut
◉ s'asseoir pour consommer sur place.

---

**chiropodist** [kɪ'rɔpədɪst] n (Brit) pédicure m/f
**chirp** [tʃəːp] n pépiement m, gazouillis m; (of crickets) stridulation f ▷ vi pépier, gazouiller; chanter, striduler
**chirpy** ['tʃəːpɪ] adj (inf) plein(e) d'entrain, tout guilleret(te)
**chisel** ['tʃɪzl] n ciseau m
**chit** [tʃɪt] n mot m, note f
**chitchat** ['tʃɪtʃæt] n bavardage m, papotage m
**chivalrous** ['ʃɪvəlrəs] adj chevaleresque
**chivalry** ['ʃɪvəlrɪ] n chevalerie f; esprit m chevaleresque
**chives** [tʃaɪvz] npl ciboulette f, civette f
**chloride** ['klɔːraɪd] n chlorure m
**chlorinate** ['klɔrɪneɪt] vt chlorer
**chlorine** ['klɔːriːn] n chlore m
**choc-ice** ['tʃɔkaɪs] n (Brit) esquimau® m
**chock** [tʃɔk] n cale f
**chock-a-block** ['tʃɔkə'blɔk], **chock-full** [tʃɔk'ful] adj plein(e) à craquer
**chocolate** ['tʃɔklɪt] n chocolat m
**choice** [tʃɔɪs] n choix m ▷ adj de choix; **by** or **from ~** par choix; **a wide ~** un grand choix
**choir** ['kwaɪəʳ] n chœur m, chorale f
**choirboy** ['kwaɪəbɔɪ] n jeune choriste m
**choke** [tʃəuk] vi étouffer ▷ vt étrangler; étouffer; (block) boucher, obstruer ▷ n (Aut) starter m
**cholera** ['kɔlərə] n choléra m
**cholesterol** [kə'lɛstərɔl] n cholestérol m
**choose** (pt **chose**, pp **chosen**) [tʃuːz, tʃəuz, 'tʃəuzn] vt choisir ▷ vi: **to ~ between** choisir entre; **to ~ from** choisir parmi; **to ~ to do** décider de faire, juger bon de faire
**choosy** ['tʃuːzɪ] adj: **(to be) ~** (faire le) difficile
**chop** [tʃɔp] vt (wood) couper (à la hache); (Culin:

*also*: **chop up**) couper (fin), émincer, hacher (en morceaux) ▷ *n* coup *m* (*de hache, du tranchant de la main*); (*Culin*) côtelette *f*; **to get the ~** (*Brit inf: project*) tomber à l'eau; (*: person: be sacked*) se faire renvoyer

▶ **chop down** *vt* (*tree*) abattre

▶ **chop off** *vt* trancher

**chopper** ['tʃɔpər] *n* (*helicopter*) hélicoptère *m*, hélico *m*

**choppy** ['tʃɔpɪ] *adj* (*sea*) un peu agité(e)

**chops** [tʃɔps] *npl* (*jaws*) mâchoires *fpl*; babines *fpl*

**chopsticks** ['tʃɔpstɪks] *npl* baguettes *fpl*

**choral** ['kɔːrəl] *adj* choral(e), chanté(e) en chœur

**chord** [kɔːd] *n* (*Mus*) accord *m*

**chore** [tʃɔːʳ] *n* travail *m* de routine; **household ~s** travaux *mpl* du ménage

**choreographer** [kɔrɪ'ɔɡrəfəʳ] *n* chorégraphe *m/f*

**choreography** [kɔrɪ'ɔɡrəfɪ] *n* chorégraphie *f*

**chorister** ['kɔrɪstəʳ] *n* choriste *m/f*

**chortle** ['tʃɔːtl] *vi* glousser

**chorus** ['kɔːrəs] *n* chœur *m*; (*repeated part of song, also fig*) refrain *m*

**chose** [tʃəuz] *pt of* **choose**

**chosen** ['tʃəuzn] *pp of* **choose**

**chow** [tʃau] *n* (*dog*) chow-chow *m*

**chowder** ['tʃaudəʳ] *n* soupe *f* de poisson

**Christ** [kraɪst] *n* Christ *m*

**christen** ['krɪsn] *vt* baptiser

**christening** ['krɪsnɪŋ] *n* baptême *m*

**Christian** ['krɪstɪən] *adj, n* chrétien(ne)

**Christianity** [krɪstɪ'ænɪtɪ] *n* christianisme *m*

**Christian name** *n* prénom *m*

**Christmas** ['krɪsməs] *n* Noël *m or f*; **happy** *or* **merry ~!** joyeux Noël!

**Christmas card** *n* carte *f* de Noël

**Christmas carol** *n* chant *m* de Noël

**Christmas Day** *n* le jour de Noël

**Christmas Eve** *n* la veille de Noël; la nuit de Noël

**Christmas Island** *n* île *f* Christmas

**Christmas pudding** *n* (*esp Brit*) Christmas *m* pudding

**Christmas tree** *n* arbre *m* de Noël

**chrome** [krəum] *n* chrome *m*

**chromium** ['krəumɪəm] *n* chrome *m*; (*also*: **chromium plating**) chromage *m*

**chromosome** ['krəuməsəum] *n* chromosome *m*

**chronic** ['krɔnɪk] *adj* chronique; (*fig: liar, smoker*) invétéré(e)

**chronicle** ['krɔnɪkl] *n* chronique *f*

**chronological** [krɔnə'lɔdʒɪkl] *adj* chronologique

**chrysanthemum** [krɪ'sænθəməm] *n* chrysanthème *m*

**chubby** ['tʃʌbɪ] *adj* potelé(e), rondelet(te)

**chuck** [tʃʌk] *vt* (*inf*) lancer, jeter; (*Brit: also*: **chuck up**: *job*) lâcher; (*: person*) plaquer

▶ **chuck out** *vt* (*inf: person*) flanquer dehors *or* à la porte; (*: rubbish etc*) jeter

**chuckle** ['tʃʌkl] *vi* glousser

**chuffed** [tʃʌft] *adj* (*Brit inf*): **to be ~ about sth** être content(e) de qch

**chug** [tʃʌɡ] *vi* faire teuf-teuf; souffler

**chum** [tʃʌm] *n* copain (copine)

**chump** ['tʃʌmp] *n* (*inf*) imbécile *m/f*, crétin(e)

**chunk** [tʃʌŋk] *n* gros morceau; (*of bread*) quignon *m*

**chunky** ['tʃʌŋkɪ] *adj* (*furniture etc*) massif(-ive); (*person*) trapu(e); (*knitwear*) en grosse laine

**Chunnel** ['tʃʌnəl] *n* = **Channel Tunnel**

**church** [tʃəːtʃ] *n* église *f*; **the C~ of England** l'Église anglicane

**churchyard** ['tʃəːtʃjɑːd] *n* cimetière *m*

**churlish** ['tʃəːlɪʃ] *adj* grossier(-ère); hargneux(-euse)

**churn** [tʃəːn] *n* (*for butter*) baratte *f*; (*also*: **milk churn**) (grand) bidon à lait

▶ **churn out** *vt* débiter

**chute** [ʃuːt] *n* goulotte *f*; (*also*: **rubbish chute**) vide-ordures *m inv*; (*Brit: children's slide*) toboggan *m*

**chutney** ['tʃʌtnɪ] *n* chutney *m*

**CIA** *n abbr* (= *Central Intelligence Agency*) CIA *f*

**CID** *n abbr* (= *Criminal Investigation Department*) ≈ P. J. *f*

**cider** ['saɪdəʳ] *n* cidre *m*

**CIF** *abbr* (= *cost, insurance and freight*) CAF

**cigar** [sɪ'ɡɑːʳ] *n* cigare *m*

**cigarette** [sɪɡə'rɛt] *n* cigarette *f*

**cigarette case** *n* étui *m* à cigarettes

**cigarette end** *n* mégot *m*

**cigarette holder** *n* fume-cigarettes *m inv*

**cigarette lighter** *n* briquet *m*

**C-in-C** *abbr* = **commander-in-chief**

**cinch** [sɪntʃ] *n* (*inf*): **it's a ~** c'est du gâteau, c'est l'enfance de l'art

**Cinderella** [sɪndə'rɛlə] *n* Cendrillon

**cine-camera** ['sɪnɪ'kæmərə] *n* (*Brit*) caméra *f*

**cine-film** ['sɪnɪfɪlm] *n* (*Brit*) film *m*

**cinema** ['sɪnəmə] *n* cinéma *m*

**cine-projector** ['sɪnɪprə'dʒɛktəʳ] *n* (*Brit*) projecteur *m* de cinéma

**cinnamon** ['sɪnəmən] *n* cannelle *f*

**cipher** ['saɪfəʳ] *n* code secret; (*fig: faceless employee etc*) numéro *m*; **in ~** codé(e)

**circa** ['səːkə] *prep* circa, environ

**circle** ['səːkl] *n* cercle *m*; (*in cinema*) balcon *m* ▷ *vi* faire *or* décrire des cercles ▷ *vt* (*surround*) entourer, encercler; (*move round*) faire le tour de, tourner autour de

**circuit** ['səːkɪt] *n* circuit *m*; (*lap*) tour *m*

**circuit board** *n* plaquette *f*

**circuitous** [səː'kjuɪtəs] *adj* indirect(e), qui fait un détour

**circular** ['səːkjulə<sup></sup>] *adj* circulaire ▷ *n* circulaire *f*; (*as advertisement*) prospectus *m*

**circulate** ['səːkjuleɪt] *vi* circuler ▷ *vt* faire circuler

**circulation** [səːkju'leɪʃən] *n* circulation *f*; (*of newspaper*) tirage *m*

**circumcise** ['səːkəmsaɪz] *vt* circoncire

**circumference** [sə'kʌmfərəns] *n* circonférence *f*

**circumflex** ['səːkəmflɛks] *n* (*also*: **circumflex accent**) accent *m* circonflexe

**circumscribe** ['sɜːkəmskraɪb] vt circonscrire

**circumspect** ['sɜːkəmspɛkt] adj circonspect(e)

**circumstances** ['sɜːkəmstənsɪz] npl circonstances fpl; (financial condition) moyens mpl, situation financière; **in** or **under the ~** dans ces conditions; **under no ~** en aucun cas, sous aucun prétexte

**circumstantial** [sɜːkəm'stænʃl] adj (report, statement) circonstancié(e); **~ evidence** preuve indirecte

**circumvent** [sɜːkəm'vɛnt] vt (rule etc) tourner

**circus** ['sɜːkəs] n cirque m; (also: **Circus**: in place names) place f

**cirrhosis** [sɪ'rəusɪs] n (also: **cirrhosis of the liver**) cirrhose f (du foie)

**CIS** n abbr (= Commonwealth of Independent States) CEI f

**cissy** ['sɪsɪ] n = **sissy**

**cistern** ['sɪstən] n réservoir m (d'eau); (in toilet) réservoir de la chasse d'eau

**citation** [saɪ'teɪʃən] n citation f; (US) P.-V m

**cite** [saɪt] vt citer

**citizen** ['sɪtɪzn] n (Pol) citoyen(ne); (resident): **the ~s of this town** les habitants de cette ville

**Citizens' Advice Bureau** ['sɪtɪznz-] n (Brit) ≈ Bureau m d'aide sociale

**citizenship** ['sɪtɪznʃɪp] n citoyenneté f; (Brit: Scol) ≈ éducation f civique

**citric** ['sɪtrɪk] adj: **~ acid** acide m citrique

**citrus fruits** ['sɪtrəs-] npl agrumes mpl

**city** ['sɪtɪ] n (grande) ville f; **the C~** la Cité de Londres (centre des affaires)

**city centre** n centre ville m

**City Hall** n (US) ≈ hôtel m de ville

**city technology college** n (Brit) établissement m d'enseignement technologique (situé dans un quartier défavorisé)

**civic** ['sɪvɪk] adj civique; (authorities) municipal(e)

**civic centre** n (Brit) centre administratif (municipal)

**civil** ['sɪvɪl] adj civil(e); (polite) poli(e), civil(e)

**civil engineer** n ingénieur civil

**civil engineering** n génie civil, travaux publics

**civilian** [sɪ'vɪlɪən] adj, n civil(e)

**civilization** [sɪvɪlaɪ'zeɪʃən] n civilisation f

**civilized** ['sɪvɪlaɪzd] adj civilisé(e); (fig) où règnent les bonnes manières, empreint(e) d'une courtoisie de bon ton

**civil law** n code civil; (study) droit civil

**civil liberties** npl libertés fpl civiques

**civil rights** npl droits mpl civiques

**civil servant** n fonctionnaire m/f

**Civil Service** n fonction publique, administration f

**civil war** n guerre civile

**civvies** ['sɪvɪz] npl: **in ~** (inf) en civil

**CJD** n abbr (= Creutzfeldt-Jakob disease) MCJ f

**cl** abbr (= centilitre) cl

**clad** [klæd] adj: **~ (in)** habillé(e) de, vêtu(e) de

**claim** [kleɪm] vt (rights etc) revendiquer; (compensation) réclamer; (assert) déclarer,

prétendre ▷ vi (for insurance) faire une déclaration de sinistre ▷ n revendication f; prétention f; (right) droit m; (for expenses) note f de frais; **(insurance) ~** demande f d'indemnisation, déclaration f de sinistre; **to put in a ~ for** (pay rise etc) demander

**claimant** ['kleɪmənt] n (Admin, Law) requérant(e)

**claim form** n (gen) formulaire m de demande

**clairvoyant** [klɛə'vɔɪənt] n voyant(e), extra-lucide m/f

**clam** [klæm] n palourde f
  ▶ **clam up** vi (inf) la boucler

**clamber** ['klæmbəʳ] vi grimper, se hisser

**clammy** ['klæmɪ] adj humide et froid(e) (au toucher), moite

**clamour, (US) clamor** ['klæməʳ] n (noise) clameurs fpl; (protest) protestations bruyantes ▷ vi: **to ~ for sth** réclamer qch à grands cris

**clamp** [klæmp] n crampon m; (on workbench) valet m; (on car) sabot m de Denver ▷ vt attacher; (car) mettre un sabot à
  ▶ **clamp down on** vt fus sévir contre, prendre des mesures draconiennes à l'égard de

**clampdown** ['klæmpdaun] n: **there has been a ~ on ...** des mesures énergiques ont été prises contre ...

**clan** [klæn] n clan m

**clandestine** [klæn'dɛstɪn] adj clandestin(e)

**clang** [klæŋ] n bruit m or fracas m métallique ▷ vi émettre un bruit or fracas métallique

**clanger** ['klæŋəʳ] n: **to drop a ~** (Brit inf) faire une boulette

**clansman** ['klænzmən] (irreg) n membre m d'un clan (écossais)

**clap** [klæp] vi applaudir ▷ vt: **to ~ (one's hands)** battre des mains ▷ n claquement m; tape f; **a ~ of thunder** un coup de tonnerre

**clapping** ['klæpɪŋ] n applaudissements mpl

**claptrap** ['klæptræp] n (inf) baratin m

**claret** ['klærət] n (vin m de) bordeaux m (rouge)

**clarification** [klærɪfɪ'keɪʃən] n (fig) clarification f, éclaircissement m

**clarify** ['klærɪfaɪ] vt clarifier

**clarinet** [klærɪ'nɛt] n clarinette f

**clarity** ['klærɪtɪ] n clarté f

**clash** [klæʃ] n (sound) choc m, fracas m; (with police) affrontement m; (fig) conflit m ▷ vi se heurter; être or entrer en conflit; (colours) jurer; (dates, events) tomber en même temps

**clasp** [klɑːsp] n (of necklace, bag) fermoir m ▷ vt serrer, étreindre

**class** [klɑːs] n (gen) classe f; (group, category) catégorie f ▷ vt classer, classifier

**class-conscious** ['klɑːs'kɔnʃəs] adj conscient(e) de son appartenance sociale

**class consciousness** n conscience f de classe

**classic** ['klæsɪk] adj classique ▷ n (author, work) classique m; (race etc) classique f

**classical** ['klæsɪkl] adj classique

**classics** ['klæsɪks] npl (Scol) lettres fpl classiques

**classification** [klæsɪfɪ'keɪʃən] n classification f

**classified** ['klæsɪfaɪd] adj (information) secret(-ète); ~ **ads** petites annonces
**classify** ['klæsɪfaɪ] vt classifier, classer
**classless society** ['klɑːslɪs-] n société f sans classes
**classmate** ['klɑːsmeɪt] n camarade m/f de classe
**classroom** ['klɑːsrum] n (salle f de) classe f
**classroom assistant** n assistant(-e) d'éducation
**classy** ['klɑːsɪ] (inf) adj classe (inf)
**clatter** ['klætəʳ] n cliquetis m ▷ vi cliqueter
**clause** [klɔːz] n clause f; (Ling) proposition f
**claustrophobia** [klɔːstrə'fəubɪə] n claustrophobie f
**claustrophobic** [klɔːstrə'fəubɪk] adj (person) claustrophobe; (place) où l'on se sent claustrophobe
**claw** [klɔː] n griffe f; (of bird of prey) serre f; (of lobster) pince f ▷ vt griffer; déchirer
**clay** [kleɪ] n argile f
**clean** [kliːn] adj propre; (clear, smooth) net(te); (record, reputation) sans tache; (joke, story) correct(e) ▷ vt nettoyer ▷ adv: **he ~ forgot** il a complètement oublié; **to come ~** (inf: admit guilt) se mettre à table; **to ~ one's teeth** se laver les dents; **~ driving licence** or (US) **record** permis où n'est portée aucune indication de contravention
  ▶ **clean off** vt enlever
  ▶ **clean out** vt nettoyer (à fond)
  ▶ **clean up** vt nettoyer; (fig) remettre de l'ordre dans ▷ vi (fig: make profit): **to ~ up on** faire son beurre avec
**clean-cut** ['kliːn'kʌt] adj (man) soigné; (situation etc) bien délimité(e), net(te), clair(e)
**cleaner** ['kliːnəʳ] n (person) nettoyeur(-euse), femme f de ménage; (also: **dry cleaner**) teinturier(-ière); (product) détachant m
**cleaner's** ['kliːnəʳz] n (also: **dry cleaner's**) teinturier m
**cleaning** ['kliːnɪŋ] n nettoyage m
**cleaning lady** n femme f de ménage
**cleanliness** ['klɛnlɪnɪs] n propreté f
**cleanly** ['kliːnlɪ] adv proprement; nettement
**cleanse** [klɛnz] vt nettoyer; purifier
**cleanser** ['klɛnzəʳ] n détergent m; (for face) démaquillant m
**clean-shaven** ['kliːn'ʃeɪvn] adj rasé(e) de près
**cleansing department** ['klɛnzɪŋ-] n (Brit) service m de voirie
**clean sweep** n: **to make a ~** (Sport) rafler tous les prix
**clean-up** ['kliːnʌp] n nettoyage m
**clear** [klɪəʳ] adj clair(e); (glass, plastic) transparent(e); (road, way) libre, dégagé(e); (profit, majority) net(te); (conscience) tranquille; (skin) frais (fraîche); (sky) dégagé(e) ▷ vt (road) dégager, déblayer; (table) débarrasser; (room etc: of people) faire évacuer; (woodland) défricher; (cheque) compenser; (Comm: goods) liquider; (Law: suspect) innocenter; (obstacle) franchir or sauter sans heurter ▷ vi (weather) s'éclaircir; (fog) se dissiper ▷ adv: **~ of** à distance de, à

l'écart de ▷ n: **to be in the ~** (out of debt) être dégagé(e) de toute dette; (out of suspicion) être lavé(e) de tout soupçon; (out of danger) être hors de danger; **to ~ the table** débarrasser la table, desservir; **to ~ one's throat** s'éclaircir la gorge; **to ~ a profit** faire un bénéfice net; **to make o.s. ~** se faire bien comprendre; **to make it ~ to sb that ...** bien faire comprendre à qn que ...; **I have a ~ day tomorrow** (Brit) je n'ai rien de prévu demain; **to keep ~ of sb/sth** éviter qn/ qch
  ▶ **clear away** vt (things, clothes etc) enlever, retirer; **to ~ away the dishes** débarrasser la table
  ▶ **clear off** vi (inf: leave) dégager
  ▶ **clear up** vi s'éclaircir, se dissiper ▷ vt ranger, mettre en ordre; (mystery) éclaircir, résoudre
**clearance** ['klɪərəns] n (removal) déblayage m; (free space) dégagement m; (permission) autorisation f
**clearance sale** n (Comm) liquidation f
**clear-cut** ['klɪə'kʌt] adj précis(e), nettement défini(e)
**clearing** ['klɪərɪŋ] n (in forest) clairière f; (Brit Banking) compensation f, clearing m
**clearing bank** n (Brit) banque f qui appartient à une chambre de compensation
**clearly** ['klɪəlɪ] adv clairement; (obviously) de toute évidence
**clearway** ['klɪəweɪ] n (Brit) route f à stationnement interdit
**cleavage** ['kliːvɪdʒ] n (of dress) décolleté m
**cleaver** ['kliːvəʳ] n fendoir m, couperet m
**clef** [klɛf] n (Mus) clé f
**cleft** [klɛft] n (in rock) crevasse f, fissure f
**clemency** ['klɛmənsɪ] n clémence f
**clement** ['klɛmənt] adj (weather) clément(e)
**clementine** ['klɛməntaɪn] n clémentine f
**clench** [klɛntʃ] vt serrer
**clergy** ['kləːdʒɪ] n clergé m
**clergyman** ['kləːdʒɪmən] (irreg) n ecclésiastique m
**clerical** ['klɛrɪkl] adj de bureau, d'employé de bureau; (Rel) clérical(e), du clergé
**clerk** [klɑːk] (US) [kləːrk] n (Brit) employé(e) de bureau; (US: salesman/woman) vendeur(-euse); **C~ of Court** (Law) greffier m (du tribunal)
**clever** ['klɛvəʳ] adj (intelligent) intelligent(e); (skilful) habile, adroit(e); (device, arrangement) ingénieux(-euse), astucieux(-euse)
**cleverly** ['klɛvəlɪ] adv (skilfully) habilement; (craftily) astucieusement
**clew** [kluː] n (US) = **clue**
**cliché** ['kliːʃeɪ] n cliché m
**click** [klɪk] vi faire un bruit sec or un déclic; (Comput) cliquer ▷ vt: **to ~ one's tongue** faire claquer sa langue; **to ~ one's heels** claquer des talons; **to ~ on an icon** cliquer sur une icône
**client** ['klaɪənt] n client(e)
**clientele** [kliːɑːn'tɛl] n clientèle f
**cliff** [klɪf] n falaise f
**cliffhanger** ['klɪfhæŋəʳ] n (TV, fig) histoire

pleine de suspense

**climactic** [klaɪ'mæktɪk] adj à son point culminant, culminant(e)

**climate** ['klaɪmɪt] n climat m

**climate change** n changement m climatique

**climax** ['klaɪmæks] n apogée m, point culminant; (sexual) orgasme m

**climb** [klaɪm] vi grimper, monter; (plane) prendre de l'altitude ▷ vt (stairs) monter; (mountain) escalader; (tree) grimper à ▷ n montée f, escalade f; **to ~ over a wall** passer par dessus un mur
  ▸ **climb down** vi (re)descendre; (Brit fig) rabattre de ses prétentions

**climb-down** ['klaɪmdaun] n (Brit) reculade f

**climber** ['klaɪmə<sup>r</sup>] n (also: **rock climber**) grimpeur(-euse), varappeur(-euse); (plant) plante grimpante

**climbing** ['klaɪmɪŋ] n (also: **rock climbing**) escalade f, varappe f

**clinch** [klɪntʃ] vt (deal) conclure, sceller

**clincher** ['klɪntʃə<sup>r</sup>] n: **that was the ~** c'est ce qui a fait pencher la balance

**cling** (pt, pp **clung**) [klɪŋ, klʌŋ] vi: **to ~ (to)** se cramponner (à), s'accrocher (à); (clothes) coller (à)

**Clingfilm®** ['klɪŋfɪlm] n film m alimentaire

**clinic** ['klɪnɪk] n clinique f; centre médical; (session: Med) consultation(s) f(pl), séance(s) f(pl); (Sport) séance(s) de perfectionnement

**clinical** ['klɪnɪkl] adj clinique; (fig) froid(e)

**clink** [klɪŋk] vi tinter, cliqueter

**clip** [klɪp] n (for hair) barrette f; (also: **paper clip**) trombone m; (Brit: also: **bulldog clip**) pince f de bureau; (holding hose etc) collier m or bague f (métallique) de serrage; (TV, Cinema) clip m ▷ vt (also: **clip together**: papers) attacher; (hair, nails) couper; (hedge) tailler

**clippers** ['klɪpəz] npl tondeuse f; (also: **nail clippers**) coupe-ongles m inv

**clipping** ['klɪpɪŋ] n (from newspaper) coupure f de journal

**clique** [kli:k] n clique f, coterie f

**cloak** [kləuk] n grande cape ▷ vt (fig) masquer, cacher

**cloakroom** ['kləukrum] n (for coats etc) vestiaire m; (Brit: W.C.) toilettes fpl

**clock** [klɔk] n (large) horloge f; (small) pendule f; **round the ~** (work etc) vingt-quatre heures sur vingt-quatre; **to sleep round the ~** or **the ~ round** faire le tour du cadran; **30,000 on the ~** (Brit Aut) 30 000 milles au compteur; **to work against the ~** faire la course contre la montre
  ▸ **clock in** or **on** (Brit) vi (with card) pointer (en arrivant); (start work) commencer à travailler
  ▸ **clock off** or **out** (Brit) vi (with card) pointer (en partant); (leave work) quitter le travail
  ▸ **clock up** vt (miles, hours etc) faire

**clockwise** ['klɔkwaɪz] adv dans le sens des aiguilles d'une montre

**clockwork** ['klɔkwə:k] n rouages mpl, mécanisme m; (of clock) mouvement m

(d'horlogerie) ▷ adj (toy, train) mécanique

**clog** [klɔg] n sabot m ▷ vt boucher, encrasser ▷ vi (also: **clog up**) se boucher, s'encrasser

**cloister** ['klɔɪstə<sup>r</sup>] n cloître m

**clone** [kləun] n clone m ▷ vt cloner

**close¹** [kləus] adj (near): **~ (to)** près (de), proche (de); (writing, texture) serré(e); (contact, link, watch) étroit(e); (examination) attentif(-ive), minutieux(-euse); (contest) très serré(e); (weather) lourd(e), étouffant(e); (room) mal aéré(e) ▷ adv près, à proximité; **~ to** (prep) près de; **~ by, ~ at hand** (adj, adv) tout(e) près; **how ~ is Edinburgh to Glasgow?** combien de kilomètres y-a-t-il entre Édimbourg et Glasgow?; **a ~ friend** un ami intime; **to have a ~ shave** (fig) l'échapper belle; **at ~ quarters** tout près, à côté

**close²** [kləuz] vt fermer; (bargain, deal) conclure ▷ vi (shop etc) fermer; (lid, door etc) se fermer; (end) se terminer, se conclure ▷ n (end) conclusion f; **to bring sth to a ~** mettre fin à qch; **what time do you ~?** à quelle heure fermez-vous?
  ▸ **close down** vt, vi fermer (définitivement)
  ▸ **close in** vi (hunters) approcher; (night, fog) tomber; **the days are closing in** les jours raccourcissent; **to ~ in on sb** cerner qn
  ▸ **close off** vt (area) boucler

**closed** [kləuzd] adj (shop etc) fermé(e); (road) fermé à la circulation

**closed-circuit** ['kləuzd'sə:kɪt] adj: **~ television** télévision f en circuit fermé

**closed shop** n organisation f qui n'admet que des travailleurs syndiqués

**close-knit** ['kləus'nɪt] adj (family, community) très uni(e)

**closely** ['kləuslɪ] adv (examine, watch) de près; **we are ~ related** nous sommes proches parents; **a ~ guarded secret** un secret bien gardé

**close season** [kləus-] n (Brit: Hunting) fermeture f de la chasse/pêche; (: Football) trêve f

**closet** ['klɔzɪt] n (cupboard) placard m, réduit m

**close-up** ['kləusʌp] n gros plan

**closing** ['kləuzɪŋ] adj (stages, remarks) final(e); **~ price** (Stock Exchange) cours m de clôture

**closing time** n heure f de fermeture

**closure** ['kləuʒə<sup>r</sup>] n fermeture f

**clot** [klɔt] n (of blood, milk) caillot m; (inf: person) ballot m ▷ vi (blood) former des caillots; (: external bleeding) se coaguler

**cloth** [klɔθ] n (material) tissu m, étoffe f; (Brit: also: **tea cloth**) torchon m; lavette f; (also: **tablecloth**) nappe f

**clothe** [kləuð] vt habiller, vêtir

**clothes** [kləuðz] npl vêtements mpl, habits mpl; **to put one's ~ on** s'habiller; **to take one's ~ off** enlever ses vêtements

**clothes brush** n brosse f à habits

**clothes line** n corde f (à linge)

**clothes peg**, (US) **clothes pin** n pince f à linge

**clothing** ['kləuðɪŋ] n = **clothes**

**clotted cream** ['klɔtɪd-] n (Brit) crème caillée

**cloud** [klaud] n nuage m ▷ vt (liquid) troubler; **to**

~ **the issue** brouiller les cartes; **every ~ has a silver lining** (*proverb*) à quelque chose malheur est bon (*proverbe*)
▶ **cloud over** *vi* se couvrir; (*fig*) s'assombrir
**cloudburst** ['klaudbə:st] *n* violente averse
**cloud-cuckoo-land** ['klaud'kuku:'lænd] *n* (*Brit*) monde *m* imaginaire
**cloudy** ['klaudɪ] *adj* nuageux(-euse), couvert(e); (*liquid*) trouble
**clout** [klaut] *n* (*blow*) taloche *f*; (*fig*) pouvoir *m* ▷ *vt* flanquer une taloche à
**clove** [kləuv] *n* clou *m* de girofle; **a ~ of garlic** une gousse d'ail
**clover** ['kləuvə<sup>r</sup>] *n* trèfle *m*
**cloverleaf** ['kləuvəli:f] *n* feuille *f* de trèfle; (*Aut*) croisement *m* en trèfle
**clown** [klaun] *n* clown *m* ▷ *vi* (*also:* **clown about, clown around**) faire le clown
**cloying** ['klɔɪɪŋ] *adj* (*taste, smell*) écœurant(e)
**club** [klʌb] *n* (*society*) club *m*; (*weapon*) massue *f*, matraque *f*; (*also:* **golf club**) club ▷ *vt* matraquer ▷ *vi*: **to ~ together** s'associer; **clubs** *npl* (*Cards*) trèfle *m*
**club car** *n* (*US Rail*) wagon-restaurant *m*
**club class** *n* (*Aviat*) classe *f* club
**clubhouse** ['klʌbhaus] *n* pavillon *m*
**club soda** *n* (*US*) eau *f* de seltz
**cluck** [klʌk] *vi* glousser
**clue** [klu:] *n* indice *m*; (*in crosswords*) définition *f*; **I haven't a ~** je n'en ai pas la moindre idée
**clued up,** (*US*) **clued in** [klu:d-] *adj* (*inf*) (*vachement*) calé(e)
**clump** [klʌmp] *n*: ~ **of trees** bouquet *m* d'arbres
**clumsy** ['klʌmzɪ] *adj* (*person*) gauche, maladroit(e); (*object*) malcommode, peu maniable
**clung** [klʌŋ] *pt, pp of* **cling**
**cluster** ['klʌstə<sup>r</sup>] *n* (petit) groupe; (*of flowers*) grappe *f* ▷ *vi* se rassembler
**clutch** [klʌtʃ] *n* (*Aut*) embrayage *m*; (*grasp*): ~**es** étreinte *f*, prise *f* ▷ *vt* (*grasp*) agripper; (*hold tightly*) serrer fort; (*hold on to*) se cramponner à
**clutter** ['klʌtə<sup>r</sup>] *vt* (*also:* **clutter up**) encombrer ▷ *n* désordre *m*, fouillis *m*
**cm** *abbr* (= *centimetre*) cm
**CNAA** *n abbr* (*Brit*: = *Council for National Academic Awards*) *organisme non universitaire délivrant des diplômes*
**CND** *n abbr* = **Campaign for Nuclear Disarmament**
**CO** *n abbr* (= *commanding officer*) Cdt; (*Brit*) = **Commonwealth Office** ▷ *abbr* (*US*) = **Colorado**
**Co.** *abbr* = **company, county**
**c/o** *abbr* (= *care of*) c/o, aux bons soins de
**coach** [kəutʃ] *n* (*bus*) autocar *m*; (*horse-drawn*) diligence *f*; (*of train*) voiture *f*, wagon *m*; (*Sport: trainer*) entraîneur(-euse); (*school: tutor*) répétiteur(-trice) ▷ *vt* (*Sport*) entraîner; (*student*) donner des leçons particulières à
**coach station** (*Brit*) *n* gare routière
**coach trip** *n* excursion *f* en car

**coagulate** [kəu'ægjuleɪt] *vt* coaguler ▷ *vi* se coaguler
**coal** [kəul] *n* charbon *m*
**coal face** *n* front *m* de taille
**coalfield** ['kəulfi:ld] *n* bassin houiller
**coalition** [kəuə'lɪʃən] *n* coalition *f*
**coalman** ['kəulmən] (*irreg*) *n* charbonnier *m*, marchand *m* de charbon
**coal mine** *n* mine *f* de charbon
**coarse** [kɔ:s] *adj* grossier(-ère), rude; (*vulgar*) vulgaire
**coast** [kəust] *n* côte *f* ▷ *vi* (*car, cycle*) descendre en roue libre
**coastal** ['kəustl] *adj* côtier(-ère)
**coaster** ['kəustə<sup>r</sup>] *n* (*Naut*) caboteur *m*; (*for glass*) dessous *m* de verre
**coastguard** ['kəustgɑ:d] *n* garde-côte *m*
**coastline** ['kəustlaɪn] *n* côte *f*, littoral *m*
**coat** [kəut] *n* manteau *m*; (*of animal*) pelage *m*, poil *m*; (*of paint*) couche *f* ▷ *vt* couvrir, enduire; ~ **of arms** *n* blason *m*, armoiries *fpl*
**coat hanger** *n* cintre *m*
**coating** ['kəutɪŋ] *n* couche *f*, enduit *m*
**co-author** ['kəu'ɔ:θə<sup>r</sup>] *n* co-auteur *m*
**coax** [kəuks] *vt* persuader par des cajoleries
**cob** [kɔb] *n see* **corn**
**cobbled** ['kɔbld] *adj* pavé(e)
**cobbler** ['kɔblə<sup>r</sup>] *n* cordonnier *m*
**cobbles, cobblestones** ['kɔblz, 'kɔblstəunz] *npl* pavés (ronds)
**COBOL** ['kəubɔl] *n* COBOL *m*
**cobra** ['kəubrə] *n* cobra *m*
**cobweb** ['kɔbweb] *n* toile *f* d'araignée
**cocaine** [kə'keɪn] *n* cocaïne *f*
**cock** [kɔk] *n* (*rooster*) coq *m*; (*male bird*) mâle *m* ▷ *vt* (*gun*) armer; **to ~ one's ears** (*fig*) dresser l'oreille
**cock-a-hoop** [kɔkə'hu:p] *adj* jubilant(e)
**cockerel** ['kɔkərl] *n* jeune coq *m*
**cock-eyed** ['kɔkaɪd] *adj* (*fig*) de travers; qui louche; qui ne tient pas debout (*fig*)
**cockle** ['kɔkl] *n* coque *f*
**cockney** ['kɔknɪ] *n* cockney *m/f* (*habitant des quartiers populaires de l'East End de Londres*), ≈ faubourien(ne)
**cockpit** ['kɔkpɪt] *n* (*in aircraft*) poste *m* de pilotage, cockpit *m*
**cockroach** ['kɔkrəutʃ] *n* cafard *m*, cancrelat *m*
**cocktail** ['kɔkteɪl] *n* cocktail *m*; **prawn ~,** (*US*) **shrimp ~** cocktail de crevettes
**cocktail cabinet** *n* (meuble-)bar *m*
**cocktail party** *n* cocktail *m*
**cocktail shaker** [-'ʃeɪkə<sup>r</sup>] *n* shaker *m*
**cocky** ['kɔkɪ] *adj* trop sûr(e) de soi
**cocoa** ['kəukəu] *n* cacao *m*
**coconut** ['kəukənʌt] *n* noix *f* de coco
**cocoon** [kə'ku:n] *n* cocon *m*
**C.O.D.** *abbr* = **cash on delivery**; (*US*) = **collect on delivery**
**cod** [kɔd] *n* morue fraîche, cabillaud *m*
**code** [kəud] *n* code *m*; (*Tel: area code*) indicatif *m*; ~ **of behaviour** règles *fpl* de conduite; ~ **of practice** déontologie *f*

511

**codeine** ['kəudi:n] n codéine f
**codger** ['kɔdʒəʳ] n: **an old ~** (Brit inf) un drôle de vieux bonhomme
**codicil** ['kɔdɪsɪl] n codicille m
**codify** ['kəudɪfaɪ] vt codifier
**cod-liver oil** ['kɔdlɪvər-] n huile f de foie de morue
**co-driver** ['kəu'draɪvəʳ] n (in race) copilote m; (of lorry) deuxième chauffeur m
**co-ed** ['kəu'ɛd] adj abbr = **coeducational** ▷ n abbr (US: female student) étudiante d'une université mixte; (Brit: school) école f mixte
**coeducational** ['kəuɛdju'keɪʃənl] adj mixte
**coerce** [kəu'ə:s] vt contraindre
**coercion** [kəu'ə:ʃən] n contrainte f
**coexistence** ['kəuɪg'zɪstəns] n coexistence f
**C. of C.** n abbr = **chamber of commerce**
**C of E** n abbr = **Church of England**
**coffee** ['kɔfɪ] n café m; **white ~**, (US) **~ with cream** (café-)crème m
**coffee bar** n (Brit) café m
**coffee bean** n grain m de café
**coffee break** n pause-café f
**coffee cake** ['kɔfɪkeɪk] n (US) = petit pain aux raisins
**coffee cup** n tasse f à café
**coffee maker** n cafetière f
**coffeepot** ['kɔfɪpɔt] n cafetière f
**coffee shop** n café m
**coffee table** n (petite) table basse
**coffin** ['kɔfɪn] n cercueil m
**C of I** n abbr = **Church of Ireland**
**C of S** n abbr = **Church of Scotland**
**cog** [kɔg] n (wheel) roue dentée; (tooth) dent f (d'engrenage)
**cogent** ['kəudʒənt] adj puissant(e), convaincant(e)
**cognac** ['kɔnjæk] n cognac m
**cogwheel** ['kɔgwi:l] n roue dentée
**cohabit** [kəu'hæbɪt] vi (formal): **to ~ (with sb)** cohabiter (avec qn)
**coherent** [kəu'hɪərənt] adj cohérent(e)
**cohesion** [kəu'hi:ʒən] n cohésion f
**cohesive** [kəu'hi:sɪv] adj (fig) cohésif(-ive)
**COI** n abbr (Brit: = Central Office of Information) service d'information gouvernemental
**coil** [kɔɪl] n rouleau m, bobine f; (one loop) anneau m, spire f; (of smoke) volute f; (contraceptive) stérilet m ▷ vt enrouler
**coin** [kɔɪn] n pièce f (de monnaie) ▷ vt (word) inventer
**coinage** ['kɔɪnɪdʒ] n monnaie f, système m monétaire
**coinbox** ['kɔɪnbɔks] n (Brit) cabine f téléphonique
**coincide** [kəuɪn'saɪd] vi coïncider
**coincidence** [kəu'ɪnsɪdəns] n coïncidence f
**coin-operated** ['kɔɪn'ɔpəreɪtɪd] adj (machine, launderette) automatique
**Coke®** [kəuk] n coca m
**coke** [kəuk] n (coal) coke m
**Col.** abbr (= colonel) Col; (US) = **Colorado**

**COLA** n abbr (US: = cost-of-living adjustment) réajustement (des salaires, indemnités etc) en fonction du coût de la vie
**colander** ['kɔləndəʳ] n passoire f (à légumes)
**cold** [kəuld] adj froid(e) ▷ n froid m; (Med) rhume m; **it's ~** il fait froid; **to be ~** (person) avoir froid; **to catch ~** prendre or attraper froid; **to catch a ~** s'enrhumer, attraper un rhume; **in ~ blood** de sang-froid; **to have ~ feet** avoir froid aux pieds; (fig) avoir la frousse or la trouille; **to give sb the ~ shoulder** battre froid à qn
**cold-blooded** ['kəuld'blʌdɪd] adj (Zool) à sang froid
**cold cream** n crème f de soins
**coldly** ['kəuldlɪ] adv froidement
**cold sore** n bouton m de fièvre
**cold sweat** n: **to be in a ~ (about sth)** avoir des sueurs froides (au sujet de qch)
**cold turkey** n (inf) manque m; **to go ~** être en manque
**Cold War** n: **the ~** la guerre froide
**coleslaw** ['kəulslɔ:] n sorte de salade de chou cru
**colic** ['kɔlɪk] n colique(s) f(pl)
**colicky** ['kɔlɪkɪ] adj qui souffre de coliques
**collaborate** [kə'læbəreɪt] vi collaborer
**collaboration** [kəlæbə'reɪʃən] n collaboration f
**collaborator** [kə'læbəreɪtəʳ] n collaborateur(-trice)
**collage** [kɔ'lɑ:ʒ] n (Art) collage m
**collagen** ['kɔlədʒən] n collagène m
**collapse** [kə'læps] vi s'effondrer, s'écrouler; (Med) avoir un malaise ▷ n effondrement m, écroulement m; (of government) chute f
**collapsible** [kə'læpsəbl] adj pliant(e), télescopique
**collar** ['kɔləʳ] n (of coat, shirt) col m; (for dog) collier m; (Tech) collier, bague f ▷ vt (inf: person) pincer
**collarbone** ['kɔləbəun] n clavicule f
**collate** [kɔ'leɪt] vt collationner
**collateral** [kə'lætərl] n nantissement m
**collation** [kə'leɪʃən] n collation f
**colleague** ['kɔli:g] n collègue m/f
**collect** [kə'lɛkt] vt rassembler; (pick up) ramasser; (as a hobby) collectionner; (Brit: call for) (passer) prendre; (mail) faire la levée de, ramasser; (money owed) encaisser; (donations, subscriptions) recueillir ▷ vi (people) se rassembler; (dust, dirt) s'amasser; **to ~ one's thoughts** réfléchir, réunir ses idées; **~ on delivery (COD)** (US Comm) payable or paiement à la livraison; **to call ~** (US Tel) téléphoner en PCV
**collected** [kə'lɛktɪd] adj: **~ works** œuvres complètes
**collection** [kə'lɛkʃən] n collection f; (of mail) levée f; (for money) collecte f, quête f
**collective** [kə'lɛktɪv] adj collectif(-ive) ▷ n collectif m
**collective bargaining** n convention collective
**collector** [kə'lɛktəʳ] n collectionneur m; (of taxes) percepteur m; (of rent, cash) encaisseur m; **~'s item** or **piece** pièce f de collection
**college** ['kɔlɪdʒ] n collège m; (of technology,

*agriculture etc*) institut *m*; **to go to ~** faire des études supérieures; **~ of education** = école normale

**collide** [kə'laɪd] *vi*: **to ~ (with)** entrer en collision (avec)

**collie** ['kɔlɪ] *n* (*dog*) colley *m*

**colliery** ['kɔlɪərɪ] *n* (*Brit*) mine *f* de charbon, houillère *f*

**collision** [kə'lɪʒən] *n* collision *f*, heurt *m*; **to be on a ~ course** aller droit à la collision; (*fig*) aller vers l'affrontement

**collision damage waiver** *n* (*Insurance*) rachat *m* de franchise

**colloquial** [kə'ləukwɪəl] *adj* familier(-ère)

**collusion** [kə'lu:ʒən] *n* collusion *f*; **in ~ with** en complicité avec

**Colo.** *abbr* (*US*) = **Colorado**

**cologne** [kə'ləun] *n* (*also*: **eau de cologne**) eau *f* de cologne

**Colombia** [kə'lɔmbɪə] *n* Colombie *f*

**Colombian** [kə'lɔmbɪən] *adj* colombien(ne) ▷ *n* Colombien(ne)

**colon** ['kəulən] *n* (*sign*) deux-points *mpl*; (*Med*) côlon *m*

**colonel** ['kə:nl] *n* colonel *m*

**colonial** [kə'ləunɪəl] *adj* colonial(e)

**colonize** ['kɔlənaɪz] *vt* coloniser

**colony** ['kɔlənɪ] *n* colonie *f*

**color** ['kʌlər] *n* (*US*) = **colour**

**Colorado beetle** [kɔlə'rɑːdəu-] *n* doryphore *m*

**colossal** [kə'lɔsl] *adj* colossal(e)

**colour,** (*US*) **color** ['kʌlər] *n* couleur *f* ▷ *vt* colorer; (*dye*) teindre; (*paint*) peindre; (*with crayons*) colorier; (*news*) fausser, exagérer ▷ *vi* (*blush*) rougir ▷ *cpd* (*film, photograph, television*) en couleur; **colours** *npl* (*of party, club*) couleurs *fpl*; **I'd like a different ~** je le voudrais dans un autre coloris

▶ **colour in** *vt* colorier

**colour bar,** (*US*) **color bar** *n* discrimination raciale (*dans un établissement etc*)

**colour-blind,** (*US*) **color-blind** ['kʌləblaɪnd] *adj* daltonien(ne)

**coloured,** (*US*) **colored** ['kʌləd] *adj* coloré(e); (*photo*) en couleur

**colour film,** (*US*) **color film** *n* (*for camera*) pellicule *f* (en) couleur

**colourful,** (*US*) **colorful** ['kʌləful] *adj* coloré(e), vif (vive); (*personality*) pittoresque, haut(e) en couleurs

**colouring,** (*US*) **coloring** ['kʌlərɪŋ] *n* colorant *m*; (*complexion*) teint *m*

**colour scheme,** (*US*) **color scheme** *n* combinaison *f* de(s) couleur(s)

**colour supplement** *n* (*Brit Press*) supplément *m* magazine

**colour television,** (*US*) **color television** *n* télévision *f* (en) couleur

**colt** [kəult] *n* poulain *m*

**column** ['kɔləm] *n* colonne *f*; (*fashion column, sports column etc*) rubrique *f*; **the editorial ~** l'éditorial *m*

**columnist** ['kɔləmnɪst] *n* rédacteur(-trice) d'une rubrique

**coma** ['kəumə] *n* coma *m*

**comb** [kəum] *n* peigne *m* ▷ *vt* (*hair*) peigner; (*area*) ratisser, passer au peigne fin

**combat** ['kɔmbæt] *n* combat *m* ▷ *vt* combattre, lutter contre

**combination** [kɔmbɪ'neɪʃən] *n* (*gen*) combinaison *f*

**combination lock** *n* serrure *f* à combinaison

**combine** [kəm'baɪn] *vt* combiner ▷ *vi* s'associer; (*Chem*) se combiner ▷ *n* ['kɔmbaɪn] association *f*; (*Econ*) trust *m*; (*also*: **combine harvester**) moissonneuse-batteuse(-lieuse) *f*; **to ~ sth with sth** (*one quality with another*) joindre *ou* allier qch à qch; **a ~d effort** un effort conjugué

**combine harvester** *n* moissonneuse-batteuse(-lieuse) *f*

**combo** ['kɔmbəu] *n* (*Jazz etc*) groupe *m* de musiciens

**combustible** [kəm'bʌstɪbl] *adj* combustible

**combustion** [kəm'bʌstʃən] *n* combustion *f*

**⊙ KEYWORD**

**come** (*pt* **came**, *pp* **-**) [kʌm, keɪm] *vi* **1** (*movement towards*) venir; **to ~ running** arriver en courant; **he's ~ here to work** il est venu ici pour travailler; **~ with me** suivez-moi; **to ~ into sight** *or* **view** apparaître

**2** (*arrive*) arriver; **to ~ home** rentrer (chez soi *or* à la maison); **we've just ~ from Paris** nous arrivons de Paris; **coming!** j'arrive!

**3** (*reach*): **to ~ to** (*decision etc*) parvenir à, arriver à; **the bill came to £40** la note s'est élevée à 40 livres; **if it ~s to it** s'il le faut, dans le pire des cas

**4** (*occur*): **an idea came to me** il m'est venu une idée; **what might ~ of it** ce qui pourrait en résulter, ce qui pourrait advenir *or* se produire

**5** (*be, become*): **to ~ loose/undone** se défaire/desserrer; **I've ~ to like him** j'ai fini par bien l'aimer

**6** (*inf: sexually*) jouir

▶ **come about** *vi* se produire, arriver

▶ **come across** *vt fus* rencontrer par hasard, tomber sur ▷ *vi*: **to ~ across well/badly** faire une bonne/mauvaise impression

▶ **come along** *vi* (*Brit: pupil, work*) faire des progrès, avancer; **~ along!** viens!; allons!, allez!

▶ **come apart** *vi* s'en aller en morceaux; se détacher

▶ **come away** *vi* partir, s'en aller; (*become detached*) se détacher

▶ **come back** *vi* revenir; (*reply*): **can I ~ back to you on that one?** est-ce qu'on peut revenir là-dessus plus tard?

▶ **come by** *vt fus* (*acquire*) obtenir, se procurer

▶ **come down** *vi* descendre; (*prices*) baisser; (*buildings*) s'écrouler; (: *be demolished*) être démoli(e)

▶ **come forward** *vi* s'avancer; (*make o.s. known*) se présenter, s'annoncer

▸ **come from** vt fus (source) venir de; (place) venir de, être originaire de
▸ **come in** vi entrer; (train) arriver; (fashion) entrer en vogue; (on deal etc) participer
▸ **come in for** vt fus (criticism etc) être l'objet de
▸ **come into** vt fus (money) hériter de
▸ **come off** vi (button) se détacher; (attempt) réussir
▸ **come on** vi (lights, electricity) s'allumer; (central heating) se mettre en marche; (pupil, work, project) faire des progrès, avancer; ~ **on!** viens!; allons!, allez!
▸ **come out** vi sortir; (sun) se montrer; (book) paraître; (stain) s'enlever; (strike) cesser le travail, se mettre en grève
▸ **come over** vt fus: **I don't know what's ~ over him!** je ne sais pas ce qui lui a pris!
▸ **come round** vi (after faint, operation) revenir à soi, reprendre connaissance
▸ **come through** vi (survive) s'en sortir; (telephone call): **the call came through** l'appel est bien parvenu
▸ **come to** vi revenir à soi ▷ vt (add up to: amount): **how much does it ~ to?** ça fait combien?
▸ **come under** vt fus (heading) se trouver sous; (influence) subir
▸ **come up** vi monter; (sun) se lever; (problem) se poser; (event) survenir; (in conversation) être soulevé
▸ **come up against** vt fus (resistance, difficulties) rencontrer
▸ **come up to** vt fus arriver à; **the film didn't ~ up to our expectations** le film nous a déçu
▸ **come up with** vt fus (money) fournir; **he came up with an idea** il a eu une idée, il a proposé quelque chose
▸ **come upon** vt fus tomber sur

**comeback** ['kʌmbæk] n (Theat) rentrée f; (reaction) réaction f; (response) réponse f
**Comecon** ['kɔmɪkɔn] n abbr (= Council for Mutual Economic Aid) COMECON m
**comedian** [kə'miːdɪən] n (comic) comique m; (Theat) comédien m
**comedienne** [kəmiːdɪ'ɛn] n comique f
**comedown** ['kʌmdaun] n déchéance f
**comedy** ['kɔmɪdɪ] n comédie f; (humour) comique m
**comet** ['kɔmɪt] n comète f
**comeuppance** [kʌm'ʌpəns] n: **to get one's ~** recevoir ce qu'on mérite
**comfort** ['kʌmfət] n confort m, bien-être m; (solace) consolation f, réconfort m ▷ vt consoler, réconforter
**comfortable** ['kʌmfətəbl] adj confortable; (person) à l'aise; (financially) aisé(e); (patient) dont l'état est stationnaire; **I don't feel very ~ about it** cela m'inquiète un peu
**comfortably** ['kʌmfətəblɪ] adv (sit) confortablement; (live) à l'aise
**comforter** ['kʌmfətər] n (US) édredon m
**comforts** ['kʌmfəts] npl aises fpl
**comfort station** n (US) toilettes fpl

**comic** ['kɔmɪk] adj (also: **comical**) comique ▷ n (person) comique m; (Brit: magazine: for children) magazine m de bandes dessinées or de BD; (: for adults) illustré m
**comical** ['kɔmɪkl] adj amusant(e)
**comic book** (US) n (for children) magazine m de bandes dessinées or de BD; (for adults) illustré m
**comic strip** n bande dessinée
**coming** ['kʌmɪŋ] n arrivée f ▷ adj (next) prochain(e); (future) à venir; **in the ~ weeks** dans les prochaines semaines
**Comintern** ['kɔmɪntəːn] n Comintern m
**comma** ['kɔmə] n virgule f
**command** [kə'mɑːnd] n ordre m, commandement m; (Mil: authority) commandement; (mastery) maîtrise f; (Comput) commande f ▷ vt (troops) commander; (be able to get) (pouvoir) disposer de, avoir à sa disposition; (deserve) avoir droit à; **to ~ sb to do** donner l'ordre or commander à qn de faire; **to have/take ~ of** avoir/prendre le commandement de; **to have at one's ~** (money, resources etc) disposer de
**command economy** n économie planifiée
**commandeer** [kɔmən'dɪər] vt réquisitionner (par la force)
**commander** [kə'mɑːndər] n chef m; (Mil) commandant m
**commander-in-chief** [kə'mɑːndərɪn'tʃiːf] n (Mil) commandant m en chef
**commanding** [kə'mɑːndɪŋ] adj (appearance) imposant(e); (voice, tone) autoritaire; (lead, position) dominant(e)
**commanding officer** n commandant m
**commandment** [kə'mɑːndmənt] n (Rel) commandement m
**command module** n (Space) module m de commande
**commando** [kə'mɑːndəu] n commando m; membre m d'un commando
**commemorate** [kə'mɛməreɪt] vt commémorer
**commemoration** [kəmɛmə'reɪʃən] n commémoration f
**commemorative** [kə'mɛmərətɪv] adj commémoratif(-ive)
**commence** [kə'mɛns] vt, vi commencer
**commend** [kə'mɛnd] vt louer; (recommend) recommander
**commendable** [kə'mɛndəbl] adj louable
**commendation** [kɔmɛn'deɪʃən] n éloge m; recommandation f
**commensurate** [kə'mɛnʃərɪt] adj: ~ **with/to** en rapport avec/selon
**comment** ['kɔmɛnt] n commentaire m ▷ vi faire des remarques or commentaires; **to ~ on** faire des remarques sur; **to ~ that** faire remarquer que; **"no ~"** "je n'ai rien à déclarer"
**commentary** ['kɔməntərɪ] n commentaire m; (Sport) reportage m (en direct)
**commentator** ['kɔmənteɪtər] n commentateur m; (Sport) reporter m
**commerce** ['kɔməːs] n commerce m
**commercial** [kə'məːʃəl] adj commercial(e) ▷ n

(*Radio, TV*) annonce *f* publicitaire, spot *m* (publicitaire)

**commercial bank** *n* banque *f* d'affaires

**commercial break** *n* (*Radio, TV*) spot *m* (publicitaire)

**commercial college** *n* école *f* de commerce

**commercialism** [kə'mə:ʃəlɪzəm] *n* mercantilisme *m*

**commercial television** *n* publicité *f* à la télévision, chaînes privées (financées par la publicité)

**commercial traveller** *n* voyageur *m* de commerce

**commercial vehicle** *n* véhicule *m* utilitaire

**commiserate** [kə'mɪzəreɪt] *vi*: **to ~ with sb** témoigner de la sympathie pour qn

**commission** [kə'mɪʃən] *n* (*committee, fee*) commission *f*; (*order for work of art etc*) commande *f* ▷ *vt* (*Mil*) nommer (à un commandement); (*work of art*) commander, charger un artiste de l'exécution de; **out of ~** (*Naut*) hors de service; (*machine*) hors service; **I get 10% ~** je reçois une commission de 10%; **~ of inquiry** (*Brit*) commission d'enquête

**commissionaire** [kəmɪʃə'nɛəʳ] *n* (*Brit: at shop, cinema etc*) portier *m* (en uniforme)

**commissioner** [kə'mɪʃənəʳ] *n* membre *m* d'une commission; (*Police*) préfet *m* (de police)

**commit** [kə'mɪt] *vt* (*act*) commettre; (*resources*) consacrer; (*to sb's care*) confier (à); **to ~ o.s. (to do)** s'engager (à faire); **to ~ suicide** se suicider; **to ~ to writing** coucher par écrit; **to ~ sb for trial** traduire qn en justice

**commitment** [kə'mɪtmənt] *n* engagement *m*; (*obligation*) responsabilité(s) (*fpl*)

**committed** [kə'mɪtɪd] *adj* (*writer, politician etc*) engagé(e)

**committee** [kə'mɪtɪ] *n* comité *m*; commission *f*; **to be on a ~** siéger dans un comité *or* une commission

**committee meeting** *n* réunion *f* de comité *or* commission

**commodity** [kə'mɒdɪtɪ] *n* produit *m*, marchandise *f*, article *m*; (*food*) denrée *f*

**commodity exchange** *n* bourse *f* de marchandises

**common** ['kɒmən] *adj* (*gen*) commun(e); (*usual*) courant(e) ▷ *n* terrain communal; **in ~** en commun; **in ~ use** d'un usage courant; **it's ~ knowledge that** il est bien connu *or* notoire que; **to the ~ good** pour le bien de tous, dans l'intérêt général

**common cold** *n*: **the ~** le rhume

**common denominator** *n* dénominateur commun

**commoner** ['kɒmənəʳ] *n* roturier(-ière)

**common ground** *n* (*fig*) terrain *m* d'entente

**common land** *n* terrain communal

**common law** *n* droit coutumier

**common-law** ['kɒmənlɔ:] *adj*: **~ wife** épouse *f* de facto

**commonly** ['kɒmənlɪ] *adv* communément,

généralement; couramment

**Common Market** *n* Marché commun

**commonplace** ['kɒmənpleɪs] *adj* banal(e), ordinaire

**commonroom** ['kɒmənrum] *n* salle commune; (*Scol*) salle des professeurs

**Commons** ['kɒmənz] *npl* (*Brit Pol*): **the (House of) ~** la chambre des Communes

**common sense** *n* bon sens

**Commonwealth** ['kɒmənwɛlθ] *n*: **the ~** le Commonwealth; *voir article*

> ● **COMMONWEALTH**
>
> ● Le *Commonwealth* regroupe 50 États
> ● indépendants et plusieurs territoires qui
> ● reconnaissent tous le souverain britannique
> ● comme chef de cette association.

**commotion** [kə'məuʃən] *n* désordre *m*, tumulte *m*

**communal** ['kɒmju:nl] *adj* (*life*) communautaire; (*for common use*) commun(e)

**commune** ['kɒmju:n] *n* (*group*) communauté *f* ▷ *vi* [kə'mju:n]: **to ~ with** (*nature*) converser intimement avec; communier avec

**communicate** [kə'mju:nɪkeɪt] *vt* communiquer, transmettre ▷ *vi*: **to ~ (with)** communiquer (avec)

**communication** [kəmju:nɪ'keɪʃən] *n* communication *f*

**communication cord** *n* (*Brit*) sonnette *f* d'alarme

**communications network** *n* réseau *m* de communications

**communications satellite** *n* satellite *m* de télécommunications

**communicative** [kə'mju:nɪkətɪv] *adj* communicatif(-ive)

**communion** [kə'mju:nɪən] *n* (*also*: **Holy Communion**) communion *f*

**communism** ['kɒmjunɪzəm] *n* communisme *m*

**communist** ['kɒmjunɪst] *adj, n* communiste *m/f*

**community** [kə'mju:nɪtɪ] *n* communauté *f*

**community centre**, (*US*) **community center** *n* foyer socio-éducatif, centre *m* de loisirs

**community chest** *n* (*US*) fonds commun

**community health centre** *n* centre médico-social

**community service** *n* ≈ travail *m* d'intérêt général, TIG *m*

**community spirit** *n* solidarité *f*

**commutation ticket** [kɒmju'teɪʃən-] *n* (*US*) carte *f* d'abonnement

**commute** [kə'mju:t] *vi* faire le trajet journalier (*de son domicile à un lieu de travail assez éloigné*) ▷ *vt* (*Law*) commuer; (*Math: terms etc*) opérer la commutation de

**commuter** [kə'mju:təʳ] *n* banlieusard(e) (*qui fait un trajet journalier pour se rendre à son travail*)

**compact** *adj* [kəm'pækt] compact(e) ▷ *n* ['kɒmpækt] contrat *m*, entente *f*; (*also*: **powder**

**compact**) poudrier *m*
**compact disc** *n* disque compact
**compact disc player** *n* lecteur *m* de disques compacts
**companion** [kəm'pænjən] *n* compagnon (compagne)
**companionship** [kəm'pænjənʃɪp] *n* camaraderie *f*
**companionway** [kəm'pænjənweɪ] *n* (Naut) escalier *m* des cabines
**company** ['kʌmpənɪ] *n* (also Comm, Mil, Theat) compagnie *f*; **he's good** – il est d'une compagnie agréable; **we have** ~ nous avons de la visite; **to keep sb** ~ tenir compagnie à qn; **to part** ~ **with** se séparer de; **Smith and C**~ Smith et Compagnie
**company car** *n* voiture *f* de fonction
**company director** *n* administrateur(-trice)
**company secretary** *n* (Brit Comm) secrétaire général (d'une société)
**comparable** ['kɔmpərəbl] *adj* comparable
**comparative** [kəm'pærətɪv] *adj* (study) comparatif(-ive); (relative) relatif(-ive)
**comparatively** [kəm'pærətɪvlɪ] *adv* (relatively) relativement
**compare** [kəm'pɛəʳ] *vt*: **to** ~ **sth/sb with** *or* **to** comparer qch/qn avec *or* à ▷ *vi*: **to** ~ (**with**) se comparer (à); être comparable (à); **how do the prices** ~? comment sont les prix?, est-ce que les prix sont comparables?; **~d with** *or* **to** par rapport à
**comparison** [kəm'pærɪsn] *n* comparaison *f*; **in** ~ (**with**) en comparaison (de)
**compartment** [kəm'pɑːtmənt] *n* (also Rail) compartiment *m*; **a non-smoking** ~ un compartiment non-fumeurs
**compass** ['kʌmpəs] *n* boussole *f*; **compasses** *npl* (Math) compas *m*; **within the** ~ **of** dans les limites de
**compassion** [kəm'pæʃən] *n* compassion *f*, humanité *f*
**compassionate** [kəm'pæʃənɪt] *adj* accessible à la compassion, au cœur charitable et bienveillant; **on** ~ **grounds** pour raisons personnelles *or* de famille
**compassionate leave** *n* congé exceptionnel (pour raisons de famille)
**compatibility** [kəmpætɪ'bɪlɪtɪ] *n* compatibilité *f*
**compatible** [kəm'pætɪbl] *adj* compatible
**compel** [kəm'pɛl] *vt* contraindre, obliger
**compelling** [kəm'pɛlɪŋ] *adj* (fig: argument) irrésistible
**compendium** [kəm'pɛndɪəm] *n* (summary) abrégé *m*
**compensate** ['kɔmpənseɪt] *vt* indemniser, dédommager ▷ *vi*: **to** ~ **for** compenser
**compensation** [kɔmpən'seɪʃən] *n* compensation *f*; (money) dédommagement *m*, indemnité *f*
**compere** ['kɔmpɛəʳ] *n* présentateur(-trice), animateur(-trice)
**compete** [kəm'piːt] *vi* (take part) concourir; (vie):

**to** ~ (**with**) rivaliser (avec), faire concurrence (à)
**competence** ['kɔmpɪtəns] *n* compétence *f*, aptitude *f*
**competent** ['kɔmpɪtənt] *adj* compétent(e), capable
**competing** [kəm'piːtɪŋ] *adj* (ideas, theories) opposé(e); (companies) concurrent(e)
**competition** [kɔmpɪ'tɪʃən] *n* (contest) compétition *f*, concours *m*; (Econ) concurrence *f*; **in** ~ **with** en concurrence avec
**competitive** [kəm'pɛtɪtɪv] *adj* (Econ) concurrentiel(le); (sports) de compétition; (person) qui a l'esprit de compétition
**competitive examination** *n* concours *m*
**competitor** [kəm'pɛtɪtəʳ] *n* concurrent(e)
**compile** [kəm'paɪl] *vt* compiler
**complacency** [kəm'pleɪsnsɪ] *n* contentement *m* de soi, autosatisfaction *f*
**complacent** [kəm'pleɪsnt] *adj* (trop) content(e) de soi
**complain** [kəm'pleɪn] *vi*: **to** ~ (**about**) se plaindre (de); (in shop etc) réclamer (au sujet de) ▶ **complain of** *vt fus* (Med) se plaindre de
**complaint** [kəm'pleɪnt] *n* plainte *f*; (in shop etc) réclamation *f*; (Med) affection *f*
**complement** ['kɔmplɪmənt] *n* complément *m*; (esp of ship's crew etc) effectif complet ▷ *vt* (enhance) compléter
**complementary** [kɔmplɪ'mɛntərɪ] *adj* complémentaire
**complete** [kəm'pliːt] *adj* complet(-ète); (finished) achevé(e) ▷ *vt* achever, parachever; (set, group) compléter; (a form) remplir
**completely** [kəm'pliːtlɪ] *adv* complètement
**completion** [kəm'pliːʃən] *n* achèvement *m*; (of contract) exécution *f*; **to be nearing** ~ être presque terminé
**complex** ['kɔmplɛks] *adj* complexe ▷ *n* (Psych, buildings etc) complexe *m*
**complexion** [kəm'plɛkʃən] *n* (of face) teint *m*; (of event etc) aspect *m*, caractère *m*
**complexity** [kəm'plɛksɪtɪ] *n* complexité *f*
**compliance** [kəm'plaɪəns] *n* (submission) docilité *f*; (agreement): ~ **with** le fait de se conformer à; **in** ~ **with** en conformité avec, conformément à
**compliant** [kəm'plaɪənt] *adj* docile, très accommodant(e)
**complicate** ['kɔmplɪkeɪt] *vt* compliquer
**complicated** ['kɔmplɪkeɪtɪd] *adj* compliqué(e)
**complication** [kɔmplɪ'keɪʃən] *n* complication *f*
**compliment** *n* ['kɔmplɪmənt] compliment *m* ▷ *vt* ['kɔmplɪment] complimenter; **compliments** *npl* compliments *mpl*, hommages *mpl*; vœux *mpl*; **to pay sb a** ~ faire *or* adresser un compliment à qn; **to** ~ **sb** (**on sth/on doing sth**) féliciter qn (pour qch/de faire qch)
**complimentary** [kɔmplɪ'mɛntərɪ] *adj* flatteur(-euse); (free) à titre gracieux
**complimentary ticket** *n* billet *m* de faveur
**compliments slip** *n* fiche *f* de transmission
**comply** [kəm'plaɪ] *vi*: **to** ~ **with** se soumettre à, se conformer à

**component** [kəm'pəunənt] *adj* composant(e),
constituant(e) ▷ *n* composant *m*, élément *m*
**compose** [kəm'pəuz] *vt* composer; (*form*): **to be
~d of** se composer de; **to ~ o.s.** se calmer, se
maîtriser; **to ~ one's features** prendre une
contenance
**composed** [kəm'pəuzd] *adj* calme, posé(e)
**composer** [kəm'pəuzə'] *n* (*Mus*) compositeur *m*
**composite** ['kɔmpəzɪt] *adj* composite; (*Bot,
Math*) composé(e)
**composition** [kɔmpə'zɪʃən] *n* composition *f*
**compost** ['kɔmpɔst] *n* compost *m*
**composure** [kəm'pəuʒə'] *n* calme *m*, maîtrise *f*
de soi
**compound** ['kɔmpaund] *n* (*Chem, Ling*) composé
*m*; (*enclosure*) enclos *m*, enceinte *f* ▷ *adj*
composé(e); (*fracture*) compliqué(e) ▷ *vt*
[kəm'paund] (*fig: problem etc*) aggraver
**compound fracture** *n* fracture compliquée
**compound interest** *n* intérêt composé
**comprehend** [kɔmprɪ'hɛnd] *vt* comprendre
**comprehension** [kɔmprɪ'hɛnʃən] *n*
compréhension *f*
**comprehensive** [kɔmprɪ'hɛnsɪv] *adj* (très)
complet(-ète); **~ policy** (*Insurance*) assurance *f*
tous risques
**comprehensive** [kɔmprɪ'hɛnsɪv],
**comprehensive school** *n* (*Brit*) *école secondaire
non sélective avec libre circulation d'une section à l'autre*,
≈ CES *m*
**compress** *vt* [kəm'prɛs] comprimer; (*text,
information*) condenser ▷ *n* ['kɔmprɛs] (*Med*)
compresse *f*
**compression** [kəm'prɛʃən] *n* compression *f*
**comprise** [kəm'praɪz] *vt* (*also*: **be comprised of**)
comprendre; (*constitute*) constituer, représenter
**compromise** ['kɔmprəmaɪz] *n* compromis *m*
▷ *vt* compromettre ▷ *vi* transiger, accepter un
compromis ▷ *cpd* (*decision, solution*) de
compromis
**compulsion** [kəm'pʌlʃən] *n* contrainte *f*, force *f*;
**under ~** sous la contrainte
**compulsive** [kəm'pʌlsɪv] *adj* (*Psych*)
compulsif(-ive); (*book, film etc*) captivant(e);
**he's a ~ smoker** c'est un fumeur invétéré
**compulsory** [kəm'pʌlsərɪ] *adj* obligatoire
**compulsory purchase** *n* expropriation *f*
**compunction** [kəm'pʌŋkʃən] *n* scrupule *m*; **to
have no ~ about doing sth** n'avoir aucun
scrupule à faire qch
**computer** [kəm'pju:tə'] *n* ordinateur *m*;
(*mechanical*) calculatrice *f*
**computer game** *n* jeu *m* vidéo
**computer-generated** [kəm'pju:tə'dʒɛnəreɪtɪd]
*adj* de synthèse
**computerize** [kəm'pju:təraɪz] *vt* (*data*) traiter
par ordinateur; (*system, office*) informatiser
**computer language** *n* langage *m* machine *or*
informatique
**computer literate** *adj* initié(e) à l'informatique
**computer peripheral** *n* périphérique *m*
**computer program** *n* programme *m*

informatique
**computer programmer** *n*
programmeur(-euse)
**computer programming** *n* programmation *f*
**computer science** *n* informatique *f*
**computer scientist** *n* informaticien(ne)
**computer studies** *npl* informatique *f*
**computing** [kəm'pju:tɪŋ] *n* informatique *f*
**comrade** ['kɔmrɪd] *n* camarade *m/f*
**comradeship** ['kɔmrɪdʃɪp] *n* camaraderie *f*
**Comsat** ['kɔmsæt] *n abbr* = **communications
satellite**
**con** [kɔn] *vt* duper; (*cheat*) escroquer ▷ *n*
escroquerie *f*; **to ~ sb into doing sth** tromper
qn pour lui faire faire qch
**concave** ['kɔn'keɪv] *adj* concave
**conceal** [kən'si:l] *vt* cacher, dissimuler
**concede** [kən'si:d] *vt* concéder ▷ *vi* céder
**conceit** [kən'si:t] *n* vanité *f*, suffisance *f*,
prétention *f*
**conceited** [kən'si:tɪd] *adj* vaniteux(-euse),
suffisant(e)
**conceivable** [kən'si:vəbl] *adj* concevable,
imaginable; **it is ~ that** il est concevable que
**conceivably** [kən'si:vəblɪ] *adv*: **he may ~ be
right** il n'est pas impossible qu'il ait raison
**conceive** [kən'si:v] *vt, vi* concevoir; **to ~ of sth/
of doing sth** imaginer qch/de faire qch
**concentrate** ['kɔnsəntreɪt] *vi* se concentrer ▷ *vt*
concentrer
**concentration** [kɔnsən'treɪʃən] *n*
concentration *f*
**concentration camp** *n* camp *m* de
concentration
**concentric** [kɔn'sɛntrɪk] *adj* concentrique
**concept** ['kɔnsɛpt] *n* concept *m*
**conception** [kən'sɛpʃən] *n* conception *f*; (*idea*)
idée *f*
**concern** [kən'sə:n] *n* affaire *f*; (*Comm*) entreprise
*f*, firme *f*; (*anxiety*) inquiétude *f*, souci *m* ▷ *vt*
(*worry*) inquiéter; (*involve*) concerner; (*relate to*) se
rapporter à; **to be ~ed (about)** s'inquiéter (de),
être inquiet(-ète) (au sujet de); **"to whom it
may ~"** "à qui de droit"; **as far as I am ~ed** en
ce qui me concerne; **to be ~ed with** (*person:
involved with*) s'occuper de; **the department ~ed**
(*under discussion*) le service en question; (*involved*)
le service concerné
**concerning** [kən'sə:nɪŋ] *prep* en ce qui
concerne, à propos de
**concert** ['kɔnsət] *n* concert *m*; **in ~** à l'unisson,
en chœur; ensemble
**concerted** [kən'sə:tɪd] *adj* concerté(e)
**concert hall** *n* salle *f* de concert
**concertina** [kɔnsə'ti:nə] *n* concertina *m* ▷ *vi* se
télescoper, se caramboler
**concerto** [kən'tʃə:təu] *n* concerto *m*
**concession** [kən'sɛʃən] *n* (*compromise*)
concession *f*; (*reduced price*) réduction *f*; **tax ~**
dégrèvement fiscal; **"~s"** tarif réduit
**concessionaire** [kənsɛʃə'nɛə'] *n*
concessionnaire *m/f*

517

**concessionary** [kən'sɛʃənrɪ] *adj* (*ticket, fare*) à tarif réduit

**conciliation** [kənsɪlɪ'eɪʃən] *n* conciliation *f*, apaisement *m*

**conciliatory** [kən'sɪlɪətrɪ] *adj* conciliateur(-trice); conciliant(e)

**concise** [kən'saɪs] *adj* concis(e)

**conclave** ['kɒnkleɪv] *n* assemblée secrète; (*Rel*) conclave *m*

**conclude** [kən'kluːd] *vt* conclure ▷ *vi* (*speaker*) conclure; (*events*): **to ~ (with)** se terminer (par)

**concluding** [kən'kluːdɪŋ] *adj* (*remarks etc*) final(e)

**conclusion** [kən'kluːʒən] *n* conclusion *f*; **to come to the ~ that** (en) conclure que

**conclusive** [kən'kluːsɪv] *adj* concluant(e), définitif(-ive)

**concoct** [kən'kɒkt] *vt* confectionner, composer

**concoction** [kən'kɒkʃən] *n* (*food, drink*) mélange *m*

**concord** ['kɒŋkɔːd] *n* (*harmony*) harmonie *f*; (*treaty*) accord *m*

**concourse** ['kɒŋkɔːs] *n* (*hall*) hall *m*, salle *f* des pas perdus; (*crowd*) affluence *f*; multitude *f*

**concrete** ['kɒŋkriːt] *n* béton *m* ▷ *adj* concret(-ète); (*Constr*) en béton

**concrete mixer** *n* bétonnière *f*

**concur** [kən'kəːʳ] *vi* être d'accord

**concurrently** [kən'kʌrntlɪ] *adv* simultanément

**concussion** [kən'kʌʃən] *n* (*Med*) commotion (cérébrale)

**condemn** [kən'dɛm] *vt* condamner

**condemnation** [kɒndɛm'neɪʃən] *n* condamnation *f*

**condensation** [kɒndɛn'seɪʃən] *n* condensation *f*

**condense** [kən'dɛns] *vi* se condenser ▷ *vt* condenser

**condensed milk** [kən'dɛnst-] *n* lait concentré (sucré)

**condescend** [kɒndɪ'sɛnd] *vi* condescendre, s'abaisser; **to ~ to do sth** daigner faire qch

**condescending** [kɒndɪ'sɛndɪŋ] *adj* condescendant(e)

**condition** [kən'dɪʃən] *n* condition *f*; (*disease*) maladie *f* ▷ *vt* déterminer, conditionner; **in good/poor ~** en bon/mauvais état; **a heart ~** une maladie cardiaque; **weather ~s** conditions *fpl* météorologiques; **on ~ that** à condition que + *sub*, à condition de

**conditional** [kən'dɪʃənl] *adj* conditionnel(le); **to be ~ upon** dépendre de

**conditioner** [kən'dɪʃənəʳ] *n* (*for hair*) baume démêlant; (*for fabrics*) assouplissant *m*

**condo** ['kɒndəu] *n* (*US inf*) = **condominium**

**condolences** [kən'dəulənsɪz] *npl* condoléances *fpl*

**condom** ['kɒndəm] *n* préservatif *m*

**condominium** [kɒndə'mɪnɪəm] *n* (*US: building*) immeuble *m* (en copropriété); (*: rooms*) appartement *m* (dans un immeuble en copropriété)

**condone** [kən'dəun] *vt* fermer les yeux sur, approuver (tacitement)

**conducive** [kən'djuːsɪv] *adj*: **~ to** favorable à, qui contribue à

**conduct** *n* ['kɒndʌkt] conduite *f* ▷ *vt* [kən'dʌkt] conduire; (*manage*) mener, diriger; (*Mus*) diriger; **to ~ o.s.** se conduire, se comporter

**conductor** [kən'dʌktəʳ] *n* (*of orchestra*) chef *m* d'orchestre; (*on bus*) receveur *m*; (*US: on train*) chef *m* de train; (*Elec*) conducteur *m*

**conductress** [kən'dʌktrɪs] *n* (*on bus*) receveuse *f*

**conduit** ['kɒndɪt] *n* conduit *m*, tuyau *m*; tube *m*

**cone** [kəun] *n* cône *m*; (*for ice-cream*) cornet *m*; (*Bot*) pomme *f* de pin, cône

**confectioner** [kən'fɛkʃənəʳ] *n* (*of cakes*) pâtissier(-ière); (*of sweets*) confiseur(-euse); **~'s (shop)** confiserie(-pâtisserie) *f*

**confectionery** [kən'fɛkʃənrɪ] *n* (*sweets*) confiserie *f*; (*cakes*) pâtisserie *f*

**confederate** [kən'fedrɪt] *adj* confédéré(e) ▷ *n* (*pej*) acolyte *m*; (*US History*) confédéré(e)

**confederation** [kənfedə'reɪʃən] *n* confédération *f*

**confer** [kən'fəːʳ] *vt*: **to ~ sth on** conférer qch à ▷ *vi* conférer, s'entretenir; **to ~ (with sb about sth)** s'entretenir (de qch avec qn)

**conference** ['kɒnfərns] *n* conférence *f*; **to be in ~** être en réunion *or* en conférence

**conference room** *n* salle *f* de conférence

**confess** [kən'fɛs] *vt* confesser, avouer ▷ *vi* (*admit sth*) avouer; (*Rel*) se confesser

**confession** [kən'fɛʃən] *n* confession *f*

**confessional** [kən'fɛʃənl] *n* confessional *m*

**confessor** [kən'fɛsəʳ] *n* confesseur *m*

**confetti** [kən'fɛtɪ] *n* confettis *mpl*

**confide** [kən'faɪd] *vi*: **to ~ in** s'ouvrir à, se confier à

**confidence** ['kɒnfɪdns] *n* confiance *f*; (*also:* **self-confidence**) assurance *f*, confiance en soi; (*secret*) confidence *f*; **to have (every) ~ that** être certain que; **motion of no ~** motion *f* de censure; **in ~** (*speak, write*) en confidence, confidentiellement; **to tell sb sth in strict ~** dire qch à qn en toute confidence

**confidence trick** *n* escroquerie *f*

**confident** ['kɒnfɪdənt] *adj* (*self-assured*) sûr(e) de soi; (*sure*) sûr

**confidential** [kɒnfɪ'dɛnʃəl] *adj* confidentiel(le); (*secretary*) particulier(-ère)

**confidentiality** ['kɒnfɪdɛnʃɪ'ælɪtɪ] *n* confidentialité *f*

**configuration** [kən'fɪgju'reɪʃən] *n* (*also Comput*) configuration *f*

**confine** [kən'faɪn] *vt* limiter, borner; (*shut up*) confiner, enfermer; **to ~ o.s. to doing sth/to sth** se contenter de faire qch/se limiter à qch

**confined** [kən'faɪnd] *adj* (*space*) restreint(e), réduit(e)

**confinement** [kən'faɪnmənt] *n* emprisonnement *m*, détention *f*; (*Mil*) consigne *f* (au quartier); (*Med*) accouchement *m*

**confines** ['kɒnfaɪnz] *npl* confins *mpl*, bornes *fpl*

**confirm** [kən'fəːm] *vt* (*report, Rel*) confirmer; (*appointment*) ratifier

**confirmation** [kɔnfə'meɪʃən] n confirmation f; ratification f
**confirmed** [kən'fə:md] adj invétéré(e), incorrigible
**confiscate** ['kɔnfɪskeɪt] vt confisquer
**confiscation** [kɔnfɪs'keɪʃən] n confiscation f
**conflagration** [kɔnflə'greɪʃən] n incendie m; (fig) conflagration f
**conflict** n ['kɔnflɪkt] conflit m, lutte f ▷ vi [kən'flɪkt] être or entrer en conflit; (opinions) s'opposer, se heurter
**conflicting** [kən'flɪktɪŋ] adj contradictoire
**conform** [kən'fɔ:m] vi: **to ~ (to)** se conformer (à)
**conformist** [kən'fɔ:mɪst] n (gen, Rel) conformiste m/f
**confound** [kən'faund] vt confondre; (amaze) rendre perplexe
**confounded** [kən'faundɪd] adj maudit(e), sacré(e)
**confront** [kən'frʌnt] vt (two people) confronter; (enemy, danger) affronter, faire face à; (problem) faire face à
**confrontation** [kɔnfrən'teɪʃən] n confrontation f
**confrontational** [kɔnfrən'teɪʃənl] adj conflictuel(le)
**confuse** [kən'fju:z] vt (person) troubler; (situation) embrouiller; (one thing with another) confondre
**confused** [kən'fju:zd] adj (person) dérouté(e), désorienté(e); (situation) embrouillé(e)
**confusing** [kən'fju:zɪŋ] adj peu clair(e), déroutant(e)
**confusion** [kən'fju:ʒən] n confusion f
**congeal** [kən'dʒi:l] vi (oil) se figer; (blood) se coaguler
**congenial** [kən'dʒi:nɪəl] adj sympathique, agréable
**congenital** [kən'dʒɛnɪtl] adj congénital(e)
**conger eel** ['kɔŋgər-] n congre m, anguille f de roche
**congested** [kən'dʒɛstɪd] adj (Med) congestionné(e); (fig) surpeuplé(e); congestionné; bloqué(e); (telephone lines) encombré(e)
**congestion** [kən'dʒɛstʃən] n (Med) congestion f; (fig: traffic) encombrement m
**conglomerate** [kən'glɔmərɪt] n (Comm) conglomérat m
**conglomeration** [kənglɔmə'reɪʃən] n groupement m; agglomération f
**Congo** ['kɔŋgəu] n (state) (république f du) Congo
**congratulate** [kən'grætjuleɪt] vt: **to ~ sb (on)** féliciter qn (de)
**congratulations** [kəngrætju'leɪʃənz] npl: **~ (on)** félicitations fpl (pour) ▷ excl: **~!** (toutes mes) félicitations!
**congregate** ['kɔŋgrɪgeɪt] vi se rassembler, se réunir
**congregation** [kɔŋgrɪ'geɪʃən] n assemblée f (des fidèles)
**congress** ['kɔŋgrɛs] n congrès m; (Pol): **C~**

Congrès m; voir article

● **Congress**
●
● Le Congress est le parlement des États-Unis. Il
● comprend la "House of Representatives" et
● le "Senate". Représentants et sénateurs sont
● élus au suffrage universel direct. Le Congrès
● se réunit au "Capitol", à Washington.

**congressman** ['kɔŋgrɛsmən] (irreg) n membre m du Congrès
**congresswoman** ['kɔŋgrɛswumən] (irreg) n membre m du Congrès
**conical** ['kɔnɪkl] adj (de forme) conique
**conifer** ['kɔnɪfər] n conifère m
**coniferous** [kə'nɪfərəs] adj (forest) de conifères
**conjecture** [kən'dʒɛktʃər] n conjecture f ▷ vt, vi conjecturer
**conjugal** ['kɔndʒugl] adj conjugal(e)
**conjugate** ['kɔndʒugeɪt] vt conjuguer
**conjugation** [kɔndʒə'geɪʃən] n conjugaison f
**conjunction** [kən'dʒʌŋkʃən] n conjonction f; **in ~ with** (conjointement) avec
**conjunctivitis** [kəndʒʌŋktɪ'vaɪtɪs] n conjonctivite f
**conjure** ['kʌndʒər] vt faire apparaître (par la prestidigitation) [kən'dʒuər] conjurer, supplier ▷ vi faire des tours de passe-passe
▶ **conjure up** vt (ghost, spirit) faire apparaître; (memories) évoquer
**conjurer** ['kʌndʒərər] n prestidigitateur m, illusionniste m/f
**conjuring trick** ['kʌndʒərɪŋ-] n tour m de prestidigitation
**conker** ['kɔŋkər] n (Brit) marron m (d'Inde)
**conk out** [kɔŋk-] vi (inf) tomber or rester en panne
**conman** ['kɔnmæn] (irreg) n escroc m
**Conn.** abbr (US) = **Connecticut**
**connect** [kə'nɛkt] vt joindre, relier; (Elec) connecter; (Tel: caller) mettre en connexion; (: subscriber) brancher; (fig) établir un rapport entre, faire un rapprochement entre ▷ vi (train): **to ~ with** assurer la correspondance avec; **to be ~ed with** avoir un rapport avec; (have dealings with) avoir des rapports avec, être en relation avec; **I am trying to ~ you** (Tel) j'essaie d'obtenir votre communication
**connecting flight** n (vol m de) correspondance f
**connection** [kə'nɛkʃən] n relation f, lien m; (Elec) connexion f; (Tel) communication f; (train etc) correspondance f; **in ~ with** à propos de; **what is the ~ between them?** quel est le lien entre eux?; **business ~s** relations d'affaires; **to miss/get one's ~** (train etc) rater/avoir sa correspondance
**connexion** [kə'nɛkʃən] n (Brit) = **connection**
**conning tower** ['kɔnɪŋ-] n kiosque m (de sous-marin)
**connive** [kə'naɪv] vi: **to ~ at** se faire le complice de

**connoisseur** [kɔnɪ'səːʳ] *n* connaisseur *m*
**connotation** [kɔnə'teɪʃən] *n* connotation *f*, implication *f*
**connubial** [kə'njuːbɪəl] *adj* conjugal(e)
**conquer** ['kɔŋkəʳ] *vt* conquérir; *(feelings)* vaincre, surmonter
**conqueror** ['kɔŋkərəʳ] *n* conquérant *m*, vainqueur *m*
**conquest** ['kɔŋkwɛst] *n* conquête *f*
**cons** [kɔnz] *npl see* **convenience; pro**
**conscience** ['kɔnʃəns] *n* conscience *f*; **in all** ~ en conscience
**conscientious** [kɔnʃɪ'ɛnʃəs] *adj* consciencieux(-euse); *(scruple, objection)* de conscience
**conscientious objector** *n* objecteur *m* de conscience
**conscious** ['kɔnʃəs] *adj* conscient(e); *(deliberate: insult, error)* délibéré(e); **to become ~ of sth/ that** prendre conscience de qch/que
**consciousness** ['kɔnʃəsnɪs] *n* conscience *f*; *(Med)* connaissance *f*; **to lose/regain ~** perdre/ reprendre connaissance
**conscript** ['kɔnskrɪpt] *n* conscrit *m*
**conscription** [kən'skrɪpʃən] *n* conscription *f*
**consecrate** ['kɔnsɪkreɪt] *vt* consacrer
**consecutive** [kən'sɛkjutɪv] *adj* consécutif(-ive); **on three ~ occasions** trois fois de suite
**consensus** [kən'sɛnsəs] *n* consensus *m*; **the ~ (of opinion)** le consensus (d'opinion)
**consent** [kən'sɛnt] *n* consentement *m* ▷ *vi*: **to ~ (to)** consentir (à); **age of ~** âge nubile (légal); **by common ~** d'un commun accord
**consenting adults** [kən'sɛntɪŋ-] *npl* personnes consentantes
**consequence** ['kɔnsɪkwəns] *n* suites *fpl*, conséquence *f*; *(significance)* importance *f*; **in ~** en conséquence, par conséquent
**consequently** ['kɔnsɪkwəntlɪ] *adv* par conséquent, donc
**conservation** [kɔnsə'veɪʃən] *n* préservation *f*, protection *f*; *(also:* **nature conservation**) défense *f* de l'environnement; **energy ~** économies *fpl* d'énergie
**conservationist** [kɔnsə'veɪʃnɪst] *n* protecteur(-trice) de la nature
**conservative** [kən'sə:vətɪv] *adj* conservateur(-trice); *(cautious)* prudent(e)
**Conservative** [kən'sə:vətɪv] *adj, n* (Brit Pol) conservateur(-trice); **the ~ Party** le parti conservateur
**conservatory** [kən'sə:vətrɪ] *n* (room) jardin *m* d'hiver; *(Mus)* conservatoire *m*
**conserve** [kən'sə:v] *vt* conserver, préserver; *(supplies, energy)* économiser ▷ *n* confiture *f*, conserve *f* (de fruits)
**consider** [kən'sɪdəʳ] *vt* (study) considérer, réfléchir à; *(take into account)* penser à, prendre en considération; *(regard, judge)* considérer, estimer; **to ~ doing sth** envisager de faire qch; **~ yourself lucky** estimez-vous heureux; **all things ~ed** (toute) réflexion faite

**considerable** [kən'sɪdərəbl] *adj* considérable
**considerably** [kən'sɪdərəblɪ] *adv* nettement
**considerate** [kən'sɪdərɪt] *adj* prévenant(e), plein(e) d'égards
**consideration** [kənsɪdə'reɪʃən] *n* considération *f*; *(reward)* rétribution *f*, rémunération *f*; **out of ~ for** par égard pour; **under ~** à l'étude; **my first ~ is my family** ma famille passe avant tout le reste
**considered** [kən'sɪdəd] *adj*: **it is my ~ opinion that ...** après avoir mûrement réfléchi, je pense que ...
**considering** [kən'sɪdərɪŋ] *prep*: **~ (that)** étant donné (que)
**consign** [kən'saɪn] *vt* expédier, livrer
**consignee** [kɔnsaɪ'ni:] *n* destinataire *m/f*
**consignment** [kən'saɪnmənt] *n* arrivage *m*, envoi *m*
**consignment note** *n* (Comm) bordereau *m* d'expédition
**consignor** [kən'saɪnəʳ] *n* expéditeur(-trice)
**consist** [kən'sɪst] *vi*: **to ~ of** consister en, se composer de
**consistency** [kən'sɪstənsɪ] *n* (thickness) consistance *f*; (fig) cohérence *f*
**consistent** [kən'sɪstənt] *adj* logique, cohérent(e); **~ with** compatible avec, en accord avec
**consolation** [kɔnsə'leɪʃən] *n* consolation *f*
**console¹** [kən'səul] *vt* consoler
**console²** ['kɔnsəul] *n* console *f*
**consolidate** [kən'sɔlɪdeɪt] *vt* consolider
**consols** ['kɔnsɔlz] *npl* (Brit Stock Exchange) rente *f* d'État
**consommé** [kən'sɔmeɪ] *n* consommé *m*
**consonant** ['kɔnsənənt] *n* consonne *f*
**consort** ['kɔnsɔ:t] *n* époux (épouse); **prince ~** prince *m* consort ▷ *vi* [kən'sɔ:t] *(often pej)*: **to ~ with sb** frayer avec qn
**consortium** [kən'sɔ:tɪəm] *n* consortium *m*, comptoir *m*
**conspicuous** [kən'spɪkjuəs] *adj* voyant(e), qui attire l'attention; **to make o.s. ~** se faire remarquer
**conspiracy** [kən'spɪrəsɪ] *n* conspiration *f*, complot *m*
**conspiratorial** [kən'spɪrə'tɔ:rɪəl] *adj* (behaviour) de conspirateur; (glance) conspirateur(-trice)
**conspire** [kən'spaɪəʳ] *vi* conspirer, comploter
**constable** ['kʌnstəbl] *n* (Brit) ≈ agent *m* de police, gendarme *m*; **chief ~** ≈ préfet *m* de police
**constabulary** [kən'stæbjulərɪ] *n* ≈ police *f*, gendarmerie *f*
**constant** ['kɔnstənt] *adj* constant(e); incessant(e)
**constantly** ['kɔnstəntlɪ] *adv* constamment, sans cesse
**constellation** [kɔnstə'leɪʃən] *n* constellation *f*
**consternation** [kɔnstə'neɪʃən] *n* consternation *f*
**constipated** ['kɔnstɪpeɪtɪd] *adj* constipé(e)
**constipation** [kɔnstɪ'peɪʃən] *n* constipation *f*

**constituency** [kən'stɪtjuənsɪ] n (Pol: area) circonscription électorale; (: electors) électorat m; voir article

**constituency party** n section locale (d'un parti)

**constituent** [kən'stɪtjuənt] n électeur(-trice); (part) élément constitutif, composant m

**constitute** ['kɒnstɪtjuːt] vt constituer

**constitution** [kɒnstɪ'tjuːʃən] n constitution f

**constitutional** [kɒnstɪ'tjuːʃnl] adj constitutionnel(le)

**constitutional monarchy** n monarchie constitutionnelle

**constrain** [kən'streɪn] vt contraindre, forcer

**constrained** [kən'streɪnd] adj contraint(e), gêné(e)

**constraint** [kən'streɪnt] n contrainte f; (embarrassment) gêne f

**constrict** [kən'strɪkt] vt rétrécir, resserrer; gêner, limiter

**construct** [kən'strʌkt] vt construire

**construction** [kən'strʌkʃən] n construction f; (fig: interpretation) interprétation f; **under ~** (building etc) en construction

**construction industry** n (industrie f du) bâtiment

**constructive** [kən'strʌktɪv] adj constructif(-ive)

**construe** [kən'struː] vt analyser, expliquer

**consul** ['kɒnsl] n consul m

**consulate** ['kɒnsjulɪt] n consulat m

**consult** [kən'sʌlt] vt consulter; **to ~ sb (about sth)** consulter qn (à propos de qch)

**consultancy** [kən'sʌltənsɪ] n service m de conseils

**consultancy fee** n honoraires mpl d'expert

**consultant** [kən'sʌltənt] n (Med) médecin consultant; (other specialist) consultant m, (expert-)conseil m ▷ cpd: **~ engineer** n ingénieur-conseil m; **~ paediatrician** n pédiatre m; **legal/management ~** conseiller m juridique/en gestion

**consultation** [kɒnsəl'teɪʃən] n consultation f; **in ~ with** en consultation avec

**consultative** [kən'sʌltətɪv] adj consultatif(-ive)

**consulting room** [kən'sʌltɪŋ-] n (Brit) cabinet m de consultation

**consume** [kən'sjuːm] vt consommer; (subj: flames, hatred, desire) consumer; **to be ~d with hatred** être dévoré par la haine; **to be ~d with desire** brûler de désir

**consumer** [kən'sjuːmər] n consommateur(-trice); (of electricity, gas etc) usager m

**consumer credit** n crédit m aux consommateurs

**consumer durables** npl biens mpl de consommation durables

**consumer goods** npl biens mpl de consommation

**consumerism** [kən'sjuːmərɪzəm] n (consumer protection) défense f du consommateur; (Econ) consumérisme m

**consumer society** n société f de consommation

**consumer watchdog** n organisme m pour la défense des consommateurs

**consummate** ['kɒnsʌmeɪt] vt consommer

**consumption** [kən'sʌmpʃən] n consommation f; **not fit for human ~** non comestible

**cont.** abbr (= continued) suite

**contact** ['kɒntækt] n contact m; (person) connaissance f, relation f ▷ vt se mettre en contact or en rapport avec; **to be in ~ with sb/sth** être en contact avec qn/qch; **business ~s** relations fpl d'affaires, contacts mpl

**contact lenses** npl verres mpl de contact

**contagious** [kən'teɪdʒəs] adj contagieux(-euse)

**contain** [kən'teɪn] vt contenir; **to ~ o.s.** se contenir, se maîtriser

**container** [kən'teɪnər] n récipient m; (for shipping etc) conteneur m

**containerize** [kən'teɪnəraɪz] vt conteneuriser

**container ship** n porte-conteneurs m inv

**contaminate** [kən'tæmɪneɪt] vt contaminer

**contamination** [kəntæmɪ'neɪʃən] n contamination f

**cont'd** abbr (= continued) suite

**contemplate** ['kɒntəmpleɪt] vt contempler; (consider) envisager

**contemplation** [kɒntəm'pleɪʃən] n contemplation f

**contemporary** [kən'tɛmpərərɪ] adj contemporain(e); (design, wallpaper) moderne ▷ n contemporain(e)

**contempt** [kən'tɛmpt] n mépris m, dédain m; **~ of court** (Law) outrage m à l'autorité de la justice

**contemptible** [kən'tɛmptəbl] adj méprisable, vil(e)

**contemptuous** [kən'tɛmptjuəs] adj dédaigneux(-euse), méprisant(e)

**contend** [kən'tɛnd] vt: **to ~ that** soutenir or prétendre que ▷ vi: **to ~ with** (compete) rivaliser avec; (struggle) lutter avec; **to have to ~ with** (be faced with) avoir affaire à, être aux prises avec

**contender** [kən'tɛndər] n prétendant(e); candidat(e)

**content** [kən'tɛnt] adj content(e), satisfait(e) ▷ vt contenter, satisfaire ▷ n ['kɒntɛnt] contenu m; (of fat, moisture) teneur f; **contents** npl (of container etc) contenu m; **(table of) ~s** table f des matières; **to be ~ with** se contenter de; **to ~ o.s. with sth/with doing sth** se contenter de qch/de faire qch

**contented** [kən'tɛntɪd] *adj* content(e),
satisfait(e)

**contentedly** [kən'tɛntɪdlɪ] *adv* avec un
sentiment de (profonde) satisfaction

**contention** [kən'tɛnʃən] *n* dispute *f*,
contestation *f*; (*argument*) assertion *f*,
affirmation *f*; **bone of ~** sujet *m* de discorde

**contentious** [kən'tɛnʃəs] *adj* querelleur(-euse);
litigieux(-euse)

**contentment** [kən'tɛntmənt] *n* contentement
*m*, satisfaction *f*

**contest** *n* ['kɔntɛst] combat *m*, lutte *f*;
(*competition*) concours *m* ▷ *vt* [kən'tɛst]
contester, discuter; (*compete for*) disputer; (*Law*)
attaquer

**contestant** [kən'tɛstənt] *n* concurrent(e); (*in
fight*) adversaire *m/f*

**context** ['kɔntɛkst] *n* contexte *m*; **in/out of ~**
dans le/hors contexte

**continent** ['kɔntɪnənt] *n* continent *m*; **the C~**
(Brit) l'Europe continentale; **on the C~** en
Europe (continentale)

**continental** [kɔntɪ'nɛntl] *adj* continental(e) ▷ *n*
(Brit) Européen(ne) (continental(e))

**continental breakfast** *n* café (*or* thé) complet

**continental quilt** *n* (Brit) couette *f*

**contingency** [kən'tɪndʒənsɪ] *n* éventualité *f*,
événement imprévu

**contingency plan** *n* plan *m* d'urgence

**contingent** [kən'tɪndʒənt] *adj* contingent(e)
▷ *n* contingent *m*; **to be ~ upon** dépendre de

**continual** [kən'tɪnjuəl] *adj* continuel(le)

**continually** [kən'tɪnjuəlɪ] *adv* continuellement,
sans cesse

**continuation** [kəntɪnju'eɪʃən] *n* continuation *f*;
(*after interruption*) reprise *f*; (*of story*) suite *f*

**continue** [kən'tɪnju:] *vi* continuer ▷ *vt*
continuer; (*start again*) reprendre; **to be ~d**
(*story*) à suivre; **~d on page 10** suite page 10

**continuing education** [kən'tɪnjuɪŋ-] *n*
formation permanente *or* continue

**continuity** [kɔntɪ'nju:ɪtɪ] *n* continuité *f*; (TV)
enchaînement *m*; (Cine) script *m*

**continuity girl** *n* (Cine) script-girl *f*

**continuous** [kən'tɪnjuəs] *adj* continu(e),
permanent(e); (Ling) progressif(-ive); **~
performance** (Cine) séance permanente; **~
stationery** (Comput) papier *m* en continu

**continuous assessment** (Brit) *n* contrôle
continu

**continuously** [kən'tɪnjuəslɪ] *adv* (*repeatedly*)
continuellement; (*uninterruptedly*) sans
interruption

**contort** [kən'tɔ:t] *vt* tordre, crisper

**contortion** [kən'tɔ:ʃən] *n* crispation *f*, torsion *f*;
(*of acrobat*) contorsion *f*

**contortionist** [kən'tɔ:ʃənɪst] *n* contorsionniste
*m/f*

**contour** ['kɔntuə'] *n* contour *m*, profil *m*; (*also:*
**contour line**) courbe *f* de niveau

**contraband** ['kɔntrəbænd] *n* contrebande *f*

▷ *adj* de contrebande

**contraception** [kɔntrə'sɛpʃən] *n*
contraception *f*

**contraceptive** [kɔntrə'sɛptɪv] *adj*
contraceptif(-ive), anticonceptionnel(le) ▷ *n*
contraceptif *m*

**contract** [*n, cpd* 'kɔntrækt, *vb* kən'trækt] *n*
contrat *m* ▷ *cpd* (*price, date*) contractuel(le);
(*work*) à forfait ▷ *vi* (*become smaller*) se contracter,
se resserrer ▷ *vt* contracter; (Comm): **to ~ to do
sth** s'engager (par contrat) à faire qch; **~ of
employment/service** contrat de travail/de
service

▶ **contract in** *vi* s'engager (par contrat); (Brit
Admin) s'affilier au régime de retraite
complémentaire

▶ **contract out** *vi* se dégager; (Brit Admin) opter
pour la non-affiliation au régime de retraite
complémentaire

**contraction** [kən'trækʃən] *n* contraction *f*;
(Ling) forme contractée

**contractor** [kən'træktə'] *n* entrepreneur *m*

**contractual** [kən'træktʃuəl] *adj* contractuel(le)

**contradict** [kɔntrə'dɪkt] *vt* contredire; (*be
contrary to*) démentir, être en contradiction avec

**contradiction** [kɔntrə'dɪkʃən] *n* contradiction *f*;
**to be in ~ with** contredire, être en
contradiction avec

**contradictory** [kɔntrə'dɪktərɪ] *adj*
contradictoire

**contraflow** ['kɔntrəfləu] *n* (Aut): **~ lane** voie *f* à
contresens; **there's a ~ system in operation
on** ... une voie a été mise en sens inverse sur ...

**contralto** [kən'træltəu] *n* contralto *m*

**contraption** [kən'træpʃən] *n* (*pej*) machin *m*,
truc *m*

**contrary¹** ['kɔntrərɪ] *adj* contraire, opposé(e) ▷ *n*
contraire *m*; **on the ~** au contraire; **unless you
hear to the ~** sauf avis contraire; **~ to what we
thought** contrairement à ce que nous pensions

**contrary²** [kən'trɛərɪ] *adj* (*perverse*)
contrariant(e), entêté(e)

**contrast** *n* ['kɔntrɑ:st] contraste *m* ▷ *vt* [kən'trɑ:
st] mettre en contraste, contraster; **in ~ to** *or*
**with** contrairement à, par opposition à

**contrasting** [kən'trɑ:stɪŋ] *adj* opposé(e),
contrasté(e)

**contravene** [kɔntrə'vi:n] *vt* enfreindre, violer,
contrevenir à

**contravention** [kɔntrə'vɛnʃən] *n*: **~ (of)**
infraction *f* (à)

**contribute** [kən'trɪbju:t] *vi* contribuer ▷ *vt*: **to ~
£10/an article to** donner 10 livres/un article à;
**to ~ to** (*gen*) contribuer à; (*newspaper*) collaborer
à; (*discussion*) prendre part à

**contribution** [kɔntrɪ'bju:ʃən] *n* contribution *f*;
(Brit: *for social security*) cotisation *f*; (*to publication*)
article *m*

**contributor** [kən'trɪbjutə'] *n* (*to newspaper*)
collaborateur(-trice); (*of money, goods*)
donateur(-trice)

**contributory** [kən'trɪbjutərɪ] *adj* (*cause*) annexe;

it was a ~ **factor in** ... ce facteur a contribué à ...
**contributory pension scheme** n (Brit)
régime m de retraite salariale
**contrite** ['kɔntraɪt] adj contrit(e)
**contrivance** [kən'traɪvəns] n (scheme)
machination f, combinaison f; (device) appareil
m, dispositif m
**contrive** [kən'traɪv] vt combiner, inventer ▷ vi:
**to ~ to do** s'arranger pour faire, trouver le
moyen de faire
**control** [kən'trəul] vt (process, machinery)
commander; (temper) maîtriser; (disease)
enrayer; (check) contrôler ▷ n maîtrise f; (power)
autorité f; **controls** npl (of machine etc)
commandes fpl; (on radio) boutons mpl de
réglage; **to take ~ of** se rendre maître de;
(Comm) acquérir une participation majoritaire
dans; **to be in ~ of** être maître de, maîtriser; (in
charge of) être responsable de; **to ~ o.s.** se
contrôler; **everything is under ~** j'ai (or il a etc)
la situation en main; **the car went out of ~** j'ai
(or il a etc) perdu le contrôle du véhicule;
**beyond our ~** indépendant(e) de notre volonté
**control key** n (Comput) touche f de commande
**controller** [kən'trəuləʳ] n contrôleur m
**controlling interest** [kən'trəulɪŋ-] n (Comm)
participation f majoritaire
**control panel** n (on aircraft, ship, TV etc) tableau m
de commandes
**control point** n (poste m de) contrôle m
**control room** n (Naut Mil) salle f des
commandes; (Radio, TV) régie f
**control tower** n (Aviat) tour f de contrôle
**control unit** n (Comput) unité f de contrôle
**controversial** [kɔntrə'və:ʃl] adj discutable,
controversé(e)
**controversy** ['kɔntrəvə:sɪ] n controverse f,
polémique f
**conurbation** [kɔnə'beɪʃən] n conurbation f
**convalesce** [kɔnvə'lɛs] vi relever de maladie, se
remettre (d'une maladie)
**convalescence** [kɔnvə'lɛsns] n convalescence f
**convalescent** [kɔnvə'lɛsnt] adj, n
convalescent(e)
**convector** [kən'vɛktəʳ] n radiateur m à
convection, appareil m de chauffage par
convection
**convene** [kən'vi:n] vt convoquer, assembler ▷ vi
se réunir, s'assembler
**convener** [kən'vi:nəʳ] n organisateur m
**convenience** [kən'vi:nɪəns] n commodité f; **at
your ~** quand or comme cela vous convient; **at
your earliest ~** (Comm) dans les meilleurs
délais, le plus tôt possible; **all modern ~s**, **all
mod cons** (Brit) avec tout le confort moderne,
tout confort
**convenience foods** npl plats cuisinés
**convenient** [kən'vi:nɪənt] adj commode; **if it is
~ to you** si cela vous convient, si cela ne vous
dérange pas
**conveniently** [kən'vi:nɪəntlɪ] adv (happen) à pic;
(situated) commodément

**convent** ['kɔnvənt] n couvent m
**convention** [kən'vɛnʃən] n convention f;
(custom) usage m
**conventional** [kən'vɛnʃənl] adj
conventionnel(le)
**convent school** n couvent m
**converge** [kən'və:dʒ] vi converger
**conversant** [kən'və:snt] adj: **to be ~ with** s'y
connaître en; être au courant de
**conversation** [kɔnvə'seɪʃən] n conversation f
**conversational** [kɔnvə'seɪʃənl] adj de la
conversation; (Comput) conversationnel(le)
**conversationalist** [kɔnvə'seɪʃnəlɪst] n
brillant(e) causeur(-euse)
**converse** ['kɔnvə:s] n contraire m, inverse m ▷ vi
[kən'və:s]: **to ~ (with sb about sth)**
s'entretenir (avec qn de qch)
**conversely** [kɔn'və:slɪ] adv inversement,
réciproquement
**conversion** [kən'və:ʃən] n conversion f; (Brit: of
house) transformation f, aménagement m;
(Rugby) transformation f
**conversion table** n table f de conversion
**convert** vt [kən'və:t] (Rel, Comm) convertir; (alter)
transformer; (house) aménager; (Rugby)
transformer ▷ n ['kɔnvə:t] converti(e)
**convertible** [kən'və:təbl] adj convertible ▷ n
(voiture f) décapotable f
**convex** ['kɔn'vɛks] adj convexe
**convey** [kən'veɪ] vt transporter; (thanks)
transmettre; (idea) communiquer
**conveyance** [kən'veɪəns] n (of goods) transport
m de marchandises; (vehicle) moyen m de
transport
**conveyancing** [kən'veɪənsɪŋ] n (Law)
rédaction f des actes de cession de propriété
**conveyor belt** [kən'veɪəʳ-] n convoyeur m tapis
roulant
**convict** vt [kən'vɪkt] déclarer (or reconnaître)
coupable ▷ n ['kɔnvɪkt] forçat m, convict m
**conviction** [kən'vɪkʃən] n (Law) condamnation
f; (belief) conviction f
**convince** [kən'vɪns] vt convaincre, persuader;
**to ~ sb (of sth/that)** persuader qn (de qch/que)
**convinced** [kən'vɪnst] adj: **~ of/that**
convaincu(e) de/que
**convincing** [kən'vɪnsɪŋ] adj persuasif(-ive),
convaincant(e)
**convincingly** [kən'vɪnsɪŋlɪ] adv de façon
convaincante
**convivial** [kən'vɪvɪəl] adj joyeux(-euse), plein(e)
d'entrain
**convoluted** ['kɔnvəlu:tɪd] adj (shape)
tarabiscoté(e); (argument) compliqué(e)
**convoy** ['kɔnvɔɪ] n convoi m
**convulse** [kən'vʌls] vt ébranler; **to be ~d with
laughter** se tordre de rire
**convulsion** [kən'vʌlʃən] n convulsion f
**coo** [ku:] vi roucouler
**cook** [kuk] vt (faire) cuire ▷ vi cuire; (person)
faire la cuisine ▷ n cuisinier(-ière)
  ▶ **cook up** vt (inf: excuse, story) inventer

523

**cookbook** ['kukbuk] *n* livre *m* de cuisine
**cooker** ['kukə$^r$] *n* cuisinière *f*
**cookery** ['kukərɪ] *n* cuisine *f*
**cookery book** *n* (*Brit*) = **cookbook**
**cookie** ['kukɪ] *n* (*US*) biscuit *m*, petit gâteau sec; (*Comput*) cookie *m*, témoin *m* de connexion
**cooking** ['kukɪŋ] *n* cuisine *f* ⊳ *cpd* (*apples, chocolate*) à cuire; (*utensils, salt*) de cuisine
**cookout** ['kukaut] *n* (*US*) barbecue *m*
**cool** [ku:l] *adj* frais (fraîche); (*not afraid*) calme; (*unfriendly*) froid(e); (*impertinent*) effronté(e); (*inf: trendy*) cool *inv* (*inf*); (: *great*) super *inv* (*inf*) ⊳ *vt, vi* rafraîchir, refroidir; **it's ~** (*weather*) il fait frais; **to keep sth ~** *or* **in a ~ place** garder *or* conserver qch au frais
  ▸ **cool down** *vi* refroidir; (*fig: person, situation*) se calmer
  ▸ **cool off** *vi* (*become calmer*) se calmer; (*lose enthusiasm*) perdre son enthousiasme
**coolant** ['ku:lənt] *n* liquide *m* de refroidissement
**cool box**, (*US*) **cooler** ['ku:lə$^r$] *n* boîte *f* isotherme
**cooling** ['ku:lɪŋ] *adj* (*breeze*) rafraîchissant(e)
**cooling tower** *n* refroidisseur *m*
**coolly** ['ku:lɪ] *adv* (*calmly*) calmement; (*audaciously*) sans se gêner; (*unenthusiastically*) froidement
**coolness** ['ku:lnɪs] *n* fraîcheur *f*; sang-froid *m*, calme *m*; froideur *f*
**coop** [ku:p] *n* poulailler *m* ⊳ *vt*: **to ~ up** (*fig*) cloîtrer, enfermer
**co-op** ['kəuɔp] *n abbr* (= *cooperative (society)*) coop *f*
**cooperate** [kəu'ɔpəreɪt] *vi* coopérer, collaborer
**cooperation** [kəuɔpə'reɪʃən] *n* coopération *f*, collaboration *f*
**cooperative** [kəu'ɔpərətɪv] *adj* coopératif(-ive) ⊳ *n* coopérative *f*
**coopt** [kəu'ɔpt] *vt*: **to ~ sb onto a committee** coopter qn pour faire partie d'un comité
**coordinate** *vt* [kəu'ɔ:dɪneɪt] coordonner ⊳ *n* [kəu'ɔdɪnət] (*Math*) coordonnée *f*; **coordinates** *npl* (*clothes*) ensemble *m*, coordonnés *mpl*
**coordination** [kəuɔ:dɪ'neɪʃən] *n* coordination *f*
**coot** [ku:t] *n* foulque *f*
**co-ownership** ['kəu'əunəʃɪp] *n* copropriété *f*
**cop** [kɔp] *n* (*inf*) flic *m*
**cope** [kəup] *vi* s'en sortir, tenir le coup; **to ~ with** (*problem*) faire face à; (*take care of*) s'occuper de
**Copenhagen** ['kəupn'heɪgən] *n* Copenhague
**copier** ['kɔpɪə$^r$] *n* (*also*: **photocopier**) copieur *m*
**co-pilot** ['kəu'paɪlət] *n* copilote *m*
**copious** ['kəupɪəs] *adj* copieux(-euse), abondant(e)
**copper** ['kɔpə$^r$] *n* cuivre *m*; (*Brit: inf: policeman*) flic *m*; **coppers** *npl* petite monnaie
**coppice** ['kɔpɪs], **copse** [kɔps] *n* taillis *m*
**copulate** ['kɔpjuleɪt] *vi* copuler
**copy** ['kɔpɪ] *n* copie *f*; (*book etc*) exemplaire *m*; (*material: for printing*) copie ⊳ *vt* copier; (*imitate*) imiter; **rough ~** (*gen*) premier jet; (*Scol*) brouillon *m*; **fair ~** version définitive; propre *m*;
  **to make good ~** (*Press*) faire un bon sujet d'article
  ▸ **copy out** *vt* copier
**copycat** ['kɔpɪkæt] *n* (*pej*) copieur(-euse)
**copyright** ['kɔpɪraɪt] *n* droit *m* d'auteur, copyright *m*; **~ reserved** tous droits (de reproduction) réservés
**copy typist** *n* dactylo *m/f*
**copywriter** ['kɔpɪraɪtə$^r$] *n* rédacteur(-trice) publicitaire
**coral** ['kɔrəl] *n* corail *m*
**coral reef** *n* récif *m* de corail
**Coral Sea** *n*: **the ~** la mer de Corail
**cord** [kɔ:d] *n* corde *f*; (*fabric*) velours côtelé; whipcord *m*; corde *f*; (*Elec*) cordon *m* (d'alimentation), fil *m* (électrique); **cords** *npl* (*trousers*) pantalon *m* de velours côtelé
**cordial** ['kɔ:dɪəl] *adj* cordial(e), chaleureux(-euse) ⊳ *n* sirop *m*; cordial *m*
**cordless** ['kɔ:dlɪs] *adj* sans fil
**cordon** ['kɔ:dn] *n* cordon *m*
  ▸ **cordon off** *vt* (*area*) interdire l'accès à; (*crowd*) tenir à l'écart
**corduroy** ['kɔ:dərɔɪ] *n* velours côtelé
**CORE** [kɔ:$^r$] *n abbr* (*US*) = **Congress of Racial Equality**
**core** [kɔ:$^r$] *n* (*of fruit*) trognon *m*, cœur *m*; (*Tech: also of earth*) noyau *m*; cœur ⊳ *vt* enlever le trognon *or* le cœur de; **rotten to the ~** complètement pourri
**Corfu** [kɔ:'fu:] *n* Corfou
**coriander** [kɔrɪ'ændə$^r$] *n* coriandre *f*
**cork** [kɔ:k] *n* (*material*) liège *m*; (*of bottle*) bouchon *m*
**corkage** ['kɔ:kɪdʒ] *n* droit payé par le client qui apporte sa propre bouteille de vin
**corked** ['kɔ:kt], (*US*) **corky** ['kɔ:kɪ] *adj* (*wine*) qui sent le bouchon
**corkscrew** ['kɔ:kskru:] *n* tire-bouchon *m*
**cormorant** ['kɔ:mərnt] *n* cormoran *m*
**corn** [kɔ:n] *n* (*Brit: wheat*) blé *m*; (*US: maize*) maïs *m*; (*on foot*) cor *m*; **~ on the cob** (*Culin*) épi *m* de maïs au naturel
**cornea** ['kɔ:nɪə] *n* cornée *f*
**corned beef** ['kɔ:nd-] *n* corned-beef *m*
**corner** ['kɔ:nə$^r$] *n* coin *m*; (*in road*) tournant *m*, virage *m*; (*Football: also*: **corner kick**) corner *m* ⊳ *vt* (*trap: prey*) acculer; (*fig*) coincer; (*Comm: market*) accaparer ⊳ *vi* prendre un virage; **to cut ~s** (*fig*) prendre des raccourcis
**corner flag** *n* (*Football*) piquet *m* de coin
**corner kick** *n* (*Football*) corner *m*
**corner shop** (*Brit*) *n* magasin *m* du coin
**cornerstone** ['kɔ:nəstəun] *n* pierre *f* angulaire
**cornet** ['kɔ:nɪt] *n* (*Mus*) cornet *m* à pistons; (*Brit: of ice-cream*) cornet (de glace)
**cornflakes** ['kɔ:nfleɪks] *npl* cornflakes *mpl*
**cornflour** ['kɔ:nflauə$^r$] *n* (*Brit*) farine *f* de maïs, maïzena® *f*
**cornice** ['kɔ:nɪs] *n* corniche *f*
**Cornish** ['kɔ:nɪʃ] *adj* de Cornouailles, cornouaillais(e)

**corn oil** n huile f de maïs
**cornstarch** ['kɔːnstɑːtʃ] n (US) farine f de maïs, maïzena® f
**cornucopia** [kɔːnjuˈkəupɪə] n corne f d'abondance
**Cornwall** ['kɔːnwəl] n Cornouailles f
**corny** ['kɔːnɪ] adj (inf) rebattu(e), galvaudé(e)
**corollary** [kəˈrɔlərɪ] n corollaire m
**coronary** ['kɔrənərɪ] n: ~ **(thrombosis)** infarctus m (du myocarde), thrombose f coronaire
**coronation** [kɔrəˈneɪʃən] n couronnement m
**coroner** ['kɔrənəʳ] n coroner m, officier de police judiciaire chargé de déterminer les causes d'un décès
**coronet** ['kɔrənɪt] n couronne f
**Corp.** abbr = **corporation**
**corporal** ['kɔːpərl] n caporal m, brigadier m ▷ adj: ~ **punishment** châtiment corporel
**corporate** ['kɔːpərɪt] adj (action, ownership) en commun; (Comm) de la société
**corporate hospitality** n arrangement selon lequel une société offre des places de théâtre, concert etc à ses clients
**corporate identity, corporate image** n (of organization) image f de la société
**corporation** [kɔːpəˈreɪʃən] n (of town) municipalité f, conseil municipal; (Comm) société f
**corporation tax** n ≈ impôt m sur les bénéfices
**corps** [kɔːʳ] (pl - [kɔːz]) n corps m; **the diplomatic ~** le corps diplomatique; **the press ~** la presse
**corpse** [kɔːps] n cadavre m
**corpuscle** ['kɔːpʌsl] n corpuscule m
**corral** [kəˈrɑːl] n corral m
**correct** [kəˈrɛkt] adj (accurate) correct(e), exact(e); (proper) correct, convenable ▷ vt corriger; **you are ~** vous avez raison
**correction** [kəˈrɛkʃən] n correction f
**correlate** ['kɔrɪleɪt] vt mettre en corrélation ▷ vi: **to ~ with** correspondre à
**correlation** [kɔrɪˈleɪʃən] n corrélation f
**correspond** [kɔrɪsˈpɔnd] vi correspondre; **to ~ to sth** (be equivalent to) correspondre à qch
**correspondence** [kɔrɪsˈpɔndəns] n correspondance f
**correspondence course** n cours m par correspondance
**correspondent** [kɔrɪsˈpɔndənt] n correspondant(e)
**corresponding** [kɔrɪsˈpɔndɪŋ] adj correspondant(e)
**corridor** ['kɔrɪdɔːʳ] n couloir m, corridor m
**corroborate** [kəˈrɔbəreɪt] vt corroborer, confirmer
**corrode** [kəˈrəud] vt corroder, ronger ▷ vi se corroder
**corrosion** [kəˈrəuʒən] n corrosion f
**corrosive** [kəˈrəuzɪv] adj corrosif(-ive)
**corrugated** ['kɔrəgeɪtɪd] adj plissé(e); ondulé(e)
**corrugated iron** n tôle ondulée
**corrupt** [kəˈrʌpt] adj corrompu(e); (Comput)

**altéré(e)** ▷ vt corrompre; (Comput) altérer; ~ **practices** (dishonesty, bribery) malversation f
**corruption** [kəˈrʌpʃən] n corruption f; (Comput) altération f (de données)
**corset** ['kɔːsɪt] n corset m
**Corsica** ['kɔːsɪkə] n Corse f
**Corsican** ['kɔːsɪkən] adj corse ▷ n Corse m/f
**cortège** [kɔːˈteɪʒ] n cortège m (gén funèbre)
**cortisone** ['kɔːtɪzəun] n cortisone f
**coruscating** ['kɔrəskeɪtɪŋ] adj scintillant(e)
**cosh** [kɔʃ] n (Brit) matraque f
**cosignatory** ['kəuˈsɪgnətərɪ] n cosignataire m/f
**cosiness** ['kəuzɪnɪs] n atmosphère douillette, confort m
**cos lettuce** ['kɔs-] n (laitue f) romaine f
**cosmetic** [kɔzˈmɛtɪk] n produit m de beauté, cosmétique m ▷ adj (preparation) cosmétique; (fig: reforms) symbolique, superficiel(le)
**cosmetic surgery** n chirurgie f esthétique
**cosmic** ['kɔzmɪk] adj cosmique
**cosmonaut** ['kɔzmənɔːt] n cosmonaute m/f
**cosmopolitan** [kɔzməˈpɔlɪtn] adj cosmopolite
**cosmos** ['kɔzmɔs] n cosmos m
**cosset** ['kɔsɪt] vt choyer, dorloter
**cost** [kɔst] (pt, pp -) n coût m ▷ vi coûter ▷ vt établir or calculer le prix de revient de; **costs** npl (Comm) frais mpl; (Law) dépens mpl; **how much does it ~?** combien ça coûte?; **it ~s £5/too much** cela coûte 5 livres/trop cher; **what will it ~ to have it repaired?** combien cela coûtera de le faire réparer?; **to ~ sb time/effort** demander du temps/un effort à qn; **it ~ him his life/job** ça lui a coûté la vie/son emploi; **at all ~s** coûte que coûte, à tout prix
**cost accountant** n analyste m/f de coûts
**co-star** ['kəustɑːʳ] n partenaire m/f
**Costa Rica** ['kɔstə'riːkə] n Costa Rica m
**cost centre** n centre m de coût
**cost control** n contrôle m des coûts
**cost-effective** ['kɔstɪ'fɛktɪv] adj rentable
**cost-effectiveness** ['kɔstɪ'fɛktɪvnɪs] n rentabilité f
**costing** ['kɔstɪŋ] n calcul m du prix de revient
**costly** ['kɔstlɪ] adj coûteux(-euse)
**cost of living** ['kɔstəv'lɪvɪŋ] n coût m de la vie ▷ adj: ~ **allowance** indemnité f de vie chère; ~ **index** indice m du coût de la vie
**cost price** n (Brit) prix coûtant or de revient
**costume** ['kɔstjuːm] n costume m; (lady's suit) tailleur m; (Brit: also: **swimming costume**) maillot m (de bain)
**costume jewellery** n bijoux mpl de fantaisie
**cosy,** (US) **cozy** ['kəuzɪ] adj (room, bed) douillet(te); (scarf, gloves) bien chaud(e); (atmosphere) chaleureux(-euse); **to be ~** (person) être bien (au chaud)
**cot** [kɔt] n (Brit: child's) lit m d'enfant, petit lit; (US: campbed) lit de camp
**cot death** n mort subite du nourrisson
**Cotswolds** ['kɔtswəuldz] npl: **the ~** région de collines du Gloucestershire
**cottage** ['kɔtɪdʒ] n petite maison (à la

525

campagne), cottage *m*

**cottage cheese** *n* fromage blanc (*maigre*)

**cottage industry** *n* industrie familiale *or* artisanale

**cottage pie** ≈ hachis *m* Parmentier

**cotton** ['kɔtn] *n* coton *m*; (*thread*) fil *m* (de coton); ~ **dress** *etc* robe *etc* en *or* de coton

▶ **cotton on** *vi* (*inf*): **to ~ on (to sth)** piger (qch)

**cotton bud** (*Brit*) *n* coton-tige ® *m*

**cotton candy** (*US*) *n* barbe *f* à papa

**cotton wool** *n* (*Brit*) ouate *f*, coton *m* hydrophile

**couch** [kautʃ] *n* canapé *m*; divan *m*; (*doctor's*) table *f* d'examen; (*psychiatrist's*) divan ▷ *vt* formuler, exprimer

**couchette** [kuː'ʃɛt] *n* couchette *f*

**couch potato** *n* (*inf*) mollasson(ne) (*qui passe son temps devant la télé*)

**cough** [kɔf] *vi* tousser ▷ *n* toux *f*; **I've got a ~** j'ai la toux

**cough drop** *n* pastille *f* pour *or* contre la toux

**cough mixture, cough syrup** *n* sirop *m* pour la toux

**cough sweet** *n* pastille *f* pour *or* contre la toux

**could** [kud] *pt of* **can²**

**couldn't** ['kudnt] = **could not**

**council** ['kaunsl] *n* conseil *m*; **city** *or* **town ~** conseil municipal; **C~ of Europe** Conseil de l'Europe

**council estate** *n* (*Brit*) (quartier *m* *or* zone *f* de) logements loués à/par la municipalité

**council house** *n* (*Brit*) maison *f* (à loyer modéré) louée par la municipalité

**councillor,** (*US*) **councilor** ['kaunslə'] *n* conseiller(-ère)

**council tax** *n* (*Brit*) impôts locaux

**counsel** ['kaunsl] *n* conseil *m*; (*lawyer*) avocat(e) ▷ *vt*: **to ~ (sb to do sth)** conseiller (à qn de faire qch); **~ for the defence/the prosecution** (avocat de la) défense/ avocat du ministère public

**counselling,** (*US*) **counseling** ['kaunslɪŋ] *n* (*Psych*) aide psychosociale

**counsellor,** (*US*) **counselor** ['kaunslə'] *n* conseiller(-ère); (*US Law*) avocat *m*

**count** [kaunt] *vt, vi* compter ▷ *n* compte *m*; (*nobleman*) comte *m*; **to ~ (up) to 10** compter jusqu'à 10; **to keep ~ of sth** tenir le compte de qch; **not ~ing the children** sans compter les enfants; **10 ~ing him** 10 avec lui, 10 en le comptant; **to ~ the cost of** établir le coût de; **it ~s for very little** cela n'a pas beaucoup d'importance; **~ yourself lucky** estimez-vous heureux

▶ **count in** *vt* (*inf*): **to ~ sb in on sth** inclure qn dans qch

▶ **count on** *vt fus* compter sur; **to ~ on doing sth** compter faire qch

▶ **count up** *vt* compter, additionner

**countdown** ['kauntdaun] *n* compte *m* à rebours

**countenance** ['kauntɪnəns] *n* expression *f* ▷ *vt* approuver

**counter** ['kauntə'] *n* comptoir *m*; (*in post office,* *bank*) guichet *m*; (*in game*) jeton *m* ▷ *vt* aller à l'encontre de, opposer; (*blow*) parer ▷ *adv*: **~ to** à l'encontre de; contrairement à; **to buy under the ~** (*fig*) acheter sous le manteau *or* en sous-main; **to ~ sth with sth/by doing sth** contrer *or* riposter à qch par qch/en faisant qch

**counteract** ['kauntər'ækt] *vt* neutraliser, contrebalancer

**counterattack** ['kauntərə'tæk] *n* contre-attaque *f* ▷ *vi* contre-attaquer

**counterbalance** ['kauntə'bæləns] *vt* contrebalancer, faire contrepoids à

**counterclockwise** ['kauntə'klɔkwaɪz] (*US*) *adv* en sens inverse des aiguilles d'une montre

**counter-espionage** ['kauntər'ɛspɪɑnɑːʒ] *n* contre-espionnage *m*

**counterfeit** ['kauntəfɪt] *n* faux *m*, contrefaçon *f* ▷ *vt* contrefaire ▷ *adj* faux (fausse)

**counterfoil** ['kauntəfɔɪl] *n* talon *m*, souche *f*

**counterintelligence** ['kauntərɪn'tɛlɪdʒəns] *n* contre-espionnage *m*

**countermand** ['kauntəmɑːnd] *vt* annuler

**countermeasure** ['kauntəmɛʒə'] *n* contre-mesure *f*

**counteroffensive** ['kauntərə'fɛnsɪv] *n* contre-offensive *f*

**counterpane** ['kauntəpeɪn] *n* dessus-de-lit *m*

**counterpart** ['kauntəpɑːt] *n* (*of document etc*) double *m*; (*of person*) homologue *m/f*

**counterproductive** ['kauntəprə'dʌktɪv] *adj* contre-productif(-ive)

**counterproposal** ['kauntəprə'pəuzl] *n* contre-proposition *f*

**countersign** ['kauntəsaɪn] *vt* contresigner

**countersink** ['kauntəsɪŋk] *vt* (*hole*) fraiser

**countess** ['kauntɪs] *n* comtesse *f*

**countless** ['kauntlɪs] *adj* innombrable

**countrified** ['kʌntrɪfaɪd] *adj* rustique, à l'air campagnard

**country** ['kʌntrɪ] *n* pays *m*; (*native land*) patrie *f*; (*as opposed to town*) campagne *f*; (*region*) région *f*, pays; **in the ~** à la campagne; **mountainous ~** pays de montagne, région montagneuse

**country and western, country and western music** *n* musique *f* country

**country dancing** *n* (*Brit*) danse *f* folklorique

**country house** *n* manoir *m*, (petit) château

**countryman** ['kʌntrɪmən] (*irreg*) *n* (*national*) compatriote *m*; (*rural*) habitant *m* de la campagne, campagnard *m*

**countryside** ['kʌntrɪsaɪd] *n* campagne *f*

**countrywide** ['kʌntrɪ'waɪd] *adj* s'étendant à l'ensemble du pays; (*problem*) à l'échelle nationale ▷ *adv* à travers *or* dans tout le pays

**county** ['kauntɪ] *n* comté *m*

**county council** *n* (*Brit*) ≈ conseil régional

**county town** *n* (*Brit*) chef-lieu *m*

**coup** [kuː'] (*pl* **-s**) [kuːz] *n* (*achievement*) beau coup; (*also*: **coup d'état**) coup d'État

**coupé** [kuː'peɪ] *n* (*Aut*) coupé *m*

**couple** ['kʌpl] *n* couple *m* ▷ *vt* (*carriages*) atteler; (*Tech*) coupler; (*ideas, names*) associer; **a ~ of** (*two*)

deux; (a few) deux ou trois
**couplet** ['kʌplɪt] n distique m
**coupling** ['kʌplɪŋ] n (Rail) attelage m
**coupon** ['ku:pɔn] n (voucher) bon m de réduction;
(detachable form) coupon m détachable, coupon-
réponse m; (Finance) coupon
**courage** ['kʌrɪdʒ] n courage m
**courageous** [kə'reɪdʒəs] adj courageux(-euse)
**courgette** [kuə'ʒet] n (Brit) courgette f
**courier** ['kurɪər] n messager m, courrier m; (for
tourists) accompagnateur(-trice)
**course** [kɔ:s] n cours m; (of ship) route f; (for golf)
terrain m; (part of meal) plat m; **first** ~ entrée f;
**of** ~ (adv) bien sûr; **(no,) of** ~ **not!** bien sûr que
non!, évidemment que non!; **in the** ~ **of** au
cours de; **in the** ~ **of the next few days** au
cours des prochains jours; **in due** ~ en temps
utile or voulu; ~ **(of action)** parti m, ligne f de
conduite; **the best** ~ **would be to** ... le mieux
serait de ...; **we have no other** ~ **but to** ... nous
n'avons pas d'autre solution que de ...; ~ **of
lectures** série f de conférences; ~ **of treatment**
(Med) traitement m
**court** [kɔ:t] n cour f; (Law) cour, tribunal m;
(Tennis) court m ▷ vt (woman) courtiser, faire la
cour à; (fig: favour, popularity) rechercher; (: death,
disaster) courir après, flirter avec; **out of** ~ (Law:
settle) à l'amiable; **to take to** ~ actionner or
poursuivre en justice; ~ **of appeal** cour d'appel
**courteous** ['kə:tɪəs] adj courtois(e), poli(e)
**courtesan** [kɔ:tɪ'zæn] n courtisane f
**courtesy** ['kə:təsɪ] n courtoisie f, politesse f;
**(by)** ~ **of** avec l'aimable autorisation de
**courtesy bus, courtesy coach** n navette
gratuite
**courtesy light** n (Aut) plafonnier m
**court-house** ['kɔ:thaus] n (US) palais m de
justice
**courtier** ['kɔ:tɪər] n courtisan m, dame f de cour
**court martial** (pl **courts martial**) n cour
martiale, conseil m de guerre
**courtroom** ['kɔ:trum] n salle f de tribunal
**court shoe** n escarpin m
**courtyard** ['kɔ:tjɑ:d] n cour f
**cousin** ['kʌzn] n cousin(e); **first** ~ cousin(e)
germain(e)
**cove** [kəuv] n petite baie, anse f
**covenant** ['kʌvənənt] n contrat m, engagement
m ▷ vt: **to** ~ **£200 per year to a charity**
s'engager à verser 200 livres par an à une œuvre
de bienfaisance
**Coventry** ['kɔvəntrɪ] n: **to send sb to** ~ (fig)
mettre qn en quarantaine
**cover** ['kʌvər] vt couvrir; (Press: report on) faire un
reportage sur; (feelings, mistake) cacher; (include)
englober; (discuss) traiter ▷ n (of book, Comm)
couverture f; (of pan) couvercle m; (over furniture)
housse f; (shelter) abri m; **covers** npl (on bed)
couvertures; **to take** ~ se mettre à l'abri; **under**
~ à l'abri; **under** ~ **of darkness** à la faveur de la
nuit; **under separate** ~ (Comm) sous pli séparé;
**£10 will** ~ **everything** 10 livres suffiront (pour

tout payer)
▸ **cover up** vt (person, object): **to** ~ **up (with)**
couvrir (de); (fig: truth, facts) occulter ▷ vi: **to** ~
**up for sb** (fig) couvrir qn
**coverage** ['kʌvərɪdʒ] n (in media) reportage m;
(Insurance) couverture f
**cover charge** n couvert m (supplément à payer)
**covering** ['kʌvərɪŋ] n couverture f, enveloppe f
**covering letter**, (US) **cover letter** n lettre
explicative
**cover note** n (Insurance) police f provisoire
**cover price** n prix m de l'exemplaire
**covert** ['kʌvət] adj (threat) voilé(e), caché(e);
(attack) indirect(e); (glance) furtif(-ive)
**cover-up** ['kʌvərʌp] n tentative f pour étouffer
une affaire
**covet** ['kʌvɪt] vt convoiter
**cow** [kau] n vache f ▷ cpd femelle ▷ vt effrayer,
intimider
**coward** ['kauəd] n lâche m/f
**cowardice** ['kauədɪs] n lâcheté f
**cowardly** ['kauədlɪ] adj lâche
**cowboy** ['kaubɔɪ] n cow-boy m
**cower** ['kauər] vi se recroqueviller; trembler
**cowshed** ['kauʃed] n étable f
**cowslip** ['kauslɪp] n (Bot) (fleur f de) coucou m
**coy** [kɔɪ] adj faussement effarouché(e) or timide
**coyote** [kɔɪ'əutɪ] n coyote m
**cozy** ['kəuzɪ] adj (US) = **cosy**
**CP** n abbr (= Communist Party) PC m
**cp.** abbr (= compare) cf
**CPA** n abbr (US) = **certified public accountant**
**CPI** n abbr (= Consumer Price Index) IPC m
**Cpl.** abbr (= corporal) C/C
**CP/M** n abbr (= Central Program for Microprocessors)
CP/M m
**c.p.s.** abbr (= characters per second) caractères/
seconde
**CPSA** n abbr (Brit: = Civil and Public Services
Association) syndicat de la fonction publique
**CPU** n abbr = **central processing unit**
**cr.** abbr = **credit; creditor**
**crab** [kræb] n crabe m
**crab apple** n pomme f sauvage
**crack** [kræk] n (split) fente f, fissure f; (in cup,
bone) fêlure f; (in wall) lézarde f; (noise)
craquement m, coup (sec); (joke) plaisanterie f;
(inf: attempt): **to have a** ~ **(at sth)** essayer (qch);
(Drugs) crack m ▷ vt fendre, fissurer; fêler;
lézarder; (whip) faire claquer; (nut) casser;
(problem) résoudre, trouver la clef de; (code)
déchiffrer ▷ cpd (athlete) de première classe,
d'élite; **to** ~ **jokes** (inf) raconter des blagues; **to
get** ~ **ing** (inf) s'y mettre, se magner
▸ **crack down on** vt fus (crime) sévir contre,
réprimer; (spending) mettre un frein à
▸ **crack up** vi être au bout de son rouleau,
flancher
**crackdown** ['krækdaun] n: ~ **(on)** (on crime)
répression f (de); (on spending) restrictions fpl (de)
**cracked** [krækt] adj (cup, bone) fêlé(e); (broken)
cassé(e); (wall) lézardé(e); (surface) craquelé(e);

(inf) toqué(e), timbré(e)
**cracker** ['krækə<sup>r</sup>] n (also: **Christmas cracker**)
pétard m; (biscuit) biscuit (salé), craquelin m; **a ~
of a …** (Brit inf) un(e) … formidable; **he's ~s** (Brit
inf) il est cinglé
**crackle** ['krækl] vi crépiter, grésiller
**crackling** ['kræklɪŋ] n crépitement m,
grésillement m; (on radio, telephone) grésillement,
friture f; (of pork) couenne f
**crackpot** ['krækpɔt] n (inf) tordu(e)
**cradle** ['kreɪdl] n berceau m ▷ vt (child) bercer;
(object) tenir dans ses bras
**craft** [krɑːft] n métier (artisanal); (cunning) ruse
f, astuce f; (boat: pl inv) embarcation f, barque f;
(plane: pl inv) appareil m
**craftsman** (irreg) ['krɑːftsmən] (irreg) n artisan m
ouvrier (qualifié)
**craftsmanship** ['krɑːftsmənʃɪp] n métier m,
habileté f
**crafty** ['krɑːftɪ] adj rusé(e), malin(-igne),
astucieux(-euse)
**crag** [kræg] n rocher escarpé
**cram** [kræm] vt (fill): **to ~ sth with** bourrer qch
de; (put): **to ~ sth into** fourrer qch dans ▷ vi (for
exams) bachoter
**cramming** ['kræmɪŋ] n (for exams) bachotage m
**cramp** [kræmp] n crampe f ▷ vt gêner, entraver;
**I've got ~ in my leg** j'ai une crampe à la jambe
**cramped** [kræmpt] adj à l'étroit, très serré(e)
**crampon** ['kræmpən] n crampon m
**cranberry** ['krænbərɪ] n canneberge f
**crane** [kreɪn] n grue f ▷ vt, vi: **to ~ forward, to ~
one's neck** allonger le cou
**cranium** (pl **crania**) ['kreɪnɪəm, 'kreɪnɪə] n boîte
crânienne
**crank** [kræŋk] n manivelle f; (person)
excentrique m/f
**crankshaft** ['kræŋkʃɑːft] n vilebrequin m
**cranky** ['kræŋkɪ] adj excentrique, loufoque;
(bad-tempered) grincheux(-euse), revêche
**cranny** ['krænɪ] n see **nook**
**crap** [kræp] n (inf!: nonsense) conneries fpl (!);
(: excrement) merde f (!); **the party was ~** la fête
était merdique (!); **to have a ~** chier (!)
**crappy** ['kræpɪ] adj (inf) merdique (!)
**crash** [kræʃ] n (noise) fracas m; (of car, plane)
collision f; (of business) faillite f; (Stock Exchange)
krach m ▷ vt (plane) écraser ▷ vi (plane) s'écraser;
(two cars) se percuter, s'emboutir; (business)
s'effondrer; **to ~ into** se jeter or se fracasser
contre; **he ~ed the car into a wall** il s'est
écrasé contre un mur avec sa voiture
**crash barrier** n (Brit Aut) rail m de sécurité
**crash course** n cours intensif
**crash helmet** n casque (protecteur)
**crash landing** n atterrissage forcé or en
catastrophe
**crass** [kræs] adj grossier(-ière), crasse
**crate** [kreɪt] n cageot m; (for bottles) caisse f
**crater** ['kreɪtə<sup>r</sup>] n cratère m
**cravat** [krə'væt] n foulard (noué autour du cou)
**crave** [kreɪv] vt, vi: **to ~ (for)** désirer

violemment, avoir un besoin physiologique de,
avoir une envie irrésistible de
**craving** ['kreɪvɪŋ] n: **~ (for)** (for food, cigarettes etc)
envie f irrésistible (de)
**crawl** [krɔːl] vi ramper; (vehicle) avancer au pas
▷ n (Swimming) crawl m; **to ~ on one's hands
and knees** aller à quatre pattes; **to ~ to sb** (inf)
faire de la lèche à qn
**crawler lane** ['krɔːlə-] n (Brit Aut) file f or voie f
pour véhicules lents
**crayfish** ['kreɪfɪʃ] n (pl inv: freshwater) écrevisse f;
(saltwater) langoustine f
**crayon** ['kreɪən] n crayon m (de couleur)
**craze** [kreɪz] n engouement m
**crazed** [kreɪzd] adj (look, person) affolé(e); (pottery,
glaze) craquelé(e)
**crazy** ['kreɪzɪ] adj fou (folle); **to go ~** devenir fou;
**to be ~ about sb/sth** (inf) être fou de qn/qch
**crazy paving** n (Brit) dallage irrégulier (en
pierres plates)
**creak** [kriːk] vi (hinge) grincer; (floor, shoes)
craquer
**cream** [kriːm] n crème f ▷ adj (colour) crème inv;
**whipped ~** crème fouettée
▶ **cream off** vt (fig) prélever
**cream cake** n (petit) gâteau à la crème
**cream cheese** n fromage m à la crème, fromage
blanc
**creamery** ['kriːmərɪ] n (shop) crémerie f; (factory)
laiterie f
**creamy** ['kriːmɪ] adj crémeux(-euse)
**crease** [kriːs] n pli m ▷ vt froisser, chiffonner
▷ vi se froisser, se chiffonner
**crease-resistant** ['kriːsrɪzɪstənt] adj
infroissable
**create** [kriː'eɪt] vt créer; (impression, fuss) faire
**creation** [kriː'eɪʃən] n création f
**creative** [kriː'eɪtɪv] adj créatif(-ive)
**creativity** [kriːeɪ'tɪvɪtɪ] n créativité f
**creator** [kriː'eɪtə<sup>r</sup>] n créateur(-trice)
**creature** ['kriːtʃə<sup>r</sup>] n créature f
**creature comforts** npl petit confort
**crèche** [krɛʃ] n garderie f, crèche f
**credence** ['kriːdns] n croyance f, foi f
**credentials** [krɪ'dɛnʃlz] npl (references) références
fpl; (identity papers) pièce f d'identité; (letters of
reference) pièces justificatives
**credibility** [krɛdɪ'bɪlɪtɪ] n crédibilité f
**credible** ['krɛdɪbl] adj digne de foi, crédible
**credit** ['krɛdɪt] n crédit m; (recognition) honneur
m; (Scol) unité f de valeur ▷ vt (Comm) créditer;
(believe: also: **give credit to**) ajouter foi à, croire;
**credits** npl (Cine) générique m; **to be in ~** (person,
bank account) être créditeur(-trice); **on ~** à crédit;
**to one's ~** à son honneur; à son actif; **to take
the ~ for** s'attribuer le mérite de; **it does him ~**
cela lui fait honneur; **to ~ sb with** (fig) prêter or
attribuer à qn; **to ~ £5 to sb** créditer (le compte
de) qn de 5 livres
**creditable** ['krɛdɪtəbl] adj honorable, estimable
**credit account** n compte m client
**credit agency** n (Brit) agence f de

renseignements commerciaux
**credit balance** n solde créditeur
**credit bureau** n (US) agence f de
renseignements commerciaux
**credit card** n carte f de crédit; **do you take ~s?**
acceptez-vous les cartes de crédit?
**credit control** n suivi m des factures
**credit crunch** n crise f du crédit
**credit facilities** npl facilités fpl de paiement
**credit limit** n limite f de crédit
**credit note** n (Brit) avoir m
**creditor** ['krɛdɪtər] n créancier(-ière)
**credit transfer** n virement m
**creditworthy** ['krɛdɪtwəːðɪ] adj solvable
**credulity** [krɪ'djuːlɪtɪ] n crédulité f
**creed** [kriːd] n croyance f; credo m, principes mpl
**creek** [kriːk] n (inlet) crique f, anse f; (US: stream)
ruisseau m, petit cours d'eau
**creel** ['kriːl] n panier m de pêche; (also: **lobster
creel**) panier à homards
**creep** (pt, pp **crept**) [kriːp, krɛpt] vi ramper;
(silently) se faufiler, se glisser; (plant) grimper
▷ n (inf: flatterer) lèche-botte m; **he's a ~** c'est un
type puant; **it gives me the ~s** cela me fait
froid dans le dos; **to ~ up on sb** s'approcher
furtivement de qn
**creeper** ['kriːpər] n plante grimpante
**creepers** ['kriːpəz] npl (US: for baby) barboteuse f
**creepy** ['kriːpɪ] adj (frightening) qui fait
frissonner, qui donne la chair de poule
**creepy-crawly** ['kriːpɪ'krɔːlɪ] n (inf) bestiole f
**cremate** [krɪ'meɪt] vt incinérer
**cremation** [krɪ'meɪʃən] n incinération f
**crematorium** (pl **crematoria**) [krɛmə'tɔːrɪəm,
-'tɔːrɪə] n four m crématoire
**creosote** ['krɪəsəut] n créosote f
**crepe** [kreɪp] n crêpe m
**crepe bandage** n (Brit) bande f Velpeau®
**crepe paper** n papier m crépon
**crept** [krɛpt] pt, pp of **creep**
**crescendo** [krɪ'ʃɛndəu] n crescendo m
**crescent** ['krɛsnt] n croissant m; (street) rue f (en
arc de cercle)
**cress** [krɛs] n cresson m
**crest** [krɛst] n crête f; (of helmet) cimier m; (of coat
of arms) timbre m
**crestfallen** ['krɛstfɔːlən] adj déconfit(e),
découragé(e)
**Crete** ['kriːt] n Crète f
**crevasse** [krɪ'væs] n crevasse f
**crevice** ['krɛvɪs] n fissure f, lézarde f, fente f
**crew** [kruː] n équipage m; (Cine) équipe f (de
tournage); (gang) bande f
**crew-cut** ['kruːkʌt] n: **to have a ~** avoir les
cheveux en brosse
**crew-neck** ['kruːnɛk] n col ras
**crib** [krɪb] n lit m d'enfant; (for baby) berceau m
▷ vt (inf) copier
**cribbage** ['krɪbɪdʒ] n sorte de jeu de cartes
**crick** [krɪk] n crampe f; **~ in the neck** torticolis m
**cricket** ['krɪkɪt] n (insect) grillon m, cri-cri m inv;
(game) cricket m

**cricketer** ['krɪkɪtər] n joueur m de cricket
**crime** [kraɪm] n crime m; **minor ~** délit mineur,
infraction mineure
**crime wave** n poussée f de la criminalité
**criminal** ['krɪmɪnl] adj, n criminel(le)
**crimp** [krɪmp] vt friser, frisotter
**crimson** ['krɪmzn] adj cramoisi(e)
**cringe** [krɪndʒ] vi avoir un mouvement de recul;
(fig) s'humilier, ramper
**crinkle** ['krɪŋkl] vt froisser, chiffonner
**cripple** ['krɪpl] n boiteux(-euse), infirme m/f ▷ vt
(person) estropier, paralyser; (ship, plane)
immobiliser; (production, exports) paralyser; **~d
with rheumatism** perclus(e) de rhumatismes
**crippling** ['krɪplɪŋ] adj (disease) handicapant(e);
(taxation, debts) écrasant(e)
**crisis** (pl **crises**) ['kraɪsɪs, -siːz] n crise f
**crisp** [krɪsp] adj croquant(e); (weather) vif (vive);
(manner etc) brusque
**crisps** [krɪsps] (Brit) npl (pommes fpl) chips fpl
**crispy** ['krɪspɪ] adj croustillant(e)
**crisscross** ['krɪskrɔs] adj entrecroisé(e), en
croisillons ▷ vt sillonner; **~ pattern** croisillons
mpl
**criterion** (pl **criteria**) [kraɪ'tɪərɪən, -'tɪərɪə] n
critère m
**critic** ['krɪtɪk] n critique m/f
**critical** ['krɪtɪkl] adj critique; **to be ~ of sb/sth**
critiquer qn/qch
**critically** ['krɪtɪklɪ] adv (examine) d'un œil
critique; (speak) sévèrement; **~ ill** gravement
malade
**criticism** ['krɪtɪsɪzəm] n critique f
**criticize** ['krɪtɪsaɪz] vt critiquer
**croak** [krəuk] vi (frog) coasser; (raven) croasser
**Croat** ['krəuæt] adj, n = **Croatian**
**Croatia** [krəu'eɪʃə] n Croatie f
**Croatian** [krəu'eɪʃən] adj croate ▷ n Croate m/f;
(Ling) croate m
**crochet** ['krəuʃeɪ] n travail m au crochet
**crock** [krɔk] n cruche f; (inf: also: **old crock**)
épave f
**crockery** ['krɔkərɪ] n vaisselle f
**crocodile** ['krɔkədaɪl] n crocodile m
**crocus** ['krəukəs] n crocus m
**croft** [krɔft] n (Brit) petite ferme
**crofter** ['krɔftər] n (Brit) fermier m
**croissant** ['krwasɑ̃] n croissant m
**crone** [krəun] n vieille bique, (vieille) sorcière
**crony** ['krəunɪ] n copain (copine)
**crook** [kruk] n escroc m; (of shepherd) houlette f
**crooked** ['krukɪd] adj courbé(e), tordu(e);
(action) malhonnête
**crop** [krɔp] n (produce) culture f; (amount produced)
récolte f; (riding crop) cravache f; (of bird) jabot m
▷ vt (hair) tondre; (animals: grass) brouter
▶ **crop up** vi surgir, se présenter, survenir
**cropper** ['krɔpər] n: **to come a ~** (inf) faire la
culbute, s'étaler
**crop spraying** [-spreɪɪŋ] n pulvérisation f des
cultures
**croquet** ['krəukeɪ] n croquet m

**cross** [krɔs] n croix f; (Biol) croisement m ▷ vt
(street etc) traverser; (arms, legs, Biol) croiser;
(cheque) barrer; (thwart: person, plan) contrarier
▷ vi: **the boat ~es from ... to ...** le bateau fait la
traversée de ... à ... ▷ adj en colère, fâché(e); **to ~
o.s.** se signer, faire le signe de (la) croix; **we
have a ~ed line** (Brit: on telephone) il y a des
interférences; **they've got their lines ~ed** (fig)
il y a un malentendu entre eux; **to be/get ~
with sb (about sth)** être en colère/(se) fâcher
contre qn (à propos de qch)
▸ **cross off** or **out** vt barrer, rayer
▸ **cross over** vi traverser
**crossbar** ['krɔsbɑːʳ] n barre transversale
**crossbow** ['krɔsbəu] n arbalète f
**crossbreed** ['krɔsbriːd] n hybride m, métis(se)
**cross-Channel ferry** ['krɔsˈtʃænl-] n ferry m qui
fait la traversée de la Manche
**cross-check** ['krɔstʃɛk] n recoupement m ▷ vi
vérifier par recoupement
**cross-country** ['krɔs'kʌntrɪ], **cross-country
race** n cross(-country) m
**cross-dressing** [krɔs'drɛsɪŋ] n travestisme m
**cross-examination** ['krɔsɪgzæmɪ'neɪʃən] n
(Law) examen m contradictoire (d'un témoin)
**cross-examine** ['krɔsɪg'zæmɪn] vt (Law) faire
subir un examen contradictoire à
**cross-eyed** ['krɔsaɪd] adj qui louche
**crossfire** ['krɔsfaɪəʳ] n feux croisés
**crossing** ['krɔsɪŋ] n croisement m, carrefour m;
(sea passage) traversée f; (also: **pedestrian
crossing**) passage clouté; **how long does the ~
take?** combien de temps dure la traversée?
**crossing guard** (US) n contractuel qui fait traverser
la rue aux enfants
**crossing point** n poste frontalier
**cross-purposes** ['krɔs'pəːpəsɪz] npl: **to be at ~
with sb** comprendre qn de travers; **we're
(talking) at ~** on ne parle pas de la même chose
**cross-question** ['krɔs'kwɛstʃən] vt faire subir
un interrogatoire à
**cross-reference** ['krɔs'rɛfrəns] n renvoi m,
référence f
**crossroads** ['krɔsrəudz] n carrefour m
**cross section** n (Biol) coupe transversale; (in
population) échantillon m
**crosswalk** ['krɔswɔːk] n (US) passage clouté
**crosswind** ['krɔswɪnd] n vent m de travers
**crosswise** ['krɔswaɪz] adv en travers
**crossword** ['krɔswəːd] n mots mpl croisés
**crotch** [krɔtʃ] n (of garment) entrejambe m; (Anat)
entrecuisse m
**crotchet** ['krɔtʃɪt] n (Mus) noire f
**crotchety** ['krɔtʃɪtɪ] adj (person) grognon(ne),
grincheux(-euse)
**crouch** [krautʃ] vi s'accroupir; (hide) se tapir;
(before springing) se ramasser
**croup** [kruːp] n (Med) croup m
**crouton** ['kruːtɔn] n croûton m
**crow** [krəu] n (bird) corneille f; (of cock) chant m
du coq, cocorico m ▷ vi (cock) chanter; (fig)
pavoiser, chanter victoire

**crowbar** ['krəubɑːʳ] n levier m
**crowd** [kraud] n foule f ▷ vt bourrer, remplir
▷ vi affluer, s'attrouper, s'entasser; **~s of
people** une foule de gens
**crowded** ['kraudɪd] adj bondé(e), plein(e); **~
with** plein de
**crowd scene** n (Cine, Theat) scène f de foule
**crown** [kraun] n couronne f; (of head) sommet m
de la tête, calotte crânienne; (of hat) fond m; (of
hill) sommet m ▷ vt (also tooth) couronner
**crown court** n (Brit) ≈ Cour f d'assises; voir article

⏺ **CROWN COURT**
⏺
⏺ En Angleterre et au pays de Galles, une _crown_
⏺ _court_ est une cour de justice où sont jugées
⏺ les affaires très graves, telles que le meurtre,
⏺ l'homicide, le viol et le vol, en présence d'un
⏺ jury. Tous les crimes et délits, quel que soit
⏺ leur degré de gravité, doivent d'abord passer
⏺ devant une "magistrates' court". Il existe
⏺ environ 90 _crown courts_.

**crowning** ['kraunɪŋ] adj (achievement, glory)
suprême
**crown jewels** npl joyaux mpl de la Couronne
**crown prince** n prince héritier
**crow's-feet** ['krəuzfiːt] npl pattes fpl d'oie (fig)
**crow's-nest** ['krəuznɛst] n (on sailing-ship) nid m
de pie
**crucial** ['kruːʃl] adj crucial(e), décisif(-ive); (also:
**crucial to**) essentiel(le) à
**crucifix** ['kruːsɪfɪks] n crucifix m
**crucifixion** [kruːsɪ'fɪkʃən] n crucifiement m,
crucifixion f
**crucify** ['kruːsɪfaɪ] vt crucifier, mettre en croix;
(fig) crucifier
**crude** [kruːd] adj (materials) brut(e); non
raffiné(e); (basic) rudimentaire, sommaire;
(vulgar) cru(e), grossier(-ière) ▷ n (also: **crude oil**)
(pétrole m) brut m
**cruel** ['kruəl] adj cruel(le)
**cruelty** ['kruəltɪ] n cruauté f
**cruet** ['kruːɪt] n huilier m; vinaigrier m
**cruise** [kruːz] n croisière f ▷ vi (ship) croiser; (car)
rouler; (aircraft) voler; (taxi) être en maraude
**cruise missile** n missile m de croisière
**cruiser** ['kruːzəʳ] n croiseur m
**cruising speed** ['kruːzɪŋ-] n vitesse f de croisière
**crumb** [krʌm] n miette f
**crumble** ['krʌmbl] vt émietter ▷ vi s'émietter;
(plaster etc) s'effriter; (land, earth) s'ébouler;
(building) s'écrouler, crouler; (fig) s'effondrer
**crumbly** ['krʌmblɪ] adj friable
**crummy** ['krʌmɪ] adj (inf) minable; (: unwell) mal
fichu(e), patraque
**crumpet** ['krʌmpɪt] n petite crêpe (épaisse)
**crumple** ['krʌmpl] vt froisser, friper
**crunch** [krʌntʃ] vt croquer; (underfoot) faire
craquer, écraser; faire crisser ▷ n (fig) instant m
or moment m critique, moment de vérité
**crunchy** ['krʌntʃɪ] adj croquant(e),

croustillant(e)

**crusade** [kruːˈseɪd] *n* croisade *f* ▷ *vi* (*fig*): **to ~ for/against** partir en croisade pour/contre

**crusader** [kruːˈseɪdəʳ] *n* croisé *m*; (*fig*): **~ (for)** champion *m* (de)

**crush** [krʌʃ] *n* (*crowd*) foule *f*, cohue *f*; (*love*): **to have a ~ on sb** avoir le béguin pour qn; (*drink*): **lemon ~** citron pressé ▷ *vt* écraser; (*crumple*) froisser; (*grind, break up: garlic, ice*) piler; (*: grapes*) presser; (*hopes*) anéantir

**crush barrier** *n* (*Brit*) barrière *f* de sécurité

**crushing** [ˈkrʌʃɪŋ] *adj* écrasant(e)

**crust** [krʌst] *n* croûte *f*

**crustacean** [krʌsˈteɪʃən] *n* crustacé *m*

**crusty** [ˈkrʌstɪ] *adj* (*bread*) croustillant(e); (*inf: person*) revêche, bourru(e); (*: remark*) irrité(e)

**crutch** [krʌtʃ] *n* béquille *f*; (*Tech*) support *m*; (*also*: **crotch**) entrejambe *m*

**crux** [krʌks] *n* point crucial

**cry** [kraɪ] *vi* pleurer; (*shout: also*: **cry out**) crier ▷ *n* cri *m*; **why are you ~ing?** pourquoi pleures-tu?; **to ~ for help** appeler à l'aide; **she had a good ~** elle a pleuré un bon coup; **it's a far ~ from …** (*fig*) on est loin de …
  ▸ **cry off** *vi* se dédire; se décommander
  ▸ **cry out** *vi* (*call out, shout*) pousser un cri ▷ *vt* crier

**crying** [ˈkraɪɪŋ] *adj* (*fig*) criant(e), flagrant(e)

**crypt** [krɪpt] *n* crypte *f*

**cryptic** [ˈkrɪptɪk] *adj* énigmatique

**crystal** [ˈkrɪstl] *n* cristal *m*

**crystal-clear** [ˈkrɪstlˈklɪəʳ] *adj* clair(e) comme de l'eau de roche

**crystallize** [ˈkrɪstəlaɪz] *vt* cristalliser ▷ *vi* (se) cristalliser; **~d fruits** (*Brit*) fruits confits

**CSA** *n abbr* = **Confederate States of America**; (*Brit*: = *Child Support Agency*) organisme pour la protection des enfants de parents séparés, qui contrôle le versement des pensions alimentaires.

**CSC** *n abbr* (= *Civil Service Commission*) commission de recrutement des fonctionnaires

**CS gas** *n* (*Brit*) gaz *m* C.S.

**CST** *abbr* (*US*: = *Central Standard Time*) fuseau horaire

**CT** *abbr* (*US*) = **Connecticut**

**ct** *abbr* = **carat**

**CTC** *n abbr* (*Brit*) = **city technology college**

**CT scanner** *n abbr* (*Med*: = *computerized tomography scanner*) scanner *m*, tomodensitomètre *m*

**cu.** *abbr* = **cubic**

**cub** [kʌb] *n* petit *m* (*d'un animal*); (*also*: **cub scout**) louveteau *m*

**Cuba** [ˈkjuːbə] *n* Cuba *m*

**Cuban** [ˈkjuːbən] *adj* cubain(e) ▷ *n* Cubain(e)

**cubbyhole** [ˈkʌbɪhəul] *n* cagibi *m*

**cube** [kjuːb] *n* cube *m* ▷ *vt* (*Math*) élever au cube

**cube root** *n* racine *f* cubique

**cubic** [ˈkjuːbɪk] *adj* cubique; **~ metre** *etc* mètre *m etc* cube; **~ capacity** (*Aut*) cylindrée *f*

**cubicle** [ˈkjuːbɪkl] *n* (*in hospital*) box *m*; (*at pool*) cabine *f*

**cuckoo** [ˈkuku:] *n* coucou *m*

**cuckoo clock** *n* (*pendule f* à) coucou *m*

**cucumber** [ˈkjuːkʌmbəʳ] *n* concombre *m*

**cud** [kʌd] *n*: **to chew the ~** ruminer

**cuddle** [ˈkʌdl] *vt* câliner, caresser ▷ *vi* se blottir l'un contre l'autre

**cuddly** [ˈkʌdlɪ] *adj* câlin(e)

**cudgel** [ˈkʌdʒl] *n* gourdin *m* ▷ *vt*: **to ~ one's brains** se creuser la tête

**cue** [kjuː] *n* queue *f* de billard; (*Theat etc*) signal *m*

**cuff** [kʌf] *n* (*Brit: of shirt, coat etc*) poignet *m*, manchette *f*; (*US: on trousers*) revers *m*; (*blow*) gifle *f* ▷ *vt* gifler; **off the ~** (*adv*) à l'improviste

**cufflinks** [ˈkʌflɪŋks] *n* boutons *m* de manchette

**cu. in.** *abbr* = **cubic inches**

**cuisine** [kwɪˈziːn] *n* cuisine *f*, art *m* culinaire

**cul-de-sac** [ˈkʌldəsæk] *n* cul-de-sac *m*, impasse *f*

**culinary** [ˈkʌlɪnərɪ] *adj* culinaire

**cull** [kʌl] *vt* sélectionner; (*kill selectively*) pratiquer l'abattage sélectif de ▷ *n* (*of animals*) abattage sélectif

**culminate** [ˈkʌlmɪneɪt] *vi*: **to ~ in** finir *or* se terminer par; (*lead to*) mener à

**culmination** [kʌlmɪˈneɪʃən] *n* point culminant

**culottes** [kjuːˈlɒts] *npl* jupe-culotte *f*

**culpable** [ˈkʌlpəbl] *adj* coupable

**culprit** [ˈkʌlprɪt] *n* coupable *m/f*

**cult** [kʌlt] *n* culte *m*

**cult figure** *n* idole *f*

**cultivate** [ˈkʌltɪveɪt] *vt* (*also fig*) cultiver

**cultivation** [kʌltɪˈveɪʃən] *n* culture *f*

**cultural** [ˈkʌltʃərəl] *adj* culturel(le)

**culture** [ˈkʌltʃəʳ] *n* (*also fig*) culture *f*

**cultured** [ˈkʌltʃəd] *adj* cultivé(e) (*fig*)

**cumbersome** [ˈkʌmbəsəm] *adj* encombrant(e), embarrassant(e)

**cumin** [ˈkʌmɪn] *n* (*spice*) cumin *m*

**cumulative** [ˈkjuːmjulətɪv] *adj* cumulatif(-ive)

**cunning** [ˈkʌnɪŋ] *n* ruse *f*, astuce *f* ▷ *adj* rusé(e), malin(-igne); (*clever: device, idea*) astucieux(-euse)

**cunt** [kʌnt] *n* (*inf!*) chatte *f* (!); (*insult*) salaud *m* (!), salope *f* (!)

**cup** [kʌp] *n* tasse *f*; (*prize, event*) coupe *f*; (*of bra*) bonnet *m*; **a ~ of tea** une tasse de thé

**cupboard** [ˈkʌbəd] *n* placard *m*

**cup final** *n* (*Brit Football*) finale *f* de la coupe

**Cupid** [ˈkjuːpɪd] *n* Cupidon *m*; (*figurine*) amour *m*

**cupidity** [kjuːˈpɪdɪtɪ] *n* cupidité *f*

**cupola** [ˈkjuːpələ] *n* coupole *f*

**cuppa** [ˈkʌpə] *n* (*Brit inf*) tasse *f* de thé

**cup tie** [ˈkʌptaɪ] *n* (*Brit Football*) match *m* de coupe

**curable** [ˈkjuːrəbl] *adj* guérissable, curable

**curate** [ˈkjuːərɪt] *n* vicaire *m*

**curator** [kjuəˈreɪtəʳ] *n* conservateur *m* (*d'un musée etc*)

**curb** [kəːb] *vt* refréner, mettre un frein à; (*expenditure*) limiter, juguler ▷ *n* (*fig*) frein *m*; (*US*) bord *m* du trottoir

**curd cheese** *n* ≈ fromage blanc

**curdle** [ˈkəːdl] *vi* (se) cailler

**curds** [kəːdz] *npl* lait caillé

531

**cure** [kjuə<sup>r</sup>] *vt* guérir; (*Culin: salt*) saler; (*: smoke*) fumer; (*: dry*) sécher ▷ *n* remède *m*; **to be ~d of sth** être guéri de qch

**cure-all** ['kjuərɔːl] *n* (*also fig*) panacée *f*

**curfew** ['kəːfjuː] *n* couvre-feu *m*

**curio** ['kjuərɪəu] *n* bibelot *m*, curiosité *f*

**curiosity** [kjuərɪ'ɔsɪtɪ] *n* curiosité *f*

**curious** ['kjuərɪəs] *adj* curieux(-euse); **I'm ~ about him** il m'intrigue

**curiously** ['kjuərɪəslɪ] *adv* curieusement; (*inquisitively*) avec curiosité; **~ enough, ...** bizarrement, ...

**curl** [kəːl] *n* boucle *f* (de cheveux); (*of smoke etc*) volute *f* ▷ *vt, vi* boucler; (*tightly*) friser
▶ **curl up** *vi* s'enrouler; (*person*) se pelotonner

**curler** ['kəːlə<sup>r</sup>] *n* bigoudi *m*, rouleau *m*; (*Sport*) joueur(-euse) de curling

**curlew** ['kəːluː] *n* courlis *m*

**curling** ['kəːlɪŋ] *n* (*sport*) curling *m*

**curling tongs**, (*US*) **curling irons** *npl* fer *m* à friser

**curly** ['kəːlɪ] *adj* bouclé(e); (*tightly curled*) frisé(e)

**currant** ['kʌrnt] *n* raisin *m* de Corinthe, raisin sec; (*fruit*) groseille *f*

**currency** ['kʌrnsɪ] *n* monnaie *f*; **foreign ~** devises étrangères, monnaie étrangère; **to gain ~** (*fig*) s'accréditer

**current** ['kʌrnt] *n* courant *m* ▷ *adj* (*common*) courant(e); (*tendency, price, event*) actuel(le); **direct/alternating ~** (*Elec*) courant continu/alternatif; **the ~ issue of a magazine** le dernier numéro d'un magazine; **in ~ use** d'usage courant

**current account** *n* (*Brit*) compte courant

**current affairs** *npl* (questions *fpl* d')actualité *f*

**current assets** *npl* (*Comm*) actif *m* disponible

**current liabilities** *npl* (*Comm*) passif *m* exigible

**currently** ['kʌrntlɪ] *adv* actuellement

**curriculum** (*pl* **-s** *or* **curricula**) [kə'rɪkjuləm, -lə] *n* programme *m* d'études

**curriculum vitae** [-'viːtaɪ] *n* curriculum vitae (CV) *m*

**curry** ['kʌrɪ] *n* curry *m* ▷ *vt*: **to ~ favour with** chercher à gagner la faveur *or* à s'attirer les bonnes grâces de; **chicken ~** curry de poulet, poulet *m* au curry

**curry powder** *n* poudre *f* de curry

**curse** [kəːs] *vi* jurer, blasphémer ▷ *vt* maudire ▷ *n* (*spell*) malédiction *f*; (*problem, scourge*) fléau *m*; (*swearword*) juron *m*

**cursor** ['kəːsə<sup>r</sup>] *n* (*Comput*) curseur *m*

**cursory** ['kəːsərɪ] *adj* superficiel(le), hâtif(-ive)

**curt** [kəːt] *adj* brusque, sec(-sèche)

**curtail** [kəː'teɪl] *vt* (*visit etc*) écourter; (*expenses etc*) réduire

**curtain** ['kəːtn] *n* rideau *m*; **to draw the ~s** (*together*) fermer *or* tirer les rideaux; (*apart*) ouvrir les rideaux

**curtain call** *n* (*Theat*) rappel *m*

**curtsey, curtsy** ['kəːtsɪ] *n* révérence *f* ▷ *vi* faire une révérence

**curvature** ['kəːvətʃə<sup>r</sup>] *n* courbure *f*

**curve** [kəːv] *n* courbe *f*; (*in the road*) tournant *m*, virage *m* ▷ *vt* courber ▷ *vi* se courber; (*road*) faire une courbe

**curved** [kəːvd] *adj* courbe

**cushion** ['kuʃən] *n* coussin *m* ▷ *vt* (*seat*) rembourrer; (*fall, shock*) amortir

**cushy** ['kuʃɪ] *adj* (*inf*): **a ~ job** un boulot de tout repos; **to have a ~ time** se la couler douce

**custard** ['kʌstəd] *n* (*for pouring*) crème anglaise

**custard powder** *n* (*Brit*) ≈ crème pâtissière instantanée

**custodial sentence** [kʌs'təudɪəl-] *n* peine *f* de prison

**custodian** [kʌs'təudɪən] *n* gardien(ne); (*of collection etc*) conservateur(-trice)

**custody** ['kʌstədɪ] *n* (*of child*) garde *f*; (*for offenders*) détention préventive; **to take sb into ~** placer qn en détention préventive; **in the ~ of** sous la garde de

**custom** ['kʌstəm] *n* coutume *f*, usage *m*; (*Law*) droit coutumier, coutume; (*Comm*) clientèle *f*

**customary** ['kʌstəmərɪ] *adj* habituel(le); **it is ~ to do it** l'usage veut qu'on le fasse

**custom-built** ['kʌstəm'bɪlt] *adj* *see* **custom-made**

**customer** ['kʌstəmə<sup>r</sup>] *n* client(e); **he's an awkward ~** (*inf*) ce n'est pas quelqu'un de facile

**customer profile** *n* profil *m* du client

**customized** ['kʌstəmaɪzd] *adj* personnalisé(e); (*car etc*) construit(e) sur commande

**custom-made** ['kʌstəm'meɪd] *adj* (*clothes*) fait(e) sur mesure; (*other goods*): *also*: **custom-built**) hors série, fait(e) sur commande

**customs** ['kʌstəmz] *npl* douane *f*; **to go through (the) ~** passer la douane

**Customs and Excise** *n* (*Brit*) administration *f* des douanes

**customs officer** *n* douanier *m*

**cut** [kʌt] (*pt, pp* **-**) *vt* couper; (*meat*) découper; (*shape, make*) tailler; couper; creuser; graver; (*reduce*) réduire; (*inf: lecture, appointment*) manquer ▷ *vi* couper; (*intersect*) se couper ▷ *n* (*gen*) coupure *f*; (*of clothes*) coupe *f*; (*of jewel*) taille *f*; (*in salary etc*) réduction *f*; (*of meat*) morceau *m*; **to ~ teeth** (*baby*) faire ses dents; **to ~ a tooth** percer une dent; **to ~ one's finger** se couper le doigt; **to get one's hair ~** se faire couper les cheveux; **I've ~ myself** je me suis coupé; **to ~ sth short** couper court à qch; **to ~ sb dead** ignorer (complètement) qn
▶ **cut back** *vt* (*plants*) tailler; (*production, expenditure*) réduire
▶ **cut down** *vt* (*tree*) abattre; (*reduce*) réduire; **to ~ sb down to size** (*fig*) remettre qn à sa place
▶ **cut down on** *vt fus* réduire
▶ **cut in** *vi* (*interrupt: conversation*): **to ~ in (on)** couper la parole (à); (*Aut*) faire une queue de poisson
▶ **cut off** *vt* couper; (*fig*) isoler; **we've been ~ off** (*Tel*) nous avons été coupés
▶ **cut out** *vt* (*picture etc*) découper; (*remove*) supprimer

▸ **cut up** *vt* découper
**cut-and-dried** ['kʌtən'draɪd] *adj* (*also:* **cut-and-dry**) tout(e) fait(e), tout(e) décidé(e)
**cutaway** ['kʌtəweɪ] *adj, n:* ~ **(drawing)** écorché *m*
**cutback** ['kʌtbæk] *n* réduction *f*
**cute** [kjuːt] *adj* mignon(ne), adorable; (*clever*) rusé(e), astucieux(-euse)
**cut glass** *n* cristal taillé
**cuticle** ['kjuːtɪkl] *n* (*on nail*): ~ **remover** repousse-peaux *m inv*
**cutlery** ['kʌtlərɪ] *n* couverts *mpl*; (*trade*) coutellerie *f*
**cutlet** ['kʌtlɪt] *n* côtelette *f*
**cutoff** ['kʌtɔf] *n* (*also:* **cutoff point**) seuil-limite *m*
**cutoff switch** *n* interrupteur *m*
**cutout** ['kʌtaut] *n* coupe-circuit *m inv*; (*paper figure*) découpage *m*
**cut-price** ['kʌt'praɪs], (US) **cut-rate** ['kʌt'reɪt] *adj* au rabais, à prix réduit
**cut-throat** ['kʌtθrəut] *n* assassin *m* ▷ *adj:* ~ **competition** concurrence *f* sauvage
**cutting** ['kʌtɪŋ] *adj* tranchant(e), coupant(e); (*fig*) cinglant(e) ▷ *n* (*Brit: from newspaper*) coupure *f* (de journal); (*from plant*) bouture *f*; (*Rail*) tranchée *f*; (*Cine*) montage *m*
**cutting edge** *n* (*of knife*) tranchant *m*; **on** *or* **at the** ~ **of** à la pointe de
**cuttlefish** ['kʌtlfɪʃ] *n* seiche *f*
**cut-up** ['kʌtʌp] *adj* affecté(e), démoralisé(e)
**CV** *n abbr* = **curriculum vitae**
**cwo** *abbr* (*Comm*) = **cash with order**
**cwt** *abbr* = **hundredweight**
**cyanide** ['saɪənaɪd] *n* cyanure *m*
**cybernetics** [saɪbə'nɛtɪks] *n* cybernétique *f*
**cyberspace** ['saɪbəspeɪs] *n* cyberespace *m*

**cyclamen** ['sɪkləmən] *n* cyclamen *m*
**cycle** ['saɪkl] *n* cycle *m*; (*bicycle*) bicyclette *f*, vélo *m* ▷ *vi* faire de la bicyclette
**cycle hire** *n* location *f* de vélos
**cycle lane, cycle path** *n* piste *f* cyclable
**cycle race** *n* course *f* cycliste
**cycle rack** *n* râtelier *m* à bicyclette
**cycling** ['saɪklɪŋ] *n* cyclisme *m*; **to go on a** ~ **holiday** (*Brit*) faire du cyclotourisme
**cyclist** ['saɪklɪst] *n* cycliste *m/f*
**cyclone** ['saɪkləun] *n* cyclone *m*
**cygnet** ['sɪgnɪt] *n* jeune cygne *m*
**cylinder** ['sɪlɪndəʳ] *n* cylindre *m*
**cylinder capacity** *n* cylindrée *f*
**cylinder head** *n* culasse *f*
**cymbals** ['sɪmblz] *npl* cymbales *fpl*
**cynic** ['sɪnɪk] *n* cynique *m/f*
**cynical** ['sɪnɪkl] *adj* cynique
**cynicism** ['sɪnɪsɪzəm] *n* cynisme *m*
**CYO** *n abbr* (*US: = Catholic Youth Organization*) ≈ JC *f*
**cypress** ['saɪprɪs] *n* cyprès *m*
**Cypriot** ['sɪprɪət] *adj* cypriote, chypriote ▷ *n* Cypriote *m/f*, Chypriote *m/f*
**Cyprus** ['saɪprəs] *n* Chypre *f*
**cyst** [sɪst] *n* kyste *m*
**cystitis** [sɪs'taɪtɪs] *n* cystite *f*
**CZ** *n abbr* (*US: = Central Zone*) zone du canal de Panama
**czar** [zɑːʳ] *n* tsar *m*
**Czech** [tʃɛk] *adj* tchèque ▷ *n* Tchèque *m/f*; (*Ling*) tchèque *m*
**Czechoslovak** [tʃɛkə'sləuvæk] *adj, n* = **Czechoslovakian**
**Czechoslovakia** [tʃɛkəslə'vækɪə] *n* Tchécoslovaquie *f*
**Czechoslovakian** [tʃɛkəslə'vækɪən] *adj* tchécoslovaque ▷ *n* Tchécoslovaque *m/f*
**Czech Republic** *n:* **the** ~ la République tchèque

**C**

# Dd

**D¹, d¹** [di:] *n* (*letter*) D, d *m*; (*Mus*): **D** ré *m*; **D for David,** (US) **D for Dog** D comme Désirée

**D²** *abbr* (*US Pol*) = **democrat; democratic**

**d²** *abbr* (*Brit: old*) = **penny**

**d.** *abbr* = **died**

**DA** *n abbr* (*US*) = **district attorney**

**dab** [dæb] *vt* (*eyes, wound*) tamponner; (*paint, cream*) appliquer (par petites touches *or* rapidement); **a ~ of paint** un petit coup de peinture

**dabble** ['dæbl] *vi:* **to ~ in** faire *or* se mêler *or* s'occuper un peu de

**Dacca** ['dækə] *n* Dacca

**dachshund** ['dækʃhund] *n* teckel *m*

**dad, daddy** [dæd, 'dædɪ] *n* papa *m*

**daddy-long-legs** [dædɪ'lɔŋlɛgz] *n* tipule *f*; faucheux *m*

**daffodil** ['dæfədɪl] *n* jonquille *f*

**daft** [dɑ:ft] *adj* (*inf*) idiot(e), stupide; **to be ~ about** être toqué(e) *or* mordu(e) de

**dagger** ['dægə<sup>r</sup>] *n* poignard *m*; **to be at ~s drawn with sb** être à couteaux tirés avec qn; **to look ~s at sb** foudroyer qn du regard

**dahlia** ['deɪljə] *n* dahlia *m*

**daily** ['deɪlɪ] *adj* quotidien(ne), journalier(-ière) ▷ *n* quotidien *m*; (*Brit: servant*) femme *f* de ménage (*à la journée*) ▷ *adv* tous les jours; **twice ~** deux fois par jour

**dainty** ['deɪntɪ] *adj* délicat(e), mignon(ne)

**dairy** ['dɛərɪ] *n* (*shop*) crémerie *f*, laiterie *f*; (*on farm*) laiterie ▷ *adj* laitier(-ière)

**dairy cow** *n* vache laitière

**dairy farm** *n* exploitation *f* pratiquant l'élevage laitier

**dairy produce** *n* produits laitiers

**dairy products** *npl* produits laitier

**dais** ['deɪs] *n* estrade *f*

**daisy** ['deɪzɪ] *n* pâquerette *f*

**daisy wheel** *n* (*on printer*) marguerite *f*

**daisy-wheel printer** ['deɪzwi:l-] *n* imprimante *f* à marguerite

**Dakar** ['dækə] *n* Dakar

**dale** [deɪl] *n* vallon *m*

**dally** ['dælɪ] *vi* musarder, flâner

**dalmatian** [dæl'meɪʃən] *n* (*dog*) dalmatien(ne)

**dam** [dæm] *n* (*wall*) barrage *m*; (*water*) réservoir

*m*, lac *m* de retenue ▷ *vt* endiguer

**damage** ['dæmɪdʒ] *n* dégâts *mpl*, dommages *mpl*; (*fig*) tort *m* ▷ *vt* endommager, abîmer; (*fig*) faire du tort à; **damages** *npl* (*Law*) dommages-intérêts *mpl*; **to pay £5000 in ~s** payer 5000 livres de dommages- intérêts; **~ to property** dégâts matériels

**damaging** ['dæmɪdʒɪŋ] *adj:* **~ (to)** préjudiciable (à), nuisible (à)

**Damascus** [də'mɑ:skəs] *n* Damas

**dame** [deɪm] *n* (*title*) *titre porté par une femme décorée de l'ordre de l'Empire Britannique ou d'un ordre de chevalerie, titre porté par la femme ou la veuve d'un chevalier ou baronnet*; (*US inf*) nana *f*; (*Theat*) vieille dame (*rôle comique joué par un homme*)

**damn** [dæm] *vt* condamner; (*curse*) maudire ▷ *n* (*inf*): **I don't give a ~** je m'en fous ▷ *adj* (*inf: also:* **damned**): **this ~ ...** ce sacré *or* foutu ...; **~ (it)!** zut!

**damnable** ['dæmnəbl] *adj* (*inf: behaviour*) odieux(-euse), détestable; (: *weather*) épouvantable, abominable

**damnation** [dæm'neɪʃən] *n* (*Rel*) damnation *f* ▷ *excl* (*inf*) malédiction!, merde!

**damning** ['dæmɪŋ] *adj* (*evidence*) accablant(e)

**damp** [dæmp] *adj* humide ▷ *n* humidité *f* ▷ *vt* (*also:* **dampen**: *cloth, rag*) humecter; (: *enthusiasm etc*) refroidir

**dampcourse** ['dæmpkɔ:s] *n* couche isolante (contre l'humidité)

**damper** ['dæmpə<sup>r</sup>] *n* (*Mus*) étouffoir *m*; (*of fire*) registre *m*; **to put a ~ on** (*fig: atmosphere, enthusiasm*) refroidir

**dampness** ['dæmpnɪs] *n* humidité *f*

**damson** ['dæmzən] *n* prune *f* de Damas

**dance** [dɑ:ns] *n* danse *f*; (*ball*) bal *m* ▷ *vi* danser; **to ~ about** sautiller, gambader

**dance floor** *n* piste *f* de danse

**dance hall** *n* salle *f* de bal, dancing *m*

**dancer** ['dɑ:nsə<sup>r</sup>] *n* danseur(-euse)

**dancing** ['dɑ:nsɪŋ] *n* danse *f*

**D and C** *n abbr* (*Med:* = *dilation and curettage*) curetage *m*

**dandelion** ['dændɪlaɪən] *n* pissenlit *m*

**dandruff** ['dændrəf] *n* pellicules *fpl*

**D & T** *n abbr* (*Brit: Scol*) = **design and technology**

**dandy** ['dændɪ] n dandy m, élégant m ▷ adj (US inf) fantastique, super

**Dane** [deɪn] n Danois(e)

**danger** ['deɪndʒəʳ] n danger m; ~! (on sign) danger!; **there is a ~ of fire** il y a (un) risque d'incendie; **in ~** en danger; **he was in ~ of falling** il risquait de tomber; **out of ~** hors de danger

**danger list** n (Med): **on the ~** dans un état critique

**danger money** n (Brit) prime f de risque

**dangerous** ['deɪndʒrəs] adj dangereux(-euse)

**dangerously** ['deɪndʒrəslɪ] adv dangereusement; **~ ill** très gravement malade, en danger de mort

**danger zone** n zone dangereuse

**dangle** ['dæŋgl] vt balancer; (fig) faire miroiter ▷ vi pendre, se balancer

**Danish** ['deɪnɪʃ] adj danois(e) ▷ n (Ling) danois m

**Danish pastry** n feuilleté m (recouvert d'un glaçage et fourré aux fruits etc)

**dank** [dæŋk] adj froid(e) et humide

**Danube** ['dænjuːb] n: **the ~** le Danube

**dapper** ['dæpəʳ] adj pimpant(e)

**Dardanelles** [daːdə'nɛlz] npl Dardanelles fpl

**dare** [dɛəʳ] vt: **to ~ sb to do** défier qn or mettre qn au défi de faire ▷ vi: **to ~ (to) do sth** oser faire qch; **I ~n't tell him** (Brit) je n'ose pas le lui dire; **I ~ say he'll turn up** il est probable qu'il viendra

**daredevil** ['dɛədɛvl] n casse-cou m inv

**Dar-es-Salaam** ['daːrɛssə'laːm] n Dar-es-Salaam, Dar-es-Salam

**daring** ['dɛərɪŋ] adj hardi(e), audacieux(-euse) ▷ n audace f, hardiesse f

**dark** [daːk] adj (night, room) obscur(e), sombre; (colour, complexion) foncé(e), sombre; (fig) sombre ▷ n: **in the ~** dans le noir; **to be in the ~ about** (fig) ignorer tout de; **after ~** après la tombée de la nuit; **it is/is getting ~** il fait nuit/commence à faire nuit

**darken** ['daːkn] vt obscurcir, assombrir ▷ vi s'obscurcir, s'assombrir

**dark glasses** npl lunettes noires

**dark horse** n (fig): **he's a ~** on ne sait pas grand-chose de lui

**darkly** ['daːklɪ] adv (gloomily) mélancoliquement; (in a sinister way) lugubrement

**darkness** ['daːknɪs] n obscurité f

**darkroom** ['daːkrʊm] n chambre noire

**darling** ['daːlɪŋ] adj, n chéri(e)

**darn** [daːn] vt repriser

**dart** [daːt] n fléchette f; (in sewing) pince f ▷ vi: **to ~ towards** (also: **make a dart towards**) se précipiter or s'élancer vers; **to ~ away/along** partir/passer comme une flèche

**dartboard** ['daːtbɔːd] n cible f (de jeu de fléchettes)

**darts** [daːts] n jeu m de fléchettes

**dash** [dæʃ] n (sign) tiret m; (small quantity) goutte f, larme f ▷ vt (throw) jeter or lancer violemment; (hopes) anéantir ▷ vi: **to ~ towards** (also: **make a dash towards**) se précipiter or se ruer vers; **a ~ of soda** un peu d'eau gazeuse
▶ **dash away** vi partir à toute allure
▶ **dash off** vi = **dash away**

**dashboard** ['dæʃbɔːd] n (Aut) tableau m de bord

**dashing** ['dæʃɪŋ] adj fringant(e)

**dastardly** ['dæstədlɪ] adj lâche

**DAT** n abbr (= digital audio tape) cassette f audio digitale

**data** ['deɪtə] npl données fpl

**database** ['deɪtəbeɪs] n base f de données

**data capture** n saisie f de données

**data processing** n traitement m (électronique) de l'information

**data transmission** n transmission f de données

**date** [deɪt] n date f; (with sb) rendez-vous m; (fruit) datte f ▷ vt dater; (person) sortir avec; **what's the ~ today?** quelle date sommes-nous aujourd'hui?; **~ of birth** date de naissance; **closing ~** date de clôture; **to ~** (adv) à ce jour; **out of ~** périmé(e); **up to ~** à la page, mis(e) à jour, moderne; **to bring up to ~** (correspondence, information) mettre à jour; (method) moderniser; (person) mettre au courant; **letter ~d 5th July** or (US) **July 5th** lettre (datée) du 5 juillet

**dated** ['deɪtɪd] adj démodé(e)

**dateline** ['deɪtlaɪn] n ligne f de changement de date

**date rape** n viol m (à l'issue d'un rendez-vous galant)

**date stamp** n timbre-dateur m

**daub** [dɔːb] vt barbouiller

**daughter** ['dɔːtəʳ] n fille f

**daughter-in-law** ['dɔːtərɪnlɔː] n belle-fille f, bru f

**daunt** [dɔːnt] vt intimider, décourager

**daunting** ['dɔːntɪŋ] adj décourageant(e), intimidant(e)

**dauntless** ['dɔːntlɪs] adj intrépide

**dawdle** ['dɔːdl] vi traîner, lambiner; **to ~ over one's work** traînasser or lambiner sur son travail

**dawn** [dɔːn] n aube f, aurore f ▷ vi (day) se lever, poindre; (fig) naître, se faire jour; **at ~** à l'aube; **from ~ to dusk** du matin au soir; **it ~ed on him that ...** il lui vint à l'esprit que ...

**dawn chorus** n (Brit) chant m des oiseaux à l'aube

**day** [deɪ] n jour m; (as duration) journée f; (period of time, age) époque f, temps m; **the ~ before** la veille, le jour précédent; **the ~ after**, **the following ~** le lendemain, le jour suivant; **the ~ before yesterday** avant-hier; **the ~ after tomorrow** après-demain; (on) **the ~ that ...** le jour où ...; **~ by ~** jour après jour; **by ~** de jour; **paid by the ~** payé(e) à la journée; **these ~s, in the present ~** de nos jours, à l'heure actuelle

**daybook** ['deɪbuk] n (Brit) main courante, brouillard m, journal m

**day boy** n (Scol) externe m

**daybreak** ['deɪbreɪk] n point m du jour

**day-care centre** ['deɪkɛə-] n (for elderly etc)

**d**

535

centre m d'accueil de jour; *(for children)* garderie f
**daydream** ['deidri:m] n rêverie f ▷ vi rêver (tout éveillé)
**day girl** n *(Scol)* externe f
**daylight** ['deilait] n (lumière f du) jour m
**daylight robbery** n: **it's ~** *(fig: inf)* c'est du vol caractérisé *or* manifeste
**daylight saving time** n *(US)* heure f d'été
**day release** n: **to be on ~** avoir une journée de congé pour formation professionnelle
**day return** n *(Brit)* billet m d'aller-retour *(valable pour la journée)*
**day shift** n équipe f de jour
**daytime** ['deitaim] n jour m, journée f
**day-to-day** ['deitə'dei] adj *(routine, expenses)* journalier(-ière); **on a ~ basis** au jour le jour
**day trip** n excursion f (d'une journée)
**day tripper** n excursionniste m/f
**daze** [deiz] vt *(drug)* hébéter; *(blow)* étourdir ▷ n: **in a ~** hébété(e), étourdi(e)
**dazed** [deizd] adj abruti(e)
**dazzle** ['dæzl] vt éblouir, aveugler
**dazzling** ['dæzliŋ] adj *(light)* aveuglant(e), éblouissant(e); *(fig)* éblouissant(e)
**DC** abbr *(Elec)* = **direct current**; *(US)* = **District of Columbia**
**DD** n abbr (= *Doctor of Divinity*) *titre universitaire*
**dd.** abbr *(Comm)* = **delivered**
**D/D** abbr = **direct debit**
**D-day** ['di:dei] n le jour J
**DDS** n abbr *(US:* = *Doctor of Dental Science; Brit:* = *Doctor of Dental Surgery) titres universitaires*
**DDT** n abbr (= *dichlorodiphenyl trichloroethane*) DDT m
**DE** abbr *(US)* = **Delaware**
**DEA** n abbr *(US:* = *Drug Enforcement Administration)* ≈ brigade f des stupéfiants
**deacon** ['di:kən] n diacre m
**dead** [dɛd] adj mort(e); *(numb)* engourdi(e), insensible; *(battery)* à plat ▷ adv *(completely)* absolument, complètement; *(exactly)* juste; **the dead** npl les morts; **he was shot ~** il a été tué d'un coup de revolver; **~ on time** à l'heure pile; **~ tired** éreinté(e), complètement fourbu(e); **to stop ~** s'arrêter pile *or* net; **the line is ~** *(Tel)* la ligne est coupée
**dead beat** adj *(inf)* claqué(e), crevé(e)
**deaden** [dɛdn] vt *(blow, sound)* amortir; *(make numb)* endormir, rendre insensible
**dead end** n impasse f
**dead-end** ['dɛdɛnd] adj: **a ~ job** un emploi *or* poste sans avenir
**dead heat** n *(Sport)*: **to finish in a ~** terminer ex aequo
**dead-letter office** [dɛd'lɛtər-] n ≈ centre m de recherche du courrier
**deadline** ['dɛdlain] n date f or heure f limite; **to work to a ~** avoir des délais stricts à respecter
**deadlock** ['dɛdlɔk] n impasse f; *(fig)*
**dead loss** n *(inf)*: **to be a ~** *(person)* n'être bon (bonne à rien); *(thing)* ne rien valoir
**deadly** ['dɛdli] adj mortel(le); *(weapon)* meurtrier(-ière); **~ dull** ennuyeux(-euse) à

mourir, mortellement ennuyeux
**deadpan** ['dɛdpæn] adj impassible; *(humour)* pince-sans-rire inv
**Dead Sea** n: **the ~** la mer Morte
**deaf** [dɛf] adj sourd(e); **to turn a ~ ear to sth** faire la sourde oreille à qch
**deaf-aid** ['dɛfeid] n *(Brit)* appareil auditif
**deaf-and-dumb** ['dɛfən'dʌm] adj sourd(e)-muet(te); **~ alphabet** alphabet m des sourds-muets
**deafen** ['dɛfn] vt rendre sourd(e); *(fig)* assourdir
**deafening** ['dɛfniŋ] adj assourdissant(e)
**deaf-mute** ['dɛfmju:t] n sourd/e-muet/te
**deafness** ['dɛfnis] n surdité f
**deal** [di:l] n affaire f, marché m ▷ vt *(pt, pp -t)* [dɛlt] *(blow)* porter; *(cards)* donner, distribuer; **to strike a ~ with sb** faire *or* conclure un marché avec qn; **it's a ~!** *(inf)* marché conclu!, tope-là!, topez-là!; **he got a bad ~ from them** ils ont mal agi envers lui; **he got a fair ~ from them** ils ont agi loyalement envers lui; **a good ~** *(a lot)* beaucoup; **a good ~ of, a great ~ of** beaucoup de, énormément de
▶ **deal in** vt fus *(Comm)* faire le commerce de, être dans le commerce de
▶ **deal with** vt fus *(Comm)* traiter avec; *(handle)* s'occuper *or* se charger de; *(be about: book etc)* traiter de
**dealer** ['di:lər] n *(Comm)* marchand m; *(Cards)* donneur m
**dealership** ['di:ləʃip] n concession f
**dealings** ['di:liŋz] npl *(in goods, shares)* opérations fpl, transactions fpl; *(relations)* relations fpl, rapports mpl
**dealt** [dɛlt] pt, pp of **deal**
**dean** [di:n] n *(Rel, Brit Scol)* doyen m; *(US Scol)* conseiller principal (conseillère principale) d'éducation
**dear** [diər] adj cher (chère); *(expensive)* cher, coûteux(-euse) ▷ n: **my ~** mon cher (ma chère) ▷ excl: **~ me!** mon Dieu!; **D~ Sir/Madam** *(in letter)* Monsieur/Madame; **D~ Mr/Mrs X** Cher Monsieur/Chère Madame X
**dearly** ['diəli] adv *(love)* tendrement; *(pay)* cher
**dearth** [də:θ] n disette f, pénurie f
**death** [dɛθ] n mort f; *(Admin)* décès m
**deathbed** ['dɛθbɛd] n lit m de mort
**death certificate** n acte m de décès
**deathly** ['dɛθli] adj de mort ▷ adv comme la mort
**death penalty** n peine f de mort
**death rate** n taux m de mortalité
**death row** [-'rəu] n *(US)* quartier m des condamnés à mort; **to be on ~** être condamné à la peine de mort
**death sentence** n condamnation f à mort
**death squad** n escadron m de la mort
**death toll** n nombre m de morts
**deathtrap** ['dɛθtræp] n endroit *or* véhicule *etc* dangereux
**deb** [dɛb] n abbr *(inf)* = **debutante**
**debar** [di'ba:r] vt: **to ~ sb from a club** *etc* exclure

qn d'un club *etc*; **to ~ sb from doing** interdire à qn de faire

**debase** [dɪ'beɪs] *vt* (*currency*) déprécier, dévaloriser; (*person*) abaisser, avilir

**debatable** [dɪ'beɪtəbl] *adj* discutable, contestable; **it is ~ whether ...** il est douteux que ...

**debate** [dɪ'beɪt] *n* discussion *f*, débat *m* ▷ *vt* discuter, débattre ▷ *vi* (*consider*): **to ~ whether** se demander si

**debauchery** [dɪ'bɔːtʃərɪ] *n* débauche *f*

**debenture** [dɪ'bentʃəʳ] *n* (*Comm*) obligation *f*

**debilitate** [dɪ'bɪlɪteɪt] *vt* débiliter

**debit** ['dɛbɪt] *n* débit *m* ▷ *vt*: **to ~ a sum to sb** *or* **to sb's account** porter une somme au débit de qn, débiter qn d'une somme

**debit balance** *n* solde débiteur

**debit card** *n* carte *f* de paiement

**debit note** *n* note *f* de débit

**debrief** [diː'briːf] *vt* demander un compte rendu de fin de mission à

**debriefing** [diː'briːfɪŋ] *n* compte rendu *m*

**debris** ['dɛbriː] *n* débris *mpl*, décombres *mpl*

**debt** [dɛt] *n* dette *f*; **to be in ~** avoir des dettes, être endetté(e); **bad ~** créance *f* irrécouvrable

**debt collector** *n* agent *m* de recouvrements

**debtor** ['dɛtəʳ] *n* débiteur(-trice)

**debug** ['diː'bʌg] *vt* (*Comput*) déboguer

**debunk** [diː'bʌŋk] *vt* (*theory, claim*) montrer le ridicule de

**debut** ['deɪbjuː] *n* début(s) *m(pl)*

**debutante** ['dɛbjutænt] *n* débutante *f*

**Dec.** *abbr* (= *December*) déc

**decade** ['dɛkeɪd] *n* décennie *f*, décade *f*

**decadence** ['dɛkədəns] *n* décadence *f*

**decadent** ['dɛkədənt] *adj* décadent(e)

**decaf** ['diːkæf] *n* (*inf*) déca *m*

**decaffeinated** [dɪ'kæfɪneɪtɪd] *adj* décaféiné(e)

**decamp** [dɪ'kæmp] *vi* (*inf*) décamper, filer

**decant** [dɪ'kænt] *vt* (*wine*) décanter

**decanter** [dɪ'kæntəʳ] *n* carafe *f*

**decarbonize** [diː'kɑːbənaɪz] *vt* (*Aut*) décalaminer

**decathlon** [dɪ'kæθlən] *n* décathlon *m*

**decay** [dɪ'keɪ] *n* (*of food, wood etc*) décomposition *f*, pourriture *f*; (*of building*) délabrement *m*; (*fig*) déclin *m*; (*also*: **tooth decay**) carie *f* (dentaire) ▷ *vi* (*rot*) se décomposer, pourrir; (*: teeth*) se carier; (*fig: city, district, building*) se délabrer; (*: civilization*) décliner; (*: system*) tomber en ruine

**decease** [dɪ'siːs] *n* décès *m*

**deceased** [dɪ'siːst] *n*: **the ~** le (la) défunt(e)

**deceit** [dɪ'siːt] *n* tromperie *f*, supercherie *f*

**deceitful** [dɪ'siːtful] *adj* trompeur(-euse)

**deceive** [dɪ'siːv] *vt* tromper; **to ~ o.s.** s'abuser

**decelerate** [diː'sɛləreɪt] *vt, vi* ralentir

**December** [dɪ'sɛmbəʳ] *n* décembre *m*; *for phrases see also* **July**

**decency** ['diːsənsɪ] *n* décence *f*

**decent** ['diːsənt] *adj* (*proper*) décent(e), convenable; **they were very ~ about it** ils se sont montrés très chics

**decently** ['diːsəntlɪ] *adv* (*respectably*) décemment, convenablement; (*kindly*) décemment

**decentralization** [diːsɛntrəlaɪ'zeɪʃən] *n* décentralisation *f*

**decentralize** [diː'sɛntrəlaɪz] *vt* décentraliser

**deception** [dɪ'sɛpʃən] *n* tromperie *f*

**deceptive** [dɪ'sɛptɪv] *adj* trompeur(-euse)

**decibel** ['dɛsɪbɛl] *n* décibel *m*

**decide** [dɪ'saɪd] *vt* (*subj: person*) décider; (*question, argument*) trancher, régler ▷ *vi* se décider, décider; **to ~ to do/that** décider de faire/que; **to ~ on** décider, se décider pour; **to ~ on doing** décider de faire; **to ~ against doing** décider de ne pas faire

**decided** [dɪ'saɪdɪd] *adj* (*resolute*) résolu(e), décidé(e); (*clear, definite*) net(te), marqué(e)

**decidedly** [dɪ'saɪdɪdlɪ] *adv* résolument; incontestablement, nettement

**deciding** [dɪ'saɪdɪŋ] *adj* décisif(-ive)

**deciduous** [dɪ'sɪdjuəs] *adj* à feuilles caduques

**decimal** ['dɛsɪməl] *adj* décimal(e) ▷ *n* décimale *f*; **to three ~ places** (jusqu')à la troisième décimale

**decimalize** ['dɛsɪməlaɪz] *vt* (*Brit*) décimaliser

**decimal point** *n* ≈ virgule *f*

**decimate** ['dɛsɪmeɪt] *vt* décimer

**decipher** [dɪ'saɪfəʳ] *vt* déchiffrer

**decision** [dɪ'sɪʒən] *n* décision *f*; **to make a ~** prendre une décision

**decisive** [dɪ'saɪsɪv] *adj* décisif(-ive); (*influence*) décisif, déterminant(e); (*manner, person*) décidé(e), catégorique; (*reply*) ferme, catégorique

**deck** [dɛk] *n* (*Naut*) pont *m*; (*of cards*) jeu *m*; (*record deck*) platine *f*; (*of bus*): **top ~** impériale *f*; **to go up on ~** monter sur le pont; **below ~** dans l'entrepont

**deckchair** ['dɛktʃɛəʳ] *n* chaise longue

**deck hand** *n* matelot *m*

**declaration** [dɛklə'reɪʃən] *n* déclaration *f*

**declare** [dɪ'klɛəʳ] *vt* déclarer

**declassify** [diː'klæsɪfaɪ] *vt* rendre accessible au public *or* à tous

**decline** [dɪ'klaɪn] *n* (*decay*) déclin *m*; (*lessening*) baisse *f* ▷ *vt* refuser, décliner ▷ *vi* décliner; (*business*) baisser; **~ in living standards** baisse du niveau de vie; **to ~ to do sth** refuser (poliment) de faire qch

**declutch** ['diː'klʌtʃ] *vi* (*Brit*) débrayer

**decode** ['diː'kəud] *vt* décoder

**decoder** [diː'kəudəʳ] *n* (*Comput, TV*) décodeur *m*

**decompose** [diːkəm'pəuz] *vi* se décomposer

**decomposition** [diːkɔmpə'zɪʃən] *n* décomposition *f*

**decompression** [diːkəm'prɛʃən] *n* décompression *f*

**decompression chamber** *n* caisson *m* de décompression

**decongestant** [diːkən'dʒɛstənt] *n* décongestif *m*

**decontaminate** [diːkən'tæmɪneɪt] *vt*

décontaminer
**decontrol** [di:kən'trəul] vt (prices etc) libérer
**décor** ['deɪkɔːʳ] n décor m
**decorate** ['dɛkəreɪt] vt (adorn, give a medal to) décorer; (paint and paper) peindre et tapisser
**decoration** [dɛkə'reɪʃən] n (medal etc, adornment) décoration f
**decorative** ['dɛkərətɪv] adj décoratif(-ive)
**decorator** ['dɛkəreɪtəʳ] n peintre m en bâtiment
**decorum** [dɪ'kɔːrəm] n décorum m, bienséance f
**decoy** ['diːkɔɪ] n piège m; **they used him as a ~ for the enemy** ils se sont servis de lui pour attirer l'ennemi
**decrease** n ['diːkriːs] diminution f ▷ vt, vi [diːkriːs] diminuer; **to be on the ~** diminuer, être en diminution
**decreasing** [diː'kriːsɪŋ] adj en voie de diminution
**decree** [dɪ'kriː] n (Pol, Rel) décret m; (Law) arrêt m, jugement m ▷ vt: **to ~ (that)** décréter (que), ordonner (que); **~ absolute** jugement définitif (de divorce); **~ nisi** jugement provisoire de divorce
**decrepit** [dɪ'krɛpɪt] adj (person) décrépit(e); (building) délabré(e)
**decry** [dɪ'kraɪ] vt condamner ouvertement, déplorer; (disparage) dénigrer, décrier
**dedicate** ['dɛdɪkeɪt] vt consacrer; (book etc) dédier
**dedicated** ['dɛdɪkeɪtɪd] adj (person) dévoué(e); (Comput) spécialisé(e), dédié(e); **~ word processor** station f de traitement de texte
**dedication** [dɛdɪ'keɪʃən] n (devotion) dévouement m; (in book) dédicace f
**deduce** [dɪ'djuːs] vt déduire, conclure
**deduct** [dɪ'dʌkt] vt: **to ~ sth (from)** déduire qch (de), retrancher qch (de); (from wage etc) prélever qch (sur), retenir qch (sur)
**deduction** [dɪ'dʌkʃən] n (deducting, deducing) déduction f; (from wage etc) prélèvement m, retenue f
**deed** [diːd] n action f, acte m; (Law) acte notarié, contrat m; **~ of covenant** (acte m de) donation f
**deem** [diːm] vt (formal) juger, estimer; **to ~ it wise to do** juger bon de faire
**deep** [diːp] adj (water, sigh, sorrow, thoughts) profond(e); (voice) grave ▷ adv: **~ in snow** recouvert(e) d'une épaisse couche de neige; **spectators stood 20 ~** il y avait 20 rangs de spectateurs; **knee-~ in water** dans l'eau jusqu'aux genoux; **4 metres ~** de 4 mètres de profondeur; **how ~ is the water?** l'eau a quelle profondeur?; **he took a ~ breath** il inspira profondément, il prit son souffle
**deepen** [diːpn] vt (hole) approfondir ▷ vi s'approfondir; (darkness) s'épaissir
**deepfreeze** ['diːp'friːz] n congélateur m ▷ vt surgeler
**deep-fry** ['diːp'fraɪ] vt faire frire (dans une friteuse)
**deeply** ['diːplɪ] adv profondément; (dig) en profondeur; (regret, interested) vivement

**deep-rooted** ['diːp'ruːtɪd] adj (prejudice) profondément enraciné(e); (affection) profond(e); (habit) invétéré(e)
**deep-sea** ['diːp'siː] adj: **~ diver** plongeur sous-marin; **~ diving** plongée sous-marine; **~ fishing** pêche hauturière
**deep-seated** ['diːp'siːtɪd] adj (belief) profondément enraciné(e)
**deep-set** ['diːpsɛt] adj (eyes) enfoncé(e)
**deep vein thrombosis** n thrombose f veineuse profonde
**deer** [dɪəʳ] n (pl inv): **the ~** les cervidés mpl; (Zool): **(red) ~** cerf m; **(fallow) ~** daim m; **(roe) ~** chevreuil m
**deerskin** ['dɪəskɪn] n peau f de daim
**deerstalker** ['dɪəstɔːkəʳ] n (person) chasseur m de cerf; (hat) casquette f à la Sherlock Holmes
**deface** [dɪ'feɪs] vt dégrader; barbouiller rendre illisible
**defamation** [dɛfə'meɪʃən] n diffamation f
**defamatory** [dɪ'fæmətrɪ] adj diffamatoire, diffamant(e)
**default** [dɪ'fɔːlt] vi (Law) faire défaut; (gen) manquer à ses engagements ▷ n (Comput: also: **default value**) valeur f par défaut; **by ~** (Law) par défaut, par contumace; (Sport) par forfait; **to ~ on a debt** ne pas s'acquitter d'une dette
**defaulter** [dɪ'fɔːltəʳ] n (on debt) débiteur défaillant
**default option** n (Comput) option f par défaut
**defeat** [dɪ'fiːt] n défaite f ▷ vt (team, opponents) battre; (fig: plans, efforts) faire échouer
**defeatism** [dɪ'fiːtɪzəm] n défaitisme m
**defeatist** [dɪ'fiːtɪst] adj, n défaitiste m/f
**defecate** ['dɛfəkeɪt] vi déféquer
**defect** ['diːfɛkt] n défaut m ▷ vi [dɪ'fɛkt]: **to ~ to the enemy/the West** passer à l'ennemi/ l'Ouest; **physical ~** malformation f, vice m de conformation; **mental ~** anomalie or déficience mentale
**defective** [dɪ'fɛktɪv] adj défectueux(-euse)
**defector** [dɪ'fɛktəʳ] n transfuge m/f
**defence**, (US) **defense** [dɪ'fɛns] n défense f; **in ~ of** pour défendre; **witness for the ~** témoin m à décharge; **the Ministry of D~**, (US) **the Department of Defense** le ministère de la Défense nationale
**defenceless** [dɪ'fɛnslɪs] adj sans défense
**defend** [dɪ'fɛnd] vt défendre; (decision, action, opinion) justifier, défendre
**defendant** [dɪ'fɛndənt] n défendeur(-deresse); (in criminal case) accusé(e), prévenu(e)
**defender** [dɪ'fɛndəʳ] n défenseur m
**defending champion** [dɪ'fɛndɪŋ-] n (Sport) champion(ne) en titre
**defending counsel** [dɪ'fɛndɪŋ-] n (Law) avocat m de la défense
**defense** [dɪ'fɛns] n (US) = **defence**
**defensive** [dɪ'fɛnsɪv] adj défensif(-ive) ▷ n défensive f; **on the ~** sur la défensive
**defer** [dɪ'fəːʳ] vt (postpone) différer, ajourner ▷ vi (submit): **to ~ to sb/sth** déférer à qn/qch, s'en

remettre à qn/qch

**deference** ['dɛfərəns] n déférence f, égards mpl; **out of** or **in ~ to** par déférence or égards pour

**defiance** [dɪ'faɪəns] n défi m; **in ~ of** au mépris de

**defiant** [dɪ'faɪənt] adj provocant(e), de défi; (person) rebelle, intraitable

**defiantly** [dɪ'faɪəntlɪ] adv d'un air (or d'un ton) de défi

**deficiency** [dɪ'fɪʃənsɪ] n (lack) insuffisance f; (: Med) carence f; (flaw) faiblesse f; (Comm) déficit m, découvert m

**deficiency disease** n maladie f de carence

**deficient** [dɪ'fɪʃənt] adj (inadequate) insuffisant(e); (defective) défectueux(-euse); **to be ~ in** manquer de

**deficit** ['dɛfɪsɪt] n déficit m

**defile** [dɪ'faɪl] vt souiller ▷ vi défiler ▷ n ['di:faɪl] défilé m

**define** [dɪ'faɪn] vt définir

**definite** ['dɛfɪnɪt] adj (fixed) défini(e), (bien) déterminé(e); (clear, obvious) net(te), manifeste; (Ling) défini(e); (certain) sûr(e); **he was ~ about it** il a été catégorique; il était sûr de son fait

**definitely** ['dɛfɪnɪtlɪ] adv sans aucun doute

**definition** [dɛfɪ'nɪʃən] n définition f; (clearness) netteté f

**definitive** [dɪ'fɪnɪtɪv] adj définitif(-ive)

**deflate** [di:'fleɪt] vt dégonfler; (pompous person) rabattre le caquet à; (Econ) provoquer la déflation de; (: prices) faire tomber or baisser

**deflation** [di:'fleɪʃən] n (Econ) déflation f

**deflationary** [di:'fleɪʃənrɪ] adj (Econ) déflationniste

**deflect** [dɪ'flɛkt] vt détourner, faire dévier

**defog** ['di:'fɔg] vt (US Aut) désembuer

**defogger** ['di:'fɔgər] n (US Aut) dispositif m anti-buée inv

**deform** [dɪ'fɔ:m] vt déformer

**deformed** [dɪ'fɔ:md] adj difforme

**deformity** [dɪ'fɔ:mɪtɪ] n difformité f

**defraud** [dɪ'frɔ:d] vt frauder; **to ~ sb of sth** soutirer qch malhonnêtement à qn; escroquer qch à qn; frustrer qn de qch

**defray** [dɪ'freɪ] vt: **to ~ sb's expenses** défrayer qn (de ses frais), rembourser or payer à qn ses frais

**defrost** [di:'frɔst] vt (fridge) dégivrer; (frozen food) décongeler

**deft** [dɛft] adj adroit(e), preste

**defunct** [dɪ'fʌŋkt] adj défunt(e)

**defuse** [di:'fju:z] vt désamorcer

**defy** [dɪ'faɪ] vt défier; (efforts etc) résister à; **it defies description** cela défie toute description

**degenerate** vi [dɪ'dʒɛnəreɪt] dégénérer ▷ adj [dɪ'dʒɛnərɪt] dégénéré(e)

**degradation** [dɛgrə'deɪʃən] n dégradation f

**degrade** [dɪ'greɪd] vt dégrader

**degrading** [dɪ'greɪdɪŋ] adj dégradant(e)

**degree** [dɪ'gri:] n degré m; (Scol) diplôme m (universitaire); **10 ~s below (zero)** 10 degrés au-dessous de zéro; **a (first) ~ in maths** (Brit)

une licence en maths; **a considerable ~ of risk** un considérable facteur or élément de risque; **by ~s** (gradually) par degrés; **to some ~, to a certain ~** jusqu'à un certain point, dans une certaine mesure

**dehydrated** [di:haɪ'dreɪtɪd] adj déshydraté(e); (milk, eggs) en poudre

**dehydration** [di:haɪ'dreɪʃən] n déshydratation f

**de-ice** ['di:'aɪs] vt (windscreen) dégivrer

**de-icer** ['di:'aɪsər] n dégivreur m

**deign** [deɪn] vi: **to ~ to do** daigner faire

**deity** ['di:ɪtɪ] n divinité f; dieu m, déesse f

**déjà vu** [deɪʒɑ:'vu:] n: **I had a sense of ~** j'ai eu une impression de déjà-vu

**dejected** [dɪ'dʒɛktɪd] adj abattu(e), déprimé(e)

**dejection** [dɪ'dʒɛkʃən] n abattement m, découragement m

**Del.** abbr (US) = **Delaware**

**del.** abbr = **delete**

**delay** [dɪ'leɪ] vt (journey, operation) retarder; (traveller, train) retarder; (payment) différer ▷ vi s'attarder ▷ n délai m, retard m; **to be ~ed** être en retard; **without ~** sans délai, sans tarder

**delayed-action** [dɪ'leɪd'ækʃən] adj à retardement

**delectable** [dɪ'lɛktəbl] adj délicieux(-euse)

**delegate** n ['dɛlɪgɪt] délégué(e) ▷ vt ['dɛlɪgeɪt] déléguer; **to ~ sth to sb/sb to do sth** déléguer qch à qn/qn pour faire qch

**delegation** [dɛlɪ'geɪʃən] n délégation f

**delete** [dɪ'li:t] vt rayer, supprimer; (Comput) effacer

**Delhi** ['dɛlɪ] n Delhi

**deli** ['dɛlɪ] n épicerie fine

**deliberate** adj [dɪ'lɪbərɪt] (intentional) délibéré(e); (slow) mesuré(e) ▷ vi [dɪ'lɪbəreɪt] délibérer, réfléchir

**deliberately** [dɪ'lɪbərɪtlɪ] adv (on purpose) exprès, délibérément

**deliberation** [dɪlɪbə'reɪʃən] n délibération f, réflexion f; (gen pl: discussion) délibérations, débats mpl

**delicacy** ['dɛlɪkəsɪ] n délicatesse f; (choice food) mets fin or délicat, friandise f

**delicate** ['dɛlɪkɪt] adj délicat(e)

**delicately** ['dɛlɪkɪtlɪ] adv délicatement; (act, express) avec délicatesse, avec tact

**delicatessen** [dɛlɪkə'tɛsn] n épicerie fine

**delicious** [dɪ'lɪʃəs] adj délicieux(-euse), exquis(e)

**delight** [dɪ'laɪt] n (grande) joie, grand plaisir ▷ vt enchanter; **she's a ~ to work with** c'est un plaisir de travailler avec elle; **a ~ to the eyes** un régal or plaisir pour les yeux; **to take ~ in** prendre grand plaisir à; **to be the ~ of** faire les délices or la joie de

**delighted** [dɪ'laɪtɪd] adj: **~ (at** or **with sth)** ravi(e) (de qch); **to be ~ to do sth/that** être enchanté(e) or ravi(e) de faire qch/que; **I'd be ~** j'en serais enchanté or ravi

**delightful** [dɪ'laɪtful] adj (person) absolument charmant(e), adorable; (meal, evening) merveilleux(-euse)

**delimit** [di:'lɪmɪt] vt délimiter

**delineate** [dɪ'lɪnɪeɪt] vt tracer, esquisser; (fig) dépeindre, décrire

**delinquency** [dɪ'lɪŋkwənsɪ] n délinquance f

**delinquent** [dɪ'lɪŋkwənt] adj, n délinquant(e)

**delirious** [dɪ'lɪrɪəs] adj (Med: fig) délirant(e); **to be ~** délirer

**delirium** [dɪ'lɪrɪəm] n délire m

**deliver** [dɪ'lɪvə<sup>r</sup>] vt (mail) distribuer; (goods) livrer; (message) remettre; (speech) prononcer; (warning, ultimatum) lancer; (free) délivrer; (Med: baby) mettre au monde; (: woman) accoucher; **to ~ the goods** (fig) tenir ses promesses

**deliverance** [dɪ'lɪvrəns] n délivrance f, libération f

**delivery** [dɪ'lɪvərɪ] n (of mail) distribution f; (of goods) livraison f; (of speaker) élocution f; (Med) accouchement m; **to take ~ of** prendre livraison de

**delivery note** n bon m de livraison

**delivery van**, (US) **delivery truck** n fourgonnette f or camionnette f de livraison

**delta** ['dɛltə] n delta m

**delude** [dɪ'lu:d] vt tromper, leurrer; **to ~ o.s.** se leurrer, se faire des illusions

**deluge** ['dɛlju:dʒ] n déluge m ▷ vt (fig): **to ~ (with)** inonder (de)

**delusion** [dɪ'lu:ʒən] n illusion f; **to have ~s of grandeur** être un peu mégalomane

**de luxe** [də'lʌks] adj de luxe

**delve** [dɛlv] vi: **to ~ into** fouiller dans

**Dem.** abbr (US Pol) = **democrat; democratic**

**demagogue** ['dɛmagɔg] n démagogue m/f

**demand** [dɪ'ma:nd] vt réclamer, exiger; (need) exiger, requérir ▷ n exigence f; (claim) revendication f; (Econ) demande f; **to ~ sth (from** or **of sb)** exiger qch (de qn), réclamer qch (à qn); **in ~** demandé(e), recherché(e); **on ~** sur demande

**demanding** [dɪ'ma:ndɪŋ] adj (person) exigeant(e); (work) astreignant(e)

**demarcation** [di:ma:'keɪʃən] n démarcation f

**demarcation dispute** n (Industry) conflit m d'attributions

**demean** [dɪ'mi:n] vt: **to ~ o.s.** s'abaisser

**demeanour**, (US) **demeanor** [dɪ'mi:nə<sup>r</sup>] n comportement m; maintien m

**demented** [dɪ'mɛntɪd] adj dément(e), fou (folle)

**demilitarized zone** [di:'mɪlɪtəraɪzd-] n zone démilitarisée

**demise** [dɪ'maɪz] n décès m

**demist** [di:'mɪst] vt (Brit Aut) désembuer

**demister** [di:'mɪstə<sup>r</sup>] n (Brit Aut) dispositif m anti-buée inv

**demo** ['dɛməu] n abbr (inf) = **demonstration**; (protest) manif f; (Comput) démonstration f

**demobilize** [di:'məubɪlaɪz] vt démobiliser

**democracy** [dɪ'mɔkrəsɪ] n démocratie f

**democrat** ['dɛməkræt] n démocrate m/f

**democratic** [dɛmə'krætɪk] adj démocratique; **the D~ Party** (US) le parti démocrate

**demography** [dɪ'mɔgrəfɪ] n démographie f

**demolish** [dɪ'mɔlɪʃ] vt démolir

**demolition** [dɛmə'lɪʃən] n démolition f

**demon** ['di:mən] n démon m ▷ cpd: **a ~ squash player** un crack en squash; **a ~ driver** un fou du volant

**demonstrate** ['dɛmənstreɪt] vt démontrer, prouver; (show) faire une démonstration de ▷ vi: **to ~ (for/against)** manifester (en faveur de/ contre)

**demonstration** [dɛmən'streɪʃən] n démonstration f; (Pol etc) manifestation f; **to hold a ~** (Pol etc) organiser une manifestation, manifester

**demonstrative** [dɪ'mɔnstrətɪv] adj démonstratif(-ive)

**demonstrator** ['dɛmənstreɪtə<sup>r</sup>] n (Pol etc) manifestant(e); (Comm: sales person) vendeur(-euse); (: car, computer etc) modèle m de démonstration

**demoralize** [dɪ'mɔrəlaɪz] vt démoraliser

**demote** [dɪ'məut] vt rétrograder

**demotion** [dɪ'məuʃən] n rétrogradation f

**demur** [dɪ'mə:<sup>r</sup>] vi: **to ~ (at sth)** hésiter (devant qch); (object) élever des objections (contre qch) ▷ n: **without ~** sans hésiter; sans faire de difficultés

**demure** [dɪ'mjuə<sup>r</sup>] adj sage, réservé(e), d'une modestie affectée

**demurrage** [dɪ'mʌrɪdʒ] n droits mpl de magasinage; surestarie f

**den** [dɛn] n (of lion) tanière f; (room) repaire m

**denationalization** [di:næʃnəlaɪ'zeɪʃən] n dénationalisation f

**denationalize** [di:'næʃnəlaɪz] vt dénationaliser

**denial** [dɪ'naɪəl] n (of accusation) démenti m; (of rights, guilt, truth) dénégation f

**denier** ['dɛnɪə<sup>r</sup>] n denier m; **15 ~ stockings** bas de 15 deniers

**denigrate** ['dɛnɪgreɪt] vt dénigrer

**denim** ['dɛnɪm] n jean m; **denims** npl (blue-)jeans mpl

**denim jacket** n veste f en jean

**denizen** ['dɛnɪzn] n (inhabitant) habitant(e); (foreigner) étranger(-ère)

**Denmark** ['dɛnma:k] n Danemark m

**denomination** [dɪnɔmɪ'neɪʃən] n (money) valeur f; (Rel) confession f; culte m

**denominator** [dɪ'nɔmɪneɪtə<sup>r</sup>] n dénominateur m

**denote** [dɪ'nəut] vt dénoter

**denounce** [dɪ'nauns] vt dénoncer

**dense** [dɛns] adj dense; (inf: stupid) obtus(e), dur(e) or lent(e) à la comprenette

**densely** ['dɛnslɪ] adv: **~ wooded** couvert(e) d'épaisses forêts; **~ populated** à forte densité (de population), très peuplé(e)

**density** ['dɛnsɪtɪ] n densité f

**dent** [dɛnt] n bosse f ▷ vt (also: **make a dent in**) cabosser; **to make a ~ in** (fig) entamer

**dental** ['dɛntl] adj dentaire

**dental floss** [-flɔs] n fil m dentaire

**dental surgeon** n (chirurgien(ne)) dentiste
**dental surgery** n cabinet m de dentiste
**dentist** ['dɛntɪst] n dentiste m/f; **~'s surgery**
(Brit) cabinet m de dentiste
**dentistry** ['dɛntɪstrɪ] n art m dentaire
**dentures** ['dɛntʃəz] npl dentier msg
**denunciation** [dɪnʌnsɪ'eɪʃən] n dénonciation f
**deny** [dɪ'naɪ] vt nier; (refuse) refuser; (disown)
renier; **he denies having said it** il nie l'avoir
dit
**deodorant** [di:'əudərənt] n désodorisant m,
déodorant m
**depart** [dɪ'pɑːt] vi partir; **to ~ from** (leave)
quitter, partir de; (fig: differ from) s'écarter de
**departed** [dɪ'pɑːtɪd] adj (dead) défunt(e); **the
(dear) ~** le défunt/la défunte/les défunts
**department** [dɪ'pɑːtmənt] n (Comm) rayon m;
(Scol) section f; (Pol) ministère m, département
m; **that's not my ~** (fig) ce n'est pas mon
domaine or ma compétence, ce n'est pas mon
rayon; **D~ of State** (US) Département d'État
**departmental** [di:pɑː'tmɛntl] adj d'une or de la
section; d'un or du ministère, d'un or du
département; **~ manager** chef m de service; (in
shop) chef de rayon
**department store** n grand magasin
**departure** [dɪ'pɑːtʃəʳ] n départ m; (fig): **~ from**
écart m par rapport à; **a new ~** une nouvelle voie
**departure lounge** n salle f de départ
**depend** [dɪ'pɛnd] vi: **to ~ (up)on** dépendre de;
(rely on) compter sur; (financially) dépendre
(financièrement) de, être à la charge de; **it ~s**
cela dépend; **~ing on the result ...** selon le
résultat ...
**dependable** [dɪ'pɛndəbl] adj sûr(e), digne de
confiance
**dependant** [dɪ'pɛndənt] n personne f à charge
**dependence** [dɪ'pɛndəns] n dépendance f
**dependent** [dɪ'pɛndənt] adj: **to be ~ (on)**
dépendre (de) ▷ n = **dependant**
**depict** [dɪ'pɪkt] vt (in picture) représenter; (in
words) (dé)peindre, décrire
**depilatory** [dɪ'pɪlətrɪ] n (also: **depilatory cream**)
dépilatoire m, crème f à épiler
**depleted** [dɪ'pliːtɪd] adj (considérablement)
réduit(e) or diminué(e)
**deplorable** [dɪ'plɔːrəbl] adj déplorable,
lamentable
**deplore** [dɪ'plɔːʳ] vt déplorer
**deploy** [dɪ'plɔɪ] vt déployer
**depopulate** [di:'pɔpjuleɪt] vt dépeupler
**depopulation** ['di:pɔpju'leɪʃən] n dépopulation
f, dépeuplement m
**deport** [dɪ'pɔːt] vt déporter, expulser
**deportation** [di:pɔː'teɪʃən] n déportation f,
expulsion f
**deportation order** n arrêté m d'expulsion
**deportee** [dɪ:pɔː'tiː] n déporté(e)
**deportment** [dɪ:'pɔːtmənt] n maintien m,
tenue f
**depose** [dɪ'pəuz] vt déposer
**deposit** [dɪ'pɔzɪt] n (Chem, Comm, Geo) dépôt m;

(of ore, oil) gisement m; (part payment) arrhes fpl,
acompte m; (on bottle etc) consigne f; (for hired
goods etc) cautionnement m, garantie f ▷ vt
déposer; (valuables) mettre or laisser en dépôt;
**to put down a ~ of £50** verser 50 livres d'arrhes
or d'acompte; laisser 50 livres en garantie
**deposit account** n compte m sur livret
**depositor** [dɪ'pɔzɪtəʳ] n déposant(e)
**depository** [dɪ'pɔzɪtərɪ] n (person) dépositaire m/
f; (place) dépôt m
**depot** ['dɛpəu] n dépôt m; (US: Rail) gare f
**depraved** [dɪ'preɪvd] adj dépravé(e), perverti(e)
**depravity** [dɪ'prævɪtɪ] n dépravation f
**deprecate** ['dɛprɪkeɪt] vt désapprouver
**deprecating** ['dɛprɪkeɪtɪŋ] adj (disapproving)
désapprobateur(-trice); (apologetic): **a ~ smile**
un sourire d'excuse
**depreciate** [dɪ'priːʃɪeɪt] vt déprécier ▷ vi se
déprécier, se dévaloriser
**depreciation** [dɪpriːʃɪ'eɪʃən] n dépréciation f
**depress** [dɪ'prɛs] vt déprimer; (press down)
appuyer sur, abaisser; (wages etc) faire baisser
**depressant** [dɪ'prɛsnt] n (Med) dépresseur m
**depressed** [dɪ'prɛst] adj (person) déprimé(e),
abattu(e); (area) en déclin, touché(e) par le sous-
emploi; (Comm: market, trade) maussade; **to get
~** se démoraliser, se laisser abattre
**depressing** [dɪ'prɛsɪŋ] adj déprimant(e)
**depression** [dɪ'prɛʃən] n (Econ) dépression f
**deprivation** [dɛprɪ'veɪʃən] n privation f; (loss)
perte f
**deprive** [dɪ'praɪv] vt: **to ~ sb of** priver qn de
**deprived** [dɪ'praɪvd] adj déshérité(e)
**dept.** abbr (= department) dép, dépt
**depth** [dɛpθ] n profondeur f; **in the ~s of** au
fond de; au cœur de; au plus profond de; **to be
in the ~s of despair** être au plus profond du
désespoir; **at a ~ of 3 metres** à 3 mètres de
profondeur; **to be out of one's ~** (Brit: swimmer)
ne plus avoir pied; (fig) être dépassé(e), nager;
**to study sth in ~** étudier qch en profondeur
**depth charge** n grenade sous-marine
**deputation** [dɛpju'teɪʃən] n députation f,
délégation f
**deputize** ['dɛpjutaɪz] vi: **to ~ for** assurer
l'intérim de
**deputy** ['dɛpjutɪ] n (replacement) suppléant(e),
intérimaire m/f; (second in command) adjoint(e);
(Pol) député m/f; (US: also: **deputy sheriff**) shérif
adjoint ▷ adj: **~ chairman** vice-président m; **~
head** (Scol) directeur(-trice) adjoint(e), sous-
directeur(-trice); **~ leader** (Brit Pol) vice-
président(e), secrétaire adjoint(e)
**derail** [dɪ'reɪl] vt faire dérailler; **to be ~ed**
dérailler
**derailment** [dɪ'reɪlmənt] n déraillement m
**deranged** [dɪ'reɪndʒd] adj: **to be (mentally) ~**
avoir le cerveau dérangé
**derby** ['dəːrbɪ] n (US) (chapeau m) melon m
**deregulate** [dɪ'rɛgjuleɪt] vt libérer, dérégler
**deregulation** [dɪrɛgju'leɪʃən] n libération f,
dérèglement m

**derelict** ['dɛrɪlɪkt] adj abandonné(e), à l'abandon
**deride** [dɪ'raɪd] vt railler
**derision** [dɪ'rɪʒən] n dérision f
**derisive** [dɪ'raɪsɪv] adj moqueur(-euse), railleur(-euse)
**derisory** [dɪ'raɪsərɪ] adj (sum) dérisoire; (smile, person) moqueur(-euse), railleur(-euse)
**derivation** [dɛrɪ'veɪʃən] n dérivation f
**derivative** [dɪ'rɪvətɪv] n dérivé m ▷ adj dérivé(e)
**derive** [dɪ'raɪv] vt: **to ~ sth from** tirer qch de; trouver qch dans ▷ vi: **to ~ from** provenir de, dériver de
**dermatitis** [də:mə'taɪtɪs] n dermatite f
**dermatology** [də:mə'tɔlədʒɪ] n dermatologie f
**derogatory** [dɪ'rɔgətərɪ] adj désobligeant(e), péjoratif(-ive)
**derrick** ['dɛrɪk] n mât m de charge, derrick m
**derv** [də:v] n (Brit) gas-oil m, diesel m
**DES** n abbr (Brit: = Department of Education and Science) ministère de l'éducation nationale et des sciences
**desalination** [di:sælɪ'neɪʃən] n dessalement m, dessalage m
**descend** [dɪ'sɛnd] vt, vi descendre; **to ~ from** descendre de, être issu(e) de; **to ~ to** s'abaisser à; **in ~ing order of importance** par ordre d'importance décroissante
  ▶ **descend on** vt fus (enemy, angry person) tomber or sauter sur; (misfortune) s'abattre sur; (gloom, silence) envahir; **visitors ~ed (up)on us** des gens sont arrivés chez nous à l'improviste
**descendant** [dɪ'sɛndənt] n descendant(e)
**descent** [dɪ'sɛnt] n descente f; (origin) origine f
**describe** [dɪs'kraɪb] vt décrire
**description** [dɪs'krɪpʃən] n description f; (sort) sorte f, espèce f; **of every ~** de toutes sortes
**descriptive** [dɪs'krɪptɪv] adj descriptif(-ive)
**desecrate** ['dɛsɪkreɪt] vt profaner
**desert** [n 'dɛzət, vb dɪ'zə:t] n désert m ▷ vt déserter, abandonner ▷ vi (Mil) déserter
**deserted** [dɪ'zə:tɪd] adj désert(e)
**deserter** [dɪ'zə:tər] n déserteur m
**desertion** [dɪ'zə:ʃən] n désertion f
**desert island** n île déserte
**deserts** [dɪ'zə:ts] npl: **to get one's just ~** n'avoir que ce qu'on mérite
**deserve** [dɪ'zə:v] vt mériter
**deservedly** [dɪ'zə:vɪdlɪ] adv à juste titre, à bon droit
**deserving** [dɪ'zə:vɪŋ] adj (person) méritant(e); (action, cause) méritoire
**desiccated** ['dɛsɪkeɪtɪd] adj séché(e)
**design** [dɪ'zaɪn] n (sketch) plan m, dessin m; (layout, shape) conception f, ligne f; (pattern) dessin, motif(s) m(pl); (of dress, car) modèle m; (art) design m, stylisme m; (intention) dessein m ▷ vt dessiner; (plan) concevoir; **to have ~s on** avoir des visées sur; **well-~ed** adj bien conçu(e); **industrial ~** esthétique industrielle
**design and technology** n (Brit: Scol) technologie f
**designate** vt ['dɛzɪgneɪt] désigner ▷ adj

['dɛzɪgnɪt] désigné(e)
**designation** [dɛzɪg'neɪʃən] n désignation f
**designer** [dɪ'zaɪnər] n (Archit, Art) dessinateur(-trice); (Industry) concepteur m, designer m; (Fashion) styliste m/f
**desirability** [dɪzaɪərə'bɪlɪtɪ] n avantage m; attrait m
**desirable** [dɪ'zaɪərəbl] adj (property, location, purchase) attrayant(e); **it is ~ that** il est souhaitable que
**desire** [dɪ'zaɪər] n désir m ▷ vt désirer, vouloir; **to ~ to do sth/that** désirer faire qch/que
**desirous** [dɪ'zaɪərəs] adj: **~ of** désireux(-euse) de
**desk** [dɛsk] n (in office) bureau m; (for pupil) pupitre m; (Brit: in shop, restaurant) caisse f; (in hotel, at airport) réception f
**desktop computer** ['dɛsktɔp-] n ordinateur m de bureau or de table
**desk-top publishing** ['dɛsktɔp-] n publication assistée par ordinateur, PAO f
**desolate** ['dɛsəlɪt] adj désolé(e)
**desolation** [dɛsə'leɪʃən] n désolation f
**despair** [dɪs'pɛər] n désespoir m ▷ vi: **to ~ of** désespérer de; **to be in ~** être au désespoir
**despatch** [dɪs'pætʃ] n, vt = **dispatch**
**desperate** ['dɛspərɪt] adj désespéré(e); (fugitive) prêt(e) à tout; (measures) désespéré, extrême; **to be ~ for sth/to do sth** avoir désespérément besoin de qch/de faire qch; **we are getting ~** nous commençons à désespérer
**desperately** ['dɛspərɪtlɪ] adv désespérément; (very) terriblement, extrêmement; **~ ill** très gravement malade
**desperation** [dɛspə'reɪʃən] n désespoir m; **in (sheer) ~** en désespoir de cause
**despicable** [dɪs'pɪkəbl] adj méprisable
**despise** [dɪs'paɪz] vt mépriser, dédaigner
**despite** [dɪs'paɪt] prep malgré, en dépit de
**despondent** [dɪs'pɔndənt] adj découragé(e), abattu(e)
**despot** ['dɛspɔt] n despote m/f
**dessert** [dɪ'zə:t] n dessert m
**dessertspoon** [dɪ'zə:tspu:n] n cuiller f à dessert
**destabilize** [di:'steɪbɪlaɪz] vt déstabiliser
**destination** [dɛstɪ'neɪʃən] n destination f
**destine** ['dɛstɪn] vt destiner
**destined** ['dɛstɪnd] adj: **to be ~ to do sth** être destiné(e) à faire qch; **~ for London** à destination de Londres
**destiny** ['dɛstɪnɪ] n destinée f, destin m
**destitute** ['dɛstɪtju:t] adj indigent(e), dans le dénuement; **~ of** dépourvu(e) or dénué(e) de
**destroy** [dɪs'trɔɪ] vt détruire; (injured horse) abattre; (dog) faire piquer
**destroyer** [dɪs'trɔɪər] n (Naut) contre-torpilleur m
**destruction** [dɪs'trʌkʃən] n destruction f
**destructive** [dɪs'trʌktɪv] adj destructeur(-trice)
**desultory** ['dɛsəltərɪ] adj (reading, conversation) décousu(e); (contact) irrégulier(-ière)
**detach** [dɪ'tætʃ] vt détacher
**detachable** [dɪ'tætʃəbl] adj amovible,

détachable

**detached** [dɪ'tætʃt] *adj* (*attitude*) détaché(e)

**detached house** *n* pavillon *m* maison(nette) (individuelle)

**detachment** [dɪ'tætʃmənt] *n* (*Mil*) détachement *m*; (*fig*) détachement, indifférence *f*

**detail** ['di:teɪl] *n* détail *m*; (*Mil*) détachement *m* ▷ *vt* raconter en détail, énumérer; (*Mil*): **to ~ sb (for)** affecter qn (à), détacher qn (pour); **in ~** en détail; **to go into ~(s)** entrer dans les détails

**detailed** ['di:teɪld] *adj* détaillé(e)

**detain** [dɪ'teɪn] *vt* retenir; (*in captivity*) détenir; (*in hospital*) hospitaliser

**detainee** [di:teɪ'ni:] *n* détenu(e)

**detect** [dɪ'tɛkt] *vt* déceler, percevoir; (*Med, Police*) dépister; (*Mil, Radar, Tech*) détecter

**detection** [dɪ'tɛkʃən] *n* découverte *f*; (*Med, Police*) dépistage *m*; (*Mil, Radar, Tech*) détection *f*; **to escape ~** échapper aux recherches, éviter d'être découvert(e); (*mistake*) passer inaperçu(e); **crime ~** le dépistage des criminels

**detective** [dɪ'tɛktɪv] *n* agent *m* de la sûreté, policier *m*; **private ~** détective privé

**detective story** *n* roman policier

**detector** [dɪ'tɛktər] *n* détecteur *m*

**détente** [deɪ'tɑ:nt] *n* détente *f*

**detention** [dɪ'tɛnʃən] *n* détention *f*; (*Scol*) retenue *f*, consigne *f*

**deter** [dɪ'tə:r] *vt* dissuader

**detergent** [dɪ'tə:dʒənt] *n* détersif *m*, détergent *m*

**deteriorate** [dɪ'tɪərɪəreɪt] *vi* se détériorer, se dégrader

**deterioration** [dɪtɪərɪə'reɪʃən] *n* détérioration *f*

**determination** [dɪtə:mɪ'neɪʃən] *n* détermination *f*

**determine** [dɪ'tə:mɪn] *vt* déterminer; **to ~ to do** résoudre de faire, se déterminer à faire

**determined** [dɪ'tə:mɪnd] *adj* (*person*) déterminé(e), décidé(e); (*quantity*) déterminé(e), établi(e); (*effort*) très gros(se); **~ to do** bien décidé à faire

**deterrence** [dɪ'tɛrns] *n* dissuasion *f*

**deterrent** [dɪ'tɛrənt] *n* effet *m* de dissuasion; force *f* de dissuasion; **to act as a ~** avoir un effet dissuasif

**detest** [dɪ'tɛst] *vt* détester, avoir horreur de

**detestable** [dɪ'tɛstəbl] *adj* détestable odieux(-euse)

**detonate** ['dɛtəneɪt] *vi* exploser ▷ *vt* faire exploser *or* détoner

**detonator** ['dɛtəneɪtər] *n* détonateur *m*

**detour** ['di:tuər] *n* détour *m*; (*US Aut: diversion*) déviation *f*

**detract** [dɪ'trækt] *vt*: **to ~ from** (*quality, pleasure*) diminuer; (*reputation*) porter atteinte à

**detractor** [dɪ'træktər] *n* détracteur(-trice)

**detriment** ['dɛtrɪmənt] *n*: **to the ~ of** au détriment de, au préjudice de; **without ~ to** sans porter atteinte *or* préjudice à, sans conséquences fâcheuses pour

**detrimental** [dɛtrɪ'mɛntl] *adj*: **~ to**

préjudiciable *or* nuisible à

**deuce** [dju:s] *n* (*Tennis*) égalité *f*

**devaluation** [dɪvælju'eɪʃən] *n* dévaluation *f*

**devalue** ['di:'vælju:] *vt* dévaluer

**devastate** ['dɛvəsteɪt] *vt* dévaster; **he was ~d by the news** cette nouvelle lui a porté un coup terrible

**devastating** ['dɛvəsteɪtɪŋ] *adj* dévastateur(-trice); (*news*) accablant(e)

**devastation** [dɛvəs'teɪʃən] *n* dévastation *f*

**develop** [dɪ'vɛləp] *vt* (*gen*) développer; (*disease*) commencer à souffrir de; (*habit*) contracter; (*resources*) mettre en valeur, exploiter; (*land*) aménager ▷ *vi* se développer; (*situation, disease: evolve*) évoluer; (*facts, symptoms: appear*) se manifester, se produire; **can you ~ this film?** pouvez-vous développer cette pellicule?; **to ~ a taste for sth** prendre goût à qch; **to ~ into** devenir

**developer** [dɪ'vɛləpər] *n* (*Phot*) révélateur *m*; (*of land*) promoteur *m*; (*also*: **property developer**) promoteur immobilier

**developing country** [dɪ'vɛləpɪŋ-] *n* pays *m* en voie de développement

**development** [dɪ'vɛləpmənt] *n* développement *m*; (*of land*) exploitation *f*; (*new fact, event*) rebondissement *m*, fait(s) nouveau(x)

**development area** *n* zone *f* à urbaniser

**deviate** ['di:vɪeɪt] *vi*: **to ~ (from)** dévier (de)

**deviation** [di:vɪ'eɪʃən] *n* déviation *f*

**device** [dɪ'vaɪs] *n* (*scheme*) moyen *m*, expédient *m*; (*apparatus*) appareil *m*, dispositif *m*; **explosive ~** engin explosif

**devil** ['dɛvl] *n* diable *m*; démon *m*

**devilish** ['dɛvlɪʃ] *adj* diabolique

**devil-may-care** ['dɛvlmeɪ'kɛər] *adj* je-m'en-foutiste

**devil's advocate** *n*: **to play devil's advocate** se faire avocat du diable

**devious** ['di:vɪəs] *adj* (*means*) détourné(e); (*person*) sournois(e), dissimulé(e)

**devise** [dɪ'vaɪz] *vt* imaginer, concevoir

**devoid** [dɪ'vɔɪd] *adj*: **~ of** dépourvu(e) de, dénué(e) de

**devolution** [di:və'lu:ʃən] *n* (*Pol*) décentralisation *f*

**devolve** [dɪ'vɔlv] *vi*: **to ~ (up)on** retomber sur

**devote** [dɪ'vəut] *vt*: **to ~ sth to** consacrer qch à

**devoted** [dɪ'vəutɪd] *adj* dévoué(e); **to be ~ to** être dévoué(e) *or* très attaché(e) à; (*book etc*) être consacré(e) à

**devotee** [dɛvəu'ti:] *n* (*Rel*) adepte *m/f*; (*Mus, Sport*) fervent(e)

**devotion** [dɪ'vəuʃən] *n* dévouement *m*, attachement *m*; (*Rel*) dévotion *f*, piété *f*

**devour** [dɪ'vauər] *vt* dévorer

**devout** [dɪ'vaut] *adj* pieux(-euse), dévot(e)

**dew** [dju:] *n* rosée *f*

**dexterity** [dɛks'tɛrɪtɪ] *n* dextérité *f*, adresse *f*

**DfEE** *n abbr* (*Brit*: = *Department for Education and Employment*) Ministère de l'éducation et de l'emploi

**dg** *abbr* (= *decigram*) dg

**diabetes** [daɪə'biːtiːz] *n* diabète *m*

**diabetic** [daɪə'bɛtɪk] *n* diabétique *m/f* ▷ *adj* (*person*) diabétique; (*chocolate, jam*) pour diabétiques

**diabolical** [daɪə'bɔlɪkl] *adj* diabolique; (*inf: dreadful*) infernal(e), atroce

**diagnose** [daɪəg'nəuz] *vt* diagnostiquer

**diagnosis** (*pl* **diagnoses**) [daɪəg'nəusɪs, -siːz] *n* diagnostic *m*

**diagonal** [daɪ'ægənl] *adj* diagonal(e) ▷ *n* diagonale *f*

**diagram** ['daɪəgræm] *n* diagramme *m*, schéma *m*

**dial** ['daɪəl] *n* cadran *m* ▷ *vt* (*number*) faire, composer; **to ~ a wrong number** faire un faux numéro; **can I ~ London direct?** puis-je *or* est-ce-que je peux avoir Londres par l'automatique?

**dial.** *abbr* = **dialect**

**dialect** ['daɪəlɛkt] *n* dialecte *m*

**dialling code** ['daɪəlɪŋ-], (US) **dial code** *n* indicatif *m* (téléphonique); **what's the ~ for Paris?** quel est l'indicatif de Paris?

**dialling tone** ['daɪəlɪŋ-], (US) **dial tone** *n* tonalité *f*

**dialogue**, (US) **dialog** ['daɪəlɔg] *n* dialogue *m*

**dialysis** [daɪ'ælɪsɪs] *n* dialyse *f*

**diameter** [daɪ'æmɪtə<sup>r</sup>] *n* diamètre *m*

**diametrically** [daɪə'mɛtrɪklɪ] *adv:* **~ opposed** (**to**) diamétralement opposé(e) (à)

**diamond** ['daɪəmənd] *n* diamant *m*; (*shape*) losange *m*; **diamonds** *npl* (*Cards*) carreau *m*

**diamond ring** *n* bague *f* de diamant(s)

**diaper** ['daɪəpə<sup>r</sup>] *n* (US) couche *f*

**diaphragm** ['daɪəfræm] *n* diaphragme *m*

**diarrhoea**, (US) **diarrhea** [daɪə'riːə] *n* diarrhée *f*

**diary** ['daɪərɪ] *n* (*daily account*) journal *m*; (*book*) agenda *m*; **to keep a ~** tenir un journal

**diatribe** ['daɪətraɪb] *n* diatribe *f*

**dice** [daɪs] *n* (*pl inv*) dé *m* ▷ *vt* (*Culin*) couper en dés *or* en cubes

**dicey** ['daɪsɪ] *adj* (*inf*): **it's a bit ~** c'est un peu risqué

**dichotomy** [daɪ'kɔtəmɪ] *n* dichotomie *f*

**dickhead** ['dɪkhɛd] *n* (*Brit inf!*) tête *f* de nœud (!)

**Dictaphone®** ['dɪktəfəun] *n* Dictaphone® *m*

**dictate** [*vb* dɪk'teɪt, *n* 'dɪkteɪt] *vt* dicter ▷ *vi:* **to ~ to** (*person*) imposer sa volonté à, régenter; **I won't be ~d to** je n'ai d'ordres à recevoir de personne ▷ *n* injonction *f*

**dictation** [dɪk'teɪʃən] *n* dictée *f*; **at ~ speed** à une vitesse de dictée

**dictator** [dɪk'teɪtə<sup>r</sup>] *n* dictateur *m*

**dictatorship** [dɪk'teɪtəʃɪp] *n* dictature *f*

**diction** ['dɪkʃən] *n* diction *f*, élocution *f*

**dictionary** ['dɪkʃənrɪ] *n* dictionnaire *m*

**did** [dɪd] *pt of* **do**

**didactic** [daɪ'dæktɪk] *adj* didactique

**didn't** ['dɪdnt] = **did not**

**die** [daɪ] *n* (*pl* **dice**) dé *m*; (*pl* **-s**) coin *m*; matrice *f*;

étampe *f* ▷ *vi* mourir; **to ~ of** *or* **from** mourir de; **to be dying** être mourant(e); **to be dying for sth** avoir une envie folle de qch; **to be dying to do sth** mourir d'envie de faire qch

▶ **die away** *vi* s'éteindre

▶ **die down** *vi* se calmer, s'apaiser

▶ **die out** *vi* disparaître, s'éteindre

**diehard** ['daɪhɑːd] *n* réactionnaire *m/f*, jusqu'au-boutiste *m/f*

**diesel** ['diːzl] *n* (*vehicle*) diesel *m*; (*also:* **diesel oil**) carburant *m* diesel, gas-oil *m*

**diesel engine** *n* moteur *m* diesel

**diesel fuel, diesel oil** *n* carburant *m* diesel

**diet** ['daɪət] *n* alimentation *f*; (*restricted food*) régime *m* ▷ *vi* (*also:* **be on a diet**) suivre un régime; **to live on a ~ of** se nourrir de

**dietician** [daɪə'tɪʃən] *n* diététicien(ne)

**differ** ['dɪfə<sup>r</sup>] *vi:* **to ~ from sth** (*be different*) être différent(e) de qch, différer de qch; **to ~ from sb over sth** ne pas être d'accord avec qn au sujet de qch

**difference** ['dɪfrəns] *n* différence *f*; (*quarrel*) différend *m*, désaccord *m*; **it makes no ~ to me** cela m'est égal, cela m'est indifférent; **to settle one's ~s** résoudre la situation

**different** ['dɪfrənt] *adj* différent(e)

**differential** [dɪfə'rɛnʃəl] *n* (*Aut, wages*) différentiel *m*

**differentiate** [dɪfə'rɛnʃɪeɪt] *vt* différencier ▷ *vi* se différencier; **to ~ between** faire une différence entre

**differently** ['dɪfrəntlɪ] *adv* différemment

**difficult** ['dɪfɪkəlt] *adj* difficile; **~ to understand** difficile à comprendre

**difficulty** ['dɪfɪkəltɪ] *n* difficulté *f*; **to have difficulties with** avoir des ennuis *or* problèmes avec; **to be in ~** avoir des difficultés, avoir des problèmes

**diffidence** ['dɪfɪdəns] *n* manque *m* de confiance en soi, manque d'assurance

**diffident** ['dɪfɪdənt] *adj* qui manque de confiance *or* d'assurance, peu sûr(e) de soi

**diffuse** *adj* [dɪ'fjuːs] diffus(e) ▷ *vt* [dɪ'fjuːz] diffuser, répandre

**dig** [dɪg] *vt* (*pt, pp* **dug** [dʌg]) (*hole*) creuser; (*garden*) bêcher ▷ *n* (*prod*) coup *m* de coude; (*fig: remark*) coup de griffe *or* de patte; (*Archaeology*) fouille *f*; **to ~ into** (*snow, soil*) creuser; **to ~ into one's pockets for sth** fouiller dans ses poches pour chercher *or* prendre qch; **to ~ one's nails into** enfoncer ses ongles dans

▶ **dig in** *vi* (*also:* **dig o.s. in**: *Mil*) se retrancher; (: *fig*) tenir bon, se braquer; (*inf: eat*) attaquer (un repas *or* un plat *etc*) ▷ *vt* (*compost*) bien mélanger à la bêche; (*knife, claw*) enfoncer; **to ~ in one's heels** (*fig*) se braquer, se buter

▶ **dig out** *vt* (*survivors, car from snow*) sortir *or* dégager (à coups de pelles *or* pioches)

▶ **dig up** *vt* déterrer

**digest** *vt* [daɪ'dʒɛst] digérer ▷ *n* ['daɪdʒɛst] sommaire *m*, résumé *m*

**digestible** [dɪ'dʒɛstəbl] *adj* digestible

**digestion** [dɪ'dʒɛstʃən] n digestion f
**digestive** [dɪ'dʒɛstɪv] adj digestif(-ive)
**digit** ['dɪdʒɪt] n (number) chiffre m (de 0 à 9); (finger) doigt m
**digital** ['dɪdʒɪtl] adj (system, recording, radio) numérique, digital(e); (watch) à affichage numérique or digital
**digital camera** n appareil m photo numérique
**digital compact cassette** n cassette f numérique
**digital TV** n télévision f numérique
**dignified** ['dɪgnɪfaɪd] adj digne
**dignitary** ['dɪgnɪtərɪ] n dignitaire m
**dignity** ['dɪgnɪtɪ] n dignité f
**digress** [daɪ'grɛs] vi: **to ~ from** s'écarter de, s'éloigner de
**digression** [daɪ'grɛʃən] n digression f
**digs** [dɪgz] npl (Brit inf) piaule f, chambre meublée
**dilapidated** [dɪ'læpɪdeɪtɪd] adj délabré(e)
**dilate** [daɪ'leɪt] vt dilater ▷ vi se dilater
**dilatory** ['dɪlətərɪ] adj dilatoire
**dilemma** [daɪ'lɛmə] n dilemme m; **to be in a ~** être pris dans un dilemme
**diligent** ['dɪlɪdʒənt] adj appliqué(e), assidu(e)
**dill** [dɪl] n aneth m
**dilly-dally** ['dɪlɪ'dælɪ] vi hésiter, tergiverser; traînasser, lambiner
**dilute** [daɪ'luːt] vt diluer ▷ adj dilué(e)
**dim** [dɪm] adj (light, eyesight) faible; (memory, outline) vague, indécis(e); (room) sombre; (inf: stupid) borné(e), obtus(e) ▷ vt (light) réduire, baisser; (US Aut) mettre en code, baisser; **to take a ~ view of sth** voir qch d'un mauvais œil
**dime** [daɪm] n (US) pièce f de 10 cents
**dimension** [daɪ'mɛnʃən] n dimension f
**-dimensional** [dɪ'mɛnʃənl] adj suffix: **two~** à deux dimensions
**diminish** [dɪ'mɪnɪʃ] vt, vi diminuer
**diminished** [dɪ'mɪnɪʃt] adj: **~ responsibility** (Law) responsabilité atténuée
**diminutive** [dɪ'mɪnjutɪv] adj minuscule, tout(e) petit(e) ▷ n (Ling) diminutif m
**dimly** ['dɪmlɪ] adv faiblement; vaguement
**dimmer** ['dɪmər] n (also: **dimmer switch**) variateur m; **dimmers** npl (US Aut: dipped headlights) phares mpl, code inv; (parking lights) feux mpl de position
**dimple** ['dɪmpl] n fossette f
**dim-witted** ['dɪm'wɪtɪd] adj (inf) stupide, borné(e)
**din** [dɪn] n vacarme m ▷ vt: **to ~ sth into sb** (inf) enfoncer qch dans la tête or la caboche de qn
**dine** [daɪn] vi dîner
**diner** ['daɪnər] n (person) dîneur(-euse); (Rail) = **dining car**; (US: eating place) petit restaurant
**dinghy** ['dɪŋgɪ] n youyou m; (inflatable) canot m pneumatique; (also: **sailing dinghy**) voilier m, dériveur m
**dingy** ['dɪndʒɪ] adj miteux(-euse), minable
**dining car** ['daɪnɪŋ-] n (Brit) voiture-restaurant f, wagon-restaurant m

**dining room** ['daɪnɪŋ-] n salle f à manger
**dining table** [daɪnɪŋ-] n table f de (la) salle à manger
**dinner** ['dɪnər] n (evening meal) dîner m; (lunch) déjeuner m; (public) banquet m; **~'s ready!** à table!
**dinner jacket** n smoking m
**dinner party** n dîner m
**dinner time** n (evening) heure f du dîner; (midday) heure du déjeuner
**dinosaur** ['daɪnəsɔːr] n dinosaure m
**dint** [dɪnt] n: **by ~ of (doing) sth** à force de (faire) qch
**diocese** ['daɪəsɪs] n diocèse m
**dioxide** [daɪ'ɔksaɪd] n dioxyde m
**Dip.** abbr (Brit) = **diploma**
**dip** [dɪp] n (slope) déclivité f; (in sea) baignade f, bain m; (Culin) ≈ sauce f ▷ vt tremper, plonger; (Brit Aut: lights) mettre en code, baisser ▷ vi plonger
**diphtheria** [dɪf'θɪərɪə] n diphtérie f
**diphthong** ['dɪfθɔŋ] n diphtongue f
**diploma** [dɪ'pləumə] n diplôme m
**diplomacy** [dɪ'pləuməsɪ] n diplomatie f
**diplomat** ['dɪpləmæt] n diplomate m
**diplomatic** [dɪplə'mætɪk] adj diplomatique; **to break off ~ relations (with)** rompre les relations diplomatiques (avec)
**diplomatic corps** n corps m diplomatique
**diplomatic immunity** n immunité f diplomatique
**dipstick** ['dɪpstɪk] n (Brit Aut) jauge f de niveau d'huile
**dipswitch** ['dɪpswɪtʃ] n (Brit Aut) commutateur m de code
**dire** [daɪər] adj (poverty) extrême; (awful) affreux(-euse)
**direct** [daɪ'rɛkt] adj direct(e); (manner, person) direct, franc (franche) ▷ vt (tell way) diriger, orienter; (letter, remark) adresser; (Cine, TV) réaliser; (Theat) mettre en scène; (order): **to ~ sb to do sth** ordonner à qn de faire qch ▷ adv directement; **can you ~ me to ...?** pouvez-vous m'indiquer le chemin de ...?
**direct cost** n (Comm) coût m variable
**direct current** n (Elec) courant continu
**direct debit** n (Brit Banking) prélèvement m automatique
**direct dialling** n (Tel) automatique m
**direct hit** n (Mil) coup m au but, touché m
**direction** [dɪ'rɛkʃən] n direction f; (Theat) mise f en scène; (Cine, TV) réalisation f; **directions** npl (to a place) indications fpl; **~s for use** mode m d'emploi; **to ask for ~s** demander sa route or son chemin; **sense of ~** sens m de l'orientation; **in the ~ of** dans la direction de, vers
**directive** [dɪ'rɛktɪv] n directive f; **a government ~** une directive du gouvernement
**direct labour** n main-d'œuvre directe; employés municipaux
**directly** [dɪ'rɛktlɪ] adv (in straight line) directement, tout droit; (at once) tout de suite,

**d**

immédiatement

**direct mail** n vente f par publicité directe

**direct mailshot** n (Brit) publicité postale

**directness** [daɪˈrɛktnɪs] n (of person, speech) franchise f

**director** [dɪˈrɛktəʳ] n directeur m; (board member) administrateur m; (Theat) metteur m en scène; (Cine, TV) réalisateur(-trice); **D~ of Public Prosecutions** (Brit) ≈ procureur général

**directory** [dɪˈrɛktərɪ] n annuaire m; (also: **street directory**) indicateur m de rues; (also: **trade directory**) annuaire du commerce; (Comput) répertoire m

**directory enquiries**, (US) **directory assistance** n (Tel: service) renseignements mpl

**dirt** [dəːt] n saleté f; (mud) boue f; **to treat sb like ~** traiter qn comme un chien

**dirt-cheap** [ˈdəːtˈtʃiːp] adj (ne) coûtant presque rien

**dirt road** n chemin non macadamisé or non revêtu

**dirty** [ˈdəːtɪ] adj sale; (joke) cochon(ne) ▷ vt salir; **~ story** histoire cochonne; **~ trick** coup tordu

**disability** [dɪsəˈbɪlɪtɪ] n invalidité f, infirmité f

**disability allowance** n allocation f d'invalidité or d'infirmité

**disable** [dɪsˈeɪbl] vt (illness, accident) rendre or laisser infirme; (tank, gun) mettre hors d'action

**disabled** [dɪsˈeɪbld] adj handicapé(e); (maimed) mutilé(e); (through illness, old age) impotent(e)

**disadvantage** [dɪsədˈvɑːntɪdʒ] n désavantage m, inconvénient m

**disadvantaged** [dɪsədˈvɑːntɪdʒd] adj (person) désavantagé(e)

**disadvantageous** [dɪsædvɑːnˈteɪdʒəs] adj désavantageux(-euse)

**disaffected** [dɪsəˈfɛktɪd] adj: **~ (to or towards)** mécontent(e) (de)

**disaffection** [dɪsəˈfɛkʃən] n désaffection f, mécontentement m

**disagree** [dɪsəˈgriː] vi (differ) ne pas concorder; (be against, think otherwise): **to ~ (with)** ne pas être d'accord (avec); **garlic ~s with me** l'ail ne me convient pas, je ne supporte pas l'ail

**disagreeable** [dɪsəˈgriːəbl] adj désagréable

**disagreement** [dɪsəˈgriːmənt] n désaccord m, différend m

**disallow** [ˈdɪsəˈlau] vt rejeter, désavouer; (Brit Football: goal) refuser

**disappear** [dɪsəˈpɪəʳ] vi disparaître

**disappearance** [dɪsəˈpɪərəns] n disparition f

**disappoint** [dɪsəˈpɔɪnt] vt décevoir

**disappointed** [dɪsəˈpɔɪntɪd] adj déçu(e)

**disappointing** [dɪsəˈpɔɪntɪŋ] adj décevant(e)

**disappointment** [dɪsəˈpɔɪntmənt] n déception f

**disapproval** [dɪsəˈpruːvəl] n désapprobation f

**disapprove** [dɪsəˈpruːv] vi: **to ~ of** désapprouver

**disapproving** [dɪsəˈpruːvɪŋ] adj désapprobateur(-trice), de désapprobation

**disarm** [dɪsˈɑːm] vt désarmer

**disarmament** [dɪsˈɑːməmənt] n désarmement m

**disarming** [dɪsˈɑːmɪŋ] adj (smile) désarmant(e)

**disarray** [dɪsəˈreɪ] n désordre m, confusion f; **in ~** (troops) en déroute; (thoughts) embrouillé(e); (clothes) en désordre; **to throw into ~** semer la confusion or le désordre dans (or parmi)

**disaster** [dɪˈzɑːstəʳ] n catastrophe f, désastre m

**disastrous** [dɪˈzɑːstrəs] adj désastreux(-euse)

**disband** [dɪsˈbænd] vt démobiliser; disperser ▷ vi se séparer; se disperser

**disbelief** [ˈdɪsbəˈliːf] n incrédulité f; **in ~** avec incrédulité

**disbelieve** [ˈdɪsbəˈliːv] vt (person) ne pas croire; (story) mettre en doute; **I don't ~ you** je veux bien vous croire

**disc** [dɪsk] n disque m; (Comput) = **disk**

**disc.** abbr (Comm) = **discount**

**discard** [dɪsˈkɑːd] vt (old things) se débarrasser de, mettre au rencart au rebut; (fig) écarter, renoncer à

**disc brake** n frein m à disque

**discern** [dɪˈsəːn] vt discerner, distinguer

**discernible** [dɪˈsəːnəbl] adj discernable, perceptible; (object) visible

**discerning** [dɪˈsəːnɪŋ] adj judicieux(-euse), perspicace

**discharge** vt [dɪsˈtʃɑːdʒ] (duties) s'acquitter de; (settle: debt) s'acquitter de, régler; (waste etc) déverser; décharger; (Elec, Med) émettre; (patient) renvoyer (chez lui); (employee, soldier) congédier, licencier; (defendant) relaxer, élargir ▷ n [ˈdɪstʃɑːdʒ] (Elec, Med) émission f; (also: **vaginal discharge**) pertes blanches; (dismissal) renvoi m; licenciement m; élargissement m; **to ~ one's gun** faire feu; **~d bankrupt** failli(e), réhabilité(e)

**disciple** [dɪˈsaɪpl] n disciple m

**disciplinary** [ˈdɪsɪplɪnərɪ] adj disciplinaire; **to take ~ action against sb** prendre des mesures disciplinaires à l'encontre de qn

**discipline** [ˈdɪsɪplɪn] n discipline f ▷ vt discipliner; (punish) punir; **to ~ o.s. to do sth** s'imposer or s'astreindre à une discipline pour faire qch

**disc jockey** n disque-jockey m (DJ)

**disclaim** [dɪsˈkleɪm] vt désavouer, dénier

**disclaimer** [dɪsˈkleɪməʳ] n démenti m, dénégation f; **to issue a ~** publier un démenti

**disclose** [dɪsˈkləuz] vt révéler, divulguer

**disclosure** [dɪsˈkləuʒəʳ] n révélation f, divulgation f

**disco** [ˈdɪskəu] n abbr discothèque f

**discolour**, (US) **discolor** [dɪsˈkʌləʳ] vt décolorer; (sth white) jaunir ▷ vi se décolorer; jaunir

**discolouration**, (US) **discoloration** [dɪskʌləˈreɪʃən] n décoloration f; jaunissement m

**discoloured**, (US) **discolored** [dɪsˈkʌləd] adj décoloré(e), jauni(e)

**discomfort** [dɪsˈkʌmfət] n malaise m, gêne f; (lack of comfort) manque m de confort

**disconcert** [dɪskənˈsəːt] vt déconcerter,

décontenancer

**disconnect** [dɪskə'nɛkt] *vt* détacher; *(Elec, Radio)* débrancher; *(gas, water)* couper

**disconnected** [dɪskə'nɛktɪd] *adj (speech, thoughts)* décousu(e), peu cohérent(e)

**disconsolate** [dɪs'kɒnsəlɪt] *adj* inconsolable

**discontent** [dɪskən'tɛnt] *n* mécontentement *m*

**discontented** [dɪskən'tɛntɪd] *adj* mécontent(e)

**discontinue** [dɪskən'tɪnjuː] *vt* cesser, interrompre; **"-d"** *(Comm)* "fin de série"

**discord** ['dɪskɔːd] *n* discorde *f*, dissension *f*; *(Mus)* dissonance *f*

**discordant** [dɪs'kɔːdənt] *adj* discordant(e), dissonant(e)

**discount** *n* ['dɪskaunt] remise *f*, rabais *m* ▷ *vt* [dɪs'kaunt] *(report etc)* ne pas tenir compte de; **to give sb a ~ on sth** faire une remise *or* un rabais à qn sur qch; **~ for cash** escompte *f* au comptant; **at a ~** avec une remise *or* réduction, au rabais

**discount house** *n (Finance)* banque *f* d'escompte; *(Comm: also:* **discount store**) magasin *m* de discount

**discount rate** *n* taux *m* de remise

**discourage** [dɪs'kʌrɪdʒ] *vt* décourager; *(dissuade, deter)* dissuader, décourager

**discouragement** [dɪs'kʌrɪdʒmənt] *n (depression)* découragement *m*; **to act as a ~ to sb** dissuader qn

**discouraging** [dɪs'kʌrɪdʒɪŋ] *adj* décourageant(e)

**discourteous** [dɪs'kəːtɪəs] *adj* incivil(e), discourtois(e)

**discover** [dɪs'kʌvər] *vt* découvrir

**discovery** [dɪs'kʌvərɪ] *n* découverte *f*

**discredit** [dɪs'krɛdɪt] *vt (idea)* mettre en doute; *(person)* discréditer ▷ *n* discrédit *m*

**discreet** [dɪ'skriːt] *adj* discret(-ète)

**discreetly** [dɪ'skriːtlɪ] *adv* discrètement

**discrepancy** [dɪ'skrɛpənsɪ] *n* divergence *f*, contradiction *f*

**discretion** [dɪ'skrɛʃən] *n* discrétion *f*; **at the ~ of** à la discrétion de; **use your own ~** à vous de juger

**discretionary** [dɪ'skrɛʃənrɪ] *adj (powers)* discrétionnaire

**discriminate** [dɪ'skrɪmɪneɪt] *vi*: **to ~ between** établir une distinction entre, faire la différence entre; **to ~ against** pratiquer une discrimination contre

**discriminating** [dɪ'skrɪmɪneɪtɪŋ] *adj* qui a du discernement

**discrimination** [dɪskrɪmɪ'neɪʃən] *n* discrimination *f*; *(judgment)* discernement *m*; **racial/sexual ~** discrimination raciale/sexuelle

**discus** ['dɪskəs] *n* disque *m*

**discuss** [dɪ'skʌs] *vt* discuter de; *(debate)* discuter

**discussion** [dɪ'skʌʃən] *n* discussion *f*; **under ~** en discussion

**disdain** [dɪs'deɪn] *n* dédain *m*

**disease** [dɪ'ziːz] *n* maladie *f*

**diseased** [dɪ'ziːzd] *adj* malade

**disembark** [dɪsɪm'baːk] *vt, vi* débarquer

**disembarkation** [dɪsɛmbaː'keɪʃən] *n* débarquement *m*

**disembodied** ['dɪsɪm'bɒdɪd] *adj* désincarné(e)

**disembowel** ['dɪsɪm'bauəl] *vt* éviscérer, étriper

**disenchanted** ['dɪsɪn'tʃaːntɪd] *adj*: **~ (with)** désenchanté(e) (de), désabusé(e) (de)

**disenfranchise** ['dɪsɪn'fræntʃaɪz] *vt* priver du droit de vote; *(Comm)* retirer la franchise à

**disengage** [dɪsɪn'geɪdʒ] *vt* dégager; *(Tech)* déclencher; **to ~ the clutch** *(Aut)* débrayer

**disentangle** [dɪsɪn'tæŋgl] *vt* démêler

**disfavour**, *(US)* **disfavor** [dɪs'feɪvər] *n* défaveur *f*; disgrâce *f*

**disfigure** [dɪs'fɪgər] *vt* défigurer

**disgorge** [dɪs'gɔːdʒ] *vt* déverser

**disgrace** [dɪs'greɪs] *n* honte *f*; *(disfavour)* disgrâce *f* ▷ *vt* déshonorer, couvrir de honte

**disgraceful** [dɪs'greɪsful] *adj* scandaleux(-euse), honteux(-euse)

**disgruntled** [dɪs'grʌntld] *adj* mécontent(e)

**disguise** [dɪs'gaɪz] *n* déguisement *m* ▷ *vt* déguiser; *(voice)* déguiser, contrefaire; *(feelings etc)* masquer, dissimuler; **in ~** déguisé(e); **to ~ o.s. as** se déguiser en; **there's no disguising the fact that ...** on ne peut pas se dissimuler que ...

**disgust** [dɪs'gʌst] *n* dégoût *m*, aversion *f* ▷ *vt* dégoûter, écœurer

**disgusted** [dɪs'gʌstɪd] *adj* dégoûté(e), écœuré(e)

**disgusting** [dɪs'gʌstɪŋ] *adj* dégoûtant(e), révoltant(e)

**dish** [dɪʃ] *n* plat *m*; **to do** *or* **wash the ~es** faire la vaisselle

▶ **dish out** *vt* distribuer

▶ **dish up** *vt* servir; *(facts, statistics)* sortir, débiter

**dishcloth** ['dɪʃklɒθ] *n (for drying)* torchon *m*; *(for washing)* lavette *f*

**dishearten** [dɪs'haːtn] *vt* décourager

**dishevelled**, *(US)* **disheveled** [dɪ'ʃɛvəld] *adj* ébouriffé(e), décoiffé(e), débraillé(e)

**dishonest** [dɪs'ɒnɪst] *adj* malhonnête

**dishonesty** [dɪs'ɒnɪstɪ] *n* malhonnêteté *f*

**dishonour**, *(US)* **dishonor** [dɪs'ɒnər] *n* déshonneur *m*

**dishonourable**, *(US)* **dishonorable** [dɪs'ɒnərəbl] *adj* déshonorant(e)

**dish soap** *n (US)* produit *m* pour la vaisselle

**dishtowel** ['dɪʃtauəl] *n (US)* torchon *m* (à vaisselle)

**dishwasher** ['dɪʃwɒʃər] *n* lave-vaisselle *m*; *(person)* plongeur(-euse)

**dishy** ['dɪʃɪ] *adj (Brit inf)* séduisant(e), sexy *inv*

**disillusion** [dɪsɪ'luːʒən] *vt* désabuser, désenchanter ▷ *n* désenchantement *m*; **to become ~ed (with)** perdre ses illusions (en ce qui concerne)

**disillusionment** [dɪsɪ'luːʒənmənt] *n* désillusionnement *m*, désillusion *f*

**disincentive** [dɪsɪn'sɛntɪv] *n*: **it's a ~** c'est démotivant; **to be a ~ to sb** démotiver qn

**disinclined** ['dɪsɪn'klaɪnd] *adj*: **to be ~ to do sth**

être peu disposé(e) *or* peu enclin(e) à faire qch

**disinfect** [dɪsɪn'fɛkt] *vt* désinfecter

**disinfectant** [dɪsɪn'fɛktənt] *n* désinfectant *m*

**disinflation** [dɪsɪn'fleɪʃən] *n* désinflation *f*

**disinformation** [dɪsɪnfə'meɪʃən] *n* désinformation *f*

**disinherit** [dɪsɪn'hɛrɪt] *vt* déshériter

**disintegrate** [dɪs'ɪntɪgreɪt] *vi* se désintégrer

**disinterested** [dɪs'ɪntrəstɪd] *adj* désintéressé(e)

**disjointed** [dɪs'dʒɔɪntɪd] *adj* décousu(e), incohérent(e)

**disk** [dɪsk] *n* (*Comput*) disquette *f*; **single-/double-sided** ~ disquette une face/double face

**disk drive** *n* lecteur *m* de disquette

**diskette** [dɪs'kɛt] *n* (*Comput*) disquette *f*

**disk operating system** *n* système *m* d'exploitation à disques

**dislike** [dɪs'laɪk] *n* aversion *f*, antipathie *f* ▷ *vt* ne pas aimer; **to take a ~ to sb/sth** prendre qn/qch en grippe; **I ~ the idea** l'idée me déplaît

**dislocate** ['dɪsləkeɪt] *vt* disloquer, déboîter; (*services etc*) désorganiser; **he has ~d his shoulder** il s'est disloqué l'épaule

**dislodge** [dɪs'lɔdʒ] *vt* déplacer, faire bouger; (*enemy*) déloger

**disloyal** [dɪs'lɔɪəl] *adj* déloyal(e)

**dismal** ['dɪzml] *adj* (*gloomy*) lugubre, maussade; (*very bad*) lamentable

**dismantle** [dɪs'mæntl] *vt* démonter; (*fort, warship*) démanteler

**dismast** [dɪs'mɑːst] *vt* démâter

**dismay** [dɪs'meɪ] *n* consternation *f* ▷ *vt* consterner; **much to my ~** à ma grande consternation, à ma grande inquiétude

**dismiss** [dɪs'mɪs] *vt* congédier, renvoyer; (*idea*) écarter; (*Law*) rejeter ▷ *vi* (*Mil*) rompre les rangs

**dismissal** [dɪs'mɪsl] *n* renvoi *m*

**dismount** [dɪs'maunt] *vi* mettre pied à terre

**disobedience** [dɪsə'biːdɪəns] *n* désobéissance *f*

**disobedient** [dɪsə'biːdɪənt] *adj* désobéissant(e), indiscipliné(e)

**disobey** [dɪsə'beɪ] *vt* désobéir à; (*rule*) transgresser, enfreindre

**disorder** [dɪs'ɔːdər] *n* désordre *m*; (*rioting*) désordres *mpl*; (*Med*) troubles *mpl*

**disorderly** [dɪs'ɔːdəlɪ] *adj* (*room*) en désordre; (*behaviour, retreat, crowd*) désordonné(e)

**disorderly conduct** *n* (*Law*) conduite *f* contraire aux bonnes mœurs

**disorganized** [dɪs'ɔːgənaɪzd] *adj* désorganisé(e)

**disorientated** [dɪs'ɔːrɪenteɪtɪd] *adj* désorienté(e)

**disown** [dɪs'əun] *vt* renier

**disparaging** [dɪs'pærɪdʒɪŋ] *adj* désobligeant(e); **to be ~ about sb/sth** faire des remarques désobligeantes sur qn/qch

**disparate** ['dɪspərɪt] *adj* disparate

**disparity** [dɪs'pærɪtɪ] *n* disparité *f*

**dispassionate** [dɪs'pæʃənət] *adj* calme, froid(e), impartial(e), objectif(-ive)

**dispatch** [dɪs'pætʃ] *vt* expédier, envoyer; (*deal with: business*) régler, en finir avec ▷ *n* envoi *m*,

expédition *f*; (*Mil, Press*) dépêche *f*

**dispatch department** *n* service *m* des expéditions

**dispatch rider** *n* (*Mil*) estafette *f*

**dispel** [dɪs'pɛl] *vt* dissiper, chasser

**dispensary** [dɪs'pɛnsərɪ] *n* pharmacie *f*; (*in chemist's*) officine *f*

**dispense** [dɪs'pɛns] *vt* distribuer, administrer; (*medicine*) préparer (et vendre); **to ~ sb from** dispenser qn de

▶ **dispense with** *vt fus* se passer de; (*make unnecessary*) rendre superflu(e)

**dispenser** [dɪs'pɛnsər] *n* (*device*) distributeur *m*

**dispensing chemist** [dɪs'pɛnsɪŋ-] *n* (*Brit*) pharmacie *f*

**dispersal** [dɪs'pəːsl] *n* dispersion *f*; (*Admin*) déconcentration *f*

**disperse** [dɪs'pəːs] *vt* disperser; (*knowledge*) disséminer ▷ *vi* se disperser

**dispirited** [dɪs'pɪrɪtɪd] *adj* découragé(e), déprimé(e)

**displace** [dɪs'pleɪs] *vt* déplacer

**displaced person** [dɪs'pleɪst-] *n* (*Pol*) personne déplacée

**displacement** [dɪs'pleɪsmənt] *n* déplacement *m*

**display** [dɪs'pleɪ] *n* (*of goods*) étalage *m*; affichage *m*; (*Comput: information*) visualisation *f*; (: *device*) visuel *m*; (*of feeling*) manifestation *f*; (*pej*) ostentation *f*; (*show, spectacle*) spectacle *m*; (*military display*) parade *f* militaire ▷ *vt* montrer; (*goods*) mettre à l'étalage, exposer; (*results, departure times*) afficher; (*pej*) faire étalage de; **on ~** (*exhibits*) exposé(e), exhibé(e); (*goods*) à l'étalage

**display advertising** *n* publicité rédactionnelle

**displease** [dɪs'pliːz] *vt* mécontenter, contrarier; **~d with** mécontent(e) de

**displeasure** [dɪs'plɛʒər] *n* mécontentement *m*

**disposable** [dɪs'pəuzəbl] *adj* (*pack etc*) jetable; (*income*) disponible; **~ nappy** (*Brit*) couche *f* à jeter, couche-culotte *f*

**disposal** [dɪs'pəuzl] *n* (*of rubbish*) évacuation *f*, destruction *f*; (*of property etc: by selling*) vente *f*; (: *by giving away*) cession *f*; (*availability, arrangement*) disposition *f*; **at one's ~** à sa disposition; **to put sth at sb's ~** mettre qch à la disposition de qn

**dispose** [dɪs'pəuz] *vt* disposer ▷ *vi*: **to ~ of** (*time, money*) disposer de; (*unwanted goods*) se débarrasser de, se défaire de; (*Comm: stock*) écouler, vendre; (*problem*) expédier

**disposed** [dɪs'pəuzd] *adj*: **~ to do** disposé(e) à faire

**disposition** [dɪspə'zɪʃən] *n* disposition *f*; (*temperament*) naturel *m*

**dispossess** ['dɪspə'zɛs] *vt*: **to ~ sb (of)** déposséder qn (de)

**disproportion** [dɪsprə'pɔːʃən] *n* disproportion *f*

**disproportionate** [dɪsprə'pɔːʃənət] *adj* disproportionné(e)

**disprove** [dɪs'pruːv] vt réfuter
**dispute** [dɪs'pjuːt] n discussion f; (also:
  **industrial dispute**) conflit m ▷ vt (question)
  contester; (matter) discuter; (victory) disputer;
  **to be in** or **under** ~ (matter) être en discussion;
  (territory) être contesté(e)
**disqualification** [dɪskwɔlɪfɪ'keɪʃən] n
  disqualification f; ~ **(from driving)** (Brit)
  retrait m du permis (de conduire)
**disqualify** [dɪs'kwɔlɪfaɪ] vt (Sport) disqualifier;
  **to** ~ **sb for sth/from doing** (status, situation)
  rendre qn inapte à qch/à faire; (authority)
  signifier à qn l'interdiction de faire; **to** ~ **sb**
  **(from driving)** (Brit) retirer à qn son permis (de
  conduire)
**disquiet** [dɪs'kwaɪət] n inquiétude f, trouble m
**disquieting** [dɪs'kwaɪətɪŋ] adj inquiétant(e),
  alarmant(e)
**disregard** [dɪsrɪ'gaːd] vt ne pas tenir compte de
  ▷ n (indifference): ~ **(for)** (feelings) indifférence f
  (pour), insensibilité f (à); (danger, money)
  mépris m (pour)
**disrepair** ['dɪsrɪ'pɛəʳ] n mauvais état; **to fall**
  **into** ~ (building) tomber en ruine; (street) se
  dégrader
**disreputable** [dɪs'rɛpjutəbl] adj (person) de
  mauvaise réputation, peu recommandable;
  (behaviour) déshonorant(e); (area) mal famé(e),
  louche
**disrepute** ['dɪsrɪ'pjuːt] n déshonneur m,
  discrédit m; **to bring into** ~ faire tomber dans
  le discrédit
**disrespectful** [dɪsrɪ'spɛktful] adj
  irrespectueux(-euse)
**disrupt** [dɪs'rʌpt] vt (plans, meeting, lesson)
  perturber, déranger
**disruption** [dɪs'rʌpʃən] n perturbation f,
  dérangement m
**disruptive** [dɪs'rʌptɪv] adj perturbateur(-trice)
**dissatisfaction** [dɪssætɪs'fækʃən] n
  mécontentement m, insatisfaction f
**dissatisfied** [dɪs'sætɪsfaɪd] adj: ~ **(with)**
  insatisfait(e) (de)
**dissect** [dɪ'sɛkt] vt disséquer; (fig) disséquer,
  éplucher
**disseminate** [dɪ'sɛmɪneɪt] vt disséminer
**dissent** [dɪ'sɛnt] n dissentiment m, différence f
  d'opinion
**dissenter** [dɪ'sɛntəʳ] n (Rel, Pol etc) dissident(e)
**dissertation** [dɪsə'teɪʃən] n (Scol) mémoire m
**disservice** [dɪs'səːvɪs] n: **to do sb a** ~ rendre un
  mauvais service à qn; desservir qn
**dissident** ['dɪsɪdnt] adj, n dissident(e)
**dissimilar** [dɪ'sɪmɪləʳ] adj: ~ **(to)** dissemblable
  (à), différent(e) (de)
**dissipate** ['dɪsɪpeɪt] vt dissiper; (energy, efforts)
  disperser
**dissipated** ['dɪsɪpeɪtɪd] adj dissolu(e),
  débauché(e)
**dissociate** [dɪ'səʊʃɪeɪt] vt dissocier; **to** ~ **o.s.**
  **from** se désolidariser de
**dissolute** ['dɪsəluːt] adj débauché(e), dissolu(e)

**dissolve** [dɪ'zɔlv] vt dissoudre ▷ vi se dissoudre,
  fondre; (fig) disparaître; **to** ~ **in(to) tears**
  fondre en larmes
**dissuade** [dɪ'sweɪd] vt: **to** ~ **sb (from)** dissuader
  qn (de)
**distance** ['dɪstns] n distance f; **what's the** ~ **to**
  **London?** à quelle distance se trouve Londres?;
  **it's within walking** ~ on peut y aller à pied; **in**
  **the** ~ au loin
**distant** ['dɪstnt] adj lointain(e), éloigné(e);
  (manner) distant(e), froid(e)
**distaste** [dɪs'teɪst] n dégoût m
**distasteful** [dɪs'teɪstful] adj déplaisant(e),
  désagréable
**Dist. Atty.** abbr (US) = **district attorney**
**distemper** [dɪs'tɛmpəʳ] n (paint) détrempe f,
  badigeon m; (of dogs) maladie f de Carré
**distended** [dɪs'tɛndɪd] adj (stomach) dilaté(e)
**distil**, (US) **distill** [dɪs'tɪl] vt distiller
**distillery** [dɪs'tɪlərɪ] n distillerie f
**distinct** [dɪs'tɪŋkt] adj distinct(e); (clear)
  marqué(e); **as** ~ **from** par opposition à, en
  contraste avec
**distinction** [dɪs'tɪŋkʃən] n distinction f; (in
  exam) mention f très bien; **to draw a** ~ **between**
  faire une distinction entre; **a writer of** ~ un
  écrivain réputé
**distinctive** [dɪs'tɪŋktɪv] adj distinctif(-ive)
**distinctly** [dɪs'tɪŋktlɪ] adv distinctement;
  (specify) expressément
**distinguish** [dɪs'tɪŋgwɪʃ] vt distinguer ▷ vi: **to** ~
  **between** (concepts) distinguer entre, faire une
  distinction entre; **to** ~ **o.s.** se distinguer
**distinguished** [dɪs'tɪŋgwɪʃt] adj (eminent,
  refined) distingué(e); (career) remarquable,
  brillant(e)
**distinguishing** [dɪs'tɪŋgwɪʃɪŋ] adj (feature)
  distinctif(-ive), caractéristique
**distort** [dɪs'tɔːt] vt déformer
**distortion** [dɪs'tɔːʃən] n déformation f
**distract** [dɪs'trækt] vt distraire, déranger
**distracted** [dɪs'træktɪd] adj (not concentrating)
  distrait(e); (worried) affolé(e)
**distraction** [dɪs'trækʃən] n distraction f,
  dérangement m; **to drive sb to** ~ rendre qn fou
  (folle)
**distraught** [dɪs'trɔːt] adj éperdu(e)
**distress** [dɪs'trɛs] n détresse f; (pain) douleur f
  ▷ vt affliger; **in** ~ (ship) en perdition; (plane) en
  détresse; **~ed area** (Brit) zone sinistrée
**distressing** [dɪs'trɛsɪŋ] adj douloureux(-euse),
  pénible, affligeant(e)
**distress signal** n signal m de détresse
**distribute** [dɪs'trɪbjuːt] vt distribuer
**distribution** [dɪstrɪ'bjuːʃən] n distribution f
**distribution cost** n coût m de distribution
**distributor** [dɪs'trɪbjutəʳ] n (gen: Tech)
  distributeur m; (Comm) concessionnaire m/f
**district** ['dɪstrɪkt] n (of country) région f; (of town)
  quartier m; (Admin) district m
**district attorney** n (US) ≈ procureur m de la
  République

549

**district council** n (Brit) = conseil municipal; voir article

● **DISTRICT COUNCIL**
●
● En Grande-Bretagne, un district council est
● une administration locale qui gère un
● "district". Les conseillers ("councillors")
● sont élus au niveau local, en général tous les
● 4 ans. Le district council est financé par des
● impôts locaux et par des subventions du
● gouvernement.

**district nurse** n (Brit) infirmière visiteuse
**distrust** [dɪs'trʌst] n méfiance f, doute m ▷ vt se méfier de
**distrustful** [dɪs'trʌstful] adj méfiant(e)
**disturb** [dɪs'tə:b] vt troubler; (inconvenience) déranger; **sorry to ~ you** excusez-moi de vous déranger
**disturbance** [dɪs'tə:bəns] n dérangement m; (political etc) troubles mpl; (by drunks etc) tapage m; **to cause a ~** troubler l'ordre public; **~ of the peace** (Law) tapage injurieux or nocturne
**disturbed** [dɪs'tə:bd] adj (worried, upset) agité(e), troublé(e); **to be emotionally ~** avoir des problèmes affectifs
**disturbing** [dɪs'tə:bɪŋ] adj troublant(e), inquiétant(e)
**disuse** [dɪs'ju:s] n: **to fall into ~** tomber en désuétude
**disused** [dɪs'ju:zd] adj désaffecté(e)
**ditch** [dɪtʃ] n fossé m; (for irrigation) rigole f ▷ vt (inf) abandonner; (person) plaquer
**dither** ['dɪðəʳ] vi hésiter
**ditto** ['dɪtəu] adv idem
**divan** [dɪ'væn] n divan m
**divan bed** n divan-lit m
**dive** [daɪv] n plongeon m; (of submarine) plongée f; (Aviat) piqué m; (pej: café, bar etc) bouge m ▷ vi plonger; **to ~ into** (bag etc) plonger la main dans; (place) se précipiter dans
**diver** ['daɪvəʳ] n plongeur m
**diverge** [daɪ'və:dʒ] vi diverger
**diverse** [daɪ'və:s] adj divers(e)
**diversification** [daɪvə:sɪfɪ'keɪʃən] n diversification f
**diversify** [daɪ'və:sɪfaɪ] vt diversifier
**diversion** [daɪ'və:ʃən] n (Brit Aut) déviation f; (distraction, Mil) diversion f
`**diversionary tactics** [daɪ'və:ʃənrɪ-] npl tactique fsg de diversion
**diversity** [daɪ'və:sɪtɪ] n diversité f, variété f
**divert** [daɪ'və:t] vt (Brit: traffic) dévier; (plane) dérouter; (train, river) détourner; (amuse) divertir
**divest** [daɪ'vɛst] vt: **to ~ sb of** dépouiller qn de
**divide** [dɪ'vaɪd] vt diviser; (separate) séparer ▷ vi se diviser; **to ~ (between** or **among)** répartir or diviser (entre); **40 ~d by 5** 40 divisé par 5
▶ **divide out** vt: **to ~ out (between** or **among)** distribuer or répartir (entre)
**divided** [dɪ'vaɪdɪd] adj (fig: country, couple)

désuni(e); (opinions) partagé(e)
**divided highway** (US) n route f à quatre voies
**divided skirt** n jupe-culotte f
**dividend** ['dɪvɪdɛnd] n dividende m
**dividend cover** n rapport m dividendes-résultat
**dividers** [dɪ'vaɪdəz] npl compas m à pointes sèches; (between pages) feuillets mpl intercalaires
**divine** [dɪ'vaɪn] adj divin(e) ▷ vt (future) prédire; (truth) deviner, entrevoir; (water, metal) détecter la présence de (par l'intermédiaire de la radiesthésie)
**diving** ['daɪvɪŋ] n plongée (sous-marine)
**diving board** n plongeoir m
**diving suit** n scaphandre m
**divinity** [dɪ'vɪnɪtɪ] n divinité f; (as study) théologie f
**division** [dɪ'vɪʒən] n division f; (Brit: Football) division f; (separation) séparation f; (Comm) service m; (Brit: Pol) vote m; (also: **division of labour**) division du travail
**divisive** [dɪ'vaɪsɪv] adj qui entraîne la division, qui crée des dissensions
**divorce** [dɪ'vɔ:s] n divorce m ▷ vt divorcer d'avec
**divorced** [dɪ'vɔ:st] adj divorcé(e)
**divorcee** [dɪvɔ:'si:] n divorcé(e)
**divot** ['dɪvət] n (Golf) motte f de gazon
**divulge** [daɪ'vʌldʒ] vt divulguer, révéler
**DIY** adj, n abbr (Brit) = **do-it-yourself**
**dizziness** ['dɪzɪnɪs] n vertige m, étourdissement m
**dizzy** ['dɪzɪ] adj (height) vertigineux(-euse); **to make sb ~** donner le vertige à qn; **I feel ~** la tête me tourne, j'ai la tête qui tourne
**DJ** n abbr = **disc jockey**
**d.j.** n abbr = **dinner jacket**
**Djakarta** [dʒə'kɑ:tə] n Djakarta
**DJIA** n abbr (US Stock Exchange) = **Dow-Jones Industrial Average**
**dl** abbr (= decilitre) dl
**DLit, DLitt** n abbr (= Doctor of Literature, Doctor of Letters) titre universitaire
**DMus** n abbr (= Doctor of Music) titre universitaire
**DMZ** n abbr = **demilitarized zone**
**DNA** n abbr (= deoxyribonucleic acid) ADN m
**DNA fingerprinting** [-'fɪŋɡəprɪntɪŋ] n technique f des empreintes génétiques
**do** abbr (= ditto) d

⊙ KEYWORD

**do** [du:] (pt **did**, pp **done**) n (inf: party etc) soirée f, fête f; (: formal gathering) réception f
▷ vb **1** (in negative constructions) non traduit; **I don't understand** je ne comprends pas
**2** (to form questions) non traduit; **didn't you know?** vous ne le saviez pas?; **what do you think?** qu'en pensez-vous?; **why didn't you come?** pourquoi n'êtes-vous pas venu?
**3** (for emphasis, in polite expressions): **people do make mistakes sometimes** on peut toujours se tromper; **she does seem rather late** je trouve qu'elle est bien en retard; **do sit down/ help yourself** asseyez-vous/servez-vous je vous

en prie; **do take care!** faites bien attention à vous!; **I Do wish I could go** j'aimerais tant y aller; **but I Do like it!** mais si, je l'aime!
**4** (*used to avoid repeating vb*): **she swims better than I do** elle nage mieux que moi; **do you agree? — yes, I do/no I don't** vous êtes d'accord? — oui/non; **she lives in Glasgow — so do I** elle habite Glasgow — moi aussi; **he didn't like it and neither did we** il n'a pas aimé ça, et nous non plus; **who broke it? — I did** qui l'a cassé? — c'est moi; **he asked me to help him and I did** il m'a demandé de l'aider, et c'est ce que j'ai fait
**5** (*in question tags*): **you like him, don't you?** vous l'aimez bien, n'est-ce pas?; **he laughed, didn't he?** il a ri, n'est-ce pas?; **I don't know him, do I?** je ne crois pas le connaître
▷ vt **1** (*gen: carry out, perform etc*) faire; (*visit: city, museum*) faire, visiter; **what are you doing tonight?** qu'est-ce que vous faites ce soir?; **what do you do?** (*job*) que faites-vous dans la vie?; **what did he do with the cat?** qu'a-t-il fait du chat?; **what can I do for you?** que puis-je faire pour vous?; **to do the cooking/ washing-up** faire la cuisine/la vaisselle; **to do one's teeth/hair/nails** se brosser les dents/se coiffer/se faire les ongles
**2** (*Aut etc: distance*) faire; (*: speed*) faire du; **we've done 200 km already** nous avons déjà fait 200 km; **the car was doing 100** la voiture faisait du 100 (à l'heure); **he can do 100 in that car** il peut faire du 100 (à l'heure) dans cette voiture-là
▷ vi **1** (*act, behave*) faire; **do as I do** faites comme moi
**2** (*get on, fare*) marcher; **the firm is doing well** l'entreprise marche bien; **he's doing well/ badly at school** ça marche bien/mal pour lui à l'école; **how do you do?** comment allez-vous?; (*on being introduced*) enchanté(e)!
**3** (*suit*) aller; **will it do?** est-ce que ça ira?
**4** (*be sufficient*) suffire, aller; **will £10 do?** est-ce que 10 livres suffiront?; **that'll do** ça suffit, ça ira; **that'll do!** (*in annoyance*) ça va or suffit comme ça!; **to make do (with)** se contenter (de)
▶ **do away with** vt fus abolir; (*kill*) supprimer
▶ **do for** vt fus (*Brit inf: clean for*) faire le ménage chez
▶ **do up** vt (*laces, dress*) attacher; (*buttons*) boutonner; (*zip*) fermer; (*renovate: room*) refaire; (*: house*) remettre à neuf; **to do o.s. up** se faire beau (belle)
▶ **do with** vt fus (*need*): **I could do with a drink/ some help** quelque chose à boire/un peu d'aide ne serait pas de refus; **it could do with a wash** ça ne lui ferait pas de mal d'être lavé; (*be connected with*): **that has nothing to do with you** cela ne vous concerne pas; **I won't have anything to do with it** je ne veux pas m'en mêler; **what has that got to do with it?** quel est le rapport?, qu'est-ce que cela vient faire là-dedans?
▶ **do without** vi s'en passer; **if you're late for tea then you'll do without** si vous êtes en retard pour le dîner il faudra vous en passer ▷ vt fus se passer de; **I can do without a car** je peux me passer de voiture

**DOA** abbr (= *dead on arrival*) décédé(e) à l'admission
**d.o.b.** abbr = **date of birth**
**doc** [dɔk] n (*inf*) toubib m
**docile** ['dəusaıl] adj docile
**dock** [dɔk] n dock m; (*wharf*) quai m; (*Law*) banc m des accusés ▷ vi se mettre à quai; (*Space*) s'arrimer ▷ vt: **they ~ed a third of his wages** ils lui ont retenu or décompté un tiers de son salaire; **docks** npl (*Naut*) docks
**dock dues** npl droits mpl de bassin
**docker** ['dɔkəʳ] n docker m
**docket** ['dɔkıt] n bordereau m; (*on parcel etc*) étiquette f or fiche f (*décrivant le contenu d'un paquet etc*)
**dockyard** ['dɔkjɑːd] n chantier m de construction navale
**doctor** ['dɔktəʳ] n médecin m, docteur m; (*PhD etc*) docteur ▷ vt (*cat*) couper; (*interfere with: food*) altérer; (*: drink*) frelater; (*: text, document*) arranger; **~'s office** (*US*) cabinet m de consultation; **call a ~!** appelez un docteur or un médecin!
**doctorate** ['dɔktərıt] n doctorat m; *voir article*

**Doctor of Philosophy** n (*degree*) doctorat m; (*person*) titulaire m/f d'un doctorat
**docudrama** ['dɔkjudrɑːmə] n (*TV*) docudrame m
**document** ['dɔkjumənt] n document m ▷ vt ['dɔkjumɛnt] documenter
**documentary** [dɔkju'mɛntərı] adj, n documentaire (*m*)
**documentation** [dɔkjumən'teıʃən] n documentation f
**DOD** n abbr (*US*) = **Department of Defense**
**doddering** ['dɔdərıŋ] adj (*senile*) gâteux(-euse)
**doddery** ['dɔdərı] adj branlant(e)
**doddle** ['dɔdl] n: **it's a ~** (*inf*) c'est simple comme bonjour, c'est du gâteau
**Dodecanese** [dəudıkə'niːz] n, **Dodecanese Islands** npl Dodécanèse m
**dodge** [dɔdʒ] n truc m; combine f ▷ vt esquiver,

éviter ▷ vi faire un saut de côté; (Sport) faire une esquive; **to ~ out of the way** s'esquiver; **to ~ through the traffic** se faufiler or faire de savantes manœuvres entre les voitures

**dodgems** ['dɔdʒəmz] npl (Brit) autos tamponneuses

**dodgy** ['dɔdʒɪ] adj (inf: uncertain) douteux(-euse); (: shady) louche

**DOE** n abbr (Brit) = **Department of the Environment**; (US) = **Department of Energy**

**doe** [dəu] n (deer) biche f; (rabbit) lapine f

**does** [dʌz] vb see **do**

**doesn't** ['dʌznt] = **does not**

**dog** [dɔg] n chien(ne) ▷ vt (follow closely) suivre de près, ne pas lâcher d'une semelle; (fig: memory etc) poursuivre, harceler; **to go to the ~s** (nation etc) aller à vau-l'eau

**dog biscuits** npl biscuits mpl pour chien

**dog collar** n collier m de chien; (fig) faux-col m d'ecclésiastique

**dog-eared** ['dɔgɪəd] adj corné(e)

**dog food** n nourriture f pour les chiens or le chien

**dogged** ['dɔgɪd] adj obstiné(e), opiniâtre

**doggy** ['dɔgɪ] n (inf) toutou m

**doggy bag** ['dɔgɪ-] n petit sac pour emporter les restes

**dogma** ['dɔgmə] n dogme m

**dogmatic** [dɔg'mætɪk] adj dogmatique

**do-gooder** [du:'gudə'] n (pej) faiseur(-euse) de bonnes œuvres

**dogsbody** ['dɔgzbɔdɪ] n (Brit) bonne f à tout faire, tâcheron m

**doily** ['dɔɪlɪ] n dessus m d'assiette

**doing** ['duɪŋ] n: **this is your ~** c'est votre travail, c'est vous qui avez fait ça

**doings** ['duɪŋz] npl activités fpl

**do-it-yourself** ['du:ɪtjɔː'self] n bricolage m

**doldrums** ['dɔldrəmz] npl: **to be in the ~** avoir le cafard; être dans le marasme

**dole** [dəul] n (Brit: payment) allocation f de chômage; **on the ~** au chômage
  ▶ **dole out** vt donner au compte-goutte

**doleful** ['dəulful] adj triste, lugubre

**doll** [dɔl] n poupée f
  ▶ **doll up** vt: **to ~ o.s. up** se faire beau (belle)

**dollar** ['dɔlə'] n dollar m

**dollop** ['dɔləp] n (of butter, cheese) bon morceau; (of cream) bonne cuillerée

**dolly** ['dɔlɪ] n poupée f

**dolphin** ['dɔlfɪn] n dauphin m

**domain** [də'meɪn] n (also fig) domaine m

**dome** [dəum] n dôme m

**domestic** [də'mɛstɪk] adj (duty, happiness) familial(e); (policy, affairs, flight) intérieur(e); (news) national(e); (animal) domestique

**domesticated** [də'mɛstɪkeɪtɪd] adj domestiqué(e); (pej) d'intérieur; **he's very ~** il participe volontiers aux tâches ménagères; question ménage, il est très organisé

**domesticity** [dəumɛs'tɪsɪtɪ] n vie f de famille

**domestic servant** n domestique m/f

**domicile** ['dɔmɪsaɪl] n domicile m

**dominant** ['dɔmɪnənt] adj dominant(e)

**dominate** ['dɔmɪneɪt] vt dominer

**domination** [dɔmɪ'neɪʃən] n domination f

**domineering** [dɔmɪ'nɪərɪŋ] adj dominateur(-trice), autoritaire

**Dominican Republic** [də'mɪnɪkən-] n République Dominicaine

**dominion** [də'mɪnɪən] n domination f; territoire m; dominion m

**domino** ['dɔmɪnəu] (pl -es) n domino m

**dominoes** ['dɔmɪnəuz] n (game) dominos mpl

**don** [dɔn] n (Brit) professeur m d'université ▷ vt revêtir

**donate** [də'neɪt] vt faire don de, donner

**donation** [də'neɪʃən] n donation f, don m

**done** [dʌn] pp of **do**

**donkey** ['dɔŋkɪ] n âne m

**donkey-work** ['dɔŋkɪwə:k] n (Brit inf) le gros du travail, le plus dur (du travail)

**donor** ['dəunə'] n (of blood etc) donneur(-euse); (to charity) donateur(-trice)

**donor card** n carte f de don d'organes

**don't** [dəunt] = **do not**

**donut** ['dəunʌt] (US) n = **doughnut**

**doodle** ['du:dl] n griffonnage m, gribouillage m ▷ vi griffonner, gribouiller

**doom** [du:m] n (fate) destin m; (ruin) ruine f ▷ vt: **to be ~ed to failure** être voué(e) à l'échec

**doomsday** ['du:mzdeɪ] n le Jugement dernier

**door** [dɔː'] n porte f; (Rail, car) portière f; **to go from ~ to ~** aller de porte en porte

**doorbell** ['dɔːbɛl] n sonnette f

**door handle** n poignée f de porte; (of car) poignée de portière

**doorknob** ['dɔːnɔb] n poignée f or bouton m de porte

**doorman** ['dɔːmən] (irreg) n (in hotel) portier m; (in block of flats) concierge m

**doormat** ['dɔːmæt] n paillasson m

**doorpost** ['dɔːpəust] n montant m de porte

**doorstep** ['dɔːstɛp] n pas m de (la) porte, seuil m

**door-to-door** ['dɔːtə'dɔː'] adj: **~ selling** vente f à domicile

**doorway** ['dɔːweɪ] n (embrasure f de) porte f

**dope** [dəup] n (inf: drug) drogue f; (: person) andouille f; (: information) tuyaux mpl, rancards mpl ▷ vt (horse etc) doper

**dopey** ['dəupɪ] adj (inf) à moitié endormi(e)

**dormant** ['dɔːmənt] adj assoupi(e), en veilleuse; (rule, law) inappliqué(e)

**dormer** ['dɔːmə'] n (also: **dormer window**) lucarne f

**dormice** ['dɔːmaɪs] npl of **dormouse**

**dormitory** ['dɔːmɪtrɪ] n (Brit) dortoir m; (US: hall of residence) résidence f universitaire

**dormouse** (pl **dormice**) ['dɔːmaus, -maɪs] n loir m

**DOS** [dɔs] n abbr (= disk operating system) DOS m

**dosage** ['dəusɪdʒ] n dose f; dosage m; (on label) posologie f

**dose** [dəus] n dose f; (Brit: bout) attaque f ▷ vt: **to ~ o.s.** se bourrer de médicaments; **a ~ of flu** une belle or bonne grippe

**dosh** [dɔʃ] (inf) n fric m
**dosser** ['dɔsəʳ] n (Brit inf) clochard(e)
**doss house** ['dɔs-] n (Brit) asile m de nuit
**DOT** n abbr (US) = **Department of**
**Transportation**
**dot** [dɔt] n point m; (on material) pois m ▷ vt: **~ted**
**with** parsemé(e) de; **on the ~** à l'heure tapante
**dotcom** [dɔt'kɔm] n point com m, pointcom m
**dot command** n (Comput) commande précédée
d'un point
**dote** [dəut]: **to ~ on** vt fus être fou (folle de)
**dot-matrix printer** [dɔt'meɪtrɪks-] n
imprimante matricielle
**dotted line** ['dɔtɪd-] n ligne pointillée; (Aut)
ligne discontinue; **to sign on the ~** signer à
l'endroit indiqué or sur la ligne pointillée; (fig)
donner son consentement
**dotty** ['dɔtɪ] adj (inf) loufoque, farfelu(e)
**double** ['dʌbl] adj double ▷ adv (fold) en deux;
(twice): **to cost ~ (sth)** coûter le double (de qch)
or deux fois plus (que qch) ▷ n double m; (Cine)
doublure f ▷ vt doubler; (fold) plier en deux ▷ vi
doubler; (have two uses): **to ~ as** servir aussi de; **~**
**five two six (5526)** (Brit Tel) cinquante-cinq –
vingt-six; **it's spelt with a ~ "l"** ça s'écrit avec
deux "l"; **on the ~**, **at the ~** au pas de course
▶ **double back** vi (person) revenir sur ses pas
▶ **double up** vi (bend over) se courber, se plier;
(share room) partager la chambre
**double bass** n contrebasse f
**double bed** n grand lit
**double-breasted** ['dʌbl'brɛstɪd] adj croisé(e)
**double-check** ['dʌbl'tʃɛk] vt, vi revérifier
**double-click** ['dʌbl'klɪk] vi (Comput) double-
cliquer
**double-clutch** ['dʌbl'klʌtʃ] vi (US) faire un
double débrayage
**double cream** n (Brit) crème fraîche épaisse
**double-cross** ['dʌbl'krɔs] vt doubler, trahir
**double-decker** ['dʌbl'dɛkəʳ] n autobus m à
impériale
**double declutch** vi (Brit) faire un double
débrayage
**double exposure** n (Phot) surimpression f
**double glazing** n (Brit) double vitrage m
**double-page** ['dʌblpeɪdʒ] adj: **~ spread**
publicité f en double page
**double parking** n stationnement m en double
file
**double room** n chambre f pour deux
**doubles** ['dʌblz] n (Tennis) double m
**double whammy** [-'wæmɪ] n (inf) double
contretemps m
**double yellow lines** npl (Brit: Aut) double bande
jaune marquant l'interdiction de stationner
**doubly** ['dʌblɪ] adv doublement, deux fois plus
**doubt** [daut] n doute m ▷ vt douter de; **no ~**
sans doute; **without (a) ~** sans aucun doute;
**beyond ~** adv indubitablement ▷ adj
indubitable; **to ~ that** douter que + sub; **I ~ it**
**very much** j'en doute fort
**doubtful** ['dautful] adj douteux(-euse); (person)

incertain(e); **to be ~ about sth** avoir des doutes
sur qch, ne pas être convaincu de qch; **I'm a bit**
**~** je n'en suis pas certain or sûr
**doubtless** ['dautlɪs] adv sans doute, sûrement
**dough** [dəu] n pâte f; (inf: money) fric m,
pognon m
**doughnut** ['dəunʌt], (US) **donut** n beignet m
**dour** [duəʳ] adj austère
**douse** [dauz] vt (with water) tremper, inonder;
(flames) éteindre
**dove** [dʌv] n colombe f
**Dover** ['dəuvəʳ] n Douvres
**dovetail** ['dʌvteɪl] n: **~ joint** assemblage m à
queue d'aronde ▷ vi (fig) concorder
**dowager** ['dauədʒəʳ] n douairière f
**dowdy** ['daudɪ] adj démodé(e), mal fagoté(e)
**Dow-Jones average** ['dau'dʒəunz-] n (US)
indice m Dow-Jones
**down** [daun] n (fluff) duvet m; (hill) colline
(dénudée) ▷ adv en bas, vers le bas; (on the
ground) par terre ▷ prep en bas de; (along) le long
de ▷ vt (enemy) abattre; (inf: drink) siffler; **to fall**
**~** tomber; **she's going ~ to Bristol** elle descend
à Bristol; **to write sth ~** écrire qch; **~ there** là-
bas (en bas), là au fond; **~ here** ici en bas; **the**
**price of meat is ~** le prix de la viande a baissé;
**I've got it ~ in my diary** c'est inscrit dans mon
agenda; **to pay £2 ~** verser 2 livres d'arrhes or en
acompte; **England is two goals ~** l'Angleterre a
deux buts de retard; **to walk ~ a hill** descendre
une colline; **to run ~ the street** descendre la
rue en courant; **to ~ tools** (Brit) cesser le travail;
**~ with X!** à bas X!
**down-and-out** ['daunəndaut] n (tramp)
clochard(e)
**down-at-heel** ['daunət'hi:l] adj (fig)
miteux(-euse)
**downbeat** ['daunbi:t] n (Mus) temps frappé
▷ adj sombre, négatif(-ive)
**downcast** ['daunkɑ:st] adj démoralisé(e)
**downer** ['daunəʳ] n (inf: drug) tranquillisant m;
**to be on a ~** (depressed) flipper
**downfall** ['daunfɔ:l] n chute f; ruine f
**downgrade** ['daungreɪd] vt déclasser
**downhearted** ['daun'hɑ:tɪd] adj découragé(e)
**downhill** ['daun'hɪl] adv (face, look) vers l'aval,
vers l'aval; (roll, go) vers le bas, en bas ▷ n (Ski: also:
**downhill race**) descente f; **to go ~** descendre;
(business) péricliter, aller à vau-l'eau
**Downing Street** ['daunɪŋ-] n (Brit): **10 ~** résidence
du Premier ministre; voir article

⬤ **DOWNING STREET**
⬤
⬤ Downing Street est une rue de Westminster (à
⬤ Londres) où se trouvent la résidence
⬤ officielle du Premier ministre et celle du
⬤ ministre des Finances. Le nom Downing Street
⬤ est souvent utilisé pour désigner le
⬤ gouvernement britannique.

**download** ['daunləud] n téléchargement m ▷ vt

(*Comput*) télécharger
**downloadable** [daun'ləudəbl] adj
téléchargeable
**down-market** ['daun'mɑːkɪt] adj (*product*) bas de
gamme *inv*
**down payment** n acompte m
**downplay** ['daunpleɪ] vt (*US*) minimiser
(l'importance de)
**downpour** ['daunpɔːʳ] n pluie torrentielle,
déluge m
**downright** ['daunraɪt] adj (*lie etc*) effronté(e);
(*refusal*) catégorique
**Downs** [daunz] npl (*Brit*): **the ~** collines crayeuses
du sud-est de l'Angleterre
**downsize** [daun'saɪz] vt réduire l'effectif de
**Down's syndrome** [daunz-] n mongolisme m,
trisomie f; **a ~ baby** un bébé mongolien or
trisomique
**downstairs** ['daun'stɛəz] adv (*on or to ground floor*)
au rez-de-chaussée; (*on or to floor below*) à l'étage
inférieur; **to come ~, to go ~** descendre
(l'escalier)
**downstream** ['daunstriːm] adv en aval
**downtime** ['dauntaɪm] n (*of machine etc*) temps
mort; (*of person*) temps d'arrêt
**down-to-earth** ['dauntu'ə:θ] adj terre à terre *inv*
**downtown** ['daun'taun] adv en ville ▷ adj (*US*):
**~ Chicago** le centre commerçant de Chicago
**downtrodden** ['dauntrɔdn] adj opprimé(e)
**down under** adv en Australie or Nouvelle
Zélande
**downward** ['daunwəd] adj, adv vers le bas; **a ~
trend** une tendance à la baisse, une
diminution progressive
**downwards** ['daunwədz] adv vers le bas
**dowry** ['dauri] n dot f
**doz.** abbr = **dozen**
**doze** [dəuz] vi sommeiller
▶ **doze off** vi s'assoupir
**dozen** ['dʌzn] n douzaine f; **a ~ books** une
douzaine de livres; **8op a ~** 8op la douzaine; **~s
of** des centaines de
**DPh, DPhil** n abbr (= Doctor of Philosophy) titre
universitaire
**DPP** n abbr (Brit) = **Director of Public
Prosecutions**
**DPT** n abbr (Med: = diphtheria, pertussis, tetanus)
DCT m
**DPW** n abbr (US) = **Department of Public Works**
**Dr.** abbr (= doctor) Dr; (in street names) = **drive**
**drab** [dræb] adj terne, morne
**draft** [drɑːft] n (*of letter, school work*) brouillon m;
(*of literary work*) ébauche f; (*of contract, document*)
version f préliminaire; (*Comm*) traite f; (*US Mil*)
contingent m; (: *call-up*) conscription f ▷ vt rédiger
le brouillon de; (*document, report*) rédiger une
version préliminaire de; (*Mil: send*) détacher; *see
also* **draught**
**drag** [dræg] vt traîner; (*river*) draguer ▷ vi
traîner ▷ n (*Aviat, Naut*) résistance f; (*inf*) casse-
pieds m/f; (*women's clothing*): **in ~** (en) travesti; **to
~ and drop** (*Comput*) glisser-poser

▶ **drag away** vt: **to ~ away (from)** arracher or
emmener de force (de)
▶ **drag on** vi s'éterniser
**dragnet** ['drægnɛt] n drège f; (*fig*) piège m,
filets mpl
**dragon** ['drægn] n dragon m
**dragonfly** ['drægənflaɪ] n libellule f
**dragoon** [drə'guːn] n (*cavalryman*) dragon m ▷ vt:
**to ~ sb into doing sth** (*Brit*) forcer qn à faire qch
**drain** [dreɪn] n égout m; (*on resources*) saignée f
▷ vt (*land, marshes*) drainer, assécher; (*vegetables*)
égoutter; (*reservoir etc*) vider ▷ vi (*water*)
s'écouler; **to feel ~ed (of energy or emotion)**
être miné(e)
**drainage** ['dreɪnɪdʒ] n (*system*) système m
d'égouts; (*act*) drainage m
**draining board** ['dreɪnɪŋ-] (*US*), **drainboard**
['dreɪnbɔːd] n égouttoir m
**drainpipe** ['dreɪnpaɪp] n tuyau m d'écoulement
**drake** [dreɪk] n canard m (mâle)
**dram** [dræm] n petit verre
**drama** ['drɑːmə] n (*art*) théâtre m, art m
dramatique; (*play*) pièce f; (*event*) drame m
**dramatic** [drə'mætɪk] adj (*Theat*) dramatique;
(*impressive*) spectaculaire
**dramatically** [drə'mætɪklɪ] adv de façon
spectaculaire
**dramatist** ['dræmətɪst] n auteur m dramatique
**dramatize** ['dræmətaɪz] vt (*events etc*)
dramatiser; (*adapt*) adapter pour la télévision
(or pour l'écran)
**drank** [dræŋk] pt of **drink**
**drape** [dreɪp] vt draper; **drapes** npl (*US*)
rideaux mpl
**draper** ['dreɪpəʳ] n (Brit) marchand(e) de
nouveautés
**drastic** ['dræstɪk] adj (*measures*) d'urgence,
énergique; (*change*) radical(e)
**drastically** ['dræstɪklɪ] adv radicalement
**draught,** (*US*) **draft** [drɑːft] n courant m d'air;
(*of chimney*) tirage m; (*Naut*) tirant m d'eau; **on ~**
(*beer*) à la pression
**draught beer** n bière f (à la) pression
**draughtboard** ['drɑːftbɔːd] n (Brit) damier m
**draughts** [drɑːfts] n (Brit: *game*) (jeu m de)
dames fpl
**draughtsman,** (*US*) **draftsman** ['drɑːftsmən]
(*irreg*) n dessinateur(-trice) (industriel(le))
**draughtsmanship,** (*US*) **draftsmanship** ['drɑː
ftsmənʃɪp] n (*technique*) dessin industriel; (*art*)
graphisme m
**draw** [drɔː] (*vb: pt* **drew,** *pp* **~n**) [druː, drɔːn] vt
tirer; (*picture*) dessiner; (*attract*) attirer; (*line,
circle*) tracer; (*money*) retirer; (*wages*) toucher;
(*comparison, distinction*): **to ~ (between)** faire
(entre) ▷ vi (*Sport*) faire match nul ▷ n match
nul; (*lottery*) loterie f; (: *picking of ticket*) tirage m
au sort; **to ~ to a close** toucher à or tirer à sa fin;
**to ~ near** vi s'approcher; approcher
▶ **draw back** vi (*move back*): **to ~ back (from)**
reculer (de)
▶ **draw in** vi (*Brit: car*) s'arrêter le long du

trottoir; (: *train*) entrer en gare *or* dans la station
▶ **draw on** *vt* (*resources*) faire appel à;
(*imagination, person*) avoir recours à, faire appel à
▶ **draw out** *vi* (*lengthen*) s'allonger ▷ *vt* (*money*)
retirer
▶ **draw up** *vi* (*stop*) s'arrêter ▷ *vt* (*document*)
établir, dresser; (*plan*) formuler, dessiner; (*chair*)
approcher

**drawback** ['drɔːbæk] *n* inconvénient *m*,
désavantage *m*

**drawbridge** ['drɔːbrɪdʒ] *n* pont-levis *m*

**drawee** [drɔːˈiː] *n* tiré *m*

**drawer** [drɔːʳ] *n* tiroir *m* ['drɔːəʳ] (*of cheque*)
tireur *m*

**drawing** ['drɔːɪŋ] *n* dessin *m*

**drawing board** *n* planche f à dessin

**drawing pin** *n* (*Brit*) punaise f

**drawing room** *n* salon *m*

**drawl** [drɔːl] *n* accent traînant

**drawn** [drɔːn] *pp of* **draw** ▷ *adj* (*haggard*) tiré(e),
crispé(e)

**drawstring** ['drɔːstrɪŋ] *n* cordon *m*

**dread** [drɛd] *n* épouvante f, effroi *m* ▷ *vt*
redouter, appréhender

**dreadful** ['drɛdful] *adj* épouvantable,
affreux(-euse)

**dream** [driːm] *n* rêve *m* ▷ *vt, vi* (*pt, pp* **-ed** *or* **-t**)
[drɛmt] rêver; **to have a ~ about sb/sth** rêver à
qn/qch; **sweet ~s!** faites de beaux rêves!
▶ **dream up** *vt* inventer

**dreamer** ['driːməʳ] *n* rêveur(-euse)

**dreamt** [drɛmt] *pt, pp of* **dream**

**dreamy** ['driːmɪ] *adj* (*absent-minded*)
rêveur(-euse)

**dreary** ['drɪərɪ] *adj* triste; monotone

**dredge** [drɛdʒ] *vt* draguer
▶ **dredge up** *vt* draguer; (*fig: unpleasant facts*)
(faire) ressortir

**dredger** ['drɛdʒəʳ] *n* (*ship*) dragueur *m*; (*machine*)
drague f; (*Brit: also:* **sugar dredger**)
saupoudreuse f

**dregs** [drɛgz] *npl* lie f

**drench** [drɛntʃ] *vt* tremper; **~ed to the skin**
trempé(e) jusqu'aux os

**dress** [drɛs] *n* robe f; (*clothing*) habillement *m*,
tenue f ▷ *vt* habiller; (*wound*) panser; (*food*)
préparer ▷ *vi*: **she ~es very well** elle s'habille
très bien; **to ~ o.s., to get ~ed** s'habiller; **to ~ a
shop window** faire l'étalage *or* la vitrine
▶ **dress up** *vi* s'habiller; (*in fancy dress*) se
déguiser

**dress circle** *n* (*Brit*) premier balcon

**dress designer** *n* modéliste *m/f*,
dessinateur(-trice) de mode

**dresser** ['drɛsəʳ] *n* (*Theat*) habilleur(-euse); (*also:*
**window dresser**) étalagiste *m/f*; (*furniture*)
vaisselier *m*; (: *US*) coiffeuse f, commode f

**dressing** ['drɛsɪŋ] *n* (*Med*) pansement *m*; (*Culin*)
sauce f, assaisonnement *m*

**dressing gown** *n* (*Brit*) robe f de chambre

**dressing room** *n* (*Theat*) loge f; (*Sport*)
vestiaire *m*

**dressing table** *n* coiffeuse f

**dressmaker** ['drɛsmeɪkəʳ] *n* couturière f

**dressmaking** ['drɛsmeɪkɪŋ] *n* couture f; travaux
*mpl* de couture

**dress rehearsal** *n* (répétition f) générale f

**dress shirt** *n* chemise f à plastron

**dressy** ['drɛsɪ] *adj* (*inf: clothes*) (qui fait) habillé(e)

**drew** [druː] *pt of* **draw**

**dribble** ['drɪbl] *vi* tomber goutte à goutte; (*baby*)
baver ▷ *vt* (*ball*) dribbler

**dried** [draɪd] *adj* (*fruit, beans*) sec (sèche); (*eggs,
milk*) en poudre

**drier** ['draɪəʳ] *n* = **dryer**

**drift** [drɪft] *n* (*of current etc*) force f; direction f; (*of
sand etc*) amoncellement *m*; (*of snow*) rafale f;
coulée f; (: *on ground*) congère f; (*general meaning*)
sens général ▷ *vi* (*boat*) aller à la dérive, dériver;
(*sand, snow*) s'amonceler, s'entasser; **to let
things ~** laisser les choses aller à la dérive; **to ~
apart** (*friends, lovers*) s'éloigner l'un de l'autre; **I
get** *or* **catch your ~** je vois en gros ce que vous
voulez dire

**drifter** ['drɪftəʳ] *n* personne f sans but dans la vie

**driftwood** ['drɪftwud] *n* bois flotté

**drill** [drɪl] *n* perceuse f; (*bit*) foret *m*; (*of dentist*)
roulette f, fraise f; (*Mil*) exercice *m* ▷ *vt* percer;
(*troops*) entraîner; (*pupils: in grammar*) faire faire
des exercices à ▷ *vi* (*for oil*) faire un *or* des
forage(s)

**drilling** ['drɪlɪŋ] *n* (*for oil*) forage *m*

**drilling rig** *n* (*on land*) tour f (de forage), derrick
*m*; (*at sea*) plate-forme f de forage

**drily** ['draɪlɪ] *adv* = **dryly**

**drink** [drɪŋk] *n* boisson f; (*alcoholic*) verre *m* ▷ *vt,
vi* (*pt* **drank**, *pp* **drunk** [dræŋk, drʌŋk]) boire; **to
have a ~** boire quelque chose, boire un verre; **a ~
of water** un verre d'eau; **would you like a ~?** tu
veux boire quelque chose?; **we had ~s before
lunch** on a pris l'apéritif
▶ **drink in** *vt* (*fresh air*) inspirer profondément;
(*story*) avaler, ne pas perdre une miette de;
(*sight*) se remplir la vue de

**drinkable** ['drɪŋkəbl] *adj* (*not dangerous*) potable;
(*palatable*) buvable

**drink-driving** ['drɪŋk'draɪvɪŋ] *n* conduite f en
état d'ivresse

**drinker** ['drɪŋkəʳ] *n* buveur(-euse)

**drinking** ['drɪŋkɪŋ] *n* (*drunkenness*) boisson f,
alcoolisme *m*

**drinking fountain** *n* (*in park etc*) fontaine
publique; (*in building*) jet *m* d'eau potable

**drinking water** *n* eau f potable

**drip** [drɪp] *n* (*drop*) goutte f; (*sound: of water etc*)
bruit *m* de l'eau qui tombe goutte à goutte;
(*Med: device*) goutte-à-goutte *m inv*; (: *liquid*)
perfusion f; (*inf: person*) lavette f, nouille f ▷ *vi*
tomber goutte à goutte; (*tap*) goutter; (*washing*)
s'égoutter; (*wall*) suinter

**drip-dry** ['drɪp'draɪ] *adj* (*shirt*) sans repassage

**drip-feed** ['drɪpfiːd] *vt* alimenter au goutte-à-
goutte *or* par perfusion

**dripping** ['drɪpɪŋ] *n* graisse f de rôti ▷ *adj*: **~ wet**

trempé(e)

**drive** [draɪv] (*pt* **drove**, *pp* **driven** [drəuv, 'drɪvn])
*n* promenade *f or* trajet *m* en voiture; (*also:*
**driveway**) allée *f*; (*energy*) dynamisme *m*,
énergie *f*; (*Psych*) besoin *m*; pulsion *f*; (*push*)
effort (concerté); campagne *f*; (*Sport*) drive *m*;
(*Tech*) entraînement *m*; traction *f*; transmission
*f*; (*Comput: also:* **disk drive**) lecteur *m* de
disquette ▷ *vt* conduire; (*nail*) enfoncer; (*push*)
chasser, pousser; (*Tech: motor*) actionner;
entraîner ▷ *vi* (*be at the wheel*) conduire; (*travel by
car*) aller en voiture; **to go for a ~** aller faire une
promenade en voiture; **it's 3 hours' ~ from
London** Londres est à 3 heures de route; **left-/
right-hand ~** (*Aut*) conduite *f* à gauche/droite;
**front-/rear-wheel ~** (*Aut*) traction *f* avant/
arrière; **to ~ sb to (do) sth** pousser *or* conduire
qn à (faire) qch; **to ~ sb mad** rendre qn fou
(folle)

▶ **drive at** *vt fus* (*fig: intend, mean*) vouloir dire, en
venir à

▶ **drive on** *vi* poursuivre sa route, continuer;
(*after stopping*) reprendre sa route, repartir ▷ *vt*
(*incite, encourage*) inciter

▶ **drive out** *vt* (*force out*) chasser

**drive-by** ['draɪvbaɪ] *n* (*also:* **drive-by shooting**)
tentative d'assassinat par coups de feu tirés d'une voiture
**drive-in** ['draɪvɪn] *adj, n* (*esp US*) drive-in *m*
**drive-in window** *n* (US) guichet-auto *m*
**drivel** ['drɪvl] *n* (*inf*) idioties *fpl*, imbécillités *fpl*
**driven** ['drɪvn] *pp of* **drive**
**driver** ['draɪvə'] *n* conducteur(-trice); (*of taxi,
bus*) chauffeur *m*
**driver's license** *n* (US) permis *m* de conduire
**driveway** ['draɪvweɪ] *n* allée *f*
**driving** ['draɪvɪŋ] *adj:* **~ rain** *n* pluie battante
▷ *n* conduite *f*
**driving force** *n* locomotive *f*, élément *m*
dynamique
**driving instructor** *n* moniteur *m* d'auto-école
**driving lesson** *n* leçon *f* de conduite
**driving licence** *n* (Brit) permis *m* de conduire
**driving school** *n* auto-école *f*
**driving test** *n* examen *m* du permis de conduire
**drizzle** ['drɪzl] *n* bruine *f*, crachin *m* ▷ *vi* bruiner
**droll** [drəul] *adj* drôle
**dromedary** ['drɔmədərɪ] *n* dromadaire *m*
**drone** [drəun] *vi* (*bee*) bourdonner; (*engine etc*)
ronronner; (*also:* **drone on**) parler d'une voix
monocorde ▷ *n* bourdonnement *m*;
ronronnement *m*; (*male bee*) faux-bourdon *m*
**drool** [dru:l] *vi* baver; **to ~ over sb/sth** (*fig*) baver
d'admiration *or* être en extase devant qn/qch
**droop** [dru:p] *vi* (*flower*) commencer à se faner;
(*shoulders, head*) tomber
**drop** [drɔp] *n* (*of liquid*) goutte *f*; (*fall*) baisse *f*; (: *in
salary*) réduction *f*; (*also:* **parachute drop**) saut
*m*; (*of cliff*) dénivellation *f*; à-pic *m* ▷ *vt* laisser
tomber; (*voice, eyes, price*) baisser; (*passenger*)
déposer ▷ *vi* (*wind, temperature, price, voice*)
tomber; (*numbers, attendance*) diminuer; **drops**
*npl* (*Med*) gouttes; **cough ~s** pastilles *fpl* pour la

toux; **a ~ of 10%** une baisse *or* réduction) de 10%;
**to ~ anchor** jeter l'ancre; **to ~ sb a line** mettre
un mot à qn

▶ **drop in** *vi* (*inf: visit*): **to ~ in (on)** faire un saut
(chez), passer (chez)

▶ **drop off** *vi* (*sleep*) s'assoupir ▷ *vt* (*passenger*)
déposer; **to ~ sb off** déposer qn

▶ **drop out** *vi* (*withdraw*) se retirer; (*student etc*)
abandonner, décrocher

**droplet** ['drɔplɪt] *n* gouttelette *f*
**dropout** ['drɔpaut] *n* (*from society*) marginal(e);
(*from university*) drop-out *m/f*, dropé(e)
**dropper** ['drɔpə'] *n* (*Med etc*) compte-gouttes
*m inv*
**droppings** ['drɔpɪŋz] *npl* crottes *fpl*
**dross** [drɔs] *n* déchets *mpl*; rebut *m*
**drought** [draut] *n* sécheresse *f*
**drove** [drəuv] *pt of* **drive** ▷ *n:* **~s of people** une
foule de gens
**drown** [draun] *vt* noyer; (*also:* **drown out:** *sound*)
couvrir, étouffer ▷ *vi* se noyer
**drowse** [drauz] *vi* somnoler
**drowsy** ['drauzɪ] *adj* somnolent(e)
**drudge** [drʌdʒ] *n* bête *f* de somme (*fig*)
**drudgery** ['drʌdʒərɪ] *n* corvée *f*
**drug** [drʌg] *n* médicament *m*; (*narcotic*) drogue *f*
▷ *vt* droguer; **to be on ~s** se droguer; **he's on ~s**
il se drogue; (*Med*) il est sous médication
**drug addict** *n* toxicomane *m/f*
**drug dealer** *n* revendeur(-euse) de drogue
**druggist** ['drʌgɪst] *n* (US) pharmacien(ne)-
droguiste
**drug peddler** *n* revendeur(-euse) de drogue
**drugstore** ['drʌgstɔ:'] *n* (US) pharmacie-
droguerie *f*, drugstore *m*
**drum** [drʌm] *n* tambour *m*; (*for oil, petrol*) bidon *m*
▷ *vt:* **to ~ one's fingers on the table** pianoter *or*
tambouriner sur la table; **drums** *npl* (*Mus*)
batterie *f*

▶ **drum up** *vt* (*enthusiasm, support*) susciter,
rallier

**drummer** ['drʌmə'] *n* (joueur *m* de) tambour *m*
**drum roll** *n* roulement *m* de tambour
**drumstick** ['drʌmstɪk] *n* (*Mus*) baguette *f* de
tambour; (*of chicken*) pilon *m*
**drunk** [drʌŋk] *pp of* **drink** ▷ *adj* ivre, soûl(e) ▷ *n*
(*also:* **drunkard**) ivrogne *m/f*; **to get ~** s'enivrer,
se soûler
**drunkard** ['drʌŋkəd] *n* ivrogne *m/f*
**drunken** ['drʌŋkən] *adj* ivre, soûl(e); (*rage, stupor*)
ivrogne, d'ivrogne; **~ driving** conduite *f* en état
d'ivresse
**drunkenness** ['drʌŋkənnɪs] *n* ivresse *f*;
ivrognerie *f*
**dry** [draɪ] *adj* sec (sèche); (*day*) sans pluie;
(*humour*) pince-sans-rire; (*uninteresting*) aride,
rébarbatif(-ive) ▷ *vt* sécher; (*clothes*) faire
sécher ▷ *vi* sécher; **on ~ land** sur la terre ferme;
**to ~ one's hands/hair/eyes** se sécher les
mains/les cheveux/les yeux

▶ **dry off** *vi, vt* sécher

▶ **dry up** *vi* (*river, supplies*) se tarir; (: *speaker*) sécher, rester sec

**dry-clean** ['draɪkli:n] vt nettoyer à sec

**dry-cleaner** ['draɪkli:nəʳ] n teinturier m

**dry-cleaner's** ['draɪkli:nəz] n teinturerie f

**dry-cleaning** ['draɪkli:nɪŋ] n (process) nettoyage m à sec

**dry dock** n (Naut) cale sèche, bassin m de radoub

**dryer** ['draɪəʳ] n (tumble-dryer) sèche-linge m inv; (for hair) sèche-cheveux m inv

**dry goods** npl (Comm) textiles mpl, mercerie f

**dry goods store** n (US) magasin m de nouveautés

**dry ice** n neige f carbonique

**dryly** ['draɪlɪ] adv sèchement, d'un ton sec

**dryness** ['draɪnɪs] n sécheresse f

**dry rot** n pourriture sèche (du bois)

**dry run** n (fig) essai m

**dry ski slope** n piste (de ski) artificielle

**DSc** n abbr (= Doctor of Science) titre universitaire

**DSS** n abbr (Brit) = **Department of Social Security**

**DST** abbr (US: = Daylight Saving Time) heure d'été

**DT** n abbr (Comput) = **data transmission**

**DTI** n abbr (Brit) = **Department of Trade and Industry**

**DTP** n abbr (= desktop publishing) PAO f

**DT's** [di:'ti:z] n abbr (inf: = delirium tremens) delirium tremens m

**dual** ['djuəl] adj double

**dual carriageway** n (Brit) route f à quatre voies

**dual-control** ['djuəlkən'trəul] adj à doubles commandes

**dual nationality** n double nationalité f

**dual-purpose** ['djuəl'pə:pəs] adj à double emploi

**dubbed** [dʌbd] adj (Cine) doublé(e); (nicknamed) surnommé(e)

**dubious** ['dju:bɪəs] adj hésitant(e), incertain(e); (reputation, company) douteux(-euse); (also: **I'm very dubious about it**) j'ai des doutes sur la question, je n'en suis pas sûr du tout

**Dublin** ['dʌblɪn] n Dublin

**Dubliner** ['dʌblɪnəʳ] n habitant(e) de Dublin, originaire m/f de Dublin

**duchess** ['dʌtʃɪs] n duchesse f

**duck** [dʌk] n canard m ▷ vi se baisser vivement, baisser subitement la tête ▷ vt plonger dans l'eau

**duckling** ['dʌklɪŋ] n caneton m

**duct** [dʌkt] n conduite f, canalisation f; (Anat) conduit m

**dud** [dʌd] n (shell) obus non éclaté; (object, tool): **it's a** ~ c'est de la camelote, ça ne marche pas ▷ adj (Brit: cheque) sans provision; (: note, coin) faux (fausse)

**due** [dju:] adj (money, payment) dû (due); (expected) attendu(e); (fitting) qui convient ▷ n dû m ▷ adv: ~ **north** droit vers le nord; **dues** npl (for club, union) cotisation f; (in harbour) droits mpl (de port); ~ **to** (because of) en raison de; (caused by) dû à; **in ~ course** en temps utile or voulu; (in the end) finalement; **the rent is ~ on the 30th** il faut payer le loyer le 30; **the train is ~ at 8 a.m.**

le train est attendu à 8 h; **she is ~ back tomorrow** elle doit rentrer demain; **he is ~ £10** on lui doit 10 livres; **I am ~ 6 days' leave** j'ai droit à 6 jours de congé; **to give sb his** or **her** ~ être juste envers qn

**due date** n date f d'échéance

**duel** ['djuəl] n duel m

**duet** [dju:'ɛt] n duo m

**duff** [dʌf] adj (Brit inf) nullard(e), nul(le)

**duffel bag, duffle bag** ['dʌfl-] n sac marin

**duffel coat, duffle coat** ['dʌfl-] n duffel-coat m

**duffer** ['dʌfəʳ] n (inf) nullard(e)

**dug** [dʌg] pt, pp of **dig**

**dugout** ['dʌgaut] n (Sport) banc m de touche

**duke** [dju:k] n duc m

**dull** [dʌl] adj (boring) ennuyeux(-euse); (slow) borné(e); (not bright) morne, terne; (sound, pain) sourd(e); (weather, day) gris(e), maussade; (blade) émoussé(e) ▷ vt (pain, grief) atténuer; (mind, senses) engourdir

**duly** ['dju:lɪ] adv (on time) en temps voulu; (as expected) comme il se doit

**dumb** [dʌm] adj muet(te); (stupid) bête; **to be struck** ~ (fig) rester abasourdie(e), être sidéré(e)

**dumbbell** ['dʌmbɛl] n (Sport) haltère m

**dumbfounded** [dʌmˈfaundɪd] adj sidéré(e)

**dummy** ['dʌmɪ] n (tailor's model) mannequin m; (mock-up) factice m, maquette f; (Sport) feinte f; (Brit: for baby) tétine f ▷ adj faux (fausse), factice

**dummy run** n essai m

**dump** [dʌmp] n tas m d'ordures; (also: **rubbish dump**) décharge (publique); (Mil) dépôt m; (Comput) listage m (de la mémoire); (inf: place) trou m ▷ vt (put down) déposer; déverser; (get rid of) se débarrasser de; (Comput) lister; (Comm: goods) vendre à perte (sur le marché extérieur); **to be (down) in the ~s** (inf) avoir le cafard, broyer du noir

**dumping** ['dʌmpɪŋ] n (Econ) dumping m; (of rubbish): **"no ~"** "décharge interdite"

**dumpling** ['dʌmplɪŋ] n boulette f (de pâte)

**dumpy** ['dʌmpɪ] adj courtaud(e), boulot(te)

**dunce** [dʌns] n âne m, cancre m

**dune** [dju:n] n dune f

**dung** [dʌŋ] n fumier m

**dungarees** [dʌŋgəˈri:z] npl bleu(s) m(pl); (for child, woman) salopette f

**dungeon** ['dʌndʒən] n cachot m

**dunk** [dʌŋk] vt tremper

**Dunkirk** [dʌnˈkə:k] n Dunkerque

**duo** ['dju:əu] n (gen: Mus) duo m

**duodenal** [dju:əu'di:nl] adj duodénal(e); ~ **ulcer** ulcère m du duodénum

**dupe** [dju:p] n dupe f ▷ vt duper, tromper

**duplex** ['dju:plɛks] n (US: also: **duplex apartment**) duplex m

**duplicate** n ['dju:plɪkət] double m, copie exacte; (copy of letter etc) duplicata m ▷ adj (copy) en double ▷ vt ['dju:plɪkeɪt] faire un double de; (on machine) polycopier; **in** ~ en deux exemplaires, en double; ~ **key** double m de la (or d'une) clé

**duplicating machine** ['dju:plɪkeɪtɪŋ-],

**duplicator** ['dju:plɪkeɪtə'] n duplicateur m
**duplicity** [dju:'plɪsɪtɪ] n duplicité f, fausseté f
**durability** [djuərə'bɪlɪtɪ] n solidité f; durabilité f
**durable** ['djuərəbl] adj durable; (clothes, metal) résistant(e), solide
**duration** [djuə'reɪʃən] n durée f
**duress** [djuə'rɛs] n: **under ~** sous la contrainte
**Durex®** ['djuərɛks] n (Brit) préservatif (masculin)
**during** ['djuərɪŋ] prep pendant, au cours de
**dusk** [dʌsk] n crépuscule m
**dusky** ['dʌskɪ] adj sombre
**dust** [dʌst] n poussière f ▷ vt (furniture) essuyer, épousseter; (cake etc): **to ~ with** saupoudrer de
▶ **dust off** vt (also fig) dépoussiérer
**dustbin** ['dʌstbɪn] n (Brit) poubelle f
**duster** ['dʌstə'] n chiffon m
**dust jacket** n jacquette f
**dustman** ['dʌstmən] (irreg) n (Brit) boueux m, éboueur m
**dustpan** ['dʌstpæn] n pelle f à poussière
**dusty** ['dʌstɪ] adj poussiéreux(-euse)
**Dutch** [dʌtʃ] adj hollandais(e), néerlandais(e) ▷ n (Ling) hollandais m, néerlandais m ▷ adv: **to go ~** or **dutch** (inf) partager les frais; **the Dutch** npl les Hollandais, les Néerlandais
**Dutch auction** n enchères fpl à la baisse
**Dutchman** ['dʌtʃmən] (irreg) n Hollandais m
**Dutchwoman** ['dʌtʃwumən] (irreg) n Hollandaise f
**dutiable** ['dju:tɪəbl] adj taxable, soumis(e) à des droits de douane
**dutiful** ['dju:tɪful] adj (child) respectueux(-euse); (husband, wife) plein(e) d'égards, prévenant(e); (employee) consciencieux(-euse)
**duty** ['dju:tɪ] n devoir m; (tax) droit m, taxe f; **duties** npl fonctions fpl; **to make it one's ~ to do sth** se faire un devoir de faire qch; **to pay ~ on sth** payer un droit or une taxe sur qch; **on ~** de service; (at night etc) de garde; **off ~** libre, pas de service or de garde
**duty-free** ['dju:tɪ'fri:] adj exempté(e) de douane,

hors-taxe; **~ shop** boutique f hors-taxe
**duty officer** n (Mil etc) officier m de permanence
**duvet** ['du:veɪ] n (Brit) couette f
**DV** abbr (= Deo volente) si Dieu le veut
**DVD** n abbr (= digital versatile or video disc) DVD m
**DVD burner** n graveur m de DVD
**DVD player** n lecteur m de DVD
**DVD writer** n graveur m de DVD
**DVLA** n abbr (Brit: = Driver and Vehicle Licensing Agency) service qui délivre les cartes grises et les permis de conduire
**DVM** n abbr (US: = Doctor of Veterinary Medicine) titre universitaire
**DVT** n abbr = **deep vein thrombosis**
**dwarf** (pl **dwarves**) [dwɔ:f, dwɔ:vz] n nain(e) ▷ vt écraser
**dwell** (pt, pp **dwelt**) [dwɛl, dwɛlt] vi demeurer
▶ **dwell on** vt fus s'étendre sur
**dweller** ['dwɛlə'] n habitant(e)
**dwelling** ['dwɛlɪŋ] n habitation f, demeure f
**dwelt** [dwɛlt] pt, pp of **dwell**
**dwindle** ['dwɪndl] vi diminuer, décroître
**dwindling** ['dwɪndlɪŋ] adj décroissant(e), en diminution
**dye** [daɪ] n teinture f ▷ vt teindre; **hair ~** teinture pour les cheveux
**dyestuffs** ['daɪstʌfs] npl colorants mpl
**dying** ['daɪɪŋ] adj mourant(e), agonisant(e)
**dyke** [daɪk] n (embankment) digue f
**dynamic** [daɪ'næmɪk] adj dynamique
**dynamics** [daɪ'næmɪks] n or npl dynamique f
**dynamite** ['daɪnəmaɪt] n dynamite f ▷ vt dynamiter, faire sauter à la dynamite
**dynamo** ['daɪnəməu] n dynamo f
**dynasty** ['dɪnəstɪ] n dynastie f
**dysentery** ['dɪsntrɪ] n dysenterie f
**dyslexia** [dɪs'lɛksɪə] n dyslexie f
**dyslexic** [dɪs'lɛksɪk] adj, n dyslexique m/f
**dyspepsia** [dɪs'pɛpsɪə] n dyspepsie f
**dystrophy** ['dɪstrəfɪ] n dystrophie f; **muscular ~** dystrophie musculaire

# Ee

**E¹, e** [i:] *n (letter)* E, e *m*; *(Mus)*: **E** mi *m*; **E for Edward**, *(US)* **E for Easy** E comme Eugène
**E²** *abbr (= east)* E ▷ *n abbr (Drugs)* = **ecstasy**
**ea.** *abbr* = **each**
**E.A.** *n abbr (US: = educational age)* niveau scolaire
**each** [i:tʃ] *adj* chaque ▷ *pron* chacun(e); **~ one** chacun(e); **~ other** l'un l'autre; **they hate ~ other** ils se détestent (mutuellement); **you are jealous of ~ other** vous êtes jaloux l'un de l'autre; **~ day** chaque jour, tous les jours; **they have 2 books ~** ils ont 2 livres chacun; **they cost £5 ~** ils coûtent 5 livres (la) pièce; **~ of us** chacun(e) de nous
**eager** ['i:gəʳ] *adj (person, buyer)* empressé(e); *(lover)* ardent(e), passionné(e); *(keen: pupil, worker)* enthousiaste; **to be ~ to do sth** *(impatient)* brûler de faire qch; *(keen)* désirer vivement faire qch; **to be ~ for** *(event)* désirer vivement; *(vengeance, affection, information)* être avide de
**eagle** ['i:gl] *n* aigle *m*
**E and OE** *abbr* = **errors and omissions excepted**
**ear** [ɪəʳ] *n* oreille *f*; *(of corn)* épi *m*; **up to one's ~s in debt** endetté(e) jusqu'au cou
**earache** ['ɪəreɪk] *n* mal *m* aux oreilles
**eardrum** ['ɪədrʌm] *n* tympan *m*
**earful** ['ɪəful] *n (inf)*: **to give sb an ~** passer un savon à qn
**earl** [ə:l] *n* comte *m*
**earlier** ['ə:lɪəʳ] *adj (date etc)* plus rapproché(e); *(edition etc)* plus ancien(ne), antérieur(e) ▷ *adv* plus tôt
**early** ['ə:lɪ] *adv* tôt, de bonne heure; *(ahead of time)* en avance; *(near the beginning)* au début ▷ *adj* précoce, qui se manifeste *(or se fait)* tôt *or* de bonne heure; *(Christians, settlers)* premier(-ière); *(reply)* rapide; *(death)* prématuré(e); *(work)* de jeunesse; **to have an ~ night/start** se coucher/ partir tôt *or* de bonne heure; **take the ~ train** prenez le premier train; **in the ~** *or* **~ in the spring/19th century** au début *or* commencement du printemps/19ème siècle; **you're ~!** tu es en avance!; **~ in the morning** tôt le matin; **she's in her ~ forties** elle a un peu plus de quarante ans *or* de la quarantaine; **at your earliest convenience** *(Comm)* dans les meilleurs délais

**early retirement** *n* retraite anticipée
**early warning system** *n* système *m* de première alerte
**earmark** ['ɪəmɑ:k] *vt*: **to ~ sth for** réserver *or* destiner qch à
**earn** [ə:n] *vt* gagner; *(Comm: yield)* rapporter; **to ~ one's living** gagner sa vie; **this ~ed him much praise, he ~ed much praise for this** ceci lui a valu de nombreux éloges; **he's ~ed his rest/reward** il mérite *or* a bien mérité *or* a bien gagné son repos/sa récompense
**earned income** [ə:nd-] *n* revenu *m* du travail
**earnest** ['ə:nɪst] *adj* sérieux(-euse) ▷ *n (also:* **earnest money**) acompte *m*, arrhes *fpl*; **in ~** *(adv)* sérieusement, pour de bon
**earnings** ['ə:nɪŋz] *npl* salaire *m*; gains *mpl*; *(of company etc)* profits *mpl*, bénéfices *mpl*
**ear, nose and throat specialist** *n* oto-rhino-laryngologiste *m/f*
**earphones** ['ɪəfəunz] *npl* écouteurs *mpl*
**earplugs** ['ɪəplʌgz] *npl* boules *fpl* Quiès®; *(to keep out water)* protège-tympans *mpl*
**earring** ['ɪərɪŋ] *n* boucle *f* d'oreille
**earshot** ['ɪəʃɔt] *n*: **out of/within ~** hors de portée/à portée de voix
**earth** [ə:θ] *n (gen, also Brit Elec)* terre *f*; *(of fox etc)* terrier *m* ▷ *vt (Brit Elec)* relier à la terre
**earthenware** ['ə:θnwɛəʳ] *n* poterie *f*; faïence *f* ▷ *adj* de *or* en faïence
**earthly** ['ə:θlɪ] *adj* terrestre; *(also:* **earthly paradise**) paradis *m* terrestre; **there is no ~ reason to think that …** il n'y a absolument aucune raison *or* pas la moindre raison de penser que …
**earthquake** ['ə:θkweɪk] *n* tremblement *m* de terre, séisme *m*
**earth-shattering** ['ə:θʃætərɪŋ] *adj* stupéfiant(e)
**earth tremor** *n* secousse *f* sismique
**earthworks** ['ə:θwə:ks] *npl* travaux *mpl* de terrassement
**earthy** ['ə:θɪ] *adj (fig)* terre à terre *inv*, truculent(e)
**earwax** ['ɪəwæks] *n* cérumen *m*
**earwig** ['ɪəwɪg] *n* perce-oreille *m*
**ease** [i:z] *n* facilité *f*, aisance *f*; *(comfort)* bien-être *m* ▷ *vt (soothe: mind)* tranquilliser; *(reduce:*

*pain, problem)* atténuer; (*: tension*) réduire; (*loosen*) relâcher, détendre; (*help pass*): **to ~ sth in/out** faire pénétrer/sortir qch délicatement *or* avec douceur, faciliter la pénétration/la sortie de qch ▷ *vi* (*situation*) se détendre; **with ~** sans difficulté, aisément; **life of ~** vie oisive; **at ~** à l'aise; (*Mil*) au repos
▶ **ease off, ease up** *vi* diminuer; (*slow down*) ralentir; (*relax*) se détendre
**easel** ['i:zl] *n* chevalet *m*
**easily** ['i:zɪlɪ] *adv* facilement; (*by far*) de loin
**easiness** ['i:sɪnɪs] *n* facilité *f*; (*of manner*) aisance *f*; nonchalance *f*
**east** [i:st] *n* est *m* ▷ *adj* (*wind*) d'est; (*side*) est *inv* ▷ *adv* à l'est, vers l'est; **the E~** l'Orient *m*; (*Pol*) les pays *mpl* de l'Est
**eastbound** ['i:stbaʊnd] *adj* en direction de l'est; (*carriageway*) est *inv*
**Easter** ['i:stə<sup>r</sup>] *n* Pâques *fpl* ▷ *adj* (*holidays*) de Pâques, pascal(e)
**Easter egg** *n* œuf *m* de Pâques
**Easter Island** *n* île *f* de Pâques
**easterly** ['i:stəlɪ] *adj* d'est
**Easter Monday** *n* le lundi de Pâques
**eastern** ['i:stən] *adj* de l'est, oriental(e); **E~ Europe** l'Europe de l'Est; **the E~ bloc** (*Pol*) les pays *mpl* de l'est
**Easter Sunday** *n* le dimanche de Pâques
**East Germany** *n* (*formerly*) Allemagne *f* de l'Est
**eastward** ['i:stwəd], **eastwards** ['i:stwədz] *adv* vers l'est, à l'est
**easy** ['i:zɪ] *adj* facile; (*manner*) aisé(e) ▷ *adv*: **to take it** *or* **things ~** (*rest*) ne pas se fatiguer; (*not worry*) ne pas (trop) s'en faire; **to have an ~ life** avoir la vie facile; **payment on ~ terms** (*Comm*) facilités *fpl* de paiement; **that's easier said than done** c'est plus facile à dire qu'à faire, c'est vite dit; **I'm ~** (*inf*) ça m'est égal
**easy chair** *n* fauteuil *m*
**easy-going** ['i:zɪ'gəʊɪŋ] *adj* accommodant(e), facile à vivre
**easy touch** *n* (*inf*): **he's an ~** c'est une bonne poire
**eat** (*pt* **ate**, *pp* **-en**) [i:t, eɪt, 'i:tn] *vt*, *vi* manger; **can we have something to ~?** est-ce qu'on peut manger quelque chose?
▶ **eat away** *vt* (*sea*) saper, éroder; (*acid*) ronger, corroder
▶ **eat away at, eat into** *vt fus* ronger, attaquer
▶ **eat out** *vi* manger au restaurant
▶ **eat up** *vt* (*food*) finir (de manger); **it ~s up electricity** ça bouffe du courant, ça consomme beaucoup d'électricité
**eatable** ['i:təbl] *adj* mangeable; (*safe to eat*) comestible
**eaten** ['i:tn] *pp* of **eat**
**eau de Cologne** ['əʊdəkə'ləʊn] *n* eau *f* de Cologne
**eaves** [i:vz] *npl* avant-toit *m*
**eavesdrop** ['i:vzdrɔp] *vi*: **to ~ (on)** écouter de façon indiscrète
**ebb** [ɛb] *n* reflux *m* ▷ *vi* refluer; (*fig: also*: **ebb**

*away*) décliner; **the ~ and flow** le flux et le reflux; **to be at a low ~** (*fig*) être bien bas(se), ne pas aller bien fort
**ebb tide** *n* marée descendante, reflux *m*
**ebony** ['ɛbənɪ] *n* ébène *f*
**e-book** ['i:buk] *n* livre *m* électronique
**ebullient** [ɪ'bʌlɪənt] *adj* exubérant(e)
**e-business** ['i:bɪznɪs] *n* (*company*) entreprise *f* électronique; (*commerce*) commerce *m* électronique
**ECB** *n abbr* (= *European Central Bank*) BCE *f* (= *Banque centrale européenne*)
**eccentric** [ɪk'sɛntrɪk] *adj*, *n* excentrique *m/f*
**ecclesiastic** [ɪkli:zɪ'æstɪk], **ecclesiastical** [ɪkli:zɪ'æstɪkl] *adj* ecclésiastique
**ECG** *n abbr* = **electrocardiogram**
**echo** ['ɛkəu] (*pl* **-es**) *n* écho *m* ▷ *vt* répéter; faire chorus avec ▷ *vi* résonner; faire écho
**éclair** ['eɪklɛə<sup>r</sup>] *n* éclair *m* (*Culin*)
**eclipse** [ɪ'klɪps] *n* éclipse *f* ▷ *vt* éclipser
**eco-** ['i:kəu] *prefix* éco-
**eco-friendly** [i:kəu'frɛndlɪ] *adj* non nuisible à *or* qui ne nuit pas à l'environnement
**ecological** [i:kə'lɔdʒɪkəl] *adj* écologique
**ecologist** [ɪ'kɔlədʒɪst] *n* écologiste *m/f*
**ecology** [ɪ'kɔlədʒɪ] *n* écologie *f*
**e-commerce** [i:kɔmə:s] *n* commerce *m* électronique
**economic** [i:kə'nɔmɪk] *adj* économique; (*profitable*) rentable
**economical** [i:kə'nɔmɪkl] *adj* économique; (*person*) économe
**economically** [i:kə'nɔmɪklɪ] *adv* économiquement
**economics** [i:kə'nɔmɪks] *n* (*Scol*) économie *f* politique ▷ *npl* (*of project etc*) côté *m or* aspect *m* économique
**economist** [ɪ'kɔnəmɪst] *n* économiste *m/f*
**economize** [ɪ'kɔnəmaɪz] *vi* économiser, faire des économies
**economy** [ɪ'kɔnəmɪ] *n* économie *f*; **economies of scale** économies d'échelle
**economy class** *n* (*Aviat*) classe *f* touriste
**economy class syndrome** *n* syndrome *m* de la classe économique
**economy size** *n* taille *f* économique
**ecosystem** ['i:kəusɪstəm] *n* écosystème *m*
**eco-tourism** [i:kəu'tuərɪzəm] *n* écotourisme *m*
**ECSC** *n abbr* (= *European Coal & Steel Community*) CECA *f* (= *Communauté européenne du charbon et de l'acier*)
**ecstasy** ['ɛkstəsɪ] *n* extase *f*; (*Drugs*) ecstasy *m*; **to go into ecstasies over** s'extasier sur
**ecstatic** [ɛks'tætɪk] *adj* extatique, en extase
**ECT** *n abbr* = **electroconvulsive therapy**
**Ecuador** ['ɛkwədɔ:<sup>r</sup>] *n* Équateur *m*
**ecumenical** [i:kju'mɛnɪkl] *adj* œcuménique
**eczema** ['ɛksɪmə] *n* eczéma *m*
**eddy** ['ɛdɪ] *n* tourbillon *m*
**edge** [ɛdʒ] *n* bord *m*; (*of knife etc*) tranchant *m*, fil *m* ▷ *vt* border ▷ *vi*: **to ~ forward** avancer petit à petit; **to ~ away from** s'éloigner furtivement

de; **on ~** (fig) crispé(e), tendu(e); **to have the ~ on** (fig) l'emporter (de justesse) sur, être légèrement meilleur que

**edgeways** ['ɛdʒweɪz] adv latéralement; **he couldn't get a word in ~** il ne pouvait pas placer un mot

**edging** ['ɛdʒɪŋ] n bordure f

**edgy** ['ɛdʒɪ] adj crispé(e), tendu(e)

**edible** ['ɛdɪbl] adj comestible; (meal) mangeable

**edict** ['iːdɪkt] n décret m

**edifice** ['ɛdɪfɪs] n édifice m

**edifying** ['ɛdɪfaɪɪŋ] adj édifiant(e)

**Edinburgh** ['ɛdɪnbərə] n Édimbourg

**edit** ['ɛdɪt] vt (text, book) éditer; (report) préparer; (film) monter; (broadcast) réaliser; (magazine) diriger; (newspaper) être le rédacteur or la rédactrice en chef de

**edition** [ɪ'dɪʃən] n édition f

**editor** ['ɛdɪtər] n (of newspaper) rédacteur(-trice), rédacteur(-trice) en chef; (of sb's work) éditeur(-trice); (also: **film editor**) monteur(-euse); **political/ foreign ~** rédacteur politique/au service étranger

**editorial** [ɛdɪ'tɔːrɪəl] adj de la rédaction, éditorial(e) ▷ n éditorial m; **the ~ staff** la rédaction

**EDP** n abbr = **electronic data processing**

**EDT** abbr (US: = Eastern Daylight Time) heure d'été de New York

**educate** ['ɛdjukeɪt] vt (teach) instruire; (bring up) éduquer; **~d at …** qui a fait ses études à …

**educated** ['ɛdjukeɪtɪd] adj (person) cultivé(e)

**educated guess** n supposition éclairée

**education** [ɛdju'keɪʃən] n éducation f; (studies) études fpl; (teaching) enseignement m, instruction f; (at university: subject etc) pédagogie f; **primary** or (US) **elementary/secondary ~** instruction f primaire/secondaire

**educational** [ɛdju'keɪʃənl] adj pédagogique; (institution) scolaire; (useful) instructif(-ive); (game, toy) éducatif(-ive); **~ technology** technologie f de l'enseignement

**Edwardian** [ɛd'wɔːdɪən] adj de l'époque du roi Édouard VII, des années 1900

**EE** abbr = **electrical engineer**

**EEG** n abbr = **electroencephalogram**

**eel** [iːl] n anguille f

**EENT** n abbr (US Med) = **eye, ear, nose and throat**

**EEOC** n abbr (US) = **Equal Employment Opportunity Commission**

**eerie** ['ɪərɪ] adj inquiétant(e), spectral(e), surnaturel(le)

**EET** abbr (= Eastern European Time) HEO (= heure d'Europe orientale)

**effect** [ɪ'fɛkt] n effet m ▷ vt effectuer; **effects** npl (Theat) effets mpl; (property) effets, affaires fpl; **to take ~** (Law) entrer en vigueur, prendre effet; (drug) agir, faire son effet; **to put into ~** (plan) mettre en application or à exécution; **to have an ~ on sb/sth** avoir or produire un effet sur qn/qch; **in ~** en fait; **his letter is to the ~ that …** sa lettre nous apprend que …

**effective** [ɪ'fɛktɪv] adj efficace; (striking: display, outfit) frappant(e), qui produit or fait de l'effet; (actual) véritable; **to become ~** (Law) entrer en vigueur, prendre effet; **~ date** date f d'effet or d'entrée en vigueur

**effectively** [ɪ'fɛktɪvlɪ] adv efficacement; (strikingly) d'une manière frappante, avec beaucoup d'effet; (in reality) effectivement, en fait

**effectiveness** [ɪ'fɛktɪvnɪs] n efficacité f

**effeminate** [ɪ'fɛmɪnɪt] adj efféminé(e)

**effervescent** [ɛfə'vɛsnt] adj effervescent(e)

**efficacy** ['ɛfɪkəsɪ] n efficacité f

**efficiency** [ɪ'fɪʃənsɪ] n efficacité f; (of machine, car) rendement m

**efficiency apartment** n (US) studio m avec coin cuisine

**efficient** [ɪ'fɪʃənt] adj efficace; (machine, car) d'un bon rendement

**efficiently** [ɪ'fɪʃəntlɪ] adv efficacement

**effigy** ['ɛfɪdʒɪ] n effigie f

**effluent** ['ɛfluənt] n effluent m

**effort** ['ɛfət] n effort m; **to make an ~ to do sth** faire or fournir un effort pour faire qch

**effortless** ['ɛfətlɪs] adj sans effort, aisé(e); (achievement) facile

**effrontery** [ɪ'frʌntərɪ] n effronterie f

**effusive** [ɪ'fjuːsɪv] adj (person) expansif(-ive); (welcome) chaleureux(-euse)

**EFL** n abbr (Scol) = **English as a Foreign Language**

**EFTA** ['ɛftə] n abbr (= European Free Trade Association) AELE f (= Association européenne de libre-échange)

**e.g.** adv abbr (= exempli gratia) par exemple, p. ex.

**egalitarian** [ɪgælɪ'tɛərɪən] adj égalitaire

**egg** [ɛg] n œuf m; **hard-boiled/soft-boiled ~** œuf dur/à la coque

▶ **egg on** vt pousser

**eggcup** ['ɛgkʌp] n coquetier m

**egg plant** ['ɛgplɑːnt] (US) n aubergine f

**eggshell** ['ɛgʃɛl] n coquille f d'œuf ▷ adj (colour) blanc cassé inv

**egg-timer** ['ɛgtaɪmər] n sablier m

**egg white** n blanc m d'œuf

**egg yolk** n jaune m d'œuf

**ego** ['iːgəʊ] n (self-esteem) amour-propre m; (Psych) moi m

**egoism** ['ɛgəʊɪzəm] n égoïsme m

**egoist** ['ɛgəʊɪst] n égoïste m/f

**egotism** ['ɛgəʊtɪzəm] n égotisme m

**egotist** ['ɛgəʊtɪst] n égocentrique m/f

**ego trip** n: **to be on an ~** être en plein délire d'autosatisfaction

**Egypt** ['iːdʒɪpt] n Égypte f

**Egyptian** [ɪ'dʒɪpʃən] adj égyptien(ne) ▷ n Égyptien(ne)

**EHIC** n abbr (= European Health Insurance Card) CEAM f

**eiderdown** ['aɪdədaʊn] n édredon m

**Eiffel Tower** ['aɪfəl-] n tour f Eiffel

**eight** [eɪt] num huit

**eighteen** [eɪ'tiːn] num dix-huit

**eighteenth** [eɪ'tiːnθ] num dix-huitième

**eighth** [eitθ] *num* huitième
**eightieth** ['eitɪɪθ] *num* quatre-vingtième
**eighty** ['eitɪ] *num* quatre-vingt(s)
**Eire** ['ɛərə] *n* République *f* d'Irlande
**EIS** *n abbr* (= *Educational Institute of Scotland*) syndicat enseignant
**either** ['aɪðə'] *adj* l'un ou l'autre; (*both, each*) chaque ▷ *pron*: ~ (**of them**) l'un ou l'autre ▷ *adv* non plus ▷ *conj*: ~ **good or bad** ou bon ou mauvais, soit bon soit mauvais; **I haven't seen** ~ **one or the other** je n'ai vu ni l'un ni l'autre; **on** ~ **side** de chaque côté; **I don't like** ~ **side** je n'aime ni l'un ni l'autre; **no, I don't** ~ moi non plus; **which bike do you want?** — ~ **will do** quel vélo voulez-vous? — n'importe lequel; **answer with** ~ **yes or no** répondez par oui ou par non
**ejaculation** [ɪdʒækju'leɪʃən] *n* (*Physiol*) éjaculation *f*
**eject** [ɪ'dʒɛkt] *vt* (*tenant etc*) expulser; (*object*) éjecter ▷ *vi* (*pilot*) s'éjecter
**ejector seat** [ɪ'dʒɛktə-] *n* siège *m* éjectable
**eke** [i:k]: **to** ~ **out** *vt* faire durer; augmenter
**EKG** *n abbr* (*US*) = **electrocardiogram**
**el** [ɛl] *n abbr* (*US inf*) = **elevated railroad**
**elaborate** [*adj* ɪ'læbərɪt, *vb* ɪ'læbəreɪt] *adj* compliqué(e), recherché(e), minutieux(-euse) ▷ *vt* élaborer ▷ *vi* entrer dans les détails
**elapse** [ɪ'læps] *vi* s'écouler, passer
**elastic** [ɪ'læstɪk] *adj*, *n* élastique (*m*)
**elastic band** *n* (*Brit*) élastique *m*
**elasticity** [ɪlæs'tɪsɪtɪ] *n* élasticité *f*
**elated** [ɪ'leɪtɪd] *adj* transporté(e) de joie
**elation** [ɪ'leɪʃən] *n* (grande) joie, allégresse *f*
**elbow** ['ɛlbəu] *n* coude *m* ▷ *vt*: **to** ~ **one's way through the crowd** se frayer un passage à travers la foule (en jouant des coudes)
**elbow grease** *n*: **to use a bit of** ~ mettre de l'huile de coude
**elder** ['ɛldə'] *adj* aîné(e) ▷ *n* (*tree*) sureau *m*; **one's** ~**s** ses aînés
**elderly** ['ɛldəlɪ] *adj* âgé(e) ▷ *npl*: **the** ~ les personnes âgées
**elder statesman** (*irreg*) *n* vétéran *m* de la politique
**eldest** ['ɛldɪst] *adj*, *n*: **the** ~ (**child**) l'aîné(e) (des enfants)
**elect** [ɪ'lɛkt] *vt* élire; (*choose*): **to** ~ **to do** choisir de faire ▷ *adj*: **the president** ~ le président désigné
**election** [ɪ'lɛkʃən] *n* élection *f*; **to hold an** ~ procéder à une élection
**election campaign** *n* campagne électorale
**electioneering** [ɪlɛkʃə'nɪərɪŋ] *n* propagande électorale, manœuvres électorales
**elector** [ɪ'lɛktə'] *n* électeur(-trice)
**electoral** [ɪ'lɛktərəl] *adj* électoral(e)
**electoral college** *n* collège électoral
**electoral roll** *n* (*Brit*) liste électorale
**electorate** [ɪ'lɛktərɪt] *n* électorat *m*
**electric** [ɪ'lɛktrɪk] *adj* électrique
**electrical** [ɪ'lɛktrɪkl] *adj* électrique

**electrical engineer** *n* ingénieur électricien
**electrical failure** *n* panne *f* d'électricité *or* de courant
**electric blanket** *n* couverture chauffante
**electric chair** *n* chaise *f* électrique
**electric cooker** *n* cuisinière *f* électrique
**electric current** *n* courant *m* électrique
**electric fire** *n* (*Brit*) radiateur *m* électrique
**electrician** [ɪlɛk'trɪʃən] *n* électricien *m*
**electricity** [ɪlɛk'trɪsɪtɪ] *n* électricité *f*; **to switch on/off the** ~ rétablir/couper le courant
**electricity board** *n* (*Brit*) ≈ agence régionale de l'E.D.F.
**electric light** *n* lumière *f* électrique
**electric shock** *n* choc *m* *or* décharge *f* électrique
**electrify** [ɪ'lɛktrɪfaɪ] *vt* (*Rail*) électrifier; (*audience*) électriser
**electro...** [ɪ'lɛktrəu] *prefix* électro...
**electrocardiogram** [ɪ'lɛktrə] *n* électrocardiogramme *m*
**electro-convulsive therapy** [ɪ'lɛktrə] *n* électrochocs *mpl*
**electrocute** [ɪ'lɛktrəkju:t] *vt* électrocuter
**electrode** [ɪ'lɛktrəud] *n* électrode *f*
**electroencephalogram** [ɪ'lɛktrəu] *n* électroencéphalogramme *m*
**electrolysis** [ɪlɛk'trɔlɪsɪs] *n* électrolyse *f*
**electromagnetic** [ɪ'lɛktrəmæg'nɛtɪk] *adj* électromagnétique
**electron** [ɪ'lɛktrɔn] *n* électron *m*
**electronic** [ɪlɛk'trɔnɪk] *adj* électronique
**electronic data processing** *n* traitement *m* électronique des données
**electronic mail** *n* courrier *m* électronique
**electronics** [ɪlɛk'trɔnɪks] *n* électronique *f*
**electron microscope** *n* microscope *m* électronique
**electroplated** [ɪ'lɛktrə'pleɪtɪd] *adj* plaqué(e) *or* doré(e) *or* argenté(e) par galvanoplastie
**electrotherapy** [ɪ'lɛktrə'θɛrəpɪ] *n* électrothérapie *f*
**elegance** ['ɛlɪgəns] *n* élégance *f*
**elegant** ['ɛlɪgənt] *adj* élégant(e)
**element** ['ɛlɪmənt] *n* (*gen*) élément *m*; (*of heater, kettle etc*) résistance *f*
**elementary** [ɛlɪ'mɛntərɪ] *adj* élémentaire; (*school, education*) primaire
**elementary school** *n* (*US*) école *f* primaire; *voir article*

⊜ **ELEMENTARY SCHOOL**
⊜
⊜ Aux États-Unis et au Canada, une *elementary*
⊜ *school* (également appelée "grade school" ou
⊜ "grammar school" aux États-Unis) est une
⊜ école publique où les enfants passent les six
⊜ à huit premières années de leur scolarité.

**elephant** ['ɛlɪfənt] *n* éléphant *m*
**elevate** ['ɛlɪveɪt] *vt* élever
**elevated railroad** ['ɛlɪveɪtɪd-] *n* (*US*) métro *m* aérien

**elevation** [ɛlɪ'veɪʃən] *n* élévation *f*; (*height*) altitude *f*

**elevator** ['ɛlɪveɪtər] *n* (*in warehouse etc*) élévateur *m*, monte-charge *m inv*; (*US: lift*) ascenseur *m*

**eleven** [ɪ'lɛvn] *num* onze

**elevenses** [ɪ'lɛvnzɪz] *npl* (*Brit*) ≈ pause-café *f*

**eleventh** [ɪ'lɛvnθ] *num* onzième; **at the ~ hour** (*fig*) à la dernière minute

**elf** (*pl* **elves**) [ɛlf, ɛlvz] *n* lutin *m*

**elicit** [ɪ'lɪsɪt] *vt*: **to ~ (from)** obtenir (de); tirer (de)

**eligible** ['ɛlɪdʒəbl] *adj* éligible; (*for membership*) admissible; **an ~ young man** un beau parti; **to be ~ for sth** remplir les conditions requises pour qch; **~ for a pension** ayant droit à la retraite

**eliminate** [ɪ'lɪmɪneɪt] *vt* éliminer

**elimination** [ɪlɪmɪ'neɪʃən] *n* élimination *f*; **by process of ~** par élimination

**elitist** [eɪ'li:tɪst] *adj* (*pej*) élitiste

**Elizabethan** [ɪlɪzə'bi:θən] *adj* élisabéthain(e)

**ellipse** [ɪ'lɪps] *n* ellipse *f*

**elliptical** [ɪ'lɪptɪkl] *adj* elliptique

**elm** [ɛlm] *n* orme *m*

**elocution** [ɛlə'kju:ʃən] *n* élocution *f*

**elongated** ['i:lɔŋgeɪtɪd] *adj* étiré(e), allongé(e)

**elope** [ɪ'ləup] *vi* (*lovers*) s'enfuir (ensemble)

**elopement** [ɪ'ləupmənt] *n* fugue amoureuse

**eloquence** ['ɛləkwəns] *n* éloquence *f*

**eloquent** ['ɛləkwənt] *adj* éloquent(e)

**else** [ɛls] *adv* d'autre; **something ~** quelque chose d'autre, autre chose; **somewhere ~** ailleurs, autre part; **everywhere ~** partout ailleurs; **everyone ~** tous les autres; **nothing ~** rien d'autre; **is there anything ~ I can do?** est-ce que je peux faire quelque chose d'autre?; **where ~?** à quel autre endroit?; **little ~** pas grand-chose d'autre

**elsewhere** [ɛls'wɛər] *adv* ailleurs, autre part

**ELT** *n abbr* (*Scol*) = **English Language Teaching**

**elucidate** [ɪ'lu:sɪdeɪt] *vt* élucider

**elude** [ɪ'lu:d] *vt* échapper à; (*question*) éluder

**elusive** [ɪ'lu:sɪv] *adj* insaisissable; (*answer*) évasif(-ive)

**elves** [ɛlvz] *npl of* **elf**

**emaciated** [ɪ'meɪsɪeɪtɪd] *adj* émacié(e), décharné(e)

**email** ['i:meɪl] *n abbr* (= *electronic mail*) (e-)mail *m*, courriel *m* ▷ *vt*: **to ~ sb** envoyer un (e-)mail *or* un courriel à qn

**email account** *n* compte *m* (e-)mail

**email address** *n* adresse *f* (e-)mail *or* électronique

**emanate** ['ɛməneɪt] *vi*: **to ~ from** émaner de

**emancipate** [ɪ'mænsɪpeɪt] *vt* émanciper

**emancipation** [ɪmænsɪ'peɪʃən] *n* émancipation *f*

**emasculate** [ɪ'mæskjuleɪt] *vt* émasculer

**embalm** [ɪm'ba:m] *vt* embaumer

**embankment** [ɪm'bæŋkmənt] *n* (*of road, railway*) remblai *m*, talus *m*; (*of river*) berge *f*, quai *m*; (*dyke*) digue *f*

**embargo** [ɪm'ba:gəu] (*pl* **-es**) *n* (*Comm, Naut*) embargo *m*; (*prohibition*) interdiction *f* ▷ *vt* frapper d'embargo, mettre l'embargo sur; **to put an ~ on sth** mettre l'embargo sur qch

**embark** [ɪm'ba:k] *vi* embarquer; **to ~ on** (s')embarquer à bord de *or* sur ▷ *vt* embarquer; **to ~ on** (*journey etc*) commencer, entreprendre; (*fig*) se lancer *or* s'embarquer dans

**embarkation** [ɛmba:'keɪʃən] *n* embarquement *m*

**embarkation card** *n* carte *f* d'embarquement

**embarrass** [ɪm'bærəs] *vt* embarrasser, gêner

**embarrassed** [ɪm'bærəst] *adj* gêné(e); **to be ~** être gêné(e)

**embarrassing** [ɪm'bærəsɪŋ] *adj* gênant(e), embarrassant(e)

**embarrassment** [ɪm'bærəsmənt] *n* embarras *m*, gêne *f*; (*embarrassing thing, person*) source *f* d'embarras

**embassy** ['ɛmbəsɪ] *n* ambassade *f*; **the French E~** l'ambassade de France

**embed** [ɪm'bɛd] *vt* enfoncer; sceller

**embellish** [ɪm'bɛlɪʃ] *vt* embellir; enjoliver

**embers** ['ɛmbəz] *npl* braise *f*

**embezzle** [ɪm'bɛzl] *vt* détourner

**embezzlement** [ɪm'bɛzlmənt] *n* détournement *m* (de fonds)

**embezzler** [ɪm'bɛzlər] *n* escroc *m*

**embitter** [ɪm'bɪtər] *vt* aigrir; envenimer

**emblem** ['ɛmbləm] *n* emblème *m*

**embodiment** [ɪm'bɔdɪmənt] *n* personnification *f*, incarnation *f*

**embody** [ɪm'bɔdɪ] *vt* (*features*) réunir, comprendre; (*ideas*) formuler, exprimer

**embolden** [ɪm'bəuldn] *vt* enhardir

**embolism** ['ɛmbəlɪzəm] *n* embolie *f*

**embossed** [ɪm'bɔst] *adj* repoussé(e), gaufré(e); **~ with** où figure(nt) en relief

**embrace** [ɪm'breɪs] *vt* embrasser, étreindre; (*include*) embrasser, couvrir, comprendre ▷ *vi* s'embrasser, s'étreindre ▷ *n* étreinte *f*

**embroider** [ɪm'brɔɪdər] *vt* broder; (*fig: story*) enjoliver

**embroidery** [ɪm'brɔɪdərɪ] *n* broderie *f*

**embroil** [ɪm'brɔɪl] *vt*: **to become ~ed (in sth)** se retrouver mêlé(e) (à qch), se laisser entraîner (dans qch)

**embryo** ['ɛmbrɪəu] *n* (*also fig*) embryon *m*

**emcee** [ɛm'si:] *n* maître *m* de cérémonie

**emend** [ɪ'mɛnd] *vt* (*text*) corriger

**emerald** ['ɛmərəld] *n* émeraude *f*

**emerge** [ɪ'mə:dʒ] *vi* apparaître; (*from room, car*) surgir; (*from sleep, imprisonment*) sortir; **it ~s that** (*Brit*) il ressort que

**emergence** [ɪ'mə:dʒəns] *n* apparition *f*; (*of nation*) naissance *f*

**emergency** [ɪ'mə:dʒənsɪ] *n* (*crisis*) cas *m* d'urgence; (*Med*) urgence *f*; **in an ~** en cas d'urgence; **state of ~** état *m* d'urgence

**emergency brake** (*US*) *n* frein *m* à main

**emergency exit** *n* sortie *f* de secours

**emergency landing** *n* atterrissage forcé

**emergency lane** n (US Aut) accotement stabilisé

**emergency road service** n (US) service m de dépannage

**emergency room** n (US: Med) urgences fpl

**emergency services** npl: **the ~** (fire, police, ambulance) les services mpl d'urgence

**emergency stop** n (Brit Aut) arrêt m d'urgence

**emergent** [ɪ'məːdʒənt] adj: **~ nation** pays m en voie de développement

**emery board** ['ɛmərɪ-] n lime f à ongles (en carton émerisé)

**emery paper** ['ɛmərɪ-] n papier m (d')émeri

**emetic** [ɪ'mɛtɪk] n vomitif m, émétique m

**emigrant** ['ɛmɪgrənt] n émigrant(e)

**emigrate** ['ɛmɪgreɪt] vi émigrer

**emigration** [ɛmɪ'greɪʃən] n émigration f

**émigré** ['ɛmɪgreɪ] n émigré(e)

**eminence** ['ɛmɪnəns] n éminence f

**eminent** ['ɛmɪnənt] adj éminent(e)

**eminently** ['ɛmɪnəntlɪ] adv éminemment, admirablement

**emissions** [ɪ'mɪʃənz] npl émissions fpl

**emit** [ɪ'mɪt] vt émettre

**emolument** [ɪ'mɔljumənt] n (often pl: formal) émoluments mpl; (fee) honoraires mpl; (salary) traitement m

**emoticon** [ɪ'məutɪkɔn] n (Comput) émoticone m

**emotion** [ɪ'məuʃən] n sentiment m; (as opposed to reason) émotion f, sentiments

**emotional** [ɪ'məuʃənl] adj (person) émotif(-ive), très sensible; (needs) affectif(-ive); (scene) émouvant(e); (tone, speech) qui fait appel aux sentiments

**emotionally** [ɪ'məuʃnəlɪ] adv (behave) émotivement; (be involved) affectivement; (speak) avec émotion; **~ disturbed** qui souffre de troubles de l'affectivité

**emotive** [ɪ'məutɪv] adj émotif(-ive); **~ power** capacité f d'émouvoir or de toucher

**empathy** ['ɛmpəθɪ] n communion f d'idées or de sentiments, empathie f; **to feel ~ with sb** se mettre à la place de qn

**emperor** ['ɛmpərər] n empereur m

**emphasis** (pl **-ases**) ['ɛmfəsɪs, -siːz] n accent m; **to lay** or **place ~ on sth** (fig) mettre l'accent sur, insister sur; **the ~ is on reading** la lecture tient une place primordiale, on accorde une importance particulière à la lecture

**emphasize** ['ɛmfəsaɪz] vt (syllable, word, point) appuyer or insister sur; (feature) souligner, accentuer

**emphatic** [ɛm'fætɪk] adj (strong) énergique, vigoureux(-euse); (unambiguous, clear) catégorique

**emphatically** [ɛm'fætɪklɪ] adv avec vigueur or énergie; catégoriquement

**empire** ['ɛmpaɪər] n empire m

**empirical** [ɛm'pɪrɪkl] adj empirique

**employ** [ɪm'plɔɪ] vt employer; **he's ~ed in a bank** il est employé de banque, il travaille dans une banque

**employee** [ɪmplɔɪ'iː] n employé(e)

**employer** [ɪm'plɔɪər] n employeur(-euse)

**employment** [ɪm'plɔɪmənt] n emploi m; **to find ~** trouver un emploi or du travail; **without ~** au chômage, sans emploi; **place of ~** lieu m de travail

**employment agency** n agence f or bureau m de placement

**employment exchange** n (Brit) agence f pour l'emploi

**empower** [ɪm'pauər] vt: **to ~ sb to do** autoriser or habiliter qn à faire

**empress** ['ɛmprɪs] n impératrice f

**emptiness** ['ɛmptɪnɪs] n vide m; (of area) aspect m désertique

**empty** ['ɛmptɪ] adj vide; (street, area) désert(e); (threat, promise) en l'air, vain(e) ▷ n (bottle) bouteille f vide ▷ vt vider ▷ vi se vider; (liquid) s'écouler; **on an ~ stomach** à jeun; **to ~ into** (river) se jeter dans, se déverser dans

**empty-handed** ['ɛmptɪ'hændɪd] adj les mains vides

**empty-headed** ['ɛmptɪ'hɛdɪd] adj écervelé(e), qui n'a rien dans la tête

**EMS** n abbr (= European Monetary System) SME m

**EMT** n abbr = **emergency medical technician**

**EMU** n abbr (= European Monetary Union) UME f

**emulate** ['ɛmjuleɪt] vt rivaliser avec, imiter

**emulsion** [ɪ'mʌlʃən] n émulsion f; (also: **emulsion paint**) peinture mate

**enable** [ɪ'neɪbl] vt: **to ~ sb to do** permettre à qn de faire, donner à qn la possibilité de faire

**enact** [ɪ'nækt] vt (Law) promulguer; (play, scene) jouer, représenter

**enamel** [ɪ'næməl] n émail m; (also: **enamel paint**) (peinture f) laque f

**enamoured** [ɪ'næməd] adj: **~ of** amoureux(-euse) de; (idea) enchanté(e) par

**encampment** [ɪn'kæmpmənt] n campement m

**encased** [ɪn'keɪst] adj: **~ in** enfermé(e) dans, recouvert(e) de

**enchant** [ɪn'tʃɑːnt] vt enchanter

**enchanting** [ɪn'tʃɑːntɪŋ] adj ravissant(e), enchanteur(-eresse)

**encircle** [ɪn'səːkl] vt entourer, encercler

**encl.** abbr (on letters etc: = enclosed) ci-joint(e); (= enclosure) PJ f

**enclose** [ɪn'kləuz] vt (land) clôturer; (space, object) entourer; (letter etc): **to ~ (with)** joindre (à); **please find ~d** veuillez trouver ci-joint

**enclosure** [ɪn'kləuʒər] n enceinte f; (in letter etc) annexe f

**encoder** [ɪn'kəudər] n (Comput) encodeur m

**encompass** [ɪn'kʌmpəs] vt encercler, entourer; (include) contenir, inclure

**encore** [ɔŋ'kɔːr] excl, n bis (m)

**encounter** [ɪn'kauntər] n rencontre f ▷ vt rencontrer

**encourage** [ɪn'kʌrɪdʒ] vt encourager; (industry, growth) favoriser; **to ~ sb to do sth** encourager qn à faire qch

**encouragement** [ɪn'kʌrɪdʒmənt] n encouragement m

**encouraging** [ɪn'kʌrɪdʒɪŋ] *adj* encourageant(e)
**encroach** [ɪn'krəutʃ] *vi:* **to ~ (up)on** empiéter sur
**encrusted** [ɪn'krʌstɪd] *adj:* **~ (with)** incrusté(e) (de)
**encyclopaedia, encyclopedia** [ɛnsaɪkləu-'piːdɪə] *n* encyclopédie *f*
**end** [ɛnd] *n* fin *f*; *(of table, street, rope etc)* bout *m*, extrémité *f*; *(of pointed object)* pointe *f*; *(of town)* bout; *(Sport)* côté *m* ▷ *vt* terminer; *(also:* **bring to an end, put an end to**) mettre fin à ▷ *vi* se terminer, finir; **from ~ to ~** d'un bout à l'autre; **to come to an ~** prendre fin; **to be at an ~** être fini(e), être terminé(e); **in the ~** finalement; **on ~** *(object)* debout, dressé(e); **to stand on ~** *(hair)* se dresser sur la tête; **for 5 hours on ~** durant 5 heures d'affilée *or* de suite; **for hours on ~** pendant des heures (et des heures); **at the ~ of the day** *(Brit fig)* en fin de compte; **to this ~, with this ~ in view** à cette fin, dans ce but
▶ **end up** *vi:* **to ~ up in** *(condition)* finir *or* se terminer par; *(place)* finir *or* aboutir à
**endanger** [ɪn'deɪndʒəʳ] *vt* mettre en danger; **an ~ed species** une espèce en voie de disparition
**endear** [ɪn'dɪəʳ] *vt:* **to ~ o.s. to sb** se faire aimer de qn
**endearing** [ɪn'dɪərɪŋ] *adj* attachant(e)
**endearment** [ɪn'dɪəmənt] *n:* **to whisper ~s** murmurer des mots *or* choses tendres; **term of ~** terme *m* d'affection
**endeavour,** *(US)* **endeavor** [ɪn'dɛvəʳ] *n* effort *m*; *(attempt)* tentative *f* ▷ *vt:* **to ~ to do** tenter *or* s'efforcer de faire
**endemic** [ɛn'dɛmɪk] *adj* endémique
**ending** ['ɛndɪŋ] *n* dénouement *m*, conclusion *f*; *(Ling)* terminaison *f*
**endive** ['ɛndaɪv] *n (curly)* chicorée *f*; *(smooth, flat)* endive *f*
**endless** ['ɛndlɪs] *adj* sans fin, interminable; *(patience, resources)* inépuisable, sans limites; *(possibilities)* illimité(e)
**endorse** [ɪn'dɔːs] *vt (cheque)* endosser; *(approve)* appuyer, approuver, sanctionner
**endorsee** [ɪndɔː'siː] *n* bénéficiaire *m/f*, endossataire *m/f*
**endorsement** [ɪn'dɔːsmənt] *n (approval)* appui *m*, aval *m*; *(signature)* endossement *m*; *(Brit: on driving licence)* contravention *f (portée au permis de conduire)*
**endorser** [ɪn'dɔːsəʳ] *n* avaliste *m*, endosseur *m*
**endow** [ɪn'dau] *vt (provide with money)* faire une donation à, doter; *(equip):* **to ~ with** gratifier de, doter de
**endowment** [ɪn'daumənt] *n* dotation *f*
**endowment mortgage** *n* hypothèque liée à une assurance-vie
**endowment policy** *n* assurance *f* à capital différé
**end product** *n (Industry)* produit fini; *(fig)* résultat *m*, aboutissement *m*
**end result** *n* résultat final
**endurable** [ɪn'djuərəbl] *adj* supportable

**endurance** [ɪn'djuərəns] *n* endurance *f*
**endurance test** *n* test *m* d'endurance
**endure** [ɪn'djuəʳ] *vt (bear)* supporter, endurer
▷ *vi (last)* durer
**end user** *n (Comput)* utilisateur final
**enema** ['ɛnɪmə] *n (Med)* lavement *m*
**enemy** ['ɛnəmɪ] *adj, n* ennemi(e); **to make an ~ of sb** se faire un(e) ennemi(e) de qn, se mettre qn à dos
**energetic** [ɛnə'dʒɛtɪk] *adj* énergique; *(activity)* très actif(-ive), qui fait se dépenser (physiquement)
**energy** ['ɛnədʒɪ] *n* énergie *f*; **Department of E~** ministère *m* de l'Énergie
**energy crisis** *n* crise *f* de l'énergie
**energy-saving** ['ɛnədʒɪ'seɪvɪŋ] *adj (policy)* d'économie d'énergie; *(device)* qui permet de réaliser des économies d'énergie
**enervating** ['ɛnəveɪtɪŋ] *adj* débilitant(e), affaiblissant(e)
**enforce** [ɪn'fɔːs] *vt (law)* appliquer, faire respecter
**enforced** [ɪn'fɔːst] *adj* forcé(e)
**enfranchise** [ɪn'fræntʃaɪz] *vt* accorder le droit de vote à; *(set free)* affranchir
**engage** [ɪn'geɪdʒ] *vt* engager; *(Mil)* engager le combat avec; *(lawyer)* prendre ▷ *vi (Tech)* s'enclencher, s'engrener; **to ~ in** se lancer dans; **to ~ sb in conversation** engager la conversation avec qn
**engaged** [ɪn'geɪdʒd] *adj (Brit: busy, in use)* occupé(e); *(betrothed)* fiancé(e); **to get ~** se fiancer; **the line's ~** la ligne est occupée; **he is ~ in research/a survey** il fait de la recherche/ une enquête
**engaged tone** *n (Brit Tel)* tonalité *f* occupé *inv*
**engagement** [ɪn'geɪdʒmənt] *n (undertaking)* obligation *f*, engagement *m*; *(appointment)* rendez-vous *m inv*; *(to marry)* fiançailles *fpl*; *(Mil)* combat *m*; **I have a previous ~** j'ai déjà un rendez-vous, je suis déjà pris(e)
**engagement ring** *n* bague *f* de fiançailles
**engaging** [ɪn'geɪdʒɪŋ] *adj* engageant(e), attirant(e)
**engender** [ɪn'dʒɛndəʳ] *vt* produire, causer
**engine** ['ɛndʒɪn] *n (Aut)* moteur *m*; *(Rail)* locomotive *f*
**engine driver** *n (Brit: of train)* mécanicien *m*
**engineer** [ɛndʒɪ'nɪəʳ] *n* ingénieur *m*; *(Brit: repairer)* dépanneur *m*; *(Navy, US Rail)* mécanicien *m*; **civil/mechanical ~** ingénieur des Travaux Publics *or* des Ponts et Chaussées/ mécanicien
**engineering** [ɛndʒɪ'nɪərɪŋ] *n* engineering *m*, ingénierie *f*; *(of bridges, ships)* génie *m*; *(of machine)* mécanique *f* ▷ *cpd:* **~ works** *or* **factory** atelier *m* de construction mécanique
**engine failure** *n* panne *f*
**engine trouble** *n* ennuis *mpl* mécaniques
**England** ['ɪŋglənd] *n* Angleterre *f*
**English** ['ɪŋglɪʃ] *adj* anglais(e) ▷ *n (Ling)* anglais *m*; **the ~** *(npl)* les Anglais; **an ~ speaker** un

**e**

anglophone

**English Channel** n: **the ~** la Manche

**Englishman** ['ɪŋglɪʃmən] (irreg) n Anglais m

**English-speaking** ['ɪŋglɪʃ'spiːkɪŋ] adj qui parle anglais; anglophone

**Englishwoman** ['ɪŋglɪʃwumən] (irreg) n Anglaise f

**engrave** [ɪn'greɪv] vt graver

**engraving** [ɪn'greɪvɪŋ] n gravure f

**engrossed** [ɪn'grəust] adj: **~ in** absorbé(e) par, plongé(e) dans

**engulf** [ɪn'gʌlf] vt engloutir

**enhance** [ɪn'hɑːns] vt rehausser, mettre en valeur; (position) améliorer; (reputation) accroître

**enigma** [ɪ'nɪgmə] n énigme f

**enigmatic** [ɛnɪg'mætɪk] adj énigmatique

**enjoy** [ɪn'dʒɔɪ] vt aimer, prendre plaisir à; (have benefit of: health, fortune) jouir de; (: success) connaître; **to ~ o.s.** s'amuser

**enjoyable** [ɪn'dʒɔɪəbl] adj agréable

**enjoyment** [ɪn'dʒɔɪmənt] n plaisir m

**enlarge** [ɪn'lɑːdʒ] vt accroître; (Phot) agrandir ▷ vi: **to ~ on** (subject) s'étendre sur

**enlarged** [ɪn'lɑːdʒd] adj (edition) augmenté(e); (Med: organ, gland) anormalement gros(se), hypertrophié(e)

**enlargement** [ɪn'lɑːdʒmənt] n (Phot) agrandissement m

**enlighten** [ɪn'laɪtn] vt éclairer

**enlightened** [ɪn'laɪtnd] adj éclairé(e)

**enlightening** [ɪn'laɪtnɪŋ] adj instructif(-ive), révélateur(-trice)

**enlightenment** [ɪn'laɪtnmənt] n édification f; éclaircissements mpl; (History): **the E~ =** le Siècle des lumières

**enlist** [ɪn'lɪst] vt recruter; (support) s'assurer ▷ vi s'engager; **~ed man** (US Mil) simple soldat m

**enliven** [ɪn'laɪvn] vt animer, égayer

**enmity** ['ɛnmɪtɪ] n inimitié f

**ennoble** [ɪ'nəubl] vt (with title) anoblir

**enormity** [ɪ'nɔːmɪtɪ] n énormité f

**enormous** [ɪ'nɔːməs] adj énorme

**enormously** [ɪ'nɔːməslɪ] adv (increase) dans des proportions énormes; (rich) extrêmement

**enough** [ɪ'nʌf] adj: **~ time/books** assez or suffisamment de temps/livres ▷ adv: **big ~** assez or suffisamment grand ▷ pron: **have you got ~?** (en) avez-vous assez?; **will five be ~?** est-ce que cinq suffiront?, est-ce qu'il y en aura assez avec cinq?; **~ to eat** assez à manger; **that's ~!** ça suffit!, assez!; **that's ~, thanks** cela suffit or c'est assez, merci; **I've had ~!** je n'en peux plus!; **I've had ~ of him** j'en ai assez de lui; **he has not worked ~** il n'a pas assez or suffisamment travaillé, il n'a pas travaillé assez or suffisamment; **~! assez!, ça suffit!; it's hot ~ (as it is)!** il fait assez chaud comme ça!; **he was kind ~ to lend me the money** il a eu la gentillesse de me prêter l'argent; **... which,** **funnily** or **oddly ~ ...** qui, chose curieuse, ...

**enquire** [ɪn'kwaɪər] vt, vi = **inquire**

**enquiry** [ɪn'kwaɪərɪ] n = **inquiry**

**enrage** [ɪn'reɪdʒ] vt mettre en fureur or en rage, rendre furieux(-euse)

**enrich** [ɪn'rɪtʃ] vt enrichir

**enrol**, (US) **enroll** [ɪn'rəul] vt inscrire ▷ vi s'inscrire

**enrolment**, (US) **enrollment** [ɪn'rəulmənt] n inscription f

**en route** [ɔn'ruːt] adv en route, en chemin; **~ for** or **to** en route vers, à destination de

**ensconced** [ɪn'skɔnst] adj: **~ in** bien calé(e) dans

**enshrine** [ɪn'ʃraɪn] vt (fig) préserver

**ensign** n (Naut) ['ɛnsən] enseigne f, pavillon m; (Mil) ['ɛnsaɪn] porte-étendard m

**enslave** [ɪn'sleɪv] vt asservir

**ensue** [ɪn'sjuː] vi s'ensuivre, résulter

**en suite** ['ɔnswiːt] adj: **with ~ bathroom** avec salle de bains en attenante

**ensure** [ɪn'ʃuər] vt assurer, garantir; **to ~ that** s'assurer que

**ENT** n abbr (= Ear, Nose and Throat) ORL f

**entail** [ɪn'teɪl] vt entraîner, nécessiter

**entangle** [ɪn'tæŋgl] vt emmêler, embrouiller; **to become ~d in sth** (fig) se laisser entraîner or empêtrer dans qch

**enter** ['ɛntər] vt (room) entrer dans, pénétrer dans; (club, army) entrer à; (profession) embrasser; (competition) s'inscrire à or pour; (sb for a competition) (faire) inscrire; (write down) inscrire, noter; (Comput) entrer, introduire ▷ vi entrer

 ▶ **enter for** vt fus s'inscrire à, se présenter pour or à

 ▶ **enter into** vt fus (explanation) se lancer dans; (negotiations) entamer; (debate) prendre part à; (agreement) conclure

 ▶ **enter on** vt fus commencer

 ▶ **enter up** vt inscrire

 ▶ **enter upon** vt fus = **enter on**

**enteritis** [ɛntə'raɪtɪs] n entérite f

**enterprise** ['ɛntəpraɪz] n (company, undertaking) entreprise f; (initiative) (esprit m d')initiative f; **free ~** libre entreprise; **private ~** entreprise privée

**enterprising** ['ɛntəpraɪzɪŋ] adj entreprenant(e), dynamique; (scheme) audacieux(-euse)

**entertain** [ɛntə'teɪn] vt amuser, distraire; (invite) recevoir (à dîner); (idea, plan) envisager

**entertainer** [ɛntə'teɪnər] n artiste m/f de variétés

**entertaining** [ɛntə'teɪnɪŋ] adj amusant(e), distrayant(e) ▷ n: **to do a lot of ~** beaucoup recevoir

**entertainment** [ɛntə'teɪnmənt] n (amusement) distraction f, divertissement m, amusement m; (show) spectacle m

**entertainment allowance** n frais mpl de représentation

**enthralled** [ɪn'θrɔːld] adj captivé(e)

**enthralling** [ɪn'θrɔːlɪŋ] adj captivant(e), enchanteur(-eresse)

**enthuse** [ɪn'θuːz] vi: **to ~ about** or **over** parler avec enthousiasme de

**enthusiasm** [ɪn'θuːzɪæzəm] n enthousiasme m

**enthusiast** [ɪnˈθuːzɪæst] n enthousiaste m/f; **a jazz** etc ~ un fervent or passionné du jazz etc
**enthusiastic** [ɪnθuːzɪˈæstɪk] adj enthousiaste; **to be ~ about** être enthousiasmé(e) par
**entice** [ɪnˈtaɪs] vt attirer, séduire
**enticing** [ɪnˈtaɪsɪŋ] adj (person, offer) séduisant(e); (food) alléchant(e)
**entire** [ɪnˈtaɪər] adj (tout) entier(-ère)
**entirely** [ɪnˈtaɪəlɪ] adv entièrement, complètement
**entirety** [ɪnˈtaɪərətɪ] n: **in its ~** dans sa totalité
**entitle** [ɪnˈtaɪtl] vt (allow): **to ~ sb to do** donner (le) droit à qn de faire; **to ~ sb to sth** donner droit à qch à qn
**entitled** [ɪnˈtaɪtld] adj (book) intitulé(e); **to be ~ to do** avoir le droit de faire
**entity** [ˈɛntɪtɪ] n entité f
**entrails** [ˈɛntreɪlz] npl entrailles fpl
**entrance** n [ˈɛntrns] entrée f ▷ vt [ɪnˈtrɑːns] enchanter, ravir; **where's the ~?** où est l'entrée?; **to gain ~ to** (university etc) être admis à
**entrance examination** n examen m d'entrée or d'admission
**entrance fee** n (to museum etc) prix m d'entrée; (to join club etc) droit m d'inscription
**entrance ramp** n (US Aut) bretelle f d'accès
**entrancing** [ɪnˈtrɑːnsɪŋ] adj enchanteur(-eresse), ravissant(e)
**entrant** [ˈɛntrnt] n (in race etc) participant(e), concurrent(e); (Brit: in exam) candidat(e)
**entreat** [ɛnˈtriːt] vt supplier
**entreaty** [ɛnˈtriːtɪ] n supplication f, prière f
**entrée** [ˈɔntreɪ] n (Culin) entrée f
**entrenched** [ɛnˈtrɛntʃt] adj retranché(e)
**entrepreneur** [ˈɔntrəprəˈnəːr] n entrepreneur m
**entrepreneurial** [ˈɔntrəprəˈnəːrɪəl] adj animé(e) d'un esprit d'entreprise
**entrust** [ɪnˈtrʌst] vt: **to ~ sth to** confier qch à
**entry** [ˈɛntrɪ] n entrée f; (in register, diary) inscription f; (in ledger) écriture f; **"no ~"** "défense d'entrer", "entrée interdite"; (Aut) "sens interdit"; **single/double ~ book-keeping** comptabilité f en partie simple/double
**entry form** n feuille f d'inscription
**entry phone** n (Brit) interphone m (à l'entrée d'un immeuble)
**entwine** [ɪnˈtwaɪn] vt entrelacer
**E-number** [ˈiːnʌmbər] n additif m (alimentaire)
**enumerate** [ɪˈnjuːməreɪt] vt énumérer
**enunciate** [ɪˈnʌnsɪeɪt] vt énoncer; prononcer
**envelop** [ɪnˈvɛləp] vt envelopper
**envelope** [ˈɛnvələup] n enveloppe f
**enviable** [ˈɛnvɪəbl] adj enviable
**envious** [ˈɛnvɪəs] adj envieux(-euse)
**environment** [ɪnˈvaɪərnmənt] n (social, moral) milieu m; (natural world): **the ~** l'environnement m; **Department of the E~** (Brit) ministère de l'Équipement et de l'Aménagement du territoire
**environmental** [ɪnvaɪərnˈmɛntl] adj (of surroundings) du milieu; (issue, disaster) écologique; **~ studies** (in school etc) écologie f
**environmentalist** [ɪnvaɪərnˈmɛntlɪst] n

écologiste m/f
**environmentally** [ɪnvaɪərnˈmɛntlɪ] adv: **~ sound/friendly** qui ne nuit pas à l'environnement
**Environmental Protection Agency** n (US) ≈ ministère m de l'Environnement
**envisage** [ɪnˈvɪzɪdʒ] vt (imagine) envisager; (foresee) prévoir
**envision** [ɪnˈvɪʒən] vt envisager, concevoir
**envoy** [ˈɛnvɔɪ] n envoyé(e); (diplomat) ministre m plénipotentiaire
**envy** [ˈɛnvɪ] n envie f ▷ vt envier; **to ~ sb sth** envier qch à qn
**enzyme** [ˈɛnzaɪm] n enzyme m
**EPA** n abbr (US) = **Environmental Protection Agency**
**ephemeral** [ɪˈfɛmərl] adj éphémère
**epic** [ˈɛpɪk] n épopée f ▷ adj épique
**epicentre**, (US) **epicenter** [ˈɛpɪsɛntər] n épicentre m
**epidemic** [ɛpɪˈdɛmɪk] n épidémie f
**epilepsy** [ˈɛpɪlɛpsɪ] n épilepsie f
**epileptic** [ɛpɪˈlɛptɪk] adj, n épileptique m/f
**epileptic fit** [ɛpɪˈlɛptɪk-] n crise f d'épilepsie
**epilogue** [ˈɛpɪlɒg] n épilogue m
**episcopal** [ɪˈpɪskəpl] adj épiscopal(e)
**episode** [ˈɛpɪsəud] n épisode m
**epistle** [ɪˈpɪsl] n épître f
**epitaph** [ˈɛpɪtɑːf] n épitaphe f
**epithet** [ˈɛpɪθɛt] n épithète f
**epitome** [ɪˈpɪtəmɪ] n (fig) quintessence f, type m
**epitomize** [ɪˈpɪtəmaɪz] vt (fig) illustrer, incarner
**epoch** [ˈiːpɒk] n époque f, ère f
**epoch-making** [ˈiːpɒkmeɪkɪŋ] adj qui fait époque
**eponymous** [ɪˈpɒnɪməs] adj de ce or du même nom, éponyme
**equable** [ˈɛkwəbl] adj égal(e), de tempérament égal
**equal** [ˈiːkwl] adj égal(e) ▷ n égal(e) ▷ vt égaler; **~ to** (task) à la hauteur de; **~ to doing** de taille à or capable de faire
**equality** [iːˈkwɔlɪtɪ] n égalité f
**equalize** [ˈiːkwəlaɪz] vt, vi (Sport) égaliser
**equalizer** [ˈiːkwəlaɪzər] n but égalisateur
**equally** [ˈiːkwəlɪ] adv également; (share) en parts égales; (treat) de la même façon; (pay) autant; (just as) tout aussi; **they are ~ clever** ils sont tout aussi intelligents
**Equal Opportunities Commission**, (US) **Equal Employment Opportunity Commission** n commission pour la non discrimination dans l'emploi
**equal sign, equals sign** n signe m d'égalité
**equanimity** [ɛkwəˈnɪmɪtɪ] n égalité f d'humeur
**equate** [ɪˈkweɪt] vt: **to ~ sth with** comparer qch à; assimiler qch à; **to ~ sth to** mettre qch en équation avec; égaler qch à
**equation** [ɪˈkweɪʃən] n (Math) équation f
**equator** [ɪˈkweɪtər] n équateur m
**Equatorial Guinea** [ɛkwəˈtɔːrɪəl ˈgɪnɪ] n Guinée équatoriale
**equestrian** [ɪˈkwɛstrɪən] adj équestre ▷ n

écuyer(-ère), cavalier(-ère)

**equilibrium** [iːkwɪˈlɪbrɪəm] n équilibre m

**equinox** [ˈiːkwɪnɒks] n équinoxe m

**equip** [ɪˈkwɪp] vt équiper; **to ~ sb/sth with** équiper or munir qn/qch de; **he is well ~ped for the job** il a les compétences or les qualités requises pour ce travail

**equipment** [ɪˈkwɪpmənt] n équipement m; (electrical etc) appareillage m, installation f

**equitable** [ˈɛkwɪtəbl] adj équitable

**equities** [ˈɛkwɪtɪz] npl (Brit Comm) actions cotées en Bourse

**equity** [ˈɛkwɪtɪ] n équité f

**equity capital** n capitaux mpl propres

**equivalent** [ɪˈkwɪvəlnt] adj équivalent(e) ▷ n équivalent m; **to be ~ to** équivaloir à, être équivalent(e) à

**equivocal** [ɪˈkwɪvəkl] adj équivoque; (open to suspicion) douteux(-euse)

**equivocate** [ɪˈkwɪvəkeɪt] vi user de faux-fuyants; éviter de répondre

**equivocation** [ɪkwɪvəˈkeɪʃən] n équivoque f

**ER** abbr (Brit: = Elizabeth Regina) la reine Élisabeth; (US: Med: = emergency room) urgences fpl

**ERA** n abbr (US Pol: = Equal Rights Amendment) amendement sur l'égalité des droits des femmes

**era** [ˈɪərə] n ère f, époque f

**eradicate** [ɪˈrædɪkeɪt] vt éliminer

**erase** [ɪˈreɪz] vt effacer

**eraser** [ɪˈreɪzəʳ] n gomme f

**erect** [ɪˈrɛkt] adj droit(e) ▷ vt construire; (monument) ériger, élever; (tent etc) dresser

**erection** [ɪˈrɛkʃən] n (Physiol) érection f; (of building) construction f; (of machinery etc) installation f

**ergonomics** [əːgəˈnɒmɪks] n ergonomie f

**ERISA** n abbr (US: = Employee Retirement Income Security Act) loi sur les pensions de retraite

**Eritrea** [ɛrɪˈtreɪə] n Érythrée f

**ERM** n abbr (= Exchange Rate Mechanism) mécanisme m des taux de change

**ermine** [ˈəːmɪn] n hermine f

**ERNIE** [ˈəːnɪ] n abbr (Brit: = Electronic Random Number Indicator Equipment) ordinateur servant au tirage des bons à lots gagnants

**erode** [ɪˈrəʊd] vt éroder; (metal) ronger

**erogenous zone** [ɪˈrɒdʒənəs-] n zone f érogène

**erosion** [ɪˈrəʊʒən] n érosion f

**erotic** [ɪˈrɒtɪk] adj érotique

**eroticism** [ɪˈrɒtɪsɪzəm] n érotisme m

**err** [əːʳ] vi se tromper; (Rel) pécher

**errand** [ˈɛrnd] n course f, commission f; **to run ~s** faire des courses; **~ of mercy** mission f de charité, acte m charitable

**errand boy** n garçon m de courses

**erratic** [ɪˈrætɪk] adj irrégulier(-ière), inconstant(e)

**erroneous** [ɪˈrəʊnɪəs] adj erroné(e)

**error** [ˈɛrəʳ] n erreur f; **typing/spelling ~** faute f de frappe/d'orthographe; **in ~** par erreur, par méprise; **~s and omissions excepted** sauf erreur ou omission

**error message** n (Comput) message m d'erreur

**erstwhile** [ˈəːstwaɪl] adj précédent(e), d'autrefois

**erudite** [ˈɛrjudaɪt] adj savant(e)

**erupt** [ɪˈrʌpt] vi entrer en éruption; (fig) éclater, exploser

**eruption** [ɪˈrʌpʃən] n éruption f; (of anger, violence) explosion f

**ESA** n abbr (= European Space Agency) ASE f (= Agence spatiale européenne)

**escalate** [ˈɛskəleɪt] vi s'intensifier; (costs) monter en flèche

**escalation** [ɛskəˈleɪʃən] n escalade f

**escalation clause** n clause f d'indexation

**escalator** [ˈɛskəleɪtəʳ] n escalier roulant

**escapade** [ɛskəˈpeɪd] n fredaine f; équipée f

**escape** [ɪˈskeɪp] n évasion f, fuite f; (of gas etc) fuite; (Tech) échappement m ▷ vi s'échapper, fuir; (from jail) s'évader; (fig) s'en tirer, en réchapper; (leak) fuir; s'échapper ▷ vt échapper à; **to ~ from** (person) échapper à; (place) s'échapper de; (fig) fuir; **to ~ to** (another place) fuir à, s'enfuir à; **to ~ to safety** se réfugier dans or gagner un endroit sûr; **to ~ notice** passer inaperçu(e); **his name ~s me** son nom m'échappe

**escape artist** n virtuose m/f de l'évasion

**escape clause** n clause f dérogatoire

**escapee** [ɪskeɪˈpiː] n évadé(e)

**escape key** n (Comput) touche f d'échappement

**escape route** n (from fire) issue f de secours; (of prisoners etc) voie empruntée pour s'échapper

**escapism** [ɪˈskeɪpɪzəm] n évasion f (fig)

**escapist** [ɪˈskeɪpɪst] adj (literature) d'évasion ▷ n personne f qui se réfugie hors de la réalité

**escapologist** [ɛskəˈpɒlədʒɪst] n (Brit) = **escape artist**

**escarpment** [ɪsˈkɑːpmənt] n escarpement m

**eschew** [ɪsˈtʃuː] vt éviter

**escort** vt [ɪˈskɔːt] escorter ▷ n [ˈɛskɔːt] (Mil) escorte f; (to dance etc): **her ~** son compagnon or cavalier; **his ~** sa compagne

**escort agency** n bureau m d'hôtesses

**Eskimo** [ˈɛskɪməu] adj esquimau(de), eskimo ▷ n Esquimau(de); (Ling) esquimau m

**ESL** n abbr (Scol) = **English as a Second Language**

**esophagus** [iːˈsɒfəgəs] n (US) = **oesophagus**

**esoteric** [ɛsəˈtɛrɪk] adj ésotérique

**ESP** n abbr = **extrasensory perception**; (Scol) = **English for Special Purposes**

**esp.** abbr = **especially**

**especially** [ɪˈspɛʃlɪ] adv (particularly) particulièrement; (above all) surtout

**espionage** [ˈɛspɪənɑːʒ] n espionnage m

**esplanade** [ɛspləˈneɪd] n esplanade f

**espouse** [ɪˈspauz] vt épouser, embrasser

**Esquire** [ɪˈskwaɪəʳ] n (Brit: abbr **Esq.**): **J. Brown, ~** Monsieur J. Brown

**essay** [ˈɛseɪ] n (Scol) dissertation f; (Literature) essai m; (attempt) tentative f

**essence** [ˈɛsns] n essence f; (Culin) extrait m; **in ~** en substance; **speed is of the ~** l'essentiel, c'est la rapidité

**essential** [ɪ'sɛnʃl] *adj* essentiel(le); *(basic)* fondamental(e); **essentials** *npl* éléments essentiels; **it is ~ that** il est essentiel *or* primordial que

**essentially** [ɪ'sɛnʃlɪ] *adv* essentiellement

**EST** *abbr (US: = Eastern Standard Time) heure d'hiver de New York*

**est.** *abbr* = **established, estimate(d)**

**establish** [ɪ'stæblɪʃ] *vt* établir; *(business)* fonder, créer; *(one's power etc)* asseoir, affermir

**established** [ɪ'stæblɪʃt] *adj* bien établi(e)

**establishment** [ɪ'stæblɪʃmənt] *n* établissement *m*; *(founding)* création *f*; *(institution)* établissement *m*; **the E~** les pouvoirs établis; l'ordre établi

**estate** [ɪ'steɪt] *n (land)* domaine *m*, propriété *f*; *(Law)* biens *mpl*, succession *f*; *(Brit: also: **housing estate**)* lotissement *m*

**estate agency** *n (Brit)* agence immobilière

**estate agent** *n (Brit)* agent immobilier

**estate car** *n (Brit)* break *m*

**esteem** [ɪ'stiːm] *n* estime *f* ▷ *vt* estimer; apprécier; **to hold sb in high ~** tenir qn en haute estime

**esthetic** [ɪs'θɛtɪk] *adj (US)* = **aesthetic**

**estimate** [*n* 'ɛstɪmət, *vb* 'ɛstɪmeɪt] *n* estimation *f*; *(Comm)* devis *m* ▷ *vt* estimer ▷ *vi (Brit Comm)*: **to ~ for** estimer, faire une estimation de; *(bid for)* faire un devis pour; **to give sb an ~ of** faire *or* donner un devis à qn pour; **at a rough ~** approximativement

**estimation** [ɛstɪ'meɪʃən] *n* opinion *f*; estime *f*; **in my ~** à mon avis, selon moi

**Estonia** [ɛ'stəʊnɪə] *n* Estonie *f*

**Estonian** [ɛ'stəʊnɪən] *adj* estonien(ne) ▷ *n* Estonien(ne); *(Ling)* estonien *m*

**estranged** [ɪs'treɪndʒd] *adj (couple)* séparé(e); *(husband, wife)* dont on s'est séparé(e)

**estrangement** [ɪs'treɪndʒmənt] *n (from wife, family)* séparation *f*

**estrogen** ['iːstrəʊdʒən] *n (US)* = **oestrogen**

**estuary** ['ɛstjuərɪ] *n* estuaire *m*

**ET** *n abbr (Brit: = Employment Training) formation professionnelle pour les demandeurs d'emploi* ▷ *abbr (US: = Eastern Time) heure de New York*

**ETA** *n abbr (= estimated time of arrival)* HPA *f (= heure probable d'arrivée)*

**et al.** *abbr (= et alii: and others)* et coll

**etc** *abbr (= et cetera)* etc

**etch** [ɛtʃ] *vt* graver à l'eau forte

**etching** ['ɛtʃɪŋ] *n* eau-forte *f*

**ETD** *n abbr (= estimated time of departure)* HPD *f (= heure probable de départ)*

**eternal** [ɪ'təːnl] *adj* éternel(le)

**eternity** [ɪ'təːnɪtɪ] *n* éternité *f*

**ether** ['iːθəʳ] *n* éther *m*

**ethereal** [ɪ'θɪərɪəl] *adj* éthéré(e)

**ethical** ['ɛθɪkl] *adj* moral(e)

**ethics** ['ɛθɪks] *n* éthique *f* ▷ *npl* moralité *f*

**Ethiopia** [iːθɪ'əʊpɪə] *n* Éthiopie *f*

**Ethiopian** [iːθɪ'əʊpɪən] *adj* éthiopien(ne) ▷ *n*

Éthiopien(ne)

**ethnic** ['ɛθnɪk] *adj* ethnique; *(clothes, food)* folklorique, exotique, *propre aux minorités ethniques non-occidentales*

**ethnic cleansing** [-'klɛnzɪŋ] *n* purification *f* ethnique

**ethnic minority** *n* minorité *f* ethnique

**ethnology** [ɛθ'nɔlədʒɪ] *n* ethnologie *f*

**ethos** ['iːθɔs] *n (system m de)* valeurs *fpl*

**e-ticket** ['iːtɪkɪt] *n* billet *m* électronique

**etiquette** ['ɛtɪkɛt] *n* convenances *fpl*, étiquette *f*

**ETV** *n abbr (US: = Educational Television) télévision scolaire*

**etymology** [ɛtɪ'mɔlədʒɪ] *n* étymologie *f*

**EU** *n abbr (= European Union)* UE *f*

**eucalyptus** [juːkə'lɪptəs] *n* eucalyptus *m*

**eulogy** ['juːlədʒɪ] *n* éloge *m*

**euphemism** ['juːfəmɪzəm] *n* euphémisme *m*

**euphemistic** [juːfə'mɪstɪk] *adj* euphémique

**euphoria** [juː'fɔːrɪə] *n* euphorie *f*

**Eurasia** [juə'reɪʃə] *n* Eurasie *f*

**Eurasian** [juə'reɪʃən] *adj* eurasien(ne); *(continent)* eurasiatique ▷ *n* Eurasien(ne)

**Euratom** [juə'rætəm] *n abbr (= European Atomic Energy Community)* EURATOM *f*

**euro** ['juərəʊ] *n (currency)* euro *m*

**Euro-** ['juərəʊ] *prefix* euro-

**Eurocrat** ['juərəʊkræt] *n* eurocrate *m/f*

**Euroland** ['juərəʊlænd] *n* Euroland *m*

**Europe** ['juərəp] *n* Europe *f*

**European** [juərə'piːən] *adj* européen(ne) ▷ *n* Européen(ne)

**European Community** *n* Communauté européenne

**European Court of Justice** *n* Cour *f* de Justice de la CEE

**European Union** *n* Union européenne

**Euro-sceptic** ['juərəʊskɛptɪk] *n* eurosceptique *m/f*

**Eurostar®** ['juərəʊstɑːʳ] *n* Eurostar® *m*

**euthanasia** [juːθə'neɪzɪə] *n* euthanasie *f*

**evacuate** [ɪ'vækjueɪt] *vt* évacuer

**evacuation** [ɪvækju'eɪʃən] *n* évacuation *f*

**evacuee** [ɪvækju'iː] *n* évacué(e)

**evade** [ɪ'veɪd] *vt* échapper à; *(question etc)* éluder; *(duties)* se dérober à

**evaluate** [ɪ'væljueɪt] *vt* évaluer

**evangelist** [ɪ'vændʒəlɪst] *n* évangéliste *m*

**evangelize** [ɪ'vændʒəlaɪz] *vt* évangéliser, prêcher l'Évangile à

**evaporate** [ɪ'væpəreɪt] *vi* s'évaporer; *(fig: hopes, fear)* s'envoler; *(anger)* se dissiper ▷ *vt* faire évaporer

**evaporated milk** [ɪ'væpəreɪtɪd-] *n* lait condensé (non sucré)

**evaporation** [ɪvæpə'reɪʃən] *n* évaporation *f*

**evasion** [ɪ'veɪʒən] *n* dérobade *f*; *(excuse)* faux-fuyant *m*

**evasive** [ɪ'veɪsɪv] *adj* évasif(-ive)

**eve** [iːv] *n*: **on the ~ of** à la veille de

**even** ['iːvn] *adj (level, smooth)* régulier(-ière);

569

(*equal*) égal(e); (*number*) pair(e) ▷ *adv* même; ~ **if** même si + *indic*; ~ **though** quand (bien) même + *cond*, alors même que + *cond*; ~ **more** encore plus; ~ **faster** encore plus vite; ~ **so** quand même; **not** ~ pas même; ~ **he was there** même lui était là; ~ **on Sundays** même le dimanche; **to break** ~ s'y retrouver, équilibrer ses comptes; **to get** ~ **with sb** prendre sa revanche sur qn
  ▶ **even out** *vi* s'égaliser
**even-handed** [iːvn'hændɪd] *adj* équitable
**evening** ['iːvnɪŋ] *n* soir *m*; (*as duration, event*) soirée *f*; **in the** ~ le soir; **this** ~ ce soir; **tomorrow/yesterday** ~ demain/hier soir
**evening class** *n* cours *m* du soir
**evening dress** *n* (*man's*) tenue *f* de soirée, smoking *m*; (*woman's*) robe *f* de soirée
**evenly** ['iːvnlɪ] *adv* uniformément, également; (*space*) régulièrement
**evensong** ['iːvnsɔŋ] *n* office *m* du soir
**event** [ɪ'vɛnt] *n* événement *m*; (*Sport*) épreuve *f*; **in the course of** ~**s** par la suite; **in the** ~ **of** en cas de; **in the** ~ en réalité, en fait; **at all** ~**s** (*Brit*): **in any** ~ en tout cas, de toute manière
**eventful** [ɪ'vɛntful] *adj* mouvementé(e)
**eventing** [ɪ'vɛntɪŋ] *n* (*Horse-Riding*) concours complet (*équitation*)
**eventual** [ɪ'vɛntʃuəl] *adj* final(e)
**eventuality** [ɪvɛntʃu'ælɪtɪ] *n* possibilité *f*, éventualité *f*
**eventually** [ɪ'vɛntʃuəlɪ] *adv* finalement
**ever** ['ɛvə**ʳ**] *adv* jamais; (*at all times*) toujours; (*in questions*): **why ~ not?** mais enfin, pourquoi pas?; **the best** ~ le meilleur qu'on ait jamais vu; **have you ~ seen it?** l'as-tu déjà vu?, as-tu eu l'occasion *or* t'est-il arrivé de le voir?; **did you ~ meet him?** est-ce qu'il vous est arrivé de le rencontrer?; **have you ~ been there?** y êtes-vous déjà allé?; **for** ~ pour toujours; **hardly** ~ ne ... presque jamais; ~ **since** (*as adv*) depuis; (*as conj*) depuis que; ~ **so pretty** si joli; **thank you** ~ **so much** merci mille fois
**Everest** ['ɛvərɪst] *n* (*also*: **Mount Everest**) le mont Everest, l'Everest *m*
**evergreen** ['ɛvəgriːn] *n* arbre *m* à feuilles persistantes
**everlasting** [ɛvə'lɑːstɪŋ] *adj* éternel(le)

**KEYWORD**

**every** ['ɛvrɪ] *adj* **1** (*each*) chaque; **every one of them** tous (sans exception); **every shop in town was closed** tous les magasins en ville étaient fermés
  **2** (*all possible*) tous (toutes) les; **I gave you every assistance** j'ai fait tout mon possible pour vous aider; **I have every confidence in him** j'ai entièrement *or* pleinement confiance en lui; **we wish you every success** nous vous souhaitons beaucoup de succès
  **3** (*showing recurrence*) tous les; **every day** tous les jours, chaque jour; **every other car** une voiture sur deux; **every other/third day** tous les deux/trois jours; **every now and then** de temps en temps

**everybody** ['ɛvrɪbɔdɪ] *pron* = **everyone**
**everyday** ['ɛvrɪdeɪ] *adj* (*expression*) courant(e), d'usage courant; (*use*) courant; (*clothes, life*) de tous les jours; (*occurrence, problem*) quotidien(ne)
**everyone** ['ɛvrɪwʌn] *pron* tout le monde, tous *pl*; ~ **knows about it** tout le monde le sait; ~ **else** tous les autres
**everything** ['ɛvrɪθɪŋ] *pron* tout; ~ **is ready** tout est prêt; **he did** ~ **possible** il a fait tout son possible
**everywhere** ['ɛvrɪwɛə**ʳ**] *adv* partout; ~ **you go you meet ...** où qu'on aille on rencontre ...
**evict** [ɪ'vɪkt] *vt* expulser
**eviction** [ɪ'vɪkʃən] *n* expulsion *f*
**eviction notice** *n* préavis *m* d'expulsion
**evidence** ['ɛvɪdns] *n* (*proof*) preuve(s) *f*(*pl*); (*of witness*) témoignage *m*; (*sign*): **to show ~ of** donner des signes de; **to give** ~ témoigner, déposer; **in** ~ (*obvious*) en évidence; en vue
**evident** ['ɛvɪdnt] *adj* évident(e)
**evidently** ['ɛvɪdntlɪ] *adv* de toute évidence; (*apparently*) apparemment
**evil** ['iːvl] *adj* mauvais(e) ▷ *n* mal *m*
**evince** [ɪ'vɪns] *vt* manifester
**evocative** [ɪ'vɔkətɪv] *adj* évocateur(-trice)
**evoke** [ɪ'vəuk] *vt* évoquer; (*admiration*) susciter
**evolution** [iːvə'luːʃən] *n* évolution *f*
**evolve** [ɪ'vɔlv] *vt* élaborer ▷ *vi* évoluer, se transformer
**ewe** [juː] *n* brebis *f*
**ex** [ɛks] *n* (*inf*): **my ex** mon ex
**ex-** [ɛks] *prefix* (*former: husband, president etc*) ex-; (*out of*): **the price ~works** le prix départ usine
**exacerbate** [ɛks'æsəbeɪt] *vt* (*pain*) exacerber, accentuer; (*fig*) aggraver
**exact** [ɪg'zækt] *adj* exact(e) ▷ *vt*: **to ~ sth (from)** (*signature, confession*) extorquer qch (à); (*apology*) exiger qch (de)
**exacting** [ɪg'zæktɪŋ] *adj* exigeant(e); (*work*) fatigant(e)
**exactitude** [ɪg'zæktɪtjuːd] *n* exactitude *f*, précision *f*
**exactly** [ɪg'zæktlɪ] *adv* exactement; ~**!** parfaitement!, précisément!
**exaggerate** [ɪg'zædʒəreɪt] *vt, vi* exagérer
**exaggeration** [ɪgzædʒə'reɪʃən] *n* exagération *f*
**exalted** [ɪg'zɔːltɪd] *adj* (*rank*) élevé(e); (*person*) haut placé(e); (*elated*) exalté(e)
**exam** [ɪg'zæm] *n abbr* (*Scol*) = **examination**
**examination** [ɪgzæmɪ'neɪʃən] *n* (*Scol, Med*) examen *m*; **to take** *or* **sit an** ~ (*Brit*) passer un examen; **the matter is under** ~ la question est à l'examen
**examine** [ɪg'zæmɪn] *vt* (*gen*) examiner; (*Scol, Law: person*) interroger; (*inspect: machine, premises*) inspecter; (*passport*) contrôler; (*luggage*) fouiller
**examiner** [ɪg'zæmɪnə**ʳ**] *n* examinateur(-trice)
**example** [ɪg'zɑːmpl] *n* exemple *m*; **for ~** par

exemple; **to set a good/bad** ~ donner le bon/mauvais exemple

**exasperate** [ɪgˈzɑːspəreɪt] vt exaspérer, agacer

**exasperated** [ɪgˈzɑːspəreɪtɪd] adj exaspéré(e)

**exasperation** [ɪgzɑːspəˈreɪʃən] n exaspération f, irritation f

**excavate** [ˈɛkskəveɪt] vt (site) fouiller, excaver; (object) mettre au jour

**excavation** [ɛkskəˈveɪʃən] n excavation f

**excavator** [ˈɛkskəveɪtəʳ] n excavateur m, excavatrice f

**exceed** [ɪkˈsiːd] vt dépasser; (one's powers) outrepasser

**exceedingly** [ɪkˈsiːdɪŋlɪ] adv extrêmement

**excel** [ɪkˈsɛl] vi exceller ▷ vt surpasser; **to** ~ **o.s.** se surpasser

**excellence** [ˈɛksələns] n excellence f

**Excellency** [ˈɛksələnsɪ] n: **His** ~ son Excellence f

**excellent** [ˈɛksələnt] adj excellent(e)

**except** [ɪkˈsɛpt] prep (also: **except for, excepting**) sauf, excepté, à l'exception de ▷ vt excepter; ~ **if/when** sauf si/quand; ~ **that** excepté que, si ce n'est que

**exception** [ɪkˈsɛpʃən] n exception f; **to take** ~ **to** s'offusquer de; **with the** ~ **of** à l'exception de

**exceptional** [ɪkˈsɛpʃənl] adj exceptionnel(le)

**exceptionally** [ɪkˈsɛpʃənəlɪ] adv exceptionnellement

**excerpt** [ˈɛksəːpt] n extrait m

**excess** [ɪkˈsɛs] n excès m; **in** ~ **of** plus de

**excess baggage** n excédent m de bagages

**excess fare** n supplément m

**excessive** [ɪkˈsɛsɪv] adj excessif(-ive)

**excess supply** n suroffre f, offre f excédentaire

**exchange** [ɪksˈtʃeɪndʒ] n échange m; (also: **telephone exchange**) central m ▷ vt: **to** ~ **(for)** échanger (contre); **could I** ~ **this, please?** est-ce que je peux échanger ceci, s'il vous plaît?; **in** ~ **for** en échange de; **foreign** ~ (Comm) change m

**exchange control** n contrôle m des changes

**exchange market** n marché m des changes

**exchange rate** n taux m de change

**excisable** [ɪkˈsaɪzəbl] adj taxable

**excise** n [ˈɛksaɪz] taxe f ▷ vt [ɛkˈsaɪz] exciser

**excise duties** npl impôts indirects

**excitable** [ɪkˈsaɪtəbl] adj excitable, nerveux(-euse)

**excite** [ɪkˈsaɪt] vt exciter

**excited** [ɪkˈsaɪtəd] adj (tout (toute)) excité(e); **to get** ~ s'exciter

**excitement** [ɪkˈsaɪtmənt] n excitation f

**exciting** [ɪkˈsaɪtɪŋ] adj passionnant(e)

**excl.** abbr = **excluding; exclusive (of)**

**exclaim** [ɪkˈskleɪm] vi s'exclamer

**exclamation** [ɛkskləˈmeɪʃən] n exclamation f

**exclamation mark,** (US) **exclamation point** n point m d'exclamation

**exclude** [ɪkˈskluːd] vt exclure

**excluding** [ɪkˈskluːdɪŋ] prep: ~ **VAT** la TVA non comprise

**exclusion** [ɪkˈskluːʒən] n exclusion f; **to the** ~ **of** à l'exclusion de

**exclusion clause** n clause f d'exclusion

**exclusion zone** n zone interdite

**exclusive** [ɪkˈskluːsɪv] adj exclusif(-ive); (club, district) sélect(e); (item of news) en exclusivité ▷ adv (Comm) exclusivement, non inclus; ~ **of VAT** TVA non comprise; ~ **of postage** (les) frais de poste non compris; **from 1st to 15th March** ~ du 1er au 15 mars exclusivement or exclu; ~ **rights** (Comm) exclusivité f

**exclusively** [ɪkˈskluːsɪvlɪ] adv exclusivement

**excommunicate** [ɛkskəˈmjuːnɪkeɪt] vt excommunier

**excrement** [ˈɛkskrəmənt] n excrément m

**excruciating** [ɪkˈskruːʃɪeɪtɪŋ] adj (pain) atroce, déchirant(e); (embarrassing) pénible

**excursion** [ɪkˈskəːʃən] n excursion f

**excursion ticket** n billet m tarif excursion

**excusable** [ɪkˈskjuːzəbl] adj excusable

**excuse** n [ɪkˈskjuːs] excuse f ▷ vt [ɪkˈskjuːz] (forgive) excuser; (justify) excuser, justifier; **to** ~ **sb from** (activity) dispenser qn de; ~ **me!** excusez-moi!, pardon!; **now if you will** ~ **me, ...** maintenant, si vous (le) permettez ...; **to make** ~**s for sb** trouver des excuses à qn; **to** ~ **o.s. for sth/for doing sth** s'excuser de/d'avoir fait qch

**ex-directory** [ˈɛksdɪˈrɛktərɪ] adj (Brit) sur la liste rouge

**execute** [ˈɛksɪkjuːt] vt exécuter

**execution** [ɛksɪˈkjuːʃən] n exécution f

**executioner** [ɛksɪˈkjuːʃnəʳ] n bourreau m

**executive** [ɪgˈzɛkjutɪv] n (person) cadre m; (managing group) bureau m; (Pol) exécutif m ▷ adj exécutif(-ive); (position, job) de cadre; (secretary) de direction; (offices) de la direction; (car, plane) de fonction

**executive director** n administrateur(-trice)

**executor** [ɪgˈzɛkjutəʳ] n exécuteur(-trice) testamentaire

**exemplary** [ɪgˈzɛmplərɪ] adj exemplaire

**exemplify** [ɪgˈzɛmplɪfaɪ] vt illustrer

**exempt** [ɪgˈzɛmpt] adj: ~ **from** exempté(e) or dispensé(e) de ▷ vt: **to** ~ **sb from** exempter or dispenser qn de

**exemption** [ɪgˈzɛmpʃən] n exemption f, dispense f

**exercise** [ˈɛksəsaɪz] n exercice m ▷ vt exercer; (patience etc) faire preuve de; (dog) promener ▷ vi (also: **to take exercise**) prendre de l'exercice

**exercise bike** n vélo m d'appartement

**exercise book** n cahier m

**exert** [ɪgˈzəːt] vt exercer, employer; (strength, force) employer; **to** ~ **o.s.** se dépenser

**exertion** [ɪgˈzəːʃən] n effort m

**ex gratia** [ˈɛksˈgreɪʃə] adj: ~ **payment** gratification f

**exhale** [ɛksˈheɪl] vt (breathe out) expirer; exhaler ▷ vi expirer

**exhaust** [ɪgˈzɔːst] n (also: **exhaust fumes**) gaz mpl d'échappement; (also: **exhaust pipe**) tuyau m d'échappement ▷ vt épuiser; **to** ~ **o.s.** s'épuiser

**exhausted** [ɪg'zɔːstɪd] *adj* épuisé(e)
**exhausting** [ɪg'zɔːstɪŋ] *adj* épuisant(e)
**exhaustion** [ɪg'zɔːstʃən] *n* épuisement *m*;
**nervous** ~ fatigue nerveuse
**exhaustive** [ɪg'zɔːstɪv] *adj* très complet(-ète)
**exhibit** [ɪg'zɪbɪt] *n* (*Art*) objet exposé, pièce
exposée; (*Law*) pièce à conviction ▷ *vt* (*Art*)
exposer; (*courage, skill*) faire preuve de
**exhibition** [ɛksɪ'bɪʃən] *n* exposition *f*; ~ **of**
**temper** manifestation *f* de colère
**exhibitionist** [ɛksɪ'bɪʃənɪst] *n*
exhibitionniste *m/f*
**exhibitor** [ɪg'zɪbɪtəʳ] *n* exposant(e)
**exhilarating** [ɪg'zɪləreɪtɪŋ] *adj* grisant(e),
stimulant(e)
**exhilaration** [ɪgzɪlə'reɪʃən] *n* euphorie *f*,
ivresse *f*
**exhort** [ɪg'zɔːt] *vt* exhorter
**ex-husband** ['ɛks'hʌzbənd] *n* ex-mari *m*
**exile** ['ɛksaɪl] *n* exil *m*; (*person*) exilé(e) ▷ *vt*
exiler; **in** ~ en exil
**exist** [ɪg'zɪst] *vi* exister
**existence** [ɪg'zɪstəns] *n* existence *f*; **to be in** ~
exister
**existentialism** [ɛgzɪs'tɛnʃlɪzəm] *n*
existentialisme *m*
**existing** [ɪg'zɪstɪŋ] *adj* (*laws*) existant(e); (*system,
regime*) actuel(le)
**exit** ['ɛksɪt] *n* sortie *f* ▷ *vi* (*Comput, Theat*) sortir;
**where's the** ~? où est la sortie?
**exit poll** *n* sondage *m* (*fait à la sortie de l'isoloir*)
**exit ramp** *n* (*US Aut*) bretelle *f* d'accès
**exit visa** *n* visa *m* de sortie
**exodus** ['ɛksədəs] *n* exode *m*
**ex officio** ['ɛksə'fɪʃɪəu] *adj, adv* d'office, de droit
**exonerate** [ɪg'zɔnəreɪt] *vt*: **to** ~ **from**
disculper de
**exorbitant** [ɪg'zɔːbɪtnt] *adj* (*price*) exorbitant(e),
excessif(-ive); (*demands*) exorbitant,
démesuré(e)
**exorcize** ['ɛksɔːsaɪz] *vt* exorciser
**exotic** [ɪg'zɔtɪk] *adj* exotique
**expand** [ɪk'spænd] *vt* (*area*) agrandir; (*quantity*)
accroître; (*influence etc*) étendre ▷ *vi* (*population,
production*) s'accroître; (*trade, etc*) se développer,
s'accroître; (*gas, metal*) se dilater, dilater; **to** ~
**on** (*notes, story etc*) développer
**expanse** [ɪk'spæns] *n* étendue *f*
**expansion** [ɪk'spænʃən] *n* (*territorial, economic*)
expansion *f*; (*of trade, influence etc*)
développement *m*; (*of production*) accroissement
*m*; (*of population*) croissance *f*; (*of gas, metal*)
expansion, dilatation *f*
**expansionism** [ɪk'spænʃənɪzəm] *n*
expansionnisme *m*
**expansionist** [ɪk'spænʃənɪst] *adj*
expansionniste
**expatriate** *n* [ɛks'pætrɪət] expatrié(e) ▷ *vt*
[ɛks'pætrɪeɪt] expatrier, exiler
**expect** [ɪk'spɛkt] *vt* (*anticipate*) s'attendre à,
s'attendre à ce que + *sub*; (*count on*) compter sur,
escompter; (*hope for*) espérer; (*require*) demander,

exiger; (*suppose*) supposer; (*await: also baby*)
attendre ▷ *vi*: **to be** ~**ing** (*pregnant woman*) être
enceinte; **to** ~ **sb to do** (*anticipate*) s'attendre à
ce que qn fasse; (*demand*) attendre de qn qu'il
fasse; **to** ~ **to do sth** penser *or* compter faire
qch, s'attendre à faire qch; **as** ~**ed** comme
prévu; **I** ~ **so** je crois que oui, je crois bien
**expectancy** [ɪks'pɛktənsɪ] *n* attente *f*; **life** ~
espérance *f* de vie
**expectant** [ɪk'spɛktənt] *adj* qui attend (quelque
chose); ~ **mother** future maman
**expectantly** [ɪk'spɛktəntlɪ] *adv* (*look, listen*) avec
l'air d'attendre quelque chose
**expectation** [ɛkspɛk'teɪʃən] *n* (*hope*) attente *f*,
espérance(s) *f(pl)*; (*belief*) attente; **in** ~ **of** dans
l'attente de, en prévision de; **against** *or*
**contrary to all** ~(**s**) contre toute attente,
contrairement à ce qu'on attendait; **to come** *or*
**live up to sb's** ~**s** répondre à l'attente *or* aux
espérances de, qn
**expedience, expediency** [ɪk'spiːdɪəns,
ɪk'spiːdɪənsɪ] *n* opportunité *f*; convenance *f* (du
moment); **for the sake of** ~ parce que c'est (*or*
c'était) plus simple *or* plus commode
**expedient** [ɪk'spiːdɪənt] *adj* indiqué(e),
opportun(e), commode ▷ *n* expédient *m*
**expedite** ['ɛkspədaɪt] *vt* hâter; expédier
**expedition** [ɛkspə'dɪʃən] *n* expédition *f*
**expeditionary force** [ɛkspə'dɪʃənrɪ-] *n* corps *m*
expéditionnaire
**expeditious** [ɛkspə'dɪʃəs] *adj* expéditif(-ive),
prompt(e)
**expel** [ɪk'spɛl] *vt* chasser, expulser; (*Scol*)
renvoyer, exclure
**expend** [ɪk'spɛnd] *vt* consacrer; (*use up*)
dépenser
**expendable** [ɪk'spɛndəbl] *adj* remplaçable
**expenditure** [ɪk'spɛndɪtʃəʳ] *n* (*act of spending*)
dépense *f*; (*money spent*) dépenses *fpl*
**expense** [ɪk'spɛns] *n* (*high cost*) coût *m*; (*spending*)
dépense *f*, frais *mpl*; **expenses** *npl* frais *mpl*;
dépenses; **to go to the** ~ **of** faire la dépense de;
**at great/little** ~ à grands/peu de frais; **at the** ~
**of** aux frais de; (*fig*) aux dépens de
**expense account** *n* (*note f* de) frais *mpl*
**expensive** [ɪk'spɛnsɪv] *adj* cher (chère),
coûteux(-euse); **to be** ~ coûter cher; **it's too** ~
ça coûte trop cher; ~ **tastes** goûts *mpl* de luxe
**experience** [ɪk'spɪərɪəns] *n* expérience *f* ▷ *vt*
connaître; (*feeling*) éprouver; **to know by** ~
savoir par expérience
**experienced** [ɪk'spɪərɪənst] *adj* expérimenté(e)
**experiment** [ɪk'spɛrɪmənt] *n* expérience *f* ▷ *vi*
faire une expérience; **to** ~ **with** expérimenter;
**to perform** *or* **carry out an** ~ faire une
expérience; **as an** ~ à titre d'expérience
**experimental** [ɪkspɛrɪ'mɛntl] *adj*
expérimental(e)
**expert** ['ɛkspəːt] *adj* expert(e) ▷ *n* expert *m*; ~ **in**
*or* **at doing sth** spécialiste de qch; **an** ~ **on sth**
un spécialiste de qch; ~ **witness** (*Law*) expert *m*
**expertise** [ɛkspəː'tiːz] *n* (grande) compétence

**expire** [ɪk'spaɪə<sup>r</sup>] vi expirer
**expiry** [ɪk'spaɪərɪ] n expiration f
**expiry date** n date f d'expiration; (on label) à utiliser avant ...
**explain** [ɪk'spleɪn] vt expliquer
  ▸ **explain away** vt justifier, excuser
**explanation** [ɛksplə'neɪʃən] n explication f; **to find an ~ for sth** trouver une explication à qch
**explanatory** [ɪk'splænətrɪ] adj explicatif(-ive)
**expletive** [ɪk'spliːtɪv] n juron m
**explicit** [ɪk'splɪsɪt] adj explicite; (definite) formel(le)
**explode** [ɪk'spləud] vi exploser ▸ vt faire exploser; (fig: theory) démolir; **to ~ a myth** détruire un mythe
**exploit** n ['ɛksplɔɪt] exploit m ▸ vt [ɪk'splɔɪt] exploiter
**exploitation** [ɛksplɔɪ'teɪʃən] n exploitation f
**exploration** [ɛksplə'reɪʃən] n exploration f
**exploratory** [ɪk'splɔrətrɪ] adj (fig: talks) préliminaire; **~ operation** (Med) intervention f (à visée) exploratrice
**explore** [ɪk'splɔː<sup>r</sup>] vt explorer; (possibilities) étudier, examiner
**explorer** [ɪk'splɔːrə<sup>r</sup>] n explorateur(-trice)
**explosion** [ɪk'spləuʒən] n explosion f
**explosive** [ɪk'spləusɪv] adj explosif(-ive) ▸ n explosif m
**exponent** [ɪk'spəunənt] n (of school of thought etc) interprète m, représentant m; (Math) exposant m
**export** vt [ɛk'spɔːt] exporter ▸ n ['ɛkspɔːt] exportation f ▸ cpd ['ɛkspɔːt] d'exportation
**exportation** [ɛkspɔː'teɪʃən] n exportation f
**exporter** [ɛk'spɔːtə<sup>r</sup>] n exportateur m
**export licence** n licence f d'exportation
**expose** [ɪk'spəuz] vt exposer; (unmask) démasquer, dévoiler; **to ~ o.s.** (Law) commettre un outrage à la pudeur
**exposed** [ɪk'spəuzd] adj (land, house) exposé(e); (Elec: wire) à nu; (pipe, beam) apparent(e)
**exposition** [ɛkspə'zɪʃən] n exposition f
**exposure** [ɪk'spəuʒə<sup>r</sup>] n exposition f; (publicity) couverture f; (Phot: speed) (temps m de) pose f; (: shot) pose; **suffering from ~** (Med) souffrant des effets du froid et de l'épuisement; **to die of ~** (Med) mourir de froid
**exposure meter** n posemètre m
**expound** [ɪk'spaund] vt exposer, expliquer
**express** [ɪk'sprɛs] adj (definite) formel(le), exprès(-esse); (Brit: letter etc) exprès inv ▸ n (train) rapide m ▸ adv (send) exprès ▸ vt exprimer; **to ~ o.s.** s'exprimer
**expression** [ɪk'sprɛʃən] n expression f
**expressionism** [ɪk'sprɛʃənɪzəm] n expressionnisme m
**expressive** [ɪk'sprɛsɪv] adj expressif(-ive)
**expressly** [ɪk'sprɛslɪ] adv expressément, formellement
**expressway** [ɪk'sprɛsweɪ] n (US) voie f express (à plusieurs files)
**expropriate** [ɛks'prəuprɪeɪt] vt exproprier

**expulsion** [ɪk'spʌlʃən] n expulsion f; renvoi m
**exquisite** [ɛk'skwɪzɪt] adj exquis(e)
**ex-serviceman** ['ɛks'səːvɪsmən] (irreg) n ancien combattant
**ext.** abbr (Tel) = **extension**
**extemporize** [ɪk'stɛmpəraɪz] vi improviser
**extend** [ɪk'stɛnd] vt (visit, street) prolonger; (deadline) reporter, remettre; (building) agrandir; (offer) présenter, offrir; (Comm: credit) accorder; (hand, arm) tendre ▸ vi (land) s'étendre
**extension** [ɪk'stɛnʃən] n (of visit, street) prolongation f; (of building) agrandissement m; (building) annexe f; (to wire, table) rallonge f; (telephone: in offices) poste m; (: in private house) téléphone m supplémentaire; **~ 3718** (Tel) poste 3718
**extension cable, extension lead** n (Elec) rallonge f
**extensive** [ɪk'stɛnsɪv] adj étendu(e), vaste; (damage, alterations) considérable; (inquiries) approfondi(e); (use) largement répandu(e)
**extensively** [ɪk'stɛnsɪvlɪ] adv (altered, damaged etc) considérablement; **he's travelled ~** il a beaucoup voyagé
**extent** [ɪk'stɛnt] n étendue f; (degree: of damage, loss) importance f; **to some ~** dans une certaine mesure; **to a certain ~** dans une certaine mesure, jusqu'à un certain point; **to a large ~** en grande partie; **to the ~ of ...** au point de ...; **to what ~?** dans quelle mesure?, jusqu'à quel point?; **to such an ~ that ...** à tel point que ...
**extenuating** [ɪk'stɛnjueɪtɪŋ] adj: **~ circumstances** circonstances atténuantes
**exterior** [ɛk'stɪərɪə<sup>r</sup>] adj extérieur(e) ▸ n extérieur m
**exterminate** [ɪk'stəːmɪneɪt] vt exterminer
**extermination** [ɪkstəːmɪ'neɪʃən] n extermination f
**external** [ɛk'stəːnl] adj externe ▸ n: **the ~s** les apparences fpl; **for ~ use only** (Med) à usage externe
**externally** [ɛk'stəːnəlɪ] adv extérieurement
**extinct** [ɪk'stɪŋkt] adj (volcano) éteint(e); (species) disparu(e)
**extinction** [ɪk'stɪŋkʃən] n extinction f
**extinguish** [ɪk'stɪŋgwɪʃ] vt éteindre
**extinguisher** [ɪk'stɪŋgwɪʃə<sup>r</sup>] n extincteur m
**extol**, (US) **extoll** [ɪk'stəul] vt (merits) chanter, prôner; (person) chanter les louanges de
**extort** [ɪk'stɔːt] vt: **to ~ sth (from)** extorquer qch (à)
**extortion** [ɪk'stɔːʃən] n extorsion f
**extortionate** [ɪk'stɔːʃnɪt] adj exorbitant(e)
**extra** ['ɛkstrə] adj supplémentaire, de plus ▸ adv (in addition) en plus ▸ n supplément m; (perk) à-coté m; (Cine, Theat) figurant(e); **wine will cost ~** le vin sera en supplément; **~ large sizes** très grandes tailles
**extra...** ['ɛkstrə] prefix extra...
**extract** vt [ɪk'strækt] extraire; (tooth) arracher; (money, promise) soutirer ▸ n ['ɛkstrækt] extrait m
**extraction** [ɪk'strækʃən] n extraction f

**extractor fan** [ık'stræktə-] n exhausteur m, ventilateur m extracteur

**extracurricular** ['ɛkstrəkə'rıkjulər] adj (Scol) parascolaire

**extradite** ['ɛkstrədaıt] vt extrader

**extradition** [ɛkstrə'dıʃən] n extradition f

**extramarital** ['ɛkstrə'mærıtl] adj extraconjugal(e)

**extramural** ['ɛkstrə'mjuərl] adj hors-faculté inv

**extraneous** [ɛk'streınıəs] adj: ~ to étranger(-ère) à

**extraordinary** [ık'strɔːdnrı] adj extraordinaire; **the ~ thing is that ...** le plus étrange or étonnant c'est que ...

**extraordinary general meeting** n assemblée f générale extraordinaire

**extrapolation** [ɛkstræpə'leıʃən] n extrapolation f

**extrasensory perception** ['ɛkstrə'sɛnsərı-] n perception f extrasensorielle

**extra time** n (Football) prolongations fpl

**extravagance** [ık'strævəgəns] n (excessive spending) prodigalités fpl; (thing bought) folie f, dépense excessive

**extravagant** [ık'strævəgənt] adj extravagant(e); (in spending: person) prodigue, dépensier(-ière); (: tastes) dispendieux(-euse)

**extreme** [ık'striːm] adj, n extrême (m); **the ~ left/right** (Pol) l'extrême gauche f/droite f; **~s of temperature** différences fpl extrêmes de température

**extremely** [ık'striːmlı] adv extrêmement

**extremist** [ık'striːmıst] adj, n extrémiste m/f

**extremity** [ık'strɛmıtı] n extrémité f

**extricate** ['ɛkstrıkeıt] vt: **to ~ sth (from)** dégager qch (de)

**extrovert** ['ɛkstrəvəːt] n extraverti(e)

**exuberance** [ıg'zjuːbərns] n exubérance f

**exuberant** [ıg'zjuːbərnt] adj exubérant(e)

**exude** [ıg'zjuːd] vt exsuder; (fig) respirer; **the charm etc he ~s** le charme etc qui émane de lui

**exult** [ıg'zʌlt] vi exulter, jubiler

**exultant** [ıg'zʌltənt] adj (shout, expression) de triomphe; **to be ~** jubiler, triompher

**exultation** [ɛgzʌl'teıʃən] n exultation f, jubilation f

**ex-wife** ['ɛkswaıf] n ex-femme f

**eye** [aı] n œil m; (of needle) trou m, chas m ▷ vt examiner; **as far as the ~ can see** à perte de vue; **to keep an ~ on** surveiller; **to have an ~ for sth** avoir l'œil pour qch; **in the public ~** en vue; **with an ~ to doing sth** (Brit) en vue de faire qch; **there's more to this than meets the ~** ce n'est pas aussi simple que cela paraît

**eyeball** ['aıbɔːl] n globe m oculaire

**eyebath** ['aıbɑːθ] n (Brit) œillère f (pour bains d'œil)

**eyebrow** ['aıbrau] n sourcil m

**eyebrow pencil** n crayon m à sourcils

**eye-catching** ['aıkætʃıŋ] adj voyant(e), accrocheur(-euse)

**eye cup** n (US) = **eyebath**

**eye drops** ['aıdrɔps] npl gouttes fpl pour les yeux

**eyeful** ['aıful] n: **to get an ~ (of sth)** se rincer l'œil (en voyant qch)

**eyeglass** ['aıglɑːs] n monocle m

**eyelash** ['aılæʃ] n cil m

**eyelet** ['aılıt] n œillet m

**eye-level** ['aılɛvl] adj en hauteur

**eyelid** ['aılıd] n paupière f

**eyeliner** ['aılaınər] n eye-liner m

**eye-opener** ['aıəupnər] n révélation f

**eye shadow** ['aıʃædəu] n ombre f à paupières

**eyesight** ['aısaıt] n vue f

**eyesore** ['aısɔːr] n horreur f, chose f qui dépare or enlaidit

**eyestrain** ['aıstreın] adj: **to get ~** se fatiguer la vue or les yeux

**eyewash** ['aıwɔʃ] n bain m d'œil; (fig) frime f

**eye witness** n témoin m oculaire

**eyrie** ['ıərı] n aire f

# Ff

**F¹, f** [ɛf] *n* (*letter*) F, f *m*; (*Mus*): **F** fa *m*; **F for Frederick**, (*US*) **F for Fox** F comme François
**F²** *abbr* (= *Fahrenheit*) F
**FA** *n abbr* (*Brit*: = *Football Association*) *fédération de football*
**FAA** *n abbr* (*US*) = **Federal Aviation Administration**
**fable** ['feɪbl] *n* fable *f*
**fabric** ['fæbrɪk] *n* tissu *m* ▷ *cpd*: ~ **ribbon** (*for typewriter*) ruban *m* (en) tissu
**fabricate** ['fæbrɪkeɪt] *vt* fabriquer, inventer
**fabrication** [fæbrɪ'keɪʃən] *n* fabrication *f*, invention *f*
**fabulous** ['fæbjuləs] *adj* fabuleux(-euse); (*inf*: *super*) formidable, sensationnel(le)
**façade** [fə'sɑːd] *n* façade *f*
**face** [feɪs] *n* visage *m*, figure *f*; (*expression*) air *m*; grimace *f*; (*of clock*) cadran *m*; (*of cliff*) paroi *f*; (*of mountain*) face *f*; (*of building*) façade *f*; (*side, surface*) face *f* ▷ *vt* faire face à; (*facts etc*) accepter; ~ **down** (*person*) à plat ventre; (*card*) face en dessous; **to lose/save ~** perdre/sauver la face; **to pull a ~** faire une grimace; **in the ~ of** (*difficulties etc*) face à, devant; **on the ~ of it** à première vue; ~ **to** ~ face à face
 ▶ **face up to** *vt fus* faire face à, affronter
**face cloth** *n* (*Brit*) gant *m* de toilette
**face cream** *n* crème *f* pour le visage
**face lift** *n* lifting *m*; (*of façade etc*) ravalement *m*, retapage *m*
**face pack** *n* (*Brit*) masque *m* (de beauté)
**face powder** *n* poudre *f* (pour le visage)
**face-saving** ['feɪsseɪvɪŋ] *adj* qui sauve la face
**facet** ['fæsɪt] *n* facette *f*
**facetious** [fə'siːʃəs] *adj* facétieux(-euse)
**face-to-face** ['feɪstə'feɪs] *adv* face à face
**face value** ['feɪs'væljuː] *n* (*of coin*) valeur nominale; **to take sth at ~** (*fig*) prendre qch pour argent comptant
**facia** ['feɪʃə] *n* = **fascia**
**facial** ['feɪʃl] *adj* facial(e) ▷ *n* soin complet du visage
**facile** ['fæsaɪl] *adj* facile
**facilitate** [fə'sɪlɪteɪt] *vt* faciliter
**facilities** [fə'sɪlɪtɪz] *npl* installations *fpl*, équipement *m*; **credit ~** facilités de paiement

**facility** [fə'sɪlɪtɪ] *n* facilité *f*
**facing** ['feɪsɪŋ] *prep* face à, en face de ▷ *n* (*of wall etc*) revêtement *m*; (*Sewing*) revers *m*
**facsimile** [fæk'sɪmɪlɪ] *n* (*exact replica*) facsimilé *m*; (*also*: **facsimile machine**) télécopieur *m*; (*transmitted document*) télécopie *f*
**fact** [fækt] *n* fait *m*; **in ~** en fait; **to know for a ~ that ...** savoir pertinemment que ...
**fact-finding** ['fæktfaɪndɪŋ] *adj*: **a ~ tour** *or* **mission** une mission d'enquête
**faction** ['fækʃən] *n* faction *f*
**factional** ['fækʃənl] *adj* de factions
**factor** ['fæktər] *n* facteur *m*; (*of sun cream*) indice *m* (de protection); (*Comm*) factor *m*, société *f* d'affacturage; (: *agent*) dépositaire *m/f* ▷ *vi* faire du factoring; **safety ~** facteur de sécurité; **I'd like a ~ 15 suntan lotion** je voudrais une crème solaire d'indice 15
**factory** ['fæktərɪ] *n* usine *f*, fabrique *f*
**factory farming** *n* (*Brit*) élevage industriel
**factory floor** *n*: **the ~** (*workers*) les ouvriers *mpl*; (*workshop*) l'usine *f*; **on the ~** dans les ateliers
**factory ship** *n* navire-usine *m*
**factual** ['fæktjuəl] *adj* basé(e) sur les faits
**faculty** ['fækəltɪ] *n* faculté *f*; (*US: teaching staff*) corps enseignant
**fad** [fæd] *n* (*personal*) manie *f*; (*craze*) engouement *m*
**fade** [feɪd] *vi* se décolorer, passer; (*light, sound*) s'affaiblir, disparaître; (*flower*) se faner
 ▶ **fade away** *vi* (*sound*) s'affaiblir
 ▶ **fade in** *vt* (*picture*) ouvrir en fondu; (*sound*) monter progressivement
 ▶ **fade out** *vt* (*picture*) fermer en fondu; (*sound*) baisser progressivement
**faeces**, (*US*) **feces** ['fiːsiːz] *npl* fèces *fpl*
**fag** [fæg] *n* (*Brit inf*: *cigarette*) clope *f*; (: *chore*): **what a ~!** quelle corvée!; (*US inf*: *homosexual*) pédé *m*
**fag end** *n* (*Brit inf*) mégot *m*
**fagged out** [fægd-] *adj* (*Brit inf*) crevé(e)
**Fahrenheit** ['fɑːrənhaɪt] *n* Fahrenheit *m inv*
**fail** [feɪl] *vt* (*exam*) échouer à; (*candidate*) recaler; (*subj: courage, memory*) faire défaut à ▷ *vi* échouer; (*supplies*) manquer; (*eyesight, health, light: also*: **be failing**) baisser, s'affaiblir; (*brakes*) lâcher; **to ~**

**to do sth** (neglect) négliger de or ne pas faire qch;
(be unable) ne pas arriver or parvenir à faire qch;
**without** ~ à coup sûr; sans faute

**failing** ['feɪlɪŋ] n défaut m ▷ prep faute de; ~ **that**
à défaut, sinon

**failsafe** ['feɪlseɪf] adj (device etc) à sûreté intégrée

**failure** ['feɪljəʳ] n échec m; (person) raté(e);
(mechanical etc) défaillance f; **his ~ to turn up** le
fait de n'être pas venu or qu'il ne soit pas venu

**faint** [feɪnt] adj faible; (recollection) vague; (mark)
à peine visible; (smell, breeze, trace) léger(-ère) ▷ n
évanouissement m ▷ vi s'évanouir; **to feel ~**
défaillir

**faintest** ['feɪntɪst] adj: **I haven't the ~ idea** je
n'en ai pas la moindre idée

**faint-hearted** ['feɪnt'hɑːtɪd] adj pusillanime

**faintly** ['feɪntlɪ] adv faiblement; (vaguely)
vaguement

**faintness** ['feɪntnɪs] n faiblesse f

**fair** [fɛəʳ] adj équitable, juste; (reasonable)
correct(e), honnête; (hair) blond(e); (skin,
complexion) pâle, blanc (blanche); (weather) beau
(belle); (good enough) assez bon(ne); (sizeable)
considérable ▷ adv: **to play ~** jouer franc jeu ▷ n
foire f; (Brit: funfair) fête (foraine); (also: **trade
fair**) foire(-exposition) commerciale; **it's not ~!**
ce n'est pas juste!; **a ~ amount of** une quantité
considérable de

**fair copy** n copie f au propre, corrigé m

**fair game** n: **to be ~ (for)** être une cible légitime
(pour)

**fairground** ['fɛəgraund] n champ m de foire

**fair-haired** [fɛə'hɛəd] adj (person) aux cheveux
clairs, blond(e)

**fairly** ['fɛəlɪ] adv (justly) équitablement; (quite)
assez; **I'm ~ sure** j'en suis quasiment or
presque sûr

**fairness** ['fɛənɪs] n (of trial etc) justice f, équité f;
(of person) sens m de la justice; **in all ~** en toute
justice

**fair play** n fair play m

**fair trade** n commerce m équitable

**fairway** ['fɛəweɪ] n (Golf) fairway m

**fairy** ['fɛərɪ] n fée f

**fairy godmother** n bonne fée

**fairy lights** npl (Brit) guirlande f électrique

**fairy tale** n conte m de fées

**faith** [feɪθ] n foi f; (trust) confiance f; (sect) culte
m, religion f; **to have ~ in sb/sth** avoir
confiance en qn/qch

**faithful** ['feɪθful] adj fidèle

**faithfully** ['feɪθfəlɪ] adv fidèlement; **yours ~**
(Brit: in letters) veuillez agréer l'expression de
mes salutations les plus distinguées

**faith healer** [-hiːləʳ] n guérisseur(-euse)

**fake** [feɪk] n (painting etc) faux m; (photo) trucage
m; (person) imposteur m ▷ adj faux (fausse) ▷ vt
(emotions) simuler; (painting) faire un faux de;
(photo) truquer; (story) fabriquer; **his illness is
a ~** sa maladie est une comédie or de la
simulation

**falcon** ['fɔːlkən] n faucon m

**Falkland Islands** ['fɔːlk</em>ənd-] npl: **the ~ les
Malouines** fpl, les îles fpl Falkland

**fall** [fɔːl] n chute f; (decrease) baisse f; (US:
autumn) automne m ▷ vi (pt **fell**, pp **-en** [fɛl,
'fɔːlən]) tomber; (price, temperature, dollar) baisser;
**falls** npl (waterfall) chute f d'eau, cascade f; **to ~
flat** (vi: on one's face) tomber de tout son long,
s'étaler; (joke) tomber à plat; (plan) échouer; **to
~ short of** (sb's expectations) ne pas répondre à; **a
~ of snow** (Brit) une chute de neige

▶ **fall apart** vi (object) tomber en morceaux; (inf:
emotionally) craquer

▶ **fall back** vi reculer, se retirer

▶ **fall back on** vt fus se rabattre sur; **to have
something to ~ back on** (money etc) avoir
quelque chose en réserve; (job etc) avoir une
solution de rechange

▶ **fall behind** vi prendre du retard

▶ **fall down** vi (person) tomber; (building)
s'effondrer, s'écrouler

▶ **fall for** vt fus (trick) se laisser prendre à; (person)
tomber amoureux(-euse) de

▶ **fall in** vi s'effondrer; (Mil) se mettre en rangs

▶ **fall in with** vt fus (sb's plans etc) accepter

▶ **fall off** vi tomber; (diminish) baisser, diminuer

▶ **fall out** vi (friends etc) se brouiller; (hair, teeth)
tomber

▶ **fall over** vi tomber (par terre)

▶ **fall through** vi (plan, project) tomber à l'eau

**fallacy** ['fæləsɪ] n erreur f, illusion f

**fallback** ['fɔːlbæk] adj: ~ **position** position f de
repli

**fallen** ['fɔːlən] pp of **fall**

**fallible** ['fæləbl] adj faillible

**fallopian tube** [fə'ləupɪən-] n (Anat) trompe f de
Fallope

**fallout** ['fɔːlaut] n retombées (radioactives)

**fallout shelter** n abri m anti-atomique

**fallow** ['fæləu] adj en jachère; en friche

**false** [fɔːls] adj faux (fausse); **under ~
pretences** sous un faux prétexte

**false alarm** n fausse alerte

**falsehood** ['fɔːlshud] n mensonge m

**falsely** ['fɔːlslɪ] adv (accuse) à tort

**false teeth** npl (Brit) fausses dents, dentier m

**falsify** ['fɔːlsɪfaɪ] vt falsifier; (accounts)
maquiller

**falter** ['fɔːltəʳ] vi chanceler, vaciller

**fame** [feɪm] n renommée f, renom m

**familiar** [fə'mɪlɪəʳ] adj familier(-ière); **to be ~
with sth** connaître qch; **to make o.s. ~ with
sth** se familiariser avec qch; **to be on ~ terms
with sb** bien connaître qn

**familiarity** [fəmɪlɪ'ærɪtɪ] n familiarité f

**familiarize** [fə'mɪlɪəraɪz] vt familiariser; **to ~
o.s. with** se familiariser avec

**family** ['fæmɪlɪ] n famille f

**family allowance** n (Brit) allocations familiales

**family business** n entreprise familiale

**family credit** n (Brit) complément familial

**family doctor** n médecin m de famille

**family life** n vie f de famille

**family man** (*irreg*) *n* père *m* de famille
**family planning** *n* planning familial
**family planning clinic** *n* centre *m* de planning familial
**family tree** *n* arbre *m* généalogique
**famine** ['fæmɪn] *n* famine *f*
**famished** ['fæmɪʃt] *adj* affamé(e); **I'm ~!** (*inf*) je meurs de faim!
**famous** ['feɪməs] *adj* célèbre
**famously** ['feɪməslɪ] *adv* (*get on*) fameusement, à merveille
**fan** [fæn] *n* (*folding*) éventail *m*; (*Elec*) ventilateur *m*; (*person*) fan *m*, admirateur(-trice); (*Sport*) supporter *m/f* ▷ *vt* éventer; (*fire, quarrel*) attiser
  ▶ **fan out** *vi* se déployer (en éventail)
**fanatic** [fə'nætɪk] *n* fanatique *m/f*
**fanatical** [fə'nætɪkl] *adj* fanatique
**fan belt** *n* courroie *f* de ventilateur
**fancied** ['fænsɪd] *adj* imaginaire
**fanciful** ['fænsɪful] *adj* fantaisiste
**fan club** *n* fan-club *m*
**fancy** ['fænsɪ] *n* (*whim*) fantaisie *f*, envie *f*; (*imagination*) imagination *f* ▷ *adj* (*luxury*) de luxe; (*elaborate: jewellery, packaging*) fantaisie *inv*; (*showy*) tape-à-l'œil *inv*; (*pretentious: words*) recherché(e) ▷ *vt* (*feel like, want*) avoir envie de; (*imagine*) imaginer; **to take a ~ to** se prendre d'affection pour; s'enticher de; **it took or caught my ~** ça m'a plu; **when the ~ takes him** quand ça lui prend; **to ~ that ...** se figurer *or* s'imaginer que ...; **he fancies her** elle lui plaît
**fancy dress** *n* déguisement *m*, travesti *m*
**fancy-dress ball** [fænsɪ'drɛs-] *n* bal masqué *or* costumé
**fancy goods** *npl* articles *mpl* (de) fantaisie
**fanfare** ['fænfɛəʳ] *n* fanfare *f* (*musique*)
**fanfold paper** ['fænfəuld-] *n* papier *m* à pliage accordéon
**fang** [fæŋ] *n* croc *m*; (*of snake*) crochet *m*
**fan heater** *n* (*Brit*) radiateur soufflant
**fanlight** ['fænlaɪt] *n* imposte *f*
**fanny** ['fænɪ] *n* (*Brit inf!*) chatte *f* (!); (*US inf*) cul *m* (!)
**fantasize** ['fæntəsaɪz] *vi* fantasmer
**fantastic** [fæn'tæstɪk] *adj* fantastique
**fantasy** ['fæntəsɪ] *n* imagination *f*, fantaisie *f*; (*unreality*) fantasme *m*
**fanzine** ['fænziːn] *n* fanzine *m*
**FAO** *n abbr* (= *Food and Agriculture Organization*) FAO *f*
**FAQ** *n abbr* (= *frequently asked question*) FAQ *f inv*, faq *f inv* ▷ *abbr* (= *free alongside quay*) FLQ
**far** [fɑːʳ] *adj* (*distant*) lointain(e), éloigné(e) ▷ *adv* loin; **the ~ side/end** l'autre côté/bout; **the ~ left/right** (*Pol*) l'extrême gauche *f*/droite *f*; **is it ~ to London?** est-ce qu'on est loin de Londres?; **it's not ~ (from here)** ce n'est pas loin (d'ici); **~ away, ~ off** au loin, dans le lointain; **~ better** beaucoup mieux; **~ from** loin de; **by ~** de loin, de beaucoup; **as ~ back as the 13th century** dès le 13e siècle; **go as ~ as the bridge** allez jusqu'au pont; **as ~ as I know** pour autant que

je sache; **how ~ is it to ...?** combien y a-t-il jusqu'à ...?; **as ~ as possible** dans la mesure du possible; **how ~ have you got with your work?** où en êtes-vous dans votre travail?
**faraway** ['fɑːrəweɪ] *adj* lointain(e); (*look*) absent(e)
**farce** [fɑːs] *n* farce *f*
**farcical** ['fɑːsɪkl] *adj* grotesque
**fare** [fɛəʳ] *n* (*on trains, buses*) prix *m* du billet; (*in taxi*) prix de la course; (*passenger in taxi*) client *m*; (*food*) table *f*, chère *f* ▷ *vi* se débrouiller; **half ~** demi-tarif; **full ~** plein tarif
**Far East** *n*: **the ~** l'Extrême-Orient *m*
**farewell** [fɛə'wɛl] *excl*, *n* adieu *m* ▷ *cpd* (*party etc*) d'adieux
**far-fetched** [fɑː'fɛtʃt] *adj* exagéré(e), poussé(e)
**farm** [fɑːm] *n* ferme *f* ▷ *vt* cultiver
  ▶ **farm out** *vt* (*work etc*) distribuer
**farmer** ['fɑːməʳ] *n* fermier(-ière), cultivateur(-trice)
**farmhand** ['fɑːmhænd] *n* ouvrier(-ière) agricole
**farmhouse** ['fɑːmhaus] *n* (maison *f* de) ferme *f*
**farming** ['fɑːmɪŋ] *n* agriculture *f*; (*of animals*) élevage *m*; **intensive ~** culture intensive
**farm labourer** *n* = **farmhand**
**farmland** ['fɑːmlænd] *n* terres cultivées *or* arables
**farm produce** *n* produits *mpl* agricoles
**farm worker** *n* = **farmhand**
**farmyard** ['fɑːmjɑːd] *n* cour *f* de ferme
**Faroe Islands** ['fɛərəu-] *npl*, **Faroes** ['fɛərəuz] *npl*: **the ~** les îles *fpl* Féroé *or* Faeroe
**far-reaching** [fɑː'riːtʃɪŋ] *adj* d'une grande portée
**far-sighted** ['fɑː'saɪtɪd] *adj* presbyte; (*fig*) prévoyant(e), qui voit loin
**fart** [fɑːt] (*inf!*) *n* pet *m* ▷ *vi* péter
**farther** ['fɑːðəʳ] *adv* plus loin ▷ *adj* plus éloigné(e), plus lointain(e)
**farthest** ['fɑːðɪst] *superlative of* **far**
**FAS** *abbr* (*Brit*: = *free alongside ship*) FLB
**fascia** ['feɪʃə] *n* (*Aut*) (garniture *f* du) tableau *m* de bord
**fascinate** ['fæsɪneɪt] *vt* fasciner, captiver
**fascinating** ['fæsɪneɪtɪŋ] *adj* fascinant(e)
**fascination** [fæsɪ'neɪʃən] *n* fascination *f*
**fascism** ['fæʃɪzəm] *n* fascisme *m*
**fascist** ['fæʃɪst] *adj*, *n* fasciste *m/f*
**fashion** ['fæʃən] *n* mode *f*; (*manner*) façon *f*, manière *f* ▷ *vt* façonner; **in ~** à la mode; **out of ~** démodé(e); **in the Greek ~** à la grecque; **after a ~** (*finish, manage etc*) tant bien que mal
**fashionable** ['fæʃnəbl] *adj* à la mode
**fashion designer** *n* (grand(e)) couturier(-ière)
**fashionista** [fœʃə'nɪstə] *n* fashionista *mf*
**fashion show** *n* défilé *m* de mannequins *or* de mode
**fast** [fɑːst] *adj* rapide; (*clock*): **to be ~** avancer; (*dye, colour*) grand *or* bon teint *inv* ▷ *adv* vite, rapidement; (*stuck, held*) solidement ▷ *n* jeûne *m* ▷ *vi* jeûner; **my watch is 5 minutes ~** ma montre avance de 5 minutes; **~ asleep**

profondément endormi; **as ~ as I can** aussi vite
que je peux; **to make a boat ~** (*Brit*) amarrer un
bateau

**fasten** ['fɑːsn] *vt* attacher, fixer; (*coat*) attacher,
fermer ▷ *vi* se fermer, s'attacher
▶ **fasten on, fasten upon** *vt fus* (*idea*) se
cramponner à

**fastener** ['fɑːsnəʳ], **fastening** ['fɑːsnɪŋ] *n*
fermeture *f*, attache *f*; (*Brit: zip fastener*)
fermeture éclair® *inv or* à glissière

**fast food** *n* fast food *m*, restauration *f* rapide

**fastidious** [fæs'tɪdɪəs] *adj* exigeant(e), difficile

**fast lane** *n* (*Aut: in Britain*) voie *f* de droite

**fat** [fæt] *adj* gros(se) ▷ *n* graisse *f*; (*on meat*) gras
*m*; (*for cooking*) matière grasse; **to live off the ~
of the land** vivre grassement

**fatal** ['feɪtl] *adj* (*mistake*) fatal(e); (*injury*)
mortel(le)

**fatalism** ['feɪtlɪzəm] *n* fatalisme *m*

**fatality** [fə'tælɪtɪ] *n* (*road death etc*) victime *f*,
décès *m*

**fatally** ['feɪtəlɪ] *adv* fatalement; (*injured*)
mortellement

**fate** [feɪt] *n* destin *m*; (*of person*) sort *m*; **to meet
one's ~** trouver la mort

**fated** ['feɪtɪd] *adj* (*person*) condamné(e); (*project*)
voué(e) à l'échec

**fateful** ['feɪtful] *adj* fatidique

**fat-free** ['fæt'friː] *adj* sans matières grasses

**father** ['fɑːðəʳ] *n* père *m*

**Father Christmas** *n* le Père Noël

**fatherhood** ['fɑːðəhud] *n* paternité *f*

**father-in-law** ['fɑːðərɪnlɔː] *n* beau-père *m*

**fatherland** ['fɑːðəlænd] *n* (*mère f*) patrie *f*

**fatherly** ['fɑːðəlɪ] *adj* paternel(le)

**fathom** ['fæðəm] *n* brasse *f* (= 1828 *mm*) ▷ *vt*
(*mystery*) sonder, pénétrer

**fatigue** [fə'tiːg] *n* fatigue *f*; (*Mil*) corvée *f*; **metal
~ fatigue** du métal

**fatness** ['fætnɪs] *n* corpulence *f*, grosseur *f*

**fatten** ['fætn] *vt, vi* engraisser

**fattening** ['fætnɪŋ] *adj* (*food*) qui fait grossir;
**chocolate is ~** le chocolat fait grossir

**fatty** ['fætɪ] *adj* (*food*) gras(se) ▷ *n* (*inf*) gros
(grosse)

**fatuous** ['fætjuəs] *adj* stupide

**faucet** ['fɔːsɪt] *n* (*US*) robinet *m*

**fault** [fɔːlt] *n* faute *f*; (*defect*) défaut *m*; (*Geo*)
faille *f* ▷ *vt* trouver des défauts à, prendre en
défaut; **it's my ~** c'est de ma faute; **to find ~
with** trouver à redire *or* à critiquer à; **at ~**
fautif(-ive), coupable; **to a ~** à l'excès

**faultless** ['fɔːltlɪs] *adj* impeccable; irréprochable

**faulty** ['fɔːltɪ] *adj* défectueux(-euse)

**fauna** ['fɔːnə] *n* faune *f*

**faux pas** ['fəu'pɑː] *n* impair *m*, bévue *f*, gaffe *f*

**favour**, (*US*) **favor** ['feɪvəʳ] *n* faveur *f*; (*help*)
service *m* ▷ *vt* (*proposition*) être en faveur de;
(*pupil etc*) favoriser; (*team, horse*) donner
gagnant; **to do sb a ~** rendre un service à qn; **in
~ of** en faveur de; **to be in ~ of sth/of doing sth**
être partisan de qch/de faire qch; **to find ~**

**with sb** trouver grâce aux yeux de qn

**favourable**, (*US*) **favorable** ['feɪvrəbl] *adj*
favorable; (*price*) avantageux(-euse)

**favourably**, (*US*) **favorably** ['feɪvrəblɪ] *adv*
favorablement

**favourite**, (*US*) **favorite** ['feɪvrɪt] *adj, n*
favori(te)

**favouritism**, (*US*) **favoritism** ['feɪvrɪtɪzəm] *n*
favoritisme *m*

**fawn** [fɔːn] *n* (*deer*) faon *m* ▷ *adj* (*also:* **fawn-
coloured**) fauve ▷ *vi:* **to ~ (up)on** flatter
servilement

**fax** [fæks] *n* (*document*) télécopie *f*; (*machine*)
télécopieur *m* ▷ *vt* envoyer par télécopie

**FBI** *n abbr* (*US: = Federal Bureau of Investigation*) FBI *m*

**FCC** *n abbr* (*US*) = **Federal Communications
Commission**

**FCO** *n abbr* (*Brit: = Foreign and Commonwealth Office*)
ministère des Affaires étrangères et du Commonwealth

**FD** *n abbr* (*US*) = **fire department**

**FDA** *n abbr* (*US: = Food and Drug Administration*) office
de contrôle des produits pharmaceutiques et alimentaires

**FE** *n abbr* = **further education**

**fear** [fɪəʳ] *n* crainte *f*, peur *f* ▷ *vt* craindre ▷ *vi:* **to
~ for** craindre pour; **to ~ that** craindre que; **~ of
heights** vertige *m*; **for ~ of** de peur que + *sub or*
de + *infinitive*

**fearful** ['fɪəful] *adj* craintif(-ive); (*sight, noise*)
affreux(-euse), épouvantable; **to be ~ of** avoir
peur de, craindre

**fearfully** ['fɪəfəlɪ] *adv* (*timidly*) craintivement;
(*inf: very*) affreusement

**fearless** ['fɪəlɪs] *adj* intrépide, sans peur

**fearsome** ['fɪəsəm] *adj* (*opponent*) redoutable;
(*sight*) épouvantable

**feasibility** [fiːzə'bɪlɪtɪ] *n* (*of plan*) possibilité *f* de
réalisation, faisabilité *f*

**feasibility study** *n* étude *f* de faisabilité

**feasible** ['fiːzəbl] *adj* faisable, réalisable

**feast** [fiːst] *n* festin *m*, banquet *m*; (*Rel: also:*
**feast day**) fête *f* ▷ *vi* festoyer; **to ~ on** se régaler
de

**feat** [fiːt] *n* exploit *m*, prouesse *f*

**feather** ['fɛðəʳ] *n* plume *f* ▷ *vt:* **to ~ one's nest**
(*fig*) faire sa pelote ▷ *cpd* (*bed etc*) de plumes

**feather-weight** ['fɛðəweɪt] *n* poids *m* plume *inv*

**feature** ['fiːtʃəʳ] *n* caractéristique *f*; (*article*)
chronique *f*, rubrique *f* ▷ *vt* (*film*) avoir pour
vedette(s) ▷ *vi* figurer (en bonne place);
**features** *npl* (*of face*) traits *mpl*; **a (special) ~ on
sth/sb** un reportage sur qch/qn; **it ~d
prominently in ...** cela a figuré en bonne place
sur *or* dans ...

**feature film** *n* long métrage

**featureless** ['fiːtʃəlɪs] *adj* anonyme, sans traits
distinctifs

**Feb.** *abbr* (= *February*) fév

**February** ['fɛbruərɪ] *n* février *m*; *for phrases see
also* **July**

**feces** ['fiːsiːz] *npl* (*US*) = **faeces**

**feckless** ['fɛklɪs] *adj* inepte

**Fed** *abbr* (*US*) = **federal; federation**

**fed** [fɛd] *pt, pp of* **feed**

**Fed.** [fɛd] *n abbr* (*US inf*) = **Federal Reserve Board**

**federal** ['fɛdərəl] *adj* fédéral(e)

**Federal Reserve Board** *n* (*US*) *organe de contrôle de la banque centrale américaine*

**Federal Trade Commission** *n* (*US*) *organisme de protection contre les pratiques commerciales abusives*

**federation** [fɛdə'reɪʃən] *n* fédération *f*

**fed up** [fɛd'ʌp] *adj*: **to be ~ (with)** en avoir marre *or* plein le dos (de)

**fee** [fi:] *n* rémunération *f*; (*of doctor, lawyer*) honoraires *mpl*; (*of school, college etc*) frais *mpl de* scolarité; (*for examination*) droits *mpl*; **entrance/ membership ~** droit d'entrée/d'inscription; **for a small ~** pour une somme modique

**feeble** ['fi:bl] *adj* faible; (*attempt, excuse*) pauvre; (*joke*) piteux(-euse)

**feeble-minded** ['fi:bl'maɪndɪd] *adj* faible d'esprit

**feed** [fi:d] *n* (*of baby*) tétée *f*; (*of animal*) nourriture *f*, pâture *f*; (*on printer*) mécanisme *m* d'alimentation ▷ *vt* (*pt, pp* **fed** [fɛd]) (*person*) nourrir; (*Brit: baby: breastfeed*) allaiter; (*: with bottle*) donner le biberon à; (*horse etc*) donner à manger à; (*machine*) alimenter; (*data etc*): **to ~ sth into** enregistrer qch dans
► **feed back** *vt* (*results*) donner en retour
► **feed on** *vt fus* se nourrir de

**feedback** ['fi:dbæk] *n* (*Elec*) effet *m* Larsen; (*from person*) réactions *fpl*

**feeder** ['fi:dəʳ] *n* (*bib*) bavette *f*

**feeding bottle** ['fi:dɪŋ-] *n* (*Brit*) biberon *m*

**feel** [fi:l] *n* (*sensation*) sensation *f*; (*impression*) impression *f* ▷ *vt* (*pt, pp* **felt** [fɛlt]) (*touch*) toucher; (*explore*) tâter, palper; (*cold, pain*) sentir; (*grief, anger*) ressentir, éprouver; (*think, believe*): **to ~ (that)** trouver que; **I ~ that you ought to do it** il me semble que vous devriez le faire; **to ~ hungry/cold** avoir faim/froid; **to ~ lonely/ better** se sentir seul/mieux; **I don't ~ well** je ne me sens pas bien; **to ~ sorry for** avoir pitié de; **it ~s soft** c'est doux au toucher; **it ~s colder here** je trouve qu'il fait plus froid ici; **it ~s like velvet** on dirait du velours, ça ressemble au velours; **to ~ like** (*want*) avoir envie de; **to ~ about** *or* **around** fouiller, tâtonner; **to get the ~ of sth** (*fig*) s'habituer à qch

**feeler** ['fi:ləʳ] *n* (*of insect*) antenne *f*; (*fig*): **to put out a ~** *or* **~s** tâter le terrain

**feeling** ['fi:lɪŋ] *n* (*physical*) sensation *f*; (*emotion, impression*) sentiment *m*; **to hurt sb's ~s** froisser qn; **~s ran high about it** cela a déchaîné les passions; **what are your ~s about the matter?** quel est votre sentiment sur cette question?; **my ~ is that ...** j'estime que ...; **I have a ~ that ...** j'ai l'impression que ...

**fee-paying school** ['fi:peɪɪŋ-] *n* établissement (d'enseignement) privé

**feet** [fi:t] *npl of* **foot**

**feign** [feɪn] *vt* feindre, simuler

**felicitous** [fɪ'lɪsɪtəs] *adj* heureux(-euse)

**fell** [fɛl] *pt of* **fall** ▷ *vt* (*tree*) abattre ▷ *n* (*Brit: mountain*) montagne *f*; (*: moorland*): **the ~s** la lande ▷ *adj*: **with one ~ blow** d'un seul coup

**fellow** ['fɛləu] *n* type *m*; (*comrade*) compagnon *m*; (*of learned society*) membre *m*; (*of university*) universitaire *m/f* (*membre du conseil*) ▷ *cpd*: **their ~ prisoners/students** leurs camarades prisonniers/étudiants; **his ~ workers** ses collègues *mpl* (de travail)

**fellow citizen** *n* concitoyen(ne)

**fellow countryman** (*irreg*) *n* compatriote *m*

**fellow feeling** *n* sympathie *f*

**fellow men** *npl* semblables *mpl*

**fellowship** ['fɛləuʃɪp] *n* (*society*) association *f*; (*comradeship*) amitié *f*, camaraderie *f*; (*Scol*) *sorte de bourse universitaire*

**fellow traveller** *n* compagnon (compagne) de route; (*Pol*) communisant(e)

**fell-walking** ['fɛlwɔ:kɪŋ] *n* (*Brit*) randonnée *f* en montagne

**felon** ['fɛlən] *n* (*Law*) criminel(le)

**felony** ['fɛlənɪ] *n* crime *m*, forfait *m*

**felt** [fɛlt] *pt, pp of* **feel** ▷ *n* feutre *m*

**felt-tip** ['fɛlttɪp-] *n* (*also:* **felt-tip pen**) stylo-feutre *m*

**female** ['fi:meɪl] *n* (*Zool*) femelle *f*; (*pej: woman*) bonne femme ▷ *adj* (*Biol, Elec*) femelle; (*sex, character*) féminin(e); (*vote etc*) des femmes; (*child etc*) du sexe féminin; **male and ~ students** étudiants et étudiantes

**female impersonator** *n* (*Theat*) travesti *m*

**feminine** ['fɛmɪnɪn] *adj* féminin(e) ▷ *n* féminin *m*

**femininity** [fɛmɪ'nɪnɪtɪ] *n* féminité *f*

**feminism** ['fɛmɪnɪzəm] *n* féminisme *m*

**feminist** ['fɛmɪnɪst] *n* féministe *m/f*

**fen** [fɛn] *n* (*Brit*): **the F~s** les plaines *fpl* du Norfolk (*anciennement marécageuses*)

**fence** [fɛns] *n* barrière *f*; (*Sport*) obstacle *m*; (*inf: person*) receleur(-euse) ▷ *vt* (*also:* **fence in**) clôturer ▷ *vi* faire de l'escrime; **to sit on the ~** (*fig*) ne pas se mouiller

**fencing** ['fɛnsɪŋ] *n* (*sport*) escrime *m*

**fend** [fɛnd] *vi*: **to ~ for o.s.** se débrouiller (tout seul)
► **fend off** *vt* (*attack etc*) parer; (*questions*) éluder

**fender** ['fɛndəʳ] *n* garde-feu *m inv*; (*on boat*) défense *f*; (*US: of car*) aile *f*

**fennel** ['fɛnl] *n* fenouil *m*

**ferment** *vi* [fə'mɛnt] fermenter ▷ *n* ['fə:mɛnt] (*fig*) agitation *f*, effervescence *f*

**fermentation** [fə:mɛn'teɪʃən] *n* fermentation *f*

**fern** [fə:n] *n* fougère *f*

**ferocious** [fə'rəuʃəs] *adj* féroce

**ferocity** [fə'rɔsɪtɪ] *n* férocité *f*

**ferret** ['fɛrɪt] *n* furet *m*
► **ferret about, ferret around** *vi* fureter
► **ferret out** *vt* dénicher

**ferry** ['fɛrɪ] *n* (*small*) bac *m*; (*large: also:* **ferryboat**) ferry(-boat *m*) ▷ *vt* transporter; **to ~ sth/sb across** *or* **over** faire traverser qch/qn

**ferryman** ['fɛrɪmən] (*irreg*) *n* passeur *m*

**fertile** ['fə:taɪl] *adj* fertile; (*Biol*) fécond(e); **~ period** période *f* de fécondité
**fertility** [fə'tɪlɪtɪ] *n* fertilité *f*; fécondité *f*
**fertility drug** *n* médicament *m* contre la stérilité
**fertilize** ['fə:tɪlaɪz] *vt* fertiliser; (*Biol*) féconder
**fertilizer** ['fə:tɪlaɪzə'] *n* engrais *m*
**fervent** ['fə:vənt] *adj* fervent(e), ardent(e)
**fervour**, (*US*)**fervor** ['fə:və'] *n* ferveur *f*
**fester** ['fɛstə'] *vi* suppurer
**festival** ['fɛstɪvəl] *n* (*Rel*) fête *f*; (*Art, Mus*) festival *m*
**festive** ['fɛstɪv] *adj* de fête; **the ~ season** (*Brit: Christmas*) la période des fêtes
**festivities** [fɛs'tɪvɪtɪz] *npl* réjouissances *fpl*
**festoon** [fɛs'tu:n] *vt*: **to ~ with** orner de
**fetch** [fɛtʃ] *vt* aller chercher; (*Brit: sell for*) rapporter; **how much did it ~?** ça a atteint quel prix?
  ▸ **fetch up** *vi* (*Brit*) se retrouver
**fetching** ['fɛtʃɪŋ] *adj* charmant(e)
**fête** [feɪt] *n* fête *f*, kermesse *f*
**fetid** ['fɛtɪd] *adj* fétide
**fetish** ['fɛtɪʃ] *n* fétiche *m*
**fetter** ['fɛtə'] *vt* entraver
**fetters** ['fɛtəz] *npl* chaînes *fpl*
**fettle** ['fɛtl] *n* (*Brit*): **in fine ~** en bonne forme
**fetus** ['fi:təs] *n* (*US*) = **foetus**
**feud** [fju:d] *n* querelle *f*, dispute *f* ▸ *vi* se quereller, se disputer; **a family ~** une querelle de famille
**feudal** ['fju:dl] *adj* féodal(e)
**feudalism** ['fju:dlɪzəm] *n* féodalité *f*
**fever** ['fi:və'] *n* fièvre *f*; **he has a ~** il a de la fièvre
**feverish** ['fi:vərɪʃ] *adj* fiévreux(-euse), fébrile
**few** [fju:] *adj* (*not many*) peu de ▸ *pron* peu; **~ succeed** il y en a peu qui réussissent, (bien) peu réussissent; **they were ~** ils étaient peu (nombreux), il y en avait peu; **a ~** (*as adj*) quelques; (*as pron*) quelques-uns(-unes); **I know a ~** j'en connais quelques-uns; **quite a ~ ...** (*adj*) un certain nombre de ..., pas mal de ...; **in the next ~ days** dans les jours qui viennent; **in the past ~ days** ces derniers jours; **every ~ days/months** tous les deux ou trois jours/mois; **a ~ more ...** encore quelques ..., quelques ... de plus
**fewer** ['fju:ə'] *adj* moins de ▸ *pron* moins; **they are ~ now** il y en a moins maintenant, ils sont moins (nombreux) maintenant
**fewest** ['fju:ɪst] *adj* le moins nombreux
**FFA** *n abbr* = **Future Farmers of America**
**FH** *abbr* (*Brit*) = **fire hydrant**
**FHA** *n abbr* (*US*: = *Federal Housing Administration*) *office fédéral du logement*
**fiancé** [fɪ'ɑ̃:ŋseɪ] *n* fiancé *m*
**fiancée** [fɪ'ɑ̃:ŋseɪ] *n* fiancée *f*
**fiasco** [fɪ'æskəu] *n* fiasco *m*
**fib** [fɪb] *n* bobard *m*
**fibre**, (*US*)**fiber** ['faɪbə'] *n* fibre *f*
**fibreboard**, (*US*)**fiberboard** ['faɪbəbɔ:d] *n* panneau *m* de fibres
**fibreglass**, (*US*)**Fiberglass®** ['faɪbəgla:s] *n*

fibre *f* de verre
**fibrositis** [faɪbrə'saɪtɪs] *n* aponévrosite *f*
**FICA** *n abbr* (*US*) = **Federal Insurance Contributions Act**
**fickle** ['fɪkl] *adj* inconstant(e), volage, capricieux(-euse)
**fiction** ['fɪkʃən] *n* romans *mpl*, littérature *f* romanesque; (*invention*) fiction *f*
**fictional** ['fɪkʃənl] *adj* fictif(-ive)
**fictionalize** ['fɪkʃnəlaɪz] *vt* romancer
**fictitious** [fɪk'tɪʃəs] *adj* fictif(-ive), imaginaire
**fiddle** ['fɪdl] *n* (*Mus*) violon *m*; (*cheating*) combine *f*; escroquerie *f* ▸ *vt* (*Brit: accounts*) falsifier, maquiller; **tax ~** fraude fiscale, combine *f* pour échapper au fisc; **to work a ~** traficoter
  ▸ **fiddle with** *vt fus* tripoter
**fiddler** ['fɪdlə'] *n* violoniste *m/f*
**fiddly** ['fɪdlɪ] *adj* (*task*) minutieux(-euse)
**fidelity** [fɪ'delɪtɪ] *n* fidélité *f*
**fidget** ['fɪdʒɪt] *vi* se trémousser, remuer
**fidgety** ['fɪdʒɪtɪ] *adj* agité(e), qui a la bougeotte
**fiduciary** [fɪ'dju:ʃɪərɪ] *n* agent *m* fiduciaire
**field** [fi:ld] *n* champ *m*; (*fig*) domaine *m*, champ; (*Sport: ground*) terrain *m*; (*Comput*) champ, zone *f*; **to lead the ~** (*Sport, Comm*) dominer; **the children had a ~ day** (*fig*) c'était un grand jour pour les enfants
**field glasses** *npl* jumelles *fpl*
**field hospital** *n* antenne chirurgicale
**field marshal** *n* maréchal *m*
**fieldwork** ['fi:ldwə:k] *n* travaux *mpl* pratiques (*or* recherches *fpl*) sur le terrain
**fiend** [fi:nd] *n* démon *m*
**fiendish** ['fi:ndɪʃ] *adj* diabolique
**fierce** [fɪəs] *adj* (*look, animal*) féroce, sauvage; (*wind, attack, person*) (très) violent(e); (*fighting, enemy*) acharné(e)
**fiery** ['faɪərɪ] *adj* ardent(e), brûlant(e), fougueux(-euse)
**FIFA** ['fi:fə] *n abbr* (= *Fédération Internationale de Football Association*) FIFA *f*
**fifteen** [fɪf'ti:n] *num* quinze
**fifteenth** [fɪf'ti:nθ] *num* quinzième
**fifth** [fɪfθ] *num* cinquième
**fiftieth** ['fɪftɪɪθ] *num* cinquantième
**fifty** ['fɪftɪ] *num* cinquante
**fifty-fifty** ['fɪftɪ'fɪftɪ] *adv* moitié-moitié; **to share ~ with sb** partager moitié-moitié avec qn ▸ *adj*: **to have a ~ chance (of success)** avoir une chance sur deux (de réussir)
**fig** [fɪg] *n* figue *f*
**fight** [faɪt] (*pt, pp* **fought** [fɔ:t]) *n* (*between persons*) bagarre *f*; (*argument*) dispute *f*; (*Mil*) combat *m*; (*against cancer etc*) lutte *f* ▸ *vt* se battre contre; (*cancer, alcoholism, emotion*) combattre, lutter contre; (*election*) se présenter à; (*Law: case*) défendre ▸ *vi* se battre; (*argue*) se disputer; (*fig*): **to ~ (for/against)** lutter (pour/contre)
  ▸ **fight back** *vi* rendre les coups; (*after illness*) reprendre le dessus ▸ *vt* (*tears*) réprimer
  ▸ **fight off** *vt* repousser; (*disease, sleep, urge*) lutter contre

**fighter** ['faɪtər] n lutteur m; (fig: plane)
chasseur m
**fighter pilot** n pilote m de chasse
**fighting** ['faɪtɪŋ] n combats mpl; (brawls)
bagarres fpl
**figment** ['fɪgmənt] n: **a ~ of the imagination**
une invention
**figurative** ['fɪgjurətɪv] adj figuré(e)
**figure** ['fɪgər] n (Drawing, Geom) figure f; (number)
chiffre m; (body, outline) silhouette f; (person's
shape) ligne f, formes fpl; (person) personnage m
▷ vt (US: think) supposer ▷ vi (appear) figurer;
(US: make sense) s'expliquer; **public ~**
personnalité f; **~ of speech** figure f de
rhétorique
  ▶ **figure on** vt fus (US): **to ~ on doing** compter
  faire
  ▶ **figure out** vt (understand) arriver à
  comprendre; (plan) calculer
**figurehead** ['fɪgəhɛd] n (Naut) figure f de proue;
(pej) prête-nom m
**figure skating** n figures imposées (en patinage),
patinage m artistique
**Fiji** ['fi:dʒi:] n, **Fiji Islands** npl (îles fpl) Fi(d)ji fpl
**filament** ['fɪləmənt] n filament m
**filch** [fɪltʃ] vt (inf: steal) voler, chiper
**file** [faɪl] n (tool) lime f; (dossier) dossier m; (folder)
dossier, chemise f; (: binder) classeur m; (Comput)
fichier m; (row) file f ▷ vt (nails, wood) limer;
(papers) classer; (Law: claim) faire enregistrer;
déposer ▷ vi: **to ~ in/out** entrer/sortir l'un
derrière l'autre; **to ~ past** défiler devant; **to ~ a
suit against sb** (Law) intenter un procès à qn
**file name** n (Comput) nom m de fichier
**filibuster** ['fɪlɪbʌstər] (esp US Pol) n (also:
**filibusterer**) obstructionniste m/f ▷ vi faire de
l'obstructionnisme
**filing** ['faɪlɪŋ] n (travaux mpl de) classement m;
**filings** npl limaille f
**filing cabinet** n classeur m (meuble)
**filing clerk** n documentaliste m/f
**Filipino** [fɪlɪ'pi:nəu] adj philippin(e) ▷ n (person)
Philippin(e); (Ling) tagalog m
**fill** [fɪl] vt remplir; (vacancy) pourvoir à ▷ n: **to
eat one's ~** manger à sa faim; **to ~ with**
remplir de
  ▶ **fill in** vt (hole) boucher; (form) remplir; (details,
  report) compléter
  ▶ **fill out** vt (form, receipt) remplir
  ▶ **fill up** vt remplir ▷ vi (Aut) faire le plein; **~ it
  up, please** (Aut) le plein, s'il vous plaît
**fillet** ['fɪlɪt] n filet m ▷ vt préparer en filets
**fillet steak** n filet m de bœuf, tournedos m
**filling** ['fɪlɪŋ] n (Culin) garniture f, farce f; (for
tooth) plombage m
**filling station** n station-service f, station f
d'essence
**fillip** ['fɪlɪp] n coup m de fouet (fig)
**filly** ['fɪlɪ] n pouliche f
**film** [fɪlm] n film m; (Phot) pellicule f, film; (of
powder, liquid) couche f, pellicule ▷ vt (scene)
filmer ▷ vi tourner; **I'd like a 36-exposure ~** je

voudrais une pellicule de 36 poses
**film star** n vedette f de cinéma
**filmstrip** ['fɪlmstrɪp] n (film m pour) projection f
fixe
**film studio** n studio m (de cinéma)
**Filofax**® ['faɪləufæks] n Filofax® m
**filter** ['fɪltər] n filtre m ▷ vt filtrer
**filter coffee** n café m filtre
**filter lane** n (Brit Aut: at traffic lights) voie f de
dégagement; (: on motorway) voie f de sortie
**filter tip** n bout m filtre
**filth** [fɪlθ] n saleté f
**filthy** ['fɪlθɪ] adj sale, dégoûtant(e); (language)
ordurier(-ère), grossier(-ière)
**fin** [fɪn] n (of fish) nageoire f; (of shark) aileron m;
(of diver) palme f
**final** ['faɪnl] adj final(e), dernier(-ière); (decision,
answer) définitif(-ive) ▷ n (Brit Sport) finale f;
**finals** npl (Scol) examens mpl de dernière année;
(US Sport) finale f; **~ demand** (on invoice etc)
dernier rappel
**finale** [fɪ'nɑ:lɪ] n finale m
**finalist** ['faɪnəlɪst] n (Sport) finaliste m/f
**finalize** ['faɪnəlaɪz] vt mettre au point
**finally** ['faɪnəlɪ] adv (eventually) enfin,
finalement; (lastly) en dernier lieu; (irrevocably)
définitivement
**finance** [faɪ'næns] n finance f ▷ vt financer;
**finances** npl finances fpl
**financial** [faɪ'nænʃəl] adj financier(-ière); **~
statement** bilan m, exercice financier
**financially** [faɪ'nænʃəlɪ] adv financièrement
**financial year** n année f budgétaire
**financier** [faɪ'nænsɪər] n financier m
**find** [faɪnd] vt (pt, pp **found** [faund]) trouver; (lost
object) retrouver ▷ n trouvaille f, découverte f; **to
~ sb guilty** (Law) déclarer qn coupable; **to ~
(some) difficulty in doing sth** avoir du mal à
faire qch
  ▶ **find out** vt se renseigner sur; (truth, secret)
  découvrir; (person) démasquer ▷ vi: **to ~ out
  about** (make enquiries) se renseigner sur; (by
  chance) apprendre
**findings** ['faɪndɪŋz] npl (Law) conclusions fpl,
verdict m; (of report) constatations fpl
**fine** [faɪn] adj (weather) beau (belle); (excellent)
excellent(e); (thin, subtle, not coarse) fin(e);
(acceptable) bien inv ▷ adv (well) très bien; (small)
fin, finement ▷ n (Law) amende f;
contravention f ▷ vt (Law) condamner à une
amende; donner une contravention à; **he's ~** il
va bien; **the weather is ~** il fait beau; **you're
doing ~** c'est bien, vous vous débrouillez bien;
**to cut it ~** calculer un peu juste
**fine arts** npl beaux-arts mpl
**fine print** n: **the ~** ce qui est imprimé en tout
petit
**finery** ['faɪnərɪ] n parure f
**finesse** [fɪ'nɛs] n finesse f, élégance f
**fine-tooth comb** ['faɪntu:θ-] n: **to go through
sth with a ~** (fig) passer qch au peigne fin or au
crible

**finger** ['fɪŋgəʳ] *n* doigt *m* ▷ *vt* palper, toucher; **index ~ index** *m*

**fingernail** ['fɪŋgəneɪl] *n* ongle *m* (de la main)

**fingerprint** ['fɪŋgəprɪnt] *n* empreinte digitale ▷ *vt* (*person*) prendre les empreintes digitales de

**fingerstall** ['fɪŋgəstɔːl] *n* doigtier *m*

**fingertip** ['fɪŋgətɪp] *n* bout *m* du doigt; (*fig*): **to have sth at one's ~s** avoir qch à sa disposition; (*knowledge*) savoir qch sur le bout du doigt

**finicky** ['fɪnɪkɪ] *adj* tatillon(ne), méticuleux(-euse), minutieux(-euse)

**finish** ['fɪnɪʃ] *n* fin *f*; (*Sport*) arrivée *f*; (*polish etc*) finition *f* ▷ *vt* finir, terminer ▷ *vi* finir, se terminer; (*session*) s'achever; **to ~ doing sth** finir de faire qch; **to ~ third** arriver *or* terminer troisième; **when does the show ~?** quand est-ce que le spectacle se termine?

▶ **finish off** *vt* finir, terminer; (*kill*) achever

▶ **finish up** *vi, vt* finir

**finishing line** ['fɪnɪʃɪŋ-] *n* ligne *f* d'arrivée

**finishing school** ['fɪnɪʃɪŋ-] *n* institution privée (*pour jeunes filles*)

**finite** ['faɪnaɪt] *adj* fini(e); (*verb*) conjugué(e)

**Finland** ['fɪnlənd] *n* Finlande *f*

**Finn** [fɪn] *n* Finnois(e), Finlandais(e)

**Finnish** ['fɪnɪʃ] *adj* finnois(e), finlandais(e) ▷ *n* (*Ling*) finnois *m*

**fiord** [fjɔːd] *n* fjord *m*

**fir** [fəːʳ] *n* sapin *m*

**fire** ['faɪəʳ] *n* feu *m*; (*accidental*) incendie *m*; (*heater*) radiateur *m* ▷ *vt* (*discharge*): **to ~ a gun** tirer un coup de feu; (*fig: interest*) enflammer, animer; (*inf: dismiss*) mettre à la porte, renvoyer ▷ *vi* (*shoot*) tirer, faire feu ▷ *cpd*: **~ hazard, ~ risk: that's a ~ hazard** *or* **risk** cela présente un risque d'incendie; **~! au feu!; on ~ en feu; to set ~ to sth, set sth on ~** mettre le feu à qch; **insured against ~** assuré contre l'incendie

**fire alarm** *n* avertisseur *m* d'incendie

**firearm** ['faɪərɑːm] *n* arme *f* à feu

**fire brigade** *n* (*régiment m de sapeurs-*) pompiers *mpl*

**fire chief** *n* (*US*) = **fire master**

**fire department** *n* (*US*) = **fire brigade**

**fire door** *n* porte *f* coupe-feu

**fire engine** *n* (*Brit*) pompe *f* à incendie

**fire escape** *n* escalier *m* de secours

**fire exit** *n* issue *f* *or* sortie *f* de secours

**fire extinguisher** *n* extincteur *m*

**fireguard** ['faɪəgɑːd] *n* (*Brit*) garde-feu *m inv*

**fire insurance** *n* assurance *f* incendie

**fireman** (*irreg*) ['faɪəmən] *n* pompier *m*

**fire master** *n* (*Brit*) capitaine *m* des pompiers

**fireplace** ['faɪəpleɪs] *n* cheminée *f*

**fireproof** ['faɪəpruːf] *adj* ignifuge

**fire regulations** *npl* consignes *fpl* en cas d'incendie

**fire screen** *n* (*decorative*) écran *m* de cheminée; (*for protection*) garde-feu *m inv*

**fireside** ['faɪəsaɪd] *n* foyer *m*, coin *m* du feu

**fire station** *n* caserne *f* de pompiers

**fire truck** *n* (*US*) = **fire engine**

**firewall** ['faɪəwɔːl] *n* (*Internet*) pare-feu *m*

**firewood** ['faɪəwud] *n* bois *m* de chauffage

**fireworks** ['faɪəwəːks] *npl* (*display*) feu(x) *m(pl)* d'artifice

**firing** ['faɪərɪŋ] *n* (*Mil*) feu *m*, tir *m*

**firing squad** *n* peloton *m* d'exécution

**firm** [fəːm] *adj* ferme ▷ *n* compagnie *f*, firme *f*; **it is my ~ belief that ...** je crois fermement que ...

**firmly** ['fəːmlɪ] *adv* fermement

**firmness** ['fəːmnɪs] *n* fermeté *f*

**first** [fəːst] *adj* premier(-ière) ▷ *adv* (*before other people*) le premier, la première; (*before other things*) en premier, d'abord; (*when listing reasons etc*) en premier lieu, premièrement; (*in the beginning*) au début ▷ *n* (*person: in race*) premier(-ière); (*Brit Scol*) mention *f* très bien; (*Aut*) première *f*; **the ~ of January** le premier janvier; **at ~** au commencement, au début; **~ of all** tout d'abord, pour commencer; **in the ~ instance** en premier lieu; **I'll do it ~ thing tomorrow** je le ferai tout de suite demain matin

**first aid** *n* premiers secours *or* soins

**first-aid kit** [fəːst'eɪd-] *n* trousse *f* à pharmacie

**first-class** ['fəːst'klɑːs] *adj* (*ticket etc*) de première classe; (*excellent*) excellent(e), exceptionnel(le); (*post*) en tarif prioritaire

**first-class mail** *n* courrier *m* rapide

**first-hand** ['fəːst'hænd] *adj* de première main

**first lady** *n* (*US*) femme *f* du président

**firstly** ['fəːstlɪ] *adv* premièrement, en premier lieu

**first name** *n* prénom *m*

**first night** *n* (*Theat*) première *f*

**first-rate** ['fəːst'reɪt] *adj* excellent(e)

**first-time buyer** ['fəːsttaɪm-] *n* personne achetant une maison ou un appartement pour la première fois

**fir tree** *n* sapin *m*

**fiscal** ['fɪskl] *adj* fiscal(e)

**fiscal year** *n* exercice financier

**fish** [fɪʃ] *n* (*pl inv*) poisson *m*; poissons *mpl* ▷ *vt, vi* pêcher; **to ~ a river** pêcher dans une rivière; **~ and chips** poisson frit et frites

**fisherman** (*irreg*) ['fɪʃəmən] *n* pêcheur *m*

**fishery** ['fɪʃərɪ] *n* pêcherie *f*

**fish factory** *n* (*Brit*) conserverie *f* de poissons

**fish farm** *n* établissement *m* piscicole

**fish fingers** *npl* (*Brit*) bâtonnets *mpl* de poisson (congelés)

**fish hook** *n* hameçon *m*

**fishing** ['fɪʃɪŋ] *n* pêche *f*; **to go ~** aller à la pêche

**fishing boat** ['fɪʃɪŋ-] *n* barque *f* de pêche

**fishing industry** ['fɪʃɪŋ-] *n* industrie *f* de la pêche

**fishing line** ['fɪʃɪŋ-] *n* ligne *f* (de pêche)

**fishing rod** ['fɪʃɪŋ-] *n* canne *f* à pêche

**fishing tackle** ['fɪʃɪŋ-] *n* attirail *m* de pêche

**fish market** *n* marché *m* au poisson

**fishmonger** ['fɪʃmʌŋgəʳ] *n* (*Brit*) marchand *m* de poisson

**fishmonger's** ['fɪʃmʌŋgəz], **fishmonger's shop** *n* (*Brit*) poissonnerie *f*

**fish slice** n (Brit) pelle f à poisson
**fish sticks** npl (US) = **fish fingers**
**fishy** ['fɪʃɪ] adj (inf) suspect(e), louche
**fission** ['fɪʃən] n fission f; **atomic** or **nuclear ~**
fission nucléaire
**fissure** ['fɪʃəʳ] n fissure f
**fist** [fɪst] n poing m
**fistfight** ['fɪstfaɪt] n pugilat m, bagarre f (à coups
de poing)
**fit** [fɪt] adj (Med, Sport) en (bonne) forme; (proper)
convenable; approprié(e) ▷ vt (subj: clothes) aller
à; (adjust) ajuster; (put in, attach) installer, poser;
adapter; (equip) équiper, garnir, munir; (suit)
convenir à ▷ vi (clothes) aller; (parts) s'adapter;
(in space, gap) entrer, s'adapter ▷ n (Med) accès m,
crise f; (of anger) accès; (of hysterics, jealousy) crise;
**~ to** (ready to) en état de; **~ for** (worthy) digne de;
(capable) apte à; **to keep ~** se maintenir en
forme; **this dress is a tight/good ~** cette robe
est un peu juste/(me) va très bien; **a ~ of
coughing** une quinte de toux; **to have a ~** (Med)
faire or avoir une crise; (inf) piquer une crise; **by
~s and starts** par à-coups
▶ **fit in** vi (add up) cadrer; (integrate) s'intégrer;
(to new situation) s'adapter
▶ **fit out** vt (Brit: also: **fit up**) équiper
**fitful** ['fɪtful] adj intermittent(e)
**fitment** ['fɪtmənt] n meuble encastré,
élément m
**fitness** ['fɪtnɪs] n (Med) forme f physique; (of
remark) à-propos m, justesse f
**fitted** ['fɪtɪd] adj (jacket, shirt) ajusté(e)
**fitted carpet** ['fɪtɪd-] n moquette f
**fitted kitchen** ['fɪtɪd-] n (Brit) cuisine équipée
**fitted sheet** ['fɪtɪd-] n drap-housse m
**fitter** ['fɪtəʳ] n monteur m; (Dressmaking)
essayeur(-euse)
**fitting** ['fɪtɪŋ] adj approprié(e) ▷ n (of dress)
essayage m; (of piece of equipment) pose f,
installation f
**fitting room** n (in shop) cabine f d'essayage
**fittings** ['fɪtɪŋz] npl installations fpl
**five** [faɪv] num cinq
**five-day week** ['faɪvdeɪ-] n semaine f de cinq
jours
**fiver** ['faɪvəʳ] n (inf: Brit) billet m de cinq livres;
(: US) billet de cinq dollars
**fix** [fɪks] vt (date, amount etc) fixer; (sort out)
arranger; (mend) réparer; (make ready: meal, drink)
préparer; (inf: game etc) truquer ▷ n: **to be in a ~**
être dans le pétrin
▶ **fix up** vt (meeting) arranger; **to ~ sb up with
sth** faire avoir qch à qn
**fixation** [fɪk'seɪʃən] n (Psych) fixation f; (fig)
obsession f
**fixed** [fɪkst] adj (prices etc) fixe; **there's a ~
charge** il y a un prix forfaitaire; **how are you ~
for money?** (inf) question fric, ça va?
**fixed assets** npl immobilisations fpl
**fixture** ['fɪkstʃəʳ] n installation f (fixe); (Sport)
rencontre f (au programme)
**fizz** [fɪz] vi pétiller

**fizzle** ['fɪzl] vi pétiller
▶ **fizzle out** vi rater
**fizzy** ['fɪzɪ] adj pétillant(e), gazeux(-euse)
**fjord** [fjɔːd] n = **fiord**
**FL, Fla.** abbr (US) = **Florida**
**flabbergasted** ['flæbəgaːstɪd] adj sidéré(e),
ahuri(e)
**flabby** ['flæbɪ] adj mou (molle)
**flag** [flæg] n drapeau m; (also: **flagstone**) dalle f
▷ vi faiblir; fléchir; **~ of convenience** pavillon
m de complaisance
▶ **flag down** vt héler, faire signe (de s'arrêter) à
**flagon** ['flægən] n bonbonne f
**flagpole** ['flægpəul] n mât m
**flagrant** ['fleɪgrənt] adj flagrant(e)
**flagship** ['flægʃɪp] n vaisseau m amiral; (fig)
produit m vedette
**flag stop** n (US: for bus) arrêt facultatif
**flair** [flɛəʳ] n flair m
**flak** [flæk] n (Mil) tir antiaérien; (inf: criticism)
critiques fpl
**flake** [fleɪk] n (of rust, paint) écaille f; (of snow, soap
powder) flocon m ▷ vi (also: **flake off**) s'écailler
**flaky** ['fleɪkɪ] adj (paintwork) écaillé(e); (skin)
desquamé(e); (pastry) feuilleté(e)
**flamboyant** [flæm'bɔɪənt] adj flamboyant(e),
éclatant(e); (person) haut(e) en couleur
**flame** [fleɪm] n flamme f
**flamingo** [flə'mɪŋgəu] n flamant m (rose)
**flammable** ['flæməbl] adj inflammable
**flan** [flæn] n (Brit) tarte f
**Flanders** ['flaːndəz] n Flandre(s) f(pl)
**flange** [flændʒ] n boudin m; collerette f
**flank** [flæŋk] n flanc m ▷ vt flanquer
**flannel** ['flænl] n (Brit: also: **face flannel**) gant m
de toilette; (fabric) flanelle f; (Brit inf) baratin m;
**flannels** npl pantalon m de flanelle
**flap** [flæp] n (of pocket, envelope) rabat m ▷ vt
(wings) battre (de) ▷ vi (sail, flag) claquer; (inf:
also: **be in a flap**) paniquer
**flapjack** ['flæpdʒæk] n (US: pancake) ≈ crêpe f;
(Brit: biscuit) galette f
**flare** [flɛəʳ] n (signal) signal lumineux; (Mil)
fusée éclairante; (in skirt etc) évasement m;
**flares** npl (trousers) pantalon m à pattes
d'éléphant
▶ **flare up** vi s'embraser; (fig: person) se mettre
en colère, s'emporter; (: revolt) éclater
**flared** ['flɛəd] adj (trousers) à jambes évasées;
(skirt) évasé(e)
**flash** [flæʃ] n éclair m; (also: **news flash**) flash m
(d'information); (Phot) flash ▷ vt (switch on)
allumer (brièvement); (direct): **to ~ sth at**
braquer qch sur; (flaunt) étaler, exhiber; (send:
message) câbler; (smile) lancer ▷ vi briller; jeter
des éclairs; (light on ambulance etc) clignoter; **a ~
of lightning** un éclair; **in a ~** en un clin d'œil;
**to ~ one's headlights** faire un appel de phares;
**he ~ed by or past** il passa (devant nous) comme
un éclair
**flashback** ['flæʃbæk] n flashback m, retour m en
arrière

**flashbulb** ['flæʃbʌlb] n ampoule f de flash
**flash card** n (Scol) carte f (support visuel)
**flashcube** ['flæʃkjuːb] n cube-flash m
**flasher** ['flæʃəʳ] n (Aut) clignotant m
**flashlight** ['flæʃlaɪt] n lampe f de poche
**flashpoint** ['flæʃpɔɪnt] n point m d'ignition;
  (fig): **to be at ~** être sur le point d'exploser
**flashy** ['flæʃɪ] adj (pej) tape-à-l'œil inv,
  tapageur(-euse)
**flask** [flɑːsk] n flacon m, bouteille f; (Chem)
  ballon m; (also: **vacuum flask**) bouteille f
  thermos®
**flat** [flæt] adj plat(e); (tyre) dégonflé(e), à plat;
  (beer) éventé(e); (battery) à plat; (denial)
  catégorique; (Mus) bémol inv; (: voice) faux
  (fausse) ⊳ n (Brit: apartment) appartement m;
  (Aut) crevaison f, pneu crevé; (Mus) bémol m; ~
  **out** (work) sans relâche; (race) à fond; **~ rate of
  pay** (Comm) salaire m fixe
**flat-footed** ['flæt'futɪd] adj: **to be ~** avoir les
  pieds plats
**flatly** ['flætlɪ] adv catégoriquement
**flatmate** ['flætmeɪt] n (Brit): **he's my ~** il
  partage l'appartement avec moi
**flatness** ['flætnɪs] n (of land) absence f de relief,
  aspect plat
**flat-screen** ['flætskriːn] adj à écran plat
**flatten** ['flætn] vt (also: **flatten out**) aplatir;
  (crop) coucher; (house, city) raser
**flatter** ['flætəʳ] vt flatter
**flatterer** ['flætərəʳ] n flatteur m
**flattering** ['flætərɪŋ] adj flatteur(-euse); (clothes
  etc) seyant(e)
**flattery** ['flætərɪ] n flatterie f
**flatulence** ['flætjuləns] n flatulence f
**flaunt** [flɔːnt] vt faire étalage de
**flavour**, (US) **flavor** ['fleɪvəʳ] n goût m, saveur f;
  (of ice cream etc) parfum m ⊳ vt parfumer,
  aromatiser; **vanilla-~ed** à l'arôme de vanille,
  vanillé(e); **what ~s do you have?** quels
  parfums avez-vous?; **to give** or **add ~ to** donner
  du goût à, relever
**flavouring**, (US) **flavoring** ['fleɪvərɪŋ] n
  arôme m (synthétique)
**flaw** [flɔː] n défaut m
**flawless** ['flɔːlɪs] adj sans défaut
**flax** [flæks] n lin m
**flaxen** ['flæksən] adj blond(e)
**flea** [fliː] n puce f
**flea market** n marché m aux puces
**fleck** [flɛk] n (of dust) particule f; (of mud, paint,
  colour) tacheture f, moucheture f ⊳ vt tacher,
  éclabousser; **brown ~ed with white** brun
  moucheté de blanc
**fled** [flɛd] pt, pp of **flee**
**fledgeling, fledgling** ['flɛdʒlɪŋ] n oisillon m
**flee** (pt, pp **fled**) [fliː, flɛd] vt fuir, s'enfuir de ⊳ vi
  fuir, s'enfuir
**fleece** [fliːs] n (of sheep) toison f; (top) (laine f)
  polaire f ⊳ vt (inf) voler, filouter
**fleecy** ['fliːsɪ] adj (blanket) moelleux(-euse);
  (cloud) floconneux(-euse)

**fleet** [fliːt] n flotte f; (of lorries, cars etc) parc m;
  convoi m
**fleeting** ['fliːtɪŋ] adj fugace, fugitif(-ive); (visit)
  très bref (brève)
**Flemish** ['flɛmɪʃ] adj flamand(e) ⊳ n (Ling)
  flamand m; **the ~** (npl) les Flamands
**flesh** [flɛʃ] n chair f
**flesh wound** [-wuːnd] n blessure superficielle
**flew** [fluː] pt of **fly**
**flex** [flɛks] n fil m or câble m électrique (souple)
  ⊳ vt (knee) fléchir; (muscles) tendre
**flexibility** [flɛksɪ'bɪlɪtɪ] n flexibilité f
**flexible** ['flɛksəbl] adj flexible; (person, schedule)
  souple
**flexitime** ['flɛksɪtaɪm], (US) **flextime**
  ['flɛkstaɪm] n horaire m variable or à la carte
**flick** [flɪk] n petit coup; (with finger) chiquenaude
  f ⊳ vt donner un petit coup à; (switch) appuyer
  sur
  ▸ **flick through** vt fus feuilleter
**flicker** ['flɪkəʳ] vi (light, flame) vaciller ⊳ n
  vacillement m; **a ~ of light** une brève lueur
**flick knife** n (Brit) couteau m à cran d'arrêt
**flicks** [flɪks] npl (inf) ciné m
**flier** ['flaɪəʳ] n aviateur m
**flies** [flaɪz] npl of **fly**
**flight** [flaɪt] n vol m; (escape) fuite f; (also: **flight
  of steps**) escalier m; **to take ~** prendre la fuite;
  **to put to ~** mettre en fuite
**flight attendant** n steward m, hôtesse f de l'air
**flight crew** n équipage m
**flight deck** n (Aviat) poste m de pilotage; (Naut)
  pont m d'envol
**flight path** n trajectoire f (de vol)
**flight recorder** n enregistreur m de vol
**flimsy** ['flɪmzɪ] adj peu solide; (clothes) trop
  léger(-ère); (excuse) pauvre, mince
**flinch** [flɪntʃ] vi tressaillir; **to ~ from** se dérober
  à, reculer devant
**fling** [flɪŋ] vt (pt, pp **flung** [flʌŋ]) jeter, lancer ⊳ n
  (love affair) brève liaison, passade f
**flint** [flɪnt] n silex m; (in lighter) pierre f (à
  briquet)
**flip** [flɪp] n chiquenaude f ⊳ vt (throw) donner
  une chiquenaude à; (switch) appuyer sur; (US:
  pancake) faire sauter; **to ~ sth over** retourner
  qch ⊳ vi: **to ~ for sth** (US) jouer qch à pile ou
  face
  ▸ **flip through** vt fus feuilleter
**flip-flops** ['flɪpflɔps] npl (esp Brit) tongs fpl
**flippant** ['flɪpənt] adj désinvolte,
  irrévérencieux(-euse)
**flipper** ['flɪpəʳ] n (of animal) nageoire f; (for
  swimmer) palme f
**flip side** n (of record) deuxième face f
**flirt** [fləːt] vi flirter ⊳ n flirteur(-euse)
**flirtation** [fləː'teɪʃən] n flirt m
**flit** [flɪt] vi voleter
**float** [fləʊt] n flotteur m; (in procession) char m;
  (sum of money) réserve f ⊳ vi flotter; (bather)
  flotter, faire la planche ⊳ vt faire flotter; (loan,
  business, idea) lancer

**floating** ['fləʊtɪŋ] *adj* flottant(e); ~ **vote** voix flottante; ~ **voter** électeur indécis

**flock** [flɔk] *n* (*of sheep*) troupeau *m*; (*of birds*) vol *m*; (*of people*) foule *f*

**floe** [fləʊ] *n* (*also*: **ice floe**) iceberg *m*

**flog** [flɔg] *vt* fouetter

**flood** [flʌd] *n* inondation *f*; (*of letters, refugees etc*) flot *m* ▷ *vt* inonder; (*Aut: carburettor*) noyer ▷ *vi* (*place*) être inondé; (*people*): **to ~ into** envahir; **to ~ the market** (*Comm*) inonder le marché; **in ~** en crue

**flooding** ['flʌdɪŋ] *n* inondation *f*

**floodlight** ['flʌdlaɪt] *n* projecteur *m* ▷ *vt* éclairer aux projecteurs, illuminer

**floodlit** ['flʌdlɪt] *pt, pp of* **floodlight** ▷ *adj* illuminé(e)

**flood tide** *n* marée montante

**floodwater** ['flʌdwɔːtəʳ] *n* eau *f* de la crue

**floor** [flɔːʳ] *n* sol *m*; (*storey*) étage *m*; (*of sea, valley*) fond *m*; (*fig: at meeting*): **the ~** l'assemblée *f*, les membres *mpl* de l'assemblée ▷ *vt* (*knock down*) terrasser; (*baffle*) désorienter; **on the ~** par terre; **ground ~**, (*US*) **first ~** rez-de-chaussée *m*; **first ~**, (*US*) **second ~** premier étage; **top ~** dernier étage; **what ~ is it on?** c'est à quel étage?; **to have the ~** (*speaker*) avoir la parole

**floorboard** ['flɔːbɔːd] *n* planche *f* (*du plancher*)

**flooring** ['flɔːrɪŋ] *n* sol *m*; (*wooden*) plancher *m*; (*material to make floor*) matériau(x) *m(pl)* pour planchers; (*covering*) revêtement *m* de sol

**floor lamp** *n* (*US*) lampadaire *m*

**floor show** *n* spectacle *m* de variétés

**floorwalker** ['flɔːwɔːkəʳ] *n* (*esp US*) surveillant *m* (de grand magasin)

**flop** [flɔp] *n* fiasco *m* ▷ *vi* (*fail*) faire fiasco; (*fall*) s'affaler, s'effondrer

**floppy** ['flɔpɪ] *adj* lâche, flottant(e) ▷ *n* (*Comput: also*: **floppy disk**) disquette *f*; ~ **hat** chapeau *m* à bords flottants

**floppy disk** *n* disquette *f*, disque *m* souple

**flora** ['flɔːrə] *n* flore *f*

**floral** ['flɔːrl] *adj* floral(e); (*dress*) à fleurs

**Florence** ['flɔrəns] *n* Florence

**florid** ['flɔrɪd] *adj* (*complexion*) fleuri(e); (*style*) plein(e) de fioritures

**florist** ['flɔrɪst] *n* fleuriste *m/f*

**florist's** ['flɔrɪsts], **florist's shop** *n* magasin *m* or boutique *f* de fleuriste

**flotation** [fləʊ'teɪʃən] *n* (*of shares*) émission *f*; (*of company*) lancement *m* (en Bourse)

**flounce** [flaʊns] *n* volant *m*
▶ **flounce out** *vi* sortir dans un mouvement d'humeur

**flounder** ['flaʊndəʳ] *n* (*Zool*) flet *m* ▷ *vi* patauger

**flour** ['flaʊəʳ] *n* farine *f*

**flourish** ['flʌrɪʃ] *vi* prospérer ▷ *vt* brandir ▷ *n* (*gesture*) moulinet *m*; (*decoration*) fioriture *f*; (*of trumpets*) fanfare *f*

**flourishing** ['flʌrɪʃɪŋ] *adj* prospère, florissant(e)

**flout** [flaʊt] *vt* se moquer de, faire fi de

**flow** [fləʊ] *n* (*of water, traffic etc*) écoulement *m*; (*tide, influx*) flux *m*; (*of orders, letters etc*) flot *m*; (*of blood, Elec*) circulation *f*; (*of river*) courant *m* ▷ *vi* couler; (*traffic*) s'écouler; (*robes, hair*) flotter

**flow chart, flow diagram** *n* organigramme *m*

**flower** ['flaʊəʳ] *n* fleur *f* ▷ *vi* fleurir; **in ~** en fleur

**flower bed** *n* plate-bande *f*

**flowerpot** ['flaʊəpɔt] *n* pot *m* (à fleurs)

**flowery** ['flaʊərɪ] *adj* fleuri(e)

**flown** [fləʊn] *pp of* **fly**

**fl. oz.** *abbr* = **fluid ounce**

**flu** [fluː] *n* grippe *f*

**fluctuate** ['flʌktjʊeɪt] *vi* varier, fluctuer

**fluctuation** [flʌktjʊ'eɪʃən] *n* fluctuation *f*, variation *f*

**flue** [fluː] *n* conduit *m*

**fluency** ['fluːənsɪ] *n* facilité *f*, aisance *f*

**fluent** ['fluːənt] *adj* (*speech, style*) coulant(e), aisé(e); **he's a ~ speaker/reader** il s'exprime/ lit avec aisance or facilité; **he speaks ~ French, he's ~ in French** il parle le français couramment

**fluently** ['fluːəntlɪ] *adv* couramment; avec aisance or facilité

**fluff** [flʌf] *n* duvet *m*; (*on jacket, carpet*) peluche *f*

**fluffy** ['flʌfɪ] *adj* duveteux(-euse); (*jacket, carpet*) pelucheux(-euse); (*toy*) en peluche

**fluid** ['fluːɪd] *n* fluide *m*; (*in diet*) liquide *m* ▷ *adj* fluide

**fluid ounce** *n* (*Brit*) = 0.028 l; 0.05 pints

**fluke** [fluːk] *n* coup *m* de veine

**flummox** ['flʌməks] *vt* dérouter, déconcerter

**flung** [flʌŋ] *pt, pp of* **fling**

**flunky** ['flʌŋkɪ] *n* larbin *m*

**fluorescent** [fluə'rɛsnt] *adj* fluorescent(e)

**fluoride** ['fluəraɪd] *n* fluor *m*

**fluorine** ['fluəriːn] *n* fluor *m*

**flurry** ['flʌrɪ] *n* (*of snow*) rafale *f*, bourrasque *f*; **a ~ of activity** un affairement soudain; **a ~ of excitement** une excitation soudaine

**flush** [flʌʃ] *n* (*on face*) rougeur *f*; (*fig: of youth etc*) éclat *m*; (*of blood*) afflux *m* ▷ *vt* nettoyer à grande eau; (*also*: **flush out**) débusquer ▷ *vi* rougir ▷ *adj* (*inf*) en fonds; (*level*): ~ **with** au ras de, de niveau avec; **to ~ the toilet** tirer la chasse (d'eau); **hot ~es** (*Med*) bouffées *fpl* de chaleur

**flushed** [flʌʃt] *adj* (tout(e)) rouge

**fluster** ['flʌstəʳ] *n* agitation *f*, trouble *m*

**flustered** ['flʌstəd] *adj* énervé(e)

**flute** [fluːt] *n* flûte *f*

**flutter** ['flʌtəʳ] *n* (*of panic, excitement*) agitation *f*; (*of wings*) battement *m* ▷ *vi* (*bird*) battre des ailes, voleter; (*person*) aller et venir dans une grande agitation

**flux** [flʌks] *n*: **in a state of ~** fluctuant sans cesse

**fly** [flaɪ] (*pt* **flew**, *pp* **flown** [fluː, fləʊn]) *n* (*insect*) mouche *f*; (*on trousers: also*: **flies**) braguette *f* ▷ *vt* (*plane*) piloter; (*passengers, cargo*) transporter (par avion); (*distance*) parcourir ▷ *vi* voler; (*passengers*) aller en avion; (*escape*) s'enfuir, fuir; (*flag*) se déployer; **to ~ open** s'ouvrir brusquement; **to ~ off the handle** s'énerver, s'emporter
▶ **fly away, fly off** *vi* s'envoler

▸**fly in** vi (plane) atterrir; **he flew in yesterday** il est arrivé hier (par avion)

▸**fly out** vi partir (par avion)

**fly-drive** ['flaɪdraɪv] n formule f avion plus voiture

**fly-fishing** ['flaɪfɪʃɪŋ] n pêche f à la mouche

**flying** ['flaɪɪŋ] n (activity) aviation f; (action) vol m ▷ adj: ~ **visit** visite f éclair inv; **with ~ colours** haut la main; **he doesn't like ~** il n'aime pas voyager en avion

**flying buttress** n arc-boutant m

**flying picket** n piquet m de grève volant

**flying saucer** n soucoupe volante

**flying squad** n (Police) brigade volante

**flying start** n: **to get off to a ~** faire un excellent départ

**flyleaf** ['flaɪliːf] n page f de garde

**flyover** ['flaɪəʊvəʳ] n (Brit: overpass) pont routier, saut-de-mouton m (Canada)

**flypast** ['flaɪpɑːst] n défilé aérien

**flysheet** ['flaɪʃiːt] n (for tent) double toit m

**flyweight** ['flaɪweɪt] n (Sport) poids m mouche

**flywheel** ['flaɪwiːl] n volant m (de commande)

**FM** abbr (Brit Mil) = **field marshal**; (Radio: = frequency modulation) FM

**FMB** n abbr (US) = **Federal Maritime Board**

**FMCS** n abbr (US: = Federal Mediation and Conciliation Services) organisme de conciliation en cas de conflits du travail

**FO** n abbr (Brit) = **Foreign Office**

**foal** [fəʊl] n poulain m

**foam** [fəʊm] n écume f; (on beer) mousse f; (also: **foam rubber**) caoutchouc m mousse; (also: **plastic foam**) mousse cellulaire or de plastique ▷ vi (liquid) écumer; (soapy water) mousser

**foam rubber** n caoutchouc m mousse

**FOB** abbr (= free on board) fob

**fob** [fɒb] n (also: **watch fob**) chaîne f, ruban m ▷ vt: **to ~ sb off with sth** refiler qch à qn

**foc** abbr (Brit) = **free of charge**

**focal** ['fəʊkl] adj (also fig) focal(e)

**focal point** n foyer m; (fig) centre m de l'attention, point focal

**focus** ['fəʊkəs] n (pl **-es**) foyer m; (of interest) centre m ▷ vt (field glasses etc) mettre au point; (light rays) faire converger ▷ vi: **to ~ (on)** (with camera) régler la mise au point (sur); (with eyes) fixer son regard (sur); (fig: concentrate) se concentrer; **out of/in ~** (picture) flou(e)/net(te); (camera) pas au point/au point

**fodder** ['fɒdəʳ] n fourrage m

**FOE** n abbr (= Friends of the Earth) AT mpl (= Amis de la Terre); (US: = Fraternal Order of Eagles) organisation charitable

**foe** [fəʊ] n ennemi m

**foetus**, (US)**fetus** ['fiːtəs] n fœtus m

**fog** [fɒg] n brouillard m

**fogbound** ['fɒgbaʊnd] adj bloqué(e) par le brouillard

**foggy** ['fɒgɪ] adj: **it's ~** il y a du brouillard

**fog lamp**, (US)**fog light** n (Aut) phare m anti-brouillard

**foible** ['fɔɪbl] n faiblesse f

**foil** [fɔɪl] vt déjouer, contrecarrer ▷ n feuille f de métal; (kitchen foil) papier m d'alu(minium); (Fencing) fleuret m; **to act as a ~ to** (fig) servir de repoussoir or de faire-valoir à

**foist** [fɔɪst] vt: **to ~ sth on sb** imposer qch à qn

**fold** [fəʊld] n (bend, crease) pli m; (Agr) parc m à moutons; (fig) bercail m ▷ vt plier; **to ~ one's arms** croiser les bras

▸**fold up** vi (map etc) se plier, se replier; (business) fermer boutique ▷ vt (map etc) plier, replier

**folder** ['fəʊldəʳ] n (for papers) chemise f; (: binder) classeur m; (brochure) dépliant m; (Comput) dossier m

**folding** ['fəʊldɪŋ] adj (chair, bed) pliant(e)

**foliage** ['fəʊlɪɪdʒ] n feuillage m

**folk** [fəʊk] npl gens mpl ▷ cpd folklorique; **folks** npl (inf: parents) famille f, parents mpl

**folklore** ['fəʊklɔːʳ] n folklore m

**folk music** n musique f folklorique; (contemporary) musique folk, folk m

**folk song** n ['fəʊksɔŋ] n chanson f folklorique; (contemporary) chanson folk inv

**follow** ['fɒləʊ] vt suivre ▷ vi suivre; (result) s'ensuivre; **to ~ sb's advice** suivre les conseils de qn; **I don't quite ~ you** je ne vous suis plus; **to ~ in sb's footsteps** emboîter le pas à qn; (fig) suivre les traces de qn; **it ~s that ...** de ce fait, il s'ensuit que ...; **to ~ suit** (fig) faire de même

▸**follow out** vt (idea, plan) poursuivre, mener à terme

▸**follow through** vt = **follow out**

▸**follow up** vt (victory) tirer parti de; (letter, offer) donner suite à; (case) suivre

**follower** ['fɒləʊəʳ] n disciple m/f, partisan(e)

**following** ['fɒləʊɪŋ] adj suivant(e) ▷ n partisans mpl, disciples mpl

**follow-up** ['fɒləʊʌp] n suite f; (on file, case) suivi m

**folly** ['fɒlɪ] n inconscience f; sottise f; (building) folie f

**fond** [fɒnd] adj (memory, look) tendre, affectueux(-euse); (hopes, dreams) un peu fou (folle); **to be ~ of** aimer beaucoup

**fondle** ['fɒndl] vt caresser

**fondly** ['fɒndlɪ] adv (lovingly) tendrement; (naïvely) naïvement

**fondness** ['fɒndnɪs] n (for things) attachement m; (for people) sentiments affectueux; **a special ~ for** une prédilection pour

**font** [fɒnt] n (Rel) fonts baptismaux; (Typ) police f de caractères

**food** [fuːd] n nourriture f

**food chain** n chaîne f alimentaire

**food mixer** n mixeur m

**food poisoning** n intoxication f alimentaire

**food processor** n robot m de cuisine

**food stamp** n (US) bon m de nourriture (pour indigents)

**foodstuffs** ['fuːdstʌfs] npl denrées fpl alimentaires

**fool** [fuːl] n idiot(e); (History: of king) bouffon m,

fou *m*; (*Culin*) mousse *f* de fruits ▷ *vt* berner, duper ▷ *vi* (*also*: **fool around**) faire l'idiot *or* l'imbécile; **to make a ~ of sb** (*ridicule*) ridiculiser qn; (*trick*) avoir *or* duper qn; **to make a ~ of o.s.** se couvrir de ridicule; **you can't ~ me** vous (ne) me la ferez pas, on (ne) me la fait pas
▶ **fool about, fool around** *vi* (*pej: waste time*) traînailler, glandouiller; (: *behave foolishly*) faire l'idiot *or* l'imbécile

**foolhardy** ['fuːlhɑːdɪ] *adj* téméraire, imprudent(e)

**foolish** ['fuːlɪʃ] *adj* idiot(e), stupide; (*rash*) imprudent(e)

**foolishly** ['fuːlɪʃlɪ] *adv* stupidement

**foolishness** ['fuːlɪʃnɪs] *n* idiotie *f*, stupidité *f*

**foolproof** ['fuːlpruːf] *adj* (*plan etc*) infaillible

**foolscap** ['fuːlskæp] *n* ≈ papier *m* ministre

**foot** (*pl* **feet**) [fut, fiːt] *n* pied *m*; (*of animal*) patte *f*; (*measure*) pied (= 30.48 *cm*; 12 *inches*) ▷ *vt* (*bill*) casquer, payer; **on ~** à pied; **to find one's feet** (*fig*) s'acclimater; **to put one's ~ down** (*Aut*) appuyer sur le champignon; (*say no*) s'imposer

**footage** ['futɪdʒ] *n* (*Cine: length*) ≈ métrage *m*; (: *material*) séquences *fpl*

**foot-and-mouth** [futənd'mauθ], **foot-and-mouth disease** *n* fièvre aphteuse

**football** ['futbɔːl] *n* (*ball*) ballon *m* (de football); (*sport: Brit*) football *m*; (: *US*) football américain

**footballer** ['futbɔːləʳ] *n* (*Brit*) = **football player**

**football ground** *n* terrain *m* de football

**football match** *n* (*Brit*) match *m* de foot(ball)

**football player** *n* footballeur(-euse), joueur(-euse) de football; (*US*) joueur(-euse) de football américain

**football pools** *npl* (*US*) ≈ loto *m* sportif, ≈ pronostics *mpl* (sur les matchs de football)

**footbrake** ['futbreɪk] *n* frein *m* à pédale

**footbridge** ['futbrɪdʒ] *n* passerelle *f*

**foothills** ['futhɪlz] *npl* contreforts *mpl*

**foothold** ['futhəuld] *n* prise *f* (de pied)

**footing** ['futɪŋ] *n* (*fig*) position *f*; **to lose one's ~** perdre pied; **on an equal ~** sur pied d'égalité

**footlights** ['futlaɪts] *npl* rampe *f*

**footman** ['futmən] (*irreg*) *n* laquais *m*

**footnote** ['futnəut] *n* note *f* (en bas de page)

**footpath** ['futpɑːθ] *n* sentier *m*; (*in street*) trottoir *m*

**footprint** ['futprɪnt] *n* trace *f* (de pied)

**footrest** ['futrɛst] *n* marchepied *m*

**footsie** ['futsɪ] *n* (*inf*): **to play ~ with sb** faire du pied à qn

**footsore** ['futsɔːʳ] *adj*: **to be ~** avoir mal aux pieds

**footstep** ['futstɛp] *n* pas *m*

**footwear** ['futwɛəʳ] *n* chaussures *fpl*

**FOR** *abbr* (= *free on rail*) franco wagon

---

🔘 KEYWORD

**for** [fɔːʳ] *prep* **1** (*indicating destination, intention, purpose*) pour; **the train for London** le train pour (*or* à destination de) Londres; **he left for Rome** il est parti pour Rome; **he went for the paper** il est allé chercher le journal; **is this for me?** c'est pour moi?; **it's time for lunch** c'est l'heure du déjeuner; **what's it for?** ça sert à quoi?; **what for?** (*why*) pourquoi?; (*to what end*) pour quoi faire?, à quoi bon?; **for sale** à vendre; **to pray for peace** prier pour la paix

**2** (*on behalf of, representing*) pour; **the MP for Hove** le député de Hove; **to work for sb/sth** travailler pour qn/qch; **I'll ask him for you** je vais lui demander pour toi; **G for George** G comme Georges

**3** (*because of*) pour; **for this reason** pour cette raison; **for fear of being criticized** de peur d'être critiqué

**4** (*with regard to*) pour; **it's cold for July** il fait froid pour juillet; **a gift for languages** un don pour les langues

**5** (*in exchange for*): **I sold it for £5** je l'ai vendu 5 livres; **to pay 50 pence for a ticket** payer un billet 50 pence

**6** (*in favour of*) pour; **are you for or against us?** êtes-vous pour ou contre nous?; **I'm all for it** je suis tout à fait pour; **vote for X** votez pour X

**7** (*referring to distance*) pendant, sur; **there are roadworks for 5 km** il y a des travaux sur *or* pendant 5 km; **we walked for miles** nous avons marché pendant des kilomètres

**8** (*referring to time*) pendant; depuis; pour; **he was away for 2 years** il a été absent pendant 2 ans; **she will be away for a month** elle sera absente (pendant) un mois; **it hasn't rained for 3 weeks** ça fait 3 semaines qu'il ne pleut pas, il ne pleut pas depuis 3 semaines; **I have known her for years** je la connais depuis des années; **can you do it for tomorrow?** est-ce que tu peux le faire pour demain?

**9** (*with infinitive clauses*): **it is not for me to decide** ce n'est pas à moi de décider; **it would be best for you to leave** le mieux serait que vous partiez; **there is still time for you to do it** vous avez encore le temps de le faire; **for this to be possible ...** pour que cela soit possible ..

**10** (*in spite of*): **for all that** malgré cela, néanmoins; **for all his work/efforts** malgré tout son travail/tous ses efforts; **for all his complaints, he's very fond of her** il a beau se plaindre, il l'aime beaucoup
▷ *conj* (*since, as: formal*) car

**forage** ['fɔrɪdʒ] *n* fourrage *m* ▷ *vi* fourrager, fouiller

**forage cap** *n* calot *m*

**foray** ['fɔreɪ] *n* incursion *f*

**forbad, forbade** [fə'bæd] *pt of* **forbid**

**forbearing** [fɔː'bɛərɪŋ] *adj* patient(e), tolérant(e)

**forbid** (*pt* **forbad(e)**, *pp* **-den**) [fə'bɪd, -'bæd, -'bɪdn] *vt* défendre, interdire; **to ~ sb to do** défendre *or* interdire à qn de faire

**forbidden** [fə'bɪdn] *adj* défendu(e)

**forbidding** [fə'bɪdɪŋ] *adj* d'aspect *or* d'allure

sévère or sombre

**force** [fɔːs] n force f ▷ vt forcer; (push) pousser (de force); **Forces** npl: **the F~s** (Brit Mil) les forces armées; **to ~ o.s. to do** se forcer à faire; **to ~ sb to do sth** forcer qn à faire qch; **in ~** (being used: rule, law, prices) en vigueur; (in large numbers) en force; **to come into ~** entrer en vigueur; **a ~ 5 wind** un vent de force 5; **the sales ~** (Comm) la force de vente; **to join ~s** unir ses forces
▶ **force back** vt (crowd, enemy) repousser; (tears) refouler
▶ **force down** vt (food) se forcer à manger

**forced** [fɔːst] adj forcé(e)

**force-feed** ['fɔːsfiːd] vt nourrir de force

**forceful** ['fɔːsful] adj énergique

**forcemeat** ['fɔːsmiːt] n (Brit Culin) farce f

**forceps** ['fɔːsɛps] npl forceps m

**forcibly** ['fɔːsəblɪ] adv par la force, de force; (vigorously) énergiquement

**ford** [fɔːd] n gué m ▷ vt passer à gué

**fore** [fɔːʳ] n: **to the ~** en évidence; **to come to the ~** se faire remarquer

**forearm** ['fɔːrɑːm] n avant-bras m inv

**forebear** ['fɔːbɛəʳ] n ancêtre m

**foreboding** [fɔːˈbəudɪŋ] n pressentiment m (néfaste)

**forecast** ['fɔːkɑːst] n prévision f; (also: **weather forecast**) prévisions fpl météorologiques, météo f ▷ vt (irreg: like **cast**) prévoir

**foreclose** [fɔːˈkləuz] vt (Law: also: **foreclose on**) saisir

**foreclosure** [fɔːˈkləuʒəʳ] n saisie f du bien hypothéqué

**forecourt** ['fɔːkɔːt] n (of garage) devant m

**forefathers** ['fɔːfɑːðəz] npl ancêtres mpl

**forefinger** ['fɔːfɪŋgəʳ] n index m

**forefront** ['fɔːfrʌnt] n: **in the ~ of** au premier rang or plan de

**forego** (pt **forewent**, pp **foregone**) [fɔːˈgəu, -ˈwɛnt, -ˈgɔn] vt renoncer à

**foregoing** ['fɔːgəuɪŋ] adj susmentionné(e) ▷ n: **the ~** ce qui précède

**foregone** ['fɔːgɔn] adj: **it's a ~ conclusion** c'est à prévoir, c'est couru d'avance

**foreground** ['fɔːgraund] n premier plan ▷ cpd (Comput) prioritaire

**forehand** ['fɔːhænd] n (Tennis) coup droit

**forehead** ['fɔrɪd] n front m

**foreign** ['fɔrɪn] adj étranger(-ère); (trade) extérieur(e); (travel) à l'étranger

**foreign body** n corps étranger

**foreign currency** n devises étrangères

**foreigner** ['fɔrɪnəʳ] n étranger(-ère)

**foreign exchange** n (system) change m; (money) devises fpl

**foreign exchange market** n marché m des devises

**foreign exchange rate** n cours m des devises

**foreign investment** n investissement m à l'étranger

**Foreign Office** n (Brit) ministère m des Affaires étrangères

**Foreign Secretary** n (Brit) ministre m des Affaires étrangères

**foreleg** ['fɔːlɛg] n patte f de devant, jambe antérieure

**foreman** (irreg) ['fɔːmən] n (in construction) contremaître m; (Law: of jury) président m (du jury)

**foremost** ['fɔːməust] adj le (la) plus en vue, premier(-ière) ▷ adv: **first and ~** avant tout, tout d'abord

**forename** ['fɔːneɪm] n prénom m

**forensic** [fəˈrɛnsɪk] adj: **~ medicine** médecine légale; **~ expert** expert m de la police, expert légiste

**foreplay** ['fɔːpleɪ] n stimulation f érotique, prélude m

**forerunner** ['fɔːrʌnəʳ] n précurseur m

**foresee** (pt **foresaw**, pp **foreseen**) [fɔːˈsiː, -ˈsɔː, -ˈsiːn] vt prévoir

**foreseeable** [fɔːˈsiːəbl] adj prévisible

**foreseen** [fɔːˈsiːn] pp of **foresee**

**foreshadow** [fɔːˈʃædəu] vt présager, annoncer, laisser prévoir

**foreshorten** [fɔːˈʃɔːtn] vt (figure, scene) réduire, faire en raccourci

**foresight** ['fɔːsaɪt] n prévoyance f

**foreskin** ['fɔːskɪn] n (Anat) prépuce m

**forest** ['fɔrɪst] n forêt f

**forestall** [fɔːˈstɔːl] vt devancer

**forestry** ['fɔrɪstrɪ] n sylviculture f

**foretaste** ['fɔːteɪst] n avant-goût m

**foretell** (pt, pp **foretold**) [fɔːˈtɛl, -ˈtəuld] vt prédire

**forethought** ['fɔːθɔːt] n prévoyance f

**foretold** [fɔːˈtəuld] pt, pp of **foretell**

**forever** [fəˈrɛvəʳ] adv pour toujours; (fig: endlessly) continuellement

**forewarn** [fɔːˈwɔːn] vt avertir

**forewent** [fɔːˈwɛnt] pt of **forego**

**foreword** ['fɔːwəːd] n avant-propos m inv

**forfeit** ['fɔːfɪt] n prix m, rançon f ▷ vt perdre; (one's life, health) payer de

**forgave** [fəˈgeɪv] pt of **forgive**

**forge** [fɔːdʒ] n forge f ▷ vt (signature) contrefaire; (wrought iron) forger; **to ~ documents/a will** fabriquer de faux papiers/un faux testament; **to ~ money** (Brit) fabriquer de la fausse monnaie
▶ **forge ahead** vi pousser de l'avant, prendre de l'avance

**forged** [fɔːdʒd] adj faux (fausse)

**forger** ['fɔːdʒəʳ] n faussaire m

**forgery** ['fɔːdʒərɪ] n faux m, contrefaçon f

**forget** (pt **forgot**, pp **forgotten**) [fəˈgɛt, -ˈgɔt, -ˈgɔtn] vt, vi oublier; **to ~ to do sth** oublier de faire qch; **to ~ about sth** (accidentally) oublier qch; (on purpose) ne plus penser à qch; **I've forgotten my key/passport** j'ai oublié ma clé/mon passeport

**forgetful** [fəˈgɛtful] adj distrait(e), étourdi(e); **~ of** oublieux(-euse) de

**forgetfulness** [fəˈgɛtfulnɪs] n tendance f aux

oublis; *(oblivion)* oubli *m*

**forget-me-not** [fə'gɛtmɪnɔt] *n* myosotis *m*

**forgive** *(pt* **forgave,** *pp* **forgiven)** [fə'gɪv, -'geɪv, - 'gɪvn] *vt* pardonner; **to ~ sb for sth/for doing sth** pardonner qch à qn/à qn de faire qch

**forgiveness** [fə'gɪvnɪs] *n* pardon *m*

**forgiving** [fə'gɪvɪŋ] *adj* indulgent(e)

**forgo** *(pt* **forwent,** *pp* **forgone)** [fɔː'gəu, -'wɛnt, - 'gɔn] *vt* = **forego**

**forgot** [fə'gɔt] *pt of* **forget**

**forgotten** [fə'gɔtn] *pp of* **forget**

**fork** [fɔːk] *n (for eating)* fourchette *f; (for gardening)* fourche *f; (of roads)* bifurcation *f; (of railways)* embranchement *m* ▷ *vi (road)* bifurquer
▶ **fork out** *(inf: pay)* *vt* allonger, se fendre de ▷ *vi* casquer

**forked** [fɔːkt] *adj (lightning)* en zigzags, ramifié(e)

**fork-lift truck** ['fɔːklɪft-] *n* chariot élévateur

**forlorn** [fə'lɔːn] *adj (person)* délaissé(e); *(deserted)* abandonné(e); *(hope, attempt)* désespéré(e)

**form** [fɔːm] *n* forme *f; (Scol)* classe *f; (questionnaire)* formulaire *m* ▷ *vt* former; *(habit)* contracter; **in the ~ of** sous forme de; **to ~ part of sth** faire partie de qch; **to be on good ~** *(Sport: fig)* être en forme; **on top ~** en pleine forme

**formal** ['fɔːməl] *adj (offer, receipt)* en bonne et due forme; *(person)* cérémonieux(-euse), à cheval sur les convenances; *(occasion, dinner)* officiel(le); *(garden)* à la française; *(Art, Philosophy)* formel(le); *(clothes)* de soirée

**formality** [fɔː'mælɪtɪ] *n* formalité *f,* cérémonie(s) *f(pl)*

**formalize** ['fɔːməlaɪz] *vt* officialiser

**formally** ['fɔːməlɪ] *adv* officiellement; formellement; cérémonieusement

**format** ['fɔːmæt] *n* format *m* ▷ *vt (Comput)* formater

**formation** [fɔː'meɪʃən] *n* formation *f*

**formative** ['fɔːmətɪv] *adj:* **~ years** années *fpl* d'apprentissage *(fig)* or de formation *(d'un enfant, d'un adolescent)*

**former** ['fɔːmə$^r$] *adj* ancien(ne); *(before n)* précédent(e); **the ~ ... the latter** le premier ... le second, celui-là ... celui-ci; **the ~ president** l'ex-président; **the ~ Yugoslavia/Soviet Union** l'ex-Yougoslavie/Union Soviétique

**formerly** ['fɔːməlɪ] *adv* autrefois

**form feed** *n (on printer)* alimentation *f* en feuilles

**formidable** ['fɔːmɪdəbl] *adj* redoutable

**formula** ['fɔːmjulə] *n* formule *f;* **F~ One** *(Aut)* Formule un

**formulate** ['fɔːmjuleɪt] *vt* formuler

**fornicate** ['fɔːnɪkeɪt] *vi* forniquer

**forsake** *(pt* **forsook,** *pp* **forsaken)** [fə'seɪk, -'suk, -'seɪkən] *vt* abandonner

**fort** [fɔːt] *n* fort *m;* **to hold the ~** *(fig)* assurer la permanence

**forte** ['fɔːtɪ] *n* (point) fort *m*

**forth** [fɔːθ] *adv* en avant; **to go back and ~** aller et venir; **and so ~** et ainsi de suite

**forthcoming** [fɔːθ'kʌmɪŋ] *adj* qui va paraître *or* avoir lieu prochainement; *(character)* ouvert(e), communicatif(-ive); *(available)* disponible

**forthright** ['fɔːθraɪt] *adj* franc (franche), direct(e)

**forthwith** ['fɔːθ'wɪθ] *adv* sur le champ

**fortieth** ['fɔːtɪɪθ] *num* quarantième

**fortification** [fɔːtɪfɪ'keɪʃən] *n* fortification *f*

**fortified wine** ['fɔːtɪfaɪd-] *n* vin liquoreux *or* de liqueur

**fortify** ['fɔːtɪfaɪ] *vt (city)* fortifier; *(person)* remonter

**fortitude** ['fɔːtɪtjuːd] *n* courage *m,* force *f* d'âme

**fortnight** ['fɔːtnaɪt] *n (Brit)* quinzaine *f,* quinze jours *mpl;* **it's a ~ since ...** il y a quinze jours que ...

**fortnightly** ['fɔːtnaɪtlɪ] *adj* bimensuel(le) ▷ *adv* tous les quinze jours

**FORTRAN** ['fɔːtræn] *n* FORTRAN *m*

**fortress** ['fɔːtrɪs] *n* forteresse *f*

**fortuitous** [fɔː'tjuːɪtəs] *adj* fortuit(e)

**fortunate** ['fɔːtʃənɪt] *adj* heureux(-euse); *(person)* chanceux(-euse); **to be ~** avoir de la chance; **it is ~ that** c'est une chance que, il est heureux que

**fortunately** ['fɔːtʃənɪtlɪ] *adv* heureusement, par bonheur

**fortune** ['fɔːtʃən] *n* chance *f; (wealth)* fortune *f;* **to make a ~** faire fortune

**fortune-teller** ['fɔːtʃəntɛlə$^r$] *n* diseuse *f* de bonne aventure

**forty** ['fɔːtɪ] *num* quarante

**forum** ['fɔːrəm] *n* forum *m,* tribune *f*

**forward** ['fɔːwəd] *adj (movement, position)* en avant, vers l'avant; *(not shy)* effronté(e); *(in time)* en avance; *(Comm: delivery, sales, exchange)* à terme ▷ *adv (also:* **forwards)** en avant ▷ *n (Sport)* avant *m* ▷ *vt (letter)* faire suivre; *(parcel, goods)* expédier; *(fig)* promouvoir, favoriser; **to look ~ to sth** attendre qch avec impatience; **to move ~** avancer; **"please ~"** "prière de faire suivre"; **~ planning** planification *f* à long terme

**forwarding address** *n* adresse *f* de réexpédition

**forward slash** *n* barre *f* oblique

**forwent** [fɔː'wɛnt] *pt of* **forgo**

**fossil** ['fɔsl] *adj, n* fossile *m;* **~ fuel** combustible *m* fossile

**foster** ['fɔstə$^r$] *vt (encourage)* encourager, favoriser; *(child)* élever *(sans adopter)*

**foster brother** *n* frère adoptif; frère de lait

**foster child** *n* enfant élevé dans une famille d'accueil

**foster mother** *n* mère adoptive; mère nourricière

**foster parent** *n* parent qui élève un enfant sans l'adopter

**fought** [fɔːt] *pt, pp of* **fight**

**foul** [faul] *adj (weather, smell, food)* infect(e); *(language)* ordurier(-ière); *(deed)* infâme ▷ *n (Football)* faute *f* ▷ *vt (dirty)* salir, encrasser; *(football player)* commettre une faute sur; *(entangle: anchor, propeller)* emmêler; **he's got a ~ temper** il a un caractère de chien

**foul play** n (Sport) jeu déloyal; (Law) acte criminel; ~ **is not suspected** la mort (or l'incendie etc) n'a pas de causes suspectes, on écarte l'hypothèse d'un meurtre (or d'un acte criminel)

**found** [faund] pt, pp of **find** ▷ vt (establish) fonder

**foundation** [faun'deɪʃən] n (act) fondation f; (base) fondement m; (also: **foundation cream**) fond m de teint; (also: **foundations** npl (of building) fondations fpl; **to lay the ~s** (fig) poser les fondements

**foundation stone** n première pierre

**founder** ['faundə'] n fondateur m ▷ vi couler, sombrer

**founding** ['faundɪŋ] adj: ~ **fathers** (esp US) pères mpl fondateurs; ~ **member** membre m fondateur

**foundry** ['faundrɪ] n fonderie f

**fount** [faunt] n source f; (Typ) fonte f

**fountain** ['fauntɪn] n fontaine f

**fountain pen** n stylo m (à encre)

**four** [fɔː'] num quatre; **on all ~s** à quatre pattes

**four-letter word** ['fɔːlɛtə-] n obscénité f, gros mot

**four-poster** ['fɔː'pəustə'] n (also: **four-poster bed**) lit m à baldaquin

**foursome** ['fɔːsəm] n partie f à quatre; sortie f à quatre

**fourteen** ['fɔː'tiːn] num quatorze

**fourteenth** ['fɔː'tiːnθ] num quatorzième

**fourth** ['fɔːθ] num quatrième ▷ n (Aut: also: **fourth gear**) quatrième f

**four-wheel drive** ['fɔːwiːl-] n (Aut: car) voiture f à quatre roues motrices; **with ~** à quatre roues motrices

**fowl** [faul] n volaille f

**fox** [fɔks] n renard m ▷ vt mystifier

**fox fur** n renard m

**foxglove** ['fɔksglʌv] n (Bot) digitale f

**fox-hunting** ['fɔkshʌntɪŋ] n chasse f au renard

**foyer** ['fɔɪeɪ] n (in hotel) vestibule m; (Theat) foyer m

**FP** n abbr (Brit) = **former pupil**; (US) = **fireplug**

**FPA** n abbr (Brit) = **Family Planning Association**

**Fr.** abbr (Rel = **father**) P; (= friar) F

**fr.** abbr (= franc) F

**fracas** ['frækɑː] n bagarre f

**fraction** ['frækʃən] n fraction f

**fractionally** ['frækʃnəlɪ] adv: ~ **smaller** etc un poil plus petit etc

**fractious** ['frækʃəs] adj grincheux(-euse)

**fracture** ['fræktʃə'] n fracture f ▷ vt fracturer

**fragile** ['frædʒaɪl] adj fragile

**fragment** ['frægmənt] n fragment m

**fragmentary** ['frægməntərɪ] adj fragmentaire

**fragrance** ['freɪɡrəns] n parfum m

**fragrant** ['freɪɡrənt] adj parfumé(e), odorant(e)

**frail** [freɪl] adj fragile, délicat(e); (person) frêle

**frame** [freɪm] n (of building) charpente f; (of human, animal) charpente, ossature f; (of picture) cadre m; (of door, window) encadrement m, chambranle m; (of spectacles: also: **frames**) monture f ▷ vt (picture) encadrer; (theory, plan)

construire, élaborer; **to ~ sb** (inf) monter un coup contre qn; ~ **of mind** disposition f d'esprit

**framework** ['freɪmwəːk] n structure f

**France** [frɑːns] n la France; **in ~** en France

**franchise** ['fræntʃaɪz] n (Pol) droit m de vote; (Comm) franchise f

**franchisee** [fræntʃaɪ'ziː] n franchisé m

**franchiser** ['fræntʃaɪzə'] n franchiseur m

**frank** [fræŋk] adj franc (franche) ▷ vt (letter) affranchir

**Frankfurt** ['fræŋkfəːt] n Francfort

**franking machine** ['fræŋkɪŋ-] n machine f à affranchir

**frankly** ['fræŋklɪ] adv franchement

**frankness** ['fræŋknɪs] n franchise f

**frantic** ['fræntɪk] adj (hectic) frénétique; (need, desire) effréné(e); (distraught) hors de soi

**frantically** ['fræntɪklɪ] adv frénétiquement

**fraternal** [frə'təːnl] adj fraternel(le)

**fraternity** [frə'təːnɪtɪ] n (club) communauté f, confrérie f; (spirit) fraternité f

**fraternize** ['frætənaɪz] vi fraterniser

**fraud** [frɔːd] n supercherie f, fraude f, tromperie f; (person) imposteur m

**fraudulent** ['frɔːdjulənt] adj frauduleux(-euse)

**fraught** [frɔːt] adj (tense: person) très tendu(e); (: situation) pénible; ~ **with** (difficulties etc) chargé(e) de, plein(e) de

**fray** [freɪ] n bagarre f; (Mil) combat m ▷ vt effilocher ▷ vi s'effilocher; **tempers were ~ed** les gens commençaient à s'énerver; **her nerves were ~ed** elle était à bout de nerfs

**FRB** n abbr (US) = **Federal Reserve Board**

**FRCM** n abbr (Brit) = **Fellow of the Royal College of Music**

**FRCO** n abbr (Brit) = **Fellow of the Royal College of Organists**

**FRCP** n abbr (Brit) = **Fellow of the Royal College of Physicians**

**FRCS** n abbr (Brit) = **Fellow of the Royal College of Surgeons**

**freak** [friːk] n (eccentric person) phénomène m; (unusual event) hasard m extraordinaire; (pej: fanatic): **health food ~** fana m/f or obsédé(e) de l'alimentation saine ▷ adj (storm) exceptionnel(le); (accident) bizarre

▸ **freak out** vi (inf: drop out) se marginaliser; (: on drugs) se défoncer

**freakish** ['friːkɪʃ] adj insolite, anormal(e)

**freckle** ['frɛkl] n tache f de rousseur

**free** [friː] adj libre; (gratis) gratuit(e); (liberal) généreux(-euse), large ▷ vt (prisoner etc) libérer; (jammed object or person) dégager; **is this seat ~?** la place est libre?; **to give sb a ~ hand** donner carte blanche à qn; ~ **and easy** sans façon, décontracté(e); **admission ~** entrée libre; ~ **(of charge)** gratuitement

**freebie** ['friːbɪ] n (inf): **it's a ~** c'est gratuit

**freedom** ['friːdəm] n liberté f

**freedom fighter** n combattant m de la liberté

**free enterprise** n libre entreprise f

**Freefone®** ['friːfəun] n numéro vert

**free-for-all** ['friːfərɔːl] *n* mêlée générale
**free gift** *n* prime *f*
**freehold** ['friːhəuld] *n* propriété foncière libre
**free kick** *n* (*Sport*) coup franc
**freelance** ['friːlɑːns] *adj* (*journalist etc*) indépendant(e), free-lance *inv*; (*work*) en free-lance ▷ *adv* en free-lance
**freeloader** ['friːləudər] *n* (*pej*) parasite *m*
**freely** ['friːlɪ] *adv* librement; (*liberally*) libéralement
**free-market economy** [friːˈmɑːkɪt-] *n* économie *f* de marché
**freemason** ['friːmeɪsn] *n* franc-maçon *m*
**freemasonry** ['friːmeɪsnrɪ] *n* franc-maçonnerie *f*
**Freepost**® ['friːpəust] *n* (*Brit*) port payé
**free-range** ['friːˈreɪndʒ] *adj* (*egg*) de ferme; (*chicken*) fermier
**free sample** *n* échantillon gratuit
**free speech** *n* liberté *f* d'expression
**free trade** *n* libre-échange *m*
**freeway** ['friːweɪ] *n* (*US*) autoroute *f*
**freewheel** [friːˈwiːl] *vi* descendre en roue libre
**freewheeling** [friːˈwiːlɪŋ] *adj* indépendant(e), libre
**free will** *n* libre arbitre *m*; **of one's own ~** de son plein gré
**freeze** [friːz] (*pt* **froze**, *pp* **frozen** [frəuz, 'frəuzn]) *vi* geler ▷ *vt* geler; (*food*) congeler; (*prices, salaries*) bloquer, geler ▷ *n* gel *m*; (*of prices, salaries*) blocage *m*
▶ **freeze over** *vi* (*river*) geler; (*windscreen*) se couvrir de givre *or* de glace
▶ **freeze up** *vi* geler
**freeze-dried** ['friːzdraɪd] *adj* lyophilisé(e)
**freezer** ['friːzər] *n* congélateur *m*
**freezing** ['friːzɪŋ] *adj*: ~ (**cold**) (*room etc*) glacial(e); (*person, hands*) gelé(e), glacé(e) ▷ *n*: **3 degrees below ~** 3 degrés au-dessous de zéro; **it's ~** il fait un froid glacial
**freezing point** *n* point *m* de congélation
**freight** [freɪt] *n* (*goods*) fret *m*, cargaison *f*; (*money charged*) fret, prix *m* du transport; ~ **forward** port dû; ~ **inward** port payé par le destinataire
**freighter** ['freɪtər] *n* (*Naut*) cargo *m*
**freight forwarder** [-fɔːwədər] *n* transitaire *m*
**freight train** *n* (*US*) train *m* de marchandises
**French** [frɛntʃ] *adj* français(e) ▷ *n* (*Ling*) français *m*; **the ~** (*npl*) les Français; **what's the ~ (word) for ...?** comment dit-on ... en français?
**French bean** *n* (*Brit*) haricot vert
**French bread** *n* pain *m* français
**French Canadian** *adj* canadien(ne) français(e) ▷ *n* Canadien(ne) français(e)
**French dressing** *n* (*Culin*) vinaigrette *f*
**French fried potatoes**, (*US*) **French fries** *npl* (pommes de terre *fpl*) frites *fpl*
**French Guiana** [-gaɪˈænə] *n* Guyane française
**French horn** *n* (*Mus*) cor *m* (d'harmonie)
**French kiss** *n* baiser profond
**French loaf** *n* ≈ pain *m*, ≈ parisien *m*
**Frenchman** ['frɛntʃmən] (*irreg*) *n* Français *m*

**French Riviera** *n*: **the ~** la Côte d'Azur
**French stick** *n* ≈ baguette *f*
**French window** *n* porte-fenêtre *f*
**Frenchwoman** ['frɛntʃwumən] (*irreg*) *n* Française *f*
**frenetic** [frəˈnɛtɪk] *adj* frénétique
**frenzy** ['frɛnzɪ] *n* frénésie *f*
**frequency** ['friːkwənsɪ] *n* fréquence *f*
**frequency modulation** *n* modulation *f* de fréquence
**frequent** *adj* ['friːkwənt] fréquent(e) ▷ *vt* [frɪˈkwɛnt] fréquenter
**frequently** ['friːkwəntlɪ] *adv* fréquemment
**fresco** ['frɛskəu] *n* fresque *f*
**fresh** [frɛʃ] *adj* frais (fraîche); (*new*) nouveau (nouvelle); (*cheeky*) familier(-ière), culotté(e); **to make a ~ start** prendre un nouveau départ
**freshen** ['frɛʃən] *vi* (*wind, air*) fraîchir
▶ **freshen up** *vi* faire un brin de toilette
**freshener** ['frɛʃnər] *n*: **skin ~** astringent *m*; **air ~** désodorisant *m*
**fresher** ['frɛʃər] *n* (*Brit University: inf*) bizuth *m*, étudiant(e) de première année
**freshly** ['frɛʃlɪ] *adv* nouvellement, récemment
**freshman** (*US: irreg*) ['frɛʃmən] *n* = **fresher**
**freshness** ['frɛʃnɪs] *n* fraîcheur *f*
**freshwater** ['frɛʃwɔːtər] *adj* (*fish*) d'eau douce
**fret** [frɛt] *vi* s'agiter, se tracasser
**fretful** ['frɛtful] *adj* (*child*) grincheux(-euse)
**Freudian** ['frɔɪdɪən] *adj* freudien(ne); ~ **slip** lapsus *m*
**FRG** *n abbr* (= *Federal Republic of Germany*) RFA *f*
**friar** ['fraɪər] *n* moine *m*, frère *m*
**friction** ['frɪkʃən] *n* friction *f*, frottement *m*
**friction feed** *n* (*on printer*) entraînement *m* par friction
**Friday** ['fraɪdɪ] *n* vendredi *m*; *for phrases see also* **Tuesday**
**fridge** [frɪdʒ] *n* (*Brit*) frigo *m*, frigidaire® *m*
**fridge-freezer** ['frɪdʒˈfriːzər] *n* réfrigérateur-congélateur *m*
**fried** [fraɪd] *pt*, *pp of* **fry** ▷ *adj* frit(e); ~ **egg** œuf *m* sur le plat
**friend** [frɛnd] *n* ami(e) ▷ *vt* (*Internet*) ajouter comme ami(e); **to make ~s with** se lier (d'amitié) avec
**friendliness** ['frɛndlɪnɪs] *n* attitude amicale
**friendly** ['frɛndlɪ] *adj* amical(e); (*kind*) sympathique, gentil(le); (*place*) accueillant(e); (*Pol: country*) ami(e) ▷ *n* (*also*: **friendly match**) match amical; **to be ~ with** être ami(e) avec; **to be ~ to** être bien disposé(e) à l'égard de
**friendly fire** *n*: **they were killed by ~** ils sont morts sous les tirs de leur propre camp
**friendly society** *n* société *f* mutualiste
**friendship** ['frɛndʃɪp] *n* amitié *f*
**fries** [fraɪz] (*esp US*) *npl* = **French fried potatoes**
**frieze** [friːz] *n* frise *f*, bordure *f*
**frigate** ['frɪgɪt] *n* (*Naut: modern*) frégate *f*
**fright** [fraɪt] *n* peur *f*, effroi *m*; **to give sb a ~** faire peur à qn; **to take ~** prendre peur, s'effrayer; **she looks a ~** elle a l'air d'un

épouvantail

**frighten** ['fraɪtn] vt effrayer, faire peur à
▸ **frighten away, frighten off** vt (birds, children etc) faire fuir, effaroucher

**frightened** ['fraɪtnd] adj: **to be ~ (of)** avoir peur (de)

**frightening** ['fraɪtnɪŋ] adj effrayant(e)

**frightful** ['fraɪtful] adj affreux(-euse)

**frightfully** ['fraɪtfəlɪ] adv affreusement

**frigid** ['frɪdʒɪd] adj frigide

**frigidity** [frɪ'dʒɪdɪtɪ] n frigidité f

**frill** [frɪl] n (of dress) volant m; (of shirt) jabot m; **without ~s** (fig) sans manières

**frilly** ['frɪlɪ] adj à fanfreluches

**fringe** [frɪndʒ] n (Brit: of hair) frange f; (edge: of forest etc) bordure f; (fig): **on the ~** en marge

**fringe benefits** npl avantages sociaux or en nature

**fringe theatre** n théâtre m d'avant-garde

**Frisbee®** ['frɪzbɪ] n Frisbee® m

**frisk** [frɪsk] vt fouiller

**frisky** ['frɪskɪ] adj vif (vive), sémillant(e)

**fritter** ['frɪtər] n beignet m
▸ **fritter away** vt gaspiller

**frivolity** [frɪ'vɒlɪtɪ] n frivolité f

**frivolous** ['frɪvələs] adj frivole

**frizzy** ['frɪzɪ] adj crépu(e)

**fro** [frəʊ] adv see **to**

**frock** [frɒk] n robe f

**frog** [frɒg] n grenouille f; **to have a ~ in one's throat** avoir un chat dans la gorge

**frogman** (irreg) ['frɒgmən] n homme-grenouille m

**frogmarch** ['frɒgmɑːtʃ] vt (Brit): **to ~ sb in/out** faire entrer/sortir qn de force

**frolic** ['frɒlɪk] n ébats mpl ▷ vi folâtrer, batifoler

O **KEYWORD**

**from** [frɒm] prep **1** (indicating starting place, origin etc) de; **where do you come from?**, **where are you from?** d'où venez-vous?; **where has he come from?** d'où arrive-t-il?; **from London to Paris** de Londres à Paris; **to escape from sb/sth** échapper à qn/qch; **a letter/telephone call from my sister** une lettre/un appel de ma sœur; **to drink from the bottle** boire à (même) la bouteille; **tell him from me that ...** dites-lui de ma part que ...

**2** (indicating time) (à partir) de; **from one o'clock to** or **until** or **till two** d'une heure à deux heures; **from January (on)** à partir de janvier

**3** (indicating distance) de; **the hotel is one kilometre from the beach** l'hôtel est à un kilomètre de la plage

**4** (indicating price, number etc) de; **prices range from £10 to £50** les prix varient entre 10 livres et 50 livres; **the interest rate was increased from 9% to 10%** le taux d'intérêt est passé de 9% à 10%

**5** (indicating difference) de; **he can't tell red from green** il ne peut pas distinguer le rouge du vert;

**to be different from sb/sth** être différent de qn/qch

**6** (because of, on the basis of): **from what he says** d'après ce qu'il dit; **weak from hunger** affaibli par la faim

**frond** [frɒnd] n fronde f

**front** [frʌnt] n (of house, dress) devant m; (of coach, train) avant m; (of book) couverture f; (promenade: also: **sea front**) bord m de mer; (Mil, Pol, Meteorology) front m; (fig: appearances) contenance f, façade f ▷ adj de devant; (page, row) premier(-ière); (seat, wheel) avant inv ▷ vi: **to ~ onto sth** donner sur qch; **in ~ (of)** devant

**frontage** ['frʌntɪdʒ] n façade f; (of shop) devanture f

**frontal** ['frʌntl] adj frontal(e)

**front bench** n (Brit: Pol) voir article

◉ **FRONT BENCH**
◉
◉ Le *front bench* est le banc du gouvernement,
◉ placé à la droite du "Speaker", ou celui du
◉ cabinet fantôme, placé à sa gauche. Ils se
◉ font face dans l'enceinte de la Chambre des
◉ communes. Par extension, *front bench*
◉ désigne les dirigeants des groupes
◉ parlementaires de la majorité et de
◉ l'opposition, qui sont appelés
◉ "frontbenchers" par opposition aux autres
◉ députés qui sont appelés "backbenchers".

**front desk** n (US: in hotel, at doctor's) réception f

**front door** n porte f d'entrée; (of car) portière f avant

**frontier** ['frʌntɪər] n frontière f

**frontispiece** ['frʌntɪspiːs] n frontispice m

**front page** n première page

**front room** n (Brit) pièce f de devant, salon m

**front runner** n (fig) favori(te)

**front-wheel drive** ['frʌntwiːl-] n traction f avant

**frost** [frɒst] n gel m, gelée f; (also: **hoarfrost**) givre m

**frostbite** ['frɒstbaɪt] n gelures fpl

**frosted** ['frɒstɪd] adj (glass) dépoli(e); (esp US: cake) glacé(e)

**frosting** ['frɒstɪŋ] n (esp US: on cake) glaçage m

**frosty** ['frɒstɪ] adj (window) couvert(e) de givre; (weather, welcome) glacial(e)

**froth** [frɒθ] n mousse f; écume f

**frown** [fraun] n froncement m de sourcils ▷ vi froncer les sourcils
▸ **frown on** vt (fig) désapprouver

**froze** [frəʊz] pt of **freeze**

**frozen** ['frəʊzn] pp of **freeze** ▷ adj (food) congelé(e); (very cold: person: Comm: assets) gelé(e)

**FRS** n abbr (Brit: = Fellow of the Royal Society) membre de l'Académie des sciences; (US: = Federal Reserve System) banque centrale américaine

**frugal** ['fruːgl] adj frugal(e)

**fruit** [fruːt] n (pl inv) fruit m

**fruiterer** ['fru:tərəʳ] n fruitier m, marchand(e) de fruits; **~'s (shop)** fruiterie f
**fruit fly** n mouche f du vinaigre, drosophile f
**fruitful** ['fru:tful] adj fructueux(-euse); (plant, soil) fécond(e)
**fruition** [fru:'ɪʃən] n: **to come to ~** se réaliser
**fruit juice** n jus m de fruit
**fruitless** ['fru:tlɪs] adj (fig) vain(e), infructueux(-euse)
**fruit machine** n (Brit) machine f à sous
**fruit salad** n salade f de fruits
**frump** [frʌmp] n mocheté f
**frustrate** [frʌs'treɪt] vt frustrer; (plot, plans) faire échouer
**frustrated** [frʌs'treɪtɪd] adj frustré(e)
**frustrating** [frʌs'treɪtɪŋ] adj (job) frustrant(e); (day) démoralisant(e)
**frustration** [frʌs'treɪʃən] n frustration f
**fry** (pt, pp **fried**) [fraɪ, -d] vt (faire) frire ▷ n: **small ~** le menu fretin
**frying pan** ['fraɪɪŋ-] n poêle f (à frire)
**FT** n abbr (Brit: = Financial Times) journal financier
**ft.** abbr = **foot; feet**
**FTC** n abbr (US) = **Federal Trade Commission**
**FTSE 100 (Share) Index** n abbr (= Financial Times Stock Exchange 100 (Share) Index) indice m Footsie des cent grandes valeurs
**fuchsia** ['fju:ʃə] n fuchsia m
**fuck** [fʌk] vt, vi (inf!) baiser (!); **~ off!** fous le camp! (!)
**fuddled** ['fʌdld] adj (muddled) embrouillé(e), confus(e)
**fuddy-duddy** ['fʌdɪdʌdɪ] adj (pej) vieux jeu inv, ringard(e)
**fudge** [fʌdʒ] n (Culin) sorte de confiserie à base de sucre, de beurre et de lait ▷ vt (issue, problem) esquiver
**fuel** [fjuəl] n (for heating) combustible m; (for engine) carburant m
**fuel oil** n mazout m
**fuel poverty** n pauvreté f énergétique
**fuel pump** n (Aut) pompe f d'alimentation
**fuel tank** n cuve f à mazout, citerne f; (in vehicle) réservoir m de or à carburant
**fug** [fʌg] n (Brit) puanteur f, odeur f de renfermé
**fugitive** ['fju:dʒɪtɪv] n fugitif(-ive)
**fulfil,** (US) **fulfill** [ful'fɪl] vt (function, condition) remplir; (order) exécuter; (wish, desire) satisfaire, réaliser
**fulfilled** [ful'fɪld] adj (person) comblé(e), épanoui(e)
**fulfilment,** (US) **fulfillment** [ful'fɪlmənt] n (of wishes) réalisation f
**full** [ful] adj plein(e); (details, hotel, bus) complet(-ète); (price) fort(e), normal(e); (busy: day) chargé(e); (skirt) ample, large ▷ adv: **to know ~ well that** savoir fort bien que; **~ (up)** (hotel etc) complet(-ète); **I'm ~ (up)** j'ai bien mangé; **~ employment/fare** plein emploi/tarif; **a ~ two hours** deux bonnes heures; **at ~ speed** à toute vitesse; **in ~** (reproduce, quote, pay) intégralement; (write name etc) en toutes lettres
**fullback** ['fulbæk] n (Rugby, Football) arrière m

**full-blooded** ['ful'blʌdɪd] adj (vigorous) vigoureux(-euse)
**full-cream** ['ful'kri:m] adj: **~ milk** (Brit) lait entier
**full-grown** ['ful'grəun] adj arrivé(e) à maturité, adulte
**full-length** ['ful'lɛŋθ] adj (portrait) en pied; (coat) long(ue); **~ film** long métrage
**full moon** n pleine lune
**full-scale** ['fulskeɪl] adj (model) grandeur nature inv; (search, retreat) complet(-ète), total(e)
**full-sized** ['ful'saɪzd] adj (portrait etc) grandeur nature inv
**full stop** n point m
**full-time** ['ful'taɪm] adj, adv (work) à plein temps ▷ n (Sport) fin f du match
**fully** ['fulɪ] adv entièrement, complètement; (at least): **~ as big** au moins aussi grand
**fully-fledged** ['fulɪ'flɛdʒd] adj (teacher, barrister) diplômé(e); (citizen, member) à part entière
**fulsome** ['fulsəm] adj (pej: praise) excessif(-ive); (: manner) exagéré(e)
**fumble** ['fʌmbl] vi fouiller, tâtonner ▷ vt (ball) mal réceptionner, cafouiller
▶ **fumble with** vt fus tripoter
**fume** [fju:m] vi (rage) rager
**fumes** [fju:mz] npl vapeurs fpl, émanations fpl, gaz mpl
**fumigate** ['fju:mɪgeɪt] vt désinfecter (par fumigation)
**fun** [fʌn] n amusement m, divertissement m; **to have ~** s'amuser; **for ~** pour rire; **it's not much ~** ce n'est pas très drôle or amusant; **to make ~ of** se moquer de
**function** ['fʌŋkʃən] n fonction f; (reception, dinner) cérémonie f, soirée officielle ▷ vi fonctionner; **to ~ as** faire office de
**functional** ['fʌŋkʃnl] adj fonctionnel(le)
**function key** n (Comput) touche f de fonction
**fund** [fʌnd] n caisse f, fonds m; (source, store) source f, mine f; **funds** npl (money) fonds mpl
**fundamental** [fʌndə'mɛntl] adj fondamental(e); **fundamentals** npl principes mpl de base
**fundamentalism** [fʌndə'mɛntəlɪzəm] n intégrisme m
**fundamentalist** [fʌndə'mɛntəlɪst] n intégriste m/f
**fundamentally** [fʌndə'mɛntəlɪ] adv fondamentalement
**funding** ['fʌndɪŋ] n financement m
**fund-raising** ['fʌndreɪzɪŋ] n collecte f de fonds
**funeral** ['fju:nərəl] n enterrement m, obsèques fpl (more formal occasion)
**funeral director** n entrepreneur m des pompes funèbres
**funeral parlour** n (Brit) dépôt m mortuaire
**funeral service** n service m funèbre
**funereal** [fju:'nɪərɪəl] adj lugubre, funèbre
**funfair** ['fʌnfɛəʳ] n (Brit) fête (foraine)
**fungus** (pl **fungi**) ['fʌŋgəs, -gaɪ] n champignon m; (mould) moisissure f

593

**funicular** [fju:'nɪkjulə<sup>r</sup>] n (also: **funicular railway**) funiculaire m

**funky** ['fʌŋkɪ] adj (music) funky inv; (inf: excellent) super inv

**funnel** ['fʌnl] n entonnoir m; (of ship) cheminée f

**funnily** ['fʌnɪlɪ] adv drôlement; (strangely) curieusement

**funny** ['fʌnɪ] adj amusant(e), drôle; (strange) curieux(-euse), bizarre

**funny bone** n endroit sensible du coude

**fun run** n course f de fond (pour amateurs)

**fur** [fə:<sup>r</sup>] n fourrure f; (Brit: in kettle etc) (dépôt m de) tartre m

**fur coat** n manteau m de fourrure

**furious** ['fjuərɪəs] adj furieux(-euse); (effort) acharné(e); **to be ~ with sb** être dans une fureur noire contre qn

**furiously** ['fjuərɪəslɪ] adv furieusement; avec acharnement

**furl** [fə:l] vt rouler; (Naut) ferler

**furlong** ['fə:lɔŋ] n = 201.17 m (terme d'hippisme)

**furlough** ['fə:ləu] n permission f, congé m

**furnace** ['fə:nɪs] n fourneau m

**furnish** ['fə:nɪʃ] vt meubler; (supply) fournir; **~ed flat** or (US) **apartment** meublé m

**furnishings** ['fə:nɪʃɪŋz] npl mobilier m, articles mpl d'ameublement

**furniture** ['fə:nɪtʃə<sup>r</sup>] n meubles mpl, mobilier m; **piece of ~** meuble m

**furniture polish** n encaustique f

**furore** [fjuə'rɔ:rɪ] n (protests) protestations fpl

**furrier** ['fʌrɪə<sup>r</sup>] n fourreur m

**furrow** ['fʌrəu] n sillon m

**furry** ['fə:rɪ] adj (animal) à fourrure; (toy) en peluche

**further** ['fə:ðə<sup>r</sup>] adj supplémentaire, autre; nouveau (nouvelle) ▷ adv plus loin; (more) davantage; (moreover) de plus ▷ vt faire avancer or progresser, promouvoir; **how much ~ is it?** quelle distance or combien reste-t-il à parcourir?; **until ~ notice** jusqu'à nouvel ordre or avis; **~ to your letter of ...** (Comm) suite à votre lettre du ...

**further education** n enseignement m postscolaire (recyclage, formation professionnelle)

**furthermore** [fə:ðə'mɔ:<sup>r</sup>] adv de plus, en outre

**furthermost** ['fə:ðəməust] adj le (la) plus éloigné(e)

**furthest** ['fə:ðɪst] superlative of **far**

**furtive** ['fə:tɪv] adj furtif(-ive)

**fury** ['fjuərɪ] n fureur f

**fuse**, (US) **fuze** [fju:z] n fusible m; (for bomb etc) amorce f, détonateur m ▷ vt, vi (metal) fondre; (fig) fusionner; (Brit: Elec): **to ~ the lights** faire sauter les fusibles or les plombs; **a ~ has blown** un fusible a sauté

**fuse box** n boîte f à fusibles

**fuselage** ['fju:zəlɑ:ʒ] n fuselage m

**fuse wire** n fusible m

**fusillade** [fju:zɪ'leɪd] n fusillade f; (fig) feu roulant

**fusion** ['fju:ʒən] n fusion f

**fuss** [fʌs] n (anxiety, excitement) chichis mpl, façons fpl; (commotion) tapage m; (complaining, trouble) histoire(s) f(pl) ▷ vi faire des histoires ▷ vt (person) embêter; **to make a ~** faire des façons (or des histoires); **to make a ~ of sb** dorloter qn

▶ **fuss over** vt fus (person) dorloter

**fusspot** ['fʌspɔt] n (inf): **don't be such a ~!** ne fais pas tant d'histoires!

**fussy** ['fʌsɪ] adj (person) tatillon(ne), difficile, chichiteux(-euse); (dress, style) tarabiscoté(e); **I'm not ~** (inf) ça m'est égal

**fusty** ['fʌstɪ] adj (old-fashioned) vieillot(te); (smell) de renfermé or moisi

**futile** ['fju:taɪl] adj futile

**futility** [fju:'tɪlɪtɪ] n futilité f

**futon** ['fu:tɔn] n futon m

**future** ['fju:tʃə<sup>r</sup>] adj futur(e) ▷ n avenir m; (Ling) futur m; **futures** npl (Comm) opérations fpl à terme; **in (the) ~** à l'avenir; **in the near/immediate ~** dans un avenir proche/immédiat

**futuristic** [fju:tʃə'rɪstɪk] adj futuriste

**fuze** [fju:z] n, vt, vi (US) = **fuse**

**fuzzy** ['fʌzɪ] adj (Phot) flou(e); (hair) crépu(e)

**fwd.** abbr = **forward**

**fwy** abbr (US) = **freeway**

**FY** abbr = **fiscal year**

**FYI** abbr = **for your information**

# Gg

**G¹, g** [dʒi:] n (letter) G, g m; (Mus): **G** sol m; **G for George** G comme Gaston

**G²** n abbr (Brit Scol: = good) b (= bien); (US Cine: = general (audience)) ≈ tous publics; (Pol: = G8) G8 m

**g.** abbr (= gram) g; (= gravity) g

**G8** abbr (Pol): **the G8 nations** le G8

**G20** n abbr (Pol) G20 m

**GA** abbr (US) = **Georgia**

**gab** [gæb] n (inf): **to have the gift of the ~** avoir la langue bien pendue

**gabble** ['gæbl] vi bredouiller; jacasser

**gaberdine** [gæbə'di:n] n gabardine f

**gable** ['geɪbl] n pignon m

**Gabon** [gə'bɔn] n Gabon m

**gad about** ['gædə'baut] vi (inf) se balader

**gadget** ['gædʒɪt] n gadget m

**Gaelic** ['geɪlɪk] adj, n (Ling) gaélique (m)

**gaffe** [gæf] n gaffe f

**gaffer** ['gæfəʳ] n (Brit: foreman) contremaître m; (Brit inf: boss) patron m

**gag** [gæg] n (on mouth) bâillon m; (joke) gag m ▷ vt (prisoner etc) bâillonner ▷ vi (choke) étouffer

**gaga** ['gɑːgɑː] adj: **to go ~** devenir gaga or gâteux(-euse)

**gaiety** ['geɪɪtɪ] n gaieté f

**gaily** ['geɪlɪ] adv gaiement

**gain** [geɪn] n (improvement) gain m; (profit) gain, profit m ▷ vt gagner; **to ~ from/by** gagner de/à; **to ~ on sb** (catch up) rattraper qn; **to ~ 3lbs (in weight)** prendre 3 livres; **to ~ ground** gagner du terrain

**gainful** ['geɪnful] adj profitable, lucratif(-ive)

**gainfully** ['geɪnfəlɪ] adv: **to be ~ employed** avoir un emploi rémunéré

**gainsay** [geɪn'seɪ] vt (irreg: like **say**) contredire; nier

**gait** [geɪt] n démarche f

**gal.** abbr = **gallon**

**gala** ['gɑːlə] n gala m; **swimming ~** grand concours de natation

**Galápagos** [gə'læpəgəs], **Galápagos Islands** npl: **the ~ (Islands)** les (îles fpl) Galapagos fpl

**galaxy** ['gæləksɪ] n galaxie f

**gale** [geɪl] n coup m de vent; **~ force 10** vent m de force 10

**gall** [gɔːl] n (Anat) bile f; (fig) effronterie f ▷ vt ulcérer, irriter

**gall.** abbr = **gallon**

**gallant** ['gælənt] adj vaillant(e), brave; (towards ladies) empressé(e), galant(e)

**gallantry** ['gæləntrɪ] n bravoure f, vaillance f; empressement m, galanterie f

**gall bladder** ['gɔːl-] n vésicule f biliaire

**galleon** ['gælɪən] n galion m

**gallery** ['gælərɪ] n galerie f; (also: **art gallery**) musée m; (: private) galerie; (for spectators) tribune f; (: in theatre) dernier balcon

**galley** ['gælɪ] n (ship's kitchen) cambuse f; (ship) galère f; (also: **galley proof**) placard m, galée f

**Gallic** ['gælɪk] adj (of Gaul) gaulois(e); (French) français(e)

**galling** ['gɔːlɪŋ] adj irritant(e)

**gallon** ['gæln] n gallon m (Brit = 4.543 l; US = 3.785 l), = 8 pints

**gallop** ['gæləp] n galop m ▷ vi galoper; **~ing inflation** inflation galopante

**gallows** ['gæləuz] n potence f

**gallstone** ['gɔːlstəun] n calcul m (biliaire)

**Gallup Poll** ['gæləp-] n sondage m Gallup

**galore** [gə'lɔːʳ] adv en abondance, à gogo

**galvanize** ['gælvənaɪz] vt galvaniser; (fig): **to ~ sb into action** galvaniser qn

**Gambia** ['gæmbɪə] n Gambie f

**gambit** ['gæmbɪt] n (fig): **(opening) ~** manœuvre f stratégique

**gamble** ['gæmbl] n pari m, risque calculé ▷ vt, vi jouer; **to ~ on the Stock Exchange** jouer en or à la Bourse; **to ~ on** (fig) miser sur

**gambler** ['gæmbləʳ] n joueur m

**gambling** ['gæmblɪŋ] n jeu m

**gambol** ['gæmbl] vi gambader

**game** [geɪm] n jeu m; (event) match m; (of tennis, chess, cards) partie f; (Hunting) gibier m ▷ adj brave; (willing): **to be ~ (for)** être prêt(e) (à or pour); **a ~ of football/tennis** une partie de football/tennis; **big ~** gros gibier; **games** npl (Scol) sport m; (sport event) jeux

**game bird** n gibier m à plume

**gamekeeper** ['geɪmkiːpəʳ] n garde-chasse m

**gamely** ['geɪmlɪ] adv vaillamment

**gamer** ['geɪməʳ] n jouer(-euse) de jeux vidéos

**game reserve** n réserve animalière

**games console** ['geɪmz-] *n* console *f* de jeux
vidéo
**game show** ['geɪmʃəu] *n* jeu télévisé
**gamesmanship** ['geɪmzmənʃɪp] *n* roublardise *f*
**gaming** ['geɪmɪŋ] *n* jeu *m*, jeux *mpl* d'argent;
(*video games*) jeux *mpl* vidéos
**gammon** ['gæmən] *n* (*bacon*) quartier *m* de lard
fumé; (*ham*) jambon fumé *or* salé
**gamut** ['gæmət] *n* gamme *f*
**gang** [gæŋ] *n* bande *f*, groupe *m*; (*of workmen*)
équipe *f*
  ▸ **gang up** *vi*: **to ~ up on sb** se liguer contre qn
**Ganges** ['gændʒiːz] *n*: **the ~** le Gange
**gangland** ['gæŋlænd] *adj*: **~ killer** tueur
professionnel du milieu; **~ boss** chef *m* de gang
**gangling** ['gæŋglɪŋ], **gangly** ['gæŋglɪ] *adj*
dégingandé(e)
**gangplank** ['gæŋplæŋk] *n* passerelle *f*
**gangrene** ['gæŋgriːn] *n* gangrène *f*
**gangster** ['gæŋstə'] *n* gangster *m*, bandit *m*
**gangway** ['gæŋweɪ] *n* passerelle *f*; (*Brit: of bus*)
couloir central
**gantry** ['gæntrɪ] *n* portique *m*; (*for rocket*) tour *f*
de lancement
**GAO** *n abbr* (*US*: = *General Accounting Office*) ≈ Cour *f*
des comptes
**gaol** [dʒeɪl] *n*, *vt* (*Brit*) = **jail**
**gap** [gæp] *n* trou *m*; (*in time*) intervalle *m*; (*fig*)
lacune *f*; vide *m*; (*difference*): **~ (between)** écart *m*
(entre)
**gape** [geɪp] *vi* (*person*) être *or* rester bouche bée;
(*hole, shirt*) être ouvert(e)
**gaping** ['geɪpɪŋ] *adj* (*hole*) béant(e)
**gap year** *n année que certains étudiants prennent pour
voyager ou pour travailler avant d'entrer à l'université*
**garage** ['gærɑːʒ] *n* garage *m*
**garage sale** *n* vide-grenier *m*
**garb** [gɑːb] *n* tenue *f*, costume *m*
**garbage** ['gɑːbɪdʒ] *n* (*US: rubbish*) ordures *fpl*,
détritus *mpl*; (*inf: nonsense*) âneries *fpl*
**garbage can** *n* (*US*) poubelle *f*, boîte *f* à ordures
**garbage collector** *n* (*US*) éboueur *m*
**garbage disposal unit** *n* broyeur *m* d'ordures
**garbage truck** *n* (*US*) camion *m* (de ramassage
des ordures), benne *f* à ordures
**garbled** ['gɑːbld] *adj* déformé(e), faussé(e)
**garden** ['gɑːdn] *n* jardin *m* ▸ *vi* jardiner;
**gardens** *npl* (*public*) jardin public; (*private*)
parc *m*
**garden centre** (*Brit*) *n* pépinière *f*, jardinerie *f*
**garden city** (*Brit*) *n* cité-jardin *f*
**gardener** ['gɑːdnə'] *n* jardinier *m*
**gardening** ['gɑːdnɪŋ] *n* jardinage *m*
**gargle** ['gɑːgl] *vi* se gargariser ▸ *n* gargarisme *m*
**gargoyle** ['gɑːgɔɪl] *n* gargouille *f*
**garish** ['gɛərɪʃ] *adj* criard(e), voyant(e)
**garland** ['gɑːlənd] *n* guirlande *f*; couronne *f*
**garlic** ['gɑːlɪk] *n* ail *m*
**garment** ['gɑːmənt] *n* vêtement *m*
**garner** ['gɑːnə'] *vt* engranger, amasser
**garnish** ['gɑːnɪʃ] (*Culin*) *vt* garnir ▸ *n* décoration *f*
**garret** ['gærɪt] *n* mansarde *f*

**garrison** ['gærɪsn] *n* garnison *f* ▸ *vt* mettre en
garnison, stationner
**garrulous** ['gærjuləs] *adj* volubile, loquace
**garter** ['gɑːtə'] *n* jarretière *f*; (*US: suspender*)
jarretelle *f*
**garter belt** *n* (*US*) porte-jarretelles *m inv*
**gas** [gæs] *n* gaz *m*; (*used as anaesthetic*): **to be
given ~** se faire endormir; (*US: gasoline*) essence
*f* ▸ *vt* asphyxier; (*Mil*) gazer; **I can smell ~** ça
sent le gaz
**Gascony** ['gæskənɪ] *n* Gascogne *f*
**gas cooker** *n* (*Brit*) cuisinière *f* à gaz
**gas cylinder** *n* bouteille *f* de gaz
**gaseous** ['gæsɪəs] *adj* gazeux(-euse)
**gas fire** *n* (*Brit*) radiateur *m* à gaz
**gas-fired** ['gæsfaɪəd] *adj* au gaz
**gash** [gæʃ] *n* entaille *f*; (*on face*) balafre *f* ▸ *vt*
taillader; balafrer
**gasket** ['gæskɪt] *n* (*Aut*) joint *m* de culasse
**gas mask** *n* masque *m* à gaz
**gas meter** *n* compteur *m* à gaz
**gasoline** ['gæsəliːn] *n* (*US*) essence *f*
**gasp** [gɑːsp] *n* halètement *m*; (*of shock etc*): **she
gave a small ~ of pain** la douleur lui coupa le
souffle ▸ *vi* haleter; (*fig*) avoir le souffle coupé
  ▸ **gasp out** *vt* (*say*) dire dans un souffle *or* d'une
voix entrecoupée
**gas pedal** *n* (*US*) accélérateur *m*
**gas ring** *n* brûleur *m*
**gas station** *n* (*US*) station-service *f*
**gas stove** *n* réchaud *m* à gaz; (*cooker*) cuisinière *f*
à gaz
**gassy** ['gæsɪ] *adj* gazeux(-euse)
**gas tank** *n* (*US Aut*) réservoir *m* d'essence
**gas tap** *n* bouton *m* (de cuisinière à gaz); (*on pipe*)
robinet *m* à gaz
**gastric** ['gæstrɪk] *adj* gastrique
**gastric ulcer** *n* ulcère *m* de l'estomac
**gastroenteritis** ['gæstrəuɛntə'raɪtɪs] *n*
gastroentérite *f*
**gastronomy** [gæs'trɔnəmɪ] *n* gastronomie *f*
**gasworks** ['gæswəːks] *n*, *npl* usine *f* à gaz
**gate** [geɪt] *n* (*of garden*) portail *m*; (*of field, at level
crossing*) barrière *f*; (*of building, town, at airport*)
porte *f*; (*of lock*) vanne *f*
**gateau** (*pl* **-x**) ['gætəu, -z] *n* gros gâteau à la
crème
**gatecrash** ['geɪtkræʃ] *vt* s'introduire sans
invitation dans
**gatecrasher** ['geɪtkræʃə'] *n* intrus(e)
**gatehouse** ['geɪthaus] *n* loge *f*
**gateway** ['geɪtweɪ] *n* porte *f*
**gather** ['gæðə'] *vt* (*flowers, fruit*) cueillir; (*pick up*)
ramasser; (*assemble: objects*) rassembler; (*: people*)
réunir; (*: information*) recueillir; (*understand*)
comprendre ▸ *vi* (*assemble*) se rassembler; (*dust*)
s'amasser; (*clouds*) s'amonceler; **to ~ (from/
that)** conclure *or* déduire (de/que); **as far as I
can ~** d'après ce que je comprends; **to ~ speed**
prendre de la vitesse
**gathering** ['gæðərɪŋ] *n* rassemblement *m*
**GATT** [gæt] *n abbr* (= *General Agreement on Tariffs and*

*Trade)* GATT *m*
**gauche** [gəʊʃ] *adj* gauche, maladroit(e)
**gaudy** ['gɔːdɪ] *adj* voyant(e)
**gauge** [geɪdʒ] *n (standard measure)* calibre *m*; *(Rail)* écartement *m*; *(instrument)* jauge *f* ▷ *vt* jauger; *(fig: sb's capabilities, character)* juger de; **to ~ the right moment** calculer le moment propice; **petrol ~,** *(US)* **gas ~** jauge d'essence
**Gaul** [gɔːl] *n (country)* Gaule *f*; *(person)* Gaulois(e)
**gaunt** [gɔːnt] *adj* décharné(e); *(grim, desolate)* désolé(e)
**gauntlet** ['gɔːntlɪt] *n (fig)*: **to throw down the ~** jeter le gant; **to run the ~ through an angry crowd** se frayer un passage à travers une foule hostile *or* entre deux haies de manifestants *etc* hostiles
**gauze** [gɔːz] *n* gaze *f*
**gave** [geɪv] *pt of* **give**
**gawky** ['gɔːkɪ] *adj* dégingandé(e), godiche
**gawp** [gɔːp] *vi*: **to ~ at** regarder bouche bée
**gay** [geɪ] *adj (homosexual)* homosexuel(le); *(slightly old-fashioned: cheerful)* gai(e), réjoui(e); *(colour)* gai, vif (vive)
**gaze** [geɪz] *n* regard *m* fixe ▷ *vi*: **to ~ at** *(vt)* fixer du regard
**gazelle** [gə'zɛl] *n* gazelle *f*
**gazette** [gə'zɛt] *n (newspaper)* gazette *f*; *(official publication)* journal officiel
**gazetteer** [gæzə'tɪər] *n* dictionnaire *m* géographique
**gazump** [gə'zʌmp] *vi (Brit) revenir sur une promesse de vente pour accepter un prix plus élevé*
**GB** *abbr* = **Great Britain**
**GBH** *n abbr (Brit Law: inf)* = **grievous bodily harm**
**GC** *n abbr (Brit: = George Cross)* distinction honorifique
**GCE** *n abbr (Brit)* = **General Certificate of Education**
**GCHQ** *n abbr (Brit: = Government Communications Headquarters) centre d'interception des télécommunications étrangères*
**GCSE** *n abbr (Brit: = General Certificate of Secondary Education) examen passé à l'âge de 16 ans sanctionnant les connaissances de l'élève;* **she's got eight ~s** elle a réussi dans huit matières aux épreuves du GCSE
**Gdns.** *abbr* = **gardens**
**GDP** *n abbr* = **gross domestic product**
**GDR** *n abbr (old: = German Democratic Republic)* RDA *f*
**gear** [gɪər] *n* matériel *m*, équipement *m*; *(Tech)* engrenage *m*; *(Aut)* vitesse *f* ▷ *vt (fig: adapt)* adapter; **top** *or* *(US)* **high/low ~** quatrième *(or* cinquième)/première vitesse; **in ~** en prise; **out of ~** au point mort; **our service is ~ed to meet the needs of the disabled** notre service répond de façon spécifique aux besoins des handicapés
  ▶ **gear up** *vi*: **to ~ up (to do)** se préparer (à faire)
**gear box** *n* boîte *f* de vitesse
**gear lever** *n* levier *m* de vitesse
**gear shift** *(US)* *n* = **gear lever**
**gear stick** *(Brit)* *n* = **gear lever**
**GED** *n abbr (US Scol)* = **general educational development**

**geese** [giːs] *npl of* **goose**
**geezer** ['giːzər] *n (Brit inf)* mec *m*
**Geiger counter** ['gaɪgə-] *n* compteur *m* Geiger
**gel** [dʒɛl] *n* gelée *f*; *(Chem)* colloïde *m*
**gelatin, gelatine** ['dʒɛlətiːn] *n* gélatine *f*
**gelignite** ['dʒɛlɪgnaɪt] *n* plastic *m*
**gem** [dʒɛm] *n* pierre précieuse
**Gemini** ['dʒɛmɪnaɪ] *n* les Gémeaux *mpl*; **to be ~** être des Gémeaux
**gen** [dʒɛn] *n (Brit inf)*: **to give sb the ~ on sth** mettre qn au courant de qch
**Gen.** *abbr (Mil: = general)* Gal
**gen.** *abbr (= general, generally)* gén
**gender** ['dʒɛndər] *n* genre *m*; *(person's sex)* sexe *m*
**gene** [dʒiːn] *n (Biol)* gène *m*
**genealogy** [dʒiːnɪ'ælədʒɪ] *n* généalogie *f*
**general** ['dʒɛnərl] *n* général *m* ▷ *adj* général(e); **in ~** en général; **the ~ public** le grand public; **~ audit** *(Comm)* vérification annuelle
**general anaesthetic,** *(US)* **general anesthetic** *n* anesthésie générale
**general delivery** *n* poste restante
**general election** *n* élection(s) législative(s)
**generalization** ['dʒɛnrəlaɪ'zeɪʃən] *n* généralisation *f*
**generalize** ['dʒɛnrəlaɪz] *vi* généraliser
**general knowledge** *n* connaissances générales
**generally** ['dʒɛnrəlɪ] *adv* généralement
**general manager** *n* directeur général
**general practitioner** *n* généraliste *m/f*
**general store** *n* épicerie *f*
**general strike** *n* grève générale
**generate** ['dʒɛnəreɪt] *vt* engendrer; *(electricity)* produire
**generation** [dʒɛnə'reɪʃən] *n* génération *f*; *(of electricity etc)* production *f*
**generator** ['dʒɛnəreɪtər] *n* générateur *m*
**generic** [dʒɪ'nɛrɪk] *adj* générique
**generosity** [dʒɛnə'rɔsɪtɪ] *n* générosité *f*
**generous** ['dʒɛnərəs] *adj* généreux(-euse); *(copious)* copieux(-euse)
**genesis** ['dʒɛnɪsɪs] *n* genèse *f*
**genetic** [dʒɪ'nɛtɪk] *adj* génétique; **~ engineering** ingénierie *m* génétique; **~ fingerprinting** système *m* d'empreinte génétique
**genetically modified** *adj (food etc)* génétiquement modifié(e)
**genetics** [dʒɪ'nɛtɪks] *n* génétique *f*
**Geneva** [dʒɪ'niːvə] *n* Genève; **Lake ~** le lac Léman
**genial** ['dʒiːnɪəl] *adj* cordial(e), chaleureux(-euse); *(climate)* clément(e)
**genitals** ['dʒɛnɪtlz] *npl* organes génitaux
**genitive** ['dʒɛnɪtɪv] *n* génitif *m*
**genius** ['dʒiːnɪəs] *n* génie *m*
**Genoa** ['dʒɛnəuə] *n* Gênes
**genocide** ['dʒɛnəusaɪd] *n* génocide *m*
**gent** [dʒɛnt] *n abbr (Brit inf)* = **gentleman**
**genteel** [dʒɛn'tiːl] *adj* de bon ton, distingué(e)
**gentle** ['dʒɛntl] *adj* doux (douce); *(breeze, touch)*

léger(-ère)

**gentleman** (*irreg*) ['dʒɛntlmən] *n* monsieur *m*; (*well-bred man*) gentleman *m*; **~'s agreement** gentleman's agreement *m*

**gentlemanly** ['dʒɛntlmənlɪ] *adj* bien élevé(e)

**gentleness** ['dʒɛntlnɪs] *n* douceur *f*

**gently** ['dʒɛntlɪ] *adv* doucement

**gentry** ['dʒɛntrɪ] *n* petite noblesse

**gents** [dʒɛnts] *n* W.-C. *mpl* (pour hommes)

**genuine** ['dʒɛnjuɪn] *adj* véritable, authentique; (*person, emotion*) sincère

**genuinely** ['dʒɛnjuɪnlɪ] *adv* sincèrement, vraiment

**geographer** [dʒɪ'ɔgrəfəʳ] *n* géographe *m/f*

**geographic** [dʒɪə'græfɪk], **geographical** [dʒɪə'græfɪkl] *adj* géographique

**geography** [dʒɪ'ɔgrəfɪ] *n* géographie *f*

**geological** [dʒɪə'lɔdʒɪkl] *adj* géologique

**geologist** [dʒɪ'ɔlədʒɪst] *n* géologue *m/f*

**geology** [dʒɪ'ɔlədʒɪ] *n* géologie *f*

**geometric** [dʒɪə'mɛtrɪk], **geometrical** [dʒɪə'mɛtrɪkl] *adj* géométrique

**geometry** [dʒɪ'ɔmɛtrɪ] *n* géométrie *f*

**Geordie** ['dʒɔːdɪ] *n* (*inf*) habitant(e) de Tyneside, originaire *m/f* de Tyneside.

**Georgia** ['dʒɔːdʒə] *n* Géorgie *f*

**Georgian** ['dʒɔːdʒən] *adj* (*Geo*) géorgien(ne) ▷ *n* Géorgien(ne); (*Ling*) géorgien *m*

**geranium** [dʒɪ'reɪnɪəm] *n* géranium *m*

**geriatric** [dʒɛrɪ'ætrɪk] *adj* gériatrique ▷ *n* patient(e) gériatrique

**germ** [dʒəːm] *n* (*Med*) microbe *m*; (*Biol: fig*) germe *m*

**German** ['dʒəːmən] *adj* allemand(e) ▷ *n* Allemand(e); (*Ling*) allemand *m*

**germane** [dʒəː'meɪn] *adj* (*formal*): **~ (to)** se rapportant (à)

**German measles** *n* rubéole *f*

**Germany** ['dʒəːmənɪ] *n* Allemagne *f*

**germination** [dʒəːmɪ'neɪʃən] *n* germination *f*

**germ warfare** *n* guerre *f* bactériologique

**gerrymandering** ['dʒɛrɪmændərɪŋ] *n* tripotage *m* du découpage électoral

**gestation** [dʒɛs'teɪʃən] *n* gestation *f*

**gesticulate** [dʒɛs'tɪkjuleɪt] *vi* gesticuler

**gesture** ['dʒɛstjəʳ] *n* geste *m*; **as a ~ of friendship** en témoignage d'amitié

🅞 KEYWORD

**get** [gɛt] (*pt, pp* **got**, *pp* **gotten**) (*US*) *vi* **1** (*become, be*) devenir; **to get old/tired** devenir vieux/fatigué, vieillir/se fatiguer; **to get drunk** s'enivrer; **to get ready/washed/shaved** *etc* se préparer/laver/raser *etc*; **to get killed** se faire tuer; **to get dirty** se salir; **to get married** se marier; **when do I get paid?** quand est-ce que je serai payé?; **it's getting late** il se fait tard

**2** (*go*): **to get to/from** aller à/de; **to get home** rentrer chez soi; **how did you get here?** comment es-tu arrivé ici?; **he got across the bridge/under the fence** il a traversé le pont/

est passé au-dessous de la barrière

**3** (*begin*) commencer *or* se mettre à; **to get to know sb** apprendre à connaître qn; **I'm getting to like him** je commence à l'apprécier; **let's get going** *or* **started** allons-y

**4** (*modal aux vb*): **you've got to do it** il faut que vous le fassiez; **I've got to tell the police** je dois le dire à la police

▷ *vt* **1**: **to get sth done** (*do*) faire qch; (*have done*) faire faire qch; **to get sth/sb ready** préparer qch/qn; **to get one's hair cut** se faire couper les cheveux; **to get the car going** *or* **to go** (faire) démarrer la voiture; **to get sb to do sth** faire faire qch à qn; **to get sb drunk** enivrer qn

**2** (*obtain: money, permission, results*) obtenir, avoir; (*buy*) acheter; (*find: job, flat*) trouver; (*fetch: person, doctor, object*) aller chercher; **to get sth for sb** procurer qch à qn; **get me Mr Jones, please** (*on phone*) passez-moi Mr Jones, s'il vous plaît; **can I get you a drink?** est-ce que je peux vous servir à boire?

**3** (*receive: present, letter*) recevoir, avoir; (*acquire: reputation*) avoir; (*prize*) obtenir; **what did you get for your birthday?** qu'est-ce que tu as eu pour ton anniversaire?; **how much did you get for the painting?** combien avez-vous vendu le tableau?

**4** (*catch*) prendre, saisir, attraper; (*hit: target etc*) atteindre; **to get sb by the arm/throat** prendre *or* saisir *or* attraper qn par le bras/à la gorge; **get him!** arrête-le!; **the bullet got him in the leg** il a pris la balle dans la jambe; **he really gets me!** il me porte sur les nerfs!

**5** (*take, move*): **to get sth to sb** faire parvenir qch à qn; **do you think we'll get it through the door?** on arrivera à le faire passer par la porte?; **I'll get you there somehow** je me débrouillerai pour t'y emmener

**6** (*catch, take: plane, bus etc*) prendre; **where do I get the train for Birmingham?** où prend-on le train pour Birmingham?

**7** (*understand*) comprendre, saisir; (*hear*) entendre; **I've got it!** j'ai compris!; **I don't get your meaning** je ne vois *or* comprends pas ce que vous voulez dire; **I didn't get your name** je n'ai pas entendu votre nom

**8** (*have, possess*): **to have got** avoir; **how many have you got?** vous en avez combien?

**9** (*illness*) avoir; **I've got a cold** j'ai le rhume; **she got pneumonia and died** elle a fait une pneumonie et elle en est morte

▸ **get about** *vi* se déplacer; (*news*) se répandre

▸ **get across** *vt*: **to get across (to)** (*message, meaning*) faire passer (à) ▷ *vi*: **to get across (to)** (*speaker*) se faire comprendre (par)

▸ **get along** *vi* (*agree*) s'entendre; (*depart*) s'en aller; (*manage*) = **get by**

▸ **get at** *vt fus* (*attack*) s'en prendre à; (*reach*) attraper, atteindre; **what are you getting at?** à quoi voulez-vous en venir?

▸ **get away** *vi* partir, s'en aller; (*escape*) s'échapper

▶ **get away with** *vt fus* (*punishment*) en être quitte pour; (*crime etc*) se faire pardonner

▶ **get back** *vi* (*return*) rentrer ▷ *vt* récupérer, recouvrer; **to get back to** (*start again*) retourner *or* revenir à; (*contact again*) recontacter; **when do we get back?** quand serons-nous de retour?

▶ **get back at** *vt fus* (*inf*): **to get back at sb** rendre la monnaie de sa pièce à qn

▶ **get by** *vi* (*pass*) passer; (*manage*) se débrouiller; **I can get by in Dutch** je me débrouille en hollandais

▶ **get down** *vi, vt fus* descendre ▷ *vt* descendre; (*depress*) déprimer

▶ **get down to** *vt fus* (*work*) se mettre à (faire); **to get down to business** passer aux choses sérieuses

▶ **get in** *vi* entrer; (*arrive home*) rentrer; (*train*) arriver ▷ *vt* (*bring in: harvest*) rentrer; (*: coal*) faire rentrer; (*: supplies*) faire des provisions de

▶ **get into** *vt fus* entrer dans; (*car, train etc*) monter dans; (*clothes*) mettre, enfiler, endosser; **to get into bed/a rage** se mettre au lit/en colère

▶ **get off** *vi* (*from train etc*) descendre; (*depart: person, car*) s'en aller; (*escape*) s'en tirer ▷ *vt* (*remove: clothes, stain*) enlever; (*send off*) expédier; (*have as leave: day, time*): **we got 2 days off** nous avons eu 2 jours de congé ▷ *vt fus* (*train, bus*) descendre de; **where do I get off?** où est-ce que je dois descendre?; **to get off to a good start** (*fig*) prendre un bon départ

▶ **get on** *vi* (*at exam etc*) se débrouiller; (*agree*): **to get on (with)** s'entendre (avec); **how are you getting on?** comment ça va? ▷ *vt fus* monter dans; (*horse*) monter sur

▶ **get on to** *vt fus* (*Brit: deal with: problem*) s'occuper de; (*contact: person*) contacter

▶ **get out** *vi* sortir; (*of vehicle*) descendre; (*news etc*) s'ébruiter ▷ *vt* sortir

▶ **get out of** *vt fus* sortir de; (*duty etc*) échapper à, se soustraire à

▶ **get over** *vt fus* (*illness*) se remettre de ▷ *vt* (*communicate: idea etc*) communiquer; (*finish*): **let's get it over (with)** finissons-en

▶ **get round** *vi*: **to get round to doing sth** se mettre (finalement) à faire qch ▷ *vt fus* contourner; (*fig: person*) entortiller

▶ **get through** *vi* (*Tel*) avoir la communication; **to get through to sb** atteindre qn ▷ *vt fus* (*finish: work, book*) finir, terminer

▶ **get together** *vi* se réunir ▷ *vt* rassembler

▶ **get up** *vi* (*rise*) se lever ▷ *vt fus* monter

▶ **get up to** *vt fus* (*reach*) arriver à; (*prank etc*) faire

**getaway** ['gɛtəweɪ] *n* fuite *f*

**getaway car** *n* voiture prévue pour prendre la fuite

**get-together** ['gɛttəgɛðəʳ] *n* petite réunion, petite fête

**get-up** ['gɛtʌp] *n* (*inf: outfit*) accoutrement *m*

**get-well card** [gɛt'wɛl-] *n* carte *f* de vœux de bon rétablissement

**geyser** ['giːzəʳ] *n* chauffe-eau *m inv*; (*Geo*) geyser *m*

**Ghana** ['gɑːnə] *n* Ghana *m*

**Ghanaian** [gɑː'neɪən] *adj* ghanéen(ne) ▷ *n* Ghanéen(ne)

**ghastly** ['gɑːstlɪ] *adj* atroce, horrible; (*pale*) livide, blême

**gherkin** ['gəːkɪn] *n* cornichon *m*

**ghetto** ['gɛtəu] *n* ghetto *m*

**ghetto blaster** [-blɑːstəʳ] *n* (*inf*) gros radiocassette

**ghost** [gəust] *n* fantôme *m*, revenant *m* ▷ *vt* (*sb else's book*) écrire

**ghostly** ['gəustlɪ] *adj* fantomatique

**ghostwriter** ['gəustraɪtəʳ] *n* nègre *m* (*fig*)

**ghoul** [guːl] *n* (*ghost*) vampire *m*

**ghoulish** ['guːlɪʃ] *adj* (*tastes etc*) morbide

**GHQ** *n abbr* (*Mil*: = *general headquarters*) GQG *m*

**GI** *n abbr* (*US inf*: = *government issue*) soldat de l'armée américaine, GI *m*

**giant** ['dʒaɪənt] *n* géant(e) ▷ *adj* géant(e), énorme; **~ (size) packet** paquet géant

**giant killer** *n* (*Sport*) équipe inconnue qui remporte un match contre une équipe renommée

**gibber** ['dʒɪbəʳ] *vi* émettre des sons inintelligibles

**gibberish** ['dʒɪbərɪʃ] *n* charabia *m*

**gibe** [dʒaɪb] *n* sarcasme *m* ▷ *vi*: **to ~ at** railler

**giblets** ['dʒɪblɪts] *npl* abats *mpl*

**Gibraltar** [dʒɪ'brɔːltəʳ] *n* Gibraltar *m*

**giddiness** ['gɪdɪnɪs] *n* vertige *m*

**giddy** ['gɪdɪ] *adj* (*dizzy*): **to be** (*or* **feel**) **~** avoir le vertige; (*height*) vertigineux(-euse); (*thoughtless*) sot(te), étourdi(e)

**gift** [gɪft] *n* cadeau *m*, présent *m*; (*donation, talent*) don *m*; (*Comm: also*: **free gift**) cadeau(-réclame) *m*; **to have a ~ for sth** avoir des dons pour *or* le don de qch

**gifted** ['gɪftɪd] *adj* doué(e)

**gift shop**, (*US*) **gift store** *n* boutique *f* de cadeaux

**gift token**, **gift voucher** *n* chèque-cadeau *m*

**gig** [gɪg] *n* (*inf: concert*) concert *m*

**gigabyte** ['dʒɪgəbaɪt] *n* gigaoctet *m*

**gigantic** [dʒaɪ'gæntɪk] *adj* gigantesque

**giggle** ['gɪgl] *vi* pouffer, ricaner sottement ▷ *n* petit rire sot, ricanement *m*

**GIGO** ['gaɪgəu] *abbr* (*Comput: inf*: = *garbage in, garbage out*) qualité d'entrée = qualité de sortie

**gild** [gɪld] *vt* dorer

**gill** [dʒɪl] *n* (*measure*) = 0.25 pints (*Brit* = 0.148 l; *US* = 0.118 l)

**gills** [gɪlz] *npl* (*of fish*) ouïes *fpl*, branchies *fpl*

**gilt** [gɪlt] *n* dorure *f* ▷ *adj* doré(e)

**gilt-edged** ['gɪltɛdʒd] *adj* (*stocks, securities*) de premier ordre

**gimlet** ['gɪmlɪt] *n* vrille *f*

**gimmick** ['gɪmɪk] *n* truc *m*; **sales ~** offre promotionnelle

**gin** [dʒɪn] *n* gin *m*

**ginger** ['dʒɪndʒəʳ] *n* gingembre *m*

▶ **ginger up** *vt* secouer; animer

**g**

**ginger ale, ginger beer** n boisson gazeuse au gingembre

**gingerbread** ['dʒɪndʒəbrɛd] n pain m d'épices

**ginger group** n (Brit) groupe m de pression

**ginger-haired** ['dʒɪndʒə'hɛəd] adj roux (rousse)

**gingerly** ['dʒɪndʒəlɪ] adv avec précaution

**gingham** ['gɪŋəm] n vichy m

**ginseng** ['dʒɪnsɛŋ] n ginseng m

**gipsy** ['dʒɪpsɪ] n = **gypsy**

**giraffe** [dʒɪ'rɑːf] n girafe f

**girder** ['gəːdə<sup>r</sup>] n poutrelle f

**girdle** ['gəːdl] n (corset) gaine f ▷ vt ceindre

**girl** [gəːl] n fille f, fillette f; (young unmarried woman) jeune fille; (daughter) fille; **an English ~** une jeune Anglaise; **a little English ~** une petite Anglaise

**girl band** n girls band m

**girlfriend** ['gəːlfrɛnd] n (of girl) amie f; (of boy) petite amie

**Girl Guide** n (Brit) éclaireuse f; (Roman Catholic) guide f

**girlish** ['gəːlɪʃ] adj de jeune fille

**Girl Scout** n (US) = **Girl Guide**

**Giro** ['dʒaɪrəu] n: **the National ~** (Brit) ≈ les comptes chèques postaux

**giro** ['dʒaɪrəu] n (bank giro) virement m bancaire; (post office giro) mandat m

**girth** [gəːθ] n circonférence f; (of horse) sangle f

**gist** [dʒɪst] n essentiel m

**give** [gɪv] (pt **gave**, pp **given** [geɪv, 'gɪvn]) n (of fabric) élasticité f ▷ vt donner ▷ vi (break) céder; (stretch: fabric) se prêter; **to ~ sb sth, ~ sth to sb** donner qch à qn; (gift) offrir qch à qn; (message) transmettre qch à qn; **to ~ sb a call/kiss** appeler/embrasser qn; **to ~ a cry/sigh** pousser un cri/un soupir; **how much did you ~ for it?** combien (l')avez-vous payé?; **12 o'clock, ~ or take a few minutes** midi, à quelques minutes près; **to ~ way** céder; (Brit Aut) donner la priorité

▸ **give away** vt donner; (give free) faire cadeau de; (betray) donner, trahir; (disclose) révéler; (bride) conduire à l'autel

▸ **give back** vt rendre

▸ **give in** vi céder ▷ vt donner

▸ **give off** vt dégager

▸ **give out** vt (food etc) distribuer; (news) annoncer ▷ vi (be exhausted: supplies) s'épuiser; (fail) lâcher

▸ **give up** vi renoncer ▷ vt renoncer à; **to ~ up smoking** arrêter de fumer; **to ~ o.s. up** se rendre

**give-and-take** ['gɪvənd'teɪk] n concessions mutuelles

**giveaway** ['gɪvəweɪ] n (inf): **her expression was a ~** son expression la trahissait; **the exam was a ~!** cet examen, c'était du gâteau! ▷ cpd: **~ prices** prix sacrifiés

**given** ['gɪvn] pp of **give** ▷ adj (fixed: time, amount) donné(e), déterminé(e) ▷ conj: **~ the circumstances ...** étant donné les circonstances ...; vu les circonstances ...; **~ that ...** étant donné que ...

**glacial** ['gleɪsɪəl] adj (Geo) glaciaire; (wind, weather) glacial(e)

**glacier** ['glæsɪə<sup>r</sup>] n glacier m

**glad** [glæd] adj content(e); **to be ~ about sth/ that** être heureux(-euse) or bien content de qch/que; **I was ~ of his help** j'étais bien content de (pouvoir compter sur) son aide or qu'il m'aide

**gladden** ['glædn] vt réjouir

**glade** [gleɪd] n clairière f

**gladioli** [glædɪ'əulaɪ] npl glaïeuls mpl

**gladly** ['glædlɪ] adv volontiers

**glamorous** ['glæmərəs] adj (person) séduisant(e); (job) prestigieux(-euse)

**glamour, (US) glamor** ['glæmə<sup>r</sup>] n éclat m, prestige m

**glance** [glɑːns] n coup m d'œil ▷ vi: **to ~ at** jeter un coup d'œil à

▸ **glance off** vt fus (bullet) ricocher sur

**glancing** ['glɑːnsɪŋ] adj (blow) oblique

**gland** [glænd] n glande f

**glandular** ['glændjulə<sup>r</sup>] adj: **~ fever** (Brit) mononucléose infectieuse

**glare** [glɛə<sup>r</sup>] n (of anger) regard furieux; (of light) lumière éblouissante; (of publicity) feux mpl ▷ vi briller d'un éclat aveuglant; **to ~ at** lancer un regard or des regards furieux à

**glaring** ['glɛərɪŋ] adj (mistake) criant(e), qui saute aux yeux

**glasnost** ['glæznɔst] n glasnost f

**glass** [glɑːs] n verre m; (also: **looking glass**) miroir m; **glasses** npl (spectacles) lunettes fpl

**glass-blowing** ['glɑːsbləuɪŋ] n soufflage m (du verre)

**glass ceiling** n (fig) plafond dans l'échelle hiérarchique au-dessus duquel les femmes ou les membres d'une minorité ethnique ne semblent pouvoir s'élever

**glass fibre** n fibre f de verre

**glasshouse** ['glɑːshaus] n serre f

**glassware** ['glɑːswɛə<sup>r</sup>] n verrerie f

**glassy** ['glɑːsɪ] adj (eyes) vitreux(-euse)

**Glaswegian** [glæs'wiːdʒən] adj de Glasgow ▷ n habitant(e) de Glasgow, natif(-ive) de Glasgow

**glaze** [gleɪz] vt (door) vitrer; (pottery) vernir; (Culin) glacer ▷ n vernis m; (Culin) glaçage m

**glazed** [gleɪzd] adj (eye) vitreux(-euse); (pottery) verni(e); (tiles) vitrifié(e)

**glazier** ['gleɪzɪə<sup>r</sup>] n vitrier m

**gleam** [gliːm] n lueur f ▷ vi luire, briller; **a ~ of hope** une lueur d'espoir

**gleaming** ['gliːmɪŋ] adj luisant(e)

**glean** [gliːn] vt (information) recueillir

**glee** [gliː] n joie f

**gleeful** ['gliːful] adj joyeux(-euse)

**glen** [glɛn] n vallée f

**glib** [glɪb] adj qui a du bagou; facile

**glide** [glaɪd] vi glisser; (Aviat, bird) planer ▷ n glissement m; vol plané

**glider** ['glaɪdə<sup>r</sup>] n (Aviat) planeur m

**gliding** ['glaɪdɪŋ] n (Aviat) vol m à voile

**glimmer** ['glɪmə<sup>r</sup>] vi luire ▷ n lueur f

**glimpse** [glɪmps] *n* vision passagère, aperçu *m*
▷ *vt* entrevoir, apercevoir; **to catch a ~ of**
entrevoir
**glint** [glɪnt] *n* éclair *m* ▷ *vi* étinceler
**glisten** ['glɪsn] *vi* briller, luire
**glitter** ['glɪtəʳ] *vi* scintiller, briller ▷ *n*
scintillement *m*
**glitz** [glɪts] *n* (*inf*) clinquant *m*
**gloat** [gləʊt] *vi*: **to ~ (over)** jubiler (à propos de)
**global** ['gləʊbl] *adj* (*world-wide*) mondial(e);
(*overall*) global(e)
**globalization** [gləʊblaɪz'eɪʃən] *n*
mondialisation *f*
**global warming** [-'wɔːmɪŋ] *n* réchauffement *m*
de la planète
**globe** [gləʊb] *n* globe *m*
**globe-trotter** ['gləʊbtrɔtəʳ] *n* globe-trotter *m*
**globule** ['glɔbjuːl] *n* (*Anat*) globule *m*; (*of water etc*) gouttelette *f*
**gloom** [gluːm] *n* obscurité *f*; (*sadness*) tristesse *f*,
mélancolie *f*
**gloomy** ['gluːmɪ] *adj* (*person*) morose; (*place,
outlook*) sombre; **to feel ~** avoir *or* se faire des
idées noires
**glorification** [glɔːrɪfɪ'keɪʃən] *n* glorification *f*
**glorify** ['glɔːrɪfaɪ] *vt* glorifier
**glorious** ['glɔːrɪəs] *adj* glorieux(-euse); (*beautiful*)
splendide
**glory** ['glɔːrɪ] *n* gloire *f*; splendeur *f* ▷ *vi*: **to ~ in**
se glorifier de
**glory hole** *n* (*inf*) capharnaüm *m*
**Glos** *abbr* (*Brit*) = **Gloucestershire**
**gloss** [glɔs] *n* (*shine*) brillant *m*, vernis *m*; (*also:
**gloss paint**) peinture brillante *or* laquée
▶ **gloss over** *vt fus* glisser sur
**glossary** ['glɔsərɪ] *n* glossaire *m*, lexique *m*
**glossy** ['glɔsɪ] *adj* brillant(e), luisant(e) ▷ *n* (*also:
**glossy magazine**) revue *f* de luxe
**glove** [glʌv] *n* gant *m*
**glove compartment** *n* (*Aut*) boîte *f* à gants,
vide-poches *m inv*
**glow** [gləʊ] *vi* rougeoyer; (*face*) rayonner; (*eyes*)
briller ▷ *n* rougeoiement *m*
**glower** ['glaʊəʳ] *vi* lancer des regards mauvais
**glowing** ['gləʊɪŋ] *adj* (*fire*) rougeoyant(e);
(*complexion*) éclatant(e); (*report, description etc*)
dithyrambique
**glow-worm** ['gləʊwəːm] *n* ver luisant
**glucose** ['gluːkəʊs] *n* glucose *m*
**glue** [gluː] *n* colle *f* ▷ *vt* coller
**glue-sniffing** ['gluːsnɪfɪŋ] *n* inhalation *f* de
colle
**glum** [glʌm] *adj* maussade, morose
**glut** [glʌt] *n* surabondance *f* ▷ *vt* rassasier;
(*market*) encombrer
**glutinous** ['gluːtɪnəs] *adj* visqueux(-euse)
**glutton** ['glʌtn] *n* glouton(ne); **a ~ for work** un
bourreau de travail
**gluttonous** ['glʌtənəs] *adj* glouton(ne)
**gluttony** ['glʌtənɪ] *n* gloutonnerie *f*; (*sin*)
gourmandise *f*
**glycerin, glycerine** ['glɪsəriːn] *n* glycérine *f*

**GM** *abbr* (= *genetically modified*) génétiquement
modifié(e)
**gm** *abbr* (= *gram*) g
**GMAT** *n abbr* (US: = *Graduate Management Admissions
Test*) examen d'admission dans la 2e cycle de
l'enseignement supérieur
**GMO** *n abbr* (= *genetically modified organism*) OGM *m*
**GMT** *abbr* (= *Greenwich Mean Time*) GMT
**gnarled** [nɑːld] *adj* noueux(-euse)
**gnash** [næʃ] *vt*: **to ~ one's teeth** grincer des
dents
**gnat** [næt] *n* moucheron *m*
**gnaw** [nɔː] *vt* ronger
**gnome** [nəʊm] *n* gnome *m*, lutin *m*
**GNP** *n abbr* = **gross national product**
**go** [gəʊ] (*pt* **went**, *pp* **gone** [wɛnt, gɔn]) *vi* aller;
(*depart*) partir, s'en aller; (*work*) marcher; (*break*)
céder; (*time*) passer; (*be sold*): **to go for £10** se
vendre 10 livres; (*become*): **to go pale/mouldy**
pâlir/moisir ▷ *n* (*pl* **goes**): **to have a go (at)**
essayer (de faire); **to be on the go** être en
mouvement; **whose go is it?** à qui est-ce de
jouer?; **to go by car/on foot** aller en voiture/à
pied; **he's going to do it** il va le faire, il est sur
le point de le faire; **to go for a walk** aller se
promener; **to go dancing/shopping** aller
danser/faire les courses; **to go looking for sb/
sth** aller *or* partir à la recherche de qn/qch; **to
go to sleep** s'endormir; **to go and see sb, go to
see sb** aller voir qn; **how is it going?** comment
ça marche?; **how did it go?** comment est-ce
que ça s'est passé?; **to go round the back/by
the shop** passer par derrière/devant le
magasin; **my voice has gone** j'ai une
extinction de voix; **the cake is all gone** il n'y a
plus de gâteau; **I'll take whatever is going**
(*Brit*) je prendrai ce qu'il y a (*or* ce que vous avez);
**... to go** (*US: food*) ... à emporter
▶ **go about** *vi* (*also:* **go around**) aller çà et là;
(*rumour*) se répandre ▷ *vt fus*: **how do I go about
this?** comment dois-je m'y prendre (pour faire
ceci)?; **to go about one's business** s'occuper
de ses affaires
▶ **go after** *vt fus* (*pursue*) poursuivre, courir
après; (*job, record etc*) essayer d'obtenir
▶ **go against** *vt fus* (*be unfavourable to*) être
défavorable à; (*be contrary to*) être contraire à
▶ **go ahead** *vi* (*make progress*) avancer; (*take place*)
avoir lieu; (*get going*) y aller
▶ **go along** *vi* aller, avancer ▷ *vt fus* longer,
parcourir; **as you go along (with your work)**
au fur et à mesure (de votre travail); **to go
along with** (*accompany*) accompagner; (*agree
with: idea*) être d'accord sur; (*: person*) suivre
▶ **go away** *vi* partir, s'en aller
▶ **go back** *vi* rentrer; revenir; (*go again*)
retourner
▶ **go back on** *vt fus* (*promise*) revenir sur
▶ **go by** *vi* (*years, time*) passer, s'écouler ▷ *vt fus*
s'en tenir à; (*believe*) en croire
▶ **go down** *vi* descendre; (*number, price, amount*)
baisser; (*ship*) couler; (*sun*) se coucher ▷ *vt fus*

**g**

descendre; **that should go down well with him** (*fig*) ça devrait lui plaire
▸ **go for** *vt fus* (*fetch*) aller chercher; (*like*) aimer; (*attack*) s'en prendre à; attaquer
▸ **go in** *vi* entrer
▸ **go in for** *vt fus* (*competition*) se présenter à; (*like*) aimer
▸ **go into** *vt fus* entrer dans; (*investigate*) étudier, examiner; (*embark on*) se lancer dans
▸ **go off** *vi* partir, s'en aller; (*food*) se gâter; (*milk*) tourner; (*bomb*) sauter; (*alarm clock*) sonner; (*alarm*) se déclencher; (*lights etc*) s'éteindre; (*event*) se dérouler ▷ *vt fus* ne plus aimer, ne plus avoir envie de; **the gun went off** le coup est parti; **to go off to sleep** s'endormir; **the party went off well** la fête s'est bien passée *or* était très réussie
▸ **go on** *vi* continuer; (*happen*) se passer; (*lights*) s'allumer ▷ *vt fus* (*be guided by: evidence etc*) se fonder sur; **to go on doing** continuer à faire; **what's going on here?** qu'est-ce qui se passe ici?
▸ **go on at** *vt fus* (*nag*) tomber sur le dos de
▸ **go on with** *vt fus* poursuivre, continuer
▸ **go out** *vi* sortir; (*fire, light*) s'éteindre; (*tide*) descendre; **to go out with sb** sortir avec qn
▸ **go over** *vi* (*ship*) chavirer ▷ *vt fus* (*check*) revoir, vérifier; **to go over sth in one's mind** repasser qch dans son esprit
▸ **go past** *vt fus*: **to go past sth** passer devant qch
▸ **go round** *vi* (*circulate: news, rumour*) circuler; (*revolve*) tourner; (*suffice*) suffire (pour tout le monde); (*visit*): **to go round to sb's** passer chez qn; aller chez qn; (*make a detour*): **to go round (by)** faire un détour (par)
▸ **go through** *vt fus* (*town etc*) traverser; (*search through*) fouiller; (*suffer*) subir; (*examine: list, book*) lire *or* regarder en détail, éplucher; (*perform: lesson*) réciter; (*: formalities*) remplir; (*: programme*) exécuter
▸ **go through with** *vt fus* (*plan, crime*) aller jusqu'au bout de
▸ **go under** *vi* (*sink: also fig*) couler; (*: person*) succomber
▸ **go up** *vi* monter; (*price*) augmenter ▷ *vt fus* gravir; (*also*: **go up in flames**) flamber, s'enflammer brusquement
▸ **go with** *vt fus* aller avec
▸ **go without** *vt fus* se passer de
**goad** [gəud] *vt* aiguillonner
**go-ahead** ['gəuəhɛd] *adj* dynamique, entreprenant(e) ▷ *n* feu vert
**goal** [gəul] *n* but *m*
**goal difference** *n* différence *f* de buts
**goalie** ['gəulı] *n* (*inf*) goal *m*
**goalkeeper** ['gəulki:pəʳ] *n* gardien *m* de but
**goal-post** [gəulpəust] *n* poteau *m* de but
**goat** [gəut] *n* chèvre *f*
**gobble** ['gɔbl] *vt* (*also*: **gobble down, gobble up**) engloutir
**go-between** ['gəubıtwi:n] *n* médiateur *m*

**Gobi Desert** ['gəubı-] *n* désert *m* de Gobi
**goblet** ['gɔblıt] *n* coupe *f*
**goblin** ['gɔblın] *n* lutin *m*
**go-cart** ['gəuka:t] *n* kart *m* ▷ *cpd*: ~ **racing** karting *m*
**god** [gɔd] *n* dieu *m*; **G~** Dieu
**god-awful** [gɔd'ɔːfəl] *adj* (*inf*) franchement atroce
**godchild** ['gɔdtʃaıld] *n* filleul(e)
**goddamn** ['gɔddæm], **goddamned** ['gɔddæmd] *excl* (*esp US inf*): ~ **(it)!** nom de Dieu! ▷ *adj* satané(e), sacré(e) ▷ *adv* sacrément
**goddaughter** ['gɔddɔːtəʳ] *n* filleule *f*
**goddess** ['gɔdıs] *n* déesse *f*
**godfather** ['gɔdfɑːðəʳ] *n* parrain *m*
**god-fearing** ['gɔdfıərıŋ] *adj* croyant(e)
**god-forsaken** ['gɔdfəseıkən] *adj* maudit(e)
**godmother** ['gɔdmʌðəʳ] *n* marraine *f*
**godparents** ['gɔdpɛərənts] *npl*: **the** ~ le parrain et la marraine
**godsend** ['gɔdsɛnd] *n* aubaine *f*
**godson** ['gɔdsʌn] *n* filleul *m*
**goes** [gəuz] *vb see* **go**
**gofer** ['gəufəʳ] *n* coursier(-ière)
**go-getter** ['gəugɛtəʳ] *n* arriviste *m/f*
**goggle** ['gɔgl] *vi*: **to** ~ **at** regarder avec des yeux ronds
**goggles** ['gɔglz] *npl* (*for skiing etc*) lunettes (protectrices); (*for swimming*) lunettes de piscine
**going** ['gəuıŋ] *n* (*conditions*) état *m* du terrain ▷ *adj*: **the** ~ **rate** le tarif (en vigueur); **a** ~ **concern** une affaire prospère; **it was slow** ~ les progrès étaient lents, ça n'avançait pas vite
**going-over** [gəuıŋ'əuvəʳ] *n* vérification *f*, révision *f*; (*inf: beating*) passage *m* à tabac
**goings-on** ['gəuıŋz'ɔn] *npl* (*inf*) manigances *fpl*
**go-kart** ['gəuka:t] *n* = **go-cart**
**gold** [gəuld] *n or m* ▷ *adj* en or; (*reserves*) d'or
**golden** ['gəuldən] *adj* (*made of gold*) en or; (*gold in colour*) doré(e)
**golden age** *n* âge *m* d'or
**golden handshake** *n* (*Brit*) prime *f* de départ
**golden rule** *n* règle *f* d'or
**goldfish** ['gəuldfıʃ] *n* poisson *m* rouge
**gold leaf** *n or m* en feuille
**gold medal** *n* (*Sport*) médaille *f* d'or
**goldmine** ['gəuldmaın] *n* mine *f* d'or
**gold-plated** ['gəuld'pleıtıd] *adj* plaqué(e) or *inv*
**goldsmith** ['gəuldsmıθ] *n* orfèvre *m*
**gold standard** *n* étalon-or *m*
**golf** [gɔlf] *n* golf *m*
**golf ball** *n* balle *f* de golf; (*on typewriter*) boule *f*
**golf club** *n* club *m* de golf; (*stick*) club *m*, crosse *f* de golf
**golf course** *n* terrain *m* de golf
**golfer** ['gɔlfəʳ] *n* joueur(-euse) de golf
**golfing** ['gɔlfıŋ] *n* golf *m*
**gondola** ['gɔndələ] *n* gondole *f*
**gondolier** [gɔndə'lıəʳ] *n* gondolier *m*
**gone** [gɔn] *pp* of **go** ▷ *adj* parti(e)
**goner** ['gɔnəʳ] *n* (*inf*): **to be a** ~ être fichu(e) *or* foutu(e)

**gong** [gɔŋ] *n* gong *m*
**good** [gud] *adj* bon(ne); (*kind*) gentil(le); (*child*)
sage; (*weather*) beau (belle) ▷ *n* bien *m*; **goods**
*npl* marchandise *f*, articles *mpl*; (*Comm etc*)
marchandises; **~! bon!, très bien!; to be ~ at**
être bon en; **to be ~ for** être bon pour; **it's ~ for
you** c'est bon pour vous; **it's a ~ thing you
were there** heureusement que vous étiez là;
**she is ~ with children/her hands** elle sait bien
s'occuper des enfants/sait se servir de ses
mains; **to feel ~** se sentir bien; **it's ~ to see you**
ça me fait plaisir de vous voir, je suis content de
vous voir; **he's up to no ~** il prépare quelque
mauvais coup; **it's no ~ complaining** cela ne
sert à rien de se plaindre; **to make ~** (*deficit*)
combler; (*losses*) compenser; **for the common
~** dans l'intérêt commun; **for ~** (*forever*) pour de
bon, une fois pour toutes; **would you be ~
enough to …?** auriez-vous la bonté *or*
l'amabilité de …?; **that's very ~ of you** c'est
très gentil de votre part; **is this any ~?** (*will it
do?*) est-ce que ceci fera l'affaire?, est-ce que cela
peut vous rendre service?; (*what's it like?*) qu'est-
ce que ça vaut?; **~s and chattels** biens *mpl* et
effets *mpl*; **a ~ deal (of)** beaucoup (de); **a ~
many** beaucoup (de); **~ morning/afternoon!**
bonjour!; **~ evening!** bonsoir!; **~ night!**
bonsoir!; (*on going to bed*) bonne nuit!
**goodbye** [gud'baɪ] *excl* au revoir!; **to say ~ to sb**
dire au revoir à qn
**good faith** *n* bonne foi
**good-for-nothing** ['gudfənʌθɪŋ] *adj* bon(ne) *or*
propre à rien
**Good Friday** *n* Vendredi saint
**good-humoured** ['gud'hju:məd] *adj* (*person*)
jovial(e); (*remark, joke*) sans malice
**good-looking** ['gud'lukɪŋ] *adj* beau (belle), bien
*inv*
**good-natured** ['gud'neɪtʃəd] *adj* (*person*) qui a un
bon naturel; (*discussion*) enjoué(e)
**goodness** ['gudnɪs] *n* (*of person*) bonté *f*; **for ~
sake!** je vous en prie!; **~ gracious!** mon Dieu!
**goods train** *n* (*Brit*) train *m* de marchandises
**goodwill** [gud'wɪl] *n* bonne volonté *f*; (*Comm*)
réputation *f* (auprès de la clientèle)
**goody-goody** ['gudɪgudɪ] *n* (*pej*) petit saint,
sainte nitouche
**gooey** ['gu:ɪ] *adj* (*Brit inf*) gluant(e)
**Google®** ['gugl] *vi, vt* googler®
**goose** (*pl* **geese**) [gu:s, gi:s] *n* oie *f*
**gooseberry** ['guzbərɪ] *n* groseille *f* à
maquereau; **to play ~** (*Brit*) tenir la chandelle
**goose bumps, goose pimples** *npl* chair *f* de
poule
**gooseflesh** ['gu:sfleʃ] *n*, **goosepimples**
['gu:spɪmplz] ▷ *npl* chair *f* de poule
**goose step** *n* (*Mil*) pas *m* de l'oie
**GOP** *n abbr* (*US Pol: inf:* = Grand Old Party) parti
républicain
**gopher** ['gəufə'] *n* = **gofer**
**gore** [gɔ:'] *vt* encorner ▷ *n* sang *m*
**gorge** [gɔ:dʒ] *n* gorge *f* ▷ *vt:* **to ~ o.s. (on)** se

gorger (de)
**gorgeous** ['gɔ:dʒəs] *adj* splendide, superbe
**gorilla** [gə'rɪlə] *n* gorille *m*
**gormless** ['gɔ:mlɪs] *adj* (*Brit inf*) lourdaud(e)
**gorse** [gɔ:s] *n* ajoncs *mpl*
**gory** ['gɔ:rɪ] *adj* sanglant(e)
**gosh** [gɔʃ] (*inf*) *excl* mince alors!
**go-slow** ['gəu'sləu] *n* (*Brit*) grève perlée
**gospel** ['gɔspl] *n* évangile *m*
**gossamer** ['gɔsəmə'] *n* (*cobweb*) fils *mpl* de la
vierge; (*light fabric*) étoffe très légère
**gossip** ['gɔsɪp] *n* (*chat*) bavardages *mpl*;
(*malicious*) commérage *m*, cancans *mpl*; (*person*)
commère *f* ▷ *vi* bavarder; cancaner, faire des
commérages; **a piece of ~** un ragot, un
racontar
**gossip column** *n* (*Press*) échos *mpl*
**got** [gɔt] *pt, pp of* **get**
**Gothic** ['gɔθɪk] *adj* gothique
**gotten** ['gɔtn] (*US*) *pp of* **get**
**gouge** [gaudʒ] *vt* (*also:* **gouge out**: *hole etc*)
évider; (*: initials*) tailler; **to ~ sb's eyes out**
crever les yeux à qn
**gourd** [guəd] *n* calebasse *f*, gourde *f*
**gourmet** ['guəmeɪ] *n* gourmet *m*, gastronome
*m/f*
**gout** [gaut] *n* goutte *f*
**govern** ['gʌvən] *vt* (*gen: Ling*) gouverner;
(*influence*) déterminer
**governess** ['gʌvənɪs] *n* gouvernante *f*
**governing** ['gʌvənɪŋ] *adj* (*Pol*) au pouvoir, au
gouvernement; **~ body** conseil *m*
d'administration
**government** ['gʌvnmənt] *n* gouvernement *m*;
(*Brit: ministers*) ministère *m* ▷ *cpd* de l'État
**governmental** [gʌvn'mɛntl] *adj*
gouvernemental(e)
**government housing** *n* (*US*) logements
sociaux
**government stock** *n* titres *mpl* d'État
**governor** ['gʌvənə'] *n* (*of colony, state, bank*)
gouverneur *m*; (*of school, hospital etc*)
administrateur(-trice); (*Brit: of prison*)
directeur(-trice)
**Govt** *abbr* (= government) gvt
**gown** [gaun] *n* robe *f*; (*of teacher, Brit: of judge*)
toge *f*
**GP** *n abbr* (*Med*) = **general practitioner; who's
your GP?** qui est votre médecin traitant?
**GPMU** *n abbr* (*Brit*) = **Graphical, Paper and Media
Union**
**GPO** *n abbr* (*Brit: old*) = **General Post Office**; (*US*)
= **Government Printing Office**
**GPS** *n abbr* (= global positioning system) GPS *m*
**gr.** *abbr* (*Comm*) = **gross**
**grab** [græb] *vt* saisir, empoigner; (*property, power*)
se saisir de ▷ *vi:* **to ~ at** essayer de saisir
**grace** [greɪs] *n* grâce *f* ▷ *vt* (*honour*) honorer;
(*adorn*) orner; **5 days' ~** un répit de 5 jours; **to
say ~** dire le bénédicité; (*after meal*) dire les
grâces; **with a good/bad ~** de bonne/mauvaise
grâce; **his sense of humour is his saving ~** il

603

se rachète par son sens de l'humour

**graceful** ['greɪsful] adj gracieux(-euse), élégant(e)

**gracious** ['greɪʃəs] adj (kind) charmant(e), bienveillant(e); (elegant) plein(e) d'élégance, d'une grande élégance; (formal: pardon etc) miséricordieux(-euse) ▷ excl: **(good)** ~! mon Dieu!

**gradation** [grə'deɪʃən] n gradation f

**grade** [greɪd] n (Comm: quality) qualité f; (size) calibre m; (type) catégorie f; (in hierarchy) grade m, échelon m; (Scol) note f; (US: school class) classe f; (: gradient) pente f ▷ vt classer; (by size) calibrer; graduer; **to make the ~** (fig) réussir

**grade crossing** n (US) passage m à niveau

**grade school** n (US) école f primaire

**gradient** ['greɪdɪənt] n inclinaison f, pente f; (Geom) gradient m

**gradual** ['grædjʊəl] adj graduel(le), progressif(-ive)

**gradually** ['grædjʊəlɪ] adv peu à peu, graduellement

**graduate** n ['grædjuɪt] diplômé(e) d'université; (US: of high school) diplômé(e) de fin d'études ▷ vi ['grædjueɪt] obtenir un diplôme d'université (or de fin d'études)

**graduated pension** ['grædjueɪtɪd-] n retraite calculée en fonction des derniers salaires

**graduation** [grædju'eɪʃən] n cérémonie f de remise des diplômes

**graffiti** [grə'fiːtɪ] n pl graffiti mpl

**graft** [grɑːft] n (Agr, Med) greffe f; (bribery) corruption f ▷ vt greffer; **hard ~** (Brit: inf) boulot acharné

**grain** [greɪn] n (single piece) grain m; (no pl: cereals) céréales fpl; (US: corn) blé m; (of wood) fibre f; **it goes against the ~** cela va à l'encontre de sa (or ma etc) nature

**gram** [græm] n gramme m

**grammar** ['græmə'] n grammaire f

**grammar school** n (Brit) ≈ lycée m

**grammatical** [grə'mætɪkl] adj grammatical(e)

**gramme** [græm] n = **gram**

**gramophone** ['græməfəun] n (Brit) gramophone m

**gran** [græn] (inf) n (Brit) mamie f (inf), mémé f (inf); **my ~** (young child speaking) ma mamie or mémé; (older child or adult speaking) ma grand-mère

**granary** ['grænərɪ] n grenier m

**grand** [grænd] adj magnifique, splendide; (terrific) magnifique, formidable; (gesture etc) noble ▷ n (inf: thousand) mille livres fpl (or dollars mpl)

**grandad** ['grændæd] (inf) n = **granddad**

**grandchild** (pl **grandchildren**) ['græntʃaɪld, 'græntʃɪldrən] n petit-fils m, petite-fille f; **grandchildren** npl petits-enfants

**granddad** ['grændæd] n (inf) papy m (inf), papi m (inf), pépé m (inf); **my ~** (young child speaking) mon papy or papi or pépé; (older child or adult speaking) mon grand-père

**granddaughter** ['grændɔːtə'] n petite-fille f

**grandeur** ['grændjə'] n magnificence f, splendeur f; (of position etc) éminence f

**grandfather** ['grændfɑːðə'] n grand-père m

**grandiose** ['grændɪəus] adj grandiose; (pej) pompeux(-euse)

**grand jury** n (US) jury m d'accusation (formé de 12 à 23 jurés)

**grandma** ['grænmɑː] n (inf) = **gran**

**grandmother** ['grænmʌðə'] n grand-mère f

**grandpa** ['grænpɑː] n (inf) = **granddad**

**grandparents** ['grændpɛərənts] npl grands-parents mpl

**grand piano** n piano m à queue

**Grand Prix** ['grɑ̃ː'priː] n (Aut) grand prix automobile

**grandson** ['grænsʌn] n petit-fils m

**grandstand** ['grændstænd] n (Sport) tribune f

**grand total** n total général

**granite** ['grænɪt] n granit m

**granny** ['grænɪ] n (inf) = **gran**

**grant** [grɑːnt] vt accorder; (a request) accéder à; (admit) concéder ▷ n (Scol) bourse f; (Admin) subside m, subvention f; **to take sth for ~ed** considérer qch comme acquis; **to take sb for ~ed** considérer qn comme faisant partie du décor; **to ~ that** admettre que

**granulated** ['grænjuleɪtɪd] adj: ~ **sugar** sucre m en poudre

**granule** ['grænjuːl] n granule m

**grape** [greɪp] n raisin m; **a bunch of ~s** une grappe de raisin

**grapefruit** ['greɪpfruːt] n pamplemousse m

**grapevine** ['greɪpvaɪn] n vigne f; **I heard it on the ~** (fig) je l'ai appris par le téléphone arabe

**graph** [grɑːf] n graphique m, courbe f

**graphic** ['græfɪk] adj graphique; (vivid) vivant(e)

**graphic designer** n graphiste m/f

**graphic equalizer** n égaliseur m graphique

**graphics** ['græfɪks] n (art) arts mpl graphiques; (process) graphisme m ▷ npl (drawings) illustrations fpl

**graphite** ['græfaɪt] n graphite m

**graph paper** n papier millimétré

**grapple** ['græpl] vi: **to ~ with** être aux prises avec

**grappling iron** ['græplɪŋ-] n (Naut) grappin m

**grasp** [grɑːsp] vt saisir, empoigner; (understand) saisir, comprendre ▷ n (grip) prise f; (fig) compréhension f, connaissance f; **to have sth within one's ~** avoir qch à sa portée; **to have a good ~ of sth** (fig) bien comprendre qch
▶ **grasp at** vt fus (rope etc) essayer de saisir; (fig: opportunity) sauter sur

**grasping** ['grɑːspɪŋ] adj avide

**grass** [grɑːs] n herbe f; (lawn) gazon m; (Brit inf: informer) mouchard(e); (: ex-terrorist) balanceur(-euse)

**grasshopper** ['grɑːshɒpə'] n sauterelle f

**grassland** ['grɑːslænd] n prairie f

**grass roots** npl (fig) base f

**grass snake** n couleuvre f

**grassy** ['grɑːsɪ] *adj* herbeux(-euse)
**grate** [greɪt] *n* grille *f* de cheminée ▷ *vi* grincer ▷ *vt* (*Culin*) râper
**grateful** ['greɪtful] *adj* reconnaissant(e)
**gratefully** ['greɪtfəlɪ] *adv* avec reconnaissance
**grater** ['greɪtəʳ] *n* râpe *f*
**gratification** [grætɪfɪ'keɪʃən] *n* satisfaction *f*
**gratify** ['grætɪfaɪ] *vt* faire plaisir à; (*whim*) satisfaire
**gratifying** ['grætɪfaɪɪŋ] *adj* agréable, satisfaisant(e)
**grating** ['greɪtɪŋ] *n* (*iron bars*) grille *f* ▷ *adj* (*noise*) grinçant(e)
**gratitude** ['grætɪtjuːd] *n* gratitude *f*
**gratuitous** [grə'tjuːɪtəs] *adj* gratuit(e)
**gratuity** [grə'tjuːɪtɪ] *n* pourboire *m*
**grave** [greɪv] *n* tombe *f* ▷ *adj* grave, sérieux(-euse)
**gravedigger** ['greɪvdɪgəʳ] *n* fossoyeur *m*
**gravel** ['grævl] *n* gravier *m*
**gravely** ['greɪvlɪ] *adv* gravement, sérieusement; **~ ill** gravement malade
**gravestone** ['greɪvstəun] *n* pierre tombale
**graveyard** ['greɪvjɑːd] *n* cimetière *m*
**gravitate** ['grævɪteɪt] *vi* graviter
**gravity** ['grævɪtɪ] *n* (*Physics*) gravité *f*; pesanteur *f*; (*seriousness*) gravité, sérieux *m*
**gravy** ['greɪvɪ] *n* jus *m* (de viande), sauce *f* (au jus de viande)
**gravy boat** *n* saucière *f*
**gravy train** *n* (*inf*): **to ride the ~** avoir une bonne planque
**gray** [greɪ] *adj* (*US*) = **grey**
**graze** [greɪz] *vi* paître, brouter ▷ *vt* (*touch lightly*) frôler, effleurer; (*scrape*) écorcher ▷ *n* écorchure *f*
**grazing** ['greɪzɪŋ] *n* (*pasture*) pâturage *m*
**grease** [griːs] *n* (*fat*) graisse *f*; (*lubricant*) lubrifiant *m* ▷ *vt* graisser; lubrifier; **to ~ the skids** (*US: fig*) huiler les rouages
**grease gun** *n* graisseur *m*
**greasepaint** ['griːspeɪnt] *n* produits *mpl* de maquillage
**greaseproof paper** ['griːspruːf-] *n* (*Brit*) papier sulfurisé
**greasy** ['griːsɪ] *adj* gras(se), graisseux(-euse); (*hands, clothes*) graisseux; (*Brit: road, surface*) glissant(e)
**great** [greɪt] *adj* grand(e); (*heat, pain etc*) très fort(e), intense; (*inf*) formidable; **they're ~ friends** ils sont très amis, ce sont de grands amis; **we had a ~ time** nous nous sommes bien amusés; **it was ~!** c'était fantastique *or* super!; **the ~ thing is that ...** ce qu'il y a de vraiment bien c'est que ...
**Great Barrier Reef** *n*: **the ~** la Grande Barrière
**Great Britain** *n* Grande-Bretagne *f*
**great-grandchild** (*pl* **-children**) [greɪt'grænʃtʃaɪld, -tʃɪldrən] *n* arrière-petit(e)-enfant
**great-grandfather** [greɪt'grænfɑːðəʳ] *n* arrière-grand-père *m*

**great-grandmother** [greɪt'grænmʌðəʳ] *n* arrière-grand-mère *f*
**Great Lakes** *npl*: **the ~** les Grands Lacs
**greatly** ['greɪtlɪ] *adv* très, grandement; (*with verbs*) beaucoup
**greatness** ['greɪtnɪs] *n* grandeur *f*
**Grecian** ['griːʃən] *adj* grec (grecque)
**Greece** [griːs] *n* Grèce *f*
**greed** [griːd] *n* (*also*: **greediness**) avidité *f*; (*for food*) gourmandise *f*
**greedily** ['griːdɪlɪ] *adv* avidement; avec gourmandise
**greedy** ['griːdɪ] *adj* avide; (*for food*) gourmand(e)
**Greek** [griːk] *adj* grec (grecque) ▷ *n* Grec (Grecque); (*Ling*) grec *m*; **ancient/modern ~** grec classique/moderne
**green** [griːn] *adj* vert(e); (*inexperienced*) (bien) jeune, naïf(-ïve); (*ecological: product etc*) écologique ▷ *n* (*colour*) vert *m*; (*on golf course*) green *m*; (*stretch of grass*) pelouse *f*; (*also*: **village green**) ≈ place *f* du village; **greens** *npl* (*vegetables*) légumes verts; **to have ~ fingers** *or* (*US*) **a ~ thumb** (*fig*) avoir le pouce vert; **G~** (*Pol*) écologiste *m/f*; **the G~ Party** le parti écologiste
**green belt** *n* (*round town*) ceinture verte
**green card** *n* (*Aut*) carte verte; (*US: work permit*) permis *m* de travail
**greenery** ['griːnərɪ] *n* verdure *f*
**greenfly** ['griːnflaɪ] *n* (*Brit*) puceron *m*
**greengage** ['griːngeɪdʒ] *n* reine-claude *f*
**greengrocer** ['griːngrəusəʳ] *n* (*Brit*) marchand *m* de fruits et légumes
**greengrocer's** ['griːngrəusəʳz], **greengrocer's shop** *n* magasin *m* de fruits et légumes
**greenhouse** ['griːnhaus] *n* serre *f*
**greenhouse effect** *n*: **the ~** l'effet *m* de serre
**greenhouse gas** *n* gaz *m* contribuant à l'effet de serre
**greenish** ['griːnɪʃ] *adj* verdâtre
**Greenland** ['griːnlənd] *n* Groenland *m*
**Greenlander** ['griːnləndəʳ] *n* Groenlandais(e)
**green light** *n*: **to give sb/sth the ~** donner le feu vert à qn/qch
**green pepper** *n* poivron (vert)
**green pound** *n* (*Econ*) livre verte
**green salad** *n* salade verte
**greet** [griːt] *vt* accueillir
**greeting** ['griːtɪŋ] *n* salutation *f*; **Christmas/birthday ~s** souhaits *mpl* de Noël/de bon anniversaire
**greeting card, greetings card** *n* carte *f* de vœux
**gregarious** [grə'gɛərɪəs] *adj* grégaire; sociable
**grenade** [grə'neɪd] *n* (*also*: **hand grenade**) grenade *f*
**grew** [gruː] *pt of* **grow**
**grey**, (*US*) **gray** [greɪ] *adj* gris(e); (*dismal*) sombre; **to go ~** (commencer à) grisonner
**grey-haired**, (*US*) **gray-haired** [greɪ'hɛəd] *adj* aux cheveux gris
**greyhound** ['greɪhaund] *n* lévrier *m*
**grid** [grɪd] *n* grille *f*; (*Elec*) réseau *m*; (*US Aut*)

**g**

intersection f (matérialisée par des marques au sol)
**griddle** ['grɪdl] n (on cooker) plaque chauffante
**gridiron** ['grɪdaɪən] n gril m
**gridlock** ['grɪdlɔk] n (traffic jam) embouteillage m
**gridlocked** ['grɪdlɔk t] adj: **to be** ~ (roads) être bloqué par un embouteillage; (talks etc) être suspendu
**grief** [gri:f] n chagrin m, douleur f; **to come to** ~ (plan) échouer; (person) avoir un malheur
**grievance** ['gri:vəns] n doléance f, grief m; (cause for complaint) grief
**grieve** [gri:v] vi avoir du chagrin; se désoler ▷ vt faire de la peine à, affliger; **to** ~ **for sb** pleurer qn; **to** ~ **at** se désoler de; pleurer
**grievous** ['gri:vəs] adj grave, cruel(le); ~ **bodily harm** (Law) coups mpl et blessures fpl
**grill** [grɪl] n (on cooker) gril m; (also: **mixed grill**) grillade(s) f(pl); (also: **grillroom**) rôtisserie f ▷ vt (Brit) griller; (inf: question) interroger longuement, cuisiner
**grille** [grɪl] n grillage m; (Aut) calandre f
**grillroom** ['grɪlrum] n rôtisserie f
**grim** [grɪm] adj sinistre, lugubre; (serious, stern) sévère
**grimace** [grɪ'meɪs] n grimace f ▷ vi grimacer, faire une grimace
**grime** [graɪm] n crasse f
**grimy** ['graɪmɪ] adj crasseux(-euse)
**grin** [grɪn] n large sourire m ▷ vi sourire; **to** ~ **(at)** faire un grand sourire (à)
**grind** [graɪnd] (pt, pp **ground** [graund]) vt écraser; (coffee, pepper etc) moudre; (US: meat) hacher; (make sharp) aiguiser; (polish: gem, lens) polir ▷ vi (car gears) grincer ▷ n (work) corvée f; **to** ~ **one's teeth** grincer des dents; **to** ~ **to a halt** (vehicle) s'arrêter dans un grincement de freins; (fig) s'arrêter, s'immobiliser; **the daily** ~ (inf) le train-train quotidien
**grinder** ['graɪndə'] n (machine: for coffee) moulin m (à café); (: for waste disposal etc) broyeur m
**grindstone** ['graɪndstəun] n: **to keep one's nose to the** ~ travailler sans relâche
**grip** [grɪp] n (handclasp) poigne f; (control) prise f; (handle) poignée f; (holdall) sac m de voyage ▷ vt saisir, empoigner; (viewer, reader) captiver; **to come to** ~**s with** se colleter avec, en venir aux prises avec; **to** ~ **the road** (Aut) adhérer à la route; **to lose one's** ~ lâcher prise; (fig) perdre les pédales, être dépassé(e)
**gripe** [graɪp] n (Med) coliques fpl; (inf: complaint) ronchonnement m, rouspétance f ▷ vi (inf) râler
**gripping** ['grɪpɪŋ] adj prenant(e), palpitant(e)
**grisly** ['grɪzlɪ] adj sinistre, macabre
**grist** [grɪst] n (fig): **it's (all)** ~ **to his mill** ça l'arrange, ça apporte de l'eau à son moulin
**gristle** ['grɪsl] n cartilage m (de poulet etc)
**grit** [grɪt] n gravillon m; (courage) cran m ▷ vt (road) sabler; **to** ~ **one's teeth** serrer les dents; **to have a piece of** ~ **in one's eye** avoir une poussière or saleté dans l'œil
**grits** [grɪts] npl (US) gruau m de maïs
**grizzle** ['grɪzl] vi (Brit) pleurnicher

**grizzly** ['grɪzlɪ] n (also: **grizzly bear**) grizzli m, ours gris
**groan** [grəun] n (of pain) gémissement m; (of disapproval, dismay) grognement m ▷ vi gémir; grogner
**grocer** ['grəusə'] n épicier m
**groceries** ['grəusərɪz] npl provisions fpl
**grocer's** ['grəusə'z], **grocer's shop, grocery** ['grəusərɪ] n épicerie f
**grog** [grɔg] n grog m
**groggy** ['grɔgɪ] adj groggy inv
**groin** [grɔɪn] n aine f
**groom** [gru:m] n (for horses) palefrenier m; (also: **bridegroom**) marié m ▷ vt (horse) panser; (fig): **to** ~ **sb for** former qn pour
**groove** [gru:v] n sillon m, rainure f
**grope** [grəup] vi tâtonner; **to** ~ **for** chercher à tâtons
**gross** [grəus] adj grossier(-ière); (Comm) brut(e) ▷ n (pl inv: twelve dozen) grosse f ▷ vt (Comm): **to** ~ **£500,000** gagner 500 000 livres avant impôt
**gross domestic product** n produit brut intérieur
**grossly** ['grəuslɪ] adv (greatly) très, grandement
**gross national product** n produit national brut
**grotesque** [grə'tɛsk] adj grotesque
**grotto** ['grɔtəu] n grotte f
**grotty** ['grɔtɪ] adj (Brit inf) minable
**grouch** [grautʃ] (inf) vi rouspéter ▷ n (person) rouspéteur(-euse)
**ground** [graund] pt, pp of **grind** ▷ n sol m, terre f; (land) terrain m, terres fpl; (Sport) terrain; (reason: gen pl) raison f; (US: also: **ground wire**) terre f ▷ vt (plane) empêcher de décoller, retenir au sol; (US Elec) équiper d'une prise de terre, mettre à la terre ▷ vi (ship) s'échouer ▷ adj (coffee etc) moulu(e); (US: meat) haché(e); **grounds** npl (gardens etc) parc m, domaine m; (of coffee) marc m; **on the** ~, **to the** ~ par terre; **below** ~ sous terre; **to gain/lose** ~ gagner/perdre du terrain; **common** ~ terrain d'entente; **he covered a lot of** ~ **in his lecture** sa conférence a traité un grand nombre de questions or la question en profondeur
**ground cloth** n (US) = **groundsheet**
**ground control** n (Aviat, Space) centre m de contrôle (au sol)
**ground floor** n (Brit) rez-de-chaussée m
**grounding** ['graundɪŋ] n (in education) connaissances fpl de base
**groundless** ['graundlɪs] adj sans fondement
**groundnut** ['graundnʌt] n arachide f
**ground rent** n (Brit) fermage m
**ground rules** npl: **the** ~ les principes mpl de base
**groundsheet** ['graundʃi:t] n (Brit) tapis m de sol
**groundsman** ['graundzmən] (irreg), (US)
**groundskeeper** ['graundzki:pə'] n (Sport) gardien m de stade
**ground staff** n équipage m au sol
**groundswell** ['graundswɛl] n lame f or vague f de fond

**ground-to-air** ['grauntu'ɛəʳ] *adj (Mil)* sol-air *inv*
**ground-to-ground** ['grauntə'graund] *adj (Mil)*
  sol-sol *inv*
**groundwork** ['graundwə:k] *n* préparation *f*
**group** [gru:p] *n* groupe *m* ▷ *vt (also:* **group**
  **together)** grouper ▷ *vi (also:* **group together)** se
  grouper
**groupie** ['gru:pɪ] *n* groupie *f*
**group therapy** *n* thérapie *f* de groupe
**grouse** [graus] *n (pl inv: bird)* grouse *f (sorte de coq*
  *de bruyère)* ▷ *vi (complain)* rouspéter, râler
**grove** [grəuv] *n* bosquet *m*
**grovel** ['grɔvl] *vi (fig):* **to ~ (before)** ramper
  (devant)
**grow** *(pt* **grew,** *pp* **-n)** [grəu, gru:, grəun] *vi (plant)*
  pousser, croître; *(person)* grandir; *(increase)*
  augmenter, se développer; *(become)* devenir; **to**
  **~ rich/weak** s'enrichir/s'affaiblir ▷ *vt* cultiver,
  faire pousser; *(hair, beard)* laisser pousser
  ▶ **grow apart** *vi (fig)* se détacher (l'un de
    l'autre)
  ▶ **grow away from** *vt fus (fig)* s'éloigner de
  ▶ **grow on** *vt fus:* **that painting is ~ing on me**
    je finirai par aimer ce tableau
  ▶ **grow out of** *vt fus (clothes)* devenir trop grand
    pour; *(habit)* perdre (avec le temps); **he'll ~ out**
    **of it** ça lui passera
  ▶ **grow up** *vi* grandir
**grower** ['grəuəʳ] *n* producteur *m*; *(Agr)*
  cultivateur(-trice)
**growing** ['grəuɪŋ] *adj (fear, amount)* croissant(e),
  grandissant(e); **~ pains** *(Med)* fièvre *f* de
  croissance; *(fig)* difficultés *fpl* de croissance
**growl** [graul] *vi* grogner
**grown** [grəun] *pp of* **grow** ▷ *adj* adulte
**grown-up** [grəun'ʌp] *n* adulte *m/f*, grande
  personne
**growth** [grəuθ] *n* croissance *f*, développement
  *m*; *(what has grown)* pousse *f*; poussée *f*; *(Med)*
  grosseur *f*, tumeur *f*
**growth rate** *n* taux *m* de croissance
**GRSM** *n abbr (Brit)* = **Graduate of the Royal**
  **Schools of Music**
**grub** [grʌb] *n* larve *f*; *(inf: food)* bouffe *f*
**grubby** ['grʌbɪ] *adj* crasseux(-euse)
**grudge** [grʌdʒ] *n* rancune *f* ▷ *vt:* **to ~ sb sth** *(in*
  *giving)* donner qch à qn à contre-cœur; *(resent)*
  reprocher qch à qn; **to bear sb a ~ (for)** garder
  rancune *or* en vouloir à qn (de); **he ~s spending**
  il rechigne à dépenser
**grudgingly** ['grʌdʒɪŋlɪ] *adv* à contre-cœur, de
  mauvaise grâce
**gruelling,** *(US)* **grueling** ['gruəlɪŋ] *adj*
  exténuant(e)
**gruesome** ['gru:səm] *adj* horrible
**gruff** [grʌf] *adj* bourru(e)
**grumble** ['grʌmbl] *vi* rouspéter, ronchonner
**grumpy** ['grʌmpɪ] *adj* grincheux(-euse)
**grunge** [grʌndʒ] *n (Mus: style)* grunge *m*
**grunt** [grʌnt] *vi* grogner ▷ *n* grognement *m*
**G-string** ['dʒi:strɪŋ] *n (garment)* cache-sexe *m inv*
**GSUSA** *n abbr* = **Girl Scouts of the United States**

**of America**
**GU** *abbr (US)* = **Guam**
**guarantee** [gærən'ti:] *n* garantie *f* ▷ *vt*
  garantir; **he can't ~ (that) he'll come** il n'est
  pas absolument certain de pouvoir venir
**guarantor** [gærən'tɔ:ʳ] *n* garant(e)
**guard** [gɑ:d] *n* garde *f*, surveillance *f*; *(squad:*
  *Boxing, Fencing)* garde *f*; *(one man)* garde *m*; *(Brit*
  *Rail)* chef *m* de train; *(safety device: on machine)*
  dispositif *m* de sûreté; *(also:* **fireguard)** garde-
  feu *m inv* ▷ *vt* garder, surveiller; *(protect):* **to ~**
  **sb/sth (against** *or* **from)** protéger qn/qch
  (contre); **to be on one's ~** *(fig)* être sur ses
  gardes
  ▶ **guard against** *vi:* **to ~ against doing sth** se
    garder de faire qch
**guard dog** *n* chien *m* de garde
**guarded** ['gɑ:dɪd] *adj (fig)* prudent(e)
**guardian** ['gɑ:dɪən] *n* gardien(ne); *(of minor)*
  tuteur(-trice)
**guard's van** ['gɑ:dz-] *n (Brit Rail)* fourgon *m*
**Guatemala** [gwɑ:tɪ'mɑ:lə] *n* Guatémala *m*
**Guernsey** ['gə:nzɪ] *n* Guernesey *m or f*
**guerrilla** [gə'rɪlə] *n* guérillero *m*
**guerrilla warfare** *n* guérilla *f*
**guess** [gɛs] *vi* deviner ▷ *vt* deviner; *(estimate)*
  évaluer; *(US)* croire, penser ▷ *n* supposition *f*,
  hypothèse *f*; **to take** *or* **have a ~** essayer de
  deviner; **to keep sb ~ing** laisser qn dans le
  doute *or* l'incertitude, tenir qn en haleine
**guesstimate** ['gɛstɪmɪt] *n (inf)* estimation *f*
**guesswork** ['gɛswə:k] *n* hypothèse *f*; **I got the**
  **answer by ~** j'ai deviné la réponse
**guest** [gɛst] *n* invité(e); *(in hotel)* client(e); **be**
  **my ~** faites comme chez vous
**guest house** ['gɛsthaus] *n* pension *f*
**guest room** *n* chambre *f* d'amis
**guff** [gʌf] *n (inf)* bêtises *fpl*
**guffaw** [gʌ'fɔ:] *n* gros rire ▷ *vi* pouffer de rire
**guidance** ['gaɪdəns] *n (advice)* conseils *mpl*;
  **under the ~ of** conseillé(e) *or* encadré(e) par,
  sous la conduite de; **vocational ~** orientation
  professionnelle; **marriage ~** conseils
  conjugaux
**guide** [gaɪd] *n (person)* guide *m/f*; *(book)* guide *m*;
  *(also:* **Girl Guide)** éclaireuse *f*; *(Roman Catholic)*
  guide *f* ▷ *vt* guider; **to be ~d by sb/sth** se
  laisser guider par qn/qch; **is there an English-**
  **speaking ~?** est-ce que l'un des guides parle
  anglais?
**guidebook** ['gaɪdbuk] *n* guide *m*; **do you have a**
  **~ in English?** est-ce que vous avez un guide en
  anglais?
**guided missile** ['gaɪdɪd-] *n* missile téléguidé
**guide dog** *n* chien *m* d'aveugle
**guided tour** *n* visite guidée; **what time does**
  **the ~ start?** la visite guidée commence à quelle
  heure?
**guidelines** ['gaɪdlaɪnz] *npl (advice)* instructions
  générales, conseils *mpl*
**guild** [gɪld] *n (History)* corporation *f*; *(sharing*
  *interests)* cercle *m*, association *f*

**g**

**guildhall** ['gɪldhɔːl] n (Brit) hôtel m de ville
**guile** [gaɪl] n astuce f
**guileless** ['gaɪllɪs] adj candide
**guillotine** ['gɪləti:n] n guillotine f; (for paper) massicot m
**guilt** [gɪlt] n culpabilité f
**guilty** ['gɪltɪ] adj coupable; **to plead ~/not ~** plaider coupable/non coupable; **to feel ~ about doing sth** avoir mauvaise conscience à faire qch
**Guinea** ['gɪnɪ] n: **Republic of ~** (République f de) Guinée f
**guinea** ['gɪnɪ] n (Brit: formerly) guinée f (= 21 shillings)
**guinea pig** ['gɪnɪ-] n cobaye m
**guise** [gaɪz] n aspect m, apparence f
**guitar** [gɪ'tɑːʳ] n guitare f
**guitarist** [gɪ'tɑːrɪst] n guitariste m/f
**gulch** [gʌltʃ] n (US) ravin m
**gulf** [gʌlf] n golfe m; (abyss) gouffre m; **the (Persian) G~** le golfe Persique
**Gulf States** npl: **the ~** (in Middle East) les pays mpl du Golfe
**Gulf Stream** n: **the ~** le Gulf Stream
**gull** [gʌl] n mouette f
**gullet** ['gʌlɪt] n gosier m
**gullibility** [gʌlɪ'bɪlɪtɪ] n crédulité f
**gullible** ['gʌlɪbl] adj crédule
**gully** ['gʌlɪ] n ravin m; ravine f; couloir m
**gulp** [gʌlp] vi avaler sa salive; (from emotion) avoir la gorge serrée, s'étrangler ▷ vt (also: **gulp down**) avaler ▷ n (of drink) gorgée f; **at one ~** d'un seul coup
**gum** [gʌm] n (Anat) gencive f; (glue) colle f; (sweet) boule f de gomme; (also: **chewing-gum**) chewing-gum m ▷ vt coller
**gumboil** ['gʌmbɔɪl] n abcès m dentaire
**gumboots** ['gʌmbuːts] npl (Brit) bottes fpl en caoutchouc
**gumption** ['gʌmpʃən] n bon sens, jugeote f
**gun** [gʌn] n (small) revolver m, pistolet m; (rifle) fusil m, carabine f; (cannon) canon m ▷ vt (also: **gun down**) abattre; **to stick to one's ~s** (fig) ne pas en démordre
**gunboat** ['gʌnbəut] n canonnière f
**gun dog** n chien m de chasse
**gunfire** ['gʌnfaɪəʳ] n fusillade f
**gunk** [gʌŋk] n (inf) saleté f
**gunman** (irreg) ['gʌnmən] n bandit armé
**gunner** ['gʌnəʳ] n artilleur m
**gunpoint** ['gʌnpɔɪnt] n: **at ~** sous la menace du pistolet (or fusil)
**gunpowder** ['gʌnpaudəʳ] n poudre f à canon
**gunrunner** ['gʌnrʌnəʳ] n trafiquant m d'armes
**gunrunning** ['gʌnrʌnɪŋ] n trafic m d'armes
**gunshot** ['gʌnʃɔt] n coup m de feu; **within ~** à portée de fusil
**gunsmith** ['gʌnsmɪθ] n armurier m
**gurgle** ['gəːgl] n gargouillis m ▷ vi gargouiller
**guru** ['guruː] n gourou m
**gush** [gʌʃ] n jaillissement m, jet m ▷ vi jaillir; (fig) se répandre en effusions
**gushing** ['gʌʃɪŋ] adj (person) trop exubérant(e) or expansif(-ive); (compliments) exagéré(e)
**gusset** ['gʌsɪt] n gousset m, soufflet m; (in tights, pants) entre-jambes m
**gust** [gʌst] n (of wind) rafale f; (of smoke) bouffée f
**gusto** ['gʌstəu] n enthousiasme m
**gusty** ['gʌstɪ] adj venteux(-euse); **~ winds** des rafales de vent
**gut** [gʌt] n intestin m, boyau m; (Mus etc) boyau ▷ vt (poultry, fish) vider; (building) ne laisser que les murs de; **guts** npl (Anat) boyaux mpl; (inf: courage) cran m; **to hate sb's ~s** ne pas pouvoir voir qn en peinture or sentir qn
**gut reaction** n réaction instinctive
**gutsy** ['gʌtsɪ] adj (person) qui a du cran; (style) qui a du punch
**gutted** ['gʌtɪd] adj: **I was ~** (inf: disappointed) j'étais carrément dégoûté
**gutter** ['gʌtəʳ] n (of roof) gouttière f; (in street) caniveau m; (fig) ruisseau m
**gutter press** n: **the ~** la presse de bas étage or à scandale
**guttural** ['gʌtərl] adj guttural(e)
**guy** [gaɪ] n (inf: man) type m; (also: **guyrope**) corde f; (figure) effigie de Guy Fawkes
**Guyana** [gaɪ'ænə] n Guyane f
**Guy Fawkes' Night** [gaɪ'fɔːks-] n voir article

---

#### ● GUY FAWKES' NIGHT

Guy Fawkes' Night, que l'on appelle également "bonfire night", commémore l'échec du complot (le "Gunpowder Plot") contre James Ist et son parlement le 5 novembre 1605. L'un des conspirateurs, Guy Fawkes, avait été surpris dans les caves du parlement alors qu'il s'apprêtait à y mettre le feu. Chaque année pour le 5 novembre, les enfants préparent à l'avance une effigie de Guy Fawkes et ils demandent aux passants "un penny pour le guy" avec lequel ils pourront s'acheter des fusées de feu d'artifice. Beaucoup de gens font encore un feu dans leur jardin sur lequel ils brûlent le "guy".

---

**guzzle** ['gʌzl] vi s'empiffrer ▷ vt avaler gloutonnement
**gym** [dʒɪm] n (also: **gymnasium**) gymnase m; (also: **gymnastics**) gym f
**gymkhana** [dʒɪm'kɑːnə] n gymkhana m
**gymnasium** [dʒɪm'neɪzɪəm] n gymnase m
**gymnast** ['dʒɪmnæst] n gymnaste m/f
**gymnastics** [dʒɪm'næstɪks] n, npl gymnastique f
**gym shoes** npl chaussures fpl de gym(nastique)
**gynaecologist**, (US) **gynecologist** [gaɪnɪ'kɔlədʒɪst] n gynécologue m/f
**gynaecology**, (US) **gynecology** [gaɪnə'kɔlədʒɪ] n gynécologie f
**gypsy** ['dʒɪpsɪ] n gitan(e), bohémien(ne) ▷ cpd: **~ caravan** n roulotte f
**gyrate** [dʒaɪ'reɪt] vi tournoyer

# Hh

**H, h** [eɪtʃ] *n (letter)* H, h *m*; **H for Harry,** (US) **H for How** H comme Henri

**habeas corpus** ['heɪbɪəs'kɔːpəs] *n (Law)* habeas corpus *m*

**haberdashery** [hæbə'dæʃərɪ] *n (Brit)* mercerie *f*

**habit** ['hæbɪt] *n* habitude *f*; *(costume: Rel)* habit *m*; *(for riding)* tenue *f* d'équitation; **to get out of/into the ~ of doing sth** perdre/prendre l'habitude de faire qch

**habitable** ['hæbɪtəbl] *adj* habitable

**habitat** ['hæbɪtæt] *n* habitat *m*

**habitation** [hæbɪ'teɪʃən] *n* habitation *f*

**habitual** [hə'bɪtjuəl] *adj* habituel(le); *(drinker, liar)* invétéré(e)

**habitually** [hə'bɪtjuəlɪ] *adv* habituellement, d'habitude

**hack** [hæk] *vt* hacher, tailler ▷ *n (cut)* entaille *f*; *(blow)* coup *m*; *(pej: writer)* nègre *m*; *(old horse)* canasson *m*

**hacker** ['hækə'] *n (Comput)* pirate *m* (informatique); (: *enthusiast)* passionné(e) *m/f* des ordinateurs

**hackles** ['hæklz] *npl:* **to make sb's ~ rise** *(fig)* mettre qn hors de soi

**hackney cab** ['hæknɪ-] *n* fiacre *m*

**hackneyed** ['hæknɪd] *adj* usé(e), rebattu(e)

**hacksaw** ['hæksɔː] *n* scie *f* à métaux

**had** [hæd] *pt, pp of* **have**

**haddock** (*pl - or -s*) ['hædək] *n* églefin *m*; **smoked ~** haddock *m*

**hadn't** ['hædnt] = **had not**

**haematology,** (US) **hematology** ['hiːmə'tɔlədʒɪ] *n* hématologie *f*

**haemoglobin,** (US) **hemoglobin** ['hiːmə'gləubɪn] *n* hémoglobine *f*

**haemophilia,** (US) **hemophilia** ['hiːmə'fɪlɪə] *n* hémophilie *f*

**haemorrhage,** (US) **hemorrhage** ['hɛmərɪdʒ] *n* hémorragie *f*

**haemorrhoids,** (US) **hemorrhoids** ['hɛmərɔɪdz] *npl* hémorroïdes *fpl*

**hag** [hæg] *n (ugly)* vieille sorcière; *(nasty)* chameau *m*, harpie *f*; *(witch)* sorcière

**haggard** ['hægəd] *adj* hagard(e), égaré(e)

**haggis** ['hægɪs] *n* haggis *m*

**haggle** ['hægl] *vi* marchander; **to ~ over** chicaner sur

**haggling** ['hæglɪŋ] *n* marchandage *m*

**Hague** [heɪg] *n*: **The ~** La Haye

**hail** [heɪl] *n* grêle *f* ▷ *vt (call)* héler; *(greet)* acclamer ▷ *vi* grêler; *(originate)*: **he ~s from Scotland** il est originaire d'Écosse

**hailstone** ['heɪlstəun] *n* grêlon *m*

**hailstorm** ['heɪlstɔːm] *n* averse *f* de grêle

**hair** [hɛə'] *n* cheveux *mpl*; *(on body)* poils *mpl*, pilosité *f*; *(of animal)* pelage *m*; *(single hair: on head)* cheveu *m*; (: *on body, of animal)* poil *m*; **to do one's ~** se coiffer

**hairband** ['hɛəbænd] *n (elasticated)* bandeau *m*; *(plastic)* serre-tête *m*

**hairbrush** ['hɛəbrʌʃ] *n* brosse *f* à cheveux

**haircut** ['hɛəkʌt] *n* coupe *f* (de cheveux)

**hairdo** ['hɛəduː] *n* coiffure *f*

**hairdresser** ['hɛədrɛsə'] *n* coiffeur(-euse)

**hairdresser's** ['hɛədrɛsə'z] *n* salon *m* de coiffure, coiffeur *m*

**hair dryer** ['hɛədraɪə'] *n* sèche-cheveux *m*, séchoir *m*

**-haired** [hɛəd] *suffix:* **fair/long~** aux cheveux blonds/longs

**hair gel** *n* gel *m* pour cheveux

**hairgrip** ['hɛəgrɪp] *n* pince *f* à cheveux

**hairline** ['hɛəlaɪn] *n* naissance *f* des cheveux

**hairline fracture** *n* fêlure *f*

**hairnet** ['hɛənɛt] *n* résille *f*

**hair oil** *n* huile *f* capillaire

**hairpiece** ['hɛəpiːs] *n* postiche *m*

**hairpin** ['hɛəpɪn] *n* épingle *f* à cheveux

**hairpin bend,** (US) **hairpin curve** *n* virage *m* en épingle à cheveux

**hair-raising** ['hɛəreɪzɪŋ] *adj* à (vous) faire dresser les cheveux sur la tête

**hair remover** *n* dépilateur *m*

**hair removing cream** *n* crème *f* dépilatoire

**hair spray** *n* laque *f* (pour les cheveux)

**hairstyle** ['hɛəstaɪl] *n* coiffure *f*

**hairy** ['hɛərɪ] *adj* poilu(e), chevelu(e); *(inf: frightening)* effrayant(e)

**Haiti** ['heɪtɪ] *n* Haïti *m*

**hake** (*pl - or -s*) [heɪk] *n* colin *m*, merlu *m*

**halcyon** ['hælsɪən] *adj* merveilleux(-euse)

**hale** [heɪl] *adj:* **~ and hearty** robuste, en

pleine santé

**half** [hɑːf] n (pl **halves** [hɑːvz]) moitié f; (of beer:
also: **half pint**) ≈ demi m; (Rail, bus: also: **half fare**)
demi-tarif m; (Sport: of match) mi-temps f; (: of
ground) moitié (du terrain) ▷ adj demi(e) ▷ adv
(à) moitié, à demi; ~ **an hour** une demi-heure;
~ **a dozen** une demi-douzaine; ~ **a pound** une
demi-livre, ≈ 250 g; **two and a** ~ deux et demi; **a
week and a** ~ une semaine et demie; ~ **(of it)** la
moitié; ~ **(of)** la moitié de; ~ **the amount of** la
moitié de; **to cut sth in** ~ couper qch en deux; ~
**past three** trois heures et demie; ~ **empty/
closed** à moitié vide/fermé; **to go halves (with
sb)** se mettre de moitié avec qn
**half-back** ['hɑːfbæk] n (Sport) demi m
**half-baked** ['hɑːfbeɪkt] adj (inf: idea, scheme) qui
ne tient pas debout
**half board** n (Brit: in hotel) demi-pension f
**half-breed** ['hɑːfbriːd] n (pej) = **half-caste**
**half-brother** ['hɑːfbrʌðəʳ] n demi-frère m
**half-caste** ['hɑːfkɑːst] n (pej) métis(se)
**half day** n demi-journée f
**half fare** n demi-tarif m
**half-hearted** ['hɑːf'hɑːtɪd] adj tiède, sans
enthousiasme
**half-hour** [hɑːf'auəʳ] n demi-heure f
**half-mast** ['hɑːf'mɑːst] n: **at** ~ (flag) en berne, à
mi-mât
**halfpenny** ['heɪpnɪ] n demi-penny m
**half-price** ['hɑːf'praɪs] adj à moitié prix ▷ adv
(also: **at half-price**) à moitié prix
**half term** n (Brit Scol) vacances fpl (de demi-
trimestre)
**half-time** [hɑːf'taɪm] n mi-temps f
**halfway** ['hɑːf'weɪ] adv à mi-chemin; **to meet
sb** ~ (fig) parvenir à un compromis avec qn; ~
**through sth** au milieu de qch
**halfway house** n (hostel) centre m de
réadaptation (pour anciens prisonniers, malades
mentaux etc); (fig): **a** ~ **(between)** une étape
intermédiaire (entre)
**half-wit** ['hɑːfwɪt] n (inf) idiot(e), imbécile m/f
**half-yearly** [hɑːf'jɪəlɪ] adv deux fois par an ▷ adj
semestriel(le)
**halibut** ['hælɪbət] n (pl inv) flétan m
**halitosis** [hælɪ'təusɪs] n mauvaise haleine
**hall** [hɔːl] n salle f; (entrance way: big) hall m;
(small) entrée f; (US: corridor) couloir m; (mansion)
château m, manoir m
**hallmark** ['hɔːlmɑːk] n poinçon m; (fig) marque f
**hallo** [hə'ləu] excl = **hello**
**hall of residence** n (Brit) pavillon m or
résidence f universitaire
**Hallowe'en, Halloween** ['hæləu'iːn] n veille f
de la Toussaint; voir article

● **HALLOWE'EN**
●
● Selon la tradition, Hallowe'en est la nuit des
● fantômes et des sorcières. En Écosse et aux
● États-Unis surtout (et de plus en plus en
● Angleterre) les enfants, pour fêter

● Hallowe'en, se déguisent ce soir-là et ils vont
● ainsi de porte en porte en demandant de
● petits cadeaux (du chocolat, etc).

**hallucination** [həluːsɪ'neɪʃən] n hallucination f
**hallucinogenic** [həluːsɪnəu'dʒɛnɪk] adj
hallucinogène
**hallway** ['hɔːlweɪ] n (entrance) vestibule m;
(corridor) couloir m
**halo** ['heɪləu] n (of saint etc) auréole f; (of sun)
halo m
**halt** [hɔːlt] n halte f, arrêt m ▷ vt faire arrêter;
(progress etc) interrompre ▷ vi faire halte,
s'arrêter; **to call a** ~ **to sth** (fig) mettre fin à qch
**halter** ['hɔːltəʳ] n (for horse) licou m
**halterneck** ['hɔːltənɛk] adj (dress) (avec) dos nu
inv
**halve** [hɑːv] vt (apple etc) partager or diviser en
deux; (reduce by half) réduire de moitié
**halves** [hɑːvz] npl of **half**
**ham** [hæm] n jambon m; (inf: also: **radio ham**)
radio-amateur m; (also: **ham actor**) cabotin(e)
**Hamburg** ['hæmbəːg] n Hambourg
**hamburger** ['hæmbəːgəʳ] n hamburger m
**ham-fisted** ['hæm'fɪstɪd], (US) **ham-handed**
['hæm'hændɪd] adj maladroit(e)
**hamlet** ['hæmlɪt] n hameau m
**hammer** ['hæməʳ] n marteau m ▷ vt (nail)
enfoncer; (fig) éreinter, démolir ▷ vi (at door)
frapper à coups redoublés; **to** ~ **a point home
to sb** faire rentrer qch dans la tête de qn
▶ **hammer out** vt (metal) étendre au marteau;
(fig: solution) élaborer
**hammock** ['hæmək] n hamac m
**hamper** ['hæmpəʳ] vt gêner ▷ n panier m
(d'osier)
**hamster** ['hæmstəʳ] n hamster m
**hamstring** ['hæmstrɪŋ] n (Anat) tendon m du
jarret
**hand** [hænd] n main f; (of clock) aiguille f;
(handwriting) écriture f; (at cards) jeu m;
(measurement: of horse) paume f; (worker)
ouvrier(-ière) ▷ vt passer, donner; **to give sb a**
~ donner un coup de main à qn; **at** ~ à portée de
la main; **in** ~ (situation) en main; (work) en cours;
**we have the situation in** ~ nous avons la
situation bien en main; **to be on** ~ (person) être
disponible; (emergency services) se tenir prêt(e) (à
intervenir); **to** ~ (information etc) sous la main, à
portée de la main; **to force sb's** ~ forcer la main
à qn; **to have a free** ~ avoir carte blanche; **to
have sth in one's** ~ tenir qch à la main; **on the
one** ~ ..., **on the other** ~ d'une part ..., d'autre
part
▶ **hand down** vt passer; (tradition, heirloom)
transmettre; (US: sentence, verdict) prononcer
▶ **hand in** vt remettre
▶ **hand out** vt distribuer
▶ **hand over** vt remettre; (powers etc)
transmettre
▶ **hand round** vt (Brit: information) faire circuler;
(: chocolates etc) faire passer

**handbag** ['hændbæg] n sac m à main
**hand baggage** n = **hand luggage**
**handball** ['hændbɔːl] n handball m
**handbasin** ['hændbeɪsn] n lavabo m
**handbook** ['hændbuk] n manuel m
**handbrake** ['hændbreɪk] n frein m à main
**h & c** abbr (Brit) = **hot and cold (water)**
**hand cream** n crème f pour les mains
**handcuffs** ['hændkʌfs] npl menottes fpl
**handful** ['hændful] n poignée f
**hand-held** ['hænd'held] adj à main
**handicap** ['hændɪkæp] n handicap m ▷ vt
handicaper; **mentally/physically ~ped**
handicapé(e) mentalement/physiquement
**handicraft** ['hændɪkrɑːft] n travail m
d'artisanat, technique artisanale
**handiwork** ['hændɪwəːk] n ouvrage m; **this
looks like his ~** (pej) ça a tout l'air d'être son
œuvre
**handkerchief** ['hæŋkətʃɪf] n mouchoir m
**handle** ['hændl] n (of door etc) poignée f; (of cup
etc) anse f; (of knife etc) manche m; (of saucepan)
queue f; (for winding) manivelle f ▷ vt toucher,
manier; (deal with) s'occuper de; (treat: people)
prendre; **"~ with care"** "fragile"; **to fly off the
~** s'énerver
**handlebar** ['hændlbɑːr] n, **handlebars**
['hændlbɑːz] npl guidon m
**handling** ['hændlɪŋ] n (Aut) maniement m;
(treatment): **his ~ of the matter** la façon dont il
a traité l'affaire
**handling charges** npl frais mpl de
manutention; (Banking) agios mpl
**hand luggage** ['hændlʌgɪdʒ] n bagages mpl à
main; **one item of ~** un bagage à main
**handmade** ['hænd'meɪd] adj fait(e) à la main
**handout** ['hændaut] n (money) aide f, don m;
(leaflet) prospectus m; (press handout)
communiqué m de presse; (at lecture)
polycopié m
**hand-picked** ['hænd'pɪkt] adj (produce) cueilli(e)
à la main; (staff etc) trié(e) sur le volet
**handrail** ['hændreɪl] n (on staircase etc) rampe f,
main courante
**handset** ['hændset] n (Tel) combiné m
**hands-free** [hændz'friː] adj mains libres inv ▷ n
(also: **hands-free kit**) kit m mains libres inv
**handshake** ['hændʃeɪk] n poignée f de main;
(Comput) établissement m de la liaison
**handsome** ['hænsəm] adj beau (belle); (gift)
généreux(-euse); (profit) considérable
**hands-on** [hændz'ɔn] adj (training, experience) sur
le tas; **she has a very ~ approach** sa politique
est de mettre la main à la pâte
**handstand** ['hændstænd] n: **to do a ~** faire
l'arbre droit
**hand-to-mouth** ['hændtə'mauθ] adj (existence)
au jour le jour
**handwriting** ['hændraɪtɪŋ] n écriture f
**handwritten** ['hændrɪtn] adj manuscrit(e),
écrit(e) à la main
**handy** ['hændɪ] adj (person) adroit(e); (close at

hand) sous la main; (convenient) pratique; **to
come in ~** être (or s'avérer) utile
**handyman** ['hændɪmæn] (irreg) n bricoleur m;
(servant) homme m à tout faire
**hang** (pt, pp **hung**) [hæŋ, hʌŋ] vt accrocher;
(criminal: pt, pp **-ed**) pendre ▷ vi pendre; (hair,
drapery) tomber ▷ n: **to get the ~ of (doing) sth**
(inf) attraper le coup pour faire qch
▶ **hang about, hang around** vi flâner, traîner
▶ **hang back** vi (hesitate): **to ~ back (from
doing)** être réticent(e) (pour faire)
▶ **hang down** vi pendre
▶ **hang on** vi (wait) attendre ▷ vt fus (depend on)
dépendre de; **to ~ on to** (keep hold of) ne pas
lâcher; (keep) garder
▶ **hang out** vt (washing) étendre (dehors) ▷ vi
pendre; (inf: live) habiter, percher; (: spend time)
traîner
▶ **hang round** vi = **hang around**
▶ **hang together** vi (argument etc) se tenir, être
cohérent(e)
▶ **hang up** vi (Tel) raccrocher ▷ vt (coat, painting
etc) accrocher, suspendre; **to ~ up on sb** (Tel)
raccrocher au nez de qn
**hangar** ['hæŋər] n hangar m
**hangdog** ['hæŋdɔg] adj (look, expression) de chien
battu
**hanger** ['hæŋər] n cintre m, portemanteau m
**hanger-on** [hæŋər'ɔn] n parasite m
**hang-glider** ['hæŋglaɪdər] n deltaplane m
**hang-gliding** ['hæŋglaɪdɪŋ] n vol m libre or sur
aile delta
**hanging** ['hæŋɪŋ] n (execution) pendaison f
**hangman** ['hæŋmən] (irreg) n bourreau m
**hangover** ['hæŋəuvər] n (after drinking) gueule f
de bois
**hang-up** ['hæŋʌp] n complexe m
**hank** [hæŋk] n écheveau m
**hanker** ['hæŋkər] vi: **to ~ after** avoir envie de
**hankering** ['hæŋkərɪŋ] n: **to have a ~ for/to do
sth** avoir une grande envie de/de faire qch
**hankie, hanky** ['hæŋkɪ] n abbr = **handkerchief**
**Hants** abbr (Brit) = **Hampshire**
**haphazard** [hæp'hæzəd] adj fait(e) au hasard,
fait(e) au petit bonheur
**hapless** ['hæplɪs] adj malheureux(-euse)
**happen** ['hæpən] vi arriver, se passer, se
produire; **what's ~ing?** que se passe-t-il?; **she
~ed to be free** il s'est trouvé (or se trouvait)
qu'elle était libre; **if anything ~ed to him** s'il
lui arrivait quoi que ce soit; **as it ~s** justement
▶ **happen on, happen upon** vt fus tomber sur
**happening** ['hæpənɪŋ] n événement m
**happily** ['hæpɪlɪ] adv heureusement; (cheerfully)
joyeusement
**happiness** ['hæpɪnɪs] n bonheur m
**happy** ['hæpɪ] adj heureux(-euse); **~ with**
(arrangements etc) satisfait(e) de; **to be ~ to do**
faire volontiers; **yes, I'd be ~ to** oui, avec plaisir
or (bien) volontiers; **~ birthday!** bon
anniversaire!; **~ Christmas/New Year!** joyeux
Noël/bonne année!

**happy-go-lucky** ['hæpɪgəʊ'lʌkɪ] *adj* insouciant(e)

**happy hour** *n* l'heure *f* de l'apéritif, *heure pendant laquelle les consommations sont à prix réduit*

**harangue** [hə'ræŋ] *vt* haranguer

**harass** ['hærəs] *vt* accabler, tourmenter

**harassed** ['hærəst] *adj* tracassé(e)

**harassment** ['hærəsmənt] *n* tracasseries *fpl*; **sexual ~** harcèlement sexuel

**harbour**, *(US)***harbor** ['hɑːbəʳ] *n* port *m* ▷ *vt* héberger, abriter; *(hopes, suspicions)* entretenir; **to ~ a grudge against sb** en vouloir à qn

**harbour dues**, *(US)***harbor dues** *npl* droits *mpl* de port

**harbour master**, *(US)***harbor master** *n* capitaine *m* du port

**hard** [hɑːd] *adj* dur(e); *(question, problem)* difficile; *(facts, evidence)* concret(-ète) ▷ *adv* *(work)* dur; *(think, try)* sérieusement; **to look ~ at** regarder fixement; *(thing)* regarder de près; **to drink ~** boire sec; **~ luck!** pas de veine!; **no ~ feelings!** sans rancune!; **to be ~ of hearing** être dur(e) d'oreille; **to be ~ done by** être traité(e) injustement; **to be ~ on sb** être dur(e) avec qn; **I find it ~ to believe that ...** je n'arrive pas à croire que ...

**hard-and-fast** ['hɑːdən'fɑːst] *adj* strict(e), absolu(e)

**hardback** ['hɑːdbæk] *n* livre relié

**hardboard** ['hɑːdbɔːd] *n* Isorel® *m*

**hard-boiled egg** ['hɑːd'bɔɪld-] *n* œuf dur

**hard cash** *n* espèces *fpl*

**hard copy** *n* *(Comput)* sortie *f* or copie *f* papier

**hard-core** ['hɑːd'kɔːʳ] *adj* *(pornography)* (dit(e)) dur(e); *(supporters)* inconditionnel(le)

**hard court** *n* *(Tennis)* court *m* en dur

**hard disk** *n* *(Comput)* disque dur

**harden** ['hɑːdn] *vt* durcir; *(steel)* tremper; *(fig)* endurcir ▷ *vi* *(substance)* durcir

**hardened** ['hɑːdnd] *adj* *(criminal)* endurci(e); **to be ~ to sth** s'être endurci(e) à qch, être (devenu(e)) insensible à qch

**hard-headed** ['hɑːd'hɛdɪd] *adj* réaliste; décidé(e)

**hard-hearted** ['hɑːd'hɑːtɪd] *adj* dur(e), impitoyable

**hard-hitting** ['hɑːd'hɪtɪŋ] *adj* *(speech, article)* sans complaisances

**hard labour** *n* travaux forcés

**hardliner** [hɑːd'laɪnəʳ] *n* intransigeant(e), dur(e)

**hard-luck story** [hɑːd'lʌk-] *n* histoire larmoyante

**hardly** ['hɑːdlɪ] *adv* *(scarcely)* à peine; *(harshly)* durement; **it's ~ the case** ce n'est guère le cas; **~ anywhere/ever** presque nulle part/jamais; **I can ~ believe it** j'ai du mal à le croire

**hardness** ['hɑːdnɪs] *n* dureté *f*

**hard-nosed** ['hɑːd'nəuzd] *adj* impitoyable, dur(e)

**hard-pressed** ['hɑːd'prɛst] *adj* sous pression

**hard sell** *n* vente agressive

**hardship** ['hɑːdʃɪp] *n* *(difficulties)* épreuves *fpl*; *(deprivation)* privations *fpl*

**hard shoulder** *n* *(Brit Aut)* accotement stabilisé

**hard-up** [hɑːd'ʌp] *adj* *(inf)* fauché(e)

**hardware** ['hɑːdwɛəʳ] *n* quincaillerie *f*; *(Comput, Mil)* matériel *m*

**hardware shop**, *(US)***hardware store** *n* quincaillerie *f*

**hard-wearing** [hɑːd'wɛərɪŋ] *adj* solide

**hard-won** ['hɑːd'wʌn] *adj* (si) durement gagné(e)

**hard-working** [hɑːd'wəːkɪŋ] *adj* travailleur(-euse), consciencieux(-euse)

**hardy** ['hɑːdɪ] *adj* robuste; *(plant)* résistant(e) au gel

**hare** [hɛəʳ] *n* lièvre *m*

**hare-brained** ['hɛəbreɪnd] *adj* farfelu(e), écervelé(e)

**harelip** ['hɛəlɪp] *n* *(Med)* bec-de-lièvre *m*

**harem** [hɑː'riːm] *n* harem *m*

**hark back** [hɑːk-] *vi*: **to ~ to** (en) revenir toujours à

**harm** [hɑːm] *n* mal *m*; *(wrong)* tort *m* ▷ *vt* *(person)* faire du mal or du tort à; *(thing)* endommager; **to mean no ~** ne pas avoir de mauvaises intentions; **there's no ~ in trying** on peut toujours essayer; **out of ~'s way** à l'abri du danger, en lieu sûr

**harmful** ['hɑːmful] *adj* nuisible

**harmless** ['hɑːmlɪs] *adj* inoffensif(-ive)

**harmonic** [hɑː'mɔnɪk] *adj* harmonique

**harmonica** [hɑː'mɔnɪkə] *n* harmonica *m*

**harmonics** [hɑː'mɔnɪks] *npl* harmoniques *mpl* or *fpl*

**harmonious** [hɑː'məunɪəs] *adj* harmonieux(-euse)

**harmonium** [hɑː'məunɪəm] *n* harmonium *m*

**harmonize** ['hɑːmənaɪz] *vt* harmoniser ▷ *vi* s'harmoniser

**harmony** ['hɑːmənɪ] *n* harmonie *f*

**harness** ['hɑːnɪs] *n* harnais *m* ▷ *vt* *(horse)* harnacher; *(resources)* exploiter

**harp** [hɑːp] *n* harpe *f* ▷ *vi*: **to ~ on about** revenir toujours sur

**harpist** ['hɑːpɪst] *n* harpiste *m/f*

**harpoon** [hɑː'puːn] *n* harpon *m*

**harpsichord** ['hɑːpsɪkɔːd] *n* clavecin *m*

**harrowing** ['hærəuɪŋ] *adj* déchirant(e)

**harsh** [hɑːʃ] *adj* *(hard)* dur(e); *(severe)* sévère; *(rough: surface)* rugueux(-euse); *(unpleasant: sound)* discordant(e); *(: light)* cru(e); *(: taste)* âpre

**harshly** ['hɑːʃlɪ] *adv* durement, sévèrement

**harshness** ['hɑːʃnɪs] *n* dureté *f*, sévérité *f*

**harvest** ['hɑːvɪst] *n* *(of corn)* moisson *f*; *(of fruit)* récolte *f*; *(of grapes)* vendange *f* ▷ *vi, vt* moissonner; récolter; vendanger

**harvester** ['hɑːvɪstəʳ] *n* *(machine)* moissonneuse *f*; *(also:* **combine harvester***)* moissonneuse-batteuse(-lieuse *f) f*

**has** [hæz] *vb see* **have**

**has-been** ['hæzbiːn] *n* *(inf: person)*: **he/she's a ~** il/elle a fait son temps or est fini(e)

**hash** [hæʃ] n (Culin) hachis m; (fig: mess) gâchis m
  ▷ n abbr (inf) = **hashish**
**hashish** ['hæʃɪʃ] n haschisch m
**hasn't** ['hæznt] = **has not**
**hassle** ['hæsl] n (inf: fuss) histoire(s) f(pl)
**haste** [heɪst] n hâte f, précipitation f; **in ~** à la
  hâte, précipitamment
**hasten** ['heɪsn] vt hâter, accélérer ▷ vi se hâter,
  s'empresser
**hastily** ['heɪstɪlɪ] adv à la hâte; (leave)
  précipitamment
**hasty** ['heɪstɪ] adj (decision, action) hâtif(-ive);
  (departure, escape) précipité(e)
**hat** [hæt] n chapeau m
**hatbox** ['hætbɔks] n carton m à chapeau
**hatch** [hætʃ] n (Naut: also: **hatchway**) écoutille f;
  (Brit: also: **service hatch**) passe-plats m inv ▷ vi
  éclore ▷ vt faire éclore; (fig: scheme) tramer,
  ourdir
**hatchback** ['hætʃbæk] n (Aut) modèle m avec
  hayon arrière
**hatchet** ['hætʃɪt] n hachette f
**hatchet job** n (inf) démolissage m
**hatchet man** (irreg) n (inf) homme m de main
**hate** [heɪt] vt haïr, détester ▷ n haine f; **to ~ to
  do** or **doing** détester faire; **I ~ to trouble you,
  but ...** désolé de vous déranger, mais ...
**hateful** ['heɪtful] adj odieux(-euse), détestable
**hater** ['heɪtər] n: cop-hater anti-flic mf; woman-
  hater misogyne m/f (haineux(-euse))
**hatred** ['heɪtrɪd] n haine f
**hat trick** n (Brit Sport, also fig): **to get a ~** réussir
  trois coups (or gagner trois matchs etc)
  consécutifs
**haughty** ['hɔːtɪ] adj hautain(e), arrogant(e)
**haul** [hɔːl] vt traîner, tirer; (by lorry) camionner;
  (Naut) haler ▷ n (of fish) prise f; (of stolen goods etc)
  butin m
**haulage** ['hɔːlɪdʒ] n transport routier
**haulage contractor** n (Brit: firm) entreprise f de
  transport (routier); (: person) transporteur
  routier
**haulier** ['hɔːlɪər], (US) **hauler** ['hɔːlər] n
  transporteur (routier), camionneur m
**haunch** [hɔːntʃ] n hanche f; **~ of venison**
  cuissot m de chevreuil
**haunt** [hɔːnt] vt (subj: ghost, fear) hanter; (: person)
  fréquenter ▷ n repaire m
**haunted** ['hɔːntɪd] adj (castle etc) hanté(e); (look)
  égaré(e), hagard(e)
**haunting** ['hɔːntɪŋ] adj (sight, music) obsédant(e)
**Havana** [hə'vænə] n La Havane

○ KEYWORD

**have** [hæv] (pt, pp **had**) aux vb **1** (gen) avoir; être;
  **to have eaten/slept** avoir mangé/dormi; **to
  have arrived/gone** être arrivé(e)/allé(e); **he
  has been promoted** il a eu une promotion;
  **having finished** or **when he had finished, he
  left** quand il a eu fini, il est parti; **we'd already
  eaten** nous avions déjà mangé

**2** (in tag questions): **you've done it, haven't you?**
  vous l'avez fait, n'est-ce pas?
**3** (in short answers and questions): **no I haven't!/yes
  we have!** mais non!/mais si!; **so I have!** ah oui!,
  oui c'est vrai!; **I've been there before, have
  you?** j'y suis déjà allé, et vous?
  ▷ modal aux vb (be obliged): **to have (got) to do
  sth** devoir faire qch, être obligé(e) de faire qch;
  **she has (got) to do it** elle doit le faire, il faut
  qu'elle le fasse; **you haven't to tell her** vous
  n'êtes pas obligé de le lui dire; (must not) ne le
  lui dites surtout pas; **do you have to book?** il
  faut réserver?
  ▷ vt **1** (possess) avoir; **he has (got) blue eyes/
  dark hair** il a les yeux bleus/les cheveux bruns
**2** (referring to meals etc): **to have breakfast**
  prendre le petit déjeuner; **to have dinner/
  lunch** dîner/déjeuner; **to have a drink**
  prendre un verre; **to have a cigarette** fumer
  une cigarette
**3** (receive) avoir, recevoir; (obtain) avoir; **may I
  have your address?** puis-je avoir votre
  adresse?; **you can have it for £5** vous pouvez
  l'avoir pour 5 livres; **I must have it for
  tomorrow** il me le faut pour demain; **to have a
  baby** avoir un bébé
**4** (maintain, allow): **I won't have it!** ça ne se
  passera pas comme ça!; **we can't have that**
  nous ne tolérerons pas ça
**5** (by sb else): **to have sth done** faire faire qch;
  **to have one's hair cut** se faire couper les
  cheveux; **to have sb do sth** faire faire qch à qn
**6** (experience, suffer) avoir; **to have a cold/flu**
  avoir un rhume/la grippe; **to have an
  operation** se faire opérer; **she had her bag
  stolen** elle s'est fait voler son sac
**7** (+noun): **to have a swim/walk** nager/se
  promener; **to have a bath/shower** prendre un
  bain/une douche; **let's have a look** regardons;
  **to have a meeting** se réunir; **to have a party**
  organiser une fête; **let me have a try** laissez-
  moi essayer
**8** (inf: dupe) avoir; **he's been had** il s'est fait
  avoir or rouler
  ▶ **have out** vt: **to have it out with sb** (settle a
  problem etc) s'expliquer (franchement) avec qn

**haven** ['heɪvn] n port m; (fig) havre m
**haven't** ['hævnt] = **have not**
**haversack** ['hævəsæk] n sac m à dos
**haves** [hævz] npl (inf): **the ~ and have-nots** les
  riches et les pauvres
**havoc** ['hævək] n ravages mpl, dégâts mpl; **to
  play ~ with** (fig) désorganiser complètement;
  détraquer
**Hawaii** [hə'waɪ:] n (îles fpl) Hawaï m
**Hawaiian** [hə'waɪjən] adj hawaïen(ne) ▷ n
  Hawaïen(ne); (Ling) hawaïen m
**hawk** [hɔːk] n faucon m ▷ vt (goods) colporter
**hawker** ['hɔːkər] n colporteur m
**hawkish** ['hɔːkɪʃ] adj belliciste
**hawthorn** ['hɔːθɔːn] n aubépine f

**h**

**hay** [heɪ] n foin m
**hay fever** n rhume m des foins
**haystack** ['heɪstæk] n meule f de foin
**haywire** ['heɪwaɪəʳ] adj (inf): **to go ~** perdre la tête; mal tourner
**hazard** ['hæzəd] n (risk) danger m, risque m; (chance) hasard m, chance f ▷ vt risquer, hasarder; **to be a health/fire ~** présenter un risque pour la santé/d'incendie; **to ~ a guess** émettre or hasarder une hypothèse
**hazardous** ['hæzədəs] adj hasardeux(-euse), risqué(e)
**hazard pay** n (US) prime f de risque
**hazard warning lights** npl (Aut) feux mpl de détresse
**haze** [heɪz] n brume f
**hazel** [heɪzl] n (tree) noisetier m ▷ adj (eyes) noisette inv
**hazelnut** ['heɪzlnʌt] n noisette f
**hazy** ['heɪzɪ] adj brumeux(-euse); (idea) vague; (photograph) flou(e)
**H-bomb** ['eɪtʃbɔm] n bombe f H
**HD** abbr (= high definition) HD (= haute définition)
**HE** abbr = **high explosive**; (Rel, Diplomacy) = **His (or Her) Excellency**
**he** [hiː] pron il; **it is he who ...** c'est lui qui ...; **here he is** le voici; **he-bear** etc ours etc mâle
**head** [hɛd] n tête f; (leader) chef m; (of school) directeur(-trice); (of secondary school) proviseur m ▷ vt (list) être en tête de; (group, company) être à la tête de; **heads** pl (on coin) (le côté) face; **~s or tails** pile ou face; **~ first** la tête la première; **~ over heels in love** follement or éperdument amoureux(-euse); **to ~ the ball** faire une tête; **10 euros a** or **per ~** 10 euros par personne; **to sit at the ~ of the table** présider la tablée; **to have a ~ for business** avoir des dispositions pour les affaires; **to have no ~ for heights** être sujet(te) au vertige; **to come to a ~** (fig: situation etc) devenir critique
▶ **head for** vt fus se diriger vers; (disaster) aller à
▶ **head off** vt (threat, danger) détourner
**headache** ['hɛdeɪk] n mal m de tête; **to have a ~** avoir mal à la tête
**headband** ['hɛdbænd] n bandeau m
**headboard** ['hɛdbɔːd] n dosseret m
**head cold** n rhume m de cerveau
**headdress** ['hɛddrɛs] n coiffure f
**headed notepaper** ['hɛdɪd-] n papier m à lettres à en-tête
**header** ['hɛdəʳ] n (Brit inf: Football) (coup m de) tête f; (: fall) chute f (or plongeon m) la tête la première
**head-first** ['hɛd'fəːst] adv (lit) la tête la première
**headhunt** ['hɛdhʌnt] vt: **she was ~ed** elle a été recrutée par un chasseur de têtes
**headhunter** ['hɛdhʌntəʳ] n chasseur m de têtes
**heading** ['hɛdɪŋ] n titre m; (subject title) rubrique f
**headlamp** ['hɛdlæmp] (Brit) n = **headlight**
**headland** ['hɛdlənd] n promontoire m, cap m
**headlight** ['hɛdlaɪt] n phare m

**headline** ['hɛdlaɪn] n titre m
**headlong** ['hɛdlɔŋ] adv (fall) la tête la première; (rush) tête baissée
**headmaster** [hɛd'mɑːstəʳ] n directeur m
**headmistress** [hɛd'mɪstrɪs] n directrice f
**head office** n siège m, bureau m central
**head-on** [hɛd'ɔn] adj (collision) de plein fouet
**headphones** ['hɛdfəunz] npl casque m (à écouteurs)
**headquarters** ['hɛdkwɔːtəz] npl (of business) bureau or siège central; (Mil) quartier général
**headrest** ['hɛdrɛst] n appui-tête m
**headroom** ['hɛdrum] n (in car) hauteur f de plafond; (under bridge) hauteur limite; dégagement m
**headscarf** ['hɛdskɑːf] (pl **headscarves** [-skɑːvz]) n foulard m
**headset** ['hɛdsɛt] n = **headphones**
**headstone** ['hɛdstəun] n pierre tombale
**headstrong** ['hɛdstrɔŋ] adj têtu(e), entêté(e)
**headteacher** [hɛd'tiːtʃəʳ] n directeur(-trice); (of secondary school) proviseur m
**head waiter** n maître m d'hôtel
**headway** ['hɛdweɪ] n: **to make ~** avancer, faire des progrès
**headwind** ['hɛdwɪnd] n vent m contraire
**heady** ['hɛdɪ] adj capiteux(-euse), enivrant(e)
**heal** [hiːl] vt, vi guérir
**health** [hɛlθ] n santé f; **Department of H~** (Brit, US) = ministère m de la Santé
**health care** n services médicaux
**health centre** n (Brit) centre m de santé
**health food** n aliment(s) naturel(s)
**health food shop** n magasin m diététique
**health hazard** n risque m pour la santé
**Health Service** n: **the ~** (Brit) = la Sécurité Sociale
**healthy** ['hɛlθɪ] adj (person) en bonne santé; (climate, food, attitude etc) sain(e)
**heap** [hiːp] n tas m, monceau m ▷ vt (also: **heap up**) entasser, amonceler; **she ~ed her plate with cakes** elle a chargé son assiette de gâteaux; **~s (of)** (inf: lots) des tas (de); **to ~ favours/praise/gifts etc on sb** combler qn de faveurs/d'éloges/de cadeaux etc
**hear** (pt, pp **heard**) [hɪəʳ, həːd] vt entendre; (news) apprendre; (lecture) assister à, écouter ▷ vi entendre; **to ~ about** entendre parler de; (have news of) avoir des nouvelles de; **did you ~ about the move?** tu es au courant du déménagement?; **to ~ from sb** recevoir des nouvelles de qn; **I've never ~d of that book** je n'ai jamais entendu parler de ce livre
▶ **hear out** vt écouter jusqu'au bout
**heard** [həːd] pt, pp of **hear**
**hearing** ['hɪərɪŋ] n (sense) ouïe f; (of witnesses) audition f; (of a case) audience f; (of committee) séance f; **to give sb a ~** (Brit) écouter ce que qn a à dire
**hearing aid** n appareil m acoustique
**hearsay** ['hɪəseɪ] n on-dit mpl, rumeurs fpl; **by ~** adv par ouï-dire

**hearse** [hə:s] n corbillard m

**heart** [hɑːt] n cœur m; **hearts** npl (Cards) cœur;
**at ~** au fond; **by ~** (learn, know) par cœur; **to have
a weak ~** avoir le cœur malade, avoir des
problèmes de cœur; **to lose/take ~** perdre/
prendre courage; **to set one's ~ on sth/on
doing sth** vouloir absolument qch/faire qch;
**the ~ of the matter** le fond du problème

**heartache** ['hɑːteɪk] n chagrin m, douleur f

**heart attack** n crise f cardiaque

**heartbeat** ['hɑːtbiːt] n battement m de cœur

**heartbreak** ['hɑːtbreɪk] n immense chagrin m

**heartbreaking** ['hɑːtbreɪkɪŋ] adj navrant(e),
déchirant(e)

**heartbroken** ['hɑːtbrəukən] adj: **to be ~** avoir
beaucoup de chagrin

**heartburn** ['hɑːtbə:n] n brûlures fpl d'estomac

**heart disease** n maladie f cardiaque

**-hearted** ['hɑːtɪd] suffix: **kind~** généreux(-euse),
qui a bon cœur

**heartening** ['hɑːtnɪŋ] adj encourageant(e),
réconfortant(e)

**heart failure** n (Med) arrêt m du cœur

**heartfelt** ['hɑːtfɛlt] adj sincère

**hearth** [hɑːθ] n foyer m, cheminée f

**heartily** ['hɑːtɪlɪ] adv chaleureusement; (laugh)
de bon cœur; (eat) de bon appétit; **to agree ~**
être entièrement d'accord; **to be ~ sick of** (Brit)
en avoir ras le bol de

**heartland** ['hɑːtlænd] n centre m, cœur m;
**France's ~s** la France profonde

**heartless** ['hɑːtlɪs] adj (person) sans cœur,
insensible; (treatment) cruel(le)

**heartstrings** ['hɑːtstrɪŋz] npl: **to tug (at) sb's ~**
toucher or faire vibrer les cordes sensibles de qn

**heartthrob** ['hɑːtθrɔb] n idole f

**heart-to-heart** ['hɑːttə'hɑːt] adj, adv à cœur
ouvert

**heart transplant** n greffe f du cœur

**heartwarming** ['hɑːtwɔːmɪŋ] adj
réconfortant(e)

**hearty** ['hɑːtɪ] adj chaleureux(-euse); (appetite)
solide; (dislike) cordial(e); (meal) copieux(-euse)

**heat** [hiːt] n chaleur f; (fig) ardeur f; feu m;
(Sport: also: **qualifying heat**) éliminatoire f;
(Zool): **in** or **on ~** (Brit) en chaleur ▷ vt chauffer
▶ **heat up** vi (liquid) chauffer; (room) se
réchauffer ▷ vt réchauffer

**heated** ['hiːtɪd] adj chauffé(e); (fig)
passionné(e), échauffé(e), excité(e)

**heater** ['hiːtə'] n appareil m de chauffage;
radiateur m; (in car) chauffage m; (water heater)
chauffe-eau m

**heath** [hiːθ] n (Brit) lande f

**heathen** ['hiːðn] adj, n païen(ne)

**heather** ['hɛðə'] n bruyère f

**heating** ['hiːtɪŋ] n chauffage m

**heat-resistant** ['hiːtrɪzɪstənt] adj résistant(e) à
la chaleur

**heat-seeking** ['hiːtsiːkɪŋ] adj guidé(e) par
infrarouge

**heatstroke** ['hiːtstrəuk] n coup m de chaleur

**heatwave** ['hiːtweɪv] n vague f de chaleur

**heave** [hiːv] vt soulever (avec effort) ▷ vi se
soulever; (retch) avoir des haut-le-cœur ▷ n
(push) poussée f; **to ~ a sigh** pousser un gros
soupir

**heaven** ['hɛvn] n ciel m, paradis m; (fig) paradis;
**~ forbid!** surtout pas!; **thank ~!** Dieu merci!;
**for ~'s sake!** (pleading) je vous en prie!;
(protesting) mince alors!

**heavenly** ['hɛvnlɪ] adj céleste, divin(e)

**heavily** ['hɛvɪlɪ] adv lourdement; (drink, smoke)
beaucoup; (sleep, sigh) profondément

**heavy** ['hɛvɪ] adj lourd(e); (work, rain, user, eater)
gros(se); (drinker, smoker) grand(e); (schedule, week)
chargé(e); **it's too ~** c'est trop lourd; **it's ~
going** ça ne va pas tout seul, c'est pénible

**heavy cream** n (US) crème fraîche épaisse

**heavy-duty** ['hɛvɪ'djuːtɪ] adj à usage intensif

**heavy goods vehicle** n (Brit) poids lourd m

**heavy-handed** ['hɛvɪ'hændɪd] adj (fig)
maladroit(e), qui manque de tact

**heavy metal** n (Mus) heavy metal m

**heavy-set** ['hɛvɪ'sɛt] adj (esp US) costaud(e)

**heavyweight** ['hɛvɪweɪt] n (Sport) poids lourd

**Hebrew** ['hiːbruː] adj hébraïque ▷ n (Ling)
hébreu m

**Hebrides** ['hɛbrɪdiːz] npl: **the ~** les Hébrides fpl

**heck** [hɛk] n (inf): **why the ~ ...?** pourquoi
diable ...?; **a ~ of a lot** une sacrée quantité; **he
has done a ~ of a lot for us** il a vraiment
beaucoup fait pour nous

**heckle** ['hɛkl] vt interpeller (un orateur)

**heckler** ['hɛklə'] n interrupteur m; élément
perturbateur

**hectare** ['hɛktɑː'] n (Brit) hectare m

**hectic** ['hɛktɪk] adj (schedule) très chargé(e); (day)
mouvementé(e); (activity) fiévreux(-euse);
(lifestyle) trépidant(e)

**he'd** [hiːd] = **he would**; **he had**

**hedge** [hɛdʒ] n haie f ▷ vi se dérober ▷ vt: **to ~
one's bets** (fig) se couvrir; **as a ~ against
inflation** pour se prémunir contre l'inflation
▶ **hedge in** vt entourer d'une haie

**hedgehog** ['hɛdʒhɔg] n hérisson m

**hedgerow** ['hɛdʒrəu] n haie(s) f(pl)

**hedonism** ['hiːdənɪzəm] n hédonisme m

**heed** [hiːd] vt (also: **take heed of**) tenir compte
de, prendre garde à

**heedless** ['hiːdlɪs] adj insouciant(e)

**heel** [hiːl] n talon m ▷ vt (shoe) retalonner; **to
bring to ~** (dog) faire venir à ses pieds; (fig:
person) rappeler à l'ordre; **to take to one's ~s**
prendre ses jambes à son cou

**hefty** ['hɛftɪ] adj (person) costaud(e); (parcel)
lourd(e); (piece, price) gros(se)

**heifer** ['hɛfə'] n génisse f

**height** [haɪt] n (of person) taille f, grandeur f; (of
object) hauteur f; (of plane, mountain) altitude f;
(high ground) hauteur, éminence f; (fig: of glory,
fame, power) sommet m; (: of luxury, stupidity)
comble m; **at the ~ of summer** au cœur de l'été;
**what ~ are you?** combien mesurez-vous?,

h

quelle est votre taille?; **of average ~** de taille
moyenne; **to be afraid of ~s** être sujet(te) au
vertige; **it's the ~ of fashion** c'est le dernier cri
**heighten** ['haɪtn] vt hausser, surélever; (fig)
augmenter
**heinous** ['heɪnəs] adj odieux(-euse), atroce
**heir** [ɛəʳ] n héritier m
**heir apparent** n héritier présomptif
**heiress** ['ɛərɛs] n héritière f
**heirloom** ['ɛəluːm] n meuble m (or bijou m or
tableau m) de famille
**heist** [haɪst] n (US inf: hold-up) casse m
**held** [hɛld] pt, pp of **hold**
**helicopter** ['hɛlɪkɒptəʳ] n hélicoptère m
**heliport** ['hɛlɪpɔːt] n (Aviat) héliport m
**helium** ['hiːlɪəm] n hélium m
**hell** [hɛl] n enfer m; **a ~ of a ...** (inf) un(e)
sacré(e) ...; **oh ~!** (inf) merde!
**he'll** [hiːl] = **he will; he shall**
**hell-bent** [hɛl'bɛnt] adj (inf): **to be ~ on doing
sth** vouloir à tout prix faire qch
**hellish** ['hɛlɪʃ] adj infernal(e)
**hello** [hə'ləu] excl bonjour!; (to attract attention)
hé!; (surprise) tiens!
**helm** [hɛlm] n (Naut) barre f
**helmet** ['hɛlmɪt] n casque m
**helmsman** ['hɛlmzmən] (irreg) n timonier m
**help** [hɛlp] n aide f; (cleaner etc) femme f de
ménage; (assistant etc) employé(e) ▷ vt, vi aider;
**~!** au secours!; **~ yourself** servez-vous; **can you
~ me?** pouvez-vous m'aider?; **can I ~ you?** (in
shop) vous désirez?; **with the ~ of** (person) avec
l'aide de; (tool etc) à l'aide de; **to be of ~ to sb**
être utile à qn; **to ~ sb (to) do sth** aider qn à
faire qch; **I can't ~ saying** je ne peux pas
m'empêcher de dire; **he can't ~ it** il n'y peut
rien
▶ **help out** vi aider ▷ vt: **to ~ sb out** aider qn
**helper** ['hɛlpəʳ] n aide m/f, assistant(e)
**helpful** ['hɛlpful] adj serviable, obligeant(e);
(useful) utile
**helping** ['hɛlpɪŋ] n portion f
**helping hand** n coup m de main; **to give sb a ~**
prêter main-forte à qn
**helpless** ['hɛlplɪs] adj impuissant(e); (baby) sans
défense
**helplessly** ['hɛlplɪslɪ] adv (watch) sans pouvoir
rien faire
**helpline** ['hɛlplaɪn] n service m d'assistance
téléphonique; (free) ≈ numéro vert
**Helsinki** ['hɛlsɪŋkɪ] n Helsinki
**helter-skelter** ['hɛltə'skɛltəʳ] n (Brit: at
amusement park) toboggan m
**hem** [hɛm] n ourlet m ▷ vt ourler
▶ **hem in** vt cerner; **to feel ~med in** (fig) avoir
l'impression d'étouffer, se sentir oppressé(e) or
écrasé(e)
**he-man** ['hiːmæn] (irreg) n (inf) macho m
**hematology** ['hiːmə'tɔlədʒɪ] n (US) =
**haematology**
**hemisphere** ['hɛmɪsfɪəʳ] n hémisphère m
**hemlock** ['hɛmlɔk] n ciguë f

**hemoglobin** ['hiːmə'gləubɪn] n (US) =
**haemoglobin**
**hemophilia** ['hiːmə'fɪlɪə] n (US) = **haemophilia**
**hemorrhage** ['hɛmərɪdʒ] n (US) =
**haemorrhage**
**hemorrhoids** ['hɛmərɔɪdz] npl (US) =
**haemorrhoids**
**hemp** [hɛmp] n chanvre m
**hen** [hɛn] n poule f; (female bird) femelle f
**hence** [hɛns] adv (therefore) d'où, de là; **2 years ~**
d'ici 2 ans
**henceforth** [hɛns'fɔːθ] adv dorénavant
**henchman** ['hɛntʃmən] (irreg) n (pej) acolyte m,
séide m
**henna** ['hɛnə] n henné m
**hen night, hen party** n soirée f entre filles
(avant le mariage de l'une d'elles)
**henpecked** ['hɛnpɛkt] adj dominé par sa
femme
**hepatitis** [hɛpə'taɪtɪs] n hépatite f
**her** [həːʳ] pron (direct) la, l' + vowel or h mute;
(indirect) lui; (stressed, after prep) elle ▷ adj son (sa),
ses pl; **I see ~** je la vois; **give ~ a book** donne-lui
un livre; **after ~** après elle; see also **me; my**
**herald** ['hɛrəld] n héraut m ▷ vt annoncer
**heraldic** [hɛ'rældɪk] adj héraldique
**heraldry** ['hɛrəldrɪ] n héraldique f; (coat of arms)
blason m
**herb** [həːb] n herbe f; **herbs** npl fines herbes
**herbaceous** [həː'beɪʃəs] adj herbacé(e)
**herbal** ['həːbl] adj à base de plantes
**herbal tea** n tisane f
**herbicide** ['həːbɪsaɪd] n herbicide m
**herd** [həːd] n troupeau m; (of wild animals, swine)
troupeau, troupe f ▷ vt (drive: animals, people)
mener, conduire; (gather) rassembler; **~ed
together** parqués (comme du bétail)
**here** [hɪəʳ] adv ici; (time) alors ▷ excl tiens!,
tenez!; **~!** (present) présent!; **~ is, ~ are** voici; **~'s
my sister** voici ma sœur; **~ he/she is** le (la)
voici; **~ she comes** la voici qui vient; **come ~!**
viens ici!; **~ and there** ici et là
**hereabouts** ['hɪərə'bauts] adv par ici, dans les
parages
**hereafter** [hɪər'ɑːftəʳ] adv après, plus tard; ci-
après ▷ n: **the ~** l'au-delà m
**hereby** [hɪə'baɪ] adv (in letter) par la présente
**hereditary** [hɪ'rɛdɪtrɪ] adj héréditaire
**heredity** [hɪ'rɛdɪtɪ] n hérédité f
**heresy** ['hɛrəsɪ] n hérésie f
**heretic** ['hɛrətɪk] n hérétique m/f
**heretical** [hɪ'rɛtɪkl] adj hérétique
**herewith** [hɪə'wɪð] adv avec ceci, ci-joint
**heritage** ['hɛrɪtɪdʒ] n héritage m, patrimoine m;
**our national ~** notre patrimoine national
**hermetically** [həː'mɛtɪklɪ] adv hermétique
**hermit** ['həːmɪt] n ermite m
**hernia** ['həːnɪə] n hernie f
**hero** ['hɪərəu] (pl -es) n héros m
**heroic** [hɪ'rəuɪk] adj héroïque
**heroin** ['hɛrəuɪn] n héroïne f (drogue)
**heroin addict** n héroïnomane m/f

**heroine** ['hɛrəʊɪn] n héroïne f (femme)
**heroism** ['hɛrəʊɪzəm] n héroïsme m
**heron** ['hɛrən] n héron m
**hero worship** n culte m (du héros)
**herring** ['hɛrɪŋ] n hareng m
**hers** [həːz] pron le (la) sien(ne), les siens (siennes); **a friend of** ~ un(e) ami(e) à elle, un(e) de ses ami(e)s; see also **mine'**
**herself** [həː'sɛlf] pron (reflexive) se; (emphatic) elle-même; (after prep) elle; see also **oneself**
**Herts** [hɑːts] abbr (Brit) = **Hertfordshire**
**he's** [hiːz] = **he is; he has**
**hesitant** ['hɛzɪtənt] adj hésitant(e), indécis(e); **to be ~ about doing sth** hésiter à faire qch
**hesitate** ['hɛzɪteɪt] vi: **to ~ (about/to do)** hésiter (sur/à faire)
**hesitation** [hɛzɪ'teɪʃən] n hésitation f; **I have no ~ in saying (that)** ... je n'hésiterais pas à dire (que) ...
**hessian** ['hɛsɪən] n (toile f de) jute m
**heterogeneous** ['hɛtərə'dʒiːnɪəs] adj hétérogène
**heterosexual** ['hɛtərəʊ'sɛksjuəl] adj, n hétérosexuel(le)
**het up** [hɛt'ʌp] adj (inf) agité(e), excité(e)
**HEW** n abbr (US: = Department of Health, Education and Welfare) ministère de la santé publique, de l'enseignement et du bien-être
**hew** [hjuː] vt tailler (à la hache)
**hex** [hɛks] (US) n sort m ▷ vt jeter un sort sur
**hexagon** ['hɛksəgən] n hexagone m
**hexagonal** [hɛk'sægənl] adj hexagonal(e)
**hey** [heɪ] excl hé!
**heyday** ['heɪdeɪ] n: **the ~ of** l'âge m d'or de, les beaux jours de
**HF** n abbr (= high frequency) HF f
**HGV** n abbr = **heavy goods vehicle**
**HI** abbr (US) = **Hawaii**
**hi** [haɪ] excl salut!; (to attract attention) hé!
**hiatus** [haɪ'eɪtəs] n trou m, lacune f; (Ling) hiatus m
**hibernate** ['haɪbəneɪt] vi hiberner
**hibernation** [haɪbə'neɪʃən] n hibernation f
**hiccough, hiccup** ['hɪkʌp] vi hoqueter ▷ n hoquet m; **to have (the) ~s** avoir le hoquet
**hick** [hɪk] n (US inf) plouc m, péquenaud(e)
**hid** [hɪd] pt of **hide**
**hidden** ['hɪdn] pp of **hide** ▷ adj: **there are no ~ extras** absolument tout est compris dans le prix; ~ **agenda** intentions non déclarées
**hide** [haɪd] (pt **hid**, pp **hidden** [hɪd, 'hɪdn]) n (skin) peau f ▷ vt cacher; (feelings, truth) dissimuler; **to ~ sth from sb** cacher qch à qn ▷ vi: **to ~ (from sb)** se cacher (de qn)
**hide-and-seek** ['haɪdən'siːk] n cache-cache m
**hideaway** ['haɪdəweɪ] n cachette f
**hideous** ['hɪdɪəs] adj hideux(-euse), atroce
**hide-out** ['haɪdaʊt] n cachette f
**hiding** ['haɪdɪŋ] n (beating) correction f, volée f de coups; **to be in ~** (concealed) se tenir caché(e)
**hiding place** n cachette f
**hierarchy** ['haɪərɑːkɪ] n hiérarchie f

**hieroglyphic** [haɪərə'glɪfɪk] adj hiéroglyphique; **hieroglyphics** npl hiéroglyphes mpl
**hi-fi** ['haɪfaɪ] adj, n abbr (= high fidelity) hi-fi f inv
**higgledy-piggledy** ['hɪgldɪ'pɪgldɪ] adv pêle-mêle, dans le plus grand désordre
**high** [haɪ] adj haut(e); (speed, respect, number) grand(e); (price) élevé(e); (wind) fort(e), violent(e); (voice) aigu(ë); (inf: person: on drugs) défoncé(e), fait(e); (: on drink) soûl(e), bourré(e); (Brit Culin: meat, game) faisandé(e); (: spoilt) avarié(e) ▷ adv haut, en haut ▷ n (weather) zone f de haute pression; **exports have reached a new** ~ les exportations ont atteint un nouveau record; **20 m** ~ haut(e) de 20 m; **to pay a ~ price for sth** payer cher pour qch; ~ **in the air** haut dans le ciel
**highball** ['haɪbɔːl] n (US) whisky m à l'eau avec des glaçons
**highboy** ['haɪbɔɪ] n (US) grande commode
**highbrow** ['haɪbraʊ] adj, n intellectuel(le)
**highchair** ['haɪtʃɛəʳ] n (child's) chaise haute
**high-class** ['haɪ'klɑːs] adj (neighbourhood, hotel) chic inv, de grand standing; (performance etc) de haut niveau
**High Court** n (Law) cour f suprême; voir article

● **HIGH COURT**
●
● Dans le système juridique anglais et gallois,
● la High Court est une cour de droit civil
● chargée des affaires plus importantes et
● complexes que celles traitées par les "county
● courts". En Écosse en revanche, la High Court
● (of Justiciary) est la plus haute cour de justice
● à laquelle les affaires les plus graves telles
● que le meurtre et le viol sont soumises et où
● elles sont jugées devant un jury.

**higher** ['haɪəʳ] adj (form of life, study etc) supérieur(e) ▷ adv plus haut
**higher education** n études supérieures
**highfalutin** [haɪfə'luːtɪn] adj (inf) affecté(e)
**high finance** n la haute finance
**high-flier, high-flyer** [haɪ'flaɪəʳ] n (fig: ambitious) ambitieux(-euse); (: gifted) personne particulièrement douée et promise à un avenir brillant
**high-flying** [haɪ'flaɪɪŋ] adj (fig) ambitieux(-euse), de haut niveau
**high-handed** [haɪ'hændɪd] adj très autoritaire; très cavalier(-ière)
**high-heeled** [haɪ'hiːld] adj à hauts talons
**high heels** npl talons hauts, hauts talons
**high jump** n (Sport) saut m en hauteur
**highlands** ['haɪləndz] npl région montagneuse; **the H~** (in Scotland) les Highlands mpl
**high-level** ['haɪlɛvl] adj (talks etc) à un haut niveau; ~ **language** (Comput) langage évolué
**highlight** ['haɪlaɪt] n (fig: of event) point culminant ▷ vt (emphasize) faire ressortir, souligner; **highlights** npl (in hair) reflets mpl
**highlighter** ['haɪlaɪtəʳ] n (pen) surligneur (lumineux)

**highly** ['haɪlɪ] adv extrêmement, très; (unlikely) fort; (recommended, skilled, qualified) hautement; ~ **paid** très bien payé(e); **to speak ~ of** dire beaucoup de bien de

**highly strung** adj nerveux(-euse), toujours tendu(e)

**High Mass** n grand-messe f

**highness** ['haɪnɪs] n hauteur f; **His/Her H~** son Altesse f

**high-pitched** [haɪ'pɪtʃt] adj aigu(ë)

**high point** n: **the ~ (of)** le clou (de), le point culminant (de)

**high-powered** ['haɪ'paʊəd] adj (engine) performant(e); (fig: person) dynamique; (: job, businessman) très important(e)

**high-pressure** ['haɪprɛʃəʳ] adj à haute pression

**high-rise** ['haɪraɪz] n (also: **high-rise block, high-rise building**) tour f (d'habitation)

**high school** n lycée m; (US) établissement m d'enseignement supérieur; voir article

⬤ **HIGH SCHOOL**
⬤
⬤ Une high school est un établissement
⬤ d'enseignement secondaire. Aux États-
⬤ Unis, il y a la "Junior High School", qui
⬤ correspond au collège, et la "Senior High
⬤ School", qui correspond au lycée. En Grande-
⬤ Bretagne, c'est un nom que l'on donne
⬤ parfois aux écoles secondaires; voir
⬤ "elementary school".

**high season** n (Brit) haute saison

**high spirits** npl pétulance f; **to be in ~** être plein(e) d'entrain

**high street** n (Brit) grand-rue f

**high-tech** ['haɪtɛk] (inf) adj de pointe

**highway** ['haɪweɪ] n (Brit) route f; (US) route nationale; **the information ~** l'autoroute f de l'information

**Highway Code** n (Brit) code m de la route

**highwayman** ['haɪweɪmən] (irreg) n voleur m de grand chemin

**hijack** ['haɪdʒæk] vt détourner (par la force) ▷ n (also: **hijacking**) détournement m (d'avion)

**hijacker** ['haɪdʒækəʳ] n auteur m d'un détournement d'avion, pirate m de l'air

**hike** [haɪk] vi faire des excursions à pied ▷ n excursion f à pied, randonnée f; (inf: in prices etc) augmentation f ▷ vt (inf) augmenter

**hiker** ['haɪkəʳ] n promeneur(-euse), excursionniste m/f

**hiking** ['haɪkɪŋ] n excursions fpl à pied, randonnée f

**hilarious** [hɪ'lɛərɪəs] adj (behaviour, event) désopilant(e)

**hilarity** [hɪ'lærɪtɪ] n hilarité f

**hill** [hɪl] n colline f; (fairly high) montagne f; (on road) côte f

**hillbilly** ['hɪlbɪlɪ] n (US) montagnard(e) du sud des USA; (pej) péquenaud m

**hillock** ['hɪlək] n petite colline, butte f

**hillside** ['hɪlsaɪd] n (flanc m de) coteau m

**hill start** n (Aut) démarrage m en côte

**hill walking** ['hɪl'wɔ:kɪŋ] n randonnée f de basse montagne

**hilly** ['hɪlɪ] adj vallonné(e), montagneux(-euse); (road) à fortes côtes

**hilt** [hɪlt] n (of sword) garde f; **to the ~** (fig: support) à fond

**him** [hɪm] pron (direct) le, l' + vowel or h mute; (stressed, indirect, after prep) lui; **I see ~** je le vois; **give ~ a book** donne-lui un livre; **after ~** après lui; see also **me**

**Himalayas** [hɪmə'leɪəz] npl: **the ~** l'Himalaya m

**himself** [hɪm'sɛlf] pron (reflexive) se; (emphatic) lui-même; (after prep) lui; see also **oneself**

**hind** [haɪnd] adj de derrière ▷ n biche f

**hinder** ['hɪndəʳ] vt gêner; (delay) retarder; (prevent): **to ~ sb from doing** empêcher qn de faire

**hindquarters** ['haɪnd'kwɔ:təz] npl (Zool) arrière-train m

**hindrance** ['hɪndrəns] n gêne f, obstacle m

**hindsight** ['haɪndsaɪt] n bon sens après coup; **with (the benefit of) ~** avec du recul, rétrospectivement

**Hindu** ['hɪndu:] n Hindou(e)

**Hinduism** ['hɪnduɪzəm] n (Rel) hindouisme m

**hinge** [hɪndʒ] n charnière f ▷ vi (fig): **to ~ on** dépendre de

**hint** [hɪnt] n allusion f; (advice) conseil m; (clue) indication f ▷ vt: **to ~ that** insinuer que ▷ vi: **to ~ at** faire une allusion à; **to drop a ~** faire une allusion or insinuation; **give me a ~** (clue) mettez-moi sur la voie, donnez-moi une indication

**hip** [hɪp] n hanche f; (Bot) fruit m de l'églantier or du rosier

**hip flask** n flacon m (pour la poche)

**hip hop** n hip hop m

**hippie, hippy** ['hɪpɪ] n hippie m/f

**hippo** ['hɪpəʊ] (pl -s) n hippopotame m

**hippopotamus** [hɪpə'pɔtəməs] (pl -es or **hippopotami** [hɪpə'pɔtəmɪ]) n hippopotame m

**hippy** ['hɪpɪ] n = **hippie**

**hire** ['haɪəʳ] vt (Brit: car, equipment) louer; (worker) embaucher, engager ▷ n location f; **for ~** à louer; (taxi) libre; **on ~** en location; **I'd like to ~ a car** je voudrais louer une voiture ▷ **hire out** vt louer

**hire car, hired car** ['haɪəd-] n (Brit) voiture f de location

**hire purchase** n (Brit) achat m (or vente f) à tempérament or crédit; **to buy sth on ~** acheter qch en location-vente

**his** [hɪz] pron le (la) sien(ne), les siens (siennes) ▷ adj son (sa), ses pl; **this is ~** c'est à lui, c'est le sien; **a friend of ~** un(e) de ses ami(e)s, un(e) ami(e) à lui; see also **mine**[1]; see also **my**

**Hispanic** [hɪs'pænɪk] adj (in US) hispano-américain(e) ▷ n Hispano-Américain(e)

**hiss** [hɪs] vi siffler ▷ n sifflement m

**histogram** ['hɪstəɡræm] n histogramme m

**historian** [hɪˈstɔːrɪən] n historien(ne)
**historic** [hɪˈstɒrɪk], **historical** [hɪˈstɒrɪkl] adj
historique
**history** [ˈhɪstərɪ] n histoire f; **medical ~** (of
patient) passé médical
**histrionics** [hɪstrɪˈɒnɪks] n gestes mpl
dramatiques, cinéma m (fig)
**hit** [hɪt] vt (pt, pp -) frapper; (knock against) cogner;
(reach: target) atteindre, toucher; (collide with: car)
entrer en collision avec, heurter; (fig: affect)
toucher; (find) tomber sur ⊳ n coup m; (success)
coup réussi; succès m; (song) chanson f à succès,
tube m; (to website) visite f; (on search engine)
résultat m de recherche; **to ~ it off with sb** bien
s'entendre avec qn; **to ~ the headlines** être à la
une des journaux; **to ~ the road** (inf) se mettre
en route
▸ **hit back** vi: **to ~ back at sb** prendre sa
revanche sur qn
▸ **hit on** vt fus (answer) trouver (par hasard);
(solution) tomber sur (par hasard)
▸ **hit out** at vt fus envoyer un coup à; (fig)
attaquer
▸ **hit upon** vt fus = **hit on**
**hit-and-miss** [ˈhɪtænd'mɪs] adj au petit
bonheur (la chance)
**hit-and-run driver** [ˈhɪtænd'rʌn-] n
chauffard m
**hitch** [hɪtʃ] vt (fasten) accrocher, attacher; (also:
**hitch up**) remonter d'une saccade ⊳ vi faire de
l'autostop ⊳ n (knot) nœud m; (difficulty)
anicroche f, contretemps m; **to ~ a lift** faire du
stop; **technical ~** incident m technique
▸ **hitch up** vt (horse, cart) atteler; see also **hitch**
**hitch-hike** [ˈhɪtʃhaɪk] vi faire de l'auto-stop
**hitch-hiker** [ˈhɪtʃhaɪkə'] n auto-stoppeur(-euse)
**hitch-hiking** [ˈhɪtʃhaɪkɪŋ] n auto-stop m, stop m
(inf)
**hi-tech** [ˈhaɪˈtɛk] adj de pointe ⊳ n high-tech m
**hitherto** [hɪðə'tuː] adv jusqu'ici, jusqu'à
présent
**hit list** n liste noire
**hitman** [ˈhɪtmæn] (irreg) n (inf) tueur m à gages
**hit-or-miss** [ˈhɪtə'mɪs] adj au petit bonheur (la
chance); **it's ~ whether ...** il est loin d'être
certain que ... + sub
**hit parade** n hit parade m
**HIV** n abbr (= human immunodeficiency virus) HIV m,
VIH m; **~-negative/positive** séronégatif(-ive)/
positif(-ive)
**hive** [haɪv] n ruche f; **the shop was a ~ of
activity** (fig) le magasin était une véritable
ruche
▸ **hive off** vt (inf) mettre à part, séparer
**hl** abbr (= hectolitre) hl
**HM** abbr (= His (or Her) Majesty) SM
**HMG** abbr (Brit) = **His (or Her) Majesty's
Government**
**HMI** n abbr (Brit Scol) = **His (or Her) Majesty's
Inspector**
**HMO** n abbr (US: = health maintenance organization)
organisme médical assurant un forfait entretien de santé

**HMS** abbr (Brit) = **His (or Her) Majesty's Ship**
**HMSO** n abbr (Brit: = His (or Her) Majesty's Stationery
Office) ≈ Imprimerie nationale
**HNC** n abbr (Brit: = Higher National Certificate)
≈ DUT m
**HND** n abbr (Brit: = Higher National Diploma)
≈ licence f de sciences et techniques
**hoard** [hɔːd] n (of food) provisions fpl, réserves fpl;
(of money) trésor m ⊳ vt amasser
**hoarding** [ˈhɔːdɪŋ] n (Brit) panneau m
d'affichage or publicitaire
**hoarfrost** [ˈhɔːfrɒst] n givre m
**hoarse** [hɔːs] adj enroué(e)
**hoax** [həuks] n canular m
**hob** [hɒb] n plaque chauffante
**hobble** [ˈhɒbl] vi boitiller
**hobby** [ˈhɒbɪ] n passe-temps favori
**hobby-horse** [ˈhɒbɪhɔːs] n cheval m à bascule;
(fig) dada m
**hobnob** [ˈhɒbnɒb] vi: **to ~ with** frayer avec,
fréquenter
**hobo** [ˈhəubəu] n (US) vagabond m
**hock** [hɒk] n (Brit: wine) vin m du Rhin; (of animal:
Culin) jarret m
**hockey** [ˈhɒkɪ] n hockey m
**hockey stick** n crosse f de hockey
**hocus-pocus** [ˈhəukəs'pəukəs] n (trickery)
supercherie f; (words: of magician) formules fpl
magiques; (: jargon) galimatias m
**hod** [hɒd] n oiseau m, hotte f
**hodgepodge** [ˈhɒdʒpɒdʒ] n = **hotchpotch**
**hoe** [həu] n houe f, binette f ⊳ vt (ground) biner;
(plants etc) sarcler
**hog** [hɒg] n porc (châtré) ⊳ vt (fig) accaparer; **to
go the whole ~** aller jusqu'au bout
**Hogmanay** [hɒgmə'neɪ] n réveillon m du jour
de l'An, Saint-Sylvestre f; voir article

● **HOGMANAY**
●
● La Saint-Sylvestre ou "New Year's Eve" se
● nomme Hogmanay en Écosse. En cette
● occasion, la famille et les amis se réunissent
● pour entendre sonner les douze coups de
● minuit et pour fêter le "first-footing", une
● coutume qui veut qu'on se rende chez ses
● amis et voisins en apportant quelque chose
● à boire (du whisky en général) et un
● morceau de charbon en gage de prospérité
● pour la nouvelle année.

**hogwash** [ˈhɒgwɒʃ] n (inf) foutaises fpl
**hoist** [hɔɪst] n palan m ⊳ vt hisser
**hoity-toity** [ˈhɔɪtɪ'tɔɪtɪ] adj (inf)
prétentieux(-euse), qui se donne
**hold** [həuld] n (pt, pp held [hɛld]) vt tenir; (contain)
contenir; (meeting) tenir; (keep back) retenir;
(believe) maintenir; considérer; (possess) avoir;
détenir ⊳ vi (withstand pressure) tenir (bon); (be
valid) valoir; (on telephone) attendre ⊳ n prise f;
(find) influence f; (Naut) cale f; **to catch** or **get
(a) ~ of** saisir; **to get ~ of** (find) trouver; **to get ~**

619

**of o.s.** se contrôler; **~ the line!** (Tel) ne quittez pas!; **to ~ one's own** (fig) (bien) se défendre; **to ~ office** (Pol) avoir un portefeuille; **to ~ firm** or **fast** tenir bon; **he ~s the view that ...** il pense que ..., d'après lui ...; **to ~ sb responsible for sth** tenir qn pour responsable de qch
▸ **hold back** vt retenir; (secret) cacher; **to ~ sb back from doing sth** empêcher qn de faire qch
▸ **hold down** vt (person) maintenir à terre; (job) occuper
▸ **hold forth** vi pérorer
▸ **hold off** vt tenir à distance ▷ vi: **if the rain ~s off** s'il ne pleut pas, s'il ne se met pas à pleuvoir
▸ **hold on** vi tenir bon; (wait) attendre; **~ on!** (Tel) ne quittez pas!; **to ~ on to sth** (grasp) se cramponner à qch; (keep) conserver or garder qch
▸ **hold out** vt offrir ▷ vi (resist): **to ~ out (against)** résister (devant), tenir bon (devant)
▸ **hold over** vt (meeting etc) ajourner, reporter
▸ **hold up** vt (raise) lever; (support) soutenir; (delay) retarder; (: traffic) ralentir; (rob) braquer
**holdall** ['həʊldɔːl] n (Brit) fourre-tout m inv
**holder** ['həʊldə<sup>r</sup>] n (container) support m; (of ticket, record) détenteur(-trice); (of office, title, passport etc) titulaire m/f
**holding** ['həʊldɪŋ] n (share) intérêts mpl; (farm) ferme f
**holding company** n holding m
**hold-up** ['həʊldʌp] n (robbery) hold-up m; (delay) retard m; (Brit: in traffic) embouteillage m
**hole** [həʊl] n trou m ▷ vt trouer, faire un trou dans; **~ in the heart** (Med) communication f interventriculaire; **to pick ~s (in)** (fig) chercher des poux (dans)
▸ **hole up** vi se terrer
**holiday** ['hɔlədɪ] n (Brit: vacation) vacances fpl; (day off) jour m de congé; (public) jour férié; **to be on ~** être en vacances; **I'm here on ~** je suis ici en vacances; **tomorrow is a ~** demain c'est fête, on a congé demain
**holiday camp** n (Brit: for children) colonie f de vacances; (also: **holiday centre**) camp m de vacances
**holiday home** n (rented) location f de vacances; (owned) résidence f secondaire
**holiday job** n (Brit) boulot m (inf) de vacances
**holiday-maker** ['hɔlədɪmeɪkə<sup>r</sup>] n (Brit) vacancier(-ière)
**holiday pay** n paie f des vacances
**holiday resort** n centre m de villégiature or de vacances
**holiday season** n période f des vacances
**holiness** ['həʊlɪnɪs] n sainteté f
**holistic** [həʊ'lɪstɪk] adj holiste, holistique
**Holland** ['hɔlənd] n Hollande f
**holler** ['hɔlə<sup>r</sup>] vi (inf) brailler
**hollow** ['hɔləʊ] adj creux(-euse); (fig) faux (fausse) ▷ n creux m; (in land) dépression f (de terrain), cuvette f ▷ vt: **to ~ out** creuser, évider
**holly** ['hɔlɪ] n houx m
**hollyhock** ['hɔlɪhɔk] n rose trémière

**Hollywood** ['hɔlɪwʊd] n Hollywood
**holocaust** ['hɔləkɔːst] n holocauste m
**hologram** ['hɔləgræm] n hologramme m
**hols** [hɔlz] npl (inf) vacances fpl
**holster** ['həʊlstə<sup>r</sup>] n étui m de revolver
**holy** ['həʊlɪ] adj saint(e); (bread, water) bénit(e); (ground) sacré(e)
**Holy Communion** n la (sainte) communion
**Holy Ghost, Holy Spirit** n Saint-Esprit m
**Holy Land** n: **the ~** la Terre Sainte
**holy orders** npl ordres (majeurs)
**homage** ['hɔmɪdʒ] n hommage m; **to pay ~ to** rendre hommage à
**home** [həʊm] n foyer m, maison f; (country) pays natal, patrie f; (institution) maison ▷ adj de famille; (Econ, Pol) national(e), intérieur(e); (Sport: team) qui reçoit; (: match, win) sur leur (or notre) terrain ▷ adv chez soi, à la maison; au pays natal; (right in: nail etc) à fond; **at ~** chez soi, à la maison; **to go (or come) ~** rentrer (chez soi), rentrer à la maison (or au pays); **I'm going ~ on Tuesday** je rentre mardi; **make yourself at ~** faites comme chez vous; **near my ~** près de chez moi
▸ **home in on** vt fus (missile) se diriger automatiquement vers or sur
**home address** n domicile permanent
**home-brew** [həʊm'bruː] n vin m (or bière f) maison
**homecoming** ['həʊmkʌmɪŋ] n retour m (au bercail)
**home computer** n ordinateur m domestique
**Home Counties** npl les comtés autour de Londres
**home economics** n économie f domestique
**home ground** n: **to be on ~** être sur son terrain
**home-grown** ['həʊmgrəʊn] adj (not foreign) du pays; (from garden) du jardin
**home help** n (Brit) aide-ménagère f
**homeland** ['həʊmlænd] n patrie f
**homeless** ['həʊmlɪs] adj sans foyer, sans abri; **the homeless** npl les sans-abri mpl
**home loan** n prêt m sur hypothèque
**homely** ['həʊmlɪ] adj (plain) simple, sans prétention; (welcoming) accueillant(e)
**home-made** [həʊm'meɪd] adj fait(e) à la maison
**home match** n match m à domicile
**Home Office** n (Brit) ministère m de l'Intérieur
**homeopathy** etc [həʊmɪ'ɔpəθɪ] (US) = **homoeopathy** etc
**home owner** ['həʊməʊnə<sup>r</sup>] n propriétaire occupant
**home page** n (Comput) page f d'accueil
**home rule** n autonomie f
**Home Secretary** n (Brit) ministre m de l'Intérieur
**homesick** ['həʊmsɪk] adj: **to be ~** avoir le mal du pays; (missing one's family) s'ennuyer de sa famille
**homestead** ['həʊmstɛd] n propriété f; (farm) ferme f
**home town** n ville natale
**home truth** n: **to tell sb a few ~s** dire ses quatre vérités à qn

**homeward** ['həʊmwəd] *adj* (*journey*) du retour
▷ *adv* = **homewards**
**homewards** ['həʊmwədz] *adv* vers la maison
**homework** ['həʊmwə:k] *n* devoirs *mpl*
**homicidal** [hɔmɪ'saɪdl] *adj* homicide
**homicide** ['hɔmɪsaɪd] *n* (*US*) homicide *m*
**homily** ['hɔmɪlɪ] *n* homélie *f*
**homing** ['həʊmɪŋ] *adj* (*device, missile*) à tête chercheuse; ~ **pigeon** pigeon voyageur
**homoeopath** ['həʊmɪəʊpæθ], (*US*) **homeopath** *n* homéopathe *m/f*
**homoeopathic**, (*US*) **homeopathic** [həʊmɪɔ'pəɪk] *adj* (*medicine*) homéopathique; (*doctor*) homéopathe
**homoeopathy**, (*US*) **homeopathy** [həʊmɪ'ɔpəθɪ] *n* homéopathie *f*
**homogeneous** [hɔməʊ'dʒi:nɪəs] *adj* homogène
**homogenize** [hə'mɔdʒənaɪz] *vt* homogénéiser
**homosexual** [hɔməʊ'sɛksjʊəl] *adj*, *n* homosexuel(le)
**Hon.** *abbr* (= *honourable, honorary*) *dans un titre*
**Honduras** [hɔn'djʊərəs] *n* Honduras *m*
**hone** [həʊn] *n* pierre *f* à aiguiser ▷ *vt* affûter, aiguiser
**honest** ['ɔnɪst] *adj* honnête; (*sincere*) franc (franche); **to be quite ~ with you** ... à dire vrai ...
**honestly** ['ɔnɪstlɪ] *adv* honnêtement; franchement
**honesty** ['ɔnɪstɪ] *n* honnêteté *f*
**honey** ['hʌnɪ] *n* miel *m*; (*inf: darling*) chéri(e)
**honeycomb** ['hʌnɪkəʊm] *n* rayon *m* de miel; (*pattern*) nid *m* d'abeilles, motif alvéolé ▷ *vt* (*fig*): **to ~ with** cribler de
**honeymoon** ['hʌnɪmu:n] *n* lune *f* de miel, voyage *m* de noces; **we're on ~** nous sommes en voyage de noces
**honeysuckle** ['hʌnɪsʌkl] *n* chèvrefeuille *m*
**Hong Kong** ['hɔŋ'kɔŋ] *n* Hong Kong
**honk** [hɔŋk] *n* (*Aut*) coup *m* de klaxon ▷ *vi* klaxonner
**Honolulu** [hɔnə'lu:lu:] *n* Honolulu
**honorary** ['ɔnərərɪ] *adj* honoraire; (*duty, title*) honorifique; ~ **degree** diplôme *m* honoris causa
**honour**, (*US*) **honor** ['ɔnə<sup>r</sup>] *vt* honorer ▷ *n* honneur *m*; **in ~ of** en l'honneur de; **to graduate with ~s** obtenir sa licence avec mention
**honourable**, (*US*) **honorable** ['ɔnərəbl] *adj* honorable
**honour-bound**, (*US*) **honor-bound** ['ɔnə'baʊnd] *adj*: **to be ~ to do** se devoir de faire
**honours degree** ['ɔnəz-] *n* (*Scol*) ≈ licence *f* avec mention; *voir article*

⬤ **HONOURS DEGREE**
⬤
⬤ Un *honours degree* est un diplôme
⬤ universitaire que l'on reçoit après trois
⬤ années d'études en Angleterre et quatre
⬤ années en Écosse. Les mentions qui

⬤ l'accompagnent sont, par ordre décroissant:
⬤ "first class" (très bien/bien), "upper second
⬤ class" (assez bien), "lower second class"
⬤ (passable), et "third class" (diplôme sans
⬤ mention). Le titulaire d'un *honours degree* a
⬤ un titre qu'il peut mettre à la suite de son
⬤ nom, par exemple: Peter Jones BA Hons; voir
⬤ "ordinary degree".

**honours list** *n* (*Brit*): *voir article*

⬤ **HONOURS LIST**
⬤
⬤ L' *honours list* est la liste des citoyens du
⬤ Royaume-Uni et du Commonwealth
⬤ auxquels le souverain confère un titre ou
⬤ une décoration. Cette liste est préparée par
⬤ le Premier ministre et paraît deux fois par
⬤ an, au Nouvel An et lors de l'anniversaire
⬤ officiel du règne du souverain. Des
⬤ personnes qui se sont distinguées dans le
⬤ monde des affaires, des sports et des médias,
⬤ ainsi que dans les forces armées, mais
⬤ également des citoyens "ordinaires" qui se
⬤ consacrent à des œuvres de charité sont
⬤ ainsi récompensées.

**Hons.** *abbr* (*Scol*) = **honours degree**
**hood** [hʊd] *n* capuchon *m*; (*of cooker*) hotte *f*; (*Brit Aut*) capote *f*; (*US Aut*) capot *m*; (*inf*) truand *m*
**hoodie** ['hʊdɪ] *n* (*top*) sweat *m* à capuche; (*youth*) jeune *m* à capuche
**hoodlum** ['hu:dləm] *n* truand *m*
**hoodwink** ['hʊdwɪŋk] *vt* tromper
**hoof** (*pl* -**s** *or* **hooves**) [hu:f, hu:vz] *n* sabot *m*
**hook** [hʊk] *n* crochet *m*; (*on dress*) agrafe *f*; (*for fishing*) hameçon *m* ▷ *vt* accrocher; (*dress*) agrafer; **off the ~** (*Tel*) décroché; ~ **and eye** agrafe; **by ~ or by crook** de gré ou de force, coûte que coûte; **to be ~ed (on)** (*inf*) être accroché(e) (par); (*person*) être dingue (de)
▶ **hook up** *vt* (*Radio, TV etc*) faire un duplex entre
**hooligan** ['hu:lɪgən] *n* voyou *m*
**hoop** [hu:p] *n* cerceau *m*; (*of barrel*) cercle *m*
**hoot** [hu:t] *vi* (*Brit: Aut*) klaxonner; (*siren*) mugir; (*owl*) hululer ▷ *vt* (*jeer at*) huer ▷ *n* huée *f*; coup *m* de klaxon; mugissement *m*; hululement *m*; **to ~ with laughter** rire aux éclats
**hooter** ['hu:tə<sup>r</sup>] *n* (*Brit Aut*) klaxon *m*; (*Naut, factory*) sirène *f*
**Hoover®** ['hu:və<sup>r</sup>] *n* (*Brit*) aspirateur *m* ▷ *vt*: **to hoover** (*room*) passer l'aspirateur dans; (*carpet*) passer l'aspirateur sur
**hooves** [hu:vz] *npl of* **hoof**
**hop** [hɔp] *vi* sauter; (*on one foot*) sauter à cloche-pied; (*bird*) sautiller ▷ *n* saut *m*
**hope** [həʊp] *vt*, *vi* espérer ▷ *n* espoir *m*; **I ~ so** je l'espère; **I ~ not** j'espère que non
**hopeful** ['həʊpfʊl] *adj* (*person*) plein(e) d'espoir; (*situation*) prometteur(-euse), encourageant(e); **I'm ~ that she'll manage to come** j'ai bon espoir qu'elle pourra venir

**hopefully** ['həupfulı] *adv (expectantly)* avec espoir, avec optimisme; *(one hopes)* avec un peu de chance; ~, **they'll come back** espérons bien qu'ils reviendront

**hopeless** ['həuplıs] *adj* désespéré(e), sans espoir; *(useless)* nul(le)

**hopelessly** ['həuplıslı] *adv (live etc)* sans espoir; ~ **confused** *etc* complètement désorienté *etc*

**hops** [hɒps] *npl* houblon *m*

**horizon** [hə'raızn] *n* horizon *m*

**horizontal** [hɒrı'zɒntl] *adj* horizontal(e)

**hormone** ['hɔːməun] *n* hormone *f*

**hormone replacement therapy** *n* hormonothérapie substitutive, traitement hormono-supplétif

**horn** [hɔːn] *n* corne *f*; *(Mus)* cor *m*; *(Aut)* klaxon *m*

**horned** [hɔːnd] *adj (animal)* à cornes

**hornet** ['hɔːnıt] *n* frelon *m*

**horny** ['hɔːnı] *adj* corné(e); *(hands)* calleux(-euse); *(inf: aroused)* excité(e)

**horoscope** ['hɒrəskəup] *n* horoscope *m*

**horrendous** [hə'rɛndəs] *adj* horrible, affreux(-euse)

**horrible** ['hɒrıbl] *adj* horrible, affreux(-euse)

**horrid** ['hɒrıd] *adj (person)* détestable; *(weather, place, smell)* épouvantable

**horrific** [hɒ'rıfık] *adj* horrible

**horrify** ['hɒrıfaı] *vt* horrifier

**horrifying** ['hɒrıfaııŋ] *adj* horrifiant(e)

**horror** ['hɒrə*r*] *n* horreur *f*

**horror film** *n* film *m* d'épouvante

**horror-struck** ['hɒrəstrʌk], **horror-stricken** ['hɒrəstrıkn] *adj* horrifié(e)

**hors d'œuvre** [ɔː'dəːvrə] *n* hors d'œuvre *m*

**horse** [hɔːs] *n* cheval *m*

**horseback** ['hɔːsbæk]: **on ~** *(adj, adv)* à cheval

**horsebox** ['hɔːsbɒks] *n* van *m*

**horse chestnut** *n (nut)* marron *m* (d'Inde); *(tree)* marronnier *m* (d'Inde)

**horse-drawn** ['hɔːsdrɔːn] *adj* tiré(e) par des chevaux

**horsefly** ['hɔːsflaı] *n* taon *m*

**horseman** ['hɔːsmən] *(irreg) n* cavalier *m*

**horsemanship** ['hɔːsmənʃıp] *n* talents *mpl* de cavalier

**horseplay** ['hɔːspleı] *n* chahut *m (blagues etc)*

**horsepower** ['hɔːspauə*r*] *n* puissance *f* (en chevaux); *(unit)* cheval-vapeur *m* (CV)

**horse-racing** ['hɔːsreısıŋ] *n* courses *fpl* de chevaux

**horseradish** ['hɔːsrædıʃ] *n* raifort *m*

**horse riding** *n (Brit)* équitation *f*

**horseshoe** ['hɔːsʃuː] *n* fer *m* à cheval

**horse show** *n* concours *m* hippique

**horse-trading** ['hɔːstreıdıŋ] *n* maquignonnage *m*

**horse trials** *npl* = **horse show**

**horsewhip** ['hɔːswıp] *vt* cravacher

**horsewoman** ['hɔːswumən] *(irreg) n* cavalière *f*

**horsey** ['hɔːsı] *adj* féru(e) d'équitation *or* de cheval; *(appearance)* chevalin(e)

**horticulture** ['hɔːtıkʌltʃə*r*] *n* horticulture *f*

**hose** [həuz] *n (also: **hosepipe**)* tuyau *m*; *(also: **garden hose**)* tuyau d'arrosage
▶ **hose down** *vt* laver au jet

**hosepipe** ['həuzpaıp] *n* tuyau *m*; *(in garden)* tuyau d'arrosage; *(for fire)* tuyau d'incendie

**hosiery** ['həuzıərı] *n* (rayon *m* des) bas *mpl*

**hospice** ['hɒspıs] *n* hospice *m*

**hospitable** ['hɒspıtəbl] *adj* hospitalier(-ière)

**hospital** ['hɒspıtl] *n* hôpital *m*; **in ~** à l'hôpital; **where's the nearest ~?** où est l'hôpital le plus proche?

**hospitality** [hɒspı'tælıtı] *n* hospitalité *f*

**hospitalize** ['hɒspıtəlaız] *vt* hospitaliser

**host** [həust] *n* hôte *m*; *(in hotel etc)* patron *m*; *(TV, Radio)* présentateur(-trice), animateur(-trice); *(large number)*: **a ~ of** une foule de; *(Rel)* hostie *f*
▷ *vt (TV programme)* présenter, animer

**hostage** ['hɒstıdʒ] *n* otage *m*

**host country** *n* pays *m* d'accueil, pays-hôte *m*

**hostel** ['hɒstl] *n* foyer *m*; *(also: **youth hostel**)* auberge *f* de jeunesse

**hostelling** ['hɒstlıŋ] *n*: **to go (youth) ~** faire une virée *or* randonnée en séjournant dans des auberges de jeunesse

**hostess** ['həustıs] *n* hôtesse *f*; *(Brit: also: **air hostess**)* hôtesse de l'air; *(TV, Radio)* animatrice *f*; *(in nightclub)* entraîneuse *f*

**hostile** ['hɒstaıl] *adj* hostile

**hostility** [hɒ'stılıtı] *n* hostilité *f*

**hot** [hɒt] *adj* chaud(e); *(as opposed to only warm)* très chaud; *(spicy)* fort(e); *(fig: contest)* acharné(e), passionné(e); *(topic)* brûlant(e); *(temper)* violent(e), passionné(e); **to be ~** *(person)* avoir chaud; *(thing)* être (très) chaud; *(weather)* faire chaud
▶ **hot up** *(Brit inf) vi (situation)* devenir tendu(e); *(party)* s'animer ▷ *vt (pace)* accélérer, forcer; *(engine)* gonfler

**hot-air balloon** [hɒt'ɛə-] *n* montgolfière *f*, ballon *m*

**hotbed** ['hɒtbɛd] *n (fig)* foyer *m*, pépinière *f*

**hotchpotch** ['hɒtʃpɒtʃ] *n (Brit)* mélange *m* hétéroclite

**hot dog** *n* hot-dog *m*

**hotel** [həu'tɛl] *n* hôtel *m*

**hotelier** [həu'tɛlıə*r*] *n* hôtelier(-ière)

**hotel industry** *n* industrie hôtelière

**hotel room** *n* chambre *f* d'hôtel

**hot flush** *n (Brit)* bouffée *f* de chaleur

**hotfoot** ['hɒtfut] *adv* à toute vitesse

**hothead** ['hɒthɛd] *n (fig)* tête brûlée

**hotheaded** [hɒt'hɛdıd] *adj* impétueux(-euse)

**hothouse** ['hɒthaus] *n* serre chaude

**hotline** ['hɒtlaın] *n (Pol)* téléphone *m* rouge, ligne directe

**hotly** ['hɒtlı] *adv* passionnément, violemment

**hotplate** ['hɒtpleıt] *n (on cooker)* plaque chauffante

**hotpot** ['hɒtpɒt] *n (Brit Culin)* ragoût *m*

**hot potato** *n (Brit inf)* sujet brûlant; **to drop sb/sth like a ~** laisser tomber qn/qch brusquement

**hot seat** n (*fig*) poste chaud
**hotspot** ['hɔtspɔt] n (*Comput: also:* **wireless hotspot**) borne f wifi, hotspot m
**hot spot** n point chaud
**hot spring** n source thermale
**hot-tempered** ['hɔt'tempəd] *adj* emporté(e)
**hot-water bottle** [hɔt'wɔ:tə-] n bouillotte f
**hot-wire** ['hɔtwaɪəʳ] vt (*inf: car*) démarrer en faisant se toucher les fils de contact
**hound** [haund] vt poursuivre avec acharnement ▷ n chien courant; **the ~s** la meute
**hour** ['auəʳ] n heure f; **at 30 miles an ~** ≈ à 50 km à l'heure; **lunch ~** heure du déjeuner; **to pay sb by the ~** payer qn à l'heure
**hourly** ['auəlɪ] *adj* toutes les heures; (*rate*) horaire; **~ paid** *adj* payé(e) à l'heure
**house** n [haus] (*pl* **-s** ['hauzɪz]) maison f; (*Pol*) chambre f; (*Theat*) salle f; auditoire m ▷ vt [hauz] (*person*) loger, héberger; **at** (*or* **to**) **my ~** chez moi; **the H~ of Commons/of Lords** (*Brit*) la Chambre des communes/des lords; *voir article*; **the H~** (**of Representatives**) (*US*) la Chambre des représentants; *voir article*; **on the ~** (*fig*) aux frais de la maison

**HOUSE OF COMMONS/OF LORDS**

⬤
⬤ Le parlement en Grande-Bretagne est
⬤ constitué de deux assemblées: la *House of*
⬤ *Commons*, présidée par le "Speaker" et
⬤ composée de plus de 600 députés (les "MP")
⬤ élus au suffrage universel direct. Ceux-ci
⬤ reçoivent tous un salaire. La Chambre des
⬤ communes siège environ 175 jours par an.
⬤ La *House of Lords*, présidée par le "Lord
⬤ Chancellor" est composée de lords dont le
⬤ titre est attribué par le souverain à vie; elle
⬤ peut amender certains projets de loi votés
⬤ par la *House of Commons*, mais elle n'est pas
⬤ habilitée à débattre des projets de lois de
⬤ finances. La *House of Lords* fait également
⬤ office de juridiction suprême en Angleterre
⬤ et au pays de Galles.

⬤ **HOUSE OF REPRESENTATIVES**

⬤
⬤ Aux États-Unis, le parlement, appelé le
⬤ "Congress", est constitué du "Senate" et de
⬤ la *House of Representatives*. Cette dernière
⬤ comprend 435 membres, le nombre de ces
⬤ représentants par État étant proportionnel
⬤ à la densité de population de cet État. Ils
⬤ sont élus pour deux ans au suffrage
⬤ universel direct et siègent au "Capitol", à
⬤ Washington D.C.

**house arrest** n assignation f à domicile
**houseboat** ['hausbəut] n bateau (aménagé en habitation)
**housebound** ['hausbaund] *adj* confiné(e) chez soi

**housebreaking** ['hausbreɪkɪŋ] n cambriolage m (avec effraction)
**house-broken** ['hausbrəukn] *adj* (*US*) = **house-trained**
**housecoat** ['hauskəut] n peignoir m
**household** ['haushəuld] n (*Admin etc*) ménage m; (*people*) famille f, maisonnée f; **~ name** nom connu de tout le monde
**householder** ['haushəuldəʳ] n propriétaire m/f; (*head of house*) chef m de famille
**househunting** ['haushʌntɪŋ] n: **to go ~** se mettre en quête d'une maison (*or* d'un appartement)
**housekeeper** ['hauski:pəʳ] n gouvernante f
**housekeeping** ['hauski:pɪŋ] n (*work*) ménage m; (*also:* **housekeeping money**) argent m du ménage; (*Comput*) gestion f (des disques)
**houseman** ['hausmən] (*irreg*) n (*Brit Med*) ≈ interne m
**house-owner** ['hausəunəʳ] n propriétaire m/f (*de maison ou d'appartement*)
**house-proud** ['hauspraud] *adj* qui tient à avoir une maison impeccable
**house-to-house** ['haustə'haus] *adj* (*enquiries etc*) chez tous les habitants (du quartier *etc*)
**house-train** ['haustreɪn] vt (*pet*) apprendre à être propre à
**house-trained** ['haustreɪnd] *adj* (*pet*) propre
**house-warming** ['hauswɔ:mɪŋ] n (*also:* **house-warming party**) pendaison f de crémaillère
**housewife** ['hauswaɪf] (*irreg*) n ménagère f; femme f au foyer
**house wine** n cuvée f maison *or* du patron
**housework** ['hauswə:k] n (travaux *mpl* du) ménage m
**housing** ['hauzɪŋ] n logement m ▷ *cpd* (*problem, shortage*) de *or* du logement
**housing association** n fondation f charitable fournissant des logements
**housing benefit** n (*Brit*) ≈ allocations *fpl* logement
**housing development,** (*Brit*) **housing estate** n (*blocks of flats*) cité f; (*houses*) lotissement m
**hovel** ['hɔvl] n taudis m
**hover** ['hɔvəʳ] vi planer; **to ~ round sb** rôder *or* tourner autour de qn
**hovercraft** ['hɔvəkra:ft] n aéroglisseur m, hovercraft m
**hoverport** ['hɔvəpɔ:t] n hoverport m
**how** [hau] *adv* comment; **~ are you?** comment allez-vous?; **~ do you do?** bonjour; (*on being introduced*) enchanté(e); **~ far is it to ...?** combien y a-t-il jusqu'à ...?; **~ long have you been here?** depuis combien de temps êtes-vous là?; **~ lovely/awful!** que *or* comme c'est joli/affreux!; **~ many/much?** combien?; **~ much time/many people?** combien de temps/gens?; **~ much does it cost?** ça coûte combien?; **~ old are you?** quel âge avez-vous?; **~ tall is he?** combien mesure-t-il?; **~ is school?** ça va à l'école?; **~ was the film?** comment était le

film?; ~'s life? (inf) comment ça va?; ~ about a drink? si on buvait quelque chose?; ~ is it that ...? comment se fait-il que ... + sub?

**however** [hau'ɛvər] conj pourtant, cependant ▷ adv de quelque façon or manière que + sub; (+ adjective) quelque or si ... que + sub; (in questions) comment; ~ I do it de quelque manière que je m'y prenne; ~ cold it is même s'il fait très froid; ~ did you do it? comment y êtes-vous donc arrivé?

**howitzer** ['hauɪtsər] n (Mil) obusier m

**howl** [haul] n hurlement m ▷ vi hurler; (wind) mugir

**howler** ['haulər] n gaffe f, bourde f

**howling** ['haulɪŋ] adj: a ~ wind or gale un vent à décorner les bœufs

**H.P.** n abbr (Brit) = **hire purchase**

**h.p.** abbr (Aut) = **horsepower**

**HQ** n abbr (= headquarters) QG m

**HR** n abbr (US) = **House of Representatives**

**hr** abbr (= hour) h

**HRH** abbr (= His (or Her) Royal Highness) SAR

**hrs** abbr (= hours) h

**HRT** n abbr = **hormone replacement therapy**

**HS** abbr (US) = **high school**

**HST** abbr (US: = Hawaiian Standard Time) heure de Hawaii

**HTML** n abbr (= hypertext markup language) HTML m

**hub** [hʌb] n (of wheel) moyeu m; (fig) centre m, foyer m

**hubbub** ['hʌbʌb] n brouhaha m

**hubcap** [hʌbkæp] n (Aut) enjoliveur m

**HUD** n abbr (US: = Department of Housing and Urban Development) ministère de l'urbanisme et du logement

**huddle** ['hʌdl] vi: to ~ together se blottir les uns contre les autres

**hue** [hju:] n teinte f, nuance f; ~ and cry n tollé (général), clameur f

**huff** [hʌf] n: in a ~ fâché(e); to take the ~ prendre la mouche

**huffy** ['hʌfɪ] adj (inf) froissé(e)

**hug** [hʌg] vt serrer dans ses bras; (shore, kerb) serrer ▷ n étreinte f; to give sb a ~ serrer qn dans ses bras

**huge** [hju:dʒ] adj énorme, immense

**hulk** [hʌlk] n (ship) vieux rafiot; (car, building) carcasse f; (person) mastodonte m, malabar m

**hulking** ['hʌlkɪŋ] adj balourd(e)

**hull** [hʌl] n (of ship) coque f; (of nuts) coque f; (of peas) cosse f

**hullabaloo** ['hʌləbə'lu:] n (inf: noise) tapage m, raffut m

**hullo** [hə'ləu] excl = **hello**

**hum** [hʌm] vt (tune) fredonner ▷ vi fredonner; (insect) bourdonner; (plane, tool) vrombir ▷ n fredonnement m; bourdonnement m; vrombissement m

**human** ['hju:mən] adj humain(e) ▷ n (also: **human being**) être humain

**humane** [hju:'meɪn] adj humain(e), humanitaire

**humanism** ['hju:mənɪzəm] n humanisme m

**humanitarian** [hju:mænɪ'tɛərɪən] adj humanitaire

**humanity** [hju:'mænɪtɪ] n humanité f

**humanly** ['hju:mənlɪ] adv humainement

**humanoid** ['hju:mənɔɪd] adj, n humanoïde m/f

**human rights** npl droits mpl de l'homme

**humble** ['hʌmbl] adj humble, modeste ▷ vt humilier

**humbly** ['hʌmblɪ] adv humblement, modestement

**humbug** ['hʌmbʌg] n fumisterie f; (Brit: sweet) bonbon m à la menthe

**humdrum** ['hʌmdrʌm] adj monotone, routinier(-ière)

**humid** ['hju:mɪd] adj humide

**humidifier** [hju:'mɪdɪfaɪər] n humidificateur m

**humidity** [hju:'mɪdɪtɪ] n humidité f

**humiliate** [hju:'mɪlɪeɪt] vt humilier

**humiliating** [hju:'mɪlɪeɪtɪŋ] adj humiliant(e)

**humiliation** [hju:mɪlɪ'eɪʃən] n humiliation f

**humility** [hju:'mɪlɪtɪ] n humilité f

**hummus** ['huməs] n houm(m)ous m

**humorist** ['hju:mərɪst] n humoriste m/f

**humorous** ['hju:mərəs] adj humoristique; (person) plein(e) d'humour

**humour**, (US) **humor** ['hju:mər] n humour m; (mood) humeur f ▷ vt (person) faire plaisir à; se prêter aux caprices de; **sense of** ~ sens m de l'humour; **to be in a good/bad** ~ être de bonne/mauvaise humeur

**humourless**, (US) **humorless** ['hu:məlɪs] adj dépourvu(e) d'humour

**hump** [hʌmp] n bosse f

**humpback** ['hʌmpbæk] n bossu(e); (Brit: also: **humpback bridge**) dos-d'âne m

**humus** ['hju:məs] n humus m

**hunch** [hʌntʃ] n bosse f; (premonition) intuition f; **I have a ~ that** j'ai (comme une vague) idée que

**hunchback** ['hʌntʃbæk] n bossu(e)

**hunched** [hʌntʃt] adj arrondi(e), voûté(e)

**hundred** ['hʌndrəd] num cent; **about a ~ people** une centaine de personnes; ~s of des centaines de; **I'm a ~ per cent sure** j'en suis absolument certain

**hundredth** [-ɪdθ] num centième

**hundredweight** ['hʌndrɪdweɪt] n (Brit) = 50.8 kg; 112 lb; (US) = 45.3 kg; 100 lb

**hung** [hʌŋ] pt, pp of **hang**

**Hungarian** [hʌŋ'gɛərɪən] adj hongrois(e) ▷ n Hongrois(e); (Ling) hongrois m

**Hungary** ['hʌŋgərɪ] n Hongrie f

**hunger** ['hʌŋgər] n faim f ▷ vi: to ~ for avoir faim de, désirer ardemment

**hunger strike** n grève f de la faim

**hungover** [hʌŋ'əuvər] adj (inf): to be ~ avoir la gueule de bois

**hungrily** ['hʌŋgrəlɪ] adv voracement; (fig) avidement

**hungry** ['hʌŋgrɪ] adj affamé(e); to be ~ avoir faim; ~ for (fig) avide de

**hung up** adj (inf) complexé(e), bourré(e) de complexes

**hunk** [hʌŋk] n gros morceau; (inf: man) beau mec

**hunt** [hʌnt] vt (seek) chercher; (criminal) pourchasser; (Sport) chasser ▷ vi (search): **to ~ for** chercher (partout); (Sport) chasser ▷ n (Sport) chasse f
  ▶ **hunt down** vt pourchasser

**hunter** ['hʌntə'] n chasseur m; (Brit: horse) cheval m de chasse

**hunting** ['hʌntɪŋ] n chasse f

**hurdle** ['hə:dl] n (for fences) claie f; (Sport) haie f; (fig) obstacle m

**hurl** [hə:l] vt lancer (avec violence); (abuse, insults) lancer

**hurling** ['hə:lɪŋ] n (Sport) genre de hockey joué en Irlande

**hurly-burly** ['hə:lɪ'bə:lɪ] n tohu-bohu m inv; brouhaha m

**hurrah, hurray** [hu'rɑ:, hu'reɪ] excl hourra!

**hurricane** ['hʌrɪkən] n ouragan m

**hurried** ['hʌrɪd] adj pressé(e), précipité(e); (work) fait(e) à la hâte

**hurriedly** ['hʌrɪdlɪ] adv précipitamment, à la hâte

**hurry** ['hʌrɪ] n hâte f, précipitation f ▷ vi se presser, se dépêcher ▷ vt (person) faire presser, faire se dépêcher; (work) presser; **to be in a ~** être pressé(e); **to do sth in a ~** faire qch en vitesse; **to ~ in/out** entrer/sortir précipitamment; **to ~ home** se dépêcher de rentrer
  ▶ **hurry along** vi marcher d'un pas pressé
  ▶ **hurry away, hurry off** vi partir précipitamment
  ▶ **hurry up** vi se dépêcher

**hurt** [hə:t] (pt, pp -) vt (cause pain to) faire mal à; (injure, fig) blesser; (damage: business, interests etc) nuire à; faire du tort à ▷ vi faire mal ▷ adj blessé(e); **my arm ~s** j'ai mal au bras; **I ~ my arm** je me suis fait mal au bras; **to ~ o.s.** se faire mal; **where does it ~?** où avez-vous mal?, où est-ce que ça vous fait mal?

**hurtful** ['hə:tful] adj (remark) blessant(e)

**hurtle** ['hə:tl] vt lancer (de toutes ses forces) ▷ vi: **to ~ past** passer en trombe; **to ~ down** dégringoler

**husband** ['hʌzbənd] n mari m

**hush** [hʌʃ] n calme m, silence m ▷ vt faire taire; **~!** chut!
  ▶ **hush up** vt (fact) étouffer

**hush-hush** [hʌʃ'hʌʃ] adj (inf) ultra-secret(-ète)

**husk** [hʌsk] n (of wheat) balle f; (of rice, maize) enveloppe f; (of peas) cosse f

**husky** ['hʌskɪ] adj (voice) rauque; (burly) costaud(e) ▷ n chien m esquimau or de traîneau

**hustings** ['hʌstɪŋz] npl (Brit Pol) plate-forme électorale

**hustle** ['hʌsl] vt pousser, bousculer ▷ n bousculade f; **~ and bustle** n tourbillon m (d'activité)

**hut** [hʌt] n hutte f; (shed) cabane f

**hutch** [hʌtʃ] n clapier m

**hyacinth** ['haɪəsɪnθ] n jacinthe f

**hybrid** ['haɪbrɪd] adj, n hybride (m)

**hydrant** ['haɪdrənt] n prise f d'eau; (also: **fire hydrant**) bouche f d'incendie

**hydraulic** [haɪ'drɔ:lɪk] adj hydraulique

**hydraulics** [haɪ'drɔ:lɪks] n hydraulique f

**hydrochloric** ['haɪdrəu'klɔrɪk] adj: **~ acid** acide m chlorhydrique

**hydroelectric** ['haɪdrəuɪ'lɛktrɪk] adj hydro-électrique

**hydrofoil** ['haɪdrəfɔɪl] n hydrofoil m

**hydrogen** ['haɪdrədʒən] n hydrogène m

**hydrogen bomb** n bombe f à hydrogène

**hydrophobia** ['haɪdrə'fəubɪə] n hydrophobie f

**hydroplane** ['haɪdrəpleɪn] n (seaplane) hydravion m; (jetfoil) hydroglisseur m

**hyena** [haɪ'i:nə] n hyène f

**hygiene** ['haɪdʒi:n] n hygiène f

**hygienic** [haɪ'dʒi:nɪk] adj hygiénique

**hymn** [hɪm] n hymne m; cantique m

**hype** [haɪp] n (inf) matraquage m publicitaire or médiatique

**hyperactive** ['haɪpər'æktɪv] adj hyperactif(-ive)

**hyperlink** ['haɪpəɪŋk] n hyperlien m

**hypermarket** ['haɪpəmɑ:kɪt] (Brit) n hypermarché m

**hypertension** ['haɪpə'tɛnʃən] n (Med) hypertension f

**hypertext** ['haɪpətɛkst] n (Comput) hypertexte m

**hyphen** ['haɪfn] n trait m d'union

**hypnosis** [hɪp'nəusɪs] n hypnose f

**hypnotic** [hɪp'nɔtɪk] adj hypnotique

**hypnotism** ['hɪpnətɪzəm] n hypnotisme m

**hypnotist** ['hɪpnətɪst] n hypnotiseur(-euse)

**hypnotize** ['hɪpnətaɪz] vt hypnotiser

**hypoallergenic** ['haɪpəuælə'dʒɛnɪk] adj hypoallergénique

**hypochondriac** [haɪpə'kɔndrɪæk] n hypocondriaque m/f

**hypocrisy** [hɪ'pɔkrɪsɪ] n hypocrisie f

**hypocrite** ['hɪpəkrɪt] n hypocrite m/f

**hypocritical** [hɪpə'krɪtɪkl] adj hypocrite

**hypodermic** [haɪpə'də:mɪk] adj hypodermique ▷ n (syringe) seringue f hypodermique

**hypotenuse** [haɪ'pɔtɪnju:z] n hypoténuse f

**hypothermia** [haɪpə'θə:mɪə] n hypothermie f

**hypothesis** (pl **hypotheses**) [haɪ'pɔθɪsɪs, -si:z] n hypothèse f

**hysterectomy** [hɪstə'rɛktəmɪ] n hystérectomie f

**hysteria** [hɪ'stɪərɪə] n hystérie f

**hysterical** [hɪ'stɛrɪkl] adj hystérique; (funny) hilarant(e); **to become ~** avoir une crise de nerfs

**hysterics** [hɪ'stɛrɪks] npl (violente) crise de nerfs; (laughter) crise de rire; **to be in/have ~** (anger, panic) avoir une crise de nerfs; (laughter) attraper un fou rire

**Hz** abbr (= hertz) Hz

# I i

**I¹, i** [aɪ] n (letter) I, i m; **I for Isaac**, (US) **I for Item** I comme Irma

**I²** [aɪ] pron je; (before vowel) j'; (stressed) moi ▷ abbr (= island, isle) I

**IA, Ia.** abbr (US) = **Iowa**

**IAEA** n abbr = **International Atomic Energy Agency**

**IBA** n abbr (Brit: = Independent Broadcasting Authority) ≈ CNCL f (= Commission nationale de la communication audio-visuelle)

**Iberian** [aɪ'bɪərɪən] adj ibérique, ibérien(ne)

**Iberian Peninsula** n: **the ~** la péninsule Ibérique

**IBEW** n abbr (US: = International Brotherhood of Electrical Workers) syndicat international des électriciens

**i/c** abbr (Brit) = **in charge**

**ICBM** n abbr (= intercontinental ballistic missile) ICBM m, engin m balistique à portée intercontinentale

**ICC** n abbr (= International Chamber of Commerce) CCI f; (US) = **Interstate Commerce Commission**

**ice** [aɪs] n glace f; (on road) verglas m ▷ vt (cake) glacer; (drink) faire rafraîchir ▷ vi (also: **ice over**) geler; (also: **ice up**) se givrer; **to put sth on ~** (fig) mettre qch en attente

**Ice Age** n ère f glaciaire

**ice axe**, (US) **ice ax** n piolet m

**iceberg** ['aɪsbəːɡ] n iceberg m; **the tip of the ~** (also fig) la partie émergée de l'iceberg

**icebox** ['aɪsbɔks] n (US) réfrigérateur m; (Brit) compartiment m à glace; (insulated box) glacière f

**icebreaker** ['aɪsbreɪkər] n brise-glace m

**ice bucket** n seau m à glace

**ice-cap** ['aɪskæp] n calotte f glaciaire

**ice-cold** [aɪs'kəuld] adj glacé(e)

**ice cream** n glace f

**ice cube** n glaçon m

**iced** [aɪst] adj (drink) frappé(e); (coffee, tea, also cake) glacé(e)

**ice hockey** n hockey m sur glace

**Iceland** ['aɪslənd] n Islande f

**Icelander** ['aɪsləndər] n Islandais(e)

**Icelandic** [aɪs'lændɪk] adj islandais(e) ▷ n (Ling) islandais m

**ice lolly** n (Brit) esquimau m

**ice pick** n pic m à glace

**ice rink** n patinoire f

**ice-skate** ['aɪsskeɪt] n patin m à glace ▷ vi faire du patin à glace

**ice skating** ['aɪsskeɪtɪŋ] n patinage m (sur glace)

**icicle** ['aɪsɪkl] n glaçon m (naturel)

**icing** ['aɪsɪŋ] n (Aviat etc) givrage m; (Culin) glaçage m

**icing sugar** n (Brit) sucre m glace

**ICJ** n abbr = **International Court of Justice**

**icon** ['aɪkɔn] n icône f

**ICR** n abbr (US) = **Institute for Cancer Research**

**ICRC** n abbr (= International Committee of the Red Cross) CICR m

**ICT** n abbr (Brit: Scol: = information and communications technology) TIC fpl

**ICU** n abbr = **intensive care unit**

**icy** ['aɪsɪ] adj glacé(e); (road) verglacé(e); (weather, temperature) glacial(e)

**ID** abbr (US) = **Idaho**

**I'd** [aɪd] = **I would; I had**

**Ida.** abbr (US) = **Idaho**

**ID card** n carte f d'identité

**IDD** n abbr (Brit Tel: = international direct dialling) automatique international

**idea** [aɪ'dɪə] n idée f; **good ~!** bonne idée!; **to have an ~ that ...** avoir idée que ...; **I have no ~** je n'ai pas la moindre idée

**ideal** [aɪ'dɪəl] n idéal m ▷ adj idéal(e)

**idealist** [aɪ'dɪəlɪst] n idéaliste m/f

**ideally** [aɪ'dɪəlɪ] adv (preferably) dans l'idéal; (perfectly): **he is ~ suited to the job** il est parfait pour ce poste; **~ the book should have ...** l'idéal serait que le livre ait ...

**identical** [aɪ'dɛntɪkl] adj identique

**identification** [aɪdɛntɪfɪ'keɪʃən] n identification f; **means of ~** pièce f d'identité

**identify** [aɪ'dɛntɪfaɪ] vt identifier ▷ vi: **to ~ with** s'identifier à

**Identikit®** [aɪ'dɛntɪkɪt] n: **~ (picture)** portrait-robot m

**identity** [aɪ'dɛntɪtɪ] n identité f

**identity card** n carte f d'identité

**identity parade** n (Brit) parade f d'identification

**identity theft** n usurpation f d'identité

**ideological** [ˌaɪdɪə'lɒdʒɪkl] *adj* idéologique
**ideology** [ˌaɪdɪ'ɒlədʒɪ] *n* idéologie *f*
**idiocy** ['ɪdɪəsɪ] *n* idiotie *f*, stupidité *f*
**idiom** ['ɪdɪəm] *n* (*language*) langue *f*, idiome *m*;
(*phrase*) expression *f* idiomatique; (*style*) style *m*
**idiomatic** [ˌɪdɪə'mætɪk] *adj* idiomatique
**idiosyncrasy** [ˌɪdɪəʊ'sɪŋkrəsɪ] *n* particularité *f*,
caractéristique *f*
**idiot** ['ɪdɪət] *n* idiot(e), imbécile *m/f*
**idiotic** [ˌɪdɪ'ɒtɪk] *adj* idiot(e), bête, stupide
**idle** ['aɪdl] *adj* (*doing nothing*) sans occupation,
désœuvré(e); (*lazy*) oisif(-ive), paresseux(-euse);
(*unemployed*) au chômage; (*machinery*) au repos;
(*question, pleasures*) vain(e), futile ▷ *vi* (*engine*)
tourner au ralenti; **to lie ~** être arrêté, ne pas
fonctionner
  ▶ **idle away** *vt*: **to ~ away one's time** passer son
  temps à ne rien faire
**idleness** ['aɪdlnɪs] *n* désœuvrement *m*; oisiveté *f*
**idler** ['aɪdlə'] *n* désœuvré(e), oisif(-ive)
**idle time** *n* (*Comm*) temps mort
**idol** ['aɪdl] *n* idole *f*
**idolize** ['aɪdəlaɪz] *vt* idolâtrer, adorer
**idyllic** [ɪ'dɪlɪk] *adj* idyllique
**i.e.** *abbr* (= *id est: that is*) c. à d., c'est-à-dire
**if** [ɪf] *conj* si ▷ *n*: **there are a lot of ifs and buts**
il y a beaucoup de si *mpl* et de mais *mpl*; **I'd be
pleased if you could do it** je serais très
heureux si vous pouviez le faire; **if necessary** si
nécessaire, le cas échéant; **if so** si c'est le cas; **if
not** sinon; **if only I could!** si seulement je
pouvais!; **if only he were here** si seulement il
était là; **if only to show him my gratitude** ne
serait-ce que pour lui témoigner ma gratitude;
*see also* **as; even**
**iffy** ['ɪfɪ] *adj* (*inf*) douteux(-euse)
**igloo** ['ɪglu:] *n* igloo *m*
**ignite** [ɪg'naɪt] *vt* mettre le feu à, enflammer
▷ *vi* s'enflammer
**ignition** [ɪg'nɪʃən] *n* (*Aut*) allumage *m*; **to
switch on/off the ~** mettre/couper le contact
**ignition key** *n* (*Aut*) clé *f* de contact
**ignoble** [ɪg'nəubl] *adj* ignoble, indigne
**ignominious** [ˌɪgnə'mɪnɪəs] *adj* honteux(-euse),
ignominieux(-euse)
**ignoramus** [ˌɪgnə'reɪməs] *n* personne *f* ignare
**ignorance** ['ɪgnərəns] *n* ignorance *f*; **to keep sb
in ~ of sth** tenir qn dans l'ignorance de qch
**ignorant** ['ɪgnərənt] *adj* ignorant(e); **to be ~ of**
(*subject*) ne rien connaître en; (*events*) ne pas être
au courant de
**ignore** [ɪg'nɔ:'] *vt* ne tenir aucun compte de;
(*mistake*) ne pas relever; (*person: pretend to not see*)
faire semblant de ne pas reconnaître; (: *pay no
attention to*) ignorer
**ikon** ['aɪkɔn] *n* = **icon**
**IL** *abbr* (*US*) = **Illinois**
**ill** [ɪl] *adj* (*sick*) malade; (*bad*) mauvais(e) ▷ *n* mal
*m* ▷ *adv*: **to speak/think ~ of sb** dire/penser du
mal de qn; **to be taken ~** tomber malade
**Ill.** *abbr* (*US*) = **Illinois**
**I'll** [aɪl] = **I will; I shall**

**ill-advised** [ˌɪləd'vaɪzd] *adj* (*decision*) peu
judicieux(-euse); (*person*) malavisé(e)
**ill-at-ease** [ˌɪlət'i:z] *adj* mal à l'aise
**ill-considered** [ˌɪlkən'sɪdəd] *adj* (*plan*)
inconsidéré(e), irréfléchi(e)
**ill-disposed** [ˌɪldɪs'pəuzd] *adj*: **to be ~ towards
sb/sth** être mal disposé(e) envers qn/qch
**illegal** [ɪ'li:gl] *adj* illégal(e)
**illegally** [ɪ'li:gəlɪ] *adv* illégalement
**illegible** [ɪ'ledʒɪbl] *adj* illisible
**illegitimate** [ˌɪlɪ'dʒɪtɪmət] *adj* illégitime
**ill-fated** [ɪl'feɪtɪd] *adj* malheureux(-euse); (*day*)
néfaste
**ill-favoured**, (*US*) **ill-favored** [ɪl'feɪvəd] *adj*
déplaisant(e)
**ill feeling** *n* ressentiment *m*, rancune *f*
**ill-gotten** ['ɪlgɔtn] *adj* (*gains etc*) mal acquis(e)
**ill health** *n* mauvaise santé
**illicit** [ɪ'lɪsɪt] *adj* illicite
**ill-informed** [ˌɪlɪn'fɔ:md] *adj* (*judgment*) erroné(e);
(*person*) mal renseigné(e)
**illiterate** [ɪ'lɪtərət] *adj* illettré(e); (*letter*) plein(e)
de fautes
**ill-mannered** [ɪl'mænəd] *adj* impoli(e),
grossier(-ière)
**illness** ['ɪlnɪs] *n* maladie *f*
**illogical** [ɪ'lɒdʒɪkl] *adj* illogique
**ill-suited** [ɪl'su:tɪd] *adj* (*couple*) mal assorti(e); **he
is ~ to the job** il n'est pas vraiment fait pour ce
travail
**ill-timed** [ɪl'taɪmd] *adj* inopportun(e)
**ill-treat** [ɪl'tri:t] *vt* maltraiter
**ill-treatment** [ɪl'tri:tmənt] *n* mauvais
traitement
**illuminate** [ɪ'lu:mɪneɪt] *vt* (*room, street*) éclairer;
(*for special effect*) illuminer; **~d sign** enseigne
lumineuse
**illuminating** [ɪ'lu:mɪneɪtɪŋ] *adj* éclairant(e)
**illumination** [ɪluːmɪ'neɪʃən] *n* éclairage *m*;
illumination *f*
**illusion** [ɪ'lu:ʒən] *n* illusion *f*; **to be under the ~
that** avoir l'illusion que
**illusive** [ɪ'lu:sɪv], **illusory** [ɪ'lu:sərɪ] *adj* illusoire
**illustrate** ['ɪləstreɪt] *vt* illustrer
**illustration** [ɪlə'streɪʃən] *n* illustration *f*
**illustrator** ['ɪləstreɪtə'] *n* illustrateur(-trice)
**illustrious** [ɪ'lʌstrɪəs] *adj* illustre
**ill will** *n* malveillance *f*
**ILO** *n abbr* (= *International Labour Organization*) OIT *f*
**ILWU** *n abbr* (*US*: = *International Longshoremen's and
Warehousemen's Union*) syndicat international des
dockers et des magasiniers
**IM** *n abbr* (= *instant message*) messagerie *f* instantée
▷ *vt* envoyer un message instantané à
**I'm** [aɪm] = **I am**
**image** ['ɪmɪdʒ] *n* image *f*; (*public face*) image de
marque
**imagery** ['ɪmɪdʒərɪ] *n* images *fpl*
**imaginable** [ɪ'mædʒɪnəbl] *adj* imaginable
**imaginary** [ɪ'mædʒɪnərɪ] *adj* imaginaire
**imagination** [ɪmædʒɪ'neɪʃən] *n* imagination *f*
**imaginative** [ɪ'mædʒɪnətɪv] *adj*

imaginatif(-ive); (*person*) plein(e)
d'imagination
**imagine** [ɪ'mædʒɪn] *vt* s'imaginer; (*suppose*)
imaginer, supposer
**imbalance** [ɪm'bæləns] *n* déséquilibre *m*
**imbecile** ['ɪmbəsiːl] *n* imbécile *m/f*
**imbue** [ɪm'bjuː] *vt*: **to ~ sth with** imprégner qch
de
**IMF** *n abbr* = **International Monetary Fund**
**imitate** ['ɪmɪteɪt] *vt* imiter
**imitation** [ɪmɪ'teɪʃən] *n* imitation *f*
**imitator** ['ɪmɪteɪtər] *n* imitateur(-trice)
**immaculate** [ɪ'mækjulət] *adj* impeccable; (*Rel*)
immaculé(e)
**immaterial** [ɪmə'tɪərɪəl] *adj* sans importance,
insignifiant(e)
**immature** [ɪmə'tjuər] *adj* (*fruit*) qui n'est pas
mûr(e); (*person*) qui manque de maturité
**immaturity** [ɪmə'tjuərɪtɪ] *n* immaturité *f*
**immeasurable** [ɪ'mɛʒrəbl] *adj*
incommensurable
**immediacy** [ɪ'miːdɪəsɪ] *n* (*of events etc*) caractère
*or* rapport immédiat; (*of needs*) urgence *f*
**immediate** [ɪ'miːdɪət] *adj* immédiat(e)
**immediately** [ɪ'miːdɪətlɪ] *adv* (*at once*)
immédiatement; **~ next to** juste à côté de
**immense** [ɪ'mɛns] *adj* immense, énorme
**immensity** [ɪ'mɛnsɪtɪ] *n* immensité *f*
**immerse** [ɪ'məːs] *vt* immerger, plonger; **to ~
sth in** plonger qch dans; **to be ~d in** (*fig*) être
plongé dans
**immersion heater** [ɪ'məːʃən-] *n* (*Brit*) chauffe-
eau *m* électrique
**immigrant** ['ɪmɪɡrənt] *n* immigrant(e); (*already
established*) immigré(e)
**immigration** [ɪmɪ'ɡreɪʃən] *n* immigration *f*
**immigration authorities** *npl* service *m* de
l'immigration
**immigration laws** *npl* lois *fpl* sur l'immigration
**imminent** ['ɪmɪnənt] *adj* imminent(e)
**immobile** [ɪ'məubaɪl] *adj* immobile
**immobilize** [ɪ'məubɪlaɪz] *vt* immobiliser
**immoderate** [ɪ'mɔdərət] *adj* immodéré(e),
démesuré(e)
**immodest** [ɪ'mɔdɪst] *adj* (*indecent*) indécent(e);
(*boasting*) pas modeste, présomptueux(-euse)
**immoral** [ɪ'mɔrl] *adj* immoral(e)
**immorality** [ɪmɔ'rælɪtɪ] *n* immoralité *f*
**immortal** [ɪ'mɔːtl] *adj*, *n* immortel(le)
**immortalize** [ɪ'mɔːtlaɪz] *vt* immortaliser
**immovable** [ɪ'muːvəbl] *adj* (*object*) fixe;
immobilier(-ière); (*person*) inflexible; (*opinion*)
immuable
**immune** [ɪ'mjuːn] *adj*: **~ (to)** immunisé(e)
(contre)
**immune system** *n* système *m* immunitaire
**immunity** [ɪ'mjuːnɪtɪ] *n* immunité *f*;
**diplomatic ~** immunité diplomatique
**immunization** [ɪmjunaɪ'zeɪʃən] *n*
immunisation *f*
**immunize** ['ɪmjunaɪz] *vt* immuniser
**imp** [ɪmp] *n* (*small devil*) lutin *m*; (*child*) petit

diable
**impact** ['ɪmpækt] *n* choc *m*, impact *m*; (*fig*)
impact
**impair** [ɪm'pɛər] *vt* détériorer, diminuer
**impaired** [ɪm'pɛəd] *adj* (*organ*, *vision*) abîmé(e),
détérioré(e); **his memory/circulation is ~** il a
des problèmes de mémoire/circulation;
**visually ~** malvoyant(e); **hearing ~**
malentendant(e); **mentally/physically ~**
intellectuellement/physiquement diminué(e)
**impale** [ɪm'peɪl] *vt* empaler
**impart** [ɪm'pɑːt] *vt* (*make known*) communiquer,
transmettre; (*bestow*) confier, donner
**impartial** [ɪm'pɑːʃl] *adj* impartial(e)
**impartiality** [ɪmpɑːʃɪ'ælɪtɪ] *n* impartialité *f*
**impassable** [ɪm'pɑːsəbl] *adj* infranchissable;
(*road*) impraticable
**impasse** [æm'pɑːs] *n* (*fig*) impasse *f*
**impassioned** [ɪm'pæʃənd] *adj* passionné(e)
**impassive** [ɪm'pæsɪv] *adj* impassible
**impatience** [ɪm'peɪʃəns] *n* impatience *f*
**impatient** [ɪm'peɪʃənt] *adj* impatient(e); **to get**
*or* **grow ~** s'impatienter
**impatiently** [ɪm'peɪʃəntlɪ] *adv* avec impatience
**impeach** [ɪm'piːtʃ] *vt* accuser, attaquer; (*public
official*) mettre en accusation
**impeachment** [ɪm'piːtʃmənt] *n* (*Law*) (mise *f*
en) accusation *f*
**impeccable** [ɪm'pɛkəbl] *adj* impeccable,
parfait(e)
**impecunious** [ɪmpɪ'kjuːnɪəs] *adj* sans
ressources
**impede** [ɪm'piːd] *vt* gêner
**impediment** [ɪm'pɛdɪmənt] *n* obstacle *m*; (*also:
**speech impediment***) défaut *m* d'élocution
**impel** [ɪm'pɛl] *vt* (*force*): **to ~ sb (to do sth)**
forcer qn (à faire qch)
**impending** [ɪm'pɛndɪŋ] *adj* imminent(e)
**impenetrable** [ɪm'pɛnɪtrəbl] *adj* impénétrable
**imperative** [ɪm'pɛrətɪv] *adj* nécessaire; (*need*)
urgent(e), pressant(e); (*tone*) impérieux(-euse)
▷ *n* (*Ling*) impératif *m*
**imperceptible** [ɪmpə'sɛptɪbl] *adj* imperceptible
**imperfect** [ɪm'pəːfɪkt] *adj* imparfait(e); (*goods
etc*) défectueux(-euse) ▷ *n* (*Ling*: *also*: **imperfect
tense**) imparfait *m*
**imperfection** [ɪmpə'fɛkʃən] *n* imperfection *f*;
défectuosité *f*
**imperial** [ɪm'pɪərɪəl] *adj* impérial(e); (*Brit*:
*measure*) légal(e)
**imperialism** [ɪm'pɪərɪəlɪzəm] *n* impérialisme *m*
**imperil** [ɪm'pɛrɪl] *vt* mettre en péril
**imperious** [ɪm'pɪərɪəs] *adj* impérieux(-euse)
**impersonal** [ɪm'pəːsənl] *adj* impersonnel(le)
**impersonate** [ɪm'pəːsəneɪt] *vt* se faire passer
pour; (*Theat*) imiter
**impersonation** [ɪmpəːsə'neɪʃən] *n* (*Law*)
usurpation *f* d'identité; (*Theat*) imitation *f*
**impersonator** [ɪm'pəːsəneɪtər] *n* imposteur *m*;
(*Theat*) imitateur(-trice)
**impertinence** [ɪm'pəːtɪnəns] *n* impertinence *f*,
insolence *f*

**impertinent** [ɪmˈpəːtɪnənt] *adj* impertinent(e), insolent(e)
**imperturbable** [ɪmpəˈtəːbəbl] *adj* imperturbable
**impervious** [ɪmˈpəːvɪəs] *adj* imperméable; (*fig*): ~ **to** insensible à; inaccessible à
**impetuous** [ɪmˈpɛtjuəs] *adj* impétueux(-euse), fougueux(-euse)
**impetus** [ˈɪmpətəs] *n* impulsion *f*; (*of runner*) élan *m*
**impinge** [ɪmˈpɪndʒ]: **to ~ on** *vt fus* (*person*) affecter, toucher; (*rights*) empiéter sur
**impish** [ˈɪmpɪʃ] *adj* espiègle
**implacable** [ɪmˈplækəbl] *adj* implacable
**implant** [ɪmˈplɑːnt] *vt* (*Med*) implanter; (*fig: idea, principle*) inculquer
**implausible** [ɪmˈplɔːzɪbl] *adj* peu plausible
**implement** *n* [ˈɪmplɪmənt] outil *m*, instrument *m*; (*for cooking*) ustensile *m* ▷ *vt* [ˈɪmplɪmɛnt] exécuter, mettre à effet
**implicate** [ˈɪmplɪkeɪt] *vt* impliquer, compromettre
**implication** [ɪmplɪˈkeɪʃən] *n* implication *f*; **by ~** indirectement
**implicit** [ɪmˈplɪsɪt] *adj* implicite; (*complete*) absolu(e), sans réserve
**implicitly** [ɪmˈplɪsɪtlɪ] *adv* implicitement; absolument, sans réserve
**implore** [ɪmˈplɔːʳ] *vt* implorer, supplier
**imply** [ɪmˈplaɪ] *vt* (*hint*) suggérer, laisser entendre; (*mean*) indiquer, supposer
**impolite** [ɪmpəˈlaɪt] *adj* impoli(e)
**imponderable** [ɪmˈpɔndərəbl] *adj* impondérable
**import** *vt* [ɪmˈpɔːt] importer ▷ *n* [ˈɪmpɔːt] (*Comm*) importation *f*; (*meaning*) portée *f*, signification *f* ▷ *cpd* [ˈɪmpɔːt] (*duty, licence etc*) d'importation
**importance** [ɪmˈpɔːtns] *n* importance *f*; **to be of great/little ~** avoir beaucoup/peu d'importance
**important** [ɪmˈpɔːtnt] *adj* important(e); **it is ~ that** il importe que, il est important que; **it's not ~** c'est sans importance, ce n'est pas important
**importantly** [ɪmˈpɔːtntlɪ] *adv* (*with an air of importance*) d'un air important; (*essentially*): **but, more ~ ...** mais, (ce qui est) plus important encore ...
**importation** [ɪmpɔːˈteɪʃən] *n* importation *f*
**imported** [ɪmˈpɔːtɪd] *adj* importé(e), d'importation
**importer** [ɪmˈpɔːtəʳ] *n* importateur(-trice)
**impose** [ɪmˈpəuz] *vt* imposer ▷ *vi*: **to ~ on sb** abuser de la gentillesse de qn
**imposing** [ɪmˈpəuzɪŋ] *adj* imposant(e), impressionnant(e)
**imposition** [ɪmpəˈzɪʃən] *n* (*of tax etc*) imposition *f*; **to be an ~ on** (*person*) abuser de la gentillesse ou la bonté de
**impossibility** [ɪmpɔsəˈbɪlɪtɪ] *n* impossibilité *f*
**impossible** [ɪmˈpɔsɪbl] *adj* impossible; **it is ~**

**for me to leave** il m'est impossible de partir
**impostor** [ɪmˈpɔstəʳ] *n* imposteur *m*
**impotence** [ˈɪmpətns] *n* impuissance *f*
**impotent** [ˈɪmpətnt] *adj* impuissant(e)
**impound** [ɪmˈpaund] *vt* confisquer, saisir
**impoverished** [ɪmˈpɔvərɪʃt] *adj* pauvre, appauvri(e)
**impracticable** [ɪmˈpræktɪkəbl] *adj* impraticable
**impractical** [ɪmˈpræktɪkl] *adj* pas pratique; (*person*) qui manque d'esprit pratique
**imprecise** [ɪmprɪˈsaɪs] *adj* imprécis(e)
**impregnable** [ɪmˈprɛgnəbl] *adj* (*fortress*) imprenable; (*fig*) inattaquable, irréfutable
**impregnate** [ˈɪmprɛgneɪt] *vt* imprégner; (*fertilize*) féconder
**impresario** [ɪmprɪˈsɑːrɪəu] *n* impresario *m*
**impress** [ɪmˈprɛs] *vt* impressionner, faire impression sur; (*mark*) imprimer, marquer; **to ~ sth on sb** faire bien comprendre qch à qn
**impressed** [ɪmˈprɛst] *adj* impressionné(e)
**impression** [ɪmˈprɛʃən] *n* impression *f*; (*of stamp, seal*) empreinte *f*; (*imitation*) imitation *f*; **to make a good/bad ~ on sb** faire bonne/mauvaise impression sur qn; **to be under the ~ that** avoir l'impression que
**impressionable** [ɪmˈprɛʃnəbl] *adj* impressionnable, sensible
**impressionist** [ɪmˈprɛʃənɪst] *n* impressionniste *m/f*
**impressive** [ɪmˈprɛsɪv] *adj* impressionnant(e)
**imprint** [ˈɪmprɪnt] *n* empreinte *f*; (*Publishing*) notice *f*; (: *label*) nom *m* (de collection *or* d'éditeur)
**imprinted** [ɪmˈprɪntɪd] *adj*: **~ on** imprimé(e) sur; (*fig*) imprimé(e) *or* gravé(e) dans
**imprison** [ɪmˈprɪzn] *vt* emprisonner, mettre en prison
**imprisonment** [ɪmˈprɪznmənt] *n* emprisonnement *m*; (*period*): **to sentence sb to 10 years' ~** condamner qn à 10 ans de prison
**improbable** [ɪmˈprɔbəbl] *adj* improbable; (*excuse*) peu plausible
**impromptu** [ɪmˈprɔmptjuː] *adj* impromptu(e) ▷ *adv* impromptu
**improper** [ɪmˈprɔpəʳ] *adj* (*wrong*) incorrect(e); (*unsuitable*) déplacé(e), de mauvais goût; (*indecent*) indécent(e); (*dishonest*) malhonnête
**impropriety** [ɪmprəˈpraɪətɪ] *n* inconvenance *f*; (*of expression*) impropriété *f*
**improve** [ɪmˈpruːv] *vt* améliorer ▷ *vi* s'améliorer; (*pupil etc*) faire des progrès
▶ **improve on, improve upon** *vt fus* (*offer*) enchérir sur
**improvement** [ɪmˈpruːvmənt] *n* amélioration *f*; (*of pupil etc*) progrès *m*; **to make ~s to** apporter des améliorations à
**improvisation** [ɪmprəvaɪˈzeɪʃən] *n* improvisation *f*
**improvise** [ˈɪmprəvaɪz] *vt, vi* improviser
**imprudence** [ɪmˈpruːdns] *n* imprudence *f*
**imprudent** [ɪmˈpruːdnt] *adj* imprudent(e)
**impudent** [ˈɪmpjudnt] *adj* impudent(e)

**impugn** [ɪmˈpjuːn] vt contester, attaquer
**impulse** [ˈɪmpʌls] n impulsion f; **on ~**
impulsivement, sur un coup de tête
**impulse buy** n achat m d'impulsion
**impulsive** [ɪmˈpʌlsɪv] adj impulsif(-ive)
**impunity** [ɪmˈpjuːnɪtɪ] n: **with ~** impunément
**impure** [ɪmˈpjuəʳ] adj impur(e)
**impurity** [ɪmˈpjuərɪtɪ] n impureté f
**IN** abbr (US) = **Indiana**

⬤ KEYWORD

**in** [ɪn] prep **1** (indicating place, position) dans; **in the
house/the fridge** dans la maison/le frigo; **in
the garden** dans le or au jardin; **in town** en
ville; **in the country** à la campagne; **in school**
à l'école; **in here/there** ici/là
**2** (with place names: of town, region, country): **in
London** à Londres; **in England** en Angleterre;
**in Japan** au Japon; **in the United States** aux
États-Unis
**3** (indicating time: during): **in spring** au
printemps; **in summer** en été; **in May/2005**
en mai/2005; **in the afternoon** (dans) l'après-
midi; **at 4 o'clock in the afternoon** à 4 heures
de l'après-midi
**4** (indicating time: in the space of) en; (: future) dans;
**I did it in 3 hours/days** je l'ai fait en 3 heures/
jours; **I'll see you in 2 weeks** or **in 2 weeks'
time** je te verrai dans 2 semaines; **once in a
hundred years** une fois tous les cent ans
**5** (indicating manner etc) à; **in a loud/soft voice** à
voix haute/basse; **in pencil** au crayon; **in
writing** par écrit; **in French** en français; **to
pay in dollars** payer en dollars; **the boy in the
blue shirt** le garçon à or avec la chemise bleue
**6** (indicating circumstances): **in the sun** au soleil;
**in the shade** à l'ombre; **in the rain** sous la
pluie; **a change in policy** un changement de
politique
**7** (indicating mood, state): **in tears** en larmes; **in
anger** sous le coup de la colère; **in despair** au
désespoir; **in good condition** en bon état; **to
live in luxury** vivre dans le luxe
**8** (with ratios, numbers): **1 in 10 households, 1
household in 10** 1 ménage sur 10; **20 pence in
the pound** 20 pence par livre sterling; **they
lined up in twos** ils se mirent en rangs (deux)
par deux; **in hundreds** par centaines
**9** (referring to people, works) chez; **the disease is
common in children** c'est une maladie
courante chez les enfants; **in (the works of)
Dickens** chez Dickens, dans (l'œuvre de)
Dickens
**10** (indicating profession etc) dans; **to be in
teaching** être dans l'enseignement
**11** (after superlative) de; **the best pupil in the
class** le meilleur élève de la classe
**12** (with present participle): **in saying this** en
disant ceci
▷ adv: **to be in** (person: at home, work) être là;
(train, ship, plane) être arrivé(e); (in fashion) être à

la mode; **to ask sb in** inviter qn à entrer; **to
run/limp** etc **in** entrer en courant/boitant etc;
**their party is in** leur parti est au pouvoir
▷ n: **the ins and outs (of)** (of proposal, situation
etc) les tenants et aboutissants (de)

**in.** abbr = **inch; inches**
**inability** [ɪnəˈbɪlɪtɪ] n incapacité f; **~ to pay**
incapacité de payer
**inaccessible** [ɪnəkˈsɛsɪbl] adj inaccessible
**inaccuracy** [ɪnˈækjurəsɪ] n inexactitude f;
manque m de précision
**inaccurate** [ɪnˈækjurət] adj inexact(e); (person)
qui manque de précision
**inaction** [ɪnˈækʃən] n inaction f, inactivité f
**inactivity** [ɪnækˈtɪvɪtɪ] n inactivité f
**inadequacy** [ɪnˈædɪkwəsɪ] n insuffisance f
**inadequate** [ɪnˈædɪkwət] adj insuffisant(e),
inadéquat(e)
**inadmissible** [ɪnədˈmɪsəbl] adj (behaviour)
inadmissible; (Law: evidence) irrecevable
**inadvertent** [ɪnədˈvəːtnt] adj (mistake)
commis(e) par inadvertance
**inadvertently** [ɪnədˈvəːtntlɪ] adv par mégarde
**inadvisable** [ɪnədˈvaɪzəbl] adj à déconseiller; **it
is ~ to** il est déconseillé de
**inane** [ɪˈneɪn] adj inepte, stupide
**inanimate** [ɪnˈænɪmət] adj inanimé(e)
**inapplicable** [ɪnˈæplɪkəbl] adj inapplicable
**inappropriate** [ɪnəˈprəuprɪət] adj
inopportun(e), mal à propos; (word, expression)
impropre
**inapt** [ɪnˈæpt] adj inapte; peu approprié(e)
**inaptitude** [ɪnˈæptɪtjuːd] n inaptitude f
**inarticulate** [ɪnɑːˈtɪkjulət] adj (person) qui
s'exprime mal; (speech) indistinct(e)
**inasmuch** [ɪnəzˈmʌtʃ] adv: **~ as** vu que, en ce
sens que
**inattention** [ɪnəˈtɛnʃən] n manque m
d'attention
**inattentive** [ɪnəˈtɛntɪv] adj inattentif(-ive),
distrait(e); négligent(e)
**inaudible** [ɪnˈɔːdɪbl] adj inaudible
**inaugural** [ɪˈnɔːgjurəl] adj inaugural(e)
**inaugurate** [ɪˈnɔːgjureɪt] vt inaugurer;
(president, official) investir de ses fonctions
**inauguration** [ɪnɔːgjuˈreɪʃən] n inauguration f;
investiture f
**inauspicious** [ɪnɔːsˈpɪʃəs] adj peu propice
**in-between** [ɪnbɪˈtwiːn] adj entre les deux
**inborn** [ɪnˈbɔːn] adj (feeling) inné(e); (defect)
congénital(e)
**inbred** [ɪnˈbrɛd] adj inné(e), naturel(le); (family)
consanguin(e)
**inbreeding** [ɪnˈbriːdɪŋ] n croisement m
d'animaux de même souche; unions
consanguines
**Inc.** abbr = **incorporated**
**Inca** [ˈɪŋkə] adj (also: **Incan**) inca inv ▷ n Inca m/f
**incalculable** [ɪnˈkælkjuləbl] adj incalculable
**incapability** [ɪnkeɪpəˈbɪlɪtɪ] n incapacité f
**incapable** [ɪnˈkeɪpəbl] adj: **~ (of)** incapable (de)

**incapacitate** [ɪnkə'pæsɪteɪt] *vt*: **to ~ sb from doing** rendre qn incapable de faire
**incapacitated** [ɪnkə'pæsɪteɪtɪd] *adj* (*Law*) frappé(e) d'incapacité
**incapacity** [ɪnkə'pæsɪtɪ] *n* incapacité *f*
**incarcerate** [ɪn'kɑːsəreɪt] *vt* incarcérer
**incarnate** *adj* [ɪn'kɑːnɪt] incarné(e) ▷ *vt* ['ɪnkɑːneɪt] incarner
**incarnation** [ɪnkɑː'neɪʃən] *n* incarnation *f*
**incendiary** [ɪn'sɛndɪərɪ] *adj* incendiaire ▷ *n* (*bomb*) bombe *f* incendiaire
**incense** *n* ['ɪnsɛns] encens *m* ▷ *vt* [ɪn'sɛns] (*anger*) mettre en colère
**incense burner** *n* encensoir *m*
**incentive** [ɪn'sɛntɪv] *n* encouragement *m*, raison *f* de se donner de la peine
**incentive scheme** *n* système *m* de primes d'encouragement
**inception** [ɪn'sɛpʃən] *n* commencement *m*, début *m*
**incessant** [ɪn'sɛsnt] *adj* incessant(e)
**incessantly** [ɪn'sɛsntlɪ] *adv* sans cesse, constamment
**incest** ['ɪnsɛst] *n* inceste *m*
**inch** [ɪntʃ] *n* pouce *m* (=25 mm; 12 in a foot); **within an ~ of** à deux doigts de; **he wouldn't give an ~** (*fig*) il n'a pas voulu céder d'un pouce
  ▸ **inch forward** *vi* avancer petit à petit
**inch tape** *n* (*Brit*) centimètre *m* (de couturière)
**incidence** ['ɪnsɪdns] *n* (*of crime, disease*) fréquence *f*
**incident** ['ɪnsɪdnt] *n* incident *m*; (*in book*) péripétie *f*
**incidental** [ɪnsɪ'dɛntl] *adj* accessoire; (*unplanned*) accidentel(le); **~ to** qui accompagne; **~ expenses** faux frais *mpl*
**incidentally** [ɪnsɪ'dɛntəlɪ] *adv* (*by the way*) à propos
**incidental music** *n* musique *f* de fond
**incident room** *n* (*Police*) salle *f* d'opérations
**incinerate** [ɪn'sɪnəreɪt] *vt* incinérer
**incinerator** [ɪn'sɪnəreɪtəʳ] *n* incinérateur *m*
**incipient** [ɪn'sɪpɪənt] *adj* naissant(e)
**incision** [ɪn'sɪʒən] *n* incision *f*
**incisive** [ɪn'saɪsɪv] *adj* incisif(-ive), mordant(e)
**incisor** [ɪn'saɪzəʳ] *n* incisive *f*
**incite** [ɪn'saɪt] *vt* inciter, pousser
**incl.** *abbr* = **including; inclusive (of)**
**inclement** [ɪn'klɛmənt] *adj* inclément(e), rigoureux(-euse)
**inclination** [ɪnklɪ'neɪʃən] *n* inclination *f*; (*desire*) envie *f*
**incline** [*n* 'ɪnklaɪn, *vb* ɪn'klaɪn] *n* pente *f*, plan incliné ▷ *vt* incliner ▷ *vi* (*surface*) s'incliner; **to ~ to** avoir tendance à; **to be ~d to do** (*want to*) être enclin(e) à faire; (*have a tendency to do*) avoir tendance à faire; **to be well ~d towards sb** être bien disposé(e) à l'égard de qn
**include** [ɪn'kluːd] *vt* inclure, comprendre; **service is/is not ~d** le service est compris/n'est pas compris
**including** [ɪn'kluːdɪŋ] *prep* y compris; **~ service**

service compris
**inclusion** [ɪn'kluːʒən] *n* inclusion *f*
**inclusive** [ɪn'kluːsɪv] *adj* inclus(e), compris(e); **~ of tax** taxes comprises; **£50 ~ of all surcharges** 50 livres tous frais compris
**inclusive terms** *npl* (*Brit*) prix tout compris
**incognito** [ɪnkɔg'niːtəu] *adv* incognito
**incoherent** [ɪnkəu'hɪərənt] *adj* incohérent(e)
**income** ['ɪnkʌm] *n* revenu *m*; (*from property etc*) rentes *fpl*; **gross/net ~** revenu brut/net; **~ and expenditure account** compte *m* de recettes et de dépenses
**income support** *n* (*Brit*) ≈ revenu *m* minimum d'insertion, RMI *m*
**income tax** *n* impôt *m* sur le revenu
**income tax inspector** *n* inspecteur *m* des contributions directes
**income tax return** *n* déclaration *f* des revenus
**incoming** ['ɪnkʌmɪŋ] *adj* (*passengers, mail*) à l'arrivée; (*government, tenant*) nouveau (nouvelle); **~ tide** marée montante
**incommunicado** ['ɪnkəmjunɪ'kɑːdəu] *adj*: **to hold sb ~** tenir qn au secret
**incomparable** [ɪn'kɔmpərəbl] *adj* incomparable
**incompatible** [ɪnkəm'pætɪbl] *adj* incompatible
**incompetence** [ɪn'kɔmpɪtns] *n* incompétence *f*, incapacité *f*
**incompetent** [ɪn'kɔmpɪtnt] *adj* incompétent(e), incapable
**incomplete** [ɪnkəm'pliːt] *adj* incomplet(-ète)
**incomprehensible** [ɪnkɔmprɪ'hɛnsɪbl] *adj* incompréhensible
**inconceivable** [ɪnkən'siːvəbl] *adj* inconcevable
**inconclusive** [ɪnkən'kluːsɪv] *adj* peu concluant(e); (*argument*) peu convaincant(e)
**incongruous** [ɪn'kɔŋgruəs] *adj* peu approprié(e); (*remark, act*) incongru(e), déplacé(e)
**inconsequential** [ɪnkɔnsɪ'kwɛnʃl] *adj* sans importance
**inconsiderable** [ɪnkən'sɪdərəbl] *adj*: **not ~** non négligeable
**inconsiderate** [ɪnkən'sɪdərət] *adj* (*action*) inconsidéré(e); (*person*) qui manque d'égards
**inconsistency** [ɪnkən'sɪstənsɪ] *n* (*of actions etc*) inconséquence *f*; (*of work*) irrégularité *f*; (*of statement etc*) incohérence *f*
**inconsistent** [ɪnkən'sɪstnt] *adj* qui manque de constance; (*work*) irrégulier(-ière); (*statement*) peu cohérent(e); **~ with** en contradiction avec
**inconsolable** [ɪnkən'səuləbl] *adj* inconsolable
**inconspicuous** [ɪnkən'spɪkjuəs] *adj* qui passe inaperçu(e); (*colour, dress*) discret(-ète); **to make o.s. ~** ne pas se faire remarquer
**inconstant** [ɪn'kɔnstnt] *adj* inconstant(e), variable
**incontinence** [ɪn'kɔntɪnəns] *n* incontinence *f*
**incontinent** [ɪn'kɔntɪnənt] *adj* incontinent(e)
**incontrovertible** [ɪnkɔntrə'vəːtəbl] *adj* irréfutable
**inconvenience** [ɪnkən'viːnjəns] *n* inconvénient

i

*m*; (*trouble*) dérangement *m* ▷ *vt* déranger; **don't ~ yourself** ne vous dérangez pas
**inconvenient** [ɪnkən'viːnjənt] *adj* malcommode; (*time, place*) mal choisi(e), qui ne convient pas; (*visitor*) importun(e); **that time is very ~ for me** c'est un moment qui ne me convient pas du tout
**incorporate** [ɪn'kɔːpəreɪt] *vt* incorporer; (*contain*) contenir ▷ *vi* fusionner; (*two firms*) se constituer en société
**incorporated** [ɪn'kɔːpəreɪtɪd] *adj*: **~ company** (*US*) ≈ société *f* anonyme
**incorrect** [ɪnkə'rɛkt] *adj* incorrect(e); (*opinion, statement*) inexact(e)
**incorrigible** [ɪn'kɔrɪdʒɪbl] *adj* incorrigible
**incorruptible** [ɪnkə'rʌptɪbl] *adj* incorruptible
**increase** *n* ['ɪnkriːs] augmentation *f* ▷ *vi, vt* [ɪn'kriːs] augmenter; **an ~ of 5%** une augmentation de 5%; **to be on the ~** être en augmentation
**increasing** [ɪn'kriːsɪŋ] *adj* croissant(e)
**increasingly** [ɪn'kriːsɪŋlɪ] *adv* de plus en plus
**incredible** [ɪn'krɛdɪbl] *adj* incroyable
**incredibly** [ɪn'krɛdɪblɪ] *adv* incroyablement
**incredulous** [ɪn'krɛdjuləs] *adj* incrédule
**increment** ['ɪnkrɪmənt] *n* augmentation *f*
**incriminate** [ɪn'krɪmɪneɪt] *vt* incriminer, compromettre
**incriminating** [ɪn'krɪmɪneɪtɪŋ] *adj* compromettant(e)
**incubate** ['ɪnkjubeɪt] *vt* (*egg*) couver, incuber ▷ *vi* (*eggs*) couver; (*disease*) couver
**incubation** [ɪnkju'beɪʃən] *n* incubation *f*
**incubation period** *n* période *f* d'incubation
**incubator** ['ɪnkjubeɪtə^r] *n* incubateur *m*; (*for babies*) couveuse *f*
**inculcate** ['ɪnkʌlkeɪt] *vt*: **to ~ sth in sb** inculquer qch à qn
**incumbent** [ɪn'kʌmbənt] *adj*: **it is ~ on him to ...** il lui appartient de ... ▷ *n* titulaire *m/f*
**incur** [ɪn'kəː^r] *vt* (*expenses*) encourir; (*anger, risk*) s'exposer à; (*debt*) contracter; (*loss*) subir
**incurable** [ɪn'kjuərəbl] *adj* incurable
**incursion** [ɪn'kəːʃən] *n* incursion *f*
**Ind.** *abbr* (*US*) = **Indiana**
**indebted** [ɪn'dɛtɪd] *adj*: **to be ~ to sb (for)** être redevable à qn (de)
**indecency** [ɪn'diːsnsɪ] *n* indécence *f*
**indecent** [ɪn'diːsnt] *adj* indécent(e), inconvenant(e)
**indecent assault** *n* (*Brit*) attentat *m* à la pudeur
**indecent exposure** *n* outrage *m* public à la pudeur
**indecipherable** [ɪndɪ'saɪfərəbl] *adj* indéchiffrable
**indecision** [ɪndɪ'sɪʒən] *n* indécision *f*
**indecisive** [ɪndɪ'saɪsɪv] *adj* indécis(e); (*discussion*) peu concluant(e)
**indeed** [ɪn'diːd] *adv* (*confirming, agreeing*) en effet, effectivement; (*for emphasis*) vraiment; (*furthermore*) d'ailleurs; **yes ~!** certainement!
**indefatigable** [ɪndɪ'fætɪgəbl] *adj* infatigable
**indefensible** [ɪndɪ'fɛnsɪbl] *adj* (*conduct*) indéfendable
**indefinable** [ɪndɪ'faɪnəbl] *adj* indéfinissable
**indefinite** [ɪn'dɛfɪnɪt] *adj* indéfini(e); (*answer*) vague; (*period, number*) indéterminé(e)
**indefinitely** [ɪn'dɛfɪnɪtlɪ] *adv* (*wait*) indéfiniment; (*speak*) vaguement, avec imprécision
**indelible** [ɪn'dɛlɪbl] *adj* indélébile
**indelicate** [ɪn'dɛlɪkɪt] *adj* (*tactless*) indélicat(e), grossier(-ière); (*not polite*) inconvenant(e), malséant(e)
**indemnify** [ɪn'dɛmnɪfaɪ] *vt* indemniser, dédommager
**indemnity** [ɪn'dɛmnɪtɪ] *n* (*insurance*) assurance *f*, garantie *f*; (*compensation*) indemnité *f*
**indent** [ɪn'dɛnt] *vt* (*text*) commencer en retrait
**indentation** [ɪndɛn'teɪʃən] *n* découpure *f*; (*Typ*) alinéa *m*; (*on metal*) bosse *f*
**indenture** [ɪn'dɛntʃə^r] *n* contrat *m* d'emploi-formation
**independence** [ɪndɪ'pɛndns] *n* indépendance *f*
**Independence Day** *n* (*US*) *fête de l'Indépendance américaine*; *voir article*

**INDEPENDENCE DAY**

L'*Independence Day* est la fête nationale aux États-Unis, le 4 juillet. Il commémore l'adoption de la déclaration d'Indépendance, en 1776, écrite par Thomas Jefferson et proclamant la séparation des 13 colonies américaines de la Grande-Bretagne.

**independent** [ɪndɪ'pɛndnt] *adj* indépendant(e); (*radio*) libre; **to become ~** s'affranchir
**independently** [ɪndɪ'pɛndntlɪ] *adv* de façon indépendante; **~ of** indépendamment de
**independent school** *n* (*Brit*) école privée
**in-depth** ['ɪndɛpθ] *adj* approfondi(e)
**indescribable** [ɪndɪ'skraɪbəbl] *adj* indescriptible
**indeterminate** [ɪndɪ'təːmɪnɪt] *adj* indéterminé(e)
**index** ['ɪndɛks] *n* (*pl* **-es**) (*in book*) index *m*; (: *in library etc*) catalogue *m* (*pl* **indices** ['ɪndɪsiːz]) (*ratio, sign*) indice *m*
**index card** *n* fiche *f*
**index finger** *n* index *m*
**index-linked** ['ɪndɛks'lɪŋkt], (*US*) **indexed** ['ɪndɛkst] *adj* indexé(e) (sur le coût de la vie *etc*)
**India** ['ɪndɪə] *n* Inde *f*
**Indian** ['ɪndɪən] *adj* indien(ne) ▷ *n* Indien(ne); **(American) ~** Indien(ne) (d'Amérique)
**Indian ink** *n* encre *f* de Chine
**Indian Ocean** *n*: **the ~** l'océan Indien
**Indian summer** *n* (*fig*) été indien, beaux jours en automne
**India paper** *n* papier *m* bible
**India rubber** *n* gomme *f*
**indicate** ['ɪndɪkeɪt] *vt* indiquer ▷ *vi* (*Brit Aut*): **to**

~ **left/right** mettre son clignotant à gauche/à droite

**indication** [ɪndɪ'keɪʃən] *n* indication *f*, signe *m*

**indicative** [ɪn'dɪkətɪv] *adj* indicatif(-ive); **to be** ~ **of sth** être symptomatique de qch ▷ *n* (*Ling*) indicatif *m*

**indicator** ['ɪndɪkeɪtəʳ] *n* (*sign*) indicateur *m*; (*Aut*) clignotant *m*

**indices** ['ɪndɪsiːz] *npl of* **index**

**indict** [ɪn'daɪt] *vt* accuser

**indictable** [ɪn'daɪtəbl] *adj* (*person*) passible de poursuites; ~ **offence** délit *m* tombant sous le coup de la loi

**indictment** [ɪn'daɪtmənt] *n* accusation *f*

**indifference** [ɪn'dɪfrəns] *n* indifférence *f*

**indifferent** [ɪn'dɪfrənt] *adj* indifférent(e); (*poor*) médiocre, quelconque

**indigenous** [ɪn'dɪdʒɪnəs] *adj* indigène

**indigestible** [ɪndɪ'dʒɛstɪbl] *adj* indigeste

**indigestion** [ɪndɪ'dʒɛstʃən] *n* indigestion *f*, mauvaise digestion

**indignant** [ɪn'dɪɡnənt] *adj*: ~ **(at sth/with sb)** indigné(e) (de qch/contre qn)

**indignation** [ɪndɪɡ'neɪʃən] *n* indignation *f*

**indignity** [ɪn'dɪɡnɪtɪ] *n* indignité *f*, affront *m*

**indigo** ['ɪndɪɡəu] *adj* indigo *inv* ▷ *n* indigo *m*

**indirect** [ɪndɪ'rɛkt] *adj* indirect(e)

**indirectly** [ɪndɪ'rɛktlɪ] *adv* indirectement

**indiscreet** [ɪndɪ'skriːt] *adj* indiscret(-ète); (*rash*) imprudent(e)

**indiscretion** [ɪndɪ'skrɛʃən] *n* indiscrétion *f*; (*rashness*) imprudence *f*

**indiscriminate** [ɪndɪ'skrɪmɪnət] *adj* (*person*) qui manque de discernement; (*admiration*) aveugle; (*killings*) commis(e) au hasard

**indispensable** [ɪndɪ'spɛnsəbl] *adj* indispensable

**indisposed** [ɪndɪ'spəuzd] *adj* (*unwell*) indisposé(e), souffrant(e)

**indisposition** [ɪndɪspə'zɪʃən] *n* (*illness*) indisposition *f*, malaise *m*

**indisputable** [ɪndɪ'spjuːtəbl] *adj* incontestable, indiscutable

**indistinct** [ɪndɪ'stɪŋkt] *adj* indistinct(e); (*memory, noise*) vague

**indistinguishable** [ɪndɪ'stɪŋgwɪʃəbl] *adj* impossible à distinguer

**individual** [ɪndɪ'vɪdjuəl] *n* individu *m* ▷ *adj* individuel(le); (*characteristic*) particulier(-ière), original(e)

**individualist** [ɪndɪ'vɪdjuəlɪst] *n* individualiste *m/f*

**individuality** [ɪndɪvɪdju'ælɪtɪ] *n* individualité *f*

**individually** [ɪndɪ'vɪdjuəlɪ] *adv* individuellement

**indivisible** [ɪndɪ'vɪzɪbl] *adj* indivisible; (*Math*) insécable

**Indo-China** ['ɪndəu'tʃaɪnə] *n* Indochine *f*

**indoctrinate** [ɪn'dɔktrɪneɪt] *vt* endoctriner

**indoctrination** [ɪndɔktrɪ'neɪʃən] *n* endoctrinement *m*

**indolent** ['ɪndələnt] *adj* indolent(e),

nonchalant(e)

**Indonesia** [ɪndə'niːzɪə] *n* Indonésie *f*

**Indonesian** [ɪndə'niːzɪən] *adj* indonésien(ne) ▷ *n* Indonésien(ne); (*Ling*) indonésien *m*

**indoor** ['ɪndɔːʳ] *adj* d'intérieur; (*plant*) d'appartement; (*swimming pool*) couvert(e); (*sport, games*) pratiqué(e) en salle

**indoors** [ɪn'dɔːz] *adv* à l'intérieur; (*at home*) à la maison

**indubitable** [ɪn'djuːbɪtəbl] *adj* indubitable, incontestable

**induce** [ɪn'djuːs] *vt* (*persuade*) persuader; (*bring about*) provoquer; (*labour*) déclencher; **to ~ sb to do sth** inciter *or* pousser qn à faire qch

**inducement** [ɪn'djuːsmənt] *n* incitation *f*; (*incentive*) but *m*; (*pej: bribe*) pot-de-vin *m*

**induct** [ɪn'dʌkt] *vt* établir dans ses fonctions; (*fig*) initier

**induction** [ɪn'dʌkʃən] *n* (*Med: of birth*) accouchement provoqué

**induction course** *n* (*Brit*) stage *m* de mise au courant

**indulge** [ɪn'dʌldʒ] *vt* (*whim*) céder à, satisfaire; (*child*) gâter ▷ *vi*: **to ~ in sth** (*luxury*) s'offrir qch, se permettre qch; (*fantasies etc*) se livrer à qch

**indulgence** [ɪn'dʌldʒəns] *n* fantaisie *f* (que l'on s'offre); (*leniency*) indulgence *f*

**indulgent** [ɪn'dʌldʒənt] *adj* indulgent(e)

**industrial** [ɪn'dʌstrɪəl] *adj* industriel(le); (*injury*) du travail; (*dispute*) ouvrier(-ière)

**industrial action** *n* action revendicative

**industrial estate** *n* (*Brit*) zone industrielle

**industrialist** [ɪn'dʌstrɪəlɪst] *n* industriel *m*

**industrialize** [ɪn'dʌstrɪəlaɪz] *vt* industrialiser

**industrial park** *n* (*US*) zone industrielle

**industrial relations** *npl* relations *fpl* dans l'entreprise

**industrial tribunal** *n* (*Brit*) ≈ conseil *m* de prud'hommes

**industrious** [ɪn'dʌstrɪəs] *adj* travailleur(-euse)

**industry** ['ɪndəstrɪ] *n* industrie *f*; (*diligence*) zèle *m*, application *f*

**inebriated** [ɪ'niːbrɪeɪtɪd] *adj* ivre

**inedible** [ɪn'edɪbl] *adj* immangeable; (*plant etc*) non comestible

**ineffective** [ɪnɪ'fɛktɪv], **ineffectual** [ɪnɪ'fɛktjuəl] *adj* inefficace; incompétent(e)

**inefficiency** [ɪnɪ'fɪʃənsɪ] *n* inefficacité *f*

**inefficient** [ɪnɪ'fɪʃənt] *adj* inefficace

**inelegant** [ɪn'ɛlɪɡənt] *adj* peu élégant(e), inélégant(e)

**ineligible** [ɪn'ɛlɪdʒɪbl] *adj* (*candidate*) inéligible; **to be ~ for sth** ne pas avoir droit à qch

**inept** [ɪ'nɛpt] *adj* inepte

**ineptitude** [ɪ'nɛptɪtjuːd] *n* ineptie *f*

**inequality** [ɪnɪ'kwɔlɪtɪ] *n* inégalité *f*

**inequitable** [ɪn'ɛkwɪtəbl] *adj* inéquitable, inique

**ineradicable** [ɪnɪ'rædɪkəbl] *adj* indéracinable, tenace

**inert** [ɪ'nəːt] *adj* inerte

**inertia** [ɪ'nəːʃə] *n* inertie *f*

**inertia-reel seat belt** [ɪˈnəːʃəˈriːl-] n ceinture f de sécurité à enrouleur
**inescapable** [ɪnɪˈskeɪpəbl] adj inéluctable, inévitable
**inessential** [ɪnɪˈsɛnʃl] adj superflu(e)
**inestimable** [ɪnˈɛstɪməbl] adj inestimable, incalculable
**inevitable** [ɪnˈɛvɪtəbl] adj inévitable
**inevitably** [ɪnˈɛvɪtəblɪ] adv inévitablement, fatalement
**inexact** [ɪnɪgˈzækt] adj inexact(e)
**inexcusable** [ɪnɪksˈkjuːzəbl] adj inexcusable
**inexhaustible** [ɪnɪgˈzɔːstɪbl] adj inépuisable
**inexorable** [ɪnˈɛksərəbl] adj inexorable
**inexpensive** [ɪnɪkˈspɛnsɪv] adj bon marché inv
**inexperience** [ɪnɪkˈspɪərɪəns] n inexpérience f, manque m d'expérience
**inexperienced** [ɪnɪkˈspɪərɪənst] adj inexpérimenté(e); **to be ~ in sth** manquer d'expérience dans qch
**inexplicable** [ɪnɪkˈsplɪkəbl] adj inexplicable
**inexpressible** [ɪnɪkˈsprɛsɪbl] adj inexprimable; indicible
**inextricable** [ɪnɪkˈstrɪkəbl] adj inextricable
**infallibility** [ɪnfæləˈbɪlɪtɪ] n infaillibilité f
**infallible** [ɪnˈfælɪbl] adj infaillible
**infamous** [ˈɪnfəməs] adj infâme, abominable
**infamy** [ˈɪnfəmɪ] n infamie f
**infancy** [ˈɪnfənsɪ] n petite enfance, bas âge; (fig) enfance, débuts mpl
**infant** [ˈɪnfənt] n (baby) nourrisson m; (young child) petit(e) enfant
**infantile** [ˈɪnfəntaɪl] adj infantile
**infant mortality** n mortalité f infantile
**infantry** [ˈɪnfəntrɪ] n infanterie f
**infantryman** [ˈɪnfəntrɪmən] (irreg) n fantassin m
**infant school** n (Brit) classes fpl préparatoires (entre 5 et 7 ans)
**infatuated** [ɪnˈfætjueɪtɪd] adj: **~ with** entiché(e) de; **to become ~ (with sb)** s'enticher (de qn)
**infatuation** [ɪnfætjuˈeɪʃən] n toquade f; engouement m
**infect** [ɪnˈfɛkt] vt (wound) infecter; (person, blood) contaminer; (fig pej) corrompre; **~ed with** (illness) atteint(e) de; **to become ~ed** (wound) s'infecter
**infection** [ɪnˈfɛkʃən] n infection f; (contagion) contagion f
**infectious** [ɪnˈfɛkʃəs] adj infectieux(-euse); (also fig) contagieux(-euse)
**infer** [ɪnˈfəːʳ] vt: **to ~ (from)** conclure (de), déduire (de)
**inference** [ˈɪnfərəns] n conclusion f, déduction f
**inferior** [ɪnˈfɪərɪəʳ] adj inférieur(e); (goods) de qualité inférieure ▷ n inférieur(e); (in rank) subalterne m/f; **to feel ~** avoir un sentiment d'infériorité
**inferiority** [ɪnfɪərɪˈɔrətɪ] n infériorité f
**inferiority complex** n complexe m d'infériorité
**infernal** [ɪnˈfəːnl] adj infernal(e)
**inferno** [ɪnˈfəːnəu] n enfer m; brasier m

**infertile** [ɪnˈfəːtaɪl] adj stérile
**infertility** [ɪnfəˈtɪlɪtɪ] n infertilité f, stérilité f
**infested** [ɪnˈfɛstɪd] adj: **~ (with)** infesté(e) (de)
**infidelity** [ɪnfɪˈdɛlɪtɪ] n infidélité f
**in-fighting** [ˈɪnfaɪtɪŋ] n querelles fpl internes
**infiltrate** [ˈɪnfɪltreɪt] vt (troops etc) faire s'infiltrer; (enemy line etc) s'infiltrer dans ▷ vi s'infiltrer
**infinite** [ˈɪnfɪnɪt] adj infini(e); (time, money) illimité(e)
**infinitely** [ˈɪnfɪnɪtlɪ] adv infiniment
**infinitesimal** [ɪnfɪnɪˈtɛsɪməl] adj infinitésimal(e)
**infinitive** [ɪnˈfɪnɪtɪv] n infinitif m
**infinity** [ɪnˈfɪnɪtɪ] n infinité f; (also Math) infini m
**infirm** [ɪnˈfəːm] adj infirme
**infirmary** [ɪnˈfəːmərɪ] n hôpital m; (in school, factory) infirmerie f
**infirmity** [ɪnˈfəːmɪtɪ] n infirmité f
**inflamed** [ɪnˈfleɪmd] adj enflammé(e)
**inflammable** [ɪnˈflæməbl] adj (Brit) inflammable
**inflammation** [ɪnfləˈmeɪʃən] n inflammation f
**inflammatory** [ɪnˈflæmətərɪ] adj (speech) incendiaire
**inflatable** [ɪnˈfleɪtəbl] adj gonflable
**inflate** [ɪnˈfleɪt] vt (tyre, balloon) gonfler; (fig: exaggerate) grossir, gonfler; (: increase) gonfler
**inflated** [ɪnˈfleɪtɪd] adj (style) enflé(e); (value) exagéré(e)
**inflation** [ɪnˈfleɪʃən] n (Econ) inflation f
**inflationary** [ɪnˈfleɪʃənərɪ] adj inflationniste
**inflexible** [ɪnˈflɛksɪbl] adj inflexible, rigide
**inflict** [ɪnˈflɪkt] vt: **to ~ on** infliger à
**infliction** [ɪnˈflɪkʃən] n: **without the ~ of pain** sans infliger de douleurs
**in-flight** [ˈɪnflaɪt] adj (refuelling) en vol; (service etc) à bord
**inflow** [ˈɪnfləu] n afflux m
**influence** [ˈɪnfluəns] n influence f ▷ vt influencer; **under the ~ of** sous l'effet de; **under the ~ of alcohol** en état d'ébriété
**influential** [ɪnfluˈɛnʃl] adj influent(e)
**influenza** [ɪnfluˈɛnzə] n grippe f
**influx** [ˈɪnflʌks] n afflux m
**info** (inf) [ˈɪnfəu] n (= information) renseignements mpl
**infomercial** [ˈɪnfəuməːʃl] (US) n (for product) publi-information f; (Pol) émission où un candidat présente son programme électoral
**inform** [ɪnˈfɔːm] vt: **to ~ sb (of)** informer or avertir qn (de) ▷ vi: **to ~ on sb** dénoncer qn, informer contre qn; **to ~ sb about** renseigner qn sur, mettre qn au courant de
**informal** [ɪnˈfɔːml] adj (person, manner, party) simple, sans cérémonie; (visit, discussion) dénué(e) de formalités; (announcement, invitation) non officiel(le); (colloquial) familier(-ère); **"dress ~"** "tenue de ville"
**informality** [ɪnfɔːˈmælɪtɪ] n simplicité f, absence f de cérémonie; caractère non officiel

**informally** [ɪnˈfɔːməlɪ] *adv* sans cérémonie, en toute simplicité; non officiellement

**informant** [ɪnˈfɔːmənt] *n* informateur(-trice)

**information** [ɪnfəˈmeɪʃən] *n* information(s) *f(pl)*; renseignements *mpl*; (*knowledge*) connaissances *fpl*; **to get ~ on** se renseigner sur; **a piece of ~** un renseignement; **for your ~** à titre d'information

**information bureau** *n* bureau *m* de renseignements

**information desk** *n* accueil *m*

**information office** *n* bureau *m* de renseignements

**information processing** *n* traitement *m* de l'information

**information technology** *n* informatique *f*

**informative** [ɪnˈfɔːmətɪv] *adj* instructif(-ive)

**informed** [ɪnˈfɔːmd] *adj* (bien) informé(e); **an ~ guess** une hypothèse fondée sur la connaissance des faits

**informer** [ɪnˈfɔːməˈ] *n* dénonciateur(-trice); (*also*: **police informer**) indicateur(-trice)

**infra dig** [ˈɪnfrəˈdɪg] *adj abbr* (*inf*: = *infra dignitatem*) au-dessous de ma (*or* sa *etc*) dignité

**infra-red** [ɪnfrəˈred] *adj* infrarouge

**infrastructure** [ˈɪnfrəstrʌktʃəˈ] *n* infrastructure *f*

**infrequent** [ɪnˈfriːkwənt] *adj* peu fréquent(e), rare

**infringe** [ɪnˈfrɪndʒ] *vt* enfreindre ▷ *vi*: **to ~ on** empiéter sur

**infringement** [ɪnˈfrɪndʒmənt] *n*: **~ (of)** infraction *f* (à)

**infuriate** [ɪnˈfjuərɪeɪt] *vt* mettre en fureur

**infuriating** [ɪnˈfjuərɪeɪtɪŋ] *adj* exaspérant(e)

**infuse** [ɪnˈfjuːz] *vt*: **to ~ sb with sth** (*fig*) insuffler qch à qn

**infusion** [ɪnˈfjuːʒən] *n* (*tea etc*) infusion *f*

**ingenious** [ɪnˈdʒiːnjəs] *adj* ingénieux(-euse)

**ingenuity** [ɪndʒɪˈnjuːɪtɪ] *n* ingéniosité *f*

**ingenuous** [ɪnˈdʒɛnjuəs] *adj* franc (franche), ouvert(e)

**ingot** [ˈɪŋgət] *n* lingot *m*

**ingrained** [ɪnˈgreɪnd] *adj* enraciné(e)

**ingratiate** [ɪnˈgreɪʃɪeɪt] *vt*: **to ~ o.s. with** s'insinuer dans les bonnes grâces de, se faire bien voir de

**ingratiating** [ɪnˈgreɪʃɪeɪtɪŋ] *adj* (*smile, speech*) insinuant(e); (*person*) patelin(e)

**ingratitude** [ɪnˈgrætɪtjuːd] *n* ingratitude *f*

**ingredient** [ɪnˈgriːdɪənt] *n* ingrédient *m*; (*fig*) élément *m*

**ingrowing** [ˈɪngrəuɪŋ], **ingrown** [ˈɪngrəun] *adj*: **~ toenail** ongle incarné

**inhabit** [ɪnˈhæbɪt] *vt* habiter

**inhabitable** [ɪnˈhæbɪtəbl] *adj* habitable

**inhabitant** [ɪnˈhæbɪtnt] *n* habitant(e)

**inhale** [ɪnˈheɪl] *vt* inhaler; (*perfume*) respirer; (*smoke*) avaler ▷ *vi* (*breathe in*) aspirer; (*in smoking*) avaler la fumée

**inhaler** [ɪnˈheɪləˈ] *n* inhalateur *m*

**inherent** [ɪnˈhɪərənt] *adj*: **~ (in *or* to)** inhérent(e) (à)

**inherently** [ɪnˈhɪərəntlɪ] *adv* (*easy, difficult*) en soi; (*lazy*) fondamentalement

**inherit** [ɪnˈhɛrɪt] *vt* hériter (de)

**inheritance** [ɪnˈhɛrɪtəns] *n* héritage *m*; (*fig*): **the situation that was his ~ as president** la situation dont il a hérité en tant que président; **law of ~** droit *m* de la succession

**inhibit** [ɪnˈhɪbɪt] *vt* (*Psych*) inhiber; (*growth*) freiner; **to ~ sb from doing** empêcher *or* retenir qn de faire

**inhibited** [ɪnˈhɪbɪtɪd] *adj* (*person*) inhibé(e)

**inhibiting** [ɪnˈhɪbɪtɪŋ] *adj* gênant(e)

**inhibition** [ɪnhɪˈbɪʃən] *n* inhibition *f*

**inhospitable** [ɪnhɔsˈpɪtəbl] *adj* inhospitalier(-ière)

**in-house** [ˈɪnˈhaus] *adj* (*system*) interne; (*training*) effectué(e) sur place *or* dans le cadre de la compagnie ▷ *adv* (*train, produce*) sur place

**inhuman** [ɪnˈhjuːmən] *adj* inhumain(e)

**inhumane** [ɪnhjuːˈmeɪn] *adj* inhumain(e)

**inimitable** [ɪˈnɪmɪtəbl] *adj* inimitable

**iniquity** [ɪˈnɪkwɪtɪ] *n* iniquité *f*

**initial** [ɪˈnɪʃl] *adj* initial(e) ▷ *n* initiale *f* ▷ *vt* parafer; **initials** *npl* initiales *fpl*; (*as signature*) parafe *m*

**initialize** [ɪˈnɪʃəlaɪz] *vt* (*Comput*) initialiser

**initially** [ɪˈnɪʃəlɪ] *adv* initialement, au début

**initiate** [ɪˈnɪʃɪeɪt] *vt* (*start*) entreprendre; amorcer; (*enterprise*) lancer; (*person*) initier; **to ~ sb into a secret** initier qn à un secret; **to ~ proceedings against sb** (*Law*) intenter une action à qn, engager des poursuites contre qn

**initiation** [ɪnɪʃɪˈeɪʃən] *n* (*into secret etc*) initiation *f*

**initiative** [ɪˈnɪʃətɪv] *n* initiative *f*; **to take the ~** prendre l'initiative

**inject** [ɪnˈdʒɛkt] *vt* (*liquid, fig: money*) injecter; (*person*): **to ~ sb with sth** faire une piqûre de qch à qn

**injection** [ɪnˈdʒɛkʃən] *n* injection *f*, piqûre *f*; **to have an ~** se faire faire une piqûre

**injudicious** [ɪndʒuˈdɪʃəs] *adj* peu judicieux(-euse)

**injunction** [ɪnˈdʒʌŋkʃən] *n* (*Law*) injonction *f*, ordre *m*

**injure** [ˈɪndʒəˈ] *vt* blesser; (*wrong*) faire du tort à; (*damage: reputation etc*) compromettre; (*feelings*) heurter; **to ~ o.s.** se blesser

**injured** [ˈɪndʒəd] *adj* (*person, leg etc*) blessé(e); (*tone, feelings*) offensé(e); **~ party** (*Law*) partie lésée

**injurious** [ɪnˈdʒuərɪəs] *adj*: **~ (to)** préjudiciable (à)

**injury** [ˈɪndʒərɪ] *n* blessure *f*; (*wrong*) tort *m*; **to escape without ~** s'en sortir sain et sauf

**injury time** *n* (*Sport*) arrêts *mpl* de jeu

**injustice** [ɪnˈdʒʌstɪs] *n* injustice *f*; **you do me an ~** vous êtes injuste envers moi

**ink** [ɪŋk] *n* encre *f*

**ink-jet printer** [ˈɪŋkdʒɛt-] *n* imprimante *f* à jet d'encre

**inkling** [ˈɪŋklɪŋ] *n* soupçon *m*, vague idée *f*

**inkpad** ['ɪŋkpæd] *n* tampon *m* encreur
**inky** ['ɪŋkɪ] *adj* taché(e) d'encre
**inlaid** ['ɪnleɪd] *adj* incrusté(e); *(table etc)*
marqueté(e)
**inland** *adj* ['ɪnlənd] intérieur(e) ▷ *adv* [ɪn'lænd] à
l'intérieur, dans les terres; ~ **waterways**
canaux *mpl* et rivières *fpl*
**Inland Revenue** *n* (Brit) fisc *m*
**in-laws** ['ɪnlɔːz] *npl* beaux-parents *mpl*; belle
famille
**inlet** ['ɪnlet] *n* (Geo) crique *f*
**inlet pipe** *n* (Tech) tuyau *m* d'arrivée
**inmate** ['ɪnmeɪt] *n* (in prison) détenu(e); (in
asylum) interné(e)
**inmost** ['ɪnməust] *adj* le (la) plus profond(e)
**inn** [ɪn] *n* auberge *f*
**innards** ['ɪnədz] *npl* (inf) entrailles *fpl*
**innate** [ɪ'neɪt] *adj* inné(e)
**inner** ['ɪnəʳ] *adj* intérieur(e)
**inner city** *n* centre *m* urbain (souffrant souvent de
délabrement, d'embouteillages etc)
**inner-city** ['ɪnəʳsɪtɪ] *adj* (schools, problems) de
quartiers déshérités
**innermost** ['ɪnəməust] *adj* le (la) plus
profond(e)
**inner tube** *n* (of tyre) chambre *f* à air
**inning** ['ɪnɪŋ] *n* (US: Baseball) tour *m* de batte;
**innings** *npl* (Cricket) tour de batte; (Brit fig): **he
has had a good ~s** il (en) a bien profité
**innocence** ['ɪnəsns] *n* innocence *f*
**innocent** ['ɪnəsnt] *adj* innocent(e)
**innocuous** [ɪ'nɔkjuəs] *adj* inoffensif(-ive)
**innovation** [ɪnəu'veɪʃən] *n* innovation *f*
**innovative** ['ɪnəu'veɪtɪv] *adj* novateur(-trice);
(product) innovant(e)
**innuendo** (pl **-es** [ɪnju'ɛndəu]) *n* insinuation *f*,
allusion (malveillante)
**innumerable** [ɪ'nju:mrəbl] *adj* innombrable
**inoculate** [ɪ'nɔkjuleɪt] *vt*: **to ~ sb with sth**
inoculer qch à qn; **to ~ sb against sth** vacciner
qn contre qch
**inoculation** [ɪnɔkju'leɪʃən] *n* inoculation *f*
**inoffensive** [ɪnə'fɛnsɪv] *adj* inoffensif(-ive)
**inopportune** [ɪn'ɔpətjuːn] *adj* inopportun(e)
**inordinate** [ɪ'nɔːdɪnət] *adj* démesuré(e)
**inordinately** [ɪ'nɔːdɪnətlɪ] *adv* démesurément
**inorganic** [ɪnɔː'gænɪk] *adj* inorganique
**in-patient** ['ɪnpeɪʃənt] *n* malade hospitalisé(e)
**input** ['ɪnput] *n* (contribution) contribution *f*;
(resources) ressources *fpl*; (Elec) énergie *f*,
puissance *f*; (of machine) consommation *f*;
(Comput) entrée *f* (de données); (: data) données
*fpl* ▷ *vt* (Comput) introduire, entrer
**inquest** ['ɪnkwɛst] *n* enquête (criminelle);
(coroner's) enquête judiciaire
**inquire** [ɪn'kwaɪəʳ] *vi* demander ▷ *vt* demander,
s'informer de; **to ~ about** s'informer de, se
renseigner sur; **to ~ when/where/whether**
demander quand/où/si
▶ **inquire after** *vt fus* demander des nouvelles
de
▶ **inquire into** *vt fus* faire une enquête sur

**inquiring** [ɪn'kwaɪərɪŋ] *adj* (mind)
curieux(-euse), investigateur(-trice)
**inquiry** [ɪn'kwaɪərɪ] *n* demande *f* de
renseignements; (Law) enquête *f*, investigation
*f*; **"inquiries"** "renseignements"; **to hold an ~
into sth** enquêter sur qch
**inquiry desk** *n* (Brit) guichet *m* de
renseignements
**inquiry office** *n* (Brit) bureau *m* de
renseignements
**inquisition** [ɪnkwɪ'zɪʃən] *n* enquête *f*,
investigation *f*; (Rel): **the I~** l'Inquisition *f*
**inquisitive** [ɪn'kwɪzɪtɪv] *adj* curieux(-euse)
**inroads** ['ɪnrəudz] *npl*: **to make ~ into** (savings,
supplies) entamer
**ins.** *abbr* = **inches**
**insane** [ɪn'seɪn] *adj* fou (folle); (Med) aliéné(e)
**insanitary** [ɪn'sænɪtərɪ] *adj* insalubre
**insanity** [ɪn'sænɪtɪ] *n* folie *f*; (Med) aliénation
(mentale)
**insatiable** [ɪn'seɪʃəbl] *adj* insatiable
**inscribe** [ɪn'skraɪb] *vt* inscrire; (book etc): **to ~
(to sb)** dédicacer (à qn)
**inscription** [ɪn'skrɪpʃən] *n* inscription *f*; (in book)
dédicace *f*
**inscrutable** [ɪn'skruːtəbl] *adj* impénétrable
**inseam** ['ɪnsiːm] *n* (US): **~ measurement**
hauteur *f* d'entre-jambe
**insect** ['ɪnsɛkt] *n* insecte *m*
**insect bite** *n* piqûre *f* d'insecte
**insecticide** [ɪn'sɛktɪsaɪd] *n* insecticide *m*
**insect repellent** *n* crème *f* anti-insectes
**insecure** [ɪnsɪ'kjuəʳ] *adj* (person) anxieux(-euse);
(job) précaire; (building etc) peu sûr(e)
**insecurity** [ɪnsɪ'kjuərɪtɪ] *n* insécurité *f*
**insensible** [ɪn'sɛnsɪbl] *adj* insensible;
(unconscious) sans connaissance
**insensitive** [ɪn'sɛnsɪtɪv] *adj* insensible
**insensitivity** [ɪnsɛnsɪ'tɪvɪtɪ] *n* insensibilité *f*
**inseparable** [ɪn'sɛprəbl] *adj* inséparable
**insert** *vt* [ɪn'səːt] insérer ▷ *n* ['ɪnsəːt] insertion *f*
**insertion** [ɪn'səːʃən] *n* insertion *f*
**in-service** ['ɪn'səːvɪs] *adj* (training) continu(e);
(course) d'initiation; de perfectionnement; de
recyclage
**inshore** [ɪn'ʃɔːʳ] *adj* côtier(-ière) ▷ *adv* près de la
côte; vers la côte
**inside** ['ɪn'saɪd] *n* intérieur *m*; (of road: Brit) côté
*m* gauche (de la route); (: US, Europe etc) côté droit
(de la route) ▷ *adj* intérieur(e) ▷ *adv* à l'intérieur,
dedans ▷ *prep* à l'intérieur de; (of time): **~ 10
minutes** en moins de 10 minutes; **insides** *npl*
(inf) intestins *mpl*; **~ information**
renseignements *mpl* à la source; **~ story**
histoire racontée par un témoin; **to go ~**
rentrer
**inside forward** *n* (Sport) intérieur *m*
**inside lane** *n* (Aut: in Britain) voie *f* de gauche; (: in
US, Europe) voie *f* de droite
**inside leg measurement** *n* (Brit) hauteur *f*
d'entre-jambe
**inside out** *adv* à l'envers; (know) à fond; **to turn**

sth ~ retourner qch
**insider** [ɪn'saɪdə<sup>r</sup>] n initié(e)
**insider dealing, insider trading** n (Stock Exchange) délit m d'initiés
**insidious** [ɪn'sɪdɪəs] adj insidieux(-euse)
**insight** ['ɪnsaɪt] n perspicacité f; (glimpse, idea) aperçu m; **to gain (an) ~ into** parvenir à comprendre
**insignia** [ɪn'sɪgnɪə] npl insignes mpl
**insignificant** [ɪnsɪg'nɪfɪknt] adj insignifiant(e)
**insincere** [ɪnsɪn'sɪə<sup>r</sup>] adj hypocrite
**insincerity** [ɪnsɪn'sɛrɪtɪ] n manque m de sincérité, hypocrisie f
**insinuate** [ɪn'sɪnjueɪt] vt insinuer
**insinuation** [ɪnsɪnju'eɪʃən] n insinuation f
**insipid** [ɪn'sɪpɪd] adj insipide, fade
**insist** [ɪn'sɪst] vi insister; **to ~ on doing** insister pour faire; **to ~ on sth** exiger qch; **to ~ that** insister pour que + sub; (claim) maintenir or soutenir que
**insistence** [ɪn'sɪstəns] n insistance f
**insistent** [ɪn'sɪstənt] adj insistant(e), pressant(e); (noise, action) ininterrompu(e)
**insofar** [ɪnsəu'fɑ:<sup>r</sup>]: ~ **as** conj dans la mesure où
**insole** ['ɪnsəul] n semelle intérieure; (fixed part of shoe) première f
**insolence** ['ɪnsələns] n insolence f
**insolent** ['ɪnsələnt] adj insolent(e)
**insoluble** [ɪn'sɔljubl] adj insoluble
**insolvency** [ɪn'sɔlvənsɪ] n insolvabilité f; faillite f
**insolvent** [ɪn'sɔlvənt] adj insolvable; (bankrupt) en faillite
**insomnia** [ɪn'sɔmnɪə] n insomnie f
**insomniac** [ɪn'sɔmnɪæk] n insomniaque m/f
**inspect** [ɪn'spɛkt] vt inspecter; (Brit: ticket) contrôler
**inspection** [ɪn'spɛkʃən] n inspection f; (Brit: of tickets) contrôle m
**inspector** [ɪn'spɛktə<sup>r</sup>] n inspecteur(-trice); (Brit: on buses, trains) contrôleur(-euse)
**inspiration** [ɪnspə'reɪʃən] n inspiration f
**inspire** [ɪn'spaɪə<sup>r</sup>] vt inspirer
**inspired** [ɪn'spaɪəd] adj (writer, book etc) inspiré(e); **in an ~ moment** dans un moment d'inspiration
**inspiring** [ɪn'spaɪərɪŋ] adj inspirant(e)
**inst.** abbr (Brit Comm) = **instant**; **of the 16th ~** du 16 courant
**instability** [ɪnstə'bɪlɪtɪ] n instabilité f
**install, (US) instal** [ɪn'stɔ:l] vt installer
**installation** [ɪnstə'leɪʃən] n installation f
**installment plan** n (US) achat m (or vente f) à tempérament or crédit
**instalment, (US) installment** [ɪn'stɔ:lmənt] n (payment) acompte m, versement partiel; (of TV serial etc) épisode m; **in ~s** (pay) à tempérament; (receive) en plusieurs fois
**instance** ['ɪnstəns] n exemple m; **for ~** par exemple; **in many ~s** dans bien des cas; **in that ~** dans ce cas; **in the first ~** tout d'abord, en premier lieu

**instant** ['ɪnstənt] n instant m ▷ adj immédiat(e), urgent(e); (coffee, food) instantané(e), en poudre; **the 10th ~** le 10 courant
**instantaneous** [ɪnstən'teɪnɪəs] adj instantané(e)
**instantly** ['ɪnstəntlɪ] adv immédiatement, tout de suite
**instant messaging** n messagerie f instantanée
**instant replay** n (US TV) retour m sur une séquence
**instead** [ɪn'stɛd] adv au lieu de cela; ~ **of** au lieu de; ~ **of sb** à la place de qn
**instep** ['ɪnstɛp] n cou-de-pied m; (of shoe) cambrure f
**instigate** ['ɪnstɪgeɪt] vt (rebellion, strike, crime) inciter à; (new ideas etc) susciter
**instigation** [ɪnstɪ'geɪʃən] n instigation f; **at sb's ~** à l'instigation de qn
**instil** [ɪn'stɪl] vt: **to ~ (into)** inculquer (à); (courage) insuffler (à)
**instinct** ['ɪnstɪŋkt] n instinct m
**instinctive** [ɪn'stɪŋktɪv] adj instinctif(-ive)
**instinctively** [ɪn'stɪŋktɪvlɪ] adv instinctivement
**institute** ['ɪnstɪtju:t] n institut m ▷ vt instituer, établir; (inquiry) ouvrir; (proceedings) entamer
**institution** [ɪnstɪ'tju:ʃən] n institution f; (school) établissement m (scolaire); (for care) établissement (psychiatrique etc)
**institutional** [ɪnstɪ'tju:ʃənl] adj institutionnel(le); ~ **care** soins fournis par un établissement médico-social
**instruct** [ɪn'strʌkt] vt instruire, former; **to ~ sb in sth** enseigner qch à qn; **to ~ sb to do** charger qn or ordonner à qn de faire
**instruction** [ɪn'strʌkʃən] n instruction f; **instructions** npl (orders) directives fpl; ~ **s for use** mode m d'emploi
**instruction book** n manuel m d'instructions
**instructive** [ɪn'strʌktɪv] adj instructif(-ive)
**instructor** [ɪn'strʌktə<sup>r</sup>] n professeur m; (for skiing, driving) moniteur m
**instrument** ['ɪnstrumənt] n instrument m
**instrumental** [ɪnstru'mɛntl] adj (Mus) instrumental(e); **to be ~ in sth/in doing sth** contribuer à qch/à faire qch
**instrumentalist** [ɪnstru'mɛntəlɪst] n instrumentiste m/f
**instrument panel** n tableau m de bord
**insubordinate** [ɪnsə'bɔ:dənɪt] adj insubordonné(e)
**insubordination** [ɪnsəbɔ:də'neɪʃən] n insubordination f
**insufferable** [ɪn'sʌfrəbl] adj insupportable
**insufficient** [ɪnsə'fɪʃənt] adj insuffisant(e)
**insufficiently** [ɪnsə'fɪʃəntlɪ] adv insuffisamment
**insular** ['ɪnsjulə<sup>r</sup>] adj insulaire; (outlook) étroit(e); (person) aux vues étroites
**insulate** ['ɪnsjuleɪt] vt isoler; (against sound) insonoriser

637

**insulating tape** ['ɪnsjuleɪtɪŋ-] n ruban isolant
**insulation** [ɪnsju'leɪʃən] n isolation f; (against sound) insonorisation f
**insulin** ['ɪnsjulɪn] n insuline f
**insult** n ['ɪnsʌlt] insulte f, affront m ▷ vt [ɪn'sʌlt] insulter, faire un affront à
**insulting** [ɪn'sʌltɪŋ] adj insultant(e), injurieux(-euse)
**insuperable** [ɪn'sju:prəbl] adj insurmontable
**insurance** [ɪn'ʃuərəns] n assurance f; **fire/life ~** assurance-incendie/-vie; **to take out ~ (against)** s'assurer (contre)
**insurance agent** n agent m d'assurances
**insurance broker** n courtier m en assurances
**insurance company** n compagnie f or société f d'assurances
**insurance policy** n police f d'assurance
**insurance premium** n prime f d'assurance
**insure** [ɪn'ʃuər] vt assurer; **to ~ (o.s.) against** (fig) parer à; **to ~ sb/sb's life** assurer qn/la vie de qn; **to be ~d for £5000** être assuré(e) pour 5000 livres
**insured** [ɪn'ʃuəd] n: **the ~** l'assuré(e)
**insurer** [ɪn'ʃuərər] n assureur m
**insurgent** [ɪn'sə:dʒənt] adj, n insurgé(e)
**insurmountable** [ɪnsə'mauntəbl] adj insurmontable
**insurrection** [ɪnsə'rekʃən] n insurrection f
**intact** [ɪn'tækt] adj intact(e)
**intake** ['ɪnteɪk] n (Tech) admission f; (consumption) consommation f; (Brit Scol): **an ~ of 200 a year** 200 admissions par an
**intangible** [ɪn'tændʒɪbl] adj intangible; (assets) immatériel(le)
**integral** ['ɪntɪgrəl] adj (whole) intégral(e); (part) intégrant(e)
**integrate** ['ɪntɪgreɪt] vt intégrer ▷ vi s'intégrer
**integrated circuit** ['ɪntɪgreɪtɪd-] n (Comput) circuit intégré
**integration** [ɪntɪ'greɪʃən] n intégration f; **racial ~** intégration raciale
**integrity** [ɪn'tɛgrɪtɪ] n intégrité f
**intellect** ['ɪntəlɛkt] n intelligence f
**intellectual** [ɪntə'lɛktjuəl] adj, n intellectuel(le)
**intelligence** [ɪn'tɛlɪdʒəns] n intelligence f; (Mil) informations fpl, renseignements mpl
**intelligence quotient** n quotient intellectuel
**Intelligence Service** n services mpl de renseignements
**intelligence test** n test m d'intelligence
**intelligent** [ɪn'tɛlɪdʒənt] adj intelligent(e)
**intelligently** [ɪn'tɛlɪdʒəntlɪ] adv intelligemment
**intelligible** [ɪn'tɛlɪdʒɪbl] adj intelligible
**intemperate** [ɪn'tɛmpərət] adj immodéré(e); (drinking too much) adonné(e) à la boisson
**intend** [ɪn'tɛnd] vt (gift etc) **to ~ sth for** destiner qch à; **to ~ to do** avoir l'intention de faire
**intended** [ɪn'tɛndɪd] adj (insult) intentionnel(le); (journey) projeté(e); (effect) voulu(e)
**intense** [ɪn'tɛns] adj intense; (person) véhément(e)

**intensely** [ɪn'tɛnslɪ] adv intensément; (moving) profondément
**intensify** [ɪn'tɛnsɪfaɪ] vt intensifier
**intensity** [ɪn'tɛnsɪtɪ] n intensité f
**intensive** [ɪn'tɛnsɪv] adj intensif(-ive)
**intensive care** n: **to be in ~** être en réanimation
**intensive care unit** n service m de réanimation
**intent** [ɪn'tɛnt] n intention f ▷ adj attentif(-ive), absorbé(e); **to all ~s and purposes** en fait, pratiquement; **to be ~ on doing sth** être (bien) décidé à faire qch
**intention** [ɪn'tɛnʃən] n intention f
**intentional** [ɪn'tɛnʃənl] adj intentionnel(le), délibéré(e)
**intently** [ɪn'tɛntlɪ] adv attentivement
**inter** [ɪn'tə:r] vt enterrer
**interact** [ɪntər'ækt] vi avoir une action réciproque; (people) communiquer
**interaction** [ɪntər'ækʃən] n interaction f
**interactive** [ɪntər'æktɪv] adj (group) interactif(-ive); (Comput) interactif, conversationnel(le)
**intercede** [ɪntə'si:d] vi: **to ~ with sb/on behalf of sb** intercéder auprès de qn/en faveur de qn
**intercept** [ɪntə'sɛpt] vt intercepter; (person) arrêter au passage
**interception** [ɪntə'sɛpʃən] n interception f
**interchange** n ['ɪntətʃeɪndʒ] (exchange) échange m; (on motorway) échangeur m ▷ vt [ɪntə'tʃeɪndʒ] échanger; mettre à la place l'un(e) de l'autre
**interchangeable** [ɪntə'tʃeɪndʒəbl] adj interchangeable
**intercity** [ɪntə'sɪtɪ] adj: **~ (train)** train m rapide
**intercom** ['ɪntəkəm] n interphone m
**interconnect** [ɪntəkə'nɛkt] vi (rooms) communiquer
**intercontinental** ['ɪntəkɔntɪ'nɛntl] adj intercontinental(e)
**intercourse** ['ɪntəkɔ:s] n rapports mpl; **sexual ~** rapports sexuels
**interdependent** [ɪntədɪ'pɛndənt] adj interdépendant(e)
**interest** ['ɪntrɪst] n intérêt m; (Comm: stake, share) participation f, intérêts mpl ▷ vt intéresser; **compound/simple ~** intérêt composé/simple; **British ~s in the Middle East** les intérêts britanniques au Moyen-Orient; **his main ~ is …** ce qui l'intéresse le plus est …
**interested** ['ɪntrɪstɪd] adj intéressé(e); **to be ~ in sth** s'intéresser à qch; **I'm ~ in going** ça m'intéresse d'y aller
**interest-free** ['ɪntrɪst'fri:] adj sans intérêt
**interesting** ['ɪntrɪstɪŋ] adj intéressant(e)
**interest rate** n taux m d'intérêt
**interface** ['ɪntəfeɪs] n (Comput) interface f
**interfere** [ɪntə'fɪər] vi: **to ~ in** (quarrel) s'immiscer dans; (other people's business) se mêler de; **to ~ with** (object) tripoter, toucher à; (plans) contrecarrer; (duty) être en conflit avec; **don't ~ ** mêlez-vous de vos affaires
**interference** [ɪntə'fɪərəns] n (gen) ingérence f; (Physics) interférence f; (Radio, TV) parasites mpl

**interfering** [ɪntə'fɪərɪŋ] *adj* importun(e)
**interim** ['ɪntərɪm] *adj* provisoire; *(post)*
intérimaire ⊳ *n*: **in the** ~ dans l'intérim
**interior** [ɪn'tɪərɪəʳ] *n* intérieur *m* ⊳ *adj*
intérieur(e); *(minister, department)* de l'intérieur
**interior decorator, interior designer** *n*
décorateur(-trice) d'intérieur
**interior design** *n* architecture *f* d'intérieur
**interjection** [ɪntə'dʒɛkʃən] *n* interjection *f*
**interlock** [ɪntə'lɔk] *vi* s'enclencher ⊳ *vt*
enclencher
**interloper** ['ɪntələupəʳ] *n* intrus(e)
**interlude** ['ɪntəluːd] *n* intervalle *m*; *(Theat)*
intermède *m*
**intermarry** [ɪntə'mærɪ] *vi* former des alliances
entre familles *(or* tribus*)*; former des unions
consanguines
**intermediary** [ɪntə'miːdɪərɪ] *n* intermédiaire
*m/f*
**intermediate** [ɪntə'miːdɪət] *adj* intermédiaire;
*(Scol: course, level)* moyen(ne)
**interment** [ɪn'təːmənt] *n* inhumation *f*,
enterrement *m*
**interminable** [ɪn'təːmɪnəbl] *adj* sans fin,
interminable
**intermission** [ɪntə'mɪʃən] *n* pause *f*; *(Theat, Cine)*
entracte *m*
**intermittent** [ɪntə'mɪtnt] *adj* intermittent(e)
**intermittently** [ɪntə'mɪtntlɪ] *adv* par
intermittence, par intervalles
**intern** *vt* [ɪn'təːn] interner ⊳ *n* ['ɪntəːn] *(US)*
interne *m/f*
**internal** [ɪn'təːnl] *adj* interne; *(dispute, reform etc)*
intérieur(e); ~ **injuries** lésions *fpl* internes
**internally** [ɪn'təːnəlɪ] *adv* intérieurement; **"not
to be taken ~"** "pour usage externe"
**Internal Revenue Service** *n (US)* fisc *m*
**international** [ɪntə'næʃənl] *adj* international(e)
⊳ *n (Brit Sport)* international *m*
**International Atomic Energy Agency** *n*
Agence Internationale de l'Énergie Atomique
**International Court of Justice** *n* Cour
internationale de justice
**international date line** *n* ligne *f* de
changement de date
**internationally** [ɪntə'næʃnəlɪ] *adv* dans le
monde entier
**International Monetary Fund** *n* Fonds
monétaire international
**international relations** *npl* relations
internationales
**internecine** [ɪntə'niːsaɪn] *adj* mutuellement
destructeur(-trice)
**internee** [ɪntəː'niː] *n* interné(e)
**Internet** [ɪntə'nɛt] *n*: **the** ~ l'Internet *m*
**Internet café** *n* cybercafé *m*
**Internet Service Provider** *n* fournisseur *m*
d'accès à Internet
**Internet user** *n* internaute *m/f*
**internment** [ɪn'təːnmənt] *n* internement *m*
**interplay** ['ɪntəpleɪ] *n* effet *m* réciproque, jeu *m*
**Interpol** ['ɪntəpɔl] *n* Interpol *m*

**interpret** [ɪn'təːprɪt] *vt* interpréter ⊳ *vi* servir
d'interprète
**interpretation** [ɪntəːprɪ'teɪʃən] *n*
interprétation *f*
**interpreter** [ɪn'təːprɪtəʳ] *n* interprète *m/f*; **could
you act as an ~ for us?** pourriez-vous nous
servir d'interprète?
**interpreting** [ɪn'təːprɪtɪŋ] *n (profession)*
interprétariat *m*
**interrelated** [ɪntərɪ'leɪtɪd] *adj* en corrélation, en
rapport étroit
**interrogate** [ɪn'tɛrəugeɪt] *vt* interroger; *(suspect
etc)* soumettre à un interrogatoire
**interrogation** [ɪntɛrəu'geɪʃən] *n* interrogation
*f*; *(by police)* interrogatoire *m*
**interrogative** [ɪntə'rɔɡətɪv] *adj*
interrogateur(-trice) ⊳ *n (Ling)* interrogatif *m*
**interrogator** [ɪn'tɛrəɡeɪtəʳ] *n*
interrogateur(-trice)
**interrupt** [ɪntə'rʌpt] *vt, vi* interrompre
**interruption** [ɪntə'rʌpʃən] *n* interruption *f*
**intersect** [ɪntə'sɛkt] *vt* couper, croiser; *(Math)*
intersecter ⊳ *vi* se croiser, se couper;
s'intersecter
**intersection** [ɪntə'sɛkʃən] *n* intersection *f*; *(of
roads)* croisement *m*
**intersperse** [ɪntə'spəːs] *vt*: **to ~ with** parsemer
de
**interstate** ['ɪntərsteɪt] *(US) n* autoroute *f* (qui
relie plusieurs États)
**intertwine** [ɪntə'twaɪn] *vt* entrelacer ⊳ *vi*
s'entrelacer
**interval** ['ɪntəvl] *n* intervalle *m*; *(Brit: Theat)*
entracte *m*; (: *Sport)* mi-temps *f*; **bright ~s** (in
weather) éclaircies *fpl*; **at ~s** par intervalles
**intervene** [ɪntə'viːn] *vi (time)* s'écouler (entre-
temps); *(event)* survenir; *(person)* intervenir
**intervention** [ɪntə'vɛnʃən] *n* intervention *f*
**interview** ['ɪntəvjuː] *n (Radio, TV)* interview *f*;
*(for job)* entrevue *f* ⊳ *vt* interviewer, avoir une
entrevue avec
**interviewee** [ɪntəvjuː'iː] *n (for job)* candidat *m (qui
passe un entretien)*; *(TV etc)* invité(e), personne
interviewée
**interviewer** ['ɪntəvjuəʳ] *n (Radio, TV)*
interviewer *m*
**intestate** [ɪn'tɛsteɪt] *adj* intestat *f inv*
**intestinal** [ɪn'tɛstɪnl] *adj* intestinal(e)
**intestine** [ɪn'tɛstɪn] *n* intestin *m*; **large ~** gros
intestin; **small ~** intestin grêle
**intimacy** ['ɪntɪməsɪ] *n* intimité *f*
**intimate** *adj* ['ɪntɪmət] intime; *(friendship)*
profond(e); *(knowledge)* approfondi(e) ⊳ *vt*
['ɪntɪmeɪt] suggérer, laisser entendre;
*(announce)* faire savoir
**intimately** ['ɪntɪmətlɪ] *adv* intimement
**intimation** [ɪntɪ'meɪʃən] *n* annonce *f*
**intimidate** [ɪn'tɪmɪdeɪt] *vt* intimider
**intimidating** [ɪn'tɪmɪdeɪtɪŋ] *adj* intimidant(e)
**intimidation** [ɪntɪmɪ'deɪʃən] *n* intimidation *f*
**into** ['ɪntu] *prep* dans; ~ **pieces/French** en
morceaux/français; **to change pounds ~**

**dollars** changer des livres en dollars; **3 ~ 9 goes 3** 9 divisé par 3 donne 3; **she's ~ opera** c'est une passionnée d'opéra

**intolerable** [ɪn'tɔlərəbl] *adj* intolérable

**intolerance** [ɪn'tɔlərns] *n* intolérance *f*

**intolerant** [ɪn'tɔlərnt] *adj*: ~ **(of)** intolérant(e) (de); (*Med*) intolérant (à)

**intonation** [ɪntəu'neɪʃən] *n* intonation *f*

**intoxicate** [ɪn'tɔksɪkeɪt] *vt* enivrer

**intoxicated** [ɪn'tɔksɪkeɪtɪd] *adj* ivre

**intoxication** [ɪntɔksɪ'keɪʃən] *n* ivresse *f*

**intractable** [ɪn'træktəbl] *adj* (*child, temper*) indocile, insoumis(e); (*problem*) insoluble; (*illness*) incurable

**intranet** [ɪn'trənɛt] *n* intranet *m*

**intransigent** [ɪn'trænsɪdʒənt] *adj* intransigeant(e)

**intransitive** [ɪn'trænsɪtɪv] *adj* intransitif(-ive)

**intra-uterine device** ['ɪntrə'juːtəraɪn-] *n* dispositif intra-utérin, stérilet *m*

**intravenous** [ɪntrə'viːnəs] *adj* intraveineux(-euse)

**in-tray** ['ɪntreɪ] *n* courrier *m* "arrivée"

**intrepid** [ɪn'trɛpɪd] *adj* intrépide

**intricacy** ['ɪntrɪkəsɪ] *n* complexité *f*

**intricate** ['ɪntrɪkət] *adj* complexe, compliqué(e)

**intrigue** [ɪn'triːg] *n* intrigue *f* ▷ *vt* intriguer ▷ *vi* intriguer, comploter

**intriguing** [ɪn'triːgɪŋ] *adj* fascinant(e)

**intrinsic** [ɪn'trɪnsɪk] *adj* intrinsèque

**introduce** [ɪntrə'djuːs] *vt* introduire; **to ~ sb (to sb)** présenter qn (à qn); **to ~ sb to** (*pastime, technique*) initier qn à; **may I ~ ...?** je vous présente ...

**introduction** [ɪntrə'dʌkʃən] *n* introduction *f*; (*of person*) présentation *f*; (*to new experience*) initiation *f*; **a letter of ~** une lettre de recommandation

**introductory** [ɪntrə'dʌktərɪ] *adj* préliminaire, introductif(-ive); **~ remarks** remarques *fpl* liminaires; **an ~ offer** une offre de lancement

**introspection** [ɪntrəu'spɛkʃən] *n* introspection *f*

**introspective** [ɪntrəu'spɛktɪv] *adj* introspectif(-ive)

**introvert** ['ɪntrəuvəːt] *adj, n* introverti(e)

**intrude** [ɪn'truːd] *vi* (*person*) être importun(e); **to ~ on** *or* **into** (*conversation etc*) s'immiscer dans; **am I intruding?** est-ce que je vous dérange?

**intruder** [ɪn'truːdəᵉ] *n* intrus(e)

**intrusion** [ɪn'truːʒən] *n* intrusion *f*

**intrusive** [ɪn'truːsɪv] *adj* importun(e), gênant(e)

**intuition** [ɪntjuː'ɪʃən] *n* intuition *f*

**intuitive** [ɪn'tjuːɪtɪv] *adj* intuitif(-ive)

**inundate** ['ɪnʌndeɪt] *vt*: **to ~ with** inonder de

**inure** [ɪn'juəᵉ] *vt*: **to ~ (to)** habituer (à)

**invade** [ɪn'veɪd] *vt* envahir

**invader** [ɪn'veɪdəᵉ] *n* envahisseur *m*

**invalid** *n* ['ɪnvəlɪd] malade *m/f*; (*with disability*) invalide *m/f* ▷ *adj* [ɪn'vælɪd] (*not valid*) invalide, non valide

**invalidate** [ɪn'vælɪdeɪt] *vt* invalider, annuler

**invalid chair** ['ɪnvəlɪd-] *n* (*Brit*) fauteuil *m* d'infirme

**invaluable** [ɪn'væljuəbl] *adj* inestimable, inappréciable

**invariable** [ɪn'vɛərɪəbl] *adj* invariable; (*fig*) immanquable

**invariably** [ɪn'vɛərɪəblɪ] *adv* invariablement; **she is ~ late** elle est toujours en retard

**invasion** [ɪn'veɪʒən] *n* invasion *f*

**invective** [ɪn'vɛktɪv] *n* invective *f*

**inveigle** [ɪn'viːgl] *vt*: **to ~ sb into (doing) sth** amener qn à (faire) qch (par la ruse *or* la flatterie)

**invent** [ɪn'vɛnt] *vt* inventer

**invention** [ɪn'vɛnʃən] *n* invention *f*

**inventive** [ɪn'vɛntɪv] *adj* inventif(-ive)

**inventiveness** [ɪn'vɛntɪvnɪs] *n* esprit inventif *or* d'invention

**inventor** [ɪn'vɛntəᵉ] *n* inventeur(-trice)

**inventory** ['ɪnvəntrɪ] *n* inventaire *m*

**inventory control** *n* (*Comm*) contrôle *m* des stocks

**inverse** [ɪn'vəːs] *adj* inverse ▷ *n* inverse *m*, contraire *m*; **in ~ proportion (to)** inversement proportionnel(le) (à)

**inversely** [ɪn'vəːslɪ] *adv* inversement

**invert** [ɪn'vəːt] *vt* intervertir; (*cup, object*) retourner

**invertebrate** [ɪn'vəːtɪbrət] *n* invertébré *m*

**inverted commas** [ɪn'vəːtɪd-] *npl* (*Brit*) guillemets *mpl*

**invest** [ɪn'vɛst] *vt* investir; (*endow*): **to ~ sb with sth** conférer qch à qn ▷ *vi* faire un investissement, investir; **to ~ in** placer de l'argent *or* investir dans; (*fig: acquire*) s'offrir, faire l'acquisition de

**investigate** [ɪn'vɛstɪgeɪt] *vt* étudier, examiner; (*crime*) faire une enquête sur

**investigation** [ɪnvɛstɪ'geɪʃən] *n* examen *m*; (*of crime*) enquête *f*, investigation *f*

**investigative** [ɪn'vɛstɪgeɪtɪv] *adj*: ~ **journalism** enquête-reportage *f*, journalisme *m* d'enquête

**investigator** [ɪn'vɛstɪgeɪtəᵉ] *n* investigateur(-trice); **private ~** détective privé

**investiture** [ɪn'vɛstɪtʃəᵉ] *n* investiture *f*

**investment** [ɪn'vɛstmənt] *n* investissement *m*, placement *m*

**investment income** *n* revenu *m* de placement

**investment trust** *n* société *f* d'investissements

**investor** [ɪn'vɛstəᵉ] *n* épargnant(e); (*shareholder*) actionnaire *m/f*

**inveterate** [ɪn'vɛtərət] *adj* invétéré(e)

**invidious** [ɪn'vɪdɪəs] *adj* injuste; (*task*) déplaisant(e)

**invigilate** [ɪn'vɪdʒɪleɪt] (*Brit*) *vt* surveiller ▷ *vi* être de surveillance

**invigilator** [ɪn'vɪdʒɪleɪtəᵉ] *n* (*Brit*) surveillant *m* (d'examen)

**invigorating** [ɪn'vɪgəreɪtɪŋ] *adj* vivifiant(e), stimulant(e)

**invincible** [ɪn'vɪnsɪbl] *adj* invincible

**inviolate** [ɪn'vaɪələt] *adj* inviolé(e)

**invisible** [ɪn'vɪzɪbl] *adj* invisible
**invisible assets** *npl* (*Brit*) actif incorporel
**invisible ink** *n* encre *f* sympathique
**invisible mending** *n* stoppage *m*
**invitation** [ɪnvɪ'teɪʃən] *n* invitation *f*; **by ~ only**
   sur invitation; **at sb's ~** à la demande de qn
**invite** [ɪn'vaɪt] *vt* inviter; (*opinions etc*)
   demander; (*trouble*) chercher; **to ~ sb (to do)**
   inviter qn (à faire); **to ~ sb to dinner** inviter qn
   à dîner
   ▶ **invite out** *vt* inviter (à sortir)
   ▶ **invite over** *vt* inviter (chez soi)
**inviting** [ɪn'vaɪtɪŋ] *adj* engageant(e),
   attrayant(e); (*gesture*) encourageant(e)
**invoice** ['ɪnvɔɪs] *n* facture *f* ▷ *vt* facturer; **to ~ sb**
   **for goods** facturer des marchandises à qn
**invoke** [ɪn'vəuk] *vt* invoquer
**involuntary** [ɪn'vɔləntrɪ] *adj* involontaire
**involve** [ɪn'vɔlv] *vt* (*entail*) impliquer; (*concern*)
   concerner; (*require*) nécessiter; **to ~ sb in** (*theft*
   *etc*) impliquer qn dans; (*activity, meeting*) faire
   participer qn à
**involved** [ɪn'vɔlvd] *adj* (*complicated*) complexe;
   **to be ~ in** (*take part*) participer à; (*be engrossed*)
   être plongé(e) dans; **to feel ~** se sentir
   concerné(e); **to become ~ in** (*in love etc*) s'engager
**involvement** [ɪn'vɔlvmənt] *n* (*personal role*) rôle
   *m*; (*participation*) participation *f*; (*enthusiasm*)
   enthousiasme *m*; (*of resources, funds*) mise *f* en jeu
**invulnerable** [ɪn'vʌlnərəbl] *adj* invulnérable
**inward** ['ɪnwəd] *adj* (*movement*) vers l'intérieur;
   (*thought*) profond(e), intime ▷ *adv* = **inwards**
**inwardly** ['ɪnwədlɪ] *adv* (*feel, think etc*)
   secrètement, en son for intérieur
**inwards** ['ɪnwədz] *adv* vers l'intérieur
**I/O** *abbr* (*Comput*: = *input/output*) E/S
**IOC** *n abbr* (= *International Olympic Committee*) CIO *m*
   (= *Comité international olympique*)
**iodine** ['aɪəudiːn] *n* iode *m*
**IOM** *abbr* = **Isle of Man**
**ion** ['aɪən] *n* ion *m*
**Ionian Sea** [aɪ'əunɪən-] *n*: **the ~** la mer Ionienne
**ioniser** ['aɪənaɪzər] *n* ioniseur *m*
**iota** [aɪ'əutə] *n* (*fig*) brin *m*, grain *m*
**IOU** *n abbr* (= *I owe you*) reconnaissance *f* de dette
**IOW** *abbr* (*Brit*) = **Isle of Wight**
**IPA** *n abbr* (= *International Phonetic Alphabet*) A.P.I *m*
**iPod**® ['aɪpɔd] *n* iPod® *m*
**IQ** *n abbr* (= *intelligence quotient*) Q.I. *m*
**IRA** *n abbr* (= *Irish Republican Army*) IRA *f*; (*US*)
   = **individual retirement account**
**Iran** [ɪ'rɑːn] *n* Iran *m*
**Iranian** [ɪ'reɪnɪən] *adj* iranien(ne) ▷ *n*
   Iranien(ne); (*Ling*) iranien *m*
**Iraq** [ɪ'rɑːk] *n* Irak *m*
**Iraqi** [ɪ'rɑːkɪ] *adj* irakien(ne) ▷ *n* Irakien(ne)
**irascible** [ɪ'ræsɪbl] *adj* irascible
**irate** [aɪ'reɪt] *adj* courroucé(e)
**Ireland** ['aɪələnd] *n* Irlande *f*; **Republic of ~**
   République *f* d'Irlande
**iris, irises** ['aɪrɪs, -ɪz] *n* iris *m*
**Irish** ['aɪrɪʃ] *adj* irlandais(e) ▷ *npl*: **the ~** les

Irlandais ▷ *n* (*Ling*) irlandais *m*; **the Irish** *npl* les
   Irlandais
**Irishman** ['aɪrɪʃmən] (*irreg*) *n* Irlandais *m*
**Irish Sea** *n*: **the ~** la mer d'Irlande
**Irishwoman** ['aɪrɪʃwumən] (*irreg*) *n* Irlandaise *f*
**irk** [əːk] *vt* ennuyer
**irksome** ['əːksəm] *adj* ennuyeux(-euse)
**IRN** *n abbr* (= *Independent Radio News*) agence de presse
   radiophonique
**IRO** *n abbr* (*US*) = **International Refugee**
   **Organization**
**iron** ['aɪən] *n* fer *m*; (*for clothes*) fer *m* à repasser
   ▷ *adj* de or en fer ▷ *vt* (*clothes*) repasser; **irons** *npl*
   (*chains*) fers *mpl*, chaînes *fpl*
   ▶ **iron out** *vt* (*crease*) faire disparaître au fer;
   (*fig*) aplanir; faire disparaître
**Iron Curtain** *n*: **the ~** le rideau de fer
**iron foundry** *n* fonderie *f* de fonte
**ironic** [aɪ'rɔnɪk], **ironical** [aɪ'rɔnɪkl] *adj*
   ironique
**ironically** [aɪ'rɔnɪklɪ] *adv* ironiquement
**ironing** ['aɪənɪŋ] *n* (*activity*) repassage *m*; (*clothes*:
   *ironed*) linge repassé; (: *to be ironed*) linge à
   repasser
**ironing board** *n* planche *f* à repasser
**ironmonger** ['aɪənmʌŋgər] *n* (*Brit*) quincaillier
   *m*; **~'s (shop)** quincaillerie *f*
**iron ore** *n* minerai *m* de fer
**ironworks** ['aɪənwəːks] *n* usine *f* sidérurgique
**irony** ['aɪrənɪ] *n* ironie *f*
**irrational** [ɪ'ræʃənl] *adj* irrationnel(le); (*person*)
   qui n'est pas rationnel
**irreconcilable** [ɪrɛkən'saɪləbl] *adj*
   irréconciliable; (*opinion*): **~ with** inconciliable
   avec
**irredeemable** [ɪrɪ'diːməbl] *adj* (*Comm*) non
   remboursable
**irrefutable** [ɪrɪ'fjuːtəbl] *adj* irréfutable
**irregular** [ɪ'rɛgjulər] *adj* irrégulier(-ière);
   (*surface*) inégal(e); (*action, event*) peu orthodoxe
**irregularity** [ɪrɛgju'lærɪtɪ] *n* irrégularité *f*
**irrelevance** [ɪ'rɛləvəns] *n* manque *m* de rapport
   *or* d'à-propos
**irrelevant** [ɪ'rɛləvənt] *adj* sans rapport, hors de
   propos
**irreligious** [ɪrɪ'lɪdʒəs] *adj* irréligieux(-euse)
**irreparable** [ɪ'rɛprəbl] *adj* irréparable
**irreplaceable** [ɪrɪ'pleɪsəbl] *adj* irremplaçable
**irrepressible** [ɪrɪ'prɛsəbl] *adj* irrépressible
**irreproachable** [ɪrɪ'prəutʃəbl] *adj* irréprochable
**irresistible** [ɪrɪ'zɪstɪbl] *adj* irrésistible
**irresolute** [ɪ'rɛzəluːt] *adj* irrésolu(e), indécis(e)
**irrespective** [ɪrɪ'spɛktɪv]: **~ of** *prep* sans tenir
   compte de
**irresponsible** [ɪrɪ'spɔnsɪbl] *adj* (*act*)
   irréfléchi(e); (*person*) qui n'a pas le sens des
   responsabilités
**irretrievable** [ɪrɪ'triːvəbl] *adj* irréparable,
   irrémédiable; (*object*) introuvable
**irreverent** [ɪ'rɛvərnt] *adj* irrévérencieux(-euse)
**irrevocable** [ɪ'rɛvəkəbl] *adj* irrévocable
**irrigate** ['ɪrɪgeɪt] *vt* irriguer

**irrigation** [ɪrɪ'geɪʃən] n irrigation f
**irritable** ['ɪrɪtəbl] adj irritable
**irritate** ['ɪrɪteɪt] vt irriter
**irritating** ['ɪrɪteɪtɪŋ] adj irritant(e)
**irritation** [ɪrɪ'teɪʃən] n irritation f
**IRS** n abbr (US) = **Internal Revenue Service**
**is** [ɪz] vb see **be**
**ISA** n abbr (Brit: = Individual Savings Account) plan m
d'épargne défiscalisé
**ISBN** n abbr (= International Standard Book Number)
ISBN m
**ISDN** n abbr (= Integrated Services Digital Network)
RNIS m
**Islam** ['ɪzlɑːm] n Islam m
**Islamic** [ɪz'lɑːmɪk] adj islamique; ~
**fundamentalists** intégristes mpl musulmans
**island** ['aɪlənd] n île f; (also: **traffic island**)
refuge m (pour piétons)
**islander** ['aɪləndəʳ] n habitant(e) d'une île,
insulaire m/f
**isle** [aɪl] n île f
**isn't** ['ɪznt] = **is not**
**isolate** ['aɪsəleɪt] vt isoler
**isolated** ['aɪsəleɪtɪd] adj isolé(e)
**isolation** [aɪsə'leɪʃən] n isolement m
**ISP** n abbr = **Internet Service Provider**
**Israel** ['ɪzreɪl] n Israël m
**Israeli** [ɪz'reɪlɪ] adj israélien(ne) ▷ n
Israélien(ne)
**issue** ['ɪʃuː] n question f, problème m; (outcome)
résultat m, issue f; (of banknotes) émission f; (of
newspaper) numéro m; (of book) publication f,
parution f; (offspring) descendance f ▷ vt (rations,
equipment) distribuer; (orders) donner; (statement)
publier, faire; (certificate, passport) délivrer; (book)
faire paraître; publier; (banknotes, cheques,
stamps) émettre, mettre en circulation ▷ vi: **to ~
from** provenir de; **at ~** en jeu, en cause; **to
avoid the ~** éluder le problème; **to take ~ with
sb (over sth)** exprimer son désaccord avec qn
(sur qch); **to make an ~ of sth** faire de qch un
problème; **to confuse** or **obscure the ~**
embrouiller la question
**Istanbul** [ɪstæn'buːl] n Istamboul, Istanbul
**isthmus** ['ɪsməs] n isthme m
**IT** n abbr = **information technology**

⬤ KEYWORD

**it** [ɪt] pron **1** (specific: subject) il (elle); (: direct object)
le (la, l'); (: indirect object) lui; **it's on the table**
c'est or il (or elle) est sur la table; **I can't find it**
je n'arrive pas à le trouver; **give it to me**
donne-le-moi
**2** (after prep): **about/from/of it** en; **I spoke to
him about it** je lui en ai parlé; **what did you
learn from it?** qu'est-ce que vous en avez
retiré?; **I'm proud of it** j'en suis fier; **I've
come from it** j'en viens; **in/to it** y; **put the
book in it** mettez-y le livre; **it's on it** c'est
dessus; **he agreed to it** il y a consenti; **did you
go to it?** (party, concert etc) est-ce que vous y êtes

allé(s)?; **above it, over it** (au-)dessus; **below it,
under it** (en-)dessous; **in front of/behind it**
devant/derrière
**3** (impersonal) il; ce, cela, ça; **it's raining** il pleut;
**it's Friday tomorrow** demain, c'est vendredi
or nous sommes, vendredi; **it's 6 o'clock** il est 6
heures; **how far is it? — it's 10 miles** c'est
loin? — c'est à 10 miles; **it's 2 hours by train**
c'est à 2 heures de train; **who is it? — it's me**
qui est-ce? — c'est moi

**ITA** n abbr (Brit: = initial teaching alphabet) alphabet
en partie phonétique utilisé pour l'enseignement de la
lecture
**Italian** [ɪ'tæljən] adj italien(ne) ▷ n Italien(ne);
(Ling) italien m
**italic** [ɪ'tælɪk] adj italique
**italics** [ɪ'tælɪks] npl italique m
**Italy** ['ɪtəlɪ] n Italie f
**itch** [ɪtʃ] n démangeaison f ▷ vi (person) éprouver
des démangeaisons; (part of body) démanger;
**I'm ~ing to do** l'envie me démange de faire
**itchy** ['ɪtʃɪ] adj qui démange; **my back is ~** j'ai le
dos qui me démange
**it'd** ['ɪtd] = **it would; it had**
**item** ['aɪtəm] n (gen) article m; (on agenda)
question f, point m; (in programme) numéro m;
(also: **news item**) nouvelle f; **~s of clothing**
articles vestimentaires
**itemize** ['aɪtəmaɪz] vt détailler, spécifier
**itemized bill** ['aɪtəmaɪzd-] n facture détaillée
**itinerant** [ɪ'tɪnərənt] adj itinérant(e); (musician)
ambulant(e)
**itinerary** [aɪ'tɪnərərɪ] n itinéraire m
**it'll** ['ɪtl] = **it will; it shall**
**ITN** n abbr (Brit: = Independent Television News) chaîne
de télévision commerciale
**its** [ɪts] adj son (sa), ses pl ▷ pron le (la) sien(ne),
les siens (siennes)
**it's** [ɪts] = **it is; it has**
**itself** [ɪt'self] pron (reflexive) se; (emphatic) lui-
même (elle-même)
**ITV** n abbr (Brit: = Independent Television) chaîne de
télévision commerciale
**IUD** n abbr = **intra-uterine device**
**I've** [aɪv] = **I have**
**ivory** ['aɪvərɪ] n ivoire m
**Ivory Coast** n Côte f d'Ivoire
**ivy** ['aɪvɪ] n lierre m
**Ivy League** n (US) voir article

⬤ **IVY LEAGUE**
⬤
⬤ L'Ivy League regroupe les huit universités les
⬤ plus prestigieuses du nord-est des États-
⬤ Unis, ainsi surnommées à cause de leurs
⬤ murs recouverts de lierre. Elles organisent
⬤ des compétitions sportives entre elles. Ces
⬤ universités sont: Brown, Columbia, Cornell,
⬤ Dartmouth College, Harvard, Princeton,
⬤ l'université de Pennsylvanie et Yale.

# J j

**J, j** [dʒeɪ] *n* (*letter*) J, j *m*; **J for Jack**, (US) **J for Jig** J comme Joseph
**JA** *n abbr* = **judge advocate**
**J/A** *n abbr* = **joint account**
**jab** [dʒæb] *vt*: **to ~ sth into** enfoncer *or* planter qch dans ▷ *n* coup *m*; (*Med: inf*) piqûre *f*
**jabber** ['dʒæbəʳ] *vt, vi* bredouiller, baragouiner
**jack** [dʒæk] *n* (*Aut*) cric *m*; (*Bowls*) cochonnet *m*; (*Cards*) valet *m*
▸ **jack in** *vt* (*inf*) laisser tomber
▸ **jack up** *vt* soulever (au cric)
**jackal** ['dʒækl] *n* chacal *m*
**jackass** ['dʒækæs] *n* (*also fig*) âne *m*
**jackdaw** ['dʒækdɔ:] *n* choucas *m*
**jacket** ['dʒækɪt] *n* veste *f*, veston *m*; (*of boiler etc*) enveloppe *f*; (*of book*) couverture *f*, jaquette *f*
**jacket potato** *n* pomme *f* de terre en robe des champs
**jack-in-the-box** ['dʒækɪnðəbɔks] *n* diable *m* à ressort
**jackknife** ['dʒæknaɪf] *n* couteau *m* de poche ▷ *vi*: **the lorry ~d** la remorque (du camion) s'est mise en travers
**jack-of-all-trades** ['dʒækəv'ɔ:ltreɪdz] *n* bricoleur *m*
**jack plug** *n* (*Brit*) jack *m*
**jackpot** ['dʒækpɔt] *n* gros lot
**Jacuzzi®** [dʒə'ku:zɪ] *n* jacuzzi® *m*
**jaded** ['dʒeɪdɪd] *adj* éreinté(e), fatigué(e)
**JAG** *n abbr* = **Judge Advocate General**
**jagged** ['dʒægɪd] *adj* dentelé(e)
**jaguar** ['dʒægjuəʳ] *n* jaguar *m*
**jail** [dʒeɪl] *n* prison *f* ▷ *vt* emprisonner, mettre en prison
**jailbird** ['dʒeɪlbə:d] *n* récidiviste *m/f*
**jailbreak** ['dʒeɪlbreɪk] *n* évasion *f*
**jailer** ['dʒeɪləʳ] *n* geôlier(-ière)
**jail sentence** *n* peine *f* de prison
**jalopy** [dʒə'lɔpɪ] *n* (*inf*) vieux clou
**jam** [dʒæm] *n* confiture *f*; (*of shoppers etc*) cohue *f*; (*also*: **traffic jam**) embouteillage *m* ▷ *vt* (*passage etc*) encombrer, obstruer; (*mechanism, drawer etc*) bloquer, coincer; (*Radio*) brouiller ▷ *vi* (*mechanism, sliding part*) se coincer, se bloquer; (*gun*) s'enrayer; **to be in a ~** (*inf*) être dans le pétrin; **to get sb out of a ~** (*inf*) sortir qn du

pétrin; **to ~ sth into** (*stuff*) entasser *or* comprimer qch dans; (*thrust*) enfoncer qch dans; **the telephone lines are ~med** les lignes (téléphoniques) sont encombrées
**Jamaica** [dʒə'meɪkə] *n* Jamaïque *f*
**Jamaican** [dʒə'meɪkən] *adj* jamaïquain(e) ▷ *n* Jamaïquain(e)
**jamb** ['dʒæm] *n* jambage *m*
**jam jar** *n* pot *m* à confiture
**jammed** [dʒæmd] *adj* (*window etc*) coincé(e)
**jam-packed** [dʒæm'pækt] *adj*: **~ (with)** bourré(e) (de)
**jam session** *n* jam session *f*
**jangle** ['dʒæŋgl] *vi* cliqueter
**janitor** ['dʒænɪtəʳ] *n* (*caretaker*) concierge *m*
**January** ['dʒænjuərɪ] *n* janvier *m*; *for phrases see also* **July**
**Japan** [dʒə'pæn] *n* Japon *m*
**Japanese** [dʒæpə'ni:z] *adj* japonais(e) ▷ *n* (*pl inv*) Japonais(e); (*Ling*) japonais *m*
**jar** [dʒɑːʳ] *n* (*stone, earthenware*) pot *m*; (*glass*) bocal *m* ▷ *vi* (*sound*) produire un son grinçant *or* discordant; (*colours etc*) détonner, jurer ▷ *vt* (*shake*) ébranler, secouer
**jargon** ['dʒɑːgən] *n* jargon *m*
**jarring** ['dʒɑːrɪŋ] *adj* (*sound, colour*) discordant(e)
**Jas.** *abbr* = **James**
**jasmin, jasmine** ['dʒæzmɪn] *n* jasmin *m*
**jaundice** ['dʒɔ:ndɪs] *n* jaunisse *f*
**jaundiced** ['dʒɔ:ndɪst] *adj* (*fig*) envieux(-euse), désapprobateur(-trice)
**jaunt** [dʒɔ:nt] *n* balade *f*
**jaunty** ['dʒɔ:ntɪ] *adj* enjoué(e), désinvolte
**Java** ['dʒɑ:və] *n* Java *f*
**javelin** ['dʒævlɪn] *n* javelot *m*
**jaw** [dʒɔ:] *n* mâchoire *f*
**jawbone** ['dʒɔ:bəun] *n* maxillaire *m*
**jay** [dʒeɪ] *n* geai *m*
**jaywalker** ['dʒeɪwɔ:kəʳ] *n* piéton indiscipliné
**jazz** [dʒæz] *n* jazz *m*
▸ **jazz up** *vt* animer, égayer
**jazz band** *n* orchestre *m* or groupe *m* de jazz
**jazzy** ['dʒæzɪ] *adj* bariolé(e), tapageur(-euse); (*beat*) de jazz
**JCB®** *n* excavatrice *f*
**JCS** *n abbr* (US) = **Joint Chiefs of Staff**

**JD** n abbr (US: = Doctor of Laws) titre universitaire; (= Justice Department) ministère de la Justice

**jealous** ['dʒeləs] adj jaloux(-ouse)

**jealously** ['dʒeləslɪ] adv jalousement

**jealousy** ['dʒeləsɪ] n jalousie f

**jeans** [dʒiːnz] npl jean m

**Jeep**® [dʒiːp] n jeep f

**jeer** [dʒɪəʳ] vi: **to ~ (at)** huer; se moquer cruellement (de), railler

**jeering** ['dʒɪərɪŋ] adj railleur(-euse), moqueur(-euse) ▷ n huées fpl

**jeers** ['dʒɪəz] npl huées fpl; sarcasmes mpl

**Jehovah's Witness** [dʒɪ'həʊvəz-] n témoin m de Jéhovah

**Jello**® ['dʒeləʊ] (US) n gelée f

**jelly** ['dʒelɪ] n (dessert) gelée f; (US: jam) confiture f

**jellyfish** ['dʒelɪfɪʃ] n méduse f

**jeopardize** ['dʒepədaɪz] vt mettre en danger or péril

**jeopardy** ['dʒepədɪ] n: **in ~** en danger or péril

**jerk** [dʒəːk] n (jolt) secousse f, saccade f; (of muscle) spasme m; (inf) pauvre type m ▷ vt (shake) donner une secousse à; (pull) tirer brusquement ▷ vi (vehicles) cahoter

**jerkin** ['dʒəːkɪn] n blouson m

**jerky** ['dʒəːkɪ] adj saccadé(e), cahotant(e)

**jerry-built** ['dʒerɪbɪlt] adj de mauvaise qualité

**jerry can** ['dʒerɪ-] n bidon m

**Jersey** ['dʒəːzɪ] n Jersey f

**jersey** ['dʒəːzɪ] n tricot m; (fabric) jersey m

**Jerusalem** [dʒə'ruːsləm] n Jérusalem

**jest** [dʒest] n plaisanterie f; **in ~** en plaisantant

**jester** ['dʒestəʳ] n (History) plaisantin m

**Jesus** ['dʒiːzəs] n Jésus; **~ Christ** Jésus-Christ

**jet** [dʒet] n (of gas, liquid) jet m; (Aut) gicleur m; (Aviat) avion m à réaction, jet m

**jet-black** ['dʒet'blæk] adj (d'un noir) de jais

**jet engine** n moteur m à réaction

**jet lag** n décalage m horaire

**jetsam** ['dʒetsəm] n objets jetés à la mer (et rejetés sur la côte)

**jet-setter** ['dʒetsetəʳ] n membre m du or de la jet set

**jet-ski** vi faire du jet-ski or scooter des mers

**jettison** ['dʒetɪsn] vt jeter par-dessus bord

**jetty** ['dʒetɪ] n jetée f, digue f

**Jew** [dʒuː] n Juif m

**jewel** ['dʒuːəl] n bijou m, joyau m; (in watch) rubis m

**jeweller, (US) jeweler** ['dʒuːələʳ] n bijoutier(-ière), joaillier m

**jeweller's, jeweller's shop** n (Brit) bijouterie f, joaillerie f

**jewellery, (US) jewelry** ['dʒuːəlrɪ] n bijoux mpl

**Jewess** ['dʒuːɪs] n Juive f

**Jewish** ['dʒuːɪʃ] adj juif (juive)

**JFK** n abbr (US) = **John Fitzgerald Kennedy International Airport**

**jib** [dʒɪb] n (Naut) foc m; (of crane) flèche f ▷ vi (horse) regimber; **to ~ at doing sth** rechigner à faire qch

**jibe** [dʒaɪb] n sarcasme m

**jiffy** ['dʒɪfɪ] n (inf): **in a ~** en un clin d'œil

**jig** [dʒɪg] n (dance, tune) gigue m

**jigsaw** ['dʒɪgsɔː] n (also: **jigsaw puzzle**) puzzle m; (tool) scie sauteuse

**jilt** [dʒɪlt] vt laisser tomber, plaquer

**jingle** ['dʒɪŋgl] n (advertising jingle) couplet m publicitaire ▷ vi cliqueter, tinter

**jingoism** ['dʒɪŋgəʊɪzəm] n chauvinisme m

**jinx** [dʒɪŋks] n (inf) (mauvais) sort

**jitters** ['dʒɪtəz] npl (inf): **to get the ~** avoir la trouille or la frousse

**jittery** ['dʒɪtərɪ] adj (inf) nerveux(-euse); **to be ~** avoir les nerfs en pelote

**jiujitsu** [dʒuː'dʒɪtsuː] n jiu-jitsu m

**job** [dʒɔb] n (chore, task) travail m, tâche f; (employment) emploi m, poste m, place f; **a part-time/full-time ~** un emploi à temps partiel/à plein temps; **he's only doing his ~** il fait son boulot; **it's a good ~ that ...** c'est heureux or c'est une chance que ... +sub; **just the ~!** (c'est) juste or exactement ce qu'il faut!

**jobber** ['dʒɔbəʳ] n (Brit Stock Exchange) négociant m en titres

**jobbing** ['dʒɔbɪŋ] adj (Brit: workman) à la tâche, à la journée

**job centre** ['dʒɔbsentəʳ] (Brit) n ≈ ANPE f, ≈ Agence nationale pour l'emploi

**job creation scheme** n plan m pour la création d'emplois

**job description** n description f du poste

**jobless** ['dʒɔblɪs] adj sans travail, au chômage ▷ npl: **the ~** les sans-emploi m inv, les chômeurs mpl

**job lot** n lot m (d'articles divers)

**job satisfaction** n satisfaction professionnelle

**job security** n sécurité f de l'emploi

**job specification** n caractéristiques fpl du poste

**Jock** [dʒɔk] n (inf: Scotsman) Écossais m

**jockey** ['dʒɔkɪ] n jockey m ▷ vi: **to ~ for position** manœuvrer pour être bien placé

**jockey box** n (US Aut) boîte f à gants, vide-poches m inv

**jockstrap** ['dʒɔkstræp] n slip m de sport

**jocular** ['dʒɔkjʊləʳ] adj jovial(e), enjoué(e); facétieux(-euse)

**jog** [dʒɔg] vt secouer ▷ vi (Sport) faire du jogging; **to ~ along** cahoter; trotter; **to ~ sb's memory** rafraîchir la mémoire de qn

**jogger** ['dʒɔgəʳ] n jogger m/f

**jogging** ['dʒɔgɪŋ] n jogging m

**john** [dʒɔn] n (US inf): **the ~** (toilet) les cabinets mpl

**join** [dʒɔɪn] vt (put together) unir, assembler; (become member of) s'inscrire à; (meet) rejoindre, retrouver; (queue) se joindre à ▷ vi (roads, rivers) se rejoindre, se rencontrer ▷ n raccord m; **will you ~ us for dinner?** vous dînerez bien avec nous?; **I'll ~ you later** je vous rejoindrai plus tard; **to ~ forces (with)** s'associer (à)

▸ **join in** vi se mettre de la partie ▷ vt fus se mêler à

▸ **join up** vi (meet) se rejoindre; (Mil) s'engager

**joiner** ['dʒɔɪnə<sup>r</sup>] (*Brit*) *n* menuisier *m*
**joinery** ['dʒɔɪnərɪ] *n* menuiserie *f*
**joint** [dʒɔɪnt] *n* (*Tech*) jointure *f*; joint *m*; (*Anat*) articulation *f*, jointure; (*Brit Culin*) rôti *m*; (*inf*: *place*) boîte *f*; (*of cannabis*) joint ▷ *adj* commun(e); (*committee*) mixte, paritaire; (*winner*) ex aequo; **~ responsibility** coresponsabilité *f*
**joint account** *n* compte joint
**jointly** ['dʒɔɪntlɪ] *adv* ensemble, en commun
**joint ownership** *n* copropriété *f*
**joint-stock company** ['dʒɔɪntstɔk-] *n* société *f* par actions
**joint venture** *n* entreprise commune
**joist** [dʒɔɪst] *n* solive *f*
**joke** [dʒəʊk] *n* plaisanterie *f*; (*also*: **practical joke**) farce *f* ▷ *vi* plaisanter; **to play a ~ on** jouer un tour à, faire une farce à
**joker** ['dʒəʊkə<sup>r</sup>] *n* plaisantin *m*, blagueur(-euse); (*Cards*) joker *m*
**joking** ['dʒəʊkɪŋ] *n* plaisanterie *f*
**jollity** ['dʒɔlɪtɪ] *n* réjouissances *fpl*, gaieté *f*
**jolly** ['dʒɔlɪ] *adj* gai(e), enjoué(e); (*enjoyable*) amusant(e), plaisant(e) ▷ *adv* (*Brit inf*) rudement, drôlement ▷ *vt* (*Brit*): **to ~ sb along** amadouer qn, convaincre *or* entraîner qn à force d'encouragements; **~ good!** (*Brit*) formidable!
**jolt** [dʒəʊlt] *n* cahot *m*, secousse *f*; (*shock*) choc *m* ▷ *vt* cahoter, secouer
**Jordan** [dʒɔːdən] *n* (*country*) Jordanie *f*; (*river*) Jourdain *m*
**Jordanian** [dʒɔːˈdeɪnɪən] *adj* jordanien(ne) ▷ *n* Jordanien(ne)
**joss stick** ['dʒɔsstɪk] *n* bâton *m* d'encens
**jostle** ['dʒɔsl] *vt* bousculer, pousser ▷ *vi* jouer des coudes
**jot** [dʒɔt] *n*: **not one ~** pas un brin
  ▸ **jot down** *vt* inscrire rapidement, noter
**jotter** ['dʒɔtə<sup>r</sup>] *n* (*Brit*) cahier *m* (de brouillon); bloc-notes *m*
**journal** ['dʒəːnl] *n* journal *m*
**journalese** [dʒəːnəˈliːz] *n* (*pej*) style *m* journalistique
**journalism** ['dʒəːnəlɪzəm] *n* journalisme *m*
**journalist** ['dʒəːnəlɪst] *n* journaliste *m/f*
**journey** ['dʒəːnɪ] *n* voyage *m*; (*distance covered*) trajet *m* ▷ *vi* voyager; **the ~ takes two hours** le trajet dure deux heures; **a 5-hour ~** un voyage de 5 heures; **how was your ~?** votre voyage s'est bien passé?
**jovial** ['dʒəʊvɪəl] *adj* jovial(e)
**jowl** [dʒaul] *n* mâchoire *f* (*inférieure*); bajoue *f*
**joy** [dʒɔɪ] *n* joie *f*
**joyful** ['dʒɔɪful], **joyous** ['dʒɔɪəs] *adj* joyeux(-euse)
**joyride** ['dʒɔɪraɪd] *vi*: **to go joyriding** faire une virée dans une voiture volée
**joyrider** ['dʒɔɪraɪdə<sup>r</sup>] *n* voleur(-euse) de voiture (*qui fait une virée dans le véhicule volé*)
**joy stick** ['dʒɔɪstɪk] *n* (*Aviat*) manche *m* à balai; (*Comput*) manche à balai, manette *f* (de jeu)
**JP** *n abbr* = **Justice of the Peace**

**Jr** *abbr* = **junior**
**JTPA** *n abbr* (*US*: = *Job Training Partnership Act*) programme gouvernemental de formation
**jubilant** ['dʒuːbɪlnt] *adj* triomphant(e), réjoui(e)
**jubilation** [dʒuːbɪˈleɪʃən] *n* jubilation *f*
**jubilee** ['dʒuːbɪliː] *n* jubilé *m*; **silver ~** (jubilé du) vingt-cinquième anniversaire
**judge** [dʒʌdʒ] *n* juge *m* ▷ *vt* juger; (*estimate*: *weight, size etc*) estimer ▷ *vi*: **judging or to ~ by his expression** d'après son expression; **as far as I can ~** autant que je puisse en juger
**judge advocate** *n* (*Mil*) magistrat *m* militaire
**judgment, judgement** ['dʒʌdʒmənt] *n* jugement *m*; (*punishment*) châtiment *m*; **in my ~** à mon avis; **to pass ~ on** (*Law*) prononcer un jugement (sur)
**judicial** [dʒuːˈdɪʃl] *adj* judiciaire; (*fair*) impartial(e)
**judiciary** [dʒuːˈdɪʃɪərɪ] *n* (pouvoir *m*) judiciaire *m*
**judicious** [dʒuːˈdɪʃəs] *adj* judicieux(-euse)
**judo** ['dʒuːdəu] *n* judo *m*
**jug** [dʒʌg] *n* pot *m*, cruche *f*
**jugged hare** ['dʒʌgd-] *n* (*Brit*) civet *m* de lièvre
**juggernaut** ['dʒʌgənɔːt] *n* (*Brit*: *huge truck*) mastodonte *m*
**juggle** ['dʒʌgl] *vi* jongler
**juggler** ['dʒʌglə<sup>r</sup>] *n* jongleur *m*
**Jugoslav** ['juːgəuˈslɑːv] *adj*, *n* = **Yugoslav**
**jugular** ['dʒʌgjulə<sup>r</sup>] *adj*: **~ (vein)** veine *f* jugulaire
**juice** [dʒuːs] *n* jus *m*; (*inf: petrol*): **we've run out of ~** c'est la panne sèche
**juicy** ['dʒuːsɪ] *adj* juteux(-euse)
**jukebox** ['dʒuːkbɔks] *n* juke-box *m*
**July** [dʒuːˈlaɪ] *n* juillet *m*; **the first of ~** le premier juillet; **(on) the eleventh of ~** le onze juillet; **in the month of ~** au mois de juillet; **at the beginning/end of ~** au début/à la fin (du mois) de juillet, début/fin juillet; **in the middle of ~** au milieu (du mois) de juillet, à la mi-juillet; **during ~** pendant le mois de juillet; **in ~ of next year** en juillet de l'année prochaine; **each or every ~** tous les ans *or* chaque année en juillet; **~ was wet this year** il a beaucoup plu cette année en juillet
**jumble** ['dʒʌmbl] *n* fouillis *m* ▷ *vt* (*also*: **jumble up, jumble together**) mélanger, brouiller
**jumble sale** *n* (*Brit*) vente *f* de charité
**jumbo** ['dʒʌmbəu] *adj* (*also*: **jumbo jet**) (avion) gros porteur (à réaction); **~ size** format maxi *or* extra-grand
**jump** [dʒʌmp] *vi* sauter, bondir; (*with fear etc*) sursauter; (*increase*) monter en flèche ▷ *vt* sauter, franchir ▷ *n* saut *m*, bond *m*; (*with fear etc*) sursaut *m*; (*fence*) obstacle *m*; **to ~ the queue** (*Brit*) passer avant son tour
  ▸ **jump about** *vi* sautiller
  ▸ **jump at** *vt fus* (*fig*) sauter sur; **he ~ed at the offer** il s'est empressé d'accepter la proposition
  ▸ **jump down** *vi* sauter (pour descendre)
  ▸ **jump up** *vi* se lever (d'un bond)
**jumped-up** ['dʒʌmptʌp] *adj* (*Brit pej*) parvenu(e)

**jumper** ['dʒʌmpə'] *n* (*Brit: pullover*) pull-over *m*; (*US: pinafore dress*) robe-chasuble *f*; (*Sport*) sauteur(-euse)

**jump leads**, (*US*) **jumper cables** *npl* câbles *mpl* de démarrage

**jump-start** ['dʒʌmpstɑːt] *vt* (*car: push*) démarrer en poussant; (*: with jump leads*) démarrer avec des câbles (de démarrage); (*fig: project, situation*) faire redémarrer promptement

**jumpy** ['dʒʌmpɪ] *adj* nerveux(-euse), agité(e)

**Jun.** *abbr* = **June; junior**

**junction** ['dʒʌŋkʃən] *n* (*Brit: of roads*) carrefour *m*; (*of rails*) embranchement *m*

**juncture** ['dʒʌŋktʃə'] *n*: **at this ~** à ce moment-là, sur ces entrefaites

**June** [dʒuːn] *n* juin *m*; *for phrases see also* **July**

**jungle** ['dʒʌŋgl] *n* jungle *f*

**junior** ['dʒuːnɪə'] *adj, n*: **he's ~ to me (by two years)**, **he's my ~ (by two years)** il est mon cadet (de deux ans), il est plus jeune que moi (de deux ans); **he's ~ to me** (*seniority*) il est en dessous de moi (dans la hiérarchie), j'ai plus d'ancienneté que lui

**junior executive** *n* cadre moyen

**junior high school** *n* (*US*) ≈ collège *m* d'enseignement secondaire; *see also* **high school**

**junior minister** *n* (*Brit*) ministre *m* sous tutelle

**junior partner** *n* associé(-adjoint) *m*

**junior school** *n* (*Brit*) école *f* primaire

**junior sizes** *npl* (*Comm*) tailles *fpl* fillettes/garçonnets

**juniper** ['dʒuːnɪpə'] *n*: **~ berry** baie *f* de genièvre

**junk** [dʒʌŋk] *n* (*rubbish*) camelote *f*; (*cheap goods*) bric-à-brac *m inv*; (*ship*) jonque *f* ▷ *vt* (*inf*) abandonner, mettre au rancart

**junk bond** *n* (*Comm*) *obligation hautement spéculative utilisée dans les OPA agressives*

**junk dealer** *n* brocanteur(-euse)

**junket** ['dʒʌŋkɪt] *n* (*Culin*) lait caillé; (*Brit inf*): **to go on a ~**, **go ~ing** voyager aux frais de la princesse

**junk food** *n* snacks vite prêts (*sans valeur nutritive*)

**junkie** ['dʒʌŋkɪ] *n* (*inf*) junkie *m*, drogué(e)

**junk mail** *n* prospectus *mpl*; (*Comput*) messages *mpl* publicitaires

**junk room** *n* (*US*) débarras *m*

**junk shop** *n* (boutique *f* de) brocanteur *m*

**Junr** *abbr* = **junior**

**junta** ['dʒʌntə] *n* junte *f*

**Jupiter** ['dʒuːpɪtə'] *n* (*planet*) Jupiter *f*

**jurisdiction** [dʒuərɪs'dɪkʃən] *n* juridiction *f*; **it falls** *or* **comes within/outside our ~** cela est/n'est pas de notre compétence *or* ressort

**jurisprudence** [dʒuərɪs'pruːdəns] *n* jurisprudence *f*

**juror** ['dʒuərə'] *n* juré *m*

**jury** ['dʒuərɪ] *n* jury *m*

**jury box** *n* banc *m* des jurés

**juryman** ['dʒuərɪmən] (*irreg*) *n* = **juror**

**just** [dʒʌst] *adj* juste ▷ *adv*: **he's ~ done it/left** il vient de le faire/partir; **~ as I expected** exactement *or* précisément comme je m'y attendais; **~ right/two o'clock** exactement *or* juste ce qu'il faut/deux heures; **we were ~ going** nous partions; **I was ~ about to phone** j'allais téléphoner; **~ as he was leaving** au moment *or* à l'instant précis où il partait; **~ before/enough/here** juste avant/assez/là; **it's ~ me/a mistake** ce n'est que moi/(rien) qu'une erreur; **~ missed/caught** manqué/attrapé de justesse; **~ listen to this!** écoutez un peu ça!; **~ ask someone the way** vous n'avez qu'à demander votre chemin à quelqu'un; **it's ~ as good** c'est (vraiment) aussi bon; **she's ~ as clever as you** elle est tout aussi intelligente que vous; **it's ~ as well that you …** heureusement que vous …; **not ~ now** pas tout de suite; **~ a minute!**, **~ one moment!** un instant (s'il vous plaît)!

**justice** ['dʒʌstɪs] *n* justice *f*; (*US: judge*) juge *m* de la Cour suprême; **Lord Chief J~** (*Brit*) premier président de la cour d'appel; **this photo doesn't do you ~** cette photo ne vous avantage pas

**Justice of the Peace** *n* juge *m* de paix

**justifiable** [dʒʌstɪ'faɪəbl] *adj* justifiable

**justifiably** [dʒʌstɪ'faɪəblɪ] *adv* légitimement, à juste titre

**justification** [dʒʌstɪfɪ'keɪʃən] *n* justification *f*

**justify** ['dʒʌstɪfaɪ] *vt* justifier; **to be justified in doing sth** être en droit de faire qch

**justly** ['dʒʌstlɪ] *adv* avec raison, justement

**justness** ['dʒʌstnɪs] *n* justesse *f*

**jut** [dʒʌt] *vi* (*also: jut out*) dépasser, faire saillie

**jute** [dʒuːt] *n* jute *m*

**juvenile** ['dʒuːvənaɪl] *adj* juvénile; (*court, books*) pour enfants ▷ *n* adolescent(e)

**juvenile delinquency** *n* délinquance *f* juvénile

**juxtapose** ['dʒʌkstəpəʊz] *vt* juxtaposer

**juxtaposition** ['dʒʌkstəpə'zɪʃən] *n* juxtaposition *f*

# Kk

**K, k** [keɪ] *n* (*letter*) K, k *m*; **K for King** K comme Kléber ▷ *abbr* (= *one thousand*) K; (*Brit*: = *Knight*) titre honorifique

**kaftan** ['kæftæn] *n* cafetan *m*

**Kalahari Desert** [kælə'hɑːrɪ-] *n* désert *m* de Kalahari

**kale** [keɪl] *n* chou frisé

**kaleidoscope** [kə'laɪdəskəup] *n* kaléidoscope *m*

**kamikaze** [kæmɪ'kɑːzɪ] *adj* kamikaze

**Kampala** [kæm'pɑːlə] *n* Kampala

**Kampuchea** [kæmpu'tʃɪə] *n* Kampuchéa *m*

**kangaroo** [kæŋgə'ruː] *n* kangourou *m*

**Kans.** *abbr* (*US*) = **Kansas**

**kaput** [kə'put] *adj* (*inf*) kaput

**karaoke** [kɑːrə'əukɪ] *n* karaoké *m*

**karate** [kə'rɑːtɪ] *n* karaté *m*

**Kashmir** [kæʃ'mɪər] *n* Cachemire *m*

**Kazakhstan** [kɑːzɑːk'stæn] *n* Kazakhstan *m*

**kB** *n abbr* (= *kilobyte*) Ko *m*

**KC** *n abbr* (*Brit Law*: = *King's Counsel*) titre donné à certains avocats; *see also* **QC**

**kd** *abbr* (*US*: = *knocked down*) en pièces détachées

**kebab** [kə'bæb] *n* kebab *m*

**keel** [kiːl] *n* quille *f*; **on an even ~** (*fig*) à flot
  ▶ **keel over** *vi* (*Naut*) chavirer, dessaler; (*person*) tomber dans les pommes

**keen** [kiːn] *adj* (*eager*) plein(e) d'enthousiasme; (*interest, desire, competition*) vif (vive); (*eye, intelligence*) pénétrant(e); (*edge*) effilé(e); **to be ~ to do** *or* **on doing sth** désirer vivement faire qch, tenir beaucoup à faire qch; **to be ~ on sth/sb** aimer beaucoup qch/qn; **I'm not ~ on going** je ne suis pas chaud pour y aller, je n'ai pas très envie d'y aller

**keenly** ['kiːnlɪ] *adv* (*enthusiastically*) avec enthousiasme; (*feel*) vivement, profondément; (*look*) intensément

**keenness** ['kiːnnɪs] *n* (*eagerness*) enthousiasme *m*; **~ to do** vif désir de faire

**keep** [kiːp] (*pt, pp* **kept** [kɛpt]) *vt* (*retain, preserve*) garder; (*hold back*) retenir; (*shop, accounts, promise, diary*) tenir; (*support*) entretenir, assurer la subsistance de; (*chickens, bees, pigs etc*) élever ▷ *vi* (*food*) se conserver; (*remain: in a certain state or place*) rester ▷ *n* (*of castle*) donjon *m*; (*food etc*): **enough for his ~** assez pour

(*assurer*) sa subsistance; **to ~ doing sth** (*continue*) continuer à faire qch; (*repeatedly*) ne pas arrêter de faire qch; **to ~ sb from doing/sth from happening** empêcher qn de faire *or* que qn (ne) fasse/que qch (n')arrive; **to ~ sb happy/a place tidy** faire que qn soit content/qu'un endroit reste propre; **to ~ sb waiting** faire attendre qn; **to ~ an appointment** ne pas manquer un rendez-vous; **to ~ a record of sth** prendre note de qch; **to ~ sth to o.s.** garder qch pour soi, tenir qch secret; **to ~ sth from sb** cacher qch à qn; **to ~ sth from happening** empêcher que qch (n')arrive *or* de se produire; **to ~ time** (*clock*) être à l'heure, ne pas retarder; **for ~s** (*inf*) pour de bon, pour toujours
  ▶ **keep away** *vt*: **to ~ sth/sb away from sb** tenir qch/qn éloigné de qn ▷ *vi*: **to ~ away (from)** ne pas s'approcher (de)
  ▶ **keep back** *vt* (*crowds, tears, money*) retenir; (*conceal: information*): **to ~ sth back from sb** cacher qch à qn ▷ *vi* rester en arrière
  ▶ **keep down** *vt* (*control: prices, spending*) empêcher d'augmenter, limiter; (*retain: food*) garder ▷ *vi* (*person*) rester assis(e); rester par terre
  ▶ **keep in** *vt* (*invalid, child*) garder à la maison; (*Scol*) consigner ▷ *vi* (*inf*): **to ~ in with sb** rester en bons termes avec qn
  ▶ **keep off** *vt* (*dog, person*) éloigner ▷ *vi* ne pas s'approcher; **if the rain ~s off** s'il ne pleut pas; **~ your hands off!** pas touche! (*inf*); **"~ off the grass"** "pelouse interdite"
  ▶ **keep on** *vi* continuer; **to ~ on doing** continuer à faire; **don't ~ on about it!** arrête (d'en parler)!
  ▶ **keep out** *vt* empêcher d'entrer ▷ *vi* (*stay out*) rester en dehors; **"~ out"** "défense d'entrer"
  ▶ **keep up** *vi* (*fig: in comprehension*) suivre ▷ *vt* continuer, maintenir; **to ~ up with sb** (*in work etc*) se maintenir au même niveau que qn; (*in race etc*) aller aussi vite que qn

**keeper** ['kiːpər] *n* gardien(ne)

**keep-fit** [kiːp'fɪt] *n* gymnastique *f* (d'entretien)

**keeping** ['kiːpɪŋ] *n* (*care*) garde *f*; **in ~ with** en harmonie avec

**keeps** [kiːps] *n*: **for ~** (*inf*) pour de bon, pour toujours

**keepsake** ['ki:pseɪk] n souvenir m
**keg** [kɛg] n barrique f, tonnelet m
**Ken.** abbr (US) = **Kentucky**
**kennel** ['kɛnl] n niche f; **kennels** npl (for boarding)
chenil m
**Kenya** ['kɛnjə] n Kenya m
**Kenyan** ['kɛnjən] adj kényan(ne) ▷ n
Kényan(ne)
**kept** [kɛpt] pt, pp of **keep**
**kerb** [kə:b] n (Brit) bordure f du trottoir
**kerb crawler** [-krɔ:lər] n personne qui accoste les
prostitué(e)s en voiture
**kernel** ['kə:nl] n amande f; (fig) noyau m
**kerosene** ['kɛrəsi:n] n kérosène m
**ketchup** ['kɛtʃəp] n ketchup m
**kettle** ['kɛtl] n bouilloire f
**key** [ki:] n; clé f; (of piano, typewriter) touche f; (on
map) légende f ▷ adj (factor, role, area) clé inv ▷ cpd
(-)clé ▷ vt (also: **key in**: text) saisir; **can I have
my ~?** je peux avoir ma clé?; **a ~ issue** un
problème fondamental
**keyboard** ['ki:bɔ:d] n clavier m ▷ vt (text) saisir
**keyboarder** ['ki:bɔ:dər] n claviste m/f
**keyed up** [ki:d'ʌp] adj: **to be (all) ~** être
surexcité(e)
**keyhole** ['ki:həul] n trou m de la serrure
**keyhole surgery** n chirurgie très minutieuse où
l'incision est minimale
**keynote** ['ki:nəut] n (Mus) tonique f; (fig) note
dominante
**keypad** ['ki:pæd] n pavé m numérique
**keyring** ['ki:rɪŋ] n porte-clés m
**keystroke** ['ki:strəuk] n frappe f
**kg** abbr (= kilogram) K
**KGB** n abbr KGB m
**khaki** ['ka:kɪ] adj, n kaki m
**kibbutz** [kɪ'buts] n kibboutz m
**kick** [kɪk] vt donner un coup de pied à ▷ vi (horse)
ruer ▷ n coup m de pied; (of rifle) recul m; (inf:
thrill): **he does it for ~s** il le fait parce que ça
l'excite, il le fait pour le plaisir; **to ~ the habit**
(inf) arrêter
  ▶ **kick around** vi (inf) traîner
  ▶ **kick off** vi (Sport) donner le coup d'envoi
**kick-off** ['kɪkɔf] n (Sport) coup m d'envoi
**kick-start** ['kɪksta:t] n (also: **kick-starter**)
lanceur m au pied
**kid** [kɪd] n (inf: child) gamin(e), gosse m/f; (animal,
leather) chevreau m ▷ vi (inf) plaisanter, blaguer
**kid gloves** npl: **to treat sb with ~** traiter qn avec
ménagement
**kidnap** ['kɪdnæp] vt enlever, kidnapper
**kidnapper** ['kɪdnæpər] n ravisseur(-euse)
**kidnapping** ['kɪdnæpɪŋ] n enlèvement m
**kidney** ['kɪdnɪ] n (Anat) rein m; (Culin) rognon m
**kidney bean** n haricot m rouge
**kidney machine** n (Med) rein artificiel
**Kilimanjaro** [kɪlɪmən'dʒa:rəu] n: **Mount ~**
Kilimandjaro m
**kill** [kɪl] vt tuer; (fig) faire échouer; détruire;
supprimer ▷ n mise f à mort; **to ~ time** tuer le
temps

▶ **kill off** vt exterminer; (fig) éliminer
**killer** ['kɪlər] n tueur(-euse); (murderer)
meurtrier(-ière)
**killer instinct** n combativité f; **to have the ~**
avoir un tempérament de battant
**killing** ['kɪlɪŋ] n meurtre m; (of group of people)
tuerie f, massacre m; (inf): **to make a ~** se
remplir les poches, réussir un beau coup ▷ adj
(inf) tordant(e)
**killjoy** ['kɪldʒɔɪ] n rabat-joie m inv
**kiln** [kɪln] n four m
**kilo** ['ki:ləu] n kilo m
**kilobyte** ['ki:ləubaɪt] n (Comput) kilo-octet m
**kilogram, kilogramme** ['kɪləugræm] n
kilogramme m
**kilometre, (US) kilometer** ['kɪləmi:tər] n
kilomètre m
**kilowatt** ['kɪləuwɔt] n kilowatt m
**kilt** [kɪlt] n kilt m
**kilter** ['kɪltər] n: **out of ~** déréglé(e), détraqué(e)
**kimono** [kɪ'məunəu] n kimono m
**kin** [kɪn] n see **next-of-kin**; **kith**
**kind** [kaɪnd] adj gentil(le), aimable ▷ n sorte f,
espèce f; (species) genre m; **would you be ~
enough to …?, would you be so ~ as to …?**
auriez-vous la gentillesse or l'obligeance de …?;
**it's very ~ of you (to do)** c'est très aimable à
vous (de faire); **to be two of a ~** se ressembler;
**in ~** (Comm) en nature; (fig): **to repay sb in ~**
rendre la pareille à qn; **~ of** (inf: rather) plutôt;
**a ~ of** une sorte de; **what ~ of …?** quelle sorte
de …?
**kindergarten** ['kɪndəga:tn] n jardin m
d'enfants
**kind-hearted** [kaɪnd'ha:tɪd] adj bon (bonne)
**kindle** ['kɪndl] vt allumer, enflammer
**kindling** ['kɪndlɪŋ] n petit bois
**kindly** ['kaɪndlɪ] adj bienveillant(e), plein(e) de
gentillesse ▷ adv avec bonté; **will you ~ …**
auriez-vous la bonté or l'obligeance de …?; **he
didn't take it ~** il l'a mal pris
**kindness** ['kaɪndnɪs] n (quality) bonté f,
gentillesse f
**kindred** ['kɪndrɪd] adj apparenté(e); **~ spirit**
âme f sœur
**kinetic** [kɪ'nɛtɪk] adj cinétique
**king** [kɪŋ] n roi m
**kingdom** ['kɪŋdəm] n royaume m
**kingfisher** ['kɪŋfɪʃər] n martin-pêcheur m
**kingpin** ['kɪŋpɪn] n (Tech) pivot m; (fig) cheville
ouvrière
**king-size** ['kɪŋsaɪz], **king-sized** ['kɪŋsaɪzd] adj
(cigarette) (format) extra-long (longue)
**king-size bed, king-sized bed** n grand lit (de
1,95 m de large)
**kink** [kɪŋk] n (of rope) entortillement m; (in hair)
ondulation f; (inf: fig) aberration f
**kinky** ['kɪŋkɪ] adj (fig) excentrique; (pej) aux
goûts spéciaux
**kinship** ['kɪnʃɪp] n parenté f
**kinsman** ['kɪnzmən] (irreg) n parent m
**kinswoman** ['kɪnzwumən] (irreg) n parente f

**kiosk** ['ki:ɔsk] n kiosque m; (Brit: also: **telephone kiosk**) cabine f (téléphonique); (also: **newspaper kiosk**) kiosque à journaux
**kipper** ['kɪpəʳ] n hareng fumé et salé
**Kirghizia** [kəːˈgɪzɪə] n Kirghizistan m
**kiss** [kɪs] n baiser m ▷ vt embrasser; **to ~ (each other)** s'embrasser; **to ~ sb goodbye** dire au revoir à qn en l'embrassant
**kissagram** ['kɪsəgræm] n baiser envoyé à l'occasion d'une célébration par l'intermédiaire d'une personne employée à cet effet
**kiss of life** n (Brit) bouche à bouche m
**kit** [kɪt] n équipement m, matériel m; (set of tools etc) trousse f; (for assembly) kit m; **tool ~** nécessaire m à outils
  ▸ **kit out** vt (Brit) équiper
**kitbag** ['kɪtbæg] n sac m de voyage or de marin
**kitchen** ['kɪtʃɪn] n cuisine f
**kitchen garden** n jardin m potager
**kitchen sink** n évier m
**kitchen unit** n (Brit) élément m de cuisine
**kitchenware** ['kɪtʃɪnwɛəʳ] n vaisselle f; ustensiles mpl de cuisine
**kite** [kaɪt] n (toy) cerf-volant m; (Zool) milan m
**kith** [kɪθ] n: **~ and kin** parents et amis mpl
**kitten** ['kɪtn] n petit chat, chaton m
**kitty** ['kɪtɪ] n (money) cagnotte f
**kiwi** ['ki:wi:] n (also: **kiwi fruit**) kiwi m
**KKK** n abbr (US) = **Ku Klux Klan**
**Kleenex®** ['kli:nɛks] n Kleenex® m
**kleptomaniac** [klɛptəu'meɪnɪæk] n kleptomane m/f
**km** abbr (= kilometre) km
**km/h** abbr (= kilometres per hour) km/h
**knack** [næk] n: **to have the ~ (of doing)** avoir le coup (pour faire); **there's a ~** il y a un coup à prendre ou une combine
**knackered** ['nækəd] adj (inf) crevé(e), nase
**knapsack** ['næpsæk] n musette f
**knave** [neɪv] n (Cards) valet m
**knead** [ni:d] vt pétrir
**knee** [ni:] n genou m
**kneecap** ['ni:kæp] n rotule f ▷ vt tirer un coup de feu dans la rotule de
**knee-deep** ['ni:'di:p] adj: **the water was ~** l'eau arrivait aux genoux
**kneel** (pt, pp **knelt**) [ni:l, nɛlt] vi (also: **kneel down**) s'agenouiller
**kneepad** ['ni:pæd] n genouillère f
**knell** [nɛl] n glas m
**knelt** [nɛlt] pt, pp of **kneel**
**knew** [nju:] pt of **know**
**knickers** ['nɪkəz] npl (Brit) culotte f (de femme)
**knick-knack** ['nɪknæk] n colifichet m
**knife** [naɪf] n (pl **knives** [naɪvz]) couteau m ▷ vt poignarder, frapper d'un coup de couteau; **~, fork and spoon** couvert m
**knife-edge** ['naɪfɛdʒ] n: **to be on a ~** être sur le fil du rasoir
**knight** [naɪt] n chevalier m; (Chess) cavalier m
**knighthood** ['naɪthud] n chevalerie f; (title): **to get a ~** être fait chevalier

**knit** [nɪt] vt tricoter; (fig): **to ~ together** unir ▷ vi tricoter; (broken bones) se ressouder; **to ~ one's brows** froncer les sourcils
**knitted** ['nɪtɪd] adj en tricot
**knitting** ['nɪtɪŋ] n tricot m
**knitting machine** n machine f à tricoter
**knitting needle** n aiguille f à tricoter
**knitting pattern** n modèle m (pour tricot)
**knitwear** ['nɪtwɛəʳ] n tricots mpl, lainages mpl
**knives** [naɪvz] npl of **knife**
**knob** [nɔb] n bouton m; (Brit): **a ~ of butter** une noix de beurre
**knobbly** ['nɔblɪ], (US) **knobby** ['nɔbɪ] adj (wood, surface) noueux(-euse); (knees) noueux
**knock** [nɔk] vt frapper; (bump into) heurter; (make: hole etc): **to ~ a hole in** faire un trou dans, trouer; (force: nail etc): **to ~ a nail into** enfoncer un clou dans; (fig: col) dénigrer ▷ vi (engine) cogner; (at door etc): **to ~ at/on** frapper à/sur ▷ n coup m; **he ~ed at the door** il frappa à la porte
  ▸ **knock down** vt renverser; (price) réduire
  ▸ **knock off** vi (inf: finish) s'arrêter (de travailler) ▷ vt (vase, object) faire tomber; (inf: steal) piquer; (fig: from price etc): **to ~ off £10** faire une remise de 10 livres
  ▸ **knock out** vt assommer; (Boxing) mettre k.-o.; (in competition) éliminer
  ▸ **knock over** vt (object) faire tomber; (pedestrian) renverser
**knockdown** ['nɔkdaun] adj (price) sacrifié(e)
**knocker** ['nɔkəʳ] n (on door) heurtoir m
**knocking** ['nɔkɪŋ] n coups mpl
**knock-kneed** [nɔk'ni:d] adj aux genoux cagneux
**knockout** ['nɔkaut] n (Boxing) knock-out m, K.-O. m; (competition) (Brit) compétition f avec épreuves éliminatoires
**knock-up** ['nɔkʌp] n (Tennis): **to have a ~** faire des balles
**knot** [nɔt] n (gen) nœud m ▷ vt nouer; **to tie a ~** faire un nœud
**knotty** ['nɔtɪ] adj (fig) épineux(-euse)
**know** [nəu] vt (pt **knew**, pp **known** [nju:, nəun]) savoir; (person, place) connaître; **to ~ that** savoir que; **to ~ how to do** savoir faire; **to ~ how to swim** savoir nager; **to ~ about/of sth** (event) être au courant de qch; (subject) connaître qch; **to get to ~ sth** (fact) apprendre qch; (place) apprendre à connaître qch; **I don't ~** je ne sais pas; **I don't ~ him** je ne le connais pas; **do you ~ where I can ...?** savez-vous où je peux ...?; **to ~ right from wrong** savoir distinguer le bon du mauvais; **as far as I ~ ...** à ma connaissance ..., autant que je sache ...
**know-all** ['nəuɔ:l] n (Brit pej) je-sais-tout m/f
**know-how** ['nəuhau] n savoir-faire m, technique f, compétence f
**knowing** ['nəuɪŋ] adj (look etc) entendu(e)
**knowingly** ['nəuɪŋlɪ] adv (on purpose) sciemment; (smile, look) d'un air entendu
**know-it-all** ['nəuɪtɔ:l] n (US) = **know-all**
**knowledge** ['nɔlɪdʒ] n connaissance f; (learning)

**k**

649

connaissances, savoir *m*; **to have no ~ of** ignorer; **not to my ~** pas à ma connaissance; **without my ~** à mon insu; **to have a working ~ of French** se débrouiller en français; **it is common ~ that** ... chacun sait que ...; **it has come to my ~ that** ... j'ai appris que ...

**knowledgeable** ['nɔlɪdʒəbl] *adj* bien informé(e)

**known** [nəun] *pp of* **know** ▷ *adj* (*thief, facts*) notoire; (*expert*) célèbre

**knuckle** ['nʌkl] *n* articulation *f* (des phalanges), jointure *f*
▸ **knuckle down** *vi* (*inf*) s'y mettre
▸ **knuckle under** *vi* (*inf*) céder

**knuckleduster** ['nʌkldʌstəʳ] *n* coup-de-poing américain

**KO** *abbr* = **knock out** ▷ *n* K.-O. *m* ▷ *vt* mettre K.-O.

**koala** [kəu'ɑːlə] *n* (*also*: **koala bear**) koala *m*

**kook** [kuːk] *n* (*US inf*) loufoque *m/f*

**Koran** [kɔ'rɑːn] *n* Coran *m*

**Korea** [kə'rɪə] *n* Corée *f*; **North/South ~** Corée du Nord/Sud

**Korean** [kə'rɪən] *adj* coréen(ne) ▷ *n* Coréen(ne)

**kosher** ['kəuʃəʳ] *adj* kascher *inv*

**Kosovar, Kosovan** ['kɔsəvɑːʳ, 'kɔsəvən] *adj* kosovar(e)

**Kosovo** ['kɔsɔvəu] *n* Kosovo *m*

**kowtow** ['kau'tau] *vi*: **to ~ to sb** s'aplatir devant qn

**Kremlin** ['krɛmlɪn] *n*: **the ~** le Kremlin

**KS** *abbr* (*US*) = **Kansas**

**Kt** *abbr* (*Brit*: = *Knight*) *titre honorifique*

**Kuala Lumpur** ['kwɑːlə'lumpuəʳ] *n* Kuala Lumpur

**kudos** ['kjuːdɔs] *n* gloire *f*, lauriers *mpl*

**Kurd** [kəːd] *n* Kurde *m/f*

**Kuwait** [ku'weɪt] *n* Koweït *m*

**Kuwaiti** [ku'weɪtɪ] *adj* koweïtien(ne) ▷ *n* Koweïtien(ne)

**kW** *abbr* (= *kilowatt*) kW

**KY, Ky.** *abbr* (*US*) = **Kentucky**

# Ll

**L¹, l** [ɛl] *n (letter)* L, l *m;* **L for Lucy,** *(US)* **L for Love** L comme Louis

**L²** *abbr* (= *lake, large*) L; (= *left*) g; *(Brit Aut: = learner)* signale un conducteur débutant

**l.** *abbr* (= *litre*) l

**LA** *n abbr (US)* = **Los Angeles** ▷ *abbr (US)* = **Louisiana**

**La.** *abbr (US)* = **Louisiana**

**lab** [læb] *n abbr* (= *laboratory*) labo *m*

**Lab.** *abbr (Canada)* = **Labrador**

**label** ['leɪbl] *n* étiquette *f;* (*brand: of record*) marque *f* ▷ *vt* étiqueter; **to ~ sb a ...** qualifier qn de ...

**labor** *etc* ['leɪbər] *(US)* = **labour** *etc*

**laboratory** [lə'bɔrətərɪ] *n* laboratoire *m*

**Labor Day** *n (US, Canada)* fête *f* du travail *(le premier lundi de septembre); voir article*

---

**● LABOR DAY**
●
● *Labor Day aux États-Unis et au Canada est*
● fixée au premier lundi de septembre.
● Instituée par le Congrès en 1894 après avoir
● été réclamée par les mouvements ouvriers
● pendant douze ans, elle a perdu une grande
● partie de son caractère politique pour
● devenir un jour férié assez ordinaire et
● l'occasion de partir pour un long week-end
● avant la rentrée des classes.

---

**laborious** [lə'bɔːrɪəs] *adj* laborieux(-euse)

**labor union** *n (US)* syndicat *m*

**Labour** ['leɪbər] *n (Brit Pol: also:* **the Labour Party**) le parti travailliste, les travaillistes *mpl*

**labour,** *(US)* **labor** ['leɪbər] *n (work)* travail *m;* (*workforce*) main-d'œuvre *f;* (*Med*) travail, accouchement *m* ▷ *vi:* **to ~ (at)** travailler dur (à), peiner (sur) ▷ *vt:* **to ~ a point** insister sur un point; **in ~** (*Med*) en travail

**labour camp,** *(US)* **labor camp** *n* camp *m* de travaux forcés

**labour cost,** *(US)* **labor cost** *n* coût *m* de la main-d'œuvre; coût de la façon

**laboured,** *(US)* **labored** ['leɪbəd] *adj* lourd(e), laborieux(-euse); (*breathing*) difficile, pénible; (*style*) lourd, embarrassé(e)

**labourer,** *(US)* **laborer** ['leɪbərər] *n* manœuvre *m;* **farm ~** ouvrier *m* agricole

**labour force,** *(US)* **labor force** *n* main-d'œuvre *f*

**labour-intensive,** *(US)* **labor-intensive** [leɪbərɪn'tɛnsɪv] *adj* intensif(-ive) en main-d'œuvre

**labour market,** *(US)* **labor market** *n* marché *m* du travail

**labour pains,** *(US)* **labor pains** *npl* douleurs *fpl* de l'accouchement

**labour relations,** *(US)* **labor relations** *npl* relations *fpl* dans l'entreprise

**labour-saving,** *(US)* **labor-saving** ['leɪbəseɪvɪŋ] *adj* qui simplifie le travail

**labour unrest,** *(US)* **labor unrest** *n* agitation sociale

**labyrinth** ['læbɪrɪnθ] *n* labyrinthe *m,* dédale *m*

**lace** [leɪs] *n* dentelle *f;* (*of shoe etc*) lacet *m* ▷ *vt* (*shoe: also:* **lace up**) lacer; (*drink*) arroser, corser

**lacemaking** ['leɪsmeɪkɪŋ] *n* fabrication *f* de dentelle

**laceration** [læsə'reɪʃən] *n* lacération *f*

**lace-up** ['leɪsʌp] *adj (shoe etc)* à lacets

**lack** [læk] *n* manque *m* ▷ *vt* manquer de; **through** *or* **for ~ of** faute de, par manque de; **to be ~ing** manquer, faire défaut; **to be ~ing in** manquer de

**lackadaisical** [lækə'deɪzɪkl] *adj* nonchalant(e), indolent(e)

**lackey** ['lækɪ] *n (also fig)* laquais *m*

**lacklustre** ['læklʌstər] *adj* terne

**laconic** [lə'kɔnɪk] *adj* laconique

**lacquer** ['lækər] *n* laque *f*

**lacy** ['leɪsɪ] *adj (made of lace)* en dentelle; (*like lace*) comme de la dentelle, qui ressemble à de la dentelle

**lad** [læd] *n* garçon *m,* gars *m;* (*Brit: in stable etc*) lad *m*

**ladder** ['lædər] *n* échelle *f;* (*Brit: in tights*) maille filée ▷ *vt, vi (Brit: tights)* filer

**laden** ['leɪdn] *adj:* **~ (with)** chargé(e) (de); **fully ~** (*truck, ship*) en pleine charge

**ladle** ['leɪdl] *n* louche *f*

**lady** ['leɪdɪ] *n* dame *f;* **"ladies and gentlemen ..."** "Mesdames (et) Messieurs ..."; **young ~** jeune fille *f;* (*married*) jeune femme *f;*

**L~ Smith** lady Smith; **the ladies' (room)** les toilettes *fpl* des dames; **a ~ doctor** une doctoresse, une femme médecin

**ladybird** ['leɪdɪbəːd], *(US)* **ladybug** ['leɪdɪbʌg] *n* coccinelle *f*

**lady-in-waiting** ['leɪdɪɪn'weɪtɪŋ] *n* dame *f* d'honneur

**lady-killer** ['leɪdɪkɪlə'] *n* don Juan *m*

**ladylike** ['leɪdɪlaɪk] *adj* distingué(e)

**ladyship** ['leɪdɪʃɪp] *n*: **your L~** Madame la comtesse (*or* la baronne *etc*)

**lag** [læg] *n* retard *m* ▷ *vi* (*also*: **lag behind**) rester en arrière, traîner; (*fig*) rester à la traîne ▷ *vt* (*pipes*) calorifuger

**lager** ['lɑːgə'] *n* bière blonde

**lager lout** *n* (*Brit inf*) jeune voyou *m* (*porté sur la boisson*)

**lagging** ['lægɪŋ] *n* enveloppe isolante, calorifuge *m*

**lagoon** [lə'guːn] *n* lagune *f*

**Lagos** ['leɪgɔs] *n* Lagos

**laid** [leɪd] *pt, pp of* **lay**

**laid back** *adj* (*inf*) relaxe, décontracté(e)

**laid up** *adj* alité(e)

**lain** [leɪn] *pp of* **lie**

**lair** [lɛə'] *n* tanière *f*, gîte *m*

**laissez-faire** [lɛseɪ'fɛə'] *n* libéralisme *m*

**laity** ['leɪətɪ] *n* laïques *mpl*

**lake** [leɪk] *n* lac *m*

**Lake District** *n*: **the ~** (*Brit*) la région des lacs

**lamb** [læm] *n* agneau *m*

**lamb chop** *n* côtelette *f* d'agneau

**lambskin** ['læmskɪn] *n* (peau *f* d')agneau *m*

**lambswool** ['læmzwul] *n* laine *f* d'agneau

**lame** [leɪm] *adj* (*also fig*) boiteux(-euse); **~ duck** (*fig*) canard boiteux

**lamely** ['leɪmlɪ] *adv* (*fig*) sans conviction

**lament** [lə'mɛnt] *n* lamentation *f* ▷ *vt* pleurer, se lamenter sur

**lamentable** ['læməntəbl] *adj* déplorable, lamentable

**laminated** ['læmɪneɪtɪd] *adj* laminé(e); (*windscreen*) (en verre) feuilleté

**lamp** [læmp] *n* lampe *f*

**lamplight** ['læmplaɪt] *n*: **by ~** à la lumière de la (*or* d'une) lampe

**lampoon** [læm'puːn] *n* pamphlet *m*

**lamppost** ['læmppəust] *n* (*Brit*) réverbère *m*

**lampshade** ['læmpʃeɪd] *n* abat-jour *m inv*

**lance** [lɑːns] *n* lance *f* ▷ *vt* (*Med*) inciser

**lance corporal** *n* (*Brit*) (soldat *m* de) première classe *m*

**lancet** ['lɑːnsɪt] *n* (*Med*) bistouri *m*

**Lancs** [læŋks] *abbr* (*Brit*) = **Lancashire**

**land** [lænd] *n* (*as opposed to sea*) terre *f* (ferme); (*country*) pays *m*; (*soil*) terre; (*piece of land*) terrain *m*; (*estate*) terre(s), domaine(s) *m(pl)* ▷ *vi* (*from ship*) débarquer; (*Aviat*) atterrir; (*fig: fall*) (re)tomber ▷ *vt* (*passengers, goods*) débarquer; (*obtain*) décrocher; **to go/travel by ~** se déplacer par voie de terre; **to own ~** être propriétaire foncier; **to ~ on one's feet** (*also fig*)

retomber sur ses pieds; **to ~ sb with sth** (*inf*) coller qch à qn

▶ **land up** *vi* atterrir, (finir par) se retrouver

**landed gentry** ['lændɪd-] *n* (*Brit*) propriétaires terriens *or* fonciers

**landfill site** ['lændfɪl-] *n* centre *m* d'enfouissement des déchets

**landing** ['lændɪŋ] *n* (*from ship*) débarquement *m*; (*Aviat*) atterrissage *m*; (*of staircase*) palier *m*

**landing card** *n* carte *f* de débarquement

**landing craft** *n* péniche *f* de débarquement

**landing gear** *n* train *m* d'atterrissage

**landing stage** *n* (*Brit*) débarcadère *m*, embarcadère *m*

**landing strip** *n* piste *f* d'atterrissage

**landlady** ['lændleɪdɪ] *n* propriétaire *f*, logeuse *f*; (*of pub*) patronne *f*

**landlocked** ['lændlɔkt] *adj* entouré(e) de terre(s), sans accès à la mer

**landlord** ['lændlɔːd] *n* propriétaire *m*, logeur *m*; (*of pub etc*) patron *m*

**landlubber** ['lændlʌbə'] *n* terrien(ne)

**landmark** ['lændmɑːk] *n* (point *m* de) repère *m*; **to be a ~** (*fig*) faire date *or* époque

**landowner** ['lændəunə'] *n* propriétaire foncier *or* terrien

**landscape** ['lænskeɪp] *n* paysage *m*

**landscape architect, landscape gardener** *n* paysagiste *m/f*

**landscape painting** *n* (*Art*) paysage *m*

**landslide** ['lændslaɪd] *n* (*Geo*) glissement *m* (de terrain); (*fig: Pol*) raz-de-marée (électoral)

**lane** [leɪn] *n* (*in country*) chemin *m*; (*in town*) ruelle *f*; (*Aut: of road*) voie *f*; (: *line of traffic*) file *f*; (*in race*) couloir *m*; **shipping ~** route *f* maritime *or* de navigation

**language** ['læŋgwɪdʒ] *n* langue *f*; (*way one speaks*) langage *m*; **what ~s do you speak?** quelles langues parlez-vous?; **bad ~** grossièretés *fpl*, langage grossier

**language laboratory** *n* laboratoire *m* de langues

**language school** *n* école *f* de langue

**languid** ['læŋgwɪd] *adj* languissant(e), langoureux(-euse)

**languish** ['læŋgwɪʃ] *vi* languir

**lank** [læŋk] *adj* (*hair*) raide et terne

**lanky** ['læŋkɪ] *adj* grand(e) et maigre, efflanqué(e)

**lanolin, lanoline** ['lænəlɪn] *n* lanoline *f*

**lantern** ['læntn] *n* lanterne *f*

**Laos** [laus] *n* Laos *m*

**lap** [læp] *n* (*of track*) tour *m* (de piste); (*of body*): **in** *or* **on one's ~** sur les genoux ▷ *vt* (*also*: **lap up**) laper ▷ *vi* (*waves*) clapoter

▶ **lap up** *vt* (*fig*) boire comme du petit-lait, se gargariser de; (: *lies etc*) gober

**La Paz** [læ'pæz] *n* La Paz *f*

**lapdog** ['læpdɔg] *n* chien *m* d'appartement

**lapel** [lə'pɛl] *n* revers *m*

**lapse** [læps] *n* défaillance *f*; (*in behaviour*) écart *m* (de conduite) ▷ *vi* (*Law*) cesser d'être en vigueur; (*contract*) expirer; (*pass*) être périmé; (*subscription*) prendre fin; **to ~ into bad habits** prendre de mauvaises habitudes; **~ of time** laps *m* de temps, intervalle *m*; **a ~ of memory** un trou de mémoire

**laptop** ['læptɔp], **laptop computer** *n* (ordinateur *m*) portable *m*

**larceny** ['lɑːsənɪ] *n* vol *m*

**larch** [lɑːtʃ] *n* mélèze *m*

**lard** [lɑːd] *n* saindoux *m*

**larder** ['lɑːdəʳ] *n* garde-manger *m inv*

**large** [lɑːdʒ] *adj* grand(e); (*person, animal*) gros (grosse); **to make ~r** agrandir; **a ~ number of people** beaucoup de gens; **by and ~** en général; **on a ~ scale** sur une grande échelle; **at ~** (*free*) en liberté; (*generally*) en général; pour la plupart; *see also* **by**

**largely** ['lɑːdʒlɪ] *adv* en grande partie; (*principally*) surtout

**large-scale** ['lɑːdʒ'skeɪl] *adj* (*map, drawing etc*) à grande échelle; (*fig*) important(e)

**lark** [lɑːk] *n* (*bird*) alouette *f*; (*joke*) blague *f*, farce *f*
▶ **lark about** *vi* faire l'idiot, rigoler

**larva** (*pl* **-e**) ['lɑːvə, -iː] *n* larve *f*

**laryngitis** [lærɪn'dʒaɪtɪs] *n* laryngite *f*

**larynx** ['lærɪŋks] *n* larynx *m*

**lasagne** [lə'zænjə] *n* lasagne *f*

**lascivious** [lə'sɪvɪəs] *adj* lascif(-ive)

**laser** ['leɪzəʳ] *n* laser *m*

**laser beam** *n* rayon *m* laser

**laser printer** *n* imprimante *f* laser

**lash** [læʃ] *n* coup *m* de fouet; (*also:* **eyelash**) cil *m* ▷ *vt* fouetter; (*tie*) attacher
▶ **lash down** *vt* attacher; amarrer; arrimer ▷ *vi* (*rain*) tomber avec violence
▶ **lash out** *vi*: **to ~ out (at** or **against sb/sth)** attaquer violemment (qn/qch); **to ~ out (on sth)** (*inf: spend*) se fendre (de qch)

**lashing** ['læʃɪŋ] *n*: **~s of** (*Brit inf: cream etc*) des masses de

**lass** [læs] (*Brit*) *n* (jeune) fille *f*

**lasso** [læ'suː] *n* lasso *m* ▷ *vt* prendre au lasso

**last** [lɑːst] *adj* dernier(-ière) ▷ *adv* en dernier; (*most recently*) la dernière fois; (*finally*) finalement ▷ *vi* durer; **~ week** la semaine dernière; **~ night** (*evening*) hier soir; (*night*) la nuit dernière; **at ~** enfin; **~ but one** avant-dernier(-ière); **the ~ time** la dernière fois; **it ~s (for) 2 hours** ça dure 2 heures

**last-ditch** ['lɑːst'dɪtʃ] *adj* ultime, désespéré(e)

**lasting** ['lɑːstɪŋ] *adj* durable

**lastly** ['lɑːstlɪ] *adv* en dernier lieu, pour finir

**last-minute** ['lɑːstmɪnɪt] *adj* de dernière minute

**latch** [lætʃ] *n* loquet *m*
▶ **latch onto** *vt fus* (*cling to: person, group*) s'accrocher à; (*idea*) se mettre en tête

**latchkey** ['lætʃkiː] *n* clé *f* (de la porte d'entrée)

**late** [leɪt] *adj* (*not on time*) en retard; (*far on in day etc*) tardif(-ive); (*: edition, delivery*) dernier(-ière);

(*recent*) récent(e), dernier; (*former*) ancien(ne); (*dead*) défunt(e) ▷ *adv* tard; (*behind time, schedule*) en retard; **to be ~** avoir du retard; **to be 10 minutes ~** avoir 10 minutes de retard; **sorry I'm ~** désolé d'être en retard; **it's too ~** il est trop tard; **to work ~** travailler tard; **~ in life** sur le tard, à un âge avancé; **of ~** dernièrement; **in ~ May** vers la fin (du mois) de mai, fin mai; **the ~ Mr X** feu M. X

**latecomer** ['leɪtkʌməʳ] *n* retardataire *m/f*

**lately** ['leɪtlɪ] *adv* récemment

**lateness** ['leɪtnɪs] *n* (*of person*) retard *m*; (*of event*) heure tardive

**latent** ['leɪtnt] *adj* latent(e); **~ defect** vice caché

**later** ['leɪtəʳ] *adj* (*date etc*) ultérieur(e); (*version etc*) plus récent(e) ▷ *adv* plus tard; **~ on today** plus tard dans la journée

**lateral** ['lætərl] *adj* latéral(e)

**latest** ['leɪtɪst] *adj* tout(e) dernier(-ière); **the ~ news** les dernières nouvelles; **at the ~** au plus tard

**latex** ['leɪtɛks] *n* latex *m*

**lath** (*pl* **-s**) [læθ, læðz] *n* latte *f*

**lathe** [leɪð] *n* tour *m*

**lather** ['lɑːðəʳ] *n* mousse *f* (de savon) ▷ *vt* savonner ▷ *vi* mousser

**Latin** ['lætɪn] *n* latin *m* ▷ *adj* latin(e)

**Latin America** *n* Amérique latine

**Latin American** *adj* latino-américain(e), d'Amérique latine ▷ *n* Latino-Américain(e)

**latitude** ['lætɪtjuːd] *n* (*also fig*) latitude *f*

**latrine** [lə'triːn] *n* latrines *fpl*

**latter** ['lætəʳ] *adj* deuxième, dernier(-ière) ▷ *n*: **the ~** ce dernier, celui-ci

**latterly** ['lætəlɪ] *adv* dernièrement, récemment

**lattice** ['lætɪs] *n* treillis *m*; treillage *m*

**lattice window** *n* fenêtre treillissée, fenêtre à croisillons

**Latvia** ['lætvɪə] *n* Lettonie *f*

**Latvian** ['lætvɪən] *adj* letton(ne) ▷ *n* Letton(ne); (*Ling*) letton *m*

**laudable** ['lɔːdəbl] *adj* louable

**laudatory** ['lɔːdətrɪ] *adj* élogieux(-euse)

**laugh** [lɑːf] *n* rire *m* ▷ *vi* rire; **(to do sth) for a ~** (faire qch) pour rire
▶ **laugh at** *vt fus* se moquer de; (*joke*) rire de
▶ **laugh off** *vt* écarter ou rejeter par une plaisanterie *ou* par une boutade

**laughable** ['lɑːfəbl] *adj* risible, ridicule

**laughing** ['lɑːfɪŋ] *adj* rieur(-euse); **this is no ~ matter** il n'y a pas de quoi rire, ça n'a rien d'amusant

**laughing gas** *n* gaz hilarant

**laughing stock** *n*: **the ~ of** la risée de

**laughter** ['lɑːftəʳ] *n* rire *m*; (*of several people*) rires *mpl*

**launch** [lɔːntʃ] *n* lancement *m*; (*boat*) chaloupe *f*; (*also:* **motor launch**) vedette *f* ▷ *vt* (*ship, rocket, plan*) lancer
▶ **launch into** *vt fus* se lancer dans
▶ **launch out** *vi*: **to ~ out (into)** se lancer (dans)

**launching** ['lɔːntʃɪŋ] *n* lancement *m*

**launder** ['lɔːndə<sup>r</sup>] vt laver; (fig: money) blanchir
**Launderette®** [lɔːn'drɛt], (US) **Laundromat®** ['lɔːndrəmæt] n laverie f (automatique)
**laundry** ['lɔːndrɪ] n (clothes) linge m; (business) blanchisserie f; (room) buanderie f; **to do the ~** faire la lessive
**laureate** ['lɔːrɪət] adj see **poet laureate**
**laurel** ['lɔrl] n laurier m; **to rest on one's ~s** se reposer sur ses lauriers
**lava** ['lɑːvə] n lave f
**lavatory** ['lævətərɪ] n toilettes fpl
**lavatory paper** n (Brit) papier m hygiénique
**lavender** ['lævəndə<sup>r</sup>] n lavande f
**lavish** ['lævɪʃ] adj (amount) copieux(-euse); (meal) somptueux(-euse); (hospitality) généreux(-euse); (person: giving freely): **~ with** prodigue de ▷ vt: **to ~ sth on sb** prodiguer qch à qn; (money) dépenser qch sans compter pour qn
**lavishly** ['lævɪʃlɪ] adv (give, spend) sans compter; (furnished) luxueusement
**law** [lɔː] n loi f; (science) droit m; **against the ~** contraire à la loi; **to study ~** faire du droit; **to go to ~** (Brit) avoir recours à la justice; **~ and order** (n) l'ordre public
**law-abiding** ['lɔːəbaɪdɪŋ] adj respectueux(-euse) des lois
**lawbreaker** ['lɔːbreɪkə<sup>r</sup>] n personne f qui transgresse la loi
**law court** n tribunal m, cour f de justice
**lawful** ['lɔːful] adj légal(e), permis(e)
**lawfully** ['lɔːfəlɪ] adv légalement
**lawless** ['lɔːlɪs] adj (action) illégal(e); (place) sans loi
**Law Lord** n (Brit) juge siégant à la Chambre des Lords
**lawmaker** ['lɔːmeɪkə<sup>r</sup>] n législateur(-trice)
**lawn** [lɔːn] n pelouse f
**lawnmower** ['lɔːnməuə<sup>r</sup>] n tondeuse f à gazon
**lawn tennis** n tennis m
**law school** n faculté f de droit
**law student** n étudiant(e) en droit
**lawsuit** ['lɔːsuːt] n procès m; **to bring a ~ against** engager des poursuites contre
**lawyer** ['lɔːjə<sup>r</sup>] n (consultant, with company) juriste m; (for sales, wills etc) ≈ notaire m; (partner, in court) ≈ avocat m
**lax** [læks] adj relâché(e)
**laxative** ['læksətɪv] n laxatif m
**laxity** ['læksɪtɪ] n relâchement m
**lay** [leɪ] pt of **lie** ▷ adj laïque; (not expert) profane ▷ vt (pt, pp **laid** [leɪd]) poser, mettre; (eggs) pondre; (trap) tendre; (plans) élaborer; **to ~ the table** mettre la table; **to ~ the facts/one's proposals before sb** présenter les faits/ses propositions à qn; **to get laid** (inf!) baiser (!), se faire baiser (!)
▶ **lay aside, lay by** vt mettre de côté
▶ **lay down** vt poser; (rules etc) établir; **to ~ down the law** (fig) faire la loi
▶ **lay in** vt accumuler, s'approvisionner en
▶ **lay into** vi (inf: attack) tomber sur; (: scold) passer une engueulade à
▶ **lay off** vt (workers) licencier

▶ **lay on** vt (water, gas) mettre, installer; (provide: meal etc) fournir; (paint) étaler
▶ **lay out** vt (design) dessiner, concevoir; (display) disposer; (spend) dépenser
▶ **lay up** vt (store) amasser; (car) remiser; (ship) désarmer; (illness) forcer à s'aliter
**layabout** ['leɪəbaut] n fainéant(e)
**lay-by** ['leɪbaɪ] n (Brit) aire f de stationnement (sur le bas-côté)
**lay days** npl (Naut) estarie f
**layer** ['leɪə<sup>r</sup>] n couche f
**layette** ['leɪɛt] n layette f
**layman** ['leɪmən] (irreg) n (Rel) laïque m; (non-expert) profane m
**lay-off** ['leɪɔf] n licenciement m
**layout** ['leɪaut] n disposition f, plan m, agencement m; (Press) mise f en page
**laze** [leɪz] vi paresser
**laziness** ['leɪzɪnɪs] n paresse f
**lazy** ['leɪzɪ] adj paresseux(-euse)
**LB** abbr (Canada) = **Labrador**
**lb.** abbr (weight) = **pound**
**lbw** abbr (Cricket: = leg before wicket) faute dans laquelle le joueur a la jambe devant le guichet
**LC** n abbr (US) = **Library of Congress**
**lc** abbr (Typ: = lower case) b.d.c.
**L/C** abbr = **letter of credit**
**LCD** n abbr = **liquid crystal display**
**Ld** abbr (Brit: = lord) titre honorifique
**LDS** n abbr (= Licentiate in Dental Surgery) diplôme universitaire; (= Latter-day Saints) Église de Jésus-Christ des Saints du dernier jour
**LEA** n abbr (Brit: = local education authority) services locaux de l'enseignement
**lead¹** [liːd] (pt, pp **led** [lɛd]) n (front position) tête f; (distance, time ahead) avance f; (clue) piste f; (to battery) raccord m; (Elec) fil m; (for dog) laisse f; (Theat) rôle principal ▷ vt (guide) mener, conduire; (induce) amener; (be leader of) être à la tête de; (Sport) être en tête de; (orchestra: Brit) être le premier violon de; (: US) diriger ▷ vi (Sport) mener, être en tête; **to ~ to** (road, pipe) mener à, conduire à; (result in) conduire à; aboutir à; **to ~ sb astray** détourner qn du droit chemin; **to be in the ~** (Sport: in race) mener, être en tête; (: in match) mener (à la marque); **to take the ~** (Sport) passer en tête, prendre la tête; mener; (fig) prendre l'initiative; **to ~ sb to believe that ...** amener qn à croire que ...; **to ~ sb to do sth** amener qn à faire qch; **to ~ the way** montrer le chemin
▶ **lead away** vt emmener
▶ **lead back** vt ramener
▶ **lead off** vi (in game etc) commencer
▶ **lead on** vt (tease) faire marcher; **to ~ sb on to** (induce) amener qn à
▶ **lead up to** vt conduire à; (in conversation) en venir à
**lead²** [lɛd] n (metal) plomb m; (in pencil) mine f
**leaded** ['lɛdɪd] adj (windows) à petits carreaux
**leaded petrol** n essence f au plomb
**leaden** ['lɛdn] adj de or en plomb

**leader** ['li:dəʳ] n (of team) chef m; (of party etc) dirigeant(e), leader m; (Sport: in league) leader; (: in race) coureur m de tête; (in newspaper) éditorial m; **they are ~s in their field** (fig) ils sont à la pointe du progrès dans leur domaine; **the L~ of the House** (Brit) le chef de la majorité ministérielle

**leadership** ['li:dəʃɪp] n (position) direction f; **under the ~ of ...** sous la direction de ...; **qualities of ~** qualités fpl de chef or de meneur

**lead-free** ['lɛdfri:] adj sans plomb

**leading** ['li:dɪŋ] adj de premier plan; (main) principal(e); (in race) de tête; **~ question** une question tendancieuse; **~ role** rôle prépondérant or de premier plan

**leading lady** n (Theat) vedette (féminine)

**leading light** n (person) sommité f, personnalité f de premier plan

**leading man** (irreg) n (Theat) vedette (masculine)

**lead pencil** [lɛd-] n crayon noir or à papier

**lead poisoning** [led-] n saturnisme m

**lead singer** [li:d-] n (in pop group) (chanteur m) vedette f

**lead time** [li:d-] n (Comm) délai m de livraison

**lead weight** [led-] n plomb m

**leaf** (pl **leaves**) [li:f, li:vz] n feuille f; (of table) rallonge f; **to turn over a new ~** (fig) changer de conduite or d'existence; **to take a ~ out of sb's book** (fig) prendre exemple sur qn
▶ **leaf through** vt (book) feuilleter

**leaflet** ['li:flɪt] n prospectus m, brochure f; (Pol, Rel) tract m

**leafy** ['li:fɪ] adj feuillu(e)

**league** [li:g] n ligue f; (Football) championnat m; (measure) lieue f; **to be in ~ with** avoir partie liée avec, être de mèche avec

**league table** n classement m

**leak** [li:k] n (out: also fig) fuite f; (in) infiltration f ▷ vi (pipe, liquid etc) fuir; (shoes) prendre l'eau; (ship) faire eau ▷ vt (liquid) répandre; (information) divulguer
▶ **leak out** vi fuir; (information) être divulgué(e)

**leakage** ['li:kɪdʒ] n (also fig) fuite f

**leaky** ['li:kɪ] adj (pipe, bucket) qui fuit, percé(e); (roof) qui coule; (shoe) qui prend l'eau; (boat) qui fait eau

**lean** [li:n] (pt, pp **-ed** or **leant** [lɛnt]) adj maigre ▷ n (of meat) maigre m ▷ vt: **to ~ sth on** appuyer qch sur ▷ vi (slope) pencher; (rest): **to ~ against** s'appuyer contre; être appuyé(e) contre; **to ~ on** s'appuyer sur
▶ **lean back** vi se pencher en arrière
▶ **lean forward** vi se pencher en avant
▶ **lean out** vi: **to ~ out (of)** se pencher au dehors (de)
▶ **lean over** vi se pencher

**leaning** ['li:nɪŋ] adj penché(e) ▷ n: **~ (towards)** penchant m (pour); **the L~ Tower of Pisa** la tour penchée de Pise

**leant** [lɛnt] pt, pp of **lean**

**lean-to** ['li:ntu:] n appentis m

**leap** [li:p] n bond m, saut m ▷ vi (pt, pp **-ed** or **leapt** [lɛpt]) bondir, sauter; **to ~ at an offer** saisir une offre
▶ **leap up** vi (person) faire un bond; se lever d'un bond

**leapfrog** ['li:pfrɔg] n jeu m de saute-mouton

**leapt** [lɛpt] pt, pp of **leap**

**leap year** n année f bissextile

**learn** (pt, pp **-ed** or **-t**) [lə:n, -t] vt, vi apprendre; **to ~ (how) to do sth** apprendre à faire qch; **we were sorry to ~ that ...** nous avons appris avec regret que ...; **to ~ about sth** (Scol) étudier qch; (hear, read) apprendre qch

**learned** ['lə:nɪd] adj érudit(e), savant(e)

**learner** ['lə:nəʳ] n débutant(e); (Brit: also: **learner driver**) (conducteur(-trice)) débutant(e)

**learning** ['lə:nɪŋ] n savoir m

**learnt** [lə:nt] pp of **learn**

**lease** [li:s] n bail m ▷ vt louer à bail; **on ~** en location
▶ **lease back** vt vendre en cession-bail

**leaseback** ['li:sbæk] n cession-bail f

**leasehold** ['li:shəuld] n (contract) bail m ▷ adj loué(e) à bail

**leash** [li:ʃ] n laisse f

**least** [li:st] adj: **the ~** (+ noun) le (la) plus petit(e), le (la) moindre; (smallest amount of) le moins de ▷ pron: **(the) ~** le moins ▷ adv (+ verb) le moins; (+ adj): **the ~** le (la) moins; **the ~ money** le moins d'argent; **the ~ expensive** le (la) moins cher (chère); **the ~ possible effort** le moins d'effort possible; **at ~** au moins; (or rather) du moins; **you could at ~ have written** tu aurais au moins pu écrire; **not in the ~** pas le moins du monde

**leather** ['lɛðəʳ] n cuir m ▷ cpd en or de cuir; **~ goods** maroquinerie f

**leave** [li:v] (vb: pt, pp **left** [lɛft]) vt laisser; (go away from) quitter; (forget) oublier ▷ vi partir, s'en aller ▷ n (time off) congé m; (Mil, also: consent) permission f; **what time does the train/bus ~?** le train/le bus part à quelle heure?; **to ~ sth to sb** (money etc) laisser qch à qn; **to be left** rester; **there's some milk left over** il reste du lait; **to ~ school** quitter l'école, terminer sa scolarité; **~ it to me!** laissez-moi faire!, je m'en occupe!; **on ~** en permission; **to take one's ~ of** prendre congé de; **~ of absence** n congé exceptionnel; (Mil) permission spéciale
▶ **leave behind** vt (also fig) laisser; (opponent in race) distancer; (forget) laisser, oublier
▶ **leave off** vt (cover, lid, heating) ne pas (re)mettre; (light) ne pas (r)allumer, laisser éteint(e); (Brit inf: stop): **to ~ off (doing sth)** s'arrêter (de faire qch)
▶ **leave on** vt (coat etc) garder, ne pas enlever; (lid) laisser dessus; (light, fire, cooker) laisser allumé(e)
▶ **leave out** vt oublier, omettre

**leaves** [li:vz] npl of **leaf**

**leavetaking** ['li:vteɪkɪŋ] n adieux mpl

**Lebanese** [lɛbə'ni:z] adj libanais(e) ▷ n (pl inv)

655

Libanais(e)

**Lebanon** ['lɛbənən] n Liban m

**lecherous** ['lɛtʃərəs] adj lubrique

**lectern** ['lɛktəːn] n lutrin m, pupitre m

**lecture** ['lɛktʃəʳ] n conférence f; (Scol) cours (magistral) ▷ vi donner des cours; enseigner ▷ vt (scold) sermonner, réprimander; **to ~ on** faire un cours (or son cours) sur; **to give a ~ (on)** faire une conférence (sur), faire un cours (sur)

**lecture hall** n amphithéâtre m

**lecturer** ['lɛktʃərəʳ] n (speaker) conférencier(-ère) f; (Brit: at university) professeur m (d'université), prof m/f de fac (inf); **assistant ~** (Brit) = assistant(e); **senior ~** (Brit) = chargé(e) d'enseignement

**lecture theatre** n = **lecture hall**

**LED** n abbr (= light-emitting diode) LED f, diode électroluminescente

**led** [lɛd] pt, pp of **lead¹**

**ledge** [lɛdʒ] n (of window, on wall) rebord m; (of mountain) saillie f, corniche f

**ledger** ['lɛdʒəʳ] n registre m, grand livre

**lee** [liː] n côté m sous le vent; **in the ~ of** à l'abri de

**leech** [liːtʃ] n sangsue f

**leek** [liːk] n poireau m

**leer** [lɪəʳ] vi: **to ~ at sb** regarder qn d'un air mauvais or concupiscent, lorgner qn

**leeward** ['liːwəd] adj, adv sous le vent ▷ n côté m sous le vent; **to ~** sous le vent

**leeway** ['liːweɪ] n (fig): **to make up ~** rattraper son retard; **to have some ~** avoir une certaine liberté d'action

**left** [lɛft] pt, pp of **leave** ▷ adj gauche ▷ adv à gauche ▷ n gauche f; **there are two ~** il en reste deux; **on the ~, to the ~** à gauche; **the L~** (Pol) la gauche

**left-hand** ['lɛfthænd] adj: **the ~ side** la gauche, le côté gauche

**left-hand drive** ['lɛfthænd-] n (Brit) conduite f à gauche; (vehicle) véhicule m avec la conduite à gauche

**left-handed** [lɛft'hændɪd] adj gaucher(-ère); (scissors etc) pour gauchers

**leftie** ['lɛftɪ] n (inf) gaucho m/f, gauchiste m/f

**leftist** ['lɛftɪst] adj (Pol) gauchiste, de gauche

**left-luggage** [lɛft'lʌɡɪdʒ], **left-luggage office** n (Brit) consigne f

**left-luggage locker** [lɛft'lʌɡɪdʒ-] n (Brit) (casier m à) consigne f automatique

**left-overs** ['lɛftəuvəz] npl restes mpl

**left wing** n (Mil, Sport) aile f gauche; (Pol) gauche f

**left-wing** ['lɛft'wɪŋ] adj (Pol) de gauche

**left-winger** ['lɛft'wɪŋɡəʳ] n (Pol) membre m de la gauche; (Sport) ailier m gauche

**lefty** ['lɛftɪ] n (inf) = **leftie**

**leg** [lɛɡ] n jambe f; (of animal) patte f; (of furniture) pied m; (Culin: of chicken) cuisse f; (of journey) étape f; **1st/2nd ~** (Sport) match m aller/retour; (of journey) 1ère/2ème étape f; **~ of lamb** (Culin) gigot m d'agneau; **to stretch one's ~s** se

dégourdir les jambes

**legacy** ['lɛɡəsɪ] n (also fig) héritage m, legs m

**legal** ['liːɡl] adj (permitted by law) légal(e); (relating to law) juridique; **to take ~ action** or **proceedings against sb** poursuivre qn en justice

**legal adviser** n conseiller(-ère) juridique

**legal holiday** (US) n jour férié

**legality** [lɪ'ɡælɪtɪ] n légalité f

**legalize** ['liːɡəlaɪz] vt légaliser

**legally** ['liːɡəlɪ] adv légalement; **~ binding** juridiquement contraignant(e)

**legal tender** n monnaie légale

**legation** [lɪ'ɡeɪʃən] n légation f

**legend** ['lɛdʒənd] n légende f

**legendary** ['lɛdʒəndərɪ] adj légendaire

**-legged** ['lɛɡɪd] suffix: **two~** à deux pattes (or jambes or pieds)

**leggings** ['lɛɡɪŋz] npl caleçon m

**leggy** ['lɛɡɪ] adj aux longues jambes

**legibility** [lɛdʒɪ'bɪlɪtɪ] n lisibilité f

**legible** ['lɛdʒəbl] adj lisible

**legibly** ['lɛdʒəblɪ] adv lisiblement

**legion** ['liːdʒən] n légion f

**legionnaire** [liːdʒə'nɛəʳ] n légionnaire m; **~'s disease** maladie f du légionnaire

**legislate** ['lɛdʒɪsleɪt] vi légiférer

**legislation** [lɛdʒɪs'leɪʃən] n législation f; **a piece of ~** un texte de loi

**legislative** ['lɛdʒɪslətɪv] adj législatif(-ive)

**legislator** ['lɛdʒɪsleɪtəʳ] n législateur(-trice)

**legislature** ['lɛdʒɪslətʃəʳ] n corps législatif

**legitimacy** [lɪ'dʒɪtɪməsɪ] n légitimité f

**legitimate** [lɪ'dʒɪtɪmət] adj légitime

**legitimize** [lɪ'dʒɪtɪmaɪz] vt légitimer

**legless** ['lɛɡlɪs] adj (Brit inf) bourré(e)

**leg-room** ['lɛɡruːm] n place f pour les jambes

**Leics** abbr (Brit) = **Leicestershire**

**leisure** ['lɛʒəʳ] n (free time) temps libre, loisirs mpl; **at ~** (tout) à loisir; **at your ~** (later) à tête reposée

**leisure centre** n (Brit) centre m de loisirs

**leisurely** ['lɛʒəlɪ] adj tranquille, fait(e) sans se presser

**leisure suit** n (Brit) survêtement m (mode)

**lemon** ['lɛmən] n citron m

**lemonade** [lɛmə'neɪd] n (fizzy) limonade f

**lemon cheese, lemon curd** n crème f de citron

**lemon juice** n jus m de citron

**lemon squeezer** [-skwiːzəʳ] n presse-citron m inv

**lemon tea** n thé m au citron

**lend** (pt, pp **lent**) [lɛnd, lɛnt] vt: **to ~ sth (to sb)** prêter qch (à qn); **could you ~ me some money?** pourriez-vous me prêter de l'argent?; **to ~ a hand** donner un coup de main

**lender** ['lɛndəʳ] n prêteur(-euse)

**lending library** ['lɛndɪŋ-] n bibliothèque f de prêt

**length** [lɛŋθ] n longueur f; (section: of road, pipe etc) morceau m, bout m; **~ of time** durée f; **what ~ is it?** quelle longueur fait-il?; **it is 2 metres**

in ~ cela fait 2 mètres de long; **to fall full ~**
tomber de tout son long; **at ~** (at last) enfin, à la
fin; (lengthily) longuement; **to go to any ~(s) to**
**do sth** faire n'importe quoi pour faire qch, ne
reculer devant rien pour faire qch
**lengthen** ['lɛŋθn] vt allonger, prolonger ▷ vi
s'allonger
**lengthways** ['lɛŋθweɪz] adv dans le sens de la
longueur, en long
**lengthy** ['lɛŋθɪ] adj (très) long (longue)
**leniency** ['li:nɪənsɪ] n indulgence f, clémence f
**lenient** ['li:nɪənt] adj indulgent(e), clément(e)
**leniently** ['li:nɪəntlɪ] adv avec indulgence or
clémence
**lens** [lɛnz] n lentille f; (of spectacles) verre m; (of
camera) objectif m
**Lent** [lɛnt] n carême m
**lent** [lɛnt] pt, pp of **lend**
**lentil** ['lɛntl] n lentille f
**Leo** ['li:əu] n le Lion; **to be ~** être du Lion
**leopard** ['lɛpəd] n léopard m
**leotard** ['li:əta:d] n justaucorps m
**leper** ['lɛpə'] n lépreux(-euse)
**leper colony** n léproserie f
**leprosy** ['lɛprəsɪ] n lèpre f
**lesbian** ['lɛzbɪən] n lesbienne f ▷ adj lesbien(ne)
**lesion** ['li:ʒən] n (Med) lésion f
**Lesotho** [lɪ'su:tu:] n Lesotho m
**less** [lɛs] adj moins de ▷ pron, adv moins ▷ prep: ~
**tax/10% discount** avant impôt/moins 10% de
remise; **~ than that/you** moins que cela/vous;
**~ than half** moins de la moitié; **~ than ever** moins
**kilo/3 metres** moins de un/d'un kilo/de 3
mètres; **~ than ever** moins que jamais; **~ and ~**
de moins en moins; **the ~ he works ...** moins il
travaille ...
**lessee** [lɛ'si:] n locataire m/f (à bail),
preneur(-euse) du bail
**lessen** ['lɛsn] vi diminuer, s'amoindrir,
s'atténuer ▷ vt diminuer, réduire, atténuer
**lesser** ['lɛsə'] adj moindre; **to a ~ extent** or
**degree** à un degré moindre
**lesson** ['lɛsn] n leçon f; **a maths ~** une leçon or
un cours de maths; **to give ~s in** donner des
cours de; **to teach sb a ~** (fig) donner une bonne
leçon à qn; **it taught him a ~** (fig) cela lui a
servi de leçon
**lessor** ['lɛsɔ:', lɛ'sɔ:'] n bailleur(-eresse)
**lest** [lɛst] conj de peur de + infinitive, de peur que
+ sub
**let** (pt, pp -) [lɛt] vt laisser; (Brit: lease) louer; **to ~**
**sb do sth** laisser qn faire qch; **to ~ sb know sth**
faire savoir qch à qn, prévenir qn de qch; **he ~**
**me go** il m'a laissé partir; **~ the water boil**
**and ...** faites bouillir l'eau et ...; **~ go** lâcher
prise; **to ~ go of sth, to ~ sth go** lâcher qch; **~'s**
**go** allons-y; **~ him come** qu'il vienne; **"to ~"**
(Brit) "à louer"
▶ **let down** vt (lower) baisser; (dress) rallonger;
(hair) défaire; (Brit: tyre) dégonfler; (disappoint)
décevoir
▶ **let go** vi lâcher prise ▷ vt lâcher

▶ **let in** vt laisser entrer; (visitor etc) faire entrer;
**what have you ~ yourself in for?** à quoi t'es-tu
engagé?
▶ **let off** vt (allow to leave) laisser partir; (not
punish) ne pas punir; (taxi driver, bus driver)
déposer; (firework etc) faire partir; (bomb) faire
exploser; (smell etc) dégager; **to ~ off steam** (fig:
inf) se défouler, décharger sa rate or bile
▶ **let on** vi (inf): **to ~ on that ....** révéler que ...,
dire que ...
▶ **let out** vt laisser sortir; (dress) élargir; (scream)
laisser échapper; (Brit: rent out) louer
▶ **let up** vi diminuer, s'arrêter
**let-down** ['lɛtdaun] n (disappointment)
déception f
**lethal** ['li:θl] adj mortel(le), fatal(e); (weapon)
meurtrier(-ère)
**lethargic** [lɛ'θɑ:dʒɪk] adj léthargique
**lethargy** ['lɛθədʒɪ] n léthargie f
**letter** ['lɛtə'] n lettre f; **letters** npl (Literature)
lettres; **small/capital ~** minuscule f/majuscule
f; **~ of credit** lettre f de crédit
**letter bomb** n lettre piégée
**letterbox** ['lɛtəbɔks] n (Brit) boîte f aux or à
lettres
**letterhead** ['lɛtəhɛd] n en-tête m
**lettering** ['lɛtərɪŋ] n lettres fpl; caractères mpl
**letter opener** n coupe-papier m
**letterpress** ['lɛtəprɛs] n (method) typographie f
**letter quality** n qualité f "courrier"
**letters patent** npl brevet m d'invention
**lettuce** ['lɛtɪs] n laitue f, salade f
**let-up** ['lɛtʌp] n répit m, détente f
**leukaemia**, (US) **leukemia** [lu:'ki:mɪə] n
leucémie f
**level** ['lɛvl] adj (flat) plat(e), plan(e), uni(e);
(horizontal) horizontal(e) ▷ n niveau m; (flat
place) terrain plat; (also: **spirit level**) niveau à
bulle ▷ vt niveler, aplanir; (gun) pointer,
braquer; (accusation): **to ~ (against)** lancer or
porter (contre) ▷ vi (inf): **to ~ with sb** être franc
(franche) avec qn; **"A" ~s** (npl: Brit)
≈ baccalauréat m; **"O" ~s** npl (Brit: formerly)
examens passés à l'âge de 16 ans sanctionnant les
connaissances de l'élève, ≈ brevet m des collèges; **a ~**
**spoonful** (Culin) une cuillerée rase; **to be ~**
**with** être au même niveau que; **to draw ~ with**
(team) arriver à égalité de points avec, égaliser
avec; arriver au même classement que; (runner,
car) arriver à la hauteur de, rattraper; **on the ~** à
l'horizontale; (fig: honest) régulier(-ière)
▶ **level off, level out** vi (prices etc) se stabiliser
▷ vt (ground) aplanir, niveler
**level crossing** n (Brit) passage m à niveau
**level-headed** [lɛvl'hɛdɪd] adj équilibré(e)
**levelling**, (US) **leveling** ['lɛvlɪŋ] adj (process,
effect) de nivellement
**level playing field** n: **to compete on a ~** jouer
sur un terrain d'égalité
**lever** ['li:və'] n levier m ▷ vt: **to ~ up/out**
soulever/extraire au moyen d'un levier
**leverage** ['li:vərɪdʒ] n (influence): **~ (on or with)**

prise f (sur)

**levity** ['lɛvɪtɪ] n manque m de sérieux, légèreté f

**levy** ['lɛvɪ] n taxe f, impôt m ▷ vt (tax) lever; (fine) infliger

**lewd** [luːd] adj obscène, lubrique

**lexicographer** [lɛksɪ'kɔgrəfəʳ] n lexicographe m/f

**lexicography** [lɛksɪ'kɔgrəfɪ] n lexicographie f

**LGV** n abbr (= Large Goods Vehicle) poids lourd

**LI** abbr (US) = **Long Island**

**liabilities** [laɪə'bɪlətɪz] npl (Comm) obligations fpl, engagements mpl; (on balance sheet) passif m

**liability** [laɪə'bɪlətɪ] n responsabilité f; (handicap) handicap m

**liable** ['laɪəbl] adj (subject): ~ **to** sujet(te) à, passible de; (responsible): ~ (**for**) responsable (de); (likely): ~ **to do** susceptible de faire; **to be ~ to a fine** être passible d'une amende

**liaise** [liː'eɪz] vi: **to ~ with** assurer la liaison avec

**liaison** [liː'eɪzɔn] n liaison f

**liar** ['laɪəʳ] n menteur(-euse)

**libel** ['laɪbl] n diffamation f; (document) écrit m diffamatoire ▷ vt diffamer

**libellous** ['laɪbləs] adj diffamatoire

**liberal** ['lɪbərl] adj libéral(e); (generous): ~ **with** prodigue de, généreux(-euse) avec ▷ n: **L~** (Pol) libéral(e)

**Liberal Democrat** n (Brit) libéral(e)-démocrate m/f

**liberality** [lɪbə'rælɪtɪ] n (generosity) générosité f, libéralité f

**liberalize** ['lɪbərəlaɪz] vt libéraliser

**liberal-minded** ['lɪbərl'maɪndɪd] adj libéral(e), tolérant(e)

**liberate** ['lɪbəreɪt] vt libérer

**liberation** [lɪbə'reɪʃən] n libération f

**liberation theology** n théologie f de libération

**Liberia** [laɪ'bɪərɪə] n Libéria m, Liberia m

**Liberian** [laɪ'bɪərɪən] adj libérien(ne) ▷ n Libérien(ne)

**liberty** ['lɪbətɪ] n liberté f; **to be at ~** (criminal) être en liberté; **at ~ to do** libre de faire; **to take the ~ of** prendre la liberté de, se permettre de

**libido** [lɪ'biːdəu] n libido f

**Libra** ['liːbrə] n la Balance; **to be ~** être de la Balance

**librarian** [laɪ'brɛərɪən] n bibliothécaire m/f

**library** ['laɪbrərɪ] n bibliothèque f

**library book** n livre m de bibliothèque

**libretto** [lɪ'brɛtəu] n livret m

**Libya** ['lɪbɪə] n Libye f

**Libyan** ['lɪbɪən] adj libyen(ne), de Libye ▷ n Libyen(ne)

**lice** [laɪs] npl of **louse**

**licence**, (US) **license** ['laɪsns] n autorisation f, permis m; (Comm) licence f; (Radio, TV) redevance f; (also: **driving licence**; US: also: **driver's license**) permis m (de conduire); (excessive freedom) licence; **import ~** licence d'importation; **produced under ~** fabriqué(e) sous licence

**licence number** n (Brit Aut) numéro m d'immatriculation

**license** ['laɪsns] n (US) = **licence** ▷ vt donner une licence à; (car) acheter la vignette de; délivrer la vignette de

**licensed** ['laɪsnst] adj (for alcohol) patenté(e) pour la vente des spiritueux, qui a une patente de débit de boissons; (car) muni(e) de la vignette

**licensee** [laɪsən'siː] n (Brit: of pub) patron(ne), gérant(e)

**license plate** n (US Aut) plaque f minéralogique

**licensing hours** (Brit) npl heures fpl d'ouvertures (des pubs)

**licentious** [laɪ'sɛnʃəs] adj licencieux(-euse)

**lichen** ['laɪkən] n lichen m

**lick** [lɪk] vt lécher; (inf: defeat) écraser, flanquer une piquette or raclée à ▷ n coup m de langue; **a ~ of paint** un petit coup de peinture; **to ~ one's lips** (fig) se frotter les mains

**licorice** ['lɪkərɪs] n = **liquorice**

**lid** [lɪd] n couvercle m; (eyelid) paupière f; **to take the ~ off sth** (fig) exposer or étaler qch au grand jour

**lido** ['laɪdəu] n piscine f en plein air, complexe m balnéaire

**lie** [laɪ] n mensonge m ▷ vi (pt, pp **-d**) (tell lies) mentir; (pt **lay**, pp **lain** [leɪ, leɪn]) (rest) être étendu(e) or allongé(e) or couché(e); (in grave) être enterré(e), reposer; (object: be situated) se trouver, être; **to ~ low** (fig) se cacher, rester caché(e); **to tell ~s** mentir

▶ **lie about, lie around** vi (things) traîner; (Brit: person) traînasser, flemmarder

▶ **lie back** vi se renverser en arrière

▶ **lie down** vi se coucher, s'étendre

▶ **lie up** vi (hide) se cacher

**Liechtenstein** ['lɪktənstaɪn] n Liechtenstein m

**lie detector** n détecteur m de mensonges

**lie-down** ['laɪdaun] n (Brit): **to have a ~** s'allonger, se reposer

**lie-in** ['laɪɪn] n (Brit): **to have a ~** faire la grasse matinée

**lieu** [luː]: **in ~ of** prep au lieu de, à la place de

**Lieut.** abbr (= lieutenant) Lt

**lieutenant** [lɛf'tɛnənt, (US) luː'tɛnənt] n lieutenant m

**lieutenant-colonel** [lɛf'tɛnənt'kə:nl, (US) luː'tɛnənt'kə:nl] n lieutenant-colonel m

**life** (pl **lives**) [laɪf, laɪvz] n vie f; **to come to ~** (fig) s'animer ▷ cpd de vie; de la vie; à vie; **true to ~** réaliste, fidèle à la réalité; **to paint from ~** peindre d'après nature; **to be sent to prison for ~** être condamné(e) (à la réclusion criminelle) à perpétuité; **country/city ~** la vie à la campagne/à la ville

**life annuity** n pension f, rente viagère

**life assurance** n (Brit) = **life insurance**

**lifebelt** ['laɪfbɛlt] n (Brit) bouée f de sauvetage

**lifeblood** ['laɪfblʌd] n (fig) élément moteur

**lifeboat** ['laɪfbəut] n canot m or chaloupe f de sauvetage

**lifebuoy** ['laɪfbɔɪ] n bouée f de sauvetage

**life expectancy** n espérance f de vie

**lifeguard** ['laɪfgɑːd] n surveillant m de baignade
**life imprisonment** n prison f à vie; (Law) réclusion f à perpétuité
**life insurance** n assurance-vie f
**life jacket** n gilet m or ceinture f de sauvetage
**lifeless** ['laɪflɪs] adj sans vie, inanimé(e); (dull) qui manque de vie or de vigueur
**lifelike** ['laɪflaɪk] adj qui semble vrai(e) or vivant(e), ressemblant(e); (painting) réaliste
**lifeline** ['laɪflaɪn] n corde f de sauvetage
**lifelong** ['laɪflɔŋ] adj de toute une vie, de toujours
**life preserver** [-prɪ'zə:vəʳ] n (US) gilet m or ceinture f de sauvetage
**lifer** ['laɪfəʳ] n (inf) condamné(e) à perpète
**life-raft** ['laɪfrɑːft] n radeau m de sauvetage
**life-saver** ['laɪfseɪvəʳ] n surveillant m de baignade
**life-saving** ['laɪfseɪvɪŋ] n sauvetage m
**life sentence** n condamnation f à vie or à perpétuité
**life-size** ['laɪfsaɪz], **life-sized** ['laɪfsaɪzd] adj grandeur nature inv
**life span** n (durée f de) vie f
**lifestyle** ['laɪfstaɪl] n style m de vie
**life-support system** n (Med) respirateur artificiel
**lifetime** ['laɪftaɪm] n: **in his ~** de son vivant; **the chance of a ~** la chance de ma (or sa etc) vie, une occasion unique
**lift** [lɪft] vt soulever, lever; (end) supprimer, lever; (steal) prendre, voler ▷ vi (fog) se lever ▷ n (Brit: elevator) ascenseur m; **to give sb a ~** (Brit) emmener or prendre qn en voiture; **can you give me a ~ to the station?** pouvez-vous m'emmener à la gare?
▶ **lift off** vi (rocket, helicopter) décoller
▶ **lift out** vt sortir; (troops, evacuees etc) évacuer par avion or hélicoptère
▶ **lift up** vt soulever
**lift-off** ['lɪftɔf] n décollage m
**ligament** ['lɪgəmənt] n ligament m
**light** [laɪt] n lumière f; (daylight) lumière, jour m; (lamp) lampe f; (Aut: rear light) feu m; (: headlamp) phare m; (for cigarette etc): **have you got a ~?** avez-vous du feu? ▷ vt (pt, pp **-ed**, pt, pp **lit** [lɪt]) (candle, cigarette, fire) allumer; (room) éclairer ▷ adj (room, colour) clair(e); (not heavy, also fig) léger(-ère); (not strenuous) peu fatigant(e) ▷ adv (travel) avec peu de bagages; **lights** npl (traffic lights) feux mpl; **to turn the ~ on/off** allumer/éteindre; **to cast or shed or throw ~ on** éclaircir; **to come to ~** être dévoilé(e) or découvert(e); **in the ~ of** à la lumière de; étant donné; **to make ~ of sth** (fig) prendre qch à la légère, faire peu de cas de qch
▶ **light up** vi s'allumer; (face) s'éclairer; (smoke) allumer une cigarette or une pipe etc ▷ vt (illuminate) éclairer, illuminer
**light bulb** n ampoule f
**lighten** ['laɪtn] vi s'éclairer ▷ vt (light up) éclairer; (make lighter) éclaircir; (make less heavy)

alléger
**lighter** ['laɪtəʳ] n (also: **cigarette lighter**) briquet m; (: in car) allume-cigare m inv; (boat) péniche f
**light-fingered** [laɪt'fɪŋgəd] adj chapardeur(-euse)
**light-headed** [laɪt'hɛdɪd] adj étourdi(e), écervelé(e)
**light-hearted** [laɪt'hɑːtɪd] adj gai(e), joyeux(-euse), enjoué(e)
**lighthouse** ['laɪthaus] n phare m
**lighting** ['laɪtɪŋ] n éclairage m; (in theatre) éclairages
**lighting-up time** [laɪtɪŋ'ʌp-] n (Brit) heure officielle de la tombée du jour
**lightly** ['laɪtlɪ] adv légèrement; **to get off ~** s'en tirer à bon compte
**light meter** n (Phot) photomètre m, cellule f
**lightness** ['laɪtnɪs] n clarté f; (in weight) légèreté f
**lightning** ['laɪtnɪŋ] n foudre f; (flash) éclair m
**lightning conductor**, (US) **lightning rod** n paratonnerre m
**lightning strike** n (Brit) grève f surprise
**light pen** n crayon m optique
**lightship** ['laɪtʃɪp] n bateau-phare m
**lightweight** ['laɪtweɪt] adj (suit) léger(-ère) ▷ n (Boxing) poids léger
**light year** ['laɪtjɪəʳ] n année-lumière f
**like** [laɪk] vt aimer (bien) ▷ prep comme ▷ adj semblable, pareil(le) ▷ n: **the ~** un(e) pareil(e) or semblable; **le (la) pareil(le)**; (pej) (d')autres du même genre or acabit; **his ~s and dislikes** ses goûts mpl or préférences fpl; **I would ~**, **I'd ~** je voudrais, j'aimerais; **would you ~ a coffee?** voulez-vous du café?; **to be/look ~ sb/sth** ressembler à qn/qch; **what's he ~?** comment est-il?; **what's the weather ~?** quel temps fait-il?; **what does it look ~?** de quoi est-ce que ça a l'air?; **what does it taste ~?** quel goût est-ce que ça a?; **that's just ~ him** c'est bien de lui, ça lui ressemble; **something ~ that** quelque chose comme ça; **do it ~ this** fais-le comme ceci; **I feel ~ a drink** je boirais bien quelque chose; **if you ~** si vous voulez; **it's nothing ~ ...** ce n'est pas du tout comme ...; **there's nothing ~ ...** il n'y a rien de tel que ...
**likeable** ['laɪkəbl] adj sympathique, agréable
**likelihood** ['laɪklɪhud] n probabilité f; **in all ~** selon toute vraisemblance
**likely** ['laɪklɪ] adj (result, outcome) probable; (excuse) plausible; **he's ~ to leave** il va sûrement partir, il risque fort de partir; **not ~!** (inf) pas de danger!
**like-minded** ['laɪk'maɪndɪd] adj de même opinion
**liken** ['laɪkən] vt: **to ~ sth to** comparer qch à
**likeness** ['laɪknɪs] n ressemblance f
**likewise** ['laɪkwaɪz] adv de même, pareillement
**liking** ['laɪkɪŋ] n (for person) affection f; (for thing) penchant m; goût m; **to take a ~ to sb** se prendre d'amitié pour qn; **to be to sb's ~** être au goût de qn, plaire à qn
**lilac** ['laɪlək] n lilas m ▷ adj lilas inv

659

**Lilo®** ['laɪləʊ] n matelas m pneumatique
**lilt** [lɪlt] n rythme m, cadence f
**lilting** ['lɪltɪŋ] adj aux cadences mélodieuses; chantant(e)
**lily** ['lɪlɪ] n lis m; ~ **of the valley** muguet m
**Lima** ['liːmə] n Lima
**limb** [lɪm] n membre m; **to be out on a** ~ (fig) être isolé(e)
**limber** ['lɪmbəʳ]: **to** ~ **up** vi se dégourdir, se mettre en train
**limbo** ['lɪmbəʊ] n: **to be in** ~ (fig) être tombé(e) dans l'oubli
**lime** [laɪm] n (tree) tilleul m; (fruit) citron vert, lime f; (Geo) chaux f
**lime juice** n jus m de citron vert
**limelight** ['laɪmlaɪt] n: **in the** ~ (fig) en vedette, au premier plan
**limerick** ['lɪmərɪk] n petit poème humoristique
**limestone** ['laɪmstəʊn] n pierre f à chaux; (Geo) calcaire m
**limit** ['lɪmɪt] n limite f ▷ vt limiter; **weight/speed** ~ limite de poids/de vitesse
**limitation** [lɪmɪ'teɪʃən] n limitation f, restriction f
**limited** ['lɪmɪtɪd] adj limité(e), restreint(e); ~ **edition** édition f à tirage limité; **to be** ~ **to** se limiter à, ne concerner que
**limited company, limited liability company** n (Brit) ≈ société f anonyme
**limitless** ['lɪmɪtlɪs] adj illimité(e)
**limousine** ['lɪməziːn] n limousine f
**limp** [lɪmp] n: **to have a** ~ boiter ▷ vi boiter ▷ adj mou (molle)
**limpet** ['lɪmpɪt] n patelle f; **like a** ~ (fig) comme une ventouse
**limpid** ['lɪmpɪd] adj limpide
**linchpin** ['lɪntʃpɪn] n esse f; (fig) pivot m
**Lincs** [lɪŋks] abbr (Brit) = **Lincolnshire**
**line** [laɪn] n (gen) ligne f; (stroke) trait m; (wrinkle) ride f; (rope) corde f; (wire) fil m; (of poem) vers m; (row, series) rangée f; (of people) file f, queue f; (railway track) voie f; (Comm: series of goods) article(s) m(pl), ligne de produits; (work) métier m ▷ vt: **to** ~ **(with)** (clothes) doubler (de); (box) garnir or tapisser (de); (subj: trees, crowd) border; **to stand in** ~ (US) faire la queue; **to cut in** ~ (US) passer avant son tour; **in his** ~ **of business** dans sa partie, dans son rayon; **on the right** ~**s** sur la bonne voie; **a new** ~ **in cosmetics** une nouvelle ligne de produits de beauté; **hold the** ~ **please** (Brit Tel) ne quittez pas; **to be in** ~ **for sth** (fig) être en lice pour qch; **in** ~ **with** en accord avec, en conformité avec; **in a** ~ aligné(e); **to bring sth into** ~ **with sth** aligner qch sur qch; **to draw the** ~ **at (doing) sth** (fig) se refuser à (faire) qch; ne pas tolérer or admettre (qu'on fasse) qch; **to take the** ~ **that** ... être d'avis or de l'opinion que ...
▶ **line up** vi s'aligner, se mettre en rang(s); (in queue) faire la queue ▷ vt aligner; (event) prévoir; (find) trouver; **to have sb/sth** ~**d up** avoir qn/qch en vue or de prévu(e)

**linear** ['lɪnɪəʳ] adj linéaire
**lined** [laɪnd] adj (paper) réglé(e); (face) marqué(e), ridé(e); (clothes) doublé(e)
**lineman** ['laɪnmən] (irreg) n (US: Rail) poseur m de rails; (: Tel) ouvrier m de ligne; (: Football) avant m
**linen** ['lɪnɪn] n linge m (de corps or de maison); (cloth) lin m
**line printer** n imprimante f (ligne par) ligne
**liner** ['laɪnəʳ] n (ship) paquebot m de ligne; (for bin) sac-poubelle m
**linesman** ['laɪnzmən] (irreg) n (Tennis) juge m de ligne; (Football) juge de touche
**line-up** ['laɪnʌp] n (US: queue) file f; (also: **police line-up**) parade f d'identification; (Sport) (composition f de l')équipe f
**linger** ['lɪŋgəʳ] vi s'attarder; traîner; (smell, tradition) persister
**lingerie** ['lænʒəriː] n lingerie f
**lingering** ['lɪŋgərɪŋ] adj persistant(e); qui subsiste; (death) lent(e)
**lingo** ['lɪŋgəʊ] (pl **-es**) n (pej) jargon m
**linguist** ['lɪŋgwɪst] n linguiste m/f; **to be a good** ~ être doué(e) pour les langues
**linguistic** [lɪŋ'gwɪstɪk] adj linguistique
**linguistics** [lɪŋ'gwɪstɪks] n linguistique f
**lining** ['laɪnɪŋ] n doublure f; (Tech) revêtement m; (: of brakes) garniture f
**link** [lɪŋk] n (connection) lien m, rapport m; (Internet) lien; (of a chain) maillon m ▷ vt relier, lier, unir; **links** npl (Golf) (terrain m de) golf m; **rail** ~ liaison f ferroviaire
▶ **link up** vt relier ▷ vi (people) se rejoindre; (companies etc) s'associer
**link-up** ['lɪŋkʌp] n lien m, rapport m; (of roads) jonction f, raccordement m; (of spaceships) arrimage m; (Radio, TV) liaison f; (: programme) duplex m
**lino** ['laɪnəʊ] n = **linoleum**
**linoleum** [lɪ'nəʊlɪəm] n linoléum m
**linseed oil** ['lɪnsiːd-] n huile f de lin
**lint** [lɪnt] n tissu ouaté (pour pansements)
**lintel** ['lɪntl] n linteau m
**lion** ['laɪən] n lion m
**lion cub** n lionceau m
**lioness** ['laɪənɪs] n lionne f
**lip** [lɪp] n lèvre f; (of cup etc) rebord m; (insolence) insolences fpl
**liposuction** ['lɪpəʊsʌkʃən] n liposuccion f
**lipread** ['lɪpriːd] vi (irreg: like **read**) lire sur les lèvres
**lip salve** [-sælv] n pommade f pour les lèvres, pommade rosat
**lip service** n: **to pay** ~ **to sth** ne reconnaître le mérite de qch que pour la forme or qu'en paroles
**lipstick** ['lɪpstɪk] n rouge m à lèvres
**liquefy** ['lɪkwɪfaɪ] vt liquéfier ▷ vi se liquéfier
**liqueur** [lɪ'kjuəʳ] n liqueur f
**liquid** ['lɪkwɪd] n liquide m ▷ adj liquide
**liquid assets** npl liquidités fpl, disponibilités fpl
**liquidate** ['lɪkwɪdeɪt] vt liquider
**liquidation** [lɪkwɪ'deɪʃən] n liquidation f; **to go**

**into** ~ déposer son bilan
**liquidator** ['lɪkwɪdeɪtə<sup>r</sup>] n liquidateur m
**liquid crystal display** n affichage m à cristaux liquides
**liquidize** ['lɪkwɪdaɪz] vt (Brit Culin) passer au mixer
**liquidizer** ['lɪkwɪdaɪzə<sup>r</sup>] n (Brit Culin) mixer m
**liquor** ['lɪkə<sup>r</sup>] n spiritueux m, alcool m
**liquorice** ['lɪkərɪs] n (Brit) réglisse m
**liquor store** (US) n magasin m de vins et spiritueux
**Lisbon** ['lɪzbən] n Lisbonne
**lisp** [lɪsp] n zézaiement m ▷ vi zézayer
**lissom** ['lɪsəm] adj souple, agile
**list** [lɪst] n liste f; (of ship) inclinaison f ▷ vt (write down) inscrire; (make list of) faire la liste de; (enumerate) énumérer; (Comput) lister ▷ vi (ship) gîter, donner de la bande; **shopping** ~ liste des courses
**listed building** ['lɪstɪd-] n (Archit) monument classé
**listed company** ['lɪstɪd-] n société cotée en Bourse
**listen** ['lɪsn] vi écouter; **to** ~ **to** écouter
**listener** ['lɪsnə<sup>r</sup>] n auditeur(-trice)
**listeria** [lɪs'tɪərɪə] n listéria f
**listing** ['lɪstɪŋ] n (Comput) listage m; (: hard copy) liste f, listing m
**listless** ['lɪstlɪs] adj indolent(e), apathique
**listlessly** ['lɪstlɪslɪ] adv avec indolence or apathie
**list price** n prix m de catalogue
**lit** [lɪt] pt, pp of **light**
**litany** ['lɪtənɪ] n litanie f
**liter** ['liːtə<sup>r</sup>] n (US) = **litre**
**literacy** ['lɪtərəsɪ] n degré m d'alphabétisation, fait m de savoir lire et écrire; (Brit: Scol) enseignement m de la lecture et de l'écriture
**literal** ['lɪtərl] adj littéral(e)
**literally** ['lɪtrəlɪ] adv littéralement; (really) réellement
**literary** ['lɪtərərɪ] adj littéraire
**literate** ['lɪtərət] adj qui sait lire et écrire; (educated) instruit(e)
**literature** ['lɪtrɪtʃə<sup>r</sup>] n littérature f; (brochures etc) copie f publicitaire, prospectus mpl
**lithe** [laɪð] adj agile, souple
**lithography** [lɪ'θɒgrəfɪ] n lithographie f
**Lithuania** [lɪθju'eɪnɪə] n Lituanie f
**Lithuanian** [lɪθju'eɪnɪən] adj lituanien(ne) ▷ n Lituanien(ne); (Ling) lituanien m
**litigate** ['lɪtɪgeɪt] vt mettre en litige ▷ vi plaider
**litigation** [lɪtɪ'geɪʃən] n litige m; contentieux m
**litmus** ['lɪtməs] n: ~ **paper** papier m de tournesol
**litre**, (US) **liter** ['liːtə<sup>r</sup>] n litre m
**litter** ['lɪtə<sup>r</sup>] n (rubbish) détritus mpl; (dirtier) ordures fpl; (young animals) portée f ▷ vt éparpiller; laisser des détritus dans; **~ed with** jonché(e) de, couvert(e) de
**litter bin** n (Brit) poubelle f
**litter lout**, (US) **litterbug** ['lɪtəbʌg] n personne qui jette des détritus par terre
**little** ['lɪtl] adj (small) petit(e); (not much): ~ **milk**

peu de lait ▷ adv peu; **a** ~ un peu (de); **a** ~ **milk** un peu de lait; **a** ~ **bit** un peu; **for a** ~ **while** pendant un petit moment; **with** ~ **difficulty** sans trop de difficulté; **as** ~ **as possible** le moins possible; ~ **by** ~ petit à petit, peu à peu; **to make** ~ **of** faire peu de cas de
**little finger** n auriculaire m, petit doigt
**little-known** ['lɪtl'nəun] adj peu connu(e)
**liturgy** ['lɪtədʒɪ] n liturgie f
**live¹** [laɪv] adj (animal) vivant(e), en vie; (wire) sous tension; (broadcast) (transmis(e)) en direct; (issue) d'actualité, brûlant(e); (unexploded) non explosé(e); ~ **ammunition** munitions fpl de combat
**live²** [lɪv] vi vivre; (reside) vivre, habiter; **to** ~ **in London** habiter (à) Londres; **where do you** ~? où habitez-vous?
▸ **live down** vt faire oublier (avec le temps)
▸ **live in** vi être logé(e) et nourri(e); être interne
▸ **live off** vt (land, fish etc) vivre de; (pej: parents etc) vivre aux crochets de
▸ **live on** vt fus (food) vivre de ▷ vi survivre; **to** ~ **on £50 a week** vivre avec 50 livres par semaine
▸ **live out** vi (Brit: students) être externe ▷ vt: **to** ~ **out one's days** or **life** passer sa vie
▸ **live together** vi vivre ensemble, cohabiter
▸ **live up** vt: **to** ~ **it up** (inf) faire la fête; mener la grande vie
▸ **live up to** vt fus se montrer à la hauteur de
**live-in** ['lɪvɪn] adj (nanny) à demeure; ~ **partner** concubin(e)
**livelihood** ['laɪvlɪhud] n moyens mpl d'existence
**liveliness** ['laɪvlɪnəs] n vivacité f, entrain m
**lively** ['laɪvlɪ] adj vif (vive), plein(e) d'entrain; (place, book) vivant(e)
**liven up** ['laɪvn-] vt (room etc) égayer; (discussion, evening) animer ▷ vi s'animer
**liver** ['lɪvə<sup>r</sup>] n foie m
**liverish** ['lɪvərɪʃ] adj qui a mal au foie; (fig) grincheux(-euse)
**Liverpudlian** [lɪvə'pʌdlɪən] adj de Liverpool ▷ n habitant(e) de Liverpool, natif(-ive) de Liverpool
**livery** ['lɪvərɪ] n livrée f
**lives** [laɪvz] npl of **life**
**livestock** ['laɪvstɒk] n cheptel m, bétail m
**live wire** [laɪv-] n (inf, fig): **to be a (real)** ~ péter le feu
**livid** ['lɪvɪd] adj livide, blafard(e); (furious) furieux(-euse), furibond(e)
**living** ['lɪvɪŋ] adj vivant(e), en vie ▷ n: **to earn** or **make a** ~ gagner sa vie; **within** ~ **memory** de mémoire d'homme
**living conditions** npl conditions fpl de vie
**living expenses** npl dépenses courantes
**living room** n salle f de séjour
**living standards** npl niveau m de vie
**living wage** n salaire m permettant de vivre (décemment)
**lizard** ['lɪzəd] n lézard m
**llama** ['lɑːmə] n lama m
**LLB** n abbr (= Bachelor of Laws) titre universitaire

**LLD** n abbr (= Doctor of Laws) titre universitaire
**LMT** abbr (US: = Local Mean Time) heure locale
**load** [ləud] n (weight) poids m; (thing carried)
chargement m, charge f; (Elec, Tech) charge ▷ vt:
**to ~ (with)** (also: **load up**: lorry, ship) charger (de);
(gun, camera) charger (avec); (Comput) charger; **a
~ of, ~s of** (fig) un or des tas de, des masses de; **to
talk a ~ of rubbish** (inf) dire des bêtises
**loaded** ['ləudɪd] adj (dice) pipé(e); (question)
insidieux(-euse); (inf: rich) bourré(e) de fric;
(: drunk) bourré
**loading bay** ['ləudɪŋ-] n aire f de chargement
**loaf** (pl **loaves**) [ləuf, ləuvz] n pain m, miche f
▷ vi (also: **loaf about, loaf around**) fainéanter,
traîner
**loam** [ləum] n terreau m
**loan** [ləun] n prêt m ▷ vt prêter; **on ~** prêté(e),
en prêt; **public ~** emprunt public
**loan account** n compte m de prêt
**loan capital** n capital m d'emprunt
**loan shark** n (inf, pej) usurier m
**loath** [ləuθ] adj: **to be ~ to do** répugner à faire
**loathe** [ləuð] vt détester, avoir en horreur
**loathing** ['ləuðɪŋ] n dégoût m, répugnance f
**loathsome** ['ləuðsəm] adj répugnant(e),
détestable
**loaves** [ləuvz] npl of **loaf**
**lob** [lɔb] vt (ball) lober
**lobby** ['lɔbɪ] n hall m, entrée f; (Pol) groupe m de
pression, lobby m ▷ vt faire pression sur
**lobbyist** ['lɔbɪɪst] n membre m/f d'un groupe de
pression
**lobe** [ləub] n lobe m
**lobster** ['lɔbstə r] n homard m
**lobster pot** n casier m à homards
**local** ['ləukl] adj local(e) ▷ n (Brit: pub) pub m or
café m du coin; **the locals** npl les gens mpl du
pays or du coin
**local anaesthetic**, (US) **local anesthetic** n
anesthésie locale
**local authority** n collectivité locale,
municipalité f
**local call** n (Tel) communication urbaine
**local government** n administration locale or
municipale
**locality** [ləu'kælɪtɪ] n région f, environs mpl;
(position) lieu m
**localize** ['ləukəlaɪz] vt localiser
**locally** ['ləukəlɪ] adv localement; dans les
environs or la région
**locate** [ləu'keɪt] vt (find) trouver, repérer;
(situate) situer; **to be ~d in** être situé à or en
**location** [ləu'keɪʃən] n emplacement m; **on ~**
(Cine) en extérieur
**loch** [lɔx] n lac m, loch m
**lock** [lɔk] n (of door, box) serrure f; (of canal) écluse
f; (of hair) mèche f, boucle f ▷ vt (with key) fermer
à clé; (immobilize) bloquer ▷ vi (door etc) fermer à
clé; (wheels) se bloquer; **~ stock and barrel** (fig)
en bloc; **on full ~** (Brit Aut) le volant tourné à
fond
▶ **lock away** vt (valuables) mettre sous clé;

(criminal) mettre sous les verrous, enfermer
▶ **lock in** vt enfermer
▶ **lock out** vt enfermer dehors; (on purpose)
mettre à la porte; (: workers) lock-outer
▶ **lock up** vt (person) enfermer; (house) fermer à
clé ▷ vi tout fermer (à clé)
**locker** ['lɔkə r] n casier m; (in station) consigne f
automatique
**locker-room** ['lɔkə ru:m] (US) n (Sport) vestiaire m
**locket** ['lɔkɪt] n médaillon m
**lockjaw** ['lɔkdʒɔ:] n tétanos m
**lockout** ['lɔkaut] n (Industry) lock-out m, grève
patronale
**locksmith** ['lɔksmɪθ] n serrurier m
**lock-up** ['lɔkʌp] n (prison) prison f; (cell) cellule f
provisoire; (also: **lock-up garage**) box m
**locomotive** [ləukə'məutɪv] n locomotive f
**locum** ['ləukəm] n (Med) suppléant(e) de
médecin etc
**locust** ['ləukəst] n locuste f, sauterelle f
**lodge** [lɔdʒ] n pavillon m (de gardien); (also:
**hunting lodge**) pavillon de chasse; (Freemasonry)
loge f ▷ vi (person): **to ~ with** être logé(e) chez,
être en pension chez; (bullet) se loger ▷ vt (appeal
etc) présenter; déposer; **to ~ a complaint** porter
plainte; **to ~ (itself) in/between** se loger dans/
entre
**lodger** ['lɔdʒə r] n locataire m/f; (with room and
meals) pensionnaire m/f
**lodging** ['lɔdʒɪŋ] n logement m; see also **board**
**lodging house** n (Brit) pension f de famille
**lodgings** ['lɔdʒɪŋz] npl chambre f, meublé m
**loft** [lɔft] n grenier m; (apartment) grenier
aménagé (en appartement) (gén dans ancien
entrepôt ou fabrique)
**lofty** ['lɔftɪ] adj élevé(e); (haughty) hautain(e);
(sentiments, aims) noble
**log** [lɔg] n (of wood) bûche f; (Naut) livre m or
journal m de bord; (of car) ≈ carte grise ▷ n abbr
(= logarithm) log m ▷ vt enregistrer
▶ **log in, log on** vi (Comput) ouvrir une session,
entrer dans le système
▶ **log off, log out** vi (Comput) clore une session,
sortir du système
**logarithm** ['lɔgərɪðm] n logarithme m
**logbook** ['lɔgbuk] n (Naut) livre m or journal m de
bord; (Aviat) carnet m de vol; (of lorry driver)
carnet de route; (of movement of goods etc) registre
m; (of car) ≈ carte grise
**log cabin** n cabane f en rondins
**log fire** n feu m de bois
**logger** ['lɔgə r] n bûcheron m
**loggerheads** ['lɔgəhedz] npl: **at ~ (with)** à
couteaux tirés (avec)
**logic** ['lɔdʒɪk] n logique f
**logical** ['lɔdʒɪkl] adj logique
**logically** ['lɔdʒɪkəlɪ] adv logiquement
**login** ['lɔgɪn] n (Comput) identifiant m
**logistics** [lɔ'dʒɪstɪks] n logistique f
**logjam** ['lɔgdʒæm] n: **to break the ~** créer une
ouverture dans l'impasse
**logo** ['ləugəu] n logo m

**loin** [lɔɪn] n (Culin) filet m, longe f; **loins** npl reins mpl

**loin cloth** n pagne m

**Loire** [lwa:] n: **the (River) ~** la Loire

**loiter** ['lɔɪtə'] vi s'attarder; **to ~ (about)** traîner, musarder; (pej) rôder

**lol** abbr (Internet, Tel: = laugh out loud) MDR (= mort(e) de vive)

**loll** [lɔl] vi (also: **loll about**) se prélasser, fainéanter

**lollipop** ['lɔlɪpɔp] n sucette f

**lollipop man/lady** (Brit: irreg) n contractuel(le) qui fait traverser la rue aux enfants; voir article

### ● LOLLIPOP MEN/LADIES

Les lollipop men/ladies sont employés pour aider les enfants à traverser la rue à proximité des écoles à l'heure où ils entrent en classe et à la sortie. On les repère facilement à cause de leur long ciré jaune et ils portent une pancarte ronde pour faire signe aux automobilistes de s'arrêter. On les appelle ainsi car la forme circulaire de cette pancarte rappelle une sucette.

**lollop** ['lɔləp] vi (Brit) avancer (or courir) maladroitement

**lolly** ['lɔlɪ] n (inf: ice) esquimau m; (: lollipop) sucette f; (: money) fric m

**Lombardy** ['lɔmbədɪ] n Lombardie f

**London** ['lʌndən] n Londres

**Londoner** ['lʌndənə'] n Londonien(ne)

**lone** [ləun] adj solitaire

**loneliness** ['ləunlɪnɪs] n solitude f, isolement m

**lonely** ['ləunlɪ] adj seul(e); (childhood etc) solitaire; (place) solitaire, isolé(e)

**lonely hearts** adj: **~ ad** petite annonce (personnelle); **~ club** club m de rencontres (pour personnes seules)

**lone parent** n parent m unique

**loner** ['ləunə'] n solitaire m/f

**lonesome** ['ləunsəm] adj seul(e), solitaire

**long** [lɔŋ] adj long (longue) ▷ adv longtemps ▷ n: **the ~ and the short of it is that ...** (fig) fin mot de l'histoire c'est que ... ▷ vi: **to ~ for sth/to do sth** avoir très envie de qch/de faire qch, attendre qch avec impatience/attendre avec impatience de faire qch; **he had ~ understood that ...** il avait compris depuis longtemps que ...; **how ~ is this river/course?** quelle est la longueur de ce fleuve/la durée de ce cours?; **6 metres ~** (long) de 6 mètres; **6 months ~** qui dure 6 mois, de 6 mois; **all night ~** toute la nuit; **he no ~er comes** il ne vient plus; **I can't stand it any ~er** je ne peux plus le supporter; **~ before** longtemps avant; **before ~** (+ future) avant peu, dans peu de temps; (+ past) peu de temps après; **~ ago** il y a longtemps; **don't be ~!** fais vite!, dépêche-toi!; **I shan't be ~** je n'en ai pas pour longtemps; **at ~ last** enfin; **in the ~ run** à la longue; finalement; **so** or **as ~**

**as** à condition que + sub

**long-distance** [lɔŋ'dɪstəns] adj (race) de fond; (call) interurbain(e)

**longer** ['lɔŋgə'] adv see **long**

**long-haired** [lɔŋ'hɛəd] adj (person) aux cheveux longs; (animal) aux longs poils

**longhand** ['lɔŋhænd] n écriture normale or courante

**long-haul** ['lɔŋhɔ:l] adj (flight) long-courrier

**longing** ['lɔŋɪŋ] n désir m, envie f; (nostalgia) nostalgie f ▷ adj plein(e) d'envie or de nostalgie

**longingly** ['lɔŋɪŋlɪ] adv avec désir or nostalgie

**longitude** ['lɔŋgɪtju:d] n longitude f

**long johns** [-dʒɔnz] npl caleçons longs

**long jump** n saut m en longueur

**long-life** [lɔŋ'laɪf] adj (batteries etc) longue durée inv; (milk) longue conservation

**long-lost** ['lɔŋlɔst] adj perdu(e) depuis longtemps

**long-range** ['lɔŋ'reɪndʒ] adj à longue portée; (weather forecast) à long terme

**longshoreman** ['lɔŋʃɔ:mən] (irreg) n (US) docker m, débardeur m

**long-sighted** ['lɔŋ'saɪtɪd] adj (Brit) presbyte; (fig) prévoyant(e)

**long-standing** ['lɔŋ'stændɪŋ] adj de longue date

**long-suffering** [lɔŋ'sʌfərɪŋ] adj empreint(e) d'une patience résignée; extrêmement patient(e)

**long-term** ['lɔŋtə:m] adj à long terme

**long wave** n (Radio) grandes ondes, ondes longues

**long-winded** [lɔŋ'wɪndɪd] adj intarissable, interminable

**loo** [lu:] n (Brit inf) w.-c mpl, petit coin

**loofah** ['lu:fə] n sorte d'éponge végétale

**look** [luk] vi regarder; (seem) sembler, paraître, avoir l'air; (building etc): **to ~ south/on to the sea** donner au sud/sur la mer ▷ n regard m; (appearance) air m, allure f, aspect m; **looks** npl (good looks) physique m, beauté f; **to ~ like** ressembler à; **it ~s like him** on dirait que c'est lui; **it ~s about 4 metres long** je dirais que ça fait 4 mètres de long; **it ~s all right to me** ça me paraît bien; **to have a ~** regarder; **to have a ~ at sth** jeter un coup d'œil à qch; **to have a ~ for sth** chercher qch; **to ~ ahead** regarder devant soi; (fig) envisager l'avenir; **~ (here)!** (annoyance) écoutez!

▶ **look after** vt fus s'occuper de, prendre soin de; (luggage etc: watch over) garder, surveiller

▶ **look around** vi regarder autour de soi

▶ **look at** vt fus regarder; (problem etc) examiner

▶ **look back** vi: **to ~ back at sth/sb** se retourner pour regarder qch/qn; **to ~ back on** (event, period) évoquer, repenser à

▶ **look down on** vt fus (fig) regarder de haut, dédaigner

▶ **look for** vt fus chercher; **we're ~ing for a hotel/restaurant** nous cherchons un hôtel/restaurant

▶ **look forward to** vt fus attendre avec

impatience; **I'm not ~ing forward to it** cette perspective ne me réjouit guère; **~ing forward to hearing from you** (*in letter*) dans l'attente de vous lire

▶ **look in** *vi*: **to ~ in on sb** passer voir qn

▶ **look into** *vt fus* (*matter, possibility*) examiner, étudier

▶ **look on** *vi* regarder (en spectateur)

▶ **look out** *vi* (*beware*): **to ~ out (for)** prendre garde (à), faire attention (à); **~ out!** attention!

▶ **look out for** *vt fus* (*seek*) être à la recherche de; (*try to spot*) guetter

▶ **look over** *vt* (*essay*) jeter un coup d'œil à; (*town, building*) visiter (rapidement); (*person*) jeter un coup d'œil à; examiner de la tête aux pieds

▶ **look round** *vt fus* (*house, shop*) faire le tour de ▷ *vi* (*turn*) regarder derrière soi, se retourner; **to ~ round for sth** chercher qch

▶ **look through** *vt fus* (*papers, book*) examiner; (: *briefly*) parcourir; (*telescope*) regarder à travers

▶ **look to** *vt fus* veiller à; (*rely on*) compter sur

▶ **look up** *vi* lever les yeux; (*improve*) s'améliorer ▷ *vt* (*word*) chercher; (*friend*) passer voir

▶ **look up to** *vt fus* avoir du respect pour

**lookout** ['lukaʊt] *n* (*tower etc*) poste *m* de guet; (*person*) guetteur *m*; **to be on the ~ (for)** guetter

**look-up table** ['lukʌp-] *n* (*Comput*) table *f* à consulter

**loom** [luːm] *n* métier *m* à tisser ▷ *vi* (*also*: **loom up**) surgir; (*event*) paraître imminent(e); (*threaten*) menacer

**loony** ['luːnɪ] *adj, n* (*inf*) timbré(e), cinglé(e) *m/f*

**loop** [luːp] *n* boucle *f*; (*contraceptive*) stérilet *m* ▷ *vt*: **to ~ sth round sth** passer qch autour de qch

**loophole** ['luːphəʊl] *n* (*fig*) porte *f* de sortie; échappatoire *f*

**loose** [luːs] *adj* (*knot, screw*) desserré(e); (*stone*) branlant(e); (*clothes*) vague, ample, lâche; (*hair*) dénoué(e), épars(e); (*not firmly fixed*) pas solide; (*animal*) en liberté, échappé(e); (*life*) dissolu(e); (*morals, discipline*) relâché(e); (*thinking*) peu rigoureux(-euse), vague; (*translation*) approximatif(-ive) ▷ *n*: **to be on the ~** être en liberté ▷ *vt* (*free: animal*) lâcher; (: *prisoner*) relâcher, libérer; (*slacken*) détendre, relâcher; desserrer; défaire; (*donner du mou a; donner du ballant à*; (*Brit: arrow*) tirer; **~ connection** (*Elec*) mauvais contact; **to be at a ~ end** *or* (*US*) **at ~ ends** (*fig*) ne pas trop savoir quoi faire; **to tie up ~ ends** (*fig*) mettre au point *or* régler les derniers détails

**loose change** *n* petite monnaie

**loose chippings** [-'tʃɪpɪŋz] *npl* (*on road*) gravillons *mpl*

**loose-fitting** ['luːsfɪtɪŋ] *adj* (*clothes*) ample

**loose-leaf** ['luːsliːf] *adj*: **~ binder** *or* **folder** classeur *m* à feuilles *or* feuillets mobiles

**loose-limbed** [luːs'lɪmd] *adj* agile, souple

**loosely** ['luːslɪ] *adv* sans serrer; (*imprecisely*) approximativement

**loosely-knit** ['luːslɪ'nɪt] *adj* élastique

**loosen** ['luːsn] *vt* desserrer, relâcher, défaire

▶ **loosen up** *vi* (*before game*) s'échauffer; (*inf: relax*) se détendre, se laisser aller

**loot** [luːt] *n* butin *m* ▷ *vt* piller

**looter** ['luːtə'] *n* pillard *m*, casseur *m*

**looting** ['luːtɪŋ] *n* pillage *m*

**lop** [lɔp] : **to ~ off** *vt* couper, trancher

**lop-sided** ['lɔp'saɪdɪd] *adj* de travers, asymétrique

**lord** [lɔːd] *n* seigneur *m*; **L~ Smith** lord Smith; **the L~** (*Rel*) le Seigneur; **my L~** (*to noble*) Monsieur le comte/le baron; (*to judge*) Monsieur le juge; (*to bishop*) Monseigneur; **good L~!** mon Dieu!

**lordly** ['lɔːdlɪ] *adj* noble, majestueux(-euse); (*arrogant*) hautain(e)

**Lords** ['lɔːdz] *npl* (*Brit: Pol*): **the (House of) ~** (*Brit*) la Chambre des Lords

**lordship** ['lɔːdʃɪp] *n* (*Brit*): **your L~** Monsieur le comte (*or* le baron *or* le Juge)

**lore** [lɔː'] *n* tradition(s) *f(pl)*

**lorry** ['lɔrɪ] *n* (*Brit*) camion *m*

**lorry driver** *n* (*Brit*) camionneur *m*, routier *m*

**lose** [luːz] (*pt, pp* **lost**) *vt* perdre; (*opportunity*) manquer, perdre; (*pursuers*) distancer, semer ▷ *vi* perdre; **I've lost my wallet/passport** j'ai perdu mon portefeuille/passeport; **to ~ (time)** (*clock*) retarder; **to ~ no time (in doing sth)** ne pas perdre de temps (à faire qch); **to get lost** (*vi*: *person*) se perdre; **my watch has got lost** ma montre est perdue

▶ **lose out** *vi* être perdant(e)

**loser** ['luːzə'] *n* perdant(e); **to be a good/bad ~** être beau/mauvais joueur

**loss** [lɔs] *n* perte *f*; **to cut one's ~es** limiter les dégâts; **to make a ~** enregistrer une perte; **to sell sth at a ~** vendre qch à perte; **to be at a ~** être perplexe *or* embarrassé(e); **to be at a ~ to do** se trouver incapable de faire

**loss adjuster** *n* (*Insurance*) responsable *m/f* de l'évaluation des dommages

**loss leader** *n* (*Comm*) article sacrifié

**lost** [lɔst] *pt, pp* *of* **lose** ▷ *adj* perdu(e); **to get ~** (*vi*) se perdre; **I'm ~** je me suis perdu; **~ in thought** perdu dans ses pensées; **~ and found property** (*n*: *US*) objets trouvés; **~ and found** (*n*: *US*) (bureau *m* des) objets trouvés

**lost property** *n* (*Brit*) objets trouvés; **~ office** *or* **department** (bureau *m* des) objets trouvés

**lot** [lɔt] *n* (*at auctions, set*) lot *m*; (*destiny*) sort *m*, destinée *f*; **the ~** (*everything*) le tout; (*everyone*) tous *mpl*, toutes *fpl*; **a ~** beaucoup; **a ~ of** beaucoup de; **~s of** des tas de; **to draw ~s (for sth)** tirer (qch) au sort

**lotion** ['ləʊʃən] *n* lotion *f*

**lottery** ['lɔtərɪ] *n* loterie *f*

**loud** [laʊd] *adj* bruyant(e), sonore; (*voice*) fort(e); (*condemnation etc*) vigoureux(-euse); (*gaudy*) voyant(e), tapageur(-euse) ▷ *adv* (*speak etc*) fort; **out ~** tout haut

**loud-hailer** [laʊd'heɪlə'] *n* porte-voix *m inv*

**loudly** ['laudlɪ] *adv* fort, bruyamment
**loudspeaker** [laud'spi:kəʳ] *n* haut-parleur *m*
**lounge** [laundʒ] *n* salon *m*; (*of airport*) salle *f*;
   (Brit: *also*: **lounge bar**) (salle de) café *m or* bar *m*
   ▷ *vi* (*also*: **lounge about, lounge around**) se
   prélasser, paresser
**lounge-bar** *n* (salle *f* de) bar *m*
**lounge suit** *n* (Brit) complet *m*; (: *on invitation*)
   "tenue de ville"
**louse** (*pl* **lice**) [laus, laɪs] *n* pou *m*
   ▶ **louse up** [lauz-] *vt* (*inf*) gâcher
**lousy** ['lauzɪ] (*inf*) *adj* (*bad quality*) infect(e),
   moche; **I feel ~** je suis mal fichu(e)
**lout** [laut] *n* rustre *m*, butor *m*
**louvre**, (US) **louver** ['lu:vəʳ] *adj* (*door, window*) à
   claire-voie
**lovable** ['lʌvəbl] *adj* très sympathique; adorable
**love** [lʌv] *n* amour *m* ▷ *vt* aimer; (*caringly, kindly*)
   aimer beaucoup; **I ~ chocolate** j'adore le
   chocolat; **to ~ to do** aimer beaucoup *or* adorer
   faire; **I'd ~ to come** cela me ferait très plaisir
   (de venir); **"15 ~"** (*Tennis*) "15 à rien *or* zéro"; **to
   be/fall in ~ with** être/tomber amoureux(-euse)
   de; **to make ~** faire l'amour; **~ at first sight** le
   coup de foudre; **to send one's ~ to sb** adresser
   ses amitiés à qn; **~ from Anne, ~, Anne**
   affectueusement, Anne; **I ~ you** je t'aime
**love affair** *n* liaison (amoureuse)
**love child** *n* (*irreg*) enfant *m/f* illégitime *or*
   naturel(le)
**loved ones** ['lʌvdwʌnz] *npl* proches *mpl* et amis
   chers
**love-hate relationship** [lʌv'heɪt-] *n* rapport
   ambigu; **they have a ~** ils s'aiment et se
   détestent à la fois
**love life** *n* vie sentimentale
**lovely** ['lʌvlɪ] *adj* (*pretty*) ravissant(e); (*friend, wife*)
   charmant(e); (*holiday, surprise*) très agréable,
   merveilleux(-euse); **we had a ~ time** c'était
   vraiment très bien, nous avons eu beaucoup de
   plaisir
**lover** ['lʌvəʳ] *n* amant *m*; (*person in love*)
   amoureux(-euse); (*amateur*): **a ~ of** un(e) ami(e)
   de, un(e) amoureux(-euse) de
**lovesick** ['lʌvsɪk] *adj* qui se languit d'amour
**love song** ['lʌvsɔŋ] *n* chanson *f* d'amour
**loving** ['lʌvɪŋ] *adj* affectueux(-euse), tendre,
   aimant(e)
**low** [ləu] *adj* bas (basse); (*quality*) mauvais(e),
   inférieur(e) ▷ *adv* bas ▷ *n* (*Meteorology*)
   dépression *f* ▷ *vi* (*cow*) mugir; **to feel ~** se sentir
   déprimé(e); **he's very ~** (*ill*) il est bien bas *or* très
   affaibli; **to turn (down) ~** (*vt*) baisser; **to be ~
   on** (*supplies etc*) être à court de; **to reach a new** *or*
   **an all-time ~** tomber au niveau le plus bas
**low-alcohol** [ləu'ælkəhɔl] *adj* à faible teneur en
   alcool, peu alcoolisé(e)
**lowbrow** ['ləubrau] *adj* sans prétentions
   intellectuelles
**low-calorie** ['ləu'kælərɪ] *adj* hypocalorique
**low-cut** ['ləukʌt] *adj* (*dress*) décolleté(e)
**low-down** ['ləudaun] *n* (*inf*): **he gave me the ~**

**(on it)** il m'a mis au courant ▷ *adj* (*mean*)
   méprisable
**lower** *adj* ['ləuəʳ] inférieur(e) ▷ *vt* ['lauəʳ]
   baisser; (*resistance*) diminuer ▷ *vi* ['lauəʳ]
   (*person*): **to ~ at sb** jeter un regard mauvais *or*
   noir à qn; (*sky, clouds*) être menaçant; **to ~ o.s.
   to** s'abaisser à
**lower sixth** (Brit) *n* (*Scol*) première *f*
**low-fat** ['ləu'fæt] *adj* maigre
**low-key** ['ləu'ki:] *adj* modéré(e), discret(-ète)
**lowland, lowlands** ['ləulənd(z)] *n(pl)*
   plaine(s) *f(pl)*
**low-level** ['ləulɛvl] *adj* bas (basse); (*flying*) à
   basse altitude
**low-loader** ['ləuləudəʳ] *n* semi-remorque *f* à
   plate-forme surbaissée
**lowly** ['ləulɪ] *adj* humble, modeste
**low-lying** [ləu'laɪɪŋ] *adj* à faible altitude
**low-paid** [ləu'peɪd] *adj* mal payé(e), aux salaires
   bas
**low-rise** ['ləuraɪz] *adj* bas(se), de faible hauteur
**low-tech** ['ləutɛk] *adj* sommaire
**loyal** ['lɔɪəl] *adj* loyal(e), fidèle
**loyalist** ['lɔɪəlɪst] *n* loyaliste *m/f*
**loyalty** ['lɔɪəltɪ] *n* loyauté *f*, fidélité *f*
**loyalty card** *n* carte *f* de fidélité
**lozenge** ['lɔzɪndʒ] *n* (*Med*) pastille *f*; (*Geom*)
   losange *m*
**LP** *n abbr* = **long-playing record**
**LPG** *n abbr* (= *liquid petroleum gas*) GPL *m*
**L-plates** ['ɛlpleɪts] *npl* (Brit) plaques *fpl*
   (obligatoires) d'apprenti conducteur
**LPN** *n abbr* (US: = *Licensed Practical Nurse*)
   infirmier(-ière) diplômé(e)
**LRAM** *n abbr* (Brit) = **Licentiate of the Royal
   Academy of Music**
**LSAT** *n abbr* (US) = **Law School Admissions Test**
**LSD** *n abbr* (= *lysergic acid diethylamide*) LSD *m*; (Brit:
   = *pounds, shillings and pence*) système monétaire en
   usage en GB jusqu'en 1971
**LSE** *n abbr* = **London School of Economics**
**LT** *abbr* (*Elec*: = *low tension*) BT
**Lt** *abbr* (= *lieutenant*) Lt.
**Ltd** *abbr* (*Comm*: *company*: = *limited*) ≈ S.A.
**lubricant** ['lu:brɪkənt] *n* lubrifiant *m*
**lubricate** ['lu:brɪkeɪt] *vt* lubrifier, graisser
**lucid** ['lu:sɪd] *adj* lucide
**lucidity** [lu:'sɪdɪtɪ] *n* lucidité *f*
**luck** [lʌk] *n* chance *f*; **bad ~** malchance *f*,
   malheur *m*; **to be in ~** avoir de la chance; **to be
   out of ~** ne pas avoir de chance; **good ~!** bonne
   chance!; **bad** *or* **hard ~!** pas de chance!
**luckily** ['lʌkɪlɪ] *adv* heureusement, par bonheur
**luckless** ['lʌklɪs] *adj* (*person*)
   malchanceux(-euse); (*trip*) marqué(e) par la
   malchance
**lucky** ['lʌkɪ] *adj* (*person*) qui a de la chance;
   (*coincidence*) heureux(-euse); (*number etc*) qui
   porte bonheur
**lucrative** ['lu:krətɪv] *adj* lucratif(-ive), rentable,
   qui rapporte
**ludicrous** ['lu:dɪkrəs] *adj* ridicule, absurde

**ludo** ['luːdəu] n jeu m des petits chevaux
**lug** [lʌg] vt traîner, tirer
**luggage** ['lʌgɪdʒ] n bagages mpl; **our ~ hasn't arrived** nos bagages ne sont pas arrivés; **could you send someone to collect our ~?** pourriez-vous envoyer quelqu'un chercher nos bagages?
**luggage lockers** npl consigne f automatique
**luggage rack** n (in train) porte-bagages m inv; (: made of string) filet m à bagages; (on car) galerie f
**luggage van**, (US) **luggage car** n (Rail) fourgon m (à bagages)
**lugubrious** [luˈguːbrɪəs] adj lugubre
**lukewarm** ['luːkwɔːm] adj tiède
**lull** [lʌl] n accalmie f; (in conversation) pause f ▷ vt: **to ~ sb to sleep** bercer qn pour qu'il s'endorme; **to be ~ed into a false sense of security** s'endormir dans une fausse sécurité
**lullaby** ['lʌləbaɪ] n berceuse f
**lumbago** [lʌmˈbeɪgəu] n lumbago m
**lumber** ['lʌmbəʳ] n (wood) bois m de charpente; (junk) bric-à-brac m inv ▷ vt (Brit inf): **to ~ sb with sth/sb** coller or refiler qch/qn à qn ▷ vi (also: **lumber about, lumber along**) marcher pesamment
**lumberjack** ['lʌmbədʒæk] n bûcheron m
**lumber room** n (Brit) débarras m
**lumber yard** n entrepôt m de bois
**luminous** ['luːmɪnəs] adj lumineux(-euse)
**lump** [lʌmp] n morceau m; (in sauce) grumeau m; (swelling) grosseur f ▷ vt (also: **lump together**) réunir, mettre en tas
**lump sum** n somme globale or forfaitaire
**lumpy** ['lʌmpɪ] adj (sauce) qui a des grumeaux; (bed) défoncé(e), peu confortable
**lunacy** ['luːnəsɪ] n démence f, folie f
**lunar** ['luːnəʳ] adj lunaire
**lunatic** ['luːnətɪk] n fou (folle), dément(e) ▷ adj fou (folle), dément(e)
**lunatic asylum** n asile m d'aliénés
**lunch** [lʌntʃ] n déjeuner m ▷ vi déjeuner; **it is his ~ hour** c'est l'heure où il déjeune; **to invite sb to** or **for ~** inviter qn à déjeuner
**lunch break, lunch hour** n pause f de midi, heure f du déjeuner
**luncheon** ['lʌntʃən] n déjeuner m
**luncheon meat** n sorte de saucisson
**luncheon voucher** n chèque-repas m, ticket-repas m
**lunchtime** ['lʌntʃtaɪm] n: **it's ~** c'est l'heure du déjeuner
**lung** [lʌŋ] n poumon m
**lung cancer** n cancer m du poumon
**lunge** [lʌndʒ] vi (also: **lunge forward**) faire un mouvement brusque en avant; **to ~ at sb** envoyer or assener un coup à qn
**lupin** ['luːpɪn] n lupin m
**lurch** [ləːtʃ] vi vaciller, tituber ▷ n écart m brusque, embardée f; **to leave sb in the ~** laisser qn se débrouiller or se dépêtrer tout(e) seul(e)
**lure** [luəʳ] n (attraction) attrait m, charme m; (in hunting) appât m, leurre m ▷ vt attirer or persuader par la ruse
**lurid** ['luərɪd] adj affreux(-euse), atroce
**lurk** [ləːk] vi se tapir, se cacher
**luscious** ['lʌʃəs] adj succulent(e), appétissant(e)
**lush** [lʌʃ] adj luxuriant(e)
**lust** [lʌst] n (sexual) désir (sexuel); (Rel) luxure f; (fig): **~ for** soif f de
  ▶ **lust after** vt fus convoiter, désirer
**luster** ['lʌstəʳ] n (US) = **lustre**
**lustful** ['lʌstful] adj lascif(-ive)
**lustre**, (US) **luster** ['lʌstəʳ] n lustre m, brillant m
**lusty** ['lʌstɪ] adj vigoureux(-euse), robuste
**lute** [luːt] n luth m
**Luxembourg** ['lʌksəmbəːg] n Luxembourg m
**luxuriant** [lʌgˈzjuərɪənt] adj luxuriant(e)
**luxurious** [lʌgˈzjuərɪəs] adj luxueux(-euse)
**luxury** ['lʌkʃərɪ] n luxe m ▷ cpd de luxe
**LV** n abbr (Brit) = **luncheon voucher**
**LW** abbr (Radio: = long wave) GO
**Lycra®** ['laɪkrə] n Lycra® m
**lying** ['laɪɪŋ] n mensonge(s) m(pl) ▷ adj (statement, story) mensonger(-ère), faux (fausse); (person) menteur(-euse)
**lynch** [lɪntʃ] vt lyncher
**lynx** [lɪŋks] n lynx m inv
**Lyons** ['ljɔ̃] n Lyon
**lyre** ['laɪəʳ] n lyre f
**lyric** ['lɪrɪk] adj lyrique
**lyrical** ['lɪrɪkl] adj lyrique
**lyricism** ['lɪrɪsɪzəm] n lyrisme m
**lyrics** ['lɪrɪks] npl (of song) paroles fpl

# Mm

**M, m** [ɛm] *n* (*letter*) M, m *m*; **M for Mary**, (*US*) **M for Mike** M comme Marcel

**M** *n abbr* (*Brit*) = **motorway**; (= *the M8*) ≈ l'A8 ▷ *abbr* (= *medium*) M

**m.** *abbr* (= *metre*) m; (= *million*) M; (= *mile*) mi

**M.A.** *n abbr* (*Scol*) = **Master of Arts** ▷ *abbr* (*US*) = **military academy**; (*US*) = **Massachusetts**

**ma** [mɑ:] (*inf*) *n* maman *f*

**mac** [mæk] *n* (*Brit*) imper(méable *m*) *m*

**macabre** [mə'kɑ:brə] *adj* macabre

**macaroni** [mækə'rəunɪ] *n* macaronis *mpl*

**macaroon** [mækə'ru:n] *n* macaron *m*

**mace** [meɪs] *n* masse *f*; (*spice*) macis *m*

**Macedonia** [mæsɪ'dəunɪə] *n* Macédoine *f*

**Macedonian** [mæsɪ'dəunɪən] *adj* macédonien(ne) ▷ *n* Macédonien(ne); (*Ling*) macédonien *m*

**machinations** [mækɪ'neɪʃənz] *npl* machinations *fpl*, intrigues *fpl*

**machine** [mə'ʃi:n] *n* machine *f* ▷ *vt* (*dress etc*) coudre à la machine; (*Tech*) usiner

**machine code** *n* (*Comput*) code *m* machine

**machine gun** *n* mitrailleuse *f*

**machine language** *n* (*Comput*) langage *m* machine

**machine-readable** [mə'ʃi:nri:dəbl] *adj* (*Comput*) exploitable par une machine

**machinery** [mə'ʃi:nərɪ] *n* machinerie *f*, machines *fpl*; (*fig*) mécanisme(s) *m(pl)*

**machine shop** *n* atelier *m* d'usinage

**machine tool** *n* machine-outil *f*

**machine washable** *adj* (*garment*) lavable en machine

**machinist** [mə'ʃi:nɪst] *n* machiniste *m/f*

**macho** ['mætʃəu] *adj* macho *inv*

**mackerel** ['mækrl] *n* (*pl inv*) maquereau *m*

**mackintosh** ['mækɪntɔʃ] *n* (*Brit*) imperméable *m*

**macro...** ['mækrəu] *prefix* macro...

**macro-economics** ['mækrəui:kə'nɔmɪks] *n* macro-économie *f*

**mad** [mæd] *adj* fou (folle); (*foolish*) insensé(e); (*angry*) furieux(-euse); **to go ~** devenir fou; **to be ~ (keen) about** *or* **on sth** (*inf*) être follement passionné de qch, être fou de qch

**Madagascar** [mædə'gæskə<sup>r</sup>] *n* Madagascar *m*

**madam** ['mædəm] *n* madame *f*; **yes ~** oui Madame; **M~ Chairman** Madame la Présidente

**madcap** ['mædkæp] *adj* (*inf*) écervelé(e)

**mad cow disease** *n* maladie *f* des vaches folles

**madden** ['mædn] *vt* exaspérer

**maddening** ['mædnɪŋ] *adj* exaspérant(e)

**made** [meɪd] *pt, pp of* **make**

**Madeira** [mə'dɪərə] *n* (*Geo*) Madère *f*; (*wine*) madère *m*

**made-to-measure** ['meɪdtə'mɛʒə<sup>r</sup>] *adj* (*Brit*) fait(e) sur mesure

**made-up** ['meɪdʌp] *adj* (*story*) inventé(e), fabriqué(e)

**madhouse** ['mædhaus] *n* (*also fig*) maison *f* de fous

**madly** ['mædlɪ] *adv* follement; **~ in love** éperdument amoureux(-euse)

**madman** ['mædmən] (*irreg*) *n* fou *m*, aliéné *m*

**madness** ['mædnɪs] *n* folie *f*

**Madrid** [mə'drɪd] *n* Madrid

**Mafia** ['mæfɪə] *n* maf(f)ia *f*

**mag** [mæg] *n abbr* (*Brit inf*: = *magazine*) magazine *m*

**magazine** [mægə'zi:n] *n* (*Press*) magazine *m*, revue *f*; (*Radio, TV*) magazine; (*Mil: store*) dépôt *m*, arsenal *m*; (*of firearm*) magasin *m*

**maggot** ['mægət] *n* ver *m*, asticot *m*

**magic** ['mædʒɪk] *n* magie *f* ▷ *adj* magique

**magical** ['mædʒɪkl] *adj* magique; (*experience, evening*) merveilleux(-euse)

**magician** [mə'dʒɪʃən] *n* magicien(ne)

**magistrate** ['mædʒɪstreɪt] *n* magistrat *m*; juge *m*; **~s' court** (*Brit*) ≈ tribunal *m* d'instance

**magnanimous** [mæg'nænɪməs] *adj* magnanime

**magnate** ['mægneɪt] *n* magnat *m*

**magnesium** [mæg'ni:zɪəm] *n* magnésium *m*

**magnet** ['mægnɪt] *n* aimant *m*

**magnetic** [mæg'nɛtɪk] *adj* magnétique

**magnetic disk** *n* (*Comput*) disque *m* magnétique

**magnetic tape** *n* bande *f* magnétique

**magnetism** ['mægnɪtɪzəm] *n* magnétisme *m*

**magnification** [mægnɪfɪ'keɪʃən] *n* grossissement *m*

**magnificence** [mæg'nɪfɪsns] *n* magnificence *f*

**magnificent** [mæg'nɪfɪsnt] *adj* superbe,

magnifique; (splendid: robe, building)
somptueux(-euse), magnifique
**magnify** ['mægnɪfaɪ] vt grossir; (sound)
amplifier
**magnifying glass** ['mægnɪfaɪɪŋ-] n loupe f
**magnitude** ['mægnɪtjuːd] n ampleur f
**magnolia** [mæg'nəʊlɪə] n magnolia m
**magpie** ['mægpaɪ] n pie f
**mahogany** [mə'hɒgənɪ] n acajou m ▷ cpd en
(bois d') acajou
**maid** [meɪd] n bonne f; (in hotel) femme f de
chambre; **old ~** (pej) vieille fille
**maiden** ['meɪdn] n jeune fille f ▷ adj (aunt etc)
non mariée; (speech, voyage) inaugural(e)
**maiden name** n nom m de jeune fille
**mail** [meɪl] n poste f; (letters) courrier m ▷ vt
envoyer (par la poste); **by ~** par la poste
**mailbag** ['meɪlbæg] n (US) sac postal; (postman's)
sacoche f
**mailbox** ['meɪlbɒks] n (US: also Comput) boîte f
aux lettres
**mailing list** ['meɪlɪŋ-] n liste f d'adresses
**mailman** ['meɪlmæn] (irreg) n (US) facteur m
**mail-order** ['meɪlɔːdəʳ] n vente f or achat m par
correspondance ▷ cpd: **~ firm** or **house** maison f
de vente par correspondance
**mailshot** ['meɪlʃɒt] n (Brit) mailing m
**mail train** n train postal
**mail truck** n (US Aut) = **mail van**
**mail van** n (Brit Aut) voiture f or fourgonnette f
des postes; (: Rail) wagon-poste m
**maim** [meɪm] vt mutiler
**main** [meɪn] adj principal(e) ▷ n (pipe) conduite
principale, canalisation f; **the ~s** (Elec) le
secteur; **the ~ thing** l'essentiel m; **in the ~**
dans l'ensemble
**main course** n (Culin) plat m de résistance
**mainframe** ['meɪnfreɪm] n (also: **mainframe**
**computer**) (gros) ordinateur, unité centrale
**mainland** ['meɪnlənd] n continent m
**mainline** ['meɪnlaɪn] adj (Rail) de grande ligne
▷ vt (drugs slang) se shooter à ▷ vi (drugs slang) se
shooter
**main line** n (Rail) grande ligne
**mainly** ['meɪnlɪ] adv principalement, surtout
**main road** n grand axe, route nationale
**mainstay** ['meɪnsteɪ] n (fig) pilier m
**mainstream** ['meɪnstriːm] n (fig) courant
principal
**main street** n rue f principale
**maintain** [meɪn'teɪn] vt entretenir; (continue)
maintenir, préserver; (affirm) soutenir; **to ~**
**that** ... soutenir que ...
**maintenance** ['meɪntənəns] n entretien m;
(Law: alimony) pension f alimentaire
**maintenance contract** n contrat m d'entretien
**maintenance order** n (Law) obligation f
alimentaire
**maisonette** [meɪzə'nɛt] n (Brit) appartement m
en duplex
**maize** [meɪz] n (Brit) maïs m
**Maj.** abbr (Mil) = **major**

**majestic** [mə'dʒɛstɪk] adj majestueux(-euse)
**majesty** ['mædʒɪstɪ] n majesté f; (title): **Your**
**M~** Votre Majesté
**major** ['meɪdʒəʳ] n (Mil) commandant m ▷ adj
(important) important(e); (most important)
principal(e); (Mus) majeur(e) ▷ vi (US Scol): **to ~**
**(in)** se spécialiser (en); **a ~ operation** (Med) une
grosse opération
**Majorca** [mə'jɔːkə] n Majorque f
**major general** n (Mil) général m de division
**majority** [mə'dʒɔrɪtɪ] n majorité f ▷ cpd (verdict,
holding) majoritaire
**make** [meɪk] vt (pt, pp made) [meɪd] faire;
(manufacture) faire, fabriquer; (earn) gagner;
(decision) prendre; (friend) se faire; (speech) faire,
prononcer; (cause to be): **to ~ sb sad** etc rendre qn
triste etc; (force): **to ~ sb do sth** obliger qn à
faire qch, faire faire qch à qn; (equal): **2 and 2 ~ 4**
2 et 2 font 4 ▷ n (manufacture) fabrication f;
(brand) marque f; **to ~ the bed** faire le lit; **to ~ a**
**fool of sb** (ridicule) ridiculiser qn; (trick) avoir or
duper qn; **to ~ a profit** faire un or des
bénéfice(s); **to ~ a loss** essuyer une perte; **to ~**
**it** (in time etc) y arriver; (succeed) réussir; **what**
**time do you ~ it?** quelle heure avez-vous?; **I ~ it**
**£249** d'après mes calculs ça fait 249 livres; **to be**
**made of** être en; **to ~ good** vi (succeed) faire son
chemin, réussir ▷ vt (deficit) combler; (losses)
compenser; **to ~ do with** se contenter de; se
débrouiller avec
▶ **make for** vt fus (place) se diriger vers
▶ **make off** vi filer
▶ **make out** vt (write out: cheque) faire; (decipher)
déchiffrer; (understand) comprendre; (see)
distinguer; (claim, imply) prétendre, vouloir faire
croire; **to ~ out a case for sth** présenter des
arguments solides en faveur de qch
▶ **make over** vt (assign): **to ~ over (to)** céder (à),
transférer (au nom de)
▶ **make up** vt (invent) inventer, imaginer;
(constitute) constituer; (parcel, bed) faire ▷ vi se
réconcilier; (with cosmetics) se maquiller, se
farder; **to be made up of** se composer de
▶ **make up for** vt fus compenser; (lost time)
rattraper
**make-believe** ['meɪkbɪliːv] n: **a world of ~** un
monde de chimères or d'illusions; **it's just ~**
c'est de la fantaisie; c'est une illusion
**makeover** ['meɪkəʊvəʳ] n (by beautician) soins mpl
de maquillage; (change of image) changement m
d'image; **to give sb a ~** relooker qn
**maker** ['meɪkəʳ] n fabricant m; (of film,
programme) réalisateur(-trice)
**makeshift** ['meɪkʃɪft] adj provisoire,
improvisé(e)
**make-up** ['meɪkʌp] n maquillage m
**make-up bag** n trousse f de maquillage
**make-up remover** n démaquillant m
**making** ['meɪkɪŋ] n (fig): **in the ~** en formation
or gestation; **to have the ~s of** (actor, athlete)
avoir l'étoffe de
**maladjusted** [mælə'dʒʌstɪd] adj inadapté(e)

**malaise** [mæ'leɪz] n malaise m
**malaria** [mə'lɛərɪə] n malaria f, paludisme m
**Malawi** [mə'lɑ:wɪ] n Malawi m
**Malay** [mə'leɪ] adj malais(e) ▷ n (person)
Malais(e); (language) malais m
**Malaya** [mə'leɪə] n Malaisie f
**Malayan** [mə'leɪən] adj, n = **Malay**
**Malaysia** [mə'leɪzɪə] n Malaisie f
**Malaysian** [mə'leɪzɪən] adj malaisien(ne) ▷ n
Malaisien(ne)
**Maldives** ['mɔ:ldaɪvz] npl: **the** ~ les Maldives fpl
**male** [meɪl] n (Biol, Elec) mâle m ▷ adj (sex,
attitude) masculin(e); (animal) mâle; (child etc) du
sexe masculin; ~ **and female students**
étudiants et étudiantes
**male chauvinist** n phallocrate m
**male nurse** n infirmier m
**malevolence** [mə'lɛvələns] n malveillance f
**malevolent** [mə'lɛvələnt] adj malveillant(e)
**malfunction** [mæl'fʌŋkʃən] n fonctionnement
défectueux
**malice** ['mælɪs] n méchanceté f, malveillance f
**malicious** [mə'lɪʃəs] adj méchant(e),
malveillant(e); (Law) avec intention criminelle
**malign** [mə'laɪn] vt diffamer, calomnier
**malignant** [mə'lɪgnənt] adj (Med) malin(-igne)
**malingerer** [mə'lɪŋgərəʳ] n simulateur(-trice)
**mall** [mɔ:l] n (also: **shopping mall**) centre
commercial
**malleable** ['mælɪəbl] adj malléable
**mallet** ['mælɪt] n maillet m
**malnutrition** [mælnju:'trɪʃən] n malnutrition f
**malpractice** [mæl'præktɪs] n faute
professionnelle; négligence f
**malt** [mɔ:lt] n malt m ▷ cpd (whisky) pur malt
**Malta** ['mɔ:ltə] n Malte f
**Maltese** [mɔ:l'ti:z] adj maltais(e) ▷ n (pl inv)
Maltais(e); (Ling) maltais m
**maltreat** [mæl'tri:t] vt maltraiter
**mammal** ['mæml] n mammifère m
**mammoth** ['mæməθ] n mammouth m ▷ adj
géant(e), monstre
**man** (pl **men**) [mæn, mɛn] n homme m; (Sport)
joueur m; (Chess) pièce f; (Draughts) pion m ▷ vt
(Naut: ship) garnir d'hommes; (machine) assurer
le fonctionnement de; (Mil: gun) servir; (: post)
être de service à; **an old** ~ un vieillard; ~ **and
wife** mari et femme
**Man.** abbr (Canada) = **Manitoba**
**manacles** ['mænəklz] npl menottes fpl
**manage** ['mænɪdʒ] vi se débrouiller; (succeed) y
arriver, réussir ▷ vt (business) gérer; (team,
operation) diriger; (control: ship) manier,
manœuvrer; (: person) savoir s'y prendre avec;
(device, things to do, career etc) arriver à se
débrouiller avec, s'en tirer avec; **to ~ to do** se
débrouiller pour faire; (succeed) réussir à faire
**manageable** ['mænɪdʒəbl] adj maniable; (task
etc) faisable; (number) raisonnable
**management** ['mænɪdʒmənt] n (running)
administration f, direction f; (people in charge: of
business, firm) dirigeants mpl, cadres mpl; (: of

hotel, shop, theatre) direction; **"under new ~"**
"changement de gérant", "changement de
propriétaire"
**management accounting** n comptabilité f de
gestion
**management consultant** n conseiller(-ère) de
direction
**manager** ['mænɪdʒəʳ] n (of business) directeur m;
(of institution etc) administrateur m; (of
department, unit) responsable m/f, chef m; (of hotel
etc) gérant m; (Sport) manager m; (of artist)
impresario m; **sales ~** responsable or chef des
ventes
**manageress** [mænɪdʒə'rɛs] n directrice f; (of
hotel etc) gérante f
**managerial** [mænɪ'dʒɪərɪəl] adj directorial(e);
(skills) de cadre, de gestion; ~ **staff** cadres mpl
**managing director** ['mænɪdʒɪŋ-] n directeur
général
**Mancunian** [mæn'kju:nɪən] adj de Manchester
▷ n habitant(e) de Manchester; natif(-ive) de
Manchester
**mandarin** ['mændərɪn] n (also: **mandarin
orange**) mandarine f; (person) mandarin m
**mandate** ['mændeɪt] n mandat m
**mandatory** ['mændətərɪ] adj obligatoire;
(powers etc) mandataire
**mandolin, mandoline** ['mændəlɪn] n
mandoline f
**mane** [meɪn] n crinière f
**maneuver** [mə'nu:vəʳ] (US) = **manoeuvre**
**manfully** ['mænfəlɪ] adv vaillamment
**manganese** [mæŋgə'ni:z] n manganèse m
**mangetout** ['mɔnʒ'tu:] n mange-tout m inv
**mangle** ['mæŋgl] vt déchiqueter; mutiler ▷ n
essoreuse f; calandre f
**mango** (pl **-es**) ['mæŋgəu] n mangue f
**mangrove** ['mæŋgrəuv] n palétuvier m
**mangy** ['meɪndʒɪ] adj galeux(-euse)
**manhandle** ['mænhændl] vt (mistreat)
maltraiter, malmener; (move by hand)
manutentionner
**manhole** ['mænhəul] n trou m d'homme
**manhood** ['mænhud] n (age) âge m d'homme;
(manliness) virilité f
**man-hour** ['mænauəʳ] n heure-homme f,
heure f de main-d'œuvre
**manhunt** ['mænhʌnt] n chasse f à l'homme
**mania** ['meɪnɪə] n manie f
**maniac** ['meɪnɪæk] n maniaque m/f; (fig) fou
(folle)
**manic** ['mænɪk] adj maniaque
**manic-depressive** ['mænɪkdɪ'prɛsɪv] adj, n
(Psych) maniaco-dépressif(-ive)
**manicure** ['mænɪkjuəʳ] n manucure f ▷ vt
(person) faire les mains à
**manicure set** n trousse f à ongles
**manifest** ['mænɪfɛst] vt manifester ▷ adj
manifeste, évident(e) ▷ n (Aviat, Naut)
manifeste m
**manifestation** [mænɪfɛs'teɪʃən] n
manifestation f

**manifesto** [mænɪˈfɛstəu] n (Pol) manifeste m
**manifold** [ˈmænɪfəuld] adj multiple, varié(e)
▷ n (Aut etc): **exhaust ~** collecteur m
d'échappement
**Manila** [məˈnɪlə] n Manille, Manila
**manila** [məˈnɪlə] adj: ~ **paper** papier m bulle
**manipulate** [məˈnɪpjuleɪt] vt manipuler;
(system, situation) exploiter
**manipulation** [mənɪpjuˈleɪʃən] n
manipulation f
**mankind** [mænˈkaɪnd] n humanité f, genre
humain
**manliness** [ˈmænlɪnɪs] n virilité f
**manly** [ˈmænlɪ] adj viril(e)
**man-made** [ˈmænˈmeɪd] adj artificiel(le); (fibre)
synthétique
**manna** [ˈmænə] n manne f
**mannequin** [ˈmænɪkɪn] n mannequin m
**manner** [ˈmænər] n manière f, façon f;
(behaviour) attitude f, comportement m;
**manners** npl: (good) ~**s** (bonnes) manières;
**bad ~s** mauvaises manières; **all ~ of** toutes
sortes de
**mannerism** [ˈmænərɪzəm] n particularité f de
langage (or de comportement), tic m
**mannerly** [ˈmænəlɪ] adj poli(e), courtois(e)
**manoeuvrable**, (US) **maneuverable** [məˈnu:
vrəbl] adj facile à manœuvrer
**manoeuvre**, (US) **maneuver** [məˈnu:vər] vt
(move) manœuvrer; (manipulate: person)
manipuler; (: situation) exploiter ▷ n manœuvre
f; **to ~ sb into doing sth** manipuler qn pour lui
faire faire qch
**manor** [ˈmænər] n (also: **manor house**) manoir m
**manpower** [ˈmænpauər] n main-d'œuvre f
**manservant** (pl **menservants**) [ˈmænsə:vənt,
ˈmɛn-] n domestique m
**mansion** [ˈmænʃən] n château m, manoir m
**manslaughter** [ˈmænslɔːtər] n homicide m
involontaire
**mantelpiece** [ˈmæntlpiːs] n cheminée f
**mantle** [ˈmæntl] n cape f; (fig) manteau m
**man-to-man** [ˈmæntəˈmæn] adj, adv d'homme
à homme
**manual** [ˈmænjuəl] adj manuel(le) ▷ n
manuel m
**manual worker** n travailleur manuel
**manufacture** [mænjuˈfæktʃər] vt fabriquer ▷ n
fabrication f
**manufactured goods** [mænjuˈfæktʃəd-] npl
produits manufacturés
**manufacturer** [mænjuˈfæktʃərər] n fabricant m
**manufacturing industries** [mænju-] npl
industries fpl de transformation
**manure** [məˈnjuər] n fumier m; (artificial)
engrais m
**manuscript** [ˈmænjuskrɪpt] n manuscrit m
**many** [ˈmɛnɪ] adj beaucoup de, de
nombreux(-euses) ▷ pron beaucoup, un grand
nombre; **how ~?** combien?; **a great ~** un grand
nombre (de); **too ~ difficulties** trop de
difficultés; **twice as ~** deux fois plus; **~ a ...**

bien des ..., plus d'un(e) ...
**Maori** [ˈmaurɪ] n Maori(e) ▷ adj maori(e)
**map** [mæp] n carte f; (of town) plan m ▷ vt
dresser la carte de; **can you show it to me on
the ~?** pouvez-vous me l'indiquer sur la carte?
▶ **map out** vt tracer; (fig: task) planifier; (career,
holiday) organiser, préparer (à l'avance); (: essay)
faire le plan de
**maple** [ˈmeɪpl] n érable m
**mar** [ma:r] vt gâcher, gâter
**marathon** [ˈmærəθən] n marathon m ▷ adj: **a ~
session** une séance-marathon
**marathon runner** n coureur(-euse) de
marathon, marathonien(ne)
**marauder** [məˈrɔːdər] n maraudeur(-euse)
**marble** [ˈmaːbl] n marbre m; (toy) bille f;
**marbles** npl (game) billes
**March** [maːtʃ] n mars m
**march** [maːtʃ] vi marcher au pas; (demonstrators)
défiler ▷ n marche f; (demonstration)
manifestation f; **to ~ out of/into** etc sortir de/
entrer dans etc (de manière décidée ou impulsive)
**marcher** [ˈmaːtʃər] n (demonstrator)
manifestant(e), marcheur(-euse)
**marching** [ˈmaːtʃɪŋ] n: **to give sb his ~ orders**
(fig) renvoyer qn; envoyer promener qn
**march-past** [ˈmaːtʃpaːst] n défilé m
**mare** [mɛər] n jument f
**marg.** [maːdʒ] n abbr (inf) = **margarine**
**margarine** [maːdʒəˈriːn] n margarine f
**margin** [ˈmaːdʒɪn] n marge f
**marginal** [ˈmaːdʒɪnl] adj marginal(e); **~ seat**
(Pol) siège disputé
**marginally** [ˈmaːdʒɪnəlɪ] adv très légèrement,
sensiblement
**marigold** [ˈmærɪgəuld] n souci m
**marijuana** [mærɪˈwaːnə] n marijuana f
**marina** [məˈriːnə] n marina f
**marinade** n [mærɪˈneɪd] marinade f ▷ vt
[ˈmærɪneɪd] = **marinate**
**marinate** [ˈmærɪneɪt] vt (faire) mariner
**marine** [məˈriːn] adj marin(e) ▷ n fusilier
marin; (US) marine m
**marine insurance** n assurance f maritime
**marital** [ˈmærɪtl] adj matrimonial(e)
**marital status** n situation f de famille
**maritime** [ˈmærɪtaɪm] adj maritime
**maritime law** n droit m maritime
**marjoram** [ˈmaːdʒərəm] n marjolaine f
**mark** [maːk] n marque f; (of skid etc) trace f; (Brit
Scol) note f; (Sport) cible f; (currency) mark m; (Brit
Tech): **M~ 2/3** 2ème/3ème série f or version f;
(oven temperature): **(gas) ~ 4** thermostat m 4 ▷ vt
(also Sport: player) marquer; (stain) tacher; (Brit
Scol) corriger, noter; (also: **punctuation marks**)
signes mpl de ponctuation; **to ~ time** marquer
le pas; **to be quick off the ~ (in doing)** (fig) ne
pas perdre de temps (pour faire); **up to the ~** (in
efficiency) à la hauteur
▶ **mark down** vt (prices, goods) démarquer,
réduire le prix de
▶ **mark off** vt (tick off) cocher, pointer

▶ **mark out** *vt* désigner
▶ **mark up** *vt* (*price*) majorer
**marked** [mɑːkt] *adj* (*obvious*) marqué(e), net(te)
**markedly** ['mɑːkɪdlɪ] *adv* visiblement, manifestement
**marker** ['mɑːkə']  *n* (*sign*) jalon *m*; (*bookmark*) signet *m*
**market** ['mɑːkɪt] *n* marché *m* ▷ *vt* (*Comm*) commercialiser; **to be on the ~** être sur le marché; **on the open ~** en vente libre; **to play the ~** jouer à la *or* spéculer en Bourse
**marketable** ['mɑːkɪtəbl] *adj* commercialisable
**market analysis** *n* analyse *f* de marché
**market day** *n* jour *m* de marché
**market demand** *n* besoins *mpl* du marché
**market economy** *n* économie *f* de marché
**market forces** *npl* tendances *fpl* du marché
**market garden** *n* (*Brit*) jardin maraîcher
**marketing** ['mɑːkɪtɪŋ] *n* marketing *m*
**marketplace** ['mɑːkɪtpleɪs] *n* place *f* du marché; (*Comm*) marché *m*
**market price** *n* prix marchand
**market research** *n* étude *f* de marché
**market value** *n* valeur marchande; valeur du marché
**marking** ['mɑːkɪŋ] *n* (*on animal*) marque *f*, tache *f*; (*on road*) signalisation *f*
**marksman** ['mɑːksmən] (*irreg*) *n* tireur *m* d'élite
**marksmanship** ['mɑːksmənʃɪp] *n* adresse *f* au tir
**mark-up** ['mɑːkʌp] *n* (*Comm: margin*) marge *f* (bénéficiaire); (: *increase*) majoration *f*
**marmalade** ['mɑːməleɪd] *n* confiture *f* d'oranges
**maroon** [mə'ruːn] *vt*: **to be ~ed** être abandonné(e); (*fig*) être bloqué(e) ▷ *adj* (*colour*) bordeaux *inv*
**marquee** [mɑː'kiː] *n* chapiteau *m*
**marquess, marquis** ['mɑːkwɪs] *n* marquis *m*
**Marrakech, Marrakesh** [mærə'keʃ] *n* Marrakech
**marriage** ['mærɪdʒ] *n* mariage *m*
**marriage bureau** *n* agence matrimoniale
**marriage certificate** *n* extrait *m* d'acte de mariage
**marriage guidance**, (*US*) **marriage counseling** *n* conseils conjugaux
**marriage of convenience** *n* mariage *m* de convenance
**married** ['mærɪd] *adj* marié(e); (*life, love*) conjugal(e)
**marrow** ['mærəu] *n* (*of bone*) moelle *f*; (*vegetable*) courge *f*
**marry** ['mærɪ] *vt* épouser, se marier avec; (*subj: father, priest etc*) marier ▷ *vi* (*also*: **get married**) se marier
**Mars** [mɑːz] *n* (*planet*) Mars *f*
**Marseilles** [mɑː'seɪ] *n* Marseille
**marsh** [mɑːʃ] *n* marais *m*, marécage *m*
**marshal** ['mɑːʃl] *n* maréchal *m*; (*US: fire, police*) ≈ capitaine *m*; (*for demonstration, meeting*) membre *m* du service d'ordre ▷ *vt* rassembler

**marshalling yard** ['mɑːʃlɪŋ-] *n* (*Rail*) gare *f* de triage
**marshmallow** [mɑːʃ'mæləu] *n* (*Bot*) guimauve *f*; (*sweet*) (pâte *f* de) guimauve
**marshy** ['mɑːʃɪ] *adj* marécageux(-euse)
**marsupial** [mɑː'suːpɪəl] *adj* marsupial(e) ▷ *n* marsupial *m*
**martial** ['mɑːʃl] *adj* martial(e)
**martial arts** *npl* arts martiaux
**martial law** *n* loi martiale
**Martian** ['mɑːʃən] *n* Martien(ne)
**martin** ['mɑːtɪn] *n* (*also*: **house martin**) martinet *m*
**martyr** ['mɑːtə'] *n* martyr(e) ▷ *vt* martyriser
**martyrdom** ['mɑːtədəm] *n* martyre *m*
**marvel** ['mɑːvl] *n* merveille *f* ▷ *vi*: **to ~ (at)** s'émerveiller (de)
**marvellous**, (*US*) **marvelous** ['mɑːvləs] *adj* merveilleux(-euse)
**Marxism** ['mɑːksɪzəm] *n* marxisme *m*
**Marxist** ['mɑːksɪst] *adj, n* marxiste (*m/f*)
**marzipan** ['mɑːzɪpæn] *n* pâte *f* d'amandes
**mascara** [mæs'kɑːrə] *n* mascara *m*
**mascot** ['mæskət] *n* mascotte *f*
**masculine** ['mæskjulɪn] *adj* masculin(e) ▷ *n* masculin *m*
**masculinity** [mæskju'lɪnɪtɪ] *n* masculinité *f*
**MASH** [mæʃ] *n abbr* (*US Mil*) = **mobile army surgical hospital**
**mash** [mæʃ] *vt* (*Culin*) faire une purée de
**mashed potato** *n*, **mashed potatoes** *npl* purée *f* de pommes de terre
**mask** [mɑːsk] *n* masque *m* ▷ *vt* masquer
**masochism** ['mæsəukɪzəm] *n* masochisme *m*
**masochist** ['mæsəukɪst] *n* masochiste *m/f*
**mason** ['meɪsn] *n* (*also*: **stonemason**) maçon *m*; (*also*: **freemason**) franc-maçon *m*
**masonic** [mə'sɔnɪk] *adj* maçonnique
**masonry** ['meɪsnrɪ] *n* maçonnerie *f*
**masquerade** [mæskə'reɪd] *n* bal masqué; (*fig*) mascarade *f* ▷ *vi*: **to ~ as** se faire passer pour
**mass** [mæs] *n* multitude *f*, masse *f*; (*Physics*) masse; (*Rel*) messe *f* ▷ *cpd* (*communication*) de masse; (*unemployment*) massif(-ive) ▷ *vi* se masser; **masses** *npl*: **the ~es** les masses; **~es of** (*inf*) des tas de; **to go to ~** aller à la messe
**Mass.** *abbr* (*US*) = **Massachusetts.**
**massacre** ['mæsəkə'] *n* massacre *m* ▷ *vt* massacrer
**massage** ['mæsɑːʒ] *n* massage *m* ▷ *vt* masser
**massive** ['mæsɪv] *adj* énorme, massif(-ive)
**mass market** *n* marché *m* grand public
**mass media** *npl* mass-media *mpl*
**mass meeting** *n* rassemblement *m* de masse
**mass-produce** ['mæsprə'djuːs] *vt* fabriquer en série
**mass production** *n* fabrication *f* en série
**mast** [mɑːst] *n* mât *m*; (*Radio, TV*) pylône *m*
**mastectomy** [mæs'tektəmɪ] *n* mastectomie *f*
**master** ['mɑːstə'] *n* maître *m*; (*in secondary school*) professeur *m*; (*in primary school*) instituteur *m*; (*title for boys*): **M~ X** Monsieur X ▷ *vt* maîtriser;

(*learn*) apprendre à fond; (*understand*) posséder parfaitement *or* à fond; **~ of ceremonies (MC)** *n* maître des cérémonies; **M~ of Arts/Science (MA/MSc)** (*n*) ≈ titulaire *m/f* d'une maîtrise (en lettres/science); **M~ of Arts/Science degree (MA/MSc)** ≈ maîtrise *f*; **M~'s degree** (*n*) ≈ maîtrise; *voir article*

### ⊕ MASTER'S DEGREE

⊕
⊕ Le *Master's degree* est un diplôme que l'on
⊕ prépare en général après le "Bachelor's
⊕ degree", bien que certaines universités
⊕ décernent un *Master's* au lieu d'un
⊕ "Bachelor's". Il consiste soit à suivre des
⊕ cours, soit à rédiger une mémoire à partir
⊕ d'une recherche personnelle, soit encore les
⊕ deux. Les principaux masters sont le "MA"
⊕ (Master of Arts), et le "MSc" (Master of
⊕ Science), qui comprennent cours et
⊕ mémoire, et le "MLitt "(Master of Letters) et
⊕ le "MPhil" (Master of Philosophy), qui
⊕ reposent uniquement sur le mémoire; voir
⊕ "doctorate".

**master disk** *n* (*Comput*) disque original
**masterful** ['mɑːstəful] *adj* autoritaire, impérieux(-euse)
**master key** *n* passe-partout *m inv*
**masterly** ['mɑːstəlɪ] *adj* magistral(e)
**mastermind** ['mɑːstəmaɪnd] *n* esprit supérieur ▷ *vt* diriger, être le cerveau de
**masterpiece** ['mɑːstəpiːs] *n* chef-d'œuvre *m*
**master plan** *n* stratégie *f* d'ensemble
**master stroke** *n* coup *m* de maître
**mastery** ['mɑːstərɪ] *n* maîtrise *f*; connaissance parfaite
**mastiff** ['mæstɪf] *n* mastiff *m*
**masturbate** ['mæstəbeɪt] *vi* se masturber
**masturbation** [mæstə'beɪʃən] *n* masturbation *f*
**mat** [mæt] *n* petit tapis; (*also:* **doormat**) paillasson *m*; (*also:* **tablemat**) set *m* de table ▷ *adj* = **matt**
**match** [mætʃ] *n* allumette *f*; (*game*) match *m*, partie *f*; (*fig*) égal(e); mariage *m*; parti *m* ▷ *vt* (*also:* **match up**) assortir; (*go well with*) aller bien avec, s'assortir à; (*equal*) égaler, valoir ▷ *vi* être assorti(e); **to be a good ~** être bien assorti(e) ▷ **match up** *vt* assortir
**matchbox** ['mætʃbɔks] *n* boîte *f* d'allumettes
**matching** ['mætʃɪŋ] *adj* assorti(e)
**matchless** ['mætʃlɪs] *adj* sans égal
**mate** [meɪt] *n* camarade *m/f* de travail; (*inf*) copain (copine); (*animal*) partenaire *m/f*, mâle (femelle); (*in merchant navy*) second *m* ▷ *vi* s'accoupler ▷ *vt* accoupler
**material** [mə'tɪərɪəl] *n* (*substance*) matière *f*, matériau *m*; (*cloth*) tissu *m*, étoffe *f*; (*information, data*) données *fpl* ▷ *adj* matériel(le); (*relevant*) pertinent(e); (*important*) essentiel(le); **materials** *npl* (*equipment*) matériaux *mpl*; **reading ~** de quoi lire, de la lecture

**materialistic** [mətɪərɪə'lɪstɪk] *adj* matérialiste
**materialize** [mə'tɪərɪəlaɪz] *vi* se matérialiser, se réaliser
**materially** [mə'tɪərɪəlɪ] *adv* matériellement; essentiellement
**maternal** [mə'təːnl] *adj* maternel(le)
**maternity** [mə'təːnɪtɪ] *n* maternité *f* ▷ *cpd* de maternité, de grossesse
**maternity benefit** *n* prestation *f* de maternité
**maternity dress** *n* robe *f* de grossesse
**maternity hospital** *n* maternité *f*
**maternity leave** *n* congé *m* de maternité
**matey** ['meɪtɪ] *adj* (*Brit: inf*) copain-copain *inv*
**math** [mæθ] *n* (*US:* = *mathematics*) maths *fpl*
**mathematical** [mæθə'mætɪkl] *adj* mathématique
**mathematician** [mæθəmə'tɪʃən] *n* mathématicien(ne)
**mathematics** [mæθə'mætɪks] *n* mathématiques *fpl*
**maths** [mæθs] *n abbr* (*Brit:* = *mathematics*) maths *fpl*
**matinée** ['mætɪneɪ] *n* matinée *f*
**mating** ['meɪtɪŋ] *n* accouplement *m*
**mating call** *n* appel *m* du mâle
**mating season** *n* saison *f* des amours
**matriarchal** [meɪtrɪ'ɑːkl] *adj* matriarcal(e)
**matrices** ['meɪtrɪsiːz] *npl of* **matrix**
**matriculation** [mətrɪkju'leɪʃən] *n* inscription *f*
**matrimonial** [mætrɪ'məunɪəl] *adj* matrimonial(e), conjugal(e)
**matrimony** ['mætrɪmənɪ] *n* mariage *m*
**matrix** (*pl* **matrices**) ['meɪtrɪks, 'meɪtrɪsiːz] *n* matrice *f*
**matron** ['meɪtrən] *n* (*in hospital*) infirmière-chef *f*; (*in school*) infirmière *f*
**matronly** ['meɪtrənlɪ] *adj* de matrone; imposant(e)
**matt** [mæt] *adj* mat(e)
**matted** ['mætɪd] *adj* emmêlé(e)
**matter** ['mætə$^r$] *n* question *f*; (*Physics*) matière *f*, substance *f*; (*content*) contenu *m*, fond *m*; (*Med: pus*) pus *m* ▷ *vi* importer; **matters** *npl* (*affairs, situation*) la situation; **it doesn't ~** cela n'a pas d'importance; (*I don't mind*) cela ne fait rien; **what's the ~?** qu'est-ce qu'il y a?, qu'est-ce qui ne va pas?; **no ~ what** quoi qu'il arrive; **that's another ~** c'est une autre affaire; **as a ~ of course** tout naturellement; **as a ~ of fact** en fait; **it's a ~ of habit** c'est une question d'habitude; **printed ~** imprimés *mpl*; **reading ~** (*Brit*) de quoi lire, de la lecture
**matter-of-fact** ['mætərəv'fækt] *adj* terre à terre, neutre
**matting** ['mætɪŋ] *n* natte *f*
**mattress** ['mætrɪs] *n* matelas *m*
**mature** [mə'tjuə$^r$] *adj* mûr(e); (*cheese*) fait(e); (*wine*) arrive(e) à maturité ▷ *vi* mûrir; (*cheese, wine*) se faire
**mature student** *n* étudiant(e) plus âgé(e) que la moyenne
**maturity** [mə'tjuərɪtɪ] *n* maturité *f*

**maudlin** ['mɔːdlɪn] *adj* larmoyant(e)
**maul** [mɔːl] *vt* lacérer
**Mauritania** [mɔːrɪ'teɪnɪə] *n* Mauritanie *f*
**Mauritius** [mə'rɪʃəs] *n* l'île *f* Maurice
**mausoleum** [mɔːsə'lɪəm] *n* mausolée *m*
**mauve** [məʊv] *adj* mauve
**maverick** ['mævrɪk] *n* (*fig*) franc-tireur *m*, non-
   conformiste *m/f*
**mawkish** ['mɔːkɪʃ] *adj* mièvre; fade
**max** *abbr* = **maximum**
**maxim** ['mæksɪm] *n* maxime *f*
**maxima** ['mæksɪmə] *npl of* **maximum**
**maximize** ['mæksɪmaɪz] *vt* (*profits etc, chances*)
   maximiser
**maximum** ['mæksɪməm] (*pl* **maxima**)
   ['mæksɪmə] *adj* maximum ▷ *n* maximum *m*
**May** [meɪ] *n* mai *m*; *for phrases see also* **July**
**may** [meɪ] (*conditional* **might**) *vi* (*indicating
   possibility*): **he ~ come** il se peut qu'il vienne; (*be
   allowed to*): **~ I smoke?** puis-je fumer?; (*wishes*):
   **~ God bless you!** (que) Dieu vous bénisse!; **~ I
   sit here?** vous permettez que je m'assoie ici?;
   **he might be there** il pourrait bien y être, il se
   pourrait qu'il y soit; **you ~ as well go** vous
   feriez aussi bien d'y aller; **I might as well go** je
   ferais aussi bien d'y aller, autant y aller; **you
   might like to try** vous pourriez (peut-être)
   essayer
**maybe** ['meɪbiː] *adv* peut-être; **~ he'll ...** peut-
   être qu'il ...; **~ not** peut-être pas
**May Day** *n* le Premier mai
**mayday** ['meɪdeɪ] *n* S.O.S *m*
**mayhem** ['meɪhɛm] *n* grabuge *m*
**mayonnaise** [meɪə'neɪz] *n* mayonnaise *f*
**mayor** [mɛə<sup>r</sup>] *n* maire *m*
**mayoress** ['mɛərɛs] *n* (*female mayor*) maire *m*;
   (*wife of mayor*) épouse *f* du maire
**maypole** ['meɪpəʊl] *n* mât enrubanné (*autour
   duquel on danse*)
**maze** [meɪz] *n* labyrinthe *m*, dédale *m*
**MB** *abbr* (*Comput*) = **megabyte**; (*Canada*)
   = **Manitoba**
**MBA** *n abbr* (= *Master of Business Administration*) *titre
   universitaire*
**MBBS, MBChB** *n abbr* (*Brit*: = *Bachelor of Medicine
   and Surgery*) *titre universitaire*
**MBE** *n abbr* (*Brit*: = *Member of the Order of the British
   Empire*) *titre honorifique*
**MBO** *n abbr* (*Brit*) = **management buyout**
**MC** *n abbr* = **master of ceremonies**
**MCAT** *n abbr* (*US*) = **Medical College Admissions
   Test**
**MD** *n abbr* (= *Doctor of Medicine*) *titre universitaire*;
   (*Comm*) = **managing director** ▷ *abbr* (*US*)
   = **Maryland**
**Md.** *abbr* (*US*) = **Maryland**
**MDT** *abbr* (*US*: = *Mountain Daylight Time*) *heure d'été
   des Montagnes Rocheuses*
**ME** *n abbr* (*US*: = *medical examiner*) médecin légiste
   *m/f*; (*Med*: = *myalgic encephalomyelitis*)
   encéphalomyélite *f* myalgique ▷ *abbr* (*US*)
   = **Maine**

**me** [miː] *pron* me, m' + *vowel or h mute*; (*stressed,
   after prep*) moi; **it's me** c'est moi; **he heard me**
   il m'a entendu; **give me a book** donnez-moi
   un livre; **it's for me** c'est pour moi
**meadow** ['mɛdəʊ] *n* prairie *f*, pré *m*
**meagre, (US) meager** ['miːgə<sup>r</sup>] *adj* maigre
**meal** [miːl] *n* repas *m*; (*flour*) farine *f*; **to go out
   for a ~** sortir manger
**meals on wheels** *npl* (*Brit*) *repas livrés à domicile aux
   personnes âgées ou handicapées*
**mealtime** ['miːltaɪm] *n* heure *f* du repas
**mealy-mouthed** ['miːlɪmaʊðd] *adj*
   mielleux(-euse)
**mean** [miːn] *adj* (*with money*) avare, radin(e);
   (*unkind*) mesquin(e), méchant(e); (*shabby*)
   misérable; (*US inf*: *animal*) méchant,
   vicieux(-euse); (: *person*) vache; (*average*)
   moyen(ne) ▷ *vt* (*pt, pp* **-t**) [mɛnt] (*signify*)
   signifier, vouloir dire; (*refer to*) faire allusion à,
   parler de; (*intend*): **to ~ to do** avoir l'intention
   de faire ▷ *n* moyenne *f*; **means** *npl* (*way, money*)
   moyens *mpl*; **by ~s of** (*instrument*) au moyen de;
   **by all ~s** je vous en prie; **to be ~t for** être
   destiné(e) à; **do you ~ it?** vous êtes sérieux?;
   **what do you ~?** que voulez-vous dire?
**meander** [mɪ'ændə<sup>r</sup>] *vi* faire des méandres; (*fig*)
   flâner
**meaning** ['miːnɪŋ] *n* signification *f*, sens *m*
**meaningful** ['miːnɪŋful] *adj* significatif(-ive);
   (*relationship*) valable
**meaningless** ['miːnɪŋlɪs] *adj* dénué(e) de sens
**meanness** ['miːnnɪs] *n* avarice *f*; mesquinerie *f*
**means test** *n* (*Admin*) contrôle *m* des conditions
   de ressources
**meant** [mɛnt] *pt, pp of* **mean**
**meantime** ['miːntaɪm] *adv* (*also*: **in the
   meantime**) pendant ce temps
**meanwhile** ['miːnwaɪl] *adv* = **meantime**
**measles** ['miːzlz] *n* rougeole *f*
**measly** ['miːzlɪ] *adj* (*inf*) minable
**measurable** ['mɛʒərəbl] *adj* mesurable
**measure** ['mɛʒə<sup>r</sup>] *vt, vi* mesurer ▷ *n* mesure *f*;
   (*ruler*) règle (graduée); **a litre ~** un litre; **some ~
   of success** un certain succès; **to take ~s to do
   sth** prendre des mesures pour faire qch
   ▸ **measure up** *vi*: **to ~ up (to)** être à la hauteur
   (de)
**measured** ['mɛʒəd] *adj* mesuré(e)
**measurements** ['mɛʒəmənts] *npl* mesures *fpl*;
   **chest/hip ~** tour *m* de poitrine/hanches; **to
   take sb's ~** prendre les mesures de qn
**meat** [miːt] *n* viande *f*; **I don't eat ~** je ne
   mange pas de viande; **cold ~s** (*Brit*) viandes
   froides; **crab ~** crabe *f*
**meatball** ['miːtbɔːl] *n* boulette *f* de viande
**meat pie** *n* pâté *m* en croûte
**meaty** ['miːtɪ] *adj* (*flavour*) de viande; (*fig:
   argument, book*) étoffé(e), substantiel(le)
**Mecca** ['mɛkə] *n* la Mecque; (*fig*): **a ~ (for)** la
   Mecque (de)
**mechanic** [mɪ'kænɪk] *n* mécanicien *m*; **can you
   send a ~?** pouvez-vous nous envoyer un

**m**

mécanicien?

**mechanical** [mɪˈkænɪkl] *adj* mécanique

**mechanical engineering** *n* (*science*) mécanique *f*; (*industry*) construction *f* mécanique

**mechanics** [məˈkænɪks] *n* mécanique *f* ▷ *npl* mécanisme *m*

**mechanism** [ˈmɛkənɪzəm] *n* mécanisme *m*

**mechanization** [mɛkənaɪˈzeɪʃən] *n* mécanisation *f*

**MEd** *n abbr* (= *Master of Education*) titre universitaire

**medal** [ˈmɛdl] *n* médaille *f*

**medallion** [mɪˈdælɪən] *n* médaillon *m*

**medallist** [ˈmɛdlɪst] *n* (*Sport*) médaillé(e)

**meddle** [ˈmɛdl] *vi*: **to ~ in** se mêler de, s'occuper de; **to ~ with** toucher à

**meddlesome** [ˈmɛdlsəm], **meddling** [ˈmɛdlɪŋ] *adj* indiscret(-ète), qui se mêle de ce qui ne le (*or* la) regarde pas; touche-à-tout *inv*

**media** [ˈmiːdɪə] *npl* media *mpl* ▷ *npl of* **medium**

**media circus** *n* (*event*) battage *m* médiatique; (*group of journalists*) cortège *m* médiatique

**mediaeval** [mɛdɪˈiːvl] *adj* = **medieval**

**median** [ˈmiːdɪən] *n* (US: *also*: **median strip**) bande médiane

**media research** *n* étude *f* de l'audience

**mediate** [ˈmiːdɪeɪt] *vi* servir d'intermédiaire

**mediation** [miːdɪˈeɪʃən] *n* médiation *f*

**mediator** [ˈmiːdɪeɪtəʳ] *n* médiateur(-trice)

**Medicaid** [ˈmɛdɪkeɪd] *n* (US) assistance médicale aux indigents

**medical** [ˈmɛdɪkl] *adj* médical(e) ▷ *n* (*also*: **medical examination**) visite médicale; (*private*) examen médical

**medical certificate** *n* certificat médical

**medical student** *n* étudiant(e) en médecine

**Medicare** [ˈmɛdɪkɛəʳ] *n* (US) régime d'assurance maladie

**medicated** [ˈmɛdɪkeɪtɪd] *adj* traitant(e), médicamenteux(-euse)

**medication** [mɛdɪˈkeɪʃən] *n* (*drugs etc*) médication *f*

**medicinal** [mɛˈdɪsɪnl] *adj* médicinal(e)

**medicine** [ˈmɛdsɪn] *n* médecine *f*; (*drug*) médicament *m*

**medicine chest** *n* pharmacie *f* (*murale ou portative*)

**medicine man** (*irreg*) *n* sorcier *m*

**medieval** [mɛdɪˈiːvl] *adj* médiéval(e)

**mediocre** [miːdɪˈəukəʳ] *adj* médiocre

**mediocrity** [miːdɪˈɔkrɪtɪ] *n* médiocrité *f*

**meditate** [ˈmɛdɪteɪt] *vi*: **to ~ (on)** méditer (sur)

**meditation** [mɛdɪˈteɪʃən] *n* méditation *f*

**Mediterranean** [mɛdɪtəˈreɪnɪən] *adj* méditerranéen(ne); **the ~ (Sea)** la (mer) Méditerranée

**medium** [ˈmiːdɪəm] *adj* moyen(ne) ▷ *n* (*pl* **media**) (*means*) moyen *m*; (*pl* **-s**) (*person*) médium *m*; **the happy ~** le juste milieu

**medium-dry** [ˈmiːdɪəmˈdraɪ] *adj* demi-sec

**medium-sized** [ˈmiːdɪəmˈsaɪzd] *adj* de taille moyenne

**medium wave** *n* (*Radio*) ondes moyennes, petites ondes

**medley** [ˈmɛdlɪ] *n* mélange *m*

**meek** [miːk] *adj* doux (douce), humble

**meet** (*pt, pp* **met**) [miːt, mɛt] *vt* rencontrer; (*by arrangement*) retrouver, rejoindre; (*for the first time*) faire la connaissance de; (*go and fetch*): **I'll ~ you at the station** j'irai te chercher à la gare; (*opponent, danger, problem*) faire face à; (*requirements*) satisfaire à, répondre à; (*bill, expenses*) régler, honorer ▷ *vi* (*friends*) se rencontrer; se retrouver; (*in session*) se réunir; (*join: lines, roads*) se joindre ▷ *n* (*Brit Hunting*) rendez-vous *m* de chasse; (*US Sport*) rencontre *f*, meeting *m*; **pleased to ~ you!** enchanté!; **nice ~ing you** ravi d'avoir fait votre connaissance

▶ **meet up** *vi*: **to ~ up with sb** rencontrer qn

▶ **meet with** *vt fus* (*difficulty*) rencontrer; **to ~ with success** être couronné(e) de succès

**meeting** [ˈmiːtɪŋ] *n* (*of group of people*) réunion *f*; (*between individuals*) rendez-vous *m*; (*formal*) assemblée *f*; (*Sport: rally*) rencontre, meeting *m*; (*interview*) entrevue *f*; **she's at** *or* **in a ~** (*Comm*) elle est en réunion; **to call a ~** convoquer une réunion

**meeting place** *n* lieu *m* de (la) réunion; (*for appointment*) lieu de rendez-vous

**mega** [ˈmɛgə] (*inf*) *adv*: **he's ~ rich** il est hyper-riche

**megabyte** [ˈmɛgəbaɪt] *n* (*Comput*) méga-octet *m*

**megaphone** [ˈmɛgəfəun] *n* porte-voix *m inv*

**megapixel** [ˈmɛgəpɪksl] *n* mégapixel *m*

**meh** [mɛ] *excl* bof

**melancholy** [ˈmɛlənkəlɪ] *n* mélancolie *f* ▷ *adj* mélancolique

**mellow** [ˈmɛləu] *adj* velouté(e), doux (douce); (*colour*) riche et profond(e); (*fruit*) mûr(e) ▷ *vi* (*person*) s'adoucir

**melodious** [mɪˈləudɪəs] *adj* mélodieux(-euse)

**melodrama** [ˈmɛləudrɑːmə] *n* mélodrame *m*

**melodramatic** [mɛlədrəˈmætɪk] *adj* mélodramatique

**melody** [ˈmɛlədɪ] *n* mélodie *f*

**melon** [ˈmɛlən] *n* melon *m*

**melt** [mɛlt] *vi* fondre; (*become soft*) s'amollir; (*fig*) s'attendrir ▷ *vt* faire fondre

▶ **melt away** *vi* fondre complètement

▶ **melt down** *vt* fondre

**meltdown** [ˈmɛltdaun] *n* fusion *f* (du cœur d'un réacteur nucléaire)

**melting point** [ˈmɛltɪŋ-] *n* point *m* de fusion

**melting pot** [ˈmɛltɪŋ-] *n* (*fig*) creuset *m*; **to be in the ~** être encore en discussion

**member** [ˈmɛmbəʳ] *n* membre *m*; (*of club, political party*) membre, adhérent(e) ▷ *cpd*: **~ country/ state** *n* pays *m*/état *m* membre

**membership** [ˈmɛmbəʃɪp] *n* (*becoming a member*) adhésion *f*; admission *f*; (*being a member*) qualité *f* de membre, fait *m* d'être membre; (*members*) membres *mpl*, adhérents *mpl*; (*number of members*) nombre *m* des membres *or* adhérents

**membership card** *n* carte *f* de membre

**membrane** [ˈmɛmbreɪn] *n* membrane *f*

**memento** [məˈmɛntəu] n souvenir m
**memo** [ˈmɛməu] n note f (de service)
**memoir** [ˈmɛmwɑːʳ] n mémoire m, étude f;
  **memoirs** npl mémoires
**memo pad** n bloc-notes m
**memorable** [ˈmɛmərəbl] adj mémorable
**memorandum** (pl **memoranda**)
  [mɛməˈrændəm, -də] n note f (de service);
  (Diplomacy) mémorandum m
**memorial** [mɪˈmɔːrɪəl] n mémorial m ▷ adj
  commémoratif(-ive)
**Memorial Day** n (US) voir article

  ● **MEMORIAL DAY**
  ●
  ● Memorial Day est un jour férié aux États-Unis,
  ● le dernier lundi de mai dans la plupart des
  ● États, à la mémoire des soldats américains
  ● morts au combat.

**memorize** [ˈmɛməraɪz] vt apprendre or retenir
  par cœur
**memory** [ˈmɛmərɪ] n (also Comput) mémoire f;
  (recollection) souvenir m; **to have a good/bad ~**
  avoir une bonne/mauvaise mémoire; **loss of ~**
  perte f de mémoire; **in ~ of** à la mémoire de
**memory card** n (for digital camera) carte f
  mémoire
**memory stick** n (Comput: flash pen) clé f USB
  (: card) carte f mémoire
**men** [mɛn] npl of **man**
**menace** [ˈmɛnɪs] n menace f; (inf: nuisance) peste f,
  plaie f ▷ vt menacer; **a public ~** un danger public
**menacing** [ˈmɛnɪsɪŋ] adj menaçant(e)
**menagerie** [mɪˈnædʒərɪ] n ménagerie f
**mend** [mɛnd] vt réparer; (darn) raccommoder,
  repriser ▷ n reprise f; **on the ~** en voie de
  guérison; **to ~ one's ways** s'amender
**mending** [ˈmɛndɪŋ] n raccommodages mpl
**menial** [ˈmiːnɪəl] adj de domestique,
  inférieur(e); subalterne
**meningitis** [mɛnɪnˈdʒaɪtɪs] n méningite f
**menopause** [ˈmɛnəupɔːz] n ménopause f
**menservants** [ˈmɛnsəːvənts] npl of **manservant**
**men's room** (US) n: **the men's room** les
  toilettes fpl pour hommes
**menstruate** [ˈmɛnstrueɪt] vi avoir ses règles
**menstruation** [mɛnstruˈeɪʃən] n menstruation f
**menswear** [ˈmɛnzwɛəʳ] n vêtements mpl
  d'hommes
**mental** [ˈmɛntl] adj mental(e); **~ illness**
  maladie mentale
**mental hospital** n hôpital m psychiatrique
**mentality** [mɛnˈtælɪtɪ] n mentalité f
**mentally** [ˈmɛntlɪ] adv: **to be ~ handicapped**
  être handicapé(e) mental(e); **the ~ ill** les
  malades mentaux
**menthol** [ˈmɛnθɔl] n menthol m
**mention** [ˈmɛnʃən] n mention f ▷ vt
  mentionner, faire mention de; **don't ~ it!** je
  vous en prie, il n'y a pas de quoi!; **I need hardly
  ~ that** ... est-il besoin de rappeler que ...?; **not**

**to ~** ..., **without ~ing** ... sans parler de ..., sans
  compter ...
**mentor** [ˈmɛntɔːʳ] n mentor m
**menu** [ˈmɛnjuː] n (set menu, Comput) menu m; (list
  of dishes) carte f; **could we see the ~?** est-ce
  qu'on peut voir la carte?
**menu-driven** [ˈmɛnjuːdrɪvn] adj (Comput)
  piloté(e) par menu
**MEP** n abbr = **Member of the European
  Parliament**
**mercantile** [ˈmaːkəntaɪl] adj marchand(e);
  (law) commercial(e)
**mercenary** [ˈmaːsɪnərɪ] adj (person) intéressé(e),
  mercenaire ▷ n mercenaire m
**merchandise** [ˈmaːtʃəndaɪz] n marchandises fpl
  ▷ vt commercialiser
**merchandiser** [ˈmaːtʃəndaɪzəʳ] n
  marchandiseur m
**merchant** [ˈmaːtʃənt] n négociant m, marchand
  m; **timber/wine ~** négociant en bois/vins,
  marchand de bois/vins
**merchant bank** n (Brit) banque f d'affaires
**merchantman** [ˈmaːtʃəntmən] (irreg) n navire
  marchand
**merchant navy**, (US) **merchant marine** n
  marine marchande
**merciful** [ˈmaːsɪful] adj miséricordieux(-euse),
  clément(e)
**mercifully** [ˈmaːsɪflɪ] adv avec clémence;
  (fortunately) par bonheur, Dieu merci
**merciless** [ˈmaːsɪlɪs] adj impitoyable, sans pitié
**mercurial** [maːˈkjuərɪəl] adj changeant(e);
  (lively) vif (vive)
**mercury** [ˈmaːkjurɪ] n mercure m
**mercy** [ˈmaːsɪ] n pitié f, merci f; (Rel)
  miséricorde f; **to have ~ on sb** avoir pitié de qn;
  **at the ~ of** à la merci de
**mercy killing** n euthanasie f
**mere** [mɪəʳ] adj simple; (chance) pur(e); **a ~ two
  hours** seulement deux heures
**merely** [ˈmɪəlɪ] adv simplement, purement
**merge** [maːdʒ] vt unir; (Comput) fusionner,
  interclasser ▷ vi (colours, shapes, sounds) se mêler;
  (roads) se joindre; (Comm) fusionner
**merger** [ˈmaːdʒəʳ] n (Comm) fusion f
**meridian** [məˈrɪdɪən] n méridien m
**meringue** [məˈræŋ] n meringue f
**merit** [ˈmɛrɪt] n mérite m, valeur f ▷ vt mériter
**meritocracy** [mɛrɪˈtɔkrəsɪ] n méritocratie f
**mermaid** [ˈmaːmeɪd] n sirène f
**merriment** [ˈmɛrɪmənt] n gaieté f
**merry** [ˈmɛrɪ] adj gai(e); **M~ Christmas!** joyeux
  Noël!
**merry-go-round** [ˈmɛrɪɡəuraund] n manège m
**mesh** [mɛʃ] n mailles fpl ▷ vi (gears) s'engrener;
  **wire ~** grillage m (métallique), treillis m
  (métallique)
**mesmerize** [ˈmɛzməraɪz] vt hypnotiser;
  fasciner
**mess** [mɛs] n désordre m, fouillis m, pagaille f;
  (muddle: of life) gâchis m; (: of economy) pagaille f;
  (dirt) saleté f; (Mil) mess m, cantine f; **to be (in)**

**a** ~ être en désordre; **to be/get o.s. in a** ~ (fig) être/se mettre dans le pétrin
▶ **mess about** or **around** (inf) vi perdre son temps
▶ **mess about** or **around with** vt fus (inf) chambarder, tripoter
▶ **mess up** vt (dirty) salir; (spoil) gâcher
▶ **mess with** (inf) vt fus (challenge, confront) se frotter à; (interfere with) toucher à
**message** ['mɛsɪdʒ] n message m; **can I leave a** ~? est-ce que je peux laisser un message?; **are there any ~s for me?** est-ce que j'ai des messages?; **to get the** ~ (fig: inf) saisir, piger
**message switching** [-swɪtʃɪŋ] n (Comput) commutation f de messages
**messenger** ['mɛsɪndʒəʳ] n messager m
**Messiah** [mɪ'saɪə] n Messie m
**Messrs, Messrs.** ['mɛsəz] abbr (on letters: = messieurs) MM
**messy** ['mɛsɪ] adj (dirty) sale; (untidy) en désordre
**Met** [mɛt] n abbr (US) = **Metropolitan Opera**
**met** [mɛt] pt, pp of **meet** ▷ adj abbr (= meteorological) météo inv
**metabolism** [mɛ'tæbəlɪzəm] n métabolisme m
**metal** ['mɛtl] n métal m ▷ cpd en métal ▷ vt empierrer
**metallic** [mɛ'tælɪk] adj métallique
**metallurgy** [mɛ'tælədʒɪ] n métallurgie f
**metalwork** ['mɛtlwəːk] n (craft) ferronnerie f
**metamorphosis** (pl **-ses**) [mɛtə'mɔːfəsɪs, -siːz] n métamorphose f
**metaphor** ['mɛtəfəʳ] n métaphore f
**metaphysics** [mɛtə'fɪzɪks] n métaphysique f
**mete** [miːt]: **to** ~ **out** vt fus infliger
**meteor** ['miːtɪəʳ] n météore m
**meteoric** [miːtɪ'ɔrɪk] adj (fig) fulgurant(e)
**meteorite** ['miːtɪəraɪt] n météorite m or f
**meteorological** [miːtɪərə'lɔdʒɪkl] adj météorologique
**meteorology** [miːtɪə'rɔlədʒɪ] n météorologie f
**meter** ['miːtəʳ] n (instrument) compteur m; (also: **parking meter**) parc(o)mètre m; (US: unit) = **metre** ▷ vt (US Post) affranchir à la machine
**methane** ['miːθeɪn] n méthane m
**method** ['mɛθəd] n méthode f; ~ **of payment** mode m or modalité f de paiement
**methodical** [mɪ'θɔdɪkl] adj méthodique
**Methodist** ['mɛθədɪst] adj, n méthodiste (m/f)
**methylated spirit** ['mɛθɪleɪtɪd-] n (Brit: also: **meths**) alcool m à brûler
**meticulous** [mɛ'tɪkjuləs] adj méticuleux(-euse)
**Met Office** ['mɛt'ɔfɪs] n (Brit): **the** ~ ≈ la Météorologie nationale
**metre**, (US) **meter** ['miːtəʳ] n mètre m
**metric** ['mɛtrɪk] adj métrique; **to go** ~ adopter le système métrique
**metrical** ['mɛtrɪkl] adj métrique
**metrication** [mɛtrɪ'keɪʃən] n conversion f au système métrique
**metric system** n système m métrique
**metric ton** n tonne f
**metro** ['mɛtrəu] n métro m

**metronome** ['mɛtrənəum] n métronome m
**metropolis** [mɪ'trɔpəlɪs] n métropole f
**metropolitan** [mɛtrə'pɔlɪtən] adj métropolitain(e); **the M~ Police** (Brit) la police londonienne
**mettle** ['mɛtl] n courage m
**mew** [mjuː] vi (cat) miauler
**mews** [mjuːz] n (Brit): ~ **cottage** maisonnette aménagée dans une ancienne écurie ou remise
**Mexican** ['mɛksɪkən] adj mexicain(e) ▷ n Mexicain(e)
**Mexico** ['mɛksɪkəu] n Mexique m
**Mexico City** n Mexico
**mezzanine** ['mɛtsəniːn] n mezzanine f; (of shops, offices) entresol m
**MFA** n abbr (US: = Master of Fine Arts) titre universitaire
**mfr** abbr = **manufacture**; **manufacturer**
**mg** abbr (= milligram) mg
**Mgr** abbr (= Monseigneur, Monsignor) Mgr; (= manager) dir
**MHR** n abbr (US) = **Member of the House of Representatives**
**MHz** abbr (= megahertz) MHz
**MI** abbr (US) = **Michigan**
**MI5** n abbr (Brit: = Military Intelligence 5) ≈ DST f
**MI6** n abbr (Brit: = Military Intelligence 6) ≈ DGSE f
**MIA** abbr (= missing in action) disparu au combat
**miaow** [miː'au] vi miauler
**mice** [maɪs] npl of **mouse**
**Mich.** abbr (US) = **Michigan**
**micro** ['maɪkrəu] n (also: **microcomputer**) micro(-ordinateur m) m
**micro...** [maɪkrəu] prefix
**microbe** ['maɪkrəub] n microbe m
**microbiology** [maɪkrəbaɪ'ɔlədʒɪ] n microbiologie f
**microchip** ['maɪkrəutʃɪp] n (Elec) puce f
**microcomputer** ['maɪkrəukəm'pjuːtəʳ] n micro-ordinateur m
**microcosm** ['maɪkrəukɔzəm] n microcosme m
**microeconomics** ['maɪkrəuiːkə'nɔmɪks] n micro-économie f
**microfiche** ['maɪkrəufiːʃ] n microfiche f
**microfilm** ['maɪkrəufɪlm] n microfilm m ▷ vt microfilmer
**microlight** ['maɪkrəulaɪt] n ULM m
**micrometer** [maɪ'krɔmɪtəʳ] n palmer m, micromètre m
**microphone** ['maɪkrəfəun] n microphone m
**microprocessor** ['maɪkrəu'prəusɛsəʳ] n microprocesseur m
**microscope** ['maɪkrəskəup] n microscope m; **under the** ~ au microscope
**microscopic** [maɪkrə'skɔpɪk] adj microscopique ▷ n
**mid** [mɪd] adj: ~ **May** la mi-mai; ~ **afternoon** le milieu de l'après-midi; **in** ~ **air** en plein ciel; **he's in his** ~ **thirties** il a dans les trente-cinq ans
**midday** [mɪd'deɪ] n midi m
**middle** ['mɪdl] n milieu m; (waist) ceinture f,

taille f ▷ adj du milieu; (average) moyen(ne); **in the ~ of the night** au milieu de la nuit; **I'm in the ~ of reading it** je suis (justement) en train de le lire

**middle age** n tranche d'âge aux limites floues, entre la quarantaine et le début du troisième âge

**middle-aged** ['mɪdl'eɪdʒd] adj d'un certain âge, ni vieux ni jeune; (pej: values, outlook) conventionnel(le), rassis(e)

**Middle Ages** npl: **the ~** le moyen âge

**middle-class** [mɪdl'klɑːs] adj bourgeois(e)

**middle class** n, **middle classes** npl: **the ~(es)** ≈ les classes moyennes

**Middle East** n: **the ~** le Proche-Orient, le Moyen-Orient

**middleman** ['mɪdlmæn] (irreg) n intermédiaire m

**middle management** n cadres moyens

**middle name** n second prénom

**middle-of-the-road** ['mɪdləvðə'rəud] adj (policy) modéré(e), du juste milieu; (music etc) plutôt classique, assez traditionnel(le)

**middle school** n (US) école pour les enfants de 12 à 14 ans, ≈ collège m; (Brit) école pour les enfants de 8 à 14 ans

**middleweight** ['mɪdlweɪt] n (Boxing) poids moyen

**middling** ['mɪdlɪŋ] adj moyen(ne)

**midge** [mɪdʒ] n moucheron m

**midget** ['mɪdʒɪt] n nain(e) ▷ adj minuscule

**midi system** ['mɪdɪ-] n chaîne f midi

**Midlands** ['mɪdləndz] npl comtés du centre de l'Angleterre

**midnight** ['mɪdnaɪt] n minuit m; **at ~** à minuit

**midriff** ['mɪdrɪf] n estomac m, taille f

**midst** [mɪdst] n: **in the ~ of** au milieu de

**midsummer** [mɪd'sʌmər] n milieu m de l'été

**midway** [mɪd'weɪ] adj, adv: **~ (between)** à mi-chemin (entre); **~ through** ... au milieu de ..., en plein(e) ...

**midweek** [mɪd'wiːk] adj du milieu de la semaine ▷ adv au milieu de la semaine, en pleine semaine

**midwife** (pl **midwives**) ['mɪdwaɪf, -vz] n sage-femme f

**midwifery** ['mɪdwɪfərɪ] n obstétrique f

**midwinter** [mɪd'wɪntər] n milieu m de l'hiver

**miffed** [mɪft] adj (inf) fâché(e), vexé(e)

**might** [maɪt] vb see **may** ▷ n puissance f, force f

**mighty** ['maɪtɪ] adj puissant(e) ▷ adv (inf) rudement

**migraine** ['miːgreɪn] n migraine f

**migrant** ['maɪgrənt] n (bird, animal) migrateur m; (person) migrant(e); nomade m/f ▷ adj migrateur(-trice); migrant(e); nomade; (worker) saisonnier(-ière)

**migrate** [maɪ'greɪt] vi migrer

**migration** [maɪ'greɪʃən] n migration f

**mike** [maɪk] n abbr (= microphone) micro m

**Milan** [mɪ'læn] n Milan

**mild** [maɪld] adj doux (douce); (reproach, infection) léger(-ère); (illness) bénin(-igne); (interest)

modéré(e); (taste) peu relevé(e) ▷ n bière légère

**mildew** ['mɪldjuː] n mildiou m

**mildly** ['maɪldlɪ] adv doucement; légèrement; **to put it ~** (inf) c'est le moins qu'on puisse dire

**mildness** ['maɪldnɪs] n douceur f

**mile** [maɪl] n mil(l)e m (= 1609 m); **to do 30 ~s per gallon** ≈ faire 9, 4 litres aux cent

**mileage** ['maɪlɪdʒ] n distance f en milles, ≈ kilométrage m

**mileage allowance** n ≈ indemnité f kilométrique

**mileometer** [maɪ'lɔmɪtər] n compteur m kilométrique

**milestone** ['maɪlstəun] n borne f; (fig) jalon m

**milieu** ['miːljɔː] n milieu m

**militant** ['mɪlɪtnt] adj, n militant(e)

**militarism** ['mɪlɪtərɪzəm] n militarisme m

**militaristic** [mɪlɪtə'rɪstɪk] adj militariste

**military** ['mɪlɪtərɪ] adj militaire ▷ n: **the ~** l'armée f, les militaires mpl

**military service** n service m (militaire ou national)

**militate** ['mɪlɪteɪt] vi: **to ~ against** militer contre

**militia** [mɪ'lɪʃə] n milice f

**milk** [mɪlk] n lait m ▷ vt (cow) traire; (fig: person) dépouiller, plumer; (: situation) exploiter à fond

**milk chocolate** n chocolat m au lait

**milk float** n (Brit) voiture f or camionnette f du or de laitier

**milking** ['mɪlkɪŋ] n traite f

**milkman** ['mɪlkmən] (irreg) n laitier m

**milk shake** n milk-shake m

**milk tooth** n dent f de lait

**milk truck** n (US) = **milk float**

**milky** ['mɪlkɪ] adj (drink) au lait; (colour) laiteux(-euse)

**Milky Way** n Voie lactée

**mill** [mɪl] n moulin m; (factory) usine f, fabrique f; (spinning mill) filature f; (flour mill) minoterie f; (steel mill) aciérie f ▷ vt moudre, broyer ▷ vi (also: **mill about**) grouiller

**millennium** (pl **-s** or **millennia**) [mɪ'lɛnɪəm, -'lɛnɪə] n millénaire m

**millennium bug** [mɪ'lɛnɪəm-] n bogue m or bug m de l'an 2000

**miller** ['mɪlər] n meunier m

**millet** ['mɪlɪt] n millet m

**milli...** ['mɪlɪ] prefix milli...

**milligram, milligramme** ['mɪlɪgræm] n milligramme m

**millilitre, (US) milliliter** ['mɪlɪliːtər] n millilitre m

**millimetre, (US) millimeter** ['mɪlɪmiːtər] n millimètre m

**milliner** ['mɪlɪnər] n modiste f

**millinery** ['mɪlɪnərɪ] n modes fpl

**million** ['mɪljən] n million m; **a ~ pounds** un million de livres sterling

**millionaire** [mɪljə'nɛər] n millionnaire m

**millionth** [-θ] num millionième

**millipede** ['mɪlɪpiːd] n mille-pattes m inv

**millstone** ['mɪlstəun] n meule f
**millwheel** ['mɪlwi:l] n roue f de moulin
**milometer** [maɪ'lɒmɪtəʳ] n = **mileometer**
**mime** [maɪm] n mime m ▷ vt, vi mimer
**mimic** ['mɪmɪk] n imitateur(-trice) ▷ vt, vi imiter, contrefaire
**mimicry** ['mɪmɪkrɪ] n imitation f; (Zool) mimétisme m
**Min.** abbr (Brit Pol) = **ministry**
**min.** abbr (= minute(s)) mn.; (= minimum) min.
**minaret** [mɪnə'ret] n minaret m
**mince** [mɪns] vt hacher ▷ vi (in walking) marcher à petits pas maniérés ▷ n (Brit Culin) viande hachée, hachis m; **he does not ~ (his) words** il ne mâche pas ses mots
**mincemeat** ['mɪnsmi:t] n hachis de fruits secs utilisés en pâtisserie; (US) viande hachée, hachis m
**mince pie** n sorte de tarte aux fruits secs
**mincer** ['mɪnsəʳ] n hachoir m
**mincing** ['mɪnsɪŋ] adj affecté(e)
**mind** [maɪnd] n esprit m ▷ vt (attend to, look after) s'occuper de; (be careful) faire attention à; (object to): **I don't ~ the noise** je ne crains pas le bruit, le bruit ne me dérange pas; **it is on my ~** cela me préoccupe; **to change one's ~** changer d'avis; **to be in two ~s about sth** (Brit) être indécis(e) or irrésolu(e) en ce qui concerne qch; **to my ~** à mon avis, selon moi; **to be out of one's ~** ne plus avoir toute sa raison; **to keep sth in ~** ne pas oublier qch; **to bear sth in ~** tenir compte de qch; **to have sb/sth in ~** avoir qn/qch en tête; **to have in ~ to do** avoir l'intention de faire; **it went right out of my ~** ça m'est complètement sorti de la tête; **to bring** or **call sth to ~** se rappeler qch; **to make up one's ~** se décider; **do you ~ if ...?** est-ce que cela vous gêne si ...?; **I don't ~** cela ne me dérange pas; (don't care) ça m'est égal; **~ you, ...** remarquez, ...; **never ~** peu importe, ça ne fait rien; (don't worry) ne vous en faîtes pas; **"~ the step"** "attention à la marche"
**mind-boggling** ['maɪndbɒglɪŋ] adj (inf) époustouflant(e), ahurissant(e)
**-minded** ['maɪndɪd] adj: **fair~** impartial(e); **an industrially~ nation** une nation orientée vers l'industrie
**minder** ['maɪndəʳ] n (child minder) gardienne f; (bodyguard) ange gardien (fig)
**mindful** ['maɪndful] adj: **~ of** attentif(-ive) à, soucieux(-euse) de
**mindless** ['maɪndlɪs] adj irréfléchi(e); (violence, crime) insensé(e); (boring: job) idiot(e)
**mine¹** [maɪn] pron le (la) mien(ne), les miens (miennes); **a friend of ~** un de mes amis, un ami à moi; **this book is ~** ce livre est à moi
**mine²** [maɪn] n mine f ▷ vt (coal) extraire; (ship, beach) miner
**mine detector** n détecteur m de mines
**minefield** ['maɪnfi:ld] n champ m de mines
**miner** ['maɪnəʳ] n mineur m
**mineral** ['mɪnərəl] adj minéral(e) ▷ n minéral m; **minerals** npl (Brit: soft drinks) boissons gazeuses (sucrées)
**mineralogy** [mɪnə'rælədʒɪ] n minéralogie f
**mineral water** n eau minérale
**minesweeper** ['maɪnswi:pəʳ] n dragueur m de mines
**mingle** ['mɪŋgl] vt mêler, mélanger ▷ vi: **to ~ with** se mêler à
**mingy** ['mɪndʒɪ] adj (inf) radin(e)
**miniature** ['mɪnətʃəʳ] adj (en) miniature ▷ n miniature f
**minibar** ['mɪnɪbɑ:ʳ] n minibar m
**minibus** ['mɪnɪbʌs] n minibus m
**minicab** ['mɪnɪkæb] n (Brit) taxi m indépendant
**minicomputer** ['mɪnɪkəm'pju:təʳ] n mini-ordinateur m
**minim** ['mɪnɪm] n (Mus) blanche f
**minima** ['mɪnɪmə] npl of **minimum**
**minimal** ['mɪnɪml] adj minimal(e)
**minimalist** ['mɪnɪməlɪst] adj, n minimaliste (m/f)
**minimize** ['mɪnɪmaɪz] vt (reduce) réduire au minimum; (play down) minimiser
**minimum** ['mɪnɪməm] n (pl **minima**) [-mə] minimum m ▷ adj minimum; **to reduce to a ~** réduire au minimum
**minimum lending rate** n (Econ) taux m de crédit minimum
**mining** ['maɪnɪŋ] n exploitation minière ▷ adj minier(-ière); de mineurs
**minion** ['mɪnjən] n (pej) laquais m; favori(te)
**mini-series** ['mɪnɪsɪəri:z] n téléfilm m en plusieurs parties
**miniskirt** ['mɪnɪskə:t] n mini-jupe f
**minister** ['mɪnɪstəʳ] n (Brit Pol) ministre m; (Rel) pasteur m ▷ vi: **to ~ to sb** donner ses soins à qn; **to ~ to sb's needs** pourvoir aux besoins de qn
**ministerial** [mɪnɪs'tɪərɪəl] adj (Brit Pol) ministériel(le)
**ministry** ['mɪnɪstrɪ] n (Brit Pol) ministère m; (Rel): **to go into the ~** devenir pasteur
**mink** [mɪŋk] n vison m
**mink coat** n manteau m de vison
**Minn.** abbr (US) = **Minnesota**
**minnow** ['mɪnəu] n vairon m
**minor** ['maɪnəʳ] adj petit(e), de peu d'importance; (Mus, poet, problem) mineur(e) ▷ n (Law) mineur(e)
**Minorca** [mɪ'nɔ:kə] n Minorque f
**minority** [maɪ'nɒrɪtɪ] n minorité f; **to be in a ~** être en minorité
**minster** ['mɪnstəʳ] n église abbatiale
**minstrel** ['mɪnstrəl] n trouvère m, ménestrel m
**mint** [mɪnt] n (plant) menthe f; (sweet) bonbon m à la menthe ▷ vt (coins) battre; **the (Royal) M~**, **the (US) M~** ≈ l'hôtel m de la Monnaie; **in ~ condition** à l'état de neuf
**mint sauce** n sauce f à la menthe
**minuet** [mɪnju'et] n menuet m
**minus** ['maɪnəs] n (also: **minus sign**) signe m moins ▷ prep moins; **12 ~ 6 equals 6** 12 moins 6 égal 6; **~ 24°C** moins 24°C
**minuscule** ['mɪnəskju:l] adj minuscule

**minute**[1] n ['mɪnɪt] minute f; (official record)
procès-verbal m, compte rendu; **minutes** npl (of
meeting) procès-verbal m, compte rendu; **it is 5
~s past 3** il est 3 heures 5; **wait a ~!** (attendez)
un instant!; **at the last ~** à la dernière minute;
**up to the ~** (fashion) dernier cri; (news) de
dernière minute; (machine, technology) de pointe

**minute**[2] adj [maɪ'njuːt] minuscule; (detailed)
minutieux(-euse)

**minute book** n registre m des procès-verbaux

**minute hand** n aiguille f des minutes

**minutely** [maɪ'njuːtlɪ] adv (by a small amount) de
peu, de manière infime; (in detail)
minutieusement, dans les moindres détails

**minutiae** [mɪ'njuːʃiː] npl menus détails

**miracle** ['mɪrəkl] n miracle m

**miraculous** [mɪ'rækjuləs] adj
miraculeux(-euse)

**mirage** ['mɪrɑːʒ] n mirage m

**mire** ['maɪər] n bourbe f, boue f

**mirror** ['mɪrər] n miroir m, glace f; (in car)
rétroviseur m ▷ vt refléter

**mirror image** n image inversée

**mirth** [mɜːθ] n gaieté f

**misadventure** [mɪsəd'vɛntʃər] n mésaventure f;
**death by ~** (Brit) décès accidentel

**misanthropist** [mɪ'zænθrəpɪst] n
misanthrope m/f

**misapply** [mɪsə'plaɪ] vt mal employer

**misapprehension** ['mɪsæprɪ'hɛnʃən] n
malentendu m, méprise f

**misappropriate** [mɪsə'prəuprɪeɪt] vt détourner

**misappropriation** ['mɪsəprəuprɪ'eɪʃən] n
escroquerie f, détournement m

**misbehave** [mɪsbɪ'heɪv] vi mal se conduire

**misbehaviour**, (US) **misbehavior**
[mɪsbɪ'heɪvjər] n mauvaise conduite

**misc.** abbr = **miscellaneous**

**miscalculate** [mɪs'kælkjuleɪt] vt mal calculer

**miscalculation** ['mɪskælkju'leɪʃən] n erreur f de
calcul

**miscarriage** ['mɪskærɪdʒ] n (Med) fausse
couche; **~ of justice** erreur f judiciaire

**miscarry** [mɪs'kærɪ] vi (Med) faire une fausse
couche; (fail: plans) échouer, mal tourner

**miscellaneous** [mɪsɪ'leɪnɪəs] adj (items, expenses)
divers(es); (selection) varié(e)

**miscellany** [mɪ'sɛlənɪ] n recueil m

**mischance** [mɪs'tʃɑːns] n malchance f; **by
(some) ~** par malheur

**mischief** ['mɪstʃɪf] n (naughtiness) sottises fpl;
(fun) farce f; (playfulness) espièglerie f; (harm) mal
m, dommage m; (maliciousness) méchanceté f

**mischievous** ['mɪstʃɪvəs] adj (playful, naughty)
coquin(e), espiègle; (harmful) méchant(e)

**misconception** ['mɪskən'sɛpʃən] n idée fausse

**misconduct** [mɪs'kɔndʌkt] n inconduite f;
**professional ~** faute professionnelle

**misconstrue** [mɪskən'struː] vt mal interpréter

**miscount** [mɪs'kaunt] vt, vi mal compter

**misdeed** ['mɪs'diːd] n méfait m

**misdemeanour**, (US) **misdemeanor** [mɪsdɪ'miː-
nər] n écart m de conduite; infraction f

**misdirect** [mɪsdɪ'rɛkt] vt (person) mal
renseigner; (letter) mal adresser

**miser** ['maɪzər] n avare m/f

**miserable** ['mɪzərəbl] adj (person, expression)
malheureux(-euse); (conditions) misérable;
(weather) maussade; (offer, donation) minable;
(failure) pitoyable; **to feel ~** avoir le cafard

**miserably** ['mɪzərəblɪ] adv (smile, answer)
tristement; (live, pay) misérablement; (fail)
lamentablement

**miserly** ['maɪzəlɪ] adj avare

**misery** ['mɪzərɪ] n (unhappiness) tristesse f; (pain)
souffrances fpl; (wretchedness) misère f

**misfire** [mɪs'faɪər] vi rater; (car engine) avoir des
ratés

**misfit** ['mɪsfɪt] n (person) inadapté(e)

**misfortune** [mɪs'fɔːtʃən] n malchance f,
malheur m

**misgiving** [mɪs'gɪvɪŋ] n (apprehension) craintes
fpl; **to have ~s about sth** avoir des doutes
quant à qch

**misguided** [mɪs'gaɪdɪd] adj malavisé(e)

**mishandle** [mɪs'hændl] vt (treat roughly)
malmener; (mismanage) mal s'y prendre pour
faire or résoudre etc

**mishap** ['mɪshæp] n mésaventure f

**mishear** [mɪs'hɪər] vt, vi (irreg: like **hear**) mal
entendre

**mishmash** ['mɪʃmæʃ] n (inf) fatras m, méli-
mélo m

**misinform** [mɪsɪn'fɔːm] vt mal renseigner

**misinterpret** [mɪsɪn'təːprɪt] vt mal interpréter

**misinterpretation** ['mɪsɪntəːprɪ'teɪʃən] n
interprétation erronée, contresens m

**misjudge** [mɪs'dʒʌdʒ] vt méjuger, se méprendre
sur le compte de

**mislay** [mɪs'leɪ] vt (irreg: like **lay**) égarer

**mislead** [mɪs'liːd] vt (irreg: like **lead**) induire en
erreur

**misleading** [mɪs'liːdɪŋ] adj trompeur(-euse)

**misled** [mɪs'lɛd] pt, pp of **mislead**

**mismanage** [mɪs'mænɪdʒ] vt mal gérer; mal s'y
prendre pour faire or résoudre etc

**mismanagement** [mɪs'mænɪdʒmənt] n
mauvaise gestion

**misnomer** [mɪs'nəumər] n terme or qualificatif
trompeur or peu approprié

**misogynist** [mɪ'sɔdʒɪnɪst] n misogyne m/f

**misplace** [mɪs'pleɪs] vt égarer; **to be ~d** (trust
etc) être mal placé(e)

**misprint** ['mɪsprɪnt] n faute f d'impression

**mispronounce** [mɪsprə'nauns] vt mal
prononcer

**misquote** ['mɪs'kwəut] vt citer erronément or
inexactement

**misread** [mɪs'riːd] vt (irreg: like **read**) mal lire

**misrepresent** [mɪsrɛprɪ'zɛnt] vt présenter sous
un faux jour

**Miss** [mɪs] n Mademoiselle; **Dear ~ Smith**
Chère Mademoiselle Smith

**miss** [mɪs] vt (fail to get, attend, see) manquer,

m

rater; (*appointment, class*) manquer; (*escape, avoid*) échapper à, éviter; (*notice loss of: money etc*) s'apercevoir de l'absence de; (*regret the absence of*): **I ~ him/it** il/cela me manque ▷ *vi* manquer ▷ *n* (*shot*) coup manqué; **we ~ed our train** nous avons raté notre train; **the bus just ~ed the wall** le bus a évité le mur de justesse; **you're ~ing the point** vous êtes à côté de la question; **you can't ~ it** vous ne pouvez pas vous tromper
▶ **miss out** *vt* (*Brit*) oublier
▶ **miss out on** *vt fus* (*fun, party*) rater, manquer; (*chance, bargain*) laisser passer

**Miss.** *abbr* (*US*) = **Mississippi**

**missal** ['mɪsl] *n* missel *m*

**misshapen** [mɪs'ʃeɪpən] *adj* difforme

**missile** ['mɪsaɪl] *n* (*Aviat*) missile *m*; (*object thrown*) projectile *m*

**missile base** *n* base *f* de missiles

**missile launcher** [-lɔːntʃəʳ] *n* lance-missiles *m*

**missing** ['mɪsɪŋ] *adj* manquant(e); (*after escape, disaster: person*) disparu(e); **to go ~** disparaître; **~ person** personne disparue, disparu(e); **~ in action** (*Mil*) porté(e) disparu(e)

**mission** ['mɪʃən] *n* mission *f*; **on a ~ to sb** en mission auprès de qn

**missionary** ['mɪʃənrɪ] *n* missionnaire *m/f*

**mission statement** *n* déclaration *f* d'intention

**missive** ['mɪsɪv] *n* missive *f*

**misspell** ['mɪs'spɛl] *vt* (*irreg: like* **spell**) mal orthographier

**misspent** ['mɪs'spɛnt] *adj*: **his ~ youth** sa folle jeunesse

**mist** [mɪst] *n* brume *f* ▷ *vi* (*also:* **mist over, mist up**) devenir brumeux(-euse); (*Brit: windows*) s'embuer

**mistake** [mɪs'teɪk] *n* erreur *f*, faute *f* ▷ *vt* (*irreg: like* **take**); (*meaning*) mal comprendre; (*intentions*) se méprendre sur; **to ~ for** prendre pour; **by ~** par erreur, par inadvertance; **to make a ~** (*in writing*) faire une faute; (*in calculating etc*) faire une erreur; **there must be some ~** il doit y avoir une erreur, se tromper; **to make a ~ about sb/sth** se tromper sur le compte de qn/sur qch

**mistaken** [mɪs'teɪkən] *pp of* **mistake** ▷ *adj* (*idea etc*) erroné(e); **to be ~** faire erreur, se tromper

**mistaken identity** *n* erreur *f* d'identité

**mistakenly** [mɪs'teɪkənlɪ] *adv* par erreur, par mégarde

**mister** ['mɪstəʳ] *n* (*inf*) Monsieur *m*; *see* **Mr**

**mistletoe** ['mɪsltəu] *n* gui *m*

**mistook** [mɪs'tuk] *pt of* **mistake**

**mistranslation** [mɪstræns'leɪʃən] *n* erreur *f* de traduction, contresens *m*

**mistreat** [mɪs'triːt] *vt* maltraiter

**mistress** ['mɪstrɪs] *n* maîtresse *f*; (*Brit: in primary school*) institutrice *f*; (: *in secondary school*) professeur *m*

**mistrust** [mɪs'trʌst] *vt* se méfier de ▷ *n*: **~ (of)** méfiance *f* (à l'égard de)

**mistrustful** [mɪs'trʌstful] *adj*: **~ (of)** méfiant(e) (à l'égard de)

**misty** ['mɪstɪ] *adj* brumeux(-euse); (*glasses, window*) embué(e)

**misty-eyed** ['mɪstɪ'aɪd] *adj* les yeux embués de larmes; (*fig*) sentimental(e)

**misunderstand** [mɪsʌndə'stænd] *vt, vi* (*irreg: like* **stand**) mal comprendre

**misunderstanding** ['mɪsʌndə'stændɪŋ] *n* méprise *f*, malentendu *m*; **there's been a ~** il y a eu un malentendu

**misunderstood** [mɪsʌndə'stud] *pt, pp of* **misunderstand** ▷ *adj* (*person*) incompris(e)

**misuse** *n* [mɪs'juːs] mauvais emploi; (*of power*) abus *m* ▷ *vt* [mɪs'juːz] mal employer; abuser de

**MIT** *n abbr* (*US*) = **Massachusetts Institute of Technology**

**mite** [maɪt] *n* (*small quantity*) grain *m*, miette *f*; (*Brit: small child*) petit(e)

**mitigate** ['mɪtɪgeɪt] *vt* atténuer; **mitigating circumstances** circonstances atténuantes

**mitigation** [mɪtɪ'geɪʃən] *n* atténuation *f*

**mitre**, (*US*) **miter** ['maɪtəʳ] *n* mitre *f*; (*Carpentry*) onglet *m*

**mitt** ['mɪt], **mitten** ['mɪtn] *n* moufle *f*; (*fingerless*) mitaine *f*

**mix** [mɪks] *vt* mélanger; (*sauce, drink etc*) préparer ▷ *vi* se mélanger; (*socialize*): **he doesn't ~ well** il est peu sociable ▷ *n* mélange *m*; **to ~ sth with sth** mélanger qch à qch; **to ~ business with pleasure** unir l'utile à l'agréable; **cake ~** préparation *f* pour gâteau
▶ **mix in** *vt* incorporer, mélanger
▶ **mix up** *vt* mélanger; (*confuse*) confondre; **to be ~ed up in sth** être mêlé(e) à qch *or* impliqué(e) dans qch

**mixed** [mɪkst] *adj* (*feelings, reactions*) contradictoire; (*school, marriage*) mixte

**mixed-ability** ['mɪkstə'bɪlɪtɪ] *adj* (*class etc*) sans groupes de niveaux

**mixed bag** *n*: **it's a (bit of a) ~** il y a (un peu) de tout

**mixed blessing** *n*: **it's a ~** cela a du bon et du mauvais

**mixed doubles** *npl* (*Sport*) double *m* mixte

**mixed economy** *n* économie *f* mixte

**mixed grill** *n* (*Brit*) assortiment *m* de grillades

**mixed marriage** *n* mariage *m* mixte

**mixed salad** *n* salade *f* de crudités

**mixed-up** [mɪkst'ʌp] *adj* (*person*) désorienté(e), embrouillé(e)

**mixer** ['mɪksəʳ] *n* (*for food*) batteur *m*, mixeur *m*; (*drink*) boisson gazeuse (*servant à couper un alcool*); (*person*): **he is a good ~** il est très sociable

**mixer tap** *n* (robinet *m*) mélangeur *m*

**mixture** ['mɪkstʃəʳ] *n* assortiment *m*, mélange *m*; (*Med*) préparation *f*

**mix-up** ['mɪksʌp] *n*: **there was a ~** il y a eu confusion

**MK** *abbr* (*Brit Tech*) = **mark**

**mk** *abbr* = **mark**

**mkt** *abbr* = **market**

**ml** *abbr* (= *millilitre(s)*) ml

**MLitt** *n abbr* (= *Master of Literature, Master of Letters*) *titre universitaire*

**MLR** *n abbr* (*Brit*) = **minimum lending rate**

**mm** *abbr* (= *millimetre*) mm

**MN** *abbr* (*Brit*) = **Merchant Navy**; (*US*)
= **Minnesota**

**MO** *n abbr* (*Med*) = **medical officer**; (*US inf*:
= *modus operandi*) méthode *f* ▷ *abbr* (*US*)
= **Missouri**

**m.o.** *abbr* = **money order**

**moan** [məʊn] *n* gémissement *m* ▷ *vi* gémir; (*inf*:
*complain*): **to ~ (about)** se plaindre (de)

**moaner** ['məʊnəʳ] *n* (*inf*) rouspéteur(-euse),
râleur(-euse)

**moaning** ['məʊnɪŋ] *n* gémissements *mpl*

**moat** [məʊt] *n* fossé *m*, douves *fpl*

**mob** [mɔb] *n* foule *f*; (*disorderly*) cohue *f*; (*pej*):
**the ~** la populace ▷ *vt* assaillir

**mobile** ['məʊbaɪl] *adj* mobile ▷ *n* (*Art*) mobile *m*;
(*Brit inf*: *mobile phone*) (téléphone *m*) portable *m*,
mobile *m*; **applicants must be ~** (*Brit*) les
candidats devront être prêts à accepter tout
déplacement

**mobile home** *n* caravane *f*

**mobile phone** *n* (téléphone *m*) portable *m*,
mobile *m*

**mobile shop** *n* (*Brit*) camion *m* magasin

**mobility** [məʊ'bɪlɪtɪ] *n* mobilité *f*

**mobilize** ['məʊbɪlaɪz] *vt*, *vi* mobiliser

**moccasin** ['mɔkəsɪn] *n* mocassin *m*

**mock** [mɔk] *vt* ridiculiser; (*laugh at*) se moquer
de ▷ *adj* faux (fausse); **mocks** *npl* (*Brit*: *Scol*)
examens blancs

**mockery** ['mɔkərɪ] *n* moquerie *f*, raillerie *f*; **to
make a ~ of** ridiculiser, tourner en dérision

**mocking** ['mɔkɪŋ] *adj* moqueur(-euse)

**mockingbird** ['mɔkɪŋbəːd] *n* moqueur *m*

**mock-up** ['mɔkʌp] *n* maquette *f*

**MOD** *n abbr* (*Brit*) = **Ministry of Defence**; *see*
**defence**

**mod** [mɔd] *adj see* **convenience**

**mod cons** ['mɔd'kɔnz] *npl abbr* (*Brit*) = **modern
conveniences**; *see* **convenience**

**mode** [məʊd] *n* mode *m*; (*of transport*) moyen *m*

**model** ['mɔdl] *n* modèle *m*; (*person: for fashion*)
mannequin *m*; (: *for artist*) modèle ▷ *vt* (*with clay
etc*) modeler ▷ *vi* travailler comme mannequin
▷ *adj* (*railway: toy*) modèle réduit *inv*; (*child,
factory*) modèle; **to ~ clothes** présenter des
vêtements; **to ~ o.s. on** imiter; **to ~ sb/sth on**
modeler qn/qch sur

**modem** ['məʊdɛm] *n* modem *m*

**moderate** [*adj, n* 'mɔdərət, *vb* 'mɔdəreɪt] *adj*
modéré(e); (*amount, change*) peu important(e)
▷ *n* (*Pol*) modéré(e) ▷ *vi* se modérer, se calmer
▷ *vt* modérer

**moderately** ['mɔdərətlɪ] *adv* (*act*) avec
modération *or* mesure; (*expensive, difficult*)
moyennement; (*pleased, happy*)
raisonnablement, assez; **~ priced** à un prix
raisonnable

**moderation** [mɔdə'reɪʃən] *n* modération *f*,
mesure *f*; **in ~** à dose raisonnable, pris(e) *or*

pratiqué(e) modérément

**moderator** ['mɔdəreɪtəʳ] *n* (*Rel*): **M~** président
*m* (*de l'Assemblée générale de l'Église presbytérienne*);
(*Pol*) modérateur *m*

**modern** ['mɔdən] *adj* moderne

**modernization** [mɔdənaɪ'zeɪʃən] *n*
modernisation *f*

**modernize** ['mɔdənaɪz] *vt* moderniser

**modern languages** *npl* langues vivantes

**modest** ['mɔdɪst] *adj* modeste

**modesty** ['mɔdɪstɪ] *n* modestie *f*

**modicum** ['mɔdɪkəm] *n*: **a ~ of** un minimum de

**modification** [mɔdɪfɪ'keɪʃən] *n* modification *f*;
**to make ~s** faire *or* apporter des modifications

**modify** ['mɔdɪfaɪ] *vt* modifier

**modish** ['məʊdɪʃ] *adj* à la mode

**Mods** [mɔdz] *n abbr* (*Brit*: = (*Honour*) *Moderations*)
*premier examen universitaire (à Oxford)*

**modular** ['mɔdjʊləʳ] *adj* (*filing, unit*) modulaire

**modulate** ['mɔdjʊleɪt] *vt* moduler

**modulation** [mɔdjʊ'leɪʃən] *n* modulation *f*

**module** ['mɔdjuːl] *n* module *m*

**mogul** ['məʊgl] *n* (*fig*) nabab *m*; (*Ski*) bosse *f*

**MOH** *n abbr* (*Brit*) = **Medical Officer of Health**

**mohair** ['məʊhɛəʳ] *n* mohair *m*

**Mohammed** [mə'hæmɛd] *n* Mahomet *m*

**moist** [mɔɪst] *adj* humide, moite

**moisten** ['mɔɪsn] *vt* humecter, mouiller
légèrement

**moisture** ['mɔɪstʃəʳ] *n* humidité *f*; (*on glass*)
buée *f*

**moisturize** ['mɔɪstʃəraɪz] *vt* (*skin*) hydrater

**moisturizer** ['mɔɪstʃəraɪzəʳ] *n* crème hydratante

**molar** ['məʊləʳ] *n* molaire *f*

**molasses** [məʊ'læsɪz] *n* mélasse *f*

**mold** *etc* [məʊld] (*US*) = **mould** *etc*

**Moldavia** [mɔl'deɪvɪə], **Moldova** [mɔl'dəʊvə] *n*
Moldavie *f*

**Moldavian** [mɔl'deɪvɪən], **Moldovan**
[mɔl'dəʊvən] *adj* moldave

**mole** [məʊl] *n* (*animal, spy*) taupe *f*; (*spot*) grain *m*
de beauté

**molecule** ['mɔlɪkjuːl] *n* molécule *f*

**molehill** ['məʊlhɪl] *n* taupinière *f*

**molest** [məʊ'lɛst] *vt* (*assault sexually*) attenter à la
pudeur de; (*attack*) molester; (*harass*) tracasser

**mollusc** ['mɔləsk] *n* mollusque *m*

**mollycoddle** ['mɔlɪkɔdl] *vt* chouchouter, couver

**Molotov cocktail** ['mɔlətɔf-] *n* cocktail *m*
Molotov

**molt** [məʊlt] *vi* (*US*) = **moult**

**molten** ['məʊltən] *adj* fondu(e); (*rock*) en fusion

**mom** [mɔm] *n* (*US*) = **mum**

**moment** ['məʊmənt] *n* moment *m*, instant *m*;
(*importance*) importance *f*; **at the ~** en ce
moment; **for the ~** pour l'instant; **in a ~** dans
un instant; **"one ~ please"** (*Tel*) "ne quittez
pas"

**momentarily** ['məʊməntrɪlɪ] *adv*
momentanément; (*US: soon*) bientôt

**momentary** ['məʊməntərɪ] *adj* momentané(e),
passager(-ère)

**momentous** [məʊ'mɛntəs] adj important(e), capital(e)

**momentum** [məʊ'mɛntəm] n élan m, vitesse acquise; (fig) dynamique f; **to gather ~** prendre de la vitesse; (fig) gagner du terrain

**mommy** ['mɒmɪ] n (US: mother) maman f

**Monaco** ['mɒnəkəʊ] n Monaco f

**monarch** ['mɒnək] n monarque m

**monarchist** ['mɒnəkɪst] n monarchiste m/f

**monarchy** ['mɒnəkɪ] n monarchie f

**monastery** ['mɒnəstərɪ] n monastère m

**monastic** [mə'næstɪk] adj monastique

**Monday** ['mʌndɪ] n lundi m; for phrases see also **Tuesday**

**monetarist** ['mʌnɪtərɪst] n monétariste m/f

**monetary** ['mʌnɪtərɪ] adj monétaire

**money** ['mʌnɪ] n argent m; **to make ~** (person) gagner de l'argent; (business) rapporter; **I've got no ~ left** je n'ai plus d'argent, je n'ai plus un sou

**money belt** n ceinture-portefeuille f

**moneyed** ['mʌnɪd] adj riche

**moneylender** ['mʌnɪlɛndər] n prêteur(-euse)

**moneymaker** ['mʌnɪmeɪkər] n (Brit: col: business) affaire lucrative

**moneymaking** ['mʌnɪmeɪkɪŋ] adj lucratif(-ive), qui rapporte (de l'argent)

**money market** n marché financier

**money order** n mandat m

**money-spinner** ['mʌnɪspɪnər] n (inf) mine f d'or (fig)

**money supply** n masse f monétaire

**Mongol** ['mɒŋgəl] n Mongol(e); (Ling) mongol m

**mongol** ['mɒŋgəl] adj, n (Med) mongolien(ne)

**Mongolia** [mɒŋ'gəʊlɪə] n Mongolie f

**Mongolian** [mɒŋ'gəʊlɪən] adj mongol(e) ▷ n Mongol(e); (Ling) mongol m

**mongoose** ['mɒŋguːs] n mangouste f

**mongrel** ['mʌŋgrəl] n (dog) bâtard m

**monitor** ['mɒnɪtər] n (TV, Comput) écran m, moniteur m; (Brit Scol) chef m de classe; (US Scol) surveillant m (d'examen) ▷ vt contrôler; (foreign station) être à l'écoute de; (progress) suivre de près

**monk** [mʌŋk] n moine m

**monkey** ['mʌŋkɪ] n singe m

**monkey nut** n (Brit) cacahuète f

**monkey wrench** n clé f à molette

**mono** ['mɒnəʊ] adj mono inv

**mono...** ['mɒnəʊ] prefix mono...

**monochrome** ['mɒnəkrəʊm] adj monochrome

**monocle** ['mɒnəkl] n monocle m

**monogamous** [mɒ'nɒgəməs] adj monogame

**monogamy** [mɒ'nɒgəmɪ] n monogamie f

**monogram** ['mɒnəgræm] n monogramme m

**monolith** ['mɒnəlɪθ] n monolithe m

**monologue** ['mɒnəlɒg] n monologue m

**monoplane** ['mɒnəpleɪn] n monoplan m

**monopolize** [mə'nɒpəlaɪz] vt monopoliser

**monopoly** [mə'nɒpəlɪ] n monopole m; **Monopolies and Mergers Commission** (Brit) commission britannique d'enquête sur les monopoles

**monorail** ['mɒnəʊreɪl] n monorail m

**monosodium glutamate** [mɒnə'səʊdɪəm 'gluː təmeɪt] n glutamate m de sodium

**monosyllabic** [mɒnəsɪ'læbɪk] adj monosyllabique; (person) laconique

**monosyllable** ['mɒnəsɪləbl] n monosyllabe m

**monotone** ['mɒnətəʊn] n ton m (or voix f) monocorde; **to speak in a ~** parler sur un ton monocorde

**monotonous** [mə'nɒtənəs] adj monotone

**monotony** [mə'nɒtənɪ] n monotonie f

**monoxide** [mɒ'nɒksaɪd] n: **carbon ~** oxyde m de carbone

**monsoon** [mɒn'suːn] n mousson f

**monster** ['mɒnstər] n monstre m

**monstrosity** [mɒns'trɒsɪtɪ] n monstruosité f, atrocité f

**monstrous** ['mɒnstrəs] adj (huge) gigantesque; (atrocious) monstrueux(-euse), atroce

**Mont.** abbr (US) = **Montana**

**montage** [mɒn'tɑːʒ] n montage m

**Mont Blanc** [mɔ̃blɑ̃] n Mont Blanc m

**month** [mʌnθ] n mois m; **every ~** tous les mois; **300 dollars a ~** 300 dollars par mois

**monthly** ['mʌnθlɪ] adj mensuel(le) ▷ adv mensuellement ▷ n (magazine) mensuel m, publication mensuelle; **twice ~** deux fois par mois

**Montreal** [mɒntrɪ'ɔːl] n Montréal

**monument** ['mɒnjumənt] n monument m

**monumental** [mɒnju'mɛntl] adj monumental(e)

**monumental mason** n marbrier m

**moo** [muː] vi meugler, beugler

**mood** [muːd] n humeur f, disposition f; **to be in a good/bad ~** être de bonne/mauvaise humeur; **to be in the ~ for** être d'humeur à, avoir envie de

**moody** ['muːdɪ] adj (variable) d'humeur changeante, lunatique; (sullen) morose, maussade

**moon** [muːn] n lune f

**moonbeam** ['muːnbiːm] n rayon m de lune

**moon landing** n alunissage m

**moonlight** ['muːnlaɪt] n clair m de lune ▷ vi travailler au noir

**moonlighting** ['muːnlaɪtɪŋ] n travail m au noir

**moonlit** ['muːnlɪt] adj éclairé(e) par la lune; **a ~ night** une nuit de lune

**moonshot** ['muːnʃɒt] n (Space) tir m lunaire

**moonstruck** ['muːnstrʌk] adj fou (folle), dérangé(e)

**moony** ['muːnɪ] adj: **to have ~ eyes** avoir l'air dans la lune or rêveur

**Moor** [mʊər] n Maure (Mauresque)

**moor** [mʊər] n lande f ▷ vt (ship) amarrer ▷ vi mouiller

**moorings** ['mʊərɪŋz] npl (chains) amarres fpl; (place) mouillage m

**Moorish** ['mʊərɪʃ] adj maure, mauresque

**moorland** ['mʊələnd] n lande f

**moose** [muːs] n (pl inv) élan m

**moot** [muːt] vt soulever ▷ adj: **~ point** point m

discutable

**mop** [mɔp] *n* balai *m* à laver; (*for dishes*) lavette *f* à vaisselle ▷ *vt* éponger, essuyer; ~ **of hair** tignasse *f*
 ▶ **mop up** *vt* éponger

**mope** [məup] *vi* avoir le cafard, se morfondre
 ▶ **mope about, mope around** *vi* broyer du noir, se morfondre

**moped** ['məupɛd] *n* cyclomoteur *m*

**MOR** *adj abbr* (*Mus*: = *middle-of-the-road*) tous publics

**moral** ['mɔrl] *adj* moral(e) ▷ *n* morale *f*; **morals** *npl* moralité *f*

**morale** [mɔ'rɑːl] *n* moral *m*

**morality** [mə'rælɪtɪ] *n* moralité *f*

**moralize** ['mɔrəlaɪz] *vi*: **to ~ (about)** moraliser (sur)

**morally** ['mɔrəlɪ] *adv* moralement

**moral victory** *n* victoire morale

**morass** [mə'ræs] *n* marais *m*, marécage *m*

**moratorium** [mɔrə'tɔːrɪəm] *n* moratoire *m*

**morbid** ['mɔːbɪd] *adj* morbide

⊙ **KEYWORD**

**more** [mɔːʳ] *adj* **1** (*greater in number etc*) plus (de), davantage (de); **more people/work (than)** plus de gens/de travail (que)
 **2** (*additional*) encore (de); **do you want (some) more tea?** voulez-vous encore du thé?; **is there any more wine?** reste-t-il du vin?; **I have no** or **I don't have any more money** je n'ai plus d'argent; **it'll take a few more weeks** ça prendra encore quelques semaines
 ▷ *pron* plus, davantage; **more than 10** plus de 10; **it cost more than we expected** cela a coûté plus que prévu; **I want more** j'en veux plus or davantage; **is there any more?** est-ce qu'il en reste?; **there's no more** il n'y en a plus; **a little more** un peu plus; **many/much more** beaucoup plus, bien davantage
 ▷ *adv* plus; **more dangerous/easily (than)** plus dangereux/facilement (que); **more and more expensive** de plus en plus cher; **more or less** plus ou moins; **more than ever** plus que jamais; **once more** encore une fois, une fois de plus; **and what's more ...** et de plus ..., et qui plus est ...

**moreover** [mɔː'rəuvəʳ] *adv* de plus

**morgue** [mɔːg] *n* morgue *f*

**MORI** ['mɔːrɪ] *n abbr* (*Brit*: = *Market & Opinion Research Institute*) institut de sondage

**moribund** ['mɔrɪbʌnd] *adj* moribond(e)

**morning** ['mɔːnɪŋ] *n* matin *m*; (*as duration*) matinée *f* ▷ *cpd* matinal(e); (*paper*) du matin; **in the ~** le matin; **7 o'clock in the ~** 7 heures du matin; **this ~** ce matin

**morning-after pill** ['mɔːnɪŋ'ɑːftə-] *n* pilule *f* du lendemain

**morning sickness** *n* nausées matinales

**Moroccan** [mə'rɔkən] *adj* marocain(e) ▷ *n*

**Morocco** [mə'rɔkəu] *n* Maroc *m*

**moron** ['mɔːrɔn] *n* idiot(e), minus *m/f*

**moronic** [mə'rɔnɪk] *adj* idiot(e), imbécile

**morose** [mə'rəus] *adj* morose, maussade

**morphine** ['mɔːfiːn] *n* morphine *f*

**morris dancing** ['mɔrɪs-] *n* (*Brit*) danses folkloriques anglaises

**Morse** [mɔːs] *n* (*also*: **Morse code**) morse *m*

**morsel** ['mɔːsl] *n* bouchée *f*

**mortal** ['mɔːtl] *adj, n* mortel(le)

**mortality** [mɔː'tælɪtɪ] *n* mortalité *f*

**mortality rate** *n* (taux *m* de) mortalité *f*

**mortar** ['mɔːtəʳ] *n* mortier *m*

**mortgage** ['mɔːgɪdʒ] *n* hypothèque *f*; (*loan*) prêt *m* (*or* crédit *m*) hypothécaire ▷ *vt* hypothéquer; **to take out a ~** prendre une hypothèque, faire un emprunt

**mortgage company** *n* (*US*) société *f* de crédit immobilier

**mortgagee** [mɔːgə'dʒiː] *n* prêteur(-euse) (sur hypothèque)

**mortgagor** ['mɔːgədʒəʳ] *n* emprunteur(-euse) (sur hypothèque)

**mortician** [mɔː'tɪʃən] *n* (*US*) entrepreneur *m* de pompes funèbres

**mortified** ['mɔːtɪfaɪd] *adj* mort(e) de honte

**mortise lock** ['mɔːtɪs-] *n* serrure encastrée

**mortuary** ['mɔːtjuərɪ] *n* morgue *f*

**mosaic** [məu'zeɪɪk] *n* mosaïque *f*

**Moscow** ['mɔskəu] *n* Moscou

**Moslem** ['mɔzləm] *adj, n* = **Muslim**

**mosque** [mɔsk] *n* mosquée *f*

**mosquito** (*pl* -**es**) [mɔs'kiːtəu] *n* moustique *m*

**mosquito net** *n* moustiquaire *f*

**moss** [mɔs] *n* mousse *f*

**mossy** ['mɔsɪ] *adj* moussu(e)

**most** [məust] *adj* (*majority of*) la plupart de; (*greatest amount of*) le plus de ▷ *pron* la plupart ▷ *adv* le plus; (*very*) très, extrêmement; **the ~** le plus; ~ **fish** la plupart des poissons; **the ~ beautiful woman in the world** la plus belle femme du monde; ~ **of** (*with plural*) la plupart de; (*with singular*) la plus grande partie de; ~ **of them** la plupart d'entre eux; ~ **of the time** la plupart du temps; **I saw ~** (*a lot but not all*) j'en ai vu la plupart; (*more than anyone else*) c'est moi qui en ai vu le plus; **at the (very)** ~ au plus; **to make the ~ of** profiter au maximum de

**mostly** ['məustlɪ] *adv* (*chiefly*) surtout, principalement; (*usually*) généralement

**MOT** *n abbr* (*Brit*) = **Ministry of Transport**; **the ~ (test)** visite technique (annuelle) obligatoire des véhicules à moteur

**motel** [məu'tɛl] *n* motel *m*

**moth** [mɔθ] *n* papillon *m* de nuit; (*in clothes*) mite *f*

**mothball** ['mɔθbɔːl] *n* boule *f* de naphtaline

**moth-eaten** ['mɔθiːtn] *adj* mité(e)

**mother** ['mʌðəʳ] *n* mère *f* ▷ *vt* (*pamper, protect*) dorloter

**mother board** *n* (*Comput*) carte-mère *f*

**m**

motherhood ['mʌðəhud] n maternité f
mother-in-law ['mʌðərɪnlɔː] n belle-mère f
motherly ['mʌðəlɪ] adj maternel(le)
mother-of-pearl ['mʌðərəv'pəːl] n nacre f
Mother's Day n fête f des Mères
mother's help n aide f or auxiliaire f familiale
mother-to-be ['mʌðətə'biː] n future maman
mother tongue n langue maternelle
mothproof ['mɔθpruːf] adj traité(e) à l'antimite
motif [məu'tiːf] n motif m
motion ['məuʃən] n mouvement m; (gesture) geste m; (at meeting) motion f; (Brit: also: **bowel motion**) selles fpl ▷ vt, vi: **to ~ (to) sb to do** faire signe à qn de faire; **to be in ~** (vehicle) être en marche; **to set in ~** mettre en marche; **to go through the ~s of doing sth** (fig) faire qch machinalement or sans conviction
motionless ['məuʃənlɪs] adj immobile, sans mouvement
motion picture n film m
motivate ['məutɪveɪt] vt motiver
motivated ['məutɪveɪtɪd] adj motivé(e)
motivation [məutɪ'veɪʃən] n motivation f
motive ['məutɪv] n motif m, mobile m ▷ adj moteur(-trice); **from the best (of) ~s** avec les meilleures intentions (du monde)
motley ['mɔtlɪ] adj hétéroclite; bigarré(e), bariolé(e)
motor ['məutəʳ] n moteur m; (Brit inf: vehicle) auto f ▷ adj moteur(-trice)
motorbike ['məutəbaɪk] n moto f
motorboat ['məutəbəut] n bateau m à moteur
motorcade ['məutəkeɪd] n cortège m d'automobiles or de voitures
motorcar ['məutəkɑː] n (Brit) automobile f
motorcoach ['məutəkəutʃ] n (Brit) car m
motorcycle ['məutəsaɪkl] n moto f
motorcycle racing n course f de motos
motorcyclist ['məutəsaɪklɪst] n motocycliste m/f
motoring ['məutərɪŋ] (Brit) n tourisme m automobile ▷ adj (accident) de voiture, de la route; **~ holiday** vacances fpl en voiture; **~ offence** infraction f au code de la route
motorist ['məutərɪst] n automobiliste m/f
motorize ['məutəraɪz] vt motoriser
motor mechanic n mécanicien m garagiste
motor oil n huile f de graissage
motor racing n (Brit) course f automobile
motor scooter n scooter m
motor trade n secteur m de l'automobile
motor vehicle n véhicule m automobile
motorway ['məutəweɪ] n (Brit) autoroute f
mottled ['mɔtld] adj tacheté(e), marbré(e)
motto (pl -es) ['mɔtəu] n devise f
mould, (US) mold [məuld] n moule m; (mildew) moisissure f ▷ vt mouler, modeler; (fig) façonner
moulder, (US) molder ['məuldəʳ] vi (decay) moisir
moulding, (US) mold ['məuldɪŋ] n (Archit) moulure f

mouldy, (US) moldy ['məuldɪ] adj moisi(e); (smell) de moisi
moult, (US) molt [məult] vi muer
mound [maund] n monticule m, tertre m
mount [maunt] n (hill) mont m, montagne f; (horse) monture f; (for picture) carton m de montage; (for jewel etc) monture ▷ vt monter; (horse) monter à; (bike) monter sur; (exhibition) organiser, monter; (picture) monter sur carton; (stamp) coller dans un album ▷ vi (inflation, tension) augmenter
  ▶ **mount up** vi s'élever, monter; (bills, problems, savings) s'accumuler
mountain ['mauntɪn] n montagne f ▷ cpd de (la) montagne; **to make a ~ out of a molehill** (fig) se faire une montagne d'un rien
mountain bike n VTT m, vélo m tout terrain
mountaineer [mauntɪ'nɪəʳ] n alpiniste m/f
mountaineering [mauntɪ'nɪərɪŋ] n alpinisme m; **to go ~** faire de l'alpinisme
mountainous ['mauntɪnəs] adj montagneux(-euse)
mountain range n chaîne f de montagnes
mountain rescue team n colonne f de secours
mountainside ['mauntɪnsaɪd] n flanc m or versant m de la montagne
mounted ['mauntɪd] adj monté(e)
mourn [mɔːn] vt pleurer ▷ vi: **to ~ for sb** pleurer qn; **to ~ for sth** se lamenter sur qch
mourner ['mɔːnəʳ] n parent(e) or ami(e) du défunt; personne f en deuil or venue rendre hommage au défunt
mourning ['mɔːnɪŋ] n deuil m ▷ cpd (dress) de deuil; **in ~** en deuil
mouse (pl mice) [maus, maɪs] n (also Comput) souris f
mouse mat n (Comput) tapis m de souris
mousetrap ['maustræp] n souricière f
moussaka [muˈsɑːkə] n moussaka f
mousse [muːs] n mousse f
moustache, (US) mustache [məsˈtɑːʃ] n moustache(s) f(pl)
mousy ['mausɪ] adj (person) effacé(e); (hair) d'un châtain terne
mouth [mauθ, pl mauðz] n bouche f; (of dog, cat) gueule f; (of river) embouchure f; (of hole, cave) ouverture f; (of bottle) goulot m; (opening) orifice m
mouthful ['mauθful] n bouchée f
mouth organ n harmonica m
mouthpiece ['mauθpiːs] n (of musical instrument) bec m, embouchure f; (spokesperson) porte-parole m inv
mouth-to-mouth ['mauθtə'mauθ] adj: **~ resuscitation** bouche à bouche m
mouthwash ['mauθwɔʃ] n eau f dentifrice
mouth-watering ['mauθwɔːtərɪŋ] adj qui met l'eau à la bouche
movable ['muːvəbl] adj mobile
move [muːv] n (movement) mouvement m; (in game) coup m; (: turn to play) tour m; (change of house) déménagement m; (change of job)

changement *m* d'emploi ▷ *vt* déplacer, bouger; (*emotionally*) émouvoir; (*Pol: resolution etc*) proposer ▷ *vi* (*gen*) bouger, remuer; (*traffic*) circuler; (*also*: **move house**) déménager; (*in game*) jouer; **can you ~ your car, please?** pouvez-vous déplacer votre voiture, s'il vous plaît?; **to ~ towards** se diriger vers; **to ~ sb to do sth** pousser *or* inciter qn à faire qch; **to get a ~ on** se dépêcher, se remuer
▸ **move about, move around** *vi* (*fidget*) remuer; (*travel*) voyager, se déplacer
▸ **move along** *vi* se pousser
▸ **move away** *vi* s'en aller, s'éloigner
▸ **move back** *vi* revenir, retourner
▸ **move forward** *vi* avancer ▷ *vt* avancer; (*people*) faire avancer
▸ **move in** *vi* (*to a house*) emménager; (*police, soldiers*) intervenir
▸ **move off** *vi* s'éloigner, s'en aller
▸ **move on** *vi* se remettre en route ▷ *vt* (*onlookers*) faire circuler
▸ **move out** *vi* (*of house*) déménager
▸ **move over** *vi* se pousser, se déplacer
▸ **move up** *vi* avancer; (*employee*) avoir de l'avancement; (*pupil*) passer dans la classe supérieure
**moveable** [mu:vəbl] *adj* = **movable**
**movement** ['mu:vmənt] *n* mouvement *m*; **~ (of the bowels)** (*Med*) selles *fpl*
**mover** ['mu:vəʳ] *n* auteur *m* d'une proposition
**movie** ['mu:vɪ] *n* film *m*; **movies** *npl*: **the ~s** le cinéma
**movie camera** *n* caméra *f*
**moviegoer** ['mu:vɪɡəuəʳ] *n* (*US*) cinéphile *m/f*
**movie theater** (*US*) *n* cinéma *m*
**moving** ['mu:vɪŋ] *adj* en mouvement; (*touching*) émouvant(e); *n* (*US*) déménagement *m*
**mow** (*pt* -**ed**, *pp* -**ed** *or* -**n**) [məu, -d, -n] *vt* faucher; (*lawn*) tondre
▸ **mow down** *vt* faucher
**mower** ['məuəʳ] *n* (*also*: **lawnmower**) tondeuse *f* à gazon
**mown** [məun] *pp of* **mow**
**Mozambique** [məuzæm'bi:k] *n* Mozambique *m*
**MP** *n abbr* (= *Military Police*) PM; (*Brit*) = **Member of Parliament**; (*Canada*) = **Mounted Police**
**MP3** *n* mp3 *m*
**MP3 player** *n* baladeur *m* numérique, lecteur *m* mp3
**mpg** *n abbr* (= *miles per gallon*) (30 mpg = 9,4 l. aux 100 km)
**m.p.h.** *abbr* (= *miles per hour*) (60 mph = 96 km/h)
**MPhil** *n abbr* (*US: = Master of Philosophy*) titre universitaire
**MPS** *n abbr* (*Brit*) = **Member of the Pharmaceutical Society**
**Mr**, (*US*) **Mr.** ['mɪstəʳ] *n*: **Mr X** Monsieur X, M. X
**MRC** *n abbr* (*Brit: = Medical Research Council*) conseil de la recherche médicale
**MRCP** *n abbr* (*Brit*) = **Member of the Royal College of Physicians**
**MRCS** *n abbr* (*Brit*) = **Member of the Royal College of Surgeons**

**MRCVS** *n abbr* (*Brit*) = **Member of the Royal College of Veterinary Surgeons**
**Mrs**, (*US*) **Mrs.** ['mɪsɪz] *n*: **~ X** Madame X, Mme X
**MS** *n abbr* (= *manuscript*) ms; (= *multiple sclerosis*) SEP *f*; (*US: = Master of Science*) titre universitaire ▷ *abbr* (*US*) = **Mississippi**
**Ms**, (*US*) **Ms.** [mɪz] *n* (*Miss or Mrs*): **Ms X** Madame X, Mme X; *voir article*

● **Ms**

*Ms* est un titre utilisé à la place de "Mrs" (Mme) ou de "Miss" (Mlle) pour éviter la distinction traditionnelle entre femmes mariées et femmes non mariées.

**MSA** *n abbr* (*US: = Master of Science in Agriculture*) titre universitaire
**MSc** *n abbr* = **Master of Science**
**MSG** *n abbr* = **monosodium glutamate**
**MSP** *n abbr* (= *Member of the Scottish Parliament*) député *m* au Parlement écossais
**MST** *abbr* (*US: = Mountain Standard Time*) heure d'hiver des Montagnes Rocheuses
**MT** *n abbr* (= *machine translation*) TM ▷ *abbr* (*US*) = **Montana**
**Mt** *abbr* (*Geo: = mount*) Mt
**mth** *abbr* (= *month*) m
**MTV** *n abbr* = **music television**
**much** [mʌtʃ] *adj* beaucoup de ▷ *adv*, *n or pron* beaucoup; **~ milk** beaucoup de lait; **we don't have ~ time** nous n'avons pas beaucoup de temps; **how ~ is it?** combien est-ce que ça coûte; **it's not ~** ce n'est pas beaucoup; **too ~** trop (de); **so ~** tant (de); **I like it very/so ~** j'aime beaucoup/tellement ça; **as ~ as** autant de; **thank you very ~** merci beaucoup; **that's ~ better** c'est beaucoup mieux; **~ to my amazement** ... à mon grand étonnement ...
**muck** [mʌk] *n* (*mud*) boue *f*; (*dirt*) ordures *fpl*
▸ **muck about** *vi* (*inf*) faire l'imbécile; (: *waste time*) traînasser; (: *tinker*) bricoler; tripoter
▸ **muck in** *vi* (*Brit inf*) donner un coup de main
▸ **muck out** *vt* (*stable*) nettoyer
▸ **muck up** *vt* (*inf: ruin*) gâcher, esquinter; (: *dirty*) salir; (: *exam, interview*) se planter à
**muckraking** ['mʌkreɪkɪŋ] *n* (*fig: inf*) déterrement *m* d'ordures
**mucky** ['mʌkɪ] *adj* (*dirty*) boueux(-euse), sale
**mucus** ['mju:kəs] *n* mucus *m*
**mud** [mʌd] *n* boue *f*
**muddle** ['mʌdl] *n* (*mess*) pagaille *f*, fouillis *m*; (*mix-up*) confusion *f* ▷ *vt* (*also*: **muddle up**) brouiller, embrouiller; **to be in a ~** (*person*) ne plus savoir où l'on en est; **to get in a ~** (*while explaining etc*) s'embrouiller
▸ **muddle along** *vi* aller son chemin tant bien que mal
▸ **muddle through** *vi* se débrouiller
**muddle-headed** [mʌdl'hedɪd] *adj* (*person*) à l'esprit embrouillé *or* confus, dans le brouillard

**muddy** ['mʌdɪ] *adj* boueux(-euse)
**mud flats** *npl* plage *f* de vase
**mudguard** ['mʌdɡɑːd] *n* garde-boue *m inv*
**mudpack** ['mʌdpæk] *n* masque *m* de beauté
**mud-slinging** ['mʌdslɪŋɪŋ] *n* médisance *f*,
  dénigrement *m*
**muesli** ['mjuːzlɪ] *n* muesli *m*
**muff** [mʌf] *n* manchon *m* ▷ *vt* (*inf: shot, catch etc*)
  rater, louper; **to ~ it** rater *or* louper son coup
**muffin** ['mʌfɪn] *n* (*roll*) petit pain rond et plat; (*cake*)
  petit gâteau au chocolat ou aux fruits
**muffle** ['mʌfl] *vt* (*sound*) assourdir, étouffer;
  (*against cold*) emmitoufler
**muffled** ['mʌfld] *adj* étouffé(e), voilé(e)
**muffler** ['mʌflər] *n* (*scarf*) cache-nez *m inv*; (*US
  Aut*) silencieux *m*
**mufti** ['mʌftɪ] *n*: **in ~** en civil
**mug** [mʌɡ] *n* (*cup*) tasse *f* (*sans soucoupe*); (: *for beer*)
  chope *f*; (*inf: face*) bouille *f*; (: *fool*) poire *f* ▷ *vt*
  (*assault*) agresser; **it's a ~'s game** (*Brit*) c'est bon
  pour les imbéciles
  ▶ **mug up** *vt* (*Brit inf: also*: **mug up on**) bosser,
  bûcher
**mugger** ['mʌɡər] *n* agresseur *m*
**mugging** ['mʌɡɪŋ] *n* agression *f*
**muggins** ['mʌɡɪnz] *n* (*inf*) ma pomme
**muggy** ['mʌɡɪ] *adj* lourd(e), moite
**mug shot** *n* (*inf: Police*) photo *f* de criminel; (: *gen:
  photo*) photo d'identité
**mulatto** (*pl* **-es**) [mjuːˈlætəu] *n* mulâtre(-esse)
**mulberry** ['mʌlbrɪ] *n* (*fruit*) mûre *f*; (*tree*)
  mûrier *m*
**mule** [mjuːl] *n* mule *f*
**mull** [mʌl]: **to ~ over** *vt* réfléchir à, ruminer
**mulled** [mʌld] *adj*: **~ wine** vin chaud
**multi...** ['mʌltɪ] *prefix* multi...
**multi-access** ['mʌltɪˈækses] *adj* (*Comput*) à accès
  multiple
**multicoloured,** (*US*) **multicolored**
  ['mʌltɪkʌləd] *adj* multicolore
**multifarious** [mʌltɪˈfɛərɪəs] *adj* divers(es),
  varié(e)
**multilateral** [mʌltɪˈlætərl] *adj* (*Pol*)
  multilatéral(e)
**multi-level** ['mʌltɪlevl] *adj* (*US*) = **multistorey**
**multimedia** ['mʌltɪˈmiːdɪə] *adj* multimédia *inv*
**multimillionaire** [mʌltɪmɪljəˈnɛər] *n*
  milliardaire *m/f*
**multinational** [mʌltɪˈnæʃənl] *n* multinationale
  *f* ▷ *adj* multinational(e)
**multiple** ['mʌltɪpl] *adj* multiple ▷ *n* multiple *m*;
  (*Brit: also*: **multiple store**) magasin *m* à
  succursales (multiples)
**multiple choice, multiple choice test** *n* QCM
  *m*, questionnaire *m* à choix multiple
**multiple crash** *n* carambolage *m*
**multiple sclerosis** [-sklɪˈrəusɪs] *n* sclérose *f* en
  plaques
**multiplex** ['mʌltɪpleks], **multiplex cinema** *n*
  (cinéma *m*) multisalles *m*
**multiplication** [mʌltɪplɪˈkeɪʃən] *n*
  multiplication *f*

**multiplication table** *n* table *f* de multiplication
**multiplicity** [mʌltɪˈplɪsɪtɪ] *n* multiplicité *f*
**multiply** ['mʌltɪplaɪ] *vt* multiplier ▷ *vi* se
  multiplier
**multiracial** [mʌltɪˈreɪʃl] *adj* multiracial(e)
**multistorey** ['mʌltɪˈstɔːrɪ] *adj* (*Brit: building*) à
  étages; (: *car park*) à étages *or* niveaux multiples
**multitude** ['mʌltɪtjuːd] *n* multitude *f*
**mum** [mʌm] *n* (*Brit*) maman *f* ▷ *adj*: **to keep ~**
  ne pas souffler mot; **~'s the word!** motus et
  bouche cousue!
**mumble** ['mʌmbl] *vt*, *vi* marmotter,
  marmonner
**mumbo jumbo** ['mʌmbəu-] *n* (*inf*) baragouin *m*,
  charabia *m*
**mummify** ['mʌmɪfaɪ] *vt* momifier
**mummy** ['mʌmɪ] *n* (*Brit: mother*) maman *f*;
  (*embalmed*) momie *f*
**mumps** [mʌmps] *n* oreillons *mpl*
**munch** [mʌntʃ] *vt*, *vi* mâcher
**mundane** [mʌnˈdeɪn] *adj* banal(e), terre à terre
  *inv*
**municipal** [mjuːˈnɪsɪpl] *adj* municipal(e)
**municipality** [mjuːnɪsɪˈpælɪtɪ] *n* municipalité *f*
**munitions** [mjuːˈnɪʃənz] *npl* munitions *fpl*
**mural** ['mjuərl] *n* peinture murale
**murder** ['mɜːdər] *n* meurtre *m*, assassinat *m* ▷ *vt*
  assassiner; **to commit ~** commettre un
  meurtre
**murderer** ['mɜːdərər] *n* meurtrier *m*, assassin *m*
**murderess** ['mɜːdərɪs] *n* meurtrière *f*
**murderous** ['mɜːdərəs] *adj* meurtrier(-ière)
**murk** [mɜːk] *n* obscurité *f*
**murky** ['mɜːkɪ] *adj* sombre, ténébreux(-euse);
  (*water*) trouble
**murmur** ['mɜːmər] *n* murmure *m* ▷ *vt*, *vi*
  murmurer; **heart ~** (*Med*) souffle *m* au cœur
**MusB, MusBac** *n abbr* (= *Bachelor of Music*) titre
  *universitaire*
**muscle** ['mʌsl] *n* muscle *m*; (*fig*) force *f*
  ▶ **muscle in** *vi* s'imposer, s'immiscer
**muscular** ['mʌskjulər] *adj* musculaire; (*person,
  arm*) musclé(e)
**muscular dystrophy** *n* dystrophie *f* musculaire
**MusD, MusDoc** *n abbr* (= *Doctor of Music*) titre
  *universitaire*
**muse** [mjuːz] *vi* méditer, songer ▷ *n* muse *f*
**museum** [mjuːˈzɪəm] *n* musée *m*
**mush** [mʌʃ] *n* bouillie *f*; (*pej*) sentimentalité *f* à
  l'eau de rose
**mushroom** ['mʌʃrum] *n* champignon *m* ▷ *vi*
  (*fig*) pousser comme un (*or* des) champignon(s)
**mushy** ['mʌʃɪ] *adj* (*vegetables, fruit*) en bouillie;
  (*movie etc*) à l'eau de rose
**music** ['mjuːzɪk] *n* musique *f*
**musical** ['mjuːzɪkl] *adj* musical(e); (*person*)
  musicien(ne) ▷ *n* (*show*) comédie musicale
**musical box** *n* = **music box**
**musical chairs** *npl* chaises musicales; (*fig*): **to
  play ~** faire des permutations
**musical instrument** *n* instrument *m* de
  musique

**music box** *n* boîte *f* à musique
**music centre** *n* chaîne compacte
**music hall** *n* music-hall *m*
**musician** [mjuːˈzɪʃən] *n* musicien(ne)
**music stand** *n* pupitre *m* à musique
**musk** [mʌsk] *n* musc *m*
**musket** [ˈmʌskɪt] *n* mousquet *m*
**muskrat** [ˈmʌskræt] *n* rat musqué
**musk rose** *n* (*Bot*) rose *f* muscade
**Muslim** [ˈmʌzlɪm] *adj, n* musulman(e)
**muslin** [ˈmʌzlɪn] *n* mousseline *f*
**musquash** [ˈmʌskwɔʃ] *n* loutre *f*; (*fur*) rat *m*
  d'Amérique, ondatra *m*
**mussel** [ˈmʌsl] *n* moule *f*
**must** [mʌst] *aux vb* (*obligation*): **I ~ do it** je dois le
  faire, il faut que je le fasse; (*probability*): **he ~ be
  there by now** il doit y être maintenant, il y est
  probablement maintenant; (*suggestion,
  invitation*): **you ~ come and see me** il faut que
  vous veniez me voir ▷ *n* nécessité *f*, impératif
  *m*; **it's a ~** c'est indispensable; **I ~ have made a
  mistake** j'ai dû me tromper
**mustache** [ˈmʌstæʃ] *n* (*US*) = **moustache**
**mustard** [ˈmʌstəd] *n* moutarde *f*
**mustard gas** *n* ypérite *f*, gaz *m* moutarde
**muster** [ˈmʌstəʳ] *vt* rassembler; (*also*: **muster
  up**: *strength, courage*) rassembler
**mustiness** [ˈmʌstɪnɪs] *n* goût *m* de moisi;
  odeur *f* de moisi *or* de renfermé
**mustn't** [ˈmʌsnt] = **must not**
**musty** [ˈmʌstɪ] *adj* qui sent le moisi *or* le
  renfermé
**mutant** [ˈmjuːtənt] *adj* mutant(e) ▷ *n* mutant *m*
**mutate** [mjuːˈteɪt] *vi* subir une mutation
**mutation** [mjuːˈteɪʃən] *n* mutation *f*
**mute** [mjuːt] *adj, n* muet(te)
**muted** [ˈmjuːtɪd] *adj* (*noise*) sourd(e), assourdi(e);
  (*criticism*) voilé(e); (*Mus*) en sourdine; (: *trumpet*)
  bouché(e)
**mutilate** [ˈmjuːtɪleɪt] *vt* mutiler

**mutilation** [mjuːtɪˈleɪʃən] *n* mutilation *f*
**mutinous** [ˈmjuːtɪnəs] *adj* (*troops*) mutiné(e);
  (*attitude*) rebelle
**mutiny** [ˈmjuːtɪnɪ] *n* mutinerie *f* ▷ *vi* se
  mutiner
**mutter** [ˈmʌtəʳ] *vt, vi* marmonner, marmotter
**mutton** [ˈmʌtn] *n* mouton *m*
**mutual** [ˈmjuːtʃuəl] *adj* mutuel(le), réciproque;
  (*benefit, interest*) commun(e)
**mutually** [ˈmjuːtʃuəlɪ] *adv* mutuellement,
  réciproquement
**Muzak®** [ˈmjuːzæk] *n* (*often pej*) musique *f*
  d'ambiance
**muzzle** [ˈmʌzl] *n* museau *m*; (*protective device*)
  muselière *f*; (*of gun*) gueule *f* ▷ *vt* museler
**MVP** *n abbr* (*US Sport*) = **most valuable player**
**MW** *abbr* (= *medium wave*) PO
**my** [maɪ] *adj* mon (ma), mes *pl*; **my house/car/
  gloves** ma maison/ma voiture/mes gants; **I've
  washed my hair/cut my finger** je me suis lavé
  les cheveux/coupé le doigt; **is this my pen or
  yours?** c'est mon stylo ou c'est le vôtre?
**Myanmar** [ˈmaɪænmɑːʳ] *n* Myanmar *m*
**myopic** [maɪˈɔpɪk] *adj* myope
**myriad** [ˈmɪrɪəd] *n* myriade *f*
**myself** [maɪˈsɛlf] *pron* (*reflexive*) me; (*emphatic*)
  moi-même; (*after prep*) moi; *see also* **oneself**
**mysterious** [mɪsˈtɪərɪəs] *adj* mystérieux(-euse)
**mystery** [ˈmɪstərɪ] *n* mystère *m*
**mystery story** *n* roman *m* à suspense
**mystic** [ˈmɪstɪk] *n* mystique *m/f* ▷ *adj* (*mysterious*)
  ésotérique
**mystical** [ˈmɪstɪkl] *adj* mystique
**mystify** [ˈmɪstɪfaɪ] *vt* (*deliberately*) mystifier;
  (*puzzle*) ébahir
**mystique** [mɪsˈtiːk] *n* mystique *f*
**myth** [mɪθ] *n* mythe *m*
**mythical** [ˈmɪθɪkl] *adj* mythique
**mythological** [mɪθəˈlɔdʒɪkl] *adj* mythologique
**mythology** [mɪˈθɔlədʒɪ] *n* mythologie *f*

# Nn

**N, n** [ɛn] *n* (*letter*) N, n *m*; **N for Nellie**, (US) **N for Nan** N comme Nicolas

**N** *abbr* (= *north*) N

**NA** *n abbr* (US: = *Narcotics Anonymous*) association d'aide aux drogués; (US) = **National Academy**

**n/a** *abbr* (= *not applicable*) n.a.; (*Comm etc*) = **no account**

**NAACP** *n abbr* (US) = **National Association for the Advancement of Colored People**

**NAAFI** ['næfɪ] *n abbr* (Brit: = *Navy, Army & Air Force Institute*) organisme responsable des magasins et cantines de l'armée

**nab** [næb] *vt* (*inf*) pincer, attraper

**NACU** *n abbr* (US) = **National Association of Colleges and Universities**

**nadir** ['neɪdɪəʳ] *n* (*Astronomy*) nadir *m*; (*fig*) fond *m*, point *m* extrême

**naff** [næf] (Brit: *inf*) *adj* nul(le)

**nag** [næg] *vt* (*scold*) être toujours après, reprendre sans arrêt ▷ *n* (*pej: horse*) canasson *m*; (*person*): **she's an awful ~** elle est constamment après lui (*or eux etc*), elle est très casse-pieds

**nagging** ['nægɪŋ] *adj* (*doubt, pain*) persistant(e) ▷ *n* remarques continuelles

**nail** [neɪl] *n* (*human*) ongle *m*; (*metal*) clou *m* ▷ *vt* clouer; **to ~ sth to sth** clouer qch à qch; **to ~ sb down to a date/price** contraindre qn à accepter *or* donner une date/un prix; **to pay cash on the ~** (Brit) payer rubis sur l'ongle

**nailbrush** ['neɪlbrʌʃ] *n* brosse *f* à ongles

**nailfile** ['neɪlfaɪl] *n* lime *f* à ongles

**nail polish** *n* vernis *m* à ongles

**nail polish remover** *n* dissolvant *m*

**nail scissors** *npl* ciseaux *mpl* à ongles

**nail varnish** *n* (Brit) = **nail polish**

**Nairobi** [naɪ'rəubɪ] *n* Nairobi

**naïve** [naɪ'iːv] *adj* naïf(-ïve)

**naïveté** [naɪ'iːvteɪ], **naivety** [naɪ'iːvɪtɪ] *n* naïveté *f*

**naked** ['neɪkɪd] *adj* nu(e); **with the ~ eye** à l'œil nu

**nakedness** ['neɪkɪdnɪs] *n* nudité *f*

**NAM** *n abbr* (US) = **National Association of Manufacturers**

**name** [neɪm] *n* nom *m*; (*reputation*) réputation *f* ▷ *vt* nommer; (*identify: accomplice etc*) citer; (*price,* date) fixer, donner; **by ~** par son nom; de nom; **in the ~ of** au nom de; **what's your ~?** comment vous appelez-vous?, quel est votre nom?; **my ~ is Peter** je m'appelle Peter; **to take sb's ~ and address** relever l'identité de qn *or* les nom et adresse de qn; **to make a ~ for o.s.** se faire un nom; **to get (o.s.) a bad ~** se faire une mauvaise réputation; **to call sb ~s** traiter qn de tous les noms

**name dropping** *n* mention (*pour se faire valoir*) du nom de personnalités qu'on connaît (*ou prétend connaître*)

**nameless** ['neɪmlɪs] *adj* sans nom; (*witness, contributor*) anonyme

**namely** ['neɪmlɪ] *adv* à savoir

**nameplate** ['neɪmpleɪt] *n* (*on door etc*) plaque *f*

**namesake** ['neɪmseɪk] *n* homonyme *m*

**nan bread** [nɑː-] *n* nan *m*

**nanny** ['nænɪ] *n* bonne *f* d'enfants

**nanny goat** *n* chèvre *f*

**nap** [næp] *n* (*sleep*) (petit) somme ▷ *vi*: **to be caught ~ping** être pris(e) à l'improviste *or* en défaut

**NAPA** *n abbr* (US: = *National Association of Performing Artists*) syndicat des gens du spectacle

**napalm** ['neɪpɑːm] *n* napalm *m*

**nape** [neɪp] *n*: **~ of the neck** nuque *f*

**napkin** ['næpkɪn] *n* serviette *f* (de table)

**Naples** ['neɪplz] *n* Naples

**Napoleonic** [nəpəulɪ'ɔnɪk] *adj* napoléonien(ne)

**nappy** ['næpɪ] *n* (Brit) couche *f*

**nappy liner** *n* (Brit) protège-couche *m*

**nappy rash** *n*: **to have ~** avoir les fesses rouges

**narcissistic** [nɑːsɪ'sɪstɪk] *adj* narcissique

**narcissus** (*pl* **narcissi**) [nɑː'sɪsəs, -saɪ] *n* narcisse *m*

**narcotic** [nɑː'kɔtɪk] *n* (Med) narcotique *m*

**narcotics** [nɑː'kɔtɪkz] *npl* (*illegal drugs*) stupéfiants *mpl*

**nark** [nɑːk] *vt* (Brit inf) mettre en rogne

**narrate** [nə'reɪt] *vt* raconter, narrer

**narration** [nə'reɪʃən] *n* narration *f*

**narrative** ['nærətɪv] *n* récit *m* ▷ *adj* narratif(-ive)

**narrator** [nə'reɪtəʳ] *n* narrateur(-trice)

**narrow** ['nærəu] *adj* étroit(e); (*fig*) restreint(e),

limité(e) ▷ *vi* (*road*) devenir plus étroit, se
rétrécir; (*gap, difference*) se réduire; **to have a ~
escape** l'échapper belle
▶ **narrow down** *vt* restreindre
**narrow gauge** *adj* (*Rail*) à voie étroite
**narrowly** ['nærəʊlɪ] *adv*: **he ~ missed injury/
the tree** il a failli se blesser/rentrer dans
l'arbre; **he only ~ missed the target** il a
manqué la cible de peu *or* de justesse
**narrow-minded** [nærəʊ'maɪndɪd] *adj* à l'esprit
étroit, borné(e); (*attitude*) borné(e)
**NAS** *n abbr* (*US*) = **National Academy of Sciences**
**NASA** ['næsə] *n abbr* (*US*: = *National Aeronautics and
Space Administration*) NASA *f*
**nasal** ['neɪzl] *adj* nasal(e)
**Nassau** ['næsɔː] *n* (*in Bahamas*) Nassau
**nastily** ['nɑːstɪlɪ] *adv* (*say, act*) méchamment
**nastiness** ['nɑːstɪnɪs] *n* (*of person, remark*)
méchanceté *f*
**nasturtium** [nəs'təːʃəm] *n* capucine *f*
**nasty** ['nɑːstɪ] *adj* (*person: malicious*) méchant(e);
(*: rude*) très désagréable; (*smell*) dégoûtant(e);
(*wound, situation*) mauvais(e), vilain(e); (*weather*)
affreux(-euse); **to turn ~** (*situation*) mal tourner;
(*weather*) se gâter; (*person*) devenir méchant; **it's
a ~ business** c'est une sale affaire
**NAS/UWT** *n abbr* (*Brit*: = *National Association of
Schoolmasters/Union of Women Teachers*) *syndicat
enseignant*
**nation** ['neɪʃən] *n* nation *f*
**national** ['næʃənl] *adj* national(e) ▷ *n* (*abroad*)
ressortissant(e); (*when home*) national(e)
**national anthem** *n* hymne national
**National Curriculum** *n* (*Brit*) *programme scolaire
commun à toutes les écoles publiques en Angleterre et au
Pays de Galles comprenant dix disciplines*
**national debt** *n* dette publique
**national dress** *n* costume national
**National Guard** *n* (*US*) milice *f* (*de volontaires*)
**National Health Service** *n* (*Brit*) *service national
de santé*, ≈ Sécurité Sociale
**National Insurance** *n* (*Brit*) ≈ Sécurité Sociale
**nationalism** ['næʃnəlɪzəm] *n* nationalisme *m*
**nationalist** ['næʃnəlɪst] *adj*, *n* nationaliste *m/f*
**nationality** [næʃə'nælɪtɪ] *n* nationalité *f*
**nationalization** [næʃnəlaɪ'zeɪʃən] *n*
nationalisation *f*
**nationalize** ['næʃnəlaɪz] *vt* nationaliser
**nationally** ['næʃnəlɪ] *adv* du point de vue
national; dans le pays entier
**national park** *n* parc national
**national press** *n* presse nationale
**National Security Council** *n* (*US*) conseil
national de sécurité
**national service** *n* (*Mil*) service *m* militaire
**National Trust** *n* (*Brit*) ≈ Caisse *f* nationale des
monuments historiques et des sites; *voir article*

◉ **NATIONAL TRUST**
◉
◉ Le *National Trust* est un organisme
◉ indépendant, à but non lucratif, dont la

◉ mission est de protéger et de mettre en
◉ valeur les monuments et les sites
◉ britanniques en raison de leur intérêt
◉ historique ou de leur beauté naturelle.

**nationwide** ['neɪʃənwaɪd] *adj* s'étendant à
l'ensemble du pays; (*problem*) à l'échelle du pays
entier ▷ *adv* à travers *or* dans tout le pays
**native** ['neɪtɪv] *n* habitant(e) du pays,
autochtone *m/f*; (*in colonies*) indigène *m/f* ▷ *adj*
du pays, indigène; (*country*) natal(e); (*language*)
maternel(le); (*ability*) inné(e); **a ~ of Russia** une
personne originaire de Russie; **a ~ speaker of
French** une personne de langue maternelle
française
**Native American** *n* Indien(ne) d'Amérique
▷ *adj* amérindien(ne)
**native speaker** *n* locuteur natif
**Nativity** [nə'tɪvɪtɪ] *n* (*Rel*): **the ~** la Nativité
**nativity play** *n* mystère *m or* miracle *m* de la
Nativité
**NATO** ['neɪtəʊ] *n abbr* (= *North Atlantic Treaty
Organization*) OTAN *f*
**natter** ['nætə'] *vi* (*Brit*) bavarder
**natural** ['nætʃrəl] *adj* naturel(le); **to die of ~
causes** mourir d'une mort naturelle
**natural childbirth** *n* accouchement *m* sans
douleur
**natural gas** *n* gaz naturel
**natural history** *n* histoire naturelle
**naturalist** ['nætʃrəlɪst] *n* naturaliste *m/f*
**naturalization** ['nætʃrəlaɪ'zeɪʃən] *n*
naturalisation *f*; acclimatation *f*
**naturalize** ['nætʃrəlaɪz] *vt* naturaliser; (*plant*)
acclimater; **to become ~d** (*person*) se faire
naturaliser
**naturally** ['nætʃrəlɪ] *adv* naturellement
**natural resources** *npl* ressources naturelles
**natural selection** *n* sélection naturelle
**natural wastage** *n* (*Industry*) départs naturels et
volontaires
**nature** ['neɪtʃə'] *n* nature *f*; **by ~** par
tempérament, de nature; **documents of a
confidential ~** documents à caractère
confidentiel
**-natured** ['neɪtʃəd] *suffix*: **ill-** qui a mauvais
caractère
**nature reserve** *n* (*Brit*) réserve naturelle
**nature trail** *n* *sentier de découverte de la nature*
**naturist** ['neɪtʃərɪst] *n* naturiste *m/f*
**naught** [nɔːt] *n* = **nought**
**naughtiness** ['nɔːtɪnɪs] *n* (*of child*)
désobéissance *f*; (*of story etc*) grivoiserie *f*
**naughty** ['nɔːtɪ] *adj* (*child*) vilain(e), pas sage;
(*story, film*) grivois(e)
**nausea** ['nɔːsɪə] *n* nausée *f*
**nauseate** ['nɔːsɪeɪt] *vt* écœurer, donner la
nausée à
**nauseating** ['nɔːsɪeɪtɪŋ] *adj* écœurant(e),
dégoûtant(e)
**nauseous** ['nɔːsɪəs] *adj* nauséabond(e),
écœurant(e); (*feeling sick*): **to be ~** avoir des

**n**

nausées
**nautical** ['nɔ:tɪkl] *adj* nautique
**nautical mile** *n* mille marin (= 1853 m)
**naval** ['neɪvl] *adj* naval(e)
**naval officer** *n* officier *m* de marine
**nave** [neɪv] *n* nef *f*
**navel** ['neɪvl] *n* nombril *m*
**navigable** ['nævɪɡəbl] *adj* navigable
**navigate** ['nævɪɡeɪt] *vt* (*steer*) diriger, piloter
▷ *vi* naviguer; (*Aut*) indiquer la route à suivre
**navigation** [nævɪ'ɡeɪʃən] *n* navigation *f*
**navigator** ['nævɪɡeɪtə'] *n* navigateur *m*
**navvy** ['nævɪ] *n* (*Brit*) terrassier *m*
**navy** ['neɪvɪ] *n* marine *f*; **Department of the
N~** (*US*) ministère *m* de la Marine
**navy-blue** ['neɪvɪ'blu:] *adj* bleu marine *inv*
**Nazi** ['nɑ:tsɪ] *adj* nazi(e) ▷ *n* Nazi(e)
**NB** *abbr* (= *nota bene*) NB; (*Canada*) = **New
Brunswick**
**NBA** *n abbr* (*US*) = **National Basketball
Association; National Boxing Association**
**NBC** *n abbr* (*US*: = *National Broadcasting Company*)
*chaîne de télévision*
**NBS** *n abbr* (*US*: = *National Bureau of Standards*) *office
de normalisation*
**NC** *abbr* (*Comm etc*) = **no charge**; (*US*) = **North
Carolina**
**NCC** *n abbr* (*Brit*: = *Nature Conservancy Council*)
*organisme de protection de la nature*; (*US*) = **National
Council of Churches**
**NCO** *n abbr* = **non-commissioned officer**
**ND, N. Dak.** *abbr* (*US*) = **North Dakota**
**NE** *abbr* (*US*) = **Nebraska; New England**
**NEA** *n abbr* (*US*) = **National Education
Association**
**neap** [ni:p] *n* (*also*: **neaptide**) mortes-eaux *fpl*
**near** [nɪə'] *adj* proche ▷ *adv* près ▷ *prep* (*also*:
**near to**) près de ▷ *vt* approcher de; **~ here/
there** près d'ici/non loin de là; **£25,000 or ~est
offer** (*Brit*) 25 000 livres à débattre; **in the ~
future** dans un proche avenir; **to come ~** *vi*
s'approcher
**nearby** [nɪə'baɪ] *adj* proche ▷ *adv* tout près, à
proximité
**Near East** *n*: **the ~** le Proche-Orient
**nearer** ['nɪərə'] *adj* plus proche ▷ *adv* plus près
**nearly** ['nɪəlɪ] *adv* presque; **I ~ fell** j'ai failli
tomber; **it's not ~ big enough** ce n'est
vraiment pas assez grand, c'est loin d'être assez
grand
**near miss** *n* collision évitée de justesse; (*when
aiming*) coup manqué de peu *or* de justesse
**nearness** ['nɪənɪs] *n* proximité *f*
**nearside** ['nɪəsaɪd] (*Aut*) *n* (*right-hand drive*) côté *m*
gauche; (*left-hand drive*) côté droit ▷ *adj* de
gauche; de droite
**near-sighted** [nɪə'saɪtɪd] *adj* myope
**neat** [ni:t] *adj* (*person, work*) soigné(e); (*room etc*)
bien tenu(e) *or* rangé(e); (*solution, plan*) habile;
(*spirits*) pur(e); **I drink it ~** je le bois sec *or* sans
eau
**neatly** ['ni:tlɪ] *adv* avec soin *or* ordre; (*skilfully*)

habilement
**neatness** ['ni:tnɪs] *n* (*tidiness*) netteté *f*;
(*skilfulness*) habileté *f*
**Nebr.** *abbr* (*US*) = **Nebraska**
**nebulous** ['nebjuləs] *adj* nébuleux(-euse)
**necessarily** ['nesɪsrɪlɪ] *adv* nécessairement;
**not ~** pas nécessairement *or* forcément
**necessary** ['nesɪsrɪ] *adj* nécessaire; **if ~** si
besoin est, le cas échéant
**necessitate** [nɪ'sesɪteɪt] *vt* nécessiter
**necessity** [nɪ'sesɪtɪ] *n* nécessité *f*; chose
nécessaire *or* essentielle; **in case of ~** en cas
d'urgence
**neck** [nek] *n* cou *m*; (*of horse, garment*) encolure *f*;
(*of bottle*) goulot *m* ▷ *vi* (*inf*) se peloter; **~ and ~** à
égalité; **to stick one's ~ out** (*inf*) se mouiller
**necklace** ['neklɪs] *n* collier *m*
**neckline** ['neklaɪn] *n* encolure *f*
**necktie** ['nektaɪ] *n* (*esp US*) cravate *f*
**nectar** ['nektə'] *n* nectar *m*
**nectarine** ['nektərɪn] *n* brugnon *m*, nectarine *f*
**née** [neɪ] *adj*: **~ Scott** née Scott
**need** [ni:d] *n* besoin *m* ▷ *vt* avoir besoin de; **to ~
to do** devoir faire; avoir besoin de faire; **you
don't ~ to go** vous n'avez pas besoin *or* vous
n'êtes pas obligé de partir; **a signature is ~ed** il
faut une signature; **to be in ~ of** *or* **have ~ of**
avoir besoin de; **£10 will meet my immediate
~s** 10 livres suffiront pour mes besoins
immédiats; **in case of ~** en cas de besoin, au
besoin; **there's no ~ to do ....** il n'y a pas lieu de
faire ..., il n'est pas nécessaire de faire ...;
**there's no ~ for that** ce n'est pas la peine, cela
n'est pas nécessaire
**needle** ['ni:dl] *n* aiguille *f*; (*on record player*) saphir
*m* ▷ *vt* (*inf*) asticoter, tourmenter
**needlecord** ['ni:dlkɔ:d] *n* (*Brit*) velours *m*
milleraies
**needless** ['ni:dlɪs] *adj* inutile; **~ to say, ...**
inutile de dire que ...
**needlessly** ['ni:dlɪslɪ] *adv* inutilement
**needlework** ['ni:dlwə:k] *n* (*activity*) travaux *mpl*
d'aiguille; (*object*) ouvrage *m*
**needn't** ['ni:dnt] = **need not**
**needy** ['ni:dɪ] *adj* nécessiteux(-euse)
**negation** [nɪ'ɡeɪʃən] *n* négation *f*
**negative** ['neɡətɪv] *n* (*Phot, Elec*) négatif *m*; (*Ling*)
terme *m* de négation ▷ *adj* négatif(-ive); **to
answer in the ~** répondre par la négative
**negative equity** *n* situation dans laquelle la valeur
d'une maison est inférieure à celle du prêt immobilier
contracté pour la payer
**neglect** [nɪ'ɡlekt] *vt* négliger; (*garden*) ne pas
entretenir; (*duty*) manquer à ▷ *n* (*of person, duty,
garden*) le fait de négliger; (*state of*) **~** abandon
*m*; **to ~ to do sth** négliger *or* omettre de faire
qch; **to ~ one's appearance** se négliger
**neglected** [nɪ'ɡlektɪd] *adj* négligé(e), à
l'abandon
**neglectful** [nɪ'ɡlektful] *adj* (*gen*) négligent(e);
**to be ~ of sb/sth** négliger qn/qch
**negligee** ['neɡlɪʒeɪ] *n* déshabillé *m*

**negligence** ['nɛglɪdʒəns] n négligence f
**negligent** ['nɛglɪdʒənt] adj négligent(e)
**negligently** ['nɛglɪdʒəntlɪ] adv par négligence;
(offhandedly) négligemment
**negligible** ['nɛglɪdʒɪbl] adj négligeable
**negotiable** [nɪ'gəʊʃɪəbl] adj négociable; **not ~**
(cheque) non négociable
**negotiate** [nɪ'gəʊʃɪeɪt] vi négocier ▷ vt
négocier; (Comm) négocier; (obstacle) franchir,
négocier; (bend in road) négocier; **to ~ with sb**
**for sth** négocier avec qn en vue d'obtenir qch
**negotiating table** [nɪ'gəʊʃɪeɪtɪŋ-] n table f des
négociations
**negotiation** [nɪgəʊʃɪ'eɪʃən] n négociation f,
pourparlers mpl; **to enter into ~s with sb**
engager des négociations avec qn
**negotiator** [nɪ'gəʊʃɪeɪtə<sup>r</sup>] n négociateur(-trice)
**Negress** ['niːgrɪs] n négresse f
**Negro** ['niːgrəʊ] adj (gen) noir(e); (music, arts)
nègre, noir ▷ n (pl **-es**) Noir(e)
**neigh** [neɪ] vi hennir
**neighbour**, (US) **neighbor** ['neɪbə<sup>r</sup>] n voisin(e)
**neighbourhood**, (US) **neighborhood**
['neɪbəhud] n (place) quartier m; (people)
voisinage m
**neighbourhood watch** n système de surveillance,
assuré par les habitants d'un même quartier
**neighbouring**, (US) **neighboring** ['neɪbərɪŋ] adj
voisin(e), avoisinant(e)
**neighbourly**, (US) **neighborly** ['neɪbəlɪ] adj
obligeant(e); (relations) de bon voisinage
**neither** ['naɪðə<sup>r</sup>] adj, pron aucun(e) (des deux), ni
l'un(e) ni l'autre ▷ conj: **- do I** moi non plus; **I**
**didn't move and ~ did Claude** je n'ai pas
bougé, (et) Claude non plus ▷ adv: **~ good nor**
**bad** ni bon ni mauvais; **~ did I refuse** (et or
mais) je n'ai pas non plus refusé; **~ of them** ni
l'un ni l'autre
**neo...** ['niːəʊ] prefix néo-
**neolithic** [niːəʊ'lɪθɪk] adj néolithique
**neologism** [nɪ'ɔlədʒɪzəm] n néologisme m
**neon** ['niːɔn] n néon m
**neon light** n lampe f au néon
**neon sign** n enseigne f (lumineuse) au néon
**Nepal** [nɪ'pɔːl] n Népal m
**nephew** ['nɛvjuː] n neveu m
**nepotism** ['nɛpətɪzəm] n népotisme m
**nerd** [nəːd] n (inf) pauvre mec m, ballot m
**nerve** [nəːv] n nerf m; (bravery) sang-froid m,
courage m; (cheek) aplomb m, toupet m; **nerves**
npl nervosité f; **he gets on my ~s** il m'énerve;
**to have a fit of ~s** avoir le trac; **to lose one's ~**
(self-confidence) perdre son sang-froid
**nerve centre** n (Anat) centre nerveux; (fig)
centre névralgique
**nerve gas** n gaz m neuroplégique
**nerve-racking** ['nəːvrækɪŋ] adj angoissant(e)
**nervous** ['nəːvəs] adj nerveux(-euse); (anxious)
inquiet(-ète), plein(e) d'appréhension; (timid)
intimidé(e)
**nervous breakdown** n dépression nerveuse
**nervously** ['nəːvəslɪ] adv nerveusement

**nervousness** ['nəːvəsnɪs] n nervosité f;
inquiétude f, appréhension f
**nervous wreck** n: **to be a ~** être une boule de
nerfs
**nervy** ['nəːvɪ] adj: **he's very ~** il a les nerfs à fleur
de peau or à vif
**nest** [nɛst] n nid m ▷ vi (se) nicher, faire son nid;
**~ of tables** table f gigogne
**nest egg** n (fig) bas m de laine, magot m
**nestle** ['nɛsl] vi se blottir
**nestling** ['nɛstlɪŋ] n oisillon m
**Net** [nɛt] n (Comput): **the ~** (Internet) le Net
**net** [nɛt] n filet m; (fabric) tulle f ▷ adj net(te) ▷ vt
(fish etc) prendre au filet; (money: person) toucher;
(: deal, sale) rapporter; **~ of tax** net d'impôt; **he**
**earns £10,000 ~ per year** il gagne 10 000 livres
net par an
**netball** ['nɛtbɔːl] n netball m
**net curtains** npl voilages mpl
**Netherlands** ['nɛðələndz] npl: **the ~** les Pays-
Bas mpl
**netiquette** ['nɛtɪkɛt] n netiquette f
**net profit** n bénéfice net
**nett** [nɛt] adj = **net**
**netting** ['nɛtɪŋ] n (for fence etc) treillis m, grillage
m; (fabric) voile m
**nettle** ['nɛtl] n ortie f
**network** ['nɛtwəːk] n réseau m ▷ vt (Radio, TV)
diffuser sur l'ensemble du réseau; (computers)
interconnecter; **there's no ~ coverage here**
(Tel) il n'y a pas de réseau ici
**neuralgia** [njuə'rældʒə] n névralgie f
**neurological** [njuərə'lɔdʒɪkl] adj neurologique
**neurosis** (pl **neuroses**) [njuə'rəusɪs, -siːz] n
névrose f
**neurotic** [njuə'rɔtɪk] adj, n névrosé(e)
**neuter** ['njuːtə<sup>r</sup>] adj neutre ▷ n neutre m ▷ vt
(cat etc) châtrer, couper
**neutral** ['njuːtrəl] adj neutre ▷ n (Aut) point
mort
**neutrality** [njuː'trælɪtɪ] n neutralité f
**neutralize** ['njuːtrəlaɪz] vt neutraliser
**neutron bomb** ['njuːtrɔn-] n bombe f à neutrons
**Nev.** abbr (US) = **Nevada**
**never** ['nɛvə<sup>r</sup>] adv (ne ...) jamais; **I ~ went** je n'y
suis pas allé; **I've ~ been to Spain** je ne suis
jamais allé en Espagne; **~ again** plus jamais; **~**
**in my life** jamais de ma vie; see also **mind**
**never-ending** [nɛvər'ɛndɪŋ] adj interminable
**nevertheless** [nɛvəðə'lɛs] adv néanmoins,
malgré tout
**new** [njuː] adj nouveau (nouvelle); (brand new)
neuf (neuve); **as good as ~** comme neuf
**New Age** n New Age m
**newbie** ['njuːbɪ] n (beginner) newbie m/f; (on
forum) nouveau(-elle)
**newborn** ['njuːbɔːn] adj nouveau-né(e)
**newcomer** ['njuːkʌmə<sup>r</sup>] n nouveau venu
(nouvelle venue)
**new-fangled** ['njuːfæŋgld] adj (pej)
ultramoderne (et farfelu(e))
**new-found** ['njuːfaund] adj de fraîche date;

**n**

(*friend*) nouveau (nouvelle)

**Newfoundland** ['nju:fənlənd] *n* Terre-Neuve *f*

**New Guinea** *n* Nouvelle-Guinée *f*

**newly** ['nju:lɪ] *adv* nouvellement, récemment

**newly-weds** ['nju:lɪwɛdz] *npl* jeunes mariés *mpl*

**new moon** *n* nouvelle lune

**newness** ['nju:nɪs] *n* nouveauté *f*; (*of fabric, clothes etc*) état neuf

**New Orleans** [-'ɔ:li:ənz] *n* la Nouvelle-Orléans

**news** [nju:z] *n* nouvelle(s) *f(pl)*; (*Radio, TV*) informations *fpl*, actualités *fpl*; **a piece of ~** une nouvelle; **good/bad ~** bonne/mauvaise nouvelle; **financial ~** (*Press, Radio, TV*) page financière

**news agency** *n* agence *f* de presse

**newsagent** ['nju:zeɪdʒənt] *n* (*Brit*) marchand *m* de journaux

**news bulletin** *n* (*Radio TV*) bulletin *m* d'informations

**newscaster** ['nju:zkɑ:stə<sup>r</sup>] *n* (*Radio, TV*) présentateur(-trice)

**news flash** *n* flash *m* d'information

**newsletter** ['nju:zlɛtə<sup>r</sup>] *n* bulletin *m*

**newspaper** ['nju:zpeɪpə<sup>r</sup>] *n* journal *m*; **daily ~** quotidien *m*; **weekly ~** hebdomadaire *m*

**newsprint** ['nju:zprɪnt] *n* papier *m* (de) journal

**newsreader** ['nju:zri:də<sup>r</sup>] *n* = **newscaster**

**newsreel** ['nju:zri:l] *n* actualités (filmées)

**newsroom** ['nju:zru:m] *n* (*Press*) salle *f* de rédaction; (*Radio, TV*) studio *m*

**news stand** *n* kiosque *m* à journaux

**newsworthy** ['nju:zwə:ðɪ] *adj*: **to be ~** valoir la peine d'être publié

**newt** [nju:t] *n* triton *m*

**new town** *n* (*Brit*) ville nouvelle

**New Year** *n* Nouvel An; **Happy ~!** Bonne Année!; **to wish sb a happy ~** souhaiter la Bonne Année à qn

**New Year's Day** *n* le jour de l'An

**New Year's Eve** *n* la Saint-Sylvestre

**New York** [-'jɔ:k] *n* New York; (*also*: **New York State**) New York *m*

**New Zealand** [-'zi:lənd] *n* Nouvelle-Zélande *f* ▷ *adj* néo-zélandais(e)

**New Zealander** [-'zi:ləndə<sup>r</sup>] *n* Néo-Zélandais(e)

**next** [nɛkst] *adj* (*in time*) prochain(e); (*seat, room*) voisin(e), d'à côté; (*meeting, bus stop*) suivant(e) ▷ *adv* la fois suivante; la prochaine fois; (*afterwards*) ensuite; **~ to** (*prep*) à côté de; **~ to nothing** presque rien; **~ time** (*adv*) la prochaine fois; **the ~ day** le lendemain, le jour suivant or d'après; **~ week** la semaine prochaine; **the ~ week** la semaine suivante; **~ year** l'année prochaine; **"turn to the ~ page"** "voir page suivante"; **~ please!** (*at doctor's etc*) au suivant!; **who's ~?** c'est à qui?; **the week after ~** dans deux semaines; **when do we meet ~?** quand nous revoyons-nous?

**next door** *adv* à côté ▷ *adj* (*neighbour*) d'à côté

**next-of-kin** ['nɛkstəv'kɪn] *n* parent *m* le plus proche

**NF** *n abbr* (*Brit Pol*: = *National Front*) ≈ FN ▷ *abbr*

(*Canada*) = **Newfoundland**

**NFL** *n abbr* (*US*) = **National Football League**

**Nfld.** *abbr* (*Canada*) = **Newfoundland**

**NG** *abbr* (*US*) = **National Guard**

**NGO** *n abbr* (*US*: = *non-governmental organization*) ONG *f*

**NH** *abbr* (*US*) = **New Hampshire**

**NHL** *n abbr* (*US*) = **National Hockey League**

**NHS** *n abbr* (*Brit*) = **National Health Service**

**NI** *abbr* = **Northern Ireland**; (*Brit*) = **National Insurance**

**Niagara Falls** [naɪˈægərə-] *npl*: **the ~** les chutes *fpl* du Niagara

**nib** [nɪb] *n* (*of pen*) (bec *m* de) plume *f*

**nibble** ['nɪbl] *vt* grignoter

**Nicaragua** [nɪkəˈrægjuə] *n* Nicaragua *m*

**Nicaraguan** [nɪkəˈrægjuən] *adj* nicaraguayen(ne) ▷ *n* Nicaraguayen(ne)

**nice** [naɪs] *adj* (*holiday, trip, taste*) agréable; (*flat, picture*) joli(e); (*person*) gentil(le); (*distinction, point*) subtil(e)

**nice-looking** ['naɪslukɪŋ] *adj* joli(e)

**nicely** ['naɪslɪ] *adv* agréablement; joliment; gentiment; subtilement; **that will do ~** ce sera parfait

**niceties** ['naɪsɪtɪz] *npl* subtilités *fpl*

**niche** [ni:ʃ] *n* (*Archit*) niche *f*

**nick** [nɪk] *n* (*indentation*) encoche *f*; (*wound*) entaille *f*; (*Brit inf*): **in good ~** en bon état ▷ *vt* (*cut*): **to ~ o.s.** se couper; (*inf: steal*) faucher, piquer; (: *Brit: arrest*) choper, pincer; **in the ~ of time** juste à temps

**nickel** ['nɪkl] *n* nickel *m*; (*US*) pièce *f* de 5 cents

**nickname** ['nɪkneɪm] *n* surnom *m* ▷ *vt* surnommer

**Nicosia** [nɪkəˈsi:ə] *n* Nicosie

**nicotine** ['nɪkəti:n] *n* nicotine *f*

**nicotine patch** *n* timbre *m* anti-tabac, patch *m*

**niece** [ni:s] *n* nièce *f*

**nifty** ['nɪftɪ] *adj* (*inf: car, jacket*) qui a du chic or de la classe; (: *gadget, tool*) astucieux(-euse)

**Niger** ['naɪdʒə<sup>r</sup>] *n* (*country, river*) Niger *m*

**Nigeria** [naɪˈdʒɪərɪə] *n* Nigéria *m or f*

**Nigerian** [naɪˈdʒɪərɪən] *adj* nigérien(ne) ▷ *n* Nigérien(ne)

**niggardly** ['nɪgədlɪ] *adj* (*person*) parcimonieux(-euse), pingre; (*allowance, amount*) misérable

**nigger** ['nɪgə<sup>r</sup>] *n* (*inf!: highly offensive*) nègre (négresse)

**niggle** ['nɪgl] *vt* tracasser ▷ *vi* (*find fault*) trouver toujours à redire; (*fuss*) n'être jamais content(e)

**niggling** ['nɪglɪŋ] *adj* tatillon(ne); (*detail*) insignifiant(e); (*doubt, pain*) persistant(e)

**night** [naɪt] *n* nuit *f*; (*evening*) soir *m*; **at ~** la nuit; **by ~** de nuit; **in the ~, during the ~** pendant la nuit; **last ~** (*evening*) hier soir; (*night-time*) la nuit dernière; **the ~ before last** avant-hier soir

**night-bird** ['naɪtbə:d] *n* oiseau *m* nocturne; (*fig*) couche-tard *m inv*, noctambule *m/f*

**nightcap** ['naɪtkæp] *n* boisson prise avant le coucher

**nightclub** *n* boîte *f* de nuit

**nightdress** ['naɪtdrɛs] *n* chemise *f* de nuit
**nightfall** ['naɪtfɔːl] *n* tombée *f* de la nuit
**nightie** ['naɪtɪ] *n* chemise *f* de nuit
**nightingale** ['naɪtɪŋɡeɪl] *n* rossignol *m*
**nightlife** ['naɪtlaɪf] *n* vie *f* nocturne
**nightly** ['naɪtlɪ] *adj* (*news*) du soir; (*by night*)
nocturne ▷ *adv* (*every evening*) tous les soirs;
(*every night*) toutes les nuits
**nightmare** ['naɪtmɛəʳ] *n* cauchemar *m*
**night porter** *n* gardien *m* de nuit, concierge *m*
de service la nuit
**night safe** *n* coffre *m* de nuit
**night school** *n* cours *mpl* du soir
**nightshade** ['naɪtʃeɪd] *n*: **deadly ~** (*Bot*)
belladone *f*
**night shift** ['naɪtʃɪft] *n* équipe *f* de nuit
**night-time** ['naɪttaɪm] *n* nuit *f*
**night watchman** (*irreg*) *n* veilleur *m* de nuit;
poste *m* de nuit
**nihilism** ['naɪɪlɪzəm] *n* nihilisme *m*
**nil** [nɪl] *n* rien *m*; (*Brit Sport*) zéro *m*
**Nile** [naɪl] *n*: **the ~** le Nil
**nimble** ['nɪmbl] *adj* agile
**nine** [naɪn] *num* neuf
**nineteen** ['naɪn'tiːn] *num* dix-neuf
**nineteenth** [naɪn'tiːnθ] *num* dix-neuvième
**ninetieth** ['naɪntɪɪθ] *num* quatre-vingt-dixième
**ninety** ['naɪntɪ] *num* quatre-vingt-dix
**ninth** [naɪnθ] *num* neuvième
**nip** [nɪp] *vt* pincer ▷ *vi* (*Brit inf*): **to ~ out/down/
up** sortir/descendre/monter en vitesse ▷ *n*
pincement *m*; (*drink*) petit verre; **to ~ into a
shop** faire un saut dans un magasin
**nipple** ['nɪpl] *n* (*Anat*) mamelon *m*, bout *m* du
sein
**nippy** ['nɪpɪ] *adj* (*Brit: person*) alerte, leste; (: *car*)
nerveux(-euse)
**nit** [nɪt] *n* (*in hair*) lente *f*; (*inf: idiot*) imbécile *m/f*,
crétin(e)
**nit-pick** ['nɪtpɪk] *vi* (*inf*) être tatillon(ne)
**nitrogen** ['naɪtrədʒən] *n* azote *m*
**nitroglycerin, nitroglycerine** ['naɪtrəʊ'ɡlɪsəri:
n] *n* nitroglycérine *f*
**nitty-gritty** ['nɪtɪ'ɡrɪtɪ] *n* (*fam*): **to get down to
the ~** en venir au fond du problème
**nitwit** ['nɪtwɪt] *n* (*inf*) nigaud(e)
**NJ** *abbr* (*US*) = **New Jersey**
**NLF** *n abbr* (= *National Liberation Front*) FLN *m*
**NLQ** *abbr* (= *near letter quality*) qualité *f* courrier
**NLRB** *n abbr* (*US*: = *National Labor Relations Board*)
*organisme de protection des travailleurs*
**NM, N. Mex.** *abbr* (*US*) = **New Mexico**

⊙ KEYWORD

**no** [nəʊ] (*pl* **noes**) *adv* (*opposite of "yes"*) non; **are
you coming? — no (I'm not)** est-ce que vous
venez? — non; **would you like some more? —
no thank you** vous en voulez encore? — non
merci
▷ *adj* (*not any*) (ne ...) pas de, (ne ...) aucun(e); **I
have no money/books** je n'ai pas d'argent/de

livres; **no student would have done it** aucun
étudiant ne l'aurait fait; **"no smoking"**
"défense de fumer"; **"no dogs"** "les chiens ne
sont pas admis"
▷ *n* non *m*; **I won't take no for an answer** il
n'est pas question de refuser

**no.** *abbr* (= *number*) n°
**nobble** ['nɔbl] *vt* (*Brit inf: bribe: person*) soudoyer,
acheter; (: *person: to speak to*) mettre le grappin
sur; (*Racing: horse, dog*) droguer (*pour l'empêcher de
gagner*)
**Nobel prize** [nəʊ'bɛl-] *n* prix *m* Nobel
**nobility** [nəʊ'bɪlɪtɪ] *n* noblesse *f*
**noble** ['nəʊbl] *adj* noble
**nobleman** ['nəʊblmən] (*irreg*) *n* noble *m*
**nobly** ['nəʊblɪ] *adv* noblement
**nobody** ['nəʊbədɪ] *pron* (ne ...) personne
**no-claims bonus** ['nəʊkleɪmz-] *n* bonus *m*
**nocturnal** [nɔk'təːnl] *adj* nocturne
**nod** [nɔd] *vi* faire un signe de (la) tête (*affirmatif
ou amical*); (*sleep*) somnoler ▷ *vt*: **to ~ one's head**
faire un signe de (la) tête; (*in agreement*) faire
signe que oui ▷ *n* signe *m* de (la) tête; **they
~ded their agreement** ils ont acquiescé d'un
signe de la tête
▷ **nod off** *vi* s'assoupir
**no-fly zone** [nəʊ'flaɪ-] *n* zone interdite (*aux
avions et hélicoptères*)
**noise** [nɔɪz] *n* bruit *m*; **I can't sleep for the ~** je
n'arrive pas à dormir à cause du bruit
**noiseless** ['nɔɪzlɪs] *adj* silencieux(-euse)
**noisily** ['nɔɪzɪlɪ] *adv* bruyamment
**noisy** ['nɔɪzɪ] *adj* bruyant(e)
**nomad** ['nəʊmæd] *n* nomade *m/f*
**nomadic** [nəʊ'mædɪk] *adj* nomade
**no man's land** *n* no man's land *m*
**nominal** ['nɔmɪnl] *adj* (*rent, fee*) symbolique;
(*value*) nominal(e)
**nominate** ['nɔmɪneɪt] *vt* (*propose*) proposer;
(*appoint*) nommer
**nomination** [nɔmɪ'neɪʃən] *n* nomination *f*
**nominee** [nɔmɪ'niː] *n* candidat agréé; personne
nommée
**non-** [nɔn] *prefix* non-
**nonalcoholic** [nɔnælkə'hɔlɪk] *adj* non
alcoolisé(e)
**nonbreakable** [nɔn'breɪkəbl] *adj* incassable
**nonce word** ['nɔns-] *n* mot créé pour l'occasion
**nonchalant** ['nɔnʃələnt] *adj* nonchalant(e)
**non-commissioned** [nɔnkə'mɪʃənd] *adj*: **~
officer** sous-officier *m*
**noncommittal** [nɔnkə'mɪtl] *adj* évasif(-ive)
**nonconformist** [nɔnkən'fɔːmɪst] *n* non-
conformiste *m/f* ▷ *adj* non-conformiste,
dissident(e)
**noncooperation** ['nɔnkəʊɔpə'reɪʃən] *n* refus *m*
de coopérer, non-coopération *f*
**nondescript** ['nɔndɪskrɪpt] *adj* quelconque,
indéfinissable
**none** [nʌn] *pron* aucun(e); **~ of you** aucun
d'entre vous, personne parmi vous; **I have ~** je

**n**

n'en ai pas; **I have ~ left** je n'en ai plus; **~ at all**
(*not one*) aucun(e); **how much milk? ~ — ~ at all**
combien de lait? — pas du tout; **he's ~ the**
**worse for it** il ne s'en porte pas plus mal
**nonentity** [nɔ'nɛntɪtɪ] *n* personne
insignifiante
**nonessential** [nɔnɪ'sɛnʃl] *adj* accessoire,
superflu(e) ▷ *n*: **~s** le superflu
**nonetheless** ['nʌnðə'lɛs] *adv* néanmoins
**nonevent** [nɔnɪ'vɛnt] *n* événement manqué
**nonexecutive** [nɔnɪg'zɛkjutɪv] *adj*: **~ director**
administrateur(-trice), conseiller(-ère) de
direction
**nonexistent** [nɔnɪg'zɪstənt] *adj* inexistant(e)
**non-fiction** [nɔn'fɪkʃən] *n* littérature *f* non
romanesque
**nonintervention** ['nɔnɪntə'vɛnʃən] *n* non-
intervention *f*
**no-no** ['nəunəu] *n* (*inf*): **it's a ~** il n'en est pas
question
**non obst.** *abbr* (= *non obstante: notwithstanding*)
nonobstant
**no-nonsense** [nəu'nɔnsəns] *adj* (*manner, person*)
plein(e) de bon sens
**nonpayment** [nɔn'peɪmənt] *n* non-paiement *m*
**nonplussed** [nɔn'plʌst] *adj* perplexe
**non-profit-making** [nɔn'prɔfɪtmeɪkɪŋ] *adj* à
but non lucratif
**nonsense** ['nɔnsəns] *n* absurdités *fpl*, idioties
*fpl*; **~!** ne dites pas d'idioties!; **it is ~ to say that**
... il est absurde de dire que ....
**nonsensical** [nɔn'sɛnsɪkl] *adj* absurde, qui n'a
pas de sens
**non-smoker** ['nɔn'sməukə'] *n* non-fumeur *m*
**non-smoking** ['nɔn'sməukɪŋ] *adj* non-fumeur
**nonstarter** [nɔn'stɑːtə'] *n*: **it`s a ~** c'est voué à
l'échec
**non-stick** ['nɔn'stɪk] *adj* qui n'attache pas
**nonstop** ['nɔn'stɔp] *adj* direct(e), sans arrêt (*or*
*escale*) ▷ *adv* sans arrêt
**nontaxable** [nɔn'tæksəbl] *adj*: **~ income**
revenu *m* non imposable
**non-U** ['nɔnjuː] *adj abbr* (*Brit inf*: = *non-upper class*)
qui ne se dit (*or* se fait) pas
**nonvolatile** [nɔn'vɔlətaɪl] *adj*: **~ memory**
(*Comput*) mémoire rémanente *or* non volatile
**nonvoting** [nɔn'vəutɪŋ] *adj*: **~ shares** actions *fpl*
sans droit de vote
**non-white** ['nɔn'waɪt] *adj* de couleur ▷ *n*
personne *f* de couleur
**noodles** ['nuːdlz] *npl* nouilles *fpl*
**nook** [nuk] *n*: **~s and crannies** recoins *mpl*
**noon** [nuːn] *n* midi *m*
**no-one** ['nəuwʌn] *pron* = **nobody**
**noose** [nuːs] *n* nœud coulant; (*hangman's*)
corde *f*
**nor** [nɔː'] *conj* = **neither** ▷ *adv* see **neither**
**norm** [nɔːm] *n* norme *f*
**normal** ['nɔːml] *adj* normal(e) ▷ *n*: **to return to**
**~** redevenir normal(e)
**normality** [nɔː'mælɪtɪ] *n* normalité *f*
**normally** ['nɔːməlɪ] *adv* normalement

**Normandy** ['nɔːməndɪ] *n* Normandie *f*
**north** [nɔːθ] *n* nord *m* ▷ *adj* nord *inv*; (*wind*) du
nord ▷ *adv* au *or* vers le nord
**North Africa** *n* Afrique *f* du Nord
**North African** *adj* nord-africain(e), d'Afrique du
Nord ▷ *n* Nord-Africain(e)
**North America** *n* Amérique *f* du Nord
**North American** *n* Nord-Américain(e) ▷ *adj*
nord-américain(e), d'Amérique du Nord
**Northants** [nɔː'θænts] *abbr* (*Brit*)
= **Northamptonshire**
**northbound** ['nɔːθbaund] *adj* (*traffic*) en
direction du nord; (*carriageway*) nord *inv*
**north-east** [nɔːθ'iːst] *n* nord-est *m*
**northerly** ['nɔːðəlɪ] *adj* (*wind, direction*) du nord
**northern** ['nɔːðən] *adj* du nord, septentrional(e)
**Northern Ireland** *n* Irlande *f* du Nord
**North Korea** *n* Corée *f* du Nord
**North Pole** *n*: **the ~** le pôle Nord
**North Sea** *n*: **the ~** la mer du Nord
**North Sea oil** *n* pétrole *m* de la mer du Nord
**northward** ['nɔːθwəd], **northwards** ['nɔː
θwədz] *adv* vers le nord
**north-west** [nɔːθ'wɛst] *n* nord-ouest *m*
**Norway** ['nɔːweɪ] *n* Norvège *f*
**Norwegian** [nɔː'wiːdʒən] *adj* norvégien(ne) ▷ *n*
Norvégien(ne); (*Ling*) norvégien *m*
**nos.** *abbr* (= *numbers*) $n^{os}$
**nose** [nəuz] *n* nez *m*; (*of dog, cat*) museau *m*; (*fig*)
flair *m* ▷ *vi* (*also*: **nose one's way**) avancer
précautionneusement; **to pay through the ~**
**(for sth)** (*inf*) payer un prix excessif (pour qch)
▶ **nose about, nose around** *vi* fouiner *or* fureter
(partout)
**nosebleed** ['nəuzbliːd] *n* saignement *m* de nez
**nose-dive** ['nəuzdaɪv] *n* (descente *f* en) piqué *m*
**nose drops** *npl* gouttes *fpl* pour le nez
**nosey** ['nəuzɪ] *adj* (*inf*) curieux(-euse)
**nostalgia** [nɔs'tældʒɪə] *n* nostalgie *f*
**nostalgic** [nɔs'tældʒɪk] *adj* nostalgique
**nostril** ['nɔstrɪl] *n* narine *f*; (*of horse*) naseau *m*
**nosy** ['nəuzɪ] (*inf*) *adj* = **nosey**
**not** [nɔt] *adv* (ne ...) pas; **he is ~ or isn't here** il
n'est pas ici; **you must ~ or mustn't do that** tu
ne dois pas faire ça; **I hope ~** j'espère que non; **~**
**at all** pas du tout; (*after thanks*) de rien; **it's too**
**late, isn't it?** c'est trop tard, n'est-ce pas?; **~**
**yet/now** pas encore/maintenant; *see also* **only**
**notable** ['nəutəbl] *adj* notable
**notably** ['nəutəblɪ] *adv* (*particularly*) en
particulier; (*markedly*) spécialement
**notary** ['nəutərɪ] *n* (*also*: **notary public**)
notaire *m*
**notation** [nəu'teɪʃən] *n* notation *f*
**notch** [nɔtʃ] *n* encoche *f*
▶ **notch up** *vt* (*score*) marquer; (*victory*)
remporter
**note** [nəut] *n* note *f*; (*letter*) mot *m*; (*banknote*)
billet *m* ▷ *vt* (*also*: **note down**) noter; (*notice*)
constater; **just a quick ~ to let you know ...**
juste un mot pour vous dire ...; **to take ~s**
prendre des notes; **to compare ~s** (*fig*)

échanger des (or leurs etc) impressions; **to take ~ of** prendre note de; **a person of ~** une personne éminente

**notebook** ['nəʊtbʊk] n carnet m; (for shorthand etc) bloc-notes m

**note-case** ['nəʊtkeɪs] n (Brit) porte-feuille m

**noted** ['nəʊtɪd] adj réputé(e)

**notepad** ['nəʊtpæd] n bloc-notes m

**notepaper** ['nəʊtpeɪpəʳ] n papier m à lettres

**noteworthy** ['nəʊtwɜːðɪ] adj remarquable

**nothing** ['nʌθɪŋ] n rien m; **he does ~** il ne fait rien; **~ new** rien de nouveau; **for ~** (free) pour rien, gratuitement; (in vain) pour rien; **~ at all** rien du tout; **~ much** pas grand-chose

**notice** ['nəʊtɪs] n (announcement, warning) avis m; (of leaving) congé m; (Brit: review: of play etc) critique f, compte rendu m ▷ vt remarquer, s'apercevoir de; **without ~** sans préavis; **advance ~** préavis m; **to give sb ~ of sth** notifier qn de qch; **at short ~** dans un délai très court; **until further ~** jusqu'à nouvel ordre; **to give ~, hand in one's ~** (employee) donner sa démission, démissionner; **to take ~ of** prêter attention à; **to bring sth to sb's ~** porter qch à la connaissance de qn; **it has come to my ~ that ...** on m'a signalé que ...; **to escape** or **avoid ~** (essayer de) passer inaperçu or ne pas se faire remarquer

**noticeable** ['nəʊtɪsəbl] adj visible

**notice board** n (Brit) panneau m d'affichage

**notification** [nəʊtɪfɪ'keɪʃən] n notification f

**notify** ['nəʊtɪfaɪ] vt: **to ~ sth to sb** notifier qch à qn; **to ~ sb of sth** avertir qn de qch

**notion** ['nəʊʃən] n idée f; (concept) notion f; **notions** npl (US: haberdashery) mercerie f

**notoriety** [nəʊtə'raɪətɪ] n notoriété f

**notorious** [nəʊ'tɔːrɪəs] adj notoire (souvent en mal)

**notoriously** [nəʊ'tɔːrɪəslɪ] adj notoirement

**Notts** [nɒts] abbr (Brit) = **Nottinghamshire**

**notwithstanding** [nɒtwɪθ'stændɪŋ] adv néanmoins ▷ prep en dépit de

**nougat** ['nuːgɑː] n nougat m

**nought** [nɔːt] n zéro m

**noun** [naʊn] n nom m

**nourish** ['nʌrɪʃ] vt nourrir

**nourishing** ['nʌrɪʃɪŋ] adj nourrissant(e)

**nourishment** ['nʌrɪʃmənt] n nourriture f

**Nov.** abbr (= November) nov

**Nova Scotia** ['nəʊvə'skəʊʃə] n Nouvelle-Écosse f

**novel** ['nɒvl] n roman m ▷ adj nouveau (nouvelle), original(e)

**novelist** ['nɒvəlɪst] n romancier m

**novelty** ['nɒvəltɪ] n nouveauté f

**November** [nəʊ'vɛmbəʳ] n novembre m; for phrases see also **July**

**novice** ['nɒvɪs] n novice m/f

**NOW** [naʊ] n abbr (US) = **National Organization for Women**

**now** [naʊ] adv maintenant ▷ conj: **~ (that)** maintenant (que); **right ~** tout de suite; **by ~** à l'heure qu'il est; **just ~** (: ): **that's the fashion**

**just ~** c'est la mode en ce moment or maintenant; **I saw her just ~** je viens de la voir, je l'ai vue à l'instant; **I'll read it just ~** je vais le lire à l'instant or dès maintenant; **~ and then, ~ and again** de temps en temps; **from ~ on** dorénavant; **in 3 days from ~** dans or d'ici trois jours; **between ~ and Monday** d'ici (à) lundi; **that's all for ~** c'est tout pour l'instant

**nowadays** ['naʊədeɪz] adv de nos jours

**nowhere** ['nəʊwɛəʳ] adv (ne ...) nulle part; **~ else** nulle part ailleurs

**no-win situation** [nəʊ'wɪn-] n impasse f; **we're in a ~** nous sommes dans l'impasse

**noxious** ['nɒkʃəs] adj toxique

**nozzle** ['nɒzl] n (of hose) jet m, lance f; (of vacuum cleaner) suceur m

**NP** n abbr = **notary public**

**nr** abbr (Brit) = **near**

**NS** abbr (Canada) = **Nova Scotia**

**NSC** n abbr (US) = **National Security Council**

**NSF** n abbr (US) = **National Science Foundation**

**NSPCC** n abbr (Brit) = **National Society for the Prevention of Cruelty to Children**

**NSW** abbr (Australia) = **New South Wales**

**NT** n abbr (= New Testament) NT m ▷ abbr (Canada) = **Northwest Territories**

**nth** [ɛnθ] adj: **for the ~ time** (inf) pour la énième fois

**nuance** ['njuːɑːns] n nuance f

**nubile** ['njuːbaɪl] adj nubile; (attractive) jeune et désirable

**nuclear** ['njuːklɪəʳ] adj nucléaire

**nuclear disarmament** n désarmement m nucléaire

**nuclear family** n famille f nucléaire

**nuclear-free zone** ['njuːklɪə'friː-] n zone f où le nucléaire est interdit

**nucleus** (pl **nuclei**) ['njuːklɪəs, 'njuːklɪaɪ] n noyau m

**NUCPS** n abbr (Brit: = National Union of Civil and Public Servants) syndicat des fonctionnaires

**nude** [njuːd] adj nu(e) ▷ n (Art) nu m; **in the ~** (tout(e)) nu(e)

**nudge** [nʌdʒ] vt donner un (petit) coup de coude à

**nudist** ['njuːdɪst] n nudiste m/f

**nudist colony** n colonie f de nudistes

**nudity** ['njuːdɪtɪ] n nudité f

**nugget** ['nʌgɪt] n pépite f

**nuisance** ['njuːsns] n: **it's a ~** c'est (très) ennuyeux or gênant; **he's a ~** il est assommant or casse-pieds; **what a ~!** quelle barbe!

**NUJ** n abbr (Brit: = National Union of Journalists) syndicat des journalistes

**nuke** [njuːk] n (inf) bombe f atomique

**null** [nʌl] adj: **~ and void** nul(le) et non avenu(e)

**nullify** ['nʌlɪfaɪ] vt invalider

**NUM** n abbr (Brit: = National Union of Mineworkers) syndicat des mineurs

**numb** [nʌm] adj engourdi(e); (with fear) paralysé(e) ▷ vt engourdir; **~ with cold** engourdi(e) par le froid, transi(e) (de froid); **~**

**n**

**with fear** transi de peur, paralysé(e) par la peur
**number** ['nʌmbəʳ] n nombre m; (numeral) chiffre
m; (of house, car, telephone, newspaper) numéro m
▷ vt numéroter; (amount to) compter; **a ~ of** un
certain nombre de; **they were seven in ~** ils
étaient (au nombre de) sept; **to be ~ed among**
compter parmi; **the staff ~s 20** le nombre
d'employés s'élève à or est de 20; **wrong ~** (Tel)
mauvais numéro
**numbered account** ['nʌmbəd-] n (in bank)
compte numéroté
**number plate** n (Brit Aut) plaque f
minéralogique or d'immatriculation
**Number Ten** n (Brit: 10 Downing Street) résidence du
Premier ministre
**numbness** ['nʌmnɪs] n torpeur f; (due to cold)
engourdissement m
**numbskull** ['nʌmskʌl] n (inf) gourde f
**numeral** ['nju:mərəl] n chiffre m
**numerate** ['nju:mərɪt] adj (Brit): **to be ~** avoir
des notions d'arithmétique
**numerical** [nju:'mɛrɪkl] adj numérique
**numerous** ['nju:mərəs] adj nombreux(-euse)
**nun** [nʌn] n religieuse f, sœur f
**nunnery** ['nʌnərɪ] n couvent m
**nuptial** ['nʌpʃəl] adj nuptial(e)
**nurse** [nə:s] n infirmière f; (also: **nursemaid**)
bonne f d'enfants ▷ vt (patient, cold) soigner;
(baby: Brit) bercer (dans ses bras); (: US) allaiter,
nourrir; (hope) nourrir
**nursery** ['nə:sərɪ] n (room) nursery f; (institution)
crèche f, garderie f; (for plants) pépinière f
**nursery rhyme** n comptine f, chansonnette f
pour enfants
**nursery school** n école maternelle
**nursery slope** n (Brit Ski) piste f pour débutants
**nursing** ['nə:sɪŋ] n (profession) profession f
d'infirmière; (care) soins mpl ▷ adj (mother) qui
allaite
**nursing home** n clinique f; (for convalescence)
maison f de convalescence or de repos; (for old
people) maison de retraite

**nurture** ['nə:tʃəʳ] vt élever
**NUS** n abbr (Brit: = National Union of Students)
syndicat des étudiants
**NUT** n abbr (Brit: = National Union of Teachers)
syndicat enseignant
**nut** [nʌt] n (of metal) écrou m; (fruit: walnut) noix f;
(: hazelnut) noisette f; (: peanut) cacahuète f (terme
générique en anglais) ▷ adj (chocolate etc) aux
noisettes; **he's ~s** (inf) il est dingue
**nutcase** ['nʌtkeɪs] n (inf) dingue m/f
**nutcrackers** ['nʌtkrækəz] npl casse-noix m inv,
casse-noisette(s) m
**nutmeg** ['nʌtmɛg] n (noix f) muscade f
**nutrient** ['nju:trɪənt] adj nutritif(-ive) ▷ n
substance nutritive
**nutrition** [nju:'trɪʃən] n nutrition f,
alimentation f
**nutritionist** [nju:'trɪʃənɪst] n nutritionniste m/f
**nutritious** [nju:'trɪʃəs] adj nutritif(-ive),
nourrissant(e)
**nuts** [nʌts] (inf) adj dingue
**nutshell** ['nʌtʃɛl] n coquille f de noix; **in a ~** en
un mot
**nutter** ['nʌtəʳ] (Brit: inf) n: **he's a complete ~** il
est complètement cinglé
**nutty** ['nʌtɪ] adj (flavour) à la noisette; (inf: person)
cinglé(e), dingue
**nuzzle** ['nʌzl] vi: **to ~ up to** fourrer son nez
contre
**NV** abbr (US) = **Nevada**
**NVQ** n abbr (Brit) = **National Vocational
Qualification**
**NWT** abbr (Canada) = **Northwest Territories**
**NY** abbr (US) = **New York**
**NYC** abbr (US) = **New York City**
**nylon** ['naɪlɔn] n nylon m ▷ adj de or en nylon;
**nylons** npl bas mpl nylon
**nymph** [nɪmf] n nymphe f
**nymphomaniac** ['nɪmfəu'meɪnɪæk] adj, n
nymphomane f
**NYSE** n abbr (US) = **New York Stock Exchange**
**NZ** abbr = **New Zealand**

# Oo

**O, o** [əʊ] *n* (*letter*) O, o *m*; (*US Scol*: = *outstanding*) tb
(= *très bien*); **O for Oliver**, (*US*) **O for Oboe** O
comme Oscar
**oaf** [əʊf] *n* balourd *m*
**oak** [əʊk] *n* chêne *m* ▷ *cpd* de *or* en (bois de)
chêne
**O&M** *n abbr* = **organization and method**
**O.A.P.** *n abbr* (*Brit*) = **old age pensioner**
**oar** [ɔːʳ] *n* aviron *m*, rame *f*; **to put** *or* **shove**
**one's ~ in** (*fig*: *inf*) mettre son grain de sel
**oarsman** ['ɔːzmən], **oarswoman** ['ɔːzwumən]
(*irreg*) *n* rameur(-euse); (*Naut*, *Sport*)
nageur(-euse)
**OAS** *n abbr* (= *Organization of American States*) OEA *f*
(= *Organisation des États américains*)
**oasis** (*pl* **oases**) [əʊ'eɪsɪs, əʊ'eɪsiːz] *n* oasis *f*
**oath** [əʊθ] *n* serment *m*; (*swear word*) juron *m*; **to**
**take the ~** prêter serment; **on** (*Brit*) *or* **under ~**
sous serment; assermenté(e)
**oatmeal** ['əʊtmiːl] *n* flocons *mpl* d'avoine
**oats** [əʊts] *n* avoine *f*
**OAU** *n abbr* (= *Organization of African Unity*) OUA *f*
(= *Organisation de l'unité africaine*)
**obdurate** ['ɔbdjurɪt] *adj* obstiné(e),
impénitent(e); intraitable
**OBE** *n abbr* (*Brit*: = *Order of the British Empire*)
distinction honorifique
**obedience** [ə'biːdɪəns] *n* obéissance *f*; **in ~ to**
conformément à
**obedient** [ə'biːdɪənt] *adj* obéissant(e); **to be ~ to**
**sb/sth** obéir à qn/qch
**obelisk** ['ɔbɪlɪsk] *n* obélisque *m*
**obese** [əʊ'biːs] *adj* obèse
**obesity** [əʊ'biːsɪtɪ] *n* obésité *f*
**obey** [ə'beɪ] *vt* obéir à; (*instructions*, *regulations*) se
conformer à ▷ *vi* obéir
**obituary** [ə'bɪtjuərɪ] *n* nécrologie *f*
**object** *n* ['ɔbdʒɪkt] objet *m*; (*purpose*) but *m*, objet;
(*Ling*) complément *m* d'objet ▷ *vi* [əb'dʒɛkt]: **to ~**
**to** (*attitude*) désapprouver; (*proposal*) protester
contre, élever une objection contre; **I ~!** je
proteste!; **he ~ed that ...** il a fait valoir *or* a
objecté que ...; **do you ~ to my smoking?** est-ce
que cela vous gêne si je fume?; **what's the ~ of**
**doing that?** quel est l'intérêt de faire cela?;
**money is no ~** l'argent n'est pas un problème

**objection** [əb'dʒɛkʃən] *n* objection *f*; (*drawback*)
inconvénient *m*; **if you have no ~** si vous n'y
voyez pas d'inconvénient; **to make** *or* **raise an**
**~** élever une objection
**objectionable** [əb'dʒɛkʃənəbl] *adj* très
désagréable; choquant(e)
**objective** [əb'dʒɛktɪv] *n* objectif *m* ▷ *adj*
objectif(-ive)
**objectivity** [ɔbdʒɪk'tɪvɪtɪ] *n* objectivité *f*
**object lesson** *n* (*fig*) (bonne) illustration
**objector** [əb'dʒɛktəʳ] *n* opposant(e)
**obligation** [ɔblɪ'geɪʃən] *n* obligation *f*, devoir *m*;
(*debt*) dette *f* (de reconnaissance); **"without ~"**
"sans engagement"
**obligatory** [ə'blɪgətərɪ] *adj* obligatoire
**oblige** [ə'blaɪdʒ] *vt* (*force*): **to ~ sb to do** obliger *or*
forcer qn à faire; (*do a favour*) rendre service à,
obliger; **to be ~d to sb for sth** être obligé(e) à
qn de qch; **anything to ~!** (*inf*) (toujours prêt à
rendre) service!
**obliging** [ə'blaɪdʒɪŋ] *adj* obligeant(e), serviable
**oblique** [ə'bliːk] *adj* oblique; (*allusion*) indirect(e)
▷ *n* (*Brit Typ*): **~ (stroke)** barre *f* oblique
**obliterate** [ə'blɪtəreɪt] *vt* effacer
**oblivion** [ə'blɪvɪən] *n* oubli *m*
**oblivious** [ə'blɪvɪəs] *adj*: **~ of** oublieux(-euse) de
**oblong** ['ɔblɔŋ] *adj* oblong(ue) ▷ *n* rectangle *m*
**obnoxious** [əb'nɔkʃəs] *adj* odieux(-euse); (*smell*)
nauséabond(e)
**o.b.o.** *abbr* (*US*) = **or best offer**; (*in classified ads*)
≈ à débattre
**oboe** ['əʊbəʊ] *n* hautbois *m*
**obscene** [əb'siːn] *adj* obscène
**obscenity** [əb'sɛnɪtɪ] *n* obscénité *f*
**obscure** [əb'skjuəʳ] *adj* obscur(e) ▷ *vt* obscurcir;
(*hide*: *sun*) cacher
**obscurity** [əb'skjuərɪtɪ] *n* obscurité *f*
**obsequious** [əb'siːkwɪəs] *adj* obséquieux(-euse)
**observable** [əb'zəːvəbl] *adj* observable;
(*appreciable*) notable
**observance** [əb'zəːvns] *n* observance *f*,
observation *f*; **religious ~s** observances
religieuses
**observant** [əb'zəːvnt] *adj* observateur(-trice)
**observation** [ɔbzə'veɪʃən] *n* observation *f*; (*by*
*police etc*) surveillance *f*

**o**

**observation post** n (Mil) poste m d'observation

**observatory** [əbˈzɔːvətrɪ] n observatoire m

**observe** [əbˈzɔːv] vt observer; (remark) faire observer or remarquer

**observer** [əbˈzɔːvəʳ] n observateur(-trice)

**obsess** [əbˈsɛs] vt obséder; **to be ~ed by** or **with sb/sth** être obsédé(e) par qn/qch

**obsession** [əbˈsɛʃən] n obsession f

**obsessive** [əbˈsɛsɪv] adj obsédant(e)

**obsolescence** [ɔbsəˈlɛsns] n vieillissement m; obsolescence f; **built-in** or **planned ~** (Comm) désuétude calculée

**obsolescent** [ɔbsəˈlɛsnt] adj obsolescent(e), en voie d'être périmé(e)

**obsolete** [ˈɔbsəliːt] adj dépassé(e), périmé(e)

**obstacle** [ˈɔbstəkl] n obstacle m

**obstacle race** n course f d'obstacles

**obstetrician** [ɔbstəˈtrɪʃən] n obstétricien(ne)

**obstetrics** [ɔbˈstɛtrɪks] n obstétrique f

**obstinacy** [ˈɔbstɪnəsɪ] n obstination f

**obstinate** [ˈɔbstɪnɪt] adj obstiné(e); (pain, cold) persistant(e)

**obstreperous** [əbˈstrɛpərəs] adj turbulent(e)

**obstruct** [əbˈstrʌkt] vt (block) boucher, obstruer; (halt) arrêter; (hinder) entraver

**obstruction** [əbˈstrʌkʃən] n obstruction f; (to plan, progress) obstacle m

**obstructive** [əbˈstrʌktɪv] adj obstructionniste

**obtain** [əbˈteɪn] vt obtenir ▷ vi avoir cours

**obtainable** [əbˈteɪnəbl] adj qu'on peut obtenir

**obtrusive** [əbˈtruːsɪv] adj (person) importun(e); (smell) pénétrant(e); (building etc) trop en évidence

**obtuse** [əbˈtjuːs] adj obtus(e)

**obverse** [ˈɔbvəːs] n (of medal, coin) côté m face; (fig) contrepartie f

**obviate** [ˈɔbvɪeɪt] vt parer à, obvier à

**obvious** [ˈɔbvɪəs] adj évident(e), manifeste

**obviously** [ˈɔbvɪəslɪ] adv manifestement; (of course): **~, he ...** or **he ~ ...** il est bien évident qu'il ...; **~!** bien sûr!; **~ not!** évidemment pas!, bien sûr que non!

**OCAS** n abbr (= Organization of Central American States) ODEAC f (= Organisation des États d'Amérique centrale)

**occasion** [əˈkeɪʒən] n occasion f; (event) événement m ▷ vt occasionner, causer; **on that ~** à cette occasion; **to rise to the ~** se montrer à la hauteur de la situation

**occasional** [əˈkeɪʒənl] adj pris(e) (or fait(e) etc) de temps en temps; (worker, spending) occasionnel(le)

**occasionally** [əˈkeɪʒənəlɪ] adv de temps en temps, quelquefois; **very ~** (assez) rarement

**occasional table** n table décorative

**occult** [ɔˈkʌlt] adj occulte ▷ n: **the ~** le surnaturel

**occupancy** [ˈɔkjupənsɪ] n occupation f

**occupant** [ˈɔkjupənt] n occupant m

**occupation** [ɔkjuˈpeɪʃən] n occupation f; (job) métier m, profession f; **unfit for ~** (house) impropre à l'habitation

**occupational** [ɔkjuˈpeɪʃənl] adj (accident, disease) du travail; (hazard) du métier

**occupational guidance** n (Brit) orientation professionnelle

**occupational hazard** n risque m du métier

**occupational pension** n retraite professionnelle

**occupational therapy** n ergothérapie f

**occupier** [ˈɔkjupaɪəʳ] n occupant(e)

**occupy** [ˈɔkjupaɪ] vt occuper; **to ~ o.s. with** or **by doing** s'occuper à faire; **to be occupied with sth** être occupé avec qch

**occur** [əˈkɔːʳ] vi se produire; (difficulty, opportunity) se présenter; (phenomenon, error) se rencontrer; **to ~ to sb** venir à l'esprit de qn

**occurrence** [əˈkʌrəns] n (existence) présence f, existence f; (event) cas m, fait m

**ocean** [ˈəuʃən] n océan m; **~s of** (inf) des masses de

**ocean bed** n fond (sous-)marin

**ocean-going** [ˈəuʃəngəuɪŋ] adj de haute mer

**Oceania** [əuʃɪˈeɪnɪə] n Océanie f

**ocean liner** n paquebot m

**ochre** [ˈəukəʳ] adj ocre

**o'clock** [əˈklɔk] adv: **it is 5 o'clock** il est 5 heures

**OCR** n abbr = **optical character reader; optical character recognition**

**Oct.** abbr (= October) oct

**octagonal** [ɔkˈtægənl] adj octogonal(e)

**octane** [ˈɔkteɪn] n octane m; **high-~ petrol** or (US) **gas** essence f à indice d'octane élevé

**octave** [ˈɔktɪv] n octave f

**October** [ɔkˈtəubəʳ] n octobre m; for phrases see also **July**

**octogenarian** [ˈɔktəudʒɪˈnɛərɪən] n octogénaire m/f

**octopus** [ˈɔktəpəs] n pieuvre f

**odd** [ɔd] adj (strange) bizarre, curieux(-euse); (number) impair(e); (left over) qui reste, en plus; (not of a set) dépareillé(e); **60-~** 60 et quelques; **at ~ times** de temps en temps; **the ~ one out** l'exception f

**oddball** [ˈɔdbɔːl] n (inf) excentrique m/f

**oddity** [ˈɔdɪtɪ] n bizarrerie f; (person) excentrique m/f

**odd-job man** [ɔdˈdʒɔb-] n (irreg) homme m à tout faire

**odd jobs** npl petits travaux divers

**oddly** [ˈɔdlɪ] adv bizarrement, curieusement

**oddments** [ˈɔdmənts] npl (Brit Comm) fins fpl de série

**odds** [ɔdz] npl (in betting) cote f; **the ~ are against his coming** il y a peu de chances qu'il vienne; **it makes no ~** cela n'a pas d'importance; **to succeed against all the ~** réussir contre toute attente; **~ and ends** de petites choses; **at ~** en désaccord

**odds-on** [ɔdzˈɔn] adj: **the ~ favourite** le grand favori; **it's ~ that he'll come** il y a toutes les chances or gros à parier qu'il vienne

**ode** [əud] n ode f

**odious** [ˈəudɪəs] adj odieux(-euse), détestable

**odometer** [ɔ'dɔmɪtər] n (US) odomètre m
**odour,** (US) **odor** ['əudər] n odeur f
**odourless,** (US) **odorless** ['əudəlɪs] adj inodore
**OECD** n abbr (= Organization for Economic Cooperation and Development) OCDE f (= Organisation de coopération et de développement économique)
**oesophagus,** (US) **esophagus** [i:'sɔfəgəs] n œsophage m
**oestrogen,** (US) **estrogen** ['i:strəudʒən] n œstrogène m

KEYWORD

**of** [ɔv, əv] prep 1 (gen) de; **a friend of ours** un de nos amis; **a boy of 10** un garçon de 10 ans; **that was kind of you** c'était gentil de votre part
2 (expressing quantity, amount, dates etc) de; **a kilo of flour** un kilo de farine; **how much of this do you need?** combien vous en faut-il?; **there were three of them** (people) ils étaient 3; (objects) il y en avait 3; **three of us went** 3 d'entre nous y sont allé(e)s; **the 5th of July** le 5 juillet; **a quarter of 4** (US) 4 heures moins le quart
3 (from, out of) en, de; **a statue of marble** une statue de or en marbre; **made of wood** (fait) en bois

**Ofcom** ['ɔfkɔm] n abbr (Brit: = Office of Communications Regulation) organe de régulation de télécommunications

**off** [ɔf] adj, adv (engine) coupé(e); (light, TV) éteint(e); (tap) fermé(e); (Brit: food) mauvais(e), avancé(e); (: milk) tourné(e); (absent) absent(e); (cancelled) annulé(e); (removed): **the lid was ~** le couvercle était retiré or n'était pas mis; (away): **to run/drive ~** partir en courant/en voiture ▷ prep de; **to be ~** (to leave) partir, s'en aller; **I must be ~** il faut que je file; **to be ~ sick** être absent pour cause de maladie; **a day ~** un jour de congé; **to have an ~ day** n'être pas en forme; **he had his coat ~** il avait enlevé son manteau; **the hook is ~** le crochet s'est détaché; le crochet n'est pas mis; **10% ~** (Comm) 10% de rabais; **5 km ~ (the road)** à 5 km (de la route); **~ the coast** au large de la côte; **a house ~ the main road** une maison à l'écart de la grand-route; **it's a long way ~** c'est loin (d'ici); **I'm ~ meat** je ne mange plus de viande; je n'aime plus la viande; **on the ~ chance** à tout hasard; **to be well/badly ~** être bien/mal loti; (financially) être aisé/dans la gêne; **~ and on, on and ~** de temps à autre; **I'm afraid the chicken is ~** (Brit: not available) je regrette, il n'y a plus de poulet; **that's a bit ~** (fig: inf) c'est un peu fort

**offal** ['ɔfl] n (Culin) abats mpl
**offbeat** ['ɔfbi:t] adj excentrique
**off-centre** [ɔf'sɛntər] adj décentré(e), excentré(e)
**off-colour** ['ɔf'kʌlər] adj (Brit: ill) malade, mal fichu(e); **to feel ~** être mal fichu
**offence,** (US) **offense** [ə'fɛns] n (crime) délit m,

infraction f; **to give ~ to** blesser, offenser; **to take ~ at** se vexer de, s'offenser de; **to commit an ~** commettre une infraction
**offend** [ə'fɛnd] vt (person) offenser, blesser ▷ vi: **to ~ against** (law, rule) contrevenir à, enfreindre
**offender** [ə'fɛndər] n délinquant(e); (against regulations) contrevenant(e)
**offending** [ə'fɛndɪŋ] adj incriminé(e)
**offense** [ə'fɛns] n (US) = **offence**
**offensive** [ə'fɛnsɪv] adj offensant(e), choquant(e); (smell etc) très déplaisant(e); (weapon) offensif(-ive) ▷ n (Mil) offensive f
**offer** ['ɔfər] n offre f, proposition f ▷ vt offrir, proposer; **to make an ~ for sth** faire une offre pour qch; **to ~ sth to sb, ~ sb sth** offrir qch à qn; **to ~ to do sth** proposer de faire qch; **"on ~"** (Comm) "en promotion"
**offering** ['ɔfərɪŋ] n offrande f
**offhand** [ɔf'hænd] adj désinvolte ▷ adv spontanément; **I can't tell you ~** je ne peux pas vous le dire comme ça
**office** ['ɔfɪs] n (place) bureau m; (position) charge f, fonction f; **doctor's ~** (US) cabinet (médical); **to take ~** entrer en fonctions; **through his good ~s** (fig) grâce à ses bons offices; **O~ of Fair Trading** (Brit) organisme de protection contre les pratiques commerciales abusives
**office automation** n bureautique f
**office bearer** n (of club etc) membre m du bureau
**office block,** (US) **office building** n immeuble m de bureaux
**office boy** n garçon m de bureau
**office hours** npl heures fpl de bureau; (US Med) heures de consultation
**office manager** n responsable administratif(-ive)
**officer** ['ɔfɪsər] n (Mil etc) officier m; (also: **police officer**) agent m (de police); (of organization) membre m du bureau directeur
**office work** n travail m de bureau
**office worker** n employé(e) de bureau
**official** [ə'fɪʃl] adj (authorized) officiel(le) ▷ n officiel m; (civil servant) fonctionnaire m/f; (of railways, post office, town hall) employé(e)
**officialdom** [ə'fɪʃldəm] n bureaucratie f
**officially** [ə'fɪʃəlɪ] adv officiellement
**official receiver** n administrateur m judiciaire, syndic m de faillite
**officiate** [ə'fɪʃɪeɪt] vi (Rel) officier; **to ~ as Mayor** exercer les fonctions de maire; **to ~ at a marriage** célébrer un mariage
**officious** [ə'fɪʃəs] adj trop empressé(e)
**offing** ['ɔfɪŋ] n: **in the ~** (fig) en perspective
**off-key** [ɔf'ki:] adj faux (fausse) ▷ adv faux
**off-licence** ['ɔflaɪsns] n (Brit: shop) débit m de vins et de spiritueux
**off-limits** [ɔf'lɪmɪts] adj (esp US) dont l'accès est interdit
**off-line** [ɔf'laɪn] adj (Comput) (en mode) autonome; (: switched off) non connecté(e)
**off-load** ['ɔfləud] vt: **to ~ sth (onto)** (goods) décharger qch (sur); (job) se décharger de qch

(sur)

**off-peak** [ɔf'piːk] adj aux heures creuses; (electricity, ticket) au tarif heures creuses

**off-putting** ['ɔfputɪŋ] adj (Brit: remark) rébarbatif(-ive); (person) rebutant(e), peu engageant(e)

**off-road vehicle** ['ɔfrəud-] n véhicule m tout-terrain

**off-season** ['ɔf'siːzn] adj, adv hors-saison inv

**offset** ['ɔfset] vt (irreg: like set); (counteract) contrebalancer, compenser ▷ n (also: **offset printing**) offset m

**offshoot** ['ɔfʃuːt] n (fig) ramification f, antenne f; (: of discussion etc) conséquence f

**offshore** [ɔf'ɔːʳ] adj (breeze) de terre; (island) proche du littoral; (fishing) côtier(-ière); **oilfield** gisement m pétrolifère en mer

**offside** ['ɔf'saɪd] n (Aut: with right-hand drive) côté droit; (: with left-hand drive) côté gauche ▷ adj (Sport) hors jeu; (Aut: in Britain) de droite; (: in US, Europe) de gauche

**offspring** ['ɔfsprɪŋ] n progéniture f

**offstage** [ɔf'steɪdʒ] adv dans les coulisses

**off-the-cuff** [ɔfðə'kʌf] adv au pied levé; de chic

**off-the-job** [ɔfðə'dʒɔb] adj: ~ **training** formation professionnelle extérieure

**off-the-peg** [ɔfðə'peg], (US) **off-the-rack** ['ɔfðə'ræk] adv en prêt-à-porter

**off-the-record** ['ɔfðə'rekɔːd] adj (remark) confidentiel(le), sans caractère officiel ▷ adv officieusement

**off-white** ['ɔfwaɪt] adj blanc cassé inv

**often** ['ɔfn] adv souvent; **how ~ do you go?** vous y allez tous les combien?; **every so ~** de temps en temps, de temps à autre; **as ~ as not** la plupart du temps

**Ofwat** ['ɔfwɔt] n abbr (Brit: = Office of Water Services) organisme qui surveille les activités des compagnies des eaux

**ogle** ['əugl] vt lorgner

**ogre** ['əugəʳ] n ogre m

**OH** abbr (US) = **Ohio**

**oh** [əu] excl ô!, oh!, ah!

**OHMS** abbr (Brit) = **On His (or Her) Majesty's Service**

**oil** [ɔɪl] n huile f; (petroleum) pétrole m; (for central heating) mazout m ▷ vt (machine) graisser

**oilcan** ['ɔɪlkæn] n burette f de graissage; (for storing) bidon m à huile

**oil change** n vidange f

**oilfield** ['ɔɪlfiːld] n gisement m de pétrole

**oil filter** n (Aut) filtre m à huile

**oil-fired** ['ɔɪlfaɪəd] adj au mazout

**oil gauge** n jauge f de niveau d'huile

**oil industry** n industrie pétrolière

**oil level** n niveau m d'huile

**oil painting** n peinture f à l'huile

**oil refinery** n raffinerie f de pétrole

**oil rig** n derrick m; (at sea) plate-forme pétrolière

**oilskins** ['ɔɪlskɪnz] npl ciré m

**oil slick** n nappe f de mazout

**oil tanker** n (ship) pétrolier m; (truck) camion-

citerne m

**oil well** n puits m de pétrole

**oily** ['ɔɪlɪ] adj huileux(-euse); (food) gras(se)

**ointment** ['ɔɪntmənt] n onguent m

**OK** abbr (US) = **Oklahoma**

**O.K., okay** ['əu'keɪ] (inf) excl d'accord! ▷ vt approuver, donner son accord à ▷ n: **to give sth one's O.K.** donner son accord à qch ▷ adj (not bad) pas mal, en règle; en bon état; sain et sauf; acceptable; **is it O.K.?, are you O.K.?** ça va?; **are you O.K. for money?** ça va or ira question argent?; **it's O.K. with** or **by me** ça me va, c'est d'accord en ce qui me concerne

**Okla.** abbr (US) = **Oklahoma**

**old** [əuld] adj vieux (vieille); (person) vieux, âgé(e); (former) ancien(ne), vieux; **how ~ are you?** quel âge avez-vous?; **he's 10 years ~** il a 10 ans, il est âgé de 10 ans; **~er brother/sister** frère/sœur aîné(e); **any ~ thing will do** n'importe quoi fera l'affaire

**old age** n vieillesse f

**old-age pensioner** n (Brit) retraité(e)

**old-fashioned** ['əuld'fæʃnd] adj démodé(e); (person) vieux jeu inv

**old maid** n vieille fille

**old people's home** n (esp Brit) maison f de retraite

**old-style** ['əuldstaɪl] adj à l'ancienne (mode)

**old-time** ['əuld'taɪm] adj du temps jadis, d'autrefois

**old-timer** [əuld'taɪməʳ] n ancien m

**old wives' tale** n conte m de bonne femme

**O-level** ['əulevl] n (in England and Wales: formerly) examen passé à l'âge de 16 ans sanctionnant les connaissances de l'élève, ≈ brevet m des collèges

**olive** ['ɔlɪv] n (fruit) olive f; (tree) olivier m ▷ adj (also: **olive-green**) (vert) olive inv

**olive oil** n huile f d'olive

**Olympic** [əu'lɪmpɪk] adj olympique; **the ~ Games, the ~s** les Jeux mpl olympiques

**OM** n abbr (Brit: = Order of Merit) titre honorifique

**Oman** [əu'mɑːn] n Oman m

**OMB** n abbr (US: = Office of Management and Budget) service conseillant le président en matière budgétaire

**omelette, omelet** ['ɔmlɪt] n omelette f; **ham/ cheese omelet(te)** omelette au jambon/ fromage

**omen** ['əumən] n présage m

**ominous** ['ɔmɪnəs] adj menaçant(e), inquiétant(e); (event) de mauvais augure

**omission** [əu'mɪʃən] n omission f

**omit** [əu'mɪt] vt omettre; **to ~ to do sth** négliger de faire qch

**omnivorous** [ɔm'nɪvrəs] adj omnivore

**ON** abbr (Canada) = **Ontario**

⭕ KEYWORD

**on** [ɔn] prep **1** (indicating position) sur; **on the table** sur la table; **on the wall** sur le or au mur; **on the left** à gauche; **I haven't any money on me** je n'ai pas d'argent sur moi

**2** (*indicating means, method, condition etc*): **on foot** à pied; **on the train/plane** (*be*) dans le train/l'avion; (*go*) en train/avion; **on the telephone/radio/television** au téléphone/à la radio/à la télévision; **to be on drugs** se droguer; **on holiday** (*Brit*): **on vacation** (*US*) en vacances; **on the continent** sur le continent
**3** (*referring to time*): **on Friday** vendredi; **on Fridays** le vendredi; **on June 20th** le 20 juin; **a week on Friday** vendredi en huit; **on arrival** à l'arrivée; **on seeing this** en voyant cela
**4** (*about, concerning*) sur, de; **a book on Balzac/physics** un livre sur Balzac/de physique
**5** (*at the expense of*): **this round is on me** c'est ma tournée
▷ *adv* **1** (*referring to dress*): **to have one's coat on** avoir (mis) son manteau; **to put one's coat on** mettre son manteau; **what's she got on?** qu'est-ce qu'elle porte?
**2** (*referring to covering*): **screw the lid on tightly** vissez bien le couvercle
**3** (*further, continuously*): **to walk etc on** continuer à marcher *etc*; **on and off** de temps à autre; **from that day on** depuis ce jour
▷ *adj* **1** (*in operation: machine*) en marche; (: *radio, TV, light*) allumé(e); (: *tap, gas*) ouvert(e); (: *brakes*) mis(e); **is the meeting still on?** (*not cancelled*) est-ce que la réunion a bien lieu?; **it was well on in the evening** c'était tard dans la soirée; **when is this film on?** quand passe ce film?
**2** (*inf*): **that's not on!** (*not acceptable*) cela ne se fait pas!; (*not possible*) pas question!

**ONC** *n abbr* (*Brit*: = *Ordinary National Certificate*) ≈ BT *m*
**once** [wʌns] *adv* une fois; (*formerly*) autrefois
▷ *conj* une fois que + *sub*; **– he had left/it was done** une fois qu'il fut parti/ que ce fut terminé; **at –** tout de suite, immédiatement; (*simultaneously*) à la fois; **all at –** (*adv*) tout d'un coup; **– a week** une fois par semaine; **– more** encore une fois; **I knew him –** je l'ai connu autrefois; **– and for all** une fois pour toutes; **– upon a time there was …** il y avait une fois …, il était une fois …
**oncoming** [ˈɒnkʌmɪŋ] *adj* (*traffic*) venant en sens inverse
**OND** *n abbr* (*Brit*: = *Ordinary National Diploma*) ≈ BTS *m*

🔘 KEYWORD

**one** [wʌn] *num* un(e); **one hundred and fifty** cent cinquante; **one by one** un(e) à *or* par un(e); **one day** un jour
▷ *adj* **1** (*sole*) seul(e), unique; **the one book which** l'unique *or* le seul livre qui; **the one man who** le seul homme qui
**2** (*same*) même; **they came in the one car** ils sont venus dans la même voiture
▷ *pron* **1**: **this one** celui-ci (celle-ci); **that one** celui-là (celle-là); **I've already got one/a red one** j'en ai déjà un(e)/un(e) rouge; **which one do you want?** lequel voulez-vous?
**2**: **one another** l'un(e) l'autre; **to look at one another** se regarder
**3** (*impersonal*) on; **one never knows** on ne sait jamais; **to cut one's finger** se couper le doigt; **one needs to eat** il faut manger
**4** (*phrases*): **to be one up on sb** avoir l'avantage sur qn; **to be at one (with sb)** être d'accord (avec qn)

**one-armed bandit** [ˈwʌnɑːmd-] *n* machine *f* à sous
**one-day excursion** [ˈwʌndeɪ-] *n* (*US*) billet *m* d'aller-retour (valable pour la journée)
**One-hundred share index** [ˈwʌnhʌndrəd-] *n* indice *m* Footsie des cent grandes valeurs
**one-man** [ˈwʌnmæn] *adj* (*business*) dirigé(e) *etc* par un seul homme
**one-man band** *n* homme-orchestre *m*
**one-off** [wʌnˈɒf] *n* (*Brit inf*) exemplaire *m* unique
▷ *adj* unique
**one-parent family** [ˈwʌnpɛərənt-] *n* famille monoparentale
**one-piece** [ˈwʌnpiːs] *adj*: **~ bathing suit** maillot *m* une pièce
**onerous** [ˈɒnərəs] *adj* (*task, duty*) pénible; (*responsibility*) lourd(e)
**oneself** [wʌnˈsɛlf] *pron* se; (*after prep, also emphatic*) soi-même; **to hurt ~** se faire mal; **to keep sth for ~** garder qch pour soi; **to talk to ~** se parler à soi-même; **by ~** tout seul
**one-shot** [wʌnˈʃɒt] (*US*) *n* = **one-off**
**one-sided** [wʌnˈsaɪdɪd] *adj* (*argument, decision*) unilatéral(e); (*judgment, account*) partial(e); (*contest*) inégal(e)
**one-time** [ˈwʌntaɪm] *adj* d'autrefois
**one-to-one** [ˈwʌntəwʌn] *adj* (*relationship*) univoque
**one-upmanship** [wʌnˈʌpmənʃɪp] *n*: **the art of ~** l'art de faire mieux que les autres
**one-way** [ˈwʌnweɪ] *adj* (*street, traffic*) à sens unique
**ongoing** [ˈɒngəʊɪŋ] *adj* en cours; (*relationship*) suivi(e)
**onion** [ˈʌnjən] *n* oignon *m*
**on-line** [ˈɒnlaɪn] *adj* (*Comput*) en ligne; (: *switched on*) connecté(e)
**onlooker** [ˈɒnlʊkəʳ] *n* spectateur(-trice)
**only** [ˈəʊnlɪ] *adv* seulement ▷ *adj* seul(e), unique
▷ *conj* seulement, mais; **an ~ child** un enfant unique; **not ~ … but also** non seulement … mais aussi; **I ~ took one** j'en ai seulement pris un, je n'en ai pris qu'un; **I saw her ~ yesterday** je l'ai vue hier encore; **I'd be ~ too pleased to help** je ne serais que trop content de vous aider; **I would come, ~ I'm very busy** je viendrais bien mais j'ai beaucoup à faire
**ono** *abbr* (*Brit*) = **or nearest offer**; (*in classified ads*) ≈ à débattre
**on-screen** [ɒnˈskriːn] *adj* à l'écran
**onset** [ˈɒnsɛt] *n* début *m*; (*of winter, old age*)

**O**

701

approche f
**onshore** ['ɔnʃɔːʳ] adj (wind) du large
**onslaught** ['ɔnslɔːt] n attaque f, assaut m
**Ont.** abbr (Canada) = **Ontario**
**on-the-job** ['ɔnðə'dʒɔb] adj: ~ **training**
formation f sur place
**onto** ['ɔntu] prep = **on to**
**onus** ['əunəs] n responsabilité f; **the ~ is upon
him to prove it** c'est à lui de le prouver
**onward** ['ɔnwəd], **onwards** ['ɔnwədz] adv
(move) en avant; **from that time ~s** à partir de
ce moment
**oops** [ups] excl houp!; **~-a-daisy!** houp-là!
**ooze** [uːz] vi suinter
**opacity** [əu'pæsɪtɪ] n opacité f
**opal** ['əupl] n opale f
**opaque** [əu'peɪk] adj opaque
**OPEC** ['əupɛk] n abbr (= Organization of Petroleum-
Exporting Countries) OPEP f
**open** ['əupn] adj ouvert(e); (car) découvert(e);
(road, view) dégagé(e); (meeting) public(-ique);
(admiration) manifeste; (question) non résolu(e);
(enemy) déclaré(e) ▷ vt ouvrir ▷ vi (flower, eyes,
door, debate) s'ouvrir; (shop, bank, museum) ouvrir;
(book etc: commence) commencer, débuter; **is it ~
to public?** est-ce ouvert au public?; **what time
do you ~?** à quelle heure ouvrez-vous?; **in the ~
(air)** en plein air; **the ~ sea** le large; **~ ground**
(among trees) clairière f; (waste ground) terrain m
vague; **to have an ~ mind (on sth)** avoir
l'esprit ouvert (sur qch)
▶ **open on to** vt fus (room, door) donner sur
▶ **open out** vt ouvrir ▷ vi s'ouvrir
▶ **open up** vt ouvrir; (blocked road) dégager ▷ vi
s'ouvrir
**open-air** [əupn'ɛəʳ] adj en plein air
**open-and-shut** [əupnən'ʃʌt] adj: ~ **case** cas m
limpide
**open day** n journée f portes ouvertes
**open-ended** [əupn'ɛndɪd] adj (fig) non limité(e)
**opener** ['əupnəʳ] n (also: **can opener, tin opener**)
ouvre-boîtes m
**open-heart surgery** [əupn'hɑːt-] n chirurgie f
à cœur ouvert
**opening** ['əupnɪŋ] n ouverture f; (opportunity)
occasion f; (work) débouché m; (job) poste
vacant
**opening hours** npl heures fpl d'ouverture
**opening night** n (Theat) première f
**open learning** n enseignement universitaire à la carte,
notamment par correspondance; (distance learning)
télé-enseignement m
**open learning centre** n centre ouvert à tous où l'on
dispense un enseignement général à temps partiel
**openly** ['əupnlɪ] adv ouvertement
**open-minded** [əupn'maɪndɪd] adj à l'esprit
ouvert
**open-necked** ['əupnnɛkt] adj à col ouvert
**openness** ['əupnnɪs] n (frankness) franchise f
**open-plan** ['əupn'plæn] adj sans cloisons
**open prison** n prison ouverte
**open sandwich** n canapé m

**open shop** n entreprise qui admet les travailleurs non
syndiqués
**Open University** n (Brit) cours universitaires par
correspondance
**opera** ['ɔpərə] n opéra m
**opera glasses** npl jumelles fpl de théâtre
**opera house** n opéra m
**opera singer** n chanteur(-euse) d'opéra
**operate** ['ɔpəreɪt] vt (machine) faire marcher,
faire fonctionner; (system) pratiquer ▷ vi
fonctionner; (drug) faire effet; **to ~ on sb (for)**
(Med) opérer qn (de)
**operatic** [ɔpə'rætɪk] adj d'opéra
**operating** ['ɔpəreɪtɪŋ] adj (Comm: costs, profit)
d'exploitation; (Med): ~ **table** table f
d'opération
**operating room** n (US: Med) salle f d'opération
**operating system** n (Comput) système m
d'exploitation
**operating theatre** n (Brit: Med) salle f
d'opération
**operation** [ɔpə'reɪʃən] n opération f; (of machine)
fonctionnement m; **to have an ~ (for)** se faire
opérer (de); **to be in ~** (machine) être en service;
(system) être en vigueur
**operational** [ɔpə'reɪʃənl] adj opérationnel(le);
(ready for use) en état de marche; **when the
service is fully ~** lorsque le service
fonctionnera pleinement
**operative** ['ɔpərətɪv] adj (measure) en vigueur
▷ n (in factory) ouvrier(-ière); **the ~ word** le mot
clef
**operator** ['ɔpəreɪtəʳ] n (of machine)
opérateur(-trice); (Tel) téléphoniste m/f
**operetta** [ɔpə'rɛtə] n opérette f
**ophthalmologist** [ɔfθæl'mɔlədʒɪst] n
ophtalmologiste m/f, ophtalmologue m/f
**opinion** [ə'pɪnjən] n opinion f, avis m; **in my ~** à
mon avis; **to seek a second ~** demander un
deuxième avis
**opinionated** [ə'pɪnjəneɪtɪd] adj aux idées bien
arrêtées
**opinion poll** n sondage m d'opinion
**opium** ['əupɪəm] n opium m
**opponent** [ə'pəunənt] n adversaire m/f
**opportune** ['ɔpətjuːn] adj opportun(e)
**opportunist** [ɔpə'tjuːnɪst] n opportuniste m/f
**opportunity** [ɔpə'tjuːnɪtɪ] n occasion f; **to take
the ~ to do** or **of doing** profiter de l'occasion
pour faire
**oppose** [ə'pəuz] vt s'opposer à; **to be ~d to sth**
être opposé(e) à qch; **as ~d to** par opposition à
**opposing** [ə'pəuzɪŋ] adj (side) opposé(e)
**opposite** ['ɔpəzɪt] adj opposé(e); (house etc) d'en
face ▷ adv en face ▷ prep en face de ▷ n opposé
m, contraire m; (of word) contraire; **"see ~ page"**
"voir ci-contre"
**opposite number** n (Brit) homologue m/f
**opposite sex** n: **the ~** l'autre sexe
**opposition** [ɔpə'zɪʃən] n opposition f
**oppress** [ə'prɛs] vt opprimer
**oppression** [ə'prɛʃən] n oppression f

**oppressive** [ə'prɛsɪv] adj oppressif(-ive)
**opprobrium** [ə'prəubrɪəm] n (formal) opprobre m
**opt** [ɔpt] vi: **to ~ for** opter pour; **to ~ to do** choisir de faire
▶ **opt out** vi (school, hospital) devenir autonome; (health service) devenir privé(e); **to ~ out of** choisir de ne pas participer à or de ne pas faire
**optical** ['ɔptɪkl] adj optique; (instrument) d'optique
**optical character reader** n lecteur m optique
**optical character recognition** n lecture f optique
**optical fibre** n fibre f optique
**optician** [ɔp'tɪʃən] n opticien(ne)
**optics** ['ɔptɪks] n optique f
**optimism** ['ɔptɪmɪzəm] n optimisme m
**optimist** ['ɔptɪmɪst] n optimiste m/f
**optimistic** [ɔptɪ'mɪstɪk] adj optimiste
**optimum** ['ɔptɪməm] adj optimum
**option** ['ɔpʃən] n choix m, option f; (Scol) matière f à option; (Comm) option; **to keep one's ~s open** (fig) ne pas s'engager; **I have no ~** je n'ai pas le choix
**optional** ['ɔpʃənl] adj facultatif(-ive); (Comm) en option; **~ extras** accessoires mpl en option, options fpl
**opulence** ['ɔpjuləns] n opulence f; abondance f
**opulent** ['ɔpjulənt] adj opulent(e); abondant(e)
**OR** abbr (US) = **Oregon**
**or** [ɔːʳ] conj ou; (with negative): **he hasn't seen or heard anything** il n'a rien vu ni entendu; **or else** sinon; ou bien
**oracle** ['ɔrəkl] n oracle m
**oral** ['ɔːrəl] adj oral(e) ▷ n oral m
**orange** ['ɔrɪndʒ] n (fruit) orange f ▷ adj orange inv
**orangeade** [ɔrɪndʒ'eɪd] n orangeade f
**orange juice** n jus m d'orange
**oration** [ɔː'reɪʃən] n discours solennel
**orator** ['ɔrətəʳ] n orateur(-trice)
**oratorio** [ɔrə'tɔːrɪəu] n oratorio m
**orb** [ɔːb] n orbe m
**orbit** ['ɔːbɪt] n orbite f ▷ vt graviter autour de; **to be in/go into ~ (round)** être/entrer en orbite (autour de)
**orbital** ['ɔːbɪtl] n (also: **orbital motorway**) périphérique f
**orchard** ['ɔːtʃəd] n verger m; **apple ~** verger de pommiers
**orchestra** ['ɔːkɪstrə] n orchestre m; (US: seating) (fauteuils mpl d')orchestre
**orchestral** [ɔː'kɛstrəl] adj orchestral(e); (concert) symphonique
**orchestrate** ['ɔːkɪstreɪt] vt (Mus, fig) orchestrer
**orchid** ['ɔːkɪd] n orchidée f
**ordain** [ɔː'deɪn] vt (Rel) ordonner; (decide) décréter
**ordeal** [ɔː'diːl] n épreuve f
**order** ['ɔːdəʳ] n ordre m; (Comm) commande f ▷ vt ordonner; (Comm) commander; **in ~** en ordre; (of document) en règle; **out of ~** (not in correct order) en désordre; (machine) hors service; (telephone)

en dérangement; **a machine in working ~** une machine en état de marche; **in ~ of size** par ordre de grandeur; **in ~ to do/that** pour faire/que + sub; **to place an ~ for sth with sb** commander qch auprès de qn, passer commande de qch à qn; **could I ~ now, please?** je peux commander, s'il vous plaît?; **to be on ~** être en commande; **made to ~** fait sur commande; **to be under ~s to do sth** avoir ordre de faire qch; **a point of ~** un point de procédure; **to the ~ of** (Banking) à l'ordre de; **to ~ sb to do** ordonner à qn de faire
**order book** n carnet m de commandes
**order form** n bon m de commande
**orderly** ['ɔːdəlɪ] n (Mil) ordonnance f; (Med) garçon m de salle ▷ adj (room) en ordre; (mind) méthodique; (person) qui a de l'ordre
**order number** n (Comm) numéro m de commande
**ordinal** ['ɔːdɪnl] adj (number) ordinal(e)
**ordinary** ['ɔːdnrɪ] adj ordinaire, normal(e); (pej) ordinaire, quelconque; **out of the ~** exceptionnel(le)
**ordinary degree** n (Scol) ≈ licence f libre; voir article

**ordinary seaman** n (Brit) matelot m
**ordinary shares** npl actions fpl ordinaires
**ordination** [ɔːdɪ'neɪʃən] n ordination f
**ordnance** ['ɔːdnəns] n (Mil: unit) service m du matériel
**Ordnance Survey map** n (Brit) ≈ carte f d'État-major
**ore** [ɔːʳ] n minerai m
**Ore., Oreg.** abbr (US) = **Oregon**
**oregano** [ɔrɪ'gɑːnəu] n origan m
**organ** ['ɔːgən] n organe m; (Mus) orgue m, orgues fpl
**organic** [ɔː'gænɪk] adj organique; (crops etc) biologique, naturel(le)
**organism** ['ɔːgənɪzəm] n organisme m
**organist** ['ɔːgənɪst] n organiste m/f
**organization** [ɔːgənaɪ'zeɪʃən] n organisation f
**organization chart** n organigramme m
**organize** ['ɔːgənaɪz] vt organiser; **to get ~d** s'organiser
**organized** ['ɔːgənaɪzd] adj (planned) organisé(e); (efficient) bien organisé
**organized crime** ['ɔːgənaɪzd-] n crime organisé, grand banditisme
**organized labour** ['ɔːgənaɪzd-] n main-d'œuvre syndiquée
**organizer** ['ɔːgənaɪzəʳ] n organisateur(-trice)
**orgasm** ['ɔːgæzəm] n orgasme m

**O**

**orgy** ['ɔːdʒɪ] n orgie f
**Orient** ['ɔːrɪənt] n: **the ~** l'Orient m
**oriental** [ɔːrɪ'ɛntl] adj oriental(e) ▷ n
Oriental(e)
**orientate** ['ɔːrɪənteɪt] vt orienter
**orientation** [ɔːrɪən'teɪʃən] n (attitudes) tendance
f; (in job) orientation f; (of building) orientation,
exposition f
**orifice** ['ɔrɪfɪs] n orifice m
**origin** ['ɔrɪdʒɪn] n origine f; **country of ~** pays m
d'origine
**original** [ə'rɪdʒɪnl] adj original(e); (earliest)
originel(le) ▷ n original m
**originality** [ərɪdʒɪ'nælɪtɪ] n originalité f
**originally** [ə'rɪdʒɪnəlɪ] adv (at first) à l'origine
**originate** [ə'rɪdʒɪneɪt] vi: **to ~ from** être
originaire de; (suggestion) provenir de; **to ~ in**
(custom) prendre naissance dans, avoir son
origine dans
**originator** [ə'rɪdʒɪneɪtər] n auteur m
**Orkney** ['ɔːknɪ] n (also: **the Orkneys, the Orkney
Islands**) les Orcades fpl
**ornament** ['ɔːnəmənt] n ornement m; (trinket)
bibelot m
**ornamental** [ɔːnə'mɛntl] adj décoratif(-ive);
(garden) d'agrément
**ornamentation** [ɔːnəmɛn'teɪʃən] n
ornementation f
**ornate** [ɔː'neɪt] adj très orné(e)
**ornithologist** [ɔːnɪ'θɔlədʒɪst] n ornithologue
m/f
**ornithology** [ɔːnɪ'θɔlədʒɪ] n ornithologie f
**orphan** ['ɔːfn] n orphelin(e) ▷ vt: **to be ~ed**
devenir orphelin
**orphanage** ['ɔːfənɪdʒ] n orphelinat m
**orthodox** ['ɔːθədɔks] adj orthodoxe
**orthopaedic**, (US) **orthopedic** [ɔːθə'piːdɪk] adj
orthopédique
**OS** abbr (Brit: = Ordnance Survey) ≈ IGN m (= Institut
géographique national); (: Naut) = **ordinary
seaman**; (: Dress) = **outsize**
**O/S** abbr = **out of stock**
**Oscar** ['ɔskər] n oscar m
**oscillate** ['ɔsɪleɪt] vi osciller
**OSHA** n abbr (US: = Occupational Safety and Health
Administration) office de l'hygiène et de la sécurité au
travail
**Oslo** ['ɔzləu] n Oslo
**ostensible** [ɔs'tɛnsɪbl] adj prétendu(e);
apparent(e)
**ostensibly** [ɔs'tɛnsɪblɪ] adv en apparence
**ostentation** [ɔstɛn'teɪʃən] n ostentation f
**ostentatious** [ɔstɛn'teɪʃəs] adj
prétentieux(-euse); ostentatoire
**osteopath** ['ɔstɪəpæθ] n ostéopathe m/f
**ostracize** ['ɔstrəsaɪz] vt frapper d'ostracisme
**ostrich** ['ɔstrɪtʃ] n autruche f
**OT** n abbr (= Old Testament) AT m
**OTB** n abbr (US: = off-track betting) paris pris en dehors
du champ de course
**O.T.E.** abbr (= on-target earnings) primes fpl sur
objectifs inclus

**other** ['ʌðər] adj autre ▷ pron: **the ~ (one)** l'autre;
**~s** (other people) d'autres ▷ adv: **~ than**
autrement que; à part; **some actor or ~** un
certain acteur, je ne sais quel acteur;
**somebody or ~** quelqu'un; **some ~ people
have still to arrive** on attend encore quelques
personnes; **the ~ day** l'autre jour; **the car was
none ~ than John's** la voiture n'était autre que
celle de John
**otherwise** ['ʌðəwaɪz] adv, conj autrement; **an ~
good piece of work** par ailleurs, un beau
travail
**OTT** abbr (inf) = **over the top**; see **top**
**Ottawa** ['ɔtəwə] n Ottawa
**otter** ['ɔtər] n loutre f
**OU** n abbr (Brit) = **Open University**
**ouch** [autʃ] excl aïe!
**ought** (pt ~) [ɔːt] aux vb: **I ~ to do it** je devrais le
faire, il faudrait que je le fasse; **this ~ to have
been corrected** cela aurait dû être corrigé; **he
~ to win** (probability) il devrait gagner; **you ~ to
go and see it** vous devriez aller le voir
**ounce** [auns] n once f (28.35g; 16 in a pound)
**our** ['auər] adj notre, nos pl; see also **my**
**ours** [auəz] pron le (la) nôtre, les nôtres; see also
**mine**[1]
**ourselves** [auə'sɛlvz] pron pl (reflexive, after
preposition) nous; (emphatic) nous-mêmes; **we
did it (all) by ~** nous avons fait ça tout seuls; see
also **oneself**
**oust** [aust] vt évincer
**out** [aut] adv dehors; (published, not at home etc)
sorti(e); (light, fire) éteint(e); (on strike) en grève
▷ vt: **to ~ sb** révéler l'homosexualité de qn; **~
here** ici; **~ there** là-bas; **he's ~** (absent) il est
sorti; (unconscious) il est sans connaissance; **to
be ~ in one's calculations** s'être trompé dans
ses calculs; **to run/back** etc **~** sortir en courant/
en reculant etc; **to be ~ and about** or (US)
**around again** être de nouveau sur pied; **before
the week was ~** avant la fin de la semaine; **the
journey ~** l'aller m; **the boat was 10 km ~** le
bateau était à 10 km du rivage; **~ loud** (adv) à
haute voix; **~ of** (prep: outside) en dehors de;
(because of: anger etc) par; (from among): **10 ~ of 10**
10 sur 10; (without): **~ of petrol** sans essence, à
court d'essence; **made ~ of wood** en or de bois;
**~ of order** (machine) en panne; (Tel: line) en
dérangement; **~ of stock** (Comm: article)
épuisé(e); (: shop) en rupture de stock
**outage** ['autɪdʒ] n (esp US: power failure) panne f or
coupure f de courant
**out-and-out** ['autəndaut] adj véritable
**outback** ['autbæk] n campagne isolée; (in
Australia) intérieur m
**outbid** [aut'bɪd] vt (irreg: like **bid**) surenchérir
**outboard** ['autbɔːd] n: **~ (motor)** (moteur m)
hors-bord m
**outbound** ['autbaund] adj: **~ (from/for)** en
partance (de/pour)
**outbreak** ['autbreɪk] n (of violence) éruption f,
explosion f; (of disease) de nombreux cas; **the ~**

**of war south of the border** la guerre qui s'est déclarée au sud de la frontière

**outbuilding** ['autbɪldɪŋ] n dépendance f

**outburst** ['autbə:st] n explosion f, accès m

**outcast** ['autkɑ:st] n exilé(e); (socially) paria m

**outclass** [aut'klɑ:s] vt surclasser

**outcome** ['autkʌm] n issue f, résultat m

**outcrop** ['autkrɔp] n affleurement m

**outcry** ['autkraɪ] n tollé (général)

**outdated** [aut'deɪtɪd] adj démodé(e)

**outdistance** [aut'dɪstəns] vt distancer

**outdo** [aut'du:] vt (irreg: like **do**) surpasser

**outdoor** [aut'dɔ:ʳ] adj de or en plein air

**outdoors** [aut'dɔ:z] adv dehors; au grand air

**outer** ['autəʳ] adj extérieur(e); ~ **suburbs** grande banlieue

**outer space** n espace m cosmique

**outfit** ['autfɪt] n équipement m; (clothes) tenue f; (inf: Comm) organisation f, boîte f

**outfitter** ['autfɪtəʳ] n (Brit): **"(gent's) ~'s"** "confection pour hommes"

**outgoing** ['autgəuɪŋ] adj (president, tenant) sortant(e); (character) ouvert(e), extraverti(e)

**outgoings** ['autgəuɪŋz] npl (Brit: expenses) dépenses fpl

**outgrow** [aut'grəu] vt (irreg: like **grow**); (clothes) devenir trop grand(e) pour

**outhouse** ['authaus] n appentis m, remise f

**outing** ['autɪŋ] n sortie f; excursion f

**outlandish** [aut'lændɪʃ] adj étrange

**outlast** [aut'lɑ:st] vt survivre à

**outlaw** ['autlɔ:] n hors-la-loi m inv ▷ vt (person) mettre hors la loi; (practice) proscrire

**outlay** ['autleɪ] n dépenses fpl; (investment) mise f de fonds

**outlet** ['autlɛt] n (for liquid etc) issue f, sortie f; (for emotion) exutoire m; (for goods) débouché m; (also: **retail outlet**) point m de vente; (US: Elec) prise f de courant

**outline** ['autlaɪn] n (shape) contour m; (summary) esquisse f, grandes lignes ▷ vt (fig: theory, plan) exposer à grands traits

**outlive** [aut'lɪv] vt survivre à

**outlook** ['autluk] n perspective f; (point of view) attitude f

**outlying** ['autlaɪɪŋ] adj écarté(e)

**outmanoeuvre** [autmə'nu:vəʳ] vt (rival etc) avoir au tournant

**outmoded** [aut'məudɪd] adj démodé(e); dépassé(e)

**outnumber** [aut'nʌmbəʳ] vt surpasser en nombre

**out-of-court** [autəv'kɔ:t] adj, adv à l'aimable

**out-of-date** [autəv'deɪt] adj (passport, ticket) périmé(e); (theory, idea) dépassé(e); (custom) désuet(-ète); (clothes) démodé(e)

**out-of-doors** ['autəv'dɔ:z] adv = **outdoors**

**out-of-the-way** ['autəvðə'weɪ] adj loin de tout; (fig) insolite

**out-of-town** [autəv'taun] adj (shopping centre etc) en périphérie

**outpatient** ['autpeɪʃənt] n malade m/f en consultation externe

**outpost** ['autpəust] n avant-poste m

**outpouring** ['autpɔ:rɪŋ] n (fig) épanchement(s) m(pl)

**output** ['autput] n rendement m, production f; (Comput) sortie f ▷ vt (Comput) sortir

**outrage** ['autreɪdʒ] n (anger) indignation f; (violent act) atrocité f, acte m de violence; (scandal) scandale m ▷ vt outrager

**outrageous** [aut'reɪdʒəs] adj atroce; (scandalous) scandaleux(-euse)

**outrider** ['autraɪdəʳ] n (on motorcycle) motard m

**outright** adv [aut'raɪt] complètement; (deny, refuse) catégoriquement; (ask) carrément; (kill) sur le coup ▷ adj ['autraɪt] complet(-ète); catégorique

**outrun** [aut'rʌn] vt (irreg: like **run**) dépasser

**outset** ['autsɛt] n début m

**outshine** [aut'ʃaɪn] vt (irreg: like **shine**); (fig) éclipser

**outside** [aut'saɪd] n extérieur m ▷ adj extérieur(e); (remote, unlikely): **an ~ chance** une (très) faible chance ▷ adv (au) dehors, à l'extérieur ▷ prep hors de, à l'extérieur de; (in front of) devant; **at the ~** (fig) au plus or maximum; ~ **left/right** n (Football) ailier gauche/droit

**outside broadcast** n (Radio, TV) reportage m

**outside lane** n (Aut: in Britain) voie f de droite; (: in US, Europe) voie de gauche

**outside line** n (Tel) ligne extérieure

**outsider** [aut'saɪdəʳ] n (in race etc) outsider m; (stranger) étranger(-ère)

**outsize** ['autsaɪz] adj énorme; (clothes) grande taille inv

**outskirts** ['autskə:ts] npl faubourgs mpl

**outsmart** [aut'smɑ:t] vt se montrer plus malin(-igne) or futé(e) que

**outspoken** [aut'spəukən] adj très franc (franche)

**outspread** [aut'sprɛd] adj (wings) déployé(e)

**outstanding** [aut'stændɪŋ] adj remarquable, exceptionnel(le); (unfinished: work, business) en suspens, en souffrance; (debt) impayé(e); (problem) non réglé(e); **your account is still ~** vous n'avez pas encore tout remboursé

**outstay** [aut'steɪ] vt: **to ~ one's welcome** abuser de l'hospitalité de son hôte

**outstretched** [aut'strɛtʃt] adj (hand) tendu(e); (body) étendu(e)

**outstrip** [aut'strɪp] vt (also fig) dépasser

**out-tray** ['auttreɪ] n courrier m "départ"

**outvote** [aut'vəut] vt: **to ~ sb (by)** mettre qn en minorité (par); **to ~ sth (by)** rejeter qch (par)

**outward** ['autwəd] adj (sign, appearances) extérieur(e); (journey) (d')aller

**outwardly** ['autwədlɪ] adv extérieurement; en apparence

**outwards** ['autwədz] adv (esp Brit) = **outward**

**outweigh** [aut'weɪ] vt l'emporter sur

**outwit** [aut'wɪt] vt se montrer plus malin que

**oval** ['əuvl] adj, n ovale m

**o**

**Oval Office** n (US: Pol) voir article

● **OVAL OFFICE**
●
● L'Oval Office est le bureau personnel du
● président des États-Unis à la Maison-
● Blanche, ainsi appelé du fait de sa forme
● ovale. Par extension, ce terme désigne la
● présidence elle-même.

**ovarian** [əu'vɛəriən] adj ovarien(ne); (cancer) des
ovaires
**ovary** ['əuvəri] n ovaire m
**ovation** [əu'veiʃən] n ovation f
**oven** ['ʌvn] n four m
**oven glove** n gant m de cuisine
**ovenproof** ['ʌvnpru:f] adj allant au four
**oven-ready** ['ʌvnrɛdi] adj prêt(e) à cuire
**ovenware** ['ʌvnwɛəʳ] n plats mpl allant au four
**over** ['əuvəʳ] adv (par-)dessus; (excessively) trop
▷ adj (or adv) (finished) fini(e), terminé(e); (too
much) en plus ▷ prep sur; par-dessus; (above) au-
dessus de; (on the other side of) de l'autre côté de;
(more than) plus de; (during) pendant; (about,
concerning): **they fell out ~ money/her** ils se
sont brouillés pour des questions d'argent/à
cause d'elle; **~ here** ici; **~ there** là-bas; **all ~**
(everywhere) partout; (finished) fini(e); **~ and ~**
**(again)** à plusieurs reprises; **~ and above** en
plus de; **to ask sb ~** inviter qn (à passer); **to go**
**~ to sb's** passer chez qn; **to fall ~** tomber; **to**
**turn sth ~** retourner qch; **now ~ to our Paris**
**correspondent** nous passons l'antenne à
notre correspondant à Paris; **the world ~** dans
le monde entier; **she's not ~ intelligent** (Brit)
elle n'est pas particulièrement intelligente
**over...** ['əuvəʳ] prefix: **overabundant**
surabondant(e)
**overact** [əuvər'ækt] vi (Theat) outrer son rôle
**overall** ['əuvərɔ:l] adj (length) total(e); (study,
impression) d'ensemble ▷ n (Brit) blouse f ▷ adv
[əuvər'ɔ:l] dans l'ensemble, en général;
**overalls** npl (boiler suit) bleus mpl (de travail)
**overall majority** n majorité absolue
**overanxious** [əuvər'æŋkʃəs] adj trop
anxieux(-euse)
**overawe** [əuvər'ɔ:] vt impressionner
**overbalance** [əuvə'bæləns] vi basculer
**overbearing** [əuvə'bɛəriŋ] adj
impérieux(-euse), autoritaire
**overboard** ['əuvəbɔ:d] adv (Naut) par-dessus
bord; **to go ~ for sth** (fig) s'emballer (pour qch)
**overbook** [əuvə'buk] vi faire du surbooking
**overcame** [əuvə'keim] pt of **overcome**
**overcapitalize** [əuvə'kæpitəlaiz] vt
surcapitaliser
**overcast** ['əuvəkɑ:st] adj couvert(e)
**overcharge** [əuvə'tʃɑ:dʒ] vt: **to ~ sb for sth** faire
payer qch trop cher à qn
**overcoat** ['əuvəkəut] n pardessus m
**overcome** [əuvə'kʌm] vt (irreg: like **come**);
(defeat) triompher de; (difficulty) surmonter ▷ adj

(emotionally) bouleversé(e); **~ with grief**
accablé(e) de douleur
**overconfident** [əuvə'kɔnfidənt] adj trop sûr(e)
de soi
**overcrowded** [əuvə'kraudid] adj bondé(e); (city,
country) surpeuplé(e)
**overcrowding** [əuvə'kraudiŋ] n
surpeuplement m; (in bus) encombrement m
**overdo** [əuvə'du:] vt (irreg: like **do**) exagérer;
(overcook) trop cuire; **to ~ it, to ~ things** (work too
hard) en faire trop, se surmener
**overdone** [əuvə'dʌn] adj (vegetables, steak) trop
cuit(e)
**overdose** ['əuvədəus] n dose excessive
**overdraft** ['əuvədrɑ:ft] n découvert m
**overdrawn** [əuvə'drɔ:n] adj (account) à découvert
**overdrive** ['əuvədraiv] n (Aut) (vitesse f)
surmultipliée f
**overdue** [əuvə'dju:] adj en retard; (bill)
impayé(e); (change) qui tarde; **that change was**
**long ~** ce changement n'avait que trop tardé
**overemphasis** [əuvər'ɛmfəsis] n: **to put an ~**
**on** accorder trop d'importance à
**overestimate** [əuvər'ɛstimeit] vt surestimer
**overexcited** [əuvərik'saitid] adj surexcité(e)
**overexertion** [əuvərig'zə:ʃən] n surmenage m
(physique)
**overexpose** [əuvərik'spəuz] vt (Phot) surexposer
**overflow** vi [əuvə'fləu] déborder ▷ n ['əuvəfləu]
trop-plein m; (also: **overflow pipe**) tuyau m
d'écoulement, trop-plein m
**overfly** [əuvə'flai] vt (irreg: like **fly**) survoler
**overgenerous** [əuvə'dʒɛnərəs] adj (person)
prodigue; (offer) excessif(-ive)
**overgrown** [əuvə'grəun] adj (garden) envahi(e)
par la végétation; **he's just an ~ schoolboy** (fig)
c'est un écolier attardé
**overhang** ['əuvə'hæŋ] vt (irreg: like **hang**)
surplomber ▷ vi faire saillie
**overhaul** vt [əuvə'hɔ:l] réviser ▷ n ['əuvəhɔ:l]
révision f
**overhead** adv [əuvə'hɛd] au-dessus ▷ adj, n
['əuvəhɛd] ▷ adj aérien(ne); (lighting) vertical(e)
▷ n (US) = **overheads**
**overhead projector** n rétroprojecteur m
**overheads** ['əuvəhɛdz] npl (Brit) frais généraux
**overhear** [əuvə'hiəʳ] vt (irreg: like **hear**) entendre
(par hasard)
**overheat** [əuvə'hi:t] vi devenir surchauffé(e);
(engine) chauffer
**overjoyed** [əuvə'dʒɔid] adj ravi(e), enchanté(e)
**overkill** ['əuvəkil] n (fig): **it would be ~** ce serait
de trop
**overland** ['əuvəlænd] adj, adv par voie de terre
**overlap** vi [əuvə'læp] se chevaucher ▷ n
['əuvəlæp] chevauchement m
**overleaf** [əuvə'li:f] adv au verso
**overload** [əuvə'ləud] vt surcharger
**overlook** [əuvə'luk] vt (have view of) donner sur;
(miss) oublier, négliger; (forgive) fermer les yeux
sur
**overlord** ['əuvəlɔ:d] n chef m suprême

**overmanning** [əuvə'mænɪŋ] n sureffectif m, main-d'œuvre f pléthorique

**overnight** adv [əuvə'naɪt] (happen) durant la nuit; (fig) soudain ▷ adj ['əuvənaɪt] d'une (or de) nuit; soudain(e); **to stay ~ (with sb)** passer la nuit (chez qn); **he stayed there ~** il y a passé la nuit; **if you travel ~ …** si tu fais le voyage de nuit …; **he'll be away ~** il ne rentrera pas ce soir

**overnight bag** n nécessaire m de voyage

**overpass** ['əuvəpɑːs] n (US: for cars) pont autoroutier; (: for pedestrians) passerelle f, pont m

**overpay** [əuvə'peɪ] vt (irreg: like **pay**); **to ~ sb by £50** donner à qn 50 livres de trop

**overplay** [əuvə'pleɪ] vt exagérer; **to ~ one's hand** trop présumer de sa situation

**overpower** [əuvə'pauəʳ] vt vaincre; (fig) accabler

**overpowering** [əuvə'pauərɪŋ] adj irrésistible; (heat, stench) suffocant(e)

**overproduction** ['əuvəprə'dʌkʃən] n surproduction f

**overrate** [əuvə'reɪt] vt surestimer

**overreact** [əuvəri:'ækt] vi réagir de façon excessive

**override** [əuvə'raɪd] vt (irreg: like **ride**); (order, objection) passer outre à; (decision) annuler

**overriding** [əuvə'raɪdɪŋ] adj prépondérant(e)

**overrule** [əuvə'ru:l] vt (decision) annuler; (claim) rejeter; (person) rejeter l'avis de

**overrun** [əuvə'rʌn] vt (irreg: like **run**); (Mil: country etc) occuper; (time limit etc) dépasser ▷ vi dépasser le temps imparti; **the town is ~ with tourists** la ville est envahie de touristes

**overseas** [əuvə'si:z] adv outre-mer; (abroad) à l'étranger ▷ adj (trade) extérieur(e); (visitor) étranger(-ère)

**oversee** [əuvə'si:] vt (irreg: like **see**) surveiller

**overseer** ['əuvəsɪəʳ] n (in factory) contremaître m

**overshadow** [əuvə'ʃædəu] vt (fig) éclipser

**overshoot** [əuvə'ʃu:t] vt (irreg: like **shoot**) dépasser

**oversight** ['əuvəsaɪt] n omission f, oubli m; **due to an ~** par suite d'une inadvertance

**oversimplify** [əuvə'sɪmplɪfaɪ] vt simplifier à l'excès

**oversleep** [əuvə'sli:p] vi (irreg: like **sleep**) se réveiller (trop) tard

**overspend** [əuvə'spɛnd] vi (irreg: like **spend**) dépenser de trop; **we have overspent by 5,000 dollars** nous avons dépassé notre budget de 5 000 dollars, nous avons dépensé 5 000 dollars de trop

**overspill** ['əuvəspɪl] n excédent m de population

**overstaffed** [əuvə'stɑ:ft] adj: **to be ~** avoir trop de personnel, être en surnombre

**overstate** [əuvə'steɪt] vt exagérer

**overstatement** [əuvə'steɪtmənt] n exagération f

**overstay** [əuvə'steɪ] vt: **to ~ one's welcome (at sb's)** abuser de l'hospitalité de qn

**overstep** [əuvə'stɛp] vt: **to ~ the mark** dépasser la mesure

**overstock** [əuvə'stɔk] vt stocker en surabondance

**overstretched** [əuvə'strɛtʃt] adj (person) débordé(e); **my budget is ~** j'ai atteint les limites de mon budget

**overstrike** n ['əuvəstraɪk] (on printer) superposition f, double frappe f ▷ vt (irreg: like **strike**) [əuvə'straɪk] surimprimer

**overt** [əu'və:t] adj non dissimulé(e)

**overtake** [əuvə'teɪk] vt (irreg: like **take**) dépasser; (Brit: Aut) dépasser, doubler

**overtaking** [əuvə'teɪkɪŋ] n (Aut) dépassement m

**overtax** [əuvə'tæks] vt (Econ) surimposer; (fig: strength, patience) abuser de; **to ~ o.s.** se surmener

**overthrow** [əuvə'θrəu] vt (irreg: like **throw**); (government) renverser

**overtime** ['əuvətaɪm] n heures fpl supplémentaires; **to do** or **work ~** faire des heures supplémentaires

**overtime ban** n refus m de faire des heures supplémentaires

**overtone** ['əuvətəun] n (also: **overtones**) note f, sous-entendus mpl

**overtook** [əuvə'tuk] pt of **overtake**

**overture** ['əuvətʃuəʳ] n (Mus, fig) ouverture f

**overturn** [əuvə'tə:n] vt renverser; (decision, plan) annuler ▷ vi se retourner

**overview** ['əuvəvju:] n vue f d'ensemble

**overweight** [əuvə'weɪt] adj (person) trop gros(se); (luggage) trop lourd(e)

**overwhelm** [əuvə'wɛlm] vt (subj: emotion) accabler, submerger; (enemy, opponent) écraser

**overwhelming** [əuvə'wɛlmɪŋ] adj (victory, defeat) écrasant(e); (desire) irrésistible; **one's ~ impression is of heat** on a une impression dominante de chaleur

**overwhelmingly** [əuvə'wɛlmɪŋlɪ] adv (vote) en masse; (win) d'une manière écrasante

**overwork** [əuvə'wə:k] n surmenage m ▷ vt surmener ▷ vi se surmener

**overwrite** [əuvə'raɪt] vt (irreg: like **write**); (Comput) écraser

**overwrought** [əuvə'rɔ:t] adj excédé(e)

**ovulation** [ɔvju'leɪʃən] n ovulation f

**owe** [əu] vt devoir; **to ~ sb sth, to ~ sth to sb** devoir qch à qn; **how much do I ~ you?** combien est-ce que je vous dois?

**owing to** ['əuɪŋtu:] prep à cause de, en raison de

**owl** [aul] n hibou m

**own** [əun] vt posséder ▷ vi (Brit): **to ~ to sth** reconnaître or avouer qch; **to ~ to having done sth** avouer avoir fait qch ▷ adj propre; **a room of my ~** une chambre à moi, ma propre chambre; **can I have it for my (very) ~?** puis-je l'avoir pour moi (tout) seul?; **to get one's ~ back** prendre sa revanche; **on one's ~** tout(e) seul(e); **to come into one's ~** trouver sa voie; trouver sa justification

**o**

▶ **own up** vi avouer

**own brand** n (Comm) marque f de distributeur

**owner** ['əunə<sup>r</sup>] n propriétaire m/f

**owner-occupier** ['əunər'ɔkjupaɪə<sup>r</sup>] n propriétaire occupant

**ownership** ['əunəʃɪp] n possession f; **it's under new ~** (shop etc) il y a eu un changement de propriétaire

**own goal** n: **he scored an ~** (Sport) il a marqué un but contre son camp; (fig) cela s'est retourné contre lui

**ox** (pl **oxen**) [ɔks, 'ɔksn] n bœuf m

**Oxbridge** ['ɔksbrɪdʒ] n (Brit) les universités d'Oxford et de Cambridge; voir article

◉ **OXBRIDGE**
◉
◉ Oxbridge, nom formé à partir des mots
◉ Ox(ford) et (Cam)bridge, s'utilise pour
◉ parler de ces deux universités comme
◉ formant un tout, dans la mesure où elles

◉ sont toutes deux les universités
◉ britanniques les plus prestigieuses et
◉ mondialement connues.

**oxen** ['ɔksən] npl of **ox**

**Oxfam** ['ɔksfæm] n abbr (Brit: = Oxford Committee for Famine Relief) association humanitaire

**oxide** ['ɔksaɪd] n oxyde m

**Oxon.** ['ɔksn] abbr (Brit: Oxoniensis) = **of Oxford**

**oxtail** ['ɔksteɪl] n: **~ soup** soupe f à la queue de bœuf

**oxygen** ['ɔksɪdʒən] n oxygène m

**oxygen mask** n masque m à oxygène

**oxygen tent** n tente f à oxygène

**oyster** ['ɔɪstə<sup>r</sup>] n huître f

**oz.** abbr = **ounce; ounces**

**ozone** ['əuzəun] n ozone m

**ozone friendly** ['əuzəunfrɛndlɪ] adj qui n'attaque pas or qui préserve la couche d'ozone

**ozone hole** n trou m d'ozone

**ozone layer** n couche f d'ozone

# Pp

**P, p** [piː] n (letter) P, p m; **P for Peter** P comme Pierre

**P** abbr = **president; prince**

**p** abbr (= page) p; (Brit) = **penny; pence**

**P.A.** n abbr = **personal assistant; public address system** ▷ abbr (US) = **Pennsylvania**

**pa** [pɑː] n (inf) papa m

**Pa.** abbr (US) = **Pennsylvania**

**p.a.** abbr = **per annum**

**PAC** n abbr (US) = **political action committee**

**pace** [peɪs] n pas m; (speed) allure f; vitesse f ▷ vi: **to ~ up and down** faire les cent pas; **to keep ~ with** aller à la même vitesse que; (events) se tenir au courant de; **to set the ~** (running) donner l'allure; (fig) donner le ton; **to put sb through his ~s** (fig) mettre qn à l'épreuve

**pacemaker** ['peɪsmeɪkə'] n (Med) stimulateur m cardiaque; (Sport: also: **pacesetter**) meneur(-euse) de train

**Pacific** [pə'sɪfɪk] n: **the ~ (Ocean)** le Pacifique, l'océan m Pacifique

**pacific** [pə'sɪfɪk] adj pacifique

**pacification** [pæsɪfɪ'keɪʃən] n pacification f

**pacifier** ['pæsɪfaɪə'] n (US: dummy) tétine f

**pacifist** ['pæsɪfɪst] n pacifiste m/f

**pacify** ['pæsɪfaɪ] vt pacifier; (soothe) calmer

**pack** [pæk] n paquet m; (bundle) ballot m; (of hounds) meute f; (of thieves, wolves etc) bande f; (of cards) jeu m; (US: of cigarettes) paquet; (back pack) sac m à dos ▷ vt (goods) empaqueter, emballer; (in suitcase etc) emballer; (box) remplir; (cram) entasser; (press down) tasser; damer; (Comput) grouper, tasser ▷ vi: **to ~ (one's bags)** faire ses bagages; **to ~ into** (room, stadium) s'entasser dans; **to send sb ~ing** (inf) envoyer promener qn

▸ **pack in** (Brit inf) vi (machine) tomber en panne ▷ vt (boyfriend) plaquer; **~ it in!** laisse tomber!

▸ **pack off** vt: **to ~ sb off to** expédier qn à

▸ **pack up** vi (Brit inf: machine) tomber en panne; (: person) se tirer ▷ vt (belongings) ranger; (goods, presents) empaqueter, emballer

**package** ['pækɪdʒ] n paquet m; (of goods) emballage m, conditionnement m; (also: **package deal**: agreement) marché global; (: purchase) forfait m; (Comput) progiciel m ▷ vt (goods) conditionner

**package holiday** n (Brit) vacances organisées

**package tour** n voyage organisé

**packaging** ['pækɪdʒɪŋ] n (wrapping materials) emballage m; (of goods) conditionnement m

**packed** [pækt] adj (crowded) bondé(e)

**packed lunch** (Brit) n repas froid

**packer** ['pækə'] n (person) emballeur(-euse); conditionneur(-euse)

**packet** ['pækɪt] n paquet m

**packet switching** [-swɪtʃɪŋ] n (Comput) commutation f de paquets

**pack ice** ['pækaɪs] n banquise f

**packing** ['pækɪŋ] n emballage m

**packing case** n caisse f (d'emballage)

**pact** [pækt] n pacte m, traité m

**pad** [pæd] n bloc(-notes m) m; (to prevent friction) tampon m; (for inking) tampon m encreur; (inf: flat) piaule f ▷ vt rembourrer ▷ vi: **to ~ in/about** etc entrer/aller et venir etc à pas feutrés

**padded** ['pædɪd] adj (jacket) matelassé(e); (bra) rembourré(e); **~ cell** cellule capitonnée

**padding** ['pædɪŋ] n rembourrage m; (fig) délayage m

**paddle** ['pædl] n (oar) pagaie f; (US: for table tennis) raquette f de ping-pong ▷ vi (with feet) barboter, faire trempette ▷ vt: **to ~ a canoe** etc pagayer

**paddle steamer** n bateau m à aubes

**paddling pool** ['pædlɪŋ-] n petit bassin

**paddock** ['pædək] n enclos m; (Racing) paddock m

**paddy** ['pædɪ] n (also: **paddy field**) rizière f

**padlock** ['pædlɔk] n cadenas m ▷ vt cadenasser

**padre** ['pɑːdrɪ] n aumônier m

**paediatrician**, (US) **pediatrician** [piːdɪə'trɪʃən] n pédiatre m/f

**paediatrics**, (US) **pediatrics** [piːdɪ'ætrɪks] n pédiatrie f

**paedophile**, (US) **pedophile** ['piːdəfaɪl] n pédophile m

**pagan** ['peɪɡən] adj, n païen(ne)

**page** [peɪdʒ] n (of book) page f; (also: **page boy**) groom m, chasseur m; (at wedding) garçon m d'honneur ▷ vt (in hotel etc) (faire) appeler

**pageant** ['pædʒənt] n spectacle m historique; grande cérémonie

**pageantry** ['pædʒəntrɪ] n apparat m, pompe f
**page break** n fin f or saut m de page
**pager** ['peɪdʒəʳ] n bip m (inf), Alphapage® m
**paginate** ['pædʒɪneɪt] vt paginer
**pagination** [pædʒɪ'neɪʃən] n pagination f
**pagoda** [pə'gəudə] n pagode f
**paid** [peɪd] pt, pp of **pay** ▷ adj (work, official)
rémunéré(e); (holiday) payé(e); **to put ~ to** (Brit)
mettre fin à, mettre par terre
**paid-up** ['peɪdʌp], (US) **paid-in** ['peɪdɪn] adj
(member) à jour de sa cotisation; (shares)
libéré(e); **~ capital** capital versé
**pail** [peɪl] n seau m
**pain** [peɪn] n douleur f; (inf: nuisance) plaie f; **to
be in ~** souffrir, avoir mal; **to have a ~ in** avoir
mal à or une douleur à or dans; **to take ~s to do**
se donner du mal pour faire; **on ~ of death** sous
peine de mort
**pained** ['peɪnd] adj peiné(e), chagrin(e)
**painful** ['peɪnful] adj douloureux(-euse);
(difficult) difficile, pénible
**painfully** ['peɪnfəlɪ] adv (fig: very) terriblement
**painkiller** ['peɪnkɪləʳ] n calmant m,
analgésique m
**painless** ['peɪnlɪs] adj indolore
**painstaking** ['peɪnzteɪkɪŋ] adj (person)
soigneux(-euse); (work) soigné(e)
**paint** [peɪnt] n peinture f ▷ vt peindre; (fig)
dépeindre; **to ~ the door blue** peindre la porte
en bleu; **to ~ in oils** faire de la peinture à
l'huile
**paintbox** ['peɪntbɔks] n boîte f de couleurs
**paintbrush** ['peɪntbrʌʃ] n pinceau m
**painter** ['peɪntəʳ] n peintre m
**painting** ['peɪntɪŋ] n peinture f; (picture)
tableau m
**paint-stripper** ['peɪntstrɪpəʳ] n décapant m
**paintwork** ['peɪntwə:k] n (Brit) peintures fpl;
(: of car) peinture f
**pair** [pɛəʳ] n (of shoes, gloves etc) paire f; (of people)
couple m; (twosome) duo m; **~ of scissors** (paire
de) ciseaux mpl; **~ of trousers** pantalon m
▶ **pair off** vi se mettre par deux
**pajamas** [pə'dʒɑ:məz] npl (US) pyjama(s) m(pl)
**Pakistan** [pɑ:kɪ'stɑ:n] n Pakistan m
**Pakistani** [pɑ:kɪ'stɑ:nɪ] adj pakistanais(e) ▷ n
Pakistanais(e)
**PAL** [pæl] n abbr (TV: = phase alternation line) PAL m
**pal** [pæl] n (inf) copain (copine)
**palace** ['pæləs] n palais m
**palatable** ['pælɪtəbl] adj bon (bonne), agréable
au goût
**palate** ['pælɪt] n palais m (Anat)
**palatial** [pə'leɪʃəl] adj grandiose, magnifique
**palaver** [pə'lɑ:vəʳ] n palabres fpl or mpl;
histoire(s) f(pl)
**pale** [peɪl] adj pâle ▷ vi pâlir ▷ n: **to be beyond
the ~** être au ban de la société; **to grow** or **turn
~** (person) pâlir; **~ blue** (adj) bleu pâle inv; **to ~
into insignificance (beside)** perdre beaucoup
d'importance (par rapport à)
**paleness** ['peɪlnɪs] n pâleur f

**Palestine** ['pælɪstaɪn] n Palestine f
**Palestinian** [pælɪs'tɪnɪən] adj palestinien(ne)
▷ n Palestinien(ne)
**palette** ['pælɪt] n palette f
**paling** ['peɪlɪŋ] n (stake) palis m; (fence) palissade f
**palisade** [pælɪ'seɪd] n palissade f
**pall** [pɔ:l] n (of smoke) voile m ▷ vi: **to ~ (on)**
devenir lassant (pour)
**pallet** ['pælɪt] n (for goods) palette f
**pallid** ['pælɪd] adj blême
**pallor** ['pæləʳ] n pâleur f
**pally** ['pælɪ] adj (inf) copain (copine)
**palm** [pɑ:m] n (Anat) paume f; (also: **palm tree**)
palmier m; (leaf, symbol) palme f ▷ vt: **to ~ sth off
on sb** (inf) refiler qch à qn
**palmist** ['pɑ:mɪst] n chiromancien(ne)
**Palm Sunday** n le dimanche des Rameaux
**palpable** ['pælpəbl] adj évident(e), manifeste
**palpitation** [pælpɪ'teɪʃən] n palpitation f
**paltry** ['pɔ:ltrɪ] adj dérisoire; piètre
**pamper** ['pæmpəʳ] vt gâter, dorloter
**pamphlet** ['pæmflət] n brochure f; (political etc)
tract m
**pan** [pæn] n (also: **saucepan**) casserole f; (also:
**frying pan**) poêle f; (of lavatory) cuvette f ▷ vi
(Cine) faire un panoramique ▷ vt (inf: book, film)
éreinter; **to ~ for gold** laver du sable aurifère
**panacea** [pænə'sɪə] n panacée f
**Panama** ['pænəmɑ:] n Panama m
**Panama Canal** n canal m de Panama
**pancake** ['pænkeɪk] n crêpe f
**Pancake Day** n (Brit) mardi gras
**pancake roll** n rouleau m de printemps
**pancreas** ['pæŋkrɪəs] n pancréas m
**panda** ['pændə] n panda m
**panda car** n (Brit) ≈ voiture f pie inv
**pandemic** [pæn'dɛmɪk] n pandémie f
**pandemonium** [pændɪ'məunɪəm] n tohu-
bohu m
**pander** ['pændəʳ] vi: **to ~ to** flatter bassement;
obéir servilement à
**p&h** abbr (US: = postage and handling) frais mpl de
port
**P&L** abbr = **profit and loss**
**p&p** abbr (Brit: = postage and packing) frais mpl de
port
**pane** [peɪn] n carreau m (de fenêtre), vitre f
**panel** ['pænl] n (of wood, cloth etc) panneau m;
(Radio, TV) panel m, invités mpl; (for interview,
exams) jury m; (official: of experts) table ronde,
comité m
**panel game** n (Brit) jeu m (radiophonique/
télévisé)
**panelling**, (US) **paneling** ['pænəlɪŋ] n boiseries
fpl
**panellist**, (US) **panelist** ['pænəlɪst] n invité(e)
(d'un panel), membre d'un panel
**pang** [pæŋ] n: **~s of remorse** pincements mpl de
remords; **~s of hunger/conscience**
tiraillements mpl d'estomac/de la conscience
**panhandler** ['pænhændləʳ] n (US inf)
mendiant(e)

**panic** ['pænɪk] n panique f, affolement m ▷ vi
s'affoler, paniquer

**panic buying** [-baɪɪŋ] n achats mpl de
précaution

**panicky** ['pænɪkɪ] adj (person) qui panique or
s'affole facilement

**panic-stricken** ['pænɪkstrɪkən] adj affolé(e)

**pannier** ['pænɪər] n (on animal) bât m; (on bicycle)
sacoche f

**panorama** [pænə'rɑːmə] n panorama m

**panoramic** [pænə'ræmɪk] adj panoramique

**pansy** ['pænzɪ] n (Bot) pensée f; (inf) tapette f,
pédé m

**pant** [pænt] vi haleter

**pantechnicon** [pæn'tɛknɪkən] n (Brit) (grand)
camion de déménagement

**panther** ['pænθər] n panthère f

**panties** ['pæntɪz] npl slip m, culotte f

**pantihose** ['pæntɪhəuz] n (US) collant m

**panto** ['pæntəu] n = **pantomime**

**pantomime** ['pæntəmaɪm] n (Brit) spectacle m
de Noël

**pantry** ['pæntrɪ] n garde-manger m inv; (room)
office m

**pants** [pænts] n (Brit: woman's) culotte f, slip m;
(: man's) slip, caleçon m; (US: trousers) pantalon m

**pantsuit** ['pæntsuːt] n (US) tailleur-pantalon m

**pantyhose** ['pæntɪhəuz] npl collant m

**papacy** ['peɪpəsɪ] n papauté f

**papal** ['peɪpəl] adj papal(e), pontifical(e)

**paparazzi** [pæpə'rætsiː] npl paparazzi mpl

**paper** ['peɪpər] n papier m; (also: **wallpaper**)
papier peint; (also: **newspaper**) journal m;
(academic essay) article m; (exam) épreuve écrite
▷ adj en or de papier ▷ vt tapisser (de papier
peint); **papers** npl (also: **identity papers**)
papiers mpl (d'identité); **a piece of** - (odd bit) un
bout de papier; (sheet) une feuille de papier; **to
put sth down on** ~ mettre qch par écrit

**paper advance** n (on printer) avance f (du) papier

**paperback** ['peɪpəbæk] n livre broché or non
relié; (small) livre m de poche ▷ adj: ~ **edition**
édition brochée

**paper bag** n sac m en papier

**paperboy** ['peɪpəbɔɪ] n (selling) vendeur m de
journaux; (delivering) livreur m de journaux

**paper clip** n trombone m

**paper handkerchief** n, **paper hankie** n (inf)
mouchoir m en papier

**paper mill** n papeterie f

**paper money** n papier-monnaie m

**paper profit** n profit m théorique

**paper shop** n (Brit) marchand m de journaux

**paperweight** ['peɪpəweɪt] n presse-papiers m
inv

**paperwork** ['peɪpəwɜːk] n papiers mpl; (pej)
paperasserie f

**papier-mâché** ['pæpɪeɪ'mæʃeɪ] n papier mâché

**paprika** ['pæprɪkə] n paprika m

**Pap test, Pap smear** ['pæp-] n (Med) frottis m

**par** [pɑːr] n pair m; (Golf) normale f du parcours;
**on a ~ with** à égalité avec, au même niveau que;

**at ~** au pair; **above/below ~** au-dessus/au-
dessous du pair; **to feel below** or **under** or **not
up to ~** ne pas se sentir en forme

**parable** ['pærəbl] n parabole f (Rel)

**parabola** [pə'ræbələ] n parabole f (Math)

**paracetamol** [pærə'siːtəmɔl] (Brit) n
paracétamol m

**parachute** ['pærəʃuːt] n parachute m ▷ vi sauter
en parachute

**parachute jump** n saut m en parachute

**parachutist** ['pærəʃuːtɪst] n parachutiste m/f

**parade** [pə'reɪd] n défilé m; (inspection) revue f;
(street) boulevard m ▷ vt (fig) faire étalage de ▷ vi
défiler; **a fashion ~** (Brit) un défilé de mode

**parade ground** n terrain m de manœuvre

**paradise** ['pærədaɪs] n paradis m

**paradox** ['pærədɔks] n paradoxe m

**paradoxical** [pærə'dɔksɪkl] adj paradoxal(e)

**paradoxically** [pærə'dɔksɪklɪ] adv
paradoxalement

**paraffin** ['pærəfɪn] n (Brit): ~ **(oil)** pétrole
(lampant); **liquid ~** huile f de paraffine

**paraffin heater** n (Brit) poêle m à mazout

**paraffin lamp** n (Brit) lampe f à pétrole

**paragon** ['pærəgən] n parangon m

**paragraph** ['pærəgrɑːf] n paragraphe m; **to
begin a new ~** aller à la ligne

**Paraguay** ['pærəgwaɪ] n Paraguay m

**Paraguayan** [pærə'gwaɪən] adj paraguayen(ne)
▷ n Paraguayen(ne)

**parallel** ['pærəlɛl] adj: ~ **(with** or **to)** parallèle
(à); (fig) analogue (à) ▷ n (line) parallèle f; (fig,
Geo) parallèle m

**paralysed** ['pærəlaɪzd] adj paralysé(e)

**paralysis** (pl **paralyses**) [pə'rælɪsɪs, -siːz] n
paralysie f

**paralytic** [pærə'lɪtɪk] adj paralytique; (Brit inf:
drunk) ivre mort(e)

**paralyze** ['pærəlaɪz] vt paralyser

**paramedic** [pærə'mɛdɪk] n auxiliaire m/f
médical(e)

**parameter** [pə'ræmɪtər] n paramètre m

**paramilitary** [pærə'mɪlɪtərɪ] adj paramilitaire

**paramount** ['pærəmaunt] adj: **of ~ importance**
de la plus haute or grande importance

**paranoia** [pærə'nɔɪə] n paranoïa f

**paranoid** ['pærənɔɪd] adj (Psych) paranoïaque;
(neurotic) paranoïde

**paranormal** [pærə'nɔːml] adj paranormal(e)

**paraphernalia** [pærəfə'neɪlɪə] n attirail m,
affaires fpl

**paraphrase** ['pærəfreɪz] vt paraphraser

**paraplegic** [pærə'pliːdʒɪk] n paraplégique m/f

**parapsychology** [pærəsaɪ'kɔlədʒɪ] n
parapsychologie f

**parasite** ['pærəsaɪt] n parasite m

**parasol** ['pærəsɔl] n ombrelle f; (at café etc)
parasol m

**paratrooper** ['pærətruːpər] n parachutiste m
(soldat)

**parcel** ['pɑːsl] n paquet m, colis m ▷ vt (also:
**parcel up**) empaqueter

**p**

▸ **parcel out** vt répartir
**parcel bomb** n (Brit) colis piégé
**parcel post** n service m de colis postaux
**parch** [pɑːtʃ] vt dessécher
**parched** [pɑːtʃt] adj (person) assoiffé(e)
**parchment** ['pɑːtʃmənt] n parchemin m
**pardon** ['pɑːdn] n pardon m; (Law) grâce f ▷ vt
pardonner à; (Law) gracier; ~! pardon!; ~
(after burping etc) excusez-moi!; **I beg your** ~! (I'm
sorry) pardon!, je suis désolé!; **(I beg your)** ~?,
(US) ~ **me?** (what did you say?) pardon?
**pare** [pɛəʳ] vt (Brit: nails) couper; (fruit etc) peler;
(fig: costs etc) réduire
**parent** ['pɛərənt] n (father) père m; (mother) mère
f; **parents** npl parents mpl
**parentage** ['pɛərəntɪdʒ] n naissance f; **of
unknown** ~ de parents inconnus
**parental** [pə'rɛntl] adj parental(e), des parents
**parent company** n société f mère
**parenthesis** (pl **parentheses**) [pə'rɛnθɪsɪs, -siːz]
n parenthèse f; **in parentheses** entre
parenthèses
**parenthood** ['pɛərənthud] n paternité f or
maternité f
**parenting** ['pɛərəntɪŋ] n le métier de parent, le
travail d'un parent
**Paris** ['pærɪs] n Paris
**parish** ['pærɪʃ] n paroisse f; (Brit: civil)
≈ commune f ▷ adj paroissial(e)
**parish council** n (Brit) ≈ conseil municipal
**parishioner** [pə'rɪʃənəʳ] n paroissien(ne)
**Parisian** [pə'rɪzɪən] adj parisien(ne), de Paris ▷ n
Parisien(ne)
**parity** ['pærɪtɪ] n parité f
**park** [pɑːk] n parc m, jardin public ▷ vt garer
▷ vi se garer; **can I** ~ **here?** est-ce que je peux
me garer ici?
**parka** ['pɑːkə] n parka m
**parking** ['pɑːkɪŋ] n stationnement m; **"no** ~"
"stationnement interdit"
**parking lights** npl feux mpl de stationnement
**parking lot** n (US) parking m, parc m de
stationnement
**parking meter** n parc(o)mètre m
**parking offence**, (US) **parking violation** n
infraction f au stationnement
**parking place** n place f de stationnement
**parking ticket** n P.-V. m
**Parkinson's** ['pɑːkɪnsənz] n (also: **Parkinson's
disease**) maladie f de Parkinson, parkinson m
**parkway** ['pɑːkweɪ] n (US) route f express (en site
vert ou aménagé)
**parlance** ['pɑːləns] n: **in common/modern** ~
dans le langage courant/actuel
**parliament** ['pɑːləmənt] n parlement m; voir
article

◉ **PARLIAMENT**
◉
◉ Le Parliament est l'assemblée législative
◉ britannique; elle est composée de deux
◉ chambres: la "House of Commons" et la

◉ "House of Lords". Ses bureaux sont les
◉ "Houses of Parliament" au palais de
◉ Westminster à Londres. Chaque Parliament
◉ est en général élu pour cinq ans. Les débats
◉ du Parliament sont maintenant retransmis à
◉ la télévision.

**parliamentary** [pɑːlə'mɛntərɪ] adj
parlementaire
**parlour**, (US) **parlor** ['pɑːləʳ] n salon m
**parlous** ['pɑːləs] adj (formal) précaire
**Parmesan** [pɑːmɪ'zæn] n (also: **Parmesan
cheese**) Parmesan m
**parochial** [pə'rəukɪəl] adj paroissial(e); (pej) à
l'esprit de clocher
**parody** ['pærədɪ] n parodie f
**parole** [pə'rəul] n: **on** ~ en liberté conditionnelle
**paroxysm** ['pærəksɪzəm] n (Med, of grief)
paroxysme m; (of anger) accès m
**parquet** ['pɑːkeɪ] n: ~ **floor(ing)** parquet m
**parrot** ['pærət] n perroquet m
**parrot fashion** adv comme un perroquet
**parry** ['pærɪ] vt esquiver, parer à
**parsimonious** [pɑːsɪ'məunɪəs] adj
parcimonieux(-euse)
**parsley** ['pɑːslɪ] n persil m
**parsnip** ['pɑːsnɪp] n panais m
**parson** ['pɑːsn] n ecclésiastique m; (Church of
England) pasteur m
**part** [pɑːt] n partie f; (of machine) pièce f; (Theat)
rôle m; (Mus) voix f; partie; (of serial) épisode m;
(US: in hair) raie f ▷ adj partiel(le) ▷ adv = **partly**
▷ vt séparer ▷ vi (people) se séparer; (crowd)
s'ouvrir; (roads) se diviser; **to take** ~ **in**
participer à, prendre part à; **to take sb's** ~
prendre le parti de qn, prendre parti pour qn;
**on his** ~ de sa part; **for my** ~ en ce qui me
concerne; **for the most** ~ en grande partie;
dans la plupart des cas; **for the better** ~ **of the
day** pendant la plus grande partie de la
journée; **to be** ~ **and parcel of** faire partie de;
**in** ~ en partie; **to take sth in good/bad** ~
prendre qch du bon/mauvais côté
▸ **part with** vt fus (person) se séparer de;
(possessions) se défaire de
**partake** [pɑː'teɪk] vi (irreg: like **take**); (formal): **to
** ~ **of sth** prendre part à qch, partager qch
**part exchange** n (Brit): **in** ~ en reprise
**partial** ['pɑːʃl] adj (incomplete) partiel(le); (unjust)
partial(e); **to be** ~ **to** aimer, avoir un faible pour
**partially** ['pɑːʃəlɪ] adv en partie, partiellement;
partialement
**participant** [pɑː'tɪsɪpənt] n (in competition,
campaign) participant(e)
**participate** [pɑː'tɪsɪpeɪt] vi: **to** ~ **(in)** participer
(à), prendre part (à)
**participation** [pɑːtɪsɪ'peɪʃən] n participation f
**participle** ['pɑːtɪsɪpl] n participe m
**particle** ['pɑːtɪkl] n particule f; (of dust) grain m
**particular** [pə'tɪkjuləʳ] adj (specific)
particulier(-ière); (special) particulier,
spécial(e); (fussy) difficile, exigeant(e); (careful)

méticuleux(-euse); **in ~** en particulier, surtout

**particularly** [pəˈtɪkjulə lɪ] *adv* particulièrement; *(in particular)* en particulier

**particulars** [pəˈtɪkjuləz] *npl* détails *mpl*; *(information)* renseignements *mpl*

**parting** [ˈpɑːtɪŋ] *n* séparation *f*; *(Brit: in hair)* raie *f* ▷ *adj* d'adieu; **his ~ shot was ...** il lança en partant....

**partisan** [pɑːtɪˈzæn] *n* partisan(e) ▷ *adj* partisan(e); de parti

**partition** [pɑːˈtɪʃən] *n* *(Pol)* partition *f*, division *f*; *(wall)* cloison *f*

**partly** [ˈpɑːtlɪ] *adv* en partie, partiellement

**partner** [ˈpɑːtnəʳ] *n* *(Comm)* associé(e); *(Sport)* partenaire *m/f*; *(spouse)* conjoint(e); *(lover)* ami(e); *(at dance)* cavalier(-ière) ▷ *vt* être l'associé *or* le partenaire *or* le cavalier de

**partnership** [ˈpɑːtnəʃɪp] *n* association *f*; **to go into ~ (with), form a ~ (with)** s'associer (avec)

**part payment** *n* acompte *m*

**partridge** [ˈpɑːtrɪdʒ] *n* perdrix *f*

**part-time** [ˈpɑːtˈtaɪm] *adj, adv* à mi-temps, à temps partiel

**part-timer** [pɑːtˈtaɪməʳ] *n* *(also: **part-time worker**)* travailleur(-euse) à temps partiel

**party** [ˈpɑːtɪ] *n* *(Pol)* parti *m*; *(celebration)* fête *f*; *(: formal)* réception *f*; *(: in evening)* soirée *f*; *(team)* équipe *f*; *(group)* groupe *m*; *(Law)* partie *f*; **dinner ~** dîner *m*; **to give** *or* **throw a ~** donner une réception; **we're having a ~ next Saturday** nous organisons une soirée *or* réunion entre amis samedi prochain; **it's for our son's birthday ~** c'est pour la fête (*or* le goûter) d'anniversaire de notre garçon; **to be a ~ to a crime** être impliqué(e) dans un crime

**party dress** *n* robe habillée

**party line** *n* *(Pol)* ligne *f* politique; *(Tel)* ligne partagée

**party piece** *n* numéro habituel

**party political broadcast** *n* *émission réservée à un parti politique.*

**pass** [pɑːs] *vt* *(time, object)* passer; *(place)* passer devant; *(friend)* croiser; *(exam)* être reçu(e) à, réussir; *(candidate)* admettre; *(overtake)* dépasser; *(approve)* approuver, accepter; *(law)* promulguer ▷ *vi* passer; *(Scol)* être reçu(e) *or* admis(e), réussir ▷ *n* *(permit)* laissez-passer *m inv*; *(membership card)* carte *f* d'accès *or* d'abonnement; *(in mountains)* col *m*; *(Sport)* passe *f*; *(Scol: also: **pass mark**)*: **to get a ~** être reçu(e) (sans mention); **to ~ sb sth** passer qch à qn; **could you ~ the salt/oil, please?** pouvez-vous me passer le sel/l'huile, s'il vous plaît?; **she could ~ for 25** on lui donnerait 25 ans; **to ~ sth through a ring** *etc* (faire) passer qch dans un anneau *etc*; **could you ~ the vegetables round?** pourriez-vous faire passer les légumes?; **things have come to a pretty ~** *(Brit)* voilà où on en est!; **to make a ~ at sb** *(inf)* faire des avances à qn

▸ **pass away** *vi* mourir

▸ **pass by** *vi* passer ▷ *vt* *(ignore)* négliger

▸ **pass down** *vt* *(customs, inheritance)* transmettre

▸ **pass on** *vi* *(die)* s'éteindre, décéder ▷ *vt* *(hand on)*: **to ~ on (to)** transmettre (à); *(: illness)* passer (à); *(: price rises)* répercuter (sur)

▸ **pass out** *vi* s'évanouir; *(Brit Mil)* sortir *(d'une école militaire)*

▸ **pass over** *vt* *(ignore)* passer sous silence

▸ **pass up** *vt* *(opportunity)* laisser passer

**passable** [ˈpɑːsəbl] *adj* *(road)* praticable; *(work)* acceptable

**passage** [ˈpæsɪdʒ] *n* *(also: **passageway**)* couloir *m*; *(gen, in book)* passage *m*; *(by boat)* traversée *f*

**passbook** [ˈpɑːsbuk] *n* livret *m*

**passenger** [ˈpæsɪndʒəʳ] *n* passager(-ère)

**passer-by** [pɑːsəˈbaɪ] *n* passant(e)

**passing** [ˈpɑːsɪŋ] *adj* *(fig)* passager(-ère); **in ~** en passant

**passing place** *n* *(Aut)* aire *f* de croisement

**passion** [ˈpæʃən] *n* passion *f*; **to have a ~ for sth** avoir la passion de qch

**passionate** [ˈpæʃənɪt] *adj* passionné(e)

**passion fruit** *n* fruit *m* de la passion

**passion play** *n* mystère *m* de la Passion

**passive** [ˈpæsɪv] *adj* *(also Ling)* passif(-ive)

**passive smoking** *n* tabagisme passif

**passkey** [ˈpɑːskiː] *n* passe *m*

**Passover** [ˈpɑːsəuvəʳ] *n* Pâque juive

**passport** [ˈpɑːspɔːt] *n* passeport *m*

**passport control** *n* contrôle *m* des passeports

**passport office** *n* bureau *m* de délivrance des passeports

**password** [ˈpɑːswəːd] *n* mot *m* de passe

**past** [pɑːst] *prep* *(in front of)* devant; *(further than)* au delà de, plus loin que; *(later than)* après ▷ *adv*: **to run ~** passer en courant ▷ *adj* passé(e); *(president etc)* ancien(ne) ▷ *n* passé *m*; **he's ~ forty** il a dépassé la quarantaine, il a plus de *or* passé quarante ans; **ten/quarter ~ eight** huit heures dix/un *or* et quart; **it's ~ midnight** il est plus de minuit, il est passé minuit; **he ran ~ me** il m'a dépassé en courant, il a passé devant moi en courant; **for the ~ few/3 days** depuis quelques/3 jours; ces derniers/3 derniers jours; **in the ~** *(gen)* dans le temps, autrefois; *(Ling)* au passé; **I'm ~ caring** je ne m'en fais plus; **to be ~ it** *(Brit inf: person)* avoir passé l'âge

**pasta** [ˈpæstə] *n* pâtes *fpl*

**paste** [peɪst] *n* pâte *f*; *(Culin: meat)* pâté *m* (à tartiner); *(: tomato)* purée *f*, concentré *m*; *(glue)* colle *f* (de pâte); *(jewellery)* strass *m* ▷ *vt* coller

**pastel** [ˈpæstl] *adj* pastel *inv* ▷ *n* *(Art: pencil)* (crayon *m*) pastel *m*; *(: drawing)* (dessin *m* au) pastel; *(colour)* ton *m* pastel *inv*

**pasteurized** [ˈpæstəraɪzd] *adj* pasteurisé(e)

**pastille** [ˈpæstl] *n* pastille *f*

**pastime** [ˈpɑːstaɪm] *n* passe-temps *m inv*, distraction *f*

**past master** *n* *(Brit)*: **to be a ~ at** être expert en

**pastor** [ˈpɑːstəʳ] *n* pasteur *m*

**pastoral** [ˈpɑːstərl] *adj* pastoral(e)

**pastry** [ˈpeɪstrɪ] *n* pâte *f*; *(cake)* pâtisserie *f*

**pasture** [ˈpɑːstʃəʳ] *n* pâturage *m*

**P**

**pasty¹** *n* ['pæstɪ] petit pâté (en croûte)
**pasty²** ['peɪstɪ] *adj* pâteux(-euse); *(complexion)* terreux(-euse)
**pat** [pæt] *vt* donner une petite tape à; *(dog)* caresser ▷ *n*: **a ~ of butter** une noisette de beurre; **to give sb/o.s. a ~ on the back** *(fig)* congratuler qn/se congratuler; **he knows it (off) ~**, *(US)* **he has it down ~** il sait cela sur le bout des doigts
**patch** [pætʃ] *n (of material)* pièce *f*; *(eye patch)* cache *m*; *(spot)* tache *f*; *(of land)* parcelle *f*; *(on tyre)* rustine *f* ▷ *vt (clothes)* rapiécer; **a bad ~** *(Brit)* une période difficile
▸ **patch up** *vt* réparer
**patchwork** ['pætʃwə:k] *n* patchwork *m*
**patchy** ['pætʃɪ] *adj* inégal(e); *(incomplete)* fragmentaire
**pate** [peɪt] *n*: **a bald ~** un crâne chauve *or* dégarni
**pâté** ['pæteɪ] *n* pâté *m*, terrine *f*
**patent** ['peɪtnt] *(US)* ['pætnt] *n* brevet *m* (d'invention) ▷ *vt* faire breveter ▷ *adj* patent(e), manifeste
**patent leather** *n* cuir verni
**patently** ['peɪtntlɪ] *adv* manifestement
**patent medicine** *n* spécialité *f* pharmaceutique
**patent office** *n* bureau *m* des brevets
**paternal** [pə'tə:nl] *adj* paternel(le)
**paternity** [pə'tə:nɪtɪ] *n* paternité *f*
**paternity leave** [pə'tə:nɪtɪ-] *n* congé *m* de paternité
**paternity suit** *n (Law)* action *f* en recherche de paternité
**path** [pɑ:θ] *n* chemin *m*, sentier *m*; *(in garden)* allée *f*; *(of planet)* course *f*; *(of missile)* trajectoire *f*
**pathetic** [pə'θɛtɪk] *adj (pitiful)* pitoyable; *(very bad)* lamentable, minable; *(moving)* pathétique
**pathological** [pæθə'lɔdʒɪkl] *adj* pathologique
**pathologist** [pə'θɔlədʒɪst] *n* pathologiste *m/f*
**pathology** [pə'θɔlədʒɪ] *n* pathologie *f*
**pathos** ['peɪθɔs] *n* pathétique *m*
**pathway** ['pɑ:θweɪ] *n* chemin *m*, sentier *m*; *(in garden)* allée *f*
**patience** ['peɪʃns] *n* patience *f*; *(Brit: Cards)* réussite *f*; **to lose (one's) ~** perdre patience
**patient** ['peɪʃnt] *n* malade *m/f*; *(of dentist etc)* patient(e) ▷ *adj* patient(e)
**patiently** ['peɪʃntlɪ] *adv* patiemment
**patio** ['pætɪəu] *n* patio *m*
**patriot** ['peɪtrɪət] *n* patriote *m/f*
**patriotic** [pætrɪ'ɔtɪk] *adj* patriotique; *(person)* patriote
**patriotism** ['pætrɪətɪzəm] *n* patriotisme *m*
**patrol** [pə'trəul] *n* patrouille *f* ▷ *vt* patrouiller dans; **to be on ~** être de patrouille
**patrol boat** *n* patrouilleur *m*
**patrol car** *n* voiture *f* de police
**patrolman** [pə'trəulmən] *(irreg)* *n (US)* agent *m* de police
**patron** ['peɪtrən] *n (in shop)* client(e); *(of charity)* patron(ne); **~ of the arts** mécène *m*
**patronage** ['pætrənɪdʒ] *n* patronage *m*, appui *m*

**patronize** ['pætrənaɪz] *vt* être (un) client *or* un habitué de; *(fig)* traiter avec condescendance
**patronizing** ['pætrənaɪzɪŋ] *adj* condescendant(e)
**patron saint** *n* saint(e) patron(ne)
**patter** ['pætə'] *n* crépitement *m*, tapotement *m*; *(sales talk)* boniment *m* ▷ *vi* crépiter, tapoter
**pattern** ['pætən] *n* modèle *m*; *(Sewing)* patron *m*; *(design)* motif *m*; *(sample)* échantillon *m*; **behaviour ~** mode *m* de comportement
**patterned** ['pætənd] *adj* à motifs
**paucity** ['pɔ:sɪtɪ] *n* pénurie *f*, carence *f*
**paunch** [pɔ:ntʃ] *n* gros ventre, bedaine *f*
**pauper** ['pɔ:pə'] *n* indigent(e); **~'s grave** fosse commune
**pause** [pɔ:z] *n* pause *f*, arrêt *m*; *(Mus)* silence *m* ▷ *vi* faire une pause, s'arrêter; **to ~ for breath** reprendre son souffle; *(fig)* faire une pause
**pave** [peɪv] *vt* paver, daller; **to ~ the way for** ouvrir la voie à
**pavement** ['peɪvmənt] *n (Brit)* trottoir *m*; *(US)* chaussée *f*
**pavilion** [pə'vɪlɪən] *n* pavillon *m*; tente *f*; *(Sport)* stand *m*
**paving** ['peɪvɪŋ] *n (material)* pavé *m*, dalle *f*; *(area)* pavage *m*, dallage *m*
**paving stone** *n* pavé *m*
**paw** [pɔ:] *n* patte *f* ▷ *vt* donner un coup de patte à; *(person: pej)* tripoter
**pawn** [pɔ:n] *n* gage *m*; *(Chess, also fig)* pion *m* ▷ *vt* mettre en gage
**pawnbroker** ['pɔ:nbrəukə'] *n* prêteur *m* sur gages
**pawnshop** ['pɔ:nʃɔp] *n* mont-de-piété *m*
**pay** [peɪ] *(pt, pp* **paid)** [peɪd] *n* salaire *m*; *(of manual worker)* paie *f* ▷ *vt* payer; *(be profitable to: also fig)* rapporter à ▷ *vi* payer; *(be profitable)* être rentable; **how much did you ~ for it?** combien l'avez-vous payé?, vous l'avez payé combien?; **I paid £5 for that ticket** j'ai payé ce billet 5 livres; **can I ~ by credit card?** est-ce que je peux payer par carte de crédit?; **to ~ one's way** payer sa part; *(company)* couvrir ses frais; **to ~ dividends** *(fig)* porter ses fruits, s'avérer rentable; **it won't ~ you to do that** vous ne gagnerez rien à faire cela; **to ~ attention (to)** prêter attention (à); **to ~ sb a visit** rendre visite à qn; **to ~ one's respects to sb** présenter ses respects à qn
▸ **pay back** *vt* rembourser
▸ **pay for** *vt fus* payer
▸ **pay in** *vt* verser
▸ **pay off** *vt (debts)* régler, acquitter; *(person)* rembourser; *(workers)* licencier ▷ *vi (scheme, decision)* se révéler payant(e); **to ~ sth off in instalments** payer qch à tempérament
▸ **pay out** *vt (money)* payer, sortir de sa poche; *(rope)* laisser filer
▸ **pay up** *vt (debts)* régler; *(amount)* payer
**payable** ['peɪəbl] *adj* payable; **to make a cheque ~ to sb** établir un chèque à l'ordre de qn
**pay-as-you-go** [ˌpeɪəzjə'gəu] *adj (mobile phone)* à

carte prépayée
**pay award** n augmentation f
**payday** n jour m de paie
**PAYE** n abbr (Brit: = pay as you earn) système de retenue des impôts à la source
**payee** [peɪˈiː] n bénéficiaire m/f
**pay envelope** n (US) paie f
**paying** [ˈpeɪɪŋ] adj payant(e); ~ **guest** hôte payant
**payload** [ˈpeɪləud] n charge f utile
**payment** [ˈpeɪmənt] n paiement m; (of bill) règlement m; (of deposit, cheque) versement m; **advance ~** (part sum) acompte m; (total sum) paiement anticipé; **deferred ~, ~ by instalments** paiement par versements échelonnés; **monthly ~** mensualité f; **in ~ for, in ~ of** en règlement de; **on ~ of £5** pour 5 livres
**payout** [ˈpeɪaut] n (from insurance) dédommagement m; (in competition) prix m
**pay packet** n (Brit) paie f
**pay phone** n cabine f téléphonique, téléphone public
**pay raise** n (US) = **pay rise**
**pay rise** n (Brit) augmentation f (de salaire)
**payroll** [ˈpeɪrəul] n registre m du personnel; **to be on a firm's ~** être employé par une entreprise
**pay slip** n (Brit) bulletin m de paie, feuille f de paie
**pay station** n (US) cabine f téléphonique
**pay television** n chaînes fpl payantes
**PBS** n abbr (US: = Public Broadcasting Service) groupement d'aide à la réalisation d'émissions pour la TV publique
**PBX** n abbr (Brit: = private branch exchange) PBX m, commutateur m privé
**PC** n abbr = **personal computer**; (Brit) = **police constable** ▷ adj abbr = **politically correct** ▷ abbr (Brit) = **Privy Councillor**
**p.c.** abbr = **per cent; postcard**
**p/c** abbr = **petty cash**
**PCB** n abbr = **printed circuit board**
**pcm** n abbr (= per calender month) par mois
**PD** n abbr (US) = **police department**
**pd** abbr = **paid**
**PDA** n abbr (= personal digital assistant) agenda m électronique
**PDQ** n abbr = **pretty damn quick**
**PDSA** n abbr (Brit) = **People's Dispensary for Sick Animals**
**PDT** abbr (US: = Pacific Daylight Time) heure d'été du Pacifique
**PE** n abbr (= physical education) EPS f ▷ abbr (Canada) = **Prince Edward Island**
**pea** [piː] n (petit) pois
**peace** [piːs] n paix f; (calm) calme m, tranquillité f; **to be at ~ with sb/sth** être en paix avec qn/qch; **to keep the ~** (policeman) assurer le maintien de l'ordre; (citizen) ne pas troubler l'ordre
**peaceable** [ˈpiːsəbl] adj paisible, pacifique
**peaceful** [ˈpiːsful] adj paisible, calme

**peacekeeper** [ˈpiːskiːpəʳ] n (force) force gardienne de la paix
**peacekeeping** [ˈpiːskiːpɪŋ] n maintien m de la paix
**peacekeeping force** n forces fpl qui assurent le maintien de la paix
**peace offering** n gage m de réconciliation; (humorous) gage de paix
**peach** [piːtʃ] n pêche f
**peacock** [ˈpiːkɔk] n paon m
**peak** [piːk] n (mountain) pic m, cime f; (of cap) visière f; (fig: highest level) maximum m; (: of career, fame) apogée m
**peak-hour** [ˈpiːkauəʳ] adj (traffic etc) de pointe
**peak hours** npl heures fpl d'affluence or de pointe
**peak period** n période f de pointe
**peak rate** n plein tarif
**peaky** [ˈpiːkɪ] adj (Brit inf) fatigué(e)
**peal** [piːl] n (of bells) carillon m; **~s of laughter** éclats mpl de rire
**peanut** [ˈpiːnʌt] n arachide f, cacahuète f
**peanut butter** n beurre m de cacahuète
**pear** [pɛəʳ] n poire f
**pearl** [pɜːl] n perle f
**peasant** [ˈpɛznt] n paysan(ne)
**peat** [piːt] n tourbe f
**pebble** [ˈpɛbl] n galet m, caillou m
**peck** [pɛk] vt (also: **peck at**) donner un coup de bec à; (food) picorer ▷ n coup m de bec; (kiss) bécot m
**pecking order** [ˈpɛkɪŋ-] n ordre m hiérarchique
**peckish** [ˈpɛkɪʃ] adj (Brit inf): **I feel ~** je mangerais bien quelque chose, j'ai la dent
**peculiar** [pɪˈkjuːlɪəʳ] adj (odd) étrange, bizarre, curieux(-euse); (particular) particulier(-ière); **~ to** particulier à
**peculiarity** [pɪkjuːlɪˈærɪtɪ] n bizarrerie f; particularité f
**pecuniary** [pɪˈkjuːnɪərɪ] adj pécuniaire
**pedal** [ˈpɛdl] n pédale f ▷ vi pédaler
**pedal bin** n (Brit) poubelle f à pédale
**pedantic** [pɪˈdæntɪk] adj pédant(e)
**peddle** [ˈpɛdl] vt colporter; (drugs) faire le trafic de
**peddler** [ˈpɛdləʳ] n colporteur m; camelot m
**pedestal** [ˈpɛdəstl] n piédestal m
**pedestrian** [pɪˈdɛstrɪən] n piéton m ▷ adj piétonnier(-ière); (fig) prosaïque, terre à terre inv
**pedestrian crossing** n (Brit) passage clouté
**pedestrianized** [pɪˈdɛstrɪənaɪzd] adj: **a ~ street** une rue piétonne
**pedestrian precinct**, (US) **pedestrian zone** n (Brit) zone piétonne
**pediatrics** [piːdɪˈætrɪks] n (US) = **paediatrics**
**pedigree** [ˈpɛdɪgriː] n ascendance f; (of animal) pedigree m ▷ cpd (animal) de race
**pedlar** [ˈpɛdləʳ] n = **peddler**
**pedophile** [ˈpiːdəufaɪl] (US) n = **paedophile**
**pee** [piː] vi (inf) faire pipi, pisser
**peek** [piːk] vi jeter un coup d'œil (furtif)

**p**

**peel** [piːl] *n* pelure *f*, épluchure *f*; (*of orange,* *lemon*) écorce *f* ▷ *vt* peler, éplucher ▷ *vi* (*paint etc*) s'écailler; (*wallpaper*) se décoller; (*skin*) peler
▶ **peel back** *vt* décoller

**peeler** ['piːlə<sup>r</sup>] *n* (*potato etc peeler*) éplucheur *m*

**peelings** ['piːlɪŋz] *npl* pelures *fpl*, épluchures *fpl*

**peep** [piːp] *n* (*Brit: look*) coup d'œil furtif; (*sound*) pépiement *m* ▷ *vi* (*Brit*) jeter un coup d'œil (furtif)
▶ **peep out** *vi* (*Brit*) se montrer (furtivement)

**peephole** ['piːphəul] *n* judas *m*

**peer** [pɪə<sup>r</sup>] *vi*: **to ~ at** regarder attentivement, scruter ▷ *n* (*noble*) pair *m*; (*equal*) pair, égal(e)

**peerage** ['pɪərɪdʒ] *n* pairie *f*

**peerless** ['pɪəlɪs] *adj* incomparable, sans égal

**peeved** [piːvd] *adj* irrité(e), ennuyé(e)

**peevish** ['piːvɪʃ] *adj* grincheux(-euse), maussade

**peg** [pɛg] *n* cheville *f*; (*for coat etc*) patère *f*; (*Brit: also*: **clothes peg**) pince *f* à linge ▷ *vt* (*clothes*) accrocher; (*Brit: groundsheet*) fixer (avec des piquets); (*fig: prices, wages*) contrôler, stabiliser

**pejorative** [pɪ'dʒɔrətɪv] *adj* péjoratif(-ive)

**Pekin** [piː'kɪn] *n*, **Peking** [piː'kɪn] ▷ *n* Pékin

**Pekinese, Pekingese** [piːkɪ'niːz] *n* pékinois *m*

**pelican** ['pɛlɪkən] *n* pélican *m*

**pelican crossing** *n* (*Brit Aut*) feu *m* à commande manuelle

**pellet** ['pɛlɪt] *n* boulette *f*; (*of lead*) plomb *m*

**pell-mell** ['pɛl'mɛl] *adv* pêle-mêle

**pelmet** ['pɛlmɪt] *n* cantonnière *f*; lambrequin *m*

**pelt** [pɛlt] *vt*: **to ~ sb (with)** bombarder qn (de) ▷ *vi* (*rain*) tomber à seaux; (*inf: run*) courir à toutes jambes ▷ *n* peau *f*

**pelvis** ['pɛlvɪs] *n* bassin *m*

**pen** [pɛn] *n* (*for writing*) stylo *m*; (*for sheep*) parc *m*; (*US inf: prison*) taule *f*; **to put ~ to paper** prendre la plume

**penal** ['piːnl] *adj* pénal(e)

**penalize** ['piːnəlaɪz] *vt* pénaliser; (*fig*) désavantager

**penal servitude** [-'səːvɪtjuːd] *n* travaux forcés

**penalty** ['pɛnltɪ] *n* pénalité *f*; sanction *f*; (*fine*) amende *f*; (*Sport*) pénalisation *f*; (*also*: **penalty kick**: *Football*) penalty *m*; (: *Rugby*) pénalité *f*; **to pay the ~ for** être pénalisé(e) pour

**penalty area** *n* (*Brit Sport*) surface *f* de réparation

**penalty clause** *n* clause pénale

**penalty kick** *n* (*Football*) penalty *m*

**penalty shoot-out** [-'ʃuːtaut] *n* (*Football*) épreuve *f* des penalties

**penance** ['pɛnəns] *n* pénitence *f*

**pence** [pɛns] *npl of* **penny**

**penchant** ['pãːʃãːŋ] *n* penchant *m*

**pencil** ['pɛnsl] *n* crayon *m*
▶ **pencil in** *vt* noter provisoirement

**pencil case** *n* trousse *f* (d'écolier)

**pencil sharpener** *n* taille-crayon(s) *m inv*

**pendant** ['pɛndnt] *n* pendentif *m*

**pending** ['pɛndɪŋ] *prep* en attendant ▷ *adj* en suspens

**pendulum** ['pɛndjuləm] *n* pendule *m*; (*of clock*) balancier *m*

**penetrate** ['pɛnɪtreɪt] *vt* pénétrer dans; (*enemy territory*) entrer en; (*sexually*) pénétrer

**penetrating** ['pɛnɪtreɪtɪŋ] *adj* pénétrant(e)

**penetration** [pɛnɪ'treɪʃən] *n* pénétration *f*

**penfriend** ['pɛnfrɛnd] *n* (*Brit*) correspondant(e)

**penguin** ['pɛŋgwɪn] *n* pingouin *m*

**penicillin** [pɛnɪ'sɪlɪn] *n* pénicilline *f*

**peninsula** [pə'nɪnsjulə] *n* péninsule *f*

**penis** ['piːnɪs] *n* pénis *m*, verge *f*

**penitence** ['pɛnɪtns] *n* repentir *m*

**penitent** ['pɛnɪtnt] *adj* repentant(e)

**penitentiary** [pɛnɪ'tɛnʃərɪ] *n* (*US*) prison *f*

**penknife** ['pɛnnaɪf] *n* canif *m*

**Penn., Penna.** *abbr* (*US*) = **Pennsylvania**

**pen name** *n* nom *m* de plume, pseudonyme *m*

**pennant** ['pɛnənt] *n* flamme *f*, banderole *f*

**penniless** ['pɛnɪlɪs] *adj* sans le sou

**Pennines** ['pɛnaɪnz] *npl*: **the ~** les Pennines *fpl*

**penny** (*pl* **pennies** *or* **pence**) ['pɛnɪ, 'pɛnɪz, pɛns] *n* (*Brit*) penny *m*; (*US*) cent *m*

**penpal** ['pɛnpæl] *n* correspondant(e)

**penpusher** ['pɛnpuʃə<sup>r</sup>] *n* (*pej*) gratte-papier *m inv*

**pension** ['pɛnʃən] *n* (*from company*) retraite *f*; (*Mil*) pension *f*
▶ **pension off** *vt* mettre à la retraite

**pensionable** ['pɛnʃnəbl] *adj* qui a droit à une retraite

**pensioner** ['pɛnʃənə<sup>r</sup>] *n* (*Brit*) retraité(e)

**pension fund** *n* caisse *f* de retraite

**pension plan** *n* plan *m* de retraite

**pensive** ['pɛnsɪv] *adj* pensif(-ive)

**pentagon** ['pɛntəgən] *n* pentagone *m*; **the P~** (*US Pol*) le Pentagone; *voir article*

● **PENTAGON**
●
● Le *Pentagon* est le nom donné aux bureaux du
● ministère de la Défense américain, situés à
● Arlington en Virginie, à cause de la forme
● pentagonale du bâtiment dans lequel ils se
● trouvent. Par extension, ce terme est
● également utilisé en parlant du ministère
● lui-même.

**pentathlon** [pɛn'tæθlən] *n* pentathlon *m*

**Pentecost** ['pɛntɪkɔst] *n* Pentecôte *f*

**penthouse** ['pɛnthaus] *n* appartement *m* (de luxe) en attique

**pent-up** ['pɛntʌp] *adj* (*feelings*) refoulé(e)

**penultimate** [pɪ'nʌltɪmət] *adj* pénultième, avant-dernier(-ière)

**penury** ['pɛnjurɪ] *n* misère *f*

**people** ['piːpl] *npl* gens *mpl*; personnes *fpl*; (*inhabitants*) population *f*; (*Pol*) peuple *m* ▷ *n* (*nation, race*) peuple *m* ▷ *vt* peupler; **I know ~ who ...** je connais des gens qui ...; **the room was full of ~** la salle était pleine de monde *or* de gens; **several ~ came** plusieurs personnes sont venues; **~ say that ...** on dit *or* les gens disent que ...; **old ~** les personnes âgées; **young ~** les jeunes; **a man of the ~** un homme du peuple

**PEP** [pɛp] *n* (= *personal equity plan*) ≈ CEA *m*

(= *compte d'épargne en actions*)

**pep** [pɛp] n (*inf*) entrain m, dynamisme m
▶ **pep up** vt (*inf*) remonter

**pepper** ['pɛpəʳ] n poivre m; (*vegetable*) poivron m
▷ vt (*Culin*) poivrer

**pepper mill** n moulin m à poivre

**peppermint** ['pɛpəmɪnt] n (*plant*) menthe
poivrée; (*sweet*) pastille f de menthe

**pepperoni** [pɛpə'rəunɪ] n *saucisson sec de porc et de
bœuf très poivré.*

**pepperpot** ['pɛpəpɔt] n poivrière f

**pep talk** ['pɛptɔ:k] n (*inf*) (petit) discours
d'encouragement

**per** [pə:ʳ] prep par; **~ hour** (*miles etc*) à l'heure;
(*fee*) (de) l'heure; **~ kilo** *etc* le kilo *etc*; **~ day/
person** par jour/personne; **~ annum** per an; **as
~ your instructions** conformément à vos
instructions

**per annum** adv par an

**per capita** adj, adv par habitant, par personne

**perceive** [pə'si:v] vt percevoir; (*notice*)
remarquer, s'apercevoir de

**per cent** adv pour cent; **a 20 ~ discount** une
réduction de 20 pour cent

**percentage** [pə'sɛntɪdʒ] n pourcentage m; **on a
~ basis** au pourcentage

**percentage point** n: **ten ~s** dix pour cent

**perceptible** [pə'sɛptɪbl] adj perceptible

**perception** [pə'sɛpʃən] n perception f; (*insight*)
sensibilité f

**perceptive** [pə'sɛptɪv] adj (*remark, person*)
perspicace

**perch** [pə:tʃ] n (*fish*) perche f; (*for bird*) perchoir m
▷ vi (se) percher

**percolate** ['pə:kəleɪt] vt, vi passer

**percolator** ['pə:kəleɪtəʳ] n percolateur m;
cafetière f électrique

**percussion** [pə'kʌʃən] n percussion f

**peremptory** [pə'rɛmptərɪ] adj péremptoire

**perennial** [pə'rɛnɪəl] adj perpétuel(le); (*Bot*)
vivace ▷ n (*Bot*) (plante f) vivace f, plante
pluriannuelle

**perfect** ['pə:fɪkt] adj parfait(e) ▷ n (*also:* **perfect
tense**) parfait m ▷ vt [pə'fɛkt] (*technique, skill,
work of art*) parfaire; (*method, plan*) mettre au
point; **he's a ~ stranger to me** il m'est
totalement inconnu

**perfection** [pə'fɛkʃən] n perfection f

**perfectionist** [pə'fɛkʃənɪst] n perfectionniste
m/f

**perfectly** ['pə:fɪktlɪ] adv parfaitement; **I'm ~
happy with the situation** cette situation me
convient parfaitement; **you know ~ well** vous
le savez très bien

**perforate** ['pə:fəreɪt] vt perforer, percer

**perforated ulcer** ['pə:fəreɪtɪd-] n (*Med*) ulcère
perforé

**perforation** [pə:fə'reɪʃən] n perforation f; (*line of
holes*) pointillé m

**perform** [pə'fɔ:m] vt (*carry out*) exécuter,
remplir; (*concert etc*) jouer, donner ▷ vi (*actor,
musician*) jouer; (*machine, car*) marcher,
fonctionner; (*company, economy*): **to ~ well/
badly** produire de bons/mauvais résultats

**performance** [pə'fɔ:məns] n représentation f,
spectacle m; (*of an artist*) interprétation f; (*Sport*:
*of car, engine*) performance f; (*of company, economy*)
résultats mpl; **the team put up a good ~**
l'équipe a bien joué

**performer** [pə'fɔ:məʳ] n artiste m/f

**performing** [pə'fɔ:mɪŋ] adj (*animal*) savant(e)

**performing arts** npl: **the ~** les arts mpl du
spectacle

**perfume** ['pə:fju:m] n parfum m ▷ vt parfumer

**perfunctory** [pə'fʌŋktərɪ] adj négligent(e), pour
la forme

**perhaps** [pə'hæps] adv peut-être; **~ he'll ...**
peut-être qu'il ...; **~ so/not** peut-être que oui/
que non

**peril** ['pɛrɪl] n péril m

**perilous** ['pɛrɪləs] adj périlleux(-euse)

**perilously** ['pɛrɪləslɪ] adv: **they came ~ close to
being caught** ils ont été à deux doigts de se
faire prendre

**perimeter** [pə'rɪmɪtəʳ] n périmètre m

**perimeter wall** n mur m d'enceinte

**period** ['pɪərɪəd] n période f; (*History*) époque f;
(*Scol*) cours m; (*full stop*) point m; (*Med*) règles fpl
▷ adj (*costume, furniture*) d'époque; **for a ~ of
three weeks** pour (une période de) trois
semaines; **the holiday ~** (*Brit*) la période des
vacances

**periodic** [pɪərɪ'ɔdɪk] adj périodique

**periodical** [pɪərɪ'ɔdɪkl] adj périodique ▷ n
périodique m

**periodically** [pɪərɪ'ɔdɪklɪ] adv périodiquement

**period pains** npl (*Brit*) douleurs menstruelles

**peripatetic** [pɛrɪpə'tɛtɪk] adj (*salesman*)
ambulant; (*Brit*: *teacher*) qui travaille dans
plusieurs établissements

**peripheral** [pə'rɪfərəl] adj périphérique ▷ n
(*Comput*) périphérique m

**periphery** [pə'rɪfərɪ] n périphérie f

**periscope** ['pɛrɪskəup] n périscope m

**perish** ['pɛrɪʃ] vi périr, mourir; (*decay*) se
détériorer

**perishable** ['pɛrɪʃəbl] adj périssable

**perishables** ['pɛrɪʃəblz] npl denrées fpl
périssables

**perishing** ['pɛrɪʃɪŋ] adj (*Brit inf*: *cold*) glacial(e)

**peritonitis** [pɛrɪtə'naɪtɪs] n péritonite f

**perjure** ['pə:dʒəʳ] vt: **to ~ o.s.** se parjurer

**perjury** ['pə:dʒərɪ] n (*Law*: *in court*) faux
témoignage m; (*breach of oath*) parjure m

**perk** [pə:k] n (*inf*) avantage m, à-côté m
▶ **perk up** vi (*inf*: *cheer up*) se ragaillardir

**perky** ['pə:kɪ] adj (*cheerful*) guilleret(te), gai(e)

**perm** [pə:m] n (*for hair*) permanente f ▷ vt: **to
have one's hair ~ed** se faire faire une
permanente

**permanence** ['pə:mənəns] n permanence f

**permanent** ['pə:mənənt] adj permanent(e);
(*job, position*) permanent, fixe; (*dye, ink*)
indélébile; **I'm not ~ here** je ne suis pas ici à

titre définitif; ~ **address** adresse habituelle
**permanently** ['pɜːmənəntlɪ] adv de façon
permanente; (move abroad) définitivement;
(open, closed) en permanence; (tired, unhappy)
constamment
**permeable** ['pɜːmɪəbl] adj perméable
**permeate** ['pɜːmɪeɪt] vi s'infiltrer ▷ vt
s'infiltrer dans; pénétrer
**permissible** [pə'mɪsɪbl] adj permis(e),
acceptable
**permission** [pə'mɪʃən] n permission f,
autorisation f; **to give sb ~ to do sth** donner à
qn la permission de faire qch
**permissive** [pə'mɪsɪv] adj tolérant(e); **the ~
society** la société de tolérance
**permit** n ['pɜːmɪt] permis m; (entrance pass)
autorisation f, laissez-passer m; (for goods)
licence f ▷ vt [pə'mɪt] permettre; **to ~ sb to do**
autoriser qn à faire, permettre à qn de faire;
**weather ~ting** si le temps le permet
**permutation** [pɜːmju'teɪʃən] n permutation f
**pernicious** [pɜː'nɪʃəs] adj pernicieux(-euse),
nocif(-ive)
**pernickety** [pə'nɪkɪtɪ] adj (inf)
pointilleux(-euse), tatillon(ne); (task)
minutieux(-euse)
**perpendicular** [pɜːpən'dɪkjulər] adj, n
perpendiculaire f
**perpetrate** ['pɜːpɪtreɪt] vt perpétrer, commettre
**perpetual** [pə'pɛtjuəl] adj perpétuel(le)
**perpetuate** [pə'pɛtjueɪt] vt perpétuer
**perpetuity** [pɜːpɪ'tjuːɪtɪ] n: **in ~** à perpétuité
**perplex** [pə'plɛks] vt (person) rendre perplexe;
(complicate) embrouiller
**perplexing** [pə'plɛksɪŋ] adj embarrassant(e)
**perquisites** ['pɜːkwɪzɪts] npl (also: **perks**)
avantages mpl annexes
**persecute** ['pɜːsɪkjuːt] vt persécuter
**persecution** [pɜːsɪ'kjuːʃən] n persécution f
**perseverance** [pɜːsɪ'vɪərns] n persévérance f,
ténacité f
**persevere** [pɜːsɪ'vɪər] vi persévérer
**Persia** ['pɜːʃə] n Perse f
**Persian** ['pɜːʃən] adj persan(e) ▷ n (Ling) persan
m; **the ~ Gulf** le golfe Persique
**Persian cat** n chat persan
**persist** [pə'sɪst] vi: **to ~ (in doing)** persister (à
faire), s'obstiner (à faire)
**persistence** [pə'sɪstəns] n persistance f,
obstination f; opiniâtreté f
**persistent** [pə'sɪstənt] adj persistant(e), tenace;
(lateness, rain) persistant; **~ offender** (Law)
multirécidiviste m/f
**persnickety** [pə'snɪkɪtɪ] adj (US inf) =
**pernickety**
**person** ['pɜːsn] n personne f; **in ~** en personne;
**on** or **about one's ~** sur soi; **~ to ~ call** (Tel)
appel m avec préavis
**personable** ['pɜːsnəbl] adj de belle prestance,
au physique attrayant
**personal** ['pɜːsnl] adj personnel(le); **~
belongings, ~ effects** effets personnels; **~**

**hygiene** hygiène f intime; **a ~ interview** un
entretien
**personal allowance** n (Tax) part f du revenu
non imposable
**personal assistant** n secrétaire personnel(le)
**personal call** n (Tel) communication f avec
préavis
**personal column** n annonces personnelles
**personal computer** n ordinateur individuel,
PC m
**personal details** npl (on form etc) coordonnées fpl
**personal identification number** n (Comput,
Banking) numéro m d'identification personnel
**personality** [pɜːsə'nælɪtɪ] n personnalité f
**personally** ['pɜːsnəlɪ] adv personnellement; **to
take sth ~** se sentir visé(e) par qch
**personal organizer** n agenda (personnel);
(electronic) agenda électronique
**personal property** n biens personnels
**personal stereo** n Walkman® m, baladeur m
**personify** [pɜː'sɒnɪfaɪ] vt personnifier
**personnel** [pɜːsə'nɛl] n personnel m
**personnel department** n service m du
personnel
**personnel manager** n chef m du personnel
**perspective** [pə'spɛktɪv] n perspective f; **to get
sth into ~** ramener qch à sa juste mesure
**perspex®** ['pɜːspɛks] n (Brit) Plexiglas® m
**perspicacity** [pɜːspɪ'kæsɪtɪ] n perspicacité f
**perspiration** [pɜːspɪ'reɪʃən] n transpiration f
**perspire** [pə'spaɪər] vi transpirer
**persuade** [pə'sweɪd] vt: **to ~ sb to do sth**
persuader qn de faire qch, amener or décider qn
à faire qch; **to ~ sb of sth/that** persuader qn de
qch/que
**persuasion** [pə'sweɪʒən] n persuasion f; (creed)
conviction f
**persuasive** [pə'sweɪsɪv] adj persuasif(-ive)
**pert** [pɜːt] adj coquin(e), mutin(e)
**pertaining** [pɜː'teɪnɪŋ]: **~ to** prep relatif(-ive) à
**pertinent** ['pɜːtɪnənt] adj pertinent(e)
**perturb** [pə'tɜːb] vt troubler, inquiéter
**perturbing** [pə'tɜːbɪŋ] adj troublant(e)
**Peru** [pə'ruː] n Pérou m
**perusal** [pə'ruːzl] n lecture (attentive)
**Peruvian** [pə'ruːvjən] adj péruvien(ne) ▷ n
Péruvien(ne)
**pervade** [pə'veɪd] vt se répandre dans, envahir
**pervasive** [pə'veɪsɪv] adj (smell) pénétrant(e);
(influence) insidieux(-euse); (gloom, ideas)
diffus(e)
**perverse** [pə'vɜːs] adj pervers(e); (contrary)
entêté(e), contrariant(e)
**perversion** [pə'vɜːʃən] n perversion f
**perversity** [pə'vɜːsɪtɪ] n perversité f
**pervert** n ['pɜːvɜːt] perverti(e) ▷ vt [pə'vɜːt]
pervertir; (words) déformer
**pessimism** ['pɛsɪmɪzəm] n pessimisme m
**pessimist** ['pɛsɪmɪst] n pessimiste m/f
**pessimistic** [pɛsɪ'mɪstɪk] adj pessimiste
**pest** [pɛst] n animal m (or insecte m) nuisible;
(fig) fléau m

**pest control** n lutte f contre les nuisibles
**pester** ['pɛstə<sup>r</sup>] vt importuner, harceler
**pesticide** ['pɛstɪsaɪd] n pesticide m
**pestilence** ['pɛstɪləns] n peste f
**pestle** ['pɛsl] n pilon m
**pet** [pɛt] n animal familier; (favourite) chouchou m ⊳ cpd (favourite) favori(e) ⊳ vt choyer; (stroke) caresser, câliner ⊳ vi (inf) se peloter; **~ lion** etc lion etc apprivoisé; **teacher's ~** chouchou m du professeur; **~ hate** bête noire
**petal** ['pɛtl] n pétale m
**peter** ['piːtə<sup>r</sup>]: **to ~ out** vi s'épuiser; s'affaiblir
**petite** [pə'tiːt] adj menu(e)
**petition** [pə'tɪʃən] n pétition f ⊳ vt adresser une pétition à ⊳ vi: **to ~ for divorce** demander le divorce
**pet name** n (Brit) petit nom
**petrified** ['pɛtrɪfaɪd] adj (fig) mort(e) de peur
**petrify** ['pɛtrɪfaɪ] vt pétrifier
**petrochemical** [pɛtrə'kɛmɪkl] adj pétrochimique
**petrodollars** ['pɛtrəudɔləz] npl pétrodollars mpl
**petrol** ['pɛtrəl] n (Brit) essence f; **I've run out of ~** je suis en panne d'essence
**petrol bomb** n cocktail m Molotov
**petrol can** n (Brit) bidon m à essence
**petrol engine** n (Brit) moteur m à essence
**petroleum** [pə'trəuliəm] n pétrole m
**petroleum jelly** n vaseline f
**petrol pump** n (Brit: in car, at garage) pompe f à essence
**petrol station** n (Brit) station-service f
**petrol tank** n (Brit) réservoir m d'essence
**petticoat** ['pɛtɪkəut] n jupon m
**pettifogging** ['pɛtɪfɔgɪŋ] adj chicanier(-ière)
**pettiness** ['pɛtɪnɪs] n mesquinerie f
**petty** ['pɛtɪ] adj (mean) mesquin(e); (unimportant) insignifiant(e), sans importance
**petty cash** n caisse f des dépenses courantes, petite caisse
**petty officer** n second-maître m
**petulant** ['pɛtjulənt] adj irritable
**pew** [pjuː] n banc m (d'église)
**pewter** ['pjuːtə<sup>r</sup>] n étain m
**Pfc** abbr (US Mil) = **private first class**
**PG** n abbr (Cine: = parental guidance) avis des parents recommandé
**PGA** n abbr = **Professional Golfers Association**
**PH** n abbr (US Mil: = Purple Heart) décoration accordée aux blessés de guerre
**PHA** n abbr (US: = Public Housing Administration) organisme d'aide à la construction
**phallic** ['fælɪk] adj phallique
**phantom** ['fæntəm] n fantôme m; (vision) fantasme m
**Pharaoh** ['fɛərəu] n pharaon m
**pharmaceutical** [fɑːmə'sjuːtɪkl] adj pharmaceutique ⊳ n: **~s** produits mpl pharmaceutiques
**pharmacist** ['fɑːməsɪst] n pharmacien(ne)
**pharmacy** ['fɑːməsɪ] n pharmacie f
**phase** [feɪz] n phase f, période f

▸ **phase in** vt introduire progressivement
▸ **phase out** vt supprimer progressivement
**Ph.D.** abbr = **Doctor of Philosophy**
**pheasant** ['fɛznt] n faisan m
**phenomena** [fə'nɔmɪnə] npl of **phenomenon**
**phenomenal** [fɪ'nɔmɪnl] adj phénoménal(e)
**phenomenon** (pl **phenomena**) [fə'nɔmɪnən, -nə] n phénomène m
**phew** [fjuː] excl ouf!
**phial** ['faɪəl] n fiole f
**philanderer** [fɪ'lændərə<sup>r</sup>] n don Juan m
**philanthropic** [fɪlən'θrɔpɪk] adj philanthropique
**philanthropist** [fɪ'lænθrəpɪst] n philanthrope m/f
**philatelist** [fɪ'lætəlɪst] n philatéliste m/f
**philately** [fɪ'lætəlɪ] n philatélie f
**Philippines** ['fɪlɪpiːnz] npl (also: **Philippine Islands**): **the ~** les Philippines fpl
**philosopher** [fɪ'lɔsəfə<sup>r</sup>] n philosophe m
**philosophical** [fɪlə'sɔfɪkl] adj philosophique
**philosophy** [fɪ'lɔsəfɪ] n philosophie f
**phishing** ['fɪʃɪŋ] n phishing m
**phlegm** [flɛm] n flegme m
**phlegmatic** [flɛg'mætɪk] adj flegmatique
**phobia** ['fəubjə] n phobie f
**phone** [fəun] n téléphone m ⊳ vt téléphoner à ⊳ vi téléphoner; **to be on the ~** avoir le téléphone; (be calling) être au téléphone
▸ **phone back** vt, vi rappeler
▸ **phone up** vt téléphoner à ⊳ vi téléphoner
**phone bill** n facture f de téléphone
**phone book** n annuaire m
**phone box**, (US) **phone booth** n cabine f téléphonique
**phone call** n coup m de fil or de téléphone
**phonecard** ['fəunkɑːd] n télécarte f
**phone-in** ['fəunɪn] n (Brit Radio, TV) programme m à ligne ouverte
**phone number** n numéro m de téléphone
**phone tapping** [-tæpɪŋ] n mise f sur écoutes téléphoniques
**phonetics** [fə'nɛtɪks] n phonétique f
**phoney** ['fəunɪ] adj faux (fausse), factice; (person) pas franc (franche) ⊳ n (person) charlatan m; fumiste m/f
**phonograph** ['fəunəgrɑːf] n (US) électrophone m
**phony** ['fəunɪ] adj, n = **phoney**
**phosphate** ['fɔsfeɪt] n phosphate m
**phosphorus** ['fɔsfərəs] n phosphore m
**photo** ['fəutəu] n photo f; **to take a ~ of** prendre en photo
**photo...** ['fəutəu] prefix photo...
**photo album** n album m de photos
**photocall** ['fəutəukɔːl] n séance f de photos pour la presse
**photocopier** ['fəutəukɔpɪə<sup>r</sup>] n copieur m
**photocopy** ['fəutəukɔpɪ] n photocopie f ⊳ vt photocopier
**photoelectric** [fəutəu'lɛktrɪk] adj photoélectrique; **~ cell** cellule f photoélectrique

**Photofit**® ['fəutəufɪt] *n* portrait-robot *m*
**photogenic** [fəutəu'dʒɛnɪk] *adj* photogénique
**photograph** ['fəutəgræf] *n* photographie *f* ▷ *vt*
photographier; **to take a ~ of sb** prendre qn en
photo
**photographer** [fə'tɔgrəfəʳ] *n* photographe *m/f*
**photographic** [fəutə'græfɪk] *adj*
photographique
**photography** [fə'tɔgrəfɪ] *n* photographie *f*
**photo opportunity** *n occasion, souvent arrangée,
pour prendre des photos d'une personnalité.*
**Photostat**® ['fəutəustæt] *n* photocopie *f*,
photostat *m*
**photosynthesis** [fəutəu'sɪnθəsɪs] *n*
photosynthèse *f*
**phrase** [freɪz] *n* expression *f*; (*Ling*) locution *f*
▷ *vt* exprimer; (*letter*) rédiger
**phrase book** *n* recueil *m* d'expressions (pour
touristes)
**physical** ['fɪzɪkl] *adj* physique; **~ examination**
examen médical; **~ exercises** gymnastique *f*
**physical education** *n* éducation *f* physique
**physically** ['fɪzɪklɪ] *adv* physiquement
**physician** [fɪ'zɪʃən] *n* médecin *m*
**physicist** ['fɪzɪsɪst] *n* physicien(ne)
**physics** ['fɪzɪks] *n* physique *f*
**physiological** [fɪzɪə'lɔdʒɪkl] *adj* physiologique
**physiology** [fɪzɪ'ɔlədʒɪ] *n* physiologie *f*
**physiotherapist** [fɪzɪəu'θɛrəpɪst] *n*
kinésithérapeute *m/f*
**physiotherapy** [fɪzɪəu'θɛrəpɪ] *n*
kinésithérapie *f*
**physique** [fɪ'ziːk] *n* (*appearance*) physique *m*;
(*health etc*) constitution *f*
**pianist** ['piːənɪst] *n* pianiste *m/f*
**piano** [pɪ'ænəu] *n* piano *m*
**piano accordion** *n* (*Brit*) accordéon *m* à touches
**Picardy** ['pɪkədɪ] *n* Picardie *f*
**piccolo** ['pɪkələu] *n* piccolo *m*
**pick** [pɪk] *n* (*tool: also:* **pick-axe**) pic *m*, pioche *f*
▷ *vt* choisir; (*gather*) cueillir; (*remove*) prendre;
(*lock*) forcer; (*scab, spot*) gratter, écorcher; **take
your ~** faites votre choix; **the ~ of** le (la)
meilleur(e) de; **to ~ a bone** ronger un os; **to ~
one's nose** se mettre les doigts dans le nez; **to ~
one's teeth** se curer les dents; **to ~ sb's brains**
faire appel aux lumières de qn; **to ~ pockets**
pratiquer le vol à la tire; **to ~ a quarrel with sb**
chercher noise à qn
▶ **pick at** *vt fus*: **to ~ at one's food** manger du
bout des dents, chipoter
▶ **pick off** *vt* (*kill*) (viser soigneusement et)
abattre
▶ **pick on** *vt fus* (*person*) harceler
▶ **pick out** *vt* choisir; (*distinguish*) distinguer
▶ **pick up** *vi* (*improve*) remonter, s'améliorer ▷ *vt*
ramasser; (*telephone*) décrocher; (*collect*) passer
prendre; (*Aut: give lift to*) prendre; (*learn*)
apprendre; (*Radio*) capter; **to ~ up speed**
prendre de la vitesse; **to ~ o.s. up** se relever; **to
~ up where one left off** reprendre là où l'on
s'est arrêté

**pickaxe,** (*US*) **pickax** ['pɪkæks] *n* pioche *f*
**picket** ['pɪkɪt] *n* (*in strike*) gréviste *m/f* participant
à un piquet de grève; piquet *m* de grève ▷ *vt*
mettre un piquet de grève devant
**picket line** *n* piquet *m* de grève
**pickings** ['pɪkɪŋz] *npl*: **there are rich ~ to be
had in** ... il y a gros à gagner dans ...
**pickle** ['pɪkl] *n* (*also:* **pickles:** *as condiment*) pickles
*mpl* ▷ *vt* conserver dans du vinaigre *or* dans de
la saumure; **in a ~** (*fig*) dans le pétrin
**pick-me-up** ['pɪkmiːʌp] *n* remontant *m*
**pickpocket** ['pɪkpɔkɪt] *n* pickpocket *m*
**pick-up** ['pɪkʌp] *n* (*also:* **pick-up truck**) pick-up *m*
*inv*; (*Brit: on record player*) bras *m* pick-up
**picnic** ['pɪknɪk] *n* pique-nique *m* ▷ *vi* pique-
niquer
**picnic area** *n* aire *f* de pique-nique
**picnicker** ['pɪknɪkəʳ] *n* pique-niqueur(-euse)
**pictorial** [pɪk'tɔːrɪəl] *adj* illustré(e)
**picture** ['pɪktʃəʳ] *n* (*also TV*) image *f*; (*painting*)
peinture *f*, tableau *m*; (*photograph*)
photo(graphie) *f*; (*drawing*) dessin *m*; (*film*) film
*m*; (*fig: description*) description *f* ▷ *vt* (*imagine*) se
représenter; (*describe*) dépeindre, représenter;
**pictures** *npl*: **the ~s** (*Brit*) le cinéma; **to take a ~
of sb/sth** prendre qn/qch en photo; **would you
take a ~ of us, please?** pourriez-vous nous
prendre en photo, s'il vous plaît?; **the overall ~**
le tableau d'ensemble; **to put sb in the ~**
mettre qn au courant
**picture book** *n* livre *m* d'images
**picture frame** *n* cadre *m*
**picture messaging** *n* picture messaging *m*,
messagerie *f* d'images
**picturesque** [pɪktʃə'rɛsk] *adj* pittoresque
**picture window** *n* baie vitrée, fenêtre *f*
panoramique
**piddling** ['pɪdlɪŋ] *adj* (*inf*) insignifiant(e)
**pie** [paɪ] *n* tourte *f*; (*of fruit*) tarte *f*; (*of meat*)
pâté *m* en croûte
**piebald** ['paɪbɔːld] *adj* pie *inv*
**piece** [piːs] *n* morceau *m*; (*of land*) parcelle *f*;
(*item*): **a ~ of furniture/advice** un meuble/
conseil; (*Draughts*) pion *m* ▷ *vt*: **to ~ together**
rassembler; **in ~s** (*broken*) en morceaux, en
miettes; (*not yet assembled*) en pièces détachées;
**to take to ~s** démonter; **in one ~** (*object*)
intact(e); **to get back all in one ~** (*person*)
rentrer sain et sauf; **a 10p ~** (*Brit*) une pièce de
10p; **~ by ~** morceau par morceau; **a six-~ band**
un orchestre de six musiciens; **to say one's ~**
réciter son morceau
**piecemeal** ['piːsmiːl] *adv* par bouts
**piece rate** *n* taux *m or* tarif *m* à la pièce
**piecework** ['piːswəːk] *n* travail *m* aux pièces *or* à
la pièce
**pie chart** *n* graphique *m* à secteurs,
camembert *m*
**Piedmont** ['piːdmɔnt] *n* Piémont *m*
**pier** [pɪəʳ] *n* jetée *f*; (*of bridge etc*) pile *f*
**pierce** [pɪəs] *vt* percer, transpercer; **to have
one's ears ~d** se faire percer les oreilles

**pierced** [pɪəst] adj (ears) percé(e)
**piercing** ['pɪəsɪŋ] adj (cry) perçant(e)
**piety** ['paɪətɪ] n piété f
**piffling** ['pɪflɪŋ] adj insignifiant(e)
**pig** [pɪg] n cochon m, porc m; (pej: unkind person) mufle m; (: greedy person) goinfre m
**pigeon** ['pɪdʒən] n pigeon m
**pigeonhole** ['pɪdʒənhəul] n casier m
**pigeon-toed** ['pɪdʒəntəud] adj marchant les pieds en dedans
**piggy bank** ['pɪgɪ-] n tirelire f
**pigheaded** ['pɪg'hɛdɪd] adj entêté(e), têtu(e)
**piglet** ['pɪglɪt] n petit cochon, porcelet m
**pigment** ['pɪgmənt] n pigment m
**pigmentation** [pɪgmən'teɪʃən] n pigmentation f
**pigmy** ['pɪgmɪ] n = **pygmy**
**pigskin** ['pɪgskɪn] n (peau f de) porc m
**pigsty** ['pɪgstaɪ] n porcherie f
**pigtail** ['pɪgteɪl] n natte f, tresse f
**pike** [paɪk] n (spear) pique f; (fish) brochet m
**pilchard** ['pɪltʃəd] n pilchard m (sorte de sardine)
**pile** [paɪl] n (pillar, of books) pile f; (heap) tas m; (of carpet) épaisseur f; **in a** ~ en tas
  ▶ **pile on** vt: **to ~ it on** (inf) exagérer
  ▶ **pile up** vi (accumulate) s'entasser, s'accumuler ▷ vt (put in heap) empiler, entasser; (accumulate) accumuler
**piles** [paɪlz] npl hémorroïdes fpl
**pile-up** ['paɪlʌp] n (Aut) télescopage m, collision f en série
**pilfer** ['pɪlfə<sup>r</sup>] vt chaparder ▷ vi commettre des larcins
**pilfering** ['pɪlfərɪŋ] n chapardage m
**pilgrim** ['pɪlgrɪm] n pèlerin m; voir article

● **PILGRIM FATHERS**
●
● Les Pilgrim Fathers ("Pères pèlerins") sont un
● groupe de puritains qui quittèrent
● l'Angleterre en 1620 pour fuir les
● persécutions religieuses. Ayant traversé
● l'Atlantique à bord du "Mayflower", ils
● fondèrent New Plymouth en Nouvelle-
● Angleterre, dans ce qui est aujourd'hui le
● Massachusetts. Ces Pères pèlerins sont
● considérés comme les fondateurs des États-
● Unis, et l'on commémore chaque année, le
● jour de "Thanksgiving", la réussite de leur
● première récolte.

**pilgrimage** ['pɪlgrɪmɪdʒ] n pèlerinage m
**pill** [pɪl] n pilule f; **the ~** la pilule; **to be on the ~** prendre la pilule
**pillage** ['pɪlɪdʒ] vt piller
**pillar** ['pɪlə<sup>r</sup>] n pilier m
**pillar box** n (Brit) boîte f aux lettres (publique)
**pillion** ['pɪljən] n (of motor cycle) siège m arrière; **to ride** ~ être derrière; (on horse) être en croupe
**pillory** ['pɪlərɪ] n pilori m ▷ vt mettre au pilori
**pillow** ['pɪləu] n oreiller m
**pillowcase** ['pɪləukeɪs], **pillowslip** ['pɪləuslɪp]

n taie f d'oreiller
**pilot** ['paɪlət] n pilote m ▷ cpd (scheme etc) pilote, expérimental(e) ▷ vt piloter
**pilot boat** n bateau-pilote m
**pilot light** n veilleuse f
**pimento** [pɪ'mɛntəu] n piment m
**pimp** [pɪmp] n souteneur m, maquereau m
**pimple** ['pɪmpl] n bouton m
**pimply** ['pɪmplɪ] adj boutonneux(-euse)
**PIN** n abbr (= personal identification number) code m confidentiel
**pin** [pɪn] n épingle f; (Tech) cheville f; (Brit: drawing pin) punaise f; (in grenade) goupille f; (Brit Elec: of plug) broche f ▷ vt épingler; **~s and needles** fourmis fpl; **to ~ sb against/to** clouer qn contre/à; **to ~ sb down** (fig) coincer qn; **to ~ sth on sb** (fig) mettre qch sur le dos de qn
  ▶ **pin down** vt (fig): **to ~ sb down** obliger qn à répondre; **there's something strange here but I can't quite ~ it down** il y a quelque chose d'étrange ici, mais je n'arrive pas exactement à savoir quoi
**pinafore** ['pɪnəfɔ:<sup>r</sup>] n tablier m
**pinafore dress** n robe-chasuble f
**pinball** ['pɪnbɔ:l] n flipper m
**pincers** ['pɪnsəz] npl tenailles fpl
**pinch** [pɪntʃ] n pincement m; (of salt etc) pincée f ▷ vt pincer; (inf: steal) piquer, chiper ▷ vi (shoe) serrer; **at a ~** à la rigueur; **to feel the ~** (fig) se ressentir des restrictions (or de la récession etc)
**pinched** [pɪntʃt] adj (drawn) tiré(e); **~ with cold** transi(e) de froid; **~ for** (short of): **~ for money** à court d'argent; **~ for space** à l'étroit
**pincushion** ['pɪnkuʃən] n pelote f à épingles
**pine** [paɪn] n (also: **pine tree**) pin m ▷ vi: **to ~ for** aspirer à, désirer ardemment
  ▶ **pine away** vi dépérir
**pineapple** ['paɪnæpl] n ananas m
**pine cone** n pomme f de pin
**ping** [pɪŋ] n (noise) tintement m
**ping-pong®** ['pɪŋpɔŋ] n ping-pong® m
**pink** [pɪŋk] adj rose ▷ n (colour) rose m; (Bot) œillet m, mignardise f
**pinking shears** ['pɪŋkɪŋ-] npl ciseaux mpl à denteler
**pin money** n (Brit) argent m de poche
**pinnacle** ['pɪnəkl] n pinacle m
**pinpoint** ['pɪnpɔɪnt] vt indiquer (avec précision)
**pinstripe** ['pɪnstraɪp] n rayure très fine
**pint** [paɪnt] n pinte f (Brit = 0,57 l; US = 0,47 l); (Brit inf) ≈ demi m, ≈ pot m
**pinup** ['pɪnʌp] n pin-up f inv
**pioneer** [paɪə'nɪə<sup>r</sup>] n explorateur(-trice); (early settler) pionnier m; (fig) pionnier, précurseur m ▷ vt être un pionnier de
**pious** ['paɪəs] adj pieux(-euse)
**pip** [pɪp] n (seed) pépin m; **pips** npl: **the ~s** (Brit: time signal on radio) le top
**pipe** [paɪp] n tuyau m, conduite f; (for smoking) pipe f; (Mus) pipeau m ▷ vt amener par tuyau; **pipes** npl (also: **bagpipes**) cornemuse f
  ▶ **pipe down** vi (inf) se taire

**P**

**pipe cleaner** n cure-pipe m
**piped music** [paɪpt-] n musique f de fond
**pipe dream** n chimère f, utopie f
**pipeline** ['paɪplaɪn] n (for gas) gazoduc m, pipeline m; (for oil) oléoduc m, pipeline; **it is in the ~** (fig) c'est en route, ça va se faire
**piper** ['paɪpəʳ] n (flautist) joueur(-euse) de pipeau; (of bagpipes) joueur(-euse) de cornemuse
**pipe tobacco** n tabac m pour la pipe
**piping** ['paɪpɪŋ] adv: **~ hot** très chaud(e)
**piquant** ['piːkənt] adj piquant(e)
**pique** [piːk] n dépit m
**piracy** ['paɪərəsɪ] n piraterie f
**pirate** ['paɪərət] n pirate m ▷ vt (CD, video, book) pirater
**pirated** ['paɪərətɪd] adj pirate
**pirate radio** n (Brit) radio f pirate
**pirouette** [pɪru'ɛt] n pirouette f ▷ vi faire une or des pirouette(s)
**Pisces** ['paɪsiːz] n les Poissons mpl; **to be ~** être des Poissons
**piss** [pɪs] vi (inf!) pisser (!); **~ off!** tire-toi! (!)
**pissed** [pɪst] (inf!) adj (Brit: drunk) bourré(e); (US: angry) furieux(-euse)
**pistol** ['pɪstl] n pistolet m
**piston** ['pɪstən] n piston m
**pit** [pɪt] n trou m, fosse f; (also: **coal pit**) puits m de mine; (also: **orchestra pit**) fosse d'orchestre; (US: fruit stone) noyau m ▷ vt: **to ~ sb against sb** opposer qn à qn; **to ~ o.s.** or **one's wits against** se mesurer à; **pits** npl (in motor racing) aire f de service
**pitapat** ['pɪtə'pæt] adv (Brit): **to go ~** (heart) battre la chamade; (rain) tambouriner
**pitch** [pɪtʃ] n (Brit Sport) terrain m; (throw) lancement m; (Mus) ton m; (of voice) hauteur f; (fig: degree) degré m; (also: **sales pitch**) baratin m, boniment m; (Naut) tangage m; (tar) poix f ▷ vt (throw) lancer; (tent) dresser; (set: price, message) adapter, positionner ▷ vi (Naut) tanguer; (fall): **to ~ into/off** tomber dans/de; **to be ~ed forward** être projeté(e) en avant; **at this ~** à ce rythme
**pitch-black** ['pɪtʃ'blæk] adj noir(e) comme poix
**pitched battle** [pɪtʃt-] n bataille rangée
**pitcher** ['pɪtʃəʳ] n cruche f
**pitchfork** ['pɪtʃfɔːk] n fourche f
**piteous** ['pɪtɪəs] adj pitoyable
**pitfall** ['pɪtfɔːl] n trappe f, piège m
**pith** [pɪθ] n (of plant) moelle f; (of orange etc) intérieur m de l'écorce; (fig) essence f; vigueur f
**pithead** ['pɪthɛd] n (Brit) bouche f de puits
**pithy** ['pɪθɪ] adj piquant(e); vigoureux(-euse)
**pitiable** ['pɪtɪəbl] adj pitoyable
**pitiful** ['pɪtɪful] adj (touching) pitoyable; (contemptible) lamentable
**pitifully** ['pɪtɪfəlɪ] adv pitoyablement; lamentablement
**pitiless** ['pɪtɪlɪs] adj impitoyable
**pittance** ['pɪtns] n salaire m de misère
**pitted** ['pɪtɪd] adj: **~ with** (chickenpox) grêlé(e) par; (rust) piqué(e) de

**pity** ['pɪtɪ] n pitié f ▷ vt plaindre; **what a ~!** quel dommage!; **it is a ~ that you can't come** c'est dommage que vous ne puissiez venir; **to have** or **take ~ on sb** avoir pitié de qn
**pitying** ['pɪtɪɪŋ] adj compatissant(e)
**pivot** ['pɪvət] n pivot m ▷ vi pivoter
**pixel** ['pɪksl] n (Comput) pixel m
**pixie** ['pɪksɪ] n lutin m
**pizza** ['piːtsə] n pizza f
**placard** ['plækɑːd] n affiche f; (in march) pancarte f
**placate** [plə'keɪt] vt apaiser, calmer
**placatory** [plə'keɪtərɪ] adj d'apaisement, lénifiant(e)
**place** [pleɪs] n endroit m, lieu m; (proper position, job, rank, seat) place f; (house) maison f, logement m; (in street names): **Laurel ~** = rue des Lauriers; (home): **at/to his ~** chez lui ▷ vt (position) placer, mettre; (identify) situer; reconnaître; **to take ~** avoir lieu; (occur) se produire; **to take sb's ~** remplacer qn; **to change ~s with sb** changer de place avec qn; **from ~ to ~** d'un endroit à l'autre; **all over the ~** partout; **out of ~** (not suitable) déplacé(e), inopportun(e); **I feel out of ~ here** je ne me sens pas à ma place ici; **in the first ~** d'abord, en premier; **to put sb in his ~** (fig) remettre qn à sa place; **he's going ~s** (fig: inf) il fait son chemin; **it is not my ~ to do it** ce n'est pas à moi de le faire; **to ~ an order with sb (for)** (Comm) passer commande à qn (de); **to be ~d** (in race, exam) se placer; **how are you ~d next week?** comment ça se présente pour la semaine prochaine?
**placebo** [plə'siːbəu] n placebo m
**place mat** n set m de table; (in linen etc) napperon m
**placement** ['pleɪsmənt] n placement m; (during studies) stage m
**place name** n nom m de lieu
**placenta** [plə'sɛntə] n placenta m
**placid** ['plæsɪd] adj placide
**placidity** [plə'sɪdɪtɪ] n placidité f
**plagiarism** ['pleɪdʒjərɪzəm] n plagiat m
**plagiarist** ['pleɪdʒjərɪst] n plagiaire m/f
**plagiarize** ['pleɪdʒjəraɪz] vt plagier
**plague** [pleɪg] n fléau m; (Med) peste f ▷ vt (fig) tourmenter; **to ~ sb with questions** harceler qn de questions
**plaice** [pleɪs] n (pl inv) carrelet m
**plaid** [plæd] n tissu écossais
**plain** [pleɪn] adj (in one colour) uni(e); (clear) clair(e), évident(e); (simple) simple, ordinaire; (frank) franc (franche); (not handsome) quelconque, ordinaire; (cigarette) sans filtre; (without seasoning etc) nature inv ▷ adv franchement, carrément ▷ n plaine f; **in ~ clothes** (police) en civil; **to make sth ~ to sb** faire clairement comprendre qch à qn
**plain chocolate** n chocolat m à croquer
**plainly** ['pleɪnlɪ] adv clairement; (frankly) carrément, sans détours
**plainness** ['pleɪnnɪs] n simplicité f

**plain speaking** n propos mpl sans équivoque; **she has a reputation for** ~ elle est bien connue pour son franc parler or sa franchise

**plaintiff** ['pleɪntɪf] n plaignant(e)

**plaintive** ['pleɪntɪv] adj plaintif(-ive)

**plait** [plæt] n tresse f, natte f ▷ vt tresser, natter

**plan** [plæn] n plan m; (scheme) projet m ▷ vt (think in advance) projeter; (prepare) organiser ▷ vi faire des projets; **to ~ to do** projeter de faire; **how long do you ~ to stay?** combien de temps comptez-vous rester?

**plane** [pleɪn] n (Aviat) avion m; (also: **plane tree**) platane m; (tool) rabot m; (Art, Math etc) plan m; (fig) niveau m, plan ▷ adj plan(e); plat(e) ▷ vt (with tool) raboter

**planet** ['plænɪt] n planète f

**planetarium** [plænɪ'tɛərɪəm] n planétarium m

**plank** [plæŋk] n planche f; (Pol) point m d'un programme

**plankton** ['plæŋktən] n plancton m

**planned economy** [plænd-] n économie planifiée

**planner** ['plænər] n planificateur(-trice); (chart) planning m; **town** or (US) **city** ~ urbaniste m/f

**planning** ['plænɪŋ] n planification f; **family** ~ planning familial

**planning permission** n (Brit) permis m de construire

**plant** [plɑːnt] n plante f; (machinery) matériel m; (factory) usine f ▷ vt planter; (bomb) déposer, poser; (microphone, evidence) cacher

**plantation** [plæn'teɪʃən] n plantation f

**plant pot** n (Brit) pot m de fleurs

**plaque** [plæk] n plaque f

**plasma** ['plæzmə] n plasma m

**plaster** ['plɑːstər] n plâtre m; (also: **plaster of Paris**) plâtre à mouler; (Brit: also: **sticking plaster**) pansement adhésif ▷ vt plâtrer; (cover): **to ~ with** couvrir de; **in ~** (Brit: leg etc) dans le plâtre

**plasterboard** ['plɑːstəbɔːd] n Placoplâtre® m

**plaster cast** n (Med) plâtre m; (model, statue) moule m

**plastered** ['plɑːstəd] adj (inf) soûl(e)

**plasterer** ['plɑːstərər] n plâtrier m

**plastic** ['plæstɪk] n plastique m ▷ adj (made of plastic) en plastique; (flexible) plastique, malléable; (art) plastique

**plastic bag** n sac m en plastique

**plastic bullet** n balle f de plastique

**plastic explosive** n plastic m

**plasticine®** ['plæstɪsiːn] n pâte f à modeler

**plate** [pleɪt] n (dish) assiette f; (sheet of metal, on door: Phot) plaque f; (Typ) cliché m; (in book) gravure f; (dental) dentier m; (Aut: number plate) plaque minéralogique; **gold/silver** ~ (dishes) vaisselle f d'or/d'argent

**plateau** (pl **-s** or **-x**) ['plætəu, -z] n plateau m

**plateful** ['pleɪtful] n assiette f, assiettée f

**plate glass** n verre m à vitre, vitre f

**platen** ['plætən] n (on typewriter, printer) rouleau m

**plate rack** n égouttoir m

**platform** ['plætfɔːm] n (at meeting) tribune f; (Brit: of bus) plate-forme f; (stage) estrade f; (Rail) quai m; (Pol) plateforme f; **the train leaves from ~ 7** le train part de la voie 7

**platform ticket** n (Brit) billet m de quai

**platinum** ['plætɪnəm] n platine m

**platitude** ['plætɪtjuːd] n platitude f, lieu commun

**platoon** [plə'tuːn] n peloton m

**platter** ['plætər] n plat m

**plaudits** ['plɔːdɪts] npl applaudissements mpl

**plausible** ['plɔːzɪbl] adj plausible; (person) convaincant(e)

**play** [pleɪ] n jeu m; (Theat) pièce f (de théâtre) ▷ vt (game) jouer à; (team, opponent) jouer contre; (instrument) jouer de; (part, piece of music, note) jouer; (CD etc) passer ▷ vi jouer; **to bring** or **call into** ~ faire entrer en jeu; ~ **on words** jeu de mots; **to** ~ **safe** ne prendre aucun risque; **to ~ a trick on sb** jouer un tour à qn; **they're ~ing at soldiers** ils jouent aux soldats; **to ~ for time** (fig) chercher à gagner du temps; **to ~ into sb's hands** (fig) faire le jeu de qn

▶ **play about, play around** vi (person) s'amuser

▶ **play along** vi (fig): **to ~ along with** (person) entrer dans le jeu de ▷ vt (fig): **to ~ sb along** faire marcher qn

▶ **play back** vt repasser, réécouter

▶ **play down** vt minimiser

▶ **play on** vt fus (sb's feelings, credulity) jouer sur; **to ~ on sb's nerves** porter sur les nerfs de qn

▶ **play up** vi (cause trouble) faire des siennes

**playact** ['pleɪækt] vi jouer la comédie

**playboy** ['pleɪbɔɪ] n playboy m

**played-out** ['pleɪd'aut] adj épuisé(e)

**player** ['pleɪər] n joueur(-euse); (Theat) acteur(-trice); (Mus) musicien(ne)

**playful** ['pleɪful] adj enjoué(e)

**playgoer** ['pleɪgəuər] n amateur(-trice) de théâtre, habitué(e) des théâtres

**playground** ['pleɪgraund] n cour f de récréation; (in park) aire f de jeux

**playgroup** ['pleɪgruːp] n garderie f

**playing card** ['pleɪɪŋ-] n carte f à jouer

**playing field** ['pleɪɪŋ-] n terrain m de sport

**playmaker** ['pleɪmeɪkər] n (Sport) joueur qui crée des occasions de marquer des buts pour ses coéquipiers.

**playmate** ['pleɪmeɪt] n camarade m/f, copain (copine)

**play-off** ['pleɪɔf] n (Sport) belle f

**playpen** ['pleɪpen] n parc m (pour bébé)

**playroom** ['pleɪruːm] n salle f de jeux

**playschool** ['pleɪskuːl] n = **playgroup**

**plaything** ['pleɪθɪŋ] n jouet m

**playtime** ['pleɪtaɪm] n (Scol) récréation f

**playwright** ['pleɪraɪt] n dramaturge m

**plc** abbr (Brit: = public limited company) ≈ SARL f

**plea** [pliː] n (request) appel m; (excuse) excuse f; (Law) défense f

**plea bargaining** n (Law) négociations entre le procureur, l'avocat de la défense et parfois le juge, pour

723

*réduire la gravité des charges.*

**plead** [pliːd] *vt* plaider; *(give as excuse)* invoquer ▷ *vi (Law)* plaider; *(beg):* **to ~ with sb (for sth)** implorer qn (d'accorder qch); **to ~ for sth** implorer qch; **to ~ guilty/not guilty** plaider coupable/non coupable

**pleasant** ['plɛznt] *adj* agréable

**pleasantly** ['plɛzntlɪ] *adv* agréablement

**pleasantry** ['plɛzntrɪ] *n (joke)* plaisanterie *f*; **pleasantries** *npl (polite remarks)* civilités *fpl*

**please** [pliːz] *excl* s'il te *(or* vous*)* plaît ▷ *vt* plaire à ▷ *vi (think fit)* faites comme il vous plaira; **my bill, ~** l'addition, s'il vous plaît; **~ don't cry!** je t'en prie, ne pleure pas!; **~ yourself!** *(inf)* (faites) comme vous voulez!

**pleased** [pliːzd] *adj:* **~ (with)** content(e) (de); **~ to meet you** enchanté (de faire votre connaissance); **we are ~ to inform you that ...** nous sommes heureux de vous annoncer que ...

**pleasing** ['pliːzɪŋ] *adj* plaisant(e), qui fait plaisir

**pleasurable** ['plɛʒərəbl] *adj* très agréable

**pleasure** ['plɛʒər] *n* plaisir *m*; **"it's a ~"** "je vous en prie"; **with ~** avec plaisir; **is this trip for business or ~?** est-ce un voyage d'affaires ou d'agrément?

**pleasure cruise** *n* croisière *f*

**pleat** [pliːt] *n* pli *m*

**plebiscite** ['plɛbɪsɪt] *n* plébiscite *m*

**plebs** [plɛbz] *npl (pej)* bas peuple

**plectrum** ['plɛktrəm] *n* plectre *m*

**pledge** [plɛdʒ] *n* gage *m*; *(promise)* promesse *f* ▷ *vt* engager; promettre; **to ~ support for sb** s'engager à soutenir qn; **to ~ sb to secrecy** faire promettre à qn de garder le secret

**plenary** ['pliːnərɪ] *adj:* **in ~ session** en séance plénière

**plentiful** ['plɛntɪful] *adj* abondant(e), copieux(-euse)

**plenty** ['plɛntɪ] *n* abondance *f*; **~ of** beaucoup de; *(sufficient)* (bien) assez de; **we've got ~ of time** nous avons largement le temps

**pleurisy** ['pluərɪsɪ] *n* pleurésie *f*

**pliable** ['plaɪəbl] *adj* flexible; *(person)* malléable

**pliers** ['plaɪəz] *npl* pinces *fpl*

**plight** [plaɪt] *n* situation *f* critique

**plimsolls** ['plɪmsəlz] *npl (Brit)* (chaussures *fpl*) tennis *fpl*

**plinth** [plɪnθ] *n* socle *m*

**PLO** *n abbr (= Palestine Liberation Organization)* OLP *f*

**plod** [plɔd] *vi* avancer péniblement; *(fig)* peiner

**plodder** ['plɔdər] *n* bûcheur(-euse)

**plodding** ['plɔdɪŋ] *adj* pesant(e)

**plonk** [plɔŋk] *(inf) n (Brit: wine)* pinard *m*, piquette *f* ▷ *vt:* **to ~ sth down** poser brusquement qch

**plot** [plɔt] *n* complot *m*, conspiration *f*; *(of story, play)* intrigue *f*; *(of land)* lot *m* de terrain, lopin *m* ▷ *vt (mark out)* tracer point par point; *(Naut)* pointer; *(make graph of)* faire le graphique de; *(conspire)* comploter ▷ *vi* comploter; **a vegetable ~** *(Brit)* un carré de légumes

**plotter** ['plɔtər] *n* conspirateur(-trice); *(Comput)*

**plough**, *(US)* **plow** [plau] *n* charrue *f* ▷ *vt (earth)* labourer; **to ~ money into** investir dans
  ▶ **plough back** *vt (Comm)* réinvestir
  ▶ **plough through** *vt fus (snow etc)* avancer péniblement dans

**ploughing**, *(US)* **plowing** ['plauɪŋ] *n* labourage *m*

**ploughman**, *(US)* **plowman** ['plaumən] *(irreg) n* laboureur *m*

**plow** [plau] *(US)* = **plough**

**ploy** [plɔɪ] *n* stratagème *m*

**pls** *abbr (= please)* SVP *m*

**pluck** [plʌk] *vt (fruit)* cueillir; *(musical instrument)* pincer; *(bird)* plumer ▷ *n* courage *m*, cran *m*; **to ~ one's eyebrows** s'épiler les sourcils; **to ~ up courage** prendre son courage à deux mains

**plucky** ['plʌkɪ] *adj* courageux(-euse)

**plug** [plʌg] *n (stopper)* bouchon *m*, bonde *f*; *(Elec)* prise *f* de courant; *(Aut: also:* **spark(ing) plug)** bougie *f* ▷ *vt (hole)* boucher; *(inf: advertise)* faire du battage pour, matraquer; **to give sb/sth a ~** *(inf)* faire de la pub pour qn/qch
  ▶ **plug in** *vt (Elec)* brancher ▷ *vi (Elec)* se brancher

**plughole** ['plʌghəul] *n (Brit)* trou *m* (d'écoulement)

**plum** [plʌm] *n (fruit)* prune *f* ▷ *adj:* **~ job** *(inf)* travail *m* en or

**plumb** [plʌm] *adj* vertical(e) ▷ *n* plomb *m* ▷ *adv (exactly)* en plein ▷ *vt* sonder
  ▶ **plumb in** *vt (washing machine)* faire le raccordement de

**plumber** ['plʌmər] *n* plombier *m*

**plumbing** ['plʌmɪŋ] *n (trade)* plomberie *f*; *(piping)* tuyauterie *f*

**plumbline** ['plʌmlaɪn] *n* fil *m* à plomb

**plume** [pluːm] *n* plume *f*, plumet *m*

**plummet** ['plʌmɪt] *vi (person, object)* plonger; *(sales, prices)* dégringoler

**plump** [plʌmp] *adj* rondelet(te), dodu(e), bien en chair ▷ *vt:* **to ~ sth (down) on** laisser tomber qch lourdement sur
  ▶ **plump for** *vt fus (inf: choose)* se décider pour
  ▶ **plump up** *vt (cushion)* battre (pour lui redonner forme)

**plunder** ['plʌndər] *n* pillage *m* ▷ *vt* piller

**plunge** [plʌndʒ] *n* plongeon *m*; *(fig)* chute *f* ▷ *vt* plonger ▷ *vi (fall)* tomber, dégringoler; *(dive)* plonger; **to take the ~** se jeter à l'eau

**plunger** ['plʌndʒər] *n* piston *m*; *(for blocked sink)* (débouchoir *m* à) ventouse *f*

**plunging** ['plʌndʒɪŋ] *adj (neckline)* plongeant(e)

**pluperfect** [pluːˈpəːfɪkt] *n (Ling)* plus-que-parfait *m*

**plural** ['pluərl] *adj* pluriel(le) ▷ *n* pluriel *m*

**plus** [plʌs] *n (also:* **plus sign)** signe *m* plus; *(advantage)* atout *m* ▷ *prep* plus; **ten/twenty ~** plus de dix/vingt; **it's a ~** c'est un atout

**plus fours** *npl* pantalon *m* (de) golf

**plush** [plʌʃ] *adj* somptueux(-euse) ▷ *n* peluche *f*

**ply** [plaɪ] *n (of wool)* fil *m*; *(of wood)* feuille *f*,

épaisseur f ▷ vt (tool) manier; (a trade) exercer
▷ vi (ship) faire la navette; **three ~ (wool)** n
laine f trois fils; **to ~ sb with drink** donner
continuellement à boire à qn
**plywood** ['plaɪwud] n contreplaqué m
**P.M.** n abbr (Brit) = **prime minister**
**p.m.** adv abbr (= post meridiem) de l'après-midi
**PMS** n abbr (= premenstrual syndrome) syndrome
prémenstruel
**PMT** n abbr (= premenstrual tension) syndrome
prémenstruel
**pneumatic** [njuːˈmætɪk] adj pneumatique
**pneumatic drill** [njuːˈmætɪk-] n marteau-
piqueur m
**pneumonia** [njuːˈməunɪə] n pneumonie f
**PO** n abbr (= Post Office) PTT fpl; (Mil) = **petty
officer**
**po** abbr = **postal order**
**POA** n abbr (Brit) = **Prison Officers' Association**
**poach** [pəutʃ] vt (cook) pocher; (steal) pêcher (or
chasser) sans permis ▷ vi braconner
**poached** [pəutʃt] adj (egg) poché(e)
**poacher** ['pəutʃəʳ] n braconnier m
**poaching** ['pəutʃɪŋ] n braconnage m
**P.O. Box** n abbr = **post office box**
**pocket** ['pɔkɪt] n poche f ▷ vt empocher; **to be
(£5) out of ~** (Brit) en être de sa poche (pour 5
livres)
**pocketbook** ['pɔkɪtbuk] n (notebook) carnet m;
(US: wallet) portefeuille m; (: handbag) sac m à
main
**pocket knife** n canif m
**pocket money** n argent m de poche
**pockmarked** ['pɔkmɑːkt] adj (face) grêlé(e)
**pod** [pɔd] n cosse f ▷ vt écosser
**podcast** n podcast m ▷ vi podcaster
**podcasting** ['pɔdkɑːstɪŋ] n podcasting m,
baladodiffusion f
**podgy** ['pɔdʒɪ] adj rondelet(te)
**podiatrist** [pɔˈdiːətrɪst] n (US) pédicure m/f
**podiatry** [pɔˈdiːətrɪ] n (US) pédicurie f
**podium** ['pəudɪəm] n podium m
**POE** n abbr = **port of embarkation; port of entry**
**poem** ['pəuɪm] n poème m
**poet** ['pəuɪt] n poète m
**poetic** [pəuˈɛtɪk] adj poétique
**poet laureate** n poète lauréat; voir article

⚫ **POET LAUREATE**

⚫ En Grande-Bretagne, le poet laureate est un
⚫ poète qui reçoit un traitement en tant que
⚫ poète de la cour et qui est officier de la
⚫ maison royale à vie. Le premier d'entre eux
⚫ fut Ben Jonson, en 1616. Jadis, le "poète
⚫ lauréat" écrivait des poèmes lors des
⚫ grandes occasions, mais cette tradition
⚫ n'est plus guère observée.

**poetry** ['pəuɪtrɪ] n poésie f
**poignant** ['pɔɪnjənt] adj poignant(e); (sharp) vif
(vive)

**point** [pɔɪnt] n (Geom, Scol, Sport, on scale) point m;
(tip) pointe f; (in time) moment m; (in space)
endroit m; (subject, idea) point, sujet m; (purpose)
but m; (also: **decimal point**): **2 ~ 3 (2.3)** 2 virgule 3
(2,3); (Brit Elec: also: **power point**) prise f (de
courant) ▷ vt (show) indiquer; (wall, window)
jointoyer; (gun etc): **to ~ sth at** braquer or
diriger qch sur ▷ vi: **to ~ at** montrer du doigt;
**points** npl (Aut) vis platinées; (Rail) aiguillage
m; **good ~s** qualités fpl; **the train stops at
Carlisle and all ~s south** le train dessert
Carlisle et toutes les gares vers le sud; **to make
a ~** faire une remarque; **to make a ~ of doing
sth** ne pas manquer de faire qch; **to make
one's ~** se faire comprendre; **to get/miss the ~**
comprendre/ne pas comprendre; **to come to
the ~** en venir au fait; **when it comes to the ~**
le moment venu; **there's no ~ (in doing)** cela
ne sert à rien (de faire); **what's the ~?** à quoi ça
sert?; **to be on the ~ of doing sth** être sur le
point de faire qch; **that's the whole ~!**
précisément!; **to be beside the ~** être à côté de
la question; **you've got a ~ there!** (c'est) juste!;
**in ~ of fact** en fait, en réalité; **~ of departure**
(also fig) point de départ; **~ of order** point de
procédure; **~ of sale** (Comm) point de vente; **to ~
to sth** (fig) signaler
▸ **point out** vt (show) montrer, indiquer;
(mention) faire remarquer, souligner
**point-blank** ['pɔɪntˈblæŋk] adv (fig)
catégoriquement; (also: **at point-blank range**) à
bout portant ▷ adj (fig) catégorique
**point duty** n (Brit): **to be on ~** diriger la
circulation
**pointed** ['pɔɪntɪd] adj (shape) pointu(e); (remark)
plein(e) de sous-entendus
**pointedly** ['pɔɪntɪdlɪ] adv d'une manière
significative
**pointer** ['pɔɪntəʳ] n (stick) baguette f; (needle)
aiguille f; (dog) chien m d'arrêt; (clue) indication
f; (advice) tuyau m
**pointless** ['pɔɪntlɪs] adj inutile, vain(e)
**point of view** n point m de vue
**poise** [pɔɪz] n (balance) équilibre m; (of head, body)
port m; (calmness) calme m ▷ vt placer en
équilibre; **to be ~d for** (fig) être prêt à
**poison** ['pɔɪzn] n poison m ▷ vt empoisonner
**poisoning** ['pɔɪznɪŋ] n empoisonnement m
**poisonous** ['pɔɪznəs] adj (snake)
venimeux(-euse); (substance, plant)
vénéneux(-euse); (fumes) toxique; (fig)
pernicieux(-euse)
**poke** [pəuk] vt (fire) tisonner; (jab with finger, stick
etc) piquer; pousser du doigt; (put): **to ~ sth
in(to)** fourrer or enfoncer qch dans ▷ n (jab)
(petit) coup; (to fire) coup m de tisonnier; **to ~
fun at sb** se moquer de qn
▸ **poke about** vi fureter
▸ **poke out** vi (stick out) sortir ▷ vt: **to ~ one's
head out of the window** passer la tête par la
fenêtre
**poker** ['pəukəʳ] n tisonnier m; (Cards) poker m

**poker-faced** ['pəukə'feɪst] *adj* au visage impassible
**poky** ['pəukɪ] *adj* exigu(ë)
**Poland** ['pəulənd] *n* Pologne *f*
**polar** ['pəulə*ʳ*] *adj* polaire
**polar bear** *n* ours blanc
**polarize** ['pəuləraɪz] *vt* polariser
**Pole** [pəul] *n* Polonais(e)
**pole** [pəul] *n* (*of wood*) mât *m*, perche *f*; (*Elec*) poteau *m*; (*Geo*) pôle *m*
**poleaxe** ['pəulæks] *vt* (*fig*) terrasser
**pole bean** *n* (*US*) haricot *m* (à rames)
**polecat** ['pəulkæt] *n* putois *m*
**Pol. Econ.** ['pɔlɪkɔn] *n abbr* = **political economy**
**polemic** [pɔ'lɛmɪk] *n* polémique *f*
**pole star** ['pəulstɑː*ʳ*] *n* étoile *f* polaire
**pole vault** ['pəulvɔːlt] *n* saut *m* à la perche
**police** [pə'liːs] *npl* police *f* ⊳ *vt* maintenir l'ordre dans; **a large number of ~ were hurt** de nombreux policiers ont été blessés
**police car** *n* voiture *f* de police
**police constable** *n* (*Brit*) agent *m* de police
**police department** *n* (*US*) services *mpl* de police
**police force** *n* police *f*, forces *fpl* de l'ordre
**policeman** [pə'liːsmən] (*irreg*) *n* agent *m* de police, policier *m*
**police officer** *n* agent *m* de police
**police record** *n* casier *m* judiciaire
**police state** *n* état policier
**police station** *n* commissariat *m* de police
**policewoman** [pə'liːswumən] (*irreg*) *n* femme-agent *f*
**policy** ['pɔlɪsɪ] *n* politique *f*; (*also*: **insurance policy**) police *f* (d'assurance); (*of newspaper, company*) politique générale; **to take out a ~** (*Insurance*) souscrire une police d'assurance
**policy holder** *n* assuré(e)
**policy-making** ['pɔlɪsɪmeɪkɪŋ] *n* élaboration *f* de nouvelles lignes d'action
**polio** ['pəulɪəu] *n* polio *f*
**Polish** ['pəulɪʃ] *adj* polonais(e) ⊳ *n* (*Ling*) polonais *m*
**polish** ['pɔlɪʃ] *n* (*for shoes*) cirage *m*; (*for floor*) cire *f*, encaustique *f*; (*for nails*) vernis *m*; (*shine*) éclat *m*, poli *m*; (*fig: refinement*) raffinement *m* ⊳ *vt* (*put polish on: shoes, wood*) cirer; (*make shiny*) astiquer, faire briller; (*fig: improve*) perfectionner
▸ **polish off** *vt* (*work*) expédier; (*food*) liquider
**polished** ['pɔlɪʃt] *adj* (*fig*) raffiné(e)
**polite** [pə'laɪt] *adj* poli(e); **it's not ~ to do that** ça ne se fait pas
**politely** [pə'laɪtlɪ] *adv* poliment
**politeness** [pə'laɪtnɪs] *n* politesse *f*
**politic** ['pɔlɪtɪk] *adj* diplomatique
**political** [pə'lɪtɪkl] *adj* politique
**political asylum** *n* asile *m* politique
**politically** [pə'lɪtɪklɪ] *adv* politiquement; **~ correct** politiquement correct(e)
**politician** [pɔlɪ'tɪʃən] *n* homme/femme politique, politicien(ne)
**politics** ['pɔlɪtɪks] *n* politique *f*
**polka** ['pɔlkə] *n* polka *f*

**polka dot** *n* pois *m*
**poll** [pəul] *n* scrutin *m*, vote *m*; (*also*: **opinion poll**) sondage *m* (d'opinion) ⊳ *vt* (*votes*) obtenir; **to go to the ~s** (*voters*) aller aux urnes; (*government*) tenir des élections
**pollen** ['pɔlən] *n* pollen *m*
**pollen count** *n* taux *m* de pollen
**pollination** [pɔlɪ'neɪʃən] *n* pollinisation *f*
**polling** ['pəulɪŋ] *n* (*Brit Pol*) élections *fpl*; (*Tel*) invitation *f* à émettre
**polling booth** *n* (*Brit*) isoloir *m*
**polling day** *n* (*Brit*) jour *m* des élections
**polling station** *n* (*Brit*) bureau *m* de vote
**pollster** ['pəulstə*ʳ*] *n* sondeur *m*, enquêteur(-euse)
**poll tax** *n* (*Brit: formerly*) ≈ impôts locaux.
**pollutant** [pə'luːtənt] *n* polluant *m*
**pollute** [pə'luːt] *vt* polluer
**pollution** [pə'luːʃən] *n* pollution *f*
**polo** ['pəuləu] *n* polo *m*
**polo-neck** ['pəuləunɛk] *adj* à col roulé ⊳ *n* (*sweater*) pull *m* à col roulé
**polo shirt** *n* polo *m*
**poly** ['pɔlɪ] *n abbr* (*Brit*) = **polytechnic**
**poly bag** *n* (*Brit inf*) sac *m* en plastique
**polyester** [pɔlɪ'estə*ʳ*] *n* polyester *m*
**polygamy** [pə'lɪgəmɪ] *n* polygamie *f*
**polygraph** ['pɔlɪgrɑːf] *n* détecteur *m* de mensonges
**Polynesia** [pɔlɪ'niːzɪə] *n* Polynésie *f*
**Polynesian** [pɔlɪ'niːzɪən] *adj* polynésien(ne) ⊳ *n* Polynésien(ne)
**polyp** ['pɔlɪp] *n* (*Med*) polype *m*
**polystyrene** [pɔlɪ'staɪriːn] *n* polystyrène *m*
**polytechnic** [pɔlɪ'tɛknɪk] *n* (*college*) IUT *m*, Institut *m* universitaire de technologie
**polythene** ['pɔlɪθiːn] *n* (*Brit*) polyéthylène *m*
**polythene bag** *n* sac *m* en plastique
**polyurethane** [pɔlɪ'juərɪθeɪn] *n* polyuréthane *m*
**pomegranate** ['pɔmɪgrænɪt] *n* grenade *f*
**pommel** ['pɔml] *n* pommeau *m* ⊳ *vt* = **pummel**
**pomp** [pɔmp] *n* pompe *f*, faste *f*, apparat *m*
**pompom** ['pɔmpɔm] *n* pompon *m*
**pompous** ['pɔmpəs] *adj* pompeux(-euse)
**pond** [pɔnd] *n* étang *m*; (*stagnant*) mare *f*
**ponder** ['pɔndə*ʳ*] *vi* réfléchir ⊳ *vt* considérer, peser
**ponderous** ['pɔndərəs] *adj* pesant(e), lourd(e)
**pong** [pɔŋ] (*Brit inf*) *n* puanteur *f* ⊳ *vi* schlinguer
**pontiff** ['pɔntɪf] *n* pontife *m*
**pontificate** [pɔn'tɪfɪkeɪt] *vi* (*fig*): **to ~ (about)** pontifier (sur)
**pontoon** [pɔn'tuːn] *n* ponton *m*; (*Brit Cards*) vingt-et-un *m*
**pony** ['pəunɪ] *n* poney *m*
**ponytail** ['pəunɪteɪl] *n* queue *f* de cheval
**pony trekking** [-trɛkɪŋ] *n* (*Brit*) randonnée *f* équestre or à cheval
**poodle** ['puːdl] *n* caniche *m*
**pooh-pooh** ['puː'puː] *vt* dédaigner
**pool** [puːl] *n* (*of rain*) flaque *f*; (*pond*) mare *f*;

(*artificial*) bassin *m*; (*also:* **swimming pool**) piscine *f*; (*sth shared*) fonds commun; (*money at cards*) cagnotte *f*; (*billiards*) poule *f*; (*Comm: consortium*) pool *m*; (*US: monopoly trust*) trust *m* ▷ *vt* mettre en commun; **pools** *npl* (*football*) = loto sportif; **typing ~**, (*US*) **secretary ~** pool *m* dactylographique; **to do the (football) ~s** (*Brit*) = jouer au loto sportif; *see also* **football pools**

**poor** [puə<sup>r</sup>] *adj* pauvre; (*mediocre*) médiocre, faible, mauvais(e) ▷ *npl*: **the ~** les pauvres *mpl*

**poorly** ['puəlɪ] *adv* pauvrement; (*badly*) mal, médiocrement ▷ *adj* souffrant(e), malade

**pop** [pɔp] *n* (*noise*) bruit sec; (*Mus*) musique *f* pop; (*inf: drink*) soda *m*; (*US inf: father*) papa *m* ▷ *vt* (*put*) fourrer, mettre (rapidement) ▷ *vi* éclater; (*cork*) sauter; **she ~ped her head out of the window** elle passa la tête par la fenêtre
  ▸ **pop in** *vi* entrer en passant
  ▸ **pop out** *vi* sortir
  ▸ **pop up** *vi* apparaître, surgir

**pop concert** *n* concert *m* pop

**popcorn** ['pɔpkɔːn] *n* pop-corn *m*

**pope** [pəup] *n* pape *m*

**poplar** ['pɔplə<sup>r</sup>] *n* peuplier *m*

**poplin** ['pɔplɪn] *n* popeline *f*

**popper** ['pɔpə<sup>r</sup>] *n* (*Brit*) bouton-pression *m*

**poppy** ['pɔpɪ] *n* (*wild*) coquelicot *m*; (*cultivated*) pavot *m*

**poppycock** ['pɔpɪkɔk] *n* (*inf*) balivernes *fpl*

**Popsicle**® ['pɔpsɪkl] *n* (*US*) esquimau *m* (*glace*)

**pop star** *n* pop star *f*

**populace** ['pɔpjuləs] *n* peuple *m*

**popular** ['pɔpjulə<sup>r</sup>] *adj* populaire; (*fashionable*) à la mode; **to be ~ (with)** (*person*) avoir du succès (auprès de); (*decision*) être bien accueilli(e) (par)

**popularity** [pɔpju'lærɪtɪ] *n* popularité *f*

**popularize** ['pɔpjuləraɪz] *vt* populariser; (*science*) vulgariser

**populate** ['pɔpjuleɪt] *vt* peupler

**population** [pɔpju'leɪʃən] *n* population *f*

**population explosion** *n* explosion *f* démographique

**populous** ['pɔpjuləs] *adj* populeux(-euse)

**pop-up** *adj* (*Comput: menu, window*) pop up *inv* ▷ *n* pop up *m inv*, fenêtre *f* pop up

**porcelain** ['pɔːslɪn] *n* porcelaine *f*

**porch** [pɔːtʃ] *n* porche *m*; (*US*) véranda *f*

**porcupine** ['pɔːkjupaɪn] *n* porc-épic *m*

**pore** [pɔː<sup>r</sup>] *n* pore *m* ▷ *vi*: **to ~ over** s'absorber dans, être plongé(e) dans

**pork** [pɔːk] *n* porc *m*

**pork chop** *n* côte *f* de porc

**pork pie** *n* pâté *m* de porc en croûte

**porn** [pɔːn] *adj* (*inf*) porno ▷ *n* (*inf*) porno *m*

**pornographic** [pɔːnə'græfɪk] *adj* pornographique

**pornography** [pɔː'nɔgrəfɪ] *n* pornographie *f*

**porous** ['pɔːrəs] *adj* poreux(-euse)

**porpoise** ['pɔːpəs] *n* marsouin *m*

**porridge** ['pɔrɪdʒ] *n* porridge *m*

**port** [pɔːt] *n* (*harbour*) port *m*; (*opening in ship*) sabord *m*; (*Naut: left side*) bâbord *m*; (*wine*) porto

*m*; (*Comput*) port *m*, accès *m* ▷ *cpd* portuaire, du port; **to ~** (*Naut*) à bâbord; **~ of call** (port d')escale *f*

**portable** ['pɔːtəbl] *adj* portatif(-ive)

**portal** ['pɔːtl] *n* portail *m*

**portcullis** [pɔːt'kʌlɪs] *n* herse *f*

**portent** ['pɔːtent] *n* présage *m*

**porter** ['pɔːtə<sup>r</sup>] *n* (*for luggage*) porteur *m*; (*doorkeeper*) gardien(ne); portier *m*

**portfolio** [pɔːt'fəuliəu] *n* portefeuille *m*; (*of artist*) portfolio *m*

**porthole** ['pɔːthəul] *n* hublot *m*

**portico** ['pɔːtɪkəu] *n* portique *m*

**portion** ['pɔːʃən] *n* portion *f*, part *f*

**portly** ['pɔːtlɪ] *adj* corpulent(e)

**portrait** ['pɔːtreɪt] *n* portrait *m*

**portray** [pɔː'treɪ] *vt* faire le portrait de; (*in writing*) dépeindre, représenter; (*subj: actor*) jouer

**portrayal** [pɔː'treɪəl] *n* portrait *m*, représentation *f*

**Portugal** ['pɔːtjugl] *n* Portugal *m*

**Portuguese** [pɔːtju'giːz] *adj* portugais(e) ▷ *n* (*pl inv*) Portugais(e); (*Ling*) portugais *m*

**Portuguese man-of-war** [-mænəv'wɔː<sup>r</sup>] *n* (*jellyfish*) galère *f*

**pose** [pəuz] *n* pose *f*; (*pej*) affectation *f* ▷ *vi* poser; (*pretend*): **to ~ as** se faire passer pour ▷ *vt* poser; (*problem*) créer; **to strike a ~** poser (pour la galerie)

**poser** ['pəuzə<sup>r</sup>] *n* question difficile *or* embarrassante; (*person*) = **poseur**

**poseur** [pəu'zə:<sup>r</sup>] *n* (*pej*) poseur(-euse)

**posh** [pɔʃ] *adj* (*inf*) chic *inv*; **to talk ~** parler d'une manière affectée

**position** [pə'zɪʃən] *n* position *f*; (*job, situation*) situation *f* ▷ *vt* mettre en place or en position; **to be in a ~ to do sth** être en mesure de faire qch

**positive** ['pɔzɪtɪv] *adj* positif(-ive); (*certain*) sûr(e), certain(e); (*definite*) formel(le), catégorique; (*clear*) indéniable, réel(le)

**positively** ['pɔzɪtɪvlɪ] *adv* (*affirmatively, enthusiastically*) de façon positive; (*inf: really*) carrément; **to think ~** être positif(-ive)

**posse** ['pɔsɪ] *n* (*US*) détachement *m*

**possess** [pə'zɛs] *vt* posséder; **like one ~ed** comme un fou; **whatever can have ~ed you?** qu'est-ce qui vous a pris?

**possession** [pə'zɛʃən] *n* possession *f*; **possessions** *npl* (*belongings*) affaires *fpl*; **to take ~ of sth** prendre possession de qch

**possessive** [pə'zɛsɪv] *adj* possessif(-ive)

**possessiveness** [pə'zɛsɪvnɪs] *n* possessivité *f*

**possessor** [pə'zɛsə<sup>r</sup>] *n* possesseur *m*

**possibility** [pɔsɪ'bɪlɪtɪ] *n* possibilité *f*; (*event*) éventualité *f*; **he's a ~ for the part** c'est un candidat possible pour le rôle

**possible** ['pɔsɪbl] *adj* possible; (*solution*) envisageable, éventuel(le); **it is ~ to do it** il est possible de le faire; **as far as ~** dans la mesure du possible, autant que possible; **if ~** si possible; **as big as ~** aussi gros que possible

**possibly** ['pɒsɪblɪ] adv (perhaps) peut-être; **if you ~ can** si cela vous est possible; **I cannot ~ come** il m'est impossible de venir

**post** [pəust] n (Brit: mail) poste f; (: collection) levée f; (: letters, delivery) courrier m; (job, situation) poste m; (pole) poteau m; (trading post) comptoir (commercial); (on internet forum) billet m, post m ▷ vt (Brit: send by post, Mil, to internet) poster; (: appoint): **to ~ to** affecter à; (notice) afficher; **by ~** (Brit) par la poste; **by return of ~** (Brit) par retour du courrier; **to keep sb ~ed** tenir qn au courant

**post...** [pəust] prefix post...; **post 1990** adj d'après 1990 ▷ adv après 1990

**postage** ['pəustɪdʒ] n tarifs mpl d'affranchissement; **~ paid** port payé; **~ prepaid** (US) franco (de port)

**postage stamp** n timbre-poste m

**postal** ['pəustl] adj postal(e)

**postal order** n mandat(-poste m) m

**postbag** ['pəustbæg] n (Brit) sac postal; (postman's) sacoche f

**postbox** ['pəustbɒks] n (Brit) boîte f aux lettres (publique)

**postcard** ['pəustkɑːd] n carte postale

**postcode** ['pəustkəud] n (Brit) code postal

**postdate** ['pəust'deɪt] vt (cheque) postdater

**poster** ['pəustə'] n affiche f

**poste restante** [pəust'rɛstɑ̃:nt] n (Brit) poste restante

**posterior** [pɒs'tɪərɪə'] n (inf) postérieur m, derrière m

**posterity** [pɒs'tɛrɪtɪ] n postérité f

**poster paint** n gouache f

**post exchange** n (US Mil) magasin m de l'armée

**post-free** [pəust'friː] adj (Brit) franco (de port)

**postgraduate** ['pəust'grædjuət] n ≈ étudiant(e) de troisième cycle

**posthumous** ['pɒstjuməs] adj posthume

**posthumously** ['pɒstjuməslɪ] adv après la mort de l'auteur, à titre posthume

**posting** ['pəustɪŋ] n (Brit) affectation f

**postman** ['pəustmən] (Brit: irreg) n facteur m

**postmark** ['pəustmɑːk] n cachet m (de la poste)

**postmaster** ['pəustmɑːstə'] n receveur m des postes

**Postmaster General** n ≈ ministre m des Postes et Télécommunications

**postmistress** ['pəustmɪstrɪs] n receveuse f des postes

**post-mortem** [pəust'mɔːtəm] n autopsie f

**postnatal** ['pəust'neɪtl] adj postnatal(e)

**post office** n (building) poste f; (organization): **the Post Office** les postes fpl

**post office box** n boîte postale

**post-paid** ['pəust'peɪd] adj (Brit) port payé

**postpone** [pəs'pəun] vt remettre (à plus tard), reculer

**postponement** [pəs'pəunmənt] n ajournement m, renvoi m

**postscript** ['pəustskrɪpt] n post-scriptum m

**postulate** ['pɒstjuleɪt] vt postuler

**posture** ['pɒstʃə'] n posture f; (fig) attitude f ▷ vi poser

**postwar** [pəust'wɔː'] adj d'après-guerre

**postwoman** [pəust'wumən] (Brit: irreg) n factrice f

**posy** ['pəuzɪ] n petit bouquet

**pot** [pɒt] n (for cooking) marmite f; casserole f; (teapot) théière f; (for coffee) cafetière f; (for plants, jam) pot m; (piece of pottery) poterie f; (inf: marijuana) herbe f ▷ vt (plant) mettre en pot; **to go to ~** (inf) aller à vau-l'eau; **~s of** (Brit inf) beaucoup de, plein de

**potash** ['pɒtæʃ] n potasse f

**potassium** [pə'tæsɪəm] n potassium m

**potato** (pl **-es**) [pə'teɪtəu] n pomme f de terre

**potato crisps**, (US) **potato chips** npl chips mpl

**potato flour** n fécule f

**potato peeler** n épluche-légumes m

**potbellied** ['pɒtbelɪd] adj (from overeating) bedonnant(e); (from malnutrition) au ventre ballonné

**potency** ['pəutnsɪ] n puissance f, force f; (of drink) degré m d'alcool

**potent** ['pəutnt] adj puissant(e); (drink) fort(e), très alcoolisé(e); (man) viril

**potentate** ['pəutnteɪt] n potentat m

**potential** [pə'tɛnʃl] adj potentiel(le) ▷ n potentiel m; **to have ~** être prometteur(-euse); ouvrir des possibilités

**potentially** [pə'tɛnʃəlɪ] adv potentiellement; **it's ~ dangerous** ça pourrait se révéler dangereux, il y a possibilité de danger

**pothole** ['pɒthəul] n (in road) nid m de poule; (Brit: underground) gouffre m, caverne f

**potholer** ['pɒthəulə'] n (Brit) spéléologue m/f

**potholing** ['pɒthəulɪŋ] n (Brit): **to go ~** faire de la spéléologie

**potion** ['pəuʃən] n potion f

**potluck** [pɒt'lʌk] n: **to take ~** tenter sa chance

**pot plant** n plante f d'appartement

**potpourri** [pəu'puri:] n pot-pourri m

**pot roast** n rôti m à la cocotte

**pot shot** ['pɒtʃɒt] n: **to take ~s at** canarder

**potted** ['pɒtɪd] adj (food) en conserve; (plant) en pot; (fig: shortened) abrégé(e)

**potter** ['pɒtə'] n potier m ▷ vi (Brit): **to ~ around** or **about** bricoler; **~'s wheel** tour m de potier

**pottery** ['pɒtərɪ] n poterie f; **a piece of ~** une poterie

**potty** ['pɒtɪ] adj (Brit inf: mad) dingue ▷ n (child's) pot m

**potty-training** ['pɒtɪtreɪnɪŋ] n apprentissage m de la propreté

**pouch** [pautʃ] n (Zool) poche f; (for tobacco) blague f; (for money) bourse f

**pouf, pouffe** [puːf] n (stool) pouf m

**poultice** ['pəultɪs] n cataplasme m

**poultry** ['pəultrɪ] n volaille f

**poultry farm** n élevage m de volaille

**poultry farmer** n aviculteur m

**pounce** [pauns] vi: **to ~ (on)** bondir (sur), fondre (sur) ▷ n bond m, attaque f

**pound** [paund] *n* livre *f* (*weight* = 453*g*, 16 *ounces*; *money* = 100 *pence*); (*for dogs, cars*) fourrière *f* ▷ *vt* (*beat*) bourrer de coups, marteler; (*crush*) piler, pulvériser; (*with guns*) pilonner ▷ *vi* (*heart*) battre violemment, taper; **half a ~ (of)** une demi-livre (de); **a five-~ note** un billet de cinq livres

**pounding** ['paundɪŋ] *n*: **to take a ~** (*fig*) prendre une râclée

**pound sterling** *n* livre *f* sterling

**pour** [pɔːʳ] *vt* verser ▷ *vi* couler à flots; (*rain*) pleuvoir à verse; **to ~ sb a drink** verser *or* servir à boire à qn; **to come ~ing in** (*water*) entrer à flots; (*letters*) arriver par milliers; (*cars, people*) affluer

▶ **pour away, pour off** *vt* vider

▶ **pour in** *vi* (*people*) affluer, se précipiter; (*news, letters*) arriver en masse

▶ **pour out** *vi* (*people*) sortir en masse ▷ *vt* vider; (*fig*) déverser; (*serve: a drink*) verser

**pouring** ['pɔːrɪŋ] *adj*: **~ rain** pluie torrentielle

**pout** [paut] *n* moue *f* ▷ *vi* faire la moue

**poverty** ['pɔvətɪ] *n* pauvreté *f*, misère *f*

**poverty line** *n* seuil *m* de pauvreté

**poverty-stricken** ['pɔvətɪstrɪkn] *adj* pauvre, déshérité(e)

**poverty trap** *n* (*Brit*) piège *m* de la pauvreté

**POW** *n abbr* = **prisoner of war**

**powder** ['paudəʳ] *n* poudre *f* ▷ *vt* poudrer; **to ~ one's nose** se poudrer; (*euphemism*) aller à la salle de bain

**powder compact** *n* poudrier *m*

**powdered milk** *n* lait *m* en poudre

**powder keg** *n* (*fig*) poudrière *f*

**powder puff** *n* houppette *f*

**powder room** *n* toilettes *fpl* (pour dames)

**powdery** ['paudərɪ] *adj* poudreux(-euse)

**power** ['pauəʳ] *n* (*strength, nation*) puissance *f*, force *f*; (*ability, Pol: of party, leader*) pouvoir *m*; (*Math*) puissance; (*of speech, thought*) faculté *f*; (*Elec*) courant *m* ▷ *vt* faire marcher, actionner; **to do all in one's ~ to help sb** faire tout ce qui est en son pouvoir pour aider qn; **the world ~s** les grandes puissances; **to be in ~** être au pouvoir

**powerboat** ['pauəbəut] *n* (*Brit*) hors-bord *m*

**power cut** *n* (*Brit*) coupure *f* de courant

**powered** ['pauəd] *adj*: **~ by** actionné(e) par, fonctionnant à; **nuclear-~ submarine** sous-marin *m* (à propulsion) nucléaire

**power failure** *n* panne *f* de courant

**powerful** ['pauəful] *adj* puissant(e); (*performance etc*) très fort(e)

**powerhouse** ['pauəhaus] *n* (*fig: person*) fonceur *m*; **a ~ of ideas** une mine d'idées

**powerless** ['pauəlɪs] *adj* impuissant(e)

**power line** *n* ligne *f* électrique

**power of attorney** *n* procuration *f*

**power point** *n* (*Brit*) prise *f* de courant

**power station** *n* centrale *f* électrique

**power steering** *n* direction assistée

**power struggle** *n* lutte *f* pour le pouvoir

**powwow** ['pauwau] *n* conciliabule *m*

**p.p.** *abbr* (= *per procurationem: by proxy*) p.p.

**PPE** *n abbr* (*Brit Scol*) = **philosophy, politics and economics**

**PPS** *n abbr* (= *post postscriptum*) PPS; (*Brit:* = *parliamentary private secretary*) parlementaire chargé de mission auprès d'un ministre

**PQ** *abbr* (*Canada*: = *Province of Quebec*) PQ

**PR** *n abbr* = **proportional representation; public relations** ▷ *abbr* (*US*) = **Puerto Rico**

**Pr.** *abbr* (= *prince*) Pce

**practicability** [præktɪkə'bɪlɪtɪ] *n* possibilité *f* de réalisation

**practicable** ['præktɪkəbl] *adj* (*scheme*) réalisable

**practical** ['præktɪkl] *adj* pratique

**practicality** [præktɪ'kælɪtɪ] *n* (*of plan*) aspect *m* pratique; (*of person*) sens *m* pratique; **practicalities** *npl* détails *mpl* pratiques

**practical joke** *n* farce *f*

**practically** ['præktɪklɪ] *adv* (*almost*) pratiquement

**practice** ['præktɪs] *n* pratique *f*; (*of profession*) exercice *m*; (*at football etc*) entraînement *m*; (*business*) cabinet *m*; clientèle *f* ▷ *vt, vi* (*US*) = **practise; in ~** (*in reality*) en pratique; **out of ~** rouillé(e); **2 hours' piano ~** 2 heures de travail *or* d'exercices au piano; **target ~** exercices de tir; **it's common ~** c'est courant, ça se fait couramment; **to put sth into ~** mettre qch en pratique

**practice match** *n* match *m* d'entraînement

**practise, (US) practice** ['præktɪs] *vt* (*work at: piano, backhand etc*) s'exercer à, travailler; (*train for: sport*) s'entraîner à; (*a sport, religion, method*) pratiquer; (*profession*) exercer ▷ *vi* s'exercer, travailler; (*train*) s'entraîner; (*lawyer, doctor*) exercer; **to ~ for a match** s'entraîner pour un match

**practised, (US) practiced** ['præktɪst] *adj* (*person*) expérimenté(e); (*performance*) impeccable; (*liar*) invétéré(e); **with a ~ eye** d'un œil exercé

**practising, (US) practicing** ['præktɪsɪŋ] *adj* (*Christian etc*) pratiquant(e); (*lawyer*) en exercice; (*homosexual*) déclaré

**practitioner** [præk'tɪʃənəʳ] *n* praticien(ne)

**pragmatic** [præg'mætɪk] *adj* pragmatique

**Prague** [prɑːg] *n* Prague

**prairie** ['prɛərɪ] *n* savane *f*; (*US*): **the ~s** la Prairie

**praise** [preɪz] *n* éloge(s) *m(pl)*, louange(s) *f(pl)* ▷ *vt* louer, faire l'éloge de

**praiseworthy** ['preɪzwɜːðɪ] *adj* digne de louanges

**pram** [præm] *n* (*Brit*) landau *m*, voiture *f* d'enfant

**prance** [prɑːns] *vi* (*horse*) caracoler

**prank** [præŋk] *n* farce *f*

**prat** [præt] *n* (*Brit inf*) imbécile *m*, andouille *f*

**prattle** ['prætl] *vi* jacasser

**prawn** [prɔːn] *n* crevette *f* (rose)

**prawn cocktail** *n* cocktail *m* de crevettes

**pray** [preɪ] *vi* prier

**prayer** [prɛəʳ] *n* prière *f*

**prayer book** n livre m de prières
**pre...** ['priː] prefix pré...; **pre-1970** adj d'avant
1970 ▷ adv avant 1970
**preach** [priːtʃ] vt, vi prêcher; **to ~ at sb** faire la
morale à qn
**preacher** ['priːtʃəʳ] n prédicateur m; (US:
clergyman) pasteur m
**preamble** [prɪ'æmbl] n préambule m
**prearranged** [priːə'reɪndʒd] adj organisé(e) or
fixé(e) à l'avance
**precarious** [prɪ'kɛərɪəs] adj précaire
**precaution** [prɪ'kɔːʃən] n précaution f
**precautionary** [prɪ'kɔːʃənrɪ] adj (measure) de
précaution
**precede** [prɪ'siːd] vt, vi précéder
**precedence** ['presɪdəns] n préséance f
**precedent** ['presɪdənt] n précédent m; **to
establish** or **set a ~** créer un précédent
**preceding** [prɪ'siːdɪŋ] adj qui précède (or
précédait)
**precept** ['priːsept] n précepte m
**precinct** ['priːsɪŋkt] n (round cathedral) pourtour
m, enceinte f; (US: district) circonscription f,
arrondissement m; **precincts** npl (neighbourhood)
alentours mpl, environs mpl; **pedestrian ~** (Brit)
zone piétonnière; **shopping ~** (Brit) centre
commercial
**precious** ['preʃəs] adj précieux(-euse) ▷ adv (inf):
**~ little** or **few** fort peu; **your ~ dog** (ironic) ton
chien chéri, ton chéri chien
**precipice** ['presɪpɪs] n précipice m
**precipitate** [prɪ'sɪpɪtɪt] adj (hasty) précipité(e)
▷ vt [prɪ'sɪpɪteɪt] précipiter
**precipitation** [prɪsɪpɪ'teɪʃən] n précipitation f
**precipitous** [prɪ'sɪpɪtəs] adj (steep) abrupt(e), à
pic
**précis** (pl ~) ['preɪsiː, -z] n résumé m
**precise** [prɪ'saɪs] adj précis(e)
**precisely** [prɪ'saɪslɪ] adv précisément
**precision** [prɪ'sɪʒən] n précision f
**preclude** [prɪ'kluːd] vt exclure, empêcher; **to ~
sb from doing** empêcher qn de faire
**precocious** [prɪ'kəuʃəs] adj précoce
**preconceived** [priːkən'siːvd] adj (idea)
préconçu(e)
**preconception** [priːkən'sepʃən] n idée
préconçue
**precondition** ['priːkən'dɪʃən] n condition f
nécessaire
**precursor** [priː'kəːsəʳ] n précurseur m
**predate** ['priː'deɪt] vt (precede) antidater
**predator** ['predətəʳ] n prédateur m, rapace m
**predatory** ['predətərɪ] adj rapace
**predecessor** ['priːdɪsesəʳ] n prédécesseur m
**predestination** [priːdestɪ'neɪʃən] n
prédestination f
**predetermine** [priːdɪ'təːmɪn] vt déterminer à
l'avance
**predicament** [prɪ'dɪkəmənt] n situation f
difficile
**predicate** ['predɪkɪt] n (Ling) prédicat m
**predict** [prɪ'dɪkt] vt prédire

**predictable** [prɪ'dɪktəbl] adj prévisible
**predictably** [prɪ'dɪktəblɪ] adv (behave, react) de
façon prévisible; **~ she didn't arrive** comme
on pouvait s'y attendre, elle n'est pas venue
**prediction** [prɪ'dɪkʃən] n prédiction f
**predispose** [priːdɪs'pəuz] vt prédisposer
**predominance** [prɪ'dɔmɪnəns] n
prédominance f
**predominant** [prɪ'dɔmɪnənt] adj
prédominant(e)
**predominantly** [prɪ'dɔmɪnəntlɪ] adv en
majeure partie; (especially) surtout
**predominate** [prɪ'dɔmɪneɪt] vi prédominer
**pre-eminent** [priː'emɪnənt] adj prééminent(e)
**pre-empt** [priː'emt] vt (Brit) acquérir par droit
de préemption; (fig) anticiper sur; **to ~ the
issue** conclure avant même d'ouvrir les débats
**pre-emptive** [prɪ'emtɪv] adj: **~ strike** attaque (or
action) préventive
**preen** [priːn] vt: **to ~ itself** (bird) se lisser les
plumes; **to ~ o.s.** s'admirer
**prefab** ['priːfæb] n abbr (= prefabricated building)
bâtiment préfabriqué
**prefabricated** [priː'fæbrɪkeɪtɪd] adj
préfabriqué(e)
**preface** ['prefəs] n préface f
**prefect** ['priːfekt] n (Brit: in school) élève chargé de
certaines fonctions de discipline; (in France) préfet m
**prefer** [prɪ'fəːʳ] vt préférer; (Law): **to ~ charges**
procéder à une inculpation; **to ~ coffee to tea**
préférer le café au thé; **to ~ doing** or **to do sth**
préférer faire qch
**preferable** ['prefrəbl] adj préférable
**preferably** ['prefrəblɪ] adv de préférence
**preference** ['prefrəns] n préférence f; **in ~ to
sth** plutôt que qch, de préférence à qch
**preference shares** npl (Brit) actions privilégiées
**preferential** [prefə'renʃəl] adj préférentiel(le); **~
treatment** traitement m de faveur
**preferred stock** [prɪ'fəːd-] npl (US) = **preference
shares**
**prefix** ['priːfɪks] n préfixe m
**pregnancy** ['pregnənsɪ] n grossesse f
**pregnancy test** n test m de grossesse
**pregnant** ['pregnənt] adj enceinte adj f; (animal)
pleine; **3 months ~** enceinte de 3 mois
**prehistoric** ['priːhɪs'tɔrɪk] adj préhistorique
**prehistory** [priː'hɪstərɪ] n préhistoire f
**prejudge** [priː'dʒʌdʒ] vt préjuger de
**prejudice** ['predʒudɪs] n préjugé m; (harm) tort
m, préjudice m ▷ vt porter préjudice à; (bias): **to
~ sb in favour of/against** prévenir qn en faveur
de/contre; **racial ~** préjugés raciaux
**prejudiced** ['predʒudɪst] adj (person) plein(e) de
préjugés; (in a matter) partial(e); (view)
préconçu(e), partial(e); **to be ~ against sb/sth**
avoir un parti-pris contre qn/qch; **to be
racially ~** avoir des préjugés raciaux
**prelate** ['prelət] n prélat m
**preliminaries** [prɪ'lɪmɪnərɪz] npl préliminaires
mpl
**preliminary** [prɪ'lɪmɪnərɪ] adj préliminaire

**prelude** ['prɛljuːd] *n* prélude *m*
**premarital** ['priːˈmærɪtl] *adj* avant le mariage; ~ **contract** contrat *m* de mariage
**premature** ['prɛmətʃuəʳ] *adj* prématuré(e); **to be ~ (in doing sth)** aller un peu (trop) vite (en faisant qch)
**premeditated** [priːˈmɛdɪteɪtɪd] *adj* prémédité(e)
**premeditation** [priːmɛdɪˈteɪʃən] *n* préméditation *f*
**premenstrual** [priːˈmɛnstruəl] *adj* prémenstruel(le)
**premenstrual tension** *n* irritabilité *f* avant les règles
**premier** ['prɛmɪəʳ] *adj* premier(-ière), principal(e) ▷ *n* (*Pol*: *Prime Minister*) premier ministre; (*Pol*: *President*) chef *m* de l'État
**premiere** ['prɛmɪɛəʳ] *n* première *f*
**Premier League** *n* première division
**premise** ['prɛmɪs] *n* prémisse *f*
**premises** ['prɛmɪsɪz] *npl* locaux *mpl*; **on the ~** sur les lieux; sur place; **business ~** locaux commerciaux
**premium** ['priːmɪəm] *n* prime *f*; **to be at a ~** (*fig*: *housing etc*) être très demandé(e), être rarissime; **to sell at a ~** (*shares*) vendre au-dessus du pair
**premium bond** *n* (*Brit*) obligation *f* à prime, bon *m* à lots
**premium deal** *n* (*Comm*) offre spéciale
**premium fuel**, (*US*) **premium gasoline** *n* super *m*
**premonition** [prɛməˈnɪʃən] *n* prémonition *f*
**preoccupation** [priːɔkjuˈpeɪʃən] *n* préoccupation *f*
**preoccupied** [priːˈɔkjupaɪd] *adj* préoccupé(e)
**prep** [prɛp] *adj abbr*: ~ **school**; = **preparatory school** ▷ *n abbr* (*Scol*: = *preparation*) étude *f*
**prepackaged** [priːˈpækɪdʒd] *adj* préempaqueté(e)
**prepaid** [priːˈpeɪd] *adj* payé(e) d'avance
**preparation** [prɛpəˈreɪʃən] *n* préparation *f*; **preparations** *npl* (*for trip, war*) préparatifs *mpl*; **in ~ for** en vue de
**preparatory** [prɪˈpærətərɪ] *adj* préparatoire; ~ **to sth/to doing sth** en prévision de qch/avant de faire qch
**preparatory school** *n* (*Brit*) école primaire privée; (*US*) lycée privé; *voir article*

⬤ **PREPARATORY SCHOOL**
⬤
⬤ En Grande-Bretagne, une *preparatory school* –
⬤ ou, plus familièrement, une *prep school* – est
⬤ une école payante qui prépare les enfants de
⬤ 7 à 13 ans aux "public schools".

**prepare** [prɪˈpɛəʳ] *vt* préparer ▷ *vi*: **to ~ for** se préparer à
**prepared** [prɪˈpɛəd] *adj*: ~ **for** préparé(e) à; ~ **to** prêt(e) à
**preponderance** [prɪˈpɔndərns] *n* prépondérance *f*
**preposition** [prɛpəˈzɪʃən] *n* préposition *f*

**prepossessing** [priːpəˈzɛsɪŋ] *adj* avenant(e), engageant(e)
**preposterous** [prɪˈpɔstərəs] *adj* ridicule, absurde
**prep school** *n* = **preparatory school**
**prerecord** ['priːrɪˈkɔːd] *vt*: ~**ed broadcast** émission *f* en différé; ~**ed cassette** cassette enregistrée
**prerequisite** [priːˈrɛkwɪzɪt] *n* condition *f* préalable
**prerogative** [prɪˈrɔgətɪv] *n* prérogative *f*
**presbyterian** [prɛzbɪˈtɪərɪən] *adj*, *n* presbytérien(ne)
**presbytery** ['prɛzbɪtərɪ] *n* presbytère *m*
**preschool** ['priːˈskuːl] *adj* préscolaire; (*child*) d'âge préscolaire
**prescribe** [prɪˈskraɪb] *vt* prescrire; ~**d books** (*Brit Scol*) œuvres *fpl* au programme
**prescription** [prɪˈskrɪpʃən] *n* prescription *f*; (*Med*) ordonnance *f*; (: *medicine*) médicament *m* (obtenu sur ordonnance); **to make up** *or* (*US*) **fill a ~** faire une ordonnance; **could you write me a ~?** pouvez-vous me faire une ordonnance?; **"only available on ~"** "uniquement sur ordonnance"
**prescription charges** *npl* (*Brit*) participation *f* fixe au coût de l'ordonnance
**prescriptive** [prɪˈskrɪptɪv] *adj* normatif(-ive)
**presence** ['prɛzns] *n* présence *f*; **in sb's ~** en présence de qn; ~ **of mind** présence d'esprit
**present** ['prɛznt] *adj* (*current*) présent(e), actuel(le) ▷ *n* cadeau *m*; (*actuality, also*: **present tense**) présent *m* ▷ *vt* [prɪˈzɛnt] présenter; (*prize, medal*) remettre; (*give*): **to ~ sb with sth** offrir qch à qn; **to be ~ at** assister à; **those ~** les présents; **at ~** en ce moment; **to give sb a ~** offrir un cadeau à qn; **to ~ sb (to sb)** présenter qn (à qn)
**presentable** [prɪˈzɛntəbl] *adj* présentable
**presentation** [prɛznˈteɪʃən] *n* présentation *f*; (*gift*) cadeau *m*, présent *m*; (*ceremony*) remise *f* du cadeau (*or* de la médaille *etc*); **on ~ of** (*voucher etc*) sur présentation de
**present-day** ['prɛzntdeɪ] *adj* contemporain(e), actuel(le)
**presenter** [prɪˈzɛntəʳ] *n* (*Brit Radio, TV*) présentateur(-trice)
**presently** ['prɛzntlɪ] *adv* (*soon*) tout à l'heure, bientôt; (*with verb in past*) peu après; (*at present*) en ce moment; (*US*: *now*) maintenant
**preservation** [prɛzəˈveɪʃən] *n* préservation *f*, conservation *f*
**preservative** [prɪˈzəːvətɪv] *n* agent *m* de conservation
**preserve** [prɪˈzəːv] *vt* (*keep safe*) préserver, protéger; (*maintain*) conserver, garder; (*food*) mettre en conserve ▷ *n* (*for game, fish*) réserve *f*; (*often pl*: *jam*) confiture *f*; (: *fruit*) fruits *mpl* en conserve
**preshrunk** ['priːˈʃrʌŋk] *adj* irrétrécissable
**preside** [prɪˈzaɪd] *vi* présider
**presidency** ['prɛzɪdənsɪ] *n* présidence *f*

P

**president** ['prezɪdənt] n président(e); (US: of company) président-directeur général, PDG m
**presidential** [prezɪ'dɛnʃl] adj présidentiel(le)
**press** [pres] n (tool, machine, newspapers) presse f; (for wine) pressoir m; (crowd) cohue f, foule f ▷ vt (push) appuyer sur; (squeeze) presser, serrer; (clothes: iron) repasser; (pursue) talonner; (insist): **to ~ sth on sb** presser qn d'accepter qch; (urge, entreat): **to ~ sb to do** or **into doing sth** pousser qn à faire qch ▷ vi appuyer, peser; se presser; **we are ~ed for time** le temps nous manque; **to ~ for sth** faire pression pour obtenir qch; **to ~ sb for an answer** presser qn de répondre; **to ~ charges against sb** (Law) engager des poursuites contre qn; **to go to ~** (newspaper) aller à l'impression; **to be in the ~** (being printed) être sous presse; (in the newspapers) être dans le journal
  ▶ **press ahead** vi = **press on**
  ▶ **press on** vi continuer
**press agency** n agence f de presse
**press clipping** n coupure f de presse
**press conference** n conférence f de presse
**press cutting** n = **press clipping**
**press-gang** ['presgæn] vt (fig): **to ~ sb into doing sth** faire pression sur qn pour qu'il fasse qch
**pressing** ['presɪn] adj urgent(e), pressant(e) ▷ n repassage m
**press officer** n attaché(e) de presse
**press release** n communiqué m de presse
**press stud** n (Brit) bouton-pression m
**press-up** ['presʌp] n (Brit) traction f
**pressure** ['preʃər] n pression f; (stress) tension f ▷ vt = **to put pressure on; to put ~ on sb (to do sth)** faire pression sur qn (pour qu'il fasse qch)
**pressure cooker** n cocotte-minute f
**pressure gauge** n manomètre m
**pressure group** n groupe m de pression
**pressurize** ['preʃəraɪz] vt pressuriser; (Brit fig): **to ~ sb (into doing sth)** faire pression sur qn (pour qu'il fasse qch)
**pressurized** ['preʃəraɪzd] adj pressurisé(e)
**prestige** [pres'tiːʒ] n prestige m
**prestigious** [pres'tɪdʒəs] adj prestigieux(-euse)
**presumably** [prɪ'zjuːməblɪ] adv vraisemblablement; **~ he did it** c'est sans doute lui (qui a fait cela)
**presume** [prɪ'zjuːm] vt présumer, supposer; **to ~ to do** (dare) se permettre de faire
**presumption** [prɪ'zʌmpʃən] n supposition f, présomption f; (boldness) audace f
**presumptuous** [prɪ'zʌmpʃəs] adj présomptueux(-euse)
**presuppose** [priːsə'pəuz] vt présupposer
**pre-tax** [priː'tæks] adj avant impôt(s)
**pretence, (US) pretense** [prɪ'tɛns] n (claim) prétention f; (pretext) prétexte m; **she is devoid of all ~** elle n'est pas du tout prétentieuse; **to make a ~ of doing** faire semblant de faire; **on** or **under the ~ of doing sth** sous prétexte de faire qch; **under false ~s** sous des prétextes fallacieux
**pretend** [prɪ'tɛnd] vt (feign) feindre, simuler ▷ vi (feign) faire semblant; (claim): **to ~ to sth** prétendre à qch; **to ~ to do** faire semblant de faire
**pretense** [prɪ'tɛns] n (US) = **pretence**
**pretension** [prɪ'tɛnʃən] n (claim) prétention f; **to have no ~s to sth/to being sth** n'avoir aucune prétention à qch/à être qch
**pretentious** [prɪ'tɛnʃəs] adj prétentieux(-euse)
**preterite** ['pretərɪt] n prétérit m
**pretext** ['priːtɛkst] n prétexte m; **on** or **under the ~ of doing sth** sous prétexte de faire qch
**pretty** ['prɪtɪ] adj joli(e) ▷ adv assez
**prevail** [prɪ'veɪl] vi (win) l'emporter, prévaloir; (be usual) avoir cours; (persuade): **to ~ (up)on sb to do** persuader qn de faire
**prevailing** [prɪ'veɪlɪn] adj (widespread) courant(e), répandu(e); (wind) dominant(e)
**prevalent** ['prevələnt] adj répandu(e), courant(e); (fashion) en vogue
**prevarication** [prɪværɪ'keɪʃən] n (usage m de) faux-fuyants mpl
**prevent** [prɪ'vɛnt] vt: **to ~ (from doing)** empêcher (de faire)
**preventable** [prɪ'vɛntəbl] adj évitable
**preventative** [prɪ'vɛntətɪv] adj préventif(-ive)
**prevention** [prɪ'vɛnʃən] n prévention f
**preventive** [prɪ'vɛntɪv] adj préventif(-ive)
**preview** ['priːvjuː] n (of film) avant-première f; (fig) aperçu m
**previous** ['priːvɪəs] adj (last) précédent(e); (earlier) antérieur(e); (question, experience) préalable; **I have a ~ engagement** je suis déjà pris(e); **~ to doing** avant de faire
**previously** ['priːvɪəslɪ] adv précédemment, auparavant
**prewar** [priː'wɔːr] adj d'avant-guerre
**prey** [preɪ] n proie f ▷ vi: **to ~ on** s'attaquer à; **it was ~ing on his mind** ça le rongeait or minait
**price** [praɪs] n prix m; (Betting: odds) cote f ▷ vt (goods) fixer le prix de; tarifer; **what is the ~ of ...?** combien coûte ...?, quel est le prix de ...?; **to go up** or **rise in ~** augmenter; **to put a ~ on sth** chiffrer qch; **to be ~d out of the market** (article) être trop cher pour soutenir la concurrence; (producer, nation) ne pas pouvoir soutenir la concurrence; **what ~ his promises now?** (Brit) que valent maintenant toutes ses promesses?; **he regained his freedom, but at a ~** il a retrouvé sa liberté, mais cela lui a coûté cher
**price control** n contrôle m des prix
**price-cutting** ['praɪskʌtɪn] n réductions fpl de prix
**priceless** ['praɪslɪs] adj sans prix, inestimable; (inf: amusing) impayable
**price list** n tarif m
**price range** n gamme f de prix; **it's within my ~** c'est dans mes prix
**price tag** n étiquette f
**price war** n guerre f des prix

**pricey** ['praɪsɪ] adj (inf) chérot inv
**prick** [prɪk] n (sting) piqûre f; (inf!) bitte f (!);
connard m (!) ▷ vt piquer; **to ~ up one's ears**
dresser or tendre l'oreille
**prickle** ['prɪkl] n (of plant) épine f; (sensation)
picotement m
**prickly** ['prɪklɪ] adj piquant(e), épineux(-euse);
(fig: person) irritable
**prickly heat** n fièvre f miliaire
**prickly pear** n figue f de Barbarie
**pride** [praɪd] n (feeling proud) fierté f; (pej) orgueil
m; (self-esteem) amour-propre m ▷ vt: **to ~ o.s.**
**on** se flatter de; s'enorgueillir de; **to take (a) ~**
**in** être (très) fier(-ère) de; **to take a ~ in doing**
mettre sa fierté à faire; **to have ~ of place** (Brit)
avoir la place d'honneur
**priest** [pri:st] n prêtre m
**priestess** ['pri:stɪs] n prêtresse f
**priesthood** ['pri:sthud] n prêtrise f, sacerdoce m
**prig** [prɪg] n poseur(-euse), fat m
**prim** [prɪm] adj collet monté inv, guindé(e)
**prima facie** ['praɪmə'feɪʃɪ] adj: **to have a ~ case**
(Law) avoir une affaire recevable
**primal** ['praɪməl] adj (first in time) primitif(-ive);
(first in importance) primordial(e)
**primarily** ['praɪmərɪlɪ] adv principalement,
essentiellement
**primary** ['praɪmərɪ] adj primaire; (first in
importance) premier(-ière), primordial(e) ▷ n
(US: election) (élection f) primaire f; voir article

**primary colour** n couleur fondamentale
**primary school** n (Brit) école f primaire; voir article

**primate** n (Rel) ['praɪmɪt] primat m; (Zool)

['praɪmeɪt] primate m
**prime** [praɪm] adj primordial(e),
fondamental(e); (excellent) excellent(e) ▷ vt
(gun, pump) amorcer; (fig) mettre au courant ▷ n:
**in the ~ of life** dans la fleur de l'âge
**Prime Minister** n Premier ministre
**primer** ['praɪmə˧] n (book) premier livre, manuel
m élémentaire; (paint) apprêt m
**prime time** n (Radio, TV) heure(s) f(pl) de grande
écoute
**primeval** [praɪ'mi:vl] adj primitif(-ive)
**primitive** ['prɪmɪtɪv] adj primitif(-ive)
**primrose** ['prɪmrəuz] n primevère f
**primus®** ['praɪməs], **primus® stove** n (Brit)
réchaud m de camping
**prince** [prɪns] n prince m
**princess** [prɪn'sɛs] n princesse f
**principal** ['prɪnsɪpl] adj principal(e) ▷ n (head
teacher) directeur m, principal m; (in play) rôle
principal; (money) principal m
**principality** [prɪnsɪ'pælɪtɪ] n principauté f
**principally** ['prɪnsɪplɪ] adv principalement
**principle** ['prɪnsɪpl] n principe m; **in ~** en
principe; **on ~** par principe
**print** [prɪnt] n (mark) empreinte f; (letters)
caractères mpl; (fabric) imprimé m; (Art) gravure
f, estampe f; (Phot) épreuve f ▷ vt imprimer;
(publish) publier; (write in capitals) écrire en
majuscules; **out of ~** épuisé(e)
▷ **print out** vt (Comput) imprimer
**printed circuit board** ['prɪntɪd-] n carte f à
circuit imprimé
**printed matter** ['prɪntɪd-] n imprimés mpl
**printer** ['prɪntə˧] n (machine) imprimante f;
(person) imprimeur m
**printhead** ['prɪnthɛd] n tête f d'impression
**printing** ['prɪntɪŋ] n impression f
**printing press** n presse f typographique
**printout** ['prɪntaut] n (Comput) sortie f
imprimante
**print wheel** n marguerite f
**prior** ['praɪə˧] adj antérieur(e), précédent(e);
(more important) prioritaire ▷ n (Rel) prieur m
▷ adv: **~ to doing** avant de faire; **without ~**
**notice** sans préavis; **to have a ~ claim to sth**
avoir priorité pour qch
**priority** [praɪ'ɔrɪtɪ] n priorité f; **to have or take ~**
**over sth/sb** avoir la priorité sur qch/qn
**priory** ['praɪərɪ] n prieuré m
**prise** [praɪz] vt: **to ~ open** forcer
**prism** ['prɪzəm] n prisme m
**prison** ['prɪzn] n prison f ▷ cpd pénitentiaire
**prison camp** n camp m de prisonniers
**prisoner** ['prɪznə˧] n prisonnier(-ière); **the ~ at**
**the bar** l'accusé(e); **to take sb ~** faire qn
prisonnier
**prisoner of war** n prisonnier(-ière) de guerre
**prissy** ['prɪsɪ] adj bégueule
**pristine** ['prɪsti:n] adj virginal(e)
**privacy** ['prɪvəsɪ] n intimité f, solitude f
**private** ['praɪvɪt] adj (not public) privé(e);
(personal) personnel(le); (house, car, lesson)

**p**

particulier(-ière); (*quiet: place*) tranquille ▷ *n* soldat *m* de deuxième classe; **"-"** (*on envelope*) "personnelle"; (*on door*) "privé"; **in ~** en privé; **in (his) ~ life** dans sa vie privée; **he is a very ~ person** il est très secret; **to be in ~ practice** être médecin (*or* dentiste *etc*) non conventionné; **~ hearing** (*Law*) audience *f* à huis-clos

**private detective** *n* détective privé

**private enterprise** *n* entreprise privée

**private eye** *n* détective privé

**private limited company** *n* (*Brit*) société *f* à participation restreinte (*non cotée en Bourse*)

**privately** ['praɪvɪtlɪ] *adv* en privé; (*within oneself*) intérieurement

**private parts** *npl* parties (génitales)

**private property** *n* propriété privée

**private school** *n* école privée

**privatize** ['praɪvɪtaɪz] *vt* privatiser

**privet** ['prɪvɪt] *n* troène *m*

**privilege** ['prɪvɪlɪdʒ] *n* privilège *m*

**privileged** ['prɪvɪlɪdʒd] *adj* privilégié(e); **to be ~ to do sth** avoir le privilège de faire qch

**privy** ['prɪvɪ] *adj*: **to be ~ to** être au courant de

**privy council** *n* conseil privé; *voir article*

**PRIVY COUNCIL**

Le *privy council* existe en Angleterre depuis l'avènement des Normands. À l'époque, ses membres étaient les conseillers privés du roi, mais en 1688 le cabinet les a supplantés. Les ministres du cabinet sont aujourd'hui automatiquement conseillers du roi, et ce titre est également accordé aux personnes qui ont occupé de hautes fonctions en politique, dans le clergé ou dans les milieux juridiques. Les pouvoirs de ces conseillers en tant que tels sont maintenant limités.

**prize** [praɪz] *n* prix *m* ▷ *adj* (*example, idiot*) parfait(e); (*bull, novel*) primé(e) ▷ *vt* priser, faire grand cas de

**prize-fighter** ['praɪzfaɪtə'] *n* boxeur professionnel

**prize-giving** ['praɪzgɪvɪŋ] *n* distribution *f* des prix

**prize money** *n* argent *m* du prix

**prizewinner** ['praɪzwɪnə'] *n* gagnant(e)

**prizewinning** ['praɪzwɪnɪŋ] *adj* gagnant(e); (*novel, essay etc*) primé(e)

**PRO** *n abbr* = **public relations officer**

**pro** [prəu] *n* (*inf: Sport*) professionnel(le) ▷ *prep* pro; **pros** *npl*: **the ~s and cons** le pour et le contre

**pro-** [prəu] *prefix* (*in favour of*) pro-

**pro-active** [prəu'æktɪv] *adj* dynamique

**probability** [prɔbə'bɪlɪtɪ] *n* probabilité *f*; **in all ~** très probablement

**probable** ['prɔbəbl] *adj* probable; **it is ~/hardly ~ that** ... il est probable/peu probable que ...

**probably** ['prɔbəblɪ] *adv* probablement

**probate** ['prəubɪt] *n* (*Law*) validation *f*, homologation *f*

**probation** [prə'beɪʃən] *n* (*in employment*) (période *f* d')essai *m*; (*Law*) liberté surveillée; (*Rel*) noviciat *m*, probation *f*; **on ~** (*employee*) à l'essai; (*Law*) en liberté surveillée

**probationary** [prə'beɪʃənrɪ] *adj* (*period*) d'essai

**probe** [prəub] *n* (*Med, Space*) sonde *f*; (*enquiry*) enquête *f*, investigation *f* ▷ *vt* sonder, explorer

**probity** ['prəubɪtɪ] *n* probité *f*

**problem** ['prɔbləm] *n* problème *m*; **to have ~s with the car** avoir des ennuis avec la voiture; **what's the ~?** qu'y a-t-il?, quel est le problème?; **I had no ~ in finding her** je n'ai pas eu de mal à la trouver; **no ~!** pas de problème!

**problematic** [prɔblə'mætɪk] *adj* problématique

**problem-solving** ['prɔbləmsɔlvɪŋ] *n* résolution *f* de problèmes; **an approach to ~** une approche en matière de résolution de problèmes

**procedure** [prə'siːdʒə'] *n* (*Admin, Law*) procédure *f*; (*method*) marche *f* à suivre, façon *f* de procéder

**proceed** [prə'siːd] *vi* (*go forward*) avancer; (*act*) procéder; (*continue*): **to ~ (with)** continuer, poursuivre; **to ~ to** aller à; passer à; **to ~ to do** se mettre à faire; **I am not sure how to ~** je ne sais pas exactement comment m'y prendre; **to ~ against sb** (*Law*) intenter des poursuites contre qn

**proceedings** [prə'siːdɪŋz] *npl* (*measures*) mesures *fpl*; (*Law: against sb*) poursuites *fpl*; (*meeting*) réunion *f*, séance *f*; (*records*) compte rendu; actes *mpl*

**proceeds** ['prəusiːdz] *npl* produit *m*, recette *f*

**process** ['prəuses] *n* processus *m*; (*method*) procédé *m* ▷ *vt* traiter ▷ *vi* (*Brit formal: go in procession*) défiler; **in ~** en cours; **we are in the ~ of doing** nous sommes en train de faire

**processed cheese** ['prəusest-] *n* ≈ fromage fondu

**processing** ['prəusesɪŋ] *n* traitement *m*

**procession** [prə'seʃən] *n* défilé *m*, cortège *m*; **funeral ~** (*on foot*) cortège funèbre; (*in cars*) convoi *m* mortuaire

**pro-choice** [prəu'tʃɔɪs] *adj* en faveur de l'avortement

**proclaim** [prə'kleɪm] *vt* déclarer, proclamer

**proclamation** [prɔklə'meɪʃən] *n* proclamation *f*

**proclivity** [prə'klɪvɪtɪ] *n* inclination *f*

**procrastinate** [prəu'kræstɪneɪt] *vi* faire traîner les choses, vouloir tout remettre au lendemain

**procrastination** [prəukræstɪ'neɪʃən] *n* procrastination *f*

**procreation** [prəukrɪ'eɪʃən] *n* procréation *f*

**Procurator Fiscal** ['prɔkjureɪtə-] *n* (*Scottish*) ≈ procureur *m* (*de la République*)

**procure** [prə'kjuə'] *vt* (*for o.s.*) se procurer; (*for sb*) procurer

**procurement** [prə'kjuəmənt] *n* achat *m*, approvisionnement *m*

**prod** [prɔd] *vt* pousser ▷ *n* (*push, jab*) petit coup, poussée *f*

**prodigal** ['prɔdɪgl] *adj* prodigue

**prodigious** [prə'dɪdʒəs] *adj* prodigieux(-euse)
**prodigy** ['prɔdɪdʒɪ] *n* prodige *m*
**produce** *n* ['prɔdjuːs] (*Agr*) produits *mpl* ▷ *vt*
[prə'djuːs] produire; (*show*) présenter; (*cause*)
provoquer, causer; (*Theat*) monter, mettre en
scène; (*TV: programme*) réaliser; (: *play, film*)
mettre en scène; (*Radio: programme*) réaliser;
(: *play*) mettre en ondes
**producer** [prə'djuːsəʳ] *n* (*Theat*) metteur *m* en
scène; (*Agr, Comm, Cine*) producteur *m*; (*TV: of
programme*) réalisateur *m*; (: *of play, film*) metteur
en scène; (*Radio: of programme*) réalisateur; (: *of
play*) metteur en ondes
**product** ['prɔdʌkt] *n* produit *m*
**production** [prə'dʌkʃən] *n* production *f*; (*Theat*)
mise *f* en scène; **to put into** ~ (*goods*)
entreprendre la fabrication de
**production agreement** *n* (*US*) accord *m* de
productivité
**production line** *n* chaîne *f* (de fabrication)
**production manager** *n* directeur(-trice) de la
production
**productive** [prə'dʌktɪv] *adj* productif(-ive)
**productivity** [prɔdʌk'tɪvɪtɪ] *n* productivité *f*
**productivity agreement** *n* (*Brit*) accord *m* de
productivité
**productivity bonus** *n* prime *f* de rendement
**Prof.** [prɔf] *abbr* (= *professor*) Prof
**profane** [prə'feɪn] *adj* sacrilège; (*lay*) profane
**profess** [prə'fɛs] *vt* professer; **I do not** ~ **to be
an expert** je ne prétends pas être spécialiste
**professed** [prə'fɛst] *adj* (*self-declared*) déclaré(e)
**profession** [prə'fɛʃən] *n* profession *f*; **the** ~**s** les
professions libérales
**professional** [prə'fɛʃənl] *n* professionnel(le)
▷ *adj* professionnel(le); (*work*) de professionnel;
**he's a** ~ **man** il exerce une profession libérale;
**to take** ~ **advice** consulter un spécialiste
**professionalism** [prə'fɛʃnəlɪzəm] *n*
professionnalisme *m*
**professionally** [prə'fɛʃnəlɪ] *adv*
professionnellement; (*Sport: play*) en
professionnel; **I only know him** ~ je n'ai avec
lui que des relations de travail
**professor** [prə'fɛsəʳ] *n* professeur *m* (*titulaire
d'une chaire*); (*US: teacher*) professeur *m*
**professorship** [prə'fɛsəʃɪp] *n* chaire *f*
**proffer** ['prɔfəʳ] *vt* (*hand*) tendre; (*remark*) faire;
(*apologies*) présenter
**proficiency** [prə'fɪʃənsɪ] *n* compétence *f*,
aptitude *f*
**proficient** [prə'fɪʃənt] *adj* compétent(e), capable
**profile** ['prəufaɪl] *n* profil *m*; **to keep a high/
low** ~ (*fig*) rester *or* être très en évidence/
discret(-ète)
**profit** ['prɔfɪt] *n* (*from trading*) bénéfice *m*;
(*advantage*) profit *m* ▷ *vi*: **to** ~ (**by** *or* **from**)
profiter (de); ~ **and loss account** compte *m* de
profits et pertes; **to make a** ~ faire un *or* des
bénéfice(s); **to sell sth at a** ~ vendre qch à
profit
**profitability** [prɔfɪtə'bɪlɪtɪ] *n* rentabilité *f*

**profitable** ['prɔfɪtəbl] *adj* lucratif(-ive),
rentable; (*fig: beneficial*) avantageux(-euse);
(: *meeting*) fructueux(-euse)
**profit centre** *n* centre *m* de profit
**profiteering** [prɔfɪ'tɪərɪŋ] *n* (*pej*)
mercantilisme *m*
**profit-making** ['prɔfɪtmeɪkɪŋ] *adj* à but lucratif
**profit margin** *n* marge *f* bénéficiaire
**profit-sharing** ['prɔfɪtʃɛərɪŋ] *n* intéressement *m*
aux bénéfices
**profits tax** *n* (*Brit*) impôt *m* sur les bénéfices
**profligate** ['prɔflɪgɪt] *adj* (*behaviour, act*)
dissolu(e); (*person*) débauché(e); (*extravagant*): ~
(**with**) prodigue (de)
**pro forma** ['prəu'fɔːmə] *adj*: ~ **invoice** facture *f*
pro-forma
**profound** [prə'faund] *adj* profond(e)
**profuse** [prə'fjuːs] *adj* abondant(e)
**profusely** [prə'fjuːslɪ] *adv* abondamment;
(*thank etc*) avec effusion
**profusion** [prə'fjuːʒən] *n* profusion *f*,
abondance *f*
**progeny** ['prɔdʒɪnɪ] *n* progéniture *f*;
descendants *mpl*
**prognosis** [prɔg'nəusɪs] (*pl* **prognoses**) *n*
pronostic *m*
**programme**, (*US*) **program** ['prəugræm] *n*
(*Comput: also Brit*) programme *m*; (*Radio, TV*)
émission *f* ▷ *vt* programmer
**programmer** ['prəugræməʳ] *n*
programmeur(-euse)
**programming**, (*US*) **programing**
['prəugræmɪŋ] *n* programmation *f*
**programming language**, (*US*) **programing
language** *n* langage *m* de programmation
**progress** *n* ['prəugrɛs] progrès *m*(*pl*) ▷ *vi*
[prə'grɛs] progresser, avancer; **in** ~ en cours; **to
make** ~ progresser, faire des progrès, être en
progrès; **as the match** ~**ed** au fur et à mesure
que la partie avançait
**progression** [prə'grɛʃən] *n* progression *f*
**progressive** [prə'grɛsɪv] *adj* progressif(-ive);
(*person*) progressiste
**progressively** [prə'grɛsɪvlɪ] *adv*
progressivement
**progress report** *n* (*Med*) bulletin *m* de santé;
(*Admin*) rapport *m* d'activité; rapport sur l'état
(d'avancement) des travaux
**prohibit** [prə'hɪbɪt] *vt* interdire, défendre; **to** ~
**sb from doing sth** défendre *or* interdire à qn de
faire qch; **"smoking -ed"** "défense de fumer"
**prohibition** [prəuɪ'bɪʃən] *n* prohibition *f*
**prohibitive** [prə'hɪbɪtɪv] *adj* (*price etc*)
prohibitif(-ive)
**project** *n* ['prɔdʒɛkt, *vb* prə'dʒɛkt] *n* (*plan*) projet
*m*, plan *m*; (*venture*) opération *f*, entreprise *f*;
(*Scol: research*) étude *f*, dossier *m* ▷ *vt* projeter ▷ *vi*
(*stick out*) faire saillie, s'avancer
**projectile** [prə'dʒɛktaɪl] *n* projectile *m*
**projection** [prə'dʒɛkʃən] *n* projection *f*;
(*overhang*) saillie *f*
**projectionist** [prə'dʒɛkʃənɪst] *n* (*Cine*)

735

projectionniste *m/f*

**projection room** *n* (*Cine*) cabine *f* de projection

**projector** [prə'dʒɛktə<sup>r</sup>] *n* (*Cine etc*) projecteur *m*

**proletarian** [prəuli'tɛərɪən] *adj* prolétarien(ne)
▷ *n* prolétaire *m/f*

**proletariat** [prəuli'tɛərɪət] *n* prolétariat *m*

**pro-life** [prəu'laɪf] *adj* contre l'avortement

**proliferate** [prə'lɪfəreɪt] *vi* proliférer

**proliferation** [prəlɪfə'reɪʃən] *n* prolifération *f*

**prolific** [prə'lɪfɪk] *adj* prolifique

**prologue** ['prəulɒg] *n* prologue *m*

**prolong** [prə'lɒŋ] *vt* prolonger

**prom** [prɒm] *n abbr* = **promenade; promenade
concert;** (*US: ball*) bal *m* d'étudiants; **the P~s**
*série de concerts de musique classique; voir article*

---

⦿ **PROM**
⦿
⦿ En Grande-Bretagne, un *promenade concert* ou
⦿ *prom* est un concert de musique classique,
⦿ ainsi appelé car, à l'origine, le public restait
⦿ debout et se promenait au lieu de rester
⦿ assis. De nos jours, une partie du public
⦿ reste debout, mais il y a également des
⦿ places assises (plus chères). Les *Proms* les
⦿ plus connus sont les Proms londoniens. La
⦿ dernière séance (the "Last Night of the
⦿ Proms") est un grand événement
⦿ médiatique où se jouent des airs
⦿ traditionnels et patriotiques.
⦿ Aux États-Unis et au Canada, le *prom* ou
⦿ *promenade* est un bal organisé par le lycée.

---

**promenade** [prɒmə'nɑːd] *n* (*by sea*) esplanade *f*,
promenade *f*

**promenade concert** *n* concert *m* (de musique
classique)

**promenade deck** *n* (*Naut*) pont *m* promenade

**prominence** ['prɒmɪnəns] *n* proéminence *f*;
importance *f*

**prominent** ['prɒmɪnənt] *adj* (*standing out*)
proéminent(e); (*important*) important(e); **he is ~
in the field of** ... il est très connu dans le
domaine de ...

**prominently** ['prɒmɪnəntlɪ] *adv* (*display, set*) bien
en évidence; **he figured ~ in the case** il a joué
un rôle important dans l'affaire

**promiscuity** [prɒmɪs'kjuːɪtɪ] *n* (*sexual*) légèreté *f*
de mœurs

**promiscuous** [prə'mɪskjuəs] *adj* (*sexually*) de
mœurs légères

**promise** ['prɒmɪs] *n* promesse *f* ▷ *vt, vi*
promettre; **to make sb a ~** faire une promesse
à qn; **a young man of ~** un jeune homme plein
d'avenir; **to ~ well** *vi* promettre

**promising** ['prɒmɪsɪŋ] *adj* prometteur(-euse)

**promissory note** ['prɒmɪsərɪ-] *n* billet *m* à ordre

**promontory** ['prɒməntrɪ] *n* promontoire *m*

**promote** [prə'məut] *vt* promouvoir; (*venture,
event*) organiser, mettre sur pied; (*new product*)
lancer; **the team was ~d to the second
division** (*Brit Football*) l'équipe est montée en 2<sup>e</sup>
division

**promoter** [prə'məutə<sup>r</sup>] *n* (*of event*)
organisateur(-trice)

**promotion** [prə'məuʃən] *n* promotion *f*

**prompt** [prɒmpt] *adj* rapide ▷ *n* (*Comput*)
message *m* (de guidage) ▷ *vt* inciter; (*cause*)
entraîner, provoquer; (*Theat*) souffler (son rôle
*or* ses répliques) à; **they're very ~** (*punctual*) ils
sont ponctuels; **at 8 o'clock ~** à 8 heures
précises; **he was ~ to accept** il a tout de suite
accepté; **to ~ sb to do** inciter *or* pousser qn à
faire

**prompter** ['prɒmptə<sup>r</sup>] *n* (*Theat*) souffleur *m*

**promptly** ['prɒmptlɪ] *adv* (*quickly*) rapidement,
sans délai; (*on time*) ponctuellement

**promptness** ['prɒmptnɪs] *n* rapidité *f*;
promptitude *f*; ponctualité *f*

**prone** [prəun] *adj* (*lying*) couché(e) (face contre
terre); (*liable*): **~ to** enclin(e) à; **to be ~ to
illness** être facilement malade; **to be ~ to an
illness** être sujet à une maladie; **she is ~ to
burst into tears if** ... elle a tendance à tomber
en larmes si ...

**prong** [prɒŋ] *n* pointe *f*; (*of fork*) dent *f*

**pronoun** ['prəunaun] *n* pronom *m*

**pronounce** [prə'nauns] *vt* prononcer ▷ *vi*: **to ~
(up)on** se prononcer sur; **how do you ~ it?**
comment est-ce que ça se prononce?; **they ~d
him unfit to drive** ils l'ont déclaré inapte à la
conduite

**pronounced** [prə'naunst] *adj* (*marked*)
prononcé(e)

**pronouncement** [prə'naunsmənt] *n*
déclaration *f*

**pronunciation** [prənʌnsɪ'eɪʃən] *n*
prononciation *f*

**proof** [pruːf] *n* preuve *f*; (*test, of book, Phot*)
épreuve *f*; (*of alcohol*) degré *m* ▷ *adj*: **~ against** à
l'épreuve de ▷ *vt* (*Brit: tent, anorak*)
imperméabiliser; **70° ~** = titrer 40 degrés

**proofreader** ['pruːfriːdə<sup>r</sup>] *n* correcteur(-trice)
(d'épreuves)

**prop** [prɒp] *n* support *m*, étai *m*; (*fig*) soutien *m*
▷ *vt* (*also:* **prop up**) étayer, soutenir; **props** *npl*
accessoires *mpl*; (*lean*): **to ~ sth against**
appuyer qch contre *or* à

**Prop.** *abbr* (*Comm*) = **proprietor**

**propaganda** [prɒpə'gændə] *n* propagande *f*

**propagation** [prɒpə'geɪʃən] *n* propagation *f*

**propel** [prə'pɛl] *vt* propulser, faire avancer

**propeller** [prə'pɛlə<sup>r</sup>] *n* hélice *f*

**propelling pencil** [prə'pɛlɪŋ-] *n* (*Brit*) porte-
mine *m inv*

**propensity** [prə'pɛnsɪtɪ] *n* propension *f*

**proper** ['prɒpə<sup>r</sup>] *adj* (*suited, right*) approprié(e),
bon (bonne); (*seemly*) correct(e), convenable;
(*authentic*) vrai(e), véritable; (*inf: real*) fini(e),
vrai(e); (*referring to place*): **the village ~** le village
proprement dit; **to go through the ~ channels**
(*Admin*) passer par la voie officielle

**properly** ['prɒpəlɪ] *adv* correctement,
convenablement; (*really*) bel et bien

**proper noun** *n* nom *m* propre
**property** ['prɔpətɪ] *n* (*possessions*) biens *mpl*; (*house etc*) propriété *f*; (*land*) terres *fpl*, domaine *m*; (*Chem etc: quality*) propriété *f*; **it's their ~** cela leur appartient, c'est leur propriété
**property developer** *n* (*Brit*) promoteur immobilier
**property owner** *n* propriétaire *m*
**property tax** *n* impôt foncier
**prophecy** ['prɔfɪsɪ] *n* prophétie *f*
**prophesy** ['prɔfɪsaɪ] *vt* prédire ▷ *vi* prophétiser
**prophet** ['prɔfɪt] *n* prophète *m*
**prophetic** [prə'fɛtɪk] *adj* prophétique
**proportion** [prə'pɔ:ʃən] *n* proportion *f*; (*share*) part *f*; partie *f* ▷ *vt* proportionner; **proportions** *npl* (*size*) dimensions *fpl*; **to be in/out of ~ to** or **with sth** être à la mesure de/hors de proportion avec qch; **to see sth in ~** (*fig*) ramener qch à de justes proportions
**proportional** [prə'pɔ:ʃənl], **proportionate** [prə'pɔ:ʃənɪt] *adj* proportionnel(le)
**proportional representation** *n* (*Pol*) représentation proportionnelle
**proposal** [prə'pəuzl] *n* proposition *f*, offre *f*; (*plan*) projet *m*; (*of marriage*) demande *f* en mariage
**propose** [prə'pəuz] *vt* proposer, suggérer; (*have in mind*): **to ~ sth/to do** or **doing sth** envisager qch/de faire qch ▷ *vi* faire sa demande en mariage; **to ~ to do** avoir l'intention de faire
**proposer** [prə'pəuzər] *n* (*Brit: of motion etc*) auteur *m*
**proposition** [prɔpə'zɪʃən] *n* proposition *f*; **to make sb a ~** faire une proposition à qn
**propound** [prə'paund] *vt* proposer, soumettre
**proprietary** [prə'praɪətərɪ] *adj* de marque déposée; **~ article** article *m* or produit *m* de marque; **~ brand** marque déposée
**proprietor** [prə'praɪətər] *n* propriétaire *m/f*
**propriety** [prə'praɪətɪ] *n* (*seemliness*) bienséance *f*, convenance *f*
**propulsion** [prə'pʌlʃən] *n* propulsion *f*
**pro rata** [prəu'rɑ:tə] *adv* au prorata
**prosaic** [prəu'zeɪɪk] *adj* prosaïque
**Pros. Atty.** *abbr* (*US*) = **prosecuting attorney**
**proscribe** [prə'skraɪb] *vt* proscrire
**prose** [prəuz] *n* prose *f*; (*Scol: translation*) thème *m*
**prosecute** ['prɔsɪkju:t] *vt* poursuivre
**prosecuting attorney** ['prɔsɪkju:tɪŋ-] *n* (*US*) procureur *m*
**prosecution** [prɔsɪ'kju:ʃən] *n* poursuites *fpl* judiciaires; (*accusing side: in criminal case*) accusation *f*; (*: in civil case*) la partie plaignante
**prosecutor** ['prɔsɪkju:tər] *n* (*lawyer*) procureur *m*; (*also*: **public prosecutor**) ministère public; (*US: plaintiff*) plaignant(e)
**prospect** *n* ['prɔspɛkt] perspective *f*; (*hope*) espoir *m*, chances *fpl* ▷ *vt, vi* [prə'spɛkt] prospecter; **prospects** *npl* (*for work etc*) possibilités *fpl* d'avenir, débouchés *mpl*; **we are faced with the ~ of leaving** nous risquons de devoir partir; **there is every ~ of an early**

**victory** tout laisse prévoir une victoire rapide
**prospecting** [prə'spɛktɪŋ] *n* prospection *f*
**prospective** [prə'spɛktɪv] *adj* (*possible*) éventuel(le); (*future*) futur(e)
**prospector** [prə'spɛktər] *n* prospecteur *m*; **gold ~** chercheur *m* d'or
**prospectus** [prə'spɛktəs] *n* prospectus *m*
**prosper** ['prɔspər] *vi* prospérer
**prosperity** [prɔ'spɛrɪtɪ] *n* prospérité *f*
**prosperous** ['prɔspərəs] *adj* prospère
**prostate** ['prɔsteɪt] *n* (*also*: **prostate gland**) prostate *f*
**prostitute** ['prɔstɪtju:t] *n* prostituée *f*; **male ~** prostitué *m*
**prostitution** [prɔstɪ'tju:ʃən] *n* prostitution *f*
**prostrate** *adj* ['prɔstreɪt] prosterné(e); (*fig*) prostré(e) ▷ *vt* [prɔ'streɪt]: **to ~ o.s. (before sb)** se prosterner (devant qn)
**protagonist** [prə'tægənɪst] *n* protagoniste *m*
**protect** [prə'tɛkt] *vt* protéger
**protection** [prə'tɛkʃən] *n* protection *f*; **to be under sb's ~** être sous la protection de qn
**protectionism** [prə'tɛkʃənɪzəm] *n* protectionnisme *m*
**protection racket** *n* racket *m*
**protective** [prə'tɛktɪv] *adj* protecteur(-trice); (*clothing*) de protection; **~ custody** (*Law*) détention préventive
**protector** [prə'tɛktər] *n* protecteur(-trice)
**protégé** ['prəuteʒeɪ] *n* protégé *m*
**protégée** ['prəuteʒeɪ] *n* protégée *f*
**protein** ['prəuti:n] *n* protéine *f*
**pro tem** [prəu'tɛm] *adv abbr* (= *pro tempore: for the time being*) provisoirement
**protest** [*n* 'prəutɛst, *vb* prə'tɛst] *n* protestation *f* ▷ *vi*: **to ~ against/about** protester contre/à propos de ▷ *vt* protester de; **to ~ (that)** protester que
**Protestant** ['prɔtɪstənt] *adj, n* protestant(e)
**protester, protestor** [prə'tɛstər] *n* (*in demonstration*) manifestant(e)
**protest march** *n* manifestation *f*
**protocol** ['prəutəkɔl] *n* protocole *m*
**prototype** ['prəutətaɪp] *n* prototype *m*
**protracted** [prə'træktɪd] *adj* prolongé(e)
**protractor** [prə'træktər] *n* (*Geom*) rapporteur *m*
**protrude** [prə'tru:d] *vi* avancer, dépasser
**protuberance** [prə'tju:bərəns] *n* protubérance *f*
**proud** [praud] *adj* fier(-ère); (*pej*) orgueilleux(-euse); **to be ~ to do sth** être fier de faire qch; **to do sb ~** (*inf*) faire honneur à qn; **to do o.s. ~** (*inf*) ne se priver de rien
**proudly** ['praudlɪ] *adv* fièrement
**prove** [pru:v] *vt* prouver, démontrer ▷ *vi*: **to ~ correct** *etc* s'avérer juste *etc*; **to ~ o.s.** montrer ce dont on est capable; **to ~ o.s./itself (to be) useful** *etc* se montrer or se révéler utile *etc*; **he was ~d right in the end** il s'est avéré qu'il avait raison
**proverb** ['prɔvə:b] *n* proverbe *m*
**proverbial** [prə'və:bɪəl] *adj* proverbial(e)
**provide** [prə'vaɪd] *vt* fournir; **to ~ sb with sth**

fournir qch à qn; **to be ~d with** (person) disposer de; (thing) être équipé(e) or muni(e) de
▶ **provide for** vt fus (person) subvenir aux besoins de; (future event) prévoir

**provided** [prə'vaɪdɪd] conj: ~ **(that)** à condition que + sub

**Providence** ['prɒvɪdəns] n la Providence

**providing** [prə'vaɪdɪŋ] conj à condition que + sub

**province** ['prɒvɪns] n province f; (fig) domaine m

**provincial** [prə'vɪnʃəl] adj provincial(e)

**provision** [prə'vɪʒən] n (supply) provision f; (supplying) fourniture f; approvisionnement m; (stipulation) disposition f; **provisions** npl (food) provisions fpl; **to make ~ for** (one's future) assurer; (one's family) assurer l'avenir de; **there's no ~ for this in the contract** le contrat ne prévoit pas cela

**provisional** [prə'vɪʒənl] adj provisoire ▷ n: **P~** (Irish Pol) Provisional m (membre de la tendance activiste de l'IRA)

**provisional licence** n (Brit Aut) permis m provisoire

**provisionally** [prə'vɪʒnəlɪ] adv provisoirement

**proviso** [prə'vaɪzəu] n condition f; **with the ~ that** à la condition (expresse) que

**Provo** ['prɒvəu] n abbr (inf) = **Provisional**

**provocation** [prɒvə'keɪʃən] n provocation f

**provocative** [prə'vɒkətɪv] adj provocateur(-trice), provocant(e)

**provoke** [prə'vəuk] vt provoquer; **to ~ sb to sth/ to do** or **into doing sth** pousser qn à qch/à faire qch

**provoking** [prə'vəukɪŋ] adj énervant(e), exaspérant(e)

**provost** ['prɒvəst] n (Brit: of university) principal m; (Scottish) maire m

**prow** [prau] n proue f

**prowess** ['prauɪs] n prouesse f

**prowl** [praul] vi (also: **prowl about, prowl around**) rôder ▷ n: **to be on the ~** rôder

**prowler** ['praulər] n rôdeur(-euse)

**proximity** [prɒk'sɪmɪtɪ] n proximité f

**proxy** ['prɒksɪ] n procuration f; **by ~** par procuration

**PRP** n abbr (= performance related pay) salaire m au rendement

**prude** [pru:d] n prude f

**prudence** ['pru:dns] n prudence f

**prudent** ['pru:dnt] adj prudent(e)

**prudish** ['pru:dɪʃ] adj prude, pudibond(e)

**prune** [pru:n] n pruneau m ▷ vt élaguer

**pry** [praɪ] vi: **to ~ into** fourrer son nez dans

**PS** n abbr (= postscript) PS m

**psalm** [sɑ:m] n psaume m

**PSAT** n abbr (US) = **Preliminary Scholastic Aptitude Test**

**PSBR** n abbr (Brit: = public sector borrowing requirement) besoins mpl d'emprunts des pouvoirs publics

**pseud** [sju:d] n (Brit inf: intellectually) pseudo-intello m; (: socially) snob m/f

**pseudo-** ['sju:dəu] prefix pseudo-

**pseudonym** ['sju:dənɪm] n pseudonyme m

**PSHE** n abbr (Brit: Scol: = personal, social and health education) cours d'éducation personnelle, sanitaire et sociale préparant à la vie adulte

**PST** abbr (US: = Pacific Standard Time) heure d'hiver du Pacifique

**PSV** n abbr (Brit) = **public service vehicle**

**psyche** ['saɪkɪ] n psychisme m

**psychiatric** [saɪkɪ'ætrɪk] adj psychiatrique

**psychiatrist** [saɪ'kaɪətrɪst] n psychiatre m/f

**psychiatry** [saɪ'kaɪətrɪ] n psychiatrie f

**psychic** ['saɪkɪk] adj (also: **psychical**) (méta)psychique; (person) doué(e) de télépathie or d'un sixième sens

**psycho** ['saɪkəu] n (inf) psychopathe m/f

**psychoanalyse** (pl **-ses**) [saɪkəu'nælɪsɪs, -si:z] n psychanalyse f

**psychoanalyst** [saɪkəu'ænəlɪst] n psychanalyste m/f

**psychological** [saɪkə'lɒdʒɪkl] adj psychologique

**psychologist** [saɪ'kɒlədʒɪst] n psychologue m/f

**psychology** [saɪ'kɒlədʒɪ] n psychologie f

**psychopath** ['saɪkəupæθ] n psychopathe m/f

**psychosis** (pl **psychoses**) [saɪ'kəusɪs, -si:z] n psychose f

**psychosomatic** [saɪkəusə'mætɪk] adj psychosomatique

**psychotherapy** [saɪkəu'θɛrəpɪ] n psychothérapie f

**psychotic** [saɪ'kɒtɪk] adj, n psychotique m/f

**PT** n abbr (Brit: = physical training) EPS f

**Pt.** abbr (in place names: = Point) Pte

**pt** abbr = pint; pints; point; points

**PTA** n abbr = **Parent-Teacher Association**

**Pte.** abbr (Brit Mil) = **private**

**PTO** abbr (= please turn over) TSVP

**PTV** abbr (US) = **pay television**

**pub** [pʌb] n abbr (= public house) pub m

**pub crawl** n (Brit inf): **to go on a ~** faire la tournée des bars

**puberty** ['pju:bətɪ] n puberté f

**pubic** ['pju:bɪk] adj pubien(ne), du pubis

**public** ['pʌblɪk] adj public(-ique) ▷ n public m; **in ~** en public; **the general ~** le grand public; **to be ~ knowledge** être de notoriété publique; **to go ~** (Comm) être coté(e) en Bourse; **to make ~** rendre public

**public address system** n (système m de) sonorisation f, sono f (col)

**publican** ['pʌblɪkən] n patron m or gérant m de pub

**publication** [pʌblɪ'keɪʃən] n publication f

**public company** n société f anonyme

**public convenience** n (Brit) toilettes fpl

**public holiday** n (Brit) jour férié

**public house** n (Brit) pub m

**publicity** [pʌb'lɪsɪtɪ] n publicité f

**publicize** ['pʌblɪsaɪz] vt (make known) faire connaître, rendre public; (advertise) faire de la publicité pour

**public limited company** n ≈ société f anonyme (SA) (cotée en Bourse)

**publicly** ['pʌblɪklɪ] *adv* publiquement, en public
**public opinion** *n* opinion publique
**public ownership** *n*: **to be taken into** ~ être
nationalisé(e), devenir propriété de l'État
**public prosecutor** *n* ≈ procureur *m (de la
République)*; **~'s office** parquet *m*
**public relations** *n or npl* relations publiques (RP)
**public relations officer** *n* responsable *m/f* des
relations publiques
**public school** *n* (Brit) école privée; (US) école
publique; *voir article*

⬤ **PUBLIC SCHOOL**
⬤
⬤ Une *public school* est un établissement
⬤ d'enseignement secondaire privé. Bon
⬤ nombre d'entre elles sont des pensionnats.
⬤ Beaucoup ont également une école primaire
⬤ qui leur est rattachée (une "prep" ou
⬤ "preparatory school") pour préparer les
⬤ élèves au cycle secondaire. Ces écoles sont
⬤ en général prestigieuses, et les frais de
⬤ scolarité sont très élevés dans les plus
⬤ connues (Westminster, Eton, Harrow).
⬤ Beaucoup d'élèves vont ensuite à
⬤ l'université, et un grand nombre entre à
⬤ Oxford ou à Cambridge. Les grands
⬤ industriels, les députés et les hauts
⬤ fonctionnaires sortent souvent de ces
⬤ écoles. Aux États-Unis, le terme "public
⬤ school" désigne tout simplement une école
⬤ publique gratuite.

**public sector** *n* secteur public
**public service vehicle** *n* (Brit) véhicule affecté
au transport de personnes
**public-spirited** [pʌblɪk'spɪrɪtɪd] *adj* qui fait
preuve de civisme
**public transport**, (US) **public transportation**
*n* transports *mpl* en commun
**public utility** *n* service public
**public works** *npl* travaux publics
**publish** ['pʌblɪʃ] *vt* publier
**publisher** ['pʌblɪʃər] *n* éditeur *m*
**publishing** ['pʌblɪʃɪŋ] *n* (industry) édition *f*; (of a
book) publication *f*
**publishing company** *n* maison *f* d'édition
**pub lunch** *n* repas *m* de bistrot
**puce** [pjuːs] *adj* puce
**puck** [pʌk] *n* (elf) lutin *m*; (Ice Hockey) palet *m*
**pucker** ['pʌkər] *vt* plisser
**pudding** ['pudɪŋ] *n* (Brit: dessert) dessert *m*,
entremets *m*; (sweet dish) pudding *m*, gâteau *m*;
(sausage) boudin *m*; **rice** ~ ≈ riz *m* au lait; **black
~**, (US) **blood ~** boudin (noir)
**puddle** ['pʌdl] *n* flaque *f* d'eau
**puerile** ['pjuəraɪl] *adj* puéril(e)
**Puerto Rico** ['pwəːtəu'riːkəu] *n* Porto Rico *f*
**puff** [pʌf] *n* bouffée *f* ▷ *vt*: **to ~ one's pipe** tirer
sur sa pipe; (also: **puff out**: sails, cheeks) gonfler
▷ *vi* sortir par bouffées; (pant) haleter; **to ~ out
smoke** envoyer des bouffées de fumée

**puffed** [pʌft] *adj* (inf: out of breath) tout(e)
essoufflé(e)
**puffin** ['pʌfɪn] *n* macareux *m*
**puff pastry**, (US) **puff paste** *n* pâte feuilletée
**puffy** ['pʌfɪ] *adj* bouffi(e), boursouflé(e)
**pugnacious** [pʌg'neɪʃəs] *adj* pugnace,
batailleur(-euse)
**pull** [pul] *n* (tug): **to give sth a** ~ tirer sur qch; (of
moon, magnet, the sea etc) attraction *f*; (fig)
influence *f* ▷ *vt* tirer; (trigger) presser; (strain:
muscle, tendon) se claquer ▷ *vi* tirer; **to ~ a face**
faire une grimace; **to ~ to pieces** mettre en
morceaux; **to ~ one's punches** (also fig)
ménager son adversaire; **to ~ one's weight** y
mettre du sien; **to ~ o.s. together** se ressaisir;
**to ~ sb's leg** (fig) faire marcher qn; **to ~ strings
(for sb)** intervenir (en faveur de qn)
▶ **pull about** *vt* (Brit: handle roughly: object)
maltraiter; (: person) malmener
▶ **pull apart** *vt* séparer; (break) mettre en pièces,
démantibuler
▶ **pull away** *vi* (vehicle: move off) partir; (draw back)
s'éloigner
▶ **pull back** *vt* (lever etc) tirer sur; (curtains) ouvrir
▷ *vi* (refrain) s'abstenir; (Mil: withdraw) se retirer
▶ **pull down** *vt* baisser, abaisser; (house)
démolir; (tree) abattre
▶ **pull in** *vi* (Aut) se ranger; (Rail) entrer en gare
▶ **pull off** *vt* enlever, ôter; (deal etc) conclure
▶ **pull out** *vi* démarrer, partir; (withdraw) se
retirer; (Aut: come out of line) déboîter ▷ *vt* (from
bag, pocket) sortir; (remove) arracher; (withdraw)
retirer
▶ **pull over** *vi* (Aut) se ranger
▶ **pull round** *vi* (unconscious person) revenir à soi;
(sick person) se rétablir
▶ **pull through** *vi* s'en sortir
▶ **pull up** *vi* (stop) s'arrêter ▷ *vt* remonter;
(uproot) déraciner, arracher; (stop) arrêter
**pulley** ['pulɪ] *n* poulie *f*
**pull-out** ['pulaut] *n* (of forces etc) retrait *m* ▷ *cpd*
(magazine, pages) détachable
**pullover** ['puləuvər] *n* pull-over *m*, tricot *m*
**pulp** [pʌlp] *n* (of fruit) pulpe *f*; (for paper) pâte *f* à
papier; (pej: also: **pulp magazines** etc) presse *f* à
sensation or de bas étage; **to reduce sth to (a)** ~
réduire qch en purée
**pulpit** ['pulpɪt] *n* chaire *f*
**pulsate** [pʌl'seɪt] *vi* battre, palpiter; (music)
vibrer
**pulse** [pʌls] *n* (of blood) pouls *m*; (of heart)
battement *m*; (of music, engine) vibrations *fpl*;
**pulses** *npl* (Culin) légumineuses *fpl*; **to feel** or
**take sb's ~** prendre le pouls à qn
**pulverize** ['pʌlvəraɪz] *vt* pulvériser
**puma** ['pjuːmə] *n* puma *m*
**pumice** ['pʌmɪs] *n* (also: **pumice stone**) pierre *f*
ponce
**pummel** ['pʌml] *vt* rouer de coups
**pump** [pʌmp] *n* pompe *f*; (shoe) escarpin *m* ▷ *vt*
pomper; (fig: inf) faire parler; **to ~ sb for
information** essayer de soutirer des

**p**

renseignements à qn
▶ **pump up** vt gonfler
**pumpkin** ['pʌmpkɪn] n potiron m, citrouille f
**pun** [pʌn] n jeu m de mots, calembour m
**punch** [pʌntʃ] n (blow) coup m de poing; (fig: force)
vivacité f, mordant m; (tool) poinçon m; (drink)
punch m ▷ vt (make a hole in) poinçonner,
perforer; (hit): **to ~ sb/sth** donner un coup de
poing à qn/sur qch; **to ~ a hole (in)** faire un
trou (dans)
▶ **punch in** vi (US) pointer (en arrivant)
▶ **punch out** vi (US) pointer (en partant)
**punch card, punched card** [pʌntʃt-] n carte
perforée
**punch-drunk** ['pʌntʃdrʌŋk] adj (Brit) sonné(e)
**punch line** n (of joke) conclusion f
**punch-up** ['pʌntʃʌp] n (Brit inf) bagarre f
**punctual** ['pʌŋktjuəl] adj ponctuel(le)
**punctuality** [pʌŋktju'ælɪtɪ] n ponctualité f
**punctually** ['pʌŋktjuəlɪ] adv ponctuellement;
**it will start ~ at 6** cela commencera à 6 heures
précises
**punctuate** ['pʌŋktjueɪt] vt ponctuer
**punctuation** [pʌŋktju'eɪʃən] n ponctuation f
**punctuation mark** n signe m de ponctuation
**puncture** ['pʌŋktʃəʳ] n (Brit) crevaison f ▷ vt
crever; **I have a ~** (Aut) j'ai (un pneu) crevé
**pundit** ['pʌndɪt] n individu m qui pontifie,
pontife m
**pungent** ['pʌndʒənt] adj piquant(e); (fig)
mordant(e), caustique
**punish** ['pʌnɪʃ] vt punir; **to ~ sb for sth/for
doing sth** punir qn de qch/d'avoir fait qch
**punishable** ['pʌnɪʃəbl] adj punissable
**punishing** ['pʌnɪʃɪŋ] adj (fig: exhausting)
épuisant(e) ▷ n punition f
**punishment** ['pʌnɪʃmənt] n punition f,
châtiment m; (fig: inf): **to take a lot of ~** (boxer)
encaisser; (car, person etc) être mis(e) à dure
épreuve
**punk** [pʌŋk] n (person: also: **punk rocker**) punk m/
f; (music: also: **punk rock**) le punk; (US inf:
hoodlum) voyou m
**punt** [pʌnt] n (boat) bachot m; (Irish) livre
irlandaise ▷ vi (Brit: bet) parier
**punter** ['pʌntəʳ] n (Brit: gambler) parieur(-euse);
(: inf) Monsieur m tout le monde; type m
**puny** ['pju:nɪ] adj chétif(-ive)
**pup** [pʌp] n chiot m
**pupil** ['pju:pl] n élève m/f; (of eye) pupille f
**puppet** ['pʌpɪt] n marionnette f, pantin m
**puppet government** n gouvernement m
fantoche
**puppy** ['pʌpɪ] n chiot m, petit chien
**purchase** ['pə:tʃɪs] n achat m; (grip) prise f ▷ vt
acheter; **to get a ~ on** trouver appui sur
**purchase order** n ordre m d'achat
**purchase price** n prix m d'achat
**purchaser** ['pə:tʃɪsəʳ] n acheteur(-euse)
**purchase tax** n (Brit) taxe f à l'achat
**purchasing power** ['pə:tʃɪsɪŋ-] n pouvoir m
d'achat

**pure** [pjuəʳ] adj pur(e); **a ~ wool jumper** un pull
en pure laine; **~ and simple** pur(e) et simple
**purebred** ['pjuəbred] adj de race
**purée** ['pjuəreɪ] n purée f
**purely** ['pjuəlɪ] adv purement
**purge** [pə:dʒ] n (Med) purge f; (Pol) épuration f,
purge ▷ vt purger; (fig) épurer, purger
**purification** [pjuərɪfɪ'keɪʃən] n purification f
**purify** ['pjuərɪfaɪ] vt purifier, épurer
**purist** ['pjuərɪst] n puriste m/f
**puritan** ['pjuərɪtən] n puritain(e)
**puritanical** [pjuərɪ'tænɪkl] adj puritain(e)
**purity** ['pjuərɪtɪ] n pureté f
**purl** [pə:l] n maille f à l'envers ▷ vt tricoter à
l'envers
**purloin** [pə:'lɔɪn] vt dérober
**purple** ['pə:pl] adj violet(te); (face) cramoisi(e)
**purport** [pə:'pɔ:t] vi: **to ~ to be/do** prétendre
être/faire
**purpose** ['pə:pəs] n intention f, but m; **on ~**
exprès; **for illustrative ~s** à titre d'illustration;
**for teaching ~s** dans un but pédagogique; **for
the ~s of this meeting** pour cette réunion; **to
no ~** en pure perte
**purpose-built** ['pə:pəs'bɪlt] adj (Brit) fait(e) sur
mesure
**purposeful** ['pə:pəsful] adj déterminé(e),
résolu(e)
**purposely** ['pə:pəslɪ] adv exprès
**purr** [pə:ʳ] n ronronnement m ▷ vi ronronner
**purse** [pə:s] n (Brit: for money) porte-monnaie m
inv, bourse f; (US: handbag) sac m (à main) ▷ vt
serrer, pincer
**purser** ['pə:səʳ] n (Naut) commissaire m du bord
**purse snatcher** [-'snætʃəʳ] n (US) voleur m à
l'arraché
**pursue** [pə'sju:] vt poursuivre; (pleasures)
rechercher; (inquiry, matter) approfondir
**pursuer** [pə'sju:əʳ] n poursuivant(e)
**pursuit** [pə'sju:t] n poursuite f; (occupation)
occupation f, activité f; **scientific ~s** recherches
fpl scientifiques; **in (the) ~ of sth** à la recherche
de qch
**purveyor** [pə'veɪəʳ] n fournisseur m
**pus** [pʌs] n pus m
**push** [pʊʃ] n poussée f; (effort) gros effort; (drive)
énergie f ▷ vt pousser; (button) appuyer sur;
(thrust): **to ~ sth (into)** enfoncer qch (dans); (fig:
product) mettre en avant, faire de la publicité
pour ▷ vi pousser; appuyer; **to ~ a door open/
shut** pousser une porte (pour l'ouvrir/pour la
fermer); **"~"** (on door) "pousser"; (on bell)
"appuyer"; **to ~ for** (better pay, conditions)
réclamer; **to be ~ed for time/money** être à
court de temps/d'argent; **she is ~ing fifty** (inf)
elle frise la cinquantaine; **at a ~** (Brit inf) à la
limite, à la rigueur
▶ **push aside** vt écarter
▶ **push in** vi s'introduire de force
▶ **push off** vi (inf) filer, ficher le camp
▶ **push on** vi (continue) continuer
▶ **push over** vt renverser

▶ **push through** *vt* (*measure*) faire voter ▷ *vi* (*in crowd*) se frayer un chemin
▶ **push up** *vt* (*total, prices*) faire monter
**push-bike** ['puʃbaɪk] *n* (*Brit*) vélo *m*
**push-button** ['puʃbʌtn] *n* bouton(-poussoir *m*) *m*
**pushchair** ['puʃtʃeəʳ] *n* (*Brit*) poussette *f*
**pusher** ['puʃəʳ] *n* (*also*: **drug pusher**) revendeur(-euse) (de drogue), ravitailleur(-euse) (en drogue)
**pushover** ['puʃəuvəʳ] *n* (*inf*): **it's a ~** c'est un jeu d'enfant
**push-up** ['puʃʌp] *n* (*US*) traction *f*
**pushy** ['puʃɪ] *adj* (*pej*) arriviste
**pussy** ['pusɪ], **pussy-cat** *n* (*inf*) minet *m*
**put** (*pt, pp* -) [put] *vt* mettre; (*place*) poser, placer; (*say*) dire, exprimer; (*a question*) poser; (*case, view*) exposer, présenter; (*estimate*) estimer; **to ~ sb in a good/bad mood** mettre qn de bonne/mauvaise humeur; **to ~ sb to bed** mettre qn au lit, coucher qn; **to ~ sb to a lot of trouble** déranger qn; **how shall I ~ it?** comment dirais-je?, comment dire?; **to ~ a lot of time into sth** passer beaucoup de temps à qch; **to ~ money on a horse** miser sur un cheval; **I ~ it to you that ...** (*Brit*) je (vous) suggère que ..., je suis d'avis que ...; **to stay ~** ne pas bouger
▶ **put about** *vi* (*Naut*) virer de bord ▷ *vt* (*rumour*) faire courir
▶ **put across** *vt* (*ideas etc*) communiquer; faire comprendre
▶ **put aside** *vt* mettre de côté
▶ **put away** *vt* (*store*) ranger
▶ **put back** *vt* (*replace*) remettre, replacer; (*postpone*) remettre; (*delay, watch, clock*) retarder; **this will ~ us back ten years** cela nous ramènera dix ans en arrière
▶ **put by** *vt* (*money*) mettre de côté, économiser
▶ **put down** *vt* (*parcel etc*) poser, déposer; (*pay*) verser; (*in writing*) mettre par écrit, inscrire; (*suppress: revolt etc*) réprimer, écraser; (*attribute*) attribuer; (*animal*) abattre; (*cat, dog*) faire piquer
▶ **put forward** *vt* (*ideas*) avancer, proposer; (*date, watch, clock*) avancer
▶ **put in** *vt* (*gas, electricity*) installer; (*complaint*) soumettre; (*time, effort*) consacrer
▶ **put in for** *vt fus* (*job*) poser sa candidature pour; (*promotion*) solliciter
▶ **put off** *vt* (*light etc*) éteindre; (*postpone*) remettre à plus tard, ajourner; (*discourage*) dissuader
▶ **put on** *vt* (*clothes, lipstick, CD*) mettre; (*light etc*) allumer; (*play etc*) monter; (*extra bus, train etc*) mettre en service; (*food, meal: provide*) servir; (: *cook*) mettre à cuire *or* à chauffer; (*weight*) prendre; (*assume: accent, manner*) prendre; (: *airs*)

se donner, prendre; (*inf: tease*) faire marcher; (*inform, indicate*): **to ~ sb on to sb/sth** indiquer qn/qch à qn; **to ~ the brakes on** freiner
▶ **put out** *vt* (*take outside*) mettre dehors; (*one's hand*) tendre; (*news, rumour*) faire courir, répandre; (*light etc*) éteindre; (*person: inconvenience*) déranger, gêner; (*Brit: dislocate*) se démettre ▷ *vi* (*Naut*): **to ~ out to sea** prendre le large; **to ~ out from Plymouth** quitter Plymouth
▶ **put through** *vt* (*Tel: caller*) mettre en communication; (: *call*) passer; (*plan*) faire accepter; **~ me through to Miss Blair** passez-moi Miss Blair
▶ **put together** *vt* mettre ensemble; (*assemble: furniture*) monter, assembler; (*meal*) préparer
▶ **put up** *vt* (*raise*) lever, relever, remonter; (*pin up*) afficher; (*hang*) accrocher; (*build*) construire, ériger; (*tent*) monter; (*umbrella*) ouvrir; (*increase*) augmenter; (*accommodate*) loger; (*incite*): **to ~ sb up to doing sth** pousser qn à faire qch; **to ~ sth up for sale** mettre qch en vente
▶ **put upon** *vt fus*: **to be ~ upon** (*imposed on*) se laisser faire
▶ **put up with** *vt fus* supporter
**putrid** ['pju:trɪd] *adj* putride
**putt** [pʌt] *vt, vi* putter ▷ *n* putt *m*
**putter** ['pʌtəʳ] *n* (*Golf*) putter *m*
**putting green** ['pʌtɪŋ-] *n* green *m*
**putty** ['pʌtɪ] *n* mastic *m*
**put-up** ['putʌp] *adj*: **~ job** coup monté
**puzzle** ['pʌzl] *n* énigme *f*, mystère *m*; (*game*) jeu *m*, casse-tête *m*; (*jigsaw*) puzzle *m*; (*also*: **crossword puzzle**) mots croisés ▷ *vt* intriguer, rendre perplexe ▷ *vi* se creuser la tête; **to ~ over** chercher à comprendre
**puzzled** ['pʌzld] *adj* perplexe; **to be ~ about sth** être perplexe au sujet de qch
**puzzling** ['pʌzlɪŋ] *adj* déconcertant(e), inexplicable
**PVC** *n abbr* (= *polyvinyl chloride*) PVC *m*
**Pvt.** *abbr* (*US Mil*) = **private**
**pw** *abbr* (= *per week*) p. sem.
**PX** *n abbr* (*US Mil*) = **post exchange**
**pygmy** ['pɪgmɪ] *n* pygmée *m/f*
**pyjamas** [pɪ'dʒɑːməz] *npl* (*Brit*) pyjama *m*; **a pair of ~** un pyjama
**pylon** ['paɪlən] *n* pylône *m*
**pyramid** ['pɪrəmɪd] *n* pyramide *f*
**Pyrenean** [pɪrə'niːən] *adj* pyrénéen(ne), des Pyrénées
**Pyrenees** [pɪrə'niːz] *npl* Pyrénées *fpl*
**Pyrex®** ['paɪrɛks] *n* Pyrex® *m* ▷ *cpd*: **Pyrex dish** plat *m* en Pyrex
**python** ['paɪθən] *n* python *m*

**p**

# Qq

**Q, q** [kju:] *n (letter)* Q, q *m*; **Q for Queen** Q comme Quintal
**Qatar** [kæ'tɑːʳ] *n* Qatar *m*, Katar *m*
**QC** *n abbr* = **Queen's Counsel**; *voir article*

**QED** *abbr* (= *quod erat demonstrandum*) CQFD
**q.t.** *n abbr (inf)* = **quiet**; **on the q.t.** discrètement
**qty** *abbr* (= *quantity*) qté
**quack** [kwæk] *n (of duck)* coin-coin *m inv*; *(pej: doctor)* charlatan *m* ▷ *vi* faire coin-coin
**quad** [kwɔd] *n abbr* = **quadruplet; quadrangle**
**quadrangle** ['kwɔdræŋgl] *n (Math)* quadrilatère *m*; *(courtyard: abbr: quad)* cour *f*
**quadruped** ['kwɔdrupɛd] *n* quadrupède *m*
**quadruple** [kwɔ'dru:pl] *adj, n* quadruple *m* ▷ *vt, vi* quadrupler
**quadruplet** [kwɔ'dru:plɪt] *n* quadruplé(e)
**quagmire** ['kwægmaɪəʳ] *n* bourbier *m*
**quail** [kweɪl] *n (Zool)* caille *f* ▷ *vi*: **to ~ at** or **before** reculer devant
**quaint** [kweɪnt] *adj* bizarre; *(old-fashioned)* désuet(-ète); *(picturesque)* au charme vieillot, pittoresque
**quake** [kweɪk] *vi* trembler ▷ *n abbr* = **earthquake**
**Quaker** ['kweɪkəʳ] *n* quaker(esse)
**qualification** [kwɔlɪfɪ'keɪʃən] *n (often pl: degree etc)* diplôme *m*; *(training)* qualification(s) *f(pl)*; *(ability)* compétence(s) *f(pl)*; *(limitation)* réserve *f*, restriction *f*; **what are your ~s?** qu'avez-vous comme diplômes?; quelles sont vos qualifications?
**qualified** ['kwɔlɪfaɪd] *adj (trained)* qualifié(e); *(professionally)* diplômé(e); *(fit, competent)* compétent(e), qualifié(e); *(limited)* conditionnel(le); **it was a ~ success** ce fut un

succès mitigé; **~ for/to do** qui a les diplômes requis pour/pour faire; qualifié pour/pour faire
**qualify** ['kwɔlɪfaɪ] *vt* qualifier; *(modify)* atténuer, nuancer; *(limit: statement)* apporter des réserves à ▷ *vi*: **to ~ (as)** obtenir son diplôme (de); **to ~ (for)** remplir les conditions requises (pour); *(Sport)* se qualifier (pour)
**qualifying** ['kwɔlɪfaɪɪŋ] *adj*: **~ exam** examen *m* d'entrée; **~ round** éliminatoires *fpl*
**qualitative** ['kwɔlɪtətɪv] *adj* qualitatif(-ive)
**quality** ['kwɔlɪtɪ] *n* qualité *f* ▷ *cpd* de qualité; **of good/poor ~** de bonne/mauvaise qualité
**quality control** *n* contrôle *m* de qualité

**quality time** *n* moments privilégiés
**qualm** [kwɑːm] *n* doute *m*; scrupule *m*; **to have ~s about sth** avoir des doutes sur qch; éprouver des scrupules à propos de qch
**quandary** ['kwɔndrɪ] *n*: **in a ~** devant un dilemme, dans l'embarras
**quango** ['kwæŋgəu] *n abbr* (Brit: = *quasi-autonomous non-governmental organization*) commission nommée par le gouvernement
**quantify** ['kwɔntɪfaɪ] *vt* quantifier
**quantitative** ['kwɔntɪtətɪv] *adj* quantitatif(-ive)
**quantity** ['kwɔntɪtɪ] *n* quantité *f*; **in ~** en grande quantité
**quantity surveyor** *n* (Brit) métreur vérificateur
**quantum leap** ['kwɔntəm-] *n (fig)* bond *m* en avant
**quarantine** ['kwɔrntiːn] *n* quarantaine *f*
**quark** [kwɑːk] *n* quark *m*

**quarrel** ['kwɒrl] n querelle f, dispute f ▷ vi se disputer, se quereller; **to have a ~ with sb** se quereller avec qn; **I've no ~ with him** je n'ai rien contre lui; **I can't ~ with that** je ne vois rien à redire à cela

**quarrelsome** ['kwɒrəlsəm] adj querelleur(-euse)

**quarry** ['kwɒrɪ] n (for stone) carrière f; (animal) proie f, gibier m ▷ vt (marble etc) extraire

**quart** [kwɔːt] n ≈ litre m

**quarter** ['kwɔːtəʳ] n quart m; (of year) trimestre m; (district) quartier m; (US, Canada: 25 cents) (pièce f de) vingt-cinq cents mpl ▷ vt partager en quartiers or en quatre; (Mil) caserner, cantonner; **quarters** npl logement m; (Mil) quartiers mpl, cantonnement m; **a ~ of an hour** un quart d'heure; **it's a ~ to 3**, (US) **it's a ~ of 3** il est 3 heures moins le quart; **it's a ~ past 3**, (US) **it's a ~ after 3** il est 3 heures et quart; **from all ~s** de tous côtés

**quarterback** ['kwɔːtəbæk] n (US Football) quarterback m/f

**quarter-deck** ['kwɔːtədɛk] n (Naut) plage f arrière

**quarter final** n quart m de finale

**quarterly** ['kwɔːtəlɪ] adj trimestriel(le) ▷ adv tous les trois mois ▷ n (Press) revue trimestrielle

**quartermaster** ['kwɔːtəmɑːstəʳ] n (Mil) intendant m militaire de troisième classe; (Naut) maître m de manœuvre

**quartet, quartette** [kwɔːˈtɛt] n quatuor m; (jazz players) quartette m

**quarto** ['kwɔːtəu] adj, n in-quarto m inv

**quartz** [kwɔːts] n quartz m ▷ cpd de or en quartz; (watch, clock) à quartz

**quash** [kwɒʃ] vt (verdict) annuler, casser

**quasi-** ['kweɪzaɪ] prefix quasi- + noun; quasi, presque + adjective

**quaver** ['kweɪvəʳ] n (Brit Mus) croche f ▷ vi trembler

**quay** [kiː] n (also: **quayside**) quai m

**Que.** abbr (Canada) = **Quebec**

**queasy** ['kwiːzɪ] adj (stomach) délicat(e); **to feel ~** avoir mal au cœur

**Quebec** [kwɪˈbɛk] n (city) Québec; (province) Québec m

**queen** [kwiːn] n (gen) reine f; (Cards etc) dame f

**queen mother** n reine mère f

**Queen's speech** n (Brit) discours m de la reine; voir article

◉ **QUEEN'S SPEECH**

Le *Queen's speech* (ou "King's speech") est le discours lu par le souverain à l'ouverture du "Parliament", dans la "House of Lords", en présence des lords et des députés. Il contient le programme de politique générale que propose le gouvernement pour la session, et il est préparé par le Premier ministre en consultation avec le cabinet.

**queer** [kwɪəʳ] adj étrange, curieux(-euse);

(suspicious) louche; (Brit: sick): **I feel ~** je ne me sens pas bien ▷ n (inf: highly offensive) homosexuel m

**quell** [kwɛl] vt réprimer, étouffer

**quench** [kwɛntʃ] vt (flames) éteindre; **to ~ one's thirst** se désaltérer

**querulous** ['kwɛrʊləs] adj (person) récriminateur(-trice); (voice) plaintif(-ive)

**query** ['kwɪərɪ] n question f; (doubt) doute m; (question mark) point m d'interrogation ▷ vt (disagree with, dispute) mettre en doute, questionner

**quest** [kwɛst] n recherche f, quête f

**question** ['kwɛstʃən] n question f ▷ vt (person) interroger; (plan, idea) remettre en question or en doute; **to ask sb a ~, to put a ~ to sb** poser une question à qn; **to bring** or **call sth into ~** remettre qch en question; **the ~ is ...** la question est de savoir ...; **it's a ~ of doing** il s'agit de faire; **there's some ~ of doing** il est question de faire; **beyond ~** sans aucun doute; **out of the ~** hors de question

**questionable** ['kwɛstʃənəbl] adj discutable

**questioner** ['kwɛstʃənəʳ] n personne f qui pose une question (or qui a posé la question etc)

**questioning** ['kwɛstʃənɪŋ] adj interrogateur(-trice) ▷ n interrogatoire m

**question mark** n point m d'interrogation

**questionnaire** [kwɛstʃəˈnɛəʳ] n questionnaire m

**queue** [kjuː] n (Brit) queue f, file f ▷ vi (also: **queue up**) faire la queue; **to jump the ~** passer avant son tour

**quibble** ['kwɪbl] vi ergoter, chicaner

**quiche** [kiːʃ] n quiche f

**quick** [kwɪk] adj rapide; (reply) prompt(e), rapide; (mind) vif (vive); (agile) agile, vif (vive) ▷ adv vite, rapidement ▷ n: **cut to the ~** (fig) touché(e) au vif; **be ~!** dépêche-toi!; **to be ~ to act** agir tout de suite

**quicken** ['kwɪkən] vt accélérer, presser; (rouse) stimuler ▷ vi s'accélérer, devenir plus rapide

**quick fix** n solution f de fortune

**quicklime** ['kwɪklaɪm] n chaux vive

**quickly** ['kwɪklɪ] adv (fast) vite, rapidement; (immediately) tout de suite

**quickness** ['kwɪknɪs] n rapidité f, promptitude f; (of mind) vivacité f

**quicksand** ['kwɪksænd] n sables mouvants

**quickstep** ['kwɪkstɛp] n fox-trot m

**quick-tempered** [kwɪkˈtɛmpəd] adj emporté(e)

**quick-witted** [kwɪkˈwɪtɪd] adj à l'esprit vif

**quid** [kwɪd] n (pl inv: Brit inf) livre f

**quid pro quo** ['kwɪdprəuˈkwəu] n contrepartie f

**quiet** ['kwaɪət] adj tranquille, calme; (not noisy: engine) silencieux(-euse); (reserved) réservé(e); (voice) bas(se); (not busy: day, business) calme; (ceremony, colour) discret(-ète) ▷ n tranquillité f, calme m; (silence) silence m ▷ vt, vi (US) = **quieten**; **keep ~!** tais-toi!; **on the ~** en secret, discrètement; **I'll have a ~ word with him** je lui en parlerai discrètement

**quieten** ['kwaɪətn] (also: **quieten down**) vi se

calmer, s'apaiser ▷ vt calmer, apaiser

**quietly** ['kwaɪətlɪ] adv tranquillement; (silently) silencieusement; (discreetly) discrètement

**quietness** ['kwaɪətnɪs] n tranquillité f, calme m; silence m

**quill** [kwɪl] n plume f (d'oie)

**quilt** [kwɪlt] n édredon m; (continental quilt) couette f

**quin** [kwɪn] n abbr = **quintuplet**

**quince** [kwɪns] n coing m; (tree) cognassier m

**quinine** [kwɪ'niːn] n quinine f

**quintet, quintette** [kwɪn'tɛt] n quintette m

**quintuplet** [kwɪn'tjuːplɪt] n quintuplé(e)

**quip** [kwɪp] n remarque piquante or spirituelle, pointe f ▷ vt: ... **he ~ped** ... lança-t-il

**quire** ['kwaɪəʳ] n ≈ main f (de papier)

**quirk** [kwəːk] n bizarrerie f; **by some ~ of fate** par un caprice du hasard

**quirky** ['kwɜːkɪ] adj singulier(-ère)

**quit** [kwɪt] (pt, pp - or -**ted**) vt quitter ▷ vi (give up) abandonner, renoncer; (resign) démissionner; **to ~ doing** arrêter de faire; **~ stalling!** (US inf) arrête de te dérober!; **notice to ~** (Brit) congé m (signifié au locataire)

**quite** [kwaɪt] adv (rather) assez, plutôt; (entirely) complètement, tout à fait; **~ new** plutôt neuf; tout à fait neuf; **she's ~ pretty** elle est plutôt jolie; **I ~ understand** je comprends très bien; **~ a few of them** un assez grand nombre d'entre eux; **that's not ~ right** ce n'est pas tout à fait juste; **not ~ as many as last time** pas tout à fait autant que la dernière fois; **~ (so)!** exactement!

**Quito** ['kiːtəu] n Quito

**quits** [kwɪts] adj: **~ (with)** quitte (envers); **let's call it ~** restons-en là

**quiver** ['kwɪvəʳ] vi trembler, frémir ▷ n (for arrows) carquois m

**quiz** [kwɪz] n (on TV) jeu-concours m (télévisé); (in magazine etc) test m de connaissances ▷ vt interroger

**quizzical** ['kwɪzɪkl] adj narquois(e)

**quoits** [kwɔɪts] npl jeu m du palet

**quorum** ['kwɔːrəm] n quorum m

**quota** ['kwəutə] n quota m

**quotation** [kwəu'teɪʃən] n citation f; (of shares etc) cote f, cours m; (estimate) devis m

**quotation marks** npl guillemets mpl

**quote** [kwəut] n citation f; (estimate) devis m ▷ vt (sentence, author) citer; (price) donner, soumettre; (shares) coter ▷ vi: **to ~ from** citer; **to ~ for a job** établir un devis pour des travaux; **quotes** npl (inverted commas) guillemets mpl; **in ~s** entre guillemets; **~ ... unquote** (in dictation) ouvrez les guillemets ... fermez les guillemets

**quotient** ['kwəuʃənt] n quotient m

**qv** abbr (= quod vide: which see) voir

**qwerty keyboard** ['kwəːtɪ-] n clavier m QWERTY

# Rr

**R, r** [ɑː[r]] *n* (*letter*) R, r *m*; **R for Robert**, (US) **R for Roger** R comme Raoul

**R** *abbr* (= *right*) dr; (= *river*) riv., fl; (= *Réaumur* (*scale*)) R; (US *Cine*: = *restricted*) interdit aux moins de 17 ans; (US *Pol*) = **republican**; (Brit) Rex, Regina

**RA** *abbr* = **rear admiral** ▷ *n abbr* (Brit) = **Royal Academy** = **Royal Academician**

**RAAF** *n abbr* = **Royal Australian Air Force**

**Rabat** [rə'bɑːt] *n* Rabat

**rabbi** ['ræbaɪ] *n* rabbin *m*

**rabbit** ['ræbɪt] *n* lapin *m* ▷ *vi*: **to ~ (on)** (Brit) parler à n'en plus finir

**rabbit hole** *n* terrier *m* (de lapin)

**rabbit hutch** *n* clapier *m*

**rabble** ['ræbl] *n* (*pej*) populace *f*

**rabid** ['ræbɪd] *adj* enragé(e)

**rabies** ['reɪbiːz] *n* rage *f*

**RAC** *n abbr* (Brit: = *Royal Automobile Club*) ≈ ACF *m*

**raccoon, racoon** [rə'kuːn] *n* raton *m* laveur

**race** [reɪs] *n* (*species*) race *f*; (*competition, rush*) course *f* ▷ *vt* (*person*) faire la course avec; (*horse*) faire courir; (*engine*) emballer ▷ *vi* (*compete*) faire la course, courir; (*hurry*) aller à toute vitesse, courir; (*engine*) s'emballer; (*pulse*) battre très vite; **the human ~** la race humaine; **to ~ in/ out** *etc* entrer/sortir *etc* à toute vitesse

**race car** *n* (US) = **racing car**

**race car driver** *n* (US) = **racing driver**

**racecourse** ['reɪskɔːs] *n* champ *m* de courses

**racehorse** ['reɪshɔːs] *n* cheval *m* de course

**racer** ['reɪsə[r]] *n* (*bike*) vélo *m* de course

**race relations** *npl* rapports *mpl* entre les races

**racetrack** ['reɪstræk] *n* piste *f*

**racial** ['reɪʃl] *adj* racial(e)

**racialism** ['reɪʃlɪzəm] *n* racisme *m*

**racialist** ['reɪʃlɪst] *adj, n* raciste (*m/f*)

**racing** ['reɪsɪŋ] *n* courses *fpl*

**racing car** *n* (Brit) voiture *f* de course

**racing driver** *n* (Brit) pilote *m* de course

**racism** ['reɪsɪzəm] *n* racisme *m*

**racist** ['reɪsɪst] *adj, n* raciste *m/f*

**rack** [ræk] *n* (*for guns, tools*) râtelier *m*; (*for clothes*) portant *m*; (*for bottles*) casier *m*; (*also*: **luggage rack**) filet *m* à bagages; (*also*: **roof rack**) galerie *f*; (*also*: **dish rack**) égouttoir *m* ▷ *vt* tourmenter; **magazine ~** porte-revues *m inv*; **shoe ~** étagère *f*

à chaussures; **toast ~** porte-toast *m*; **to ~ one's brains** se creuser la cervelle; **to go to ~ and ruin** (*building*) tomber en ruine; (*business*) péricliter

▶ **rack up** *vt* accumuler

**racket** ['rækɪt] *n* (*for tennis*) raquette *f*; (*noise*) tapage *m*, vacarme *m*; (*swindle*) escroquerie *f*; (*organized crime*) racket *m*

**racketeer** [rækɪ'tɪə[r]] *n* (*esp US*) racketteur *m*

**racquet** ['rækɪt] *n* raquette *f*

**racy** ['reɪsɪ] *adj* plein(e) de verve, osé(e)

**RADA** [rɑː'də] *n abbr* (Brit) = **Royal Academy of Dramatic Art**

**radar** ['reɪdɑː[r]] *n* radar *m* ▷ *cpd* radar *inv*

**radar trap** *n* (Aut: *police*) contrôle *m* radar

**radial** ['reɪdɪəl] *adj* (*also*: **radial-ply**) à carcasse radiale

**radiance** ['reɪdɪəns] *n* éclat *m*, rayonnement *m*

**radiant** ['reɪdɪənt] *adj* rayonnant(e); (*Physics*) radiant(e)

**radiate** ['reɪdɪeɪt] *vt* (*heat*) émettre, dégager ▷ *vi* (*lines*) rayonner

**radiation** [reɪdɪ'eɪʃən] *n* rayonnement *m*; (*radioactive*) radiation *f*

**radiation sickness** *n* mal *m* des rayons

**radiator** ['reɪdɪeɪtə[r]] *n* radiateur *m*

**radiator cap** *n* bouchon *m* de radiateur

**radiator grill** *n* (Aut) calandre *f*

**radical** ['rædɪkl] *adj* radical(e)

**radii** ['reɪdɪaɪ] *npl of* **radius**

**radio** ['reɪdɪəʊ] *n* radio *f* ▷ *vi*: **to ~ to sb** envoyer un message radio à qn ▷ *vt* (*information*) transmettre par radio; (*one's position*) signaler par radio; (*person*) appeler par radio; **on the ~** à la radio

**radioactive** ['reɪdɪəʊ'æktɪv] *adj* radioactif(-ive)

**radioactivity** ['reɪdɪəʊæk'tɪvɪtɪ] *n* radioactivité *f*

**radio announcer** *n* annonceur *m*

**radio cassette** *n* radiocassette *m*

**radio-controlled** ['reɪdɪəʊkən'trəʊld] *adj* radioguidé(e)

**radiographer** [reɪdɪ'ɔgrəfə[r]] *n* radiologue *m/f* (*technicien*)

**radiography** [reɪdɪ'ɔgrəfɪ] *n* radiographie *f*

**radiologist** [reɪdɪ'ɔlədʒɪst] *n* radiologue *m/f*

*(médecin)*
**radiology** [reɪdɪˈɔlədʒɪ] *n* radiologie *f*
**radio station** *n* station *f* de radio
**radio taxi** *n* radio-taxi *m*
**radiotelephone** [ˈreɪdɪəuˈtɛlɪfəun] *n* radiotéléphone *m*
**radiotherapist** [ˈreɪdɪəuˈθɛrəpɪst] *n* radiothérapeute *m/f*
**radiotherapy** [ˈreɪdɪəuˈθɛrəpɪ] *n* radiothérapie *f*
**radish** [ˈrædɪʃ] *n* radis *m*
**radium** [ˈreɪdɪəm] *n* radium *m*
**radius** (*pl* **radii**) [ˈreɪdɪəs, -ɪaɪ] *n* rayon *m*; (*Anat*) radius *m*; **within a ~ of 50 miles** dans un rayon de 50 milles
**RAF** *n abbr* (*Brit*) = **Royal Air Force**
**raffia** [ˈræfɪə] *n* raphia *m*
**raffish** [ˈræfɪʃ] *adj* dissolu(e), canaille
**raffle** [ˈræfl] *n* tombola *f* ▷ *vt* mettre comme lot dans une tombola
**raft** [rɑːft] *n* (*craft: also:* **life raft**) radeau *m*; (*logs*) train *m* de flottage
**rafter** [ˈrɑːftəʳ] *n* chevron *m*
**rag** [ræg] *n* chiffon *m*; (*pej: newspaper*) feuille *f*, torchon *m*; (*for charity*) attractions organisées par les étudiants au profit d'œuvres de charité ▷ *vt* (*Brit*) chahuter, mettre en boîte; **rags** *npl* haillons *mpl*; **in ~s** (*person*) en haillons; (*clothes*) en lambeaux
**rag-and-bone man** [rægənˈbəunmæn] (*irreg*) *n* chiffonnier *m*
**ragbag** [ˈrægbæg] *n* (*fig*) ramassis *m*
**rag doll** *n* poupée *f* de chiffon
**rage** [reɪdʒ] *n* (*fury*) rage *f*, fureur *f* ▷ *vi* (*person*) être fou (folle) de rage; (*storm*) faire rage, être déchaîné(e); **to fly into a ~** se mettre en rage; **it's all the ~** cela fait fureur
**ragged** [ˈrægɪd] *adj* (*edge*) inégal(e), qui accroche; (*clothes*) en loques; (*cuff*) effiloché(e); (*appearance*) déguenillé(e)
**raging** [ˈreɪdʒɪŋ] *adj* (*sea, storm*) en furie; (*fever, pain*) violent(e); **~ toothache** rage *f* de dents; **in a ~ temper** dans une rage folle
**rag trade** *n* (*inf*): **the ~** la confection

⬤ **RAG WEEK**
◦
◦ *Rag Week*, est une semaine où les étudiants
◦ se déguisent et collectent de l'argent pour
◦ les œuvres de charité. Toutes sortes
◦ d'animations sont organisées à cette
◦ occasion (marches sponsorisées, spectacles
◦ de rue etc). Des magazines (les "rag mags")
◦ contenant des plaisanteries osées sont
◦ vendus dans les rues, également au profit
◦ des œuvres. Enfin, la plupart des universités
◦ organisent un bal (le "rag ball").

**raid** [reɪd] *n* (*Mil*) raid *m*; (*criminal*) hold-up *m inv*; (*by police*) descente *f*, rafle *f* ▷ *vt* faire un raid sur *or* un hold-up dans *or* une descente dans
**raider** [ˈreɪdəʳ] *n* malfaiteur *m*
**rail** [reɪl] *n* (*on stair*) rampe *f*; (*on bridge, balcony*)

balustrade *f*; (*of ship*) bastingage *m*; (*for train*) rail *m*; **rails** *npl* rails *mpl*, voie ferrée; **by ~** en train, par le train
**railcard** [ˈreɪlkɑːd] *n* (*Brit*) carte *f* de chemin de fer; **young person's ~** carte *f* jeune
**railing** [ˈreɪlɪŋ] *n*, **railings** [ˈreɪlɪŋz] ▷ *npl* grille *f*
**railway** [ˈreɪlweɪ], (US) **railroad** [ˈreɪlrəud] *n* chemin *m* de fer; (*track*) voie *f* ferrée
**railway engine** *n* locomotive *f*
**railway line** *n* (*Brit*) ligne *f* de chemin de fer; (*track*) voie ferrée
**railwayman** [ˈreɪlweɪmən] (*irreg*) *n* cheminot *m*
**railway station** *n* (*Brit*) gare *f*
**rain** [reɪn] *n* pluie *f* ▷ *vi* pleuvoir; **in the ~** sous la pluie; **it's ~ing** il pleut; **it's ~ing cats and dogs** il pleut à torrents
**rainbow** [ˈreɪnbəu] *n* arc-en-ciel *m*
**raincoat** [ˈreɪnkəut] *n* imperméable *m*
**raindrop** [ˈreɪndrɔp] *n* goutte *f* de pluie
**rainfall** [ˈreɪnfɔːl] *n* chute *f* de pluie; (*measurement*) hauteur *f* des précipitations
**rainforest** [ˈreɪnfɔrɪst] *n* forêt tropicale
**rainproof** [ˈreɪnpruːf] *adj* imperméable
**rainstorm** [ˈreɪnstɔːm] *n* pluie torrentielle
**rainwater** [ˈreɪnwɔːtəʳ] *n* eau *f* de pluie
**rainy** [ˈreɪnɪ] *adj* pluvieux(-euse)
**raise** [reɪz] *n* augmentation *f* ▷ *vt* (*lift*) lever, hausser; (*end: siege, embargo*) lever; (*build*) ériger; (*increase*) augmenter; (*morale*) remonter; (*standards*) améliorer; (*a protest, doubt*) provoquer, causer; (*a question*) soulever; (*cattle, family*) élever; (*crop*) faire pousser; (*army, funds*) rassembler; (*loan*) obtenir; **to ~ one's glass to sb/sth** porter un toast en l'honneur de qn/qch; **to ~ one's voice** élever la voix; **to ~ sb's hopes** donner de l'espoir à qn; **to ~ a laugh/a smile** faire rire/sourire
**raisin** [ˈreɪzn] *n* raisin sec
**Raj** [rɑːdʒ] *n*: **the ~** l'empire *m* (*aux Indes*)
**rajah** [ˈrɑːdʒə] *n* radja(h) *m*
**rake** [reɪk] *n* (*tool*) râteau *m*; (*person*) débauché *m* ▷ *vt* (*garden*) ratisser; (*fire*) tisonner; (*with machine gun*) balayer ▷ *vi*: **to ~ through** (*fig: search*) fouiller (dans)
**rake-off** [ˈreɪkɔf] *n* (*inf*) pourcentage *m*
**rakish** [ˈreɪkɪʃ] *adj* dissolu(e); cavalier(-ière)
**rally** [ˈrælɪ] *n* (*Pol etc*) meeting *m*, rassemblement *m*; (*Aut*) rallye *m*; (*Tennis*) échange *m* ▷ *vt* rassembler, rallier; (*support*) gagner ▷ *vi* se rallier; (*sick person*) aller mieux; (*Stock Exchange*) reprendre
▶ **rally round** *vi* venir en aide ▷ *vt fus* se rallier à; venir en aide à
**rallying point** [ˈrælɪɪŋ-] *n* (*Mil*) point *m* de ralliement
**RAM** [ræm] *n abbr* (*Comput*: = *random access memory*) mémoire vive
**ram** [ræm] *n* bélier *m* ▷ *vt* (*push*) enfoncer; (*soil*) tasser; (*crash into: vehicle*) emboutir; (*: lamppost etc*) percuter; (*in battle*) éperonner
**Ramadan** [ræməˈdæn] *n* Ramadan *m*
**ramble** [ˈræmbl] *n* randonnée *f* ▷ *vi* (*walk*) se

promener, faire une randonnée; (*pej: also:* **ramble on**) discourir, pérorer

**rambler** ['ræmblə<sup>r</sup>] *n* promeneur(-euse), randonneur(-euse); (*Bot*) rosier grimpant

**rambling** ['ræmblɪŋ] *adj* (*speech*) décousu(e); (*house*) plein(e) de coins et de recoins; (*Bot*) grimpant(e)

**RAMC** *n abbr* (*Brit*) = **Royal Army Medical Corps**

**ramification** [ræmɪfɪ'keɪʃən] *n* ramification *f*

**ramp** [ræmp] *n* (*incline*) rampe *f*; (*Aut*) dénivellation *f*; (*in garage*) pont *m*; **on/off** ~ (*US Aut*) bretelle *f* d'accès

**rampage** [ræm'peɪdʒ] *n*: **to be on the** ~ se déchaîner ▷ *vi*: **they went rampaging through the town** ils ont envahi les rues et ont tout saccagé sur leur passage

**rampant** ['ræmpənt] *adj* (*disease etc*) qui sévit

**rampart** ['ræmpɑːt] *n* rempart *m*

**ram raiding** [-reɪdɪŋ] *n* pillage d'un magasin en enfonçant la vitrine avec une voiture volée

**ramshackle** ['ræmʃækl] *adj* (*house*) délabré(e); (*car etc*) déglingué(e)

**RAN** *n abbr* = **Royal Australian Navy**

**ran** [ræn] *pt of* **run**

**ranch** [rɑːntʃ] *n* ranch *m*

**rancher** ['rɑːntʃə<sup>r</sup>] *n* (*owner*) propriétaire *m* de ranch; (*ranch hand*) cowboy *m*

**rancid** ['rænsɪd] *adj* rance

**rancour,** (*US*) **rancor** ['ræŋkə<sup>r</sup>] *n* rancune *f*, rancœur *f*

**R&B** *n abbr* = **rhythm and blues**

**R&D** *n abbr* (= *research and development*) R-D *f*

**random** ['rændəm] *adj* fait(e) or établi(e) au hasard; (*Comput, Math*) aléatoire ▷ *n*: **at** ~ au hasard

**random access memory** *n* (*Comput*) mémoire vive, RAM *f*

**R&R** *n abbr* (*US Mil*) = **rest and recreation**

**randy** ['rændɪ] *adj* (*Brit inf*) excité(e); lubrique

**rang** [ræŋ] *pt of* **ring**

**range** [reɪndʒ] *n* (*of mountains*) chaîne *f*; (*of missile, voice*) portée *f*; (*of products*) choix *m*, gamme *f*; (*also:* **shooting range**) champ *m* de tir; (: *indoor*) stand *m* de tir; (*also:* **kitchen range**) fourneau *m* (de cuisine) ▷ *vt* (*place*) mettre en rang, placer; (*roam*) parcourir ▷ *vi*: **to** ~ **over** couvrir; **to** ~ **from ... to** aller de ... à; **price** ~ éventail *m* des prix; **do you have anything else in this price** ~? avez-vous autre chose dans ces prix?; **within (firing)** ~ à portée (de tir); **~d left/right** (*text*) justifié à gauche/à droite

**ranger** ['reɪndʒə<sup>r</sup>] *n* garde *m* forestier

**Rangoon** [ræŋ'guːn] *n* Rangoon

**rank** [ræŋk] *n* rang *m*; (*Mil*) grade *m*; (*Brit: also:* **taxi rank**) station *f* de taxis ▷ *vi*: **to** ~ **among** compter or se classer parmi ▷ *vt*: **I** ~ **him sixth** je le place sixième ▷ *adj* (*smell*) nauséabond(e); (*hypocrisy, injustice etc*) flagrant(e); **he's a** ~ **outsider** il n'est vraiment pas dans la course; **the** ~**s** (*Mil*) la troupe; **the** ~ **and file** (*fig*) la masse, la base; **to close** ~**s** (*Mil: fig*) serrer les rangs

**rankle** ['ræŋkl] *vi* (*insult*) rester sur le cœur

**ransack** ['rænsæk] *vt* fouiller (à fond); (*plunder*) piller

**ransom** ['rænsəm] *n* rançon *f*; **to hold sb to** ~ (*fig*) exercer un chantage sur qn

**rant** [rænt] *vi* fulminer

**ranting** ['ræntɪŋ] *n* invectives *fpl*

**rap** [ræp] *n* petit coup sec; tape *f*; (*music*) rap *m* ▷ *vt* (*door*) frapper sur or à; (*table etc*) taper sur

**rape** [reɪp] *n* viol *m*; (*Bot*) colza *m* ▷ *vt* violer

**rape oil, rapeseed oil** ['reɪp(siːd)] *n* huile *f* de colza

**rapid** ['ræpɪd] *adj* rapide

**rapidity** [rə'pɪdɪtɪ] *n* rapidité *f*

**rapidly** ['ræpɪdlɪ] *adv* rapidement

**rapids** ['ræpɪdz] *npl* (*Geo*) rapides *mpl*

**rapist** ['reɪpɪst] *n* auteur *m* d'un viol

**rapport** [ræ'pɔː<sup>r</sup>] *n* entente *f*

**rapt** [ræpt] *adj* (*attention*) extrême; **to be** ~ **in contemplation** être perdu(e) dans la contemplation

**rapture** ['ræptʃə<sup>r</sup>] *n* extase *f*, ravissement *m*; **to go into** ~**s over** s'extasier sur

**rapturous** ['ræptʃərəs] *adj* extasié(e); frénétique

**rare** [rɛə<sup>r</sup>] *adj* rare; (*Culin: steak*) saignant(e)

**rarebit** ['rɛəbɪt] *n see* **Welsh rarebit**

**rarefied** ['rɛərɪfaɪd] *adj* (*air, atmosphere*) raréfié(e)

**rarely** ['rɛəlɪ] *adv* rarement

**raring** ['rɛərɪŋ] *adj*: **to be** ~ **to go** (*inf*) être très impatient(e) de commencer

**rarity** ['rɛərɪtɪ] *n* rareté *f*

**rascal** ['rɑːskl] *n* vaurien *m*

**rash** [ræʃ] *adj* imprudent(e), irréfléchi(e) ▷ *n* (*Med*) rougeur *f*, éruption *f*; (*of events*) série *f* (noire); **to come out in a** ~ avoir une éruption

**rasher** ['ræʃə<sup>r</sup>] *n* fine tranche (de lard)

**rasp** [rɑːsp] *n* (*tool*) lime *f* ▷ *vt* (*speak: also:* **rasp out**) dire d'une voix grinçante

**raspberry** ['rɑːzbərɪ] *n* framboise *f*

**raspberry bush** *n* framboisier *m*

**rasping** ['rɑːspɪŋ] *adj*: ~ **noise** grincement *m*

**Rastafarian** [ræstə'fɛərɪən] *adj, n* rastafari (*m/f*)

**rat** [ræt] *n* rat *m*

**ratable** ['reɪtəbl] *adj see* **rateable value**

**ratchet** ['rætʃɪt] *n*: ~ **wheel** roue *f* à rochet

**rate** [reɪt] *n* (*ratio*) taux *m*, pourcentage *m*; (*speed*) vitesse *f*, rythme *m*; (*price*) tarif *m* ▷ *vt* (*price*) évaluer, estimer; (*people*) classer; (*deserve*) mériter; **rates** *npl* (*Brit: property tax*) impôts locaux; **to** ~ **sb/sth as** considérer qn/qch comme; **to** ~ **sb/sth among** classer qn/qch parmi; **to** ~ **sb/sth highly** avoir une haute opinion de qn/qch; **at a** ~ **of 60 kph** à une vitesse de 60 km/h; **at any** ~ en tout cas; ~ **of exchange** taux or cours *m* du change; ~ **of flow** débit *m*; ~ **of return** (taux de) rendement *m*; **pulse** ~ fréquence *f* des pulsations

**rateable value** ['reɪtəbl-] *n* (*Brit*) valeur locative imposable

**ratepayer** ['reɪtpeɪə<sup>r</sup>] *n* (*Brit*) contribuable *m/f* (payant les impôts locaux)

**rather** ['rɑːðə<sup>r</sup>] *adv* (*somewhat*) assez, plutôt; (*to*

**r**

*some extent)* un peu; **it's ~ expensive** c'est assez cher; *(too much)* c'est un peu cher; **there's ~ a lot** il y en a beaucoup; **I would** *or* **I'd ~ go** j'aimerais mieux *or* je préférerais partir; **I had ~ go** il vaudrait mieux que je parte; **I'd ~ not leave** j'aimerais mieux ne pas partir; **or ~** *(more accurately)* ou plutôt; **I ~ think he won't come** je crois bien qu'il ne viendra pas

**ratification** [rætɪfɪ'keɪʃən] *n* ratification *f*

**ratify** ['rætɪfaɪ] *vt* ratifier

**rating** ['reɪtɪŋ] *n (assessment)* évaluation *f; (score)* classement *m; (Finance)* cote *f; (Naut: category)* classe *f; (: sailor: Brit)* matelot *m;* **ratings** *npl (Radio)* indice(s) *m(pl)* d'écoute; *(TV)* Audimat® *m*

**ratio** ['reɪʃɪəu] *n* proportion *f;* **in the ~ of 100 to 1** dans la proportion de 100 contre 1

**ration** ['ræʃən] *n* ration *f ▷ vt* rationner; **rations** *npl (food)* vivres *mpl*

**rational** ['ræʃənl] *adj* raisonnable, sensé(e); *(solution, reasoning)* logique; *(Med: person)* lucide

**rationale** [ræʃə'nɑːl] *n* raisonnement *m;* justification *f*

**rationalization** [ræʃnəlaɪ'zeɪʃən] *n* rationalisation *f*

**rationalize** ['ræʃnəlaɪz] *vt* rationaliser; *(conduct)* essayer d'expliquer *or* de motiver

**rationally** ['ræʃnəlɪ] *adv* raisonnablement; logiquement

**rationing** ['ræʃnɪŋ] *n* rationnement *m*

**rat pack** ['rætpæk] *n (Brit inf)* journalistes *mpl* de la presse à sensation

**rat poison** *n* mort-aux-rats *f inv*

**rat race** *n* foire *f* d'empoigne

**rattan** [ræ'tæn] *n* rotin *m*

**rattle** ['rætl] *n (of door, window)* battement *m; (of coins, chain)* cliquetis *m; (of train, engine)* bruit *m* de ferraille; *(for baby)* hochet *m; (of sports fan)* crécelle *f ▷ vi* cliqueter; *(car, bus):* **to ~ along** rouler en faisant un bruit de ferraille *▷ vt* agiter (bruyamment); *(inf: disconcert)* décontenancer; *(: annoy)* embêter

**rattlesnake** ['rætlsneɪk] *n* serpent *m* à sonnettes

**ratty** ['rætɪ] *adj (inf)* en rogne

**raucous** ['rɔːkəs] *adj* rauque

**raucously** ['rɔːkəslɪ] *adv* d'une voix rauque

**raunchy** ['rɔːntʃɪ] *adj (inf: voice, image, act)* sexy; *(scenes, film)* lubrique

**ravage** ['rævɪdʒ] *vt* ravager

**ravages** ['rævɪdʒɪz] *npl* ravages *mpl*

**rave** [reɪv] *vi (in anger)* s'emporter; *(with enthusiasm)* s'extasier; *(Med)* délirer *▷ n (inf: party)* rave *f,* soirée *f* techno *▷ adj (scene, culture, music)* rave, techno *▷ cpd:* **~ review** *(inf)* critique *f* dithyrambique

**raven** ['reɪvən] *n* grand corbeau

**ravenous** ['rævənəs] *adj* affamé(e)

**ravine** [rə'viːn] *n* ravin *m*

**raving** ['reɪvɪŋ] *adj:* **he's ~ mad** il est complètement cinglé

**ravings** ['reɪvɪŋz] *npl* divagations *fpl*

**ravioli** [rævɪ'əulɪ] *n* ravioli *mpl*

**ravish** ['rævɪʃ] *vt* ravir

**ravishing** ['rævɪʃɪŋ] *adj* enchanteur(-eresse)

**raw** [rɔː] *adj (uncooked)* cru(e); *(not processed)* brut(e); *(sore)* à vif, irrité(e); *(inexperienced)* inexpérimenté(e); *(weather, day)* froid(e) et humide; **~ deal** *(inf: bad bargain)* sale coup *m; (: unfair treatment):* **to get a ~ deal** être traité(e) injustement; **~ materials** matières premières

**Rawalpindi** [rɔːl'pɪndɪ] *n* Rawalpindi

**raw material** *n* matière première

**ray** [reɪ] *n* rayon *m;* **~ of hope** lueur *f* d'espoir

**rayon** ['reɪɔn] *n* rayonne *f*

**raze** [reɪz] *vt (also:* **raze to the ground)** raser

**razor** ['reɪzə'] *n* rasoir *m*

**razor blade** *n* lame *f* de rasoir

**razzle** ['ræzl], **razzle-dazzle** ['ræzl'dæzl] *n (Brit inf):* **to go on the ~(-dazzle)** faire la bringue

**razzmatazz** ['ræzmə'tæz] *n (inf)* tralala *m,* tapage *m*

**RC** *abbr* = **Roman Catholic**

**RCAF** *n abbr* = **Royal Canadian Air Force**

**RCMP** *n abbr* = **Royal Canadian Mounted Police**

**RCN** *n abbr* = **Royal Canadian Navy**

**RD** *abbr (US)* = **rural delivery**

**Rd** *abbr* = **road**

**RDC** *n abbr (Brit)* = **rural district council**

**RE** *n abbr (Brit)* = **religious education;** *(Brit Mil)* = **Royal Engineers**

**re** [riː] *prep* concernant

**reach** [riːtʃ] *n* portée *f,* atteinte *f; (of river etc)* étendue *f ▷ vt* atteindre, arriver à; *(conclusion, decision)* parvenir à *▷ vi* s'étendre; *(stretch out hand):* **to ~ up/down** *etc (for sth)* lever/baisser *etc* le bras (pour prendre qch); **to ~ sb by phone** joindre qn par téléphone; **out of/within ~** *(object)* hors de/à portée; **within easy ~ (of)** *(place)* à proximité (de), proche (de)
▶ **reach out** *vt* tendre *▷ vi:* **to ~ out (for)** allonger le bras (pour prendre)

**react** [riː'ækt] *vi* réagir

**reaction** [riː'ækʃən] *n* réaction *f*

**reactionary** [riː'ækʃənrɪ] *adj, n* réactionnaire *(m/f)*

**reactor** [riː'æktə'] *n* réacteur *m*

**read** *(pt, pp* **~)** [riːd, rɛd] *vi* lire *▷ vt* lire; *(understand)* comprendre, interpréter; *(study)* étudier; *(meter)* relever; *(subj: instrument etc)* indiquer, marquer; **to take sth as ~** *(fig)* considérer qch comme accepté; **do you ~ me?** *(Tel)* est-ce que vous me recevez?
▶ **read out** *vt* lire à haute voix
▶ **read over** *vt* relire
▶ **read through** *vt (quickly)* parcourir; *(thoroughly)* lire jusqu'au bout
▶ **read up** *vt,* **read up on** *vt fus* étudier

**readable** ['riːdəbl] *adj* facile à or agréable à lire

**reader** ['riːdə'] *n* lecteur(-trice); *(book)* livre *m* de lecture; *(Brit: at university)* maître *m* de conférences

**readership** ['riːdəʃɪp] *n (of paper etc)* (nombre *m* de) lecteurs *mpl*

**readily** ['rɛdɪlɪ] *adv* volontiers, avec empressement; *(easily)* facilement
**readiness** ['rɛdɪnɪs] *n* empressement *m*; **in ~** *(prepared)* prêt(e)
**reading** ['ri:dɪŋ] *n* lecture *f*; *(understanding)* interprétation *f*; *(on instrument)* indications *fpl*
**reading lamp** *n* lampe *f* de bureau
**reading room** *n* salle *f* de lecture
**readjust** [ri:ə'dʒʌst] *vt* rajuster; *(instrument)* régler de nouveau ▷ *vi (person)*: **to ~ (to)** se réadapter (à)
**ready** ['rɛdɪ] *adj* prêt(e); *(willing)* prêt, disposé(e); *(quick)* prompt(e); *(available)* disponible ▷ *n*: **at the ~** *(Mil)* prêt à faire feu; *(fig)* tout(e) prêt(e); **~ for use** prêt à l'emploi; **to be ~ to do sth** être prêt à faire qch; **when will my photos be ~?** quand est-ce que mes photos seront prêtes?; **to get ~** *(as vi)* se préparer; *(as vt)* préparer
**ready cash** *n* (argent *m*) liquide *m*
**ready-cooked** ['rɛdɪ'kukd] *adj* précuit(e)
**ready-made** ['rɛdɪ'meɪd] *adj* tout(e) faite(e)
**ready-mix** ['rɛdɪmɪks] *n (for cakes etc)* préparation *f* en sachet
**ready reckoner** [-'rɛknə'] *n (Brit)* barème *m*
**ready-to-wear** ['rɛdɪtə'wɛə'] *adj* (en) prêt-à-porter
**reagent** [ri:'eɪdʒənt] *n* réactif *m*
**real** [rɪəl] *adj (world, life)* réel(le); *(genuine)* véritable; *(proper)* vrai(e) ▷ *adv (US inf: very)* vraiment; **in ~ life** dans la réalité
**real ale** *n* bière traditionnelle
**real estate** *n* biens fonciers *or* immobiliers
**realism** ['rɪəlɪzəm] *n* réalisme *m*
**realist** ['rɪəlɪst] *n* réaliste *m/f*
**realistic** [rɪə'lɪstɪk] *adj* réaliste
**reality** [ri:'ælɪtɪ] *n* réalité *f*; **in ~** en réalité, en fait
**reality TV** *n* téléréalité *f*
**realization** [rɪəlaɪ'zeɪʃən] *n (awareness)* prise *f* de conscience; *(fulfilment: also: of asset)* réalisation *f*
**realize** ['rɪəlaɪz] *vt (understand)* se rendre compte de, prendre conscience de; *(a project, Comm: asset)* réaliser
**really** ['rɪəlɪ] *adv* vraiment; **~?** vraiment?, c'est vrai?
**realm** [rɛlm] *n* royaume *m*; *(fig)* domaine *m*
**real-time** ['ri:ltaɪm] *adj (Comput)* en temps réel
**realtor** ['rɪəltɔ:'] *n (US)* agent immobilier
**ream** [ri:m] *n* rame *f (de papier)*; **reams** *npl (fig: inf)* des pages et des pages
**reap** [ri:p] *vt* moissonner; *(fig)* récolter
**reaper** ['ri:pə'] *n (machine)* moissonneuse *f*
**reappear** [ri:ə'pɪə'] *vi* réapparaître, reparaître
**reappearance** [ri:ə'pɪərəns] *n* réapparition *f*
**reapply** [ri:ə'plaɪ] *vi*: **to ~ for** *(job)* faire une nouvelle demande d'emploi concernant; reposer sa candidature à; *(loan, grant)* faire une nouvelle demande de
**reappraisal** [ri:ə'preɪzl] *n* réévaluation *f*
**rear** [rɪə'] *adj* de derrière, arrière *inv*; *(Aut: wheel etc)* arrière ▷ *n* arrière *m*, derrière *m* ▷ *vt (cattle, family)* élever ▷ *vi (also: **rear up**: animal)* se cabrer

**rear admiral** *n* vice-amiral *m*
**rear-engined** ['rɪər'ɛndʒɪnd] *adj (Aut)* avec moteur à l'arrière
**rearguard** ['rɪəgɑ:d] *n* arrière-garde *f*
**rearmament** [ri:'ɑ:məmənt] *n* réarmement *m*
**rearrange** [ri:ə'reɪndʒ] *vt* réarranger
**rear-view mirror** *n (Aut)* rétroviseur *m*
**rear-wheel drive** *n (Aut)* traction *f* arrière
**reason** ['ri:zn] *n* raison *f* ▷ *vi*: **to ~ with sb** raisonner qn, faire entendre raison à qn; **the ~ for/why** la raison de/pour laquelle; **to have ~ to think** avoir lieu de penser; **it stands to ~ that** il va sans dire que; **she claims with good ~ that ...** elle affirme à juste titre que ...; **all the more ~ why** raison de plus pour + *infinitive or* pour que + *sub*; **within ~** dans les limites du raisonnable
**reasonable** ['ri:znəbl] *adj* raisonnable; *(not bad)* acceptable
**reasonably** ['ri:znəblɪ] *adv (behave)* raisonnablement; *(fairly)* assez; **one can ~ assume that ...** on est fondé à *or* il est permis de supposer que ...
**reasoned** ['ri:znd] *adj (argument)* raisonné(e)
**reasoning** ['ri:znɪŋ] *n* raisonnement *m*
**reassemble** [ri:ə'sɛmbl] *vt* rassembler; *(machine)* remonter
**reassert** [ri:ə'sə:t] *vt* réaffirmer
**reassurance** [ri:ə'ʃuərəns] *n (factual)* assurance *f*, garantie *f*; *(emotional)* réconfort *m*
**reassure** [ri:ə'ʃuə'] *vt* rassurer; **to ~ sb of** donner à qn l'assurance répétée de
**reassuring** [ri:ə'ʃuərɪŋ] *adj* rassurant(e)
**reawakening** [ri:ə'weɪknɪŋ] *n* réveil *m*
**rebate** ['ri:beɪt] *n (on product)* rabais *m*; *(on tax etc)* dégrèvement *m*; *(repayment)* remboursement *m*
**rebel** ['rɛbl] *n* rebelle *m/f* ▷ *vi* [rɪ'bɛl] se rebeller, se révolter
**rebellion** [rɪ'bɛljən] *n* rébellion *f*, révolte *f*
**rebellious** [rɪ'bɛljəs] *adj* rebelle
**rebirth** [ri:'bə:θ] *n* renaissance *f*
**rebound** *vi* [rɪ'baund] *(ball)* rebondir ▷ *n* ['ri:baund] rebond *m*
**rebuff** [rɪ'bʌf] *n* rebuffade *f* ▷ *vt* repousser
**rebuild** [ri:'bɪld] *vt (irreg: like **build**)* reconstruire
**rebuke** [rɪ'bju:k] *n* réprimande *f*, reproche *m* ▷ *vt* réprimander
**rebut** [rɪ'bʌt] *vt* réfuter
**rebuttal** [rɪ'bʌtl] *n* réfutation *f*
**recalcitrant** [rɪ'kælsɪtrənt] *adj* récalcitrant(e)
**recall** [rɪ'kɔ:l] *vt* rappeler; *(remember)* se rappeler, se souvenir de ▷ *n* ['ri:kɔl] rappel *m*; *(ability to remember)* mémoire *f*; **beyond ~** *adj* irrévocable
**recant** [rɪ'kænt] *vi* se rétracter; *(Rel)* abjurer
**recap** ['ri:kæp] *n* récapitulation *f* ▷ *vt, vi* récapituler
**recapture** [ri:'kæptʃə'] *vt* reprendre; *(atmosphere)* recréer
**recede** [rɪ'si:d] *vi* s'éloigner; reculer
**receding** [rɪ'si:dɪŋ] *adj (forehead, chin)* fuyant(e); **~ hairline** front dégarni
**receipt** [rɪ'si:t] *n (document)* reçu *m*; *(for parcel etc)*

r

accusé *m* de réception; (*act of receiving*) réception *f*; **receipts** *npl* (*Comm*) recettes *fpl*; **to acknowledge ~ of** accuser réception de; **we are in ~ of** ... nous avons reçu ...; **can I have a ~, please?** je peux avoir un reçu, s'il vous plaît?

**receivable** [rɪ'siːvəbl] *adj* (*Comm*) recevable; (: *owing*) à recevoir

**receive** [rɪ'siːv] *vt* recevoir; (*guest*) recevoir, accueillir; **"~d with thanks"** (*Comm*) "pour acquit"; **R~d Pronunciation:** *voir article*

⬤ **RECEIVED PRONUNCIATION**
⬤
⬤ En Grande-Bretagne, la *Received Pronunciation*
⬤ ou "RP" est une prononciation de la langue
⬤ anglaise qui, récemment encore, était
⬤ surtout associée à l'aristocratie et à la
⬤ bourgeoisie, mais qui maintenant est en
⬤ général considérée comme la prononciation
⬤ correcte.

**receiver** [rɪ'siːvər] *n* (*Tel*) récepteur *m*, combiné *m*; (*Radio*) récepteur; (*of stolen goods*) receleur *m*; (*for bankruptcies*) administrateur *m* judiciaire

**receivership** [rɪ'siːvəʃɪp] *n*: **to go into ~** être placé sous administration judiciaire

**recent** ['riːsnt] *adj* récent(e); **in ~ years** au cours de ces dernières années

**recently** ['riːsntlɪ] *adv* récemment; **as ~ as** pas plus tard que; **until ~** jusqu'à il y a peu de temps encore

**receptacle** [rɪ'sɛptɪkl] *n* récipient *m*

**reception** [rɪ'sɛpʃən] *n* réception *f*; (*welcome*) accueil *m*, réception

**reception centre** *n* (*Brit*) centre *m* d'accueil

**reception desk** *n* réception *f*

**receptionist** [rɪ'sɛpʃənɪst] *n* réceptionniste *m/f*

**receptive** [rɪ'sɛptɪv] *adj* réceptif(-ive)

**recess** [rɪ'sɛs] *n* (*in room*) renfoncement *m*; (*for bed*) alcôve *f*; (*secret place*) recoin *m*; (*Pol etc*: *holiday*) vacances *fpl*; (*US Law*: *short break*) suspension *f* d'audience; (*Scol*: *esp US*) récréation *f*

**recession** [rɪ'sɛʃən] *n* (*Econ*) récession *f*

**recessionista** [rɪsɛʃə'nɪstə] *n* recessionista *m/f*

**recharge** [riː'tʃɑːdʒ] *vt* (*battery*) recharger

**rechargeable** [riː'tʃɑːdʒəbl] *adj* rechargeable

**recipe** ['rɛsɪpɪ] *n* recette *f*

**recipient** [rɪ'sɪpɪənt] *n* (*of payment*) bénéficiaire *m/f*; (*of letter*) destinataire *m/f*

**reciprocal** [rɪ'sɪprəkl] *adj* réciproque

**reciprocate** [rɪ'sɪprəkeɪt] *vt* retourner, offrir en retour ▷ *vi* en faire autant

**recital** [rɪ'saɪtl] *n* récital *m*

**recite** [rɪ'saɪt] *vt* (*poem*) réciter; (*complaints etc*) énumérer

**reckless** ['rɛkləs] *adj* (*driver etc*) imprudent(e); (*spender etc*) insouciant(e)

**recklessly** ['rɛkləslɪ] *adv* imprudemment; avec insouciance

**reckon** ['rɛkən] *vt* (*count*) calculer, compter; (*consider*) considérer, estimer; (*think*): **I ~ (that)**

... je pense (que) ..., j'estime (que) ... ▷ *vi*: **he is somebody to be ~ed with** il ne faut pas le sous-estimer; **to ~ without sb/sth** ne pas tenir compte de qn/qch
▶ **reckon on** *vt fus* compter sur, s'attendre à

**reckoning** ['rɛknɪŋ] *n* compte *m*, calcul *m*; estimation *f*; **the day of ~** le jour du Jugement

**reclaim** [rɪ'kleɪm] *vt* (*land*: *from sea*) assécher; (: *from forest*) défricher; (: *with fertilizer*) amender; (*demand back*) réclamer (le remboursement *or* la restitution de); (*waste materials*) récupérer

**reclamation** [rɛklə'meɪʃən] *n* (*of land*) amendement *m*; assèchement *m*; défrichement *m*

**recline** [rɪ'klaɪn] *vi* être allongé(e) *or* étendu(e)

**reclining** [rɪ'klaɪnɪŋ] *adj* (*seat*) à dossier réglable

**recluse** [rɪ'kluːs] *n* reclus(e), ermite *m*

**recognition** [rɛkəg'nɪʃən] *n* reconnaissance *f*; **in ~ of** en reconnaissance de; **to gain ~** être reconnu(e); **transformed beyond ~** méconnaissable

**recognizable** ['rɛkəgnaɪzəbl] *adj*: **~ (by)** reconnaissable (à)

**recognize** ['rɛkəgnaɪz] *vt*: **to ~ (by/as)** reconnaître (à/comme étant)

**recoil** [rɪ'kɔɪl] *vi* (*person*): **to ~ (from)** reculer (devant) ▷ *n* (*of gun*) recul *m*

**recollect** [rɛkə'lɛkt] *vt* se rappeler, se souvenir de

**recollection** [rɛkə'lɛkʃən] *n* souvenir *m*; **to the best of my ~** autant que je m'en souvienne

**recommend** [rɛkə'mɛnd] *vt* recommander; **can you ~ a good restaurant?** pouvez-vous me conseiller un bon restaurant?; **she has a lot to ~ her** elle a beaucoup de choses en sa faveur

**recommendation** [rɛkəmɛn'deɪʃən] *n* recommandation *f*

**recommended retail price** [rɛkə'mɛndɪd-] *n* (*Brit*) prix conseillé

**recompense** ['rɛkəmpɛns] *vt* récompenser; (*compensate*) dédommager ▷ *n* récompense *f*; dédommagement *m*

**reconcilable** ['rɛkənsaɪləbl] *adj* (*ideas*) conciliable

**reconcile** ['rɛkənsaɪl] *vt* (*two people*) réconcilier; (*two facts*) concilier, accorder; **to ~ o.s. to** se résigner à

**reconciliation** [rɛkənsɪlɪ'eɪʃən] *n* réconciliation *f*; conciliation *f*

**recondite** [rɪ'kɒndaɪt] *adj* abstrus(e), obscur(e)

**recondition** [riːkən'dɪʃən] *vt* remettre à neuf; réviser entièrement

**reconnaissance** [rɪ'kɒnɪsns] *n* (*Mil*) reconnaissance *f*

**reconnoitre**, (*US*) **reconnoiter** [rɛkə'nɔɪtər] (*Mil*) *vt* reconnaître ▷ *vi* faire une reconnaissance

**reconsider** [riːkən'sɪdər] *vt* reconsidérer

**reconstitute** [riː'kɒnstɪtjuːt] *vt* reconstituer

**reconstruct** [riːkən'strʌkt] *vt* (*building*) reconstruire; (*crime, system*) reconstituer

**reconstruction** [riːkən'strʌkʃən] *n* reconstruction *f*; reconstitution *f*

**reconvene** [riːkən'viːn] vt reconvoquer ▷ vi se réunir or s'assembler de nouveau

**record** n ['rɛkɔːd] rapport m, récit m; (of meeting etc) procès-verbal m; (register) registre m; (file) dossier m; (Comput) article m; (also: **police record**) casier m judiciaire; (Mus: disc) disque m; (Sport) record m ▷ adj record inv ▷ vt [rɪ'kɔːd] (set down) noter; (relate) rapporter; (Mus: song etc) enregistrer; **public ~s** archives fpl; **to keep a ~ of** noter; **to keep the ~ straight** (fig) mettre les choses au point; **he is on ~ as saying that ...** il a déclaré en public que ...; **Italy's excellent ~** les excellents résultats obtenus par l'Italie; **off the ~** adj officieux(-euse) ▷ adv officieusement; **in ~ time** dans un temps record

**record card** n (in file) fiche f

**recorded delivery** [rɪ'kɔːdɪd-] n (Brit Post): **to send sth ~** ≈ envoyer qch en recommandé

**recorded delivery letter** [rɪ'kɔːdɪd-] n (Brit Post) ≈ lettre recommandée

**recorder** [rɪ'kɔːdəʳ] n (Law) avocat nommé à la fonction de juge; (Mus) flûte f à bec

**record holder** n (Sport) détenteur(-trice) du record

**recording** [rɪ'kɔːdɪŋ] n (Mus) enregistrement m

**recording studio** n studio m d'enregistrement

**record library** n discothèque f

**record player** n tourne-disque m

**recount** [rɪ'kaunt] vt raconter

**re-count** n ['riːkaunt] (Pol: of votes) nouveau décompte (des suffrages) ▷ vt [riː'kaunt] recompter

**recoup** [rɪ'kuːp] vt: **to ~ one's losses** récupérer ce qu'on a perdu, se refaire

**recourse** [rɪ'kɔːs] n recours m; expédient m; **to have ~ to** recourir à, avoir recours à

**recover** [rɪ'kʌvəʳ] vt récupérer ▷ vi (from illness) se rétablir; (from shock) se remettre; (country) se redresser

**re-cover** [riː'kʌvəʳ] vt (chair etc) recouvrir

**recovery** [rɪ'kʌvərɪ] n récupération f; rétablissement m; (Econ) redressement m

**recreate** [riːkrɪ'eɪt] vt recréer

**recreation** [rɛkrɪ'eɪʃən] n (leisure) récréation f, détente f

**recreational** [rɛkrɪ'eɪʃənl] adj pour la détente, récréatif(-ive)

**recreational drug** [rɛkrɪ'eɪʃənl-] n drogue récréative

**recreational vehicle** [rɛkrɪ'eɪʃənl-] n (US) camping-car m

**recrimination** [rɪkrɪmɪ'neɪʃən] n récrimination f

**recruit** [rɪ'kruːt] n recrue f ▷ vt recruter

**recruiting office** [rɪ'kruːtɪŋ-] n bureau m de recrutement

**recruitment** [rɪ'kruːtmənt] n recrutement m

**rectangle** ['rɛktæŋgl] n rectangle m

**rectangular** [rɛk'tæŋgjuləʳ] adj rectangulaire

**rectify** ['rɛktɪfaɪ] vt (error) rectifier, corriger; (omission) réparer

**rector** ['rɛktəʳ] n (Rel) pasteur m; (in Scottish

universities) personnalité élue par les étudiants pour les représenter

**rectory** ['rɛktərɪ] n presbytère m

**rectum** ['rɛktəm] n (Anat) rectum m

**recuperate** [rɪ'kjuːpəreɪt] vi (from illness) se rétablir

**recur** [rɪ'kəːʳ] vi se reproduire; (idea, opportunity) se retrouver; (symptoms) réapparaître

**recurrence** [rɪ'kəːrns] n répétition f; réapparition f

**recurrent** [rɪ'kəːrnt] adj périodique, fréquent(e)

**recurring** [rɪ'kəːrɪŋ] adj (problem) périodique, fréquent(e); (Math) périodique

**recyclable** [riː'saɪkləbl] adj recyclable

**recycle** [riː'saɪkl] vt, vi recycler

**recycling** [riː'saɪklɪŋ] n recyclage m

**red** [rɛd] n rouge m; (Pol: pej) rouge m/f ▷ adj rouge; (hair) roux (rousse); **in the ~** (account) à découvert; (business) en déficit

**red alert** n alerte f rouge

**red-blooded** [rɛd'blʌdɪd] adj (inf) viril(e), vigoureux(-euse)

⊛ **REDBRICK UNIVERSITY**

⊛
⊛ Une redbrick university, ainsi nommée à cause
⊛ du matériau de construction répandu à
⊛ l'époque (la brique), est une université
⊛ britannique provinciale construite assez
⊛ récemment, en particulier fin XIXe-début
⊛ XXe siècle. Il y en a notamment une à
⊛ Manchester, une à Liverpool et une à Bristol.
⊛ Ce terme est utilisé pour établir une
⊛ distinction avec les universités les plus
⊛ anciennes et traditionnelles.

**red carpet treatment** n réception f en grande pompe

**Red Cross** n Croix-Rouge f

**redcurrant** ['rɛdkʌrənt] n groseille f (rouge)

**redden** ['rɛdn] vt, vi rougir

**reddish** ['rɛdɪʃ] adj rougeâtre; (hair) plutôt roux (rousse)

**redecorate** [riː'dɛkəreɪt] vt refaire à neuf, repeindre et retapisser

**redeem** [rɪ'diːm] vt (debt) rembourser; (sth in pawn) dégager; (fig, also Rel) racheter

**redeemable** [rɪ'diːməbl] adj rachetable; remboursable, amortissable

**redeeming** [rɪ'diːmɪŋ] adj (feature) qui sauve, qui rachète (le reste)

**redefine** [riːdɪ'faɪn] vt redéfinir

**redemption** [rɪ'dɛmʃən] n (Rel) rédemption f; **past or beyond ~** (situation) irrémédiable; (place) qui ne peut plus être sauvé(e); (person) irrécupérable

**redeploy** [riːdɪ'plɔɪ] vt (Mil) redéployer; (staff, resources) reconvertir

**redeployment** [riːdɪ'plɔɪmənt] n redéploiement m; reconversion f

**redevelop** [riːdɪ'vɛləp] vt rénover

**redevelopment** [riːdɪ'vɛləpmənt] n

**r**

rénovation *f*
**red-haired** [rɛdˈhɛəʳd] *adj* roux (rousse)
**red-handed** [rɛdˈhændɪd] *adj*: **to be caught ~**
être pris(e) en flagrant délit *or* la main dans le
sac
**redhead** [ˈrɛdhɛd] *n* roux (rousse)
**red herring** *n* (*fig*) diversion *f*, fausse piste
**red-hot** [rɛdˈhɔt] *adj* chauffé(e) au rouge,
brûlant(e)
**redirect** [riːdaɪˈrɛkt] *vt* (*mail*) faire suivre
**redistribute** [riːdɪˈstrɪbjuːt] *vt* redistribuer
**red-letter day** [ˈrɛdlɛtə-] *n* grand jour, jour
mémorable
**red light** *n*: **to go through a ~** (*Aut*) brûler un
feu rouge
**red-light district** [ˈrɛdlaɪt-] *n* quartier mal
famé
**red meat** *n* viande *f* rouge
**redness** [ˈrɛdnɪs] *n* rougeur *f*; (*of hair*) rousseur *f*
**redo** [riːˈduː] *vt* (*irreg: like* **do**) refaire
**redolent** [ˈrɛdələnt] *adj*: **~ of** qui sent; (*fig*) qui
évoque
**redouble** [riːˈdʌbl] *vt*: **to ~ one's efforts**
redoubler d'efforts
**redraft** [riːˈdrɑːft] *vt* remanier
**redress** [rɪˈdrɛs] *n* réparation *f* ▷ *vt* redresser; **to**
**~ the balance** rétablir l'équilibre
**Red Sea** *n*: **the ~** la mer Rouge
**redskin** [ˈrɛdskɪn] *n* Peau-Rouge *m/f*
**red tape** *n* (*fig*) paperasserie (administrative)
**reduce** [rɪˈdjuːs] *vt* réduire; (*lower*) abaisser; **"~**
**speed now"** (*Aut*) "ralentir"; **to ~ sth by/to**
réduire qch de/à; **to ~ sb to tears** faire pleurer
qn
**reduced** [rɪˈdjuːst] *adj* réduit(e); **"greatly ~**
**prices"** "gros rabais"; **at a ~ price** (*goods*) au
rabais; (*ticket etc*) à prix réduit
**reduction** [rɪˈdʌkʃən] *n* réduction *f*; (*of price*)
baisse *f*; (*discount*) rabais *m*; réduction; **is there**
**a ~ for children/students?** y a-t-il une
réduction pour les enfants/les étudiants?
**redundancy** [rɪˈdʌndənsɪ] *n* (*Brit*) licenciement
*m*, mise *f* au chômage; **compulsory ~**
licenciement; **voluntary ~** départ *m* volontaire
**redundancy payment** *n* (*Brit*) indemnité *f* de
licenciement
**redundant** [rɪˈdʌndnt] *adj* (*Brit: worker*)
licencié(e), mis(e) au chômage; (*detail, object*)
superflu(e); **to be made ~** (*worker*) être licencié,
être mis au chômage
**reed** [riːd] *n* (*Bot*) roseau *m*; (*Mus: of clarinet etc*)
anche *f*
**re-educate** [riːˈɛdjukeɪt] *vt* rééduquer
**reedy** [ˈriːdɪ] *adj* (*voice, instrument*) ténu(e)
**reef** [riːf] *n* (*at sea*) récif *m*, écueil *m*
**reek** [riːk] *vi*: **to ~ (of)** puer, empester
**reel** [riːl] *n* bobine *f*; (*Tech*) dévidoir *m*; (*Fishing*)
moulinet *m*; (*Cine*) bande *f*; (*dance*) quadrille
écossais ▷ *vt* (*Tech*) bobiner; (*also*: **reel up**)
enrouler ▷ *vi* (*sway*) chanceler; **my head is ~ing**
j'ai la tête qui tourne
▸ **reel in** *vt* (*fish, line*) ramener

▸ **reel off** *vt* (*say*) énumérer, débiter
**re-election** [riːɪˈlɛkʃən] *n* réélection *f*
**re-enter** [riːˈɛntəʳ] *vt* (*also Space*) rentrer dans
**re-entry** [riːˈɛntrɪ] *n* (*also Space*) rentrée *f*
**re-export** *vt* [ˈriːˈɪksˈpɔːt] réexporter ▷ *n*
[riːˈɛkspɔːt] marchandise réexportée; (*act*)
réexportation *f*
**ref** [rɛf] *n abbr* (*inf: = referee*) arbitre *m*
**ref.** *abbr* (*Comm*: = *with reference to*) réf
**refectory** [rɪˈfɛktərɪ] *n* réfectoire *m*
**refer** [rɪˈfəːʳ] *vt*: **to ~ sth to** (*dispute, decision*)
soumettre qch à; **to ~ sb to** (*inquirer, patient*)
adresser qn à; (*reader: to text*) renvoyer qn à ▷ *vi*:
**to ~ to** (*allude to*) parler de, faire allusion à;
(*consult*) se reporter à; (*apply to*) s'appliquer à;
**~ring to your letter** (*Comm*) en réponse à votre
lettre; **he ~red me to the manager** il m'a dit
de m'adresser au directeur
**referee** [rɛfəˈriː] *n* arbitre *m*; (*Tennis*) juge-
arbitre *m*; (*Brit: for job application*) répondant(e)
▷ *vt* arbitrer
**reference** [ˈrɛfrəns] *n* référence *f*, renvoi *m*;
(*mention*) allusion *f*, mention *f*; (*for job application:*
*letter*) références; lettre *f* de recommandation;
(: *person*) répondant(e); **with ~ to** en ce qui
concerne; (*Comm: in letter*) me référant à;
**"please quote this ~"** (*Comm*) "prière de
rappeler cette référence"
**reference book** *n* ouvrage *m* de référence
**reference library** *n* bibliothèque *f* d'ouvrages à
consulter
**reference number** *n* (*Comm*) numéro *m* de
référence
**referendum** (*pl* **referenda**) [rɛfəˈrɛndəm, -də] *n*
référendum *m*
**referral** [rɪˈfəːrəl] *n* soumission *f*; **she got a ~ to**
**a specialist** elle a été adressée à un spécialiste
**refill** *vt* [riːˈfɪl] remplir à nouveau; (*pen, lighter etc*)
recharger ▷ *n* [ˈriːfɪl] (*for pen etc*) recharge *f*
**refine** [rɪˈfaɪn] *vt* (*sugar, oil*) raffiner; (*taste*)
affiner; (*idea, theory*) peaufiner
**refined** [rɪˈfaɪnd] *adj* (*person, taste*) raffiné(e)
**refinement** [rɪˈfaɪnmənt] *n* (*of person*)
raffinement *m*
**refinery** [rɪˈfaɪnərɪ] *n* raffinerie *f*
**refit** (*Naut*) *n* [ˈriːfɪt] remise *f* en état ▷ *vt* [riːˈfɪt]
remettre en état
**reflate** [riːˈfleɪt] *vt* (*economy*) relancer
**reflation** [riːˈfleɪʃən] *n* relance *f*
**reflationary** [riːˈfleɪʃənrɪ] *adj* de relance
**reflect** [rɪˈflɛkt] *vt* (*light, image*) réfléchir, refléter;
(*fig*) refléter ▷ *vi* (*think*) réfléchir, méditer; **it ~s**
**badly on him** cela le discrédite; **it ~s well on**
**him** c'est tout à son honneur
**reflection** [rɪˈflɛkʃən] *n* réflexion *f*; (*image*) reflet
*m*; (*criticism*): **~ on** critique *f* de; atteinte *f* à; **on ~**
réflexion faite
**reflector** [rɪˈflɛktəʳ] *n* (*also Aut*) réflecteur *m*
**reflex** [ˈriːflɛks] *adj*, *n* réflexe (*m*)
**reflexive** [rɪˈflɛksɪv] *adj* (*Ling*) réfléchi(e)
**reform** [rɪˈfɔːm] *n* réforme *f* ▷ *vt* réformer
**reformat** [riːˈfɔːmæt] *vt* (*Comput*) reformater

**Reformation** [rɛfə'meɪʃən] n: **the** ~ la Réforme
**reformatory** [rɪ'fɔːmətərɪ] n (US) centre m
d'éducation surveillée
**reformed** [rɪ'fɔːmd] adj amendé(e), assagi(e)
**reformer** [rɪ'fɔːməʳ] n réformateur(-trice)
**refrain** [rɪ'freɪn] vi: **to** ~ **from doing** s'abstenir
de faire ▷ n refrain m
**refresh** [rɪ'frɛʃ] vt rafraîchir; (subj: food, sleep etc)
redonner des forces à
**refresher course** [rɪ'frɛʃə-] n (Brit) cours m de
recyclage
**refreshing** [rɪ'frɛʃɪŋ] adj (drink) rafraîchissant(e);
(sleep) réparateur(-trice); (fact, idea etc) qui
réjouit par son originalité or sa rareté
**refreshment** [rɪ'frɛʃmənt] n: **for some** ~ (eating)
pour se restaurer or sustenter; **in need of** ~
(resting etc) ayant besoin de refaire ses forces
**refreshments** [rɪ'frɛʃmənts] npl
rafraîchissements mpl
**refrigeration** [rɪfrɪdʒə'reɪʃən] n réfrigération f
**refrigerator** [rɪ'frɪdʒəreɪtəʳ] n réfrigérateur m,
frigidaire m
**refuel** [riː'fjuəl] vt ravitailler en carburant ▷ vi
se ravitailler en carburant
**refuge** ['rɛfjuːdʒ] n refuge m; **to take** ~ **in** se
réfugier dans
**refugee** [rɛfjuˈdʒiː] n réfugié(e)
**refugee camp** n camp m de réfugiés
**refund** n ['riːfʌnd] remboursement m ▷ vt
[rɪ'fʌnd] rembourser
**refurbish** [riː'fəːbɪʃ] vt remettre à neuf
**refurnish** [riː'fəːnɪʃ] vt remeubler
**refusal** [rɪ'fjuːzəl] n refus m; **to have first** ~ **on
sth** avoir droit de préemption sur qch
**refuse¹** ['rɛfjuːs] n ordures fpl, détritus mpl
**refuse²** [rɪ'fjuːz] vt, vi refuser; **to** ~ **to do sth**
refuser de faire qch
**refuse collection** n ramassage m d'ordures
**refuse disposal** n élimination f des ordures
**refusenik** [rɪ'fjuːznɪk] n refuznik m/f
**refute** [rɪ'fjuːt] vt réfuter
**regain** [rɪ'geɪn] vt (lost ground) regagner;
(strength) retrouver
**regal** ['riːɡl] adj royal(e)
**regale** [rɪ'ɡeɪl] vt: **to** ~ **sb with sth** régaler qn de
qch
**regalia** [rɪ'ɡeɪlɪə] n insignes mpl de la royauté
**regard** [rɪ'ɡɑːd] n respect m, estime f,
considération f ▷ vt considérer; **to give one's
~s to** faire ses amitiés à; **"with kindest ~s"**
"bien amicalement"; **as ~s, with ~ to** en ce qui
concerne
**regarding** [rɪ'ɡɑːdɪŋ] prep en ce qui concerne
**regardless** [rɪ'ɡɑːdlɪs] adv quand même; ~ **of**
sans se soucier de
**regatta** [rɪ'ɡætə] n régate f
**regency** ['riːdʒənsɪ] n régence f
**regenerate** [rɪ'dʒɛnəreɪt] vt régénérer ▷ vi se
régénérer
**regent** ['riːdʒənt] n régent(e)
**reggae** ['rɛɡeɪ] n reggae m
**régime** [reɪ'ʒiːm] n régime m

**regiment** ['rɛdʒɪmənt] n régiment m ▷ vt
['rɛdʒɪmɛnt] imposer une discipline trop stricte
à
**regimental** [rɛdʒɪ'mɛntl] adj d'un régiment
**regimentation** [rɛdʒɪmɛn'teɪʃən] n
réglementation excessive
**region** ['riːdʒən] n région f; **in the** ~ **of** (fig) aux
alentours de
**regional** ['riːdʒənl] adj régional(e)
**regional development** n aménagement m du
territoire
**register** ['rɛdʒɪstəʳ] n registre m; (also: **electoral
register**) liste électorale ▷ vt enregistrer,
inscrire; (birth) déclarer; (vehicle) immatriculer;
(luggage) enregistrer; (letter) envoyer en
recommandé; (subj: instrument) marquer ▷ vi
s'inscrire; (at hotel) signer le registre; (make
impression) être (bien) compris(e); **to** ~ **for a
course** s'inscrire à un cours; **to** ~ **a protest**
protester
**registered** ['rɛdʒɪstəd] adj (design) déposé(e);
(Brit: letter) recommandé(e); (student, voter)
inscrit(e)
**registered company** n société immatriculée
**registered nurse** n (US) infirmier(-ière)
diplômé(e) d'État
**registered office** n siège social
**registered trademark** n marque déposée
**registrar** ['rɛdʒɪstrɑːʳ] n officier m de l'état civil;
secrétaire m/f général
**registration** [rɛdʒɪs'treɪʃən] n (act)
enregistrement m; (of student) inscription f; (Brit
Aut: also: **registration number**) numéro m
d'immatriculation
**registry** ['rɛdʒɪstrɪ] n bureau m de
l'enregistrement
**registry office** ['rɛdʒɪstrɪ-] n (Brit) bureau m de
l'état civil; **to get married in a** ~ ~ se marier à
la mairie
**regret** [rɪ'ɡrɛt] n regret m ▷ vt regretter; **to** ~
**that** regretter que + sub; **we** ~ **to inform you
that** ... nous sommes au regret de vous
informer que ...
**regretfully** [rɪ'ɡrɛtfəlɪ] adv à or avec regret
**regrettable** [rɪ'ɡrɛtəbl] adj regrettable,
fâcheux(-euse)
**regrettably** [rɪ'ɡrɛtəblɪ] adv (drunk, late)
fâcheusement; ~, **he** ... malheureusement, il ...
**regroup** [riː'ɡruːp] vt regrouper ▷ vi se
regrouper
**regt** abbr = **regiment**
**regular** ['rɛɡjuləʳ] adj régulier(-ière); (usual)
habituel(le), normal(e); (listener, reader) fidèle;
(soldier) de métier; (Comm: size) ordinaire ▷ n
(client etc) habitué(e)
**regularity** [rɛɡju'lærɪtɪ] n régularité f
**regularly** ['rɛɡjuləlɪ] adv régulièrement
**regulate** ['rɛɡjuleɪt] vt régler
**regulation** [rɛɡju'leɪʃən] n (rule) règlement m;
(adjustment) réglage m ▷ cpd réglementaire
**rehabilitate** [riːə'bɪlɪteɪt] vt (criminal) réinsérer;
(drug addict) désintoxiquer; (invalid) rééduquer

r

753

**rehabilitation** ['riːəbɪlɪ'teɪʃən] n (of offender) réhabilitation f; (of addict) réadaptation f; (of disabled) rééducation f, réadaptation f

**rehash** [riː'hæʃ] vt (inf) remanier

**rehearsal** [rɪ'hɜːsəl] n répétition f; **dress ~** (répétition) générale f

**rehearse** [rɪ'hɜːs] vt répéter

**rehouse** [riː'hauz] vt reloger

**reign** [reɪn] n règne m ▷ vi régner

**reigning** ['reɪnɪŋ] adj (monarch) régnant(e); (champion) actuel(le)

**reimburse** [riːɪm'bɜːs] vt rembourser

**rein** [reɪn] n (for horse) rêne f; **to give sb free ~** (fig) donner carte blanche à qn

**reincarnation** [riːɪnkɑː'neɪʃən] n réincarnation f

**reindeer** ['reɪndɪəʳ] n (pl inv) renne m

**reinforce** [riːɪn'fɔːs] vt renforcer

**reinforced concrete** [riːɪn'fɔːst-] n béton armé

**reinforcement** [riːɪn'fɔːsmənt] n (action) renforcement m

**reinforcements** [riːɪn'fɔːsmənts] npl (Mil) renfort(s) m(pl)

**reinstate** [riːɪn'steɪt] vt rétablir, réintégrer

**reinstatement** [riːɪn'steɪtmənt] n réintégration f

**reissue** [riː'ɪʃjuː] vt (book) rééditer; (film) ressortir

**reiterate** [riː'ɪtəreɪt] vt réitérer, répéter

**reject** n ['riːdʒɛkt] (Comm) article m de rebut ▷ vt [rɪ'dʒɛkt] refuser; (Comm: goods) mettre au rebut; (idea) rejeter

**rejection** [rɪ'dʒɛkʃən] n rejet m, refus m

**rejoice** [rɪ'dʒɔɪs] vi: **to ~ (at or over)** se réjouir (de)

**rejoinder** [rɪ'dʒɔɪndəʳ] n (retort) réplique f

**rejuvenate** [rɪ'dʒuːvəneɪt] vt rajeunir

**rekindle** [riː'kɪndl] vt rallumer; (fig) raviver

**relapse** [rɪ'læps] n (Med) rechute f

**relate** [rɪ'leɪt] vt (tell) raconter; (connect) établir un rapport entre ▷ vi: **to ~ to** (connect) se rapporter à; **to ~ to sb** (interact) entretenir des rapports avec qn

**related** [rɪ'leɪtɪd] adj apparenté(e); **~ to** (subject) lié(e) à

**relating to** [rɪ'leɪtɪŋ-] prep concernant

**relation** [rɪ'leɪʃən] n (person) parent(e); (link) rapport m, lien m; **relations** npl (relatives) famille f; **diplomatic/international ~s** relations diplomatiques/internationales; **in ~ to** en ce qui concerne; par rapport à; **to bear no ~ to** être sans rapport avec

**relationship** [rɪ'leɪʃənʃɪp] n rapport m, lien m; (personal ties) relations fpl, rapports; (also: **family relationship**) lien de parenté; (affair) liaison f; **they have a good ~** ils s'entendent bien

**relative** ['rɛlətɪv] n parent(e) ▷ adj relatif(-ive); (respective) respectif(-ive); **all her ~s** toute sa famille

**relatively** ['rɛlətɪvlɪ] adv relativement

**relax** [rɪ'læks] vi (muscle) se relâcher; (person: unwind) se détendre; (calm down) se calmer ▷ vt relâcher; (mind, person) détendre

**relaxation** [riːlæk'seɪʃən] n relâchement m; (of mind) détente f; (recreation) détente, délassement m; (entertainment) distraction f

**relaxed** [rɪ'lækst] adj relâché(e); détendu(e)

**relaxing** [rɪ'læksɪŋ] adj délassant(e)

**relay** ['riːleɪ] n (Sport) course f de relais ▷ vt (message) retransmettre, relayer

**release** [rɪ'liːs] n (from prison, obligation) libération f; (of gas etc) émission f; (of film etc) sortie f; (new recording) disque m; (device) déclencheur m ▷ vt (prisoner) libérer; (book, film) sortir; (report, news) rendre public, publier; (gas etc) émettre, dégager; (free: from wreckage etc) dégager; (Tech: catch, spring etc) déclencher; (let go: person, animal) relâcher; (: hand, object) lâcher; (: grip, brake) desserrer; **to ~ one's grip** or **hold** lâcher prise; **to ~ the clutch** (Aut) débrayer

**relegate** ['rɛləgeɪt] vt reléguer; (Brit Sport): **to be ~d** descendre dans une division inférieure

**relent** [rɪ'lɛnt] vi se laisser fléchir

**relentless** [rɪ'lɛntlɪs] adj implacable; (non-stop) continuel(le)

**relevance** ['rɛləvəns] n pertinence f; **~ of sth to sth** rapport m entre qch et qch

**relevant** ['rɛləvənt] adj (question) pertinent(e); (corresponding) approprié(e); (fact) significatif(-ive); (information) utile; **~ to** ayant rapport à, approprié à

**reliability** [rɪlaɪə'bɪlɪtɪ] n sérieux m; fiabilité f

**reliable** [rɪ'laɪəbl] adj (person, firm) sérieux(-euse), fiable; (method, machine) fiable; (news, information) sûr(e)

**reliably** [rɪ'laɪəblɪ] adv: **to be ~ informed** savoir de source sûre

**reliance** [rɪ'laɪəns] n: **~ (on)** (trust) confiance f (en); (dependence) besoin m (de), dépendance f (de)

**reliant** [rɪ'laɪənt] adj: **to be ~ on sth/sb** dépendre de qch/qn

**relic** ['rɛlɪk] n (Rel) relique f; (of the past) vestige m

**relief** [rɪ'liːf] n (from pain, anxiety) soulagement m; (help, supplies) secours m(pl); (of guard) relève f; (Art, Geo) relief m; **by way of light ~** pour faire diversion

**relief map** n carte f en relief

**relief road** n (Brit) route f de délestage

**relieve** [rɪ'liːv] vt (pain, patient) soulager; (fear, worry) dissiper; (bring help) secourir; (take over from: gen) relayer; (: guard) relever; **to ~ sb of sth** débarrasser qn de qch; **to ~ sb of his command** (Mil) relever qn de ses fonctions; **to ~ o.s.** (euphemism) se soulager, faire ses besoins

**relieved** [rɪ'liːvd] adj soulagé(e); **to be ~ that ...** être soulagé que ...; **I'm ~ to hear it** je suis soulagé de l'entendre

**religion** [rɪ'lɪdʒən] n religion f

**religious** [rɪ'lɪdʒəs] adj religieux(-euse); (book) de piété

**religious education** n instruction religieuse

**relinquish** [rɪ'lɪŋkwɪʃ] vt abandonner; (plan, habit) renoncer à

**relish** ['rɛlɪʃ] n (Culin) condiment m; (enjoyment)

délectation f ▷ vt (food etc) savourer; **to ~ doing** se délecter à faire

**relive** [riːˈlɪv] vt revivre

**reload** [riːˈləud] vt recharger

**relocate** [riːləuˈkeɪt] vt (business) transférer ▷ vi se transférer, s'installer or s'établir ailleurs; **to ~ in** (déménager et) s'installer or s'établir à, se transférer à

**reluctance** [rɪˈlʌktəns] n répugnance f

**reluctant** [rɪˈlʌktənt] adj peu disposé(e), qui hésite; **to be ~ to do sth** hésiter à faire qch

**reluctantly** [rɪˈlʌktəntlɪ] adv à contrecœur, sans enthousiasme

**rely on** [rɪˈlaɪ-] vt fus (be dependent on) dépendre de; (trust) compter sur

**remain** [rɪˈmeɪn] vi rester; **to ~ silent** garder le silence; **I ~, yours faithfully** (Brit: in letters) je vous prie d'agréer, Monsieur etc l'assurance de mes sentiments distingués

**remainder** [rɪˈmeɪndəʳ] n reste m; (Comm) fin f de série

**remaining** [rɪˈmeɪnɪŋ] adj qui reste

**remains** [rɪˈmeɪnz] npl restes mpl

**remake** [ˈriːmeɪk] n (Cine) remake m

**remand** [rɪˈmɑːnd] n: **on ~** en détention préventive ▷ vt: **to be ~ed in custody** être placé(e) en détention préventive

**remand home** n (Brit) centre m d'éducation surveillée

**remark** [rɪˈmɑːk] n remarque f, observation f ▷ vt (faire) remarquer, dire; (notice) remarquer; **to ~ on sth** faire une or des remarque(s) sur qch

**remarkable** [rɪˈmɑːkəbl] adj remarquable

**remarkably** [rɪˈmɑːkəblɪ] adv remarquablement

**remarry** [riːˈmærɪ] vi se remarier

**remedial** [rɪˈmiːdɪəl] adj (tuition, classes) de rattrapage

**remedy** [ˈrɛmədɪ] n: **~ (for)** remède m (contre or à) ▷ vt remédier à

**remember** [rɪˈmɛmbəʳ] vt se rappeler, se souvenir de; (send greetings): **~ me to him** saluez-le de ma part; **I ~ seeing it, I ~ having seen it** je me rappelle l'avoir vu or que je l'ai vu; **she ~ed to do it** elle a pensé à le faire; **~ me to your wife** rappelez-moi au bon souvenir de votre femme

**remembrance** [rɪˈmɛmbrəns] n souvenir m; mémoire f

**Remembrance Day** [rɪˈmɛmbrəns-] n (Brit) ≈ (le jour de) l'Armistice m, ≈ le 11 novembre; voir article

**remind** [rɪˈmaɪnd] vt: **to ~ sb of sth** rappeler qch à qn; **to ~ sb to do** faire penser à qn à faire, rappeler à qn qu'il doit faire; **that ~s me!** j'y pense!

**reminder** [rɪˈmaɪndəʳ] n (Comm: letter) rappel m; (note etc) pense-bête m; (souvenir) souvenir m

**reminisce** [rɛmɪˈnɪs] vi: **to ~ (about)** évoquer ses souvenirs (de)

**reminiscences** [rɛmɪˈnɪsnsɪz] npl réminiscences fpl, souvenirs mpl

**reminiscent** [rɛmɪˈnɪsnt] adj: **~ of** qui rappelle, qui fait penser à

**remiss** [rɪˈmɪs] adj négligent(e); **it was ~ of me** c'était une négligence de ma part

**remission** [rɪˈmɪʃən] n rémission f; (of debt, sentence) remise f; (of fee) exemption f

**remit** [rɪˈmɪt] vt (send: money) envoyer

**remittance** [rɪˈmɪtns] n envoi m, paiement m

**remnant** [ˈrɛmnənt] n reste m, restant m; (of cloth) coupon m; **remnants** npl (Comm) fins fpl de série

**remonstrate** [ˈrɛmənstreɪt] vi: **to ~ (with sb about sth)** se plaindre (à qn de qch)

**remorse** [rɪˈmɔːs] n remords m

**remorseful** [rɪˈmɔːsful] adj plein(e) de remords

**remorseless** [rɪˈmɔːslɪs] adj (fig) impitoyable

**remote** [rɪˈməut] adj éloigné(e), lointain(e); (person) distant(e); (possibility) vague; **there is a ~ possibility that ...** il est tout juste possible que ...

**remote control** n télécommande f

**remote-controlled** [rɪˈməutkənˈtrəuld] adj téléguidé(e)

**remotely** [rɪˈməutlɪ] adv au loin; (slightly) très vaguement

**remould** [ˈriːməuld] n (Brit: tyre) pneu m rechapé

**removable** [rɪˈmuːvəbl] adj (detachable) amovible

**removal** [rɪˈmuːvəl] n (taking away) enlèvement m; suppression f; (Brit: from house) déménagement m; (from office: dismissal) renvoi m; (of stain) nettoyage m; (Med) ablation f

**removal man** (irreg) n (Brit) déménageur m

**removal van** n (Brit) camion m de déménagement

**remove** [rɪˈmuːv] vt enlever, retirer; (employee) renvoyer; (stain) faire partir; (abuse) supprimer; (doubt) chasser; **first cousin once ~d** cousin(e) au deuxième degré

**remover** [rɪˈmuːvəʳ] n (for paint) décapant m; (for

r

*varnish*) dissolvant *m*; **make-up ~** démaquillant *m*

**remunerate** [rɪ'mjuːnəreɪt] *vt* rémunérer

**remuneration** [rɪmjuːnə'reɪʃən] *n* rémunération *f*

**Renaissance** [rɪ'neɪsɑ̃s] *n*: **the ~** la Renaissance

**rename** [riː'neɪm] *vt* rebaptiser

**rend** (*pt, pp* **rent**) [rɛnd, rɛnt] *vt* déchirer

**render** ['rɛndə<sup>r</sup>] *vt* rendre; (*Culin: fat*) clarifier

**rendering** ['rɛndərɪŋ] *n* (*Mus etc*) interprétation *f*

**rendezvous** ['rɔndɪvuː] *n* rendez-vous *m inv* ▷ *vi* opérer une jonction, se rejoindre; **to ~ with sb** rejoindre qn

**renegade** ['rɛnɪɡeɪd] *n* renégat(e)

**renew** [rɪ'njuː] *vt* renouveler; (*negotiations*) reprendre; (*acquaintance*) renouer

**renewable** [rɪ'njuːəbl] *adj* renouvelable; **~ energy, ~s** énergies renouvelables

**renewal** [rɪ'njuːəl] *n* renouvellement *m*; reprise *f*

**renounce** [rɪ'nauns] *vt* renoncer à; (*disown*) renier

**renovate** ['rɛnəveɪt] *vt* rénover; (*work of art*) restaurer

**renovation** [rɛnə'veɪʃən] *n* rénovation *f*; restauration *f*

**renown** [rɪ'naun] *n* renommée *f*

**renowned** [rɪ'naund] *adj* renommé(e)

**rent** [rɛnt] *pt, pp of* **rend** ▷ *n* loyer *m* ▷ *vt* louer; (*car, TV*) louer, prendre en location; (*also:* **rent out**: *car, TV*) louer, donner en location

**rental** ['rɛntl] *n* (*for television, car*) (prix *m* de) location *f*

**rent boy** *n* (*Brit inf*) jeune prostitué

**renunciation** [rɪnʌnsɪ'eɪʃən] *n* renonciation *f*; (*self-denial*) renoncement *m*

**reopen** [riː'əupən] *vt* rouvrir

**reorder** [riːˈɔːdə<sup>r</sup>] *vt* commander de nouveau; (*rearrange*) réorganiser

**reorganize** [riːˈɔːɡənaɪz] *vt* réorganiser

**rep** [rɛp] *n abbr* (*Comm*) = **representative**; (*Theat*) = **repertory**

**Rep.** *abbr* (*US Pol*) = **representative; republican**

**repair** [rɪ'pɛə<sup>r</sup>] *n* réparation *f* ▷ *vt* réparer; **in good/bad ~** en bon/mauvais état; **under ~** en réparation; **where can I get this ~ed?** où est-ce que je peux faire réparer ceci?

**repair kit** *n* trousse *f* de réparations

**repair man** (*irreg*) *n* réparateur *m*

**repair shop** *n* (*Aut etc*) atelier *m* de réparations

**repartee** [rɛpɑː'tiː] *n* repartie *f*

**repast** [rɪ'pɑːst] *n* (*formal*) repas *m*

**repatriate** [riː'pætrɪeɪt] *vt* rapatrier

**repay** [riː'peɪ] *vt* (*irreg: like* **pay**); (*money, creditor*) rembourser; (*sb's efforts*) récompenser

**repayment** [riː'peɪmənt] *n* remboursement *m*; récompense *f*

**repeal** [rɪ'piːl] *n* (*of law*) abrogation *f*; (*of sentence*) annulation *f* ▷ *vt* abroger; annuler

**repeat** [rɪ'piːt] *n* (*Radio, TV*) reprise *f* ▷ *vt* répéter; (*pattern*) reproduire; (*promise, attack, also Comm: order*) renouveler; (*Scol: a class*) redoubler ▷ *vi* répéter; **can you ~ that, please?** pouvez-vous répéter, s'il vous plaît?

**repeatedly** [rɪ'piːtɪdlɪ] *adv* souvent, à plusieurs reprises

**repeat prescription** *n* (*Brit*): **I'd like a ~** je voudrais renouveler mon ordonnance

**repel** [rɪ'pɛl] *vt* repousser

**repellent** [rɪ'pɛlənt] *adj* repoussant(e) ▷ *n*: **insect ~** insectifuge *m*; **moth ~** produit *m* antimite(s)

**repent** [rɪ'pɛnt] *vi*: **to ~ (of)** se repentir (de)

**repentance** [rɪ'pɛntəns] *n* repentir *m*

**repercussions** [riːpə'kʌʃənz] *npl* répercussions *fpl*

**repertoire** ['rɛpətwɑː<sup>r</sup>] *n* répertoire *m*

**repertory** ['rɛpətərɪ] *n* (*also:* **repertory theatre**) théâtre *m* de répertoire

**repertory company** *n* troupe théâtrale permanente

**repetition** [rɛpɪ'tɪʃən] *n* répétition *f*

**repetitious** [rɛpɪ'tɪʃəs] *adj* (*speech*) plein(e) de redites

**repetitive** [rɪ'pɛtɪtɪv] *adj* (*movement, work*) répétitif(-ive); (*speech*) plein(e) de redites

**replace** [rɪ'pleɪs] *vt* (*put back*) remettre, replacer; (*take the place of*) remplacer; (*Tel*): **"~ the receiver"** "raccrochez"

**replacement** [rɪ'pleɪsmənt] *n* replacement *m*; (*substitution*) remplacement *m*; (*person*) remplaçant(e)

**replacement part** *n* pièce *f* de rechange

**replay** ['riːpleɪ] *n* (*of match*) match rejoué; (*of tape, film*) répétition *f*

**replenish** [rɪ'plɛnɪʃ] *vt* (*glass*) remplir (de nouveau); (*stock etc*) réapprovisionner

**replete** [rɪ'pliːt] *adj* rempli(e); (*well-fed*): **~ (with)** rassasié(e) (de)

**replica** ['rɛplɪkə] *n* réplique *f*, copie exacte

**reply** [rɪ'plaɪ] *n* réponse *f* ▷ *vi* répondre; **in ~ (to)** en réponse (à); **there's no ~** (*Tel*) ça ne répond pas

**reply coupon** *n* coupon-réponse *m*

**report** [rɪ'pɔːt] *n* rapport *m*; (*Press etc*) reportage *m*; (*Brit: also:* **school report**) bulletin *m* (scolaire); (*of gun*) détonation *f* ▷ *vt* rapporter, faire un compte rendu de; (*Press etc*) faire un reportage sur; (*notify: accident*) signaler; (*: culprit*) dénoncer ▷ *vi* (*make a report*) faire un rapport; (*for newspaper*) faire un reportage (sur); **I'd like to ~ a theft** je voudrais signaler un vol; (*present o.s.*): **to ~ (to sb)** se présenter (chez qn); **it is ~ed that** on dit or annonce que; **it is ~ed from Berlin that** on nous apprend de Berlin que

**report card** *n* (*US, Scottish*) bulletin *m* (scolaire)

**reportedly** [rɪ'pɔːtɪdlɪ] *adv*: **she is ~ living in Spain** elle habiterait en Espagne; **he ~ told them to ...** il leur aurait dit de ...

**reported speech** *n* (*Ling*) discours indirect

**reporter** [rɪ'pɔːtə<sup>r</sup>] *n* reporter *m*

**repose** [rɪ'pəuz] *n*: **in ~** en or au repos

**repossess** [riːpə'zɛs] *vt* saisir

**repossession order** [ri:pə'zɛʃən-] *n* ordre *m* de reprise de possession

**reprehensible** [rɛprɪ'hɛnsɪbl] *adj* répréhensible

**represent** [rɛprɪ'zɛnt] *vt* représenter; *(view, belief)* présenter, expliquer; *(describe):* **to ~ sth as** présenter *or* décrire qch comme; **to ~ to sb that** expliquer à qn que

**representation** [rɛprɪzɛn'teɪʃən] *n* représentation *f*; **representations** *npl* *(protest)* démarche *f*

**representative** [rɛprɪ'zɛntətɪv] *n* représentant(e); *(Comm)* représentant(e) (de commerce); *(US Pol)* député *m* ▷ *adj* représentatif(-ive), caractéristique

**repress** [ri'prɛs] *vt* réprimer

**repression** [ri'prɛʃən] *n* répression *f*

**repressive** [ri'prɛsɪv] *adj* répressif(-ive)

**reprieve** [ri'pri:v] *n* *(Law)* grâce *f*; *(fig)* sursis *m*, délai *m* ▷ *vt* gracier; accorder un sursis *or* un délai à

**reprimand** ['rɛprɪmɑ:nd] *n* réprimande *f* ▷ *vt* réprimander

**reprint** *n* ['ri:prɪnt] réimpression *f* ▷ *vt* [ri:'prɪnt] réimprimer

**reprisal** [ri'praɪzl] *n* représailles *fpl*; **to take ~s** user de représailles

**reproach** [ri'prəutʃ] *n* reproche *m* ▷ *vt:* **to ~ sb with sth** reprocher qch à qn; **beyond ~** irréprochable

**reproachful** [ri'prəutʃful] *adj* de reproche

**reproduce** [ri:prə'dju:s] *vt* reproduire ▷ *vi* se reproduire

**reproduction** [ri:prə'dʌkʃən] *n* reproduction *f*

**reproductive** [ri:prə'dʌktɪv] *adj* reproducteur(-trice)

**reproof** [ri'pru:f] *n* reproche *m*

**reprove** [ri'pru:v] *vt* *(action)* réprouver; *(person):* **to ~ (for)** blâmer (de)

**reproving** [ri'pru:vɪŋ] *adj* réprobateur(-trice)

**reptile** ['rɛptaɪl] *n* reptile *m*

**Repub.** *abbr* *(US Pol)* = **republican**

**republic** [ri'pʌblɪk] *n* république *f*

**republican** [ri'pʌblɪkən] *adj, n* républicain(e)

**repudiate** [ri'pju:dɪeɪt] *vt* *(ally, behaviour)* désavouer; *(accusation)* rejeter; *(wife)* répudier

**repugnant** [ri'pʌgnənt] *adj* répugnant(e)

**repulse** [ri'pʌls] *vt* repousser

**repulsion** [ri'pʌlʃən] *n* répulsion *f*

**repulsive** [ri'pʌlsɪv] *adj* repoussant(e), répulsif(-ive)

**reputable** ['rɛpjutəbl] *adj* de bonne réputation; *(occupation)* honorable

**reputation** [rɛpju'teɪʃən] *n* réputation *f*; **to have a ~ for** être réputé(e) pour; **he has a ~ for being awkward** il a la réputation de ne pas être commode

**repute** [ri'pju:t] *n* (bonne) réputation

**reputed** [ri'pju:tɪd] *adj* réputé(e); **he is ~ to be rich/intelligent** *etc* on dit qu'il est riche/intelligent *etc*

**reputedly** [ri'pju:tɪdlɪ] *adv* d'après ce qu'on dit

**request** [ri'kwɛst] *n* demande *f*; *(formal)* requête

*f* ▷ *vt:* **to ~ (of** *or* **from sb)** demander (à qn); **at the ~ of** à la demande de

**request stop** *n* *(Brit: for bus)* arrêt facultatif

**requiem** ['rɛkwɪəm] *n* requiem *m*

**require** [ri'kwaɪə<sup>r</sup>] *vt* *(need: subj: person)* avoir besoin de; *(: thing, situation)* nécessiter, demander; *(want)* exiger; *(order):* **to ~ sb to do sth/sth of sb** exiger que qn fasse qch/qch de qn; **if ~d** s'il le faut; **what qualifications are ~d?** quelles sont les qualifications requises?; **~d by law** requis par la loi

**required** [ri'kwaɪəd] *adj* requis(e), voulu(e)

**requirement** [ri'kwaɪəmənt] *n* *(need)* exigence *f*; besoin *m*; *(condition)* condition *f* (requise)

**requisite** ['rɛkwɪzɪt] *n* chose *f* nécessaire ▷ *adj* requis(e), nécessaire; **toilet ~s** accessoires *mpl* de toilette

**requisition** [rɛkwɪ'zɪʃən] *n:* **~ (for)** demande *f* (de) ▷ *vt* *(Mil)* réquisitionner

**reroute** [ri:'ru:t] *vt* *(train etc)* dérouter

**resale** ['ri:'seɪl] *n* revente *f*

**resale price maintenance** *n* vente au détail à prix imposé

**resat** [ri:'sæt] *pt, pp of* **resit**

**rescind** [ri'sɪnd] *vt* annuler; *(law)* abroger; *(judgment)* rescinder

**rescue** ['rɛskju:] *n* *(from accident)* sauvetage *m*; *(help)* secours *mpl* ▷ *vt* sauver; **to come to sb's ~** venir au secours de qn

**rescue party** *n* équipe *f* de sauvetage

**rescuer** ['rɛskjuə<sup>r</sup>] *n* sauveteur *m*

**research** [ri'sə:tʃ] *n* recherche(s) *f(pl)* ▷ *vt* faire des recherches sur ▷ *vi:* **to ~ (into sth)** faire des recherches (sur qch); **a piece of ~** un travail de recherche; **~ and development (R & D)** recherche-développement (R-D)

**researcher** [ri'sə:tʃə<sup>r</sup>] *n* chercheur(-euse)

**research work** *n* recherches *fpl*

**resell** [ri:'sɛl] *vt* *(irreg: like* **sell***)* revendre

**resemblance** [ri'zɛmbləns] *n* ressemblance *f*; **to bear a strong ~ to** ressembler beaucoup à

**resemble** [ri'zɛmbl] *vt* ressembler à

**resent** [ri'zɛnt] *vt* éprouver du ressentiment de, être contrarié(e) par

**resentful** [ri'zɛntful] *adj* irrité(e), plein(e) de ressentiment

**resentment** [ri'zɛntmənt] *n* ressentiment *m*

**reservation** [rɛzə'veɪʃən] *n* *(booking)* réservation *f*; *(doubt, protected area)* réserve *f*; *(Brit Aut: also:* **central reservation***)* bande médiane; **to make a ~ (in an hotel/a restaurant/on a plane)** réserver *or* retenir une chambre/une table/une place; **with ~s** *(doubts)* avec certaines réserves

**reservation desk** *n* *(US: in hotel)* réception *f*

**reserve** [ri'zə:v] *n* réserve *f*; *(Sport)* remplaçant(e) ▷ *vt* *(seats etc)* réserver, retenir; **reserves** *npl* *(Mil)* réservistes *mpl*; **in ~** en réserve

**reserve currency** *n* monnaie *f* de réserve

**reserved** [ri'zə:vd] *adj* réservé(e)

**reserve price** *n* *(Brit)* mise *f* à prix, prix *m* de départ

r

**reserve team** n (*Brit Sport*) deuxième équipe f
**reservist** [rɪˈzəːvɪst] n (*Mil*) réserviste m
**reservoir** [ˈrɛzəvwɑːʳ] n réservoir m
**reset** [riːˈsɛt] vt (*irreg: like* **set**) remettre; (*clock, watch*) mettre à l'heure; (*Comput*) remettre à zéro
**reshape** [riːˈʃeɪp] vt (*policy*) réorganiser
**reshuffle** [riːˈʃʌfl] n: **Cabinet ~** (*Pol*) remaniement ministériel
**reside** [rɪˈzaɪd] vi résider
**residence** [ˈrɛzɪdəns] n résidence f; **to take up ~** s'installer; **in ~** (*queen etc*) en résidence; (*doctor*) résidant(e)
**residence permit** n (*Brit*) permis m de séjour
**resident** [ˈrɛzɪdənt] n (*of country*) résident(e); (*of area, house*) habitant(e); (*in hotel*) pensionnaire ▷ adj résidant(e)
**residential** [rɛzɪˈdɛnʃəl] adj de résidence; (*area*) résidentiel(le); (*course*) avec hébergement sur place
**residential school** n internat m
**residue** [ˈrɛzɪdjuː] n reste m; (*Chem, Physics*) résidu m
**resign** [rɪˈzaɪn] vt (*one's post*) se démettre de ▷ vi démissionner; **to ~ o.s. to** (*endure*) se résigner à
**resignation** [rɛzɪɡˈneɪʃən] n (*from post*) démission f; (*state of mind*) résignation f; **to tender one's ~** donner sa démission
**resigned** [rɪˈzaɪnd] adj résigné(e)
**resilience** [rɪˈzɪlɪəns] n (*of material*) élasticité f; (*of person*) ressort m
**resilient** [rɪˈzɪlɪənt] adj (*person*) qui réagit, qui a du ressort
**resin** [ˈrɛzɪn] n résine f
**resist** [rɪˈzɪst] vt résister à
**resistance** [rɪˈzɪstəns] n résistance f
**resistant** [rɪˈzɪstənt] adj: **~ (to)** résistant(e) (à)
**resit** vt [riːˈsɪt] (*Brit: pt, pp* **resat**) (*exam*) repasser ▷ n [ˈriːsɪt] deuxième session f (*d'un examen*)
**resolute** [ˈrɛzəluːt] adj résolu(e)
**resolution** [rɛzəˈluːʃən] n résolution f; **to make a ~** prendre une résolution
**resolve** [rɪˈzɔlv] n résolution f ▷ vt (*decide*): **to ~ to do** résoudre *or* décider de faire; (*problem*) résoudre
**resolved** [rɪˈzɔlvd] adj résolu(e)
**resonance** [ˈrɛzənəns] n résonance f
**resonant** [ˈrɛzənənt] adj résonnant(e)
**resort** [rɪˈzɔːt] n (*seaside town*) station f balnéaire; (*for skiing*) station de ski; (*recourse*) recours m ▷ vi: **to ~ to** avoir recours à; **in the last ~** en dernier ressort
**resound** [rɪˈzaund] vi: **to ~ (with)** retentir (de)
**resounding** [rɪˈzaundɪŋ] adj retentissant(e)
**resource** [rɪˈsɔːs] n ressource f; **resources** npl ressources; **natural ~s** ressources naturelles; **to leave sb to his** (*or* **her**) **own ~s** (*fig*) livrer qn à lui-même (*or* elle-même)
**resourceful** [rɪˈsɔːsful] adj ingénieux(-euse), débrouillard(e)
**resourcefulness** [rɪˈsɔːsfəlnɪs] n ressource f
**respect** [rɪsˈpɛkt] n respect m; (*point, detail*): **in**

**some ~s** à certains égards ▷ vt respecter; **respects** npl respects, hommages mpl; **to have** *or* **show ~ for sb/sth** respecter qn/qch; **out of ~ for** par respect pour; **with ~ to** en ce qui concerne; **in ~ of** sous le rapport de, quant à; **in this ~** sous ce rapport, à cet égard; **with due ~ I** ... malgré le respect que je vous dois, je ...
**respectability** [rɪspɛktəˈbɪlɪtɪ] n respectabilité f
**respectable** [rɪsˈpɛktəbl] adj respectable; (*quite good: result etc*) honorable; (*player*) assez bon (bonne)
**respectful** [rɪsˈpɛktful] adj respectueux(-euse)
**respective** [rɪsˈpɛktɪv] adj respectif(-ive)
**respectively** [rɪsˈpɛktɪvlɪ] adv respectivement
**respiration** [rɛspɪˈreɪʃən] n respiration f
**respirator** [ˈrɛspɪreɪtəʳ] n respirateur m
**respiratory** [ˈrɛspərətərɪ] adj respiratoire
**respite** [ˈrɛspaɪt] n répit m
**resplendent** [rɪsˈplɛndənt] adj resplendissant(e)
**respond** [rɪsˈpɔnd] vi répondre; (*react*) réagir
**respondent** [rɪsˈpɔndənt] n (*Law*) défendeur(-deresse)
**response** [rɪsˈpɔns] n réponse f; (*reaction*) réaction f; **in ~ to** en réponse à
**responsibility** [rɪspɔnsɪˈbɪlɪtɪ] n responsabilité f; **to take ~ for sth/sb** accepter la responsabilité de qch/d'être responsable de qn
**responsible** [rɪsˈpɔnsɪbl] adj (*liable*): **~ (for)** responsable (de); (*person*) digne de confiance; (*job*) qui comporte des responsabilités; **to be ~ to sb (for sth)** être responsable devant qn (de qch)
**responsibly** [rɪsˈpɔnsɪblɪ] adv avec sérieux
**responsive** [rɪsˈpɔnsɪv] adj (*student, audience*) réceptif(-ive); (*brakes, steering*) sensible
**rest** [rɛst] n repos m; (*stop*) arrêt m, pause f; (*Mus*) silence m; (*support*) support m, appui m; (*remainder*) reste m, restant m ▷ vi se reposer; (*be supported*): **to ~ on** appuyer *or* reposer sur; (*remain*) rester ▷ vt (*lean*): **to ~ sth on/against** appuyer qch sur/contre; **the ~ of them** les autres; **to set sb's mind at ~** tranquilliser qn; **it ~s with him to** c'est à lui de; **~ assured that** ... soyez assuré que ...
**restart** [riːˈstɑːt] vt (*engine*) remettre en marche; (*work*) reprendre
**restaurant** [ˈrɛstərɔŋ] n restaurant m
**restaurant car** n (*Brit Rail*) wagon-restaurant m
**rest cure** n cure f de repos
**restful** [ˈrɛstful] adj reposant(e)
**rest home** n maison f de repos
**restitution** [rɛstɪˈtjuːʃən] n (*act*) restitution f; (*reparation*) réparation f
**restive** [ˈrɛstɪv] adj agité(e), impatient(e); (*horse*) rétif(-ive)
**restless** [ˈrɛstlɪs] adj agité(e); **to get ~** s'impatienter
**restlessly** [ˈrɛstlɪslɪ] adv avec agitation
**restock** [riːˈstɔk] vt réapprovisionner
**restoration** [rɛstəˈreɪʃən] n (*of building*) restauration f; (*of stolen goods*) restitution f

**restorative** [rɪ'stɔrətɪv] *adj* reconstituant(e) ▷ *n* reconstituant *m*

**restore** [rɪ'stɔːʳ] *vt* (*building*) restaurer; (*sth stolen*) restituer; (*peace, health*) rétablir; **to ~ to** (*former state*) ramener à

**restorer** [rɪ'stɔːrəʳ] *n* (*Art etc*) restaurateur(-trice) (d'œuvres d'art)

**restrain** [rɪs'treɪn] *vt* (*feeling*) contenir; (*person*): **to ~ (from doing)** retenir (de faire)

**restrained** [rɪs'treɪnd] *adj* (*style*) sobre; (*manner*) mesuré(e)

**restraint** [rɪs'treɪnt] *n* (*restriction*) contrainte *f*; (*moderation*) retenue *f*; (*of style*) sobriété *f*; **wage ~** limitations salariales

**restrict** [rɪs'trɪkt] *vt* restreindre, limiter

**restricted area** [rɪs'trɪktɪd-] *n* (*Aut*) zone *f* à vitesse limitée

**restriction** [rɪs'trɪkʃən] *n* restriction *f*, limitation *f*

**restrictive** [rɪs'trɪktɪv] *adj* restrictif(-ive)

**restrictive practices** *npl* (*Industry*) pratiques *fpl* entravant la libre concurrence

**rest room** *n* (*US*) toilettes *fpl*

**restructure** [riː'strʌktʃəʳ] *vt* restructurer

**result** [rɪ'zʌlt] *n* résultat *m* ▷ *vi*: **to ~ (from)** résulter (de); **to ~ in** aboutir à, se terminer par; **as a ~ it is too expensive** il en résulte que c'est trop cher; **as a ~ of** à la suite de

**resultant** [rɪ'zʌltənt] *adj* résultant(e)

**resume** [rɪ'zjuːm] *vt* (*work, journey*) reprendre; (*sum up*) résumer ▷ *vi* (*work etc*) reprendre

**résumé** ['reɪzjuːmeɪ] *n* (*summary*) résumé *m*; (*US: curriculum vitae*) curriculum vitae *m inv*

**resumption** [rɪ'zʌmpʃən] *n* reprise *f*

**resurgence** [rɪ'səːdʒəns] *n* réapparition *f*

**resurrection** [rɛzə'rɛkʃən] *n* résurrection *f*

**resuscitate** [rɪ'sʌsɪteɪt] *vt* (*Med*) réanimer

**resuscitation** [rɪsʌsɪ'teɪʃən] *n* réanimation *f*

**retail** ['riːteɪl] *n* (*vente f au*) détail *m* ▷ *adj* de or au détail ▷ *adv* au détail ▷ *vt* vendre au détail ▷ *vi*: **to ~ at 10 euros** se vendre au détail à 10 euros

**retailer** ['riːteɪləʳ] *n* détaillant(e)

**retail outlet** *n* point *m* de vente

**retail price** *n* prix *m* de détail

**retail price index** *n* ≈ indice *m* des prix

**retain** [rɪ'teɪn] *vt* (*keep*) garder, conserver; (*employ*) engager

**retainer** [rɪ'teɪnəʳ] *n* (*servant*) serviteur *m*; (*fee*) acompte *m*, provision *f*

**retaliate** [rɪ'tælɪeɪt] *vi*: **to ~ (against)** se venger (de); **to ~ (on sb)** rendre la pareille (à qn)

**retaliation** [rɪtælɪ'eɪʃən] *n* représailles *fpl*, vengeance *f*; **in ~ for** par représailles pour

**retaliatory** [rɪ'tælɪətərɪ] *adj* de représailles

**retarded** [rɪ'tɑːdɪd] *adj* retardé(e)

**retch** [rɛtʃ] *vi* avoir des haut-le-cœur

**retentive** [rɪ'tɛntɪv] *adj*: **~ memory** excellente mémoire

**rethink** ['riː'θɪŋk] *vt* repenser

**reticence** ['rɛtɪsns] *n* réticence *f*

**reticent** ['rɛtɪsnt] *adj* réticent(e)

**retina** ['rɛtɪnə] *n* rétine *f*

**retinue** ['rɛtɪnjuː] *n* suite *f*, cortège *m*

**retire** [rɪ'taɪəʳ] *vi* (*give up work*) prendre sa retraite; (*withdraw*) se retirer, partir; (*go to bed*) (aller) se coucher

**retired** [rɪ'taɪəd] *adj* (*person*) retraité(e)

**retirement** [rɪ'taɪəmənt] *n* retraite *f*

**retirement age** *n* âge *m* de la retraite

**retiring** [rɪ'taɪərɪŋ] *adj* (*person*) réservé(e); (*chairman etc*) sortant(e)

**retort** [rɪ'tɔːt] *n* (*reply*) riposte *f*; (*container*) cornue *f* ▷ *vi* riposter

**retrace** [riː'treɪs] *vt* reconstituer; **to ~ one's steps** revenir sur ses pas

**retract** [rɪ'trækt] *vt* (*statement, claws*) rétracter; (*undercarriage, aerial*) rentrer, escamoter ▷ *vi* se rétracter; rentrer

**retractable** [rɪ'træktəbl] *adj* escamotable

**retrain** [riː'treɪn] *vt* recycler ▷ *vi* se recycler

**retraining** [riː'treɪnɪŋ] *n* recyclage *m*

**retread** *vt* [riː'trɛd] (*Aut: tyre*) rechaper ▷ *n* ['riːtrɛd] pneu rechapé

**retreat** [rɪ'triːt] *n* retraite *f* ▷ *vi* battre en retraite; (*flood*) reculer; **to beat a hasty ~** (*fig*) partir avec précipitation

**retrial** [riː'traɪəl] *n* nouveau procès

**retribution** [rɛtrɪ'bjuːʃən] *n* châtiment *m*

**retrieval** [rɪ'triːvəl] *n* récupération *f*; réparation *f*; recherche *f* et extraction *f*

**retrieve** [rɪ'triːv] *vt* (*sth lost*) récupérer; (*situation, honour*) sauver; (*error, loss*) réparer; (*Comput*) rechercher

**retriever** [rɪ'triːvəʳ] *n* chien *m* d'arrêt

**retroactive** [rɛtrəu'æktɪv] *adj* rétroactif(-ive)

**retrograde** ['rɛtrəgreɪd] *adj* rétrograde

**retrospect** ['rɛtrəspɛkt] *n*: **in ~** rétrospectivement, après coup

**retrospective** [rɛtrə'spɛktɪv] *adj* rétrospectif(-ive); (*law*) rétroactif(-ive) ▷ *n* (*Art*) rétrospective *f*

**return** [rɪ'təːn] *n* (*going or coming back*) retour *m*; (*of sth stolen etc*) restitution *f*; (*recompense*) récompense *f*; (*Finance: from land, shares*) rapport *m*; (*report*) relevé *m*, rapport ▷ *cpd* (*journey*) de retour; (*Brit: ticket*) aller et retour; (*match*) retour ▷ *vi* (*person etc: come back*) revenir; (: *go back*) retourner ▷ *vt* rendre; (*bring back*) rapporter; (*send back*) renvoyer; (*put back*) remettre; (*Pol: candidate*) élire; **returns** *npl* (*Comm*) recettes *fpl*; (*Finance*) bénéfices *mpl*; (: *returned goods*) marchandises renvoyées; **many happy ~s (of the day)!** bon anniversaire!; **by ~ (of post)** par retour (du courrier); **in ~ (for)** en échange (de); **a ~ (ticket) for …** un billet aller et retour pour …

**returnable** [rɪ'təːnəbl] *adj* (*bottle etc*) consigné(e)

**returner** [rɪ'təːnəʳ] *n* femme qui reprend un travail après avoir élevé ses enfants

**returning officer** [rɪ'təːnɪŋ-] *n* (*Brit Pol*) président *m* de bureau de vote

**return key** *n* (*Comput*) touche *f* de retour

**return ticket** *n* (*esp Brit*) billet *m* aller-retour

**reunion** [riːˈjuːnɪən] n réunion f
**reunite** [riːjuːˈnaɪt] vt réunir
**reuse** [riːˈjuːz] vt réutiliser
**rev** [rɛv] n abbr = **revolution**; (Aut) tour m ▷ vt (also: **rev up**) emballer ▷ vi (also: **rev up**) s'emballer
**Rev.** abbr = **reverend**
**revaluation** [riːvæljuˈeɪʃən] n réévaluation f
**revamp** [riːˈvæmp] vt (house) retaper; (firm) réorganiser
**rev counter** n (Brit) compte-tours m inv
**Revd.** abbr = **reverend**
**reveal** [rɪˈviːl] vt (make known) révéler; (display) laisser voir
**revealing** [rɪˈviːlɪŋ] adj révélateur(-trice); (dress) au décolleté généreux or suggestif
**reveille** [rɪˈvælɪ] n (Mil) réveil m
**revel** [ˈrɛvl] vi: **to ~ in sth/in doing** se délecter de qch/à faire
**revelation** [rɛvəˈleɪʃən] n révélation f
**reveller** [ˈrɛvləʳ] n fêtard m
**revelry** [ˈrɛvlrɪ] n festivités fpl
**revenge** [rɪˈvɛndʒ] n vengeance f; (in game etc) revanche f ▷ vt venger; **to take ~ (on)** se venger (sur)
**revengeful** [rɪˈvɛndʒful] adj vengeur(-eresse), vindicatif(-ive)
**revenue** [ˈrɛvənjuː] n revenu m
**reverberate** [rɪˈvəːbəreɪt] vi (sound) retentir, se répercuter; (light) se réverbérer
**reverberation** [rɪvəːbəˈreɪʃən] n répercussion f; réverbération f
**revere** [rɪˈvɪəʳ] vt vénérer, révérer
**reverence** [ˈrɛvərəns] n vénération f, révérence f
**Reverend** [ˈrɛvərənd] adj vénérable; (in titles): **the ~ John Smith** (Anglican) le révérend John Smith; (Catholic) l'abbé (John) Smith; (Protestant) le pasteur (John) Smith
**reverent** [ˈrɛvərənt] adj respectueux(-euse)
**reverie** [ˈrɛvərɪ] n rêverie f
**reversal** [rɪˈvəːsl] n (of opinion) revirement m; (of order) renversement m; (of direction) changement m
**reverse** [rɪˈvəːs] n contraire m, opposé m; (back) dos m, envers m; (of paper) verso m; (of coin) revers m; (Aut: also: **reverse gear**) marche f arrière ▷ adj (order, direction) opposé(e), inverse ▷ vt (order, position) changer, inverser; (direction, policy) changer complètement de; (decision) annuler; (roles) renverser; (car) faire marche arrière avec; (Law: judgment) réformer ▷ vi (Brit Aut) faire marche arrière; **to go into ~** faire marche arrière; **in ~ order** en ordre inverse
**reverse video** n vidéo m inverse
**reversible** [rɪˈvəːsəbl] adj (garment) réversible; (procedure) révocable
**reversing lights** [rɪˈvəːsɪŋ-] npl (Brit Aut) feux mpl de marche arrière or de recul
**reversion** [rɪˈvəːʃən] n retour m
**revert** [rɪˈvəːt] vi: **to ~ to** revenir à, retourner à
**review** [rɪˈvjuː] n revue f; (of book, film) critique f; (of situation, policy) examen m, bilan m; (US:

examination) examen ▷ vt passer en revue; faire la critique de; examiner; **to come under ~** être révisé(e)
**reviewer** [rɪˈvjuːəʳ] n critique m
**revile** [rɪˈvaɪl] vt injurier
**revise** [rɪˈvaɪz] vt réviser, modifier; (manuscript) revoir, corriger ▷ vi (study) réviser; **~d edition** édition revue et corrigée
**revision** [rɪˈvɪʒən] n révision f; (revised version) version corrigée
**revitalize** [riːˈvaɪtəlaɪz] vt revitaliser
**revival** [rɪˈvaɪvəl] n reprise f; (recovery) rétablissement m; (of faith) renouveau m
**revive** [rɪˈvaɪv] vt (person) ranimer; (custom) rétablir; (economy) relancer; (hope, courage) raviver, faire renaître; (play, fashion) reprendre ▷ vi (person) reprendre connaissance; (: from ill health) se rétablir; (hope etc) renaître; (activity) reprendre
**revoke** [rɪˈvəuk] vt révoquer; (promise, decision) revenir sur
**revolt** [rɪˈvəult] n révolte f ▷ vi se révolter, se rebeller ▷ vt révolter, dégoûter
**revolting** [rɪˈvəultɪŋ] adj dégoûtant(e)
**revolution** [rɛvəˈluːʃən] n révolution f; (of wheel etc) tour m, révolution
**revolutionary** [rɛvəˈluːʃənrɪ] adj, n révolutionnaire (m/f)
**revolutionize** [rɛvəˈluːʃənaɪz] vt révolutionner
**revolve** [rɪˈvɔlv] vi tourner
**revolver** [rɪˈvɔlvəʳ] n revolver m
**revolving** [rɪˈvɔlvɪŋ] adj (chair) pivotant(e); (light) tournant(e)
**revolving door** n (porte f à) tambour m
**revue** [rɪˈvjuː] n (Theat) revue f
**revulsion** [rɪˈvʌlʃən] n dégoût m, répugnance f
**reward** [rɪˈwɔːd] n récompense f ▷ vt: **to ~ (for)** récompenser (de)
**rewarding** [rɪˈwɔːdɪŋ] adj (fig) qui (en) vaut la peine, gratifiant(e); **financially ~** financièrement intéressant(e)
**rewind** [riːˈwaɪnd] vt (irreg: like **wind**); (watch) remonter; (tape) réembobiner
**rewire** [riːˈwaɪəʳ] vt (house) refaire l'installation électrique de
**reword** [riːˈwəːd] vt formuler or exprimer différemment
**rewritable** [riːˈraɪtəbl] adj (CD, DVD) réinscriptible
**rewrite** [riːˈraɪt] (pt **rewrote**, pp **rewritten**) vt récrire
**Reykjavik** [ˈreɪkjəviːk] n Reykjavik
**RFD** abbr (US Post) = **rural free delivery**
**Rh** abbr (= rhesus) Rh
**rhapsody** [ˈræpsədɪ] n (Mus) rhapsodie f; (fig) éloge délirant
**rhesus negative** [ˈriːsəs-] adj (Med) de rhésus négatif
**rhesus positive** [ˈriːsəs-] adj (Med) de rhésus positif
**rhetoric** [ˈrɛtərɪk] n rhétorique f
**rhetorical** [rɪˈtɔrɪkl] adj rhétorique

**rheumatic** [ruːˈmætɪk] *adj* rhumatismal(e)
**rheumatism** [ˈruːmətɪzəm] *n* rhumatisme *m*
**rheumatoid arthritis** [ˈruːmətɔɪd-] *n*
polyarthrite *f* chronique
**Rhine** [raɪn] *n*: **the (River)** ~ le Rhin
**rhinestone** [ˈraɪnstəun] *n* faux diamant
**rhinoceros** [raɪˈnɔsərəs] *n* rhinocéros *m*
**Rhodes** [rəudz] *n* Rhodes *f*
**Rhodesia** [rəuˈdiːʒə] *n* Rhodésie *f*
**Rhodesian** [rəuˈdiːʒən] *adj* rhodésien(ne) ▷ *n*
Rhodésien(ne)
**rhododendron** [rəudəˈdɛndrn] *n*
rhododendron *m*
**rhubarb** [ˈruːbɑːb] *n* rhubarbe *f*
**rhyme** [raɪm] *n* rime *f*; (*verse*) vers *mpl* ▷ *vi*: to ~
**(with)** rimer (avec); **without ~ or reason** sans
rime ni raison
**rhythm** [ˈrɪðm] *n* rythme *m*
**rhythmic** [ˈrɪðmɪk], **rhythmical** [ˈrɪðmɪkl] *adj*
rythmique
**rhythmically** [ˈrɪðmɪklɪ] *adv* avec rythme
**rhythm method** *n* méthode *f* des températures
**RI** *n abbr* (*Brit*) = **religious instruction** ▷ *abbr* (*US*)
= **Rhode Island**
**rib** [rɪb] *n* (*Anat*) côte *f* ▷ *vt* (*mock*) taquiner
**ribald** [ˈrɪbəld] *adj* paillard(e)
**ribbed** [rɪbd] *adj* (*knitting*) à côtes; (*shell*) strié(e)
**ribbon** [ˈrɪbən] *n* ruban *m*; **in ~s** (*torn*) en
lambeaux
**rice** [raɪs] *n* riz *m*
**rice field** [ˈraɪsfiːld] *n* rizière *f*
**rice pudding** *n* riz *m* au lait
**rich** [rɪtʃ] *adj* riche; (*gift, clothes*)
somptueux(-euse); **the ~** (*npl*) les riches *mpl*;
**riches** *npl* richesses *fpl*; **to be ~ in sth** être riche
en qch
**richly** [ˈrɪtʃlɪ] *adv* richement; (*deserved, earned*)
largement, grandement
**rickets** [ˈrɪkɪts] *n* rachitisme *m*
**rickety** [ˈrɪkɪtɪ] *adj* branlant(e)
**rickshaw** [ˈrɪkʃɔː] *n* pousse(-pousse) *m inv*
**ricochet** [ˈrɪkəʃeɪ] *n* ricochet *m* ▷ *vi* ricocher
**rid** [rɪd] (*pt, pp* ~) *vt*: **to ~ sb of** débarrasser qn de;
**to get ~ of** se débarrasser de
**riddance** [ˈrɪdns] *n*: **good ~!** bon débarras!
**ridden** [ˈrɪdn] *pp of* **ride**
**riddle** [ˈrɪdl] *n* (*puzzle*) énigme *f* ▷ *vt*: **to be ~d
with** être criblé(e) de; (*fig*) être en proie à
**ride** [raɪd] (*pt* **rode**, *pp* **ridden**) [rəud, ˈrɪdn] *n*
promenade *f*, tour *m*; (*distance covered*) trajet *m*
▷ *vi* (*as sport*) monter (à cheval), faire du cheval;
(*go somewhere: on horse, bicycle*) aller (à cheval *or*
bicyclette *etc*); (*travel: on bicycle, motor cycle, bus*)
rouler ▷ *vt* (*a horse*) monter; (*distance*) parcourir,
faire; **we rode all day/all the way** nous
sommes restés toute la journée en selle/avons
fait tout le chemin en selle *or* à cheval; **to ~ a
horse/bicycle** monter à cheval/à bicyclette;
**can you ~ a bike?** est-ce que tu sais monter à
bicyclette?; **to ~ at anchor** (*Naut*) être à l'ancre;
**horse/car ~** promenade *or* tour à cheval/en
voiture; **to go for a ~** faire une promenade (en

voiture *or* à bicyclette *etc*); **to take sb for a ~** (*fig*)
faire marcher qn; (*cheat*) rouler qn
▶ **ride out** *vt*: **to ~ out the storm** (*fig*)
surmonter les difficultés
**rider** [ˈraɪdə²] *n* cavalier(-ière); (*in race*) jockey *m*;
(*on bicycle*) cycliste *m/f*; (*on motorcycle*)
motocycliste *m/f*; (*in document*) annexe *f*, clause
additionnelle
**ridge** [rɪdʒ] *n* (*of hill*) faîte *m*; (*of roof, mountain*)
arête *f*; (*on object*) strie *f*
**ridicule** [ˈrɪdɪkjuːl] *n* ridicule *m*; dérision *f* ▷ *vt*
ridiculiser, tourner en dérision; **to hold sb/sth
up to ~** tourner qn/qch en ridicule
**ridiculous** [rɪˈdɪkjuləs] *adj* ridicule
**riding** [ˈraɪdɪŋ] *n* équitation *f*
**riding school** *n* manège *m*, école *f* d'équitation
**rife** [raɪf] *adj* répandu(e); **~ with** abondant(e) en
**riffraff** [ˈrɪfræf] *n* racaille *f*
**rifle** [ˈraɪfl] *n* fusil *m* (à canon rayé) ▷ *vt* vider,
dévaliser
▶ **rifle through** *vt fus* fouiller dans
**rifle range** *n* champ *m* de tir; (*indoor*) stand *m* de
tir
**rift** [rɪft] *n* fente *f*, fissure *f*; (*fig: disagreement*)
désaccord *m*
**rig** [rɪg] *n* (*also*: **oil rig**: *on land*) derrick *m*; (*: at sea*)
plate-forme pétrolière ▷ *vt* (*election etc*) truquer
▶ **rig out** *vt* (*Brit*) habiller; (*: pej*) fringuer, attifer
▶ **rig up** *vt* arranger, faire avec des moyens de
fortune
**rigging** [ˈrɪgɪŋ] *n* (*Naut*) gréement *m*
**right** [raɪt] *adj* (*true*) vrai, exact(e); (*correct*) bon
(bonne); (*suitable*) approprié(e), convenable;
(*just*) juste, équitable; (*morally good*) bien *inv*; (*not
left*) droit(e) ▷ *n* (*moral good*) bien *m*; (*title, claim*)
droit *m*; (*not left*) droite *f* ▷ *adv* (*answer*)
correctement; (*treat*) bien, comme il faut; (*not
on the left*) à droite ▷ *vt* redresser ▷ *excl* bon!;
**rights** *npl* (*Comm*) droits *mpl*; **the ~ time** (*precise*)
l'heure exacte; (*not wrong*) la bonne heure; **do
you have the ~ time?** avez-vous l'heure juste *or*
exacte?; **to be ~** (*person*) avoir raison; (*answer*)
être juste *or* correct(e); **to get sth ~** ne pas se
tromper sur qch; **let's get it ~ this time!**
essayons de ne pas nous tromper cette fois-ci!;
**you did the ~ thing** vous avez bien fait; **to put
a mistake ~** (*Brit*) rectifier une erreur; **by ~s** en
toute justice; **on the ~** à droite; **~ and wrong** le
bien et le mal; **to be in the ~** avoir raison; **film
~s** droits d'adaptation cinématographique; **~
now** en ce moment même; (*immediately*) tout de
suite; **~ before/after** juste avant/après; **~
against the wall** tout contre le mur; **~ ahead**
tout droit; droit devant; **~ in the middle** en
plein milieu; **~ away** immédiatement; **to go ~
to the end of sth** aller jusqu'au bout de qch
**right angle** *n* (*Math*) angle droit
**righteous** [ˈraɪtʃəs] *adj* droit(e), vertueux(-euse);
(*anger*) justifié(e)
**righteousness** [ˈraɪtʃəsnɪs] *n* droiture *f*, vertu *f*
**rightful** [ˈraɪtful] *adj* (*heir*) légitime
**rightfully** [ˈraɪtfəlɪ] *adv* à juste titre,

r

légitimement

**right-hand** ['raɪthænd] *adj:* **the ~ side** la droite

**right-hand drive** *n* (*Brit*) conduite *f* à droite; (*vehicle*) véhicule *m* avec la conduite à droite

**right-handed** [raɪt'hændɪd] *adj* (*person*) droitier(-ière)

**right-hand man** ['raɪthænd-] (*irreg*) *n* bras droit *m* (*fig*)

**rightly** ['raɪtlɪ] *adv* bien, correctement; (*with reason*) à juste titre; **if I remember ~** (*Brit*) si je me souviens bien

**right-minded** ['raɪt'maɪndɪd] *adj* sensé(e), sain(e) d'esprit

**right of way** *n* (*on path etc*) droit *m* de passage; (*Aut*) priorité *f*

**rights issue** *n* (*Stock Exchange*) émission préférentielle *or* de droit de souscription

**right wing** *n* (*Mil, Sport*) aile droite; (*Pol*) droite *f*

**right-wing** [raɪt'wɪŋ] *adj* (*Pol*) de droite

**right-winger** [raɪt'wɪŋər] *n* (*Pol*) membre *m* de la droite; (*Sport*) ailier droit

**rigid** ['rɪdʒɪd] *adj* rigide; (*principle, control*) strict(e)

**rigidity** [rɪ'dʒɪdɪtɪ] *n* rigidité *f*

**rigidly** ['rɪdʒɪdlɪ] *adv* rigidement; (*behave*) inflexiblement

**rigmarole** ['rɪgmərəul] *n* galimatias *m*, comédie *f*

**rigor** ['rɪgər] *n* (*US*) = **rigour**

**rigor mortis** ['rɪgə'mɔ:tɪs] *n* rigidité *f* cadavérique

**rigorous** ['rɪgərəs] *adj* rigoureux(-euse)

**rigorously** ['rɪgərəslɪ] *adv* rigoureusement

**rigour,** (*US*) **rigor** ['rɪgər] *n* rigueur *f*

**rig-out** ['rɪgaut] *n* (*Brit inf*) tenue *f*

**rile** [raɪl] *vt* agacer

**rim** [rɪm] *n* bord *m*; (*of spectacles*) monture *f*; (*of wheel*) jante *f*

**rimless** ['rɪmlɪs] *adj* (*spectacles*) à monture invisible

**rind** [raɪnd] *n* (*of bacon*) couenne *f*; (*of lemon etc*) écorce *f*, zeste *m*; (*of cheese*) croûte *f*

**ring** [rɪŋ] (*pt* **rang**, *pp* **rung**) [ræŋ, rʌŋ] *n* anneau *m*; (*on finger*) bague *f*; (*also:* **wedding ring**) alliance *f*; (*for napkin*) rond *m*; (*of people, objects*) cercle *m*; (*of spies*) réseau *m*; (*of smoke etc*) rond *m*; (*arena*) piste *f*, arène *f*; (*for boxing*) ring *m*; (*sound of bell*) sonnerie *f*; (*telephone call*) coup *m* de téléphone ▷ *vi* (*telephone, bell*) sonner; (*person: by telephone*) téléphoner; (*ears*) bourdonner; (*also:* **ring out**: *voice, words*) retentir ▷ *vt* (*Brit Tel: also:* **ring up**) téléphoner à, appeler; **to ~ the bell** sonner; **to give sb a ~** (*Tel*) passer un coup de téléphone *or* de fil à qn; **that has the ~ of truth about it** cela sonne vrai; **the name doesn't ~ a bell (with me)** ce nom ne me dit rien

▶ **ring back** *vt, vi* (*Brit Tel*) rappeler

▶ **ring off** *vi* (*Brit Tel*) raccrocher

▶ **ring up** (*Brit*) *vt* (*Tel*) téléphoner à, appeler

**ring binder** *n* classeur *m* à anneaux

**ring finger** *n* annulaire *m*

**ringing** ['rɪŋɪŋ] *n* (*of bell*) tintement *m*; (*louder: also:* **of telephone**) sonnerie *f*; (*in ears*)

bourdonnement *m*

**ringing tone** *n* (*Brit Tel*) tonalité *f* d'appel

**ringleader** ['rɪŋli:dər] *n* (*of gang*) chef *m*, meneur *m*

**ringlets** ['rɪŋlɪts] *npl* anglaises *fpl*

**ring road** *n* (*Brit*) rocade *f*; (*motorway*) périphérique *m*

**ring tone** ['rɪŋtəun] *n* (*on mobile*) sonnerie *f* (*de téléphone portable*)

**rink** [rɪŋk] *n* (*also:* **ice rink**) patinoire *f*; (*for roller-skating*) skating *m*

**rinse** [rɪns] *n* rinçage *m* ▷ *vt* rincer

**Rio** ['ri:əu], **Rio de Janeiro** ['ri:əudədʒə'nɪərəu] *n* Rio de Janeiro

**riot** ['raɪət] *n* émeute *f*, bagarres *fpl* ▷ *vi* (*demonstrators*) manifester avec violence; (*population*) se soulever, se révolter; **a ~ of colours** une débauche *or* orgie de couleurs; **to run ~** se déchaîner

**rioter** ['raɪətər] *n* émeutier(-ière), manifestant(e)

**riot gear** *n:* **in ~** casqué et portant un bouclier

**riotous** ['raɪətəs] *adj* tapageur(-euse); tordant(e)

**riotously** ['raɪətəslɪ] *adv:* **~ funny** tordant(e)

**riot police** *n* forces *fpl* de police intervenant en cas d'émeute; **hundreds of ~** des centaines de policiers casqués et armés

**RIP** *abbr* (= *rest in peace*) RIP

**rip** [rɪp] *n* déchirure *f* ▷ *vt* déchirer ▷ *vi* se déchirer

▶ **rip off** *vt* (*inf: cheat*) arnaquer

▶ **rip up** *vt* déchirer

**ripcord** ['rɪpkɔ:d] *n* poignée *f* d'ouverture

**ripe** [raɪp] *adj* (*fruit*) mûr(e); (*cheese*) fait(e)

**ripen** ['raɪpn] *vt* mûrir ▷ *vi* mûrir; se faire

**ripeness** ['raɪpnɪs] *n* maturité *f*

**rip-off** ['rɪpɔf] *n* (*inf*): **it's a ~!** c'est du vol manifeste!, c'est de l'arnaque!

**riposte** [rɪ'pɔst] *n* riposte *f*

**ripple** ['rɪpl] *n* ride *f*, ondulation *f*; (*of applause, laughter*) cascade *f* ▷ *vi* se rider, onduler ▷ *vt* rider, faire onduler

**rise** [raɪz] *n* (*slope*) côte *f*, pente *f*; (*hill*) élévation *f*; (*increase: in wages: Brit*) augmentation *f*; (: *in prices, temperature*) hausse *f*, augmentation; (*fig: to power etc*) ascension *f* ▷ *vi* (*pt* **rose**, *pp* **-n**) [rəuz, rɪzn] s'élever, monter; (*prices, numbers*) augmenter, monter; (*waters, river*) monter; (*sun, wind, person: from chair, bed*) se lever; (*also:* **rise up**: *tower, building*) s'élever; (: *rebel*) se révolter, se rebeller; (*in rank*) s'élever; **~ to power** montée *f* au pouvoir; **to give ~ to** donner lieu à; **to ~ to the occasion** se montrer à la hauteur

**risen** ['rɪzn] *pp of* **rise**

**rising** ['raɪzɪŋ] *adj* (*increasing: number, prices*) en hausse; (*tide*) montant(e); (*sun, moon*) levant(e) ▷ *n* (*uprising*) soulèvement *m*, insurrection *f*

**rising damp** *n* humidité *f* (*montant des fondations*)

**rising star** *n* (*also fig*) étoile montante

**risk** [rɪsk] *n* risque *m*, danger *m*; (*deliberate*) risque ▷ *vt* risquer; **to take** *or* **run the ~ of**

**doing** courir le risque de faire; **at ~ en** danger; **at one's own ~** à ses risques et périls; **it's a fire/health ~** cela présente un risque d'incendie/pour la santé; **I'll ~ it** je vais risquer le coup

**risk capital** n capital-risque m

**risky** ['rɪskɪ] adj risqué(e)

**risqué** ['riːskeɪ] adj (joke) risqué(e)

**rissole** ['rɪsəʊl] n croquette f

**rite** [raɪt] n rite m; **the last ~s** les derniers sacrements

**ritual** ['rɪtjʊəl] adj rituel(le) ▷ n rituel m

**rival** ['raɪvl] n rival(e); (in business) concurrent(e) ▷ adj rival(e); qui fait concurrence ▷ vt (match) égaler; (compete with) être en concurrence avec; **to ~ sb/sth in** rivaliser avec qn/qch de

**rivalry** ['raɪvlrɪ] n rivalité f; (in business) concurrence f

**river** ['rɪvəʳ] n rivière f; (major: also fig) fleuve m ▷ cpd (port, traffic) fluvial(e); **up/down ~** en amont/aval

**riverbank** ['rɪvəbæŋk] n rive f, berge f

**riverbed** ['rɪvəbɛd] n lit m (de rivière or de fleuve)

**riverside** ['rɪvəsaɪd] n bord m de la rivière or du fleuve

**rivet** ['rɪvɪt] n rivet m ▷ vt riveter; (fig) river, fixer

**riveting** ['rɪvɪtɪŋ] adj (fig) fascinant(e)

**Riviera** [rɪvɪ'ɛərə] n: **the (French) ~** la Côte d'Azur; **the Italian ~** la Riviera (italienne)

**Riyadh** [rɪ'jɑːd] n Riyad

**RMT** n abbr (= Rail, Maritime and Transport) syndicat des transports

**RN** n abbr = **registered nurse**; (Brit) = **Royal Navy**

**RNA** n abbr (= ribonucleic acid) ARN m

**RNLI** n abbr (Brit: = Royal National Lifeboat Institution) ≈ SNSM f

**RNZAF** n abbr = **Royal New Zealand Air Force**

**RNZN** n abbr = **Royal New Zealand Navy**

**road** [rəʊd] n route f; (in town) rue f; (fig) chemin, voie f ▷ cpd (accident) de la route; **main ~** grande route; **major/minor ~** route principale or à priorité/voie secondaire; **it takes four hours by ~** il y a quatre heures de route; **which ~ do I take for ...?** quelle route dois-je prendre pour aller à ...?; **"~ up"** (Brit) "attention travaux"

**road accident** n accident m de la circulation

**roadblock** ['rəʊdblɔk] n barrage routier

**road haulage** n transports routiers

**roadhog** ['rəʊdhɔg] n chauffard m

**road map** n carte routière

**road rage** n comportement très agressif de certains usagers de la route

**road safety** n sécurité routière

**roadside** ['rəʊdsaɪd] n bord m de la route, bas-côté m ▷ cpd (situé(e) etc) au bord de la route; **by the ~** au bord de la route

**road sign** ['rəʊdsaɪn] n panneau m de signalisation

**road sweeper** ['rəʊdswiːpəʳ] n (Brit: person) balayeur(-euse)

**road tax** n (Brit Aut) taxe f sur les automobiles

**road user** n usager m de la route

**roadway** ['rəʊdweɪ] n chaussée f

**roadworks** ['rəʊdwəːks] npl travaux mpl (de réfection des routes)

**roadworthy** ['rəʊdwəːðɪ] adj en bon état de marche

**roam** [rəʊm] vi errer, vagabonder ▷ vt parcourir, errer par

**roar** [rɔːʳ] n rugissement m; (of crowd) hurlements mpl; (of vehicle, thunder, storm) grondement m ▷ vi rugir; hurler; gronder; **to ~ with laughter** rire à gorge déployée

**roaring** ['rɔːrɪŋ] adj: **a ~ fire** une belle flambée; **a ~ success** un succès fou; **to do a ~ trade** faire des affaires en or

**roast** [rəʊst] n rôti m ▷ vt (meat) (faire) rôtir; (coffee) griller, torréfier

**roast beef** n rôti m de bœuf, rosbif m

**roasting** ['rəʊstɪŋ] n (inf): **to give sb a ~** sonner les cloches à qn

**rob** [rɔb] vt (person) voler; (bank) dévaliser; **to ~ sb of sth** voler or dérober qch à qn; (fig: deprive) priver qn de qch

**robber** ['rɔbəʳ] n bandit m, voleur m

**robbery** ['rɔbərɪ] n vol m

**robe** [rəʊb] n (for ceremony etc) robe f; (also: **bathrobe**) peignoir m; (US: rug) couverture f ▷ vt revêtir (d'une robe)

**robin** ['rɔbɪn] n rouge-gorge m

**robot** ['rəʊbɔt] n robot m

**robotics** [rə'bɔtɪks] n robotique m

**robust** [rəʊ'bʌst] adj robuste; (material, appetite) solide

**rock** [rɔk] n (substance) roche f, roc m; (boulder) rocher m, roche; (US: small stone) caillou m; (Brit: sweet) ≈ sucre m d'orge ▷ vt (swing gently: cradle) balancer; (: child) bercer; (shake) ébranler, secouer ▷ vi se balancer, être ébranlé(e) or secoué(e); **on the ~s** (drink) avec des glaçons; (ship) sur les écueils; (marriage etc) en train de craquer; **to ~ the boat** (fig) jouer les trouble-fête

**rock and roll** n rock (and roll) m, rock'n'roll m

**rock-bottom** ['rɔk'bɔtəm] n (fig) niveau le plus bas ▷ adj (fig: prices) sacrifié(e); **to reach** or **touch ~** (price, person) tomber au plus bas

**rock climber** n varappeur(-euse)

**rock climbing** n varappe f

**rockery** ['rɔkərɪ] n (jardin m de) rocaille f

**rocket** ['rɔkɪt] n fusée f; (Mil) fusée, roquette f; (Culin) roquette ▷ vi (prices) monter en flèche

**rocket launcher** [-lɔːnʃə] n lance-roquettes m inv

**rock face** n paroi rocheuse

**rock fall** n chute f de pierres

**rocking chair** ['rɔkɪŋ-] n fauteuil m à bascule

**rocking horse** ['rɔkɪŋ-] n cheval m à bascule

**rocky** ['rɔkɪ] adj (hill) rocheux(-euse); (path) rocailleux(-euse); (unsteady: table) branlant(e)

**Rocky Mountains** npl: **the ~** les (montagnes fpl) Rocheuses fpl

**rod** [rɔd] n (metallic) tringle f; (Tech) tige f;

**r**

(wooden) baguette f; (also: **fishing rod**) canne f à pêche

**rode** [rəud] pt of **ride**

**rodent** ['rəudnt] n rongeur m

**rodeo** ['rəudɪəu] n rodéo m

**roe** [rəu] n (species: also: **roe deer**) chevreuil m; (of fish: also: **hard roe**) œufs mpl de poisson; **soft ~** laitance f

**roe deer** n chevreuil m; chevreuil femelle

**rogue** [rəug] n coquin(e)

**roguish** ['rəugɪʃ] adj coquin(e)

**role** [rəul] n rôle m

**role-model** ['rəulmɔdl] n modèle m à émuler

**role play**, **role playing** n jeu m de rôle

**roll** [rəul] n rouleau m; (of banknotes) liasse f; (also: **bread roll**) petit pain; (register) liste f; (sound: of drums etc) roulement m; (movement: of ship) roulis m ▷ vt rouler; (also: **roll up**: string) enrouler; (also: **roll out**: pastry) étendre au rouleau, abaisser ▷ vi rouler; (wheel) tourner; **cheese ~ ≈** sandwich m au fromage (dans un petit pain)

▶ **roll about**, **roll around** vi rouler çà et là; (person) se rouler par terre

▶ **roll by** vi (time) s'écouler, passer

▶ **roll in** vi (mail, cash) affluer

▶ **roll over** vi se retourner

▶ **roll up** vi (inf: arrive) arriver, s'amener ▷ vt (carpet, cloth, map) rouler; (sleeves) retrousser; **to ~ o.s. up into a ball** se rouler en boule

**roll call** n appel m

**roller** ['rəulə'] n rouleau m; (wheel) roulette f; (for road) rouleau compresseur; (for hair) bigoudi m

**Rollerblades**® ['rəulə'bleɪdz] npl patins mpl en ligne

**roller blind** n (Brit) store m

**roller coaster** n montagnes fpl russes

**roller skates** npl patins mpl à roulettes

**roller-skating** ['rəulə'skeɪtɪŋ] n patin m à roulettes; **to go ~** faire du patin à roulettes

**rollicking** ['rɔlɪkɪŋ] adj bruyant(e) et joyeux(-euse); (play) bouffon(ne); **to have a ~ time** s'amuser follement

**rolling** ['rəulɪŋ] adj (landscape) onduleux(-euse)

**rolling mill** n laminoir m

**rolling pin** n rouleau m à pâtisserie

**rolling stock** n (Rail) matériel roulant

**roll-on-roll-off** ['rəulɔn'rəulɔf] adj (Brit: ferry) roulier(-ière)

**roly-poly** ['rəulɪ'pəulɪ] n (Brit Culin) roulé m à la confiture

**ROM** [rɔm] n abbr (Comput: = read-only memory) mémoire morte, ROM f

**Roman** ['rəumən] adj romain(e) ▷ n Romain(e)

**Roman Catholic** adj, n catholique (m/f)

**romance** [rə'mæns] n (love affair) idylle f; (charm) poésie f; (novel) roman m à l'eau de rose

**Romanesque** [rəumə'nɛsk] adj roman(e)

**Romania** [rəu'meɪnɪə] = **Rumania**

**Romanian** [rəu'meɪnɪən] adj, n see **Rumanian**

**Roman numeral** n chiffre romain

**romantic** [rə'mæntɪk] adj romantique; (novel, attachment) sentimental(e)

**romanticism** [rə'mæntɪsɪzəm] n romantisme m

**Romany** ['rɔmənɪ] adj de bohémien ▷ n bohémien(ne); (Ling) romani m

**Rome** [rəum] n Rome

**romp** [rɔmp] n jeux bruyants ▷ vi (also: **romp about**) s'ébattre, jouer bruyamment; **to ~ home** (horse) arriver bon premier

**rompers** ['rɔmpəz] npl barboteuse f

**rondo** ['rɔndəu] n (Mus) rondeau m

**roof** [ru:f] n toit m; (of tunnel, cave) plafond m ▷ vt couvrir (d'un toit); **the ~ of the mouth** la voûte du palais

**roof garden** n toit-terrasse m

**roofing** ['ru:fɪŋ] n toiture f

**roof rack** n (Aut) galerie f

**rook** [ruk] n (bird) freux m; (Chess) tour f ▷ vt (inf: cheat) rouler, escroquer

**rookie** ['rukɪ] n (inf: esp Mil) bleu m

**room** [ru:m] n (in house) pièce f; (also: **bedroom**) chambre f (à coucher); (in school etc) salle f; (space) place f; **rooms** npl (lodging) meublé m; **"~s to let"**, (US) **"~s for rent"** "chambres à louer"; **is there ~ for this?** est-ce qu'il y a de la place pour ceci?; **to make ~ for sb** faire de la place à qn; **there is ~ for improvement** on peut faire mieux

**rooming house** ['ru:mɪŋ-] n (US) maison f de rapport

**roommate** ['ru:mmeɪt] n camarade m/f de chambre

**room service** n service m des chambres (dans un hôtel)

**room temperature** n température ambiante; **"serve at ~"** (wine) "servir chambré"

**roomy** ['ru:mɪ] adj spacieux(-euse); (garment) ample

**roost** [ru:st] n juchoir m ▷ vi se jucher

**rooster** ['ru:stə'] n coq m

**root** [ru:t] n (Bot, Math) racine f; (fig: of problem) origine f, fond m ▷ vi (plant) s'enraciner; **to take ~** (plant, idea) prendre racine

▶ **root about** vi (fig) fouiller

▶ **root for** vt fus (inf) applaudir

▶ **root out** vt extirper

**root beer** n (US) sorte de limonade à base d'extraits végétaux

**rope** [rəup] n corde f; (Naut) cordage m ▷ vt (box) corder; (tie up or together) attacher; (climbers: also: **rope together**) encorder; (area: also: **rope off**) interdire l'accès de; (: divide off) séparer; **to ~ sb in** (fig) embringuer qn; **to know the ~s** (fig) être au courant, connaître les ficelles

**rope ladder** n échelle f de corde

**ropey** ['rəupɪ] adj (inf) pas fameux(-euse) or brillant(e); **I feel a bit ~ today** c'est pas la forme aujourd'hui

**rosary** ['rəuzərɪ] n chapelet m

**rose** [rəuz] pt of **rise** ▷ n rose f; (also: **rosebush**) rosier m; (on watering can) pomme f ▷ adj rose

**rosé** ['rəuzeɪ] n rosé m

**rosebed** ['rəuzbɛd] n massif m de rosiers

**rosebud** ['rəuzbʌd] n bouton m de rose
**rosebush** ['rəuzbuʃ] n rosier m
**rosemary** ['rəuzmərɪ] n romarin m
**rosette** [rəu'zɛt] n rosette f; (larger) cocarde f
**ROSPA** ['rɒspə] n abbr (Brit) = **Royal Society for the Prevention of Accidents**
**roster** ['rɒstəʳ] n: **duty ~** tableau m de service
**rostrum** ['rɒstrəm] n tribune f (pour un orateur etc)
**rosy** ['rəuzɪ] adj rose; **a ~ future** un bel avenir
**rot** [rɒt] n (decay) pourriture f; (fig: pej: nonsense) idioties fpl, balivernes fpl ▷ vt, vi pourrir; **to stop the ~** (Brit fig) rétablir la situation; **dry ~** pourriture sèche (du bois); **wet ~** pourriture (du bois)
**rota** ['rəutə] n liste f, tableau m de service; **on a ~ basis** par roulement
**rotary** ['rəutərɪ] adj rotatif(-ive)
**rotate** [rəu'teɪt] vt (revolve) faire tourner; (change round: crops) alterner; (: jobs) faire à tour de rôle ▷ vi (revolve) tourner
**rotating** [rəu'teɪtɪŋ] adj (movement) tournant(e)
**rotation** [rəu'teɪʃən] n rotation f; **in ~** à tour de rôle
**rote** [rəut] n: **by ~** machinalement, par cœur
**rotor** ['rəutəʳ] n rotor m
**rotten** ['rɒtn] adj (decayed) pourri(e); (dishonest) corrompu(e); (inf: bad) mauvais(e), moche; **to feel ~** (ill) être mal fichu(e)
**rotting** ['rɒtɪŋ] adj pourrissant(e)
**rotund** [rəu'tʌnd] adj rondelet(te); arrondi(e)
**rouble,** (US) **ruble** ['ru:bl] n rouble m
**rouge** [ru:ʒ] n rouge m (à joues)
**rough** [rʌf] adj (cloth, skin) rêche, rugueux(-euse); (terrain) accidenté(e); (path) rocailleux(-euse); (voice) rauque, rude; (person, manner: coarse) rude, fruste; (: violent) brutal(e); (district, weather) mauvais(e); (sea) houleux(-euse); (plan) ébauché(e); (guess) approximatif(-ive) ▷ n (Golf) rough m ▷ vt: **to ~ it** vivre à la dure; **the sea is ~ today** la mer est agitée aujourd'hui; **to have a ~ time (of it)** en voir de dures; **~ estimate** approximation f; **to play ~** jouer avec brutalité; **to sleep ~** (Brit) coucher à la dure; **to feel ~** (Brit) être mal fichu(e)
▸ **rough out** vt (draft) ébaucher
**roughage** ['rʌfɪdʒ] n fibres fpl diététiques
**rough-and-ready** ['rʌfən'redɪ] adj (accommodation, method) rudimentaire
**rough-and-tumble** ['rʌfən'tʌmbl] n agitation f
**roughcast** ['rʌfkɑ:st] n crépi m
**rough copy, rough draft** n brouillon m
**roughen** ['rʌfn] vt (a surface) rendre rude or rugueux(-euse)
**rough justice** n justice f sommaire
**roughly** ['rʌflɪ] adv (handle) rudement, brutalement; (speak) avec brusquerie; (make) grossièrement; (approximately) à peu près, en gros; **~ speaking** en gros
**roughness** ['rʌfnɪs] n (of cloth, skin) rugosité f; (of person) rudesse f; brutalité f
**roughshod** ['rʌfʃɒd] adv: **to ride ~ over** ne tenir aucun compte de

**rough work** n (at school etc) brouillon m
**roulette** [ru:'lɛt] n roulette f
**Roumania** etc [ru:'meɪnɪə] = **Romania** etc
**round** [raund] adj rond(e) ▷ n rond m, cercle m; (Brit: of toast) tranche f; (duty: of policeman, milkman etc) tournée f; (: of doctor) visites fpl; (game: of cards, in competition) partie f; (Boxing) round m; (of talks) série f ▷ vt (corner) tourner; (bend) prendre; (cape) doubler ▷ prep autour de ▷ adv: **right ~, all ~** tout autour; **in ~ figures** en chiffres ronds; **to go the ~s** (disease, story) circuler; **the daily ~** (fig) la routine quotidienne; **~ of ammunition** cartouche f; **~ of applause** applaudissements mpl; **~ of drinks** tournée f; **~ of sandwiches** (Brit) sandwich m; **the long way ~** (par) le chemin le plus long; **all (the) year ~** toute l'année; **it's just ~ the corner** c'est juste après le coin; (fig) c'est tout près; **to ask sb ~** inviter qn (chez soi); **I'll be ~ at 6 o'clock** je serai là à 6 heures; **to go ~** faire le tour or un détour; **to go ~ to sb's (house)** aller chez qn; **to go ~ an obstacle** contourner un obstacle; **go ~ the back** passez par derrière; **to go ~ a house** visiter une maison, faire le tour d'une maison; **enough to go ~** assez pour tout le monde; **she arrived ~ (about) noon** (Brit) elle est arrivée vers midi; **~ the clock** 24 heures sur 24
▸ **round off** vt (speech etc) terminer
▸ **round up** vt rassembler; (criminals) effectuer une rafle de; (prices) arrondir (au chiffre supérieur)
**roundabout** ['raundəbaut] n (Brit Aut) rond-point m (à sens giratoire); (at fair) manège m (de chevaux de bois) ▷ adj (route, means) détourné(e)
**rounded** ['raundɪd] adj arrondi(e); (style) harmonieux(-euse)
**rounders** ['raundəz] npl (game) ≈ balle f au camp
**roundly** ['raundlɪ] adv (fig) tout net, carrément
**round-shouldered** ['raund'ʃəuldəd] adj au dos rond
**round trip** n (voyage m) aller et retour m
**roundup** ['raundʌp] n rassemblement m; (of criminals) rafle f; **a ~ of the latest news** un rappel des derniers événements
**rouse** [rauz] vt (wake up) réveiller; (stir up) susciter, provoquer; (interest) éveiller; (suspicions) susciter, éveiller
**rousing** ['rauzɪŋ] adj (welcome) enthousiaste
**rout** [raut] n (Mil) déroute f ▷ vt mettre en déroute
**route** [ru:t] n itinéraire m; (of bus) parcours m; (of trade, shipping) route f; **"all ~s"** (Aut) "toutes directions"; **the best ~ to London** le meilleur itinéraire pour aller à Londres
**route map** n (Brit: for journey) croquis m d'itinéraire; (for trains etc) carte f du réseau
**routine** [ru:'ti:n] adj (work) ordinaire, courant(e); (procedure) d'usage ▷ n (habits) habitudes fpl; (pej) train-train m; (Theat) numéro m; **daily ~** occupations journalières
**roving** ['rəuvɪŋ] adj (life) vagabond(e)
**roving reporter** n reporter volant

**r**

**row**[1] [rəu] n (line) rangée f; (of people, seats, Knitting) rang m; (behind one another: of cars, people) file f ▷ vi (in boat) ramer; (as sport) faire de l'aviron ▷ vt (boat) faire aller à la rame or à l'aviron; **in a ~** (fig) d'affilée

**row**[2] [rau] n (noise) vacarme m; (dispute) dispute f, querelle f; (scolding) réprimande f, savon m ▷ vi (also: **to have a row**) se disputer, se quereller

**rowboat** ['rəubəut] n (US) canot m (à rames)

**rowdiness** ['raudɪnɪs] n tapage m, chahut m; (fighting) bagarre f

**rowdy** ['raudɪ] adj chahuteur(-euse); bagarreur(-euse) ▷ n voyou m

**rowdyism** ['raudɪɪzəm] n tapage m, chahut m

**rowing** ['rəuɪŋ] n canotage m; (as sport) aviron m

**rowing boat** n (Brit) canot m (à rames)

**rowlock** ['rɔlək] n (Brit) dame f de nage, tolet m

**royal** ['rɔɪəl] adj royal(e)

**Royal Academy, Royal Academy of Arts** n (Brit) l'Académie f royale des Beaux-Arts; voir article

### ● ROYAL ACADEMY (OF ARTS)

● La Royal Academy ou Royal Academy of Arts,
● fondée en 1768 par George III pour
● encourager la peinture, la sculpture et
● l'architecture, est située à Burlington
● House, sur Piccadilly. Une exposition des
● œuvres d'artistes contemporains a lieu tous
● les étés. L'Académie dispense également des
● cours en peinture, sculpture et architecture.

**Royal Air Force** n (Brit) armée de l'air britannique

**royal blue** adj bleu roi inv

**royalist** ['rɔɪəlɪst] adj, n royaliste m/f

**Royal Navy** n (Brit) marine de guerre britannique

**royalty** ['rɔɪəltɪ] n (royal persons) (membres mpl de la) famille royale; (payment: to author) droits mpl d'auteur; (: to inventor) royalties fpl

**RP** n abbr (Brit: = received pronunciation) prononciation f standard

**RPI** n abbr = **retail price index**

**rpm** abbr (= revolutions per minute) t/mn (= = tours/minute)

**RR** abbr (US) = **railroad**

**RRP** abbr = **recommended retail price**

**RSA** n abbr (Brit) = **Royal Society of Arts; Royal Scottish Academy**

**RSI** n abbr (Med: = repetitive strain injury) microtraumatisme permanent

**RSPB** n abbr (Brit: = Royal Society for the Protection of Birds) ≈ LPO f

**RSPCA** n abbr (Brit: = Royal Society for the Prevention of Cruelty to Animals) ≈ SPA f

**R.S.V.P.** abbr (= répondez s'il vous plaît) RSVP

**RTA** n abbr (= road traffic accident) accident m de la route

**Rt. Hon.** abbr (Brit: = Right Honourable) titre donné aux députés de la Chambre des communes

**Rt Rev.** abbr (= Right Reverend) très révérend

**rub** [rʌb] n (with cloth) coup m de chiffon or de torchon; (on person) friction f; **to give sth a ~** donner un coup de chiffon or de torchon à qch ▷ vt frotter; (person) frictionner; (hands) se frotter; **to ~ sb up** (Brit) or **to ~ sb** (US) **the wrong way** prendre qn à rebrousse-poil

▶ **rub down** vt (body) frictionner; (horse) bouchonner

▶ **rub in** vt (ointment) faire pénétrer

▶ **rub off** vi partir; **to ~ off on** déteindre sur

▶ **rub out** vt effacer ▷ vi s'effacer

**rubber** ['rʌbə[r]] n caoutchouc m; (Brit: eraser) gomme f (à effacer)

**rubber band** n élastique m

**rubber bullet** n balle f en caoutchouc

**rubber gloves** npl gants mpl en caoutchouc

**rubber plant** n caoutchouc m (plante verte)

**rubber ring** n (for swimming) bouée f (de natation)

**rubber stamp** n tampon m

**rubber-stamp** [rʌbə'stæmp] vt (fig) approuver sans discussion

**rubbery** ['rʌbərɪ] adj caoutchouteux(-euse)

**rubbish** ['rʌbɪʃ] n (from household) ordures fpl; (fig: pej) choses fpl sans valeur; camelote f; (nonsense) bêtises fpl, idioties fpl ▷ vt (Brit inf) dénigrer, rabaisser; **what you've just said is ~** tu viens de dire une bêtise

**rubbish bin** n (Brit) boîte f à ordures, poubelle f

**rubbish dump** n (Brit: in town) décharge publique, dépotoir m

**rubbishy** ['rʌbɪʃɪ] adj (Brit inf) qui ne vaut rien, moche

**rubble** ['rʌbl] n décombres mpl; (smaller) gravats mpl; (Constr) blocage m

**ruble** ['ruːbl] n (US) = **rouble**

**ruby** ['ruːbɪ] n rubis m

**RUC** n abbr (Brit) = **Royal Ulster Constabulary**

**rucksack** ['rʌksæk] n sac m à dos

**ructions** ['rʌkʃənz] npl grabuge m

**rudder** ['rʌdə[r]] n gouvernail m

**ruddy** ['rʌdɪ] adj (face) coloré(e); (inf: damned) sacré(e), fichu(e)

**rude** [ruːd] adj (impolite: person) impoli(e); (: word, manners) grossier(-ière); (shocking) indécent(e), inconvenant(e); **to be ~ to sb** être grossier envers qn

**rudely** ['ruːdlɪ] adv impoliment; grossièrement

**rudeness** ['ruːdnɪs] n impolitesse f; grossièreté f

**rudiment** ['ruːdɪmənt] n rudiment m

**rudimentary** [ruːdɪ'mentərɪ] adj rudimentaire

**rue** [ruː] vt se repentir de, regretter amèrement

**rueful** ['ruːful] adj triste

**ruff** [rʌf] n fraise f, collerette f

**ruffian** ['rʌfɪən] n brute f, voyou m

**ruffle** ['rʌfl] vt (hair) ébouriffer; (clothes) chiffonner; (water) agiter; (fig: person) émouvoir, faire perdre son flegme à; **to get ~d** s'énerver

**rug** [rʌg] n petit tapis; (Brit: blanket) couverture f

**rugby** ['rʌgbɪ] n (also: **rugby football**) rugby m

**rugged** ['rʌgɪd] adj (landscape) accidenté(e); (features, character) rude; (determination) farouche

**rugger** ['rʌgə[r]] n (Brit inf) rugby m

**ruin** ['ruːɪn] n ruine f ▷ vt ruiner; (spoil: clothes)

abîmer; (: *event*) gâcher; **ruins** *npl* (*of building*)
ruine(s); **in ~s** en ruine
**ruination** [ru:ɪ'neɪʃən] *n* ruine *f*
**ruinous** ['ru:ɪnəs] *adj* ruineux(-euse)
**rule** [ru:l] *n* règle *f*; (*regulation*) règlement *m*;
(*government*) autorité *f*, gouvernement *m*;
(*dominion etc*): **under British ~** sous l'autorité
britannique ▷ *vt* (*country*) gouverner; (*person*)
dominer; (*decide*) décider ▷ *vi* commander;
décider; (*Law*): **to ~ against/in favour of/on**
statuer contre/en faveur de/sur; **to ~ that**
(*umpire, judge etc*) décider que; **it's against the ~s**
c'est contraire au règlement; **by ~ of thumb** à
vue de nez; **as a ~** normalement, en règle
générale
▶ **rule out** *vt* exclure; **murder cannot be ~d**
**out** l'hypothèse d'un meurtre ne peut être
exclue
**ruled** [ru:ld] *adj* (*paper*) réglé(e)
**ruler** ['ru:lə<sup>r</sup>] *n* (*sovereign*) souverain(e); (*leader*)
chef *m* (d'État); (*for measuring*) règle *f*
**ruling** ['ru:lɪŋ] *adj* (*party*) au pouvoir; (*class*)
dirigeant(e) ▷ *n* (*Law*) décision *f*
**rum** [rʌm] *n* rhum *m* ▷ *adj* (*Brit inf*) bizarre
**Rumania** [ru:'meɪnɪə] *n* Roumanie *f*
**Rumanian** [ru:'meɪnɪən] *adj* roumain(e) ▷ *n*
Roumain(e); (*Ling*) roumain *m*
**rumble** ['rʌmbl] *n* grondement *m*; (*of stomach,*
*pipe*) gargouillement *m* ▷ *vi* gronder; (*stomach,*
*pipe*) gargouiller
**rumbustious** [rʌm'bʌstʃəs], **rumbunctious**
[rʌm'bʌŋkʃəs] *adj* (*US: person*) exubérant(e)
**rummage** ['rʌmɪdʒ] *vi* fouiller
**rumour**, (*US*) **rumor** ['ru:mə<sup>r</sup>] *n* rumeur *f*, bruit
*m* (qui court) ▷ *vt*: **it is ~ed that** le bruit court
que
**rump** [rʌmp] *n* (*of animal*) croupe *f*
**rumple** ['rʌmpl] *vt* (*hair*) ébouriffer; (*clothes*)
chiffonner, friper
**rump steak** *n* romsteck *m*
**rumpus** ['rʌmpəs] *n* (*inf*) tapage *m*, chahut *m*;
(*quarrel*) prise *f* de bec; **to kick up a ~** faire toute
une histoire
**run** [rʌn] (*pt* **ran**, *pp* **~**) [ræn, rʌn] *n* (*race*) course *f*;
(*outing*) tour *m* or promenade *f* (en voiture);
(*distance travelled*) parcours *m*, trajet *m*; (*series*)
suite *f*, série *f*; (*Theat*) série de représentations;
(*Ski*) piste *f*; (*Cricket, Baseball*) point *m*; (*in tights,*
*stockings*) maille filée, échelle *f* ▷ *vt* (*business*)
diriger; (*competition, course*) organiser; (*hotel,*
*house*) tenir; (*race*) participer à; (*Comput: program*)
exécuter; (*force through: rope, pipe*): **to ~ sth**
**through** faire passer qch à travers; (*to pass:*
*hand, finger*): **to ~ sth over** promener or passer
qch sur; (*water, bath*) faire couler; (*Press: feature*)
publier ▷ *vi* courir; (*pass: road etc*) passer; (*work:*
*machine, factory*) marcher; (*bus, train*) circuler;
(*continue: play*) se jouer, être à l'affiche;
(: *contract*) être valide or en vigueur; (*slide: drawer*
*etc*) glisser; (*flow: river, bath, nose*) couler; (*colours,*
*washing*) déteindre; (*in election*) être candidat, se
présenter; **at a ~** au pas de course; **to go for a ~**

aller courir or faire un peu de course à pied; (*in*
*car*) faire un tour or une promenade (en voiture);
**to break into a ~** se mettre à courir; **a ~ of luck**
une série de coups de chance; **to have the ~ of**
**sb's house** avoir la maison de qn à sa
disposition; **there was a ~ on** (*meat, tickets*) les
gens se sont rués sur; **in the long ~** à la longue,
à longue échéance; **in the short ~** à brève
échéance, à court terme; **on the ~** en fuite; **to**
**make a ~ for it** s'enfuir; **I'll ~ you to the**
**station** je vais vous emmener or conduire à la
gare; **to ~ errands** faire des commissions; **the**
**train ~s between Gatwick and Victoria** le
train assure le service entre Gatwick et Victoria;
**the bus ~s every 20 minutes** il y a un autobus
toutes les 20 minutes; **it's very cheap to ~** (*car,*
*machine*) c'est très économique; **to ~ on petrol**
*or* (*US*) **gas/on diesel/off batteries** marcher à
l'essence/au diesel/sur piles; **to ~ for**
**president** être candidat à la présidence; **to ~ a**
**risk** courir un risque; **their losses ran into**
**millions** leurs pertes se sont élevées à plusieurs
millions; **to be ~ off one's feet** (*Brit*) ne plus
savoir où donner de la tête
▶ **run about** *vi* (*children*) courir çà et là
▶ **run across** *vt fus* (*find*) trouver par hasard
▶ **run after** *vt fus* (*to catch up*) courir après; (*chase*)
poursuivre
▶ **run around** *vi* = **run about**
▶ **run away** *vi* s'enfuir
▶ **run down** *vi* (*clock*) s'arrêter (faute d'avoir été
remonté) ▷ *vt* (*Aut: knock over*) renverser; (*Brit:*
*reduce: production*) réduire progressivement;
(: *factory/shop*) réduire progressivement la
production/l'activité de; (*criticize*) critiquer,
dénigrer; **to be ~ down** (*tired*) être fatigué(e) or à
plat
▶ **run in** *vt* (*Brit: car*) roder
▶ **run into** *vt fus* (*meet: person*) rencontrer par
hasard; (: *trouble*) se heurter à; (*collide with*)
heurter; **to ~ into debt** contracter des dettes
▶ **run off** *vi* s'enfuir ▷ *vt* (*water*) laisser
s'écouler; (*copies*) tirer
▶ **run out** *vi* (*person*) sortir en courant; (*liquid*)
couler; (*lease*) expirer; (*money*) être épuisé(e)
▶ **run out of** *vt fus* se trouver à court de; **I've ~**
**out of petrol** *or* (*US*) **gas** je suis en panne
d'essence
▶ **run over** *vt* (*Aut*) écraser ▷ *vt fus* (*revise*) revoir,
reprendre
▶ **run through** *vt fus* (*recap*) reprendre, revoir;
(*play*) répéter
▶ **run up** *vi*: **to ~ up against** (*difficulties*) se
heurter à ▷ *vt*: **to ~ up a debt** s'endetter
**runaround** ['rʌnəraund] *n* (*inf*): **to give sb the ~**
rester très évasif
**runaway** ['rʌnəweɪ] *adj* (*horse*) emballé(e); (*truck*)
fou (folle); (*person*) fugitif(-ive); (*child*)
fugueur(-euse); (*inflation*) galopant(e)
**rundown** ['rʌndaun] *n* (*Brit: of industry etc*)
réduction progressive
**rung** [rʌŋ] *pp of* **ring** ▷ *n* (*of ladder*) barreau *m*

**r**

**run-in** ['rʌnɪn] n (inf) accrochage m, prise f de bec
**runner** ['rʌnəʳ] n (in race: person) coureur(-euse);
(: horse) partant m; (on sledge) patin m; (for drawer
etc) coulisseau m; (carpet: in hall etc) chemin m
**runner bean** n (Brit) haricot m (à rames)
**runner-up** [rʌnərˈʌp] n second(e)
**running** ['rʌnɪŋ] n (in race etc) course f; (of business,
organization) direction f, gestion f; (of event)
organisation f; (of machine etc) marche f,
fonctionnement m ▷ adj (water) courant(e);
(commentary) suivi(e); **6 days** ~ 6 jours de suite;
**to be in/out of the** ~ **for sth** être/ne pas être
sur les rangs pour qch
**running commentary** n commentaire détaillé
**running costs** npl (of business) frais mpl de
gestion; (of car): **the** ~ **are high** elle revient cher
**running head** n (Typ, Comput) titre courant
**running mate** n (US Pol) candidat à la vice-
présidence
**runny** ['rʌnɪ] adj qui coule
**run-off** ['rʌnɔf] n (in contest, election) deuxième
tour m; (extra race etc) épreuve f supplémentaire
**run-of-the-mill** ['rʌnəvðə'mɪl] adj ordinaire,
banal(e)
**runt** [rʌnt] n avorton m
**run-through** ['rʌnθru:] n répétition f, essai m
**run-up** ['rʌnʌp] n (Brit): ~ **to sth** période f
précédant qch
**runway** ['rʌnweɪ] n (Aviat) piste f (d'envol or
d'atterrissage)
**rupee** [ru:'pi:] n roupie f
**rupture** ['rʌptʃəʳ] n (Med) hernie f ▷ vt: **to** ~ **o.s.**
se donner une hernie
**rural** ['ruərl] adj rural(e)
**ruse** [ru:z] n ruse f
**rush** [rʌʃ] n course précipitée; (of crowd, Comm:
sudden demand) ruée f; (hurry) hâte f; (of anger, joy)
accès m; (current) flot m; (Bot) jonc m; (for chair)
paille f ▷ vt (hurry) transporter or envoyer
d'urgence; (attack: town etc) prendre d'assaut;
(Brit inf: overcharge) estamper; faire payer ▷ vi se
précipiter; **don't** ~ **me!** laissez-moi le temps de
souffler!; **to** ~ **sth off** (do quickly) faire qch à la
hâte; (send) envoyer qch d'urgence; **is there
any** ~ **for this?** est-ce urgent?; **we've had a** ~ **of
orders** nous avons reçu une avalanche de
commandes; **I'm in a** ~ **(to do)** je suis vraiment
pressé (de faire); **gold** ~ ruée vers l'or
▶ **rush through** vt fus (work) exécuter à la hâte
▷ vt (Comm: order) exécuter d'urgence
**rush hour** n heures fpl de pointe or d'affluence
**rush job** n travail urgent
**rush matting** n natte f de paille
**rusk** [rʌsk] n biscotte f
**Russia** ['rʌʃə] n Russie f
**Russian** ['rʌʃən] adj russe ▷ n Russe m/f; (Ling)
russe m
**rust** [rʌst] n rouille f ▷ vi rouiller
**rustic** ['rʌstɪk] adj rustique ▷ n (pej) rustaud(e)
**rustle** ['rʌsl] vi bruire, produire un bruissement
▷ vt (paper) froisser; (US: cattle) voler
**rustproof** ['rʌstpru:f] adj inoxydable
**rustproofing** ['rʌstpru:fɪŋ] n traitement m
antirouille
**rusty** ['rʌstɪ] adj rouillé(e)
**rut** [rʌt] n ornière f; (Zool) rut m; **to be in a** ~ (fig)
suivre l'ornière, s'encroûter
**rutabaga** [ru:tə'beɪgə] n (US) rutabaga m
**ruthless** ['ru:θlɪs] adj sans pitié, impitoyable
**ruthlessness** ['ru:θlɪsnɪs] n dureté f, cruauté f
**RV** abbr (= revised version) traduction anglaise de la Bible
de 1885 ▷ n abbr (US) = **recreational vehicle**
**rye** [raɪ] n seigle m
**rye bread** n pain m de seigle

# Ss

**S, s** [ɛs] n (letter) S, s m; (US Scol: satisfactory)
≈ assez bien; **S for Sugar** S comme Suzanne
**S** abbr (= south, small) S; (= saint) St
**SA** n abbr = **South Africa; South America**
**Sabbath** ['sæbəθ] n (Jewish) sabbat m; (Christian)
dimanche m
**sabbatical** [sə'bætɪkl] adj: ~ **year** année f
sabbatique
**sabotage** ['sæbəta:ʒ] n sabotage m ▷ vt saboter
**saccharin, saccharine** ['sækərɪn] n
saccharine f
**sachet** ['sæʃeɪ] n sachet m
**sack** [sæk] n (bag) sac m ▷ vt (dismiss) renvoyer,
mettre à la porte; (plunder) piller, mettre à sac;
**to give sb the ~** renvoyer qn, mettre qn à la
porte; **to get the ~** être renvoyé(e) or mis(e) à la
porte
**sackful** ['sækful] n: **a ~ of** un (plein) sac de
**sacking** ['sækɪŋ] n toile f à sac; (dismissal)
renvoi m
**sacrament** ['sækrəmənt] n sacrement m
**sacred** ['seɪkrɪd] adj sacré(e)
**sacred cow** n (fig) chose sacro-sainte
**sacrifice** ['sækrɪfaɪs] n sacrifice m ▷ vt sacrifier;
**to make ~s (for sb)** se sacrifier or faire des
sacrifices (pour qn)
**sacrilege** ['sækrɪlɪdʒ] n sacrilège m
**sacrosanct** ['sækrəusæŋkt] adj sacro-saint(e)
**sad** [sæd] adj (unhappy) triste; (deplorable) triste,
fâcheux(-euse); (inf: pathetic: thing) triste,
lamentable; (: person) minable
**sadden** ['sædn] vt attrister, affliger
**saddle** ['sædl] n selle f ▷ vt (horse) seller; **to be
~d with sth** (inf) avoir qch sur les bras
**saddlebag** ['sædlbæg] n sacoche f
**sadism** ['seɪdɪzəm] n sadisme m
**sadist** ['seɪdɪst] n sadique m/f
**sadistic** [sə'dɪstɪk] adj sadique
**sadly** ['sædlɪ] adv tristement; (unfortunately)
malheureusement; (seriously) fort
**sadness** ['sædnɪs] n tristesse f
**sado-masochism** [seɪdəu'mæsəkɪzəm] n
sadomasochisme m
**s.a.e.** n abbr (Brit: = stamped addressed envelope)
enveloppe affranchie pour la réponse
**safari** [sə'fɑːrɪ] n safari m

**safari park** n réserve f
**safe** [seɪf] adj (out of danger) hors de danger, en
sécurité; (not dangerous) sans danger; (cautious)
prudent(e); (sure: bet) assuré(e) ▷ n coffre-fort
m; ~ **from** à l'abri de; ~ **and sound** sain(e) et
sauf (sauve); **(just) to be on the ~ side** pour
plus de sûreté, par précaution; **to play ~** ne
prendre aucun risque; **it is ~ to say that ...** on
peut dire sans crainte que ...; ~ **journey!** bon
voyage!
**safe bet** n: **it was a ~** ça ne comportait pas trop
de risques; **it's a ~ that he'll be late** il y a
toutes les chances pour qu'il soit en retard
**safe-breaker** ['seɪfbreɪkəʳ] n (Brit) perceur m de
coffre-fort
**safe-conduct** [seɪf'kɔndʌkt] n sauf-conduit m
**safe-cracker** ['seɪfkrækəʳ] n = **safe-breaker**
**safe-deposit** ['seɪfdɪpɔzɪt] n (vault) dépôt m de
coffres-forts; (box) coffre-fort m
**safeguard** ['seɪfgɑːd] n sauvegarde f, protection
f ▷ vt sauvegarder, protéger
**safe haven** n zone f de sécurité
**safekeeping** ['seɪf'kiːpɪŋ] n bonne garde
**safely** ['seɪflɪ] adv (assume, say) sans risque
d'erreur; (drive, arrive) sans accident; **I can ~
say ...** je peux dire à coup sûr ...
**safe passage** n: **to grant sb ~** accorder un
laissez-passer à qn
**safe sex** n rapports sexuels protégés
**safety** ['seɪftɪ] n sécurité f; ~ **first!** la sécurité
d'abord!
**safety belt** n ceinture f de sécurité
**safety catch** n cran m de sûreté or sécurité
**safety net** n filet m de sécurité
**safety pin** n épingle f de sûreté or de nourrice
**safety valve** n soupape f de sûreté
**saffron** ['sæfrən] n safran m
**sag** [sæg] vi s'affaisser, fléchir; (hem, breasts)
pendre
**saga** ['sɑːgə] n saga f; (fig) épopée f
**sage** [seɪdʒ] n (herb) sauge f; (person) sage m
**Sagittarius** [sædʒɪ'tɛərɪəs] n le Sagittaire; **to be
~** être du Sagittaire
**sago** ['seɪgəu] n sagou m
**Sahara** [sə'hɑːrə] n: **the ~ (Desert)** le (désert du)
Sahara m

**S**

**Sahel** [sæ'hɛl] n Sahel m
**said** [sɛd] pt, pp of **say**
**Saigon** [saɪ'gɒn] n Saigon
**sail** [seɪl] n (on boat) voile f; (trip): **to go for a ~**
faire un tour en bateau ▷ vt (boat) manœuvrer,
piloter ▷ vi (travel: ship) avancer, naviguer;
(: passenger) aller or se rendre (en bateau); (set off)
partir, prendre la mer; (Sport) faire de la voile;
**they ~ed into Le Havre** ils sont entrés dans le
port du Havre
  ▶ **sail through** vi, vt fus (fig) réussir haut la main
**sailboat** ['seɪlbəut] n (US) bateau m à voiles,
voilier m
**sailing** ['seɪlɪŋ] n (Sport) voile f; **to go ~** faire de la
voile
**sailing boat** n bateau m à voiles, voilier m
**sailing ship** n grand voilier
**sailor** ['seɪləʳ] n marin m, matelot m
**saint** [seɪnt] n saint(e)
**saintly** ['seɪntlɪ] adj saint(e), plein(e) de bonté
**sake** [seɪk] n: **for the ~ of** (out of concern for) pour
(l'amour de), dans l'intérêt de; (out of
consideration for) par égard pour; (in order to achieve)
pour plus de, par souci de; **arguing for
arguing's ~** discuter pour (le plaisir de)
discuter; **for heaven's ~!** pour l'amour du ciel!;
**for the ~ of argument** à titre d'exemple
**salad** ['sæləd] n salade f; **tomato ~** salade de
tomates
**salad bowl** n saladier m
**salad cream** n (Brit) (sorte f de) mayonnaise f
**salad dressing** n vinaigrette f
**salad oil** n huile f de table
**salami** [sə'lɑ:mɪ] n salami m
**salaried** ['sælərɪd] adj (staff) salarié(e), qui
touche un traitement
**salary** ['sælərɪ] n salaire m, traitement m
**salary scale** n échelle f des traitements
**sale** [seɪl] n vente f; (at reduced prices) soldes mpl;
**sales** npl (total amount sold) chiffre m de ventes;
**"for ~"** "à vendre"; **on ~** en vente; **on ~ or
return** vendu(e) avec faculté de retour;
**closing-down** or **liquidation ~** (US) liquidation
f (avant fermeture); **~ and lease back** n cession-
bail f
**saleroom** ['seɪlru:m] n salle f des ventes
**sales assistant**, (US) **sales clerk** n
vendeur(-euse)
**sales conference** n réunion f de vente
**sales drive** n campagne commerciale,
animation f des ventes
**sales force** n (ensemble m du) service des ventes
**salesman** ['seɪlzmən] (irreg) n (in shop) vendeur
m; (representative) représentant m de commerce
**sales manager** n directeur commercial
**salesmanship** ['seɪlzmənʃɪp] n art m de la vente
**salesperson** ['seɪlzpə:sn] (irreg) n (in shop)
vendeur(-euse)
**sales rep** n (Comm) représentant(e) m/f
**sales tax** n (US) taxe f à l'achat
**saleswoman** ['seɪlzwumən] (irreg) n (in shop)
vendeuse f

**salient** ['seɪlɪənt] adj saillant(e)
**saline** ['seɪlaɪn] adj salin(e)
**saliva** [sə'laɪvə] n salive f
**sallow** ['sæləu] adj cireux(-euse)
**sally forth**, **sally out** ['sælɪ-] vi partir plein(e)
d'entrain
**salmon** ['sæmən] n (pl inv) saumon m
**salmon trout** n truite saumonée
**salon** ['sælɒn] n salon m
**saloon** [sə'lu:n] n (US) bar m; (Brit Aut) berline f;
(ship's lounge) salon m
**SALT** [sɔ:lt] n abbr (= Strategic Arms Limitation Talks/
Treaty) SALT m
**salt** [sɔ:lt] n sel m ▷ vt saler ▷ cpd de sel; (Culin)
salé(e); **an old ~** un vieux loup de mer
  ▶ **salt away** vt mettre de côté
**salt cellar** n salière f
**salt-free** ['sɔ:lt'fri:] adj sans sel
**saltwater** ['sɔ:lt'wɔ:təʳ] adj (fish etc) (d'eau) de
mer
**salty** ['sɔ:ltɪ] adj salé(e)
**salubrious** [sə'lu:brɪəs] adj salubre
**salutary** ['sæljutərɪ] adj salutaire
**salute** [sə'lu:t] n salut m; (of guns) salve f ▷ vt
saluer
**salvage** ['sælvɪdʒ] n (saving) sauvetage m; (things
saved) biens sauvés or récupérés ▷ vt sauver,
récupérer
**salvage vessel** n bateau m de sauvetage
**salvation** [sæl'veɪʃən] n salut m
**Salvation Army** [sæl'veɪʃən-] n Armée f du
Salut
**salver** ['sælvəʳ] n plateau m de métal
**salvo** ['sælvəu] n salve f
**Samaritan** [sə'mærɪtən] n: **the ~s** (organization)
≈ S.O.S. Amitié
**same** [seɪm] adj même ▷ pron: **the ~** le (la)
même, les mêmes; **the ~ book as** le même livre
que; **on the ~ day** le même jour; **at the ~ time**
en même temps; (yet) néanmoins; **all** or just
**the ~** tout de même, quand même; **they're one
and the ~** (person/thing) c'est une seule et même
personne/chose; **to do the ~** faire de même, en
faire autant; **to do the ~ as sb** faire comme qn;
**and the ~ to you!** et à vous de même!; (after
insult) toi-même!; **~ here!** moi aussi!; **the ~
again!** (in bar etc) la même chose!
**sample** ['sɑ:mpl] n échantillon m; (Med)
prélèvement m ▷ vt (food, wine) goûter; **to take a
~** prélever un échantillon; **free ~** échantillon
gratuit
**sanatorium** (pl **sanatoria**) [sænə'tɔ:rɪəm, -rɪə] n
sanatorium m
**sanctify** ['sæŋktɪfaɪ] vt sanctifier
**sanctimonious** [sæŋktɪ'məunɪəs] adj
moralisateur(-trice)
**sanction** ['sæŋkʃən] n approbation f, sanction f
▷ vt cautionner, sanctionner; **sanctions** npl
(Pol) sanctions; **to impose economic ~s on** or
**against** prendre des sanctions économiques
contre
**sanctity** ['sæŋktɪtɪ] n sainteté f, caractère sacré

**sanctuary** ['sæŋktjuərɪ] *n* (*holy place*) sanctuaire *m*; (*refuge*) asile *m*; (*for wildlife*) réserve *f*

**sand** [sænd] *n* sable *m* ▷ *vt* sabler; (*also*: **sand down**: *wood etc*) poncer

**sandal** ['sændl] *n* sandale *f*

**sandbag** ['sændbæg] *n* sac *m* de sable

**sandblast** ['sændblɑːst] *vt* décaper à la sableuse

**sandbox** ['sændbɒks] *n* (*US: for children*) tas *m* de sable

**sand castle** ['sændkɑːsl] *n* château *m* de sable

**sand dune** *n* dune *f* de sable

**sander** ['sændə$^r$] *n* ponceuse *f*

**S&M** *n abbr* (= *sadomasochism*) sadomasochisme *m*

**sandpaper** ['sændpeɪpə$^r$] *n* papier *m* de verre

**sandpit** ['sændpɪt] *n* (*Brit: for children*) tas *m* de sable

**sands** [sændz] *npl* plage *f* (de sable)

**sandstone** ['sændstəun] *n* grès *m*

**sandstorm** ['sændstɔːm] *n* tempête *f* de sable

**sandwich** ['sændwɪtʃ] *n* sandwich *m* ▷ *vt* (*also*: **sandwich in**) intercaler; **~ed between** pris en sandwich entre; **cheese/ham** ~ sandwich au fromage/jambon

**sandwich board** *n* panneau *m* publicitaire (porté par un homme-sandwich)

**sandwich course** *n* (*Brit*) cours *m* de formation professionnelle

**sandy** ['sændɪ] *adj* sablonneux(-euse); couvert(e) de sable; (*colour*) sable *inv*, blond roux *inv*

**sane** [seɪn] *adj* (*person*) sain(e) d'esprit; (*outlook*) sensé(e), sain(e)

**sang** [sæŋ] *pt of* **sing**

**sanguine** ['sæŋgwɪn] *adj* optimiste

**sanitarium** (*pl* **sanitaria**) [sænɪ'tɛərɪəm, -rɪə] *n* (*US*) = **sanatorium**

**sanitary** ['sænɪtərɪ] *adj* (*system, arrangements*) sanitaire; (*clean*) hygiénique

**sanitary towel**, (*US*) **sanitary napkin** ['sænɪtərɪ-] *n* serviette *f* hygiénique

**sanitation** [sænɪ'teɪʃən] *n* (*in house*) installations *fpl* sanitaires; (*in town*) système *m* sanitaire

**sanitation department** *n* (*US*) service *m* de voirie

**sanity** ['sænɪtɪ] *n* santé mentale; (*common sense*) bon sens

**sank** [sæŋk] *pt of* **sink**

**San Marino** ['sænmə'riːnəu] *n* Saint-Marin *m*

**Santa Claus** [sæntə'klɔːz] *n* le Père Noël

**Santiago** [sæntɪ'ɑːgəu] *n* (*also*: **Santiago de Chile**) Santiago (du Chili)

**sap** [sæp] *n* (*of plants*) sève *f* ▷ *vt* (*strength*) saper, miner

**sapling** ['sæplɪŋ] *n* jeune arbre *m*

**sapphire** ['sæfaɪə$^r$] *n* saphir *m*

**sarcasm** ['sɑːkæzm] *n* sarcasme *m*, raillerie *f*

**sarcastic** [sɑː'kæstɪk] *adj* sarcastique

**sarcophagus** (*pl* **sarcophagi**) [sɑː'kɔfəgəs, -gaɪ] *n* sarcophage *m*

**sardine** [sɑː'diːn] *n* sardine *f*

**Sardinia** [sɑː'dɪnɪə] *n* Sardaigne *f*

**Sardinian** [sɑː'dɪnɪən] *adj* sarde ▷ *n* Sarde *m/f*; (*Ling*) sarde *m*

**sardonic** [sɑː'dɔnɪk] *adj* sardonique

**sari** ['sɑːrɪ] *n* sari *m*

**SARS** ['sɑːz] *n abbr* = **severe acute respiratory syndrome**

**sartorial** [sɑː'tɔːrɪəl] *adj* vestimentaire

**SAS** *n abbr* (*Brit Mil*: = *Special Air Service*) ≈ GIGN *m*

**SASE** *n abbr* (*US*: = *self-addressed stamped envelope*) enveloppe affranchie pour la réponse

**sash** [sæʃ] *n* écharpe *f*

**sash window** *n* fenêtre *f* à guillotine

**Sask.** *abbr* (*Canada*) = **Saskatchewan**

**sat** [sæt] *pt, pp of* **sit**

**Sat.** *abbr* (= *Saturday*) sa

**Satan** ['seɪtn] *n* Satan *m*

**satanic** [sə'tænɪk] *adj* satanique, démoniaque

**satchel** ['sætʃl] *n* cartable *m*

**sated** ['seɪtɪd] *adj* repu(e); blasé(e)

**satellite** ['sætəlaɪt] *adj*, *n* satellite *m*

**satellite dish** *n* antenne *f* parabolique

**satellite navigation system** *n* système *m* de navigation par satellite

**satellite television** *n* télévision *f* par satellite

**satiate** ['seɪʃɪeɪt] *vt* rassasier

**satin** ['sætɪn] *n* satin *m* ▷ *adj* en or de satin, satiné(e); **with a ~ finish** satiné(e)

**satire** ['sætaɪə$^r$] *n* satire *f*

**satirical** [sə'tɪrɪkl] *adj* satirique

**satirist** ['sætɪrɪst] *n* (*writer*) auteur *m* satirique; (*cartoonist*) caricaturiste *m/f*

**satirize** ['sætɪraɪz] *vt* faire la satire de, satiriser

**satisfaction** [sætɪs'fækʃən] *n* satisfaction *f*

**satisfactory** [sætɪs'fæktərɪ] *adj* satisfaisant(e)

**satisfied** ['sætɪsfaɪd] *adj* satisfait(e); **to be ~ with sth** être satisfait de qch

**satisfy** ['sætɪsfaɪ] *vt* satisfaire, contenter; (*convince*) convaincre, persuader; **to ~ the requirements** remplir les conditions; **to ~ sb (that)** convaincre qn (que); **to ~ o.s. of sth** vérifier qch, s'assurer de qch

**satisfying** ['sætɪsfaɪɪŋ] *adj* satisfaisant(e)

**SAT(s)** *n abbr* (*US*) = **Scholastic Aptitude Test(s)**

**satsuma** [sæt'suːmə] *n* satsuma *f*

**saturate** ['sætʃəreɪt] *vt*: **to ~ (with)** saturer (de)

**saturated fat** ['sætʃəreɪtɪd-] *n* graisse saturée

**saturation** [sætʃə'reɪʃən] *n* saturation *f*

**Saturday** ['sætədɪ] *n* samedi *m*; *for phrases see also* **Tuesday**

**sauce** [sɔːs] *n* sauce *f*

**saucepan** ['sɔːspən] *n* casserole *f*

**saucer** ['sɔːsə$^r$] *n* soucoupe *f*

**saucy** ['sɔːsɪ] *adj* impertinent(e)

**Saudi Arabia** *n* Arabie *f* Saoudite

**Saudi (Arabian)** ['saudi] *adj* saoudien(ne) ▷ *n* Saoudien(ne)

**sauna** ['sɔːnə] *n* sauna *m*

**saunter** ['sɔːntə$^r$] *vi*: **to ~ to** aller en flânant *or* se balader jusqu'à

**sausage** ['sɔsɪdʒ] *n* saucisse *f*; (*salami etc*) saucisson *m*

**sausage roll** *n* friand *m*

**sauté** ['səuteɪ] *adj* (*Culin: potatoes*) sauté(e);

**S**

(: *onions*) revenu(e) ▷ *vt* faire sauter; faire revenir

**sautéed** ['səuteɪd] *adj* sauté(e)

**savage** ['sævɪdʒ] *adj* (*cruel, fierce*) brutal(e), féroce; (*primitive*) primitif(-ive), sauvage ▷ *n* sauvage *m/f* ▷ *vt* attaquer férocement

**savagery** ['sævɪdʒrɪ] *n* sauvagerie *f*, brutalité *f*, férocité *f*

**save** [seɪv] *vt* (*person, belongings*) sauver; (*money*) mettre de côté, économiser; (*time*) (faire) gagner; (*keep*) garder; (*Comput*) sauvegarder; (*Sport: stop*) arrêter; (*avoid: trouble*) éviter ▷ *vi* (*also:* **save up**) mettre de l'argent de côté ▷ *n* (*Sport*) arrêt *m* (du ballon); ▷ *prep* sauf, à l'exception de; **it will ~ me an hour** ça me fera gagner une heure; **to ~ face** sauver la face; **God ~ the Queen!** vive la Reine!

**saving** ['seɪvɪŋ] *n* économie *f* ▷ *adj*: **the ~ grace of** ce qui rachète; **savings** *npl* économies *fpl*; **to make ~s** faire des économies

**savings account** *n* compte *m* d'épargne

**savings and loan association** (*US*) *n* ≈ société *f* de crédit immobilier

**savings bank** *n* caisse *f* d'épargne

**saviour**, (*US*) **savior** ['seɪvjər] *n* sauveur *m*

**savour**, (*US*) **savor** ['seɪvər] *n* saveur *f*, goût *m* ▷ *vt* savourer

**savoury**, (*US*) **savory** ['seɪvərɪ] *adj* savoureux(-euse); (*dish: not sweet*) salé(e)

**savvy** ['sævɪ] *n* (*inf*) jugeote *f*

**saw** [sɔː] *pt of* **see** ▷ *n* (*tool*) scie *f* ▷ *vt* (*pt* **-ed**, *pp* **-ed** *or* **-n** [sɔːn]) scier; **to ~ sth up** débiter qch à la scie

**sawdust** ['sɔːdʌst] *n* sciure *f*

**sawmill** ['sɔːmɪl] *n* scierie *f*

**sawn** [sɔːn] *pp of* **saw**

**sawn-off** ['sɔːnɔf], **sawed-off** ['sɔːdɔf] (*US*) *adj*: **~ shotgun** carabine *f* à canon scié

**sax** [sæks] (*inf*) *n* saxo *m*

**saxophone** ['sæksəfəun] *n* saxophone *m*

**say** [seɪ] *n*: **to have one's ~** dire ce qu'on a à dire ▷ *vt* (*pt, pp* **said**) [sɛd] dire; **to have a ~** avoir voix au chapitre; **could you ~ that again?** pourriez-vous répéter ce que vous venez de dire?; **to ~ yes/no** dire oui/non; **she said (that) I was to give you this** elle m'a chargé de vous remettre ceci; **my watch ~s 3 o'clock** ma montre indique 3 heures, il est 3 heures à ma montre; **shall we ~ Tuesday?** disons mardi?; **that doesn't ~ much for him** ce n'est pas vraiment à son honneur; **when all is said and done** en fin de compte, en définitive; **there is something** *or* **a lot to be said for it** cela a des avantages; **that is to ~** c'est-à-dire; **to ~ nothing of** sans compter; **~ that ...** mettons *or* disons que ...; **that goes without ~ing** cela va sans dire, cela va de soi

**saying** ['seɪɪŋ] *n* dicton *m*, proverbe *m*

**SBA** *n abbr* (*US*) = *Small Business Administration*) *organisme d'aide aux PME*

**SC** *n abbr* (*US*) = **supreme court** ▷ *abbr* (*US*) = **South Carolina**

**s/c** *abbr* = **self-contained**

**scab** [skæb] *n* croûte *f*; (*pej*) jaune *m*

**scabby** ['skæbɪ] *adj* croûteux(-euse)

**scaffold** ['skæfəld] *n* échafaud *m*

**scaffolding** ['skæfəldɪŋ] *n* échafaudage *m*

**scald** [skɔːld] *n* brûlure *f* ▷ *vt* ébouillanter

**scalding** ['skɔːldɪŋ] *adj* (*also:* **scalding hot**) brûlant(e), bouillant(e)

**scale** [skeɪl] *n* (*of fish*) écaille *f*; (*Mus*) gamme *f*; (*of ruler, thermometer etc*) graduation *f*, échelle (graduée); (*of salaries, fees etc*) barème *m*; (*of map, also size, extent*) échelle ▷ *vt* (*mountain*) escalader; (*fish*) écailler; **scales** *npl* balance *f*; (*larger*) bascule *f*; (*also:* **bathroom scales**) pèse-personne *m inv*; **pay ~** échelle des salaires; **~ of charges** tableau *m* des tarifs; **on a large ~** sur une grande échelle, en grand; **to draw sth to ~** dessiner qch à l'échelle; **small-~ model** modèle réduit

▶ **scale down** *vt* réduire

**scaled-down** [skeɪld'daun] *adj* à échelle réduite

**scale drawing** *n* dessin *m* à l'échelle

**scale model** *n* modèle *m* à l'échelle

**scallion** ['skæljən] *n* oignon *m*; (*US: salad onion*) ciboule *f*; (: *shallot*) échalote *f*; (: *leek*) poireau *m*

**scallop** ['skɔləp] *n* coquille *f* Saint-Jacques; (*Sewing*) feston *m*

**scalp** [skælp] *n* cuir chevelu ▷ *vt* scalper

**scalpel** ['skælpl] *n* scalpel *m*

**scalper** ['skælpər] *n* (*US inf: of tickets*) revendeur *m* de billets

**scam** [skæm] *n* (*inf*) arnaque *f*

**scamp** [skæmp] *vt* bâcler

**scamper** ['skæmpər] *vi*: **to ~ away**, **~ off** détaler

**scampi** ['skæmpɪ] *npl* langoustines (frites), scampi *mpl*

**scan** [skæn] *vt* (*examine*) scruter, examiner; (*glance at quickly*) parcourir; (*poetry*) scander; (*TV, Radar*) balayer ▷ *n* (*Med*) scanographie *f*

**scandal** ['skændl] *n* scandale *m*; (*gossip*) ragots *mpl*

**scandalize** ['skændəlaɪz] *vt* scandaliser, indigner

**scandalous** ['skændələs] *adj* scandaleux(-euse).

**Scandinavia** [skændɪ'neɪvɪə] *n* Scandinavie *f*

**Scandinavian** [skændɪ'neɪvɪən] *adj* scandinave ▷ *n* Scandinave *m/f*

**scanner** ['skænər] *n* (*Radar, Med*) scanner *m*, scanographe *m*; (*Comput*) scanner

**scant** [skænt] *adj* insuffisant(e)

**scantily** ['skæntɪlɪ] *adv*: **~ clad** *or* **dressed** vêtu(e) du strict minimum

**scanty** ['skæntɪ] *adj* peu abondant(e), insuffisant(e), maigre

**scapegoat** ['skeɪpgəut] *n* bouc *m* émissaire

**scar** [skɑːr] *n* cicatrice *f* ▷ *vt* laisser une cicatrice *or* une marque à

**scarce** [skɛəs] *adj* rare, peu abondant(e); **to make o.s. ~** (*inf*) se sauver

**scarcely** ['skɛəslɪ] *adv* à peine, presque pas; **~ anybody** pratiquement personne; **I can ~ believe it** j'ai du mal à le croire

**scarcity** ['skɛəsɪtɪ] n rareté f, manque m, pénurie f

**scarcity value** n valeur f de rareté

**scare** [skɛəʳ] n peur f, panique f ▷ vt effrayer, faire peur à; **to ~ sb stiff** faire une peur bleue à qn; **bomb ~** alerte f à la bombe
▶ **scare away, scare off** vt faire fuir

**scarecrow** ['skɛəkrəu] n épouvantail m

**scared** ['skɛəd] adj: **to be ~** avoir peur

**scaremonger** ['skɛəmʌŋgəʳ] n alarmiste m/f

**scarf** (pl **scarves**) [skɑ:f, skɑ:vz] n (long) écharpe f; (square) foulard m

**scarlet** ['skɑ:lɪt] adj écarlate

**scarlet fever** n scarlatine f

**scarper** ['skɑ:pəʳ] vi (Brit inf) ficher le camp

**scarves** [skɑ:vz] npl of **scarf**

**scary** ['skɛərɪ] adj (inf) effrayant(e); (film) qui fait peur

**scathing** ['skeɪðɪŋ] adj cinglant(e), acerbe; **to be ~ about sth** être très critique vis-à-vis de qch

**scatter** ['skætəʳ] vt éparpiller, répandre; (crowd) disperser ▷ vi se disperser

**scatterbrained** ['skætəbreɪnd] adj écervelé(e), étourdi(e)

**scattered** ['skætəd] adj épars(e), dispersé(e)

**scatty** ['skætɪ] adj (Brit inf) loufoque

**scavenge** ['skævəndʒ] vi (person): **to ~ (for)** faire les poubelles (pour trouver); **to ~ for food** (hyenas etc) se nourrir de charognes

**scavenger** ['skævəndʒəʳ] n éboueur m

**SCE** n abbr = **Scottish Certificate of Education**

**scenario** [sɪ'nɑ:rɪəu] n scénario m

**scene** [si:n] n (Theat, fig etc) scène f; (of crime, accident) lieu(x) m(pl), endroit m; (sight, view) spectacle m, vue f; **behind the ~s** (also fig) dans les coulisses; **to make a ~** (inf: fuss) faire une scène or toute une histoire; **to appear on the ~** (also fig) faire son apparition, arriver; **the political ~** la situation politique

**scenery** ['si:nərɪ] n (Theat) décor(s) m(pl); (landscape) paysage m

**scenic** ['si:nɪk] adj scénique; offrant de beaux paysages or panoramas

**scent** [sɛnt] n parfum m, odeur f; (fig: track) piste f; (sense of smell) odorat m ▷ vt parfumer; (smell: also fig) flairer; (also: **to put** or **throw sb off the scent**: fig) mettre qn sur une mauvaise piste

**sceptic, (US) skeptic** ['skɛptɪk] n sceptique m/f

**sceptical, (US) skeptical** ['skɛptɪkl] adj sceptique

**scepticism, (US) skepticism** ['skɛptɪsɪzəm] n scepticisme m

**sceptre, (US) scepter** ['sɛptəʳ] n sceptre m

**schedule** ['ʃɛdju:l] (US) ['skɛdju:l] n programme m, plan m; (of trains) horaire m; (of prices etc) barème m, tarif m ▷ vt prévoir; **as ~d** comme prévu; **on ~** à l'heure (prévue); à la date prévue; **to be ahead of/behind ~** avoir de l'avance/du retard; **we are working to a very tight ~** notre programme de travail est très serré or intense; **everything went according to ~** tout s'est passé comme prévu

**scheduled** ['ʃɛdju:ld, (US) 'skɛdju:ld] adj (date, time) prévu(e), indiqué(e); (visit, event) programmé(e), prévu; (train, bus, stop, flight) régulier(-ière)

**scheduled flight** n vol régulier

**schematic** [skɪ'mætɪk] adj schématique

**scheme** [ski:m] n plan m, projet m; (method) procédé m; (plot) complot m, combine f; (arrangement) arrangement m, classification f; (pension scheme etc) régime m ▷ vt, vi comploter, manigancer; **colour ~** combinaison f de(s) couleurs

**scheming** ['ski:mɪŋ] adj rusé(e), intrigant(e) ▷ n manigances fpl, intrigues fpl

**schism** ['skɪzəm] n schisme m

**schizophrenia** [skɪtsə'fri:nɪə] n schizophrénie f

**schizophrenic** [skɪtsə'frɛnɪk] adj schizophrène

**scholar** ['skɔləʳ] n érudit(e); (pupil) boursier(-ère)

**scholarly** ['skɔləlɪ] adj érudit(e), savant(e)

**scholarship** ['skɔləʃɪp] n érudition f; (grant) bourse f (d'études)

**school** [sku:l] n (gen) école f; (secondary school) collège m; lycée m; (in university) faculté f; (US: university) université f; (of fish) banc m ▷ cpd scolaire ▷ vt (animal) dresser

**school age** n âge m scolaire

**schoolbook** ['sku:lbuk] n livre m scolaire or de classe

**schoolboy** ['sku:lbɔɪ] n écolier m; (at secondary school) collégien m; lycéen m

**schoolchildren** ['sku:ltʃɪldrən] npl écoliers mpl; (at secondary school) collégiens mpl; lycéens mpl

**schooldays** ['sku:ldeɪz] npl années fpl de scolarité

**schoolgirl** ['sku:lgə:l] n écolière f; (at secondary school) collégienne f; lycéenne f

**schooling** ['sku:lɪŋ] n instruction f, études fpl

**school-leaver** ['sku:lli:vəʳ] n (Brit) jeune qui vient de terminer ses études secondaires

**schoolmaster** ['sku:lmɑ:stəʳ] n (primary) instituteur m; (secondary) professeur m

**schoolmistress** ['sku:lmɪstrɪs] n (primary) institutrice f; (secondary) professeur m

**school report** n (Brit) bulletin m (scolaire)

**schoolroom** ['sku:lru:m] n (salle f de) classe f

**schoolteacher** ['sku:lti:tʃəʳ] n (primary) instituteur(-trice); (secondary) professeur m

**schoolyard** ['sku:lja:d] n (US) cour f de récréation

**schooner** ['sku:nəʳ] n (ship) schooner m, goélette f; (glass) grand verre (à xérès)

**sciatica** [saɪ'ætɪkə] n sciatique f

**science** ['saɪəns] n science f; **the ~s** les sciences; (Scol) les matières fpl scientifiques

**science fiction** n science-fiction f

**scientific** [saɪən'tɪfɪk] adj scientifique

**scientist** ['saɪəntɪst] n scientifique m/f; (eminent) savant m

**sci-fi** ['saɪfaɪ] n abbr (inf: = science fiction) SF f

**Scilly Isles** ['sɪlɪ'aɪlz], **Scillies** ['sɪlɪz] npl: **the ~** les Sorlingues fpl, les îles fpl Scilly

**S**

**scintillating** ['sɪntɪleɪtɪŋ] *adj* scintillant(e), étincelant(e); (*wit etc*) brillant(e)

**scissors** ['sɪzəz] *npl* ciseaux *mpl*; **a pair of** ~ une paire de ciseaux

**sclerosis** [sklɪ'rəʊsɪs] *n* sclérose *f*

**scoff** [skɒf] *vt* (*Brit inf: eat*) avaler, bouffer ▷ *vi*: **to** ~ **(at)** (*mock*) se moquer (de)

**scold** [skəʊld] *vt* gronder, attraper, réprimander

**scolding** ['skəʊldɪŋ] *n* réprimande *f*

**scone** [skɒn] *n* *sorte de petit pain rond au lait*

**scoop** [sku:p] *n* pelle *f* (à main); (*for ice cream*) boule *f* à glace; (*Press*) reportage exclusif *or* à sensation
  ▶ **scoop out** *vt* évider, creuser
  ▶ **scoop up** *vt* ramasser

**scooter** ['sku:tər] *n* (*motor cycle*) scooter *m*; (*toy*) trottinette *f*

**scope** [skəʊp] *n* (*capacity: of plan, undertaking*) portée *f*, envergure *f*; (: *of person*) compétence *f*, capacités *fpl*; (*opportunity*) possibilités *fpl*; **within the** ~ **of** dans les limites de; **there is plenty of** ~ **for improvement** (*Brit*) cela pourrait être beaucoup mieux

**scorch** [skɔ:tʃ] *vt* (*clothes*) brûler (légèrement), roussir; (*earth, grass*) dessécher, brûler

**scorched earth policy** ['skɔ:tʃt-] *n* politique *f* de la terre brûlée

**scorcher** ['skɔ:tʃər] *n* (*inf: hot day*) journée *f* torride

**scorching** ['skɔ:tʃɪŋ] *adj* torride, brûlant(e)

**score** [skɔ:r] *n* score *m*, décompte *m* des points; (*Mus*) partition *f* ▷ *vt* (*goal, point*) marquer; (*success*) remporter; (*cut: leather, wood, card*) entailler, inciser ▷ *vi* marquer des points; (*Football*) marquer un but; (*keep score*) compter les points; **on that** ~ sur ce chapitre, à cet égard; **to have an old** ~ **to settle with sb** (*fig*) avoir un (vieux) compte à régler avec qn; **a** ~ **of** (*twenty*) vingt; ~**s of** (*fig*) des tas de; **to** ~ **6 out of 10** obtenir 6 sur 10
  ▶ **score out** *vt* rayer, barrer, biffer

**scoreboard** ['skɔ:bɔ:d] *n* tableau *m*

**scorecard** ['skɔ:ka:d] *n* (*Sport*) carton *m*, feuille *f* de marque

**scoreline** ['skɔ:laɪn] *n* (*Sport*) score *m*

**scorer** ['skɔ:rər] *n* (*Football*) auteur *m* du but; buteur *m*; (*keeping score*) marqueur *m*

**scorn** [skɔ:n] *n* mépris *m*, dédain *m* ▷ *vt* mépriser, dédaigner

**scornful** ['skɔ:nful] *adj* méprisant(e), dédaigneux(-euse)

**Scorpio** ['skɔ:pɪəʊ] *n* le Scorpion; **to be** ~ être du Scorpion

**scorpion** ['skɔ:pɪən] *n* scorpion *m*

**Scot** [skɒt] *n* Écossais(e)

**Scotch** [skɒtʃ] *n* whisky *m*, scotch *m*

**scotch** [skɒtʃ] *vt* faire échouer; enrayer; étouffer

**Scotch tape®** (*US*) *n* scotch® *m*, ruban adhésif

**scot-free** ['skɒt'fri:] *adj*: **to get off** ~ s'en tirer sans être puni(e); s'en sortir indemne

**Scotland** ['skɒtlənd] *n* Écosse *f*

**Scots** [skɒts] *adj* écossais(e)

**Scotsman** ['skɒtsmən] (*irreg*) *n* Écossais *m*

**Scotswoman** ['skɒtswumən] (*irreg*) *n* Écossaise *f*

**Scottish** ['skɒtɪʃ] *adj* écossais(e); **the** ~ **National Party** le parti national écossais; **the** ~ **Parliament** le Parlement écossais

**scoundrel** ['skaundrl] *n* vaurien *m*

**scour** ['skauər] *vt* (*clean*) récurer; frotter; décaper; (*search*) battre, parcourir

**scourer** ['skauərər] *n* tampon abrasif *or* à récurer; (*powder*) poudre *f* à récurer

**scourge** [skə:dʒ] *n* fléau *m*

**scout** [skaut] *n* (*Mil*) éclaireur *m*; (*also:* **boy scout**) scout *m*; **girl** ~ (*US*) guide *f*
  ▶ **scout around** *vi* chercher

**scowl** [skaul] *vi* se renfrogner, avoir l'air maussade; **to** ~ **at** regarder de travers

**scrabble** ['skræbl] *vi* (*claw*): **to** ~ **(at)** gratter; **to** ~ **about** *or* **around for sth** chercher qch à tâtons ▷ *n*: **S~®** Scrabble® *m*

**scraggy** ['skrægɪ] *adj* décharné(e), efflanqué(e), famélique

**scram** [skræm] *vi* (*inf*) ficher le camp

**scramble** ['skræmbl] *n* (*rush*) bousculade *f*, ruée *f* ▷ *vi* grimper/descendre tant bien que mal; **to** ~ **for** se bousculer *or* se disputer pour (avoir); **to go scrambling** (*Sport*) faire du trial

**scrambled eggs** ['skræmbld-] *npl* œufs brouillés

**scrap** [skræp] *n* bout *m*, morceau *m*; (*fight*) bagarre *f*; (*also:* **scrap iron**) ferraille *f* ▷ *vt* jeter, mettre au rebut; (*fig*) abandonner, laisser tomber ▷ *vi* se bagarrer; **scraps** *npl* (*waste*) déchets *mpl*; **to sell sth for** ~ vendre qch à la casse *or* à la ferraille

**scrapbook** ['skræpbuk] *n* album *m*

**scrap dealer** *n* marchand *m* de ferraille

**scrape** [skreɪp] *vt, vi* gratter, racler ▷ *n*: **to get into a** ~ s'attirer des ennuis
  ▶ **scrape through** *vi* (*exam etc*) réussir de justesse
  ▶ **scrape together** *vt* (*money*) racler ses fonds de tiroir pour réunir

**scraper** ['skreɪpər] *n* grattoir *m*, racloir *m*

**scrap heap** *n* tas *m* de ferraille; (*fig*): **on the** ~ au rancart *or* rebut

**scrap merchant** *n* (*Brit*) marchand *m* de ferraille

**scrap metal** *n* ferraille *f*

**scrap paper** *n* papier *m* brouillon

**scrappy** ['skræpɪ] *adj* fragmentaire, décousu(e)

**scrap yard** *n* parc *m* à ferrailles; (*for cars*) cimetière *m* de voitures

**scratch** [skrætʃ] *n* égratignure *f*, rayure *f*; (*on paint*) éraflure *f*; (*from claw*) coup *m* de griffe ▷ *vt* (*rub*) (se) gratter; (*record*) rayer; (*paint etc*) érafler; (*with claw, nail*) griffer; (*Comput*) effacer ▷ *vi* (se) gratter; **to start from** ~ partir de zéro; **to be up to** ~ être à la hauteur

**scratch card** *n* carte *f* à gratter

**scrawl** [skrɔ:l] *n* gribouillage *m* ▷ *vi* gribouiller

**scrawny** ['skrɔ:nɪ] *adj* décharné(e)

**scream** [skri:m] *n* cri perçant, hurlement *m* ▷ *vi* crier, hurler; **to be a ~** (*inf*) être impayable; **to ~ at sb to do sth** crier *or* hurler à qn de faire qch

**scree** [skri:] *n* éboulis *m*

**screech** [skri:tʃ] *n* cri strident, hurlement *m*; (*of tyres, brakes*) crissement *m*, grincement *m* ▷ *vi* hurler; crisser, grincer

**screen** [skri:n] *n* écran *m*; (*in room*) paravent *m*; (*Cine, TV*) écran; (*fig*) écran, rideau *m* ▷ *vt* masquer, cacher; (*from the wind etc*) abriter, protéger; (*film*) projeter; (*candidates etc*) filtrer; (*for illness*): **to ~ sb for sth** faire subir un test de dépistage de qch à qn

**screen editing** [-'ɛdɪtɪŋ] *n* (*Comput*) édition *f or* correction *f* sur écran

**screening** ['skri:nɪŋ] *n* (*of film*) projection *f*; (*Med*) test *m* (*or tests*) de dépistage; (*for security*) filtrage *m*

**screen memory** *n* (*Comput*) mémoire *f* écran

**screenplay** ['skri:npleɪ] *n* scénario *m*

**screen saver** *n* (*Comput*) économiseur *m* d'écran

**screen test** *n* bout *m* d'essai

**screw** [skru:] *n* vis *f*; (*propeller*) hélice *f* ▷ *vt* (*also:* **screw in**) visser; (*inf!: woman*) baiser (!); **to ~ sth to the wall** visser qch au mur; **to have one's head ~ed on** (*fig*) avoir la tête sur les épaules
▶ **screw up** *vt* (*paper etc*) froisser; (*inf: ruin*) bousiller; **to ~ up one's eyes** se plisser les yeux; **to ~ up one's face** faire la grimace

**screwdriver** ['skru:draɪvəʳ] *n* tournevis *m*

**screwed-up** ['skru:d'ʌp] *adj* (*inf*): **to be ~** être paumé(e)

**screwy** ['skru:ɪ] *adj* (*inf*) dingue, cinglé(e)

**scribble** ['skrɪbl] *n* gribouillage *m* ▷ *vt* gribouiller, griffonner; **to ~ sth down** griffonner qch

**scribe** [skraɪb] *n* scribe *m*

**script** [skrɪpt] *n* (*Cine etc*) scénario *m*, texte *m*; (*in exam*) copie *f*; (*writing*) (écriture *f*) script *m*

**scripted** ['skrɪptɪd] *adj* (*Radio, TV*) préparé(e) à l'avance

**Scripture** ['skrɪptʃəʳ] *n* Écriture sainte

**scriptwriter** ['skrɪptraɪtəʳ] *n* scénariste *m/f*, dialoguiste *m/f*

**scroll** [skrəul] *n* rouleau *m* ▷ *vt* (*Comput*) faire défiler (sur l'écran)

**scrotum** ['skrəutəm] *n* scrotum *m*

**scrounge** [skraundʒ] (*inf*) *vt*: **to ~ sth (off or from sb)** se faire payer qch (par qn), emprunter qch (à qn) ▷ *vi*: **to ~ on sb** vivre aux crochets de qn

**scrounger** ['skraundʒəʳ] *n* parasite *m*

**scrub** [skrʌb] *n* (*clean*) nettoyage *m* (à la brosse); (*land*) broussailles *fpl* ▷ *vt* (*floor*) nettoyer à la brosse; (*pan*) récurer; (*washing*) frotter; (*reject*) annuler

**scrubbing brush** ['skrʌbɪŋ-] *n* brosse dure

**scruff** [skrʌf] *n*: **by the ~ of the neck** par la peau du cou

**scruffy** ['skrʌfɪ] *adj* débraillé(e)

**scrum** ['skrʌm], **scrummage** ['skrʌmɪdʒ] *n* mêlée *f*

**scruple** ['skru:pl] *n* scrupule *m*; **to have no ~s about doing sth** n'avoir aucun scrupule à faire qch

**scrupulous** ['skru:pjuləs] *adj* scrupuleux(-euse)

**scrupulously** ['skru:pjuləslɪ] *adv* scrupuleusement; **to be ~ honest** être d'une honnêteté scrupuleuse

**scrutinize** ['skru:tɪnaɪz] *vt* scruter, examiner minutieusement

**scrutiny** ['skru:tɪnɪ] *n* examen minutieux; **under the ~ of sb** sous la surveillance de qn

**scuba** ['sku:bə] *n* scaphandre *m* (autonome)

**scuba diving** ['sku:bə-] *n* plongée sous-marine

**scuff** [skʌf] *vt* érafler

**scuffle** ['skʌfl] *n* échauffourée *f*, rixe *f*

**scullery** ['skʌlərɪ] *n* arrière-cuisine *f*

**sculptor** ['skʌlptəʳ] *n* sculpteur *m*

**sculpture** ['skʌlptʃəʳ] *n* sculpture *f*

**scum** [skʌm] *n* écume *f*, mousse *f*; (*pej: people*) rebut *m*, lie *f*

**scupper** ['skʌpəʳ] *vt* (*Brit*) saborder

**scurrilous** ['skʌrɪləs] *adj* haineux(-euse), virulent(e); calomnieux(-euse)

**scurry** ['skʌrɪ] *vi* filer à toute allure; **to ~ off** détaler, se sauver

**scurvy** ['skə:vɪ] *n* scorbut *m*

**scuttle** ['skʌtl] *n* (*Naut*) écoutille *f*; (*also:* **coal scuttle**) seau *m* (à charbon) ▷ *vt* (*ship*) saborder ▷ *vi* (*scamper*): **to ~ away, ~ off** détaler

**scythe** [saɪð] *n* faux *f*

**SD, S. Dak.** *abbr* (*US*) = **South Dakota**

**SDI** *n abbr* (= *Strategic Defense Initiative*) IDS *f*

**SDLP** *n abbr* (*Brit Pol*) = **Social Democratic and Labour Party**

**sea** [si:] *n* mer *f* ▷ *cpd* marin(e), de (la) mer, maritime; **on the ~** (*boat*) en mer; (*town*) au bord de la mer; **by** *or* **beside the ~** (*holiday, town*) au bord de la mer; **by ~** par mer, en bateau; **out to ~** au large; **(out) at ~** en mer; **heavy** *or* **rough ~(s)** grosse mer, mer agitée; **a ~ of faces** (*fig*) une multitude de visages; **to be all at ~** (*fig*) nager complètement

**sea bed** *n* fond *m* de la mer

**sea bird** *n* oiseau *m* de mer

**seaboard** ['si:bɔ:d] *n* côte *f*

**sea breeze** *n* brise *f* de mer

**seafarer** ['si:fɛərəʳ] *n* marin *m*

**seafaring** ['si:fɛərɪŋ] *adj* (*life*) de marin; **~ people** les gens *mpl* de mer

**seafood** ['si:fu:d] *n* fruits *mpl* de mer

**sea front** ['si:frʌnt] *n* bord *m* de mer

**seagoing** ['si:gəuɪŋ] *adj* (*ship*) de haute mer

**seagull** ['si:gʌl] *n* mouette *f*

**seal** [si:l] *n* (*animal*) phoque *m*; (*stamp*) sceau *m*, cachet *m*; (*impression*) cachet, estampille *f* ▷ *vt* sceller; (*envelope*) coller; (*: with seal*) cacheter; (*decide: sb's fate*) décider (de); (*: bargain*) conclure; **~ of approval** approbation *f*
▶ **seal off** *vt* (*close*) condamner; (*forbid entry to*) interdire l'accès de

**sea level** *n* niveau *m* de la mer

**sealing wax** ['si:lɪŋ-] *n* cire *f* à cacheter

**S**

**sea lion** n lion m de mer

**sealskin** ['si:lskɪn] n peau f de phoque

**seam** [si:m] n couture f; (of coal) veine f, filon m;
  **the hall was bursting at the ~s** la salle était
  pleine à craquer

**seaman** ['si:mən] (irreg) n marin m

**seamanship** ['si:mənʃɪp] n qualités fpl de marin

**seamless** ['si:mlɪs] adj sans couture(s)

**seamy** ['si:mɪ] adj louche, mal famé(e)

**seance** ['seɪɔns] n séance f de spiritisme

**seaplane** ['si:pleɪn] n hydravion m

**seaport** ['si:pɔ:t] n port m de mer

**search** [sə:tʃ] n (for person, thing, Comput)
  recherche(s) f(pl); (of drawer, pockets) fouille f;
  (Law: at sb's home) perquisition f ▷ vt fouiller;
  (examine) examiner minutieusement; scruter
  ▷ vi: **to ~ for** chercher; **in ~ of** à la recherche de
  ▶ **search through** vt fus fouiller

**search engine** n (Comput) moteur m de
  recherche

**searcher** ['sə:tʃər] n chercheur(-euse)

**searching** ['sə:tʃɪŋ] adj (look, question)
  pénétrant(e); (examination) minutieux(-euse)

**searchlight** ['sə:tʃlaɪt] n projecteur m

**search party** n expédition f de secours

**search warrant** n mandat m de perquisition

**searing** ['sɪərɪŋ] adj (heat) brûlant(e); (pain)
  aigu(ë)

**seashore** ['si:ʃɔ:r] n rivage m, plage f, bord m de
  (la) mer; **on the ~** sur le rivage

**seasick** ['si:sɪk] adj: **to be ~** avoir le mal de mer

**seaside** ['si:saɪd] n bord m de mer

**seaside resort** n station f balnéaire

**season** ['si:zn] n saison f ▷ vt assaisonner,
  relever; **to be in/out of ~** être/ne pas être de
  saison; **the busy ~** (for shops) la période de
  pointe; (for hotels etc) la pleine saison; **the open
  ~** (Hunting) la saison de la chasse

**seasonal** ['si:znl] adj saisonnier(-ière)

**seasoned** ['si:znd] adj (wood) séché(e); (fig:
  worker, actor, troops) expérimenté(e); **a ~
  campaigner** un vieux militant, un vétéran

**seasoning** ['si:znɪŋ] n assaisonnement m

**season ticket** n carte f d'abonnement

**seat** [si:t] n siège m; (in bus, train: place) place f;
  (Parliament) siège; (buttocks) postérieur m; (of
  trousers) fond m ▷ vt faire asseoir, placer; (have
  room for) avoir des places assises pour, pouvoir
  accueillir; **are there any ~s left?** est-ce qu'il
  reste des places?; **to take one's ~** prendre place;
  **to be ~ed** être assis; **please be ~ed** veuillez
  vous asseoir

**seat belt** n ceinture f de sécurité

**seating** ['si:tɪŋ] n sièges fpl, places assises

**seating capacity** ['si:tɪŋ-] n nombre m de
  places assises

**sea urchin** n oursin m

**sea water** n eau f de mer

**seaweed** ['si:wi:d] n algues fpl

**seaworthy** ['si:wə:ðɪ] adj en état de naviguer

**SEC** n abbr (US: = Securities and Exchange Commission)
  ≈ COB f (= Commission des opérations de Bourse)

**sec.** abbr (= second) sec

**secateurs** [sɛkə'tə:z] npl sécateur m

**secede** [sɪ'si:d] vi faire sécession

**secluded** [sɪ'klu:dɪd] adj retiré(e), à l'écart

**seclusion** [sɪ'klu:ʒən] n solitude f

**second¹** ['sɛkənd] num deuxième, second(e)
  ▷ adv (in race etc) en seconde position ▷ n (unit of
  time) seconde f; (Aut: also: **second gear**) seconde;
  (in series, position) deuxième m/f, second(e);
  (Comm: imperfect) article m de second choix; (Brit
  Scol) ≈ licence f avec mention ▷ vt (motion)
  appuyer; **seconds** npl (inf: food) rab m (inf);
  **Charles the S~** Charles II; **just a ~!** une
  seconde!, un instant!; (stopping sb) pas si vite!; **~
  floor** (Brit) deuxième (étage) m; (US) premier
  (étage) m; **to ask for a ~ opinion** (Med)
  demander l'avis d'un autre médecin

**second²** [sɪ'kɔnd] vt (employee) détacher, mettre
  en détachement

**secondary** ['sɛkəndərɪ] adj secondaire

**secondary school** n (age 11 to 15) collège m; (age 15
  to 18) lycée m

**second-best** [sɛkənd'bɛst] n deuxième choix m;
  **as a ~** faute de mieux

**second-class** ['sɛkənd'klɑ:s] adj de deuxième
  classe; (Rail) de seconde (classe); (Post) au tarif
  réduit; (pej) de qualité inférieure ▷ adv (Rail) en
  seconde; (Post) au tarif réduit; **~ citizen**
  citoyen(ne) de deuxième classe

**second cousin** n cousin(e) issu(e) de germains

**seconder** ['sɛkəndər] n personne f qui appuie
  une motion

**second-guess** ['sɛkənd'gɛs] vt (predict) (essayer
  d')anticiper; **they're still trying to ~ his
  motives** ils essaient toujours de comprendre
  ses raisons

**second hand** n (on clock) trotteuse f

**secondhand** ['sɛkənd'hænd] adj d'occasion;
  (information) de seconde main ▷ adv (buy)
  d'occasion; **to hear sth ~** apprendre qch
  indirectement

**second-in-command** ['sɛkəndɪnkə'mɑ:nd] n
  (Mil) commandant m en second; (Admin)
  adjoint(e), sous-chef m

**secondly** ['sɛkəndlɪ] adv deuxièmement;
  **firstly ... ~ ...** d'abord ... ensuite ... or de plus ...

**secondment** [sɪ'kɔndmənt] n (Brit)
  détachement m

**second-rate** ['sɛkənd'reɪt] adj de deuxième
  ordre, de qualité inférieure

**second thoughts** npl: **to have ~** changer d'avis;
  **on ~** or **thought** (US) à la réflexion

**secrecy** ['si:krəsɪ] n secret m; **in ~** en secret

**secret** ['si:krɪt] adj secret(-ète) ▷ n secret m; **in ~**
  (adv) en secret, secrètement, en cachette; **to
  keep sth ~ from sb** cacher qch à qn, ne pas
  révéler qch à qn; **to make no ~ of sth** ne pas
  cacher qch; **keep it ~** n'en parle à personne

**secret agent** n agent secret

**secretarial** [sɛkrɪ'tɛərɪəl] adj de secrétaire, de
  secrétariat

**secretariat** [sɛkrɪ'tɛərɪət] n secrétariat m

**secretary** ['sɛkrətrɪ] n secrétaire m/f; (Comm) secrétaire général; **S~ of State** (US Pol) ≈ ministre m des Affaires étrangères; **S~ of State (for)** (Brit Pol) ministre m (de)

**secretary-general** ['sɛkrətrɪ'dʒɛnərl] n secrétaire général

**secrete** [sɪ'kriːt] vt (Anat, Biol, Med) sécréter; (hide) cacher

**secretion** [sɪ'kriːʃən] n sécrétion f

**secretive** ['siːkrətɪv] adj réservé(e); (pej) cachottier(-ière), dissimulé(e)

**secretly** ['siːkrɪtlɪ] adv en secret, secrètement, en cachette

**secret police** n police secrète

**secret service** n services secrets

**sect** [sɛkt] n secte f

**sectarian** [sɛk'tɛərɪən] adj sectaire

**section** ['sɛkʃən] n section f; (department) section; (Comm) rayon m; (of document) section, article m, paragraphe m; (cut) coupe f ▷ vt sectionner; **the business** etc ~ (Press) la page des affaires etc

**sector** ['sɛktər] n secteur m

**secular** ['sɛkjulər] adj laïque

**secure** [sɪ'kjuər] adj (free from anxiety) sans inquiétude, sécurisé(e); (firmly fixed) solide, bien attaché(e) (or fermé(e) etc); (in safe place) en lieu sûr, en sûreté ▷ vt (fix) fixer, attacher; (get) obtenir, se procurer; (Comm: loan) garantir; **to make sth ~** bien fixer or attacher qch; **to ~ sth for sb** obtenir qch pour qn, procurer qch à qn

**secured creditor** [sɪ'kjuəd-] n créancier(-ière), privilégié(e)

**security** [sɪ'kjuərɪtɪ] n sécurité f, mesures fpl de sécurité; (for loan) caution f, garantie f; **securities** npl (Stock Exchange) valeurs fpl, titres mpl; **to increase** or **tighten ~** renforcer les mesures de sécurité; **~ of tenure** stabilité f d'un emploi, titularisation f

**Security Council** n: **the ~** le Conseil de sécurité

**security forces** npl forces fpl de sécurité

**security guard** n garde chargé de la sécurité; (transporting money) convoyeur m de fonds

**security risk** n menace f pour la sécurité de l'état (or d'une entreprise etc)

**sedan** [sə'dæn] n (US Aut) berline f

**sedate** [sɪ'deɪt] adj calme; posé(e) ▷ vt donner des sédatifs à

**sedation** [sɪ'deɪʃən] n (Med) sédation f; **to be under ~** être sous calmants

**sedative** ['sɛdɪtɪv] n calmant m, sédatif m

**sedentary** ['sɛdntrɪ] adj sédentaire

**sediment** ['sɛdɪmənt] n sédiment m, dépôt m

**sedition** [sɪ'dɪʃən] n sédition f

**seduce** [sɪ'djuːs] vt séduire

**seduction** [sɪ'dʌkʃən] n séduction f

**seductive** [sɪ'dʌktɪv] adj séduisant(e); (smile) séducteur(-trice); (fig: offer) alléchant(e)

**see** [siː] (pt **saw**, pp **seen** [sɔː, siːn]) vt (gen) voir; (accompany): **to ~ sb to the door** reconduire or raccompagner qn jusqu'à la porte ▷ vi voir ▷ n évêché m; **to ~ that** (ensure) veiller à ce que + sub,

faire en sorte que + sub, s'assurer que; **there was nobody to be ~n** il n'y avait pas un chat; **let me ~** (show me) fais(-moi) voir; (let me think) voyons (un peu); **to go and ~ sb** aller voir qn; **~ for yourself** voyez vous-même; **I don't know what she ~s in him** je ne sais pas ce qu'elle lui trouve; **as far as I can ~** pour autant que je puisse en juger; **~ you!** au revoir!, à bientôt!; **~ you soon/later/tomorrow!** à bientôt/plus tard/demain!

▸ **see about** vt fus (deal with) s'occuper de

▸ **see off** vt accompagner (à l'aéroport etc)

▸ **see out** vt (take to door) raccompagner à la porte

▸ **see through** vt mener à bonne fin ▷ vt fus voir clair dans

▸ **see to** vt fus s'occuper de, se charger de

**seed** [siːd] n graine f; (fig) germe m; (Tennis etc) tête f de série; **to go to ~** (plant) monter en graine; (fig) se laisser aller

**seedless** ['siːdlɪs] adj sans pépins

**seedling** ['siːdlɪŋ] n jeune plant m, semis m

**seedy** ['siːdɪ] adj (shabby) minable, miteux(-euse)

**seeing** ['siːɪŋ] conj: **~ (that)** vu que, étant donné que

**seek** [siːk] (pt, pp **sought** [sɔːt]) vt chercher, rechercher; **to ~ advice/help from sb** demander conseil/de l'aide à qn

▸ **seek out** vt (person) chercher

**seem** [siːm] vi sembler, paraître; **there ~s to be ...** il semble qu'il y a ..., on dirait qu'il y a ...; **it ~s (that) ...** il semble que ...; **what ~s to be the trouble?** qu'est-ce qui ne va pas?

**seemingly** ['siːmɪŋlɪ] adv apparemment

**seen** [siːn] pp of **see**

**seep** [siːp] vi suinter, filtrer

**seer** [sɪər] n prophète (prophétesse) voyant(e)

**seersucker** ['sɪəsʌkər] n cloqué m, étoffe cloquée

**seesaw** ['siːsɔː] n (jeu m de) bascule f

**seethe** [siːð] vi être en effervescence; **to ~ with anger** bouillir de colère

**see-through** ['siːθruː] adj transparent(e)

**segment** ['sɛgmənt] n segment m; (of orange) quartier m

**segregate** ['sɛgrɪgeɪt] vt séparer, isoler

**segregation** [sɛgrɪ'geɪʃən] n ségrégation f

**Seine** [seɪn] n: **the (River) ~** la Seine

**seismic** ['saɪzmɪk] adj sismique

**seize** [siːz] vt (grasp) saisir, attraper; (take possession of) s'emparer de; (opportunity) saisir; (Law) saisir

▸ **seize on** vt fus saisir, sauter sur

▸ **seize up** vi (Tech) se gripper

▸ **seize upon** vt fus = **seize on**

**seizure** ['siːʒər] n (Med) crise f, attaque f; (of power) prise f; (Law) saisie f

**seldom** ['sɛldəm] adv rarement

**select** [sɪ'lɛkt] adj choisi(e), d'élite; (hotel, restaurant, club) chic inv, sélect inv ▷ vt sélectionner, choisir; **a ~ few** quelques privilégiés

**selection** [sɪ'lɛkʃən] n sélection f, choix m

777

**selection committee** n comité m de sélection
**selective** [sɪ'lɛktɪv] adj sélectif(-ive); (school) à recrutement sélectif
**selector** [sɪ'lɛktə<sup>r</sup>] n (person) sélectionneur(-euse); (Tech) sélecteur m
**self** [sɛlf] n (pl **selves**) [sɛlvz]: **the ~** le moi inv ▷ prefix auto-
**self-addressed** ['sɛlfə'drɛst] adj: ~ **envelope** enveloppe f à mon (or votre etc) nom
**self-adhesive** [sɛlfəd'hiːzɪv] adj autocollant(e)
**self-assertive** [sɛlfə'səːtɪv] adj autoritaire
**self-assurance** [sɛlfə'ʃuərəns] n assurance f
**self-assured** [sɛlfə'ʃuəd] adj sûr(e) de soi, plein(e) d'assurance
**self-catering** [sɛlf'keɪtərɪŋ] adj (Brit: flat) avec cuisine, où l'on peut faire sa cuisine; (: holiday) en appartement (or chalet etc) loué
**self-centred**, (US) **self-centered** [sɛlf'sɛntəd] adj égocentrique
**self-cleaning** [sɛlf'kliːnɪŋ] adj autonettoyant(e).
**self-confessed** [sɛlfkən'fɛst] adj (alcoholic etc) déclaré(e), qui ne s'en cache pas
**self-confidence** [sɛlf'kɔnfɪdns] n confiance f en soi
**self-confident** [sɛlf'kɔnfɪdnt] adj sûr(e) de soi, plein(e) d'assurance
**self-conscious** [sɛlf'kɔnʃəs] adj timide, qui manque d'assurance
**self-contained** [sɛlfkən'teɪnd] adj (Brit: flat) avec entrée particulière, indépendant(e)
**self-control** [sɛlfkən'trəul] n maîtrise f de soi
**self-defeating** [sɛlfdɪ'fiːtɪŋ] adj qui a un effet contraire à l'effet recherché
**self-defence**, (US) **self-defense** [sɛlfdɪ'fɛns] n autodéfense f; (Law) légitime défense f
**self-discipline** [sɛlf'dɪsɪplɪn] n discipline personnelle
**self-drive** [sɛlf'draɪv] adj (Brit): ~ **car** voiture f de location
**self-employed** [sɛlfɪm'plɔɪd] adj qui travaille à son compte
**self-esteem** [sɛlfɪ'stiːm] n amour-propre m
**self-evident** [sɛlf'ɛvɪdnt] adj évident(e), qui va de soi
**self-explanatory** [sɛlfɪk'splænətrɪ] adj qui se passe d'explication
**self-governing** [sɛlf'ɡʌvənɪŋ] adj autonome
**self-help** ['sɛlf'hɛlp] n initiative personnelle, efforts personnels
**self-importance** [sɛlfɪm'pɔːtns] n suffisance f
**self-indulgent** [sɛlfɪn'dʌldʒənt] adj qui ne se refuse rien
**self-inflicted** [sɛlfɪn'flɪktɪd] adj volontaire
**self-interest** [sɛlf'ɪntrɪst] n intérêt personnel
**selfish** ['sɛlfɪʃ] adj égoïste
**selfishness** ['sɛlfɪʃnɪs] n égoïsme m
**selfless** ['sɛlflɪs] adj désintéressé(e)
**selflessly** ['sɛlflɪslɪ] adv sans penser à soi
**self-made man** ['sɛlfmeɪd-] n self-made man m
**self-pity** [sɛlf'pɪtɪ] n apitoiement m sur soi-même

**self-portrait** [sɛlf'pɔːtreɪt] n autoportrait m
**self-possessed** [sɛlfpə'zɛst] adj assuré(e)
**self-preservation** ['sɛlfprɛzə'veɪʃən] n instinct m de conservation
**self-raising** [sɛlf'reɪzɪŋ], (US) **self-rising** [sɛlf'raɪzɪŋ] adj: ~ **flour** farine f pour gâteaux (avec levure incorporée)
**self-reliant** [sɛlfrɪ'laɪənt] adj indépendant(e)
**self-respect** [sɛlfrɪs'pɛkt] n respect m de soi, amour-propre m
**self-respecting** [sɛlfrɪs'pɛktɪŋ] adj qui se respecte
**self-righteous** [sɛlf'raɪtʃəs] adj satisfait(e) de soi, pharisaïque
**self-rising** [sɛlf'raɪzɪŋ] adj (US) = **self-raising**
**self-sacrifice** [sɛlf'sækrɪfaɪs] n abnégation f
**self-same** ['sɛlfseɪm] adj même
**self-satisfied** [sɛlf'sætɪsfaɪd] adj content(e) de soi, suffisant(e)
**self-sealing** [sɛlf'siːlɪŋ] adj (envelope) autocollant(e)
**self-service** [sɛlf'səːvɪs] adj, n libre-service (m), self-service (m)
**self-styled** ['sɛlfstaɪld] adj soi-disant inv
**self-sufficient** [sɛlfsə'fɪʃənt] adj indépendant(e)
**self-supporting** [sɛlfsə'pɔːtɪŋ] adj financièrement indépendant(e)
**self-tanning** ['sɛlf'tænɪŋ] adj: ~ **cream** or **lotion** etc autobronzant m
**self-taught** [sɛlf'tɔːt] adj autodidacte
**sell** (pt, pp **sold**) [sɛl, səuld] vt vendre ▷ vi se vendre; **to ~** or **for 10 euros** se vendre 10 euros; **to ~ sb an idea** (fig) faire accepter une idée à qn
 ▶ **sell off** vt liquider
 ▶ **sell out** vi: **to ~ out (of sth)** (use up stock) vendre tout son stock (de qch); **to ~ out (to)** (Comm) vendre son fonds or son affaire (à) ▷ vt vendre tout son stock de; **the tickets are all sold out** il ne reste plus de billets
 ▶ **sell up** vi vendre son fonds or son affaire
**sell-by date** ['sɛlbaɪ-] n date f limite de vente
**seller** ['sɛlə<sup>r</sup>] n vendeur(-euse), marchand(e); **~'s market** marché m à la hausse
**selling price** ['sɛlɪŋ-] n prix m de vente
**Sellotape®** ['sɛləuteɪp] n (Brit) scotch® m
**sellout** ['sɛlaut] n trahison f, capitulation f; (of tickets): **it was a ~** tous les billets ont été vendus
**selves** [sɛlvz] npl of **self**
**semantic** [sɪ'mæntɪk] adj sémantique
**semantics** [sɪ'mæntɪks] n sémantique f
**semaphore** ['sɛməfɔː<sup>r</sup>] n signaux mpl à bras; (Rail) sémaphore m
**semblance** ['sɛmblns] n semblant m
**semen** ['siːmən] n sperme m
**semester** [sɪ'mɛstə<sup>r</sup>] n (esp US) semestre m
**semi...** ['sɛmɪ] prefix semi-, demi-; à demi, à moitié ▷ n: **semi** = **semidetached house**
**semi-breve** ['sɛmɪbriːv] n (Brit) ronde f
**semicircle** ['sɛmɪsəːkl] n demi-cercle m
**semicircular** ['sɛmɪ'səːkjulə<sup>r</sup>] adj en demi-cercle, semi-circulaire

**semicolon** [sɛmɪ'kəʊlən] n point-virgule m
**semiconductor** [sɛmɪkən'dʌktəʳ] n semi-conducteur m
**semiconscious** [sɛmɪ'kɔnʃəs] adj à demi conscient(e)
**semidetached** [sɛmɪdɪ'tætʃt], **semidetached house** n (Brit) maison jumelée or jumelle
**semi-final** [sɛmɪ'faɪnl] n demi-finale f
**seminar** ['sɛmɪnɑ:ʳ] n séminaire m
**seminary** ['sɛmɪnərɪ] n (Rel: for priests) séminaire m
**semiprecious** [sɛmɪ'prɛʃəs] adj semi-précieux(-euse)
**semiquaver** ['sɛmɪkweɪvəʳ] n (Brit) double croche f
**semiskilled** [sɛmɪ'skɪld] adj: ~ **worker** ouvrier(-ière) spécialisé(e)
**semi-skimmed** ['sɛmɪ'skɪmd] adj demi-écrémé(e)
**semitone** ['sɛmɪtəʊn] n (Mus) demi-ton m
**semolina** [sɛmə'li:nə] n semoule f
**SEN** n abbr (Brit) = **State Enrolled Nurse**
**Sen., sen.** abbr = **senator; senior**
**senate** ['sɛnɪt] n sénat m; (US): **the S~** le Sénat; voir article

⊚ S E N A T E
⊚
⊚ Le *Senate* est la chambre haute du
⊚ "Congress", le parlement des États-Unis. Il
⊚ est composé de 100 sénateurs, 2 par État,
⊚ élus au suffrage universel direct tous les 6
⊚ ans, un tiers d'entre eux étant renouvelé
⊚ tous les 2 ans.

**senator** ['sɛnɪtəʳ] n sénateur m
**send** (pt, pp **sent**) [sɛnd, sɛnt] vt envoyer; **to ~ by post** or (US) **mail** envoyer or expédier par la poste; **to ~ sb for sth** envoyer qn chercher qch; **to ~ word that ...** faire dire que ...; **she ~s (you) her love** elle vous adresse ses amitiés; **to ~ sb to Coventry** (Brit) mettre qn en quarantaine; **to ~ sb to sleep** endormir qn; **to ~ sb into fits of laughter** faire rire qn aux éclats; **to ~ sth flying** envoyer valser qch
▶ **send away** vt (letter, goods) envoyer, expédier
▶ **send away for** vt fus commander par correspondance, se faire envoyer
▶ **send back** vt renvoyer
▶ **send for** vt fus envoyer chercher; faire venir; (by post) se faire envoyer, commander par correspondance
▶ **send in** vt (report, application, resignation) remettre
▶ **send off** vt (goods) envoyer, expédier; (Brit Sport: player) expulser or renvoyer du terrain
▶ **send on** vt (Brit: letter) faire suivre; (luggage etc: in advance) (faire) expédier à l'avance
▶ **send out** vt (invitation) envoyer (par la poste); (emit: light, heat, signal) émettre
▶ **send round** vt (letter, document etc) faire circuler

▶ **send up** vt (person, price) faire monter; (Brit: parody) mettre en boîte, parodier
**sender** ['sɛndəʳ] n expéditeur(-trice)
**send-off** ['sɛndɔf] n: **a good ~** des adieux chaleureux
**Senegal** [sɛnɪ'gɔ:l] n Sénégal m
**Senegalese** [sɛnɪgə'li:z] adj sénégalais(e) ▷ n (pl inv) Sénégalais(e)
**senile** ['si:naɪl] adj sénile
**senility** [sɪ'nɪlɪtɪ] n sénilité f
**senior** ['si:nɪəʳ] adj (older) aîné(e), plus âgé(e); (high-ranking) de haut niveau; (of higher rank): **to be ~ to sb** être le supérieur de qn ▷ n (older): **she is 15 years his ~** elle est son aînée de 15 ans, elle est plus âgée que lui de 15 ans; (in service) personne f qui a plus d'ancienneté; **P. Jones ~** P. Jones père
**senior citizen** n personne f du troisième âge
**senior high school** n (US) ≈ lycée m
**seniority** [si:nɪ'ɔrɪtɪ] n priorité f d'âge, ancienneté f; (in rank) supériorité f (hiérarchique)
**sensation** [sɛn'seɪʃən] n sensation f; **to create a ~** faire sensation
**sensational** [sɛn'seɪʃənl] adj qui fait sensation; (marvellous) sensationnel(le)
**sense** [sɛns] n sens m; (feeling) sentiment m; (meaning) sens, signification f; (wisdom) bon sens ▷ vt sentir, pressentir; **senses** npl raison f; **it makes ~** c'est logique; **there is no ~ in (doing) that** cela n'a pas de sens; **to come to one's ~s** (regain consciousness) reprendre conscience; (become reasonable) revenir à la raison; **to take leave of one's ~s** perdre la tête
**senseless** ['sɛnslɪs] adj insensé(e), stupide; (unconscious) sans connaissance
**sense of humour**, (US) **sense of humor** n sens m de l'humour
**sensibility** [sɛnsɪ'bɪlɪtɪ] n sensibilité f; **sensibilities** npl susceptibilité f
**sensible** ['sɛnsɪbl] adj sensé(e), raisonnable; (shoes etc) pratique
**sensitive** ['sɛnsɪtɪv] adj: ~ **(to)** sensible (à); **he is very ~ about it** c'est un point très sensible (chez lui)
**sensitivity** [sɛnsɪ'tɪvɪtɪ] n sensibilité f
**sensual** ['sɛnsjuəl] adj sensuel(le)
**sensuous** ['sɛnsjuəs] adj voluptueux(-euse), sensuel(le)
**sent** [sɛnt] pt, pp of **send**
**sentence** ['sɛntns] n (Ling) phrase f; (Law: judgment) condamnation f, sentence f; (: punishment) peine f ▷ vt: **to ~ sb to death/to 5 years** condamner qn à mort/à 5 ans; **to pass ~ on sb** prononcer une peine contre qn
**sentiment** ['sɛntɪmənt] n sentiment m; (opinion) opinion f, avis m
**sentimental** [sɛntɪ'mɛntl] adj sentimental(e)
**sentimentality** [sɛntɪmɛn'tælɪtɪ] n sentimentalité f, sensiblerie f
**sentry** ['sɛntrɪ] n sentinelle f, factionnaire m
**sentry duty** n: **to be on ~** être de faction

**S**

**Seoul** [səul] n Séoul
**separable** ['sɛprəbl] adj séparable
**separate** [adj 'sɛprɪt, vb 'sɛpəreɪt] adj séparé(e);
(organization) indépendant(e); (day, occasion, issue)
différent(e) ▷ vt séparer; (distinguish) distinguer
▷ vi se séparer; **~ from** distinct(e) de; **under ~
cover** (Comm) sous pli séparé; **to ~ into** diviser
en
**separately** ['sɛprɪtlɪ] adv séparément
**separates** ['sɛprɪts] npl (clothes) coordonnés mpl
**separation** [sɛpə'reɪʃən] n séparation f
**Sept.** abbr (= September) sept
**September** [sɛp'tɛmbə'] n septembre m; for
phrases see also **July**
**septic** ['sɛptɪk] adj septique; (wound) infecté(e);
**to go ~** s'infecter
**septicaemia** [sɛptɪ'si:mɪə] n septicémie f
**septic tank** n fosse f septique
**sequel** ['si:kwl] n conséquence f; séquelles fpl;
(of story) suite f
**sequence** ['si:kwəns] n ordre m, suite f; (in film)
séquence f; (dance) numéro m; **in ~** par ordre,
dans l'ordre, les uns après les autres; **~ of
tenses** concordance f des temps
**sequential** [sɪ'kwɛnʃəl] adj: **~ access** (Comput)
accès séquentiel
**sequin** ['si:kwɪn] n paillette f
**Serb** [sə:b] adj, n = **Serbian**
**Serbia** ['sə:bɪə] n Serbie f
**Serbian** ['sə:bɪən] adj serbe ▷ n Serbe m/f; (Ling)
serbe m
**Serbo-Croat** ['sə:bəu'krəuæt] n (Ling) serbo-
croate m
**serenade** [sɛrə'neɪd] n sérénade f ▷ vt donner
une sérénade à
**serene** [sɪ'ri:n] adj serein(e), calme, paisible
**serenity** [sə'rɛnɪtɪ] n sérénité f, calme m
**sergeant** ['sɑ:dʒənt] n sergent m; (Police)
brigadier m
**sergeant major** n sergent-major m
**serial** ['sɪərɪəl] n feuilleton m ▷ adj (Comput:
interface, printer) série inv; (: access) séquentiel(le)
**serialize** ['sɪərɪəlaɪz] vt publier (or adapter) en
feuilleton
**serial killer** n meurtrier m tuant en série
**serial number** n numéro m de série
**series** ['sɪərɪz] n série f; (Publishing) collection f
**serious** ['sɪərɪəs] adj sérieux(-euse); (accident etc)
grave; **are you ~ (about it)?** parlez-vous
sérieusement?
**seriously** ['sɪərɪəslɪ] adv sérieusement; (hurt)
gravement; **~ rich/difficult** (inf: extremely)
drôlement riche/difficile; **to take sth/sb ~**
prendre qch/qn au sérieux
**seriousness** ['sɪərɪəsnɪs] n sérieux m, gravité f
**sermon** ['sə:mən] n sermon m
**serrated** [sɪ'reɪtɪd] adj en dents de scie
**serum** ['sɪərəm] n sérum m
**servant** ['sə:vənt] n domestique m/f; (fig)
serviteur (servante)
**serve** [sə:v] vt (employer etc) servir, être au service
de; (purpose) servir à; (customer, food, meal) servir;

(subj: train) desservir; (apprenticeship) faire,
accomplir; (prison term) faire; purger ▷ vi (Tennis)
servir; (be useful): **to ~ as/for/to do** servir de/à/à
faire ▷ n (Tennis) service m; **are you being ~d?**
est-ce qu'on s'occupe de vous?; **to ~ on a
committee/jury** faire partie d'un comité/jury;
**it ~s him right** c'est bien fait pour lui; **it ~s my
purpose** cela fait mon affaire
  ▶ **serve out, serve up** vt (food) servir
**server** [sə:və'] n (Comput) serveur m
**service** ['sə:vɪs] n (gen) service m; (Aut) révision f;
(Rel) office m ▷ vt (car etc) réviser; **services** npl
(Econ: tertiary sector) (secteur m) tertiaire m,
secteur des services; (Brit: on motorway) station-
service f; (Mil): **the S~s** (npl) les forces armées;
**to be of ~ to sb, to do sb a ~** rendre service à qn;
**~ included/not included** service compris/non
compris; **to put one's car in for ~** donner sa
voiture à réviser; **dinner ~** service de table
**serviceable** ['sə:vɪsəbl] adj pratique, commode
**service area** n (on motorway) aire f de services
**service charge** n (Brit) service m
**service industries** npl les industries fpl de
service, les services mpl
**serviceman** ['sə:vɪsmən] (irreg) n militaire m
**service station** n station-service f
**serviette** [sə:vɪ'ɛt] n (Brit) serviette f (de table)
**servile** ['sə:vaɪl] adj servile
**session** ['sɛʃən] n (sitting) séance f; (Scol) année f
scolaire (or universitaire); **to be in ~** siéger, être
en session or en séance
**session musician** n musicien(ne) de studio
**set** [sɛt] (pt, pp **set**) n série f, assortiment m; (of
tools etc) jeu m; (Radio, TV) poste m; (Tennis) set m;
(group of people) cercle m, milieu m; (Cine) plateau
m; (Theat: stage) scène f; (: scenery) décor m;
(Math) ensemble m; (Hairdressing) mise f en plis
▷ adj (fixed) fixe, déterminé(e); (ready) prêt(e)
▷ vt (place) mettre, poser, placer; (fix, establish)
fixer; (: record) établir; (assign: task, homework)
donner; (exam) composer; (adjust) régler; (decide:
rules etc) fixer, choisir; (Typ) composer ▷ vi (sun)
se coucher; (jam, jelly, concrete) prendre; (bone) se
ressouder; **to be ~ on doing** être résolu(e) à
faire; **to be all ~ to do** être (fin) prêt(e) pour
faire; **to be (dead) ~ against** être (totalement)
opposé à; **he's ~ in his ways** il n'est pas très
souple, il tient à ses habitudes; **to ~ to music**
mettre en musique; **to ~ on fire** mettre le feu à;
**to ~ free** libérer; **to ~ sth going** déclencher
qch; **to ~ the alarm clock for seven o'clock**
mettre le réveil à sonner à sept heures; **to ~ sail**
partir, prendre la mer; **a ~ phrase** une
expression toute faite, une locution; **a ~ of
false teeth** un dentier; **a ~ of dining-room
furniture** une salle à manger
  ▶ **set about** vt fus (task) entreprendre, se mettre
à; **to ~ about doing sth** se mettre à faire qch
  ▶ **set aside** vt mettre de côté; (time) garder
  ▶ **set back** vt (in time): **to ~ back (by)** retarder
(de); (place): **a house ~ back from the road** une
maison située en retrait de la route

▶ **set down** vt (subj: bus, train) déposer
▶ **set in** vi (infection, bad weather) s'installer; (complications) survenir, surgir; **the rain has ~ in for the day** c'est parti pour qu'il pleuve toute la journée
▶ **set off** vi se mettre en route, partir ▷ vt (bomb) faire exploser; (cause to start) déclencher; (show up well) mettre en valeur, faire valoir
▶ **set out** vi: **to ~ out (from)** partir (de) ▷ vt (arrange) disposer; (state) présenter, exposer; **to ~ out to do** entreprendre de faire; avoir pour but or intention de faire
▶ **set up** vt (organization) fonder, créer; (monument) ériger; **to ~ up shop** (fig) s'établir, s'installer
**setback** ['sɛtbæk] n (hitch) revers m, contretemps m; (in health) rechute f
**set menu** n menu m
**set square** n équerre f
**settee** [sɛ'tiː] n canapé m
**setting** ['sɛtɪŋ] n cadre m; (of jewel) monture f; (position: of controls) réglage m
**setting lotion** n lotion f pour mise en plis
**settle** ['sɛtl] vt (argument, matter, account) régler; (problem) résoudre; (Med: calm) calmer; (colonize: land) coloniser ▷ vi (bird, dust etc) se poser; (sediment) se déposer; **to ~ to sth** se mettre sérieusement à qch; **to ~ for sth** accepter qch, se contenter de qch; **to ~ on sth** opter or se décider pour qch; **that's ~d then** alors, c'est d'accord!; **to ~ one's stomach** calmer des maux d'estomac
▶ **settle down** vi (get comfortable) s'installer; (become calmer) se calmer; se ranger
▶ **settle in** vi s'installer
▶ **settle up** vi: **to ~ up with sb** régler (ce que l'on doit à) qn
**settlement** ['sɛtlmənt] n (payment) règlement m; (agreement) accord m; (colony) colonie f; (village etc) village m, hameau m; **in ~ of our account** (Comm) en règlement de notre compte
**settler** ['sɛtlər] n colon m
**setup** ['sɛtʌp] n (arrangement) manière f dont les choses sont organisées; (situation) situation f, allure f des choses
**seven** ['sɛvn] num sept
**seventeen** [sɛvn'tiːn] num dix-sept
**seventeenth** [sɛvn'tiːnθ] num dix-septième
**seventh** ['sɛvnθ] num septième
**seventieth** ['sɛvntɪɪθ] num soixante-dixième
**seventy** ['sɛvntɪ] num soixante-dix
**sever** ['sɛvər] vt couper, trancher; (relations) rompre
**several** ['sɛvərl] adj, pron plusieurs pl; **~ of us** plusieurs d'entre nous; **~ times** plusieurs fois
**severance** ['sɛvərəns] n (of relations) rupture f
**severance pay** n indemnité f de licenciement
**severe** [sɪ'vɪər] adj (stern) sévère, strict(e); (serious) grave, sérieux(-euse); (hard) rigoureux(-euse), dur(e); (plain) sévère, austère
**severely** [sɪ'vɪəlɪ] adv sévèrement; (wounded, ill) gravement

**severity** [sɪ'vɛrɪtɪ] n sévérité f; gravité f; rigueur f
**sew** (pt **-ed**, pp **-n**) [səu, səud, səun] vt, vi coudre
▶ **sew up** vt (re)coudre; **it is all ~n up** (fig) c'est dans le sac or dans la poche
**sewage** ['suːɪdʒ] n vidange(s) f(pl)
**sewage works** n champ m d'épandage
**sewer** ['suːər] n égout m
**sewing** ['səuɪŋ] n couture f; (item(s)) ouvrage m
**sewing machine** n machine f à coudre
**sewn** [səun] pp of **sew**
**sex** [sɛks] n sexe m; **to have ~ with** avoir des rapports (sexuels) avec
**sex act** n acte sexuel
**sex appeal** n sex-appeal m
**sex education** n éducation sexuelle
**sexism** ['sɛksɪzəm] n sexisme m
**sexist** ['sɛksɪst] adj sexiste
**sex life** n vie sexuelle
**sex object** n femme-objet f, objet sexuel
**sextet** [sɛks'tɛt] n sextuor m
**sexual** ['sɛksjuəl] adj sexuel(le); **~ assault** attentat m à la pudeur; **~ harassment** harcèlement sexuel
**sexual intercourse** n rapports sexuels
**sexuality** [sɛksju'ælɪtɪ] n sexualité f
**sexy** ['sɛksɪ] adj sexy inv
**Seychelles** [seɪ'ʃel(z)] npl: **the ~** les Seychelles fpl
**SF** n abbr (= science fiction) SF f
**SG** n abbr (US) = **Surgeon General**
**Sgt** abbr (= sergeant) Sgt
**shabbiness** ['ʃæbɪnɪs] n aspect miteux; mesquinerie f
**shabby** ['ʃæbɪ] adj miteux(-euse); (behaviour) mesquin(e), méprisable
**shack** [ʃæk] n cabane f, hutte f
**shackles** ['ʃæklz] npl chaînes fpl, entraves fpl
**shade** [ʃeɪd] n ombre f; (for lamp) abat-jour m inv; (of colour) nuance f, ton m; (US: window shade) store m; (small quantity): **a ~ of** un soupçon de ▷ vt abriter du soleil, ombrager; **shades** npl (US: sunglasses) lunettes fpl de soleil; **in the ~** à l'ombre; **a ~ smaller** un tout petit peu plus petit
**shadow** ['ʃædəu] n ombre f ▷ vt (follow) filer; **without** or **beyond a ~ of doubt** sans l'ombre d'un doute
**shadow cabinet** n (Brit Pol) cabinet parallèle formé par le parti qui n'est pas au pouvoir
**shadowy** ['ʃædəuɪ] adj ombragé(e); (dim) vague, indistinct(e)
**shady** ['ʃeɪdɪ] adj ombragé(e); (fig: dishonest) louche, véreux(-euse)
**shaft** [ʃɑːft] n (of arrow, spear) hampe f; (Aut, Tech) arbre m; (of mine) puits m; (of lift) cage f; (of light) rayon m, trait m; **ventilator ~** conduit m d'aération or de ventilation
**shaggy** ['ʃægɪ] adj hirsute; en broussaille
**shake** [ʃeɪk] (pt **shook**, pp **shaken** [ʃuk, 'ʃeɪkn]) vt secouer; (bottle, cocktail) agiter; (house, confidence) ébranler ▷ vi trembler ▷ n secousse f; **to ~ one's head** (in refusal etc) dire or faire non de la

**S**

tête; (in dismay) secouer la tête; **to ~ hands with sb** serrer la main à qn

▸ **shake off** vt secouer; (pursuer) se débarrasser de

▸ **shake up** vt secouer

**shake-up** ['ʃeɪkʌp] n grand remaniement

**shakily** ['ʃeɪkɪlɪ] adv (reply) d'une voix tremblante; (walk) d'un pas mal assuré; (write) d'une main tremblante

**shaky** ['ʃeɪkɪ] adj (hand, voice) tremblant(e); (building) branlant(e), peu solide; (memory) chancelant(e); (knowledge) incertain(e)

**shale** [ʃeɪl] n schiste argileux

**shall** [ʃæl] aux vb: **I ~ go** j'irai; **~ I open the door?** j'ouvre la porte?; **I'll get the coffee, ~ I?** je vais chercher le café, d'accord?

**shallot** [ʃə'lɔt] n (Brit) échalote f

**shallow** ['ʃæləu] adj peu profond(e); (fig) superficiel(le), qui manque de profondeur

**sham** [ʃæm] n frime f; (jewellery, furniture) imitation f ▷ adj feint(e), simulé(e) ▷ vt feindre, simuler

**shambles** ['ʃæmblz] n confusion f, pagaïe f, fouillis m; **the economy is (in) a complete ~** l'économie est dans la confusion la plus totale

**shambolic** [ʃæm'bɔlɪk] adj (inf) bordélique

**shame** [ʃeɪm] n honte f ▷ vt faire honte à; **it is a ~ (that/to do)** c'est dommage (que + sub/de faire); **what a ~!** quel dommage!; **to put sb/sth to ~** (fig) faire honte à qn/qch

**shamefaced** ['ʃeɪmfeɪst] adj honteux(-euse), penaud(e)

**shameful** ['ʃeɪmful] adj honteux(-euse), scandaleux(-euse)

**shameless** ['ʃeɪmlɪs] adj éhonté(e), effronté(e); (immodest) impudique

**shampoo** [ʃæm'puː] n shampooing m ▷ vt faire un shampooing à; **~ and set** shampooing et mise f en plis

**shamrock** ['ʃæmrɔk] n trèfle m (emblème national de l'Irlande)

**shandy** ['ʃændɪ] n bière panachée

**shan't** [ʃɑːnt] = **shall not**

**shantytown** ['ʃæntɪtaun] n bidonville m

**SHAPE** [ʃeɪp] n abbr (= Supreme Headquarters Allied Powers, Europe) quartier général des forces alliées en Europe

**shape** [ʃeɪp] n forme f ▷ vt façonner, modeler; (clay, stone) donner forme à; (statement) formuler; (sb's ideas, character) former; (sb's life) déterminer; (course of events) influer sur le cours de ▷ vi (also: **shape up**: events) prendre tournure; (: person) faire des progrès, s'en sortir; **to take ~** prendre forme or tournure; **in the ~ of a heart** en forme de cœur; **I can't bear gardening in any ~ or form** je déteste le jardinage sous quelque forme que ce soit; **to get o.s. into ~** (re)trouver la forme

**-shaped** [ʃeɪpt] suffix: **heart~** en forme de cœur

**shapeless** ['ʃeɪplɪs] adj informe, sans forme

**shapely** ['ʃeɪplɪ] adj bien proportionné(e), beau (belle)

**share** [ʃɛər] n (thing received, contribution) part f; (Comm) action f ▷ vt partager; (have in common) avoir en commun; **to ~ out (among or between)** partager (entre); **to ~ in** (joy, sorrow) prendre part à; (profits) participer à, avoir part à; (work) partager

**share capital** n capital social

**share certificate** n certificat m or titre m d'action

**shareholder** ['ʃeəhəuldər] n (Brit) actionnaire m/f

**share index** n indice m de la Bourse

**shark** [ʃɑːk] n requin m

**sharp** [ʃɑːp] adj (razor, knife) tranchant(e), bien aiguisé(e); (point, voice) aigu(ë); (nose, chin) pointu(e); (outline, increase) net(te); (curve, bend) brusque; (cold, pain) vif (vive); (taste) piquant(e), âcre; (Mus) dièse; (person: quick-witted) vif (vive), éveillé(e); (: unscrupulous) malhonnête ▷ n (Mus) dièse m ▷ adv: **at 2 o'clock** ~ à 2 heures pile or tapantes; **turn ~ left** tournez immédiatement à gauche; **to be ~ with sb** être brusque avec qn; **look ~!** dépêche-toi!

**sharpen** ['ʃɑːpn] vt aiguiser; (pencil) tailler; (fig) aviver

**sharpener** ['ʃɑːpnər] n (also: **pencil sharpener**) taille-crayon(s) m inv; (also: **knife sharpener**) aiguisoir m

**sharp-eyed** [ʃɑːp'aɪd] adj à qui rien n'échappe

**sharpish** ['ʃɑːpɪʃ] adv (Brit inf: quickly) en vitesse

**sharply** ['ʃɑːplɪ] adv (turn, stop) brusquement; (stand out) nettement; (criticize, retort) sèchement, vertement

**sharp-tempered** [ʃɑːp'tempəd] adj prompt(e) à se mettre en colère

**sharp-witted** [ʃɑːp'wɪtɪd] adj à l'esprit vif, malin(-igne)

**shatter** ['ʃætər] vt fracasser, briser, faire voler en éclats; (fig: upset) bouleverser; (: ruin) briser, ruiner ▷ vi voler en éclats, se briser, se fracasser

**shattered** ['ʃætəd] adj (overwhelmed, grief-stricken) bouleversé(e); (inf: exhausted) éreinté(e)

**shatterproof** ['ʃætəpruːf] adj incassable

**shave** [ʃeɪv] vt raser ▷ vi se raser ▷ n: **to have a ~** se raser

**shaven** ['ʃeɪvn] adj (head) rasé(e)

**shaver** ['ʃeɪvər] n (also: **electric shaver**) rasoir m électrique

**shaving** ['ʃeɪvɪŋ] n (action) rasage m

**shaving brush** n blaireau m

**shaving cream** n crème f à raser

**shaving foam** n mousse f à raser

**shavings** ['ʃeɪvɪŋz] npl (of wood etc) copeaux mpl

**shaving soap** n savon m à barbe

**shawl** [ʃɔːl] n châle m

**she** [ʃiː] pron elle; **there ~ is** la voilà; **~-elephant** etc éléphant m etc femelle

**sheaf** (pl **sheaves**) [ʃiːf, ʃiːvz] n gerbe f

**shear** [ʃɪər] vt (pt **-ed**, pp **-ed** or **shorn** [ʃɔːn]) (sheep) tondre

▸ **shear off** vt tondre; (branch) élaguer

**shears** ['ʃɪəz] npl (for hedge) cisaille(s) f(pl)

**sheath** [ʃiːθ] *n* gaine *f*, fourreau *m*, étui *m*; *(contraceptive)* préservatif *m*
**sheathe** [ʃiːð] *vt* gainer; *(sword)* rengainer
**sheath knife** *n* couteau *m* à gaine
**sheaves** [ʃiːvz] *npl of* **sheaf**
**shed** [ʃɛd] *n* remise *f*, resserre *f*; *(Industry, Rail)* hangar *m* ▷ *vt (pt, pp* **-)** *(leaves, fur etc)* perdre; *(tears)* verser, répandre; *(workers)* congédier; **to ~ light on** *(problem, mystery)* faire la lumière sur
**she'd** [ʃiːd] = **she had; she would**
**sheen** [ʃiːn] *n* lustre *m*
**sheep** [ʃiːp] *n (pl inv)* mouton *m*
**sheepdog** ['ʃiːpdɔg] *n* chien *m* de berger
**sheep farmer** *n* éleveur *m* de moutons
**sheepish** ['ʃiːpɪʃ] *adj* penaud(e), timide
**sheepskin** ['ʃiːpskɪn] *n* peau *f* de mouton
**sheepskin jacket** *n* canadienne *f*
**sheer** [ʃɪəʳ] *adj (utter)* pur(e), pur et simple; *(steep)* à pic, abrupt(e); *(almost transparent)* extrêmement fin(e) ▷ *adv* à pic, abruptement; **by ~ chance** par pur hasard
**sheet** [ʃiːt] *n (on bed)* drap *m*; *(of paper)* feuille *f*; *(of glass, metal etc)* feuille, plaque *f*
**sheet feed** *n (on printer)* alimentation *f* en papier (feuille à feuille)
**sheet lightning** *n* éclair *m* en nappe(s)
**sheet metal** *n* tôle *f*
**sheet music** *n* partition(s) *f(pl)*
**sheik, sheikh** [ʃeɪk] *n* cheik *m*
**shelf** *(pl* **shelves)** [ʃɛlf, ʃɛlvz] *n* étagère *f*, rayon *m*; **set of shelves** rayonnage *m*
**shelf life** *n (Comm)* durée *f* de conservation (avant la vente)
**shell** [ʃɛl] *n (on beach)* coquillage *m*; *(of egg, nut etc)* coquille *f*; *(explosive)* obus *m*; *(of building)* carcasse *f* ▷ *vt (crab, prawn etc)* décortiquer; *(peas)* écosser; *(Mil)* bombarder (d'obus)
▸ **shell out** *vi (inf)*: **to ~ out (for)** casquer (pour)
**she'll** [ʃiːl] = **she will; she shall**
**shellfish** ['ʃɛlfɪʃ] *n (pl inv: crab etc)* crustacé *m*; *(: scallop etc)* coquillage *m* ▷ *npl (as food)* fruits *mpl* de mer
**shell suit** *n* survêtement *m*
**shelter** ['ʃɛltəʳ] *n* abri *m*, refuge *m* ▷ *vt* abriter, protéger; *(give lodging to)* donner asile à ▷ *vi* s'abriter, se mettre à l'abri; **to take ~ (from)** s'abriter (de)
**sheltered** ['ʃɛltəd] *adj (life)* retiré(e), à l'abri des soucis; *(spot)* abrité(e)
**sheltered housing** *n* foyers *mpl (pour personnes âgées ou handicapées)*
**shelve** [ʃɛlv] *vt (fig)* mettre en suspens *or* en sommeil
**shelves** ['ʃɛlvz] *npl of* **shelf**
**shelving** ['ʃɛlvɪŋ] *n (shelves)* rayonnage(s) *m(pl)*
**shepherd** ['ʃɛpəd] *n* berger *m* ▷ *vt (guide)* guider, escorter
**shepherdess** ['ʃɛpədɪs] *n* bergère *f*
**shepherd's pie** ['ʃɛpədz-] *n* ≈ hachis *m* Parmentier
**sherbet** ['ʃəːbət] *n (Brit: powder)* poudre acidulée; *(US: water ice)* sorbet *m*

**sheriff** ['ʃɛrɪf] *(US)* *n* shérif *m*
**sherry** ['ʃɛrɪ] *n* xérès *m*, sherry *m*
**she's** [ʃiːz] = **she is; she has**
**Shetland** ['ʃɛtlənd] *n (also:* **the Shetlands, the Shetland Isles** *or* **Islands)** les îles *fpl* Shetland
**Shetland pony** *n* poney *m* des îles Shetland
**shield** [ʃiːld] *n* bouclier *m*; *(protection)* écran *m* de protection ▷ *vt*: **to ~ (from)** protéger (de *or* contre)
**shift** [ʃɪft] *n (change)* changement *m*; *(work period)* période *f* de travail; *(of workers)* équipe *f*, poste *m* ▷ *vt* déplacer, changer de place; *(remove)* enlever ▷ *vi* changer de place, bouger; **the wind has ~ed to the south** le vent a tourné au sud; **a ~ in demand** *(Comm)* un déplacement de la demande
**shift key** *n (on typewriter)* touche *f* de majuscule
**shiftless** ['ʃɪftlɪs] *adj* fainéant(e)
**shift work** *n* travail *m* par roulement; **to do ~** travailler par roulement
**shifty** ['ʃɪftɪ] *adj* sournois(e); *(eyes)* fuyant(e)
**Shiite** ['ʃiːaɪt] *n* Chiite *m/f* ▷ *adj* chiite
**shilling** ['ʃɪlɪŋ] *n (Brit)* shilling *m (= 12 old pence; 20 in a pound)*
**shilly-shally** ['ʃɪlɪʃælɪ] *vi* tergiverser, atermoyer
**shimmer** ['ʃɪməʳ] *n* miroitement *m*, chatoiement *m* ▷ *vi* miroiter, chatoyer
**shin** [ʃɪn] *n* tibia *m* ▷ *vi*: **to ~ up/down a tree** grimper dans un/descendre d'un arbre
**shindig** ['ʃɪndɪg] *n (inf)* bamboula *f*
**shine** [ʃaɪn] *(pt, pp* **shone)** [ʃɔn] *n* éclat *m*, brillant *m* ▷ *vi* briller ▷ *vt (torch)*: **to ~ on** braquer sur; *(polish: pt, pp* **-d)** faire briller *or* reluire
**shingle** ['ʃɪŋgl] *n (on beach)* galets *mpl*; *(on roof)* bardeau *m*
**shingles** ['ʃɪŋglz] *n (Med)* zona *m*
**shining** ['ʃaɪnɪŋ] *adj* brillant(e)
**shiny** ['ʃaɪnɪ] *adj* brillant(e)
**ship** [ʃɪp] *n* bateau *m*; *(large)* navire *m* ▷ *vt* transporter (par mer); *(send)* expédier (par mer); *(load)* charger, embarquer; **on board ~** à bord
**shipbuilder** ['ʃɪpbɪldəʳ] *n* constructeur *m* de navires
**shipbuilding** ['ʃɪpbɪldɪŋ] *n* construction navale
**ship chandler** [-'tʃɑːndləʳ] *n* fournisseur *m* maritime, shipchandler *m*
**shipment** ['ʃɪpmənt] *n* cargaison *f*
**shipowner** ['ʃɪpəunəʳ] *n* armateur *m*
**shipper** ['ʃɪpəʳ] *n* affréteur *m*, expéditeur *m*
**shipping** ['ʃɪpɪŋ] *n (ships)* navires *mpl*; *(traffic)* navigation *f*; *(the industry)* industrie navale; *(transport)* transport *m*
**shipping agent** *n* agent *m* maritime
**shipping company** *n* compagnie *f* de navigation
**shipping lane** *n* couloir *m* de navigation
**shipping line** *n* = **shipping company**
**shipshape** ['ʃɪpʃeɪp] *adj* en ordre impeccable
**shipwreck** ['ʃɪprɛk] *n* épave *f*; *(event)* naufrage *m* ▷ *vt*: **to be ~ed** faire naufrage
**shipyard** ['ʃɪpjɑːd] *n* chantier naval
**shire** ['ʃaɪəʳ] *n (Brit)* comté *m*

**S**

**shirk** [ʃəːk] *vt* esquiver, se dérober à
**shirt** [ʃəːt] *n* chemise *f*; *(woman's)* chemisier *m*;
**in ~ sleeves** en bras de chemise
**shirty** ['ʃəːtɪ] *adj* (*Brit inf*) de mauvais poil
**shit** [ʃɪt] *excl* (*inf*!) merde (!)
**shiver** ['ʃɪvə<sup>r</sup>] *n* frisson *m* ▷ *vi* frissonner
**shoal** [ʃəʊl] *n* (*of fish*) banc *m*
**shock** [ʃɔk] *n* (*impact*) choc *m*, heurt *m*; (*Elec*)
secousse *f*, décharge *f*; (*emotional*) choc; (*Med*)
commotion *f*, choc ▷ *vt* (*scandalize*) choquer,
scandaliser; (*upset*) bouleverser; **suffering
from ~** (*Med*) commotionné(e); **it gave us a ~** ça
nous a fait un choc; **it came as a ~ to hear that
...** nous avons appris avec stupeur que ...
**shock absorber** [-əbzɔːbə<sup>r</sup>] *n* amortisseur *m*
**shocker** ['ʃɔkə<sup>r</sup>] *n* (*inf*): **the news was a real ~ to
him** il a vraiment été choqué par cette nouvelle
**shocking** ['ʃɔkɪŋ] *adj* (*outrageous*) choquant(e),
scandaleux(-euse); (*awful*) épouvantable
**shockproof** ['ʃɔkpruːf] *adj* anti-choc *inv*
**shock therapy, shock treatment** *n* (*Med*)
(traitement *m* par) électrochoc(s) *m(pl)*
**shock wave** *n* (*also fig*) onde *f* de choc
**shod** [ʃɔd] *pt, pp of* **shoe; well-~** bien chaussé(e)
**shoddy** ['ʃɔdɪ] *adj* de mauvaise qualité, mal
fait(e)
**shoe** [ʃuː] *n* chaussure *f*, soulier *m*; (*also:*
**horseshoe**) fer *m* à cheval; (*also:* **brake shoe**)
mâchoire *f* de frein ▷ *vt* (*pt, pp* **shod**) [ʃɔd] (*horse*)
ferrer
**shoebrush** ['ʃuːbrʌʃ] *n* brosse *f* à chaussures
**shoehorn** ['ʃuːhɔːn] *n* chausse-pied *m*
**shoelace** ['ʃuːleɪs] *n* lacet *m* (de soulier)
**shoemaker** ['ʃuːmeɪkə<sup>r</sup>] *n* cordonnier *m*,
fabricant *m* de chaussures
**shoe polish** *n* cirage *m*
**shoeshop** ['ʃuːʃɔp] *n* magasin *m* de chaussures
**shoestring** ['ʃuːstrɪŋ] *n*: **on a ~** (*fig*) avec un
budget dérisoire; avec des moyens très
restreints
**shoetree** ['ʃuːtriː] *n* embauchoir *m*
**shone** [ʃɔn] *pt, pp of* **shine**
**shoo** [ʃuː] *excl* allez, ouste! ▷ *vt* (*also:* **shoo away,
shoo off**) chasser
**shook** [ʃuk] *pt of* **shake**
**shoot** [ʃuːt] (*pt, pp* **shot**) [ʃɔt] *n* (*on branch, seedling*)
pousse *f*; (*shooting party*) partie *f* de chasse ▷ *vt*
(*game: hunt*) chasser; (*: aim at*) tirer; (*: kill*)
abattre; (*person*) blesser/tuer d'un coup de fusil
(*or* de revolver); (*execute*) fusiller; (*arrow*) tirer;
(*gun*) tirer un coup de; (*Cine*) tourner ▷ *vi* (*with
gun, bow*): **to ~ (at)** tirer (sur); (*Football*) shooter,
tirer; **to ~ past sb** passer en flèche devant qn;
**to ~ in/out** entrer/sortir comme une flèche
▶ **shoot down** *vt* (*plane*) abattre
▶ **shoot up** *vi* (*fig: prices etc*) monter en flèche
**shooting** ['ʃuːtɪŋ] *n* (*shots*) coups *mpl* de feu;
(*attack*) fusillade *f*; (*murder*) homicide *m* (*à l'aide
d'une arme à feu*); (*Hunting*) chasse *f*; (*Cine*)
tournage *m*
**shooting range** *n* stand *m* de tir
**shooting star** *n* étoile filante

**shop** [ʃɔp] *n* magasin *m*; (*workshop*) atelier *m* ▷ *vi*
(*also:* **go shopping**) faire ses courses *or* ses
achats; **repair ~** atelier de réparations; **to talk
~** (*fig*) parler boutique
▶ **shop around** *vi* faire le tour des magasins
(pour comparer les prix); (*fig*) se renseigner
avant de choisir *or* décider
**shopaholic** [ʃɔpə'hɔlɪk] *n* (*inf*) personne qui achète
sans pouvoir s'arrêter
**shop assistant** *n* (*Brit*) vendeur(-euse)
**shop floor** *n* (*Brit: fig*) ouvriers *mpl*
**shopkeeper** ['ʃɔpkiːpə<sup>r</sup>] *n* marchand(e),
commerçant(e)
**shoplift** ['ʃɔplɪft] *vi* voler à l'étalage
**shoplifter** ['ʃɔplɪftə<sup>r</sup>] *n* voleur(-euse) à l'étalage
**shoplifting** ['ʃɔplɪftɪŋ] *n* vol *m* à l'étalage
**shopper** ['ʃɔpə<sup>r</sup>] *n* personne *f* qui fait ses
courses, acheteur(-euse)
**shopping** ['ʃɔpɪŋ] *n* (*goods*) achats *mpl*,
provisions *fpl*
**shopping bag** *n* sac *m* (à provisions)
**shopping centre,** (*US*) **shopping center** *n*
centre commercial
**shopping mall** *n* centre commercial
**shopping trolley** *n* (*Brit*) Caddie® *m*
**shop-soiled** ['ʃɔpsɔɪld] *adj* défraîchi(e), qui a
fait la vitrine
**shop window** *n* vitrine *f*
**shore** [ʃɔː<sup>r</sup>] *n* (*of sea, lake*) rivage *m*, rive *f* ▷ *vt*: **to ~
(up)** étayer; **on ~** à terre
**shore leave** *n* (*Naut*) permission *f* à terre
**shorn** [ʃɔːn] *pp of* **shear** ▷ *adj*: **~ of** dépouillé(e)
de
**short** [ʃɔːt] *adj* (*not long*) court(e); (*soon finished*)
court, bref (brève); (*person, step*) petit(e); (*curt*)
brusque, sec (sèche); (*insufficient*) insuffisant(e)
▷ *n* (*also:* **short film**) court métrage; (*Elec*) court-
circuit *m*; **to be ~ of sth** être à court de *or*
manquer de qch; **to be in ~ supply** manquer,
être difficile à trouver; **I'm 3 ~** il m'en manque
3; **in ~** bref; en bref; **~ of doing** à moins de faire;
**everything ~ of** tout sauf; **it is ~ for** c'est
l'abréviation *or* le diminutif de; **a ~ time ago** il
y a peu de temps; **in the ~ term** à court terme;
**to cut ~** (*speech, visit*) abréger, écourter; (*person*)
couper la parole à; **to fall ~ of** ne pas être à la
hauteur de; **to run ~ of** arriver à court de, venir
à manquer de; **to stop ~** s'arrêter net; **to stop ~
of** ne pas aller jusqu'à
**shortage** ['ʃɔːtɪdʒ] *n* manque *m*, pénurie *f*
**shortbread** ['ʃɔːtbred] *n* ≈ sablé *m*
**short-change** [ʃɔːt'tʃeɪndʒ] *vt*: **to ~ sb** ne pas
rendre assez à qn
**short-circuit** [ʃɔːt'səːkɪt] *n* court-circuit *m* ▷ *vt*
court-circuiter ▷ *vi* se mettre en court-circuit
**shortcoming** ['ʃɔːtkʌmɪŋ] *n* défaut *m*
**shortcrust pastry** ['ʃɔːtkrʌst-], **short pastry** *n*
(*Brit*) pâte brisée
**shortcut** ['ʃɔːtkʌt] *n* raccourci *m*
**shorten** ['ʃɔːtn] *vt* raccourcir; (*text, visit*) abréger
**shortening** ['ʃɔːtnɪŋ] *n* (*Culin*) matière grasse
**shortfall** ['ʃɔːtfɔːl] *n* déficit *m*

**shorthand** ['ʃɔːthænd] *n* (*Brit*) sténo(graphie) *f*;
**to take sth down in** ~ prendre qch en sténo
**shorthand notebook** *n* bloc *m* sténo
**shorthand typist** *n* (*Brit*) sténodactylo *m/f*
**shortlist** ['ʃɔːtlɪst] *n* (*Brit: for job*) liste *f* des
candidats sélectionnés
**short-lived** ['ʃɔːt'lɪvd] *adj* de courte durée
**shortly** ['ʃɔːtlɪ] *adv* bientôt, sous peu
**shortness** ['ʃɔːtnɪs] *n* brièveté *f*
**short notice** *n*: **at** ~ au dernier moment
**shorts** [ʃɔːts] *npl*: (**a pair of**) ~ un short
**short-sighted** [ʃɔːt'saɪtɪd] *adj* (*Brit*) myope; (*fig*)
qui manque de clairvoyance
**short-sleeved** [ʃɔːt'sliːvd] *adj* à manches
courtes
**short-staffed** [ʃɔːt'stɑːft] *adj* à court de
personnel
**short-stay** [ʃɔːt'steɪ] *adj* (*car park*) de courte
durée
**short story** *n* nouvelle *f*
**short-tempered** [ʃɔːt'tempəd] *adj* qui
s'emporte facilement
**short-term** ['ʃɔːttɜːm] *adj* (*effect*) à court terme
**short time** *n*: **to work** ~, **to be on** ~ (*Industry*) être
en chômage partiel, travailler à horaire réduit
**short wave** *n* (*Radio*) ondes courtes
**shot** [ʃɔt] *pt, pp of* **shoot** ▷ *n* coup *m* (de feu);
(*shotgun pellets*) plombs *mpl*; (*try*) coup, essai *m*;
(*injection*) piqûre *f*; (*Phot*) photo *f*; **to be a good/**
**poor** ~ (*person*) tirer bien/mal; **to fire a** ~ **at sb/**
**sth** tirer sur qn/qch; **to have a** ~ **at (doing) sth**
essayer de faire qch; **like a** ~ comme une flèche;
(*very readily*) sans hésiter; **to get** ~ **of sb/sth** (*inf*)
se débarrasser de qn/qch; **a big** ~ (*inf*) un gros
bonnet
**shotgun** ['ʃɔtgʌn] *n* fusil *m* de chasse
**should** [ʃud] *aux vb*: **I** ~ **go now** je devrais partir
maintenant; **he** ~ **be there now** il devrait être
arrivé maintenant; **I** ~ **go if I were you** si j'étais
vous j'irais; **I** ~ **like to** volontiers, j'aimerais
bien; ~ **he phone** ... si jamais il téléphone ...
**shoulder** ['ʃəuldər] *n* épaule *f*; (*Brit: of road*): **hard**
~ accotement *m* ▷ *vt* (*fig*) endosser, se charger
de; **to look over one's** ~ regarder derrière soi
(en tournant la tête); **to rub ~s with sb** (*fig*)
côtoyer qn; **to give sb the cold** ~ (*fig*) battre
froid à qn
**shoulder bag** *n* sac *m* à bandoulière
**shoulder blade** *n* omoplate *f*
**shoulder strap** *n* bretelle *f*
**shouldn't** ['ʃudnt] = **should not**
**shout** [ʃaut] *n* cri *m* ▷ *vt* crier ▷ *vi* crier, pousser
des cris; **to give sb a** ~ appeler qn
▶ **shout down** *vt* huer
**shouting** ['ʃautɪŋ] *n* cris *mpl*
**shouting match** *n* (*inf*) engueulade *f*,
empoignade *f*
**shove** [ʃʌv] *vt* pousser; (*inf: put*): **to** ~ **sth in**
fourrer *or* ficher qch dans ▷ *n* poussée *f*; **he ~d**
**me out of the way** il m'a écarté en me
poussant
▶ **shove off** *vi* (*Naut*) pousser au large; (*fig: col*)

ficher le camp
**shovel** ['ʃʌvl] *n* pelle *f* ▷ *vt* pelleter, enlever (*or*
enfourner) à la pelle
**show** [ʃəu] (*pt* -**ed**, *pp* -**n**) [ʃəun] *n* (*of emotion*)
manifestation *f*, démonstration *f*; (*semblance*)
semblant *m*, apparence *f*; (*exhibition*) exposition
*f*, salon *m*; (*Theat, TV*) spectacle *m*; (*Cine*) séance *f*
▷ *vt* montrer; (*film*) passer; (*courage etc*) faire
preuve de, manifester; (*exhibit*) exposer ▷ *vi* se
voir, être visible; **can you** ~ **me where it is,**
**please?** pouvez-vous me montrer où c'est?; **to**
**ask for a** ~ **of hands** demander que l'on vote à
main levée; **to be on** ~ être exposé(e); **it's just**
**for** ~ c'est juste pour l'effet; **who's running**
**the** ~ **here?** (*inf*) qui est-ce qui commande ici?;
**to** ~ **sb to his seat/to the door** accompagner
qn jusqu'à sa place/la porte; **to** ~ **a profit/loss**
(*Comm*) indiquer un bénéfice/une perte; **it just**
**goes to** ~ **that** ... ça prouve bien que ...
▶ **show in** *vt* faire entrer
▶ **show off** *vi* (*pej*) crâner ▷ *vt* (*display*) faire
valoir; (*pej*) faire étalage de
▶ **show out** *vt* reconduire à la porte
▶ **show up** *vi* (*stand out*) ressortir; (*inf: turn up*) se
montrer ▷ *vt* démontrer; (*unmask*) démasquer,
dénoncer; (*flaw*) faire ressortir
**showbiz** ['ʃəubɪz] *n* (*inf*) showbiz *m*
**show business** *n* le monde du spectacle
**showcase** ['ʃəukeɪs] *n* vitrine *f*
**showdown** ['ʃəudaun] *n* épreuve *f* de force
**shower** ['ʃauər] *n* (*for washing*) douche *f*; (*rain*)
averse *f*; (*of stones etc*) pluie *f*, grêle *f*; (*US: party*)
réunion organisée pour la remise de cadeaux ▷ *vi*
prendre une douche, se doucher ▷ *vt*: **to** ~ **sb**
**with** (*gifts etc*) combler qn de; (*abuse etc*) accabler
qn de; (*missiles*) bombarder qn de; **to have** *or*
**take a** ~ prendre une douche, se doucher
**shower cap** *n* bonnet *m* de douche
**shower gel** *n* gel *m* douche
**showerproof** ['ʃauəpruːf] *adj* imperméable
**showery** ['ʃauərɪ] *adj* (*weather*) pluvieux(-euse)
**showground** ['ʃəugraund] *n* champ *m* de foire
**showing** ['ʃəuɪŋ] *n* (*of film*) projection *f*
**show jumping** [-dʒʌmpɪŋ] *n* concours *m*
hippique
**showman** ['ʃəumən] (*irreg*) *n* (*at fair, circus*) forain
*m*; (*fig*) comédien *m*
**showmanship** ['ʃəumənʃɪp] *n* art *m* de la mise
en scène
**shown** [ʃəun] *pp of* **show**
**show-off** ['ʃəuɔf] *n* (*inf: person*) crâneur(-euse),
m'as-tu-vu(e)
**showpiece** ['ʃəupiːs] *n* (*of exhibition etc*) joyau *m*,
clou *m*; **that hospital is a** ~ cet hôpital est un
modèle du genre
**showroom** ['ʃəurum] *n* magasin *m* *or* salle *f*
d'exposition
**show trial** *n* grand procès *m* médiatique (*qui fait*
*un exemple*)
**showy** ['ʃəuɪ] *adj* tapageur(-euse)
**shrank** [ʃræŋk] *pt of* **shrink**
**shrapnel** ['ʃræpnl] *n* éclats *mpl* d'obus

**shred** [ʃrɛd] n (gen pl) lambeau m, petit morceau;
(fig: of truth, evidence) parcelle f ▷ vt mettre en
lambeaux, déchirer; (documents) détruire; (Culin:
grate) râper; (: lettuce etc) couper en lanières
**shredder** ['ʃrɛdə'] n (for vegetables) râpeur m; (for
documents, papers) déchiqueteuse f
**shrewd** [ʃruːd] adj astucieux(-euse), perspicace;
(business person) habile
**shrewdness** ['ʃruːdnɪs] n perspicacité f
**shriek** [ʃriːk] n cri perçant or aigu, hurlement m
▷ vt, vi hurler, crier
**shrift** [ʃrɪft] n: **to give sb short** ~ expédier qn
sans ménagements
**shrill** [ʃrɪl] adj perçant(e), aigu(ë), strident(e)
**shrimp** [ʃrɪmp] n crevette grise
**shrine** [ʃraɪn] n châsse f; (place) lieu m de
pèlerinage
**shrink** (pt **shrank**, pp **shrunk**) [ʃrɪŋk, ʃræŋk,
ʃrʌŋk] vi rétrécir; (fig) diminuer; (also: **shrink
away**) reculer ▷ vt (wool) (faire) rétrécir ▷ n (inf:
pej) psychanalyste m/f; **to ~ from (doing) sth**
reculer devant (la pensée de faire) qch
**shrinkage** ['ʃrɪŋkɪdʒ] n (of clothes)
rétrécissement m
**shrink-wrap** ['ʃrɪŋkræp] vt emballer sous film
plastique
**shrivel** ['ʃrɪvl] (also: **shrivel up**) vt ratatiner,
flétrir ▷ vi se ratatiner, se flétrir
**shroud** [ʃraud] n linceul m ▷ vt: **~ed in mystery**
enveloppé(e) de mystère
**Shrove Tuesday** ['ʃrəuv-] n (le) Mardi gras
**shrub** [ʃrʌb] n arbuste m
**shrubbery** ['ʃrʌbərɪ] n massif m d'arbustes
**shrug** [ʃrʌg] n haussement m d'épaules ▷ vt, vi:
**to ~ (one's shoulders)** hausser les épaules
▶ **shrug off** vt faire fi de; (cold, illness) se
débarrasser de
**shrunk** [ʃrʌŋk] pp of **shrink**
**shrunken** ['ʃrʌŋkn] adj ratatiné(e)
**shudder** ['ʃʌdə'] n frisson m, frémissement m
▷ vi frissonner, frémir
**shuffle** ['ʃʌfl] vt (cards) battre; **to ~ (one's feet)**
traîner les pieds
**shun** [ʃʌn] vt éviter, fuir
**shunt** [ʃʌnt] vt (Rail: direct) aiguiller; (: divert)
détourner ▷ vi: **to ~ (to and fro)** faire la navette
**shunting yard** ['ʃʌntɪŋ-] n voies fpl de garage or
de triage
**shush** [ʃuʃ] excl chut!
**shut** (pt, pp ~) [ʃʌt] vt fermer ▷ vi (se) fermer
▶ **shut down** vt fermer définitivement;
(machine) arrêter ▷ vi fermer définitivement
▶ **shut off** vt couper, arrêter
▶ **shut out** vt (person, cold) empêcher d'entrer;
(noise) éviter d'entendre; (block: view) boucher;
(: memory of sth) chasser de son esprit
▶ **shut up** vi (inf: keep quiet) se taire ▷ vt (close)
fermer; (silence) faire taire
**shutdown** ['ʃʌtdaun] n fermeture f
**shutter** ['ʃʌtə'] n volet m; (Phot) obturateur m
**shuttle** ['ʃʌtl] n navette f; (also: **shuttle service**)
(service m de) navette f ▷ vi (vehicle, person) faire

la navette ▷ vt (passengers) transporter par un
système de navette
**shuttlecock** ['ʃʌtlkɔk] n volant m (de badminton)
**shuttle diplomacy** n navettes fpl diplomatiques
**shy** [ʃaɪ] adj timide; **to fight ~ of** se dérober
devant; **to be ~ of doing sth** hésiter à faire qch,
ne pas oser faire qch ▷ vi: **to ~ away from
doing sth** (fig) craindre de faire qch
**shyness** ['ʃaɪnɪs] n timidité f
**Siam** [saɪˈæm] n Siam m
**Siamese** [saɪəˈmiːz] adj: **~ cat** chat siamois mpl;
**~ twins** (frères mpl) siamois mpl, (sœurs fpl)
siamoises fpl
**Siberia** [saɪˈbɪərɪə] n Sibérie f
**siblings** ['sɪblɪŋz] npl (formal) frères et sœurs mpl
(de mêmes parents)
**Sicilian** [sɪˈsɪlɪən] adj sicilien(ne) ▷ n
Sicilien(ne)
**Sicily** ['sɪsɪlɪ] n Sicile f
**sick** [sɪk] adj (ill) malade; (Brit: vomiting): **to be ~**
vomir; (humour) noir(e), macabre; **to feel ~**
avoir envie de vomir, avoir mal au cœur; **to fall
~** tomber malade; **to be (off) ~** être absent(e)
pour cause de maladie; **a ~ person** un(e)
malade; **to be ~ of** (fig) en avoir assez de
**sick bag** ['sɪkbæg] n sac m vomitoire
**sick bay** n infirmerie f
**sick building syndrome** n maladie dûe à la
climatisation, l'éclairage artificiel etc des bureaux
**sicken** ['sɪkn] vt écœurer ▷ vi: **to be ~ing for sth**
(cold, flu etc) couver qch
**sickening** ['sɪknɪŋ] adj (fig) écœurant(e),
révoltant(e), répugnant(e)
**sickle** ['sɪkl] n faucille f
**sick leave** n congé m de maladie
**sickle-cell anaemia** ['sɪklsɛl-] n anémie f à
hématies falciformes, drépanocytose f
**sickly** ['sɪklɪ] adj maladif(-ive),
souffreteux(-euse); (causing nausea) écœurant(e)
**sickness** ['sɪknɪs] n maladie f; (vomiting)
vomissement(s) m(pl)
**sickness benefit** n (prestations fpl de
l')assurance-maladie f
**sick note** n (from parents) mot m d'absence; (from
doctor) certificat médical
**sick pay** n indemnité f de maladie (versée par
l'employeur)
**sickroom** ['sɪkruːm] n infirmerie f
**side** [saɪd] n côté m; (of animal) flanc m; (of lake,
road) bord m; (of mountain) versant m; (fig: aspect)
côté, aspect m; (team: Sport) équipe f; (TV:
channel) chaîne f ▷ adj (door, entrance) latéral(e)
▷ vi: **to ~ with sb** prendre le parti de qn, se
ranger du côté de qn; **by the ~ of** au bord de; **~
by ~** côte à côte; **the right/wrong ~** le bon/
mauvais côté, l'endroit/l'envers m; **they are on
our ~** ils sont avec nous; **from all ~s** de tous
côtés; **to rock from ~ to ~** se balancer; **to take
~s (with)** prendre parti (pour); **a ~ of beef** ≈ un
quartier de bœuf
**sideboard** ['saɪdbɔːd] n buffet m
**sideboards** ['saɪdbɔːdz] (Brit), **sideburns**

['saɪdbə:nz] *npl* (*whiskers*) pattes *fpl*
**sidecar** ['saɪdkɑ:ʳ] *n* side-car *m*
**side dish** *n* (plat *m* d')accompagnement *m*
**side drum** *n* (*Mus*) tambour plat, caisse claire
**side effect** *n* effet *m* secondaire
**sidekick** ['saɪdkɪk] *n* (*inf*) sous-fifre *m*
**sidelight** ['saɪdlaɪt] *n* (*Aut*) veilleuse *f*
**sideline** ['saɪdlaɪn] *n* (*Sport*) (ligne *f* de) touche *f*; (*fig*) activité *f* secondaire
**sidelong** ['saɪdlɔŋ] *adj*: **to give sb a ~ glance** regarder qn du coin de l'œil
**side order** *n* garniture *f*
**side plate** *n* petite assiette
**side road** *n* petite route, route transversale
**sidesaddle** ['saɪdsædl] *adv* en amazone
**sideshow** ['saɪdʃəu] *n* attraction *f*
**sidestep** ['saɪdstɛp] *vt* (*question*) éluder; (*problem*) éviter ▷ *vi* (*Boxing etc*) esquiver
**side street** *n* rue transversale
**sidetrack** ['saɪdtræk] *vt* (*fig*) faire dévier de son sujet
**sidewalk** ['saɪdwɔ:k] *n* (*US*) trottoir *m*
**sideways** ['saɪdweɪz] *adv* de côté
**siding** ['saɪdɪŋ] *n* (*Rail*) voie *f* de garage
**sidle** ['saɪdl] *vi*: **to ~ up (to)** s'approcher furtivement (de)
**SIDS** [sɪdz] *n abbr* (= *sudden infant death syndrome*) mort subite du nourrisson, mort *f* au berceau
**siege** [si:dʒ] *n* siège *m*; **to lay ~ to** assiéger
**siege economy** *n* économie *f* de (temps de) siège
**Sierra Leone** [sɪ'ɛrəlɪ'əun] *n* Sierra Leone *f*
**sieve** [sɪv] *n* tamis *m*, passoire *f* ▷ *vt* tamiser, passer (au tamis)
**sift** [sɪft] *vt* passer au tamis *or* au crible; (*fig*) passer au crible ▷ *vi* (*fig*): **to ~ through** passer en revue
**sigh** [saɪ] *n* soupir *m* ▷ *vi* soupirer, pousser un soupir
**sight** [saɪt] *n* (*faculty*) vue *f*; (*spectacle*) spectacle *m*; (*on gun*) mire *f* ▷ *vt* apercevoir; **in ~** visible; (*fig*) en vue; **out of ~** hors de vue; **at ~** (*Comm*) à vue; **at first ~** à première vue, au premier abord; **I know her by ~** je la connais de vue; **to catch ~ of sb/sth** apercevoir qn/qch; **to lose ~ of sb/sth** perdre qn/qch de vue; **to set one's ~s on sth** jeter son dévolu sur qch
**sighted** ['saɪtɪd] *adj* qui voit; **partially ~** qui a un certain degré de vision
**sightseeing** ['saɪtsi:ɪŋ] *n* tourisme *m*; **to go ~** faire du tourisme
**sightseer** ['saɪtsi:əʳ] *n* touriste *m/f*
**sign** [saɪn] *n* (*gen*) signe *m*; (*with hand etc*) signe, geste *m*; (*notice*) panneau *m*, écriteau *m*; (*also*: **road sign**) panneau de signalisation ▷ *vt* signer; **as a ~ of** en signe de; **it's a good/bad ~** c'est bon/mauvais signe; **plus/minus ~** signe plus/moins; **there's no ~ of a change of mind** rien ne laisse présager un revirement; **he was showing ~s of improvement** il commençait visiblement à faire des progrès; **to ~ one's name** signer; **where do I ~?** où dois-je signer?

▶ **sign away** *vt* (*rights etc*) renoncer officiellement à
▶ **sign for** *vt fus* (*item*) signer le reçu pour
▶ **sign in** *vi* signer le registre (en arrivant)
▶ **sign off** *vi* (*Radio*, *TV*) terminer l'émission
▶ **sign on** *vi* (*Mil*) s'engager; (*Brit*: *as unemployed*) s'inscrire au chômage; (*enrol*) s'inscrire ▷ *vt* (*Mil*) engager; (*employee*) embaucher; **to ~ on for a course** s'inscrire pour un cours
▶ **sign out** *vi* signer le registre (en partant)
▶ **sign over** *vt*: **to ~ sth over to sb** céder qch par écrit à qn
▶ **sign up** *vt* (*Mil*) engager ▷ *vi* (*Mil*) s'engager; (*for course*) s'inscrire
**signal** ['sɪgnl] *n* signal *m* ▷ *vi* (*Aut*) mettre son clignotant ▷ *vt* (*person*) faire signe à; (*message*) communiquer par signaux; **to ~ a left/right turn** (*Aut*) indiquer *or* signaler que l'on tourne à gauche/droite; **to ~ to sb (to do sth)** faire signe à qn (de faire qch)
**signal box** *n* (*Rail*) poste *m* d'aiguillage
**signalman** [sɪgnlmən] *n* (*Rail*) aiguilleur *m*
**signatory** ['sɪgnətərɪ] *n* signataire *m/f*
**signature** ['sɪgnətʃəʳ] *n* signature *f*
**signature tune** *n* indicatif musical
**signet ring** ['sɪgnət-] *n* chevalière *f*
**significance** [sɪg'nɪfɪkəns] *n* signification *f*; importance *f*; **that is of no ~** ceci n'a pas d'importance
**significant** [sɪg'nɪfɪkənt] *adj* significatif(-ive); (*important*) important(e), considérable
**significantly** [sɪg'nɪfɪkəntlɪ] *adv* (*improve*, *increase*) sensiblement; (*smile*) d'un air entendu, éloquemment; **~, ...** fait significatif, ...
**signify** ['sɪgnɪfaɪ] *vt* signifier
**sign language** *n* langage *m* par signes
**signpost** ['saɪnpəust] *n* poteau indicateur
**Sikh** [si:k] *adj*, *n* Sikh *m/f*
**silage** ['saɪlɪdʒ] *n* (*fodder*) fourrage vert; (*method*) ensilage *m*
**silence** ['saɪlns] *n* silence *m* ▷ *vt* faire taire, réduire au silence
**silencer** ['saɪlənsəʳ] *n* (*Brit*: *on gun*, *Aut*) silencieux *m*
**silent** ['saɪlnt] *adj* silencieux(-euse); (*film*) muet(te); **to keep** *or* **remain ~** garder le silence, ne rien dire
**silently** ['saɪlntlɪ] *adv* silencieusement
**silent partner** *n* (*Comm*) bailleur *m* de fonds, commanditaire *m*
**silhouette** [sɪlu:'ɛt] *n* silhouette *f* ▷ *vt*: **~d against** se profilant sur, se découpant contre
**silicon** ['sɪlɪkən] *n* silicium *m*
**silicon chip** ['sɪlɪkən-] *n* puce *f* électronique
**silicone** ['sɪlɪkəun] *n* silicone *f*
**silk** [sɪlk] *n* soie *f* ▷ *cpd* de *or* en soie
**silky** ['sɪlkɪ] *adj* soyeux(-euse)
**sill** [sɪl] *n* (*also*: **windowsill**) rebord *m* (de la fenêtre); (*of door*) seuil *m*; (*Aut*) bas *m* de marche
**silly** ['sɪlɪ] *adj* stupide, sot(te), bête; **to do something ~** faire une bêtise
**silo** ['saɪləu] *n* silo *m*

**S**

**silt** [sɪlt] n vase f; limon m
**silver** ['sɪlvə'] n argent m; (money) monnaie f (en pièces d'argent); (also: **silverware**) argenterie f ▷ adj (made of silver) d'argent, en argent; (in colour) argenté(e); (car) gris métallisé inv
**silver-plated** [sɪlvə'pleɪtɪd] adj plaqué(e) argent
**silversmith** ['sɪlvəsmɪθ] n orfèvre m/f
**silverware** ['sɪlvəwɛə'] n argenterie f
**silver wedding, silver wedding anniversary** n noces fpl d'argent
**silvery** ['sɪlvrɪ] adj argenté(e)
**SIM card** abbr (= subscriber identity module card) carte f SIM
**similar** ['sɪmɪlə'] adj: ~ **(to)** semblable (à)
**similarity** [sɪmɪ'lærɪtɪ] n ressemblance f, similarité f
**similarly** ['sɪmɪləlɪ] adv de la même façon, de même
**simile** ['sɪmɪlɪ] n comparaison f
**simmer** ['sɪmə'] vi cuire à feu doux, mijoter
▶ **simmer down** vi (fig: inf) se calmer
**simper** ['sɪmpə'] vi minauder
**simpering** ['sɪmprɪŋ] adj stupide
**simple** ['sɪmpl] adj simple; **the ~ truth** la vérité pure et simple
**simple interest** n (Math, Comm) intérêts mpl simples
**simple-minded** [sɪmpl'maɪndɪd] adj simplet(te), simple d'esprit
**simpleton** ['sɪmpltən] n nigaud(e), niais(e)
**simplicity** [sɪm'plɪsɪtɪ] n simplicité f
**simplification** [sɪmplɪfɪ'keɪʃən] n simplification f
**simplify** ['sɪmplɪfaɪ] vt simplifier
**simply** ['sɪmplɪ] adv simplement; (without fuss) avec simplicité; (absolutely) absolument
**simulate** ['sɪmjuleɪt] vt simuler, feindre
**simulation** [sɪmju'leɪʃən] n simulation f
**simultaneous** [sɪməl'teɪnɪəs] adj simultané(e)
**simultaneously** [sɪməl'teɪnɪəslɪ] adv simultanément
**sin** [sɪn] n péché m ▷ vi pécher
**Sinai** ['saɪneɪaɪ] n Sinaï m
**since** [sɪns] adv, prep depuis ▷ conj (time) depuis que; (because) puisque, étant donné que, comme; ~ **then, ever ~** depuis ce moment-là; ~ **Monday** depuis lundi; **(ever) ~ I arrived** depuis mon arrivée, depuis que je suis arrivé
**sincere** [sɪn'sɪə'] adj sincère
**sincerely** [sɪn'sɪəlɪ] adv sincèrement; **Yours ~** (at end of letter) veuillez agréer, Monsieur (or Madame) l'expression de mes sentiments distingués or les meilleurs
**sincerity** [sɪn'sɛrɪtɪ] n sincérité f
**sine** [saɪn] n (Math) sinus m
**sinew** ['sɪnju:] n tendon m; **sinews** npl muscles mpl
**sinful** ['sɪnful] adj coupable
**sing** (pt **sang**, pp **sung**) [sɪŋ, sæŋ, sʌŋ] vt, vi chanter
**Singapore** [sɪŋgə'pɔ:'] n Singapour m
**singe** [sɪndʒ] vt brûler légèrement; (clothes)

roussir
**singer** ['sɪŋə'] n chanteur(-euse)
**Singhalese** [sɪŋə'li:z] adj = **Sinhalese**
**singing** ['sɪŋɪŋ] n (of person, bird) chant m; façon f de chanter; (of kettle, bullet, in ears) sifflement m
**single** ['sɪŋgl] adj seul(e), unique; (unmarried) célibataire; (not double) simple ▷ n (Brit: also: **single ticket**) aller m (simple); (record) 45 tours m; **singles** npl (Tennis) simple m; (US: single people) célibataires m/fpl; **not a ~ one was left** il n'en est pas resté un(e), seul(e); **every ~ day** chaque jour sans exception
▶ **single out** vt choisir; (distinguish) distinguer
**single bed** n lit m d'une personne or à une place
**single-breasted** ['sɪŋglbrɛstɪd] adj droit(e)
**Single European Market** n: **the ~** le marché unique européen
**single file** n: **in ~** en file indienne
**single-handed** [sɪŋgl'hændɪd] adv tout(e) seul(e), sans (aucune) aide
**single-minded** [sɪŋgl'maɪndɪd] adj résolu(e), tenace
**single parent** n parent unique (or célibataire; **single-parent family** famille monoparentale
**single room** n chambre f à un lit or pour une personne
**singles bar** n (esp US) bar m de rencontres pour célibataires
**single-sex school** [sɪŋgl'sɛks-] n école f non mixte
**singlet** ['sɪŋglɪt] n tricot m de corps
**single-track road** [sɪŋgl'træk-] n route f à voie unique
**singly** ['sɪŋglɪ] adv séparément
**singsong** ['sɪŋsɔŋ] adj (tone) chantant(e) ▷ n (songs): **to have a ~** chanter quelque chose (ensemble)
**singular** ['sɪŋgjulə'] adj singulier(-ière); (odd) singulier, étrange; (outstanding) remarquable; (Ling) (au) singulier, du singulier ▷ n (Ling) singulier m; **in the feminine ~** au féminin singulier
**singularly** ['sɪŋgjuləlɪ] adv singulièrement; étrangement
**Sinhalese** [sɪnhə'li:z] adj cingalais(e)
**sinister** ['sɪnɪstə'] adj sinistre
**sink** [sɪŋk] (pt **sank**, pp **sunk**) [sæŋk, sʌŋk] n évier m; (washbasin) lavabo m ▷ vt (ship) (faire) couler, faire sombrer; (foundations) creuser; (piles etc): **to ~ sth into** enfoncer qch dans ▷ vi couler, sombrer; (ground etc) s'affaisser; **to ~ into sth** (chair) s'enfoncer dans qch; **he sank into a chair/the mud** il s'est enfoncé dans un fauteuil/la boue; **a ~ing feeling** un serrement de cœur
▶ **sink in** vi s'enfoncer, pénétrer; (explanation) rentrer (inf), être compris; **it took a long time to ~ in** il a fallu longtemps pour que ça rentre
**sinking fund** n fonds mpl d'amortissement
**sink unit** n bloc-évier m
**sinner** ['sɪnə'] n pécheur(-eresse)
**Sinn Féin** [ʃɪn'feɪn] n Sinn Féin m (parti politique

irlandais qui soutient l'IRA)

**Sino~** ['saɪnəu] *prefix* sino-

**sinuous** ['sɪnjuəs] *adj* sinueux(-euse)

**sinus** ['saɪnəs] *n* (*Anat*) sinus *m inv*

**sip** [sɪp] *n* petite gorgée ▷ *vt* boire à petites gorgées

**siphon** ['saɪfən] *n* siphon *m* ▷ *vt* (*also:* **siphon off**) siphonner; (: *fig: funds*) transférer; (: *illegally*) détourner

**sir** [səʳ] *n* monsieur *m*; **S~ John Smith** sir John Smith; **yes ~** oui Monsieur; **Dear S~** (*in letter*) Monsieur

**siren** ['saɪərn] *n* sirène *f*

**sirloin** ['səːlɔɪn] *n* (*also:* **sirloin steak**) aloyau *m*

**sirloin steak** *n* bifteck *m* dans l'aloyau

**sirocco** [sɪ'rɔkəu] *n* sirocco *m*

**sisal** ['saɪsəl] *n* sisal *m*

**sissy** ['sɪsɪ] *n* (*inf: coward*) poule mouillée

**sister** ['sɪstəʳ] *n* sœur *f*; (*nun*) religieuse *f*, (bonne) sœur; (*Brit: nurse*) infirmière *f* en chef ▷ *cpd*: **~ organization** organisation *f* sœur; **~ship** sister(-)ship *m*

**sister-in-law** ['sɪstərɪnlɔ:] *n* belle-sœur *f*

**sit** (*pt, pp* **sat**) [sɪt, sæt] *vi* s'asseoir; (*be sitting*) être assis(e); (*assembly*) être en séance, siéger; (*for painter*) poser; (*dress etc*) tomber ▷ *vt* (*exam*) passer, se présenter à; **to ~ tight** ne pas bouger
- ▶ **sit about, sit around** *vi* être assis(e) *or* rester à ne rien faire
- ▶ **sit back** *vi* (*in seat*) bien s'installer, se carrer
- ▶ **sit down** *vi* s'asseoir; **to be ~ting down** être assis(e)
- ▶ **sit in** *vi*: **to ~ in on a discussion** assister à une discussion
- ▶ **sit on** *vt fus* (*jury, committee*) faire partie de
- ▶ **sit up** *vi* s'asseoir; (*straight*) se redresser; (*not go to bed*) rester debout, ne pas se coucher

**sitcom** ['sɪtkɔm] *n abbr* (*TV:* = *situation comedy*) sitcom *f*, comédie *f* de situation

**sit-down** ['sɪtdaun] *adj*: **a ~ strike** une grève sur le tas; **a ~ meal** un repas assis

**site** [saɪt] *n* emplacement *m*, site *m*; (*also:* **building site**) chantier *m* ▷ *vt* placer

**sit-in** ['sɪtɪn] *n* (*demonstration*) sit-in *m inv*, occupation *f* de locaux

**siting** ['saɪtɪŋ] *n* (*location*) emplacement *m*

**sitter** ['sɪtəʳ] *n* (*for painter*) modèle *m*; (*also:* **babysitter**) baby-sitter *m/f*

**sitting** ['sɪtɪŋ] *n* (*of assembly etc*) séance *f*; (*in canteen*) service *m*

**sitting member** *n* (*Pol*) parlementaire *m/f* en exercice

**sitting room** *n* salon *m*

**sitting tenant** *n* (*Brit*) locataire occupant(e)

**situate** ['sɪtjueɪt] *vt* situer

**situated** ['sɪtjueɪtɪd] *adj* situé(e)

**situation** [sɪtju'eɪʃən] *n* situation *f*; **"~s vacant/ wanted"** (*Brit*) "offres/demandes d'emploi"

**situation comedy** *n* (*Theat*) comédie *f* de situation

**six** [sɪks] *num* six

**six-pack** ['sɪkspæk] *n* (*esp US*) pack *m* de six

canettes

**sixteen** [sɪks'tiːn] *num* seize

**sixteenth** [sɪks'tiːnθ] *num* seizième

**sixth** ['sɪksθ] *num* sixième ▷ *n*: **the upper/ lower ~** (*Brit Scol*) la terminale/la première

**sixth form** *n* (*Brit*) ≈ classes *fpl* de première et de terminale

**sixth-form college** *n* lycée *n'ayant que des classes de première et de terminale*

**sixtieth** ['sɪkstɪɪθ] *num* soixantième

**sixty** ['sɪkstɪ] *num* soixante

**size** [saɪz] *n* dimensions *fpl*; (*of person*) taille *f*; (*of clothing*) taille; (*of shoes*) pointure *f*; (*of estate, area*) étendue *f*; (*of problem*) ampleur *f*; (*of company*) importance *f*; (*glue*) colle *f*; **I take ~ 14** (*of dress etc*) ≈ je prends du 42 *or* la taille 42; **the small/ large ~** (*of soap powder etc*) le petit/grand modèle; **it's the ~ of ...** c'est de la taille (*or* grosseur) de ..., c'est grand (*or* gros) comme ...; **cut to ~** découpé(e) aux dimensions voulues
- ▶ **size up** *vt* juger, jauger

**sizeable** ['saɪzəbl] *adj* (*object, building, estate*) assez grand(e); (*amount, problem, majority*) assez important(e)

**sizzle** ['sɪzl] *vi* grésiller

**SK** *abbr* (*Canada*) = **Saskatchewan**

**skate** [skeɪt] *n* patin *m*; (*fish: pl inv*) raie *f* ▷ *vi* patiner
- ▶ **skate over, skate around** *vt* (*problem, issue*) éluder

**skateboard** ['skeɪtbɔːd] *n* skateboard *m*, planche *f* à roulettes

**skateboarding** ['skeɪtbɔːdɪŋ] *n* skateboard *m*

**skater** ['skeɪtəʳ] *n* patineur(-euse)

**skating** ['skeɪtɪŋ] *n* patinage *m*

**skating rink** *n* patinoire *f*

**skeleton** ['skɛlɪtn] *n* squelette *m*; (*outline*) schéma *m*

**skeleton key** *n* passe-partout *m*

**skeleton staff** *n* effectifs réduits

**skeptic** ['skɛptɪk] (*US*) = **sceptic**

**skeptical** ['skɛptɪkl] (*US*) = **sceptical**

**sketch** [skɛtʃ] *n* (*drawing*) croquis *m*, esquisse *f*; (*outline plan*) aperçu *m*; (*Theat*) sketch *m*, saynète *f* ▷ *vt* esquisser, faire un croquis *or* une esquisse de; (*plan etc*) esquisser

**sketch book** *n* carnet *m* à dessin

**sketch pad** *n* bloc *m* à dessin

**sketchy** ['skɛtʃɪ] *adj* incomplet(-ète), fragmentaire

**skew** [skjuː] *n* (*Brit*): **on the ~** de travers, en biais

**skewer** ['skjuːəʳ] *n* brochette *f*

**ski** [skiː] *n* ski *m* ▷ *vi* skier, faire du ski

**ski boot** *n* chaussure *f* de ski

**skid** [skɪd] *n* dérapage *m* ▷ *vi* déraper; **to go into a ~** déraper

**skid mark** *n* trace *f* de dérapage

**skier** ['skiːəʳ] *n* skieur(-euse)

**skiing** ['skiːɪŋ] *n* ski *m*; **to go ~** (aller) faire du ski

**ski instructor** *n* moniteur(-trice) de ski

**ski jump** *n* (*ramp*) tremplin *m*; (*event*) saut *m* à skis

**skilful**, *(US)* **skillful** ['skɪlful] *adj* habile, adroit(e)
**skilfully**, *(US)* **skillfully** ['skɪlfəlɪ] *adv* habilement, adroitement
**ski lift** *n* remonte-pente *m inv*
**skill** [skɪl] *n* *(ability)* habileté *f*, adresse *f*, talent *m*; *(requiring training)* compétences *fpl*
**skilled** [skɪld] *adj* habile, adroit(e); *(worker)* qualifié(e)
**skillet** ['skɪlɪt] *n* poêlon *m*
**skillful** *etc* ['skɪlful] *(US)* = **skilful** *etc*
**skim** [skɪm] *vt* *(milk)* écrémer; *(soup)* écumer; *(glide over)* raser, effleurer ▷ *vi*: **to ~ through** *(fig)* parcourir
**skimmed milk** [skɪmd-], *(US)* **skim milk** *n* lait écrémé
**skimp** [skɪmp] *vt* *(work)* bâcler, faire à la va-vite; *(cloth etc)* lésiner sur
**skimpy** ['skɪmpɪ] *adj* étriqué(e); maigre
**skin** [skɪn] *n* peau *f* ▷ *vt* *(fruit etc)* éplucher; *(animal)* écorcher; **wet** *or* **soaked to the ~** trempé(e) jusqu'aux os
**skin-deep** ['skɪn'diːp] *adj* superficiel(le)
**skin diver** *n* plongeur(-euse) sous-marin(e)
**skin diving** *n* plongée sous-marine
**skinflint** ['skɪnflɪnt] *n* grippe-sou *m*
**skin graft** *n* greffe *f* de peau
**skinhead** ['skɪnhɛd] *n* skinhead *m*
**skinny** ['skɪnɪ] *adj* maigre, maigrichon(ne)
**skin test** *n* cuti *f* (-réaction) *f*
**skintight** ['skɪntaɪt] *adj* *(dress etc)* collant(e), ajusté(e)
**skip** [skɪp] *n* petit bond *or* saut; *(Brit: container)* benne *f* ▷ *vi* gambader, sautiller; *(with rope)* sauter à la corde ▷ *vt* *(pass over)* sauter; **to ~ school** *(esp US)* faire l'école buissonnière
**ski pants** *npl* pantalon *m* de ski
**ski pass** *n* forfait-skieur(s) *m*
**ski pole** *n* bâton *m* de ski
**skipper** ['skɪpəʳ] *n* *(Naut, Sport)* capitaine *m*; *(in race)* skipper *m* ▷ *vt* *(boat)* commander; *(team)* être le chef de
**skipping rope** ['skɪpɪŋ-], *(US)* **skip rope** *n* corde *f* à sauter
**ski resort** *n* station *f* de sports d'hiver
**skirmish** ['skəːmɪʃ] *n* escarmouche *f*, accrochage *m*
**skirt** [skəːt] *n* jupe *f* ▷ *vt* longer, contourner
**skirting board** ['skəːtɪŋ-] *n* *(Brit)* plinthe *f*
**ski run** *n* piste *f* de ski
**ski slope** *n* piste *f* de ski
**ski suit** *n* combinaison *f* de ski
**skit** [skɪt] *n* sketch *m* satirique
**ski tow** *n* = **ski lift**
**skittle** ['skɪtl] *n* quille *f*; **skittles** *(game)* (jeu *m* de) quilles *fpl*
**skive** [skaɪv] *vi* *(Brit inf)* tirer au flanc
**skulk** [skʌlk] *vi* rôder furtivement
**skull** [skʌl] *n* crâne *m*
**skullcap** ['skʌlkæp] *n* calotte *f*
**skunk** [skʌŋk] *n* mouffette *f*; *(fur)* sconse *m*
**sky** [skaɪ] *n* ciel *m*; **to praise sb to the skies** porter qn aux nues

**sky-blue** [skaɪ'bluː] *adj* bleu ciel *inv*
**skydiving** ['skaɪdaɪvɪŋ] *n* parachutisme *m (en chute libre)*
**sky-high** ['skaɪ'haɪ] *adv* très haut ▷ *adj* exorbitant(e); **prices are ~** les prix sont exorbitants
**skylark** ['skaɪlɑːk] *n* *(bird)* alouette *f* (des champs)
**skylight** ['skaɪlaɪt] *n* lucarne *f*
**skyline** ['skaɪlaɪn] *n* *(horizon)* (ligne *f* d')horizon *m*; *(of city)* ligne des toits
**Skype®** [skaɪp] *(Internet, Tel)* *n* Skype® ▷ *vt* contacter via Skype®
**skyscraper** ['skaɪskreɪpəʳ] *n* gratte-ciel *m inv*
**slab** [slæb] *n* plaque *f*; *(of stone)* dalle *f*; *(of wood)* bloc *m*; *(of meat, cheese)* tranche épaisse
**slack** [slæk] *adj* *(loose)* lâche, desserré(e); *(slow)* stagnant(e); *(careless)* négligent(e), peu sérieux(-euse) *or* consciencieux(-euse); *(Comm: market)* peu actif(-ive); *(: demand)* faible; *(period)* creux(-euse) ▷ *n* *(in rope etc)* mou *m*; **business is ~** les affaires vont mal
**slacken** ['slækn] *(also:* **slacken off)** *vi* ralentir, diminuer ▷ *vt* relâcher
**slacks** [slæks] *npl* pantalon *m*
**slag** [slæg] *n* scories *fpl*
**slag heap** *n* crassier *m*
**slag off** *(Brit: inf)* *vt* dire du mal de
**slain** [sleɪn] *pp* of **slay**
**slake** [sleɪk] *vt* *(one's thirst)* étancher
**slalom** ['slɑːləm] *n* slalom *m*
**slam** [slæm] *vt* *(door)* (faire) claquer; *(throw)* jeter violemment, flanquer; *(inf: criticize)* éreinter, démolir ▷ *vi* claquer
**slammer** ['slæməʳ] *n* *(inf)*: **the ~** la taule
**slander** ['slɑːndəʳ] *n* calomnie *f*; *(Law)* diffamation *f* ▷ *vt* calomnier; diffamer
**slanderous** ['slɑːndrəs] *adj* calomnieux(-euse); diffamatoire
**slang** [slæŋ] *n* argot *m*
**slanging match** ['slæŋɪŋ-] *n* *(Brit inf)* engueulade *f*, empoignade *f*
**slant** [slɑːnt] *n* inclinaison *f*; *(fig)* angle *m*, point *m* de vue
**slanted** ['slɑːntɪd] *adj* tendancieux(-euse)
**slanting** ['slɑːntɪŋ] *adj* en pente, incliné(e); couché(e)
**slap** [slæp] *n* claque *f*, gifle *f*; *(on the back)* tape *f* ▷ *vt* donner une claque *or* une gifle *(or* une tape) à; **to ~ on** *(paint)* appliquer rapidement ▷ *adv* *(directly)* tout droit, en plein
**slapdash** ['slæpdæʃ] *adj* *(work)* fait(e) sans soin *or* à la va-vite; *(person)* insouciant(e), négligent(e)
**slaphead** ['slæphɛd] *n* *(Brit inf)* chauve
**slapstick** ['slæpstɪk] *n* *(comedy)* grosse farce *(style tarte à la crème)*
**slap-up** ['slæpʌp] *adj* *(Brit)*: **a ~ meal** un repas extra *or* fameux
**slash** [slæʃ] *vt* entailler, taillader; *(fig: prices)* casser
**slat** [slæt] *n* *(of wood)* latte *f*, lame *f*
**slate** [sleɪt] *n* ardoise *f* ▷ *vt* *(fig: criticize)* éreinter, démolir

**slaughter** ['slɔ:təʳ] n carnage m, massacre m; (of animals) abattage m ▷ vt (animal) abattre; (people) massacrer

**slaughterhouse** ['slɔ:təhaus] n abattoir m

**Slav** [sla:v] adj slave

**slave** [sleɪv] n esclave m/f ▷ vi (also: **slave away**) trimer, travailler comme un forçat; **to ~ (away) at sth/at doing sth** se tuer à qch/à faire qch

**slave driver** n (inf: pej) négrier(-ière)

**slave labour** n travail m d'esclave; **it's just ~** (fig) c'est de l'esclavage

**slaver** ['slævəʳ] vi (dribble) baver

**slavery** ['sleɪvərɪ] n esclavage m

**Slavic** ['slævɪk] adj slave

**slavish** ['sleɪvɪʃ] adj servile

**slavishly** ['sleɪvɪʃlɪ] adv (copy) servilement

**Slavonic** [slə'vɔnɪk] adj slave

**slay** (pt **slew**, pp **slain**) [sleɪ, slu:, sleɪn] vt (literary) tuer

**sleazy** ['sli:zɪ] adj miteux(-euse), minable

**sled** [slɛd] (US) = **sledge**

**sledge** [slɛdʒ] n luge f

**sledgehammer** ['slɛdʒhæməʳ] n marteau m de forgeron

**sleek** [sli:k] adj (hair, fur) brillant(e), luisant(e); (car, boat) aux lignes pures or élégantes

**sleep** [sli:p] n sommeil m ▷ vi (pt, pp **slept**) [slɛpt] dormir; (spend night) dormir, coucher ▷ vt: **we can ~ 4** on peut coucher or loger 4 personnes; **to go to ~** s'endormir; **to have a good night's ~** passer une bonne nuit; **to put to ~** (patient) endormir; (animal: euphemism: kill) piquer; **to ~ lightly** avoir le sommeil léger; **to ~ with sb** (have sex) coucher avec qn
  ▶ **sleep around** vi coucher à droite et à gauche
  ▶ **sleep in** vi (oversleep) se réveiller trop tard; (on purpose) faire la grasse matinée
  ▶ **sleep together** vi (have sex) coucher ensemble

**sleeper** ['sli:pəʳ] n (person) dormeur(-euse); (Brit Rail: on track) traverse f; (: train) train-couchettes m; (: carriage) wagon-lits m, voiture-lits f; (: berth) couchette f

**sleepily** ['sli:pɪlɪ] adv d'un air endormi

**sleeping** ['sli:pɪŋ] adj qui dort, endormi(e)

**sleeping bag** n sac m de couchage

**sleeping car** n wagon-lits m, voiture-lits f

**sleeping partner** n (Brit Comm) = **silent partner**

**sleeping pill** n somnifère m

**sleeping sickness** n maladie f du sommeil

**sleepless** ['sli:plɪs] adj: **a ~ night** une nuit blanche

**sleeplessness** ['sli:plɪsnɪs] n insomnie f

**sleepover** ['sli:pəuvəʳ] n nuit f chez un copain or une copine; **we're having a ~ at Jo's** nous allons passer la nuit chez Jo

**sleepwalk** ['sli:pwɔ:k] vi marcher en dormant

**sleepwalker** ['sli:pwɔ:kəʳ] n somnambule m/f

**sleepy** ['sli:pɪ] adj qui a envie de dormir; (fig) endormi(e); **to be** or **feel ~** avoir sommeil, avoir envie de dormir

**sleet** [sli:t] n neige fondue

**sleeve** [sli:v] n manche f; (of record) pochette f

**sleeveless** ['sli:vlɪs] adj (garment) sans manches

**sleigh** [sleɪ] n traîneau m

**sleight** [slaɪt] n: **~ of hand** tour m de passe-passe

**slender** ['slɛndəʳ] adj svelte, mince; (fig) faible, ténu(e)

**slept** [slɛpt] pt, pp of **sleep**

**sleuth** [slu:θ] n (inf) détective (privé)

**slew** [slu:] vi (also: **slew round**) virer, pivoter ▷ pt of **slay**

**slice** [slaɪs] n tranche f; (round) rondelle f; (utensil) spatule f; (also: **fish slice**) pelle f à poisson ▷ vt couper en tranches (or en rondelles); **~d bread** pain m en tranches

**slick** [slɪk] adj (skilful) bien ficelé(e); (salesperson) qui a du bagout, mielleux(-euse) ▷ n (also: **oil slick**) nappe f de pétrole, marée noire

**slid** [slɪd] pt, pp of **slide**

**slide** [slaɪd] (pt, pp **slid**) [slɪd] n (in playground) toboggan m; (Phot) diapositive f; (Brit: also: **hair slide**) barrette f; (microscope slide) (lame f) porte-objet m; (in prices) chute f, baisse f ▷ vt (faire) glisser ▷ vi glisser; **to let things ~** (fig) laisser les choses aller à la dérive

**slide projector** n (Phot) projecteur m de diapositives

**slide rule** n règle f à calcul

**sliding** ['slaɪdɪŋ] adj (door) coulissant(e); **~ roof** (Aut) toit ouvrant

**sliding scale** n échelle f mobile

**slight** [slaɪt] adj (slim) mince, menu(e); (frail) frêle; (trivial) faible, insignifiant(e); (small) petit(e), léger(-ère); (before n) ▷ n offense f, affront m ▷ vt (offend) blesser, offenser; **the ~est** le (or la) moindre; **not in the ~est** pas le moins du monde, pas du tout

**slightly** ['slaɪtlɪ] adv légèrement, un peu; **~ built** fluet(te)

**slim** [slɪm] adj mince ▷ vi maigrir; (diet) suivre un régime amaigrissant

**slime** [slaɪm] n vase f; substance visqueuse

**slimming** ['slɪmɪŋ] n amaigrissement m ▷ adj (diet, pills) amaigrissant(e), pour maigrir; (food) qui ne fait pas grossir

**slimy** ['slaɪmɪ] adj visqueux(-euse), gluant(e); (covered with mud) vaseux(-euse)

**sling** [slɪŋ] n (Med) écharpe f; (for baby) porte-bébé m; (weapon) fronde f, lance-pierre m ▷ vt (pt, pp **slung**) [slʌŋ] lancer, jeter; **to have one's arm in a ~** avoir le bras en écharpe

**slink** (pt, pp **slunk**) [slɪŋk, slʌŋk] vi: **to ~ away** or **off** s'en aller furtivement

**slinky** ['slɪŋkɪ] adj (clothes) moulant(e)

**slip** [slɪp] n faux pas; (mistake) erreur f, bévue f; (underskirt) combinaison f; (of paper) petite feuille, fiche f ▷ vt (slide) glisser ▷ vi (slide) glisser; (decline) baisser; (move smoothly): **to ~ into/out of** se glisser or se faufiler dans/hors de; **to let a chance ~ by** laisser passer une occasion; **to ~ sth on/off** enfiler/enlever qch; **it ~ped from her hand** cela lui a glissé des mains; **to give sb the ~** fausser compagnie à

**S**

qn; **a ~ of the tongue** un lapsus
▸ **slip away** vi s'esquiver
▸ **slip in** vt glisser
▸ **slip out** vi sortir
▸ **slip up** vi faire une erreur, gaffer
**slip-on** ['slɪpɒn] adj facile à enfiler; **~ shoes** mocassins mpl
**slipped disc** [slɪpt-] n déplacement m de vertèbre
**slipper** ['slɪpər] n pantoufle f
**slippery** ['slɪpərɪ] adj glissant(e); (fig: person) insaisissable
**slip road** n (Brit: to motorway) bretelle f d'accès
**slipshod** ['slɪpʃɒd] adj négligé(e), peu soigné(e)
**slip-up** ['slɪpʌp] n bévue f
**slipway** ['slɪpweɪ] n cale f (de construction or de lancement)
**slit** [slɪt] n fente f; (cut) incision f; (tear) déchirure f ▷ vt (pt, pp ~) fendre; couper, inciser; déchirer; **to ~ sb's throat** trancher la gorge à qn
**slither** ['slɪðər] vi glisser, déraper
**sliver** ['slɪvər] n (of glass, wood) éclat m; (of cheese, sausage) petit morceau
**slob** [slɒb] n (inf) rustaud(e)
**slog** [slɒg] n (Brit: effort) gros effort; (: work) tâche fastidieuse ▷ vi travailler très dur
**slogan** ['sləʊgən] n slogan m
**slop** [slɒp] vi (also: **slop over**) se renverser; déborder ▷ vt répandre; renverser
**slope** [sləʊp] n pente f, côte f; (side of mountain) versant m; (slant) inclinaison f ▷ vi: **to ~ down** être or descendre en pente; **to ~ up** monter
**sloping** ['sləʊpɪŋ] adj en pente, incliné(e); (handwriting) penché(e)
**sloppy** ['slɒpɪ] adj (work) peu soigné(e), bâclé(e); (appearance) négligé(e), débraillé(e); (film etc) sentimental(e)
**slosh** [slɒʃ] vi (inf): **to ~ about** or **around** (children) patauger; (liquid) clapoter
**sloshed** [slɒʃt] adj (inf: drunk) bourré(e)
**slot** [slɒt] n fente f; (fig: in timetable, Radio, TV) créneau m, plage f ▷ vt: **to ~ sth into** encastrer or insérer qch dans ▷ vi: **to ~ into** s'encastrer or s'insérer dans
**sloth** [sləʊθ] n (vice) paresse f; (Zool) paresseux m
**slot machine** n (Brit: vending machine) distributeur m (automatique), machine f à sous; (for gambling) appareil m or machine à sous
**slot meter** n (Brit) compteur m à pièces
**slouch** [slaʊtʃ] vi avoir le dos rond, être voûté(e)
▸ **slouch about, slouch around** vi traîner à ne rien faire
**Slovak** ['sləʊvæk] adj slovaque ▷ n Slovaque m/f; (Ling) slovaque m; **the ~ Republic** la République slovaque
**Slovakia** [sləʊˈvækɪə] n Slovaquie f
**Slovakian** [sləʊˈvækɪən] adj, n = **Slovak**
**Slovene** [sləʊˈviːn] adj slovène ▷ n Slovène m/f; (Ling) slovène m
**Slovenia** [sləʊˈviːnɪə] n Slovénie f
**Slovenian** [sləʊˈviːnɪən] adj, n = **Slovene**

**slovenly** ['slʌvənlɪ] adj sale, débraillé(e), négligé(e)
**slow** [sləʊ] adj lent(e); (watch): **to be ~** retarder ▷ adv lentement ▷ vt, vi ralentir; **"~"** (road sign) "ralentir"; **at a ~ speed** à petite vitesse; **to be ~ to act/decide** être lent à agir/décider; **my watch is 20 minutes ~** ma montre retarde de 20 minutes; **business is ~** les affaires marchent au ralenti; **to go ~** (driver) rouler lentement; (in industrial dispute) faire la grève perlée
▸ **slow down** vi ralentir
**slow-acting** [sləʊˈæktɪŋ] adj qui agit lentement, à action lente
**slowcoach** ['sləʊkəʊtʃ] n (Brit inf) lambin(e)
**slowly** ['sləʊlɪ] adv lentement
**slow motion** n: **in ~** au ralenti
**slowness** ['sləʊnɪs] n lenteur f
**slowpoke** ['sləʊpəʊk] n (US inf) = **slowcoach**
**sludge** [slʌdʒ] n boue f
**slug** [slʌg] n limace f; (bullet) balle f
**sluggish** ['slʌgɪʃ] adj (person) mou (molle), lent(e); (stream, engine, trading) lent(e); (business, sales) stagnant(e)
**sluice** [sluːs] n écluse f; (also: **sluice gate**) vanne f ▷ vt: **to ~ down** or **out** laver à grande eau
**slum** [slʌm] n (house) taudis m; **slums** npl (area) quartiers mpl pauvres
**slumber** ['slʌmbər] n sommeil m
**slump** [slʌmp] n baisse soudaine, effondrement m; (Econ) crise f ▷ vi s'effondrer, s'affaisser
**slung** [slʌŋ] pt, pp of **sling**
**slunk** [slʌŋk] pt, pp of **slink**
**slur** [sləːr] n bredouillement m; (smear): **~ (on)** atteinte f (à); insinuation f (contre) ▷ vt mal articuler; **to be a ~ on** porter atteinte à
**slurp** [sləːp] vt, vi boire à grand bruit
**slurred** [sləːd] adj (pronunciation) inarticulé(e), indistinct(e)
**slush** [slʌʃ] n neige fondue
**slush fund** n caisse noire, fonds secrets
**slushy** ['slʌʃɪ] adj (snow) fondu(e); (street) couvert(e) de neige fondue; (Brit: fig) à l'eau de rose
**slut** [slʌt] n souillon f
**sly** [slaɪ] adj (person) rusé(e); (smile, expression, remark) sournois(e); **on the ~** en cachette
**smack** [smæk] n (slap) tape f; (on face) gifle f ▷ vt donner une tape à; (on face) gifler; (on bottom) donner la fessée à ▷ vi: **to ~ of** avoir des relents de, sentir ▷ adv (inf): **it fell ~ in the middle** c'est tombé en plein milieu or en plein dedans; **to ~ one's lips** se lécher les babines
**smacker** ['smækər] n (inf: kiss) bisou m or bise f sonore; (: Brit: pound note) livre f; (: US: dollar bill) dollar m
**small** [smɔːl] adj petit(e); (letter) minuscule ▷ n: **the ~ of the back** le creux des reins; **to get** or **grow ~er** diminuer; **to make ~er** (amount, income) diminuer; (object, garment) rapetisser; **a ~ shopkeeper** un petit commerçant
**small ads** npl (Brit) petites annonces

**small arms** *npl* armes individuelles
**small business** *n* petit commerce, petite affaire
**small change** *n* petite *or* menue monnaie
**smallholder** ['smɔːlhəʊldə<sup>r</sup>] *n* (*Brit*) petit cultivateur
**smallholding** ['smɔːlhəʊldɪŋ] *n* (*Brit*) petite ferme
**small hours** *npl*: **in the ~** au petit matin
**smallish** ['smɔːlɪʃ] *adj* plutôt *or* assez petit(e)
**small-minded** [smɔːl'maɪndɪd] *adj* mesquin(e)
**smallpox** ['smɔːlpɒks] *n* variole *f*
**small print** *n* (*in contract etc*) clause(s) imprimée(s) en petits caractères
**small-scale** ['smɔːlskeɪl] *adj* (*map, model*) à échelle réduite, à petite échelle; (*business, farming*) peu important(e), modeste
**small talk** *n* menus propos
**small-time** ['smɔːltaɪm] *adj* (*farmer etc*) petit(e); **a ~ thief** un voleur à la petite semaine
**small-town** ['smɔːltaʊn] *adj* provincial(e)
**smarmy** ['smɑːmɪ] *adj* (*Brit pej*) flagorneur(-euse), lécheur(-euse)
**smart** [smɑːt] *adj* élégant(e), chic *inv*; (*clever*) intelligent(e); (*pej*) futé(e); (*quick*) vif (vive), prompt(e) ▷ *vi* faire mal, brûler; **the ~ set** le beau monde; **to look ~** être élégant(e); **my eyes are ~ing** j'ai les yeux irrités *or* qui me piquent
**smart card** ['smɑːt'kɑːd] *n* carte *f* à puce
**smart phone** *n* smartphone *m*
**smarten up** ['smɑːtn-] *vi* devenir plus élégant(e), se faire beau (belle) ▷ *vt* rendre plus élégant(e)
**smash** [smæʃ] *n* (*also*: **smash-up**) collision *f*, accident *m*; (*Mus*) succès foudroyant; (*sound*) fracas *m* ▷ *vt* casser, briser, fracasser; (*opponent*) écraser; (*hopes*) ruiner, détruire; (*Sport*: *record*) pulvériser ▷ *vi* se briser, se fracasser; s'écraser ▶ **smash up** *vt* (*car*) bousiller; (*room*) tout casser dans
**smashing** ['smæʃɪŋ] *adj* (*inf*) formidable
**smattering** ['smætərɪŋ] *n*: **a ~ of** quelques notions de
**smear** [smɪə<sup>r</sup>] *n* (*stain*) tache *f*; (*mark*) trace *f*; (*Med*) frottis *m*; (*insult*) calomnie *f* ▷ *vt* enduire; (*make dirty*) salir; (*fig*) porter atteinte à; **his hands were ~ed with oil/ink** il avait les mains maculées de cambouis/d'encre
**smear campaign** *n* campagne *f* de dénigrement
**smear test** *n* (*Brit Med*) frottis *m*
**smell** [smɛl] (*pt, pp* **smelt** *or* **-ed**) [smɛlt, smɛld] *n* odeur *f*; (*sense*) odorat *m* ▷ *vt* sentir ▷ *vi* (*pej*) sentir mauvais; (*food etc*): **to ~ (of)** sentir; **it ~s good** ça sent bon
**smelly** ['smɛlɪ] *adj* qui sent mauvais, malodorant(e)
**smelt** [smɛlt] *pt, pp of* **smell** ▷ *vt* (*ore*) fondre
**smile** [smaɪl] *n* sourire *m* ▷ *vi* sourire
**smiling** ['smaɪlɪŋ] *adj* souriant(e)
**smirk** [smə:k] *n* petit sourire suffisant *or* affecté
**smith** [smɪθ] *n* maréchal-ferrant *m*; forgeron *m*
**smithy** ['smɪðɪ] *n* forge *f*
**smitten** ['smɪtn] *adj*: **~ with** pris(e) de;

**frappé(e) de**
**smock** [smɒk] *n* blouse *f*, sarrau *m*
**smog** [smɒg] *n* brouillard mêlé de fumée
**smoke** [sməʊk] *n* fumée *f* ▷ *vt, vi* fumer; **to have a ~** fumer une cigarette; **do you ~?** est-ce que vous fumez?; **do you mind if I ~?** ça ne vous dérange pas que je fume?; **to go up in ~** (*house etc*) brûler; (*fig*) partir en fumée
**smoke alarm** *n* détecteur *m* de fumée
**smoked** [sməʊkt] *adj* (*bacon, glass*) fumé(e)
**smokeless fuel** ['sməʊklɪs-] *n* combustible non polluant
**smokeless zone** ['sməʊklɪs-] *n* (*Brit*) zone *f* où l'usage du charbon est réglementé
**smoker** ['sməʊkə<sup>r</sup>] *n* (*person*) fumeur(-euse); (*Rail*) wagon *m* fumeurs
**smoke screen** *n* rideau *m* *or* écran *m* de fumée; (*fig*) paravent *m*
**smoke shop** *n* (*US*) (bureau *m* de) tabac *m*
**smoking** ['sməʊkɪŋ] *n*: **"no ~"** (*sign*) "défense de fumer"; **to give up ~** arrêter de fumer
**smoking compartment**, (*US*) **smoking car** *n* wagon *m* fumeurs
**smoky** ['sməʊkɪ] *adj* enfumé(e); (*taste*) fumé(e)
**smolder** ['sməʊldə<sup>r</sup>] *vi* (*US*) = **smoulder**
**smoochy** ['smuːtʃɪ] *adj* (*inf*) langoureux(-euse)
**smooth** [smuːð] *adj* lisse; (*sauce*) onctueux(-euse); (*flavour, whisky*) moelleux(-euse); (*cigarette*) doux (douce); (*movement*) régulier(-ière), sans à-coups *or* heurts; (*landing, takeoff*) en douceur; (*flight*) sans secousses; (*pej: person*) doucereux(-euse), mielleux(-euse) ▷ *vt* (*also*: **smooth out**) lisser, défroisser; (*creases, difficulties*) faire disparaître ▶ **smooth over** *vt*: **to ~ things over** (*fig*) arranger les choses
**smoothly** ['smuːðlɪ] *adv* (*easily*) facilement, sans difficulté(s); **everything went ~** tout s'est bien passé
**smother** ['smʌðə<sup>r</sup>] *vt* étouffer
**smoulder**, (*US*) **smolder** ['sməʊldə<sup>r</sup>] *vi* couver
**SMS** *n abbr* (= *short message service*) SMS *m*
**SMS message** *n* (message *m*) SMS *m*
**smudge** [smʌdʒ] *n* tache *f*, bavure *f* ▷ *vt* salir, maculer
**smug** [smʌg] *adj* suffisant(e), content(e) de soi
**smuggle** ['smʌgl] *vt* passer en contrebande *or* en fraude; **to ~ in/out** (*goods etc*) faire entrer/sortir clandestinement *or* en fraude
**smuggler** ['smʌglə<sup>r</sup>] *n* contrebandier(-ière)
**smuggling** ['smʌglɪŋ] *n* contrebande *f*
**smut** [smʌt] *n* (*grain of soot*) grain de suie; (*mark*) tache *f* de suie; (*in conversation etc*) obscénités *fpl*
**smutty** ['smʌtɪ] *adj* (*fig*) grossier(-ière), obscène
**snack** [snæk] *n* casse-croûte *m inv*; **to have a ~** prendre un en-cas, manger quelque chose (de léger)
**snack bar** *n* snack(-bar) *m*
**snag** [snæg] *n* inconvénient *m*, difficulté *f*
**snail** [sneɪl] *n* escargot *m*
**snake** [sneɪk] *n* serpent *m*

**snap** [snæp] n (sound) claquement m, bruit sec; (photograph) photo f, instantané m; (game) sorte de jeu de bataille ▷ adj subit(e), fait(e) sans réfléchir ▷ vt (fingers) faire claquer; (break) casser net; (photograph) prendre un instantané de ▷ vi se casser net or avec un bruit sec; (fig: person) craquer; (speak sharply) parler d'un ton brusque; **to ~ open/shut** s'ouvrir/se refermer brusquement; **to ~ one's fingers at** (fig) se moquer de; **a cold ~** (of weather) un refroidissement soudain de la température

▸ **snap at** vt fus (subj: dog) essayer de mordre

▸ **snap off** vt (break) casser net

▸ **snap up** vt sauter sur, saisir

**snap fastener** n bouton-pression m

**snappy** ['snæpɪ] adj prompt(e); (slogan) qui a du punch; **make it ~!** (inf: hurry up) grouille-toi!, magne-toi!

**snapshot** ['snæpʃɒt] n photo f, instantané m

**snare** [snɛəʳ] n piège m ▷ vt attraper, prendre au piège

**snarl** [snɑːl] n grondement m or grognement m féroce ▷ vi gronder ▷ vt: **to get ~ed up** (wool, plans) s'emmêler; (traffic) se bloquer

**snatch** [snætʃ] n (fig) vol m; (small amount): **~es of** des fragments mpl or bribes fpl de ▷ vt saisir (d'un geste vif); (steal) voler ▷ vi: **don't ~!** doucement!; **to ~ a sandwich** manger or avaler un sandwich à la hâte; **to ~ some sleep** arriver à dormir un peu

▸ **snatch up** vt saisir, s'emparer de

**snazzy** ['snæzɪ] adj (inf: clothes) classe inv, chouette

**sneak** [sniːk] (US: pt **snuck**) vi: **to ~ in/out** entrer/sortir furtivement or à la dérobée ▷ vt: **to ~ a look at sth** regarder furtivement qch ▷ n (inf: pej: informer) faux jeton; **to ~ up on sb** s'approcher de qn sans faire de bruit

**sneakers** ['sniːkəz] npl tennis mpl, baskets fpl

**sneaking** ['sniːkɪŋ] adj: **to have a ~ feeling or suspicion that ...** avoir la vague impression que ...

**sneaky** ['sniːkɪ] adj sournois(e)

**sneer** [snɪəʳ] n ricanement m ▷ vi ricaner, sourire d'un air sarcastique; **to ~ at sb/sth** se moquer de qn/qch avec mépris

**sneeze** [sniːz] n éternuement m ▷ vi éternuer

**snide** [snaɪd] adj sarcastique, narquois(e)

**sniff** [snɪf] n reniflement m ▷ vi renifler ▷ vt renifler, flairer; (glue, drug) sniffer, respirer

▸ **sniff at** vt fus: **it's not to be ~ed at** il ne faut pas cracher dessus, ce n'est pas à dédaigner

**sniffer dog** ['snɪfə-] n (Police) chien dressé pour la recherche d'explosifs et de stupéfiants

**snigger** ['snɪgəʳ] n ricanement m; rire moqueur ▷ vi ricaner

**snip** [snɪp] n (cut) entaille f; (piece) petit bout; (Brit: inf: bargain) (bonne) occasion or affaire f ▷ vt couper

**sniper** ['snaɪpəʳ] n (marksman) tireur embusqué

**snippet** ['snɪpɪt] n bribes fpl

**snivelling** ['snɪvlɪŋ] adj larmoyant(e), pleurnicheur(-euse)

**snob** [snɒb] n snob m/f

**snobbery** ['snɒbərɪ] n snobisme m

**snobbish** ['snɒbɪʃ] adj snob inv

**snog** [snɒg] vi (inf) se bécoter

**snooker** ['snuːkəʳ] n sorte de jeu de billard

**snoop** [snuːp] vi: **to ~ on sb** espionner qn; **to ~ about** fureter

**snooper** ['snuːpəʳ] n fureteur(-euse)

**snooty** ['snuːtɪ] adj snob inv, prétentieux(-euse)

**snooze** [snuːz] n petit somme ▷ vi faire un petit somme

**snore** [snɔːʳ] vi ronfler ▷ n ronflement m

**snoring** ['snɔːrɪŋ] n ronflement(s) m(pl)

**snorkel** ['snɔːkl] n (of swimmer) tuba m

**snort** [snɔːt] n grognement m ▷ vi grogner; (horse) renâcler ▷ vt (inf: drugs) sniffer

**snotty** ['snɒtɪ] adj morveux(-euse)

**snout** [snaut] n museau m

**snow** [snəu] n neige f ▷ vi neiger ▷ vt: **to be ~ed under with work** être débordé(e) de travail

**snowball** ['snəubɔːl] n boule f de neige

**snowbound** ['snəubaund] adj enneigé(e), bloqué(e) par la neige

**snow-capped** ['snəukæpt] adj (peak, mountain) couvert(e) de neige

**snowdrift** ['snəudrɪft] n congère f

**snowdrop** ['snəudrɔp] n perce-neige m

**snowfall** ['snəufɔːl] n chute f de neige

**snowflake** ['snəufleɪk] n flocon m de neige

**snowman** ['snəumæn] (irreg) n bonhomme m de neige

**snowplough**, (US) **snowplow** ['snəuplau] n chasse-neige m inv

**snowshoe** ['snəuʃuː] n raquette f (pour la neige)

**snowstorm** ['snəustɔːm] n tempête f de neige

**snowy** ['snəuɪ] adj neigeux(-euse); (covered with snow) enneigé(e)

**SNP** n abbr (Brit Pol) = **Scottish National Party**

**snub** [snʌb] vt repousser, snober ▷ n rebuffade f

**snub-nosed** [snʌb'nəuzd] adj au nez retroussé

**snuck** [snʌk] (US) pt, pp of **sneak**

**snuff** [snʌf] n tabac m à priser ▷ vt (also: **snuff out**: candle) moucher

**snuff movie** n (inf) film pornographique qui se termine par le meurtre réel de l'un des acteurs

**snug** [snʌg] adj douillet(te), confortable; (person) bien au chaud; **it's a ~ fit** c'est bien ajusté(e)

**snuggle** ['snʌgl] vi: **to ~ down in bed/up to sb** se pelotonner dans son lit/contre qn

**SO** abbr (Banking) = **standing order**

🅞 KEYWORD

**so** [səu] adv **1** (thus, likewise) ainsi, de cette façon; **if so** si oui; **so do** or **have I** moi aussi; **it's 5 o'clock — so it is!** il est 5 heures — en effet! or c'est vrai!; **I hope/think so** je l'espère/le crois; **so far** jusqu'ici, jusqu'à maintenant; (in past) jusque-là; **quite so!** exactement!, c'est bien ça!; **even so** quand même, tout de même

**2** (in comparisons etc: to such a degree) si, tellement;

**so big (that)** si or tellement grand (que); **she's not so clever as her brother** elle n'est pas aussi intelligente que son frère
**3**: **so much** (adj, adv) tant (de); **I've got so much work** j'ai tant de travail; **I love you so much** je vous aime tant; **so many** tant (de)
**4** (phrases): **10 or so** à peu près or environ 10; **so long!** (inf: goodbye) au revoir!, à un de ces jours!; **so to speak** pour ainsi dire; **so (what)?** (inf) (bon) et alors?, et après?
▷ conj **1** (expressing purpose): **so as to do** pour faire, afin de faire; **so (that)** pour que or afin que + sub
**2** (expressing result) donc, par conséquent; **so that** si bien que, de (telle) sorte que; **so that's the reason!** c'est donc (pour) ça!; **so you see, I could have gone** alors tu vois, j'aurais pu y aller

**soak** [səuk] vt faire or laisser tremper; (drench) tremper ▷ vi tremper; **to be ~ed through** être trempé jusqu'aux os
  ▶ **soak in** vi pénétrer, être absorbé(e)
  ▶ **soak up** vt absorber
**soaking** ['səukɪŋ] adj (also: **soaking wet**) trempé(e)
**so-and-so** ['səuənsəu] n (somebody) un(e) tel(le)
**soap** [səup] n savon m
**soapflakes** ['səupfleɪks] npl paillettes fpl de savon
**soap opera** n feuilleton télévisé (quotidienneté réaliste ou embellie)
**soap powder** n lessive f, détergent m
**soapsuds** ['səupsʌds] npl mousse f de savon
**soapy** ['səupɪ] adj savonneux(-euse)
**soar** [sɔːr] vi monter (en flèche), s'élancer; (building) s'élancer; **~ing prices** prix qui grimpent
**sob** [sɔb] n sanglot m ▷ vi sangloter
**s.o.b.** n abbr (US inf!: = son of a bitch) salaud m (!)
**sober** ['səubər] adj qui n'est pas (or plus) ivre; (serious) sérieux(-euse), sensé(e); (moderate) mesuré(e); (colour, style) sobre, discret(-ète)
  ▶ **sober up** vt dégriser ▷ vi se dégriser
**sobriety** [sə'braɪətɪ] n (not being drunk) sobriété f; (seriousness, sedateness) sérieux m
**sob story** n (inf: pej) histoire larmoyante
**Soc.** abbr (= society) Soc
**so-called** ['səu'kɔːld] adj soi-disant inv
**soccer** ['sɔkər] n football m
**soccer pitch** n terrain m de football
**soccer player** n footballeur m
**sociable** ['səuʃəbl] adj sociable
**social** ['səuʃl] adj social(e); (sociable) sociable ▷ n (petite) fête
**social climber** n arriviste m/f
**social club** n amicale f, foyer m
**Social Democrat** n social-démocrate m/f
**social insurance** n (US) sécurité sociale
**socialism** ['səuʃəlɪzəm] n socialisme m
**socialist** ['səuʃəlɪst] adj, n socialiste (m/f)
**socialite** ['səuʃəlaɪt] n personnalité mondaine

**socialize** ['səuʃəlaɪz] vi voir or rencontrer des gens, se faire des amis; **to ~ with** (meet often) fréquenter; (get to know) lier connaissance or parler avec
**social life** n vie sociale; **how's your ~?** est-ce que tu sors beaucoup?
**socially** ['səuʃəlɪ] adv socialement, en société
**social networking** [-'nɛtwəːkɪŋ] n réseaux mpl sociaux
**social science** n sciences humaines
**social security** n aide sociale
**social services** npl services sociaux
**social welfare** n sécurité sociale
**social work** n assistance sociale
**social worker** n assistant(e) sociale(e)
**society** [sə'saɪətɪ] n société f; (club) société, association f; (also: **high society**) (haute) société, grand monde ▷ cpd (party) mondain(e)
**socio-economic** ['səusɪəuiːkə'nɔmɪk] adj socioéconomique
**sociological** [səusɪə'lɔdʒɪkl] adj sociologique
**sociologist** [səusɪ'ɔlədʒɪst] n sociologue m/f
**sociology** [səusɪ'ɔlədʒɪ] n sociologie f
**sock** [sɔk] n chaussette f ▷ vt (inf: hit) flanquer un coup à; **to pull one's ~s up** (fig) se secouer (les puces)
**socket** ['sɔkɪt] n cavité f; (Elec: also: **wall socket**) prise f de courant; (: for light bulb) douille f
**sod** [sɔd] n (of earth) motte f; (Brit inf!) con m (!), salaud m (!)
  ▶ **sod off** vi: **~ off!** (Brit inf!) fous le camp!, va te faire foutre! (!)
**soda** ['səudə] n (Chem) soude f; (also: **soda water**) eau f de Seltz; (US: also: **soda pop**) soda m
**sodden** ['sɔdn] adj trempé(e), détrempé(e)
**sodium** ['səudɪəm] n sodium m
**sodium chloride** n chlorure m de sodium
**sofa** ['səufə] n sofa m, canapé m
**sofa bed** n canapé-lit m
**Sofia** ['səufɪə] n Sofia
**soft** [sɔft] adj (not rough) doux (douce); (not hard) doux, mou (molle); (not loud) doux, léger(-ère); (kind) doux, gentil(le); (weak) indulgent(e); (stupid) stupide, débile
**soft-boiled** ['sɔftbɔɪld] adj (egg) à la coque
**soft drink** n boisson non alcoolisée
**soft drugs** npl drogues douces
**soften** ['sɔfn] vt (r)amollir; (fig) adoucir ▷ vi se ramollir; (fig) s'adoucir
**softener** ['sɔfnər] n (water softener) adoucisseur m; (fabric softener) produit assouplissant
**soft fruit** n (Brit) baies fpl
**soft furnishings** npl tissus mpl d'ameublement
**soft-hearted** [sɔft'hɑːtɪd] adj au cœur tendre
**softly** ['sɔftlɪ] adv doucement; (touch) légèrement; (kiss) tendrement
**softness** ['sɔftnɪs] n douceur f
**soft option** n solution f de facilité
**soft sell** n promotion f de vente discrète
**soft target** n cible f facile
**soft toy** n jouet m en peluche
**software** ['sɔftwɛər] n (Comput) logiciel m,

**S**

software *m*
**software package** *n* (*Comput*) progiciel *m*
**soggy** ['sɔgɪ] *adj* (*clothes*) trempé(e); (*ground*) détrempé(e)
**soil** [sɔɪl] *n* (*earth*) sol *m*, terre *f* ▷ *vt* salir; (*fig*) souiller
**soiled** [sɔɪld] *adj* sale; (*Comm*) défraîchi(e)
**sojourn** ['sɔdʒəːn] *n* (*formal*) séjour *m*
**solace** ['sɔlɪs] *n* consolation *f*, réconfort *m*
**solar** ['səulər] *adj* solaire
**solarium** (*pl* **solaria**) [sə'lɛərɪəm, -rɪə] *n* solarium *m*
**solar panel** *n* panneau *m* solaire
**solar plexus** [-'plɛksəs] *n* (*Anat*) plexus *m* solaire
**solar power** *n* énergie *f* solaire
**solar system** *n* système *m* solaire
**sold** [səuld] *pt*, *pp* of **sell**
**solder** ['səuldər] *vt* souder (*au fil à souder*) ▷ *n* soudure *f*
**soldier** ['səuldʒər] *n* soldat *m*, militaire *m* ▷ *vi*: **to ~ on** persévérer, s'accrocher; **toy ~** petit soldat
**sold out** *adj* (*Comm*) épuisé(e)
**sole** [səul] *n* (*of foot*) plante *f*; (*of shoe*) semelle *f*; (*fish: pl inv*) sole *f* ▷ *adj* seul(e), unique; **the ~ reason** la seule et unique raison
**solely** ['səullɪ] *adv* seulement, uniquement; **I will hold you ~ responsible** je vous en tiendrai pour seul responsable
**solemn** ['sɔləm] *adj* solennel(le); (*person*) sérieux(-euse), grave
**sole trader** *n* (*Comm*) chef *m* d'entreprise individuelle
**solicit** [sə'lɪsɪt] *vt* (*request*) solliciter ▷ *vi* (*prostitute*) racoler
**solicitor** [sə'lɪsɪtər] *n* (*Brit: for wills etc*) ≈ notaire *m*; (: *in court*) ≈ avocat *m*
**solid** ['sɔlɪd] *adj* (*strong, sound, reliable: not liquid*) solide; (*not hollow: mass*) compact(e); (: *metal, rock, wood*) massif(-ive); (*meal*) consistant(e), substantiel(le); (*vote*) unanime ▷ *n* solide *m*; **to be on ~ ground** être sur la terre ferme; (*fig*) être en terrain sûr; **we waited two ~ hours** nous avons attendu deux heures entières
**solidarity** [sɔlɪ'dærɪtɪ] *n* solidarité *f*
**solid fuel** *n* combustible *m* solide
**solidify** [sə'lɪdɪfaɪ] *vi* se solidifier ▷ *vt* solidifier
**solidity** [sə'lɪdɪtɪ] *n* solidité *f*
**solid-state** ['sɔlɪdsteɪt] *adj* (*Elec*) à circuits intégrés
**soliloquy** [sə'lɪləkwɪ] *n* monologue *m*
**solitaire** [sɔlɪ'tɛər] *n* (*gem, Brit: game*) solitaire *m*; (*US: card game*) réussite *f*
**solitary** ['sɔlɪtərɪ] *adj* solitaire
**solitary confinement** *n* (*Law*) isolement *m* (cellulaire)
**solitude** ['sɔlɪtjuːd] *n* solitude *f*
**solo** ['səuləu] *n* solo *m* ▷ *adv* (*fly*) en solitaire
**soloist** ['səuləuɪst] *n* soliste *m/f*
**Solomon Islands** ['sɔləmən-] *npl*: **the ~** les (îles *fpl*) Salomon *fpl*
**solstice** ['sɔlstɪs] *n* solstice *m*
**soluble** ['sɔljubl] *adj* soluble

**solution** [sə'luːʃən] *n* solution *f*
**solve** [sɔlv] *vt* résoudre
**solvency** ['sɔlvənsɪ] *n* (*Comm*) solvabilité *f*
**solvent** ['sɔlvənt] *adj* (*Comm*) solvable ▷ *n* (*Chem*) (dis)solvant *m*
**solvent abuse** *n* usage *m* de solvants hallucinogènes
**Somali** [səu'mɑːlɪ] *adj* somali(e), somalien(ne) ▷ *n* Somali(e), Somalien(ne)
**Somalia** [səu'mɑːlɪə] *n* (République *f* de) Somalie *f*
**Somaliland** [səu'mɑːlɪlænd] *n* Somaliland *m*
**sombre**, (*US*) **somber** ['sɔmbər] *adj* sombre, morne

⊙ **KEYWORD**

**some** [sʌm] *adj* **1** (*a certain amount or number of*): **some tea/water/ice cream** du thé/de l'eau/de la glace; **some children/apples** des enfants/ pommes; **I've got some money but not much** j'ai de l'argent mais pas beaucoup
**2** (*certain: in contrasts*): **some people say that ...** il y a des gens qui disent que ...; **some films were excellent, but most were mediocre** certains films étaient excellents, mais la plupart étaient médiocres
**3** (*unspecified*): **some woman was asking for you** il y avait une dame qui vous demandait; **he was asking for some book (or other)** il demandait un livre quelconque; **some day** un de ces jours; **some day next week** un jour la semaine prochaine; **after some time** après un certain temps; **at some length** assez longuement; **in some form or other** sous une forme ou une autre, sous une forme quelconque
▷ *pron* **1** (*a certain number*) quelques-un(e)s, certain(e)s; **I've got some** (*books etc*) j'en ai (quelques-uns); **some (of them) have been sold** certains ont été vendus
**2** (*a certain amount*) un peu; **I've got some** (*money, milk*) j'en ai (un peu); **would you like some?** est-ce que vous en voulez?, en voulez-vous?; **could I have some of that cheese?** pourrais-je avoir un peu de ce fromage?; **I've read some of the book** j'ai lu une partie du livre
▷ *adv*: **some 10 people** quelque 10 personnes, 10 personnes environ

**somebody** ['sʌmbədɪ] *pron* = **someone**
**someday** ['sʌmdeɪ] *adv* un de ces jours, un jour ou l'autre
**somehow** ['sʌmhau] *adv* d'une façon ou d'une autre; (*for some reason*) pour une raison ou une autre
**someone** ['sʌmwʌn] *pron* quelqu'un; **~ or other** quelqu'un, je ne sais qui
**someplace** ['sʌmpleɪs] *adv* (*US*) = **somewhere**
**somersault** ['sʌməsɔːlt] *n* culbute *f*, saut périlleux ▷ *vi* faire la culbute *or* un saut périlleux; (*car*) faire un tonneau

**something** ['sʌmθɪŋ] *pron* quelque chose *m*; ~ **interesting** quelque chose d'intéressant; ~ **to do** quelque chose à faire; **he's ~ like me** il est un peu comme moi; **it's ~ of a problem** il y a là un problème

**sometime** ['sʌmtaɪm] *adv* (*in future*) un de ces jours, un jour ou l'autre; (*in past*): ~ **last month** au cours du mois dernier

**sometimes** ['sʌmtaɪmz] *adv* quelquefois, parfois

**somewhat** ['sʌmwɔt] *adv* quelque peu, un peu

**somewhere** ['sʌmwɛəʳ] *adv* quelque part; ~ **else** ailleurs, autre part

**son** [sʌn] *n* fils *m*

**sonar** ['səʊnɑːʳ] *n* sonar *m*

**sonata** [sə'nɑːtə] *n* sonate *f*

**song** [sɔŋ] *n* chanson *f*; (*of bird*) chant *m*

**songbook** ['sɔŋbʊk] *n* chansonnier *m*

**songwriter** ['sɔŋraɪtəʳ] *n* auteur-compositeur *m*

**sonic** ['sɔnɪk] *adj* (*boom*) supersonique

**son-in-law** ['sʌnɪnlɔː] *n* gendre *m*, beau-fils *m*

**sonnet** ['sɔnɪt] *n* sonnet *m*

**sonny** ['sʌnɪ] *n* (*inf*) fiston *m*

**soon** [suːn] *adv* bientôt; (*early*) tôt; ~ **afterwards** peu après; **quite ~** sous peu; **how ~ can you do it?** combien de temps vous faut-il pour le faire, au plus pressé?; **how ~ can you come back?** quand *or* dans combien de temps pouvez-vous revenir, au plus tôt?; **see you ~!** à bientôt!; *see also* **as**

**sooner** ['suːnəʳ] *adv* (*time*) plus tôt; (*preference*): **I would ~ do that** j'aimerais autant *or* je préférerais faire ça; ~ **or later** tôt ou tard; **no ~ said than done** sitôt dit, sitôt fait; **the ~ the better** le plus tôt sera le mieux; **no ~ had we left than …** à peine étions-nous partis que …

**soot** [sʊt] *n* suie *f*

**soothe** [suːð] *vt* calmer, apaiser

**soothing** ['suːðɪŋ] *adj* (*ointment etc*) lénitif(-ive), lénifiant(e); (*tone, words etc*) apaisant(e); (*drink, bath*) relaxant(e)

**SOP** *n abbr* = **standard operating procedure**

**sop** [sɔp] *n*: **that's only a ~** c'est pour nous (*or* les *etc*) amadouer

**sophisticated** [sə'fɪstɪkeɪtɪd] *adj* raffiné(e), sophistiqué(e); (*machinery*) hautement perfectionné(e), très complexe; (*system etc*) très perfectionné(e), sophistiqué

**sophistication** [səfɪstɪ'keɪʃən] *n* raffinement *m*, niveau *m* (de) perfectionnement *m*

**sophomore** ['sɔfəmɔːʳ] *n* (*US*) étudiant(e) de seconde année

**soporific** [sɔpə'rɪfɪk] *adj* soporifique ▷ *n* somnifère *m*

**sopping** ['sɔpɪŋ] *adj* (*also*: **sopping wet**) tout(e) trempé(e)

**soppy** ['sɔpɪ] *adj* (*pej*) sentimental(e)

**soprano** [sə'prɑːnəʊ] *n* (*voice*) soprano *m*; (*singer*) soprano *m/f*

**sorbet** ['sɔːbeɪ] *n* sorbet *m*

**sorcerer** ['sɔːsərəʳ] *n* sorcier *m*

**sordid** ['sɔːdɪd] *adj* sordide

**sore** [sɔːʳ] *adj* (*painful*) douloureux(-euse), sensible; (*offended*) contrarié(e), vexé(e) ▷ *n* plaie *f*; **to have a ~ throat** avoir mal à la gorge; **it's a ~ point** (*fig*) c'est un point délicat

**sorely** ['sɔːlɪ] *adv* (*tempted*) fortement

**sorrel** ['sɔrəl] *n* oseille *f*

**sorrow** ['sɔrəʊ] *n* peine *f*, chagrin *m*

**sorrowful** ['sɔrəʊful] *adj* triste

**sorry** ['sɔrɪ] *adj* désolé(e); (*condition, excuse, tale*) triste, déplorable; (*sight*) désolant(e); ~! pardon!, excusez-moi!; ~? pardon?; **to feel ~ for sb** plaindre qn; **I'm ~ to hear that …** je suis désolé(e) *or* navré(e) d'apprendre que …; **to be ~ about sth** regretter qch

**sort** [sɔːt] *n* genre *m*, espèce *f*, sorte *f*; (*make: of coffee, car etc*) marque *f* ▷ *vt* (*also*: **sort out**: *select which to keep*) trier; (*classify*) classer; (*tidy*) ranger; (*letters etc*) trier; (*Comput*) trier; **what ~ do you want?** quelle sorte *or* quel genre voulez-vous?; **what ~ of car?** quelle marque de voiture?; **I'll do nothing of the ~!** je ne ferai rien de tel!; **it's ~ of awkward** (*inf*) c'est plutôt gênant
 ▷ **sort out** *vt* (*problem*) résoudre, régler

**sortie** ['sɔːtɪ] *n* sortie *f*

**sorting office** ['sɔːtɪŋ-] *n* (*Post*) bureau *m* de tri

**SOS** *n* SOS *m*

**so-so** ['səʊsəʊ] *adv* comme ci comme ça

**soufflé** ['suːfleɪ] *n* soufflé *m*

**sought** [sɔːt] *pt, pp* of **seek**

**sought-after** ['sɔːtɑːftəʳ] *adj* recherché(e)

**soul** [səʊl] *n* âme *f*; **the poor ~ had nowhere to sleep** le pauvre n'avait nulle part où dormir; **I didn't see a ~** je n'ai vu (absolument) personne

**soul-destroying** ['səʊldɪstrɔɪɪŋ] *adj* démoralisant(e)

**soulful** ['səʊlful] *adj* plein(e) de sentiment

**soulless** ['səʊllɪs] *adj* sans cœur, inhumain(e)

**soul mate** *n* âme *f* sœur

**soul-searching** ['səʊlsɜːtʃɪŋ] *n*: **after much ~, I decided …** j'ai longuement réfléchi avant de décider …

**sound** [saʊnd] *adj* (*healthy*) en bonne santé, sain(e); (*safe, not damaged*) solide, en bon état; (*reliable, not superficial*) sérieux(-euse), solide; (*sensible*) sensé(e) ▷ *adv*: ~ **asleep** profondément endormi(e) ▷ *n* (*noise, volume*) son *m*; (*louder*) bruit *m*; (*Geo*) détroit *m*, bras *m* de mer ▷ *vt* (*alarm*) sonner; (*also*: **sound out**: *opinions*) sonder ▷ *vi* sonner, retentir; (*fig: seem*) sembler (être); **to be of ~ mind** être sain(e) d'esprit; **I don't like the ~ of it** ça ne me dit rien qui vaille; **to ~ one's horn** (*Aut*) klaxonner, actionner son avertisseur; **to ~ like** ressembler à; **it ~s as if …** il semblerait que …, j'ai l'impression que …
 ▷ **sound off** *vi* (*inf*): **to ~ off (about)** la ramener (sur)

**sound barrier** *n* mur *m* du son

**sound bite** *n* phrase toute faite (*pour être citée dans les médias*)

**sound effects** *npl* bruitage *m*

**sound engineer** *n* ingénieur *m* du son

**sounding** ['saʊndɪŋ] *n* (*Naut etc*) sondage *m*

**S**

**sounding board** n (Mus) table f d'harmonie; (fig): **to use sb as a ~ for one's ideas** essayer ses idées sur qn

**soundly** ['saundlɪ] adv (sleep) profondément; (beat) complètement, à plate couture

**soundproof** ['saundpru:f] vt insonoriser ▷ adj insonorisé(e)

**sound system** n sono(risation) f

**soundtrack** ['saundtræk] n (of film) bande f sonore

**sound wave** n (Physics) onde f sonore

**soup** [su:p] n soupe f, potage m; **in the ~** (fig) dans le pétrin

**soup course** n potage m

**soup kitchen** n soupe f populaire

**soup plate** n assiette creuse or à soupe

**soupspoon** ['su:pspu:n] n cuiller f à soupe

**sour** ['sauəʳ] adj aigre, acide; (milk) tourné(e), aigre; (fig) acerbe, aigre; revêche; **to go** or **turn ~** (milk, wine) tourner; (fig: relationship, plans) mal tourner; **it's ~ grapes** c'est du dépit

**source** [sɔ:s] n source f; **I have it from a reliable ~ that** je sais de source sûre que

**south** [sauθ] n sud m ▷ adj sud inv; (wind) du sud ▷ adv au sud, vers le sud; **(to the) ~ of** au sud de; **to travel ~** aller en direction du sud

**South Africa** n Afrique f du Sud

**South African** adj sud-africain(e) ▷ n Sud-Africain(e)

**South America** n Amérique f du Sud

**South American** adj sud-américain(e) ▷ n Sud-Américain(e)

**southbound** ['sauθbaund] adj en direction du sud; (carriageway) sud inv

**south-east** [sauθ'i:st] n sud-est m

**South-East Asia** n le Sud-Est asiatique

**southerly** ['sʌðəlɪ] adj du sud; au sud

**southern** ['sʌðən] adj (du) sud; méridional(e); **with a ~ aspect** orienté(e) or exposé(e) au sud; **the ~ hemisphere** l'hémisphère sud or austral

**South Korea** n Corée f du Sud

**South of France** n: **the ~** le Sud de la France, le Midi

**South Pole** n Pôle m Sud

**South Sea Islands** npl: **the ~** l'Océanie f

**South Seas** npl: **the ~** les mers fpl du Sud

**South Vietnam** n Viêt-Nam m du Sud

**South Wales** n sud m du Pays de Galles

**southward** ['sauθwəd], **southwards** ['sauθwədz] adv vers le sud

**south-west** [sauθ'wɛst] n sud-ouest m

**souvenir** [su:və'nɪəʳ] n souvenir m (objet)

**sovereign** ['sɔvrɪn] adj, n souverain(e)

**sovereignty** ['sɔvrɪntɪ] n souveraineté f

**soviet** ['səuvɪət] adj soviétique

**Soviet Union** n: **the ~** l'Union f soviétique

**sow¹** [səu] (pt **-ed**, pp **-n**) [səun] vt semer

**sow²** n [sau] truie f

**soya** ['sɔɪə], (US) **soy** [sɔɪ] n: **~ bean** graine f de soja; **~ sauce** sauce f au soja

**sozzled** ['sɔzld] adj (Brit inf) paf inv

**spa** [spa:] n (town) station thermale; (US: also:

**health spa**) établissement m de cure de rajeunissement

**space** [speɪs] n (gen) espace m; (room) place f; espace; (length of time) laps m de temps ▷ cpd spatial(e) ▷ vt (also: **space out**) espacer; **to clear a ~ for sth** faire de la place pour qch; **in a confined ~** dans un espace réduit or restreint; **in a short ~ of time** dans peu de temps; **(with)in the ~ of an hour** en l'espace d'une heure

**space bar** n (on typewriter) barre f d'espacement

**spacecraft** ['speɪskrɑ:ft] n engin or vaisseau spatial

**spaceman** ['speɪsmæn] (irreg) n astronaute m, cosmonaute m

**spaceship** ['speɪsʃɪp] n = **spacecraft**

**space shuttle** n navette spatiale

**spacesuit** ['speɪssu:t] n combinaison spatiale

**spacewoman** ['speɪswumən] (irreg) n astronaute f, cosmonaute f

**spacing** ['speɪsɪŋ] n espacement m; **single/double ~** (Typ etc) interligne m simple/double

**spacious** ['speɪʃəs] adj spacieux(-euse), grand(e)

**spade** [speɪd] n (tool) bêche f, pelle f; (child's) pelle; **spades** npl (Cards) pique m

**spadework** ['speɪdwə:k] n (fig) gros m du travail

**spaghetti** [spə'gɛtɪ] n spaghetti mpl

**Spain** [speɪn] n Espagne f

**spam** [spæm] n (Comput) spam m

**span** [spæn] n (of bird, plane) envergure f; (of arch) portée f; (in time) espace m de temps, durée f ▷ vt enjamber, franchir; (fig) couvrir, embrasser

**Spaniard** ['spænjəd] n Espagnol(e)

**spaniel** ['spænjəl] n épagneul m

**Spanish** ['spænɪʃ] adj espagnol(e), d'Espagne ▷ n (Ling) espagnol m; **the Spanish** npl les Espagnols; **~ omelette** omelette f à l'espagnole

**spank** [spæŋk] vt donner une fessée à

**spanner** ['spænəʳ] n (Brit) clé f (de mécanicien)

**spar** [spa:ʳ] n espar m ▷ vi (Boxing) s'entraîner

**spare** [spɛəʳ] adj de réserve, de rechange; (surplus) de or en trop, de reste ▷ n (part) pièce f de rechange, pièce détachée ▷ vt (do without) se passer de; (afford to give) donner, accorder, passer; (not hurt) épargner; (not use) ménager; **to ~ (surplus)** en surplus, de trop; **there are 2 going ~ (Brit)** il y en a 2 de disponible; **to ~ no expense** ne pas reculer devant la dépense; **can you ~ the time?** est-ce que vous avez le temps?; **there is no time to ~** il n'y a pas de temps à perdre; **I've a few minutes to ~** je dispose de quelques minutes

**spare part** n pièce f de rechange, pièce détachée

**spare room** n chambre f d'ami

**spare time** n moments mpl de loisir

**spare tyre**, (US) **spare tire** n (Aut) pneu m de rechange

**spare wheel** n (Aut) roue f de secours

**sparing** ['spɛərɪŋ] adj: **to be ~ with** ménager

**sparingly** ['spɛərɪŋlɪ] adv avec modération

**spark** [spa:k] n étincelle f; (fig) étincelle, lueur f

**sparkle** ['spa:kl] n scintillement m,

étincellement m, éclat m ▷ vi étinceler,
scintiller; (bubble) pétiller
**sparkler** ['spɑːklə'] n cierge m magique
**sparkling** ['spɑːklɪŋ] adj étincelant(e),
scintillant(e); (wine) mousseux(-euse),
pétillant(e); (water) pétillant(e), gazeux(-euse)
**spark plug** n bougie f
**sparring partner** ['spɑːrɪŋ-] n sparring-partner
m; (fig) vieil(le) ennemi(e)
**sparrow** ['spærəu] n moineau m
**sparse** [spɑːs] adj clairsemé(e)
**spartan** ['spɑːtən] adj (fig) spartiate
**spasm** ['spæzəm] n (Med) spasme m; (fig) accès m
**spasmodic** [spæz'mɔdɪk] adj (fig)
intermittent(e)
**spastic** ['spæstɪk] n handicapé(e) moteur
**spat** [spæt] pt, pp of **spit** ▷ n (US) prise f de bec
**spate** [speɪt] n (fig): ~ **of** avalanche f or torrent m
de; **in** ~ (river) en crue
**spatial** ['speɪʃl] adj spatial(e)
**spatter** ['spætə'] n éclaboussure(s) f(pl) ▷ vt
éclabousser ▷ vi gicler
**spatula** ['spætjulə] n spatule f
**spawn** [spɔːn] vt pondre; (pej) engendrer ▷ vi
frayer ▷ n frai m
**SPCA** n abbr (US: = Society for the Prevention of Cruelty
to Animals) ≈ SPA f
**SPCC** n abbr (US) = **Society for the Prevention of
Cruelty to Children**
**speak** (pt **spoke**, pp **spoken**) [spiːk, spəuk,
'spəukn] vt (language) parler; (truth) dire ▷ vi
parler; (make a speech) prendre la parole; **to ~ to
sb/of** or **about sth** parler à qn/de qch; **I don't ~
French** je ne parle pas français; **do you ~
English?** parlez-vous anglais?; **can I ~ to ...?**
est-ce que je peux parler à ...?; **~ing!** (on
telephone) c'est moi-même!; **to ~ one's mind**
dire ce que l'on pense; **it ~s for itself** c'est
évident; **~ up!** parle plus fort!; **he has no
money to ~ of** il n'a pas d'argent
▶ **speak for** vt fus: **to ~ for sb** parler pour qn;
**that picture is already spoken for** (in shop) ce
tableau est déjà réservé
**speaker** ['spiːkə'] n (in public) orateur m; (also:
**loudspeaker**) haut-parleur m; (for stereo etc)
baffle m, enceinte f; (Pol): **the S~** (Brit) le président
de la Chambre des communes or des représentants; (US)
le président de la Chambre; **are you a Welsh ~?**
parlez-vous gallois?
**speaking** ['spiːkɪŋ] adj parlant(e); **French-~
people** les francophones; **to be on ~ terms** se
parler
**spear** [spɪə'] n lance f ▷ vt transpercer
**spearhead** ['spɪəhɛd] n fer m de lance; (Mil)
colonne f d'attaque ▷ vt (attack etc) mener
**spearmint** ['spɪəmɪnt] n (Bot etc) menthe verte
**spec** [spɛk] n (Brit inf): **on** ~ à tout hasard; **to
buy on** ~ acheter avec l'espoir de faire une
bonne affaire
**special** ['spɛʃl] adj spécial(e) ▷ n (train) train
spécial; **take ~ care** soyez particulièrement
prudents; **nothing** ~ rien de spécial; **today's ~**

(at restaurant) le plat du jour
**special agent** n agent secret
**special correspondent** n envoyé spécial
**special delivery** n (Post): **by** ~ en express
**special effects** npl (Cine) effets spéciaux
**specialist** ['spɛʃəlɪst] n spécialiste m/f; **heart ~**
cardiologue m/f
**speciality** [spɛʃɪ'ælɪtɪ] n (Brit) spécialité f
**specialize** ['spɛʃəlaɪz] vi: **to ~ (in)** se spécialiser
(dans)
**specially** ['spɛʃlɪ] adv spécialement,
particulièrement
**special needs** npl (Brit) difficultés fpl
d'apprentissage scolaire
**special offer** n (Comm) réclame f
**special school** n (Brit) établissement m
d'enseignement spécialisé
**specialty** ['spɛʃəltɪ] n (US) = **speciality**
**species** ['spiːʃiːz] n (pl inv) espèce f
**specific** [spə'sɪfɪk] adj (not vague) précis(e),
explicite; (particular) particulier(-ière); (Bot,
Chem etc) spécifique; **to be ~ to** être particulier
à, être le or un caractère (or les caractères)
spécifique(s) de
**specifically** [spə'sɪfɪklɪ] adv explicitement,
précisément; (intend, ask, design) expressément,
spécialement; (exclusively) exclusivement,
spécifiquement
**specification** [spɛsɪfɪ'keɪʃən] n spécification f;
stipulation f; **specifications** npl (of car, building
etc) spécification
**specify** ['spɛsɪfaɪ] vt spécifier, préciser; **unless
otherwise specified** sauf indication contraire
**specimen** ['spɛsɪmən] n spécimen m,
échantillon m; (Med: of blood) prélèvement m;
(: of urine) échantillon m
**specimen copy** n spécimen m
**specimen signature** n spécimen m de
signature
**speck** [spɛk] n petite tache, petit point; (particle)
grain m
**speckled** ['spɛkld] adj tacheté(e), moucheté(e)
**specs** [spɛks] npl (inf) lunettes fpl
**spectacle** ['spɛktəkl] n spectacle m; **spectacles**
npl (Brit) lunettes fpl
**spectacle case** n (Brit) étui m à lunettes
**spectacular** [spɛk'tækjulə'] adj spectaculaire
▷ n (Cine etc) superproduction f
**spectator** [spɛk'teɪtə'] n spectateur(-trice)
**spectator sport** n: **football is a great ~** le
football est un sport qui passionne les foules
**spectra** ['spɛktrə] npl of **spectrum**
**spectre**, (US) **specter** ['spɛktə'] n spectre m,
fantôme m
**spectrum** (pl **spectra**) ['spɛktrəm, -rə] n spectre
m; (fig) gamme f
**speculate** ['spɛkjuleɪt] vi spéculer; (try to guess):
**to ~ about** s'interroger sur
**speculation** [spɛkju'leɪʃən] n spéculation f;
conjectures fpl
**speculative** ['spɛkjulətɪv] adj spéculatif(-ive)
**speculator** ['spɛkjuleɪtə'] n spéculateur(-trice)

**S**

**sped** [spɛd] *pt, pp of* **speed**
**speech** [spi:tʃ] *n* (*faculty*) parole *f*; (*talk*) discours *m*, allocution *f*; (*manner of speaking*) façon *f* de parler, langage *m*; (*language*) langage *m*; (*enunciation*) élocution *f*
**speech day** *n* (*Brit Scol*) distribution *f* des prix
**speech impediment** *n* défaut *m* d'élocution
**speechless** ['spi:tʃlɪs] *adj* muet(te)
**speech therapy** *n* orthophonie *f*
**speed** [spi:d] *n* vitesse *f*; (*promptness*) rapidité *f* ▷ *vi* (*pt, pp* **sped**) [spɛd] (*Aut: exceed speed limit*) faire un excès de vitesse; **to ~ along/by** *etc* aller/passer *etc* à toute vitesse; **at ~** (*Brit*) rapidement; **at full** *or* **top ~** à toute vitesse *or* allure; **at a ~ of 70 km/h** à une vitesse de 70 km/h; **shorthand/typing ~s** nombre *m* de mots à la minute en sténographie/dactylographie; **a five-~ gearbox** une boîte cinq vitesses
  ▸ **speed up** (*pt, pp* **-ed up**) *vi* aller plus vite, accélérer ▷ *vt* accélérer
**speedboat** ['spi:dbəut] *n* vedette *f*, hors-bord *m inv*
**speedily** ['spi:dɪlɪ] *adv* rapidement, promptement
**speeding** ['spi:dɪŋ] *n* (*Aut*) excès *m* de vitesse
**speed limit** *n* limitation *f* de vitesse, vitesse maximale permise
**speedometer** [spɪ'dɔmɪtər] *n* compteur *m* (de vitesse)
**speed trap** *n* (*Aut*) piège *m* de police pour contrôle de vitesse
**speedway** *n* (*Sport*) piste *f* de vitesse pour motos; (*also:* **speedway racing**) épreuve(s) *f*(*pl*) de vitesse de motos
**speedy** [spi:dɪ] *adj* rapide, prompt(e)
**speleologist** [spɛlɪ'ɔlədʒɪst] *n* spéléologue *m/f*
**spell** [spɛl] *n* (*also:* **magic spell**) sortilège *m*, charme *m*; (*period of time*) (courte) période ▷ *vt* (*pt, pp* **spelt** *or* **-ed**) [spɛlt, spɛld] (*in writing*) écrire, orthographier; (*aloud*) épeler; (*fig*) signifier; **to cast a ~ on sb** jeter un sort à qn; **he can't ~** - il fait des fautes d'orthographe; **how do you ~ your name?** comment écrivez-vous votre nom?; **can you ~ it for me?** pouvez-vous me l'épeler?
  ▸ **spell out** *vt* (*explain*): **to ~ sth out for sb** expliquer qch clairement à qn
**spellbound** ['spɛlbaund] *adj* envoûté(e), subjugué(e)
**spellchecker** ['speltʃekər] *n* (*Comput*) correcteur *m* or vérificateur *m* orthographique
**spelling** ['spɛlɪŋ] *n* orthographe *f*
**spelt** [spɛlt] *pt, pp of* **spell**
**spend** (*pt, pp* **spent**) [spɛnd, spɛnt] *vt* (*money*) dépenser; (*time, life*) passer; (*devote*) consacrer; **to ~ time/money/effort on sth** consacrer du temps/de l'argent/de l'énergie à qch
**spending** ['spɛndɪŋ] *n* dépenses *fpl*; **government ~** les dépenses publiques
**spending money** *n* argent *m* de poche
**spending power** *n* pouvoir *m* d'achat
**spendthrift** ['spɛndθrɪft] *n* dépensier(-ière)

**spent** [spɛnt] *pt, pp of* **spend** ▷ *adj* (*patience*) épuisé(e), à bout; (*cartridge, bullets*) vide; **~ matches** vieilles allumettes
**sperm** [spə:m] *n* spermatozoïde *m*; (*semen*) sperme *m*
**sperm bank** *n* banque *f* du sperme
**sperm whale** *n* cachalot *m*
**spew** [spju:] *vt* vomir
**sphere** [sfɪər] *n* sphère *f*; (*fig*) sphère, domaine *m*
**spherical** ['sfɛrɪkl] *adj* sphérique
**sphinx** [sfɪŋks] *n* sphinx *m*
**spice** [spaɪs] *n* épice *f* ▷ *vt* épicer
**spick-and-span** ['spɪkən'spæn] *adj* impeccable
**spicy** ['spaɪsɪ] *adj* épicé(e), relevé(e); (*fig*) piquant(e)
**spider** ['spaɪdər] *n* araignée *f*; **~'s web** toile *f* d'araignée
**spiel** [spi:l] *n* laïus *m inv*
**spike** [spaɪk] *n* pointe *f*; (*Elec*) pointe de tension; (*Bot*) épi *m*; **spikes** *npl* (*Sport*) chaussures *fpl* à pointes
**spike heel** *n* (*US*) talon *m* aiguille
**spiky** ['spaɪkɪ] *adj* (*bush, branch*) épineux(-euse); (*animal*) plein(e) de piquants
**spill** (*pt, pp* **spilt** *or* **-ed**) [spɪl, -t, -d] *vt* renverser; répandre ▷ *vi* se répandre; **to ~ the beans** (*inf*) vendre la mèche; (: *confess*) lâcher le morceau
  ▸ **spill out** *vi* sortir à flots, se répandre
  ▸ **spill over** *vi* déborder
**spillage** ['spɪlɪdʒ] *n* (*of oil*) déversement *m* (accidentel)
**spilt** [spɪlt] *pt, pp of* **spill**
**spin** [spɪn] (*pt, pp* **spun**) [spʌn] *n* (*revolution of wheel*) tour *m*; (*Aviat*) (chute *f* en) vrille *f*; (*trip in car*) petit tour, balade *f*; (*on ball*) effet *m* ▷ *vt* (*wool etc*) filer; (*wheel*) faire tourner; (*Brit: clothes*) essorer ▷ *vi* (*turn*) tourner, tournoyer; **to ~ a yarn** débiter une longue histoire; **to ~ a coin** (*Brit*) jouer à pile ou face
  ▸ **spin out** *vt* faire durer
**spina bifida** ['spaɪnə'bɪfɪdə] *n* spina-bifida *m inv*
**spinach** ['spɪnɪtʃ] *n* épinard *m*; (*as food*) épinards *mpl*
**spinal** ['spaɪnl] *adj* vertébral(e), spinal(e)
**spinal column** *n* colonne vertébrale
**spinal cord** *n* moelle épinière
**spindly** ['spɪndlɪ] *adj* grêle, filiforme
**spin doctor** *n* (*inf*) *personne employée pour présenter un parti politique sous un jour favorable*
**spin-dry** ['spɪn'draɪ] *vt* essorer
**spin-dryer** [spɪn'draɪər] *n* (*Brit*) essoreuse *f*
**spine** [spaɪn] *n* colonne vertébrale; (*thorn*) épine *f*, piquant *m*
**spine-chilling** ['spaɪntʃɪlɪŋ] *adj* terrifiant(e)
**spineless** ['spaɪnlɪs] *adj* invertébré(e); (*fig*) mou (molle), sans caractère
**spinner** ['spɪnər] *n* (*of thread*) fileur(-euse)
**spinning** ['spɪnɪŋ] *n* (*of thread*) filage *m*; (*by machine*) filature *f*
**spinning top** *n* toupie *f*
**spinning wheel** *n* rouet *m*
**spin-off** ['spɪnɔf] *n* sous-produit *m*; avantage

inattendu

**spinster** ['spɪnstə<sup>r</sup>] n célibataire f; vieille fille

**spiral** ['spaɪərl] n spirale f ▷ adj en spirale ▷ vi (fig: prices etc) monter en flèche; **the inflationary ~** la spirale inflationniste

**spiral staircase** n escalier m en colimaçon

**spire** ['spaɪə<sup>r</sup>] n flèche f, aiguille f

**spirit** ['spɪrɪt] n (soul) esprit m, âme f; (ghost) esprit, revenant m; (mood) esprit, état m d'esprit; (courage) courage m, énergie f; **spirits** npl (drink) spiritueux mpl, alcool m; **in good ~s** de bonne humeur; **in low ~s** démoralisé(e); **community ~** solidarité f; **public ~** civisme m

**spirit duplicator** n duplicateur m à alcool

**spirited** ['spɪrɪtɪd] adj vif (vive), fougueux(-euse), plein(e) d'allant

**spirit level** n niveau m à bulle

**spiritual** ['spɪrɪtjuəl] adj spirituel(le); (religious) religieux(-euse) ▷ n (also: **Negro spiritual**) spiritual m

**spiritualism** ['spɪrɪtjuəlɪzəm] n spiritisme m

**spit** [spɪt] n (for roasting) broche f; (spittle) crachat m; (saliva) salive f ▷ vi (pt, pp **spat**) [spæt] cracher; (sound) crépiter; (rain) crachiner

**spite** [spaɪt] n rancune f, dépit m ▷ vt contrarier, vexer; **in ~ of** en dépit de, malgré

**spiteful** ['spaɪtful] adj malveillant(e), rancunier(-ière)

**spitroast** ['spɪt'rəust] vt faire rôtir à la broche

**spitting** ['spɪtɪŋ] n: **"~ prohibited"** "défense de cracher" ▷ adj: **to be the ~ image of sb** être le portrait tout craché de qn

**spittle** ['spɪtl] n salive f; bave f; crachat m

**spiv** [spɪv] n (Brit inf) chevalier m d'industrie, aigrefin m

**splash** [splæʃ] n (sound) plouf m; (of colour) tache f ▷ vt éclabousser ▷ vi (also: **splash about**) barboter, patauger

▶ **splash out** vi (Brit) faire une folie

**splashdown** ['splæʃdaun] n amerrissage m

**splay** [spleɪ] adj: **~footed** marchant les pieds en dehors

**spleen** [spli:n] n (Anat) rate f

**splendid** ['splɛndɪd] adj splendide, superbe, magnifique

**splendour**, (US) **splendor** ['splɛndə<sup>r</sup>] n splendeur f, magnificence f

**splice** [splaɪs] vt épisser

**splint** [splɪnt] n attelle f, éclisse f

**splinter** ['splɪntə<sup>r</sup>] n (wood) écharde f; (metal) éclat m ▷ vi (wood) se fendre; (glass) se briser

**splinter group** n groupe dissident

**split** [splɪt] (pt, pp **split**) n fente f, déchirure f; (fig: Pol) scission f ▷ vt fendre, déchirer; (party) diviser; (work, profits) partager, répartir ▷ vi (break) se fendre, se briser; (divide) se diviser; **let's ~ the difference** coupons la poire en deux; **to do the ~s** faire le grand écart

▶ **split up** vi (couple) se séparer, rompre; (meeting) se disperser

**split-level** ['splɪtlɛvl] adj (house) à deux or plusieurs niveaux

**split peas** npl pois cassés

**split personality** n double personnalité f

**split second** n fraction f de seconde

**splitting** ['splɪtɪŋ] adj: **a ~ headache** un mal de tête atroce

**splutter** ['splʌtə<sup>r</sup>] vi bafouiller; postillonner

**spoil** (pt, pp **-ed** or **spoilt**) [spɔɪl, -d, -t] vt (damage) abîmer; (mar) gâcher; (child) gâter; (ballot paper) rendre nul ▷ vi: **to be ~ing for a fight** chercher la bagarre

**spoils** [spɔɪlz] npl butin m

**spoilsport** ['spɔɪlspɔːt] n trouble-fête m/f inv, rabat-joie m inv

**spoilt** [spɔɪlt] pt, pp of **spoil** ▷ adj (child) gâté(e); (ballot paper) nul(le)

**spoke** [spəuk] pt of **speak** ▷ n rayon m

**spoken** ['spəukn] pp of **speak**

**spokesman** ['spəuksmən] (irreg) n porte-parole m inv

**spokesperson** ['spəukspə:sn] (irreg) n porte-parole m inv

**spokeswoman** ['spəukswumən] (irreg) n porte-parole m inv

**sponge** [spʌndʒ] n éponge f; (Culin: also: **sponge cake**) ≈ biscuit m de Savoie ▷ vt éponger ▷ vi: **to ~ off** or **on** vivre aux crochets de

**sponge bag** n (Brit) trousse f de toilette

**sponge cake** n ≈ biscuit m de Savoie

**sponger** ['spʌndʒə<sup>r</sup>] n (pej) parasite m

**spongy** ['spʌndʒɪ] adj spongieux(-euse)

**sponsor** ['spɔnsə<sup>r</sup>] n (Radio, TV, Sport) sponsor m; (for application) parrain m, marraine f; (Brit: for fund-raising event) donateur(-trice) m ▷ vt (programme, competition etc) parrainer, patronner, sponsoriser; (Pol: bill) présenter; (new member) parrainer; (fund-raiser) faire un don à; **I ~ed him at 3p a mile** (in fund-raising race) je me suis engagé à lui donner 3p par mile

**sponsorship** ['spɔnsəʃɪp] n sponsoring m; patronage m, parrainage m; dons mpl

**spontaneity** [spɔntə'neɪɪtɪ] n spontanéité f

**spontaneous** [spɔn'teɪnɪəs] adj spontané(e)

**spoof** [spu:f] n (parody) parodie f; (trick) canular m

**spooky** ['spu:kɪ] adj (inf) qui donne la chair de poule

**spool** [spu:l] n bobine f

**spoon** [spu:n] n cuiller f

**spoon-feed** ['spu:nfi:d] vt nourrir à la cuiller; (fig) mâcher le travail à

**spoonful** ['spu:nful] n cuillerée f

**sporadic** [spə'rædɪk] adj sporadique

**sport** [spɔːt] n sport m; (amusement) divertissement m; (person) chic type m/chic fille f ▷ vt (wear) arborer; **indoor/outdoor ~s** sports en salle/de plein air; **to say sth in ~** dire qch pour rire

**sporting** ['spɔːtɪŋ] adj sportif(-ive); **to give sb a ~ chance** donner sa chance à qn

**sport jacket** n (US) = **sports jacket**

**sports car** n voiture f de sport

**sports centre** (Brit) n centre sportif

**sports ground** n terrain m de sport
**sports jacket** n (Brit) veste f de sport
**sportsman** ['spɔːtsmən] (irreg) n sportif m
**sportsmanship** ['spɔːtsmənʃɪp] n esprit sportif, sportivité f
**sports page** n page f des sports
**sports utility vehicle** n véhicule m de loisirs (de type SUV)
**sportswear** ['spɔːtswɛəʳ] n vêtements mpl de sport
**sportswoman** ['spɔːtswumən] (irreg) n sportive f
**sporty** ['spɔːtɪ] adj sportif(-ive)
**spot** [spɔt] n tache f; (dot: on pattern) pois m; (pimple) bouton m; (place) endroit m, coin m; (also: **spot advertisement**) message m publicitaire; (small amount): **a ~ of** un peu de ▷ vt (notice) apercevoir, repérer; **on the ~** sur place, sur les lieux; (immediately) sur le champ; **to put sb on the ~** (fig) mettre qn dans l'embarras; **to come out in ~s** se couvrir de boutons, avoir une éruption de boutons
**spot check** n contrôle intermittent
**spotless** ['spɔtlɪs] adj immaculé(e)
**spotlight** ['spɔtlaɪt] n projecteur m; (Aut) phare m auxiliaire
**spot-on** [spɔt'ɔn] adj (Brit inf) en plein dans le mille
**spot price** n prix m sur place
**spotted** ['spɔtɪd] adj tacheté(e), moucheté(e); à pois; ~ **with** tacheté(e) de
**spotty** ['spɔtɪ] adj (face) boutonneux(-euse)
**spouse** [spauz] n époux (épouse)
**spout** [spaut] n (of jug) bec m; (of liquid) jet m ▷ vi jaillir
**sprain** [spreɪn] n entorse f, foulure f ▷ vt: **to ~ one's ankle** se fouler or se tordre la cheville
**sprang** [spræŋ] pt of **spring**
**sprawl** [sprɔːl] vi s'étaler ▷ n: **urban ~** expansion urbaine; **to send sb ~ing** envoyer qn rouler par terre
**spray** [spreɪ] n jet m (en fines gouttelettes); (from sea) embruns mpl; (aerosol) vaporisateur m, bombe f; (for garden) pulvérisateur m; (of flowers) petit bouquet ▷ vt vaporiser, pulvériser; (crops) traiter ▷ cpd (deodorant etc) en bombe or atomiseur
**spread** [sprɛd] (pt, pp **spread**) n (distribution) répartition f; (Culin) pâte f à tartiner; (inf: meal) festin m; (Press, Typ: two pages) double page f ▷ vt (paste, contents) étendre, étaler; (rumour, disease) répandre, propager; (repayments) échelonner, étaler; (wealth) répartir ▷ vi s'étendre; se répandre; se propager; (stain) s'étaler; **middle-age** ~ embonpoint m (pris avec l'âge)
  ▶ **spread out** vi (people) se disperser
**spread-eagled** ['sprɛdiːgld] adj: **to be** or **lie ~** être étendu(e) bras et jambes écartés
**spreadsheet** ['sprɛdʃiːt] n (Comput) tableur m
**spree** [spriː] n: **to go on a ~** faire la fête
**sprig** [sprɪg] n rameau m
**sprightly** ['spraɪtlɪ] adj alerte

**spring** [sprɪŋ] (pt **sprang** [spræŋ], pp **sprung** [sprʌŋ]) n (season) printemps m; (leap) bond m, saut m; (coiled metal) ressort m; (bounciness) élasticité f; (of water) source f ▷ vi bondir, sauter ▷ vt: **to ~ a leak** (pipe etc) se mettre à fuir; **he sprang the news on me** il m'a annoncé la nouvelle de but en blanc; **in ~, in the ~** au printemps; **to ~ from** provenir de; **to ~ into action** passer à l'action; **to walk with a ~ in one's step** marcher d'un pas souple
  ▶ **spring up** vi (problem) se présenter, surgir; (plant, buildings) surgir de terre
**springboard** ['sprɪŋbɔːd] n tremplin m
**spring-clean** [sprɪŋ'kliːn] n (also: **spring-cleaning**) grand nettoyage de printemps
**spring onion** n (Brit) ciboule f, cive f
**spring roll** n rouleau m de printemps
**springtime** ['sprɪŋtaɪm] n printemps m
**springy** ['sprɪŋɪ] adj élastique, souple
**sprinkle** ['sprɪŋkl] vt (pour) répandre; verser; **to ~ water on, ~ with water** etc asperger d'eau etc; **to ~ sugar** etc **on, ~ with sugar** etc saupoudrer de sucre etc; **~d with** (fig) parsemé(e) de
**sprinkler** ['sprɪŋkləʳ] n (for lawn etc) arroseur m; (to put out fire) diffuseur m d'extincteur automatique d'incendie
**sprinkling** ['sprɪŋklɪŋ] n (of water) quelques gouttes fpl; (of salt) pincée f; (of sugar) légère couche
**sprint** [sprɪnt] n sprint m ▷ vi courir à toute vitesse; (Sport) sprinter
**sprinter** ['sprɪntəʳ] n sprinteur(-euse)
**sprite** [spraɪt] n lutin m
**spritzer** ['sprɪtsəʳ] n boisson à base de vin blanc et d'eau de Seltz
**sprocket** ['sprɔkɪt] n (on printer etc) picot m
**sprout** [spraut] vi germer, pousser
**sprouts** [sprauts] npl (also: **Brussels sprouts**) choux mpl de Bruxelles
**spruce** [spruːs] n épicéa m ▷ adj net(te), pimpant(e)
  ▶ **spruce up** vt (smarten up: room etc) apprêter; **to ~ o.s. up** se faire beau (belle)
**sprung** [sprʌŋ] pp of **spring**
**spry** [spraɪ] adj alerte, vif (vive)
**SPUC** n abbr = **Society for the Protection of Unborn Children**
**spud** [spʌd] n (inf: potato) patate f
**spun** [spʌn] pt, pp of **spin**
**spur** [spəːʳ] n éperon m; (fig) aiguillon m ▷ vt (also: **spur on**) éperonner; aiguillonner; **on the ~ of the moment** sous l'impulsion du moment
**spurious** ['spjuərɪəs] adj faux (fausse)
**spurn** [spəːn] vt repousser avec mépris
**spurt** [spəːt] n jet m; (of blood) jaillissement m; (of energy) regain m, sursaut m ▷ vi jaillir, gicler; **to put in** or **on a ~** (runner) piquer un sprint; (fig: in work etc) donner un coup de collier
**sputter** ['spʌtəʳ] vi = **splutter**
**spy** [spaɪ] n espion(ne) ▷ vi: **to ~ on** espionner, épier ▷ vt (see) apercevoir ▷ cpd (film, story)

d'espionnage

**spying** ['spaɪɪŋ] n espionnage m

**Sq.** abbr (in address) = **square**

**sq.** abbr (Math etc) = **square**

**squabble** ['skwɒbl] n querelle f, chamaillerie f ▷ vi se chamailler

**squad** [skwɒd] n (Mil, Police) escouade f, groupe m; (Football) contingent m; **flying ~** (Police) brigade volante

**squad car** n (Brit Police) voiture f de police

**squaddie** ['skwɒdɪ] n (Mil: inf) troufion m, bidasse m

**squadron** ['skwɒdrn] n (Mil) escadron m; (Aviat, Naut) escadrille f

**squalid** ['skwɒlɪd] adj sordide, ignoble

**squall** [skwɔːl] n rafale f, bourrasque f

**squalor** ['skwɒləʳ] n conditions fpl sordides

**squander** ['skwɒndəʳ] vt gaspiller, dilapider

**square** [skwɛəʳ] n carré m; (in town) place f; (US: block of houses) îlot m, pâté m de maisons; (instrument) équerre f ▷ adj carré(e); (honest) honnête, régulier(-ière); (inf: ideas, tastes) vieux jeu inv, qui retarde ▷ vt (arrange) régler; arranger; (Math) élever au carré; (reconcile) concilier ▷ vi (agree) cadrer, s'accorder; **all ~** quitte; à égalité; **a ~ meal** un repas convenable; **2 metres ~** (de) 2 mètres sur 2; **1 ~ metre** 1 mètre carré; **we're back to ~ one** (fig) on se retrouve à la case départ

▶ **square up** vi (Brit: settle) régler; **to ~ up with sb** régler ses comptes avec qn

**square bracket** n (Typ) crochet m

**squarely** ['skwɛəlɪ] adv carrément; (honestly, fairly) honnêtement, équitablement

**square root** n racine carrée

**squash** [skwɒʃ] n (Brit: drink): **lemon/orange ~** citronnade f/orangeade f; (Sport) squash m; (US: vegetable) courge f ▷ vt écraser

**squat** [skwɒt] adj petit(e) et épais(se), ramassé(e) ▷ vi (also: **squat down**) s'accroupir; (on property) squatter, squattériser

**squatter** ['skwɒtəʳ] n squatter m

**squawk** [skwɔːk] vi pousser un or des gloussement(s)

**squeak** [skwiːk] n (of hinge, wheel etc) grincement m; (of shoes) craquement m; (of mouse etc) petit cri aigu ▷ vi (hinge, wheel) grincer; (mouse) pousser un petit cri

**squeaky** ['skwiːkɪ] adj grinçant(e); **to be ~ clean** (fig) être au-dessus de tout soupçon

**squeal** [skwiːl] vi pousser un or des cri(s) aigu(s) or perçant(s); (brakes) grincer

**squeamish** ['skwiːmɪʃ] adj facilement dégoûté(e); facilement scandalisé(e)

**squeeze** [skwiːz] n pression f; (also: **credit squeeze**) encadrement m du crédit, restrictions fpl de crédit ▷ vt presser; (hand, arm) serrer ▷ vi: **to ~ past/under sth** se glisser avec (beaucoup de) difficulté devant/sous qch; **a ~ of lemon** quelques gouttes de citron

▶ **squeeze out** vt exprimer; (fig) soutirer

**squelch** [skwɛltʃ] vi faire un bruit de succion;

patauger

**squib** [skwɪb] n pétard m

**squid** [skwɪd] n calmar m

**squiggle** ['skwɪgl] n gribouillis m

**squint** [skwɪnt] vi loucher ▷ n: **he has a ~** il louche, il souffre de strabisme; **to ~ at sth** regarder qch du coin de l'œil; (quickly) jeter un coup d'œil à qch

**squire** ['skwaɪəʳ] n (Brit) propriétaire terrien

**squirm** [skwəːm] vi se tortiller

**squirrel** ['skwɪrəl] n écureuil m

**squirt** [skwəːt] n jet m ▷ vi jaillir, gicler ▷ vt faire gicler

**Sr** abbr = **senior**; = **sister**

**SRC** n abbr (Brit: = Students' Representative Council) ≈ CROUS m

**Sri Lanka** [srɪ'læŋkə] n Sri Lanka m

**SRN** n abbr (Brit) = **State Registered Nurse**

**SRO** abbr (US) = **standing room only**

**SS** abbr (= steamship) S/S

**SSA** n abbr (US: = Social Security Administration) organisme de sécurité sociale

**SST** n abbr (US) = **supersonic transport**

**ST** abbr (US: = Standard Time) heure officielle

**St** abbr = **saint**; **street**

**stab** [stæb] n (with knife etc) coup m (de couteau etc); (of pain) lancée f; (inf: try): **to have a ~ at (doing) sth** s'essayer à (faire) qch ▷ vt poignarder; **to ~ sb to death** tuer qn à coups de couteau

**stabbing** ['stæbɪŋ] n: **there's been a ~** quelqu'un a été attaqué à coups de couteau ▷ adj (pain, ache) lancinant(e)

**stability** [stə'bɪlɪtɪ] n stabilité f

**stabilization** [steɪbəlaɪ'zeɪʃən] n stabilisation f

**stabilize** ['steɪbəlaɪz] vt stabiliser ▷ vi se stabiliser

**stabilizer** ['steɪbəlaɪzəʳ] n stabilisateur m

**stable** ['steɪbl] n écurie f ▷ adj stable; **riding ~s** centre m d'équitation

**staccato** [stə'kɑːtəu] adv staccato ▷ adj (Mus) piqué(e); (noise, voice) saccadé(e)

**stack** [stæk] n tas m, pile f ▷ vt empiler, entasser; **there's ~s of time** (Brit inf) on a tout le temps

**stadium** ['steɪdɪəm] n stade m

**staff** [stɑːf] n (work force) personnel m; (Brit Scol: also: **teaching staff**) professeurs mpl, enseignants mpl, personnel enseignant; (servants) domestiques mpl; (Mil) état-major m; (stick) perche f, bâton m ▷ vt pourvoir en personnel

**staffroom** ['stɑːfruːm] n salle f des professeurs

**Staffs** abbr (Brit) = **Staffordshire**

**stag** [stæg] n cerf m; (Brit Stock Exchange) loup m

**stage** [steɪdʒ] n scène f; (platform) estrade f; (point) étape f, stade m; (profession): **the ~** le théâtre ▷ vt (play) monter, mettre en scène; (demonstration) organiser; (fig: recovery etc) effectuer; **in ~s** par étapes, par degrés; **to go through a difficult ~** traverser une période difficile; **in the early ~s** au début; **in the final**

**S**

**~s** à la fin
**stagecoach** ['steɪdʒkəʊtʃ] *n* diligence *f*
**stage door** *n* entrée *f* des artistes
**stage fright** *n* trac *m*
**stagehand** ['steɪdʒhænd] *n* machiniste *m*
**stage-manage** ['steɪdʒmænɪdʒ] *vt* (*fig*) orchestrer
**stage manager** *n* régisseur *m*
**stagger** ['stægəʳ] *vi* chanceler, tituber ▷ *vt* (*person: amaze*) stupéfier; bouleverser; (*hours, holidays*) étaler, échelonner
**staggering** ['stægərɪŋ] *adj* (*amazing*) stupéfiant(e), renversant(e)
**staging post** ['steɪdʒɪŋ-] *n* relais *m*
**stagnant** ['stægnənt] *adj* stagnant(e)
**stagnate** [stæg'neɪt] *vi* stagner, croupir
**stagnation** [stæg'neɪʃən] *n* stagnation *f*
**stag night, stag party** *n* enterrement *m* de vie de garçon
**staid** [steɪd] *adj* posé(e), rassis(e)
**stain** [steɪn] *n* tache *f*; (*colouring*) colorant *m* ▷ *vt* tacher; (*wood*) teindre
**stained glass** [steɪnd-] *n* (*decorative*) verre coloré; (*in church*) vitraux *mpl*; **~ window** vitrail *m*
**stainless** ['steɪnlɪs] *adj* (*steel*) inoxydable
**stainless steel** *n* inox *m*, acier *m* inoxydable
**stain remover** *n* détachant *m*
**stair** [stɛəʳ] *n* (*step*) marche *f*
**staircase** ['stɛəkeɪs] *n* = **stairway**
**stairs** [stɛəz] *npl* escalier *m*; **on the ~** dans l'escalier
**stairway** ['stɛəweɪ] *n* escalier *m*
**stairwell** ['stɛəwɛl] *n* cage *f* d'escalier
**stake** [steɪk] *n* pieu *m*, poteau *m*; (*Comm: interest*) intérêts *mpl*; (*Betting*) enjeu *m* ▷ *vt* risquer, jouer; (*also: **stake out**: area*) marquer, délimiter; **to be at ~** être en jeu; **to have a ~ in sth** avoir des intérêts (en jeu) dans qch; **to ~ a claim (to sth)** revendiquer (qch)
**stakeout** ['steɪkaʊt] *n* surveillance *f*; **to be on a ~** effectuer une surveillance
**stalactite** ['stæləktaɪt] *n* stalactite *f*
**stalagmite** ['stæləgmaɪt] *n* stalagmite *f*
**stale** [steɪl] *adj* (*bread*) rassis(e); (*food*) pas frais (fraîche); (*beer*) éventé(e); (*smell*) de renfermé; (*air*) confiné(e)
**stalemate** ['steɪlmeɪt] *n* pat *m*; (*fig*) impasse *f*
**stalk** [stɔːk] *n* tige *f* ▷ *vt* traquer ▷ *vi*: **to ~ out/off** sortir/partir d'un air digne
**stall** [stɔːl] *n* (*Brit: in street, market etc*) éventaire *m*, étal *m*; (*in stable*) stalle *f* ▷ *vt* (*Aut*) caler; (*fig: delay*) retarder ▷ *vi* (*Aut*) caler; (*fig*) essayer de gagner du temps; **stalls** *npl* (*Brit: in cinema, theatre*) orchestre *m*; **a newspaper/flower ~** un kiosque à journaux/de fleuriste
**stallholder** ['stɔːlhəʊldəʳ] *n* (*Brit*) marchand(e) en plein air
**stallion** ['stæljən] *n* étalon *m* (*cheval*)
**stalwart** ['stɔːlwət] *n* partisan *m* fidèle
**stamen** ['steɪmɛn] *n* étamine *f*
**stamina** ['stæmɪnə] *n* vigueur *f*, endurance *f*
**stammer** ['stæməʳ] *n* bégaiement *m* ▷ *vi* bégayer
**stamp** [stæmp] *n* timbre *m*; (*also: **rubber stamp**) tampon *m*; (*mark, also fig*) empreinte *f*; (*on document*) cachet *m* ▷ *vi* (*also: **stamp one's foot**) taper du pied ▷ *vt* (*letter*) timbrer; (*with rubber stamp*) tamponner
▸ **stamp out** *vt* (*fire*) piétiner; (*crime*) éradiquer; (*opposition*) éliminer
**stamp album** *n* album *m* de timbres(-poste)
**stamp collecting** [-kəlɛktɪŋ] *n* philatélie *f*
**stamp duty** *n* (*Brit*) droit *m* de timbre
**stamped addressed envelope** *n* (*Brit*) enveloppe affranchie pour la réponse
**stampede** [stæm'piːd] *n* ruée *f*; (*of cattle*) débandade *f*
**stamp machine** *n* distributeur *m* de timbres
**stance** [stæns] *n* position *f*
**stand** [stænd] (*pt, pp* **stood**) [stʊd] *n* (*position*) position *f*; (*for taxis*) station *f* (de taxis); (*Mil*) résistance *f*; (*structure*) guéridon *m*; support *m*; (*Comm*) étalage *m*, stand *m*; (*Sport: also: **stands**) tribune *f*; (*also: **music stand**) pupitre *m* ▷ *vi* être or se tenir (debout); (*rise*) se lever, se mettre debout; (*be placed*) se trouver; (*remain: offer etc*) rester valable ▷ *vt* (*place*) mettre, poser; (*tolerate, withstand*) supporter; (*treat, invite*) offrir, payer; **to make a ~** prendre position; **to take a ~ on an issue** prendre position sur un problème; **to ~ for parliament** (*Brit*) se présenter aux élections (*comme candidat à la députation*); **to ~ guard** or **watch** (*Mil*) monter la garde; **it ~s to reason** c'est logique; cela va de soi; **as things ~** dans l'état actuel des choses; **to ~ sb a drink/meal** payer à boire/à manger à qn; **I can't ~ him** je ne peux pas le voir
▸ **stand aside** *vi* s'écarter
▸ **stand back** *vi* (*move back*) reculer, s'écarter
▸ **stand by** *vi* (*be ready*) se tenir prêt(e) ▷ *vt fus* (*opinion*) s'en tenir à; (*person*) ne pas abandonner, soutenir
▸ **stand down** *vi* (*withdraw*) se retirer; (*Law*) renoncer à ses droits
▸ **stand for** *vt fus* (*signify*) représenter, signifier; (*tolerate*) supporter, tolérer
▸ **stand in for** *vt fus* remplacer
▸ **stand out** *vi* (*be prominent*) ressortir
▸ **stand up** *vi* (*rise*) se lever, se mettre debout
▸ **stand up for** *vt fus* défendre
▸ **stand up to** *vt fus* tenir tête à, résister à
**stand-alone** ['stændələʊn] *adj* (*Comput*) autonome
**standard** ['stændəd] *n* (*norm*) norme *f*, étalon *m*; (*level*) niveau *m* (voulu); (*criterion*) critère *m*; (*flag*) étendard *m* ▷ *adj* (*size etc*) ordinaire, normal(e); (*model, feature*) standard *inv*; (*practice*) courant(e); (*text*) de base; **standards** *npl* (*morals*) morale *f*, principes *mpl*; **to be** or **come up to ~** être du niveau voulu or à la hauteur; **to apply a double ~** avoir or appliquer deux poids deux mesures
**standardization** [stændədaɪ'zeɪʃən] *n* standardisation *f*
**standardize** ['stændədaɪz] *vt* standardiser

**standard lamp** n (Brit) lampadaire m
**standard of living** n niveau m de vie
**standard time** n heure légale
**stand-by** ['stændbaɪ] n remplaçant(e) ▷ adj (provisions) de réserve; **to be on** ~ se tenir prêt(e) (à intervenir); (doctor) être de garde
**stand-by generator** n générateur m de secours
**stand-by passenger** n passager(-ère) en stand-by or en attente
**stand-by ticket** n (Aviat) billet m stand-by
**stand-in** ['stændɪn] n remplaçant(e); (Cine) doublure f
**standing** ['stændɪŋ] adj debout inv; (permanent) permanent(e); (rule) immuable; (army) de métier; (grievance) constant(e), de longue date ▷ n réputation f, rang m, standing m; (duration): **of 6 months'** ~ qui dure depuis 6 mois; **of many years'** ~ qui dure or existe depuis longtemps; **he was given a ~ ovation** on s'est levé pour l'acclamer; **it's a ~ joke** c'est un vieux sujet de plaisanterie; **a man of some ~** un homme estimé
**standing committee** n commission permanente
**standing order** n (Brit: at bank) virement m automatique, prélèvement m bancaire; **standing orders** npl (Mil) règlement m
**standing room** n places fpl debout
**stand-off** ['stændɔf] n (esp US: stalemate) impasse f
**stand-offish** [stænd'ɔfɪʃ] adj distant(e), froid(e)
**standpat** ['stændpæt] adj (US) inflexible, rigide
**standpipe** ['stændpaɪp] n colonne f d'alimentation
**standpoint** ['stændpɔɪnt] n point m de vue
**standstill** ['stændstɪl] n: **at a** ~ à l'arrêt; (fig) au point mort; **to come to a** ~ s'immobiliser, s'arrêter
**stank** [stæŋk] pt of **stink**
**stanza** ['stænzə] n strophe f; couplet m
**staple** ['steɪpl] n (for papers) agrafe f; (chief product) produit m de base ▷ adj (food, crop, industry etc) de base principal(e) ▷ vt agrafer
**stapler** ['steɪplə'] n agrafeuse f
**star** [stɑː'] n étoile f; (celebrity) vedette f ▷ vi: **to ~ (in)** être la vedette (de) ▷ vt (Cine) avoir pour vedette; **4-~ hotel** hôtel m à 4 étoiles; **2-~ petrol** (Brit) essence f ordinaire; **4-~ petrol** (Brit) super m; **stars** npl: **the ~s** (Astrology) l'horoscope m
**star attraction** n grande attraction
**starboard** ['stɑːbəd] n tribord m; **to ~** à tribord
**starch** [stɑːtʃ] n amidon m; (in food) fécule f
**starched** ['stɑːtʃt] adj (collar) amidonné(e), empesé(e)
**starchy** ['stɑːtʃɪ] adj riche en féculents; (person) guindé(e)
**stardom** ['stɑːdəm] n célébrité f
**stare** [stɛə'] n regard m fixe ▷ vi: **to ~ at** regarder fixement
**starfish** ['stɑːfɪʃ] n étoile f de mer
**stark** [stɑːk] adj (bleak) désolé(e), morne; (simplicity, colour) austère; (reality, poverty) nu(e)

▷ adv: ~ **naked** complètement nu(e)
**starkers** ['stɑːkəz] adj: **to be** ~ (Brit inf) être à poil
**starlet** ['stɑːlɪt] n (Cine) starlette f
**starlight** ['stɑːlaɪt] n: **by** ~ à la lumière des étoiles
**starling** ['stɑːlɪŋ] n étourneau m
**starlit** ['stɑːlɪt] adj étoilé(e); illuminé(e) par les étoiles
**starry** ['stɑːrɪ] adj étoilé(e)
**starry-eyed** [stɑːrɪ'aɪd] adj (innocent) ingénu(e)
**Stars and Stripes** npl: **the** ~ la bannière étoilée
**star sign** n signe zodiacal or du zodiaque
**star-studded** ['stɑːstʌdɪd] adj: **a ~ cast** une distribution prestigieuse
**start** [stɑːt] n commencement m, début m; (of race) départ m; (sudden movement) sursaut m; (advantage) avance f, avantage m ▷ vt commencer; (cause: fight) déclencher; (rumour) donner naissance à; (fashion) lancer; (found: business, newspaper) lancer, créer; (engine) mettre en marche ▷ vi (begin) commencer; (begin journey) partir, se mettre en route; (jump) sursauter; **when does the film ~?** à quelle heure est-ce que le film commence?; **at the** ~ au début; **for a** ~ d'abord, pour commencer; **to make an early** ~ partir or commencer de bonne heure; **to ~ doing** or **to do sth** se mettre à faire qch; **to ~ (off) with ...** (firstly) d'abord ...; (at the beginning) au commencement ...
  ▶ **start off** vi commencer; (leave) partir
  ▶ **start out** vi (begin) commencer; (set out) partir
  ▶ **start over** vi (US) recommencer
  ▶ **start up** vi (car) démarrer ▷ vt (fight) déclencher; (business) créer; (car) mettre en marche
**starter** ['stɑːtə'] n (Aut) démarreur m; (Sport: official) starter m; (: runner, horse) partant m; (Brit Culin) entrée f
**starting handle** ['stɑːtɪŋ-] n (Brit) manivelle f
**starting point** ['stɑːtɪŋ-] n point m de départ
**starting price** ['stɑːtɪŋ-] n prix initial
**startle** ['stɑːtl] vt faire sursauter; donner un choc à
**startling** ['stɑːtlɪŋ] adj surprenant(e), saisissant(e)
**star turn** n (Brit) vedette f
**starvation** [stɑː'veɪʃən] n faim f, famine f; **to die of** ~ mourir de faim or d'inanition
**starve** [stɑːv] vi mourir de faim ▷ vt laisser mourir de faim; **I'm starving** je meurs de faim
**stash** [stæʃ] vt (inf): **to ~ sth away** planquer qch
**state** [steɪt] n état m; (Pol) État; (pomp): **in ~** en grande pompe ▷ vt (declare) déclarer, affirmer; (specify) indiquer, spécifier; **States** npl: **the S~s** les États-Unis; **to be in a ~** être dans tous ses états; ~ **of emergency** état d'urgence; ~ **of mind** état d'esprit; **the ~ of the art** l'état actuel de la technologie (or des connaissances)
**state control** n contrôle m de l'État
**stated** ['steɪtɪd] adj fixé(e), prescrit(e)
**State Department** n (US) Département m d'État, ≈ ministère m des Affaires étrangères

S

**state education** n (Brit) enseignement public
**stateless** ['steɪtlɪs] adj apatride
**stately** ['steɪtlɪ] adj majestueux(-euse), imposant(e)
**stately home** ['steɪtlɪ-] n manoir m or château m (ouvert au public)
**statement** ['steɪtmənt] n déclaration f; (Law) déposition f; (Econ) relevé m; **official ~** communiqué officiel; **~ of account, bank ~** relevé de compte
**state-owned** ['steɪtəʊnd] adj étatisé(e)
**States** [steɪts] npl: **the ~** les États-Unis mpl
**state school** n école publique
**statesman** ['steɪtsmən] (irreg) n homme m d'État
**statesmanship** ['steɪtsmənʃɪp] n qualités fpl d'homme d'État
**static** ['stætɪk] n (Radio) parasites mpl; (also: **static electricity**) électricité f statique ▷ adj statique
**station** ['steɪʃən] n gare f; (also: **police station**) poste m or commissariat m (de police); (Mil) poste m (militaire); (rank) condition f, rang m ▷ vt placer, poster; **action ~s** postes de combat; **to be ~ed in** (Mil) être en garnison à
**stationary** ['steɪʃnərɪ] adj à l'arrêt, immobile
**stationer** ['steɪʃənər] n papetier(-ière)
**stationer's, stationer's shop** n (Brit) papeterie f
**stationery** ['steɪʃnərɪ] n papier m à lettres, petit matériel de bureau
**station wagon** n (US) break m
**statistic** [stə'tɪstɪk] n statistique f
**statistical** [stə'tɪstɪkl] adj statistique
**statistics** [stə'tɪstɪks] n (science) statistique f
**statue** ['stætjuː] n statue f
**statuesque** [stætju'ɛsk] adj sculptural(e)
**statuette** [stætju'ɛt] n statuette f
**stature** ['stætʃər] n stature f; (fig) envergure f
**status** ['steɪtəs] n position f, situation f; (prestige) prestige m; (Admin, official position) statut m
**status quo** [-'kwəʊ] n: **the ~** le statu quo
**status symbol** n marque f de standing, signe extérieur de richesse
**statute** ['stætjuːt] n loi f; **statutes** npl (of club etc) statuts mpl
**statute book** n ≈ code m, textes mpl de loi
**statutory** ['stætjʊtrɪ] adj statutaire, prévu(e) par un article de loi; **~ meeting** assemblée constitutive or statutaire
**staunch** [stɔːntʃ] adj sûr(e), loyal(e) ▷ vt étancher
**stave** [steɪv] n (Mus) portée f ▷ vt: **to ~ off** (attack) parer; (threat) conjurer
**stay** [steɪ] n (period of time) séjour m; (Law): **~ of execution** sursis m à statuer ▷ vi rester; (reside) loger; (spend some time) séjourner; **to ~ put** ne pas bouger; **to ~ with friends** loger chez des amis; **to ~ the night** passer la nuit
▶ **stay away** vi (from person, building) ne pas s'approcher; (from event) ne pas venir

▶ **stay behind** vi rester en arrière
▶ **stay in** vi (at home) rester à la maison
▶ **stay on** vi rester
▶ **stay out** vi (of house) ne pas rentrer; (strikers) rester en grève
▶ **stay up** vi (at night) ne pas se coucher
**staying power** ['steɪɪŋ-] n endurance f
**STD** n abbr (= sexually transmitted disease) MST f; (Brit: = subscriber trunk dialling) l'automatique m
**stead** [stɛd] n (Brit): **in sb's ~** à la place de qn; **to stand sb in good ~** être très utile or servir beaucoup à qn
**steadfast** ['stɛdfɑːst] adj ferme, résolu(e)
**steadily** ['stɛdɪlɪ] adv (regularly) progressivement; (firmly) fermement; (walk) d'un pas ferme; (fixedly: look) sans détourner les yeux
**steady** ['stɛdɪ] adj stable, solide, ferme; (regular) constant(e), régulier(-ière); (person) calme, pondéré(e) ▷ vt assurer, stabiliser; (nerves) calmer; (voice) assurer; **a ~ boyfriend** un petit ami; **to ~ oneself** reprendre son aplomb
**steak** [steɪk] n (meat) bifteck m, steak m; (fish, pork) tranche f
**steakhouse** ['steɪkhaʊs] n ≈ grill-room m
**steal** (pt **stole**, pp **stolen**) [stiːl, stəʊl, 'stəʊln] vt, vi voler; (move) se faufiler, se déplacer furtivement; **my wallet has been stolen** on m'a volé mon portefeuille
▶ **steal away, steal off** vi s'esquiver
**stealth** [stɛlθ] n: **by ~** furtivement
**stealthy** ['stɛlθɪ] adj furtif(-ive)
**steam** [stiːm] n vapeur f ▷ vt passer à la vapeur; (Culin) cuire à la vapeur ▷ vi fumer; (ship): **to ~ along** filer; **under one's own ~** (fig) par ses propres moyens; **to run out of ~** (fig: person) caler; être à bout; **to let off ~** (fig: inf) se défouler
▶ **steam up** vi (window) se couvrir de buée; **to get ~ed up about sth** (fig: inf) s'exciter à propos de qch
**steam engine** n locomotive f à vapeur
**steamer** ['stiːmər] n (bateau m à) vapeur m; (Culin) ≈ couscoussier m
**steam iron** n fer m à repasser à vapeur
**steamroller** ['stiːmrəʊlər] n rouleau compresseur
**steamship** ['stiːmʃɪp] n = **steamer**
**steamy** ['stiːmɪ] adj humide; (window) embué(e); (sexy) torride
**steed** [stiːd] n (literary) coursier m
**steel** [stiːl] n acier m ▷ cpd d'acier
**steel band** n steel band m
**steel industry** n sidérurgie f
**steel mill** n aciérie f, usine f sidérurgique
**steelworks** ['stiːlwəːks] n aciérie f
**steely** ['stiːlɪ] adj (determination) inflexible; (eyes, gaze) d'acier
**steep** [stiːp] adj raide, escarpé(e); (price) très élevé(e), excessif(-ive) ▷ vt (faire) tremper
**steeple** ['stiːpl] n clocher m
**steeplechase** ['stiːpltʃeɪs] n steeple(-chase) m
**steeplejack** ['stiːpldʒæk] n réparateur m de

clochers et de hautes cheminées
**steeply** ['sti:plɪ] *adv* en pente raide
**steer** [stɪə<sup>r</sup>] *n* bœuf *m* ▷ *vt* diriger; (*boat*)
gouverner; (*lead: person*) guider, conduire ▷ *vi*
tenir le gouvernail; **to ~ clear of sb/sth** (*fig*)
éviter qn/qch
**steering** ['stɪərɪŋ] *n* (*Aut*) conduite *f*
**steering column** *n* (*Aut*) colonne *f* de direction
**steering committee** *n* comité *m* d'organisation
**steering wheel** *n* volant *m*
**stellar** ['stɛlə<sup>r</sup>] *adj* stellaire
**stem** [stɛm] *n* (*of plant*) tige *f*; (*of leaf, fruit*) queue
*f*; (*of glass*) pied *m* ▷ *vt* contenir, endiguer;
(*attack, spread of disease*) juguler
▸ **stem from** *vt fus* provenir de, découler de
**stem cell** *n* cellule *f* souche
**stench** [stɛntʃ] *n* puanteur *f*
**stencil** ['stɛnsl] *n* stencil *m*; pochoir *m* ▷ *vt*
polycopier
**stenographer** [stɛ'nɔgrəfə<sup>r</sup>] *n* (*US*) sténographe
*m/f*
**stenography** [stɛ'nɔgrəfɪ] *n* (*US*)
sténo(graphie) *f*
**step** [stɛp] *n* pas *m*; (*stair*) marche *f*; (*action*)
mesure *f*, disposition *f* ▷ *vi*: **to ~ forward/back**
faire un pas en avant/arrière, avancer/reculer;
**steps** *npl* (*Brit*) = **stepladder**; **~ by ~** pas à pas;
(*fig*) petit à petit; **to be in/out of ~ (with)** (*fig*)
aller dans le sens (de)/être déphasé(e) (par
rapport à)
▸ **step down** *vi* (*fig*) se retirer, se désister
▸ **step in** *vi* (*fig*) intervenir
▸ **step off** *vt fus* descendre de
▸ **step over** *vt fus* enjamber
▸ **step up** *vt* (*production, sales*) augmenter;
(*campaign, efforts*) intensifier
**step aerobics**® *npl* step® *m*
**stepbrother** ['stɛpbrʌðə<sup>r</sup>] *n* demi-frère *m*
**stepchild** ['stɛptʃaɪld] (*pl* **-ren**) *n* beau-fils *m*,
belle-fille *f*
**stepdaughter** ['stɛpdɔ:tə<sup>r</sup>] *n* belle-fille *f*
**stepfather** ['stɛpfɑ:ðə<sup>r</sup>] *n* beau-père *m*
**stepladder** ['stɛplædə<sup>r</sup>] *n* (*Brit*) escabeau *m*
**stepmother** ['stɛpmʌðə<sup>r</sup>] *n* belle-mère *f*
**stepping stone** ['stɛpɪŋ-] *n* pierre *f* de gué; (*fig*)
tremplin *m*
**stepsister** ['stɛpsɪstə<sup>r</sup>] *n* demi-sœur *f*
**stepson** ['stɛpsʌn] *n* beau-fils *m*
**stereo** ['stɛrɪəu] *n* (*sound*) stéréo *f*; (*hi-fi*) chaîne *f*
stéréo ▷ *adj* (*also:* **stereophonic**)
stéréo(phonique); **in ~** en stéréo
**stereotype** ['stɛrɪətaɪp] *n* stéréotype *m* ▷ *vt*
stéréotyper
**sterile** ['stɛraɪl] *adj* stérile
**sterility** [stɛ'rɪlɪtɪ] *n* stérilité *f*
**sterilization** [stɛrɪlaɪ'zeɪʃən] *n* stérilisation *f*
**sterilize** ['stɛrɪlaɪz] *vt* stériliser
**sterling** ['stə:lɪŋ] *adj* sterling *inv*; (*silver*) de bon
aloi, fin(e); (*fig*) à toute épreuve, excellent(e) ▷ *n*
(*currency*) livre *f* sterling *inv*; **a pound ~** une livre
sterling
**sterling area** *n* zone *f* sterling *inv*

**stern** [stə:n] *adj* sévère ▷ *n* (*Naut*) arrière *m*,
poupe *f*
**sternum** ['stə:nəm] *n* sternum *m*
**steroid** ['stɪərɔɪd] *n* stéroïde *m*
**stethoscope** ['stɛθəskəup] *n* stéthoscope *m*
**stevedore** ['sti:vədɔ:<sup>r</sup>] *n* docker *m*, débardeur *m*
**stew** [stju:] *n* ragoût *m* ▷ *vt, vi* cuire à la
casserole; **~ed tea** thé trop infusé; **~ed fruit**
fruits cuits *or* en compote
**steward** ['stju:əd] *n* (*Aviat, Naut, Rail*) steward *m*;
(*in club etc*) intendant *m*; (*also:* **shop steward**)
délégué syndical
**stewardess** ['stju:ədɛs] *n* hôtesse *f*
**stewardship** ['stju:ədʃɪp] *n* intendance *f*
**stewing steak** ['stju:ɪŋ-], (*US*) **stew meat** *n*
bœuf *m* à braiser
**St. Ex.** *abbr* = **stock exchange**
**stg** *abbr* = **sterling**
**stick** [stɪk] (*pt, pp* **stuck**) [stʌk] *n* bâton *m*; (*for
walking*) canne *f*; (*of chalk etc*) morceau *m* ▷ *vt*
(*glue*) coller; (*thrust*): **to ~ sth into** piquer *or*
planter *or* enfoncer qch dans; (*inf: put*) mettre,
fourrer; (*: tolerate*) supporter ▷ *vi* (*adhere*) tenir,
coller; (*remain*) rester; (*get jammed: door, lift*) se
bloquer; **to get hold of the wrong end of the ~**
(*Brit fig*) comprendre de travers; **to ~ to** (*one's
promise*) s'en tenir à; (*principles*) rester fidèle à
▸ **stick around** *vi* (*inf*) rester (dans les parages)
▸ **stick out** *vi* dépasser, sortir ▷ *vt*: **to ~ it out**
(*inf*) tenir le coup
▸ **stick up** *vi* dépasser, sortir
▸ **stick up for** *vt fus* défendre
**sticker** ['stɪkə<sup>r</sup>] *n* auto-collant *m*
**sticking plaster** ['stɪkɪŋ-] *n* sparadrap *m*,
pansement adhésif
**sticking point** ['stɪkɪŋ-] *n* (*fig*) point *m* de
friction
**stick insect** *n* phasme *m*
**stickleback** ['stɪklbæk] *n* épinoche *f*
**stickler** ['stɪklə<sup>r</sup>] *n*: **to be a ~ for** être
pointilleux(-euse) sur
**stick shift** *n* (*US Aut*) levier *m* de vitesses
**stick-up** ['stɪkʌp] *n* (*inf*) braquage *m*, hold-up *m*
**sticky** ['stɪkɪ] *adj* poisseux(-euse); (*label*)
adhésif(-ive); (*fig: situation*) délicat(e)
**stiff** [stɪf] *adj* (*gen*) raide, rigide; (*door, brush*)
dur(e); (*difficult*) difficile, ardu(e); (*cold*) froid(e),
distant(e); (*strong, high*) fort(e), élevé(e) ▷ *adv*: **to
be bored/scared/frozen ~** s'ennuyer à mourir/
être mort(e) de peur/froid; **to be** *or* **feel ~**
(*person*) avoir des courbatures; **to have a ~ back**
avoir mal au dos; **~ upper lip** (*Brit: fig*) flegme *m*
(*typiquement britannique*)
**stiffen** ['stɪfn] *vt* raidir, renforcer ▷ *vi* se raidir;
se durcir
**stiff neck** *n* torticolis *m*
**stiffness** ['stɪfnɪs] *n* raideur *f*
**stifle** ['staɪfl] *vt* étouffer, réprimer
**stifling** ['staɪflɪŋ] *adj* (*heat*) suffocant(e)
**stigma** ['stɪgmə] (*Bot, Med, Rel*) (*pl* **-ta**) [stɪg'mɑ:
tə] (*fig*), **stigmas** *n* stigmate *m*
**stile** [staɪl] *n* échalier *m*

**stiletto** [stɪˈlɛtəu] n (Brit: also: **stiletto heel**) talon m aiguille

**still** [stɪl] adj (motionless) immobile; (calm) calme, tranquille; (Brit: mineral water etc) non gazeux(-euse) ▷ adv (up to this time) encore, toujours; (even) encore; (nonetheless) quand même, tout de même ▷ n (Cine) photo f; **to stand ~** rester immobile, ne pas bouger; **keep ~!** ne bouge pas!; **he ~ hasn't arrived** il n'est pas encore arrivé, il n'est toujours pas arrivé

**stillborn** [ˈstɪlbɔːn] adj mort-né(e)

**still life** n nature morte

**stilt** [stɪlt] n échasse f; (pile) pilotis m

**stilted** [ˈstɪltɪd] adj guindé(e), emprunté(e)

**stimulant** [ˈstɪmjulənt] n stimulant m

**stimulate** [ˈstɪmjuleɪt] vt stimuler

**stimulating** [ˈstɪmjuleɪtɪŋ] adj stimulant(e)

**stimulation** [stɪmjuˈleɪʃən] n stimulation f

**stimulus** (pl **stimuli**) [ˈstɪmjuləs, ˈstɪmjulaɪ] n stimulant m; (Biol, Psych) stimulus m

**sting** [stɪŋ] n piqûre f; (organ) dard m; (inf: confidence trick) arnaque m ▷ vt, vi (pt, pp **stung**) [stʌŋ] piquer; **my eyes are ~ing** j'ai les yeux qui piquent

**stingy** [ˈstɪndʒɪ] adj avare, pingre, chiche

**stink** [stɪŋk] n puanteur f ▷ vi (pt **stank**, pp **stunk**) [stæŋk, stʌŋk] puer, empester

**stinker** [ˈstɪŋkəʳ] n (inf: problem, exam) vacherie f; (person) dégueulasse m/f

**stinking** [ˈstɪŋkɪŋ] adj (fig: inf) infect(e); **~ rich** bourré(e) de pognon

**stint** [stɪnt] n part f de travail ▷ vi: **to ~ on** lésiner sur, être chiche de

**stipend** [ˈstaɪpɛnd] n (of vicar etc) traitement m

**stipendiary** [staɪˈpɛndɪərɪ] adj: **~ magistrate** juge m de tribunal d'instance

**stipulate** [ˈstɪpjuleɪt] vt stipuler

**stipulation** [stɪpjuˈleɪʃən] n stipulation f, condition f

**stir** [stəːʳ] n agitation f, sensation f ▷ vt remuer ▷ vi remuer, bouger; **to give sth a ~** remuer qch; **to cause a ~** faire sensation

▸ **stir up** vt exciter; (trouble) fomenter, provoquer

**stir-fry** [ˈstəːfraɪ] vt faire sauter ▷ n: **vegetable ~** légumes sautés à la poêle

**stirring** [ˈstəːrɪŋ] adj excitant(e); émouvant(e)

**stirrup** [ˈstɪrəp] n étrier m

**stitch** [stɪtʃ] n (Sewing) point m; (Knitting) maille f; (Med) point de suture; (pain) point de côté ▷ vt coudre, piquer; (Med) suturer

**stoat** [stəut] n hermine f (avec son pelage d'été)

**stock** [stɔk] n réserve f, provision f; (Comm) stock m; (Agr) cheptel m, bétail m; (Culin) bouillon m; (Finance) valeurs fpl, titres mpl; (Rail: also: **rolling stock**) matériel roulant; (descent, origin) souche f ▷ adj (fig: reply etc) courant(e); classique ▷ vt (have in stock) avoir, vendre; **well-~ed** bien approvisionné(e) or fourni(e); **in ~** en stock, en magasin; **out of ~** épuisé(e); **to take ~** (fig) faire le point; **~s and shares** valeurs (mobilières), titres; **government ~** fonds publics

▸ **stock up** vi: **to ~ up (with)** s'approvisionner (en)

**stockade** [stɔˈkeɪd] n palissade f

**stockbroker** [ˈstɔkbrəukəʳ] n agent m de change

**stock control** n (Comm) gestion f des stocks

**stock cube** n (Brit Culin) bouillon-cube m

**stock exchange** n Bourse f (des valeurs)

**stockholder** [ˈstɔkhəuldəʳ] n (US) actionnaire m/f

**Stockholm** [ˈstɔkhəum] n Stockholm

**stocking** [ˈstɔkɪŋ] n bas m

**stock-in-trade** [ˈstɔkɪnˈtreɪd] n (fig): **it's his ~** c'est sa spécialité

**stockist** [ˈstɔkɪst] n (Brit) stockiste m

**stock market** n Bourse f, marché financier

**stock phrase** n cliché m

**stockpile** [ˈstɔkpaɪl] n stock m, réserve f ▷ vt stocker, accumuler

**stockroom** [ˈstɔkruːm] n réserve f, magasin m

**stocktaking** [ˈstɔkteɪkɪŋ] n (Brit Comm) inventaire m

**stocky** [ˈstɔkɪ] adj trapu(e), râblé(e)

**stodgy** [ˈstɔdʒɪ] adj bourratif(-ive), lourd(e)

**stoic** [ˈstəuɪk] n stoïque m/f

**stoical** [ˈstəuɪkl] adj stoïque

**stoke** [stəuk] vt garnir, entretenir; chauffer

**stoker** [ˈstəukəʳ] n (Rail, Naut etc) chauffeur m

**stole** [stəul] pt of **steal** ▷ n étole f

**stolen** [ˈstəuln] pp of **steal**

**stolid** [ˈstɔlɪd] adj impassible, flegmatique

**stomach** [ˈstʌmək] n estomac m; (abdomen) ventre m ▷ vt supporter, digérer

**stomachache** [ˈstʌməkeɪk] n mal m à l'estomac or au ventre

**stomach pump** n pompe stomacale

**stomach ulcer** n ulcère m à l'estomac

**stomp** [stɔmp] vi: **to ~ in/out** entrer/sortir d'un pas bruyant

**stone** [stəun] n pierre f; (pebble) caillou m, galet m; (in fruit) noyau m; (Med) calcul m; (Brit: weight) = 6.348 kg; 14 pounds ▷ cpd de or en pierre ▷ vt (person) lancer des pierres sur, lapider; (fruit) dénoyauter; **within a ~'s throw of the station** à deux pas de la gare

**Stone Age** n: **the ~** l'âge m de pierre

**stone-cold** [ˈstəunˈkəuld] adj complètement froid(e)

**stoned** [stəund] adj (inf: drunk) bourré(e); (: on drugs) défoncé(e)

**stone-deaf** [ˈstəunˈdɛf] adj sourd(e) comme un pot

**stonemason** [ˈstəunmeɪsn] n tailleur m de pierre(s)

**stonewall** [stəunˈwɔːl] vi faire de l'obstruction ▷ vt faire obstruction à

**stonework** [ˈstəunwəːk] n maçonnerie f

**stony** [ˈstəunɪ] adj pierreux(-euse), rocailleux(-euse)

**stood** [stud] pt, pp of **stand**

**stooge** [stuːdʒ] n (inf) larbin m

**stool** [stuːl] n tabouret m

**stoop** [stuːp] vi (also: **have a stoop**) être voûté(e);

(also: **stoop down**: bend) se baisser, se courber;
(fig): **to ~ to sth/doing sth** s'abaisser jusqu'à
qch/jusqu'à faire qch
**stop** [stɔp] n arrêt m; (short stay) halte f; (in
punctuation) point m ▷ vt arrêter; (break off)
interrompre; (also: **put a stop to**) mettre fin à;
(prevent) empêcher ▷ vi s'arrêter; (rain, noise etc)
cesser, s'arrêter; **could you ~ here/at the
corner?** arrêtez-vous ici/au coin, s'il vous plaît;
**to ~ doing sth** cesser or arrêter de faire qch; **to ~
sb (from) doing sth** empêcher qn de faire qch;
**to ~ dead** vi s'arrêter net; **~ it!** arrête!
▶ **stop by** vi s'arrêter (au passage)
▶ **stop off** vi faire une courte halte
▶ **stop up** vt (hole) boucher
**stopcock** ['stɔpkɔk] n robinet m d'arrêt
**stopgap** ['stɔpgæp] n (person) bouche-trou m;
(also: **stopgap measure**) mesure f intérimaire
**stoplights** ['stɔplaɪts] npl (Aut) signaux mpl de
stop, feux mpl arrière
**stopover** ['stɔpəʊvəʳ] n halte f; (Aviat) escale f
**stoppage** ['stɔpɪdʒ] n arrêt m; (of pay) retenue f;
(strike) arrêt m de travail; (obstruction) obstruction f
**stopper** ['stɔpəʳ] n bouchon m
**stop press** n nouvelles fpl de dernière heure
**stopwatch** ['stɔpwɔtʃ] n chronomètre m
**storage** ['stɔːrɪdʒ] n emmagasinage m; (of
nuclear waste etc) stockage m; (in house) rangement
m; (Comput) mise f en mémoire or réserve
**storage heater** n (Brit) radiateur m électrique
par accumulation
**store** [stɔːʳ] n (stock) provision f, réserve f; (depot)
entrepôt m; (Brit: large shop) grand magasin; (US:
shop) magasin m ▷ vt emmagasiner; (nuclear
waste etc) stocker; (information) enregistrer; (in
filing system) classer, ranger; (Comput) mettre en
mémoire; **stores** npl (food) provisions f; **who
knows what is in ~ for us?** qui sait ce que
l'avenir nous réserve or ce qui nous attend?; **to
set great/little ~ by sth** faire grand cas/peu de
cas de qch
▶ **store up** vt mettre en réserve, emmagasiner
**storehouse** ['stɔːhaus] n entrepôt m
**storekeeper** ['stɔːkiːpəʳ] n (US) commerçant(e)
**storeroom** ['stɔːruːm] n réserve f, magasin m
**storey**, (US) **story** ['stɔːrɪ] n étage m
**stork** [stɔːk] n cigogne f
**storm** [stɔːm] n tempête f; (thunderstorm) orage
m ▷ vi (fig) fulminer ▷ vt prendre d'assaut
**storm cloud** n nuage m d'orage
**storm door** n double-porte (extérieure)
**stormy** ['stɔːmɪ] adj orageux(-euse)
**story** ['stɔːrɪ] n histoire f; récit m; (Press: article)
article m; (: subject) affaire f; (US) = **storey**
**storybook** ['stɔːrɪbuk] n livre m d'histoires or de
contes
**storyteller** ['stɔːrɪtɛləʳ] n conteur(-euse)
**stout** [staut] adj (strong) solide; (brave) intrépide;
(fat) gros(se), corpulent(e) ▷ n bière brune
**stove** [stəuv] n (for cooking) fourneau m; (: small)
réchaud m; (for heating) poêle m; **gas/electric ~**
(cooker) cuisinière f à gaz/électrique

**stow** [stəu] vt ranger; cacher
**stowaway** ['stəuəwei] n passager(-ère)
clandestin(e)
**straddle** ['strædl] vt enjamber, être à cheval sur
**strafe** [strɑːf] vt mitrailler
**straggle** ['strægl] vi être (or marcher) en
désordre; **~d along the coast** disséminé(e) tout
au long de la côte
**straggler** ['stræglәʳ] n traînard(e)
**straggling** ['stræglɪŋ], **straggly** ['stræglɪ] adj
(hair) en désordre
**straight** [streit] adj droit(e); (hair) raide; (frank)
honnête, franc (franche); (simple) simple;
(Theat: part, play) sérieux(-euse); (inf: heterosexual)
hétéro inv ▷ adv (tout) droit; (drink) sec, sans eau
▷ n: **the ~** (Sport) la ligne droite; **to put** or **get ~**
mettre en ordre, mettre de l'ordre dans; (fig)
mettre au clair; **let's get this ~** mettons les
choses au point; **10 ~ wins** 10 victoires d'affilée;
**to go ~ home** rentrer directement à la maison;
**~ away, ~ off** (at once) tout de suite; **~ off, ~ out**
sans hésiter
**straighten** ['streitn] vt ajuster; (bed) arranger
▶ **straighten out** vt (fig) débrouiller; **to ~
things out** arranger les choses
▶ **straighten up** vi (stand up) se redresser; (tidy)
ranger
**straighteners** ['streitnәz] npl (for hair) lisseur m
**straight-faced** [streit'feist] adj impassible
▷ adv en gardant son sérieux
**straightforward** [streit'fɔːwәd] adj simple;
(frank) honnête, direct(e)
**strain** [strein] n (Tech) tension f; pression f;
(physical) effort m; (mental) tension (nerveuse);
(Med) entorse f; (streak, trace) tendance f;
élément m; (breed: of plants) variété f; (: of animals)
race f; (of virus) souche f ▷ vt (stretch) tendre
fortement; (fig: resources etc) mettre à rude
épreuve, grever; (hurt: back etc) se faire mal à;
(filter) passer, filtrer; (vegetables) égoutter ▷ vi
peiner, fournir un gros effort; **strains** npl (Mus)
accords mpl, accents mpl; **he's been under a lot
of ~** il a traversé des moments difficiles, il est
très éprouvé nerveusement
**strained** [streind] adj (muscle) froissé(e); (laugh
etc) forcé(e), contraint(e); (relations) tendu(e)
**strainer** ['streinәʳ] n passoire f
**strait** [streit] n (Geo) détroit m; **straits** npl: **to be
in dire ~s** (fig) avoir de sérieux ennuis
**straitjacket** ['streitdʒækit] n camisole f de
force
**strait-laced** [streit'leist] adj collet monté inv
**strand** [strænd] n (of thread) fil m, brin m; (of rope)
toron m; (of hair) mèche f ▷ vt (boat) échouer
**stranded** ['strændid] adj en rade, en plan
**strange** [streindʒ] adj (not known) inconnu(e);
(odd) étrange, bizarre
**strangely** ['streindʒlɪ] adv étrangement,
bizarrement; see also **enough**
**stranger** ['streindʒәʳ] n (unknown) inconnu(e);
(from somewhere else) étranger(-ère); **I'm a ~ here**
je ne suis pas d'ici

**S**

**strangle** ['stræŋgl] vt étrangler
**stranglehold** ['stræŋglhəuld] n (fig) emprise totale, mainmise f
**strangulation** [stræŋgju'leɪʃən] n strangulation f
**strap** [stræp] n lanière f, courroie f, sangle f; (of slip, dress) bretelle f ▷ vt attacher (avec une courroie etc)
**straphanging** ['stræphæŋɪŋ] n (fait m de) voyager debout (dans le métro etc)
**strapless** ['stræplɪs] adj (bra, dress) sans bretelles
**strapped** [stræpt] adj: **to be ~ for cash** (inf) être à court d'argent
**strapping** ['stræpɪŋ] adj bien découplé(e), costaud(e)
**strappy** [stræpɪ] adj (dress) à bretelles; (sandals) à lanières
**Strasbourg** ['stræzbə:g] n Strasbourg
**strata** ['strɑ:tə] npl of **stratum**
**stratagem** ['strætɪdʒəm] n stratagème m
**strategic** [strə'ti:dʒɪk] adj stratégique
**strategist** ['strætɪdʒɪst] n stratège m
**strategy** ['strætɪdʒɪ] n stratégie f
**stratosphere** ['strætəsfɪər] n stratosphère f
**stratum** (pl **strata**) ['strɑ:təm, 'strɑ:tə] n strate f, couche f
**straw** [strɔ:] n paille f; **that's the last ~!** ça c'est le comble!
**strawberry** ['strɔ:bərɪ] n fraise f; (plant) fraisier m
**stray** [streɪ] adj (animal) perdu(e), errant(e); (scattered) isolé(e) ▷ vi s'égarer; **~ bullet** balle perdue
**streak** [stri:k] n bande f, filet m; (in hair) raie f; (fig: of madness etc): **a ~ of** une or des tendance(s) à ▷ vt zébrer, strier ▷ vi: **to ~ past** passer à toute allure; **to have ~s in one's hair** s'être fait faire des mèches; **a winning/losing ~** une bonne/mauvaise série or période
**streaker** ['stri:kər] n streaker(-euse)
**streaky** ['stri:kɪ] adj zébré(e), strié(e)
**streaky bacon** n (Brit) ≈ lard m (maigre)
**stream** [stri:m] n (brook) ruisseau m; (current) courant m, flot m; (of people) défilé ininterrompu, flot ▷ vt (Scol) répartir par niveau ▷ vi ruisseler; **to ~ in/out** entrer/sortir à flots; **against the ~** à contre courant; **on ~** (new power plant etc) en service
**streamer** ['stri:mər] n serpentin m, banderole f
**stream feed** n (on photocopier etc) alimentation f en continu
**streamline** ['stri:mlaɪn] vt donner un profil aérodynamique à; (fig) rationaliser
**streamlined** ['stri:mlaɪnd] adj (Aviat) fuselé(e), profilé(e); (Aut) aérodynamique; (fig) rationalisé(e)
**street** [stri:t] n rue f; **the back ~s** les quartiers pauvres; **to be on the ~s** (homeless) être à la rue or sans abri
**streetcar** ['stri:tkɑ:r] n (US) tramway m
**street cred** [-krɛd] n (inf): **to have ~** être branché(e)

**street lamp** n réverbère m
**street light** n réverbère m
**street lighting** n éclairage public
**street map, street plan** n plan m des rues
**street market** n marché m à ciel ouvert
**streetwise** ['stri:twaɪz] adj (inf) futé(e), réaliste
**strength** [strεŋθ] n force f; (of girder, knot etc) solidité f; (of chemical solution) titre m; (of wine) degré m d'alcool; **on the ~ of** en vertu de; **at full ~** au grand complet; **below ~** à effectifs réduits
**strengthen** ['strεŋθən] vt renforcer; (muscle) fortifier; (building, Econ) consolider
**strenuous** ['strɛnjuəs] adj vigoureux(-euse), énergique; (tiring) ardu(e), fatigant(e)
**stress** [strɛs] n (force, pressure) pression f; (mental strain) tension (nerveuse), stress m; (accent) accent m; (emphasis) insistance f ▷ vt insister sur, souligner; (syllable) accentuer; **to lay great ~ on sth** insister beaucoup sur qch; **to be under ~** être stressé(e)
**stressed** [strɛst] adj (tense) stressé(e); (syllable) accentué(e)
**stressful** ['strɛsful] adj (job) stressant(e)
**stretch** [strɛtʃ] n (of sand etc) étendue f; (of time) période f ▷ vi s'étirer; (extend): **to ~ to** or **as far as** s'étendre jusqu'à; (be enough: money, food): **to ~ to** aller pour ▷ vt tendre, étirer; (spread) étendre; (fig) pousser (au maximum); **at a ~** d'affilée; **to ~ a muscle** se distendre un muscle; **to ~ one's legs** se dégourdir les jambes ▷ **stretch out** vi s'étendre ▷ vt (arm etc) allonger, tendre; (to spread) étendre; **to ~ out for sth** allonger la main pour prendre qch
**stretcher** ['strɛtʃər] n brancard m, civière f
**stretcher-bearer** ['strɛtʃəbɛərər] n brancardier m
**stretch marks** npl (on skin) vergetures fpl
**stretchy** ['strɛtʃɪ] adj élastique
**strewn** [stru:n] adj: **~ with** jonché(e) de
**stricken** ['strɪkən] adj très éprouvé(e); dévasté(e); (ship) très endommagé(e); **~ with** frappé(e) or atteint(e) de
**strict** [strɪkt] adj strict(e); **in ~ confidence** tout à fait confidentiellement
**strictly** ['strɪktlɪ] adv strictement; **~ confidential** strictement confidentiel(le); **~ speaking** à strictement parler
**stride** [straɪd] n grand pas, enjambée f ▷ vi (pt **strode**) [strəud] marcher à grands pas; **to take in one's ~** (fig: changes etc) accepter sans sourciller
**strident** ['straɪdnt] adj strident(e)
**strife** [straɪf] n conflit m, dissensions fpl
**strike** [straɪk] (pt, pp **struck**) [strʌk] n grève f; (of oil etc) découverte f; (attack) raid m ▷ vt frapper; (oil etc) trouver, découvrir; (make: agreement, deal) conclure ▷ vi faire grève; (attack) attaquer; (clock) sonner; **to go on** or **come out on ~** se mettre en grève, faire grève; **to ~ a match** frotter une allumette; **to ~ a balance** (fig) trouver un juste milieu

▸ **strike back** vi (Mil, fig) contre-attaquer
▸ **strike down** vt (fig) terrasser
▸ **strike off** vt (from list) rayer; (: doctor etc) radier
▸ **strike out** vt rayer
▸ **strike up** vt (Mus) se mettre à jouer; **to ~ up a friendship with** se lier d'amitié avec
**strikebreaker** ['straɪkbreɪkə'] n briseur m de grève
**striker** ['straɪkə'] n gréviste m/f; (Sport) buteur m
**striking** ['straɪkɪŋ] adj frappant(e), saisissant(e); (attractive) éblouissant(e)
**strimmer**® ['strɪmə'] n (Brit) coupe-bordures m
**string** [strɪŋ] n ficelle f, fil m; (row: of beads) rang m; (: of onions, excuses) chapelet m; (: of people, cars) file f; (Mus) corde f; (Comput) chaîne f ▷ vt (pt, pp **strung**) [strʌŋ]: **to ~ out** échelonner; **to ~ together** enchaîner; **the strings** npl (Mus) les instruments mpl à cordes; **to pull ~s** (fig) faire jouer le piston; **to get a job by pulling ~s** obtenir un emploi en faisant jouer le piston; **with no ~s attached** (fig) sans conditions
**string bean** n haricot vert
**stringed instrument** [strɪŋ(d)-], **string instrument** n (Mus) instrument m à cordes
**stringent** ['strɪndʒənt] adj rigoureux(-euse); (need) impérieux(-euse)
**string quartet** n quatuor m à cordes
**strip** [strɪp] n bande f; (Sport) tenue f ▷ vt (undress) déshabiller; (paint) décaper; (fig) dégarnir, dépouiller; (also: **strip down**: machine) démonter ▷ vi se déshabiller; **wearing the Celtic ~** en tenue du Celtic
▸ **strip off** vt (paint etc) décaper ▷ vi (person) se déshabiller
**strip cartoon** n bande dessinée
**stripe** [straɪp] n raie f, rayure f; (Mil) galon m
**striped** [straɪpt] adj rayé(e), à rayures
**strip light** n (Brit) (tube m au) néon m
**stripper** ['strɪpə'] n strip-teaseuse f
**strip-search** ['strɪpsə:tʃ] n fouille corporelle (en faisant se déshabiller la personne) ▷ vt: **to ~ sb** fouiller qn (en le faisant se déshabiller)
**striptease** ['strɪpti:z] n strip-tease m
**stripy** ['straɪpɪ] adj rayé(e)
**strive** (pt **strove**, pp **striven**) [straɪv, strəuv, 'strɪvn] vi: **to ~ to do/for sth** s'efforcer de faire/ d'obtenir qch
**strobe** [strəub] n (also: **strobe light**) stroboscope m
**strode** [strəud] pt of **stride**
**stroke** [strəuk] n coup m; (Med) attaque f; (caress) caresse f; (Swimming: style) (sorte f de) nage f; (of piston) course f ▷ vt caresser; **at a ~** d'un (seul) coup; **on the ~ of 5** à 5 heures sonnantes; **a ~ of luck** un coup de chance; **a 2-~ engine** un moteur à 2 temps
**stroll** [strəul] n petite promenade ▷ vi flâner, se promener nonchalamment; **to go for a ~** aller se promener or faire un tour
**stroller** ['strəulə'] n (US: for child) poussette f
**strong** [strɔŋ] adj (gen) fort(e); (healthy) vigoureux(-euse); (heart, nerves) solide; (distaste,

desire) vif (vive); (drugs, chemicals) puissant(e)
▷ adv: **to be going ~** (company) marcher bien; (person) être toujours solide; **they are 50 ~** ils sont au nombre de 50
**strong-arm** ['strɔŋɑ:m] adj (tactics, methods) musclé(e)
**strongbox** ['strɔŋbɔks] n coffre-fort m
**stronghold** ['strɔŋhəuld] n forteresse f, fort m; (fig) bastion m
**strongly** ['strɔŋlɪ] adv fortement, avec force; vigoureusement; solidement; **I feel ~ about it** c'est une question qui me tient particulièrement à cœur; (negatively) j'y suis profondément opposé(e)
**strongman** ['strɔŋmæn] (irreg) n hercule m, colosse m; (fig) homme m à poigne
**strongroom** ['strɔŋru:m] n chambre forte
**stroppy** ['strɔpɪ] adj (Brit inf) contrariant(e), difficile
**strove** [strəuv] pt of **strive**
**struck** [strʌk] pt, pp of **strike**
**structural** ['strʌktʃrəl] adj structural(e); (Constr) de construction; affectant les parties portantes
**structurally** ['strʌktʃrəlɪ] adv du point de vue de la construction
**structure** ['strʌktʃə'] n structure f; (building) construction f
**struggle** ['strʌgl] n lutte f ▷ vi lutter, se battre; **to have a ~ to do sth** avoir beaucoup de mal à faire qch
**strum** [strʌm] vt (guitar) gratter de
**strung** [strʌŋ] pt, pp of **string**
**strut** [strʌt] n étai m, support m ▷ vi se pavaner
**strychnine** ['strɪkni:n] n strychnine f
**stub** [stʌb] n (of cigarette) bout m, mégot m; (of ticket etc) talon m ▷ vt: **to ~ one's toe (on sth)** se heurter le doigt de pied (contre qch)
▸ **stub out** vt écraser
**stubble** ['stʌbl] n chaume m; (on chin) barbe f de plusieurs jours
**stubborn** ['stʌbən] adj têtu(e), obstiné(e), opiniâtre
**stubby** ['stʌbɪ] adj trapu(e); gros(se) et court(e)
**stucco** ['stʌkəu] n stuc m
**stuck** [stʌk] pt, pp of **stick** ▷ adj (jammed) bloqué(e), coincé(e); **to get ~** se bloquer or coincer
**stuck-up** [stʌk'ʌp] adj prétentieux(-euse)
**stud** [stʌd] n (on boots etc) clou m; (collar stud) bouton m de col; (earring) petite boucle d'oreille; (of horses: also: **stud farm**) écurie f, haras m; (also: **stud horse**) étalon m ▷ vt (fig): **~ded with** parsemé(e) or criblé(e) de
**student** ['stju:dənt] n étudiant(e) ▷ adj (life) estudiantin(e), étudiant(e), d'étudiant; (residence, restaurant) universitaire; (loan, movement) étudiant, universitaire d'étudiant; **law/medical ~** étudiant en droit/ médecine
**student driver** n (US) (conducteur(-trice)) débutant(e)
**students' union** n (Brit: association) ≈ union f des étudiants; (: building) ≈ foyer m des étudiants

S

**studied** ['stʌdɪd] adj étudié(e), calculé(e)
**studio** ['stju:dɪəu] n studio m, atelier m; (TV etc) studio
**studio flat**, (US) **studio apartment** n studio m
**studious** ['stju:dɪəs] adj studieux(-euse), appliqué(e); (studied) étudié(e)
**studiously** ['stju:dɪəslɪ] adv (carefully) soigneusement
**study** ['stʌdɪ] n étude f; (room) bureau m ▷ vt étudier; (examine) examiner ▷ vi étudier, faire ses études; **to make a ~ of sth** étudier qch, faire une étude de qch; **to ~ for an exam** préparer un examen
**stuff** [stʌf] n (gen) chose(s) f(pl), truc m; (belongings) affaires fpl, trucs; (substance) substance f ▷ vt rembourrer; (Culin) farcir; (inf: push) fourrer; (animal: for exhibition) empailler; **my nose is ~ed up** j'ai le nez bouché; **get ~ed!** (inf!) va te faire foutre! (!); **~ed toy** jouet m en peluche
**stuffing** ['stʌfɪŋ] n bourre f, rembourrage m; (Culin) farce f
**stuffy** ['stʌfɪ] adj (room) mal ventilé(e) or aéré(e); (ideas) vieux jeu inv
**stumble** ['stʌmbl] vi trébucher; **to ~ across** or **on** (fig) tomber sur
**stumbling block** ['stʌmblɪŋ-] n pierre f d'achoppement
**stump** [stʌmp] n souche f; (of limb) moignon m ▷ vt: **to be ~ed** sécher, ne pas savoir que répondre
**stun** [stʌn] vt (blow) étourdir; (news) abasourdir, stupéfier
**stung** [stʌŋ] pt, pp of **sting**
**stunk** [stʌŋk] pp of **stink**
**stunned** [stʌnd] adj assommé(e); (fig) sidéré(e)
**stunning** ['stʌnɪŋ] adj (beautiful) étourdissant(e); (news etc) stupéfiant(e)
**stunt** [stʌnt] n tour m de force; (in film) cascade f, acrobatie f; (publicity) truc m publicitaire; (Aviat) acrobatie f ▷ vt retarder, arrêter
**stunted** ['stʌntɪd] adj rabougri(e)
**stuntman** ['stʌntmæn] (irreg) n cascadeur m
**stupefaction** [stju:pɪ'fækʃən] n stupéfaction f, stupeur f
**stupefy** ['stju:pɪfaɪ] vt étourdir; abrutir; (fig) stupéfier
**stupendous** [stju:'pɛndəs] adj prodigieux(-euse), fantastique
**stupid** ['stju:pɪd] adj stupide, bête
**stupidity** [stju:'pɪdɪtɪ] n stupidité f, bêtise f
**stupidly** ['stju:pɪdlɪ] adv stupidement, bêtement
**stupor** ['stju:pər] n stupeur f
**sturdy** ['stə:dɪ] adj (person, plant) robuste, vigoureux(-euse); (object) solide
**sturgeon** ['stə:dʒən] n esturgeon m
**stutter** ['stʌtər] n bégaiement m ▷ vi bégayer
**sty** [staɪ] n (of pigs) porcherie f
**stye** [staɪ] n (Med) orgelet m
**style** [staɪl] n style m; (of dress etc) genre m; (distinction) allure f, cachet m, style; (design)

modèle m; **in the latest ~** à la dernière mode; **hair ~** coiffure f
**stylish** ['staɪlɪʃ] adj élégant(e), chic inv
**stylist** ['staɪlɪst] n (hair stylist) coiffeur(-euse); (literary stylist) styliste m/f
**stylized** ['staɪlaɪzd] adj stylisé(e)
**stylus** (pl **styli** or **-es**) ['staɪləs, -laɪ] n (of record player) pointe f de lecture
**Styrofoam®** ['staɪrəfəum] n (US) polystyrène expansé ▷ adj en polystyrène
**suave** [swɑ:v] adj doucereux(-euse), onctueux(-euse)
**sub** [sʌb] n abbr = **submarine; subscription**
**sub...** [sʌb] prefix sub..., sous-
**subcommittee** ['sʌbkəmɪtɪ] n sous-comité m
**subconscious** [sʌb'kɔnʃəs] adj subconscient(e) ▷ n subconscient m
**subcontinent** [sʌb'kɔntɪnənt] n: **the (Indian) ~** le sous-continent indien
**subcontract** n ['sʌb'kɔntrækt] contrat m de sous-traitance ▷ vt [sʌbkən'trækt] sous-traiter
**subcontractor** ['sʌbkən'træktər] n sous-traitant m
**subdivide** [sʌbdɪ'vaɪd] vt subdiviser
**subdivision** ['sʌbdɪvɪʒən] n subdivision f
**subdue** [səb'dju:] vt subjuguer, soumettre
**subdued** [səb'dju:d] adj contenu(e), atténué(e); (light) tamisé(e); (person) qui a perdu de son entrain
**sub-editor** ['sʌb'ɛdɪtər] n (Brit) secrétaire m/f de (la) rédaction
**subject** n ['sʌbdʒɪkt] sujet m; (Scol) matière f ▷ vt [səb'dʒɛkt]: **to ~ to** soumettre à; exposer à; **to be ~ to** (law) être soumis(e) à; (disease) être sujet(te) à; **~ to confirmation in writing** sous réserve de confirmation écrite; **to change the ~** changer de conversation
**subjection** [səb'dʒɛkʃən] n soumission f, sujétion f
**subjective** [səb'dʒɛktɪv] adj subjectif(-ive)
**subject matter** n sujet m; (content) contenu m
**sub judice** [sʌb'dju:dɪsɪ] adj (Law) devant les tribunaux
**subjugate** ['sʌbdʒugeɪt] vt subjuguer
**subjunctive** [səb'dʒʌŋktɪv] adj subjonctif(-ive) ▷ n subjonctif m
**sublet** [sʌb'lɛt] vt sous-louer
**sublime** [sə'blaɪm] adj sublime
**subliminal** [sʌb'lɪmɪnl] adj subliminal(e)
**submachine gun** ['sʌbmə'ʃi:n-] n mitraillette f
**submarine** [sʌbmə'ri:n] n sous-marin m
**submerge** [səb'mə:dʒ] vt submerger; immerger ▷ vi plonger
**submersion** [səb'mə:ʃən] n submersion f; immersion f
**submission** [səb'mɪʃən] n soumission f; (to committee etc) présentation f
**submissive** [səb'mɪsɪv] adj soumis(e)
**submit** [səb'mɪt] vt soumettre ▷ vi se soumettre
**subnormal** [sʌb'nɔ:ml] adj au-dessous de la normale; (person) arriéré(e)
**subordinate** [sə'bɔ:dɪnət] adj (junior) subalterne;

(*Grammar*) subordonné(e) ▷ *n* subordonné(e)

**subpoena** [səb'pi:nə] (*Law*) *n* citation *f*,
assignation *f* ▷ *vt* citer *or* assigner (à
comparaître)

**subroutine** [sʌbruː'tiːn] *n* (*Comput*) sous-
programme *m*

**subscribe** [səb'skraɪb] *vi* cotiser; **to ~ to** (*opinion,
fund*) souscrire à; (*newspaper*) s'abonner à; être
abonné(e) à

**subscriber** [səb'skraɪbəʳ] *n* (*to periodical, telephone*)
abonné(e)

**subscript** ['sʌbskrɪpt] *n* (*Typ*) indice inférieur

**subscription** [səb'skrɪpʃən] *n* (*to fund*)
souscription *f*; (*to magazine etc*) abonnement *m*;
(*membership dues*) cotisation *f*; **to take out a ~ to**
s'abonner à

**subsequent** ['sʌbsɪkwənt] *adj* ultérieur(e),
suivant(e); **~ to** *prep* à la suite de

**subsequently** ['sʌbsɪkwəntlɪ] *adv* par la suite

**subservient** [səb'sɜːvɪənt] *adj*
obséquieux(-euse)

**subside** [səb'saɪd] *vi* (*land*) s'affaisser; (*flood*)
baisser; (*wind, feelings*) tomber

**subsidence** [səb'saɪdns] *n* affaissement *m*

**subsidiarity** [səbsɪdɪ'ærɪtɪ] *n* (*Pol*) subsidiarité *f*

**subsidiary** [səb'sɪdɪərɪ] *adj* subsidiaire;
accessoire; (*Brit Scol: subject*) complémentaire
▷ *n* filiale *f*

**subsidize** ['sʌbsɪdaɪz] *vt* subventionner

**subsidy** ['sʌbsɪdɪ] *n* subvention *f*

**subsist** [səb'sɪst] *vi*: **to ~ on sth** (arriver à) vivre
avec *or* subsister avec qch

**subsistence** [səb'sɪstəns] *n* existence *f*,
subsistance *f*

**subsistence allowance** *n* indemnité *f* de séjour

**subsistence level** *n* niveau *m* de vie minimum

**substance** ['sʌbstəns] *n* substance *f*; (*fig*)
essentiel *m*; **a man of ~** un homme jouissant
d'une certaine fortune; **to lack ~** être plutôt
mince (*fig*)

**substance abuse** *n* abus *m* de substances
toxiques

**substandard** [sʌb'stændəd] *adj* (*goods*) de
qualité inférieure, qui laisse à désirer; (*housing*)
inférieur(e) aux normes requises

**substantial** [səb'stænʃl] *adj* substantiel(le); (*fig*)
important(e)

**substantially** [səb'stænʃəlɪ] *adv*
considérablement; en grande partie

**substantiate** [səb'stænʃɪeɪt] *vt* étayer, fournir
des preuves à l'appui de

**substitute** ['sʌbstɪtjuːt] *n* (*person*)
remplaçant(e); (*thing*) succédané *m* ▷ *vt*: **to ~
sth/sb for** substituer qch/qn à, remplacer par
qch/qn

**substitute teacher** *n* (*US*) suppléant(e)

**substitution** [sʌbstɪ'tjuːʃən] *n* substitution *f*

**subterfuge** ['sʌbtəfjuːdʒ] *n* subterfuge *m*

**subterranean** [sʌbtə'reɪnɪən] *adj* souterrain(e)

**subtitled** ['sʌbtaɪtld] *adj* sous-titré(e)

**subtitles** ['sʌbtaɪtlz] *npl* (*Cine*) sous-titres *mpl*

**subtle** ['sʌtl] *adj* subtil(e)

**subtlety** ['sʌtltɪ] *n* subtilité *f*

**subtly** ['sʌtlɪ] *adv* subtilement

**subtotal** [sʌb'təutl] *n* total partiel

**subtract** [səb'trækt] *vt* soustraire, retrancher

**subtraction** [səb'trækʃən] *n* soustraction *f*

**subtropical** [sʌb'trɔpɪkl] *adj* subtropical(e)

**suburb** ['sʌbəːb] *n* faubourg *m*; **the ~s** la
banlieue

**suburban** [sə'bəːbən] *adj* de banlieue,
suburbain(e)

**suburbia** [sə'bəːbɪə] *n* la banlieue

**subvention** [səb'vɛnʃən] *n* (*subsidy*) subvention *f*

**subversion** [səb'vəːʃən] *n* subversion *f*

**subversive** [səb'vəːsɪv] *adj* subversif(-ive)

**subway** ['sʌbweɪ] *n* (*Brit: underpass*) passage
souterrain; (*US: railway*) métro *m*

**sub-zero** [sʌb'zɪərəu] *adj* au-dessous de zéro

**succeed** [sək'siːd] *vi* réussir ▷ *vt* succéder à; **to
~ in doing** réussir à faire

**succeeding** [sək'siːdɪŋ] *adj* suivant(e), qui suit
(*or* suivent *or* suivront *etc*)

**success** [sək'sɛs] *n* succès *m*; réussite *f*

**successful** [sək'sɛsful] *adj* qui a du succès;
(*candidate*) choisi(e), agréé(e); (*business*) prospère,
qui réussit; (*attempt*) couronné(e) de succès; **to
be ~ (in doing)** réussir (à faire)

**successfully** [sək'sɛsfəlɪ] *adv* avec succès

**succession** [sək'sɛʃən] *n* succession *f*; **in ~**
successivement; **3 years in ~** 3 ans de suite

**successive** [sək'sɛsɪv] *adj* successif(-ive); **on 3 ~
days** 3 jours de suite *or* consécutifs

**successor** [sək'sɛsəʳ] *n* successeur *m*

**succinct** [sək'sɪŋkt] *adj* succinct(e), bref (brève)

**succulent** ['sʌkjulənt] *adj* succulent(e) ▷ *n*
(*Bot*): **~s** plantes grasses

**succumb** [sə'kʌm] *vi* succomber

**such** [sʌtʃ] *adj* tel (telle); (*of that kind*): **~ a book**
un livre de ce genre *or* pareil, un tel livre; (*so
much*): **~ courage** un tel courage ▷ *adv* si; **~
books** des livres de ce genre *or* pareils, de tels
livres; **~ a long trip** un si long voyage; **~ good
books** de si bons livres; **~ a long trip that** un
voyage si *or* tellement long que; **~ a lot of**
tellement *or* tant de; **making ~ a noise that**
faisant un tel bruit que *or* tellement de bruit
que; **~ a long time ago** il y a si *or* tellement
longtemps; **~ as** (*like*) tel (telle) que, comme; **a
noise ~ as to** un bruit de nature à; **~ books as I
have** les quelques livres que j'ai; **as ~** (*adv*) en
tant que tel (telle), à proprement parler

**such-and-such** ['sʌtʃənsʌtʃ] *adj* tel ou tel (telle
ou telle)

**suchlike** ['sʌtʃlaɪk] *pron* (*inf*): **and ~** et le reste

**suck** [sʌk] *vt* sucer; (*breast, bottle*) téter; (*pump,
machine*) aspirer

**sucker** ['sʌkəʳ] *n* (*Bot, Zool, Tech*) ventouse *f*; (*inf*)
naïf(-ïve), poire *f*

**suckle** ['sʌkl] *vt* allaiter

**sucrose** ['suːkrəuz] *n* saccharose *m*

**suction** ['sʌkʃən] *n* succion *f*

**suction pump** *n* pompe aspirante

**Sudan** [suː'dɑːn] *n* Soudan *m*

S

**Sudanese** [suːdəˈniːz] *adj* soudanais(e) ▷ *n*
Soudanais(e)

**sudden** [ˈsʌdn] *adj* soudain(e), subit(e); **all of a**
**~** soudain, tout à coup

**sudden-death** [sʌdnˈdɛθ] *n*: **~ play-off** *partie*
*supplémentaire pour départager les adversaires*

**suddenly** [ˈsʌdnlɪ] *adv* brusquement, tout à
coup, soudain

**sudoku** [sʊˈdəʊkuː] *n* sudoku *m*

**suds** [sʌdz] *npl* eau savonneuse

**sue** [suː] *vt* poursuivre en justice, intenter un
procès à ▷ *vi*: **to ~ (for)** intenter un procès
(pour); **to ~ for divorce** engager une procédure
de divorce; **to ~ sb for damages** poursuivre qn
en dommages-intérêts

**suede** [sweɪd] *n* daim *m*, cuir suédé ▷ *cpd* de
daim

**suet** [ˈsuɪt] *n* graisse *f* de rognon *or* de bœuf

**Suez Canal** [ˈsuːɪz-] *n* canal *m* de Suez

**suffer** [ˈsʌfər] *vt* souffrir, subir; (*bear*) tolérer,
supporter, subir ▷ *vi* souffrir; **to ~ from** (*illness*)
souffrir de, avoir; **to ~ from the effects of**
**alcohol/a fall** se ressentir des effets de l'alcool/
des conséquences d'une chute

**sufferance** [ˈsʌfərns] *n*: **he was only there on ~**
sa présence était seulement tolérée

**sufferer** [ˈsʌfərər] *n* malade *m/f*; victime *m/f*

**suffering** [ˈsʌfərɪŋ] *n* souffrance(s) *f(pl)*

**suffice** [səˈfaɪs] *vi* suffire

**sufficient** [səˈfɪʃənt] *adj* suffisant(e); **~ money**
suffisamment d'argent

**sufficiently** [səˈfɪʃəntlɪ] *adv* suffisamment,
assez

**suffix** [ˈsʌfɪks] *n* suffixe *m*

**suffocate** [ˈsʌfəkeɪt] *vi* suffoquer; étouffer

**suffocation** [sʌfəˈkeɪʃən] *n* suffocation *f*; (*Med*)
asphyxie *f*

**suffrage** [ˈsʌfrɪdʒ] *n* suffrage *m*; droit *m* de
suffrage *or* de vote

**suffuse** [səˈfjuːz] *vt* baigner, imprégner; **the**
**room was ~d with light** la pièce baignait dans
la lumière *or* était imprégnée de lumière

**sugar** [ˈʃʊɡər] *n* sucre *m* ▷ *vt* sucrer

**sugar beet** *n* betterave sucrière

**sugar bowl** *n* sucrier *m*

**sugar cane** *n* canne *f* à sucre

**sugar-coated** [ˈʃʊɡəˈkəʊtɪd] *adj* dragéifié(e)

**sugar lump** *n* morceau *m* de sucre

**sugar refinery** *n* raffinerie *f* de sucre

**sugary** [ˈʃʊɡərɪ] *adj* sucré(e)

**suggest** [səˈdʒɛst] *vt* suggérer, proposer;
(*indicate*) sembler indiquer; **what do you ~ I do?**
que vous me suggérez de faire?

**suggestion** [səˈdʒɛstʃən] *n* suggestion *f*

**suggestive** [səˈdʒɛstɪv] *adj* suggestif(-ive)

**suicidal** [suɪˈsaɪdl] *adj* suicidaire

**suicide** [ˈsuɪsaɪd] *n* suicide *m*; **to commit ~** se
suicider; **~ bombing** attentat *m* suicide; *see also*
**commit**

**suicide bomber** *n* kamikaze *m/f*

**suit** [suːt] *n* (*man's*) costume *m*, complet *m*;
(*woman's*) tailleur *m*, ensemble *m*; (*Cards*) couleur

*f*; (*lawsuit*) procès *m* ▷ *vt* (*subj: clothes, hairstyle*)
aller à; (*be convenient for*) convenir à; (*adapt*): **to ~**
**sth to** adapter *or* approprier qch à; **to be ~ed to**
**sth** (*suitable for*) être adapté(e) *or* approprié(e) à
qch; **well ~ed** (*couple*) faits l'un pour l'autre,
très bien assortis; **to bring a ~ against sb**
intenter un procès contre qn; **to follow ~** (*fig*)
faire de même

**suitable** [ˈsuːtəbl] *adj* qui convient;
approprié(e), adéquat(e); **would tomorrow be**
**~?** est-ce que demain vous conviendrait?; **we**
**found somebody ~** nous avons trouvé la
personne qu'il nous faut

**suitably** [ˈsuːtəblɪ] *adv* comme il se doit (*or* se
devait *etc*), convenablement

**suitcase** [ˈsuːtkeɪs] *n* valise *f*

**suite** [swiːt] *n* (*of rooms, also Mus*) suite *f*;
(*furniture*): **bedroom/dining room ~** (ensemble
*m* de) chambre *f* à coucher/salle *f* à manger; **a**
**three-piece ~** un salon (canapé et deux
fauteuils)

**suitor** [ˈsuːtər] *n* soupirant *m*, prétendant *m*

**sulfate** [ˈsʌlfeɪt] *n* (*US*) = **sulphate**

**sulfur** [ˈsʌlfər] (*US*) *n* = **sulphur**

**sulk** [sʌlk] *vi* bouder

**sulky** [ˈsʌlkɪ] *adj* boudeur(-euse), maussade

**sullen** [ˈsʌlən] *adj* renfrogné(e), maussade;
morne

**sulphate**, (*US*) **sulfate** [ˈsʌlfeɪt] *n* sulfate *m*;
**copper ~** sulfate de cuivre

**sulphur**, (*US*) **sulfur** [ˈsʌlfər] *n* soufre *m*

**sulphur dioxide** *n* anhydride sulfureux

**sulphuric**, (*US*) **sulfuric** [sʌlˈfjuərɪk] *adj*: **~ acid**
acide *m* sulfurique

**sultan** [ˈsʌltən] *n* sultan *m*

**sultana** [sʌlˈtɑːnə] *n* (*fruit*) raisin (sec) de
Smyrne

**sultry** [ˈsʌltrɪ] *adj* étouffant(e)

**sum** [sʌm] *n* somme *f*; (*Scol etc*) calcul *m*
▷ **sum up** *vt* résumer; (*evaluate rapidly*)
récapituler ▷ *vi* résumer

**Sumatra** [suˈmɑːtrə] *n* Sumatra

**summarize** [ˈsʌməraɪz] *vt* résumer

**summary** [ˈsʌmərɪ] *n* résumé *m* ▷ *adj* (*justice*)
sommaire

**summer** [ˈsʌmər] *n* été *m* ▷ *cpd* d'été, estival(e);
**in (the) ~** en été, pendant l'été

**summer camp** *n* (*US*) colonie *f* de vacances

**summer holidays** *npl* grandes vacances

**summerhouse** [ˈsʌməhaʊs] *n* (*in garden*)
pavillon *m*

**summertime** [ˈsʌmətaɪm] *n* (*season*) été *m*

**summer time** *n* (*by clock*) heure *f* d'été

**summery** [ˈsʌmərɪ] *adj* estival(e); d'été

**summing-up** [sʌmɪŋˈʌp] *n* résumé *m*,
récapitulation *f*

**summit** [ˈsʌmɪt] *n* sommet *m*; (*also*: **summit**
**conference**) (conférence *f* au) sommet *m*

**summon** [ˈsʌmən] *vt* appeler, convoquer; **to ~ a**
**witness** citer *or* assigner un témoin
▷ **summon up** *vt* rassembler, faire appel à

**summons** [ˈsʌmənz] *n* citation *f*, assignation *f*

▷ vt citer, assigner; **to serve a ~ on sb** remettre une assignation à qn

**sumo** ['suːməu] n: ~ **wrestling** sumo m

**sump** [sʌmp] n (Brit Aut) carter m

**sumptuous** ['sʌmptjuəs] adj somptueux(-euse)

**Sun.** abbr (= Sunday) dim

**sun** [sʌn] n soleil m; **in the ~** au soleil; **to catch the ~** prendre le soleil; **everything under the ~** absolument tout

**sunbathe** ['sʌnbeɪð] vi prendre un bain de soleil

**sunbeam** ['sʌnbiːm] n rayon m de soleil

**sunbed** ['sʌnbɛd] n lit pliant; (with sun lamp) lit à ultra-violets

**sunblock** ['sʌnblɔk] n écran m total

**sunburn** ['sʌnbəːn] n coup m de soleil

**sunburned** ['sʌnbəːnd], **sunburnt** ['sʌnbəːnt] adj bronzé(e), hâlé(e); (painfully) brûlé(e) par le soleil

**sun cream** n crème f (anti-)solaire

**sundae** ['sʌndeɪ] n sundae m, coupe glacée

**Sunday** ['sʌndɪ] n dimanche m; for phrases see also **Tuesday**

**Sunday paper** n journal m du dimanche; voir article

⬤ **SUNDAY PAPER**
⬤
⬤ Les Sunday papers sont une véritable
⬤ institution en Grande-Bretagne. Il y a des
⬤ "quality Sunday papers" et des "popular
⬤ Sunday papers", et la plupart des quotidiens
⬤ ont un journal du dimanche qui leur est
⬤ associé, bien que leurs équipes de rédacteurs
⬤ soient différentes. Les quality Sunday
⬤ papers ont plusieurs suppléments et
⬤ magazines; voir "quality press" et "tabloid
⬤ press".

**Sunday school** n ≈ catéchisme m

**sundial** ['sʌndaɪəl] n cadran m solaire

**sundown** ['sʌndaun] n coucher m du soleil

**sundries** ['sʌndrɪz] npl articles divers

**sundry** ['sʌndrɪ] adj divers(e), différent(e); **all and ~** tout le monde, n'importe qui

**sunflower** ['sʌnflauəʳ] n tournesol m

**sung** [sʌŋ] pp of **sing**

**sunglasses** ['sʌnglɑːsɪz] npl lunettes fpl de soleil

**sunk** [sʌŋk] pp of **sink**

**sunken** ['sʌŋkn] adj (rock, ship) submergé(e); (cheeks) creux(-euse); (bath) encastré(e)

**sunlamp** ['sʌnlæmp] n lampe f à rayons ultra-violets

**sunlight** ['sʌnlaɪt] n (lumière f du) soleil m

**sunlit** ['sʌnlɪt] adj ensoleillé(e)

**sun lounger** n chaise longue

**sunny** ['sʌnɪ] adj ensoleillé(e); (fig) épanoui(e), radieux(-euse); **it is ~** il fait (du) soleil, il y a du soleil

**sunrise** ['sʌnraɪz] n lever m du soleil

**sun roof** n (Aut) toit ouvrant

**sunscreen** ['sʌnskriːn] n crème f solaire

**sunset** ['sʌnsɛt] n coucher m du soleil

**sunshade** ['sʌnʃeɪd] n (lady's) ombrelle f; (over table) parasol m

**sunshine** ['sʌnʃaɪn] n (lumière f du) soleil m

**sunspot** ['sʌnspɔt] n tache f solaire

**sunstroke** ['sʌnstrəuk] n insolation f, coup m de soleil

**suntan** ['sʌntæn] n bronzage m

**suntan lotion** n lotion f or lait m solaire

**suntanned** ['sʌntænd] adj bronzé(e)

**suntan oil** n huile f solaire

**suntrap** ['sʌntræp] n coin très ensoleillé

**super** ['suːpəʳ] adj (inf) formidable

**superannuation** [suːpərænjuˈeɪʃən] n cotisations fpl pour la pension

**superb** [suːˈpəːb] adj superbe, magnifique

**Super Bowl** n (US Sport) Super Bowl m

**supercilious** [suːpəˈsɪlɪəs] adj hautain(e), dédaigneux(-euse)

**superconductor** [suːpəkənˈdʌktəʳ] n supraconducteur m

**superficial** [suːpəˈfɪʃəl] adj superficiel(le)

**superficially** [suːpəˈfɪʃəlɪ] adv superficiellement

**superfluous** [suˈpəːfluəs] adj superflu(e)

**superglue** ['suːpəgluː] n colle forte

**superhighway** ['suːpəhaɪweɪ] n (US) voie f express (à plusieurs files); **the information ~** la super-autoroute de l'information

**superhuman** [suːpəˈhjuːmən] adj surhumain(e)

**superimpose** ['suːpərɪmˈpəuz] vt superposer

**superintend** [suːpərɪnˈtɛnd] vt surveiller

**superintendent** [suːpərɪnˈtɛndənt] n directeur(-trice); (Police) ≈ commissaire m

**superior** [suˈpɪərɪəʳ] adj supérieur(e); (Comm: goods, quality) de qualité supérieure; (smug) condescendant(e), méprisant(e) ▷ n supérieur(e); **Mother S~** (Rel) Mère supérieure

**superiority** [supɪərɪˈɔrɪtɪ] n supériorité f

**superlative** [suˈpəːlətɪv] adj sans pareil(le), suprême ▷ n (Ling) superlatif m

**superman** ['suːpəmæn] (irreg) n surhomme m

**supermarket** ['suːpəmɑːkɪt] n supermarché m

**supermodel** ['suːpəmɔdl] n top model m

**supernatural** [suːpəˈnætʃərəl] adj surnaturel(le) ▷ n: **the ~** le surnaturel

**supernova** [suːpəˈnəuvə] n supernova f

**superpower** ['suːpəpauəʳ] n (Pol) superpuissance f

**supersede** [suːpəˈsiːd] vt remplacer, supplanter

**supersonic** ['suːpəˈsɔnɪk] adj supersonique

**superstar** ['suːpəstɑːʳ] n (Cine etc) superstar f; (Sport) superchampion(ne) ▷ adj (status, lifestyle) de superstar

**superstition** [suːpəˈstɪʃən] n superstition f

**superstitious** [suːpəˈstɪʃəs] adj superstitieux(-euse)

**superstore** ['suːpəstɔːʳ] n (Brit) hypermarché m, grande surface

**supertanker** ['suːpətæŋkəʳ] n pétrolier géant, superpétrolier m

**supertax** ['suːpətæks] n tranche supérieure de l'impôt

**S**

**supervise** ['su:pəvaɪz] vt (*children etc*) surveiller; (*organization, work*) diriger

**supervision** [su:pə'vɪʒən] n surveillance f; (*monitoring*) contrôle m; (*management*) direction f; **under medical ~** sous contrôle du médecin

**supervisor** ['su:pəvaɪzər] n surveillant(e); (*in shop*) chef m de rayon; (*Scol*) directeur(-trice) de thèse

**supervisory** ['su:pəvaɪzərɪ] adj de surveillance

**supine** ['su:paɪn] adj couché(e) or étendu(e) sur le dos

**supper** ['sʌpər] n dîner m; (*late*) souper m; **to have ~** dîner; souper

**supplant** [sə'plɑ:nt] vt supplanter

**supple** ['sʌpl] adj souple

**supplement** n ['sʌplɪmənt] supplément m ⊳ vt [sʌplɪ'mɛnt] ajouter à, compléter

**supplementary** [sʌplɪ'mɛntərɪ] adj supplémentaire

**supplementary benefit** n (*Brit*) allocation f supplémentaire d'aide sociale

**supplier** [sə'plaɪər] n fournisseur m

**supply** [sə'plaɪ] vt (*provide*) fournir; (*equip*): **to ~ (with)** approvisionner or ravitailler (en); fournir (en); (*system, machine*): **to ~ sth (with sth)** alimenter qch (en qch); (*a need*) répondre à ⊳ n provision f, réserve f; (*supplying*) approvisionnement m; (*Tech*) alimentation f; **supplies** npl (*food*) vivres mpl; (*Mil*) subsistances fpl; **office supplies** fournitures fpl de bureau; **to be in short ~** être rare, manquer; **the electricity/water/gas ~** l'alimentation f en électricité/eau/gaz; **~ and demand** l'offre f et la demande; **it comes supplied with an adaptor** il (or elle) est pourvu(e) d'un adaptateur

**supply teacher** n (*Brit*) suppléant(e)

**support** [sə'pɔ:t] n (*moral, financial etc*) soutien m, appui m; (*Tech*) support m, soutien ⊳ vt soutenir, supporter; (*financially*) subvenir aux besoins de; (*uphold*) être pour, être partisan de, appuyer; (*Sport: team*) être pour; **to ~ o.s.** (*financially*) gagner sa vie

**supporter** [sə'pɔ:tər] n (*Pol etc*) partisan(e); (*Sport*) supporter m

**supporting** [sə'pɔ:tɪŋ] adj (*wall*) d'appui

**supporting role** n second rôle m

**supportive** [sə'pɔ:tɪv] adj: **my family were very ~** ma famille m'a été d'un grand soutien

**suppose** [sə'pəuz] vt, vi supposer; imaginer; **to be ~d to do/be** être censé(e) faire/être; **I don't ~ she'll come** je suppose qu'elle ne viendra pas, cela m'étonnerait qu'elle vienne

**supposedly** [sə'pəuzɪdlɪ] adv soi-disant

**supposing** [sə'pəuzɪŋ] conj si, à supposer que + sub

**supposition** [sʌpə'zɪʃən] n supposition f, hypothèse f

**suppository** [sə'pɔzɪtrɪ] n suppositoire m

**suppress** [sə'prɛs] vt (*revolt, feeling*) réprimer; (*information*) faire disparaître; (*scandal, yawn*) étouffer

**suppression** [sə'prɛʃən] n suppression f, répression f

**suppressor** [sə'prɛsər] n (*Elec etc*) dispositif m antiparasite

**supremacy** [su'prɛməsɪ] n suprématie f

**supreme** [su'pri:m] adj suprême

**Supreme Court** n (*US*) Cour f suprême

**supremo** [su'pri:məu] n grand chef

**Supt.** abbr (*Police*) = **superintendent**

**surcharge** ['sə:tʃɑ:dʒ] n surcharge f; (*extra tax*) surtaxe f

**sure** [ʃuər] adj (*gen*) sûr(e); (*definite, convinced*) sûr, certain(e) ⊳ adv (*inf: US*): **that ~ is pretty, that's ~ pretty** c'est drôlement joli(e); **~!** (*of course*) bien sûr!; **~ enough** effectivement; **I'm not ~ how/why/when** je ne sais pas très bien comment/pourquoi/quand; **to be ~ of o.s.** être sûr de soi; **to make ~ of sth/that** s'assurer de qch/que, vérifier qch/que

**sure-fire** ['ʃuəfaɪər] adj (*inf*) certain(e), infaillible

**sure-footed** [ʃuə'futɪd] adj au pied sûr

**surely** ['ʃuəlɪ] adv sûrement; certainement; **~ you don't mean that!** vous ne parlez pas sérieusement!

**surety** ['ʃuərətɪ] n caution f; **to go** or **stand ~ for sb** se porter caution pour qn

**surf** [sə:f] n (*waves*) ressac m ⊳ vt: **to ~ the Net** surfer sur Internet, surfer sur le net

**surface** ['sə:fɪs] n surface f ⊳ vt (*road*) poser un revêtement sur ⊳ vi remonter à la surface; (*fig*) faire surface; **on the ~** (*fig*) au premier abord; **by ~ mail** par voie de terre; (*by sea*) par voie maritime

**surface area** n superficie f, aire f

**surface mail** n courrier m par voie de terre (or maritime)

**surface-to-surface** ['sə:fɪstə'sə:fɪs] adj (*Mil*) sol-sol inv

**surfboard** ['sə:fbɔ:d] n planche f de surf

**surfeit** ['sə:fɪt] n: **a ~ of** un excès de; une indigestion de

**surfer** ['sə:fər] n (*in sea*) surfeur(-euse); **web** or **net ~** internaute m/f

**surfing** ['sə:fɪŋ] n surf m

**surge** [sə:dʒ] n (*of emotion*) vague f; (*Elec*) pointe f de courant ⊳ vi déferler; **to ~ forward** se précipiter (en avant)

**surgeon** ['sə:dʒən] n chirurgien m

**Surgeon General** n (*US*) chef m du service fédéral de la santé publique

**surgery** ['sə:dʒərɪ] n chirurgie f; (*Brit: room*) cabinet m (de consultation); (*also:* **surgery hours**) heures fpl de consultation; (*of MP etc*) permanence f (*où le député etc reçoit les électeurs etc*); **to undergo ~** être opéré(e)

**surgery hours** npl (*Brit*) heures fpl de consultation

**surgical** ['sə:dʒɪkl] adj chirurgical(e)

**surgical spirit** n (*Brit*) alcool m à 90°

**surly** ['sə:lɪ] adj revêche, maussade

**surmise** [sə:'maɪz] vt présumer, conjecturer

**surmount** [sə:'maunt] vt surmonter

**surname** ['sə:neɪm] n nom m de famille

**surpass** [səˈpɑːs] *vt* surpasser, dépasser
**surplus** [ˈsəːpləs] *n* surplus *m*, excédent *m* ▷ *adj*
en surplus, de trop; (*Comm*) excédentaire; **it is ~
to our requirements** cela dépasse nos besoins;
**~ stock** surplus *m*
**surprise** [səˈpraɪz] *n* (*gen*) surprise *f*;
(*astonishment*) étonnement *m* ▷ *vt* surprendre,
étonner; **to take by ~** (*person*) prendre au
dépourvu; (*Mil: town, fort*) prendre par surprise
**surprised** [səˈpraɪzd] *adj* (*look, smile*) surpris(e),
étonné(e); **to be ~** être surpris
**surprising** [səˈpraɪzɪŋ] *adj* surprenant(e),
étonnant(e)
**surprisingly** [səˈpraɪzɪŋlɪ] *adv* (*easy, helpful*)
étonnamment, étrangement; **(somewhat) ~**,
**he agreed** curieusement, il a accepté
**surrealism** [səˈrɪəlɪzəm] *n* surréalisme *m*
**surrealist** [səˈrɪəlɪst] *adj, n* surréaliste (*m/f*)
**surrender** [səˈrɛndəʳ] *n* reddition *f*, capitulation
*f* ▷ *vi* se rendre, capituler ▷ *vt* (*claim, right*)
renoncer à
**surrender value** *n* valeur *f* de rachat
**surreptitious** [sʌrəpˈtɪʃəs] *adj* subreptice,
furtif(-ive)
**surrogate** [ˈsʌrəgɪt] *n* (*Brit: substitute*) substitut *m*
▷ *adj* de substitution, de remplacement; **a food
~** un succédané alimentaire; **~ coffee** ersatz *m*
*or* succédané *m* de café
**surrogate mother** *n* mère porteuse *or* de
substitution
**surround** [səˈraund] *vt* entourer; (*Mil etc*)
encercler
**surrounding** [səˈraundɪŋ] *adj* environnant(e)
**surroundings** [səˈraundɪŋz] *npl* environs *mpl*,
alentours *mpl*
**surtax** [ˈsəːtæks] *n* surtaxe *f*
**surveillance** [səːˈveɪləns] *n* surveillance *f*
**survey** *n* [ˈsəːveɪ] enquête *f*, étude *f*; (*in house
buying etc*) inspection *f*, (*rapport m d'*)expertise *f*;
(*of land*) levé *m*; (*comprehensive view: of situation etc*)
vue *f* d'ensemble ▷ *vt* [səːˈveɪ] (*situation*) passer
en revue; (*examine carefully*) inspecter; (*building*)
expertiser; (*land*) faire le levé de; (*look at*)
embrasser du regard
**surveying** [səˈveɪɪŋ] *n* arpentage *m*
**surveyor** [səˈveɪəʳ] *n* (*of building*) expert *m*; (*of
land*) (arpenteur *m*) géomètre *m*
**survival** [səˈvaɪvl] *n* survie *f*; (*relic*) vestige *m*
▷ *cpd* (*course, kit*) de survie
**survive** [səˈvaɪv] *vi* survivre; (*custom etc*)
subsister ▷ *vt* (*accident etc*) survivre à, réchapper
de; (*person*) survivre à
**survivor** [səˈvaɪvəʳ] *n* survivant(e)
**susceptible** [səˈsɛptəbl] *adj*: **~ (to)** sensible (à);
(*disease*) prédisposé(e) (à)
**suspect** *adj, n* [ˈsʌspɛkt] suspect(e) ▷ *vt* [səsˈpɛkt]
soupçonner, suspecter
**suspected** [səsˈpɛktɪd] *adj*: **a ~ terrorist** une
personne soupçonnée de terrorisme; **he had a
~ broken arm** il avait une supposée fracture du
bras
**suspend** [səsˈpɛnd] *vt* suspendre

**suspended animation** [səsˈpɛndɪd-] *n*: **in a
state of ~** en hibernation
**suspended sentence** [səsˈpɛndɪd-] *n* (*Law*)
condamnation *f* avec sursis
**suspender belt** [səsˈpɛndə-] *n* (*Brit*) porte-
jarretelles *m inv*
**suspenders** [səsˈpɛndəz] *npl* (*Brit*) jarretelles *fpl*;
(*US*) bretelles *fpl*
**suspense** [səsˈpɛns] *n* attente *f*, incertitude *f*; (*in
film etc*) suspense *m*; **to keep sb in ~** tenir qn en
suspens, laisser qn dans l'incertitude
**suspension** [səsˈpɛnʃən] *n* (*gen, Aut*) suspension
*f*; (*of driving licence*) retrait *m* provisoire
**suspension bridge** *n* pont suspendu
**suspicion** [səsˈpɪʃən] *n* soupçon(s) *m(pl)*; **to be
under ~** être considéré(e) comme suspect(e),
être suspecté(e); **arrested on ~ of murder**
arrêté sur présomption de meurtre
**suspicious** [səsˈpɪʃəs] *adj* (*suspecting*)
soupçonneux(-euse), méfiant(e); (*causing
suspicion*) suspect(e); **to be ~ of** *or* **about sb/sth**
avoir des doutes à propos de qn/sur qch, trouver
qn/qch suspect(e)
**suss out** [ˈsʌsˈaut] *vt* (*Brit inf: discover*) supputer;
(: *understand*) piger
**sustain** [səsˈteɪn] *vt* soutenir; supporter;
corroborer; (*subj: food*) nourrir, donner des forces
à; (*damage*) subir; (*injury*) recevoir
**sustainable** [səsˈteɪnəbl] *adj* (*rate, growth*) qui
peut être maintenu(e); (*development*) durable
**sustained** [səsˈteɪnd] *adj* (*effort*) soutenu(e),
prolongé(e)
**sustenance** [ˈsʌstɪnəns] *n* nourriture *f*; moyens
*mpl* de subsistance
**suture** [ˈsuːtʃəʳ] *n* suture *f*
**SUV** *n abbr* (*esp US: = sports utility vehicle*) SUV *m*,
véhicule *m* de loisirs
**SW** *abbr* (= *short wave*) OC
**swab** [swɔb] *n* (*Med*) tampon *m*; prélèvement *m*
▷ *vt* (*Naut: also:* **swab down**) nettoyer
**swagger** [ˈswægəʳ] *vi* plastronner, parader
**swallow** [ˈswɔləu] *n* (*bird*) hirondelle *f*; (*of food
etc*) gorgée *f* ▷ *vt* avaler; (*fig: story*) gober
▷ **swallow up** *vt* engloutir
**swam** [swæm] *pt of* **swim**
**swamp** [swɔmp] *n* marais *m*, marécage *m* ▷ *vt*
submerger
**swampy** [ˈswɔmpɪ] *adj* marécageux(-euse)
**swan** [swɔn] *n* cygne *m*
**swank** [swæŋk] *vi* (*inf*) faire de l'épate
**swan song** *n* (*fig*) chant *m* du cygne
**swap** [swɔp] *n* échange *m*, troc *m* ▷ *vt*: **to ~ (for)**
échanger (contre), troquer (contre)
**SWAPO** [ˈswɑːpəu] *n abbr* (= *South-West Africa
People's Organization*) SWAPO *f*
**swarm** [swɔːm] *n* essaim *m* ▷ *vi* (*bees*) essaimer;
(*people*) grouiller; **to be ~ing with** grouiller de
**swarthy** [ˈswɔːðɪ] *adj* basané(e), bistré(e)
**swashbuckling** [ˈswɔʃbʌklɪŋ] *adj* (*film*) de cape
et d'épée
**swastika** [ˈswɔstɪkə] *n* croix gammée
**SWAT** *n abbr* (*US: = Special Weapons and Tactics*)

**S**

≈ CRS f

**swat** [swɔt] vt écraser ▷ n (Brit: also: **fly swat**) tapette f

**swathe** [sweɪð] vt: **to ~ in** (bandages, blankets) embobiner de

**swatter** ['swɔtəʳ] n (also: **fly swatter**) tapette f

**sway** [sweɪ] vi se balancer, osciller; tanguer ▷ vt (influence) influencer ▷ n (rule, power): **~ (over)** emprise f (sur); **to hold ~ over sb** avoir de l'emprise sur qn

**Swaziland** ['swɑːzɪlænd] n Swaziland m

**swear** [swɛəʳ] (pt **swore**, pp **sworn**) [swɔːʳ, swɔːn] vt, vi jurer; **to ~ to sth** jurer de qch; **to ~ an oath** prêter serment
▸ **swear in** vt assermenter

**swearword** ['swɛəwɜːd] n gros mot, juron m

**sweat** [swɛt] n sueur f, transpiration f ▷ vi suer; **in a ~** en sueur

**sweatband** ['swɛtbænd] n (Sport) bandeau m

**sweater** ['swɛtəʳ] n tricot m, pull m

**sweatshirt** ['swɛtʃəːt] n sweat-shirt m

**sweatshop** ['swɛtʃɔp] n atelier m où les ouvriers sont exploités

**sweaty** ['swɛtɪ] adj en sueur, moite or mouillé(e) de sueur

**Swede** [swiːd] n Suédois(e)

**swede** [swiːd] n (Brit) rutabaga m

**Sweden** ['swiːdn] n Suède f

**Swedish** ['swiːdɪʃ] adj suédois(e) ▷ n (Ling) suédois m

**sweep** [swiːp] (pt, pp **swept**) [swɛpt] n coup m de balai; (curve) grande courbe; (range) champ m; (also: **chimney sweep**) ramoneur m ▷ vt balayer; (subj: current) emporter; (subj: fashion, craze) se répandre dans ▷ vi avancer majestueusement or rapidement; s'élancer; s'étendre
▸ **sweep away** vt balayer; entraîner; emporter
▸ **sweep past** vi passer majestueusement or rapidement
▸ **sweep up** vt, vi balayer

**sweeper** ['swiːpəʳ] n (person) balayeur m; (machine) balayeuse f; (Football) libéro m

**sweeping** ['swiːpɪŋ] adj (gesture) large; circulaire; (changes, reforms) radical(e); **a ~ statement** une généralisation hâtive

**sweepstake** ['swiːpsteɪk] n sweepstake m

**sweet** [swiːt] n (Brit: pudding) dessert m; (candy) bonbon m ▷ adj doux (douce); (not savoury) sucré(e); (fresh) frais (fraîche), pur(e); (kind) gentil(le); (baby) mignon(ne) ▷ adv: **to smell ~** sentir bon; **to taste ~** avoir un goût sucré; **~ and sour** adj aigre-doux (douce)

**sweetbread** ['swiːtbrɛd] n ris m de veau

**sweetcorn** ['swiːtkɔːn] n maïs doux

**sweeten** ['swiːtn] vt sucrer; (fig) adoucir

**sweetener** ['swiːtnəʳ] n (Culin) édulcorant m

**sweetheart** ['swiːthɑːt] n amoureux(-euse)

**sweetly** ['swiːtlɪ] adv (smile) gentiment; (sing, play) mélodieusement

**sweetness** ['swiːtnɪs] n douceur f; (of taste) goût sucré

**sweet pea** n pois m de senteur

**sweet potato** n patate douce

**sweetshop** ['swiːtʃɔp] n (Brit) confiserie f

**sweet tooth** n: **to have a ~** aimer les sucreries

**swell** [swɛl] (pt **-ed**, pp **swollen** or **-ed**) ['swəulən] n (of sea) houle f ▷ adj (US: inf: excellent) chouette ▷ vt (increase) grossir, augmenter ▷ vi (increase) grossir, augmenter; (sound) s'enfler; (Med: also: **swell up**) enfler

**swelling** ['swɛlɪŋ] n (Med) enflure f; (: lump) grosseur f

**sweltering** ['swɛltərɪŋ] adj étouffant(e), oppressant(e)

**swept** [swɛpt] pt, pp of **sweep**

**swerve** [swəːv] vi (to avoid obstacle) faire une embardée or un écart; (off the road) dévier

**swift** [swɪft] n (bird) martinet m ▷ adj rapide, prompt(e)

**swiftly** ['swɪftlɪ] adv rapidement, vite

**swig** [swɪg] n (inf: drink) lampée f

**swill** [swɪl] n pâtée f ▷ vt (also: **swill out**, **swill down**) laver à grande eau

**swim** [swɪm] (pt **swam**, pp **swum**) [swæm, swʌm] n: **to go for a ~** aller nager or se baigner ▷ vi nager; (Sport) faire de la natation; (fig: head, room) tourner ▷ vt traverser (à la nage); (distance) faire (à la nage); **to ~ a length** nager une longueur; **to go ~ming** aller nager

**swimmer** ['swɪməʳ] n nageur(-euse)

**swimming** ['swɪmɪŋ] n nage f, natation f

**swimming baths** npl (Brit) piscine f

**swimming cap** n bonnet m de bain

**swimming costume** n (Brit) maillot m (de bain)

**swimmingly** ['swɪmɪŋlɪ] adv: **to go ~** (wonderfully) se dérouler à merveille

**swimming pool** n piscine f

**swimming trunks** npl maillot m de bain

**swimsuit** ['swɪmsuːt] n maillot m (de bain)

**swindle** ['swɪndl] n escroquerie f ▷ vt escroquer

**swindler** ['swɪndləʳ] n escroc m

**swine** [swaɪn] n (pl inv) pourceau m, porc m; (inf!) salaud m (!)

**swine flu** n grippe f porcine

**swing** [swɪŋ] (pt, pp **swung**) [swʌŋ] n (in playground) balançoire f; (movement) balancement m, oscillations fpl; (change in opinion etc) revirement m; (Mus) swing m; rythme m ▷ vt balancer, faire osciller; (also: **swing round**) tourner, faire virer ▷ vi se balancer, osciller; (also: **swing round**) virer, tourner; **a ~ to the left** (Pol) un revirement en faveur de la gauche; **to be in full ~** battre son plein; **to get into the ~ of things** se mettre dans le bain; **the road ~s south** la route prend la direction sud

**swing bridge** n pont tournant

**swing door** n (Brit) porte battante

**swingeing** ['swɪndʒɪŋ] adj (Brit) écrasant(e); considérable

**swinging** ['swɪŋɪŋ] adj rythmé(e); entraînant(e); (fig) dans le vent; **~ door** (US) porte battante

**swipe** [swaɪp] n grand coup; gifle f ▷ vt (hit) frapper à toute volée; gifler; (inf: steal) piquer;

*(credit card etc)* faire passer (dans la machine)
**swipe card** n carte f magnétique
**swirl** [swəːl] n tourbillon m ▷ vi tourbillonner, tournoyer
**swish** [swɪʃ] adj *(Brit inf: smart)* rupin(e) ▷ vi *(whip)* siffler; *(skirt, long grass)* bruire
**Swiss** [swɪs] adj suisse ▷ n *(pl inv)* Suisse(-esse)
**Swiss French** adj suisse romand(e)
**Swiss German** adj suisse-allemand(e)
**Swiss roll** n gâteau roulé
**switch** [swɪtʃ] n *(for light, radio etc)* bouton m; *(change)* changement m, revirement m ▷ vt *(change)* changer; *(exchange)* intervertir; *(invert)*: **to ~ (round** or **over)** changer de place
  ▸ **switch off** vt éteindre; *(engine, machine)* arrêter; **could you ~ off the light?** pouvez-vous éteindre la lumière?
  ▸ **switch on** vt allumer; *(engine, machine)* mettre en marche; *(Brit: water supply)* ouvrir
**switchback** ['swɪtʃbæk] n *(Brit)* montagnes fpl russes
**switchblade** ['swɪtʃbleɪd] n *(also:* **switchblade knife)** couteau m à cran d'arrêt
**switchboard** ['swɪtʃbɔːd] n *(Tel)* standard m
**switchboard operator** n *(Tel)* standardiste m/f
**Switzerland** ['swɪtsələnd] n Suisse f
**swivel** ['swɪvl] vi *(also:* **swivel round)** pivoter, tourner
**swollen** ['swəulən] pp of **swell** ▷ adj *(ankle etc)* enflé(e)
**swoon** [swuːn] vi se pâmer
**swoop** [swuːp] n *(by police etc)* rafle f, descente f; *(of bird etc)* descente f en piqué ▷ vi *(bird: also:* **swoop down)** descendre en piqué, piquer
**swop** [swɔp] n, vt = **swap**
**sword** [sɔːd] n épée f
**swordfish** ['sɔːdfɪʃ] n espadon m
**swore** [swɔːʳ] pt of **swear**
**sworn** [swɔːn] pp of **swear** ▷ adj *(statement, evidence)* donné(e) sous serment; *(enemy)* juré(e)
**swot** [swɔt] vt, vi bûcher, potasser
**swum** [swʌm] pp of **swim**
**swung** [swʌŋ] pt, pp of **swing**
**sycamore** ['sɪkəmɔːʳ] n sycomore m
**sycophant** ['sɪkəfænt] n flagorneur(-euse)
**sycophantic** [sɪkə'fæntɪk] adj flagorneur(-euse)
**Sydney** ['sɪdnɪ] n Sydney
**syllable** ['sɪləbl] n syllabe f
**syllabus** ['sɪləbəs] n programme m; **on the ~** au programme
**symbol** ['sɪmbl] n symbole m
**symbolic** [sɪm'bɔlɪk], **symbolical** [sɪm'bɔlɪkl] adj symbolique
**symbolism** ['sɪmbəlɪzəm] n symbolisme m
**symbolize** ['sɪmbəlaɪz] vt symboliser
**symmetrical** [sɪ'mɛtrɪkl] adj symétrique
**symmetry** ['sɪmɪtrɪ] n symétrie f
**sympathetic** [sɪmpə'θɛtɪk] adj *(showing pity)* compatissant(e); *(understanding)* bienveillant(e), compréhensif(-ive); **~ towards** bien disposé(e) envers

**sympathetically** [sɪmpə'θɛtɪklɪ] adv avec compassion *(or* bienveillance)
**sympathize** ['sɪmpəθaɪz] vi: **to ~ with sb** plaindre qn; *(in grief)* s'associer à la douleur de qn; **to ~ with sth** comprendre qch
**sympathizer** ['sɪmpəθaɪzəʳ] n *(Pol)* sympathisant(e)
**sympathy** ['sɪmpəθɪ] n *(pity)* compassion f; **sympathies** npl *(support)* soutien m; **in ~ with** en accord avec; *(strike)* en or par solidarité avec; **with our deepest ~** en vous priant d'accepter nos sincères condoléances
**symphonic** [sɪm'fɔnɪk] adj symphonique
**symphony** ['sɪmfənɪ] n symphonie f
**symphony orchestra** n orchestre m symphonique
**symposium** [sɪm'pəuzɪəm] n symposium m
**symptom** ['sɪmptəm] n symptôme m; indice m
**symptomatic** [sɪmptə'mætɪk] adj symptomatique
**synagogue** ['sɪnəgɔg] n synagogue f
**sync** [sɪŋk] n *(inf)*: **in/out of ~** bien/mal synchronisé(e); **they're in ~ with each other** *(fig)* le courant passe bien entre eux
**synchromesh** [sɪŋkrəu'mɛʃ] n *(Aut)* synchronisation f
**synchronize** ['sɪŋkrənaɪz] vt synchroniser ▷ vi: **to ~ with** se produire en même temps que
**synchronized swimming** ['sɪŋkrənaɪzd-] n natation synchronisée
**syncopated** ['sɪŋkəpeɪtɪd] adj syncopé(e)
**syndicate** ['sɪndɪkɪt] n syndicat m, coopérative f; *(Press)* agence f de presse
**syndrome** ['sɪndrəum] n syndrome m
**synonym** ['sɪnənɪm] n synonyme m
**synonymous** [sɪ'nɔnɪməs] adj: **~ (with)** synonyme (de)
**synopsis** *(pl* **synopses)** [sɪ'nɔpsɪs, -siːz] n résumé m, synopsis m or f
**syntax** ['sɪntæks] n syntaxe f
**synthesis** *(pl* **syntheses)** ['sɪnθəsɪs, -siːz] n synthèse f
**synthesizer** ['sɪnθəsaɪzəʳ] n *(Mus)* synthétiseur m
**synthetic** [sɪn'θɛtɪk] adj synthétique ▷ n matière f synthétique; **synthetics** npl textiles artificiels
**syphilis** ['sɪfɪlɪs] n syphilis f
**syphon** ['saɪfən] n, vb = **siphon**
**Syria** ['sɪrɪə] n Syrie f
**Syrian** ['sɪrɪən] adj syrien(ne) ▷ n Syrien(ne)
**syringe** [sɪ'rɪndʒ] n seringue f
**syrup** ['sɪrəp] n sirop m; *(Brit: also:* **golden syrup)** mélasse raffinée
**syrupy** ['sɪrəpɪ] adj sirupeux(-euse)
**system** ['sɪstəm] n système m; *(order)* méthode f; *(Anat)* organisme m
**systematic** [sɪstə'mætɪk] adj systématique; méthodique
**system disk** n *(Comput)* disque m système
**systems analyst** n analyste-programmeur m/f

**S**

# Tt

**T, t** [tiː] *n* (*letter*) T, t *m*; **T for Tommy** T comme Thérèse

**TA** *n abbr* (*Brit*) = **Territorial Army**

**ta** [tɑː] *excl* (*Brit inf*) merci!

**tab** [tæb] *n abbr* = **tabulator** ▷ *n* (*loop on coat etc*) attache *f*; (*label*) étiquette *f*; (*on drinks can etc*) languette *f*; **to keep ~s on** (*fig*) surveiller

**tabby** ['tæbɪ] *n* (*also*: **tabby cat**) chat(te) tigré(e)

**table** ['teɪbl] *n* table *f* ▷ *vt* (*Brit: motion etc*) présenter; **to lay** *or* **set the ~** mettre le couvert *or* la table; **to clear the ~** débarrasser la table; **league ~** (*Brit Football, Rugby*) classement *m* (du championnat); **~ of contents** table des matières

**tablecloth** ['teɪblklɔθ] *n* nappe *f*

**table d'hôte** [tɑːbl'dəut] *adj* (*meal*) à prix fixe

**table football** *n* baby-foot *m*

**table lamp** *n* lampe décorative *or* de table

**tablemat** ['teɪblmæt] *n* (*for plate*) napperon *m*, set *m*; (*for hot dish*) dessous-de-plat *m inv*

**table salt** *n* sel fin *or* de table

**tablespoon** ['teɪblspuːn] *n* cuiller *f* de service; (*also*: **tablespoonful**: *as measurement*) cuillerée *f* à soupe

**tablet** ['tæblɪt] *n* (*Med*) comprimé *m*; (: *for sucking*) pastille *f*; (*of stone*) plaque *f*; **~ of soap** (*Brit*) savonnette *f*

**table tennis** *n* ping-pong *m*, tennis *m* de table

**table wine** *n* vin *m* de table

**tabloid** ['tæblɔɪd] *n* (*newspaper*) quotidien *m* populaire; *voir article*

### ● TABLOID PRESS

●

● Le terme *tabloid press* désigne les journaux
● populaires de demi-format où l'on trouve
● beaucoup de photos et qui adoptent un style
● très concis. Ce type de journaux vise des
● lecteurs s'intéressant aux faits divers ayant
● un parfum de scandale; voir "quality press"

**taboo** [tə'buː] *adj, n* tabou (*m*)

**tabulate** ['tæbjuleɪt] *vt* (*data, figures*) mettre sous forme de table(s)

**tabulator** ['tæbjuleɪtə'] *n* tabulateur *m*

**tachograph** ['tækəgrɑːf] *n* tachygraphe *m*

**tachometer** [tæ'kɔmɪtə'] *n* tachymètre *m*

**tacit** ['tæsɪt] *adj* tacite

**taciturn** ['tæsɪtəːn] *adj* taciturne

**tack** [tæk] *n* (*nail*) petit clou; (*stitch*) point *m* de bâti; (*Naut*) bord *m*, bordée *f*; (*fig*) direction *f* ▷ *vt* (*nail*) clouer; (*sew*) bâtir ▷ *vi* (*Naut*) tirer un *or* des bord(s); **to change ~** virer de bord; **on the wrong ~** (*fig*) sur la mauvaise voie; **to ~ sth on to (the end of) sth** (*of letter, book*) rajouter qch à la fin de qch

**tackle** ['tækl] *n* matériel *m*, équipement *m*; (*for lifting*) appareil *m* de levage; (*Football, Rugby*) plaquage *m* ▷ *vt* (*difficulty, animal, burglar*) s'attaquer à; (*person: challenge*) s'expliquer avec; (*Football, Rugby*) plaquer

**tacky** ['tækɪ] *adj* collant(e); (*paint*) pas sec (sèche); (*inf: shabby*) moche; (*pej: poor-quality*) minable; (: *showing bad taste*) ringard(e)

**tact** [tækt] *n* tact *m*

**tactful** ['tæktful] *adj* plein(e) de tact

**tactfully** ['tæktfəlɪ] *adv* avec tact

**tactical** ['tæktɪkl] *adj* tactique; **~ error** erreur *f* de tactique

**tactician** [tæk'tɪʃən] *n* tacticien(ne)

**tactics** ['tæktɪks] *n, npl* tactique *f*

**tactless** ['tæktlɪs] *adj* qui manque de tact

**tactlessly** ['tæktlɪslɪ] *adv* sans tact

**tadpole** ['tædpəul] *n* têtard *m*

**Tadzhikistan** [tædʒɪkɪ'stɑːn] *n* = **Tajikistan**

**taffy** ['tæfɪ] *n* (*US*) (bonbon *m* au) caramel *m*

**tag** [tæg] *n* étiquette *f*; **price/name ~** étiquette (portant le prix/le nom)
  ▸ **tag along** *vi* suivre

**Tahiti** [tɑː'hiːtɪ] *n* Tahiti *m*

**tail** [teɪl] *n* queue *f*; (*of shirt*) pan *m* ▷ *vt* (*follow*) suivre, filer; **tails** *npl* (*suit*) habit *m*; **to turn ~** se sauver à toutes jambes; *see also* **head**
  ▸ **tail away, tail off** *vi* (*in size, quality etc*) baisser peu à peu

**tailback** ['teɪlbæk] *n* (*Brit*) bouchon *m*

**tail coat** *n* habit *m*

**tail end** *n* bout *m*, fin *f*

**tailgate** ['teɪlgeɪt] *n* (*Aut*) hayon *m* arrière

**tail light** *n* (*Aut*) feu *m* arrière

**tailor** ['teɪlə'] *n* tailleur *m* (*artisan*) ▷ *vt*: **to ~ sth (to)** adapter qch exactement (à); **~'s (shop)**

(boutique f de) tailleur m

**tailoring** ['teɪlərɪŋ] n (cut) coupe f

**tailor-made** ['teɪlə'meɪd] adj fait(e) sur mesure; (fig) conçu(e) spécialement

**tailwind** ['teɪlwɪnd] n vent m arrière inv

**taint** [teɪnt] vt (meat, food) gâter; (fig: reputation) salir

**tainted** ['teɪntɪd] adj (food) gâté(e); (water, air) infecté(e); (fig) souillé(e)

**Taiwan** ['taɪ'wɑːn] n Taïwan (no article)

**Taiwanese** [taɪwə'niːz] adj taïwanais(e) ▷ n inv Taïwanais(e)

**Tajikistan** [tædʒɪkɪ'stɑːn] n Tadjikistan m/f

**take** [teɪk] (pt **took**, pp **-n**) [tuk, 'teɪkn] vt prendre; (gain: prize) remporter; (require: effort, courage) demander; (tolerate) accepter, supporter; (hold: passengers etc) contenir; (accompany) emmener, accompagner; (bring, carry) apporter, emporter; (exam) passer, se présenter à; (conduct: meeting) présider ▷ vi (dye, fire etc) prendre ▷ n (Cine) prise f de vues; **to ~ sth from** (drawer etc) prendre qch dans; (person) prendre qch à; **I ~ it that** je suppose que; **I took him for a doctor** je l'ai pris pour un docteur; **to ~ sb's hand** prendre qn par la main; **to ~ for a walk** (child, dog) emmener promener; **to be ~n ill** tomber malade; **to ~ it upon o.s. to do sth** prendre sur soi de faire qch; **~ the first (street) on the left** prenez la première à gauche; **it won't ~ long** ça ne prendra pas longtemps; **I was quite ~n with her/it** elle/cela m'a beaucoup plu

▶ **take after** vt fus ressembler à

▶ **take apart** vt démonter

▶ **take away** vt (carry off) emporter; (remove) enlever; (subtract) soustraire ▷ vi: **to ~ away from** diminuer

▶ **take back** vt (return) rendre, rapporter; (one's words) retirer

▶ **take down** vt (building) démolir; (dismantle: scaffolding) démonter; (letter etc) prendre, écrire

▶ **take in** vt (deceive) tromper, rouler; (understand) comprendre, saisir; (include) couvrir, inclure; (lodger) prendre; (orphan, stray dog) recueillir; (dress, waistband) reprendre

▶ **take off** vi (Aviat) décoller ▷ vt (remove) enlever; (imitate) imiter, pasticher

▶ **take on** vt (work) accepter, se charger de; (employee) prendre, embaucher; (opponent) accepter de se battre contre

▶ **take out** vt sortir; (remove) enlever; (invite) sortir avec; (licence) prendre, se procurer; **to ~ sth out of** enlever qch de; (out of drawer etc) prendre qch dans; **don't ~ it out on me!** ne t'en prends pas à moi!; **to ~ sb out to a restaurant** emmener qn au restaurant

▶ **take over** vt (business) reprendre ▷ vi: **to ~ over from sb** prendre la relève de qn

▶ **take to** vt fus (person) se prendre d'amitié pour; (activity) prendre goût à; **to ~ to doing sth** prendre l'habitude de faire qch

▶ **take up** vt (one's story) reprendre; (dress)

raccourcir; (occupy: time, space) prendre, occuper; (engage in: hobby etc) se mettre à; (accept: offer, challenge) accepter; (absorb: liquids) absorber ▷ vi: **to ~ up with sb** se lier d'amitié avec qn

**takeaway** ['teɪkəweɪ] (Brit) adj (food) à emporter ▷ n (shop, restaurant) ≈ magasin m qui vend des plats à emporter

**take-home pay** ['teɪkhəum-] n salaire net

**taken** ['teɪkən] pp of **take**

**takeoff** ['teɪkɔf] n (Aviat) décollage m

**takeout** ['teɪkaut] adj, n (US) = **takeaway**

**takeover** ['teɪkəuvər] n (Comm) rachat m

**takeover bid** n offre publique d'achat, OPA f

**takings** ['teɪkɪŋz] npl (Comm) recette f

**talc** [tælk] n (also: **talcum powder**) talc m

**tale** [teɪl] n (story) conte m, histoire f; (account) récit m; (pej) histoire; **to tell ~s** (fig) rapporter

**talent** ['tælnt] n talent m, don m

**talented** ['tæləntɪd] adj doué(e), plein(e) de talent

**talent scout** n découvreur m de vedettes (or joueurs etc)

**talisman** ['tælɪzmən] n talisman m

**talk** [tɔːk] n (a speech) causerie f, exposé m; (conversation) discussion f; (interview) entretien m, propos mpl; (gossip) racontars mpl (pej) ▷ vi parler; (chatter) bavarder; **talks** npl (Pol etc) entretiens mpl; conférence f; **to give a ~** faire un exposé; **to ~ about** parler de; (converse) s'entretenir or parler de; **~ing of films, have you seen …?** à propos de films, as-tu vu …?; **to ~ sb out of/into doing** persuader qn de ne pas faire/de faire; **to ~ shop** parler métier or affaires

▶ **talk over** vt discuter (de)

**talkative** ['tɔːkətɪv] adj bavard(e)

**talking point** ['tɔːkɪŋ-] n sujet m de conversation

**talking-to** ['tɔːkɪŋtu] n: **to give sb a good ~** passer un savon à qn

**talk show** n (TV, Radio) émission-débat f

**tall** [tɔːl] adj (person) grand(e); (building, tree) haut(e); **to be 6 feet ~** ≈ mesurer 1 mètre 80; **how ~ are you?** combien mesurez-vous?

**tallboy** ['tɔːlbɔɪ] n (Brit) grande commode

**tallness** ['tɔːlnɪs] n grande taille; hauteur f

**tall story** n histoire f invraisemblable

**tally** ['tælɪ] n compte m ▷ vi: **to ~ (with)** correspondre (à); **to keep a ~ of sth** tenir le compte de qch

**talon** ['tælən] n griffe f; (of eagle) serre f

**tambourine** [tæmbə'riːn] n tambourin m

**tame** [teɪm] adj apprivoisé(e); (fig: story, style) insipide

**Tamil** ['tæmɪl] adj tamoul(e) or tamil(e) ▷ n Tamoul(e) or Tamil(e); (Ling) tamoul m or tamil m

**tamper** ['tæmpər] vi: **to ~ with** toucher à (en cachette ou sans permission)

**tampon** ['tæmpən] n tampon m hygiénique or périodique

**tan** [tæn] n (also: **suntan**) bronzage m ▷ vt, vi

**t**

bronzer, brunir ▷ adj (colour) marron clair inv; **to get a ~** bronzer

**tandem** ['tændəm] n tandem m

**tandoori** [tæn'duərɪ] adj tandouri

**tang** [tæŋ] n odeur (or saveur) piquante

**tangent** ['tændʒənt] n (Math) tangente f; **to go off at a ~** (fig) partir dans une digression

**tangerine** [tændʒə'riːn] n mandarine f

**tangible** ['tændʒəbl] adj tangible; **~ assets** biens réels

**Tangier** [tæn'dʒɪər] n Tanger

**tangle** ['tæŋgl] n enchevêtrement m ▷ vt enchevêtrer; **to get in(to) a ~** s'emmêler

**tango** ['tæŋgəu] n tango m

**tank** [tæŋk] n réservoir m; (for processing) cuve f; (for fish) aquarium m; (Mil) char m d'assaut, tank m

**tankard** ['tæŋkəd] n chope f

**tanker** ['tæŋkər] n (ship) pétrolier m, tanker m; (truck) camion-citerne m; (Rail) wagon-citerne m

**tankini** [tæn'kɪnɪ] n tankini m

**tanned** [tænd] adj bronzé(e)

**tannin** ['tænɪn] n tanin m

**tanning** ['tænɪŋ] n (of leather) tannage m

**tannoy®** ['tænɔɪ] n (Brit) haut-parleur m; **over the tannoy** par haut-parleur

**tantalizing** ['tæntəlaɪzɪŋ] adj (smell) extrêmement appétissant(e); (offer) terriblement tentant(e)

**tantamount** ['tæntəmaunt] adj: **~ to** qui équivaut à

**tantrum** ['tæntrəm] n accès m de colère; **to throw a ~** piquer une colère

**Tanzania** [tænzə'nɪə] n Tanzanie f

**Tanzanian** [tænzə'nɪən] adj tanzanien(ne) ▷ n Tanzanien(ne)

**tap** [tæp] n (on sink etc) robinet m; (gentle blow) petite tape ▷ vt frapper or taper légèrement; (resources) exploiter, utiliser; (telephone) mettre sur écoute; **on ~** (beer) en tonneau; (fig: resources) disponible

**tap dancing** ['tæpdɑːnsɪŋ] n claquettes fpl

**tape** [teɪp] n (for tying) ruban m; (also: **magnetic tape**) bande f (magnétique); (cassette) cassette f; (sticky) Scotch® m ▷ vt (record) enregistrer (au magnétoscope or sur cassette); (stick) coller avec du Scotch®; **on ~** (song etc) enregistré(e)

**tape measure** n mètre m à ruban

**taper** ['teɪpər] n cierge m ▷ vi s'effiler

**tape recorder** n magnétophone m

**tapered** ['teɪpəd], **tapering** ['teɪpərɪŋ] adj fuselé(e), effilé(e)

**tapestry** ['tæpɪstrɪ] n tapisserie f

**tape-worm** ['teɪpwəːm] n ver m solitaire, ténia m

**tapioca** [tæpɪ'əukə] n tapioca m

**tappet** ['tæpɪt] n (Aut) poussoir m (de soupape)

**tar** [tɑː] n goudron m; **low-/middle-~ cigarettes** cigarettes fpl à faible/moyenne teneur en goudron

**tarantula** [tə'ræntjulə] n tarentule f

**tardy** ['tɑːdɪ] adj tardif(-ive)

**target** ['tɑːgɪt] n cible f; (fig: objective) objectif m; **to be on ~** (project) progresser comme prévu

**target practice** n exercices mpl de tir (à la cible)

**tariff** ['tærɪf] n (Comm) tarif m; (taxes) tarif douanier

**tarmac** ['tɑːmæk] n (Brit: on road) macadam m; (Aviat) aire f d'envol ▷ vt (Brit) goudronner

**tarnish** ['tɑːnɪʃ] vt ternir

**tarot** ['tærəu] n tarot m

**tarpaulin** [tɑː'pɔːlɪn] n bâche goudronnée

**tarragon** ['tærəgən] n estragon m

**tart** [tɑːt] n (Culin) tarte f; (Brit inf: pej: prostitute) poule f ▷ adj (flavour) âpre, aigrelet(te)
  ▶ **tart up** vt (inf): **to ~ o.s. up** se faire beau (belle); (: pej) s'attifer

**tartan** ['tɑːtn] n tartan m ▷ adj écossais(e)

**tartar** ['tɑːtər] n (on teeth) tartre m

**tartar sauce, tartare sauce** n sauce f tartare

**task** [tɑːsk] n tâche f; **to take to ~** prendre à partie

**task force** n (Mil, Police) détachement spécial

**taskmaster** ['tɑːskmɑːstər] n: **he's a hard ~** il est très exigeant dans le travail

**Tasmania** [tæz'meɪnɪə] n Tasmanie f

**tassel** ['tæsl] n gland m; pompon m

**taste** [teɪst] n goût m; (fig: glimpse, idea) idée f, aperçu m ▷ vt goûter ▷ vi: **to ~ of** (fish etc) avoir le or un goût de; **it ~s like fish** ça a un or le goût de poisson, on dirait du poisson; **what does it ~ like?** quel goût ça a?; **you can ~ the garlic (in it)** on sent bien l'ail; **to have a ~ of sth** goûter (à) qch; **can I have a ~?** je peux goûter?; **to have a ~ for sth** aimer qch, avoir un penchant pour qch; **to be in good/bad** or **poor ~** être de bon/ mauvais goût

**taste bud** n papille f

**tasteful** ['teɪstful] adj de bon goût

**tastefully** ['teɪstfəlɪ] adv avec goût

**tasteless** ['teɪstlɪs] adj (food) insipide; (remark) de mauvais goût

**tasty** ['teɪstɪ] adj savoureux(-euse), délicieux(-euse)

**tattered** ['tætəd] adj see **tatters**

**tatters** ['tætəz] npl: **in ~** (also: **tattered**) en lambeaux

**tattoo** [tə'tuː] n tatouage m; (spectacle) parade f militaire ▷ vt tatouer

**tatty** ['tætɪ] adj (Brit inf) défraîchi(e), en piteux état

**taught** [tɔːt] pt, pp of **teach**

**taunt** [tɔːnt] n raillerie f ▷ vt railler

**Taurus** ['tɔːrəs] n le Taureau; **to be ~** être du Taureau

**taut** [tɔːt] adj tendu(e)

**tavern** ['tævən] n taverne f

**tawdry** ['tɔːdrɪ] adj (d'un mauvais goût) criard

**tawny** ['tɔːnɪ] adj fauve (couleur)

**tax** [tæks] n (on goods etc) taxe f; (on income) impôts mpl, contributions fpl ▷ vt taxer; imposer; (fig: patience etc) mettre à l'épreuve; **before/after ~** avant/après l'impôt; **free of ~** exonéré(e) d'impôt

**taxable** ['tæksəbl] adj (income) imposable

**tax allowance** n part f du revenu non imposable, abattement m à la base

**taxation** [tæk'seɪʃən] n taxation f; impôts mpl, contributions fpl; **system of ~** système fiscal

**tax avoidance** n évasion fiscale

**tax collector** n percepteur m

**tax disc** n (Brit Aut) vignette f (automobile)

**tax evasion** n fraude fiscale

**tax exemption** n exonération fiscale, exemption f d'impôts

**tax exile** n personne qui s'expatrie pour raisons fiscales

**tax-free** ['tæksfri:] adj exempt(e) d'impôts

**tax haven** n paradis fiscal

**taxi** ['tæksɪ] n taxi m ▷ vi (Aviat) rouler (lentement) au sol

**taxidermist** ['tæksɪdə:mɪst] n empailleur(-euse) (d'animaux)

**taxi driver** n chauffeur m de taxi

**tax inspector** n (Brit) percepteur m

**taxi rank**, (Brit) **taxi stand** n station f de taxis

**tax payer** [-peɪə'] n contribuable m/f

**tax rebate** n ristourne f d'impôt

**tax relief** n dégrèvement or allègement fiscal, réduction f d'impôt

**tax return** n déclaration f d'impôts or de revenus

**tax year** n année fiscale

**TB** n abbr = **tuberculosis**

**tbc** abbr = **to be confirmed**

**TD** n abbr (US) = **Treasury Department**; (: Football) = **touchdown**

**tea** [ti:] n thé m; (Brit: snack: for children) goûter m; **high ~** (Brit) collation combinant goûter et dîner

**tea bag** n sachet m de thé

**tea break** n (Brit) pause-thé f

**teacake** ['ti:keɪk] n (Brit) ≈ petit pain aux raisins

**teach** (pt, pp **taught**) [ti:tʃ, tɔ:t] vt: **to ~ sb sth, to ~ sth to sb** apprendre qch à qn; (in school etc) enseigner qch à qn ▷ vi enseigner; **it taught him a lesson** (fig) ça lui a servi de leçon

**teacher** ['ti:tʃə'] n (in secondary school) professeur m; (in primary school) instituteur(-trice); **French ~** professeur de français

**teacher training college** n (for primary schools) ≈ école normale d'instituteurs; (for secondary schools) collège m de formation pédagogique (pour l'enseignement secondaire)

**teaching** ['ti:tʃɪŋ] n enseignement m

**teaching aids** npl supports mpl pédagogiques

**teaching hospital** n (Brit) C.H.U. m, centre m hospitalo-universitaire

**teaching staff** n (Brit) enseignants mpl

**tea cosy** n couvre-théière m

**teacup** ['ti:kʌp] n tasse f à thé

**teak** [ti:k] n teck m ▷ adj en or de teck

**tea leaves** npl feuilles fpl de thé

**team** [ti:m] n équipe f; (of animals) attelage m
▸ **team up** vi: **to ~ up (with)** faire équipe (avec)

**team games** npl jeux mpl d'équipe

**teamwork** ['ti:mwə:k] n travail m d'équipe

**tea party** n thé m (réception)

**teapot** ['ti:pɔt] n théière f

**tear¹** ['tɪə'] n larme f; **in ~s** en larmes; **to burst into ~s** fondre en larmes

**tear²** [tɛə'] (pt **tore**, pp **torn**) [tɔː', tɔːn] n déchirure f ▷ vt déchirer ▷ vi se déchirer; **to ~ to pieces** or **to bits** or **to shreds** mettre en pièces; (fig) démolir
▸ **tear along** vi (rush) aller à toute vitesse
▸ **tear apart** vt (also fig) déchirer
▸ **tear away** vt: **to ~ o.s. away (from sth)** (fig) s'arracher (de qch)
▸ **tear down** vt (building, statue) démolir; (poster, flag) arracher
▸ **tear off** vt (sheet of paper etc) arracher; (one's clothes) enlever à toute vitesse
▸ **tear out** vt (sheet of paper, cheque) arracher
▸ **tear up** vt (sheet of paper etc) déchirer, mettre en morceaux or pièces

**tearaway** ['tɛərəweɪ] n (inf) casse-cou m inv

**teardrop** ['tɪədrɔp] n larme f

**tearful** ['tɪəful] adj larmoyant(e)

**tear gas** ['tɪə-] n gaz m lacrymogène

**tearoom** ['ti:ru:m] n salon m de thé

**tease** [ti:z] n taquin(e) ▷ vt taquiner; (unkindly) tourmenter

**tea set** n service m à thé

**teashop** ['ti:ʃɔp] n (Brit) salon m de thé

**teaspoon** ['ti:spu:n] n petite cuiller; (also: **teaspoonful**: as measurement) ≈ cuillerée f à café

**tea strainer** n passoire f (à thé)

**teat** [ti:t] n tétine f

**teatime** ['ti:taɪm] n l'heure f du thé

**tea towel** n (Brit) torchon m (à vaisselle)

**tea urn** n fontaine f à thé

**tech** [tɛk] n abbr (inf) = **technology**; **technical college**

**technical** ['tɛknɪkl] adj technique

**technical college** n C.E.T. m, collège m d'enseignement technique

**technicality** [tɛknɪ'kælɪtɪ] n technicité f; (detail) détail m technique; **on a legal ~** à cause de (or grâce à) l'application à la lettre d'une subtilité juridique; pour vice de forme

**technically** ['tɛknɪklɪ] adv techniquement; (strictly speaking) en théorie, en principe

**technician** [tɛk'nɪʃən] n technicien(ne)

**technique** [tɛk'ni:k] n technique f

**techno** ['tɛknəu] n (Mus) techno f

**technocrat** ['tɛknəkræt] n technocrate m/f

**technological** [tɛknə'lɔdʒɪkl] adj technologique

**technologist** [tɛk'nɔlədʒɪst] n technologue m/f

**technology** [tɛk'nɔlədʒɪ] n technologie f

**teddy** ['tɛdɪ], **teddy bear** n ours m (en peluche)

**tedious** ['ti:dɪəs] adj fastidieux(-euse)

**tedium** ['ti:dɪəm] n ennui m

**tee** [ti:] n (Golf) tee m

**teem** [ti:m] vi: **to ~ (with)** grouiller (de); **it is ~ing (with rain)** il pleut à torrents

**teen** [ti:n] adj = **teenage** ▷ n (US) = **teenager**

**teenage** ['ti:neɪdʒ] adj (fashions etc) pour jeunes, pour adolescents; (child) qui est adolescent(e)

**teenager** ['ti:neɪdʒə'] n adolescent(e)

**teens** [ti:nz] *npl*: **to be in one's ~** être adolescent(e)

**tee-shirt** ['ti:ʃəːt] *n* = **T-shirt**

**teeter** ['ti:təʳ] *vi* chanceler, vaciller

**teeth** [ti:θ] *npl of* **tooth**

**teethe** [ti:ð] *vi* percer ses dents

**teething ring** ['ti:ðɪŋ-] *n* anneau *m* (*pour bébé qui perce ses dents*)

**teething troubles** ['ti:ðɪŋ-] *npl* (*fig*) difficultés initiales

**teetotal** ['ti:'təutl] *adj* (*person*) qui ne boit jamais d'alcool

**teetotaller**, (*US*) **teetotaler** ['ti:'təutləʳ] *n* personne *f* qui ne boit jamais d'alcool

**TEFL** ['tɛfl] *n abbr* = **Teaching of English as a Foreign Language**

**Teflon®** ['tɛflɔn] *n* Téflon® *m*

**Teheran** [tɛə'raːn] *n* Téhéran *f*

**tel.** *abbr* (= *telephone*) tél

**Tel Aviv** ['tɛlə'vi:v] *n* Tel Aviv

**telecast** ['tɛlɪkaːst] *vt* télédiffuser, téléviser

**telecommunications** ['tɛlɪkəmju:nɪ'keɪʃənz] *n* télécommunications *fpl*

**teleconferencing** [tɛlɪ'kɔnfərənsɪŋ] *n* téléconférence(s) *f(pl)*

**telegram** ['tɛlɪgræm] *n* télégramme *m*

**telegraph** ['tɛlɪgraːf] *n* télégraphe *m*

**telegraphic** [tɛlɪ'græfɪk] *adj* télégraphique

**telegraph pole** ['tɛlɪgraːf-] *n* poteau *m* télégraphique

**telegraph wire** *n* fil *m* télégraphique

**telepathic** [tɛlɪ'pæθɪk] *adj* télépathique

**telepathy** [tə'lɛpəθɪ] *n* télépathie *f*

**telephone** ['tɛlɪfəun] *n* téléphone *m* ▷ *vt* (*person*) téléphoner à; (*message*) téléphoner; **to have a ~** (*Brit*): **to be on the ~** (*subscriber*) être abonné(e) au téléphone; **to be on the ~** (*be speaking*) être au téléphone

**telephone book** *n* = **telephone directory**

**telephone booth**, (*Brit*) **telephone box** *n* cabine *f* téléphonique

**telephone call** *n* appel *m* téléphonique

**telephone directory** *n* annuaire *m* (du téléphone)

**telephone exchange** *n* central *m* (téléphonique)

**telephone number** *n* numéro *m* de téléphone

**telephone operator** *n* téléphoniste *m/f*, standardiste *m/f*

**telephone tapping** [-tæpɪŋ] *n* mise *f* sur écoute

**telephonist** [tə'lɛfənɪst] *n* (*Brit*) téléphoniste *m/f*

**telephoto** ['tɛlɪfəutəu] *adj*: **~ lens** téléobjectif *m*

**teleprinter** ['tɛlɪprɪntəʳ] *n* téléscripteur *m*

**telesales** ['tɛlɪseɪlz] *npl* télévente *f*

**telescope** ['tɛlɪskəup] *n* télescope *m* ▷ *vi* se télescoper ▷ *vt* télescoper

**telescopic** [tɛlɪ'skɔpɪk] *adj* télescopique; (*umbrella*) à manche télescopique

**Teletext®** ['tɛlɪtɛkst] *n* télétexte *m*

**telethon** ['tɛlɪθɔn] *n* téléthon *m*

**televise** ['tɛlɪvaɪz] *vt* téléviser

**television** ['tɛlɪvɪʒən] *n* télévision *f*; **on ~** à la télévision

**television licence** *n* (*Brit*) redevance *f* (de l'audio-visuel)

**television programme** *n* émission *f* de télévision

**television set** *n* poste *m* de télévision, téléviseur *m*

**telex** ['tɛlɛks] *n* télex *m* ▷ *vt* (*message*) envoyer par télex; (*person*) envoyer un télex à ▷ *vi* envoyer un télex

**tell** (*pt, pp* **told**) [tɛl, təuld] *vt* dire; (*relate: story*) raconter; (*distinguish*): **to ~ sth from** distinguer qch de ▷ *vi* (*talk*): **to ~ of** parler de; (*have effect*) se faire sentir, se voir; **to ~ sb to do** dire à qn de faire; **to ~ sb about sth** (*place, object etc*) parler de qch à qn; (*what happened etc*) raconter qch à qn; **to ~ the time** (*know how to*) savoir lire l'heure; **can you ~ me the time?** pourriez-vous me dire l'heure?; (**I**) **~ you what**, ... écoute, ...; **I can't ~ them apart** je n'arrive pas à les distinguer

▶ **tell off** *vt* réprimander, gronder

▶ **tell on** *vt fus* (*inform against*) dénoncer, rapporter contre

**teller** ['tɛləʳ] *n* (*in bank*) caissier(-ière)

**telling** ['tɛlɪŋ] *adj* (*remark, detail*) révélateur(-trice)

**telltale** ['tɛlteɪl] *n* rapporteur(-euse) ▷ *adj* (*sign*) éloquent(e), révélateur(-trice)

**telly** ['tɛlɪ] *n abbr* (*Brit inf*: = *television*) télé *f*

**temerity** [tə'mɛrɪtɪ] *n* témérité *f*

**temp** [tɛmp] *n* (*Brit*: = *temporary worker*) intérimaire *m/f* ▷ *vi* travailler comme intérimaire

**temper** ['tɛmpəʳ] *n* (*nature*) caractère *m*; (*mood*) humeur *f*; (*fit of anger*) colère *f* ▷ *vt* (*moderate*) tempérer, adoucir; **to be in a ~** être en colère; **to lose one's ~** se mettre en colère; **to keep one's ~** rester calme

**temperament** ['tɛmprəmənt] *n* (*nature*) tempérament *m*

**temperamental** [tɛmprə'mɛntl] *adj* capricieux(-euse)

**temperance** ['tɛmpərns] *n* modération *f*; (*in drinking*) tempérance *f*

**temperate** ['tɛmprət] *adj* modéré(e); (*climate*) tempéré(e)

**temperature** ['tɛmprətʃəʳ] *n* température *f*; **to have** *or* **run a ~** avoir de la fièvre

**temperature chart** *n* (*Med*) feuille *f* de température

**tempered** ['tɛmpəd] *adj* (*steel*) trempé(e)

**tempest** ['tɛmpɪst] *n* tempête *f*

**tempestuous** [tɛm'pɛstjuəs] *adj* (*fig*) orageux(-euse); (: *person*) passionné(e)

**tempi** ['tɛmpi:] *npl of* **tempo**

**template** ['tɛmplɪt] *n* patron *m*

**temple** ['tɛmpl] *n* (*building*) temple *m*; (*Anat*) tempe *f*

**templet** ['tɛmplɪt] *n* = **template**

**tempo** (*pl* **-s** *or* **tempi**) ['tɛmpəu, 'tɛmpi:] *n*

tempo *m*; *(fig: of life etc)* rythme *m*
**temporal** ['tɛmpərl] *adj* temporel(le)
**temporarily** ['tɛmpərərɪlɪ] *adv* temporairement; provisoirement
**temporary** ['tɛmpərərɪ] *adj* temporaire, provisoire; *(job, worker)* temporaire; ~ **secretary** (secrétaire *f*) intérimaire *f*; **a** ~ **teacher** un professeur remplaçant *or* suppléant
**temporize** ['tɛmpəraɪz] *vi* atermoyer; transiger
**tempt** [tɛmpt] *vt* tenter; **to** ~ **sb into doing** induire qn à faire; **to be ~ed to do sth** être tenté(e) de faire qch
**temptation** [tɛmp'teɪʃən] *n* tentation *f*
**tempting** ['tɛmptɪŋ] *adj* tentant(e); *(food)* appétissant(e)
**ten** [tɛn] *num* dix ▷ *n*: ~**s of thousands** des dizaines *fpl* de milliers
**tenable** ['tɛnəbl] *adj* défendable
**tenacious** [tə'neɪʃəs] *adj* tenace
**tenacity** [tə'næsɪtɪ] *n* ténacité *f*
**tenancy** ['tɛnənsɪ] *n* location *f*; état *m* de locataire
**tenant** ['tɛnənt] *n* locataire *m/f*
**tend** [tɛnd] *vt* s'occuper de; *(sick etc)* soigner ▷ *vi*: **to** ~ **to do** avoir tendance à faire; *(colour)*: **to** ~ **to** tirer sur
**tendency** ['tɛndənsɪ] *n* tendance *f*
**tender** ['tɛndə$^r$] *adj* tendre; *(delicate)* délicat(e); *(sore)* sensible; *(affectionate)* tendre, doux (douce) ▷ *n* *(Comm: offer)* soumission *f*; *(money)*: **legal** ~ cours légal ▷ *vt* offrir; **to** ~ **one's resignation** donner sa démission; **to put in a** ~ **(for)** faire une soumission (pour); **to put work out to** ~ *(Brit)* mettre un contrat en adjudication
**tenderize** ['tɛndəraɪz] *vt* *(Culin)* attendrir
**tenderly** ['tɛndəlɪ] *adv* tendrement
**tenderness** ['tɛndənɪs] *n* tendresse *f*; *(of meat)* tendreté *f*
**tendon** ['tɛndən] *n* tendon *m*
**tenement** ['tɛnəmənt] *n* immeuble *m* (de rapport)
**Tenerife** [tɛnə'ri:f] *n* Ténérife *f*
**tenet** ['tɛnət] *n* principe *m*
**Tenn.** *abbr* *(US)* = **Tennessee**
**tenner** ['tɛnə$^r$] *n* *(Brit inf)* billet *m* de dix livres
**tennis** ['tɛnɪs] *n* tennis *m* ▷ *cpd* *(club, match, racket, player)* de tennis
**tennis ball** *n* balle *f* de tennis
**tennis court** *n* (court *m* de) tennis *m*
**tennis elbow** *n* *(Med)* synovite *f* du coude
**tennis match** *n* match *m* de tennis
**tennis player** *n* joueur(-euse) de tennis
**tennis racket** *n* raquette *f* de tennis
**tennis shoes** *npl* (chaussures *fpl* de) tennis *mpl*
**tenor** ['tɛnə$^r$] *n* *(Mus)* ténor *m*; *(of speech etc)* sens général
**tenpin bowling** ['tɛnpɪn-] *n* *(Brit)* bowling *m* (à 10 quilles)
**tense** [tɛns] *adj* tendu(e); *(person)* tendu, crispé(e) ▷ *n* *(Ling)* temps *m* ▷ *vt* *(tighten: muscles)* tendre
**tenseness** ['tɛnsnɪs] *n* tension *f*

**tension** ['tɛnʃən] *n* tension *f*
**tent** [tɛnt] *n* tente *f*
**tentacle** ['tɛntəkl] *n* tentacule *m*
**tentative** ['tɛntətɪv] *adj* timide, hésitant(e); *(conclusion)* provisoire
**tenterhooks** ['tɛntəhuks] *npl*: **on** ~ sur des charbons ardents
**tenth** [tɛnθ] *num* dixième
**tent peg** *n* piquet *m* de tente
**tent pole** *n* montant *m* de tente
**tenuous** ['tɛnjuəs] *adj* ténu(e)
**tenure** ['tɛnjuə$^r$] *n* *(of property)* bail *m*; *(of job)* période *f* de jouissance; statut *m* de titulaire
**tepid** ['tɛpɪd] *adj* tiède
**Ter.** *abbr* = **terrace**
**term** [tə:m] *n* *(limit)* terme *m*; *(word)* terme, mot *m*; *(Scol)* trimestre *m*; *(Law)* session *f* ▷ *vt* appeler; **terms** *npl* *(conditions)* conditions *fpl*; *(Comm)* tarif *m*; ~ **of imprisonment** peine *f* de prison; **his** ~ **of office** la période où il était en fonction; **in the short/long** ~ à court/long terme; **"easy ~s"** *(Comm)* "facilités de paiement"; **to come to ~s with** *(problem)* faire face à; **to be on good ~s with** bien s'entendre avec, être en bons termes avec
**terminal** ['tə:mɪnl] *adj* terminal(e); *(disease)* dans sa phase terminale; *(patient)* incurable ▷ *n* *(Elec)* borne *f*; *(for oil, ore etc, also Comput)* terminal *m*; *(also:* **air terminal)** aérogare *f*; *(Brit: also:* **coach terminal)** gare routière
**terminally** ['tə:mɪnlɪ] *adv*: **to be ~ ill** être condamné(e)
**terminate** ['tə:mɪneɪt] *vt* mettre fin à; *(pregnancy)* interrompre ▷ *vi*: **to ~ in** finir en *or* par
**termination** [tə:mɪ'neɪʃən] *n* fin *f*; cessation *f*; *(of contract)* résiliation *f*; ~ **of pregnancy** *(Med)* interruption *f* de grossesse
**termini** ['tə:mɪnaɪ] *npl* *of* **terminus**
**terminology** [tə:mɪ'nɔlədʒɪ] *n* terminologie *f*
**terminus** *(pl* **termini)** ['tə:mɪnəs, 'tə:mɪnaɪ] *n* terminus *m inv*
**termite** ['tə:maɪt] *n* termite *m*
**term paper** *n* *(US University)* dissertation trimestrielle
**terrace** ['tɛrəs] *n* terrasse *f*; *(Brit: row of houses)* rangée *f* de maisons *(attenantes les unes aux autres)*; **the ~s** *(Brit Sport)* les gradins *mpl*
**terraced** ['tɛrəst] *adj* *(garden)* en terrasses; *(in a row: house)* attenant(e) aux maisons voisines
**terracotta** ['tɛrə'kɔtə] *n* terre cuite
**terrain** [tɛ'reɪn] *n* terrain *m* (sol)
**terrestrial** [tɪ'rɛstrɪəl] *adj* terrestre
**terrible** ['tɛrɪbl] *adj* terrible, atroce; *(weather, work)* affreux(-euse), épouvantable
**terribly** ['tɛrɪblɪ] *adv* terriblement; *(very badly)* affreusement mal
**terrier** ['tɛrɪə$^r$] *n* terrier *m* *(chien)*
**terrific** [tə'rɪfɪk] *adj* *(very great)* fantastique, incroyable, terrible; *(wonderful)* formidable, sensationnel(le)
**terrified** ['tɛrɪfaɪd] *adj* terrifié(e); **to be ~ of sth**

**t**

avoir très peur de qch
**terrify** ['tɛrɪfaɪ] vt terrifier
**terrifying** ['tɛrɪfaɪɪŋ] adj terrifiant(e)
**territorial** [tɛrɪ'tɔːrɪəl] adj territorial(e)
**territorial waters** npl eaux territoriales
**territory** ['tɛrɪtərɪ] n territoire m
**terror** ['tɛrəʳ] n terreur f
**terrorism** ['tɛrərɪzəm] n terrorisme m
**terrorist** ['tɛrərɪst] n terroriste m/f
**terrorist attack** n attentat m terroriste
**terrorize** ['tɛrəraɪz] vt terroriser
**terse** [təːs] adj (style) concis(e); (reply) laconique
**tertiary** ['təːʃərɪ] adj tertiaire; ~ education (Brit) enseignement m postscolaire
**TESL** ['tɛsl] n abbr = **Teaching of English as a Second Language**
**test** [tɛst] n (trial, check) essai m; (: of goods in factory) contrôle m; (of courage etc) épreuve f; (Med) examen m; (Chem) analyse f; (exam: of intelligence etc) test m (d'aptitude); (Scol) interrogation f de contrôle; (also: **driving test**) (examen du) permis m de conduire ▷ vt essayer; contrôler; mettre à l'épreuve; examiner; analyser; tester; faire subir une interrogation à; **to put sth to the ~** mettre qch à l'épreuve
**testament** ['tɛstəmənt] n testament m; **the Old/New T~** l'Ancien/le Nouveau Testament
**test ban** n (also: **nuclear test ban**) interdiction f des essais nucléaires
**test case** n (Law) affaire f qui fait jurisprudence
**testes** ['tɛstiːz] npl testicules mpl
**test flight** n vol m d'essai
**testicle** ['tɛstɪkl] n testicule m
**testify** ['tɛstɪfaɪ] vi (Law) témoigner, déposer; **to ~ to sth** (Law) attester qch; (gen) témoigner de qch
**testimonial** [tɛstɪ'məunɪəl] n (Brit: reference) recommandation f; (gift) témoignage m d'estime
**testimony** ['tɛstɪmənɪ] n (Law) témoignage m, déposition f
**testing** ['tɛstɪŋ] adj (situation, period) difficile
**test match** n (Cricket, Rugby) match international
**testosterone** [tɛs'tɔstərəun] n testostérone f
**test paper** n (Scol) interrogation écrite
**test pilot** n pilote m d'essai
**test tube** n éprouvette f
**test-tube baby** ['tɛsttjuːb-] n bébé-éprouvette m
**testy** ['tɛstɪ] adj irritable
**tetanus** ['tɛtənəs] n tétanos m
**tetchy** ['tɛtʃɪ] adj hargneux(-euse)
**tether** ['tɛðəʳ] vt attacher ▷ n: **at the end of one's ~** à bout (de patience)
**Tex.** abbr (US) = **Texas**
**text** [tɛkst] n texte m; (on mobile phone) texto m, SMS m inv ▷ vt (inf) envoyer un texto or SMS à
**textbook** ['tɛkstbuk] n manuel m
**textile** ['tɛkstaɪl] n textile m

**text message** n texto m, SMS m inv
**text messaging** [-'mɛsɪdʒɪŋ] n messagerie textuelle
**textual** ['tɛkstjuəl] adj textuel(le)
**texture** ['tɛkstʃəʳ] n texture f; (of skin, paper etc) grain m
**TGIF** abbr (inf) = **thank God it's Friday**
**TGWU** n abbr (Brit: = Transport and General Workers' Union) syndicat de transporteurs
**Thai** [taɪ] adj thaïlandais(e) ▷ n Thaïlandais(e); (Ling) thaï m
**Thailand** ['taɪlænd] n Thaïlande f
**Thames** [tɛmz] n: **the (River)** ~ la Tamise
**than** [ðæn, ðən] conj que; (with numerals): **more ~ 10/once** plus de 10/d'une fois; **I have more/less ~ you** j'en ai plus/moins que toi; **she has more apples ~ pears** elle a plus de pommes que de poires; **it is better to phone ~ to write** il vaut mieux téléphoner (plutôt) qu'écrire; **she is older ~ you think** elle est plus âgée que tu le crois; **no sooner did he leave ~ the phone rang** il venait de partir quand le téléphone a sonné
**thank** [θæŋk] vt remercier, dire merci à; **thanks** npl remerciements mpl ▷ excl merci!; **~ you (very much)** merci (beaucoup); **~ heavens, ~ God** Dieu merci; **~s to** (prep) grâce à
**thankful** ['θæŋkful] adj: **~ (for)** reconnaissant(e) (de); **~ for/that** (relieved) soulagé(e) de/que
**thankfully** ['θæŋkfəlɪ] adv avec reconnaissance; avec soulagement; (fortunately) heureusement; **~ there were few victims** il y eut fort heureusement peu de victimes
**thankless** ['θæŋklɪs] adj ingrat(e)
**Thanksgiving** ['θæŋksɡɪvɪŋ], **Thanksgiving Day** n jour m d'action de grâce

🅞 KEYWORD

**that** [ðæt] adj (demonstrative: pl **those**) ce, cet + vowel or h mute, cette f; **that man/woman/book** cet homme/cette femme/ce livre; (not this) cet homme-là/cette femme-là/ce livre-là; **that one** celui-là (celle-là)
▷ pron **1** (demonstrative: pl **those**) ce; (not this one) cela, ça; (that one) celui (celle); **who's that?** qui est-ce?; **what's that?** qu'est-ce que c'est?; **is that you?** c'est toi?; **I prefer this to that** je préfère ceci à cela or ça; **that's what he said** c'est or voilà ce qu'il a dit; **will you eat all that?** tu vas manger tout ça?; **that is (to say)** c'est-à-dire, à savoir; **at or with that, he ...** là-dessus, il ...; **do it like that** fais-le comme ça
**2** (relative: subject) qui; (: object) que; (: after prep) lequel (laquelle), lesquels (lesquelles) pl; **the book that I read** le livre que j'ai lu; **the books that are in the library** les livres qui sont dans la bibliothèque; **all that I have** tout ce que j'ai; **the box that I put it in** la boîte dans laquelle je l'ai mis; **the people that I spoke to** les gens auxquels or à qui j'ai parlé; **not that I know of** pas à ma connaissance

**3** (*relative: of time*) où; **the day that he came** le jour où il est venu
▷ *conj* que; **he thought that I was ill** il pensait que j'étais malade
▷ *adv* (*demonstrative*): **I don't like it that much** ça ne me plaît pas tant que ça; **I didn't know it was that bad** je ne savais pas que c'était si *or* aussi mauvais; **that high** aussi haut; si haut; **it's about that high** c'est à peu près de cette hauteur

**thatched** [θætʃt] *adj* (*roof*) de chaume; **~ cottage** chaumière *f*
**Thatcherism** ['θætʃərɪzəm] *n* thatchérisme *m*
**thaw** [θɔ:] *n* dégel *m* ▷ *vi* (*ice*) fondre; (*food*) dégeler ▷ *vt* (*food*) (faire) dégeler; **it's ~ing** (*weather*) il dégèle

 **KEYWORD**

**the** [ði:, ðə] *def art* **1** (*gen*) le, la *f*, l' + *vowel or h mute*, les *pl* (*NB: à + le(s) =* **au(x)**; *de + le =* **du**; *de + les =* **des**); **the boy/girl/ink** le garçon/la fille/l'encre; **the children** les enfants; **the history of the world** l'histoire du monde; **give it to the postman** donne-le au facteur; **to play the piano/flute** jouer du piano/de la flûte
**2** (+ *adj to form n*) le, la *f*, l' + *vowel or* h mute, les *pl*; **the rich and the poor** les riches et les pauvres; **to attempt the impossible** tenter l'impossible
**3** (*in titles*): **Elizabeth the First** Elisabeth première; **Peter the Great** Pierre le Grand
**4** (*in comparisons*): **the more he works, the more he earns** plus il travaille, plus il gagne de l'argent; **the sooner the better** le plus tôt sera le mieux

**theatre,** (US) **theater** ['θɪətəʳ] *n* théâtre *m*; (*also:* **lecture theatre**) amphithéâtre *m*, amphi *m* (*inf*); (*Med: also:* **operating theatre**) salle *f* d'opération
**theatre-goer,** (US) **theater-goer** ['θɪətəgəʊəʳ] *n* habitué(e) du théâtre
**theatrical** [θɪ'ætrɪkl] *adj* théâtral(e); **~ company** troupe *f* de théâtre
**theft** [θɛft] *n* vol *m* (*larcin*)
**their** [ðɛəʳ] *adj* leur, leurs *pl*; *see also* **my**
**theirs** [ðɛəz] *pron* le (la) leur, les leurs; **it is ~** c'est à eux; **a friend of ~** un de leurs amis; *see also* **mine¹**
**them** [ðɛm, ðəm] *pron* (*direct*) les; (*indirect*) leur; (*stressed, after prep*) eux (elles); **I see ~** je les vois; **give ~ the book** donne-leur le livre; **give me a few of ~** donnez m'en quelques uns (*or* quelques unes); *see also* **me**
**theme** [θi:m] *n* thème *m*
**theme park** *n* parc *m* à thème
**theme song** *n* chanson principale
**themselves** [ðəm'sɛlvz] *pl pron* (*reflexive*) se; (*emphatic, after prep*) eux-mêmes (elles-mêmes); **between ~** entre eux (elles); *see also* **oneself**
**then** [ðɛn] *adv* (*at that time*) alors, à ce moment-

là; (*next*) puis, ensuite; (*and also*) et puis ▷ *conj* (*therefore*) alors, dans ce cas ▷ *adj*: **the ~ president** le président d'alors *or* de l'époque; **by ~** (*past*) à ce moment-là; (*future*) d'ici là; **from ~ on** dès lors; **before ~** avant; **until ~** jusqu'à ce moment-là, jusque-là; **and ~ what?** et puis après?; **what do you want me to do ~?** (*afterwards*) que veux-tu que je fasse ensuite?; (*in that case*) bon alors, qu'est-ce que je fais?
**theologian** [θɪə'ləudʒən] *n* théologien(ne)
**theological** [θɪə'lɔdʒɪkl] *adj* théologique
**theology** [θɪ'ɔlədʒɪ] *n* théologie *f*
**theorem** ['θɪərəm] *n* théorème *m*
**theoretical** [θɪə'rɛtɪkl] *adj* théorique
**theorize** ['θɪəraɪz] *vi* élaborer une théorie; (*pej*) faire des théories
**theory** ['θɪərɪ] *n* théorie *f*
**therapeutic** [θɛrə'pju:tɪk] *adj* thérapeutique
**therapist** ['θɛrəpɪst] *n* thérapeute *m/f*
**therapy** ['θɛrəpɪ] *n* thérapie *f*

 **KEYWORD**

**there** [ðɛəʳ] *adv* **1**: **there is, there are** il y a; **there are 3 of them** (*people, things*) il y en a 3; **there is no-one here/no bread left** il n'y a personne/il n'y a plus de pain; **there has been an accident** il y a eu un accident
**2** (*referring to place*) là, là-bas; **it's there** c'est là(-bas); **in/on/up/down there** là-dedans/là-dessus/là-haut/en bas; **he went there on Friday** il y est allé vendredi; **to go there and back** faire l'aller-retour; **I want that book there** je veux ce livre-là; **there he is!** le voilà!
**3**: **there, there** (*esp to child*) allons, allons!

**thereabouts** ['ðɛərə'bauts] *adv* (*place*) par là, près de là; (*amount*) environ, à peu près
**thereafter** [ðɛər'ɑ:ftəʳ] *adv* par la suite
**thereby** ['ðɛəbaɪ] *adv* ainsi
**therefore** ['ðɛəfɔ:ʳ] *adv* donc, par conséquent
**there's** ['ðɛəz] = **there is; there has**
**thereupon** [ðɛərə'pɔn] *adv* (*at that point*) sur ce; (*formal: on that subject*) à ce sujet
**thermal** ['θə:ml] *adj* thermique; **~ paper/printer** papier *m*/imprimante *f* thermique; **~ underwear** sous-vêtements *mpl* en Thermolactyl®
**thermodynamics** ['θə:mədaɪ'næmɪks] *n* thermodynamique *f*
**thermometer** [θə'mɔmɪtəʳ] *n* thermomètre *m*
**thermonuclear** ['θə:məu'nju:klɪəʳ] *adj* thermonucléaire
**Thermos**® ['θə:məs] *n* (*also:* **Thermos flask**) thermos® *m or f inv*
**thermostat** ['θə:məustæt] *n* thermostat *m*
**thesaurus** [θɪ'sɔ:rəs] *n* dictionnaire *m* synonymique
**these** [ði:z] *pl pron* ceux-ci (celles-ci) ▷ *pl adj* ces; (*not those*): **~ books** ces livres-ci
**thesis** (*pl* **theses**) ['θi:sɪs, 'θi:si:z] *n* thèse *f*
**they** [ðeɪ] *pl pron* ils (elles); (*stressed*) eux (elles); **~**

say that ... (it is said that) on dit que ...
**they'd** [ðeɪd] = **they had; they would**
**they'll** [ðeɪl] = **they shall; they will**
**they're** [ðɛəʳ] = **they are**
**they've** [ðeɪv] = **they have**
**thick** [θɪk] adj épais(se); (crowd) dense; (stupid) bête, borné(e) ▷ n: **in the ~ of** au beau milieu de, en plein cœur de; **it's 20 cm ~** ça a 20 cm d'épaisseur
**thicken** ['θɪkn] vi s'épaissir ▷ vt (sauce etc) épaissir
**thicket** ['θɪkɪt] n fourré m, hallier m
**thickly** ['θɪklɪ] adv (spread) en couche épaisse; (cut) en tranches épaisses; **~ populated** à forte densité de population
**thickness** ['θɪknɪs] n épaisseur f
**thickset** [θɪk'sɛt] adj trapu(e), costaud(e)
**thick-skinned** [θɪk'skɪnd] adj (fig) peu sensible
**thief** (pl **thieves**) [θi:f, θi:vz] n voleur(-euse)
**thieving** ['θi:vɪŋ] n vol m (larcin)
**thigh** [θaɪ] n cuisse f
**thighbone** ['θaɪbəʊn] n fémur m
**thimble** ['θɪmbl] n dé m (à coudre)
**thin** [θɪn] adj mince; (skinny) maigre; (soup) peu épais(se); (hair, crowd) clairsemé(e); (fog) léger(-ère) ▷ vt (hair) éclaircir; (also: **thin down**: sauce, paint) délayer ▷ vi (fog) s'éclaircir; (also: **thin out**: crowd) se disperser; **his hair is ~ning** il se dégarnit
**thing** [θɪŋ] n chose f; (object) objet m; (contraption) truc m; **things** npl (belongings) affaires fpl; **first ~ (in the morning)** à la première heure, tout de suite (le matin); **last ~ (at night), he ...** juste avant de se coucher, il ...; **the ~ is ...** c'est que ...; **for one ~** d'abord; **the best ~ would be to** le mieux serait de; **how are ~s?** comment ça va?; **to have a ~ about** (be obsessed by) être obsédé(e) par; (hate) détester; **poor ~!** le (or la) pauvre!
**think** (pt, pp **thought**) [θɪŋk, θɔ:t] vi penser, réfléchir ▷ vt penser, croire; (imagine) s'imaginer; **to ~ of** penser à; **what do you ~ of it?** qu'en pensez-vous?; **what did you ~ of them?** qu'avez-vous pensé d'eux?; **to ~ about sth/sb** penser à qch/qn; **I'll ~ about it** je vais y réfléchir; **to ~ of doing** avoir l'idée de faire; **I ~ so/not** je crois or pense que oui/non; **to ~ well of** avoir une haute opinion de; **~ again!** attention, réfléchis bien!; **to ~ aloud** penser tout haut
  ▶ **think out** vt (plan) bien réfléchir à; (solution) trouver
  ▶ **think over** vt bien réfléchir à; **I'd like to ~ things over** (offer, suggestion) j'aimerais bien y réfléchir un peu
  ▶ **think through** vt étudier dans tous les détails
  ▶ **think up** vt inventer, trouver
**thinking** ['θɪŋkɪŋ] n: **to my (way of) ~** selon moi
**think tank** n groupe m de réflexion
**thinly** ['θɪnlɪ] adv (cut) en tranches fines; (spread) en couche mince
**thinness** ['θɪnnɪs] n minceur f; maigreur f
**third** [θə:d] num troisième ▷ n troisième m/f; (fraction) tiers m; (Aut) troisième (vitesse) f; (Brit Scol: degree) ≈ licence f avec mention passable; **a ~ of** le tiers de
**third-degree burns** ['θə:dɪdɡri:-] npl brûlures fpl au troisième degré
**thirdly** ['θə:dlɪ] adv troisièmement
**third party insurance** n (Brit) assurance f au tiers
**third-rate** ['θə:d'reɪt] adj de qualité médiocre
**Third World** n: **the ~** le Tiers-Monde
**thirst** [θə:st] n soif f
**thirsty** ['θə:stɪ] adj qui a soif, assoiffé(e); (work) qui donne soif; **to be ~** avoir soif
**thirteen** [θə:'ti:n] num treize
**thirteenth** [-'ti:nθ] num treizième
**thirtieth** ['θə:tɪɪθ] num trentième
**thirty** ['θə:tɪ] num trente

🔵 **KEYWORD**

**this** [ðɪs] adj (demonstrative: pl **these**) ce, cet + vowel or h mute, cette f; **this man/woman/book** cet homme/cette femme/ce livre; (not that) cet homme-ci/cette femme-ci/ce livre-ci; **this one** celui-ci (celle-ci); **this time** cette fois-ci; **this time last year** l'année dernière à la même époque; **this way** (in this direction) par ici; (in this fashion) de cette façon, ainsi
  ▷ pron (demonstrative: pl **these**) ce; (not that one) celui-ci (celle-ci), ceci; **who's this?** qui est-ce?; **what's this?** qu'est-ce que c'est?; **I prefer this to that** je préfère ceci à cela; **they were talking of this and that** ils parlaient de choses et d'autres; **this is where I live** c'est ici que j'habite; **this is what he said** voici ce qu'il a dit; **this is Mr Brown** (in introductions) je vous présente Mr Brown; (in photo) c'est Mr Brown; (on telephone) ici Mr Brown
  ▷ adv (demonstrative): **it was about this big** c'était à peu près de cette grandeur or grand comme ça; **I didn't know it was this bad** je ne savais pas que c'était si or aussi mauvais

**thistle** ['θɪsl] n chardon m
**thong** [θɔŋ] n lanière f
**thorn** [θɔ:n] n épine f
**thorny** ['θɔ:nɪ] adj épineux(-euse)
**thorough** ['θʌrə] adj (search) minutieux(-euse); (knowledge, research) approfondi(e); (work, person) consciencieux(-euse); (cleaning) à fond
**thoroughbred** ['θʌrəbrɛd] n (horse) pur-sang m inv
**thoroughfare** ['θʌrəfɛəʳ] n rue f; **"no ~"** (Brit) "passage interdit"
**thoroughgoing** ['θʌrəɡəʊɪŋ] adj (analysis) approfondi(e); (reform) profond(e)
**thoroughly** ['θʌrəlɪ] adv (search) minutieusement; (study) en profondeur; (clean) à fond; (very) tout à fait; **he ~ agreed** il était tout à fait d'accord
**thoroughness** ['θʌrənɪs] n soin (méticuleux)
**those** [ðəʊz] pl pron ceux-là (celles-là) ▷ pl adj

ces; (not these): ~ **books** ces livres-là

**though** [ðəu] conj bien que + sub, quoique + sub ▷ adv pourtant; **even ~** quand bien même + conditional; **it's not easy,** ~ pourtant, ce n'est pas facile

**thought** [θɔːt] pt, pp of **think** ▷ n pensée f; (idea) idée f; (opinion) avis m; (intention) intention f; **after much ~** après mûre réflexion; **I've just had a ~** je viens de penser à quelque chose; **to give sth some ~** réfléchir à qch

**thoughtful** ['θɔːtful] adj (deep in thought) pensif(-ive); (serious) réfléchi(e); (considerate) prévenant(e)

**thoughtfully** ['θɔːtfəlɪ] adv pensivement; avec prévenance

**thoughtless** ['θɔːtlɪs] adj qui manque de considération

**thoughtlessly** ['θɔːtlɪslɪ] adv inconsidérément

**thought-provoking** ['θɔːtprəvəukɪŋ] adj stimulant(e)

**thousand** ['θauzənd] num mille; **one ~** mille; **two ~** deux mille; **~s of** des milliers de

**thousandth** ['θauzəntθ] num millième

**thrash** [θræʃ] vt rouer de coups; (as punishment) donner une correction à; (inf: defeat) battre à plate(s) couture(s)
  ▸ **thrash about** vi se débattre
  ▸ **thrash out** vt débattre de

**thrashing** ['θræʃɪŋ] n: **to give sb a ~; = to thrash sb**

**thread** [θrɛd] n fil m; (of screw) pas m, filetage m ▷ vt (needle) enfiler; **to ~ one's way between** se faufiler entre

**threadbare** ['θrɛdbɛər] adj râpé(e), élimé(e)

**threat** [θrɛt] n menace f; **to be under ~ of** être menacé(e) de

**threaten** ['θrɛtn] vi (storm) menacer ▷ vt: **to ~ sb with sth/to do** menacer qn de qch/de faire

**threatening** ['θrɛtnɪŋ] adj menaçant(e)

**three** [θriː] num trois

**three-dimensional** [θriːdɪ'mɛnʃənl] adj à trois dimensions; (film) en relief

**threefold** ['θriːfəuld] adv: **to increase ~** tripler

**three-piece suit** ['θriːpiːs-] n complet m (avec gilet)

**three-piece suite** n salon m (canapé et deux fauteuils)

**three-ply** [θriː'plaɪ] adj (wood) à trois épaisseurs; (wool) trois fils inv

**three-quarters** [θriː'kwɔːtəz] npl trois-quarts mpl; **~ full** aux trois-quarts plein

**three-wheeler** [θriː'wiːlər] n (car) voiture f à trois roues

**thresh** [θrɛʃ] vt (Agr) battre

**threshing machine** ['θrɛʃɪŋ-] n batteuse f

**threshold** ['θrɛʃhəuld] n seuil m; **to be on the ~ of** (fig) être au seuil de

**threshold agreement** n (Econ) accord m d'indexation des salaires

**threw** [θruː] pt of **throw**

**thrift** [θrɪft] n économie f

**thrifty** ['θrɪftɪ] adj économe

**thrill** [θrɪl] n (excitement) émotion f, sensation forte; (shudder) frisson m ▷ vi tressaillir, frissonner ▷ vt (audience) électriser

**thrilled** [θrɪld] adj: **~ (with)** ravi(e) de

**thriller** ['θrɪlər] n film m (or roman m or pièce f) à suspense

**thrilling** ['θrɪlɪŋ] adj (book, play etc) saisissant(e); (news, discovery) excitant(e)

**thrive** (pt **-d** or **throve**, pp **-d** or **thriven**) [θraɪv, θrəuv, 'θrɪvn] vi pousser or se développer bien; (business) prospérer; **he ~s on it** cela lui réussit

**thriving** ['θraɪvɪŋ] adj vigoureux(-euse); (business, community) prospère

**throat** [θrəut] n gorge f; **to have a sore ~** avoir mal à la gorge

**throb** [θrɔb] n (of heart) pulsation f; (of engine) vibration f; (of pain) élancement m ▷ vi (heart) palpiter; (engine) vibrer; (pain) lanciner; (wound) causer des élancements; **my head is ~bing** j'ai des élancements dans la tête

**throes** [θrəuz] npl: **in the ~ of** au beau milieu de; en proie à; **in the ~ of death** à l'agonie

**thrombosis** [θrɔm'bəusɪs] n thrombose f

**throne** [θrəun] n trône m

**throng** [θrɔŋ] n foule f ▷ vt se presser dans

**throttle** ['θrɔtl] n (Aut) accélérateur m ▷ vt étrangler

**through** [θruː] prep à travers; (time) pendant, durant; (by means of) par, par l'intermédiaire de; (owing to) à cause de ▷ adj (ticket, train, passage) direct(e) ▷ adv à travers; **(from) Monday ~ Friday** (US) de lundi à vendredi; **to let sb ~** laisser passer qn; **to put sb ~ to sb** (Tel) passer qn à qn; **to be ~** (Brit; Tel) avoir la communication; (esp US: have finished) avoir fini; **"no ~ traffic"** (US) "passage interdit"; **"no ~ road"** (Brit) "impasse"

**throughout** [θruː'aut] prep (place) partout dans; (time) durant tout(e) le (la) ▷ adv partout

**throughput** ['θruːput] n (of goods, materials) quantité de matières premières utilisée; (Comput) débit m

**throve** [θrəuv] pt of **thrive**

**throw** [θrəu] n jet m; (Sport) lancer m ▷ vt (pt **threw**, pp **-n**) [θruː, θrəun] lancer, jeter; (Sport) lancer; (rider) désarçonner; (fig) décontenancer; (pottery) tourner; **to ~ a party** donner une réception
  ▸ **throw about, throw around** vt (litter etc) éparpiller
  ▸ **throw away** vt jeter; (money) gaspiller
  ▸ **throw in** vt (Sport: ball) remettre en jeu; (include) ajouter
  ▸ **throw off** vt se débarrasser de
  ▸ **throw out** vt jeter; (reject) rejeter; (person) mettre à la porte
  ▸ **throw together** vt (clothes, meal etc) assembler à la hâte; (essay) bâcler
  ▸ **throw up** vi vomir

**throwaway** ['θrəuəweɪ] adj à jeter

**throwback** ['θrəubæk] n: **it's a ~ to** ça nous etc ramène à

**t**

**throw-in** ['θrəʊɪn] n (Sport) remise f en jeu
**thrown** [θrəʊn] pp of **throw**
**thru** [θruː] (US) = **through**
**thrush** [θrʌʃ] n (Zool) grive f; (Med: esp in children) muguet m; (: in women: Brit) muguet vaginal
**thrust** [θrʌst] n (Tech) poussée f ▷ vt (pt, pp **thrust**) pousser brusquement; (push in) enfoncer
**thrusting** ['θrʌstɪŋ] adj dynamique; qui se met trop en avant
**thud** [θʌd] n bruit sourd
**thug** [θʌg] n voyou m
**thumb** [θʌm] n (Anat) pouce m ▷ vt (book) feuilleter; **to ~ a lift** faire de l'auto-stop, arrêter une voiture; **to give sb/sth the ~s up/~s down** donner/refuser de donner le feu vert à qn/qch
  ▶ **thumb through** vt (book) feuilleter
**thumb index** n répertoire m (à onglets)
**thumbnail** ['θʌmneɪl] n ongle m du pouce
**thumbnail sketch** n croquis m
**thumbtack** ['θʌmtæk] n (US) punaise f (clou)
**thump** [θʌmp] n grand coup; (sound) bruit sourd ▷ vt cogner sur ▷ vi cogner, frapper
**thunder** ['θʌndər] n tonnerre m ▷ vi tonner; (train etc): **to ~ past** passer dans un grondement or un bruit de tonnerre
**thunderbolt** ['θʌndəbəʊlt] n foudre f
**thunderclap** ['θʌndəklæp] n coup m de tonnerre
**thunderous** ['θʌndrəs] adj étourdissant(e)
**thunderstorm** ['θʌndəstɔːm] n orage m
**thunderstruck** ['θʌndəstrʌk] adj (fig) abasourdi(e)
**thundery** ['θʌndərɪ] adj orageux(-euse)
**Thursday** ['θəːzdɪ] n jeudi m; see also **Tuesday**
**thus** [ðʌs] adv ainsi
**thwart** [θwɔːt] vt contrecarrer
**thyme** [taɪm] n thym m
**thyroid** ['θaɪrɔɪd] n thyroïde f
**tiara** [tɪ'ɑːrə] n (woman's) diadème m
**Tibet** [tɪ'bɛt] n Tibet m
**Tibetan** [tɪ'bɛtən] adj tibétain(e) ▷ n Tibétain(e); (Ling) tibétain m
**tibia** ['tɪbɪə] n tibia m
**tic** [tɪk] n tic (nerveux)
**tick** [tɪk] n (sound: of clock) tic-tac m; (mark) coche f; (Zool) tique f; (Brit inf): **in a ~** dans un instant; (Brit inf: credit): **to buy sth on ~** acheter qch à crédit ▷ vi faire tic-tac ▷ vt (item on list) cocher; **to put a ~ against sth** cocher qch
  ▶ **tick off** vt (item on list) cocher; (person) réprimander, attraper
  ▶ **tick over** vi (Brit: engine) tourner au ralenti; (: fig) aller or marcher doucettement
**ticker tape** ['tɪkə-] n bande f de téléscripteur; (US: in celebrations) ≈ serpentin m
**ticket** ['tɪkɪt] n billet m; (for bus, tube) ticket m; (in shop: on goods) étiquette f; (: from cash register) reçu m, ticket; (for library) carte f; (also: **parking ticket**) contravention f, p.-v. m; (US Pol) liste électorale (soutenue par un parti); **to get a (parking) ~** (Aut) attraper une contravention (pour stationnement illégal)
**ticket agency** n (Theat) agence f de spectacles

**ticket barrier** n (Brit: Rail) portillon m automatique
**ticket collector** n contrôleur(-euse)
**ticket holder** n personne munie d'un billet
**ticket inspector** n contrôleur(-euse)
**ticket machine** n billetterie f automatique
**ticket office** n guichet m, bureau m de vente des billets
**tickle** ['tɪkl] n chatouillement m ▷ vi chatouiller ▷ vt chatouiller; (fig) plaire à; faire rire
**ticklish** ['tɪklɪʃ] adj (person) chatouilleux(-euse); (which tickles: blanket) qui chatouille; (: cough) qui irrite; (problem) épineux(-euse)
**tidal** ['taɪdl] adj à marée
**tidal wave** n raz-de-marée m inv
**tidbit** ['tɪdbɪt] n (esp US) = **titbit**
**tiddlywinks** ['tɪdlɪwɪŋks] n jeu m de puce
**tide** [taɪd] n marée f; (fig: of events) cours m ▷ vt: **to ~ sb over** dépanner qn; **high/low ~** marée haute/basse
**tidily** ['taɪdɪlɪ] adv avec soin, soigneusement
**tidiness** ['taɪdɪnɪs] n bon ordre; goût m de l'ordre
**tidy** ['taɪdɪ] adj (room) bien rangé(e); (dress, work) net (nette), soigné(e); (person) ordonné(e), qui a de l'ordre; (: in character) soigneux(-euse); (mind) méthodique ▷ vt (also: **tidy up**) ranger; **to ~ o.s. up** s'arranger
**tie** [taɪ] n (string etc) cordon m; (Brit: also: **necktie**) cravate f; (fig: link) lien m; (Sport: draw) égalité f de points; match nul; (: match) rencontre f; (US Rail) traverse f ▷ vt (parcel) attacher; (ribbon) nouer ▷ vi (Sport) faire match nul; finir à égalité de points; **"black/white ~"** "smoking/habit de rigueur"; **family ~s** liens de famille; **to ~ sth in a bow** faire un nœud à or avec qch; **to ~ a knot in sth** faire un nœud à qch
  ▶ **tie down** vt attacher; (fig): **to ~ sb down to** contraindre qn à accepter; **to feel ~d down** (by relationship) se sentir coincé(e)
  ▶ **tie in** vi: **to ~ in (with)** (correspond) correspondre (à)
  ▶ **tie on** vt (Brit: label etc) attacher (avec une ficelle)
  ▶ **tie up** vt (parcel) ficeler; (dog, boat) attacher; (prisoner) ligoter; (arrangements) conclure; **to be ~d up** (busy) être pris(e) or occupé(e)
**tie-break** ['taɪbreɪk], **tie-breaker** ['taɪbreɪkər] n (Tennis) tie-break m; (in quiz) question f subsidiaire
**tie-on** ['taɪɒn] adj (Brit: label) qui s'attache
**tie-pin** ['taɪpɪn] n (Brit) épingle f de cravate
**tier** [tɪər] n gradin m; (of cake) étage m
**Tierra del Fuego** [tɪ'ɛrədɛl'fweɪgəʊ] n Terre f de Feu
**tie tack** n (US) épingle f de cravate
**tiff** [tɪf] n petite querelle
**tiger** ['taɪgər] n tigre m
**tight** [taɪt] adj (rope) tendu(e), raide; (clothes) étroit(e), très juste; (budget, programme, bend) serré(e); (control) strict(e), sévère; (inf: drunk) ivre, rond(e) ▷ adv (squeeze) très fort; (shut) à bloc, hermétiquement; **to be packed ~** (suitcase)

être bourré(e); (*people*) être serré(e); **hold ~!** accrochez-vous bien!

**tighten** ['taɪtn] *vt* (*rope*) tendre; (*screw*) resserrer; (*control*) renforcer ▷ *vi* se tendre; se resserrer

**tightfisted** [taɪt'fɪstɪd] *adj* avare

**tight-lipped** ['taɪt'lɪpt] *adj*: **to be ~ (about sth)** (*silent*) ne pas desserrer les lèvres *or* les dents (au sujet de qch); **she was ~ with anger** elle pinçait les lèvres de colère

**tightly** ['taɪtlɪ] *adv* (*grasp*) bien, très fort

**tightrope** ['taɪtrəʊp] *n* corde *f* raide

**tights** [taɪts] *npl* (*Brit*) collant *m*

**tigress** ['taɪgrɪs] *n* tigresse *f*

**tilde** ['tɪldə] *n* tilde *m*

**tile** [taɪl] *n* (*on roof*) tuile *f*; (*on wall or floor*) carreau *m* ▷ *vt* (*floor, bathroom etc*) carreler

**tiled** [taɪld] *adj* en tuiles; carrelé(e)

**till** [tɪl] *n* caisse (enregistreuse) ▷ *vt* (*land*) cultiver ▷ *prep, conj* = **until**

**tiller** ['tɪlər] *n* (*Naut*) barre *f* (du gouvernail)

**tilt** [tɪlt] *vt* pencher, incliner ▷ *vi* pencher, être incliné(e) ▷ *n* (*slope*) inclinaison *f*; **to wear one's hat at a ~** porter son chapeau incliné sur le côté; **(at) full ~** à toute vitesse

**timber** ['tɪmbər] *n* (*material*) bois *m* de construction; (*trees*) arbres *mpl*

**time** [taɪm] *n* temps *m*; (*epoch: often pl*) époque *f*, temps; (*by clock*) heure *f*; (*moment*) moment *m*; (*occasion, also Math*) fois *f*; (*Mus*) mesure *f* ▷ *vt* (*race*) chronométrer; (*programme*) minuter; (*visit*) fixer; (*remark etc*) choisir le moment de; **a long ~** un long moment, longtemps; **four at a ~** quatre à la fois; **for the ~ being** pour le moment; **from ~ to ~** de temps en temps; **~ after ~, ~ and again** bien des fois; **at ~s** parfois; **in ~** (*soon enough*) à temps; (*after some time*) avec le temps, à la longue; (*Mus*) en mesure; **in a week's ~** dans une semaine; **in no ~** en un rien de temps; **any ~** n'importe quand; **on ~** à l'heure; **to be 30 minutes behind/ahead of ~** avoir 30 minutes de retard/d'avance; **by the ~ he arrived** quand il est arrivé, le temps qu'il arrive + *sub*; **5 ~s 5** 5 fois 5; **what ~ is it?** quelle heure est-il?; **what ~ do you make it?** quelle heure avez-vous?; **what ~ is the museum/ shop open?** à quelle heure ouvre le musée/ magasin?; **to have a good ~** bien s'amuser; **we** (*or* **they** *etc*) **had a hard ~** ça a été difficile *or* pénible; **~'s up!** c'est l'heure!; **I've no ~ for it** (*fig*) cela m'agace; **he'll do it in his own (good) ~** (*without being hurried*) il le fera quand il en aura le temps; **he'll do it in** *or* (*US*) **on his own ~** (*out of working hours*) il le fera à ses heures perdues; **to be behind the ~s** retarder (sur son temps)

**time-and-motion study** ['taɪmənd'məʊʃən-] *n* étude *f* des cadences

**time bomb** *n* bombe *f* à retardement

**time clock** *n* horloge pointeuse

**time-consuming** ['taɪmkənsjuːmɪŋ] *adj* qui prend beaucoup de temps

**time difference** *n* décalage *m* horaire

**time frame** *n* délais *mpl*

**time-honoured, (US) time-honored** ['taɪmɔnəd] *adj* consacré(e)

**timekeeper** ['taɪmkiːpər] *n* (*Sport*) chronomètre *m*

**time lag** *n* (*Brit*) décalage *m*; (: *in travel*) décalage horaire

**timeless** ['taɪmlɪs] *adj* éternel(le)

**time limit** *n* limite *f* de temps, délai *m*

**timely** ['taɪmlɪ] *adj* opportun(e)

**time off** *n* temps *m* libre

**timer** ['taɪmər] *n* (*in kitchen*) compte-minutes *m inv*; (*Tech*) minuteur *m*

**time-saving** ['taɪmseɪvɪŋ] *adj* qui fait gagner du temps

**timescale** ['taɪmskeɪl] *n* délais *mpl*

**time-share** ['taɪmʃeər] *n* maison *f/* appartement *m* en multipropriété

**time-sharing** ['taɪmʃeərɪŋ] *n* (*Comput*) temps partagé

**time sheet** *n* feuille *f* de présence

**time signal** *n* signal *m* horaire

**time switch** *n* (*Brit*) minuteur *m*; (: *for lighting*) minuterie *f*

**timetable** ['taɪmteɪbl] *n* (*Rail*) (indicateur *m*) horaire *m*; (*Scol*) emploi *m* du temps; (*programme of events etc*) programme *m*

**time zone** *n* fuseau *m* horaire

**timid** ['tɪmɪd] *adj* timide; (*easily scared*) peureux(-euse)

**timidity** [tɪ'mɪdɪtɪ] *n* timidité *f*

**timing** ['taɪmɪŋ] *n* minutage *m*; (*Sport*) chronométrage *m*; **the ~ of his resignation** le moment choisi pour sa démission

**timing device** *n* (*on bomb*) mécanisme *m* de retardement

**timpani** ['tɪmpənɪ] *npl* timbales *fpl*

**tin** [tɪn] *n* étain *m*; (*also*: **tin plate**) fer-blanc *m*; (*Brit: can*) boîte *f* (de conserve); (: *for baking*) moule *m* (à gâteau); (*for storage*) boîte *f*; **a ~ of paint** un pot de peinture

**tinfoil** ['tɪnfɔɪl] *n* papier *m* d'étain *or* d'aluminium

**tinge** [tɪndʒ] *n* nuance *f* ▷ *vt*: **~d with** teinté(e) de

**tingle** ['tɪŋgl] *n* picotement *m*; frisson *m* ▷ *vi* picoter; (*person*) avoir des picotements

**tinker** ['tɪŋkər] *n* rétameur ambulant; (*gipsy*) romanichel *m*

▷ **tinker with** *vt fus* bricoler, rafistoler

**tinkle** ['tɪŋkl] *vi* tinter ▷ *n* (*inf*): **to give sb a ~** passer un coup de fil à qn

**tin mine** *n* mine *f* d'étain

**tinned** [tɪnd] *adj* (*Brit: food*) en boîte, en conserve

**tinnitus** ['tɪnɪtəs] *n* (*Med*) acouphène *m*

**tinny** ['tɪnɪ] *adj* métallique

**tin opener** [-'əʊpnər] *n* (*Brit*) ouvre-boîte(s) *m*

**tinsel** ['tɪnsl] *n* guirlandes *fpl* de Noël (*argentées*)

**tint** [tɪnt] *n* teinte *f*; (*for hair*) shampooing colorant ▷ *vt* (*hair*) faire un shampooing colorant à

**tinted** ['tɪntɪd] *adj* (*hair*) teint(e); (*spectacles, glass*) teinté(e)

**tiny** ['taɪnɪ] *adj* minuscule

**tip** [tɪp] *n* (*end*) bout *m*; (*protective: on umbrella etc*)

embout m; (gratuity) pourboire m; (Brit: for coal)
terril m; (Brit: for rubbish) décharge f; (advice)
tuyau m ▷ vt (waiter) donner un pourboire à;
(tilt) incliner; (overturn: also: **tip over**) renverser;
(empty: also: **tip out**) déverser; (predict: winner etc)
pronostiquer; **he ~ped out the contents of
the box** il a vidé le contenu de la boîte; **how
much should I ~?** combien de pourboire est-ce
qu'il faut laisser?
  ▶ **tip off** vt prévenir, avertir
**tip-off** ['tɪpɔf] n (hint) tuyau m
**tipped** ['tɪpt] adj (Brit: cigarette) (à bout) filtre inv;
**steel~** à bout métallique, à embout de métal
**Tipp-Ex®** ['tɪpɛks] n (Brit) Tipp-Ex® m
**tipple** ['tɪpl] (Brit) vi picoler ▷ n: **to have a ~**
boire un petit coup
**tipster** ['tɪpstər] n (Racing) pronostiqueur m
**tipsy** ['tɪpsɪ] adj un peu ivre, éméché(e)
**tiptoe** ['tɪptəu] n: **on ~** sur la pointe des pieds
**tiptop** ['tɪptɔp] adj: **in ~ condition** en excellent
état
**tirade** [taɪ'reɪd] n diatribe f
**tire** ['taɪər] n (US) = **tyre** ▷ vt fatiguer ▷ vi se
fatiguer
  ▶ **tire out** vt épuiser
**tired** ['taɪəd] adj fatigué(e); **to be/feel/look ~**
être/se sentir/avoir l'air fatigué; **to be ~ of** en
avoir assez de, être las (lasse) de
**tiredness** ['taɪədnɪs] n fatigue f
**tireless** ['taɪəlɪs] adj infatigable, inlassable
**tire pressure** (US) = **tyre pressure**
**tiresome** ['taɪsəm] adj ennuyeux(-euse)
**tiring** ['taɪərɪŋ] adj fatigant(e)
**tissue** ['tɪʃuː] n tissu m; (paper handkerchief)
mouchoir m en papier, kleenex® m
**tissue paper** n papier m de soie
**tit** [tɪt] n (bird) mésange f; (inf: breast) nichon m;
**to give ~ for tat** rendre coup pour coup
**titanium** [tɪ'teɪnɪəm] n titane m
**titbit** ['tɪtbɪt] n (food) friandise f; (before meal)
amuse-gueule m inv; (news) potin m
**titillate** ['tɪtɪleɪt] vt titiller, exciter
**titivate** ['tɪtɪveɪt] vt pomponner
**title** ['taɪtl] n titre m; (Law: right): ~ **(to)** droit m (à)
**title deed** n (Law) titre (constitutif) de propriété
**title page** n page f de titre
**title role** n rôle principal
**titter** ['tɪtər] vi rire (bêtement)
**tittle-tattle** ['tɪtltætl] n bavardages mpl
**titular** ['tɪtjulər] adj (in name only) nominal(e)
**tizzy** ['tɪzɪ] n: **to be in a ~** être dans tous ses états
**T-junction** ['tiː'dʒʌŋkʃən] n croisement m en T
**TM** n abbr = **trademark; transcendental
meditation**
**TN** abbr (US) = **Tennessee**
**TNT** n abbr (= trinitrotoluene) TNT m

◯ KEYWORD

**to** [tuː, tə] prep (with noun/pronoun) **1** (direction) à;
(towards) vers; envers; **to go to France/
Portugal/London/school** aller en France/au

Portugal/à Londres/à l'école; **to go to
Claude's/the doctor's** aller chez Claude/le
docteur; **the road to Edinburgh** la route
d'Édimbourg
**2** (as far as) (jusqu')à; **to count to 10** compter
jusqu'à 10; **from 40 to 50 people** de 40 à 50
personnes
**3** (with expressions of time): **a quarter to 5** 5
heures moins le quart; **it's twenty to 3** il est 3
heures moins vingt
**4** (for, of) de; **the key to the front door** la clé de
la porte d'entrée; **a letter to his wife** une lettre
(adressée) à sa femme
**5** (expressing indirect object) à; **to give sth to sb**
donner qch à qn; **to talk to sb** parler à qn; **it
belongs to him** cela lui appartient, c'est à lui;
**to be a danger to sb** être dangereux(-euse)
pour qn
**6** (in relation to) à; **3 goals to 2** 3 (buts) à 2; **30
miles to the gallon** ≈ 9,4 litres aux cent (km)
**7** (purpose, result): **to come to sb's aid** venir au
secours de qn, porter secours à qn; **to sentence
sb to death** condamner qn à mort; **to my
surprise** à ma grande surprise
  ▷ prep (with vb) **1** (simple infinitive): **to go/eat**
aller/manger
**2** (following another vb): **to want/try/start to do**
vouloir/essayer de/commencer à faire
**3** (with vb omitted): **I don't want to** je ne veux
pas
**4** (purpose, result) pour; **I did it to help you** je l'ai
fait pour vous aider
**5** (equivalent to relative clause): **I have things to do**
j'ai des choses à faire; **the main thing is to try**
l'important est d'essayer
**6** (after adjective etc): **ready to go** prêt(e) à partir;
**too old/young to ...** trop vieux/jeune pour ...
  ▷ adv: **push/pull the door to** tirez/poussez la
porte; **to go to and fro** aller et venir

**toad** [təud] n crapaud m
**toadstool** ['təudstuːl] n champignon
(vénéneux)
**toady** ['təudɪ] vi flatter bassement
**toast** [təust] n (Culin) pain grillé, toast m; (drink,
speech) toast ▷ vt (Culin) faire griller; (drink to)
porter un toast à; **a piece or slice of ~** un toast
**toaster** ['təustər] n grille-pain m inv
**toastmaster** ['təustmɑːstər] n animateur m
pour réceptions
**toast rack** n porte-toast m inv
**tobacco** [tə'bækəu] n tabac m; **pipe ~** tabac à
pipe
**tobacconist** [tə'bækənɪst] n marchand(e) de
tabac; ~**'s (shop)** (bureau m de) tabac m
**Tobago** [tə'beɪgəu] n see **Trinidad and Tobago**
**toboggan** [tə'bɔgən] n toboggan m; (child's)
luge f
**today** [tə'deɪ] adv, n (also fig) aujourd'hui (m);
**what day is it ~?** quel jour sommes-nous
aujourd'hui?; **what date is it ~?** quelle est la
date aujourd'hui?; ~ **is the 4th of March**

aujourd'hui nous sommes le 4 mars; **a week ago** ~ il y a huit jours aujourd'hui

**toddler** ['tɔdlə<sup>r</sup>] n enfant m/f qui commence à marcher, bambin m

**toddy** ['tɔdɪ] n grog m

**to-do** [tə'du:] n (fuss) histoire f, affaire f

**toe** [təu] n doigt m de pied, orteil m; (of shoe) bout m ▷ vt: **to ~ the line** (fig) obéir, se conformer; **big ~** gros orteil; **little ~** petit orteil

**TOEFL** n abbr = **Test(ing) of English as a Foreign Language**

**toehold** ['təuhəuld] n prise f

**toenail** ['təuneɪl] n ongle m de l'orteil

**toffee** ['tɔfɪ] n caramel m

**toffee apple** n (Brit) pomme caramélisée

**tofu** ['təufu:] n fromage m de soja

**toga** ['təugə] n toge f

**together** [tə'gɛðə<sup>r</sup>] adv ensemble; (at same time) en même temps; **~ with** (prep) avec

**togetherness** [tə'gɛðənɪs] n camaraderie f; intimité f

**toggle switch** ['tɔgl-] n (Comput) interrupteur m à bascule

**Togo** ['təugəu] n Togo m

**togs** [tɔgz] npl (inf: clothes) fringues fpl

**toil** [tɔɪl] n dur travail, labeur m ▷ vi travailler dur; peiner

**toilet** ['tɔɪlət] n (Brit: lavatory) toilettes fpl, cabinets mpl ▷ cpd (bag, soap etc) de toilette; **to go to the ~** aller aux toilettes; **where's the ~?** où sont les toilettes?

**toilet bag** n (Brit) nécessaire m de toilette

**toilet bowl** n cuvette f des W.-C.

**toilet paper** n papier m hygiénique

**toiletries** ['tɔɪlətrɪz] npl articles mpl de toilette

**toilet roll** n rouleau m de papier hygiénique

**toilet water** n eau f de toilette

**to-ing and fro-ing** ['tu:ɪŋən'frəuɪŋ] n (Brit) allées et venues fpl

**token** ['təukən] n (sign) marque f, témoignage m; (metal disc) jeton m; (voucher) bon m, coupon m ▷ adj (fee, strike) symbolique; **by the same ~** (fig) de même; **book/record ~** (Brit) chèque-livre/-disque m

**tokenism** ['təukənɪzəm] n (Pol): **it's just ~** c'est une politique de pure forme

**Tokyo** ['təukjəu] n Tokyo

**told** [təuld] pt, pp of **tell**

**tolerable** ['tɔlərəbl] adj (bearable) tolérable; (fairly good) passable

**tolerably** ['tɔlərəblɪ] adv: **~ good** tolérable

**tolerance** ['tɔlərns] n (also Tech) tolérance f

**tolerant** ['tɔlərnt] adj: **~ (of)** tolérant(e) (à l'égard de)

**tolerate** ['tɔləreɪt] vt supporter; (Med,: Tech) tolérer

**toleration** [tɔlə'reɪʃən] n tolérance f

**toll** [təul] n (tax, charge) péage m ▷ vi (bell) sonner; **the accident ~ on the roads** le nombre des victimes de la route

**tollbridge** ['təulbrɪdʒ] n pont m à péage

**toll call** n (US Tel) appel m (à) longue distance

**toll-free** ['təul'fri:] adj (US) gratuit(e) ▷ adv gratuitement

**tomato** [tə'mɑːtəu] (pl **-es**) n tomate f

**tomato sauce** n sauce f tomate

**tomb** [tu:m] n tombe f

**tombola** [tɔm'bəulə] n tombola f

**tomboy** ['tɔmbɔɪ] n garçon manqué

**tombstone** ['tu:mstəun] n pierre tombale

**tomcat** ['tɔmkæt] n matou m

**tomorrow** [tə'mɔrəu] adv, n (also fig) demain (m); **the day after ~** après-demain; **a week ~** demain en huit; **~ morning** demain matin

**ton** [tʌn] n tonne f (Brit: = 1016 kg; US = 907 kg; metric = 1000 kg); (Naut: also: **register ton**) tonneau m (= 2.83 cu.m); **~s of** (inf) des tas de

**tonal** ['təunl] adj tonal(e)

**tone** [təun] n ton m; (of radio, Brit Tel) tonalité f ▷ vi (also: **tone in**) s'harmoniser
  ▶ **tone down** vt (colour, criticism) adoucir; (sound) baisser
  ▶ **tone up** vt (muscles) tonifier

**tone-deaf** [təun'dɛf] adj qui n'a pas d'oreille

**toner** ['təunə<sup>r</sup>] n (for photocopier) encre f

**Tonga** [tɔŋə] n îles fpl Tonga

**tongs** [tɔŋz] npl pinces fpl; (for coal) pincettes fpl; (for hair) fer m à friser

**tongue** [tʌŋ] n langue f; **~ in cheek** (adv) ironiquement

**tongue-tied** ['tʌŋtaɪd] adj (fig) muet(te)

**tonic** ['tɔnɪk] n (Med) tonique m; (Mus) tonique f; (also: **tonic water**) Schweppes® m

**tonight** [tə'naɪt] adv, n cette nuit; (this evening) ce soir; **(I'll) see you ~!** à ce soir!

**tonnage** ['tʌnɪdʒ] n (Naut) tonnage m

**tonne** [tʌn] n (Brit: metric ton) tonne f

**tonsil** ['tɔnsl] n amygdale f; **to have one's ~s out** se faire opérer des amygdales

**tonsillitis** [tɔnsɪ'laɪtɪs] n amygdalite f; **to have ~** avoir une angine or une amygdalite

**too** [tu:] adv (excessively) trop; (also) aussi; **it's ~ sweet** c'est trop sucré; **I went ~** moi aussi, j'y suis allé; **~ much** (as adv) trop; (as adj) trop de; **~ many** (adj) trop de; **~ bad!** tant pis!

**took** [tuk] pt of **take**

**tool** [tu:l] n outil m; (fig) instrument m ▷ vt travailler, ouvrager

**tool box** n boîte f à outils

**tool kit** n trousse f à outils

**toot** [tu:t] n coup m de sifflet (or de klaxon) ▷ vi siffler; (with car-horn) klaxonner

**tooth** (pl **teeth**) [tu:θ, ti:θ] n (Anat, Tech) dent f; **to have a ~ out** or (US) **pulled** se faire arracher une dent; **to brush one's teeth** se laver les dents; **by the skin of one's teeth** (fig) de justesse

**toothache** ['tu:θeɪk] n mal m de dents; **to have ~** avoir mal aux dents

**toothbrush** ['tu:θbrʌʃ] n brosse f à dents

**toothpaste** ['tu:θpeɪst] n (pâte f) dentifrice m

**toothpick** ['tu:θpɪk] n cure-dent m

**tooth powder** n poudre f dentifrice

**top** [tɔp] n (of mountain, head) sommet m; (of page, ladder) haut m; (of list, queue) commencement m;

833

(*of box, cupboard, table*) dessus *m*; (*lid: of box, jar*) couvercle *m*; (: *of bottle*) bouchon *m*; (*toy*) toupie *f*; (*Dress: blouse etc*) haut; (: *of pyjamas*) veste *f* ▷ *adj* du haut; (*in rank*) premier(-ière); (*best*) meilleur(e) ▷ *vt* (*exceed*) dépasser; (*be first in*) être en tête de; **at the ~ of the stairs/page/street** en haut de l'escalier/de la page/de la rue; **from ~ to bottom** de fond en comble; **on ~ of** sur; (*in addition to*) en plus de; **from ~ to toe** (*Brit*) de la tête aux pieds; **at the ~ of the list** en tête de liste; **at the ~ of one's voice** à tue-tête; **at ~ speed** à toute vitesse; **over the ~** (*inf: behaviour etc*) qui dépasse les limites
  ▶ **top up** (*Brit*), **top off** *vt* (*bottle*) remplir; (*salary*) compléter; **to ~ up one's mobile (phone)** recharger son compte
**topaz** ['təupæz] *n* topaze *f*
**top-class** ['tɔp'klɑːs] *adj* de première classe; (*Sport*) de haute compétition
**topcoat** ['tɔpkəut] *n* pardessus *m*
**topflight** ['tɔpflaɪt] *adj* excellent(e)
**top floor** *n* dernier étage
**top hat** *n* haut-de-forme *m*
**top-heavy** [tɔp'hɛvɪ] *adj* (*object*) trop lourd(e) du haut
**topic** ['tɔpɪk] *n* sujet *m*, thème *m*
**topical** ['tɔpɪkl] *adj* d'actualité
**topless** ['tɔplɪs] *adj* (*bather etc*) aux seins nus; **~ swimsuit** monokini *m*
**top-level** ['tɔplɛvl] *adj* (*talks*) à l'échelon le plus élevé
**topmost** ['tɔpməust] *adj* le (la) plus haut(e)
**top-notch** ['tɔp'nɔtʃ] *adj* (*inf*) de premier ordre
**topography** [tə'pɔgrəfɪ] *n* topographie *f*
**topping** ['tɔpɪŋ] *n* (*Culin*) couche de crème, fromage etc qui recouvre un plat
**topple** ['tɔpl] *vt* renverser, faire tomber ▷ *vi* basculer; tomber
**top-ranking** ['tɔpræŋkɪŋ] *adj* très haut placé(e)
**top-secret** ['tɔp'siːkrɪt] *adj* ultra-secret(-ète)
**top-security** ['tɔpsə'kjuərɪtɪ] *adj* (*Brit*) de haute sécurité
**topsy-turvy** ['tɔpsɪ'təːvɪ] *adj*, *adv* sens dessus-dessous
**top-up** ['tɔpʌp] *n* (*for mobile phone*) recharge *f*, minutes *fpl*; **would you like a ~?** je vous en remets or rajoute?
**top-up card** *n* (*for mobile phone*) recharge *f*
**top-up loan** *n* (*Brit*) prêt *m* complémentaire
**torch** [tɔːtʃ] *n* torche *f*; (*Brit: electric*) lampe *f* de poche
**tore** [tɔːʳ] *pt of* **tear²**
**torment** *n* ['tɔːmɛnt] tourment *m* ▷ *vt* [tɔː'mɛnt] tourmenter; (*fig: annoy*) agacer
**torn** [tɔːn] *pp of* **tear²** ▷ *adj*: **~ between** (*fig*) tiraillé(e) entre
**tornado** [tɔː'neɪdəu] (*pl* **-es**) *n* tornade *f*
**torpedo** [tɔː'piːdəu] (*pl* **-es**) *n* torpille *f*
**torpedo boat** *n* torpilleur *m*
**torpor** ['tɔːpəʳ] *n* torpeur *f*
**torrent** ['tɔrnt] *n* torrent *m*
**torrential** [tɔ'rɛnʃl] *adj* torrentiel(le)

**torrid** ['tɔrɪd] *adj* torride; (*fig*) ardent(e)
**torso** ['tɔːsəu] *n* torse *m*
**tortoise** ['tɔːtəs] *n* tortue *f*
**tortoiseshell** ['tɔːtəʃɛl] *adj* en écaille
**tortuous** ['tɔːtjuəs] *adj* tortueux(-euse)
**torture** ['tɔːtʃəʳ] *n* torture *f* ▷ *vt* torturer
**torturer** ['tɔːtʃərəʳ] *n* tortionnaire *m*
**Tory** ['tɔːrɪ] *adj*, *n* (*Brit Pol*) tory *m/f*, conservateur(-trice)
**toss** [tɔs] *vt* lancer, jeter; (*Brit: pancake*) faire sauter; (*head*) rejeter en arrière ▷ *vi*: **to ~ up for sth** (*Brit*) jouer qch à pile ou face ▷ *n* (*movement: of head etc*) mouvement soudain; (*of coin*) tirage *m* à pile ou face; **to ~ a coin** jouer à pile ou face; **to ~ and turn** (*in bed*) se tourner et se retourner; **to win/lose the ~** gagner/perdre à pile ou face; (*Sport*) gagner/perdre le tirage au sort
**tot** [tɔt] *n* (*Brit: drink*) petit verre; (*child*) bambin *m*
  ▶ **tot up** *vt* (*Brit: figures*) additionner
**total** ['təutl] *adj* total(e) ▷ *n* total *m* ▷ *vt* (*add up*) faire le total de, additionner; (*amount to*) s'élever à; **in ~** au total
**totalitarian** [təutælɪ'tɛərɪən] *adj* totalitaire
**totality** [təu'tælɪtɪ] *n* totalité *f*
**totally** ['təutəlɪ] *adv* totalement
**tote bag** [təut-] *n* fourre-tout *m inv*
**totem pole** ['təutəm-] *n* mât *m* totémique
**totter** ['tɔtəʳ] *vi* chanceler; (*object, government*) être chancelant(e)
**touch** [tʌtʃ] *n* contact *m*, toucher *m*; (*sense, skill: of pianist etc*) toucher; (*fig: note, also Football*) touche *f* ▷ *vt* (*gen*) toucher; (*tamper with*) toucher à; **the personal ~** la petite note personnelle; **to put the finishing ~es to sth** mettre la dernière main à qch; **a ~ of** (*fig*) un petit peu de; **une touche de; in ~ with** en contact or rapport avec; **to get in ~ with** prendre contact avec; **I'll be in ~** je resterai en contact; **to lose ~** (*friends*) se perdre de vue; **to be out of ~ with events** ne pas être au courant de ce qui se passe
  ▶ **touch down** *vi* (*Aviat*) atterrir; (*on sea*) amerrir
  ▶ **touch on** *vt fus* (*topic*) effleurer, toucher
  ▶ **touch up** *vt* (*paint*) retoucher
**touch-and-go** ['tʌtʃən'gəu] *adj* incertain(e); **it was ~ whether we did it** nous avons failli ne pas le faire
**touchdown** ['tʌtʃdaun] *n* (*Aviat*) atterrissage *m*; (*on sea*) amerrissage *m*; (*US Football*) essai *m*
**touched** [tʌtʃt] *adj* (*moved*) touché(e); (*inf*) cinglé(e)
**touching** ['tʌtʃɪŋ] *adj* touchant(e), attendrissant(e)
**touchline** ['tʌtʃlaɪn] *n* (*Sport*) (ligne *f* de) touche *f*
**touch screen** *n* (*Tech*) écran tactile; **~ mobile** (*téléphone*) portable *m* à écran tactile; **~ technology** technologie *f* à écran tactile
**touch-sensitive** ['tʌtʃsɛnsɪtɪv] *adj* (*keypad*) à effleurement; (*screen*) tactile
**touch-type** ['tʌtʃtaɪp] *vi* taper au toucher
**touchy** ['tʌtʃɪ] *adj* (*person*) susceptible

**tough** [tʌf] *adj* dur(e); *(resistant)* résistant(e),
solide; *(meat)* dur, coriace; *(firm)* inflexible;
*(journey)* pénible; *(task, problem, situation)* difficile;
*(rough)* dur ▷ *n (gangster etc)* dur *m*; **~ luck!** pas de
chance!; tant pis!

**toughen** ['tʌfn] *vt* rendre plus dur(e) (*or* plus
résistant(e) *or* plus solide)

**toughness** ['tʌfnɪs] *n* dureté *f*; résistance *f*;
solidité *f*

**toupee** ['tuːpeɪ] *n* postiche *m*

**tour** ['tuəʳ] *n* voyage *m*; *(also:* **package tour**)
voyage organisé; *(of town, museum)* tour *m*, visite
*f*; *(by band)* tournée *f* ▷ *vt* visiter; **to go on a ~ of**
*(museum, region)* visiter; **to go on ~** partir en
tournée

**tour guide** *n (person)* guide *m/f*

**touring** ['tuərɪŋ] *n* voyages *mpl* touristiques,
tourisme *m*

**tourism** ['tuərɪzm] *n* tourisme *m*

**tourist** ['tuərɪst] *n* touriste *m/f* ▷ *adv (travel)* en
classe touriste ▷ *cpd* touristique; **the ~ trade** le
tourisme

**tourist class** *n (Aviat)* classe *f* touriste

**tourist office** *n* syndicat *m* d'initiative

**tournament** ['tuənəmənt] *n* tournoi *m*

**tourniquet** ['tuənɪkeɪ] *n (Med)* garrot *m*

**tour operator** *n (Brit)* organisateur *m* de
voyages, tour-opérateur *m*

**tousled** ['tauzld] *adj (hair)* ébouriffé(e)

**tout** [taut] *vi*: **to ~ for** essayer de raccrocher,
racoler; **to ~ sth (around)** *(Brit)* essayer de
placer *or* (re)vendre qch ▷ *n (Brit: ticket tout)*
revendeur *m* de billets

**tow** [tou] *n*: **to give sb a ~** *(Aut)* remorquer qn
▷ *vt* remorquer; *(caravan, trailer)* tracter; **"on ~",**
(US) **"in ~"** *(Aut)* "véhicule en remorque"
▶ **tow away** *vt (subj: police)* emmener à la
fourrière; *(: breakdown service)* remorquer

**toward** [tə'wɔːd], **towards** [tə'wɔːdz] *prep* vers;
*(of attitude)* envers, à l'égard de; *(of purpose)* pour;
**~(s) noon/the end of the year** vers midi/la fin
de l'année; **to feel friendly ~(s) sb** être bien
disposé envers qn

**towel** ['tauəl] *n* serviette *f* (de toilette); *(also:* **tea
towel**) torchon *m*; **to throw in the ~** *(fig)* jeter
l'éponge

**towelling** ['tauəlɪŋ] *n (fabric)* tissu-éponge *m*

**towel rail**, (US) **towel rack** *n* porte-serviettes *m*
*inv*

**tower** ['tauəʳ] *n* tour *f* ▷ *vi (building, mountain)* se
dresser (majestueusement); **to ~ above** *or* **over
sb/sth** dominer qn/qch

**tower block** *n (Brit)* tour *f* (d'habitation)

**towering** ['tauərɪŋ] *adj* très haut(e), imposant(e)

**towline** ['təulaɪn] *n* (câble *m* de) remorque *f*

**town** [taun] *n* ville *f*; **to go to ~** aller en ville;
*(fig)* y mettre le paquet; **in the ~** dans la ville, en
ville; **to be out of ~** *(person)* être en déplacement

**town centre** *n (Brit)* centre *m* de la ville, centre-
ville *m*

**town clerk** *n* ≈ secrétaire *m/f* de mairie

**town council** *n* conseil municipal

**town crier** [-'kraɪəʳ] *n (Brit)* crieur public

**town hall** *n* ≈ mairie *f*

**townie** ['tauni] *n (Brit inf)* citadin(e)

**town plan** *n* plan *m* de ville

**town planner** *n* urbaniste *m/f*

**town planning** *n* urbanisme *m*

**township** ['taunʃɪp] *n* banlieue noire *(établie sous
le régime de l'apartheid)*

**townspeople** ['taunzpiːpl] *npl* citadins *mpl*

**towpath** ['təupɑːθ] *n* (chemin *m* de) halage *m*

**towrope** ['təurəup] *n* (câble *m* de) remorque *f*

**tow truck** *n (US)* dépanneuse *f*

**toxic** ['tɔksɪk] *adj* toxique

**toxic asset** *n (Econ)* actif *m* toxique

**toxic bank** *n (Econ)* bad bank *f*, banque *f* toxique

**toxin** ['tɔksɪn] *n* toxine *f*

**toy** [tɔɪ] *n* jouet *m*
▶ **toy with** *vt fus* jouer avec; *(idea)* caresser

**toyshop** ['tɔɪʃɔp] *n* magasin *m* de jouets

**trace** [treɪs] *n* trace *f* ▷ *vt (draw)* tracer, dessiner;
*(follow)* suivre la trace de; *(locate)* retrouver;
**without ~** *(disappear)* sans laisser de traces;
**there was no ~ of it** il n'y en avait pas trace

**trace element** *n* oligo-élément *m*

**trachea** [trə'kɪə] *n (Anat)* trachée *f*

**tracing paper** ['treɪsɪŋ-] *n* papier-calque *m*

**track** [træk] *n (mark)* trace *f*; *(path: gen)* chemin
*m*, piste *f*; *(: of bullet etc)* trajectoire *f*; *(: of suspect,
animal)* piste *f*; *(Rail)* voie ferrée, rails *mpl*; *(on tape,
Comput, Sport)* piste *f*; *(on CD)* piste *f*; *(on record)*
plage *f* ▷ *vt* suivre la trace *or* la piste de; **to keep
~ of** suivre; **to be on the right ~** *(fig)* être sur la
bonne voie
▶ **track down** *vt (prey)* trouver et capturer; *(sth
lost)* finir par retrouver

**tracker dog** ['trækə-] *n (Brit) chien dressé pour suivre
une piste*

**track events** *npl (Sport)* épreuves *fpl* sur piste

**tracking station** ['trækɪŋ-] *n (Space)* centre *m*
d'observation de satellites

**track meet** *n (US)* réunion sportive sur piste

**track record** *n*: **to have a good ~** *(fig)* avoir fait
ses preuves

**tracksuit** ['træksuːt] *n* survêtement *m*

**tract** [trækt] *n (Geo)* étendue *f*, zone *f*; *(pamphlet)*
tract *m*; **respiratory ~** *(Anat)* système *m*
respiratoire

**traction** ['trækʃən] *n* traction *f*

**tractor** ['træktəʳ] *n* tracteur *m*

**trade** [treɪd] *n* commerce *m*; *(skill, job)* métier *m*
▷ *vi* faire du commerce ▷ *vt (exchange)*: **to ~ sth
(for sth)** échanger qch (contre qch); **to ~ with/
in** faire du commerce avec/le commerce de;
**foreign ~** commerce extérieur
▶ **trade in** *vt (old car etc)* faire reprendre

**trade barrier** *n* barrière commerciale

**trade deficit** *n* déficit extérieur

**Trade Descriptions Act** *n (Brit) loi contre les
appellations et la publicité mensongères*

**trade discount** *n* remise *f* au détaillant

**trade fair** *n* foire(-exposition) commerciale

**trade-in** ['treɪdɪn] *n* reprise *f*

**t**

**trade-in price** n prix m à la reprise
**trademark** ['treɪdmɑːk] n marque f de fabrique
**trade mission** n mission commerciale
**trade name** n marque déposée
**trade-off** ['treɪdɔf] n (exchange) échange f; (balancing) équilibre m
**trader** ['treɪdəʳ] n commerçant(e), négociant(e)
**trade secret** n secret m de fabrication
**tradesman** ['treɪdzmən] (irreg) n (shopkeeper) commerçant m; (skilled worker) ouvrier qualifié
**trade union** n syndicat m
**trade unionist** [-'juːnjənɪst] n syndicaliste m/f
**trade wind** n alizé m
**trading** ['treɪdɪŋ] n affaires fpl, commerce m
**trading estate** n (Brit) zone industrielle
**trading stamp** n timbre-prime m
**tradition** [trə'dɪʃən] n tradition f; **traditions** npl coutumes fpl, traditions
**traditional** [trə'dɪʃənl] adj traditionnel(le)
**traffic** ['træfɪk] n trafic m; (cars) circulation f
  ▷ vi: **to ~ in** (pej: liquor, drugs) faire le trafic de
**traffic calming** [-'kɑːmɪŋ] n ralentissement m de la circulation
**traffic circle** n (US) rond-point m
**traffic island** n refuge m (pour piétons)
**traffic jam** n embouteillage m
**trafficker** ['træfɪkəʳ] n trafiquant(e)
**traffic lights** npl feux mpl (de signalisation)
**traffic offence** n (Brit) infraction f au code de la route
**traffic sign** n panneau m de signalisation
**traffic violation** n (US) = **traffic offence**
**traffic warden** n contractuel(le)
**tragedy** ['trædʒədɪ] n tragédie f
**tragic** ['trædʒɪk] adj tragique
**trail** [treɪl] n (tracks) trace f, piste f; (path) chemin m, piste; (of smoke etc) traînée f ▷ vt (drag) traîner, tirer; (follow) suivre ▷ vi traîner; (in game, contest) être en retard; **to be on sb's ~** être sur la piste de qn
  ▶ **trail away, trail off** vi (sound, voice) s'évanouir; (interest) disparaître
  ▶ **trail behind** vi traîner, être à la traîne
**trailer** ['treɪləʳ] n (Aut) remorque f; (US) caravane f; (Cine) bande-annonce f
**trailer truck** n (US) (camion m) semi-remorque m
**train** [treɪn] n train m; (in underground) rame f; (of dress) traîne f; (Brit: series): ~ **of events** série f d'événements ▷ vt (apprentice, doctor etc) former; (Sport) entraîner; (dog) dresser; (memory) exercer; (point: gun etc): **to ~ sth on** braquer qch sur ▷ vi recevoir sa formation; (Sport) s'entraîner; **one's ~ of thought** le fil de sa pensée; **to go by ~** voyager par le train or en train; **what time does the ~ from Paris get in?** à quelle heure arrive le train de Paris?; **is this the ~ for ...?** c'est bien le train pour ...?; **to ~ sb to do sth** apprendre à qn à faire qch; (employee) former qn à faire qch
**train attendant** n (US) employé(e) des wagons-lits

**trained** [treɪnd] adj qualifié(e), qui a reçu une formation; dressé(e)
**trainee** [treɪ'niː] n stagiaire m/f; (in trade) apprenti(e)
**trainer** ['treɪnəʳ] n (Sport) entraîneur(-euse); (of dogs etc) dresseur(-euse); **trainers** npl (shoes) chaussures fpl de sport
**training** ['treɪnɪŋ] n formation f; (Sport) entraînement m; (of dog etc) dressage m; **in ~** (Sport) à l'entraînement; (fit) en forme
**training college** n école professionnelle; (for teachers) ≈ école normale
**training course** n cours m de formation professionnelle
**training shoes** npl chaussures fpl de sport
**train wreck** n (fig) épave f; **he's a complete ~** c'est une épave
**traipse** [treɪps] vi (se) traîner, déambuler
**trait** [treɪt] n trait m (de caractère)
**traitor** ['treɪtəʳ] n traître m
**trajectory** [trə'dʒɛktərɪ] n trajectoire f
**tram** [træm] n (Brit: also: **tramcar**) tram(way) m
**tramline** ['træmlaɪn] n ligne f de tram(way)
**tramp** [træmp] n (person) vagabond(e), clochard(e); (inf: pej: woman): **to be a ~** être coureuse ▷ vi marcher d'un pas lourd ▷ vt (walk through: town, streets) parcourir à pied
**trample** ['træmpl] vt: **to ~ (underfoot)** piétiner; (fig) bafouer
**trampoline** ['træmpəliːn] n trampoline m
**trance** [trɑːns] n transe f; (Med) catalepsie f; **to go into a ~** entrer en transe
**tranquil** ['træŋkwɪl] adj tranquille
**tranquillity** [træŋ'kwɪlɪtɪ] n tranquillité f
**tranquillizer, (US) tranquilizer** ['træŋkwɪlaɪzəʳ] n (Med) tranquillisant m
**transact** [træn'zækt] vt (business) traiter
**transaction** [træn'zækʃən] n transaction f; **transactions** npl (minutes) actes mpl; **cash ~** transaction au comptant
**transatlantic** ['trænzət'læntɪk] adj transatlantique
**transcend** [træn'sɛnd] vt transcender; (excel over) surpasser
**transcendental** [trænsɛn'dɛntl] adj: ~ **meditation** méditation transcendantale
**transcribe** [træn'skraɪb] vt transcrire
**transcript** ['trænskrɪpt] n transcription f (texte)
**transcription** [træn'skrɪpʃən] n transcription f
**transept** ['trænsɛpt] n transept m
**transfer** n ['trænsfəʳ] (gen, also Sport) transfert m; (Pol: of power) passation f; (of money) virement m; (picture, design) décalcomanie f; (: stick-on) autocollant m ▷ vt [træns'fəːʳ] transférer; passer; virer; décalquer; **to ~ the charges** (Brit Tel) téléphoner en P.C.V.; **by bank ~** par virement bancaire
**transferable** [træns'fəːrəbl] adj transmissible, transférable; **"not ~"** "personnel"
**transfer desk** n (Aviat) guichet m de transit
**transfix** [træns'fɪks] vt transpercer; (fig): **~ed with fear** paralysé(e) par la peur

**transform** [træns'fɔ:m] *vt* transformer
**transformation** [trænsfə'meɪʃən] *n*
transformation *f*
**transformer** [træns'fɔ:mə<sup>r</sup>] *n* (*Elec*)
transformateur *m*
**transfusion** [træns'fju:ʒən] *n* transfusion *f*
**transgress** [træns'grɛs] *vt* transgresser
**transient** ['trænzɪənt] *adj* transitoire,
éphémère
**transistor** [træn'zɪstə<sup>r</sup>] *n* (*Elec*: *also*: **transistor radio**) transistor *m*
**transit** ['trænzɪt] *n*: **in ~** en transit
**transit camp** *n* camp *m* de transit
**transition** [træn'zɪʃən] *n* transition *f*
**transitional** [træn'zɪʃənl] *adj* transitoire
**transitive** ['trænzɪtɪv] *adj* (*Ling*) transitif(-ive)
**transit lounge** *n* (*Aviat*) salle *f* de transit
**transitory** ['trænzɪtərɪ] *adj* transitoire
**translate** [trænz'leɪt] *vt*: **to ~ (from/into)**
traduire (du/en); **can you ~ this for me?**
pouvez-vous me traduire ceci?
**translation** [trænz'leɪʃən] *n* traduction *f*; (*Scol*: *as opposed to prose*) version *f*
**translator** [trænz'leɪtə<sup>r</sup>] *n* traducteur(-trice)
**translucent** [trænz'lu:snt] *adj* translucide
**transmission** [trænz'mɪʃən] *n* transmission *f*
**transmit** [trænz'mɪt] *vt* transmettre; (*Radio, TV*)
émettre
**transmitter** [trænz'mɪtə<sup>r</sup>] *n* émetteur *m*
**transparency** [træns'pɛərnsɪ] *n* (*Brit Phot*)
diapositive *f*
**transparent** [træns'pærnt] *adj* transparent(e)
**transpire** [træns'paɪə<sup>r</sup>] *vi* (*become known*): **it finally ~d that ...** on a finalement appris que
...; (*happen*) arriver
**transplant** *vt* [træns'plɑ:nt] transplanter;
(*seedlings*) repiquer ⊳ *n* ['trænsplɑ:nt] (*Med*)
transplantation *f*; **to have a heart ~** subir une
greffe du cœur
**transport** *n* ['trænspɔ:t] transport *m* ⊳ *vt*
[træns'pɔ:t] transporter; **public ~** transports en
commun; **Department of T~** (*Brit*) ministère *m*
des Transports
**transportation** [trænspɔ:'teɪʃən] *n* (*moyen m*
de) transport *m*; (*of prisoners*) transportation *f*;
**Department of T~** (*US*) ministère *m* des
Transports
**transport café** *n* (*Brit*) ≈ routier *m*
**transpose** [træns'pəuz] *vt* transposer
**transsexual** [trænz'sɛksjuəl] *adj, n*
transsexuel(le)
**transverse** ['trænzvə:s] *adj* transversal(e)
**transvestite** [trænz'vɛstaɪt] *n* travesti(e)
**trap** [træp] *n* (*snare, trick*) piège *m*; (*carriage*)
cabriolet *m* ⊳ *vt* prendre au piège; (*immobilize*)
bloquer; (*confine*) coincer; **to set** *or* **lay a ~ (for sb)** tendre un piège (à qn); **to shut one's ~** (*inf*)
la fermer
**trap door** *n* trappe *f*
**trapeze** [trə'pi:z] *n* trapèze *m*
**trapper** ['træpə<sup>r</sup>] *n* trappeur *m*
**trappings** ['træpɪŋz] *npl* ornements *mpl*;

attributs *mpl*
**trash** [træʃ] *n* (*pej*: *goods*) camelote *f*; (: *nonsense*)
sottises *fpl*; (*US*: *rubbish*) ordures *fpl*
**trash can** *n* (*US*) poubelle *f*
**trashy** ['træʃɪ] *adj* (*inf*) de camelote, qui ne vaut
rien
**trauma** ['trɔ:mə] *n* traumatisme *m*
**traumatic** [trɔ:'mætɪk] *adj* traumatisant(e)
**travel** ['trævl] *n* voyage(s) *m(pl)* ⊳ *vi* voyager;
(*move*) aller, se déplacer; (*news, sound*) se
propager ⊳ *vt* (*distance*) parcourir; **this wine
doesn't ~ well** ce vin voyage mal
**travel agency** *n* agence *f* de voyages
**travel agent** *n* agent *m* de voyages
**travel brochure** *n* brochure *f* touristique
**travel insurance** *n* assurance-voyage *f*
**traveller**, (*US*) **traveler** ['trævlə<sup>r</sup>] *n*
voyageur(-euse); (*Comm*) représentant *m* de
commerce
**traveller's cheque**, (*US*) **traveler's check** *n*
chèque *m* de voyage
**travelling**, (*US*) **traveling** ['trævlɪŋ] *n* voyage(s)
*m(pl)* ⊳ *adj* (*circus, exhibition*) ambulant(e) ⊳ *cpd*
(*bag, clock*) de voyage; (*expenses*) de déplacement
**travelling salesman**, (*US*) **traveling salesman**
(*irreg*) *n* voyageur *m* de commerce
**travelogue** ['trævəlɔg] *n* (*book, talk*) récit *m* de
voyage; (*film*) documentaire *m* de voyage
**travel-sick** ['trævlsɪk] *adj*: **to get ~** avoir le mal
de la route (*or* de mer *or* de l'air)
**travel sickness** *n* mal *m* de la route (*or* de mer *or*
de l'air)
**traverse** ['trævəs] *vt* traverser
**travesty** ['trævəstɪ] *n* parodie *f*
**trawler** ['trɔ:lə<sup>r</sup>] *n* chalutier *m*
**tray** [treɪ] *n* (*for carrying*) plateau *m*; (*on desk*)
corbeille *f*
**treacherous** ['trɛtʃərəs] *adj* traître(sse); (*ground,
tide*) dont il faut se méfier; **road conditions
are ~** l'état des routes est dangereux
**treachery** ['trɛtʃərɪ] *n* traîtrise *f*
**treacle** ['tri:kl] *n* mélasse *f*
**tread** [trɛd] *n* (*step*) pas *m*; (*sound*) bruit *m* de pas;
(*of tyre*) chape *f*, bande *f* de roulement ⊳ *vi* (*pt*
**trod**, *pp* **trodden**) [trɔd, 'trɔdn] marcher
▸ **tread on** *vt fus* marcher sur
**treadle** ['trɛdl] *n* pédale *f* (*de machine*)
**treas.** *abbr* = **treasurer**
**treason** ['tri:zn] *n* trahison *f*
**treasure** ['trɛʒə<sup>r</sup>] *n* trésor *m* ⊳ *vt* (*value*) tenir
beaucoup à; (*store*) conserver précieusement
**treasure hunt** *n* chasse *f* au trésor
**treasurer** ['trɛʒərə<sup>r</sup>] *n* trésorier(-ière)
**treasury** ['trɛʒərɪ] *n* trésorerie *f*; **the T~**, (*US*) **the
T~ Department** ≈ le ministère des Finances
**treasury bill** *n* bon *m* du Trésor
**treat** [tri:t] *n* petit cadeau, petite surprise ⊳ *vt*
traiter; **it was a ~** ça m'a (*or* nous a *etc*) vraiment
fait plaisir; **to ~ sb to sth** offrir qch à qn; **to ~
sth as a joke** prendre qch à la plaisanterie
**treatise** ['tri:tɪz] *n* traité *m* (*ouvrage*)
**treatment** ['tri:tmənt] *n* traitement *m*; **to have**

**t**

**~ for sth** (*Med*) suivre un traitement pour qch
**treaty** ['tri:tɪ] *n* traité *m*
**treble** ['trɛbl] *adj* triple ▷ *n* (*Mus*) soprano *m* ▷ *vt*, *vi* tripler
**treble clef** *n* clé *f* de sol
**tree** [tri:] *n* arbre *m*
**tree-lined** ['tri:laɪnd] *adj* bordé(e) d'arbres
**treetop** ['tri:tɔp] *n* cime *f* d'un arbre
**tree trunk** *n* tronc *m* d'arbre
**trek** [trɛk] *n* (*long walk*) randonnée *f*; (*tiring walk*) longue marche, trotte *f* ▷ *vi* (*as holiday*) faire de la randonnée
**trellis** ['trɛlɪs] *n* treillis *m*, treillage *m*
**tremble** ['trɛmbl] *vi* trembler
**trembling** ['trɛmblɪŋ] *n* tremblement *m* ▷ *adj* tremblant(e)
**tremendous** [trɪ'mɛndəs] *adj* (*enormous*) énorme; (*excellent*) formidable, fantastique
**tremendously** [trɪ'mɛndəslɪ] *adv* énormément, extrêmement + *adjective*; formidablement
**tremor** ['trɛmər] *n* tremblement *m*; (*also:* **earth tremor**) secousse *f* sismique
**trench** [trɛntʃ] *n* tranchée *f*
**trench coat** *n* trench-coat *m*
**trench warfare** *n* guerre *f* de tranchées
**trend** [trɛnd] *n* (*tendency*) tendance *f*; (*of events*) cours *m*; (*fashion*) mode *f*; **~ towards/away from doing** tendance à faire/à ne pas faire; **to set the ~** donner le ton; **to set a ~** lancer une mode
**trendy** ['trɛndɪ] *adj* (*idea, person*) dans le vent; (*clothes*) dernier cri *inv*
**trepidation** [trɛpɪ'deɪʃən] *n* vive agitation
**trespass** ['trɛspəs] *vi*: **to ~ on** s'introduire sans permission dans; (*fig*) empiéter sur; **"no ~ing"** "propriété privée", "défense d'entrer"
**trespasser** ['trɛspəsər] *n* intrus(e); **"~s will be prosecuted"** "interdiction d'entrer sous peine de poursuites"
**trestle** ['trɛsl] *n* tréteau *m*
**trestle table** *n* table *f* à tréteaux
**trial** ['traɪəl] *n* (*Law*) procès *m*, jugement *m*; (*test: of machine etc*) essai *m*; (*worry*) souci *m*; **trials** *npl* (*unpleasant experiences*) épreuves *fpl*; (*Sport*) épreuves éliminatoires; **horse ~s** concours *m* hippique; **~ by jury** jugement par jury; **to be sent for ~** être traduit(e) en justice; **to be on ~** passer en jugement; **by ~ and error** par tâtonnements
**trial balance** *n* (*Comm*) balance *f* de vérification
**trial basis** *n*: **on a ~** pour une période d'essai
**trial period** *n* période *f* d'essai
**trial run** *n* essai *m*
**triangle** ['traɪæŋgl] *n* (*Math, Mus*) triangle *m*
**triangular** [traɪ'æŋgjulər] *adj* triangulaire
**triathlon** [traɪ'æθlən] *n* triathlon *m*
**tribal** ['traɪbl] *adj* tribal(e)
**tribe** [traɪb] *n* tribu *f*
**tribesman** ['traɪbzmən] *n* membre *m* de la tribu
**tribulation** [trɪbju'leɪʃən] *n* tribulation *f*, malheur *m*
**tribunal** [traɪ'bju:nl] *n* tribunal *m*
**tributary** ['trɪbjutərɪ] *n* (*river*) affluent *m*

**tribute** ['trɪbju:t] *n* tribut *m*, hommage *m*; **to pay ~ to** rendre hommage à
**trice** [traɪs] *n*: **in a ~** en un clin d'œil
**trick** [trɪk] *n* (*magic*) tour *m*; (*joke, prank*) tour, farce *f*; (*skill, knack*) astuce *f*; (*Cards*) levée *f* ▷ *vt* attraper, rouler; **to play a ~ on sb** jouer un tour à qn; **to ~ sb into doing sth** persuader qn par la ruse de faire qch; **to ~ sb out of sth** obtenir qch de qn par la ruse; **it's a ~ of the light** c'est une illusion d'optique causée par la lumière; **that should do the ~** (*fam*) ça devrait faire l'affaire
**trickery** ['trɪkərɪ] *n* ruse *f*
**trickle** ['trɪkl] *n* (*of water etc*) filet *m* ▷ *vi* couler en un filet *or* goutte à goutte; **to ~ in/out** (*people*) entrer/sortir par petits groupes
**trick question** *n* question-piège *f*
**trickster** ['trɪkstər] *n* arnaqueur(-euse), filou *m*
**tricky** ['trɪkɪ] *adj* difficile, délicat(e)
**tricycle** ['traɪsɪkl] *n* tricycle *m*
**trifle** ['traɪfl] *n* bagatelle *f*; (*Culin*) ≈ diplomate *m* ▷ *adv*: **a ~ long** un peu long ▷ *vi*: **to ~ with** traiter à la légère
**trifling** ['traɪflɪŋ] *adj* insignifiant(e)
**trigger** ['trɪgər] *n* (*of gun*) gâchette *f*
  ▶ **trigger off** *vt* déclencher
**trigonometry** [trɪgə'nɔmətrɪ] *n* trigonométrie *f*
**trilby** ['trɪlbɪ] *n* (*Brit: also:* **trilby hat**) chapeau mou, feutre *m*
**trill** [trɪl] *n* (*of bird, Mus*) trille *m*
**trilogy** ['trɪlədʒɪ] *n* trilogie *f*
**trim** [trɪm] *adj* net(te); (*house, garden*) bien tenu(e); (*figure*) svelte ▷ *n* (*haircut etc*) légère coupe; (*embellishment*) finitions *fpl*; (*on car*) garnitures *fpl* ▷ *vt* (*cut*) couper légèrement; (*decorate*): **to ~ (with)** décorer (de); (*Naut: a sail*) gréer; **to keep in (good) ~** maintenir en (bon) état
**trimmings** ['trɪmɪŋz] *npl* décorations *fpl*; (*extras: gen Culin*) garniture *f*
**Trinidad and Tobago** ['trɪnɪdæd-] *n* Trinité et Tobago *f*
**Trinity** ['trɪnɪtɪ] *n*: **the ~** la Trinité
**trinket** ['trɪŋkɪt] *n* bibelot *m*; (*piece of jewellery*) colifichet *m*
**trio** ['tri:əu] *n* trio *m*
**trip** [trɪp] *n* voyage *m*; (*excursion*) excursion *f*; (*stumble*) faux pas ▷ *vi* faire un faux pas, trébucher; (*go lightly*) marcher d'un pas léger; **on a ~** en voyage
  ▶ **trip up** *vi* trébucher ▷ *vt* faire un croc-en-jambe à
**tripartite** [traɪ'pɑ:taɪt] *adj* triparti(e)
**tripe** [traɪp] *n* (*Culin*) tripes *fpl*; (*pej: rubbish*) idioties *fpl*
**triple** ['trɪpl] *adj* triple ▷ *adv*: **~ the distance/the speed** trois fois la distance/la vitesse
**triple jump** *n* triple saut *m*
**triplets** ['trɪplɪts] *npl* triplés(-ées)
**triplicate** ['trɪplɪkət] *n*: **in ~** en trois exemplaires
**tripod** ['traɪpɔd] *n* trépied *m*
**Tripoli** ['trɪpəlɪ] *n* Tripoli

**tripper** ['trɪpəʳ] *n* (*Brit*) touriste *m/f*; excursionniste *m/f*

**tripwire** ['trɪpwaɪəʳ] *n* fil *m* de déclenchement

**trite** [traɪt] *adj* banal(e)

**triumph** ['traɪʌmf] *n* triomphe *m* ▷ *vi*: **to ~ (over)** triompher (de)

**triumphal** [traɪ'ʌmfl] *adj* triomphal(e)

**triumphant** [traɪ'ʌmfənt] *adj* triomphant(e)

**trivia** ['trɪvɪə] *npl* futilités *fpl*

**trivial** ['trɪvɪəl] *adj* insignifiant(e); (*commonplace*) banal(e)

**triviality** [trɪvɪ'ælɪtɪ] *n* caractère insignifiant; banalité *f*

**trivialize** ['trɪvɪəlaɪz] *vt* rendre banal(e)

**trod** [trɒd] *pt of* **tread**

**trodden** [trɒdn] *pp of* **tread**

**trolley** ['trɒlɪ] *n* chariot *m*

**trolley bus** *n* trolleybus *m*

**trollop** ['trɒləp] *n* prostituée *f*

**trombone** [trɒm'bəun] *n* trombone *m*

**troop** [tru:p] *n* bande *f*, groupe *m* ▷ *vi*: **to ~ in/ out** entrer/sortir en groupe; **troops** *npl* (*Mil*) troupes *fpl*; (: *men*) hommes *mpl*, soldats *mpl*; **~ing the colour** (*Brit*: *ceremony*) le salut au drapeau

**troop carrier** *n* (*plane*) avion *m* de transport de troupes; (*Naut*: *also*: **troopship**) transport *m* (*navire*)

**trooper** ['tru:pəʳ] *n* (*Mil*) soldat *m* de cavalerie; (*US*: *policeman*) ≈ gendarme *m*

**troopship** ['tru:pʃɪp] *n* transport *m* (*navire*)

**trophy** ['trəufɪ] *n* trophée *m*

**tropic** ['trɒpɪk] *n* tropique *m*; **in the ~s** sous les tropiques; **T~ of Cancer/Capricorn** tropique du Cancer/Capricorne

**tropical** ['trɒpɪkl] *adj* tropical(e)

**trot** [trɒt] *n* trot *m* ▷ *vi* trotter; **on the ~** (*Brit*: *fig*) d'affilée

▶ **trot out** *vt* (*excuse, reason*) débiter; (*names, facts*) réciter les uns après les autres

**trouble** ['trʌbl] *n* difficulté(s) *f(pl)*, problème(s) *m(pl)*; (*worry*) ennuis *mpl*, soucis *mpl*; (*bother, effort*) peine *f*; (*Pol*) conflit(s) *m(pl)*, troubles *mpl*; (*Med*): **stomach** *etc* **~** troubles gastriques *etc* ▷ *vt* (*disturb*) déranger, gêner; (*worry*) inquiéter ▷ *vi*: **to ~ to do** prendre la peine de faire; **troubles** *npl* (*Pol etc*) troubles; (*personal*) ennuis, soucis; **to be in ~** avoir des ennuis; (*ship, climber etc*) être en difficulté; **to have ~ doing sth** avoir du mal à faire qch; **to go to the ~ of doing** se donner le mal de faire; **it's no ~!** je vous en prie!; **please don't ~ yourself** je vous en prie, ne vous dérangez pas!; **the ~ is ...** le problème, c'est que ...; **what's the ~?** qu'est-ce qui ne va pas?

**troubled** ['trʌbld] *adj* (*person*) inquiet(-ète); (*times, life*) agité(e)

**trouble-free** ['trʌblfri:] *adj* sans problèmes *or* ennuis

**troublemaker** ['trʌblmeɪkəʳ] *n* élément perturbateur, fauteur *m* de troubles

**troubleshooter** ['trʌblʃu:təʳ] *n* (*in conflict*) conciliateur *m*

**troublesome** ['trʌblsəm] *adj* (*child*) fatigant(e), difficile; (*cough*) gênant(e)

**trouble spot** *n* point chaud (*fig*)

**troubling** ['trʌblɪŋ] *adj* (*times, thought*) inquiétant(e)

**trough** [trɒf] *n* (*also*: **drinking trough**) abreuvoir *m*; (*also*: **feeding trough**) auge *f*; (*depression*) creux *m*; (*channel*) chenal *m*; **~ of low pressure** (*Meteorology*) dépression *f*

**trounce** [trauns] *vt* (*defeat*) battre à plates coutures

**troupe** [tru:p] *n* troupe *f*

**trouser press** *n* presse-pantalon *m inv*

**trousers** ['trauzəz] *npl* pantalon *m*; **short ~** (*Brit*) culottes courtes

**trouser suit** *n* (*Brit*) tailleur-pantalon *m*

**trousseau** (*pl* **-x** *or* **-s**) ['tru:səu, -z] *n* trousseau *m*

**trout** [traut] *n* (*pl inv*) truite *f*

**trowel** ['trauəl] *n* truelle *f*; (*garden tool*) déplantoir *m*

**truant** ['truənt] *n*: **to play ~** (*Brit*) faire l'école buissonnière

**truce** [tru:s] *n* trêve *f*

**truck** [trʌk] *n* camion *m*; (*Rail*) wagon *m* à plate-forme; (*for luggage*) chariot *m* (à bagages)

**truck driver** *n* camionneur *m*

**trucker** ['trʌkəʳ] *n* (*esp US*) camionneur *m*

**truck farm** *n* (*US*) jardin maraîcher

**trucking** ['trʌkɪŋ] *n* (*esp US*) transport routier

**trucking company** *n* (*US*) entreprise *f* de transport (routier)

**truck stop** (*US*) *n* routier *m*, restaurant *m* de routiers

**truculent** ['trʌkjulənt] *adj* agressif(-ive)

**trudge** [trʌdʒ] *vi* marcher lourdement, se traîner

**true** [tru:] *adj* vrai(e); (*accurate*) exact(e); (*genuine*) vrai, véritable; (*faithful*) fidèle; (*wall*) d'aplomb; (*beam*) droit(e); (*wheel*) dans l'axe; **to come ~** se réaliser; **~ to life** réaliste

**truffle** ['trʌfl] *n* truffe *f*

**truly** ['tru:lɪ] *adv* vraiment, réellement; (*truthfully*) sans mentir; (*faithfully*) fidèlement; **yours ~** (*in letter*) je vous prie d'agréer, Monsieur (*or* Madame *etc*), l'expression de mes sentiments respectueux

**trump** [trʌmp] *n* atout *m*; **to turn up ~s** (*fig*) faire des miracles

**trump card** *n* atout *m*; (*fig*) carte maîtresse *f*

**trumped-up** [trʌmpt'ʌp] *adj* inventé(e) (de toutes pièces)

**trumpet** ['trʌmpɪt] *n* trompette *f*

**truncated** [trʌŋ'keɪtɪd] *adj* tronqué(e)

**truncheon** ['trʌntʃən] *n* bâton *m* (d'agent de police); matraque *f*

**trundle** ['trʌndl] *vt, vi*: **to ~ along** rouler bruyamment

**trunk** [trʌŋk] *n* (*of tree, person*) tronc *m*; (*of elephant*) trompe *f*; (*case*) malle *f*; (*US Aut*) coffre *m*; **trunks** *npl* (*also*: **swimming trunks**) maillot *m or* slip *m* de bain

**trunk call** *n* (*Brit Tel*) communication

**t**

839

interurbaine

**trunk road** *n* (*Brit*) ≈ (route *f*) nationale *f*

**truss** [trʌs] *n* (*Med*) bandage *m* herniaire ▷ *vt*: **to ~ (up)** (*Culin*) brider

**trust** [trʌst] *n* confiance *f*; (*responsibility*): **to place sth in sb's ~** confier la responsabilité de qch à qn; (*Law*) fidéicommis *m*; (*Comm*) trust *m* ▷ *vt* (*rely on*) avoir confiance en; (*entrust*): **to ~ sth to sb** confier qch à qn; (*hope*): **to ~ (that)** espérer (que); **to take sth on ~** accepter qch les yeux fermés; **in ~** (*Law*) par fidéicommis

**trust company** *n* société *f* fiduciaire

**trusted** ['trʌstɪd] *adj* en qui l'on a confiance

**trustee** [trʌsˈtiː] *n* (*Law*) fidéicommissaire *m/f*; (*of school etc*) administrateur(-trice)

**trustful** ['trʌstful] *adj* confiant(e)

**trust fund** *n* fonds *m* en fidéicommis

**trusting** ['trʌstɪŋ] *adj* confiant(e)

**trustworthy** ['trʌstwəːðɪ] *adj* digne de confiance

**trusty** ['trʌstɪ] *adj* fidèle

**truth** [truːθ, *pl* truːðz] *n* vérité *f*

**truthful** ['truːθful] *adj* (*person*) qui dit la vérité; (*answer*) sincère; (*description*) exact(e), vrai(e)

**truthfully** ['truːθfəlɪ] *adv* sincèrement, sans mentir

**truthfulness** ['truːθfəlnɪs] *n* véracité *f*

**try** [traɪ] *n* essai *m*, tentative *f*; (*Rugby*) essai ▷ *vt* (*attempt*) essayer, tenter; (*test: sth new: also*: **try out**) essayer, tester; (*Law: person*) juger; (*strain*) éprouver ▷ *vi* essayer; **to ~ to do** essayer de faire; (*seek*) chercher à faire; **to ~ one's (very) best** *or* **one's (very) hardest** faire de son mieux; **to give sth a ~** essayer qch

▶ **try on** *vt* (*clothes*) essayer; **to ~ it on** (*fig*) tenter le coup, bluffer

▶ **try out** *vt* essayer, mettre à l'essai

**trying** ['traɪɪŋ] *adj* pénible

**tsar** [zɑːʳ] *n* tsar *m*

**T-shirt** ['tiːʃəːt] *n* tee-shirt *m*

**T-square** ['tiːskwɛəʳ] *n* équerre *f* en T

**tsunami** [tsʊˈnɑːmɪ] *n* tsunami *m*

**TT** *adj abbr* (*Brit inf*) = **teetotal** ▷ *abbr* (*US*) = **Trust Territory**

**tub** [tʌb] *n* cuve *f*; (*for washing clothes*) baquet *m*; (*bath*) baignoire *f*

**tuba** ['tjuːbə] *n* tuba *m*

**tubby** ['tʌbɪ] *adj* rondelet(te)

**tube** [tjuːb] *n* tube *m*; (*Brit: underground*) métro *m*; (*for tyre*) chambre *f* à air; (*inf: television*): **the ~** la télé

**tubeless** ['tjuːblɪs] *adj* (*tyre*) sans chambre à air

**tuber** ['tjuːbəʳ] *n* (*Bot*) tubercule *m*

**tuberculosis** [tjubəːkjuˈləusɪs] *n* tuberculose *f*

**tube station** *n* (*Brit*) station *f* de métro

**tubing** ['tjuːbɪŋ] *n* tubes *mpl*; **a piece of ~** un tube

**tubular** ['tjuːbjuləʳ] *adj* tubulaire

**TUC** *n abbr* (*Brit*: = *Trades Union Congress*) confédération *f* des syndicats britanniques

**tuck** [tʌk] *n* (*Sewing*) pli *m*, rempli *m* ▷ *vt* (*put*) mettre

▶ **tuck away** *vt* cacher, ranger; (*money*) mettre de côté; (*building*): **to be ~ed away** être caché(e)

▶ **tuck in** *vt* rentrer; (*child*) border ▷ *vi* (*eat*) manger de bon appétit; attaquer le repas

▶ **tuck up** *vt* (*child*) border

**tuck shop** *n* (*Brit Scol*) boutique *f* à provisions

**Tuesday** ['tjuːzdɪ] *n* mardi *m*; (**the date**) **today is ~ 23rd March** nous sommes aujourd'hui le mardi 23 mars; **on ~** mardi; **on ~s** le mardi; **every ~** tous les mardis, chaque mardi; **every other ~** un mardi sur deux; **last/next ~** mardi dernier/prochain; **~ next** mardi qui vient; **the following ~** le mardi suivant; **a week/fortnight on ~, ~ week/fortnight** mardi en huit/quinze; **the ~ before last** l'autre mardi; **the ~ after next** mardi en huit; **~ morning/lunchtime/afternoon/evening** mardi matin/midi/après-midi/soir; **~ night** mardi soir; (*overnight*) la nuit de mardi (à mercredi); **~'s newspaper** le journal de mardi

**tuft** [tʌft] *n* touffe *f*

**tug** [tʌg] *n* (*ship*) remorqueur *m* ▷ *vt* tirer (sur)

**tug-of-love** [tʌgəvˈlʌv] *n* lutte acharnée entre parents divorcés pour avoir la garde d'un enfant

**tug-of-war** [tʌgəvˈwɔːʳ] *n* lutte *f* à la corde

**tuition** [tjuːˈɪʃən] *n* (*Brit: lessons*) leçons *fpl*; (*: private*) cours particuliers; (*US: fees*) frais *mpl* de scolarité

**tulip** ['tjuːlɪp] *n* tulipe *f*

**tumble** ['tʌmbl] *n* (*fall*) chute *f*, culbute *f* ▷ *vi* tomber, dégringoler; (*somersault*) faire une *or* des culbute(s) ▷ *vt* renverser, faire tomber; **to ~ to sth** (*inf*) réaliser qch

**tumbledown** ['tʌmbldaun] *adj* délabré(e)

**tumble dryer** *n* (*Brit*) séchoir *m* (à linge) à air chaud

**tumbler** ['tʌmbləʳ] *n* verre (droit), gobelet *m*

**tummy** ['tʌmɪ] *n* (*inf*) ventre *m*

**tumour**, (*US*) **tumor** ['tjuːməʳ] *n* tumeur *f*

**tumult** ['tjuːmʌlt] *n* tumulte *m*

**tumultuous** [tjuːˈmʌltjuəs] *adj* tumultueux(-euse)

**tuna** ['tjuːnə] *n* (*pl inv: also*: **tuna fish**) thon *m*

**tune** [tjuːn] *n* (*melody*) air *m* ▷ *vt* (*Mus*) accorder; (*Radio, TV, Aut*) régler, mettre au point; **to be in/out of ~** (*instrument*) être accordé/désaccordé; (*singer*) chanter juste/faux; **to be in/out of ~ with** (*fig*) être en accord/désaccord avec; **she was robbed to the ~ of £30,000** (*fig*) on lui a volé la jolie somme de 10 000 livres

▶ **tune in** *vi* (*Radio, TV*): **to ~ in (to)** se mettre à l'écoute (de)

▶ **tune up** *vi* (*musician*) accorder son instrument

**tuneful** ['tjuːnful] *adj* mélodieux(-euse)

**tuner** ['tjuːnəʳ] *n* (*radio set*) tuner *m*; **piano-~** accordeur *m* de pianos

**tuner amplifier** *n* ampli-tuner *m*

**tungsten** ['tʌŋstn] *n* tungstène *m*

**tunic** ['tjuːnɪk] *n* tunique *f*

**tuning** ['tjuːnɪŋ] *n* réglage *m*

**tuning fork** *n* diapason *m*

**Tunis** ['tjuːnɪs] *n* Tunis

**Tunisia** [tju:'nɪzɪə] n Tunisie f
**Tunisian** [tju:'nɪzɪən] adj tunisien(ne) ▷ n
Tunisien(ne)
**tunnel** ['tʌnl] n tunnel m; (in mine) galerie f ▷ vi
creuser un tunnel (or une galerie)
**tunnel vision** n (Med) rétrécissement m du
champ visuel; (fig) vision étroite des choses
**tunny** ['tʌnɪ] n thon m
**turban** ['tə:bən] n turban m
**turbid** ['tə:bɪd] adj boueux(-euse)
**turbine** ['tə:baɪn] n turbine f
**turbo** ['tə:bəu] n turbo m
**turbojet** [tə:bəu'dʒɛt] n turboréacteur m
**turboprop** [tə:bəu'prɔp] n (engine)
turbopropulseur m
**turbot** ['tə:bət] n (pl inv) turbot m
**turbulence** ['tə:bjuləns] n (Aviat) turbulence f
**turbulent** ['tə:bjulənt] adj turbulent(e); (sea)
agité(e)
**tureen** [tə'ri:n] n soupière f
**turf** [tə:f] n gazon m; (clod) motte f (de gazon)
▷ vt gazonner; **the T~** le turf, les courses fpl
▸ **turf out** vt (inf) jeter; jeter dehors
**turf accountant** n (Brit) bookmaker m
**turgid** ['tə:dʒɪd] adj (speech) pompeux(-euse)
**Turin** [tjuə'rɪn] n Turin
**Turk** [tə:k] n Turc (Turque)
**Turkey** ['tə:kɪ] n Turquie f
**turkey** ['tə:kɪ] n dindon m, dinde f
**Turkish** ['tə:kɪʃ] adj turc (turque) ▷ n (Ling)
turc m
**Turkish bath** n bain turc
**Turkish delight** n loukoum m
**turmeric** ['tə:mərɪk] n curcuma m
**turmoil** ['tə:mɔɪl] n trouble m,
bouleversement m
**turn** [tə:n] n tour m; (in road) tournant m;
(tendency: of mind, events) tournure f; (performance)
numéro m; (Med) crise f, attaque f ▷ vt tourner;
(collar, steak) retourner; (age) atteindre; (shape:
wood, metal) tourner; (milk) faire tourner;
(change): **to ~ sth into** changer qch en ▷ vi
(object, wind, milk) tourner; (person: look back) se
(re)tourner; (reverse direction) faire demi-tour;
(change) changer; (become) devenir; **to ~ into** se
changer en, se transformer en; **a good ~** un
service; **a bad ~** un mauvais tour; **it gave me
quite a ~** ça m'a fait un coup; **"no left ~"** (Aut)
"défense de tourner à gauche"; **~ left/right at
the next junction** tournez à gauche/droite au
prochain carrefour; **it's your ~** c'est (à) votre
tour; **in ~** à son tour; à tour de rôle; **to take ~s**
se relayer; **to take ~s at** faire à tour de rôle; **at
the ~ of the year/century** à la fin de l'année/
du siècle; **to take a ~ for the worse** (situation,
events) empirer; **his health** or **he has taken a ~
for the worse** son état s'est aggravé
▸ **turn about** vi faire demi-tour; faire un demi-
tour
▸ **turn around** vi (person) se retourner ▷ vt
(object) tourner
▸ **turn away** vi se détourner, tourner la tête ▷ vt

(reject: person) renvoyer; (: business) refuser
▸ **turn back** vi revenir, faire demi-tour
▸ **turn down** vt (refuse) rejeter, refuser; (reduce)
baisser; (fold) rabattre
▸ **turn in** vi (inf: go to bed) aller se coucher ▷ vt
(fold) rentrer
▸ **turn off** vi (from road) tourner ▷ vt (light, radio
etc) éteindre; (tap) fermer; (engine) arrêter; **I
can't ~ the heating off** je n'arrive pas à
éteindre le chauffage
▸ **turn on** vt (light, radio etc) allumer; (tap) ouvrir;
(engine) mettre en marche; **I can't ~ the
heating on** je n'arrive pas à allumer le
chauffage
▸ **turn out** vt (light, gas) éteindre; (produce: goods,
novel, good pupils) produire ▷ vi (voters, troops) se
présenter; **to ~ out to be ...** s'avérer ..., se
révéler ...
▸ **turn over** vi (person) se retourner ▷ vt (object)
retourner; (page) tourner
▸ **turn round** vi faire demi-tour; (rotate) tourner
▸ **turn to** vt fus: **to ~ to sb** s'adresser à qn
▸ **turn up** vi (person) arriver, se pointer (inf); (lost
object) être retrouvé(e) ▷ vt (collar) remonter;
(radio, heater) mettre plus fort
**turnabout** ['tə:nəbaut], **turnaround**
['tə:nəraund] n volte-face f inv
**turncoat** ['tə:nkəut] n renégat(e)
**turned-up** ['tə:ndʌp] adj (nose) retroussé(e)
**turning** ['tə:nɪŋ] n (in road) tournant m; **the
first ~ on the right** la première (rue or route) à
droite
**turning circle** n (Brit) rayon m de braquage
**turning point** n (fig) tournant m, moment
décisif
**turning radius** n (US) = **turning circle**
**turnip** ['tə:nɪp] n navet m
**turnout** ['tə:naut] n (nombre m de personnes
dans l')assistance f; (of voters) taux m de
participation
**turnover** ['tə:nəuvə'] n (Comm: amount of money)
chiffre m d'affaires; (: of goods) roulement m; (of
staff) renouvellement m, changement m; (Culin)
sorte de chausson; **there is a rapid ~ in staff** le
personnel change souvent
**turnpike** ['tə:npaɪk] n (US) autoroute f à péage
**turnstile** ['tə:nstaɪl] n tourniquet m (d'entrée)
**turntable** ['tə:nteɪbl] n (on record player) platine f
**turn-up** ['tə:nʌp] n (Brit: on trousers) revers m
**turpentine** ['tə:pəntaɪn] n (also: **turps**) (essence
f de) térébenthine f
**turquoise** ['tə:kwɔɪz] n (stone) turquoise f ▷ adj
turquoise inv
**turret** ['tʌrɪt] n tourelle f
**turtle** ['tə:tl] n tortue marine
**turtleneck** ['tə:tlnɛk], **turtleneck sweater** n
pullover m à col montant
**Tuscany** ['tʌskənɪ] n Toscane f
**tusk** [tʌsk] n défense f (d'éléphant)
**tussle** ['tʌsl] n bagarre f, mêlée f
**tutor** ['tju:tə'] n (Brit Scol: in college)
directeur(-trice) d'études; (private teacher)

**t**

841

précepteur(-trice)

**tutorial** [tjuː'tɔːrɪəl] *n* (*Scol*) (séance *f* de) travaux *mpl* pratiques

**tuxedo** [tʌk'siːdəu] *n* (*US*) smoking *m*

**TV** [tiː'viː] *n abbr* (= *television*) télé *f*, TV *f*

**TV dinner** *n* plateau-repas surgelé

**twaddle** ['twɔdl] *n* balivernes *fpl*

**twang** [twæŋ] *n* (*of instrument*) son vibrant; (*of voice*) ton nasillard ▷ *vi* vibrer ▷ *vt* (*guitar*) pincer les cordes de

**tweak** [twiːk] *vt* (*nose*) tordre; (*ear, hair*) tirer

**tweed** [twiːd] *n* tweed *m*

**tweezers** ['twiːzəz] *npl* pince *f* à épiler

**twelfth** [twɛlfθ] *num* douzième

**Twelfth Night** *n* la fête des Rois

**twelve** [twɛlv] *num* douze; **at ~ (o'clock)** à midi; (*midnight*) à minuit

**twentieth** ['twɛntɪɪθ] *num* vingtième

**twenty** ['twɛntɪ] *num* vingt

**twerp** [twəːp] *n* (*inf*) imbécile *m/f*

**twice** [twaɪs] *adv* deux fois; **~ as much** deux fois plus; **~ a week** deux fois par semaine; **she is ~ your age** elle a deux fois ton âge

**twiddle** ['twɪdl] *vt, vi*: **to ~ (with) sth** tripoter qch; **to ~ one's thumbs** (*fig*) se tourner les pouces

**twig** [twɪg] *n* brindille *f* ▷ *vt, vi* (*inf*) piger

**twilight** ['twaɪlaɪt] *n* crépuscule *m*; (*morning*) aube *f*; **in the ~** dans la pénombre

**twill** [twɪl] *n* sergé *m*

**twin** [twɪn] *adj, n* jumeau(-elle) ▷ *vt* jumeler

**twin-bedded room** ['twɪn'bɛdɪd-] *n* = **twin room**

**twin beds** *npl* lits *mpl* jumeaux

**twin-carburettor** ['twɪnkɑːbju'rɛtə'] *adj* à double carburateur

**twine** [twaɪn] *n* ficelle *f* ▷ *vi* (*plant*) s'enrouler

**twin-engined** [twɪn'ɛndʒɪnd] *adj* bimoteur; **~ aircraft** bimoteur *m*

**twinge** [twɪndʒ] *n* (*of pain*) élancement *m*; (*of conscience*) remords *m*

**twinkle** ['twɪŋkl] *n* scintillement *m*; pétillement *m* ▷ *vi* scintiller; (*eyes*) pétiller

**twin room** *n* chambre *f* à deux lits

**twin town** *n* ville jumelée

**twirl** [twəːl] *n* tournoiement *m* ▷ *vt* faire tournoyer ▷ *vi* tournoyer

**twist** [twɪst] *n* torsion *f*, tour *m*; (*in wire, flex*) tortillon *m*; (*bend: in road*) tournant *m*; (*in story*) coup *m* de théâtre ▷ *vt* tordre; (*weave*) entortiller; (*roll around*) enrouler; (*fig*) déformer ▷ *vi* s'entortiller; s'enrouler; (*road, river*) serpenter; **to ~ one's ankle/wrist** (*Med*) se tordre la cheville/le poignet

**twisted** ['twɪstɪd] *adj* (*wire, rope*) entortillé(e); (*ankle, wrist*) tordu(e), foulé(e); (*fig: logic, mind*) tordu

**twit** [twɪt] *n* (*inf*) crétin(e)

**twitch** [twɪtʃ] *n* (*pull*) coup sec, saccade *f*; (*nervous*) tic *m* ▷ *vi* se convulser; avoir un tic

**Twitter**® ['twɪtə'] *n* Twitter® ▷ *vi* twitter

**two** [tuː] *num* deux; **~ by ~, in ~s** par deux; **to put ~ and ~ together** (*fig*) faire le rapprochement

**two-bit** [tuː'bɪt] *adj* (*esp US inf, pej*) de pacotille

**two-door** [tuː'dɔː'] *adj* (*Aut*) à deux portes

**two-faced** [tuː'feɪst] *adj* (*pej: person*) faux (fausse)

**twofold** ['tuːfəuld] *adv*: **to increase ~** doubler ▷ *adj* (*increase*) de cent pour cent; (*reply*) en deux parties

**two-piece** ['tuː'piːs] *n* (*also*: **two-piece suit**) (costume *m*) deux-pièces *m inv*; (*also*: **two-piece swimsuit**) (maillot *m* de bain) deux-pièces

**two-seater** [tuː'siːtə'] *n* (*plane*) (avion *m*) biplace *m*; (*car*) voiture *f* à deux places

**twosome** ['tuːsəm] *n* (*people*) couple *m*

**two-stroke** ['tuːstrəuk] *n* (*also*: **two-stroke engine**) moteur *m* à deux temps ▷ *adj* à deux temps

**two-tone** ['tuː'təun] *adj* (*in colour*) à deux tons

**two-way** ['tuː'weɪ] *adj* (*traffic*) dans les deux sens; **~ radio** émetteur-récepteur *m*

**TX** *abbr* (*US*) = **Texas**

**tycoon** [taɪ'kuːn] *n*: **(business) ~** gros homme d'affaires

**type** [taɪp] *n* (*category*) genre *m*, espèce *f*; (*model*) modèle *m*; (*example*) type *m*; (*Typ*) type, caractère *m* ▷ *vt* (*letter etc*) taper (à la machine); **what ~ do you want?** quel genre voulez-vous?; **in bold/italic ~** en caractères gras/en italiques

**typecast** ['taɪpkɑːst] *adj* condamné(e) à toujours jouer le même rôle

**typeface** ['taɪpfeɪs] *n* police *f* (de caractères)

**typescript** ['taɪpskrɪpt] *n* texte dactylographié

**typeset** ['taɪpsɛt] *vt* composer (*en imprimerie*)

**typesetter** ['taɪpsɛtə'] *n* compositeur *m*

**typewriter** ['taɪpraɪtə'] *n* machine *f* à écrire

**typewritten** ['taɪprɪtn] *adj* dactylographié(e)

**typhoid** ['taɪfɔɪd] *n* typhoïde *f*

**typhoon** [taɪ'fuːn] *n* typhon *m*

**typhus** ['taɪfəs] *n* typhus *m*

**typical** ['tɪpɪkl] *adj* typique, caractéristique

**typically** ['tɪpɪklɪ] *adv* (*as usual*) comme d'habitude; (*characteristically*) typiquement

**typify** ['tɪpɪfaɪ] *vt* être caractéristique de

**typing** ['taɪpɪŋ] *n* dactylo(graphie) *f*

**typing error** *n* faute *f* de frappe

**typing pool** *n* pool *m* de dactylos

**typist** ['taɪpɪst] *n* dactylo *m/f*

**typo** ['taɪpəu] *n abbr* (*inf*: = *typographical error*) coquille *f*

**typography** [taɪ'pɔgrəfɪ] *n* typographie *f*

**tyranny** ['tɪrənɪ] *n* tyrannie *f*

**tyrant** ['taɪrənt] *n* tyran *m*

**tyre**, (*US*) **tire** ['taɪə'] *n* pneu *m*

**tyre pressure** *n* (*Brit*) pression *f* (de gonflage)

**Tyrol** [tɪ'rəul] *n* Tyrol *m*

**Tyrrhenian Sea** [tɪ'riːnɪən-] *n*: **the ~** la mer Tyrrhénienne

**tzar** [zɑː'] *n* = **tsar**

# Uu

**U, u** [juː] n (letter) U, u m; **U for Uncle** U comme Ursule

**U** n abbr (Brit Cine: = universal) ≈ tous publics

**UAW** n abbr (US: = United Automobile Workers) syndicat des ouvriers de l'automobile

**UB40** n abbr (Brit: = unemployment benefit form 40) numéro de référence d'un formulaire d'inscription au chômage; par extension, le bénéficiaire

**U-bend** ['juːbɛnd] n (Brit Aut) coude m, virage m en épingle à cheveux; (in pipe) coude

**ubiquitous** [juːˈbɪkwɪtəs] adj doué(e) d'ubiquité, omniprésent(e)

**UCAS** ['juːkæs] n abbr (Brit) = **Universities and Colleges Admissions Service**

**UDA** n abbr (Brit) = **Ulster Defence Association**

**UDC** n abbr (Brit) = **Urban District Council**

**udder** ['ʌdəʳ] n pis m, mamelle f

**UDI** n abbr (Brit Pol) = **unilateral declaration of independence**

**UDR** n abbr (Brit) = **Ulster Defence Regiment**

**UEFA** [juːˈeɪfə] n abbr (= Union of European Football Associations) UEFA f

**UFO** ['juːfəu] n abbr (= unidentified flying object) ovni m

**Uganda** [juːˈgændə] n Ouganda m

**Ugandan** [juːˈgændən] adj ougandais(e) ▷ n Ougandais(e)

**UGC** n abbr (Brit: = University Grants Committee) commission d'attribution des dotations aux universités

**ugh** [əːh] excl pouah!

**ugliness** ['ʌglɪnɪs] n laideur f

**ugly** ['ʌglɪ] adj laid(e), vilain(e); (fig) répugnant(e)

**UHF** abbr (= ultra-high frequency) UHF

**UHT** adj abbr = **ultra-heat treated**; ~ **milk** lait m UHT or longue conservation

**UK** n abbr = **United Kingdom**

**Ukraine** [juːˈkreɪn] n Ukraine f

**Ukrainian** [juːˈkreɪnɪən] adj ukrainien(ne) ▷ n Ukrainien(ne); (Ling) ukrainien m

**ulcer** ['ʌlsəʳ] n ulcère m; **mouth** ~ aphte f

**Ulster** ['ʌlstəʳ] n Ulster m

**ulterior** [ʌlˈtɪərɪəʳ] adj ultérieur(e); ~ **motive** arrière-pensée f

**ultimate** ['ʌltɪmət] adj ultime, final(e); (authority) suprême ▷ n: **the ~ in luxury** le

summum du luxe

**ultimately** ['ʌltɪmətlɪ] adv (at last) en fin de compte; (fundamentally) finalement; (eventually) par la suite

**ultimatum** (pl **-s** or **ultimata**) [ʌltɪˈmeɪtəm, -tə] n ultimatum m

**ultrasonic** [ʌltrəˈsɔnɪk] adj ultrasonique

**ultrasound** ['ʌltrəsaund] n (Med) ultrason m

**ultraviolet** ['ʌltrəˈvaɪəlɪt] adj ultraviolet(te)

**umbilical** [ʌmbɪˈlaɪkl] adj: ~ **cord** cordon ombilical

**umbrage** ['ʌmbrɪdʒ] n: **to take** ~ prendre ombrage, se froisser

**umbrella** [ʌmˈbrelə] n parapluie m; (for sun) parasol m; (fig): **under the** ~ **of** sous les auspices de; chapeauté(e) par

**umlaut** ['umlaut] n tréma m

**umpire** [ʌmpaɪəʳ] n arbitre m; (Tennis) juge m de chaise ▷ vt arbitrer

**umpteen** [ʌmpˈtiːn] adj je ne sais combien de; **for the ~th time** pour la nième fois

**UMW** n abbr (= United Mineworkers of America) syndicat des mineurs

**UN** n abbr = **United Nations**

**unabashed** [ʌnəˈbæʃt] adj nullement intimidé(e)

**unabated** [ʌnəˈbeɪtɪd] adj non diminué(e)

**unable** [ʌnˈeɪbl] adj: **to be** ~ **to** ne (pas) pouvoir, être dans l'impossibilité de; (not capable) être incapable de

**unabridged** [ʌnəˈbrɪdʒd] adj complet(-ète), intégral(e)

**unacceptable** [ʌnəkˈseptəbl] adj (behaviour) inadmissible; (price, proposal) inacceptable

**unaccompanied** [ʌnəˈkʌmpənɪd] adj (child, lady) non accompagné(e); (singing, song) sans accompagnement

**unaccountably** [ʌnəˈkauntəblɪ] adv inexplicablement

**unaccounted** [ʌnəˈkauntɪd] adj: **two passengers are ~ for** on est sans nouvelles de deux passagers

**unaccustomed** [ʌnəˈkʌstəmd] adj inaccoutumé(e), inhabituel(le); **to be ~ to sth** ne pas avoir l'habitude de qch

**unacquainted** [ʌnəˈkweɪntɪd] adj: **to be ~ with**

ne pas connaître

**unadulterated** [ʌnə'dʌltəreɪtɪd] *adj* pur(e), naturel(le)

**unaffected** [ʌnə'fɛktɪd] *adj* (*person, behaviour*) naturel(le); (*emotionally*): **to be ~ by** ne pas être touché(e) par

**unafraid** [ʌnə'freɪd] *adj*: **to be ~** ne pas avoir peur

**unaided** [ʌn'eɪdɪd] *adj* sans aide, tout(e) seul(e)

**unanimity** [juːnə'nɪmɪtɪ] *n* unanimité *f*

**unanimous** [juː'nænɪməs] *adj* unanime

**unanimously** [juː'nænɪməslɪ] *adv* à l'unanimité

**unanswered** [ʌn'ɑːnsəd] *adj* (*question, letter*) sans réponse

**unappetizing** [ʌn'æpɪtaɪzɪŋ] *adj* peu appétissant(e)

**unappreciative** [ʌnə'priːʃɪətɪv] *adj* indifférent(e)

**unarmed** [ʌn'ɑːmd] *adj* (*person*) non armé(e); (*combat*) sans armes

**unashamed** [ʌnə'ʃeɪmd] *adj* sans honte; impudent(e)

**unassisted** [ʌnə'sɪstɪd] *adj* non assisté(e) ▷ *adv* sans aide, tout(e) seul(e)

**unassuming** [ʌnə'sjuːmɪŋ] *adj* modeste, sans prétentions

**unattached** [ʌnə'tætʃt] *adj* libre, sans attaches

**unattended** [ʌnə'tɛndɪd] *adj* (*car, child, luggage*) sans surveillance

**unattractive** [ʌnə'træktɪv] *adj* peu attrayant(e); (*character*) peu sympathique

**unauthorized** [ʌn'ɔːθəraɪzd] *adj* non autorisé(e), sans autorisation

**unavailable** [ʌnə'veɪləbl] *adj* (*article, room, book*) (qui n'est) pas disponible; (*person*) (qui n'est) pas libre

**unavoidable** [ʌnə'vɔɪdəbl] *adj* inévitable

**unavoidably** [ʌnə'vɔɪdəblɪ] *adv* inévitablement

**unaware** [ʌnə'wɛəʳ] *adj*: **to be ~ of** ignorer, ne pas savoir, être inconscient(e) de

**unawares** [ʌnə'wɛəz] *adv* à l'improviste, au dépourvu

**unbalanced** [ʌn'bælənst] *adj* déséquilibré(e)

**unbearable** [ʌn'bɛərəbl] *adj* insupportable

**unbeatable** [ʌn'biːtəbl] *adj* imbattable

**unbeaten** [ʌn'biːtn] *adj* invaincu(e); (*record*) non battu(e)

**unbecoming** [ʌnbɪ'kʌmɪŋ] *adj* (*unseemly: language, behaviour*) malséant(e), inconvenant(e); (*unflattering: garment*) peu seyant(e)

**unbeknown** [ʌnbɪ'nəun], **unbeknownst** [ʌnbɪ'nəunst] *adv*: **~ to** à l'insu de

**unbelief** [ʌnbɪ'liːf] *n* incrédulité *f*

**unbelievable** [ʌnbɪ'liːvəbl] *adj* incroyable

**unbelievingly** [ʌnbɪ'liːvɪŋlɪ] *adv* avec incrédulité

**unbend** [ʌn'bɛnd] (*irreg: like* **bend**) *vi* se détendre ▷ *vt* (*wire*) redresser, détordre

**unbending** [ʌn'bɛndɪŋ] *adj* (*fig*) inflexible

**unbiased, unbiassed** [ʌn'baɪəst] *adj* impartial(e)

**unblemished** [ʌn'blɛmɪʃt] *adj* impeccable

**unblock** [ʌn'blɔk] *vt* (*pipe*) déboucher; (*road*) dégager

**unborn** [ʌn'bɔːn] *adj* à naître

**unbounded** [ʌn'baundɪd] *adj* sans bornes, illimité(e)

**unbreakable** [ʌn'breɪkəbl] *adj* incassable

**unbridled** [ʌn'braɪdld] *adj* débridé(e), déchaîné(e)

**unbroken** [ʌn'brəukn] *adj* intact(e); (*line*) continu(e); (*record*) non battu(e)

**unbuckle** [ʌn'bʌkl] *vt* déboucler

**unburden** [ʌn'bəːdn] *vt*: **to ~ o.s.** s'épancher, se livrer

**unbutton** [ʌn'bʌtn] *vt* déboutonner

**uncalled-for** [ʌn'kɔːldfɔːʳ] *adj* déplacé(e), injustifié(e)

**uncanny** [ʌn'kænɪ] *adj* étrange, troublant(e)

**unceasing** [ʌn'siːsɪŋ] *adj* incessant(e), continu(e)

**unceremonious** [ʌnsɛrɪ'məunɪəs] *adj* (*abrupt, rude*) brusque

**uncertain** [ʌn'səːtn] *adj* incertain(e); (*hesitant*) hésitant(e); **we were ~ whether ...** nous ne savions pas vraiment si ...; **in no ~ terms** sans équivoque possible

**uncertainty** [ʌn'səːtntɪ] *n* incertitude *f*, doutes *mpl*

**unchallenged** [ʌn'tʃælɪndʒd] *adj* (*gen*) incontesté(e); (*information*) non contesté(e); **to go ~** ne pas être contesté

**unchanged** [ʌn'tʃeɪndʒd] *adj* inchangé(e)

**uncharitable** [ʌn'tʃærɪtəbl] *adj* peu charitable

**uncharted** [ʌn'tʃɑːtɪd] *adj* inexploré(e)

**unchecked** [ʌn'tʃɛkt] *adj* non réprimé(e)

**uncivilized** [ʌn'sɪvɪlaɪzd] *adj* non civilisé(e); (*fig*) barbare

**uncle** ['ʌŋkl] *n* oncle *m*

**unclear** [ʌn'klɪəʳ] *adj* (qui n'est) pas clair(e) *or* évident(e); **I'm still ~ about what I'm supposed to do** je ne sais pas encore exactement ce que je dois faire

**uncoil** [ʌn'kɔɪl] *vt* dérouler ▷ *vi* se dérouler

**uncomfortable** [ʌn'kʌmfətəbl] *adj* inconfortable, peu confortable; (*uneasy*) mal à l'aise, gêné(e); (*situation*) désagréable

**uncomfortably** [ʌn'kʌmfətəblɪ] *adv* inconfortablement; d'un ton *etc* gêné *or* embarrassé; désagréablement

**uncommitted** [ʌnkə'mɪtɪd] *adj* (*attitude, country*) non engagé(e)

**uncommon** [ʌn'kɔmən] *adj* rare, singulier(-ière), peu commun(e)

**uncommunicative** [ʌnkə'mjuːnɪkətɪv] *adj* réservé(e)

**uncomplicated** [ʌn'kɔmplɪkeɪtɪd] *adj* simple, peu compliqué(e)

**uncompromising** [ʌn'kɔmprəmaɪzɪŋ] *adj* intransigeant(e), inflexible

**unconcerned** [ʌnkən'səːnd] *adj* (*unworried*): **to be ~ (about)** ne pas s'inquiéter (de)

**unconditional** [ʌnkən'dɪʃənl] *adj* sans

conditions
**uncongenial** [ˌʌnkən'dʒiːnɪəl] *adj* peu agréable
**unconnected** [ˌʌnkə'nɛktɪd] *adj* (*unrelated*): ~
**(with)** sans rapport (avec)
**unconscious** [ʌn'kɒnʃəs] *adj* sans connaissance,
évanoui(e); (*unaware*): ~ **(of)** inconscient(e) (de)
▷ *n*: **the ~** l'inconscient *m*; **to knock sb ~**
assommer qn
**unconsciously** [ʌn'kɒnʃəslɪ] *adv*
inconsciemment
**unconstitutional** [ˌʌnkɒnstɪ'tjuːʃənl] *adj*
anticonstitutionnel(le)
**uncontested** [ˌʌnkən'tɛstɪd] *adj* (*champion*)
incontesté(e); (*Pol: seat*) non disputé(e)
**uncontrollable** [ˌʌnkən'trəʊləbl] *adj* (*child, dog*)
indiscipliné(e); (*temper, laughter*) irrépressible
**uncontrolled** [ˌʌnkən'trəʊld] *adj* (*laughter, price
rises*) incontrôlé(e)
**unconventional** [ˌʌnkən'vɛnʃənl] *adj* peu
conventionnel(le)
**unconvinced** [ˌʌnkən'vɪnst] *adj*: **to be ~** ne pas
être convaincu(e)
**unconvincing** [ˌʌnkən'vɪnsɪŋ] *adj* peu
convaincant(e)
**uncork** [ʌn'kɔːk] *vt* déboucher
**uncorroborated** [ˌʌnkə'rɒbəreɪtɪd] *adj* non
confirmé(e)
**uncouth** [ʌn'kuːθ] *adj* grossier(-ière), fruste
**uncover** [ʌn'kʌvəʳ] *vt* découvrir
**unctuous** ['ʌŋktjuəs] *adj* onctueux(-euse),
mielleux(-euse)
**undamaged** [ʌn'dæmɪdʒd] *adj* (*goods*) intact(e),
en bon état; (*fig: reputation*) intact
**undaunted** [ʌn'dɔːntɪd] *adj* non intimidé(e),
inébranlable
**undecided** [ˌʌndɪ'saɪdɪd] *adj* indécis(e),
irrésolu(e)
**undelivered** [ˌʌndɪ'lɪvəd] *adj* non remis(e), non
livré(e)
**undeniable** [ˌʌndɪ'naɪəbl] *adj* indéniable,
incontestable
**under** ['ʌndəʳ] *prep* sous; (*less than*) (de) moins de;
au-dessous de; (*according to*) selon, en vertu de
▷ *adv* au-dessous; en dessous; **from ~ sth** de
dessous *or* de sous qch; ~ **there** là-dessous; **in ~
2 hours** en moins de 2 heures; ~ **anaesthetic**
sous anesthésie; ~ **discussion** en discussion; ~
**the circumstances** étant donné les
circonstances; ~ **repair** en (cours de) réparation
**under...** ['ʌndəʳ] *prefix* sous-
**underage** [ˌʌndər'eɪdʒ] *adj* qui n'a pas l'âge
réglementaire
**underarm** ['ʌndərɑːm] *adv* par en-dessous ▷ *adj*
(*throw*) par en-dessous; (*deodorant*) pour les
aisselles
**undercapitalized** [ˌʌndə'kæpɪtəlaɪzd] *adj* sous-
capitalisé(e)
**undercarriage** ['ʌndəkærɪdʒ] *n* (*Brit Aviat*)
train *m* d'atterrissage
**undercharge** [ˌʌndə'tʃɑːdʒ] *vt* ne pas faire payer
assez à
**underclass** ['ʌndəklɑːs] *n* ≈ quart-monde *m*

**underclothes** ['ʌndəkləʊðz] *npl* sous-
vêtements *mpl*; (*women's only*) dessous *mpl*
**undercoat** ['ʌndəkəʊt] *n* (*paint*) couche *f* de fond
**undercover** [ˌʌndə'kʌvəʳ] *adj* secret(-ète),
clandestin(e)
**undercurrent** ['ʌndəkʌrnt] *n* courant sous-
jacent
**undercut** [ˌʌndə'kʌt] *vt* (*irreg: like* **cut**) vendre
moins cher que
**underdeveloped** ['ʌndədɪ'vɛləpt] *adj* sous-
développé(e)
**underdog** ['ʌndədɔg] *n* opprimé *m*
**underdone** [ˌʌndə'dʌn] *adj* (*Culin*) saignant(e);
(: *pej*) pas assez cuit(e)
**underestimate** ['ʌndər'ɛstɪmeɪt] *vt* sous-
estimer, mésestimer
**underexposed** ['ʌndərɪks'pəʊzd] *adj* (*Phot*)
sous-exposé(e)
**underfed** [ˌʌndə'fɛd] *adj* sous-alimenté(e)
**underfoot** [ˌʌndə'fʊt] *adv* sous les pieds
**under-funded** ['ʌndə'fʌndɪd] *adj*: **to be ~**
(*organization*) ne pas être doté(e) de fonds
suffisants
**undergo** [ˌʌndə'gəʊ] *vt* (*irreg: like* **go**) subir;
(*treatment*) suivre; **the car is ~ing repairs** la
voiture est en réparation
**undergraduate** [ˌʌndə'grædjuɪt] *n* étudiant(e)
(qui prépare la licence) ▷ *cpd*: ~ **courses** cours
*mpl* préparant à la licence
**underground** ['ʌndəgraʊnd] *adj* souterrain(e);
(*fig*) clandestin(e) ▷ *n* (*Brit: railway*) métro *m*;
(*Pol*) clandestinité *f*
**undergrowth** ['ʌndəgrəʊθ] *n* broussailles *fpl*,
sous-bois *m*
**underhand** [ˌʌndə'hænd], **underhanded**
[ˌʌndə'hændɪd] *adj* (*fig*) sournois(e), en dessous
**underinsured** [ˌʌndərɪn'ʃʊəd] *adj* sous-assuré(e)
**underlie** [ˌʌndə'laɪ] *vt* (*irreg: like* **lie**) être à la base
de; **the underlying cause** la cause sous-
jacente
**underline** [ˌʌndə'laɪn] *vt* souligner
**underling** ['ʌndəlɪŋ] *n* (*pej*) sous-fifre *m*,
subalterne *m*
**undermanning** [ˌʌndə'mænɪŋ] *n* pénurie *f* de
main-d'œuvre
**undermentioned** [ˌʌndə'mɛnʃənd] *adj*
mentionné(e) ci-dessous
**undermine** [ˌʌndə'maɪn] *vt* saper, miner
**underneath** [ˌʌndə'niːθ] *adv* (en) dessous ▷ *prep*
sous, au-dessous de
**undernourished** [ˌʌndə'nʌrɪʃt] *adj* sous-
alimenté(e)
**underpaid** [ˌʌndə'peɪd] *adj* sous-payé(e)
**underpants** ['ʌndəpænts] *npl* caleçon *m*, slip *m*
**underpass** ['ʌndəpɑːs] *n* (*Brit: for pedestrians*)
passage souterrain; (: *for cars*) passage inférieur
**underpin** [ˌʌndə'pɪn] *vt* (*argument, case*) étayer
**underplay** [ˌʌndə'pleɪ] *vt* (*Brit*) minimiser
**underpopulated** [ˌʌndə'pɒpjuleɪtɪd] *adj* sous-
peuplé(e)
**underprice** [ˌʌndə'praɪs] *vt* vendre à un prix
trop bas

**u**

**underprivileged** [ʌndə'prɪvɪlɪdʒd] *adj* défavorisé(e)

**underrate** [ʌndə'reɪt] *vt* sous-estimer, mésestimer

**underscore** [ʌndə'skɔːʳ] *vt* souligner

**underseal** [ʌndə'siːl] *vt* (*Brit*) traiter contre la rouille

**undersecretary** ['ʌndə'sɛkrətrɪ] *n* sous-secrétaire *m*

**undersell** [ʌndə'sɛl] *vt* (*irreg: like* **sell**: *competitors*) vendre moins cher que

**undershirt** ['ʌndəʃəːt] *n* (*US*) tricot *m* de corps

**undershorts** ['ʌndəʃɔːts] *npl* (*US*) caleçon *m*, slip *m*

**underside** ['ʌndəsaɪd] *n* dessous *m*

**undersigned** ['ʌndə'saɪnd] *adj, n* soussigné(e) *m/f*

**underskirt** ['ʌndəskəːt] *n* (*Brit*) jupon *m*

**understaffed** [ʌndə'stɑːft] *adj* qui manque de personnel

**understand** [ʌndə'stænd] *vt, vi* (*irreg: like* **stand**) comprendre; **I don't ~** je ne comprends pas; **I ~ that** ... je me suis laissé dire que ..., je crois comprendre que ...; **to make o.s. understood** se faire comprendre

**understandable** [ʌndə'stændəbl] *adj* compréhensible

**understanding** [ʌndə'stændɪŋ] *adj* compréhensif(-ive) ▷ *n* compréhension *f*; (*agreement*) accord *m*; **to come to an ~ with sb** s'entendre avec qn; **on the ~ that** ... à condition que ...

**understate** [ʌndə'steɪt] *vt* minimiser

**understatement** ['ʌndəsteɪtmənt] *n*: **that's an ~** c'est (bien) peu dire, le terme est faible

**understood** [ʌndə'stud] *pt, pp of* **understand** ▷ *adj* entendu(e); (*implied*) sous-entendu(e)

**understudy** ['ʌndəstʌdɪ] *n* doublure *f*

**undertake** [ʌndə'teɪk] *vt* (*irreg: like* **take**: *job, task*) entreprendre; (*duty*) se charger de; **to ~ to do sth** s'engager à faire qch

**undertaker** ['ʌndəteɪkəʳ] *n* (*Brit*) entrepreneur *m* des pompes funèbres, croque-mort *m*

**undertaking** ['ʌndəteɪkɪŋ] *n* entreprise *f*; (*promise*) promesse *f*

**undertone** ['ʌndətəun] *n* (*low voice*): **in an ~** à mi-voix; (*of criticism etc*) nuance cachée

**undervalue** [ʌndə'væljuː] *vt* sous-estimer

**underwater** [ʌndə'wɔːtəʳ] *adv* sous l'eau ▷ *adj* sous-marin(e)

**underway** [ʌndə'weɪ] *adj*: **to be ~** (*meeting, investigation*) être en cours

**underwear** ['ʌndəwɛəʳ] *n* sous-vêtements *mpl*; (*women's only*) dessous *mpl*

**underweight** [ʌndə'weɪt] *adj* d'un poids insuffisant; (*person*) (trop) maigre

**underwent** [ʌndə'wɛnt] *pt of* **undergo**

**underworld** ['ʌndəwəːld] *n* (*of crime*) milieu *m*, pègre *f*

**underwrite** [ʌndə'raɪt] *vt* (*Finance*) garantir; (*Insurance*) souscrire

**underwriter** ['ʌndəraɪtəʳ] *n* (*Insurance*)

souscripteur *m*

**undeserving** [ʌndɪ'zəːvɪŋ] *adj*: **to be ~ of** ne pas mériter

**undesirable** [ʌndɪ'zaɪərəbl] *adj* peu souhaitable; (*person, effect*) indésirable

**undeveloped** [ʌndɪ'vɛləpt] *adj* (*land, resources*) non exploité(e)

**undies** ['ʌndɪz] *npl* (*inf*) dessous *mpl*, lingerie *f*

**undiluted** ['ʌndaɪ'luːtɪd] *adj* pur(e), non dilué(e)

**undiplomatic** ['ʌndɪplə'mætɪk] *adj* peu diplomatique, maladroit(e)

**undischarged** ['ʌndɪs'tʃɑːdʒd] *adj*: **~ bankrupt** failli(e) non réhabilité(e)

**undisciplined** [ʌn'dɪsɪplɪnd] *adj* indiscipliné(e)

**undisguised** ['ʌndɪs'gaɪzd] *adj* (*dislike, amusement etc*) franc (franche)

**undisputed** ['ʌndɪs'pjuːtɪd] *adj* incontesté(e)

**undistinguished** ['ʌndɪs'tɪŋgwɪʃt] *adj* médiocre, quelconque

**undisturbed** [ʌndɪs'təːbd] *adj* (*sleep*) tranquille, paisible; **to leave ~** ne pas déranger

**undivided** [ʌndɪ'vaɪdɪd] *adj*: **can I have your ~ attention?** puis-je avoir toute votre attention?

**undo** [ʌn'duː] *vt* (*irreg: like* **do**) défaire

**undoing** [ʌn'duːɪŋ] *n* ruine *f*, perte *f*

**undone** [ʌn'dʌn] *pp of* **undo** ▷ *adj*: **to come ~** se défaire

**undoubted** [ʌn'dautɪd] *adj* indubitable, certain(e)

**undoubtedly** [ʌn'dautɪdlɪ] *adv* sans aucun doute

**undress** [ʌn'drɛs] *vi* se déshabiller ▷ *vt* déshabiller

**undrinkable** [ʌn'drɪŋkəbl] *adj* (*unpalatable*) imbuvable; (*poisonous*) non potable

**undue** [ʌn'djuː] *adj* indu(e), excessif(-ive)

**undulating** ['ʌndjuleɪtɪŋ] *adj* ondoyant(e), onduleux(-euse)

**unduly** [ʌn'djuːlɪ] *adv* trop, excessivement

**undying** [ʌn'daɪɪŋ] *adj* éternel(le)

**unearned** [ʌn'əːnd] *adj* (*praise, respect*) immérité(e); **~ income** rentes *fpl*

**unearth** [ʌn'əːθ] *vt* déterrer; (*fig*) dénicher

**unearthly** [ʌn'əːθlɪ] *adj* surnaturel(le); (*hour*) indu(e), impossible

**uneasy** [ʌn'iːzɪ] *adj* mal à l'aise, gêné(e); (*worried*) inquiet(-ète); (*feeling*) désagréable; (*peace, truce*) fragile; **to feel ~ about doing sth** se sentir mal à l'aise à l'idée de faire qch

**uneconomic** ['ʌniːkə'nɔmɪk], **uneconomical** ['ʌniːkə'nɔmɪkl] *adj* peu économique; peu rentable

**uneducated** [ʌn'ɛdjukeɪtɪd] *adj* sans éducation

**unemployed** [ʌnɪm'plɔɪd] *adj* sans travail, au chômage ▷ *n*: **the ~** les chômeurs *mpl*

**unemployment** [ʌnɪm'plɔɪmənt] *n* chômage *m*

**unemployment benefit**, (*US*) **unemployment compensation** *n* allocation *f* de chômage

**unending** [ʌn'ɛndɪŋ] *adj* interminable

**unenviable** [ʌn'ɛnvɪəbl] *adj* peu enviable

**unequal** [ʌn'iːkwəl] *adj* inégal(e)

**unequalled**, (*US*) **unequaled** [ʌn'iːkwəld] *adj*

inégalé(e)

**unequivocal** [ʌnɪ'kwɪvəkl] *adj* (*answer*) sans équivoque; (*person*) catégorique

**unerring** [ʌn'ə:rɪŋ] *adj* infaillible, sûr(e)

**UNESCO** [ju:'nɛskəu] *n abbr* (= *United Nations Educational, Scientific and Cultural Organization*) UNESCO *f*

**unethical** [ʌn'ɛθɪkl] *adj* (*methods*) immoral(e); (*doctor's behaviour*) qui ne respecte pas l'éthique

**uneven** [ʌn'i:vn] *adj* inégal(e); (*quality, work*) irrégulier(-ière)

**uneventful** [ʌnɪ'vɛntful] *adj* tranquille, sans histoires

**unexceptional** [ʌnɪk'sɛpʃənl] *adj* banal(e), quelconque

**unexciting** [ʌnɪk'saɪtɪŋ] *adj* pas passionnant(e)

**unexpected** [ʌnɪk'spɛktɪd] *adj* inattendu(e), imprévu(e)

**unexpectedly** [ʌnɪk'spɛktɪdlɪ] *adv* (*succeed*) contre toute attente; (*arrive*) à l'improviste

**unexplained** [ʌnɪk'spleɪnd] *adj* inexpliqué(e)

**unexploded** [ʌnɪk'spləudɪd] *adj* non explosé(e) *or* éclaté(e)

**unfailing** [ʌn'feɪlɪŋ] *adj* inépuisable; infaillible

**unfair** [ʌn'fɛəʳ] *adj*: ~ **(to)** injuste (envers); **it's ~ that ...** il n'est pas juste que ...

**unfair dismissal** *n* licenciement abusif

**unfairly** [ʌn'fɛəlɪ] *adv* injustement

**unfaithful** [ʌn'feɪθful] *adj* infidèle

**unfamiliar** [ʌnfə'mɪlɪəʳ] *adj* étrange, inconnu(e); **to be ~ with sth** mal connaître qch

**unfashionable** [ʌn'fæʃnəbl] *adj* (*clothes*) démodé(e); (*place*) peu chic *inv*; (*district*) déshérité(e), pas à la mode

**unfasten** [ʌn'fɑ:sn] *vt* défaire; (*belt, necklace*) détacher; (*open*) ouvrir

**unfathomable** [ʌn'fæðəməbl] *adj* insondable

**unfavourable**, (*US*) **unfavorable** [ʌn'feɪvrəbl] *adj* défavorable

**unfavourably**, (*US*) **unfavorably** [ʌn'feɪvrəblɪ] *adv*: **to look ~ upon** ne pas être favorable à

**unfeeling** [ʌn'fi:lɪŋ] *adj* insensible, dur(e)

**unfinished** [ʌn'fɪnɪʃt] *adj* inachevé(e)

**unfit** [ʌn'fɪt] *adj* (*physically: ill*) en mauvaise santé; (: *out of condition*) pas en forme; (*incompetent*): ~ **(for)** impropre (à); (*work, service*) inapte (à)

**unflagging** [ʌn'flægɪŋ] *adj* infatigable, inlassable

**unflappable** [ʌn'flæpəbl] *adj* imperturbable

**unflattering** [ʌn'flætərɪŋ] *adj* (*dress, hairstyle*) qui n'avantage pas; (*remark*) peu flatteur(-euse)

**unflinching** [ʌn'flɪntʃɪŋ] *adj* stoïque

**unfold** [ʌn'fəuld] *vt* déplier; (*fig*) révéler, exposer ▷ *vi* se dérouler

**unforeseeable** [ʌnfɔ:'si:əbl] *adj* imprévisible

**unforeseen** ['ʌnfɔ:'si:n] *adj* imprévu(e)

**unforgettable** [ʌnfə'gɛtəbl] *adj* inoubliable

**unforgivable** [ʌnfə'gɪvəbl] *adj* impardonnable

**unformatted** [ʌn'fɔ:mætɪd] *adj* (*disk, text*) non formaté(e)

**unfortunate** [ʌn'fɔ:tʃnət] *adj* malheureux(-euse); (*event, remark*) malencontreux(-euse)

**unfortunately** [ʌn'fɔ:tʃnətlɪ] *adv* malheureusement

**unfounded** [ʌn'faundɪd] *adj* sans fondement

**unfriendly** [ʌn'frɛndlɪ] *adj* peu aimable, froid(e), inamical(e)

**unfulfilled** [ʌnful'fɪld] *adj* (*ambition, prophecy*) non réalisé(e); (*desire*) insatisfait(e); (*promise*) non tenu(e); (*terms of contract*) non rempli(e); (*person*) qui n'a pas su se réaliser

**unfurl** [ʌn'fə:l] *vt* déployer

**unfurnished** [ʌn'fə:nɪʃt] *adj* non meublé(e)

**ungainly** [ʌn'geɪnlɪ] *adj* gauche, dégingandé(e)

**ungodly** [ʌn'gɔdlɪ] *adj* impie; **at an ~ hour** à une heure indue

**ungrateful** [ʌn'greɪtful] *adj* qui manque de reconnaissance, ingrat(e)

**unguarded** [ʌn'gɑ:dɪd] *adj*: ~ **moment** moment *m* d'inattention

**unhappily** [ʌn'hæpɪlɪ] *adv* tristement; (*unfortunately*) malheureusement

**unhappiness** [ʌn'hæpɪnɪs] *n* tristesse *f*, peine *f*

**unhappy** [ʌn'hæpɪ] *adj* triste, malheureux(-euse); (*unfortunate: remark etc*) malheureux(-euse); (*not pleased*): ~ **with** mécontent(e) de, peu satisfait(e) de

**unharmed** [ʌn'hɑ:md] *adj* indemne, sain(e) et sauf (sauve)

**UNHCR** *n abbr* (= *United Nations High Commission for Refugees*) HCR *m*

**unhealthy** [ʌn'hɛlθɪ] *adj* (*gen*) malsain(e); (*person*) maladif(-ive)

**unheard-of** [ʌn'hə:dɔv] *adj* inouï(e), sans précédent

**unhelpful** [ʌn'hɛlpful] *adj* (*person*) peu serviable; (*advice*) peu utile

**unhesitating** [ʌn'hɛzɪteɪtɪŋ] *adj* (*loyalty*) spontané(e); (*reply, offer*) immédiat(e)

**unholy** [ʌn'həulɪ] *adj*: **an ~ alliance** une alliance contre nature; **he got home at an ~ hour** il est rentré à une heure impossible

**unhook** [ʌn'huk] *vt* décrocher; dégrafer

**unhurt** [ʌn'hə:t] *adj* indemne, sain(e) et sauf (sauve)

**unhygienic** ['ʌnhaɪ'dʒi:nɪk] *adj* antihygiénique

**UNICEF** ['ju:nɪsɛf] *n abbr* (= *United Nations International Children's Emergency Fund*) UNICEF *m*, FISE *m*

**unicorn** ['ju:nɪkɔ:n] *n* licorne *f*

**unidentified** [ʌnaɪ'dɛntɪfaɪd] *adj* non identifié(e); *see also* **UFO**

**uniform** ['ju:nɪfɔ:m] *n* uniforme *m* ▷ *adj* uniforme

**uniformity** [ju:nɪ'fɔ:mɪtɪ] *n* uniformité *f*

**unify** ['ju:nɪfaɪ] *vt* unifier

**unilateral** [ju:nɪ'lætərəl] *adj* unilatéral(e)

**unimaginable** [ʌnɪ'mædʒɪnəbl] *adj* inimaginable, inconcevable

**unimaginative** [ʌnɪ'mædʒɪnətɪv] *adj* sans imagination

**u**

**unimpaired** [ʌnɪm'pɛəd] adj intact(e)
**unimportant** [ʌnɪm'pɔːtənt] adj sans importance
**unimpressed** [ʌnɪm'prɛst] adj pas impressionné(e)
**uninhabited** [ʌnɪn'hæbɪtɪd] adj inhabité(e)
**uninhibited** [ʌnɪn'hɪbɪtɪd] adj sans inhibitions; sans retenue
**uninjured** [ʌn'ɪndʒəd] adj indemne
**uninspiring** [ʌnɪn'spaɪərɪŋ] adj peu inspirant(e)
**unintelligent** [ʌnɪn'tɛlɪdʒənt] adj inintelligent(e)
**unintentional** [ʌnɪn'tɛnʃənəl] adj involontaire
**unintentionally** [ʌnɪn'tɛnʃnəlɪ] adv sans le vouloir
**uninvited** [ʌnɪn'vaɪtɪd] adj (guest) qui n'a pas été invité(e)
**uninviting** [ʌnɪn'vaɪtɪŋ] adj (place) peu attirant(e); (food) peu appétissant(e)
**union** ['juːnjən] n union f; (also: **trade union**) syndicat m ▷ cpd du syndicat, syndical(e)
**unionize** ['juːnjənaɪz] vt syndiquer
**Union Jack** n drapeau du Royaume-Uni
**Union of Soviet Socialist Republics** n (formerly) Union f des républiques socialistes soviétiques
**union shop** n entreprise où tous les travailleurs doivent être syndiqués
**unique** [juː'niːk] adj unique
**unisex** ['juːnɪsɛks] adj unisexe
**Unison** ['juːnɪsn] n (trade union) grand syndicat des services publics en Grande-Bretagne
**unison** ['juːnɪsn] n: **in** ~ à l'unisson, en chœur
**unit** ['juːnɪt] n unité f; (section: of furniture etc) élément m, bloc m; (team, squad) groupe m, service m; **production** ~ atelier m de fabrication; **kitchen** ~ élément de cuisine; **sink** ~ bloc-évier m
**unit cost** n coût m unitaire
**unite** [juː'naɪt] vt unir ▷ vi s'unir
**united** [juː'naɪtɪd] adj uni(e); (country, party) unifié(e); (efforts) conjugué(e)
**United Arab Emirates** npl Émirats Arabes Unis
**United Kingdom** n Royaume-Uni m
**United Nations, United Nations Organization** n (Organisation f des) Nations unies
**United States, United States of America** n États-Unis mpl
**unit price** n prix m unitaire
**unit trust** n (Brit Comm) fonds commun de placement, FCP m
**unity** ['juːnɪtɪ] n unité f
**Univ.** abbr = **university**
**universal** [juːnɪ'vəːsl] adj universel(le)
**universe** ['juːnɪvəːs] n univers m
**university** [juːnɪ'vəːsɪtɪ] n université f ▷ cpd (student, professor) d'université; (education, year, degree) universitaire
**unjust** [ʌn'dʒʌst] adj injuste
**unjustifiable** ['ʌndʒʌstɪ'faɪəbl] adj injustifiable
**unjustified** [ʌn'dʒʌstɪfaɪd] adj injustifié(e);

(text) non justifié(e)
**unkempt** [ʌn'kɛmpt] adj mal tenu(e), débraillé(e); mal peigné(e)
**unkind** [ʌn'kaɪnd] adj peu gentil(le), méchant(e)
**unkindly** [ʌn'kaɪndlɪ] adv (treat, speak) avec méchanceté
**unknown** [ʌn'nəʊn] adj inconnu(e); ~ **to me** sans que je le sache; ~ **quantity** (Math, fig) inconnue f
**unladen** [ʌn'leɪdn] adj (ship, weight) à vide
**unlawful** [ʌn'lɔːful] adj illégal(e)
**unleaded** [ʌn'lɛdɪd] n (also: **unleaded petrol**) essence f sans plomb
**unleash** [ʌn'liːʃ] vt détacher; (fig) déchaîner, déclencher
**unleavened** [ʌn'lɛvnd] adj sans levain
**unless** [ʌn'lɛs] conj: ~ **he leaves** à moins qu'il (ne) parte; ~ **we leave** à moins de partir, à moins que nous (ne) partions; ~ **otherwise stated** sauf indication contraire; ~ **I am mistaken** si je ne me trompe
**unlicensed** [ʌn'laɪsnst] adj (Brit) non patenté(e) pour la vente des spiritueux
**unlike** [ʌn'laɪk] adj dissemblable, différent(e) ▷ prep à la différence de, contrairement à
**unlikelihood** [ʌn'laɪklɪhud] adj improbabilité f
**unlikely** [ʌn'laɪklɪ] adj (result, event) improbable; (explanation) invraisemblable
**unlimited** [ʌn'lɪmɪtɪd] adj illimité(e)
**unlisted** ['ʌn'lɪstɪd] adj (US Tel) sur la liste rouge; (Stock Exchange) non coté(e) en Bourse
**unlit** [ʌn'lɪt] adj (room) non éclairé(e)
**unload** [ʌn'ləʊd] vt décharger
**unlock** [ʌn'lɔk] vt ouvrir
**unlucky** [ʌn'lʌkɪ] adj (person) malchanceux(-euse); (object, number) qui porte malheur; **to be** ~ (person) ne pas avoir de chance
**unmanageable** [ʌn'mænɪdʒəbl] adj (unwieldy: tool, vehicle) peu maniable; (: situation) inextricable
**unmanned** [ʌn'mænd] adj sans équipage
**unmannerly** [ʌn'mænəlɪ] adj mal élevé(e), impoli(e)
**unmarked** [ʌn'mɑːkt] adj (unstained) sans marque; ~ **police car** voiture de police banalisée
**unmarried** [ʌn'mærɪd] adj célibataire
**unmask** [ʌn'mɑːsk] vt démasquer
**unmatched** [ʌn'mætʃt] adj sans égal(e)
**unmentionable** [ʌn'mɛnʃnəbl] adj (topic) dont on ne parle pas; (word) qui ne se dit pas
**unmerciful** [ʌn'məːsɪful] adj sans pitié
**unmistakable, unmistakeable** [ʌnmɪs'teɪkəbl] adj indubitable; qu'on ne peut pas ne pas reconnaître
**unmitigated** [ʌn'mɪtɪgeɪtɪd] adj non mitigé(e), absolu(e), pur(e)
**unnamed** [ʌn'neɪmd] adj (nameless) sans nom; (anonymous) anonyme
**unnatural** [ʌn'nætʃrəl] adj non naturel(le); (perversion) contre nature

unnecessary [ʌn'nɛsəsərɪ] adj inutile, superflu(e)

unnerve [ʌn'nɜːv] vt faire perdre son sang-froid à

unnoticed [ʌn'nəʊtɪst] adj inaperçu(e); to go ~ passer inaperçu

UNO ['juːnəʊ] n abbr = United Nations Organization

unobservant [ʌnəb'zɜːvnt] adj pas observateur(-trice)

unobtainable [ʌnəb'teɪnəbl] adj (Tel) impossible à obtenir

unobtrusive [ʌnəb'truːsiv] adj discret(-ète)

unoccupied [ʌn'ɔkjʊpaɪd] adj (seat, table, Mil) libre; (house) inoccupé(e)

unofficial [ʌnə'fɪʃl] adj (news) officieux(-euse), non officiel(le); (strike) ≈ sauvage

unopposed [ʌnə'pəʊzd] adj sans opposition

unorthodox [ʌn'ɔːθədɔks] adj peu orthodoxe

unpack [ʌn'pæk] vi défaire sa valise, déballer ses affaires ▷ vt (suitcase) défaire; (belongings) déballer

unpaid [ʌn'peɪd] adj (bill) impayé(e); (holiday) non-payé(e), sans salaire; (work) non rétribué(e); (worker) bénévole

unpalatable [ʌn'pælətəbl] adj (truth) désagréable (à entendre)

unparalleled [ʌn'pærəlɛld] adj incomparable, sans égal

unpatriotic ['ʌnpætrɪ'ɔtɪk] adj (person) manquant de patriotisme; (speech, attitude) antipatriotique

unplanned [ʌn'plænd] adj (visit) imprévu(e); (baby) non prévu(e)

unpleasant [ʌn'plɛznt] adj déplaisant(e), désagréable

unplug [ʌn'plʌg] vt débrancher

unpolluted [ʌnpə'luːtɪd] adj non pollué(e)

unpopular [ʌn'pɔpjʊləʳ] adj impopulaire; to make o.s. ~ (with) se rendre impopulaire (auprès de)

unprecedented [ʌn'prɛsɪdɛntɪd] adj sans précédent

unpredictable [ʌnprɪ'dɪktəbl] adj imprévisible

unprejudiced [ʌn'prɛdʒʊdɪst] adj (not biased) impartial(e); (having no prejudices) qui n'a pas de préjugés

unprepared [ʌnprɪ'pɛəd] adj (person) qui n'est pas suffisamment préparé(e); (speech) improvisé(e)

unprepossessing ['ʌnpriːpə'zɛsɪŋ] adj peu avenant(e)

unpretentious [ʌnprɪ'tɛnʃəs] adj sans prétention(s)

unprincipled [ʌn'prɪnsɪpld] adj sans principes

unproductive [ʌnprə'dʌktɪv] adj improductif(-ive); (discussion) stérile

unprofessional [ʌnprə'fɛʃənl] adj (conduct) contraire à la déontologie

unprofitable [ʌn'prɔfɪtəbl] adj non rentable

UNPROFOR [ʌn'prəʊfɔːʳ] n abbr (= United Nations Protection Force) FORPRONU f

unprotected ['ʌnprə'tɛktɪd] adj (sex) non protégé(e)

unprovoked [ʌnprə'vəʊkt] adj (attack) sans provocation

unpunished [ʌn'pʌnɪʃt] adj impuni(e); to go ~ rester impuni

unqualified [ʌn'kwɔlɪfaɪd] adj (teacher) non diplômé(e), sans titres; (success) sans réserve, total(e); (disaster) total(e)

unquestionably [ʌn'kwɛstʃənəblɪ] adv incontestablement

unquestioning [ʌn'kwɛstʃənɪŋ] adj (obedience, acceptance) inconditionnel(le)

unravel [ʌn'rævl] vt démêler

unreal [ʌn'rɪəl] adj irréel(le); (extraordinary) incroyable

unrealistic ['ʌnrɪə'lɪstɪk] adj (idea) irréaliste; (estimate) peu réaliste

unreasonable [ʌn'riːznəbl] adj qui n'est pas raisonnable; to make ~ demands on sb exiger trop de qn

unrecognizable [ʌn'rɛkəgnaɪzəbl] adj pas reconnaissable

unrecognized [ʌn'rɛkəgnaɪzd] adj (talent, genius) méconnu(e); (Pol: régime) non reconnu(e)

unrecorded [ʌnrɪ'kɔːdɪd] adj non enregistré(e)

unrefined [ʌnrɪ'faɪnd] adj (sugar, petroleum) non raffiné(e)

unrehearsed [ʌnrɪ'hɜːst] adj (Theat etc) qui n'a pas été répété(e); (spontaneous) spontané(e)

unrelated [ʌnrɪ'leɪtɪd] adj sans rapport; (people) sans lien de parenté

unrelenting [ʌnrɪ'lɛntɪŋ] adj implacable; acharné(e)

unreliable [ʌnrɪ'laɪəbl] adj sur qui (or quoi) on ne peut pas compter, peu fiable

unrelieved [ʌnrɪ'liːvd] adj (monotony) constant(e), uniforme

unremitting [ʌnrɪ'mɪtɪŋ] adj inlassable, infatigable, acharné(e)

unrepeatable [ʌnrɪ'piːtəbl] adj (offer) unique, exceptionnel(le)

unrepentant [ʌnrɪ'pɛntənt] adj impénitent(e)

unrepresentative ['ʌnrɛprɪ'zɛntətɪv] adj: ~ (of) peu représentatif(-ive) (de)

unreserved [ʌnrɪ'zɜːvd] adj (seat) non réservé(e); (approval, admiration) sans réserve

unreservedly [ʌnrɪ'zɜːvɪdlɪ] adv sans réserve

unresponsive [ʌnrɪs'pɔnsɪv] adj insensible

unrest [ʌn'rɛst] n agitation f, troubles mpl

unrestricted [ʌnrɪ'strɪktɪd] adj illimité(e); to have ~ access to avoir librement accès or accès en tout temps à

unrewarded [ʌnrɪ'wɔːdɪd] adj pas récompensé(e)

unripe [ʌn'raɪp] adj pas mûr(e)

unrivalled, (US) unrivaled [ʌn'raɪvəld] adj sans égal, incomparable

unroll [ʌn'rəʊl] vt dérouler

unruffled [ʌn'rʌfld] adj (person) imperturbable; (hair) qui n'est pas ébouriffé(e)

unruly [ʌn'ruːlɪ] adj indiscipliné(e)

849

**unsafe** [ʌn'seɪf] *adj* (*in danger*) en danger; (*journey, car*) dangereux(-euse); (*method*) hasardeux(-euse); ~ **to drink/eat** non potable/comestible

**unsaid** [ʌn'sɛd] *adj*: **to leave sth** ~ passer qch sous silence

**unsaleable**, (*US*) **unsalable** [ʌn'seɪləbl] *adj* invendable

**unsatisfactory** ['ʌnsætɪs'fæktərɪ] *adj* peu satisfaisant(e), qui laisse à désirer

**unsavoury**, (*US*) **unsavory** [ʌn'seɪvərɪ] *adj* (*fig*) peu recommandable, répugnant(e)

**unscathed** [ʌn'skeɪðd] *adj* indemne

**unscientific** ['ʌnsaɪən'tɪfɪk] *adj* non scientifique

**unscrew** [ʌn'skru:] *vt* dévisser

**unscrupulous** [ʌn'skru:pjuləs] *adj* sans scrupules

**unseat** [ʌn'si:t] *vt* (*rider*) désarçonner; (*fig: official*) faire perdre son siège à

**unsecured** ['ʌnsɪ'kjuəd] *adj*: ~ **creditor** créancier(-ière) sans garantie

**unseeded** [ʌn'si:dɪd] *adj* (*Sport*) non classé(e)

**unseemly** [ʌn'si:mlɪ] *adj* inconvenant(e)

**unseen** [ʌn'si:n] *adj* (*person*) invisible; (*danger*) imprévu(e)

**unselfish** [ʌn'sɛlfɪʃ] *adj* désintéressé(e)

**unsettled** [ʌn'sɛtld] *adj* (*restless*) perturbé(e); (*unpredictable*) instable; incertain(e); (*not finalized*) non résolu(e)

**unsettling** [ʌn'sɛtlɪŋ] *adj* qui a un effet perturbateur

**unshakable, unshakeable** [ʌn'ʃeɪkəbl] *adj* inébranlable

**unshaven** [ʌn'ʃeɪvn] *adj* non *or* mal rasé(e)

**unsightly** [ʌn'saɪtlɪ] *adj* disgracieux(-euse), laid(e)

**unskilled** [ʌn'skɪld] *adj*: ~ **worker** manœuvre *m*

**unsociable** [ʌn'səuʃəbl] *adj* (*person*) peu sociable; (*behaviour*) qui manque de sociabilité

**unsocial** [ʌn'səuʃl] *adj* (*hours*) en dehors de l'horaire normal

**unsold** [ʌn'səuld] *adj* invendu(e), non vendu(e)

**unsolicited** [ʌnsə'lɪsɪtɪd] *adj* non sollicité(e)

**unsophisticated** [ʌnsə'fɪstɪkeɪtɪd] *adj* simple, naturel(le)

**unsound** [ʌn'saund] *adj* (*health*) chancelant(e); (*floor, foundations*) peu solide; (*policy, advice*) peu judicieux(-euse)

**unspeakable** [ʌn'spi:kəbl] *adj* indicible; (*awful*) innommable

**unspoiled** ['ʌn'spɔɪld], **unspoilt** ['ʌn'spɔɪlt] *adj* (*place*) non dégradé(e)

**unspoken** [ʌn'spəukn] *adj* (*word*) qui n'est pas prononcé(e); (*agreement, approval*) tacite

**unstable** [ʌn'steɪbl] *adj* instable

**unsteady** [ʌn'stɛdɪ] *adj* mal assuré(e), chancelant(e), instable

**unstinting** [ʌn'stɪntɪŋ] *adj* (*support*) total(e), sans réserve; (*generosity*) sans limites

**unstuck** [ʌn'stʌk] *adj*: **to come** ~ se décoller; (*fig*) faire fiasco

**unsubstantiated** ['ʌnsəb'stænʃɪeɪtɪd] *adj* (*rumour*) qui n'est pas confirmé(e); (*accusation*) sans preuve

**unsuccessful** [ʌnsək'sɛsful] *adj* (*attempt*) infructueux(-euse); (*writer, proposal*) qui n'a pas de succès; (*marriage*) malheureux(-euse), qui ne réussit pas; **to be** ~ (*in attempting sth*) ne pas réussir; ne pas avoir de succès; (*application*) ne pas être retenu(e)

**unsuccessfully** [ʌnsək'sɛsfəlɪ] *adv* en vain

**unsuitable** [ʌn'su:təbl] *adj* qui ne convient pas, peu approprié(e); (*time*) inopportun(e)

**unsuited** [ʌn'su:tɪd] *adj*: **to be** ~ **for** *or* **to** être inapte *or* impropre à

**unsung** ['ʌnsʌŋ] *adj*: **an** ~ **hero** un héros méconnu

**unsupported** [ʌnsə'pɔ:tɪd] *adj* (*claim*) non soutenu(e); (*theory*) qui n'est pas corroboré(e)

**unsure** [ʌn'ʃuəʳ] *adj* pas sûr(e); **to be** ~ **of o.s.** ne pas être sûr de soi, manquer de confiance en soi

**unsuspecting** [ʌnsə'spɛktɪŋ] *adj* qui ne se méfie pas

**unsweetened** [ʌn'swi:tnd] *adj* non sucré(e)

**unswerving** [ʌn'swə:vɪŋ] *adj* inébranlable

**unsympathetic** ['ʌnsɪmpə'θɛtɪk] *adj* hostile; (*unpleasant*) antipathique; ~ **to** indifférent(e) à

**untangle** [ʌn'tæŋgl] *vt* démêler, débrouiller

**untapped** [ʌn'tæpt] *adj* (*resources*) inexploité(e)

**untaxed** [ʌn'tækst] *adj* (*goods*) non taxé(e); (*income*) non imposé(e)

**unthinkable** [ʌn'θɪŋkəbl] *adj* impensable, inconcevable

**unthinkingly** [ʌn'θɪŋkɪŋlɪ] *adv* sans réfléchir

**untidy** [ʌn'taɪdɪ] *adj* (*room*) en désordre; (*appearance, person*) débraillé(e); (*person: in character*) sans ordre, désordonné; débraillé; (*work*) peu soigné(e)

**untie** [ʌn'taɪ] *vt* (*knot, parcel*) défaire; (*prisoner, dog*) détacher

**until** [ən'tɪl] *prep* jusqu'à; (*after negative*) avant ▷ *conj* jusqu'à ce que + *sub*, en attendant que + *sub*; (*in past, after negative*) avant que + *sub*; ~ **he comes** jusqu'à ce qu'il vienne, jusqu'à son arrivée; ~ **now** jusqu'à présent, jusqu'ici; ~ **then** jusque-là; **from morning** ~ **night** du matin au soir *or* jusqu'au soir

**untimely** [ʌn'taɪmlɪ] *adj* inopportun(e); (*death*) prématuré(e)

**untold** [ʌn'təuld] *adj* incalculable; indescriptible

**untouched** [ʌn'tʌtʃt] *adj* (*not used etc*) tel(le) quel(le), intact(e); (*safe: person*) indemne; (*unaffected*): ~ **by** indifférent(e) à

**untoward** [ʌntə'wɔ:d] *adj* fâcheux(-euse), malencontreux(-euse)

**untrained** ['ʌn'treɪnd] *adj* (*worker*) sans formation; (*troops*) sans entraînement; **to the** ~ **eye** à l'œil non exercé

**untrammelled** [ʌn'træmld] *adj* sans entraves

**untranslatable** [ʌntrænz'leɪtəbl] *adj* intraduisible

**untrue** [ʌn'tru:] *adj* (*statement*) faux (fausse)

**untrustworthy** [ʌn'trʌstwə:ðɪ] adj (person) pas digne de confiance, peu sûr(e)
**unusable** [ʌn'ju:zəbl] adj inutilisable
**unused¹** [ʌn'ju:zd] adj (new) neuf (neuve)
**unused²** [ʌn'ju:st] adj: **to be ~ to sth/to doing sth** ne pas avoir l'habitude de qch/de faire qch
**unusual** [ʌn'ju:ʒuəl] adj insolite, exceptionnel(le), rare
**unusually** [ʌn'ju:ʒuəlɪ] adv exceptionnellement, particulièrement
**unveil** [ʌn'veɪl] vt dévoiler
**unwanted** [ʌn'wɒntɪd] adj (child, pregnancy) non désiré(e); (clothes etc) à donner
**unwarranted** [ʌn'wɒrəntɪd] adj injustifié(e)
**unwary** [ʌn'wɛərɪ] adj imprudent(e)
**unwavering** [ʌn'weɪvərɪŋ] adj inébranlable
**unwelcome** [ʌn'wɛlkəm] adj importun(e); **to feel ~** se sentir de trop
**unwell** [ʌn'wɛl] adj indisposé(e), souffrant(e); **to feel ~** ne pas se sentir bien
**unwieldy** [ʌn'wi:ldɪ] adj difficile à manier
**unwilling** [ʌn'wɪlɪŋ] adj: **to be ~ to do** ne pas vouloir faire
**unwillingly** [ʌn'wɪlɪŋlɪ] adv à contrecœur, contre son gré
**unwind** [ʌn'waɪnd] (irreg: like **wind**) vt dérouler ▷ vi (relax) se détendre
**unwise** [ʌn'waɪz] adj imprudent(e), peu judicieux(-euse)
**unwitting** [ʌn'wɪtɪŋ] adj involontaire
**unwittingly** [ʌn'wɪtɪŋlɪ] adv involontairement
**unworkable** [ʌn'wə:kəbl] adj (plan etc) inexploitable
**unworthy** [ʌn'wə:ðɪ] adj indigne
**unwrap** [ʌn'ræp] vt défaire; ouvrir
**unwritten** [ʌn'rɪtn] adj (agreement) tacite
**unzip** [ʌn'zɪp] vt ouvrir (la fermeture éclair de); (Comput) dézipper

🅞 KEYWORD

**up** [ʌp] prep: **he went up the stairs/the hill** il a monté l'escalier/la colline; **the cat was up a tree** le chat était dans un arbre; **they live further up the street** ils habitent plus haut dans la rue; **go up that road and turn left** remontez la rue et tournez à gauche
▷ vi (inf): **she upped and left** elle a fichu le camp sans plus attendre
▷ adv **1** en haut; en l'air; (upwards, higher): **up in the sky/the mountains** (là-haut) dans le ciel/les montagnes; **put it a bit higher up** mettez-le un peu plus haut; **to stand up** (get up) se lever, se mettre debout; (be standing) être debout; **up there** là-haut; **up above** au-dessus; **"this side up"** "haut"
**2**: **to be up** (out of bed) être levé(e); (prices) avoir augmenté or monté; (finished): **when the year was up** à la fin de l'année; **time's up** c'est l'heure
**3**: **up to** (as far as) jusqu'à; **up to now** jusqu'à présent

**4**: **to be up to** (depending on): **it's up to you** c'est à vous de décider; (equal to): **he's not up to it** (job, task etc) il n'en est pas capable; (inf: be doing): **what is he up to?** qu'est-ce qu'il peut bien faire?
**5** (phrases): **he's well up in** or **on ...** (Brit: knowledgeable) il s'y connaît en ...; **up with Leeds United!** vive Leeds United!; **what's up?** (inf) qu'est-ce qui ne va pas?; **what's up with him?** (inf) qu'est-ce qui lui arrive?
▷ n: **ups and downs** hauts et bas mpl

**up-and-coming** [ʌpənd'kʌmɪŋ] adj plein(e) d'avenir or de promesses
**upbeat** ['ʌpbi:t] n (Mus) levé m; (in economy, prosperity) amélioration f ▷ adj (optimistic) optimiste
**upbraid** [ʌp'breɪd] vt morigéner
**upbringing** ['ʌpbrɪŋɪŋ] n éducation f
**upcoming** ['ʌpkʌmɪŋ] adj tout(e) prochain(e)
**update** [ʌp'deɪt] vt mettre à jour
**upend** [ʌp'ɛnd] vt mettre debout
**upfront** [ʌp'frʌnt] adj (open) franc (franche) ▷ adv (pay) d'avance; **to be ~ about sth** ne rien cacher de qch
**upgrade** [ʌp'greɪd] vt (person) promouvoir; (job) revaloriser; (property, equipment) moderniser
**upheaval** [ʌp'hi:vl] n bouleversement m; (in room) branle-bas m; (event) crise f
**uphill** [ʌp'hɪl] adj qui monte; (fig: task) difficile, pénible ▷ adv (face, look) en amont, vers l'amont; (go, move) vers le haut, en haut; **to go ~** monter
**uphold** [ʌp'həuld] vt (irreg: like **hold**) maintenir; soutenir
**upholstery** [ʌp'həulstərɪ] n rembourrage m; (cover) tissu m d'ameublement; (of car) garniture f
**upkeep** ['ʌpki:p] n entretien m
**upmarket** [ʌp'mɑ:kɪt] adj (product) haut de gamme inv; (area) chic inv
**upon** [ə'pɒn] prep sur
**upper** ['ʌpəʳ] adj supérieur(e); du dessus ▷ n (of shoe) empeigne f
**upper class** n: **the ~** ≈ la haute bourgeoisie
**upper-class** [ʌpə'klɑ:s] adj de la haute société, aristocratique; (district) élégant(e), huppé(e); (accent, attitude) caractéristique des classes supérieures
**uppercut** ['ʌpəkʌt] n uppercut m
**upper hand** n: **to have the ~** avoir le dessus
**Upper House** n: **the ~** (in Britain) la Chambre des Lords, la Chambre haute; (in France, in the US etc) le Sénat
**uppermost** ['ʌpəməust] adj le (la) plus haut(e), en dessus; **it was ~ in my mind** j'y pensais avant tout autre chose
**upper sixth** n terminale f
**Upper Volta** [-'vɒltə] n Haute Volta
**upright** ['ʌpraɪt] adj droit(e); (fig) droit, honnête ▷ n montant m
**uprising** ['ʌpraɪzɪŋ] n soulèvement m, insurrection f

**u**

851

**uproar** ['ʌprɔːʳ] *n* tumulte *m*, vacarme *m*; (*protests*) protestations *fpl*

**uproarious** [ʌp'rɔːrɪəs] *adj* (*event etc*) désopilant(e); ~ **laughter** un brouhaha de rires

**uproot** [ʌp'ruːt] *vt* déraciner

**upset** *n* ['ʌpset] dérangement *m* ▷ *vt* [ʌp'sɛt] (*irreg: like* **set**: *glass etc*) renverser; (*plan*) déranger; (*person: offend*) contrarier; (: *grieve*) faire de la peine à; bouleverser ▷ *adj* [ʌp'sɛt] contrarié(e); peiné(e); (*stomach*) détraqué(e), dérangé(e); **to get ~** (*sad*) devenir triste; (*offended*) se vexer; **to have a stomach ~** (*Brit*) avoir une indigestion

**upset price** *n* (*US, Scottish*) mise *f* à prix, prix *m* de départ

**upsetting** [ʌp'sɛtɪŋ] *adj* (*offending*) vexant(e); (*annoying*) ennuyeux(-euse)

**upshot** ['ʌpʃɔt] *n* résultat *m*; **the ~ of it all was that ...** il a résulté de tout cela que ...

**upside down** ['ʌpsaɪd-] *adv* à l'envers; **to turn sth ~** (*fig: place*) mettre sens dessus dessous

**upstage** ['ʌp'steɪdʒ] *vt*: **to ~ sb** souffler la vedette à qn

**upstairs** [ʌp'stɛəz] *adv* en haut ▷ *adj* (*room*) du dessus, d'en haut ▷ *n*: **the ~** l'étage *m*; **there's no ~** il n'y a pas d'étage

**upstart** ['ʌpstɑːt] *n* parvenu(e)

**upstream** [ʌp'striːm] *adv* en amont

**upsurge** ['ʌpsəːdʒ] *n* (*of enthusiasm etc*) vague *f*

**uptake** ['ʌpteɪk] *n*: **he is quick/slow on the ~** il comprend vite/est lent à comprendre

**uptight** [ʌp'taɪt] *adj* (*inf*) très tendu(e), crispé(e)

**up-to-date** ['ʌptə'deɪt] *adj* moderne; (*information*) très récent(e)

**upturn** ['ʌptəːn] *n* (*in economy*) reprise *f*

**upturned** ['ʌptəːnd] *adj* (*nose*) retroussé(e)

**upward** ['ʌpwəd] *adj* ascendant(e); vers le haut ▷ *adv* vers le haut; (*more than*): ~ **of** plus de; **and ~** et plus, et au-dessus

**upwardly-mobile** ['ʌpwədlɪ'məubaɪl] *adj* à mobilité sociale ascendante

**upwards** ['ʌpwədz] *adv* vers le haut; (*more than*): ~ **of** plus de; **and ~** et plus, et au-dessus

**URA** *n abbr* (*US*) = **Urban Renewal Administration**

**Ural Mountains** ['juərəl-] *npl*: **the ~** (*also:* **the Urals**) les monts *mpl* Oural, l'Oural *m*

**uranium** [juə'reɪnɪəm] *n* uranium *m*

**Uranus** [juə'reɪnəs] *n* Uranus *f*

**urban** ['əːbən] *adj* urbain(e)

**urban clearway** *n* rue *f* à stationnement interdit

**urbane** [əː'beɪn] *adj* urbain(e), courtois(e)

**urbanization** [əːbənaɪ'zeɪʃən] *n* urbanisation *f*

**urchin** ['əːtʃɪn] *n* gosse *m*, garnement *m*

**Urdu** ['uədu:] *n* ourdou *m*

**urge** [əːdʒ] *n* besoin (impératif), envie (pressante) ▷ *vt* (*caution etc*) recommander avec insistance; (*person*): **to ~ sb to do** exhorter qn à faire, pousser qn à faire, recommander vivement à qn de faire
  ▶ **urge on** *vt* pousser, presser

**urgency** ['əːdʒənsɪ] *n* urgence *f*; (*of tone*) insistance *f*

**urgent** ['əːdʒənt] *adj* urgent(e); (*plea, tone*) pressant(e)

**urgently** ['əːdʒəntlɪ] *adv* d'urgence, de toute urgence; (*need*) sans délai

**urinal** ['juərɪnl] *n* (*Brit: place*) urinoir *m*

**urinate** ['juərɪneɪt] *vi* uriner

**urine** ['juərɪn] *n* urine *f*

**URL** *abbr* (= *uniform resource locator*) URL *f*

**urn** [əːn] *n* urne *f*; (*also:* **tea urn**) fontaine *f* à thé

**Uruguay** ['juərəgwaɪ] *n* Uruguay *m*

**Uruguayan** [juərə'gwaɪən] *adj* uruguayen(ne) ▷ *n* Uruguayen(ne)

**US** *n abbr* = **United States**

**us** [ʌs] *pron* nous; *see also* **me**

**USA** *n abbr* = **United States of America**; (*Mil*) = **United States Army**

**usable** ['ju:zəbl] *adj* utilisable

**USAF** *n abbr* = **United States Air Force**

**usage** ['ju:zɪdʒ] *n* usage *m*

**USCG** *n abbr* = **United States Coast Guard**

**USDA** *n abbr* = **United States Department of Agriculture**

**USDAW** ['ʌzdɔː] *n abbr* (*Brit*: = *Union of Shop, Distributive and Allied Workers*) syndicat du commerce de détail et de la distribution

**USDI** *n abbr* = **United States Department of the Interior**

**use** *n* [ju:s] emploi *m*, utilisation *f*; usage *m*; (*usefulness*) utilité *f* ▷ *vt* [ju:z] se servir de, utiliser, employer; **in ~** en usage; **out of ~** hors d'usage; **to be of ~** servir, être utile; **to make ~ of sth** utiliser qch; **ready for ~** prêt à l'emploi; **it's no ~** ça ne sert à rien; **to have the ~ of** avoir l'usage de; **what's this ~d for?** à quoi est-ce que ça sert?; **she ~d to do it** elle le faisait (autrefois), elle avait coutume de le faire; **to be ~d to** avoir l'habitude de, être habitué(e) à; **to get ~d to** s'habituer à
  ▶ **use up** *vt* finir, épuiser; (*food*) consommer

**used** [ju:zd] *adj* (*car*) d'occasion

**useful** ['ju:sful] *adj* utile; **to come in ~** être utile

**usefulness** ['ju:sfəlnɪs] *n* utilité *f*

**useless** ['ju:slɪs] *adj* inutile; (*inf: person*) nul(le)

**user** ['ju:zəʳ] *n* utilisateur(-trice), usager *m*

**user-friendly** ['ju:zə'frɛndlɪ] *adj* convivial(e), facile d'emploi

**username** ['ju:zəneɪm] *nom m* d'utilisateur

**USES** *n abbr* = **United States Employment Service**

**usher** ['ʌʃəʳ] *n* placeur *m* ▷ *vt*: **to ~ sb in** faire entrer qn

**usherette** [ʌʃə'rɛt] *n* (*in cinema*) ouvreuse *f*

**USIA** *n abbr* = **United States Information Agency**

**USM** *n abbr* = **United States Mail; United States Mint**

**USN** *n abbr* = **United States Navy**

**USP** *n abbr* = **unique selling proposition**

**USPHS** *n abbr* = **United States Public Health Service**

**USPO** *n abbr* = **United States Post Office**
**USS** *abbr* = **United States Ship (or Steamer)**
**USSR** *n abbr* = **Union of Soviet Socialist Republics**
**usu.** *abbr* = **usually**
**usual** ['juːʒuəl] *adj* habituel(le); **as ~** comme d'habitude
**usually** ['juːʒuəlɪ] *adv* d'habitude, d'ordinaire
**usurer** ['juːʒərəʳ] *n* usurier(-ière)
**usurp** [juːˈzəːp] *vt* usurper
**UT** *abbr* (*US*) = **Utah**
**utensil** [juːˈtɛnsl] *n* ustensile *m*; **kitchen ~s** batterie *f* de cuisine
**uterus** ['juːtərəs] *n* utérus *m*
**utilitarian** [juːtɪlɪˈtɛərɪən] *adj* utilitaire
**utility** [juːˈtɪlɪtɪ] *n* utilité *f*; (*also*: **public utility**) service public

**utility room** *n* buanderie *f*
**utilization** [juːtɪlaɪˈzeɪʃən] *n* utilisation *f*
**utilize** ['juːtɪlaɪz] *vt* utiliser; (*make good use of*) exploiter
**utmost** ['ʌtməust] *adj* extrême, le (la) plus grand(e) ▷ *n*: **to do one's ~** faire tout son possible; **of the ~ importance** d'une importance capitale, de la plus haute importance
**utter** ['ʌtəʳ] *adj* total(e), complet(-ète) ▷ *vt* prononcer, proférer; (*sounds*) émettre
**utterance** ['ʌtrns] *n* paroles *fpl*
**utterly** ['ʌtəlɪ] *adv* complètement, totalement
**U-turn** ['juːˈtəːn] *n* demi-tour *m*; (*fig*) volte-face *f inv*
**Uzbekistan** [ʌzbɛkɪˈstaːn] *n* Ouzbékistan *m*

u

# V

**V, v** [viː] *n (letter)* V, v *m*; **V for Victor** V comme Victor

**v.** *abbr* = **verse**; (= *vide*) v.; (= *versus*) vs; (= *volt*) V

**VA, Va.** *abbr (US)* = **Virginia**

**vac** [væk] *n abbr (Brit inf)* = **vacation**

**vacancy** ['veɪkənsɪ] *n (Brit: job)* poste vacant; *(room)* chambre *f* disponible; **"no vacancies"** "complet"

**vacant** ['veɪkənt] *adj (post)* vacant(e); *(seat etc)* libre, disponible; *(expression)* distrait(e)

**vacant lot** *n* terrain inoccupé; *(for sale)* terrain à vendre

**vacate** [və'keɪt] *vt* quitter

**vacation** [və'keɪʃən] *n (esp US)* vacances *fpl*; **to take a ~** prendre des vacances; **on ~** en vacances

**vacation course** *n* cours *mpl* de vacances

**vacationer** [və'keɪʃənəʳ], **(US) vacationist** [və'keɪʃənɪst] *n* vacancier(-ière)

**vaccinate** ['væksɪneɪt] *vt* vacciner

**vaccination** [væksɪ'neɪʃən] *n* vaccination *f*

**vaccine** ['væksiːn] *n* vaccin *m*

**vacuum** ['vækjum] *n* vide *m*

**vacuum bottle** *n (US)* = **vacuum flask**

**vacuum cleaner** *n* aspirateur *m*

**vacuum flask** *n (Brit)* bouteille *f* thermos®

**vacuum-packed** ['vækjumpækt] *adj* emballé(e) sous vide

**vagabond** ['vægəbɔnd] *n* vagabond(e); *(tramp)* chemineau *m*, clochard(e)

**vagary** ['veɪgərɪ] *n* caprice *m*

**vagina** [və'dʒaɪnə] *n* vagin *m*

**vagrancy** ['veɪgrənsɪ] *n* vagabondage *m*

**vagrant** ['veɪgrənt] *n* vagabond(e), mendiant(e)

**vague** [veɪg] *adj* vague, imprécis(e); *(blurred: photo, memory)* flou(e); **I haven't the ~st idea** je n'en ai pas la moindre idée

**vaguely** ['veɪglɪ] *adv* vaguement

**vain** [veɪn] *adj (useless)* vain(e); *(conceited)* vaniteux(-euse); **in ~** en vain

**valance** ['væləns] *n (of bed)* tour *m* de lit

**valedictory** [vælɪ'dɪktərɪ] *adj* d'adieu

**valentine** ['væləntaɪn] *n (also: **valentine card**)* carte *f* de la Saint-Valentin

**Valentine's Day** ['væləntaɪnz-] *n* Saint-Valentin *f*

**valet** ['vælɪt] *n* valet *m* de chambre

**valet parking** *n* parcage *m* par les soins du personnel (de l'hôtel *etc*)

**valet service** *n (for clothes)* pressing *m*; *(for car)* nettoyage complet

**valiant** ['væliənt] *adj* vaillant(e), courageux(-euse)

**valid** ['vælɪd] *adj (document)* valide, valable; *(excuse)* valable

**validate** ['vælɪdeɪt] *vt (contract, document)* valider; *(argument, claim)* prouver la justesse de, confirmer

**validity** [və'lɪdɪtɪ] *n* validité *f*

**valise** [və'liːz] *n* sac *m* de voyage

**valley** ['vælɪ] *n* vallée *f*

**valour, (US) valor** ['væləʳ] *n* courage *m*

**valuable** ['væljuəbl] *adj (jewel)* de grande valeur; *(time, help)* précieux(-euse)

**valuables** ['væljuəblz] *npl* objets *mpl* de valeur

**valuation** [vælju'eɪʃən] *n* évaluation *f*, expertise *f*

**value** ['væljuː] *n* valeur *f* ▷ *vt (fix price)* évaluer, expertiser; *(appreciate)* apprécier; *(cherish)* tenir à; **values** *npl (principles)* valeurs *fpl*; **you get good ~ (for money) in that shop** vous en avez pour votre argent dans ce magasin; **to lose (in) ~** *(currency)* baisser; *(property)* se déprécier; **to gain (in) ~** *(currency)* monter; *(property)* prendre de la valeur; **to be of great ~ to sb** *(fig)* être très utile à qn

**value added tax** [-'ædɪd-] *n (Brit)* taxe *f* à la valeur ajoutée

**valued** ['væljuːd] *adj (appreciated)* estimé(e)

**valuer** ['væljuəʳ] *n* expert *m* (en estimations)

**valve** [vælv] *n (in machine)* soupape *f*; *(on tyre)* valve *f*; *(in radio)* lampe *f*; *(Med)* valve, valvule *f*

**vampire** ['væmpaɪəʳ] *n* vampire *m*

**van** [væn] *n (Aut)* camionnette *f*; *(Brit Rail)* fourgon *m*

**V and A** *n abbr (Brit)* = **Victoria and Albert Museum**

**vandal** ['vændl] *n* vandale *m/f*

**vandalism** ['vændəlɪzəm] *n* vandalisme *m*

**vandalize** ['vændəlaɪz] *vt* saccager

**vanguard** ['vængɑːd] *n* avant-garde *m*

**vanilla** [və'nɪlə] *n* vanille *f* ▷ *cpd (ice cream)* à la vanille

**vanish** ['vænɪʃ] *vi* disparaître
**vanity** ['vænɪtɪ] *n* vanité *f*
**vanity case** *n* sac *m* de toilette
**vantage** ['vɑːntɪdʒ] *n*: **~ point** bonne position
**vaporize** ['veɪpəraɪz] *vt* vaporiser ▷ *vi* se vaporiser
**vapour**, *(US)* **vapor** ['veɪpə<sup>r</sup>] *n* vapeur *f*; *(on window)* buée *f*
**variable** ['vɛərɪəbl] *adj* variable; *(mood)* changeant(e) ▷ *n* variable *f*
**variance** ['vɛərɪəns] *n*: **to be at ~ (with)** être en désaccord (avec); *(facts)* être en contradiction (avec)
**variant** ['vɛərɪənt] *n* variante *f*
**variation** [vɛərɪ'eɪʃən] *n* variation *f*; *(in opinion)* changement *m*
**varicose** ['værɪkəus] *adj*: **~ veins** varices *fpl*
**varied** ['vɛərɪd] *adj* varié(e), divers(e)
**variety** [və'raɪətɪ] *n* variété *f*; *(quantity)* nombre *m*, quantité *f*; **a wide ~ of ...** une quantité *or* un grand nombre de ... (différent(e)s *or* divers(es)); **for a ~ of reasons** pour diverses raisons
**variety show** *n* (spectacle *m* de) variétés *fpl*
**various** ['vɛərɪəs] *adj* divers(e), différent(e); *(several)* divers, plusieurs; **at ~ times** *(different)* en diverses occasions; *(several)* à plusieurs reprises
**varnish** ['vɑːnɪʃ] *n* vernis *m*; *(for nails)* vernis (à ongles) ▷ *vt* vernir; **to ~ one's nails** se vernir les ongles
**vary** ['vɛərɪ] *vt, vi* varier, changer; **to ~ with** *or* **according to** varier selon
**varying** ['vɛərɪɪŋ] *adj* variable
**vase** [vɑːz] *n* vase *m*
**vasectomy** [væ'sɛktəmɪ] *n* vasectomie *f*
**Vaseline®** ['væsɪliːn] *n* vaseline *f*
**vast** [vɑːst] *adj* vaste, immense; *(amount, success)* énorme
**vastly** ['vɑːstlɪ] *adv* infiniment, extrêmement
**vastness** ['vɑːstnɪs] *n* immensité *f*
**VAT** [væt] *n abbr (Brit: = value added tax)* TVA *f*
**vat** [væt] *n* cuve *f*
**Vatican** ['vætɪkən] *n*: **the ~** le Vatican
**vatman** ['vætmæn] *(irreg) n (Brit inf)* contrôleur *m* de la T.V.A.
**vault** [vɔːlt] *n (of roof)* voûte *f*; *(tomb)* caveau *m*; *(in bank)* salle *f* des coffres; chambre forte; *(jump)* saut *m* ▷ *vt (also:* **vault over)** sauter (d'un bond)
**vaunted** ['vɔːntɪd] *adj*: **much-~** tant célébré(e)
**VC** *n abbr* = **vice-chairman**; *(Brit: = Victoria Cross)* distinction militaire
**VCR** *n abbr* = **video cassette recorder**
**VD** *n abbr* = **venereal disease**
**VDU** *n abbr* = **visual display unit**
**veal** [viːl] *n* veau *m*
**veer** [vɪə<sup>r</sup>] *vi* tourner; *(car, ship)* virer
**veg.** [vɛdʒ] *n abbr (Brit inf)* = **vegetable**; **vegetables**
**vegan** ['viːgən] *n* végétalien(ne)
**vegeburger** ['vɛdʒɪbəːgə<sup>r</sup>] *n* burger végétarien
**vegetable** ['vɛdʒtəbl] *n* légume *m* ▷ *adj* végétal(e)

**vegetable garden** *n* (jardin *m*) potager *m*
**vegetarian** [vɛdʒɪ'tɛərɪən] *adj, n* végétarien(ne); **do you have any ~ dishes?** avez-vous des plats végétariens?
**vegetate** ['vɛdʒɪteɪt] *vi* végéter
**vegetation** [vɛdʒɪ'teɪʃən] *n* végétation *f*
**vegetative** ['vɛdʒɪtətɪv] *adj (lit)* végétal(e); *(fig)* végétatif(-ive)
**veggieburger** ['vɛdʒɪbəːgə<sup>r</sup>] *n* = **vegeburger**
**vehemence** ['viːɪməns] *n* véhémence *f*, violence *f*
**vehement** ['viːɪmənt] *adj* violent(e), impétueux(-euse); *(impassioned)* ardent(e)
**vehicle** ['viːɪkl] *n* véhicule *m*
**vehicular** [vɪ'hɪkjulə<sup>r</sup>] *adj*: **"no ~ traffic"** "interdit à tout véhicule"
**veil** [veɪl] *n* voile *m* ▷ *vt* voiler; **under a ~ of secrecy** *(fig)* dans le plus grand secret
**veiled** [veɪld] *adj* voilé(e)
**vein** [veɪn] *n* veine *f*; *(on leaf)* nervure *f*; *(fig: mood)* esprit *m*
**Velcro®** ['vɛlkrəu] *n* velcro® *m*
**vellum** ['vɛləm] *n (writing paper)* vélin *m*
**velocity** [vɪ'lɔsɪtɪ] *n* vitesse *f*, vélocité *f*
**velour, velours** [və'luə<sup>r</sup>] *n* velours *m*
**velvet** ['vɛlvɪt] *n* velours *m*
**vending machine** ['vɛndɪŋ-] *n* distributeur *m* automatique
**vendor** ['vɛndə<sup>r</sup>] *n* vendeur(-euse); **street ~** marchand ambulant
**veneer** [və'nɪə<sup>r</sup>] *n* placage *m* de bois; *(fig)* vernis *m*
**venerable** ['vɛnərəbl] *adj* vénérable
**venereal** [vɪ'nɪərɪəl] *adj*: **~ disease** maladie vénérienne
**Venetian blind** [vɪ'niːʃən-] *n* store vénitien
**Venezuela** [vɛnɛ'zweɪlə] *n* Venezuela *m*
**Venezuelan** [vɛnɛ'zweɪlən] *adj* vénézuélien(ne) ▷ *n* Vénézuélien(ne)
**vengeance** ['vɛndʒəns] *n* vengeance *f*; **with a ~** *(fig)* vraiment, pour de bon
**vengeful** ['vɛndʒful] *adj* vengeur(-geresse)
**Venice** ['vɛnɪs] *n* Venise
**venison** ['vɛnɪsn] *n* venaison *f*
**venom** ['vɛnəm] *n* venin *m*
**venomous** ['vɛnəməs] *adj* venimeux(-euse)
**vent** [vɛnt] *n* conduit *m* d'aération; *(in dress, jacket)* fente *f* ▷ *vt (fig: one's feelings)* donner libre cours à
**ventilate** ['vɛntɪleɪt] *vt (room)* ventiler, aérer
**ventilation** [vɛntɪ'leɪʃən] *n* ventilation *f*, aération *f*
**ventilation shaft** *n* conduit *m* de ventilation *or* d'aération
**ventilator** ['vɛntɪleɪtə<sup>r</sup>] *n* ventilateur *m*
**ventriloquist** [vɛn'trɪləkwɪst] *n* ventriloque *m/f*
**venture** ['vɛntʃə<sup>r</sup>] *n* entreprise *f* ▷ *vt* risquer, hasarder ▷ *vi* s'aventurer, se risquer; **a business ~** une entreprise commerciale; **to ~ to do sth** se risquer à faire qch
**venture capital** *n* capital-risque *m*
**venue** ['vɛnjuː] *n* lieu *m*; *(of conference etc)* lieu de

**V**

855

la réunion (or manifestation etc); (of match) lieu de la rencontre

**Venus** ['vi:nəs] n (planet) Vénus f

**veracity** [və'ræsɪtɪ] n véracité f

**veranda, verandah** [və'rændə] n véranda f

**verb** [və:b] n verbe m

**verbal** ['və:bl] adj verbal(e); (translation) littéral(e)

**verbally** ['və:bəlɪ] adv verbalement

**verbatim** [və:'beɪtɪm] adj, adv mot pour mot

**verbose** [və:'bəus] adj verbeux(-euse)

**verdict** ['və:dɪkt] n verdict m; ~ **of guilty/not guilty** verdict de culpabilité/de non-culpabilité

**verge** [və:dʒ] n bord m; "**soft –s**" (Brit) "accotements non stabilisés"; **on the ~ of doing** sur le point de faire
  ▶ **verge on** vt fus approcher de

**verger** ['və:dʒəʳ] n (Rel) bedeau m

**verification** [verɪfɪ'keɪʃən] n vérification f

**verify** ['verɪfaɪ] vt vérifier

**veritable** ['verɪtəbl] adj véritable

**vermin** ['və:mɪn] npl animaux mpl nuisibles; (insects) vermine f

**vermouth** ['və:məθ] n vermouth m

**vernacular** [və'nækjuləʳ] n langue f vernaculaire, dialecte m

**versatile** ['və:sətaɪl] adj polyvalent(e)

**verse** [və:s] n vers mpl; (stanza) strophe f; (in Bible) verset m; **in ~** en vers

**versed** [və:st] adj: **(well-)~ in** versé(e) dans

**version** ['və:ʃən] n version f

**versus** ['və:səs] prep contre

**vertebra** (pl **-e**) ['və:tɪbrə, -bri:] n vertèbre f

**vertebrate** ['və:tɪbrɪt] n vertébré m

**vertical** ['və:tɪkl] adj vertical(e) ▷ n verticale f

**vertically** ['və:tɪklɪ] adv verticalement

**vertigo** ['və:tɪgəu] n vertige m; **to suffer from ~** avoir des vertiges

**verve** [və:v] n brio m; enthousiasme m

**very** ['verɪ] adv très ▷ adj: **the ~ book which** le livre même que; **the ~ thought (of it)** ... rien que d'y penser ...; **at the ~ end** tout à la fin; **the ~ last** le tout dernier; **at the ~ least** au moins; **~ well** très bien; **~ little** très peu; **~ much** beaucoup

**vespers** ['vespəz] npl vêpres fpl

**vessel** ['vesl] n (Anat, Naut) vaisseau m; (container) récipient m; see also **blood**

**vest** [vest] n (Brit: underwear) tricot m de corps; (US: waistcoat) gilet m ▷ vt: **to ~ sb with sth, to ~ sth in sb** investir qn de qch

**vested interest** n: **to have a ~ in doing** avoir tout intérêt à faire; **vested interests** npl (Comm) droits acquis

**vestibule** ['vestɪbju:l] n vestibule m

**vestige** ['vestɪdʒ] n vestige m

**vestry** ['vestrɪ] n sacristie f

**Vesuvius** [vɪ'su:vɪəs] n Vésuve m

**vet** [vet] n abbr (Brit: = veterinary surgeon) vétérinaire m/f; (US: = veteran) ancien(ne) combattant(e) ▷ vt examiner minutieusement; (text) revoir; (candidate) se renseigner

soigneusement sur, soumettre à une enquête approfondie

**veteran** ['vetərn] n vétéran m; (also: **war veteran**) ancien combattant ▷ adj: **she's a ~ campaigner for** ... cela fait très longtemps qu'elle lutte pour ...

**veteran car** n voiture f d'époque

**veterinarian** [vetrɪ'neərɪən] n (US) = **veterinary surgeon**

**veterinary** ['vetrɪnərɪ] adj vétérinaire

**veterinary surgeon** ['vetrɪnərɪ-] (Brit) n vétérinaire m/f

**veto** ['vi:təu] n (pl **-es**) veto m ▷ vt opposer son veto à; **to put a ~ on** mettre (or opposer) son veto à

**vetting** ['vetɪŋ] n: **positive ~** enquête f de sécurité

**vex** [veks] vt fâcher, contrarier

**vexed** [vekst] adj (question) controversé(e)

**VFD** n abbr (US) = **voluntary fire department**

**VG** n abbr (Brit: Scol etc: = very good) tb (= très bien)

**VHF** abbr (= very high frequency) VHF

**VI** abbr (US) = **Virgin Islands**

**via** ['vaɪə] prep par, via

**viability** [vaɪə'bɪlɪtɪ] n viabilité f

**viable** ['vaɪəbl] adj viable

**viaduct** ['vaɪədʌkt] n viaduc m

**vial** ['vaɪəl] n fiole f

**vibes** [vaɪbz] npl (inf): **I get good/bad ~ about it** je le sens bien/ne le sens pas; **there are good/bad ~ between us** entre nous le courant passe bien/ne passe pas

**vibrant** ['vaɪbrnt] adj (sound, colour) vibrant(e)

**vibraphone** ['vaɪbrəfəun] n vibraphone m

**vibrate** [vaɪ'breɪt] vi: **to ~ (with)** vibrer (de); (resound) retentir (de)

**vibration** [vaɪ'breɪʃən] n vibration f

**vibrator** [vaɪ'breɪtəʳ] n vibromasseur m

**vicar** ['vɪkəʳ] n pasteur m (de l'Église anglicane)

**vicarage** ['vɪkərɪdʒ] n presbytère m

**vicarious** [vɪ'keərɪəs] adj (pleasure, experience) indirect(e)

**vice** [vaɪs] n (evil) vice m; (Tech) étau m

**vice-** [vaɪs] prefix vice-

**vice-chairman** [vaɪs'tʃeəmən] (irreg) n vice-président(e)

**vice-chancellor** [vaɪs'tʃɑːnsələʳ] n (Brit) ≈ président(e) d'université

**vice-president** [vaɪs'prezɪdənt] n vice-président(e)

**viceroy** ['vaɪsrɔɪ] n vice-roi m

**vice squad** n ≈ brigade mondaine

**vice versa** ['vaɪsɪ'və:sə] adv vice versa

**vicinity** [vɪ'sɪnɪtɪ] n environs mpl, alentours mpl

**vicious** ['vɪʃəs] adj (remark) cruel(le), méchant(e); (blow) brutal(e); (dog) méchant(e), dangereux(-euse); **a ~ circle** un cercle vicieux

**viciousness** ['vɪʃəsnɪs] n méchanceté f, cruauté f; brutalité f

**vicissitudes** [vɪ'sɪsɪtju:dz] npl vicissitudes fpl

**victim** ['vɪktɪm] n victime f; **to be the ~ of** être victime de

**victimization** [vɪktɪmaɪ'zeɪʃən] n brimades fpl; représailles fpl
**victimize** ['vɪktɪmaɪz] vt brimer; exercer des représailles sur
**victor** ['vɪktə<sup>r</sup>] n vainqueur m
**Victorian** [vɪk'tɔːrɪən] adj victorien(ne)
**victorious** [vɪk'tɔːrɪəs] adj victorieux(-euse)
**victory** ['vɪktərɪ] n victoire f; **to win a ~ over sb** remporter une victoire sur qn
**video** ['vɪdɪəu] n (video film) vidéo f; (also: **video cassette**) vidéocassette f; (also: **video cassette recorder**) magnétoscope m ▷ vt (with recorder) enregistrer; (with camera) filmer ▷ cpd vidéo inv
**video camera** n caméra f vidéo inv
**video cassette** n vidéocassette f
**video cassette recorder** n = **video recorder**
**videodisc** ['vɪdɪəudɪsk] n vidéodisque m
**video game** n jeu m vidéo inv
**video nasty** n vidéo à caractère violent ou pornographique
**videophone** ['vɪdɪəufəun] n visiophone m, vidéophone m
**video recorder** n magnétoscope m
**video recording** n enregistrement m (en) vidéo inv
**video shop** n vidéoclub m
**video tape** n bande f vidéo inv; (cassette) vidéocassette f
**video wall** n mur m d'images vidéo
**vie** [vaɪ] vi: **to ~ with** lutter avec, rivaliser avec
**Vienna** [vɪ'ɛnə] n Vienne
**Vietnam, Viet Nam** ['vjɛt'næm] n Viêt-nam or Vietnam m
**Vietnamese** [vjɛtnə'miːz] adj vietnamien(ne) ▷ n (pl inv) Vietnamien(ne); (Ling) vietnamien m
**view** [vjuː] n vue f; (opinion) avis m, vue ▷ vt voir, regarder; (situation) considérer; (house) visiter; **on ~** (in museum etc) exposé(e); **in full ~ of sb** sous les yeux de qn; **to be within ~ (of sth)** être à portée de vue (de qch); **an overall ~ of the situation** une vue d'ensemble de la situation; **in my ~** à mon avis; **in ~ of the fact that** étant donné que; **with a ~ to doing sth** dans l'intention de faire qch
**viewdata** ['vjuːdeɪtə] n (Brit) télétexte m (version téléphonique)
**viewer** ['vjuːə<sup>r</sup>] n (viewfinder) viseur m; (small projector) visionneuse f; (TV) téléspectateur(-trice)
**viewfinder** ['vjuːfaɪndə<sup>r</sup>] n viseur m
**viewpoint** ['vjuːpɔɪnt] n point m de vue
**vigil** ['vɪdʒɪl] n veille f; **to keep ~** veiller
**vigilance** ['vɪdʒɪləns] n vigilance f
**vigilant** ['vɪdʒɪlənt] adj vigilant(e)
**vigilante** [vɪdʒɪ'læntɪ] n justicier ou membre d'un groupe d'autodéfense
**vigorous** ['vɪgərəs] adj vigoureux(-euse)
**vigour**, (US) **vigor** ['vɪgə<sup>r</sup>] n vigueur f
**vile** [vaɪl] adj (action) vil(e); (smell, food) abominable; (temper) massacrant(e)
**vilify** ['vɪlɪfaɪ] vt calomnier, vilipender
**villa** ['vɪlə] n villa f

**village** ['vɪlɪdʒ] n village m
**villager** ['vɪlɪdʒə<sup>r</sup>] n villageois(e)
**villain** ['vɪlən] n (scoundrel) scélérat m; (Brit: criminal) bandit m; (in novel etc) traître m
**VIN** n abbr (US) = **vehicle identification number**
**vinaigrette** [vɪneɪ'grɛt] n vinaigrette f
**vindicate** ['vɪndɪkeɪt] vt défendre avec succès; justifier
**vindication** [vɪndɪ'keɪʃən] n: **in ~ of** pour justifier
**vindictive** [vɪn'dɪktɪv] adj vindicatif(-ive), rancunier(-ière)
**vine** [vaɪn] n vigne f; (climbing plant) plante grimpante
**vinegar** ['vɪnɪgə<sup>r</sup>] n vinaigre m
**vine grower** n viticulteur m
**vine-growing** ['vaɪngrəuɪŋ] adj viticole ▷ n viticulture f
**vineyard** ['vɪnjɑːd] n vignoble m
**vintage** ['vɪntɪdʒ] n (year) année f, millésime m ▷ cpd (car) d'époque; (wine) de grand cru; **the 1970 ~** le millésime 1970
**vinyl** ['vaɪnl] n vinyle m
**viola** [vɪ'əulə] n alto m
**violate** ['vaɪəleɪt] vt violer
**violation** [vaɪə'leɪʃən] n violation f; **in ~ of** (rule, law) en infraction à, en violation de
**violence** ['vaɪələns] n violence f; (Pol etc) incidents violents
**violent** ['vaɪələnt] adj violent(e); **a ~ dislike of sb/sth** une aversion profonde pour qn/qch
**violently** ['vaɪələntlɪ] adv violemment; (ill, angry) terriblement
**violet** ['vaɪələt] adj (colour) violet(te) ▷ n (plant) violette f
**violin** [vaɪə'lɪn] n violon m
**violinist** [vaɪə'lɪnɪst] n violoniste m/f
**VIP** n abbr (= very important person) VIP m
**viper** ['vaɪpə<sup>r</sup>] n vipère f
**viral** ['vaɪərəl] adj viral(e)
**virgin** ['vəːdʒɪn] n vierge f ▷ adj vierge; **she is a ~** elle est vierge; **the Blessed V~** la Sainte Vierge
**virginity** [vəː'dʒɪnɪtɪ] n virginité f
**Virgo** ['vəːgəu] n la Vierge; **to be ~** être de la Vierge
**virile** ['vɪraɪl] adj viril(e)
**virility** [vɪ'rɪlɪtɪ] n virilité f
**virtual** ['vəːtjuəl] adj (Comput, Physics) virtuel(le); (in effect): **it's a ~ impossibility** c'est quasiment impossible; **the ~ leader** le chef dans la pratique
**virtually** ['vəːtjuəlɪ] adv (almost) pratiquement; **it is ~ impossible** c'est quasiment impossible
**virtual reality** n (Comput) réalité virtuelle
**virtue** ['vəːtjuː] n vertu f; (advantage) mérite m, avantage m; **by ~ of** en vertu or raison de
**virtuosity** [vəːtju'ɒsɪtɪ] n virtuosité f
**virtuoso** [vəːtju'əuzəu] n virtuose m/f
**virtuous** ['vəːtjuəs] adj vertueux(-euse)
**virulent** ['vɪrulənt] adj virulent(e)
**virus** ['vaɪərəs] n (Med, Comput) virus m
**visa** ['viːzə] n visa m

**V**

**vis-à-vis** [viːzə'viː] *prep* vis-à-vis de

**viscount** ['vaɪkaunt] *n* vicomte *m*

**viscous** ['vɪskəs] *adj* visqueux(-euse), gluant(e)

**vise** [vaɪs] *n* (*US Tech*) = **vice**

**visibility** [vɪzɪ'bɪlɪtɪ] *n* visibilité *f*

**visible** ['vɪzəbl] *adj* visible; **~ exports/imports** exportations/importations *fpl* visibles

**visibly** ['vɪzəblɪ] *adv* visiblement

**vision** ['vɪʒən] *n* (*sight*) vue *f*, vision *f*; (*foresight, in dream*) vision

**visionary** ['vɪʒənrɪ] *n* visionnaire *m/f*

**visit** ['vɪzɪt] *n* visite *f*; (*stay*) séjour *m* ▷ *vt* (*person: US: also:* **visit with**) rendre visite à; (*place*) visiter; **on a private/official ~** en visite privée/officielle

**visiting** ['vɪzɪtɪŋ] *adj* (*speaker, team*) invité(e), de l'extérieur

**visiting card** *n* carte *f* de visite

**visiting hours** *npl* heures *fpl* de visite

**visitor** ['vɪzɪtə<sup>r</sup>] *n* visiteur(-euse); (*to one's house*) invité(e); (*in hotel*) client(e)

**visitor centre,** (*US*) **visitor center** *n* hall *m* or centre *m* d'accueil

**visitors' book** *n* livre *m* d'or; (*in hotel*) registre *m*

**visor** ['vaɪzə<sup>r</sup>] *n* visière *f*

**VISTA** ['vɪstə] *n abbr* (= *Volunteers in Service to America*) *programme d'assistance bénévole aux régions pauvres*

**vista** ['vɪstə] *n* vue *f*, perspective *f*

**visual** ['vɪzjuəl] *adj* visuel(le)

**visual aid** *n* support visuel (pour l'enseignement)

**visual arts** *npl* arts *mpl* plastiques

**visual display unit** *n* console *f* de visualisation, visuel *m*

**visualize** ['vɪzjuəlaɪz] *vt* se représenter; (*foresee*) prévoir

**visually** ['vɪzjuəlɪ] *adv* visuellement; **~ handicapped** handicapé(e) visuel(le)

**visually-impaired** ['vɪzjuəliːm'pɛə<sup>r</sup>d] *adj* malvoyant(e)

**vital** ['vaɪtl] *adj* vital(e); **of ~ importance (to sb/sth)** d'une importance capitale (pour qn/qch)

**vitality** [vaɪ'tælɪtɪ] *n* vitalité *f*

**vitally** ['vaɪtəlɪ] *adv* extrêmement

**vital statistics** *npl* (*of population*) statistiques *fpl* démographiques; (*inf: woman's*) mensurations *fpl*

**vitamin** ['vɪtəmɪn] *n* vitamine *f*

**vitiate** ['vɪʃɪeɪt] *vt* vicier

**vitreous** ['vɪtrɪəs] *adj* (*china*) vitreux(-euse); (*enamel*) vitrifié(e)

**vitriolic** [vɪtrɪ'ɔlɪk] *adj* (*fig*) venimeux(-euse)

**viva** ['vaɪvə] *n* (*also:* **viva voce**) (*examen*) oral

**vivacious** [vɪ'veɪʃəs] *adj* animé(e), qui a de la vivacité

**vivacity** [vɪ'væsɪtɪ] *n* vivacité *f*

**vivid** ['vɪvɪd] *adj* (*account*) frappant(e), vivant(e); (*light, imagination*) vif (vive)

**vividly** ['vɪvɪdlɪ] *adv* (*describe*) d'une manière vivante; (*remember*) de façon précise

**vivisection** [vɪvɪ'sɛkʃən] *n* vivisection *f*

**vixen** ['vɪksn] *n* renarde *f*; (*pej: woman*) mégère *f*

**viz** [vɪz] *abbr* (= *videlicet: namely*) à savoir, c. à d.

**VLF** *abbr* = **very low frequency**

**V-neck** ['viːnɛk] *n* décolleté *m* en V

**VOA** *n abbr* (= *Voice of America*) voix *f* de l'Amérique (*émissions de radio à destination de l'étranger*)

**vocabulary** [vəu'kæbjulərɪ] *n* vocabulaire *m*

**vocal** ['vəukl] *adj* vocal(e); (*articulate*) qui n'hésite pas à s'exprimer, qui sait faire entendre ses opinions; **vocals** *npl* voix *fpl*

**vocal cords** *npl* cordes vocales

**vocalist** ['vəukəlɪst] *n* chanteur(-euse)

**vocation** [vəu'keɪʃən] *n* vocation *f*

**vocational** [vəu'keɪʃənl] *adj* professionnel(le); **~ guidance/training** orientation/formation professionnelle

**vociferous** [və'sɪfərəs] *adj* bruyant(e)

**vodka** ['vɔdkə] *n* vodka *f*

**vogue** [vəug] *n* mode *f*; (*popularity*) vogue *f*; **to be in ~** être en vogue *or* à la mode

**voice** [vɔɪs] *n* voix *f*; (*opinion*) avis *m* ▷ *vt* (*opinion*) exprimer, formuler; **in a loud/soft ~** à voix haute/basse; **to give ~ to** exprimer

**voice mail** *n* (*system*) messagerie *f* vocale, boîte *f* vocale; (*device*) répondeur *m*

**voice-over** ['vɔɪsəuvə<sup>r</sup>] *n* voix off *f*

**void** [vɔɪd] *n* vide *m* ▷ *adj* (*invalid*) nul(le); (*empty*): **~ of** vide de, dépourvu(e) de

**voile** [vɔɪl] *n* voile *m* (*tissu*)

**vol.** *abbr* (= *volume*) vol

**volatile** ['vɔlətaɪl] *adj* volatil(e); (*fig: person*) versatile; (: *situation*) explosif(-ive)

**volcanic** [vɔl'kænɪk] *adj* volcanique

**volcano** (*pl* **-es**) [vɔl'keɪnəu] *n* volcan *m*

**volition** [və'lɪʃən] *n*: **of one's own ~** de son propre gré

**volley** ['vɔlɪ] *n* (*of gunfire*) salve *f*; (*of stones etc*) pluie *f*, volée *f*; (*Tennis etc*) volée

**volleyball** ['vɔlibɔːl] *n* volley(-ball) *m*

**volt** [vəult] *n* volt *m*

**voltage** ['vəultɪdʒ] *n* tension *f*, voltage *m*; **high/low ~** haute/basse tension

**voluble** ['vɔljubl] *adj* volubile

**volume** ['vɔljuːm] *n* volume *m*; (*of tank*) capacité *f*; **~ one/two** (*of book*) tome un/deux; **his expression spoke ~s** son expression en disait long

**volume control** *n* (*Radio, TV*) bouton *m* de réglage du volume

**volume discount** *n* (*Comm*) remise *f* sur la quantité

**voluminous** [və'luːmɪnəs] *adj* volumineux(-euse)

**voluntarily** ['vɔləntrɪlɪ] *adv* volontairement; bénévolement

**voluntary** ['vɔləntərɪ] *adj* volontaire; (*unpaid*) bénévole

**voluntary liquidation** *n* (*Comm*) dépôt *m* de bilan

**voluntary redundancy** *n* (*Brit*) départ *m* volontaire (*en cas de licenciements*)

**volunteer** [vɔlən'tɪəʳ] n volontaire m/f ▷ vt (information) donner spontanément ▷ vi (Mil) s'engager comme volontaire; **to ~ to do** se proposer pour faire

**voluptuous** [və'lʌptjuəs] adj voluptueux(-euse)

**vomit** ['vɔmɪt] n vomissure f ▷ vt, vi vomir

**voracious** [və'reɪʃəs] adj vorace; (reader) avide

**vote** [vəut] n vote m, suffrage m; (votes cast) voix f, vote; (franchise) droit m de vote ▷ vt (bill) voter; (chairman) élire; (propose): **to ~ that** proposer que +sub ▷ vi voter; **to put sth to the ~, to take a ~ on sth** mettre qch aux voix, procéder à un vote sur qch; **~ for** or **in favour of/against** vote pour/contre; **to ~ to do sth** voter en faveur de faire qch; **~ of censure** motion f de censure; **~ of thanks** discours m de remerciement

**voter** ['vəutəʳ] n électeur(-trice)

**voting** ['vəutɪŋ] n scrutin m, vote m

**voting paper** n (Brit) bulletin m de vote

**voting right** n droit m de vote

**vouch** [vautʃ]: **to ~ for** vt fus se porter garant de

**voucher** ['vautʃəʳ] n (for meal, petrol, gift) bon m; (receipt) reçu m; **travel ~** bon m de transport

**vow** [vau] n vœu m, serment m ▷ vi jurer; **to take** or **make a ~ to do sth** faire le vœu de faire qch

**vowel** ['vauəl] n voyelle f

**voyage** ['vɔɪɪdʒ] n voyage m par mer, traversée f; (by spacecraft) voyage

**voyeur** [vwɑ:jəːʳ] n voyeur m

**VP** n abbr = **vice-president**

**vs** abbr (= versus) vs

**VSO** n abbr (Brit: = Voluntary Service Overseas) ≈ coopération civile

**VT, Vt.** abbr (US) = **Vermont**

**vulgar** ['vʌlgəʳ] adj vulgaire

**vulgarity** [vʌl'gærɪtɪ] n vulgarité f

**vulnerability** [vʌlnərə'bɪlɪtɪ] n vulnérabilité f

**vulnerable** ['vʌlnərəbl] adj vulnérable

**vulture** ['vʌltʃəʳ] n vautour m

V

# W w

**W, w** ['dʌblju:] *n* (*letter*) W, w *m*; **W for William**
W comme William

**W** *abbr* (= *west*) O; (*Elec*: = *watt*) W

**WA** *abbr* (*US*) = **Washington**

**wad** [wɔd] *n* (*of cotton wool, paper*) tampon *m*; (*of banknotes etc*) liasse *f*

**wadding** ['wɔdɪŋ] *n* rembourrage *m*

**waddle** ['wɔdl] *vi* se dandiner

**wade** [weɪd] *vi*: **to ~ through** marcher dans, patauger dans; (*fig: book*) venir à bout de ▷ *vt* passer à gué

**wafer** ['weɪfə<sup>r</sup>] *n* (*Culin*) gaufrette *f*; (*Rel*) pain *m* d'hostie; (*Comput*) tranche *f* (de silicium)

**wafer-thin** ['weɪfə'θɪn] *adj* ultra-mince, mince comme du papier à cigarette

**waffle** ['wɔfl] *n* (*Culin*) gaufre *f*; (*inf*) rabâchage *m*; remplissage *m* ▷ *vi* parler pour ne rien dire; faire du remplissage

**waffle iron** *n* gaufrier *m*

**waft** [wɔft] *vt* porter ▷ *vi* flotter

**wag** [wæg] *vt* agiter, remuer ▷ *vi* remuer; **the dog ~ged its tail** le chien a remué la queue

**wage** [weɪdʒ] *n* (*also*: **wages**) salaire *m*, paye *f* ▷ *vt*: **to ~ war** faire la guerre; **a day's ~s** un jour de salaire

**wage claim** *n* demande *f* d'augmentation de salaire

**wage differential** *n* éventail *m* des salaires

**wage earner** [-ə:nə<sup>r</sup>] *n* salarié(e); (*breadwinner*) soutien *m* de famille

**wage freeze** *n* blocage *m* des salaires

**wage packet** *n* (*Brit*) (enveloppe *f* de) paye *f*

**wager** ['weɪdʒə<sup>r</sup>] *n* pari *m* ▷ *vt* parier

**waggle** ['wægl] *vt, vi* remuer

**wagon, waggon** ['wægən] *n* (*horse-drawn*) chariot *m*; (*Brit Rail*) wagon *m* (de marchandises)

**wail** [weɪl] *n* gémissement *m*; (*of siren*) hurlement *m* ▷ *vi* gémir; (*siren*) hurler

**waist** [weɪst] *n* taille *f*, ceinture *f*

**waistcoat** ['weɪskəut] *n* (*Brit*) gilet *m*

**waistline** ['weɪstlaɪn] *n* (tour *m* de) taille *f*

**wait** [weɪt] *n* attente *f* ▷ *vi* attendre; **to ~ for sb/ sth** attendre qn/qch; **to keep sb ~ing** faire attendre qn; **~ for me, please** attendez-moi, s'il vous plaît; **~ a minute!** un instant!;

**"repairs while you ~"** "réparations minute"; **I can't ~ to ...** (*fig*) je meurs d'envie de ...; **to lie in ~ for** guetter

▶ **wait behind** *vi* rester (à attendre)

▶ **wait on** *vt fus* servir

▶ **wait up** *vi* attendre, ne pas se coucher; **don't ~ up for me** ne m'attendez pas pour aller vous coucher

**waiter** ['weɪtə<sup>r</sup>] *n* garçon *m* (de café), serveur *m*

**waiting** ['weɪtɪŋ] *n*: **"no ~"** (*Brit Aut*) "stationnement interdit"

**waiting list** *n* liste *f* d'attente

**waiting room** *n* salle *f* d'attente

**waitress** ['weɪtrɪs] *n* serveuse *f*

**waive** [weɪv] *vt* renoncer à, abandonner

**waiver** ['weɪvə<sup>r</sup>] *n* dispense *f*

**wake** [weɪk] (*pt* **woke** *or* **-d**, *pp* **woken** *or* **waked** [wəuk, 'wəukn]) *vt* (*also*: **wake up**) réveiller ▷ *vi* (*also*: **wake up**) se réveiller ▷ *n* (*for dead person*) veillée *f* mortuaire; (*Naut*) sillage *m*; **to ~ up to sth** (*fig*) se rendre compte de qch; **in the ~ of** (*fig*) à la suite de; **to follow in sb's ~** (*fig*) marcher sur les traces de qn

**waken** ['weɪkn] *vt, vi* = **wake**

**Wales** [weɪlz] *n* pays *m* de Galles; **the Prince of ~** le prince de Galles

**walk** [wɔ:k] *n* promenade *f*; (*short*) petit tour; (*gait*) démarche *f*; (*path*) chemin *m*; (*in park etc*) allée *f*; (*pace*): **at a quick ~** d'un pas rapide ▷ *vi* marcher; (*for pleasure, exercise*) se promener ▷ *vt* (*distance*) faire à pied; (*dog*) promener; **10 minutes' ~ from** à 10 minutes de marche de; **to go for a ~** se promener; faire un tour; **from all ~s of life** de toutes conditions sociales; **I'll ~ you home** je vais vous raccompagner chez vous

▶ **walk out** *vi* (*go out*) sortir; (*as protest*) partir (en signe de protestation); (*strike*) se mettre en grève; **to ~ out on sb** quitter qn

**walkabout** ['wɔ:kəbaut] *n*: **to go (on a) ~** (*VIP*) prendre un bain de foule

**walker** ['wɔ:kə<sup>r</sup>] *n* (*person*) marcheur(-euse)

**walkie-talkie** ['wɔ:kɪ'tɔ:kɪ] *n* talkie-walkie *m*

**walking** ['wɔ:kɪŋ] *n* marche *f* à pied; **it's within ~ distance** on peut y aller à pied

**walking holiday** *n* vacances passées à faire de

la randonnée

**walking shoes** *npl* chaussures *fpl* de marche

**walking stick** *n* canne *f*

**Walkman®** ['wɔːkmən] *n* Walkman® *m*

**walk-on** ['wɔːkɔn] *adj* (*Theat: part*) de figurant(e)

**walkout** ['wɔːkaut] *n* (*of workers*) grève-surprise *f*

**walkover** ['wɔːkəuvəʳ] *n* (*inf*) victoire *f or* examen *m etc* facile

**walkway** ['wɔːkweɪ] *n* promenade *f*, cheminement piéton

**wall** [wɔːl] *n* mur *m*; (*of tunnel, cave*) paroi *f*; **to go to the ~** (*fig: firm etc*) faire faillite
  ▶ **wall in** *vt* (*garden etc*) entourer d'un mur

**wall cupboard** *n* placard mural

**walled** [wɔːld] *adj* (*city*) fortifié(e)

**wallet** ['wɔlɪt] *n* portefeuille *m*; **I can't find my ~** je ne retrouve plus mon portefeuille

**wallflower** ['wɔːlflauəʳ] *n* giroflée *f*; **to be a ~** (*fig*) faire tapisserie

**wall hanging** *n* tenture (murale), tapisserie *f*

**wallop** ['wɔləp] *vt* (*Brit inf*) taper sur, cogner

**wallow** ['wɔləu] *vi* se vautrer; **to ~ in one's grief** se complaire à sa douleur

**wallpaper** ['wɔːlpeɪpəʳ] *n* papier peint ▷ *vt* tapisser

**wall-to-wall** ['wɔːltə'wɔːl] *adj*: **~ carpeting** moquette *f*

**walnut** ['wɔːlnʌt] *n* noix *f*; (*tree, wood*) noyer *m*

**walrus** (*pl* **walrus** *or* **-es**) ['wɔːlrəs] *n* morse *m*

**waltz** [wɔːlts] *n* valse *f* ▷ *vi* valser

**wan** [wɔn] *adj* pâle; triste

**wand** [wɔnd] *n* (*also*: **magic wand**) baguette *f* (magique)

**wander** ['wɔndəʳ] *vi* (*person*) errer, aller sans but; (*thoughts*) vagabonder; (*river*) serpenter ▷ *vt* errer dans

**wanderer** ['wɔndərəʳ] *n* vagabond(e)

**wandering** ['wɔndrɪŋ] *adj* (*tribe*) nomade; (*minstrel, actor*) ambulant(e)

**wane** [weɪn] *vi* (*moon*) décroître; (*reputation*) décliner

**wangle** ['wæŋgl] (*Brit inf*) *vt* se débrouiller pour avoir; carotter ▷ *n* combine *f*, magouille *f*

**wanker** ['wæŋkəʳ] *n* (*inf!*) branleur *m* (!)

**want** [wɔnt] *vt* vouloir; (*need*) avoir besoin de; (*lack*) manquer de ▷ *n* (*poverty*) pauvreté *f*, besoin *m*; **wants** *npl* (*needs*) besoins *mpl*; **to ~ to do** vouloir faire; **to ~ sb to do** vouloir que qn fasse; **you're ~ed on the phone** on vous demande au téléphone; **"cook ~ed"** "on demande un cuisinier"; **for ~ of** par manque de, faute de

**want ads** *npl* (*US*) petites annonces

**wanted** ['wɔntɪd] *adj* (*criminal*) recherché(e) par la police

**wanting** ['wɔntɪŋ] *adj*: **to be ~ (in)** manquer (de); **to be found ~** ne pas être à la hauteur

**wanton** ['wɔntn] *adj* capricieux(-euse), dévergondé(e)

**war** [wɔːʳ] *n* guerre *f*; **to go to ~** se mettre en guerre; **to make ~ (on)** faire la guerre (à)

**warble** ['wɔːbl] *n* (*of bird*) gazouillis *m* ▷ *vi* gazouiller

**war cry** *n* cri *m* de guerre

**ward** [wɔːd] *n* (*in hospital*) salle *f*; (*Pol*) section électorale; (*Law: child: also*: **ward of court**) pupille *m/f*
  ▶ **ward off** *vt* parer, éviter

**warden** ['wɔːdn] *n* (*Brit: of institution*) directeur(-trice); (*of park, game reserve*) gardien(ne); (*Brit: also*: **traffic warden**) contractuel(le); (*of youth hostel*) responsable *m/f*

**warder** ['wɔːdəʳ] *n* (*Brit*) gardien *m* de prison

**wardrobe** ['wɔːdrəub] *n* (*cupboard*) armoire *f*; (*clothes*) garde-robe *f*; (*Theat*) costumes *mpl*

**warehouse** ['wɛəhaus] *n* entrepôt *m*

**wares** [wɛəz] *npl* marchandises *fpl*

**warfare** ['wɔːfɛəʳ] *n* guerre *f*

**war game** *n* jeu *m* de stratégie militaire

**warhead** ['wɔːhɛd] *n* (*Mil*) ogive *f*

**warily** ['wɛərɪlɪ] *adv* avec prudence, avec précaution

**warlike** ['wɔːlaɪk] *adj* guerrier(-ière)

**warm** [wɔːm] *adj* chaud(e); (*person, thanks, welcome, applause*) chaleureux(-euse); (*supporter*) ardent(e), enthousiaste; **it's ~** il fait chaud; **I'm ~** j'ai chaud; **to keep sth ~** tenir qch au chaud; **with my ~est thanks/congratulations** avec mes remerciements/mes félicitations les plus sincères
  ▶ **warm up** *vi* (*person, room*) se réchauffer; (*water*) chauffer; (*athlete, discussion*) s'échauffer ▷ *vt* (*food*) (faire) réchauffer; (*water*) (faire) chauffer; (*engine*) faire chauffer

**warm-blooded** ['wɔːm'blʌdɪd] *adj* (*Zool*) à sang chaud

**war memorial** *n* monument *m* aux morts

**warm-hearted** [wɔːm'hɑːtɪd] *adj* affectueux(-euse)

**warmly** ['wɔːmlɪ] *adv* (*dress*) chaudement; (*thank, welcome*) chaleureusement

**warmonger** ['wɔːmʌŋgəʳ] *n* belliciste *m/f*

**warmongering** ['wɔːmʌŋgrɪŋ] *n* propagande *f* belliciste, bellicisme *m*

**warmth** [wɔːmθ] *n* chaleur *f*

**warm-up** ['wɔːmʌp] *n* (*Sport*) période *f* d'échauffement

**warn** [wɔːn] *vt* avertir, prévenir; **to ~ sb (not) to do** conseiller à qn de (ne pas) faire

**warning** ['wɔːnɪŋ] *n* avertissement *m*; (*notice*) avis *m*; (*signal*) avertisseur *m*; **without (any) ~** (*suddenly*) inopinément; (*without notifying*) sans prévenir; **gale ~** (*Meteorology*) avis de grand vent

**warning light** *n* avertisseur lumineux

**warning triangle** *n* (*Aut*) triangle *m* de présignalisation

**warp** [wɔːp] *n* (*Textiles*) chaîne *f* ▷ *vi* (*wood*) travailler, se voiler *or* gauchir ▷ *vt* voiler; (*fig*) pervertir

**warpath** ['wɔːpɑːθ] *n*: **to be on the ~** (*fig*) être sur le sentier de la guerre

**W**

**warped** [wɔːpt] *adj* (*wood*) gauchi(e); (*fig*) perverti(e)

**warrant** ['wɔrnt] *n* (*guarantee*) garantie *f*; (*Law*: *to arrest*) mandat *m* d'arrêt; (: *to search*) mandat de perquisition ▷ *vt* (*justify, merit*) justifier

**warrant officer** *n* (*Mil*) adjudant *m*; (*Naut*) premier-maître *m*

**warranty** ['wɔrəntɪ] *n* garantie *f*; **under ~** (*Comm*) sous garantie

**warren** ['wɔrən] *n* (*of rabbits*) terriers *mpl*, garenne *f*

**warring** ['wɔːrɪŋ] *adj* (*nations*) en guerre; (*interests etc*) contradictoire, opposé(e)

**warrior** ['wɔrɪəʳ] *n* guerrier(-ière)

**Warsaw** ['wɔːsɔː] *n* Varsovie

**warship** ['wɔːʃɪp] *n* navire *m* de guerre

**wart** [wɔːt] *n* verrue *f*

**wartime** ['wɔːtaɪm] *n*: **in ~** en temps de guerre

**wary** ['wɛərɪ] *adj* prudent(e); **to be ~ about** *or* **of doing sth** hésiter beaucoup à faire qch

**was** [wɔz] *pt of* **be**

**wash** [wɔʃ] *vt* laver, (*sweep, carry: sea etc*) emporter, entraîner; (: *ashore*) rejeter ▷ *vi* se laver; (*sea*): **to ~ over/against sth** inonder/baigner qch ▷ *n* (*paint*) badigeon *m*; (*clothes*) lessive *f*; (*washing programme*) lavage *m*; (*of ship*) sillage *m*; **to give sth a ~** laver qch; **to have a ~** se laver, faire sa toilette; **he was ~ed overboard** il a été emporté par une vague

  ▶ **wash away** *vt* (*stain*) enlever au lavage; (*subj: river etc*) emporter

  ▶ **wash down** *vt* laver; laver à grande eau

  ▶ **wash off** *vi* partir au lavage

  ▶ **wash up** *vi* (*Brit*) faire la vaisselle; (*US: have a wash*) se débarbouiller

**Wash.** *abbr* (*US*) = **Washington**

**washable** ['wɔʃəbl] *adj* lavable

**washbasin** ['wɔʃbeɪsn] *n* lavabo *m*

**washer** ['wɔʃəʳ] *n* (*Tech*) rondelle *f*, joint *m*

**washing** ['wɔʃɪŋ] *n* (*Brit: linen etc: dirty*) linge *m*; (: *clean*) lessive *f*

**washing line** *n* (*Brit*) corde *f* à linge

**washing machine** *n* machine *f* à laver

**washing powder** *n* (*Brit*) lessive *f* (en poudre)

**Washington** ['wɔʃɪŋtən] *n* (*city, state*) Washington *m*

**washing-up** [wɔʃɪŋˈʌp] *n* (*Brit*) vaisselle *f*

**washing-up liquid** *n* (*Brit*) produit *m* pour la vaisselle

**wash-out** ['wɔʃaut] *n* (*inf*) désastre *m*

**washroom** ['wɔʃrum] *n* (*US*) toilettes *fpl*

**wasn't** ['wɔznt] = **was not**

**Wasp, WASP** [wɔsp] *n abbr* (*US inf:* = *White Anglo-Saxon Protestant*) surnom, souvent péjoratif, donné à l'américain de souche anglo-saxonne, aisé et de tendance conservatrice

**wasp** [wɔsp] *n* guêpe *f*

**waspish** ['wɔspɪʃ] *adj* irritable

**wastage** ['weɪstɪdʒ] *n* gaspillage *m*; (*in manufacturing, transport etc*) déchet *m*

**waste** [weɪst] *n* gaspillage *m*; (*of time*) perte *f*; (*rubbish*) déchets *mpl*; (*also*: **household waste**)

ordures *fpl* ▷ *adj* (*energy, heat*) perdu(e); (*food*) inutilisé(e); (*land, ground: in city*) à l'abandon; (: *in country*) inculte, en friche; (*leftover*): **~ material** déchets ▷ *vt* gaspiller; (*time, opportunity*) perdre; **wastes** *npl* étendue *f* désertique; **it's a ~ of money** c'est de l'argent jeté en l'air; **to go to ~** être gaspillé(e); **to lay ~** (*destroy*) dévaster

  ▶ **waste away** *vi* dépérir

**wastebasket** ['weɪstbɑːskɪt] *n* = **wastepaper basket**

**waste disposal, waste disposal unit** *n* (*Brit*) broyeur *m* d'ordures

**wasteful** ['weɪstful] *adj* gaspilleur(-euse); (*process*) peu économique

**waste ground** *n* (*Brit*) terrain *m* vague

**wasteland** ['weɪstlənd] *n* terres *fpl* à l'abandon; (*in town*) terrain(s) *m(pl)* vague(s)

**wastepaper basket** ['weɪstpeɪpə-] *n* corbeille *f* à papier

**waste pipe** *n* (*tuyau m de*) vidange *f*

**waste products** *npl* (*Industry*) déchets *mpl* (de fabrication)

**waster** ['weɪstəʳ] *n* (*inf*) bon(ne) à rien

**watch** [wɔtʃ] *n* montre *f*; (*act of watching*) surveillance *f*; (*guard: Mil*) sentinelle *f*; (: *Naut*) homme *m* de quart; (*Naut: spell of duty*) quart *m* ▷ *vt* (*look at*) observer; (: *match, programme*) regarder; (*spy on, guard*) surveiller; (*be careful of*) faire attention à ▷ *vi* regarder; (*keep guard*) monter la garde; **to keep a close ~ on sb/sth** surveiller qn/qch de près; **to keep ~** faire le guet; **~ what you're doing** fais attention à ce que tu fais

  ▶ **watch out** *vi* faire attention

**watchband** ['wɔtʃbænd] *n* (*US*) bracelet *m* de montre

**watchdog** ['wɔtʃdɔg] *n* chien *m* de garde; (*fig*) gardien(ne)

**watchful** ['wɔtʃful] *adj* attentif(-ive), vigilant(e)

**watchmaker** ['wɔtʃmeɪkəʳ] *n* horloger(-ère)

**watchman** ['wɔtʃmən] (*irreg*) *n* gardien *m*; (*also*: **night watchman**) veilleur *m* de nuit

**watch stem** *n* (*US*) remontoir *m*

**watch strap** ['wɔtʃstræp] *n* bracelet *m* de montre

**watchword** ['wɔtʃwəːd] *n* mot *m* de passe

**water** ['wɔːtəʳ] *n* eau *f* ▷ *vt* (*plant, garden*) arroser ▷ *vi* (*eyes*) larmoyer; **a drink of ~** un verre d'eau; **in British ~s** dans les eaux territoriales Britanniques; **to pass ~** uriner; **to make sb's mouth ~** mettre l'eau à la bouche de qn

  ▶ **water down** *vt* (*milk etc*) couper avec de l'eau; (*fig: story*) édulcorer

**water closet** *n* (*Brit*) w.-c. *mpl*, waters *mpl*

**watercolour**, (*US*) **watercolor** ['wɔːtəkʌləʳ] *n* aquarelle *f*; **watercolours** *npl* couleurs *fpl* pour aquarelle

**water-cooled** ['wɔːtəkuːld] *adj* à refroidissement par eau

**watercress** ['wɔːtəkres] *n* cresson *m* (de

fontaine)

**waterfall** ['wɔ:təfɔ:l] n chute f d'eau

**waterfront** ['wɔ:frʌnt] n (seafront) front m de mer; (at docks) quais mpl

**water heater** n chauffe-eau m

**water hole** n mare f

**water ice** n (Brit) sorbet m

**watering can** ['wɔ:tərɪŋ-] n arrosoir m

**water level** n niveau m de l'eau; (of flood) niveau des eaux

**water lily** n nénuphar m

**waterline** ['wɔ:təlaɪn] n (Naut) ligne f de flottaison

**waterlogged** ['wɔ:təlɒgd] adj détrempé(e); imbibé(e) d'eau

**water main** n canalisation f d'eau

**watermark** ['wɔ:təmɑ:k] n (on paper) filigrane m

**watermelon** ['wɔ:təmɛlən] n pastèque f

**water polo** n water-polo m

**waterproof** ['wɔ:təpru:f] adj imperméable

**water-repellent** ['wɔ:tərɪ'pɛlnt] adj hydrofuge

**watershed** ['wɔ:təʃɛd] n (Geo) ligne f de partage des eaux; (fig) moment m critique, point décisif

**water-skiing** ['wɔ:təski:ɪŋ] n ski m nautique

**water softener** n adoucisseur m d'eau

**water tank** n réservoir m d'eau

**watertight** ['wɔ:tətaɪt] adj étanche

**water vapour** n vapeur f d'eau

**waterway** ['wɔ:təweɪ] n cours m d'eau navigable

**waterworks** ['wɔ:təwə:ks] npl station f hydraulique

**watery** ['wɔ:tərɪ] adj (colour) délavé(e); (coffee) trop faible

**watt** [wɒt] n watt m

**wattage** ['wɒtɪdʒ] n puissance f or consommation f en watts

**wattle** ['wɒtl] n clayonnage m

**wave** [weɪv] n vague f; (of hand) geste m, signe m; (Radio) onde f; (in hair) ondulation f; (fig: of enthusiasm, strikes etc) vague ▷ vi faire signe de la main; (flag) flotter au vent; (grass) ondoyer ▷ vt (handkerchief) agiter; (stick) brandir; (hair) onduler; **short/medium ~** (Radio) ondes courtes/moyennes; **long ~** (Radio) grandes ondes; **the new ~** (Cine, Mus) la nouvelle vague; **to ~ goodbye to sb** dire au revoir de la main à qn

▸ **wave aside**

▸ **wave away** vt (fig: suggestion, objection) rejeter, repousser; (: doubts) chasser; (person): **to ~ sb aside** faire signe à qn de s'écarter

**waveband** ['weɪvbænd] n bande f de fréquences

**wavelength** ['weɪvlɛŋθ] n longueur f d'ondes

**waver** ['weɪvəʳ] vi vaciller; (voice) trembler; (person) hésiter

**wavy** ['weɪvɪ] adj (hair, surface) ondulé(e); (line) onduleux(-euse)

**wax** [wæks] n cire f; (for skis) fart m ▷ vt cirer; (car) lustrer; (skis) farter ▷ vi (moon) croître

**waxworks** ['wækswə:ks] npl personnages mpl

de cire; musée m de cire

**way** [weɪ] n chemin m, voie f; (path, access) passage m; (distance) distance f; (direction) chemin, direction f; (manner) façon f, manière f; (habit) habitude f, façon; (condition) état m; **which ~? — this ~/that ~** par où or de quel côté? **— par ici/par là**; **to crawl one's ~ to ...** ramper jusqu'à ...; **to lie one's ~ out of it** s'en sortir par un mensonge; **to lose one's ~** perdre son chemin; **on the ~ (to)** en route (pour); **to be on one's ~** être en route; **to be in the ~** bloquer le passage; (fig) gêner; **to keep out of sb's ~** éviter qn; **it's a long ~ away** c'est loin d'ici; **the village is rather out of the ~** le village est plutôt à l'écart or isolé; **to go out of one's ~ to do** (fig) se donner beaucoup de mal pour faire; **to be under ~** (work, project) être en cours; **to make ~ (for sb/sth)** faire place (à qn/qch), s'écarter pour laisser passer (qn/qch); **to get one's own ~** arriver à ses fins, **put it the right ~ up** (Brit) mettez-le dans le bon sens; **to be the wrong ~ round** être à l'envers, ne pas être dans le bon sens; **he's in a bad ~** il va mal; **in a ~** dans un sens; **by the ~** à propos; **in some ~s** à certains égards; d'un côté; **in the ~ of** en fait de, comme; **by ~ of** (through) en passant par, via; (as a sort of) en guise de; **"~ in"** (Brit) "entrée"; **"~ out"** (Brit) "sortie"; **the ~ back** le chemin du retour; **this ~ and that** par-ci par-là; **"give ~"** (Brit Aut) "cédez la priorité"; **no ~!** (inf) pas question!

**waybill** ['weɪbɪl] n (Comm) récépissé m

**waylay** [weɪ'leɪ] vt (irreg: like **lay**) attaquer; (fig): **I got waylaid** quelqu'un m'a accroché

**wayside** ['weɪsaɪd] n bord m de la route; **to fall by the ~** (fig) abandonner; (morally) quitter le droit chemin

**way station** n (US Rail) petite gare; (: fig) étape f

**wayward** ['weɪwəd] adj capricieux(-euse), entêté(e)

**W.C.** n abbr (Brit: = water closet) w.-c. mpl, waters mpl

**WCC** n abbr (= World Council of Churches) COE m (Conseil œcuménique des Églises)

**we** [wi:] pl pron nous

**weak** [wi:k] adj faible; (health) fragile; (beam etc) peu solide; (tea, coffee) léger(-ère); **to grow ~(er)** s'affaiblir, faiblir

**weaken** ['wi:kn] vi faiblir ▷ vt affaiblir

**weak-kneed** ['wi:k'ni:d] adj (fig) lâche, faible

**weakling** ['wi:klɪŋ] n gringalet m; faible m/f

**weakly** ['wi:klɪ] adj chétif(-ive) ▷ adv faiblement

**weakness** ['wi:knɪs] n faiblesse f; (fault) point m faible

**wealth** [wɛlθ] n (money, resources) richesse(s) f(pl); (of details) profusion f

**wealth tax** n impôt m sur la fortune

**wealthy** ['wɛlθɪ] adj riche

**wean** [wi:n] vt sevrer

**weapon** ['wɛpən] n arme f; **~s of mass destruction** armes fpl de destruction massive

**W**

863

**wear** [wɛə<sup>r</sup>] (*pt* **wore**, *pp* **worn**) [wɔː<sup>r</sup>, wɔːn] *n*
(*use*) usage *m*; (*deterioration through use*) usure *f*
▷ *vt* (*clothes*) porter; (*put on*) mettre; (*beard etc*)
avoir; (*damage: through use*) user ▷ *vi* (*last*) faire de
l'usage; (*rub etc through*) s'user; **sports/baby~**
vêtements *mpl* de sport/pour bébés; **evening ~**
tenue *f* de soirée; **~ and tear** usure *f*; **to ~ a hole
in sth** faire (à la longue) un trou dans qch
▶ **wear away** *vt* user, ronger ▷ *vi* s'user, être
rongé(e)
▶ **wear down** *vt* user; (*strength*) épuiser
▶ **wear off** *vi* disparaître
▶ **wear on** *vi* se poursuivre; passer
▶ **wear out** *vt* user; (*person, strength*) épuiser
**wearable** ['wɛərəbl] *adj* mettable
**wearily** ['wɪərɪlɪ] *adv* avec lassitude
**weariness** ['wɪərɪnɪs] *n* épuisement *m*,
lassitude *f*
**wearisome** ['wɪərɪsəm] *adj* (*tiring*) fatigant(e);
(*boring*) ennuyeux(-euse)
**weary** ['wɪərɪ] *adj* (*tired*) épuisé(e); (*dispirited*) las
(lasse); abattu(e) ▷ *vt* lasser ▷ *vi*: **to ~ of** se
lasser de
**weasel** ['wiːzl] *n* (*Zool*) belette *f*
**weather** ['wɛðə<sup>r</sup>] *n* temps *m* ▷ *vt* (*wood*) faire
mûrir; (*storm: lit, fig*) essuyer; (*crisis*) survivre à;
**what's the ~ like?** quel temps fait-il?; **under
the ~** (*fig: ill*) mal fichu(e)
**weather-beaten** ['wɛðəbiːtn] *adj* (*person*)
hâlé(e); (*building*) dégradé(e) par les intempéries
**weather forecast** *n* prévisions *fpl*
météorologiques, météo *f*
**weatherman** ['wɛðəmæn] (*irreg*) *n*
météorologue *m*
**weatherproof** ['wɛðəpruːf] *adj* (*garment*)
imperméable; (*building*) étanche
**weather report** *n* bulletin *m* météo, météo *f*
**weather vane** [-veɪn] *n* = **weather cock**
**weave** (*pt* **wove**, *pp* **woven**) [wiːv, wəuv, 'wəuvn]
*vt* (*cloth*) tisser; (*basket*) tresser ▷ *vi* (*fig: pt, pp*
**weaved**) (*move in and out*) se faufiler
**weaver** ['wiːvə<sup>r</sup>] *n* tisserand(e)
**weaving** ['wiːvɪŋ] *n* tissage *m*
**web** [wɛb] *n* (*of spider*) toile *f*; (*on duck's foot*)
palmure *f*; (*fig*) tissu *m*; (*Comput*): **the (World-
Wide) W~** le Web
**web address** *n* adresse *f* Web
**webbed** ['wɛbd] *adj* (*foot*) palmé(e)
**webbing** ['wɛbɪŋ] *n* (*on chair*) sangles *fpl*
**webcam** ['wɛbkæm] *n* webcam *f*
**weblog** ['wɛblɔg] *n* blog *m*, blogue *m*
**web page** *n* (*Comput*) page *f* Web
**website** ['wɛbsaɪt] *n* (*Comput*) site *m* web
**wed** [wɛd] (*pt, pp* **-ded**) *vt* épouser ▷ *vi* se marier
▷ *n*: **the newly--s** les jeunes mariés
**we'd** [wiːd] = **we had; we would**
**wedded** ['wɛdɪd] *pt, pp* of **wed**
**wedding** ['wɛdɪŋ] *n* mariage *m*
**wedding anniversary** *n* anniversaire *m* de
mariage; **silver/golden ~** noces *fpl* d'argent/
d'or
**wedding day** *n* jour *m* du mariage

**wedding dress** *n* robe *f* de mariée
**wedding present** *n* cadeau *m* de mariage
**wedding ring** *n* alliance *f*
**wedge** [wɛdʒ] *n* (*of wood etc*) coin *m*; (*under door
etc*) cale *f*; (*of cake*) part *f* ▷ *vt* (*fix*) caler; (*push*)
enfoncer, coincer
**wedge-heeled shoes** ['wɛdʒhiːld-] *npl*
chaussures *fpl* à semelles compensées
**wedlock** ['wɛdlɔk] *n* (*union f du*) mariage *m*
**Wednesday** ['wɛdnzdɪ] *n* mercredi *m*; *for phrases
see also* **Tuesday**
**wee** [wiː] *adj* (*Scottish*) petit(e); tout(e) petit(e)
**weed** [wiːd] *n* mauvaise herbe ▷ *vt* désherber
▶ **weed out** *vt* éliminer
**weedkiller** ['wiːdkɪlə<sup>r</sup>] *n* désherbant *m*
**weedy** ['wiːdɪ] *adj* (*man*) gringalet
**week** [wiːk] *n* semaine *f*; **once/twice a ~** une
fois/deux fois par semaine; **in two ~s' time**
dans quinze jours; **a ~ today/on Tuesday**
aujourd'hui/mardi en huit
**weekday** ['wiːkdeɪ] *n* jour *m* de semaine;
(*Comm*) jour ouvrable; **on ~s** en semaine
**weekend** [wiːk'ɛnd] *n* week-end *m*
**weekend case** *n* sac *m* de voyage
**weekly** ['wiːklɪ] *adv* une fois par semaine,
chaque semaine ▷ *adj, n* hebdomadaire (*m*)
**weep** [wiːp] (*pt, pp* **wept**) [wɛpt] *vi* (*person*)
pleurer; (*Med: wound etc*) suinter
**weeping willow** ['wiːpɪŋ-] *n* saule pleureur
**weepy** ['wiːpɪ] *n* (*inf: film*) mélo *m*
**weft** [wɛft] *n* (*Textiles*) trame *f*
**weigh** [weɪ] *vt, vi* peser; **to ~ anchor** lever
l'ancre; **to ~ the pros and cons** peser le pour et
le contre
▶ **weigh down** *vt* (*branch*) faire plier; (*fig: with
worry*) accabler
▶ **weigh out** *vt* (*goods*) peser
▶ **weigh up** *vt* examiner
**weighbridge** ['weɪbrɪdʒ] *n* pont-bascule *m*
**weighing machine** ['weɪɪŋ-] *n* balance *f*,
bascule *f*
**weight** [weɪt] *n* poids *m* ▷ *vt* alourdir; (*fig: factor*)
pondérer; **sold by ~** vendu au poids; **to put on/
lose ~** grossir/maigrir; **~s and measures** poids
et mesures
**weighting** ['weɪtɪŋ] *n*: **~ allowance** indemnité *f*
de résidence
**weightlessness** ['weɪtlɪsnɪs] *n* apesanteur *f*
**weightlifter** ['weɪtlɪftə<sup>r</sup>] *n* haltérophile *m*
**weightlifting** ['weɪtlɪftɪŋ] *n* haltérophilie *f*
**weight training** *n* musculation *f*
**weighty** ['weɪtɪ] *adj* lourd(e)
**weir** [wɪə<sup>r</sup>] *n* barrage *m*
**weird** [wɪəd] *adj* bizarre; (*eerie*) surnaturel(le)
**weirdo** ['wɪədəu] *n* (*inf*) type *m* bizarre
**welcome** ['wɛlkəm] *adj* bienvenu(e) ▷ *n* accueil
*m* ▷ *vt* accueillir; (*also*: **bid welcome**) souhaiter
la bienvenue à; (*be glad of*) se réjouir de; **to be ~**
être le (la) bienvenu(e); **to make sb ~** faire bon
accueil à qn; **you're ~ to try** vous pouvez
essayer si vous voulez; **you're ~!** (*after thanks*) de
rien, il n'y a pas de quoi

**welcoming** ['wɛlkəmɪŋ] *adj* accueillant(e); (*speech*) d'accueil
**weld** [wɛld] *n* soudure f ▷ *vt* souder
**welder** ['wɛldə*ʳ*] *n* (*person*) soudeur m
**welding** ['wɛldɪŋ] *n* soudure f (autogène)
**welfare** ['wɛlfɛə*ʳ*] *n* (*wellbeing*) bien-être m; (*social aid*) assistance sociale
**welfare state** *n* État-providence m
**welfare work** *n* travail social
**well** [wɛl] *n* puits m ▷ *adv* bien ▷ *adj*: **to be ~** aller bien ▷ *excl* eh bien!; (*relief also*) bon!; (*resignation*) enfin!; **~ done!** bravo!; **I don't feel ~** je ne me sens pas bien; **get ~ soon!** remets-toi vite!; **to do ~** bien réussir; (*business*) prospérer; **to think ~ of sb** penser du bien de qn; **as ~** (*in addition*) aussi, également; **you might as ~ tell me** tu ferais aussi bien de me le dire; **as ~ as** aussi bien que *or* de; en plus de; **~, as I was saying** … donc, comme je disais …
▷ **well up** *vi* (*tears, emotions*) monter
**we'll** [wiːl] = **we will; we shall**
**well-behaved** ['wɛlbɪ'heɪvd] *adj* sage, obéissant(e)
**well-being** ['wɛl'biːɪŋ] *n* bien-être m
**well-bred** ['wɛl'brɛd] *adj* bien élevé(e)
**well-built** ['wɛl'bɪlt] *adj* (*house*) bien construit(e); (*person*) bien bâti(e)
**well-chosen** ['wɛl'tʃəuzn] *adj* (*remarks, words*) bien choisi(e), pertinent(e)
**well-deserved** ['wɛldɪ'zəːvd] *adj* (*bien*) mérité(e)
**well-developed** ['wɛldɪ'vɛləpt] *adj* (*girl*) bien fait(e)
**well-disposed** ['wɛldɪs'pəuzd] *adj*: **~ to(wards)** bien disposé(e) envers
**well-dressed** ['wɛl'drɛst] *adj* bien habillé(e), bien vêtu(e)
**well-earned** ['wɛl'əːnd] *adj* (*rest*) bien mérité(e)
**well-groomed** [-'gruːmd] *adj* très soigné(e)
**well-heeled** ['wɛl'hiːld] *adj* (*inf: wealthy*) fortuné(e), riche
**wellies** ['wɛlɪz] (*inf*) *npl* (*Brit*) = **wellingtons**
**well-informed** ['wɛlɪn'fɔːmd] *adj* (*having knowledge of sth*) bien renseigné(e); (*having general knowledge*) cultivé(e)
**Wellington** ['wɛlɪŋtən] *n* Wellington
**wellingtons** ['wɛlɪŋtənz] *npl* (*also:* **wellington boots**) bottes fpl en caoutchouc
**well-kept** ['wɛl'kɛpt] *adj* (*house, grounds*) bien tenu(e), bien entretenu(e); (*secret*) bien gardé(e); (*hair, hands*) soigné(e)
**well-known** ['wɛl'nəun] *adj* (*person*) bien connu(e)
**well-mannered** ['wɛl'mænəd] *adj* bien élevé(e)
**well-meaning** ['wɛl'miːnɪŋ] *adj* bien intentionné(e)
**well-nigh** ['wɛl'naɪ] *adv*: **~ impossible** pratiquement impossible
**well-off** ['wɛl'ɔf] *adj* aisé(e), assez riche
**well-paid** [wɛl'peɪd] *adj* bien payé(e)
**well-read** ['wɛl'rɛd] *adj* cultivé(e)
**well-spoken** ['wɛl'spəukn] *adj* (*person*) qui parle

bien; (*words*) bien choisi(e)
**well-stocked** ['wɛl'stɔkt] *adj* bien approvisionné(e)
**well-timed** ['wɛl'taɪmd] *adj* opportun(e)
**well-to-do** ['wɛltə'duː] *adj* aisé(e), assez riche
**well-wisher** ['wɛlwɪʃə*ʳ*] *n* ami(e), admirateur(-trice); **scores of ~s had gathered** de nombreux amis et admirateurs s'étaient rassemblés; **letters from ~s** des lettres d'encouragement
**well-woman clinic** ['wɛlwumən-] *n* centre prophylactique et thérapeutique pour femmes
**Welsh** [wɛlʃ] *adj* gallois(e) ▷ *n* (*Ling*) gallois m; **the Welsh** *npl* (*people*) les Gallois
**Welsh Assembly** *n* Parlement gallois
**Welshman** ['wɛlʃmən] (*irreg*) *n* Gallois m
**Welsh rarebit** *n* croûte f au fromage
**Welshwoman** ['wɛlʃwumən] (*irreg*) *n* Galloise f
**welter** ['wɛltə*ʳ*] *n* fatras m
**went** [wɛnt] *pt of* **go**
**wept** [wɛpt] *pt, pp of* **weep**
**were** [wəː*ʳ*] *pt of* **be**
**we're** [wɪə*ʳ*] = **we are**
**weren't** [wəːnt] = **were not**
**werewolf** (*pl* **-wolves**) ['wɪəwulf, -wulvz] *n* loup-garou m
**west** [wɛst] *n* ouest m ▷ *adj* (*wind*) d'ouest; (*side*) ouest *inv* ▷ *adv* à *or* vers l'ouest; **the W~** l'Occident m, l'Ouest
**westbound** ['wɛstbaund] *adj* en direction de l'ouest; (*carriageway*) ouest *inv*
**West Country** *n*: **the ~** le sud-ouest de l'Angleterre
**westerly** ['wɛstəlɪ] *adj* (*situation*) à l'ouest; (*wind*) d'ouest
**western** ['wɛstən] *adj* occidental(e), de *or* à l'ouest ▷ *n* (*Cine*) western m
**westerner** ['wɛstənə*ʳ*] *n* occidental(e)
**westernized** ['wɛstənaɪzd] *adj* occidentalisé(e)
**West German** (*formerly*) *adj* ouest-allemand(e) ▷ *n* Allemand(e) de l'Ouest
**West Germany** *n* (*formerly*) Allemagne f de l'Ouest
**West Indian** *adj* antillais(e) ▷ *n* Antillais(e)
**West Indies** [-'ɪndɪz] *npl* Antilles fpl
**Westminster** ['wɛstmɪnstə*ʳ*] *n* (*Brit Parliament*) Westminster m
**westward** ['wɛstwəd], **westwards** ['wɛstwədz] *adv* vers l'ouest
**wet** [wɛt] *adj* mouillé(e); (*damp*) humide; (*soaked: also:* **wet through**) trempé(e); (*rainy*) pluvieux(-euse) ▷ *vt*: **to ~ one's pants** *or* **o.s.** mouiller sa culotte, faire pipi dans sa culotte; **to get ~** se mouiller; **"~ paint"** "attention peinture fraîche"
**wet blanket** *n* (*fig*) rabat-joie m *inv*
**wetness** ['wɛtnɪs] *n* humidité f
**wetsuit** ['wɛtsuːt] *n* combinaison f de plongée
**we've** [wiːv] = **we have**
**whack** [wæk] *vt* donner un grand coup à
**whacked** [wækt] *adj* (*Brit inf: tired*) crevé(e)
**whale** [weɪl] *n* (*Zool*) baleine f

W

865

**whaler** ['weɪlə<sup>r</sup>] n (ship) baleinier m
**whaling** ['weɪlɪŋ] n pêche f à la baleine
**wharf** (pl **wharves**) [wɔ:f, wɔ:vz] n quai m

 **KEYWORD**

**what** [wɔt] adj **1** (in questions) quel(le); **what size is he?** quelle taille fait-il?; **what colour is it?** de quelle couleur est-ce?; **what books do you need?** quels livres vous faut-il?
**2** (in exclamations): **what a mess!** quel désordre!; **what a fool I am!** que je suis bête!
▷ pron **1** (interrogative) que; de/à/en etc quoi; **what are you doing?** que faites-vous?, qu'est-ce que vous faites?; **what is happening?** qu'est-ce qui se passe?, que se passe-t-il?; **what are you talking about?** de quoi parlez-vous?; **what are you thinking about?** à quoi pensez-vous?; **what is it called?** comment est-ce que ça s'appelle?; **what about me?** et moi?; **what about doing ...?** et si on faisait ...?
**2** (relative: subject) ce qui; (: direct object) ce que; (: indirect object) ce à quoi, ce dont; **I saw what you did/was on the table** j'ai vu ce que vous avez fait/ce qui était sur la table; **tell me what you remember** dites-moi ce dont vous vous souvenez; **what I want is a cup of tea** ce que je veux, c'est une tasse de thé
▷ excl (disbelieving) quoi!, comment!

**whatever** [wɔt'ɛvə<sup>r</sup>] adj: **take ~ book you prefer** prenez le livre que vous préférez, peu importe lequel; **~ book you take** quel que soit le livre que vous preniez ▷ pron: **do ~ is necessary** faites (tout) ce qui est nécessaire; **~ happens** quoi qu'il arrive; **no reason ~ or whatsoever** pas la moindre raison; **nothing ~ or whatsoever** rien du tout
**whatsoever** [wɔtsəu'ɛvə<sup>r</sup>] adj see **whatever**
**wheat** [wi:t] n blé m, froment m
**wheatgerm** ['wi:tdʒə:m] n germe m de blé
**wheatmeal** ['wi:tmi:l] n farine bise
**wheedle** ['wi:dl] vt: **to ~ sb into doing sth** cajoler or enjôler qn pour qu'il fasse qch; **to ~ sth out of sb** obtenir qch de qn par des cajoleries
**wheel** [wi:l] n roue f; (Aut: also: **steering wheel**) volant m; (Naut) gouvernail m ▷ vt (pram etc) pousser, rouler ▷ vi (birds) tournoyer; (also: **wheel round**: person) se retourner, faire volte-face
**wheelbarrow** ['wi:lbærəu] n brouette f
**wheelbase** ['wi:lbeɪs] n empattement m
**wheelchair** ['wi:ltʃɛə<sup>r</sup>] n fauteuil roulant
**wheel clamp** n (Aut) sabot m (de Denver)
**wheeler-dealer** ['wi:lə'di:lə<sup>r</sup>] n (pej) combinard(e), affairiste m/f
**wheelie-bin** ['wi:lɪbɪn] n (Brit) poubelle f à roulettes
**wheeling** ['wi:lɪŋ] n: **~ and dealing** (pej) manigances fpl, magouilles fpl
**wheeze** [wi:z] n respiration bruyante

(d'asthmatique) ▷ vi respirer bruyamment
**wheezy** ['wi:zɪ] adj sifflant(e)

**KEYWORD**

**when** [wen] adv quand; **when did he go?** quand est-ce qu'il est parti?
▷ conj **1** (at, during, after the time that) quand, lorsque; **she was reading when I came in** elle lisait quand or lorsque je suis entré
**2** (on, at which): **on the day when I met him** le jour où je l'ai rencontré
**3** (whereas) alors que; **I thought I was wrong when in fact I was right** j'ai cru que j'avais tort alors qu'en fait j'avais raison

**whenever** [wɛn'ɛvə<sup>r</sup>] adv quand donc ▷ conj quand; (every time that) chaque fois que; **I go ~ I can** j'y vais quand or chaque fois que je le peux
**where** [wɛə<sup>r</sup>] adv, conj où; **this is ~** c'est là que; **~ are you from?** d'où venez vous?
**whereabouts** ['wɛərəbauts] adv où donc ▷ n: **nobody knows his ~** personne ne sait où il se trouve
**whereas** [wɛər'æz] conj alors que
**whereby** [wɛə'baɪ] adv (formal) par lequel (or laquelle etc)
**whereupon** [wɛərə'pɔn] adv sur quoi, et sur ce
**wherever** [wɛər'ɛvə<sup>r</sup>] adv où donc ▷ conj où que + sub; **sit ~ you like** asseyez-vous (là) où vous voulez
**wherewithal** ['wɛəwɪðɔ:l] n: **the ~ (to do sth)** les moyens mpl (de faire qch)
**whet** [wɛt] vt aiguiser
**whether** ['wɛðə<sup>r</sup>] conj si; **I don't know ~ to accept or not** je ne sais pas si je dois accepter ou non; **it's doubtful ~** il est peu probable que + sub; **~ you go or not** que vous y alliez ou non
**whey** ['weɪ] n petit-lait m

**KEYWORD**

**which** [wɪtʃ] adj **1** (interrogative: direct, indirect) quel(le); **which picture do you want?** quel tableau voulez-vous?; **which one?** lequel (laquelle)?
**2**: **in which case** auquel cas; **we got there at 8pm, by which time the cinema was full** quand nous sommes arrivés à 20h, le cinéma était complet
▷ pron **1** (interrogative) lequel (laquelle), lesquels (lesquels) pl; **I don't mind which** peu importe lequel; **which (of these) are yours?** lesquels sont à vous?; **tell me which you want** dites-moi lesquels or ceux que vous voulez
**2** (relative: subject) qui; (: object) que; sur/vers etc lequel (laquelle); (NB: à + lequel = **auquel**; de + lequel = **duquel**); **the apple which you ate/which is on the table** la pomme que vous avez mangée/qui est sur la table; **the chair on which you are sitting** la chaise sur laquelle vous êtes assis; **the book of which you spoke** le livre

dont vous avez parlé; **he said he knew, which is true/I was afraid of** il a dit qu'il le savait, ce qui est vrai/ce que je craignais; **after which** après quoi

**whichever** [wɪtʃ'ɛvə<sup>r</sup>] *adj*: **take ~ book you prefer** prenez le livre que vous préférez, peu importe lequel; **~ book you take** quel que soit le livre que vous preniez; **~ way you** de quelque façon que vous + *sub*

**whiff** [wɪf] *n* bouffée *f*; **to catch a ~ of sth** sentir l'odeur de qch

**while** [waɪl] *n* moment *m* ▷ *conj* pendant que; (*as long as*) tant que; (*as, whereas*) alors que; (*though*) bien que + *sub*, quoique + *sub*; **for a ~** pendant quelque temps; **in a ~** dans un moment; **all the ~** pendant tout ce temps-là; **we'll make it worth your ~** nous vous récompenserons de votre peine
▶ **while away** *vt* (*time*) (faire) passer

**whilst** [waɪlst] *conj* = **while**

**whim** [wɪm] *n* caprice *m*

**whimper** ['wɪmpə<sup>r</sup>] *n* geignement *m* ▷ *vi* geindre

**whimsical** ['wɪmzɪkl] *adj* (*person*) capricieux(-euse); (*look*) étrange

**whine** [waɪn] *n* gémissement *m*; (*of engine, siren*) plainte stridente ▷ *vi* gémir, geindre, pleurnicher; (*dog, engine, siren*) gémir

**whip** [wɪp] *n* fouet *m*; (*for riding*) cravache *f*; (*Pol: person*) chef *m* de file (*assurant la discipline dans son groupe parlementaire*) ▷ *vt* fouetter; (*snatch*) enlever (*or* sortir) brusquement
▶ **whip up** *vt* (*cream*) fouetter; (*inf: meal*) préparer en vitesse; (*stir up: support*) stimuler; (*: feeling*) attiser, aviver; *voir article*

**whiplash** ['wɪplæʃ] *n* (*Med: also:* **whiplash injury**) coup *m* du lapin

**whipped cream** [wɪpt-] *n* crème fouettée

**whipping boy** ['wɪpɪŋ-] *n* (*fig*) bouc *m* émissaire

**whip-round** ['wɪpraund] *n* (*Brit*) collecte *f*

**whirl** [wəːl] *n* tourbillon *m* ▷ *vi* tourbillonner; (*dancers*) tournoyer ▷ *vt* faire tourbillonner; faire tournoyer

**whirlpool** ['wəːlpuːl] *n* tourbillon *m*

**whirlwind** ['wəːlwɪnd] *n* tornade *f*

**whirr** [wəː<sup>r</sup>] *vi* bruire; ronronner; vrombir

**whisk** [wɪsk] *n* (*Culin*) fouet *m* ▷ *vt* (*eggs*) fouetter, battre; **to ~ sb away** *or* **off** emmener

qn rapidement

**whiskers** ['wɪskəz] *npl* (*of animal*) moustaches *fpl*; (*of man*) favoris *mpl*

**whisky,** (*Irish, US*) **whiskey** ['wɪskɪ] *n* whisky *m*

**whisper** ['wɪspə<sup>r</sup>] *n* chuchotement *m*; (*fig: of leaves*) bruissement *m*; (*rumour*) rumeur *f* ▷ *vt, vi* chuchoter

**whispering** ['wɪspərɪŋ] *n* chuchotement(s) *m(pl)*

**whist** [wɪst] *n* (*Brit*) whist *m*

**whistle** ['wɪsl] *n* (*sound*) sifflement *m*; (*object*) sifflet *m* ▷ *vi* siffler ▷ *vt* siffler, siffloter

**whistle-stop** ['wɪslstɔp] *adj*: **to make a ~ tour of** (*Pol*) faire la tournée électorale des petits patelins de

**Whit** [wɪt] *n* la Pentecôte

**white** [waɪt] *adj* blanc (blanche); (*with fear*) blême ▷ *n* blanc *m*; (*person*) blanc (blanche); **to turn** *or* **go ~** (*person*) pâlir, blêmir; (*hair*) blanchir; **the ~s** (*washing*) le linge blanc; **tennis ~s** tenue *f* de tennis

**whitebait** ['waɪtbeɪt] *n* blanchaille *f*

**whiteboard** ['waɪtbɔːd] *n* tableau *m* blanc; **interactive ~** tableau *m* (blanc) interactif

**white coffee** *n* (*Brit*) café *m* au lait, (café) crème *m*

**white-collar worker** ['waɪtkɔlə-] *n* employé(e) de bureau

**white elephant** *n* (*fig*) objet dispendieux et superflu

**white goods** *npl* (*appliances*) (gros) électroménager *m*; (*linen etc*) linge *m* de maison

**white-hot** [waɪt'hɔt] *adj* (*metal*) incandescent(e)

**White House** *n* (*US*): **the ~** la Maison-Blanche; *voir article*

**white lie** *n* pieux mensonge

**whiteness** ['waɪtnɪs] *n* blancheur *f*

**white noise** *n* son *m* blanc

**whiteout** ['waɪtaut] *n* jour blanc

**white paper** *n* (*Pol*) livre blanc

**whitewash** ['waɪtwɔʃ] *n* (*paint*) lait *m* de chaux ▷ *vt* blanchir à la chaux; (*fig*) blanchir

**whiting** ['waɪtɪŋ] *n* (*pl inv: fish*) merlan *m*

**Whit Monday** *n* le lundi de Pentecôte

**Whitsun** ['wɪtsn] *n* la Pentecôte

**whittle** ['wɪtl] *vt*: **to ~ away, to ~ down** (*costs*) réduire, rogner

**whizz** [wɪz] *vi* aller (*or* passer) à toute vitesse

**whizz kid** *n* (*inf*) petit prodige

**WHO** *n abbr* (= World Health Organization) OMS *f* (Organisation mondiale de la Santé)

**who** [huː] *pron* qui

**whodunit** [huːˈdʌnɪt] *n* (*inf*) roman policier

W

**whoever** [hu:'ɛvəʳ] *pron:* ~ **finds it** celui (celle) qui le trouve (, qui que ce soit), quiconque le trouve; **ask ~ you like** demandez à qui vous voulez; ~ **he marries** qui que ce soit *or* quelle que soit la personne qu'il épouse; ~ **told you that?** qui a bien pu vous dire ça?, qui donc vous a dit ça?

**whole** [həul] *adj (complete)* entier(-ière), tout(e); *(not broken)* intact(e), complet(-ète) ▷ *n (entire unit)* tout *m*; *(all)*: **the ~ of** la totalité de, tout(e) le (la); **the ~ lot (of it)** tout; **the ~ lot (of them)** tous (sans exception); **the ~ of the time** tout le temps; **the ~ of the town** la ville tout entière; **on the ~, as a ~** dans l'ensemble

**wholefood** ['həulfu:d] *n*, **wholefoods** ['həulfu:dz] *npl* aliments complets

**wholehearted** [həul'hɑ:tɪd] *adj* sans réserve(s), sincère

**wholeheartedly** [həul'hɑ:tɪdlɪ] *adv* sans réserve; **to agree ~** être entièrement d'accord

**wholemeal** ['həulmi:l] *adj (Brit: flour, bread)* complet(-ète)

**wholesale** ['həulseɪl] *n* (vente *f* en) gros *m* ▷ *adj (price)* de gros; *(destruction)* systématique

**wholesaler** ['həulseɪləʳ] *n* grossiste *m/f*

**wholesome** ['həulsəm] *adj* sain(e); *(advice)* salutaire

**wholewheat** ['həulwi:t] *adj* = **wholemeal**

**wholly** ['həulɪ] *adv* entièrement, tout à fait

 KEYWORD

**whom** [hu:m] *pron* **1** *(interrogative)* qui; **whom did you see?** qui avez-vous vu?; **to whom did you give it?** à qui l'avez-vous donné?
**2** *(relative)* que; à/de *etc* qui; **the man whom I saw/to whom I spoke** l'homme que j'ai vu/à qui j'ai parlé

**whooping cough** ['hu:pɪŋ-] *n* coqueluche *f*

**whoops** [wu:ps] *excl (also:* **whoops-a-daisy**) oups!, houp-là!

**whoosh** [wuʃ] *vi:* **the skiers ~ed past** les skieurs passèrent dans un glissement rapide

**whopper** ['wɔpəʳ] *n (inf: lie)* gros bobard; (: *large thing)* monstre *m*, phénomène *m*

**whopping** ['wɔpɪŋ] *adj (inf: big)* énorme

**whore** [hɔ:ʳ] *n (inf: pej)* putain *f*

KEYWORD

**whose** [hu:z] *adj* **1** *(possessive: interrogative)*: **whose book is this?, whose is this book?** à qui est ce livre?; **whose pencil have you taken?** à qui est le crayon que vous avez pris?, c'est le crayon de qui que vous avez pris?; **whose daughter are you?** de qui êtes-vous la fille?
**2** *(possessive: relative)*: **the man whose son you rescued** l'homme dont *or* de qui vous avez sauvé le fils; **the girl whose sister you were speaking to** la fille à la sœur de qui *or* de laquelle vous parliez; **the woman whose car**

**was stolen** la femme dont la voiture a été volée
▷ *pron* à qui; **whose is this?** à qui est ceci?; **I know whose it is** je sais à qui c'est

**Who's Who** ['hu:z'hu:] *n* ≈ Bottin Mondain

KEYWORD

**why** [waɪ] *adv* pourquoi; **why is he late?** pourquoi est-il en retard?; **why not?** pourquoi pas?
▷ *conj:* **I wonder why he said that** je me demande pourquoi il a dit ça; **that's not why I'm here** ce n'est pas pour ça que je suis là; **the reason why** la raison pour laquelle
▷ *excl* eh bien!, tiens!; **why, it's you!** tiens, c'est vous!; **why, that's impossible!** voyons, c'est impossible!

**whyever** [waɪ'ɛvəʳ] *adv* pourquoi donc, mais pourquoi

**WI** *n abbr (Brit:* = Women's Institute) amicale de femmes au foyer ▷ *abbr (Geo)* = **West Indies**; *(US)* = **Wisconsin**

**wick** [wɪk] *n* mèche *f (de bougie)*

**wicked** ['wɪkɪd] *adj* méchant(e); *(mischievous: grin, look)* espiègle, malicieux(-euse); *(crime)* pervers(e); *(terrible: prices, weather)* épouvantable; *(inf: very good)* génial(e) *(inf)*

**wicker** ['wɪkəʳ] *n* osier *m*; *(also:* **wickerwork**) vannerie *f*

**wicket** ['wɪkɪt] *n (Cricket: stumps)* guichet *m*; (: *grass area)* espace compris entre les deux guichets

**wicket keeper** *n (Cricket)* gardien *m* de guichet

**wide** [waɪd] *adj* large; *(area, knowledge)* très étendu(e); *(choice)* grand(e) ▷ *adv:* **to open ~** ouvrir tout grand; **to shoot ~** tirer à côté; **it is 3 metres ~** cela fait 3 mètres de large

**wide-angle lens** ['waɪdæŋgl-] *n* objectif *m* grand-angulaire

**wide-awake** [waɪdə'weɪk] *adj* bien éveillé(e)

**wide-eyed** [waɪd'aɪd] *adj* aux yeux écarquillés; *(fig)* naïf(-ïve), crédule

**widely** ['waɪdlɪ] *adv (different)* radicalement; *(spaced)* sur une grande étendue; *(believed)* généralement; *(travel)* beaucoup; **to be ~ read** *(author)* être beaucoup lu(e); *(reader)* avoir beaucoup lu, être cultivé(e)

**widen** ['waɪdn] *vt* élargir ▷ *vi* s'élargir

**wideness** ['waɪdnɪs] *n* largeur *f*

**wide open** *adj* grand(e) ouvert(e)

**wide-ranging** [waɪd'reɪndʒɪŋ] *adj (survey, report)* vaste; *(interests)* divers(e)

**widespread** ['waɪdsprɛd] *adj (belief etc)* très répandu(e)

**widget** ['wɪdʒɪt] *n (Comput)* widget *m*

**widow** ['wɪdəu] *n* veuve *f*

**widowed** ['wɪdəud] *adj (qui est devenu(e))* veuf (veuve)

**widower** ['wɪdəuəʳ] *n* veuf *m*

**width** [wɪdθ] *n* largeur *f*; **it's 7 metres in** ~ cela fait 7 mètres de large

**widthways** ['wɪdθweɪz] *adv* en largeur

**wield** [wiːld] *vt* (*sword*) manier; (*power*) exercer

**wife** (*pl* **wives**) [waɪf, waɪvz] *n* femme *f*, épouse *f*

**WiFi** ['waɪfaɪ] *n abbr* (= *wireless fidelity*) WiFi *m*
▷ *adj* (*hot spot, network*) WiFi *inv*

**wig** [wɪg] *n* perruque *f*

**wigging** ['wɪgɪŋ] *n* (*Brit inf*) savon *m*, engueulade *f*

**wiggle** ['wɪgl] *vt* agiter, remuer ▷ *vi* (*loose screw etc*) branler; (*worm*) se tortiller

**wiggly** ['wɪglɪ] *adj* (*line*) ondulé(e)

**wild** [waɪld] *adj* sauvage; (*sea*) déchaîné(e); (*idea, life*) fou (folle); (*behaviour*) déchaîné(e), extravagant(e); (*inf: angry*) hors de soi, furieux(-euse); (*: enthusiastic*): **to be ~ about** être fou (folle) *or* dingue de ▷ *n*: **the ~** la nature; **wilds** *npl* régions *fpl* sauvages

**wild card** *n* (*Comput*) caractère *m* de remplacement

**wildcat** ['waɪldkæt] *n* chat *m* sauvage

**wildcat strike** *n* grève *f* sauvage

**wilderness** ['wɪldənɪs] *n* désert *m*, région *f* sauvage

**wildfire** ['waɪldfaɪə<sup>r</sup>] *n*: **to spread like ~** se répandre comme une traînée de poudre

**wild-goose chase** [waɪld'guːs-] *n* (*fig*) fausse piste

**wildlife** ['waɪldlaɪf] *n* faune *f* (et flore *f*)

**wildly** ['waɪldlɪ] *adv* (*behave*) de manière déchaînée; (*applaud*) frénétiquement; (*hit, guess*) au hasard; (*happy*) follement

**wiles** [waɪlz] *npl* ruses *fpl*, artifices *mpl*

**wilful**, (US) **willful** ['wɪlful] *adj* (*person*) obstiné(e); (*action*) délibéré(e); (*crime*) prémédité(e)

**KEYWORD**

**will** [wɪl] *aux vb* **1** (*forming future tense*): **I will finish it tomorrow** je le finirai demain; **I will have finished it by tomorrow** je l'aurai fini d'ici demain; **will you do it? — yes I will/no I won't** le ferez-vous? — oui/non; **you won't lose it, will you?** vous ne le perdrez pas, n'est-ce pas?

**2** (*in conjectures, predictions*): **he will** *or* **he'll be there by now** il doit être arrivé à l'heure qu'il est; **that will be the postman** ça doit être le facteur

**3** (*in commands, requests, offers*): **will you be quiet!** voulez-vous bien vous taire!; **will you help me?** est-ce que vous pouvez m'aider?; **will you have a cup of tea?** voulez-vous une tasse de thé?; **I won't put up with it!** je ne le tolérerai pas!

▷ *vt* (*pt, pp* **willed**): **to will sb to do** souhaiter ardemment que qn fasse; **he willed himself to go on** par un suprême effort de volonté, il continua

▷ *n* volonté *f*; (*document*) testament *m*; **to do sth** **of one's own free will** faire qch de son propre gré; **against one's will** à contre-cœur

**willful** ['wɪlful] *adj* (US) = **wilful**

**willing** ['wɪlɪŋ] *adj* de bonne volonté, serviable ▷ *n*: **to show** ~ faire preuve de bonne volonté; **he's ~ to do it** il est disposé à le faire, il veut bien le faire

**willingly** ['wɪlɪŋlɪ] *adv* volontiers

**willingness** ['wɪlɪŋnɪs] *n* bonne volonté

**will-o'-the-wisp** ['wɪləðə'wɪsp] *n* (*also fig*) feu follet *m*

**willow** ['wɪləu] *n* saule *m*

**willpower** ['wɪl'pauə<sup>r</sup>] *n* volonté *f*

**willy-nilly** ['wɪlɪ'nɪlɪ] *adv* bon gré mal gré

**wilt** [wɪlt] *vi* dépérir

**Wilts** [wɪlts] *abbr* (Brit) = **Wiltshire**

**wily** ['waɪlɪ] *adj* rusé(e)

**wimp** [wɪmp] *n* (*inf*) mauviette *f*

**win** [wɪn] (*pt, pp* **won**) [wʌn] *n* (*in sports etc*) victoire *f* ▷ *vt* (*battle, money*) gagner; (*prize, contract*) remporter; (*popularity*) acquérir ▷ *vi* gagner

▶ **win over** *vt* convaincre

▶ **win round** *vt* gagner, se concilier

**wince** [wɪns] *n* tressaillement *m* ▷ *vi* tressaillir

**winch** [wɪntʃ] *n* treuil *m*

**Winchester disk** ['wɪntʃɪstə-] *n* (*Comput*) disque *m* Winchester

**wind¹** [wɪnd] *n* (*also Med*) vent *m*; (*breath*) souffle *m* ▷ *vt* (*take breath away*) couper le souffle à; **the ~(s)** (*Mus*) les instruments *mpl* à vent; **into** *or* **against the ~** contre le vent; **to get ~ of sth** (*fig*) avoir vent de qch; **to break ~** avoir des gaz

**wind²** (*pt, pp* **wound**) [waɪnd, waund] *vt* enrouler; (*wrap*) envelopper; (*clock, toy*) remonter ▷ *vi* (*road, river*) serpenter

▶ **wind down** *vt* (*car window*) baisser; (*fig: production, business*) réduire progressivement

▶ **wind up** *vt* (*clock*) remonter; (*debate*) terminer, clôturer

**windbreak** ['wɪndbreɪk] *n* brise-vent *m inv*

**windcheater** ['wɪndtʃiːtə<sup>r</sup>], (US) **windbreaker** ['wɪndbreɪkə<sup>r</sup>] *n* anorak *m*

**winder** ['waɪndə<sup>r</sup>] *n* (Brit: *on watch*) remontoir *m*

**windfall** ['wɪndfɔːl] *n* coup *m* de chance

**wind farm** *n* ferme *f* éolienne

**winding** ['waɪndɪŋ] *adj* (*road*) sinueux(-euse); (*staircase*) tournant(e)

**wind instrument** *n* (*Mus*) instrument *m* à vent

**windmill** ['wɪndmɪl] *n* moulin *m* à vent

**window** ['wɪndəu] *n* fenêtre *f*; (*in car, train: also*: **windowpane**) vitre *f*; (*in shop etc*) vitrine *f*

**window box** *n* jardinière *f*

**window cleaner** *n* (*person*) laveur(-euse) de vitres

**window dressing** *n* arrangement *m* de la vitrine

**window envelope** *n* enveloppe *f* à fenêtre

**window frame** *n* châssis *m* de fenêtre

**window ledge** *n* rebord *m* de la fenêtre

**window pane** *n* vitre *f*, carreau *m*

**W**

**window seat** n (in vehicle) place f côté fenêtre
**window-shopping** ['wɪndəuʃɔpɪŋ] n: **to go ~**
faire du lèche-vitrines
**windowsill** ['wɪndəusɪl] n (inside) appui m de la
fenêtre; (outside) rebord m de la fenêtre
**windpipe** ['wɪndpaɪp] n gosier m
**wind power** n énergie éolienne
**windscreen** ['wɪndskriːn] n pare-brise m inv
**windscreen washer** n lave-glace m inv
**windscreen wiper**, (US) **windshield wiper**
[-waɪpəʳ] n essuie-glace m inv
**windshield** ['wɪndʃiːld] (US) n = **windscreen**
**windsurfing** ['wɪndsəːfɪŋ] n planche f à voile
**windswept** ['wɪndswɛpt] adj balayé(e) par le
vent
**wind tunnel** n soufflerie f
**windy** ['wɪndɪ] adj (day) de vent, venteux(-euse);
(place, weather) venteux; **it's ~** il y a du vent
**wine** [waɪn] n vin m ▷ vt: **to ~ and dine sb** offrir
un dîner bien arrosé à qn
**wine bar** n bar m à vin
**wine cellar** n cave f à vins
**wine glass** n verre m à vin
**wine list** n carte f des vins
**wine merchant** n marchand(e) de vins
**wine tasting** [-teɪstɪŋ] n dégustation f (de vins)
**wine waiter** n sommelier m
**wing** [wɪŋ] n aile f; (in air force) groupe m
d'escadrilles; **wings** npl (Theat) coulisses fpl
**winger** ['wɪŋəʳ] n (Sport) ailier m
**wing mirror** n (Brit) rétroviseur latéral
**wing nut** n papillon m, écrou m à ailettes
**wingspan** ['wɪŋspæn], **wingspread**
['wɪŋsprɛd] n envergure f
**wink** [wɪŋk] n clin m d'œil ▷ vi faire un clin
d'œil; (blink) cligner des yeux
**winkle** [wɪŋkl] n bigorneau m
**winner** ['wɪnəʳ] n gagnant(e)
**winning** ['wɪnɪŋ] adj (team) gagnant(e); (goal)
décisif(-ive); (charming) charmeur(-euse)
**winning post** n poteau m d'arrivée
**winnings** ['wɪnɪŋz] npl gains mpl
**winsome** ['wɪnsəm] adj avenant(e),
engageant(e)
**winter** ['wɪntəʳ] n hiver m ▷ vi hiverner; **in ~** en
hiver
**winter sports** npl sports mpl d'hiver
**wintertime** ['wɪntətaɪm] n hiver m
**wintry** ['wɪntrɪ] adj hivernal(e)
**wipe** [waɪp] n coup m de torchon (or de chiffon or
d'éponge); **to give sth a ~** donner un coup de
torchon/de chiffon/d'éponge à qch ▷ vt
essuyer; (erase: tape) effacer; **to ~ one's nose** se
moucher
▶ **wipe off** vt essuyer
▶ **wipe out** vt (debt) éteindre, amortir; (memory)
effacer; (destroy) anéantir
▶ **wipe up** vt essuyer
**wire** ['waɪəʳ] n fil m (de fer); (Elec) fil électrique;
(Tel) télégramme m ▷ vt (fence) grillager; (house)
faire l'installation électrique de; (also: **wire up**)
brancher; (person: send telegram to) télégraphier à

**wire brush** n brosse f métallique
**wire cutters** [-kʌtəz] npl cisaille f
**wireless** ['waɪəlɪs] n (Brit) télégraphie f sans fil;
(set) T.S.F. f
**wire netting** n treillis m métallique, grillage m
**wire service** n (US) revue f de presse (par
téléscripteur)
**wire-tapping** ['waɪə'tæpɪŋ] n écoute f
téléphonique
**wiring** ['waɪərɪŋ] n (Elec) installation f
électrique
**wiry** ['waɪərɪ] adj noueux(-euse), nerveux(-euse)
**Wis.** abbr (US) = **Wisconsin**
**wisdom** ['wɪzdəm] n sagesse f; (of action)
prudence f
**wisdom tooth** n dent f de sagesse
**wise** [waɪz] adj sage, prudent(e); (remark)
judicieux(-euse); **I'm none the ~r** je ne suis
pas plus avancé(e) pour autant
▶ **wise up** vi (inf): **to ~ up to** commencer à se
rendre compte de
**...wise** [waɪz] suffix: **time~** en ce qui concerne le
temps, question temps
**wisecrack** ['waɪzkræk] n sarcasme m
**wish** [wɪʃ] n (desire) désir m; (specific desire)
souhait m, vœu m ▷ vt souhaiter, désirer,
vouloir; **best ~es** (on birthday etc) meilleurs
vœux; **with best ~es** (in letter) bien
amicalement; **give her my best ~es** faites-lui
mes amitiés; **to ~ sb goodbye** dire au revoir à
qn; **he ~ed me well** il m'a souhaité bonne
chance; **to ~ to do/sb to do** désirer or vouloir
faire/que qn fasse; **to ~ for** souhaiter; **to ~ sth
on sb** souhaiter qch à qn
**wishbone** ['wɪʃbəun] n fourchette f
**wishful** ['wɪʃful] adj: **it's ~ thinking** c'est
prendre ses désirs pour des réalités
**wishy-washy** ['wɪʃɪ'wɔʃɪ] adj (inf: person) qui
manque de caractère falot(e); (: ideas, thinking)
faiblard(e)
**wisp** [wɪsp] n fine mèche (de cheveux); (of smoke)
mince volute f; **a ~ of straw** un fétu de paille
**wistful** ['wɪstful] adj mélancolique
**wit** [wɪt] n (also: **wits**: intelligence) intelligence f,
esprit m; (presence of mind) présence f d'esprit;
(wittiness) esprit; (person) homme/femme
d'esprit; **to be at one's ~s' end** (fig) ne plus
savoir que faire; **to have one's ~s about one**
avoir toute sa présence d'esprit, ne pas perdre la
tête; **to ~** adv à savoir
**witch** [wɪtʃ] n sorcière f
**witchcraft** ['wɪtʃkrɑːft] n sorcellerie f
**witch doctor** n sorcier m
**witch-hunt** ['wɪtʃhʌnt] n chasse f aux sorcières

🔵 KEYWORD

**with** [wɪð, wɪθ] prep **1** (in the company of) avec; (at
the home of) chez; **we stayed with friends** nous
avons logé chez des amis; **I'll be with you in a
minute** je suis à vous dans un instant
**2** (descriptive): **a room with a view** une chambre

avec vue; **the man with the grey hat/blue eyes** l'homme au chapeau gris/aux yeux bleus **3** (*indicating manner, means, cause*): **with tears in her eyes** les larmes aux yeux; **to walk with a stick** marcher avec une canne; **red with anger** rouge de colère; **to shake with fear** trembler de peur; **to fill sth with water** remplir qch d'eau

**4** (*in phrases*): **I'm with you** (*I understand*) je vous suis; **to be with it** (*inf: up-to-date*) être dans le vent

**withdraw** [wɪθ'drɔ:] *vt* (*irreg: like* **draw**) retirer ▷ *vi* se retirer; (*go back on promise*) se rétracter; **to ~ into o.s.** se replier sur soi-même
**withdrawal** [wɪθ'drɔ:əl] *n* retrait *m*; (*Med*) état *m* de manque
**withdrawal symptoms** *npl*: **to have ~** être en état de manque, présenter les symptômes *mpl* de sevrage
**withdrawn** [wɪθ'drɔ:n] *pp of* **withdraw** ▷ *adj* (*person*) renfermé(e)
**withdrew** [wɪθ'dru:] *pt of* **withdraw**
**wither** ['wɪðə*r*] *vi* se faner
**withered** ['wɪðəd] *adj* fané(e), flétri(e); (*limb*) atrophié(e)
**withhold** [wɪθ'həuld] *vt* (*irreg: like* **hold**: *money*) retenir; (*decision*) remettre; **to ~ (from)** (*permission*) refuser (à); (*information*) cacher (à)
**within** [wɪð'ɪn] *prep* à l'intérieur de ▷ *adv* à l'intérieur; **~ his reach** à sa portée; **~ sight of** en vue de; **~ a mile of** à moins d'un mille de; **~ the week** avant la fin de la semaine; **~ an hour from now** d'ici une heure; **to be ~ the law** être légal(e) *or* dans les limites de la légalité
**without** [wɪð'aut] *prep* sans; **~ a coat** sans manteau; **~ speaking** sans parler; **~ anybody knowing** sans que personne ne sache; **to go** *or* **do ~ sth** se passer de qch
**withstand** [wɪθ'stænd] *vt* (*irreg: like* **stand**) résister à
**witness** ['wɪtnɪs] *n* (*person*) témoin *m*; (*evidence*) témoignage *m* ▷ *vt* (*event*) être témoin de; (*document*) attester l'authenticité de; **to bear ~ to sth** témoigner de qch; **~ for the prosecution/defence** témoin à charge/à décharge; **to ~ to sth/having seen sth** témoigner de qch/d'avoir vu qch
**witness box**, (*US*) **witness stand** *n* barre *f* des témoins
**witticism** ['wɪtɪsɪzəm] *n* mot *m* d'esprit
**witty** ['wɪtɪ] *adj* spirituel(le), plein(e) d'esprit
**wives** [waɪvz] *npl of* **wife**
**wizard** ['wɪzəd] *n* magicien *m*
**wizened** ['wɪznd] *adj* ratatiné(e)
**wk** *abbr* = **week**
**Wm.** *abbr* = **William**
**WMD.** *abbr* = **weapons of mass destruction**
**WO** *n abbr* = **warrant officer**
**wobble** ['wɔbl] *vi* trembler; (*chair*) branler
**wobbly** ['wɔblɪ] *adj* tremblant(e), branlant(e)
**woe** [wəu] *n* malheur *m*

**woeful** ['wəuful] *adj* (*sad*) malheureux(-euse); (*terrible*) affligeant(e)
**wok** [wɔk] *n* wok *m*
**woke** [wəuk] *pt of* **wake**
**woken** ['wəukn] *pp of* **wake**
**wolf** (*pl* **wolves**) [wulf, wulvz] *n* loup *m*
**woman** (*pl* **women**) ['wumən, 'wɪmɪn] *n* femme *f* ▷ *cpd*: **~ doctor** femme *f* médecin; **~ friend** amie *f*; **~ teacher** professeur *m* femme; **young ~** jeune femme; **women's page** (*Press*) page *f* des lectrices
**womanize** ['wumənaɪz] *vi* jouer les séducteurs
**womanly** ['wumənlɪ] *adj* féminin(e)
**womb** [wu:m] *n* (*Anat*) utérus *m*
**women** ['wɪmɪn] *npl of* **woman**
**won** [wʌn] *pt, pp of* **win**
**wonder** ['wʌndə*r*] *n* merveille *f*, miracle *m*; (*feeling*) émerveillement *m* ▷ *vi*: **to ~ whether/why** se demander si/pourquoi; **to ~ at** (*surprise*) s'étonner de; (*admiration*) s'émerveiller de; **to ~ about** songer à; **it's no ~ that** il n'est pas étonnant que + *sub*
**wonderful** ['wʌndəful] *adj* merveilleux(-euse)
**wonderfully** ['wʌndəfəlɪ] *adv* (+ *adj*) merveilleusement; (+ *vb*) à merveille
**wonky** ['wɔŋkɪ] *adj* (*Brit inf*) qui ne va *or* ne marche pas très bien
**wont** [wəunt] *n*: **as is his/her ~** comme de coutume
**won't** [wəunt] = **will not**
**woo** [wu:] *vt* (*woman*) faire la cour à
**wood** [wud] *n* (*timber, forest*) bois *m* ▷ *cpd* de bois, en bois
**wood carving** *n* sculpture *f* en *or* sur bois
**wooded** ['wudɪd] *adj* boisé(e)
**wooden** ['wudn] *adj* en bois; (*fig: actor*) raide; (*: performance*) qui manque de naturel
**woodland** ['wudlənd] *n* forêt *f*, région boisée
**woodpecker** ['wudpɛkə*r*] *n* pic *m* (*oiseau*)
**wood pigeon** *n* ramier *m*
**woodwind** ['wudwɪnd] *n* (*Mus*) bois *m*; **the ~** les bois *mpl*
**woodwork** ['wudwə:k] *n* menuiserie *f*
**woodworm** ['wudwə:m] *n* ver *m* du bois; **the table has got ~** la table est piquée des vers
**woof** [wuf] *n* (*of dog*) aboiement *m* ▷ *vi* aboyer; **~, ~!** oua, oua!
**wool** [wul] *n* laine *f*; **to pull the ~ over sb's eyes** (*fig*) en faire accroire à qn
**woollen**, (*US*) **woolen** ['wulən] *adj* de *or* en laine; (*industry*) lainier(-ière) ▷ *n*: **~s** lainages *mpl*
**woolly**, (*US*) **wooly** ['wulɪ] *adj* laineux(-euse); (*fig: ideas*) confus(e)
**woozy** ['wu:zɪ] *adj* (*inf*) dans les vapes
**word** [wə:d] *n* mot *m*; (*spoken*) mot, parole *f*; (*promise*) parole; (*news*) nouvelles *fpl* ▷ *vt* rédiger, formuler; **~ for ~** (*repeat*) mot pour mot; (*translate*) mot à mot; **what's the ~ for "pen" in French?** comment dit-on "pen" en français?; **to put sth into ~s** exprimer qch; **in other ~s** en d'autres termes; **to have a ~ with sb**

W

toucher un mot à qn; **to have ~s with sb** (*quarrel with*) avoir des mots avec qn; **to break/keep one's ~** manquer à sa parole/tenir (sa) parole; **I'll take your ~ for it** je vous crois sur parole; **to send ~ of** prévenir de; **to leave ~ (with sb/ for sb) that ...** laisser un mot (à qn/pour qn) disant que ...

**wording** ['wəːdɪŋ] *n* termes *mpl*, langage *m*; (*of document*) libellé *m*

**word of mouth** *n*: **by** *or* **through ~** de bouche à oreille

**word-perfect** ['wəːd'pəːfɪkt] *adj*: **he was ~ (in his speech** *etc*)**, his speech** *etc* **was ~** il savait son discours *etc* sur le bout du doigt

**word processing** *n* traitement *m* de texte

**word processor** [-prəʊsɛsəʳ] *n* machine *f* de traitement de texte

**wordwrap** ['wəːdræp] *n* (*Comput*) retour *m* (automatique) à la ligne

**wordy** ['wəːdɪ] *adj* verbeux(-euse)

**wore** [wɔːʳ] *pt of* **wear**

**work** [wəːk] *n* travail *m*; (*Art, Literature*) œuvre *f* ▷ *vi* travailler; (*mechanism*) marcher, fonctionner; (*plan etc*) marcher; (*medicine*) agir ▷ *vt* (*clay, wood etc*) travailler; (*mine etc*) exploiter; (*machine*) faire marcher *or* fonctionner; (*miracles etc*) faire; **works** *n* (*Brit: factory*) usine *f* ▷ *npl* (*of clock, machine*) mécanisme *m*; **how does this ~?** comment est-ce que ça marche?; **the TV isn't ~ing** la télévision est en panne *or* ne marche pas; **to go to ~** aller travailler; **to set to ~, to start ~** se mettre à l'œuvre; **to be at ~ (on sth)** travailler (sur qch); **to be out of ~** être au chômage *or* sans emploi; **to ~ hard** travailler dur; **to ~ loose** se défaire, se desserrer; **road ~s** travaux *mpl* (d'entretien des routes)
  ▸ **work on** *vt fus* travailler à; (*principle*) se baser sur
  ▸ **work out** *vi* (*plans etc*) marcher; (*Sport*) s'entraîner ▷ *vt* (*problem*) résoudre; (*plan*) élaborer; **it ~s out at £100** ça fait 100 livres
  ▸ **work up** *vt*: **to get ~ed up** se mettre dans tous ses états

**workable** ['wəːkəbl] *adj* (*solution*) réalisable

**workaholic** [wəːkə'hɔlɪk] *n* bourreau *m* de travail

**workbench** ['wəːkbɛntʃ] *n* établi *m*

**worked up** [wəːkt-] *adj*: **to get ~** se mettre dans tous ses états

**worker** ['wəːkəʳ] *n* travailleur(-euse), ouvrier(-ière); **office ~** employé(e) de bureau

**work experience** *n* stage *m*

**workforce** ['wəːkfɔːs] *n* main-d'œuvre *f*

**work-in** ['wəːkɪn] *n* (*Brit*) occupation *f* d'usine *etc* (*sans arrêt de la production*)

**working** ['wəːkɪŋ] *adj* (*day, tools etc, conditions*) de travail; (*wife*) qui travaille; (*partner, population*) actif(-ive); **in ~ order** en état de marche; **a ~ knowledge of English** une connaissance toute pratique de l'anglais

**working capital** *n* (*Comm*) fonds *mpl* de roulement

**working class** *n* classe ouvrière ▷ *adj*: **working-class** ouvrier(-ière), de la classe ouvrière

**working man** (*irreg*) *n* travailleur *m*

**working party** *n* (*Brit*) groupe *m* de travail

**working week** *n* semaine *f* de travail

**work-in-progress** ['wəːkɪn'prəʊɡrɛs] *n* (*Comm*) en-cours *m inv*; (*: value*) valeur *f* des en-cours

**workload** ['wəːkləʊd] *n* charge *f* de travail

**workman** ['wəːkmən] (*irreg*) *n* ouvrier *m*

**workmanship** ['wəːkmənʃɪp] *n* métier *m*, habileté *f*; facture *f*

**workmate** ['wəːkmeɪt] *n* collègue *m/f*

**work of art** *n* œuvre *f* d'art

**workout** ['wəːkaʊt] *n* (*Sport*) séance *f* d'entraînement

**work permit** *n* permis *m* de travail

**workplace** ['wəːkpleɪs] *n* lieu *m* de travail

**works council** *n* comité *m* d'entreprise

**worksheet** ['wəːkʃiːt] *n* (*Scol*) feuille *f* d'exercices; (*Comput*) feuille *f* de programmation

**workshop** ['wəːkʃɔp] *n* atelier *m*

**work station** *n* poste *m* de travail

**work study** *n* étude *f* du travail

**work surface** *n* plan *m* de travail

**worktop** ['wəːktɔp] *n* plan *m* de travail

**work-to-rule** ['wəːktə'ruːl] *n* (*Brit*) grève *f* du zèle

**world** [wəːld] *n* monde *m* ▷ *cpd* (*champion*) du monde; (*power, war*) mondial(e); **all over the ~** dans le monde entier, partout dans le monde; **to think the ~ of sb** (*fig*) ne jurer que par qn; **what in the ~ is he doing?** qu'est-ce qu'il peut bien être en train de faire?; **to do sb a ~ of good** faire le plus grand bien à qn; **W~ War One/ Two, the First/Second W~ War** la Première/ Deuxième Guerre mondiale; **out of this ~** *adj* extraordinaire

**World Cup** *n*: **the ~** (*Football*) la Coupe du monde

**world-famous** [wəːld'feɪməs] *adj* de renommée mondiale

**worldly** ['wəːldlɪ] *adj* de ce monde

**world music** *n* world music *f*

**World Series** *n*: **the ~** (*US: Baseball*) le championnat national de baseball

**world-wide** ['wəːld'waɪd] *adj* universel(le) ▷ *adv* dans le monde entier

**World-Wide Web** *n*: **the ~** le Web

**worm** [wəːm] *n* (*also:* **earthworm**) ver *m*

**worn** [wɔːn] *pp of* **wear** ▷ *adj* usé(e)

**worn-out** ['wɔːnaut] *adj* (*object*) complètement usé(e); (*person*) épuisé(e)

**worried** ['wʌrɪd] *adj* inquiet(-ète); **to be ~ about sth** être inquiet au sujet de qch

**worrier** ['wʌrɪəʳ] *n* inquiet(-ète)

**worrisome** ['wʌrɪsəm] *adj* inquiétant(e)

**worry** ['wʌrɪ] *n* souci *m* ▷ *vt* inquiéter ▷ *vi* s'inquiéter, se faire du souci; **to ~ about** *or* **over sth/sb** se faire du souci pour *or* à propos de qch/ qn

**worrying** ['wʌrɪɪŋ] *adj* inquiétant(e)

**worse** [wəːs] *adj* pire, plus mauvais(e) ▷ *adv*

plus mal ▷ *n* pire *m*; **to get ~** (*condition, situation*) empirer, se dégrader; **a change for the ~** une détérioration; **he is none the ~ for it** il ne s'en porte pas plus mal; **so much the ~ for you!** tant pis pour vous!

**worsen** ['wəːsn] *vt, vi* empirer

**worse off** *adj* moins à l'aise financièrement; (*fig*): **you'll be ~ this way** ça ira moins bien de cette façon; **he is now ~ than before** il se retrouve dans une situation pire qu'auparavant

**worship** ['wəːʃɪp] *n* culte *m* ▷ *vt* (*God*) rendre un culte à; (*person*) adorer; **Your W~** (Brit: *to mayor*) Monsieur le Maire; (: *to judge*) Monsieur le Juge

**worshipper** ['wəːʃɪpər] *n* adorateur(-trice); (*in church*) fidèle *m/f*

**worst** [wəːst] *adj* le (la) pire, le (la) plus mauvais(e) ▷ *adv* le plus mal ▷ *n* pire *m*; **at ~** au pis aller; **if the ~ comes to the ~** si le pire doit arriver

**worst-case** ['wəːstkeɪs] *adj*: **the ~ scenario** le pire scénario *or* cas de figure

**worsted** ['wustɪd] *n*: (**wool**) ~ laine peignée

**worth** [wəːθ] *n* valeur *f* ▷ *adj*: **to be ~** valoir; **how much is it ~?** ça vaut combien?; **it's ~ it** cela en vaut la peine, ça vaut la peine; **it is ~ one's while (to do)** ça vaut le coup (*inf*) (de faire); **50 pence ~ of apples** (pour) 50 pence de pommes

**worthless** ['wəːθlɪs] *adj* qui ne vaut rien

**worthwhile** ['wəːθ'waɪl] *adj* (*activity*) qui en vaut la peine; (*cause*) louable; **a ~ book** un livre qui vaut la peine d'être lu

**worthy** ['wəːðɪ] *adj* (*person*) digne; (*motive*) louable; **~ of** digne de

KEYWORD

**would** [wud] *aux vb* **1** (*conditional tense*): **if you asked him he would do it** si vous le lui demandiez, il le ferait; **if you had asked him he would have done it** si vous le lui aviez demandé, il l'aurait fait

**2** (*in offers, invitations, requests*): **would you like a biscuit?** voulez-vous un biscuit?; **would you close the door please?** voulez-vous fermer la porte, s'il vous plaît?

**3** (*in indirect speech*): **I said I would do it** j'ai dit que je le ferais

**4** (*emphatic*): **it WOULD have to snow today!** naturellement il neige aujourd'hui! *or* il fallait qu'il neige aujourd'hui!

**5** (*insistence*): **she wouldn't do it** elle n'a pas voulu *or* elle a refusé de le faire

**6** (*conjecture*): **it would have been midnight** il devait être minuit; **it would seem so** on dirait bien

**7** (*indicating habit*): **he would go there on Mondays** il y allait le lundi

**would-be** ['wudbiː] *adj* (*pej*) soi-disant
**wouldn't** ['wudnt] = **would not**
**wound**[1] [wuːnd] *n* blessure *f* ▷ *vt* blesser; **~ed in**

**the leg** blessé à la jambe
**wound**[2] [waund] *pt, pp of* **wind**[2]
**wove** [wəuv] *pt of* **weave**
**woven** ['wəuvn] *pp of* **weave**
**WP** *n abbr* = **word processing; word processor** ▷ *abbr* (Brit *inf*) = **weather permitting**
**WPC** *n abbr* (Brit) = **woman police constable**
**wpm** *abbr* (= *words per minute*) mots/minute
**WRAC** *n abbr* (Brit: = *Women's Royal Army Corps*) *auxiliaires féminines de l'armée de terre*
**WRAF** *n abbr* (Brit: = *Women's Royal Air Force*) *auxiliaires féminines de l'armée de l'air*
**wrangle** ['ræŋgl] *n* dispute *f* ▷ *vi* se disputer
**wrap** [ræp] *n* (*stole*) écharpe *f*; (*cape*) pèlerine *f* ▷ *vt* (*also*: **wrap up**) envelopper; (*parcel*) emballer; (*wind*) enrouler; **under ~s** (*fig*: *plan, scheme*) secret(-ète)
**wrapper** ['ræpər] *n* (*on chocolate etc*) papier *m*; (Brit: *of book*) couverture *f*
**wrapping** ['ræpɪŋ] *n* (*of sweet, chocolate*) papier *m*; (*of parcel*) emballage *m*
**wrapping paper** *n* papier *m* d'emballage; (*for gift*) papier cadeau
**wrath** [rɔθ] *n* courroux *m*
**wreak** [riːk] *vt* (*destruction*) entraîner; **to ~ havoc** faire des ravages; **to ~ vengeance on** se venger de, exercer sa vengeance sur
**wreath** [riːθ, *pl* riːðz] *n* couronne *f*
**wreck** [rɛk] *n* (*sea disaster*) naufrage *m*; (*ship*) épave *f*; (*vehicle*) véhicule accidentée; (*pej*: *person*) loque (humaine) ▷ *vt* démolir; (*ship*) provoquer le naufrage de; (*fig*) briser, ruiner
**wreckage** ['rɛkɪdʒ] *n* débris *mpl*; (*of building*) décombres *mpl*; (*of ship*) naufrage *m*
**wrecker** ['rɛkər] *n* (US: *breakdown van*) dépanneuse *f*
**WREN** [rɛn] *n abbr* (Brit) *membre du WRNS*
**wren** [rɛn] *n* (Zool) troglodyte *m*
**wrench** [rɛntʃ] *n* (Tech) clé *f* (à écrous); (*tug*) violent mouvement de torsion; (*fig*) déchirement *m* ▷ *vt* tirer violemment sur, tordre; **to ~ sth from** arracher qch (violemment) à *or* de
**wrest** [rɛst] *vt*: **to ~ sth from sb** arracher *or* ravir qch à qn
**wrestle** ['rɛsl] *vi*: **to ~ (with sb)** lutter (avec qn); **to ~ with** (*fig*) se débattre avec, lutter contre
**wrestler** ['rɛslər] *n* lutteur(-euse)
**wrestling** ['rɛslɪŋ] *n* lutte *f*; (*also*: **all-in wrestling**: Brit) catch *m*
**wrestling match** *n* rencontre *f* de lutte (*or* de catch)
**wretch** [rɛtʃ] *n* pauvre malheureux(-euse); **little ~!** (*often humorous*) petit(e) misérable!
**wretched** ['rɛtʃɪd] *adj* misérable; (*inf*) maudit(e)
**wriggle** ['rɪgl] *n* tortillement *m* ▷ *vi* (*also*: **wriggle about**) se tortiller
**wring** (*pt, pp* **wrung**) [rɪŋ, rʌŋ] *vt* tordre; (*wet clothes*) essorer; (*fig*): **to ~ sth out of** arracher qch à
**wringer** ['rɪŋər] *n* essoreuse *f*
**wringing** ['rɪŋɪŋ] *adj* (*also*: **wringing wet**) tout

**W**

mouillé(e), trempé(e)

**wrinkle** ['rɪŋkl] n (on skin) ride f; (on paper etc) pli m ▷ vt rider, plisser ▷ vi se plisser

**wrinkled** ['rɪŋkld], **wrinkly** ['rɪŋklɪ] adj (fabric, paper) froissé(e), plissé(e); (surface) plissé; (skin) ridé(e), plissé

**wrist** [rɪst] n poignet m

**wristband** ['rɪstbænd] n (Brit: of shirt) poignet m; (: of watch) bracelet m

**wrist watch** ['rɪstwɔtʃ] n montre-bracelet f

**writ** [rɪt] n acte m judiciaire; **to issue a ~ against sb, to serve a ~ on sb** assigner qn en justice

**writable** ['raɪtəbl] adj (CD, DVD) inscriptible

**write** (pt **wrote**, pp **written**) [raɪt, rəut, 'rɪtn] vt, vi écrire; (prescription) rédiger; **to ~ sb a letter** écrire une lettre à qn

▶ **write away** vi: **to ~ away for** (information) (écrire pour) demander; (goods) (écrire pour) commander

▶ **write down** vt noter; (put in writing) mettre par écrit

▶ **write off** vt (debt) passer aux profits et pertes; (project) mettre une croix sur; (depreciate) amortir; (smash up: car etc) démolir complètement

▶ **write out** vt écrire; (copy) recopier

▶ **write up** vt rédiger

**write-off** ['raɪtɔf] n perte totale; **the car is a ~** la voiture est bonne pour la casse

**write-protect** ['raɪtprə'tekt] vt (Comput) protéger contre l'écriture

**writer** ['raɪtəʳ] n auteur m, écrivain m

**write-up** ['raɪtʌp] n (review) critique f

**writhe** [raɪð] vi se tordre

**writing** ['raɪtɪŋ] n écriture f; (of author) œuvres fpl; **in ~** par écrit; **in my own ~** écrit(e) de ma main

**writing case** n nécessaire m de correspondance

**writing desk** n secrétaire m

**writing paper** n papier m à lettres

**written** ['rɪtn] pp of **write**

**WRNS** n abbr (Brit: = Women's Royal Naval Service) auxiliaires féminines de la marine

**wrong** [rɔŋ] adj (incorrect) faux (fausse); (incorrectly chosen: number, road etc) mauvais(e); (not suitable) qui ne convient pas; (wicked) mal; (unfair) injuste ▷ adv mal ▷ n tort m ▷ vt faire du tort à, léser; **to be ~** (answer) être faux (fausse); (in doing/saying) avoir tort (de dire/ faire); **you are ~ to do it** tu as tort de le faire; **it's ~ to steal, stealing is ~** c'est mal de voler; **you are ~ about that, you've got it ~** tu te trompes; **to be in the ~** avoir tort; **what's ~?** qu'est-ce qui ne va pas?; **there's nothing ~** tout va bien; **what's ~ with the car?** qu'est-ce qu'elle a, la voiture?; **to go ~** (person) se tromper; (plan) mal tourner; (machine) se détraquer; **I took a ~ turning** je me suis trompé de route

**wrongdoer** ['rɔŋduːəʳ] n malfaiteur m

**wrong-foot** [rɔŋ'fut] vt (Sport) prendre à contre-pied; (fig) prendre au dépourvu

**wrongful** ['rɔŋful] adj injustifié(e); **~ dismissal** (Industry) licenciement abusif

**wrongly** ['rɔŋlɪ] adv à tort; (answer, do, count) mal, incorrectement; (treat) injustement

**wrong number** n (Tel): **you have the ~** vous vous êtes trompé de numéro

**wrong side** n (of cloth) envers m

**wrote** [rəut] pt of **write**

**wrought** [rɔːt] adj: **~ iron** fer forgé

**wrung** [rʌŋ] pt, pp of **wring**

**WRVS** n abbr (Brit: = Women's Royal Voluntary Service) auxiliaires féminines bénévoles au service de la collectivité

**wry** [raɪ] adj désabusé(e)

**wt.** abbr (= weight) pds.

**WV, W.Va.** abbr (US) = **West Virginia**

**WWW** n abbr = **World-Wide Web**

**WY, Wyo.** abbr (US) = **Wyoming**

**WYSIWYG** ['wɪzɪwɪg] abbr (Comput: = what you see is what you get) ce que vous voyez est ce que vous aurez

**X, x** [ɛks] *n* (*letter*) X, x *m*; (*Brit Cine: formerly*) film interdit aux moins de 18 ans; **X for Xmas** X comme Xavier

**Xerox®** [ˈzɪərɔks] *n* (*also:* **Xerox machine**) photocopieuse *f*; (*photocopy*) photocopie *f* ▷ *vt* photocopier

**XL** *abbr* (= *extra large*) XL

**Xmas** [ˈɛksməs] *n abbr* = **Christmas**

**X-rated** [ˈɛksˈreɪtɪd] *adj* (*US: film*) interdit(e) aux moins de 18 ans

**X-ray** [ˈɛksreɪ] *n* (*ray*) rayon *m* X; (*photograph*) radio(graphie) *f* ▷ *vt* radiographier

**xylophone** [ˈzaɪləfəun] *n* xylophone *m*

# Yy

**Y, y** [waɪ] n (letter) Y, y m; **Y for Yellow,** (US) **Y for Yoke** Y comme Yvonne

**yacht** [jɔt] n voilier m; (motor, luxury yacht) yacht m

**yachting** ['jɔtɪŋ] n yachting m, navigation f de plaisance

**yachtsman** ['jɔtsmən] (irreg) n yacht(s)man m

**yam** [jæm] n igname f

**Yank** [jæŋk], **Yankee** ['jæŋkɪ] n (pej) Amerloque m/f, Ricain(e)

**yank** [jæŋk] vt tirer d'un coup sec

**yap** [jæp] vi (dog) japper

**yard** [jɑːd] n (of house etc) cour f; (US: garden) jardin m; (measure) yard m (= 914 mm; 3 feet); **builder's ~** chantier m

**yard sale** n (US) brocante f (dans son propre jardin)

**yardstick** ['jɑːdstɪk] n (fig) mesure f, critère m

**yarn** [jɑːn] n fil m; (tale) longue histoire

**yawn** [jɔːn] n bâillement m ▷ vi bâiller

**yawning** ['jɔːnɪŋ] adj (gap) béant(e)

**yd.** abbr = **yard; yards**

**yeah** [jɛə] adv (inf) ouais

**year** [jɪəʳ] n an m, année f; (Scol etc) année f; **every ~** tous les ans, chaque année; **this ~** cette année; **a** or **per ~** par an; **~ in, ~ out** année après année; **to be 8 ~s old** avoir 8 ans; **an eight-~-old child** un enfant de huit ans

**yearbook** ['jɪəbuk] n annuaire m

**yearly** ['jɪəlɪ] adj annuel(le) ▷ adv annuellement; **twice ~** deux fois par an

**yearn** [jəːn] vi: **to ~ for sth/to do** aspirer à qch/à faire

**yearning** ['jəːnɪŋ] n désir ardent, envie f

**yeast** [jiːst] n levure f

**yell** [jɛl] n hurlement m, cri m ▷ vi hurler

**yellow** ['jɛləu] adj, n jaune (m)

**yellow fever** n fièvre f jaune

**yellowish** ['jɛləuɪʃ] adj qui tire sur le jaune, jaunâtre (pej)

**Yellow Pages®** npl (Tel) pages fpl jaunes

**Yellow Sea** n: **the ~** la mer Jaune

**yelp** [jɛlp] n jappement m; glapissement m ▷ vi japper; glapir

**Yemen** ['jɛmən] n Yémen m

**yen** [jɛn] n (currency) yen m; (craving): **~ for/to do** grande envie de/de faire

**yeoman** ['jəumən] (irreg) n: **Y~ of the Guard** hallebardier m de la garde royale

**yes** [jɛs] adv oui; (answering negative question) si ▷ n oui m; **to say ~ (to)** dire oui (à)

**yesterday** ['jɛstədɪ] adv, n hier (m); **~ morning/ evening** hier matin/soir; **the day before ~** avant-hier; **all day ~** toute la journée d'hier

**yet** [jɛt] adv encore; (in questions) déjà ▷ conj pourtant, néanmoins; **it is not finished ~** ce n'est pas encore fini or toujours pas fini; **must you go just ~?** dois-tu déjà partir?; **have you eaten ~?** vous avez déjà mangé?; **the best ~** le meilleur jusqu'ici or jusque-là; **as ~** jusqu'ici, encore; **a few days ~** encore quelques jours; **~ again** une fois de plus

**yew** [juː] n if m

**Y-fronts®** ['waɪfrʌnts] npl (Brit) slip m kangourou

**YHA** n abbr (Brit) = **Youth Hostels Association**

**Yiddish** ['jɪdɪʃ] n yiddish m

**yield** [jiːld] n production f, rendement m; (Finance) rapport m ▷ vt produire, rendre, rapporter; (surrender) céder ▷ vi céder; (US Aut) céder la priorité; **a ~ of 5%** un rendement de 5%

**YMCA** n abbr (= Young Men's Christian Association) ≈ union chrétienne de jeunes gens (UCJG)

**yob** ['jɔb], **yobbo** ['jɔbəu] n (Brit inf) loubar(d) m

**yodel** ['jəudl] vi faire des tyroliennes, jodler

**yoga** ['jəugə] n yoga m

**yoghurt, yogurt** ['jɔgət] n yaourt m

**yoke** [jəuk] n joug m ▷ vt (also: **yoke together**: oxen) accoupler

**yolk** [jəuk] n jaune m (d'œuf)

**yonder** ['jɔndəʳ] adv là(-bas)

**yonks** [jɔŋks] npl (inf): **for ~** très longtemps; **we've been here for ~** ça fait une éternité qu'on est ici; **we were there for ~** on est resté là pendant des lustres

**Yorks** [jɔːks] abbr (Brit) = **Yorkshire**

⊙ KEYWORD

**you** [juː] pron **1** (subject) tu; (polite form) vous; (plural) vous; **you are very kind** vous êtes très gentil; **you French enjoy your food** vous

autres Français, vous aimez bien manger; **you and I will go** toi et moi *or* vous et moi, nous irons; **there you are!** vous voilà!
**2** (*object: direct, indirect*) te, t' + *vowel*; vous; **I know you** je te *or* vous connais; **I gave it to you** je te l'ai donné, je vous l'ai donné
**3** (*stressed*) toi; vous; **I told you to do it** c'est à toi *or* vous que j'ai dit de le faire
**4** (*after prep, in comparisons*) toi; vous; **it's for you** c'est pour toi *or* vous; **she's younger than you** elle est plus jeune que toi *or* vous
**5** (*impersonal: one*) on; **fresh air does you good** l'air frais fait du bien; **you never know** on ne sait jamais; **you can't do that!** ça ne se fait pas!

**you'd** [ju:d] = **you had; you would**
**you'll** [ju:l] = **you will; you shall**
**young** [jʌŋ] *adj* jeune ▷ *npl* (*of animal*) petits *mpl*; (*people*): **the** ~ les jeunes, la jeunesse; **a** ~ **man** un jeune homme; **a** ~ **lady** (*unmarried*) une jeune fille, une demoiselle; (*married*) une jeune femme *or* dame; **my ~er brother** mon frère cadet; **the ~er generation** la jeune génération
**younger** [jʌŋgə<sup>r</sup>] *adj* (*brother etc*) cadet(te)
**youngish** ['jʌŋɪʃ] *adj* assez jeune
**youngster** ['jʌŋstə<sup>r</sup>] *n* jeune *m/f*; (*child*) enfant *m/f*
**your** [jɔ:<sup>r</sup>] *adj* ton (ta), tes *pl*; (*polite form, pl*) votre, vos *pl*; *see also* **my**
**you're** [juə<sup>r</sup>] = **you are**
**yours** [jɔ:z] *pron* le (la) tien(ne), les tiens (tiennes); (*polite form, pl*) le (la) vôtre, les vôtres;

**is it ~?** c'est à toi (*or* à vous)?; **a friend of** ~ un(e) de tes (*or* de vos) amis; *see also* **faithfully; sincerely**
**yourself** [jɔ:'sɛlf] *pron* (*reflexive*) te; (: *polite form*) vous; (*after prep*) toi; vous; (*emphatic*) toi-même; **you ~ told me** c'est vous qui me l'avez dit, vous me l'avez dit vous-même; *see also* **oneself**
**yourselves** [jɔ:'sɛlvz] *pl pron* vous; (*emphatic*) vous-mêmes; *see also* **oneself**
**youth** [ju:θ] *n* jeunesse *f*; (*young man*) (*pl* **-s**) [ju:ðz] jeune homme *m*; **in my ~** dans ma jeunesse, quand j'étais jeune
**youth club** *n* centre *m* de jeunes
**youthful** ['ju:θful] *adj* jeune; (*enthusiasm etc*) juvénile; (*misdemeanour*) de jeunesse
**youthfulness** ['ju:θfəlnɪs] *n* jeunesse *f*
**youth hostel** *n* auberge *f* de jeunesse
**youth movement** *n* mouvement *m* de jeunes
**you've** [ju:v] = **you have**
**yowl** [jaul] *n* hurlement *m*; miaulement *m* ▷ *vi* hurler; miauler
**YT** *abbr* (*Canada*) = **Yukon Territory.**
**Yugoslav** ['ju:gəuslɑ:v] *adj* (*Hist*) yougoslave ▷ *n* Yougoslave *m/f*
**Yugoslavia** [ju:gəu'slɑ:vɪə] *n* (*Hist*) Yougoslavie *f*
**Yugoslavian** [ju:gəu'slɑ:vɪən] *adj* (*Hist*) yougoslave
**yuppie** ['jʌpɪ] *n* yuppie *m/f*
**YWCA** *n abbr* (= *Young Women's Christian Association*) union chrétienne féminine

**y**

# Zz

**Z, z** [zɛd, (US) ziː] n (letter) Z, z m; **Z for Zebra** Z comme Zoé

**Zambia** ['zæmbɪə] n Zambie f

**Zambian** ['zæmbɪən] adj zambien(ne) ▷ n Zambien(ne)

**zany** ['zeɪnɪ] adj farfelu(e), loufoque

**zap** [zæp] vt (Comput) effacer

**zeal** [ziːl] n (revolutionary etc) ferveur f; (keenness) ardeur f, zèle m

**zealot** ['zɛlət] n fanatique m/f

**zealous** ['zɛləs] adj fervent(e); ardent(e), zélé(e)

**zebra** ['ziːbrə] n zèbre m

**zebra crossing** n (Brit) passage clouté or pour piétons

**zenith** ['zɛnɪθ] n (Astronomy) zénith m; (fig) zénith, apogée m

**zero** ['zɪərəu] n zéro m ▷ vi: **to ~ in on** (target) se diriger droit sur; **5° below ~** 5 degrés au-dessous de zéro

**zero hour** n l'heure f H

**zero option** n (Pol): **the ~** l'option f zéro

**zero-rated** ['ziːrəureɪtɪd] adj (Brit) exonéré(e) de TVA

**zest** [zɛst] n entrain m, élan m; (of lemon etc) zeste m

**zigzag** ['zɪgzæg] n zigzag m ▷ vi zigzaguer, faire des zigzags

**Zimbabwe** [zɪm'bɑːbwɪ] n Zimbabwe m

**Zimbabwean** [zɪm'bɑːbwɪən] adj zimbabwéen(ne) ▷ n Zimbabwéen(ne)

**Zimmer®** ['zɪməʳ] n (also: **Zimmer frame**) déambulateur m

**zinc** [zɪŋk] n zinc m

**Zionism** ['zaɪənɪzəm] n sionisme m

**Zionist** ['zaɪənɪst] adj sioniste ▷ n Sioniste m/f

**zip** [zɪp] n (also: **zip fastener**) fermeture f éclair® or à glissière; (energy) entrain m ▷ vt (file) zipper; (also: **zip up**) fermer (avec une fermeture éclair®)

**zip code** n (US) code postal

**zip file** n (Comput) fichier m zip inv

**zipper** ['zɪpəʳ] n (US) = **zip**

**zit** [zɪt] (inf) n bouton m

**zither** ['zɪðəʳ] n cithare f

**zodiac** ['zəudɪæk] n zodiaque m

**zombie** ['zɒmbɪ] n (fig): **like a ~** avec l'air d'un zombie, comme un automate

**zone** [zəun] n zone f

**zoo** [zuː] n zoo m

**zoological** [zuə'lɒdʒɪkl] adj zoologique

**zoologist** [zu'ɒlədʒɪst] n zoologiste m/f

**zoology** [zu'ɒlədʒɪ] n zoologie f

**zoom** [zuːm] vi: **to ~ past** passer en trombe; **to ~ in (on sb/sth)** (Phot, Cine) zoomer (sur qn/qch)

**zoom lens** n zoom m, objectif m à focale variable

**zucchini** [zuː'kiːnɪ] n (US) courgette f

**Zulu** ['zuːluː] adj zoulou ▷ n Zoulou m/f

**Zürich** ['zjuərɪk] n Zurich

# Grammar
# Grammaire

# Using the grammar

The Grammar section deals systematically and comprehensively with all the information you will need in order to communicate accurately in French. The user-friendly layout explains the grammar point on a left-hand page, leaving the facing page free for illustrative examples. The numbers, → ❶ etc, direct you to the relevant example in every case.

The Grammar section also provides invaluable guidance on the danger of translating English structures by identical structures in French. Use of Numbers and Punctuation are important areas covered towards the end of the section. Finally, the index lists the main words and grammatical terms in both English and French.

# Abbreviations

| | |
|---|---|
| fem. | feminine |
| infin. | infinitive |
| masc. | masculine |
| perf. | perfect |
| plur. | plural |
| qch | quelque chose |
| qn | quelqu'un |
| sb | somebody |
| sing. | singular |
| sth | something |

# Irregular Verbs

## Contents

# Examples

## Simple Tenses: formation

In French the simple tenses are:

      Present → ①
      Imperfect → ②
      Future → ③
      Conditional → ④
      Past Historic → ⑤
      Present Subjunctive → ⑥
      Imperfect Subjunctive → ⑦

They are formed by adding endings to a verb stem. The endings show the number and person of the subject of the verb → ⑧

The stem and endings of regular verbs are totally predictable. The following sections show all the patterns for regular verbs. For irregular verbs see page 74 onwards.

## Regular Verbs

There are three regular verb patterns (called conjugations), each identifiable by the ending of the infinitive:

      First conjugation verbs end in **-er** e.g. **donner** to give

      Second conjugation verbs end in **-ir** e.g. **finir** to finish

      Third conjugation verbs end in **-re** e.g. **vendre** to sell

These three conjugations are treated in order on the following pages.

# Examples

**❶** je donne

I give
I am giving
I do give

**❷** je donnais

I gave
I was giving
I used to give

**❸** je donnerai

I shall give
I shall be giving

**❹** je donnerais

I should/would give
I should/would be giving

**❺** je donnai

I gave

**❻** (que) je donne

(that) I give/gave

**❼** (que) je donnasse

(that) I gave

**❽** je donne
nous donnons
je donnerais
nous donnerions

I give
we give
I would give
we would give

# Verbs

## Simple Tenses: First Conjugation

The stem is formed as follows:

| TENSE | FORMATION | EXAMPLE |
|---|---|---|
| Present | | |
| Imperfect | | |
| Past Historic | infinitive minus -er | donn- |
| Present Subjunctive | | |
| Imperfect Subjunctive | | |
| Future | infinitive | donner- |
| Conditional | | |

To the appropriate stem add the following endings:

| | | **1** PRESENT | **2** IMPERFECT | **3** PAST HISTORIC |
|---|---|---|---|---|
| | 1st person | -e | -ais | -ai |
| sing. | 2nd person | -es | -ais | -as |
| | 3rd person | -e | -ait | -a |
| | 1st person | -ons | -ions | -âmes |
| plur. | 2nd person | -ez | -iez | -âtes |
| | 3rd person | -ent | -aient | -èrent |

| | | **4** PRESENT SUBJUNCTIVE | **5** IMPERFECT SUBJUNCTIVE |
|---|---|---|---|
| | 1st person | -e | -asse |
| sing. | 2nd person | -es | -asses |
| | 3rd person | -e | -ât |
| | 1st person | -ions | -assions |
| plur. | 2nd person | -iez | -assiez |
| | 3rd person | -ent | -assent |

| | | **6** FUTURE | **7** CONDITIONAL |
|---|---|---|---|
| | 1st person | -ai | -ais |
| sing. | 2nd person | -as | -ais |
| | 3rd person | -a | -ait |
| | 1st person | -ons | -ions |
| plur. | 2nd person | -ez | -iez |
| | 3rd person | -ont | -aient |

# Examples

**❶ PRESENT**
je donne
tu donnes
il donne
elle donne
nous donnons
vous donnez
ils donnent
elles donnent

**❷ IMPERFECT**
je donnais
tu donnais
il donnait
elle donnait
nous donnions
vous donniez
ils donnaient
elles donnaient

**❸ PAST HISTORIC**
je donnai
tu donnas
il donna
elle donna
nous donnâmes
vous donnâtes
ils donnèrent
elles donnèrent

**❹ PRESENT SUBJUNCTIVE**
je donne
tu donnes
il donne
elle donne
nous donnions
vous donniez
ils donnent
elles donnent

**❺ IMPERFECT SUBJUNCTIVE**
je donnasse
tu donnasses
il donnât
elle donnât
nous donnassions
vous donnassiez
ils donnassent
elles donnassent

**❻ FUTURE**
je donnerai
tu donneras
il donnera
elle donnera
nous donnerons
vous donnerez
ils donneront
elles donneront

**❼ CONDITIONAL**
je donnerais
tu donnerais
il donnerait
elle donnerait
nous donnerions
vous donneriez
ils donneraient
elles donneraient

## Simple Tenses: Second Conjugation

The stem is formed as follows:

| TENSE | FORMATION | EXAMPLE |
|---|---|---|
| Present | | |
| Imperfect | | |
| Past Historic | infinitive minus –ir | fin- |
| Present Subjunctive | | |
| Imperfect Subjunctive | | |
| Future | infinitive | finir- |
| Conditional | | |

To the appropriate stem add the following endings:

| | | ❶ PRESENT | ❷ IMPERFECT | ❸ PAST HISTORIC |
|---|---|---|---|---|
| | 1st person | -is | -issais | -is |
| sing. | 2nd person | -is | -issais | -is |
| | 3rd person | -it | -issait | -it |
| | 1st person | -issons | -issions | -îmes |
| plur. | 2nd person | -issez | -issiez | -îtes |
| | 3rd person | -issent | -issaient | -irent |

| | | ❹ PRESENT SUBJUNCTIVE | ❺ IMPERFECT SUBJUNCTIVE |
|---|---|---|---|
| | 1st person | -isse | -isse |
| sing. | 2nd person | -isses | -isses |
| | 3rd person | -isse | -ît |
| | 1st person | -issions | -issions |
| plur. | 2nd person | -issiez | -issiez |
| | 3rd person | -issent | -issent |

| | | ❻ FUTURE | ❼ CONDITIONAL |
|---|---|---|---|
| | 1st person | -ai | -ais |
| sing. | 2nd person | -as | -ais |
| | 3rd person | -a | -ait |
| | 1st person | -ons | -ions |
| plur. | 2nd person | -ez | -iez |
| | 3rd person | -ont | -aient |

# Examples

**1 PRESENT**
je finis
tu finis
il finit
elle finit
nous finissons
vous finissez
ils finissent
elles finissent

**2 IMPERFECT**
je finissais
tu finissais
il finissait
elle finissait
nous finissions
vous finissiez
ils finissaient
elles finissaient

**3 PAST HISTORIC**
je finis
tu finis
il finit
elle finit
nous finîmes
vous finîtes
ils finirent
elles finirent

**4 PRESENT SUBJUNCTIVE**
je finisse
tu finisses
il finisse
elle finisse
nous finissions
vous finissiez
ils finissent
elles finissent

**5 IMPERFECT SUBJUNCTIVE**
je finisse
tu finisses
il finît
elle finît
nous finissions
vous finissiez
ils finissent
elles finissent

**6 FUTURE**
je finirai
tu finiras
il finira
elle finira
nous finirons
vous finirez
ils finiront
elles finiront

**7 CONDITIONAL**
je finirais
tu finirais
il finirait
elle finirait
nous finirions
vous finiriez
ils finiraient
elles finiraient

11

## Simple Tenses: Third Conjugation

The stem is formed as follows:

| TENSE | FORMATION | EXAMPLE |
|---|---|---|
| Present | | |
| Imperfect | | |
| Past Historic | infinitive minus -re | vend- |
| Present Subjunctive | | |
| Imperfect Subjunctive | | |
| Future | infinitive minus -e | vendr- |
| Conditional | | |

To the appropriate stem add the following endings:

| | | ① PRESENT | ② IMPERFECT | ③ PAST HISTORIC |
|---|---|---|---|---|
| | 1st person | -s | -ais | -is |
| sing. | 2nd person | -s | -ais | -is |
| | 3rd person | – | -ait | -it |
| | 1st person | -ons | -ions | -îmes |
| plur. | 2nd person | -ez | -iez | -îtes |
| | 3rd person | -ent | -aient | -irent |

| | | ④ PRESENT SUBJUNCTIVE | ⑤ IMPERFECT SUBJUNCTIVE |
|---|---|---|---|
| | 1st person | -e | -isse |
| sing. | 2nd person | -es | -isses |
| | 3rd person | -e | -ît |
| | 1st person | -ions | -issions |
| plur. | 2nd person | -iez | -issiez |
| | 3rd person | -ent | -issent |

| | | ⑥ FUTURE | ⑦ CONDITIONAL |
|---|---|---|---|
| | 1st person | -ai | -ais |
| sing. | 2nd person | -as | -ais |
| | 3rd person | -a | -ait |
| | 1st person | -ons | -ions |
| plur. | 2nd person | -ez | -iez |
| | 3rd person | -ont | -aient |

# Examples

**❶ PRESENT**
je vends
tu vends
il vend
elle vend
nous vendons
vous vendez
ils vendent
elles vendent

**❷ IMPERFECT**
je vendais
tu vendais
il vendait
elle vendait
nous vendions
vous vendiez
ils vendaient
elles vendaient

**❸ PAST HISTORIC**
je vendis
tu vendis
il vendit
elle vendit
nous vendîmes
vous vendîtes
ils vendirent
elles vendirent

**❹ PRESENT SUBJUNCTIVE**
je vende
tu vendes
il vende
elle vende
nous vendions
vous vendiez
ils vendent
elles vendent

**❺ IMPERFECT SUBJUNCTIVE**
je vendisse
tu vendisses
il vendît
elle vendît
nous vendissions
vous vendissiez
ils vendissent
elles vendissent

**❻ FUTURE**
je vendrai
tu vendras
il vendra
elle vendra
nous vendrons
vous vendrez
ils vendront
elles vendront

**❼ CONDITIONAL**
je vendrais
tu vendrais
il vendrait
elle vendrait
nous vendrions
vous vendriez
ils vendraient
elles vendraient

## First Conjugation Spelling Irregularities

Before certain endings, the stems of some '-er' verbs may change slightly.

Below, and on subsequent pages, the verb types are identified, and the changes described are illustrated by means of a representative verb.

| | |
|---|---|
| Verbs ending: | **-cer** |
| Change: | **c** becomes **ç** before **a** or **o** |
| Tenses affected: | Present, Imperfect, Past Historic, Imperfect Subjunctive, Present Participle |
| Model: | **lancer** to throw → ❶ |

Why the change occurs:  A cedilla is added to the **c** to retain its soft [s] pronunciation before the vowels **a** and **o**.

| | |
|---|---|
| Verbs ending: | **-ger** |
| Change: | **g** becomes **ge** before **a** or **o** |
| Tenses affected: | Present, Imperfect, Past Historic, Imperfect Subjunctive, Present Participle |
| Model: | **manger** to eat → ❷ |

Why the change occurs:  An **e** is added after the **g** to retain its soft [ʒ] pronunciation before the vowels **a** and **o**.

# Examples

**①** INFINITIVE
**lancer**

PRESENT PARTICIPLE
**lançant**

PRESENT
je lance
tu lances
il/elle lance
nous **lançons**
vous lancez
ils/elles lancent

IMPERFECT
je **lançais**
tu **lançais**
il/elle **lançait**
nous lancions
vous lanciez
ils/elles **lançaient**

PAST HISTORIC
je **lançai**
tu **lanças**
il/elle **lança**
nous **lançâmes**
vous **lançâtes**
ils/elles lancèrent

IMPERFECT SUBJUNCTIVE
je **lançasse**
tu **lançasses**
il/elle **lançât**
nous **lançassions**
vous **lançassiez**
ils/elles **lançassent**

**②** INFINITIVE
**manger**

PRESENT PARTICIPLE
**mangeant**

PRESENT
je mange
tu manges
il/elle mange
nous **mangeons**
vous mangez
ils/elles mangent

IMPERFECT
je **mangeais**
tu **mangeais**
il/elle **mangeait**
nous mangions
vous mangiez
ils/elles **mangeaient**

PAST HISTORIC
je **mangeai**
tu **mangeas**
il/elle **mangea**
nous **mangeâmes**
vous **mangeâtes**
ils/elles mangèrent

IMPERFECT SUBJUNCTIVE
je **mangeasse**
tu **mangeasses**
il/elle **mangeât**
nous **mangeassions**
vous **mangeassiez**
ils/elles **mangeassent**

## First Conjugation Spelling Irregularities *continued*

| | |
|---|---|
| Verbs ending | **-eler** |
| Change: | **-l** doubles before **-e**, **-es**, **-ent** and throughout the Future and Conditional tenses |
| Tenses affected: | Present, Present Subjunctive, Future, Conditional |
| Model: | **appeler** to call → ❶ |
| EXCEPTIONS: | **geler** to freeze; **peler** to peel → like **mener** (page 18) |

| | |
|---|---|
| Verbs ending | **-eter** |
| Change: | **-t** doubles before **-e**, **-es**, **-ent** and throughout the Future and Conditional tenses |
| Tenses affected: | Present, Present Subjunctive, Future, Conditional |
| Model: | **jeter** to throw → ❷ |
| EXCEPTIONS: | **acheter** to buy; **haleter** to pant → like **mener** (page 18) |

| | |
|---|---|
| Verbs ending | **-yer** |
| Change: | **y** changes to **i** before **-e**, **-es**, **-ent** and throughout the Future and Conditional tenses |
| Tenses affected: | Present, Present Subjunctive, Future, Conditional |
| Model: | **essuyer** to wipe → ❸ |

The change described is optional for verbs ending in **-ayer**
e.g. **payer** to pay; **essayer** to try.

# Examples

**1** PRESENT (+ SUBJUNCTIVE)
j'**appelle**
tu **appelles**
il/elle **appelle**
nous appelons
(appelions)
vous appelez
(appeliez)
ils/elles **appellent**

FUTURE
j'**appellerai**
tu **appelleras**
il **appellera** *etc*

CONDITIONAL
j'**appellerais**
tu **appellerais**
il **appellerait** *etc*

**2** PRESENT (+ SUBJUNCTIVE)
je **jette**
tu **jettes**
il/elle **jette**
nous jetons
(jetions)
vous jetez
(jetiez)
ils/elles **jettent**

FUTURE
je **jetterai**
tu **jetteras**
il **jettera** *etc*

CONDITIONAL
je **jetterais**
tu **jetterais**
il **jetterait** *etc*

**3** PRESENT (+ SUBJUNCTIVE)
j'**essuie**
tu **essuies**
il/elle **essuie**
nous essuyons
(essuyions)
vous essuyez
(essuyiez)
ils/elles **essuient**

FUTURE
j'**essuierai**
tu **essuieras**
il **essuiera** *etc*

CONDITIONAL
j'**essuierais**
tu **essuierais**
il **essuierait** *etc*

## First Conjugation Spelling Irregularities *continued*

| | |
|---|---|
| Verbs ending | **mener**, **peser**, **lever** *etc* |
| Change: | **e** changes to **è**, before **-e**, **-es**, **-ent** and throughout the Future and Conditional tenses |
| Tenses affected: | Present, Present Subjunctive, Future, Conditional |
| Model: | **mener** to lead → ❶ |

| | |
|---|---|
| Verbs like: | **céder**, **régler**, **espérer** *etc* |
| Change: | **é** changes to **è** before **-e**, **-es**, **-ent** |
| Tenses affected: | Present, Present Subjunctive |
| Model: | **céder** to yield → ❷ |

# Examples

**1** PRESENT (+ SUBJUNCTIVE)
je **mène**
tu **mènes**
il/elle **mène**
nous menons
     (menions)
vous menez
     (meniez)
ils/elles **mènent**

FUTURE
je **mènerai**
tu **mèneras**
il **mènera** *etc*

CONDITIONAL
je **mènerais**
tu **mènerais**
il **mènerait** *etc*

**2** PRESENT (+ SUBJUNCTIVE)
je **cède**
tu **cèdes**
il/elle **cède**
nous cédons
     (cédions)
vous cédez
     (cédiez)
ils/elles **cèdent**

## The Imperative

The imperative is the form of the verb used to give commands or orders. It can be used politely, as in English 'Shut the door, please'.

The imperative is the same as the present tense **tu**, **nous** and **vous** forms without the subject pronouns:

> **donne**\* give        **finis** finish        **vends** sell
> \* The final 's' of the present tense of first conjugation verbs is dropped, except before **y** and **en** → ❶

> **donnons** let's give    **finissons** let's finish    **vendons** let's sell

> **donnez** give        **finissez** finish        **vendez** sell

The imperative of irregular verbs is given in the verb tables, page 74 onwards.

Position of object pronouns with the imperative:
- in *positive* commands: they follow the verb and are attached to it by hyphens → ❷
- in *negative* commands: they precede the verb and are not attached to it → ❸

For the order of object pronouns, see page 170.

For reflexive verbs – e.g. **se lever** to get up – the object pronoun is the reflexive pronoun → ❹

# Examples

**1** Compare:

| | |
|---|---|
| Tu donnes de l'argent à Paul | You give (some) money to Paul |
| and: | |
| Donne de l'argent à Paul | Give (some) money to Paul |

**2**

| | |
|---|---|
| Excusez-moi | Excuse me |
| Envoyons-les-leur | Let's send them to them |
| Crois-nous | Believe us |
| Expliquez-le-moi | Explain it to me |
| Attendons-la | Let's wait for her/it |
| Rends-la-lui | Give it back to him/her |

**3**

| | |
|---|---|
| Ne me dérange pas | Don't disturb me |
| Ne leur en parlons pas | Let's not speak to them about it |
| Ne les appelons pas | Let's not call them |
| N'y pense plus | Don't think about it any more |
| Ne leur répondez pas | Don't answer them |
| Ne la lui rends pas | Don't give it back to him/her |

**4**

| | |
|---|---|
| Lève-toi | Get up |
| Ne te lève pas | Don't get up |
| Dépêchons-nous | Let's hurry |
| Ne nous affolons pas | Let's not panic |
| Levez-vous | Get up |
| Ne vous levez pas | Don't get up |

## Compound Tenses: formation

In French the compound tenses are:

Perfect  → ❶
Pluperfect  → ❷
Future Perfect  → ❸
Conditional Perfect  → ❹
Past Anterior  → ❺
Perfect Subjunctive  → ❻
Pluperfect Subjunctive  → ❼

They consist of the past participle of the verb together with an auxiliary verb. Most verbs take the auxiliary **avoir**, but some take **être** (see page 28).

Compound tenses are formed in exactly the same way for both regular and irregular verbs, the only difference being that irregular verbs may have an irregular past participle.

## The Past Participle

For all compound tenses you need to know how to form the past participle of the verb. For regular verbs this is as follows:

First conjugation:  replace the **-er** of the infinitive by **-é**  → ❽

Second conjugation:  replace the **-ir** of the infinitive by **-i**  → ❾

Third conjugation:  replace the **-re** of the infinitive by **-u**  → ❿

See page 50 for agreement of past participles.

# Examples

| with **avoir** | with **être** |
|---|---|
| **1** j'ai donné  I gave, have given | je suis tombé  I fell, have fallen |
| **2** j'avais donné  I had given | j'étais tombé  I had fallen |
| **3** j'aurai donné  I shall have given | je serai tombé  I shall have fallen |
| **4** j'aurais donné  I should/would have given | je serais tombé  I should/would have fallen |
| **5** j'eus donné  I had given | je fus tombé  I had fallen |
| **6** (que) j'aie donné  (that) I gave, have given | (que) je sois tombé  (that) I fell, have fallen |
| **7** (que) j'eusse donné  (that) I had given | (que) je fusse tombé  (that) I had fallen |

**8** **donner** to give → **donné** given

**9** **finir** to finish → **fini** finished

**10** **vendre** to sell → **vendu** sold

## Compound Tenses: formation *continued*

### Verbs taking the auxiliary avoir

PERFECT TENSE
The present tense of **avoir** plus the past participle → ❶

PLUPERFECT TENSE
The imperfect tense of **avoir** plus the past participle → ❷

FUTURE PERFECT
The future tense of **avoir** plus the past participle → ❸

CONDITIONAL PERFECT
The conditional of **avoir** plus the past participle → ❹

PAST ANTERIOR
The past historic of **avoir** plus the past participle → ❺

PERFECT SUBJUNCTIVE
The present subjunctive of **avoir** plus the past participle → ❻

PLUPERFECT SUBJUNCTIVE
The imperfect subjunctive of **avoir** plus the past participle → ❼

For how to form the past participle of regular verbs see page 22. The past participle of irregular verbs is given for each verb in the verb tables, page 74 onwards.

The past participle must agree in number and in gender with any preceding direct object (see page 50).

# Examples

**1** PERFECT

| | |
|---|---|
| j'ai donné | nous avons donné |
| tu as donné | vous avez donné |
| il/elle a donné | ils/elles ont donné |

**2** PLUPERFECT

| | |
|---|---|
| j'avais donné | nous avions donné |
| tu avais donné | vous aviez donné |
| il/elle avait donné | ils/elles avaient donné |

**3** FUTURE PERFECT

| | |
|---|---|
| j'aurai donné | nous aurons donné |
| tu auras donné | vous aurez donné |
| il/elle aura donné | ils/elles auront donné |

**4** CONDITIONAL PERFECT

| | |
|---|---|
| j'aurais donné | nous aurions donné |
| tu aurais donné | vous auriez donné |
| il/elle aurait donné | ils/elles auraient donné |

**5** PAST ANTERIOR

| | |
|---|---|
| j'eus donné | nous eûmes donné |
| tu eus donné | vous eûtes donné |
| il/elle eut donné | ils/elles eurent donné |

**6** PERFECT SUBJUNCTIVE

| | |
|---|---|
| j'aie donné | nous ayons donné |
| tu aies donné | vous ayez donné |
| il/elle ait donné | ils/elles aient donné |

**7** PLUPERFECT SUBJUNCTIVE

| | |
|---|---|
| j'eusse donné | nous eussions donné |
| tu eusses donné | vous eussiez donné |
| il/elle eût donné | ils/elles eussent donné |

## Compound Tenses: formation *continued*

### Verbs taking the auxiliary être

**PERFECT TENSE**
The present tense of **être** plus the past participle → ❶

**PLUPERFECT TENSE**
The imperfect tense of **être** plus the past participle → ❷

**FUTURE PERFECT**
The future tense of **être** plus the past participle → ❸

**CONDITIONAL PERFECT**
The conditional of **être** plus the past participle → ❹

**PAST ANTERIOR**
The past historic of **être** plus the past participle → ❺

**PERFECT SUBJUNCTIVE**
The present subjunctive of **être** plus the past participle → ❻

**PLUPERFECT SUBJUNCTIVE**
The imperfect subjunctive of **être** plus the past participle → ❼

For how to form the past participle of regular verbs see page 22. The past participle of irregular verbs is given for each verb in the verb tables, page 74 onwards.

For agreement of past participles, see page 50.

For a list of verbs and verb types that take the auxiliary **être**, see page 28.

# Examples

**1 PERFECT**

| | |
|---|---|
| je suis tombé(e) | nous sommes tombé(e)s |
| tu es tombé(e) | vous êtes tombé(e)(s) |
| il est tombé | ils sont tombés |
| elle est tombée | elles sont tombées |

**2 PLUPERFECT**

| | |
|---|---|
| j'étais tombé(e) | nous étions tombé(e)s |
| tu étais tombé(e) | vous étiez tombé(e)(s) |
| il était tombé | ils étaient tombés |
| elle était tombée | elles étaient tombées |

**3 FUTURE PERFECT**

| | |
|---|---|
| je serai tombé(e) | nous serons tombé(e)s |
| tu seras tombé(e) | vous serez tombé(e)(s) |
| il sera tombé | ils seront tombés |
| elle sera tombée | elles seront tombées |

**4 CONDITIONAL PERFECT**

| | |
|---|---|
| je serais tombé(e) | nous serions tombé(e)s |
| tu serais tombé(e) | vous seriez tombé(e)(s) |
| il serait tombé | ils seraient tombés |
| elle serait tombée | elles seraient tombées |

**5 PAST ANTERIOR**

| | |
|---|---|
| je fus tombé(e) | nous fûmes tombé(e)s |
| tu fus tombé(e) | vous fûtes tombé(e)(s) |
| il fut tombé | ils furent tombés |
| elle fut tombée | elles furent tombées |

**6 PERFECT SUBJUNCTIVE**

| | |
|---|---|
| je sois tombé(e) | nous soyons tombé(e)s |
| tu sois tombé(e) | vous soyez tombé(e)(s) |
| il soit tombé | ils soient tombés |
| elle soit tombée | elles soient tombées |

**7 PLUPERFECT SUBJUNCTIVE**

| | |
|---|---|
| je fusse tombé(e) | nous fussions tombé(e)s |
| tu fusses tombé(e) | vous fussiez tombé(e)(s) |
| il fût tombé | ils fussent tombés |
| elle fût tombée | elles fussent tombées |

27

## Compound Tenses *continued*

### The following verbs take the auxiliary être

Reflexive verbs (see page 30) → ①

The following intransitive verbs (i.e. verbs which cannot take a direct object), largely expressing motion or a change of state:

| | |
|---|---|
| **aller** to go → ② | **passer** to pass |
| **arriver** to arrive; to happen | **rentrer** to go back/in |
| **descendre** to go/come down | **rester** to stay → ⑤ |
| **devenir** to become | **retourner** to go back |
| **entrer** to go/come in | **revenir** to come back |
| **monter** to go/come up | **sortir** to go/come out |
| **mourir** to die → ③ | **tomber** to fall |
| **naître** to be born | **venir** to come → ⑥ |
| **partir** to leave → ④ | |

Of these, the following are conjugated with **avoir** when used transitively (i.e. with a direct object):

**descendre** to bring/take down
**entrer** to bring/take in
**monter** to bring/take up → ⑦
**passer** to pass; to spend → ⑧
**rentrer** to bring/take in
**retourner** to turn over
**sortir** to bring/take out → ⑨

ⓘ Note that the past participle must show an agreement in number and gender whenever the auxiliary is **être** except for reflexive verbs where the reflexive pronoun is the indirect object (see page 50).

# Examples

**1** je me suis arrêté(e)  I stopped
elle s'est trompée  she made a mistake
tu t'es levé(e)  you got up
ils s'étaient battus  they had fought (one another)

**2** elle est allée  she went

**3** ils sont morts  they died

**4** vous êtes partie  you left (*addressing a female person*)

vous êtes parties  you left (*addressing more than one female person*)

**5** nous sommes resté(e)s  we stayed

**6** elles étaient venues  they (*female*) had come

**7** Il a monté les valises  He's taken up the cases

**8** Nous avons passé trois semaines chez elle  We spent three weeks at her place

**9** Avez-vous sorti la voiture?  Have you taken the car out?

## Reflexive Verbs

A reflexive verb is one accompanied by a reflexive pronoun,
e.g. **se lever** to get up; **se laver** to wash (oneself).
The reflexive pronouns are:

|  | SINGULAR | PLURAL |
|---|---|---|
| 1st person | me (m') | nous |
| 2nd person | te (t') | vous |
| 3rd person | se (s') | se (s') |

The forms shown in brackets are used before a vowel, an **h** 'mute', or the
pronoun **y** → ❶

> In positive commands, **te** changes to **toi** → ❷
>
> The reflexive pronoun 'reflects back' to the subject, but it is not
> always translated in English → ❸
>
> The plural pronouns are sometimes translated as 'one another',
> 'each other' (the *reciprocal* meaning) → ❹
>
> The reciprocal meaning may be emphasized by **l'un(e) l'autre (les
> un(e)s les autres)** → ❺

Simple tenses of reflexive verbs are conjugated in exactly the same way
as those of non-reflexive verbs except that the reflexive pronoun is always
used. Compound tenses are formed with the auxiliary **être**. A sample
reflexive verb is conjugated in full on pages 34 and 35.

For agreement of past participles, see page 32.

## Position of Reflexive Pronouns

In constructions other than the imperative affirmative the pronoun
comes before the verb → ❻

In the imperative affirmative, the pronoun follows the verb and is
attached to it by a hyphen → ❼

# Examples

① Je m'ennuie  
   Elle s'habille  
   Ils s'y intéressent  

I'm bored  
She's getting dressed  
They are interested in it  

② Assieds-toi  
   Tais-toi  

Sit down  
Be quiet  

③ Je me prépare  
   Nous nous lavons  
   Elle se lève  

I'm getting (myself) ready  
We're washing (ourselves)  
She gets up  

④ Nous nous parlons  
   Ils se ressemblent  

We speak to each other  
They resemble one another  

⑤ Ils se regardent l'un l'autre  

They are looking at each other  

⑥ Je me couche tôt  
   Comment vous appelez-vous?  
   Il ne s'est pas rasé  
   Ne te dérange pas pour nous  

I go to bed early  
What is your name?  
He hasn't shaved  
Don't put yourself out on our account  

⑦ Dépêche-toi  
   Renseignons-nous  
   Asseyez-vous  

Hurry (up)  
Let's find out  
Sit down

## Reflexive Verbs *continued*

### Past Participle Agreement

In most reflexive verbs the reflexive pronoun is a *direct* object pronoun → ❶

When a direct object accompanies the reflexive verb the pronoun is then the *indirect* object → ❷

The past participle of a reflexive verb agrees in number and gender with a direct object which *precedes* the verb (usually, but not always, the reflexive pronoun) → ❸

The past participle does not change if the direct object follows the verb → ❹

Here are some common reflexive verbs:

| | |
|---|---|
| **s'en aller**  to go away | **se hâter**  to hurry |
| **s'amuser**  to enjoy oneself | **se laver**  to wash (oneself) |
| **s'appeler**  to be called | **se lever**  to get up |
| **s'arrêter**  to stop | **se passer**  to happen |
| **s'asseoir**  to sit (down) | **se promener**  to go for a walk |
| **se baigner**  to go swimming | **se rappeler**  to remember |
| **se blesser**  to hurt oneself | **se ressembler**  to resemble each other |
| **se coucher**  to go to bed | **se retourner**  to turn round |
| **se demander**  to wonder | **se réveiller**  to wake up |
| **se dépêcher**  to hurry | **se sauver**  to run away |
| **se diriger**  to make one's way | **se souvenir de**  to remember |
| **s'endormir**  to fall asleep | **se taire**  to be quiet |
| **s'ennuyer**  to be/get bored | **se tromper**  to be mistaken |
| **se fâcher**  to get angry | **se trouver**  to be (situated) |
| **s'habiller**  to dress (oneself) | |

# Examples

**1** Je m'appelle — I'm called (*literally*: I call myself)
Asseyez-vous — Sit down (*literally*: Seat yourself)
Ils se lavent — They wash (themselves)

**2** Elle se lave les mains — She's washing her hands (*literally*: She's washing to herself the hands)

Je me brosse les dents — I brush my teeth
Nous nous envoyons des cadeaux à Noël — We send presents to each other at Christmas

**3** 'Je me suis endormi' s'est-il excusé — 'I fell asleep', he apologized
Pauline s'est dirigée vers la sortie — Pauline made her way towards the exit

Ils se sont levés vers dix heures — They got up around ten o'clock
Elles se sont excusées de leur erreur — They apologized for their mistake
Est-ce que tu t'es blessée, Cécile? — Have you hurt yourself, Cécile?

**4** Elle s'est lavé les cheveux — She (has) washed her hair
Nous nous sommes serré la main — We shook hands
Christine s'est cassé la jambe — Christine has broken her leg

## Reflexive Verbs *continued*

Conjugation of: **se laver** to wash (oneself)

### 1 SIMPLE TENSES

#### PRESENT

| | |
|---|---|
| je me lave | nous nous lavons |
| tu te laves | vous vous lavez |
| il/elle se lave | ils/elles se lavent |

#### IMPERFECT

| | |
|---|---|
| je me lavais | nous nous lavions |
| tu te lavais | vous vous laviez |
| il/elle se lavait | ils/elles se lavaient |

#### FUTURE

| | |
|---|---|
| je me laverai | nous nous laverons |
| tu te laveras | vous vous laverez |
| il/elle se lavera | ils/elles se laveront |

#### CONDITIONAL

| | |
|---|---|
| je me laverais | nous nous laverions |
| tu te laverais | vous vous laveriez |
| il/elle se laverait | ils/elles se laveraient |

#### PAST HISTORIC

| | |
|---|---|
| je me lavai | nous nous lavâmes |
| tu te lavas | vous vous lavâtes |
| il/elle se lava | ils/elles se lavèrent |

#### PRESENT SUBJUNCTIVE

| | |
|---|---|
| je me lave | nous nous lavions |
| tu te laves | vous vous laviez |
| il/elle se lave | ils/elles se lavent |

#### IMPERFECT SUBJUNCTIVE

| | |
|---|---|
| je me lavasse | nous nous lavassions |
| tu te lavasses | vous vous lavassiez |
| il/elle se lavât | ils/elles se lavassent |

## Reflexive Verbs *continued*

Conjugation of: **se laver** to wash (oneself)

### 2 COMPOUND TENSES

#### PERFECT

| | |
|---|---|
| je me suis lavé(e) | nous nous sommes lavé(e)s |
| tu t'es lavé(e) | vous vous êtes lavé(e)(s) |
| il/elle s'est lavé(e) | ils/elles se sont lavé(e)s |

#### PLUPERFECT

| | |
|---|---|
| je m'étais lavé(e) | nous nous étions lavé(e)s |
| tu t'étais lavé(e) | vous vous étiez lavé(e)(s) |
| il/elle s'était lavé(e) | ils/elles s'étaient lavé(e)s |

#### FUTURE PERFECT

| | |
|---|---|
| je me serai lavé(e) | nous nous serons lavé(e)s |
| tu te seras lavé(e) | vous vous serez lavé(e)(s) |
| il/elle se sera lavé(e) | ils/elles se seront lavé(e)s |

#### CONDITIONAL PERFECT

| | |
|---|---|
| je me serais lavé(e) | nous nous serions lavé(e)s |
| tu te serais lavé(e) | vous vous seriez lavé(e)(s) |
| il/elle se serait lavé(e) | ils/elles se seraient lavé(e)s |

#### PAST ANTERIOR

| | |
|---|---|
| je me fus lavé(e) | nous nous fûmes lavé(e)s |
| tu te fus lavé(e) | vous vous fûtes lavé(e)(s) |
| il/elle se fut lavé(e) | ils/elles se furent lavé(e)s |

#### PERFECT SUBJUNCTIVE

| | |
|---|---|
| je me sois lavé(e) | nous nous soyons lavé(e)s |
| tu te sois lavé(e) | vous vous soyez lavé(e)(s) |
| il/elle se soit lavé(e) | ils/elles se soient lavé(e)s |

#### PLUPERFECT SUBJUNCTIVE

| | |
|---|---|
| je me fusse lavé(e) | nous nous fussions lavé(e)s |
| tu te fusses lavé(e) | vous vous fussiez lavé(e)(s) |
| il/elle se fût lavé(e) | ils/elles se fussent lavé(e)s |

## The Passive

In the passive, the subject *receives* the action (e.g. I was hit) as opposed to *performing* it (e.g. I hit him). In English the verb 'to be' is used with the past participle. In French the passive is formed in exactly the same way, i.e.:
> a tense of **être** + *past participle*.

The past participle agrees in number and gender with the subject → **1**

A sample verb is conjugated in the passive voice on pages 38 and 39.

The indirect object in French cannot become the subject in the passive:
> in quelqu'un m'a donné un livre the indirect object **m'** cannot
> become the subject of a passive verb (unlike English: someone
> gave me a book → I was given a book).

The passive meaning is often expressed in French by:
- **on** plus a verb in the active voice → **2**
- a reflexive verb (see page 30) → **3**

# Examples

**①** Philippe a été récompensé — Philippe has been rewarded
Son travail est très admiré — His work is greatly admired
Ils le feront pourvu qu'ils soient payés — They'll do it provided they're paid
Les enfants seront punis — The children will be punished
Cette mesure aurait été critiquée si ... — This measure would have been criticized if ...
Les portes avaient été fermées — The doors had been closed

**②** On leur a envoyé une lettre — They were sent a letter
On nous a montré le jardin — We were shown the garden
On m'a dit que ... — I was told that ...

**③** Ils se vendent 3 euros (la) pièce — They are sold for 3 euros each
Ce mot ne s'emploie plus — This word is no longer used

## The Passive *continued*

Conjugation of: **être aimé** to be liked

### PRESENT

| | |
|---|---|
| je suis aimé(e) | nous sommes aimé(e)s |
| tu es aimé(e) | vous êtes aimé(e)(s) |
| il/elle est aimé(e) | ils/elles sont aimé(e)s |

### IMPERFECT

| | |
|---|---|
| j'étais aimé(e) | nous étions aimé(e)s |
| tu étais aimé(e) | vous étiez aimé(e)(s) |
| il/elle était aimé(e) | ils/elles étaient aimé(e)s |

### FUTURE

| | |
|---|---|
| je serai aimé(e) | nous serons aimé(e)s |
| tu seras aimé(e) | vous serez aimé(e)(s) |
| il/elle sera aimé(e) | ils/elles seront aimé(e)s |

### CONDITIONAL

| | |
|---|---|
| je serais aimé(e) | nous serions aimé(e)s |
| tu serais aimé(e) | vous seriez aimé(e)(s) |
| il/elle serait aimé(e) | ils/elles seraient aimé(e)s |

### PAST HISTORIC

| | |
|---|---|
| je fus aimé(e) | nous fûmes aimé(e)s |
| tu fus aimé(e) | vous fûtes aimé(e)(s) |
| il/elle fut aimé(e) | ils/elles furent aimé(e)s |

### PRESENT SUBJUNCTIVE

| | |
|---|---|
| je sois aimé(e) | nous soyons aimé(e)s |
| tu sois aimé(e) | vous soyez aimé(e)(s) |
| il/elle soit aimé(e) | ils/elles soient aimé(e)s |

### IMPERFECT SUBJUNCTIVE

| | |
|---|---|
| je fusse aimé(e) | nous fussions aimé(e)s |
| tu fusses aimé(e) | vous fussiez aimé(e)(s) |
| il/elle fût aimé(e) | ils/elles fussent aimé(e)s |

# Verbs

## The Passive *continued*

Conjugation of: **être aimé** to be liked

### PERFECT

| | |
|---|---|
| j'ai été aimé(e) | nous avons été aimé(e)s |
| tu as été aimé(e) | vous avez été aimé(e)(s) |
| il/elle a été aimé(e) | ils/elles ont été aimé(e)s |

### PLUPERFECT

| | |
|---|---|
| j'avais été aimé(e) | nous avions été aimé(e)s |
| tu avais été aimé(e) | vous aviez été aimé(e)(s) |
| il/elle avait été aimé(e) | ils/elles avaient été aimé(e)s |

### FUTURE PERFECT

| | |
|---|---|
| j'aurai été aimé(e) | nous aurons été aimé(e)s |
| tu auras été aimé(e) | vous aurez été aimé(e)(s) |
| il/elle aura été aimé(e) | ils/elles auront été aimé(e)s |

### CONDITIONAL PERFECT

| | |
|---|---|
| j'aurais été aimé(e) | nous aurions été aimé(e)s |
| tu aurais été aimé(e) | vous auriez été aimé(e)(s) |
| il/elle aurait été aimé(e) | ils/elles auraient été aimé(e)s |

### PAST ANTERIOR

| | |
|---|---|
| j'eus été aimé(e) | nous eûmes été aimé(e)s |
| tu eus été aimé(e) | vous eûtes été aimé(e)(s) |
| il/elle eut été aimé(e) | ils/elles eurent été aimé(e)s |

### PERFECT SUBJUNCTIVE

| | |
|---|---|
| j'aie été aimé(e) | nous ayons été aimé(e)s |
| tu aies été aimé(e) | vous ayez été aimé(e)(s) |
| il/elle ait été aimé(e) | ils/elles aient été aimé(e)s |

### PLUPERFECT SUBJUNCTIVE

| | |
|---|---|
| j'eusse été aimé(e) | nous eussions été aimé(e)s |
| tu eusses été aimé(e) | vous eussiez été aimé(e)(s) |
| il/elle eût été aimé(e) | ils/elles eussent été aimé(e)s |

## Impersonal Verbs

Impersonal verbs are used only in the infinitive and in the third person singular with the subject pronoun **il**, generally translated as 'it'.

e.g.  il pleut  it's raining
  il est facile de dire que ...  it's easy to say that ...

The most common impersonal verbs are:

| INFINITIVE | CONSTRUCTIONS |
|---|---|
| **s'agir** | il s'agit de + *noun*  → ❶ |
| | it's a question/matter of something, it's about something |
| | il s'agit de + *infinitive*  → ❷ |
| | it's a question/matter of doing; somebody must do |
| **falloir** | il faut + *noun object* (+ *indirect object*)  → ❸ |
| | (somebody) needs something, something is necessary (to somebody) |
| | il faut + *infinitive* (+ *indirect object*)  → ❹ |
| | it is necessary to do |
| | il faut que + *subjunctive*  → ❺ |
| | it is necessary to do, somebody must do |
| **grêler** | il grêle  it's hailing |
| **neiger** | il neige  it's snowing     → ❻ |
| **pleuvoir** | il pleut  it's raining |
| **tonner** | il tonne  it's thundering |
| **valoir mieux** | il vaut mieux + *infinitive*  → ❼ |
| | it's better to do |
| | il vaut mieux que + *subjunctive*  → ❽ |
| | it's better to do/that somebody does |

# Examples

① Il ne s'agit pas d'argent

It isn't a question/matter of
money

De quoi s'agit-il?

What is it about?

Il s'agit de la vie d'une famille au
début du siècle

It's about the life of a family at
the turn of the century

② Il s'agit de faire vite

We must act quickly

③ Il faut du courage pour faire ça

One needs courage to do that

Il me faut une chaise de plus

I need an extra chair

④ Il faut partir

It is necessary to leave
We/I/You must leave*

Il me fallait prendre une décision

I had to make a decision

⑤ Il faut que vous partiez

You must leave

Il faudrait que je fasse mes valises

I ought to pack my cases

⑥ Il pleuvait à verse

It was pouring with rain

⑦ Il vaut mieux refuser

It's better to refuse
You/He/I had better refuse*

Il vaudrait mieux rester

You/We/She had better stay*

⑧ Il vaudrait mieux que nous ne
venions pas

It would be better if we didn't
come
We'd better not come

* The translation here obviously depends on context

41

## Impersonal Verbs

The following verbs are also commonly used in impersonal constructions:

| INFINITIVE | CONSTRUCTIONS |
|---|---|
| avoir | **il y a** + *noun* → ① <br> there is/are |
| être | **il est** + *noun* → ② <br> it is, there are (*very literary style*) <br> **il est** + *adjective* + **de** + *infinitive* → ③ <br> it is |
| faire | **il fait** + *adjective of weather* → ④ <br> it is <br> **il fait** + *noun depicting weather/dark/light etc* → ⑤ <br> it is |
| manquer | **il manque** + *noun* (+ *indirect object*) → ⑥ <br> there is/are ... missing, something is missing |
| paraître | **il paraît que** + *subjunctive* → ⑦ <br> it seems/appears that <br> **il paraît** + *indirect object* + **que** + *indicative* → ⑧ <br> it seems/appears to somebody that |
| rester | **il reste** + *noun* (+ *indirect object*) → ⑨ <br> there is/are ... left, (somebody) has something left |
| sembler | **il semble que** + *subjunctive* → ⑩ <br> it seems/appears that <br> **il semble** + *indirect object* + **que** + *indicative* → ⑪ <br> it seems/appears to somebody that |
| suffire | **il suffit de** + *infinitive* → ⑫ <br> it is enough to do <br> **il suffit de** + *noun* → ⑬ <br> something is enough, it only takes something |

# Examples

1. Il y a du pain (qui reste) — There is some bread (left)
   Il n'y avait pas de lettres ce matin — There were no letters this morning

2. Il est dix heures — It's ten o'clock
   Il est des gens qui … — There are (some) people who …

3. Il était inutile de protester — It was useless to protest
   Il est facile de critiquer — Criticizing is easy

4. Il fait beau/mauvais — It's lovely/horrible weather

5. Il faisait du soleil/du vent — It was sunny/windy
   Il fait jour/nuit — It's light/dark

6. Il manque deux tasses — There are two cups missing / Two cups are missing
   Il manquait un bouton à sa chemise — His shirt had a button missing

7. Il paraît qu'ils partent demain — It appears they are leaving tomorrow

8. Il nous paraît certain qu'il aura du succès — It seems certain to us that he'll be successful

9. Il reste deux miches de pain — There are two loaves left
   Il lui restait cinquante euros — He/She had fifty euros left

10. Il semble que vous ayez raison — It seems that you are right

11. Il me semblait qu'il conduisait trop vite — It seemed to me (that) he was driving too fast

12. Il suffit de téléphoner pour réserver une place — It is enough to reserve a seat by phone

13. Il suffit d'une seule erreur pour tout gâcher — One single error is enough to ruin everything

## The Infinitive

The infinitive is the form of the verb found in dictionary entries meaning 'to ... ', e.g. **donner** to give; **vivre** to live.

There are three main types of verbal construction involving the infinitive:
- with no linking preposition → ❶
- with the linking preposition **à** (see also page 64) → ❷
- with the linking preposition **de** (see also page 64) → ❸

### Verbs followed by an infinitive with no linking preposition

**devoir**, **pouvoir**, **savoir**, **vouloir** and **falloir** (i.e. modal auxiliary verbs: page 52 → ❶).

**valoir mieux**: see Impersonal Verbs, page 40.

verbs of seeing or hearing e.g. **voir** to see; **entendre** to hear → ❹

intransitive verbs of motion e.g. **aller** to go; **descendre** to come/go down → ❺

**envoyer** to send → ❻

**faillir** → ❼

**faire** → ❽

**laisser** to let, allow → ❾

The following common verbs:

| | |
|---|---|
| **adorer** to love | **espérer** to hope → ⓮ |
| **aimer** to like, love → ❿ | **oser** to dare → ⓯ |
| **aimer mieux** to prefer → ⓫ | **préférer** to prefer |
| **compter** to expect | **sembler** to seem → ⓰ |
| **désirer** to wish, want → ⓬ | **souhaiter** to wish |
| **détester** to hate → ⓭ | |

# Examples

1. Voulez-vous attendre? — Would you like to wait?

2. J'apprends à nager — I'm learning to swim

3. Essayez de venir — Try to come

4. Il nous a vus arriver — He saw us arriving
   On les entend chanter — You can hear them singing

5. Allez voir Nicolas — Go and see Nicholas
   Descends leur demander — Go down and ask them

6. Je l'ai envoyé les voir — I sent him to see them

7. J'ai failli tomber — I almost fell

8. Ne me faites pas rire! — Don't make me laugh!
   J'ai fait réparer ma voiture — I've had my car repaired

9. Laissez-moi passer — Let me pass

10. Il aime nous accompagner — He likes to come with us

11. J'aimerais mieux le choisir moi-même — I'd rather choose it myself

12. Elle ne désire pas venir — She doesn't wish to come

13. Je déteste me lever le matin — I hate getting up in the morning

14. Espérez-vous aller en vacances? — Are you hoping to go on holiday?

15. Nous n'avons pas osé y retourner — We haven't dared go back

16. Vous semblez être inquiet — You seem to be worried

## The Infinitive: Set Expressions

The following are set in French with the meaning shown:

> aller chercher to go for, to go and get → ①
> envoyer chercher to send for → ②
> entendre dire que to hear it said that → ③
> entendre parler de to hear of/about → ④
> faire entrer to show in → ⑤
> faire sortir to let out → ⑥
> faire venir to send for → ⑦
> laisser tomber to drop → ⑧
> vouloir dire to mean → ⑨

### The Perfect Infinitive

The perfect infinitive is formed using the auxiliary verb **avoir** or **être** as appropriate with the past participle of the verb → ⑩

The perfect infinitive is found:
- following the preposition **après** after → ⑪
- following certain verbal constructions → ⑫

# Examples

**1** Va chercher tes photos — Go and get your photos
Il est allé chercher Alexandre — He's gone to get Alexander

**2** J'ai envoyé chercher un médecin — I've sent for a doctor

**3** J'ai entendu dire qu'il est malade — I've heard it said that he's ill

**4** Je n'ai plus entendu parler de lui — I didn't hear anything more (said) of him

**5** Fais entrer nos invités — Show our guests in

**6** J'ai fait sortir le chat — I've let the cat out

**7** Je vous ai fait venir parce que … — I sent for you because …

**8** Il a laissé tomber le vase — He dropped the vase

**9** Qu'est-ce que cela veut dire? — What does that mean?

**10** avoir fini — to have finished
être allé — to have gone
s'être levé — to have got up

**11** Après avoir pris cette décision, il nous a appelé — After making/having made that decision, he called us
Après être sorties, elles se sont dirigées vers le parking — After leaving/having left, they headed for the car park
Après nous être levé(e)s, nous avons lu les journaux — After getting up/having got up, we read the papers

**12** pardonner à qn d'avoir fait — to forgive sb for doing/having done
remercier qn d'avoir fait — to thank sb for doing/having done
regretter d'avoir fait — to be sorry for doing/having done

## The Present Participle

### Formation

First conjugation:
Replace the -er of the infinitive by -ant → ①
- Verbs ending in -cer: c changes to ç → ②
- Verbs ending in -ger: g changes to ge → ③

Second conjugation:
Replace the -ir of the infinitive by -issant → ④

Third conjugation:
Replace the -re of the infinitive by -ant → ⑤

For irregular present participles, see irregular verbs, page 74 onwards.

### Uses

The present participle has a more restricted use in French than in English.

Used as a verbal form, the present participle is invariable. It is found:
- on its own, where it corresponds to the English present participle → ⑥
- following the preposition en → ⑦
- ⓘ Note, in particular, the construction:
  *verb + en + present participle*
  which is often translated by an English phrasal verb, i.e. one followed by a preposition like 'to run down', 'to bring up' → ⑧

Used as an adjective, the present participle agrees in number and gender with the noun or pronoun → ⑨
- ⓘ Note, in particular, the use of **ayant** and **étant** – the present participles of the auxiliary verbs **avoir** and **être** – with a past participle → ⑩

# Examples

1. donner to give → donnant giving

2. lancer to throw → lançant throwing

3. manger to eat → mangeant eating

4. finir to finish → finissant finishing

5. vendre to sell → vendant selling

6. David, habitant près de Paris, a la possibilité de ...
   David, living near Paris, has the opportunity of ...

   Elle, pensant que je serais fâché, a dit ...
   She, thinking that I would be angry, said ...

   Ils m'ont suivi, criant à tue-tête
   They followed me, shouting at the top of their voices

7. En attendant sa sœur, Richard s'est endormi
   While waiting for his sister, Richard fell asleep

   Téléphone-nous en arrivant chez toi
   Phone us when you get home

   En appuyant sur ce bouton, on peut ...
   By pressing this button, you can ...

   Il s'est blessé en essayant de sauver un chat
   He hurt himself trying to rescue a cat

8. sortir en courant
   to run out (*literally*: to go out running)

   avancer en boîtant
   to limp along (*literally*: to go forward limping)

9. le soleil couchant
   the setting sun

   une lumière éblouissante
   a dazzling light

   ils sont dégoûtants
   they are disgusting

   elles étaient étonnantes
   they were surprising

10. Ayant mangé plus tôt, il a pu ...
    Having eaten earlier, he was able to ...

    Étant arrivée en retard, elle a dû ...
    Having arrived late, she had to ...

## Past Participle Agreement

Like adjectives, a past participle must sometimes agree in number and gender with a noun or pronoun. For the rules of agreement, see below. Example: **donné**

|         | MASCULINE | FEMININE |
|---------|-----------|----------|
| SING.   | donné     | donn**ée** |
| PLUR.   | donné**s** | donn**ées** |

When the masculine singular form already ends in **-s**, no further **s** is added in the masculine plural, e.g. **pris** taken.

### Rules of Agreement in Compound Tenses

When the auxiliary verb is **avoir**:

> The past participle remains in the masculine singular form, unless a direct object precedes the verb. The past participle then agrees in number and gender with the preceding direct object → **1**

When the auxiliary verb is **être**:

> The past participle of a non-reflexive verb agrees in number and gender with the subject → **2**
> The past participle of a reflexive verb agrees in number and gender with the reflexive pronoun, if the pronoun is a direct object → **3**
> No agreement is made if the reflexive pronoun is an indirect object → **4**

### The Past Participle as an adjective

The past participle agrees in number and gender with the noun or pronoun → **5**

# Examples

1. Voici le livre que vous avez demandé — Here's the book you asked for
   Laquelle avaient-elles choisie? — Which one had they chosen?
   Ces amis? Je les ai rencontrés à Édimbourg — Those friends? I met them in Edinburgh
   Il a gardé toutes les lettres qu'elle a écrites — He has kept all the letters she wrote

2. Est-ce que ton frère est allé à l'étranger? — Did your brother go abroad?
   Elle était restée chez elle — She had stayed at home
   Ils sont partis dans la matinée — They left in the morning
   Mes cousines sont revenues hier — My cousins came back yesterday

3. Tu t'es rappelé d'acheter du pain, Georges? — Did you remember to buy bread, Georges?
   Martine s'est demandée pourquoi il l'appelait — Martine wondered why he was calling her
   'Lui at moi nous nous sommes cachés' a-t-elle dit — 'He and I hid,' she said
   Les vendeuses se sont mises en grève — The shop assistants have gone on strike
   Vous vous êtes brouillés? — Have you fallen out with each other?

   Les enfants s'étaient entraidés — The children had helped one another

4. Elle s'est lavé les mains — She washed her hands
   Ils se sont parlé pendant des heures — They talked to each other for hours

5. à un moment donné — at a given time
   la porte ouverte — the open door
   ils sont bien connus — they are well-known
   elles semblent fatiguées — they seem tired

## Modal Auxiliary Verbs

In French, the modal auxiliary verbs are: **devoir**, **pouvoir**, **savoir**, **vouloir** and **falloir**.

They are followed by a verb in the infinitive and have the following meanings:

**devoir**   to have to, must → ❶
to be due to → ❷
*in the conditional/conditional perfect*:
should/should have, ought/ought to have → ❸

**pouvoir**  to be able to, can → ❹
to be allowed to, can, may → ❺
*indicating possibility*: may/might/could → ❻

**savoir**   to know how to, can → ❼

**vouloir**   to want/wish to → ❽
to be willing to, will → ❾
*in polite phrases* → ❿

**falloir**   to be necessary: see Impersonal Verbs, page 40.

# Examples

1. Je dois leur rendre visite
   Elle a dû partir
   Il a dû regretter d'avoir parlé

   I must visit them
   She (has) had to leave
   He must have been sorry he
     spoke

2. Vous devez revenir demain

   Je devais attraper le train de
     neuf heures mais ...

   You're due (to come) back
     tomorrow
   I was (supposed) to catch the
     nine o'clock train but ...

3. Je devrais le faire
   J'aurais dû m'excuser

   I ought to do it
   I ought to have apologized

4. Il ne peut pas lever le bras
   Pouvez-vous réparer cette
     montre?

   He can't raise his arm
   Can you mend this watch?

5. Puis-je les accompagner?

   May I go with them?

6. Il peut encore changer d'avis
   Cela pourrait être vrai

   He may change his mind yet
   It could/might be true

7. Savez-vous conduire?
   Je ne sais pas faire une omelette

   Can you drive?
   I don't know how to make an
     omelette

8. Elle veut rester encore un jour

   She wants to stay another day

9. Ils ne voulaient pas le faire

   Ma voiture ne veut pas démarrer

   They wouldn't do it
   They weren't willing to do it
   My car won't start

10. Voulez-vous boire quelque chose?

    Would you like something to
      drink?

# Verbs

## Use of Tenses

### The Present

Unlike English, French does not distinguish between the simple present (e.g. I smoke, he reads, we live) and the continuous present (e.g. I am smoking, he is reading, we are living) → ①

To emphasize continuity, the following constructions may be used:
**être en train de faire**, **être à faire** to be doing → ②

French uses the present tense where English uses the perfect in the following cases:
- with certain prepositions of time – notably **depuis** for/since – when an action begun in the past is continued in the present → ③
  Note, however, that the perfect is used as in English when the verb is negative or the action has been completed → ④
- in the construction **venir de faire** to have just done → ⑤

### The Future

The future is generally used as in English, but note the following:

Immediate future time is often expressed by means of the present tense of **aller** plus an infinitive → ⑥

In time clauses expressing future action, French uses the future where English uses the present → ⑦

### The Future Perfect

Used as in English to mean 'shall/will have done' → ⑧

In time clauses expressing future action, where English uses the perfect tense → ⑨

# Examples

**1**
| | |
|---|---|
| Je fume | I smoke *or* I am smoking |
| Il lit | He reads *or* He is reading |
| Nous habitons | We live *or* We are living |

**2**
| | |
|---|---|
| Il est en train de travailler | He's (busy) working |

**3**
| | |
|---|---|
| Paul apprend à nager depuis six mois | Paul's been learning to swim for six months (and still is) |
| Je suis debout depuis sept heures | I've been up since seven |
| Il y a longtemps que vous attendez? | Have you been waiting long? |
| Voilà deux semaines que nous sommes ici | That's two weeks we've been here (now) |

**4**
| | |
|---|---|
| Ils ne se sont pas vus depuis des mois | They haven't seen each other for months |
| Elle est revenue il y a un an | She came back a year ago |

**5**
| | |
|---|---|
| Elisabeth vient de partir | Elizabeth has just left |

**6**
| | |
|---|---|
| Tu vas tomber si tu ne fais pas attention | You'll fall if you're not careful |
| Il va manquer le train | He's going to miss the train |
| Ça va prendre une demi-heure | It'll take half an hour |

**7**
| | |
|---|---|
| Quand il viendra vous serez en vacances | When he comes you'll be on holiday |
| Faites-nous savoir aussitôt qu'elle arrivera | Let us know as soon as she arrives |

**8**
| | |
|---|---|
| J'aurai fini dans une heure | I shall have finished in an hour |

**9**
| | |
|---|---|
| Quand tu auras lu ce roman, rends-le-moi | When you've read the novel, give it back to me |
| Je partirai dès que j'aurai fini | I'll leave as soon as I've finished |

## Use of Tenses *continued*

### The Imperfect

The imperfect describes:
- an action (or state) in the past without definite limits in time  → ❶
- habitual action(s) in the past (often translated by means of 'would' or 'used to')  → ❷

French uses the imperfect tense where English uses the pluperfect in the following cases:
- with certain prepositions of time – notably **depuis** for/since – when an action begun in the remoter past was continued in the more recent past  → ❸

  Note, however, that the pluperfect is used as in English, when the verb is negative or the action has been completed  → ❹
  - in the construction **venir de faire** to have just done  → ❺

### The Perfect

The perfect is used to recount a completed action or event in the past. Note that this corresponds to a perfect tense or a simple past tense in English  → ❻

### The Past Historic

Only ever used in *written, literary* French, the past historic recounts a completed action in the past, corresponding to a simple past tense in English  → ❼

### The Past Anterior

This tense is used instead of the pluperfect when a verb in another part of the sentence is in the past historic. That is:
- in time clauses, after conjunctions like: **quand, lorsque** when; **dès que, aussitôt que** as soon as; **après que** after  → ❽
- after **à peine** hardly, scarcely  → ❾

### The Subjunctive

In spoken French, the present subjunctive generally replaces the imperfect subjunctive. See also page 58 onwards.

# Examples

①  Elle regardait par la fenêtre    She was looking out of the window

Il pleuvait quand je suis sorti de chez moi    It was raining when I left the house

Nos chambres donnaient sur la plage    Our rooms overlooked the beach

②  Quand il était étudiant, il se levait à l'aube    When he was a student he got up at dawn

Nous causions des heures entières    We would talk for hours on end

Elle te taquinait, n'est-ce pas?    She used to tease you, didn't she?

③  Nous habitions à Londres depuis deux ans    We had been living in London for two years (and still were)

Il était malade depuis 2004    He had been ill since 2004

Il y avait assez longtemps qu'il le faisait    He had been doing it for quite a long time

④  Voilà un an que je ne l'avais pas vu    I hadn't seen him for a year

Il y avait une heure qu'elle était arrivée    She had arrived one hour before

⑤  Je venais de les rencontrer    I had just met them

⑥  Nous sommes allés au bord de la mer    We went/have been to the seaside

Il a refusé de nous aider    He (has) refused to help us

La voiture ne s'est pas arrêtée    The car didn't stop/hasn't stopped

⑦  Le roi mourut en 1592    The king died in 1592

⑧  Quand il eut fini, il se leva    When he had finished, he got up

⑨  À peine eut-il fini de parler qu'on frappa à la porte    He had scarcely finished speaking when there was a knock at the door

## The Subjunctive: when to use it

For how to form the subjunctive see page 6 onwards.

The subjunctive is used :

After certain conjunctions:

| | |
|---|---|
| quoique ⎤<br>bien que ⎦ | although → ① |
| pour que ⎤<br>afin que ⎦ | so that → ② |
| pourvu que | provided that → ③ |
| jusqu'à ce que | until → ④ |
| avant que (... ne) | before → ⑤ |
| à moins que (... ne) | unless → ⑥ |
| de peur que (... ne) ⎤<br>de crainte que (... ne) ⎦ | for fear that, lest → ⑦ |

ⓘ Note that the **ne** following the conjunctions in examples ⑤ to ⑦ has no translation value. It is often omitted in spoken informal French.

After the conjunctions:

| | |
|---|---|
| de sorte que ⎤<br>de façon que<br>de manière que ⎦ | so that (*indicating a purpose*) → ⑧ |

When these conjunctions introduce a result and not a purpose, the subjunctive is not used → ⑨

After impersonal constructions which express necessity, possibility etc:

| | |
|---|---|
| il faut que ⎤<br>il est nécessaire que ⎦ | it is necessary that → ⑩ |
| il est possible que | it is possible that → ⑪ |
| il semble que | it seems that, it appears that → ⑫ |
| il vaut mieux que | it is better that → ⑬ |
| il est dommage que | it's a pity that, it's a shame that → ⑭ |

# Examples

1. Bien qu'il fasse beaucoup d'efforts, il est peu récompensé

   Although he makes a lot of effort, he isn't rewarded for it

2. Demandez un reçu afin que vous puissiez être remboursé

   Ask for a receipt so that you can get a refund

3. Nous partirons ensemble pourvu que Sylvie soit d'accord

   We'll leave together provided Sylvie agrees

4. Reste ici jusqu'à ce que nous revenions

   Stay here until we come back

5. Je le ferai avant que tu ne partes

   I'll do it before you leave

6. Ce doit être Paul, à moins que je ne me trompe

   That must be Paul, unless I'm mistaken

7. Parlez bas de peur qu'on ne vous entende

   Speak softly for fear that someone hears you

8. Retournez-vous de sorte que je vous voie

   Turn round so that I can see you

9. Il refuse de le faire de sorte que je dois le faire moi-même

   He refuses to do it so that I have to do it myself

10. Il faut que je vous parle immédiatement

    I must speak to you right away
    It is necessary that I speak to you right away

11. Il est possible qu'ils aient raison

    They may be right
    It's possible that they are right

12. Il semble qu'elle ne soit pas venue

    It appears that she hasn't come

13. Il vaut mieux que vous restiez chez vous

    It's better that you stay at home

14. Il est dommage qu'elle ait perdu cette adresse

    It's a shame/a pity that she's lost the address

## The Subjunctive: when to use it *continued*

After verbs of:
- wishing
  **vouloir que**
  **désirer que**       to wish that, want → ❶
  **souhaiter que**

- fearing
  **craindre que**
  **avoir peur que**     to be afraid that → ❷

  ⓘ Note that ne in the first phrase of example ❷ has no translation value. It is often omitted in spoken informal French.

- ordering, forbidding, allowing
  **ordonner que**      to order that → ❸
  **défendre que**      to forbid that → ❹
  **permettre que**     to allow that → ❺

- opinion, expressing uncertainty
  **croire que**
  **penser que**        to think that → ❻
  **douter que**        to doubt that → ❼

- emotion (e.g. regret, shame, pleasure)
  **regretter que**       to be sorry that → ❽
  **être content/surpris** *etc* **que** to be pleased/surprised *etc* that → ❾

After a superlative → ❿

After certain adjectives expressing some sort of 'uniqueness' → ⓫
    **dernier ... qui/que**      last ... who/that
    **premier ... qui/que**    first ... who/that
    **meilleur ... qui/que**   best ... who/that
    **seul ... qui/que**
    **unique ... qui/que**     only ... who/that

# Examples

**1**   Nous voulons qu'elle soit contente

We want her to be happy (*literally*: We want that she is happy)

Désirez-vous que je le fasse?

Do you want me to do it?

**2**   Il craint qu'il ne soit trop tard

He's afraid it may be too late

Avez-vous peur qu'il ne revienne pas?

Are you afraid that he won't come back?

**3**   Il a ordonné qu'ils soient désormais à l'heure

He has ordered that they be on time from now on

**4**   Elle défend que vous disiez cela

She forbids you to say that

**5**   Permettez que nous vous aidions

Allow us to help you

**6**   Je ne pense pas qu'ils soient venus

I don't think they came

**7**   Nous doutons qu'il ait dit la vérité

We doubt that he told the truth

**8**   Je regrette que vous ne puissiez pas venir

I'm sorry that you cannot come

**9**   Je suis content que vous les aimiez

I'm pleased that you like them

**10**   la personne la plus sympathique que je connaisse

the nicest person I know

l'article le moins cher que j'aie jamais acheté

the cheapest item I have ever bought

**11**   Voici la dernière lettre qu'elle m'ait écrite

This is the last letter she wrote to me

David est la seule personne qui puisse me conseiller

David is the only person who can advise me

## The Subjunctive: when to use it *continued*

After:
>     si ( ... ) que  however → ❶
>     qui que  whoever → ❷
>     quoi que  whatever → ❸

After **que** in the following:
- to form the 3^{rd} person imperative or to express a wish → ❹
- when **que** has the meaning 'if', replacing **si** in a clause → ❺
- when **que** has the meaning 'whether' → ❻

In relative clauses following certain types of indefinite and negative construction → ❼/❽

In set expressions → ❾

# Examples

**1** si courageux qu'il soit      however brave he may be
si peu que ce soit      however little it is

**2** Qui que vous soyez,      Whoever you are, go away!
  allez-vous-en!

**3** Quoi que nous fassions, ...      Whatever we do, ...

**4** Qu'il entre!      Let him come in!
Que cela vous serve de leçon!      Let that be a lesson to you!

**5** S'il fait beau et que tu te sentes      If it's nice and you're feeling
  mieux, nous irons ...      better, we'll go ...

**6** Que tu viennes ou non, je ...      Whether you come or not, I ...

**7** Il cherche une maison qui ait      He's looking for a house which
  une piscine      has a swimming pool
         *(subjunctive used since such a*
         *house may or may not exist)*

J'ai besoin d'un livre qui décrive      I need a book which describes
  l'art du mime      the art of mime
         *(subjunctive used since such a*
         *book may or may not exist)*

**8** Je n'ai rencontré personne qui      I haven't met anyone who
  la connaisse      knows her
Il n'y a rien qui puisse vous      There's nothing that can
  empêcher de ...      prevent you from ...

**9** Vive le roi!      Long live the king!
Que Dieu vous bénisse!      God bless you!

## Verbs governing à and de

The following lists (pages 64 to 72) contain common verbal constructions using the prepositions à and **de**

Note the following abbreviations:

| | |
|---|---|
| *infin.* | *infinitive* |
| *perf. infin.* | *perfect infinitive*\* |
| **qch** | quelque chose |
| **qn** | quelqu'un |
| sb | somebody |
| sth | something |

| | |
|---|---|
| **accuser qn de qch/de** + *perf. infin.* | to accuse sb of sth/of doing, having done → ❶ |
| **accoutumer qn à qch/à** + *infin.* | to accustom sb to sth/to doing |
| **acheter qch à qn** | to buy sth from sb/for sb → ❷ |
| **achever de** + *infin.* | to end up doing |
| **aider qn à** + *infin.* | to help sb to do → ❸ |
| **s'amuser à** + *infin.* | to have fun doing |
| **s'apercevoir de qch** | to notice sth → ❹ |
| **apprendre qch à qn** | to teach sb sth |
| **apprendre à** + *infin.* | to learn to do → ❺ |
| **apprendre à qn à** + *infin.* | to teach sb to do → ❻ |
| **s'approcher de qn/qch** | to approach sb/sth → ❼ |
| **arracher qch à qn** | to snatch sth from sb → ❽ |
| **(s')arrêter de** + *infin.* | to stop doing → ❾ |
| **arriver à** + *infin.* | to manage to do → ❿ |
| **assister à qch** | to attend sth, be at sth |
| **s'attendre à** + *infin.* | to expect to do → ⓫ |
| **blâmer qn de qch/de** + *perf. infin.* | to blame sb for sth/for having done → ⓬ |
| **cacher qch à qn** | to hide sth from sb → ⓭ |
| **cesser de** + *infin.* | to stop doing → ⓮ |

\* For formation see page 46

# Examples

1. Il m'a accusé d'avoir menti — He accused me of lying

2. Marie-Christine leur a acheté deux billets — Marie-Christine bought two tickets from/for them

3. Aidez-moi à porter ces valises — Help me to carry these cases

4. Il ne s'est pas aperçu de son erreur — He didn't notice his mistake

5. Elle apprend à lire — She's learning to read

6. Je lui apprends à nager — I'm teaching him/her to swim

7. Elle s'est approchée de moi, en disant ... — She approached me, saying ...

8. Le voleur lui a arraché l'argent — The thief snatched the money from him/her

9. Arrêtez de faire du bruit! — Stop making so much noise!

10. Le professeur n'arrive pas à se faire obéir de sa classe — The teacher couldn't manage to control the class

11. Est-ce qu'elle s'attendait à le voir? — Was she expecting to see him?

12. Je ne la blâme pas de l'avoir fait — I don't blame her for doing it

13. Cache-les-leur! — Hide them from them!

14. Est-ce qu'il a cessé de pleuvoir? — Has it stopped raining?

## Verbs governing à and de *continued*

| | |
|---|---|
| **changer de qch** | to change sth → ❶ |
| **se charger de qch/de** + *infin.* | to see to sth/undertake to do |
| **chercher à** + *infin.* | to try to do |
| **commander à qn de** + *infin.* | to order sb to do → ❷ |
| **commencer à/de** + *infin.* | to begin to do, to start to do → ❸ |
| **conseiller à qn de** + *infin.* | to advise sb to do → ❹ |
| **consentir à qch/à** + *infin.* | to agree to sth/to do → ❺ |
| **continuer à/de** + *infin.* | to continue to do |
| **craindre de** + *infin.* | to be afraid to do/of doing |
| **décider de** + *infin.* | to decide to → ❻ |
| **se décider à** + *infin.* | to make up one's mind to do |
| **défendre à qn de** + *infin.* | to forbid sb to do → ❼ |
| **demander qch à qn** | to ask sb sth/for sth → ❽ |
| **demander à qn de** + *infin.* | to ask sb to do → ❾ |
| **se dépêcher de** + *infin.* | to hurry to do |
| **dépendre de qn/qch** | to depend on sb/sth |
| **déplaire à qn** | to displease sb → ❿ |
| **désobéir à qn** | to disobey sb → ⓫ |
| **dire à qn de** + *infin.* | to tell sb to do → ⓬ |
| **dissuader qn de** + *infin.* | to dissuade sb from doing |
| **douter de qch** | to doubt sth |
| **se douter de qch** | to suspect sth |
| **s'efforcer de** + *infin.* | to strive to do |
| **empêcher qn de** + *infin.* | to prevent sb from doing → ⓭ |
| **emprunter qch à qn** | to borrow sth from sb → ⓮ |
| **encourager qn à** + *infin.* | to encourage sb to do → ⓯ |
| **enlever qch à qn** | to take sth away from sb |
| **enseigner qch à qn** | to teach sb sth |
| **enseigner à qn à** + *infin.* | to teach sb to do |
| **entreprendre de** + *infin.* | to undertake to do |
| **essayer de** + *infin.* | to try to do → ⓰ |
| **eviter de** + *infin.* | to avoid doing → ⓱ |

# Examples

1. J'ai changé d'avis/de robe
   Il faut changer de train à
   Toulouse

   I changed my mind/my dress
   You have to change trains at
   Toulouse

2. Il leur a commandé de tirer

   He ordered them to shoot

3. Il commence à neiger

   It's starting to snow

4. Il leur a conseillé d'attendre

   He advised them to wait

5. Je n'ai pas consenti à l'aider

   I haven't agreed to help him/her

6. Qu'est-ce que vous avez décidé
   de faire?

   What have you decided to do?

7. Je leur ai défendu de sortir

   I've forbidden them to go out

8. Je lui ai demandé l'heure
   Il lui a demandé un livre

   I asked him/her the time
   He asked him/her for a book

9. Demande à Alain de le faire

   Ask Alan to do it

10. Leur attitude lui déplaît

    He/She doesn't like their
    attitude

11. Ils lui désobéissent souvent

    They often disobey him/her

12. Dites-leur de se taire

    Tell them to be quiet

13. Le bruit m'empêche de travailler

    The noise is preventing me from
    working

14. Puis-je vous emprunter ce stylo?

    May I borrow this pen from you?

15. Elle encourage ses enfants à
    être indépendants

    She encourages her children to
    be independent

16. Essayez d'arriver à l'heure

    Try to arrive on time

17. Il évite de lui parler

    He avoids speaking to him/her

67

## Verbs governing à and de *continued*

| | |
|---|---|
| s'excuser de qch/de + *(perf.) infin.* | to apologize for sth/for doing, having done → ❶ |
| exceller à + *infin.* | to excel at doing |
| se fâcher de qch | to be annoyed at sth |
| feindre de + *infin.* | to pretend to do → ❷ |
| féliciter qn de qch/de + *(perf.) infin.* | to congratulate sb on sth/on doing, having done → ❸ |
| se fier à qn | to trust sb → ❹ |
| finir de + *infin.* | to finish doing → ❺ |
| forcer qn à + *infin.* | to force sb to do |
| habituer qn à + *infin.* | to accustom sb to doing |
| s'habituer à + *infin.* | to get/be used to doing → ❻ |
| se hâter de + *infin.* | to hurry to do |
| hésiter à + *infin.* | to hesitate to do |
| interdire à qn de + *infin.* | to forbid sb to do → ❼ |
| s'intéresser à qn/qch/à + *infin.* | to be interested in sb/sth/in doing → ❽ |
| inviter qn à + *infin.* | to invite sb to do → ❾ |
| jouer à (+ *sports, games*) | to play → ❿ |
| jouer de (+ *musical instruments*) | to play → ⓫ |
| jouir de qch | to enjoy sth → ⓬ |
| jurer de + *infin.* | to swear to do |
| louer qn de qch | to praise sb for sth |
| manquer à qn | to be missed by sb → ⓭ |
| manquer de qch | to lack sth |
| manquer de + *infin.* | to fail to do → ⓮ |
| se marier à qn | to marry sb |
| se méfier de qn | to distrust sb |
| menacer de + *infin.* | to threaten to do → ⓯ |
| mériter de + *infin.* | to deserve to do → ⓰ |
| se mettre à + *infin.* | to begin to do |
| se moquer de qn/qch | to make fun of sb/sth |
| négliger de + *infin.* | to fail to do |

# Examples

1. Je m'excuse d'être (arrivé) en retard

   I apologize for being/arriving late

2. Elle feint de dormir

   She's pretending to be asleep

3. Je l'ai félicitée d'avoir gagné

   I congratulated her on winning

4. Je ne me fie pas à ces gens-là

   I don't trust those people

5. Avez-vous fini de lire ce journal?

   Have you finished reading this newspaper?

6. Il s'est habitué à boire moins de café

   He got used to drinking less coffee

7. Il a interdit aux enfants de jouer avec des allumettes

   He's forbidden the children to play with matches

8. Elle s'intéresse beaucoup au sport

   She's very interested in sport

9. Il m'a invitée à dîner

   He invited me for dinner

10. Elle joue au tennis et au hockey

    She plays tennis and hockey

11. Il joue du piano et de la guitare

    He plays the piano and the guitar

12. Il jouit d'une santé solide

    He enjoys good health

13. Tu manques à tes parents

    Your parents miss you

14. Je ne manquerai pas de le lui dire

    I'll be sure to tell him/her about it

15. Elle a menacé de démissionner tout de suite

    She threatened to resign straight away

16. Ils méritent d'être promus

    They deserve to be promoted

## Verbs governing à and de *continued*

| | |
|---|---|
| nuire à qch | to harm sth, to do damage to sth → ❶ |
| obéir à qn | to obey sb |
| obliger qn à + *infin.* | to oblige/force sb to do → ❷ |
| s'occuper de qch/qn | to look after sth/sb → ❸ |
| offrir de + *infin.* | to offer to do → ❹ |
| omettre de + *infin.* | to fail to do |
| ordonner à qn de + *infin.* | to order sb to do → ❺ |
| ôter qch à qn | to take sth away from sb |
| oublier de + *infin.* | to forget to do |
| pardonner qch à qn | to forgive sb for sth |
| pardonner à qn de + *perf. infin.* | to forgive sb for having done → ❻ |
| parvenir à + *infin.* | to manage to do |
| se passer de qch | to do/go without sth → ❼ |
| penser à qn/qch | to think about sb/sth → ❽ |
| permettre qch à qn | to allow sb sth |
| permettre à qn de + *infin.* | to allow sb to do → ❾ |
| persister à + *infin.* | to persist in doing |
| persuader qn de + *infin.* | to persuade sb to do → ❿ |
| se plaindre de qch | to complain about sth |
| plaire à qn | to please sb → ⓫ |
| pousser qn à + *infin.* | to urge sb to do |
| prendre qch à qn | to take sth from sb → ⓬ |
| préparer qn à + *infin.* | to prepare sb to do |
| se préparer à + *infin.* | to get ready to do |
| prier qn de + *infin.* | to beg sb to do |
| profiter de qch/de + *infin.* | to take advantage of sth/of doing |
| promettre à qn de + *infin.* | to promise sb to do → ⓭ |
| proposer de + *infin.* | to suggest doing → ⓮ |
| punir qn de qch | to punish sb for sth → ⓯ |
| récompenser qn de qch | to reward sb for sth |
| réfléchir à qch | to think about sth |
| refuser de + *infin.* | to refuse to do → ⓰ |

1. Ce mode de vie va nuire à sa santé — This lifestyle will damage her health

2. Il les a obligés à faire la vaisselle — He forced them to do the washing-up

3. Je m'occupe de ma nièce — I'm looking after my niece

4. Stuart a offert de nous accompagner — Stuart has offered to go with us

5. Les soldats leur ont ordonné de se rendre — The soldiers ordered them to give themselves up

6. Est-ce que tu as pardonné à Charles de t'avoir menti? — Have you forgiven Charles for lying to you?

7. Je me suis passé d'électricité pendant plusieurs jours — I did without electricity for several days

8. Je pense souvent à toi — I often think about you

9. Permettez-moi de continuer, s'il vous plaît — Allow me to go on, please

10. Elle nous a persuadés de rester — She persuaded us to stay

11. Ce genre de film lui plaît — He/she likes this kind of film

12. Je lui ai pris son mobile — I took his mobile phone from him

13. Ils ont promis à Pascale de venir — They promised Pascale that they would come

14. J'ai proposé de les inviter — I suggested inviting them

15. Il a été puni de sa malhonnêteté — He has been punished for his dishonesty

16. Il a refusé de coopérer — He has refused to cooperate

## Verbs governing à and de *continued*

| | |
|---|---|
| **regretter de** + *perf. infin.* | to regret doing, having done → ❶ |
| **remercier qn de qch/de** + *perf. infin.* | to thank sb for sth/for doing, having done → ❷ |
| **renoncer à qch/à** + *infin.* | to give sth up/give up doing |
| **reprocher qch à qn** | to reproach sb with/for sth → ❸ |
| **résister à qch** | to resist sth → ❹ |
| **résoudre de** + *infin.* | to resolve to do |
| **ressembler à qn/qch** | to look/be like sb/sth → ❺ |
| **réussir à** + *infin.* | to manage to do → ❻ |
| **rire de qn/qch** | to laugh at sb/sth |
| **risquer de** + *infin.* | to risk doing → ❼ |
| **servir à qch/à** + *infin.* | to be used for sth/for doing → ❽ |
| **se servir de qch** | to use sth; to help oneself to sth → ❾ |
| **songer à** + *infin.* | to think of doing |
| **se souvenir de qn/qch/de** + *perf. infin.* | to remember sb/sth/doing, having done → ❿ |
| **succéder à qn** | to succeed sb |
| **survivre à qn** | to outlive sb → ⓫ |
| **tâcher de** + *infin.* | to try to do → ⓬ |
| **tarder à** + *infin.* | to delay doing → ⓭ |
| **tendre à** + *infin.* | to tend to do |
| **tenir à** + *infin.* | to be keen to do → ⓮ |
| **tenter de** + *infin.* | to try to do → ⓯ |
| **se tromper de qch** | to be wrong about sth → ⓰ |
| **venir de*** + *infin.* | to have just done → ⓱ |
| **vivre de qch** | to live on sth |
| **voler qch à qn** | to steal sth from sb |

* See also Use of Tenses, pages 54 and 56

# Examples

1. Je regrette de ne pas l'avoir vue plus souvent quand elle était ici

   I regret not having seen her more while she was here

2. Nous les avons remerciés de leur gentillesse

   We thanked them for their kindness

3. On lui reproche son manque d'enthousiasme

   They're reproaching him for his lack of enthusiasm

4. Comment résistez-vous à la tentation?

   How do you resist temptation?

5. Elles ressemblent beaucoup à leur mère

   They look very like their mother

6. Vous avez réussi à me convaincre

   You've managed to convince me

7. Vous risquez de tomber en faisant cela

   You risk falling doing that

8. Ce bouton sert à régler le volume

   This knob is (used) for adjusting the volume

9. Il s'est servi d'un tournevis pour l'ouvrir

   He used a screwdriver to open it

10. Vous vous souvenez de Lucienne? Il ne se souvient pas de l'avoir perdu

    Do you remember Lucienne? He doesn't remember losing it

11. Elle a survécu à son mari

    She outlived her husband

12. Tâchez de ne pas être en retard!

    Try not to be late!

13. Il n'a pas tardé à prendre une décision

    He was not long in taking a decision

14. Elle tient à le faire elle-même

    She's keen to do it herself

15. J'ai tenté de la comprendre

    I've tried to understand her

16. Je me suis trompé de route

    I took the wrong road

17. Mon père vient de téléphoner
    Nous venions d'arriver

    My father's just phoned
    We had just arrived

## Irregular Verbs

The verbs listed opposite and conjugated on pages 76 to 131 provide the main patterns for irregular verbs. The verbs are grouped opposite according to their infinitive ending (except **avoir** and **être**), and are shown in the following tables in alphabetical order.

In the tables, the most important irregular verbs are given in their most common simple tenses, together with the imperative and the present participle.

The auxiliary (**avoir** or **être**) is also shown for each verb, together with the past participle, to enable you to form all the compound tenses, as on pages 24 and 26.

For a fuller list of irregular verbs, the reader is referred to Collins Easy Learning French Verbs, which shows you how to conjugate some 2000 French verbs.

avoir
être

'-er':  aller
envoyer

'-ir':  acquérir
bouillir
courir
cueillir
dormir
fuir
haïr
mourir
ouvrir
partir
sentir
servir
sortir
tenir
venir
vêtir

'-oir':  s'asseoir
devoir
falloir
pleuvoir
pouvoir
recevoir
savoir
valoir
voir
vouloir

'-re':  battre
boire
connaître
coudre
craindre
croire
croître
cuire
dire
écrire
faire
lire
mettre
moudre
naître
paraître
plaire
prendre
résoudre
rire
rompre
suffire
suivre
se taire
vaincre
vivre

# acquérir (to acquire)

|  | PRESENT |  | IMPERFECT |
|---|---|---|---|
|  | j'acquiers |  | j'acquérais |
| tu | acquiers | tu | acquérais |
| il | acquiert | il | acquérait |
| nous | acquérons | nous | acquérions |
| vous | acquérez | vous | acquériez |
| ils | acquièrent | ils | acquéraient |

|  | FUTURE |  | CONDITIONAL |
|---|---|---|---|
|  | j'acquerrai |  | j'acquerrais |
| tu | acquerras | tu | acquerrais |
| il | acquerra | il | acquerrait |
| nous | acquerrons | nous | acquerrions |
| vous | acquerrez | vous | acquerriez |
| ils | acquerront | ils | acquerraient |

|  | PRESENT SUBJUNCTIVE |  | PAST HISTORIC |
|---|---|---|---|
|  | j'acquière |  | j'acquis |
| tu | acquières | tu | acquis |
| il | acquière | il | acquit |
| nous | acquérions | nous | acquîmes |
| vous | acquériez | vous | acquîtes |
| ils | acquièrent | ils | acquirent |

---

**PAST PARTICIPLE**
acquis

**IMPERATIVE**
acquiers
acquérons
acquérez

**PRESENT PARTICIPLE**
acquérant

**AUXILIARY**
avoir

# aller (to go)

| | PRESENT | | IMPERFECT |
|---|---|---|---|
| je | **vais** | | j'allais |
| tu | **vas** | tu | allais |
| il | **va** | il | allait |
| nous | allons | nous | allions |
| vous | allez | vous | alliez |
| ils | **vont** | ils | allaient |

| | FUTURE | | CONDITIONAL |
|---|---|---|---|
| | j'**irai** | | j'**irais** |
| tu | **iras** | tu | **irais** |
| il | **ira** | il | **irait** |
| nous | **irons** | nous | **irions** |
| vous | **irez** | vous | **iriez** |
| ils | **iront** | ils | **iraient** |

| | PRESENT SUBJUNCTIVE | | PAST HISTORIC |
|---|---|---|---|
| | j'**aille** | | j'allai |
| tu | **ailles** | tu | allas |
| il | **aille** | il | alla |
| nous | allions | nous | allâmes |
| vous | alliez | vous | allâtes |
| ils | **aillent** | ils | allèrent |

---

| PAST PARTICIPLE | IMPERATIVE |
|---|---|
| allé | **va** |
| | allons |
| | allez |

| PRESENT PARTICIPLE | AUXILIARY |
|---|---|
| allant | **être** |

# s'asseoir (to sit down)

| | PRESENT | | IMPERFECT |
|---|---|---|---|
| je | m'assieds or assois | je | m'asseyais |
| tu | t'assieds or assois | tu | t'asseyais |
| il | s'assied or assoit | il | s'asseyait |
| nous | nous asseyons or assoyons | nous | nous asseyions |
| vous | vous asseyez or assoyez | vous | vous asseyiez |
| ils | s'asseyent or assoient | ils | s'asseyaient |

| | FUTURE | | CONDITIONAL |
|---|---|---|---|
| je | m'assiérai | je | m'assiérais |
| tu | t'assiéras | tu | t'assiérais |
| il | s'assiéra | il | s'assiérait |
| nous | nous assiérons | nous | nous assiérions |
| vous | vous assiérez | vous | vous assiériez |
| ils | s'assiéront | ils | s'assiéraient |

| | PRESENT SUBJUNCTIVE | | PAST HISTORIC |
|---|---|---|---|
| je | m'asseye | je | m'assis |
| tu | t'asseyes | tu | t'assis |
| il | s'asseye | il | s'assit |
| nous | nous asseyions | nous | nous assîmes |
| vous | vous asseyiez | vous | vous assîtes |
| ils | s'asseyent | ils | s'assirent |

---

**PAST PARTICIPLE**
assis

**IMPERATIVE**
assieds-toi
asseyons-nous
asseyez-vous

**PRESENT PARTICIPLE**
s'asseyant

**AUXILIARY**
être

# avoir (to have)

| | PRESENT | | IMPERFECT |
|---|---|---|---|
| | j'ai | | j'avais |
| tu | as | tu | avais |
| il | a | il | avait |
| nous | avons | nous | avions |
| vous | avez | vous | aviez |
| ils | ont | ils | avaient |

| | FUTURE | | CONDITIONAL |
|---|---|---|---|
| | j'aurai | | j'aurais |
| tu | auras | tu | aurais |
| il | aura | il | aurait |
| nous | aurons | nous | aurions |
| vous | aurez | vous | auriez |
| ils | auront | ils | auraient |

| | PRESENT SUBJUNCTIVE | | PAST HISTORIC |
|---|---|---|---|
| | j'aie | | j'eus |
| tu | aies | tu | eus |
| il | ait | il | eut |
| nous | ayons | nous | eûmes |
| vous | ayez | vous | eûtes |
| ils | aient | ils | eurent |

---

**PAST PARTICIPLE**
eu

**IMPERATIVE**
aie
ayons
ayez

**PRESENT PARTICIPLE**
ayant

**AUXILIARY**
avoir

# battre (to beat)

| | PRESENT | | | IMPERFECT |
|---|---|---|---|---|
| je | **bats** | | je | battais |
| tu | **bats** | | tu | battais |
| il | **bat** | | il | battait |
| nous | battons | | nous | battions |
| vous | battez | | vous | battiez |
| ils | battent | | ils | battaient |

| | FUTURE | | | CONDITIONAL |
|---|---|---|---|---|
| je | battrai | | je | battrais |
| tu | battras | | tu | battrais |
| il | battra | | il | battrait |
| nous | battrons | | nous | battrions |
| vous | battrez | | vous | battriez |
| ils | battront | | ils | battraient |

| | PRESENT SUBJUNCTIVE | | | PAST HISTORIC |
|---|---|---|---|---|
| je | batte | | je | battis |
| tu | battes | | tu | battis |
| il | batte | | il | battit |
| nous | battions | | nous | battîmes |
| vous | battiez | | vous | battîtes |
| ils | battent | | ils | battirent |

---

**PAST PARTICIPLE**
battu

**IMPERATIVE**
**bats**
battons
battez

**PRESENT PARTICIPLE**
battant

**AUXILIARY**
**avoir**

# boire (to drink)

| | PRESENT | | IMPERFECT |
|---|---|---|---|
| je | bois | je | **buvais** |
| tu | bois | tu | **buvais** |
| il | boit | il | **buvait** |
| nous | **buvons** | nous | **buvions** |
| vous | **buvez** | vous | **buviez** |
| ils | **boivent** | ils | **buvaient** |

| | FUTURE | | CONDITIONAL |
|---|---|---|---|
| je | boirai | je | boirais |
| tu | boiras | tu | boirais |
| il | boira | il | boirait |
| nous | boirons | nous | boirions |
| vous | boirez | vous | boiriez |
| ils | boiront | ils | boiraient |

| | PRESENT SUBJUNCTIVE | | PAST HISTORIC |
|---|---|---|---|
| je | **boive** | je | **bus** |
| tu | **boives** | tu | **bus** |
| il | **boive** | il | **but** |
| nous | **buvions** | nous | **bûmes** |
| vous | **buviez** | vous | **bûtes** |
| ils | **boivent** | ils | **burent** |

---

**PAST PARTICIPLE**
**bu**

**IMPERATIVE**
bois
**buvons**
**buvez**

**PRESENT PARTICIPLE**
**buvant**

**AUXILIARY**
**avoir**

# bouillir (to boil)

| | PRESENT | | IMPERFECT |
|---|---|---|---|
| je | **bous** | je | **bouillais** |
| tu | **bous** | tu | **bouillais** |
| il | **bout** | il | **bouillait** |
| nous | **bouillons** | nous | **bouillions** |
| vous | **bouillez** | vous | **bouilliez** |
| ils | **bouillent** | ils | **bouillaient** |

| | FUTURE | | CONDITIONAL |
|---|---|---|---|
| je | bouillirai | je | bouillirais |
| tu | bouilliras | tu | bouillirais |
| il | bouillira | il | bouillirait |
| nous | bouillirons | nous | bouillirions |
| vous | bouillirez | vous | bouilliriez |
| ils | bouilliront | ils | bouilliraient |

| | PRESENT SUBJUNCTIVE | | PAST HISTORIC |
|---|---|---|---|
| je | **bouille** | je | bouillis |
| tu | **bouilles** | tu | bouillis |
| il | **bouille** | il | bouillit |
| nous | **bouillions** | nous | bouillîmes |
| vous | **bouilliez** | vous | bouillîtes |
| ils | **bouillent** | ils | bouillirent |

| PAST PARTICIPLE | IMPERATIVE |
|---|---|
| bouilli | **bous** |
| | **bouillons** |
| | **bouillez** |

| PRESENT PARTICIPLE | AUXILIARY |
|---|---|
| **bouillant** | **avoir** |

# connaître (to know)

| | PRESENT | | IMPERFECT |
|---|---|---|---|
| je | connais | je | connaissais |
| tu | connais | tu | connaissais |
| il | connaît | il | connaissait |
| nous | connaissons | nous | connaissions |
| vous | connaissez | vous | connaissiez |
| ils | connaissent | ils | connaissaient |

| | FUTURE | | CONDITIONAL |
|---|---|---|---|
| je | connaîtrai | je | connaîtrais |
| tu | connaîtras | tu | connaîtrais |
| il | connaîtra | il | connaîtrait |
| nous | connaîtrons | nous | connaîtrions |
| vous | connaîtrez | vous | connaîtriez |
| ils | connaîtront | ils | connaîtraient |

| | PRESENT SUBJUNCTIVE | | PAST HISTORIC |
|---|---|---|---|
| je | connaisse | je | connus |
| tu | connaisses | tu | connus |
| il | connaisse | il | connut |
| nous | connaissions | nous | connûmes |
| vous | connaissiez | vous | connûtes |
| ils | connaissent | ils | connurent |

---

**PAST PARTICIPLE**
connu

**IMPERATIVE**
connais
connaissons
connaissez

**PRESENT PARTICIPLE**
connaissant

**AUXILIARY**
avoir

# coudre (to sew)

| | PRESENT | | | IMPERFECT |
|---|---|---|---|---|
| je | couds | | je | cousais |
| tu | couds | | tu | cousais |
| il | coud | | il | cousait |
| nous | cousons | | nous | cousions |
| vous | cousez | | vous | cousiez |
| ils | cousent | | ils | cousaient |

| | FUTURE | | | CONDITIONAL |
|---|---|---|---|---|
| je | coudrai | | je | coudrais |
| tu | coudras | | tu | coudrais |
| il | coudra | | il | coudrait |
| nous | coudrons | | nous | coudrions |
| vous | coudrez | | vous | coudriez |
| ils | coudront | | ils | coudraient |

| | PRESENT SUBJUNCTIVE | | | PAST HISTORIC |
|---|---|---|---|---|
| je | couse | | je | cousis |
| tu | couses | | tu | cousis |
| il | couse | | il | cousit |
| nous | cousions | | nous | cousîmes |
| vous | cousiez | | vous | cousîtes |
| ils | cousent | | ils | cousirent |

---

**PAST PARTICIPLE**
cousu

**IMPERATIVE**
couds
cousons
cousez

**PRESENT PARTICIPLE**
cousant

**AUXILIARY**
avoir

# courir (to run)

| | PRESENT | | IMPERFECT |
|---|---|---|---|
| je | cours | je | courais |
| tu | cours | tu | courais |
| il | court | il | courait |
| nous | courons | nous | courions |
| vous | courez | vous | couriez |
| ils | courent | ils | couraient |

| | FUTURE | | CONDITIONAL |
|---|---|---|---|
| je | courrai | je | courrais |
| tu | courras | tu | courrais |
| il | courra | il | courrait |
| nous | courrons | nous | courrions |
| vous | courrez | vous | courriez |
| ils | courront | ils | courraient |

| | PRESENT SUBJUNCTIVE | | PAST HISTORIC |
|---|---|---|---|
| je | coure | je | courus |
| tu | coures | tu | courus |
| il | coure | il | courut |
| nous | courions | nous | courûmes |
| vous | couriez | vous | courûtes |
| ils | courent | ils | coururent |

---

**PAST PARTICIPLE**
couru

**IMPERATIVE**
cours
courons
courez

**PRESENT PARTICIPLE**
courant

**AUXILIARY**
avoir

# craindre (to fear)

| | PRESENT | | | IMPERFECT |
|---|---|---|---|---|
| je | crains | | je | craignais |
| tu | crains | | tu | craignais |
| il | craint | | il | craignait |
| nous | craignons | | nous | craignions |
| vous | craignez | | vous | craigniez |
| ils | craignent | | ils | craignaient |

| | FUTURE | | | CONDITIONAL |
|---|---|---|---|---|
| je | craindrai | | je | craindrais |
| tu | craindras | | tu | craindrais |
| il | craindra | | il | craindrait |
| nous | craindrons | | nous | craindrions |
| vous | craindrez | | vous | craindriez |
| ils | craindront | | ils | craindraient |

| | PRESENT SUBJUNCTIVE | | | PAST HISTORIC |
|---|---|---|---|---|
| je | craigne | | je | craignis |
| tu | craignes | | tu | craignis |
| il | craigne | | il | craignit |
| nous | craignions | | nous | craignîmes |
| vous | craigniez | | vous | craignîtes |
| ils | craignent | | ils | craignirent |

---

**PAST PARTICIPLE**
craint

**IMPERATIVE**
crains
craignons
craignez

**PRESENT PARTICIPLE**
craignant

**AUXILIARY**
avoir

Note that verbs ending in **-eindre** and **-oindre** are conjugated similarly

# croire (to believe)

| | PRESENT | | IMPERFECT |
|---|---|---|---|
| je | crois | je | **croyais** |
| tu | crois | tu | **croyais** |
| il | **croit** | il | **croyait** |
| nous | **croyons** | nous | **croyions** |
| vous | **croyez** | vous | **croyiez** |
| ils | croient | ils | **croyaient** |

| | FUTURE | | CONDITIONAL |
|---|---|---|---|
| je | croirai | je | croirais |
| tu | croiras | tu | croirais |
| il | croira | il | croirait |
| nous | croirons | nous | croirions |
| vous | croirez | vous | croiriez |
| ils | croiront | ils | croiraient |

| | PRESENT SUBJUNCTIVE | | PAST HISTORIC |
|---|---|---|---|
| je | croie | je | **crus** |
| tu | croies | tu | **crus** |
| il | croie | il | **crut** |
| nous | **croyions** | nous | **crûmes** |
| vous | **croyiez** | vous | **crûtes** |
| ils | croient | ils | **crurent** |

---

**PAST PARTICIPLE**
**cru**

**IMPERATIVE**
crois
**croyons**
**croyez**

**PRESENT PARTICIPLE**
**croyant**

**AUXILIARY**
**avoir**

# croître (to grow)

| | PRESENT | | IMPERFECT |
|---|---|---|---|
| je | croîs | je | croissais |
| tu | croîs | tu | croissais |
| il | croît | il | croissait |
| nous | croissons | nous | croissions |
| vous | croissez | vous | croissiez |
| ils | croissent | ils | croissaient |

| | FUTURE | | CONDITIONAL |
|---|---|---|---|
| je | croîtrai | je | croîtrais |
| tu | croîtras | tu | croîtrais |
| il | croîtra | il | croîtrait |
| nous | croîtrons | nous | croîtrions |
| vous | croîtrez | vous | croîtriez |
| ils | croîtront | ils | croîtraient |

| | PRESENT SUBJUNCTIVE | | PAST HISTORIC |
|---|---|---|---|
| je | croisse | je | crûs |
| tu | croisses | tu | crûs |
| il | croisse | il | crût |
| nous | croissions | nous | crûmes |
| vous | croissiez | vous | crûtes |
| ils | croissent | ils | crûrent |

---

**PAST PARTICIPLE**
crû

**IMPERATIVE**
croîs
croissons
croissez

**PRESENT PARTICIPLE**
croissant

**AUXILIARY**
avoir

# cueillir (to pick)

| | PRESENT | | IMPERFECT |
|---|---|---|---|
| je | cueille | je | cueillais |
| tu | cueilles | tu | cueillais |
| il | cueille | il | cueillait |
| nous | cueillons | nous | cueillions |
| vous | cueillez | vous | cueilliez |
| ils | cueillent | ils | cueillaient |

| | FUTURE | | CONDITIONAL |
|---|---|---|---|
| je | cueillerai | je | cueillerais |
| tu | cueilleras | tu | cueillerais |
| il | cueillera | il | cueillerait |
| nous | cueillerons | nous | cueillerions |
| vous | cueillerez | vous | cueilleriez |
| ils | cueilleront | ils | cueilleraient |

| | PRESENT SUBJUNCTIVE | | PAST HISTORIC |
|---|---|---|---|
| je | cueille | je | cueillis |
| tu | cueilles | tu | cueillis |
| il | cueille | il | cueillit |
| nous | cueillions | nous | cueillîmes |
| vous | cueilliez | vous | cueillîtes |
| ils | cueillent | ils | cueillirent |

| PAST PARTICIPLE | IMPERATIVE |
|---|---|
| cueilli | cueille |
| | cueillons |
| | cueillez |

| PRESENT PARTICIPLE | AUXILIARY |
|---|---|
| cueillant | avoir |

# cuire (to cook)

| | PRESENT | | IMPERFECT |
|---|---|---|---|
| je | cuis | je | cuisais |
| tu | cuis | tu | cuisais |
| il | cuit | il | cuisait |
| nous | cuisons | nous | cuisions |
| vous | cuisez | vous | cuisiez |
| ils | cuisent | ils | cuisaient |

| | FUTURE | | CONDITIONAL |
|---|---|---|---|
| je | cuirai | je | cuirais |
| tu | cuiras | tu | cuirais |
| il | cuira | il | cuirait |
| nous | cuirons | nous | cuirions |
| vous | cuirez | vous | cuiriez |
| ils | cuiront | ils | cuiraient |

| | PRESENT SUBJUNCTIVE | | PAST HISTORIC |
|---|---|---|---|
| je | cuise | je | cuisis |
| tu | cuises | tu | cuisis |
| il | cuise | il | cuisit |
| nous | cuisions | nous | cuisîmes |
| vous | cuisiez | vous | cuisîtes |
| ils | cuisent | ils | cuisirent |

---

**PAST PARTICIPLE**
cuit

**IMPERATIVE**
cuis
cuisons
cuisez

**PRESENT PARTICIPLE**
cuisant

**AUXILIARY**
avoir

Note that **nuire** (to harm) is conjugated similarly, but past participle is **nui**

# devoir (to have to, to owe)

| | PRESENT | | IMPERFECT |
|---|---|---|---|
| je | dois | je | devais |
| tu | dois | tu | devais |
| il | doit | il | devait |
| nous | devons | nous | devions |
| vous | devez | vous | deviez |
| ils | doivent | ils | devaient |

| | FUTURE | | CONDITIONAL |
|---|---|---|---|
| je | devrai | je | devrais |
| tu | devras | tu | devrais |
| il | devra | il | devrait |
| nous | devrons | nous | devrions |
| vous | devrez | vous | devriez |
| ils | devront | ils | devraient |

| | PRESENT SUBJUNCTIVE | | PAST HISTORIC |
|---|---|---|---|
| je | doive | je | dus |
| tu | doives | tu | dus |
| il | doive | il | dut |
| nous | devions | nous | dûmes |
| vous | deviez | vous | dûtes |
| ils | doivent | ils | durent |

---

| PAST PARTICIPLE | IMPERATIVE |
|---|---|
| dû | dois |
| | devons |
| | devez |

| PRESENT PARTICIPLE | AUXILIARY |
|---|---|
| devant | avoir |

# dire (to say, to tell)

| | PRESENT | | | IMPERFECT |
|---|---|---|---|---|
| je | dis | | je | disais |
| tu | dis | | tu | disais |
| il | dit | | il | disait |
| nous | disons | | nous | disions |
| vous | dites | | vous | disiez |
| ils | disent | | ils | disaient |

| | FUTURE | | | CONDITIONAL |
|---|---|---|---|---|
| je | dirai | | je | dirais |
| tu | diras | | tu | dirais |
| il | dira | | il | dirait |
| nous | dirons | | nous | dirions |
| vous | direz | | vous | diriez |
| ils | diront | | ils | diraient |

| | PRESENT SUBJUNCTIVE | | | PAST HISTORIC |
|---|---|---|---|---|
| je | dise | | je | dis |
| tu | dises | | tu | dis |
| il | dise | | il | dit |
| nous | disions | | nous | dîmes |
| vous | disiez | | vous | dîtes |
| ils | disent | | ils | dirent |

| PAST PARTICIPLE | IMPERATIVE |
|---|---|
| dit | dis |
| | disons |
| | dites |

| PRESENT PARTICIPLE | AUXILIARY |
|---|---|
| disant | avoir |

Note that **interdire** (to forbid) is conjugated similarly, but the second person plural of the present tense is **vous interdisez**

# dormir (to sleep)

| | PRESENT | | IMPERFECT |
|---|---|---|---|
| je | dors | je | dormais |
| tu | dors | tu | dormais |
| il | dort | il | dormait |
| nous | dormons | nous | dormions |
| vous | dormez | vous | dormiez |
| ils | dorment | ils | dormaient |

| | FUTURE | | CONDITIONAL |
|---|---|---|---|
| je | dormirai | je | dormirais |
| tu | dormiras | tu | dormirais |
| il | dormira | il | dormirait |
| nous | dormirons | nous | dormirions |
| vous | dormirez | vous | dormiriez |
| ils | dormiront | ils | dormiraient |

| | PRESENT SUBJUNCTIVE | | PAST HISTORIC |
|---|---|---|---|
| je | dorme | je | dormis |
| tu | dormes | tu | dormis |
| il | dorme | il | dormit |
| nous | dormions | nous | dormîmes |
| vous | dormiez | vous | dormîtes |
| ils | dorment | ils | dormirent |

| PAST PARTICIPLE | IMPERATIVE |
|---|---|
| dormi | dors |
| | dormons |
| | dormez |

| PRESENT PARTICIPLE | AUXILIARY |
|---|---|
| dormant | avoir |

# écrire (to write)

| | PRESENT | | IMPERFECT |
|---|---|---|---|
| | j'écris | | j'**écrivais** |
| tu | écris | tu | **écrivais** |
| il | écrit | il | **écrivait** |
| nous | **écrivons** | nous | **écrivions** |
| vous | **écrivez** | vous | **écriviez** |
| ils | **écrivent** | ils | **écrivaient** |

| | FUTURE | | CONDITIONAL |
|---|---|---|---|
| | j'écrirai | | j'écrirais |
| tu | écriras | tu | écrirais |
| il | écrira | il | écrirait |
| nous | écrirons | nous | écririons |
| vous | écrirez | vous | écririez |
| ils | écriront | ils | écriraient |

| | PRESENT SUBJUNCTIVE | | PAST HISTORIC |
|---|---|---|---|
| | j'**écrive** | | j'**écrivis** |
| tu | **écrives** | tu | **écrivis** |
| il | **écrive** | il | **écrivit** |
| nous | **écrivions** | nous | **écrivîmes** |
| vous | **écriviez** | vous | **écrivîtes** |
| ils | **écrivent** | ils | **écrivirent** |

---

| PAST PARTICIPLE | IMPERATIVE |
|---|---|
| écrit | écris |
| | **écrivons** |
| | **écrivez** |

| PRESENT PARTICIPLE | AUXILIARY |
|---|---|
| écrivant | avoir |

# envoyer (to send)

| | PRESENT | | IMPERFECT |
|---|---|---|---|
| | j'envoie | | j'envoyais |
| tu | envoies | tu | envoyais |
| il | envoie | il | envoyait |
| nous | envoyons | nous | envoyions |
| vous | envoyez | vous | envoyiez |
| ils | envoient | ils | envoyaient |

| | FUTURE | | CONDITIONAL |
|---|---|---|---|
| | j'**enverrai** | | j'**enverrais** |
| tu | **enverras** | tu | **enverrais** |
| il | **enverra** | il | **enverrait** |
| nous | **enverrons** | nous | **enverrions** |
| vous | **enverrez** | vous | **enverriez** |
| ils | **enverront** | ils | **enverraient** |

| | PRESENT SUBJUNCTIVE | | PAST HISTORIC |
|---|---|---|---|
| | j'envoie | | j'envoyai |
| tu | envoies | tu | envoyas |
| il | envoie | il | envoya |
| nous | envoyions | nous | envoyâmes |
| vous | envoyiez | vous | envoyâtes |
| ils | envoient | ils | envoyèrent |

---

| PAST PARTICIPLE | IMPERATIVE |
|---|---|
| envoyé | envoie |
| | envoyons |
| | envoyez |

| PRESENT PARTICIPLE | AUXILIARY |
|---|---|
| envoyant | **avoir** |

# être (to be)

| | PRESENT | | IMPERFECT |
|---|---|---|---|
| je | suis | | j'étais |
| tu | es | tu | étais |
| il | est | il | était |
| nous | sommes | nous | étions |
| vous | êtes | vous | étiez |
| ils | sont | ils | étaient |

| | FUTURE | | CONDITIONAL |
|---|---|---|---|
| je | serai | je | serais |
| tu | seras | tu | serais |
| il | sera | il | serait |
| nous | serons | nous | serions |
| vous | serez | vous | seriez |
| ils | seront | ils | seraient |

| | PRESENT SUBJUNCTIVE | | PAST HISTORIC |
|---|---|---|---|
| je | sois | je | fus |
| tu | sois | tu | fus |
| il | soit | il | fut |
| nous | soyons | nous | fûmes |
| vous | soyez | vous | fûtes |
| ils | soient | ils | furent |

---

**PAST PARTICIPLE**
été

**IMPERATIVE**
sois
soyons
soyez

**PRESENT PARTICIPLE**
étant

**AUXILIARY**
avoir

# faire (to do, to make)

| | PRESENT | | IMPERFECT |
|---|---|---|---|
| je | fais | je | faisais |
| tu | fais | tu | faisais |
| il | fait | il | faisait |
| nous | faisons | nous | faisions |
| vous | faites | vous | faisiez |
| ils | font | ils | faisaient |

| | FUTURE | | CONDITIONAL |
|---|---|---|---|
| je | ferai | je | ferais |
| tu | feras | tu | ferais |
| il | fera | il | ferait |
| nous | ferons | nous | ferions |
| vous | ferez | vous | feriez |
| ils | feront | ils | feraient |

| | PRESENT SUBJUNCTIVE | | PAST HISTORIC |
|---|---|---|---|
| je | fasse | je | fis |
| tu | fasses | tu | fis |
| il | fasse | il | fit |
| nous | fassions | nous | fîmes |
| vous | fassiez | vous | fîtes |
| ils | fassent | ils | firent |

PAST PARTICIPLE
fait

IMPERATIVE
fais
faisons
faites

PRESENT PARTICIPLE
faisant

AUXILIARY
avoir

# falloir (to be necessary)

**PRESENT**
il faut

**IMPERFECT**
il fallait

**FUTURE**
il faudra

**CONDITIONAL**
il faudrait

**PRESENT SUBJUNCTIVE**
il faille

**PAST HISTORIC**
il fallut

---

**PAST PARTICIPLE**
fallu

**IMPERATIVE**
*not used*

**PRESENT PARTICIPLE**
*not used*

**AUXILIARY**
avoir

# fuir (to flee)

| | PRESENT | | IMPERFECT |
|---|---|---|---|
| je | fuis | je | **fuyais** |
| tu | fuis | tu | **fuyais** |
| il | fuit | il | **fuyait** |
| nous | **fuyons** | nous | **fuyions** |
| vous | **fuyez** | vous | **fuyiez** |
| ils | **fuient** | ils | **fuyaient** |

| | FUTURE | | CONDITIONAL |
|---|---|---|---|
| je | fuirai | je | fuirais |
| tu | fuiras | tu | fuirais |
| il | fuira | il | fuirait |
| nous | fuirons | nous | fuirions |
| vous | fuirez | vous | fuiriez |
| ils | fuiront | ils | fuiraient |

| | PRESENT SUBJUNCTIVE | | PAST HISTORIC |
|---|---|---|---|
| je | **fuie** | je | fuis |
| tu | **fuies** | tu | fuis |
| il | **fuie** | il | fuit |
| nous | **fuyions** | nous | fuîmes |
| vous | **fuyiez** | vous | fuîtes |
| ils | **fuient** | ils | fuirent |

---

| PAST PARTICIPLE | IMPERATIVE |
|---|---|
| fui | fuis |
| | **fuyons** |
| | **fuyez** |

| PRESENT PARTICIPLE | AUXILIARY |
|---|---|
| **fuyant** | **avoir** |

# haïr (to hate)

| | PRESENT | | IMPERFECT |
|---|---|---|---|
| je | hais | je | haïssais |
| tu | hais | tu | haïssais |
| il | hait | il | haïssait |
| nous | haïssons | nous | haïssions |
| vous | haïssez | vous | haïssiez |
| ils | haïssent | ils | haïssaient |

| | FUTURE | | CONDITIONAL |
|---|---|---|---|
| je | haïrai | je | haïrais |
| tu | haïras | tu | haïrais |
| il | haïra | il | haïrait |
| nous | haïrons | nous | haïrions |
| vous | haïrez | vous | haïriez |
| ils | haïront | ils | haïraient |

| | PRESENT SUBJUNCTIVE | | PAST HISTORIC |
|---|---|---|---|
| je | haïsse | je | haïs |
| tu | haïsses | tu | haïs |
| il | haïsse | il | haït |
| nous | haïssions | nous | haïmes |
| vous | haïssiez | vous | haïtes |
| ils | haïssent | ils | haïrent |

---

| PAST PARTICIPLE | IMPERATIVE |
|---|---|
| haï | hais |
| | haïssons |
| | haïssez |

| PRESENT PARTICIPLE | AUXILIARY |
|---|---|
| haïssant | avoir |

# lire (to read)

| | PRESENT | | | IMPERFECT |
|---|---|---|---|---|
| je | lis | | je | lisais |
| tu | lis | | tu | lisais |
| il | lit | | il | lisait |
| nous | lisons | | nous | lisions |
| vous | lisez | | vous | lisiez |
| ils | lisent | | ils | lisaient |

| | FUTURE | | | CONDITIONAL |
|---|---|---|---|---|
| je | lirai | | je | lirais |
| tu | liras | | tu | lirais |
| il | lira | | il | lirait |
| nous | lirons | | nous | lirions |
| vous | lirez | | vous | liriez |
| ils | liront | | ils | liraient |

| | PRESENT SUBJUNCTIVE | | | PAST HISTORIC |
|---|---|---|---|---|
| je | lise | | je | lus |
| tu | lises | | tu | lus |
| il | lise | | il | lut |
| nous | lisions | | nous | lûmes |
| vous | lisiez | | vous | lûtes |
| ils | lisent | | ils | lurent |

---

**PAST PARTICIPLE**
lu

**PRESENT PARTICIPLE**
lisant

**IMPERATIVE**
lis
lisons
lisez

**AUXILIARY**
avoir

# mettre (to put)

| | PRESENT | | IMPERFECT |
|---|---|---|---|
| je | **mets** | je | mettais |
| tu | **mets** | tu | mettais |
| il | **met** | il | mettait |
| nous | mettons | nous | mettions |
| vous | mettez | vous | mettiez |
| ils | mettent | ils | mettaient |

| | FUTURE | | CONDITIONAL |
|---|---|---|---|
| je | mettrai | je | mettrais |
| tu | mettras | tu | mettrais |
| il | mettra | il | mettrait |
| nous | mettrons | nous | mettrions |
| vous | mettrez | vous | mettriez |
| ils | mettront | ils | mettraient |

| | PRESENT SUBJUNCTIVE | | PAST HISTORIC |
|---|---|---|---|
| je | mette | je | **mis** |
| tu | mettes | tu | **mis** |
| il | mette | il | **mit** |
| nous | mettions | nous | **mîmes** |
| vous | mettiez | vous | **mîtes** |
| ils | mettent | ils | **mirent** |

---

**PAST PARTICIPLE**
mis

**IMPERATIVE**
**mets**
mettons
mettez

**PRESENT PARTICIPLE**
mettant

**AUXILIARY**
**avoir**

# moudre (to grind)

| | PRESENT | | IMPERFECT |
|---|---|---|---|
| je | mouds | je | moulais |
| tu | mouds | tu | moulais |
| il | moud | il | moulait |
| nous | moulons | nous | moulions |
| vous | moulez | vous | mouliez |
| ils | moulent | ils | moulaient |

| | FUTURE | | CONDITIONAL |
|---|---|---|---|
| je | moudrai | je | moudrais |
| tu | moudras | tu | moudrais |
| il | moudra | il | moudrait |
| nous | moudrons | nous | moudrions |
| vous | moudrez | vous | moudriez |
| ils | moudront | ils | moudraient |

| | PRESENT SUBJUNCTIVE | | PAST HISTORIC |
|---|---|---|---|
| je | moule | je | moulus |
| tu | moules | tu | moulus |
| il | moule | il | moulut |
| nous | moulions | nous | moulûmes |
| vous | mouliez | vous | moulûtes |
| ils | moulent | ils | moulurent |

---

| PAST PARTICIPLE | IMPERATIVE |
|---|---|
| moulu | mouds |
| | moulons |
| | moulez |

| PRESENT PARTICIPLE | AUXILIARY |
|---|---|
| moulant | avoir |

# mourir (to die)

| | PRESENT | | IMPERFECT |
|---|---|---|---|
| je | meurs | je | mourais |
| tu | meurs | tu | mourais |
| il | meurt | il | mourait |
| nous | mourons | nous | mourions |
| vous | mourez | vous | mouriez |
| ils | meurent | ils | mouraient |

| | FUTURE | | CONDITIONAL |
|---|---|---|---|
| je | mourrai | je | mourrais |
| tu | mourras | tu | mourrais |
| il | mourra | il | mourrait |
| nous | mourrons | nous | mourrions |
| vous | mourrez | vous | mourriez |
| ils | mourront | ils | mourraient |

| | PRESENT SUBJUNCTIVE | | PAST HISTORIC |
|---|---|---|---|
| je | meure | je | mourus |
| tu | meures | tu | mourus |
| il | meure | il | mourut |
| nous | mourions | nous | mourûmes |
| vous | mouriez | vous | mourûtes |
| ils | meurent | ils | moururent |

---

**PAST PARTICIPLE**
mort

**IMPERATIVE**
meurs
mourons
mourez

**PRESENT PARTICIPLE**
mourant

**AUXILIARY**
être

# naître (to be born)

| | PRESENT | | IMPERFECT |
|---|---|---|---|
| je | **nais** | je | **naissais** |
| tu | **nais** | tu | **naissais** |
| il | naît | il | **naissait** |
| nous | **naissons** | nous | **naissions** |
| vous | **naissez** | vous | **naissiez** |
| ils | **naissent** | ils | **naissaient** |

| | FUTURE | | CONDITIONAL |
|---|---|---|---|
| je | naîtrai | je | naîtrais |
| tu | naîtras | tu | naîtrais |
| il | naîtra | il | naîtrait |
| nous | naîtrons | nous | naîtrions |
| vous | naîtrez | vous | naîtriez |
| ils | naîtront | ils | naîtraient |

| | PRESENT SUBJUNCTIVE | | PAST HISTORIC |
|---|---|---|---|
| je | **naisse** | je | naquis |
| tu | **naisses** | tu | naquis |
| il | **naisse** | il | naquit |
| nous | **naissions** | nous | naquîmes |
| vous | **naissiez** | vous | naquîtes |
| ils | **naissent** | ils | naquirent |

---

| PAST PARTICIPLE | IMPERATIVE |
|---|---|
| **né** | **nais** |
| | **naissons** |
| | **naissez** |

| PRESENT PARTICIPLE | AUXILIARY |
|---|---|
| **naissant** | **être** |

# ouvrir (to open)

| | PRESENT | | IMPERFECT |
|---|---|---|---|
| | j'ouvre | | j'ouvrais |
| tu | ouvres | tu | ouvrais |
| il | ouvre | il | ouvrait |
| nous | ouvrons | nous | ouvrions |
| vous | ouvrez | vous | ouvriez |
| ils | ouvrent | ils | ouvraient |

| | FUTURE | | CONDITIONAL |
|---|---|---|---|
| | j'ouvrirai | | j'ouvrirais |
| tu | ouvriras | tu | ouvrirais |
| il | ouvrira | il | ouvrirait |
| nous | ouvrirons | nous | ouvririons |
| vous | ouvrirez | vous | ouvririez |
| ils | ouvriront | ils | ouvriraient |

| | PRESENT SUBJUNCTIVE | | PAST HISTORIC |
|---|---|---|---|
| | j'ouvre | | j'ouvris |
| tu | ouvres | tu | ouvris |
| il | ouvre | il | ouvrit |
| nous | ouvrions | nous | ouvrîmes |
| vous | ouvriez | vous | ouvrîtes |
| ils | ouvrent | ils | ouvrirent |

---

| PAST PARTICIPLE | IMPERATIVE |
|---|---|
| ouvert | ouvre |
| | ouvrons |
| | ouvrez |

| PRESENT PARTICIPLE | AUXILIARY |
|---|---|
| ouvrant | avoir |

Note that **offrir** (to offer) and **souffrir** (to suffer) are conjugated similarly

# paraître (to appear)

| | PRESENT | | IMPERFECT |
|---|---|---|---|
| je | parais | je | paraissais |
| tu | parais | tu | paraissais |
| il | paraît | il | paraissait |
| nous | paraissons | nous | paraissions |
| vous | paraissez | vous | paraissiez |
| ils | paraissent | ils | paraissaient |

| | FUTURE | | CONDITIONAL |
|---|---|---|---|
| je | paraîtrai | je | paraîtrais |
| tu | paraîtras | tu | paraîtrais |
| il | paraîtra | il | paraîtrait |
| nous | paraîtrons | nous | paraîtrions |
| vous | paraîtrez | vous | paraîtriez |
| ils | paraîtront | ils | paraîtraient |

| | PRESENT SUBJUNCTIVE | | PAST HISTORIC |
|---|---|---|---|
| je | paraisse | je | parus |
| tu | paraisses | tu | parus |
| il | paraisse | il | parut |
| nous | paraissions | nous | parûmes |
| vous | paraissiez | vous | parûtes |
| ils | paraissent | ils | parurent |

| PAST PARTICIPLE | IMPERATIVE |
|---|---|
| paru | parais |
| | paraissons |
| | paraissez |

| PRESENT PARTICIPLE | AUXILIARY |
|---|---|
| paraissant | avoir |

# partir (to leave)

| | PRESENT | | IMPERFECT |
|---|---|---|---|
| je | **pars** | je | **partais** |
| tu | **pars** | tu | **partais** |
| il | **part** | il | **partait** |
| nous | **partons** | nous | **partions** |
| vous | **partez** | vous | **partiez** |
| ils | **partent** | ils | **partaient** |

| | FUTURE | | CONDITIONAL |
|---|---|---|---|
| je | partirai | je | partirais |
| tu | partiras | tu | partirais |
| il | partira | il | partirait |
| nous | partirons | nous | partirions |
| vous | partirez | vous | partiriez |
| ils | partiront | ils | partiraient |

| | PRESENT SUBJUNCTIVE | | PAST HISTORIC |
|---|---|---|---|
| je | **parte** | je | partis |
| tu | **partes** | tu | partis |
| il | **parte** | il | partit |
| nous | **partions** | nous | partîmes |
| vous | **partiez** | vous | partîtes |
| ils | **partent** | ils | partirent |

---

**PAST PARTICIPLE**
parti

**IMPERATIVE**
**pars**
**partons**
**partez**

**PRESENT PARTICIPLE**
**partant**

**AUXILIARY**
**être**

# plaire (to please)

| | PRESENT | | IMPERFECT |
|---|---|---|---|
| je | plais | je | plaisais |
| tu | plais | tu | plaisais |
| il | plaît | il | plaisait |
| nous | plaisons | nous | plaisions |
| vous | plaisez | vous | plaisiez |
| ils | plaisent | ils | plaisaient |

| | FUTURE | | CONDITIONAL |
|---|---|---|---|
| je | plairai | je | plairais |
| tu | plairas | tu | plairais |
| il | plaira | il | plairait |
| nous | plairons | nous | plairions |
| vous | plairez | vous | plairiez |
| ils | plairont | ils | plairaient |

| | PRESENT SUBJUNCTIVE | | PAST HISTORIC |
|---|---|---|---|
| je | plaise | je | plus |
| tu | plaises | tu | plus |
| il | plaise | il | plut |
| nous | plaisions | nous | plûmes |
| vous | plaisiez | vous | plûtes |
| ils | plaisent | ils | plurent |

---

**PAST PARTICIPLE**
plu

**IMPERATIVE**
plais
plaisons
plaisez

**PRESENT PARTICIPLE**
plaisant

**AUXILIARY**
avoir

# pleuvoir (to rain)

| | PRESENT | | | IMPERFECT |
|---|---|---|---|---|
| il | pleut | | il | pleuvait |

| | FUTURE | | | CONDITIONAL |
|---|---|---|---|---|
| il | pleuvra | | il | pleuvrait |

| | PRESENT SUBJUNCTIVE | | | PAST HISTORIC |
|---|---|---|---|---|
| il | pleuve | | il | plut |

---

| PAST PARTICIPLE | IMPERATIVE |
|---|---|
| plu | *not used* |

| PRESENT PARTICIPLE | AUXILIARY |
|---|---|
| pleuvant | avoir |

# pouvoir (to be able to)

| | PRESENT | | | IMPERFECT |
|---|---|---|---|---|
| je | peux* | | je | pouvais |
| tu | peux | | tu | pouvais |
| il | peut | | il | pouvait |
| nous | pouvons | | nous | pouvions |
| vous | pouvez | | vous | pouviez |
| ils | peuvent | | ils | pouvaient |

| | FUTURE | | | CONDITIONAL |
|---|---|---|---|---|
| je | pourrai | | je | pourrais |
| tu | pourras | | tu | pourrais |
| il | pourra | | il | pourrait |
| nous | pourrons | | nous | pourrions |
| vous | pourrez | | vous | pourriez |
| ils | pourront | | ils | pourraient |

| | PRESENT SUBJUNCTIVE | | | PAST HISTORIC |
|---|---|---|---|---|
| je | puisse | | je | pus |
| tu | puisses | | tu | pus |
| il | puisse | | il | put |
| nous | puissions | | nous | pûmes |
| vous | puissiez | | vous | pûtes |
| ils | puissent | | ils | purent |

---

| PAST PARTICIPLE | IMPERATIVE |
|---|---|
| pu | *not used* |

| PRESENT PARTICIPLE | AUXILIARY |
|---|---|
| pouvant | avoir |

\* In questions **puis-je?** is used

# prendre (to take)

| | PRESENT | | IMPERFECT |
|---|---|---|---|
| je | prends | je | **prenais** |
| tu | prends | tu | **prenais** |
| il | prend | il | **prenait** |
| nous | **prenons** | nous | **prenions** |
| vous | **prenez** | vous | **preniez** |
| ils | **prennent** | ils | **prenaient** |

| | FUTURE | | CONDITIONAL |
|---|---|---|---|
| je | prendrai | je | prendrais |
| tu | prendras | tu | prendrais |
| il | prendra | il | prendrait |
| nous | prendrons | nous | prendrions |
| vous | prendrez | vous | prendriez |
| ils | prendront | ils | prendraient |

| | PRESENT SUBJUNCTIVE | | PAST HISTORIC |
|---|---|---|---|
| je | **prenne** | je | pris |
| tu | **prennes** | tu | pris |
| il | **prenne** | il | prit |
| nous | **prenions** | nous | prîmes |
| vous | **preniez** | vous | prîtes |
| ils | **prennent** | ils | prirent |

| PAST PARTICIPLE | IMPERATIVE |
|---|---|
| pris | prends |
| | prenons |
| | prenez |

| PRESENT PARTICIPLE | AUXILIARY |
|---|---|
| prenant | avoir |

# recevoir (to receive)

| | PRESENT | | IMPERFECT |
|---|---|---|---|
| je | reçois | je | recevais |
| tu | reçois | tu | recevais |
| il | reçoit | il | recevait |
| nous | recevons | nous | recevions |
| vous | recevez | vous | receviez |
| ils | reçoivent | ils | recevaient |

| | FUTURE | | CONDITIONAL |
|---|---|---|---|
| je | recevrai | je | recevrais |
| tu | recevras | tu | recevrais |
| il | recevra | il | recevrait |
| nous | recevrons | nous | recevrions |
| vous | recevrez | vous | recevriez |
| ils | recevront | ils | recevraient |

| | PRESENT SUBJUNCTIVE | | PAST HISTORIC |
|---|---|---|---|
| je | reçoive | je | reçus |
| tu | reçoives | tu | reçus |
| il | reçoive | il | reçut |
| nous | recevions | nous | reçûmes |
| vous | receviez | vous | reçûtes |
| ils | reçoivent | ils | reçurent |

| PAST PARTICIPLE | IMPERATIVE |
|---|---|
| reçu | reçois |
| | recevons |
| | recevez |

| PRESENT PARTICIPLE | AUXILIARY |
|---|---|
| recevant | avoir |

# résoudre (to solve)

| | PRESENT | | | IMPERFECT |
|---|---|---|---|---|
| je | **résous** | | je | **résolvais** |
| tu | **résous** | | tu | **résolvais** |
| il | **résout** | | il | **résolvait** |
| nous | **résolvons** | | nous | **résolvions** |
| vous | **résolvez** | | vous | **résolviez** |
| ils | **résolvent** | | ils | **résolvaient** |

| | FUTURE | | | CONDITIONAL |
|---|---|---|---|---|
| je | **résoudrai** | | je | **résoudrais** |
| tu | **résoudras** | | tu | **résoudrais** |
| il | **résoudra** | | il | **résoudrait** |
| nous | **résoudrons** | | nous | **résoudrions** |
| vous | **résoudrez** | | vous | **résoudriez** |
| ils | **résoudront** | | ils | **résoudraient** |

| | PRESENT SUBJUNCTIVE | | | PAST HISTORIC |
|---|---|---|---|---|
| je | **résolve** | | je | **résolus** |
| tu | **résolves** | | tu | **résolus** |
| il | **résolve** | | il | **résolut** |
| nous | **résolvions** | | nous | **résolûmes** |
| vous | **résolviez** | | vous | **résolûtes** |
| ils | **résolvent** | | ils | **résolurent** |

---

| PAST PARTICIPLE | IMPERATIVE |
|---|---|
| résolu | **résous** |
| | **résolvons** |
| | **résolvez** |

| PRESENT PARTICIPLE | AUXILIARY |
|---|---|
| résolvant | **avoir** |

# rire (to laugh)

| | PRESENT | | IMPERFECT |
|---|---|---|---|
| je | ris | je | riais |
| tu | ris | tu | riais |
| il | **rit** | il | riait |
| nous | rions | nous | riions |
| vous | riez | vous | riiez |
| ils | rient | ils | riaient |

| | FUTURE | | CONDITIONAL |
|---|---|---|---|
| je | rirai | je | rirais |
| tu | riras | tu | rirais |
| il | rira | il | rirait |
| nous | rirons | nous | ririons |
| vous | rirez | vous | ririez |
| ils | riront | ils | riraient |

| | PRESENT SUBJUNCTIVE | | PAST HISTORIC |
|---|---|---|---|
| je | rie | je | **ris** |
| tu | ries | tu | **ris** |
| il | rie | il | **rit** |
| nous | riions | nous | **rîmes** |
| vous | riiez | vous | **rîtes** |
| ils | rient | ils | **rirent** |

---

**PAST PARTICIPLE**
**ri**

**IMPERATIVE**
ris
rions
riez

**PRESENT PARTICIPLE**
riant

**AUXILIARY**
**avoir**

# rompre (to break)

| | PRESENT | | IMPERFECT |
|---|---|---|---|
| je | romps | je | rompais |
| tu | romps | tu | rompais |
| il | **rompt** | il | rompait |
| nous | rompons | nous | rompions |
| vous | rompez | vous | rompiez |
| ils | rompent | ils | rompaient |

| | FUTURE | | CONDITIONAL |
|---|---|---|---|
| je | romprai | je | romprais |
| tu | rompras | tu | romprais |
| il | rompra | il | romprait |
| nous | romprons | nous | romprions |
| vous | romprez | vous | rompriez |
| ils | rompront | ils | rompraient |

| | PRESENT SUBJUNCTIVE | | PAST HISTORIC |
|---|---|---|---|
| je | rompe | je | rompis |
| tu | rompes | tu | rompis |
| il | rompe | il | rompit |
| nous | rompions | nous | rompîmes |
| vous | rompiez | vous | rompîtes |
| ils | rompent | ils | rompirent |

| PAST PARTICIPLE | IMPERATIVE |
|---|---|
| rompu | romps |
| | rompons |
| | rompez |

| PRESENT PARTICIPLE | AUXILIARY |
|---|---|
| rompant | **avoir** |

# savoir (to know)

| | PRESENT | | IMPERFECT |
|---|---|---|---|
| je | sais | je | savais |
| tu | sais | tu | savais |
| il | sait | il | savait |
| nous | savons | nous | savions |
| vous | savez | vous | saviez |
| ils | savent | ils | savaient |

| | FUTURE | | CONDITIONAL |
|---|---|---|---|
| je | saurai | je | saurais |
| tu | sauras | tu | saurais |
| il | saura | il | saurait |
| nous | saurons | nous | saurions |
| vous | saurez | vous | sauriez |
| ils | sauront | ils | sauraient |

| | PRESENT SUBJUNCTIVE | | PAST HISTORIC |
|---|---|---|---|
| je | sache | je | sus |
| tu | saches | tu | sus |
| il | sache | il | sut |
| nous | sachions | nous | sûmes |
| vous | sachiez | vous | sûtes |
| ils | sachent | ils | surent |

---

**PAST PARTICIPLE**
su

**IMPERATIVE**
sache
sachons
sachez

**PRESENT PARTICIPLE**
sachant

**AUXILIARY**
avoir

# sentir (to feel, to smell)

| | PRESENT | | | IMPERFECT |
|---|---|---|---|---|
| je | sens | | je | sentais |
| tu | sens | | tu | sentais |
| il | sent | | il | sentait |
| nous | sentons | | nous | sentions |
| vous | sentez | | vous | sentiez |
| ils | sentent | | ils | sentaient |

| | FUTURE | | | CONDITIONAL |
|---|---|---|---|---|
| je | sentirai | | je | sentirais |
| tu | sentiras | | tu | sentirais |
| il | sentira | | il | sentirait |
| nous | sentirons | | nous | sentirions |
| vous | sentirez | | vous | sentiriez |
| ils | sentiront | | ils | sentiraient |

| | PRESENT SUBJUNCTIVE | | | PAST HISTORIC |
|---|---|---|---|---|
| je | sente | | je | sentis |
| tu | sentes | | tu | sentis |
| il | sente | | il | sentit |
| nous | sentions | | nous | sentîmes |
| vous | sentiez | | vous | sentîtes |
| ils | sentent | | ils | sentirent |

---

**PAST PARTICIPLE**
senti

**IMPERATIVE**
sens
sentons
sentez

**PRESENT PARTICIPLE**
sentant

**AUXILIARY**
avoir

# servir (to serve)

| | PRESENT | | | IMPERFECT |
|---|---|---|---|---|
| je | sers | | je | servais |
| tu | sers | | tu | servais |
| il | sert | | il | servait |
| nous | servons | | nous | servions |
| vous | servez | | vous | serviez |
| ils | servent | | ils | servaient |

| | FUTURE | | | CONDITIONAL |
|---|---|---|---|---|
| je | servirai | | je | servirais |
| tu | serviras | | tu | servirais |
| il | servira | | il | servirait |
| nous | servirons | | nous | servirions |
| vous | servirez | | vous | serviriez |
| ils | serviront | | ils | serviraient |

| | PRESENT SUBJUNCTIVE | | | PAST HISTORIC |
|---|---|---|---|---|
| je | serve | | je | servis |
| tu | serves | | tu | servis |
| il | serve | | il | servit |
| nous | servions | | nous | servîmes |
| vous | serviez | | vous | servîtes |
| ils | servent | | ils | servirent |

---

**PAST PARTICIPLE**
servi

**IMPERATIVE**
sers
servons
servez

**PRESENT PARTICIPLE**
servant

**AUXILIARY**
avoir

# sortir (to go, to come out)

| | PRESENT | | | IMPERFECT |
|---|---|---|---|---|
| je | **sors** | | je | **sortais** |
| tu | **sors** | | tu | **sortais** |
| il | **sort** | | il | **sortait** |
| nous | **sortons** | | nous | **sortions** |
| vous | **sortez** | | vous | **sortiez** |
| ils | **sortent** | | ils | **sortaient** |

| | FUTURE | | | CONDITIONAL |
|---|---|---|---|---|
| je | sortirai | | je | sortirais |
| tu | sortiras | | tu | sortirais |
| il | sortira | | il | sortirait |
| nous | sortirons | | nous | sortirions |
| vous | sortirez | | vous | sortiriez |
| ils | sortiront | | ils | sortiraient |

| | PRESENT SUBJUNCTIVE | | | PAST HISTORIC |
|---|---|---|---|---|
| je | **sorte** | | je | sortis |
| tu | **sortes** | | tu | sortis |
| il | **sorte** | | il | sortit |
| nous | **sortions** | | nous | sortîmes |
| vous | **sortiez** | | vous | sortîtes |
| ils | **sortent** | | ils | sortirent |

---

**PAST PARTICIPLE**
sorti

**IMPERATIVE**
**sors**
**sortons**
**sortez**

**PRESENT PARTICIPLE**
sortant

**AUXILIARY**
être

# suffire (to be enough)

| | PRESENT | | IMPERFECT |
|---|---|---|---|
| je | suffis | je | **suffisais** |
| tu | suffis | tu | **suffisais** |
| il | suffit | il | **suffisait** |
| nous | **suffisons** | nous | **suffisions** |
| vous | **suffisez** | vous | **suffisiez** |
| ils | **suffisent** | ils | **suffisaient** |

| | FUTURE | | CONDITIONAL |
|---|---|---|---|
| je | suffirai | je | suffirais |
| tu | suffiras | tu | suffirais |
| il | suffira | il | suffirait |
| nous | suffirons | nous | suffirions |
| vous | suffirez | vous | suffiriez |
| ils | suffiront | ils | suffiraient |

| | PRESENT SUBJUNCTIVE | | PAST HISTORIC |
|---|---|---|---|
| je | **suffise** | je | **suffis** |
| tu | **suffises** | tu | **suffis** |
| il | **suffise** | il | **suffit** |
| nous | **suffisions** | nous | **suffîmes** |
| vous | **suffisiez** | vous | **suffîtes** |
| ils | **suffisent** | ils | **suffirent** |

---

**PAST PARTICIPLE**
**suffi**

**IMPERATIVE**
suffis
**suffisons**
**suffisez**

**PRESENT PARTICIPLE**
**suffisant**

**AUXILIARY**
avoir

# suivre (to follow)

| | PRESENT | | IMPERFECT |
|---|---|---|---|
| je | **suis** | je | suivais |
| tu | **suis** | tu | suivais |
| il | **suit** | il | suivait |
| nous | suivons | nous | suivions |
| vous | suivez | vous | suiviez |
| ils | suivent | ils | suivaient |

| | FUTURE | | CONDITIONAL |
|---|---|---|---|
| je | suivrai | je | suivrais |
| tu | suivras | tu | suivrais |
| il | suivra | il | suivrait |
| nous | suivrons | nous | suivrions |
| vous | suivrez | vous | suivriez |
| ils | suivront | ils | suivraient |

| | PRESENT SUBJUNCTIVE | | PAST HISTORIC |
|---|---|---|---|
| je | suive | je | suivis |
| tu | suives | tu | suivis |
| il | suive | il | suivit |
| nous | suivions | nous | suivîmes |
| vous | suiviez | vous | suivîtes |
| ils | suivent | ils | suivirent |

---

**PAST PARTICIPLE**
**suivi**

**IMPERATIVE**
**suis**
suivons
suivez

**PRESENT PARTICIPLE**
suivant

**AUXILIARY**
**avoir**

# se taire (to stop talking)

| | PRESENT | | | IMPERFECT |
|---|---|---|---|---|
| je | me tais | | je | me taisais |
| tu | te tais | | tu | te taisais |
| il | se tait | | il | se taisait |
| nous | nous taisons | | nous | nous taisions |
| vous | vous taisez | | vous | vous taisiez |
| ils | se taisent | | ils | se taisaient |

| | FUTURE | | | CONDITIONAL |
|---|---|---|---|---|
| je | me tairai | | je | me tairais |
| tu | te tairas | | tu | te tairais |
| il | se taira | | il | se tairait |
| nous | nous tairons | | nous | nous tairions |
| vous | vous tairez | | vous | vous tairiez |
| ils | se tairont | | ils | se tairaient |

| | PRESENT SUBJUNCTIVE | | | PAST HISTORIC |
|---|---|---|---|---|
| je | me taise | | je | me tus |
| tu | te taises | | tu | te tus |
| il | se taise | | il | se tut |
| nous | nous taisions | | nous | nous tûmes |
| vous | vous taisiez | | vous | vous tûtes |
| ils | se taisent | | ils | se turent |

---

**PAST PARTICIPLE**
tu

**IMPERATIVE**
tais-toi
taisons-nous
taisez-vous

**PRESENT PARTICIPLE**
se taisant

**AUXILIARY**
être

# tenir (to hold)

| | PRESENT | | IMPERFECT |
|---|---|---|---|
| je | tiens | je | tenais |
| tu | tiens | tu | tenais |
| il | tient | il | tenait |
| nous | tenons | nous | tenions |
| vous | tenez | vous | teniez |
| ils | tiennent | ils | tenaient |

| | FUTURE | | CONDITIONAL |
|---|---|---|---|
| je | tiendrai | je | tiendrais |
| tu | tiendras | tu | tiendrais |
| il | tiendra | il | tiendrait |
| nous | tiendrons | nous | tiendrions |
| vous | tiendrez | vous | tiendriez |
| ils | tiendront | ils | tiendraient |

| | PRESENT SUBJUNCTIVE | | PAST HISTORIC |
|---|---|---|---|
| je | tienne | je | tins |
| tu | tiennes | tu | tins |
| il | tienne | il | tint |
| nous | tenions | nous | tînmes |
| vous | teniez | vous | tîntes |
| ils | tiennent | ils | tinrent |

---

**PAST PARTICIPLE**
tenu

**IMPERATIVE**
tiens
tenons
tenez

**PRESENT PARTICIPLE**
tenant

**AUXILIARY**
avoir

# vaincre (to defeat)

| | PRESENT | | | IMPERFECT |
|---|---|---|---|---|
| je | vaincs | | je | vainquais |
| tu | vaincs | | tu | vainquais |
| il | vainc | | il | vainquait |
| nous | **vainquons** | | nous | **vainquions** |
| vous | **vainquez** | | vous | **vainquiez** |
| ils | **vainquent** | | ils | **vainquaient** |

| | FUTURE | | | CONDITIONAL |
|---|---|---|---|---|
| je | vaincrai | | je | vaincrais |
| tu | vaincras | | tu | vaincrais |
| il | vaincra | | il | vaincrait |
| nous | vaincrons | | nous | vaincrions |
| vous | vaincrez | | vous | vaincriez |
| ils | vaincront | | ils | vaincraient |

| | PRESENT SUBJUNCTIVE | | | PAST HISTORIC |
|---|---|---|---|---|
| je | **vainque** | | je | **vainquis** |
| tu | **vainques** | | tu | **vainquis** |
| il | **vainque** | | il | **vainquit** |
| nous | **vainquions** | | nous | **vainquîmes** |
| vous | **vainquiez** | | vous | **vainquîtes** |
| ils | **vainquent** | | ils | **vainquirent** |

| PAST PARTICIPLE | IMPERATIVE |
|---|---|
| vaincu | vaincs |
| | **vainquons** |
| | **vainquez** |

| PRESENT PARTICIPLE | AUXILIARY |
|---|---|
| **vainquant** | **avoir** |

# valoir (to be worth)

|  | PRESENT |  | IMPERFECT |
|---|---|---|---|
| je | vaux | je | valais |
| tu | vaux | tu | valais |
| il | vaut | il | valait |
| nous | valons | nous | valions |
| vous | valez | vous | valiez |
| ils | valent | ils | valaient |

|  | FUTURE |  | CONDITIONAL |
|---|---|---|---|
| je | vaudrai | je | vaudrais |
| tu | vaudras | tu | vaudrais |
| il | vaudra | il | vaudrait |
| nous | vaudrons | nous | vaudrions |
| vous | vaudrez | vous | vaudriez |
| ils | vaudront | ils | vaudraient |

|  | PRESENT SUBJUNCTIVE |  | PAST HISTORIC |
|---|---|---|---|
| je | vaille | je | valus |
| tu | vailles | tu | valus |
| il | vaille | il | valut |
| nous | valions | nous | valûmes |
| vous | valiez | vous | valûtes |
| ils | vaillent | ils | valurent |

---

**PAST PARTICIPLE**
valu

**IMPERATIVE**
vaux
valons
valez

**PRESENT PARTICIPLE**
valant

**AUXILIARY**
avoir

# venir (to come)

| | PRESENT | | IMPERFECT |
|---|---|---|---|
| je | viens | je | venais |
| tu | viens | tu | venais |
| il | vient | il | venait |
| nous | venons | nous | venions |
| vous | venez | vous | veniez |
| ils | viennent | ils | venaient |

| | FUTURE | | CONDITIONAL |
|---|---|---|---|
| je | viendrai | je | viendrais |
| tu | viendras | tu | viendrais |
| il | viendra | il | viendrait |
| nous | viendrons | nous | viendrions |
| vous | viendrez | vous | viendriez |
| ils | viendront | ils | viendraient |

| | PRESENT SUBJUNCTIVE | | PAST HISTORIC |
|---|---|---|---|
| je | vienne | je | vins |
| tu | viennes | tu | vins |
| il | vienne | il | vint |
| nous | venions | nous | vînmes |
| vous | veniez | vous | vîntes |
| ils | viennent | ils | vinrent |

---

**PAST PARTICIPLE**
venu

**IMPERATIVE**
viens
venons
venez

**PRESENT PARTICIPLE**
venant

**AUXILIARY**
être

# vêtir (to dress)

| | PRESENT | | IMPERFECT |
|---|---|---|---|
| je | vêts | je | vêtais |
| tu | vêts | tu | vêtais |
| il | vêt | il | vêtait |
| nous | vêtons | nous | vêtions |
| vous | vêtez | vous | vêtiez |
| ils | vêtent | ils | vêtaient |

| | FUTURE | | CONDITIONAL |
|---|---|---|---|
| je | vêtirai | je | vêtirais |
| tu | vêtiras | tu | vêtirais |
| il | vêtira | il | vêtirait |
| nous | vêtirons | nous | vêtirions |
| vous | vêtirez | vous | vêtiriez |
| ils | vêtiront | ils | vêtiraient |

| | PRESENT SUBJUNCTIVE | | PAST HISTORIC |
|---|---|---|---|
| je | vête | je | vêtis |
| tu | vêtes | tu | vêtis |
| il | vête | il | vêtit |
| nous | vêtions | nous | vêtîmes |
| vous | vêtiez | vous | vêtîtes |
| ils | vêtent | ils | vêtirent |

| PAST PARTICIPLE | IMPERATIVE |
|---|---|
| vêtu | vêts |
| | vêtons |
| | vêtez |

| PRESENT PARTICIPLE | AUXILIARY |
|---|---|
| vêtant | avoir |

# vivre (to live)

| | PRESENT | | IMPERFECT |
|---|---|---|---|
| je | **vis** | je | vivais |
| tu | **vis** | tu | vivais |
| il | **vit** | il | vivait |
| nous | vivons | nous | vivions |
| vous | vivez | vous | viviez |
| ils | vivent | ils | vivaient |

| | FUTURE | | CONDITIONAL |
|---|---|---|---|
| je | vivrai | je | vivrais |
| tu | vivras | tu | vivrais |
| il | vivra | il | vivrait |
| nous | vivrons | nous | vivrions |
| vous | vivrez | vous | vivriez |
| ils | vivront | ils | vivraient |

| | PRESENT SUBJUNCTIVE | | PAST HISTORIC |
|---|---|---|---|
| je | vive | je | **vécus** |
| tu | vives | tu | **vécus** |
| il | vive | il | **vécut** |
| nous | vivions | nous | **vécûmes** |
| vous | viviez | vous | **vécûtes** |
| ils | vivent | ils | **vécurent** |

| PAST PARTICIPLE | IMPERATIVE |
|---|---|
| **vêcu** | **vis** |
| | vivons |
| | vivez |

| PRESENT PARTICIPLE | AUXILIARY |
|---|---|
| **vivant** | **avoir** |

# voir (to see)

| | PRESENT | | IMPERFECT |
|---|---|---|---|
| je | vois | je | voyais |
| tu | vois | tu | voyais |
| il | voit | il | voyait |
| nous | voyons | nous | voyions |
| vous | voyez | vous | voyiez |
| ils | voient | ils | voyaient |

| | FUTURE | | CONDITIONAL |
|---|---|---|---|
| je | verrai | je | verrais |
| tu | verras | tu | verrais |
| il | verra | il | verrait |
| nous | verrons | nous | verrions |
| vous | verrez | vous | verriez |
| ils | verront | ils | verraient |

| | PRESENT SUBJUNCTIVE | | PAST HISTORIC |
|---|---|---|---|
| je | voie | je | vis |
| tu | voies | tu | vis |
| il | voie | il | vit |
| nous | voyions | nous | vîmes |
| vous | voyiez | vous | vîtes |
| ils | voient | ils | virent |

| PAST PARTICIPLE | IMPERATIVE |
|---|---|
| vu | vois |
| | voyons |
| | voyez |

| PRESENT PARTICIPLE | AUXILIARY |
|---|---|
| voyant | avoir |

# vouloir (to wish, to want)

| | PRESENT | | IMPERFECT |
|---|---|---|---|
| je | veux | je | voulais |
| tu | veux | tu | voulais |
| il | veut | il | voulait |
| nous | voulons | nous | voulions |
| vous | voulez | vous | vouliez |
| ils | veulent | ils | voulaient |

| | FUTURE | | CONDITIONAL |
|---|---|---|---|
| je | voudrai | je | voudrais |
| tu | voudras | tu | voudrais |
| il | voudra | il | voudrait |
| nous | voudrons | nous | voudrions |
| vous | voudrez | vous | voudriez |
| ils | voudront | ils | voudraient |

| | PRESENT SUBJUNCTIVE | | PAST HISTORIC |
|---|---|---|---|
| je | veuille | je | voulus |
| tu | veuilles | tu | voulus |
| il | veuille | il | voulut |
| nous | voulions | nous | voulûmes |
| vous | vouliez | vous | voulûtes |
| ils | veuillent | ils | voulurent |

**PAST PARTICIPLE**
voulu

**IMPERATIVE**
veuille
veuillons
veuillez

**PRESENT PARTICIPLE**
voulant

**AUXILIARY**
avoir

# Nouns

## The Gender of Nouns

In French, all nouns are either masculine or feminine, whether denoting people, animals or things. Unlike English, there is no neuter gender for inanimate objects and abstract nouns.

Gender is largely unpredictable and has to be learnt for each noun. However, the following guidelines will help you determine the gender for certain types of nouns:

Nouns denoting male people and animals are usually – but not always – masculine, e.g.
**un homme** a man
**un taureau** a bull
**un infirmier** a (*male*) nurse
**un cheval** a horse

Nouns denoting female people and animals are usually – but not always – feminine, e.g.
**une fille** a girl
**une vache** a cow
**une infirmière** a nurse
**une brebis** a ewe

Some nouns are masculine *or* feminine depending on the sex of the person to whom they refer, e.g.
**un camarade** a (*male*) friend
**une camarade** a (*female*) friend
**un Belge** a Belgian (*man*)
**une Belge** a Belgian (*woman*)

Other nouns referring to either men or women have only one gender which applies to both, e.g.
**un professeur** a teacher
**une personne** a person
**une sentinelle** a sentry
**un témoin** a witness
**une victime** a victim
**une recrue** a recruit

Sometimes the ending of the noun indicates its gender. Shown below are some of the most important to guide you:

## Masculine endings

| -age | le courage courage; le rinçage rinsing |
| | EXCEPTIONS: une cage a cage; une image a picture; la nage swimming; une page a page; une plage a beach; une rage a rage |
| -ment | le commencement the beginning |
| | EXCEPTION: une jument a mare |
| -oir | un couloir a corridor; un miroir a mirror |
| -sme | le pessimisme pessimism; l'enthousiasme enthusiasm |

## Feminine endings

| -ance, -anse | la confiance confidence; la danse dancing |
| -ence, -ense | la prudence caution; la défense defence |
| | EXCEPTION: le silence silence |
| -ion | une région a region; une addition a bill |
| | EXCEPTIONS: un pion a pawn; un espion a spy |
| -oire | une baignoire a bath(tub) |
| -té, -tié | la beauté beauty; la moitié half |

Suffixes which differentiate between male and female are shown on pages 134 and 136.

The following words have different meanings depending on gender:

| | |
|---|---|
| le crêpe crêpe | la crêpe pancake |
| le livre book | la livre pound |
| le manche handle | la manche sleeve |
| le mode method | la mode fashion |
| le moule mould | la moule mussel |
| le page page(boy) | la page page (*in book*) |
| le physique physique | la physique physics |
| le poêle stove | la poêle frying pan |
| le somme nap | la somme sum |
| le tour turn | la tour tower |
| le voile veil | la voile sail |

# Nouns

## Gender: the Formation of Feminines

As in English, male and female are sometimes differentiated by the use of two quite separate words, e.g.

> **mon oncle** my uncle
> **ma tante** my aunt
> **un taureau** a bull
> **une vache** a cow

There are, however, some words in French which show this distinction by the form of their ending:

> Some nouns add an **e** to the masculine singular form to form the feminine → ➊

> If the masculine singular form already ends in **-e**, no further **e** is added in the feminine → ➋

> Some nouns undergo a further change when **e** is added. These changes occur regularly and are shown on page 136.

### Feminine forms to note

| MASCULINE | FEMININE | |
|-----------|----------|---|
| un âne | une ânesse | donkey |
| le comte | la comtesse | count/countess |
| le duc | la duchesse | duke/duchess |
| un Esquimau | une Esquimaude | Eskimo |
| le fou | la folle | madman/madwoman |
| le Grec | la Grecque | Greek |
| un hôte | une hôtesse | host/hostess |
| le jumeau | la jumelle | twin |
| le maître | la maîtresse | master/mistress |
| le prince | la princesse | prince/princess |
| le tigre | la tigresse | tiger/tigress |
| le traître | la traîtresse | traitor |
| le Turc | la Turque | Turk |
| le vieux | la vieille | old man/old woman |

# Examples

**1** un ami            a (*male*) friend
une amie         a (*female*) friend
un employé     a (*male*) employee
une employée    a (*female*) employee
un Français       a Frenchman
une Française     a Frenchwoman

**2** un élève         a (*male*) pupil
une élève        a (*female*) pupil
un collègue      a (*male*) colleague
une collègue     a (*female*) colleague
un camarade    a (*male*) friend
une camarade   a (*female*) friend

## Regular feminine endings

The following are regular feminine endings:

| MASC. SING. | FEM. SING. |
|---|---|
| -f | -ve → ❶ |
| -x | -se → ❷ |
| -eur | -euse → ❸ |
| -teur | -teuse → ❹ |
| | -trice → ❺ |

Some nouns double the final consonant before adding **e**:

| MASC. SING. | FEM. SING. |
|---|---|
| -an | -anne → ❻ |
| -en | -enne → ❼ |
| -on | -onne → ❽ |
| -et | -ette → ❾ |
| -el | -elle → ❿ |

Some nouns add an accent to the final syllable before adding **e**:

| MASC. SING. | FEM. SING. |
|---|---|
| -er | -ère → ⑪ |

## Pronunciation and feminine endings

This is dealt with on page 244.

# Examples

1. un sportif a sportsman        une sportive a sportswoman
   un veuf a widower             une veuve a widow

2. un époux a husband           une épouse a wife
   un amoureux a man in love    une amoureuse a woman in love

3. un danseur a dancer          une danseuse a dancer
   un voleur a thief            une voleuse a thief

4. un menteur a liar            une menteuse a liar
   un chanteur a singer         une chanteuse a singer

5. un acteur an actor           une actrice an actress
   un conducteur a driver       une conductrice a driver

6. un paysan a countryman       une paysanne a countrywoman

7. un Parisien a Parisian (*man*)   une Parisienne a Parisian (*woman*)

8. un baron a baron             une baronne a baroness

9. le cadet the youngest (child)   la cadette the youngest (child)

10. un intellectuel an intellectual   une intellectuelle an intellectual

11. un étranger a foreigner      une étrangère a foreigner
    le dernier the last (one)    la dernière the last (one)

## The Formation of Plurals

Most nouns add **s** to the singular form → ❶

When the singular form already ends in -**s**, -**x** or -**z**, no further **s** is added → ❷

For nouns ending in -**au**, -**eau** or -**eu**, the plural ends in -**aux**, -**eaux** or -**eux** → ❸
EXCEPTIONS: **pneu** tyre   (*plural*: **pneus**)
            **bleu** bruise   (*plural*: **bleus**)

For nouns ending in -**al** or -**ail**, the plural ends in -**aux** → ❹
EXCEPTIONS: **bal** ball   (*plural*: **bals**)
            **festival** festival   (*plural*: **festivals**)
            **chandail** sweater   (*plural*: **chandails**)
            **détail** detail   (*plural*: **détails**)

Forming the plural of compound nouns is complicated and you are advised to check each one individually in a dictionary.

### Irregular plural forms

Some masculine nouns ending in -**ou** add **x** in the plural. These are:

| | | |
|---|---|---|
| **bijou** jewel | **genou** knee | **joujou** toy |
| **caillou** pebble | **hibou** owl | **pou** louse |
| **chou** cabbage | | |

Some other nouns are totally unpredictable. The most important of these are:

| SINGULAR | | PLURAL |
|---|---|---|
| **œil** | eye | **yeux** |
| **ciel** | sky | **cieux** |
| **Monsieur** | Mr | **Messieurs** |
| **Madame** | Mrs | **Mesdames** |
| **Mademoiselle** | Miss | **Mesdemoiselles** |

### Pronunciation of plural forms

This is dealt with on page 244.

# Examples

**1**
| le jardin | the garden |
| les jardins | the gardens |
| une voiture | a car |
| des voitures | (some) cars |
| l'hôtel | the hotel |
| les hôtels | the hotels |

**2**
| un bois | a wood |
| des bois | (some) woods |
| une voix | a voice |
| des voix | (some) voices |
| le gaz | the gas |
| les gaz | the gases |

**3**
| un tuyau | a pipe |
| des tuyaux | (some) pipes |
| le chapeau | the hat |
| les chapeaux | the hats |
| le feu | the fire |
| les feux | the fires |

**4**
| le journal | the newspaper |
| les journaux | the newspapers |
| un travail | a job |
| des travaux | (some) jobs |

## The Definite Article

**le (l')/la (l'), les**

|         | WITH MASC. NOUN | WITH FEM. NOUN |     |
|---------|-----------------|----------------|-----|
| SING.   | le (l')         | la (l')        | the |
| PLUR.   | les             | les            | the |

The gender and number of the noun determines the form of the article → ❶

**le** and **la** change to **l'** before a vowel or an h 'mute' → ❷

For uses of the definite article see page 142.

**à + le/la (l'), à + les**

|         | WITH MASC. NOUN | WITH FEM. NOUN |
|---------|-----------------|----------------|
| SING.   | au (à l')       | à la (à l')    |
| PLUR.   | aux             | aux            |

The definite article combines with the preposition **à**, as shown above. You should pay particular attention to the masculine singular form **au**, and both plural forms **aux**, since these are not visually the sum of their parts → ❸

**de + le/la (l'), de + les**

|         | WITH MASC. NOUN | WITH FEM. NOUN |
|---------|-----------------|----------------|
| SING.   | du (de l')      | de la (de l')  |
| PLUR.   | des             | des            |

The definite article combines with the preposition **de**, as shown above. You should pay particular attention to the masculine singular form **du**, and both plural forms **des**, since these are not visually the sum of their parts → ❹

# Examples

| MASCULINE | FEMININE |
|---|---|

**1** le train  the train
le garçon  the boy
les hôtels  the hotels
les professeurs  the teachers

la gare  the station
la fille  the girl
les écoles  the schools
les femmes  the women

**2** l'acteur  the actor
l'effet  the effect
l'ingrédient  the ingredient
l'objet  the object
l'univers  the universe
l'hôpital  the hospital

l'actrice  the actress
l'eau  the water
l'idée  the idea
l'ombre  the shadow
l'usine  the factory
l'heure  the time

**3** au cinéma  at/to the cinema

à l'employé  to the employee
à l'hôpital  at/to the hospital
aux étudiants  to the students

à la bibliothèque  at/to the library
à l'infirmière  to the nurse
à l'hôtesse  to the hostess
aux maisons  to the houses

**4** du bureau  from/of the office

de l'auteur  from/of the author

de l'hôte  from/of the host
des États-Unis  from/of the United States

de la réunion  from/of the meeting
de l'Italienne  from/of the Italian woman
de l'horloge  of the clock
des vendeuses  from/of the saleswomen

## Uses of the Definite Article

While the definite article is used in much the same way in French as it is in English, its use is more widespread in French. Unlike English the definite article is also used:

with abstract nouns, except when following certain prepositions → ①

in generalizations, especially with plural or uncountable* nouns → ②

with names of countries → ③
EXCEPTIONS: no article with countries following **en** to/in → ④

with parts of the body → ⑤
'Ownership' is often indicated by an indirect object pronoun or a reflexive pronoun → ⑥

in expressions of quantity/rate/price → ⑦

with titles/ranks/professions followed by a proper name → ⑧

The definite article is *not* used with nouns in apposition → ⑨

* An uncountable noun is one which cannot be used in the plural or with an indefinite article, e.g. **l'acier** steel; **le lait** milk.

# Examples

1. Les prix montent — Prices are rising
   L'amour rayonne dans ses yeux — Love shines in his eyes
   BUT:
   avec plaisir — with pleasure
   sans espoir — without hope

2. Je n'aime pas le café — I don't like coffee
   Les enfants ont besoin d'être aimés — Children need to be loved

3. le Japon — Japan
   la France — France
   l'Italie — Italy
   les Pays-Bas — The Netherlands

4. aller en Écosse — to go to Scotland
   Il travaille en Allemagne — He works in Germany

5. Tournez la tête à gauche — Turn your head to the left
   J'ai mal à la gorge — My throat is sore, I have a sore throat

6. La tête me tourne — My head is spinning
   Elle s'est brossé les dents — She brushed her teeth

7. 4 euros le mètre/le kilo/la douzaine/la pièce — 4 euros a metre/a kilo/a dozen/each
   rouler à 80 km à l'heure — to go at 50 mph
   payé à l'heure/au jour/au mois — paid by the hour/by the day/by the month

8. le roi Georges III — King George III
   le capitaine Darbeau — Captain Darbeau
   le docteur Rousseau — Dr Rousseau
   Monsieur le président — Mr Chairman/President

9. Victor Hugo, grand écrivain du dix-neuvième siècle — Victor Hugo, a great author of the nineteenth century
   Joseph Leblanc, inventeur et entrepreneur, a été le premier ... — Joseph Leblanc, an inventor and entrepreneur, was the first ...

143

## The Partitive Article

The partitive article has the sense of 'some' or 'any', although the French is not always translated in English.

### Forms of the partitive

du (de l')/de la (de l'), des

|  | WITH MASC. NOUN | WITH FEM. NOUN |  |
|---|---|---|---|
| SING. | du (de l') | de la (de l') | some, any |
| PLUR. | des | des | some, any |

The gender and number of the noun determines the form of the partitive → ①

The forms shown in brackets (de l') are used before a vowel or an h 'mute' → ②

des becomes de (d' + *vowel*) before an adjective → ③
EXCEPTION:  if the adjective and noun are seen as forming one unit → ④

In negative sentences de (d' + *vowel*) is used for both genders, singular and plural → ⑤
EXCEPTION:  after ne ... que 'only', the positive forms above are used → ⑥

# Examples

1. Avez-vous du sucre? — Have you any sugar?
   J'ai acheté de la farine et de la margarine — I bought (some) flour and margarine
   Il a mangé des gâteaux — He ate some cakes
   Est-ce qu'il y a des lettres pour moi? — Are there (any) letters for me?

2. Il me doit de l'argent — He owes me (some) money
   C'est de l'histoire ancienne — That's ancient history

3. Il a fait de gros efforts pour nous aider — He made a great effort to help us
   Cette région a de belles églises — This region has some beautiful churches

4. des grandes vacances — summer holidays
   des jeunes gens — young people

5. Je n'ai pas de nourriture/d'argent — I don't have any food/money
   Vous n'avez pas de timbres/d'œufs? — Have you no stamps/eggs?
   Je ne mange jamais de viande/d'omelettes — I never eat meat/omelettes
   Il ne veut plus de visiteurs/d'eau — He doesn't want any more visitors/water

6. Il ne boit que du thé/de la bière/de l'eau — He only drinks tea/beer/water
   Je n'ai que des problèmes avec cette machine — I have nothing but trouble with this machine

# Articles

## The Indefinite Article

un/une, des

| | WITH MASC. NOUN | WITH FEM. NOUN | |
|---|---|---|---|
| SING. | un | une | a |
| PLUR. | des | des | some |

**des** is also the plural of the partitive article (see page 144).

In negative sentences, **de** (d' + *vowel*) is used for both singular and plural → ❶

The indefinite article is used in French largely as it is in English *except*:

there is no article when a person's profession is being stated → ❷

EXCEPTION: the article *is* present following **ce** (c' + *vowel*) → ❸

the English article is not translated by **un/une** in constructions like 'what a surprise', 'what an idiot' → ❹

in structures of the type given in example ❺ the article **un/une** is used in French and not translated in English → ❺

# Examples

1. Je n'ai pas de livre/d'enfants

   I don't have a book/(any) children

2. Il est professeur
   Ma mère est infirmière

   He's a teacher
   My mother's a nurse

3. C'est un médecin
   Ce sont des acteurs

   He's/She's a doctor
   They're actors

4. Quelle surprise!
   Quel dommage!

   What a surprise!
   What a shame!

5. avec une grande sagesse/un courage admirable
   Il a fait preuve d'un sang-froid incroyable
   un produit d'une qualité incomparable

   with great wisdom /admirable courage
   He showed incredible calmness

   a product of incomparable quality

## Adjectives

Most adjectives agree in number and in gender with the noun or pronoun.

### The formation of feminines

Most adjectives add an **e** to the masculine singular form → ❶

If the masculine singular form already ends in **-e**, no further **e** is added → ❷

Some adjectives undergo a further change when **e** is added. These changes occur regularly and are shown on page 150.

Irregular feminine forms are shown on page 152.

### The formation of plurals

The plural of both regular and irregular adjectives is formed by adding an **s** to the masculine or feminine singular form, as appropriate → ❸

When the masculine singular form already ends in **-s** or **-x**, no further **s** is added → ❹

For masculine singulars ending in **-au** and **-eau**, the masculine plural is **-aux** and **-eaux** → ❺

For masculine singulars ending in **-al**, the masculine plural is **-aux** → ❻
EXCEPTIONS:  final    (*masculine plural* **finals**)
                      fatal    (*masculine plural* **fatals**)
                      naval    (*masculine plural* **navals**)

### Pronunciation of feminine and plural adjectives

This is dealt with on page 244.

# Examples

**①**

| | |
|---|---|
| mon frère aîné | my elder brother |
| ma sœur aînée | my elder sister |
| le petit garçon | the little boy |
| la petite fille | the little girl |
| un sac gris | a grey bag |
| une chemise grise | a grey shirt |
| un bruit fort | a loud noise |
| une voix forte | a loud voice |

**②**

| | |
|---|---|
| un jeune homme | a young man |
| une jeune femme | a young woman |
| l'autre verre | the other glass |
| l'autre assiette | the other plate |

**③**

| | |
|---|---|
| le dernier train | the last train |
| les derniers trains | the last trains |
| une vieille maison | an old house |
| de vieilles maisons | old houses |
| un long voyage | a long journey |
| de longs voyages | long journeys |
| la rue étroite | the narrow street |
| les rues étroites | the narrow streets |

**④**

| | |
|---|---|
| un diplomate français | a French diplomat |
| des diplomates français | French diplomats |
| un homme dangereux | a dangerous man |
| des hommes dangereux | dangerous men |

**⑤**

| | |
|---|---|
| le nouveau professeur | the new teacher |
| les nouveaux professeurs | the new teachers |
| un chien esquimau | a husky (*literally*: an Eskimo dog) |
| des chiens esquimaux | huskies (*literally*: Eskimo dogs) |

**⑥**

| | |
|---|---|
| un ami loyal | a loyal friend |
| des amis loyaux | loyal friends |
| un geste amical | a friendly gesture |
| des gestes amicaux | friendly gestures |

# Adjectives

## Regular feminine endings

| MASC SING. | FEM. SING. | EXAMPLES |
|---|---|---|
| -f | -ve | neuf, vif → ① |
| -x | -se | heureux, jaloux → ② |
| -eur | -euse | travailleur, flâneur → ③ |
| -teur | -teuse | flatteur, menteur → ④ |
| | -trice | destructeur, séducteur → ⑤ |

EXCEPTIONS: bref: see page 152
doux, faux, roux, vieux: see page 152
extérieur, inférieur, intérieur, meilleur, supérieur:
all add e to the masculine
enchanteur: *fem.* = enchanteresse

| MASC SING. | FEM. SING. | EXAMPLES |
|---|---|---|
| -an | -anne | paysan → ⑥ |
| -en | -enne | ancien, parisien → ⑦ |
| -on | -onne | bon, breton → ⑧ |
| -as | -asse | bas, las → ⑨ |
| -et* | -ette | muet, violet → ⑩ |
| -el | -elle | annuel, mortel → ⑪ |
| -eil | -eille | pareil, vermeil → ⑫ |

EXCEPTION: ras: *fem.* = rase

| MASC SING. | FEM. SING. | EXAMPLES |
|---|---|---|
| -et* | -ète | secret, complet → ⑬ |
| -er | -ète | étranger, fier → ⑭ |

* Note that there are two feminine endings for masculine adjectives ending in -et.

# Examples

1. un résultat positif — a positive result
   une attitude positive — a positive attitude

2. d'un ton sérieux — in a serious tone (of voice)
   une voix sérieuse — a serious voice

3. un enfant trompeur — a deceitful child
   une déclaration trompeuse — a misleading statement

4. un tableau flatteur — a flattering picture
   une comparaison flatteuse — a flattering comparison

5. un geste protecteur — a protective gesture
   une couche protectrice — a protective layer

6. un problème paysan — a farming problem
   la vie paysanne — country life

7. un avion égyptien — an Egyptian plane
   une statue égyptienne — an Egyptian statue

8. un bon repas — a good meal
   de bonne humeur — in a good mood

9. un plafond bas — a low ceiling
   à voix basse — in a low voice

10. un travail net — a clean piece of work
    une explication nette — a clear explanation

11. un homme cruel — a cruel man
    une remarque cruelle — a cruel remark

12. un livre pareil — such a book
    en pareille occasion — on such an occasion

13. un regard inquiet — an anxious look
    une attente inquiète — an anxious wait

14. un goût amer — a bitter taste
    une amère déception — a bitter disappointment

# Adjectives

## Adjectives with irregular feminine forms

| MASC SING. | FEM. SING. | |
|---|---|---|
| aigu | aiguë | sharp; high-pitched → ① |
| ambigu | ambiguë | ambiguous |
| beau (bel*) | belle | beautiful |
| bénin | bénigne | benign |
| blanc | blanche | white |
| bref | brève | brief, short → ② |
| doux | douce | soft; sweet |
| épais | épaisse | thick |
| esquimau | esquimaude | Eskimo |
| faux | fausse | wrong |
| favori | favorite | favourite → ③ |
| fou (fol*) | folle | mad |
| frais | fraîche | fresh → ④ |
| franc | franche | frank |
| gentil | gentille | kind |
| grec | grecque | Greek |
| gros | grosse | big |
| jumeau | jumelle | twin → ⑤ |
| long | longue | long |
| malin | maligne | malignant |
| mou (mol*) | molle | soft |
| nouveau (nouvel*) | nouvelle | new |
| nul | nulle | no |
| public | publique | public → ⑥ |
| roux | rousse | red-haired |
| sec | sèche | dry |
| sot | sotte | foolish |
| turc | turque | Turkish |
| vieux (vieil*) | vieille | old |

\* This form is used when the following word begins with a vowel or an **h** 'mute' → ⑦

# Examples

1. un son aigu — a high-pitched sound
   une douleur aiguë — a sharp pain

2. un bref discours — a short speech
   une brève rencontre — a short meeting

3. mon sport favori — my favourite sport
   ma chanson favorite — my favourite song

4. du pain frais — fresh bread
   de la crème fraîche — fresh cream

5. mon frère jumeau — my twin brother
   ma sœur jumelle — my twin sister

6. un jardin public — a (public) park
   l'opinion publique — public opinion

7. un bel appartement — a beautiful flat
   le nouvel ordinateur — the new computer
   un vieil arbre — an old tree
   un bel habit — a beautiful outfit
   un nouvel harmonica — a new harmonica
   un vieil hôtel — an old hotel

# Adjectives

## Comparatives and Superlatives

### Comparatives

These are formed using the following constructions:

      **plus ... (que)** more ... (than) → ❶
      **moins ... (que)** less ... (than) → ❷
      **aussi ... que** as ... as → ❸
      **si ... que\*** as ... as → ❹

\* used mainly after a negative

### Superlatives

These are formed using the following constructions:

      **le/la/les plus ... (que)** the most ... (that) → ❺
      **le/la/les moins ... (que)** the least ... (that) → ❻

When the possessive adjective is present, two constructions are possible → ❼

After a superlative the preposition **de** is often translated as 'in' → ❽

If a clause follows a superlative, the verb is in the subjunctive → ❾

### Adjectives with irregular comparatives/superlatives

| ADJECTIVE | COMPARATIVE | SUPERLATIVE |
|---|---|---|
| **bon** | **meilleur** | **le meilleur** |
| good | better | the best |
| **mauvais** | **pire** or **plus mauvais** | **le pire** or **le plus mauvais** |
| bad | worse | the worst |
| **petit** | **moindre\*** or **plus petit** | **le moindre\*** or **le plus petit** |
| small | smaller; lesser | the smallest; the least |

\* used only with abstract nouns

Comparative and superlative adjectives agree in number and in gender with the noun, just like any other adjective → ❿

# Examples

1. une raison plus grave — a more serious reason
   Elle est plus petite que moi — She is smaller than me

2. un film moins connu — a less well-known film
   C'est moins cher qu'il ne pense — It's cheaper than he thinks

3. Robert était aussi inquiet que moi — Robert was as worried as I was
   Cette ville n'est pas aussi grande que Bordeaux — This town isn't as big as Bordeaux

4. Ils ne sont pas si contents que ça — They aren't as happy as all that

5. le guide le plus utile — the most useful guidebook
   la voiture la plus petite — the smallest car
   les plus grandes maisons — the biggest houses

6. le mois le moins agréable — the least pleasant month
   la fille la moins forte — the weakest girl
   les peintures les moins chères — the least expensive paintings

7. Mon désir le plus cher est de voyager — My dearest wish is to travel
   Mon plus cher désir est de voyager

8. la plus grande gare de Londres — the biggest station in London
   l'habitant le plus âgé du village/ de la région — the oldest inhabitant in the village/in the area

9. la personne la plus gentille que je connaisse — the nicest person I know

10. les moindres difficultés — the least difficulties
    la meilleure qualité — the best quality

## Demonstrative Adjectives

ce (cet)/cette, ces

|  | MASCULINE | FEMININE | |
|---|---|---|---|
| SING. | ce (cet) | cette | this; that |
| PLUR. | ces | ces | these; those |

Demonstrative adjectives agree in number and gender with the noun → ❶

**cet** is used when the following word begins with a vowel or an h 'mute' → ❷

For emphasis or in order to distinguish between people or objects, **-ci** or **-là** is added to the noun:  **-ci** indicates proximity (usually translated 'this') and **là** distance 'that' → ❸

1. Ce stylo ne marche pas | This/That pen isn't working

   Comment s'appelle cette entreprise? | What's this/that company called?

   Ces livres sont les miens | These/Those books are mine

   Ces couleurs sont plus jolies | These/Those colours are nicer

2. cet oiseau | this/that bird

   cet article | this/that article

   cet homme | this/that man

3. Combien coûte ce manteau-ci? | How much is this coat?

   Je voudrais cinq de ces pommes-là | I'd like five of those apples

   Est-ce que tu reconnais cette personne-là? | Do you recognize that person?

   Mettez ces vêtements-ci dans cette valise-là | Put these clothes in that case

   Ce garçon-là appartient à ce groupe-ci | That boy belongs to this group

## Interrogative Adjectives

**quel/quelle, quels/quelles?**

|          | MASCULINE | FEMININE  |                |
|----------|-----------|-----------|----------------|
| SING.    | quel?     | quelle?   | what?; which?  |
| PLUR.    | quels?    | quelles?  | what?; which?  |

Interrogative adjectives agree in number and gender with the noun → ❶

The forms shown above are also used in indirect questions → ❷

## Exclamatory Adjectives

**quel/quelle, quels/quelles!**

|          | MASCULINE | FEMININE  |            |
|----------|-----------|-----------|------------|
| SING.    | quel!     | quelle!   | what (a)!  |
| PLUR.    | quels!    | quelles!  | what!      |

Exclamatory adjectives agree in number and gender with the noun → ❸

For other exclamations, see page 214.

# Examples

**1** Quel genre d'homme est-ce?     What type of man is he?
Quelle est leur décision?     What is their decision?
Vous jouez de quels instruments?     What instruments do you play?
Quelles offres avez-vous reçues?     What offers have you received?
Quel vin recommandez-vous?     Which wine do you recommend?
Quelles couleurs préférez-vous?     Which colours do you prefer?

**2** Je ne sais pas à quelle heure il est arrivé     I don't know what time he arrived
Dites-moi quels sont les livres les plus chers     Tell me which books are the most expensive

**3** Quel dommage!     What a pity!
Quelle idée!     What an idea!
Quels livres intéressants vous avez!     What interesting books you have!
Quelles jolies fleurs!     What nice flowers!

# Adjectives

## Possessive Adjectives

| WITH SING. NOUN | | WITH PLUR. NOUN | |
|---|---|---|---|
| MASC. | FEM. | MASC./FEM. | |
| mon | ma (mon) | mes | my |
| ton | ta (ton) | tes | your |
| son | sa (son) | ses | his; her; its |
| notre | notre | nos | our |
| votre | votre | vos | your |
| leur | leur | leurs | their |

Possessive adjectives agree in number and gender with the noun, not with the owner → ❶

The forms shown in brackets are used when the following word begins with a vowel or an **h** 'mute' → ❷

**son**, **sa**, **ses** have the additional meaning of 'one's' → ❸

# Examples

① Catherine a oublié son parapluie — Catherine has left her umbrella
Paul cherche sa montre — Paul's looking for his watch
Mon frère et ma sœur habitent à Glasgow — My brother and sister live in Glasgow
Est-ce que tes voisins ont vendu leur voiture? — Did your neighbours sell their car?
Rangez vos affaires — Put your things away

② mon appareil-photo — my camera
ton histoire — your story
son erreur — his/her mistake
mon autre sœur — my other sister

③ perdre son équilibre — to lose one's balance
présenter ses excuses — to offer one's apologies

# Adjectives

## Position of Adjectives

French adjectives usually follow the noun → ❶

Adjectives of colour or nationality *always* follow the noun → ❷

As in English, demonstrative, possessive, numerical and interrogative adjectives precede the noun → ❸

The adjectives **autre** (other) and **chaque** (each, every) precede the noun → ❹

The following common adjectives can precede the noun:

| | |
|---|---|
| **beau** beautiful | **jeune** young |
| **bon** good | **joli** pretty |
| **court** short | **long** long |
| **dernier** last | **mauvais** bad |
| **grand** great | **petit** small |
| **gros** big | **tel** such (a) |
| **haut** high | **vieux** old |

The meaning of the following adjectives varies according to their position:

| | BEFORE NOUN | AFTER NOUN |
|---|---|---|
| **ancien** | former | old, ancient → ❺ |
| **brave** | good | brave → ❻ |
| **cher** | dear (*beloved*) | expensive → ❼ |
| **grand** | great | tall → ❽ |
| **même** | same | very → ❾ |
| **pauvre** | poor (*wretched*) | poor (*not rich*) → ❿ |
| **propre** | own | clean → ⓫ |
| **seul** | single, sole | on one's own → ⓬ |
| **simple** | mere, simple | simple, easy → ⓭ |
| **vrai** | real | true → ⓮ |

Adjectives following the noun are linked by **et** → ⓯

# Examples

① le chapitre suivant — the following chapter
l'heure exacte — the right time

② une cravate rouge — a red tie
un mot français — a French word

③ ce dictionnaire — this dictionary
mon père — my father
le premier étage — the first floor
deux exemples — two examples
quel homme? — which man?

④ une autre fois — another time
chaque jour — every day

⑤ un ancien collègue — a former colleague
l'histoire ancienne — ancient history

⑥ un brave homme — a good man
un homme brave — a brave man

⑦ mes chers amis — my dear friends
une robe chère — an expensive dress

⑧ un grand peintre — a great painter
un homme grand — a tall man

⑨ la même réponse — the same answer
vos paroles mêmes — your very words

⑩ cette pauvre femme — that poor woman
une nation pauvre — a poor nation

⑪ ma propre vie — my own life
une chemise propre — a clean shirt

⑫ une seule réponse — a single reply
une femme seule — a woman on her own

⑬ un simple regard — a mere look
un problème simple — a simple problem

⑭ la vraie raison — the real reason
les faits vrais — the true facts

⑮ un acte lâche et trompeur — a cowardly, deceitful act
un acte lâche, trompeur et ignoble — a cowardly, deceitful and ignoble act

163

## Personal Pronouns

|  | SUBJECT PRONOUNS | |
| --- | --- | --- |
|  | SINGULAR | PLURAL |
| 1st person | je (j') I | nous we |
| 2nd person | tu you | vous you |
| 3rd person (*masc.*) | il he; it | ils they |
| (*fem.*) | elle she; it | elles they |

**je** changes to **j'** before a vowel, an **h** 'mute', or the pronoun **y** → ❶

**tu/vous**
**Vous**, as well as being the second person plural, is also used when addressing one person. As a general rule, use **tu** only when addressing a friend, a child, a relative, someone you know very well, or when invited to do so. In all other cases use **vous**. For singular and plural uses of **vous**, see example ❷

**il/elle; ils/elles**
The form of the 3rd person pronouns reflects the number and gender of the noun(s) they replace, referring to animals and things as well as to people. **Ils** also replaces a combination of masculine and feminine nouns → ❸

Sometimes stressed pronouns replace the subject pronouns, see page 172.

# Examples

**❶** J'arrive!      I'm just coming!
J'en ai trois      I've got three of them
J'hésite à le déranger      I hesitate to disturb him
J'y pense souvent      I often think about it

**❷** Compare:

Vous êtes certain, Monsieur Leclerc?      Are you sure, Mr Leclerc?

and:

Vous êtes certains, les enfants?      Are you sure, children?

Compare:

Vous êtes partie quand, Estelle?      When did you leave, Estelle?

and:

Estelle et Sophie – vous êtes parties quand?      Estelle and Sophie – when did you leave?

**❸** Où logent ton père et ta mère quand ils vont à Rome?      Where do your father and mother stay when they go to Rome?

Donne-moi le journal et les lettres quand ils arriveront      Give me the newspaper and the letters when they arrive

# Pronouns

## Personal Pronouns *continued*

|  | DIRECT OBJECT PRONOUNS | |
|---|---|---|
|  | SINGULAR | PLURAL |
| 1ˢᵗ person | **me (m')** me | **nous** us |
| 2ⁿᵈ person | **te (t')** you | **vous** you |
| 3ʳᵈ person (*masc.*) | **le (l')** him; it | **ils** them |
| (*fem.*) | **la (l')** her; it | **elles** them |

The forms shown in brackets are used before a vowel, an **h** 'mute', or the pronoun **y** → **①**

In positive commands **me** and **te** change to **moi** and **toi** except before **en** or **y** → **②**

**le** sometimes functions as a 'neuter' pronoun, referring to an idea or information contained in a previous statement or question. It is often not translated → **③**

### Position of direct object pronouns

In constructions other than the imperative affirmative, the pronoun comes before the verb → **④**

The same applies when the verb is in the infinitive → **⑤**

In the imperative affirmative, the pronoun follows the verb and is attached to it by a hyphen → **⑥**

For further information, see Order of Object Pronouns, page 170.

### Reflexive Pronouns

These are dealt with under reflexive verbs, page 30.

# Examples

**1** Il m'a vu
He saw me

Je ne t'oublierai jamais
I'll never forget you

Ça l'habitue à travailler seul
That gets him/her used to working on his/her own

Je veux l'y accoutumer
I want to accustom him/her to it

**2** Avertis-moi de ta décision
Inform me of your decision

Avertis-m'en
Inform me of it

**3** Il n'est pas là. — Je le sais bien.
He isn't there. — I know that.

Aidez-moi si vous le pouvez
Help me if you can

Elle viendra demain. — Je l'espère bien.
She'll come tomorrow. — I hope so.

**4** Je t'aime
I love you

Les voyez-vous?
Can you see them?

Elle ne nous connaît pas
She doesn't know us

Est-ce que tu ne les aimes pas?
Don't you like them?

Ne me faites pas rire
Don't make me laugh

**5** Puis-je vous aider?
May I help you?

**6** Aidez-moi
Help me

Suivez-nous
Follow us

# Pronouns

## Personal Pronouns *continued*

|  | INDIRECT OBJECT PRONOUNS | |
|---|---|---|
|  | SINGULAR | PLURAL |
| 1st person | me (m') | nous |
| 2nd person | te (t') | vous |
| 3rd person (*masc.*) | lui | leur |
| (*fem.*) | lui | leur |

me and te change to m' and t' before a vowel or an h 'mute' → ①

In positive commands, me and te change to moi and toi except before en → ②

The pronouns shown in the above table replace the preposition à + *noun*, where the noun is a person or an animal → ③

The verbal construction affects the translation of the pronoun → ④

## Position of indirect object pronouns

In constructions other than the imperative affirmative, the pronoun comes before the verb → ⑤

The same applies when the verb is in the infinitive → ⑥

In the imperative affirmative, the pronoun follows the verb and is attached to it by a hyphen → ⑦

For further information, see Order of Object Pronouns, page 170.

## Reflexive Pronouns

These are dealt with under reflexive verbs, page 30.

# Examples

**1** Tu m'as donné ce livre — You gave me this book
Ils t'ont caché les faits — They hid the facts from you

**2** Donnez-moi du sucre — Give me some sugar
Donnez-m'en — Give me some
Garde-toi assez d'argent — Keep enough money for yourself
Garde-t'en assez — Keep enough for yourself

**3** J'écris à Suzanne — I'm writing to Suzanne
Je lui écris — I'm writing to her
Donne du lait au chat — Give the cat some milk
Donne-lui du lait — Give it some milk

**4** arracher qch à qn: — to snatch sth from sb:
Un voleur m'a arraché mon porte-monnaie — A thief snatched my purse from me
promettre qch à qn: — to promise sb sth:
Il leur a promis un cadeau — He promised them a present
demander à qn de faire: — to ask sb to do:
Elle nous avait demandé de revenir — She had asked us to come back

**5** Elle vous a écrit — She's written to you
Vous a-t-elle écrit? — Has she written to you?
Il ne nous parle pas — He doesn't speak to us
Est-ce que cela ne vous intéresse pas? — Doesn't it interest you?
Ne leur répondez pas — Don't answer them

**6** Voulez-vous leur envoyer l'adresse? — Do you want to send them the address?

**7** Répondez-moi — Answer me
Donnez-nous la réponse — Tell us the answer

## Personal Pronouns *continued*

### Order of object pronouns

When two object pronouns of different persons come before the verb, the order is: indirect before direct, i.e.

| | | | |
|---|---|---|---|
| me | | | |
| te | | le | |
| nous | before | la | → ① |
| vous | | les | |

When two 3rd person object pronouns come before the verb, the order is: direct before indirect, i.e.

| | | | |
|---|---|---|---|
| le | | | |
| la | before | lui | → ② |
| les | | leur | |

When two object pronouns come after the verb (i.e. in the imperative affirmative), the order is: direct before indirect, i.e.

| | | | |
|---|---|---|---|
| | | moi | |
| | | toi | |
| le | | lui | |
| la | before | nous | → ③ |
| les | | vous | |
| | | leur | |

The pronouns **y** and **en** (see pages 176 and 174) always come last → ④

# Examples

1. Dominique vous l'envoie demain — Dominique's sending it to you tomorrow

   Est-ce qu'il te les a montrés? — Has he shown them to you?
   Ne me le dis pas — Don't tell me (it)
   Il ne veut pas nous la prêter — He won't lend it to us

2. Elle le leur a emprunté — She borrowed it from them
   Je les lui ai lus — I read them to him/her
   Ne la leur donne pas — Don't give it to them
   Je voudrais les lui rendre — I'd like to give them back to him/her

3. Rends-les-moi — Give them back to me
   Donnez-le-nous — Give it to us
   Apportons-les-leur — Let's take them to them

4. Donnez-leur-en — Give them some
   Je l'y ai déposé — I dropped him there
   Ne nous en parlez plus — Don't speak to us about it any more

## Personal Pronouns *continued*

| | STRESSED OR DISJUNCTIVE PRONOUNS | |
|---|---|---|
| | SINGULAR | PLURAL |
| 1st person | **moi** me | **nous** us |
| 2nd person | **toi** you | **vous** you |
| 3rd person (*masc.*) | **lui** him; it | **eux** them |
| (*fem.*) | **elle** her; it | **elles** them |
| (*reflexive*) | **soi** oneself | |

These pronouns are used:
- after prepositions → **1**
- on their own → **2**
- following **c'est**, **ce sont** it is → **3**
- for emphasis, especially where contrast is involved → **4**
- when the subject consists of two or more pronouns → **5**
- when the subject consists of a pronoun and a noun → **6**
- in comparisons → **7**
- before relative pronouns → **8**

For particular emphasis **-même** (*singular*) or **-mêmes** (*plural*) is added to the pronoun → **9**

| | |
|---|---|
| **moi-même** myself | **nous-mêmes** ourselves |
| **toi-même** yourself | **vous-même** yourself |
| **lui-même** himself; itself | **vous-mêmes** yourselves |
| **elle-même** herself; itself | **eux-mêmes** themselves |
| **soi-même** oneself | **elles-mêmes** themselves |

## Examples

**①**  Je pense à toi
 Partez sans eux
 C'est pour elle
 Assieds-toi à côté de lui
 Venez avec moi
 Il a besoin de nous

 I think about you
 Leave without them
 This is for her
 Sit beside him
 Come with me
 He needs us

**②**  Qui a fait cela? — Lui.
 Qui est-ce qui gagne? — Moi.

 Who did that? — He did.
 Who's winning? — Me.

**③**  C'est toi, Simon? — Non, c'est
 moi, David.
 Qui est-ce? — Ce sont eux.

 Is that you, Simon? — No, it's
 me, David.
 Who is it? — It's them.

**④**  Ils voyagent séparément: lui par
 le train, elle en autobus
 Toi, tu ressembles à ton père,
 eux pas
 Il n'a pas l'air de s'ennuyer, lui!

 They travel separately: he by
 train and she by bus
 You look like your father, they
 don't
 He doesn't look bored!

**⑤**  Lui et moi partons demain
 Ni vous ni elles ne pouvez rester

 He and I are leaving tomorrow
 Neither you nor they can stay

**⑥**  Mon père et elle ne s'entendent
 pas

 My father and she don't get on

**⑦**  plus jeune que moi
 Il est moins grand que toi

 younger than me
 He's smaller than you (are)

**⑧**  Moi, qui étais malade, je n'ai pas
 pu les accompagner
 Ce sont eux qui font du bruit,
 pas nous

 I, who was ill, couldn't go with
 them
 They're the ones making the
 noise, not us

**⑨**  Je l'ai fait moi-même

 I did it myself

# Pronouns

## The pronoun en

**en** replaces the preposition **de** + *noun* → ❶

The verbal construction can affect the translation → ❷

**en** also replaces the partitive article (English = some, any) + *noun* → ❸

In expressions of quantity en represents the noun → ❹

Position:  **en** comes before the verb, except in positive commands when it follows and is attached to the verb by a hyphen → ❺

**en** follows other object pronouns → ❻

# Examples

**1** Il est fier de son succès — He's proud of his success
Il en est fier — He's proud of it
Elle est sortie du cinéma — She came out of the cinema
Elle en est sortie — She came out (of it)
Je suis couvert de peinture — I'm covered in paint
J'en suis couvert — I'm covered in it
Il a beaucoup d'amis — He has lots of friends
Il en a beaucoup — He has lots (of them)

**2** avoir besoin de qch: — to need sth:
J'en ai besoin — I need it/them
avoir peur de qch: — to be afraid of sth:
J'en ai peur — I'm afraid of it/them

**3** Avez-vous de l'argent? — Do you have any money?
En avez-vous? — Do you have any?
Je veux acheter des timbres — I want to buy some stamps
Je veux en acheter — I want to buy some

**4** J'ai deux crayons — I've two pencils
J'en ai deux — I've two (of them)
Combien de sœurs as-tu? — J'en ai trois. — How many sisters do you have? — I have three.

**5** Elle en a discuté avec moi — She discussed it with me
En êtes-vous content? — Are you pleased with it/them?
Je veux an garder trois — I want to keep three of them
N'en parlez plus — Don't talk about it any more
Prenez-en — Take some
Soyez-en fier — Be proud of it/them

**6** Donnez-leur-en — Give them some
Il m'en a parlé — He spoke to me about it

## The pronoun y

y replaces the preposition **à** + *noun* → ❶

The verbal construction can affect the translation → ❷

y also replaces the prepositions **dans** and **sur** + *noun* → ❸

y can also mean 'there' → ❹

Position: y comes before the verb, except in positive commands when it follows and is attached to the verb by a hyphen → ❺

y follows other object pronouns → ❻

# Examples

① Ne touchez pas à ce bouton — Don't touch this switch
   N'y touchez pas — Don't touch it
   Il participe aux concerts — He takes part in the concerts
   Il y participe — He takes part (in them)

② penser à qch: — to think about sth:
     J'y pense souvent — I often think about it
   consentir à qch: — to agree to sth:
     Tu y as consenti? — Have you agreed to it?

③ Mettez-les dans la boîte — Put them in the box
   Mettez-les-y — Put them in it
   Il les a mis sur les étagères — He put them on the shelves
   Il les y a mis — He put them on them
   J'ai placé de l'argent sur ce compte — I've put money into this account
   J'y ai placé de l'argent — I've put money into it

④ Elle y passe tout l'été — She spends the whole summer there

⑤ Il y a ajouté du sucre — He added sugar to it
   Elle n'y a pas écrit son nom — She hasn't written her name on it
   Comment fait-on pour y aller? — How do you get there?
   N'y pense plus! — Don't give it another thought!
   Restez-y — Stay there
   Réfléchissez-y — Think it over

⑥ Elle m'y a conduit — She drove me there
   Menez-nous-y — Take us there

## Indefinite Pronouns

The following are indefinite pronouns:

**aucun(e)** none, not any → ❶
**certain(e)s** some, certain → ❷
**chacun(e)** each (one); everybody → ❸
**on** one, you; somebody; they, people; we (*informal use*) → ❹
**personne** nobody → ❺
**plusieurs** several → ❻
**quelque chose** something; anything → ❼
**quelques-un(e)s** some, a few → ❽
**quelqu'un** somebody; anybody → ❾
**rien** nothing → ❿
**tout** all; everything → ⓫
**tous (toutes)** all → ⓬
**l'un(e) ... l'autre** (the) one ... the other
**les un(e)s ... les autres** some ... others → ⓭

**aucun(e), personne, rien**
When used as subject or object of the verb, these require the word **ne** placed immediately before the verb. Note that **aucun** further needs the pronoun **en** when used as an object → ⓮

**quelque chose, rien**
When qualified by an adjective, these pronouns require the preposition **de** before the adjective → ⓯

# Examples

1. Combien en avez-vous? — Aucun. — How many have you got? — None.

2. Certains pensent que ... — Some (people) think that ...

3. Chacune de ces boîtes est pleine — Each of these boxes is full
   Chacun son tour! — Everybody in turn!

4. On voit l'église de cette fenêtre — You can see the church from this window

   En semaine on se couche tôt — During the week they/we go to bed early

   Est-ce qu'on lui a permis de rester? — Was he/she allowed to stay?

5. Qui voyez-vous? — Personne. — Who can you see? — Nobody.

6. Ils sont plusieurs — There are several of them

7. Mange donc quelque chose! — Eat something!
   Tu as vu quelque chose? — Did you see anything?

8. Je connais quelques-uns de ses amis — I know some of his/her friends

9. Quelqu'un a appelé — Somebody called (out)
   Tu as vu quelqu'un? — Did you see anybody?

10. Qu'est-ce que tu as dans la main? — What have you got in your hand?
    — Rien. — — Nothing.

11. Il a tout gâché — He has spoiled everything
    Tout va bien — All's well

12. Tu les as tous? — Do you have all of them?
    Elles sont toutes venues — They all came

13. Les uns sont satisfaits, les autres pas — Some are satisfied, (the) others aren't

14. Je ne vois personne — I can't see anyone
    Rien ne lui plaît — Nothing pleases him/her
    Aucune des entreprises ne veut ... — None of the companies wants ...
    Il n'en a aucun — He hasn't any (of them)

15. quelque chose de grand — something big
    rien d'intéressant — nothing interesting

## Relative Pronouns

**qui** who; which
**que** who(m); which
These are subject and direct object pronouns that introduce a clause and refer to people or things.

| | PEOPLE | THINGS |
|---|---|---|
| SUBJECT | **qui** | **qui** |
| | who, that → ❶ | which, that → ❸ |
| DIRECT OBJECT | **que (qu')** | **que (qu')** |
| | who(m), that → ❷ | which, that → ❹ |

**que** changes to **qu'** before a vowel → ❷/❹

You cannot omit the object relative pronoun in French as you can in English → ❷/❹

After a preposition:
When referring to people, use **qui** → ❺
EXCEPTIONS: after **parmi** 'among' and **entre** 'between' use **lesquels/ lesquelles**; see below → ❻

When referring to things, use forms of **lequel**:

| | MASCULINE | FEMININE | |
|---|---|---|---|
| SING. | **lequel** | **laquelle** | which |
| PLUR. | **lesquels** | **lesquelles** | which |

The pronoun agrees in number and gender with the noun → ❼

After the prepositions **à** and **de**, **lequel** and **lesquel(le)s** contract as follows:
**à + lequel** → **auquel**
**à + lesquels** → **auxquels** → ❽
**à + lesquelles** → **auxquelles**

**de + lequel** → **duquel**
**de + lesquels** → **desquels** → ❾
**de + lesquelles** → **desquelles**

# Examples

1. Mon frère, qui a vingt ans, est à l'université

   My brother, who's twenty, is at university

2. Les amis que je vois le plus sont ...

   Lucienne, qu'il connaît depuis longtemps, est ...

   The friends (that) I see most are ...

   Lucienne, whom he has known for a long time, is ...

3. Il y a un escalier qui mène au toit

   There's a staircase which leads to the roof

4. La maison que nous avons achetée a ...

   Voici le cadeau qu'elle m'a envoyé

   The house (which) we've bought has ...

   This is the present (that) she sent me

5. la personne à qui il parle

   la personne avec qui je voyage

   les enfants pour qui je l'ai acheté

   the person he's talking to

   the person with whom I travel

   the children for whom I bought it

6. Il y avait des jeunes, parmi lesquels Robert

   les filles entre lesquelles j'étais assis

   There were some young people, Robert among them

   the girls between whom I was sitting

7. le torchon avec lequel il l'essuie

   la table sur laquelle je l'ai mis

   les moyens par lesquels il l'accomplit

   les pièces pour lesquelles elle est connue

   the cloth with which he's wiping it

   the table on which I put it

   the means by which he achieves it

   the plays for which she is famous

8. le magasin auquel il livre ces marchandises

   the shop to which he delivers these goods

9. les injustices desquelles il se plaint

   the injustices about which he's complaining

181

# Pronouns

## Relative Pronouns *continued*

**quoi** which, what

> When the relative pronoun does not refer to a specific noun, **quoi** is used after a preposition → ❶

**dont** whose, of whom, of which

> **dont** often (but not always) replaces **de qui**, **duquel**, **de laquelle**, and **desquel(le)s** → ❷

> It cannot replace **de qui**, **duquel** *etc* in the construction *preposition + noun +* **de qui/duquel** → ❸

# Examples

**1** C'est en quoi vous vous trompez
À quoi, j'ai répondu …

That's where you're wrong
To which I replied, …

**2** la femme dont (= *de qui*) la
voiture est garée en face
un prix dont (= *de qui*) je suis fier
un ami dont (= *de qui*) je connais
le frère
les enfants dont (= *de qui*) vous
vous occupez
le film dont (= *duquel*) il a parlé
la fenêtre dont (= *de laquelle*) les
rideaux sont tirés
des garçons dont (= *desquels*) j'ai
oublié les noms
les maladies dont (= *desquelles*)
il souffre

the woman whose car is parked
opposite
an award I am proud of
a friend whose brother I know

the children you look after

the film of which he spoke
the window the curtains of
which are drawn
boys whose names I've
forgotten
the illnesses he suffers from

**3** une personne sur l'aide de qui on
peut compter
les enfants aux parents de qui
j'écris
la maison dans le jardin
de laquelle il y a …

a person whose help one can
rely on
the children to whose parents
I'm writing
the house in whose garden
there is …

## Relative Pronouns *continued*

**ce qui, ce que** that which, what

These are used when the relative pronoun does not refer to a specific noun, and they are often translated as 'what' (*literally*: that which):

**ce qui** is used as the subject → ❶

**ce que**\* is used as the direct object → ❷

\* **que** changes to **qu'** before a vowel → ❷

Note the construction:
**tout ce qui**
**tout ce que**       everything/all that → ❸

**de** + **ce que** → **ce dont** → ❹

*preposition* + **ce que** → **ce** + *preposition* + **quoi** → ❺

When **ce qui**, **ce que** etc, refers to a previous clause the translation is 'which' → ❻

# Examples

1. Ce qui m'intéresse ne l'intéresse pas forcément

   What interests me doesn't necessarily interest him

   Je n'ai pas vu ce qui s'est passé

   I didn't see what happened

2. Ce que j'aime c'est la musique classique

   What I like is classical music

   Montrez-moi ce qu'il vous a donné

   Show me what he gave you

3. Tout ce qui reste c'est ...

   All that's left is ...

   Donnez-moi tout ce que vous avez

   Give me everything you have

4. Il risque de perdre ce dont il est si fier

   He risks losing what he's so proud of

   Voilà ce dont il s'agit

   That's what it's about

5. Ce n'est pas ce à quoi je m'attendais

   It's not what I was expecting

   Ce à quoi je m'intéresse particulièrement c'est ...

   What I'm particularly interested in is ...

6. Il est d'accord, ce qui m'étonne

   He agrees, which surprises me

   Il a dit qu'elle ne venait pas, ce que nous savions déjà

   He said she wasn't coming, which we already knew

# Pronouns

## Interrogative Pronouns

These pronouns are used in direct questions:
> **qui?** who; whom?
> **que?** what?
> **quoi?** what?

The form of the pronoun depends on:
- whether it refers to people or to things
- whether it is the subject or object of the verb, or if it comes after a preposition

**Qui** and **que** have longer forms, as shown in the tables below.

Referring to people:

| SUBJECT | **qui?** | who? → **1** |
| | **qui est-ce qui?** | |
| OBJECT | **qui?** | who(m)? → **2** |
| | **qui est-ce que*?** | |
| AFTER PREPOSITIONS | **qui?** | who(m)? → **3** |

Referring to things:

| SUBJECT | **qu'est-ce qui?** | what? → **4** |
| OBJECT | **que*?** | what? → **5** |
| | **qu'est-ce que*?** | |
| AFTER PREPOSITIONS | **quoi?** | what? → **6** |

* **que** changes to **qu'** before a vowel → **2**/**5**

# Examples

1. Qui vient?　　　　　　　　　　Who's coming?
   Qui est-ce qui vient?

2. Qui vois-tu?　　　　　　　　　Who(m) can you see?
   Qui est-ce que tu vois?
   Qui a-t-elle rencontré?　　　　　Who(m) did she meet?
   Qui est-ce qu'elle a rencontré?

3. De qui parle-t-il?　　　　　　　Who's he talking about?
   Pour qui est ce livre?　　　　　　Who's this book for?
   À qui avez-vous écrit?　　　　　　To whom did you write?

4. Qu'est-ce qui se passe?　　　　　What's happening?
   Qu'est-ce qui a vexé Paul?　　　　What upset Paul?

5. Que faites-vous?　　　　　　　　What are you doing?
   Qu'est-ce que vous faites?
   Qu'a-t-il dit?　　　　　　　　　What did he say?
   Qu'est-ce qu'il a dit?

6. À quoi cela sert-il?　　　　　　　What's that used for?
   De quoi a-t-on parlé?　　　　　　What was the discussion about?
   Sur quoi vous basez-vous?　　　　What do you base it on?

## Interrogative Pronouns *continued*

These pronouns are used in indirect questions:

**qui** who; whom
**ce qui** what
**ce que** what
**quoi** what

The form of the pronoun depends on:
- whether it refers to people or to things
- whether it is the subject or object of the verb, or if it comes after a preposition

Referring to people: use **qui** in all instances → **1**

Referring to things:

| SUBJECT | **ce qui** | what → **2** |
| OBJECT | **ce que*** | what → **3** |
| AFTER PREPOSITIONS | **quoi?** | what → **4** |

* **que** changes to **qu'** before a vowel → **3**

# Examples

**1** Demande-lui qui est venu — Ask him who came
Je me demande qui ils ont vu — I wonder who they saw
Dites-moi qui vous préférez — Tell me who you prefer
Elle ne sait pas à qui s'adresser — She doesn't know who to apply to
Demandez-leur pour qui elles travaillent — Ask them who they work for

**2** Il se demande ce qui se passe — He's wondering what's happening

Je ne sais pas ce qui vous fait croire que … — I don't know what makes you think that …

**3** Raconte-nous ce que tu as fait — Tell us what you did
Je me demande ce qu'elle pense — I wonder what she's thinking

**4** On ne sait pas de quoi vivent ces animaux — We don't know what these animals live on
Je vais lui demander à quoi il fait allusion — I'm going to ask him what he's hinting at

## Interrogative Pronouns *continued*

lequel/laquelle, lesquels/lesquelles?

|  | MASCULINE | FEMININE |  |
|---|---|---|---|
| SING. | lequel? | laquelle? | which (one)? |
| PLUR. | lesquels? | lesquelles? | which (ones)? |

The pronoun agrees in number and gender with the noun it refers to → ❶

The same forms are used in indirect questions → ❷

After the prepositions à and de, lequel and lesquel(le)s contract as follows:

> à + lequel? → auquel?
> à + lesquels? → auxquels?
> à + lesquelles? → auxquelles?
>
> de + lequel? → duquel?
> de + lesquels? → desquels?
> de + lesquelles? → desquelles?

# Examples

① J'ai choisi un livre. — Lequel?
   Laquelle de ces valises est la
     vôtre?
   Amenez quelques amis.
     — Lesquels?
   Lesquelles de vos sœurs sont
     mariées?

I've chosen a book. — Which one?
Which of these cases is yours?

Bring some friends. — Which
  ones?
Which of your sisters are
  married?

② Je me demande laquelle des
     maisons est la leur
   Dites-moi lesquels d'entre eux
     étaient là

I wonder which is their house

Tell me which of them were
  there

## Possessive Pronouns

Singular:

| MASCULINE | FEMININE | |
|---|---|---|
| le mien | la mienne | mine |
| le tien | la tienne | yours |
| le sien | la sienne | his; hers; its |
| le nôtre | la nôtre | ours |
| le vôtre | la vôtre | yours |
| le leur | la leur | theirs |

Plural:

| MASCULINE | FEMININE | |
|---|---|---|
| le miens | la miennes | mine |
| le tiens | la tiennes | yours |
| le siens | la siennes | his; hers; its |
| le nôtres | la nôtres | ours |
| le vôtres | la vôtres | yours |
| le leurs | la leurs | theirs |

The pronoun agrees in number and gender with the noun it replaces, not with the owner → ❶

Alternative translations are 'my own', 'your own' etc; **le sien**, **la sienne** *etc* may also mean 'one's own' → ❷

After the prepositions **à** and **de** the articles **le** and **les** are contracted in the normal way (see page 140):

> à + le mien → au mien
> à + les miens → aux miens     → ❸
> à + les miennes → aux miennes

> de + le mien → du mien
> de + les miens → des miens     → ❹
> de + les miennes → des miennes

# Examples

**1** Demandez à Carole si ce stylo est le sien

Ask Carole if this pen is hers

Quelle équipe a gagné – la leur ou la nôtre?

Which team won – theirs or ours?

Mon portable est plus rapide que le tien

My laptop is faster than yours

Richard a pris mes affaires pour les siennes

Richard mistook my belongings for his

Si tu n'as pas de DVDs, emprunte les miens

If you don't have any DVDs, borrow mine

Nos maisons sont moins grandes que les vôtres

Our houses are smaller than yours

**2** Est-ce que leur entreprise est aussi grande que la vôtre?

Is their company as big as your own?

Leurs prix sont moins élevés que les nôtres

Their prices are lower than our own

Le bonheur des autres importe plus que le sien

Other people's happiness matters more than one's own

**3** Pourquoi préfères-tu ce manteau au mien?

Why do you prefer this coat to mine?

Quelles maisons ressemblent aux leurs?

Which houses resemble theirs?

**4** Leur voiture est garée à côté de la tienne

Their car is parked next to yours

Vos livres sont au-dessus des miens

Your books are on top of mine

## Demonstrative Pronouns

**celui/celle, ceux/celles**

|  | MASCULINE | FEMININE |  |
|---|---|---|---|
| SING. | **celui** | **celle** | the one |
| PLUR. | **ceux** | **celles** | the ones |

The pronoun agrees in number and gender with the noun it replaces → ①

Uses:

- preceding a relative pronoun, meaning 'the one(s) who/which' → ①
- preceding the preposition **de**, meaning 'the one(s) belonging to', 'the one(s) of' → ②
- with **-ci** and **-là**, for emphasis or to distinguish between two things:

|  | MASCULINE | FEMININE |  |  |
|---|---|---|---|---|
| SING. | **celui-ci** | **celle-ci** | this (one) | → ③ |
| PLUR. | **ceux-ci** | **celles-ci** | these (ones) |  |

|  | MASCULINE | FEMININE |  |  |
|---|---|---|---|---|
| SING. | **celui-là** | **celle-là** | that (one) | → ③ |
| PLUR. | **ceux-là** | **celles-là** | those (ones) |  |

- an additional meaning of **celui-ci/celui-là** *etc* is 'the former/the latter'.

# Examples

**1** Lequel? — Celui qui parle à Anne.

Which man? — The one who's talking to Anne.

Quelle robe désirez-vous? — Celle qui est en vitrine.

Which dress do you want? — The one which is in the window.

Est-ce que ces livres sont ceux qu'il t'a donnés?

Are these the books that he gave you?

Quelles filles? — Celles que nous avons vues hier.

Which girls? — The ones we saw yesterday.

Cet article n'est pas celui dont vous m'avez parlé

This article isn't the one you spoke to me about

**2** Ce jardin est plus grand que celui de mes parents

This garden is bigger than my parents' (garden)

Est-ce que ta fille est plus âgée que celle de Gabrielle?

Is your daughter older than Gabrielle's (daughter)?

Je préfère les chiens de Paul à ceux de Roger

I prefer Paul's dogs to Roger's (dogs)

Comparez vos réponses à celles de votre voisin

Compare your answers with your neighbour's (answers)

les montagnes d'Écosse et celles du pays de Galles

the mountains of Scotland and those of Wales

**3** Quel tailleur préférez-vous: celui-ci ou celui-là?

Which suit do you prefer: this one or that one?

Cette chemise a deux poches mais celle-la n'en a pas

This shirt has two pockets but that one has none

Quels œufs choisirais-tu: ceux-ci ou ceux-là?

Which eggs would you choose: these (ones) or those (ones)?

De toutes mes jupes, celle-ci me va le mieux

Of all my skirts, this one fits me best

## Demonstrative Pronouns *continued*

**ce (c')** it, that

> Usually used with **être**, in the expressions **c'est, c'était, ce sont** *etc* → ❶
>
> Note the spelling **ç**, when followed by the letter **a** → ❷
>
> Uses:
> - to identify a person or object → ❸
> - for emphasis → ❹
> - as a neuter pronoun, referring to a statement, idea *etc* → ❺

**ce qui, ce que, ce dont** *etc*:   see Relative Pronouns (page 184), and
Interrogative Pronouns (page 188).

**cela, ça** it, that

> **cela** and **ça** are used as 'neuter' pronouns, referring to a
> statement, an idea, an object → ❻
>
> In everyday spoken language **ça** is used in preference to **cela**.

**ceci** this → ❼

> **ceci** is not used as often as 'this' in English; **cela, ça** are often used
> where we use 'this'.

# Examples

**1** C'est ...                    It's/That's ...
C'était moi                    It was me

**2** Ça été la cause de ...        It has been cause of ...

**3** Qui est-ce?                   Who is it?; Who's this/that?;
Who's he/she?

C'est lui/mon frère/nous       It's/That's him/my brother/us
Ce sont eux                    It's them
C'est une infirmière*          She's a nurse
Ce sont des professeurs*       They're teachers
Qu'est-ce que c'est?           What's this/that?
Qu'est-ce que c'est que ça?    What's that?
C'est une agrafeuse            It's a stapler
Ce sont des trombones          They're paper clips

**4** C'est moi qui ai téléphoné    It was me who phoned
Ce sont les enfants qui importent   It's the children who matter
le plus                           most

**5** C'est très intéressant        That's/It's very interesting
Ce serait dangereux            That/It would be dangerous

**6** Ça ne fait rien              It doesn't matter
À quoi bon faire ça?           What's the use of doing that?
Cela ne compte pas             That doesn't count
Cela demande du temps          It/That takes time

**7** À qui est ceci?              Whose is this?
Ouvrez-le comme ceci           Open it like this

* See pages 146 and 147 for the use of the article when stating a person's
profession

## Adverbs

### Formation

Most adverbs are formed by adding **-ment** to the feminine form of the adjective → ①

**-ment** is added to the *masculine* form when the masculine form ends in **-é**, **-i** or **-u** → ②
EXCEPTION: gai → ③

Occasionally the **u** changes to **û** before **-ment** is added → ④

If the adjective ends in **-ant** or **-ent**, the adverb ends in **-amment** or **-emment** → ⑤
EXCEPTIONS: lent, présent → ⑥

### Irregular Adverbs

| ADJECTIVE | ADVERB |
|---|---|
| **aveugle** blind | **aveuglément** blindly |
| **bon** good | **bien** well → ⑦ |
| **bref** brief | **brièvement** briefly |
| **énorme** enormous | **énormément** enormously |
| **exprès** express | **expressément** expressly → ⑧ |
| **gentil** kind | **gentiment** kindly |
| **mauvais** bad | **mal** badly → ⑨ |
| **meilleur** better | **mieux** better |
| **pire** worse | **pis** worse |
| **précis** precise | **précisément** precisely |
| **profond** deep | **profondément** deeply → ⑩ |
| **traître** treacherous | **traîtreusement** treacherously |

### Adjectives used as adverbs

Certain adjectives are used adverbially. These include: **bas, bon, cher, clair, court, doux, droit, dur, faux, ferme, fort, haut, mauvais** and **net** → ⑪

# Examples

**1** MASC./FEM. ADJECTIVE
heureux/heureuse fortunate
franc/franche frank
extrême/extrême extreme

ADVERB
heureusement fortunately
franchement frankly
extrêmement extremely

**2** MASC. ADJECTIVE
désespéré desperate
vrai true
résolu resolute

ADVERB
désespérément desperately
vraiment truly
résolument resolutely

**3** gai cheerful

gaiement or gaîment cheerfully

**4** continu continuous

continûment continuously

**5** constant constant
courant fluent
évident obvious
fréquent frequent

constamment constantly
couramment fluently
évidemment obviously
fréquemment frequently

**6** lent slow
présent present

lentement slowly
présentement presently

**7** Elle travaille bien

She works well

**8** Il a expressément défendu qu'on
parte

He has expressly forbidden us to
leave

**9** un emploi mal payé

a badly paid job

**10** J'ai été profondément ému

I was deeply moved

**11** parler bas/haut
coûter cher
voir clair
travailler dur
chanter faux
sentir bon/mauvais

to speak softly/loudly
to be expensive
to see clearly
to work hard
to sing off key
to smell nice/horrible

# Adverbs

## Position of Adverbs

When the adverb accompanies a verb in a simple tense, it generally follows the verb → ①

When the adverb accompanies a verb in a compound tense, it generally comes between the auxiliary verb and the past participle → ②

Some adverbs, however, follow the past participle → ③

When the adverb accompanies an adjective or another adverb it generally precedes the adjective/adverb → ④

## Comparatives of Adverbs

These are formed using the following constructions:

    **plus ... (que)** more ... (than) → ⑤
    **moins ... (que)** less ... (than) → ⑥
    **aussi ... que** as ... as → ⑦
    **si ... que\*** as ... as → ⑧

\*  used mainly after a negative

## Superlatives of Adverbs

These are formed using the following constructions:

    **le plus ... (que)** the most ... (that) → ⑨
    **le moins ... (que)** the least ... (that) → ⑩

## Adverbs with irregular comparatives/superlatives

| ADVERB | COMPARATIVE | SUPERLATIVE |
|---|---|---|
| **beaucoup** a lot | **plus** more | **le plus** (the) most |
| **bien** well | **mieux** better | **le mieux** (the) best |
| **mal** badly | **pis/plus mal** worse | **le pis/plus mal** (the) worst |
| **peu** little | **moins** less | **le moins** (the) least |

# Examples

**①** Il dort encore  
    Je pense souvent à toi

He's still asleep  
I often think about you

**②** Ils sont déjà partis  
    J'ai toujours cru que ...  
    J'ai presque fini  
    Il a trop mangé

They've already gone  
I've always thought that ...  
I'm almost finished  
He's eaten too much

**③** On les a vus partout  
    Elle est revenue hier

We saw them everywhere  
She came back yesterday

**④** un très beau chemisier  
    une femme bien habillée  
    beaucoup plus vite  
    peu souvent

a very nice blouse  
a well-dressed woman  
much faster  
not very often

**⑤** plus vite  
    plus régulièrement  
    Elle chante plus fort que moi

more quickly  
more regularly  
She sings louder than I do

**⑥** moins facilement  
    moins souvent  
    Nous nous voyons moins  
      fréquemment qu'auparavant

less easily  
less often  
We see each other less  
  frequently than before

**⑦** Faites-le aussi vite que possible  
    Il en sait aussi long que nous

Do it as quickly as possible  
He knows as much about it as  
  we do

**⑧** Ce n'est pas si loin que je pensais

It's not as far as I thought

**⑨** Marianne court le plus vite

Marianne runs fastest

**⑩** Le plus tôt que je puisse venir  
    c'est samedi

The earliest that I can come is  
  Saturday

**⑪** C'est l'auteur que je connais le  
    moins bien

He's the writer I'm least familiar  
  with

# Adverbs

## Common adverbs and their usage

Some common adverbs:

**assez** enough; quite → ① *See also below*
**aussi** also, too; as → ②
**autant** as much → ③ *See also below*
**beaucoup** a lot; much → ④ *See also below*
**bien** well; very; very much; 'indeed' → ⑤ *See also below*
**combien** how much; how many → ⑥ *See also below*
**comme** how; what → ⑦
**déjà** already; before → ⑧
**encore** still; yet; more; even → ⑨
**moins** less → ⑩ *See also below*
**peu** little, not much; not very → ⑪ *See also below*
**plus** more → ⑫ *See also below*
**si** so; such → ⑬
**tant** so much → ⑭ *See also below*
**toujours** always; still → ⑮
**trop** too much; too → ⑯ *See also below*

**assez**, **autant**, **beaucoup**, **combien** *etc* are used in the construction *adverb* + **de** + *noun* with the following meanings:

**assez de** enough → ⑰
**autant de** as much; as many; so much; so many
**beaucoup de** a lot of
**combien de** how much; how many
**moins de** less; fewer → ⑰
**peu de** little, not much; few, not many
**plus de** more
**tant de** so much; so many
**trop de** too much; too many

**bien** can be followed by a partitive article (see page 144) plus a noun to mean *a lot of*; *a good many* → ⑱

# Examples

1. Avez-vous assez chaud? — Are you warm enough?
   Il est assez tard — It's quite late

2. Je préfère ça aussi — I prefer it too
   Elle est aussi grande que moi — She is as tall as I am

3. Je voyage autant que lui — I travel as much as him

4. Tu lis beaucoup? — Do you read a lot?
   C'est beaucoup plus loin? — Is it much further?

5. Bien joué! — Well played!
   Je suis bien content que ... — I'm very pleased that ...
   Il s'est bien amusé — He enjoyed himself very much
   Je l'ai bien fait — I DID do it

6. Combien coûte ce livre? — How much is this book?
   Vous êtes combien? — How many of you are there?

7. Comme tu es jolie! — How pretty you look!
   Comme il fait beau! — What lovely weather!

8. Je l'ai déjà fait — I've already done it
   Êtes-vous déjà allé en France? — Have you been to France before?

9. J'en ai encore deux — I've still got two
   Elle n'est pas encore là — She isn't there yet
   Encore du café, Alain? — More coffee, Alan?
   Encore mieux! — Even better!

10. Travaillez moins! — Work less!
    Je suis moins étonné que toi — I'm less surprised than you are

11. Elle mange peu — She doesn't eat very much
    C'est peu important — It's not very important

12. Il se détend plus — He relaxes more
    Elle est plus timide que Sophie — She is shyer than Sophie

13. Simon est si charmant — Simon is so charming
    une si belle vue — such a lovely view

14. Elle l'aime tant — She loves him so much

15. Il dit toujours ça! — He always says that!
    Tu le vois toujours? — Do you still see him?

16. J'ai trop mangé — I've eaten too much
    C'est trop cher — It's too expensive

17. assez d'argent/de livres — enough money/books
    moins de temps/d'amis — less time/fewer friends

18. bien du mal/des gens — a lot of harm/a good many people

# Prepositions

On the following pages you will find some of the most frequent uses of prepositions in French. Particular attention is paid to cases where usage differs markedly from English. It is often difficult to give an English equivalent for French prepositions, since usage does vary so much between the two languages.

In the list below, the broad meaning of the preposition is given on the left, with examples of usage following.

Prepositions are dealt with in alphabetical order, except à, de and en which are shown first.

## à

| | |
|---|---|
| at | **lancer qch à qn** to throw sth at sb |
| | **il habite à St Pierre** he lives at St Pierre |
| | **à 2 euros (la) pièce** (at) 2 euros each |
| | **à 100 km à l'heure** at 100 km per hour |
| | |
| in | **à la campagne** in the country |
| | **à Londres** in London |
| | **au lit** in bed (*also* to bed) |
| | **un livre à la main** with a book in his/her hand |
| | |
| on | **un tableau au mur** a picture on the wall |
| | |
| to | **aller au cinéma** to go to the cinema |
| | **donner qch à qn** to give sth to sb |
| | **le premier/dernier à faire** the first/last to do |
| | **demander qch à qn** to ask sb sth |
| | |
| from | **arracher qch à qn** to snatch sth from sb |
| | **acheter qch à qn** to buy sth from sb |
| | **cacher qch à qn** to hide sth from sb |
| | **emprunter qch à qn** to borrow sth from sb |
| | **prendre qch à qn** to take sth from sb |
| | **voler qch à qn** to steal sth from sb |

# Prepositions

| | |
|---|---|
| *descriptive* | **la femme au chapeau vert** the woman with the green hat |
| | **un garçon aux yeux bleus** a boy with blue eyes |
| *manner, means* | **à l'ancienne** in the old-fashioned way |
| | **fait à la main** handmade |
| | **à bicyclette/cheval** by bicycle/on horseback |
| | (*but note other forms of transport used with* **en** *and* **par**) |
| | **à pied** on foot |
| | **chauffer au gaz** to heat with/by gas |
| | **à pas lents** with slow steps |
| | **cuisiner au beurre** to cook with butter |
| *time, date*: at, in | **à minuit** at midnight |
| | **à trois heures cinq** at five past three |
| | **au 20ème siècle** in the 20<sup>th</sup> century |
| | **à Noël/Pâques** at Christmas/Easter |
| *distance* | **à 6 km d'ici** (at a distance of) 6 km from here |
| | **à deux pas de chez moi** just a step from my place |
| *destined for* | **une tasse à thé** a teacup |
| | (*compare* **une tasse de thé**) |
| | **un service à café** a coffee service |
| *after certain adjectives* | **son écriture est difficile à lire** his writing is difficult to read |
| | (*compare the usage with* **de**, *page 206*) |
| | **prêt à tout** ready for anything |
| *after certain verbs* | see page 64 |

# Prepositions

## de

| | |
|---|---|
| from | **venir de Londres** to come from London |
| | **du matin au soir** from morning till night |
| | **du 21 juin au 5 juillet** from 21$^{st}$ June till 5$^{th}$ July |
| | **de 10 à 15** from 10 to 15 |
| belonging to, of | **un ami de la famille** a friend of the family |
| | **les vents d'automne** the autumn winds |
| contents, composition, material | **une boîte d'allumettes** a box of matches |
| | **une tasse de thé** a cup of tea |
| | (compare **une tasse à thé**) |
| | **une robe de soie** a silk dress |
| manner | **d'une façon irrégulière** in an irregular way |
| | **d'un seul coup** at one go |
| quality | **la société de consommation** the consumer society |
| | **des objets de valeur** valuable items |
| comparative + a number | **Il y avait plus/moins de cent personnes** There were more/fewer than a hundred people |
| in (after superlatives) | **la plus/moins belle ville du monde** the most/least beautiful city in the world |
| after certain adjectives | **surpris de voir** surprised to see |
| | **Il est difficile d'y accéder** Access is difficult |
| | (compare the usage with **à**, page 205) |
| after certain verbs | see page 64 |

# Prepositions

## en

| | |
|---|---|
| to, in, on (*place*) | **en ville** in/to town<br>**en pleine mer** on the open sea<br>**en France** in/to France<br>  (*note that masculine countries use* **à**) |
| in (*dates, months*) | **en 2007** in 2007<br>**en janvier** in January |
| transport | **en voiture** by car<br>**en avion** by plane<br>  (*but note usage of* **à** *and* **par** *in other expressions*) |
| language | **en français** in French |
| duration | **Je le ferai en trois jours** I'll do it in three days<br>(i.e. I'll take 3 days to do it: *compare* **dans trois jours**) |
| material | **un bracelet en or** a bracelet made of gold<br>  (*note that the use of* **en** *stresses the material more than the use of* **de**)<br>**consister en** to consist of |
| in the manner of, like a | **parler en vrai connaisseur** to speak like a real connoisseur<br>**déguisé en cowboy** dressed up as a cowboy |
| + present participle | **il l'a vu en passant devant la porte**<br>he saw it as he came past the door |

# Prepositions

## avant

| | |
|---|---|
| before | **Il est arrivé avant toi** He arrived before you |
| + *infinitive* (*add* **de**) | **Je vais finir ça avant de manger** I'm going to finish this before eating |
| *preference* | **la santé avant tout** health above everything |

## chez

| | |
|---|---|
| *at the home of* | **chez lui/moi** at his/my house<br>**être chez soi** to be at home<br>**venez chez nous** come round to our place |
| *at/to* (*a shop*) | **chez le boucher** at/to the butcher's |
| *in* (*a person, among a group of people or animals*) | **Ce que je n'aime pas chez lui c'est son ...** What I don't like in him is his ...<br>**chez les fourmis** among ants |

## dans

| | |
|---|---|
| *position* | **dans une boîte** in(to) a box |
| *circumstance* | **dans son enfance** in his childhood |
| *future time* | **dans trois jours** in three days' time (*compare* **en trois jours**, *page 207*) |

## depuis

| | |
|---|---|
| *since* (*time/place*) | **depuis mardi** since Tuesday<br>**Il pleut depuis Paris** It's been raining since Paris |
| *for* | **Il habite cette maison depuis 3 ans** He's been living in this house for 3 years (*note tense*) |

# Prepositions

## dès

| | |
|---|---|
| *past time* | **dès mon enfance** since my childhood |
| *future time* | **Je le ferai dès mon retour** I'll do it as soon as I get back |

## entre

| | |
|---|---|
| between | **entre 8 et 10** between 8 and 10 |
| among | **Jean et Pierre, entre autres** Jean and Pierre, among others |
| *reciprocal* | **s'aider entre eux** to help each other (out) |

## d'entre

| | |
|---|---|
| of, among | **trois d'entre eux** three of them |

## par

| | |
|---|---|
| by (*agent of passive*) | **renversé par une voiture** knocked down by a car<br>**tué par la foudre** killed by lightning |
| *weather conditions* | **par un beau jour d'été** on a lovely summer's day |
| by (means of) | **par un couloir/sentier** by a corridor/path<br>**par le train** by train (*but see also* à *and* en)<br>**par l'intermédiaire de M. Duval** through Mr Duval |
| *distribution* | **deux par deux** two by two<br>**par groupes de dix** in groups of ten<br>**deux fois par jour** twice a day |

# Prepositions

## pour

| | |
|---|---|
| for | **C'est pour vous** It's for you |
| | **C'est pour demain** It's for tomorrow |
| | **une chambre pour 2 nuits** a room for 2 nights |
| | **Pour un enfant, il se débrouille bien** |
| | For a child he manages very well |
| | **Il part pour l'Espagne** He's leaving for Spain |
| | **Il l'a fait pour vous** He did it for you |
| | **Il lui a donné 5 euros pour ce livre** |
| | He gave him 5 euros for this book |
| | **Je ne suis pas pour cette idée** I'm not for that idea |
| | **Pour qui me prends-tu?** Who do you take me for? |
| | **Il passe pour un idiot** He's taken for a fool |
| *+ infinitive:* (in order) to | **Elle se pencha pour le ramasser** |
| | She bent down to pick it up |
| | **C'est trop fragile pour servir de siège** |
| | It's too fragile to be used as a seat |
| to(wards) | **être bon/gentil pour qn** to be kind to sb |
| *with prices, time* | **pour 30 euros d'essence** 30 euros' worth of petrol |
| | **J'en ai encore pour une heure** |
| | I'll be another hour (at it) yet |

## sans

| | |
|---|---|
| without | **sans eau** without water |
| | **sans ma femme** without my wife |
| *+ infinitive* | **sans compter les autres** without counting the others |

# Prepositions

## sauf

| | |
|---|---|
| except (for) | **tous sauf lui** all except him<br>**sauf quand il pleut** except when it's raining |
| barring | **sauf imprévu** barring the unexpected<br>**sauf avis contraire** unless you hear to the contrary |

## sur

| | |
|---|---|
| on | **sur le siège** on the seat<br>**sur l'armoire** on top of the wardrobe<br>**sur le mur** on (top of) the wall<br>(*if the meaning is* 'hanging on the wall' *use* **à**, *page 204*)<br>**sur votre gauche** on your left<br>**être sur le point de faire** to be on the point of doing |
| on (to) | **mettez-le sur la table** put it on the table |
| out of, by (*proportion*) | **8 sur 10** 8 out of 10<br>**un automobiliste sur 5** one motorist in 5<br>**la pièce fait 2 mètres sur 3** the room measures 2 metres by 3 |

## Conjunctions

There are conjunctions which introduce a main clause, such as **et** (and), **mais** (but), **si** (if), **ou** (or) and so on, and those which introduce subordinate clauses like **parce que** (because), **pendant que** (while), **après que** (after) and so on. They are all used in much the same way as in English, but the following points are of note:

> Some conjunctions in French require a following subjunctive, see page 58

> Some conjunctions are 'split' in French like 'both ... and', 'either ... or' in English:

> **et ... et** both ... and → ❶
> **ni ... ni ... ne** neither ... nor → ❷
> **ou (bien) ... ou (bien)** either ... or (else) → ❸
> **soit ... soit** either ... or → ❹

> **si + il(s)** → **s'il(s)** → ❺

> **que**
> - meaning *that* → ❻
> - replacing another conjunction → ❼
> - replacing **si**, see page 62
> - in comparisons, meaning 'as', 'than' → ❽
> - followed by the subjunctive, see page 62

> **aussi** (so, therefore):  the subject and verb are inverted if the subject is a pronoun → ❾

# Examples

1. Ces fleurs poussent et en été et en hiver — These flowers grow in both summer and winter

2. Ni lui ni elle ne sont venus — Neither he nor she came
   Ils n'ont ni argent ni nourriture — They have neither money nor food

3. Elle doit être ou naïve ou stupide — She must be either naïve or stupid

   Ou bien il m'évite ou bien il ne me reconnaît pas — Either he's avoiding me or else he doesn't recognize me

4. Il faut choisir soit l'un soit l'autre — You have to choose either one or the other

5. Je ne sais pas s'il vient/s'ils viennent — I don't know if he's coming/if they're coming
   Dis-moi s'il y a des erreurs — Tell me if there are any mistakes
   Votre passeport, s'il vous plaît — Your passport, please

6. Il dit qu'il t'a vu — He says (that) he saw you
   Est-ce qu'elle sait que vous êtes là? — Does she know that you're here?

7. Quand tu seras plus grand et que tu auras une maison à toi, ... — When you're older and you have a house of your own, ...
   Comme il pleuvait et que je n'avais pas de parapluie, ... — As it was raining and I didn't have an umbrella, ...

8. Ils n'y vont pas aussi souvent que nous — They don't go there as often as we do
   Il les aime plus que jamais — He likes them more than ever
   L'argent est moins lourd que le plomb — Silver is lighter than lead

9. Ceux-ci sont plus rares, aussi coûtent-ils cher — These ones are rarer, so they're expensive

# Sentence structure

## Word Order

Word order in French is largely the same as in English, except for the
following points. Most of these have already been dealt with under the
appropriate part of speech, but are summarized here along with other
instances not covered elsewhere.

> Object pronouns nearly always come before the verb → ①
> For details, see pages 166 to 170
>
> Certain adjectives come after the noun → ②
> For details, see page 162
>
> Adverbs accompanying a verb in a simple tense usually follow the
> verb → ③
> For details, see page 200
>
> After **aussi** (so, therefore), **à peine** (hardly), **peut-être** (perhaps),
> the verb and subject are inverted → ④
>
> After the relative pronoun **dont** (whose), word order can affect
> the meaning → ⑤
> For details, see page 182
>
> In exclamations, **que** and **comme** do not affect the normal word
> order → ⑥
>
> Following direct speech:
> - the *verb + subject* order is inverted to become *subject + verb* → ⑦
> - with a pronoun subject, the verb and pronoun are linked by
>   a hyphen → ⑧
> - when the verb ends in a vowel in the 3rd person singular, **-t-** is
>   inserted between the pronoun and the verb → ⑨

For word order in negative sentences, see page 216.

For word order in interrogative sentences, see pages 220 and 222.

# Examples

**①** Je les vois!      I can see them!
Il me l'a donné      He gave it to me

**②** une ville française      a French town
du vin rouge      some red wine

**③** Il pleut encore      It's still raining
Elle m'aide quelquefois      She sometimes helps me

**④** Il vit tout seul, aussi fait-il ce qu'il veut      He lives alone, so he does what he likes
À peine la pendule avait-elle sonné trois heures que …      Hardly had the clock struck three when …
Peut-être avez-vous raison      Perhaps you're right

**⑤** Compare:
un homme dont je connais la fille      a man whose daughter I know
and:
un homme dont la fille me connaît      a man whose daughter knows me
If the person (or object) 'owned' is the object of the verb, the order is:
**dont** + *verb* + *noun* (*first sentence*)
If the person (or object) 'owned' is the subject of the verb, the order is:
**dont** + *noun* + *verb* (*second sentence*)
Note also:
l'homme dont elle est la fille      the man whose daughter she is

**⑥** Qu'il fait chaud!      How warm it is!
Que je suis content de vous voir!      How pleased I am to see you!
Comme c'est cher      How expensive it is!
Que tes voisins sont gentils!      How kind your neighbours are!

**⑦** « Je pense que oui » a dit Luc      ' I think so,' said Luke
« Ça ne fait rien » répondit Julie      'It doesn't matter,' Julie replied

**⑧** « Quelle horreur! » me suis-je exclamé      'How awful!' I exclaimed

**⑨** « Pourquoi pas? » a-t-elle demandé      'Why not?' she asked
« Si c'est vrai », continua-t-il …      'If it's true', he went on …

# Sentence structure

## Negatives

The following are the most common negative pairs:

> ne ... **pas**  not
> ne ... **point** (*literary*)  not
> ne ... **rien**  nothing
> ne ... **personne**  nobody
> ne ... **plus**  no longer, no more
> ne ... **jamais**  never
> ne ... **que**  only
> ne ... **aucun(e)**  no
> ne ... **nul(le)**  no
> ne ... **nulle part**  nowhere
> ne ... **ni**  neither ... nor
> ne ... **ni ... ni**  neither ... nor

### Word order

In simple tenses and the imperative:
- **ne** precedes the verb (and any object pronouns) and the second element follows the verb → **❶**

In compound tenses:
- ne ... **pas**, ne ... **point**, ne ... **rien**, ne ... **plus**, ne ... **jamais**, ne ... **guère** follow the pattern:
  ne + *auxiliary verb* + **pas** + *past participle* → **❷**
- ne ... **personne**, ne ... **que**, ne ... **aucun(e)**, ne ... **nul(le)**, ne ... **nulle part**, ne ... **ni** (... **ni**) follow the pattern:
  ne + *auxiliary verb* + *past participle* + **personne** → **❸**

With a verb in the infinitive:
- **ne ... pas**, **ne ... point** (*etc*, see above) come together → **❹**

For use of **rien**, **personne** and **aucun** as pronouns, see page 178.

# Examples

① Je ne fume pas — I don't smoke
Ne changez rien — Don't change anything
Je ne vois personne — I can't see anybody
Nous ne nous verrons plus — We won't see each other any more

Il n'arrive jamais à l'heure — He never arrives on time
Il n'avait qu'une valise — He only had one suitcase
Je n'ai reçu aucune réponse — I have received no reply
Il ne boit ni ne fume — He neither drinks nor smokes
Ni mon fils ni ma fille ne les connaissaient — Neither my son nor my daughter knew them

② Elle n'a pas fait ses devoirs — She hasn't done her homework
Ne vous a-t-il rien dit? — Didn't he say anything to you?
Ils n'avaient jamais vu une si belle maison — They had never seen such a beautiful house

③ Tu n'as guère changé — You've hardly changed

Je n'ai parlé à personne — I haven't spoken to anybody
Il n'avait mangé que la moitié du repas — He had only eaten half the meal
Elle ne les a trouvés nulle part — She couldn't find them anywhere
Il ne l'avait ni vu ni entendu — He had neither seen nor heard him

④ Il essayait de ne pas rire — He was trying not to laugh

## Negatives *continued*

These are the most common combinations of negative particles:

> **ne ... plus jamais** → ①
> **ne ... plus personne** → ②
> **ne ... plus rien** → ③
> **ne ... plus ni ... ni ...** → ④
> **ne ... jamais personne** → ⑤
> **ne ... jamais rien** → ⑥
> **ne ... jamais que** → ⑦
> **ne ... jamais ni ... ni ...** → ⑧
> **(ne ... pas) non plus** → ⑨

### non and pas

**non** (no) is the usual negative response to a question → ⑩
It is often translated as 'not' → ⑪

**pas** is generally used when a distinction is being made, or for emphasis → ⑫
It is often translated as 'not' → ⑬

# Examples

1. Je ne le ferai plus jamais — I'll never do it again

2. Je ne connais plus personne à Rouen — I don't know anybody in Rouen any more

3. Ces marchandises ne valaient plus rien — Those goods were no longer worth anything

4. Ils n'ont plus ni chats ni chiens — They no longer have either cats or dogs

5. On n'y voit jamais personne — You never see anybody there

6. Ils ne font jamais rien d'intéressant — They never do anything interesting

7. Je n'ai jamais parlé qu'à sa femme — I've only ever spoken to his wife

8. Il ne m'a jamais ni écrit ni téléphoné — He has never either written to me or phoned me

9. Ils n'ont pas d'enfants et nous non plus — They don't have any children and neither do we
   Je ne les aime pas. — Moi non plus. — I don't like them. — Neither do I/ I don't either.

10. Vous voulez nous accompagner? — Non. — Do you want to come with us? — No (I don't).

11. Tu viens ou non? — Are you coming or not?
    J'espère que non — I hope not

12. Ma sœur aime le ski, moi pas — My sister likes skiing, I don't

13. Qui a fait ça? — Pas moi! — Who did that? — Not me!
    Est-il de retour? — Pas encore. — Is he back? — Not yet.
    Tu as froid? — Pas du tout. — Are you cold? — Not at all.

# Sentence structure

## Question forms: direct

There are four ways of forming direct questions in French:

by inverting the normal word order so that *pronoun subject + verb* becomes *verb + pronoun subject*. A hyphen links the verb and pronoun → ❶

- When the subject is a noun, a pronoun is inserted after the verb and linked to it by a hyphen → ❷
- When the verb ends in a vowel in the third person singular, **-t-** is inserted before the pronoun → ❸

by maintaining the word order *subject + verb*, but by using a rising intonation at the end of the sentence → ❹

by inserting **est-ce que** before the construction *subject + verb* → ❺

by using an interrogative word at the beginning of the sentence, together with inversion or the **est-ce que** form above → ❻

# Examples

① Aimez-vous la France?            Do you like France?
  Avez-vous fini?                  Have you finished?
  Est-ce possible?                 Is it possible?
  Est-elle restée?                 Did she stay?
  Part-on tout de suite?           Are we leaving right away?

② Tes parents sont-ils en vacances?   Are your parents on holiday?
  Jean-Benoît est-il parti?           Has Jean-Benoît left?

③ A-t-elle de l'argent?             Has she any money?
  La pièce dure-t-elle longtemps?   Does the play last long?
  Mon père a-t-il téléphoné?        Has my father phoned?

④ Il l'a fini                       He's finished it
  Il l'a fini?                      Has he finished it?
  Robert va venir                   Robert's coming
  Robert va venir?                  Is Robert coming?

⑤ Est-ce que tu la connais?         Do you know her?
  Est-ce que tes parents sont       Have your parents come back
    revenus d'Italie?                 from Italy?

⑥ Quel train prends-tu?            ⎤
  Quel train est-ce que tu prends?  ⎦ What train are you getting?
  Lequel est-ce que ta sœur préfère? ⎤
  Lequel ta sœur préfère-t-elle?    ⎦ Which one does your sister prefer?
  Quand êtes-vous arrivé?          ⎤
  Quand est-ce que vous êtes        ⎦ When did you arrive?
    arrivé?
  Pourquoi ne sont-ils pas venus?  ⎤
  Pourquoi est-ce qu'ils ne sont pas ⎦ Why haven't they come?
    venus?

# Sentence structure

## Question forms: indirect

An indirect question is one that is 'reported', e.g. 'he asked me what the time was'; 'tell me which way to go'. Word order in indirect questions is as follows:

> *interrogative word + subject + verb* → ❶

> when the subject is a noun, and not a pronoun, the subject and verb are often inverted → ❷

## n'est-ce pas

This is used wherever English would use 'isn't it?', 'don't they?', 'weren't we?', 'is it?' and so on tagged on to the end of a sentence → ❸

## oui and si

**Oui** is the word for 'yes' in answer to a question put in the affirmative → ❹

**Si** is the word for 'yes' in answer to a question put in the negative or to contradict a negative statement → ❺

# Examples

1. Je me demande s'il viendra — I wonder if he'll come
   Je ne sais pas à quoi ça sert — I don't know what it's for
   Dites-moi quel autobus va à la gare — Tell me which bus goes to the station
   Il m'a demandé combien d'argent j'avais — He asked me how much money I had

2. Elle ne sait pas à quelle heure commence le film — She doesn't know what time the film starts
   Je me demande où sont mes clés — I wonder where my keys are
   Elle nous a demandé comment allait notre père — She asked us how our father was
   Je ne sais pas ce que veulent dire ces mots — I don't know what these words mean

3. Il fait chaud, n'est-ce pas? — It's warm, isn't it?
   Vous n'oublierez pas, n'est-ce pas? — You won't forget, will you?

4. Tu l'as fait? — Oui. — Have you done it? — Yes (I have).

5. Tu ne l'as pas fait? — Si. — Haven't you done it? — Yes (I have).

# Numbers

| Cardinal (one, two *etc*) | | Ordinal (first, second *etc*) | |
|---|---|---|---|
| zéro | 0 | | |
| un (une) | 1 | premier (première) | 1$^{er}$, 1$^{ère}$ |
| deux | 2 | deuxième, second(e) | 2$^{ème}$ |
| trois | 3 | troisième | 3$^{ème}$ |
| quatre | 4 | quatrième | 4$^{ème}$ |
| cinq | 5 | cinquième | 5$^{ème}$ |
| six | 6 | sixième | 6$^{ème}$ |
| sept | 7 | septième | 7$^{ème}$ |
| huit | 8 | huitième | 8$^{ème}$ |
| neuf | 9 | neuvième | 9$^{ème}$ |
| dix | 10 | dixième | 10$^{ème}$ |
| onze | 11 | onzième | 11$^{ème}$ |
| douze | 12 | douzième | 12$^{ème}$ |
| treize | 13 | treizième | 13$^{ème}$ |
| quatorze | 14 | quatorzième | 14$^{ème}$ |
| quinze | 15 | quinzième | 15$^{ème}$ |
| seize | 16 | seizième | 16$^{ème}$ |
| dix-sept | 17 | dix-septième | 17$^{ème}$ |
| dix-huit | 18 | dix-huitième | 18$^{ème}$ |
| dix-neuf | 19 | dix-neuvième | 19$^{ème}$ |
| vingt | 20 | vingtième | 20$^{ème}$ |
| vingt et un (une) | 21 | vingt et unième | 21$^{ème}$ |
| vingt-deux | 22 | vingt-deuxième | 22$^{ème}$ |
| vingt-trois | 23 | vingt-troisième | 23$^{ème}$ |
| trente | 30 | trentième | 30$^{ème}$ |
| quarante | 40 | quarantième | 40$^{ème}$ |
| cinquante | 50 | cinquantième | 50$^{ème}$ |
| soixante | 60 | soixantième | 60$^{ème}$ |
| soixante-dix | 70 | soixante-dixième | 70$^{ème}$ |
| soixante et onze | 71 | soixante et onzième | 71$^{ème}$ |
| soixante-douze | 72 | soixante-douzième | 72$^{ème}$ |
| quatre-vingts | 80 | quatre-vingtième | 80$^{ème}$ |
| quatre-vingt-un (une) | 81 | quatre-vingt-unième | 81$^{ème}$ |
| quatre-vingt-dix | 90 | quatre-vingt-dixième | 90$^{ème}$ |
| quatre-vingt-onze | 91 | quatre-vingt-onzième | 91$^{ème}$ |

# Numbers

## Cardinal

| | |
|---|---|
| cent | 100 |
| cent un (une) | 101 |
| cent deux | 102 |
| cent dix | 110 |
| cent quarante-deux | 142 |
| deux cents | 200 |
| deux cent un (une) | 201 |
| deux cent deux | 202 |
| trois cents | 300 |
| quatre cents | 400 |
| cinq cents | 500 |
| six cents | 600 |
| sept cents | 700 |
| huit cents | 800 |
| neuf cents | 900 |
| mille | 1000 |
| mille un (une) | 1001 |
| mille deux | 1002 |
| deux mille | 2000 |
| cent mille | 100.000 |
| un million | 1.000.000 |
| deux millions | 2.000.000 |

## Ordinal

| | |
|---|---|
| centième | 100ème |
| cent unième | 101ème |
| cent deuxième | 102ème |
| cent dixième | 110ème |
| cent quarante-deuxième | 142ème |
| deux centième | 200ème |
| deux cent unième | 201ème |
| deux cent deuxième | 202ème |
| trois centième | 300ème |
| quatre centième | 400ème |
| cinq centième | 500ème |
| six centième | 600ème |
| sept centième | 700ème |
| huit centième | 800ème |
| neuf centième | 900ème |
| millième | 1000ème |
| mille unième | 1001ème |
| mille deuxième | 1002ème |
| deux millième | 2000ème |
| cent millième | 100.000ème |
| millionième | 1.000.000ème |
| deux millionième | 2.000.000ème |

## Fractions

| | |
|---|---|
| un demi, une demie | a half |
| un tiers | a third |
| deux tiers | two thirds |
| un quart | a quarter |
| trois quarts | three quarters |
| un cinquième | one fifth |
| cinq et trois quarts | five and three quarters |

## Others

| | |
|---|---|
| zéro virgule cinq (0,5) | 0.5 |
| un virgule trois (1,3) | 1.3 |
| dix pour cent | 10% |
| deux plus deux | $2+2$ |
| deux moins deux | $2-2$ |
| deux fois deux | $2 \times 2$ |
| deux divisé par deux | $2 \div 2$ |

ⓘ Note the use of points with large numbers and commas with fractions, i.e. the opposite of English usage.

## Other Uses

**-aine** denoting approximate numbers:

    une douzaine (de pommes) about a dozen (apples)

    une quinzaine (d'hommes) about fifteen (men)

    des centaines de personnes hundreds of people

    BUT: un millier (de voitures) about a thousand (cars)

measurements:

    vingt mètres carrés 20 square metres

    vingt mètres cubes 20 cubic metres

    un pont long de quarante mètres a bridge 40 metres long

    avoir trois mètres de large/de haut to be 3 metres wide/high

miscellaneous:

    Il habite au dix He lives at number 10

    C'est au chapitre sept It's in chapter 7

    (C'est) à la page 17 (It's) on page 17

    (Il habite) au septième étage (He lives) on the 7th floor

    Il est arrivé le septième He came in 7th

    échelle au vingt-cinq millième scale 1:25,000

## Telephone numbers

Je voudrais Édimbourg trois cent trente, vingt-deux, dix

  I would like Edinburgh 330 22 10

Je voudrais le soixante-cinq, treize, vingt-deux, zéro deux

  Could you get me 65 13 22 02

Poste trois cent trente-cinq Extension number 335

Poste vingt-deux, trente-trois Extension number 22 33

ⓘ In French, telephone numbers are broken down into groups of two or three numbers (never four), and are not spoken separately as in English. They are also written in groups of two or three numbers.

# Calendar

## Dates

| | |
|---|---|
| Quelle est la date d'aujourd'hui? | |
| Quel jour sommes-nous? | What's the date today? |

| | |
|---|---|
| C'est ... | It's the ... |
| Nous sommes ... | |
| ... le premier février | ... 1st of February |
| ... le deux février | ... 2nd of February |
| ... le vingt-huit février | ... 28th of February |

| | |
|---|---|
| Il vient le sept mars | He's coming on the 7th of March |

ⓘ Use cardinal numbers except for the first of the month.

## Years

| | |
|---|---|
| Elle est née en 1930 | She was born in 1930 |
| le douze février mille neuf cent trente | (on) 12th February 1930 |
| le douze février mil neuf cent trente | |

ⓘ There are two ways of expressing the year (see last example). Note the spelling of **mil** (one thousand) in dates.

## Other expressions

| | |
|---|---|
| dans les années cinquante | during the fifties |
| au vingtième siècle | in the twentieth century |
| en mai | in May |
| lundi (quinze) | on Monday (the 15th) |
| le lundi | on Mondays |
| dans dix jours | in 10 days' time |
| il y a dix jours | 10 days ago |

# Time

| Quelle heure est-il? | What time is it? |
|---|---|
| Il est ... | It's ... |

| | |
|---|---|
| 00.00 | minuit **midnight, twelve o'clock** |
| 00.10 | minuit dix, zéro heure dix |
| 00.15 | minuit et quart, zéro heure quinze |
| 00.30 | minuit et demi, zéro heure trente |
| 00.45 | une heure moins (le) quart, zéro heure quarante-cinq |
| 01.00 | une heure du matin **one a.m., one o'clock in the morning** |
| 01.10 | une heure dix (du matin) |
| 01.15 | une heure et quart, une heure quinze |
| 01.30 | une heure et demie, une heure trente |
| 01.45 | deux heures moins (le) quart, une heure quarante cinq |
| 01.50 | deux heures moins dix, une heure cinquante |
| 01.59 | deux heures moins une, une heure cinquante-neuf |
| 12.00 | midi, douze heures **noon, twelve o'clock** |
| 12.30 | midi et demi, douze heures trente |
| 13.00 | une heure de l'après-midi, treize heures **one p.m., one o'clock in the afternoon** |
| 01.30 | une heure et demie (de l'après-midi), treize heures trente |
| 19.00 | sept heures du soir, dix-neuf heures **seven p.m., seven o'clock in the evening** |
| 19.30 | sept heures et demie (du soir), dix-neuf heures trente |

# Examples

| | |
|---|---|
| À quelle heure venez-vous?<br> — À sept heures. | What time are you coming?<br> — At seven o'clock. |
| Les bureaux sont fermés de midi à quatorze heures | The offices are closed from twelve until two |
| à deux heures du matin/de l'après-midi | at two o'clock in the morning/ afternoon; at two a.m./p.m. |
| à sept heures du soir | at seven o'clock in the evening; at seven p.m. |
| à cinq heures précises *or* pile | at five o'clock sharp |
| vers neuf heures | about nine o'clock |
| peu avant/après midi | shortly before/after noon |
| entre huit et neuf heures | between eight and nine o'clock |
| Il est plus de trois heures et demie | It's after half past three |
| Il faut y être à dix heures au plus tard/au plus tôt | You have to be there by ten o'clock at the latest/earliest |
| Ne venez pas plus tard que onze heures moins le quart | Come no later than a quarter to eleven |
| Il en a pour une demi-heure | He'll be half an hour (at it) |
| Elle est restée sans connaissance pendant un quart d'heure | She was unconscious for (a) quarter of an hour |
| Je les attends depuis une heure | I've been waiting for them for an hour/since one o'clock |
| Ils sont partis il y a quelques minutes | They left a few minutes ago |
| Je l'ai fait en vingt minutes | I did it in twenty minutes |
| Le train arrive dans une heure | The train arrives in an hour('s time) |
| Combien de temps dure ce film? | How long does this film last? |

# Translation problems

Beware of translating word for word. While on occasion this is quite possible, quite often it is not. The need for caution is illustrated by the following:

> English phrasal verbs (i.e. verbs followed by a preposition) e.g. 'to run away', 'to fall down' are often translated by one word in French → ①
>
> English verbal constructions often contain a preposition where none exists in French, or vice versa → ②
>
> Two or more prepositions in English may have a single rendering in French → ③
>
> A word which is singular in English may be plural in French, or vice versa → ④
>
> French has no equivalent of the possessive construction denoted by -'s/-s' → ⑤

See also at/in/to, page 234.

The following pages look at some specific problems.


## -ing

This is translated in a variety of ways in French:

> 'to be ...-ing' is translated by a simple verb → ⑥
> EXCEPTION: when a physical position is denoted, a past participle is used → ⑦
>
> in the construction 'to see/hear sb ...-ing', use an infinitive or **qui** + *verb* → ⑧

'-ing' can also be translated by:
- an infinitive, see page 44 → ⑨
- a perfect infinitive, see page 46 → ⑩
- a present participle, see page 48 → ⑪
- a noun → ⑫

# Examples

**1** s'enfuir — to run away
tomber — to fall down
céder — to give in

**2** payer — to pay for
regarder — to look at
écouter — to listen to
obéir à — to obey
nuire à — to harm
manquer de — to lack

**3** s'étonner de — to be surprised at
satisfait de — satisfied with
voler qch à — to steal sth from
apte à — capable of; fit for

**4** les bagages — the luggage
ses cheveux — his/her hair
le bétail — the cattle
mon pantalon — my trousers

**5** la voiture de mon frère — my brother's car (*literally*: ... of my brother)

la chambre des enfants — the children's bedroom (*literally*: ... of the children)

**6** Il part demain — He's leaving tomorrow
Je lisais un roman — I was reading a novel

**7** Elle est assise là-bas — She's sitting over there
Il était couché par terre — He was lying on the ground

**8** Je les vois venir — I can see them coming
Je les vois qui viennent
Je l'ai entendue chanter — I heard her singing
Je l'ai entendue qui chantait

**9** J'aime aller au cinéma — I like going to the cinema
Arrêtez de parler! — Stop talking!
Au lieu de répondre — Instead of answering
Avant de partir — Before leaving

**10** Après avoir ouvert la boîte, il ... — After opening the box, he ...

**11** Étant plus timide que moi, elle ... — Being shyer than me, she ...

**12** Le ski me maintient en forme — Skiing keeps me fit

# Translation problems

## to be

'to be' is generally translated by **être** → ❶

When physical location is implied, **se trouver** may be used → ❷

In set expressions, describing physical and emotional conditions, **avoir** is used:
        **avoir chaud/froid** to be warm/cold
        **avoir faim/soif** to be hungry/thirsty
        **avoir peur/honte** to be afraid/ashamed
        **avoir tort/raison** to be wrong/right

Describing the weather, e.g. what's the weather like?, it's windy/sunny, use **faire** → ❸

For ages, e.g. he is 6, use **avoir** → ❹

For state of health, e.g. he's unwell, how are you?, use **aller** → ❺

## it is, it's

'It is' and 'it's' are usually translated by **il/elle est**, when referring to a noun → ❻

For expressions of time, also use **il est** → ❼

To describe the weather, e.g. it's windy, see above.

In the construction: it is difficult/easy to do sth, use **il est** → ❽

In all other constructions, use **c'est** → ❾

## can, be able

Physical ability is expressed by **pouvoir** → ❿

If the meaning is 'to know how to', use **savoir** → ⓫

'can' + a 'verb of hearing or seeing etc' in English is not translated in French → ⓬

# Examples

1. Il est tard — It's late
   C'est peu probable — It's not very likely

2. Où se trouve la gare? — Where's the station?
   Quel temps fait-il? — What's the weather like?

3. Il fait beau/mauvais/du vent — It's lovely/miserable/windy

4. Quel âge avez-vous? — How old are you?
   J'ai quinze ans — I'm fifteen

5. Comment allez-vous? — How are you?
   Je vais très bien — I'm very well
   Où est mon parapluie? — Il est là, dans le coin. — Where's my umbrella? — It's there, in the corner.

6. Descends la valise si elle n'est pas trop lourde — Bring down the case if it isn't too heavy

7. Quelle heure est-il? — Il est sept heures et demie. — What's the time? — It's half past seven.

8. Il est difficile de répondre à cette question — It's difficult to reply to this question

9. C'est moi qui ne l'aime pas — It's me who doesn't like him
   C'est Charles/ma mère qui l'a dit — It's Charles/my mother who said so

   C'est ici que je les ai achetés — It's here that I bought them
   C'est parce que la poste est fermée que ... — It's because the post office is closed that ...

10. Pouvez-vous atteindre cette étagère? — Can you reach up to that shelf?

11. Elle ne sait pas nager — She can't swim
    Je ne vois rien — I can't see anything

12. Il les entendait — He could hear them

233

# Translation problems

**to** (*see also below*)

'to' is generally translated by **à**, see page 204 → ❶

In time expressions, e.g. 10 to 6, use **moins** → ❷

When the meaning is 'in order to', use **pour** → ❸

Following a verb, as in 'to try to do', 'to like to do', see pages 44 and 64

'easy/difficult/impossible' etc to do:  the preposition used depends on whether a specific noun is referred to → ❹ or not → ❺

## at/in/to

With feminine countries, use **en** → ❻

With masculine countries, use **au** (**aux** with plural countries) → ❼

With towns, use **à** → ❽

'at/to the butcher's/grocer's' etc: use **à** + *noun* designating the shop, or **chez** + *noun* designating the shopkeeper → ❾

'at/to the dentist's/doctor's' etc: use **chez** → ❿

'at/to -'s/-s' house': use **chez** → ⑪

## there is/there are

Both are translated by **il y a** → ⑫

# Examples

1. Donne le livre à Patrick — Give the book to Patrick

2. dix heures moins cinq — five to ten
   à sept heures moins le quart — at a quarter to seven

3. Je l'ai fait pour vous aider — I did it to help you
   Il se pencha pour nouer son lacet — He bent down to tie his shoelace

4. Ce livre est difficile à lire — This book is difficult to read

5. Il est difficile de comprendre leurs raisons — It's difficult to understand their reasons

6. Il est allé en France/en Suisse — He has gone to France/to Switzerland

   un village en Norvège/en Belgique — a village in Norway/in Belgium

7. Êtes-vous allé au Canada/au Danemark/aux États-Unis? — Have you been to Canada/to Denmark/to the United States?
   une ville au Japon/au Brésil — a town in Japan/in Brazil

8. Il est allé à Vienne/à Bruxelles — He has gone to Vienna/to Brussels
   Il habite à Londres/à Genève — He lives in London/in Geneva
   Ils logent dans un hôtel à St Pierre — They're staying in a hotel at St Pierre

9. Je l'ai acheté à l'épicérie — I bought it at the grocer's
   Je l'ai acheté chez l'épicier
   Elle est allée à la boulangerie — She's gone to the baker's
   Elle est allée chez le boulanger

10. J'ai un rendez-vous chez le dentiste — I've an appointment at the dentist's
    Il est allé chez le médecin — He has gone to the doctor's

11. chez Christian — at/to Christian's house
    chez les Pagot — at/to the Pagots' house

12. Il y a quelqu'un à la porte — There's somebody at the door
    Il y a cinq livres sur la table — There are five books on the table

## General Points

### Activity of the lips

The lips play a very important part in French. When a vowel is described as having 'rounded' lips, the lips are slightly drawn together and pursed, as when an English speaker expresses exaggerated surprise with the vowel 'ooh!' Equally, if the lips are said to be 'spread', the corners are pulled firmly back towards the cheeks, tending to reveal the front teeth.

In English, lip position is not important, and vowel sounds tend to merge because of this. In French, the activity of the lips means that every vowel sound is clearly distinct from every other.

### No diphthongs

A diphthong is a glide between two vowel sounds in the same syllable. In English, there are few 'pure' vowel sounds, but largely diphthongs instead. Although speakers of English may think they produce one vowel sound in the word 'day', in fact they use a diphthong, which in this instance is a glide between the vowels [e] and [ɪ]: [deɪ]. In French the tension maintained in the lips, tongue and the mouth in general prevents diphthongs occurring, as the vowel sound is kept constant throughout. Hence the French word corresponding to the above example, 'dé', is pronounced with no final [ɪ] sound, but is phonetically represented thus: [de].

### Consonants

In English, consonants are often pronounced with a degree of laxness that can result in their practically disappearing altogether although not strictly 'silent'. In a relaxed pronunciation of a word such as 'hat', the 't' is often scarcely heard, or is replaced by a 'glottal stop' (a sort of jerk in the throat). This never occurs in French, where consonants are always given their full value.

## Pronunciation of Consonants

Some consonants are pronounced almost exactly as in English:
[b, p, f, v, g, k, m, w].

Most others are similar to English, but slight differences should be noted.

| | EXAMPLES | HINTS ON PRONUNCIATION |
|---|---|---|
| [d] | dinde | The tip of the tongue touches the upper |
| [t] | tente | front teeth and not the roof of the mouth |
| [n] | nonne | as in English |
| [l] | Lille | |
| | | |
| [s] | tous ça | The tip of the tongue is down behind the |
| [z] | zéro rose | bottom front teeth, lower than in English |
| | | |
| [ʃ] | chose tache | Like the 'sh' of English 'shout' |
| | | |
| [ʒ] | je gilet beige | Like the 's' of English 'measure' |
| | | |
| [j] | yeux paille | Like the 'y' of English 'yes' |

Three consonants are not heard in English:

| | | |
|---|---|---|
| [ʀ] | rare venir | 'r' is often silent in English, e.g. farm. In French the [ʀ] is never silent, unless it follows an e at the end of a word e.g. chercher. To pronounce it, try to make a short sound like gargling. Similar, too, to the Scottish pronunciation of 'loch' |
| | | |
| [ɲ] | vigne agneau | Similar to the 'ni' of the English word 'Spaniard' |
| | | |
| [ɥ] | huile lueur | Like a very rapid [y] (see page 239) followed immediately by the next vowel of the word |

## Pronunciation of Vowels

| | EXAMPLES | HINTS ON PRONUNCIATION |
|---|---|---|
| [a] | patte plat amour | Similar to the vowel in English 'pat' |
| [ɑ] | bas pâte | Longer than the sound above, it resembles the English exclamation of surprise 'ah!' Similar, too, to the English vowel in 'car' without the final 'r' sound |
| [ɛ] | lait jouet merci | Similar to the English vowel in 'pet'. Beware of using the English diphthong [eɪ] as in 'pay' |
| [e] | été jouer | A pure vowel, again quite different from the diphthong in English 'pay' |
| [ə] | le premier | Similar to the English sound in 'butter' when the 'r' is not pronounced |
| [i] | ici vie lycée | The lips are well spread towards the cheeks while uttering this sound. Shorter than the English vowel in 'see' |
| [ɔ] | mort homme | The lips are well rounded while producing a sound similar to the 'o' of English 'cot' |
| [o] | mot dôme eau | A pure vowel with strongly rounded lips quite different from the diphthong in the English words 'bone', 'low' |

# Pronunciation

| EXAMPLES | HINTS ON PRONUNCIATION |
|---|---|
| [u] gen**ou** r**ou**e | A pure vowel with strongly rounded lips. Similar to the English 'ooh!' of surprise |
| [y] r**u**e vêt**u** | Often the most difficult for English speakers to produce: round your lips and try to pronounce [i] (see page 238). There is no [j] sound (see page 237) as there is in English 'pure' |
| [œ] s**œu**r b**eu**rre | Similar to the vowel in English 'fir' or 'murmur', but without the 'r' sound and with the lips more strongly rounded |
| [ø] p**eu** d**eu**x | To pronounce this, try to say [e] (see page 238) with the lips strongly rounded |

## Nasal Vowels

These are spelt with a vowel followed by a 'nasal' consonant – **n** or **m**. The production of nasal vowels really requires the help of a teacher or a recording of the sound. However, to help you, the vowel is pronounced by allowing the air from the lungs to come partly down the nose and partly through the mouth, and the **n** or **m** is not pronounced at all.

| | |
|---|---|
| [ɑ̃] l**en**t s**an**g d**an**s | In each case, the vowel shown in the |
| [ɛ̃] mat**in** pl**ein** | phonetic symbol is pronounced as |
| [ɔ̃] n**on** p**on**t | described above, but air is allowed to come |
| [œ̃] br**un** **un** parf**um** | through the nose as well as the mouth |

# Pronunciation

## From Spelling to Sounds

Although it may not seem so at first sight, there are some fairly precise 'rules' which can help you to know how to pronounce French words from their spelling.

### Vowels

| SPELLING | PRONOUNCED | EXAMPLES |
|---|---|---|
| a, à | [a] | chatte table à |
| a, â | [ɑ] | pâte pas |
| er, é | [e] | été marcher |
| e, è, ê | [ɛ] | fenêtre fermer chère |
| e | [ə] | double fenêtre |
| i, î, y | [i] | lit abîmer lycée |
| o, ô | [o] | pot trop dôme |
| o | [ɔ] | sotte orange |
| u, û | [y] | battu fût pur |

### Vowel Groups

There are several groups of vowels in French spelling which are regularly pronounced in the same way:

| SPELLING | PRONOUNCED | EXAMPLES |
|---|---|---|
| ai | [ɛ] *or* [e] | maison marchai faire |
| ail | [aj] | portail |
| ain, aim, (e)in, im | [ɛ̃] | pain faim frein impair |
| au | [o] | auberge landau |
| an, am, en, em | [ɑ̃] | plan ample entrer temps |
| eau | [o] | bateau eau |
| eu | [œ] *or* [ø] | feu peur |
| euil(le), ueil | [œj] | feuille recueil |
| oi, oy | [wa] | voir voyage |
| on, om | [ɔ̃] | ton compter |
| ou | [u] | hibou outil |
| œu | [œ] | sœur cœur |
| ue | [y] | rue |
| un, um | [œ̃] | brun parfum |

# Pronunciation

Added to these are the many groups of letters occurring at the end of words, where their pronunciation is predictable, bearing in mind the tendency (see page 242) of final consonants to remain silent.

| TYPICAL WORDS | PRONUNCIATION OF FINAL SYLLABLE |
|---|---|
| pas, mât, chat | [ɑ] or [a] |
| marcher, marchez, marchais, marchait, baie, valet, mes, fumée | [e] or [ɛ] |
| nid | [i] |
| chaud, vaut, faux, sot, tôt, Pernod, dos, croc | [o] |
| bout, bijoux, sous, boue | [u] |
| fut, fût, crus, crûs | [y] |
| queue, heureux, bleus | [ø] |
| en, vend, vent, an, sang, grand, dans | [ɑ̃] |
| fin, feint, frein, vain | [ɛ̃] |
| on, pont, fond, avons | [ɔ̃] |
| brun, parfum | [œ̃] |

## From Spelling to Sounds *continued*

### Consonants

Final consonants are usually silent → ①

**n** or **m** at the end of a syllable or word are silent, but they have the effect of 'nasalizing' the preceding vowel(s) (see page 239 on Nasal Vowels).

The letter **h** is either 'silent' ('mute') or 'aspirate' when it begins a word. When silent, the word behaves as though it started with a vowel and takes a liaison with the preceding word where appropriate.

When the **h** is aspirate, no liaison is made → ②

There is no way of predicting which words start with which sort of **h** – this simply has to be learnt with each word

The following consonants in spelling have predictable pronunciations: b, d, f, k, l, p, r, t, v, w, x, y, z.

Others vary:

| SPELLING | PRONOUNCED | ENGLISH EXAMPLES |
|---|---|---|
| **c** + a, o, u | [k] | can cot cut → ③ |
| + l, r | | class cram |
| **c** + e, i, y | [s] | ceiling ice → ④ |
| **ç** + a, o, u | [s] | ceiling ice → ⑤ |
| **ch** | [ʃ] | shop lash → ⑥ |
| **g** + a, o, u | [g] | gate got gun → ⑦ |
| + l, r | | glass gramme |
| **g** + e, i, y | [ʒ] | leisure → ⑧ |
| **gn** | [ɲ] | companion onion → ⑨ |
| **j** | [ʒ] | measure → ⑩ |
| **q, qu** | [k] | quay kit → ⑪ |
| **s** (*between vowels*) | [z] | rose → ⑫ |
| **s** (*elsewhere*) | [s] | sit |
| **th** | [t] | Thomas → ⑬ |
| **t** in **-tion** | [s] | sit → ⑭ |

# Examples

**1** éclat [ekla]  nez [ne]
chaud [ʃo]  aider [ɛde]

**2** silent h:  aspirate h:
des hôtels [de zotɛl]  des haricots [de aʀiko]

**3** café [kafe]  côte [kot]  culture [kyltyʀ]
classe [klas]  croûte [kʀut]

**4** ceci [səsi]  cil [sil]  cycliste [siklist]

**5** ça [sa]  garçon [gaʀsɔ̃]  déçu [desy]

**6** chat [ʃa]  riche [ʀiʃ]

**7** gare [gaʀ]  gourde [guʀd]  aigu [ɛgy]
glaise [glɛz]  gramme [gʀam]

**8** gemme [ʒem]  gilet [ʒilɛ]  gymnaste [ʒimnast]

**9** vigne [viɲ]  oignon [ɔɲɔ̃]

**10** joli [ʒɔli]  Jules [ʒyl]

**11** quiche [kiʃ]  quitter [kite]

**12** sable [sablə]  maison [mɛzɔ̃]

**13** théâtre [teɑtʀ]  Thomas [tɔma]

**14** nation [nasjɔ̃]  action [aksjɔ̃]

## Feminine Forms and Pronunciation

For adjectives and nouns ending in a vowel in the masculine, the addition of an **e** to form the feminine does not alter the pronunciation → ①

If the masculine ends with a silent consonant, generally **-d**, **-s**, **-r** or **-t**, the consonant is sounded in the feminine → ②
This also applies when the final consonant is doubled before the addition of the feminine **e** → ③

If the masculine ends in a nasal vowel and a silent **n**, e.g. **-an**, **-on**, **-in**, the vowel is no longer nasalized and the **-n** is pronounced in the feminine → ④
This also applies when the final **-n** is doubled before the addition of the feminine **e** → ⑤

Where the masculine and feminine forms have totally different endings (see pages 136 and 150), the pronunciation of course varies accordingly → ⑥

## Plural Forms and Pronunciation

The addition of **s** or **x** to form regular plurals generally does not affect pronunciation → ⑦

Where liaison has to be made, the final **-s** or **-x** of the plural form is pronounced → ⑧

Where the masculine singular and plural forms have totally different endings (see pages 138 and 148), the pronunciation of course varies accordingly → ⑨

Note the change in pronunciation in the following nouns:

| SINGULAR | PLURAL |
|---|---|
| bœuf [bœf] ox | bœufs [bø] oxen |
| œuf [œf] egg | œufs [ø] eggs |
| os [ɔs] bone | os [o] bones |

# Examples

| ADJECTIVES | NOUNS |
|---|---|

**1** joli [ʒɔli] → jolie [ʒɔli]
  déçu [desy] → déçue [desy]

un ami [ami] → une amie [ami]
un employé [ɑ̃plwaje] →
  une employée [ɑ̃plwaje]

**2** chaud [ʃo] → chaude [ʃod]

  français [fRɑ̃sɛ] →
  française [fRɑ̃sɛz]
  inquiet [ɛ̃kjɛ] →
  inquiète [ɛ̃kjɛt]

un étudiant [etydjɑ̃] →
  une étudiante [etydjɑ̃t]
un Anglais [ɑ̃glɛ] →
  une Anglaise [ɑ̃glɛz]
un étranger [etRɑ̃ʒe] →
  une étrangère [etRɑ̃ʒeR]

**3** violet [vjɔlɛ] → violette [vjɔlɛt]

  gras [gRɑ] → grasse [gRɑs]

le cadet [kadɛ] →
  la cadette [kadɛt]

**4** plein [plɛ̃] → pleine [plɛn]

  fin [fɛ̃] → fine [fin]

  brun [bRœ̃] → brune [bRyn]

le souverain [suvRɛ̃] →
  la souveraine [suvRɛn]
Le Persan [pɛRsɑ̃] →
  la Persane [pɛRsan]
le voisin [vwazɛ̃] →
  la voisine [vwazin]

**5** canadien [kanadjɛ̃] →
  canadienne [kanadjɛn]
  breton [bRətɔ̃] →
  bretonne [bRətɔn]

le paysan [peizɑ̃] →
  la paysanne [peizan]
le baron [baRɔ̃] →
  la baronne [baRɔn]

**6** vif [vif] → vive [viv]
  traître [tRɛtRə] →
  traîtresse [tRɛtRɛs]

le veuf [vœf] → la veuve [vœv]
le maître [mɛtRə] →
  la maîtresse [mɛtRɛs]

**7** beau [bo] → beaux [bo]

la maison [mɛzɔ̃] →
  les maisons [mɛzɔ̃]

**8** des anciens élèves
  [de zɑ̃sjɛ zelɛv]

de beaux arbres
  [də bo zaRbR(ə)]

**9** amical [amikal] →
  amicaux [amiko]

un journal [ʒuRnal] →
  des journaux [ʒuRno]

## The Alphabet

| | | |
|---|---|---|
| A, a [ɑ] | J, j [ʒi] | S, s [ɛs] |
| B, b [be] | K, k [ka] | T, t [te] |
| C, c [se] | L, l [ɛl] | U, u [y] |
| D, d [de] | M, m [ɛm] | V, v [ve] |
| E, e [ə] | N, n [ɛn] | W, w [dubləve] |
| F, f [ɛf] | O, o [o] | X, x [iks] |
| G, g [ʒe] | P, p [pe] | Y, y [igʀɛk] |
| H, h [aʃ] | Q, q [ky] | Z, z [zɛd] |
| I, i [i] | R, r [ɛʀ] | |

Capital letters are used as in English except for the following:

adjectives of nationality
e.g. une ville espagnole a Spanish town
un auteur français a French author

languages
e.g. Parlez-vous anglais? Do you speak English?
Il parle français et allemand He speaks French and German

days of the week:
**lundi** Monday
**mardi** Tuesday
**mercredi** Wednesday
**jeudi** Thursday
**vendredi** Friday
**samedi** Saturday
**dimanche** Sunday

months of the year:
**janvier** January
**février** February
**mars** March
**avril** April
**mai** May
**juin** June

**juillet** July
**août** August
**septembre** September
**octobre** October
**novembre** November
**décembre** December

# Index

The following index lists comprehensively both grammatical terms and key words in French and English contained in this book.

# Index

# Index

# Index

# Index

# Index

# Index

# Index